JEWISH WRITERS
OF THE
TWENTIETH CENTURY

JEWISH WRITERS
OF THE
TWENTIETH CENTURY

Editor
SORREL KERBEL

Assistant Editors
MURIEL EMANUEL
LAURA PHILLIPS

FITZROY DEARBORN
An imprint of the Taylor and Francis Group
NEW YORK · LONDON

Published in 2003 by
Fitzroy Dearborn
An Imprint of the Taylor and Francis Group
29 West 35th Street
New York, NY 10001
www.routledge-ny.com

Published in Great Britain by
Fitzroy Dearborn
An Imprint of the Taylor and Francis Group
11 New Fetter Lane
London EC4P 4EE
www.routledge.co.uk

10 9 8 7 6 5 4 3 2 1

British Library and Library of Congress Cataloging-in-Publication Data are available.

Library of Congress Cataloging-in-Publication Data

Jewish writers of the twentieth century / editor, Sorrel Kerbel ;
assistant editors, Muriel Emanuel, Laura Phillips.
p. cm.
Includes bibliographical references and index.
ISBN 1-57958-313-X (alk. paper)
1. Jewish literature – Bio-bibliography. 2. Jewish literature – 20th century – History and criticism. I. Title: Jewish writers of the 20th century. II. Kerbel, Sorrel. III. Emanuel, Muriel IV. Phillips, Laura.
PN842.J48 2003
809'.88924 – dc21 2002152950

Typeset by Servis Filmsetting Ltd, Manchester England
Printed in the United States of America on acid-free paper.

CONTENTS

Editor's Note *page* vii
Advisers and Contributors ix
Alphabetical List of Writers xi
Chronological List of Writers xv

Introductory Surveys

American-Jewish Literature 3
British-Jewish Literature 7
Hebrew Literature in the 20th Century 10
Holocaust Writing 13
Yiddish Writing in the 20th Century 17

Writers 23

Title Index 647
Notes on Contributors 685

EDITOR'S NOTE

This reference work aims to recover the rich history of Jewish creative writers worldwide in the 20th century and make visible their diverse accomplishments, examining in particular the Jewish themes in their work. We begin the century with Theodor Herzl, the father of Zionism who was also a dramatist, and the masters of Yiddish, Mendele Moykher Sforim, Sholem Aleichem, and the father of Yiddish theatre, Avrom Goldfaden, as well as the pioneers of Hebrew in the new century, H.N. Bialik, M.Y. Berdyczewski and Y.H. Brenner. We end the century with contemporary writers such as the American Allegra Goodman, the Israeli Savyon Liebrecht, and the Dutch Harry Mulisch, all still writing happily into the 21st century.

Many brilliant writers are included in this book: household names like Proust and Kafka, the Dadaist Tristan Tzara, the dramatist Ionesco, and the Russian poet Il'ia Erenburg; Nobel laureates of literature: S.Y. Agnon, Saul Bellow, Joseph Brodsky, Elias Canetti, Boris Pasternak, Nelly Sachs, Nadine Gordimer, and Imre Kertész, and the Nobel laureate of peace, Elie Wiesel; humorists such as Woody Allen, Ephraim Kishon, and Leo Rosten. So many lives have been affected by experiences in the Shoa: Henri Nathansen of Denmark committed suicide rather than endure, a pattern later followed by Primo Levi and Paul Celan. Others died in the camps: Max Jacob, Janusz Korczak, Gertrude Kolmar, and Isaak Babel'. Survivors such as Elie Wiesel, Aharon Appelfeld, Rose Ausländer, Ka-Tzetnik 135633 (Yechiel Dinur), Piotr Rawicz, and the hidden child Judith Herzberg, lived to write eloquently of their experiences.

We have unfortunately not been able to include the many writers who have written only one memoir/ journal/testimony to the period of the Holocaust. Because of this we have included an introductory essay on Holocaust writing by Sue Vice. Other introductory essays are on the rise and decline of Yiddish literature by Joel Berkowitz, and on the phenomenal rise of Hebrew writing in the 20th century by Leon Yudkin who comments on the many Israeli poets, novelists, and dramatists who have flourished, especially since the founding of the State of Israel. Many of these Israeli writers appear here in a reference work for the first time. Mark Shechner focuses on the flourishing of Jewish writing in America, and Bryan Cheyette writes on British-Jewish writing.

Defining who is a Jew proved to be a challenge. Anyone who was born a Jew qualified for inclusion, even if he or she had subsequently converted or otherwise dissociated himself or herself from Jewish life. Muriel Rukeyser suggests that "to be a Jew in the twentieth century/ is to be offered a gift. If you refuse/ wishing to be invisible, you choose/ death of the spirit, the stone insanity". Conversion was and is after all an aspect of Jewish experience. In the aftermath of Nuremberg, a person with only one Jewish parent qualifies for inclusion. We accepted as Jewish anyone who identified themselves as a Jew, or was perceived as such by others. Aharon Appelfeld has said that he has always loved "assimilated Jews, because that was where the Jewish character, and also, perhaps, Jewish fate, was concentrated with the greatest force".

Although this is a book on Jewish writers, it does not try to define what constitutes Jewish writing. Is it simply writing by Jewish writers? Are those included good writers who happen to be Jewish, and does their Jewishness contribute to their success? Jews have always been devoted to the reading and writing of books, but 19th-century Jews would not have easily recognized as "Jewish writing" much of what was written in the 20th century. There had always been a rich tradition of literacy and scholarship, which was translated in the 20th century into secular imaginative literature. Does it need to be in a Jewish language, i.e. Yiddish or Hebrew? Patently not, because we have included writers from all over the world, writing in their vernacular languages. Many of these writers characterized a certain urban rootlessness, a sense of alienation or psychological estrangement, deracination and marginality which became central to much 20th-century literature. As Jabès said, "I have been wandering for 2,000 years". Sometimes it is the sense of the little man (Mendele Moykher Sforim's *Dos kleyne mentshele*), the luftmensch (dreamer), the vulnerable shlemiel, or even a wise fool, who is a victim of the more confident world, that suggests a kind of Jewishness. In many works, it is a depiction of Yiddishkeit, a way of living in the lost world of the shtetl, or in the ghettos of New York or London's East End. But for many writers, assimilated into the larger population, it was necessary to be discreet, to express themselves as Jews with great reserve. This applied to many English Jewish writers and to several French Jewish writers, where the obligation was "to be a man in the street and a Jew at home", as well as to Soviet Jews where there was active discrimination against Jews like Brodsky or Mandel'shtam.

After the Holocaust or Shoa, it was a sense of Zakhor, the ethical duty to remember, that needed to be fulfilled and which gave integrity to those who had witnessed the terrible events. And after the Shoa, the sense of the dispossessed and suffering was even more important, yet the flame of hope survived. As Rose Ausländer wrote: "I, survivor/ of the horror/ write with words/ life". For Brazilian Moacyr Scliar, the rediscovery of ethnic identity was important because "Jewishness is a condition one cannot escape, one that carries within itself the strength to endure." Above all, Jewish writing may be characterized by the need to understand what it is to be a mentsh, a humane person, with a heightened consciousness or sensitivity to oppression, in the apartheid era of Nadine Gordimer's South Africa, in Ariel Dorfman's Chile, or in David Grossman's Israel.

Freud is reputed to have said that "conscience is a Jewish invention". So it is appropriate that Philip Roth's *Operation Shylock* ends with the line, "Let your Jewish conscience be your guide." Perhaps the best advice is from George Eliot, quoting from J.S. Mill's *On Liberty*: "from the freedom of individual men to persist in idiosyncracies, the world may be enriched. Why should we not apply this argument to the idiosyncracy of a nation, and pause in our haste to shoot it down?" *(On the Jewish Problem)*.

Of course we could not include every writer who deserved to be here, and had a real tussle in deciding who was worthy of inclusion. Given the comparatively uncharted nature of this subject, *Jewish Writers of the Twentieth Century* cannot hope to be completely comprehensive. However, the inclusion of the longer survey articles should ensure that many interesting issues are raised, and that lesser-known individuals as well as the 19th-century pioneers, are mentioned.

There may be inconsistencies in the transliteration of places and names. Accepted usage is followed in most cases, but there are many problems: places and countries had different names at different periods. A preference has been given to works in the English language when recommending books for Further Reading, but many others have been listed. We have tried, where possible, to include the translator of the works listed under Selected Writings, where we have tried to list the most important and significant works.

Acknowledgements

I was fortunate to be able to complete the task of this book, begun with Muriel Emanuel in 1994, but aborted when the previous publishers closed their London office in 1995. This project was revived in 1999 when it was greeted enthusiastically by Roda Morrison of Fitzroy Dearborn, with Muriel Emanuel and Laura Phillips as wonderful assistant editors. Since then it has blossomed and finally reached publication because these professional people were dedicated to the project, set it into motion, and worked energetically, remaining committed to its progress. I thank them all, as well all those scholars and specialists who have written for the book and were so generous with their time in giving advice and answering queries. I would also like to thank my husband Jack, my family, and many others, including Alan Todres in Chicago, Dorothée van Tendeloo, librarians at the British Library and the Institute for the Translation of Hebrew Literature, Tel Aviv, Dr Glenda Abrahams of Oxford, Professor Tami Hess of the Hebrew University, Professor Yael Feldman of New York, and of course the original board of advisers, Dr Risa Domb of Cambridge who co-opted some of her best students to write essays, the late Professor Eduard Goldstücker of Prague, Professor Gabriel Josipovici of Sussex, and Dr Stephen Lehmann, Philadelphia, and Professor Simon Sibelman, Wisconsin. The essay on Patrick Modiano was first published in *Contemporary World Writers*, 2nd edition, edited by Tracy Chevalier (Detroit and London: St James Press, 1993).

SORREL KERBEL

ADVISERS

Hugh Denman
Risa Domb
Eduard Goldstücker
Gabriel Josipovici
Stephen Lehmann
Simon Sibelman
Leon I. Yudkin

CONTRIBUTORS

Béa Aaronson
Nathan Abrams
Edward A. Abramson
Tamar Agnon
Hephzibah Anderson
Jennifer Andrews
Tali Asher
Alex Auswaks
Mark Axelrod
Hamutal Bar-Yosef
Marion Baraitser
Gerd Bayer
Helen Beer
Wendy H. Bergoffen
Joel Berkowitz
Jane Blevins
Felicity Bloch
Cecil Bloom
Saskia Brown
Justin Cammy
Bryan H. Cheyette
Dafna Clifford
Marge Clouts
Uri Cohen
Zafrira Lidovsky Cohen
Clara Corona
David Coward
Victoria Cox
Richard Crownshaw
William Cutter
Tish Dace
Jeremy Dauber
Barry Davis
Gerald de Groot
Hugh Denman
Claude Desmarais
Lynne Diamond-Nigh
Gennady Estraikh
Moris Farhi
Yael S. Feldman
Hannah Berliner Fischthal
Shelley Fisher Fishkin
Richard Freadman
Albert H. Friedlander
Mark Gelber
Lydia M. Gil
Nora Glickman
Michael Gluzman
Barry Goldensohn
Chanita Goodblatt
Alex Gordon
Linda Grant
Nancy Grey
Elvira Groezinger
Dan Gunn
Birgit Haas
Jay L. Halio
Kathryn Hellerstein
Hannan Hever
Matthew Hoffman
Dara Horn
Peter Hutchinson
Carol Iancu
Wilma Iggers

Steven Jaron
G. Matthew Jenkins
Stephen Karpowitz
Devra Kay
Ray Keenoy
Steven G. Kellman
Sorrel Kerbel
Ilona Klein
Jerome Klinkowitz
Krisztina Koenen
Matthias Konzett
Mark Krupnick
Mervyn Lebor
Marcia Leveson
Jennifer Levi
Gabriel Levin
Tamara Levine
Ward B. Lewis
Dagmar C. G. Lorenz
Lev Loseff
Orly Lubin
Tom Lundskær-Nielsen
Barbara Mann
Marta Marzanska
Daphne Meijer
Giulia Miller
Valerie Minogue
Tomasz Mirkowicz
Michael Mitchell
Craig Monk
Robert A. Morace
Paul Morris
David Nathan
Matthew Nesvisky
Ranen Omer-Sherman
Leonard Orr
Avraham Oz
Gary Pacernick
Valentina Polukhina
Dina Porat
Leonard Prager
Victor J. Ramraj
Norman Ravvin
Wendy Robbins
David Rock
Juanita Rothman
Joshua Rubenstein
Rachel Rubinstein
Anthony Rudolf
Geoff Sadler
Gwynne Schrire
Michael J. Schwartz
Ziva Shamir
Mark Shechner
Joseph Sherman
Batya Shimony
David Shneer
Maxim D. Shrayer
Gerald S. Smith
Reuven Snir
David Solway
Ezra Spicehandler
Ilan Stavans
Louise Sylvester
Jeanie M. Tietjen
Michael True
Richard Tuerk
Hamutal Tzamir
Shai Tzur
Heather Valencia
Dorothée van Tendeloo
Jeffrey Veidlinger
Sue Vice
Elvira Lato Vinti
Manfred Voigts
Jeroen Vullings
Stephen Wade
Diane Wakoski
Anat Weissman
Sally Whyte
Katarzyna Wieclawska
Shira Wolosky
Tamra Wright
Anny Wynchank
Leon I. Yudkin

ALPHABETICAL LIST OF WRITERS

Walter Abish
Dannie Abse
S.Y. Agnon
Lea Aini
Woody Allen
Ruth Almog
Nissim Aloni
Natan Alterman
A. Alvarez
Yehuda Amichai
Eli Amir
An-ski
Aharon Appelfeld
Max Apple
Sholem Asch
Max Aub
Rose Ausländer
Paul Auster
David Avidan
Leah Ayalon

Isaak Emmanuilovich Babel'
Eduard Bagritskii
Shimon Ballas
Benny Barbash
(Joseph) Alexander Baron
Dvora Baron
Hanokh Bartov
Giorgio Bassani
Jurek Becker
Maya Bejerano
Saul Bellow
Yitzhak Ben-Ner
Netiva Ben-Yehuda
Micha Yosef Berdyczewski
Dovid Bergelson
Steven Berkoff
Chaim Bermant
Hayyim Nahman Bialik
Maxim Biller
Jean-Richard Bloch
Yosef Hayyim Brenner
Hermann Broch
Max Brod
Harold Brodkey
Joseph Brodsky
E.M. Broner
Anita Brookner

Abraham Cahan
Elias Canetti
Veza Canetti
T. Carmi
Orly Castel-Bloom
Paul Celan
Hélène Cixous
Sydney Clouts
Albert Cohen
Leonard Cohen

Der Nister
Alfred Döblin
E.L. Doctorow
Ariel Dorfman
Alicia Dujovne Ortiz
G.L. Durlacher
Andrea Dworkin

Stanley Elkin
Leslie Epstein
Il'ia Erenburg
Esther
Nissim Ezekiel

Ruth Fainlight
Moris Farhi
Raymond Federman
Itsik Fefer
Elaine Feinstein
Edna Ferber
Lion Feuchtwanger
Leslie A. Fiedler
Harvey Fierstein
Ida Fink
Edmond Fleg
Erich Fried
Bruce Jay Friedman

Romain Gary
Mordkhe Gebirtig
Alberto Gerchunoff
Jozef Habib Gerez
Karen Gershon
Amir Gilboa

Allen Ginsberg
Natalia Ginzburg
Arn Glants-Leyeles
Margo Glantz
Yankev Glatshteyn
Nora Glickman
Uri Nissan Gnessin
Leah Goldberg
Isaac Goldemberg
Avrom Goldfaden
Louis Golding
Gerardo Mario Goloboff
Allegra Goodman
Nadine Gordimer
Yankev Gordin
Chaim Grade
Uri Zvi Greenberg
David Grossman
Vasilii Semenovich Grossman
Batya Gur
Zali Gurevitch
Haim Guri

Shmuel Halkin
Moyshe-Leyb Halpern
Marek Halter
Shulamith Hareven
Ronald Harwood
Hayim Hazaz
Herman Heijermans
Joseph Heller
Lillian Hellman
Yehudit Hendel
Judith Herzberg
Theodor Herzl
Stefan Heym
Edgar Hilsenrath
Perets Hirshbein
Yoel Hoffman
John Hollander

Eugène Ionesco

Edmond Jabès
Max Jacob
Dan Jacobson
Howard Jacobson
Ruth Prawer Jhabvala
Erica Jong
Gabriel Josipovici

Ka-Tzetnik 135633
Franz Kafka
Amalia Kahana-Carmon
Yoram Kaniuk
Avrom Karpinovich
Menke Katz
Steve Katz
Yehudit Katzir
Yehoshua Kenaz
Imre Kertész
Danilo Kiš
Egon Erwin Kisch
Ephraim Kishon
A.M. Klein
Ivan Klíma
Arthur Koestler
Gertrud Kolmar
György Konrád
Bernard Kops
Janusz Korczak
Jerzy Kosinski
Abba Kovner
Karl Kraus
Esther Kreitman
Moyshe Kulbak
Stanley Kunitz
Tony Kushner

Jiří Langer
Shulamit Lapid
Else Lasker-Schüler
Irving Layton
Bolesław Leśmian
Carlo Levi
Primo Levi
Hanoch Levin
H. Leyvik
Serge Liberman
Savyon Liebrecht
Jakov Lind
Clarice Lispector
Emanuel Litvinoff
Simon Louvish
Armand Lunel
Arnošt Lustig

Norman Mailer
Bernard Malamud
David Mamet
Osip Mandel'shtam
Itsik Manger
Mani Leyb
Wolf Mankowitz
Anna Margolin
Wallace Markfield
Perets Markish
Ronit Matalon
André Maurois
Aharon Megged
Albert Memmi
Mendele Moykher Sforim
Sami Michael
Anne Michaels
George Mikes
Arthur Miller
Sarah Gertrude Millin
Marga Minco
Patrick Modiano
Kadye Molodovski

Elsa Morante
Alberto Moravia
Marcel Möring
Harry Mulisch

Henri Nathansen

Clifford Odets
Tillie Olsen
Joseph Opatoshu
George Oppen
Yitzhak Orpaz
Amos Oz
Cynthia Ozick

Dan Pagis
Grace Paley
Dorothy Parker
Boris Pasternak
Georges Perec
S.J. Perelman
Yitskhok-Leyb Perets
Lily Perry
Leo Perutz
Marge Piercy
Dovid Pinski
Robert Pinsky
Harold Pinter
Chaim Potok
Gabriel Yehoshua Preil
Giorgio Pressburger
Marcel Proust

Esther Raab
Rachel
Carl Rakosi
Frederic Raphael
Yonatan Ratosh
Dalia Ravikovitch
Piotr Rawicz
Avrom Reyzen
Charles Reznikoff
Adrienne Rich
Mordecai Richler
Laura Riding
Isaac Rosenberg
Chava Rosenfarb
Isaac Rosenfeld
Moris Rosenfeld
Leo Rosten
Henry Roth
Joseph Roth
Philip Roth
Jerome Rothenberg
Bernice Rubens
Adolf Rudnicki
Muriel Rukeyser

Umberto Saba
Nelly Sachs
Pinhas Sadeh
J.D. Salinger
Maurice Samuel
Nathalie Sarraute
Robert Schindel
Zalkind-Zalmen Schneour
Arthur Schnitzler
Bruno Schulz
David Schütz
Delmore Schwartz
André Schwarz-Bart
Marcel Schwob
Moacyr Scliar
Will Self
Maurice Sendak
Yaakov Shabtai
Peter Shaffer
Nathan Shaham
David Shahar
Meir Shalev
Moshe Shamir
Karl Shapiro
Lamed Shapiro
Martin Sherman
Yuval Shimoni
Avraham Shlonsky
Sholem Aleichem (Sholem Rabinovitsh)
Yeshayohu (Shaye) Shpigl (Isaiah Spiegel)
David Shrayer-Petrov
Jon Silkin
Neil Simon
Clive Sinclair
Isaac Bashevis Singer
Israel Joshua Singer
Boris Abramovich Slutskii
Yehoshua Sobol
Susan Sontag
Muriel Spark
Art Spiegelman
André Spire
Ilan Stavans
Gertrude Stein
George Steiner
Tom Stoppard
Julian Stryjkowski
Ronald Sukenick
Abraham Sutzkever
Italo Svevo

Benjamin Tammuz
C.P. Taylor
Saul Tchernichovski
Friedrich Torberg
Lionel Trilling
Malka Heifetz Tussman
Julian Tuwim
Tristan Tzara

Leon Uris

Berthold Viertel
Claude Vigée
David Vogel

Yona Wallach
Edward Lewis Wallant
Jakob Wassermann
Ernst Weiss
Daniel Weissbort
Isaac Meier Weissenberg
Franz Werfel
Arnold Wesker
Nathanael West
Elie Wiesel
Meir Wieseltier
Léon de Winter
Adele Wiseman
Leonard Sidney Woolf
Herman Wouk

A.B. Yehoshua
Avot Yeshurun
Anzia Yezierska
S. Yizhar

Nathan Zach
Israel Zangwill
Zelda
Louis Zukofsky
Arnold Zweig
Stefan Zweig
Fay Zwicky

CHRONOLOGICAL LIST OF WRITERS

1836–1917	Mendele Moykher Sforim
1840–1908	Avrom Goldfaden
1851–1915	Yitskhok-Leyb Perets
1853–1909	Yankev Gordin
1859–1916	Sholem Aleichem
1860–1951	Abraham Cahan
1860–1904	Theodor Herzl
1861–1928	Italo Svevo
1862–1923	Moris Rosenfeld
1862–1931	Arthur Schnitzler
1863–1920	An-ski
1864–1924	Herman Heijermans
1864–1926	Israel Zangwill
1865–1921	Micha Yosef Berdyczewski
1867–1905	Marcel Schwob
1868–1944	Henri Nathansen
1868–1966	André Spire
1869–1945	Else Lasker-Schüler
1872–1959	Dovid Pinski
1872–1922	Marcel Proust
1873–1934	Hayyim Nahman Bialik
1873–1934	Jakob Wassermann
1874–1963	Edmond Fleg
1874–1936	Karl Kraus
1874–1946	Gertrude Stein
1875–1943	Saul Tchernichovski
1876–1944	Max Jacob
1876–1953	Avrom Reyzen
1877–1942	Mordkhe Gebirtig
1877/78–1937	Bolesław Leśmian
1878–1957	Alfred Döblin
1878–1942	Janusz Korczak
1878–1948	Lamed Shapiro
1879–1913	Uri Nissan Gnessin
*c.*1880–1940	Esther
1880–1957	Sholem Asch
1880–1948	Perets Hirshbein
1880–1969	Leonard Sidney Woolf
1881–1921	Yosef Hayyim Brenner
1881–1938	Isaac Meier Weissenberg
1881–1942	Stefan Zweig
1882–1957	Leo Perutz
1882–1940	Ernst Weiss
1883–1924	Franz Kafka
1883–1953	Mani Leyb
1883–1957	Umberto Saba
1884–1952	Dovid Bergelson
1884–1947	Jean-Richard Bloch
1884–1968	Max Brod
1884–1950	Der Nister
1884–1958	Lion Feuchtwanger
1884–1950	Alberto Gerchunoff
1885–1968	Edna Ferber
1885–1948	Egon Erwin Kisch
1885–1967	André Maurois
1885–1953	Berthold Viertel
*c.*1885–1970	Anzia Yezierska
1886–1951	Hermann Broch
1886–1932	Moyshe-Leyb Halpern
1886–1954	Joseph Opatoshu
1887–1956	Dvora Baron
1887–1952	Anna Margolin
1887–1959	Zalkind-Zalmen Schneour
1887–1968	Arnold Zweig
1888–1970	S.Y. Agnon
1888–1962	H. Leyvik
1888–1968	Sarah Gertrude Millin
1889–1966	Arn Glants-Leyeles
1890–1960	Boris Pasternak
1890–1931	Rachel
1890–1918	Isaac Rosenberg
1890–1945	Franz Werfel
1891–1967	Il'ia Erenburg
1891–1954	Esther Kreitman
1891–1938	Osip Mandel'shtam
1891–1970	Nelly Sachs
1891–1944	David Vogel
1892–1977	Armand Lunel
1892–1942	Bruno Schulz
1893–1967	Dorothy Parker
1893–1944	Israel Joshua Singer
1893?–1987	Malka Heifetz Tussman
1894–1940	Isaak Emmanuilovich Babel'
1894–1943	Gertrud Kolmar
1894–1943	Jiří Langer
1894–1975	Kadye Molodovski
1894–1981	Esther Raab
1894–1976	Charles Reznikoff
1894–1939	Joseph Roth
1894–1953	Julian Tuwim
1895–1934	Eduard Bagritskii
1895–1981	Albert Cohen
1895–1958	Louis Golding
1895–1952	Perets Markish

1895–1972	Maurice Samuel
1896–1971	Yankev Glatshteyn
1896–1981	Uri Zvi Greenberg
1896–1940	Moyshe Kulbak
1896–1963	Tristan Tzara
1897–1963	Veza Canetti
1897–1960	Shmuel Halkin
1898–1973	Hayim Hazaz
1900–1952	Itsik Fefer
1900–1999	Nathalie Sarraute
1900–1973	Avraham Shlonsky
1901–1969	Itsik Manger
1901–1991	Laura Riding
1902–1975	Carlo Levi
1903–1972	Max Aub
1903–	Carl Rakosi
1903–1940	Nathanael West
1904–1979	S.J. Perelman
1904–1991	Isaac Bashevis Singer
1904–1992	Avot Yeshurun
1904–1978	Louis Zukofsky
1905–1994	Elias Canetti
1905–1964	Vasilii Semenovich Grossman
1905–1983	Arthur Koestler
1905–	Stanley Kunitz
1905–1996	Julian Stryjkowski
1905–1975	Lionel Trilling
1906–1984	Lillian Hellman
1906–1991	Menke Katz
1906–1963	Clifford Odets
1906–1995	Henry Roth
1906–1990	Yeshayohu Shpigl
1907–1988	Rose Ausländer
1907–1990	Alberto Moravia
1908–1984	George Oppen
1908–1981	Yonatan Ratosh
1908–1997	Leo Rosten
1908–1979	Friedrich Torberg
1909–1972	A.M. Klein
1910–1970	Natan Alterman
1910–1982	Chaim Grade
1911–1970	Leah Goldberg
1911–1993	Gabriel Yehoshua Preil
1912–1994	Eugène Ionesco
1912–1991	Edmond Jabès
1912–	Irving Layton
1912–1987	George Mikes
1912–1985	Elsa Morante
1912–1990	Adolf Rudnicki
1912 or 1913–	Tillie Olsen
1913–2001	Stefan Heym
1913–1980	Muriel Rukeyser
1913–1966	Delmore Schwartz
1913–2000	Karl Shapiro
1913–	Abraham Sutzkever
1914–1980	Romain Gary
1914–1986	Bernard Malamud
1914–1984	Zelda
1915–	Saul Bellow
1915–	Emanuel Litvinoff
1915–	Arthur Miller
1915–	Herman Wouk
1916–2000	Giorgio Bassani
1916–1991	Natalia Ginzburg
1916–	S. Yizhar
before 1917–2001	Ka-Tzetnik 135633
1917–1999	Alexander Baron
1917–	Leslie A. Fiedler
1917–1984	Amir Gilboa
1918–	Avrom Karpinovich
1918–1987	Abba Kovner
1918–1956	Isaac Rosenfeld
1918–	Muriel Spark
1919–1987	Primo Levi
1919–1982	Piotr Rawicz
1919–	J.D. Salinger
1919–1986	Boris Abramovich Slutskii
1919–1989	Benjamin Tammuz
1920–1970	Paul Celan
1920–	Aharon Megged
1920–	Albert Memmi
1920–	Marga Minco
1921–	Ida Fink
1921–1988	Erich Fried
1921–	Moshe Shamir
1921–	Claude Vigée
1922–	Grace Paley
1923–	Dannie Abse
1923–1993	Karen Gershon
1923–	Nadine Gordimer
1923–	Haim Guri
1923–1999	Joseph Heller
1923–	Norman Mailer
1923–	Yitzhak Orpaz
1923–	Chava Rosenfarb
1924–2000	Yehuda Amichai
1924–	Nissim Ezekiel
1924–	Ephraim Kishon
1924–1998	Wolf Mankowitz
1924–	Leon Uris
1925–1994	T. Carmi
1925–1977	Clarice Lispector
1925–	Nathan Shaham
1926–1998	Nissim Aloni
1926–	Hanokh Bartov
1926–1982	Sydney Clouts
1926–	Jozef Habib Gerez
1926–1997	Allen Ginsberg
1926–	Yehudit Hendel
1926–	Edgar Hilsenrath
1926–	Bernard Kops
1926–	Arnošt Lustig
1926–2002	Wallace Markfield
1926–	Sami Michael
1926–	Peter Shaffer
1926–1997	David Shahar
1926–1962	Edward Lewis Wallant
1927–	Ruth Prawer Jhabvala
1927–	Jakov Lind
1927–	Harry Mulisch

1927–	Neil Simon
1928–	Netiva Ben-Yehuda
1928–	Anita Brookner
1928–1996	G.L. Durlacher
1928–	Raymond Federman
1928–	Cynthia Ozick
1928–	Bernice Rubens
1928–	André Schwarz-Bart
1928–	Maurice Sendak
1928–	Elie Wiesel
1928–1992	Adele Wiseman
1929–	A. Alvarez
1929–1998	Chaim Bermant
1929–	John Hollander
1929–	Dan Jacobson
1929–	Imre Kertész
1929–2002	Chaim Potok
1929–	Adrienne Rich
1929–1994	Pinhas Sadeh
1929–	George Steiner
1929–1981	C.P. Taylor
1930–	Shimon Ballas
1930–1996	Harold Brodkey
1930–	E.M. Broner
1930–1995	Stanley Elkin
1930–	Elaine Feinstein
1930–	Bruce Jay Friedman
1930–	Margo Glantz
1930–	Shulamith Hareven
1930–	Amalia Kahana-Carmon
1930–	Yoram Kaniuk
1930–1986	Dan Pagis
1930–	Harold Pinter
1930–1997	Jon Silkin
1930–	Nathan Zach
1931–	Walter Abish
1931–	E.L. Doctorow
1931–	Ruth Fainlight
1931–	Ivan Klíma
1931–	Frederic Raphael
1931–2001	Mordecai Richler
1931–	Jerome Rothenberg
1932–	Aharon Appelfeld
1932–	Ronald Sukenick
1932–	Arnold Wesker
1933–1995	David Avidan
1933–	György Konrád
1933–1991	Jerzy Kosinski
1933–	Philip Roth
1933–	Susan Sontag
1933–	Fay Zwicky
1934–	Leonard Cohen
1934–	Ronald Harwood
1934–	Judith Herzberg
1934–	Shulamit Lapid
1934–1981	Yaakov Shabtai
1935–	Woody Allen
1935–	Moris Farhi
1935–	Steve Katz
1935–1989	Danilo Kiš
1935–	Daniel Weissbort
1936–	Ruth Almog
1936–	Marek Halter
1936–1982	Georges Perec
1936–	Marge Piercy
1936–	Dalia Ravikovitch
1936–	David Shrayer-Petrov
1936–	A.B. Yehoshua
1937–	Eli Amir
1937–1997	Jurek Becker
1937–	Yitzhak Ben-Ner
1937–	Steven Berkoff
1937–	Hélène Cixous
1937–	Yoel Hoffman
1937–	Yehoshua Kenaz
1937–	Giorgio Pressburger
1937–	Moacyr Scliar
1937–	Tom Stoppard
1938–	Leslie Epstein
1938–	Martin Sherman
1939–	Gerardo Mario Goloboff
1939–	Amos Oz
1939–	Yehoshua Sobol
1940–1996	Joseph Brodsky
1940–	Alicia Dujovne Ortiz
1940–	Gabriel Josipovici
1940–	Robert Pinsky
1941–	Max Apple
1941–	David Schütz
1941–	Meir Wieseltier
1942–	Ariel Dorfman
1942–	Howard Jacobson
1942–	Erica Jong
1942–	Serge Liberman
1943–1999	Hanoch Levin
1944–	Nora Glickman
1944–	Robert Schindel
1944–1985	Yona Wallach
1945–	Isaac Goldemberg
1945–	Patrick Modiano
1946–	Andrea Dworkin
1947–	Paul Auster
1947–	Batya Gur
1947–	Simon Louvish
1947–	David Mamet
1948–	Savyon Liebrecht
1948–	Meir Shalev
1948–	Clive Sinclair
1948–	Art Spiegelman
1949–	Maya Bejerano
1949–	Zali Gurevitch
1950–	Leah Ayalon
1951–	Benny Barbash
1953–	Lily Perry
1954–	Harvey Fierstein
1954–	David Grossman
1954–	Léon de Winter
1955–	Yuval Shimoni
1956–	Tony Kushner
1957–	Marcel Möring

1958–	Anne Michaels
1959–	Ronit Matalon
1960–	Maxim Biller
1960–	Orly Castel-Bloom
1961–	Will Self
1961–	Ilan Stavans
1962–	Lea Aini
1963–	Yehudit Katzir
1967–	Allegra Goodman

INTRODUCTORY SURVEYS

American-Jewish Literature

Roughly between 1945 and 1965 the terrain of American literature underwent a sea change in which Jewish writers, critics, and intellectuals played a key role. American fiction was essentially "Europeanized", and Jewish writers and thinkers, in touch with European trends, bore a portion of the responsibility for the new direction. To document this change one could simply enumerate the names of those novelists, poets, playwrights, and critics who starred on the American literary stage during this period, or list the journals, starting with *Partisan Review* and *Commentary*, that became the vehicles of a new sensibility. But then the names are well-known; history has recorded the Jewish moment, long since past, in American letters. Where did it come from, what did it consist of, why should it have flourished precisely when it did?

One immediate answer is obvious – it was bound to happen. The children and grandchildren of butchers, grocers, peddlers, junk dealers, garment workers, even rabbis and scholars, came of age all at once in a kind of Jewish baby-boom and elbowed their way into the cultural arena by the force of their ambitions and the keenness of their intellects. Demographically, the garment industry in the 20th century gave birth to more writers, scholars, critics, and professors than any other American profession, including the ministry. Like the illegal immigration into Palestine after World War II that broke the back of the British mandate there, the Jewish literary arrival in the United States was the cultural by-product of a generational movement, and nothing short of an American version of the Nuremberg laws was going to prevent it. Given the special Jewish affinity for literacy and learning, Jews in any society will rise into elite literary circles when granted the opportunity. As "people of the book", Jews were once people of the holy texts and their vast commentaries, but since the Enlightenment they have become the people of all textual forms, and it is no more outlandish to see the novel as a contemporary Torah than to see the law firm as a modern development of the Bet Din or rabbinic court.

The rise of Jews into artistic and intellectual circles in the United States also correlates with the improvement of their economic circumstances, as the children of merchants and workers, in waves of generational ascent, percolated upwards into the arts. With money made in business came the leisure of the children to paint, sculpt, dance, act, play, compose, write, weave, or throw clay. It also corresponded with the postwar opening of doors. After the Shoah it was inevitable that social barriers would wither away, especially the reprehensible quota systems that permitted only so many Jews into the elite universities, the medical and law schools, and the tenured faculties.

We are bound to view the rise of the Jewish novelist as basically that: an arrival, an emergence, a maturation, the literary harvest of a social growth. But if we have learned anything at all from history it is that all complex events are, to borrow a phrase from Freud, "overdetermined", the result of many vectors in fortuitous intersection. The arrival of the Jewish writer at the heart of American letters was such an event, and conditioned as it was by simple social factors, it also displayed features that are not so neatly explained. One is the explosiveness with which so many talented Jews rose to the top. To a native New Yorker, the literary scene in 1945, especially as viewed through journals of opinion, must have looked like Ellis Island just after a docking – all these gabbling, animated, contentious Jews where just moments ago one saw only mannerly Gentiles. The metaphor of immigration here is more than symbolic. The Jewish moment in literature was also connected to the intellectual migration that brought refugees from Hitler and Stalin to America, largely New York City, and created a whole new culture in art, critical theory, music, and psychoanalysis. The fall of Paris, it is sometimes said, was the rise of New York, and New York was the locus of the new literary intellectual life to which the Jews were contributors.

The intellectual migration accounts for a feature of the new literature that renders it different in spirit and tone from the writing produced by Jews before World War II. The new literature is more contemporary in its gestures – at first brooding, introspective, tragic, occasionally neurotic, painfully selfconscious, demonstratively Kafkaesque, morosely Dostoevskian – a far cry from work Jewish writers were producing before the war, which was closer to the habits and manners, the boldness and panorama, of American realism. Before the war Jewish culture produced the likes of Abraham Cahan, Anzia Yezierska, Sholom Ash, Michael Gold, Clifford Odets, and Daniel Fuchs, who wrote novels and plays largely in the native realist mode. In all their writing, dollops of social realism swam in bowls of sentiment like sour cream in borscht. Only Henry Roth's tormented and symbolist *Call It Sleep* and the novelistic dreamscapes of Nathanael West could be taken for harbingers of the modernism that was to emerge late on.

With Saul Bellow and *Dangling Man* in 1944, however, a new writing appeared to be at hand, one that was more controlled, inner-directed, and selfconscious. It took other writers a few years to catch up with Bellow's sultry interiority and cunning stylistics, but by the mid-1950s Bernard Malamud, Isaac Rosenfeld, Norman Mailer, and others less well remembered as fiction writers now, such as Meyer Liben, Delmore Schwartz, Michael Seide, Lionel Trilling, and Paul Goodman, could be seen grappling with the subtleties of literary form and the intricacies of a human spirit whose basic agendas of desire were always unconscious and perverse. (The novels and stories of Harold Brodkey, which did not reach their full flowering until late in the century, represent the fullest development of the line of neurotic-as-hero.) To be sure, the technical advance represented by this writing was not so thoroughgoing as to make it appear strikingly modernist in, say, the manner of Joyce or Proust or Faulkner or Nabokov. The cunning and playfulness – the proto-hypertextuality – of Nabokov would be always beyond them. The modernity lay in their inward gaze and the discovery of the heart as the battlefield of history.

Other words beside "emergence" might characterize this 20-year moment from 1945 to 1965. Breakthrough is one, implying the release of pent-up energy and the collapse of obstacles. Another is renaissance, suggesting a renewal, a resurrection, a rebirth. The new writing comes into focus as a literature of turmoil and confusion, crisis and conversion, death and rebirth, conditions that determine its manner and sometimes its explicit themes. Its writers are all converts of one variety or another, and their writing is the testament of their conversions.

I am tempted to say that *conversion* constitutes the single most comprehensive "theme" of contemporary Jewish writing, though the word "theme" might be reserved for an author's explicitly drawn concerns – the "theme", say, of life on the Lower East Side or the struggles between father and son, husband and wife, tradition and change, etc. For the most part the impulse to change is less a theme than a field of force, a property of the soul itself that draws the world around it into its own shape, much as gravity gives shape to space. It is the shape of despair as well as the shape of possibility. The Jewish writer is straining at the limits of not just expression but being. His discontent gives him motive, contour, and line. The Shoah had something to do with this – how could it not? One's own people had been murdered, and a part of oneself had died with them. Though many postwar writers and intellectuals were estranged from Jewish culture, having grown up with the socialist rejection of religious Judaism, they were not insensible of the fact that only an ocean divided them from Auschwitz and that but for an accident of birth and the vagaries of immigration they themselves were the victims of the Final Solution. Yet it is a curious fact that the first generation of postwar writers did not write much about either the Shoah or the founding of Israel. The Shoah was a hidden wound, shrouded in darkness and suffered in silence, felt everywhere but expressed virtually nowhere. Theirs was a survivor's literature, in which relief and liberation are tinged with guilt and dread.

Nor was Israel readily available to the American literary imagination – certainly not to writers who had not experienced it directly – but it had lodged in the heart, in some deep chambers from which it could exert a tug upon other centres of the mind. (Meyer Levin, now scarcely remembered, proves to be a significant exception. A conspicuously Jewish Jew with commitments to Zionism, he stood apart from the emerging culture of merely personal angst and literary modernism.) I would suggest that the Jewish writers, though pointedly ignoring these great events as themes for their fiction, were symbolizing them in the lives they lived and the moods they expressed in their writing. Death and rebirth were very much the implied subjects of their literary expression, and if their explicit themes were commonly local, domestic, and removed from the catastrophic and the monumental, the deeper tonalities of their fiction were profoundly determined by world-historical events. It was not for nothing that Bernard Malamud called his 1961 novel *A New Life*, and though the scene of renewal was a small town in Oregon, the idea of the new life had resonances far beyond the fields and meadows of Willamette Valley. To take yet another phrase from Freud, something like a displacement of affect took place; feelings about unspoken and unspeakable subjects were displaced onto the overt themes of Malamud's writing.

But if great dramas of death and rebirth provided the mood and the music of postwar Jewish writing, yet another great drama affected intellectuals more directly and provided an explicit crisis – the collapse of the revolutionary dreams of their youths. A number of the writers who continue to matter to us – Saul Bellow, Norman Mailer, Lionel Trilling – had grown up with visions of socialism (or communism or Trotskyism) dancing in their heads like sugar plums and after the war threw in the red towel and sought redemption elsewhere. Their careers traced out an arc of commitment, recoil, and conversion. The ex-communist or ex-Trotskyist or ex-socialist or even ex-liberal was as typical a Jewish figure of that generation as, say, the ex-Torah scholar (exemplified in Abraham Cahan's David Levinsky) was typical of the immigrant generation. The recent (1990s) tone of anti-Left zealotry that has crept into the late novels of Philip Roth (*American Pastoral*, *I Married a Communist*, *The Human Stain*) marks him as a belated product of the genre, though he is a generation younger than the other writers in this group.

The postwar generation of Jewish writers and social thinkers had been nurtured in the hothouse climate of social unrest and revolutionary zeal of the 1930s. Throughout that decade event after event came along to spoil dreams of an ideal socialist order, capped off by the revelations that the Soviet Union had failed utterly as the embodiment of Man's Hope. In the climate of crisis that came in the wake of these revelations, writers and intellectuals faced the dilemma of how to bury their revolutionism while preserving their iconoclasm. It was in the effort to resolve that dilemma that a remarkable history of personal changes unfolded, shaping the careers of a generation and leaving a profound mark on our literature and our thought. Both the critical intelligence and the creative impulse flowered during the twilight of American Marxism, as the conversion of intellectuals from sectarians to individuals released geysers of creative and intellectual power.

Most of the major Jewish writers of this era brought their careers to a point at the moment of abandoning old faiths. But the writers who generated the most excitement were not simply those who changed their minds, but rather those who transformed themselves through ordeals of conversion and redemption. From Isaac Rosenfeld's 1946 novel *Passage from Home* and Lionel Trilling's novel *The Middle of the Journey* (1947), to Saul Bellow's *The Adventures of Augie March* (1953), *Henderson the Rain King* (1959) and his play *The Last Analysis* (1964), Allen Ginsberg's *Howl* (1956), Norman Mailer's *Advertisements for Myself* (1959) and, a generation later, Philip Roth's *Portnoy's Complaint* (1969), a single note rings clear from book to book – I am not, I can no longer be, the man I was. It is not to be wondered that when these writers took stock of their situations, many discovered in psychoanalysis or other psychotherapies formulas for their shock and substitutes for the therapies of social redemption they could no longer support. As a releasing agent for the imagination and as a royal road to the American ethic of self-improvement, therapeutic nostrums became both guides to the perplexed and bridges to the New World. Such novels were allegories of crisis and change that, by a logic that is as strange as it is fascinating, were a generation's tickets to the American heartland.

One illustrative instance may stand for the larger movement. What are we to make of a writer who started out in the 1930s with the Spartacus Youth League and the Young People's Socialist League during its brief phase as a revolutionary Trotskyist organization and wound up 30 years later humouring the public with the antics of Moses Herzog, failed scholar and cuckolded husband, who goes about half-dazed in a striped jacket and straw boater trying to understand how he lost out?

I mean of course Saul Bellow, a case in point of the artist as convert, whose labours at self-transformation, self-transcendence really, provide the basic impulse and drama of his writing. Bellow came onto the scene in the 1940s as a writer of depression. *Dangling Man* in 1944 and *The Victim* in 1947 are depressed and depressing books. Perhaps to match his mood or to symbolize the times, the young Bellow – he was 29 in 1944 – had apprenticed himself to Fedor Dostoevskii and tailored his imagination to the poetic half-light of czarist St Petersburg, taking the plot of *The Victim* from Dostoevskii's novella, "The Eternal Husband". The impulse to Russianize the imagination was thoroughgoing; not only was it a rule of style, it was the very character Bellow and his friends, the Chicago Dostoevskians – Isaac Rosenfeld and Oscar Tarcov – assumed in the 1940s when they embarked for New York to seek their fortunes. These attitudes hardly need justifying – 1944 was a tragic year world-wide, especially if you were Jewish, and to assume a depressive literary posture was to do no more than take note of what was going on.

What seems noteworthy now about both *Dangling Man* and *The Victim* is not their plots, which could have been anything at all that suited Bellow's state of mind, but their rhythmic and melodic tonalities – their keening timbres and languorous cadences – in short, their funereal music. This is both intentional – at 29 Bellow was a coming master of his narrative medium – and involuntary – he was writing out of a powerful sense of despair. Behind this despair lay both the Shoah, unspoken but symbolized, and a shattered vision, a lost optimism.

Upon finishing *The Victim*, Bellow embarked on an ambitious novel to be titled *The Crab and the Butterfly*. The novel was suppressed and we know little about it except for a fragment that was published separately in 1950 as the story "The Trip to Galena". We can only surmise why Bellow suppressed the novel, and my guess is that it cut too close to the bone and gave too much away. Many elements that would be properly distanced and impersonalized in *The Adventures of Augie March* were too raw in the uncompleted novel. "The Trip to Galena" provides us with clues about what that might be. It is the frantic monologue of one Weyl, a patient in a mental hospital whose tale of a trip to Illinois decomposes into a ramble, spinning off a froth of metaphysics – wild speculations on shoes and garters, murder and mass murder, conduct and the depths of life. Weyl is a manic-depressive who bursts out of his iron lethargy while telling his story to a fellow patient and sinks in again once he is finished. It sounds like one of the false awakenings recorded by psychologist Oliver Sacks. In the midst of his mad rambles occur some lines that are symptomatic of what Bellow was trying to do in *The Crab and the Butterfly* and *Augie March*:

> You heard me tell my old aunt a while back when she asked me what I wanted, that I didn't want to be sad any more. I meant it to the letter. That being sad is being disfigured, and the first reply I feel like making to it is good fast kick in the wind.
>
> I didn't want to be sad anymore.

By 1953, when Bellow published *Augie March*, his public disposition was anything but sad – it was upbeat, up-tempo, boosterishly American. He had abandoned the soulful cello for maracas, turned in his dirges for rhumbas, exchanged his Shostakovich for Xavier Cugat. "I am an American, Chicago born." In its rambling free-style structure it is bumptiously American, resembling in its high spirits, its vivid adventures, its larger-than-life characters, a *Huckleberry Finn* in Chicago. So promotional was the design of the book that a few critics were prone to take it for Bellow's rejection of his own past and a statement that henceforth he could no longer be counted among the alienated.

Augie March was a classic conversion book – a testimonial to a new faith – the first of several Bellow would write, exhibiting all the classic symptoms of a testimonial – the overstatement, the note of protest, the uncommon vividness. That conversion had both public and private meanings. Publicly, it was a testament of de-Russification and acceptance of the terms and conditions of being an American at last. It was a public burning of Old World manners – the gabardines of alienation and mourning that had been draped, like a caftan, over his previous books. Bellow had sat Shiva long enough and was fretting to start life anew. The early 1950s were, moreover, the time for such affirmations. *Augie March* in 1953 came a year after a famous symposium conducted by *Partisan Review* magazine in which 25 writers and intellectuals, many of whom had once identified with radical causes, sang hallelujah to "Our Country and Our Culture". And then, of course, in 1953, there was Israel, embattled but indisputably there, and while Bellow would not write of it until many years later, in *To Jerusalem and*

Back, it was, one now imagines, yet another source of the high spirits that permeated *The Adventures of Augie March*. Its hero may have been American, Chicago-born, but its author was a Canadian-born son of Jewish immigrants.

Bellow's writing from *Augie March* in 1953 through *The Last Analysis* and *Herzog* in 1964, then, is conversion literature, conversion away from his youthful Dostoevskianism and all that it implied – brooding, languor, guilt, alienation, a sense of life as bizarre and irrational, and of the self as wilful and perverse – toward an Americanism brimming with high spirits, can-do, and futurity. The irony of such an Americanization was that it was facilitated by a discipline invented by Wilhelm Reich, the German-Jewish sexologist who by the end of his career had become a crackpot – a cancer quack, a rain maker, egomaniac, and UFO hunter whose youthful ideas about sex in culture had been eclipsed by his quixotic charges into biophysics and his doomed quests for the cosmic Shangri-La. For a writer like Bellow, afflicted with the curse of irony, the only recourse in dealing with this phase of his life was to treat it as comedy and farce, as he did in both *Seize the Day* (1956) and *Henderson the Rain King* (1959), even though it was the comedy of trying to stay alive and in command of his powers. The confusions and bewilderment this quest entailed have been highlighted in Bellow's writing all along; he was in the 1950s far less rational or settled a writer than most people think, and has been at his best as a writer when most desperate and uncertain.

Conversion is hardly a uniquely Jewish drama. The churning heart and the fragile ego, the sense of incompleteness or of shame that lead one to change one's life, are universally if not evenly distributed throughout the tribes of mankind. The very drama of the modern novel itself is the drama of conversion, the imagination engaged by the tropes of becoming. But the Jewish people, plunged suddenly into the modern world in the last two centuries and subject to assaults from without and upheavals from within, have been subject to the forces of conversion in greater numbers and with greater force than other cultures. Is not Zionism a conversion, a movement of the soul projected onto history and decked out with the paraphernalia of a social and historical force – land, weapons, a government, an ideology? Was not the Yiddishist movement that brought the remarkable flowering of Yiddish literature, drama, and culture to life in the early decades of the 20th century also a conversion, or perhaps the external sign of some interior rearrangement in the furniture of the soul? Was not the romance of Marxism and the withdrawal from it? The Hasidic movement of the 18th century and its modernizing counterpart, the *Haskalah* or Enlightenment?

It would be a wonder if the trials of Jewish history were not reflected in literature and were not indeed the very heart and soul of it, not only in its themes but in its very character as a form of human expression – its nervousness, its vividness, its fluxions of emotion. This may seem a commonplace, though one fails to see much evidence of it in the endless stream of books, essays, and monographs that all too often treat Jewish writing as the voice of timeless verities and Jewish writers as particularly insightful into what is generically human or profoundly spiritual or broadly "humanistic" in humankind. The Jew, by virtue of being ancient, is endowed with the faculty of being deep or wise.

Of course, if trouble doesn't bring wisdom, what does? And especially in an American literary culture dominated from time to time by a peculiar Anglo-Saxon depthlessness, the Jewish writer may in fact be drawing his water from deeper wells. It is not a position I would care to press too hard against now. We do have – did have – Hawthorne, Melville, Whitman, and Poe a century ago to show us that the Anglo-Saxon mind was honeycombed with secret vestibules. But we also have the undying cult of Ernest Hemingway to testify that fishing, hunting, drinking, and womanizing are spiritual bedrock.

I would say of Bernard Malamud that in honour of all that seemed to be rabbinical in him, we have not yet fully measured the side of him that was unsettled and confused; we may yet have to temper our reverence for him in order to gain a full appreciation of him. In books such as *Pictures of Fidelman*, *Dubin's Lives*, and *God's Grace*, Malamud took off the gabardines and donned some shocking outfits. So too, with Bellow, whose restlessness has been more conspicuous, we have been a little loathe to take the turmoil in his books at face value – as being of their essence rather than as, say, tests of the Bellovian hero's "humanity", an ascription that is sometimes hard to pin down in terms of actual behaviour. Roth has presented a different case – a careening turbulence receding at first into wise passiveness and from there into clinical depression, in virtue of which he has not yet stood widely accused of wisdom or depth, though as the road of excess leads to the palace of wisdom, those charges are bound to crop up.

Finally, the literature that has been called Jewish-American is a decidedly Romantic, as opposed to Classical, literature: egotistical, self-assertive, spontaneous, and undisciplined (though sometimes painstakingly composed to give the appearance of spontaneity and undiscipline), naked in its appetites, unembarrassed in its need, and sometimes fanatical in its demands upon the reader. Classicism is an ethos of being, Romanticism one of becoming, and it is the trials and exactions of becoming that Jewish-American writers in our time have excelled in expressing. That the possibility of transforming the self should be an integral, even basic, ingredient of such a literature should not surprise us; Jewishness itself, in all its variousness and possibility, is the great surprise. Jewish writers, in their alarm, their uncertainty, and their Protean changeability, are heralds indeed, bringing the strange news about our strange selves.

MARK SHECHNER

Further Reading

Alter, Robert, *After the Tradition: Essays on Modern Jewish Writing*, New York: Dutton, 1969

Chametzky, Jules, John Felstiner, Hilene Flanzbaum, Kathryn Hellerstein (editors), *Jewish American Literature: A Norton Anthology*, New York and London: W.W. Norton & Company, 2001

Fiedler, Leslie, *To the Gentiles*, New York: Stein and Day, 1972

Finkelstein, Norman, *The Ritual of New Creation: Jewish Tradition and Contemporary Literature*, Albany: State University of New York Press, 1992

Furman, Andrew, *Contemporary Jewish American Writers and the Multicultural Dilemma: The Return of the Exiled*, Syracuse, New York: Syracuse University Press, 2000

Guttmann, Allen, *The Jewish Writer in America: Assimilation and the Crisis of Identity*, New York: Oxford University Press, 1971

Malin, Irving (editor), *Contemporary American-Jewish Literature: Critical Essays*, Bloomington: Indiana University Press, 1973

Shechner, Mark, *After the Revolution: Studies in the Contemporary Jewish-American Imagination*, Bloomington: Indiana University Press, 1987

Shechner, Mark, *The Conversion of the Jews and Other Essays*, London: Macmillan, 1990

British-Jewish Literature

There exists a commonplace perception, despite a good deal of evidence to the contrary, that Jewish writers in Britain do not exist. Such disbelief is shared by a surprisingly disparate group of bedfellows from newspaper reviewers to academic critics. Workaday literary journalists in Britain treat the Jewishness of British-born writers as a form of embarrassment; a guilty secret to be passed over with unseemly haste or to be ignored altogether. Jewish history, after all, is meant to take place on the battlefields of the Middle East, or the capitals of Europe, or the urban centres of America, not in the heartlands of the British bourgeoisie. The English Literature academic establishment, on the other hand, has long since subsumed writers from most of the globe – especially from the United States, Australia, Canada, Ireland, New Zealand, Scotland, and Wales – into the canon of "English" letters. No wonder that Jewish writers have either been smothered under this rubric or, more usually, simply been left out in the cold. Judaic literary scholars also look for their inspiration and their canonical writers in the supposedly more authentic fields of Hebrew and Yiddish literature or, at a stretch, in the American-Jewish Diaspora. From the narrow perspective of ignominious exile and national rebirth, European writers are divided retrospectively into those who published before and after the death camps, with Britain occupying a strangely untouched space on the sidelines.

The perception that Jewish writing in Britain is outlandish at best and an impossibility at worst runs deep and has created an understandable sense of inferiority. Part of the reason for this perceived inferiority is that, around a century ago, British-Jewish literature was, in effect, suffocated at birth. Two outstanding writers, Amy Levy (1861–89) and Isaac Rosenberg (1890–1918), both lived desperately short lives and only in the past few decades has the true promise of their writings begun to be realized. The premature deaths of Levy and Rosenberg continue to cast a shadow over their modern-day compatriots although some, such as Jon Silkin, have courageously tried to write poetry as if Rosenberg, especially, had achieved something like his enormous potential. At the moment, Amy Levy is the subject of innumerable doctoral studies and one recently published biography and it is clear that she, too, is being reinvented for a future generation.

Not that British-Jewish writers haven't, over the years, also engaged in a good deal of self-inflicted mutilation. Brian Glanville, in the late 1950s, wrote *The Bankrupts* (1958) which caused a similar prolonged and hostile communal reaction to that of Philip Roth's collection of stories, *Goodbye, Columbus* (1959). Roth, in his autobiography, describes the "bruising" public reaction to his fiction as constituting "not the end of my imagination's involvement with the Jews, let alone an excommunication, but the real beginning of my thraldom. My humiliation . . . was the luckiest break I could have had. I was branded" (*The Facts: A Novelist's Autobiography*, 1988). Glanville, on the other hand, did end his imaginative involvement with the Jews after the publication of *Diamond* (1962). Although he had defended himself rigorously, even astutely relating *The Bankrupts* to Amy Levy's *Reuben Sachs* (1888), Glanville subsequently became a sports journalist and publishes novels primarily about Italy. Ironically enough, it is Glanville who is often characterized as initiating a "new wave" of British-Jewish literature in the 1960s which included writers such as Frederic Raphael, Gerda Charles, and Alexander Baron. Charles, however, perhaps the most unequivocally Jewish of writers, has not published a novel since *The Destiny Waltz* (1971), and Raphael's fiction seems to be increasingly written with one eye on the screenplay. The best of these writers, Alexander Baron, author of *The Lowlife* (1963), certainly deserves greater attention than he has received in recent years. Bernice Rubens is the great survivor from this "new wave", buoyed up by her Booker prize-winning *The Elected Member* (1969).

If the field of British-Jewish writing is littered with the walking wounded, no wonder it seems hardly to exist at all. The very notion of a discrete "British-Jewish literature" is often vehemently rejected by its authors as the severest form of marginalization. There is clearly something quite profound about English culture, which saps the confidence of its writers who happen also to be Jews. Ever since Israel Zangwill refused to be "shut up in the ghetto", as he put it, Jewish writers in Britain have been made to feel distinctly uncomfortable with their Jewishness. To succeed in the wider culture authors as diverse as Harold Pinter and Anita Brookner have had to write out or write implicitly about their sense of Jewishness. After publishing his collection of stories, *Hearts of Gold* (1979), which won a Somerset Maughan Award, Clive Sinclair was immediately proclaimed – along with Martin Amis and Ian McEwan – as one of a clutch of "new nasties". But whereas Amis and McEwan can accentuate their seriousness by writing about the Holocaust, Sinclair, when he writes about Israel, only reinforces his marginality. When he makes Sweden's August Strindberg the subject of *Augustus Rex* (1992), however, Sinclair is once again lauded as a "universal" writer (largely because Sinclair's Strindberg is a cunningly disguised "Jew"). By definition, when a Jew writes about Jewishness he or she is perceived to be self-serving, parochial and / or hysterical. When a non-Jew writes about Jewishness, on the other hand, they are ambitiously demonstrating their "range" to the world.

All this, needless to say, has nothing to do with Jewishness and everything to do with the Britishness of the wider culture. It is almost as if Jewish writers in Britain have had to fight Britishness throughout their careers and, sometimes, Britishness wins. The walking wounded have lost the fight. Many of the writers who thrive in Britain, such as Dan Jacobson, Gabriel Josipovici, or George Steiner, are not British-born and can therefore stand back from the fray. Of course Steiner's "homeland", as he puts it, is "the text". It could hardly be England. One can chart the career of a writer such as Dan Jacobson from his early South African novels and stories to *The God-Fearer* (1992), whose only real setting is an imaginary homeland. Josipovici, on the other hand, has moved from the cosmopolitan modernism of his early fiction to a more explicitly Judaic understanding of the world. These writers, for obvious reasons, do not have to conform to the dominant precepts of British culture. Others are not so lucky.

What is it about Britishness that is so deforming? For what seems self-evident about British-Jewish writing is the apparent difficulty which it has in absorbing a monolithic Britishness. Whereas American Jews can constantly reinvent themselves using prevalent American mythologies, English national culture is made up of a peculiarly homogenous unchanging idea of the past. British Jews, as Philip Dodd has argued, "were invited to take their place, and become spectators of a culture already complete and represented for them by its trustees". In contrast, the American-Jewish writer is able constantly to re-imagine or re-mythologize their relationship to a European past in a much less harmonious manner. If this "normative" Britishness contrasts starkly with the mobility and Protean nature of American culture, then it also has some distinct attributes. Unlike its American counterpart, the very impossibility of absorbing the Jewish past into a territorial Britishness has forced British-Jewish writers to look elsewhere.

The most interesting British-Jewish writers, it seems to me, have overcome a communal sense of inferiority by transcending their Britishness. This, to some extent, has been enforced. The bombing of the East End of London during World War II has meant that many writers no longer have a concrete sense of place. Emanuel Litvinoff, in his preface to his *Journey through a Small Planet* (1972), makes explicit the extent to which his East End memoir is a selfconscious reconstruction of a place that no longer exists. For this reason, his subsequent trilogy moves from the East End of London to the impact of the Russian Revolution and the horrors of Stalinism. To survive as a writer Litvinoff was forced to write about the world of his fathers. Pinter's determined universalism and modernist deracination, therefore, has a real historical subtext. The publication of his early novel, *The Dwarfs* (1990), makes explicit the importance of the social and cultural milieu of Hackney to Pinter's writing. The novel was written originally between 1952 and 1956, and the intense seriousness of the three gifted Jewish men who feature in it indicates something of the flavour of Pinter's background. European literature and philosophy overwhelms this youthful novel and shows the extent that, from the beginning, Pinter wished to transfigure his parochial Britishness. Arnold Wesker and Bernard Kops have, perhaps, been more deeply wounded than Pinter by the loss of their East End surroundings. The specificities of their background seem, in many ways, to have been the very lifeblood of their most characteristic plays.

Rather than the playwrights, it is the writers of fiction who have had the tools to create and realize alternative homelands in their work. Elaine Feinstein has, I believe, led the way in this regard. During the past two decades Feinstein, for the most part, has centred her tight, poetic novels on a largely imaginary but historically specific central Europe. Paradoxically, when she does write directly about her British antecedents, in *The Survivors* (1982), she is unable to go beyond the restrictions inherent in the conventional family saga novel form. The deceptive looseness of her poetry gives her a good deal more space to examine the particularities of her British-Jewish background. Ironically enough, her early novels were thought of as a species of contemporary "Gothic" – along with fiction by Angela Carter, J.G. Ballard, and Emma Tennant – but she was quick to differentiate herself from this fashionable genre. Feinstein argued that contemporary "Gothic" was a "steely rejection of humanism, a fashionable resistance to compassion which I believe is as much a luxury of our English innocence as the euphoria of the flower generation" (see Conrad, 1982). Her career as a writer has, precisely, gone beyond such "English innocence".

Only when she became the translator of the poetry of Marina Tsvetaeva and, later, of Margarita Aliger, Yunna Moritz, and Bella Akhmadulina, did Feinstein discover her voice as a "European" writer. In this sense, her writing was selfconsciously opposed to another early influential group of Essex University poets (including Lee Harwood and Tom Pickard) who wished to foreground their common "Britishness" and "de-Europeanize" themselves. As a woman writer, Feinstein has situated "magical" father-enchanters at the heart of her fiction. These figures are always thoroughly ambiguous, both breathing "life" into her female protagonists and, at the same time, threatening to make them "dead with dependence". In *The Shadow Master* (1978), the 17th-century Jewish false messiah,

Sabbatai Zevi, is the ultimate historical expression of this double-edged enchantment. By the time of her *The Border* (1984) and *Loving Brecht* (1992), Feinstein was to situate Walter Benjamin and Bertolt Brecht in this "magical" role. If the source of this life-giving "magic" is the "music of words", as suggested in *The Circle* (1970), then male writers are peculiarly uncertain embodiments of this imaginative "refuge" for her female personae.

In *The Border* Walter Benjamin – "a Marxist who is not a materialist" – is a "mystical" synthesizing figure which the novel deliberately fragments. Set in Vienna before the Anschluss, this work is written as a triptych in diary and epistolary form and this allows for three equally passionate accounts of an erotic triangle. Far from a single, male consciousness, the multiple, hallucinatory sense of reality in this novel – which is split along the lines of gender, poetic emotion, and scientific reason – comes into play even when the main characters are faced with the threat of Nazism. The Spanish border at Port Bou in 1940, where Benjamin committed suicide, by the end signifies both his tragically fixed place in history and his internal fissures which are writ large in the novel. This is acknowledged in the form of *The Border*, which reads an arbitrary version of its own story back from a contemporary perspective.

By situating a great many different kinds of texts in a historical novel Feinstein, above all, establishes the possibilities for re-imagining a European past in terms of limitless "magical" word-play as well as acknowledging the insurmountable "borders" of history. But this is not, as Mark Shechner has argued, merely a "journey of self-integration" into the European past for the Jewish novelist. On the contrary, it is the lack of a sense of "integration" into an historical other-world that many British-Jewish writers highlight in their fiction. Clive Sinclair, in particular, is important in this regard. From his earliest collections of short stories, *Hearts of Gold* (1979) and *Bedbugs* (1982), Sinclair has attempted to "write fiction that owes nothing to any English antecedents" and has, therefore, selfconsciously located his "national" history as a Jew in Israel, America, and Eastern Europe (see Cheyette, 1984). At the same time, Sinclair's fiction is playfully aware of the dangers of solipsism in this displacement of an "English" identity onto a Judaized "imaginary homeland". "Ashkenazia", collected in *Bedbugs*, is both a fictitious Yiddish-speaking country situated somewhere in central Europe and, also, the sum of Sinclair's writer-narrator:

> Many of my fellow-countrymen do not believe in the existence of God. I am more modest. I do not believe in myself. What proof can I have when no one reads what I write? There you have it; my words are the limit of my world. You will therefore smile at this irony; I have been commissioned by our government to write the official English-language *Guide to Ashkenazia*.

By the end of this story, all that remains of "Ashkenazia" is a "field of wooden skeletons" and Sinclair's deranged persona truly becomes bounded by his words, "Now the world will listen to me, for I am the guide to Ashkenazia. I am Ashkenazia." This conflation of selfhood with nationhood is, on one level, the necessary solipsistic response of an author who displaces an historical narrative onto what Philip Roth has called a "useful fiction". For the post-Holocaust writer, however, an "imaginary homeland" cannot merely be constituted by words alone as Europe is littered with "fields of wooden skeletons". A purely textual "Ashkenazia" is an act of writerly megalomania precisely because Sinclair's narrator thinks that he can bring these "skeletons" to life. This simultaneous need to imagine more interesting homelands, which can never be fully possessed by the writer, is the subject of Sinclair's early fiction.

"The Promised Land", for instance, is a story told by a fool – or "shlemiel" – who wishes to possess Hannah Ratskin, who lives in Tel Aviv. Considered an "irrelevance" by Hannah who loves a handsome Israeli warrior, Ami Ben Tur, the "schlemiel" of the story is in a state of unrequited love that also defines his diasporic relationship with the actual "promised land" of Israel. The opening line of the story is (*pace* Melville) "Call me Schlemiel" and Sinclair's narrator later expands, lewdly, on this reference to *Moby-Dick*. A non-Hebrew-speaking Jew in Israel is, according to this story, the ultimate outsider, "I am Jewish but my tongue is not circumcised." Unlike the writer-narrator in "Ashkenazia", who deludes himself into making a "homeland" out of language, Sinclair's "schlemiel" turns into a Nazi-rapist by thinking that his sense of displacement can have an all too literal biological solution.

In his *Diaspora Blues: A View of Israel* (1987), Sinclair defines himself as having a "dual loyalty" to "the language of England and the history of Israel" and argues that, for a writer, there is "something to be gained from having a language but no history, a history but no language". Unlike his relation to England, his interest in Israel has provided him with a "narrative" in which to situate himself. His first two novels, *Blood Libels* (1985) and *Cosmetic Effects* (1989), take to its logical conclusion the reproductive union, in his stories, of selfhood with nationhood. Both novels, that is, are personal histories that have national consequences. As in one of Sinclair's later stories, "Kayn Aynhoreh", hypochondria is the natural condition of those who place the imagination at the centre of nationhood.

With the publication of *Cosmetic Effects*, the centrality of the imagination in the creation of historical and political "facts" becomes the novel's subject. This can be seen especially in the involvement of Sinclair's protagonist, Jonah Isaacson – a teacher of Film Studies at the University of St Albans – with the making of a biblical Western in Israel called *The Six Pointed Star*. The producer of this film, Lewis Falcon (based on John Ford), is quite explicit about the fictionality of his "America":

> Every people has its story . . . which is not the same as its history. It is this story that roots them on the land, that sustains their sense of identity. It may not be the truth, but it is believed. I have lived all my life in the twentieth century, I am not ignorant of the importance of truth, but I am an artist and my first responsibility is to the story – the story of the American people.

Sinclair's own short story called "America" anticipated

Falcon by showing that the idea of America, based on a series of puns and word-plays, is always liable to reinterpretation. The depiction in *Cosmetic Effects* of "America", as being not only a nation-state but a "state of mind", interestingly reverses Philip Roth's well-known account of the difficulties of writing American fiction. For Roth, "the American writer in the middle of the twentieth century has his hands full in trying to understand, describe and then make *credible* much of American reality. It stupefies, it sickens, it infuriates, and finally it is even a kind of embarrassment to one's meagre imagination" (Roth, 1985). For Sinclair, the issue is not whether he can "make credible" the world that surrounds him, but whether he can make it *incredible*.

Whereas Feinstein and Sinclair have led the way in transcending and transfiguring their Britishness, Howard Jacobson, from a different perspective, has decided to face head on the thorny question of Britishness in his fiction. His *Coming from Behind* (1983) and *Peeping Tom* (1984) both directly confront a definition of Jewishness based on an excessive regard for the Britishness of others. For this reason they are not, strictly, "Jewish" novels but, more accurately, they are anti-Gentile novels. That is Jacobson's protagonists define themselves throughout as the opposite to the English gentility (in both senses of the word). Sefton Goldberg in *Coming from Behind*, Jacobson's campus novel, is Jewish because he hates *goyische* soccer; the English countryside; small towns and midland polytechnics; British rail; students; Cambridge; women; homosexuals; you name it. He is not Jewish because he attends a synagogue.

In *Peeping Tom* Jacobson cleverly turns this negative definition of Jewishness into the subject of his novel. Barney Fugelman discovers that he needs Thomas Hardy's "goyische greenery" to exist. The Victorian rural novelist, Hardy, is Barney's polar opposite in the novel: "Pity the poor Jew. Let him gentrify and ruralize himself all he likes . . . he will never know what it is to take a turn around the garden." But Barney also *is* Hardy (or, at least, his reincarnation). He becomes Hardy because he is part of a "culture" that he feels isn't really his own. In other words, Jacobson's fictional protagonists define themselves negatively in terms of their supposed Gentile "others".

Fugelman is someone steeped in a culture from which he also feels alienated. Jacobson's skill is to concentrate on Fugelman's realization that he is nothing without Hardy's alien rural community. *Peeping Tom* is, above all, a study in cultural masochism. What Jacobson highlights is the extent to which Jews, who had come to love English culture, were caught in a double bind. He argues that Jews can participate in this culture – through the English language – but that they have a precarious foot-hold in it. This is a particularly painful contradiction for Jacobson, as he thinks of himself as a Leavisite who is meant to be one of the custodians of culture. But, as a "Jew", he can always be expelled from that which he loves. Only with *The Very Model of a Man* (1992), a rewriting of the story of Cain and Abel, and *Roots Schmoots: Journeys among Jews* (1993), does Jacobson, finally, fill the vacuum of his protagonists' aggressively empty selves.

It takes a writer like Jacobson, rather like a prize-fighter, to take Britishness on at its own game. As a Leavisite he can out-culture the English and add the Bible, in *The Very Model of a Man*, to a spurious Great Tradition of British-Jewish literature. His novel, *The Mighty Walzer* (1999), rewrites Charles Dickens using material from his Manchester-Jewish childhood. Other writers are more crafty. Jonathan Wilson's collection of stories, *Schoom* (1993), for instance, is set in London, Jerusalem, and Boston, and makes no pretence at being at home in any one of these cities. A typical story, "From Shanghai", is about an obsessive Uncle, who emigrates from Shanghai to Britain in the 1950s, and turns out to have lost his wife and child in World War II. The transformation of the Uncle's collection of Hans Andersen into a shrine for his family is poignantly recounted. Many of Wilson's characters similarly traverse a number of differing cultures and continents and are no longer bounded by the Britishness of their parents. His more recent novel *The Hiding Room* (1995) is set in pre-war Palestine and reimagines Britishness from an early Zionist perspective. As with British literature in general, both Jacobson and Wilson use their Jewishness to extend the range of the novel in English well beyond its more parochial concerns. The fact that so many contemporary Jewish writers seem to be no longer restricted by a disabling Britishness makes, one can only hope, for less sense of inferiority in the future.

BRYAN H. CHEYETTE

Further Reading

Dodd, Philip, "Englishness and the National Culture" in *Englishness and Culture 1880–1920*, edited by Robert Colls and Philip Dodd, London: Croom Helm, 1986

Cheyette, Bryan, " 'On the Edge of the Imagination': Clive Sinclair Interviewed by Bryan Cheyette", *Jewish Quarterly*, 31/3–4 (1984): 26–29

Conradi, Peter, "Elaine Feinstein: Life and Novels", *Literary Review* (April 1982)

Roth, Philip, "Writing American Fiction" in his *Reading Myself and Others*, revised edition, New York and London: Penguin, 1985

Shechner, Mark, *The Conversion of the Jews and Other Essays*, London: Macmillan, and New York: St Martin's Press, 1990

Hebrew Literature in the 20th Century

The situation of Hebrew literature at the beginning of the modern era was problematic for a number of reasons. The range had been limited, both in subject matter and in means of expression. Although in many and various centres, in medieval times, the literature was extensive, from the time of the Renaissance onwards the focus had narrowed and the output was principally legal, liturgical, and ethical. Earlier traditions of storytelling, secular poetry, philosophy, and science had been largely left to other languages. The language of Hebrew expression, too, had suffered from a lack of vernacular usage or, in strictly literary terms, from the close adhesion to the classical models. The Enlightenment movement of the 18th century, originating in Germany, and then shifting to central and, later, to eastern Europe, adopted European models of secular poetic expression, but strictly adhered to a biblical lexicon in its reaching out to a revival of the classical. No fiction was admitted at this stage, and a very high-minded but artificial language was taken up. There were very few readers for this material, even after periodical literature was introduced in the 1780s. The east European writers from the middle of the 19th century could broaden the range. They, after all, had wider range of readers, as they operated within a Jewish society, the Pale of Settlement. It was at this time that novel writing was introduced, first in the form of satire and the epistolary novels of Joseph Perl and Isaac Erter, and then with the romantic writing of Avraham Mapu. Gradually a notion of imitation of reality was coming to the fore.

However, it was really only in the 1880s that Hebrew began to shift into a sort of recognizable modern expression. Significantly, the rise of modern Hebrew literature almost exactly parallels that of Yiddish. Most of the practitioners were bilingual. Hebrew was the ideal, the historical precedent for the classical. But Yiddish was the lingua franca, and reached out to the mass of readers. It was only when writers began to import the flexibility of code from Yiddish into Hebrew, thus introducing adaptability and range into the lexicon that Hebrew could accommodate, that an interesting and readable text became possible – what the great poet H.N. Bialik labelled the "nusah", i.e. the accepted, textual model. The modern literature marked the entry of Jewish writers into the world around them, importing the rhythms of natural speech, the representation of society, and the confrontation with the world. If it was executed in Yiddish, it could be imported into Hebrew, the language generally of first choice, although deeply problematic. But Hebrew had to be written as though it were Yiddish, alive as a language of total register, broad in range. For this, the restriction of deploying biblical layers only was abandoned for an all-encompassing Hebrew of all periods, including the related language, the popularly used Aramaic, and calquing Yiddish expressions, many of which had originally derived from Hebrew anyway. Such a writer as Mendele Moykher Sforim (1836–1917) moved from the Hebrew writing of the Enlightenment to the creation of the classical Yiddish tale, satirical, humorous, and structured, to an imitation of that new model in Hebrew. This then became the standard for the Hebrew fiction of subsequent generations.

As in most literatures, Hebrew poetry preceded prose. Indeed, there has never been a period, and scarcely a significant Jewish centre, when and where Hebrew poetry was not composed. There is the great biblical tradition, where parallelism is the structural key and mark of recognition. Then came Midrashic piyut (religious, liturgical poetry) and alphabetic acrostic. Classical Arabic prosody was taken as the model in Spain and the successor Sephardi tradition in medieval times reached even into the modern period, and there were alternative models in the Ashkenazi traditions. And then with the *Haskalah* (the Hebrew Enlightenment), classical European poetry, especially German, was adopted as the model for imitation. In the new schools however, the environment was Slavic.

Initially the principal Hebrew poets imitated the great poets in Russian and Polish. But soon they began to break away. The greatest of all, H.N. Bialik (1873–1934), produced a form of free verse from the 1890s onwards. As with the new Hebrew fiction, the Hebrew poets were bilingual, and were very familiar with the literary environment of the times. Bialik combined an intimate association with all strands of the Hebrew tradition with a personalized, post-Romantic, even "decadent" slant. His predominant line was affirmative and nationalist, asserting the Jewish tradition as well as the new Zionism. But he was also individualistic, despairing, and nihilistic. He seemed both to praise the old tradition, but also to mourn its passing. He also saw himself in all his own limitations as representative of what was now dead. Saul Tchernichovski (1875–1943) seemed more obviously rebellious, technically innovative, and widely educated in various literatures, as well as heretical and challenging. The way was open for new voices in Hebrew poetry, and these came in the form of new rhythms, linguistic invention, personal statement, and, later, a renewed confrontation with the ancient and now revived Land of Israel.

Whereas such writers as Mendele had been innovative linguistically and formally, as well as thematically and structurally, they had still, in the main, remained voices of the Jewish collective. Most of the prominent writers, Yiddish and Hebrew, had related themselves to the wider social and historical situation of Jews around the world. Even when their major thrust can be seen now as individual, they were often understood as representative voices, as we can see in the case of Bialik, who was hailed as the "national poet".

Yet the fictional successors of Mendele were sometimes very different in tone from their mentor. Although Y.H. Brenner (1881–1921), for example, lauded Mendele to the skies, and described him as a forerunner of the New and as the first real Modern Hebrew writer, his own writing is frankly personalised, highly individualistic and introverted. It is with Brenner and many others, such as U.N. Gnessin (1879–1913) and M.Y. Berdyczewski (1865–1921), that Hebrew fiction really came into its own as the repository of great psychological fiction. The central characters are no longer stereotypes or social delegates, but created individuals. In order to set this new man/woman on the Hebrew stage, Hebrew fiction leapt into the forefront of the world vanguard. Stream-of-consciousness technique was taken up by writers such as Brenner, and even more by Gnessin, as early as in any other world literature. The narrative voice was not necessarily Jewish in any but an incidental sense. And the central concerns of the fictional characters, as well as those of the narrator, were existential and personal. A new sort of literary language had to be found, albeit a Hebrew one, and albeit one that recognized the contemporary reality, which took in the tragic situation of the Jews. The Jew was indeed marginalized, even within the context of European civilization. He had to find another mode of expression that might take him into an alternative sphere of influence; into, for example, the Hebrew society that was arising from a new Jewish presence within the Palestine of the decaying Ottoman Empire, soon to be subsumed under the British Mandate.

This was the transitional phase for Hebrew literature, in terms of location and attitude. The foundations had been laid. The language and the forms had been created. Modernism had been invented and absorbed. And yet there were problems everywhere. Where were the Jews to be? Where did they belong, and how were the authors to write? The emergent generation of writers were spanning the worlds of the decaying Diaspora and the nascent Israel. In the Diaspora, the shtetl was witnessing its death throes, through compulsion in the Soviet Union, through exclusivist nationalism, as in Poland, through assimilation emigration and change of identity everywhere. On the other hand, there was the emergent but uncrystallized cohesion discernible in the Land of Israel. This was not yet an independent state, and the character of this entity was unformed, many branched, slightly chaotic and uncertain. The principal writers of this phase were to reflect some of these difficulties and moods. S.Y. Agnon (1888–1970) and Hayim Hazaz (1898–1973) were two of the leading prose writers who bestrode the two worlds, bringing something of each to the other. They were both innovators, formally and linguistically, and in their novels, stories, novellas, and fables they imported a consciousness of the Jewish past into the shaping of a new nation. Their language had a foothold in the past while embracing and helping to create a potential and emergent national entity.

Hebrew literature, just like any other minority literature, did not exist in a vacuum. It was constantly buffeted by the major currents in a sea of world events – social, political, historical, and cultural. There had never been as massive a social transformation as that which was created by World War I. The scale of destruction was enormous, as well as the concomitant dislocation, alteration of frontiers, fall of empires, and shift of peoples. This applied to the Jews too, to the Jews indeed even more so, as they were so widespread. Their literature necessarily reflected all this, and especially Hebrew literature had a social, as well as a historical and cultural, role to play.

Because of the destruction and dislocation of the Jewish communities in eastern Europe, the mass migration westwards, and the resultant tendencies of cultural assimilation, the only saving remnant of Hebrew creativity was confined to Palestine. Here the Balfour Declaration and the responsible mandated power held out the hope of the creation of a Hebrew society and thus of a Hebrew literature that would arise on its own territory. This literature would be established on earlier foundations of course, but it would also mark out new paths. And indeed, within the decade of the 1920s, there was an enormous movement of Hebrew creativity from Europe to Palestine. Most of the journals relocated to Palestine/Israel, and some of the greatest of the Hebrew writers finally moved to the land that had been the material of aspiration and dreams from afar for so long.

For this greatest of all revolutionary situations an equally revolutionary form of expression seemed appropriate. A new land, a new language (as far as Hebrew was now spoken and adopted for the first time in 2000 years as a language of total register), and a new society had emerged. This situation demanded revised approaches, and fresh literary tools too, if it was not to be condemned as irrelevant and footling. Thus a transformed Hebrew literature was born. This literature, especially the poetry, came to be known as Expressionist, in the wake of the German poetry of the early part of the century. Such poetry was particularly taken up by U.Z. Greenberg (1896–1981) in his postwar phase both in Yiddish and Hebrew, but also by Avraham Shlonsky (1900–73) and Yitzhak Lamdan (1900–55), who sought an equivalent in verse for the violence of the events and moods they were recording. This verse sang not of green pastures and fine landscapes, but of death, war and machinery, mass production, and the modern environment. This was territory that had been marked out in Yiddish too by Yiddish poets such as Perets Markish (1895–1952) and Melech Ravitch (1893–1976) in their Warsaw phase in the 1920s. It was a tendency that had been specifically associated with German literature, as well as German painting.

These were writers with a European background. But the generation was also notable for being the first that was writing the language of exclusive nationhood. Hebrew had come into its own as a national language, and could thus become richer, more expressive, more rooted, and more natural, unimpeded (in theory) by the interference of clusters of foreign elements. The new Palestinian authors could take special delight in renewed contact with the earth. A full range of linguistic virtuosity was created by the prose writer S. Yizhar (1916–), the most linguistically inventive of Israeli fiction writers, revelling in the conjuring up of the landscape, as well as in rhetorical analyses of uncertain states of mind, through a rediscovered internal monologue technique.

Although political events do not necessarily coincide with literary watersheds, we do have to note the change of perception moving into the literature of the post-1948 generation, i.e. those literary generations that flourished within the independent state of Israel. Within Israel's early birth pains, the notion of statehood was naturally the prime point of reference for fiction and poetry. The most notable writers of this phase are known as the "sabra" (native-born Israeli) or the "Palmach" (Israeli defence units) writers. Their subject matter is predominantly the new Israel, the war situation, the new immigrants, the new borders, institutions such as kibbutz and *histadrut* (Israeli trade union organization), and the Hebrew language and emergent culture. Moshe Shamir (1921–) was an eminent representative of this trend, in the journals that he established and in the novels that he composed. Foremost among the novelists of the genre, he also created what became known as the sabra hero, the man (always a male) without roots outside the Land, without too much diasporic conflict, without the heavy load of Jewish historical consciousness, strong, decisive, and limited in horizons. Shamir, Yizhar, and poets such as Haim Guri (1923–) set down markers for a Hebrew literature of the state of Israel. But more introspective poets too, such as Yehuda Amichai (1924–2000) and Nathan Zach (1930–), also wrote a new sort of Hebrew poetry, one that was idiomatic and colloquial, and freed themselves from the Europeanized conventions of such notable poets as Natan Alterman (1910–70) and Shlonsky by attempting to represent a specifically young Israeli situation. This situation was dislocated from origin and family (Amichai) and from society (Zach, confronting the individual in himself). Despite the fact that the sabra writing constituted a new and specifically Israeli voice in the history of Hebrew literature, and that it seemed to spring from the collective need and call to action of the Israeli writer, it did not take long for a new perception of its function to arise. There were other voices who thought of the sabra style as restrictive and its range limited. Even the selfsame writers who had been associated with this general tendency later seemed to want to move off in a different direction. Shamir's novels of the 1960s found sabra heroes expressing dissatisfaction with the constraints imposed upon them. Aharon Megged (1920–) and Benjamin Tammuz (1919–89) created fictional characters who sought out places beyond the frontiers of the new state, frontiers not exclusively geographical, but also spiritual. We must of course be careful not to confuse the narrator with the author, and thus to assume that the voice of a fictionally represented character is that of the writer behind the page. Yet, nevertheless, this substitution does sometimes inevitably take place. What was also introduced into the Hebrew prose of the late 1950s and 1960s was a confessional note, where autobiography is represented as fiction. This is particularly so in the writing of Pinhas Sadeh (1929–1994), in which the first-person narrator expresses explicit dissatisfaction with the prevalent mode of Israeli discourse, and seeks pastures beyond the immediate radius of apparently current concerns. His own concern is with issues that pertain to all mankind, questions of good and evil, confrontation with God and the ultimate, and is accompanied by supreme indifference towards transient matters, such as national boundaries, issues of sovereignty, and all things parochial.

This tendency was taken up by the notable fiction writers of the new wave, such as A.B. Yehoshua (1936–) and Amos Oz (1939–), whose writing moved from short stories or novellas to novels, and whose concerns relate both specifically to Israel as well as to humanity and the human condition beyond. Both writers have experimented with form and content, constantly employing different techniques of fictional representation in order to capture a polyvocal re-creation of situations local and present, as well as foreign and past.

But there are other voices too, some that have been less prevalent in the brief history of Modern Hebrew literature: Oriental voices, Arab voices, and the voices of women. A. Shammas (1950–) has written a major novel in Hebrew, very much from an Arab point of view. Amalia Kahana-Carmon (1930–) was a forerunner to a specifically feminine form of writing from the 1960s. Now the female element in current Hebrew fiction is dominant. Such writers as Orly Castel-Bloom (1960–), Yehudit Katzir (1963–), and Savyon Liebrecht (1948–) have introduced alternative concerns into Hebrew fiction. Poets like Dalia Ravikovitch (1936–) and Yona Wallach (1944–85) have written poetry of a perception and highly tuned feeling that is specifically and engagingly feminine. The overall picture of current Hebrew literature has been transformed.

The range of Hebrew literature emerging at the outset of the 21st century is very varied. Fashions have been superseded within much less than the normal generational span, so that we have several generations and modes operating within the same market simultaneously. Yizhar has recently been producing a succession of new works, echoing the past in the present day. At the same time, experiments are being conducted indicating dissatisfaction with current techniques of representation, and seeking new means in the setting out of the fictional material. Yoel Hoffman (1937–) and Yuval Shimoni (1955–), among others, have been experimenting with variations of format, as well as with different types of narrative style – intermingling layers of reportage, flashbacks, direct speech, graphic design, representations of silence, and solicited reader response – both to attract attention, and to produce effects of difference. There has also been a revival in Hebrew drama, coincident with the crystallization of levels of Israeli argot, although the death in 1999 of the greatest of Israeli dramatists, Hanoch Levin (1943–99) was a major loss to creative theatre. Israeli literature rejoices at least in a multiplicity of styles, forms, and structures, the classical jostling with the postmodern, and the traditional with the experimental. No single mode remains unquestionably pre-eminent.

LEON I. YUDKIN

Further Reading

Alter, Robert, *Defenses of the Imagination*, Philadelphia: Jewish Publication Society of America, 1977

Mintz, Alan (editor), *The Boom in Contemporary Israeli Fiction*, Hanover and London: Brandeis University Press, 1997

Yudkin, Leon, *1948 and After: Aspects of Israeli Fiction*, Journal of Semitic Studies: Manchester, 1984

Yudkin, Leon, *Beyond Sequence: Current Israeli Fiction and its Context*, London: Symposium Press, 1992

Yudkin, Leon, *A Home Within: Varieties of Jewish Expression in Modern Fiction*, London: Symposium Press, 1996

Yudkin, Leon, *Public Crisis and Literary Response: The Adjustment of Modern Jewish Literature*. Paris: Éditions Suger, 2001

Holocaust Writing

This literary category is unusual in having a historical subject as its uniting focus, and it encompasses a variety of genres that are usually seen as not only distinct but mutually exclusive: history and poetry, testimony and fiction. These boundaries are shown to be porous under pressure from the subject itself. Work written during the Holocaust years by Jewish writers is often read as authentic documentation due to temporal proximity and lack of retrospection. Such work most obviously includes diaries, but there are also letters (Etty Hillesum's *Letters from Westerbork* (1986) written by an assimilated young Dutchwoman from the transit camp near Amsterdam), poems (Miklós Radnóti's were found with his dead body in a mass grave, in the pockets of his coat), and testimonies (collections were made of accounts by, for instance, the "Teheran Children", who arrived in Palestine in 1943 after years spent first under the Nazis and then the Soviets). Published Holocaust diaries are largely by writers who did not survive the war, but who felt impelled, either collectively or individually, to record the destruction of their communities and the deformation of their lives. Such works range from the publicly-focused *The Warsaw Diary of Adam Czerniakow: Prelude to Doom* (1979) kept by the chairman of the Warsaw Ghetto Judenrat who committed suicide in 1942; to the lengthy *Chronicle of the Łódź Ghetto, 1941–1944* (1984, edited by Lucjan Dobroszycki) which was commissioned by the ghetto chairman, Chaim Rumkowski, and consists of accounts of daily life written by several ghetto inmates.

These works are less well-known than the diaries of individuals. Even Chaim Kaplan's *Scroll of Agony* (1965), a diary of the Warsaw Ghetto from 1939 until Kaplan's deportation in 1942, has a strong sense of a particular viewpoint and individual tone despite Kaplan's stated aim to write impersonally. Kaplan's uncannily accurate predictions of the fate of Poland's Jews make his diary especially striking; as early as September 1939 he notes down Hitler's stated vow to "exterminate" the Jewish people. The picture of Kaplan constructed by the reader of his diary is somewhat contradictory. He is a religious man, the founder of a yeshiva, whose biblical knowledge informs his writing, yet his approach is modern and secular, particularly in his analysis of the Nazis' ideological motivation. Kaplan is also an *Ostjude*, born in White Russia, yet one who admits his own suspicion of Polish Jews. Despite these intriguing ambiguities and its individual narration, Kaplan's diary remains little known because of his religious bent and documentary view of life in a Polish ghetto. Anne Frank, by contrast, was an assimilated German-born teenager living in Amsterdam. Although totally determined by the events of the Holocaust, her situation – two years spent hiding in an attic with only the radio and glances out of the window to link her to the outside – means that her *Diary of a Young Girl* (1952; reissued in a critical edition 1989) focuses on her inner life and familial relations. Similarly, the recently published *The Diaries of Victor Klemperer, I Shall Bear Witness: 1933–41* (1998) are more likely to appeal to the general Western reader – whether Jewish or not. These diaries recount years spent in hiding by a cultured, assimilated Berliner who was married to a Gentile woman and was related to the musical Klemperer family. Although Victor Klemperer's diaries are also unique documents – no other diaries written by Jews living in Nazi Germany have survived – they issue from a mainstream cultural tradition, unlike either Avraham Tory's *Surviving the Holocaust: The Kovno Ghetto Diary* (1990) or the Dutch Moshe Flinker's *Young Moshe's Diary: The Spiritual Torment of a Jewish Boy in Nazi Europe* (1965). Critics have argued that the respective background and assumptions of Anne Frank and the Orthodox, God-fearing Moshe Flinker lead to their viewing the same events quite differently, which disrupts any idea of individual diaries offering straightforward historical documentation.

Holocaust testimony and memoir are more obviously literary in language and construction. As they are retrospective, there is a bigger distance than in a chronicle or diary between the narrator and the protagonist. For instance, Elie Wiesel's distance from the events described in his testimony *Night* (1960) is signalled by the author's adoption of a French version of the character's Hebrew name, Eliezer; while Primo Levi in his memoir *If This is a Man* (1959) finds the gap between life in the Lager and that as a free man so great that he remarks that as he sits at his desk he can hardly believe what he is describing. The distinction made here between testimony and memoir is to some extent artificial, but rests on the difference between a stark deposition and a more meditative account.

Wiesel has claimed that the Holocaust testimony is the literary genre bequeathed to the reading world by survivors; while of course the notion of authentic testimony – the author can be identified with the protagonist – predates World War II, Wiesel is right to emphasize the survivor's impetus to narrate. The very term "testimony" suggests a sworn legal statement, a presentation of evidence before a court. Levi likewise records nightmares he had in the Lager that no one would believe the story he had to tell, and his chillingly ironized version of the Shema which acts as an epigraph to *If This is a Man* makes listening as much of an obligation as telling:

> Consider that this has been:
> I commend these words to you.
> Engrave them on your hearts
> When you are in your house, when you walk on your way
> When you go to bed, when you rise.
> Repeat them to your children.
> Or may your house crumble,
> Disease render you powerless,
> Your offspring avert their faces from you.

Levi's invocation of this central daily prayer is striking given his non-religious viewpoint: he was arrested as a resistance fighter, and his cultural codes are scientific (he was a chemist) and literary (he struggles to remember Dante in Auschwitz). The prayer is directed at the human reader rather than at an absent God; the first person commandment issues in Levi's version from the survivor and not from God, as it does in the prayer. This is the original on which Levi bases his secularized version:

> These words that I
> command you today shall be upon
> your heart. Repeat them to your
> children, and talk about them when
> you sit in your home, and when you
> lie down, and when you rise up.
> Hold fast to them as a sign upon
> your hand, and let them be as
> reminders before your eyes. Write

> them upon the doorposts of your
> home and at your gates.

Levi's method is rather different from Wiesel's use of the same device of the reversed prayer in *Night*. As well as the curse he delivers – "Never shall I forget that night, the first night in camp, which has turned my life into one long night, seven times cursed and seven times sealed" – and an ironized blessing for mud, Wiesel offers a death-camp version of the Aleinu. Instead of the usual sabbath prayer, which runs:

> It is our duty to praise the Lord of all,
> to recognize the greatness of the creator of first things,
> who has chosen us from all peoples by giving us his Torah

we read:

> How could I say to him, "Blessed art Thou, Eternal, Master of the Universe, Who chose us from among the races to be tortured day and night, to see our fathers, our mothers, our brothers, end in the crematory? Praised by Thy Holy Name, Thou Who hast chosen us to be butchered on thine altar?

It is a common trope in Holocaust writing to transform chosenness by God into scenes of being chosen by the Nazis, either on the ramp at Auschwitz or during later selections for the gas chambers. Interestingly in *Night* this palpable fury at God does not end in repudiation, and the book charts a dialogue between the boy Eliezer and the God he had previously worshipped without question. It is almost as if *Night* acts as a version – again ironized – of a Talmudic puzzle set in the "orchard" mentioned at the beginning of the text; yet the end appears to record the death of the text's protagonist, who looks into a mirror and sees there the face of a corpse, although its narrator survives. The balance here between brutally secular and apparently irrelevant religious discourses is unusual and significant.

Holocaust fiction by survivors might be described as the next most authentic category, although once more it complicates the apparently simple opposition between authentic fact and false fiction. This is even true of a case such as Jerzy Kosinski's novel *The Painted Bird*, published in 1965 at a time when readers and critics were not always happy to separate survivor biography and survivor fiction. Kosinski never claimed that *The Painted Bird* was anything other than a novel, and its brutal version of magic realism set during the Holocaust years bears this designation out. However, although he had survived the war in hiding in occupied Poland, Kosinski embellished his own account of what had happened to him to fit with the experiences of the nameless boy in his novel, who is separated from his parents and undergoes terrible cruelty at the hands of local peasantry in an unnamed east European country. It is easy now to dismiss Kosinski's self-mythifications as extra-textual and irrelevant, but Kosinski's great fictional success was reduced to the scandal of a false autobiography through particular reader expectations.

Thirty years later, readers are accustomed to more sophisticated generic distinctions where Holocaust writing is concerned, for instance in relation to Ida Fink's collections of short stories *A Scrap of Time and Other Stories* (1987) and *Traces* (1997), and her novel *The Journey* (1992). Although the author biography given on all three texts does link Fink to the events she describes – she was born in Poland in 1921, spent the war in hiding, and then left for Israel in 1957 – it is never clear, as with Kosinski, just what the link is between her experiences and the stories she relates. Moreover, Fink's texts are published as fiction. It seems that such a categorization frees up Fink to represent a variety of viewpoints, rather than limiting her to the first person and to her own life – even if we read the first-person novel *The Journey* as autobiographical fiction. Fiction also allows Fink to experiment with form and style. For instance, in *A Scrap of Time and Other Stories* the text is constructed out of "scraps" of memory and hearsay. Some stories are in the first person, but might be from the point of view of a male narrator or older woman who cannot be identified with the author. The scraps try through their fragmentariness to represent the unrepresentable: no overview, complete tales or explanations are offered, and progression through the war is shared out among different characters. Many stories end either in the middle of events or just before the moment of death. In the story "Night of Surrender", for example, it is not a personal surrender but the end of the war that is recounted. The same scenarios are replayed throughout the collection: many feature a person who allows a mother or child to be taken to death alone, a child or dog who does not betray, a person in hiding who sees "scraps" of the whole, a person after the war who tries to tell what has happened. *A Scrap of Time* is not autobiography but rather the biography of a community, and this can best be accomplished fictively.

The role of fiction in writing by Holocaust survivors is varied. In Louis Begley's *Wartime Lies* (1991), for instance, the tale of a young boy, Maciek, in hiding in Aryan Warsaw during the war, must be told in the form of a novel to convey the toll taken on Maciek's ability to distinguish fact from fiction. Maciek's Gentile persona becomes indistinguishable from his original subjectivity, suggesting a complex and indirect link for Begley – also a survivor – and this text. Aharon Appelfeld's Holocaust novels are also the work of a survivor, who as a child hid in the woods of Ukraine during the war and then moved to Israel; but his writings bear little relation to the precise details of his biography. Although Appelfeld's novels are historically specific, they are not always historically accurate representations of Jews in Europe on the brink of catastrophe. Rather, they work by associative, imagistic logic and require the reader to fill in the gaps. His novels – such as *Badenheim 1939* (1980) and *To the Land of the Cattails* (1986; as *To the Land of the Reeds*, 1994) – are troubling allegories of the Holocaust. The self-concerned Jews of *Badenheim 1939* are on holiday in an Austrian resort, and ignore warning signs such as posters advertising work in Poland, the appearance of government health officials, and the gradual encircling of the resort with barbed wire. Finally these people allow themselves to be herded onto a train headed east. One character ominously sees the filthy state of the goods vehicles which make up their train as a good sign, meaning they cannot be going far: but of course the reader knows better. Similarly, *To the Land of the Cattails* ends at the moment when the characters get onto a train; for Appelfeld, genocidal violence itself is outside the frame of representation and can only be implied, not shown.

Although he is a poet, Paul Celan's writings are perhaps most similar to those of survivor novelists in offering not the authenticity of testimony, although Celan too is a survivor, but a rhetorically constructed sincerity. Celan's work flies in the face of Theodor Adorno's dictum that lyric poetry after Auschwitz is impossible. His best-known poem is "Death-Fugue", written originally in German, like all his work: German was Celan's mother-tongue, but also that of his mother's murderers, a paradox that is a source of both anxiety and strength in his work.

Celan's style is condensed, repetitive and allusive, drawing on historical and literary antecedents as well as his own wordplay. This obviously makes its translation into English difficult, but the poet Michael Hamburger has made prize-winning efforts to do so (*Poems of Paul Celan*, 1995). "Death Fugue" juxtaposes Germany's dual heritage: the "golden hair" of Goethe's Margarete and the "ashen hair" of a Jewish Shulamith. The poem recounts a nightmarish vision in which a man writes and "plays with serpents" while around him "his Jews" must "dig for a grave". The poem's anguished persona insistently enacts a double "compulsive repetition" (a phrase from Celan's poem "... And No Kind Of"): "death is a master from Germany", and "Black milk of daybreak we drink you at night", placing its action in a ghostly death-camp where sustenance is poison and time is out of joint. Celan's poem "Psalm" offers another image for the unspeakable in addressing the God who has reversed his creation of humanity out of dust:

A nothing
were we, are we, will
we remain, blooming:
No-one's-rose.

Although it seems in this poem that only the victims themselves can speak "the purple word" with their own blood, as "no-one" else is there to remember them, the first-person plural of this poem and "Death Fugue" suggests that Celan is their witness too.

At a further temporal remove from the events themselves are writings by second-generation survivors. Such work is extremely varied, and includes Art Spiegelman's cartoon testimony *Maus* (1986 and 1991) as well as novels by the Israeli novelist David Grossman (*See Under – Love*, 1989) and the Canadian Anne Michaels (*Fugitive Pieces*, 1997). *Maus* is a 2-volume cartoon history of Spiegelman's parents' experiences during the war, told by Vladek Spiegelman – the father – to his son Art, who narrates the story both as a character within the tale and by recasting the Holocaust story into animal form. The ingeniously simple device of representing Jews as mice, Germans as cats, Poles as pigs, and Americans as dogs (other small parts are taken by British fish, gypsy butterflies, and French frogs) both satirizes and reproduces the Nazis' racialized categories. *Maus* is autobiography as well as biography, as the ambiguous subtitle of the first volume, *A Survivor's Tale*, suggests: is this Vladek surviving Auschwitz, or Art surviving Vladek? Anne Michaels's novel is also about survivor parents passing on the effects of trauma on to their children. *Fugitive Pieces* is a meticulously researched account of the rescue of Jakob Beer – a young Polish Jew whose parents and sister were killed during the war – by Athos Roussos, a Greek archaeologist; Beer's adult life in Canada; and, after Beer's death, the search for his diaries and papers by a young acolyte, himself the son of survivors. Electing not to appropriate any detailed horror, rather like Appelfeld's work, *Fugitive Pieces* infuses human loss and memory into descriptions of landscape, weather, and ancient history. As the first novel of a poet, this book conveys the enormity of the Holocaust and its legacy in an oblique and stylized way.

The final category of Holocaust literature by Jewish writers is that of fiction by non-survivors who are also not the descendants of survivors. This is, naturally, a growing category, and if we include in it writers whose work is even partly concerned with the Holocaust it would already constitute a long list, ranging from Philip Roth (*The Ghost Writer*, 1979) and Saul Bellow (*Mr Sammler's Planet*, 1970) to Cynthia Ozick (*The Shawl*, 1989) and Joseph Skibell (*A Blessing on the Moon*, 1997). Ozick's novel is unusual in depicting not only the life of Rosa, an elderly Holocaust survivor living in Miami, but also flashbacks to the death of her infant daughter in Auschwitz: most novelists shy away from showing camp life itself.

The case of Binjamin Wilkomirski's *Fragments: Memories of a Childhood 1939–1948* (1996) at first appeared to be a Holocaust testimony of an almost unprecedented kind. This text was originally published, first in German and then in English, as the memoir of a child-survivor of the Holocaust: a Jewish boy who was born in Latvia, lost his entire family and was imprisoned in Majdanek and Auschwitz. Wilkomirski's public pronouncements on the subject confirmed details from the text; he claimed to have been adopted by a Swiss couple after the war, who urged him never to think back to his troubled past. Yet the efforts of a Swiss journalist and author of another Holocaust novel, Daniel Ganzfried, have since shown that "Binjamin Wilkomirski" is at best the pen-name or alter-ego of the Swiss musician Bruno Doessekker, who was born in 1941, is not Jewish, and never left neutral Switzerland during the war. It seems that Doessekker's troubled infancy as an illegitimate child consigned to orphanages and eventually put up for adoption has been transmuted into a Holocaust biography. This is a very curious case, partly because of the "Holocaust envy" it suggests: Doessekker, who seems firmly to believe that he really is Binjamin Wilkomirski, has effected an overwhelming identification with the suffering of Jewish children during the war. On the other hand, *Fragments* is a very accomplished and striking work that will in time undoubtedly become well-known as a Holocaust novel. Its strengths lie in the depiction of the Holocaust world and death camps from a child's viewpoint, forcing the reader to re-view genocide through innocent eyes; and in reconstructing the logic of memory, which works ahistorically, out of order, and does not always understand what it recalls. The story of the unmasking of Binjamin Wilkomirski as Bruno Doessekker also brings home some literary-critical points to readers: it is very hard to determine whether a work is "authentic" or not from internal evidence; and fictional accounts of the Holocaust may have their own particular force when we try to understand that world.

Finally, mention must be made of the recent award of the Nobel Prize for Literature to the Hungarian Imre Kertész whose *Sorstalanság* (1975; translated as *Fateless*) and other works draw upon his experiences in Auschwitz and Buchenwald.

SUE VICE

Further Reading

Clendinnen, Inga, *Reading the Holocaust*, Cambridge and New York: Cambridge University Press, 1999

Horowitz, Sara R., *Voicing the Void: Muteness and Memory in Holocaust Fiction*, Albany: State University of New York Press, 1997

Lang, Berel (editor), *Writing and the Holocaust*, New York: Holmes and Meier, 1988

Langer, Lawrence L., *The Holocaust and the Literary Imagination*, New Haven, Connecticut: Yale University Press, 1975

Langer, Lawrence L. (editor), *Art from the Ashes: A Holocaust Anthology*, Oxford and New York: Oxford University Press, 1995

Leak, Andrew and George Paizis (editors), *The Holocaust and the Text: Speaking the Unspeakable*, London: Macmillan, and New York: St Martin's Press, 2000

Rosenfeld, Alvin H., *A Double Dying: Reflections on Holocaust Literature*, Bloomington: Indiana University Press, 1980

Schiff, Hilda (editor), *Holocaust Poetry*, London: Fount, and New York: St Martin's Press, 1995

Vice, Sue, *Holocaust Fiction*, London and New York: Routledge, 2000

Young, James E., *Writing and Rewriting the Holocaust*, Bloomington: Indiana University Press, 1988

Yiddish Writing in the 20th Century

As the 20th century began, Yiddish literature was in the midst of a remarkable flowering. Many of its major currents followed in the footsteps of trends that had been developing over the previous four decades. In 1862, Alexander Tsederboym introduced a new Yiddish supplement, *Kol mevaser* [The Voice of the Herald], to his Odessa Hebrew literary journal *Hamelits* [The Advocate]. The new journal immediately became an important forum for Yiddish writers. Sholem Yankev Abramovitsh, in the guise of his literary persona Mendele Moykher Sforim [Mendele the Bookpeddler], would inaugurate what many regard as the beginnings of modern Yiddish literature with his novel *Dos kleyne mentshele* [The Little Man], serialized in *Kol mevaser* in 1864–65. His satirical attacks on hypocrisy and parochialism run throughout his major work: the play *Di takse* [The Tax]; the fictionalized memoir *Shloyme reb khayms* [Shloyme Son of Chaim]; and the novels *Dos vintshfingerl* [The Magic Ring], *Fishke der krumer* [Fishke the Lame], *Di klyatshe* [The Nag], and *Masoes binyomin hashlishi* [The Travels of Benjamin the Third]. Abramovitsh pioneered both modern Yiddish and Hebrew literature, having rewritten many of his own works into Hebrew, and then incorporated many of the changes into revisions of the original Yiddish texts.

One of his most ardent supporters was Sholem Rabinovitsh, who in 1888 issued a new journal of Yiddish belles-lettres, *Di yidishe folks-bibliotek* [The Jewish People's Library], for which he commissioned writing from the most notable Yiddish writers of the day. Among them was Sholem Aleichem, the pseudonym under which Rabinovitsh would become beloved by Yiddish speakers worldwide. In his masterpieces, such as *Tevye der milkhiker* [Tevye the Dairyman], *Menakhem mendl*, and *Motl peysi dem khazns* [Motl the Cantor's Son], he perfected an intimate style of storytelling. Sholem Aleichem enjoyed far greater success as a writer of fiction than of drama, but several of his plays, such as *Dos groyse gevins* [The Jackpot] and *Shver tsu zayn a yid* [It's Hard to be a Jew], enjoyed posthumous success.

One of the writers whose Yiddish debut appeared in Sholem Aleichem's *Yidishe folks-bibliotek* was Yitskhok-Leyb Perets, a lawyer turned civil servant who in the 1890s would soon found his own literary journals, *Yontev bletlekh* [Holiday Pages] and *Yidishe bibliotek* [Yiddish Library]. These journals, along with Mordkhe Spektor's *Hoyz-fraynd* [Home Companion], published a growing body of secular Yiddish literature. Perets became best known as a master craftsman of the short story, often championing the causes of ordinary men and women, yet with ambivalent endings that suggest a double edge to the narratives. Perets brought that same spirit to his neo-Hasidic stories, recasting tales of rebbes and their followers in a modern vein, as in "Oyb nisht nokh hekher" [If Not Higher] and "Tsvishn tsvey berg" [Between Two Mountains]. Late in his career, he also experimented with symbolist techniques, which inform his mystical dramas *Bay nakht oyfn altn mark* [A Night in the Old Market] and *Di goldene keyt* [The Golden Chain]. Collectively, Abramovitsh, Sholem Aleichem, and Perets are known as the "classic" Yiddish writers, who in varied, complementary ways laid the foundation for modern Yiddish literature.

In the theatre, Avrom Goldfaden was a one-man "classic". Already a published Hebrew and Yiddish poet by the time he began writing plays, Goldfaden formed a professional company in Romania in 1876, and then proceeded to provide its dramatic and musical repertoire. For the next few years, his output was dominated by farces and musical comedies, often with an eye to combating fanaticism and superstition, as in *Di tsvey kuni lemls* [The Two Kuni Lemls] and *Di kishef-makherin* [The Sorceress]. His troupe quickly met with competition, when playwrights Joseph Lateiner and Moyshe Hurwitz formed their own ensembles. Like Goldfaden, they borrowed plots, characters, and melodies from various European cultures – and from each other.

After Yiddish theatre was officially banned in the Russian empire in 1883, many Yiddish actors and playwrights went westward. Some three million eastern European Jews would make similar journeys in the next three decades, establishing major Jewish communities in western Europe and the Americas. New York emerged as the most important centre of Yiddish theatre from the mid-1880s to World War I, although other American cities served as important regional centres, and Yiddish theatre thrived in London during the same period. Along with the founding trio of professional Yiddish theatre, other important early dramatists included Nokhem Meyer Shaykevitsh, or Shomer, also a prolific and popular novelist; Anshl Shor, Moyshe Shor, and Moyshe Zeifert. Sigmund Feinman and Boris Thomashefsky, star actors from this period, also enjoyed success as playwrights.

A new voice emerged in Yiddish drama in the early 1890s. Yankev Gordin, newly arrived in New York from his native Ukraine, deplored the melodramas and musical comedies that dominated the Yiddish theatre of his time, and set out to reform the Yiddish stage with plays inspired by contemporary masters such as Ibsen and Hauptmann. Gordin's first play, *Siberia* (1891), was hailed as little short of revolutionary, and for the next two decades he led a school of Yiddish dramaturgy structured in the tradition of the well-made play. Gordin often tailored roles to specific actors: for example, *Der yidisher kenig lir* [The Jewish King Lear] for Jacob Adler; *Khasye di yesoyme* [Khasye the Orphan] for Keni Liptzin; *Got, mentsh un tayvl* [God, Man, and Devil] for David Kessler; and *Sappho* for Bertha Kalish. Gordin's most successful followers, Leon Kobrin and Zalmen Libin (Israel Zalmen Hurwitz), both wrote fiction as well as drama. Melodrama writers who learned from Gordin's craftsmanship included Nokhem Rakov, Moyshe Rikhter, Harry Sackler, Max Gable, and Isidore Zolatarevsky.

The new century brought new Yiddish newspapers, literary journals, and publishers to eastern Europe. One of the earliest and most influential periodicals was *Der fraynd* [The Friend], founded in St Petersburg in 1903 and soon followed by others in Odessa, Warsaw, and elsewhere. Warsaw emerged as the most important centre of Yiddish in eastern Europe, and Perets continued to be a seminal figure not just for his literary output, but for his support of other writers, who made pilgrimages to seek out the master's advice. Avrom Reyzen would become popular with his simple, singable poems and gift of storytelling. Hersh Dovid Nomberg's early short stories gained him a reputation as an original stylist, and, with his friend Perets, would make an important contribution to the Yiddish Language Conference in Czernowitz in 1908. I.M. Weissenberg voiced an unsentimental view of the shtetl. Jonah Rosenfeld probed individual psychology. Dovid Pinski, a committed socialist, wrote sympathetically of the Jewish working class in his stories and plays. Jacob Dinezon, Perets's close friend and secretary, became popular with his sentimental fiction. Lamed Shapiro explored traditional themes in a modern style. Ultimately, Sholem Asch, whom we will encounter again in America, would become the most prolific and famous of all the Perets disciples, after his first full-length work, *Dos shtetl* [The Shtetl] (1904), landed him solidly on the literary map. From that point on, Asch poured out a steady stream of writings, including the controversial play *God of Vengeance*, a tale of sin v. redemption set in a brothel.

After Perets's death in 1915, Yiddish writers attempted at least partially to fill the literary void by founding a writers' club at 13 Tlomatckie Street in Warsaw. While elder statesmen such as Nomberg looked down upon the young modernists, the latter were injecting Yiddish letters in Poland with extraordinary vitality. The generation's leaders included poet and playwright Aaron Tseytlin, critic and memoirist Y.Y. Trunk, and I.J. Singer, who gained early renown as a prose craftsman and foreign correspondent for the New York *Forverts* (*Jewish Daily Forward*). Warsaw was also developing a vital publishing scene, at the centre of which stood such critics as Nakhmen Mayzel at *Literarishe bleter* [Literary Pages], Noah Prilutski, and Ba'al Makhshoves (Isidore Elyashev).

Three other frequent visitors to the writers' club formed the writers' group *Di khalyastre* [The Gang] in 1922. Perets Markish, Melekh Ravitch, and Uri Zvi Greenberg would soon go off in different geographical and aesthetic directions, but for a short time, the group's exuberant use of expressionist techniques brought an anti-aesthetic challenge to Yiddish letters. Seven years later, the literary scholar and critic Zalmen Reyzen heralded the arrival of *Yung vilne* [Young Vilna]. The group focused on poetry, but in its three issues of *Yung vilne* there was no attempt to articulate common ideas that united the writers, including Shmerke Kaczerginsky, Leyzer Volf, Hirsch Glick, Chaim Grade, and Avrom Sutskever (Abraham Sutzkever). The latter two would become among the most important postwar Yiddish writers.

In 1920 Warsaw witnessed the most sensational event the Yiddish theatre has known: the Vilna Troupe's production of An-ski's (Shloyme Zaynvl Rapoport) *Der dibek* [The Dybbuk]. An-ski had led the Jewish Ethnographic Expedition of 1912–14 inside the Pale of Settlement in czarist Russia, which collected a wealth of ethnographic, historical, and literary material. As An-ski wandered, he began to conceive his drama, a tapestry of Jewish folk belief into which a tale of romance and spirit possession is woven. Following in the spirit of Perets and An-ski, Polish Yiddish drama – as well as film, which would flourish in Poland in the 1930s – would always display a strong spiritual component. Aaron Tseytlin and Jacob Preger used Jewish folklore, legend, and history to theatrical effect, the former in such dramas as *Shabse tsvi*, the latter in *Simkhe plakhte*. Alter Kacyzne's *Der dukus* [The Duke], Fishl Bimko's *Ganovim* [Thieves], and Mark Arnshteyn's *Der vilner balebesl* [The Little Landlord from Vilna] are among the high points of Yiddish drama in interwar Poland.

The Warsaw Art Theatre (VYKT), led by Zygmunt Turkow and his wife Ida Kaminska, established a repertoire that combined European classics with original Yiddish dramas. In 1929, Mikhl Vaykhert, who had trained in Max Reinhardt's drama school in Vienna, founded the Culture League Drama Studio, which would soon produce enough graduates to form a company. The result, Yung Teater, championed an experimental approach aimed at creating an intimate relationship between actors and audience. Its productions included *Mississippi*, about race relations in the United States, and Vaykhert's *Trupe tanentsap*, a play-within-a-play about the early days of the professional Yiddish theatre. An alternative to the mainstream companies was the cabaret revue form known as *kleynkunst*, which reached its heights at Azazel in Warsaw, and Moyshe Broderzon's Ararat in Łódź, where Broderzon, Shimen Dzigan, and Yisroel Shumakher dazzled audiences with their comic wit.

The turn of the century witnessed an explosion of Yiddish publishing in the United States. Between 1885 and 1914, more than 150 Yiddish publications of different kinds would appear in New York alone; among them were papers such as *Di fraye arbeter shtime* [The Free Worker's Voice] and *Di arbeter tsaytung* [The Worker's Paper]. The socialist daily *Der forverts* (now a weekly) and the socialist monthly *Di tsukunft* [The Future] both began publication in the 1890s and continue to operate. The Yiddish press offered articles on every facet of life in the United States and beyond, advice on personal matters, and entertainment in both its news coverage and various forms of literature. Literary and theatrical critics became associated with specific newspapers: Joel Entin at the *Tog* [Day], Alexander Mukdoiny at the *Morgn zhurnal* [Morning Paper], the *Frayhayt*'s [Freedom's] Nokhem Buchwald, and Abraham Cahan and Hillel Rogoff at the *Forverts*. To this list must be added the dean of Yiddish critics, Shmuel Niger.

American Yiddish writing was initially dominated by poetry. In an age when a rapidly swelling immigrant population toiled long hours to earn a meagre living, the so-called "sweatshop poets" won fame for their songs of protest and lament. Foremost among this group was Moris Rosenfeld, whose own experience as a labourer and gift for fluid rhyme helped him move audiences with such poems as "Mayn yingele" [My Little Boy] and "Der svet-shap" [The Sweatshop]. Fellow labour poets Moris Vintshevski, Dovid Edelshtat, and Joseph Bovshover added their plaintive lyrics to Rosenfeld's, giving voice to the travails of masses of ordinary Jews.

From its formation in 1907, *Di yunge* (the Young Ones) announced a break with proletarian poetry. *Di yunge* eschewed politically engaged art, and were inspired by the modernist experimentation being carried out in other European languages. Its leading poets included Mani Leyb, master of evocative sound in verse whose crowning achievements were the sonnets he penned late in life; H. Leyvik, whose life and work seemed to embody grace in the face of deep suffering; Moyshe Leyb Halpern, who channelled his fiery temperament into brilliant experiments with poetic form and content; Zishe Landau, advocate of "pure" poetry; Reuben Ayzland, and Joseph Rolnick.

While *Di yunge* did not stay together for long, its writers continued to influence the next generation. Seeds of a new movement were sown by A. Leyeles's (Arn Glants-Leyeles's) first book of poems, *Labirint* [Labyrinth], 1918. His radical break with the forms of Yiddish poetry then prevalent alienated most of his contemporaries, with at least two notable exceptions: Yankev Glatshteyn and N.B. Minkov. In 1919 the three writers issued a manifesto as the introduction to a new journal, *Inzikh* [In Oneself], which included their poems and those of kindred spirits. From then until its last issue in 1940, *Inzikh* would publish some hundred or so writers, including fellow *Inzikhistn* (Introspectivists) Celia Dropkin and Judd L. Teller.

In the 1920s, a group of poets known as Proletpen began working in direct opposition to the individualistic approach of the Introspectivists, and in the spirit of the socially committed art of the era. The Proletpen writers published in such Communist organs as *Frayhayt* and *Der hamer* [The Hammer], but saw their ranks dwindle after the *Frayhayt*'s party-line, anti-Zionist response to anti-Jewish riots in Hebron in 1929. Those who continued their affiliation with Proletpen, such as Zishe Vaynper, Zelig Dorfman, Moyshe Nadir, and Menke Katz, frequently probed issues such as racism, poverty, and other contemporary social problems in their work.

Many other poets were less clearly affiliated with one particular movement. In addition to his verse, Avrom Lyesin would make an impact as longstanding editor of the journal *Di tsukunft*. Yehoash (Solomon Bloomgarten) was a fine nature poet whose translation of the Tanakh remains one of the great achievements of Yiddish letters. I.J. Schwartz, another accomplished translator, produced polished Yiddish versions of *Hamlet* and *Julius Caesar*, as well as the first epic American Yiddish poem, *Kentucky*. Anna Margolin brought together disparate cultural references in work influenced by the Imagists.

Eventually, some of the best-known Yiddish literature came from prose writers based in New York. Sholem Asch was truly a citizen of the world, but spent long stretches in America, where the settings of his work often alternated between the "Old Country" and the new. Examples of the former include *Kidish hashem* [Sanctification of God's Name], set during a wave of massacres in 17th-century Poland; the trilogy *Three Cities*, depicting events leading up to the Russian revolution; and *Der tilim yid* (*Salvation*). Asch's new surroundings inspired him to apply similar scrutiny to American Jewish life, as in *Moses* and *East River*. Like Asch, Joseph Opatoshu emigrated from Poland to New York, where he became a lifelong contributor to the daily *Der tog* from its founding in 1914. In his masterpiece, *In poylishe velder* [In the Polish Woods], Opatoshu showed a people caught up in the decline of Hasidism, the rise of the *Haskalah* [The Enlightenment], and struggles for Polish independence.

Another immigrant from Poland whose reputation preceded him to the United States was I.J. Singer, who in the 1930s and 1940s produced several major social novels of Jewish life in Europe: *Yoshe kalb* [Yoshe the Calf], set in a Hasidic court, was an enormous success both in its own right and in a stage adaptation by Maurice Schwartz; *Di brider ashkenazi* [The Brothers Ashkenazi], an epic story of Jewish industrialists in Łódź, and *Di mishpokhe karnovski*

[The Carnovsky Family], the story of German Jews in the grip of the Nazis. When Singer died suddenly in 1944, his younger brother Isaac began to step out of his shadow – and into his shoes as a contributor to the *Forverts*. Isaac Bashevis Singer gained early attention with such works as *Der sotn in goray* (*Satan in Goray*) and *Di familye Moshkat* (The FamilyMoskat), and somewhat later with *Der kuntsn-makher fun lublin* (*The Magician of Lublin*) and *Der knekht* (*The Slave*). Yet Singer, the most widely translated Yiddish writer and winner of the Nobel Prize for Literature in 1978, is best known as a master of short stories energized by irreverence and the supernatural, as in "Gimpel the Fool", "Yentl the Yeshiva Boy", and "The Last Demon".

In the interwar period, New York's Second Avenue became known as "the Yiddish Broadway". The king of Second Avenue was Maurice Schwartz, who formed an ensemble in 1918 that would soon become world-famous as the Yiddish Art Theatre. Over the next three decades, in addition to Yiddish translations of European classics and new interpretations of Yiddish classics, Schwartz would stage works by a new generation of Yiddish playwrights, starting with Perets Hirshbein, who had earlier directed and written for a repertory company in Odessa. In dramas such as *Grine felder* [Green Fields] and *A farvorfn vinkl* [A Far-flung Corner] Hirshbein displayed an understated quality rarely seen among his predecessors. Other Russian Jewish émigrés would help him build a new type of dramatic repertoire. Leyvik added to his achievements in verse with both poetic dramas such as *Der goylem* [The Golem] and naturalistic prose works such as *Shmates* [Rags] and *Shop*. Osip Dimov began his career writing symbolist stories in Russian, and his 1907 play *Shma yisroel* [Hear, O Israel] was performed in both Russian and Yiddish. After emigrating to New York, he enjoyed international success with such works as *Yoshke musikant* [Yoshke the Musician].

The theatrical counterpart to Proletpen was the Artef (from the Yiddish acronym for the Workers' Theatre Collective), which opened its doors in 1928 with a production of Soviet Yiddish playwright Beynush Shteyman's *Bam toyer* [At the Gate]. The company established itself as the radical alternative to the Yiddish Art Theatre and other commercial houses with its innovative productions of such works as an adaptation of Yisroel Aksenfeld's *Der ershter yidisher rekrut in rusland* (*Rekrutn*) [The First Jewish Recruits in Russia (Recruits)]; Sholem Aleichem's *200,000*; and H. Leyvick's *Keytn* [Chains].

In the first years following the Russian Revolution of 1917, the new Soviet Union state offered Yiddish writers an unprecedented opportunity to join a state-supported and funded Yiddish artistic, literary, and scholarly enterprises. This situation proved attractive to many artists, and just as such émigrés as Gor'kii and Prokofiev returned to the Soviet Union, so did Yiddish writers Der Nister (Pinkhes Kahanovitch), Leyb Kvitko, Dovid Hofshteyn, Perets Markish, and Dovid Bergelson. In addition, a number of important figures living elsewhere immigrated and became Soviet citizens, among them literary historians Max Erik and Meir Viner, critic Nokhem Shtif, and poet and playwright Moyshe Kulbak.

This hospitable atmosphere quickly bore fruit. A literary circle in Kiev issued the literary journal *Baginen* [Dawn] in 1919 and *Eygns* [Our Own] in 1918 and 1920, featuring fiction by Bergelson, Der Nister, and Alter Kacyzne; drama by Beynush Shteyman; and poetry by such writers as Hofshteyn, Kadye Molodovski, Kvitko, and Markish, each producing expressionistic poetry along the lines of other Yiddish writing being written at the same time in New York and Poland. Other important Soviet Yiddish literary journals included *Shtrom* [Stream], *Di royte velt* [The Red World], and *Der shtern* [The Star]. But the Moscow-based *Der emes* [The Truth], the organ of the Jewish Section, would come to reflect a different approach to Soviet Yiddish literature. In the pages of *Der emes*, critic Moyshe Litvakov sternly took to task such writers as Markish and Kvitko for not adhering to the goals of the new literature. Writers were forced to apologize for their "errors" and then, if they wanted to survive, censor their own work in future. In the end, though, such efforts hardly mattered. Even Litvakov perished in the purges of the 1930s, as did Kulbak, Erik, poet Izi Kharik, and literary historian Israel Tsinberg.

Nevertheless, the Soviet Union remained a leading centre of Yiddish writing from the 1920s to 1941. The leading prose stylist was Dovid Bergelson, the most important modernist writer in Yiddish literature, who began making his presence felt with the story "Der toyber" [The Deaf One] and the novella *Arum vakzal* [Around the Depot]. Bergelson became a founder of the Kiev Culture League between 1917 and 1919, and served as editor on a number of journals and newspapers. After a sojourn abroad, Bergelson settled in Moscow in 1934, and in the 1930s published what would be his last major work: *Bam dnieper* [By the Dnieper]. Other masterpieces of Soviet Yiddish fiction include Kulbak's *Zelmenyaner* [The Zelmenyaner Clan] and Der Nister's *Di mishpokhe mashber* (*The Family Mashber*). Before the censorial cloud descended on Soviet writers and stifled their creativity, Soviet Yiddish literature could boast extraordinary achievements in poetry: the lyric verse of Dovid Hofshteyn, the rhythmic innovations of Kulbak, the brilliant imagery and epic sweep of Perets Markish, the charming children's poems of Leyb Kvitko, the fluid versification of Itsik Fefer, and the emotional sweep of Shmuel Halkin.

Ultimately, no Yiddish artist, no matter how loyal to Stalin, was safe. Shloyme Mikhoels, the brilliant actor and chairman of the Jewish Anti-Fascist Committee during World War II, was murdered by the Stalinist regime in 1948. And on 12 August 1952, the Tishe b'Av of Yiddish literature, the remaining leading lights of Soviet Yiddish writing, including Hoftsheyn, Bergelson, Kvitko, and Fefer, were rounded up and executed.

The Soviet Yiddish theatre reached similar heights and sunk to similar depths. Yiddish troupes would be established in Minsk, Riga, Kharkov, and elsewhere, but the most famous was the Moscow troupe founded by Alexander Granovsky, who in 1919 founded the Yiddish Chamber Theatre of Petrograd. The troupe soon came to the attention of critic Avrom Efros, who invited the actors to Moscow to inaugurate a new Jewish emancipation centred on a renaissance of theatrical art. In 1920 the renamed Yiddish State Theatre (best known by its Russian acronym, Goset) began to stage landmark productions in Moscow, including

Goldfaden's *Di kishef-makherin*, Sholem Aleichem's *Dos groyse gevins*, Mendele's *Masoes binyomin hashlishi*, Perets's *Bay nakht oyfn altn mark*, and *King Lear*. At the heart of the company, which remained active until 1948, was the acting partnership of Mikhoels and Binyomen Zuskin.

After World War II the Yiddish writers who survived, or who had already lived elsewhere by the time the war broke out, now wrote for an audience greatly diminished in number, and the Yiddish readership would further shrink as survivors migrated to areas less nurturing of Yiddish culture than pre-war eastern Europe had been. Nevertheless, several of the most important writers in modern Yiddish literature would remain active for decades after the Holocaust. New York remained an important centre, where the work of such writers as Glatshteyn, Leyvik, and Isaac Bashevis Singer often reflected on the destruction of European Jewry. They were joined by Chaim Grade, in such prose works as *Der mames shabosim* [My Mother's Sabbath Days], *Di agune* [The Abandoned Wife], and *Tsemakh atlas*. Mordkhe Shtrigler, long-time editor of the *Forverts*, also wrote novels based on his experience in the Holocaust. And the 1960s saw the start of a modest resurgence of Soviet Yiddish literature: fiction by Elye Shekhtman, Moyshe Altman, and Nathan Zabara, poetry by Moyshe Teyf, Hirsh Osherovitsh, Motl Grubian, and Shloyme Roytman, and the journal *Sovetish heymland* [Soviet Homeland], edited by Aaron Vergelis.

Avrom Sutskever would come to stand at the centre of the Yiddish literary circle in Israel. He had chronicled the Vilna ghetto in his poetry during the Nazi occupation, when he and fellow *Yung vilne* member Shmerke Kaczerginski risked their lives to preserve material from the YIVO Institute for Jewish Research. They continued their efforts after the war, and Sutskever soon settled in Israel, where he founded and edited the literary journal *Di goldene keyt* [The Golden Chain] (1949–95). Other noteworthy Yiddish writing in Israel includes poetry by Binem Heler, Rivke Basman, Yankev Shargel, and Yoysef Kerler, and prose by Rokhl Oyerbakh, Yeshayohu Shpigl, Yosl Birshteyn, and Mordkhe Tsanin.

Yiddish literature has followed the migrations of the Jews to various corners of the globe. Melekh Ravitsh eventually settled in Montreal, home of a vibrant Yiddish cultural circle that included poet Rokhl Korn and writers Y.Y. Segal, Yehuda Elberg, and Chava Rosenfarb. Y.M. Sherman, Yerakhmiel Feldman, and Nekhemye Levinski stand out among South African Yiddish prose writers, and David Fram and David Volpe among its poets. Whereas South African Yiddish culture was dominated by *litvaks* (Lithuanians), Poland served as the main pipeline to Australia, where editor and story writer Pinkhes Goldhar arrived from Łódź in 1926. There were, too, Herz Bergner, a novelist from Warsaw; essayists Yitskhok Kahn and Yehoshua Rappoport, prose writer Moyshe Ajzenbud, and poet and playwright Abraham Cykiert, and other poets who wrote of the "Old Country", the Holocaust, and the immigrant experience. Halfway across the world, Yiddish writers active in Buenos Aires included storyteller Berl Greenberg, critics Jacob Botoshansky and Shmuel Rozhansky, and poet Kehos Kliger. Paris became the most important western European centre after the war, the home of short-story writer Menukhe Ram, novelist Mendel Mann, poet Moyshe Shulshteyn, and dramatist Khayim Sloves.

Just as 20th-century Yiddish writing had its roots in the 19th century, its reach extends into the 21st. A number of authors, mostly born after World War II, have been producing original Yiddish fiction and poetry since the 1980s. Notable among them are prose writers Boris Sandler (New York, originally Moldova) and Hirshe-Dovid Menkes (Wales, originally Brooklyn); poets Lev Berinski (Akko, originally Moldova and Russia), Velvl Chernin (Israel, originally Russia), and Yitskhok Niborski (Paris, originally Argentina); and playwright Miriam Hoffman (New York, originally Łódź).

Brief as this essay has been, it illustrates several key characteristics of 20th-century Yiddish literature. First, its development was extremely compressed. Other European literatures have had centuries to develop. Jewish society, on the other hand, placed firm strictures on its writers and readers, so that secular Yiddish writing only began to sprout its first buds at the end of the 18th century, and even then under often inhospitable conditions. In essence, then, modern Yiddish literature had under a century – from the 1860s to World War II – in which to reach full flower. During that time, its writers absorbed or otherwise reacted to the major trends and writers in other Western cultures, in a range of responses from translation, imitation, parody, and at times brilliant reinventions that wedded established literary conventions to sensibilities shaped by Yiddish language and culture.

Most Yiddish writers have been bilingual at the very least, and frequently polyglots. Many began their literary careers in Hebrew and moved to Yiddish, which held out the promise of a much larger readership and more flexible vernacular. Some continued to produce in both these tongues, while others gravitated to Hebrew after starting in Yiddish. Even writers who produce exclusively in Yiddish often drew upon Hebrew and Aramaic, the languages of the canonical Jewish religious texts. Other languages coloured Yiddish writing as well. A writer's native region tends to influence his Yiddish vocabulary, so that Sholem Aleichem's writing is peppered with Russian and Ukrainian words, Isaac Bashevis Singer's with Polish. The cultural trappings also play a significant role. The shadow of Gogol' hovers over Sholem Aleichem, Polish symbolists inspire Perets, and Walt Whitman might understandably be seen as the patron saint of the poets of *Di yunge*.

Yiddish literature constantly transgresses boundaries of geography, genre, and era. Its writers were constantly on the move – often forced to move by persecution, war, or dire poverty. While many clearly bore the stamp of certain cultural centres, others led endlessly peripatetic existences. Writers as mobile as Goldfaden, Melekh Ravitsh, Leyb Malakh, and Daniel Charney can hardly be said to belong to any one locale, or even to two or three. Any attempt to divide modern Yiddish literature into periods runs into similar obstacles. Many of the most important writers at the start of the century had already been active for decades, and even seemingly clear transformations, such as the Russian Revolution, do not mark completely new breaks. At least in the early years of the new state, much of the literature produced by "Soviet" Yiddish writers had few "Soviet" features whatsoever.

Arranging modern Yiddish literature by genre hardly makes matters any simpler. Besides the loss of focus on the character of Yiddish literature in any given cultural milieu, such a scheme would have difficulty accounting for how frequently Yiddish writers move from one type of writing to another. Glatshteyn and Manger are celebrated primarily as poets, but both wrote noteworthy fiction and criticism. Manger, Kulbak, and Leyvik brought their lyric gifts to writing for the stage. Prolific dramatists such as Kobrin and Pinski also wrote fiction and criticism. And the writers who shuttled between belles-lettres and journalism are too numerous to count. To make matters even more interesting, Yiddish writers used endless pseudonyms.

20th-century Yiddish literature was both localized and international; moved the masses to tears, the intellectuals to thought, and the activists to action; drew upon world literature and then enriched it in turn. Yiddish literature bore witness to the mass migrations, political upheavals, persecution, and mass murders that the Jews endured. In so doing, it stands as one of the richest and most powerful expressions of the modern Jewish experience.

JOEL BERKOWITZ

Further Reading

Frieden, Ken, *Classic Yiddish Fiction*, Albany: State University of New York Press, 1995

Goldberg, I., *Unzer dramaturgye*, New York: YKUF and Yekhiel Levenstein Bukh-Komitet, 1961

Goldman, Eric A., *Visions, Images, and Dreams: Yiddish Film Past and Present*, Ann Arbor, Michigan: UMI Research Press, 1983

Gorin, B., *Di geshikhte fun yidishn teater*, 2 vols, New York: Mayzel, 1923

Harshav, Benjamin, *The Meaning of Yiddish*, Berkeley: University of California Press, 1990

Harshav, Benjamin and Barbara Harshav, *American Yiddish Poetry: A Bilingual Anthology*, Berkeley: University of California Press, 1986

Hoberman, J., *Bridge of Light: Yiddish Film between Two Worlds*, New York: Museum of Modern Art–Schocken, 1991

Howe, Irving, *World of Our Fathers*, New York: Harcourt Brace, 1976; as *The Immigrant Jews of New York, 1881 to the Present*, London: Routledge, 1976

Howe, Irving, Ruth R. Wisse, and Khone Shmeruk (editors), *The Penguin Book of Modern Yiddish Verse*, New York and London: Viking, 1987

Hrushovski, Binyomin, Avrom Sutskever, and Khone Shmeruk (editors), *A shpigl af a shteyn*, Tel Aviv: Perets, 1964

Leksikon fun der nayer yidisher literatur, 8 vols, New York: Congress for Jewish Culture, 1958–81

Liptzin, Solomon, *A History of Yiddish Literature*, New York: Jonathan David, 1972

Madison, Charles A., *Jewish Publishing in America: The Impact of Jewish Writing on American Culture*, New York: Sanhedrin Press, 1976

Mark, Yudel, "Yiddish Literature" in *The Jews: Their History*, 4th edition, edited by Louis Finkelstein, vol. 2: *The Jews: Their Religion and Culture*, New York: Schocken, 1970

Mayzel, Nakhman, *Noente un eygene*, New York: YKUF, 1957

Niger, Shmuel, *Dertseylers un romanistn*, New York: CYCO, 1946

Niger, Shmuel, *Yidishe shrayber in sovet-rusland*, New York: CYCO, 1956

Perlmutter, Sholem, *Yidishe dramaturgn un teater-kompozitors*, New York: YKUF, 1952

Ravitsh, Melekh, *Mayn leksikon*, 5 vols, Montreal and Tel Aviv, 1945–80

Roskies, David G., *A Bridge of Longing: The Lost Art of Yiddish Storytelling*, Cambridge, Massachusetts: Harvard University Press, 1995

Sandrow, Nahma, *Vagabond Stars: A World History of Yiddish Theater*, New York: Harper and Row, 1977

Shatsky, Jacob (editor), *Arkhiv far der geshikhte fun yidishn teater un drame*, Vilna: YIVO, 1930

Shmeruk, Chone, "Yiddish Literature in the USSR" in *The Jews in Soviet Russia since 1917*, 3rd edition, edited Lionel Kochan, Oxford and New York: Oxford University Press, 1978

Yidisher teater tsvishn beyde velt-milkhomes, 2 vols, New York: Congress for Jewish Culture, 1968

Zinberg, Israel, *A History of Jewish Literature*, translated by Bernard Martin, 12 vols, Cincinnati: Hebrew Union College–Ktav, 1975

Zylbercweig, Zalmen, *Leksikon fun yidishn teater*, 6 vols, New York: Elisheva, 1931–70

WRITERS

A

Abish, Walter

Austrian-born US fiction writer, 1931–

Born in Vienna, 24 December 1931. Son of middle-class Adolph (a businessman) and Frieda (née Rubin). Family fled to Nice after the Anschluss, 1938. Left France by boat for Shanghai just ten days before German invasion of France, 1940. Moved to Israel, 1949. Served in Israeli army, studied architecture. Married Cecile Gelb (scupltor and photographer), 1956. Lived briefly in England. Came to New York, 1957. Became US citizen, 1960. Worked in urban planning. Published first book, a poetry collection *Duel Site*, 1970. Adjunct Professor at State University of New York Empire State College, 1975; Writer in Residence, Wheaton College, spring 1977; Visiting Butler Professor of English at State University of New York at Buffalo, autumn 1977; lecturer in English, Columbia University, 1979–86; Guest Professor, Yale University, spring 1985 and Brown University, spring 1986; visiting writer, Cooper Union, spring 1984. Many awards, including Fellow of New Jersey State Council for the Arts, 1972; Rose Isabel Williams Foundation Grant, 1974; Ingram Merrill Foundation Grant, 1977; Fellow of National Endowment for the Arts, 1979 and 1985; Guggenheim Fellowship, 1981; CAPS Grant, 1981; PEN/Faulkner Award, 1981; DAAD Fellowship, Deutscher Akademischer Austauschdienst, Berlin, 1987; John D. MacArthur Foundation Fellowship, 1987–92; Award of Merit Medal for the Novel, American Academy and Institute of Arts and Letters, 1991.

Selected Writings

Novels
Alphabetical Africa, 1974
How German Is It, 1980
Eclipse Fever, 1993

Short Stories
Minds Meet, 1975
In the Future Perfect, 1977
99: The New Meaning, 1990

Poetry
Duel Site, 1970

Further Reading

Arias-Mission, Alain, "The Puzzle of Walter Abish: In The Future Perfect", *Sub-Stance*, 27 (1980): 115–24
Arias-Mission, Alain, "The New Novel and Television Culture: Reflections on Walter Abish's *How German Is It*", *Fiction International*, 17/1 (1986): 152–64
Bradbury, Malcolm, Introduction to Abish's *In the Future Perfect*, London: Faber, 1984
Butler, Christopher, "Scepticism and Experimental Fiction", *Essays in Criticism*, 36 (January 1985): 47–67
Butler, Christopher, "Walter Abish and the Questioning of the Reader", in *Facing Texts: Encounters between Contemporary Writers and Critics*, edited by Heide Ziegler, Durham, North Carolina: Duke University Press, 1988
Caramello, Charles, *Silverless Mirrors: Book, Self and Postmodern American Fiction*, Tallahassee: Florida State University Press, 1983
Durand, Regis, "The Disposition of the Familiar (Walter Abish)", in *Representation and Performance in Postmodern Fiction*, edited by Maurice Couturier, Montpellier: Université Paul Valéry, 1983
Houen, Alexander, "Plotting a 'Terrorism' of Postmodern Fiction", *Yearbook of English Studies*, 30 (2000), 202–20
Karl, Frederick, *American Fictions, 1940–1980*, New York: Harper and Row, 1983
Klinkowitz, Jerome, *Fiction International*, 4–5 (1975): 93–100
Klinkowitz, Jerome, *The Life of Fiction*, Urbana: University of Illinois Press, 1977
Klinkowitz, Jerome, "Walter Abish and the Surfaces of Life", *Georgia Review*, 35 (Summer 1981): 416–20
Klinkowitz, Jerome, *The Self-Apparent Word: Fiction as Language/Language as Fiction*, Carbondale: Southern Illinois University Press, 1984
Klinkowitz, Jerome, "Experimental Realism", in *Postmodern Fiction: A Bio-Bibliographical Guide*, edited by Larry McCaffery, New York: Greenwood, 1986
McCaffery, Larry and Sinda Gregory, *Alive and Writing: Interviews with American Authors of the 1980s*, Urbana: University of Illinois Press, 1987
McHale, Brian, *Postmodernist Fiction*, London and New York: Methuen, 1987
Martin, Richard, "Walter Abish's Fictions: Perfect Unfamiliarity, Familiar Imperfections" *Journal of American Studies*, 17/2 (1983): 229–41
Peyser, Thomas, "How Global Is It: Walter Abish and the Fiction of Globalization", *Contemporary Literature*, 40.2 (Summer, 1999), 240–62
Saalman, Dieter, "Walter Abish's *How German Is It*: Language and the Crisis of Human Behaviour", *Critique* (Spring 1985): 105–21

Schirato, Anthony, "The Politics of Writing and Being Written: A Study of Walter Abish's *How German Is It*", *Novel*, 24 (Autumn 1990): 69–85
Schirato, Anthony, "Comic Politics and the Politics of the Comic: Walter Abish's *Alphabetical Africa*", *Critique: Studies in Contemporary Fiction* 33/2 (Winter 1992)
Siegle, Robert, "On the Subject of Walter Abish and Kathy Acker", *Literature and Psychology*, 33/3–4 (1987): 38–58
Tanner, Tony, "Present Imperfect: A Note on the Work of Walter Abish", *Granta* (Spring 1979): 65–71
Updike, John, *Picked-Up Pieces*, New York: Knopf, 1975; London: Deutsch, 1976
van Delden, Maarten, "Walter Abish's *How German Is It*: Postmodernism and the Past", *Salmagundi*, 85–86 (Winter–Spring 1990): 172–94
van Delden, Maarten, "An Interview with Walter Abish on *Eclipse Fever*", *Annals of Scholarship* 10/3–4 (1993)
van Delden, Maarten, "Crossing the Great Divide: Rewritings of the U.S.-Mexican Encounter in Walter Abish and Richard Roderiguez", *Studies in Twentieth-Century Literature*, 25/1 (Winter, 2001): 118–39
Varsava, Jerry A., "Walter Abish and the Topographies of Desire" in *Contingent Meanings: Postmodern Fiction, Mimesis and the Reader*, Tallahassee: Florida State University Press, 1990
Wotipka, Paul, "Walter Abish's *How German Is It:* Representing the Postmodern", *Contemporary Literature*, 30 (Winter 1989): 503–17

Walter Abish is often seen in the context of postmodern American fiction, in the company of such experimental American writers of the late 1960s and 1970s as Donald Barthelme, John Hawkes, Robert Coover, Gilbert Sorrentino, Don DeLillo, and John Barth. But it may be much more fruitful to place Abish in connection with a different group. He is far closer in a number of ways to the many writers of the 20th century who have been displaced by wars and politics, by their religious, ethnic, and religious differences. These writers often must adapt their writing to languages not their own, live in physical and cultural exile, always the minority, the other, and often particularly attentive to isolation, language, and the conditions of exile, even when treated with black humour and complex games. With this in mind, it is perhaps most appropriate to see Abish in the company of such writers as Vladimir Nabokov, Aharon Appelfeld, Milan Kundera, Georges Perec, Italo Calvino, and Samuel Beckett.

Abish was born in Vienna in 1931 and before the end of the decade fled Hitler's Europe for Shanghai. Here the wartime refugees remained a fragmented, multinational and multilingual community apart, never assimilated into Chinese culture or country, kept away from Chinese language and friendships. The Europeans maintained their former languages, national divisions, social hierarchies and habits, overlooking the poverty, violence, and brutality around them. After the war Abish emigrated to Israel and served in the Tank Corps in the Israeli Defence Services. He claims that it was while walking across the parade grounds "when quite suddenly the idea of becoming a writer flashed through my mind. A moment of pure exhilaration". He moved to the United States and became an American citizen in 1960, publishing primarily in avant-garde magazines and teaching creative writing at Columbia University. He published volumes of poems and short stories as well as three novels. His most acclaimed novel, *How German Is It*, is the work by Abish of greatest interest to Jewish literature, although it does not focus on Jewish characters or even allude to Jews except most obliquely.

How German Is It/Wie Deutsch Ist Es is a novel about the Holocaust set in present-day Germany, the new Germany that is desperately trying to forget the crimes of the war, to repress national memory and transform national identity. Ulrich Hargenau, a difficult but critically admired novelist, has returned to his hometown of Brumholdstein after many years of self-exile in Paris. Brumholdstein is named after the fictional philosopher Brumhold, still alive and honoured (based on the philosopher and Nazi sympathizer Martin Heidegger, whose ideas and specialized terminology are archly placed throughout the omniscient narrator's descriptions). The "New Germany" is on the "edge of forgetfulness", where complicity in the extermination of the Jews and memory of the war years has been repressed in an attempt at a "state of the forgetting of being" (Heidegger's *Seinsvergessenheit*). The original name of the town, Durst, because it was associated with forced labour and death camps, was covered over by the new name of Brumholdstein, just as the new, glittery boutiques and galleries are built over mass graves, sometimes embarrassingly uncovered during construction. The people of the nearby town of Daemling remember the railroad carriages passing and "an occasional scarecrow face framed in the tiny cutout window of a freight car... Some people of Daemling maintained that thousands upon thousands of people were being shipped to Durst. What they would do there was anyone's guess. Work at the I. G. Farben plant? Who knows. Best not to ask. Best not to pry into this matter."

Any mention of the camps and the victims brings a whiff of death and shame before the boosters of the New Germany of the economic miracle. The mayor makes a speech favourably contrasting the popular novelist Bernard Feig to the angst-ridden writing of Ulrich Hargenau: "His novels, the mayor said, are not immersed in the past, and the characters in his books are all happily free of that all too familiar obsession with the 1940–45 period of our life. Great applause." A waiter, Franz, is making a matchstick model of the concentration camp at Durst and when he asks for the plans in the public library, the reference librarian walks away from him, leaving him baffled.

The brilliance and subtle device of the omniscient third-person narrator undercutting everything related to the New Germany by constant reference to the Nazi years makes every set of innocent questions seem like the interrogation of prisoners. A list of the great German authors ends with Thomas Mann and the narrator asks, "why not Mann? He remains *echt Deutsch* despite his dubious decision to abandon his country at its greatest time of need . . . Absolutely no irony intended." Every attempt to honour Brumhold recalls his collaboration ("it was only five minutes brisk walk to the university, where old Brumhold was still teaching philosophy after an enforced period of idleness, the result of too many speeches in the '30s and early '40s, speeches that dealt with the citizen's responsibilities to the New Order"). How German is the German language? "Has it not once again, by brushing against so many foreign substances, so many foreign languages and experiences, acquired foreign impurities . . . ?" The refrain of "a glorious German summer" combines the present summer of the story with the summer of 1944 when Hargenau's father was executed ("What was the summer of 1944 like? Active. Certainly, active"). Italicized questions recur throughout the novel, as whole paragraphs, as interrogations for the readers, and sometimes the plural "we" voice representing the collective thinking appears (as in "We Germans . . .").

How German Is It is a powerful and chilling book about the Holocaust, about memory and forgetting, about Germany, about guilt and collaboration, and about silence and the desire to repress. It has affinities with the fiction of Israeli novelist Aharon Applefeld (especially *Badenheim 1939* and *The Iron Tracks*). After the experience of reading *How German Is It*, one's response to Abish's other works – the early experimental stories, the extended work of Oulipian constraints *Alphabetical Africa*, or the odd use of "found sources" such as *99: The New Meaning* – takes on a darker set of associations, and adds to the complexity of reading the literature of trauma, oppression, war, and genocide.

LEONARD ORR

Abse, Dannie

British poet and dramatist, 1923–

Born Daniel Abse in Cardiff, 22 September 1923. Studied at Marlborough Road Elementary School, St Illtyd's College, and University of South Wales and Monmouthshire, Cardiff; then at King's College, London, and Westminster Hospital; qualified as physician 1950; Member of the Royal College of Surgeons, Licentiate of the Royal College of Physicians. Served in Royal Air Force, 1951–54: squadron leader. Married Joan Mercer, 1951; one son and two daughters. Specialist in charge of chest clinic, Central London Medical Establishment, 1954–89. Senior Fellow in Humanities, Princeton University, 1973–74. Editor, *Poetry and Poverty* magazine, London, 1949–54. President, Poetry Society, 1978–92. Many awards, including the Foyle Award, 1960; Welsh Arts Council Award, 1971, 1987, and, for play, 1980; Cholmondeley Award, 1985. DLitt, University of Wales, Cardiff, 1989; Fellowship of Welsh Academy, 1981; Fellowship of Royal Society of Literature, 1983.

Selected Writings

Poetry
After Every Green Thing, 1948
Walking under Water, 1952
Tenants of the House: Poems 1951–1956, 1957
Poems, Golders Green, 1962
Dannie Abse: A Selection, 1963
A Small Desperation, 1968
Demo, 1969
Selected Poems, 1970
Funland: A Poem in Nine Parts, 1971
Corgi Modern Poets in Focus 4, with others, edited by Jeremy Robson, 1972
Funland and Other Poems, 1973
Lunchtime, 1974
Penguin Modern Poets 26, with D.J. Enright and Michael Longley, 1975
Collected Poems 1948–1976, 1977
Way Out in the Centre, 1981; as *One-Legged on Ice*, 1983
Ask the Bloody Horse, 1986; as *Sky in Narrow Streets*, 1987
White Coat, Purple Coat: Collected Poems 1948–1988, 1989
Remembrance of Crimes Past, 1990
On the Evening Road, 1994
Selected Poems, 1994
Welsh Retrospective, 1997
Arcadia, One Mile, 1998
Be Seated, Thou, 2000
Encounters, 2001

Plays
Fire in Heaven, 1948; as *Is the House Shut?*, 1964; as *In the Cage*, 1967
Hands around the Wall, 1950
House of Cowards, 1960
The Eccentric, 1961
Gone, 1962; as *Gone in January*, 1977
The Joker, 1962; as *The Courting of Essie Glass*, 1981
Three Questor Plays, 1967
The Dogs of Pavlov, 1969
Funland, 1975
Pythagoras, 1976; as *Pythagoras Smith from Row G*, 1990
The View from Row G (includes *House of Cowards*, *The Dogs of Pavlov*, and *Pythagoras Smith*), 1990

Radio Plays: *Conform or Die*, 1957; *No Telegrams, No Thunder*, 1962; *You Can't Say Hello to Anybody*, 1964; *A Small Explosion*, 1964; *The Courting of Essie Glass*, 1975

Novels
Ash on a Young Man's Sleeve, 1954
Some Corner of an English Field, 1956
O. Jones, O. Jones, 1970
There Was a Young Man from Cardiff, 1991
The Strange Case of Dr Simmonds and Dr Glas, 2002

Other
Editor, with Elizabeth Jennings and Stephen Spender, *New Poems 1956*, 1956
Editor, with Howard Sergeant, *Mavericks*, 1957
Editor, *European Verse*, 1964
Medicine on Trial, 1968
Editor, *Corgi Modern Poets in Focus 1,3,5*, 1973
Editor, *Thirteen Poets*, 1973
A Poet in the Family, 1974; 2nd revised edition as *Goodbye, Twentieth Century: An Autobiography*, 2001
Editor, *Poetry Supplement, Christmas*, 1975
Editor, *Poetry Dimension 2–5*, 1978

Editor, *My Medical School*, 1978
Editor, *The Best of the Poetry Year 6–7*, 1980
Miscellany One, 1981
A Strong Dose of Myself, 1983
Editor, *Wales in Verse*, 1983
Under the Influence Of, 1984
Editor, *Doctors and Patients*, 1984
Editor, with Joan Abse, *Voices in the Gallery*, 1986
Journals from the Ant Heap, 1986
Editor, with Joan Abse, *The Music Lover's Literary Companion*, 1988
Editor, *The Hutchinson Book of Post-War British Poetry*, 1989
Editor, with Anne Stevenson, *The Gregory Anthology*, 1994
Intermittent Journals, 1994
Editor, *Twentieth Century Anglo-Welsh Poetry*, 1997

Further Reading

Interviews in *The Guardian* (31 January 1978); *Good Housekeeping* (May 1981); *The Times* (28 February 1983); and *Sunday Times Magazine* (22 May 1983)
Adcock, Fleur, *Ambit*, 70, 1977
Cohen, Joseph (editor), *The Poetry of Dannie Abse: Critical Essays and Reminiscences*, London: Robson, 1983
Curtis, Tony, *Dannie Abse*, Cardiff: University of Wales Press, 1985
Curtis, Tony, *The New Welsh Review*, 22 (1993)
Hoffman, Daniel, "Doctor and Magus in the Work of Dannie Abse", *Literature and Medicine*, 3 (1984)
Oxley, William, *The Inner Tapestry: Literary Essays*, Salzburg: Institut für Anglistik und Amerikanistik, University of Salzburg, 1985
Soniat, Katherine, *Spirit* (Spring–Summer 1989)
Ward, J.P., "Science, Poetry: Approaches to Redgrove, Abse and Ammons", *Poesis* (Fall 1984)
Winegarten, Renee, *Jewish Chronicle Literary Supplement* (24 December 1982)

Dannie Abse was born in Cardiff, Wales, to Jewish parents. A leading British poet, he is also a successful novelist and playwright, and has developed an individual style of conversational openness and varied range. Witty and entertaining, his poems are also capable of biting, uncomfortable insights. A medical doctor most of his life, Abse is fascinated by the conflict between science and art, and more specifically between the scientist as authoritarian controller and individual self-assertion.

Though raised in the Jewish faith, Abse found religion unappealing, true awareness arriving only with the first news of the concentration camps. "Yes", Abse comments in *A Poet in the Family*, "Auschwitz made me more of a Jew than Moses did". Even so, some inkling of his people's sufferings dawned on him as a child in the synagogue, and is recalled in his first novel *Ash on a Young Man's Sleeve.*

> As they murmured their long incantations, I saw in their large dark eyes that infinite, that mute animal sadness, as in the liquid eyes of fugitives everywhere. I was eleven years old then: I could not have named all of this but I knew it . . . I knew it all.

Recognition of the Holocaust nightmare and his own narrow escape from it has exercised a potent effect on Abse's writing ever since. Equally significant has been his support for the State of Israel. In 1948, he wrote one of his best-known poems, "Song – After the Hebrew of Dov Shamir", in Israel's honour. The fact that "Shamir" was Abse's own invention doesn't detract from his admiration for the infant state, or diminish the real merits of the poem. Ironically, soon after writing it Abse received a letter from T.S. Eliot, who urged him to make more "Shamir" translations, as they were better than Abse's own work! Since then, his commitment to Israel has remained firm; while visiting the United States in 1973, he followed the Yom Kippur war on television with a personal involvement. "It is as if my own life was endangered", he remarks in *A Strong Dose of Myself*, and later on, "I become a Jew the moment I hear the word *Israel* spoken by one not Jewish".

Fire in Heaven, the verse-play he wrote in the late 1940s, presents its leading character with the awful choice of murdering his own family or having his entire village massacred. While the play itself is flawed, the sinister theme clearly derives from atrocities committed in Europe shortly before, and similar concerns recur in the poems. In "Postmark", from *Poems, Golders Green*, sight of an official stamp on an envelope suggests unpleasant associations with death. In *A Small Desperation* (which also contains "On the Beach", a protest against the Vietnam War), "A Night Out" describes how Abse and his wife watch a Polish film on the Nazi death-camps. "Later, uneasy, in the velvet dark/ we peered through the cut-out oblong window/ at the split drama of our nightmares:/ images of Auschwitz, almost authentic,/ the human obscenity in close-up". Troubled, the couple return home and make love, as if to shut out the horrifying images they have seen. "No More Mozart", from *Funland and Other Poems* tells of Abse's 1970 visit to Germany, where he lies awake, hearing in the noise of the wind outside – "the far Jew-sounds of railway trucks".

Almost worse than the genocide is the knowledge that the same destructive impulses lie close beneath the surface, and may be released at any time by unscrupulous authority. As a Jew, Abse is aware of the murderous instincts harboured by his neighbours, and as a doctor he distrusts the godlike power his white-coated colleagues are allowed to exercise. These forebodings are powerfully expressed in his plays. *The Dogs of Pavlov* is based on a psychological experiment carried out at Yale University, where, in order to test "obedience to evil commands", an electric chair is rigged up and "subjects" selected to apply electric shock to a "victim" when he fails to answer questions correctly. The "electric chair" is a fake and the "victim" an actor whose pain is imaginary, but none of this alters Abse's chilling revelation that ordinary people are ready to inflict pain on others for the purposes of scientific experiment. The drama gains a personal dimension in the tormented relationship between Kurt and Sally as torturer and victim, and its dehumanizing effect on them both. In the manipulative power wielded by the doctors Abse suggests a link with "experiments" in the

Nazi death-camps, a link that many playgoers were reluctant to admit.

Set in a mental hospital, *Pythagoras* follows the battle of wits between the superintendent Dr Aquillus and one of his patients, a disturbed stage magician who believes himself the reincarnation of the Greek scientist/artist Pythagoras. Their struggle echoes Abse's own situation; as doctor and writer, he wears the white coat and the magician's purple cloak. In fact, at one point the two men are confused, Pythagoras posing as Aquillus and "recreating" him as a psychopathic patient. The climax is reached when Pythagoras confronts Aquillus and collapses; afterwards he recovers and becomes "normal", but his creative individuality is lost, and with it his humanity. Both plays demonstrate the dangers of scientists "acting God", and indicate the darker hidden depths that lie within us all.

This said, Abse's work is far from gloomy. His writing is peppered with jokes and marked by a wry, self-deprecating humour, and his novel *O. Jones, O. Jones* is given a mostly comic treatment, while his short play *The Eccentric* has an amusing portrait of a Jewish shopkeeper who refuses to sell his customers what they want. As he sees it, he is acting in their interest, helping them to experience self-denial. "God doesn't say yes to everything", Goldstein comments. "Maybe that's what makes a man."

Recent years have seen Abse return to his Jewish roots, visiting Israel and studying Hebrew writers. Later collections include several poems that draw on Yiddish humour for their inspiration. "Of Rabbi Yose", "Snake", "Of Itzig and His Dog", and "Street Scene" from *Way Out in the Centre*, and the "Joke" that opens *Ask the Bloody Horse*, together with "Uncle Isidore" and "Tales of Schatz" from the earlier *Poems*, mark a new direction in his writing. The latter collection also includes translations from Hebrew writers, factual echoes of the earlier "Dov Shamir" poem. Yet the shadow of Auschwitz persists. In "Exit", one of his most moving poems, Abse describes the death of his mother in hospital. Contemplating her final suffering, a Holocaust image comes to mind, "but what will spring from this/ unredeemed, needless degradation/ this concentration camp for one?"

GEOFF SADLER

Agnon, S.Y.

Polish-born Israeli fiction writer, 1888–1970

Born Shmuel Yosef Halevi Czaczkes in Buczacz, 17 July 1888; father rabbi, scholar, and fur merchant. Studied at private schools and Baron Hirsch School. Lived in Palestine, 1907–13; secretary of Jewish court in Jaffa and secretary of Jewish National Council. Lecturer and tutor in Hebrew literature, Germany, 1913–24, then returned to Palestine. Married Esther Marx; one son, one daughter. Member of Hebrew Language Academy: President 1950–70. Many awards, including Bialik Prize, 1934, 1954; Ussisskin Prize, 1950; Israel Prize, 1954 and 1958; Nobel Prize for Literature, shared with Nelly Sachs, 1966. President, Mekitzei Nirdamim, 1950. Died in Jerusalem, 17 February 1970.

Selected Writings

Fiction

Agunot [Forsaken Wives], 1908
Toyten-tants [Death Dance], 1911
Vehayah heakov lemishor [And the Crooked Shall Be Made Straight], 1912
Givat hahol [The Hill of Sand], 1920
Besod yesharim [Among the Pious], 1921
Mehamat hametsik [From the Wrath of the Oppressor], 1921
Al kapot hamanul [Upon the Handles of the Lock], 1922
Polin [Poland], 1925
Maaseh rabi gadiel hatinok [The Tale of Little Reb Gadiel], 1925
Hashanim hatovot [The Good Years], 1925
Agadat hasofer [The Legend of the Scribe], 1929
Kol sipurav [Collected Stories], 11 vols, 1931–52
Hakhnasat kalah, 2 vols, 1931; as *The Bridal Canopy*, translated by I.M. Lask, 1967
Meaz umeatah [From Then and From Now], 1931
Sipurei ahavim [Love Stories], 1931
Elu veelu, 1932; as *Dwelling Place of My People: Sixteen Stories of the Chassidim*, translated by J. Weinberg and H. Russell, 1983
Beshuvah vanahat [In Peace and Tranquility], 1935
Sipur pashut, 1935; as *A Simple Story*, translated by Hillel Halkin, 1985
Bilvav yamim, 1935; as *In the Heart of the Seas*, translated by I.M. Lask, 1948
Sefer, sofer vesipur [Book, Scribe, and Tale], 1938
Oreah nata lalun, 1939; as *A Guest for the Night*, translated by Misha Louvish, 1968
Shevuat emunim, 1943; as *Two Tales: The Betrothed and Edo and Enam*, translated by Walter Lever, 1966
Sipurim veagadot [Stories and Legends], 1944
Temol shilshom, 1945; as *Only Yesterday*, translated by Barbara Harshav, 2000; in part as *Kelev chutsot*, 1950
Samukh venireh [Close and Apparent], 1950
Ad heinah [Until Now], 1952
Leahar haseudah [After the Meal], 1963
Selected Stories, 1970
Twenty-One Stories, translated by Nahum N. Glatzer, 1970; as *Selection*, 1977
Shirah, 1971; as *Shira*, translated by Zeva Shapiro, 1989
Pithei devarim [Opening Remarks], 1977
Takhrikh shel sipurim [A Collection of Stories], 1984
A Book that was Lost and Other Stories, translated by Alan Mintz and Anne Golomb Hoffman, 1995

Other

Yamim noraim, 1938; as *Days of Awe, Being a Treasury of Traditions, Legends, and Learned Commentaries*, translated by M. Galpert, 1948
Atem reitem, 1959; as *Present at Sinai: The Giving of the Law*, translated by M. Swirsky, 1994
Sifreihim shel tsadikim [Books of the Zaddiks], 1961
Speech at the Nobel Banquet, 1967
Meatsmi el atsmi [From Me to Me], 1976
Esterlain yekirati: mikhtavim [Estherlein My Darling] (letters 1924–31), 1983

Kurzweil, Agnon, Greenberg: Letters, edited by Lillian Dabby-Goury, 1987

Further Reading

Aberbach, David, *At the Handles of the Lock: Themes in the Fiction of S.J. Agnon*, Oxford and New York: Oxford University Press, 1984
Band, Arnold J., *Nostalgia and Nightmare: A Study in the Fiction of S.Y. Agnon*, Berkeley: University of California Press, and London: Cambridge University Press, 1968
Ben-Dov, Nitza, *Agnon's Art of Indirection: Uncovering Latent Content in the Fiction of S.Y. Agnon*, Leiden and New York: Brill, 1993
Fisch, Harold, *S.Y. Agnon*, New York: Ungar, 1975
Hochman, Baruch, *The Fiction of S.Y. Agnon*, Ithaca, New York: Cornell University Press, 1970
Hoffman, Anne Golomb, *Between Exile and Return: S.Y. Agnon and the Drama of Writing*, Albany: State University of New York Press, 1991
Patterson, David and Glenda Abramson (editors), *Tradition and Trauma: Studies in the Fiction of S.J. Agnon*, Boulder, Colorado: Westview Press, 1994
Prooftexts, vol. 11, special issue on Agnon celebrating the centenary of his birth, with critical studies by N. Ben-Dov, Y. Feldman, A. Mintz, D. Miron and others, 1987
Shaked, Gershon, *Shmuel Yosef Agnon: A Revolutionary Traditionalist*, New York: New York University Press, 1989
Yudkin, Leon I. (editor), *Agnon: Texts and Contexts in English Translation*, New York: Wiener, 1988

Agnon is considered by many readers and writers to be the greatest Modern Hebrew prose writer, and the Nobel Prize, which he won in 1966, expressed international recognition of his extraordinary achievement. The author who in his personal life moved between various centres, old and new, of Jewish history, built his oeuvre around the tension between the irremediably broken past and the complexity of the modern Jewish condition. In the story "Tehilah" we read, "I stood at times among the worshippers, at times among those who question". His own dilemma: how to remain "within the system" (Agnon's term for religious observance) in a modern world, may seem archaic. Yet one can also consider it as inextricably linked to the struggle of Modern Hebrew itself, "the revival of a literature and a language from the past for a revived Jewish nation".

According to the Israeli writer Amos Oz every true writer becomes a writer because of a trauma experienced in youth or childhood. "Beyond all differences in talent", he writes, "the trauma, the rift, in Agnon's soul was deeper and more painful", and this rift is caused by one fundamental uncertainty: "There is One Who hears our prayers or there is not. There is Justice and there is a Judge or there is not." A.G. Hoffman and A. Mintz point out the universal resonance of these questions, and they refer to such writers as James Joyce and William Faulkner, who, like Agnon, explore the issue of humankind's aloneness "through the particular and unfamiliar – and often exotic and arcane – materials of their national and regional cultures".

In Agnon's case this "national" culture is not even shared by all speakers of Modern Hebrew today, as his texts are layered with meaning, drawing upon a vast range of traditional concepts, textual references, and poetic images contained within biblical and post-biblical literature. His own pen name, Agnon, which the young Shmuel Yosef Czaczkes adopted during his first stay in Palestine, is an example of his ironic appropriation of Jewish tradition. It is an adaptation of the title of the first story he published there in 1908, "Agunot". Agnon took the legal term "agunah", literally an abandoned Jewish wife who can't remarry because no divorce has been issued, and he used this symbol of an eternally indeterminate figure, at once belonging to and standing apart from the community, to carve out his own place on the Hebrew literary scene from the start. For the rest of his career Agnon remained conscious of his literary persona, carefully crafting it so as to create links between his personal life and important events and concepts in Jewish history.

Agnon's early work consists of short stories and novellas in a wide variety of styles, ranging from romantic to expressionistic, mystical to realist. According to some critics it is in the short prose form that the author most distinguished himself. Although Jerusalem occupies a central place in his oeuvre, Agnon also situated some of his stories in other places in Erets Israel, most notably "Hill of Sand", which takes place in Jaffa, and "From Lodging to Lodging". In the latter we follow a restless narrator on an impossible search for an ideal place to live. However, the problem lies with him, not with the place. "When I saw the house and the yard, I was glad and I had doubts. I was glad that a man in the Land of Israel had all this, and I had my doubts that this place was for me."

In 1913 Agnon left Palestine for Germany, and although not intentionally, this visit turned into a sojourn of more than ten years. There he established relationships with many important figures of the German-Jewish intelligentsia, such as Franz Rosenzweig, Gershom Scholem, and Martin Buber, who all had a lasting influence on his work. His encounter with the businessman and bibliophile Salman Schocken, who would start the famous publishing house, played a decisive role in Agnon's further career.

The destruction of Agnon's house, and with it his whole library, in 1924, prompted the writer to return to Palestine, where he settled in Talpiyot, on the outskirts of Jerusalem, yet another example of his deliberate choice of a place just outside the centre. In the riots of 1929 Agnon lost his home and his books for the second time. In the opening paragraph of "The Sign" he ties together the various instances of loss and rebuilding affecting his life:

> In the year when the news reached us that all the Jews in my town had been killed, I was living in a certain section of Jerusalem, in a house I had built for myself after the disturbances of 1929 (5629 – which numerically is equal to "The Eternity of Israel"). On the night when the Arabs destroyed my home, I vowed that if God would save me from the hands of the enemy and I should live, I would build a house in this particular neighbourhood which the Arabs had tried to destroy.

Agnon's fictional landscape is filled with people running around in dread and despair. Many of his most memorable characters are weighed down by feelings of guilt: Isaac Kumer in *Only Yesterday*, who deserted both his hometown and his family, or the protagonist of *A Guest for the Night* who left his family and a safe home in the Land of Israel. Perhaps the most guilt-ridden of all is Manfred Herbst, the adulterous protagonist of *Shira*. But, in the thematic logic of the novel, adultery only serves as a means to lure Herbst, a bourgeois academic, into the arms of Shira (a woman's name that means "poetry" in Hebrew), who incorporates both love and death, health and disease. The phrase "Flesh such as yours will not soon be forgotten", which is conjured up time and again, serves as the leitmotiv of the novel. Its real theme is, in Robert Alter's words "the indissoluble bond between eros and thanatos". The novel, which remained unfinished when Agnon died in 1970, can be regarded as his artistic testament, "his vision of the role of art in human reality".

DOROTHÉE VAN TENDELOO

Aini, Lea

Israeli poet and fiction writer, 1962–

Born in Tel Aviv, 1962. Moved with her family to Bat-Yam, 1966. After army service, had various jobs for two years. Studied Hebrew language and literature at college for teachers in Tel Aviv, but never worked as teacher. Published first poems in 1986. Member of editorial staff of daily newspaper *Al Hamishmar*, 1987–91. Lectures for victims of rape and sexual abuse; conducted a self-expression workshop for cerebral palsy sufferers, 1998. Married; one daughter. Received prizes for two volumes of poetry; award from Tel Aviv Fund for Literature, 1993; Prime Minister's Prize, 1994.

Selected Writings

Poetry
Diokan [Portrait], 1988
Keisarit hapirion hamedumeh [Empress of the Imagined Fertility], 1990

Fiction
Giborei kayits [Summer Heroes], 1991
Geut hahol [Sand Tide], 1992
Tikrah li milemata [Call Me from Downstairs], 1994
Mar arnav mehapes avoda [Mr Rabbit's Job Hunt], 1994
Hei, yuli [Hi, Yuli], 1995
Mishehi tsricha lihiot kan [Someone Must Be Here], 1995
Hetsi veananas [Half-Pint and Wandercloud/Octopina], 1996
Hardufim o sipurim muralim al ahava [Oleanders or Poisoned Love Stories], 1997
Ashtoret, 1999
Shir ani, shir immah [Song Me, Song Mummy], 2000

Works in English translation
"Shower", *Modern Hebrew Literature*, new series 8–9 (Spring/Fall 1992)
"White", *Modern Hebrew Literature*, new series 13 (Fall/Winter 1994)
"Until the Entire Guard Has Passed", *Jerusalem Post Magazine* (28 July 1995)

Further Reading

Domb, Risa (editor), *New Women's Writing from Israel*, London: Vallentine Mitchell, 1996
Glazer, Miriyam (editor), *Dreaming the Actual: Contemporary Fiction and Poetry by Israeli Women Writers*, Albany: State University of New York Press, 2000
Hoffman, Haya (editor), *A Chance beyond Bombs: An Anthology of Modern Hebrew Peace Poems*, New Delhi and London: Penguin, 1998
Kaufman, Shirley, Galit Hasan-Rokem and Tamar S. Hess (editors), *The Defiant Muse: Hebrew Feminist Poems*, New York: Feminist Press, 1999; London: Loki, 2000
Lentin, Ronit, *Israel and the Daughters of the Shoah*, New York: Berghahn, 2000
Yudkin, Leon, *Public Crisis and Literary Response: The Adjustment of Modern Jewish Literature*: Paris: Suger, 2001

Lea Aini is a writer in various media, whose work quickly struck a chord in the Israeli reading public. Her first prose work (she had already published two volumes of poetry), appeared in 1991, *Giborei kayits* [Summer Heroes]. This is a collection of stories set in a poor and decaying part of southern Tel Aviv, where the social reality of Israel's underclass works out its life in an atmosphere of cramped bickering. However, the world of Aini's figures, whether conveyed in first or third person, is not confined to the immediate environment. It always partakes of another realm, suggested by the imaginative flight of the fictional character, and it so permeates that life and being that it becomes difficult to draw a line of division between reality and fantasy. There emerges a portrait throughout the author's opus of a tension between logical concerns and human relations. The first works against the second, which acts as the driving force in the character's life, and it is the restraint of logical elements that then imposes its stark rule on the outcome in a rather depressing existence.

The author's first full-length fiction, the novel *Geut hahol* [Sand Tide], is a first-person account of a young woman, prematurely widowed when her husband is killed in an army training accident. But, unlike many of her contemporaries, the narrator here is so obsessed by her own man that she finds difficulty in coming to terms with any sort of normality without him, and her narrative is in fact a monologue addressed to him.

Aini's second novel, *Mishehi tsricha lihiot kan* [Someone Must Be Here], is a gritty amalgamation of the surreal and the naturalistic. Set in contemporary Tel Aviv, the narrative is related by the 17-year-old Gila, and constitutes a monologue. It reveals an unusual view of the world on the part of a fiction-obsessed post-adolescent who works in a bookshop, and who merges her identity in the world and characters of the writers whom she handles. As Dubek says at the outset, she is so much part of the world of print that she bears the marks on her hands of the fresh newspapers that she discharges into the shop, and she is "intoxicated" by it.

That Aini is willing to experiment with form and subject-matter is established by the volume of stories *Hardufim* [Oleanders] in 1997. There is here a variety of settings and plots, confirming the irony and surrealistic undercurrent of what could be seen as apparently romantic. Although Aini's texts are set in Israel, and in a central sector of its geography, her themes and literary texture are not typical of the mainstream of Israeli culture. The atmosphere is seamy, the stance not overtly ideological. The environment, the after effects of the Holocaust, the ethnic mix resulting from the immigration of the Jewish populations of so many lands, are seen as naturally assumed, rather than explicated. The sexual tension brought about by pressures, internal and external, those connected with family and career, are dissipated if not resolved, in the first and title story of the collection.

Aini captures the current scene in middle Israel. She achieves this through penetration into the heart of the commonplace, and through the use of an admixture of contemporary Israeli argot and literary Hebrew. There are ellipses not only of language, but of sense and context. For example, a presented dialogue can reflect a given moment in considerable detail, but then years can pass in the implied narrative without a mention. The effect is like a landscape lit up by occasional flashes of light. Much is suggested by implication in the narrative gaps in this portrait of the mundane and the (particularly female) concerns of the average Israeli. But, more than anything else, what we have here is an obsessive preoccupation with loneliness. The principal figure, characteristically female, remains stranded in splendid isolation, and is compelled to find a *modus vivendi* within the world that inevitably will not submit to her will. The Aini character is introverted, strange, and unwilling to articulate feeling. But that feeling is internalized, and it becomes the text of the narrative. The search for love is covered over, as in the image of the sabra fruit as exemplifying the sabra person; prickly on the outside, but sugary within. The search for love is conveyed to the reader in the description of the criteria for genuine love. These criteria are constantly modified and refined, but they keep bubbling up insistently. They are movingly invoked in the story "Ping Pong", an apparent representation of the way that feelings, banter, and attempted thrusts of communication pass back and forth. The stories are suggestive rather than fully explicated and spelled out. We get flashes of the commonplace, life as it is lived and felt. The stories do not cheer on the whole. They present love, or what may pass for a kind of love, with its physical attachment and dependence, despair at the loss of the loved object and the life that was carried by the partner, and death, in despair's wake. And then, there is the inevitable and unpromising continuation that follows. The world is a world of new immigrants as well as native-born Israelis, of young people, whose hope wanes with middle age, and of old people who fear death, of the poor who aspire to a more lavish lifestyle, and a world too of foolish flummeries. It is a world where women wait for men, and then suffer for the results of the contact. It is a world of the Levantine State that is also Israel. This is conveyed through the medium of the monologue addressed to an imagined auditor/reader in the intimate language of immediacy and idiom.

Not only are there few links with the tradition of Modern Hebrew literature, there is hardly any contemporary literary source discernible in Aini's writing. It seems to emerge from itself, and to be preoccupied with itself and the pictures that it draws in texts devoid of allusiveness. Aini's stories have created themselves, and live in their own space. As a representative of the new proletarian fiction, Aini has heralded a wave of such "kitchen sink" writing, so popular in the Britain of the 1950s.

LEON I. YUDKIN

Allen, Woody

US writer, dramatist, scriptwriter, film director, actor, 1935–

Born Allen Stewart Konigsberg in Brooklyn, New York, 1 December 1935. Studied at New York University and City College of New York, 1953; did not graduate. Worked variously as gag writer for newspaper and television personalities, staff writer for National Broadcasting Corporation, night club, television and film artist, and film director. Married, first, Heulene Rosen, 1954; divorced 1960; second, Louise Lasser, 1966; divorced; third, Soon Yi Previn, 1997; two adopted children; one child with Mia Farrow; several adopted children. Many awards and nominations for books and films, including Sylvana Award, 1957; Oscar, 1977 (for directing and for screenplay), 1986 (for screenplay); O. Henry Award, 1978.

Selected Writings

Screenplays
What's New, Pussycat, 1965
Take the Money and Run, with Mickey Rose, 1969
Bananas, with Mickey Rose, 1971
Everything You Always Wanted to Know about Sex, 1972
Sleeper, with Marshall Brickman, 1973
Love and Death, 1975
Annie Hall, with Marshall Brickman, 1977
Interiors, 1978
Manhattan, with Marshall Brickman, 1979
Stardust Memories, 1980
A Midsummer Night's Sex Comedy, 1982
Zelig, 1983
Broadway Danny Rose, 1984
The Purple Rose of Cairo, 1985
Hannah and Her Sisters, 1986
Radio Days, 1987
September, 1987
Another Woman, 1988
Crimes and Misdemeanors, 1989
Oedipus Wrecks, 1989
Alice, 1990
Shadows and Fog, 1992
Husbands and Wives, 1992
Manhattan Murder Mystery, 1993
Bullets over Broadway, 1994
Mighty Aphrodite, 1995

Everyone Says I Love You, 1996
Deconstructing Harry, 1997
Celebrity, 1998
Sweet and Lowdown, 1999
Small Time Crooks, 2000
The Curse of the Jade Scorpion, 2001
Hollywood Ending, 2002

Plays
From A to Z, with Herbert Farjeon and others, 1960
Don't Drink the Water, 1966
Play It Again, Sam, 1969
Death: A Comedy in One Act, 1975
God: A Comedy in One Act, 1975
The Floating Light Bulb, 1982

Prose
Getting Even, 1971
Without Feathers, 1972
Side Effects, 1975
Non-Being and Somethingness, 1978
The Lunatic's Tale, 1986
The Complete Prose, 1991
The Illustrated Woody Allen Reader, 1993

Numerous television shows including *The Tonight Show* and *Your Show of Shows*

Further Reading

Adler, Bill and Jerry Feinman, *Woody Allen: Clown Prince of American Humor*, New York: Pinnacle, 1975
Baxter, John, *Woody Allen: A Biography*, London: HarperCollins, 1998; New York: Carroll and Graf, 1999
Björkman, Stig, *Woody Allen on Woody Allen*, London: Faber, 1994; New York: Grove Press, 1995
Blake, Richard A., *Woody Allen: Profane and Sacred*, Lanham, Maryland: Scarecrow Press, 1995
Brode, Douglas, *Woody Allen: His Films and Career*, Secaucus, New Jersey: Citadel Press, 1985, London: Columbus, 1986; as *The Films of Woody Allen*, revised and updated, New York: Carol, 1991
Curry, Renee R. (editor), *Perspectives on Woody Allen*, New York: G.K. Hall, and London: Prentice Hall, 1996
Fox, Julian, *Woody: Movies from Manhattan*, London: Batsford, and Woodstock, New York: Overlook Press, 1996
Guthrie, Lee, *Woody Allen: A Biography*, New York: Drake, 1978
Lax, Eric, *On Being Funny: Woody Allen and Comedy*, New York: Charterhouse, 1975; as *Woody Allen and His Comedy*, London: Elm Tree, 1976
Lax, Eric, *Woody Allen: A Biography*, New York: Knopf, and London: Jonathan Cape, 1991
Meade, Marion, *The Unruly Life of Woody Allen*, London: Weidenfeld and Nicolson, and New York: Scribner, 2000
Palmer, Myles, *Woody Allen: An Illustrated Biography*, London and New York: Proteus, 1980
Wernblad, Annette, *Brooklyn Is Not Expanding: Woody Allen's Comic Universe*, Rutherford, New Jersey: Fairleigh Dickinson University Press, 1992
Yacowar, Maurice, *Loser Take All: The Comic Art of Woody Allen*, New York: Ungar, 1979; revised edition, Oxford: Roundhouse, 1991

Allen's concerns with Jewishness in his major work are always difficult to access as his dominant methods are the application of parody and irony. His work also spans several genres and he freely makes intertextual reference to both film and literary narrative. His representation of Jewish people and culture, as with Philip Roth, is always open to criticism in terms of his flippancy and easy sarcasm. But in the essays and pastiches of his three prose collections there is a more explicit demonstration of the tendency to merge his personal surreal vision with established New York liberal humanism.

Allen in the essays is playful with many established stereotypes of the Jewish intellectual. In "Remembering Needleman" he parodies the style of the literary memoir: "It is easy to remember the public Needleman. Brilliant, committed, the author of Styles and Modes. But it is the private Needleman I will always fondly recall, the Sandor Needleman who was never without some favourite hat." But equally, he writes grand-scale metanarratives of the Jewishness in the secular culture of American letters. Often he textualizes the Representative Jew, as in Zelig, in which Zelig melts into every identity around him, or in Alvy Singer, whom Eric Lax notes as "the most Jewish of all his screen characters, a man obsessed with paranoia, guilt, sexual hang-ups, death and childhood fantasies".

Yet paradoxically Allen, even within parody and pastiche of literary genres and cultural types, still writes within certain irresistible Jewish traditions, as in his *Death: A Comedy*, in which his character is Kleinman (little man) and very much the *nebbish* of the films (text in *Without Feathers*). In the essays and articles he also spoofs Hasidic tales, Viennese psychology, posturing philosophy and the bookish, literary milieu which has been so common in his screenplays. Julian Fox notes that in Allen's work for highbrow periodicals, he was writing for an audience "which didn't demand . . . that his humour be instantly comprehensible". Of course, that highbrow base in the audience has also always been the target of his humour, but the laughs are always from love, and never from loathing.

It is in his film writing that we have the most intense and extended representation of Jewishness – both secular and religious. Often, Allen takes over the parable as a site of comedy and satire, but this is often mixed with distorted autobiography. Thus we have the powerful guilt-generating mother figure of *Oedipus Wrecks* (a segment of *New York Stories*), the raucous but loving family of *Radio Days*, and the recurrent anti-heroes deep in analysis and angst, often artistic individuals, from Alvy Singer to Harry. In fact, his statements about the Jewish elements in the films are minimal, and their relation to autobiography is always fraught with difficulty for the critic. But he has made occasional comments on this, as when asked about the "goy" being introduced into a Jewish family (*Oedipus Wrecks*) he notes, "the sheer stupidity of insisting that your child not marry out of the religion. I just think that's atrocious".

But Allen's preoccupations have always been with more

universally fundamental protagonists and their dilemmas, and the dogmas of Judaism have been prominent only through the distortions and simplifications of comedy; thus Allen is not afraid to write the "cheap laugh" by including visual jokes about the appearance of rabbis, or adapting the wit and irony of the one-liner to a serious theme. His early influences were the slapstick of the Marx Brothers, together with the wryness of Milton Berle and the Catskill comedy-circuit family humour of Allen's nightclub years. This combination makes for much of the comedic success in his best work.

Ultimately, Allen celebrates and often poeticizes a certain ideology and lifestyle which is intimately embedded in Manhattan and in the third-generation immigrant communities, communities in which the professional classes clamour for intellectual and artistic stimulation as part of constructing life's values. Hence his sets often involve a book-lined study, music recitals and theatre, art exhibitions and long conversations on philosophy. His work reflects those values: the bedrock of the Jewish New York circles who read and discuss the *New York Review of Books* and the latest Saul Bellow. The characters are, however, usually aspirants to a higher being, a fulfilment always within range, perhaps typified by Allen's own cultural habits such as his comments on his reading: "I still read a lot. But I have never read a lot for pleasure".

STEPHEN WADE

Almog, Ruth

Israeli fiction writer, 1936–

Born in Petah Tikvah, 15 May 1936. Studied at Teachers Seminary, Jerusalem 1954–55; Tel Aviv University, 1959–65, BA in literature and philosophy. Military service, 1956–58. Taught at various high schools, 1959–67. Assistant to literary editor of *Haaretz* from 1967; taught script writing, Tel Aviv University, 1989, and creative writing, Hebrew University, Jerusalem, for one year. Married Aharon Almog, 1959; two daughters. Awards include Le'ev Prize for Children and Youth Literature, Ministry of Education, 1985; Haifa University Prize for Youth Book, 1986; Brenner Prize, 1989.

Selected Writings

Short Stories

Hasdei halayla shel margerita [Marguerita's Nightly Charities], 1969
Aharei tu bishvat [After Tubishvat], 1979
Nashim [Women], 1986
Shrinking, 1986; in *Six Israeli Novellas*, edited by Gershon Shaked, 1999
Die Blaue Frau [The Blue Woman], 1992
Tikun omanuti [Invisible Mending], 1993

Novels

Beerets gezirah [The Exile], 1970
Et hazar vehaoyev [The Stranger and the Foe], 1980
Mavet Bageshem, 1982; as *Death in the Rain*, translated by Dalya Bilu, 1993
Shorshei avir [Roots of Air], 1993
Meahev mushlam [A Perfect Lover], with Esther Ettinger, 1995

For Children

The Prince of the Rhinoceri, 1976
Naphy nasikh hakarnafim [Naphy], 1979
Tzoanim bapardes [Gypsies in the Orange Grove], 1986
Kadur hakesef [The Silver Ball], 1986
Gilgil, 1986
The Wonderbird, 1991
Rakefet, ahavati harishonah [Rakefet, My First Love], 1992
Gilgil rotsa kelev [Gilgil Wants a Dog], 1998
Hamasa sheli im alex [My Journey with Alex], 1998
Balut hapele shel kamila [The Wonder Acorn], 1999

Further Reading

Feldman, Yael S., *No Room of their Own: Gender and Nation in Israeli Women's Fiction*, New York: Columbia University Press, 1999; Hebrew edition, Tel Aviv: Hakibuts hameuhad, 2001
Shaked, Gerson, introduction to *Six Israeli Novellas*, edited by Shaked, Boston: David R. Godine, 1999
Shirav, Peninah, *Ketiva Lo Tamah: 'Emdat Siha Vi-Yitsuge Nashiyut Bi-Yetsirotam Shel Yehudit Hendel, Amalyah Kahana-Karmon, ve-Rut Almog* [Non Innocent Writing: Discourse Position and Female Representations in Works by Yehudit Hendel, Amalia Kahana-Carmon and Ruth Almog], Tel Aviv: Hakibuts hameuhad, 1998
Siegel, Richard and Tamar Sofer (editors), *The Writer in the Jewish Community: An Israeli/North American Dialogue*, Rutherford, New Jersey: Fairleigh Dickinson University Press, 1993
Sokoloff, Naomi B., Anne Lapidus Lerner and Anita Norich (editors), *Gender and Text in Modern Hebrew and Yiddish Literature*, New York: Jewish Theological Seminary of America, 1992

Almog's early work keeps close to her roots where the locale of Petah Tikvah, its fauna and flora, and the background of her extended orthodox Jewish family make a strong appearance. She talks of her near idyllic childhood surrounded by farmyard life. When the author was 14 her father died and much of this changed. The title story from *Aharei tu bishvat* (translated as "After Arbor Day" in *Stories from Women Writers in Israel*) reflects this loss, disappointment and irredeemable sadness. She is one of the few Israeli women authors to enter the world of childhood in her writing, both in a Proustian longing to remember and retrace lost time, and in creating award-winning children's books. The fate of children during wartime is a major fascination.

She claims to feel distinctly "marginal" as a woman writer in modern Israeli society. The culture of war that pervades the ethos, structure, and history of the society since the Six Day War of 1967, remains outside any possible first-hand experience of women. Unable to embrace the entirety of national life, the scope of her writing (and her claim extends to women's writing in general) is resultantly confined to family life, female experience, or relations between the sexes.

Her collection of short stories, *Nashim* [Women] explores the process of women's seeking freedom from a patriarchal society. This is frequently represented by an intransigent father figure, or unattainable oedipal love. The costs of this freedom are great, resulting in an overwhelming sense of guilt and loss, and the absence of love, creativity, or sexual fulfilment. In the story *Shrinking* Almog portrays a vision of loneliness appeased only by Abigail's care of the neighbourhood cats, and her solace in listening to music. Clearly her thankless and obdurate father denies her any sense of self-worth. The plot is constructed by an accumulation of images of lights and colours, of interactions that portray her increasing sense of disappointment.

Almog studied philosophy, and this plays a significant role in her work. Her chapter "Polemos and Polemics" in *The Writer in the Jewish Community* from 1993 discusses the "stigma of female marginality" which forms her credo of women's writing: "As I matured as a writer, I realized with growing intensity that if my artistic efforts were not also an act of subversion – in the broadest sense of the word – I would not be satisfied". This subversion is manifest in the important innovations women have introduced into Israeli literature: "they have penetrated more deeply into the human experience – illness, death, madness, servitude [the stuff of their prose]". Her protagonists address the issues of life and its meaning, existential freedoms and choices. Suicide as supreme existential alternative is introduced through the maternal line of characters, grappling with emotional abuse. She shows her concern with female insanity and its relationship to artistic madness. Frequently the maternal figure is shown as free-spirited to the point of losing her hold on the practical world.

Mavet bageshem (translated as *Death in the Rain*) explores the value and meaning of life through the leitmotif of death. This is reinforced by numerous intertexts (explicit and implicit references to other authors and their works within the literary text). Most significant of these is the American poet Hart Crane, who committed suicide age 32.

Using the postmodern reflection on the metanarrative, Almog discusses the purpose and process of writing itself. It's a multi-vocal novel, where individual narrative voices progress the plot-line, a device explored frequently in Israeli literature of this period, especially by Amos Oz in *Black Box*, A.B. Yehoshua in *The Lover*, and David Grossman in *The Smile of the Lamb*. Here is the added sophistication of letters and fragments, letters within letters, some presented posthumously, reflecting on life in death, and death in life. There is a panorama of characters from modern Israeli society. Each explores, through the free-association of the psychoanalytical method, their own aims and defences, life-force motivations, and attitudes to death. Using the Home as a metonymy for the Land, Almog explores the questions of Exile and Homeland. She includes a character raised but not born in Israel, Yanis the Greek, who lends an objective view on Israel and Jewish history, on the Outsider and the Chosen People: Jews are "a people haunted by death". This is a barren story, where children do not survive and are not given a voice. Since the central protagonist, Elisheva, has claimed that children are one's only consolation, the means of overcoming loneliness, this is clearly an indictment of the characters and their choices. "Not that need explains anything – it's the ends of our actions that illuminate them . . .". This sentence, spoken by Yanis, highlights Almog's philosophy.

The subversive elements emerge as the women are misunderstood by the men, treated with triviality or selfishness, and denied the possibility of self-actualization through generous love or maternal fulfilment. Elisheva finally meets her demands for creativity by conspiring to involve Professor Licht, the love of her life who had disappointed and abandoned her, in writing her life story. She thus achieves a coalescing of man's voice and woman's voice, shifting the important boundaries.

With the publication of her novel *Shorshei avir* [Roots of Air] in 1993, Almog takes a determined step to enter the male prerogative of the "virile, political novel". The genre of novel rather than short story is an act of assertiveness, a sign of wrestling with broader issues. She uses the prism of history to deal with questions of determinism, to explore the confluence of personal and national legacy.

This work continues the narrative switch of her previous novel, with chapters narrated by alternating protagonists in Book One. The first is Mira, exploring and evaluating the emotional legacy of her mother, a woman wracked by hysteria and disturbing fantasy. The second is her maternal great-grandfather, Lavdovi, a passionate Zionist and immigrant; these chapters combine historical, psychological, and ideological perspectives.

In Book Two Mira's autobiographic narrative splits open: Almog changes from the intimacy of first-person narrator when the recollection becomes too painful, to third-person narration, lending distance and external wisdom, to reflect the protagonist as divided self. This device recalls Yehuda Amichai's novel *Not of This Time, Not of This Place*, where dual narratives play out simultaneously. Shifting the locale from Israel to Europe maintains this division, while yet evading the fulfilment the protagonist Mira has been seeking. Mira is a far more active persona than previously seen in Almog's work. She decides to leave her native home, and by association the volatile and dependent world of her maternal background. She chooses to explore the masculine world of her father, only to find the aggressive controlling forces perpetuated by her husband. She is faced with double motivations and impossible choices, her road to freedom strewn with emotional turmoil and continued male oppression.

In *Tikun omanuti* [Invisible Mending] Almog is able to explore how women can find redemption and free-spiritedness through art and creativity. The constraints of the traditional world and its practices are subverted and overturned: in the title story this is represented by the young girl, Hephtzibah, repairing the obligatory tear made in her pinafore, a sign of mourning when her father dies, in an "artistic fashion". The Hebrew title can be translated as "artistic" or "invisible" mending, emphasizing the female need for finding inner peace through creative fulfilment. Almog illustrates her thesis that through the prism of beauty, art, or creativity, adversity in life can become poignant and bearable, the pain enriching and elevating. She artistically mends the life stories of her characters.

Ruth Almog has been responsible for the evolution of the New Hebrew Woman in Israeli literature. This persona is very different from the New Hebrew of Israeli male literature; Almog needs to deconstruct this male ideal through education. Her literature does not aim for happy endings, yet the process of self-analysis and assertiveness, of working through both the maternal and paternal role models, leads to a new construct of protagonist, reaching ever closer to centre stage of society.

TAMARA LEVINE

Aloni, Nissim

Israeli dramatist, fiction writer, and translator
1926–1998

Born in Tel Aviv, 24 August 1926. Served in Israeli Army, 1948. Studied history and French culture, Hebrew University, Jerusalem; did not graduate. Stories published in *Bemahane*, Israeli army weekly journal. Founder and Director, *Teatron haonot*, Tel Aviv, 1963. Awarded Israel Prize for Theatre, 1996. Died in Tel Aviv, 13 June 1998.

Selected Writings

Plays
Akhzar mikol hamelekh [Most Cruel of All the Kings], 1953
Bigdei hamelekh hahadashim [The Emperor's New Clothes], 1961
Arlekino [Harlequin], 1963
Hanesikhah haamerikait, 1963; as *The American Princess*, translated by Richard Flantz, 1980
Hamahapekhah vehatarnegolet [The Revolution and the Chicken], 1964
Hakalah vetsiad haparparim, 1967; as *The Bride and the Butterfly Hunter*, translated by Valerie Arnon, 1998
Napoleon – hai o met [Napoleon, Dead or Alive], 1967
Hadodah liza [Aunt Lisa], 1968
Hatsoanim miyafo [The Gypsies of Jaffa], 1971
Sar ehad laazazel [That Scapegoat], 1973
Eddy king [Eddy King], 1975
Haniftar mitparea [The Deceased Goes Wild], 1980
Reshimot shel hatul rehov [Notes of an Alley Cat], 1996

Short Stories
Hayanshuf [The Owl], 1975

Further Reading

Aharoni, Rachel, *Ha Ya'ar Sheba-beten: 'al Mahazot Nisim Aloni*, Tel Aviv: Tag, 1997
Avigal, S., "Nissim Aloni's Theatre of Mirrors and Reflections", *Theatron* (1975–76)
Nathan, Moshe, *Kishuf Neged Mavet: Ha Te'atron shel Nisim Aloni*, Tel Aviv: Hakibuts hameuhad, 1996
Porat, Z., "The Tragic-comedy of Fulfilment in Nissim Aloni's Plays", *Ariel*, 32 (1973)

Although Nissim Aloni took an active part in the 1948 war, and soon afterwards began to publish numerous short stories in the Israeli army weekly, he is not commonly associated with writers and dramatists of his own age group, most of whom reigned over the Israeli stage in the late 1940s and early 1950s with pieces of work in the socialist realist tradition. His first play, *Akhzar mikol hamelekh* [Most Cruel of All the Kings] (produced by Habima Theatre in 1953), which was based on the biblical account of the division of the Hebrew kingdoms, attempted to construct a new dramatic style of historical themes rendered through poetic idiom.

Aloni studied history and French culture at the Hebrew University in Jerusalem, then spent a year in Paris, where he became closely acquainted with the new European drama. This had a crucial influence on his plays. Upon his return to Israel he developed a journalistic career, and in 1961, wrote and directed his second play, *Bigdei hamelekh hahadashim* [The Emperor's New Clothes], a modern symbolic sequel to Hans Andersen's fairy tale, in which the boy-poet who cries "the king is naked" is drawn into the network of complex political plots in the court of the Emperor. He emerges as an opportunistic politician, who cynically marries the Emperor's lesbian daughter in order to succeed the shivering Emperor (who contracts pneumonia and dies), but is finally exposed by his former girlfriend, who has waited for him, pure and faithful, all this time. The play was one of the first to introduce into Israeli drama the modernist influences of existentialist plays, and in particular the dramatic idiom of modernist playwrights such as Michel de Ghelderode and Friedrich Dürrenmatt. Aloni's language, possibly his most original artistic achievement, developed a personal lyrical rhythm, at once mysterious and highly accessible.

In 1963 he was among the founders of the Seasons Theatre, a theatrical venture that lasted for about four years, where he produced one of his major plays, *The American Princess*. Acclaimed as one of Israel's foremost dramatists during the 1960s and early 1970s, he wrote and produced plays for most of the country's major companies. *Hamahapekhah vehatarnegolet* [The Revolution and the Chicken] (1964) is a dramatic reworking of a Mark Twain story about the remote Pitcairn Island whose inhabitants spend their days rolling a rock into the sea. *The Bride and the Butterfly Hunter* (1967) is a stylized one-act play, written as an illustration to a painting by Aloni's friend, the artist Yossl Bergner: a poetic dialogue between a bride hiding in a garden from her flute-player bridegroom (who communicates with her solely through his music), and an intriguing butterfly catcher. The anachronistic *Napoleon – hai o met* [Napoleon, Dead or Alive] (1967), written during the euphoric days following the sweeping victory of Israel in the Six Day War, is an anti-militaristic historical drama in which Napoleon claims his promised resurrection to escape hell and correct his errors and unfinished military projects upon earth. It is the only play of Aloni's in which his poetic imagination crosses the line between the world of the living and the land of the dead. Once Aloni allows himself to compromise the domain of rationalism by crossing the boundaries of metaphysics he gives shelter to histrionic fantasies. He releases on stage a host of wild demons and colourful dramatic characters from the storehouse of the Commedia dell'Arte (a major source that shaped his comic vision), all rushing frantically after Napoleon, who chases his military career through the European battlefields of the 19th century. In spite of the elaborate dramatic fireworks and embellishments that veil his deeply covert political statements, the trauma of the 1967 war may have returned his attention to the local cultural landscapes, which he had abandoned in his early 1960s plays. Thus *Hadodah liza* [Aunt Lisa] (1968) is a mystery play uncovering a murder plot that occurred in pre-Israeli Palestine, reading aristocratic degeneration into an allegedly socialist-plebeian cultural context, whereas *Hatsoanim miyafo* [The Gypsies of Jaffa] (1971) is a romantic story of love and death occurring against the background of the mysterious ancient Mediterranean seaport. *Sar ehad laazazel* [That Scapegoat] (1973) is a lyrical spy-farce, ridiculing the popular myths and practices of secret agents. *Eddy king* (1975), Aloni's last full-length play, brings to light a dormant theme haunting several of his earlier pieces, such as *The American Princess*, *Aunt Lisa* or *The Gypsies of Jaffa*: a modern rendering of the Oedipus story, which is set here in the guise of an American mafia plot.

Aloni was critically acclaimed both for his plays and for his translations of drama into a lively, exuberant Hebrew, but his most popular and influential works were his satirical sketches and songs written for the highly successful comic trio *Hagashash hahiver* [The Pale Pathfinder], which had an enormous impact on idiomatic Hebrew slang. Aloni directed most of his plays himself, as well as directing other, mainly comic plays (particularly French farces). His work has been translated into French and English. Two years before his death, Aloni was awarded the prestigious Israel Prize for his life achievement in the theatre.

AVRAHAM OZ

Alterman, Natan

Polish-born Israeli poet, dramatist, essayist, and translator, 1910–1970

Born in Warsaw, 10 March 1910. Family moved to Moscow, 1914; later lived in Kiev and Kishinev before emigrating to Palestine in 1925; settled in Tel Aviv. Studied in Paris and Nancy, BSc in agronomy, 1932. Married actress Rachel Markus, 1935; one daughter. Returned to Palestine, 1934. Journalist on *Haaretz*, 1934–43, and later on *Davar* and *Maariv*. Awards include Tschernichowski Prize, 1947 and 1967; Bialik Prize, 1957; Israel Prize for Literature, 1968. Died in Tel Aviv, 11 March 1970.

Selected Writings

Poetry
Kokhavim bahuts [Stars Outside], 1938
Simhat aniyyim [Joy of the Poor], 1941
The Tenth Chick, 1943
Shirei makot mitsrayyim [Songs of the Plagues of Egypt], 1944
The Seventh Column, 2 vols, 1948–54
Ir hayonah [The Wailing City], 1957
The Singing Book of Friendship, 1958
Poems of Ten Brothers, 1961
The Writings, 4 vols, 1961–62
Hagigat hakayits [Summer Festival], 1965
Bamaagal [In the Circle], 1971
Hahut hameshulash [The Triple Thread], 1971
Sefer hahidot [The Book of Riddles], 1971
Collected Works, 1971–79
Regaim [Moments], 1973
The Silver Platter: Selected Poems, 1974
Pizmonim veshirei zemer [Refrains and Songs], 1976
Selected Poems, translated by Robert Friend, 1978

Plays
Kinneret, kinneret [Galilee, Galilee], 1962
Pundak haruhot [The Inn of the Ghosts], 1962
Mishpat pythagoras [Pythagoras's Trial], 1965
Ester hamalka [Queen Esther], 1966
Last Days of Or, 1990

Other
Translator, *The Merry Wives of Windsor*, by William Shakespeare
Translator, *Phaedre*, by Racine
Hamasikhah haaharonah [The Final Mask], 1968
Translator, *Shlomo hamelekh veshalmai hasandlar*, by Samuel Gronemann, 1975; original title *Der Weise und der Narr: König Salomo und der Schuster*
Little Tel Aviv, 1981

Further Reading

Burnshaw, Stanley, T. Carmi and Ezra Spicehandler (editors and translators), *The Modern Hebrew Poem Itself*, New York: Holt Rinehart and Winston, 1965
Carmi, T. (editor and translator), *The Penguin Book of Hebrew Verse*, London: Penguin, and New York: Viking, 1981
Dorman, Menahem, *Natan Alterman: pirkey biyographiyah* [Natan Alterman: Biographical Episodes], Tel Aviv: Hakibuts hameuhad, 1991
Laor, Dan, *Hashofar vehaherev: masot al Natan Alterman* [The Trumpet and the Sword: Essays on Natan Alterman], Tel Aviv: Hakibuts hameuhad, 1983
Mintz, Ruth Finer (editor), *Modern Hebrew Poetry*, Berkeley: University of California Press, 1966
Penueli, S.Y. and A. Ukhmani (editors), *Anthology of Modern Hebrew Poetry*, Tel Aviv: Institute for the Translation of Hebrew Literature, 1966
Silberschlag, Eisig, *From Renaissance to Renaissance*, 2 vols, New York: Ktav, 1973–77
Zimmerman, Shoshanah, *Lefanekha teumim: al haikaron hamekhonan beyitsirat Natan Alterman* [Twins Before You: On the Underlying Principle in the Work of Natan Alterman], Oraniom: Hotsaat hamidrashah, 1997

Natan Alterman was one the most sophisticated poets in Israel to tackle the theme of national identity in modern Israel, and he is considered the poetic spokesman for *Dor Hapalmah*, the generation that fought for Israel's independence. Beginning his career during the period of the British mandate in Palestine and publishing up until his death a few years after the watershed of the Six Day War in 1967, Alterman wrote poetry that expressed the various national struggles that dominated discourse in Israel over the course of his lifetime, such as the fight against the British mandate, the battles for survival against the new state's Arab neighbours, and the dilemma of the new Israeli identity in the face of a rapidly industrializing state.

Alterman, an imagist poet greatly influenced by French and Russian modernist poets as well as the work of earlier Hebrew poets such as Avraham Shlonsky, chose to depict these conflicts and compromises in the form of poems that strike a balance between the universal and the personal, often borrowing images and phrases from earlier Jewish sources to turn them on their heads or to bring additional layers of meaning to his work. Although he was not born in Israel, he was among the first major Israeli poets to spend his entire adult life in the new land, and this freshness of the near-native Israeli experience plays a large role in his poetic appeal. For example, while Hebrew poets through the ages have traditionally aimed their city-related lyrics at Jerusalem, Alterman directs his at Tel Aviv. His poems often have the unpretentious air of folk ballads, describing but not overly elevating ordinary people.

Unlike much modern poetry, most of Alterman's poems are written according to metre and rhyme schemes. Instead of giving the poems an artificial sound, this strictness of form tends to bring out the sort of unexpected figures for which Alterman is justly famous. Alterman's greatest gift as a poet is perhaps his virtuosity with original and creative metaphors, sometimes to the point where his poems are nearly overwhelmed by them. In Alterman's poetry, trees wear earrings, silence whistles, a child returns to his mother like a rolling ball, and "rumors of non-consolation, like wind" can "rock bridges like a line of cradles". Unlike many earlier Hebrew poets, Alterman wrote mainly in a colloquial style, imitating the diction of everyday speech.

Alterman shares his main poetic themes with those of many modernist poets in western languages: the end of innocence, as well as the yearning for nature and a primeval life in the uncontrolled and hostile city. Alterman saw these ideas as clashes between two worlds, one idyllic (childhood, nature, love) and one difficult and painful (ageing, city life, loss of love), and his poems seek to explore the precise moment of the clash between these two worlds. What distinguishes his work is the smoothness with which he often integrated these themes into the Jewish and, after the 1948 founding of the state, the Israeli experience. His collection, *Simhat aniyyim* [Joy of the Poor] from 1941, imposes the theme of loss of innocence and yearning for nature onto Jewish folkoric motifs, using phrase patterns familiar from poetic books of the Bible and from Jewish liturgy. *Shirei makot mitsrayyim* [Songs of the Plagues of Egypt] from 1944, borrows directly from the Hebrew Bible by using the Ten Plagues as an allegory for periods of violence in human history. Later *Ir hayonah* [The Wailing City] deals explicitly with the birth of the state of Israel and with the sufferings and struggles of the generations of the Holocaust, and the battles for independence against the British and then the neighbouring Arab states. *Sefer hahidot* [The Book of Riddles], published posthumously in 1971, returns to Alterman's earliest themes, admitting with the wisdom of a mature poet that while one may never solve life's mysteries, one also cannot abandon the search for answers.

Alterman's poetry has tremendous scope, but much of it can be divided into poetry that is mainly literary or personal (that is, poetry that does not clearly refer to external public events) and poetry with more political ends. Alterman is well-known in Israel as a political and national poet who recorded Israel's wars and struggles with an unrestrained rhetoric, and for today's readers, many of his lyrics concerning both the Holocaust and Israel's wars are anything but subtle. In the poem "Mikol haamim" [From All Peoples], Alterman, borrowing from Jewish liturgy that speaks of God choosing the people of Israel from all peoples, describes the slaughter of Jewish boys and girls by speaking in their voices: "We know/ that Thou didst choose us from all children / To be slaughtered before the Throne of Glory . . . " In his poetry concerning the experiences of the Jewish people, Alterman holds little back.

In Israeli circles, Alterman's best-known poem is most likely "Magash hakesef" [The Silver Platter], which has long been read at memorial services and national ceremonies in Israel honouring the country's fallen soldiers. The poem's title comes from a dictum from Israel's first president, Hayyim Weizmann: "A state is not given to a people on a silver platter". The poem offers a romantic and generalized image of the country approaching the dawn of a new age, concluding with a generic boy and girl who emerge from this halcyon dawn to announce that "We are the silver platter on whom the State of Israel was given to you". It is difficult for most readers today to avoid interpreting this poem at least slightly ironically; that is, to read the poem as if the speaker is presenting this loss of young life as tragedy rather than heroism. Did the poet intend the poem "Magash hakesef" as a tribute to fallen soldiers, as the state has ceremonially interpreted it, or is it an ironic statement about the undervalued lives of Israel's young citizens?

Part of the poem's strength lies in its ambiguity on this subject, its ability to be interpreted in either way. This ambiguity is emblematic of Alterman's work, and it is perhaps one of the main reasons why his poetry has a great capacity to appeal to its readers both in periods of Zionist fervour and periods of disenchantment with the Zionist dream.

DARA HORN

Alvarez, A.

British poet and fiction writer, 1929–

Born Alfred Alvarez in London, 5 August 1929. Educated at Oundle School, Northamptonshire; Corpus Christi College, Oxford, BA 1952, MA 1956; Princeton University (Procter Visiting Fellow, 1953–54); Harvard University (Rockefeller Fellow, 1955); University of New Mexico, Albuquerque (D.H. Lawrence Fellow, 1958). Gauss Lecturer, Princeton University, 1957–58; Visiting Professor, Brandeis University, 1960, and State University of New York, 1966. Married, first, Ursula Barr, 1956 (marriage dissolved, 1961), one son; second, Anne Adams, 1966, one son, one daughter. Poetry critic and poetry editor, *Observer*, 1956–66; editor, *Journal of Education*, 1957; drama critic, *New Statesman*, 1958–60. Awards include Vachel Lindsay prize, 1961.

Selected Writings

Poetry
(*Poems*), 1952
The End of It, 1958
Twelve Poems, 1968
Lost, 1968
Penguin Modern Poets 18, with Roy Fuller and Anthony Thwaite, 1970
Apparition, 1971
The Legacy, 1972
Autumn to Autumn and Selected Poems 1953–1976, 1978

Novels
Hers, 1974
Hunt, 1978
Day of Atonement, 1991

Other
The Shaping Spirit: Studies in Modern English and American Poets, 1958; as *Stewards of Excellence*, 1958
The School of Donne, 1961
Editor, *The New Poetry*, 1962
Under Pressure: The Artist and Society: Eastern Europe and the USA, 1965
Beyond All This Fiddle: Essays 1955–1967, 1968
The Anarchist (screenplay), 1969
The Savage God: A Study of Suicide, 1971
Beckett, 1973
Life after Marriage: Scenes from Divorce, 1982; as *Life after Marriage: Love in an Age of Divorce*, 1982
The Biggest Game in Town, 1983
Offshore: A North Sea Journey, 1986
Feeding the Rat: Profile of a Climber, 1988
Rainforest, with Charles Blackman, 1988
Editor, *Faber Book of Modern European Poetry*, 1992
Night: An Exploration of Night Life, Night Language, Sleep and Dreams, 1995
Where Did It All Go Right? (autobiography), 1999
Poker: Bets, Bluffs and Bad Beats, 2001

Further Reading

Guardian, 18 December 1999; 8 March 2000 (interview); 14 April 2001
Hamilton, Ian, interview in *New Review*, March 1978
Holbrook, David, "Out of the Ash: Different Views of the 'Death Camp': Sylvia Plath, Al Alvarez and Viktor Frankl", *Human World*, 5 (1971)
Holden, Anthony and Frank Kermode (editors), *The Mind Has Mountains: a.alvarez@lxx*, Cambridge: Los Poetry Press, 1999
Observer, 18 March 2001
Times Literary Supplement, 28 January 2000

An acknowledged literary scholar, Alvarez has published studies on Donne, Beckett, Plath, American and English poetry, and on the political role of the writer. He played a major role in bringing the work of eastern European poets to the West. Editor of the influential and controversial anthology, *The New Poetry*, he called for a rejection of the English "disease" of "gentility". The collapse of the old civilized order rendered the "decency and politeness" of the poetry of the inhibited and "provincial" man next door obsolete. It was to be replaced with individual emotion and experience at its very limit under the pressures of the "extreme conditions" (two world wars, the Holocaust, and the threat of nuclear war) of the 20th century. This poetry would reflect what he referred to as the "new seriousness".

Alvarez has published several books of poetry. He writes, "I am sure that real poetry only comes from a live core, a real voice, which one finds by living outside the self". His verse is elegant, exhibits precision of form, and shows the influence of Donne, Eliot, and Plath. A number of his poems deal with the limit experiences of death and disintegration, consuming anger, lament, loss, and love. For example, in his elegy to his father ("A Cemetery in New Mexico") grief and self-knowledge are powerfully combined, and in "Mourning and Melancholia" violent feelings are given voice. The tone of much of his poetry is harsh and confessional as he attempts to capture the most fleeting of emotions. He sets stringent standards for "the new poetry" and it could be argued that he often appears to fail his own gentility test.

The Savage God: A Study of Suicide (1971) explores the relationship of artistic creativity to madness. Alvarez chronicles his own depression and suicide attempt, examines suicide in literature, and includes a passionate essay on his friend, Sylvia Plath's life and poetry. His explanation of Plath's suicide made the intimate relationship between the poet and her husband, Ted Hughes, public. Thirty years later, Alvarez recorded his failure to help Plath when she asked him to – "I wasn't up to her despair and it scared me". He has continued to promote the significance of her work and defends her use of the Holocaust as a vehicle for articulating her personal situation.

Alpine rock and mountain climbing, North Sea oilrigs, and playing poker for high stakes have satisfied Alvarez's obsessive need for "testing" himself in dangerous situations. He wrote about these risky activities for the *New Yorker*, later published as books. Alvarez has played poker at the highest level (World Poker Championships in 1994 and 1995) and this love of cards has led to two volumes on the game. This intimate knowledge of the tensions and excitement of the poker table are used to good effect in his novel *Hunt*, with its particularly evocative smoky poker scenes which convey something of being caught up in the sheer thrill of the game. Alvarez has also written a book about divorce, and a study of our experience of night.

Alvarez's family is Sephardi in origin and he grew up in comfortable and fashionable Hampstead, north London. At boarding school he experienced anti-Semitism, and devoted himself to study and developing his sporting prowess as a boxer and rugby player. While he recounts his early and continuing awareness of being Jewish, this is largely a reflection of his difference being noted by others, and his writings evidence little explicit knowledge of Jewish belief and practice. For example, in his poem, "A Cemetery in New Mexico", he writes about his father's funeral, "there were Hebrew prayers I didn't understand", and there is little reference to Jewish communal life in his work.

Alvarez uses the Holocaust as the shady background for his novel *Hers*, where Julie, the Oxbridge professor Charles Stone's German wife slowly recovers from the shattering of her early life by the Nazis and the invading Russians. The professor is a wonderful creation as the scholar who explains that "after all, I always respond to literature more than to life", and who seems to feel through literary quotations. Julie's lover is the young research student, Sam Green, who is rapidly losing faith in the value of the genteel academic life. Green, the son of a businessman, a public school educated assimilated English Jew, still has to explain that he is English and not a refugee. When she claims that they are a "new Frieda and Lawrence", he replies, "A Jewish Lawrence. Don't forget that. It's very important." His claim not to be restricted in his life by dietary laws and so on is responded to with the condemnation that he's not even a very good Jew! Green allows Alvarez to explore English anti-Semitism ("In England a Jew's a foreigner and that's that") where the bottom line is that, "Jews aren't gentlemen" and "it's just not done to be Jewish".

Green's family is portrayed as a caricature of north London Jewry, complete with Yiddishisms. In a similar way, a number of his other characters, such as the poker player and undercover agent Abe in the novel *Hunt*, border on being negative stereotypes, in this case of the money grabbing, pushy American Jew.

Alvarez is a multifaceted writer and critic whose work has explored the loneliness and fragility of disintegrating relationships and just how easily tempted his characters are to risk all and reject their shallow suburban lives. His interest in the "the world of action, where people take real risks with their bodies or machinery or money", is in stark contrast to the Anglo-Jewish world of his father, "who had spent his life in a business he didn't care for and had never been anywhere". It might even be construed as an "extreme" form of assimilation. At the centre of his writing is the tension between the English literary tradition and his ambivalent identity as a "never completely at home" Jew in England. He describes his identity as a "Londoner but not as an Englishman", a recognition of this exclusion of the "English" Jew. Alvarez at 70, in his recent autobiography, describes his first 30 years as "purgatory" and the next 40 as "blissful".

PAUL MORRIS

Amichai, Yehuda

German-born Israeli poet, 1924–2000

Born Yehuda Pfeuffer in Würzburg, 1924; emigrated to Palestine, 1935. Studied at Bet Sefer Maaleh, Jerusalem, and Hebrew University, Jerusalem. Served with Jewish Brigade of British army during World War II, and as infantryman in Israeli War of Independence: sergeant major in reserve. Married, first, Tamar Horn; one son; second, Hanna Sokolov; one son and one daughter. Teacher of Hebrew literature and scripture in secondary schools, Jerusalem; visiting poet, University of California, Berkeley, 1971, 1976; Dorot Visiting Fellowship, 1983–84, and visiting poet, 1987, New York University. Many awards, including Shlonsky Prize; Acum Prize (twice); Bialik Prize; Israel Prize; Brenner Prize, 1985; Agnon Prize, 1986. Honorary doctorate, Hebrew University, 1990. Distinguished Associate Fellow, American Academy of Arts and Sciences. Died in Jerusalem, 22 September 2000.

Selected Writings

Poetry

Akhshav ubeyamim haakherim [Now and in Other Days], 1955
Bemerhak shetey tikvot [Two Hopes Away], 1958
Beginah hatsiburit [In the Park], 1959
Shirim 1948–1962 [Poetry 1948–1962], 1962/63
Selected Poems, translated by Assia Gutmann, 1968; as *Poems*, 1969
Akhshav baraash [Now in the Turmoil], 1968
Selected Poems, translated by Ted Hughes, Assia Gutmann, and Harold Schimmel, 1971
Velo al menat lizkor [And Not in Order to Remember], 1971
Songs of Jerusalem and Myself, translated by Harold Schimmel, 1973
Meachorei kol zeh mistater osher gadol [Behind All This Hides Great Happiness], 1974
Masot binyamin haaharon mitudelah, as *Travels of a Latter-Day Benjamin of Tudela*, translated by Ruth Nevo, 1977; as *Travels* (bilingual edition), translated by Ruth Nevo, 1986
Amen, translated by the author and Ted Hughes, 1978
On New Year's Day, Next to a House Being Built, 1979
Time, translated by the author and Ted Hughes, 1979
Love Poems (bilingual edition), various translators, 1981
Sheat hahesed [Hour of Charity], 1982
Great Tranquillity: Questions and Answers, translated by Glenda Abramson and Tudor Parfitt, 1983
Meadam atah veel adam tashuv [From Man You Come, and to Man You Will Return], 1985
The Selected Poetry of Yehuda Amichai, edited and translated by Stephen Mitchell and Chana Bloch, 1986; as *Selected Poems*, 1988
Shirei yerushalayim/Poems of Jerusalem (bilingual edition), translated by Alizah Orbakh, 1987
Gam haegrof hayah paam yad petuhah, 1989; as *Even a Fist Was Once an Open Palm with Fingers*, translated by Barbara Harshav and Benjamin Harshav, 1991
Yehuda Amichai: A Life of Poetry, 1948–1994, translated by Barbara Harshav, 1994
More Love Poems, various translators, 1994

Plays

Masa leninveh [Journey to Nineveh], 1962
Paamonim verakavot, 1963; translated as *Bells and Trains*, 1966

Fiction

Beruah hanoraah hazot, 1961; as *The World Is a Room (and Other Stories)*, translated by Elinor Grumet *et al.*, 1984

Lo meakhshav, lo mikan, 1963; as *Not of This Time, Not of This Place*, translated by Shlomo Katz, 1968
Miyitneni malon [Hotel in the Wilderness], 1971

Other
Mah shekarah leroni binyu york, 1968
Editor, with Allen Mandelbaum, *The Syrian–African Rift and Other Poems*, 1980
Editor, with Allen Mandelbaum, *Points of Departure*, 1982
Sefer halaylah hagadol [The Big Night-Time Book], 1988
Has translated works by Rolf Hochhuth and Else Lasker-Schüler

Further Reading

Abramson, Glenda, *The Writing of Yehuda Amichai: A Thematic Approach*, Albany: State University of New York Press, 1989
Cargas, Harry James, "An Interview with Yehuda Amichai", *Webster Review*, 2/1 (1975)
Flinker, Noam, "Saul and David in the Early Poetry of Yehuda Amichai" in *The David Myth in Western Literature*, edited by Raymond-Jean Frontain and Jan Wojcik, West Lafayette, Indiana: Purdue University Press, 1980
Halkin, Hillel, "The Poet as Prose Writer", *Ariel*, 61 (1985)
Hirsch, Edward, "Poet at the Window", *American Poetry Review*, 10/3 (1981)
Kahn, Sholom J., "Yehuda Amichai", *Literature East and West*, 14/1 (1970)
Levy, Shimon, "Elements of Poetic Self-Awareness in Modern Poetry", *Modern Hebrew Literature*, 3 (1976)
Mazar, Yari, "Farewell to Arms and Sentimentality: Reflections of Israel's Wars in Yehuda Amichai's Poetry", *World Literature Today*, 60/1 (1986)
Scharf, Nili Gold, "Images in Transformation in the Recent Poetry of Yehuda Amichai", *Prooftexts*, 4/2 (1984)
Sokoloff, Naomi B., "On Amichai's 'El male rahamin'", *Prooftexts*, 4/2 (1984)
Stiller, Nikki, "In the Great Wilderness", *Parnassus: Poetry in Review*, 11/2 (Fall 1983–Summer 1984)

For long Israel's foremost poet, Amichai was a prolific writer, with numerous volumes of poetry, two plays, and some fiction. His work was initially not well received by the older generation of critics. They failed to understand him or to appreciate his talent. Critics questioned his meaning and intention, which they found relatively obscure. Amichai's voice was that of a young intellectual, familiar with European ideas of chaos, disillusionment and the nightmares of the 20th century. His critics thought these were signs of existentialism, nihilism, individualism, and a loss of the Jewish nature of their world. Yet Amichai managed to reach his public directly, without the mediation of established critics.

His poetry in fact was a link between old and new. He once said "I was destined to be planted between two generations. A sort of 'double agent' ". Being born in Germany, he did not belong to the modern Israeli generation, and, indeed, had an orthodox education. He is described by some as an optimist. Mati Megged sees the source of this optimism in "childhood" and "love", two themes prominent throughout his oeuvre. Nathan Zach and Dan Miron both noted the element of illusion, expressed consciously in Amichai's optimism. While Zach presents Amichai as a love poet, they both stress that Amichai, aware of the nightmarish quality of existence, and the loneliness in a sheltered world that has been shattered, escapes into illusion. Although influenced by European poets like Georg Trakl, Else Lasker-Schüler, and Dylan Thomas, his poetry is unique, and the sources of his verse are rooted in personal experience.

Amichai is steeped in traditional wisdom, and generations of learning. However, everything in this new continent, with its amazing smells, colours, light, textures, sits in strong contrast with Amichai's European past. In Jerusalem – its markets, Hasidic people, houses, stones, tombs, cemeteries – the boy (Amichai) is enchanted by the exotic landscape, its wild dance of exuberance. Amichai embraces the Levant, and the Levant falls in love. Love is a central theme; it is the key to his life, the quest and the attainment are the meaning of his earthly embodiment.

Amichai tries to fulfil his father's wishes – to protect him from the trauma of war, paradoxically resulting in his own service as a soldier. In "My Father", a sonnet, we find combined two of the poet's main subjects, war and his father:

My father was four years in their war
And he didn't hate his enemies or love them
But I know that already there on the battlefield
He was building me daily out of his tranquilities
So few, which he gathered
Between the bombs and smoke
And put into his ragged knapsack
With the leftovers of his mother's hardening cake
And with his eyes he gathered the nameless dead
The many dead he gathered for my sake
So that I should know them with his glance and love
them
And not die like them in terror . . .
He filled his eyes with them and he erred:
I depart for all my wars.

The son expresses tenderness towards the father; he is touched by his father's care and love for him. The mother's love is sheltering, a protective shield. She is apparent in much of his writing, and his love for her reflects and multiplies her love for him. Shielded by that love, but gaining experience, losing innocence, the boy steps out, a necessary step in becoming a "Man" (or I should say "Mensh"). He remains sweet somehow, along the years, expressing much love for his aging, dying mother in many of the later poems.

When it comes to the girls in his life, he refuses to mature fully. He remains flirtatious, craving, yearning for the perfect maiden. Composing walls of ancient stones, biblical landscapes, with the unforgettable flavour of young thighs, the boy is determined, "I want them all". Scenes that sweeten his memories are present in "The Man Who Travelled": "Remember him fondly because he called me out of the classroom in the middle of a lesson/ a beautiful woman is waiting for you in the garden/ And he quietened the noisy children".

There is a solid quality to the man behind the poems, a kindness. His inability to mature as regards girls can easily be forgiven. After all he is a harmless old grandfather, pure in heart, ticking away like an old, yet reliable, German clock. He is defiantly in love with life, creations, fields, houses, romantically spreading his metaphors, mingling past/ present, war/love, mother/father, women/men. Dichotomies play a major part in his drama.

Love serves as a reassuring factor, providing security to face a century of fear and detachment. Amichai's poetry is human, his values harmonious. "In This Valley":

But this valley is a chance
To start again without dying. To love
Without forgetting the other love
And to be like the breeze passing it now
Though it was not meant for it.

What Amichai brings to literature is the mingling of a refreshing, unique quality with ancient tradition. The magic is a combination of simplicity, vivid metaphorical language, with the ordinary and traditional. His ability is to be present at once in two realities, the surface superficial, and a deeper reality, enjoying his simultaneous journey on both levels. (The notion of journeying recurs throughout his work.) Arieh Sachs talks about "a kind of superabundance, sometimes overabundance in his work . . . a feeling that the richness of the metaphorical display sometimes exceeds the emotional matter with which it is designed to deal."

With his mellow, human, stable way, whether in human relationships or in his political attitudes, Amichai looks toward peace and coexistence with the other, seeking a middle way to bridge the opposites. Amichai was the most popular poet in Israel, widely read by people of all ages, and it was not surprising that when Rabin and Peres received the Nobel Peace Prize in Oslo, Amichai read his poem "Wildpeace":

Let it come
Like wildflowers
Suddenly, because the field
Must have it: Wildpeace.

Rabin also read part of "God Takes Pity on Kindergarten Children":

On grownups, He won't take pity anymore.
He leaves them alone
Sometimes they have to crawl on all fours
In the blazing sand
To get to the first-aid station
Dripping blood.

Amichai once said, "When I was young, the country was young . . . my personal history has coincided with a larger history. For me it's always been one and the same." Ted Hughes, Amichai's friend and translator, noted that he "begins to look more and more like a truly major poet . . . there is a depth, breadth, and weighty momentum in these subtle and intricate poems of his, like the undersong of a people."

TAMAR AGNON

Amir, Eli

Iraqi-born Israeli fiction writer, 1937–

Born in Baghdad, 1937. Family emigrated to Israel, 1950; initially sent to a *maabarah* (transit camp), later settled on kibbutz Mishmar Ha'Emek. Studied at Hebrew University, Jerusalem, BA in Arabic language and literature, and Middle Eastern studies. Served in Israeli army as officer in tank corps and intelligence corps. Married, three children. Adviser to Prime Minister on East Jerusalem Arab affairs, 1955–68; civil servant, rising to Deputy Director General, Ministry of Immigrant Absorption, 1968–84; then, since 1984, Director General, Youth Immigration, Jewish Agency for Israel, Jerusalem. Served as emissary of Sephardi Federation in United States. Regular contributor to newspapers and journals, lecturer, broadcaster, and television personality. Many awards, including Prize for Jewish Literature, Mexico 1985; Am Oved Publisher's Best-selling Award, 1992; David Sala Award, 1993; Am Oved Jubilee Literature Prize, 1994; award of Association for the Promotion of Research, Literature, and Art, 1994.

Selected Writings

Novels
Tarnegol kapparot, 1983; as *Scapegoat*, translated by Dalia Bilu, 1988
Mafriah hayonim, 1992; translated as *Farewell, Baghdad*, 1993
Ahavat shaul [Saul's Love], 1998

Further Reading

Berg, Nancy E., *Exile from Exile: Israeli Writers from Iraq*, Albany: State University of New York Press, 1996
Snir, Reuven, "Baghdad My Beloved City", *Haaretz* (23 April 1993)
Snir, Reuven, "Arabic Literature of Iraqi Jews: The Dynamics of the Jewish Cultural System and the Relationship with the Arabic Cultural System", *Miqqedem Umiyyam*, 6 (1995)
Snir, Reuven, "Zionism as Reflected in Arabic and Hebrew Belles Lettres of Iraqi Jewry", *Peamim: Studies in Oriental Jewry*, 73 (Autumn 1997)

Arab culture has always been an integral part of Amir's background; he even concentrated on Arabic language and literature at Hebrew University. Yet he never wrote in Arabic, though in recent years he has been showing his talent as traditional *ḥakawāṭī* (story-teller) in televised Arabic programmes. He made his literary debut in the mid-1970s with part of his memoirs titled *Tarnegol kappara* [Fowl of Atonement] included in a reader for students (edited by A. Shatal). Eight years later it would be the nucleus for his first quasi-autobiographical novel with the slightly different title *Tarnegol kapparot* [Fowl of Atonements] in 1983. Described by the *Jerusalem Post* as "casually turning a flashlight into a dark corner of a field and catching the eyes of a ferocious beast", the novel immediately proved to be one of the Hebrew bestsellers of the 1980s. The protagonist Nuri, a young boy of Iraqi origin, is sent from the *maabarah* to get his education in Kiryat Oranim, a kibbutz in Jezreel Valley established by Polish pioneers. Nuri's struggle to become one of "them" – the arrogant Ashkenazi aristocrat sabra youth ("the regionals") – epitomizes the conflict between East and West, and between the original values of the oriental immigrants and the Ashkenazi values forced upon them. As he came to the kibbutz accompanied by "the whole Jewish Baghdad", Nuri was reassuring himself that the painful process through which he acquired his new identity did not come on the expense of his original identity. Amir, writing in *Ba-Maracha*, considers the novel as "settling accounts with myself and with Zionism", but Zionist narrative dominates it and the fate of Nuri is dictated by Ashkenazi western values. Surprisingly enough, immigrants from Ethiopia and Russia also found in the novel an expression of their agonies of uprooting and immigration. The writer Aharon Megged says that the novel is "one of the significant treasures of Jewish culture, like the stories of the Jewish villages in Poland and Russia".

Strongly coloured by what Eric Hobsbawm called "invented tradition", the core of Amir's second novel *Mafriah hayonim* (*Farewell, Baghdad*), is the desire of the Iraqi Jews to return to their ancient homeland. Referring to the relationship of past to present, Amir says that "it is a mixture that can hardly be returned into its original components . . . I told my story through my anxiety about the fate of Israeli society". The panoramic novel, a kind of *Bildungsroman* based on the author's childhood in Iraq in the 1940s, is related through the eyes of the protagonist Kabi Imari while he is attaining puberty. Highlighting the historical events on the eve of the mass immigration, it depicts the complicated relationship of the Jews with their Muslim neighbours and abounds in sensual descriptions of almost every corner of the Arab Jewish life in the colourful exotic streets and alleys of Baghdad. "When writing this Hebrew novel", Amir recalls, "I imagined myself listening in one ear to my father telling it to me in Arabic". Described in *Moznayin* as "one of the most important achievements of Hebrew literature in recent years", the novel is populated by dynamic figures reflecting the diversity of characters in an *Arabian Nights* Baghdad. The events of the plot are flavoured with the music of the Egyptian singer and composer Muḥammad 'Abd al-Wahhāb (1901–91) and the Jewish singer Salīma Murād Bāsha (1905–74), as well as erotic belly-dancing with the dancer Bahiyya, seductive prostitutes, adventurous sailing on the river, summer nights on the roofs, rich cousins, smells of spices, and the sexual dreams of the adolescent narrator whose fantasies includes Rashelle, his uncle's wife, the teacher Sylvia, and Amira, Abu Edwar's daughter, who would end, like him, in a kibbutz. Again *Moznayin*: "Within the rich and the varied social mosaic of the novel each character represents a type, trait and also a particular way of approaching the national and existential questions raised". However, one may raise doubts concerning the reliability of the communist teacher Salīm Afandī presented as a *carpe diem* hedonist, while all evidence proves that the communist option was no less popular at the time than the Zionist one. Asked why only in his second novel did he return to his childhood, Amir replies that "the confrontation with the figure of the father was difficult", especially against the background of the collapse of his own father following the immigration. While in Iraq Kabi's father, Salman, was dreaming of growing rice in the Hula Valley, but soon after he kissed the sacred soil of the "promised land", his dreams were shattered on the rock of reality. Unlike him, the mother, Umm Kabi, who was opposed to the emigration, shows a marvellous ability of adjustment. Still, the disappointment is mingled with a gleam of hope – the birth of Salman's first sabra son is presented by the implied author as signifying a first step in a new start. In a personal communication Amir reveals that he is in the process of writing a third novel which will complete a trilogy corresponding to the well-known Cairo trilogy of the Egyptian novelist Najīb Maḥfūẓ. This trilogy will cover what he describes as "the Via Dolorosa of being an Israeli and devoting myself to this society".

Meanwhile, Amir surprised his readers with a third novel, *Ahavat shaul* [Saul's Love], departing from his own fictionalized experiences and the autobiographical alter egos Nuri and Kabi. Appealing to Israeli mainstream readers, it touches on Ashkenazim, Sepharadim of the Old Yishuv, Oriental Jews, the Israeli army, and the Holocaust in addition to a plot with clear soap opera tendencies. One critic wrote that "Amir compensates his heroes and readers with plenty of tasty food, sexual encounters steeped with fresh Hebrew songs, tours which are full of love of the land, and praises of the gathering of the Jewish immigrants". Also noteworthy in the novel is the implied author's clear outlook regarding the territorial price Israel should pay for peace in the Middle East.

Propagating the central myths of Zionism – the kibbutz, the Aliyah, and the Israeli army – Amir has been considered since the mid-1990s one of the established canonical Hebrew writers. Amir's novels show profound awareness of the injustice done to the oriental Jews, but at the same time they refer to the mitigating circumstances through which the Zionist vision was carried out. The founders of the kibbutz themselves had rebelled against their original culture with the aim of "overturning the pyramid", as Dolek, in charge of the fertilizer section in "Fowl of Atonements" puts it (Dolek had abandoned his doctoral studies in physics). Amir in the *Jerusalem Post Magazine* expresses his appreciation of the way the kibbutz absorbed the newcomers and the values it represents. "No other immigrant society in the modern era has registered", says Amir, "a comparable success or social revolution in absorbing nearly two million immigrants, in difficult economic condition and while fighting five wars". Attempting to bridge between East and West, Amir is trying in his novels to fulfil Jacques Derrida's ideal "to speak the other's language without renouncing his own". Yet, more than any other author of Iraqi origin, his writings illustrate the adoption of the master Zionist narrative.

REUVEN SNIR

An-ski

Russian folklorist, ethnographer, and dramatist, 1863–1920

Born Shloyme [Solomon] Zaynvl Rapoport in Chashniki in the Vitebsk gubernija, Belorussia, 1863. Received a traditional education and learned the locksmith and book-binding trades. Left home, 1879; became acquainted with Khayim Zhitlovski, who remained a lifelong friend. Was attracted to the ideas of the Narodnaja Volja movement, worked among the people in Latvia, Central Russia, and Ukraine. Returned to St Petersburg, 1892; wrote articles for the Narodnik journal *Russkoje Bogatstvo*. Left Russia, 1892, lived in Germany and Switzerland. Lived in Paris, 1894–1904; secretary to Pjotr Lavrov, revolutionary and theoretician of Narodnichestvo or Populism. Returned increasingly to Yiddish cultural life. Founder member of Socialist-Revolutionary (SR) Party, 1902. Returned to St Petersburg, 1905; editor of *Evreiskij Mir*. Joined the Jewish Ethnographic Society in St Petersburg and led an ethnographic expedition to study Jewish life and culture in Volhynia and Podolia, 1912–14; organized relief committees for Jewish war victims during World War I. Elected Deputy for the SR Party to the All-Russian Constituent Assembly, 1917. Fled St Petersburg, 1918; settled in Warsaw. Founded a Jewish ethnographic society in Vilna (Vilnius), 1919. Died in Warsaw, 8 November 1920.

Selected Writings

Plays

V dvadtsat' let [At the Age of Twenty], 1892; as *Der hungeriker (a skitse)* [The Hungry Lad (A Sketch)], in *Gezamlte shriftn*, vol. 14, 1915: 71–100

Foter un zun [Father and Son], 1906

Tsvishn tsvey veltn (der dibek): a dramatishe legende in fir aktn [Between Two Worlds (the Dybbuk): A Dramatic Legend in Four Acts], in *Gezamlte shriftn*, vol. 2, 1920–25; as *The Dybbuk*, translated by Henry G. Alsberg and Winifred Katzin, 1926; as *The Dybbuk*, translated and edited by Joseph C. Landis, in *The Dybbuk and Other Great Yiddish Plays*, 1966

In a konspirativer dire [In a Revolutionary Apartment], *Der zeyde* [The Grandfather], *Tog un nakht* [Day and Night], completed by Alter Katsine, in *Gezamlte shriftn*, vol. 3, 1920–25

The Dybbuk and Other Writings, edited by David G. Roskies, translated by Golda Werman and others, 1992

Other

Di shvue [The Oath (the Bundist Anthem)], 1902, in *Mir trogn a gezang (Favorite Yiddish Songs of Our Generation)*, edited by Khane Gordon Mlotek

Khurbn galitsye: der yidisher khurbn fun poyln, galitsye un bukovine [The Destruction of Galicia: The Destruction of the Jews of Poland, Galicia, and the Bukovina], in *Gezamlte shriftn*, vols 4–6, 1920–25

Further Reading

Beukers, Mariëlla and Renée Waale (editors), *Tracing An-sky: Jewish Collections from the State Ethnographic Museum in St Petersburg*, Zwolle: Waanders, 1992

Roskies, David G., "The Maskil as Folk Hero", *Prooftexts*, 10/2 (1990): 219–35

Roskies, David G., Introduction to *The Dybbuk and Other Writings*, edited by Roskies, New York: Schocken, 1992

Roskies, David G., "S. Ansky and the Paradigm of Return" in *The Uses of Tradition: Jewish Continuity in the Modern Era*, edited by Jacob Wertheimer, New York: Jewish Theological Seminary of America, 1992

Sandrow, Nahma, *Vagabond Stars: A World History of Yiddish Theater*, revised edition, Syracuse, New York: Syracuse University Press, 1996: 216–21, 276–77

Shloyme Zaynvl Rapoport is better known by his pen-name An-ski (or Anski, An-sky), a name that may have been derived from his mother's first name, Anna or Khane, or may alternatively have been simply invented by his Russian associate and mentor Gleb Uspenskij. An-ski is famous principally for his play, *Der dibek* (*The Dybbuk*) which has been more frequently performed in translation than any other Yiddish play and became the source of one of the most successful Yiddish films. In addition he is remembered as the author of *Di shvue* [The Oath] which became the anthem of the Jewish Labour Bund.

Der dibek was originally titled *Tsvishn tsvey veltn* [Between Two Worlds] and An-ski's life and thought were characterized by his liminal position between Hasidism and Orthodoxy, between tradition and modernity, between his Jewishness and his commitment to cosmopolitan socialism. Linguistically he also spanned two contrasting spheres, being as much at home in the Russian language as he was in Yiddish.

The central unifying dynamic of An-ski's life was his strong sense of identity with the common people. After becoming disillusioned at a tender age with the possibility of reforming Judaism in the spirit of the *Haskalah*, he was attracted to the revolutionary and populist Narodnaja Volja movement. During a major part of his adult life he lived and worked among the Latvian, Russian, and Ukrainian working class contributing articles and stories to the Russian radical press. Only subsequently were many of these works translated into Yiddish. Typical of his writings of this period was the *ocherk* or sketch *V dvadtsat' let* [At the Age of Twenty] dating from 1892. The Yiddish version entitled *Der hungeriker (a skitse)* [The Hungry Lad (a Sketch)] was published in his *Gezamlte shriftn* (1915). An English version is to be found in *The Dybbuk and Other Writings* (1992). The 20-year-old protagonist moves in radical Russian circles, is uncomfortable about his Jewish origins and ekes out a living from private tutoring, but his money is exhausted and he has nothing to eat. He is too proud to ask for help and his friends are too preoccupied with the fate of the sick children of a destitute washerwoman to recognize that he is dying of hunger. When he collapses he is taken to the home of an aunt whom he has been avoiding. As he recovers, he is surprised to realize that his friends like his aunt and do not despise her imperfect Russian.

However, the Dreyfus trials began to disillusion An-ski concerning the possibility of universalist solutions to Jewish problems and this process was much accelerated by the pogroms of 1903 and especially those that followed the failed 1905 revolution. With Zhitlovski's encouragement An-ski looked increasingly towards his Jewish roots and turned his attention increasingly to Yiddish folklore. It was at this period that he came under the literary influence of Perets's mixture of satire and neo-romanticism. By 1911, collecting Jewish folklore materials had become for him a national imperative. He joined the Jewish Ethnographic Society in St Petersburg founded by Shimen Dubnov and thought of Jewish folklore as a new Torah of the people, both an aesthetic and a moral basis for modern Jewish culture. In 1912 he became leader of the ethnographic expedition financed by Baron Naftali Horace Guenzburg. The expedition visited over 70 *shtetlekh* in Podolia, Volhynia, and the Kiev gubernija, where they recorded thousands of folktales and folksongs as well as taking innumerable photographs and collecting ritual objects. This work was brought to an abrupt end by the outbreak of World War I. Much of the assembled material was seized by the Bolsheviks in 1918 and was long believed to have been irretrievably lost, but since the collapse of communism in Russia much has been recovered and successfully exhibited in Israel, Germany, and the United States. During the war An-ski's unique combination of deep understanding of the shtetl and impeccable Russian enabled him to play an invaluable role in affording relief to both Austrian and Russian Jews who had become refugees as a result of the hostilities. This activity was reflected in his *Khurbn galitsye* [The Destruction of Galicia], extracts of which in Werman's translation are included in *The Dybbuk and Other Writings*. This work forms one of the most moving accounts of Jewish suffering during World War I and subsequently became a source of inspiration to Emanuel Ringelblum and other Holocaust diarists. Impressions formed both during the expedition and in the course of An-ski's wartime relief work were incorporated into his most famous work, *Der dibek*, on which he began work in 1914. The play first appeared in a Hebrew translation by Khayim Nakhmen Byalik in 1918. During the turmoil of the revolution the Yiddish original was lost and An-ski was obliged to recreate the text from Byalik's version. The premiere performance was given by the famed Vilner trupe and took place in Warsaw on 9 December 1920, following the 30 days of mourning for An-ski's death.

Der dibek is set in the enclosed Hasidic world of the early 19th century, still remote from the modern world. It is a world of superstition, but also one with a deep sense of the immediacy of the divine and the miraculous. Two poor yeshive-bokherim (rabbinical academy students), swear that if it should happen that one of them should have a son and the other a daughter, then they will be betrothed. One of them soon dies, while the other, Sender, forgetful of his oath, becomes a rich and respected khosid. His daughter, Leye, and the yeshive-bokher, Khonen, who lodges in their house and who (unknown to all) is the son of Sender's dead friend, fall in love. As a poor student, Khonen has no chance of winning Leye's hand and Sender betroths Lee to the timid son of a rich merchant. In a desperate attempt to force fate he tries to make gold by means of Kabbalistic magic and falls dead while invoking Satan. He falls dead when he hears the news that Sender has betrothed Leye to a rich suitor. On the day of the wedding Leye visits her mother's grave in order to invite her to the wedding and falls in a faint on the fresh grave of Khonen. During the wedding ceremony the *dibek/dybbuk* or departed spirit of Khonen enters Leye's body. Leye is taken to the aged Miropoler *rebe*. On the eve of the modern era the *rebe*'s powers are waning. Nevetheless he succeeds in consulting both the *dibek* and Sender's friend and the broken promise comes to light. The *rebe* imposes upon Sender penitence and a fine to be distributed among the poor. He is finally able to drive out the *dibek* from Leye's body, but she cannot bear to part from Khonen's spirit and falls dead. The outcome is foreseen by the mystical figure of the Meshulekh or messenger who is constantly present on the stage and comments often ambiguously on events. *Der dibek* inspired two operas and a ballet and has been filmed three times, most notably in 1937 by Michał Waszyński in an expressionistic style using a screenplay brilliantly adapted from An-ski's play by the Yiddish poet Alter Katsizne.

HUGH DENMAN

Appelfeld, Aharon

Romanian-born Israeli fiction writer 1932–

Born in Czernowitz, 1932. Sent to concentration camp, 1940; escaped and spent three years in hiding in Ukraine; joined Soviet army. Wandered through Europe, arriving in Palestine 1946. Served in Israeli army. Studied Hebrew and Yiddish literature at Hebrew University, Jerusalem. Married with children. Visiting Fellowship for Israeli Writers, St Cross College, Oxford, 1967–68; visiting lecturer, School of Oriental and African Studies, London, and Oxford and Cambridge universities, 1984. Currently lecturer in Hebrew literature, Beer Sheva University. Many awards, including Prime Minister's Prize for Creative Writing, 1969; Anne Frank Literary Prize (twice); Brenner Prize, 1975; Milo Prize; Israel Prize, 1983; Jerusalem Prize; H.H. Wingate Literary Award, 1987, 1989; Harold U. Ribelow Prize, 1987.

Selected Writings

Short Stories
In the Wilderness, various translators, 1965
Kefor al haarets [Frost on the Land], 1965
Bekomat hakarka [At Ground Level], 1968
Hamishah sipurim [Five Stories], 1969
Adnei hanahar [The River Banks], 1971
Kemeah edim: mivchar [Like a Hundred Witnesses: A Selection], 1975

Novels
Haor vehakutonet [The Skin and the Gown], 1971
Keishon haayin [Like the Pupil of an Eye], 1973
Tor hapelaot, 1978; as *The Age of Wonders*, translated by Dalya Bilu, 1981
Badenheim, ir nofesh, 1979; as *Badenheim 1939*, translated by Dalya Bilu, 1980
1946, 1980
Mihvat haor [Searing Light], 1980

"Hapsiga" [The Summit], 1982; as *The Retreat*, translated by Dalya Bilu, 1984
Bartfus ben almavet, 1983; as *The Immortal Bartfuss*, translated by Jeffrey M. Green, 1988
Hakutonet vehapasim [The Shirt and the Stripes], 1983; as *Tzili, the Story of a Life*, translated by Dalya Bilu, 1983
Beet uveonah ahat [At One and the Same Time], 1985; as *The Healer*, translated by Jeffrey M. Green, 1990
"El erets hagomeh"; as *To the Land of the Cattails*, translated by Jeffrey M. Green, 1986
Ritspat esh [Tongue of Fire], 1988
"Al kol hapeshaim"; as *For Every Sin*, translated by Jeffrey M. Green, 1989
Katerinah, 1989; as *Katerina*, translated by Jeffrey M. Green, 1992
Mesilat barzel, 1991; as *The Iron Tracks*, translated by Jeffrey M. Green, 1998
Timyon [Oblivion], 1993; as *The Conversion*, translated by Jeffrey M. Green, 1998
Ad nefesh, unpublished; as *Unto the Soul*, translated by Jeffrey M. Green, 1994
Laish, 1994
Ad sheyaaleh amud hashahar [Until the Light of Dawn], 1995
Kol asher ahavti [All I Have Loved], 1999

Other
Editor, *From the World of Rabbi Nahman of Bratslav*, 1973
Masot beguf rishon [Essays in First Person], 1979
"After the Holocaust", translated by Jeffrey M. Green, in *Writing and the Holocaust*, edited by Berel Lang, 1988
Beyond Despair: Three Lectures and a Conversation with Philip Roth, translated by Jeffrey M. Green, 1994
Sipur hayim [(The) Story of a Life], 1999
Od hayom gadol [It is Yet High Day], 2001

Further Reading

Bercovitch, Sacvan (moderator), *What Is Jewish in Jewish Literature? A Symposium with Israeli Writers, Aharon Appelfeld and Yoav Elstein*, Cambridge, Massachusetts: Harvard University Library, 1993
Chertok, Chaim, "Appelfeld and Affirmation," *Ariel*, 61 (1985)
Chertok, Chaim, "Aharon Appelfeld, Not to the Left, Not to the Right" in *We Are All Close: Conversations with Israeli Writers*, New York: Fordham University Press, 1989
Dudai, Rina, "Literary Device Used for Effects of Subtlety and Restraint in Emotion-Loaded Narrative Text: 'The Burn of Light', by A. Appelfeld", *Hebrew Linguistics* (January 1990)
Ezrahi, Sidra DeKoven, "Aharon Appelfeld: The Search for a Language", *Studies in Contemporary Jewry*, 1 (1984)
Furstenberg, Rochelle, "The Shirt and the Stripes", *Modern Hebrew Literature*, 9/1–2 (1983)
Hatley, James, "Impossible Mourning: Two Attempts to Remember Annihilation", *Centennial Review*, 35/3 (1991): 445
Langer, Lawrence, "Aharon Appelfeld and the Uses of Language and Silence" in *Remembering for the Future*, edited by Yehuda Bauer *et al.*, Oxford: Pergamon Press, 1989
Lewis, Stephen, *Art Out of Agony: The Holocaust Theme in Literature, Sculpture and Film*, Montreal: CBC Enterprises, 1984
Wisse, Ruth R., "Aharon Appelfeld, Survivor", *Commentary*, 76 (1983): 74–76

Unlike that other internationally famous writer and survivor from Czernowitz in the Bukovina, Paul Celan, who chose to write in German, Aharon Appelfeld has chosen to write his hugely significant novels in Hebrew, the language of his adopted country. Yet his work remains closer to that of his compatriot Celan than to that of most contemporary Israeli novelists. Appelfeld is one of the foremost writers whose work emerges out of first-hand experience of the Holocaust, yet one who is also intensely aware of what the calls the "untranslatable" nature of that experience.

In interview, Appelfeld has stated:

> I survived as a child, I came to Israel . . . It is unbelievable. To tell this story is an unbelievable thing. I do not believe it. How can other people believe it? So you have to put some *reason* on it. So to make it first of all *lower*, you know, to lower it. Because too much drama is in it.

The quietness of Appelfeld's characteristic tone, the formal inventiveness of his novels, the refusal of any simple moral judgement – all these follow from this perceived need not to dramatize the events of the 1930s and 1940s, but on the contrary to dedramatize them. Appelfeld continues:

> What happened to Jews is not tragic. It is something beyond tragic. If we are saying tragic it means it has to be somewhere focused in the individual. What happened to Jews in the Second World War is beyond tragic. It is untranslatable in your mind. We are not able to think about the death of an individual, a close person. How can we think about a hundred or a thousand people? So this is really the difficulty – technical and of content – of writing.

For Appelfeld, the intractability of the past is attributable not so much to its obscurity or darkness as to its traumatic brightness: "This is really the question about the Holocaust. It's an air you cannot breathe. It's too hot. It's like the sun. You cannot breathe. You cannot look at it."

Most of Appelfeld's novels deal with the period up to the deportation of the Jews, when this "sun" is already shining brightly. In *Badenheim 1939* Jewish holiday-makers are returning to a preferred resort, and to their private obsessions and rituals. They hardly seem bothered that the "Sanitation Department" is gradually sealing off the town, so that in the novel's closing sentence, as the holiday-makers are being loaded onto trains for "transfer", an impresario announces, "If the coaches are so dirty it must mean that we have not far to go". Pain is not described here so much as it is enjoined in the reader, who is appalled not just by the characters' insouciance, but by the way in which the narrative colludes with this insouciance, nowhere explicitly naming the "sun" now climbing on the horizon. Appelfeld's writing is often described as "ironic", but is always one wise step short of simple irony, forgoing irony's knowing winks and nods. The narrator is no more perspicacious here than the protagonists. The utter tranquillity and almost fairy-tale stillness of the prose lulls the reader just as the resort has lulled its holiday-makers. The rising Nazi menace, aiming at extirpation of the whole, is itself like a hole in language – Appelfeld's language included. Whence the darkness in Appelfeld's novels? As if from the heart of the light which is invading and illuminating his prose.

In *The Retreat* the characters have withdrawn from society to eradicate the flaws in their personalities, which they hope will lead to a new purity of person and performance, ignoring the strict irrelevance of any such perfection, when their society will be "perfected" by the removal of their very lives. In *To the Land of the Cattails* and in *The Healer* a trip is made from Vienna back towards the homeland of the Carpathian mountains, in the hope that some reconnection with the fertile lands of origin, and their healing powers, may bring physical and psychic renewal, a journey which can succeed only in so far as it ignores the strict irrelevance of any such inner health when Nazi society is about to "purify" itself of all such nostalgic notions.

In what may be Appelfeld's finest novel, *The Age of Wonders*, it is the irrelevance not just of the protagonist's father's literary endeavours which is revealed. It is the redundancy of virtually a whole novelistic tradition which is embodied in this novel's broken form. For in Book I a young Viennese Jewish boy, Bruno, is gradually growing towards consciousness and separation, through a narrative told in the first person, in a way typical of the *Bildungsroman* or "novel of formation". Just as he is starting to exercise real judgement and discrimination, he is summoned to the temple with his mother and his people, where he is about to become the absolute object – not subject – of discrimination: "By the next day we were on the cattle train hurtling south". This narrative of growth, truncated, is followed by a blank page, as if the author has turned his hand against his own creation and craft, followed by a very different narrative, told in the third person, of a man, whom we only gradually learn to be the Bruno of Book I, who has returned to his home town, "Many Years Later, When Everything Was Over", and who is now struggling and failing to reconnect with his past.

In the gap between the first- and third-person narratives, the former so traditionally full of burgeoning consciousness and interiority, the latter so emptied of these selfsame qualities, is to be found Appelfeld's intense awareness of the artistic implications of what he himself suffered as a child. It is as if, in the blank heart of his novel, the bright sun of persecution had burnt a hole. Returning to his hometown, finding to his horror that things have remained remarkably the same, Bruno lacks even the words of Paul Celan to describe the experience: "Look around", as Celan writes in the poem "Speak, You Also", "look how it all leaps alive –/ where death is! Alive!" It remains only for Bruno's author to absorb the conclusion that Celan draws from these lines, and to make them the very ground of his fiction: "He speaks truly who speaks the shade".

DAN GUNN

Apple, Max

US fiction writer, scriptwriter, and critic 1941–

Born Max Isaac Apple in Grand Rapids, Michigan, 22 October 1941. Studied at University of Michigan, BA 1963; Stanford University, 1964; PhD 1970. Assistant Professor of Literature and Humanities, Reed College, Portland, Oregon, to 1971; Assistant Professor, 1972–76, Associate Professor, 1976–80, Professor of English since 1980, Rice University, Houston, Texas. Contributed stories to *Esquire*, *Mademoiselle*, *American Review*, *Georgia Review*, and other journals. Married, first, Debra (died); one daughter, one son; second, Talya Fishman, two daughters. Many awards, including National Endowment for the Humanities Younger Humanists Fellowship, 1971; *Hadassah* Magazine, Ribalous Awards for Best Jewish Fiction, 1985.

Selected Writings

Short Stories
The Oranging of America and Other Stories, 1976
Three Stories, 1983
Free Agents, 1984

Novels
Zip: A Novel of the Left and the Right, 1978
The Propheteers, 1987
Roommates: My Grandfather's Story, 1994
I Love Gootie: My Grandmother's Story, 1998

Other
Studies in English, with others, 1975
Mom, The Flag and Apple Pie: Great American Writers on Great American Things, 1976
Editor, *Southwest Fiction*, 1980

Further Reading

Apple, Max, "Marxism and Comedy", *Studies in English*, 61/1 (1975)
Hundey, Patrick D., "Triggering the Imagination: An Interview with Max Apple", *Southwest Review*, 65 (1979)
Klinkowitz, Jerome, "Ritual: Max Apple's History of Our Times" in *Structuring the Void: The Struggle for Subject in Contemporary American Fiction*, Durham, North Carolina: Duke University Press, 1992
McCaffery, Larry and Sinda Gregory, "Max Apple", *Alive and Writing: Interviews with American Authors of the 1980s*, Urbana: University of Illinois Press, 1987
Wilde, Alan, "Dayanu: Max Apple and the Ethics of Sufficiency" in *Middle Grounds: Studies in Contemporary American Fiction*, Philadelphia: University of Pennsylvania Press, 1987

Max Apple's childhood in Grand Rapids, Michigan, provides the two distinct sources for his work. On the one hand, from the American midwest he was ideally positioned to experience the commercial franchising of his country as he grew up, from the mass marketing of food by name brands (particularly the Post and Kellogg cereal empires) to the uniformity of motel accommodations (the Howard Johnson's chain), and even fantasy (such as Disneyland). Apple's perspective on this phenomenon is comic but also gently critical, thanks to his other main influence: having been raised by his grandparents, early 20th-century Jewish immigrants from Lithuania. He has written books about each of them, in the same exuberant style of his fiction that itself combines an understanding of American popular culture with an appreciation of almost ghetto-style extended family life.

The Oranging of America and Other Stories was Apple's first collection, much of it written during his doctoral studies in American literature and years as a young assistant professor of English, first at Reed College and then Rice University (where he would continue a full academic career). Its title piece takes the well known national motel franchise, Howard Johnson's (noted for its distinctive orange roofs), and creates a fictive founder for it: an actual Howard Johnson who travels across America seeking mystical guidance for where to stop. Where he stops, another motel is built, satisfying mythic needs of a population at large. The key to Apple's method here is its mixture of fact and fantasy. There really are thousands of Howard Johnson's motels, as familiar to readers as anything from their commercialized country, which is the intended effect of the chain's mass marketing. That the spokesman is a fiction, a character as invented as Uncle Ben (for cooked rice) or Aunt Jemima (for pancake mix), hardly matters – until Apple takes that fiction to its next level by fleshing out a character as part of the chain's creation story. Given such life, the character assumes credibility, even more so when he interacts with an actual figure such as Robert Frost. Yet is Frost, known through his poems and even more so from his legendary cultural status, any more real to readers than Howard Johnson? It is on this higher level of speculation, where art and history intermix in a form known as the metafictive historiographic, that the action of Apple's story takes place.

Zip, the first of Apple's novels, locates his metafictive dabbling in American history and popular culture within a more stably understood context, that of his protagonist's life in an extended family of Jewish immigrants from Lithuania (something the author's later autobiographical volumes establish as a direct borrowing from experience). The narrator is Ira Goldstein, and his story is as much about his family as his larger historical times. Both give him problems: the family because it refuses to assimilate to more common American values, America itself because it refuses to deal rationally with history. As a doctoral student of American culture, Apple knows that sport is one way individuals can emerge from the ghetto and become figures of the larger culture. Hence Ira becomes the manager of a young Hispanic boxer named Jesús, whose iconic name serves as a further irony for Ira's extended family. The ultimate prize fight involves contenders of a higher order, FBI Director J. Edgar Hoover and Cuban President Fidel Castro. In real life, the Hoover–Castro rivalry took on comic-book proportion; one of the appealing factors in *Zip* is how little the author has to exaggerate these character's foibles in order to create hilarious comedy.

Free Agents is another collection on the order of *The Oranging of America*, though in addition to his fun with popular culture Apple begins exploring the personal themes that would lead him to write a pair of autobiographical books about living with his grandparents. The key to this latter technique is finding a metaphor that can both contain otherwise overflowing emotions and direct them to the production of imaginative insight. "Bridging", the author's most successful story in this mode, uses the innocent device of a father following his daughter's progress from Brownies to the Girl Scouts as a way of coming to terms with his wife's death. Each process is a ritual, Apple understands. As in his more light-hearted satires of popular culture, he appreciates how such rituals help people understand change, especially changes where the transitions can be painful.

Ritual is exceptionally important in Apple's second novel, *The Propheteers*. The focus here is the accomplishment of Walt Disney – like Howard Johnson a brand name, but unlike him an actual person whom America at large (rather than just Apple) has made into a mythic personage. Disney has become so because he understands how the country needs a national shrine and that he is the person most qualified to provide it, thanks to his success in creating the most popular image of the century, Mickey Mouse. "More kids know the Mouse than Jesus Christ," Disney observes. "We could build a religion, a college, an atom-powered village – anything we want". As a combination of all three, he builds Disneyworld in Orlando, a site that associates with human quests from Ponce de León's fountain of youth to the astronauts in America's space programme. To give his story a dramatic element, Apple introduces similar plots being pursued by cereal king C.W. Post and frozen food magnate Clarence Birdseye. Howard Johnson and his retinue make a brief appearance as well, contributing to Apple's theme of how rituals are effective when applied to specific purposes, but things of great mischief when given life and allowed to intermix – a reminder of what happened when Ira Goldstein's prize fighter became a factor for both Hoover and Castro.

Roommates in 1994 and *I Love Gootie* in 1998 are Apple's tributes not just to his grandparents, who raised him, but to the unique contribution family members from another culture can provide. The term "roommates" is an effective example, for Apple's grandfather, nicknamed Rocky, was a roommate at two key stages in the author's life, neither of which would customarily include a cohabitor of this age. First, when Apple was a college student, Rocky was sent along as a protector of sorts – after all, he was retired and available, while his grandson was heading off to a radically counter-cultural world where his family, not even yet fully assimilated into traditional America, feared for the worst. But more than a generation later Rocky, still healthy at age 103, moved in with his grandson's family when their wife and mother died (the situation earlier described in "Bridging"). In his second volume, the author describes his grandmother, only apparently quieter than her husband. She, he recounts, was less the feisty one and more of a wise woman who made an agreement with her grandson: he would teach her about America, while she taught him about the old ways back home, devices that let Apple discern the mythic force of both cultures as they appear in interface.

Jerome Klinkowitz

Asch, Sholem

Polish-born US fiction writer and dramatist, 1880–1957

Also known as Sholem Ash, Sholom Ash, or Shalom Asch. Born in Kutno, Poland, 1 January 1880. Married Blime-Matl (Madzshe) Shapiro (Mathilda Spiro), 1901; four children. Studied at religious schools until 1897; taught himself German; moved to Włocławek, where he earned a living teaching Hebrew and writing letters for illiterate villagers. In 1900, encouraged by Y.L. Perets, settled in Warsaw and became professional writer. Travelled in Europe, 1905–06, Palestine, 1907, and United States, 1909–10; lived in France, 1912–14. Settled in United States, 1914, and lived in New York until 1923; became US citizen, 1920. Contributor to *Haynt*, *Fraynd* (St Petersburg), and *Forverts* (New York). Returned to Poland 1923; settled in France 1925. Honorary President, Yiddish PEN Club, 1932. Visited Palestine several times during 1920s and 1930s; returned to United States, 1938. Lived in London and Nice, 1953–55. Emigrated to Israel 1956; settled in Bat Yam. Awarded Polonia Restituta, 1932; Anisfield–Wolf Award, 1946. Died in London, 10 July 1957.

Selected Writings

Novels

Dos shtetl, 1904; as *The Little Town*, translated by Meyer Levin (in *Tales of My People*), 1948
Erd [Earth], 1910
Amerika, 1911; as *America*, translated by James Fuchs, 1918
Reb shloyme nogid [Wealthy Shloyme], 1913
Meri, 1913
Der veg tsu zikh [The Road to Oneself], 1914
Motke ganiv, 1916; as *Mottke the Thief*, translated by Willa and Edwin Muir, 1935
Onkl mozes, 1918; as *Uncle Moses*, translated by Isaac Goldberg, 1920 and by Elsa Krauch (in *Three Novels*), 1938
Kidish hashem [Sanctification of God's Name], 1919; as *Kiddush Hashem: An Epic of 1648*, translated by Rufus Learsi (Isaac Goldberg), 1926
Toyt urteyl [Death Sentence] or *Elektrik tsher*, 1923; as *Judge Not*, translated by Elsa Krauch (in *Three Novels*), 1938
Di muter, 1925; as *The Mother*, translated by Nathan Ausubel, 1930 and by Elsa Krauch, 1937
Di kishif-makherin fun kastilye [The Witch of Castille], 1926
Khayim leyderers tsurik-kumen, 1927; as *Chaim Lederer's Return*, translated by Elsa Krauch (in *Three Novels*), 1938
Farn mabl [Before the Flood]: *Peterburg*, 1929, *Varshe*, 1930, *Moskve*, 1931; as *Three Cities: A Trilogy*, translated by Willa and Edwin Muir, 1933
Gots gefangene: der goyrl fun a froy [God's Captives: The Fate of a Woman], 1933
Der tilim yid, 1934; as *Salvation*, translated by Willa and Edwin Muir, 1934
Baym opgrunt, 1937; in USA as *The War Goes On*, translated by Willa and Edwin Muir, 1936; in UK as *The Calf of Paper*, 1936
Dos gezang fun tol, 1938; as *Song of the Valley*, translated by Elsa Krauch, 1939
Der man fun natseres, 1943; as *The Nazarene*, translated by Maurice Samuel, 1939
The Apostle, translated by Maurice Samuel, 1943
Ist River, 1946; as *East River*, translated by A.H. Gross, 1946
Mary, translated by Leo Steinberg, 1949
Moyshe, 1951; as *Moses*, translated by Maurice Samuel, 1951
Grosman un zun, 1954; as *A Passage in the Night*, translated by Maurice Samuel, 1953
Der novi, 1955; as *The Prophet*, translated by Arthur Saul Soper, 1955

Short Stories

Sipurim [Stories], 1902
In a shlekhter tsayt [In a Bad Time], 1903
Yugend [Youth], 1908
Mayselekh fun khumish, 1913; as *In the Beginning*, translated by Caroline Cunningham, 1935
Amerikaner dertseylungen [American Stories], 1918
Khorbm poyln [Catastrophe in Poland], 1918
Children of Abraham: The Short Stories of Sholem Asch, translated by Maurice Samuel, 1942
Der brenendiker dorn [The Burning Bush], 1946
Tales of my People, translated by Meyer Levin, 1948
From Many Countries: The Collected Short Stories of Sholem Asch, translated by Maurice Samuel and Meyer Levin, 1958

Plays

Amnon un Tamar [Amnon and Tamar], 1907
Got fun nekome, 1907; as *God of Vengeance*, translated by Isaac Goldberg, 1918
Motke ganiv [Mottke the Thief], 1921
Dramatishe shriftn [Plays], 1922
Toyt urteyl [Death Sentence], 1924
Shabbetai Zvi: A Tragedy in 3 Acts, translated by F. Whyte and G.R. Noyes, 1930
Naye dramen [New Plays], 1930

Other

Rückblick [Looking Back], 1930
What I Believe, translated by Maurice Samuel, 1941; as *My Personal Faith*, 1942
One Destiny: An Epistle to the Christians, translated by Milton Hindus, 1945
Briv [Letters], 1980

Further Reading

Brodwin, Stanley, "History and Martyrology Tragedy: The Jewish Experience in Sholem Asch and André Schwartz Bart", *Twentieth Century Literature*, 40/1 (1994)
Fischthal, Hannah Berliner, "Christianity as a Consistent Area of Investigation in Sholem Asch's Works Prior to *The Nazarene*", *Yiddish*, 9/2 (1994)
Fischthal, Hannah Berliner, "Abraham Cahan and Sholem Asch", *Yiddish*, 11/1–2 (1998)

Jeshurin, Ephim, "Sholem Asch Bibliografie" in *Sholem Asch fun der noent* [Face to Face with Sholem Asch], by Shloyme Rosenberg, Miami, Florida: Shoulzon, 1958: 375–96
Liptzin, Solomon, *The Flowering of Yiddish Literature*, New York: Yoseloff, 1963
Liptzin, Solomon, *A History of Yiddish Literature*, New York: Jonathan David, 1972
Madison, Charles A., *Yiddish Literature: Its Scope and Major Writers*, New York: Ungar, 1968
Nemoy, Leon, *Catalogue of Hebrew and Yiddish Manuscripts and Books from the Library of Sholem Asch*, New Haven, Connecticut: Yale University Library, 1945
Siegel, Ben, *The Controversial Sholem Asch: An Introduction to his Fiction*, Bowling Green, Ohio: Bowling Green University Popular Press, 1976

Of all Yiddish writers, Sholem Asch, who was brought up in a Hasidic family in Kutno, Poland, is probably the most concerned with Jewish themes, especially faith. Y.L. Perets's favourite disciple, Asch was the most popular and important Yiddish writer in the first half of the 20th century. His prodigious body of work, encompassing novels, dramas, stories, essays, and poetry, presents a history of Jewish life from antiquity to the 1950s. His early stories and novellas, notably *Dos shtetl* (*The Little Town*) and *Reb shloyme nogid* [Wealthy Shloyme], are lyrical, idyllic depictions of the shtetl. In the first novella, Asch writes lovingly of the joys centred around the family of Reb Yekhazkl, a wealthy, and observant, merchant. The serenity of Shabes in particular unites all Jews: after hearing the Rebbe's speech:

> a loving, sweet faith enveloped everything, and Jews held each others' hands . . . The holiness soared over the heads of the crowd. It poured out the open window into God's mysterious creation, and everything in the whole world was lifted out of its weekday plainness, everything was elevated and made sacred.

Asch quickly ventured into works broader in scope. His drama *Got fun nekome* (*God of Vengeance*), takes place in a Jewish brothel. Yankl, the owner, purchases a Torah scroll in an attempt to ensure his daughter's purity, but this does not prevent her from running away with one of the prostitutes. Asch also portrayed the Jewish underworld in *Motke ganiv* (*Mottke the Thief*), written first as a novel and then as a drama. Even in these realistic works, Asch always stresses his characters' idealism, their striving to become better Jews and better people. Yankl was heartbroken that his daughter Rivkele did not agree to marry the respectable bridegroom, a Talmudic scholar, he had brought home for her. "The Torah has been defiled", he laments. Motke, too, tries to escape his own sordid past when he falls in love with a virtuous woman.

Asch explored Old Testament topics in biblical stories, in his play *Amnon un tamar*, in his translation of the Book of Ruth, and in later novels *Moyshe* (*Moses*) and *Der novi* (*The Prophet*). An ardent Zionist, Asch wrote about Palestine in shorter works and in his novel *Dos gezang fun tol* (*Song of the Valley*), in which he delineates the countless hardships, including hunger, vicious insects, and lack of supplies, that 70 heroic pioneers encountered in the 1920s and 1930s when they came to drain the swamps, plough the earth, and settle in the Land of Israel. This new country "was to serve as a model for the new truly-social order of things; there were to be neither oppressors nor oppressed, neither employers nor employed – a model state of affairs, indeed, and one which all the world would do well to emulate."

Farn mabl (*Three Cities*), Asch's first bestseller in English translation, is a grandiose account of Jewish life between 1910–20 in three distinct societies: St Petersburg, Warsaw, and Moscow. Zachary Mirkin, a wealthy Russian Jew, ties the threads together as he travels through the cities, searching for a solution and meaning to all the tragedies that have befallen the Jews. In spite of his terrible disillusionment with the so-called liberation of Poland and with the Russian Revolution, with "the fine dreams that had been so brutally liquidated by reality", however, Mirkin decides "to begin all over again", to continue to pursue his ideals.

Asch additionally wrote many works about Jews in America, including *Amerikaner dertseylungen* [American Stories], *Onkl mozes* (*Uncle Moses*), *Di muter* (*The Mother*), *Toyt-urteyl* (*Judge Not*), *Khayim leyderers tsurikkumen* (*Chaim Lederer's Return*), *Grosman un zun* (*A Passage in the Night*), and *Ist River* (*East River*). Asch became an American citizen in 1920, and he always praised the country for its opportunities and for its absence of European cynicism, among the other freedoms. He was well aware of the difficulties, especially for immigrants, but these problems were surmountable. In *Uncle Moses*, for example, the second generation of Jewish Americans profits in every way from their parents' toil. America, asserts Nathan Davidowsky, the crippled scholar in *East River*, has "the highest moral order yet achieved in the world".

Asch was most interested in intense Jewish faith, and particularly its extremes of martyrdom and messianism. In *Kidish hashem*, one of the first historical novels in Yiddish literature, and taking place during Chmelnitzky's slaughter of a half million Jews in Ukraine in the 17th century, Asch presents different levels of martyrdom, of dying for the sake of the Almighty. The holy Jewish tailor selling "faith" during that tragic era is one of Asch's most significant symbolic figures. There are many Jewish martyrs in *Di kishifmakherin fun kastilyen* [Witch of Castile], set in Rome during the Spanish Inquisition, but the most important is the young Madonna-like Jephtha. In *Der tilim yid* (*Salvation*), Yekhiel is a saintly Hasidic Rebbe. Asch's most exalted character, Yeshua ben Yoysef of *Der man fun natseres* (*The Nazarene*), is both a messianic figure and a Jewish martyr.

This novel, absolutely Jewish in theme and tone, was followed in translation by *The Apostle*, about Paul of Tarsus, and then by *Mary*, about the mother of Jesus. Asch wished to demonstrate Christianity's debt to Judaism, to emphasize common roots. These works achieved critical acclaim and bestseller status in English translation in the United States and Britain, but were bitterly attacked by some influential Yiddish critics, notably the editor of *Forverts*, Abraham Cahan. While these were written during the Holocaust years, Asch also published Ghetto stories, later gathered together and published as *Der brenendiker dorn* [The Burning Bush].

Asch created works of unprecedented range in Yiddish literature; at least three are extraordinary by any standards: *Salvation*, *The Nazarene*, and *East River*. Asch features extremely idealistic, religious Jews who struggle with the turmoil and sinfulness of earthly life in order to better mankind. Neither Rebbe Yekhiel, nor Rebbe Yeshua, nor the Orthodox Moshe Wolf Davidowsky can bear to see suffering of any kind, and they work to ameliorate other people's sorrows. They push the confines of traditional Judaism, and they find that their faith is flexible enough to allow them to transcend rigidity. Yekhiel, for example, helps his mother in the market even though rigid Orthodoxy tells him this is sinful behaviour for a boy. Yeshua accepts followers from other nations, even though they are ignorant of Jewish rituals. And in *East River*, Asch's American masterpiece, Moshe Wolf Davidowsky suffers terrible shame when his son Irving jilts Rachel, daughter of his dying friend, and marries Irish Mary McCarthy instead. Yet he learns to embrace his Catholic daughter-in-law and grandchild, and he even takes them into his own home after his son abandons them. In his dying prayers, devout Moshe Wolf reminds God that: "You yourself commanded that we be merciful to all Your creation." Asch illuminates the greatness of souls like his. In all of his works, Sholem Asch idealized the person of pure heart and faith.

HANNAH BERLINER FISCHTHAL

Aub, Max

French-born Mexican dramatist, fiction writer, and essayist, 1903–1972

Born in Paris, 2 June 1903; moved with his family to Valencia, Spain, 1914. Attended high school, Valencia, then began to write fiction and drama in Spanish. Worked as travelling salesman. Married Perpetua (Peua) Barjau, 1926. Joined Spanish Socialist Workers Party, 1929. Cultural attaché in Paris and assistant to André Malraux, 1938; wrote script for film, *Sierra de Teruel*. Left Spain for France, 1939. Denounced as Jew in Paris, 1940; in concentration camps in France and Djelfa, Algiers; press attaché for Mexican Council in Marseilles, 1941; sought political asylum and settled in Mexico, 1942. Lectured for Unesco at Hebrew University, Jerusalem, 1966. Visited Spain, 1969 and 1972. Chevalier, Ordre des Arts et des Lettres, 1972. Died in Mexico, 22 July 1972. Published journals *Sala de espera* [The Waiting Room], 1948–51; *Los sesanta* [The Sixties], 1964–65; *El Correo de Euclides* [Euclides' Mail], 1959.

Selected Writings

Novels
Geografía [Geography], 1929
Fábula verde [Green Fable], 1932
Luis Álvarez Petreña, 1934
Campo cerrado [Closed Field], 1943
Campo de sangre [Field of Blood], 1945
Campo abierto [Open Field], 1951
Yo vivo [I, Alive], 1953
Las buenas intenciones [The Good Intentions], 1954
Jusep Torres Campalans, 1958, as *Jusep Torres Campalans*, translated by Herbert Weinstock, 1962
La calle de Valverde, 1961
Campo del moro [Field of the Moor], 1963
Juego de cartas [Card Game], 1964
Campo francés [French Field], 1965
Campo de los almendros [Almond Field], 1968
Últimos cuentos de la guerra de España [Last Stories of the Spanish Civil War], 1969
Novelas escogidas [Chosen Novels], 1970

Short Stories
No son cuentos [They Are Not Stories], 1951
Cuentos ciertos, Ciertos cuentos [True Stories, Certain Stories], 1955
Cuentos mexicanos (con pilón) [Mexican Stories (with a Tip)], 1959
La verdadera historia de la muerte de Francisco Franco y otros cuentos [The True Story of the Death of Francisco Franco and Other Stories], 1960
El zopilote y otros cuentos mexicanos [The Vulture and Other Mexican Stories], 1964
Historias de mala muerte [Awful Stories], 1965

Plays
Teatro incompleto [Incomplete Theatre], 1931
Espejo de avaricia [Mirror of Avarice], 1935
La vida conyugal [Married Life], 1943
San Juan, 1943
Morir por cerrar los ojos [To Die by Closing One's Eyes], 1944
El rapto de Europa o Siempre se puede hacer algo [The Abduction of Europe or You Can Always Find a Way], 1946
Cara y cruz [Heads and Tales], 1948
De algun tiempo a esta parte [From Those Days to the Present Time], 1949
Deseada, 1950
No, 1952
Tres monólogos y uno solo verdadero [Three Monologues, One Truth], 1956
Del amor [On Love], 1960
Las vueltas [The Turns], 1965
El cerco [The Fence], 1968
Teatro completo [Complete Theatre], 1968
Retrato de un general visto de medio cuerpo y vuelto hacia la izquierda [Portrait of a General from the Waist Upwards and Turning to the Left], 1969
Los muertos [The Dead] 1971
El desconfiado prodigioso y otras obras [The Prodigious Cynic and Other Stories], 1971

Poetry
Los poemas cotidianos, 1929
A, 1933
Diario de Djelfa [Djelfa Diary], 1944
Antología traducida [Translated Anthology], 1963

Versiones y subversiones [Versions and Subversions], 1971
Imposible Sinaí, 1982

Other
Proyecto de estructura para un teatro nacional y escuela nacional de baile [Project of a Structure for a National Theatre and for a National Dance School], 1936
La poesía española contemporánea [Spanish Contemporary Poetry], 1954
Algunas prosas [Some Prose], 1954
Crimenes ejemplares [Exemplary Crimes], 1957
Heine, 1957
Poesía mexicana (1950–1960), 1960
Mis páginas mejores [My Best Pages], 1966
Hablo como hombre [I Speak as a Man], 1967
Pruebas [Proofs], 1967
América Latina, 1967
Enero en Cuba, 1969
La gallina ciega: diario español, 1971
Conversaciones con Buñuel, 1985
Diarios, 1939–1972, edited by Manuel Aznar Soler, 1998

Further Reading
Borrás, Angel A., *El teatro del exilio de Max Aub*, Seville: Universidad de Seville, 1975
Fundación Max Aub website <www.maxaub.org> (including extensive bibliography)
Glickman, Nora, "El entredicho de Librada y los Diarios de Max Aub" in *Prosa y Poesía: Homenaje en Honor a Gonzalo Sobejano*, Madrid: Gredos, 2000: 124–34
Glickman, Nora, "Los Diarios de Max Aub", *Raíces* (January 2000)
Irizarry, Estelle, *La broma literaria en nuestros días: Max Aub, Francisco Ayala, Ricardo Gullón, Carlos Ripoll, César Tiempo*, New York: Eliseo Torres, 1979
Isasi Angulo, Amando Carlos, *Diálogos del teatro español de la postguerra: entrevistas con Max Aub . . .*, Madrid: AYUSO, 1974
Longoria, Francisco A., *El arte narrativo de Max Aub*, Madrid: Playor, 1977
López, Estela R., *El teatro de Max Aub*, Rio Piedras: Editorial Universitaria, Universidad de Puerte Rico, 1976
Monleón, José, *El teatro de Max Aub*, Madrid: Taurus, 1971
Monti, Silvia, *Sala d'attesa: il teatro incompiuto di Max Aub*, Rome: Bulzoni, 1992
Moraleda García, Pilar, *Temas y técnicas del teatro menor de Max Aub*, Córdoba: Universidad de Córdoba, 1989
Soldevila Durante, Ignacio, *La obra narrativa de Max Aub (1929–1969)*, Madrid: Gredos, 1973

Max Aub, best remembered for his polemical and controversial views, was born in Paris on 2 June 1903, the son of a French mother and German father, both agnostic, of Jewish descent. In 1914 his family moved to Valencia, Spain, where he went to high school and began to write fiction and theatre in Spanish. Rather than attending university like his bohemian contemporaries (Buñuel, Dalí, García Lorca), Aub chose "the school of life" and became a travelling salesman for his father's business, with the purpose of becoming economically independent, of satisfying his passion for reading, and of familiarizing himself with the culture of his adopted country. In 1926 he married Perpetua (Peua) Barjau, who was a determining influence throughout his life.

His early production of "vanguardist", "dehumanized" literature seemed to follow contemporary trends. Aub, however, was not only concerned with aesthetic innovation, detached from the social realities of his time, since he continued his activities as a political militant, and in 1929 joined the Spanish Socialist Workers Party. During this period he published *Los poemas cotidianos*, and collaborated on several journals: *Alfar*, *Carmen*, and *Verso y Prosa*. He also published two novels, *Geografía* and *Fábula verde*, and at the Valencia university theatre he wrote and directed *El Búho* and other plays in 1935 and 1936.

Aub's permanent frontiersman condition turned him into a symbol of his time. He is partly French, German, and Jewish, although he described himself as "escritor español y ciudadano mexicano". His conflicts regarding politics put him always on the defensive, since he does not totally defend any particular political view.

The first change towards a more socially responsible literature appeared in the journal *Azor*, with the serial publication of his novel *Luis Álvarez Petreña*. The protagonist is a vanguardist writer who puts an end to his crisis of values by committing suicide.

The Spanish Civil War had the effect of fusing Aub's aesthetics with his social and human preoccupations. In 1938, as a cultural attaché in Paris, he was assistant to French writer André Malraux in the filming of *Sierra de Teruel*, the script of which he wrote and translated into Spanish. In 1939 Aub left Spain for France. During this year he wrote *Campo cerrado*, the first novel of *El laberinto mágico* cycle, based on the Spanish Civil War. But in 1940, while in Paris, he was anonymously and falsely denounced as "a German subject (Jewish), a notorious communist and revolutionary", and dragged through jails and concentration camps in France and Algiers for several years. The poems of *Diario de Djelfa* and his novel *Campo de sangre* were produced during this period. In 1941 the Mexican Council named him press attaché in Marseilles, and in 1942 it offered him political asylum in Mexico.

In spite of Aub's feelings about Mexico's xenophobic attitude, his *Diarios* reflect his successful adaptation to Mexico's cultural life as fiction and film writer, theatre director and translator. His *Diarios* also reflect his harsh self-criticism. During his years in Mexico he produced 30 one-act plays and 12 three-act plays, poetry, and criticism. He contributed to the newspapers *El Excelsior* and *El Nacional*, worked as scriptwriter with Luis Buñuel, and founded a journal *Sala de espera*, producing 30 issues between 1948 and 1951. In 1957 he recorded the series *Voz viva de México* and the *Voz viva de América Latina* (edited by the Universidad Nacional Autónoma de México), and he directed the Radio Universidad programme for six years. Over the next 25 years his production was vast: the six novels and the numerous stories of *El laberinto mágico*, and other novels such as *La calle de Valverde*. In 1958 appeared an exhibition followed by the biography of an unknown painter, *Jusep Torres Campalans*, which disconcerted the critics. This homonymous novel became world famous, as one of the best artistic-literary spoofs of the 20th century.

In 1966 Unesco sent him to teach a course at the Hebrew University. His experience, rather than helping him embrace his Judaism, had the opposite effect of reinforcing his affiliation with his adopted countries, Spain and Mexico. His apocryphal collection *Imposible Sinaí* derives from this experience in Israel. In these poems supposedly written by Jewish and Palestinian victims of the Six Day War, Aub defends the Sephardic culture and the *ladino* (Judeo-Spanish) language, as opposed to the majority Ashkenazi culture prevalent in Israel.

Aub's Cuban experience from his 1967 participation in the First Congreso de Intelectuales in Havana, resulted in the publication of his diary *Enero en Cuba*.

During his last years he created a journal – *Los sesenta* – in which he invited writers above 60 to collaborate. In 1968 he began his biography of Buñuel, which was published posthumously in 1985. His 1969 visit to Spain resulted in his bitter diary *La gallina ciega*, and in his realization that his years of exile had separated him forever from the young generations, who ignored him, and from his own friends, who distanced themselves from him. During his second and last visit to Spain, in 1972, his health had already become very frail, as he had been stricken with diabetes.

In 1972, perhaps to make up for past injustices, France named him Chevalier des Arts et des Lettres. Aub died in Mexico on 22 July 1972. Since 1997, the Fundación Max Aub, from Segorbe, Castellón, has organized an annual tribute to Aub's life and work.

NORA GLICKMAN

Ausländer, Rose

Romanian-born German poet, 1907–1988

Born in Czernowitz, 11 May 1907. Studied literature and philosophy, Czernowitz University. Emigrated to United States, 1921; in New York, 1923. Visited Constantin Brunner in Berlin, 1928; editorial work for Czernowitz newspapers from 1931; taught English and worked as secretary in chemical factory. Escaped deportation from ghetto by working in a library. In New York as correspondent and translator, 1946; regained US citizenship, 1948; settled in Düsseldorf, 1965. Awards include Droste-Hülshoff Prize, 1967; Andreas Gryphius Prize, 1977; Ida Dehmel Prize, 1977; Gandersheim Literature Prize; Bavarian Academy of Fine Arts Prize, 1984. Died in Düsseldorf, 3 January 1988.

Selected Writings

Collection
Gesammelte Werke [Collected Works], 8 vols, 1984–90

Poetry
Der Regenbogen [The Rainbow], 1939
Blinder Sommer [Blind Summer], 1965
Inventar [Inventory], 1972
Andere Zeichen [Other Signs], 1974
36 Gerechte [36 Righteous Ones], 1975
Noch ist Raum [There's Still Space], 1976
Aschensommer [Summer of Ashes], 1977
Doppelspiel [Game of Doubles], 1977
Es ist alles anders [Everything has Changed], 1977
Selected Poems, translated by Ewald Osers, 1977
Mutterland [Motherland], 1978
Es bleibt noch viel zu sagen [There's Still a Lot to Say], 1978
Ein Stück weiter [One More Piece], 1979
Im Atemhaus wohnen [To Live in the House of Breath], 1979
Einen Drachen reiten [To Ride a Dragon], 1980
Einverständnis [Approval], 1980
Mein Atem heisst jetzt [My Breath is Called Now], 1981
Südlich wartet ein wärmeres Land [In the South Awaits a Warmer Land], 1982
Mein Venedig versinkt nicht [My Venice is Not Sinking], 1982
Ich zähl die Sterne meiner Worte [I Count the Stars of My Words], 1983
Festtag in Manhattan [Holiday in Manhattan], 1987
Ich spiele noch [I'm Still Playing], 1987
Freundschaft mit der Mondin [Friendship with the Lady Moon], 1987
Der Traum hat offene Augen: unveröffentlichte Gedichte 1965–78 [The Open-Eyed Dream: Unpublished Poems 1965–78], 1987
Wir ziehen mit den dunklen Flüssen [We Drift with the Dark Rivers], 1993
Denn wo ist Heimat [For Where is Home], 1994
Der Mohn ist noch nicht rot [The Poppy is Not Yet Red], 1994
The Forbidden Tree: englische Gedichte [The Forbidden Tree: English Poems], 1995

Further Reading

Beil, Claudia, *Sprache als Heimat: jüdische Tradition und Exilerfahrung in der Lyrik von Nelly Sachs und Rose Ausländer* [Language as Homeland: Jewish Tradition and the Experience of Exile in the Poetry of Nelly Sachs and Rose Ausländer], Munich: Tuduv, 1991

Braun, Helmut (editor), *Rose Ausländer: Materialien zu Leben und Werk* [Rose Ausländer: Materials on Her Life and Work], Frankfurt: Fischer, 1991

Eichmann-Leutenegger, Beatrice, "'Ich möchte mich ins wahre Leben schreiben . . .': Zum Leben der Dichterin Rose Ausländer, 1901–1988" [On the Life of the Poet Rose Ausländer], *Orientierung*, 52/8 (1988)

Glenn, Jerry, "Blumenworte / Kriegsgestammel: The Poetry of Rose Ausländer" [Words of Flowers / Stuttering of War: The Poetry of Rose Ausländer], *Modern Austrian Literature*, 12/3–4 (1979)

Helfrich, Cilly, *Es ist ein Aschensommer in der Welt* [This is a Summer of Ashes in the World], Weinheim: Beltz Quadriga, 1995 (biography)

Köhl, Gabriele, *Die Bedeutung der Sprache in der Lyrik Rose Ausländers* [The Meaning of Language in the Poetry of Rose Ausländer], Pfaffenweiler: Centaurus, 1993

Lehmann, Annette Jael, *Im Zeichen der Shoah: Aspekte der Dichtungs- und Sprachkrise bei Rose Ausländers und Nelly Sachs* [Under the Influence of the Shoah:

Aspects of the Crisis in Poetry and Language in the Work of Rose Ausländer and Nelly Sachs], Tübingen: Stauffenburg, 1999

Weissenberger, Klaus, "Rose Auslaender" in *Deutschsprachige Exilliteratur seit 1933* [The Literature of Exile in German since 1933], vol. 2, edited by John M. Spalek and Joseph Strelka, Bern: Francke, 1989

Rose Ausländer's oeuvre has either been overshadowed by her fellow-Romanian Paul Celan's poetical achievements, or it has been reduced by persistently comparing it with the poetry of other Jewish women poets of her generation – Nelly Sachs, Gertrud Kolmar, and Hilde Domin. Although these poets share a common Jewish cultural heritage and they have all attempted to come to terms with and give some sort of a response to the Shoah and to exile, their poetic answers differ considerably. As the critic H. Bender points out, it is time to pull Ausländer out of this shadow and to focus on the development and stature of her creativity. The range of her poetry pivots on a central existential condition she had to confront from early on: that of a Shoah survivor, a "Jüdische Zigeunerin" (Jewish Gypsy) doomed to live in exile. In her poetry there are few direct references to the Shoah since she felt completely inadequate to face the brutality and absurdity of this reality. The only possibly adequate reaction she envisioned was one of helpless pain: "Was wir besitzen: eine Klagewand/ and der die Fluten unser Tränen brechen" [What we possess is a Wailing Wall/ where the flowing of our tears breaks]. Her poetic answer stems from her determination not to be overwhelmed by this pain, therefore to somewhat remove that tragic reality in order to affirm, in line with Jewish tradition, the value of life.

Ausländer lived through the Shoah hidden in the Czernowitz ghetto. In the collection "Ghettomotive", written between 1939 and 1942 in a romantic and classical tradition, the reality of the Shoah is not communicated. Writing became a corroboration of her being alive, her sole form of survival which meant escape from reality. She found some comfort in the German poetic tradition with which she was familiar, an alternative ideal to the tragic existence she was living through. After the war she had to confront circumstances no less devastating: the destruction and irretrievable loss of her native land and the doom of exile: "Nun heisst die Heimat: wandern müssen" [Now my country means to wander]. Many are the poems, throughout the years, where Ausländer evokes that "Heimat": the Bukowina as a place of ideal childhood, of positive memories, of natural beauty, and of an intercultural and harmonious society. Its loss, in the poem "Verbrämt" [Adorned], is compared to leprosy, a disease that makes one weak, guilty, and above all an outsider constantly concerned with hiding the condition. Coming to terms with this loss and its painful consequence, exile, the par excellence condition of her own people, becomes the challenge of her life and of her creative expression. Significantly, she felt the need to symbolize this emotional and physical condition in maintaining, after her divorce, her husband's last name.

Living in exile implied a loss of identity, a searching for other roots, for another "Heimat", that Ausländer desperately tried to find in the United States where she even wrote poems in English. This experiment, however, did not last long; a decisive event – the death of her mother – drastically changed the course of this quest. With the death of her mother Ausländer lost the last tie with her origins, with her native and mother tongue. "Die Musik ist zerbrochen" [The Music is Shattered], claims the lyrical "I", in a new essential style. Yet it is this very fracture that forced her radically to rethink the concept of "Heimat", to find roots elsewhere and to discover in her own Jewish heritage other sources of identity. She drew from the biblical and Kabbalistic tradition and found in the creative and divine concept of language a new source. After having fully accepted the destruction – "Mein Vaterland ist tot/ sie haben es begraben/ im Feuer" [My native land is dead/ they have buried it/ in fire], the poet realizes that there still is one inner, indestructible root to which she can always refer, in which she can always find shelter: her mother tongue. "Ich lebe in meinem Mutterland/ Wort" [I live in my motherland/ Word]. As Claudia Beil points out, the word "Mutterland" that replaces her forever lost "Vaterland", becomes her new "Heimat".

Like a bird, a recurrent Kabbalistic metaphor in her poetry, the lyrical I finds identity in perpetual wandering, in "Unterwegssein" [being on the way] and in giving expression to this condition: "Ich bin nicht/ ich werde und stehe ein/ für das unverlässliche Leben" [I am not/ I become and answer for/ the unreliable life]. In the creative act the lyrical I overcomes exile, fully accepting, in line with the teachings of her philosophical fathers Spinoza and Constantin Brunner, the constant transformation of reality. Life is no longer bound to a specific place, to a "Heimat": "Ich wohne nicht/ ich lebe" [I don't live anywhere/ I live]. Only language, the Kabbalistic "Tree", can ensure the bird a certain degree of emotional safety and become the searching impulse for "Das atmende Wort" [the breathing word]. The duty of the writer is, in line with the Kabbalistic tradition, to restore through language things to their real nature. This implies an intense immersion in reality, a giving up of one's self, a becoming an instrument of language, a means for the poetic word. Through the poetic act the lyrical I takes part in the divine creative process and writing poetry becomes an affirmation of life: "Ich überlebende/ des Grauens/ schreibe aus Worten/ Leben" [I, survivor/ of the horror/ write with words/ life].

The resulting importance of language helps us to understand her problematic choice to spend the last years of her life in Germany. It was her only remedy to the threat, repeatedly expressed in the poetic production of the 1970s, of losing her mother tongue. In a deep sense Rose Ausländer did not return to Germany – the dramatic self-confinement in bed, in the last 11 years of her life, confirms it . She only returned to her "Heimat", her native tongue. That this language, was, of all things, one of the persecutors, made it even more urgent and imperative to affirm, to the very end and in memory of the dead, the will to survive: "Mein Volk/ mein Sandvolk/ mein Grasvolk/ wir lassen uns nichet vernichten" [my people/ my sand people/ my grass people/ we are not letting them exterminate us].

ELVIRA LATO VINTI

Auster, Paul

US fiction writer and poet, 1947–

Born in Newark, New Jersey, 3 February 1947. Studied at Columbia University, BA 1969, MA 1970. Spent four years in France writing and working as translator. Married, first, Lydia Davis, 1974; second, Siri Hustvedt, 1981; two children. Worked as merchant seaman, census taker, and teacher. Taught creative writing, Princeton University, 1986–90. Many awards, including Ingram Merrill Foundation Grant, for poetry, 1975, 1982; PEN Translation Center Grant, 1977; Morton Dauwen Zabel Award, American Academy of Arts and Letters, 1990; Chevalier de l'Ordre des Arts et Lettres, 1991; Prix Médicis Etranger, 1993.

Selected Writings

Novels
City of Glass, 1985, *Ghosts*, 1986, and *The Locked Room*, 1986; together as *The New York Trilogy*, 1987
In the Country of Last Things, 1987
Moon Palace, 1989
The Music of Chance, 1990
Leviathan, 1992
Mr Vertigo, 1994
Timbuktu: A Novel, 1999

Poetry
Unearth: Poems 1970–72, 1974
Wall Writing: Poems 1971–75, 1976
Fragments from Cold, 1977
Facing the Music, 1980
Disappearances: Selected Poems, 1988
Ground Work: Selected Poems and Essays, 1970–1979, 1990
Selected Poems, 1998

Play
Eclipse, 1977

Other
Translator, *A Little Anthology of Surrealist Poems*, 1972
Translator, *Fits and Starts: Selected Poems of Jacques Dupin*, 1974
Translator, *The Uninhabited: Selected Poems of André de Bouchet*, 1976
Translator (with Lydia Davis), *Jean-Paul Sartre: Life Situations*, 1977
White Spaces, 1980
The Invention of Solitude, 1982
Editor, *The Random House Book of Twentieth-Century French Poetry*, 1982
The Art of Hunger and Other Essays, 1982; as *The Art of Hunger: Essays, Prefaces, Interviews*, 1992
Translator, *A Tomb for Anatole*, by Stéphane Mallarmé, 1983
Translator, *The Notebooks of Joseph Joubert: A Selection*, 1983
Translator, *Vicious Circles*, by Maurice Blanchot, 1985
Translator, *On the High Wire*, by Philippe Petit, 1985
Translator (with Margit Rowell), *Joan Miró: Selected Writings*, 1986
Auggie Wren's Christmas Story, 1990
The Red Notebook and Other Writings, 1995
Smoke and *Blue in the Face* (two films), 1995
Why Write?, 1996
Hand to Mouth: A Chronicle of Early Failure, 1997
La Solitude du labyrinthe (essays and interviews), with Gérard de Cortanze, 1997
Lulu on the Bridge, 1998

Further Reading

Barone, Dennis (editor), *Beyond the Red Notebook: Essays on Paul Auster*, Philadelphia: University of Pennsylvania Press, 1995
Drenttel, William, *Paul Auster: A Comprehensive Bibliographic Checklist of Published Works, 1968–1994*, New York: Delos Press, 1994
Herzogenrath, Bernd, *An Art of Desire: Reading Paul Auster*, Amsterdam: Rodopi, 1999
Holzapfel, Anne M., *The New York Trilogy: Whodunit? Tracking the Structure of Paul Auster's Anti-detective Novels*, Frankfurt and New York: Peter Lang, 1996
Jackson, Kevin, "You are About to Read a True Story", *The Independent*, London (22 April 1995)
Rowen, Norma, "The Detective in Search of the Lost Tongue of Adam: Paul Auster's 'City of Glass'", *Critique: Studies in Contemporary Fiction*, 32/4 (Summer 1991): 224
Varvogli, Aliki, *The World that is the Book: Paul Auster's Fiction*, Liverpool: Liverpool University Press, 2001

Paul Auster's Jewishness arguably manifests itself through an engagement with the Holocaust's impact on language and memory in the post-Holocaust world. In other words, Auster's concern is with that event's challenge to literary representation. As it is only occasionally mentioned in his prose works, or alluded to in the earlier poetry that marked a first and distinct stage in his writing career, the Holocaust is more of a present absence. This is not to say that the Holocaust is an over-determining aspect of Auster's writing, nor of Jewishness *per se*, but this event in history has shaped his literature.

Written as a letter from a post-apocalyptic city, whose author's survival is uncertain, and evoking scenes from the Warsaw ghetto, *In the Country of Last Things* invokes the ghetto diaries that survived the Holocaust and, often, their authors. The character Anna Blume travels to this city in search of her lost brother, a journalist who went to report on conditions there but who disappeared while on assignment. Her letter is testimony to what she finds there. The evocation of the ghetto as opposed to its direct allusion signals an immediate problem of historical representation in the face of the Holocaust. In particular, Auster dramatizes Anna's struggle to witness and write before the genocidal process swallows her up too. The closing distance between her position as writer and the victims of whom she writes is illuminated by her self-identification to a precarious community of rabbis: "'I'm Jewish, too,' I blurted out. 'My name is Anna Blume'". In this she announces not only her identity but also the condition of writing that stems from that identity. Each scene of death witnessed and written about prefigures the possible fate of the narrator. For Anna, then, writing is a form of self-wounding. "That is what I mean by being wounded: you cannot merely see, for each thing somehow belongs to you, is part of the story unfolding inside you". The more she writes the closer she comes to her death, but writing is also an affirmation of her existence. As we do not know whether she survived her attempted escape from the ghettoized city, her writing is all that is left of her. However, this letter is unreliable proof of what once was, given the difficulties of translating the traumatic nature of what has been seen (witnessed) in the ghetto into language, of writing the unspeakable. So, like the historic ghetto scribes, chroniclers, and diarists, upon whom Auster undoubtedly bases his narrator, Anna very much writes at the limits of existence and exists at the limits of her writing.

If *In the Country of Last Things* dramatizes the inception of a crisis of language, narrativity, and, by extension, memory, in the face of the Holocaust, but also an attempted inscription and remembrance of that event, then *The Invention of Solitude* registers, theorizes, and strives to work through the transmission of that crisis to post-Holocaust writing. *The Invention of Solitude* dramatizes the problems of what might be called second generation Holocaust memory – a collective memory shared by those who did not necessarily witness the Holocaust, in one form or another, but who have inherited the burden of remembering from those who did. Auster shows us that the trauma of the event, as it passes from living memory, has not necessarily lessened over time. *The Invention of Solitude* is comprised of two parts: "Portrait of an Invisible Man" and "The Book of Memory". "Portrait of an Invisible Man" is Auster's meditation on the death of his father: a biography, an autobiography, but also an act of memorialization. The second part of the book, "The Book of Memory", theorizes the problems of a collective remembrance of the Holocaust. It too is an act of memorialization, but one that is cast in doubt. Given the problems of representing such an event to memory and writing, Auster offers a commentary on his own text that holds in check the claims of its theory and practice of memory-work and prevents such work from assuming a false sense of completion. More fundamentally, this commentary questions the ability of language itself to live up to the task assigned it. As Auster concludes in his essay on Edmond Jabès's *The Book of Questions* (in *The Art of Hunger*):

> To Jabès, nothing can be written about the Holocaust unless writing itself is first put into question. If language is to be pushed to the limit, then the writer must condemn himself to an exile of doubt, to a desert of uncertainty. What he must do, in effect, is create a poetics of absence. The dead cannot be brought back to life. But they can be heard, and their voices live in the Book.

In light of the concerns of "The Book of Memory", "Portrait of an Invisible Man", cannot but help resonate with the Holocaust. It is as though the Holocaust has caused a wound in language and memory, whatever is remembered and written after that event.

City of Glass (the first part of *The New York Trilogy*) reports that collective memories of the Holocaust have not lost their disruptive resonance. In *City of Glass*, Daniel Quinn, posing as a detective by the name of Paul Auster, is hired by Peter Stillman to protect him from his father (just released from prison). Stillman senior was imprisoned for incarcerating his son for nine years in the hopes that, without contact with this world, he would remember the language of a previous one, Eden, as though it were somehow a deep, genetic memory. For Stillman senior, the Fall from Eden, and more specifically from an Adamic language in which words created the very things they stood for – went "straight to the quick of the world" – has meant that "words no longer correspond to the world . . . Hence, every time we try to speak of what we see, we speak falsely, distorting the very thing we are trying to represent".

Stillman senior has returned to New York to continue his experiments with language. He hopes to reverse the Fall, in a modern-day Tower of Babel project, by inventing a language to rename broken things which no longer correspond to their original names. Auster implies it is modernity, and more specifically the Holocaust, rather than pre-history, that has left language in ruins – shattered by what it has to represent. Picking over these ruins, renaming broken things, and therefore repairing language, Stillman sees broken objects, but Quinn, following him, sees broken people – those refused by society, impoverished, and existing on its margins. Stillman's failure to recognize and name the abject is a lesson in Holocaust memorialization. For it is the indeterminacies of language which allow the generation of a varied reality, rather than one truth at the expense of another, one that will refuse history's refused again.

Auster's 1999 novel *Timbuktu* narrates, from the consciousness of a dog owned by the son of Holocaust survivors, a journey to the kingdom of death, "Timbuktu". Willy, the son, arrives there (dies) first, later to be joined by Mr Bones (the dog). This, then, is a book about the elongated process of dying, in which existence prefigures death. Death is a place associated with Poland, from where Willy's parents escaped the Holocaust. Willy dies outside the former house of Edgar Allan Poe, the place he names Poe-land. Through this chain of association, American literature is overshadowed by death, and death is overshadowed by the Holocaust. Death occupies that literature as an irredeemably negative space that cannot be fully known but which continues to structure that literature including *Timbuktu: A Novel* itself.

RICHARD CROWNSHAW

Avidan, David

Israeli poet, 1933–1995

Born in Tel Aviv, February 1933. Studied literature and philosophy at the Hebrew University. Began publishing poetry in early 1950s. Awards include Abraham Woursell Prize from the University of Vienna, Prime Minister's Prize (twice), and Bialik Prize, 1994. Died 11 May 1995.

Selected Writings

Poetry
Berazim arufei sefatayim [Lipless Faucets], 1954
Beayot ishiot [Personal Problems], 1957/59
Sikum beinayim [Interim], 1960
Shirei lahats [Pressure Poems], 1962
Mashehu bishvil mishehu [Something for Somebody], 1964
Shirim bilti efshariim [Impossible Poems], 1968
Diyun veheshbon ishi al masa LSD [Personal Report on an LSD Trip], 1968
Shirim hitsoniim [External Poems], 1970
Shirim shimushiim [Used Poems], 1973
Hapsikhiater haelektroni sheli [My Electronic Psychiatrist], 1974
Shirei milhamah vemehaah [Poems of War and Protest], 1976
Shirei ahava vemin [Poems of Love and Sex], 1976
Tishdoret milavyan rigul [Cryptograms from a Telstar], 1976
Shirim ekroniim [Axiomatic Poems], 1978
Energia meshurbetet [Scribbled Energy], 1979
Sefer haefsharuyot [The Book of Possibilities], 1985
Avidanium 20, 1987
Hamifrats haaharon [The Last Gulf], 1991

For Children
Dani mehunani benyu york [Gifted Danny in New York], 1993
Rosh leshualim [Foxes' Heads], 1994

Plays
The End of the Season is the End of the World, 1962
Carambole, 1965

Further Reading

Ohel, Hayim, *Shaar lashirah hatseirah: segulot hashirah hatseirah: nituah yetsirot mishel hameshorerim: David Avidan, Hayim Guri, Natan Zakh, Yehudah Amichai, Dalyah Rabikovits, Ben-Tsiyon Tomer*, Tel Aviv: Tserikover, 1993

Avidan belongs chronologically to the poets of the establishment of the State of Israel. This generation created a new poetic journey, whose model was essentially Anglo-Saxon, as opposed to the Russo-German model that influenced Natan Alterman, Leah Goldberg, and Avraham Shlonsky. The poetry of Avidan is daring and innovative by both Israeli and international standards. He was perceived as avant-garde and did not publish through recognized publishing houses.

In his poetry there are no escape routes to nostalgia, redemption, religiosity, or the search for beauty. The alternative that his poetry suggests is "That which justifies more than any/ the loneliness, the great despair/ the odd bearing of a yoke/ the great loneliness and the great despair/ is the simple decisive fact/ that in essence we have nowhere to go . . ." ("A Proxy").

Avidan's poetry is known for its dynamic struggle against the static, struggling for survival amid a changing world and language. It is often polemical, tending to repetition and to the logical and linguistical dismantling of routine phrases of speech. Avidan describes himself as a poet "single-drafter" ("Had tiyutay") or "single rough copy" ("Had tiyutathi"). He confesses to writing the poem in one act and without drafts. This shows us his preference for speed, for the spontaneous: "If I did not write quickly, I would not be writing even one word", he observes in "Fast and a Lot".

Avidan dramatizes the image of the poet. His poetry lacks actual biographical material. The image of the poet (the "I" of the speaker) is very Tel Avivian, and simultaneously seems alien to its time and place. His poetry includes linguistic innovation, using different combinations of language (the language of the Bible, secular language, slang, foreign languages). He often combines two words in one and especially in circumstances in which the resonance that finishes the first word identifies with the sound that opens the second word (for example, *Arochtavah detested her droppings*). This serves to speed up the poem.

Avidan began writing poetry at school, publishing his first poems in the communist journal *Voice of the People*. His earliest poems reveal a number of key subjects that were to preoccupy him: the relationship between the poet and mass society; the relationship between the political and the intimate and the role of the poet to be the voice of the epoch; the pursuit of avant-garde; and the unclear relationship between the serious and prosaic in existing texts.

The tendency towards conceptual radicalism, linguistic virtuosity, and preservation of traditional forms of poetry from the standpoint of rhyme and metre characterize his poetry in the first period of his creativity – *Lipless Faucets* in 1954 to *Something for Someone* in 1964. Unlike others of his generation, Avidan refrained from free verse and safeguarded rhythmic regularity in the first period of his work. He breaks the monotony of rhyme by means of syntax, intense pauses, and the quality of dialogue: "Then we will ride in the strangulated streets, like horses, and the road is hot, it breathes below us, and we will run to the light, and we will slip dying, and we will inseminate women in the square opposite the sun" (from "Suddenly"). His attitude to his predecessor, Alterman, is one of veneration, imitation, controversy, parody, and play. The image of the wanderer used by Alterman is translated into "they who go at night, go, go, on the long and dirty highways" (the first lines of the poem "Visiting Card"). Avidan is the "User Poet": his link to the poetic tradition, to the materials of language, and the reality of his predecessors is that of perspective, interpretation, and change. After the period of *Something for Someone* he focuses primarily on the canonization of his own poetry; his earlier texts become parody or pastiche.

In the years 1968–74 Avidan published "experimental-laboratory" poems in the books *Impossible Poems*, *Personal Report on an LSD Trip*, *External Poems*, and *My Electronic Psychiatrist*. In these years, his poems place at their centre of attention problems of consciousness, identity, and language. *External Poems* is based on the Rorschach tests and TAT that are used for psychological diagnosis. *My Electronic Psychiatrist* consists of eight authentic conversations with a computer (according to the subtitle) by means of the computer software program "Aliza". Avidan is a poet who creates stubborn dialogue with a hard core of modernism in "real time". His modernistic perception is linked also to the centrality of technology, computerization, and communication as legitimate themes of poetry. The dovetailing between the naivety of the innovative technological veneration and the scientific facts with the criticism of the fundamental assumptions of modernism is one of the riddles that Avidan's poetry places before us. The spark of his poetry adds to popular culture – Avidan seeks "an audience of pop groups" for his poetry and not a crowd of "conventional poetry readers". It constructs an image of the poet-hero of culture, the journalistic, the visual art, and the cinematic, whose role is to accompany, document, and to be as a prophet of the modern. Avidan is a poet with one leg rooted in modernism, the other in postmodern manifestation.

From the chronological standpoint, the book *Used Poems* in 1973 actually belongs to the "experimental-laboratory" period, but, contrasted with the books that he wrote in the 1970s, the book synthesizes the tendencies that were exposed in this period. The poems are "utilitarian" in the sense that they are objects that need "to work". This book appears to be liberated from the direct conflict of the poetry of the previous generation and from the "anti-poetical" poetry of the second period (an exception is the poem "A Modest Contribution to the Theory of Poetry", which becomes a direct argument with academic discussions on the subject of the definition of a poem). "Now is the Time" opens with the lines: "Now is the time to begin something that will not be finished, in short lines and long verse," and finishes: "Now is the right moment to give it to him fast and deep, but the matter is not simple and already there is no one with whom to speak, not with a man nearby nor with another man".

Avidan's poetry in *Cryptograms from a Telstar*, *The Book of Possibilities*, and *The Last Gulf* is characterized by the development of the theme of futuristic prophecy and the exchange of an existentialist vocabulary for that of the futuristic escapist. The futuristic theme is in essence a transformation of the theme of longing for immortality and yearning for connection with the possible other person, if not in our world we are in other possible worlds. In "Iron Ration" he describes himself "ascending weakly from death, with eyes stuck together from sleep" and "exchanging words in their language . . . in another thousand years" with people of the new world who live "without law and order".

Most critics consider the period of *Something for Somebody* to be Avidan's strongest, though there are some who say that his later poetry was weakened and eroded by linguistic games and excessive chatter. "What is there for an old man in his life? He gets up in the morning, and morning does not arise in him" (from "Sudden Evening") – these are the inalienable goods of Israeli culture.

ANAT WEISSMAN
translated by Rachel M. Paul

Ayalon, Leah

Israeli poet and short-story writer, 1950–

Born in Jerusalem, 10 January 1950, the seventh generation of a German family who settled there. Studied at the Hebrew University, BA in Hebrew and Comparative Literature. Has worked for more than 25 years for the Jewish National Library in Jerusalem. Also a part-time journalist and critic. Awarded the Jerusalem Prize, several prizes from the Hebrew University and has twice received an award from the Israeli Prime Minister.

Selected Writings

Poetry
Mitahat lamayim [Under the Water], 1983
Zehu gan-eden [This is Paradise], 1984
Uba hayareah uba halaylah [And the Moon Came and the Night Came], 1987
Daniel Daniel, 1988
Kamelot, 1995
Kan beitsim [A Nest of Eggs], 1998
"A Closed Place", "Wonderings and an Absurd Shattering", "Happiness?" "Second Woman and Insecurity", *Modern Hebrew Literature*, 13/3–4 (1998): 21–23
Lynch, 2000

Stories
Mashehu kiyyumi [Something Existential], 1991

Novel
Habilti musariyim [The Immorals], 1996

Further Reading

Ayalon, Leah, "Leave Me Alone" (in response to Dorit Meirovitch's article from *Hadarim*), *Haaretz* (22 January 1993)
Kafri, Yehudit, "Unique Poetry", *Al hamishmar* (24 May 1985)
Matalon, Ronit, "Riding to Nothingness", *Haaretz sefarim* (3 July 1996)
Meirovitch, Dorit, "I Who Touches Things: on Leah Ayalon's Poetry", *Hadarim*, 10 (Winter 1993): 163–68
Netzer, Ruth, "A Murder in a Ginger Dress", *Itton 77*, 120 (March 1990): 13
Snir, Leah, "Walking in Scarred Forests", *Moznayim*, 62/7–8 (October–November 1988): 76–77
Snir, Leah, "Like in a Movie Theatre", *Maariv* (30 December 1988)
Zevi, Azza, "The Purple Rose of Cairo", *Haaretz* (4 January 1989)

Ayalon has been a distinctive voice in Israeli poetry for the last two decades, with her idiosyncratic, surreal, "hallucinated," almost esoteric poetics, reminiscent of Sylvia Plath, Anne Sexton, and, in Israeli poetry, of Yona Wallach. In Ayalon's poems, different semantic fields and language registers are joined together to create a strange, wild, and often disturbing poetic language. Elements from prosaic, mundane reality are set alongside intimate situations to create a surreal, dream-like, violent, and somewhat magical world.

Ayalon's world is made of two kinds of materials. The first is the forces of nature – the sea, the stars, the moon, the wind, and the lightning – which accumulate symbolic and metonymic meanings throughout the poems, as the speaker's self-projections as well as those of rivals:

The presence of the house
near a bay that creates a slashing sea
which attacks and withdraws furiously on the shore
affects me.

(from *Under the Water*)

The second ingredient of Ayalon's world is Hollywood movies. She imagines herself as Jayne Mansfield or Marilyn Monroe, her lover as Rhett Butler or Paul Newman; she drives a Chevrolet or Porsche, wears sexy black dresses, drinks Budweiser or Coca-Cola, and is surrounded by strong motorcyclists and mafia men, as is evident in *Daniel Daniel*:

I wanted to enter with a face like Jayne Mansfield's
in a black sleek sexy one-piece bathing suit

Being a metaphor – or a substitute – for the real world, Ayalon's poetic world gives way to, and is ruled by primordial, chaotic instincts and desires; it recognizes no restrictions of law or morality. Two axes of desires and instincts are being enacted and re-enacted in the poems: one is that of the speaker's love and passion for her male lover. Hers is a mythical love (as she admits: "This love will be a myth"), which usually begins as yearning, total dedication and dependence on him but gradually turns into violent obsession, possessiveness, envy, hatred, revenge, and murder. The speaker's monologues thus vacillate between extreme tenderness and extreme violence, from naive romanticism to unrelenting sado-masochism. Again *Daniel Daniel*:

I wanted to lean on you
to enter your thoughts
your feelings
your body
to enter deep into you
so you won't belong to any other woman.

She is thus not only beyond morality and the law, but also, like a super-woman, above and beyond all ordinary, mortal people:

What's in me
a complete justification of Cain
covered despair
and unexplained power.

(*A Nest of Eggs*)

But behind this demonic, mythical, cruel *femme fatale* is a tortured and vulnerable girl, perpetually hungry for love, and behind the romantic and sexual desire is the spoiled love between mother and daughter. In her second book, *This is Paradise* (which significantly was written first), the lonely golden girl takes it upon herself to re-raise her childhood self. She thus re-imagines herself as a loved girl ("she is so pretty/ tiny golden/ lily in her mouth/ sea in her ear/ and a seashell") – and, at the same time, as her own better mother, who wishes she could "transform myself into her". But here, too, the corrective, redeeming experience turns sour and the good, nourishing mother is suddenly bad and cruel.

The speaker is thus divided or hopelessly broken into two or more selves (and her recent books seem to be more concerned with this division):

And my feelings what are they I thought
when they move in two opposite directions
dissecting

(*Kamelot*)

Significantly, the girl's hunger for love is rendered in an insatiable hunger for food, and Ayalon's poems are often filled to bursting with lists of edibles, often sweets, and most frequently milk and eggs.

Being idiosyncratic and personal, Ayalon's poems seem to imply or hide a real, particular and concrete, even confessional "I" (who often refers to specific, renowned people and places). At the same time, it is a mysterious, distant, clearly incommunicative and inaccessible "I" – not even accessible through the poems (or especially not through them). Ayalon's poems allude to the particular "I" that is Leah Ayalon, the Author outside and "before" the text, at the same time that they keep "her" distant, unreachable, and inapprehensible – even illusionary, imagined, or invented. The title of her first book, *Under the Water*, conveys this elusive duality: voiceless existence and communication in an underworld that is visible (and parallel) to the earthly and human world, yet sealed and detached from it. Thus, the question arises as to the nature and meaning of this poetry: is it intimate and confessional, and therefore chaotic (and essentially cathartic)? What are the relationships between the concrete and the metaphorical in it? Are the realistic and intimate elements metaphors for a personal, mental experience – or are the figural and surreal elements metaphors for the real (personal and intimate) condition?

This confusion may explain the ambivalence of critics towards Ayalon, mainly regarding her personal life: on the one hand, they emphasize her somewhat peculiar position – her orthodox background and hearing disability – while on the other hand they attempt to not let that affect their reading. Oddly enough, Ayalon herself often adds to the confusion in her critical articles, in which she argues with, criticizes, and "corrects" her critics. Indeed, Ayalon writes poetry that purposefully seems *as if it were* confessional and intimate. Thus, at the same time that Ayalon's poetry does construct a female subject that is the fragmented, narcissistic, suffering woman, the strong impression of confessional poetry emanates also the figure of Ayalon-the-poet as the fantasy – or perhaps, a mock-parody of the fantasy – of this suffering female Author.

HAMUTAL TZAMIR

B

Babel', Isaak Emmanuilovich

Russian fiction writer and dramatist, 1894–1940

Born in Odessa, 30 June 1894 to Feiga and Man Yitzkhovich Bobel, a dealer in agricultural machinery. Pseudonyms Bab-El and Kirill Vasilevich Lyutov. Witnessed pogrom in Odessa, 1905. Private Jewish education in Hebrew, Bible and Talmud; then educated at the Nicholas I Commercial School, Odessa, 1906–11. Attended Beilis trial, 1911. Graduated from Kiev Institute of Financial and Business Studies, 1916. Contributed to Gor'kii's magazine, *Letopis*, 1916. Served briefly on the Romanian front, 1917. Worked for Cheka, as translator for counter-intelligence, 1917. Contributed to Gor'kii's newspaper, *Novaya zhizn*, and Petrograd newspaper *Zhizn iskusstva*, 1918. Served in food requisitioning detachments during Civil War. Assigned to Budyonny's 1st Cavalry (Cossacks) as a supply officer in the Polish campaign of 1920; returned ill. Married Evgeniia Borisovna Gronfein, 1919; daughter Nathalie (both emigrated to Paris, 1925); second daughter, Lidiya, by Antonina Pirozhkova. Son, Mikhail, with Tamara Kashirina. Worked with Sergei Eisenstein on filmscripts. Permitted to visit Paris in 1927 and 1932. Witnessed brutal collectivization and famine in Ukraine, 1930. Lived in Molodenovo, outside Moscow, 1932. Attended First Congress of Soviet Writers, 1934, and Congress of Soviets, Moscow, 1935; attended International Writer's Congress for the Defence of Culture in Paris, 1935, with Boris Pasternak. Received *dacha* (country house) in Peredelkino as leading writer, 1936. Arrested 13 May 1939, charged with spying. Executed in Lubyanka prison, 15 January 1940 (death certificate states: "died under unknown circumstances, 17 March 1941"). Posthumously exonerated, 1954.

Selected Writings

Collections

Collected Stories, edited and translated by Walter Morrison, 1955
Izbrannoe [Selected Works], 1957
Izbrannye proizvedeniia [Selected Works], 2 vols, 1988
Sochineniia [Works], edited by A.N. Pirozhkova, 2 vols, 1990
Collected Stories, translated by David McDuff, 1994
The Complete Works of Isaac Babel, edited by Nathalie Babel, translated by Peter Constantine, 2002

Fiction

Na pole chesti [On the Field of Honour], 1920
Konarmiia, 1926; as *Red Cavalry*, translated by John Harland, 1929; also translated by Walter Morrison in *Collected Stories*, 1955; by Andrew R MacAndrew in *Liubka the Cossack and Other Stories*, 1963; and by David McDuff in *Collected Stories*, 1994
Bluzhdaiushchie zvezdy: rasskaz dlia kino [Wandering Stars: A Cine-Story], 1926
Istoriia moei golubiatni [The Story of My Dovecote], 1926
Benia Krik: kinopovest', 1926; as *Benya Krik: A Film-Novel*, translated by Ivor Montague and S.S. Nolbandov, 1935
Korol' [The King], 1926
Evreiskie rasskazy [Jewish Tales], 1927
Odesskie rasskazy [Odessa Tales], 1931; as *Tales of Odessa*, translated by Walter Morrison in *Collected Stories*, 1955; and by David McDuff in *Collected Stories*, 1994
Benya Krik, The Gangster, and Other Stories, edited and translated by Avrahm Yarmolinsky, 1948
Liubka the Cossack and Other Stories, edited and translated by Andrew R. MacAndrew, 1963
You Must Know Everything: Stories 1915–1937, edited by Nathalie Babel, translated by Max Hayward, 1969
Detstvo i drugie rasskazy [Childhood and Other Stories], edited by Efraim Sicher, 1979

Plays

Zakat, 1927; as *Sunset*, translated by Raymond Rosenthal and Mirra Ginsburg, 1960
Mariia, 1935; as *Marya*, translated by Michael Glenny and Harold Shukman, in *Three Soviet Plays*, edited by Glenny, 1966

Other

Isaac Babel: The Lonely Years 1925–1939: Unpublished Stories and Private Correspondence, edited by Nathalie Babel, translated by Andrew R. MacAndrew and Max Hayward, 1964
The Forgotten Prose, edited and translated by Nicholas Stroud, 1978; as *Zabytyi Babel*, 1979
1920 Diary, edited by Carol J. Avins, translated by H.T. Willetts, 1995

Further Reading

Carden, Patricia, *The Art of Isaac Babel*, Ithaca, New York: Cornell University Press, 1972
Danow, David K., "A Poetics of Inversion: The Non-Dialogic Aspect in Isaac Babel's *Red Cavalry*", *Modern Language Review*, 86/4 (1991)

Ehre, Milton, *Isaac Babel*, Boston: Twayne, 1986
Falen, James E., *Isaac Babel, Russian Master of the Short Story*, Knoxville: University of Tennessee Press, 1974
Gillespie, David, *The Twentieth-Century Russian Novel: An Introduction*, Oxford: Berg, 1996
Luck, Christopher, *Figures of War and Fields of Honour: Isaak Babel's Red Cavalry*, Keele, Staffordshire: Keele University Press, 1995
Luplow, Carol, *Isaac Babel's Red Cavalry*, Ann Arbor, Michigan: Ardis, 1982
Mendelsohn, Danuta, *Metaphor in Babel's Short Stories*, Ann Arbor, Michigan: Ardis, 1982
Rougle, Charles (editor), *Red Cavalry: A Critical Companion*, Evanston, Illinois, Northwestern University Press, 1996
Schreurs, Marc, *Procedures of Montage in Isaak Babel's Red Cavalry*, Amsterdam: Rodopi, 1989
Sicher, Efraim, "Art as Metaphor, Epiphany, and Aesthetic Statement: The Short Stories of Babel", *Modern Language Review*, 77/2 (1982): 387–96
Sicher, Efraim, "The Road to a Red Cavalry: Myth and Mythology in the Works of Babel", *Slavonic and East European Review*, 60 (1982): 528–46
Sicher, Efraim, *Style and Structure in the Prose of Isaak Babel*, Columbus, Ohio: Slavica, 1986
Sicher, Efraim, *Jews in Russian Literature after the October Revolution: Writers and Artists between Hope and Apostasy*, Cambridge: Cambridge University Press, 1995
Stora-Sandor, Judith, *Isaac Babel' 1894–1941: l'Homme et l'oeuvre*, Paris: Klincksieck, 1968

"Do not bother the reader with explanations", Babel' once told his colleague Dmitri Furmanov. Influenced by Maupassant and Chekhov, Babel' achieves much through little in an economy of words. Today, he is credited with being the master of Soviet stylists. He was indeed an anomaly: an intellectual, humane, pacifist Jew fighting for the Communist cause in the ranks of Cossack horsemen, coming to terms with the Cossack ethos of physical violence. The Yiddish expression, "a Cossack in a *succah* [fragile temporary dwelling]" (equivalent to the English phrase "a bull in a china shop"), illustrates how the Cossack was perceived as the arch-enemy of the Jew. Babel''s view is more consonant with Tolstoi's representation of the Cossack as having a primitive energy, a simplicity, moving with speed and grace on his horse. At the end of "After the Battle" the narrator prays for "the simplest of proficiencies – the ability to kill my fellow-men", and, in "My First Goose", "my heart, stained with bloodshed, . . . brimmed over."

Babel''s stories are tinged with violence and cruelty yet retain a kind of lyrical joy. When the Cossacks are about to attack in "Zamoste", "the raw dawn flowed over us like waves of chloroform. Green rockets soared . . . shuddered in the air, scattered like rose leaves beneath the moon, and went out." A simple story is transcended, dissolved in a multitude of implication. When Babel' describes a woman removing a man's troublesome tooth, "Sasha went over to him with her wobbling breasts . . . and took out of his black mouth a long tooth that was swaying there like a birch by a bare highway." We are led from the commonplace towards the shock of new knowledge in the beauty of the lyric image.

The enigma remains: Babel''s Red Cavalry are Cossacks fighting for the revolution, yet were the instrument and symbol of czarist repression. As a supply officer under General Budyonny in the 1920 campaign, Babel' experienced for himself the Cossacks' power over the Jewish world. Yet he was committed to secular life, and broke with Jewish tradition by joining the Revolution. It was while he was in Odessa convalescing from asthma after the campaign, that he wrote *Red Cavalry* and *Tales of Odessa*. Both these works aroused the wrath of General Budyonny who issued a denunciation of this vilification. Yet in a letter (1926) to his mother and sister who had fled to Belgium, Babel' rejects "the memories of the last 200 years": "We must decorate our houses with gaiety, not with *tsoros* [troubles]." His first biographer, Judith Stora-Sandor, wrote that "his literary sensibility was French, his vision was Jewish and his fate was all too Russian".

In his first story, "Old Shloyme", published in Kiev in 1913, Babel' reveals a younger generation rejecting traditional Jewish values, a theme enunciated also in "The Rabbi's Son". Here Elijah, son of the Rabbi of Zhitomir, who has joined the revolutionary cause despite his parents' protests, lies dying, his possessions strewn about him, "pages of the Song of Songs and revolver cartridges". Babel' describes the scene, "the wilderness of war yawned beyond the window", and as they bury him, the narrator feels a sense of companionship, "I was there beside my brother". There is nothing superfluous in the writing; brevity is achieved by tight control.

Gor'kii published two of Babel''s stories in his journal, *Letopis*, in 1916, and was his protector for many years. These stories were indicted as obscene, but the courthouse was timeously burned down by revolutionaries, so the records were destroyed. Shocking and outspoken, one story describes how Rimma performs an abortion on her sister in the bathroom of their Moscow flat; the other, equally outrageous for the time, shows how an Odessa Jew evades the police when he lacks a residence permit, by spending the night with a Russian prostitute.

Babel' grew up among the Jews of Nikolayev and Odessa during the reign of Nicholas II; it was a time of anti-Semitism, pogroms, the Beilis trial, and a life outside the Pale of Settlement. Yet in Odessa, the cosmopolitan Black Sea port, Jewish life flourished. It was also a time of the *Haskalah* (Enlightenment) and the birth of modern Hebrew poetry. Raised in a Yiddish-speaking home, with a knowledge of Hebrew, Babel' chose nonetheless to write in Russian. (Although six of his stories appeared in Hebrew translation, "edited by the author", in the only issue of *Bereshit*, a Hebrew journal published in 1926.)

When Babel' describes the Jews in the Moldavanko ghetto in Odessa, it is quite different to the poor Jews of the shtetl. Here are the jovial types who "bubbled over with cheap wine", the ordinary firemen, dairy farmers, and gangsters. Benya Krik, the gangster, is a "lion [who] could spend the night with a Russian woman and satisfy her" ("How It Was Done in Odessa"). He forgets for a while he has "spectacles on [his] nose and autumn in [his] heart". Benya tells his bereaved aunt with delightful humour that, while "everyone makes mistakes", God has made a terrible one "in settling the Jews in Russia". "How would it hurt if the Jews lived in Switzerland, where they would be surrounded by first-class lakes, mountain air, and nothing but Frenchies!" Benya's sister in "The King" is Deborah, "a virgin of forty summers who suffered from goitre". Most of the story describes her wedding feast, and the "accidental" but opportune fire, engineered by Krik, at the police station (reminiscent of the fire at the courthouse in Babel''s own life story). Yet the Joycean epiphany at the story's end utterly transforms it, as Deborah urges her new and faint-hearted husband to the nuptial chamber: "like a cat she was, that holding a mouse in her jaws, tests it gently with her teeth".

Tsudechkis complains in "Liubka the Cossack" that the Jews are "in the hands of pharaoh". Their bondage of pogrom and discrimination is exacerbated by the fact that their taskmasters are often Jews, like Liubka. When the boy in "The Story of My Dovecot" achieves top marks at school and deserves to get into secondary school, a bribe from the wealthy Jewish corn-dealer gets his marks changed, and young Ephrussi Junior gets into the school instead. The narrator believes that, "like all Jews I was short, weakly, and had headaches from studying". When the boy finally achieves school-entrance, he has vanquished not only the Russian boys, but "I had vanquished the sons of our own vulgar parvenus". After the pogrom, the ten-year-old boy finds his grandfather dead; a victim this time of the peasants, and a procession bearing the Cross.

Jewish life in Odessa is brilliantly portrayed in the autobiographical story, "Awakening", where everyone in their circle has their children taught music. For, after all, from Odessa came Mischa Elman, Efrem Zimbalist, Ossip Gabrilowitsch and, above all, Jascha Heifetz. So the father sends his reluctant lad of 14 to Mr Zagursky, who "ran a factory of infant prodigies". But laden with the payment for a month's tuition, the boy walks near the harbour. "To learn to swim was my dream." But the "hydrophobia of my ancestors – Spanish rabbis and Frankfurt money-changers – dragged me to the bottom". However, the local "water-god" takes pity on him, in exchange for the roubles, and teaches him to swim. He also reads the boy's writings and points out that he lacks a feeling for nature, doesn't know the names of trees and birds. (Yiddish has, in fact, only two names for flowers, the rose and the violet, the rest are simply "blumen"!) When, finally, Zagursky arrives at the house to complain about the truant, he hides in the privy until late that night. Then, as he walks to his grandmother, "The moonlight congealed on bushes unknown to me, on trees that had no name. Some anonymous bird emitted a whistle . . ." His ignorance of the natural world is a handicap to be overcome.

In the increasingly repressive Zeitgeist of the 1930s, Babel' stopped publishing. When Soviet writer Vera Imber asked what his plans were, he replied that he intended to buy a goat. He was not a successful playwright. *Sunset* (produced in 1927) was not revived after a brief production at the Moscow Arts Theatre. *Marya* (1935) was banned while still in rehearsal. Harassed, and called upon to explain his silence, he said he was searching for a new language and a new form. Babel''s "conspiracy of silence" could not be endured, for Stalin believed, correctly, that silence was also a form of criticism. With Gor'kii's continued patronage and support, Babel' survived the purges, but was arrested early on 13 May 1939, preventing the publication of his *New Stories*. As he was led away, he was said to have declared: "They did not let me finish". All his diaries, notes, manuscripts, and letters were confiscated and destroyed. Lionel Trilling records unconfirmed reports by former camp inmates that he died of typhus or was executed on 17 March 1941, but it is now known that he was executed in the Lubyanka prison on 15 January 1940.

In 1954 Babel' was posthumously exonerated. His works were published, but subsequently ignored. In 1964 his daughter Nathalie, who had escaped to Paris with her mother in 1925, published his correspondence as *The Lonely Years 1925–1939*.

SORREL KERBEL

Bagritskii, Eduard

Russian poet, 1895–1934

Born Eduard Godelevich Dziubin in Odessa, 3 November 1895. Studied at Zhukovsky School; graduated from Odessa School of Land Surveying, 1915. Began publishing under pseudonym, 1913. Episodic existence until 1917. Contributor to Odessa's literary publications, 1915–17. Served briefly in Provisional Government law enforcement; participant in General Baratov's military expedition to Persia, 1917–18. Returned to Odessa, 1918. Joined Red Army, 1919; worked for Ukrainian division of IuGROSTA. Married Lidia Gustavovna Suok, 1920; one son, the poet Vsevolod Bagritskii (1922–42). Visited Moscow, 1924–25; moved to Kuntsevo, suburb of Moscow, 1925. Member of *Pereval* group; member of LTsK (Literary Centre of Constructivists), 1926–30. Member of editorial board of *Literaturnaia gazeta*, 1932–34. Chief poetry editor, Federatsia Publishing House. Joined MAPP (Moscow Association of Proletarian Writers), 1930. Moved to central Moscow, became housebound by illness. Died in Moscow, 16 February 1934 and given official funeral.

Selected Writings

Collections

Sobranie sochinenii v dvukh tomakh [Collected Works in 2 Volumes], 1938 (vol. 2 never appeared)
Stikhotvoreniia [Poems], 1940
Izbrannoe [Selected Works], 1948
Stikhotvoreniia i poèmy [Short and Long Poems], 1964
Stikhotvoreniia i poèmy [Short and Long Poems], 1984
Stikhotvoreniia i poèmy [Short and Long Poems], 2000

Poetry

Iugo-Zapad [South-West], 1928
Zvezda mordvina [The Mordvinian's Star], 1931
Duma pro Opanasa [The Lay of Opanas], 1932
Izbrannye stikhi [Selected Poems], 1932

Pobediteli [Victors], 1932
Posledniia noch' [The Last Night], 1932
Oisgeveilte lider un poemes (in Yiddish), translated by Ia. A. Zeldin, 1940

Other
Duma pro Opanasa [The Lay of Opanas] (opera libretto), 1935
Eduard Bagritskii. Alymanakh [Eduard Bagritskii: Almanac], 1936

Many translations into Russian, including works by Mikola Bazhan, Robert Burns, Itsik Fefer, Nazym Hikmet, Arthur Rimbaud

Further Reading

Bagritskaia, L.G. (editor), *Eduard Bagritskii: vospominaniia sovremennikov*, Moscow: Sovetskii pisatel', 1973
Cavaion, Danilo, Ebracità come memoria oscura (Eduard Bagrickij)", *Memoria e poesia: Storia e letteratura degli ebrei russi nell'età moderna*, Rome: Carucci editore, 1988
Kowalski, Luba Halat, "Eduard Bagritsky: A Biographical Sketch with Three Unpublished Works", *Russian Literature Triquarterly*, 8 (1974)
Kuniaev, Stanislav, "Legenda i vremia", *Dvadtsat' dva*, 14 (September 1980)
L'vov, Arkadii, "Vernost' i otstupnichestvo Eduarda Bagritskogo", *Utolenie pechal'iu: opyt issledovaniia evreiskoi mental'nosti*, New York: Vremia i my, 1983
Rosslyn, Wendy, "Bagritskii's *Duma pro Opanasa*: The Poem and Its Context", *Canadian-American Slavic Studies*, 11/3 (Fall 1977): 388–405
Shrayer, Maxim D., *Russian Poet/Soviet Jew: The Legacy of Eduard Bagritskii*, Lanham, Maryland: Rowman and Littlefield, 2000 (includes English translations)
Sinel'nikov, Mikhail, "Ptitselov: k stoletiiu Eduarda Bagritskogo", *Moskovskie novosti*, (29 October–5 November 1995)

Owing to his unique talent, the epoch, the place in which he was born and formed as a poet, and also to the legend-proof brevity of his career, Eduard Bagritskii cuts a most controversial and colourful figure among the Russian-Jewish poets of the Soviet period. His career mirrors that of his close friend Isaak Babel', and in some respects Bagritskii was the Babel' of Russian poetry. Bagritskii's Soviet literary legend reduced his multifarious poetic heritage to a standard set of anthologized poems and ideologically correct topics. Furthermore, his Jewish theme remained a forbidden subject even at the height of Khrushchev's thaw. Ironically, the fact of Bagritskii's Jewishness was given full billing only in those instances when he became the object of violent anti-Semitic attacks. To Soviet (and post-Soviet) Judeophobes, Bagritskii's career as a Russian-Jewish writer symbolized everything that supposedly went wrong with Russian culture after the Bolshevik revolution.

Bagritskii's short life typifies the destinies of Russia's Jewish artists born in the late 1890s and early 1900s. Bagritskii was raised in Odessa in a family where Judaic traditions were respected, while the lifestyle was that of secularized urban bourgeoisie. As a teenager, he experienced first-hand both the pogroms of 1905 and the czarist anti-Semitic quotas. Bagritskii welcomed the February 1917 revolution and served in the law-enforcement organs created by the Provisional Government. Following the end of the civil war in European Russia, Bagritskii rejoined Odessa's cultural life. He married a non-Jew, Lidia Suok, in 1920, and their son Vsevolod was born in 1922. In 1925, upon the insistence of his friends, Bagritskii moved to Moscow. In a relatively short time, he gained wide acceptance and admiration. The asthmatic (and probably tubercular) Bagritskii spent his latter years confined to his apartment in the centre of Moscow, writing, editing, and mentoring younger writers.

In 1925 he published his best known work, the epic poem "Duma pro Opanas" [The Lay of Opanas]. Its protagonist, Commissar Iosif Kogan, dies by the hand of the Ukrainian peasant Opanas who is fighting in the anarchist army of Nestor Makhno. A visceral anti-Semite, Opanas refers to Kogan as "Kogan-zhid" ("Kogan the Yid") and wears a fur coat that had previously belonged to a rabbi whom Opanas murdered. In contrast to Opanas's marked anti-Semitism, Kogan is only nominally a Jew. His distinct Jewish traits are his physical features, telling last name, and stern loyalty to the revolution and the Party. While Kogan identifies himself only as a communist, Opanas regards him primarily as a "Yid" who stands in the way of peasant happiness. Bagritskii's epic poem is superb at exploring and exposing linkages between Jewish participation in the revolution and civil war and explosions of anti-Semitism among the peasant masses caught between the gears of history.

In 1930 Bagritskii wrote "Origin", a militant monologue of a Russian Jew at odds with his familial past and upbringing. "Origin" tells a terrifying story of a Jewish childhood and youth in which things went awry every step of the way. Remarkably, and despite the continuous efforts of his kinsmen to "dry him out with Matzos", to "deceive him with the candle", the Jewish youth retains his capacity to question his condition and to protest. This inborn gift, which he terms "Jewish disbelief", impels him to flee. Does one find a Soviet discourse of Jewish self-hatred in "Origin"? Yes and no. Descriptions such as this sketch of a Jewish girl would make many readers cringe: "lice-eaten braids;/ A jutting collar bone;/ Pimples; a mouth, greased with herring/ And a horsy curve of the neck". What redeems "Origin" is the realization that even in his protest against, as well as his de-aesthetization of the traditional Jewish life, the protagonist preserves a Jewish mindset. Emblematically Jewish is the protagonist's restlessness, his unceasing questioning of himself and his milieu.

Bagritskii's greatest contribution is the narrative poem "February", the story of the traumatic formation of a Russian-Jewish identity in a time of historical and political cataclysms. The poem has emerged as the single work by a Russian-Jewish author most maligned by anti-Semitic critics. "February" is set in Odessa in the 1900s and 1910s. The protagonist, a timid Jewish dreamer, is desperately in love with a girl who comes from an upper-class non-Jewish family. The distance between the two is prohibitive. The Slavic girl refuses even to speak with him, and threatens to enlist the help of a nearby police officer. Then the February 1917 revolution turns the protagonist's life around. An equal citizen of a temporarily democratic Russia, he now works in the law enforcement agencies created in place of the czarist police force. These proud words of the protagonist have enraged many an anti-Semite: "My Judaic pride sang,/ Like a string stretched to its limit . . ." Accompanied by a unit of sailors, the protagonist raids an illicit house of prostitution and arrests three Jewish gangsters. In one of the bedrooms, in bed with a gangster, he also discovers his former beloved. Shocked and enraged by her metamorphosis into a prostitute, the young man offers to pay her for sex. "Have pity . . . I don't want the money", is the prostitute's plea. Both cruel and passionate in his revenge, the protagonist throws her the money and has sexual intercourse with her. In the poem's closing monologue, the protagonist expresses a tortured hope of harmony between Jews and Russians: "Maybe my night seed/ Will fertilize your desert."

Bagritskii wrote "February" when he realized that his hopes for the disappearance of anti-Semitism were but a beautiful dream, light years away from the reality of interethnic relations in the Soviet Union. Reading the protagonist's final monologue, one cannot help but think of its biblical intonation and imagery, and particularly of two chapters in the Book of Isaiah. Bagritskii's romantic viewpoint conflates the enduring Judaic idea of Jews as divinely chosen to carry out a historical mission and a short-lived Soviet ideal of Jews living in harmony with other nations. In Isaiah 35:1–2, and later, in Isaiah 51:3, the prophet brings forth an image of a transformed and beautified desert, an image that crowns Bagritskii's poem, but not the history of Russia's Jews.

Famous on the early Soviet literary scene, Bagritskii has influenced several generations of Russian poets, from Pavel Vasil'ev to Joseph Brodsky. At the beginning of the 21st century, Bagritskii stands as a brave transgressor of boundaries – Jewish, Russian, and Soviet. It is the task of tomorrow's students of Jewish literature to embrace his legacy.

MAXIM D. SHRAYER

Ballas, Shimon

Iraqi-born Israeli fiction writer and editor, 1930–

Born in Baghdad, 6 March 1930. Emigrated to Israel, 1951. Served in Israeli defence forces, 1952–53. Editor for Arab affairs, *Kol Haam*, *c.*1954–60. Married M. Gila, 1959; one daughter. Studied Arabic literature, the Sorbonne; PhD 1974. Professor, 1975, and Chair, Department of Arabic, 1982–85, University of Haifa. Editor, *al-Karmil*, since 1991; visiting professor, the Sorbonne, 1986. Awarded Prime Minister's Prize, 1978 and 1993.

Selected Writings

Novels
Hamaabarah [The Camp], 1964
Ashab mebagdad [Ashab from Baghdad], 1970
The Shoes of Tanboury, 1970
Hitbaharut [Clarification], 1972
Ḥeder naul [A Locked Room], 1980
Ḥoref aḥaron [Last Winter], 1984
Hayoresh [The Heir], 1987
Vehu aher [And He is Other], 1991
Lo bimkoma [Not in her Place], 1994
Solo, 1998
Tel Aviv Mizraḥ [Tel Aviv East], 1998

Short Stories
Mul haḥomah [In Front of the Wall], 1969
Bair hataḥtit [In Death Town], 1979
Otot stav [Signs of Autumn], 1992; as *Nudhur al-Kharīf*, 1997

Other
Editor/translator, *Palestinian Stories*, 1969
Arab Literature under the Shadow of War [in Arabic], 1978; translated as *La littérature arabe et le conflit au proche-orient, 1948–1973*, 1980
Secular Trends in Arab Literature [in Arabic], 1993
Editor, with R. Snir, *Studies in Canonical and Popular Arabic Literature*, 1998

Further Reading

Alcalay, Ammiel, *After Jews and Arabs: Remaking Levantine Culture*, Minneapolis: University of Minnesota Press, 1993
Berg, Nancy E., *Exile from Exile: Israeli Writers from Iraq*, Albany: State University of New York Press, 1996
Snir, Reuven, "We Were like Those Who Dream: Iraqi-Jewish Writers in Israel in the 1950s", *Prooftexts*, 11 (1991)
Snir, Reuven, "Intersecting Circles between Hebrew and Arabic Literature" in *Ever and Arav: Contacts between Arabic Literature and Jewish Literature in the Middle Ages and Modern Times*, edited by Yosef Tobi, Tel Aviv: Afikim, 1998
Snir, Reuven, "Shimon Ballas and the Canon of Hebrew Literature", *Iton 77* (April 1998)
Taha, Ibrahim, "Signs of Autumn", *Aleh Siyah*, 34 (Summer 1994)
Yahil-Max, M., "The Third Position", *Iton 77* (August/September 1987)

"I am an Arab Jew", says Shimon Ballas. "I write in Hebrew, and I belong here. This does not mean, however, that I have given up my cultural origins, and my cultural origins are Arab". Born as "a Jew by chance", in his words, in the Christian quarter of Baghdad, Ballas grew to adopt a secular cosmopolitan world view. He was educated at the Alliance where he mastered Arabic and French; the latter was his window to world literature. He even attributes his membership of the Communist Party, when he was 16, as being triggered by reading in French Jack London's *The Iron Heel*. Yet, Arabic literature, especially by Gibran Khalil Gibran and Ṭāhā Ḥusayn, proved to be his major inspiration. Besides publishing essays on movies and making translations, he wrote in Iraq short stories and even a detective novel; however he burned them before emigrating to Israel, an act which he would later greatly rue.

Ballas's emigration to Israel in 1951 was by no means motivated by Zionism. His first preference was France and he had even been chosen for a scholarship to study in the Sorbonne, but this dream would materialize only about 20 years later when Paris would become for him a second homeland. In Israel the transit camp (*maabarah*) experience and his communist activities would inspire his literary production. Joining the Communist Party, he served for six years as editor for Arab Affairs of the Party's Hebrew organ, *Kol Haam*, and started to publish Arabic short stories. In one of them, "Uḥibbu al-Ḥayāt" [I Love Life], although he is facing deprivation of the very means of living, the protagonist does not give up his principles. After leaving the party in 1961, he has devoted himself ever since to literary writing, academic research, and translation.

Ballas's first novel, on the experiences of the transit camps, was completed in Arabic but, before publication, he decided to switch over to Hebrew writing. He devoted himself to Hebrew, reading thoroughly the Bible, the Mishnah, and later concentrating on S.Y. Agnon and other Hebrew works. When he found himself capable, he rewrote the novel in Hebrew and published it as *Hamaabarah* [The Camp], the first novel written by an Iraqi Jewish author. Explaining his switch over to Hebrew, he says that he felt that in Arabic he was facing a contradiction and was isolating himself from the society in which he was living (he would return to literary Arabic writing only when he translated two of his stories into Arabic in *Nudhur al-Kharīf* [Signs of Autumn]). *Hamaabarah* depicts the tragedy of the oriental immigrants who had been uprooted from their homes and thrown into poverty with insufficient resources for living. His approach traversed the material level to deal with the cultural deprivation of the oriental Jews whose most esteemed moral and cultural values were rejected. Being thrown into a hostile environment which felt contempt for their original culture, they were labelled as exceptional, thereby becoming victims of an organized and institutionalized process of adaptation to a new culture in which Arabic language, literature, and music were considered inferior and "weapons" of the enemy. Surprisingly enough, the novel was very well received by critics, some of whom even praised Ballas as representing the oriental Jews, who preserved Hebrew throughout the generations, though he arrived in Israel without knowing Hebrew at all. Shortly after the publication of *Hamaabarah* he completed a sequel novel, *Tel aviv mizraḥ* [Tel Aviv East]; however, due to the patronizing and dismissive attitude of the literary establishment its publication was delayed until 1998.

In *Vehu aher* [And He Is Other], Ballas presents his views on the fate of Iraqi Jews through the story of several non-Zionist Jewish Iraqi intellectuals. One of them, to whom the title of the novel alludes, is Aḥmad Hārūn Sawsan whose figure is based on the well-known Aḥmad Nissīm Sūsa (1900–82), who converted to Islam. Another figure, As'ad Nissīm, is reminiscent of Anwar Sha'ūl (1904–84), one of the founders of the art of the Iraqi short story and owner and editor of *al-Ḥāṣid* [The Reaper], the most influential Iraqi literary journal in the 1930s. *Otot stav* [Signs of Autumn] is a kind of sequel to the novel, at least with respect to the vision in both of them. It consists of three long short stories, each symbolizing a necessary component for the longed-for Ballasian utopia. Based on autobiographical material, the first story, "Iyya", depicts the Iraqi Jews in the late 1940s, before their departure from their beloved ancient homeland, from the point of view of a Muslim maid named Zakiyya, nicknamed "Iyya". The second story, "Signs of Autumn", centred on the cosmopolitan figure of Ḥusnī Manṣūr, is based on the figure of the Egyptian Ḥusayn Fawzī (1900–88), well-known for his books that use the mythical figure of al-Sindibad from *Arabian Nights*. The third story, "In the Gates of Kandinski", is about Yaqob Reshef, a Jewish painter immigrant from Russia torn between the values of the surrounding society and his idealistic aspirations. Failing to pass "the Gates of Kandinski", he died two days before the beginning of the new year. The three protagonists illustrate three central components of Israeli culture, each of them related to the town where the events of the story take place: Baghdad/Arab culture; Paris/Western culture and Tel-Aviv/Israeli culture.

Although concentrating on the role of Arab culture in Israel, Ballas's literary project is much more comprehensive in accompanying the readers into unknown fictional realms. In *Hitbahart* [Clarification] the protagonist is an Iraqi Jew not participating in the 1973 war. Iraqi characters also appear in his short stories, such as in the collection *Mul hahomah* [In Front of the Wall]. *Ḥeder naul* [A Locked Room] deals with a Palestinian architect returning home for a visit. In *Ḥoref aḥaron* [Last Winter] the focus is on Middle Eastern exiles in Paris, especially Henri Curiel, a Jewish communist of Egyptian origin. *Hayoresh* [The Heir] is a self-referential novel in which Ballas's academic professionalism finds its best manifestation. *Lo bimkoma* [Not in her Place] has feminist implications, and the protagonist of *Solo* [Solo] is based on the life of Yaqob (James) Sanua (1839–1912), a Jewish dramatist who was considered as the father of Egyptian theatre. Experiencing alienation and estrangement, most of Ballas' protagonists, or better anti-heroes, are outsiders living on the margins of society, not willing to compromise their principles. Preaching a new connection between identity, language, and territory, Ballas de-mystifies Hebrew, attempting to "un-Jew" it, in a process of "deterritorialization" accompanied by simultaneous "reterritorialization". Master Zionist narrative, in his view, is an Ashkenazi ideology that developed in a different culture and surroundings, and came to claim its stake in the Middle East with no acceptance of the environment.

Ballas is considered by a new generation of critics and scholars to be a prophetic voice challenging, since the mid-1960s, Ashkenazi western-oriented Hebrew literature's reluctance to accept the legitimacy of Arab culture. Only after demarcating new boundaries for the Hebrew literary canon, in which cosmopolitan humanistic values will be combined with oriental and western values, according to Ballas, will Israeli society be able to boast a particular original culture that expresses the aspirations of all its citizens – Jewish, Muslim, and Christian.

REUVEN SNIR

Barbash, Benny

Israeli dramatist, screenwriter, and fiction writer, 1951–

Born in Beer Sheva, 8 August 1951; both parents civil servants. Served in Israeli army, 1969–80; severely wounded in Yom Kippur War, 1973. After recovery enlisted in regular army; served in administrative and command positions until leaving as lieutenant colonel. Joined Peace Now movement, becoming leading activist. Graduated from Tel Aviv University with degree in history. Began writing film scripts, 1982. Writes dramas, television series, novels, and articles for Israeli newspapers. Won Critics Prize at Venice Film Festival for screenplay of *Beyond the Walls*, 1984. Lives in Kvar Neter, near Natanya.

Selected Writings

Novels
Hayekitsah hagedolah [The Big Awakening], 1982
My First Sony, 1994; as *My First Sony*, translated by Dalya Bilu, 1999
Matzavim potentsia veimpotentsia [Potent and Impotent Situations], 2000

Plays
The Moon is Down, 1986
My First Sony, 1997

Television Series: *Sitton*, 1995; *Basic Training*, still running

Other
Translator, *Black Comedy*, by Peter Shaffer, 1987
Several Israeli feature films including *Beyond the Walls*, 1984 and *Ehad meshelanu* [One of Us], 1986 which won Israeli Oscars for directing, scriptwriting, and acting

Further Reading
Naveh, Hanna, "Things Fall Apart", *Modern Hebrew Literature*, new series, 14 (Spring/Summer 1995)

Barbash established his reputation as a playwright and filmmaker, especially with two films, *Beyond the Walls* and *One of Us*. He was a founder member of the Peace Now movement, formed after the 1982 Israeli invasion of Lebanon, in protest against the treatment of Arabs by Israeli soldiers. Barbash and those officers with him were apprehensive about the possible conflict between their military roles and their involvement in this movement. They felt very strongly that, as Barbash said then, "we are gradually losing our humanity. The local community are becoming objects in our eyes – at best mere objects, at worst something to be degraded and humiliated". This background highlights the position taken by a majority of Israeli secular authors during the last quarter of the 20th century. The pattern can be recognized in the life history of among others Amos Oz, A.B. Yehoshua, and David Grossman. Most were prominent in left-wing protests. Through their writing, these authors prepared the way for an acceptance of their philosophy of peace.

Beyond the Walls presents Arab political prisoners and Jewish criminals placed alongside each other in an Israeli maximum-security prison. In this harsh environment tensions and reconciliation are played out where both sets of prisoners appear as victims of a manipulative warden. They unite in a hunger strike to challenge prison authorities. Barbash has set the play on a human plane, with a strong moral and political backdrop. He maintains that Israelis and Arabs share a common destiny. Directed by his brother Uri Barbash, it won the Critics Prize at the 1984 Venice Film Festival and was nominated for the Best Foreign Film at the American Academy Awards.

He turned to the novel with *My First Sony*. Through a child's perspective, Barbash presents an intensely personal rendition of life in Israel. He uses the device of capturing conversations on a Sony tape recorder, given to the young Yotam by his father Assaf. The novel works on multiple layers, attempting to comprehend the collective biography of Israel by presenting individual issues as they interface with historical ones. It pulses with humour and poignancy, directly reporting conversations beyond the ken of Yotam. He records every family conversation, public or private, in his presence or after he's gone to sleep; he hides under beds, behind walls and on the veranda to tape intimate tales; he tapes the family's therapy session at the Adler Institute and Assaf's meetings with his clients. By using the tape recorder, Yotam presents a total witness of the past, bringing unmodified events to memory with the same tension and urgency with which they occurred. The recordings have a primary, unadapted, and indisputable truth about them. Little by little events, physical and emotional, impinge on the child's consciousness. His psychological development operates as the moving force in these sounds and dissonances of childhood.

Various structures govern this work, despite its apparent freewheeling sense of unbound associations and stream-of-consciousness. The characters in Yotam's complex and dysfunctional family represent a "slice of life" of Israeli society. Their individual stories unfold: Assaf's parents' experiences in war-torn Europe; his brothers' obsessions with either new-found religious observance or successful but intolerant capitalism. Assaf, the unfulfilled writer, desperate to reaffirm his talents and masculinity, causes great heartache to his family. Barbash presents Assaf as a keen supporter of the Peace Now movement. Alma, Yotam's mother, is originally from South America, and her family's biography chronicles a different set of Diaspora and Israeli experiences.

Structured around the annual Passover Seders (festive dinners), the novel is Yotam's attempt to find order ("seder" means "order" in Hebrew) in his life as his family network unravels before his eyes. Thus these exceptional events charged with tales and retellings are presented by reports of conversations, and by a wonderful series of photomontages orchestrated and collected by Assaf's mother. Her albums provide a governing structure of their own, as she photographs each of the Seders, beginning in Europe before the war. Memory and its ownership are debated, as Yotam's grandfather tells how he first fell in love with Grandma.

One of the finest results of recording the events is the possibility of catching older people in their younger lives, and recapturing voices even after death. Yotam captures silences on his tape, and returns to ponder these almost as much as the conversations and arguments. He records breathing, as with Alma's mother in her final illness, and thus learns even what "death smells like". He records his family's admixture of languages and sayings, using them to great humorous effect, as when Grandpa runs around the cemetery trying to chase the cows out "and all the time he shouted at them, *kishta*, and *ruhu*, and *lehu*, but they were Dutch cows and they didn't understand Yiddish and Arabic and Hebrew, and they only scattered more and more . . ." This layering of discourse through the story, the "Spanish words that jump into Mom's mouth when she's angry", represents the multilingual reality of Israel.

This novel reveals the bigger picture of the Holocaust, "Grandma's Holocaust" as Yotam names it, and its part in the collective memory of Israel. During moments when her cultural background comes to the fore, and the suffering and abuse pales a little, Grandma lists all the disorderly elements in Israel that "wouldn't have happened in Germany". Alma is incensed at a Holocaust survivor who opposes her views, denying that his status gives him authority. But we are never allowed to ignore the impact of the Holocaust, both on the survivors and the next generation. In a powerful sequence Yotam relates the different testimonials of survivors whose memoirs his father is ghostwriting. Assaf too is overwhelmed by the anguish of their efforts:

> because these poor people, as Dad said once to Mom, want to translate their experiences into a language which hasn't yet been invented and will probably never be invented, and they rummage in the meagre and narrow lexicon of words available to us, trying to find the formula which will express what they've been through.

There is the central theme of Boundary, the protest group Alma energetically supports, from both the immediate political scenario of Yesh Gevul (meaning "there is a border" or "limit") to the more complex theme of boundaries in the work, questioning whether the characters can exercise restraint and keep within some boundary of respect for others and their points of view. Within the language, this continuum of run-on sentences is an example of absence of boundary, of an impelling need to rush from one painful or humorous thought to another, as the associations well up in Yotam's mind.

In the final scenario, the theme of responsibility is highlighted. Barbash captures the essence of Survivor Syndrome: abandonment and loss shift the weight of responsibility to the children. This book begins mid-sentence and ends mid-sentence. It resonates with the ongoing discourse of Israel and its diverse inhabitants.

TAMARA LEVINE

Baron, (Joseph) Alexander

British fiction writer, 1917–1999

Born Alec Bernstein, 4 December 1917, into a working-class Jewish family in Hackney, London. Studied at Grocers' Company School. Became member of Young Communist League. Assistant editor of left-wing newspaper *Tribune*, 1938–39. Served as infantry sergeant in Sicily and Normandy during World War II. Journalist and freelance writer from 1948. Editor of left-wing magazine *New Theatre*, 1946–49. Dramatized classic novels for BBC. Married Delorez Salzedo, 1960; one son. Died 5 December 1999.

Selected Writings

Novels
From the City, from the Plough, 1948
The Wine of Etna, 1950
There's No Home, 1950
Rosie Hogarth, 1951
With Hope, Farewell, 1952
The Human Kind, 1953
The Golden Princess, 1954
Queen of the East, 1956
Seeing Life, 1958
The Lowlife, 1963
Strip Jack Naked, 1966
King Dido, 1969
The In-Between Time, 1971
Gentle Folk, 1976
Franco is Dying, 1977

Alexander Baron's career exemplifies the fragility of literary reputation. Acclaimed and praised in the late 1940s and 1950s by, among others, V.S. Pritchett, Tyrone Guthrie, P.H. Newby, Arthur Helliwell, C.P. Snow, and Pamela Hansford Johnson, in various articles of the time he was linked with and compared to Graham Greene, Sinclair Lewis, Maupassant, and Hemingway, but by 1997 he is referred to in Ian Sinclair's book about London, *Lights Out for the Territory*, as one of the "reforgotten". His last novel *Franco is Dying* was published in 1977.

Between 1948 when his first book *From the City, from the Plough* was published and his last, Baron produced 14 volumes covering a wide range of subject matter, but it is with his three war volumes and, to a lesser extent, his London novels that he is most closely associated. These works were forged out of his direct experiences as a working-class Jewish boy in London's East End, and as an infantryman in World War II.

Like so many Jews of his generation and background, Baron was politically active, taking part as a teenager in the anti-fascist (and in the London context specifically anti-Mosley) struggle. He was a member of the Communist Party in the late 1930s, but left in the postwar years, having become increasingly disillusioned by its functioning as an arm of the Soviets in the Cold War.

The compassion that dictated his politics also informed his fiction. It was concern for the human condition, especially the under-privileged, downtrodden, or exploited, that he sets out to illustrate and explore in his best work. His model was Dickens. His deeply felt social concerns led him occasionally (fortunately rarely) to weaken his effects by being too overtly didactic.

Baron wished to be regarded as a writer in English, not as

a "Jewish writer". None of the main characters in his war trilogy is Jewish, and although some of the protagonists of his London novels are Jews his only work with a specifically Jewish theme *With Hope, Farewell* is one of his least successful. The story follows Mark Strong, from pre- to post-World War II years, including service as a fighter pilot, in his attempt to come to terms with his outsider or "other" status, which he strongly resents. Unfortunately, the characters remain stuck to the page and ultimately the work is too didactic. The novel ends on a Panglossian view of mankind's future, a view which Baron himself would probably have found unrealistic as he became increasingly less utopian in outlook. The lack of verisimilitude may also have resulted from Baron's complicated attitude towards his own Jewishness and his consciousness of his heritage.

In 1963 he declared "I wasn't Bar mitzvah and I knew nothing of the Jewish religion until in recent years I studied it from the outside." And he wrote in the *Jewish Quarterly*:

> I bring to my job a complicated mixture of perceptions, impulses, peculiarities of temperament, reflexes, ideas, ethics, that determine the kind of writer I am; and many of these things are determined, in turn, by the fact that I am Jewish. Only part of my consciousness was shaped in my own lifetime. Much of it is the product of centuries of experience of the whole Jewish people.
>
> Centuries of Jewish experience have cast a special light for its inheritors upon all human phenomena. When an Anglo-Jewish writer looks upon life, he sees it – whether he knows it or not – in the additional clarity, in the particular hue, with which this light endows it.

One of the distinguishing features of his war trilogy and his London novels is their realism. In writing about what he knew and experienced Baron recreates it for the reader. And his perspective was in contrast to much major British fiction of the time. This was particularly so of the war books. Written from the point of view of the private soldier and noncommissioned officer they portray much more general experiences and attitudes than are offered by such works as Evelyn Waugh's *Sword of Honour* trilogy. This, plus the quality of his descriptive powers sets them apart from other novels of the time and many considered, and still do consider, them to be the best fiction to have emerged in Britain from World War II.

But Baron's range was considerable. He indulged in historical recreation, like *Queen of the East*, the story of Zenobia and Aurelian, set around 258 CE, and *The Golden Princess*, the background to which is Cortés's conquest of Mexico in the early 16th century. His last novel *Franco is Dying*, as its title implies, is set in and explores the complications of a society undergoing significant political and social change.

In addition to his literary output Baron also produced original TV plays, radio plays, movie scripts, and most famously between 1967 and 1988 adaptations of classics for TV, taking in Dumas, Conrad, Tolstoi, Scott, Kipling, Dickens, Austen, and Thackeray among others. Many of these adaptations are considered classics in their own right and are used as study props in school literary classes.

In all of this work Baron eschewed postmodern tropes. Not for him self-referential exercises, the inclusion of contemporary or near contemporary characters to impose an element of faction, the splitting of time sequence, or any of the many devices of alienation. Baron was almost premodernist. He wrote in a direct, easy to follow, classical style, and mainly employed linear narrative. To this extent his work is not fashionable and combined with his innate shyness, which inhibited him from actively promoting his work, is probably the reason for the comparative neglect he has suffered in recent years.

The D-Day anniversary saw some revival of interest in Baron and there have been recent republications of some of his books. His best work is beautifully written and structured, with fully rounded identifiable characters shown at their most dignified and absurd, most noble and most savage. It deserves to outlast fashion.

GERALD DE GROOT

Baron, Dvora

Russian-born Israeli fiction writer, 1887–1956

Born in Ozdah, Belorussia, 1887. Brought up in Lithuanian shtetl where her father, a Hasidic rabbi, considered education important even for girls. Began to write at early age; first stories published, 1903. Emigrated to Palestine, 1911. Married Yosef Aharonovitz, Labour Zionist leader and editor of *Hapoel Hatsair*; one daughter. Lived in Egypt during World War I. Literary editor of *Hapoel Hatsair* until 1937. Awarded Bialik Prize twice. Died in Tel Aviv, 1956.

Selected Writings

Short Stories
Sipurim [Stories], 1926
Ketanot [Small Things], 1933
Mah shehayah [What has Been], 1939
Leet atah: sipurim [For the Time Being: Stories], 1942
Misham [From over There: Stories], 1945
Halavan [The Bricklayer], 1946
Shavririm: sipurim [Fragments: Stories], 1948
Parshiyot [Chapters], 1951
Hulyot: sipurim [Chains: Stories], 1952
Meemesh [Last Night], 1954
Agav-orha: asufah meizvonah [By the Way: A Collection of Unpublished Stories], 1960
The Thorny Path, translated by Joseph Schachter, 1969
Hagolim [The Exiles], 1970
Sheloshah sipurim, 1974; as *Three Stories*, 1975
Early Chapters, 1988
Keritut vesipurim aherim [Divorce and Other Stories], 1997
The First Day and Other Stories, translated by Chana Kronfeld and Naomi Seidman, 2001

Further Reading

Anderson, Benedict, *Imagined Communities: Reflections on the Origin and Spread of Nationalism*, London: Verso, 1983; revised edition, 1991

Butler, Judith, *Bodies That Matter: On the Discursive Limits of "Sex"*, New York and London: Routledge, 1993
Gilbert, Sandra M. and Susan Gubar, *The Madwoman in the Attic: The Woman Writer and the Nineteenth-Century Literary Imagination*, New Haven, Connecticut: Yale University Press, 1979; 2nd edition, 2000
Lieblich, Amia, *Conversations with Dvora: An Experimental Biography of the First Modern Hebrew Woman Writer*, translated by Naomi Seidman, edited by Chana Kronfeld and Naomi Seidman, Berkeley: University of California Press, 1997 (Hebrew original, 1991)
Lubin, Orly, *A Woman Reading Women*, Haifa University Press (in preparation)
Pagis, Ada (editor), *Dvora Baron: A Selection of Critical Essays on Her Literary Prose* (in Hebrew), Tel Aviv: Am Oved, 1974
Seidman, Naomi, *A Marriage Made in Heaven: The Sexual Politics of Hebrew and Yiddish*, Berkeley: University of California Press, 1997
Wallenrod, Reuben, *The Literature of Modern Israel*, New York: Abelard Schuman, 1956

Dvora Baron was immediately accepted into the Hebrew literary arena not "only" as a welcome addition to the small group of women writers, but also as a valuable writer within the newly forming Hebrew canon. Her depictions of the condition of women within Jewish religious laws and social norms were accepted as pointing to much-needed changes. Discrimination against women by Rabbinic law, their lack of education and total dependence on the men of the family, the priority of childbearing (specifically of boys), and the humiliation in divorce, are some of the major topics of Baron's stories, which explore the new woman in the new society. Baron was perceived, by virtue of the themes of her stories, as one of the first feminist writers in Hebrew literature.

However, the critics did not fail to note, and sometimes to condemn, her peculiar portrayal of Diaspora township life, and her virtual neglect of life in Erets Israel. Gershon Shaked, for example, writes that "her world of motifs was indeed rather limited" – exclusively to the Lithuanian township. But the critics were confused: on the one hand, hers was perceived as "work of quality" worthy of inclusion within the national canon; but on the other hand Baron's preoccupation seemed to be "moulding human life from within the tiny dimensions of everyday banality" (Ben-Zvi Saar). Baron's description of daily life in the Diasporic township, focusing on events such as marriage, giving birth, dying, or falling in love, full of "trivia" and "minutiae", pose a problem: How to reconcile the quality of the writing, which merits inclusion in the canon, with the "unimportant" story-lines and the avoidance of the real crucial topic – the new Jewish settlement in Palestine?

The presence of the hegemonic national perspective in the texts still calls for a formulation to make it the metanarrative of Baron's work. The numerous attempts by critics to "resolve" the problem rest largely upon identification of her work's universalistic aspect, whereby they attach her to the camp of national writers. Thus, Lachover writes on "the tension between the concrete reality and its details, and its universal signification"; Nurit Govrin claims Baron exhibits in her writing "the indignation at the world order from the viewpoint of the disinherited, the women in particular"; Ben-Zvi Saar affirms that "the objects of everyday reality are imbued with symbolism" which highlights the cruelty of existence; and in Dan Miron's view, not only is private experience subjugated to mythological, a-historical universal aspects, but social and national experience is perceived as shallow. The "feminine minutiae", then, serve mainly as building blocks of the metanarrative, national or universal. The critics seek to "heal" the disjointed stories by unifying the author's entire creative oeuvre, and to remedy the historical fragmentation and rectify the break between the private and national by universalistic harmony.

In contrast, a feminist reading of Baron searches for a different structure through which women can be inserted into the national narrative. Access to the national Zionist discourse is blocked: the national story of the imagined political community has no place for women, for it is the story of a masculine fraternity wherein the woman is the image of the nation through portrayal of the nation as mother. The motherland is depicted as female body whose molestation by strangers vindicates its inhabitants in going to its defence; woman's entry into the imaginary national community is achieved through her substitution by imagery. Baron offers a variety of other modes through which women participate in the national effort, and thus manages to "promote" women's experience from the margins to the centre of the story and, hence, the national cultural canon.

The novel *Hagolim* [The Exiles], comprises two novellas and tells the story of a group of Tel Aviv people exiled to Alexandria by the Turks in World War I, who then return to continue their life in the "new neighbourhood". Significantly, 28 out of 37 chapters have women at their core. The men appear to be doing the important things but turn out to be "women": passive exiled, as they actually have no power, and are exposed as marginal to world events which take over and determine their lives. The women, on the other hand, busy cooking, match-making, and raising children are the ones "weaving" the community (in Gilbert and Gubar's terminology) through their peripheral doings, saving the refugees' lives with their food which is medicine, and maintaining communal togetherness through their solidarity. Female stereotypical positioning turns out to be source of power. Thus in this novel, as in other stories, Baron erects two systems counterpoised against one another: the house and the building, both *Bayit* in Hebrew. She uses *Bayit* to denote both "the private house: home" and "the national building" – women's participation in the national building is through the private home.

But not only themes structure the different outlook on communal life; even the time axis is different, and follows that of women's experience: the deportation from Jaffa occurs not on a certain date and hour, but when "in Mrs Rotstein's kitchen the practice of frying mince balls had just ended, and the tiny woman stood beside the stove preparing fresh compote". The time axis is broken, fragmented, but this alternative time continuity inserts women, through their activities and daily structure of life, into national life.

Baron gives voice to that which has yet to be represented – the female historical story. To do that, she gives voice to yet another silenced element – the Diasporic site, which the women both remember and adapt to now, in Alexandria. This new historical narrative is not a chronological, factual narrative with a beginning, middle, and end. The women's stories never end, and their gossipy memories take no linear path, but "intercut" according to their minds' flaws; even the novel itself is fragmented, "pieced" together, as in Elaine Showalter's description of quilt-narrative. In other stories the women's world is focused on the material, corporeal body. In "The Thorny Path" the protagonist is paralyzed, and controls her world through her gazing eye, in a manner that makes her paralysis almost a blessing, if not actually self-induced. In "Fragments" again an almost self-induced broken leg changes the girl's fate, although her body remains a barrier between herself and her community and husband, and finally is analogized to the body of her beloved cow, whom she treats as a daughter.

Baron uses, then, a plethora of stereotypes to create in her stories an alternative communal experience: that of women. The home and female chores become a constituent of nationality; the stereotypical mode of women's reading and telling stories become an alternative form of creating – inventing – his(her)story of national participation; and the body, the ultimate symbol of womanhood, becomes the major site of the constitution of the female subject as she who does not have to give up her corporeality in order to become part of nationality.

ORLY LUBIN

Bartov, Hanokh

Israeli fiction writer, 1926–

Born in Petah Tikvah, 13 August 1926. Served in Jewish Brigade of British army, 1943–46, then Israeli army, 1947–49. Studied history and sociology, Hebrew University, Jerusalem, 1946–51. Married Yehudith Schimmer, 1946; one son, one daughter. Taught in high schools, 1951–55; news editor, and later foreign correspondent in the United States, for *Lamerkhav Daily*, 1956–60; wrote personal view column for *Lamerkhav Daily* and *Maariv Daily*, 1960–90; member of board of Israel Broadcasting Authority, 1965–66 and 1969–72, and of Hebrew Writers' Association, 1968–72. Counsellor for cultural affairs, Israeli Embassy, London, 1966–68. President, International Theatre Institute, 1976–80; member of board, 1968–72, and President since 1990, Israel PEN Centre. Many awards, including Ussishkin Prize, 1955; Prime Minister's Prize, 1974; Bialik Prize, 1985; Israel Efrat Prize, 1995.

Selected Writings

Novels
Haheshbon vehanefesh [The Reckoning and the Soul], 1953
Shesh kenafayim laehad [Each One had Six Wings], 1954
Pittzei bagrut [Pains of Growth], 1965; as *The Brigade*, translated by David S. Segal, 1968
Shel mi ata yeled?, 1970; as *Whose Little Boy are You?*, translated by Hillel Halkin, 1978
Habaday [The Lying Man], 1975
Beemtsa haroman [In the Middle of it All], 1984
Zeh ishi medaber [Ishi Speaking], 1990
Regel ahat bahuts [Halfway Out], 1994

Short Stories
Hashuk hakatan [The Little Market], 1957
Lev hakhamim [The Heart of the Wise], 1962
Ahot rehokah [Distant Sister], 1973
Yehudi katan [A Little Jew], 1980
Mazal ayalah [Ayala's Star], 1988
Mavet bepurim [Death on Purim], 1992

Plays
Shesh kenafayim laehad, 1958; as *Every One Had Six Wings*, 1971
Sa habaytah yonatan [Jonathan, Go Home], 1962
Agada hayah [Living Legend], 1989

Other
Arbaa isreelim vekhol [Four Israelis all over America], 1963
Isreelim bahatsar St James's, 1969; as *An Israeli at the Court of St James's*, translated by Ruth Aronson, 1971
Translator, *Maseotay im dodati*, translation of *Travels with My Aunt* by Graham Greene, 1971
DADO, 48 Shanim veod 20 yom [DADO, 48 years and 20 more days], 1978
Translator, *Mimosa*, by Zhang Xianliang, 1985
Yarid bemoskva [A Fair in Moscow], 1988
Ani lo hatsabar hamitologi [I am Not the Mythological Sabra], 1995

Further Reading

Yudkin, Leon I., *Escape into Siege: A Survey of Israeli Literature Today*, London and Boston: Routledge and Kegan Paul, 1974

Bartov's writing can be tied essentially to the generation of the Israeli state. His writing has accompanied the early years, has etched its movement, and its uncertain grasp of its own self. The writer himself has located the centre of his literary concerns as "the question of an Israeli identity in a country that as yet has no clear identity of its own." The reasons for this amorphous sense lie in the nature of the land, its people, and its strange history with its rapid, inorganic transformation over such a short period. It is only recently that Israel has become a mainly Jewish territory, with Hebrew as a revived and now predominant, as well as official, language. The Jewish population, even though in its majority it is now native born, hails from places all over the world, so the roots of individual denizens are embedded elsewhere as well as in the surface soil of the new country. The architecture is new and unstable, the landscape has been transformed, and the people shaken up. No wonder then that any representative picture of the society therein must be unsteady and uncrystallized. This is what Bartov seeks to convey in a long series of novels that take the story through from the traumatic ingathering of exiles to the alienated quest for other sources of identity among contemporary Israelis. Although he himself is Israeli (born in Petah Tikvah), and served in the British army's Jewish Brigade in World War II, and then later fought in Israel's War of Independence, he is primarily interested in charting the adjustments and maladjustments of all the elements, and in seeing the larger picture.

His first notable published work, a novel which was dramatized, and later rewritten, was *Shesh kenafayim laehad* [Each One had Six Wings]. This tells of immigrant adjustment to the infant state, to its primitive housing, to its wartime conditions, to the population transformation. We are introduced to a campsite, in just the way that the bereft immigrants are, in all its rickety, ramshackle condition. The housing, such as it is, is prefabricated, and thus lacks solidity, and any sense of a past. This is the new Israel. But Israel, even at this stage, is divided between the older and the newer. There are the veterans and the new arrivals, from various places, with all the implications of stratification, of relative privilege, and thus of resentment too. Certainly, there is a sense of "us" and "them", or of "ours" and "yours". Amnon, the kibbutznik, can instruct the "greeners", particularly the children, in the ways of what was to be their new life. However, as we are to see more clearly in the course of events, these "new" people are individuals with a past, with memories, and a history. They cannot be expected to adapt within moments in a way that would entail the jettisoning of all that baggage, even if others consider it otiose or negative, when what is required is state building and the unification of all these elements into something that is recognizable as the new Hebrew society. The situation is described from many points of view. The veterans tend to believe that the immigrants should consider themselves lucky for having any sort of home, especially one provided by others, i.e. by the veterans themselves. But what is this housing other than that abandoned by Arabs fleeing in defeat? Some of the rehoused just feel abandoned themselves.

Bartov uses his own biography to create his novels throughout his literary career. This we can see in a novel about the Jewish Brigade and its own part in the war against the Nazis, *Pitsei bagrut* (*The Brigade*). This is a story told in the first person that declares itself in the acknowledgements to be based on fact, although fictionalized and now incorporated in a work that must be considered fictional. It is a bitter account of the fighting and the horrific encounter with a Europe on which the narrator would like, by the end of the novel while still a life-hungry 19 year old, to turn his back. He is already a full-blooded Israeli (before the state), and wants only the companionship of his own kind, and his own home. But it is also a time and a scene of the encounter with another kind of compatriot, the survivors of the Holocaust, who tell of another, incomprehensible reality that adds a further dimension to the author's knowledge of the world, and to his own writing. It also gives an added meaning to what Bartov had understood about what Israel stands for. But we also have stated the sense of unbreachable community achieved only in his early past, and which has stayed with him for life. It is only from the ties of the very early, and, for him, ultimately formative years, that he shares a common fate with a specific group to which he still pays allegiance. No subsequent attachment has replaced that initial one. As he says of his time in the army: "In my two army years I got friendly with one person or another. But I found no genuine comrade, not only during that period. But from the time that I was torn away from the circle in which my youth developed, I had no other real friend."

Another strand in the author's own life tale takes us back further in time, to his childhood and birthplace in Petah Tikvah. This is related in *Shel mi ata yeled?* (*Whose Little Boy are You?*), a re-creation of the small, early Hebrew colony near Tel Aviv. But in later novels Bartov also tells of others, also from his own initial circle of intimates, and whose stories assist in the building up of Israel's story. In the course of a half century of creativity, Bartov still relates to the ongoing issue of an Israeli identity in the process of formation, with an increasing complexity and sophistication.

LEON I. YUDKIN

Bassani, Giorgio

Italian fiction writer, 1916–2000

Born in Bologna, 4 April 1916. Studied at Bologna University; graduated 1939. Imprisoned during World War II; member of resistance from 1943, using *nom de guerre* "Giacomo Marchi". Married Valeria Sinigallia, 1943; one son and one daughter. Lived in Ferrara until 1943. Settled in Rome, 1945; worked as scriptwriter and film dubbing editor; editor, Feltrinelli publishers, Milan, 1958–64; lecturer in History of Theatre, Academy of Dramatic Art, Rome, 1957–68; Vice President, Radiotelevisione Italiana, Rome, 1964–65. Editor, *Botteghe Oscure*, Rome, 1948–60; co-editor, *Paragone*, Milan, 1953–55. President, from 1966, and later Honorary President, Italia Nostra. Many awards, including Veillon Prize, 1956; Strega Prize, 1956; Viareggio Prize, 1962; Campiello Prize, 1969; Sachs Prize, 1969; Bagutta Prize, 1983. Died in Rome, 13 April 2000.

Selected Writings

Novels

Una città di pianura [A City of the Plain], 1940

La passeggiata prima di cena [A Stroll before Dinner], 1953

Gli ultimi anni di Clelia Trotti [The Last Years of Clelia Trotti], 1955

Cinque storie ferraresi, 1956; as *A Prospect of Ferrara*, translated by Isabel Quigly, 1962; as *Five Stories of Ferrara*, translated by William Weaver, 1971

Gli occhiali d'oro, 1958; as *The Gold-Rimmed Spectacles*, translated by Isabel Quigly, 1960; as *The Gold-Rimmed Eyeglasses*, translated by William Weaver (with *The Smell of Hay*), 1975

Una notte del '43 [One Night in 1943], 1960

Il giardino dei Finzi-Contini, 1962; as *The Garden of the Finzi-Continis*, translated by Isabel Quigly, 1965

Dietro la porta, 1964; as *Behind the Door*, translated by William Weaver, 1972

Due novelle [Two Novellas], 1965
L'airone, 1968; as *The Heron*, translated by William Weaver, 1970
L'odore del fieno, 1972; as *The Smell of Hay*, translated by William Weaver (with *The Gold-Rimmed Eyeglasses*), 1975
Il romanzo di Ferrara [The Ferrara Cycle], 1974
Di là dal cuore [From There to the Heart], 1984

Poetry
Storie dei poveri amanti e altri versi [Stories of the Poor Lovers and Other Verses], 1946
Te lucis ante, 1947
Un'altra libertà [Another Freedom], 1951
L'alba ai vetri: poesie 1942–50 [The Dawn at the Windows: Poems 1942–50], 1963
Epitaffio [Epitaph], 1974
In gran segreto [Deep Secret], 1978
In rima e senza [In Rhyme and Without], 1982
Rolls Royce and Other Poems (bilingual edition), various translators, 1982

Other
The Stranger's Hands (screenplay), with Guy Elmes and Graham Greene, 1954
Le parole preparate e altri scritti di letteratura [Prepared Words and Other Writings of Literature], 1966

Further Reading
Bastianutti, Diego L., "Giorgio Bassani: The Record of a Confession", *Queen's Quarterly*, 88/4 (1981)
Canadian Journal of Italian Studies, special issue, 1 (1977–78)
Cicioni, Mirna, "Insiders and Outsiders: Discourses of Oppression in Giorgio Bassani's *Gli occhiali d'oro*", *Italian Studies*, 41 (1986)
Hughes, H. Stuart, *Prisoners of Hope: The Silver Age of the Italian Jews, 1924–1974*, Cambridge, Massachusetts: Harvard University Press, 1983
Radcliff-Umstead, Douglas, *The Exile into Eternity: A Study of the Narrative Writings of Giorgio Bassani*, Rutherford, New Jersey: Fairleigh Dickinson University Press, 1987

Giorgio Bassani holds a notable place in the panorama of 20th-century Italian literature, not just for the obvious merit of his writing but also for the fact that he is the only one among the great contemporary Italian writers of Jewish descent who, far from dissimulating his own origins or "recovering them" (often through a painful and difficult process usually triggered by Italian fascism's anti-Semitic policies after 1938), explicitly affirms them. Born in Bologna, he finished his university studies in Arts in 1939, just managing to get round the anti-Jewish legislation (*le legge razziali*/ "racial laws") in force since 1938. His family belonged to the well-off Jewish bourgeoisie of Ferrara, the northern Italian city within whose walls the writer spent his childhood and adolescence. Having established itself over the centuries as one of the most conspicuous centres of Italian Judaism, Ferrara, uniquely for Italy, had seen many Jews from the 19th century onwards become landowners, which explains the support they gave – no differently from the Catholic landowners – to rising fascism, perceived as able to protect them from the violent claims of their labourers. This circumstance and the generally more open link with their historic faith distinguishes Ferrara's Jewish community from the prevalently secular and decidedly anti-fascist Jews of Turin (cf. Carlo Levi, Natalia Ginzburg, Primo Levi). It also explains how the trauma caused by the previously unsuspected anti-Semitic politics of the regime was particularly devastating here even if its effect was extremely strong throughout Italy, where Jews had taken an active part in the process of forming the new Italian state which, from 1860, allowed them to climb to the highest rungs of the social ladder, even in politics. The pain of an incomprehensible exclusion and shock at the terrible progress of events provided the emotive hinterland for the marvellously poignant *Il giardino dei Finzi-Contini* (1962; translated in 1963 as *The Garden of the Finzi-Continis*, and successfully filmed by Visconti). This work established Bassani's success. From within a walled garden-universe – a renewed metaphor for a ghetto which has been transfigured and is the object of a love–hate relationship – the novel leads through what for Italian and European Jews were the phases of a progressive and unstoppable horror: discrimination, isolation, capture, extermination. The rich Finzi-Contini family – criticized by their fellow Jews in Ferrara for their aristocratic lifestyle and for their failure to join the fascists – open the gates of their house and garden to the young Jews who had been expelled as a result of racial politics from the town's societies and institutions. This provides the frame of the love of the main character and narrator for the beautiful and gentle Micol Finzi-Contini, whose rejection of the possibility of love presages her own imminent destruction, together with that of her people.

Perhaps the most celebrated of Bassani's novels, *The Garden of the Finzi-Continis* is in reality only a chapter of an ideal autobiography bounded by the minimum and topographically precise space of the city through the six stages of *Il romanzo di Ferrara* [The Ferrara Cycle], which explores an interior universe forced into an awareness of the diversity and harshness of the outside world. Bassani worked from 1937 to 1981 to produce this ample fresco whose layers – *Cinque storie ferraresi* (*A Prospect of Ferrara*), *Gli occhiali d'oro* (*The Gold-Rimmed Spectacles*), *Il giardino dei Finzi-Contini*, *Dietro la porta* (*Behind the Door*), *L'airone* (*The Heron*), and *L'odore di fieno* (*The Smell of Hay*) – constitute a complex tale. It is a tale that unwinds without order or temporal sequence through separate stories stretching back from the 1920s and 1930s to the beginning of the century, before leaping forward to 1943 and 1944 and beyond, and whose characters chase after one another from one tale to the next, outlining the ancient Jewish tragedy, which is the tragedy of diversity rejected and persecuted. It is no coincidence that the decisive moment also in stylistic terms is represented in this Ferrara cycle by *The Gold-Rimmed Spectacles*, where the main character, a respected doctor, loses his position and respectability and is driven to suicide on account of his homosexuality, which manifests itself to his fellow citizens through his unbridled passion for a cynical young man. Dr Fadigati's tragedy is consummated at the same time as the anti-Semitic campaign breaks out in the press and the young narrator, feeling himself to be similar to Fadigati in his solitude, perceives the same mechanism in the old doctor's rejection by his fellow citizens as that which provokes the marginalization of the Jews. This feeling of exclusion is also central to *Behind the Door*, which deals with the turmoil of adolescence.

The Ferrara Cycle is closed in a sense by the main characters of the story "Una lapide in via Mazzini" ("A Memorial Tablet in via Mazzini") from *Cinque storie ferraresi*: Geo Josz, who reappears in Ferrara in August 1945 as the sole survivor of the 183 members of the Ferrara community deported by the Germans two years earlier, and of *The Heron*, the landowner Edgardo Limentani. Both symbolize the bewilderment of feeling oneself to be different, this time in the postwar period: Geo Josz can no longer live in Ferrara because he embodies the embarrassing memory of which the city (and the whole country?) now wishes to be rid; Edgardo Limentani in turn cannot manage to integrate himself back into an environment that has apparently returned to normality, and yields to a suicidal impulse. The Ferrara Cycle is the long tale of a city and a world, of a Jewish community that is rich and contradictory. It is an analysis of fascism, and of fascism in Ferrara in particular, and the story of an unspeakably painful and unhealable wound.

CLARA CORONA

Becker, Jurek

Polish-born German fiction writer and scriptwriter, 1937–1997

Born in Łódź, 30 September 1937. In Łódź ghetto and, later, Ravensbrück concentration camp, 1942–45. Studied at Humboldt University, Berlin, 1957–60, and at Filmhochschule, Potsdam-Babelsberg. Married and divorced; three sons. Member, Socialist Unity Party in East Germany, 1957; expelled 1976; resigned from Writers' Union 1976; settled in West Germany. Visited United States, 1977; writer in residence, Oberlin College, Ohio, 1978; Cornell University, 1984; University of Texas, Austin, 1987. Visiting professor, Essen University, 1978, and Augsburg University, 1982–83; resident writer, Bergen-Enkheim, 1987. Lived in Kreuzberg, West Berlin, until his death. Awards include Heinrich Mann Prize, 1971; Silver Bear, Berlin Film Festival, 1974; National Prize for Literature, German Democratic Republic, 1975; Adolf Grimme Prize, 1987 and 1988; Bayerischer Fernsehpreis, 1991; Thomas Mann Award, 1991. Died in Frankfurt am Main, 14 March 1997.

Selected Writings

Novels

Jacob der Lügner, 1969; as *Jacob the Liar*, translated by Melvin Kornfeld, 1975; as screenplay, 1973
Irreführung der Behörden [Leading the Authorities Astray], 1973
Der Boxer [The Boxer], 1976
Schlaflose Tage, 1978; as *Sleepless Days*, translated by Leila Vennewitz, 1979
Aller Welt Freund [Friend to All the World], 1982
Bronsteins Kinder, 1986; as *Bronstein's Children*, translated by Leila Vennewitz, 1988
Amanda herzlos [Heartless Amanda], 1992

Short Stories

Nach der ersten Zukunft [After the Initial Future], 1980
Erzählungen, 1986
Die beliebteste Familiengeschichte und andere Erzählungen [The Favourite Family Story and Other Stories], 1992
Five Stories, edited by David Rock, 1993

Plays

Neuner, 1991
Many plays for television, including *Liebling Kreuzberg* [Darling Kreuzberg], 1990; and *Wir sind auch nur ein Volk* [We Are After All Just a People], 1995

Other

Warnung vor dem Schriftsteller [Warning against the Writer], 1990 (three lectures)
Ende des Grössenwahns [End of Megalomania], 1996

Further Reading

Arnold, Heinz Ludwig (editor), *Jurek Becker*, Munich: Text + Kritik, 1992
Brown, Russell E., "Radios and Trees: A Note to Jurek Becker's Ghetto Fiction", *Germanic Notes*, 19/1–2 (1988)
Brown, Russell E., "Jurek Becker's Holocaust Fiction: A Father and Son Survive", *Critique: Studies in Contemporary Fiction* (Spring 1989)
Gilman, Sander L., "Jüdischer Literaten und deutsche Literatur: Antisemitismus und verborgene Sprache der Juden am Beispiel von Jurek Becker und Edgar Hilsenrath", *Zeitschrift für Deutsche Philologie*, 107/2 (1988)
Heidelberger-Leonard, Irene (editor), *Jurek Becker*, Frankfurt: Suhrkamp, 1992
Johnson, Susan M., *The Works of Jurek Becker: A Thematic Analysis*, New York: Peter Lang, 1988
Riordan, Colin (editor), *Jurek Becker*, Cardiff: University of Wales Press, 1998
Rock, David, *Jurek Becker: A Jew Who became a German?*, Oxford: Berg, 2000
Seminar, special issue, 19/4 (1983)
Zipser, Richard A., "Interview with Jurek Becker" and "Jurek Becker: Writer with a Cause", *Dimension*, 11/3 (1978)

With the publication of his first novel, *Jacob der Lügner* (*Jacob the Liar*), Jurek Becker's reputation grew rapidly from that of a relatively unknown writer of East German filmscripts to that of a prize-winning novelist of international standing. Though his Jewish works relate to his childhood experiences in the Lodz ghetto and in concentration camps, Becker claimed to have almost no memories of this time, admitting that his works set in this period were largely the product of his own imagination, his father's sparse anecdotes, and historical research. *Jacob the Liar* is thus a remarkable reconstruction of the lost world of his childhood in a story about an unheroic hero in a Polish ghetto during World War II. Through his fictitious radio, the shopkeeper Jakob Heym is able to give his desperate fellow Jews hope by supplying them with "news" about the Russian advance. In the narrative technique and style of *Jacob the Liar*, and of *Die beliebteste Familiengeschichte und andere Erzählungen* [The Favourite Family Story and Other Stories], Becker recreates something of the Yiddish oral tradition of storytelling, and in the novel, too, he weaves Yiddish words and Old Testament imagery into a language in which he "tried to transfer some of the rules of colloquial Yiddish to High German". The first-person narrator, unlike Becker an adult survivor of the Holocaust, avoids sensational brutality and tells his story of everyday life in the ghetto in a disarmingly casual, humorous, conversational tone, making this a unique Holocaust tale; his frequent touches of gentle irony and humour create distance and avoid sentimentality, but also bring home the horror of the historical situation. The form of the novel underlines its central theme of hope as resistance to barbarity by employing techniques associated with Jewish culture in order to affirm its survival against its attempted destruction by the Nazis.

The young Becker was hailed by critics as the East German heir of Aleichem and Singer, yet in his essay "My Way of Being a Jew", the author resisted the label of "Jewish" writer, denying any attachment to Judaism (he was an atheist). His other fictional works on Jewish themes are, though, partly a search for his lost Jewish identity via linguistic constructs, an attempt to unlock his own suppressed memories. In "The Wall", for instance, an adult narrator pretends to become a child again and to re-experience events in a ghetto through the eyes of himself as a five-year-old. In such works, Becker articulates the voice of his own possible childhood, exploring conceivable versions of the past, possible dimensions of his own forgotten experiences, and of his Jewish origins, through fiction.

The notion of the past living on in the present is central to the two later novels, *Der Boxer* [The Boxer] and *Bronsteins Kinder* [Bronstein's Children], and Becker is probably unique among German writers in relating the problem of coming to terms with Nazism from the perspective of Jewish victims rather than Nazi perpetrators. *Der Boxer* demonstrates the inability of a Holocaust survivor to overcome his psychological scars, despite his efforts to obliterate his Jewish identity. His attempt to shield his son from the past also has tragic consequences. The father's reticence is that of the Jew as Holocaust survivor and leads to the tragic breakdown of communication with his son who suddenly leaves his East German home and is eventually killed fighting for Israel in the Six Day War. By choosing a Jewish identity for himself in the Jewish state of Israel, the son corresponds closely to the definition of a Jew given by Becker in his essay, "My Jewishness", when he claimed that the question of belonging to a group of people such as the Jews involved an act of individual free will, an intellectual decision.

The plot of *Bronsteins Kinder* opens up new dimensions in terms of Jewish themes and Holocaust repercussions: here, a Jewish victim of Nazi oppression becomes the oppressor who takes revenge on his former persecutor, a guard from the Neuengamme concentration camp. The novel is narrated from the perspective of the victim's son, Hans, a citizen of the GDR who was born after the Holocaust and tries to ignore his Jewish identity only to discover that he is unable to disconnect himself from his father's fate as life-long victim. Through his narrator, Becker reflects on the difficulties facing children of Jewish victims of the Holocaust in adjusting to life in Germany and trying to live as "Germans": despite his desire to be and feel like a German, Hans develops a sense of Jewish identity. Both *Der Boxer* and *Bronsteins Kinder* are novels with strong parallels to Becker's own life, yet they are not confessional autobiography but improvisatory models, representing just two of several possible situations and views of life.

With his novels and stories, Becker restored to modern German literature some of the characteristics of Jewish-German writing that had been missing for some 50 years: melancholy wit, intellectual sharpness, poignancy, casual yet finely detailed realism, and a unique ability as raconteur. One of his great contributions to Holocaust literature is the fact that, in all his works, he portrayed his characters as active subjects not as objects, avoiding the stereotypical portrayal of Jews as passive victims. Also without precedent among East or West German postwar writers was Becker's portrayal of sensitive Jewish issues unclouded by sentimentality or prejudice: he posed the delicate questions which others in Germany felt unable to ask. His novels also suggest that many Jews had become too dependent on the Shoah for their sense of identity, and that being a victim could bring with it its own deformities, as in the case of Arno Bronstein who dies of a heart-attack in his attempt to turn the tables on his former guard. This outcome endorses Becker's view that attitudes and emotions rooted in the past are deformities which prevent survivors from living life to the full in the present and ultimately destroy them. During the 1970s and 1980s, Becker also saw evidence of such ugliness in the actions of the Jewish state, Israel. Yet this controversial standpoint, partly shaped by his GDR experiences, represented only one (temporary) side of the coin. By the 1990s, his views on Israeli politics had turned *volte face*: he found the arguments of the Palestinians for their own state on Israeli territory unconvincing, affirming the Jewish need for a "secure refuge" in the light of what had happened throughout history.

DAVID ROCK

Bejerano, Maya

Israeli poet and fiction writer, 1949–

Born Maya Schwarzman on Kibbutz Ailon, Haifa, 23 February 1949. Studied at Bar-Ilan University, Tel Aviv, BA in literature and philosophy 1974; Hebrew University, Jerusalem, degree in librarianship 1977. Military service, 1967–69. Married, 1983, divorced, 1988; one daughter. Librarian, Tel Aviv Public Library. Many awards including

Prime Minister's Prize, 1986 and 1994; Bernstein Prize, 1989; Israel Literature Prize for Poetry, 1992.

Selected Writings

Poetry
Bat yaana [Ostrich], 1978
Hahom vehakor [The Heat and the Cold], 1981
Ibbud netunim 52: shishah maamarim umaamar al mosad [Data Processing 52: Six Essays and Essay about Institution], 1982
Shirat hatsipporim [Song of the Birds], 1985
Kol [Voice], 1987
Retsef hashirim [Collected Poems], 1987
Livyatan [Whale], 1990
Mizmorei iyyov [The Hymns of Job], 1993
Anaseh lagaat betabbur bitni [Trying to Touch my Belly-Button], 1997
Hayofi hu kaas [Beauty is Rage], 2001

Fiction
Hasimlah ha-kehullah vesokhen habittuah [The Blue Dress and the Insurance Agent] (short stories and a play), 1993

Translations
Two poems from *The Heat and the Cold* ("Data Processing 16" and "I'm in a Hurry"), *Modern Hebrew Literature*, 7/3–4 (1982)
Four poems from *Ostrich* ("Word Processing 1", "Word Processing 2", "Word Processing 3", "Word Processing 4"), *Modern Hebrew Literature (New Series)*, 1 (Fall/Winter) (1988)
Six poems from *Ostrich* ("Salambo", "Data Processing no. 15", "Gainsborough", "Ostrich", "The Tibetan Princess", "Data Processing 48: The Heat and the Cold"), *Tel Aviv Review*, 1 January 1988
Poems appear in *The Defiant Muse: Hebrew Feminist Poems from Antiquity to the Present*, edited by Shirley Kaufman, Galit Hasan-Rokem, and Tamar S. Hess, 1999

Other
Ishi ahuvi [My Man, My Love], 1989 (poems set to music, sung by Shlomith Aharon)
Haperah hasakran [The Curious Flower], 1993

Further Reading

Gurevitch, Zali, "Poetry as Alternative", *Davar*, 1/1 (1982)
Gurevitch, Zali, "The Belly-Button of Memory", *Moznayim*, 73 (January 1990): 53–54
Hever, Hannan, "Conditions of Swing and [Its] Hollow", *Siman Kriah*, 11 (May 1980): 142–44
Interview in *Makom*, 1 (1985)
Kubovy, Miri, "The Fraction of Consciousness and Classification of Imagination", *Moznayim* (February–March 1987)
Lahav, Avner, "A Wonderful Journey", *Haakhshav*, 51–54 (1987)
Leshem, Giora, "'Video-poesy' as a New Step", *Moznayim*, 55/6 (1982)
Snir, Leah, "A Magical Forest", *Davar*, 1/7 (1988)
Weichart, Rafi, "Beauty and Suffering from the Veins of Poetry", *Now*, 1 (1994)

One of the leading Israeli/Hebrew poets since the 1970s, Bejerano has published nine poetry books and one collection of short stories and a play. Her poetry is somewhere between modernism and postmodernism. She shares modernism's fascination with technology, with time, and with the figure of the poet as bearing the torch of wisdom, and postmodernism's juxtapositions of quotations and images from high and popular culture and preoccupation with language as a productive force. Bejerano elaborates the poetic projects of her 1950s–60s predecessors. In her poetry one sees Yona Wallach's long stychic structures and "totalistic" enterprise, David Avidan's preoccupation with technology as a new mode of being and thinking, and Meir Wieseltier's political and critical probing of the place and responsibilities of poetry.

In her early work, Bejerano wrote two alternate types of poetry. Her first collection, *Ostrich*, consists of relatively conventional lyrical poetry, in which short and quite musical poems are focused around a specific experience or mood. Mostly these are epiphanic moments of fantasy or revelation ("At First There Was Rain", "Lizard", "Cranes") or surreal scenes of legendary characters ("Salambo", "Gainsborough", "The Tibetan Princess"). Next to these poems, however, are the "data processing" poems – a genre or a poetic mode that Bejerano "invented" and developed in her subsequent books and with which she is primarily identified. These are long, amorphic, randomly numbered sequences of poems that break the boundaries of conventional poetry in terms of language, structure, and thematics, and, as their title designates, are concerned with the computer-like procedure of processing. Rather than a way to extricate logic from chaotic reality (or to impose order on it), these poems introduce a verbal procedure that constantly, actively shifts back and forth between objective reality and rich, free imagination, between concrete situations in the world and the perceiving and creative mind.

The computer becomes the model for the process of writing/making poetry, and the very tension – or rather, the inherent circulation and interdependency – between subject and object, between the objective world and human perception – are at stake. Rather than attempting to describe, reflect, or react to the world, Bejerano's poetry creates or gives birth to her own world – one that is at once autonomous and communicative, separate from the real world and connected to it – like the blood circulation in the body or, indeed, like giving birth:

> [Let's] suppose that the whole world is standing opposite
> to me; no, actually, the whole world opposite to the whole
> world – opposite to me as first person, in a birthing slant
> ("Data Processing 31")

Throughout Bejerano's poetry the two worlds – the speaker/poet and the world/reader – are in constant tension, which, however complex and multifaceted, is often formulated in gendered relationships. In Bejerano's first poem, "Ostrich" (which opens her first book of the same name), the (female) ostrich, true to its traditional characteristic as coward, wants "the shutters to be closed/ covered with flowery plastic cover", in order to preserve "domestic happiness". But at the end:

comes the day of the ostrich
and she rai-
ses her head, loo-
king at her suitor, ex-
cuses herself
and walks away.

In the poem "I'm in a hurry" (in *The Heat and the Cold*) the speaker politely rejects her addressee (the reader?) because she is engulfed in her own pleasure and internal voices:

I'm in a hurry and won't be able to talk pleasantly
for my whole body is in pleasantness,
and my tongue is mute for your friendly conversation
my voice draws into itself
long chords and within it thousands of goblins
sing my pleasantness

In another poem, however, this tension becomes a violent struggle for life (writing) or death (silence): "My problem in writing is to create/ conditions of sling and [its] hollow."

In *Data Processing 52*, the admiration and use of computer technology as a model for poetry and being expands to an admiring exploration of a state institution (the Social Security Department in Jerusalem) and the ways that people and institutions produce, feed on, and transform one another. In *Song of the Birds* Bejerano replaces the data processing with the encyclopedic project of classifying the world into categories (cycles) of "marvelous people", "marvelous places", "marvelous plants", etc. The speaker – "a ray of light, a short voice frequency" on her way to the "star of the mind/soul" – is the watching mind that finds echoes of herself in everything from nature to technology and science ("once in a hundred years the bamboo blossoms, like me"). Eventually she wants to learn how to "come home"; the knowledge she acquired is practically divine – like seeing God ("for we saw and did not die/ . . . / for we touched ourselves and returned to life").

Bejerano's next books are concerned precisely with such journeys "back home" – to (new) "life" or to the "star of the mind/soul" – journeys in which the personal explorations of love and desire (in *Voice* and *Whale*), of pain (in *The Hymns of Job*) and of birth/memories (in *Trying to Touch my Belly Button*) are intertwined with questions of (divine) knowledge, (Godless?) fate, and language.

In *Voice* (1987) Bejerano returns to lyric poetry and appears as a concrete person/body in intimate, erotic situations. This physical, "wordless" closeness is precisely what leads her to examine, throughout the book, the "possibility of negation and absence": "the no within the extended yes/ the black within the white colour" – within oneself as between people. Inseparable from this is the question of presence and absence within language – the gap between signifier and signified, between words and things, which leads to the materialization of the words, on the one hand (in the cycle "Constants and Variables") and to the desire to transcend it, on the other ("each name is a pillory on the original, unbound movement of freedom"). In the cycle "Sex, Car, and Then Love" (in *Whale*) love is a cinematographic, semi-epic, and semi-comic road trip (or life-trip) – with a comics-style "green-eyed, green-lip, green-legged and chest" young lover. The cycle *The Hymns of Job* examines the relationship between suffering and poetry – "the poetic aptitude as a bundle of ropes ["ropes" also = "pain"]/ was piling up at the bottom on the boat" – through Job's fate that is "divided like two halves of a fruit,/ . . . God and His negative" in the Land of Uz, "the land of paper that flies in the wind of Times." The speaker is eventually re-born as Job, thrown "from the belly of God, the belly of suffering" into a new life cycle, with an eye like an "inverted memory of a baby,/ foreseeing." This "inverted memory of a baby" lies at the heart of *Trying to Touch my Belly Button*: an attempt to remember what cannot be remembered but only imagined, invented as a given origin – being born. Bejerano's latest book, *Beauty is Rage*, is concerned with the direct gaze at others, the overt confrontation with faces – of a dead father, of fellow poets, of the battered woman on television, of Lady Poetry who faces her untamed fighting-bull image in the mirror.

HAMUTAL TZAMIR

Bellow, Saul

Canadian-born US fiction writer and critic, 1915–

Born in Lachine, Quebec, 10 June 1915. Moved with his family to Montreal and then, in 1924, Chicago. Studied at University of Chicago, 1933–35; Northwestern University, Evanston, Illinois, 1935–37, BS in sociology and anthropology 1937. Postgraduate work in anthropology at University of Wisconsin, Madison, 1937. Served in merchant marine, 1944–45. Married, first, Anita Goshkin, 1937; divorced, one son; second, Alexandra Tschacbasov, 1956, divorced; one son; third, Susan Glassman, 1961; divorced, one son; fourth, Alexandra Ionescu Tulcea, 1975; divorced; fifth, Janis Freedman, 1989, one son. Worked as schoolteacher, 1938–42; member of editorial department, "Great Books" project, *Encyclopaedia Britannica*, Chicago, 1943–44; freelance editor and reviewer, New York, 1945–46. Numerous academic posts, including assistant professor of English, University of Minnesota, Minneapolis, 1948–49; visiting lecturer, New York University, 1950–52; creative writing fellow, Princeton University, 1952–53; Professor, and Chairman of Committee on Social Thought, University of Chicago, 1970–76. Romanes Lecturer, 1990; Professor of English and University Professor, Boston University, 1999–2000. Numerous awards and fellowships, including National Book Award, 1954, 1965, 1971; Jewish Heritage Award, 1968; member, American Academy of Arts and Letters, 1970; Pulitzer Prize, 1976; Nobel Prize for Literature, 1976; Commandeur, Légion d'Honneur, 1983; Commandeur, Ordre des Arts et des Lettres, 1985.

Selected Writings

Novels
Dangling Man, 1944
The Victim, 1947
The Adventures of Augie March, 1953
Henderson the Rain King, 1959

Herzog, 1964
Mr Sammler's Planet, 1970
Humboldt's Gift, 1975
The Dean's December, 1982
More Die of Heartbreak, 1987
Ravelstein, 2000

Short Stories and Novellas
Seize the Day, with Three Short Stories and a One-Act Play, 1956
Mosby's Memoirs and Other Stories, 1968
Him with His Foot in His Mouth and Other Stories, 1984
A Theft, 1989
The Bellarosa Connection, 1989
Something to Remember Me By: Three Tales, 1991
The Actual, 1997

Plays
The Wrecker, included in *Seize the Day*, 1956
Scenes from Humanitas: A Farce, in *Partisan Review*, 29 (1962)
The Last Analysis, 1965
Under the Weather (A Wen, Orange Souffle, Out from Under), 1966

Other
"The Jewish Writer and the English Literary Tradition", *Commentary*, 8 (October 1949): 366–67
"Laughter in the Ghetto", *Saturday Review of Literature* (30 May 1953): 15
Dessins, by Jesse Reichek; text by Bellow and Christian Zervos, 1960
Recent American Fiction: A Lecture, 1963
Editor, *Great Jewish Short Stories*, 1963
Like You're Nobody: The Letters of Louis Gallo to Saul Bellow, 1961–1962, plus Oedipus-Schmoedipus, The Story That Started It All, 1966
The Portable Saul Bellow, 1974
Technology and the Frontiers of Knowledge (lectures), with others, 1975
To Jerusalem and Back: A Personal Account, 1976
Nobel Lecture, 1977
It All Adds Up: From the Dim Past to the Uncertain Future: A Nonfiction Collection, 1994

Further Reading

Bach, Gerhard (editor), *The Critical Response to Saul Bellow*, Westport, Connecticut: Greenwood Press, 1995
Bigler, Walter, *Figures of Madness in Saul Bellow's Longer Fiction*, Bern: Peter Lang, 1998
Bloom, Harold (editor), *Saul Bellow*, New York: Chelsea House, 1986
Cronin, Gloria L. and Blaine H. Hall, *Saul Bellow: An Annotated Bibliography*, New York: Garland, 1987
Cronin, Gloria L. and Ben Siegel (editors), *Conversations with Saul Bellow*, Jackson: University Press of Mississippi, 1994
Dutton, Robert R., *Saul Bellow*, New York: Twayne, 1971
Eichelberger, Julia, *Prophets of Recognition: Ideology and the Individual in Novels by Ralph Ellison, Toni Morrison, Saul Bellow, and Eudora Welty*, Baton Rouge: Louisiana State University Press, 1999
Friedrich, Marianne M., *Character and Narration in the Short Fiction of Saul Bellow*, New York: Peter Lang, 1995
Glenday, Michael K., *Saul Bellow and the Decline of Humanism*, London: Macmillan, 1990
Goldman, L.H., *Saul Bellow's Moral Vision: A Critical Study of the Jewish Experience*, New York: Irvington, 1983
Hollahan, Eugene (editor), *Saul Bellow and the Struggle at the Center*, New York: AMS Press, 1996
Hyland, Peter, *Saul Bellow*, New York: St Martin's Press, 1992
Kulshrestha, Chirantan, *Saul Bellow: The Problem of Affirmation*, New Delhi: Arnold–Heinemann, 1978
Miller, Ruth, *Saul Bellow: A Biography of the Imagination*, New York: St Martin's Press, 1991
Pifer, Ellen, *Saul Bellow against the Grain*, Philadelphia: University of Pennsylvania Press, 1990
Rodrigues, Eusebio L., *Quest for the Human: An Exploration of Saul Bellow's Fiction*, Lewisburg, Pennsylvania: Bucknell University Press, 1981
Sarma, G.V.L.N. (editor), *A Garland to Saul Bellow*, Machilipatnam, India: Triveni, 1980
Tanner, Tony, *Saul Bellow*, Edinburgh: Oliver and Boyd, 1965; New York: Barnes and Noble, 1967
Wasserman, Harriet, *Handsome Is: Adventures with Saul Bellow: A Memoir*, New York: Fromm, 1997
Wilson, Jonathan, *On Bellow's Planet: Readings from the Dark Side*, Rutherford, New Jersey: Fairleigh Dickinson University Press, 1985

Saul Bellow is recognized as one of the most important writers in English in the 20th century. In addition to novels, he has written critically acclaimed short fiction, dramas, and nonfiction. Although he has repeatedly said that he does not want to be considered a Jewish author, his works are mostly about Jews, and even the ones about non-Jews, such as *Henderson the Rain King*, have, critics argue, Jewish themes. And in his nonfiction work, *To Jerusalem and Back*, he shows his commitment to Israel.

His first two novels – *Dangling Man*, the story of an American man during World War II waiting for the draft and finally volunteering, and *The Victim*, the tale of a Jew and an anti-Semitic Gentile, both of whom are, in a sense, victims – won him a reputation as an author of great power although they were not very popular. *The Adventures of Augie March* brought him wider acclaim and the National Book Award. This picaresque tale tells of Augie's adventures in and around Chicago and ranging into Mexico and Europe. It examines the Chicago underworld, a topic that reappears in *Humboldt's Gift*, which won the Pulitzer Prize and which immediately preceded his winning the Nobel Prize for Literature. It also involves Augie's meeting with Trotskii while Augie is in Mexico trying to help a woman train eagles to hunt iguanas.

Henderson the Rain King at first also appears to be a kind of picaresque, tracing Henderson's journey from his pig farm in America to the wilds of Africa, where he becomes a rain king. Yet in the course of his fabulous journey, Henderson is able to tame the voice inside him that constantly says, "*I want, I want, I want*", and achieve a higher kind of transcendence.

Seize the Day is a novella about Tommy Wilhelm, who views himself as a failure and whose very successful physician father also views him as a failure. Out of work and separated from his wife, Tommy tries desperately to make money in lard futures so that he can pay his debts and support his children, whom he loves tremendously. When he loses all of his money, he begs his father for help and is rejected. He ends up in a funeral home mourning for a man he does not know in such a way that the real mourners are jealous. As many critics read the short novel, Tommy has reached the bottom; he now has nowhere to go but up.

Herzog also deals with a man who loves his daughter, June, but no longer lives with Madeleine, the child's mother. Herzog moves from a position of intense anxiety, one in which hospitalization for mental illness seems appropriate, to one of growing calm and stability. He travels to Chicago, ostensibly to visit his child but also while contemplating killing Madeleine and Valentine Gersbach, the man who committed adultery with Herzog's wife. He gets arrested for possessing a gun after a truck rear-ends a car he is driving with his daughter as passenger. He ends up in the peace of a huge old house he owns in Ludeyville, a rural retreat in Massachusetts. There, he seems to be regaining his strength and health.

In *Mr Sammler's Planet* Bellow treats a Holocaust survivor, Mr Sammler, who now lives in a New York City that has become nightmarish in many ways. Mr Sammler sees people at their worst in Europe and later witnesses the Israeli War for Independence, yet he retains his faith in humanity.

Like Herzog, in *Humboldt's Gift* Charlie Citrine is separated from his wife and tremendously fond of his daughters. He was once a kind of protégé to Von Humboldt Fleisher, a paranoid but gifted poet based loosely on American Jewish poet Delmore Schwartz. Humboldt died in poverty. Now a successful playwright, Citrine lives well in Chicago, but gets involved with Rinaldo Cantabile, a minor gangster whom Citrine thinks has cheated him in cards. When Citrine refuses to pay a gambling debt, Cantabile terrifies him until he pays.

Citrine develops money troubles because of what he feels are his ex-wife's exorbitant demands. He travels to New York with Renata, his mistress. From there, they are supposed to travel to Europe together. When he hears that his brother is to have surgery, he gives Renata money and sends her ahead, but when he arrives in Europe, he finds Renata's mother and Renata's son but no Renata. Eventually, Citrine discovers that Renata has run off with and married one of her other lovers. Citrine remains taking care of the son as his money begins to dwindle. Then, Cantabile finds Citrine and tells him about a very successful movie based on an idea that Citrine and Humboldt created and that Citrine told Cantabile about. Citrine uses a still-sealed package that he inherited from Humboldt to prove that he and Humboldt created the tale and as a result gets enough money to solve many of his problems. At the novel's end, he reburies Humboldt.

In *The Dean's December* Bellow paints the horror that communism produced in Romania and compares it with a nightmarish Chicago riddled with corruption and crime. Corde, the dean, spends December in Bucharest, where his wife's family lives. At the book's end, the dean and his wife, Minna, return to America. His wife, an astronomer, goes to an observatory to view the stars. Corde too sees the stars there and ultimately realizes that there is a kind of "equilibrium" in the universe and that what he views is part of himself.

Summarizing the plots of Bellow's works hardly does them justice. They are intellectual and allusive, often with highly educated thinkers as protagonists. Even his short stories such as "Mosby's Memoirs" and his late short novels such as *The Actual* often immerse the reader in intellectual exercises trying to keep up with the minds of their characters. Although Bellow's works often deal with unpleasant realities, they remain basically optimistic about the human situation and about the possibility of people making choices that enable them to triumph over the forces that try to control them.

RICHARD TUERK

Ben-Ner, Yitzhak

Israeli fiction writer, 1937–

Born in Kfar Yehoshua, 1937. Studied literature and drama at Tel Aviv University. Lived in the United States, 1978–80. Edits and presents radio and television programmes, writes screenplays and plays; also a film critic and journalist. Awards include the Agnon-Jerusalem Prize, 1981; Berenstein and Ramat Gan municipal literary prizes; first prize at Theatroneto Festival, 1990.

Selected Writings

Fiction
Beikvot maveer hasadot [After the Field-Burner], 1967
Haish misham 1967; as *The Man from There*, translated by Dorothea Shefer, 1970
Shkiah kafrit, 1976; as *Rustic Sunset and Other Stories*, translated by Robert Whitehill, 1998
Kishona [Kishona], 1978
Aharei hageshem [After the Rain], 1979
Yedidi emanuel veani [My Friend Emmanuel and I], 1979
Erets rehokah [A Far Land], 1981
Protokol [Protocol], 1983
Malakhim baim [Angels are Coming], 1987
Taatuon [A Slight Deception], 1989
Jeans [Jeans, a Dog], 1991
Boker shel shotim [Morning of Fools], 1992
Dubim vayaar [Bears and Woods], 1995
Mitham oyev [Enemy Scope], 1997

Films and Television: *Again, Forever*, 1985; *Atalia*, 1986; *The Class Queen*, 1988; *Winter Games*, 1989; *Nili*, 1996; *Enemy Scope*, 1999

Plays
David August, 1983
Taatuon, 1990

A Far Land, 1992
Morning of Fools, 1992
Uri Muri, 1999

Further Reading

Krinski, Aviva, *Maarkhei shiur lehoraet "shekiah kafrit" meet Yitzhak Ben-Ner*, Tel Aviv: Or'am, 1984
Tammuz, Benjamin and Leon Yudkin (editors), *Meetings with the Angel: Seven Stories from Israel*, London: Deutsch, 1973

Yitzhak Ben-Ner expresses and portrays poignant and sharp emotions using very simple language, and it is this simplicity that emphasizes the depth of what he is describing. Disturbing and moving psychological complexities appear in a plot that often seems bare and uneventful. In *Haish misham* (*The Man from There*), for example, the protagonist who remains nameless finds himself stranded in an Arab town during the 1947 War of Independence. Although most of the plot consists of the protagonist lying ill in bed or walking around the town, his observations and various talks with different characters combine to create a rich and sensitive prose that deals not only with political issues but also human relations and how they change under various circumstances either on neutral territory or in war zones. Similarly the short story "Kolnoa" ("Cinema") tells the simple tale of an uncle and nephew who work in a print shop. Yet it could be interpreted as a tale that reveals a great deal about the nature of human existence and in particular the fear and loneliness that accompanies it. "Cinema" was published in 1976 in a book of eight short stories entitled *Shkiah kafrit* (*Rustic Sunset*). It was written however in the years 1967 and 1976, and three of the stories ("Roman zair" ["Dime Novel"], "Shmoneh eser hadashim" ["Eighteen Months"] and "Nikole") are about characters who are somehow affected by the 1973 Yom Kippur War. "Mishakim behoref" ("Games in Winter") and more importantly "Cinema" differ from these and the other stories by being introspective accounts of an adult reflecting on his youth. On the other hand, the era following the Yom Kippur War was one of national depression and vulnerability. There was a feeling of "aloneness" and this "aloneness" can be detected in "Cinema", although in a completely indirect manner – so indirect that the war is not even mentioned and one can only assume that it is a factor.

"Cinema" is told through the eyes of a young man who remembers his holidays spent at his uncle's printing shop in Tel Aviv. The uncle is obsessed by cinema and spends most of his time watching films. He has been deserted by his wife, whom he still waits for in vain. After 12 years she finally returns, but the uncle, incapable of communicating with her, avoids the reunion by going to the cinema. After the uncle retires, the nephew and protagonist takes over the running of the shop. The whole story describes characters who are trapped by their surroundings and who are unable to make any real progress. The motif of the cinema underlines the act of escapism, and the uncle's futile waiting for a long lost wife demonstrates how people can so often place themselves in hopeless situations. Furthermore, his rejection of her when she finally does return shows how the waiting was far more powerful than the actual realization, and how the uncle was using this waiting as a means of escape.

The title story of this volume, "Rustic Sunset", concerns a man slowly preparing himself for the moment of death. This preparation is shown to the reader symbolically as the protagonist himself experiences the finality of death through others. In other words, his constant contact with death acts as a reminder of his own preparation. This is paralleled by the protagonist's relationship to the village itself, for although he lives in it he continues to harbour feelings of longing for it. The village is both near and far in his mind in the same way as the experience of death is both within him and beyond him. Indeed it has been said of Ben-Ner's work that the settings are always a dominant factor: "Cinema", "Rustic Sunset", and to an extent *The Man from There* demonstrate this. In the latter the protagonist is in a town that is both neutral and biased, and lives with people who seem neither for nor against his presence. This blurring remains even after the finality of Israel's victory over Palestine.

Similarly this blurring of biased affinities can be found in Ben-Ner's more recent novel *Mitham oyev* [Enemy Scope]. Here the protagonist Slutzky is sent to the West Bank by the Israeli government to try to uncover secret anti-government organizations such as those that supposedly engineered the assassination of Yitzhak Rabin. Slutzky, who is in fact Rabin's former and therefore disgraced bodyguard, agrees to this government mission as a means of repentance. However, Slutzky, a former orthodox Jew, finds himself torn between the gallant protection of his country's leader and the wishes of his previous community. Certainly this problem acts as a reflection of the social and political complexities within Israel. *The Man from There* on the other hand acts as a reflection of how such a simple thing such as friendship between two people can be marred and threatened by national pride. In both stories Ben-Ner writes with insight and sensitivity.

GIULIA MILLER

Ben-Yehuda, Netiva

Israeli fiction writer, 1928–

Born in Tel Aviv, 1928. Was member of an elite Palmach unit in 1948 War of Independence. After leaving army, studied at Bezalel Art Academy, Jerusalem, 1949, and in London. Returned to Jerusalem; studied Hebrew and Philosophy at the Hebrew University. Works as freelance editor.

Selected Writings

Novels
1948: Bein hasfirot [1948: Between the Calendars], 1981
Mibaad leavotot [Through the Binding Ropes], 1985
Yerushalayim mibifnokho [Jerusalem from the Inside], 1988
Keshepartsah hamedinah [When the War Broke Out], 1991

Other

Hamilon leivrit meduberet [The World Dictionary of Hebrew Slang], with Dan Ben-Amotz, 1972

Hamilon leivrit meduberet II [The World Dictionary of Hebrew Slang, part 2], with Dan Ben-Amotz, 1982

Brakhot uklalot [Blessings and Curses], 1984

Otobiografiah beshir vezemer [Autobiography in Poem and Song], 1990

Further Reading

Feldman, Yael S., *No Room of their Own: Gender and Nation in Israeli Women's Fiction*, New York: Columbia University Press, 1999; Hebrew edition, Tel Aviv: Hakibuts hameuhad, 2001

Netiva Ben-Yehuda is unique among the writers of her generation not only by her late entry into the Israeli writing scene (1981, when she was in her fifties), but also because of her life-long devotion to the cause of spoken Hebrew. Her uniqueness does not stem from these factors alone, however. Though she has become something of a media figure since the 1980s, she had hardly been recognized before as a professional writer. Rather, Ben-Yehuda, "Tiva" to her many friends, had long been identified as a living emblem of the myth of the Palmach, those legendary elite units that spearheaded the struggle for Israel's independence in 1947–48. Indeed, Ben-Yehuda had for many years embodied precisely that heroic voluntarism and utter loyalty to the "Jewish national rebirth in its homeland" that had been the hallmark of the Palmach since 1948. She was also known for her sharp tongue and scathing humour – qualities that stood her in good stead when she finally came into her own as a writer.

Simultaneously, however, Ben-Yehuda was ahead of her time: her bold sexual permissiveness stood out in a period marked by sexual puritanism. In a way, she brazenly carried out her own private sexual revolution, living (rather than writing) through the body, in an age that locked up both body and emotions "in the cellar", to use Shulamit Hareven's useful metaphor from her 1972 novel, *City of Many Days*.

Fearlessness, physical prowess, and total devotion were thus some of the features distinguishing this young officer, whose military specialities included topography, reconnaissance, and demolition. Yet, for later generations, it was mainly Ben-Yehuda's fearlessness that captured the imagination, expressed now not in military pursuits but in the battle for the soul of the Hebrew language. A few years after independence, and after studying at home and abroad (art, language, and philosophy), Ben-Yehuda became a freelance editor, openly fighting the chasm between the spoken Hebrew developed in the Palmach, marked by humorous slang and linguistic inventiveness, and the elevated, highly stylized standards required then by Hebrew belles lettres. Her devotion to this matter resulted in the publication, in 1972, of *The World Dictionary of Hebrew Slang*. Indeed, this hilariously irreverent book, co-authored with another palmachnik, the late writer and satirist Dan Ben-Amotz, added another layer to the cultural idiosyncrasy of that legendary generation.

Traces of this early work can be found in her later Palmach trilogy, published between 1981 and 1991. As indicated by the title of the first of these books, *1948: Bein hasfirot* [1948: Between Calendars], she still experienced 1948 as a momentous breach in history, a transition of tremendous magnitude (which the English translation, "Between the Calendars", unfortunately fails to convey). She chose to express this traumatic experience through an idiosyncratic language, colloquially repetitious and associative, at times preserving slang and idiomatic Hebrew of days gone by – which did not make her writing easy to digest. Nor did its generic hybridity: "This book is not history", she said in the brief preface, nor fiction, not even memoirs. It is "a report from the field," she argued in her next book, *Through the Binding Ropes*, a "worm's eye view" of a low-ranking soldier.

Those readers who were willing, however, to ignore the author's disclaimers (and many other masks woven into the narration itself), found themselves not only in the presence of a garrulous but consummate storyteller, but in the current of a gripping narrative. Moreover, they slowly realized that this was a subversive telling of a major chapter in the Israeli national narrative – the "collective memory" of the 1948 War of Independence. In fact, the Palmach trilogy as a whole contributed to the process of de-mythologization of the past that has been taking place in Israel since the early 1980s. Apparently, it was no accident that Ben-Yehuda's confessional memoirs coincided with the work of the Israeli "new historians." Her books functioned as a courageous corrective by a first-hand witness, reducing the myth of a glorious past to human, and at times petty, proportions. Among the rest, they also expressed remorse about the attitude of the native young fighters towards the Yiddish-speaking new immigrant soldiers, whose foreign manners and diasporic language were often the object of ridicule and misapprehension (see especially the third part, *When the War Broke Out*).

At the same time, however, this rewriting also coincided with the revisionist feminist research that gained momentum in the 1980s. In fact, the second volume of the trilogy directly challenged – as implied by its title – the Israeli public conversation over the *Akedah*, The Binding of Isaac (Genesis 22). Ben-Yehuda's unique contribution to this discourse was the foregrounding, perhaps for the first time in Israeli culture, of the *Titshaks*, in her language, the female Isaacs of Israel's wars. Yet her critique goes much further than that. Although this aspect of Ben-Yehuda's work was not readily detected, a close reading of her texts uncovers a subversive exposure of the gap between the Palmach's promise for "sexual equality" and the reality in its ranks. As I have shown in my recent study, *No Room of their Own*, the whole "plot" of the Palmach trilogy stems from and revolves around a personal trauma caused by this gap. Half camouflaged by the narrator's rhetoric, the conflict between the slogan "inscribed" on the flag of Zionist ideology and the sexism carried out by its propagators nevertheless emerges as the hidden motivation behind this telling, as well as the cause behind the author's 30-year-long reticence.

YAEL S. FELDMAN

Berdyczewski, Micha Yosef (later Bin-Gorion)

Russian writer, 1865–1921

Born in Medzibezh, Podolia, 1865, son of a line of Hasidic rabbis. Traditional religious education. First marriage (1883–85) ended in divorce, when father-in-law would not tolerate his modern attitudes. Studied at Volozhin Yeshiva, 1885–86. Left for Breslau, Germany, studying at the university and liberal rabbinic seminary, 1890–92. Moved to Berlin, 1892. Studied in Bern 1894–96. Settled in Berlin 1911. One of the most important leaders of the movement of thinkers "The Young" (Hatseirim) who rejected systematic definitions of Jewish experience. Married dentist Rachel Romberg; son Emanuel Bin-Gorion. Returned to Pale of Settlement only once after his migration westward. Died in Berlin, 1921.

Selected Writings

Collections
Kol kitvei [Collected Works], 20 vols, 1921–25
Yidishe ksuvim [Collected Yiddish Works], 1924

Fiction
"Hetsits venifga", 1888
Urba parah [The Raven Flies], 1900
Mahanayim [Two Camps], 1900
Miriam, 1921

Essays
"Reshut hayahid bead harabbim", 1892
"Shinui arakhin" [The Transvaluation of Values], 1890s
"Mishnat hasidim" [The Teachings of Hasidim], 1899
"Lisheelat hatarbut" [The Question of Culture], 1902
"Inyenei lashon" [On the Nature of (Hebrew) Language], 1908

Folklore and Related Work
Meotsar haaggadah, 2 vols, 1913
Mimekor yisroel, 5 vols, 1930–45
Yeshu ben hanan [Jesus Son of Hanan], 1958?
Shaul ufaul [Saul or Paul], 1971

Further Reading

Almagor, Dan and Samuel Fishman, *Nahlat M.Y.B.* (The Heritage of M.Y. Berdyczewski), Tel Aviv: Hakibuts hameuhad, 1982
Band, Arnold, "The Ahad Ha'am and Berdyczewsky Polarity" in *At the Crossroads: Essays on Ahad Ha-am*, edited by Jacques Kornberg, Albany: State University of New York Press, 1983
Bin-Gorion, Emanuel, *The Reader of Generations (Stories, Essays, Legends of Berdyczewski)*, Tel Aviv: Reshafim, 1981
Cutter, William, "Language Matters", *Hebrew Studies*, 39 (1998)
Govrin, Nurit, *Alienation and Regeneration*, translated by John Glucker, Tel Aviv: MOD, 1989
Holtzman, Avner, *Essays on Micha Josef Berdyczewski*, Tel Aviv: Reshafim, 1993
Holtzman, Avner, *Towards the Tear in the Heart: Micha Josef Berdyczewski, the Formative Years (1886–1902)*, Tel Aviv: Mosad Bialik, 1995

Micha Yosef Berdyczewski is one of the great and exhilarating figures of modern Jewish letters. A writer little known in Britain or America, he represents a phase in modern Jewish thought that is implicit in Jewish modernity, and his work represents the major issues of modern Jewish identity. He was a near reclusive intellectual, a product of the Jewish Enlightenment that created the great break away from the eastern European tradition that we understand as dominating Jewish religious life from the 18th century until the Holocaust. Major leaders of the modern Zionist movement credit him with a mysterious and extravagant influence on their ability to reject the thinking of their parents' past, and yet he was a sceptic with regard to political movements and even cynical about their promise. This scepticism he shared with the man who became one of his true intimates, Yosef Hayyim Brenner, the radical and obstreperous novelist and essayist with whom he corresponded for several years.

Berdyczewski's novels and stories told of the turbulence of the young eastern European intellectual struggling to break from home and past; it was a turbulence he shared, though he never substituted an ideological program for his lost innocence. He rejected the tendency of his colleagues to refashion Jewish norms into modern secular terms, to re-imagine without turmoil the language and attitude of the classic Jewish positions. This, among other issues, caused a rift between him and Ahad Ha'am (Asher Ginsburg). The rift is reflected in Berdyczewski's correspondence with the great editor and thinker which was published in the journal they both edited, *Hashiloah*. Some of Berdyczewski's essays seem today wooden in style and format, petulant and occasionally ungrounded in important contextual realities of which their author was certainly aware. Though he was uniquely cosmopolitan, visiting museums, reading widely, immersing himself in the language of the Berlin he so loved, his essays sometimes seem strangely de-contextualized – as if he did not know that swirling around him were the projects of Durkheim, Freud, Buber, Herman Cohen, and others. From other sources we can safely assume his intellectually cosmopolitan range.

Berdyczewski seems to have been more at home in a "Gentile" milieu, staying far away from the centres of Jewish community authority, and certainly keeping his distance from any particular form of Jewish religious life. His formal company with Jews seems to have been limited to a small group of men who gathered around a weekly luncheon table (stammtisch) in Berlin just before and after World War I. Many of these figures were in the publishing industry, and Berdyczewski was frequently trying to promote his material. In spite of his reclusiveness, it is noteworthy that many of the leading figures from the Jewish world tried to meet with him, to share ideas and – as it were – to receive his blessing for their work.

He carried on a prodigious correspondence with many major figures of the period, and while much of that correspondence has now been read and analysed, more work remains to be done in order for us to gain a clearer understanding of his influence. There has been a modest renaissance of interest in Berdyczewski through major Israeli thinkers such as Avner Holtzman and Menachem Brinker; and the occasional American treatment of his work is always suggestive and illuminating. (Alan Mintz, David Biale, Arnold Band, and this writer routinely make reference to his work.)

Among other interesting anomalies in Berdyczewski's thinking was his affinity with Hasidism as an essentially vibrant and authentic expression of Jewish life – unselfconscious and uncontaminated by the deleterious influences of rationalization within modernity. It is as if the great thinker and author said: "None of this makes any sense, but if you must appreciate something in Judaism, it might as well be simple, basic and honest." To this end he published several essays on Hasidism, included Hasidic lore in his research projects, and managed to embed some Hasidic themes within one genre of his short stories. In a significant critique of the work of Martin Buber, he chastised the world figure with a tendency to create his own version of the Hasidic story – a kind of Germanizing literariness – which contaminated a genuine understanding of the "real thing". But he had something critical to say about any people who sought to "essentialize" the object of their desire, whether it was Buber, or Bialik's view of the rabbinic tradition, or modern Reform Judaism. Each of these modern Jewish projects wound up conceptualizing a kind of Jewish essence, which ran counter to Berdyczewski's organic, anthropological perspective on the Jewish experience.

Those who did derive these essences emerged as the more obvious leaders and interpreters of Jewish experience, as if we moderns are always seeking definition and clarity, whether it be Leo Baeck, Martin Buber, Hayyim Nahman Bialik, or Ahad Ha'am. The colossal prominence of each of these thinkers as against the standing of Berdyczewski's thought in our contemporary world, says a little about his own failures, and a great deal about our need for clarity and definition. But the traces of Berdyczewski's work and thought remain among the most interesting traces of any thinker in the 20th century, and bear continued study and scholarly enthusiasm.

WILLIAM CUTTER

Bergelson, Dovid

Russian writer, 1884–1952

Born in Okrimova, near Uman, 12 August 1884. Attended religious schools; privately educated in secular subjects. After parents' death lived with brothers in Kiev, Odessa, and Warsaw. Studied Hebrew and Russian literature as external university student; studied dentistry, 1909, but never practised. Co-editor, with N. Meisel, *Der yidisher almanakh*, 1910; literary editor, *Di yidishe velt*, journal, Vilna (Vilnius), from 1912; founder/director, Yidishe Kultur Lige, cultural organization, *c*.1918; co-editor of their journals *Oyfgang*, 1919, and *Eygns*, 1920. Settled in Berlin 1920; co-editor, with Der Nister, *Milgroym*, 1922–23; editor, *In shpan*. Travelled extensively from 1924, to Romania, USSR, Paris, USA, Poland, Copenhagen. Correspondent for *Der emes* (Moscow) and *Morgn frayhayt* (New York); regular contributor to *Forverts* (New York) until 1926 and from 1926 *Frayhayt* newspaper. Settled in Moscow, 1934; arrested in 1949 for anti-fascist activities; executed 12 August 1952.

Selected Writings

Collections
Geklibene verk [Selected Works], 1949
Ale verk [Complete Works], 1961

Novels
Arum vakzal [Around the Depot], 1909
Nokh alemen, 1913; as *When All is Said and Done*, translated by Bernard Martin, 1977
In a fargrebter shtot [In a Backwoods Town], 1919
Opgang, 1920; as *Descent*, translated by Joseph Sherman, 1999
Mides-hadin [Strict Justice], 1929
Bam dnieper [By the Dnieper], 2 vols, 1932–36
Birebidzshaner: dertseylung [Birebidzschaner: The Story], 1934
Dimdumin, 1946

Short Stories
Mayse Bikhl [Little Story Book], 1922
Collected Works, 1922–23, 1924
Shturemteg [Stormy Days], 1928
Tzugvintn [Winds of Change], 1929
Der toyber [The Deaf One]; as *Di broyt mil* [The Bread Mill], dramatized version, 1930
Velt-oys, velt-ayn [Out with the Old, In with the New], 1930
Naye dertseylungen [New Stories], 1947
Tsvey veltn [Two Worlds], 1953
"Joseph Shur, The Hole through which Life Slips" and "Civil War" in *Ashes out of Hope*, edited by Irving Howe and Eliezer Greenberg, 1977
The Stories of Dovid Bergelson: Yiddish Short Fiction from Russia, translated by Golda Werman, 1996

Plays
Prints reuveni [Prince Reuveni], performed 1946
Mir viln lebn [We Want to Live], 1946

Further Reading

Harshav, Benjamin, *The Meaning of Yiddish*, Berkeley: University of California Press, 1990
Harshav, Benjamin, *Language in Time of Revolution*, Berkeley: University of California Press, 1993
Howe, Irving and Eliezer Greenberg (editors), *A Treasury of Yiddish Stories*, New York: Schocken, 1973
Howe, Irving and Eliezer Greenberg, *Ashes Out of Hope: Fiction by Soviet Yiddish Writers*, New York: Schocken, 1977
Madison, Charles A., *Yiddish Literature: Its Scope and Major Writers*, New York: Schocken, 1971
Nakhimovsky, Alice Stone, *Russian-Jewish Literature and Identity*, Baltimore: Johns Hopkins University Press, 1992

Roskies, David G., *A Bridge of Longing: The Lost Art of Yiddish Storytelling*, Cambridge, Massachusetts: Harvard University Press, 1995
Sicher, Efraim, *Jews in Russian Literature after the October Revolution*, Cambridge and New York: Cambridge University Press, 1995
Waxman, Meyer, *A History of Jewish Literature*, 2nd edition, vol. 4, New York: T. Yoseloff, 1971
Wisse, Ruth R. (editor), *A Shtetl and Other Yiddish Novellas*, New York: Behrman House, 1973

Bergelson was recognized from his earliest publications as one of the major literary talents of his generation. In the stories and novels of the years before the October Revolution, he developed a unique Yiddish style designed to express the spiritual malaise of the Jewish youth of the small towns scattered across the Ukraine after the failure of the 1905 revolution. Bergelson was especially concerned with the lost and wasted lives of the young people who, as a result of their secular education and fluency in the Russian language, felt they had outgrown the intellectual and economic limitations of the shtetl, but were prevented by both state-sponsored and popular anti-Semitism from integrating into mainstream Russian society. Their frustrated eagerness to be part of the modern world beyond the narrow confines of traditional Jewish life found its supreme expression in Bergelson's creation of the character Mirl Hurvitz, the protagonist of his most famous novel, *Nokh alemen* (*When All is Said and Done*). Mirl is exceptional for being the first female character to hold centre stage in a Yiddish novel, as well as being the first to reject the roles of wife and mother in her search for meaning in her life. She represents the young woman in the transitional phase between tradition and modernity; intelligent and educated, but also passive and neurotic. Unlike many other writers in Yiddish, Hebrew, and non-Jewish-languages, Bergelson never wrote about the shtetl in terms of praise for the piety, suffering, and humility of its religious inhabitants. As he made clear in a 1930 essay, his conviction had always been that "it was time to leave the shtetl". Nonetheless, the Jewish towns of his youth remained the fundamental inspiration for Bergelson's work, despite his years of wandering and exile, and despite being reviled in his Soviet period.

Throughout his career, Bergelson was much exercised by the question of the artist's role in society, especially that of the Yiddish writer caught in the conflicting socio-political movements of assimilation, Zionism, and revolution. Under the combined pressure of personal and historical circumstances, he set out his thoughts as they evolved, in a series of essays that illustrate the arguments of the day about the major issues facing Russian Jewry, subjects that he treated imaginatively in his prose fiction as well as theoretically in his extensive journalistic production. The existential search for meaning that had ravaged the lives of the passive and tormented heroes of his pre-revolutionary stories gave way to characters meant to embody the certainties prescribed by the Communist Party. However, as the 1930s wore on, Bergelson was increasingly attacked in the Soviet Yiddish press for devising plots and protagonists that not only failed to measure up to the demands of socialist realism, but secretly revealed sympathy and abiding affection for the discredited Jewish ways that the October Revolution had consigned firmly to the past.

In the first of his theoretical articles on the relation between art and society in revolutionary times, Bergelson reveals his doubts about whether the Yiddish writer could speak with assurance and authority about a new world which he did not fully understand, and indeed, whether he could even find the words with which to do so. Inextricably rooted in and formed by the Jewish religion and nearly 1000 years of European Jewish history, Yiddish was not designed to serve the political ends now required of it. The first source of anxiety was the lack of appropriate images (*bilder*), untainted by association with the banished social order, with which to construct metaphors equal to the task of describing the new reality and assisting the reader in the task of radically reorganizing society. Bergelson was fearful of losing the established Yiddish readership by writing a denatured Yiddish without Hebrew words and idioms taken from religious customs. Equally, he was afraid of becoming irrelevant to younger readers who disdained narratives about the dead world of the shtetl, and preferred to read Russian anyway. Moreover, he never forgot his "bourgeois" background, a fact which made him vulnerable to dismissive criticism by the guardians of the proletariat dictatorship. Thus he was torn between the desire of the Yiddish artist to address the complex situation of his people without ambiguity, and the imperative of conforming to the dictates of the party. Ultimately, what was most damaging for Bergelson's integrity as a writer was his inability to confront the moral and aesthetic implications of trying to write about the Revolution without relating the brutality of the regime to Jewish ethics. These dilemmas are at the heart of the often contradictory, self-defeating artistic and private decisions Bergelson made.

In "Three Centres", a pivotal article that paved the way for his return to Moscow, Bergelson announced that, in his view, the Soviet Union was the only country where Yiddish had an assured future as a living language. Only the working classes, he maintained, saw in Yiddish an inseparable part of their identity and therefore retained their loyalty to it, unlike the American Jews, for whom English was a necessary means of assimilation into bourgeois society, or the Polish Jews, who were too religious, Zionist, or just backward to be interested in innovative forms of literature. Curiously, the bold declarations of his theoretical writings are not matched by similar daring in his prose fiction. The stories and the novel *Mides-hadin* [Strict Justice] which date from his Berlin period (1921–33) are marred in varying degrees by a lack of psychological subtlety and realism in the characterization, and plots that conform to predictable patterns. The material dealt with falls into two main categories: the civil war in Ukraine which he tried to approach without focusing on the pogroms (in which he and his family suffered), but rather emphasizing the obligation for the Jews to accept the inevitable triumph of Bolshevik power; and the lives of Russian-Jewish refugees in Berlin in the unequal battle with the painful disorientation of exile. "Tsvishn emigrantn" [Among Émigrés] in the collection *Shturemteg* [Stormy Days] combines the themes of the role of the writer as witness to his people's suffering, and the psychological damage wrought by war and exile. "In pansion fun di dray shvester" [In the Boarding House of the Three Sisters] and "Shvester" [Sisters] in *Velt-oys, velt-ayn* show Bergelson doing what he did better than almost any other Yiddish writer of his generation: create vivid, believable, complex female characters around whom the narrative develops. Because, however, his vision of a totalitarian dictatorship as a propitious environment for Yiddish culture proved aberrant, the work of his mature years was distorted by the limits imposed by Stalinist ideology. *Bam dnieper*, a two-volume autobiographical novel, arguably marks the nadir of the long process of debasement of Bergelson's talent. Nevertheless, his earlier writings distinguish Bergelson as an outstanding Yiddish stylist and sensitive portraitist of the children of the shtetl in their myriad struggles to survive the battering of 20th-century history.

DAFNA CLIFFORD

Berkoff, Steven

British dramatist, 1937–

Born in London, 3 August 1937. Educated at Hackney Downs Grammar School; Webber-Douglas Academy of Dramatic Art, 1958–59; École Jacques Lecoq, Paris, 1965. Married Shelley Lee in 1976. Actor in repertory in Nottingham, Liverpool, Coventry, and at Citizens' Theatre, Glasgow, for six years; founding director, London Theatre Group, 1973, which has produced many of his plays; actor and director in own plays and other works and films.

Selected Writings

Plays
In the Penal Colony, 1968
Metamorphosis, 1968
Agamemnon, 1971
The Trial, 1971
Knock at the Manor Gate, 1972
Miss Julie versus Expressionism, 1973
The Fall of the House of Usher, 1974
East, 1975
Greek, 1980
West, 1980
Decadence, 1981
Lunch, 1983 (first produced as *Mr Prufrock's Songs*, 1974)
The Tell-Tale Heart, 1985
Acapulco, 1986
Kvetch, 1986
Sink the Belgrano!, 1986
Massage, 1987
The Trial; Metamorphosis; In the Penal Colony: Three Theatre Adaptations from Franz Kafka, 1988
Decadence and Other Plays, 1989
The Collected Plays, 2 vols, 1994; as *Plays One* and *Plays Two*, 1996
Messiah, 2000
Plays Three, 2000

Fiction
Gross Intrusion and Other Stories, 1979
Graft: Tales of an Actor, 1998

Other
Steven Berkoff's America, 1988
A Prisoner in Rio, 1989
I am Hamlet, 1989
Coriolanus in Deutschland, 1992
The Theatre of Steven Berkoff, 1992
Overview, 1994
Meditations on Metamorphosis, 1995
Free Association: An Autobiography, 1996
Shakespeare's Villains, 1998
Richard II in New York, 1999
Sixty, 2000

Steven Berkoff is a playwright, prolific author and mesmerizing actor/director. He was born in Stepney, London to a family of Romanian Jewish background. His education was completed at the Webber-Douglas drama school and the famous École Jacques Lecoq in Paris which is a "university of mime and mimemic choreography". Berkoff has over many years established himself as one of the most innovative, intriguing, controversial, and unconventional members of the British theatrical scene.

As a writer his plays have covered every aspect of "la vie humaine", and a quantity of his work has been inspired by Greek mythology and the work of Edgar Allan Poe and Franz Kafka. It is virtually impossible to separate the writer from the actor as Berkoff performs in much of his own work. However his acting of other roles including those in Shakespeare, or as Hitler in the TV series based on Herman Wouk's *War and Remembrance*, have always left an indelible impression on those who have witnessed his extraordinary performances as either anti-heroes or psychotic villains.

Berkoff's acting is both hypnotic and threatening; always on the verge of getting out of control, permanently "on the edge", as are many of his plays. The language of his theatrical oeuvre is unpretentious, except when pretentiousness is part of the dramatic language; street vernacular is often foul and discomfiting but is written with intelligence, wit, and clarity. Little of this deliberate theatricality is to be found in his books, which are the work of a man of deep sensibility and culture.

His own portrayals are inspired by his work and training in mime and physical theatre, and his roles have been taken over by such performers as the great Russian dancer Mikhail Baryshnikov and Roman Polanski in the playwright's now greatly admired adaptation of Kafka's *Metamorphosis*. He admits to writing for a young public in the style and street-language to which they respond. His is not commercial theatre, his plays are written to be performed today for a contemporary and socially aware audience. Will they be retained for posterity?

It is safe to assume that the literary works – as opposed to his work as a playwright – will become standard works for theatrical study. The books, which include *I am Hamlet*, *Meditations on Metamorphosis*, and *Coriolanus in*

Deutschland, illustrate in human terms what it is to be both writer, director and actor vis-a-vis the rest of the world, what it is to create and convince, and what it is to experience critical animosity. Berkoff and the theatrical press have had stormy relationships; nevertheless a new Berkoff play is an event even for the most jaded pundit.

The Edinburgh Festival has always welcomed Berkoff, and the Scottish capital has been the scene for some of his most successful productions. One of the UK's most eminent theatre critics, Jack Tinker, stated that "there is simply no actor today with Berkoff's charismatic daring, both physical and vocal . . . to say this is a tour de force is to rob the phrase of all its meaning. It is a unique theatrical experience." In a long review in the *Financial Times* in August 1993 Anthony Thorncroft wrote, "Edgar Allan Poe and Steven Berkoff: a marriage made in Heaven or perhaps for some spectators Purgatory . . . So Berkoff performing Poe's *Tell Tale Heart* is an awesome experience . . . Berkoff brings death to life." The above reviews refer to his show *One Man*.

However it is probably through the first part of his autobiography, *Free Association*, that the real Steven Berkoff is encountered, for the theatrical persona and the real character of the writer are so completely at odds with each other. This is probably illustrated most clearly in the cover of his autobiography which shows a portrait of the actor with one side as himself, the other in full and disquieting make-up as Adolf Hitler.

Berkoff's Jewishness is apparent in his books, rarely in his plays. Unusually for the postwar generation of English Jews who made up what could be loosely termed the "London School" – Arnold Wesker, Harold Pinter, Bernard Kops, Wolf Mankowitz, and Lionel Bart – Berkoff is a fighter for his people. Although he states that he is English of Jewish origins, his outspoken love and admiration for the State of Israel and his people is rare and welcome. In a very moving passage in his autobiography Berkoff tells of being invited to recite the words of Eleazar of Massada to a group of tourists and wished that his mother "could have seen this wondrous land".

So, is Berkoff primarily an actor, director, or writer? In his case one aspect cannot be separated from another and is probably best summed up in his own words from the introduction to *I am Hamlet*: "No other play gives an actor such words of compassion, charm, wisdom, wit, moral force, insight and philosophy. The actor needs to feel those things within his own breast and to touch these words is to set alight a small flame within himself."

SALLY WHYTE

Bermant, Chaim

Polish-born British fiction writer and journalist, 1929–1998

Born in Breslev, 26 February 1929. Lived in Barovke, Latvia, 1933–38; father was last rabbi of Barovke. Traditional Jewish education. Moved with his family to Glasgow, 1938. Studied at Glasgow Yeshiva (rabbinical college), 1949–51; Glasgow University, MA 1955, MLitt 1960; London School of Economics, MSc 1957. Married artist Judith Weil, 1957; two sons and two daughters. Schoolmaster, 1955–57; economist 1957–58; scriptwriter for television, Glasgow and London, 1958–60; wrote for the *Daily Telegraph*, *Observer*, and *Newsweek*; feature writer, *Jewish Chronicle*, 1964 until his death. Awarded *Jewish Quarterly* Wingate Award for non-fiction, 1977. Died in London, 20 January 1998.

Selected Writings

Novels
Jericho Sleep Alone, 1964
Berl Make Tea, 1965
Ben Preserve Us, 1965
Diary of an Old Man, 1966
Swinging in the Rain, 1967
Here Endeth the Lesson, 1969
Now Dowager, 1971
Roses are Blooming in Picardy, 1972
The Last Supper, 1973
The Second Mrs Whitberg, 1976
The Squire of Bor Shachor, 1977
Now Newman was Old, 1978
The Patriarch, 1981
The House of Women, 1983
Dancing Bear, 1984
Titch, 1987
The Companion, 1988

Television Plays: *Pews*, 1980; *The Party*, 1981; *The Mole*, 1982; *There's One Born Every Minute*, 1983

Other
Israel, 1967
Troubled Eden: An Anatomy of British Jewry, 1969
The Cousinhood: The Anglo-Jewish Gentry, 1971
The Walled Garden: The Saga of Jewish Family Life and Tradition, 1974
Point of Arrival: A Study of London's East End, 1975
Coming Home, 1976
The Jews, 1977
Ebla: An Archaeological Enigma, with Michael Weitzmann, 1979
Belshazzar: A Cat's Story for Humans, 1982
What's the Joke? A Study of Jewish Humour through the Ages, 1986
Lord Jakobovits: The Authorised Biography of the Chief Rabbi, 1990
Murmurings of a Licensed Heretic, 1990
Genesis: A Latvian Childhood (intended first volume of autobiography, published posthumously), 1998
On the Other Hand, 2000

Further Reading

"Chaim Bermant" (obituary), *The Times* (23 January 1998)
Frankel, William, "He was the Son of a Preacher Man", *Jewish Chronicle* (20 June 2000)
Wheatcroft, Geoffrey, "Community Living", *New Statesman* (12 June 2000)

Journalist, historian, and the author of more than 20 novels, Chaim Bermant was best known as British Jewry's leading columnist and commentator. Bermant, son of a rabbi and shochet, was born in Poland, lived in Latvia and Glasgow, and spent most of his adult life with his family in Hampstead Garden Suburb, London. Although he was a yeshiva student and maintained traditional Jewish observances, he was often critical of the orthodox and ultra-orthodox rabbinate, particularly over issues of "fundamentalist" interpretation, and the blurring of the lines between politics and religion.

For more than 20 years he penned his outspoken "On the Other Hand" column in the *Jewish Chronicle,* frequently addressing fraught and controversial issues in a forthright and provocative fashion. In his column, syndicated in Jewish newspapers around the world, he deliberated on the Palestinians, human rights abuses in Israel, Jewish political extremism, the religious politics and practices of British Jews, religious bigotry, and Jewish spirituality. In his writings he stressed the moral dimensions of the Jewish tradition – a tradition deeper than remembering the Holocaust – with its long history of tolerance and humanity, a tradition that he was anxious was in danger of being lost or compromised. Two collections of his journalism, *Murmurings of a Licensed Heretic* and *On the Other Hand*, have been published.

In 1969 Bermant wrote *Troubled Eden*, a perceptive analysis of the relations between the various sectors of British Jewry, against the background of the history of immigration. He detailed the communal tensions and institutional rivalry, and portrayed a defensive leadership, which considered the "community" under siege by assimilation, modern scholarship, and new ideas and practices, all forces that threatened to lure away the young. His fascination with class, and in particular aristocracy, included an interest in the Anglo-Jewish elite. His accessible study, *The Cousinhood: The Anglo-Jewish Gentry*, traces the history and relationships between families, such as the Cohens, the Rothschilds, and the Montefiores, and their influence on English society. His other books on Anglo-Jewry include a study of changing immigrant communities in *Point of Arrival: A Study of London's East End*, and a generally sympathetic but occasionally critical biography, *Lord Jacobovits*.

Often critical of Israeli policies, and of the right-wing and religious elements in particular, Bermant remained a lifelong supporter of Jewish settlement in Israel. He spent time there before university, and moved there twice with his family, in the 1970s and again in the1980s. Bermant's experiences in Israel are reflected in his autobiography, *Coming Home*, and in his book, *Israel*. The culture gap experienced by many new immigrants to Israel is humorously reported in his novel, *The Squire of Bor Shachor*.

Bermant wrote books on modern Jewish experience (*The Jews*), on Jewish humour (*What's the Joke?*), and on Jewish family life and traditions (*The Walled Garden*). Before his death he completed the first book of his planned five-volume autobiography, *Genesis: A Latvian Childhood* (1998), which traces his first nine years, ending with the family leaving for Scotland before the outbreak of World War II. This account, framed by the seasons, of the now vanished rural shtetl life is centred on the village market and the bathhouse, with its cast of weird and wonderful characters.

Bermant's life and experience were creatively and imaginatively recast in many of his novels. In his first book, *Jericho Sleep Alone*, Jericho Broch is a young man from an orthodox Glasgow family. He joins a religious Zionist youth group, spends time on their training farm, travels to Israel, and later studies at Glasgow University. Jericho considers becoming a rabbi, and his cousin writes for the *Guardian*, the *Observer*, and the *Jewish Chronicle* and has just published his first novel! This story of youthful confusion and lack of direction includes a powerful evocation of his native Glasgow, returned to in other novels (*The Patriarch* and *The Second Mrs Whitberg*). His unhappy teaching experience in a secondary modern school in Essex is put to good use in *Here Endeth the Lesson*.

A number of his novels focus on tensions within Jewish families, and between the generations (*Ben Preserve Us*, *Swinging in the Rain*, *The Patriarch*, *The House of Women*, and *The Last Supper*), and a number of themes are repeated, such as the young protagonist sleeping with his aunt (*Dancing Bear*, *The Patriarch*). In *Diary of an Old Man*, he focuses on the weaknesses of old age and the prejudices that the elderly experience, as we follow Cyril through a cold winter month, sharing his loneliness and feeling his decreasing grip on reality. In *Roses are Blooming in Picardy* and *Now Newman was Old*, Bermant sensitively creates elderly characters who reflect on their lives and loves amid the difficulties of failing memory and other frailties.

Bermant imaginatively explores Jewish identity at the margins, in a family where only a residue of Jewish experience remains (*The House of Women*), where the protagonist may not be Jewish at all (*Dancing Bear*), where Jewish identity and conversion are questioned (*Now Dowager*), and in a man's search for his past after the Holocaust (*Titch*).

Referring to his early novels, Bermant includes himself among the "Golders Green novelists". These were the Jewish writers of north London who wrote about mostly prosperous and materialistic middle-class, and, in Bermant's case, orthodox, Jewish life in the suburbs. Chaim Raphael characterized *Now Dowager* "as if Sholem Aleichem had been rewritten by P.G. Wodehouse" and it would seem an apposite comment for many of his novels. Bermant is not only a competent novelist but a very funny one. The humour is of context and situation, and his characters, while sometimes down, are rarely beaten. His fluently and engagingly written books are optimistic (love and friendship are always possibilities), do raise serious issues, and are eminently readable, and, although most of his characters are Jewish, their perplexities, problems, and relationships are universal.

Bermant wrote that in Latvia he was a Pole, in Poland a Lett, in Scotland a foreigner, and in Israel he became a Scot, but the truth is that underlying these nationalist labels he was a Jew, certain in his identity. And it is from this certainty that he was sufficiently confident to ask difficult questions, challenge the ruling authorities, and share the exuberance of his rich Jewish spirit.

PAUL MORRIS

Bialik, Hayyim Nahman

Russian poet, fiction writer, and essayist, 1873–1934

Born in Radi, Ukraine, 11 January 1873. Studied at Volozhin Talmudic Academy, Lithuania. Settled in Odessa, 1891. Married Manya Auerbach, 1893. Moved to Zhitomir; taught Hebrew in Jewish schools, 1896–1900. Returned to Odessa, 1900; founded Moriah publishing house. Settled in Warsaw, 1904; literary editor, *Hashiloah*, Warsaw, 1904–09. Regular contributor of poems to several journals. Participated in Zionist congresses, 1907, 1913, 1921, 1931. Moved to Berlin, 1921; founded Dvir publishing house. Emigrated to Palestine, 1924; settled in Tel Aviv. President, Hebrew Writers' Union and Hebrew Language Council, Jerusalem. Died in Vienna, 4 July 1934.

Selected Writings

Poetry
Poems, 1901
Poems, 1908
Poems from the Hebrew, edited by Leonard V. Snowman, 1924
The Writings of H.N. Bialik, 1924
Aggadat shloshah vearbaah [The Legend of Three and Four], 1930
Poems and Songs, 1933
Collected Poems: Critical Edition, 1938
The Writings of H.N. Bialik, 4 vols, 1938
Far over the Sea, translated by Jessie E. Sampter, 1939
Hayyim Nachman Bialik: Complete Poetic Works (includes bibliography), edited by I. Ephros, 1948
Selected Poems, translated by Maurice Samuel, 1972
Chaim Nahman Bialik: Selected Poems, translated by Ruth Nevo, 1981
Shirot Bialik: A New and Annotated Translation of Hayyim Nahman Bialik's Epic Poem, translated by Steven L. Jacobs, 1987
The Poems of Bialik, 1987

Other
Rabbinic Lore: sefer haagadah, 1908–11
Translator, *Don Quixote*, 1912
Translator, *William Tell*, 1923
Editor, *Collected Works of Solomon ibn Gabirol*, 1924
Editor, *Collected Works of Moses ibn Ezra*, 1928
Lectures and Ad devarim shebeal, 2 vols, 1935
And it Came to Pass: Legends and Stories about King David and King Solomon, translated by Herbert Danby, 1938
Letters: iggerot, 5 vols, 1938–39
Aftergrowth and Other Stories, translated by I.M. Lask, 1939
Knight of Onions and Knight of Garlic, translated by Herbert Danby, 1939
The Hebrew Book: An Essay, translated by Minnie Halkin, 1951
The Book of Legends, translated by William G. Braude, 1992
Random Harvest: The Novellas of Bialik, edited by David Patterson and Ezra Spicehandler, 1999
A Bialik Treasury: Selections from the Works of Hayyim Nahman Bialik, edited by Jacob E. Segal, no date

Further Reading

Aberbach, David, *Bialik*, London: Halban, and New York: Grove Press, 1988
Breslauer, S. Daniel, *The Hebrew Poetry of Hayyim Nahman Bialik*, Lewiston, New York, and Lampeter, Dyfed: Mellen Press, 1991
Burnshaw, Stanley, T. Carmi and Ezra Spicehandler (editors and translators), *The Modern Hebrew Poem Itself*, New York: Holt Rinehart and Winston, 1965
Goell, Yohai, *Bibliography of Modern Hebrew Literature in English Translation*, Jerusalem and New York: Israel Universities Press, 1968
Ovadyahu, Mordechai (editor), *Bialik Speaks: Words from the Poet's Lips, Clues to the Man*, translated by A. El-Dror, New York: Herzl Press, 1969

Hayyim Nahman Bialik is the greatest modern Hebrew poet. Born in a small Ukrainian village whose lush environment was to colour his lyric poetry throughout much of his career, he was raised in Zhitomir by his grandfather after his father's untimely death when Bialik was about six years old. The move to Zhitomir's densely settled and unaesthetic lumber dealers' suburb had a traumatic effect upon the imaginative child. His grandfather was a pious, learned Hasid who treated his gifted but mischievous grandchild (whom in his odd way he dearly loved) with the severity meted out to children of the time: "Spare the rod, spoil the child."

During his adolescence, Bialik discovered the literature of the *Haskalah* (the Jewish Enlightenment) and began to question the restrictive traditional life of the Jewish shtetl (small town). Determined to leave Zhitomir to obtain a secular education, he was led to believe that the curriculum of the famous Volozhin Yeshiva included some secular subjects. He prevailed upon his grandfather to send him to Volozhin. Arriving there at the age of 16, he discovered that the school had remained a traditional Talmudic academy that excluded secular studies. Nevertheless, the new spirit of the Enlightenment had permeated its student body. Bialik soon became a leading figure of the students' literary society that aimed at a synthesis of the traditional with modernity. Several members of the society were admirers of the cultural nationalist and Zionist essayist Ahad Ha'am, who urged a secular ethnical-nationalist reading of the Jewish past. Influenced by August Comte, Ahad Ha'am had advocated the translation of Jewish religious customs and values into a modern secularist nationalist ones. Bialik became a devout Ahad Ha'amist and soon decided to leave Volozhin for Odessa, the centre of the Ahad Ha'am cultural national movement. Yet Volozhin had done the young Bialik a great service. At Volozhin he learned enough Russian to begin appreciating Russian poetry, particularly by the works of Samuel Frug, a romantic Russian Jewish poet whose Yiddish and Russian verse frequently dealt with Jewish national and religious themes.

He arrived in Odessa, a shy teenager still dressed in the traditional Jewish garb. He was able to contact a number of proto-Zionist Hebrew writers and intellectuals and showed his notebook crammed with callow poems to H.Y. Ravnitsky, editor of *Hapardes,* an Ahad Ha'mist literary review. Ravnitsky was impressed by "To the Bird", one of Bialik's romantic Zionist poems and agreed to publish it.

Unable to find employment in Odessa, he returned to his grandfather's home in Zhitomir. His later recollection of his stay in Odessa during his twenties was as a period of frustration and deep despair. He felt himself trapped in a civilization that was moribund. In later poems the image of his stern grandfather is presented as a composite of a Godfearing venerable sage representing an ancient and venerable tradition on the one hand, and, on the other, an aged man declining into senility. This ambivalent view of the tradition pervades much of his poetry until the early 1900s.

During this period Bialik entered an arranged marriage to a daughter of a prominent lumber merchant. He was engaged for some time in his father-in-law's forestry business. Many of his later novellas and short stories depict the lives and struggles of the Jewish foresters or the lumber merchants, their love/hate relationship with their non-Jewish neighbours and employees (*Random Harvest*). Bialik gained the reputation as the foremost Hebrew poet of his generation. He wrote either lyrical nature poetry or cultural ethnic verse animated with proto-Zionist convictions. His long poem "The Talmud Student" reflected his ambivalence toward the asceticism of Orthodox Judaism and its irrelevance in a modern world and yet expressed his admiration for its deep commitment to a religious way of life. Under the influence of Russian poetry, Bialik abandoned the older syllabic poetry that prevailed in Hebrew literature during the *Haskalah* for the tonal syllabic metres employed in Russian poetry. He tended to use conventional poetic genres (odes, lyrical poems, etc.), though he experimented with the use of varying metres within the same poem. He had great command of the resources of Hebrew literature of all ages and possessed an extraordinary skill with rhyme.

In the 1890s an economic crisis in Russia compelled him to quit the forestry trade and became a Hebrew teacher – an experience that ultimately led him to produce or edit Hebrew school texts and children's poems (among them *The Book of Legends*) suitable for the many modern Hebrew schools that had now begun spreading in Russia. His old dream of moving to Odessa, a major centre of Hebrew literature, was finally realized when he was offered the position of head teacher in a new Ahad Ha'amist elementary school established in that city. In 1900 he and his wife moved to Odessa, the beautiful modern city on the shores of the Black Sea. Except for a period of about a year when he served as the literary editor of *Hashiloah* in Warsaw, he lived in Odessa until 1924. In Odessa and Warsaw he composed his major works including many long poems. "The Pool" is a long nature poem of exquisite beauty in which the pond symbolizes the psyche of the artist. "The Dead of the Desert" is based upon a Talmudic legend that the generation of the Exodus from Egypt condemned to die in the desert and not enter the Promised Land actually still lives asleep in the desert awaiting redemption. This poem employs a Promethean-like theme. The dead arise in different periods of Jewish history in rebellion against God's decree and attempt to wrest redemption from Him only to be repelled by the deity and forced to return to their eternal sleep. "In the City of Slaughter" forms a stark description of the well-known pogrom in Kishinev, and Bialik castigates the Jews for their passive cowering before their assailants and cries out against God who in an age of disbelief is helplessly bankrupt and unable to save His people. Translated into Yiddish and Russian, this long poem inspired Jewish youth to organize self-defence militias to protect Jews from further massacres. "The Scroll of Fire" is a symbolist poem based on an ancient Jewish legend about the storing away of the sacred fire (inspiration, courage) once lit on the altar of the Temple, so that it be preserved and ultimately restored when Israel would be redeemed. The protagonist is a young man (the poet?) who sets out to discover the fire, but when, after many frustrating encounters and tribulations, he finally discovers it he is distracted by the sight of a luscious maiden (Eros, personal fulfilment as opposed to national commitment) and drops the brand of fire into a swirling river and thus fails to bring about the redemption. He nevertheless persists in his quest for salvation.

World War I and the Russian Revolution which followed in its wake destroyed the great cultural renaissance of Russian Jewry. Bialik abandoned Russia and migrated first to Berlin (1921), where he transferred the publishing house he had founded in Odessa, and then to Tel Aviv, Palestine (1924), where he became the cultural mentor of the growing Jewish community there.

Despite his deep Zionist convictions, Bialik wrote only a few poems in Tel Aviv. The immigrant culture of that city was no match for the eastern European world and its rooted Jewish culture destroyed by the communist revolution. The revival of spoken Hebrew – a project to which he devoted so much effort – also created a serious poetic crisis for those Hebrew poets who like Bialik accented their Hebrew in the old eastern European manner and not in the Sephardic accent which was used in Palestine. Bialik wrote several poems circumventing the problem by employing so-called biblical cadences – among them, "Departure", an unfinished biographical poem composed during the last years of his life. He also wrote a truly magnificent symbolist poem, the "Legend of the Three and Four" – set in the days of King Solomon, but its veiled theme was the hope that the revival of the Jewish National Home would lead to a synthesis between Judaism and western culture.

Bialik was not a prolific writer, but he nevertheless was one of the greatest Hebrew poets in all of Jewish history. He published several poems in Yiddish but stubbornly wrote most of his works in Hebrew, believing that Yiddish was doomed to die out in eastern Europe but that Hebrew would enjoy the revival he and Ahad Ha'am had hoped for in the reborn Jewish national home. The decimation of eastern European Jewry in World War II unfortunately proved him right.

Bialik was not only a skilled poet but a superb short-story writer. He also wrote and/or published Hebrew textbooks, edited and issued collections of modern Hebrew poetry, and together with his collaborator Y.H. Ravitsk, published a brilliant anthology of Talmudic legends. He translated several acts of Shakespeare's *Julius Caesar*, Schiller's *The*

Robbers, and an abridged version of Cervantes's *Don Quixote*. His literary legacy also includes a series of brilliant essays. As a tough but intelligent editor he had a lasting impact on most of his younger contemporaries, many of whom became important Hebrew writers in the generation which succeeded his own.

He died suddenly in 1934 in Vienna after he had undergone surgery.

EZRA SPICEHANDLER

Biller, Maxim

Czechoslovak-born German journalist and fiction writer, 1960–

Born in Prague, 25 August 1960. Moved with his family to West Germany in 1970; studied German literature, history, and philosophy in Hamburg and Munich; MA, 1983–84; journalism school, Munich, 1984. Freelance writer and journalist since 1985; columnist for journal *Tempo*; member of editorial board of *Jewish Quarterly*, 1996–97; columnist for *Die Zeit* since 1996. Awarded Tukan Prize, 1994; Otto Stoessel Prize, 1996; Prize of the Europäische Feuilletons, 1996.

Selected Writings

Stories
Wenn ich einmal reich und tot bin [When I'll be Rich and Dead], 1990
Die Tempojahre [The Tempo Years], 1991
Land der Väter und Verräter [Land of Fathers and Traitors], 1994
Harlem Holocaust, 1998
Die Tochter [The Daughter], 2000

Essays and Interviews
Aufbruch nach Deutschland: Sechzehn Foto-Essays, edited by Sybille Bergemann *et al.*, 1993
Brauchen wir eine neue Gruppe 47? Interviews mit Joachim Kaiser und Maxim Biller: 55 Fragebögen zur deutschen Literatur, edited by Joachim Leser and Georg Guntermann, 1995

Further Reading

Becker, Peter von, "Ein Buch dieser Jahre und Tage", *Süddeutsche Zeitung* (4 April 1990)
Feinberg, Anat, "Abiding in a Haunted Land: The Issue of Heimat in Contemporary German-Jewish Writing", *New German Critique*, 70 (1997)
Gilman, Sander L., *Jews in Today's German Culture*, Bloomington: Indiana University Press, 1995
Gilman, Sander L. and Karen Remmler (editors), *Reemerging Jewish Culture in Germany: Life and Literature since 1989*, New York: New York University Press, 1994
Goetz, Rainald, "Alles was knallt", *Der Spiegel* (6 January 1992)
Koch, Gertrud, "Corporate Identities: Zur Prosa von Dische, Biller und Seligmann", *Babylon*, 7 (1990)
Köppen, Manuel, "Auschwitz im Blick der zweiten Generation: Tendenzen der Gegenwartsprosa (Biller, Grossman, Schindel)" in *Kunst und Literatur nach Auschwitz*, edited by Köppen *et al.*, Berlin: Schmidt, 1993
Nolden, Thomas, "Contemporary German Jewish Literature", *German Life and Letters*, 47/1 (1994)
Nolden, Thomas, *Junge jüdische Literatur: Konzentrisches Schreiben in der Gegenwart*, Würzburg: Königshausen und Neumann, 1995
Seibt, Gustav, "Der letzte Augenblick der Unschuld", epilogue to Biller's *Harlem Holocaust*, Cologne: Kiepenheuer und Witsch, 1998
Shelliem, Jochanan, "Maxim Biller. Ein Gespräch", *Listen*, 20 (1990)

Maxim Biller – who describes himself as "Deutscher wider Willen" [German against his will] – is one of the most important representatives of the new generation of Jewish writers who emerged in the 1980s. They were the children and grandchildren of the survivors of the Holocaust who for various reasons had decided not to turn their backs on Germany. Like many of his contemporaries, Biller raises the question as to which role he is supposed to play in society. Equipped with an extraordinary selfconsciousness, he sets off to attack and disavow the hypocrisy with which, according to Biller, the Germans deal with their recent past. In his column in the journal *Tempo*, which significantly bears the title "Hundert Zeilen Hasse" [Hundred Lines of Hatred], he seeks open confrontation with his contemporaries, including the Jews who have adapted themselves to Germany. He repeatedly states that all their lies are getting on his nerves. Also, his position towards the German Holocaust memorial is characterized by undisguised aggressiveness:

> etwas ist faul, wenn sie [die Deutschen, BH] sich immer wieder auf diese offene exhibitionistische Art an etwas berauschen, das jedem anderen Volk so peinlich wäre, daß es alles dafür täte, es vergessen zu machen. [There is something wrong about constantly indulging in an exhibitionist attitude, a topic which would be so embarrassing for every other nation that it would do everything to forget].

Biller quickly became the prototype of the new Jewish writer generation. His assaults on literature and society are collected in *Die Tempojahre* [The Tempo Years], a book that shows this new Jewish attitude. Instead of taking on the classical Jewish role of the victim, Biller prefers to express his feelings and thoughts without restraint. The German writer Rainald Goetz views him as an *agent provocateur* of the literary scene and welcomes Biller's uncompromisingly critical attitude towards the *Gähnomat-Kritiker* (yawn-machine-critics):

> Und es gibt eben Maxim Biller, der haut da überall sauber drauf. Und zwar mit dem goldrichtigen Hammer einer unmittelbaren Vernunft, die nicht dauernd noch sich selbst höchst selbstquälerisch in Frage stellt. [And there is Maxim Biller who hits the nail right on the head, using the

appropriate hammer of a reasoning that does not always masochistically cast doubt on itself.]

His first collection of short stories *Wenn ich einmal reich und tot bin* [When I'll be Rich and Dead] immediately gained the full attention of the literary critics. Through his shockingly open and provocative narrations, he unveils both Jewish and German self-delusions and hypocrisies. Biller sketches cliché-laden portraits of typical Jews who had become rich, wealthy, famous, and successful members of postwar Germany. In his parable-like stories, celebrities – such as the chairman of the Zentralrat deutscher Juden or the president of the Federal Republic of Germany – can easily be detected: facts and fiction merge into one another. In *Land der Väter und Verräter* [Land of Fathers and Traitors], Biller's overall cynical attitude becomes even more obvious. Again, Biller depicts the neuroses of his contemporaries when they face the horrors of the Third Reich and emphasizes that an entirely unprejudiced approach to the past is needed. Can something positive spring from such a self-tormenting manner of handling the Holocaust, he asks himself and adds: "Sie sollten . . . begreifen, dass eine freundliche, offene Nation nie aus dem Horror entstehen kann, sondern aus einem Traum." [They should understand . . . that an open and friendly nation can never develop out of horror but out of a dream.]

His latest book, *Harlem Holocaust*, is written as a novel within a novel. Employing the technique of the fictive editor, Biller claims in the epilogue that the whole story is the product of a Jew named Warzawski. Biller himself, however, wishes to be detached from a grotesque, at times off-puttingly obscene, story as it is allegedly just a document. The lack of taste and the constant violation of taboos are nothing more than the pointless efforts of the Jewish "wannabee-author" Warzawski. Nonetheless the novel offers a very sharp-sighted kaleidoscope of the double-mindedness in present-day Germany.

Although Biller is at times criticized for his provocative mixture of "Shoah und Scheisse" (Thomas Miessgang), he can undoubtedly be regarded as one of the most outstanding figures among contemporary Jewish writers.

BIRGIT HAAS

Bloch, Jean-Richard

French essayist, fiction writer, and critic, 1884–1947

Born 1884 into secular but culturally Jewish family in Paris. Stirred into greater awareness of Jewish heritage by Dreyfus affair. Studied at the Sorbonne, *agrégé* in history, 1907. Married Marguerite Herzog, sister of the writer André Maurois. Founded or co-founded three journals: *L'Effort Libre,* 1910; *Europe* (with Romain Rolland), 1924; and *Ce Soir* (with Louis Aragon), 1937. Taught history in secondary schools in Lons-le-Saunier and Poitiers until 1910, when he began to devote himself to writing. Nominated to the Institut français de Florence, 1913. Visited Palestine, 1925. Left Paris to escape deportation, 1941; spent remaining years of World War II in Moscow, working for Radio Free France. Returned to Paris, 1945; resumed editorship of *Ce Soir.* Appointed Councillor of the Republic, 1946. Died in Paris, 1947.

Selected Writings

Novels and Essays

Lévy: premier livre de contes, 1912

. . . *et Cie,* 1918; as . . . *and Co.*, translated by C.K. Scott-Moncrieff, 1929

Carnaval est mort: premiers essais pour mieux comprendre mon temps [Carnival is Dead: First Essays towards a Better Understanding of My Time], 1920

La Nuit kurde, 1920; as *A Night in Kurdistan*, translated by Stephen Haden-Guest, 1931

À la découverte du monde connu [Discovering the Known World], 1924

Sur un cargo [On a Cargo Boat], 1924

Première journée à Rufisque [First Day at Rufisque], 1926

Forces du monde: drame écrit pour un musicien d'après une nouvelle du comte de Gobineau [Forces of the World: Drama Written for a Musician Based on a Short Story by Count Gobineau], 1927

Le Dernier Empereur [The Last Emperor], 1927

Les Chasses de Renaut [Renaut's Hunts], 1927

Cacaouettes et bananes [Peanuts and Bananas], 1929

Destin du théâtre [Fate / Destiny of the Theatre], 1930

Destin du siècle: seconds essais pour mieux comprendre mon temps [The Century's Destiny: Second Essays to Better Understand my Time], 1931

Sybilla, 1932

Offrande à la politique: troisièmes essais pour mieux comprendre mon temps [Offering to Politics], 1933

L'anoblissement en France au temps de François Ier: essai d'une définition de la condition juridique et sociale de la noblesse au début du XVIe siècle, 1934

Espagne, Espagne! [Spain, Spain!], 1936

Naissance d'une culture: quatrièmes essais pour mieux comprendre mon temps [Birth of a Culture], 1936

Chantez avec nous! [Sing with Us!], 1945

Moscou–Paris [Moscow–Paris], 1947

De la France trahie à la France en armes [From France Betrayed to France at War], 1949

L'Homme du communisme: portrait de Staline [Man of Communism: Portrait of Stalin], 1949

"Le Robinson juif" [The Jewish Robinson], *Europe*, 495 (1970)

Other

Bloch, Jean-Richard and Romain Rolland, *Deux hommes se recontrent: correspondance . . . 1910–1918*, 1964

Further Reading

Abraham, Pierre, *Les Trois Frères* [The Three Brothers], Paris: Les Editeurs Français Réunis, 1971

Albertini, Jean, *Avez-vous lu Jean-Richard Bloch?* [Have You Read Jean-Richard Bloch?], Paris: Sociales, 1981

Aragon, Louis (editor), *Les Plus Belles Pages de Jean-Richard Bloch* [Jean-Richard Bloch's Best Pages], Paris: La Bibliothèque Française, 1948

Blum, Antoinette, "L'Altérité du Juif dans l'oeuvre de Jean-Richard Bloch" [The Otherness of the Jew in the Work of Jean-Richard Bloch] in *Europa Provincia Mundi: Essays in Comparative Literature and European Studies*, edited by Joep Leerssen and Karl Ulrich Syndram, Amsterdam: Rodopi, 1992

Études Jean-Richard Bloch, *Journal of the Association Études Jean-Richard Bloch Europe*, March–April 1957, June 1966 (special issues)

Gorilovics, Tivadar (editor), *Retrouver Jean-Richard Bloch* [Rediscovering Jean-Richard Bloch], Debrecen: Kossuth Lajos Tudományegyetem, 1994

Prochasson, Christophe, "L'Effort libre de Jean-Richard Bloch", *Cahiers Georges Sorel*, 5 (1987)

Trebitsch, Michel, preface to *Destin du siècle*, by Bloch, Paris: Presses Universitaires de France, 1996

Jean-Richard Bloch is best known in contemporary France as an intellectual who divided his time between political activism and writing. His curiosity and energy inspired him to explore many genres of writing, including novels, plays, essays, and journalistic articles, all of which were marked by his politics. Despite his prolific writing, only two fictional works address Judaism and Jewish identity: the short story *Lévy* and the novel . . . *et Cie* (. . . *and Co.*). Another short story, "Une Irruption de nouveaux Dieux" [An Irruption of New Gods], also mentions Jewish identity, but only within the context of mocking all organized religion in France. Therefore, while the story does mention the Jewish religion, it does not engage with larger questions of Jewish identity as do the other two works. In addition to these short stories, Bloch presented a speech for the inauguration of the Hebrew University of Jerusalem in 1925, and wrote about Jewish identity in his collection of essays, *Destin du siècle*. While perhaps not immediately apparent, Bloch's Jewish identity both directly and indirectly informs all his writing and his brand of intellectualism.

Bloch's family originated from Alsace, and there is evidence of their presence on both sides in France dating back to the Revolution. Bloch grew up in a non-religious, but culturally Jewish, home. His father, a Polytéchnicien who worked as a chief engineer for the Ponts et Chaussées, stressed a rational and sceptical, rather than a religious approach to life. The Dreyfus affair profoundly marked Bloch's adolescence. His brother, Pierre Abraham, wrote that whereas his older brother, Marcel, was beaten by other students at school, Jean-Richard became quiet, pale, and experienced terrible headaches. Indeed, the Dreyfus affair and the question of French-Jewish identity dominate both *Lévy* and . . . *et Cie*.

Written in 1910, *Lévy* tells the story of a small Jewish community's struggle with integration into France during the most heated moments of the Dreyfus affair and then some ten years later. This story exemplifies both Bloch's strong belief in integration and his understanding of the identity crisis it provokes. The first part of the story, which occurs on the eve of Colonel Henry's suicide, portrays the realities of life for Mr Lévy and his family. Children mock him and shout "Death to the Jews" when they see him; the few other Jews in the community complain about their persecution and exclusion; and, in a moment of anti-Semitic passion, Lévy's shop is burnt down by an uncontrollable crowd which threatens to drown his children and rape his wife. Ten years later, however, the situation has changed completely. Lévy is now fully integrated into the town, he has been elected to the local government, and his business is thriving. His son attends the most prestigious public school in France, the École Normale Supérieure. Yet for all the success that this integration has brought, Lévy bemoans the fact that the younger generation no longer practices Judaism or even considers itself culturally Jewish. For this reason, he ponders the need to bring about a "new Affair", which would remind the young of their origins. While Bloch suggests that the best solution to coping with anti-Semitic discrimination is for the Jewish community to stay put, not flee persecution, and create its place in society, this solution is not without tension. While "staying put" eventually creates an atmosphere of tolerance, this same climate of tolerance also entails the loss of cultural and religious identity for the Jews.

Bloch examines the French-Jewish identity question in more depth in his "Balzacien" novel . . . *et Cie*, published in 1918. Once again, Bloch represents Jewish identity in France as a delicate balance and ultimate struggle between old traditions and modernity, exclusion and inclusion, and the preservation of versus the loss of identity. . . . *et Cie*, whose plot was inspired by his in-laws' experiences, follows the Simlers, a Jewish family of cloth manufacturers from Strasbourg, over three generations after they opt to remain French in the wake of the loss of Alsace and Lorraine to the Prussians in 1871. The Simlers face initial isolation and exclusion from the local anti-Semitic merchants. Over time, however, they are accepted by the villagers, and their business thrives. Although the Simlers seem happy to belong in the new town, they continue to separate themselves from certain aspects of mainstream Frenchness, particularly intermarriage. When one of the Simler sons falls in love with a non-Jew, the family, which has grown increasingly secular and distant from its religious roots, nevertheless pressures him to marry a Jewish cousin and "remain faithful to the family" rather than pursue his own happiness. The Simler family comes to represent tradition in the face of modernity, and to provide an example of how such traditional ideology fares when confronted with change. Bloch elucidates this same theme in his parallel portrayal of the class struggle between the factory workers and the owners, whose paternalist system of running their business becomes increasingly outmoded, ineffectual, and inhumane. For Bloch, the Simler patriarchs represent the Old World, their children a transitional generation, and their grandchildren the coming age of modernity.

Bloch saw the Jew as a universal figure. In "Le Robinson juif", he states that the Jew should be the "Oriental in the Occident, the Occidental in the Orient". For him, the Jew would be a "universal witness, a spectator of others and himself". Bloch understood the figure of the Jew as representative of the modern man, about whom he writes in *Destin du siècle*. He claims that while Christian morality pertains to the individual, Jewish morality pertains to the society. The Jew, in Bloch's mind, would help to bring disparate groups together, toward a universalism that would bring peace. This image of the Jew coincides with Bloch's belief in socialism and communism, which marked his entire oeuvre as well as his life.

Bloch left Paris in 1941 to escape deportation to the concentration camps. He spent the war years in Moscow working at Radio Free France. He returned to Paris in 1945, where he died in 1947.

NANCY GREY

Brenner, Yosef Hayyim

Russian fiction writer, 1881–1921

Born in Novi Mlini, Ukraine, 1881. Received religious education but as young man joined Jewish socialist movement, the Bund, and later became Zionist. Published first short story, 1900. Served in Russian imperial army, 1902–04, but at outbreak of Russo–Japanese War, 1904, escaped to London. Worked as typesetter, and edited *Hameorer*, 1906. Moved to L'viv, 1908; edited *Revivim*. Contributed to journals of the Second Aliyah, writing in both Hebrew and Yiddish. Emigrated to Palestine, 1909. Worked as agricultural labourer on Kibbutz Hadera; moved to Jaffa, 1915; taught Hebrew literature at Herzlia High School. After Jews were driven out of Jaffa by Ottoman authorities, moved to Jerusalem, where he edited *Haadamah* from 1920. Active in Poalei Zion movement; founder member of Histadrut labour union, 1920. Killed by Arab rioters, 2 May 1921.

Selected Writings

Fiction

Meemek akhor [From the Valley of Trouble], 1901
Bahoref [In Winter], 1904
Misaviv lanekudah [Around the Point], 1904
Min hametser, 1909; as *Out of the Depths*, translated by David Patterson, 1992
Atsabim, 1910; as *Nerves* in *Eight Great Hebrew Short Novels*, edited by Alan Lelchuk and Gershon Shaked, 1983
Mikan umikan [From Here and There], 1911
Hamotsa [The Way Out], 1919
Shekhol vekishalon, 1920; as *Breakdown and Bereavement*, translated by Hillel Halkin, 1971
Ketavim [Collected Works], edited by Menachem Dorman, 1977
Haketavim hayidiyim / Di Yiddishe shriftn [The Yiddish Writings], edited by Yitzhak Bacon, 1985

Further Reading

Brinker, Menahem, *Ad ha-simt ah ha-teveryanit* [Narrative Art and Social Thought in Y.H. Brenner's Work], Tel Aviv: Am Oved, 1990
Even, Josef, *Omanut ha-sipur shel Y.H. Brenner* [Y.H. Brenner's Craft of Fiction], Jerusalem: Mossad Bialik, 1977
Shaked, Gershon, *Le-lo motsa: al Y.H. Brenner, M.Y. Berdishevski, G. Shofman ve-A.N. Gnessin* [Dead End: Studies in Y.H. Brenner, M.Y. Berdyczewski, G. Shofman, and A.N. Gnessin], Tel Aviv: Hotsaat hakibuts hameuhad, 1973

Yosef Hayyim Brenner is the apotheosis of a group of Hebrew writers in the late 19th and early 20th centuries known in Hebrew as the *telushim*, or "uprooted ones". These writers were the heirs of the *Haskalah*, or Hebrew Enlightenment, a Jewish cultural movement that strove to break down the barriers between European Jews and European culture. The *telushim* wrote in still-developing modern Hebrew and largely turned their backs on the religious beliefs and practices of their parents, yet they found that once they had abandoned the traditional Jewish community, they could find no place to replant themselves.

For some, Zionism was the answer, and many left Europe to build new lives in the land of Israel. But Brenner's was the first and most strident voice to claim that Zion itself was not all the Jews had hoped it would be, and that the damage done to the Jewish spirit in exile could not be so easily repaired. Most of Brenner's fiction depicts the agonies of daily life in primitive Palestine, underscoring the physical suffering and moral corruption of Jews who had supposedly achieved redemption. In his essay "Hazhanr haerets yisreeli" [The Land-of-Israel Genre], he severely criticized writers who tried to beautify the Zionist experiment at the expense of depicting reality. Yet his work often leaves its readers room to believe that hope may spring from despair.

A journalist, critic, translator, teacher, editor, Labor Zionist, and socialist, Brenner was a realist both in the style and content of his writing, and his fiction is perhaps best described as psychological realism. In Hebrew letters he was most influenced by M.Y. Berdyczewski and by S.Y. Abramovitch (Mendele Moykher Sforim), both of whom, Berdyczewski through naturalism and Abramovitch through satire, criticized the weaknesses of the Jews in improving their own conditions. From other languages, Brenner found inspiration in the German philosopher Friedrich Nietzsche, and in Russian authors such as Tolstoi and particularly Dostoevskii who focused on the private agonies of the alienated individual.

Unlike many of his contemporaries in Hebrew, particularly poets such as Bialik, Brenner did not attempt to write in an elevated Hebrew style. His language is gritty and earthy, resorting to biblical references only rarely and mainly for ironic effect. While some Hebrew novelists used highbrow biblical language in their dialogue because the spoken language had not yet taken hold, Brenner struggled to imitate the way real people spoke, borrowing from Aramaic and other sources to expand the boundaries of the developing modern language. His dialogue, which he uses prolifically, is littered with stutterings, ellipses, repetitions, and the difficulties of ordinary people in expressing their feelings. Aiming for honesty above all else, Brenner often employs the confessional monologue. His protagonists are largely intellectual, self-reflective anti-heroes who share many traits later prominent in European existentialist characters, and a strong autobiographical strain runs through his work. His fiction is fragmented and episodic, and this makes much of his work seem unpolished or even clumsy.

Brenner, however, believed in literature as a social rather than an aesthetic instrument, and he was firmly dedicated to showing his readers not only what life was, but what it wasn't and what it should be.

Brenner's most important fiction work by far is his psychological realist novel *Shekhol vekhishalon* (translated as *Breakdown and Bereavement*). Brenner's best-known translation into Hebrew was Dostoevskii's *Crime and Punishment*, and several parallels exist between Dostoevskii's novel and *Breakdown and Bereavement*, particularly in their young, overeducated, underutilized, and anguished protagonists. *Breakdown and Bereavement*'s anti-hero is Yehezkel Hefetz, a 29-year-old immigrant to Palestine from Russia who has already despaired of Palestine, left for western European cities, failed to find solace there, and returned. Hefetz is a typical alienated character in many ways. But in Palestine, where individual identity plays no part in the collective utopian dream, Hefetz's rather normal post-adolescent angst – aggravated by Palestine-inflicted health problems such as malaria and a below-the-belt injury that leaves him wounded sexually – escalates into a full-blown nervous breakdown as Hefetz finds himself in a world where suffering must be sufficiently noble to evoke sympathy. Cowering under the crushing blows of physical and mental demolition in Palestine, Hefetz can only think to himself, "what an amateur he was at suffering!" At the novel's end, Hefetz reconciles himself to life in Palestine, but while the novel does not leave its readers in despair, it does challenge them to confront the weaknesses that both life in exile and the return from it have imposed upon the Jewish people.

Much of Brenner's fiction centres around this conflict between the individual Jew and the collective. His earliest short novel, *Bahoref* [In Winter] from 1903, written in the style of a confessional memoir, describes a young man's departure from his traditional religious upbringing and his inability to find solace after his irreparable loss of faith. Brenner's novella *Atsabim* (translated as *Nerves*), is largely the monologue of another anti-hero, a disenchanted immigrant to the land of Israel who recounts to a friend his disillusioning journey there, crippled by corruption among Jews and non-Jews alike. Brenner's story *Hamotsa* [The Way Out] deals with another anti-hero, a Zionist pioneer forced to deal with a flood of Jewish refugees into a settlement in Palestine during the World War I, where corruption and apathy reign and the weak protagonist's only redeeming act is to bury the diseased dead infant of one of the refugees, a task described in the most unromantic and devastating detail. While Brenner's novella *Min hametsar* (translated as *Out of the Depths*) does not take place in Palestine, it shares the worldview of Brenner's other works as it describes a failed strike among Jewish immigrant workers from Russia at a Jewish newspaper in London.

Brenner may have been a realist, but he was not a pessimist. His dedication to the land he so often criticized was ultimately demonstrated by his death at the hands of Arab rioters as he defended a Jewish outpost. In his lifetime he inspired many followers as a critic favouring Labor Zionism, and he was an artist for whom life and art were tightly intertwined. Like the author, Brenner's protagonists maintain their potential to pursue the idealist dream. Founding political Zionist Theodor Herzl's motto was "If you will it, it is no legend", but Brenner's might be the rabbinic proverb, "You are not required to complete the work, but neither are you free to desist from it."

DARA HORN

Broch, Hermann

Austrian-born US fiction writer, 1886–1951

Born in Vienna, 11 November 1886. Studied at Vienna Institute for Weaving Technology, 1903–06, and at Technical University of Vienna, 1906–07. Administrator for International Red Cross during World War I. Managed father's factory, Teesdorf, 1908–27. Married Franziska von Rothermann, 1910; divorced, 1925; one son. Reviewer for *Moderne Welt*, Vienna, 1919; studied mathematics, philosophy, and psychology, University of Vienna, 1926–30. Arrested and detained by Nazis, 1938; rescued, partly because of intervention of James Joyce; emigrated to Britain; settled in London. Emigrated to United States, becoming involved in refugee work, 1940; naturalized US citizen, 1944. Fellow, Seabrook College, Yale University, 1949. Guggenheim Fellowship, 1940; member, American Academy of Arts and Letters, 1942. Died in New Haven, Connecticut, 30 May 1951.

Selected Writings

Collections

Gesammelte Werke, edited by Felix Stössinger *et al.*, 10 vols, 1953–61

Kommentierte Werkausgabe, edited by Paul Michael Lützeler, 13 vols, 1974–81

Fiction

Die Schlafwandler, 1931–32; as *The Sleepwalkers*, translated by Willa Muir and Edwin Muir, 1932, and by John J. White, 2000

Die unbekannte Grösse, 1933; as *The Unknown Quantity*, translated by Willa Muir and Edwin Muir, 1935

Die Verzauberung, 1934; as *The Spell*, translated by H.F. Broch de Rothermann, 1987

Der Tod des Vergil, 1945; as *The Death of Virgil*, translated by Jean Starr Untermeyer, 1945

Die Schuldlosen, 1950; as *The Guiltless*, translated by Ralph Manheim, 1974

Der Versucher [The Tempter], in *Gesammelte Werke*, vol. 4, 1953

Bergroman [Mountain Novel], edited by Frank Kress and Hans Albert Maier, 4 vols, 1969

Barbara und andere Novellen, edited by P.M. Lützeler, 1973

Short Stories

Der Meeresspiegel, 1933; as *Sea Level*, translated by E.W. Herd, 1966

Verlorener Sohn, 1933; as *Lost Son*, translated by E.W. Herd, 1966

Die Heimkehr des Vergil, 1937; as *The Homecoming of Vergil*, translated by E.W. Herd, 1966
Short Stories, translated by E.W. Herd, 1966

Plays
Die Entsühnung [The Atonement], 1934
Aus der Luft gegriffen; oder die Geschäfte des Baron Laborde [Plucked from the Air; or, The Affairs of Baron Laborde], 1981

Other
"Hofmannsthal und seine Zeit", 1955; as *Hugo von Hofmannsthal and His Times: The European Imagination*, translated by Michael P. Steinberg, 1984
Zur Universitätsreform [On University Reform], edited by G. Wienold, 1969
Gedanken zur Politik [Thoughts on Politics], edited by D. Hildebrand, 1970
Briefwechsel 1930–1951, with Daniel Brody, edited by Bertold Hack and Marietta Kleiss, 1971
Völkerbund-Resolution, edited by P.M. Lützeler, 1973
Menschenrecht und Demokratie: Politische Schriften [The Rights of Man and Democracy], edited by P.M. Lützeler, 1978
Briefe über Deutschland, 1945–1949: Die Korrespondenz mit Volkmar von Zühlsdorff, edited by P.M. Lützeler, 1986
Das Teesdorfer Tagebuch für Eva von Allesch, edited by P.M. Lützeler, 1995
Briefwechsel, 1946 bis 1951, with Hannah Arendt, edited by P.M. Lützeler, 1996
Psychische Selbstbiographie, edited by P.M. Lützeler, 1999

Further Reading
Arendt, Hannah, *Men in Dark Times*, New York: Harcourt Brace, 1968; London: Jonathan Cape, 1970
Dowden, Stephen D. (editor), *Hermann Broch: Literature, Philosophy, Politics: The Yale Broch Symposium 1986*, Columbia, South Carolina: Camden House, 1988
Durzak, Manfred, *Hermann Broch, der Dichter und seine Zeit*, Stuttgart: Kohlhammer, 1968
Hatfield, Henry, *Crisis and Continuity in Modern German Fiction*, Ithaca, New York: Cornell University Press, 1969
Kessler, Michael and P.M. Lützeler (editors), *Hermann Broch: Das dichterische Werk, neue Interpretationen*, Tübingen: Stauffenburg, 1987
Lützeler, P.M., *Hermann Broch: A Biography*, London: Quartet, 1987 (German original, 1985)
Ritzer, Monika, *Hermann Broch und die Kulturkrise des frühen 20. Jahrhunderts*, Stuttgart: Metzler, 1988
Roethke, Gisela, *Zur Symbolik in Hermann Brochs Werken*, Tübingen: Francke, 1992
Schlant, Ernestine, *Hermann Broch*, Boston: Twayne, 1978

As the son of a textile manufacturer, Broch followed his father's footsteps in the first instance, running the business from 1908 until 1927. Simultaneously, he began to educate himself in philosophy and history and published several essays on art and literature, while his friendship with Franz Blei opened the doors to the literary circles of Vienna. Broch grew up in the Vienna of the "gay apocalypse" (E. Schlant), at first taking no or little interest in political and socioeconomic issues. He made acquaintances with Robert Musil, Franz Werfel, and Karl Kraus, whom he held in very high esteem. From 1927 he lived as a freelance writer in Vienna and South Austria. Although Broch and Musil did not always agree on literary matters, they nonetheless gave recognition to the value of each other's work.

After Austria's occupation by the Nazis, Broch was taken into custody for political reasons: as a liberal writer, he was feared by the Nazis. Ignoring an order to return to Vienna, he managed to escape at the very last minute. Although his custody had been relatively short, it had a markedly traumatic effect on Broch who wrote:

> Ich habe einen schweren Choc erlitten, und er hat mich in einem Zustand getroffen, der durch die vorhergehenden zwei Jahre schon völlig deroutiert gewesen war. [I have suffered from a shock which further impacted on a state of mind that had already been devastated by the previous two years.]

During the weeks following this he became even more bitter when he realized that in the meantime most of his Jewish friends had either left Austria or had been arrested. In the streets, he encountered a good deal of hatred: "was ich da an Spiessbürgergemeinheit und-niedertracht erlebt habe, ist schlechterdings unschilderbar." [The meanness of the Philistines I encountered can hardly be described.] In 1938, he managed to emigrate via England to America where he stayed for the rest of his life living on modest grants.

In Broch's eyes, literature was closely interlinked with a philosophical criticism of his times. As a consequence, his whole writing was concentrated on the problem of the *Wertezerfall* (the disintegration of values). For Broch, modernism was not only the reason for the dissolution of traditional values, but also caused a splintering of the brain which split up into pure art, science, religion, and politics. Instead of furthering the disintegration both of communal values and of the self, Broch proposed the institution of a central value that should infuse each individual with directives and a goal. In the face of Hitler's Germany and his forced exile this goal became the preservation of human dignity and of human life, anchored in a constitutional framework.

His first novel trilogy, *Die Schlafwandler* (*The Sleepwalkers*), analyses the historical development of the period dating from the Bismarck era until the end of World War I, presenting this as an epoch of disintegrating values. All three protagonists, the Prussian Junker Pasenow, the petty bourgeois Esch, and the Alsatian profiteer Hugenau are representatives of different stages of the moral decay of society. In *Die Verzauberung* (*The Spell*), Broch shows how a false prophet uses mass psychology to mislead the inhabitants of a small mountain village, culminating in a collective suicide.

Broch began writing his major novel, *Der Tod des Vergil* (*The Death of Virgil*) in the spring of 1937. He continued working on this text during his custody in 1938 and then in the USA, before finally finishing it in 1945. This novel was to gain him international attention for the first time. It describes the last 24 hours of Vergil's life, correlating these to the death of art. Vergil's existence becomes a paradigm of the modern writer who finds himself in an epoch of decline, an epoch during which art has long become useless. Using the technique of the inner monologue, the novel elaborates on the moral responsibility of art in times of totalitarianism and slaughter.

Broch's cycle of the so-called Zodiak stories which, after alterations and amendments, became the novel *Die Schuldlosen* (*The Guiltless*), provides us with a scathing image of a number of indifferent characters and their actions. Based on Einstein's theory of relativity, Broch dissolves three-dimensionality into a multi-dimensionality that mirrors the progressive disintegration of reality.

Although Broch received relatively little attention for his literary works during his lifetime, his novels rank him among the novelists of world renown. His theoretical works on philosophy, art, and politics earned him a reputation as a humanist who was persistently trying to conceive of a concrete utopia.

BIRGIT HAAS

Brod, Max

Czech-Austrian-born Israeli fiction writer, dramatist, and biographer, 1884–1968

Born in Prague, 27 May 1884. Studied law at Prague University, graduated 1907. Married Eva Taussig. Worked as a civil servant in the postal service, 1907–24; arts editor of *Prager Tageblatt*; also a composer. Founder member, National Council for Czech Jews, 1918. Despite his friend Franz Kafka's wish to have his writings destroyed after his death, Brod preserved and promoted Kafka's works, and wrote the first biography of him. Became a Zionist; emigrated to Palestine, 1939; settled in Tel Aviv. Appointed adviser to the Habimah Theatre. Died in Tel Aviv, 20 December 1968.

Selected Writings

Novels

Die That [The Action], 1905
Tod den Toten! [Death to the Dead!], 1906
Schloss Nornepygge: der Roman des Indifferenten [Nornepygge Castle: The Novel of the Indifferent Man], 1908
Ein tschechisches Dienstmädchen [A Czech Servant Girl], 1909
Jüdinnen [Jewesses], 1911
Arnold Beer: das Schicksal eines Juden [Arnold Beer: The Fate of a Jew], 1912
Tycho Brahes Weg zu Gott, 1915; as *The Redemption of Tycho Brahe*, translated by Felix Warren Crosse, 1928
Ausgewählte Romane und Novellen [Selected Novels and Novellas], 6 vols, 1915–19
Das grosse Wagnis [The Great Dare], 1918
August Nachreiters Attentat [August Nachreiter's Outrage], 1921
Franzi; oder, eine Liebe zweiten Ranges [Franzi; or, A Second Class Love], 1922
Leben mit einer Göttin [Life with a Goddess], 1923
Rëubeni, Fürst der Juden, 1925; as *Rëubeni, Prince of the Jews: A Tale of the Renaissance*, translated by Hannah Waller, 1928
David Rëubeni in Portugal, 1927
Die Frau, nach der man sich sehnt, 1927; as *Three Loves*, translated by Jacob Wittmer Hartmann, 1929
Zauberreich der Liebe, 1928; as *The Kingdom of Love*, translated by Eric Sutton, 1930
Stefan Rott; oder, das Jahr der Entscheidung [Stefan Rott; or, The Year of Decision], 1931
Die Frau, die nicht enttäuscht [The Woman Who Does Not Disappoint], 1933
Annerl, 1936
Novellen aus Böhmen [Novellas from Bohemia], 1936
Abenteuer in Japan [Adventure in Japan], 1938
Der Hügel ruft [The Call of the Hill], 1942
Galilei in Gefangenschaft [Galileo Imprisoned], 1948
Unambo: Roman aus dem jüdisch-arabischen Krieg, 1949; as *Unambo: A Novel of the War in Israel*, translated by Ludwig Lewisohn, 1952
Der Meister, 1951; as *The Master*, translated by Heinz Norden, 1951
Beinahe ein Vorzugsschüler oder Pièce Touchée [Almost at the Top of the Class], 1952
Der Sommer, den man zurückwünscht [The Summer One Wishes Would Return], 1952
Ein Abenteuer Napoleons und andere Novellen [Napoleon's Adventure and Other Novellas], 1954
Armer Cicero [Poor Cicero], 1955
Rebellische Herzen [Rebellious Hearts], 1957; as *Prager Tagblatt: Roman aus jungen Jahren* [Prager Tagblatt: A Novel from Early Years], 1968
Mira: ein Roman um Hofmannsthal [Mira: A Novel about Hofmannsthal], 1958
Jugend im Nebel [Youth in Fog], 1959
Die verbotene Frau [The Forbidden Woman], 1960
Die Rosenkoralle [Pink Coral], 1961
Der Ritter Laberius schafft sich aus der Welt [Knight Laberius Removes Himself from the World], 1964

Short Stories

Experimente: Vier Geschichten [Experiments: Four Stories], 1907
Weiberwirtschaft: Drei Erzählungen [Henhouse: Three Stories], 1913
Durchbruch ins Wunder: Erzählungen [Breakthrough to the Miraculous], 1962

Poetry

Der Weg des Verliebten [The Way of One in Love], 1907
Das gelobte Land [The Promised Land], 1917
Das Buch der Liebe [The Book of Love], 1921

Plays

Abschied von der Jugend: ein romantisches Lustspiel [Goodbye to Youth: A Romantic Comedy], 1912
Die Retterin [The Saviour], 1914
Die Höhe des Gefühls [The Height of Feeling], 1918

Eine Königin Esther [Queen Esther], 1918
Die Fälscher [The Forger], 1920
Klarissas halbes Herz [Clarissa's Best Friend], 1924
Prozess Bunterbart [The Bunterbart Case], 1924
Lord Byron kommt aus der Mode [Lord Byron Goes out of Fashion], 1929

Other
Der jüdische Dichter deutscher Zunge [The Jewish Poet of German Tongue], 1913
Über die Schönheit hässlicher Bilder [On the Beauty of Ugly Pictures], 1913
Die dritte Phase des Zionismus [The Three Phases of Zionism], 1917
Sozialismus im Zionismus [Socialism in Zionism], 1920
Heidentum, Christentum, Judentum: ein Bekenntnisbuch, 2 vols, 1921, as *Paganism, Christianity, Judaism*, translated by William Wolff, 1970
Leoš Janáček: Leben und Werk [Leoš Janáček: Life and Work], 1925
Zionismus als Weltanschauung [Zionism as a World View], with Felix Weltsch, 1925
Liebe im Film [Love in Film], with Rudolf Thomas, 1930
Heinrich Heine, 1934; as *Heinrich Heine: The Artist in Revolt*, translated by Joseph Witriol, 1956
Rassentheorie und Judentum [Racial Theory and Judaism], 1936
Franz Kafka: Eine Biographie: Erinnerungen und Dokumente, 1937; as *The Biography of Franz Kafka*, translated by G. Humphreys-Roberts, 1947; and as *Franz Kafka: A Biography*, translated by Humpreys-Roberts and Richard Winston, 1960
Das Diesseitswunder oder die jüdische Idee und ihre Verwirklichung [The Jewish Idea and its Fulfilment], 1939
Saul melek Yisrael [Saul, King of Israel], 1944
Diesseits und Jenseits [Here and Beyond], 2 vols, 1947–48
Franz Kafkas Glauben und Lehre: Kafka und Tolstoi: Eine Studie [Franz Kafka's Beliefs and Teachings: Kafka and Tolstoi: A Study], 1948
Die Musik Israels, 1951; as *Israel's Music*, translated by Toni Volcani, 1951
Franz Kafka als wegweisende Gestalt [Franz Kafka's Revolutionary Structure], 1951
Streitbares Leben: Autobiographie [Contentious Life: Autobiography], 1960; enlarged and revised as *Streitbares Leben 1884–1968*, 1969
Gustav Mahler: Beispiel einer deutsch–jüdischen Symbiose [Gustav Mahler: An Example of a German–Jewish Symbiosis], 1961
Die verkaufte Braut: der abenteuerliche Lebensroman des Textdichters Karel Sabina [The Bartered Bride: The Adventurous Life Story of the Writer Karel Sabina], 1962
Das Schloss: Nach Franz Kafkas gleichnamigem Roman [The Castle: From Franz Kafka's Novel of the Same Name], 1964
Johannes Reuchlin und sein Kampf: eine historische Monographie [Johannes Reuchlin and His Struggle: A Historical Monograph], 1965
Der Prager Kreis [The Prague Circle], 1966
Gesang einer Giftschlange: Wirrnis und Auflichtung [The Song of a Serpent: Confusion and Illumination], 1966
Das Unzerstörbare [The Indestructible], 1968
Von der Unsterblichkeit der Seele [On the Immortality of the Soul], 1969

Further Reading

Demetz, Peter, *Prague in Black and Gold: The History of a City*, London: Allen Lane, and New York: Hill and Wang, 1997
Gelber, Mark H., "Max Brod's Zionist Writings", *Year Book of the Leo Baeck Institute*, 33 (1988)
Gelber, Mark H., "Indifferentism, Anti-Semitism, the Holocaust and Zionism: Thomas Mann and Max Brod", *Tel Aviver Jahrbuch für deutsche Geschichte*, 20 (1991)
Gold, Hugo (editor), *Max Brod: ein Gedenkbuch*, Tel Aviv: Olamenu, 1969
Kayser, Werner and Horst Gronemeyer (editors), *Max Brod*, Hamburg: Christians, 1972
Pawel, Ernst, *The Nightmare of Reason: A Life of Franz Kafka*, New York: Farrar Straus, and London: Harvill Press, 1984
Pazi, Margarita, *Max Brod: Werke und Persönlichkeit* [Max Brod: Works and Personality], Bonn: Bouvier, 1970
Pazi, Margarita (editor), *Max Brod 1884–1968: Untersuchungen zu Max Brods literarischen und philosophischen Schriften*, New York: Peter Lang, 1987
Weltsch, Robert, *Max Brod and His Age*, New York: Leo Baeck Institute, 1970 (lecture)
Wessling, Berndt W., *Max Brod: ein Porträt zum 100. Geburtstag*, Gerlingen: Bleicher, 1984

Max Brod was a prolific and successful writer and a major Jewish figure of the 20th century. Taking his entire career into account, it is fair to label him a veritable renaissance man. He is best remembered for his devotion to his close friend, Franz Kafka, and for his untiring efforts to secure a permanent place in the Western literary canon for him. Brod encouraged Kafka to publish literary works while the latter was alive. After Kafka's death, Brod edited and published Kafka's unpublished writings, wrote the first Kafka biography, and several separate studies, focusing on the Jewish and universal literary and religious significance of his friend's work.

Brod was the dominating and most energetic figure of a Prague Circle of writers for many years, and he published feverishly in virtually every literary genre. He wrote philosophical works, composed music and was also a librettist. Brod's efforts to have Czech literature, for example Jaroslav Hašek's *The Good Soldier Švejk*, published or presented in Germany complemented his goal of promoting the literary careers of local young talent, such as that of Franz Werfel. Also, he was instrumental in having Leoš Janáček's operas performed throughout Europe.

Although his first literary works were characterized by pessimism and indifferentism, a concept of decadence he developed in his early writings and first major novel, *Schloss*

Nornepygge: der Roman des Indifferenten [Nornepygge Castle: The Novel of the Indifferent Man], Brod gradually came to believe that human beings do have ethical tasks to perform that lend significance to their lives. This reorientation complemented his changing views about Judaism and the Jewish people. Influenced decisively by his Zionist friend Hugo Bergmann, and by the visits and lectures of Martin Buber and Nathan Birnbaum in Prague, Brod distanced himself from the assimilationist ethos he had absorbed in his parental home and at school, and he embraced Zionism before World War I. This change set the tone for much of his literary output for the rest of his life. He wrote many Zionist essays and books and became well known as a Zionist polemicist, who promoted a special version of Zionism humanism. Brod saw Zionism as one of the major universal movements of human salvation. For him, it was a new kind of nationalism, which would purify the negative elements found in other nationalist movements. Zionism could be successful only if it accomplished its particularist goals together with the goals of universal justice and general human reconciliation and peace. His Zionist convictions also propelled him in the direction of Jewish activism. He helped found the National Council for Czech Jews in 1918, and he served as its vice-president for many years.

Brod's Jewish and Zionist ideas and interests came to expression in his poetry, plays, and novels. For example, his volume of poetry entitled *Das gelobte Land* [The Promised Land] in 1917, contained several poems that indicate the direction of his Jewish development. In "Hebräische Lektion" [Hebrew Lesson], the first lines read:

> Dreissig Jahre alt bin ich geworden,
> Eh ich begann, die Sprache meines Volkes zu lernen
> Da war es mir, als sei ich dreissig Jahre taub gewesen.
> [I was thirty years old
> Before I began to learn the language of my people,
> It seemed to me, as if for thirty years I had been deaf]

The poem entitled "Schule für galizische Flüchtlingskinder" [School for the Children of Galician Refugees] praises and encourages the refugee girls whom Brod actually taught as part of an effort to assist Jewish refugees from the Eastern Front who arrived in Prague during World War I. The motto of the poem is a quotation from the Talmud. In his major novel, *Tycho Brahes Weg zu Gott* (*The Redemption of Tycho Brahe*), the character Rabbi Löw says that the just man is not permitted to wait for redemption. Rather he can contribute to bringing redemption by joining in God's work. The righteous of the world exist in order to serve and support God. In later works, such as *Rëubeni, Fürst der Juden* (*Rëubeni, Prince of the Jews: A Tale of the Renaissance*) and *Diesseits und Jenseits* [Here and Beyond], the view is expressed that the sense of Messianism was to inspire the amelioration of this world, given all of its negative, anti-human aspects. In the novel *Zauberreich der Liebe* (*The Kingdom of Love*) the protagonist visits the Land of Israel, and the work in general vigorously praises the kibbutz as paradise on earth, as the concrete realization of Brod's socialist-humanist Zionist vision.

Brod was perturbed about the problematical middle position of the Jewish writer caught between German culture and Jewish identity. In his essay "Der jüdische Dichter deutscher Zunge" he formulated the concept of "Distanzliebe" (love from a distance) in order to explore this situation. Brod's love for German culture from a distance was a way to maintain his Germanic cultural allegiances, while professing his ultimate belonging to the Jewish people. He applied this concept graphically later on in literary works, for example in his novel *Die Frau, die nicht enttäauscht* [The Woman Who Does Not Disappoint], and also in his major biography of the German-Jewish poet, Heinrich Heine.

During the last phase of his life in Tel Aviv Brod played an important role in determining the artistic direction of the Jewish national theatre, Habima, by serving as its dramaturgical director. He also continued to incorporate philosophical dimensions and ethical debates into his novels. In *Unambo*, a complex novel about the 1948 War of Independence, Brod sought to measure the justice of the war against the background of the Holocaust, on one hand, and the legitimate rights and aspirations of the native Palestinian-Arab population, on the other.

MARK GELBER

Brodkey, Harold

US fiction writer, poet, and essayist, 1930–1996

Born Aaron Roy Weintrub in Staunton, Illinois, 25 October 1930. Mother died before he was two; adopted by cousins, Joseph and Doris Brodkey. Studied at Harvard University, graduated in 1952. Settled in New York. Contributor to the *New Yorker* and *American Poetry Review*. Married, first, Joanna Brown, one daughter; divorced 1960; second, Ellen Schwamm. Many awards, including Prix de Rome, 1959; Brandeis University Creative Arts Award, 1974; O. Henry Short Story Prize, 1975 and 1976. Died 26 January 1996.

Selected Writings

Novels
The Runaway Soul, 1991
Profane Friendship, 1994

Short Stories
First Love and Other Sorrows, 1957
Women and Angels, 1985
Stories in an Almost Classical Mode, 1988; as *The Abundant Dreamer*, 1989
The World is the Home of Love and Death, 1997

Other
A Poem about Testimony and Argument, 1986
This Wild Darkness: The Story of My Death, 1996
My Venice, 1998
Sea Battles on Dry Land: Essays, 1999

Further Reading

Adams, Robert M., review of *The Runaway Soul*, *New York Review of Books* (21 November 1991)

Bawer, Bruce, "A Genius for Publicity", *New Criterion*, 7/4 (December 1988)
Enright, D.J., "Jews, Have Pity!", review of *Women and Angels*, *New York Review of Books* (26 September 1987)
Hitchens, Christopher, "The Drive and the Drivel: For Fans Only: The Last Work of Harold Brodkey", *Washington Post* (20 October 1997)
Hoffman, Eva, review of *This Wild Darkness*, *New York Times* (27 October 1996)
Hollinghurst, Alan, review of *Profane Friendship*, *Washington Post* (6 March 1994)
Howard, Richard, "Almost Classic: Harold Brodkey's Solipsism", *New Republic* (12 July 1993)
Iannone, Carol, "The Brodkey Question", *Commentary*, 87/4 (April 1989)
Marx, Bill, review of *The World is the Home of Love and Death*, *Boston Globe* (9 November 1997)
Passaro, Vince, review of *Profane Friendship*, *Newsday* (8 March 1994)
Rothstein, Edward, review of *Stories in an Almost Classical Mode*, *New York Review of Books* (15 February 1990)
Schwamm, Ellen, "I Felt that I Had Met My Destiny", *The Times*, London (4 November 1996)
Thomas, D.M., review of *The Runaway Soul*, *New York Times Book Review* (10 November 1991)
Wood, Michael, review of *Profane Friendship*, *New York Times Book Review* (27 March 1994)

When Harold Brodkey learned in spring 1993 that he was dying of AIDS he was incredulous. His last exposure to homosexual contact had been 1977, some 16 years before, and he had assumed himself to have passed safely beyond the latency period of the disease but he was mistaken. Brodkey first became aware of the disease when he became gravely ill with *pneumocystis carinii pneumonia*, a common opportunistic disease among AIDS sufferers. During his medical struggle with *pneumocystis*, which bought him a two-year reprieve, Brodkey elected to die in public before an international audience, by means of a series of reports on himself for the *New Yorker*, for which he was then writing film reviews. Those articles were then compiled into a book, *This Wild Darkness: The Story of My Death*, in which Brodkey explained himself to the world, even as he thumbed his nose at it.

For years, Brodkey had borne the reputation of a tease and a con, whose promise, it was thought, based on a handful of stories that boasted more knowledge of the erotic life than anyone since James Joyce, would not be realized. He was infamous for passages so purple, and so blue, that they made more mundane considerations, like character and plot, seem disposable; for a cinéma vérité approach to sex that had reading about it take longer than performing it; for the Proustian memoir-novel he was *not* writing; and for the preening solipsism and aggressive public relations that grated on everyone within earshot. With an early volume of short stories, *First Love and Other Sorrows* in 1958, a basket of disjecta membra some 27 years later, *Women and Angels*, and a roundup of the scattered bones, *Stories in an Almost Classical Mode*, Brodkey acquired the reputation of an underachiever: extravagant talent and small product, who invited dismissals that were the flip side of the envy he aroused. Imagine a writer who could prophesy to *People Magazine* a coming "Brodkey dictatorship in letters".

Then in 1991 Brodkey published his prodigious memoir/novel *The Runaway Soul*, which was billed as a fragment of the 300,000–600,000 word manuscript from which it was culled. An encyclopedia of family dysfunction, a hairball of tangled emotions, a child's story veined with adult erotic knowledge, it fell short of securing Brodkey's dictatorship, but did give notice that he intended to be formidable, even if his instinct for plot was as unruly as his gift for language was abundant. The book needed, reviewers agreed, a sharp pair of scissors. It was followed by *Profane Friendship* and three posthumous volumes: *This Wild Darkness*, *The World is the Home of Love and Death*, and *Sea Battles on Dry Land: Essays*. The promise, it appears, had been kept.

From start to finish, Brodkey's writing was close to the bone, his life providing the tawdry material and his prose the promise of magic transformation. From the stories in *First Love and Early Sorrows* through *Runaway Soul* to *This Wild Darkness*, Brodkey was captivated by the dramatically enlarged and aggrandized self. The world came shadowed by anger, blood, and betrayal, and mystical mother love, and shaded too in "a certain shade of red brick – a dark, almost melodious red, sombre and riddled with blue" in St Louis, Missouri, where Brodkey grew up. His latter-day enchantment with Hollywood was of a piece with his light-struck self-portraits. In this Brodkey would exemplify and sum up the Jewish writers of his generation. Like his contemporaries, Saul Bellow, Philip Roth, Allen Ginsberg, and Norman Mailer, he would consecrate his writing to the self, which was to be regarded as the greatest of all mysteries, the elusive trophy to be tracked down, captured, and brought home for display.

Brodkey's self-obsession was honestly come by. He was a bartered child: from one dysfunctional Jewish family to another. In *This Wild Darkness* Brodkey tells how his mother died "of a curse laid on her by her father, a wonder-working rabbi . . . When I was barely two, she died painfully, over a period of months, either of peritonitis from a bungled abortion or from cancer, depending on who related the story." His father, Max Weintrub, "an illiterate local junk man, a semi-pro prizefighter in his youth and unhealably violent", sold him to relatives, Joe and Doris Brodkey, for $300. The Brodkeys in turn, both suffering perennially from physical ailments, were obsessed with him sexually on account of his beauty. Joe Brodkey, suffering from heart disease, approached Harold for two years, while he was 12 and 13, while Doris Brodkey, in the background and aware, cheered her husband on. Brodkey believes that he killed his stepfather with his steadfast refusals: "He turned his face to the wall, telling me I was a cold fish – because I would not sex around with him. He was lecherous and strange."

In *The Runaway Soul*, the Brodkeys become the Silenowiczes of Alton, Illinois, and the story is scaled up to Homeric proportions and beyond, at 835 pages. The book's victim-hero, Wiley Silenowicz, will lament/boast:

> I am a shattered guy, a shallow boy, a battered person . . . Perhaps I might begin to escape now. Maybe I won't make it. Maybe I will always be sad and mostly silent. It is likely I won't live too long. I gave my childhood and youth away. Still, the main thing is not to show how hurt you are and how hard it is for you to go on at the moment. You don't want to be mainly a structure of blame, of accusation – of exhaustion.

Of course, an unhappy childhood is the novelist's birthright; how many great novels, from Dickens's *David Copperfield* to Joyce's *A Portrait of the Artist*, have been rooted in the miseries of childhood? Of course what distinguished their work as writers was the formal control they exercised over their sorrows, something that Brodkey usually chose to walk away from.

One particular sexual interlude, between Wiley Silenowicz and a luscious Harvard coed, is described over the course of 87 pages, which is more than one-tenth of the book's length. The scene is doubly performative, for the character as well as the author, who is out to make a demonstration of literary athleticism as gruelling and obstinate as the sexual athleticism of his hero, who is also, transparently, himself. One early reviewer said of Brodkey's first stories, "Skin has manhole-size pores; clay has mica shards you could find your reflection in; an emotion will have twelve different states of being."

Brodkey taught himself how to play those states of being like a musical scale. In his stories, from beginning to end, in his marvellous film reviews for the *New Yorker*, in the early pages of *Profane Friendship*, an operatic story of erotic attraction between American and Italian youths in Venice, he could be almost religiously lyrical and exquisitely attuned to the quivers of tenderness and budding eros, to the lights and shadows of emotion, the dance and flutter of language. As a Jewish writer, Brodkey reminds us that at a certain phase of Jewish selfconsciousness in America, the choice between Hebraist and Hellenist modes of consciousness was no choice at all: what Hellenism had to offer, training in sensation and taste, was not only more attractive, but for a writer of a certain age, it was the only option available. If that was the case, you made the best of it, and Harold Brodkey would prove to be America's most dramatic example of a Baroque sensibility that flowered among Jewish writers whose Jewish inheritance was not substantial enough to nourish a modern literary imagination.

MARK SHECHNER

Brodsky, Joseph

Russian-born US poet, 1940–1996

Born Iosif Aleksandrovich Brodskii in Leningrad, 24 May 1940; educated at schools in Leningrad to age 15. Married; one son and one daughter. Convicted as a "social parasite" in 1964 and served 20 months of a five-year sentence of internal exile in the far north; in 1972 exiled by the Soviet government and emigrated to United States; became US citizen in 1977. Taught at the University of Michigan, 1972–73, 1974–80; and at various colleges in New York state and Massachusetts. Professor of literature, Mount Holyoke College, 1980–96. Wrote some of his later prose and poetry in English. Many awards including the Nobel Prize for Literature, 1987. Member, American Academy of Arts and Letters (resigned in protest over the honorary membership of Evgenii Evtushenko, 1987); US Poet Laureate, 1991–92. Died in New York, 28 January 1996.

Selected Writings

Poetry

Stikhotvoreniia i poemy [Longer and Shorter Poems], 1965
Elegy to John Donne and Other Poems, translated by Nicholas Bethell, 1967
Ostanovka v pustyne [A Halt in the Wilderness], 1970
Selected Poems, translated by George L. Kline, foreword by W.H. Auden, 1973
Konets prekrasnoi epokhi: Stikhotvoreniia 1964–1971 [The End of the Belle Epoque: Poems 1964–1971], 1977
Chast' rechi: stikhotvoreniia 1972–1976, 1977; as *A Part of Speech*, translated by Anthony Hecht *et al.*, 1980
Rimskie elegii [Roman Elegies], 1982
Novye stansy k Avguste: stikhi M.B. 1962–1982 [New Stanzas to Augusta: Poems to M.B. 1962–1982], 1983
Uraniia [Urania], 1987
To Urania (selected poems), 1988
Chast' rechi: izbrannye stikhi 1962–1989 [A Part of Speech: Selected Poems 1962–1989], 1990
Osennii krik iastreba [The Hawk's Cry in Autumn], 1990
Primechaniia paporotnika [A Fern's Commentary], 1990
Stikhotvoreniia [Poems], 1990
Bog sokhraniaet vse [God Preserves All Things], 1991
Kholmy: bol'shie stikhotvoreniia i poemy [Hills: Longer Poems], 1991
Forma vremeni [The Form of Time] 2 vols, 1992 (vol. 2 includes essays and plays)
Sochineniia Iosifa Brodskogo [Works], 4 vols, 1992–95
V okrestnostiakh Atlantidy: novye stikhotvoreniia [In the Environs of Atlantis: New Poems], 1995
Peizazh s navodneniem [Landscape with a Flood], 1996
So Forth (poems in English), 1996
Sochineniia Iosifa Brodskogo [Works], 6 vols, 1997–2000

Plays

Mramor, 1984; as *Marbles: A Play in Three Acts*, translated by Alan Myers, 1989
Demokratiia/Démocratie (bilingual edition in Russian and French), 1990; as *Democracy*, translated by Alan Myers, 1990

Other

Editor, with Carl Proffer, *Modern Russian Poets on Poetry: Blok, Mandelstam, Pasternak, Mayakovsky, Gumilev, Tsvetaeva*, 1982
Less than One: Selected Essays, 1986
The Nobel Lecture, 1988
Editor, *An Age Ago: A Selection of Nineteenth-Century Russian Poetry*, translated by Alan Myers, 1988
Razmerom podlinnike [In the Meter of the Original], 1990
Watermark, 1992

On Grief and Reason, 1995
Conversations with Joseph Brodsky: A Poet's Journey Through the 20th Century, edited by Solomon Volkov, 1998

Further Reading

Bethea, David M., *Joseph Brodsky and the Creation of Exile*, Princeton, New Jersey: Princeton University Press, 1994
Etkind, Efim, *The Trial of Joseph Brodsky*, London: Overseas Publications, 1988
Loseff, Lev and Valentina Polukhina (editors), *Brodsky's Poetics and Aesthetics*, London: Macmillan, and New York: St Martin's Press, 1990
Polukhina, Valentina, *Joseph Brodsky: A Poet for Our Time*, Cambridge: Cambridge University Press, 1989
Polukhina, Valentina, *Brodsky through the Eyes of His Contemporaries*, London: Macmillan, and New York: St Martin's Press, 1992

After the Nobel award in 1987, an anonymous admirer chalked on the wall of a home in St Petersburg: HERE LIVED IOSIF BRODSKII, THE POET. Almost immediately the message changed giving the phrase an elegiacally anti-Semitic character: HERE IS THE YID IOSIF BRODSKII, THE POET (zdes' zhid poet Iosif Brodskii). But was Joseph Brodsky really a "Yid"? This question defies an unequivocal answer.

In his mature years Brodsky coined a lapidary formulaic answer, which he used in interviews: "I am a Jew, a Russian poet, and an American citizen". Citizenship is the easiest to explain. After forcible emigration from the Soviet Union in 1972 Brodsky settled in the United States. A Jewish component entered his cultural universum to the same degree that it enters Western civilization at large, i.e. as the Old Testament received in the light of the New Testament. His expansive "Isaac and Abraham" (1963) indicates that. Although this poem contains some allegorical hints at the tragic plight of Jewish people in the Diaspora and the Holocaust, its main theme, Abraham's unfulfilled sacrifice, is based on existentialist interpretations in the works of Kierkegaard, a Christian thinker, and Shestov.

Brodsky never declared any formal religious affiliation. His relationship with Christianity remained ambiguous: he called himself "a Christian by correspondence". He wrote many poems featuring New Testament imagery, including the powerful "Farewell, Mlle Veronique" (1967), and "Nunc Dimittis" (1972); he wrote a Christmas poem every year, but his treatment of Christian subjects was tinged with agnosticism, being irreverent, even blasphemous.

Although the family name reveals roots in the Ukrainian town of Brody, the centre of rabbinical scholarship, by the time Joseph was born, two generations of his family had already been assimilated. Even if Aleksandr and Maria Brodsky wanted to maintain some degree of Jewishness in their family life, that would have been impossible during the Soviet era, when all religion was crushed. Soviet citizens of Jewish extraction in the cities led lives in no way different from their Gentile neighbours. As a child Brodsky had no opportunity to learn anything about Judaism or Jewishness, Hebrew, or much Yiddish, which he humorously used in his "Two Hours in the Empty Tank" (1965) as a mock-German language.

Besides "Isaac and Abraham", which invokes Jewish topics only tangentially, there are just two short poems on this subject in Brodsky's copious output: "The Jewish Cemetery near Leningrad" (1958) and "Liejyklos" (1971). The former is a youthful work; Brodsky never included it in his collections. The latter is a part of the "Lithuanian Divertimento" cycle and is, possibly, related to memories of his maternal grandfather, who was a tailor from Vilna (Vilnius):

> To be born a century ago
> and over the down bedding, airing,
> through a window see a garden grow
> and Catherine's crosses, twin domes soaring;
> be embarrassed for Mother, hiccup
> when the brandished lorgnettes scrutinize
> and push a cart with rubbish heaped up
> along the ghetto's yellow alleys . . .
> then shape Jew's ringlets into sideburns
> and off, on to the New World like a shot,
> puking in waves as the engine churns.

Central to Brodsky's idea of himself was his poetic vocation: "a Russian poet". He said in his Nobel lecture: "[A] poet always knows that . . . the voice of the Muse is, in reality, the dictate of the language; . . . he is the language's means toward the continuation of its existence." The notion of language as a force shaping an individual's worldview, the idea that it is not logic but the grammar of the mother tongue that shapes an individual's thinking occurs numerous times in Brodsky's work. According to the poet's own reminiscences he received the first impulse to this language-worship in 1965 when he read W.H. Auden. Mid-century linguistics and Wittgenstein's philosophy also influenced this line of thinking. In "1972", a poem which was to be his credo, he declared:

> Listen, my boon brethren and my enemies!
> What I've done, I've done not for fame or memories
> in this era of radio waves and cinemas,
> but for the sake of my native tongue and letters.

If his native tongue was the crux of his identity and if he had no religious or cultural affinity with the Jewish people, one might think that the third part of Brodsky's tripartite formula ("I am a Jew . . .") was due exclusively to anti-Semitism. As Brodsky wrote in his autobiographical essay "Less than One" (1976), he dated the beginning of his self-awareness back to the moment when, at the age of seven, he came to the school library to enroll and the librarian asked his "nationality": "I was seven years old and knew very well that I was a Jew, but I told the attendant that I didn't know". Thirty years later, trying to make out his feelings as a first-grader, Brodsky comes to the conclusion that he was embarrassed not by his parentage but by the word itself, "Jew" (*yevrei*), which it seemed to him had the "status of a four-letter word or like a name for VD". However, in Brodsky's case, it would be incorrect to reduce the Jewish element in his self-identity to the anti-Semitic environment which by mockery, hostility, and social limitations forced Jewishness on this off-spring of a long-assimilated family. The totality of his autobiographical statements in essays, poems, and interviews reveals how *little* anti-Semitism he personally suffered, whether of the everyday variety or through the state policies. This can be explained in part by his sense of independence, and by the fact that he dropped out of school and never aspired toward a career where the special quotas for Jews applied.

When in 1964 the KGB and Communist Party targeted Brodsky for persecution, they tried to depict him as a Jew who hated everything Russian, insinuating that Brodsky hated the Russian people and in private conversations "called them *hazyrim* (swine)". Brodsky was sentenced to five years of internal exile in the Archangel region, where he worked as a farm hand at a state farm. He remembered his relationship with the local peasants as nearly idyllic without a hint of anti-Semitism.

However politically incorrect, studying what Brodsky had to say about his Jewishness one cannot help coming to the conclusion that it was for him primarily an anthropological quality. At the end of his life, answering a friend, Brodsky said: "One has to be very cautious about the problem of anti-Semitism. In essence, anti-Semitism is just one of the forms of racism. And we all are racists to a degree. There are some faces we don't like. Some kinds of beauty." Then to the question, "How were you reared – as a Jew or as a Russian?," he replied, "When I was asked about my nationality, I naturally answered that I was Jewish. But that didn't happen often. Nobody had to ask since I can't say 'r'." (Many Russian Jews use the uvular "r" instead of the Russian rolling one.) Brodsky usually describes a Jewish profile as crow-like: "Crow, a bird who is Jewish . . ." – a frequent visitor to his poetic texts. "I am a Jew. One hundred per cent. It is impossible to be more Jewish than I am. Dad, mom – no doubts. Without a dash of admixture. But I don't think of myself as being Jewish just because of that. I know that there is a certain absolutism in my thinking. As far as faith is concerned, if I had to describe for myself a Supreme Being, I'd say that God is arbitrary force. And this is what the God of the Old Testament is. I feel that very strongly. I feel that precisely, without any proofs whatsoever." How can one reconcile this statement with his notion of himself as a Russian poet *par excellence*, whose personality could be construed only through the rules of Russian grammar? He was indeed a poet who once said of himself: "My very existence is a paradox."

LEV LOSEFF

Broner, E.M.

US fiction writer, poet, and dramatist, 1930–

Born Esther Masserman in Detroit, 8 July 1930; parents were Russian immigrants. Studied at Wayne State University, Detroit, BA 1950, MFA 1962; and at Union Graduate School, PhD 1978. Married; four children. Lecturer in English and writer in residence, Wayne State University, from 1964; lecturer at various institutions, including Ohio State University, Columbia University, New York University, and Sarah Lawrence College; also lecturer in creative writing and women's studies, University of Haifa. Awards include O. Henry Award.

Selected Writings

Novels
Her Mothers, 1975
A Weave of Women, 1978

Plays
Summer is a Foreign Land, 1966
Colonel Higginson, musical with M. Zieve, 1968
The Body Parts of Margaret Fuller, 1976

Other
Journal-Nocturnal, and Seven Stories, 1968
Editor, with Cathy N. Davidson, *The Lost Tradition: Mothers and Daughters in Literature*, 1980
The Telling (includes "The Women's Haggadah", with Naomi Nimrod), 1993
Mornings and Mourning: A Kaddish Journal, 1994
Bringing Home the Light: A Jewish Woman's Handbook of Rituals, 1999

Further Reading

Dalton, Elizabeth, "Books in Review: Journal / Nocturnal and Seven Stories", *Commentary*, 47/4 (April 1969)
Glazer, Miriyam, "Orphans of Culture and History: Gender and Spirituality in Contemporary Jewish-American Women's Novels", *Tulsa Studies in Women's Literature*, 13/1 (Spring 1994): 127
Kamel, Rose Yalow, *Aggravating the Conscience: Jewish-American Literary Mothers in the Promised Land*, New York: Peter Lang, 1988
Robson, Ruthmann, "A Conversation with E.M. Broner", *Kalliope*, 7 (1985)
Shapiro, Ann R. (editor), *Jewish American Women Writers: A Bio-Bibliographical and Critical Sourcebook*, Westport, Connecticut: Greenwood Press, 1994
Weinthal, Edith C., "The Image of the City in E.M. Broner's *A Weave of Women*", *Response: A Contemporary Jewish Review* (Fall 1993)

Throughout E.M. Broner's novels, essays, stories, and plays, she consistently articulates a form of dwelling-in-displacement, a radical Jewish identity expressed as a condition of dislocation. Meditating on the meaning of the near-sacrifice of Isaac, a narrative retold in the *Akedah* on a daily basis in the synagogue, for a Jewish feminist, she muses:

> death is very close to us in the shul . . . Does every man in turn, feel bound, tethered . . . in danger? . . . There is something worse. That is to stand behind a curtain stretched on metal poles. Contained or partitioned, I am invisible. Worse than the binding is this unbinding, this disconnection, this being pushed out of one's inheritance.

In Judaism, the concept of boundaries and partitions are

meant to sanctify everyday experience, not degrade it. But in Broner's oeuvre, this paradigm represents a painful estrangement, which might be called a diaspora of the border or partition. Raised in the Conservative movement, she has been dedicated for many years to a feminist reconstruction of Judaism, has written a significant body of poetry, novels, short stories, and creative liturgies that interrogate the existential and spiritual exile of women within Judaism. In 1966 she published her first work, a verse play called *Summer is a Foreign Land*, concerning the death of a Russian Jewish matriarch who possesses magical gifts, which was soon followed by collections of short stories, and the novels *Her Mothers* and *A Weave of Women* which both appeared in the mid-1970s.

An important nonfiction work, *The Telling*, which includes "The Women's Haggadah", narrates the history of a community of Jewish women in New York and their efforts to create the first women's seders. The 1976 New York women's Passover ritual meal was based on a feminist *Haggadah*, structured around a gathering of elders and daughters asking and answering questions about their legacy as women, a text that Broner co-wrote with Naomi Nimrod in Israel the previous year. In subsequent decades, the women's seder (the text was printed by *Ms.* magazine and was widely circulated as stapled pages entitled "The Stolen Legacy") and other new rituals have had a significant impact on the evolution of Jewish feminism in North America. Such practices often lead to combative encounters with traditional institutions. For instance, after the death of her father in 1987, Broner attempted to say *Kaddish* in a small American synagogue. Because Orthodox Jewish tradition precludes the participation of women in a *minyan*, she was called *zona*, or whore, and forced to pray behind makeshift partitions known as the *mekhitzah*. Eventually she prevailed and earned the respect of at least some of the congregants, a story that is told in *Mornings and Mourning: A Kaddish Journal*.

As she relates in *The Telling*, her experience of dislocatedness in Israel intensified her awareness that "we had to correct memory and history and myth with new myth, with revision, with data." This epiphany culminated in Broner's most fully realized work of fiction to date, the 1978 novel *A Weave of Women*. Broner's attempts to grapple with the misogynist nature of Israeli society, and other ethical dimensions of its existence, were unprecedented in pre-Intifada Jewish-American writing. Embodying a spirit of theological activism, *A Weave of Women*, is a raw fable of communal transgression, liturgical revision, and resistance, a novel that reveals its author's commitment to wrestling with the difficult Jewish burden of the Text:

> With *Weave* I had ancient books with me, I had a lot of Biblical literature. Before I wrote that book I wrote a note to myself: "I want to do holy writing and make a special calendar for women, and I want to speak in a priestly voice." That was my note to myself. I had it pinned up on the wall so I wouldn't deviate . . . I am both out of the tradition and a maker of tradition.

The novel's speculative journey toward a brave new world of transnational, utopian womanhood is set in a "stone house" under siege, in a tense Jerusalem patently unfriendly to their quest and torn by conflict between Arabs and Jews, the Left and the Right, the religious and secular. As the novel progresses, new crises and catastrophes in the lives of the women as individuals and as a group inspire the innovations of new rituals much like the currents of Broner's subsequent work. While much concerned with the marginalization of women in Judaism, the novel also directly engages with the tangible reality of the Jewish state. Besides episodes that portray state institutions such as the military and police, religious hegemony comes under attack in the novel, specifically the orthodox laws concerning divorce, reproduction, and other rights of women. In *A Weave of Women*, woman's ritual is directed toward the scars inflicted by patriarchy and making the collective's members whole through new/old liturgies, even if this desire is masked with gently humorous irony: "They are all virgins again."

Like Jerome Rothenberg's ethnopoetic recoveries of the esoteric in Judaism, Broner strives to investigate the sexual and spiritual grounds of Judaism, toward a textual recovery of what has been lost to post-Enlightenment Jewish culture. Deeply conversant with alternative traditions within Judaism, the novel contains rituals, demons, exorcisms, transubstantiations, resurrections, and above all, a return to language as an agency of healing. In many ways the activities of the women in this novel serve as a blueprint for what actually followed, the production of new prayer books by the Reform and Reconstructionist movements, feminist haggadot for use at women's as well as conventional family seders, and particularly the recent publication of the poet and Hebraist Marcia Falk's *The Book of Blessings* and Broner's own handbook of rituals, *Bringing Home the Light*. Her true significance as a Jewish-American writer resides in her tenacious dedication to imaginative ways of creating liturgies and rituals that incorporate women's life experience and feminist understandings of the community.

RANEN OMER-SHERMAN

Brookner, Anita

British fiction writer, 1928–

Born in London, 16 July 1928. Studied history at King's College, London; PhD in art history at Courtauld Institute, London; some post-graduate years in Paris; first woman to be Slade Professor, Cambridge, 1967–68; Reader at Courtauld Institute, 1977–88; Fellow, King's College, 1990. Won Booker Prize for *Hotel du Lac*, 1984. Awarded CBE (Commander, Order of the British Empire), 1990.

Selected Writings

Novels

A Start in Life, 1981; as *The Debut*, New York, 1981
Providence, 1982
Look at Me, 1983
Hotel du Lac, 1984
Family and Friends, 1985
A Misalliance, 1986; as *The Misalliance*, 1987

A Friend from England, 1987
Latecomers, 1987
Lewis Percy, 1989
Brief Lives, 1990
A Closed Eye, 1991
Fraud, 1992
A Family Romance, 1993
A Private View, 1994
Incidents in the Rue Laugier, 1995
Altered States, 1996
Visitors, 1997
Falling Slowly, 1998
Undue Influence, 1999
The Bay of Angels, 2001
The Next Big Thing, 2002

Other
Several volumes on art history, including works on Greuze, Watteau, and Jacques-Louis David
Soundings: Studies in Art and Literature, 1997
Romanticism and its Discontents, 2000

Further Reading

Baxter, Gisèle Marie, "Clothes, Men and Books: Cultural Experiences and Identity in the Early Novels of Anita Brookner", *English*, 42 (1993): 125–39, especially 129
Cheyette, Brian, "Moroseness and Englishness", *Jewish Quarterly* (Spring 1995)
Fisher-Wirth, Ann, "Hunger Art: The Novels of Anita Brookner", *Twentieth Century Literature*, 41 (1995): 1–15
Galef, David, "You Aren't What You Eat: Anita Brookner's Dilemma", *Journal of Popular Culture*, 28 (1994): 1–7
Guppy, Shusha, "The Art of Fiction XCVIII: Anita Brookner", *The Paris Review*, 29 (1987): 146–69
Haffenden, John, Interview with Anita Brookner, *Literary Review* (September 1984)
Haffenden, John, *Novelists in Interview*, London: Methuen, 1985
Hosmer, Robert J. Jr, *Contemporary British Women Writers: Texts and Strategies*, London: Macmillan, and New York: St Martin's Press, 1993
Kenyon, Olga, *Women Novelists Today: A Survey of English Writing in the Seventies and Eighties*, Brighton, Sussex: Harvester Press, 1988
Shechner, Mark, *The Conversion of the Jews and Other Essays*, London: Macmillan, and New York: St Martin's Press, 1990
Skinner, John, *The Fictions of Anita Brookner: Illusions of Romance*, London: Macmillan, and New York: St Martin's Press, 1992
Waugh, Patricia, *Feminine Fictions: Revisiting the Postmodern*, London: Routledge, 1989

Brookner has said she does not wish to be "ghettoized", and deplores any "Jewish eagerness to reclaim lost souls". Instead, she prefers to be known as an "English" writer, and has indeed achieved fame and recognition as one of the most accomplished writers of English fiction. She is known for her elegant turn of phrase and elegiac description of mood, often a deep well of inner loneliness. She initially gained eminence in the field of art history, with a passionate espousal of French 18th-century painters such as Watteau, Greuze, and David.

Few of her readers are aware of her Jewish background. Her mother was born in England to Polish-Jewish immigrants and her father was a Polish Jew. "I think my parents' lives were blighted – and in some sense mine is too – largely by the fact . . . of being strangers in England, not quite understanding what was happening and being done to them" (Haffenden, 1984). "You're never really free of your own history, are you?" (interview with Paul Bailey, BBC, 1988). "I have never learned the custom of the country, because we were Jews, tribal and alien" (Kenyon, 1988).

Many writers in Britain have been made to feel uncomfortable with their Jewishness, so it is hardly surprising to find that Brookner rarely writes overtly about Jews. Yet her characters are often refugees who inhabit the outsider's world of London's St John's Wood. They may even have arrived as children on a train from Germany during the war (*Latecomers*). In Brookner's first novel, *A Start in Life*, Ruth Weiss's grandmother has "a sad European past", is surrounded by the dark, heavy pieces of furniture brought from Berlin, and enjoys, as a source of warmth and security, the food she knew back home – the buttermilk, rye-bread, caraway-seeds, cucumbers. Skinner (1992) has highlighted Brookner's concern with food, seeing the shared meal as a form of communion. A Jewish critic would have no difficulty in also perceiving the significance of food as the primary achievement of the nurturing Jewish mother. The Jewish father's duty, on the other hand, is to provide spiritual sustenance (in Brookner's novels, via the book). In many of her fictions, the steady father figure is a kindly bookseller who, significantly, learned his trade and acquired his stock in Europe, the old country. The Weiss family has not yet become much anglicized. (Georg is now George, as Meyer becomes May in *Visitors*.) The alienated and introspective narrator is 40-year-old Dr Ruth Weiss, her carefully chosen name suggesting the biblical Ruth "amid the alien corn", and the purity of the innocent Snow-white (Weiss). Ruth's initiation in this Bildungsroman begins with a meal in a Paris restaurant where "for the very first time she ate lobster, forbidden on her father's side" (a reference to the laws of Kashrut which prohibit shellfish).

Brookner's later novels disguise most references to Jewishness, but in *Family and Friends*, after Sofka's death, her son impulsively covers his mother's looking-glass (a Jewish custom after a death), and recites from Proverbs 31:10 – "A virtuous woman who can find?" In *A Family Romance*, the assimilated matriarch Toni Ferber is nonetheless angry when her daughter-in-law attempts to have a Catholic mass said for her son. Cheyette (1995) comments that "with even Anita Brookner making explicit the Jewishness of her characters in *A Family Romance* . . . the future seems full of promise for British Jewish writing".

But in *Latecomers* there is nary a mention of the fact that the protagonists are two Jewish *Kindertransport* survivors who suffer survivor guilt. We are aware of the Shoah only in its absence. Hartmann has come to terms with survival by "consigning certain memories to the dust", and sedating himself at night to ensure untroubled sleep. But Fibich is troubled by haunting memories, of separation from his parents at the train station, and returns to Berlin in a journey to redeem the past. As he squeezes through the narrow door on his underground journey ("so like a symbolic birth that he laughed") we are relieved that he has come through, albeit as a latecomer, to some sense of belonging and peace.

Brookner prefers discretion to disclosure. She says of Jane Austen what could as well be applied to her own writing: "I think she made a tremendous far-reaching decision to leave certain things out." The words "Jew" or "Jewish" rarely occur in Brookner's writing (any more than they do in Kafka's), but it is time that she was recognized as a quintessentially Anglo-Jewish writer. It may have proved easier for her to reach an English audience by drawing a discreet veil over her many Jewish characters. Her people are subject to doubt and dislocation, despondency and alienation; they are aware, like her, "of what it is like to be lonely, perceptive, an observer" (interview with Richard Mayne, Radio 4, October 1984). Shechner (1990) describes this condition as "ghetto cosmopolitanism", "a frame of mind which gives rise to moods or tonalities . . . seen as particularly Jewish, an ambivalence towards oneself and others". At the same time Brookner mirrors the way in which British Jewry has preferred to keep a low profile. Her writing epitomizes the way in which it has been easier for some Jews in Britain to assimilate within society. Yet they may find themselves with a poignant sense of loss, the loss of Jewish warmth and community while enduring the contradictions of Diaspora life.

SORREL KERBEL

C

Cahan, Abraham

Lithuanian-born US fiction writer, 1860–1951

Born in Podberezy, near Vilna (Vilnius), 7 July 1860. Attended teacher's seminary in Vilna; espoused Russian revolutionary ideals. Fled from Russian police and settled in New York, 1882. Became correspondent for various Russian periodicals, and edited *Di naye tsayt*, *Arbeter tsaytung*, and *Tsukunft*. Wrote English stories and articles for the *Workmen's Advocate*, the *Sun*, the *World*, and the *Evening Post*. Apprenticeship for four years as police reporter for *Commercial Advertiser*. Founder of *Forverts* (*Jewish Daily Forward*), 1897: editor for 50 years. Member of Socialist Party for many years. Visited Palestine, 1925. Died in New York, 31 August 1951.

Selected Writings

Novels (written in English)
Yekl, A Tale of the New York Ghetto, 1896
The Imported Bridegroom and Other Stories of the New York Ghetto, 1898
The White Terror and the Red: A Novel of Revolutionary Russia, 1905
The Rise of David Levinsky, 1917

Other
Refoel naaritsokh: an ertsehlung vegen a stolyer vos iz gekumen tsum seykhl [Naarizokh: A Story of a Carpenter Who Came to his Senses], 1907
Historye fun di fereynigte shtaaten [History of the United States], 2 vols, 1910–12
Di neshome yeseyre un feni's khasanim [The Extra Sabbath Soul and Fanny's Bridegrooms], 1913
Der toydt fun ivan ilitsh: ertsehlung fun leo tolstoy: iberzetst fun rusishen fun abraham cahan mit kritishe erklerungen fun dem iberzetser [The Death of Ivan Ilych: Story by Leo Tolstoi, Translated from the Russian by Abraham Cahan with Critical Comments by the Translator], 1918
Editor, *Hear the Other Side: A Symposium of Democratic Socialist Opinion*, 1934
Palestina [Palestine], 1934
Editor, *Socialism, Fascism, Communism*, 1934
Rashel: a biografye [Rachel: A Biography], 1938
Sholem aschs nayer veg [Sholem Asch's New Path], 1941
Bleter fun mayn lebn [Pages from my Life], 5 vols, 1926–31; vols 1-2 as *The Education of Abraham Cahan*, translated by Leon Stein *et al.*, 1969
Grandma Never Lived in America: The New Journalism of Abraham Cahan, edited by Moses Rischin, 1985

Further Reading

Chametzky, Jules, *From the Ghetto: The Fiction of Abraham Cahan*, Amherst: University of Massachusetts Press, 1977
Fischthal, Hannah Berliner, "Abraham Cahan and Sholem Asch", *Yiddish*, 11/1–2 (1998)
Goldstein, Yaacov N., *Jewish Socialists in the United States: The Cahan Debate 1925–26*, Brighton: Sussex Academic Press, 1998
Guttmann, Allen, *The Jewish Writer in America: Assimilation and the Crisis of Identity*, New York: Oxford University Press, 1971
Howe, Irving, *World of Our Fathers*, New York: Harcourt Brace, 1976; as *The Immigrant Jews of New York*, London: Routledge, 1976
Jeshurin, Ephim H., *Avrom Kahan Bibliografye*, New York, 1941
Marovitz, Sanford E., *Abraham Cahan*, New York: Twayne, 1996
Marovitz, Sanford E. and Lewis Fried, "Abraham Cahan 1860–1951: An Annotated Bibliography", *American Literary Realism 1870–1940*, 3 (Summer 1970)
Rosenfeld, Isaac, "America, Land of the Sad Millionaire", *Commentary*, 14 (August 1952)
Sanders, Ronald, *The Downtown Jews: Portraits of an Immigrant Generation*, New York: Harper and Row, 1969
Saul, Scott, *Homing Pidgins: Immigrant Tongues, Immanent Bodies in Abraham Cahan's Yekl*, Stanford, California: Stanford University Press, 1995
Walden, Daniel (editor), *On Being Jewish: American Jewish Writers from Cahan to Bellow*, Greenwich, Connecticut: Fawcett, 1974

Like many other Russian-educated Jewish intellectuals who fled Russia in the 1880s, Abraham Cahan shifted to Yiddish in America to reach the Jewish worker. Uniquely, he also had notable success in English. "Russian was the embodiment of his intellectual life, Yiddish of the emotional, English of the fascinating and rich 'other' world" is an apt summary that helps explain "his more casual attitude towards writing in Yiddish than in English" (Chametzky). In his autobiography, Cahan tells of a visit to his wealthy Petersburg relations where he "conversed with the children in Russian and envied their inability to speak Yiddish". The same youth would give the first socialist lecture in Yiddish in America and edit the greatest Yiddish newspaper in the New World. Ironically, however, he wrote better in English than in Yiddish.

Cahan's first extensive fiction was a didactic Yiddish novel entitled *Refoel Naaritsokh Becomes a Socialist*, published in parts in 1894 in the socialist *Arbeter tsaytung* [Worker's Newspaper]. In book form it was called *Refoel Naaritsokh: A Story of a Carpenter Who Came to his Senses*. Though weighted down with socialist theorizing, this work draws vitality from its idiom. Here is the innocent hero speaking at a socialist meeting where he is humoured for his naivety:

> Ikh kum haynt gor mit a naye min kashe . . . es vet zikh efsher klepn vi an arbes tsum vant mit dem redners lektshur. Ober ikh muz mikh ton dos maynike. Di kashe shteyt mir shoyn lang vi a beyndl fun a hekht in haldz. Hakitser hamayse, ikh vel a fule nit brayen, ikh volt veln visn, tsu vos darft ir zayn apikorsim?
> – an eksplosyon fun gelekhter.
>
> [I have a new kind of question this time and possibly it will have nothing to do with the lecture. But I must have my say. This question has been sticking in my throat for some time. Short and sweet, I won't take long, I want to know Why do you have to be unbelievers?
> – An explosion of laughter.]

This same question in a variety of forms echoes in much of Cahan's fiction.

Extended works of the imagination in Yiddish – *Di neshome yeseyre* [The Extra Sabbath Soul], *Feni's khasanim* [Fanny's Bridegrooms], and *Bleter fun mayn lebn*, his five-volume autobiography partially excepted – were not to flow from Cahan's pen. Encouraged by William Dean Howells, a foremost figure in American letters, as well as by his success with *Refoel Naaritsokh*, Cahan published his first English novel (actually long short story), *Yekl: A Tale of the New York Ghetto*, in 1896. Though praised by Howells, the story of the painful transformation of Yekl into Jake was not widely read. It continues to be of immense interest to students of the immigrant novel, in which genre it was a pioneer. Numerous critics have remarked on the grating representation of the protagonist's broken English, though Cahan's efforts at portraying a crude and unsympathetic hero merit praise.

Cahan published short fiction in respected American journals. "The Imported Bridegroom" is rich in ironies, again playing on old world/new world conflicts, as does "Circumstances", an honest portrait of a Russian-Jewish intellectual woman turned proletarian. "The Apostate of Chego-Chegg", "Tzinchadzi of the Catskills", and "Rabbi Eliezer's Christmas" all deal with lost worlds and the search for meaning in new ones. Michalina, the *meshumedeste* [apostate] longs for the warmth of Jewish life, but cannot desert her Gentile husband. The Circassian Tzinchadzi has ceased to yearn, leaving him stranded in an emotional desert. Rabbi Eliezer, a scribe and micrography artist in Russia, keeps a miserable newsstand in America, where machines have replaced his manual skills.

Delving into early memories, Cahan in 1905 published *The White Terror and the Red*, a vivid account of the Russian revolutionary movement before and after the assassination of Czar Alexander II. Despite its acute tendentiousness and romanticizing of its heroes and their impossible ideals, this work can still grip a present-day reader. Central to the novel is the revolutionary's dilemma vis à vis "the Jewish question", so hotly debated for decades. The Jewish revolutionary Elkin, deviating from the path of his nihilist comrades, decides to organize emigration to America. Clara, the heroine, tells him: "The right place for a revolutionist is here, in Russia", and he replies: "So many Jewish revolutionists have sacrificed their lives by 'going to the people' – to the Russian people. It's about time some of us at least went to our own people. They need us, Clara." Yet when Elkin is caught and imprisoned, so great is his revolutionary ardour that he claims to be happy at his incarceration. "It is sweet to be suffering for liberty", he says.

In *The Rise of David Levinsky*, Cahan's "classic novel of the urban immigrant experience" (Moses Rischin), the hero's opening self-assessment – masking at least a kernel of the author's consciousness as well – adumbrates the entire novel:

> When I take a look at my inner identity it impresses me as being precisely the same as it was thirty or forty years ago. My present station, power, the amount of worldly happiness at my command, and the rest of it, seem to be devoid of significance.

Leaving one's homeland – even the harshest – often entailed the loss of cultural and spiritual values which were somehow not duplicated in the new land. An indefinable feeling of purposelessness could gnaw away at the heart of powerful men like David Levinsky, whose brilliant business success came to seem hollow.

It is as a public figure, and principally as editor for half a century of the New York *Daily Forward* that Cahan is most remembered. After his visit to Palestine in 1925, Cahan – who was not a Zionist – wrote a series of articles that viewed Jewish efforts at nation-building in a positive light, thereby starting a debate that effectively neutralized the American Jewish labour movement's opposition to Zionism. Cahan can also be credited for his early opposition to Soviet totalitarianism.

Nevertheless, as the pejorative Yiddish word *eybkahanizm* [Abe-Cahanism], reminds us, this extraordinary man had many enemies. Yiddishists, for instance, accused him of being "anti-Yiddish", and from their vantage point, of course, he was.

LEONARD PRAGER

Canetti, Elias

Bulgarian-born fiction writer and essayist, 1905–1994

Born in Ruse, 25 July 1905, into Ladino-speaking Sephardi business family. Taken to Manchester, 1911. Studied at schools in Britain, then in Austria (after father died in 1912), Switzerland, and Germany; University of Vienna, PhD in chemistry 1929. Married, first, Venetiana (Veza) Taubner-Calderon, 1934 (died 1963); second, Hera Buschor, 1971; one daughter. Lived in Britain from 1939 and after World War II in Zürich also. Many awards, including the Foreign Book Prize (France), 1949; Vienna Prize, 1966; Great Austrian State Prize, 1967; Bavarian Academy of Fine Arts Prize, 1969; Büchner Prize, 1972; Nelly Sachs Prize, 1975; Keller Prize, 1977; Nobel Prize for Literature, 1981; Kafka Prize, 1981. Honorary doctorates from University of Manchester, 1975, and University of Munich, 1976. Died in Zürich, 14 August 1994.

Canetti, Veza

Austrian fiction writer, 1897–1963

Born Venetiana Taubner-Calderon in Vienna, 21 November 1897. Frequent visits to England, where her half-brother, Maurice Calderon lived, until outbreak of World War I; worked as a translator and a private school teacher after 1918; met Elias Canetti, 1924; published stories in *Arbeiter-Zeitung*, 1932–33; married Elias Canetti, 1934; emigrated to Paris, November 1938, and to London, January 1939. Destroyed most of her unpublished work, 1956. Died 1 May 1963.

Selected Writings – Elias Canetti

Fiction

Die Blendung, 1936 (banned in Germany); in UK as *Auto-da-Fé*, 1946; in US as *The Tower of Babel*, 1947, translated by C.V. Wedgwood
Der Ohrenzeuge: 50 Charaktere, 1974; as *Earwitness: Fifty Characters*, translated by Joachim Neugroschel, 1979

Plays

Hochzeit, 1932; as *The Wedding*, translated by Gitta Honegger, 1986
Komödie der Eitelkeit, 1950; as *Comedy of Vanity*, translated by Gitta Honegger, 1983
Die Befristeten, 1964; as *The Numbered*, translated by Carol Stewart, 1956; translated as *Life-Terms*, with *Comedy of Vanity*, 1983
Dramen, 1964

Other

Translator, *Leidweg der Liebe* [Love's Pilgrimage], by Upton Sinclair, 1930
Translator, *Das Geld schreibt: eine Studie über die amerikanische Literatur* [Money Writes: A Study of American Literature], by Upton Sinclair, 1930
Translator, *Alkohol*, by Upton Sinclair, 1932
Fritz Wotruba, 1955
Masse und Macht, 1960; as *Crowds and Power*, translated by Carol Stewart, 1962
Welt im Kopf, 1962
Aufzeichnungen 1942–1948, 1965
Die Stimmen von Marrakesch: Aufzeichnungen nach einer Reise, 1967; as *The Voices of Marrakesh: A Record of a Visit*, translated by J.A. Underwood, 1978
Der andere Prozess: Kafkas Briefe an Felice, 1969; as *Kafka's Other Trial: The Letters to Felice*, translated by Christopher Middleton, 1974
Alle vergeudete Verehrung: Aufzeichnungen 1949–1960 [All Wasted Veneration], 1970
Die gespaltene Zukunft: Aufsätze und Gespräche [The Divided Future], 1972
Macht und Überleben: drei Essays [Power and Survival], 1972
Die Provinz des Menschen: Aufzeichnungen 1942–1972, 1973; as *The Human Province*, translated by Joachim Neugroschel, 1978
Das Gewissen der Worte: Essays, 1975; as *The Conscience of Words*, translated by Joachim Neugroschel, 1979
Der Überlebende [The Survivor], 1975
Der Beruf des Dichters [The Poet's Profession], 1976
Die gerettete Zunge: Geschichte einer Jugend, 1977; as *The Tongue Set Free: Remembrance of a European Childhood*, translated by Joachim Neugroschel, 1979; in *The Memoirs of Elias Canetti*, 1999
Die Fackel im Ohr: Lebensgeschichte 1921–1931, 1980; as *The Torch in My Ear*, translated by Joachim Neugroschel, 1982; in *The Memoirs of Elias Canetti*, 1999
Das Augenspiel: Lebensgeschichte 1931–1937, 1985; as *The Play of the Eyes*, translated by Ralph Manheim, 1986; in *The Memoirs of Elias Canetti*, 1999
Das Geheimherz der Uhr: Aufzeichnungen 1973–1985, 1987; as *The Secret Heart of the Clock: Notes, Aphorisms, Fragments 1973–1985*, translated by Joel Agee, 1989
Die Fliegenpein, 1992; as *The Agony of Flies*, translated by H.F. Broch de Rothermann, 1994
Notes from Hampstead: The Writer's Notes, 1954–1971, translated by John Hargraves, 1998
The Memoirs of Elias Canetti, 1999

Selected Writings – Veza Canetti

Fiction

Die gelbe Strasse, 1990; as *Yellow Street*, translated by Ian Mitchell, 1990
Geduld bringt Rosen [Patience Brings Roses], 1992
Die Schildkröten, 1999; as *The Tortoises*, translated by Ian Mitchell, 2001
Der Fund: Erzählungen und Stücke [The Find: Stories and Plays], 2001

Play

Der Oger [The Ogre], 1991

Further Reading

Barnouw, Dagmar, "Doubting Death: On Elias Canetti's Drama *The Deadlined*", *Mosaic*, 7/2 (1974)
Cohen, Yair, "Elias Canetti: Exile and the German Language", *German Life and Letters*, 42/1 (October 1988)
Darby, David (editor), *Critical Essays on Elias Canetti*, New York: G.K. Hall, 2000
Düssel, Reinhard, "Aspects of Confucianism in Elias Canetti's Notes and Essays", *Tamkang Review* (Autumn 1987–Summer 1988)

Falk, Thomas H., *Elias Canetti*, New York: Twayne, 1993
Honegger, Gitta, "Acoustic Masks: Strategies and Language in the Theater of Canetti, Bernhard and Handke", *Modern Austrian Literature*, 18/2 (1985)
Hulse, Michael (translator), *Essays in Honor of Elias Canetti*, New York: Farrar Straus and Giroux, 1987
Kimball, Roger, "Becoming Elias Canetti", *New Criterion*, 5/1 (September 1986)
Lorenz, Dagmar C.G., "Feminism and Socialism in Vienna (Veza Canetti)", in *Keepers of the Motherland: German Texts by Jewish Women Writers*, Lincoln: University of Nebraska Press, 1997
Modern Austrian Literature, special issue, 16/3–4 (1983)
Parry, Idris, "Elias Canetti's Novel *Die Blendung*" in *Essays on German Literature*, edited by F. Norman, London: University of London Institute of German Studies, 1965
Preece, Julian, "The Rediscovered Writings of Veza Magd-Canetti: On the Psychology of Subservience", *Modern Austrian Literature*, 28/2 (1995)
Russell, Peter, "The Vision of Man in Elias Canetti's *Die Blendung*", *German Life and Letters*, 28 (1974–75)
Sacharoff, Mark, "Grotesque Comedy in Canetti's *Auto-da-Fé*", *Critique: Studies in Modern Fiction*, 14/1 (1972)
Stenberg, Peter, "Remembering Times Past: Canetti, Sperber, and 'A World That Is No More' ", *Seminar* (November 1981)
Thompson, Edward, "Elias Canetti's *Die Blendung* and the Changing Image of Madness", *German Life and Letters*, 26 (1972–73)
Thorpe, Kathleen, "Notes on *Die Blendung* by Elias Canetti", *Theoria* (October 1986)

Elias Canetti first received significant critical attention in 1960 for the publication of his socio-anthropological study *Masse und Macht* (*Crowds and Power*). His multi-volume autobiography later won him popular success. *Masse und Macht* and *Die Blendung* (*Auto-da-Fé*), his sole novel, have received the bulk of scholarly attention, and account for his stature as an important 20th-century writer and thinker, but offer little insight into his Jewish identity.

Canetti understood his Sephardic background to be a cultural, linguistic, and religious heritage in the service of humanistic ideas. These views culminate in his enmity with death ("Todfeindschaft"), i.e., his fight against death's intrusion into, and thus control of, our lives. The key element in this fight, in his view, is metamorphosis, the human capacity for transformation and regeneration, a notion that includes embracing other cultures. This explains the writer's assumption of the position of the free individual: "In order to be free, the conditions that determine existence must be accepted, so that they can later be surpassed" (Vilém Flusser).

That Canetti explored and took part in cultures outside his own, thereby rejecting essentialist notions of Jewish identity, is clear in the following, from *Die Provinz des Menschen* (*The Human Province*):

> The greatest intellectual temptation in my life, the only one I have to fight very hard against is: to be a total Jew . . . I scorned my friends for tearing loose from the enticements of many nations and blindly becoming Jews again, simply Jews. How hard it is for me now not to emulate them. The new dead, those dead long before their time, plead with one, and who has the heart to say no to them? But aren't the new dead everywhere, on all sides, in every nation? . . . Can't I still belong to all of them, as before, and nevertheless be a Jew?

The author's discussion of his Jewish-German heritage further underscores this position, as he maintains his special ties to German culture, despite the recent past, because the German language and its people share in a kinship with the rest of the world:

> The language of my intellect will remain German – because I am Jewish. Whatever remains of the land which has been laid to waste in every way – I wish to preserve it in me as a Jew. *Their* destiny too is mine; but I bring along a universal human legacy. I want to give back to their language what I owe it. I want to contribute to their having something that others can be grateful for.

Further expressions of Canetti's Jewish identity are to be found in *Die Stimmen von Marrakesch* (*The Voices of Marrakesh*) and his three-volume autobiography. In the first volume of the autobiography, *Die gerettete Zunge* (*The Tongue Set Free*), Canetti contemplates his mother's sense of pride in her Sephardic heritage, and states that, unlike her, he extends this emotion to all of humanity. Jewish themes in this volume underline Canetti's experience of the Jewish oral tradition, and highlight Ruse as a model for peaceful interaction between diverse ethnic groups. For example, in one scene the Roma not only are included in the Sabbath by receiving alms, but are made the centre of the occasion by the portrayal of their proud entrance into the Canetti family courtyard.

Canetti's mother was of major importance in shaping his personality. She was a fiercely independent woman who rejected restrictions placed upon her by others. For instance, she picked fruit on the Sabbath to console her son, thereby placing human gestures above laws.

Another important role model in the writer's life was Dr Sonne, perhaps better known as the Hebrew poet Abraham ben Yitzhak (or ben Jizchak), who is portrayed in the third volume of the autobiography, *Das Augenspiel* (*The Play of the Eyes*). Sonne is the embodiment of the good person ("der gute Mensch"), and his conception of Spain (based on a knowledge of its literature, history, and languages), did not divide that country into ethnicities in conflict, but rather stressed how these can complement and mutually benefit one another.

In *The Voices of Marrakesh*, Canetti's account of a trip to Morocco in 1954, the author describes his affinity for the residents of the Jewish quarter. He celebrates and identifies with not only the city's Sephardic, but also Muslim cultural heritage. Thus, his work illustrates the common ties among humans and encourages an identification with others that promotes mutual respect, recognition, and tolerance.

While critical acclaim came late in Canetti's career, his first wife Veza Canetti, despite increased distribution and consideration of her work since the 1990s, has yet to receive due attention. Canetti termed this lack of a reception of her work "unnatural" because he considered her to be an extremely accomplished writer. She deserves recognition for all four of her fictional works, which are richer and more varied than those of her husband.

Although no clear statements outline Veza Canetti's Jewish identity, her writing provides insight into the connections between her sociopolitical views and those of Austrian Social Democracy, and demonstrates the importance of her Jewish identity. The combination of empathy and critical distance is a striking characteristic of her writing. Her work focuses on female figures who suffer either because of their birth into an underprivileged socioeconomic class, or at the hands of others, mainly ruthless dowry-hunters. However, in the stories of *Die gelbe Strasse* (*The Yellow Street*) and *Geduld bringt Rosen* [Patience Brings Roses], as well as in the play *Der Oger* [The Ogre], the female characters are varied. Yet most retain their dignity regardless of the hardships they endure.

Despite the quality of her writing, Veza Canetti was forced to use pseudonyms to have her work published in the anti-Semitic climate of 1930s Vienna. Among the pseudonyms she chose, those of Veza Magd (maid) and Veronika Knecht (servant) symbolize her respect for women regardless of class.

It is in her posthumously published work *Die Schildkröten* [The Tortoises], that Veza Canetti deals with a specifically Jewish theme, namely the fictionalized account of the months between the Anschluss in the spring of 1938, and the Canettis' own escape from Austria later that same year. In a noticeably harsher and less detached tone than that of her earlier works, she vividly portrays the struggle of Jewish citizens to maintain human dignity amid the dehumanizing actions of the Nazis. The metaphor of the tortoise, unable to leave its protective shell without dying, is used to express the dilemma of two groups: those who go into exile, and those who find it impossible to leave their homes. The novella also unmasks Nazi posturing, propaganda, and ideology – in the character of the SA-man Pilz (fungus) – as the rapaciousness of the morally bankrupt unleashed by the Hitler regime. This text also bears witness to the furious pace with which Jewish citizens of Austria were robbed of their rights, their property, and ultimately their lives.

Both Veza and Elias Canetti identified with and expressed their Jewish identity while placing their ties to humanity at large at the forefront of their work.

CLAUDE DESMARAIS

Carmi, T.

US-born Israeli poet, 1925–1994

Born Carmi Charney in New York City, 31 December 1925 to a Hebrew-speaking family. Received an intensive Hebrew education in Jewish parochial schools. Spent three years in Tel Aviv, returning to USA, 1939. Settled in Israel, 1946. Studied at Yeshiva University, New York, BA, 1946; Columbia University, New York, 1946; the Sorbonne, 1946–47; Hebrew University, Jerusalem, 1949–51. Served in the Israeli Defence Forces, 1947–49: Captain. Married, first, Shoshana Heiman, one child; second, Tamara Rikman, one child; third, Lilach Peled, one child. Served as counsellor at Jewish orphanage in France, housing survivors, 1946. Co-editor, *Massa*, Tel Aviv, 1952–54; editor, *Orot*, Jerusalem, 1955, and *Ariel*, 1971–74; editor, Sifriyat Poalim Publishers, Tel Aviv, 1957–62, and Am Oved Publishers, Tel Aviv, 1963–70; Ziskind Visiting Professor, Brandeis University, Waltham, Massachusetts, 1970; Associate Professor, Institute for Arts and Communications, Tel Aviv University, 1973; Visiting Fellow, Oxford Centre for Postgraduate Hebrew Studies, 1974–76; Poet in Residence, Hebrew University, Spring 1977; from 1978 Visiting Professor of Hebrew Literature, Hebrew Union College, Jewish Institute of Religion, Jerusalem; Visiting Professor, Stanford University, California, 1979. Many awards including Shlonsky prize, 1958; Littauer Foundation grant, 1971, 1989; Matz Foundation grant, 1971; Brenner Prize, 1972; Prime Minister's Prize, 1973; Jewish Book Council Kovner award, 1978; *Present Tense*, Kenneth Smilen award, for translation; 1982, Guggenheim Fellowship, 1987; Bialik Prize, 1990. Died in Jerusalem, 21 November 1994

Selected Writings

Poetry

Mum vehalom [Wound and Dream], 1951
Eyn perahim shehorim [There Are No Black Flowers], 1953
Sheleg biyerushalayim [Snow in Jerusalem], 1956
Hayam haaharon [The Last Sea], 1958
Nahash haneboshet, 1961; translated as *The Brass Serpent*, by Dan Moraes, 1964
Haunikorn mistakel bamarah [The Unicorn Looks in the Mirror], 1967
Teviah [The Claim], 1967
Davar aher: shirim 1959–1969 [Selected Poems 1951–69], 1970
"Somebody Like You", translated by Stephen Mitchell, 1971
Hitnatslut hamehaber [Author's Apology], 1974
Selected Poems, translated by Stephen Mitchell, 1976
El erets aheret [Into Another Land], 1977
Leyad even hatoim, 1981; translated as *At the Stone of Losses*, 1983
Ahat hi li [One to Me], 1985
Shirim min haazuvah [Poems of the Azuvah], 1988
Emet vehovah: shirim [Truth and Consequence], 1993
Shirim: mivhar 1951–1994 [Collected Poems 1952–1994], 1994
Poems included in *The Modern Hebrew Poem Itself*, 1965 and 1989; and in *The Penguin Book of Hebrew Verse*, 1981

Plays

The Firstborn, from the play by Christopher Fry, 1958
Herr Puntila und sein Knecht Matti (Hebrew version), from the play by Bertolt Brecht, 1962
Pantagleize (Hebrew version), from the play by Michel de Ghelderode, 1963

A Midsummer Night's Dream (Hebrew version), from the play by William Shakespeare, 1964
Antigone (Hebrew version), from the Robert Fitzgerald and Dudley Fitts version of the play by Sophocles, 1969
Measure for Measure (Hebrew version), from the play by William Shakespeare, 1979
La Folle de Chaillot (Hebrew version), from the play by Jean Giraudoux, 1979
Hamlet (Hebrew version), from the play by William Shakespeare, 1981
Much Ado About Nothing (Hebrew version), from the play by William Shakespeare, 1983
Cyrano de Bergerac (Hebrew version), from the play by Edmond Rostand, 1986
Othello (Hebrew version), from the play by William Shakespeare, 1991

Also made Hebrew versions of the following works for stage production: *Spoon River Anthology* by Edgar Lee Masters, *Noé* by André Obey, *Rosencrantz and Guildenstern Are Dead* by Tom Stoppard, *The Beaux' Stratagem* by George Farquhar, *The Zoo Story* by Edward Albee, *Look Back in Anger* by John Osborne, *The Hostage* by Brendan Behan, *The Little Foxes* by Lillian Hellman.

Further Reading

Levy, Shimon, "Elements of Poetic Self-Awareness in Modern Poetry", *Modern Hebrew Literature*, 3 (1976)
Schulman, Grace, " 'The Voice Inside': Translating the Poetry of T. Carmi", in *Translating Poetry: The Double Labyrinth*, edited by Daniel Weissbort, Iowa City: University of Iowa Press, 1989

Carmi was a prolific poet and translator, one of the few poets born in the United States who wrote in Hebrew. His first volume *Mum vehalom* [Wound and Dream] (1951) has all the characteristics of the work of a young poet. Carmi included only four of its poems in his *Collected Poems 1952–1994* (1994). He retained "Wound and Dream", which serves as a foretaste of his views on the *ars poetica*:

My left hand is under your head
My right grates the scratch;
You were betrothed to me with a wound and a dream,
Without mercy, without loving grace.

The speaker is unable to sustain his love. His dream is spoiled by his wound. The woman addressed also represents the poet's muse. The poetic act is simultaneously an embrace and a scratching of a wound. (*Mum*, in Hebrew, denotes a blemish or defect.) The dream is impaired by the artist's awareness that the translation of the dream into words always falls short of the thing in itself.

Carmi's poetry is replete with allusions to biblical, rabbinical, and kabbalistic themes and texts. His frequent manipulation of the tension between the sacred subtext underlying his secular texts affords him opportunities for ironic interplay. In a poem bearing the superscription of a quotation by Robert Graves: "The muse is the perpetual other woman," he writes:

Hatsarah (the enemy, the trouble, the second wife), the other . . .
The beloved, the traitor, the bosom of mystery
Who covers my voice (inspiration)
With a goat's pelt.

The harlot, the peddler, my possession.
Who waves the scarlet thread
In her window
("To . . .", *Collected Poems*)

Michal, King David's wife, had covered her *terafim* (house gods) with a goat's pelt, placing them in David's bed to deceive Saul as to his whereabouts (I Samuel, 19: 13–17). The pelt alludes, perhaps, to the kid's skin with which Rebecca covered Jacob's arms so that they may seem as hairy as Esau's – and thus deceive Isaac, leading him to bless Jacob instead of Esau, – or perhaps to the whore's price of a goat's skin that Judah gave to Tamar (Genesis, 38: 12–27). The scarlet thread is the sign with which Rachel, the harlot, marked her residence so that the Israelites attacking at Jericho might spare her life (Joshua, 2:18–20). All these are ruses used by temptresses to silence the real voice of the artist.

Carmi believed that modern Hebrew poets must relate to what Eliot had called "the tradition". "I live within a specific tradition", he argued, "I am permitted, even obliged, to utilize it. I wish that the relationship between what is written today in poetry be like the relationship between Bartok and Beethoven."

A second characteristic of his poetry is recourse to the concrete – a technique he learned from the British and American imagists and from several Hebrew poets (e.g. David Vogel and Leah Goldberg). At times he can be ironically whimsical:

You are slippery [the original Hebrew reads: My slippery one]
You slide through my fingers
Like a cake of soap
Into the drain (eddy) of the tub.
I grope and fumble in vain.
Only after the many waters run out,
I find you at the bottom,
Pure and shining,
White [or a shining moon] in the white sky.
(*Into Another Land*)

The white, shimmering, evasive cake of soap reminds the lover, taking a shower in a distant city, of his evasive, white-rounded love. His groping after the soap recalls her mystery, her charm, and physical beauty. The "many waters" refer both to her elusiveness and to the sea that separates the two.

Another aspect of his *ars poetica* appears in "First I Will Sing":

First I will sing (say poetry). Then, I might speak.
Repeating words I have already said

Like a person studying his features at dawn,
I shall return to my silences

Just like the moon decreases,
I shall publicly brandish the bird of weeping

Like a child drawing his sword on Purim,
I will return to (woo) your closed hands . . .

And I will sing. First I will sing. Wrap my words
In paper bags like pomegranates.
And then, perhaps we will speak
(*Selected Poems 1951–1969*)

The pomegranate is the symbol of the poetic word – red and bursting with juice and seed – it must be wrapped in paper bags against the buffeting of the weather. Art is a rich but a delicate and vulnerable private matter. The poet may partially "brandish his sword of weeping" – his hidden "wound", but only "like a child drawing his sword on Purim". Purim is the time of masquerading, and the child's sword is made of cardboard.

On occasion, Carmi dealt with social and political themes but always shunned placard verse. His second volume *There Are No Black Flowers* (1953) is a dramatic poem in several voices and reflects his painful encounter with children who survived the Holocaust. It telescopes the tragedy of the Shoah into a series of dramatic monologues. The agony of the speakers, their sense of loss mixed with feelings of guilt, are projected against the background of the indifference of society (embodied in the polite officialese of French bureaucrats who order that the home be evacuated so that it can be replaced by an atomic plant). A Far Eastern bamboo tree looms as a recurrent image of alienation and hopelessness. The poem closes in an optimistic note. Rene hears wind blowing music through the bamboo shoots and sees "how suddenly the almond tree runs along the [director's] window in the perfumed snow and bursts into her room, its amazing abundance invading her heart with its white buds – there are no black flowers" (*Selected Poems 1951–1969*).

His last two volumes of verse: *Poems of the Azuvah* (1988) and *Truth and Consequence* (1993), are deeply pessimistic. *Haazuvah* is a double-entendre with two meanings in Hebrew: (1) forsaken, desolation and (2) forsaken one (f) (i.e. the abandoned wife). *Poems of the Azuvah* has two central themes: first, the devastation felt by the speaker as he grows older, is plagued with disease, and suffers the loss of friends; secondly, the theme of his latest divorce, the abandonment of his wife and home. The volume is dedicated to the memory of Dan Pagis.

In *Truth and Consequence* Carmi returns to the problem of authentic art. In "The Whole Truth" the speaker contends: "I'm the liar/ and search for the truth" and concludes: "But if you tell me/ that I am a liar/ I would be quite insulted". "To Him Who is Far and Near" was published after Carmi learned that he was dying of cancer:

In the distance C
The train's whistle is heard
Like the wail of a baby;
The note on the wall dangles
Like burnt-out hyssop:
The crab's line in the damp sand
Looks like a secret code
Of a submarine secret agent.

The view is from a hospital bed. The note on the wall is the diagnostic chart, conjuring up an association with the petitionary notes inserted in the Western Wall pleading for heavenly mercy. The cancer (the crab) works as an undercover agent leaving its traces on the sand.

Close by
The malignant growth
(radius 2.7)
Looks like a malignant growth.
Shalom, I say
Shalom to Him who is near and far

Shalom means peace and is used as greeting and farewell. The patient is aware of his possible death/departure, but still hopes for peace/healing? Carmi died in 1994.

EZRA SPICEHANDLER

Castel-Bloom, Orly

Israeli fiction writer, 1960–

Born in Tel Aviv, 1960, to French-speaking Jewish-Egyptian parents. Completed army training, then studied film at Tel Aviv University. Wrote for Channel One television. Divorced, two children; lives in Tel Aviv. Awards include Tel Aviv Prize, 1990; Prime Minister's Prize, 1992; Natan Alterman Prize, 1996.

Selected Writings

Stories
Lo rahok Mimerkaz hair [Not Far from the Centre of Town], 1987
Svivah oyenet [Hostile Surroundings], 1989
"How Can you Lose your Cool, When the Kinneret is as Calm as a Pool", *Modern Hebrew Literature*, new series, 6 (Spring–Summer 1991)
Sipurim bilti retsuim [Unbidden Stories], 1993
"The Woman Who Gave Birth to Twins and Disgraced Herself!", "The Woman Who Went Looking for a Walkie Talkie", and "The Woman Who Wanted to Kill Someone" in *The Best of Ariel: A Celebration of Contemporary Israeli Prose and Art*, 2 (1995)
Zikhronot netushim [Abandoned Memories], 1998

Novels
Heikhan ani nimtset [Where Am I], 1990
Dolly City 1992; as *Dolly City*, translated by Dalya Bilu, 1997
Hamina lisa [The Mina Lisa], 1995
Hasefer Hahadash Shel Orly Castel-Bloom [Taking the Trend], 1998

For Children
Shneinu nitnaheg yafeh [Let's Behave Ourselves], 1997

Further Reading

Abromowitz, Molly, "Doctors: The Plot Thickens", *Jews and Medicine* (June–July 1999)

Baraitser, Marion, "Playing with a Dolly Can Be Dangerous", *Jewish Chronicle Literary Supplement* (February 1997)

Esterik, Chris van, "A Different Goy on the Cross Every Day", *NRC Handelsblad* (March 1994)

Feinberg, Anat, "What an Intoxicating Madness!", *Modern Hebrew Literature*, new series (Spring–Autumn 1992)

Figes, Eva, "Go along for the Ride", *Jewish Chronicle* (March 1997)

Galea, Claudine, "Joyce's Little Girl", *La Marseillaise* (June 1995)

Gurevitch, David, "Postmodernism in Israeli Literature in the 80s and 90s", *Modern Hebrew Literature*, new series, 15 (Autumn–Winter 1995)

Miron, Dan, "A Handbook to a New Prose Language", *Modern Hebrew Literature*, new series (Autumn 1994)

Richler, Noah, "Young Israelis: Interviews with Writers of a New Generation", *Jewish Quarterly*, 45/2 (Summer 1998): 18

Schwartz, Yigal, "Alice in Tel Aviv", *Modern Hebrew Literature*, 6 (Spring–Summer 1991): 18–19

Orly Castel-Bloom is the high priestess of the postmodern revolution of young Israeli writers that began in the mid-1980s. She has a cult following not only in Israel, but also in France, the Netherlands, and Germany, a following which appreciates her satires on Israeli Arabophobia, the ultra-Orthodox movement and the bureaucracy of Israeli political life. She is a controversial writer. Some argue that her writing style is merely provocative, others that she has broken new ground and has changed the face of "learned" Hebrew literature by using a language that beats its verbal rhythm on a hollow tin can, reflecting the sound of the harsh reality of Tel Aviv, and exposing the shallowness of modern life. It is clear she writes about Israel from a position of protest and anger, inventing a literary language to express this, which deliberately uses the flat, harsh, and violent language of the cartoon and the world of punk, which does not expect to understand or interpret the world. She draws from, and parodies, many sources – for example, from the work of Pinter – its uncertainty, its living in the moment in order to forget the past – to the surreal fables of Kafka and silent Dada films. "My work is based on the political, or social, or maybe even personal feeling I have that nothing lasts. It's a very Israel situation. Very post-modern." The writer furthermore states she is describing a "post spiritual state of the soul".

Her fiction is not concerned with exploring her roots:

> I feel maybe because I am Jewish, I don't have roots . . . My parents were from Egypt and not Europe . . . I felt guilty that none of my family died in the Holocaust . . . And clinging to roots brings violence . . . I don't want to be a victim of the political situation . . . I want to float above circumstances and to look at life from a distance. This is also a way to feel free.

Her first novel, *Where am I*, presents the mid-life crisis of a capricious, penniless divorcee with no status, who always finds herself in a flawed and violent relationship with her society and its bureaucracy. The chilling hilarity of the encounters is expressed in the "mechanical, alienated speech rhythms and apathetic and provocative tone" that reflects the protagonist's "infantile sociopathic attitude" (Schwartz). There are amusing and frightening meetings, both real and imaginary, between the rich and powerful, and the poor and the outcast, who like the protagonist, live on the margins of society. "The heroine crosses the boundaries of dream and reality, passes across the screen like a cinema star who jilts film, public and fame in order to join a spectator sitting in the first row, who she has subtly fallen in love with" (Galea).

Castel-Bloom's second novel, *Dolly City*, forces us to react to the horror of a "cancerous" city life that is apocalyptic and futuristic. "We shriek with both laughter and horror, for once the reader realises that the protagonist, Doctor Dolly is a metaphor for Israel, it becomes clear that the novel is a modern biblical parable, a scathing social satirical fantasy not unlike Swift's or Kafka's – with the Yiddishe-mamma complex as its theme" (Baraitser). "I wanted to show that motherhood is like art" – by this Castel-Bloom means that motherhood is obsessive and alienating. As in the work of Canetti and Musil, a character such as Mother Dolly fights to protect her adopted son from the sickness of modern existence by building a fortress against it. Locations are important in her books. *Dolly City* is set in a chaotic, lunatic, and agitated high-rise cityscape – part Tel Aviv, part London and Paris, where Doctor Dolly slices up various animals for investigation in her apartment. Here she brings an abandoned, shivering infant boy she happens on by the roadside. As Boy grows, she treats him, in her deluded self-involved state, as one of her experiments. She carves the map of Israel into his back, the borders enlarging as he grows. Miraculously, with the help of a saintly aunt and earthy grandmother, the boy manages to survive into adulthood, and even to save his mother from a suicide attempt. He joins the navy, then the army, tries to hijack an airplane to escape, fails, and we last see him escaping into the desert, chased by police. Castel-Bloom seems to be suggesting that perhaps Israel can be cured of the overwhelming need to control borders and to kill for it.

Castel-Bloom's third novel, *Hamina lisa*, parodies melodrama, soap opera, and stock film fantasies. The writer debates the nature of the artistic process through the grotesque character of a 203-year-old crone, Flora, who eats scripts to extract the essence of "script substance", which exists at the end of time, and which is accessed through a process of remembrance that begins at a moment of poetic blindness and takes place in a timelessness of floating unease. The Mona Lisa of high art becomes secularized into the bourgeois Mina Lisa, a housewife who writes scripts that Flora devours. Mina is the granddaughter-in-law to the old crone, who feeds the old woman scripts in order to fuel her and Mina's flight to the artistic time zone of "the Time Police". Mina Lisa chooses not to learn how to become "mother of the year", or how to write an instant script, but to enter an experience of somnambulance that borders on madness, in which a script is transformed into great art by the way reality refutes illusion, and illusion refutes reality.

The latest novel, *Taking the Trend*, is a witty "nonsense" book, written in the style of a stand-up comic, satirizing the emptiness of postmodern trends. Castel-Bloom's stories are odd tales of alienation set in suburbia – bizarre modern-day fables of the extraordinary, or "morality tales for an amoral world" (Richler). The tales in *Unbidden Stories* are deliberately very short, an artistic area where she reigns supreme. "In many ways [they] are like animated movies . . . [that] portray a violent and cruel reality with humour. They are highly-strung, compulsively repetitive, but still light, funny and philosophically and linguistically playful" (Miron).

MARION BARAITSER

Celan, Paul

Romanian poet and translator, 1920–1970

Born Paul Antschel in Czernowitz, 23 November 1920. Studied at Czernowitz Gymnasium; medical school of Tours University, 1938–39; Czernowitz University, 1939–41. Parents interned and murdered by Nazis, 1942. Worked as field surgeon in psychiatric unit, then left for Vienna. Studied for Licence ès Lettres, Paris, 1950. Married Gisèle Lestrange, 1952. Settled in Paris; lectured in German at École Normale Supérieure. Awards include Bremen Literary Prize, 1958; Büchner Prize, 1960; North Rhine Westphalia Prize, 1964. Committed suicide, 20 April 1970.

Selected Writings

Collections
Gedichte, 2 volumes, 1975
Gesammelte Werke, edited by Beda Allemann and Stefan Reichert, 5 vols, 1983; vol. 3 as *Collected Prose*, translated by Rosemarie Waldrop, 1986
Gedichte 1938–1944, 1985

Poetry
Der Sand aus den Urnen [The Sand from the Urns], 1948
Mohn und Gedächtnis, 1952; as *Poppy and Memory*, translated by Michael Hamburger, 1988
Von Schwelle zu Schwelle, 1955; as *From Threshold to Threshold*, translated by Michael Hamburger, 1988
Sprachgitter, 1959; as *Language Mesh*, translated by Michael Hamburger, 1988
Die Niemandsrose, 1963; as *The No-one's Rose*, translated by Michael Hamburger, 1988
Atemwende [Breath Change], 1967
Totnauberg, 1968
Fadensonnen [Thread-suns], 1968
Lichtzwang [Light Compulsion], 1970
Speech-Grille and Selected Poems, translated by Joachim Neugroschel, 1971
Schneepart [Snow-share], 1971
Selected Poems, translated by Michael Hamburger and Christopher Middleton, 1972
Nineteen Poems, translated by Michael Hamburger, 1972
Zeitgehoft: Späte Gedichte aus dem Nachlass [Time-hoped], 1976
Poems, translated by Michael Hamburger, 1980
65 Poems, translated by Brian Lynch and Peter Jankowsky, 1985
Thirty-Two Poems, translated by Michael Hamburger, 1985
Last Poems, translated by Katharine Washburn and Margaret Guillemin, 1986

Other
Edgar Jené und der Traum vom Traume [Edgar Jené and the Dream-Dream], 1948
Der Meridian, 1961
Übertragungen aus dem Russischen [Translations from the Russian], 1986
Translator of works by many authors, including Chekhov, Lermontov, Rimbaud, and Shakespeare

Further Reading

Arnold, H.L. (editor), Celan issue of *Text + Kritik*, 53–54 (1977)
Arnold, H.L. (editor), Celan issue of *Acts: A Journal of New Writing*, 8–9 (1988)
Burger, Hermann, *Paul Celan: Auf der Suche nach der verlorenen Sprache* [Paul Celan: Searching for Lost Language], Zürich and Munich: Artemis, 1974
Chalfen, Israel, *Paul Celan: A Biography of His Youth*, New York: Persea, 1991 (German original, 1979)
Colin, Amy, *Paul Celan: Holograms of Darkness*, Bloomington: Indiana University Press, 1991
Felstiner, John, *Paul Celan: Poet, Survivor, Jew*, New Haven, Connecticut: Yale University Press, 1995
Glenn, Jerry, *Paul Celan*, New York: Twayne, 1973
Lyon, James K, "The Poetry of Paul Celan: An Approach", *Germanic Review*, 39/1 (January 1964)
Pilling, John, *A Reader's Guide to Fifty Modern European Poets*, London: Heinemann, and New York: Barnes and Noble, 1982
Samuels, Clarise, *Holocaust Visions: Surrealism and Existentialism in the Poetry of Paul Celan*, Columbia, South Carolina: Camden House, 1993

Even his principal English translator, Michael Hamburger, has admitted that Celan's work is extremely challenging for the scholar and indeed for the general reader of poetry: "Paul Celan's work confronts us with difficulty and paradox." Celan's fundamental statement about his poetry is that language is all he has left: that is, after the trauma of the Shoah and the murder of his parents. It is clear that Celan has come to represent the quintessential Jewish poet of the post-Nazi era in the mode of existential angst. His poetry confronts the unspeakable on purely ontological terms.

John Pilling locates some of the difficulty of the syntax and patterns of meaning thus: "Celan saw himself as a poet of dialogue, an explorer and interpreter of the space in which a dialogue might take place." This hermetic quality in Celan is inextricably bound with his tendency to create a personal neologistic diction at times, and to write a text in search of its perfect reader, as if theoretically, there will be an ideal reader for each written statement. In this syntactical and lexical difficulty, Celan has no intention to write about the death camps or any other suffering of the Jewish people in an explicit, realistic way. In fact, his tendency to use silence as much as utterance is possibly related to what Pilling calls his "origins in the Hasidic communities of Eastern Europe".

His early poetry sets the method which intensifies as the work goes on. The reader looks in vain for a logical, linear progression of thought and word: "Any reader familiar with the kind of poetry whose progression is one of imagery rather than argument will know how to read the earlier poems" (Hamburger). The lyrics in the first three volumes are a dazzling, powerful fusion of literariness and transmuted autobiographical catharsis. Many poems seek to assimilate the fact of Celan's mother's brutal murder (she was shot in the neck) with the condition of life itself, as in "The Travelling Companion" in which the line, "Your mother's soul whips on the sharks at the bow" as part of a visionary image of negation and death, places his deep loss at the heart of an existential crisis.

Celan's most anthologized poem, "Death Fugue", illustrates the method of subversion and surreal menace inherent in his dark and elusive poetry, with its refrain of "Black milk at daybreak we drink you at night". This establishes much of the approach to poetry which came later in the profound and disturbing poems of *Thread-suns* and *Light Compulsion*. Often in these collections, poems explore the resonances of Old Testament language and rhetoric with a deeply personal statement of annihilation. Poems such as "Psalm" convey this relentless potency of creative negation of life-belonging: "A nothing/ we were, are, shall/ remain, flowering/ the nothing-, the/ no-one's rose."

In this haunting minimalism, Celan is close to Beckett's examination of the elements of being and the terror of a receding sense of meaning in experience and in others. But Celan is more concerned with the need to allow the undervoice of the poet in the creative process to emerge unhindered by external reference. A poem such as "There was Earth inside Them" at once conveys a vague suggestion of the horrific images of Jews digging their own graves in a concentration camp, while also avoiding actual detail: that is, Celan stretches the awful images of "They dug and dug, so their day/ went by for them . . ." into a more universal evocation of the negation of the self.

This is not to deny an occasional poem with a more overt and accessible historical and topographical reference, as we have "Think of It" from *Thread-suns*. Here, Celan evokes the "bog soldier" at Massada who "teaches himself home" in the "wire", and then, having fixed the poem in that dual time-reference of two crucial events in Jewish history, he extends the metaphor of land and earth into the clay of being itself, and when he talks of "your own self" having a bit of habitable earth, he condenses several strands of Jewish identity and history into a very short poem.

Celan's work has come to represent a core text for theoretical perspectives on the nature of language and its opposite, silence, and so logically to the prayer and dialogue of man and God, in addition to language as truth. In George Steiner's magisterial work on translation, *After Babel*, Celan is taken as an instance of such difficulties being apparent in the task of the translator. Partly through this perception of Celan's importance in that context, Steiner says, elsewhere, that the "shared after-death of the Holocaust" gave us "one of the indispensable poems of the German language" and he sees Celan as the catalyst.

STEPHEN WADE

Cixous, Hélène

French dramatist and literary theorist, 1937–

Born in Oran, Algeria, 5 June 1937. Raised in a German Ashkenazi / North African Sephardi household. Secondary education in Algiers. Married Guy Berger, 1955; divorced; one daughter and two sons (one died 1961). Moved to Paris, 1955; studied English literature; Doctorat des lettres, 1968 (thesis on James Joyce). Has taught at many universities, including Bordeaux, 1962, the Sorbonne, 1965–67, and Nanterre. Co-founder, with Gérard Genette and Tzvetan Todorov, of structuralist periodical *Journal poétique*, 1968. Professor of English literature since 1968, and founder-director of Centre de Recherche en Études Féminines since 1974, University of Paris VII, St Vincennes. Participated in Groupe Information Prison (GIP), with Michel Foucault and others, putting on performances in front of prisons; beaten at a demonstration in Nancy, 1971. Joined Association internationale pour la défense des artistes (AIDA); participated in campaigns for Václav Havel and Wei Jingsheng, 1977. With Foucault and Jacques Derrida, formed first Commission Nationale des Lettres, but resigned after a year, 1981–82. Made several trips to Khmer Rouge camps on Cambodian–Thai border, and to India, 1986. Member of board, International Parliament of Writers, 1994. Many awards include Prix Médicis, 1969; Southern Cross of Brazil, 1989; Légion d'Honneur, 1994.

Selected Writings

Plays

La Pupille [The Pupil], 1972

Portrait de Dora, 1976; as *Portrait of Dora* in *Benmussa Directs*, translated by Anita Barrows, 1979

Le Nom d'Oedipe: chant du corps interdit (libretto), 1978; translated as *The Name of Oedipus* in *Women's Theater in French*, 1991

La Prise de l'école de Madhubaï [The Taking of Madhubaï's School], 1983

Celui que ne parle pas [He Who is Silent], 1984

L'Histoire terrible mais inachevée de Norodom Sihanouk, roi du Cambodge, 1985; as *The Terrible but Unfinished Story of Norodom Sihanouk, King of Cambodia*, translated by Juliet Flower MacCannell, Judith Pike, and Lillie Groth, 1994

Théâtre (includes *Portrait de Dora*; *La Prise de l'école de Madhubaï*), 1986

L'Indiade; ou, l'Inde de leurs rêves, 1987

Karine Saporta, Peter Greenaway, with Daniel Dobbels and Bérénice Reynaud, 1990

On ne part pas, on ne revient pas [One Does Not Leave nor Return], 1991

Fiction
Le Prénom de Dieu [God's Forename], 1967
Dedans, 1969; as *Inside*, translated by Carol Barko, 1986
Le Troisième Corps, 1970; as *The Third Body*, translated by Keith Cohen, 1999
Les Commencements [The Beginnings], 1970
Un Vrai Jardin [A Real Garden], 1971
Neutre [Neuter], 1972
Tombe [Tomb; Fall], 1973
Portrait du soleil [Portrait of the Sun], 1974
Révolutions pour plus d'un Faust [Revolutions for More than One Faust], 1975
Un K incompréhensible: Pierre Goldman, 1975
Souffles [Breaths], 1975
La [The Feminine], 1976
Partie [Gone], 1976
Angst, 1977; as *Angst*, translated by Jo Levy, 1985
Préparatifs de noces au delà de l'abîme [Wedding Preparations beyond the Abyss], 1978
Vivre l'orange / To Live the Orange (bilingual edition), 1979
Anankè, 1979
Illa, 1980
With; ou, l'art de l'innocence [With; or, the Art of Innocence], 1981
Limonade tout était si infini [Lemonade Everything So Infinite], 1982
Le Livre de Promethea, 1983; as *The Book of Promethea*, translated by Betsy Wing, 1991
La Bataille d'Arcachon [The Battle of Arcachon], 1986
Manne aux Mandelstams aux Mandelas, 1988; as *Manna, for the Mandelstams, for the Mandelas*, translated by Catherine MacGillivray, 1994
Jours de l'an, 1990; as *First Days of the Year*, translated by Catherine MacGillivray, 1998
L'Ange au secret [The Angel with a Secret], 1991
Déluge [Flood], 1992
La Fiancée juive [The Jewish Fiancée], 1995
Messie [Messiah], 1996

Television Play: *La Nuit miraculeuse* [The Miraculous Night], with Ariane Mnouchkine, 1989

Radio Play: *Amour d'une délicatesse* [Love of a Delicacy], 1982

Other
L'Exil de James Joyce; ou, l'art du remplacement, 1968; as *The Exile of James Joyce*, translated by Sally A.J. Purcell, 1972
Les États-Unis d'aujourd'hui [The USA Today], with Pierre Dommergues and Mariane Debouzy, 1969
Prénoms de personne [No One's Forenames], 1974
La Jeune née, with Catherine Clément, 1975; as *The Newly Born Woman*, translated by Betsy Wing, 1986
La Venue à l'écriture [Coming to Writing], with Madeleine Gagnon and Annie Leclerc, 1977
Rykiel, with Madeleine Chapsal and Sonia Rykiel, edited by Daniele Flis, 1985
Entre l'Écriture [Between; Enters Writing], 1986
Writing Differences: Readings from the Seminar of Hélène Cixous, edited by Susan Sellers (includes "Extreme Fidelity"), 1988
L'Heure de Clarice Lispector, 1989; as *Reading with Clarice Lispector*, translated by Verena Andermatt Conley, 1990
Coming to Writing and Other Essays, edited by Deborah Jenson, translated by Sarah Cornell, 1991
Readings: The Poetics of Blanchot, Joyce, Kafka, Kleist, Lispector, and Tsvetayeva, translated by Verena Andermatt Conley, 1991
Three Steps on the Ladder of Writing: A Lecture Series, translated by Sarah Cornell and Susan Sellers, 1993
Beethoven à jamais; ou l'existence de Dieu [Beethoven for Ever; or, The Existence of God], 1993
The Hélène Cixous Reader, edited by Susan Sellers, 1994
Rootprints: Memory and Life Writing, with Mireille Calle-Gruber, translated by Eric Prenowitz, 1997
Or: les lettres de mon père [Gold: My Father's Letters], 1997
Stigmata: Escaping Texts, 1998

Further Reading
Carpenter, Deborah W., "Hélène Cixous's North African Origin: Writing *L'Orange*", *Revue CELFAN / CELFAN Review*, 6/1 (November 1986)
Conley, Verena Andermatt, *Hélène Cixous: Writing the Feminine*, Lincoln: University of Nebraska Press, 1984
Duren, Brian, "Cixous's Exorbitant Texts", *Sub-Stance*, 10 (1981)
Evans, Martha Noel, "Portrait of Dora: Freud's Case History as Reviewed by Hélène Cixous", *Sub-Stance*, 11 (1982)
Gibbs, Anna, "Cixous and Gertrude Stein", *Meanjin*, 38/3 (September 1979)
Jacobus, Lee A. and Regina Barreca (editors), *Hélène Cixous: Critical Impressions*, Amsterdam: Gordon and Breach, 1999
Jones, Ann Rosalind, "Writing and Body: Toward an Understanding of *l'Écriture féminine*", *French Studies*, 35 (Summer 1981)
Kuhn, Annette, "Introduction to Hélène Cixous's 'Castration or Decapitation?' ", *Signs*, 7/1 (Autumn 1981)
Makward, Christiane (interview), *Sub-Stance* (Autumn 1976)
Moi, Toril, "Cixous: An Imaginary Utopia" in Moi's *Sexual / Textual Politics: Feminist Literary Theory*, London: Methuen, 1985
Savona, Jeannette Laillou, "In Search of a Feminist Theater: *Portrait of Dora*" in *Feminine Focus: The New Women Playwrights*, edited by Enoch Brater, New York and Oxford: Oxford University Press, 1989
Wilcox, Helen (editor), *The Body and the Text: Hélène Cixous, Reading and Teaching*, New York: St Martin's Press, and London: Harvester Wheatsheaf, 1990
Wilson, Ann, "History and Hysteria: Writing the Body in *Portrait of Dora* and *Signs of Life*", *Modern Drama*, 32/1 (March 1989): 73

For Cixous writing is living. In *With; ou, l'art de l'innocence*, she reveals: "I need writing; I need to surprise myself living

. . . I need writing thinking of living; I write celebrating living . . . I need writing to celebrate living . . . " Whether poetry, prose, essays, literary criticism, or theatre works, all of her writing breathes with the same thirst for life and understanding. The enigmatic immediacy of her style is nurtured by the urgent need to decipher what cannot be said.

Akin to the Talmud, which never offers any closure and gathers meaning as it is written, Cixous's books are "like life and history, heterogeneous chapters in a single vast book whose ending [she] will never know." No one fragment carries the totality of the message. In an interview published in *Rootprints*, Cixous explains:

> My mother always told me about my Talmudist great-grandfathers . . . The Talmud is as infinite in its commentaries as our experience of sexual difference and its translations . . . I must be a Talmudist of "reality" . . . In the Talmud the words are written; in my book the words are not there. It is by dint of contemplating and listening that I see words appear. That's it. That is how writing begins for me.

In her fictional texts, Cixous works with philosophical contents within a poetic form that unravels the mysteries of subjectivity. From a psychoanalytical and cultural conception of femininity, nurtured by the work of Jacques Lacan and Jacques Derrida, she does not ask "who am I?", "qui suis-je," but "who are I?", "qui sont-je", thus weaving the dream, "sont-je =songe= dream," into the making of identity. The "I" is always in difference.

The Zakhor (importance of remembering) lives inside Cixous's creative energy: memory, identity, and writing are linked. In the preface to *The Hélène Cixous Reader*, edited for the English-speaking world, she explains: "When I write, language remembers . . . I inscribe an additional memory in language, a memory in progress."

In *Neutre*, the text of the poem "Holocauste" offers itself as "un drap plein de sans" [a sheet full of nothing]. The homophony "sans/sang" [nothing or without/blood] propels us to the realm of life, death and nothingness. Cixous loves to play with words. She enriches language with verbs like "appalir", which contains "pâlir" [pale] and "appeler" [call], adjectives such as "virtueux", which plays on "vertueux" [virtuous] and the Latin prefix "vir" meaning man. In "Holocauste" Cixous creates a dark, airless atmosphere where "la lumière des dents" [the light of teeth – in memory of Edgar Allan Poe] looms like a grinning death, and where names and age are no more. In a "delirium of ashes", within "the skin of smoke", she asks the question "Who am I?" What does it mean to be human after the Holocaust?

> si, sans nom, sans force, sans âge et sans
> voir, suis, manquant d'air et de ressource,
> manquant de lumière et d'espace et de
> temps aussi, pourtant non sans désir et
> mouvement, mais les membres retranchés
> du tronc,
> Neutre donc,
> En viens-je à engendrer moi-même,
> Qui suis-je?
> . . .
> épaisse peau de fumée
> . . .
> le cendrier, un drap plein de cendres
> quand on coule la lessive
> la mord un drap plein de sans et dans
> la nuit, la lumière des dents
>
> [if, nameless, powerless, ageless and sightless,
> am, lacking air and resources,
> lacking light and space and also time, and yet not
> without desire and
> movement, but the limbs cut from
> the trunk,
> Neuter therefore,
> Come to engender myself,
> Who am I?
> . . .
> thick skin of smoke
> . . .
> the ashtray, a sheet full of ashes
> when you pour the washing
> bites it a sheet full of nothing and in
> the night,
> the light of teeth
> . . .]

Dedans (*Inside*), Cixous's first full-length work of fiction, won the Prix Médicis in 1969. Centring on the dimensions of identity within her relationship to loss and death, this novel is nurtured by the father. Cixous's father died of tuberculosis when she was 11. For Cixous loss and the need for reparation are key motivating forces in her writing. This is the tikkun (mystical correction of the world) dimension of all her writings. Cixous wrote *Dedans* "inside the father". In part 1, the "I" is inside a body demarcated by physical limitations: "Skin, I am inside that skin, stretched out between its lips and fingers". In part 2, Cixous escapes from the incarcerating power of boundaries: "I have forgotten forms and limits." The same sense of loss nurtures *Déluge*, which, within the power of a biblical flood, tells of the experience of personal loss at the end of a love relationship and projects the "compulsory murder" of the self.

La Jeune née (*The Newly Born Woman*), written with Catherine Clément, is her most widely known text. It contains Cixous's ground-breaking essay "Sorties". Cixous fights against the image of woman as a construct of the prevailing phallocentric system. She reclaims feminine identity within this system and undermines the masculine order, a theme Cixous develops in *Angst* which presents the newly born woman inside a language depicted as "a web of metaphors" spun by the masculine "il" (he) to entrap her. Woman must find a place for herself within the masculine order. Between poetry and prose, prose and poetic prose, Cixous's words destabilize order.

Published the same year as *La Jeune née*, *Souffles* [Breaths] is a series of fictional texts that pertains to loss in relation to the mother, and deals with the rebirth of a self that is both female and feminine. The voice belongs to "the time when the soul still speaks flesh. This is the enigma: softness is born from strength. And now, who is to be born?" The voice ("la voix," feminine in French) says: "I am there. And everything is there."

In *La* [The Feminine] Cixous offers the portrait of a feminine writer. Beyond the limits of censorship, feminine writing overcomes reason which is depicted as "the enemy" of life. Cixous's "écriture féminine" draws on the unconscious, plays the music of the body, its needs and pleasures, ultimately to liberate language and love. Feminine writing is one of Cixous's gifts to world literature. It exhorts women to write their body, "écrire le corps", and asks them to reclaim the uncharted continent of their sexuality. As the "art of singing the abyss" feminine writing is a celebration of life and the unknown.

In *Vivre l'orange / To Live the Orange* Cixous's text is presented in both English and French. She revised the English translation herself. A rich and juicy example of Cixous's feminine writing, *Vivre l'orange* expands the borders of the self. Written as an homage to Clarice Lispector, the Brazilian Jewish author whom Cixous discovered in 1978, and whose work touched the core of Cixous's feminine exploration, this symbiotic, osmotic book humouristically recounts Cixous's contemplation of an orange, with numerous linguistic jewels which "un-forget, un-silence, unearth, unblind and un-deafen" the self. " Orange" becomes "Oranje", the "I" born in Oran. Then, "Oran" slides to "Iran" when Cixous empathizes with the plight of women in that country. *Vivre l'orange* uses the interstitiality of language rooted in the Hebrew language to unlock new meanings, and discover new territories of expression.

The immediacy of Cixous's language vibrates in each word: "The orange is a moment . . . the infinite immensity of the moment . . . The orange is a beginning; starting out from the orange all voyages are possible." Those journeys are also those of interpretation. The text plays on multiple meanings as in the Midrash. Thus, "Oran's Jews" become "orange juice", as the sap of identity ejaculates from the fruit of her origins. Language is sexual. It can give birth to the self, in all its different manifestations.

Love is primordial in Cixous's work. In *Limonade tout était si infini*, a title borrowed from Kafka's dying words, the feminine subject strives to write a love letter against the raging war of "men-men". In *Le Livre de Promethea*, a book of love where Promethea is the source of writing, love, like writing, can invent, lie, wound, and kill. Whether in "Extreme Fidelity", where Cixous clarifies her view of sex and gender differences as "economies" that can coexist "as equals", or in *Jours de l'an*, which expresses the truth of the body and manipulates language to find alternative ways of expressing love, love is a life-death force that energizes all of Cixous's works. She eroticizes the text to such an extent that the text becomes sexual itself: it is the world of the "sext", one of Cixous's strongest and most resonant neologisms, because, as we can read in "Holocauste", "la. retire s'aime (sème)", that is "the Letter loves itself (sows)." The sexual dimension of language is onanist at first, and then implicates the other.

This brief sampling of Hélène Cixous's work demonstrates how deep and versatile, strong and sensual she can be. The "unlimited territory" of language is her playground, her world, the locus of her identity. Only writing can convey the truth about identity, and that is the true Jewish dimension of her work. Sexuality, Love, Loss, Death, and Rebirth become the muscling forces of her being in writing. They choreograph the ballet of her life as a Jewish woman, daughter, wife, lover, and writer, in order to "regain the body" and dance the dance of language, "because we are born inside language."

BÉA AARONSON

Clouts, Sydney

South African poet, 1926–1982

Born in Cape Town, 10 January 1926. Studied at South African College School. Served in South African Corps of Signals, 1944–45. Studied at University of Cape Town, BA 1947, and Rhodes University, MA 1971; research fellow, Institute for Study of English in Africa, Grahamstown, 1969–71; British Council reading and lecture tour of South Africa, 1974; also worked as literary agent and librarian. Married Marjorie Leftwich, 1952; three sons. Moved to London, 1961. Awards include Olive Schreiner Poetry Prize, 1968; Ingrid Jonker Poetry Prize, 1968. Died in London, 31 July 1982

Selected Writings

Poetry
One Life, 1966
Collected Poems, edited by Marjorie Clouts and Cyril Clouts, 1984
In *New Coin Poetry* [Grahamstown] (20 June 1984); (posthumously published fragments)

Further Reading

Butler, Guy and Ruth Harnett (editors), *English in Africa*, Sydney Clouts memorial issue, 11/2 (October 1984)
Coetzee, J.M., *White Writing: On the Culture of Letters in South Africa*, New Haven, Connecticut: Yale University Press, 1988
Glenn, Ian, "Sydney Clouts: Our Pen-Insular Poet", *English Academy Review*, 3 (1985): 127
Goddard, Kevin, entry in *Encyclopedia of Post-Colonial Literatures in English*, edited by Eugene Benson and L.W. Conolly, London: Routledge, 1994
Joubert, Susan, "The Unresolved Shibboleth", *Theoria*, 75 (May 1990)
Radio Programme, *Living Poet Series: Sydney Clouts*, BBC Radio (28 March 1969)
Skinner, Douglas Reid, "Revealing Riches Gradually: The Composite Clouts", *Contrast*, 59 (15/3) (Winter 1985): 77
Van Wyk Smith, M., *Shades of Adamastor: Africa and the Portuguese Connection: An Anthology of Poetry*, Grahamstown: Institute for the Study of English in Africa, 1988
Watson, Stephen, *Selected Essays 1980–1990*, Cape Town: Carrefour Press, 1990

The lyrical, enigmatic, and profound poetry of Sydney Clouts has been given detailed scrutiny by South African writers and academics, attempting interpretations of his "breadth, power and conciseness" and his "drive towards transcendence, his concentration on the thisness of things and his . . . compression of language". They have also debated and contested comments such as "the purest poetic talent to have worked in South Africa since Roy Campbell", "South Africa's most intellectual poet", and "most original poet". All these English-speaking South African commentators focus on Clouts's stature in relation to what has been called by J.M. Coetzee "the burden assumed by the South African poet of European culture: the burden of finding a home in Africa for a consciousness formed in and by a language whose history lies on another continent".

Clouts himself said in an interview:

> I wanted to create a South African poetry and a new language for it – an aboriginal language which fulfils not present but future aspirations . . . I am obsessed with this secret language which Africa will produce out of English. But I am not aboriginally African. I am a South African Jewish writer who writes in English.

This rare reference to his Jewishness has not been taken up by most critics, who were not interested in it; nor was it easily visible in his poetry. Only a perceptive short piece by Tony Dinner in the *Jewish Chronicle* in 1995 urges a proper recognition outside South Africa of Clouts's poems "which convey a most powerful concatenation of feelings and ideas". Four of Clouts's poems were chosen for *Voices from the Ark: The Modern Jewish Poets* by Howard Schwartz and Anthony Rudolf.

Clouts's father was born in Inverness, Scotland, but the family emigrated to South Africa in his early youth. He became a highly respected Cape Town advocate, and was president of the Cape Town Jewish Historical Society for many years. Clouts's South African-born mother was a member of the Friedlander family, who were among the founders of the town of De Aar. She too was well-known and well-respected for her wide variety of activities in the Cape Town Jewish community. Sydney Clouts was born and grew up in Cape Town, on the slopes of Table Mountain. "That mountain is an absolute part of my being", he commented. The South African poet and academic Guy Butler wrote that Clouts "took the cosmos for his theme, but viewed it mainly from the Cape Peninsula".

The Jewish hunger for interpretation, and deep philosophical concern with the idea of "oneness", may well have influenced Clouts's desire for, in the words of a BBC broadcast in 1969, "a fresh consciousness, not so much to restore the once viable textures of God, nature and man, but to reconstitute, to rearrange if it can, all meanings around fresh ignition points".

The 17th-century mystic Thomas Traherne could feel the totality of himself within the reality of supernatural being, but for Clouts the steady contemplation of the smallest objects, each particle a universe, is an almost frightening sensation of eye and object fusing, becoming part of an "ache of incompleteness".

> "Of Thomas Traherne and the Pebble Outside"
> Ghosts of the sun race on the approaching sea.
> In the air Traherne's Contentments shine.
> A jewelled Garden gazed at him.
> What shall be said of Paradise?
> Obscure vermilion heats the dim pebble I hold.
> The long rock-sheltered surges flash with spume.
> I have read firm poems of God.
> Good friend, you perceived bright angels.
> This heathen bit of the world lies warm in my palm.

Clouts acknowledges an apartness, yet strives for a unity, which he states "seems impossible, but is the only really desirable end beyond art".

Clouts's poems of the 1950s, some of great lyrical simplicity, are filled with the "beauty and menace" of South Africa in the grip of apartheid. What he wanted, "the full penetrant eye", was also turned to more specifically Jewish themes. His poem "The Eye" moves from its third line, "millions done to death with grass in sight", into a fusion of evil, history, and silent picnic, in a startling and original way. Rabbi Akiba bristles with burning in a way that cannot be paraphrased. Clouts draws very widely on world history and mythology, but biblical references (to Samuel, Job, Jerusalem) are also woven through his poetry. Guy Butler comments that "his favourite philosophers are Pre-Socratics, his deepest insights are Mosaic". As an exile, in his own Diaspora of incomplete belonging, he wrote both of Europe as a museum of dead cultures, and of a doom-laden South Africa. (His passionate commitment to the English language precluded any ideas of settling in Israel.)

Ruth Harnett has written a very scholarly and insightful commentary on Clouts's recurring theme of the journey of the mind. "The vehicle to this tenor" in several poems is the image of discovery, relating to the sea voyages of exploration round Africa. Three powerful poems refer to the Portuguese Prince Henry the Navigator, whom Clouts admired as "a man of intense vision, who chose not a life of ease but a life of profound devotion to the understanding of the unknown. He knew the oneness of the universe". That description epitomizes the Jewish Clouts himself, except that "He strove to know" must replace "He knew".

Susan Joubert posits that like Prince Henry, who was a man in possession of fluent, cultural language, Clouts himself feared that his own English language could malfunction in Africa as a "shibboleth"; her idea was inspired by the opening stanzas of "Prince Henry the Navigator": "At the summit of perception/ a blackness starts to rise:/ raw images of darkness/ unkempt alarming skies/ that can torment the sturdy mind/ to grief or shibboleth". This fear, she suggests, led to Clouts's search for "a new language" for Africa, and to the use in some of his poems indigenous people as personae – Afrikaners embedded in their land, the so-called Cape Coloured man of the "Hotknife" poems, and then – in "Firebowl" – the Kalahari Bushmen celebrating their Fire Dance, which is a poem of aboriginal incantation, and an astonishing use of Clouts's ideal of "a coiled rhythmic spring of sound".

Certainly, the commanding powers of poetic language, and the intractability of the object ("a world-word disjunction"), led Clouts to the innovative language and spatial design most excitingly realized in "Residuum", which is, according to Joubert, "revelatory in terms of his whole poetic development". However, the sheer exuberance and delight of his many sea and animal-inspired poems are what may be celebrated most of all.

MARGE CLOUTS

Cohen, Albert

Greek-born French fiction writer, 1895–1981

Born in Corfu, 16 August 1895. Family emigrated to France, 1900; settled in Marseilles. Studied law and literature, Geneva, 1914–19. Married, first, Élisabeth Brocher, daughter of a Protestant minister, 1919; one daughter; second, Marianne Goss, 1931; third, Bella Berkowich, 1955. Editor, *La Revue juive*, Geneva, 1925; worked for International Labour Office, Geneva, 1926–30. Chaim Weizmann's personal representative in Paris, 1939; fled to London, May 1940, serving as official advisor to the Jewish Agency for Palestine then as legal adviser to Intergovernmental Committee on Refugees, 1944. Returned to Geneva in 1947 and worked for the International Refugee Organization and the ILO. Retired 1952. Died in Geneva, 17 October 1981.

Selected Writings

Collection
Oeuvres, edited by Christel Peyrefitte and Bella Cohen, 1993

Novels
Solal, 1930; as *Solal of the Solals*, translated by Wilfred Benson, 1933
Mangeclous, 1938; as *Nailcruncher*, translated by Vyvyan Holland, 1940
Belle du Seigneur, 1968; as *Belle du Seigneur*, translated by David Coward, 1995
Les Valeureux, 1969

Poetry
Paroles juives [Jewish Words], 1921

Other
Ézéchiel (play), 1930
Le Livre de ma mère, 1954; as *Book of my Mother*, translated by Bella Cohen, with a foreword by David Coward, 1997
Ô vous, frères humains, 1972
Carnets 1978, 1979

Further Reading

Auroy, Carole, *Albert Cohen: une quête solaire* [Albert Cohen: A Lone Quest], Paris: Presses de l'Université de Paris-Sorbonne, 1996
Bensoussan, A., "L'Image du Sépharade dans l'oeuvre d'Albert Cohen" [The Image of the Sephardic in the Work of Albert Cohen], *Les Temps Modernes*, 394 (1979)
Blot, Jean, *Albert Cohen*, Paris: Balland, 1986; revised edition, 1995
Cohen, Bella, *Albert Cohen, mythe et realité*, Paris: Gallimard, 1991
Goitein-Galperin, D.R., *Visage de mon peuple: essai sur Albert Cohen* [Face of My People], Paris: Nizet, 1982
Goitein-Galperin, D.R., *Albert Cohen: visions du sacré*, Paris: L'Atelier Albert Cohen, 1994
Les Nouveaux Cahiers, special issue (Winter 1995)
Valbert, Gerard, *Albert Cohen, le seigneur*, Paris: Grasset, 1990

Albert Cohen, who held a Turkish passport until 1919 when he became a Swiss citizen, claimed the language of France as his *patrie.* As a writer, he preferred the expressive to the analytical tradition of French literature. He set Villon, Ronsard, Rabelais, and Montaigne above the classical 17th century, was left unmoved by the 18th, and in the 19th preferred Stendhal to Flaubert. But his tastes were also cosmopolitan. The Bible left a permanent mark on both his sensibility and his style, and he admired Dickens and Tolstoi for their clear-eyed, tolerant humanity. As a contributor to the *Nouvelle Revue Française* and editor of the short-lived *Revue juive*, he was aware of the direction of postwar intellectualism, but remained unenthused by Freud, Marx, and surrealism. In his own writing, both as a poet (*Paroles juives*) and a playwright (*Ézéchiel*), he ignored the themes and manner of contemporary poetry and theatre. Instead, he drew close to the sensuous language and sinuous spirituality of the Old Testament to celebrate the Jewish people in his own fluid, incantatory, but far from uncritical terms.

With *Solal* in 1930, he emerged as a novelist of vast ambition. Solal is one of nature's princes. From humble beginnings, he achieves high political office and the love of women. Yet he despises his success which has been secured at the expense of his Jewish roots. With reckless abandon, he throws it away, becomes an outcast (neither good works nor the love of Aude can save him) and kills himself, only to be magically resurrected and made to live on and face "the miracle of his defeat". *Solal*, a *Bildungsroman* which turns into a love story and an allegory, derives its dramatic tension from the conflict between assimilation and betrayal. The tone is lightened by the "Valeureux" (the "Valiant of France"), a chorus of five rumbustious cousins who represent the life-enhancing good humour that Cohen admired in the Jewish tradition. But Solal is already what he will continue to be: a tragic figure, incapable of choosing between Reason and Belief, East and West, Love and Death.

Solal was well reviewed and its success encouraged Cohen to cast it as the first of a series of novels, provisionally entitled *Solal et les Solal* (*Solal of the Solals*), which would confront his hero with new tests to his divided loyalties. In *Mangeclous* (*Nailcruncher*), Solal has once more scaled the heights: not yet 40, he is Under-Secretary General of the League of Nations. The chaos created by the "Valeureux" is an embarrassment which revives the dilemma he had failed to resolve in *Solal*. His western head tells him that the world will be saved through intellect and the law of nations. Yet he knows instinctively that a better solution will come from Faith, which he cannot acquire, and the Law of Moses, which he reveres. Unable to build a bridge between his Jewish and westernized selves, he invests his idealism in love.

But even as he sets out to seduce Ariane Deume, the knowledge that she will find him irresistible leads to self-disgust. The novel ends as the seduction is about to begin.

Exiled to London in 1940, Cohen was forced to abandon Solal and published only occasional pieces in wartime magazines, notably his homage, "Churchill d'Angleterre" [Churchill of England]. He later revised one essay on the death of his mother in 1943 which became the poignant *Le Livre de ma mère* (*Book of my Mother*), but *Belle du Seigneur*, announced in *Mangeclous*, did not appear until 1968. *Les Valeureux*, issued separately at the behest of his publisher, completed the saga. Enriched by new strains of high comedy, acid observation, social satire, and allegory, it traces Solal's doomed attempt to rescue the world through political action and, when this fails, to save himself through love. But love proves as illusory as he had foreseen. He can no more live love than he can defend his people against the fascist threat in the Europe of 1937. His epic journey ends because "it is time", and Solal, impaled on his human dilemma, dies defiant but defeated. His story, spread over a million and a half words, forms one of the great novel cycles of the 20th century.

Cohen's last books, *Ô vous, frères humains* (a revised version of another wartime essay) and *Carnets 1978* returned to the meditative register of *Le Livre de ma mère*. The first recalls his introduction to anti-Semitism at the age of ten and develops a creed of tolerance and fraternal love that, in 1979, he once more locates in our shared mortality. Man's inhumanity to Man is endless, but the realization that all must die, that the living are tomorrow's dead, can be the beginning of pity and universal communion. It was a human solution, for, like Solal, Cohen, a lucid, unsentimental idealist, never found a faith to match his reverence for the Law of Moses.

DAVID COWARD

Cohen, Leonard

Canadian poet, 1934–

Born Leonard Norman Cohen in Montreal, 21 September 1934. Educated at McGill University, BA 1955; Columbia University. Lived with Suzanne Elrod for several years; two children. Composer and singer: has given concerts in Canada, the United States, and Europe. Many awards including McGill University Literary Award, 1956; Canada Council Award, 1960; Quebec Literary Award, 1964; Governor-General's Award, 1969 (refused); Canadian Authors Association Award, 1985.

Selected Writings

Poetry
Let Us Compare Mythologies, 1956
The Spice-Box of Earth, 1961
Flowers for Hitler, 1964
Parasites of Heaven, 1966
Selected Poems 1956–1968, 1968
Leonard Cohen's Song Book, 1969
Five Modern Canadian Poets, with others, 1970
The Energy of Slaves, 1972
Death of a Lady's Man (poetry and prose), 1978
Wise Publications, 1978
Two Views, 1980
Book of Mercy, 1984
Stranger Music: Selected Poems and Songs, 1993

Novels
The Favourite Game, 1963
Beautiful Losers, 1966

Plays
The New Step, 1972
Sisters of Mercy: A Journey into the Words and Music of Leonard Cohen, 1973
A Man Was Killed, with Irving Layton, *Canadian Theatre Review* (Spring 1977)

Recordings
The Songs of Leonard Cohen, 1968; *Songs from a Room*, 1969; *Songs of Love and Hate*, 1971; *Live Songs*, 1973; *New Skin for the Old Ceremony*, 1974; *The Best of Leonard Cohen*, 1975; *Death of a Ladies' Man*, 1977; *Recent Songs*, 1979; *Various Positions*, 1985; *I'm Your Man*, 1987; *The Future*, 1992; *Ten New Songs*, 2001

Further Reading

Dorman, Loranne S. and Clive L. Rawlins, *Leonard Cohen: Prophet of the Heart*, London: Omnibus Press, 1990
Gnarowski, Michael (editor), *Leonard Cohen: The Artist and His Critics*, Toronto: McGraw Hill Ryerson, 1976
Morley, Patricia A., *The Immoral Moralists: Hugh MacLennan and Leonard Cohen*, Toronto: Clarke Irwin, 1972
Ondaatje, Michael, *Leonard Cohen*, Toronto: McClelland and Stewart, 1970
Scobie, Stephen, *Leonard Cohen*, Vancouver: Douglas and McIntyre, 1978
Whiteman, Bruce, entry in *The Annotated Bibliography of Canada's Major Authors*, vol. 2, edited by Robert Lecker and Jack David, Downsview: Ontario, ECW Press, 1980

Leonard Cohen's influence on the Canadian literary scene, though once substantial, has faded, especially during the years his artistic energy has been devoted to songwriting. The era when young Jewish writers, and young poets of a certain urban bohemian stripe, sought him out as a mentor, is largely over. And one might guess from the lyric of his 1992 song "The Future" that Cohen himself has tired of this role, as he bemoans "all the lousy little poets / coming round / trying to sound like Charlie Manson."

Part of the legacy of Cohen's art for Canadian writers and readers is his talent for entering an array of cultural scenes, deriving from each of them lasting literary art before shifting gears and abandoning one persona for the next. His early accomplishments in Montreal came in connection with the McGill University teacher and poet Louis Dudek, who initiated Cohen into the late modern imagist tradition and gave him the opportunity to publish the early poems, that became part of his first collection, *Let Us Compare Mythologies*. Cohen's next step was into the jazz- and beat-inflected coffee-house scene of Montreal, where he was able to try out his penchant for marrying word to song. His early collections, *The Spice-Box of Earth* and *Flowers for Hitler*, assured him a readership and a reputation as a precocious, provocative voice.

Trying his hand as a novelist, Cohen produced two of the finer examples of postwar Canadian prose – the lyrical *Bildungsroman The Favourite Game* in 1963, and the much rawer *Beautiful Losers* in 1966, which stands as a testament to the counterculture in the way that Allen Ginsberg's *Howl*, Jack Kerouac's *On the Road*, and William Burroughs's *Naked Lunch* do in American letters. It could be argued that no other book by a Canadian so accurately prophesies what would become the Canadian postmodern, or better, post-colonial, predicament. *Beautiful Losers* focuses on Kateri Tekakwitha – a 17th-century Mohawk girl who died near Montreal and has been beatified by the Vatican for the miraculous events associated with her. It portrays the hybrid history of Quebec, where English, French, Mohawk, and in a later context, Jewish culture have become so famously entangled. "I wanted Fifth Avenue to remember its Indian trails", the novel's ever-ironic narrator intones, including the entire continent in the historical tableau he offers his reader.

The year of *Beautiful Losers*' appearance roughly matches Cohen's move to New York, and his commitment to the folk music scene of Greenwich Village as well as to the underground cultural explosion whose capital was the Chelsea Hotel. The song lyrics he penned for early albums, such as *The Songs of Leonard Cohen* and *Songs from a Room*, are as stark and plain as the finger-picking tablature that provides their score. In this era of his musical output he was an odder Bob Dylan, a less soulful Van Morrison, a more street savvy Nick Drake, forcing his love of popular forms into the most serious of artistic shapes. The song lyrics on his early records have entered the canon of Cohen's literary output, in part because of the 1993 collection *Stranger Music: Selected Poems and Songs*, which presents his poetry and song lyrics as a single body of work, as if they were merely opposite sides of the same hand. This approach to his work is supported by Cohen's own habit of transforming poems into songs: in the 1966 *Parasites of Heaven*, early versions of the lyrics for "Suzanne", "The Master Song", and "Fingerprints" appear.

But the focus on songwriting, and the attendant rigours of performance and recording, has been matched by a gradual move away from the popular reading audience Cohen created for himself with his early poetry and novels. In the 1965 documentary, *Ladies and Gentleman, Mr Leonard Cohen*, the author can be seen reading to a huge, rapt audience of pre-hippie, pre-folky, neatly coifed youth. He reads somewhat difficult, always lyrical poems, framing them with a wise patter he may be copying from Lenny Bruce. Soon enough, this sort of scene would be unthinkable in Canada. With much of his time spent in Greece or New York, and his poetic vision darkening, Cohen jettisoned his role as literary avatar as he pursued his musician's persona. The books of the 1970s were unforgiving, often self-loathing, but in certain ways, the most challenging poetic work of his career. *The Energy of Slaves* in 1972 must have struck many of Cohen's fans as a surprise, and possibly as an affront. Its back cover displays a photo that appeared on his *Live Songs* record – the poet leaning, apparently on a bathroom wall, head shaved, eyes at once dead and flinty, a cigar in his long-fingered hand. The poems address the reader as "you" in a way that we've come to think of as self-reflexive, or postmodern. The mood is anguished:

> Welcome to these lines
> There is a war on
> but I'll try to make you comfortable
> Don't follow my conversation
> it's just nervousness

Canada is far from the poet's mind, though his own mentor, Irving Layton, merits a mention in one short comic piece. This is the poetry of an international exile, a failed revolutionary, a disheartened lover: "*Who could have foretold / the heart grows old* / from touching others".

More has been made of the publishing history of Cohen's next book of new poetry than of its contents. *Death of a Lady's Man* was submitted, reportedly withdrawn, rethought, and finally published as a kind of divided text, with poems and prose pieces on one page, facing the poet's own interpretive comments, themselves often poetic in their diffident rewriting of the piece they respond to. "*Is there a modern reader that can measure up to this page?*" one afterthought asks. Or, another proclaims more simply, "*This fails.*" At roughly the time of the publication of *Death of a Lady's Man* Cohen released a similarly titled record, produced, full of 1950s swagger, by Phil Spector. With these two works, Cohen launched himself against his audience, though with hindsight the poetry of *Death of a Lady's Man* seems prescient of much recent poetry. Young musicians have also found much to inspire them in the melodic wall of sound – at times elated and at others sad – offered up in the songs included on *Death of a Ladies' Man*.

In his last book of new poetry, *Book of Mercy*, Cohen points toward the spiritual yearnings of his recent Buddhist discipline. This book of psalmlike pieces is, however, deeply Jewish in its lyricism, its meditations on Jerusalem, and its use of biblical imagery. The result is a slim book of great meditative power.

In recent press and documentary appearances, Cohen asserts his old adage that a writer must "blacken the pages", but this assertion has not led to much in the way of recent published poetry. Buddhism and song-writing have been the focus of Cohen's discipline, while life in Los Angeles has made him only a sometime visitor in his old home of Montreal.

NORMAN RAVVIN

D

Der Nister

Russian fiction writer, 1884–1950

Born Pinkhes Kahanovitsh in Berdichev, Ukraine, 1884. Associated with Zionist socialist groups. Attended the Poale Zion conference, 1905. Settled in Kiev to avoid serving in the czarist army, 1908; visited Warsaw, 1910; left Soviet Union for Kovno and Berlin, 1922, and then lived in Hamburg, 1924–25. Settled in Kharkov, 1926. Spent war years in Tashkent and Moscow in penury. Arrested in 1949. Died in prison hospital, 1950.

Selected Writings

Gedanken un motivn [Thoughts and Motives], 1907
Hekher fun der erd [Higher than the Earth], 1910
Gezang un gebet [Song and Prayer], 1912
Gedakht [Contemplations], 2 vols, 1922
Fun mayne giter [From My Estates], 1929
Unter a ployt [Under a Fence], 1929
Dray hoyptshtet [Three Capitals], 1934
Di mishpokhe mashber, 1939; as *The Family Mashber*, translated by Leonard Wolf, 1948
Korbones [Victims], 1943
Fun finftn yor [From the Fifth Year], 1964

Further Reading

Bechtel, Delphine, *Der Nister's Work 1970–1929: A Study of a Yiddish Symbolist*, New York: Peter Lang, 1990
Maggs, Peter B., *The Mandelstam and "Der Nister" Files: An Introduction to Stalin-Era Prison and Labor Camp Records*, Armonk, New York: M.E. Sharpe, 1996
Shmeruk, Khone, essay in *The Field of Yiddish*, edited by Uriel Weinreich, 2nd collection, The Hague: Mouton, 1965

Der Nister (in Yiddish, "the concealed one") was one of a select band of Yiddish writers who succeeded in creating a uniquely Jewish and Yiddish literary landscape. Influenced above all in the field of Yiddish literature by Y.L. Perets he worked the vein of Jewish mysticism to produce an extraordinary atmosphere of mysterious depth in his best work. On this work it is hard to better Joachim Neugroschel's comment: "The language, an authentic, colloquial Yiddish, is alive with a hypnotic and mellow lyricism, flows along in strange, meandering sentences. We are left on a hazy verge of something, a brink overlooking the ultimate reality, that we can only sense with the pre-rational strata of the mind, but cannot capture with logic or human discourse."

In retrospect we can see that Der Nister was present at several crucial encounters of the previously intellectually cut-off Ashkenazi world with contemporary ideas and historical movements. First with the late-romantic fascination with folk culture, second with Symbolism, and finally with "Cultural Bolshevism". His earliest work in Yiddish, after some poetry in Hebrew, draws on a youth and childhood spent among mystics and Kabbalists. His father was a famously other-worldly seller of smoked fish while an elder brother became a Bratslaver Hasid. Although his early work, on the borders of prose and poetry (*Gedanken un motivn* [Thoughts and Motives], 1907, and *Hekher fun der erd* [Higher than the Earth], 1910), was widely seen as wilfully obscure, it nevertheless established a name for him as a unique writer, respectfully incorporating the mystical and the mystical folktale (after Rabbi Nachman) tradition into a contemporary Yiddish literature that was essentially secular in outlook.

The core of his work in this style, though, was collected in *Gedakht* published in Berlin in 1922, partly translated in Neugroschel's *Yene velt* in 1976. While Perets's treatment of the same sources is always somehow still concrete and evokes a reality, Der Nister, inspired by the Symbolists' programme of remaking humanity through art marches us alongside nameless archetypal figures like "The Wanderer" or "The Giant" through fearful desert and forest landscapes on bizarre quests: to make demons acquire human feelings or exploring the everyday life of anthropomorphized star-constellations in "In der vayn-keler" [In the Wine-Cellar]. The head simply reels, although perhaps the spiritual programme of Der Nister is best understood in the story "In vald" ["The Fool and the Forest Demon"] where a simpleton who has lived long years in the forest as the lowly servant of a demon one day takes off and is reclaimed from his bondage by a beautiful forest sprite and awakens from all foolishness.

The head is made to reel, and reeling, hypnotized by language and by images, a higher appreciation of consciousness may be achieved and man re-made by the new religion, art. Again in contrast to Perets, Der Nister also mines elements from non-Jewish, from Classical and Slavic literatures, for his synthesis.

Der Nister's quest for spiritual knowledge was of course carried out against the background of world war, revolution and their vast consequences especially for Russian and Yiddish literature. Returning to the Soviet Union from a German exile that had been precipitated by post-revolutionary pogroms and hunger he was to find his style of writing had very much gone out of favour. In fact one particular variety of crime against socialist realism was even named "*dernisterizm*". His cycle of mystical-Symbolist work in its pure form ends with *Fun mayne giter* [From My Estates] (1929), part-translated in Leftwich's *Anthology of Modern Yiddish Literature* (1974), where a character called "Der Nister" has to feed his own fingers to a hungry bear, eternal symbol of violent and aggrieved Russia. The story is set in a place where people have to literally eat mud and filth, but Der Nister succeeds in moving to another land where the mud is perceived as gold, which is wonderful until he arranges a great ball where the bear appears again and turns the gold back to mud and he ends up in poverty and the mad-house. Der Nister himself was to spend his time in the Soviet Union in great poverty and difficulty. He eventually brought himself to write more realistic, documentary accounts such as *Dray hoyptshtet* [Three Capitals] (1934), which concerns Moscow, Kharkov (then the Ukrainian capital), and Leningrad. In 1943 he published *Korbones* [Victims] a pamphlet of three accounts of the destruction of Polish Jewry. In 1948 he was arrested and died in 1950 in detention.

However, he also managed to produce rather heroically a three-volume novel of which two volumes and a long fragment survived, the celebrated and fascinating *Di mishpokhe mashber* (1939, first volume only), translated as *The Family Mashber* in 1948 (first two volumes). For most readers this is probably the best place to start with this author as within its more realistic framework one is nevertheless introduced to a powerful moral landscape of mature Hasidic pietism. Unlike many other authors, or even perhaps many of those who claim this inheritance today in their various American, Jerusalem, and European ghettoes, Der Nister really manages to transmit a sense of spiritual nobility of a particular, unique, and strange kind, particularly in his portraits of the troubled but highly charismatic Uncle Luzi – whose life is spent trying to atone for a heretical grandfather who was a follower of Shabbatai Zvi, the notorious false Messiah – and the even more troubled Sruli Gol. *The Family Mashber* is also an essential text for getting a sense of life in the crowded Jewish-Polish-Ukrainian borderlands of czarist Russia with, among other things, its depictions of otherwise rarely-mentioned professions of the time such as the "dog-killer" and the paid breaker of arms or the helpful widow-woman who attends to the conveniently premature death of unwanted children. In *Mashber* Der Nister captures, better than many other writers, the older Jewish life with all its close-communal warmth, with all its mystery and misery intact. It is a story built out of long-reflected-upon autobiographical experiences, as in the figure of Luzi who, like Der Nister's own elder brother, joins the despised and fanatical Bratslaver Hasids, followers of Rabbi Nachman – "their days were spent in prayer, and their nights lying on the graves of the town's holy men". No doubt one of the reasons that Der Nister was able to publish the first volume at least of *Mashber* in the Soviet Union was the realistic to the point of grotesque description of former ways and types. Sruli Gol, for example, has a twisted and difficult personality because he was ostracized as a presumed illegitimate child, a *mamzer*, a powerful stigma in the traditional Jewish world. Similarly, the bizarre Polish landowner featured in the book is so emotionally attached to his prize pigs that he feeds them to death. Nevertheless among the pathological types is a shining and unforgettable vision of the pre-Soviet Russian-Jewish world.

RAY KEENOY

Döblin, Alfred

German-born poet and fiction writer, 1878–1957

Born in Stettin, 10 August 1878; family moved to Berlin, 1888. Studied medicine, receiving doctorate, 1905, with thesis on a psychiatric subject. Opened own practice, 1911. Married Erna Reiss, 1912. Military doctor in Alsace, 1914–18; member of Independent Social Democratic Party of Germany (USPD), 1919, before joining Social Democratic Party of Germany (SPD). Awarded Fontane Prize, 1916; Chairman of the Schutzverbandes Deutscher Schriftsteller (Association for the Interests of German Writers), 1924; became member of "1925 Group" and, in 1928, of Creative Writing Section of Prussian Academy of Arts. Resigned from Academy after Nazi seizure of power, 1933; fled via Switzerland to France, where granted citizenship. Took part in International Congress for Defence of Culture, Paris, 1935. Emigrated to New York, 1940. Joined Catholic Church, 1941. Returned to Germany, 1945, as officer in French army. Publisher, *Das Goldene Tor*, 1946–51. Co-founded Mainz Academy of Sciences and Literature, 1949, honorary chairman, 1953; also honorary chairman of Free Academy of Fine Arts in Hamburg. Died in Emmendingen, 26 June 1957.

Selected Writings

Collections

Ausgewählte Werke, 31 volumes, 1960–
Die Zeitlupe: Kleine Prosa, 1962
Die Vertreibung der Gespenster [The Exorcism of Ghosts], 1968
Gesammelte Erzählungen, 1971
Ein Kerl muss eine Meinung haben [A Fellow Must Have an Opinion], 1976

Fiction

Die Ermordung einer Butterblume und andere Erzählungen [The Murder of a Buttercup and Other Stories], 1913
Die drei Sprünge des Wang-lun, 1915; as *The Three Leaps of Wang-lun*, translated by C.D. Godwin, 1991
Die Lobensteiner reisen nach Böhmen [The Lobensteiner Travel to Bohemia], 1917
Wadzeks Kampf mit der Dampfturbine [Wadzek's Struggle with the Steam Turbine], 1918
Der schwarze Vorhang: Roman von den Worten und Zufällen [The Black Curtain], 1919
Wallenstein, 2 volumes, 1920
Blaubart und Miss Ilsebill [Bluebeard and Miss Ilsebill], 1923
Berge, Meere und Giganten [Mountains, Seas, and Giants], 1924; 2nd edition as *Giganten*, 1932
Die beiden Freudinnen und ihr Giftmord [The Two Girl Friends and Their Poisoning], 1925

Feldzeugmeister Cratz, Der Kaplan, Zwei Erzählungen, 1926
Manas: Epische Dichtung, 1927
Berlin Alexanderplatz: Die Geschichte von Franz Biberkopf, 1929; as *Alexanderplatz, Berlin: The Story of Franz Biberkopf*, translated by Eugène Jolas, 1931
Babylonische Wandrung; oder, Hochmut kommt vor dem Fall [Babylonian Tour; or, Pride Goes before a Fall], 1934
Pardon wird nicht gegeben, 1935; as *Men without Mercy*, translated by Trevor Blewitt and Phyllis Blewitt, 1937
Die Fahrt ins Land ohne Tod [Journey to the Land without Death], 1937; as *Das Land ohne Tod*, 1947
Der blaue Tiger [The Blue Tiger], 1938
Bürger und Soldaten 1918 [Townspeople and Soldiers], 1939
Der neue Urwald [The New Primeval Forest], 1948
November 1918: Eine deutsche Revolution, 1948–50 (trilogy); as *A People Betrayed* and *Karl and Rosa*, translated by John E. Woods, 1983
Der Oberst und der Dichter; oder, Das menschliche Herz [The Colonel and the Poet; or, The Human Heart], 1946
Heitere Magie: zwei Erzählungen [Merry Magic], 1948
Hamlet; oder, die lange Nacht nimmt ein Ende [Hamlet; or, The Long Night Comes to an End], 1956
Amazonas: Romantrilogie (includes *Das Land ohne Tod*; *Der blaue Tiger*; *Der neue Urwald*), 1988

Plays
Lydia und Mäxchen: Tiefe Verbeugung in einem Akt, 1906
Lusitania, 1920
Die Nonnen von Kemnade [The Nuns of Kemnade], 1923
Die Ehe [Marriage], 1931

Other
"Gedächtnisstörungen bei der Korsakoffschen Psychose" [Memory Disturbance in Korsakoff's Psychosis] (medicine dissertation), University of Freiburg im Breisgau, 1905
Gespräche mit Kalypso über die Liebe und die Musik [Conversations with Calypso on Love and Music], 1910
Der deutsche Maskenball [The German Masked Ball], 1921
Staat und Schriftsteller [The State and the Author], 1921
Reise in Polen, 1926; as *Journey to Poland*, translated by Joachim Neugroschel, 1991
Das Ich über der Natur, 1927
Alfred Döblin: Im Buch, Zu Haus, Auf der Strasse [Alfred Döblin in His Books, At Home, On the Street], with Oskar Loerke, 1928
Der Bau des epischen Werkes [The Structure of the Epic Work], 1929
Wissen und Verändern! Offene Briefe an einem jungen Menschen [Know and Change! Open Letters to a Young Person], 1931
Unser Dasein [Our Existence], 1933
Jüdische Erneuerung [Jewish Renewal], 1933
Flucht und Sammlung des Judenvolks: Aufsätze und Erzählungen [Flight and Gathering of the Jewish People], 1935
Der historische Roman und Wir [The Historical Novel and Us], 1936
Die deutsche Literatur: Ein Dialog zwischen Politik und Kunst [German Literature: A Dialogue between Politics and Art], 1938
Der Nürnberger Lehrprozess, 1946
Der unsterbliche Mensch: Ein Religionsgespräch [The Immortal Human Being], 1946; with *Der Kampf mit dem Engel: Religionsgespräch* [Struggle with the Angel], 1980
Die literarische Situation [The Literary Situation], 1947
Unsere Sorge: der Mensch [Our Concern: Mankind], 1948
Schicksalsreise: Bericht und Bekenntnis, 1949; as *Destiny's Journey*, translated by Edna McCown, 1992
Die Dichtung, ihre Natur und ihre Rolle [Poetry, its Nature and Role], 1950

Further Reading

Dollenmayer, David B., *The Berlin Novels of Alfred Döblin*, Berkeley: University of California Press, 1988
Keller, Otto, *Döblins Montageroman als Epos der Moderne* [Döblin's Novel of Montage as an Epic of the Modern], Munich: Fink, 1980
Kiesel, Helmuth, *Literarische Trauerarbeit: Das Exil- und Spätwerk Alfred Döblins* [Literary Labour of Sorrow: The Work of Albert Döblin in Exile and Later Life], Tübingen: Niemeyer, 1986
Links, Roland, *Alfred Döblin: Leben und Werk* [Albert Döblin: His Life and Work], East Berlin: Volk und Wissen, 1965; 2nd edition, 1976
Meyer, Jochen (editor), *Alfred Döblin, 1878–1978: Eine Ausstellung des Deutschen Literaturarchivs im Schiller-Nationalmuseum* (exhibition catalogue), Munich: Kosel, 1978
Müller-Salget, Klaus, *Alfred Döblin: Werk und Entwicklung* [Albert Döblin: His Work and Development], Bonn: Bouvier, 1972; 2nd edition, 1988
Prangel, Matthias, *Alfred Döblin*, Stuttgart: Metzler, 1973; 2nd edition, 1987
Ziolkowski, Theodore, *Dimensions of the Modern Novel: German Texts and European Contexts*, Princeton, New Jersey: Princeton University Press, 1969

From the start, Döblin's relationship to Judaism and the religious was dichotomous and tense in the extreme. His father came from a fully assimilated family, while his mother's upbringing was Orthodox. As a result of his father leaving the family destitute, Döblin's bond with his mother became stronger, but the atmosphere of Berlin, imperial yet modern, loosened the religious ties and in 1912, as he began to discover his literary identity, he left Berlin's Jewish community. Nevertheless, his work continued to be influenced by religious dimensions. In 1919 he wrote the following in the almanac entitled *Die Erhebung*: "The most important facet of religions is the binding of the individual, not to a metaphysical principle but by the telling of fascinating tales to a group, folk, race." But, "towns live in a completely artificially socially constructed world . . . myth and God are immediately unmasked and groundless here." Yet the first sentence of the essay reads: "It is not the case that God is dead to non-believers." Döblin did, however, distance himself from Judaism: "These formulas and ancient legends mean nothing to me, or too little. The world is richer and darker than these legends suggest." A year later, his prose piece entitled "Die Flucht aus dem Himmel", a poetic representation of the relationship of God, Mary, and Jesus appeared in the second almanac. In 1941 he was received into the Catholic Church.

Döblin's first major novel, *Die drei Sprünge des Wang-lun* (*The Three Leaps of Wang-lun*), was published in 1915, although the manuscript had been finished as early as March 1913. In May 1913 the Expressionist periodical *Der Sturm* published a short essay which nevertheless soon came to be known as the "Berliner Programm", in which Döblin set out his goals and which was understood as the direct antithesis of the already well-known Thomas Mann: no psychology, no emergence of the author as individual and creator. "The hegemony of the author must be broken; the fanaticism of self-abnegation can never be pursued too far." Pegasus was outstripped by technology: "The subject of the novel is the inanimate reality. The reader, confronted, fully independently, by a shaped, designed course of events may judge, but not the author." This serves to contradict the basic principle of narrative literature: "The whole may not appear as spoken, but as it is." The major novels, which Döblin now published in quick succession, *Die drei Sprünge des Wang-lun*, *Wadzeks Kampf mit der Dampfturbine*, *Wallenstein*, and *Berge, Meere und Giganten*, novels which were set in the most diverse times and places – including the future – were read as the redemption of this modern programme, which had broken with the classical narrative tradition.

Döblin was now one of the most important authors of the Weimar Republic as an exponent of modern, factual, science-orientated, and politically left-liberal literature. The year 1929 saw the publication of *Berlin Alexanderplatz: Die Geschichte von Franz Biberkopf*, a book to which the designation "novel" scarcely does justice. It was written between 1925 and 1929 and described the eventful life of a proletarian in these years, with Döblin interspersing contemporary newspaper reports and non-literary documents. The cover of this unique major publishing success refers to the "very clear instruction": "One does not start one's life with good words and intentions; one starts with recognition and understanding, and with the right neighbour." This novel, which had previously been serialized in the *Frankfurter Zeitung*, was adapted as a radio play and filmed in 1931 with Heinrich George in the leading role. *Berlin Alexanderplatz* became the most famous Berlin novel of the era.

Alongside this novel evolved the quite different *Das Ich über der Natur*, in which Döblin completes a spiritual reorientation. "There are only beings with a living soul in nature; even the chemical-physical nature has a living soul." His religious affinities now came clearly to the fore: "The world is enduring and becomes real through a super-reality, which stems from the original self, the original consciousness." Without defending an anti-scientific belief, Döblin demands here a discipline extending beyond the current level of science and hopes for the "rebirth of the principle science of theology". *Wissen und Verändern! Offene Briefe an einen jungen Menschen* followed in 1931. In this work Döblin describes the position of the intellectual alongside the worker and his political organizations as an ideological and, at least in part, religious socialism. *Unser Dasein* (1933) was an attempt to determine the position of humankind between biology and theology. As early as 1924 Döblin had written: "I intend to show what this epoch is beyond the humanistic field of vision."

Döblin expanded the last chapter of *Unser Dasein* and published it in 1933 under the title *Jüdische Erneuerung*. Again and again he dealt with Jewish themes, particularly Zionism and eastern European Judaism. In autumn 1924, in response to anti-Semitic violence in the east of Berlin, he embarked on a long journey through Poland, which he recorded in *Reise in Polen*. Here he saw and experienced how faith has the power to form communities, a power that simultaneously heightened his distance from "western" Judaism and drove him to almost anti-Semitic expression. In two subsequent works, *Jüdische Erneuerung* and *Flucht und Sammlung des Judenvolks*, he dealt with a now highly topical political issue: he considered Zionism concentrated on Palestine to be inadequate and he followed in the footsteps of Nathan Birnbaum in embracing territorialism, which also considered other countries such as Angola in the question of "ingathering" of the Jews. Now he regarded liberation of the Jews as a "deception" and acknowledged: "Hideously, shamefully, the story of the Jews and the Germans is ending. They were caught in a trap." As was only to be expected, he moved between the frequently feuding fronts of communists and Zionists. At the same time, one sentence makes clear how far he had distanced himself from his earlier view of the world: "One should not deny that we no longer have any true joy in simple technology and science." His preoccupation with the "Jewish question", which was always at the same time a preoccupation with his own past, accelerated the process of profound change which Döblin had been experiencing since 1933.

In 1933 Döblin left Germany. His books were burnt "and the Jew in me along with my name. . . . Thus am I honoured." In Paris he was active in both politics and publishing and was one of the few granted French citizenship. During this period he was working on the trilogy which later became known as *November 1918*. In 1940 he fled to the USA, where he lived in extremely difficult conditions and worked for the film industry. His reception into the Catholic Church, which did not become common knowledge until 1945, disappointed many of his friends when he returned to Baden-Baden in 1945. *Das Goldene Tor*, the journal he published, was no longer able to cover the newly emerging spiritual currents such as Existentialism. His deteriorating health worsened his financial and personal situation. He was so disappointed with the restorative tendencies of the fledgling Federal Republic of Germany that in 1953 he returned to Paris. His last major novel *Hamlet; oder, die lange Nacht nimmt ein Ende* appeared in 1956; this was a novel cycle in which he used the fate of a war survivor to portray the father–son conflict as well as a highly problematic mother–son relationship. The breadth of Döblin's work reflects the author's ability relentlessly to represent the world's contradictions, without creating, being able to create, or needing to create a synthesis or conciliation.

MANFRED VOIGTS
translated by Karen Goulding

Doctorow, E.L.

US fiction writer, 1931–

Born Edgar Lawrence Doctorow in New York City, 6 January 1931. Studied at Bronx High School of Science; Kenyon College, Gambier, Ohio, BA in philosophy 1952; Columbia University, 1952–53. Served in US army, 1953–55. Married Helen Setzer, 1954; two daughters and one son. Editor, New American Library, New York, 1960–64; editor in chief, 1964–69, and publisher, 1969, Dial Press, New York. Member of faculty, Sarah Lawrence College, Bronxville, New York, 1971–78; Adjunct Professor of English, 1982–86, and since 1987 Glucksman Professor of American and English Letters, New York University. Writer in residence, University of California, Irvine, 1969–70; Creative Writing Fellow, Yale University School of Drama, 1974–75; Visiting Professor, University of Utah, Salt Lake City, 1975; Visiting Senior Fellow, Princeton University, 1980–81. Director, Authors Guild of America and American PEN Center. Many awards, including Guggenheim Fellowship, 1972; Creative Artists Public Service grant, 1973; National Book Critics Circle Award, 1976, 1990; American Academy Award, 1976, and Howells Medal, 1990; American Book Award, 1986; PEN Faulkner Award, 1990. Member, American Academy of Arts and Letters, 1984.

Selected Writings

Novels
Welcome to Hard Times, 1960; as *Bad Man from Bodie*, 1961
Big as Life, 1966
The Book of Daniel, 1971
Ragtime, 1975
Loon Lake, 1980
World's Fair, 1985
Billy Bathgate, 1989
Poets and Presidents, 1994
The Waterworks, 1994
City of God, 2000

Short Stories
Lives of the Poets: Six Stories and a Novella, 1984

Plays
Drinks before Dinner, 1979
Daniel, 1983

Other
American Anthem, 1982
Eric Fischl: Scenes and Sequences: Fifty-Eight Monotypes, 1990
Conversations with E.L. Doctorow, edited by Christopher D. Morris, 1999

Further Reading

Harter, Carol C. and James R. Thompson, *E.L. Doctorow*, Boston: Twayne, 1990
Levine, Paul, *E.L. Doctorow*, London: Methuen, 1985
Morris, Christopher D., *Models of Misrepresentation: On the Fiction of E.L. Doctorow*, Jackson: University Press of Mississippi, 1991
Parks, John G., *E.L. Doctorow*, New York: Continuum Press, 1991
Tokarczyk, Michelle M., *E.L. Doctorow: An Annotated Bibliography*, New York: Garland, 1988
Tokarczyk, Michelle M., *E.L. Doctorow's Skeptical Commitment*, New York: Peter Lang, 2000
Trenner, Richard (editor), *E.L. Doctorow: Essays and Conversations*, Princeton, New Jersey: Ontario Review Press, 1983

E.L. Doctorow is indisputably one of the most gifted American novelists of his generation, yet he is not as salient as such coevals as Philip Roth, Joseph Heller, Saul Bellow, or Bernard Malamud, to say nothing of the non-Jewish contingent such as Updike or Styron. This is because he is a master stylist without an individual voice. One cannot recognize or define a Doctorow sentence. Each new novel is a departure in form and substance from the previous, delighting the literati and the academy, who have showered him with prestigious awards, but depriving the general reader of the comfort of familiarity.

There are nonetheless persistent tropes; especially the exploration of key periods of American history, a deep and philosophical probing into existential significance, and, for the most part, the weaving of historical, and sometimes contemporary, figures into the fictional narrative, occasionally verging on the edge of "faction". None of this is unique. Examples can be found in the work of the other novelists mentioned above, but the intensity and extent to which Doctorow combines and exploits these traits is very much his own.

His first novel, *Welcome to Hard Times*, was a Western (filmed with Henry Fonda in the lead) written in a plain allegorical style suited to its exploration of good and evil, and the tension between honour, duty, and survival that a frontier society magnifies. This was followed six years later by the kind of complete departure that Doctorow devotees have now come to take for granted, into the realm of science fiction. The book was *Big as Life*, a satirical take on a future New York which was really a comment on the present one, and which introduced another theme that was to be found in much subsequent work – his fascination with, and ambivalence towards, the Big Apple.

There have been long gaps between his publications, paying witness to the amount of craft and care that each work receives, but his third novel *The Book of Daniel* established his reputation as a major writer. It can also be said to have had a "Jewish" theme insofar as it was based on the 1950s trial of the Rosenberg atom spies. Told mainly from the point of view of the spies' children, it was a literary *tour de force*, employing Joycean stream of consciousness, shifts in perspective, and above all revealing a concern and compassion for those caught up innocently and unwillingly in the irresistible tide of history. The metaphorical implication was obvious, and as well as being a caustic exploration of the then contemporary American political scene it was a moving experience. Certainly for many years Doctorow considered it his best work, although to his regret it cost him his friendship with the Rosenberg children. It was nominated for a National Book Award.

His muse turning in a different direction then produced his most popular and acclaimed work, *Ragtime* (successfully filmed with James Cagney and Pat O'Brien playing elderly versions of their famous personae). Dealing imaginatively with an historical event and including an array of figures from the first decades of the 20th century, including at least two Jews, Houdini and Freud, the novel examines an early example of black consciousness, contrasting the inescapable trap in which self-assertive African-Americans found themselves with such money-making escapades as the illusions of a Houdini. It earned Doctorow both the first National Book Critics Circle award for fiction (1976) and the Arts and Letters award of the American Academy and National Institute of Arts and Letters.

Two subsequent works of fiction, *Loon Lake* in 1980 and *Lives of the Poets: Six Stories and a Novella* in 1984, continued his experiments with style and form, and his exploration of the American experience. The novella in *Lives of the Poets* was set in New York's SoHo and *Loon Lake* dealt with the years of the Great Depression and was Doctorow's contribution to the literary examination and questioning of the American dream. Neither work achieved much popularity. Nor did his next novel, *World's Fair*, an experiment in the memoir form, which nevertheless had critical acclaim and received the 1986 American Book Award.

Billy Bathgate in 1989 was stylistically closer to *Ragtime* and enjoyed considerable sales. It is not without significance that both these novels are closer to straightforward linear narrative than any of Doctorow's other works from, and including, *The Book of Daniel*. As with all his work it is quintessentially American, following as it does the eponymous fictional and opportunistic hero who becomes the right-hand man of the historical gangster Dutch Schultz. The opportunities for commenting on the implications of the singular phenomenon of the gangster as public figure and icon were seized with consummate skill.

With his latest work, *City of God*, Doctorow has produced one of his most absorbing, analytical, and challenging works. A mystery which is never solved (the disappearance of the cross from a neighbourhood church which is subsequently found on the roof of the synagogue of an advanced Jewish sect), the novel traces the loss of faith of the church's priest until he joins (possibly through infatuation with its woman rabbi) the sect. The sect itself is highly unorthodox, having conceived of "Evolutionary Judaism" which is an attempt to get back to the essential ethical basis of the religion and while not shedding tradition, rejecting the implausible myths that have accumulated over aeons. "God" is seen as the fulfilment, rather than the origin of man's destiny. In this book Doctorow employs all his mimetic skills, with first-person narratives by all the main characters and bringing on to stage, Einstein, Wittgenstein, Frank Sinatra, and the author himself. He uses his own background to give authenticity to New York Jewish speech patterns and attitudes. Among other themes are the improbability that the combination of circumstances for life as we know it could have come about by chance; the seemingly meaningless or cruel nature of natural phenomena; similarly for man-made events (especially the Holocaust); a satirical look at deconstruction (based on popular songs or "standards"); and in a typically postmodern self-referential manner it is also a book about the writing of a book – this book. And above all else it is ludic. While never allowing the reader to lose sight of the seriousness of the themes or the depths of the analyses, it keeps the reader constantly amused.

It is impossible to predict what Doctorow will offer in the future other than to say it will differ from anything that has gone before. His versatility may inhibit his contemporary popularity, but his work will outlast many whose current standing is higher in the literary marketplace.

GERALD DE GROOT

Dorfman, Ariel

Chilean fiction writer and essayist, 1942–

Born in Buenos Aires, Argentina, 6 May 1942. Lived with his family in the United States, 1943–53; moved to Chile, 1954; became Chilean citizen, 1967. Graduated from University of Chile, Santiago, with a degree in philosophy 1967. Married María Angélica Malinarich, 1966; two sons. Research scholar, University of California, Berkeley, 1968–69; Professor of Spanish-American studies, University of Chile, 1970–73. Exiled from Chile by Pinochet regime, 1973. Research Fellow, Friedrich Ebert Stiftung, West Germany, 1974–76; taught Spanish-American literature at the Sorbonne, 1975–76; University of Amsterdam, 1976–80; Fellow, Woodrow Wilson Center for International Scholars, Washington, DC, 1980–81; Visiting Fellow, Institute for Policy Studies, Washington, DC, 1981–84; Visiting Professor, University of Maryland, College Park, 1983; Visiting Professor, 1984, and since 1985 (spring semesters) Professor of Literature and Latin American Studies, Duke University, Durham, North Carolina. Has contributed frequently to *Los Angeles Times*, the *Nation*, and *Village Voice*. Many awards, including Chile Films Award, for screenplay, 1972; *La Opinión* Ampliado Sudamericana Prize, 1973; Israeli Alternative Theatre Festival Prize, 1987; Kennedy Center–American Express New American Plays Award, 1988; *Time Out* Award, 1991; Olivier Award, for play, 1992.

Selected Writings

Fiction

Moros en la costa, 1973; as *Hard Rain*, translated by the author and George R. Shivers, 1990
Cría ojos, 1979; as *My House is on Fire*, translated by the author and George R. Shivers, 1990
Viudas, 1981; as *Widows*, translated by Stephen Kessler, 1983
La última canción de Manuel Sendero, 1982; as *The Last Song of Manuel Sendero*, translated by the author and George R. Shivers, 1987
Dorando la pildora, 1985
Travesía: cuentos, 1986
Cuentos para militares: la batalla de los colores y otros cuentos, 1986
Máscaras, 1988; as *Mascara*, 1988

Konfidenz, 1994
The Nanny and the Iceberg, 1999
Terapia, in Portuguese, 1999; in Spanish, 2001; translated as *Blake's Therapy*, 2001

Plays
Widows, 1988
Death and the Maiden, 1991; translated as *La muerte y la doncella*, 1992
Reader, 1992
Resistance Trilogy: Widows, Death and the Maiden, Reader, 1998

Poetry
Aus den Augen verlieren / Desaparecer, 1979; as *Missing*, translated by Edith Grossman, 1982
Pruebas al canto, 1980
Pastel de choclo, 1986
Last Waltz in Santiago and Other Poems of Exile and Disappearance, translated by the author and Edith Grossman, 1988

Other
El absurdo entre cuatro paredes: el teatro de Harold Pinter, 1968
Imaginación y violencia en América, 1970; selections in *Some Write to the Future*, translated by the author and George R. Shivers, 1991
Para leer al Pato Donald, with Armand Mattelart, 1971; as *How to Read Donald Duck: Imperialist Ideology in the Disney Comic*, translated by David Kunzle, 1975
Ensayos quemados en Chile: inocencia y neocolonialismo, 1974
Superman y sus amigos del alma, with Manuel Jofré, 1974
La última aventura del llanero solitario, 1979
Reader's Nuestro que estás en la tierra: ensayos sobre el imperialismo cultural, 1980; translated as *The Empire's Old Clothes: What the Lone Ranger, Babar, and Other Innocent Heroes Do to Our Minds*, 1983; as *Patos, elefantes y héroes: la infancia como subdesarrollo*, 1985
Hacia la liberación del lector latinoamericano, 1984; selections in *Some Write to the Future*, translated by the author and George R. Shivers, 1991
Sin ir más lejos, 1986
La rebelión de los conejos mágicos, 1987
Chile from Within, 1973–1988, with Marco Antonio de la Parra, 1990
Missing Continents, 1994
Heading South, Looking North: A Bilingual Journey, 1998; as *Rumba al sur, descendo el norte: un romance in dos linguas*, 1998

Further Reading

Alcides Jofre, Manuel, "La muerte y la doncella de Ariel Dorfman: transición democrática y crisis de la memoria", *Atenea*, 469 (1984)
Barr, Lois Baer, "Deconstructing Authoritarian Codes: Ariel Dorfman" in her *Isaac Unbound: Patriarchal Traditions in the Latin American Jewish Novel*, Tempe: Arizona State University Center for Latin American Studies, 1995
Boyers, Peggy and Juan Carlos Lértora, "Ideology, Exile, Language: An Interview with Ariel Dorfman", *Salmagundi* (Spring–Summer 1989)
Butler, Cornelia, "Roasting Donald Duck: Alternative Comics and Photonovels in Latin America", *Journal of Popular Culture*, 18/1 (1984)
Claro-Mayo, Juan, "Dorfman, cuentista comprometido", *Revista iberoamericana*, 114–115 (1981)
Glickman, Nora, "Ariel Dorfman" in *Tradition and Innovation: Reflections on Latin American Jewish Writing*, edited by Robert DiAntonio and Nora Glickman, Albany: State University of New York Press, 1993
Graham-Yooll, Andrew, "Dorfman: A Case of Conscience", *Index on Censorship*, 20/6 (June 1991)
Incledon, John, "Liberating the Reader: A Conversation with Ariel Dorfman", *Chasqui*, 20/1 (1990)
Kafka, Paul, "On Exile and Return: An Interview with Ariel Dorfman", *Bloomsbury Review*, 9/6 (1989)
Oropesa, Salvador A., *La obra de Ariel Dorfman: ficción y crítica*, Madrid: Pliegos, 1992
Wisenberg, S.L., "Ariel Dorfman: A Conversation", *Another Chicago Magazine*, 18 (1988)

One of Latin America's most prolific writers, Ariel Dorfman forcefully resists the categorization of "Jewish writer". He prefers to be known as a Chilean or Latin American writer, a designation supported by the lack of Jewish figures and themes in his fiction. The experience of exile and his commitment to human rights have clearly marked his writing, and, for some, this suffices to claim him for Jewish literature.

Dorfman's grandparents and their children moved to Argentina in the early part of the 20th century from pogrom-infested eastern Europe, thanks in part to the efforts of Baron de Hirch's Jewish Colonization Association. His father, Adolfo Dorfman became a professor at the Universidad de la Plata in Buenos Aires, but in 1943 resigned his academic position after the military coup that eventually took control of the university. Feeling threatened by the new pro-Axis government, the Dorfmans decided to emigrate to the US. The family lived in New York for ten years until McCarthyism forced them once again into exile. In 1954, the Dorfmans took up permanent residence in Chile. Ariel Dorfman became a naturalized Chilean citizen in 1967, and participated actively in Chilean politics until forced to emigrate in 1973, owing to his outspoken resistance to the government of Augusto Pinochet.

Although Dorfman grew up speaking both Spanish and English, his early fiction and critical prose were written in Spanish. He addresses the issues of exile, politics, language, and identity in his recent memoir *Heading South, Looking North: A Bilingual Journey*, written in English. This elegant and complex autobiography is one of the few spaces in which Dorfman meditates – albeit briefly – on his Jewish background.

Published at the height of political turmoil in Chile, Dorfman's first novel, *Moros en la costa* (*Hard Rain*), is a collage of fictitious newspaper articles, filmscripts, book reviews, encyclopedia entries, and other short forms, depicting the political situation in Chile during the last months of

Salvador Allende's socialist government. Although the text was edited significantly for the English translation, the original mood of resistance to political and aesthetic despotism remains intact.

His second novel, *Viudas* (*Widows*) is set in a small town in Greece about to be invaded by Nazi troops during World War II. The women courageously resist the military invasion even in the face of the barbaric acts committed against their families. Alternative readings of this text have been suggested, specifically as pertaining to the Shoah experience and the civilian "disappearances" under military dictatorships in Latin America.

Dorfman formally introduces a Jewish protagonist in his third novel, *La última canción de Manuel Sendero* (*The Last Song of Manuel Sendero*), yet there are no specific Jewish themes other than the recurrent experience of exile that allows the main character to be portrayed as a "wandering Jew". Forced exile and resistance continued to emerge in his fiction. *Konfidenz* is a political allegory set in Paris shortly before the Nazi occupation. Dorfman's vocation for playwriting is evident in the dialogue of this novel in which suspense takes precedence over contemplation, forging a tense atmosphere of fright and betrayal.

After years of pondering issues of deterritorialization and self-identity, Dorfman's fiction has taken a lighter turn. *The Nanny and the Iceberg*, written in English, deals with post-Pinochet Chilean politics, yet, unlike his earlier fiction, the tone is comic, almost farcical. The same lightness characterizes his latest novel, *Blake's Therapy*, a treatise on avarice about a man who has everything except inner peace. Unable to eat or sleep, Graham Blake embarks on a radical experimental therapy that turns his life into an infinite succession of reflections, an internal panoptikon.

Dorfman's phenomenally successful plays do not address issues of Jewish identity any more than his novels. His best-known play, *Death and the Maiden*, is a powerful psychological thriller about power, torture, and revenge. A woman confronts a man whom she believes to have been her torturer 15 years earlier during a military regime and is determined to take revenge. The universal theme of this play makes it plausible to perceive in it echoes of post-Shoah literature or even a subtle commentary on the Arab–Israeli conflict. A film version directed by Roman Polanski was released in 1994.

His latest film project is *Dead Line*, an adaptation of his *Last Waltz in Santiago*, a collection of poetry detailing tales of government abuse and terror campaigns in Chile.

LYDIA M. GIL

Dujovne Ortiz, Alicia

Argentine fiction writer and journalist, 1940–

Born in Buenos Aires, 1940, daughter of a Spanish Christian mother and a Russian Jewish father. Moved to Paris at onset of military dictatorship, 1978, remaining there until 1998. Has contributed to *La Nación* and *La Opinión* of Buenos Aires, *El Excelsior* of Mexico City, and *Le Monde*, Paris. Returned to Buenos Aires, 1998.

Selected Writings

Novels

El buzón de la esquina [The Corner Mailbox], 1977
El agujero en la tierra [The Hole in the Earth], 1983
L'arbre de la gitane [The Gypsy's Tree], 1990; as *Vamos a Vladivostok* [Let's Go to Vladivostok], 1990; as *El árbol de la gitana*, 1997
Mireya, 1998; as *Femme Couleur Tango* [Woman Colour Tango], 1998

Short Stories

Orejas invisibles para el rumor de nuestros pasos [Invisible Ears for the Murmur of Our Steps], 1966
Recetas, florecillas y otros contentos [Recipes, Little Flowers and Other Joys], 1973
Wara, la petite indienne de l'Altiplano [Wara, the Little Indian of the Altiplano], 1983

Poetry

El mapa del olvidado tesoro [The Map of Forgotten Treasure], 1967

Other

María Elena Walsh, 1982
Buenos Aires, 1984
Le Mexique, le Guatemala, with Nanon Gardin, 1984
Le sourire des dauphins [The Smile of the Dolphins], 1989
Bogota, 1991
Maradona, c'est moi, 1993; as *Maradona soy yo*, 1993
Eva Perón: La biografía, 1995; as *Eva Perón*, translated by Shawn Fields, 1996

Further Reading

Glickman, Nora, "Andando se hacen los caminos de Alicia Dujovne Ortiz", *Revista Iberoamericana*, 191 (April–June 2000)
Kaplan, Karen, "The Poetics of Displacement in Alicia Dujovne Ortiz' *Buenos Aires*", *Discourse*, 8 (1985–86); 9 (1986–87)
Senkman, Leonardo, "Las tribulaciones de una centaura argentina exiliada en Paris", *Noaj*, 1/1 (August 1987)

The building of a genealogical tree to unravel the labyrinth of one's own family roots is a substantial element prevalent in the writings of a large number of Jewish-Latin American authors such as Isaac Chocrón, Marcos Aguinis, and Ricardo Feierstein, who descend from immigrants who had been expelled from their countries because of racial persecution and economic deprivation. At times the sagas they write are faithful to history; other times, as in the case of Mario Szichman, they are apocryphal satires, or, as in Moacyr Scliar's case, they go back to a remote, even biblical past before recalling the memories of closer generations.

This fervent search into the past is also the most important propellant of a Jewish feminine literature, that begins in the 1960s and reaches its height in contemporary letters. The authors are daughters and granddaughters of immigrants who turn to the past in order to build their genealogical tree: Alicia Freilich Segal, Sabina Berman, Margo Glanz, Alicia Steimberg, Manuela Fingueret, and numerous stories and poems by writers such as Angelina Muñiz, Teresa

Porzekansky, Aída Gelbrunk, Luisa Futoransky, Diana Raznovich, Elisa Lerner, and Nora Glickman.

Alicia Dujovne Ortiz belongs to the above group of Latin American women, who especially in Argentina and Mexico have been part of a literary "boom". The fact that a large number of them are of Jewish origin has caused them to reveal their conflicted identities in autobiographical, satirical, feminist, and intellectual fiction.

Born in Buenos Aires in 1940, Dujovne Ortiz moved to Paris at the onset of the military dictatorship in her country (1978–83) and remained there until 1998. As a journalist she contributed to *La Nación* and *La Opinión* of Buenos Aires, *El Excelsior* of Mexico City and *Le Monde* of Paris. Her style is characterized by the use of parody and humour as forms of escape.

Dujovne's initial writing period is marked by her use of a baroque, bright, and sensual language. *El agujero en la tierra* [The Hole in the Earth], written during the worst decade of violence in Argentina, reveals not only an intricate personal history, but is also a metaphor of a country being torn from its roots. Dujovne's condition as an exile and a Jew becomes an important theme during her years in France. Starting from her collection of stories – *Orejas invisibles para el rumor de nuestros pasos* [Invisible Ears for the Murmur of Our Steps] and *Recetas, florecillas y otros contentos* [Recipes, Little Flowers and Other Joys] – Dujovne poeticizes ordinary sensations and simple elements of everyday life: she addresses the coconut, the eucalyptus tree, the balcony, the tango. Here the poetic voice discovers love, sex, and its own erotic dimension.

The leitmotif of the map appears in Dujovne's first novel, *El buzón de la esquina* [The Corner Mailbox], where the narrator provides the reader with a map of her neighbourhood in Buenos Aires. But the city here could be any city, as the novel is a journey into the protagonist's inner growth from adolescence to womanhood in her struggle for independence. The Jewish theme appears here in the character of Jrein, a "cabalist" of a Jewish neighbourhood in Buenos Aires.

The poems Dujovne included in *El mapa del olvidado tesoro* [The Map of the Forgotten Treasure] encompass a Latin American map of Bolivia, Peru, Brazil, Chile, and Argentina, moving from childhood to youth, from past history to present times.

Dujovne wrote a collection of metaphysical essays, *Buenos Aires*, describing the dilemmas that confront a Buenos Aires native. Here she discusses the male gaze as opposed to the female; the European stare, vis-à-vis the South American perspective, the contrast between the inner city and the surrounding neighbourhoods. Buenos Aires is seen as a melting pot, a rootless, immigrant metropolis.

Unlike the novels located in the city, *El agujero en la tierra* is set in the countryside. Again, Dujovne's preoccupation concerns the fate of the immigrants in their move from the large city to a small village in the province.

Vamos a Vladivostok [Let's go to Vladivostok] later called *El árbol de la gitana* [The Gypsy's Tree] was first published in French in 1990. It is a testimonial novel in which Dujovne reinvents the history of her parents' families. Often forced to explain the double identity she had embraced, Dujovne shows here her concern with conflicts, of belonging to two worlds: Russian-Jewish on her father's side and Spanish-Christian on her mother's.

Her years of exile forced her to adopt a more authentic attitude towards her writing. While she used more sensual images and concrete language before she left Argentina, exile led her to a more introspective level of writing and to incorporating expressions of pain, without losing her humour as a means of gaining knowledge and distance from herself. The anguish of having lost her place of origin turned in time into a reconciliation with her exile: "I would have dreamt to be a writer of the land, but I was left without a land. And I think that from that moment on I began to write with my own voice – of a woman without a land."

The idea of searching into the past turned into an obsession. From her own biography and that of her ancestors, she builds a saga inhabited by most diverse characters. Her double fragmented identity as a writer with two religions, who writes in two languages, is magnified during the years of voluntary exile. The writing of *El árbol de la gitana* as a fictionalized autobiography has the effect of resolving the author's obsessive preoccupation with repeating fragments of her past experiences. It is an historic fresco that recomposes scattered fragments of her familiar roots. To identify herself through her characters from various lineages – famous and anonymous, Jewish and Christian, persecutors and persecuted – Dujovne places them in different countries and periods.

Her father's only consolation on his deathbed is to leave his memoirs to his daughter as a legacy of his frustrated ambition to be a writer. Only at the end of the novel can Dujovne make sense of a chain of dispersed memories, to tie the scattered anecdotes that lost sense from being told over and over again. Finally, in Israel she finds the necessary connection with all her ancestry.

For Dujovne Ortiz writing and everyday life go hand in hand. The mission of the exiled person is to collect fragments from the past, scattered throughout the world. When one leaves it is not to return, and if one returns it is not to the same land one left.

NORA GLICKMAN

Durlacher, G.L.

German-born Dutch writer, 1928–1996

Born Gerhard Leopold Durlacher in Baden-Baden, 10 July 1928. Fled with family from Nazi Germany to Rotterdam, 1937. Home bombed and made uninhabitable, 14 May 1940; moved to Apeldoorn. Detained with family, 1942, and sent to Auschwitz via Westerbork. Parents died in Auschwitz; he survived by chance. Studied and lectured in sociology at the Sociology Institute of the University of Amsterdam. Married; three daughters, eldest being another writer, Jessica Durlacher; also father-in-law of writer Léon de Winter. Took early retirement, 1983; made writing debut, 1985. Received AKO-Literatuurprijs, 1994, Swiss Anne Frank Prize, 1994. Died in Haarlem, 2 July 1996.

Selected Writings

Collection
Verzameld werk [Collected Work], 1997

Fiction
Strepen aan de hemel, 1985; as *Stripes in the Sky*, translated by Susan Massoty, 1991
Drenkeling: Kinderjaren in het Derde Rijk, 1987; as *Drowning: Growing Up in the Third Reich*, translated by Susan Massoty, 1993
De zoektocht, 1991; as *The Search*, translated by Susan Massoty, 1998
Quarantaine: verhalen [Quarantine], 1993
Niet verstaan: verhalen [Not Understood], 1995

Further Reading

Muller, Elianne, *G.L. Durlacher, Drenkeling, Quarantaine*, Laren, The Netherlands: Walvaboek, 1995
Scherphuis, Ageeth *et al.*, *Met haat valt niet te leven: krantenstukken door G.L. Durlacher*, Amsterdam: Meulenhoff, 1998

G.L. Durlacher used to be a sociologist, not a writer. For years he taught at the Sociology Institute of the University of Amsterdam. He suppressed his experiences as a child in the war and as a young man in the postwar Netherlands. He never talked about those; almost no one knew what had happened to him.

Until 1983. At that time he took early retirement from the university. In 1981, after hesitating for a long time, he had read Walter Laqueur's *The Terrible Secret* and Martin Gilbert's *Auschwitz and the Allies*, studies about how the Allies reacted to the persecution of Jews in Nazi Germany. He went into therapy and discovered a wealth of experiences hidden in his memory. All sorts of painful memories of events, feelings, and situations from Auschwitz spilled out. He couldn't do anything but write them down.

Gerhard Leopold Durlacher was born in 1928 in Baden-Baden in south Germany. His first name was changed to Gerard in the Netherlands when in 1937 his parents fled there and settled in Rotterdam. After the bombardment of Rotterdam, the family moved to Apeldoorn in eastern Holland. In 1942 Gerard and his parents were picked up in Apeldoorn and via Westerbork and Terezin were sent to Auschwitz-Birkenau where his parents were killed. Gerard escaped death when in 1944 the so-called *Familienlager* was cleared out and all the boys who appeared to be employable were sent to the men's barracks, the so-called *Männerlager*. There he witnessed the liberation of Auschwitz in January of 1945.

Gerard returned to the Netherlands, finished high school, and studied political science. For years he didn't speak about his experiences, However, the images and experiences kept haunting him. When he was a well-known author, he referred to this: "I kept everything under lock and key much too long. My wife knew a few things, but I couldn't talk about it. I knew that I would break down."

In 1985 this led to his autobiographical debut *Strepen aan de hemel* (*Stripes in the Sky*), an account of his experiences in Birkenau and his trip back to the Netherlands in 1945. Almost immediately this small book was regarded as a special addition to the large amount of survivor literature that was then and still is being published in the Netherlands. The careful descriptions and polished style were very well received by the critics as well as by the Dutch readers. Soon the book appeared in other European countries. The title came from the contrails that the Allied aircraft left behind in the sky when they bombarded factories near Auschwitz. *Stripes in the Sky* ends with Durlacher's return to sleepy Apeldoorn where no one in his family returned and practically no one remembered who he was.

Two years later appeared *Drenkeling* (*Drowning*), an evocation of his youth in Baden-Baden during the period when many fell under the spell of National Socialism. In 1994 he received the Swiss Anne-Frank-Preis for this book. When the English translation appeared, the London *Independent* wrote that *Drenkeling* was written in "a mood of acceptance mixed with deep sorrow".

In *De zoektocht* (*The Search*) of 1991 Durlacher related his attempts to find the boys with whom he had stayed in the *Männerlager*. A mere handful of the 87 adolescent boys had survived. In 1986 he visited his former comrades in Israel and the United States to see how their lives had turned out. During these trips, Durlacher was followed by the well-known Dutch documentary maker Cherry Duyns who filmed and recorded the individual encounters and the final reunion of the "boys" at the Beit Terezin museum in Israel.

When the English translation of *De zoektocht* was published, Durlacher's British colleague, the author Theo Konin, wrote in a review: "The longing to forget and the duty to remember: these are the haunting themes of Durlacher's search for his past, and those who shared in its horrors. Durlacher offers us a victory for the human spirit."

Durlacher continued to publish. His next book *Quarantaine* [Quarantine] appeared in 1993. The older man described how as a young man he returned totally shattered from the camps. *Quarantine* starts where *Stripes in the Sky* stops. He described succinctly the chilliness and lack of understanding in the postwar Netherlands for what the Jewish survivors had experienced. The Dutch were full of their own experiences after five years of German occupation and the hungry winter of 1944–45; in their world there was no room for stories about Auschwitz.

Niet verstaan, the collection of short stories published in 1995, was about the 1950s, when Durlacher was a young student trying to find his way in Dutch society. It is a book of suffocating loneliness.

One wonders whether Durlacher actually enjoyed writing. In an interview he once said:

> I don't want to, I have to. For me it's not only a question of history as it took place. What I want to convey – and perhaps it's very naïve – is that there still is hope, that there are people who retain their dignity. I know that everyone carries terrible elements within himself and can be a small fascist, so to speak, but thank God there are people who can overcome these aspects within themselves or experience them only in their imagination. That idealism of hope must nevertheless be asserted.

Durlacher was extremely surprised about his success in the Netherlands and in the rest of Europe. He permitted a television crew to go along when he returned to his birthplace in Germany, but he thought this interest in himself and his private life rather strange. He said that he "never wrote anything with the purpose of being literature. But if it turns out well and people experience what I write as beautiful, then I'm pleased."

Durlacher was disturbed at comparisons between himself and Primo Levi, another former prisoner in Auschwitz. According to Durlacher, the fact that two people were in the same place did not mean that they had the same experiences or would draw the same conclusions from what happened to them. Durlacher did not share Levi's dark view of the world after Auschwitz.

After his sudden death in 1996, it appeared that he had completed the first chapters of a novel, *Van Tivoli tot Danang*. It would have been his first non-autobiographical work. The fragment is included in his *Verzameld werk* [Collected Work].

Daphne Meijer
translated by Jeannette Ringold

Dworkin, Andrea

US fiction writer and political activist, 1946–

Born in Camden, New Jersey, 26 September 1946. Studied at Bennington College, BA 1968. Worked as waitress, receptionist, factory worker, political organizer, and teacher. Contributor to various journals including *America Report*, *Gay Community News*, and *Village Voice*, particularly on issues of radical feminism.

Selected Writings

Novels
Ice and Fire, 1986
Mercy, 1990

Short Stories
The New Woman's Broken Heart, 1980

Other
Woman Hating: A Radical Look at Sexuality, 1974
Last Days of Hot Slit: A Radical Look at Sexual Polarity, 1974
Our Blood: Prophecies and Discourses on Sexual Politics, 1976
Marx and Gandhi were Liberals: Feminism and the "Radical" Left, 1977
Why So-called Radical Men Love and Need Pornography, 1978
Take back the Night: Women on Pornography, 1980
Pornography: Men Possessing Women, 1981
Right-Wing Women: The Politics of Domesticated Females, 1983
Intercourse, 1987
Pornography and Civil Rights: A New Day for Women's Equality, with Catharine A. MacKinnon, 1988
Letters from a War Zone: Writings, 1976–1987, 1988
Editor, with Catharine A. MacKinnon, *In Harm's Way: The Pornography Civil Rights Hearings*, 1997
Life and Death, 1997 (collection of articles)
Scapegoat: The Jews, Israel, and Women's Liberation, 2000

Further Reading

Jenefsky, Cindy and Ann Russo, *Without Apology: Andrea Dworkin's Art and Politics*, Boulder, Colorado: Westview Press, 1998

Andrea Dworkin has built a formidable reputation as America's leading radical feminist. Her work as a chronicler of and campaigner against pornography, rape, prostitution, and violence against women has led her to be reviled, particularly by the sex industry and by sexual libertarians who saw in her a puritan backlash against the sexual revolution. But she continues to capture the allegiance of new generations of feminists compelled by her uncompromising accounts of women's brutalization by men. Dworkin's Jewishness had formed no particular feature of her work, but in 2000 she published what she considered to be her major work, nine years in the writing. *Scapegoat: The Jews, Israel, and Women's Liberation* is a hugely ambitious work, perhaps even more controversial than any she had written before, which sought to analyse the similarities between the victimization of the Jews and of women.

Dworkin was born into a traditional, Jewish Zionist household in New Jersey. Throughout her childhood she attended Hebrew school and wanted to become a rabbi. In 1965, when she was 18, Dworkin was arrested at an anti-Vietnam demonstration at the United Nations in New York and sent to the Women's House of Detention in Greenwich Village – where she was given a brutal internal examination. A violent marriage in Amsterdam led her to develop a radical-feminist critique of pornography in her first book, *Woman Hating*. In 1978 she addressed the historic rally in San Francisco, when women attending the first feminist conference on pornography held a Take Back the Night march, shutting down the city's sex district for a few hours. Together with anti-porn campaigner Catharine MacKinnon, Dworkin went on to attempt to pass legislation embodying the legal principle that pornography violates the civil liberties of women, creating a rift between herself and civil rights campaigners who saw the proposed legislation as a threat to the First and Fourteenth Amendments.

Dworkin's own writing, together with interviews she has given, has always led the public to believe that her studies of violence against women derived from her own personal experience, but with the publication of *Scapegoat* she revealed that there was an earlier source. At the age of ten she had witnessed a relative, who had been in the Kraków ghetto, Plaszow, Auschwitz-Birkenau, and Buchenwald, having what Dworkin called a "flashback" of her experiences. This was her first introduction to the Holocaust. As a student at Bennington College she read the transcripts of the Nuremberg trials in the library. She told a newspaper:

> I checked it out and it was all true, what [she] had told me, so I've been very involved in trying to learn about the

> Holocaust and trying to understand it, which is probably pointless. I have read Holocaust material you might say compulsively, over a life time. I might go through six months when I won't read it and a few months when I will and I have been doing that since I was a kid.

With the publication of *Scapegoat*, dedicated to her father, Harry Dworkin, the intellectual source of Dworkin's radical programme became apparent. The book derived from a visit she paid to Israel in 1988. She made a direct comparison between anti-Semitism and sexism, between Zionism and women's liberation. Unexpectedly for some readers on the Left, she applauded Jews for demanding, and fighting for, their own country, which she saw as a logical consequence of centuries of violence:

> the Israelis are my guys . . . a miracle of self-determination and courage. Well, they took the land because they had to. I continue to believe that they (we) had to; but brutality has become institutionalized in Israel as expressions of male dominance and state sovereignty – over Jewish / Israeli women as well as over Palestinian men and women.

She analysed the politics of the Middle East conflict in terms of gender, seeing a line of causality beginning with the victimization of Jewish men in pogroms, leading to their desire for the shoring up of their masculinity through fighting back and creating a Jewish state. That masculinity was further defined in relation both to Israeli women and to their enemies, Arab men, who because of their own emasculation as a result of their victimization by the Israeli army, were to take out their aggression on the weakest in their own society, Arab women.

Dworkin then argued that women's position in all societies was analogous to that of Jews, that they were the scapegoats for male violence and frustration. If the Jews had a plan, which was to defend themselves against aggression, to carve out their own space in the world, why not women? As Dworkin saw it, women had the right, for example, to kill men who had physically abused them without paying a legal penalty; they had the right to demand territory. When asked how a woman-only country would operate, what peoples it would have to displace, and how it could be prevented from finding its own scapegoats to oppress, Dworkin has replied that she agreed that such a country would, like Israel itself, be no utopia but that without a debate within feminism about how the country could be made to work, these questions can never be resolved.

Dworkin generates more hostility than any other well-known feminist, much of it in revulsion not only against her ideas but also her physical appearance, with her weight a recurrent theme of most newspaper interviews. Yet she has attracted unlikely support: from John Berger who describes her as "perhaps the most misrepresented writer in the western world. Her words bleed with love and her vision is oracular." In her favour, she has survived to continue to write and be published long after other feminists of her generation have fallen silent or been silenced by indifference or mental illness. Reading *Scapegoat* it becomes clear that her endurance is partly due to her early training as a scholar of Judaism.

LINDA GRANT

E

Elkin, Stanley

US fiction writer, 1930–1995

Born in New York, 11 May 1930. Studied at the University of Illinois, Urbana, 1948–60, BA 1952, MA 1953, PhD in English 1961. Served in the US Army 1955–57. Married Joan Jacobson in 1953; two sons and one daughter. Lecturer in English, Washington University, St Louis, 1960–95; Merle Kling Professor of Modern Letters from 1983. Visiting Professor, Smith College, 1964–65; University of California, Santa Barbara, 1967; University of Wisconsin, Milwaukee, 1969; Yale University, 1975; Boston University, 1976. Many awards, including Guggenheim Fellowship, 1966; Rockefeller Fellowship 1968; Rosenthal Foundation Award, 1980; National Book Critics Circle Award, 1983; Brandeis University Creative Arts Award, 1986. Died in St Louis, Missouri, 31 May 1995.

Selected Writings

Novels
Boswell: A Modern Comedy, 1964
A Bad Man, 1967
The Dick Gibson Show, 1971
The Franchiser, 1976
George Mills, 1982
The Magic Kingdom, 1985
The Rabbi of Lud, 1987
The MacGuffin, 1991
Mrs Ted Bliss, 1995

Short Stories
Criers and Kibitzers, Kibitzers and Criers, 1968
The Making of Ashenden, 1972
Searchers and Seizures, 1973; as *Alex and the Gypsy*, 1977
The Living End, 1979
Early Elkin, 1985
Van Gogh's Room at Arles, 1993

Plays
The Coffee Room, 1987
The Six-Year-Old Man, 1987

Other
Editor, *Stories from the Sixties*, 1971
Stanley Elkin's Greatest Hits, 1980
Editor, *The Best American Short Stories*, with Shannon Ravenel, 1980
Why I Live Where I Live, 1983
Pieces of Soap: Literary Essays, 1992

Further Reading

Bailey, Peter J., *Reading Stanley Elkin*, Urbana: University of Illinois Press, 1985
Bargen, Doris G., *The Fiction of Stanley Elkin*, Bern: Peter Lang, 1979
Dougherty, David C., *Stanley Elkin*, Boston: Twayne, 1990
Guttmann, Allen, *The Jewish Writer in America: Assimilation and the Crisis of Identity*, New York: Oxford University Press, 1971
LeClair, Thomas, "The Obsessional Fiction of Stanley Elkin", *Contemporary Literature* (Spring 1976)
Saltzman, Arthur M., *Designs of Darkness in Contemporary American Fiction*, Philadelphia: University of Pennsylvania Press, 1990
Saltzman, Arthur M., *The Novel in the Balance*, Columbia: University of South Carolina Press, 1993

Born in New York and raised in Chicago, Stanley Elkin stands at a slight remove from the more familiar Jewish-American milieu of his contemporaries Bernard Malamud and Philip Roth. Yet this relative distance from more traditional subject matter allows a new dimension to develop in his fiction, that of a world created less by social fact than by language. From the midwestern heartland he returned for childhood visits to relatives in Brooklyn, and with his parents spent part of each summer at a New Jersey seaside resort area, thus experiencing the worlds of Malamud and Roth, yet from a perspective more likely to encourage a comic rather than a tragic attitude. The author's ability to let characters define themselves in their speaking voices also recalls a heritage of listening to adults talk, especially when that talk involved renewing old cultural bonds. That Elkin's father was a salesman only deepened the son's appreciation of what strength lay in verbal dexterity, of how an entire world of identities and desires could be created by a motivated voice.

Among Elkin's earliest short stories, collected in 1985 as *Early Elkin*, appears the character Feldman. In "A Sound of Distant Thunder", Feldman sells fine china in a declining business district, the surrounding neighbourhood of which is becoming an African-American ghetto. Throughout the day's action, Feldman is on edge – about the weather, the business decline, and the general weariness of trying to market quality merchandise to a public that wants only trendily advertised wares. At the story's end his worse fears seem to be coming true, as sounds approaching from the distance suggest how urban rioting and looting may be underway. If there is, readers can surmise a possible cause for this effect, because earlier in the story Feldman has been hostile to some young black customers whose intentions have been sincere (if unintelligible to the harried shopkeeper). Yet the story's point is not to make a racial judgement against anyone. Instead, Elkin's art has been to dramatize his character's existence through speech alone, specifically the self-defining aria that the salesman performs as he pulls out all the stops in promoting his fine china to a white customer who could care less.

Elkin's novels are devoted to similar self-definition by language. Each has a noteworthy central character from whom an entire world emanates. In *Boswell*, it is a seeker of notoriety who creates a life for himself by courting celebrities; in *A Bad Man*, another businessman named Feldman appears, this time one who finds conventional life so unchallenging that he conspires to have himself imprisoned (and so face tougher tests); the protagonist of *The Dick Gibson Show* is a self-created "radio personality", while the central character in *The Franchiser* uses manic energy to hold together a far-flung business empire while struggling to coordinate a more personal corporate entity, which is his body as afflicted with multiple sclerosis. That Elkin's talent for verbal definition is practically unlimited becomes clear in *George Mills*, in which a thousand years' worth of characters with this unassuming name (and with unexceptional lives to match) manage to make recognizable subjects of themselves.

By mid-career Elkin himself became ill with multiple sclerosis, a slow but eventually terminal degenerative disease that added a certain pathos to his otherwise rambunctious sense of literary comedy. In *The Living End* he presents a triptych of related novellas in which a liquor store owner named Ellerbee is robbed and murdered, only to join his murderer in the afterlife where the two of them and a murdered store clerk help God and Christ adjust the philosophies of Heaven and Hell. *The Magic Kingdom* in 1985 is set back on earth, but only literally so; figuratively its locale is Walt Disney World in Florida, where a group of terminally ill children are taken on a wish-fulfilling trip. "It breaks your heart", one of the tour supervisors says, referring not to the poor dying children but to the ravaged state of a generally ageing populace drawn to the amusement park:

> Imperfection everywhere, everywhere. Not like in nature. What, you think stars show their age? Oceans, the sky? No fear! Only in man, only in woman. Trees never look a day older. The mountains are better off for each million years. Everywhere, everywhere. Bodies mismanaged, malfeasanced, gone off. Like styles, like fashions gone off. It's this piecemeal surrender to time, kids. You can't hold on to your baby teeth. Scissors cut paper, paper covers rock, rock smashes scissors. A bite of candy causes tooth decay, and jawlines that were once firm slip off like shoreline lost to the sea. Noses balloon, amok as a cancer. Bellies swell up and muscles go down. Hip and thighs widen like jodhpurs. My God, children, we look like were dressed for the horseback! (And everywhere, everywhere, there's this clumsy imbalance. You see these old, sluggish bodies on thin-looking legs, like folks carrying packages piled too high. Or like birds puffed out, skewed, out of sorts with their foundations.)

It is the energy of language that carries this vision from nature to humankind and back to nature again, anchored by the mantra of "everywhere, everywhere", a reminder of how widespread and unresolvable the problem is. "It is as if we've been nickel-and-dimed by the elements", Elkin's spokesperson concludes, and it is his aria to this effect that makes readers think they should agree.

In his last decade of life Elkin wrote a last collection of stories (*Van Gogh's Room at Arles*) to accompany his first, *Criers and Kibitzers, Kibitzers and Criers* and three more novels. *The Rabbi of Lud* examines the death industry in a New Jersey town famous for its funerals and burials; *The MacGuffin* propels itself with shoptalk, the ultimate refinement of the author's talent for popular arias; *Mrs Ted Bliss* is about the title character who, as a widow, defines herself by doing what she has to do. This last condition is what has interested Elkin from the start, harking back to the shopkeeper Feldman in "A Sound of Distant Thunder," who even though hopelessly removed from the social reality around him and from the practicality of making a sale, still manages to express an identity through his voice.

JEROME KLINKOWITZ

Epstein, Leslie

US fiction writer, 1938–

Born in Los Angeles, 4 May 1938. Studied at Yale University, BA 1960; Oxford University, diploma 1962; University of California, MA 1963. Married Ilene Gradman, 1969; three children. Lecturer, Queens College of the City University of New York, 1965–67; Assistant Professor of English, 1976, and currently Director of Creative Writing Program at Boston University. Awarded Rhodes scholarship, 1960–62; National Endowment for the Arts grant, 1972; Fulbright Fellow, 1972–73; CAPS grant, 1976–77; Guggenheim Fellow, 1977–78.

Selected Writings

Novels
P.D. Kimerakov, 1975
King of the Jews: A Novel of the Holocaust, 1979
Regina, 1982
Pinto and Sons, 1990
Pandaemonium, 1997

Short Stories
The Steinway Quintet plus Four, 1976
Goldkorn Tales, 1985
Ice Fire Water: A Leib Goldkorn Cocktail, 1999

Further Reading

Alter, Robert, "A Fable of Power: Review of *King of the Jews*", *New York Times Book Review* (4 February 1979)
Lydon, Susan, review of *Regina*, *Village Voice* (18 January 1983)
Pollitt, Katha, review of *The Steinway Quintet*, *New York Times Book Review* (10 August 1975)
Smith, Daniel, "A Cold, Comic Heart", *Atlantic Unbound* (20 October 1999) [online]

Stade, George, "Parallels are Everywhere: Review of *Regina*", *New York Times Book Review* (21 November 1982)

Stamford, Anne Marie, review of *P.D. Kimerakov*, *Best Sellers* (August 1975)

Wisse, Ruth R., "Fairy Tale: Review of *King of the Jews*", *Commentary* (May 1979)

Leslie Epstein occupies an unusual place among American Jewish novelists. For one thing, he is among the very few such writers – Budd Schulberg being the only other who comes to mind – who was born into the world of Hollywood filmmakers but who opted to write fiction that would ultimately win respect among the so-called East Coast literary establishment. Traversing a well-trodden path in reverse, however, is not Epstein's only distinction, for he was also a pioneer among Americans daring to write about the Holocaust. He remains one of the very few to treat this grimmest of subjects with archness, irony, and humour.

Epstein's best-known book – though arguably not his greatest achievement – is *King of the Jews*. The novel concerns the doomed efforts of a community of Jews in a fictional Polish town to survive the Nazi occupation and deportations. The book startled readers with its aura of magic realism, its heightened sense of absurdity, and its black (and even slapstick) humour. *King of the Jews* also generated controversy for daring to address one of the most painfully divisive aspects of the Jewish response to Nazism, namely the institution of the *Judenrat*. These were the Jewish councils established at the behest of the Germans to administer affairs in the ghettos and eventually to assist in the round-ups of Jews for labour camps and worse. While Epstein obviously makes it clear his Jewish characters have been thrust into an impossible, not to say abominable set of circumstances, he also shows many of them – most notably the titular Jewish Council head I.C. Trumpelman – behaving appallingly.

Many readers naturally enough were repelled by Epstein's depiction of the "king of the ghetto" and his collaboration with his Nazi overlords. But others admired the novel for its maturity of vision. Regarding the use of the Holocaust in fiction, Epstein himself is on record as suggesting "the real sin [is] sentimentalizing the Holocaust and asking for emotions that haven't been earned."

Beyond the groundbreaking achievement of *King of the Jews*, Epstein can also take pride in creating one of the most original and engaging figures in all of American-Jewish fiction, and as well a character who possesses one of the most distinctive voices in contemporary literature. This character is Leib Goldkorn, whom Epstein introduced in *The Steinway Quintet*, a collection of short stories. In 1985 Goldkorn reappeared in *Goldkorn Tales*, a trio of novellas, one of which was an expansion of the debut "Steinway" story. Goldkorn's next appearance was in the three novellas called *Ice Fire Water* in 1999.

That Leib Goldkorn strains credibility merely acknowledges the incredibility of the century throughout which his long life extends. Born in the Austro-Hungarian Empire in 1901, Goldkorn is a flautist, the composer of an unproduced opera called *Esther, the Jewish Girl at the Persian Court*, a member of the chamber group at the Steinway Restaurant in New York's Lower East Side, an occasional performer on musical water tumblers in subway stations and on sidewalks, and an all-round classic schlemiel. Not that this innocent little nobody doesn't rub up against history. Before eventually settling in New York, for example, Goldkorn witnesses an assassination attempt on Hitler's life (indeed, he inadvertently averts it), travels to Brazil with Arturo Toscanini and almost (but not quite) prevents the Japanese attack on Pearl Harbor.

In *Ice Fire Water* Goldkorn is unwittingly involved with a phone-sex operator with the unfortunate name of Crystal Knight, and in the book's most hilarious running gag, he plots a meeting with Michiko Kakutani, the real-life chief book reviewer of the *New York Times*, whom Goldkorn is convinced is of Norwegian origin. (Ms Kakutani is Japanese–American.) Here in his own inimitable voice is Goldkorn at the Oak Room of Manhattan's Plaza Hotel, where he has just accosted a blonde whom he has mistaken for Michiko Kakutani:

> I shall make a tall story shorter. Mistaken identity. Mild indiscretion. Understandable error. Why, then, especially after hearing my explanation that I have taken the wrong pig by the tail, does she create such a stigma? Or strike with one's weighty purse, and on the noggin, a nonagenarian? Or send flying, for a faux pas, his Panama hat? This is an overreaction, in my opinion. Luckily, the pianist, and the bassist, too, break into a lively melody – "Oklahoma" – Sooner State, mining interests, natural gas – in order to distract the teatime guests from the hullabaloo. At my table slivovitz awaits. Thoughtfully uncorked. Chin-chin! And still, in the parts of propagation, the bonfire burns. Skoal! To my Norse nymph! On and on the seconds hand goes tick-ticking by. Is it my imagination, or is the boulevard without falling into shade, into shadow? Cheers, friends! Down to the hatch!

In other adventures Goldkorn scores music for Hollywood producer Darryl F. Zanuck, gets involved in a Nazi spy plot with Carmen Miranda, and stumbles onto the set of a South Seas adventure film starring Esther Williams and Victor Mature. Indeed, the Goldkorn stories are not the only place where Epstein's Hollywood background and his interest in European Jewry converge. In a 1997 extravaganza of a novel called *Pandaemonium*, the actor Peter Lorre (born Laszlo Lowenstein), who is one of the novel's narrators, agonizes over the fate of the Jews in Nazi Germany even as he struggles to complete his role in a miserable B feature directed by a mad Hollywood monster called Rudolph von Beckmann. Other real-life personages who feature in *Pandaemonium* include Philip and Julius Epstein, respectively Leslie Epstein's father and uncle and the authors of such screenplays as *Casablanca* and *Yankee Doodle Dandy*. Suffice to say that Epstein's surreal blend of low comedy and horrific bloodletting works considerably less well in this novel than it did in *King of the Jews*.

Like a number of his other novels (*P.D. Kimerakov*, *Pinto and Sons*, *Regina*), *Pandaemonium* earned Epstein some respectful reviews but few readers. Which is to say that for all of his obvious talent and risk-taking imagination, Epstein is far from everyone's cup of tea. Yet often enough Epstein's efforts have yielded original and rewarding literature.

MATTHEW NESVISKY

Erenburg, Il'ia

Russian fiction writer, poet and journalist, 1891–1967

Born Il'ia Grigor'evich Erenburg in Kiev, 27 January 1891. Family settled in Moscow, 1895; on the barricades during 1905 Revolution; joined the Social Democrats, 1906, under the influence of Nikolai Bukharin. Forced to flee, settled in Paris 1908–17; returned to Russia in summer of 1917, but in 1918 sided with the White Russians. One daughter, born 1911. Married Liubov' Kozintseva, 1919. Lived in Berlin, 1921–24; in Paris 1925–40. Delegate to First Congress of Soviet writers in Moscow, 1934. Correspondent for *Izvestia* in the Spanish Civil War, 1936–39. Returned to Moscow from Paris in July 1940, after the German occupation. World War II correspondent, 1941–45. His pamphlets against the Nazis distributed to millions of Soviet soldiers. Visited Canada and the US, 1946. Vice President, World Peace Council, 1950–67; Deputy of the Supreme Soviet of the USSR, 1950–67. Awards include the Stalin Prize, 1942 and 1948; International Lenin Peace Prize, 1952; Order of Lenin (twice); Order of the Red Star. Died in Moscow, 31 August 1967.

Selected Writings

Collections
Polnoe sobranie sochinenii, 8 vols, 1927–28
Sobranie sochinenii, 9 vols, 1962–67

Fiction
Neobychainye pokhozhdeniia Khulio Khurenito i ego uchenikov, 1922; as *The Extraordinary Adventures of Julio Jurenito and His Disciples*, translated by Usick Vanzler, 1930; as *Julio Jurenito*, translated by Anna Bostock and Yvonne Kapp, 1958
Shifs-Karta [The Steamship Ticket], 1922
Trest D E [Trust D E], 1923
Liubov' Zhanny Nei, 1924; as *The Love of Jeanne Ney*, translated by Helen Chrouschoff Matheson, 1929
Burnaia zhizn' Lazika Roitshvanetsa, 1928; translated as *The Stormy Life of Lasik Roitschwantz*, 1960; as *The Stormy Life of Laz Roitshvants*, translated by Alec Brown, 1965
Desiat' loshadinykh sil, 1929; as *The Life of the Automobile*, translated by Joachim Neugroschel, 1976
Den' vtoroi, 1934; as *Out of Chaos*, translated by Alexander Bakshy, 1934; as *The Second Day*, translated by Liv Tudge, 1984
"Padenie Parizha", *Roman-gazeta*, 3–5, 1942; as *The Fall of Paris*, translated by Gerard Shelley, 1942
Buria, 1948; as *The Storm*, translated by Eric Hartley and Tatiana Shebunina, 1949; also by J. Fineberg, 1949
Deviatyi val, 1951; as *The Ninth Wave*, translated by Tatiana Shebunina and Joseph Castle, 1955
Ottepel', 1954; as *The Thaw*, translated by Manya Harari, 1955

Poetry
Stikhi [Poems], 1910
Ia zhivu [I am Alive], 1911
Opustoshaiushchaia liubov' [A Devastating Love], 1922
Vernost' [Loyalty], 1941
Stikhi o voine [War Poems], 1943
Derevo [Wood], 1946
Stikhi, 1938–58, 1959

Play
Zolotoe serdtse; Veter [Golden Heart; Wind], 1922

Essays and Memoirs
Portrety russkikh poetov [Portraits of Russian Poets], 1922
Perechityvaia Chekhova, 1960; as *Chekhov, Stendhal, and Other Essays*, translated by Anna Bostock, Yvonne Kapp and Tatiana Shebunina, 1962
Liudi, Gody, Zhizn', 1961–66; translated as *Men, Years, Life*, 1962; as *Memoirs*, 1964
Childhood and Youth, 1891–1917, translated by Anna Bostock and Yvonne Kapp, 1962
First Years of Revolution, 1918–21, translated by Anna Bostock and Yvonne Kapp, 1962
Truce, 1921–33, translated by Tatiana Shebunina, 1963
Eve of War, 1933–41, translated by Tatiana Shebunina, 1963
The War, 1941–45, translated by Tatiana Shebunina, 1964
Post-War Years, 1945–54, translated by Tatiana Shebunina and Yvonne Kapp, 1966
Editor, *Chernaia kniga*, 1980, with Vasilii Grossman; as *The Complete Black Book of Russian Jewry*, translated by David Paterson, 2001
V smertnyi chas (Stat'i 1918–19) [At the Hour of Death (Articles, 1918–19)], 1996

Further Reading

Goldberg, Anatol, *Ilya Ehrenburg: Writing, Politics, and the Art of Survival*, London: Weidenfeld and Nicolson, and New York: Viking, 1984
Klimenko, Michael, *Ehrenburg: An Attempt at a Literary Portrait*, New York: Peter Lang, 1990
Laychuk, Julian L., *Ilya Ehrenburg: An Idealist in an Age of Realism*, New York: Peter Lang, 1991
Rubenstein, Joshua, *Tangled Loyalties: The Life and Times of Ilya Ehrenburg*, New York: Basic Books, 1996
Sicher, Ephraim, *Jews in Russian Literature after the October Revolution: Writers and Artists between Hope and Apostasy*, Cambridge: Cambridge University Press, 1995

Il'ia Erenburg's Jewish passions and commitments have long been at the heart of the controversies that surround his career as a Soviet writer. His survival under Stalin, when so many Jewish cultural figures disappeared – among them scores of his friends – casts a shadow over his reputation and was a cause for rumour and accusation. There was even an unfounded suspicion that Erenburg had betrayed his Jewish origins. Nothing could have been further from the truth. As he made clear in his first novel *The Extraordinary*

Adventures of Julio Jurenito and His Disciples, the role of the Jews was to dissent, to say "no" when everyone else says "yes". He liked to compare the role of Jewish writers in world literature to a "spoonful of tar in a barrel of honey". It was they who provide a measure of scepticism, even when scepticism "poorly fits in with society's needs". Erenburg identified with this tradition.

Jewish themes can be found throughout his work. His second book of poems, *I am Alive*, which was written in Paris, contains the explicitly Zionist poem "To the Jewish People", in which he concludes that Jews have no place in Europe and should return to the land of Israel. It would not be the last time Erenburg expressed such an acute premonition.

He returned to Russia four months before the October Revolution and witnessed revolutionary violence and civil war, including pogroms in Ukraine, where tens of thousands of Jews perished. This experience influenced his subsequent writing. He despised the logic of reactionary anti-Semitism. "If Jewish blood could cure", he bitterly observed in September 1919, "then Russia would be a flourishing country." *Julio Jurenito*, written immediately upon his return to western Europe in 1921, contains a chapter foretelling the Holocaust; the Jews of Europe are consumed by bonfires as European leaders watch from nearby bleachers. He returned to this theme in the short story "The Old Furrier" in 1928, describing how fear envelops Kiev's Jewish neighbourhoods when White forces wrest control of the city. And his only fully Jewish novel, *The Stormy Life of Lasik Roitschwantz*, tells the story of a poor, misunderstood tailor whom everyone abuses. Whether he lives in communist Moscow or bourgeois Paris, Lasik tries in vain to find a place for himself in the broader secular world. His language and exploits, his stories, even his death make Erenburg's hero an exemplary Jewish victim. Imprisoned and exiled, Lasik ends his life in Palestine.

But none of this work adequately foretells Erenburg's profound response to the Holocaust. Throughout the 1930s, as he covered the threat of fascism in western Europe for *Izvestia*, Erenburg often alluded to Hitler's special hatred for the Jews. During World War II, Erenburg contributed more than 2000 articles to the Soviet press. As a regular columnist for the army newspaper *Red Star*, he took it upon himself to teach the Soviet people to hate the Germans. And he often highlighted Jewish heroism and suffering. The soldiers constantly responded, describing atrocities they discovered as they pushed the Nazis out of the country. In 1943 Erenburg tried to publish an anthology called *One Hundred Letters* in French and in Russian. The French edition was published, but the regime forbade publication of the Russian one; it contained too much material about Jewish suffering.

Erenburg made a point of befriending Jewish partisans, among them the Yiddish poet Avrom Sutskever (Abraham Sutzkever) who had survived the Vilna (Vilnius) ghetto and was brought to Moscow in 1944. Erenburg wrote a famous portrait of Sutskever in *Pravda*, highlighting his poem "Kol Nidre" about a father who kills his son rather than allowing the Germans to torture him. Erenburg also visited Kiev soon after the city's liberation and wrote the first poem about Babi Yar, where many of his own relatives had been slaughtered. Writing in *Pravda* in December 1944, with Soviet troops poised to invade East Prussia, Erenburg declared that the Nazis' greatest crime was the destruction of six million Jews.

But his most significant response to Nazi massacres came in 1943, when he began compiling material for *The Black Book*, an anthology about the Holocaust on Soviet territory. Together with the front-line correspondent Vasilii Grossman, Erenburg assembled a group of two dozen Jewish and non-Jewish writers, who, under the auspices of the Jewish Anti-Fascist Committee, gathered documents and first-hand testimony in newly liberated cities and towns.

Erenburg had genuine hopes that *The Black Book* would appear in the Soviet Union. He wanted to demonstrate the depth of Jewish suffering and counter domestic anti-Semitism. But by 1945, he understood that the regime was weary of hearing about the Jews. Stalin soon banned publication of *The Black Book* and it did not appear in print until 1980, when it was published by Yad Vashem in Jerusalem. Still, Erenburg tried to remind his readers of the Holocaust. His novel *The Storm* in 1948 carried a vivid description of a Nazi massacre. And in his next novel, *The Ninth Wave*, a Jewish war veteran visits the mass grave of his relatives at Babi Yar only to be abused by an anti-Semitic neighbour. Appearing at a moment of terrifying official anti-Semitism, this passage was the only depiction of popular anti-Semitism to appear in a Soviet novel.

After Stalin's death, Erenburg did not hesitate to focus on anti-Semitism even more. *The Thaw*, which lent its name to that period of Soviet history, was the first work of literature to contain direct references to the Doctors' Plot, when Soviet society had been overwhelmed by suspicions against the Jews. Even in the essay "Re-Reading Chekhov" in 1959, Erenburg found a way to criticize contemporary Soviet anti-Semitism by writing about Chekhov's response to the Dreyfus affair. In 1960 Erenburg was responsible for publication of the Russian-language edition of *The Diary of Anne Frank*. And his memoirs *Men, Years, Life*, which came out in instalments from 1960 to 1965, contained many pages about anti-Semitism and the Holocaust and helped to revive Jewish national feeling in the years before the Six Day War in 1967. As Erenburg defiantly declared in a speech on his 70th birthday, "I am a Russian writer. But as long as a single anti-Semite remains on earth, I will answer the question of nationality with pride: a Jew."

JOSHUA RUBENSTEIN

Esther

Russian writer, educator, newspaper editor, *c*.1880–1940

Born Malke Lifshits in Minsk, White Russia, around 1880, into a family of Maskilim, followers of the Berlin Enlightenment. Universally known either as Esther Frumkin or by one forename, Esther. Educated at a Gymnasium, and at Berlin University. Teacher in a girls' school for professional subjects. Joined the Bund (the Jewish Trade Union Movement) in 1901. Became St Petersburg correspondent for their daily Yiddish newspaper *Der veker* [The Awakener], which later became *Di folkstsaytung* [The People's Newspaper]. Arrested many times between 1910 and 1914, was forced to flee abroad, becoming an important member of the international Bund. Married, first, an engineer, Frumkin, around 1910; one daughter, Freydl; husband died, 1916; second, a rabbi and Zionist, Vibnin, 1916; divorced, 1917. A controversial figure at the First Jewish Language Conference in Czernowitz, 1908, where she led the Bund delegation. Rose to prominence in Russian politics when she became leader of the Leftist breakaway group of the Bund that joined the national Communist Party in 1920. In 1921 became the only woman among the leaders of the Kombund that formed a Central Bureau in Moscow under Yevsektsie, the Jewish section of the Communist Party. Championed Jewish secular schools in Russia with teaching in Yiddish rather than Russian or Hebrew. Arrested 1938, and disappeared in a Stalinist prison camp around 1940. Exact date of death unknown.

Selected Writings

Di naye tsayt, 4 (1909) (personal record of the 1908 Czernowitz Language Conference)
Tsu der frage vegn der yidisher folkshul [On the Question of the Jewish Public School], 1910
Hirsh Lekert, 1922
Lenin's Writings (in Yiddish), with Moyshe Litvakov, 8 vols, 1925
Biography of Lenin, 1925–26

Further Reading

Berger, Lili, *Nisht farendikte bletlekh* [Unfinished Pages], Tel Aviv: Yisroel-bukh, 1982
Di ershte yidishe shprakh-konferents, tchernovits, 1908 [The First Yiddish Language Conference, Czernowitz, 1908], Vilna: Yivo, 1931
Di tschernovitser shprakh-konferents [The Czernowitz Language Conference], Vilna, 1908
Schwarz, Solomon M., *The Jews in the Soviet Union*, Syracuse, New York: Syracuse University Press, 1951
Shepherd, Naomi, *A Price below Rubies: Jewish Women as Rebels and Radicals*, Cambridge, Massachusetts: Harvard University Press, 1993

Esther (born Malke Lifshits), was a leading political figure in revolutionary Russia until her arrest in 1938 and subsequent demise in a Stalinist prison camp. She was ambitious and achieved high political office. She was very much a woman of the revolutionary times in which she lived, and had attained a high level of Jewish education, studying the sacred texts in their original Hebrew.

As a successful propagandist, she was constantly adapting to events and circumstances. She was aware of the presentation of her own self-image, and shifted identity by adopting different names that were appropriate at the time. During her student days, she changed her Jewish forename, Malke (Hebrew = queen) to the secular, if not Christian, Maria, after meeting Avrom Liessin, a poet and socialist propagandist who introduced Esther to the women's workers' circles in Minsk. In 1901, she joined the Bund, in which women were able to rise to the highest ranks, and became St Petersburg correspondent for their daily Yiddish newspaper *Der veker* which became *Di folkstsaytung*. As a proponent of Yiddish, she was an important participant in the 1908 Czernowitz Language Conference, a gathering of international scholars, writers, and intellectuals who debated whether Hebrew or Yiddish should be established as the national Jewish language. Esther led the Bund delegation, which at one point walked out of the Conference en masse in disgust at the Zionist view in favour of Hebrew. She caused endless controversy and bitter feeling that lasted beyond her death. Yiddish had been established as the language of socialism in Russia. A record of the Conference was published in Vilna in 1908 (reprinted 1931) and her own personal record was published in *Di naye tsayt* (1909).

From the time she joined the Bund, she reverted to the Jewish name, Esther, by which she became known internationally. Like other socialists of the time, she used only her forename, not her family name. With the name Esther, she took on the attributes of the popular 5th-century BCE Jewish heroine, Queen Esther, who saved the Jews in Babylon from the tyrant Xerxes. It seems that Esther saw herself and wished others to see her as a heroic force for good and a saviour of her people. In 1910 she married an engineer and socialist named Frumkin, taking his surname. In spite of her public ambitions, Esther never shirked her personal duties; when her sister Gute died in childbirth, she helped her brother-in-law, the well-known Bundist, Vaynshtayn to bring up the two children, as well as her own daughter. Frumkin died in 1916, and Esther and their daughter, Freydl, moved to Astroban where Esther began work as a teacher. There she fell in love with a Zionist rabbi called Vibnin, and they married. But in 1917, following the Russian Revolution, she divorced him out of political correctness. It was inappropriate for a Bundist, and therefore an opponent of Zionism and a champion of secularism and Yiddish over Hebrew, to be married to a religious leader and a Zionist. Conversely a wife of Esther's political allegiances would have brought nothing but embarrassment to the Astroban rabbi. Esther returned to Minsk where she became editor of the daily Bundist newspaper *Der veker* but, deciding to write as Esther Vibnin-Frumkin, she was nicknamed "The Rebetsn" (The Rabbi's wife) which mocked her religious nature. She rapidly dropped the surname, using only the name Esther, and was sufficiently well-known to be represented only by the first and last letters of the name Esther, joined with a dash, E–R, on the title page of her book *Tsu der frage vegn der yidisher folkshul* [On the Question of the Jewish Public School]. Her name appears in the same abbreviated form in her newspaper articles between 1910 and 1913, suggesting a necessity for anonymity which is borne out by her being arrested several times during this period and having to flee abroad, becoming an important member of the international Bund.

At the beginning of World War I Esther returned to Russia and took over the editorship of the main Bund forum, *Der veker*, rose to prominence in the Bund movement, and after the revolution came to hold high rank. She became an extreme exponent of Soviet Bolshevik Communism, which led the Bund to regard her as a traitor to this day. From 1918 the left arm of the Bund, to which Esther belonged, began to detach itself from the right, and while the left worked to strengthen itself, it weakened the Bund in general. In 1920 the Bund split into two parts, with Esther herself the leader of the left that joined with the Russian Communist Party. Many angry Bundists left politics for good. In truth Esther and her party became puppets of the Communist Party. In 1921 Esther, the only woman among six men in the Central Bureau in Moscow of Yevsektsie, the Jewish section of the Communist Party, hoped to save the Bund, but to no avail. The Bund was dissolved in 1921. Yevsektsie was brought to an end in January 1930, and by 1938, all its leaders, including Esther, had been arrested.

Without doubt, Esther's contribution to the fight for Yiddish and Yiddish scholarship was one of the greatest ever. She vigorously opposed the Communist Party's bid for Jews to replace Yiddish with Russian. Her views can be seen in her longest published work, *On the Question of the Jewish Public School*. This was her plan for Jewish secular education in which she advocated education for all in subjects that were practically applicable and taught in the everyday Jewish language, Yiddish. At a time when her publisher was also publishing prestigious academic works by the great new wave of Yiddish linguists such as Borokhov and Weinreich, Esther puts the sociolinguistic argument that Yiddish is indeed a language, not a dialect, as it had been described by its critics. She argues that, although Hebrew is without doubt a beautiful language with a highly structured grammar, it has suffered the fate of other classical languages such as Greek and Latin, and is dead, while Yiddish is alive in the mouths of the people. Her passionate defence of Yiddish in Chapter 3 rejects the necessity to enter into linguistic proofs to prove the importance of Yiddish as a language, although she does provide a linguistic argument that she draws from scholarly sources in order to support her argument that Yiddish stands as a language in its own right and has nothing to be ashamed of linguistically.

A Yiddish novel by Lili Berger published in Israel in 1982 entitled *Nisht farendikte bletlekh* [Unfinished Pages], set in a Stalinist prison camp, provides a fictional version of what may have happened to Esther after her arrest.

In 1965 E. Folkovitsh wrote of Esther in the *Folks-shtime* [People's Voice], 22 May 1965:

> A bourgeois philosopher . . . once said that a normal person is one who eats, drinks, sleeps and does not think about what tomorrow will bring. Esther had every possibility to be a "normal" person. She did not wish to be one.

DEVRA KAY

Ezekiel, Nissim

Indian poet and playwright, 1924–

Born in Bombay, 16 December 1924. Studied at the University of Bombay, MA 1947. Married Daisy Jacob, 1952; three daughters. Lecturer in English, Khalsa College, Bombay, 1947–48. Lived in London 1948–52; visited USA 1957 and 1967. Editor, *Quest*, Bombay. Contributor to various journals including *Encounter*, *Spectator*, *Poetry Review* and *A Review of English Literature*. Professor of English and Vice-Principal, Mithibai College of Arts, Bombay, 1961–62. Visiting Professor at various universities including Leeds and Chicago. Reader in American Literature, University of Bombay from 1972. Awards include R.K. Lagu Prize, University of Bombay, 1947; Fairfield Foundation Grant, 1957; National Academy Award, 1983; Padma Shree, 1988.

Selected Writings

Poetry
A Time to Change and Other Poems, 1952
Sixty Poems, 1953
The Third, 1958
The Unfinished Man, 1960
The Exact Time: Poems 1960–64, 1965
Hymns in Darkness, 1976
Selected Poems, 1965–75, 1976
Latterday Psalms, 1982
Collected Poems, 1952–88, 1989

Plays
Three Plays, 1969
Song of Deprivation, 1969
Don't Call it Suicide: A Tragedy, 1993

Other
Editor, *A New Look at Communism*, 1963
Editor, *Young Commonwealth Poets, 1965*, 1965
Editor, *Writing in India*, 1965
Editor, *A Martin Luther King Reader*, 1969
Editor, *The Face*, 1971
The Actor: A Sad and Funny Story for Children of Most Ages, 1974
Editor, *Artists Today*, 1987
Editor, with Meenakshi Mukherjee, *Another India: An Anthology of Indian Fiction and Poetry*, 1991
Selected Prose, 1992

Further Reading

Bharucha, Nilufer and Vrinda Nabar (editors), *Mapping Cultural Spaces: Post Colonial Indian Literature in English: Essays in Honour of Nissim Ezekiel*, New Delhi: Vision, 1998
Chindhade, Shirish, *Five Indian English Poets: Nissim Ezekiel, A.K. Ramanujan, Arun Kolatkar, Dilip Chitre, R. Parthasarathy*, New Delhi: Atlantic, 1996
Das, B.K., *The Horizon of Nissim Ezekiel's Poetry*, Delhi: BR, 1995
Dwivedi, Suresh Chandra (editor), *Perspectives on Nissim Ezekiel*, New Delhi: KM, 1989
King, Bruce, *Three Indian Poets: Nissim Ezekiel, A.K. Ramanujan, Dom Moraes*, Madras, Oxford, and New York: Oxford University Press, 1991
Kurup, P.K.J, *Contemporary Indian Poetry in English with Special Reference to the Poetry of Nissim Ezekiel*, New Delhi: Atlantic, 1991
Raghunandan, Lakshmi, *Contemporary Indian Poetry in*

English: Nissim Ezekiel, Kamala Das, R. Parthasarathy and A.K. Ramanujan , New Delhi: Reliance, 1990
Rahman, Anisur, *Form and Value in the Poetry of Nissim Ezekiel*, New Delhi: Abhinav, 1990
Raja Rao, R., *Nissim Ezekiel: The Authorised Biography*, New Delhi and New York: Viking, 2000
Sharma, T.R., *Essays on Nissim Ezekiel*, Meerut: Shalab Prakashan, 1994
Wieland, James, *The Ensphering Mind: A Comparative Study of Derek Walcott,Christopher Okigbo, A.D. Hope, Allen Curnow, A.M. Klein and Nissim Ezekiel*, Washington, DC: Three Continents Press, 1988

Nissim Ezekiel, academic, literary critic, and playwright, is one of India's leading poets. He was born into a Bene Israel family in Bombay (Mumbai), and his Jewish identity and background have been central to his writing. At home in his beloved native city, Ezekiel reports that he has always been aware of belonging to his "own community". "Not being a Hindu . . . makes me a natural outsider", he writes. Ezekiel has made it clear that living in India, in Bombay ("I was born here and belong"), has been a conscious choice when so many members of Bene Israel have migrated to Israel. This commitment and sense of critical distance are integral elements in his unique, "cultural insider-outsider", view of contemporary Indian life.

Ezekiel was one of the first poets to choose to write in English as an "Indian" in post-Independence India. Since the early 1950s his work has played a major role in forging an Indian poetry in English and establishing this genre as a recognized part of the literature of modern India. He is the noted mentor of younger poets and founder of the "Bombay school of English poetry".

Ezekiel's poetry creates a new Indian voice for the humanistic, English-speaking, educated city-dweller, focusing on the realities of urban experience. He records conflict and frustration in family and professional life, marriage, love affairs, sex, moral dilemmas, spiritual alienation and confusion, deprivation and decay, and the struggle to make sense of changing values in postcolonial India. This middle-class life with its desire for stability, order, and control amid swirling chaos is portrayed with humour and honesty and without romanticism.

His poetry is controlled and displays a striking clarity. Written in traditional verse forms as well as free verse, it has a limited metrical range. There are irony and satire often with the lightest touch. Much of his work appears conversational and confessional as Ezekiel publicly explores the inner workings of his life and that of his family, in a poetic process he refers to as "therapeutic". His cultural detachment is evident in his kindly poems of everyday educated Indian folk. A number of these are written as monologues in "Indian English" (Bombayia), a language the grammar and resonance of which he brilliantly captures. He explores the personal and political frailties and failures of the ordinary man with wit, and in a way that, while not revolutionary, supports individual liberty, and opposes injustice and naive nationalism.

As a student Ezekiel was influenced by the nationalist leader, M.N. Roy and was an active member of his Radical Communist Party. Later, he claimed that it was Roy's teachings that led him to reject his religious faith in favour of rationalism and atheism. But his new faith turned inwards; as he counsels, if you cannot save the world, "redeem yourself".

Ezekiel is a noted religious poet, promoting spirituality beyond the different religious mythologies. He addresses those who acknowledge the spiritual aridity of liberalism. What sort of salvation is there for the modern urbanite whose faith in the old traditions is lost and who can no longer believe in the saving power of Marxism? There is a tone of lament and envy as he describes the superstitions of the peasants and their blind faith. He writes in a biblical vein, quoting, paraphrasing, and questioning the form and content of the King James Version of the Bible – "how spiritual the language, how fiery and human in the folly of its feelings". There are also references to Hindu scriptures (Vedas, Gita, and Upanishads), and to the Islamic and Christian traditions. He challenges god for being "so elusive", active in Egypt, and so inactive at Auschwitz, where it made little difference whether one had prayed or not.

Ezekiel is cynical of saints and gurus, portrayed as corrupt as himself and the rest of us, all in dire need of redemption. We cannot be saved by simple belief or unbelief, but perhaps only by a light, provocative, and progressive piety. His is a theology that recognizes that "just as the sceptic and the believer are found together so are spirituality and sensuality".

Ezekiel is known for his explicit "love" poems, which celebrate sex, within, but mostly outside of, marriage, with a series of remembered and imagined lovers. Illicit and often impersonal sex is tinged with guilt and experienced as "the taste of sin", perhaps the legacy of his Roman Catholic schooling. But sex always offers the promise of salvation, that is sex as an alternative, miraculous, and secular redemption beyond oneself and the constraints of family, caste, and situation. The world appears rational and ordered, but in sex, Ezekiel discovers the counterweight to his rational worldview. Sex is a holy ritual "in the temple" that "saves lovers", at least for a while, before they return to their bonds, or despair. The only true antidote to restlessness, appetite, and the life of "duplicities", flattery, and that "charade of passion and possession" is the purity of the "religious life", more Christian monastic or Hindu than Jewish.

Although Ezekiel refers to "my Jewish consciousness" and the certainty of his Jewish identity, he writes little explicitly about Jewish life. In his poem, "Jewish Wedding in Bombay", he writes of his own wedding. "Not solemn or beautiful", he records, the gap between the orthodox traditional ceremonies and the beliefs and practices of those there – modern himself, he has a "progressive" mother and a "liberal" father. In his correspondence with his friend, A.K. Ramanujan, he later claims that this poem is about personal failure rather than a judgement on an outdated Judaism. Ezekiel writes that he was accused at school of "killing Christ" and was fearful of Muslim and Hindu boys ("Background Casually"). In a 1996 interview, however, Ezekiel contended that as an Indian Jew he had never experienced anti-Semitism. A little later, the same interviewer asked him if he thought that the obsessive interest in sex in his poetry was due to his Jewish background!

Ezekiel writes that his concern with his Jewish identity came after he returned from England and he was forced to confront his Indian identity. He partially resolved these tensions by becoming self-consciously Jewish but a vocal non-Zionist. Ezekiel's poetry explicates these complexities of Indian Jewish identity in India. Currently he lives in a clinic in Bombay and suffers from Alzheimer's disease.

PAUL MORRIS

F

Fainlight, Ruth

US poet, 1931–

Born in New York, 2 May 1931. Settled in England, 1946. Studied at Birmingham and Brighton colleges of art. Married the writer Alan Sillitoe, 1959; one son, one daughter. Poet in Residence, Vanderbilt University, Tennessee, 1985, 1990. Poetry Editor, *European Judaism*. Served on the Council of the Poetry Society; member, Writers in Prison Committee, British PEN. Awards include Cholmondeley Award for Poets, 1994.

Selected Writings

Poetry
A Forecast, a Fable, 1958
Cages, 1966
18 Poems from 1966, 1967
To See the Matter Clearly and Other Poems, 1968
Poems, with Alan Sillitoe and Ted Hughes, 1971
The Region's Violence, 1973
21 Poems, 1973
Another Full Moon, 1976
Sibyls and Others, 1980
Climates, 1983
Fifteen to Infinity, 1983
Selected Poems, 1987
Three Poems, 1988
The Knot, 1990
Sibyls, 1991
This Time of Year, 1993
Selected Poems, 1995
Sugar-Paper Blue, 1997
Poems, 1999

Short Stories
Daylife and Nightlife, 1971
Dr Clock's Last Case, 1994

Other
Translator, *All Citizens are Soldiers*, by Lope de Vega, 1969
Translator, *Navigations*, by Sophia de Mello Breyner Andresen, 1983
Editor, *Harry Fainlight: Selected Poems*, 1986
Translator, *Marine Rose*, by Sophia de Mello Breyner Andresen, 1987
The Dancer Hotoke, 1991
The European Story, 1993

Further Reading

Bogen, Nancy, *How to Write Poetry*, New York: Arco, 1991
Couzyn, Jeni (editor), *The Bloodaxe Book of Contemporary Women Poets*, Newcastle: Bloodaxe, 1985

Ruth Fainlight was born in New York, the daughter of a British father and an American mother with Russian-Jewish ancestry. Although a successful writer of short stories, dramatist/librettist, and translator, she is best known for her poetry, whose modern style blends subtle image-making with toughness of expression. Her verse pinpoints routine thoughts and actions with striking immediacy, while invoking an imagined ancestry of earlier female oracles and prophetesses. A writer of rare originality, she resists easy definition, and her poetry bears witness to her dislike of being categorized. In "Vertical", from *Another Full Moon*, she praises the liberating power of her writing which enables her to escape from the pigeon-holing tendency. "I am released by language . . . / which sets me free/ From whomsoever's definition:/ Jew. Woman. Poet." Clearly, Fainlight does not wish to be described purely as a Jewish writer, and her poetry shows equivocal views on modern Israel and historical Zionism; indeed, Zionist opinions are more forcibly expressed by her non-Jewish husband Alan Sillitoe in one of his novels. Fainlight combines ethnic, female, and literary elements in uneasy balance within her own complex personality, but there can be no doubt that her Jewish heritage is a potent factor in her work. Just as the feminist role is revealed by repeated invocations of the moon and the catalogue of sibyls and rebels in her writing, so the Jewish aspect of her nature is shown through the many biblical accounts and references, and the race-memory of oppression and the Holocaust that colour her poetry. *To See the Matter Clearly* includes such poems as the reflective "The Spirit Moving on the Face of the Waters" with its echoes of Genesis, and in "Gloria" presents a frightening muse that leads the poet "to the burning-place". In "Sleep-Learning" Fainlight watches her drowsing child, and ponders on the dreams he has inherited from his persecuted ancestors.

With *The Region's Violence* her writing becomes more fiercely questioning, God and the Old Testament subjected to a merciless feminist critique in poems such as "Lilith", where Adam's companion is punished with exile for thinking herself his equal. Her image of the Jewish God as a vindictive male chauvinist is matched by her mocking comparison of Adam's phallus with the serpent in the

Garden of Eden. The biblical oppression of her sex is seen as continuing with Christ in the New Testament, Fainlight pondering on the Velasquez portrait and the hard-worked Martha's "sad, resentful gaze" as she is overlooked in favour of her more spiritual sister. In "My Grandparents" she moves closer to home, considering ancestors of her own who died, victims of persecution, before she was born. Fainlight sees herself as their monument, the one surviving reminder of their suffering, "the museum's prize,/ Memorial to their legend." *Another Full Moon,* which contains the self-assertive "Vertical", is also notable for "My Position in the History of the Twentieth Century" where she reflects on her good fortune in being somewhere else when Hitler was killing Jews in Europe:

> Lucky to live where it was not dangerous
> To look like me (no need for a yellow star.)
> My good fortune took me far from the Holocaust
> – Though it's easy to imagine how it feels
> To read those scrawls on the station's tiled wall . . .
> I flaunt my being manifest
> To whoever wishes to read the signs.

Sibyls and Others preoccupies itself mainly with the feminist concerns of oracular utterance and female mystery whose price is the loss of freedom, but even here Fainlight presents "The Hebrew Sibyl" who prophesies for those about to die, and in "Sibyl of the Waters" imagines the daughter of Noah witnessing the nakedness of her father and seeing in the flood "the nakedness of God". *Fifteen to Infinity* finds her digging deeper into her ancestral past, the Bible and the Talmud searched for "Miriam's Well" and "Susannah and the Elders" where Fainlight again champions the rebellious Susannah, and depicts the horror of Tamar's rape in "Sister, Sister". In "Archive Film" images of the Holocaust return, the truck-borne Auschwitz victims on their way to oblivion likened to short-lived flowers, while "Red Message" ponders on the race-memory inherited by the living from "lives gone into the earth like water,/ poured for ritual." "The Mount of Olives", written following a visit to Israel, has Fainlight in an unusually reverential mood, deciding that "Eternity has staked its claim/ to the hills around Jerusalem." In *Sugar-Paper Blue*, which also includes some prose pieces, the poet studies Genesis while commenting ruefully on the problems of ageing. In "Dinah" she recalls with sadness the tale of a girl's ravishment and the revenge massacre by her brothers, in a way that appears to draw parallels with the present-day conflict in the Middle East, and in "Queen of the Nile" indicates possible reconciliation as "Black Sarah" accompanies the three Marys on a legendary voyage to eventual sainthood. "Horns" describes her own experience of racist bullying as a child, while in "Sugar-Paper Blue" she weaves a subtle web of poetic images that move from her immigrant relatives in New York to the Russian poet Anna Akhmatova, imprisoned in the very house where Fainlight herself is staying while on a visit to the Soviet Union. Not simply Jewish, or female, or a poet, Ruth Fainlight is all of them and more, and this threefold heritage is reflected in her writing from first to last.

GEOFF SADLER

Farhi, Moris (Musa)

Turkish-born British fiction writer, 1935–

Born in Ankara, 5 July 1935. Studied at Istanbul American College, BA in Humanities 1954; graduated from Royal Academy of Dramatic Art, London, 1956. Became British citizen in 1964. Married, first, Monique Hassid, 1957; divorced; second, Nina Sievers, née Gould, 1978; one stepdaughter, Rachel Sievers. Actor with several touring and repertory companies. Began writing in 1960s; scriptwriter for BBC Television and Independent Television, 1960–83; novelist from 1983. Chairperson, Writers in Prison Committee, British PEN, 1994–97, and International PEN, 1997–2000. Awarded MBE for services to literature, 2001. Elected an International Vice-President of PEN, 2001; Fellow of the Royal Society of Literature, 2001.

Selected Writings

Novels
The Pleasure of Your Death, 1972
The Last of Days, 1983
Journey through the Wilderness, 1989
Children of the Rainbow, 1999

Play
From the Ashes of Thebes (in verse), 1969

Film
The Primitives, 1960

Short Story
"Lentils in Paradise" in *The Slow Mirror and Other Stories: New Fiction by Jewish Writers*, edited by Sonja Lyndon and Sylvia Paskin, 1996

Further Reading

Gee, Sue, "A Humanitarian Epic", *Jewish Quarterly*, 46/176 (Winter 1999–2000)
Graham-Yooll, Andrew, "In Search of Saint George", *London Magazine*, 30/5–6 (August–September 1990)
Mirkowicz, Tomasz, "Pisarz powinien być jak kasiarz" [A Writer Should be Like a Safecracker], *Midrasz*, 38 (June 2000) (interview)
Rudolf, Anthony, "Heresies", *London Magazine*, 30/5–6 (August–September 1990)

It has been often said that the power of the Old Testament derives from the two kinds of texts found in it, representing two different traditions: the lay and the priestly, the popular and the spiritual. The same can be said of Moris Farhi's fiction.

Born in Ankara, Turkey, to a Sephardi family, Farhi pursued an acting career upon arriving in Britain, then turned to writing TV scripts, contributing episodes to such popular series as *Man in a Suitcase*, *The Onedin Line*, and *Return of the Saint*. It is thus not surprising that his first novel, *The Pleasure of Your Death*, was a fast-paced thriller with vivid scenery, sharp dialogue, and a cast of colourful characters. Played out against the exotic backdrop of Iceland's lava fields, it pitched a group of former Dutch Resistance members and an exuberant half-Turkish

American stuntman and part-time private detective against Nazis planning to reestablish the Third Reich.

The Pleasure of Your Death is entertainment at its best. Farhi's second novel, *The Last of Days*, set in the aftermath of the Yom Kippur War, in which Israel suffered heavy casualties, transcends the entertainment genre by its scope, authenticity, and acute assessment of the geopolitical situation in the Middle East. "Every Jew [has] the vision of the Last of Days", says Sanbat Abraham, an Ethiopian Jewess raised in Israel and working for Mossad. This apocalyptic pessimism is echoed by Boaz Ben-Ya'ir, Colonel in the Israeli Defense Forces, who allies himself with his Jordanian counterpart to stop a fundamentalist Arab terrorist organization from destroying Mecca with a nuclear bomb, a cataclysm for which Israel would be blamed, and which would unleash a *jihad* leading to its annihilation. A Jew from Salonika, Boaz is haunted by a tragic past – his mother died in Auschwitz, his partisan father was killed by the Nazis, and his sister gruesomely murdered by Syrian soldiers. Boaz, in many instances, reflects the author's emotional scars: although Jews in Turkey did not suffer persecution, numerous members of his Salonika-born mother's family perished in Auschwitz.

Daniel Brac, the protagonist of *Journey through the Wilderness*, with which Farhi more than completed his transition to serious fiction, shares Boaz's roots and angst: Daniel's mother, too, died in Auschwitz, his three young sisters were brutally murdered by the Ustashi, his scholarly father, having joined the partisans, was executed by the SS. But here the similarity ends: while the young Boaz made his way to Palestine and fought for the creation of the State of Israel, Daniel, befriended and brought up by monks, became a Christian, a restorer of old paintings ("What can one create after the gas chambers?"), and gradually atrophied into a man paralyzed by fear, unable even to avenge his father whose murderer he finds in South America. To redeem himself, to become a whole man, Daniel must first accept his Jewishness, then acquire spiritual enlightenment. He does so eventually when he dons the chasuble of a martyred priest and is transformed into the mythical Inca hero, Manku Yupanqui. Thereafter, he leads the Andean Indians on their great march for dignity and freedom.

Setting the novel in an unnamed South American country, and deliberately using archetypal characters whom he suffuses with individuality and raw passion – the folk-singer who has attained fame in the West but wants to return to her roots; the Indian security chief who has achieved power but who, hateful of his origins, despises himself and the world; the aristocrat who turns Marxist revolutionary, but holds in contempt the indigenes he leads; the baby-faced sadist, Angel of Death – Farhi offers a tale of redemption and hope which in itself becomes the archetypal South American novel. This is a work that blends past and present, myth and actuality, in the best tradition of magical realism.

Farhi's fourth novel, the epic *Children of the Rainbow*, also champions the down-trodden, the weak, the oppressed; this time the forgotten victims of the Holocaust, the Roma. This haunting tale begins with the birth of a Gypsy boy at the Birkenau extermination camp. Smuggled out by a Red Cross worker, placed in an orphanage, and adopted by a Swiss couple, he discovers, years later, his Gypsy roots, becomes the leader of his people, still relentlessly persecuted all over Europe, and leads them on two quests: one for Romanestan, their mythical homeland, the other for their equally mythical holy book, the Gypsy Bible. It is that holy writ, painstakingly recreated by Farhi from Romany myths, Genesis, Hindu lore, and his own imagination, that shows fiction can be inspired, that it can achieve the scope and power of divine revelation. Farhi explains this quality of his writing in the following way:

> When I was researching *The Last of Days* someone told me expert safecrackers would rub their fingers on sandpaper, so that the skin would come off and the nerves would be exposed, and they would actually feel the click as they turned the dial on the safe. That has always stayed with me as a formative image for a writer. To be able to express raw emotions you have to sandpaper your whole being, so that all your nerves are exposed. If you can achieve that, you can acquire a more spiritual vision, and that gives another dimension to your work.

Farhi's works have been published in Italian, Dutch, Hebrew, Romanian, Galician, Turkish, Polish, German, and Arabic.

TOMASZ MIRKOWICZ

Federman, Raymond

French-born US fiction writer and poet, 1928–

Born in Paris, 15 May 1928, to Simon Federman, painter, and wife Marguerite (née Epstein). Family perished in Holocaust. Emigrated to United States, 1947; became citizen, 1953. Studied at Columbia University, BA 1957; University of California, Los Angeles, MA 1959, PhD in French 1963. Served as Sergeant in 82nd Airborne Division, Korea, 1951–54. Married Erica Hubscher, 1960; one daughter. Jazz saxophonist, 1947–50. Assistant Professor, University of California, 1959–64; from 1964 taught at State University of New York, Buffalo: from 1994 Melodia E. Jones Chair of Literature. Visiting Professor, Hebrew University, Jerusalem, 1982–83. Co-director, Fiction Collective, New York. Awards include Guggenheim Fellowship, 1966; Frances Steloff Prize and *Panache* Experimental Fiction Prize, 1972; Fulbright Fellowship to Israel, 1982–83; American Book Award 1986.

Selected Writings

Novels

Double or Nothing: A Real Fictitious Discourse, 1971
Amer Eldorado, 1974
Take It or Leave It: An Exaggerated Second-hand Tale to be Read Aloud either Standing or Sitting, 1976
The Voice in the Closet / La Voix dans le cabinet de Debaras, 1979
The Rigmarole of Contrariety, 1982
The Twofold Vibration, 1982
Smiles on Washington Square: A Love Story of Sorts, 1985; new edition, 1994

To Whom it May Concern, 1990
A Version of My Life, 1993
La Fourrure de ma Tante Rachel, 1996; as *Aunt Rachel's Fur: A Novel Improvised in Sad Laughter*, translated by Federman and Patricia Privat-Standley, 2001
Twilight of the Bums, 2001

Poetry
Among the Beasts / Parmi Les Monstres, 1967
Me Too, 1975
Loves, 1986
Playtexts / Spieltexte, 1989
Duel-l, 1991
Now Then / Nun Denn, 1992

Other
Translator, *Postal Cards*, by Jacques Temple, 1964
Journey to Chaos: Samuel Beckett's Early Fiction, 1965
Translator, *Temporary Landscapes*, by Yvonne Caroutch, 1965
Editor, *Cinq Nouvelles Nouvelles*, 1970
Samuel Beckett: His Works and His Critics: An Essay in Bibliography, with John Fletcher, 1970
"Surfiction", *Partisan Review*, 1973
Editor, *Surfiction: Fiction Now and Tomorrow*, 1975; revised edition, 1981
"Imagination as Plagiarism", *New Literary History*, 1977
Editor, with Lawrence Graver, *Samuel Beckett: The Critical Heritage*, 1979
Editor, with Tom Bishop, *Samuel Beckett*, 1985
Translator, with Genevieve James, *Detachment*, by Michel Serres, 1989
Critifiction: Postmodern Essays, 1993
Eine Version meines Lebens, 1993
Surfiction: der Weg der Literatur, 1993
Editor, with Bill Howe, *Sam Changed Tense*, 1995
The Supreme Indecision of the Writer, 1995
Loose Shoes: A Life Story of Sorts, 2000

Further Reading

Cornis-Pop, Marcel, "Narrative Disarticulation and the Voice in the Closet Complex in Raymond Federman's Fiction", *Critique: Studies in Contemporary Fiction* (Winter 1988)
Dowling, David, "Raymond Federman's America: Take It or Leave It", *Contemporary Literature*, 30/3 (Autumn 1989)
Erdpohl, Evamaria, *Criteria of Identity: A Comparative Analysis of Raymond Federman's "The Voice in the Closet" and Selected Works by Jasper Johns*, Frankfurt and New York: Peter Lang, 1992
Hartl, Thomas, *Raymond Federman's Real Fictitious Discourses: Formulating Yet Another Paradox*, Lewiston, New York: Mellen Press, 1995
Kutnik, Jerzy, *The Novel as Performance: The Fiction of Ronald Sukenick and Raymond Federman*, Carbondale: Southern Illinois University Press, 1986
LeClair, Tom and Larry McCaffery (editors), *Anything Can Happen: Interviews with Contemporary American Novelists*, Urbana: University of Illinois Press, 1983
McCaffery, Larry, Thomas Hartl and Doug Rice (editors), *Federman A to X-X-X-X: A Recyclopedic Narrative*, San Diego, California: San Diego State University Press, 1998

When I wrote to tell him I was doing this entry, Raymond Federman sent back the following words: "me a Jewish writer? since when?" In the tradition of the Talmud, his entire work is a circumlocution of that God whose name is not permitted to be said. But for Federman this is not Yahweh but His demonic analogue, the Holocaust, the central event of Federman's existence, which at once annihilated his past and everything associated with it – family, identity, country, language, memories – and at the same time created an eternal present of the new. What can be more Jewish, more orthodox, than refusing to name the all-powerful, the ineffable? In fact, Federman will not even accept the name of "survivor of the Holocaust." He consistently calls himself a survivor of the post-Holocaust.

But while refusing to name it explicitly, it is there everywhere, allusively, symbolically, in opposition, straight on, formed by every conceivable literary trope to image(ine) a void that humans can neither know nor name, for the very act of so doing trivializes it, returns it to a human level with which it has no possible relationship. It is for this reason that Federman rejects Elie Wiesel's works of excavated hope, Spielberg's redemptions in *Schindler's List* ("How come neither my mother nor my sisters made Schindler's list? They were there. I know they were there. There are records of that. I am sure my mother and my sisters would have done a good job in Schindler's factory making Pots & Pans"), and the very existence of the Holocaust Museum, where he vows he will never go. It is slipped into every narrative, such as in the following section from the e-book *Twilight of the Bums*:

> The old men walking along, ahead of them another bridge rising into the fogbank, and beyond it on a siding, a line of boxcars [digression: as he glances at the boxcars the smaller one recalls, for no specific reason, that in France, boxcars carry this inscription: 40 hommes ou 20 chevaux (40 men or 20 horses).]

And it is this opposition between human and non-human that explains the breaking of scatological and pornographic taboos, literary, philosophical, and psychological conventions and boundaries, that we find in Federman's *oeuvre*. For in some miraculous way, he emerged from the experience not scarred by bitterness and hate, but with a Gargantuan amoral appetite that ingests, devours, and makes his everything that gives life.

The "true" story (as I have been able to ascertain it) is as follows: when Federman was a young adolescent living in France with his Jewish family, the Nazis arrived at their apartment. As the family heard their boots on the stairs, Federman's mother shoved Raymond into a closet stuffed with junk. In so doing she saved him, but she, her husband, and Federman's two sisters were taken to concentration camps where they all died. In that closet, he defecates on some old newspaper, and that shit becomes the fertilizer of his re-birth. Young Federman made his way across the Atlantic, lived in Detroit, played jazz, and eventually ended up in California where he did a doctorate in literature, becoming in the meantime an international expert on (and friend of) Samuel Beckett, to whom his work owes much. Eventually he took a position as Distinguished Professor of French, English, Comparative Literature, Creative Writing, and Poetics at the State University of New York in Buffalo, from which he has just recently retired. In the meantime, he has written a plethora of novels, plays, poems, theory, and hybrids, winning prizes for *Double or Nothing*, a nomination for the Prix Médicis for *Amer Eldorado*, and the American Book Award for *Smiles on Washington Square*.

This postmodern Heraclitus, thus, fashions his writing on axes of opposition that annihilate seemingly contradictory polarities. Nothing holds the stasis of truth, all is provisional, dissolving into its opposite, gobbling up the past, predicting the future. Time and notions of authority, ownership and individuality are abolished: absence/presence, birth/death, shit/manna, real/fictitious, fidelity/promiscuity, French/English, teller/told.

He is "born voiceless", but in one of his many pseudonyms, Moinous, he gives voice to that silence:

> Moinous is probably the result of that complicity, of that tacit accord that took place between Federman and his mother when, that morning of July 1942, she pushed him into the junk closet. It is perhaps from this gesture [that Federman has never really wanted or been able to explain to himself, probably through fear of ruining its beauty], that Moinous was born: Me: Raymond We: my absent ones. It was perhaps at that precise moment that Moinous began to exist and that he became the nameless voice that would speak later, for those whose voice had been snuffed out forever" *Brother, she says, write the poem I will whisper to you* . . . Moinous, the silent and prostrate voice at the beginning: *But he's afraid that if he writes it the words will not come out right*, until Federman realizes, many years and misadventures later, why he was spared: *And again I'll sit beside the ashes and try to scoop them in the palm of my hand, so they can speak to me and tell me what happened after I was abandoned.* It was from that time that that voice began to express itself and Federman affirm himself as a poet and novelist.

The transgression of the taboo against naming takes on megalomaniac proportions in Federman's writings, as he both defies God and seeks to fashion and refashion an identity for himself. Not content with just the One name and the One identity, he flip-flops Federman to get Namredef, melds himself and others into Moinous, translates Federman, the FeatherMan (quill) into the *Hombre della Pluma*, the *Homme* [Nom] *de Plume*, always beginning and ending with the irreducible facticity of writing as origin, inscription, salvation, and being. His most explicit evocation, *The Voice in the Closet*, typographically mimics the closet experience and tells "the whole story crossed out my family parenthetically xxxx into typographical symbols".

To the univocal, ordered, and predestined world of the Old Testament God, Federman opposes randomness and chance, affirming that survival is simply a question of good or bad luck, and that no one deserves (or doesn't) to be alive. Two of his most famous books, *Double or Nothing* and *Take It or Leave It* suggest this idea of play and risk. As an experimental writer, they are at the heart of his craft. Coherent psychology is replaced by proliferating voices, names are overrun by numbers, plots are fragmented and iterated in multiple forms, motivation is virtually absent, as is extended narrative and plot. French and English weave in and out of each other, with sprinklings of German folded in. Instead of controlled, lucid discourse, we have infinite proliferations and Joycean carnivals of logorrhoea that erupt in the rampant life-force of sexuality and engulf the works of previous times and other writers, all without citation.

This vitality, coupled with a zero degree of lack of sentimentality, characterizes all his work. In "Concerning a Close Friend" (*Loose Shoes* (e-book)), Federman sums it up perfectly: "He learned early in life that laughter is always tragic. And so, to save himself, he invented the laugh laughing at the laugh. And then he flopped among the daisies."

LYNNE DIAMOND-NIGH

Fefer, Itsik

Russian poet, 1900–1952

Born in Shpola, Ukraine. Worked in a printing shop aged 12. In 1917 joined the Bund and became trade-union activist; joined Communist Party, 1919; served in Red Army. From 1927 occupied central positions in Soviet literary organizations; was leading figure in Jewish Anti-fascist Committee, created during World War II; arrested in 1948 together with other members of the Committee. Executed 12 August 1952.

Selected Writings

Poetry
Shpener [Splinters], 1922
Vegn zikh un azoyne vi ikh, 1924
Proste trit, 1924
A shteyn tsu a shteyn, 1925
Geklibene verk, 1928
Gezamlte verk, 1932
Lider un poemes, 1934
Geklibene verk, 1938
Birobidzhaner lider, 1939
Geklibns, 1940
Milkhome-balades, 1943
Shayn un opshayn, 1946
Afsnay, 1948
Lider, balades, poemes, 1967

Further Reading

Rubenstein, Joshua and Vladimir P. Naumov (editors), *Stalin's Secret Pogrom*, New Haven, Connecticut: Yale University Press, 2001
Shmeruk, Khone (editor), *A shpigl oyf a shteyn: An Anthology of Poetry and Prose by Twelve Soviet Yiddish Writers*, Jerusalem: Hotsaat sefarim a. sh. Y.L. Magnes, ha universitah haivrit, 1987

Revolutions always treasure young people and despise the older generations, and the Bolshevik Revolution was no exception. Among the Yiddish writers, too, young people were promoted to central positions. The most prominent among these Yiddish "children of the revolution" was Itsik Fefer. On 4 June 1918 – we know exactly the date – he wrote his first poem. His literary career began properly in 1922, when he joined in Kiev the group of young Yiddish literary talents, called the *Vidervuks* [New Growth]; their mentor was Dovid Hofshteyn, then the most popular Yiddish poet in Ukraine. The same year, the appearance of Fefer's small collection, *Shpener* [Splinters], established him as a rising literary star. In 1922 he also formulated his literary credo of *proste reyd* (simple speech). In the early 1920s, Soviet Yiddish literature lacked prose writers. Poetry, particularly avant-garde poetry, swamped the literary pages of all Soviet Yiddish periodicals. This phenomenon worried the editors and critics, wary of the fact that the bulk of Yiddish readers could not understand this kind of literature. Everyone, on the other hand, could understand Fefer's *proste reyd*. He was no ivory tower writer. In 1927 we find Fefer among the founding members of the Jewish Section of the All-Ukrainian Union of Proletarian Writers. Fefer became one of the leaders of the section and one of the editors of its journal, *Prolit* [Proletarian Literature].

In 1929 Fefer published a poetic cycle under the title "Manure in Bloom". It was presented as a travel log, dedicated to the author's trip to his home shtetl. Fefer meets there young pioneers and Comsomol members. The former dive-keeper trades in needlework rather than in vodka and girls, and her only son is in the Red Army. The poet's former *melamed* (religious teacher) is dead, and his daughter ran away with a *goy*. The *shames* (synagogue sexton) dreams about a position at the local party committee. Not very much is left of the old shtetl, of the "synagogue, goats, shops and mud". Fefer is happy to see the transformation:

> I'm standing in a festive mood, seeing
> how in the noise of years
> here, in the manure, in pain,
> a world is being born.

He obviously believes that the shtetl can be revitalized as a centre of Soviet Jewish life and culture, where a new – Soviet Jewish – nation will be built. True, in the 1930s he will concentrate mostly on another Jewish nation-building project – the Birobidzhan utopia.

The complete centralization of the Soviet "writing industry", that is, the creation of the Writers' Union, increased the importance of the communist poet and apparatchik Fefer. He represented Yiddish literature on the governing bodies of the union. The Soviet Yiddish press characterized him as an embodiment of the best qualities of a poet who had been brought up by the party. In 1934, on the eve of the First All-Union Congress of Soviet Writers, Fefer edited the *Almanac of Soviet Yiddish Writers*. Instead of an introduction, he published his poem "Between Sky and Ice", glorifying the expedition of the *SS Cheliuskin*. The polar expedition of the *Cheliuskin*, which was crushed in the ice, attracted attention of millions and gave rise to a vast body of writing. The Arctic subject-matter fitted perfectly the socialist-realist thematic base: mastery over nature, technological progress, patriotism, optimism, leadership of the party, Stalin and heroism. In Fefer's poem, Stalin appears as the main decision-maker and Teacher: ". . . he already sees the directions which the world will follow / and shows the world the way with his hand". Stalin appears as the Teacher also in Fefer's later poem called "Stalin". This sample of Yiddish poetic Newspeak is written in the form of interviews with a few Soviet celebrities, including two Jewish ones: the violinist David Oistrakh and the chess-player Mikhail Botvinik. These "questions and answers" had to reveal the pivotal role of Stalin, the Teacher of Soviet people.

> Oh, Oistrakh, my Fatherland is proud of you!
> Who teaches you to weave the sounds,
> to make the red polished, ordinary wood
> to speak the language of our life?
>
> Oistrakh answers with young, modest pride:
> Stalin gave me the breath of life,
> therefore the red, ordinary wood breathes
> and charms, like the charms of our life.

Fefer's books can be used as a reader in Soviet Jewish – and general Soviet – history. Like a Poet Laureate of a kind he wrote for virtually all state occasions and campaigns. Not many Yiddish writers could compete with him in the mastery of adopting the official discourse to the spoken language. At the same time, he penned many lyrical poems, such as "A Shy Girl", which is about his infatuation with "the girl who is peeling potatoes" and has "flaxen hair". A slim volume of his lyrics would show us a different poet, only distantly related to the tireless communist rhymester Fefer.

In 1943 Fefer, together with the popular Yiddish actor Solomon Mikhoels, visited the United States, Canada, Mexico, and England. This unprecedented tour helped mobilize pro-Soviet support. National pride runs through his poetry of that period. The poem "I am a Jew" is the best-known sample of such Soviet Jewish patriotism. He includes in his Soviet Jewish genealogy such figures as Bar Kochba, King Solomon, Baruch Spinoza, Isaac Levitan, Yakov Sverdlov, and Lazar Kaganovich.

In 1946 Fefer wrote his poem "Epitaph":

> When I remain on my own with the naked earth,
> when the Jewish cemetery takes my old bones,
> I hope a passer-by, noticing my fence
> and seeing the grass which grows from my body,
> will tell the living wind:
> He was a *mensch*, he served his people!

The master of "simple speech", Fefer perceived himself, and was praised by critics, as a popular poet. In reality, however, he was one of many Soviet court poets, producing easy-to-understand-and-memorize texts for glorifying Stalin and Stalinism. He was useful as long as the Soviet Union had considerable Yiddish-speaking masses. In the late 1940s, after the Holocaust and assimilation had decimated this section of the Soviet population, he became redundant.

Moreover, he and his ilk were seen as an obstacle to achieving the complete assimilation. The regime no longer needed communists who cherished the anachronistic hope of being buried in a Jewish cemetery.

GENNADY ESTRAIKH

Feinstein, Elaine

British fiction writer and poet 1930–

Born Elaine Cooklin in Bootle, Lancashire, 24 October 1930. Studied at Cambridge University, BA in English 1952; MA 1955. Married Arnold Feinstein, 1956; three sons. Member of editorial staff, Cambridge University Press, 1960–62. Lecturer in English, Bishop's Stortford Training College, Hertfordshire 1963–66; lecturer in literature, University of Essex, 1967–70; writer in residence, British Council, Singapore, 1993. Fellow, Royal Society of Literature, 1980. Many awards, including Daisy Miller Award for Fiction, 1971; Kelus Prize, 1978; Cholmondeley Award for Poets, 1990; three Arts Council translation awards; Society of Authors Travelling Bursary, 1992.

Selected Writings

Poetry
In a Green Eye, 1966
The Magic Apple Tree, 1971
At the Edge, 1972
The Celebrants and Other Poems, 1973
Some Unease and Angels: Selected Poems, 1977
The Feast of Euridice, 1980
Badlands, 1986
City Music, 1990
Selected Poems, 1994
Daylight, 1997
Gold, 2000

Novels
The Circle, 1970
The Amberstone Exit, 1972
The Glass Alembic, 1973; as *The Crystal Garden*, 1974
Children of the Rose, 1975
The Ecstasy of Dr Miriam Garner, 1976
The Shadow Master, 1978
The Survivors, 1982
The Border, 1984
Mother's Girl, 1988
All You Need, 1989
Loving Brecht, 1992
Dreamers, 1994
Lady Chatterley's Confession, 1995
Dark Inheritance, 2000

Short Stories
Matters of Chance, 1972
The Silent Areas, 1980

Plays
Foreign Girls, 1993
Winter Meeting, 1994

Radio: *Echoes*, 1980; *A Late Spring*, 1981; *A Day Off*, 1983; *Marina Tsvetayeva: A Life*, 1985; *If I Ever Get on my Feet Again*, 1987; *The Man in her Life*, 1990

Television: *Breath*, 1975; *Lunch*, 1981; *A Brave Face*, 1985; *A Passionate Woman*, 1990

Other
Translator, *The Selected Poems of Marina Tsvetayeva*, 1971; revised 1993
Translator, *Three Russian Poets: Margarite Aliger, Yunna Moritz, Bella Akhmadulina*, 1976
Editor, with Fay Weldon, *New Stories*, 1979
Bessie Smith, 1986
A Captive Lion: The Life of Marina Tsvetayeva, 1987
Lawrence and the Women: The Intimate Life of D.H. Lawrence, 1993
Pushkin: A Biography, 1998
Editor, *After Pushkin: Versions of the Poems of Pushkin by Contemporary Poets*, 1999
Ted Hughes: The Life of a Poet, 2001

Further Reading

Conradi, Peter, "An Interview with Elaine Feinstein", *Literary Review*, 1 (April 1982)
Davie, Donald, *Under Briggflatts: A History of Poetry in Great Britain 1960–1988*, Manchester: Carcanet, and Chicago: University of Chicago Press, 1989
Lawson, Peter, "Way Out in the Centre: In Conversation with Elaine Feinstein", *Jewish Quarterly* 181 (2001)
Schmidt, Michael, "Interview", *PN Review* (November–December 1997)
Schmidt, Michael and Peter Jones (editors), *British Poetry since 1970: A Critical Survey*, Manchester: Carcanet, and New York: Persea, 1980

Poet, novelist, literary biographer, critic, and translator, Elaine Feinstein is a noted English writer. Although describing herself as having three strikes against her – being Jewish, a woman, and from the North of England – she is included in the *Oxford Book of English Verse* (edited by Christopher Ricks, 1999), and is the recipient of a number of major awards and prizes for her work. Feinstein is the author of a dozen books of poetry, five biographies, three books of translations of poetry, and 14 novels.

Even if Feinstein's novel writing began, as she reports, as an extension of her verse, she is now an acknowledged contemporary British novelist. She writes of the lives of the middle class, with most of her work narrated by women protagonists. Although she records her own experience of anti-Semitism as being social rather than political and "really very little", many of her Jewish characters do experience various levels of overt and more subtle anti-Semitism. In *All You Need*, for example, Cambridge educated Nell's mother reports that she "married one didn't I?", a Jew, that is. Her mother explains that her father's family, "aren't properly English, are they? I know they were all born here, but it isn't the same." Not Jewish, nor fully comfortable with Jews, Nell does feel at home in the smells of her childhood, the smells of the foods of eastern Europe. Nell's ambiguous

"Jewish" identity is contrasted with that of her Bishop's Avenue cousin, Mark, whose "public-school cadences . . . were deliberately anglicised more than her own". Theo Walloon, Nell's Jewish lover, understands his own Jewishness as not being based on blood but on his not fitting in anywhere (even in a synagogue in "some *judenrein* bit of the Midlands"), although using the Third Reich's definition of Jewish identity, he recognizes her as sharing something significant with him.

In *The Border*, Inge and Hans Wendler, a young Jewish couple (although there is a suggestion that Hans's mother is not Jewish) leave Vienna following the Anschluss. Their escape to Paris, their time there, and their flight to the Spanish border are described, and the narrative includes the suicide at the border by their companion, Walter Benjamin. Feinstein uses a range of fictional documents including Hans's and Inge's diaries and Hans's poetry and letters, as vehicles for the narrative. The novel records the terrible strains and tensions of being refugees ("We were separate because we were Jews and because we were foreigners") in a hostile France and having their lives and relationship tragically disrupted beyond remedy.

Mother's Girl is also set against the background of the war. Halina, sent to England as a child refugee from Hungary, makes her way to Cambridge as a student. As an outsider, she speculates that "because I came from central Europe, and the embarrassing curiosity about my being Jewish", she has become "less probing" – "I came close to escaping the class system altogether". Feinstein's own outsider status is used skilfully to convey English class mores. *Children of the Rose* examines the nature of memory and responsibility as Jewish refugees return to Poland 30 years after the end of the war amid discussions, debates, and trials in France of wartime collaboration with the Nazis.

Jewish identity in England is explicated in *The Survivors*. The novel is set in Feinstein's native Liverpool; issues of assimilation, acculturation, and tradition are portrayed, and the alternatives explored, through the lives of two Jewish immigrant families in a rapidly changing Britain, from World War I, via the Depression and World War II, to the mid-1950s. The granddaughter of a Talmudic scholar, Feinstein grew up in an orthodox Jewish home, and one of the themes of her fiction is religion and spirituality, although not of the orthodox type. (*The Ecstasy of Dr Miriam Garner* and *The Shadow Master* were influenced by Isaac Bashevis Singer.)

Feinstein is best known for her poetry, which conveys a range of emotions and moods, from despair to the blackest humour. Her verse is crisp, direct, sharp, and unsentimental. Her themes are relationships ("Separations", "Bonds"), family ("Birthday", "Mother"), friendship ("Companionship"), and the balance between engagement and withdrawal. A number of poems deal explicitly with women's perspectives and Jewish themes. The separation and experiential gaps – linguistic and cultural – between the generations of English Jews ("Rose", "Against Winter") are set against the sharing of three generations at the Passover Seder table ("Eclipse"), although precisely what is shared beyond presence at the table remains unclear. "Exile" is the title of three different poems that are dedicated to, and refer to, three different experiences of exile. "Annus Mirabilis 1989" gives a sense of the difficulties of understanding the persistence of European anti-Semitism in a report of a cabaret show in Hungary where laughter and applause are engendered by the stage murder of a Jew. The poem "Allegiance" contrasts the Jewish poet's love ("taste") of Israel with her English friend's tourist responses in a powerful account of Jewish attachments to the country. Her poems powerfully evoke the feel and tenor of those she loves ("Tony", "Rose"). "Rose", for example, is a caring and sympathetic portrait of her mother-in-law. A number of poems deal with religion ("Prayer", "The Celebrants", "Against Winter").

Feinstein's passion for Russian literature led her to publish two volumes of her translations of Marina Tsvetayeva's poetry, and a well-received biography of this Russian poet. She has also translated the poetry of Margarite Aliger, Yunna Moritz, and Bella Akhmadulina. Her work has played a major role in the English-language reception of these writers. More recently her biography of Pushkin (1998) appeared. This Russian interest has been of central importance to Feinstein's development as a poet, as she credits the discovery of her "own voice" to the experience of translating poetry from Russian to English. Her Jewish identity too appears to have been intensified by being "English" in Russia aware that being "Jewish" there would be a very different experience.

Feinstein eloquently explores the tensions of being Jewish and English. She writes of the not quite at-homeness of the English Jew in England and refers to their allegiances to other people and places – to Holocaust survivors and victims, to Israel and Russia, and to family, ceremony, and traditions. But alongside these seeming barriers to full integration in England there is a sustained celebration in her novels and poetry of English literary culture, Cambridge, the freedoms of living in a relatively tolerant society, of England. Feinstein insists that for a Jew it is a "privilege" to live in England.

PAUL MORRIS

Ferber, Edna

US fiction writer and journalist, 1885–1968

Born in Kalamazoo, Michigan, 15 August 1885. Moved with family to Ottumwa, Iowa; Chicago; and later to Appleton, Wisconsin. Educated at Ryan High School, Appleton. Worked as reporter for *Appleton Daily Crescent*, *Milwaukee Journal*, and *Chicago Tribune*. War correspondent during World War II. Visited Israel, *c.*1954. Many awards, including Pulitzer Prize, 1924. Died 16 April 1968.

Selected Writings

Novels

Dawn O'Hara: The Girl who Laughed, 1911

Roast Beef, Medium: The Business Adventures of Emma McChesney and her Son, Jock, 1913

Personality Plus: Some Experiences of Emma McChesney and her Son, Jock, 1914

Emma McChesney and Co, 1915
Fanny Herself, 1917
The Girls, 1921
Old Man Minick: A Short Story, and *Minick: A Play*, with George S. Kaufman, 1924
So Big, 1924
Show Boat, 1926
Mother Knows Best: A Fiction Book, 1927
Cimarron, 1930
American Beauty, 1931
Come and Get It, 1935
Nobody's in Town, 1938
Saratoga Trunk, 1941
Great Son, 1945
Your Town, 1948
Giant, 1952
Ice Palace, 1958

Short Stories
Buttered Side Down, 1912
Cheerful, By Request, 1918
Half Portions, 1920
Gigolo, 1922
They Brought their Women, 1933
No Room at the Inn, 1941
One Basket: Thirty-one Short Stories, 1947

Plays
Our Mrs McChesney, with George V. Hobart, 1915
$1200 a Year, with Newman Levy, 1920
Minick, with George S. Kaufman, 1924
The Eldest: A Drama of American Life, 1925
The Royal Family, with George S. Kaufman, 1927
Dinner at Eight, with George S. Kaufman, 1932
Stage Door, with George S. Kaufman, 1936
The Land is Bright, with George S. Kaufman, 1941
Bravo!, with George S. Kaufman, 1948

Other
A Peculiar Treasure, 1939
A Kind of Magic, 1963

Further Reading

Brenni, Vito J. and B.L. Spencer, "Edna Ferber: A Selected Bibliography", *Bulletin of Bibliography*, 22 (1958)
Burstein, Janet Handler, *Writing Mothers, Writing Daughters: Tracing the Maternal in Stories by American Jewish Women*, Urbana: University of Illinois Press, 1996
Gilbert, Julie Goldsmith, *Ferber: A Biography*, New York: Doubleday, 1978
Horowitz, Stephen J. and Miriam J. Landsman, "The Americanization of Edna: A Study of Ms Ferber's Jewish Identity", *Studies in American Jewish Literature*, 2 (1982)
Lichtenstein, Diane Marilyn, *Writing their Nations: The Tradition of Nineteenth-Century American Jewish Women Writers*, Bloomington: Indiana University Press, 1992
Shapiro, Ann R. (editor), *Jewish American Women Writers: A Bio-Bibliographical and Critical Sourcebook*, Westport, Connecticut: Greenwood Press, 1994
Wilson, Christopher, *White Collar Fictions: Class and Social Representation in American Literature, 1885–1925*, Athens: University of Georgia Press, 1992

Among readers in the United States and abroad, Ferber is less known for her Jewish identity than for her vivid portrayals of American regional life in the first half of the 20th century. Of her many publications and collaborations, only a handful address Jewish themes. As she indicates in her first autobiography, *A Peculiar Treasure*, Ferber saw herself as "an American, a writer, a Jew". Jewishness was not distinct from her Americanness. To the contrary, she believed the two were mutually constitutive. Though, she admits, "being a Jew makes it tougher to get on, and I like that".

The anti-Semitism Ferber experienced as a child in the small town of Ottumwa, Iowa, provided her with a heightened understanding of prejudice, an understanding she later drew upon in constructing characters of varying races, classes, and backgrounds in American culture. A background in journalism provided her with powers of keen observation, intense research, and indefatigable interest to portray the lives of everyday Americans, many of whom are ambitious women. Ferber attributes her writerly instincts to her Jewish identity: "Two thousand years of persecution have made the Jew quick to sympathy, quick-witted (he'd better be), tolerant, humanly understanding". Just as she felt her Jewish identity was inextricably tied to her American identity, Ferber believed that to tell the story of struggling, hard-working Americans was, in large measure, to tell a Jewish story.

Though best known for such popular novels as *So Big*, *Show Boat*, *Cimarron*, and *Giant*, Ferber's short story, "The Girl Who Went Right" (published in *Cheerful, by Request*) and her 1917 novel, *Fanny Herself*, dramatize two women's inner conflicts to assert a Jewish identity in American, middle-class culture. Rachel Wiletzky, in "The Girl Who Went Right", becomes a saleswoman in a large, upscale department store with hopes of transcending her humble "West Side" origins as a shop clerk at "Halsted Street Bazaar." While her vibrantly rosy cheeks and soft, delicate hands suggest "five generations of ancestors who have sat with their hands folded in their laps" studying Talmud, Rachel feels she must repress that history, that identity, in order to compete successfully for employment and acceptance outside the Jewish community. She must quiet her "ghetto voice", patch holes in her old shirtwaists, and keep sick babies and heating bills separate from her work life uptown. Despite her attempts to disguise her shabbiness and her origins (she goes so far as to lie about her name), the promises of class mobility do not outweigh the emptiness Rachel finds in this "real" world full of phonies. By the end of the story, she no longer feels compelled to choose between an American and a Jewish identity and asserts proudly, "I am Rachel Wiletzky".

Jewishness is not merely a religious identity for Rachel (or Ferber, who was decidedly secular), but a quality of character – a dramatic performance of difference. To distinguish herself from the other girls waiting for interviews, Rachel conjures "that latent dramatic force which is a heritage of her race" and insists, "I'm different." Ferber believed her

Jewish heritage marked her as "especially privileged", and the vibrancy of her female characters emanates from qualities she attributes to Jews – "adaptability, nervous energy, ambition to succeed and a desire to be liked".

In *Fanny Herself*, Ferber examines how Jewish identity enables, rather than limits, social and economic mobility in the American marketplace. In the small midwestern town of Winnebago, Wisconsin, Fanny Brandeis gains valuable business experience, working alongside her mother in the family store. Their labour marks them as working class (among the non-Jewish community), despite their material comforts, and aligns them with the "Russian" Jews of the community, despite their Hungarian-German ancestry. Ferber takes pains to detail the hierarchy within the Jewish community and its adherence to American, middle-class values of male professionalism and female domestication. "Jewish women" in Winnebago, the narrator tells us "did not work thus. Their husbands worked for them, or their sons, or their brothers." Fanny's skill in identifying the "wants and needs" of the working-class farmer enables her to "work her way up" as a successful businesswoman and designer. In the process, she (like Rachel) initially finds her Jewish heritage a "handicap", lies about her background, and ascends the ladder of success. Ferber describes Fanny's Jewishness as "temperamental, or emotional, or dramatic, or historic, or all four". As much as Fanny wants to privilege her business acumen, Ferber insists that her "race, religion, training, [and] natural impulses" are the *basis* for her success, not handicaps.

The paucity of contemporary critical interest in Ferber's canon does not bespeak the genuine success she achieved in her lifetime. Christopher Wilson notes that "from the 1920s to World War II, she would become one of Doubleday's highest-paid authors". Only a handful of scholars has turned its attention to Ferber and, of this group, an even smaller number remarks on her contributions as a Jewish writer. Steven Horowitz and Miriam Landsman suggest that "Edna Ferber was probably the most popular Jewish American author in history". No small accomplishment. Diane Lichtenstein believes Ferber carried the themes of 19th-century, Jewish American women's writing into the 20th by "transform[ing] the myths of True and Jewish womanhood into the fearless, invincible pioneer woman". Carol Batker reads the work of Ferber, Anzia Yezierska, and Fannie Hurst together to locate the intersections and boundaries of class, ethnic identity, and immigration in Jewish women's fiction of the 1920s.

As Ferber insists in her autobiography, "All my life I have been inordinately proud of being a Jew. But I have felt that one should definitely not brag about it." Perhaps Ferber universalized the qualities she ascribed to Jewish identity in order not to "brag" and, more importantly, to assert that Jewish Americans are integral members of the American community.

WENDY H. BERGOFFEN

Feuchtwanger, Lion

German fiction writer, dramatist, and critic, 1884–1958

Born in Munich, 7 July 1884. Studied philology, history, and anthropology at universities of Berlin and Munich, 1903–07, PhD 1907. Married Marta Loeffler, 1912; one daughter died in infancy. Freelance writer and theatre critic from 1907; settled in Berlin, 1925. Exiled to France, 1933; settled in Sanary-sur-Mer; in detention camps, 1939–40. Fled to United States, 1940; settled in Los Angeles. Many awards, including National Prize, First Class, for Art and Literature of the German Democratic Republic, 1953. Died in Los Angeles, 21 December 1958.

Selected Writings

Novels

Die Einsamen: zwei Skizzen [The Lonely Ones: Two Sketches], 1903
Der tönerne Gott [The God of Clay], 1910
Die hässliche Herzogin, 1923; as *The Ugly Duchess*, translated by Willa Muir and Edwin Muir, 1928
Jud Süss, 1925; as *Jew Süss: A Historical Romance*, translated by Willa Muir and Edwin Muir, 1926; as *Power*, 1926
Erfolg: drei Jahre Geschichte einer Provinz, 2 vols, 1930; as *Success: Three Years in the Life of a Province*, translated by Willa Muir and Edwin Muir, 1930
Der jüdische Krieg, 1932; as *Josephus*, translated by Willa Muir and Edwin Muir, 1932
Die Geschwister Oppermann, 1933; as *The Oppermanns*, translated by James Cleugh, 1934
Marianne in Indien und sieben andere Erzählungen, 1934; as *Marianne in India*, translated by Basil Creighton, 1935; as *Little Tales*, 1935
Die Söhne, 1935; as *The Jew of Rome*, translated by Willa Muir and Edwin Muir, 1936
Der falsche Nero, 1936; as *The Pretender*, translated by Willa Muir and Edwin Muir, 1937
Zwei Erzählungen [Two Stories], 1938
Der Wartesaal Trilogie [The Waiting Room Trilogy], 1939
Der Tag wird kommen, 1940; as *Josephus and the Emperor*, translated from the German manuscript by Caroline Oram, 1942, as *The Day Will Come*, 1944; as *Simone*, translated by G.A. Hermann, 1944
Exil, 1940; as *Paris Gazette*, translated by Willa Muir and Edwin Muir, 1940
Die Brüder Lautensack, 1944; as *Double, Double, Toil and Trouble*, translated by Caroline Oram, 1943; as *The Lautensack Brothers*, 1944
Venedig (Texas) und vierzehn andere Erzählungen [Venice (Texas) and Fourteen Other Stories], 1946
Waffen für Amerika, 1947; as *Die Füchse im Weinberg*, 2 vols, 1947; as *Proud Destiny*, translated by Moray Firth, 1947
Odysseus and the Swine and Other Stories, translated by Barrows Mussey, 1949; original German published as *Odysseus und die Schweine und zwölf andere Erzählungen*, 1950
Goya; oder, Der arge Weg der Erkenntnis, 1951; as *This is*

the Hour, translated by H.T. Lowe-Porter and Frances Fawcett, 1951
Narrenweisheit; oder, Tod und Verklärung des Jean-Jacques Rousseau, 1952; as *'Tis Folly to be Wise; or, Death and Transfiguration of Jean-Jacques Rousseau*, translated by Frances Fawcett, 1953
Spanische Ballade, 1955; as *Die Jüdin von Toledo*, 1955; as *Raquel, the Jewess of Toledo*, translated by Eithne Wilkins and Ernst Kaiser, 1956
Jefta und seine Tochter, 1957; as *Jephta and his Daughter*, translated by Eithne Wilkins and Ernst Kaiser, 1958

Plays
Kleine Dramen: Joel, König Saul, das Weib des Urias, Der arme Heinrich, Donna Bianca, Die Brant von Korinth [Joel, King Saul, The Woman of Urias, Poor Henry, Donna Bianca, The Bride of Corinth], 2 vols, 1905–06
Der Fetisch [The Fetish], 1907
Ein feste Burg ist unser Gott [A Mighty Fortress is Our God], 1911
Julia Farnese, 1915
Pierrots Herrentraum: Pantomime, 1916
Vasantasena: Nach dem Indischen des Königs Sudraka [Vasantasena: From the Hindu of King Sudraka], 1916
Jud Süss, 1917
Warren Hastings, Gouverneur von Inden, 1916; reworked with Bertolt Brecht as *Kalkutta, 4 Mai*, 1925; as *Warren Hastings*, translated by Willa Muir and Edwin Muir in *Two Anglo-Saxon Plays*, 1928
Der König und die Tänzerin [The King and the Dancing-Girl], 1917
Friede: Ein burleskes Spiel: Nach den "Acharnern" und der "Eirene" des Aristophanes [Peace: A Burlesque after Aristophanes], 1917
Appius und Virginia, 1918
Die Kriegsgefangenen, 1919; as *Prisoners of War*, translated by Emma D. Ashton in *Three Plays*, 1934
Thomas Wendt: ein dramatischer Roman, 1919
Der Amerikaner; oder, Die entzauberte Stadt [The American: or, The Town That Lost its Magic], 1921
Der Frauenverkäufer: ein Spiel in drei Akten nach Calderon [The Woman-Seller: A Play in Three Acts after Calderon], 1923
Der holländische Kaufmann, 1923; as *The Dutch Merchant*, translated by Emma D. Ashton in *Three Plays*, 1934
Wird Hill amnestiert? [Will Hill Be Pardoned?], 1923
Leben Eduards des Zweiten von England (nach Marlowe): Historie, with Bertolt Brecht, 1924; as *Edward II*, translated by Eric Bentley, 1966; as *The Life of Edward II of England*, translated by Jean Benedetti, 1970
Die Petroleuminseln in *Drei angelsächsische Stücke*, 1927; as *The Oil Islands*, translated by Willa Muir and Edwin Muir in *Two Anglo-Saxon Plays*, 1928
Stücke in Prosa [Plays in Prose], 1936
Stücke in Versen [Plays in Verse], 1954
Die Witwe Capet, 1956; as *The Widow Capet*, 1956
Die Gesichte der Simone Machard, with Bertolt Brecht, 1957; as *The Visions of Simone Machard*, translated by Carl Richard Mueller, 1965

Poetry
PEP: J.L. Wetcheeks amerikanisches Liederbuch, 1928; as *PEP: J.L. Wetcheek's American Songbook*, translated by Dorothy Thompson and Sinclair Lewis, 1929

Other
Heinrich Heines "Der Rabbi von Bacharach": eine kritische Studie [Heinrich Heine's "The Rabbi from Bacharach": A Critical Study], 1907
Die Aufgabe des Judentums [The Task of the Jews], with Arnold Zweig, 1933
Moskau 1937: ein Reisebericht für meine Freunde, 1937; as *Moscow 1937: My Visit Described for my Friends*, translated by Irene Josephy, 1937
Unholdes Frankreich: meine Erlebnisse unter der Regierung Pétain, 1942; as *Der Teufel in Frankreich*; as *The Devil in France: My Encounter with him in the Summer of 1940*, translated by Elisabeth Abbott, 1941
Centum Opuscula: eine Auswahl [100 Short Works: A Selection], edited by Wolfgang Berndt, 1956
Das Haus der Desdemona; oder, Grösse und Grenzen der historischen Dichtung, edited by Fritz Zschech, 1961; as *The House of Desdemona; or The Laurels and Limitations of Historical Fiction*, translated by Harold A. Basilius, 1963

Further Reading
Jeske, Wolfgang and Peter Zahn, *Lion Feuchtwanger oder der arge Weg der Erkenntis: Eine Biographie*, Stuttgart: Metzler, 1984
Kahn, Lothar, *Mirrors of the Jewish Mind*, Chapter 6, New York: Yoseloff, 1968
Kahn, Lothar, *Insight and Action: The Life and Work of Lion Feuchtwanger*, Rutherford, New Jersey: Fairleigh Dickinson University Press, 1975
Köpke, Wulf, *Lion Feuchtwanger*, Munich: Beck 1983
Müller-Funk, Wolfgang, "Bibliographie zu Lion Feuchtwanger", *Text + Kritik*, 79/80 (1983)
Spalek, John M. (editor), *Lion Feuchtwanger: The Man, his Ideas, his Work: A Collection of Critical Essays*, Los Angeles: Hennessey and Ingalls, 1972
Spalek, John M. and Sandra H. Hawrylchak, *Lion Feuchtwanger: A Bibliographic Handbook*, 4 vols, Munich: Saur, 1998–

Lion Feuchtwanger was the master of the historical novel and his work sheds much light both on the historical characters he portrayed and on the events he depicted. Altogether, he wrote 16 full-length novels and about a dozen plays. The major novels were mostly on Jewish subjects. He was very popular in the United States where two million of his books have been sold in hardback but, remarkably, there are claims that some ten million of his books have been sold in Russia. He developed late as a novelist and his first best-seller came when he was 40. This was *Jud Süss* (*Jew Süss* in Britain and *Power* in USA) which he had first written as a play in 1917. *Jud Süss* is based on the life of an 18th-century court financier, Joseph Süss Oppenheimer. It deals with the issues of conversion and anti-Semitism. Süss pandered to the rapacious and sensual Duke of Württenberg. His rise to power as the duke's financial adviser was meteoric, only for him eventually to be discarded and to lose his life on the scaffold. This novel reflected Feuchtwanger's concern with the struggle of Jews in the Diaspora, a theme that he retained for a number of subsequent novels. In 1940 Goebbels made *Jud Süss* into a viciously anti-Semitic film. It had previously been filmed in Britain in 1934 with Conrad Veidt in the title role.

Feuchtwanger's next important effort was a trilogy based on the life of Jewish historian, Flavius Josephus, whom he saw as a man fully rooted in Jewish faith and culture. The basic human conflict between nationalism and internationalism intrigued Feuchtwanger and he placed this conflict within Josephus' soul. *Der jüdische Krieg* (*Josephus*) deals in dramatic fashion with Josephus' life under Nero's and Vespasian's rule and it describes his personal ambition and his turbulent life in Rome, Galilee, and Jerusalem. Josephus is depicted as a cowardly character trying to make the best of all worlds especially in his efforts for friendship with the enemies of the Jews. *Die Söhne* (*The Jew of Rome*) is less dramatic. The novel begins with the death of Vespasian and focuses on Josephus' return to Jerusalem, raising some questions about the future of Judea. *Der Tag wird kommen* (*The Day Will Come* in Britain and *Josephus and the Emperor* in USA), the last of the trilogy, is about Domitian's reign and the latter's conflict with the Jewish God. Josephus is surrounded by enemies, Domitian and others, but he is resented too by his own people because he courted Rome and because of his writings. The story considers also the mess Josephus made of his life.

Die Geschwister Oppenmann (*The Oppermanns*) is the middle book of another trilogy entitled *Der Wartesaal* [The Waiting Room], but Jewish themes are absent in the other two. It is set in Germany between the two world wars. The Oppermanns are a family of furniture manufacturers and the powerful story focuses on three brothers and one sister. It is perceptive in its portrayal of the threats to and the fate of German Jewry as it describes how the family fell victim to the Nazis. There is a chilling account of the Nazi youth movement.

Two other novels are on Jewish subjects. *Spanische Ballade* (*Raquel, the Jewess of Toledo*) is set in the Golden Age of Spanish Jewry and features the relationship between Judaism, Christianity, and Islam. King Alfonso of Castile loves Raquel, the beautiful daughter of Yehuda who becomes Alfonso's adviser. Yehuda is the principal character and the story encompasses his rise to power as well as the love affair. It ends with the murders of both father and daughter and with Alfonso's transformation. Feuchtwanger's objective here was to show how the magic of such an ill-natured king could attract even those who understood his destructiveness and how evil can radiate from war and adventure. Feuchtwanger's last novel was *Jefta und seine Tochter* (*Jephta and his Daughter*) based on the biblical story in the Book of Judges. He was fascinated by Jephta's vow and depicts him as the rebellious man who stood alone fighting all his battles within himself. One other book, *Die hässliche Herzogin* (*The Ugly Duchess*) touched on a Jewish theme. The novel contained Jewish characters and revealed Feuchtwanger's concern for his people's fate. Their oppressed condition was understood by the clever Duchess, herself a sufferer as a result of some physical birth defects. She brought Jews into her realm to improve its economy, but she was later unable to prevent pogroms.

Feuchtwanger believed it was essential for Jews to share a common mentality and attitude and it was important also to understand the differences between good and evil and between happiness and unhappiness. He was not an observant Jew but his fiction shows he had a great respect for Jewish tradition and a great concern for the future of Jewry. He won many honours late in life and was nominated for the Nobel Prize for Literature just before he died.

Feuchtwanger wrote a number of articles on Jewish topics. "Gesprache mit dem wigen Juden" [Conversations with the Wandering Jew] was an optimistic examination of Jewish life in Germany and in "Die Verjudung der Abendlandischen Literatur" [The Judaization of Western Literature] he put forward the thesis that Judaism was spiritually part of tradition and historical consciousness. He was never a supporter of Zionism although he did see it had some advantages. In "Nationalismus und Judentum" [Nationalism and Judaism] he argued that the elements necessary for a proper Jewish life – a land, a common race, a common history, and a common language – were missing.

Among the non-Jewish historical characters used by Feuchtwanger in his fiction was Hitler. This choice was especially perceptive because the book based on Hitler's abortive 1923 *putsch* was written in 1930. *Erfolg* (*Success*) was a satire on a figure of fun, Rudolf Kutzner, who was easily recognized as the rising demagogue. *Erfolg* was perhaps the first anti-Nazi novel in world literature.

CECIL BLOOM

Fiedler, Leslie A.

US critic and fiction writer, 1917–

Born Leslie Aaron Fiedler in Newark, New Jersey, 8 March 1917. Studied at New York University, BA 1938; University of Wisconsin, Madison, MA 1939, PhD 1941. Married, first, Margaret Shipley, 1939; second, Sally Smith Anderson, 1973; six children. Has taught at University of Montana, 1941–65; State University of New York, Buffalo, since 1965. Rockefeller Fellow, Harvard University, 1946–47; Fulbright Lecturer, universities of Rome and Bologna, 1951–53, and Athens, 1961–62; Visiting Professor, Princeton University, 1956–57, University of Sussex, 1967–68, Yale University, 1969, University of Vincennes, 1971. Awarded Guggenheim Fellowship, 1970–71; National Book Critics Circle Ivan Sandrof Lifetime Achievement Award, 1998.

Selected Writings

Fiction

Pull Down Vanity and Other Stories, 1963
The Second Stone, 1963
Back to China, 1965
The Last Jew in America, 1966
Nude Croquet and Other Stories, 1969
The Messengers Will Come No More, 1974

Essays and Criticism
An End to Innocence, 1955
Love and Death in the American Novel, 1960
No! In Thunder, 1960
The Return of the Vanishing American, 1968
Being Busted, 1969
The Collected Essays, 2 vols, 1971
Cross the Border – Close the Gap, 1972
The Stranger in Shakespeare, 1972
The Leslie Fiedler Reader, 1977
Freaks: Myths and Images of the Secret Self, 1978
What Was Literature?, 1982
Fiedler on the Roof: Essays on Literature and Jewish Identity, 1991
Tyranny of the Normal: Essays on Bioethics, Theology and Myth, 1996

Further Reading

Kellman, Steven G. and Irving Malin (editors), *Leslie Fiedler and American Culture*, Newark: University of Delaware Press, 1999
McGowan, John, "Leslie A. Fiedler" in *Modern American Critics since 1955*, edited by Gregory S. Jay, Detroit: Gale, 1988 (Dictionary of Literary Biography, vol. 67)
Winchell, Mark Royden, *Leslie Fiedler*, Boston: Twayne, 1985

Leslie Fiedler, during the course of his long career, has managed continually to re-direct the field of American studies, prompting, for instance, the move away from postwar New Criticism, and anticipating the current focus on cultural studies and multiculturalism in the academy. He has done this while explicitly defining himself as a Jewish-American critic and scholar who was preoccupied for a good part of his career with Jewish-American writers. Fiedler was responsible to a great degree for reviving the reputations of such forgotten writers as Nathanael West and Henry Roth, has himself written fiction that featured Jewish characters and dealt explicitly with the Jewish experience in America, and has used Jewishness as a critical lens through which to read the Legend of the Grail Knight, Shakespeare, James Joyce, and the genre of science fiction.

The controversial (and still perhaps his best known) essay that launched Fiedler's reputation as a literary and critical maverick was published in the *Partisan Review* in June 1948, and was entitled "Come Back to the Raft Ag'in, Huck Honey!" The essay's thesis argued that the flight from civilization that characterizes so many classic American texts is actually a flight towards wilderness and towards a homosocial bonding of white and dark-skinned men, represented famously by Huck and Jim, Natty Bumppo and Chingachgook, Ishmael and Queequeg. Fiedler expanded this analysis in his influential *Love and Death in the American Novel*, the impact of which in the field of American studies was immense. Fiedler's brand of psychosexual, mytho-historical criticism was a breath of fresh air in an academic environment increasingly bogged down in "close reading" without reference to theoretical or historical context. Fiedler had written a PhD dissertation on John Donne, had then re-invented the study and teaching of the most classic American texts, and now proceeded to turn toward Jewish-American literature.

Most of Fiedler's essays on Jewish topics have been collected in the section entitled "To the Gentiles", in volume 2 of his *Collected Essays*, published in 1971. Many others can be found in his 1991 collection entitled *Fiedler on the Roof: Essays on Literature and Jewish Identity*. He wrote on such "Jewish" subjects as Ethel and Julius Rosenberg, Lionel Trilling, Simone Weil, and the *Partisan Review*. He became particularly interested in the vast body of cultural production that he termed the "middlebrow", which, he argued, had become the special province of the Jewish writer. The Jew in America, he proclaimed, had come to stand in for the American experience; the Jewish writer, in turn, had become the creator and mediator of American popular culture: the Superman comic strip, science fiction, Marjorie Morningstar, and Holden Caulfield, Fiedler was the first to point out, had all been created by Jews. Fiedler's best essays on the topic of Jewish literature and the Jewish writer are "The Jew in the American Novel", "Negro and Jew", and "Master of Dreams: The Jew in a Gentile World". But Jewish-American literature, Fiedler began to argue, was a genre that was ephemeral by nature. By 1991, Fiedler would write in his preface to *Fiedler on the Roof*:

> The very success of Jewish-American writers in thus becoming mouthpieces for all of America meant their disappearance as Jews, their assimilation into the anonymous mainstream of our culture . . . In any case, by the late sixties, though many of them continued to write and would for the next couple of decades, Jewish-American writers had ceased to seem central.

Fiedler, however, used Jewish culture as a referent and employed a Jewish sensibility even when he addressed such canonical writers as Shakespeare and Joyce. In *The Stranger in Shakespeare* Fiedler devoted a chapter to *The Merchant of Venice* (the "stranger" in Shakespeare is, in Fiedler's argument, Jew, black, and woman). The collection *Fiedler on the Roof* showcases his interest in Leopold Bloom, the Jewish protagonist of Joyce's *Ulysses* (in "Bloom on Joyce; or, Jokey for Jacob", and "Joyce and Jewish Consciousness"), as well as his provocative reading of the centrality of Jewishness to that most "goyish" of myths, the Grail Legend (in "Why is the Grail Knight Jewish?"). The connecting thread throughout his critical career has been Fiedler's enduring interest in otherness and outsiders, and the geographical and cultural margins, as embodied by the American West, in the stranger, the black, the Jew, the Indian (in *The Return of the Vanishing American*), and the "freak" (in *Freaks: Myths and Images of the Secret Self*). As John McGowan asserts, Fiedler's work has constantly concerned itself with "people on the margin of culture who embody its deepest fears and deepest urges".

Fiedler's own fiction also taps into his general concern with the alienated and marginalized, and his more particular concern with the Jew in America. "The Last Jew in America" takes place in the fictional Lewis and Clark City, located somewhere between Montana and Idaho. One of the three first Jewish men to settle the city is dying in a Catholic hospital, and the second tries to convince the third to organize a bedside Yom Kippur service for the dying man. The subject of the story, as of many of Fiedler's works of fiction, is the cultural and spiritual impoverishment of the city's (and America's) assimilated and secularized Jews. Even Jacob Moskowitz, the protagonist of the story, who thinks of himself as the "last Jew in America" no longer observes the tenets of his faith, and his only childhood memory is of deliberately breaking the Yom Kippur fast. The stories "Pull Down Vanity" and "Nude Croquet", as well as Fiedler's first novel *The Second Stone*, all deal with the theme of love among the intellectuals, most of whom, in Fiedler's fictional universe, happen to be Jewish.

In his famous 1969 essay "*Chutzpah* and *Pudeur*" Fiedler identified these two terms – one the Yiddish term for nerve or gall, and the other a French term for delicacy or gentility – as signifying the polarity in "our very understanding of what constitutes art and literature". He called most literary theory "*pudique*" – too genteel, bashful, obscuring. He issued a mandate for more "*chutzpahdik*" criticism; and indeed, among Fiedler's contributions to the field of literary studies has been the introduction of the feisty persona of the *chutzpahdik* critic. He helped to make Jewish-American literature a worthy subject of study, and inversely, transformed Jewishness into the literary critic's cultural asset.

RACHEL RUBINSTEIN

Fierstein, Harvey

US dramatist and actor, 1954–

Born Harvey Forbes Fierstein in Brooklyn, New York, 6 June 1954. Educated at Pratt Institute, Brooklyn, BFA 1973. Drag performer and actor from 1970; professional debut at Club 82 and La Mama Experimental Theatre Club, New York, 1971; roles in more than 60 plays and in several films. Many awards, including grants from Rockefeller and Ford foundations; Creative Artists Public Services grant; Obie, 1982; Tony, 1983 (for writing and acting), 1984; Oppenheimer Award, 1983; Drama Desk Award, 1983 (for writing and acting); Dramatists Guild Hull–Warriner Award, 1983; Los Angeles Drama Critics Circle Award, 1984; Ace Award, 1988.

Selected Writings

Plays
In Search of the Cobra Jewels, 1972
Freaky Pussy, 1973
Flatbush Tosca, 1975
The International Stud, 1978
Fugue in a Nursery, 1979
Widows and Children First!, 1979
Torch Song Trilogy: Three Plays, 1981
Spookhouse, 1982
La Cage aux Folles, 1983
Manny and Jake, 1987
Safe Sex, 1987
Forget Him, 1988
Legs Diamond, with Charles Suppon, 1988

Screenplays: *Torch Song Trilogy*, 1989; *The Celluloid Closet*, 1996

Further Reading

Furtado, Ken and Nancy Hellner, *Gay and Lesbian American Plays: An Annotated Bibliography*, Metuchen, New Jersey: Scarecrow Press, 1993
Helbing, Terry, *Gay and Lesbian Plays Today*, Portsmouth, New Hampshire: Heinemann, 1993

Harvey Fierstein was born in Brooklyn, New York, in 1954; his father was a handkerchief manufacturer and his mother a school librarian. He began his theatrical career at the age of 11, when he became a founding member of a drama group that met at the local Gallery Players Community Theater in Brooklyn. In 1973 he graduated from the Pratt Institute with a BFA.

As both writer and performer, Fierstein is best known for the three one-act plays he wrote between 1976 and 1979 that tell of Arnold Beckoff and his homosexual experiences in the AIDS era. These plays, namely *The International Stud*, *Fugue in a Nursery*, and *Widows and Children First!*, are known collectively as *Torch Song Trilogy* and were first produced in small Broadway theatres. In 1981 the modest production in which Fierstein was starring was transferred to Broadway where it became one of the longest ever running Broadway shows, clocking up 1222 performances. Fierstein became the first person to win Tony awards for best play (as writer) as well as best performer for the same production. He repeated his stage characterization of Arnold Beckoff for the substantially rewritten and condensed 1988 film version.

His performance is distinguished by daring, provocative humour which he delivers in an outrageously camp rasp of a voice that spits out challenge after challenge, while managing to combine poignancy with sharp, observational wit. Typically cynical is this line from *Torch Song Trilogy*: "Face it, a thing of beauty is a joy till sunrise." Fierstein's plays are daring because of their content. He deals with the difficult, controversial issues of homosexuality and its place in today's world and brings it to the consciousness of a mainstream audience. When he claimed to be the first "real live out-of-the-closet queer on Broadway" he was declaring not only his willingness to be a pioneer, but his acceptance of all the risks and responsibility that came with it. His unapologetic, direct language underlines the vulnerability of his situation, but it does not offend. It is clear that he understands ridicule and humiliation, even physical danger, so he has nothing to lose. The transference of *Torch Song Trilogy* from stage to film and its general release further increased and widened the audience base. Fierstein's book *La Cage aux Folles* based on the play by the French writer Jean Poiret and the ensuing film which was then made into a Broadway and West End musical reached an audience of vast proportions and was a great mainstream success. The sympathetic, yet unsentimental story of ageing homosexual lovers whose 20 years of domestic tranquillity are shattered when a son, of one of the couple, fathered during a one-night heterosexual fling, decides to the marry the daughter of a right-wing politician who wishes to meet the boy's parents. Fierstein's gay characters are affectionately portrayed and empathy is struck between them and an appreciative audience.

Fierstein's work is brave, but he is fortunate that his openness came at a time when such revelation, such public confession, was ready to be accepted into a culturally sophisticated New York society and some way beyond. His audiences welcomed his honesty and were fascinated by the inside views of a risky world that had been lived in fearful shadows. With Fierstein as catalyst, it could be acknowledged that another way of life existed as real and as natural as the heterosexual world:

> Try to imagine the world the other way around. Imagine that every movie, book, magazine, TV show, newspaper, commercial, billboard told you that you should be homosexual. But you know you're not and you know that for you this is right.

Yet he has acknowledged that the situation has not changed for many homosexuals today and his involvement with gay rights continues.

At the beginning of a new millennium, Fierstein has become part of the consciousness of the American public. In the *New York Times Magazine* of 28 May 2000, David France reviews the play *An Inconvenient Woman* which is about a soldier who is murdered because he is thought to be gay, but is in fact a heterosexual man who has fallen in love with a transsexual. France writes: "The fact is that Winchell [the hero], killed for being gay, wasn't gay, at least not in the traditional Harvey Fierstein sense of the word". Fierstein has come to represent the epitome of a gay man and has established a comfortable, acceptable image of homosexuality that is universally definable.

Safe Sex established him as a writer without the performance element. It is, as one might expected, about the gay world and gay love and his voice is as distinctive as ever in its outspoken, crude, but painfully honest humour. He is certainly a unique force for gay rights and shows how much art can reflect and influence life in a way that can challenge and even change the attitudes of a generation.

He revealed his views on his Jewish roots in 1995 when he appeared on Bill Maher's television talk show, *Politically Incorrect*. A panellist suggested that Fierstein must be in favour of menorahs (the candelabra used during the Jewish winter festival of Chanukah) being displayed alongside Christmas trees in public locations in the city. Fierstein disputed this and said that neither should be displayed and that though he is a Jew, he is also an atheist. He views religion as an intellectual and moral choice, while he identifies his sexuality as an unequivocal physical truth that is the essence of his being.

DEVRA KAY

Fink, Ida

Polish-born Israeli fiction writer and dramatist, 1921–

Born in Zbaraz, 11 January 1921. Studied piano at Conservatory of Music, Lwów; studies interrupted by outbreak of war between Nazi Germany and Soviet Union, 1941. Relocated to ghetto in Zbaraz, but escaped and survived war using papers indicating "Aryan" identity. Married Bruno Fink, 1948; one daughter. Emigrated to Israel, 1957. Worked for Yad Vashem, Tel Aviv, 1960–71; music librarian at Goethe Institute, Tel Aviv, 1971–83. Many awards, including Anne Frank Prize, 1985; Wizo Literary Prize, 1990; German Workers Union Television Prize, 1982.

Selected Writings

Fiction

Skrawek czasu, 1983; as *A Scrap of Time and Other Stories*, translated by Madeline Levine and Francine Prose, 1987

Podroz, 1990; as *The Journey*, translated by Joanna Weschler and Francine Prose, 1992

Traces: Stories, translated by Philip Boehm and Francine Prose, 1997

Plays

The Table, 1983; as radio play, 1971; as television play, 1981

A Trace, 1990

Further Reading

Adamiec, Marek, "*Skrawek czasu* Idy Fink" [*A Scrap of Time* of Ida Fink] in *W: Swiadectwa i powroty nieludzkiego czasu* [Testimonies and Returns of the Unhuman Time], edited by Jerzy Swiech, Lublin: Lublin University Press, 1990

Deveson, Richard, "Fictional Truth", *New Statesman* (27 September 1988)

Gorczynska, Renata, "A Scrap of Time and Other Stories", *Polish Review*, 29/4 (1984)

Horowitz, Sara R., *Voicing the Void: Muteness and Memory in Holocaust Fiction*, Albany: State University of New York Press, 1997

Kaplan, Johanna, "Bad Dreams", *New York Times Book Review* (15 December 1987)

Kiec, Izolda, *The Way of Ida Fink to the Dramatic Form*, Poznań: Poznań University Press, 1993

Maliszewska, Magdalena, "Testimony of Ida Fink", *Znak*, 11 (1988)

Merkin, Daphne, "A Stratagem of Survival", *Los Angeles Times Book Review* (21 September 1992)

Pilling, Jayne, "Acts of Excavation", *Times Literary Supplement* (26 August 1988)

Shaked, Gershon, "Shem, Ha-Mishak: Histardut" [The Name of the Play: Survival], *Yedi'ot Aharonot* (6 and 13 August 1983)

Wróbel, Józef, *Tematy żydowskie w prozie polskiej, 1939–1987* [Jewish Themes in Polish Literature], Kraków: Universitas, 1991

"I think that authenticity is the most important element in Holocaust literature", writes Israeli author Ida Fink. Born in Poland in 1921, she survived the war, escaping the ghetto in her hometown of Zbaraz with the Aryan documents of a Polish girl. Her own experience of having to forge and sustain a fiction to survive, of subverting the real (authentic) self in a fiction, shapes Fink's narrative universe. Authenticity is made as complex as it is urgent because of the destruction of her family and friends in Poland during the time of the Shoah. Fink is writing as survivor-witness from the "ruins of memory", against genocidal silence into language, inscribing "fear and despair, their loneliness and hope . . . their struggle for life while facing death . . . on the periphery of catastrophe."

Fink emigrated to Israel in 1957, and worked from 1960 to 1971 at Yad Vashem documenting the experiences and memories of other Jewish survivors. According to a biographical essay in *Contemporary Authors*, she delayed writing about her own experiences for more than ten years "in order to achieve the emotional distance that would allow her to write in the proper voice". Central and significant to her desire for an authentic narrative witness, she writes in Polish. Her first published collection of stories, *Skrawek czasu* in 1983 was translated to English in 1987 as *A Scrap of Time and Other Stories*. The stories are carefully constructed portraits of Zbaraz beginning in September 1939, when Poland fell to Nazi Germany. Fink translates memory into story in the language of those killed, achieving a nuanced fidelity to experience consistent with her desire for authenticity.

In the English-language version (translated by Madeline Levine and Francine Prose), these short stories, or scraps, are translated with attention to the volume and tone of the narrator, usually first-person. The stories unfold from a singular point of view, often that of a young girl, close to Fink's age at the time, keeping the focus and movement quieter, more intimate than the terror and chaos she is witnessing. The seeming simplicity of the narration preserves the sense of individuality in the face of a dehumanizing assault on Jewish life. By inscribing access to private thoughts in the comprehensive presence of annihilation, Fink writes against the genocidal erasure of a meaningful identity.

But it, too, is a kind of double life. This persistence of the private and individual cannot alter the fate of the lives it recalls. The stories of murdered friends and family are scraps indeed, pieces torn from a larger fabric; these scraps, however, bits and remainders, achieve a new significance because they are a new measure of the catastrophe. "A Scrap of Time", the first in the collection, begins by redefining time – a force memory defies (remembering over hours, days, years) and with which it must contend (forgetting over hours, days, years). As not-forgetting is the injunction after the Shoah, Fink redefines time to address the enormous rent and loss from 1939 onwards, narrating how radically it has altered language. Fink writes:

> Today, digging around in the ruins of memory, I found it fresh and untouched by forgetfulness. This time was measured not in months but in a word – we no longer said "in the beautiful month of May, but "after the first 'action,' or the second, or right before the third." We had different measures of time, we different ones, always different . . . we, who because of our difference were condemned once again, as we had been before in our history, we were condemned once again during this time measured not in months nor by the rising and setting of the sun, but by a word – "action," a word signifying movement, a word you would use about a novel or a play.

Fink simultaneously intones a continuum of specifically Jewish suffering (condemned once again) and the singularity of the catastrophic losses life and culture sustained in the Nazi campaign for a world *judenrein*.

That knowledge requires a new understanding of history, and therefore of language, as the scribe and archivist of history. That the new history is composed not of sustained and epic poetry or prose, but represented most authentically in precisely-conceived scraps, is both a lament for what is lost, as well as a bid for how one might accurately remember radical suffering. Fink speaks to language as well as memory here, looking into the eye of the word "action" for its textual identity: from action, one does something. If a woman takes "action", she is sure to change a thing or two. But Fink reverses this action, turning it into a terminal and fatal movement, conveying the Nazi perversion onto language – a beautiful May morning become an action, no longer a beautiful event but an action – *Arbeit macht frei*. The point of reference is no longer the sun or moon or seasons, calendar or clock; lives are no longer marked by these conventional referents. Rather, in the same way that lived experience was altered by the catastrophe, so too is language. There is an inaccurate desolation that characterizes a text clinging to an hour or day in such a time; further, that kind of inaccuracy in diction and form further silences the actual experiences of those who suffered. To claim the correct language, then, is to remember with veracity, to make language by experience, to leave memory's trace in the collective text.

JEANIE M. TIETJEN

Fleg, Edmond

Swiss-born French poet, essayist, and dramatist, 1874–1963

Born Edmond Flegheimer in Geneva, 26 November 1874. Studied at schools in Geneva and at the Sorbonne; *licence de lettres*. Became theatre critic and dramatist in Paris; outlook affected by Dreyfus affair, 1894–1906, and first three Zionist congresses, 1897–99. Married Madeleine Bernheim, 1907; two sons. Volunteered for Foreign Legion in World War I; Croix de Guerre, 1918. Became French citizen, 1921. Honorary President of Éclaireurs Israélites de France; member of Alliance Israélite Universelle; founding member of committee of l'Amitié judéo-chrétienne; member of National Committee of Writers. Forest in Israel dedicated in his honour, 1952. Died 1963.

Selected Writings

Le Message [The Message], 1904
La Bête [The Beast], 1910
Libretto for Ernest Bloch's *Macbeth*, 1910
Écoute Israël [Hear Israel], 1913–21
Le Mur des pleurs: poème, 1919; as *The Wall of Weeping*, translated by Humbert Wolfe, 1929
Le Psaume de la terre promise [The Psalm of the Promised Land], 1919
Editor, *Anthologie juive des origines à nos jours*, 1921; as

The Jewish Anthology, translated by Maurice Samuel, 1925
La Terre de promesses [The Land of Promises], 1924
Le Juif du Pape [The Pope's Jew], 1925
L'Enfant prophète, 1926; as *The Boy Prophet*, translated by D.L. Orna, 1928
Moïse raconté par les Sages, 1928; as *The Life of Moses*, translated by Stephen Haden Guest, 928
Pourquoi je suis juif, 1928; as *Why I am a Jew*, translated by Louise Waterman Wise, 1929, and by Victor Gollancz, 1943
Le Marchand de Paris [The Paris Merchant], 1929
Salomon, 1930; as *The Life of Solomon*, translated by Viola Gerard Garvin, 1930
Ma Palestine, 1932; as *The Land of Promise*, translated by Louise Waterman Wise, 1933
Jesus, raconté par le Juif errant, 1933; as *Jesus, Told by the Wandering Jew*, translated by Phyllis Mégroz, 1934
Libretto for Georges Enesco's *Oedipe*, 1936 (first performance)
Apocalypse, 1938
L'Éternel est Notre Dieu [The Lord is God], 1940
L'Éternel est Un [The Lord is One], 1945
Et Tu Aimeras l'Éternel [And You Shall Love the Lord], 1948
Nous de l'Espérance [We, of Hope], 1949
La Terre que Dieu habite, 1953; as *The Land in which God Dwells*, 1955
Vers le Monde qui vient [Towards the Coming World], 1960
Le Chant nouveau [The New Song], 1971

Further Reading

Elbaz, André E., "L'Évolution d'Edmond Fleg à la suite de l'affaire Dreyfus", *Archives juives*, 9 (1972–73)
Elbaz, André E. (editor), *Correspondance d'Edmond Fleg pendant l'affaire Dreyfus*, Paris: Nizet, 1976
Roussel, Odile, *Un Itinéraire spiritual: Edmond Fleg*, Paris: La Pensée Universelle, 1978

Edmond Fleg's writing exemplifies the philosophy of emancipated, modern Judaism in the pre-Holocaust era. His Jewishness was intricately interwoven with his European, or more specifically, French, identity, and this hybridity constitutes his primary contribution to and vision for Jewish literature. Although Fleg was born Swiss, he always maintained strong ties with France. His parents, both of Alsacian origin, encouraged him to pursue his studies in Paris, which he did at the age of 18. After applying for French citizenship in 1921, he wrote to his close friend Ernest Bloch:

> [my application] is the natural result of a twenty-five year evolution and of four and a half years spent in French uniform. I feel, very strongly, the Jewish tradition and the French tradition merging in me; I see them taking shape in my work, as in my sensitivity; and I feel that they will continue to blend into the soul of my children. It is a great moment in my life.

Indeed, Fleg felt that each identity complemented and enhanced the other, both in his life and his literature.

Fleg's life provides a rich example of constructions of identity and feelings of national allegiance under the Third Republic. Although Fleg's French naturalization was the logical result of the way he felt himself to be more French than Swiss, what is fascinating about his example is that in addition to his desire to be a French citizen in compliance with the norms of the Third Republic, he insisted on adhering to his religious affiliation in a public way, an ideological contradiction to that which he aspired to become. Similar to his contemporaries, Fleg incorporated his particular Jewish identity into his public persona. He participated in the French Jewish literary renaissance movement that began in 1925 and reached its apogee in 1928. What distinguished Fleg from his peers, however, was his desire and ability to go *beyond* questions of national versus ethnic affiliations. He considered his identity not only within the parameters of Judaism, but more importantly, within the larger context of a Jewish–Christian dialogue. He defined himself as a Jew, but not in opposition to French or Christian identity. Rather, Fleg defined his Judaism in conjunction with and in relation to Frenchness. He was able to define himself publicly as a Jew only once he understood Judaism's relationship to France and Christianity.

Fleg's interest in Jewish identity began in 1897 when the Dreyfus affair, and the rampant anti-Semitism that accompanied it, caused him to rethink and postpone his French naturalization. In 1921 Fleg compiled the *Anthologie juive* (*The Jewish Anthology*), a collection of writing by, for, and about Jews. This anthology served to "give a succinct idea not only of Israel's literary tradition, but also its historic, religious, judicial, philosophical, moral, sentimental, and political traditions, from the Middle Ages to today." The *Anthologie*, which is no longer in print, followed the history of the Jewish people, from Genesis up to 1920. Fleg incorporated texts from selected time periods to illustrate the history and culture of the Jewish people.

Of all the events in Fleg's life that had an impact on the ways in which he conceived of his Jewish identity, the most important one was the birth of his first son in 1908. This event catalysed his desire to examine his own life as a Jew and to transcend his mortality to become a part of his living ancestry. Fleg wished to pass on his Jewish identity to his son in *L'Enfant prophète* (*The Boy Prophet*), a semi-autobiographical work that traced a small boy's discovery of what it meant to be Jewish in France. *L'Enfant prophète* emblematized the ways in which assimilated Jews in France may have struggled with their own identities within the context of the Third Republic.

Fleg went on to dedicate his best-known work, *Pourquoi je suis juif* (*Why I am a Jew*) to his as-yet-unborn grandson in 1928. About this work, Gilbert Werndorfer stated that Fleg "describes the universality of the Jewish message and the urgency for future generations to stay close to its precepts which are the source of the Jewish people's power and durability. Fleg guides his unborn grandson, who symbolizes future generations, and gently directs him to the pure path which so inspires the Jewish message: humanism."

Fleg continued his discussion of Judaism within a comparative context of Christianity and Judaism in his play, *Le*

Juif du Pape [The Pope's Jew]. Once again, Fleg stressed the important similarities between these religions. Influenced by Isaiah, Fleg stated:

> Both the Jew and Christian believe that, in order to enter the celestial kingdom, they must try to establish it down here: the Jew waits for the Messiah to come, the Christian waits for the Messiah to come back; and, as I indicated in *The Pope's Jew*, in this wait lies the same hope.

In addition to essays, plays, poetry, and novels, Fleg also wrote in hybrid genres. *Jésus raconté par le Juif errant* (*Jesus, Told by the Wandering Jew*), for example, combined the personal memoir with third-person narrative as well as biblical interpretation. Similar to *Le Juif du Pape*, this work stressed the topoi common to both Judaism and Christianity. Again, Fleg framed these similarities in terms of hope for world peace. Fleg's use of many genres allowed him to express different parts of his identity, but it is in the space found between genres that he finally conveyed a complete identity as a French and Jewish author. Fleg wrote within the French tradition, constantly conscious of and influenced by Jewish literary tradition. His intellectual project demanded that he utilize several genres in the hope of creating a single new genre – that of French-Jewish writing.

NANCY GREY

Fried, Erich

Austrian-born British poet, fiction writer, and dramatist, 1921–1988

Born in Vienna, 6 May 1921. Emigrated to United Kingdom, 1938; settled in London. Married, first, Maria Marburg, 1944; divorced; second, Nan Spence, 1951; divorced; third, Katherine Boswell, 1965; divorced; two sons, two daughters. Worked as chemist, librarian, editor, translator, and freelance writer. Co-editor of periodical *Blick in die Welt*, London, 1950–52; programme assistant and commentator for BBC Radio German Service, 1952–68. Many awards, including International Publishers' Prize, 1977; Austrian Würdigungspreis für Literatur, 1973; Bremer Literaturpreis, 1983; Georg Büchner Preis, 1987. Died in Baden-Baden, Germany, 22 November 1988.

Selected Writings

Poetry
Deutschland: Gedichte [Germany: Poems], 1944
Österreich: Gedichte [Austria: Poems], 1946
Gedichte [Poems], 1958
Reich der Steine: Zyklische Gedichte [Realm of Stones], 1963
Überlegungen [Reflections], 1964
Warngedichte [Poems of Warning], 1964
Indizienbeweise [Circumstantial Evidence], 1966
Und Vietnam und . . . 41 Gedichte [And Vietnam and . . . 41 Poems], 1966
Anfechtungen: 50 Gedichte [Arguments: 50 Poems], 1967
Zeitfragen: Gedichte [Contemporary Questions: Poems], 1967
Befreiung von der Flucht: Gedichte und Gegengedichte [Deliverance from Flight: Poems and Counter-Poems], 1968
Last Honours, translated by George Rapp, 1968
Die Beine der Grösseren Lügen: 51 Gedichte [Legs of the Bigger Lies: 51 Poems], 1969
On Pain of Seeing, translated by George Rapp, 1969
Unter Nebenfeinden: 50 Gedichte [Under Neighbouring Enemies: 50 Poems], 1970
Aufforderung zur Unruhe [Challenge to Restlessness], 1972
Die Freiheit den Mund aufzumachen: 48 Gedichte [The Freedom to Open One's Mouth: 48 Poems], 1972
Gegengift: 49 Gedichte und ein Zyklus [Antidote: 49 Poems and One Cycle], 1974
Höre, Israel! [Hear O Israel], 1974
So kam ich unter die Deutschen [Thus I Found Myself among the Germans], 1977
Die bunten Getüme: 70 Gedichte [Coloured Costumes: 70 Poems], 1978
100 Gedichte ohne Vaterland, 1978; as *100 Poems without a Country*, translated by Stuart Hood, 1978
Liebesgedichte [Love Poems], 1979
Lebensschatten: Gedichte [Shadows of Life: Poems], 1981
Zur Zeit und zur Unzeit: Gedichte [Timely and Untimely: Poems], 1981
Das Nahe suchen [Seeking the Near], 1982
Es ist was es ist: Gedichte [It is What It Is], 1983
Beunruhigungen: Gedichte [Causes for Restlessness], 1984
In die Sinne einradiert [Engraved into the Senses], 1985
Um Klarheit: Gedichte gegen das Vergessen [Concerning Clarity: Poems against Forgetting], 1985
Frühe Gedichte [Early Poems], 1986
Wächst das Rettende auch? Gedichte für den Frieden [Is Salvation Growing Too? Poems for Peace], 1986
Am Rand unsere Lebenszeit [At the Boundary of our Lifetime], 1987
Gegen das Vergessen [Lest we Forget], 1987
Vorübungen für Wunder [(Preliminary) Exercises/Studies for Wonder], 1987
Unverwundenes: Liebe, Trauer, Widersprüche [Not yet Overcome], 1988
Einblicke, Durchblicke: Fundstücke und Werkstattberichte aus dem Nachlass [Insights and Findings: Reports from the Laboratory of the Unpublished Works], 1993

Novels
Ein Soldat und ein Mädchen [A Soldier and a Girl], 1960

Short Stories
Kinder und Narren, 1965; as *Children and Fools*, translated by Martin Chambers, 1992
Fast alles Mögliche [Almost Everything Possible], 1975
Das Unmass aller Dinge [The Excess of All Things], 1982

Other
They Fight in the Dark: The Story of Austria's Youth, 1944
Translator, *Unter dem Milchwald* (*Under Milk Wood*), by Dylan Thomas, 1958

Translator, *Ein verdienter Staatsmann*, by T.S. Eliot, 1959
Translator, *Der verbindliche Liebhaber*, by Graham Greene, 1960
Translator, *Die Bacchantinnen*, by Euripides, 1960
Translator, *Ein Sommernachtstraum* (*A Midsummers Night's Dream*), by William Shakespeare, 1964
Arden muss sterben; as *Arden Must Die*, translated by Geoffrey Skelton, 1967
Angst und Trost: Erzählungen und Gedichte über Juden und Nazis [Fear and Consolation: Stories and Poems about Jews and Nazis], 1983
Translator, *Lysistrata*, by Aristophanes, 1985

Further Reading

Fried-Boswell, Catherine and Volker Kaukoreit (editors), *Erich Fried: ein Leben in Bildern und Geschichten*, Berlin: Wagenbach, 1996
Goodbody, Axel, "Erich Fried – German, Jew, British and Socialist: The Composite Identity of an Austrian Émigré" in *From High Priests to Desecrators: Contemporary Austrian Writers*, edited by Ricarda Schmidt and Moray McGowan, Sheffield: Sheffield Academic Press, 1993
Kane, Martin, "From Solipsism to Engagement: The Development of Erich Fried as a Political Poet", *Forum for Modern Language Studies*, 21 (1985)
Lawrie, Steven W., *Erich Fried: A Writer without a Country*, New York: Peter Lang, 1996

"Erich Fried wrote some of the worst poems of our time, and he wrote some of the best poems" stated the critic Helmud Mader in *Die Zeit* in 1968. And he added "I refer to his political, his public poems." No one could ever be neutral about Fried: Fried himself fought against his own work. His "Poems and Counter Poems" of 1968 challenged a work published in 1958 which contained his work between 1946 and 1957. Thus, an early poem about the exodus: "they sent out the wild soldiers/ into the desert sand/ no messenger" is balanced by a post-Six Day War poem: "Since Moses/ it is considered good/ that Egyptians die/ their death/ is seen as just punishment. The war against them/ should be different/ than all other wars . . ." Fried did not want to deny his past work, but insisted upon showing progress within himself. Fried's *Hear O Israel* carries the motto: "When you were persecuted/ I was one of you./ How can I remain this/ when you are the persecutors?" In his Bremen Prize acceptance speech "I Must not Accustom Myself" he cited his poem "Entwöhnung" [Weaning]:

> I should not murder
> I should not betray
> I know that
> I must learn a third law: I must not accustom myself . . .
> If I even just accustom myself to the beginning
> I begin to accustom myself to the end.

Erich Fried grew up in the "red" Vienna, which was also the city of Sigmund Freud, Max Reinhardt, and Karl Kraus. When he was six, he saw the Justizpalast burn to the ground while the stretchers of the dead and wounded moved past him. That world changed, and his father was beaten to death by the Gestapo in 1938. Erich escaped to London and was a labourer, a chemist, a librarian, a worker in a glass factory – always to support his writings. And he was always a rebel. He wrote: "I decided then, if I should survive, to become a writer fighting against fascism, racism, against the expulsion of the innocent." Fried joined the communist-dominated Free German Cultural Association but broke with them by 1945. He had begun writing in 1939, and his poetry attracted attention, in part because of its political commitment. As a BBC commentator, he sympathized with but was also critical of the developments of socialism in Europe. The younger generation followed him closely, and his speeches and poetry readings attracted a large public. As *Der Spiegel* noted: "the poems of Fried are a tool which demystifies the developments of our time. They illuminate their hidden depths and bring them out into the area where they can be recognised."

The body of his work is impressive. More than 50 books, some of them great love poetry; any number of essays, lectures, reviews; well received radio plays; and, just as important, his great translations of English texts into German. A number of his Shakespeare translations were taught in the schools. This earned him the Schiller Förder Prize in Stuttgart. Fried's Dylan Thomas texts are marvels of style and perception, and he also translated T.S. Eliot, Sylvia Plath, J.M. Synge, Arnold Wesker, and a variety of American writers.

Fried only wrote one novel, *Ein Soldat und ein Mädchen* [A Soldier and a Girl], most of it written when he was a young man, but published only in 1960. It is a strange tale, almost incoherent, with autobiographical aspects, and yet deeply moving. As the story of Helga, the concentration camp criminal sentenced to death, and of the American soldier who guards her before her execution, it carries all of the tensions of the post-Auschwitz time into a human situation that cannot simply decide upon guilt and innocence. It is a profoundly disturbing book.

Nevertheless, one has to turn back to Fried's prose and poetry and to his own life in order to understand the impact he made on our time. His work contained a biblical dimension, and his parables are almost rabbinic. In a memorable retelling of Cain and Abel, it is Abel, in the end, who kills Cain. Fried's life included priests and rabbis, communists and neo-fascists; and he changed them more than they changed him. The Hebrew concept of *tikkun ha-olam*, the task of changing the world, lived in his writings and in his daily life. As he once wrote: "Whoever desires/ that the world/ should remain as it is/ does not desire/ that it remains."

ALBERT H. FRIEDLANDER

Friedman, Bruce Jay

US fiction writer and dramatist, 1930–

Born in New York City, 26 April 1930. Studied at De Witt Clinton High School, Bronx, New York; University of Missouri, Columbia, 1947–51, Bachelor of Journalism

1951. Served in the US Air Force, 1951–53: Lieutenant. Married, first, Ginger Howard, 1954; divorced 1977; three children; second, Patricia J. O' Donohue, 1983; one daughter. Editorial director, Magazine Management Company, New York, 1953–56. Visiting Professor of Literature, York College, City University of New York, 1974–76.

Selected Writings

Novels
Stern, 1962
A Mother's Kisses, 1964
The Dick, 1970
About Harry Towns, 1974
Tokyo Woes, 1985
Violencia, 1988
The Current Climate, 1990
The Slightly Older Guy, 1995
A Father's Kisses: A Novel, 1996

Short Stories
Far from the City of Class and Other Stories, 1963
Black Angels, 1966
Let's Hear It for a Beautiful Guy and Other Works of Short Fiction, 1984
The Collected Short Fiction of Bruce Jay Friedman, 1995

Plays
23 Pat O'Brien Movies, 1966
Scuba Duba: A Tense Comedy in Two Acts, 1967
A Mother's Kisses, 1968
Steambath, 1970
First Offenders, with Jacques Levy, 1973
A Foot in the Door, 1979

Screenplays: *The Owl and the Pussycat*, 1971; *Stir Crazy*, 1980; *Doctor Detroit*, 1983; *Splash*, 1984

Other
Editor, *Black Humor*, 1965
The Lonely Guy's Book of Life, 1978

Further Reading

Klein, M., "Further Notes on the Dereliction of Culture: Edward Lewis Wallant and Bruce Jay Friedman" in *Contemporary America-Jewish Literature*, edited by Irving Malin, Bloomington: Indiana University Press, 1973
Schulz, Max F., *Bruce Jay Friedman*, New York: Twayne, 1974

Bruce Jay Friedman is a remarkably prolific writer. Since publishing his first novel, *Stern*, in 1962 he has produced at least eight novels, several collections of short stories and short fiction (mostly culled from the *New Yorker*, *Harpers*, *Esquire*, and *Playboy*) several screenplays, a few stage plays, works of criticism, and journalism, and edited a couple of anthologies, and yet he is little known outside his native United States.

He has been very active, and presumably financially successful as a writer for the movies, including among his credits such box-office successes as *Stir Crazy*. His lack of a high profile outside the United States may be due to his being overshadowed by an outstanding conglomeration of coevals, both Jewish and non-Jewish, such as Philip Roth, Joseph Heller, Thomas Pynchon, John Barth, John Updike, and Vladimir Nabokov, all of whom were at one time classified as practitioners of "Black Humor", a taxonomy Friedman himself first coined. It was the title he gave to an anthology he edited in 1965 which included, in addition to works by himself, pieces by Terry Southern, J.P. Donleavy, Edward Albee, John Barth, Nabokov, Pynchon, Celine, and Heller among others – all authors who shared a jaundiced view of their contemporary world, which they considered a cosmic joke, but who found delight in the absurdities and coincidences they observed, and expressed their vision with deadly serious, often surrealistic, humour. This was in contrast to the existentialist approach of their immediate predecessors of the 1950s, such as Bellow, Malamud, and Mailer.

Until then Friedman had enjoyed critical but little commercial success and as a family man money was a major concern. *Black Humor* sold well. Although taken up for a short while as a useful umbrella under which to include a number of then-contemporary writers, Friedman always rejected the use of "Black Humor" as an all-embracing description given the diversity of techniques employed by the writers he included. For his own work he preferred the term "tense comedy".

His fiction is quintessentially American and for the most part New York Jewish. Beginning with *Stern* virtually all his main protagonists are Jewish males who do not share the conventional assumptions of either their co-religionists or their middle-class neighbours. In bucking trends or following his own logic the Friedman hero often has to contend with a devouring virago mother and / or an inconstant wife, and always a preposterous world of chance, indirection, and odd coincidence – a *reductio ad absurdum* world.

Perhaps another reason for the lack of fame, indeed for the most part lack of publication, outside the United States, is the highly parochial nature of many of his references. Typical is a 1963 story "When You're Excused, You're Excused". A semi-conventional New York Jew, Mr Kessler, invokes strict theology in order to justify his attendance at the gym on Yom Kippur. This is done on grounds of health needs ("when you're excused, you're excused") but leads through the same rationalization to a night of sex with a girl named Irish, drunkenness, eating ham, smoking marijuana, hiding a dead cop, and being kissed by a homosexual black man. However his ethnic pride is finally aroused when he violently assaults a man who fails to recognize the existence of an unknown Jewish baseball player "Phumblin' Phil' Weintraub". As Kessler says "I may have been excused, but I wasn't that excused."

Friedman's protagonists do not judge, do not express a point of view. Rather they observe and react, making the best of the hazardous, apparently meaningless, obviously absurd, journey we all have to undertake. From *Stern* in 1962 to *A Father's Kisses* in 1996 this has been a constant motif. It also informs his successful off-Broadway plays *Scuba Duba* and *Steambath*. In all his work outside of screenplays Friedman casts a critical eye over the social, religious, and commercial conventions of his society. In *Steambath*, for instance, a New York public steambath is used as symbol of purgatory. It is run by a Puerto Rican (Marty), who seems to be God, and who has a Jewish assistant Gottleib ("The lover of God") .

In common with other writers of the 1960s Friedman was initially criticized for lack of constructive views by the Knight on a White Charger school of literary evaluation, but with the passing of time and the ubiquity of his kind of vision such voices are hardly heard. Despite his large output he does not receive the academic or critical attention or acclaim of some of the other writers included in his *Black Humor* anthology. He has ploughed a narrower field than most of them and has often seemed to be repeating himself with some concomitant loss of verve and energy. One of his most successful novels, *About Harry Towns*, was followed in 1990 by *The Current Climate* in which Harry reappears at age 57. The sequel, while it had its comic moments, was generally seen to be a poor follow-up to the original.

Friedman combines surrealism with vaudevillian humour in a straightforward narrative delivered in simple, often demotic, language. Critics have compared him to Pinter, Mamet, Woody Allen, and Salinger and similarities can be discerned in much of his writing. It is not that he is imitative, rather that he shares a viewpoint and a sensibility with others maturing in the same environment and reacting in much the same way. As Max Schulz puts it in the only extended analysis of his work, "[it] is the response of a sensitive individual to America at mid-century – to a culture defined by the movies and television, by billboards and flashing neon signs, by psychology textbooks and pornographic paperbacks . . . by assassinations and the Vietnam War . . ."

Friedman is by no means at the end of his career, and given the fertility of his talent we may not yet have seen the best of him. In the meantime we have an excellent writer who has cast a valuable, objective, always amusing, eye on the contemporary American scene and given us a handful of first-rate novels and short stories.

GERALD DE GROOT

G

Gary, Romain

Russian-born French fiction writer, 1914–1980

Born Roman Kacew in Moscow, 8 May 1914. Pseudonyms: Émile Ajar, Shatan Bogat, René Deville, Fosco Sinibaldi. Moved with mother to Vilna (Vilnius), 1917, and to Poland, 1921. Emigrated to France, 1927; settled in Nice. Studied law in Aix-en-Provence, 1933, and in Paris, 1934. Studied aviation and served in French air force; after French surrender, 1940, joined Free French forces in London. Married the actress Jean Seberg, 1963; divorced. Returned to France and became diplomat: in Paris, 1948; Berne, 1949; La Paz, 1956; Los Angeles, as Consul-General, 1956–61. Awarded Prix Goncourt, 1956 and 1975. Committed suicide in Paris, 2 December 1980.

Selected Writings

Novels

Forest of Anger, translated by Viola Gerard Garvin, 1944; original French as *Éducation Européenne*, 1945; as *A European Education* and *Nothing Important Ever Dies*, 1960

Tulipe [Tulip], 1946

Le Grand Vestiaire, 1948; as *The Company of Men*, translated by Joseph Barnes, 1950

Les Racines du ciel, 1956; as *The Roots of Heaven*, translated by Jonathan Griffin, 1958

L'Homme à la colombe [The Man with the Dove], 1958 (as Fosco Sinibaldi)

Lady L., 1963 (adapted from the English, 1959)

Le Mangeur d'Étoiles, 1966; as *The Talent Scout*, translated by John Markham Beach, 1961

The Ski Bum, 1966; as *Adieu Gary Cooper*, translated by the author, 1969

La Danse de Gengis Cohn, 1967; as *The Dance of Gengis Cohn*, translated by the author and Camilla Sykes, 1969

La Tête coupable, 1968; as *The Guilty Head*, 1969

Europa, 1972; as *Europa*, translated by R.G. Bray and Barbara Bray, 1978

Les Enchanteurs, 1973; as *The Enchanters*, translated by Helen Eustis, 1975

Gros-Câlin, 1974 (as Émile Ajar)

Les Têtes de Stéphanie, 1974 (as Shatan Bogat); as *Direct Flight to Allah*, translated by J. Maxwell Brownjohn, 1975

Au-delà de cette limite votre ticket n'est plus valable, 1975; as *Your Ticket is No Longer Valid* and *The Way Out*, translated by Sophie Wilkins, 1977

La Vie devant soi, 1975 (as Émile Ajar); as *The Life before Us*, translated by Ralph Manheim, 1986

L'Angoisse du roi Salomon, 1979 (as Émile Ajar); as *King Solomon*, translated by Barbara Wright, 1983

Les Cerfs-volants [The Kites], 1980

Other

La Promesse de l'aube, 1960; as *Promise at Dawn*, translated by John Markham Beach, 1962

Pour Sganarelle, recherche d'un roman et d'un personnage [For Sganarelle: Research on a Novel and a Character], 1965

La Nuit sera calme [The Night Will be Calm], 1974

Vie et Mort d'Émile Ajar [Life and Death of Émile Ajar], 1981

Further Reading

Bayard, Pierre, *Il était deux fois Romain Gary* [Twice upon a Time Romain Gary], Paris: Presses Universitaires de France, 1990

Bona, Dominique, *Romain Gary*, Paris: Mercure de France, 1987

Huston, Nancy, *Tombeau de Romain Gary* [Romain Gary's Tomb], Arles: Actes Sud, 1995

Lehrmann, Chanan, *L'Élément juif dans la Littérature Française*, 2nd edition, 2 vols, Paris: Albin Michel, 1960–61; as *The Jewish Element in French Literature*, translated by George Klin, Rutherford, New Jersey: Fairleigh Dickinson University Press, 1971

Livres de France, special issue, 18/3 (1967)

Mehlman, Jeffrey, "The Holocaust Comedies of 'Émile Ajar'" in *Genealogies of the Text: Literature, Psychoanalysis and Politics in Modern France*, Cambridge: Cambridge University Press, 1995

When it came to discussing his Jewish identity, Romain Gary was wont to convey his bad temper. To his life-long friend François Bondy, he recounted how once he had been approached by the Israeli editors of a *Who's Who in World Jewry* who were considering him for an entry. As instructed he filled out the questionnaire, sent it to Tel Aviv, and awaited a response. It turned out that according to the editors he did not possess the qualities necessary to be included.

> They are, you understand, more watchful than Rosenberg and Himmler . . . They determine who has the right and who doesn't have the right to the gas chamber . . . So I get pissed off, I remind them that my mother was Mosaic, Jewish, that it's the mother, it appears, who counts for *us*, and that if they don't get me into the *Who's Who*, I'm going to make a public stink . . . Dead silence and then I'm made the object of a very courteous diplomatic visit in the proper meaning of the term during which I'm given an hour of theological, official, and technical explanations which amount to that over there the law determines who has the right to the gas chamber and who doesn't have the right . . . The Germans, in this sense, were broader minded.

When Bondy asked him what it meant to be a Jew, Gary remarked, "It is a way of making myself annoyed". Judaism in Gary's writings is not a self-evident, unproblematical subject. As his bilious conversation with Bondy suggests, Gary perceived the Jew in himself with despair. This is reflected in his novels, where in an awkward, sometimes erotic relationship made all the more challenging for its verbal charm and wit, Judaism mixes, fraternally at moments, with Christianity; Jews with blacks and Arabs; and the elderly with the young. Author, too, fuses with hero.

One source of renewed creativity in Gary's novels is the frequent use of a pseudonym. Among them are Fosco Sinibaldi, Shatan Bogat, or, most famously, Émile Ajar, author of four of Gary's last works and recipient, like Gary himself in 1956 for *The Roots of Heaven*, of the Prix Goncourt for *The Life before Us*. Gary's nephew Paul Pavlowitch was said to be the author of Ajar's memoir, *Pseudo*; a real, fictional author (Pavlowitch) had plausibly replaced the fictional one (Ajar), thereby proliferating confusion among Ajar's readers. The patronymic "Gary" is itself a fabrication, the author having been named Roman Kacew after his presumed father whom he never knew.

One motif in his novels, associated with the multiple use of a pseudonym as a protective measure, is the hiding place. In *Forest of Anger*, written between bombing raids as a pilot in General De Gaulle's Free France and hailed by Sartre as possibly the greatest novel of the Resistance, an adolescent, Janek Twardowski and his father, a member of the Polish underground, dig a hole in the wood outside of Vilna in which Janek hides before he himself becomes a partisan. The child hero of the autobiographical *Promise at Dawn*, a tribute to the author's mother, constucts a forest refuge in which he escapes the madness of the adult world. In one of the novels signed Émile Ajar, *The Life before Us*, Madame Rosa, an elderly Jewish woman who had worked as a prostitute and who had been deported to Auschwitz, and who now takes on orphaned children of younger Jewish, Arab, Vietnamese, and black prostitutes, keeps a "Jew hole", her "secondary residence", in the basement of her building in Paris' Belleville quarter where she hides – long after the end of the war – when she senses the threat of a round-up. In the final Ajar novel, *King Solomon*, a young man goes to work for the ageing hero, Salomon Rubinstein, who directs a telephone help line for other senior citizens. Jeannot answers the call of an old friend of Monsieur Salomon from the war years, a faded singer in the Fréhel mode called Mademoiselle Cora, from whom he learns that Monsieur Salomon had hidden, "as a Jew", in the basement of a building along the Champs-Elysées.

Judaism as theme or character appears in many of Gary's novels. References can be minor, but they are no less moving for their brevity. In *Forest of Anger*, for instance, one Friday evening in the hideout of the young Polish partisans Yankel Cukier puts on his tallis and begins to pray. However, only in mid-career does Judaism, and precisely the Shoah, enter Gary's novels with force. *The Dance of Gengis Cohn*, dated Warsaw 1966, tells the story of a dibbuk, in life a Jewish comedian in Berlin cabarets, who following the war takes possession of the conscience of Schatz, the German soldier responsible for his murder. (The "Jew hole" here assumes a negative value; it is the grave-pit Cohn and the other Jews were forced to dig before being shot.) Cohn makes Schatz learn Yiddish, eat kosher, and recite the *Kaddish*; it seems that the Jew controls the former Nazi's mind. We learn, however, that Cohn is in fact at the mercy of the body he inhabits. Gary resolves their perverse mutual dependence by intervening directly into the narrative, explaining the origins of this sadistic allegory of postwar memory: that following a visit to Warsaw's museum of the resistance with his then wife, the American actress Jean Seberg, Gary fainted, overcome by his self-identification with the Jews of the ghetto with whom he had previously not sympathized.

The Kites, Gary's final novel, recalls the anti-fascist stance of his first, *Forest of Anger*. Set in France shortly before, during, and after World War II, it relates the relationship of Ludo and his uncle Ambroise Fleury, a kite-maker. In protest of the July 1942 Vel' d'Hiv' round-up of Parisian Jews, Fleury makes seven kites in the shape of Jewish stars, each yellow, and sets them aflight. The Germans arrest him. After being released from a short detention Fleury flees to the village of Le Chambon-sur-Lignon, whence he sends his nephew a photograph of himself surrounded by children with a message on the back that reads, "Everything *here* is fine. *Here* was underlined." It is only after the war that Ludo learns that it was in Chambon-sur-Lignon that the Protestant pastor André Trocmé and his wife, along with the other villagers, had protected Jewish children from deportation. The novel begins with the dedication, "To Memory", and it ends with Ludo's recollection of Trocmé and the others, "for one could not put it any better".

In 1980 Gary refused the Prix Paul-Morand, newly established by the French Academy, unwilling to associate himself with the "Petainist" personality of the writer after whom the prize was called. The same year he had *The Kites* sent to each of his fellow Companions of the Liberation. In December he was found dead, in his apartment on the rue du Bac in Paris, a bullet wound to the mouth. A suicide note lay nearby. In the end the novelist who had so effectively used irony to oppose the intellectual hypocrisy and political malfeasance of his age turned that very derisive sensibility upon himself; he wore a red bath robe, the better to camouflage the blood he believed would be running from his head.

In June 1981, to the astonishment of his readers, a French press agency revealed that the novelists Émile Ajar and Romain Gary were one and the same person. *Life and Death of Émile Ajar*, dated 21 March 1979, appeared in July. In this brief testament Gary recalled the theory of the novel he had developed in the 1965 essay *Pour Sganarelle*, which argues against Sartre's engaged literature and the "totalitarianism" of the New Novel, the dominant literary forms of the postwar decades in France. His ideal novel, he wrote, would be a "total novel" in which it would be impossible to distinguish real-life author from his fictional hero. His ideal hero, he specified, would be modelled after the picaro, the 18th-century adventurer known as much for his legendary personality as for his beautiful works. In life as in death Gary came to fit the description.

STEVEN JARON

Gebirtig, Mordkhe

Polish poet and songwriter, 1877–1942

Born in Kraków, 4 May 1877. Limited education in religious schools; worked as carpenter all his life; self-taught in music. Married Blume (Blumke) Lindenbaum; three daughters, Bashke, Shifre, and Liola (among whom Liola became a folksinger). Suffered heart attack, 1907, and consequent diabetes. Active in Jewish socialist movement. Served in Austro-Hungarian army, as medical orderly in Kraków, during World War I. After Nazi and Soviet invasions, 1939, imprisoned in ghettos of Kraków and later in Lagiewniki. Murdered, along with Blume, Bashke, and Liola, en route to Belzec, 4 June 1942.

Selected Writings

Poetry
Folkstimlekh [For Plain People], 1920
Mayne lider [My Songs], edited by M. Kipnis, 1936
Undzer shtetl brent [Our Town is on Fire], 1938
S'Brent, 1946
Geklibende lider, 1954
Mordkhe Gebirtig zingt, 1964
Mordechai Gebirtig: Jiddische Lieder, edited by Manfred Lemm, 1994
Mayn Fayfele: umbekante lider, 1997
Mordechai Gebirtig Songbook, edited by Velvel Pasternak, 1999
Anthology of Yiddish Folksongs, vol. 5: *The Mordechai Gebirtig Volume*, edited by Sinai Leichter, 2000

Further Reading

Gross, Natan, *Zydowski Bard: Gaweda o Zyciu i Tworczosci Mordechaja Gebirtiga* [Jewish Bard: Literary Conversation about the Life and Work of Mordechai Gebirtig], Kraków: Ksiegarnia Akademicka, 2000
Leftwich, Joseph (editor), *The Golden Peacock: An Anthology of Yiddish Poetry*, Cambridge, Massachusetts: Sci-Art, 1939
Mark, Bernard, *Di umgekumene shrayber fun di getos un lagern in zayere verk*, Warsaw: Yiddish Bukh, 1954
Schneider, Gertrude (editor), *Mordechai Gebirtig: His Poetic and Musical Legacy*, Westport, Connecticut: Praeger, 2000

Gebirtig was a *chansonnier* or troubadour, in the tradition of the minnesingers of medieval times, and of 19th-century bards such as Berl Broder, Velvel Zbarazhov, and Mark Warshavsky. His poems without music also contained the timbre and rhythm of song and, like his predecessors, his music was a fusion of Hasidic melody, chazanic prayer, and Slavic dance. He could paint superb pictures, and his songs were like photographs taken with a clear lens and at an illuminating angle. He did not use symbolism and metaphor, unlike many of his contemporary poets, nor did he seek to participate in or to elevate Jewish tradition. On the contrary, he sought to demystify it. His birds were not like the mythical golden Peacock, but ordinary ones who, as in "Di zun iz fargangen" [The Sun has Set], would talk to him, and reflect his sadness or hopes. In his almost unselfconscious poetry there is little strain, and a directness and honesty. Where there was musical accompaniment, it was mostly his, though he could not write music. He would compose it on his *fujarka* (shepherd's pipe) and his friends, Julius Hoffman or Barukh Sperber, would write down the musical notation. Sperber also wrote the music for three of his songs. His first book, *Folkstimlekh* [For Plain People] had no music, but by 1936, when the second collection, *Mayne lider* [My Songs] was published, his tunes were too well known for them not to be included. Gebirtig's songs and his life were one, reflecting the times in which he lived in such a clear and stark way that they were taken as folksongs, and sung anonymously, often by street singers who would tour the Jewish courtyards. Gebirtig's identification with these singers was absolute, as shown in "Der zinger fun noyt" [The Singer of Want].

The early Gebirtig was a socialist and an internationalist. This was reinforced by his experience in World War I when, as a medical orderly in Kraków, he treated wounded soldiers of all nationalities of the Austro-Hungarian empire. He listened to the songs that the soldiers sang, and used the tunes for his own poems. Separation through war, the sadness of lovers parted forever, the plight of the orphan and the injured were constant themes. Two poems, "A royte tsaykhn" [A Red Sign] and "Krigs-invalid" [War Wounded], deal with the "rewards" of war with biting sarcasm.

Gebirtig was outstanding in his depiction of social life, and particularly poverty. The images and situations are precise, with no trace of sentimentality, as with the woman bagel seller arrested for selling without a licence in "Di oreme kremerke" [The Poor Saleswoman], or the exploited and abused Jewish housemaid in "Bay gvirim a dinstmoyd tsu zayn" [To be a Maid for Rich People]. The nostalgia in popular songs, such as "Moyshele, mayn fraynd" and "Kinder yorn" [Childhood Years], seems to have arisen from his sense of vulnerability and the fragility of life, which had begun with his heart attack in 1907 and the onset of diabetes, and was reinforced by the experience of World War I. It was intensified by the suicide of his close friend Mordkhe Erlich in 1934, and in "Di nakht kumt tsu shvebn" [The Night Floats Down], he wrote: "Another night has passed/ Another day has come/ So the two chase each other" and each day simply brought death closer. These words were to find an echo in one of his last poems (written in May 1942) "In geto": "And so you lie, in terror and in fear/ hunted and degraded like slaves –/ And so our days draw out / our sleepless nights".

The most beloved of Gebirtig's songs are the character portraits, such as "Reyzele" with its delicate depiction of young love, or "Motele", where the father berates his young son for his misbehaviour. Here, the music is well integrated, it reflects the sing-song rhythm of the study in the heder and yeshiva, for which the boy is unenthusiastic. Many of Gebirtig's songs were concerned with childhood in all its phases, from the many lullabies to the joys and deprivations of childhood, and the attempts by children to come to terms with death. In "Mamenyu mayne" [Dear Mother, Mine], the child hopes he will meet his dead father when the Messiah comes, and the dead are resurrected.

One of the most interesting areas of Polish-Jewish life satirized by Gebirtig was the push of modernization and acculturation. In "Kh'vil nisht aza khosn" [I Don't Want such a Bridegroom] the girl rejects a potential match because he's too old-fashioned. In "Kum leybke, tantsn" [Come Leybke, Dance] the girl requires that her partner learns the tango or the Charleston. The presence of these independent-minded women in Gebirtig's songs is also a reflection of that modernization. Gebirtig celebrated all the rites of passage in Jewish life, but also displayed sympathy for those outside. In "Avreml der marvikher" [Avreml the Pickpocket] he depicts a loveable rogue, whose circumstances drove him to petty crime. In "Di gefalene" [The Fallen Woman], he gives a sympathetic portrait of a prostitute.

Not only did Gebirtig reflect the life of Polish Jews, he also reflected their death. His last poems were like a series x-rays into the Jewish soul under the Nazi yoke. As with many, writing was a form of consolation. Sometimes, to reawaken creativity was enough, as in "Ikh hob shoyn lang . . ." [It's been so long . . .], where he hopes his muse will soon awaken. The poetry of this last period oscillates between personal despair and collective hope, feelings that coexisted within him and many others. The fact that Gebirtig and others were concerned to pursue and to preserve their poetry during this period reinforces this sense of constructive and collective optimism. There will always be others who will be able to read it afterwards. His most unmediated poem of despair, as the title announces, is "Minutn fun yoesh" [Moments of Despair] written in September 1940. The heavens are closed to the cries of humanity, and he finally realizes that "there is no justice, there is no God". Clearly, he fought against this mood, as is evident from "Minutn fun betokhn" [Moments of Confidence] written at the beginning of October, with its hope in the fall of the Nazis and the possibility of revenge. This, and "Undzer shtetl brent" [Our Town is Burning] – written originally as a protest and call to arms against Polish anti-Semitism – became anthems of resistance. Virtually all of Gebirtig's songs were in the minor key, characteristic of the sad and downbeat mood, in contrast to the more optimistic major key. Gebirtig's last song, the painfully ironic "S'iz gut" [It's Good] was, however, wholly in the major mode, and an allegro instruction is given. It is his final celebration, and at the same time a final castigation of the shortsightedness of the victims – his fellow Jews. Shortly afterwards, he was shot on his way to be deported to the Belzec death camp. No doubt, he knew the end was near, and so this song can be seen as a *danse macabre*, part of his threnody for the murdered Jews of Poland.

BARRY DAVIS

Gerchunoff, Alberto

Russian-born Argentine fiction writer, 1884–1950

Born in Proskurov, Ukraine, 1884. Emigrated with family to Argentina, 1890; settled first in Buenos Aires and then in Moisés Ville, one of first settlements of Baron Maurice de Hirsch's Jewish Colonization Association, in province of Entre Ríos. Father killed there by gaucho. Later settled in Buenos Aires; joined staff of daily newspaper *La Nación*, 1908; worked as editor of *La Nación* and *El Mundo*. Founder and President of Argentine Writers Association; active as radical Zionist and socialist. Awarded third Argentinian National Prize for Literature, 1927. Died 1950.

Selected Writings

Fiction

Los gauchos judíos, 1910; as *The Jewish Gauchos of the Pampas*, translated by Prudencio de Pereda, 1955
Cuentos de ayer, 1919
El hombre importante, 1934
La clínica del Dr Mefistófeles, 1937
In *Tropical Synagogues: Short Stories by Jewish-Latin American Writers*, edited by Ilan Stavans, 1994
In *The Silver Candelabra and Other Stories: A Century of Jewish Argentine Literature*, edited and translated by Rita Gardiol, 1997

Other

La jofaina maravillosa: agenda cervantina, 1922
La asamblea de la bohardilla, 1925
El hombre que habló en la Sorbona, 1926
Pequeñas prosas, 1926
Enrique Heine, el poeta de nuestra intimidad, 1927
Los amores de Baruj Spinoza, 1932
Entre Ríos, mi país, 1950
Retorno de Don Quijote, 1951
El pino y la palmera, 1952

Further Reading

Aizenberg, Edna, "Parricide in the Pampa: Deconstructing Gerchunoff and his Jewish Gauchos", *Folio*, 17 (1987): 24–39
Barchilón, José, *Gerchunoff, Bufano*, San Juan, Argentina: Editorial Sanjuanian, 1973
Cúneo, Dardo, *El romanticismo politico*, Buenos Aires: Transición, 1955
Gordon, Marjorie Salgado, entry on Gerchunoff in *Jewish Writers of Latin America: A Dictionary*, edited by Darrell B. Lockhart, New York: Garland, 1997
Gover de Nasatsky, Miryam Esther, *Bibliografia de Alberto Gerchunoff*, Buenos Aires: Fondo Nacional de las Artes–Sociedad Hebraica Argentina, 1976

Jaroslavsky de Lowy, Sara, *Alberto Gerchunoff: vida y obra, bibliografia, antologia*, New York: Hispanic Institute, 1957
Kantor, Manuel, *Alberto Gerchunoff*, Buenos Aires: Ejecutivo Sudamericano del Congreso Judio Mundial, 1969
Lindstrom, Naomi, *Jewish Issues in Argentine Literature: From Gerchunoff to Szichman*, Columbia: University of Missouri Press, 1989
Sadow, Stephen A., "*A Jewish Gaucho* by Alberto Gerchunoff" in *King David's Harp: Autobiographical Essays by Jewish Latin American Writers*, edited by Sadow, Albuquerque: University of New Mexico Press, 1999
Stavans, Ilan, foreword to *The Jewish Gauchos of the Pampas*, by Gerchunoff, New York: Abelard Schuman, 1955
Stavans, Ilan, introduction to *Tropical Synagogues: Short Stories by Jewish-Latin American Writers*, New York: Holmes and Meier, 1994

Writers and critics attribute the founding of Jewish-Argentine writing to Alberto Gerchunoff, and *Encyclopedia Judaica* cites his most popular work, *Los gauchos judíos* (*The Jewish Gauchos of the Pampas*), as "the first work of literary value to be written in Spanish by a Jew in modern times". His integrationist politics and idealized vision of Argentina as "Zion" have made this cornerstone position somewhat contested. Contemporary readers place Gerchunoff's writing in historical context – amid Argentine nationalist fervour in the 1910s and 1920s and against the anti-Semitism of *Semana Tragíca* ("Tragic Week"), a pogrom directed against the Jewish community – and charge him with understating the tension between Jews and non-Jews in Argentine culture. *Los gauchos judíos* is "unreliable as documentation of social conditions", Naomi Lindstrom explains, but "may offer testimony to the dreams that shape social thought." Gerchunoff inscribes his vision of Argentina as the Promised Land for the Jews and constructs a hybrid Jewish-Argentine identity in the *gaucho judío*.

Several of the short vignettes collected in *Los gauchos judíos* were published serially in *La Nación* in 1908. As part of Argentina's centennial celebration of independence, Leopoldo Lugones commissioned Gerchunoff to publish these pieces together as "commemorative material". These loosely-connected stories of Jewish life in the agricultural colonies express Gerchunoff's sincere appreciation for his adopted homeland. His melding of *gaucho* (cowboy) and shtetl traditions figures a successful model of acculturation and enables a biblical "return to the land" for his eastern European immigrant characters. Gerchunoff frames the text with a quote from the Passover *Haggadah*: "With the strength of His arm, God liberated us from Pharaoh in Egypt." In doing so, he links Jewish and Argentine remembrances of liberation.

"In the Beginning" solidifies immigration to Argentina as a second Exodus. With assistance from the Jewish Colonization Association, supported by the philanthropy of Baron Maurice de Hirsch, Jews could leave the poverty and religious intolerance of eastern Europe behind in search of the "Promised Land" on "Spanish soil". "If we return to that life", as farmers closely tied to the land, one character exclaims, "we will be going back to our old mode of life, our true one!" Reb Favel Duglach is an enigmatic *gaucho judío*, interweaving "Argentine epics of bravery" with "stories of the Bible" and asserting, for Gerchunoff's non-Jewish readers, the assimilability of Jewish immigrants to Argentine *gaucho* culture.

Writing from the cosmopolitan centre of Buenos Aires, Gerchunoff argues for the peaceful integration of Jews on the pampas (interior agricultural regions) as well as in the cities. "The Case of the Stolen Horse" explores anti-Semitism among the colonists, when a *gaucho* accuses Don Abraham of stealing his horse. Rather than endure threats of violence, Don Abraham pays for the horse, despite his innocence. "The Gaucho is not the same as a Russian *mujik*, but he himself is still the same Jew, and apparently the situation doesn't change." Here, as in his other writings, Gerchunoff offers an accommodationist solution: "Patience, like suffering is the ennobling gift and treasure of the sorry race of Job!"

While critics reject the "romanticized" and "idealized" portraits in *Los gauchos judíos*, Gerchunoff's personal writings indicate that such representations illustrate an ideological project. "Wouldn't it be interesting", he queries in an autobiographical selection, "to show Judaism redeemed from the share of slavery, martyrdom, and stoicism that usually plunges it into abjection?" He inscribes idyllic versions of acculturation because he believes they will become reality. "In Argentina, Jews, redeemed from injustice and religious stereotypes, will lose their generally accepted profile. On this soil, they will be gradually freed from the whip of persecution."

Gerchunoff does not openly challenge Argentine anti-Semitism in writing until the Spanish translation of Ludwig Lewisohn's *Rebirth of Israel* appeared prior to World War II. His belief in Argentina as the new "Zion" prevented him initially from supporting the State of Israel. With shifts in Argentine politics in the 1930s, Gerchunoff began speaking out – in his personal addresses and writings – on the centrality and specificity of Jewish identity. His dream of Argentina as the Promised Land fragmented in response to heightened xenophobia and nationalist fervour. *El pino y la palmera* [The Pine and the Palm Tree], a posthumous collection of writings, places Argentine Jews in a continuum with Sephardim in Spain; acknowledges Gerchunoff's respect for Sholem Aleichem; and defines "traditional Jewish optimism as simply a sombre faith in better times for the Jew".

Gerchunoff is best remembered, as Ilan Stavans notes, for his "beautiful and meticulously measured Castilian prose", described by critics as "lyrical", "rhapsodic", and "sumptuous" in *Los gauchos judíos*. He succeeded in inserting the experiences of Spanish-speaking Jews in 20th-century history and earned an esteemed place in Argentine letters. After Gerchunoff's death, Jorge Luis Borges lauded him as "the perfect friend of the Spanish dictionary" with "infallible literary precision".

WENDY H. BERGOFFEN

Gerez, Jozef Habib

Turkish poet, essayist, and artist, 1926–

Born in Istanbul, 14 June 1926. Studied at Kabataş High School for Boys; Faculty of Law, Istanbul; Fine Arts Academy, Istanbul. First exhibition, 1961; director of Modern Art Gallery, 1965–70. Numerous awards (for poetry and for painting), including European Academy Award for Services to Art, 1998; honorary membership of six academies in various countries; honorary consulship of Academy of Europe.

Selected Writings

Poetry
Gönülden Damlalar [Droplets from the Heart], 1952
Renklerin Akını [Assault of Colours], 1954
Savrulan Zaman [Winnowed Time], 1955
Meyhaneden Çıkan Kıral [The King Who Came Out of the Tavern], 1956
Acılı Bitimler [Sorrowful Endings], 1960
Seni Yaşamak [Living You], 1963
Daraçılar [Narrow Angles], 1965
Ölü Nokta [Dead Point], 1966
Arayış İçinde [Searching], 1967
Büyük Güzel [Great Beauty], 1969
On İki Kavim / On ıki Tablo [Twelve Tribes / Twelve Paintings], 1986

Anthologies
Başını Alıp Giden Dünya [The World Going Its Own Way], 1970
Yaşama Sevinci [Joy of Living], 1983
Gökyüzüne Gülen Güller [Roses Smiling at the Sky], 1986
Yaşamın Ayak İzleri [Footprints of Life], 1998
Özlem Yorgunu [Wearied by Desire], 2000
Art is My Destiny, 2000

Other
Rüzgâra Söylenenler [Told to the Wind], 1988
Yaşamın Tadı Tuzu Sanat [The Taste and Salt of Life is Art], 1998

Further Reading

Schwartz, Howard and Anthony Rudolf (editors), *Voices within the Ark: The Modern Jewish Poets*, New York: Avon, 1980

A protégé of Turkey's renowned Jewish historian and polymath, Avram Galante (1873–1961), Gerez believes that the objective of art must be "to inculcate human beings with love, friendship and fraternity without any distinction of race and religion". In pursuit of this belief, he has taken the oath, composed like a charter and prominently displayed in his home, that, for as long as he lives, he will be "servant and slave to art". Moreover, having chosen art as his way of life, he has forsaken such commitments as marriage and children.

Gerez, by virtue of his dual gifts, has gained the reputation of being "poetry's painter" and "painting's poet". Many of his poems have been translated into French and Italian; a collection in English, *Art is My Destiny*, was published in 2000.

Gerez defines the "purity" of poetry with a paradox: "poems are lies that tell the truth". Most of his poems pursue humanitarian themes and the imperative for social justice as the requisite for universal peace. This pastoral principle is further enhanced by Gerez's esteem for science and mankind's general hunger for knowledge. In his view, without these factors, an artist, particularly a poet, would never fulfil his potential in terms of the range and depth of universal themes.

Turkish poets have the benefit of being influenced by at least four important traditions: the classical *divan* poetry, much favoured, over a number of centuries, by the Ottoman court; folk poetry, the simpler, unstylized people's poetry which offered the alternative to *divan* poetry; the *tekke*, religious poetry, of which the works of the mystic Mevlânâ Celâleddin-i Rumi have achieved an international following; and the Europeanized poetry. (In addition to these, the traditions of Arabic and Farsi poetry also generate considerable influence.) Two poets, the prolific Nâzım Hikmet – indisputably one of the 20th century's giants – and the quite unprolific Orhan Veli Kanık – author of only a slim, single volume – combining, almost imperceptibly, these rich influences have created a new, modern tradition. The new generation of Turkish poets has carried this tradition to unimaginable heights.

Gerez belongs to this new generation. He works in the modern tradition and uses free verse. His poems on love and the joys of everyday life carry strong sensibilities of *divan* poetry; while his adoration of Nature and compassion for a suffering humanity attains some of the mystic dimensions of *tekke* poetry.

Gerez is also a formidable columnist. His 500-odd prose articles cover the full spectrum of his interests and many aspects of life in Turkey. Some pursue his notions on social justice and universal peace; others serve as contemplations on aspects of poetry and art, poets and artists; yet others deal with Jewish themes and Jewish personalities. Such articles as his anecdotes on Galante, his brief biographies on other famous Turkish Jews such as the poet İsak Ferera (1883–1933) and the journalist Nesim Benbanaste (1939–92), his commemoration of Atatürk's 16th death anniversary as well as his analysis of that statesman's genius, and his reports on the Jewish communities of the provincial cities of Edirne and Çorlu, have become classics of their kind.

Whereas Gerez's poetry has yet to reach an international readership, he has a growing reputation as a painter of great originality. He started painting in 1960. Since 1961, the year of his first exhibition, in Istanbul, he has exhibited at more than 100 venues, 27 of them in France and Italy. Gerez started painting by experimenting with colours, studying their hues, thinning and thickening them to produce marbling effects. Later, by drawing tree trunks and forests over these explorations, he gradually moved from the abstract to the figurative. Later still, when he started producing canvases that combined these styles, he began to be classified first as an expressionist, then as a post-expressionist. He himself refuses to be subsumed to any category. A painter seeking universal appeal must, in his view, eschew a particular school and pursue "a pluralism of styles". He has, however, a mystical attachment to colours. He believes composition, even if near perfect, would not in itself guarantee masterpieces; great art can only be achieved by harmonizing warm colours with cold colours; thus a weaker colour can be animated with a stronger one, and a harsh colour moderated by a soft counterpart. This, he would hasten to add, is how Nature weaves its miracles.

MORIS FARHI

Gershon, Karen

German-born British poet, 1923–1993

Born Kate Loewenthal in Bielefeld, 29 August 1923, into liberal Jewish family. Joined Zionist youth movement; left Germany on *Kindertransport*, 1938; family killed in concentration camp in Riga, Latvia. Left first foster home, in Scotland, to work as domestic servant and office clerk in Leeds. Rejected scholarship to Edinburgh University; continued to work as house-mother and matron in progressive boarding schools. Married artist Val Tripp, 1948; four children. Settled in Ilminster, Somerset. Emigrated to Israel, 1969; returned to England, 1975; settled in Cornwall. Awards include Pioneer Women Award, 1968. Died in London, 24 March 1993.

Selected Writings

Poetry
Selected Poems, 1966
Legacies and Encounters, 1972
First Meeting, 1974
My Daughters, My Sisters, 1975
Jepthah's Daughter, 1978
Coming Back from Babylon, 1979
Collected Poems, 1990

Novels
Burn Helen, 1980
The Bread of Exile, 1985
The Fifth Generation, 1987

Other
We Came as Children, 1966
Postscript: A Collective Account of the Lives of Jews in West Germany since the Second World War, 1969
A Lesser Child: An Autobiography, 1994 (German original 1992)

Further Reading

"Karen Gershon", obituary, *The Times* (15 April 1993)

Karen Gershon was described in her obituary as a lone voice in the Holocaust poetry of the 1960s, and certainly her exploration of the implications of memory and guilt place her work in the mainstream of Holocaust writing in Britain in that period. Yet surprisingly there has been an alarming neglect of her work in the critical surveys of the poetry of the postwar period. It is difficult to find her work represented in major anthologies also; F.E.S. Finn included a few poems in his *Poets of the Sixties* in 1970, but she was never included in the influential anthologies. Even in reappraisals of the 1960s and 1970s, her work remains occluded from view and hard to find. Yet, in terms of periodical publication and reviewing by peers, Gershon's poetry was very prominent for a decade or more, and her voice strikingly original.

Gershon came to England after the removal of her family to a concentration camp, and her new life was restless and varied; she was house-mother, scholarship student, translator, and Zionist. But her writing has certain constants: a focus on explorative questioning of mankind's nature and relation to the concepts of good and evil; family relationships and a darker, mostly generalized strand of quasi-philosophical speculation. But it must be noted that her achievements in autobiography were remarkable, and her book, *A Lesser Child*, is arguably one of the most insightful memoirs of the Jewish literary and artistic aspirational self within the incipient Nazi regime. In that book, she relates her early ventures into writing (in German) and disarmingly alludes to influences on her sense of self-worth. She was told that her poem submitted for a youth group theme was "too serious, it doesn't fit in".

This seriousness became, of course, one of her sustaining strengths. Her poems written as early as the *Selected Poems* (1966) show her enviable command of insistent and rhetorical rhyming and metrics, particularly in the sequence "The Children's Exodus", which establishes a plangent, intensely haunting tone and metrical power in lines such as "At Dovercourt the winter sea/ was like God's mercy vast and wild". In her early poetry there is a quality of Blakean simplicity approaching unspeakable subjects with no fear of missing the emotional mark. Perhaps her most widely-known poem, "I Was Not There", is so successful because it has that rare quality of directness and literalness that is increasingly avoided in a postmodern age of complexity and intertextual allusion.

The later poetry is capable of a similar rhetorical effect, stemming often from sonorous statements of biblical syntax and diction. She was never too cautious with a bare and rough-hewn end-rhyme, and this adds a dimension of the prophetic and didactic to her later writing. In "Cain" for instance, we have Miltonic seriousness in "*Accursed and cast out/ from holy leisure/ the parents lived in doubt.*" The moral seriousness is most explanatory of the Jewish preoccupation with memory in her poetry. Indeed, the centrality of memory in all its manifestations in the Jewish nature, perhaps accounts for the extraordinary emotional velocity of her autobiographical poems, and in this she universalizes a moment of selfhood and revelation of man's capacity for evil. Her couplets in these poems of a Jewish consciousness include such existential assertions as "In fear and pride I walked alone/ as if I were an enemy/ and each stone seemed to look at me/ there is no rancour in a stone". Paradoxically, her stylistic technique has a lot in common with the English dissenting, preaching, visionary tradition, and indeed her intellectual enterprise has the capacity to include statements about Christian belief alongside Judaism.

Equally, Gershon's poetry is markedly successful in confronting the oppositions of modernity: the paradox of the need for human friendship and the undermining of faith and trust in the massive macrocosmic ideologies working to efface human feeling. Writing of her father, she accepts him "with every blemish" and in other places she even asserts the necessary solitude, away from family ties and the claims of others: "Now I am glad to be one whom people ignore."

Gershon's is a voice of terrible honesty in her writing of her Jewishness, and she manages to perpetuate the viewpoint of the child in her, juxtaposed with the maturing intellect and the sensibility living among strangers. The persistence of memory might be noted as the one recurrent theme in her work, and this memory expresses itself in relation both to Jewish victimization and to the unanswerable questions of the "Final solution". But her individuation of this persistent pain will always be the appeal of her work: "Whenever I sit in a train/ I see my parents in a truck/ events in themselves innocent/ bring their experiences back." This illustrates that the outstanding poetic power in Gershon's work is that of literal honesty and simplicity, rather than the stretches and demands of intricate metaphor.

STEPHEN WADE

Gilboa, Amir

Polish-born Israeli poet and editor, 1917–1984

Born in Radzywilow, 30 September 1917. Emigrated illegally to Palestine, 1937. Worked in kibbutzim and stone quarries. Entire family perished in Holocaust. Served in Jewish Brigade of British army during World War II; participated in transfer of Jews from Netherlands to Palestine, 1945. Fought in Israel's War of Independence, 1948. Worked as editor in publishing house. Many awards, including Israel Prize, Bialik Award, 1971; Bertha and Irving Neuman Hebrew Literary Award, 1984. Died in Tel Aviv, 1984.

Selected Writings

Poetry

Laot [For the Sign], 1942
Sheva rashuyot [Seven Dominions], 1949
Shirim baboker, baboker [Poems Very Early in the Morning], 1953
Gili's Water Man, 1963
Kehulim veadumim [Blues and Reds], 1963
Ratsiti likhtov siftei yeshenim [I Wanted to Write the Lips of Sleepers], 1968
Ayalah ashalah otakh [Hind, I Shall Send Thee Off], 1973
The Light of Lost Suns, translated by Shirley Kaufman and Shlomith Rimmon, 1979
Hakol holekh [Anything Goes], 1985
Collected Poems, 2 vols, 1987

Further Reading

Bargad, Warren, *"To Write the Lips of Sleepers": The Poetry of Amir Gilboa*, Cincinnati: Hebrew Union College Press, 1994
Burnshaw, Stanley, T. Carmi and Ezra Spicehandler (editors and translators), *The Modern Hebrew Poem Itself*, New York: Holt Rinehart and Winston, 1965
Tsalka, Dan, *Amir Gilboa: Mivhar shirim udevarim al yetsirato*, Tel Aviv: Mahbarot leshirah, 1962
Yudkin, Leon I., "Israeli Poetry: Gilboa, Amichai and Zach" in *Escape into Siege: A Survey of Israeli Literature Today*, London and Boston: Routledge and Kegan Paul, 1974

From the start, Gilboa was associated with the school of symbolist poetry led by Avraham Shlonsky, which enjoyed hegemonic status in the field of Hebrew poetry in Palestine during the 1930s and 1940s, and published his work in editions of *Yalkut Hareim* which featured many of the school's new generation of poets such as Galai, Rabin, and Tannai. But even then he stood out on account of his expressive writing, which maintained a closeness to the expressionistic tradition in Hebrew writing headed by Uri Zvi Greenberg. The symbol – which lies at the heart of symbolist poetry – appears in Gilboa as a hybrid symbol which is subservient at once to both the tradition of sublimation of the universal symbol as well as the corporeal expressive tradition. The typical idiom of his early writing is prayer and a mystical appeal to a supreme divine entity. In his poem "Ki az etsak" [For Then Shall I Shout] he focuses on the human shout as the essence of expression and on pain as affirmation of the physical and corporeal existence of the poetic subject: "On miserable times and hours dripping bitterness./ And on groping with my hand, with my foot, with my forehead – I knew: I am cold./ And a tongue was sent me contrariwise."

Gilboa served in the British army during World War II and his writing then concerned his experiences fighting in the North African desert. The space of the desert is a point of departure for a mystical ascent that transforms the pain and loss at war, especially that of his relatives killed in the Holocaust, into a single conglomerate. For example, a poem written in el-Agiela: "A strip of your dreams, a road,/ Shimmering with the desert's golden locks [. . .] Like a dream to me is – the night/ Which out of blood clots wove/ A scarf for my sister-bride." These poems appeared in *Sheva rashuyot* [Seven Dominions], in which he also included the poems he had written during the struggle for Israel's independence. With these latter poems Gilboa achieved the status of a major figure in Israeli poetry. Among other things the book includes the poem "Molidei haor" [Begetters of Light], which is a complex attempt to search for metaphysical values of light in a situation of conflict and collective violence. Gilboa examines its Messianic potential and drives in an ecstatic rhythm towards the conclusion, in which the blood of those fallen in war and the mystical nationalist light commingle in an iconography that is Christian and Messianic: "The dazzling light – / Its crystal drops the blood has/ Embedded in the diadems of the boys/ And has enclappered in bells of gold/ News of the birth in the mountains."

Gilboa is also one of those who helped establish the figure of the living dead in the poetry of the period. This refers to a description of the victim as someone who continues to live, and as someone whose private physical death makes it possible to preserve the essential values of the collective in his life after death. The forefathers killed in the Holocaust are those who appear as the living in the poem "Laylah, bekarahat hayaar" [Night in the Forest Clearing] in order to enjoin vengeance upon their posterity as the last resort of hope. However, Gilboa later also wrote poetry that undermines the symbol of the living dead. He introduced the idea of private existential representation of the fallen in war, in the course of delineating a biting critical representation of the mythical figure of the living dead.

Shirim baboker baboker [Poems Very Early in the Morning] includes a poem that begins with the line "My brother came back from the field." It is a parody on the return of the warrior from the battlefield and the reception accorded to him by his brother. But the brother's preoccupation with the glory of collective valour blinds him from seeing that his silent brother has actually died in the war. The reception turns out to be just another act of homicide, in a biblical quotation taken from the story of Cain and Abel.

Gilboa has written other poems that offer re-readings of biblical myths. In this spirit he rewrites the story of Isaac's sacrifice in "Yitshak". This critical writing links Gilboa with the collective poetry of the generation of the struggle for independence in the 1940s and 1950s, and the existential ironic poetry of "the generation of statehood" in the 1950s and 1960s.

In the mid-1960s there was a shift in his poetry, which began with poems that appeared in the final section of the comprehensive compendium *Kehulim veadumim* [Blues and Reds], which was published in 1963. The Kabbalistic elements that had permeated his work began to predominate. His work drew closer to writing in the rhythms of speech, and towards an "I" wearing an impersonal mask. Such poems are included in *Ratsiti likhtov siftei yeshenim* [I Wanted to Write the Lips of Sleepers]. The language of prayer intensifies and is tinged with a profound anxiety. These poems lead towards a far-reaching abstraction, with the music of each overflowing line turning them into a modernistic psalmist text. "And in the morning of a gilded day, I awaked. There before me, Jerusalem./ And I see I see with tens of thousands of eyes." An impressive follow-up came with *Ayalah ashalah otakh* [Hind, I Shall Send Thee Off]. Here Gilboa develops a poetic structure of quasi-biblical language in a modernist version. The musicality of the poems is overwhelming: "Mine city. I shall again not be able/ To enter into thy gates my city/ Without my city my people inside thee." The symbolic writing posits female figures as its object, whose erotic characteristics Gilboa uses to develop a complex and conflict-ridden moral statement:

> Hind, I shall send thee off to the wolves who not in the
>   forest are they
> In the city too upon sidewalks thou shalt flee before
>   them alarmed
> Thy eyes comely shall envy me that I seest thou how
> You flutter in fright and your soul
> Thee I into the face of presumption shall send
> War is no more for me
> My heart goes out, hind, to the sight of you blood-
>   wounded in the dawn bleeding.

Gilboa produces an expressive statement, which undermines the traditional model of the female figure as a symbol of the nation and concludes unequivocally that war – both personal and national – is not for him.

After Gilboa's death in 1984, a selection of poems was published as *Hakol holekh* [Anything Goes], subtitled "Diary Notes in Late Season." These poems are fragmented, the inter-flow between one line and the next becomes the crux of the poem's drama. Gilboa employs this abstract and intermittent mode of expression in order to re-read all his writing in sober retrospect. Now, in the face of current events and the poetry of protest against the War of Lebanon of 1982, he re-reads his own poetry and political stance of the past: "I once went to the plaza and it/ Was a self-delusion which deluded/ Others too and I was glad/ That I went to the plaza now".

HANNAN HEVER

Ginsberg, Allen

US poet, 1926–1997

Born Newark, New Jersey, 3 June 1926. Studied at Columbia University, BA 1948. Worked as spot welder, dishwasher, on various cargo ships, as literary agent, reporter, copy boy, night porter, book reviewer for *Newsweek*, market research consultant. Instructor, University of British Columbia, Vancouver, 1963; founder and treasurer, Committee on Poetry Foundation, 1966–97; organizer, Gathering of the Tribes for a Human Be-In, San Francisco, 1967; co-founder, 1974, co-director, and teacher, Jack Kerouac School of Disembodied Poetics, Naropa Institute, Boulder, Colorado, 1974–97. Read poems and gave lectures at universities, coffee houses, and art galleries around the world. Appeared in numerous films, including *Pull My Daisy*, 1960; *Couch*, 1964; *Wholly Communion*, *Chappaqua* and *Allen for Allen*, all 1965; *It Was 20 Years Ago Today*, 1987; *Heavy Petting*, 1988; *John Bowles: The Complete Outsider* and *Jonas in the Desert*, both 1994. Narrator of television film *Kaddish*, 1977. Many awards, including Guggenheim Fellowship, 1963; National Book Award, 1974; Poetry Society of America Gold Medal, 1986; Before Columbus Foundation Award (for lifetime achievement), 1990; Chevalier de l'Ordre des Artes et des Lettres, 1992; Fellowship, American Academy of Arts and Sciences, 1992. Died in New York, 5 April 1997.

Selected Writings

Poetry

Howl and Other Poems, 1956; revised edition 1971; 40th anniversary edition, 1996
Siesta in Xbalba and Return to the States, 1956
Empty Mirror: Early Poems, 1961
Kaddish and Other Poems, 1961
A Strange New Cottage in Berkeley, 1963
Penguin Modern Poets 5, with Lawrence Ferlinghetti and Gregory Corso, 1963
Reality Sandwiches, 1963
The Change, 1963
Kral Majales, 1965

Prose Contribution to Cuban Revolution, 1966
Wichita Vortex Sutra, 1966
TV Baby Poems, 1967
Airplane Dreams: Compositions from Journals, 1968
Ankor Wat, with Alexandra Lawrence, 1968
Message II, 1968
Planet News, 1968
Scrap Leaves, Hasty Scribbles, 1968
The Heart is a Clock, 1968
Wales – A Visitation, July 29, 1967, 1968
For the Soul of the Planet is Wakening, 1970
Notes after an Evening with William Carlos Williams, 1970
The Moments Return, 1970
Ginsberg's Improvised Poetics, 1971
Bixby Canyon Ocean Path Word Breeze, 1972
Iron Horse, 1972
New Year Blues, 1972
Open Head, 1972
The Fall of America: Poems of These States 1965–1971, 1972
The Gates of Wrath: Rhymed Poems, 1972
First Blues: Rags, Ballads and Harmonium Songs, 1971–1974, 1975
Sad Dust Glories: Poems during Work Summer in Woods, 1975
Careless Love: Two Rhymes, 1978
Mind Breaths: Poems 1972–1977, 1978
Mostly Sitting Haiku, 1978; revised edition, 1979
Poems All over the Place: Mostly Seventies, 1978
Straight Hearts' Delight: Love Poems and Selected Letters, 1947–1980, with Peter Orlovsky, 1980
Plutonian Ode: Poems, 1977–1980, 1982
Collected Poems, 1947–1980, 1984; expanded edition as *Collected Poems, 1947–1985*, 1995
Many Loves, 1984
Old Love Story, 1986
White Shroud: Poems 1980–1985, 1986
Collected Poems, edited by Michael Fournier, 1992
Kaddish: For Naomi Ginsberg 1894–1956, 1992
Cosmopolitan Greetings: Poems 1986–1992, 1994
Making It Up: Poetry Composed at St Mark's Church on May 9, 1979, with Kenneth Koch, 1994
Poems, Interviews, Photographs, 1994
Illuminated Poems, 1996
Selected Poems, 1947–1995, 1996
Luminous Dreams, 1997
Death and Fame Poems, 1993–1997, 1999

Plays
Don't Go Away Mad in *Pardon Me, Sir, But is My Eye Hurting Your Elbow?*, edited by Bob Booker and George Foster, 1968
No Chanting in the Court! Allen Ginsberg at the Conspiracy Trial, edited by Judy Gumbo, 1969/70
Kaddish, 1972
The Hydrogen Jukebox, 1990

Other
Translator, with others, *Poems and Antipoems*, by Nicholas Parra, 1967
Indian Journals: March 1962–May 1963: Notebooks, Diary, Blank Pages, Writings, 1970
Allen Verbatim: Lectures on Poetry, Politics, Consciousness, 1974
Chicago Trial Testimony, 1975
Composed on the Tongue: Literary Conversations 1967–1977, 1980
Letters to William Burroughs 1953–1957, 1982
Allen Ginsberg: Photographs, 1991
Snapshot Poetics: A Photographic Memoir of the Beat Era, 1993
Journals Mid-Fifties 1954–1958, 1995
Deliberate Prose: Selected Essays 1952–1995, 1996
Family Business: Selected Letters Between a Father and a Son, by Allen Ginsberg and Louis Ginsberg, edited by Michael Schumacher, 2001

Further Reading

Caveney, Graham, *Screaming with Joy: The Life of Allen Ginsberg*, New York: Broadway, 1999
Clarke, Thomas, "Interview with Allen Ginsberg, 1966" in *Beat Writers at Work: The Paris Review Interviews*, edited by George Plimpton, New York: Modern Library, and London: Harvill Press, 1999
Dowden, George, *Allen Ginsberg: The Man/The Poet on Entering Earth Decade His Seventh*, Montreal: Alpha Beat Press, 1990
Kostelanetz, Richard (editor), "An Interview with Ginsberg", *American Writing Today*, Troy, New York: Whitston, 1991
Kramer, Jane, *Allen Ginsberg in America*, New York: Random House, 1968
Merrill, Thomas F., *Allen Ginsberg*, New York: Twayne, 1969
Miles, Barry, *Two Lectures on the Work of Allen Ginsberg*, London: Turret, 1992
Miles, Barry, *Ginsberg: A Biography*, New York: Simon and Schuster, and London: Viking, 1989
Morgan, Bill, *The Works of Allen Ginsberg, 1941–1994: A Descriptive Bibliography*, Westport, Connecticut: Greenwood Press, 1995
Morgan, Bill, *The Response to Allen Ginsberg 1926–1994: A Bibliography of Secondary Sources*, Westport, Connecticut: Greenwood Press, 1996
Mottram, Eric, *Allen Ginsburg in the Sixties*, Brighton, East Sussex and Seattle: Unicorn Bookshop, 1972
Podhoretz, Norman, *Ex-Friends: Falling Out with Allen Ginsberg, Lionel and Diana Trilling, Lillian Hellman, Hannah Arendt, and Norman Mailer*, New York: Free Press, 1999
Portuges, Paul, *The Visionary Poetics of Allen Ginsberg*, Santa Barbara, California: Ross Erikson, 1978
Schneeman, George and Anne Waldman, *Homage to Allen G.*, New York: Granary, 1997
Schumacher, Michael, *Dharma Lion: A Critical Biography of Allen Ginsberg*, New York: St Martin's Press, 1992
Simpson, Louis, *A Revolution in Taste: Studies of Dylan Thomas, Allen Ginsberg, Sylvia Plath, and Robert Lowell*, New York: Macmillan, 1978
Whitmer, Peter O., with Bruce VanWyngarden: *Aquarius*

Revisited: Seven Who Created the Sixties Counterculture That Changed America, New York: Macmillan, 1987
Young, Allen, *Gay Sunshine Interview: Allen Ginsberg with Allen Young*, Bolinas, California: Grey Fox Press, 1974

Ginsberg's early influences were his father's teaching and writing of poetry, childhood exposure to the English Romantics and Milton, and his family's secular, Jewish, Marxist outlook as partly evidenced by their support for his initial university course as a labour lawyer.

The next layer of seminal literary influences was Blake, Whitman, and Ginsberg's first meeting with the successful Beat writer, Jack Kerouac. From Blake and Whitman, Ginsberg gained models for his role as Old Testament prophet, subversive and pacifistic critic of American technocracy, but also developed a critical understanding of the homogenous political and spiritual "fall" of the nation. Making use of Whitman's visionary, long-lined, large-scaled poems, he also embraced Blake's sense of ecstatic experience encapsulated in symbolism and song. It is intriguing that he also quotes fascist-sympathizer Ezra Pound as an influence (see "Improvisation in Beijing"), but this is presumably connected with Pound's rejection of capitalism ("usury"), vital defence of poetry, and a possible empathy with Pound in his trial for treason. Through Kerouac, Ginsberg realized that writing could be a full-time career and began to identify with the West Coast "beat" style and its interest in jazz rhythms, being up-beat, "beat", or a finished generation. He also met William Burroughs, Neal Cassady, and Peter Orlovsky, with whom Ginsberg came out as homosexual, and was perceived as a Jewish radical in this early grouping.

Although he embraced Buddhism and later Eastern meditation systems, Ginsberg never explored the equivalent traditions within Jewish culture. Yet he was identified as a Jewish gay in Prague where the police beat him up in the 1960s. Again central to his description of his New Jersey childhood is an evocation of Jewish New York immigrant life as expressed in "Kaddish" and "The White Shroud". Ginsberg's views were anti-authoritarian, pro-spiritual, democratic and egalitarian. Hence in the playfully named poem "Hymmnn", he translates the *Kaddish* by subverting the Jewish idea of making a distinction between the sacred and profane and blesses the holiness of the "madhouse", "Paranoia" and "homosexuality".

His first major successful poem, "Howl", was a scream of rage against the destructive effects of materialism and technology, America viewed as an urban Hell of tortured souls. "I saw the best minds of my generation destroyed by madness, starving hysterical naked." The homo- and hetero-erotic relations outlined in "Howl" involved Ginsberg and his publisher, Lawrence Ferlinghetti in the first of many obscenity proceedings. In the first section of "Howl" Ginsberg imagines a relentless series of cameos of sensitive individuals heading towards suicide. This is a 300-line boundless sentence, evoking the breadth of American destructiveness, each cameo punctuated by the word "who". He addresses and empathizes with a murderer, Carl Solomon, suffering in Rockland mental hospital, "ah, Carl, while you are not safe I am not safe". The Judaic element is, however, limited to God as "El", a suicide as "meat for the synagogue", and the Christian appropriation from Psalms "eli . . . lamma *sabachtani*". These references are part of a strategy for placing destroyed minds in a context of hallucinogenic and religious experiences. In the second section the cause of spiritual destruction is repetitively identified as Moloch. Yet this is taken from Milton and Blake who had also previously used this symbol of a false materialist god from the Torah.

His second major poem, "Kaddish", was the sanctification of the life of his mother, Naomi Ginsberg. The methodology of this poem works as a mixture of direct address to his dead mother, stream of consciousness, details of her personal history, conversation, Jewish family life, and prayer. He juxtaposes the ancient *Kaddish* against the modernity of Ray Charles screaming the blues, historical and family events, Naomi's movement from Russia, and Stalin's purges, immigrant life on Orchard Street, and Naomi's paranoid obsession that in America she is being persecuted by Hitler, but also by members of her own family. Again the large scale boundless form represents the crazy chaos of her life and the modern world. There is a recurring motif of a flash of light symbolizing her life-span, an intense experience of pain and spiritual illumination, but also the Nagasaki explosion as constant features in Ginsberg's consciousness (see also "Nagasaki Days").

During the 1960s and subsequently Ginsberg emerged as the older generation rebel, criticizing America's Cold War nuclear politics as in "War Profit Litany". He became associated with other Jewish protest writers, such as Norman Mailer, Bob Dylan, and Abbie Hoffman in their assault on American policy in Vietnam (see "Going to Chicago"). Ginsberg always continued the stance of protest as in "Plutonian Ode" where he linked "Radioactive Nemesis", several biblical names for God, and "whirlpools of star spume silver-thin as hairs of Einstein". Jewish themes often emerge in several of Ginsberg's minor poems where the paradoxes of ethnic ties are put within a cosmopolitan context. In "NY Youth Call Annunciation" he addresses "all you Jewish boy friends" in N.Y. "show . . . your sex", but there is no preference for Jewish gays, for the same call is subsequently made to "black boys", Puerto Ricans, Amerindians, and Italians.

Again in "Yiddishe Kopf" in 1991 Ginsberg lists contradictory and irrational reasons for identifying as Jewish. He is Jewish because "violent Zionists make my blood boil", "Jewish because Buddhist", "Jewish because monotheist Jews Catholics, Moslems're intolerable intolerant", "Oy such Messhuggeneh absolutes". He mimics Yiddish humour to satirize extremists from a range of ideological divides, while his underlying values again appear to be universalist. He subverts Arab–Israeli polarities in the "Jaweh and Allah Battle" of 1974 by identifying mirror images of racial and theological parallels and stereotypes. Both Gods "Terrible", "Awful", both "hook-nosed", their followers "Zalmon Schacter" and "Suffi Sam", "Irgun Al Fatah." The poem relies on juxtaposing opposing organizations and ideologies, only reconciled in the final line, reminiscent of the end of T.S. Eliot's *Wasteland*, "SHALOM SHANTIH SALAAM." Clownish, sometimes publicly naked doing yoga, yet of rabbinic appearance, Ginsberg always retained a sense of outrage at moral corruption and thus in one of his last poems "Elephant in the Meditation Hall" he exposed dishonesty in a range of left-wing ideologies and religions of the East. He always remained subversive of icons, retaining his iconoclast's position as an icon for post-1960s subversives.

MERVYN LEBOR

Ginzburg, Natalia

Italian fiction writer, poet, dramatist, and essayist, 1916–1991

Born in Palermo, 14 July 1916, to Giuseppe Levi, Jewish professor of anatomy at Turin University, and Lydia, his Catholic wife. Moved with family to Turin, 1919. Studied at home and at schools in Turin, then in Faculty of Letters, Turin University, 1935; left before graduating. Married, first, Leone Ginzburg, Russian expatriate writer and political activist, 1938; three children. Exiled to Pizzoli, in Abruzzo, 1940; returned to Rome after fall of Mussolini, 1943; went into hiding in Rome, then in Florence, 1944; husband died while political prisoner in Rome, 1944; returned to Rome after Liberation. Worked for Einaudi, publishers, Rome and Turin, 1944–49. Married, second, Gabriele Baldini, 1950; settled in Rome, 1952. Moved to London, where Baldini became director of Italian Institute, 1959; returned to Rome, where Baldini became professor of English literature at Rome University, 1961. Baldini died, 1969. Elected to lower house of Parliament, as independent left-wing deputy, 1983. Awards include Tempo Prize 1947; Veillon Prize, 1952; Viareggio Prize, 1957; Chianciano Prize, 1961; Strega Prize, 1963; Marzotto Prize, 1965; Bargutta Prize, 1983. Died of cancer in Rome, 8 October 1991.

Selected Writings

Collection

Opere [Works], edited by Cesare Garboli, 2 vols, 1986–87

Novels

Giulietta [Julietta] (as Natalia Levi), 1934
I bambini [The Children] (as Natalia Levi), 1934
Un'assenza [An Absence] (as Natalia Levi), 1934
Casa al mare [House by the Sea] (as Alessandra Tornimparte), 1937
La strada che va in città (as Alessandra Tornimparte), 1942, revised edition, 1945; as *The Road to the City*, translated by Frances Frenaye in *The Road to the City: Two Novelettes*, 1949
È stato così, 1947; as *The Dry Heart*, translated by Frances Frenaye in *The Road to the City: Two Novelettes*, 1949
Tutti i nostri ieri, 1952; translated by Angus Davidson as *Dead Yesterdays*, 1956, as *A Light for Fools*, 1957; republished as *All Our Yesterdays*, 1985
Valentino (includes *Valentino*, *La madre*, and *Sagittario*), 1957
Le voci della sera, 1961; edited by S. Pacifici, 1971, and by Alan Bullock, 1982; as *Voices in the Evening*, translated by D.M. Low, 1963
Lessico famigliare, 1963; as *Family Sayings*, translated by D.M. Low, 1967; revised 1984
Cinque romanzi brevi [Five Short Novels], 1964
Mio marito [My Husband], 1964
Caro Michele, 1973; translated by Sheila Cudahy as *No Way*, 1974, as *Dear Michael*, 1975
Borghesia, 1977; as *Borghesia* in *Family: Two Novellas*, translated by Beryl Stockman, 1988
Famiglia, 1977; as *Family* in *Family: Two Novellas*, translated by Beryl Stockman, 1988
La famiglia Manzoni, 1983; as *The Manzoni Family*, translated by Marie Evans, 1987
La città e la casa, 1984; as *The City and the House*, translated by Dick Davis, 1987
Four Novellas (includes *Valentino*, *Sagittarius*, *Family*, and *Borghesia*), translated by Avril Bardoni and Beryl Stockman, 1990
The Things We Used to Say, translated by Judith Woolf, 1997

Plays

Ti ho sposato per allegria [I Married You for Fun], 1965
L'inserzione in *Ti ho sposato per allegria e altre commedie* [I Married You for Fun and Other Plays], 1968; as *The Advertisement*, translated by Henry Reed, 1969
Paese di mare e altre commedie [A Town by the Sea and Other Plays], 1973
La poltrona [The Armchair] in *Opere*, vol. 2, 1987
L'intervista [The Interview], 1989
Teatro [Theatre], includes *L'intervista* [The Interview], *La poltrona* [The Armchair], *Dialogo* [Conversation], *Paese di mare* [Town of the Sea], *La porta sbagliata* [The Wrong Door], *La parrucca* [The Wig], 1990
Il cormorano [The Cormorant], 1991

Other

Translator, *La strada di Swann* [Swann's Way], by Marcel Proust, 1946
Le piccole virtù, 1962; as *The Little Virtues*, translated by Dick Davis, 1985
Ma devi domandarmi, 1970; as *Never Must You Ask Me*, translated by Isabel Quigly, 1973
Vita immaginaria [Imaginary Life], 1974
Editor, *La carta del cielo: racconti*, by Mario Soldati, 1980
Editor, *Diari, 1927–1961*, by Antonio Delfini, 1982
La mia psicanalisi: tre racconti [My Psychoanalysis: Three Short Stories], 1983
Translator, *La signora Bovary*, by Gustave Flaubert, 1983
Serena Cruz; o La vera giustizia [Serena Cruz; or, True Justice], 1990

Further Reading

Borri, Giancarlo, *Natalia Ginzburg*, Rimini: Luise, 1999
Bullock, Allan, *Natalia Ginzburg: Human Relationships in a Changing World*, New York and Oxford: Berg, 1991
Cappetti, Carla, "Natalia Ginzburg" in *European Writers*, edited by George Stade, New York: Scribner, 1991
Giffuni, Cathe, "A Bibliography of the Writings of Natalia Ginzburg", *Bulletin of Bibliography*, 50/2 (1993)
Gordon, Mary, "Surviving History", *New York Times* (25 March 1990)

Heiney, Donald, "Natalia Ginzburg: The Fabric of Voices", *Iowa Review*, 1/4 (1970)
Hughes, Henry Stuart, *Prisoners of Hope: The Silver Age of the Italian Jews*, Cambridge, Massachusetts: Harvard University Press, 1983
Lobner, Corinna del Greco, "A Lexicon for Both Sexes: Natalia Ginzburg and the Family Saga" in *Contemporary Women Writers in Italy: A Modern Renaissance*, edited by Santo L. Arico, Amherst: University of Massachusetts Press, 1990
Merry, Bruce, *Women in Modern Italian Literature: Four Studies Based on the Work of Grazia Deledda, Alba de Cespedes, Natalia Ginzburg and Dacia Maraini*, Townsville, Australia: Department of Modern Languages, James Cook University of North Queensland, 1990
O'Healy, Anne-Marie, "Natalia Ginzburg and the Family", *Canadian Journal of Italian Studies*, 9 (1986): 21–36
Piclardi, Rosetta, "Forms and Figures in the Novels of Natalia Ginzburg", *World Literature Today*, 53 (1979)
Salmagundi, special issue, 96 (Autumn 1992)
Soave Bowe, Clotilde, "The Narrative Strategy of Natalia Ginzburg", *Modern Language Review*, 68 (1973)
Wood, Sharon, "Memory, Melancholy and Melodrama in Natalia Ginzburg 1916–1991" in *Italian Women's Writing, 1860–1994*, London: Athlone Press, 1995

Natalia Ginzburg was born Natalia Levi on 14 July 1916 in Palermo, the city in which her father taught anatomy. Her mother, a Catholic, descended from a cultivated and progressive family from Milan: the writer's grandfather, a lawyer, was a socialist and the friend of Filippo Turati, one of the most eminent figures in Italian socialism. On her father's side Natalia was Jewish, even though Giuseppe Levi, a descendent of a dynasty of bankers from Trieste, was not religious, any more than his wife was, for that matter: "neither the one nor the other practised religion, in one sense or in another. Neither the one nor the other ever set foot in a church or a temple", she tells us in the *Autodizionario degli autori italiani* [Autodictionary of Italian Authors]. Natalia's childhood and adolescence, therefore, are characterized by the absolute distance that was kept from religion, a matter that was not, however, alien to her sensibility and that was interwoven with the problem of her own identity. She resolved this problem over the course of time with originality and inventiveness, according to a line of development that was to lead her from a state of "unbelonging" to her acquiring "dual citizenship", Jewish and Catholic, in which the latter did not limit the full and conscious affirmation of the former. This path set the tempo for both her private and artistic life, until the two dimensions met in her characteristically clear and subdued writing, with its blend of irony and wisdom, in her capacity to capture everyday life's little exemplary gestures. Ginzburg's social and intellectual education took place in Turin, where her father had been transferred as early as 1919. The town hosted an assimilated Jewish minority actively involved in the intellectual professions and important in Piedmont's anti-fascist tradition, among whose ranks were numbered members of the writer's family and their entourage: Carlo Levi, Vittorio Foa, her brothers Mario, Gino and Alberto Levi, her husband Leone Ginzburg, and her brother-in-law Adriano Olivetti.

As a young girl at home she witnessed the first phase of the opposition to fascism (Mussolini came to power in 1922 and consolidated his dictatorship in 1925) in a feeling of conspiracy, in an intuitive idea of secrecy in which she was included through being told to be silent and yet at the same time excluded through the protective and prudent lies of her mother. Writing was her true interest even then: first she wrote poetry, and towards the age of 16 she practised writing short stories. It was thanks to one of these that she came into direct contact with Leone Ginzburg, a Russian Jew who had become a naturalized Italian, an anti-fascist, and an intellectual of the first rank (he played a vital role in the birth of the publishing house Einaudi, where some of the greatest Italian writers, including Natalia Ginzburg, were to write and work). She was to marry Leone Ginzburg in 1938, the year of the proclamation of the racial laws through which she lost the possibility of publishing her work – some of her short stories had already appeared from 1934 onwards – under her own name. Indeed *La strada che va in città* (*The Road to the City*) – a novel that she wrote during the three years she spent in confinement together with her husband in a small village in Abruzzo – came out under the pseudonym Alessandra Tornimparte. They were hard years which culminated in the death of her husband, in prison in Rome, in 1944; years in which Ginzburg experienced what it was like to be persecuted, forced to live in secrecy and to be uprooted as a Jew. Nonetheless, there is no place in her short stories and in her novels for Jews and Jewishness until 1952, in the evocative novel *Tutti i nostri ieri* (*All Our Yesterdays*), where for the first time she introduces, in the framework of the war, some Jewish characters: a Serbian family and a "Turk" who is given no better connotation and is defined only by the terror of being discovered – and deported – that animates him. Until that point, being a Jew, just like being a woman, had constituted a hurdle yet to be crossed in her writing. It had seemed to her that neither her environment, nor her city, nor her femininity were capable of producing literature. After the events of the war and all the previous experiences had been decanted, and thanks to a new marriage, to the scholar of English literature Gabriele Baldini, and to life in a new city – Rome – Ginzburg was finally able to bring her private universe into her poetic one. After *Sagittario* (from *Valentino*), in which a Jewish character appears who is portrayed with greater detail and realism – the Polish Jew Dr Chaim Wesser who, after being hidden during the persecution by an Italian family, decides when the war ends to stay on in Italy – and *Le voci della sera* (*Voices in the Evening*, written in London on a wave of acute homesickness) she wrote the highly successful autobiographical novel *Lessico famigliare* (*Family Sayings*) and seemed to complete the process of reconciling her internal contradictions.

She then continued her work as a writer, concentrating once again above all on the theme of the family. Her first collection of essays, *Le piccole virtù* (*The Little Virtues*) in 1962 contains significant observations on how Jews recognize one another through a kind of common environmental *quid*, an "air of home", and on the stubborn way she feels Jewish every time this identity appears threatened. Taken as a whole, however, Ginzburg's Jewishness appears to be a starting point towards a strong humanitarianism in which we also meet her as a Catholic, a communist, and a woman. Her sense of Jewishness, which was also always far from any Zionist tendencies, seems to be in the end a kind of ecumenical spiritual citizenship.

CLARA CORONA

Glants-Leyeles, Arn (Aaron Glanz-Leyeles)

Polish poet, dramatist, and essayist, 1889–1966

Born Arn Glants in Włocławek, 5 March 1889; moved with his family to Łódź, 1892; educated in his father's *talmed toyre* and at the local Russian commercial Gymnasium; emigrated to London, 1905; acted as London correspondent for *Der nayer veg* (Vilna), attended lectures at the University of London and became an active member of the SS (Socialist-Zionist) party; emigrated to New York, 1909; studied literature at Columbia University, 1910–13. Was an ardent supporter of Yiddish education, helped to found Yiddish schools in New York, Chicago, and western Canada and lectured on Yiddish literature; for 50 years contributed articles to the New York Yiddish daily, *Der tog*. Prose appeared under his own name, A. Glants, and poetry under the pseudonym, A. Leyeles. With Yankev Glatshteyn and Nokhem-Borekh Minkov co-founded the In zikh or Introspectivist movement of Yiddish poetry and the journal *Inzikh*, 1919. Visited Israel in 1964. Awarded the H. Leyvik prize and an honorary degree from Hebrew Union College, 1965. Died in New York, 30 December 1966.

Selected Writings

Collection
Opklayb: lider, poemes, drames [Collected Works: verse, long poems and dramas], 1968

Poetry
Labirint: lider [Labyrinth: Poems], 1918
Yungharbst [Young-Autumn], 1922
Rondos un andere lider [Rondeaux and Other Poems], 1926
Fabyus lind: lider un poemes [Fabius Lind: verse and long poems], 1937
A yid oyfn yam: lider un poemen [A Jew in the Sea: Verse and Long Poems], 1947
Baym fus fun barg: lider un poemes [At the Foot of the Mountain: Verse and Long Poems], 1957
Amerike un ikh [America and I], 1963
In *American Yiddish Poetry: A Bilingual Anthology*, edited and translated by Benjamin Harshav and Barbara Harshav, 1986
In *The Penguin Book of Modern Yiddish Verse*, edited by Irving Howe, Ruth R. Wisse, and Khone Shmeruk, 1987

Plays
Shloyme moylkhe: dramatishe poeme in tsen bilder [Solomon Molcho: Verse Drama in Ten Tableaux], 1926
Asher lemlekh [Asher Lemlekh], 1927

Other
Der Territorialismus ist die einzige Lösung der Judenfrage [Territorialism is the Only Solution to the Jewish Question] (in German), 1913
Velt un vort: literarishe un andere eseyen [World and Word: Literary and Other Essays], 1958
"My Literary Memories" and "Leonardo and Judas", in *The Way We Think: A Collection of Essays from the Yiddish*, edited and translated by Joseph Leftwich, 1969

Further Reading

Harshav, Benjamin, *The Meaning of Yiddish*, Berkeley: University of California Press, 1990
Liptzin, Solomon, *The Maturing of Yiddish Literature*, New York: Jonathan David, 1970

Arn Glants began publishing his earliest poems in 1914 under the name A. Leyeles in the *Fraye arbeter-shtime* [Free Worker's Voice], while continuing to sign his journalistic work with his real name. In 1918 Yankev Glatshteyn and Nokhem-Borekh Minkov, at that time still students, came to Glants-Leyeles (as he is these days normally known), with their poems and together with him developed the ideology and poetics of a new modernist trend. In his first collection of poems, *Labirint*, published the same year, Glants-Leyeles can be seen moving away from the neo-romantic style of his predecessors towards the innovations that were to become characteristic of the Introspectivist movement in whose foundation and theoretical underpinning he played so dominant a role. In 1920 appeared *In zikh: a zamlung introspektive lider* [In Oneself: An Anthology of Introspective Poems] which contained the manifesto of the new movement which sees truth not in external reality, but in a succession of impressions filtered through the psychological prism of the individual consciousness and which maintains that "an illusion is often more real than the cluster of external appearances we call life". Above all, and this is what constitutes the major break with the practice of the earlier movement known as *Di yunge* or the Young Ones, the manifesto calls for the uniqueness of the experience to be reflected in unique dictions. The manifesto announces, among other things, that in future all Yiddish words including those of Hebrew origin are to be spelled phonetically. In this, together with all the Inzikhists, Glants-Leyeles was employing what he liked to call the "naturalistic orthography" that was effectively more or less identical to "Soviet"-Yiddish spelling. Glatshteyn and Minkov also signed, but the manifesto was largely the work of Glants-Leyeles. These ideas were reinforced in 1923, in an essay on technique published in *Inzikh*, in which Glants-Leyeles was scathing in his rejection of the shallow, cloying diminutives of the "hartsenyu, kroynenyu"-school of popular Yiddish poetry.

Glants-Leyeles was strongly influenced by Russian symbolism and neo-romanticism. As in the case of Glatshteyn, Glants-Leyeles's verse moves freely between modernist inventiveness, more overtly Jewish themes, and more conservative forms. A master of Provençal and Italian metres that he learned from the Russian Symbolists and the German Impressionists, he wrote sonnets, villanelles, rondeaux, poems in ottava rima and invented his own strophic patterns. At the same time he was a forceful advocate of American themes and created a variety of American-influenced but original and rhythmically intense free verse forms. Glants-Leyeles demanded the use of simple and precise language rather than traditionally mellifluous diction. He advocated the use of free verse, though not as an exclusive method, and called for sharp, condensed images and a completely free choice of themes. His own thematic material is taken from many sources, including Buddhism, psychoanalysis, American architecture, the Russian Revolution, the scriptures, Baudelaire, and the Holocaust. With his lifelong friend H. Leyvik (who had originally been associated with *Di yunge*) Glants-Leyeles shared a proclivity for mysticism and certain of his poems contemplate the numinous immanence of animals and things in a manner that is comparable with Rilke's early *Dinggedichte*. In 1926 Glants-Leyeles published his *Rondos un andere lider*, which ironically desentimentalized personal experience and celebrated the architecture, multifarious life, and power of New York City in a manner that invites comparison with the strident urbanism of German *Asphaltdichtung* or with what Moyshe Kulbak was to do for Berlin seven years later in his *Disner tshayld harold* [The Childe Harold of Disna]. The collection included the famous free-verse "In sobvey" poems, which gave kaleidoscopic expression to the powerful synesthetic sensations of rush-hour travel on the New York subway.

The historical dramas *Shloyme moylkhe* (1926) and *Asher lemlekh* (1927), which are set against a wide variety of medieval backgrounds, show Glants-Leyeles's concern for Jewish destiny across the centuries and debate different strategies of Jewish survival in a hostile environment. The protagonist of his *Fabyus lind* (1937) is a sort of alter ego who presents an increasingly pessimistic view of man's destiny in an alienated urban world. *Fabyus lind* is a kaleidoscopic diary of a contemporary, in which the personal and the social, the trivial and the metaphysical alternate, matched by an ostensibly random alternation of a broad spectrum of formal and free verse. This concept of kaleidoscopic method brought together several modern principles: the psychology of the stream of consciousness, the multidimensional nature of modern life, simultaneity of experience, fragmented representation rather than full description, and the conscious organization of a poem as a "fugue" or a " symphony" of heterogeneous elements. The Holocaust led him in the direction of greater conservatism and a return to more Jewish themes, again in a manner that is paralleled in the career of Glatshteyn. *A yid oyfn yam* [A Jew in the Sea] (1947), which was composed as the magnitude of the catastrophe was becoming apparent, recorded his feelings of guilt for having survived.

HUGH DENMAN

Glantz, Margo

Mexican fiction writer, critic, and translator, 1930–

Born in Mexico City, 28 January 1930; parents both immigrants from Ukraine. Studied at Universidad Nacional Autónoma de México, MA in modern letters, history of art, and drama; at the Sorbonne, PhD in letters, 1958; history of art at the Louvre; English literature at Central London Polytechnic. Married twice; two children. Director, Cultural Institute of Mexico–Israel, 1964–67; director of publications and libraries in Department of Public Education, 1982; director of literature, Instituto Nacional de Bellas Artes, 1983–86; cultural attaché at Mexican Embassy, London, 1986–88; professor emeritus, Faculty of Philosophy and Letters, Universidad Nacional Autónoma, since 1995. Member of Mexican Academy of Language since 1995. Numerous visiting professorships; Regent Scholar, Irvine University, 1986; Welford Thompson lecturer, Cambridge University, 1993; Council of the Humanities Fellow, Princeton University, 1994; member of advisory council, Program in Latin American Studies, Princeton University, 1998. Has translated works by Antonin Artaud, Georges Bataille, Henry Fielding, Jerzy Grotowski, and Tennessee Williams into Spanish. Contributor to journals, such as *Filosofía y Letras* and *Revista Iberoamericana*; to newspapers, including *Unomasuno* and *La Jornada*; and to radio programmes. Awarded Magda Donato Prize, 1982; Premio Xavier Villaurrutia, 1984; Premio Universidad Nacional, 1991; Guggenheim Fellowship and Rockefeller Foundation grant, 1996; Guggenheim Scholarship, 1998.

Selected Writings

Novels

Las mil y una calorías: novela dietética [One Thousand and One Calories: A Dietetic Novel], 1978
Doscientas ballenas azules [Two Hundred Blue Whales], 1979
No pronunciarás [Thou Shalt Not Say], 1980
Las genealogías, 1981; as *The Family Tree: An Illustrated Novel*, translated by Susan Bassnett, 1991
Síndrome de naufragios [Shipwreck Syndrome], 1984
Apariciones [Apparitions], 1996

Short Stories

La guerra de los hermanos: leyenda de la Coyolxauhqui [The Brothers' War], 1982
"Todas las rosas" [All the Roses] in *Mujeres en espejo: Narradoras latinoamericanas siglo XX* [Ladies in the Mirror: Latin-American Women Writers] vol. 2, 1985

Other

Tennessee Williams y el teatro norteamericano [Tennessee Williams and North American Theatre], 1964
Viajes en México: crónicas extranjeras [Travels in Mexico: Foreign Chronicles], 1964
Onda y escritura en México: Jóvenes de 20 a 33 [The New Wave and Writing in Mexico: Young Writers from 20 to 33], 1971
Un folletín realizado: la aventura del Conde de Raousset-Boulbon en México, 1973

Repeticiones: ensayos sobre literatura mexicana [Repetitions: Essays on Mexican Literature], 1979
Intervención y pretexto: ensayos de literatura comparada e iberoamericana [Intervention and Excuse: Essays about Comparative and Spanish-American Literature], 1981
El día de tu boda [Your Wedding Day], 1982
La lengua en la mano [With Tongue in Hand], 1983
De la amorosa inclinación a enredarse en cabellos [On the Amorous Inclination to Get Entangled in Tresses], 1984
Erosiones [Erosions], 1984
Borrones y borradores: ensayos de literatura colonial [Jottings and Sketches: Essays on Colonial Literature], 1992
Notas y commentarios sobre Álvar Núñez Cabeza de Vaca [Notes and Commentaries about Álvar Núñez Cabeza de Vaca], 1992
Esguince de cintura: ensayos sobre narrativa mexicana del siglo XX [Twist: Essays on Twentieth-Century Mexican Narrative], 1994
Editor, *La Malinche, sus padres y sus hijos* [Malinche, her Parents and her Children], 1994
Huérfanos y bandidos: los bandidos de Río Frío [The Bandits of Río Frío], 1995
Introduction to edition of *Parayso occidental* by Carlos de Sigüenza y Góngora (1684), 1995
Introduction to edition of *Segundo volumen de sus obras* [Second Volume of Her Works], by Juana Inés de la Cruz, 1995
Sor Juana Inés de la Cruz: ¿hagiografía o autobiografía? [Sor Juana Inés de la Cruz: Hagiography or Autobiography?], 1995
Rulfo y Gorostiza: discurso de recepción a la Academia Mexicana de la Lengua, 1996
Sor Juana Inés de la Cruz: saberes y placeres [Sor Juana Inés de la Cruz: Wisdom and Pleasure], 1996
Editor, *Del fistol a la linterna: homenaje a José Tomás de Cuéllar y Manuel Payno en el centario de su merte (1894–1994)*, 1997
Editor, *Sor Juana Inés de la Cruz y sus contemporáneos* [Sor Juana Inés de la Cruz and her Contemporaries], 1998
Sor Juana: la comparación y la hipérbole [Sor Juana: Comparison and Hyperbole], 1999

Further Reading

Agosín, Marjorie, "Dialogando *Las genealogías* de Margo Glantz", in her *Las hacedoras: mujer, imagen, escritura*, Santiago: Cuarto Propio, 1993
Agosín, Marjorie (editor), *The House of Memory: Stories by Jewish Women Writers of Latin America*, New York: Feminist Press, 1999
Eltit, Diamela, "El Alertado y Riesgoso Cuerpo de la Letra", *Debate Feminista*, 9/17 (1998): 269–72
Franco, Jean, "Cuerpos en pedazos", *Debate feminista*, 9/17 (1998)
García Pinto, Magdalena, "Entrevista con Margo Glantz" in *Historias íntimas: conversaciones con diez escritoras latinoamericanas*, Hanover, New Hampshire: Ediciones del Norte, 1988; translated by Magdalena García Pinto and Trudy Balch as *Women Writers of Latin America: Intimate Histories*, Austin: University of Texas Press, 1991
García Pinto, Magdalena, "La problemática de la sexualidad en la escritura de Margo Glantz", *Coloquio Internacional: escritura y sexualidad en la literatura hispanoamericana, Poitiers, 1987*, Madrid: Centre de Recherches Latino-Americaines / Fundamentos / Espiral Hispanoamericana, 1990
Glickman, Nora, "Margo Glantz" in *Tradition and Innovation: Reflections on Latin American Jewish Writing*, edited by Robert DiAntonio and Nora Glickman, Albany: State University of New York Press, 1993
Gliemmo, Graciela, "La transgresión que no cesa", *Feminaria*, Buenos Aires, 3/6 (1990)
Gliemmo, Graciela, "Margo Glantz" in *Las huellas de la memoria: entrevista a escritores latinoamericanos* [The Trace of Memory: Interviews with Latin American Writers], Buenos Aires: Beas, 1994
Jörgensen, Beth Ellen, "Margo Glantz, Tongue in Hand" in *Reinterpreting the Spanish American Essay: Women Writers of the 19th and 20th Centuries*, edited by Doris Meyer, Austin: University of Texas Press, 1995
Lindstrom, Naomi, "*No pronunciarás* de Margo Glantz: los nombres como señas de la imaginación cultural", *Revista Iberoamericana*, 56/151 (1990)
Lorenzano, Sandra, "Del amoroso enredo en la literatura", *Debate Feminista*, 9/17 (1998)
Mansour, Mónica, "Apariciones", *Debate Feminista*, 9/17 (1998)
Miller, Beth Kurti, *A la sombra del volcán: conversaciones sobre la narrativa mexicana actual*, Guadalajara: Universidad de Guadalajara / Universidad Veracruzana / Instituto Nacional de Bellas Artes, 1990
Otero-Krauthammer, Elizabeth, "Integración de la identidad judía en *Las genealogías* de Margo Glantz", *Revista Iberoamericana*, 51/130–131 (1985)
Pasternac, Nora, "La escritura fragmentaria", *Sin imágenes falsas, sin falsos espejos: narradoras mexicanas del siglo XX*, edited by Aralia López González, Mexico City: El Colegio de México, 1995
Pfeiffer, Erna, "Tenemos que reescribir el mundo: Margo Glantz" in *Entrevistas: diez escritoras mexicanas desde bastidores*, Frankfurt: Vervuert, 1992
Senkman, Leonardo, "Jewish Latin American Writers and Collective Memory" in *Tradition and Innovation: Reflections on Latin American Jewish Writing*, edited by Robert DiAntonio and Nora Glickman, Albany: State University of New York Press, 1993
Valenzuela, Luisa, "Mis Brujas Favoritas" in *Theory and Practice of Feminist Literary Criticism*, edited by Gabriela Mora and Karen S. Van Hooft, Ypsilanti, Michigan: Bilingual Press, 1982

Margo Glantz's oeuvre manifests a *mestizaje* or hybridity in both style and context, making the Jewish aspects of her writing inextricable from the Mexican. Her writing displays a fusion of genres and themes that challenges canonical classification.

Glantz's first novel, *Las mil y una calorías* [One Thousand

and One Calories] is an avant-garde tapestry of puns and humorous quotes that questions the aesthetic ideals of unity and uniformity. She follows this trend in *Doscientas ballenas azules* [Two Hundred Blue Whales] with a lyrical yet fragmentary style that would become characteristic of her writing, challenging, once again, generic expectations.

Glantz, the daughter of the renowned Yiddish poet Yaacov (Jacobo) Glantz, begins to ponder Jewish issues in *No pronunciarás* [Thou Shalt Not Say], a literary exploration of the act of naming and prohibition. While some critics have linked her text *De la amorosa inclinación a enredarse en cabellos* [On the Amorous Inclination to Get Entangled in Tresses] to a biblical theme, it is evident that this polymorphic work is yet another manifestation of the crisis of literary genres in her oeuvre. According to Chilean critic and novelist Diamela Eltit, in this text "Glantz examines icons and 'monstrous' figures that touch upon the contemporary imagination". Eltit defines Glantz's tapestry of genres as the product of her relentless determination "to hold on to diverse structures in which the foreign and the personal are interchanged, and where the fragment and the whole confront each other with the same vertigo as an entangled head of hair".

Síndrome de naufragios [Shipwreck Syndrome] is, according to Glantz, "a novel without characters" in which the protagonists are forces of nature, from the biblical flood to ordinary hurricanes. The autobiographical component is also present, for Glantz acknowledges that it is also "the story of a divorce".

Glantz's most celebrated novel, *Las genealogías* (*The Family Tree*), is a tender examination of her Jewish and Mexican heritages. Somewhere between novel, documentary, and autobiography, *Las genealogías* intertwines memories of her family's life in czarist Russia and their arrival in Mexico after the Soviet Revolution with her own experiences of growing up in a Jewish – yet secular – household in predominantly Catholic Mexico. This "biography of exiles" chronicles the processes of transculturation, and places Glantz in the role of cultural mediator between the Jewish and the Mexican. It can also be read as a literary genealogy, for Glantz ascertains her father's prominent place in Yiddish letters and among Mexican intellectuals, while situating herself on the periphery of both worlds.

Glantz's determination with searching for unity in fragmentation – a pursuit reminiscent of the work of French feminist Monique Wittig – is further evidenced in her latest novel *Apariciones* [Apparitions], an exploration of eroticism, from its human to its divine manifestations. The text gravitates from the contemporary to the colonial period, merging the two areas of research that have characterized Glantz's academic writing.

Glantz has achieved great notoriety in the field of Mexican colonial literature, specifically as the leading scholar on the writings of Sor Juana Inés de la Cruz (1651(?)–95). In *Borrones y borradores* [Jottings and Sketches] she examines the metaphors of colonial writing in an attempt to forge a continuity between colonial and contemporary writing, while in *Sor Juana Inés de la Cruz: ¿hagiografía o autobiografía?* [Sor Juana Inés de la Cruz: Hagiography or Autobiography?] Glantz analyses the concept of autobiography in the light of an era in which religious and social discourses were inextricably linked. She retakes this theme in her 1999 book, *Sor Juana: la comparación y la hipérbole* [Sor Juana: Comparison and Hyperbole]. She also examines the impact of fame and the hyperbolic definition of greatness as applied to the historical figure of Sor Juana, specifically in the Baroque letters.

LYDIA M. GIL

Glatshteyn, Yankev (Jacob Glatstein)

Polish-born poet, fiction writer, and critic, 1896–1971

Born in Lublin, 1896. Emigrated with his family to United States, 1914. Married Nettie Bush, 1919; three children. Began writing at an early age. First poems appeared in *Poezye*, 1919. Inaugurated the Inzikhist or "Introspectivist" tendency in America's Yiddish poetry with Arn Glants-Leyeles and N.B. Minkov; journal *Inzikh* appeared irregularly, 1920–39. Worked as columnist for the New York Yiddish daily, the *Day-Morning Journal*. Left wife; became Fanny Mazel's companion, 1952. Contributed regular column, "In tokh genumen", to the weekly *Idisher kemfer*, 1945–57. Died in New York City, 19 November 1971.

Selected Writings

Poetry
Yankev Glatshteyn, 1921
Fraye ferzn [Free Verse], 1926
Kredos [Credos], 1929
Yidishstaytshn [Yiddish Meanings], 1937
Gedenklider [Remembrance Poems], 1943
Shtralendike yidn [Radiant Jews], 1946
Dem tatns shotn [My Father's Shadow], 1953
Fun mayn gantser mi [Of All My Labour: Collected Poems], 1956
Di freyd fun yidishn vort [The Joy of the Yiddish Word], 1961
A yid fun lublin [A Jew from Lublin], 1966
Kh'tu dermonen [I Remind], 1967
Poems, edited and translated by Etta Blum, 1970
Gezangen fun rekhts tsu links [Songs from Right to Left], 1971
The Selected Poems of Jacob Glatstein, translated by Ruth Whitman, 1972
Selected Poems of Yankev Glatshteyn, translated and edited by Richard J. Fein, 1987
I Keep Recalling: The Holocaust Poems of Jacob Glatstein, translated by Barnett Zumoff, 1993

For Children
Emil un Karl [Emil and Karl], 1940

Other
Ven yash iz geforn [When Yash Went Away], 1938; as *Homeward Bound*, translated by Abraham Goldstein, 1969
Ven yash iz gekumen [When Yash Arrived], 1940; as *Homecoming at Twilight*, translated by Norbert Guterman, 1962

Editor, with S. Niger and Hilel Rogof, *Finf un zibetsik yor yidishe prese in amerike, 1870–1945* [Seventy-Five Years of the Yiddish Press in America], 1945
In tokh genumen: eseyen [Sum and Substance: Essays], 4 vols, 1947–60
Mit mayne fartogbikher [With My Books at Dawn], 1963
Oyf greyte temes [On Prepared Topics], 1967
Editor, with Israel Knox and Samuel Margoshes, *Anthology of Holocaust Literature*, 1969
In der velt mit yidish: eseyen [In the World with Yiddish], 1972
Prost un poshet: literarishe eseyen [Plain and Simple: Literary Essays], 1978

Further Reading

Deitch, Mattes, *Yankev Glatshteyn: der yid fun lid*, Tel Aviv: Perets, 1963
Faerstein, Ch., in *Judaism*, 14 (1965)
Greenberg, Eliezer, *Yankev Glatshteyns freyd fun yidishn vort*, New York: Tsiko, 1964
Gutman, Saul, *Traditsye un banayung: eseyen 1944–1966*, New York: Matones, 1967
Hadda, Janet, *Yankev Glatshteyn*, Boston: Twayne, 1980
Sadan, Dov, bibliographical notes, in Glatshteyn's *Mi-kol amali: shirim u-po'emot* (translation of *Fun mayn gantser mi*), Jerusalem: Mosad Byalik, 1964
Starkman, Moyshe (editor), *Hemshekh antologye fun amerikaner-yidisher dikhtung 1918–1943*, New York: Hemshekh, 1945

Given the breadth and depth of Yankev Glatshteyn's (Jacob Glatstein's) writing, this essay must of necessity be highly selective. Though Glatshteyn was a noted essayist and novelist as well as a poet, it is primarily for his poetry that he is known to students of Yiddish literature, and this essay will correspondingly focus on this aspect of his literary output. In lieu of a biographical or directly chronological approach, four ways of looking at Glatshteyn's poetry will be suggested, with brief analyses of representative poems for each.

The first approach is to view Glatshteyn as an Inzikhist or Introspectivist; that is, as the founding member he was of one of the most important aesthetic movements in the history of Yiddish poetry. The Inzikhists, who released their manifesto in 1920, advocated a modernist engagement with free verse and a highly individualistic experimentation with word, sound, and form which resulted in work quite different from the smooth poetic lines of *Di yunge* (the Young Ones) or the calls for social reform of the sweatshop poets.

Much of Glatshteyn's early work, particularly the poetry in his first collection, *Yankev Glatshteyn*, can be seen in this Inzikhist mould. Take, for example, "Tirtl-toybn" [Turtle-Doves], in which the poet's link to his schoolboy past is effectively and instantaneously accomplished by his contemplation of a word, and of the series of sounds which constitute that word: "Suddenly -/ cheder years and a word -/ just one word:/ Turtledoves./ It won't go away:/ Supple crinkle of *turtle*,/ its caressing wrinkle./ Oh, turtledoves/ turtledoves./ Turtle-turtle/turtledoves." (Fein, 1987). Or "Tsela-Tseldi" [Tsela-Tseldi], which discusses the rejuvenative possibilities of sheer sound: "Tsela-tseldi,/Tsela-tseldi – nimble body,/ To the cymb of cymbals/ You become a nimble doe,/ a lithe hare" (Fein, 1987). Here the rejuvenation affects not merely the creature addressed by the poet, but the poet himself, and, by extension, the reader – a poetical proof of the potency of Inzikhist stylistics.

To consider Glatshteyn as simply a technical or formal innovator, however, is to fail to give him his due as a master of mood and psychology. In one of his finest poems, "Ovntbroyt" [Evening Bread], published in *Fraye ferzn* [Free Verse], the very first few lines, "Pregnant, plump, abundant, warm/ bread is on the table./ Silently,/ guests gather at the table:/ I and she and still another she" (Fein, 1987) effectively juxtapose spare, dehumanized description of individuals with an almost tumescent characterization of the meal they are about to share. With remarkable economy, the lines foreshadow the complex love/hate relationships that Glatshteyn goes on to sketch among the three. At times, as in "A toyt-sharade" [A Death Charade], Glatshteyn is able to use formalist structures to further psychological considerations; in using the word "toyt" ("dead" or "death") 15 times in 20 lines, he both stresses the universality of the death experience and the ultimate numbness and alienation that sustained contemplation of such an experience must provide.

Although Glatshteyn's voice was forged in the fires of a movement which apotheosized the individuality of poetic expression, much of his work can also be seen as an attempt to speak in a national voice. This is particularly the case with his Holocaust poetry, written before, during, and after World War II. As early as 1938, Glatshteyn had seen the writing on the wall, and in his biting "A gute nakht, velt" [Good Night, World], written in 1938 but published in *Gedenklider* [Remembrance Poems], 1943, he blisteringly announces the failure of all attempts to grapple with or to accept external European culture in the face of anti-Semitism, and proudly advocates a return to Jewish culture on his own terms: "Good night, wide world/ great, stinking world./ Not you, but I slam the gate. With the long gabardine, with the yellow patch – burning -/ with proud stride/ I decide –: I am going back to the ghetto/ [. . .] Prussian pig and hate-filled Pole; Jew-killers, land of guzzle and gorge./ [. . .] Back to my kerosene, tallowed shadows,/ eternal October, minute stars,/ to my warped streets and hunch-backed lanterns,/ my worn-out pages of the Prophets,/ my Gemaras, to arduous/ Talmudic debates, to lucent, exegetic Yiddish,/ to Rabbinical Law, to deep-deep meaning, to duty, to what is right" (Fein, 1987).

Glatshteyn's return to Jewish forms and concepts can also be seen in "Nisht di meysim loybn got" [The Dead Don't Praise God], from *Shtralendike yidn* [Radiant Jews]. In this poem, whose title is taken from the Hallel, the traditional prayer of praise offered by Jews to God on holidays, Glatshteyn describes a communal rejection of the covenant between God and his chosen people in the face of the Holocaust: "We accepted the Torah on Sinai,/ And in Lublin we gave it back./ The dead don't praise God –/ The Torah was given for Life./ And just as we all stood together/ At the giving of the Torah,/ So indeed did we all die in Lublin" (Zumoff, 1993). Referring explicitly to the Jewish legend that all Jews who had ever lived and were yet to be born were also present at the giving of the Torah on Mount Sinai, the

Yiddish poet who witnessed the destruction of European Jewry from afar in America audaciously creates a unified Jewish presence which suffers and perishes together: "All those who had stood on Mount Sinai/ And accepted the Torah/ Took upon themselves the holy deaths./ We want to die together with our entire people,/ We want to become dead once again,/ Wailed the souls" (Zumoff, 1993).

Even this communal memory, however, is often expressed in individual voice, of the poet's and others', and Glatshteyn's skills in playing with historical figures and adopting historical personae, both within and without the Jewish community, should be particularly noted even within the course of this brief essay. Unsurprisingly, Glatshteyn's attentions were particularly drawn to writers and poets, and his portraits of Rabbi Nachman of Bratslav, the great Hasidic storyteller of the 19th century, and Li Po, the 8th-century Chinese poet, are particularly compelling, and in fact allow us to revisit some of the themes we saw earlier.

For example, Glatshteyn's Nachman, in "Der bratslaver tsu zayn soyfer" ([From Nakhman of Bratslav to His Scribe], in *Remembrance Poems*), blends principles of traditional Hasidic thought and doctrine, such as the movement's emphasis on music and unification with the Divine essence, with the modernist poet's interest and joy in the sounds of words and his frustration at an inability to capture the precise expression he wants. ("So, seize it – now –/ How wonderful it is –/ One – oneness./ One and only One –/ All – Oneness./ And again and again – Oneness./ [. . .] I'll break your bones/ If you don't get that tune./ If you lose any part of it – a word, or even a letter./ It's got to be as simple as this –/ Di-dana-di." (Fein, 1987). On the other hand, the later Li Po poems, such as "Mit li tai po" ([After Li Tai Po], in *A yid fun lublin* [A Jew from Lublin]) provide a moody, psychologized look at the poet's strained relationship with his wife, to whom he is unfaithful, which is somehow evocative of the sparer "Ovntbroyt": "Driven by curiosity to sample strange beds,/ Without restraint,/ He finds his own wife is very like/ The sobering mockery/ You hear when you tap the empty pitcher" (Whitman, 1972).

As such, these varied ways of looking at Glatshteyn's poetry can be used either singly or in combination to approach this brilliant poet's large and varied body of work.

JEREMY DAUBER

Glickman, Nora

Argentine writer, 1944–

Born in Bernasconi, La Pampa, 23 July 1944. Married Henry Glickman, 1964; three children. Studied in Argentina, Israel, United Kingdom; MA at Columbia University; PhD in comparative literature at New York University 1972. Professor of Latin American literature, Queens College, City University of New York. Vice President, City University of New York Academy for Sciences and Humanities; member of board, Latin American Jewish Studies Association. Several awards for research on contemporary fiction of Latin America; from Memorial Foundation for Jewish Culture, 1980, Research Foundation for Jewish Culture, 1994; Jerome Foundation Drama Award, 1994; National Foundation for Jewish Culture Award, 1995.

Selected Writings

Fiction

Uno de sus Juanes y otros cuentos [One of her Johns], 1983

Mujeres, memorias, malogros, 1991

Plays

Antología de teatro de Nora Glickman, 2000

Other

"The Image of the Jew in Brazilian and Argentinian Literature" (PhD dissertation), New York University, 1972

Leib Malach y la trata de blancas, 1984

Editor and translator, *Argentine Jewish Fiction* (*Modern Jewish Studies*), 1993

Editor, *Argentine Jewish Literature: Critical Essays* (*Modern Jewish Studies*), 1993

Editor, with Robert DiAntonio,, *Tradition and Innovation: Reflections on Latin American Jewish Writing*, 1993

Editor, with Gloria F. Waldman, *Argentine Jewish Theatre: A Critical Anthology*, 1996

"Discovering Self in History: Aida Bortnik and Gerardo Goloboff" in *Jewish Diaspora in Latin America: New Studies in History and Literature*, edited by D. Sheining and L. Barr, 1996

The Jewish White Slave Trade and the Untold Story of Raquel Liberman, 2000

"Los Diarios de Max Aub", *Raíces* (January 2000)

"Andando se hacen los caminos de Alicia Dujovne Ortiz", *Revista Iberoamericana*, 191 (April–June 2000)

"El entredicho de la 'Librada': reconstrucción de un cuento de Max Aub" in *Prosa y poesía: homenaje a Gonzalo Sobejano*, edited by Jean François Botrel *et al.*, Madrid: Gredos, 2001

Further Reading

Baumgarten, Murray, "Urban Life and Jewish Memory in the Tales of Moacyr Scliar and Nora Glickman" in *Tradition and Innovation: Reflections on Latin American Jewish Writing*, edited by Robert DiAntonio and Nora Glickman, Albany: State University of New York Press, 1993

Bausset-Orcutt, Monica, "Nora Glickman: Diaspora and Identity in 'Liturgies' and 'Blanca Días' ", *Modern Jewish Studies*, 12/4 (1995): 98–107

Cox, Victoria, " Nora Glickman: Between Several Cultures", *Buenos Aires Herald* (4 June 1995)

Dellepìane, Angela, "Un Bildungsroman feminino", *Confluencie* (Fall 2000): 130–34

Lampert, Zohra, " 'A Day in New York': A Narrative on the Process of Staging Nora Glickman's Play as a One-Woman Show" (MA thesis), CUNY Graduate Center

Lindstrom, Naomi, *Jewish Issues in Argentina Literature: From Gerchunoff to Szichman*, Columbia: University of Missouri Press, 1989

Lockhart, Darrell B., "Review of *Mujeres, memorias, malagros*", *Chasqui*, 21/1 (1992)

Martínez, Elena M., "La problematica de la mujer en los textos de Julia Ortiz Gaffen, Mireya Robles y Nora Glickman" in *New Voices in Latin American Literature*, edited by Miguel Falquez-Certain, New York: Ollantay Center for the Arts, 1993
"Review of *Mujeres, memorias, malogros*", *World Literature Today*, 65/4 (1991)
Schiminovich, Flora H., "Noticias de suburbio: una vision utopica de relacion entre mujeres" in *En un acto: antología de teatro femenino latinamericano*, Medellín, Colombia: Editorial Universidad de Antioquia, 1995
Schiminovich, Flora, "Una propuesta utópia de comunión entre mujeres" in *Antología crítica del teatro breve hispanoamericano, 1948–1993*, edited by María Mercedes Jaramillo and Mario Yepes, Medellín, Colombia: Editorial Universidad de Antioquia, 1997
Schneider, Judith Morganroth, "Una lectura femenina y judía de dos escritoras *judeoargentinas*: Nora Glickman y Alicia Steimberg", *Alba de America: Critica Literaria de la Literatura de Latinoamerica, Siglo XX* (1990) [1992]: 319–27
Schneider, Judith Morganroth, "Forjando nuevas alianzas feministas en la diáspora latinoamericana: Esmeralda Santiago y Nora Glickman, dos escritoras latinas de los suburbios de Nueva York", in *Exilios femeninos*, Huelva: Servicios de Publicaciones de la Universidad de Huelva, 1999: 293–302
Schneider, Judith Morganroth, "Mestizas judeolatinoamericanas: La construcción de identidades diaspóricas femeninas en el teatro de Nora Glickman" in *Actas del Coloquio Internacional: La mujer latinoamericana y su cultura en los umbrales del próximo milenio: teoría, historia y crítica*, Casa de las Américas, Universidad Autónoma Metropolitana-Iztapalapa de México, and Universidad de Buenos Aires (in press)
Torres-Saillant, Silvio, *Hispanic Immigrant Writers and the Family*, New York: Ollantay Center for the Arts, 1994

Nora Glickman was born in Argentina, in the province of La Pampa. She traces her origins to her Russian grandparents who settled in the Pampas and were known as Jewish "gauchos". Glickman emigrated from Argentina to Israel and England, then to the United States where she completed her graduate studies. She received her MA at Columbia University and her PhD in comparative literature at New York University. She is Professor of Latin American literature, drama, and cinema at Queens College of the City University of New York.

Glickman has won recognition in the United States and Latin America as an author of short stories and plays, and has lectured and published extensively on contemporary Latin American literature and drama. Over the years she has continued her studies on the work of the Spanish writer Max Aub and has concentrated most of her research on the image of the Jew in Brazilian and Latin American literature. Her book *Leib Malach y la trata de blancas*, a monographic study on the ramification of the Jewish prostitution trade from Poland to Argentina, includes a translation (written with Rosalí a Rosembuj) from the Yiddish of Leib Malach's play *Ibergus* [Regeneration].

Glickman edited two volumes of the annual *Modern Jewish Studies / Yiddish* which were dedicated to Argentine Jewish fiction and criticism respectively. Her co-edition (with Roberto DiAntonio) of *Tradition and Innovation: Reflections on Latin American Jewish Writing* examines works of fiction and literary criticism. In her writings Glickman explores themes of exile and conflicting cultural identity. Her interest in the immigrant experience and in characters who constantly cross borders arises in part from her condition as a writer who does not belong to the mainstream. She thus offers a unique perspective on marginal female characters such as Raquel Liberman, a Polish immigrant who had the courage to denounce publicly the Zwi Migdal – a criminal traffickers' organization. Liberman's recently discovered letters shed new light on the relationship between immigration and prostitution in the first decades of the 20th century. The full documentation and testimonies are present in Glickman's book, *The Jewish White Slave Trade and the Untold Story of Raquel Liberman.*

Glickman's stories explore similar themes as those treated in her plays. *Uno de sus Juanes* [One of her Johns] is a collection of 18 stories in which the author examines issues of gender, identity, and the experience of the Jewish immigrants who settled in Argentina; among them, "El último de los colonos" [The Last of the Colonists] has appeared in various anthologies. Many of these stories question the cultural values that determine the roles of men and women in society. The title of the book itself inverts the stereotype of the Don Juan, observing love and desire from the woman's perspective.

Mujeres, memorias, malogros is a collection of stories divided into three parts. The first takes place in the late 19th century in a Jewish colony created as a result of the vision of Baron Maurice de Hirsch, a philanthropist who established Jewish agricultural communities for those who suffered persecution in eastern Europe. In this section, the protagonist is a young woman who ventures outside her closely knit circle, and discovers her sexuality. Stories such as "Incendio en la chacra" [Fire at the Farm] and "Los años de varón" [Years as a Boy] take place among Jewish settlers. "El barco" [The Boat] deals with rupture and the desire to transcend. It builds a bridge to cross into the world of adults, and into another territory – life in North America.

The second part of the book focuses on lifestyles in a modern society. Stories such as "Fantasía planetaria" [Planetary fantasy], "Autopistas Newyorkinas" [New York Highways], and "Tag Sale", explore the position of women in a consumer-oriented society in which brand names at once overwhelm and impose a limited view of the world.

Jewish culture and the Yiddish stage have had an impact on Glickman's work. Just as in her short stories, her plays endeavour to discover the effects produced by the mixture of cultures through her own dual heritage. She has written on contemporary Argentine dramatists of Jewish background such as Ricardo Halac, Jorge Goldemberg, Diana Raznovich, and Aída Bortnik who share a multicultural experience. Her collection (edited with Gloria Walden) of seven plays in English translation, *Argentine Jewish Theatre: A Critical Anthology*, selects representative plays from the turn of the century to the present (from Samuel Eichelbaum to Osvaldo Dragún).

Glickman's plays are collected in an anthology entitled *Teatro: cuatro obras*. The first two are "Latino" plays, based on life in New York. *Noticias de suburbio* [Suburban News] was the winner of a Jerome Foundation Drama Award, and was staged at the Theatre for the New City, in Manhattan. Its optimistic, almost utopian view of the bond formed among Hispanic women of different social and economic backgrounds that transcend their socioeconomic limitations sets Glickman apart from other "Latino" writers in the United States. *Un día en Nueva York* [A Day in New York], initially performed by Zohra Lampert as a monologue, was developed for the Bridge Theatre into a four-character play. It continues to explore the Hispanic immigrant experience, this time from the vantage point of a Jewish-Latina, inspired by an old Polish immigrant who, like Candide, learns to cultivate her own garden in order to survive in New York.

The subject of *Liturgias* [Liturgies] centres on the contemporary crypto-Judaic experience in New Mexico, which raises issues of questionable identities. Using metatheatrical techniques (a puppet show in this case) the stories of *converso* Jews and martyrs of the Inquisition are brought to the foreground.

As in *Liturgias*, the fourth play in this anthology, *Una tal Raquel* [A Certain Raquel], based on the life of Raquel Liberman, also resorts to metatheatrical techniques: the performance of a 1920s play within a play is used both as illustration and as a symbol of prejudice and oppression, which can be vindicated only by the power of individual conviction. In 1990 this play toured New York, Mexico, and Belgium with the Latino Teatro-Taller of Cornell University.

In examining contemporary issues, Glickman points to many of the problems of modern society with great candour, humanity, and humour, although she is well aware of the limitations society has imposed on her as a Hispanic woman writer. By comparing the process of writing with that of giving birth, Glickman reaffirms the value of woman as creator. Her portrayal of the hardships suffered by immigrants and the Jewish Diaspora are not devoid of the magic present in everyday life. Throughout her work Glickman weaves into her narrative her unique perspective on the contemporary postcolonial experience.

VICTORIA COX

Gnessin, Uri Nissan

Russian fiction writer, critic, journalist, and translator, 1879–1913

Born in Starodub, Ukraine, 1879; father a rabbi. Studied in father's yeshiva, where Yosef Brenner was also a student. Self-educated in secular subjects, including classic and modern languages and literatures. Began to write and edit at early age. Began publishing, with Brenner, a literary monthly and a literary weekly for a small number of friends and readers, 1894. Joined editorial staff of Hebrew newspaper *Hazefirah*, Warsaw, 1895, contributing poems, literary criticism, stories, and translations. Moved to Vilna (Vilnius), 1896; worked for periodical *Hazeman*; then went to Kiev; plans to found Hebrew literary organ and publishing house failed. Moved to London, 1907; there helped Brenner to publish Hebrew periodical *Hameorer*, which soon failed; spent several months in Palestine; returned to Russia, 1908. Wrote critical essays under pseudonym U. Esthersohn, and translated works by Baudelaire, Chekhov, Heinrich Heine, and others into Hebrew. Died after heart attack in Warsaw, 1913.

Selected Writings

Collections

Kol kitvei U.N. Genesin [Complete Works], 1 vol., 1914
Kitvei Uri Nisan Genesin [Works of U. N. Gnessin], 3 vols, 1946
Kol kitvei [Collected Works], 2 vols, 1982

Fiction

Zilelei hahayyim [The Shadows of Life], 1904
Hatsidah, 1905; as *Sideways* in *Eight Great Hebrew Short Novels*, edited by Alan Lelchuk and Gershon Shaked, 1983
Beynatayyim [In the Meantime], 1906
"Baganim" [In the Gardens], 1909
Beterem [Beforehand], 1909
"Ketatah" [A Quarrel], 1912
Etsel [By the Way], 1913; republished 1965

Further Reading

Bacon, Yitzhak, *Brener U-Genesin Ke-Sofrim Du-Leshoniyim* [Brenner and Gnesin as Bi-Lingual Writers], Beer Sheva, Israel: Hakatedrah leyidish, Universitat Ben-Guryon, 1986
Bar-Yosef, Hamutal, *Metaforot usemalim biyetsirato shel Genesin* [Metaphors and Symbols in Gnessin's Stories], Tel Aviv: Hakibuts hameuhad, 1987
Benshalom, Benzion, *Uri Nissan Gnessin*, Kraków, 1935
Brandwein, Naftali Chaim, *Meshorer hashekiah: Uri Nisan Genesin umasekhet yetsirato*, Jerusalem: Mas, 1964
Brenner, Yosef (editor), *Ha-Tsidah* (memorial volume), Jerusalem, 1913/14
Fishman, Z., article in *Ha-Toren*, 10 (1923)
Miron, Dan, *Hahim Be-Apo Shel Ha-Netsah: Yetsirato Shel Uri Nisan Genesin: Hamishah Mahazore iyunim* [Posterity Hooked: The Travail and Achievement of Uri Nissan Gnessin: A Study in Five Cycles], Jerusalem: Mosad Byalik, 1997
Nashkes S., essay in *Kitvei Uri Nisan Gnessin*, vol. 3, Merhavya, Israel: Sifriyat Poalim, 1946
Penueli S.Y., *Brenner u-Gnessin ba-Sippur ha-Ivri: shel Reshit ha-Meah ha-Esrim*, Tel Aviv: Tel Aviv University, 1965
Rattock, Lily (editor), *Uri Nissan Gnessin: Mivhar Ma-amre Bikoret al Yetsirato* [Uri Nissan Gnessin: A Selection of Critical Essays on his Literary Prose], Tel Aviv: Am Oved, 1977
Steinhardt, Deborah, "The Modernist Enterprise of Uri Nissan Gnessin: Gnessin's Narrative Technique in the Context of Hebrew Fiction of the Late Nineteenth and Early Twentieth Centuries" (dissertation), University of California, 1989

Zmora, Israel, *Ha-Mesapper Kav le-Kav, Uri Nisan Genessin*, Tel Aviv: Mahberot lesifrut, 1951

Uri Nissan Gnessin deserves recognition as the most important pioneer of the genre of aesthetically focused psychological fiction in Modern Hebrew prose. Gnessin was part of the late 19th- and early 20th-century generation of Hebrew authors known as *telushim*, or "uprooted ones" – heirs to the *Haskalah*, or Jewish Enlightenment – in Europe who largely abandoned the faith and practices of traditional Jewish life, only to find themselves equally uncomfortable or unwanted in the secular world. In Gnessin's short lifetime, he managed to catapult Modern Hebrew literature from a series of fictionalized polemics to a truly aesthetic enterprise while accurately expressing the dilemmas of his own generation.

Gnessin was a key figure among the *telushim*. Like that of the other writers in this group, his work owes a great deal to the Hebrew writer M.Y. Berdyczewski (1865–1921), who introduced into Modern Hebrew fiction the theme that preoccupied Gnessin: the alienated Jew who struggles to find his place in the world after facing doubts about traditional or small-town life. Like Berdyczewski, Gnessin shuns social or ideological debates, depicting these problems instead through the filter of highly personal experiences. Gnessin was also closely associated, both personally and in a literary sense, with the influential Hebrew author Yosef Hayyim Brenner until their friendship ebbed on literary grounds. Brenner believed in Hebrew literature as a didactic instrument, whereas Gnessin felt that polemics in fiction detracted from literature's main aesthetic focus. It is this difference that distinguished Gnessin from his contemporaries in Hebrew letters and makes his contribution to Hebrew literature both unique and crucial. In focusing all of his energies on literature itself rather than on propagating a moral message, Gnessin vastly expanded the powers of the Hebrew language for expressing subtle actions and emotions, developing a personal style that continues to leave its impact on Hebrew literature to this day.

Gnessin was the first to import into Hebrew literature certain modernist European literary techniques such as stream of consciousness, interior monologue, and narrative intimacy, the latter being an intense literary focus on small ordinary details in order to strengthen the reader's impression of a character, to the point where these details (a hand on the back of a chair, an impression in a snowdrift, a glass of milk) form a complex web of psychological symbols and hints from which the reader may draw conclusions about the characters and their interactions. Gnessin is also credited with giving Hebrew the equivalent of the present continuous tense, a verb tense lacking in traditional Hebrew, through his technique of modifying verbs with adjectival phrases. This accomplishment underscores the importance of time in Gnessin's work. His characters wrestle with their memories of the irretrievable past and their hopes for an impossible future, caught in a never-ending and often empty or unhappy present. Gnessin's sentences are very long and carefully constructed, often creating full scenes in themselves. His sensory descriptions are exceptionally vivid, and he makes particularly strong use of colours to create settings that match the characters' internal moods. Gnessin translated Anton Chekhov's works into Hebrew, and his own fiction bears the influence of Chekhov and that of other European writers who came to focus less on plot than on the interaction between their characters' interior worlds and the often inadequate actual worlds they live in. Characters express their alienation in Gnessin's work through physical wandering, stunted relationships, unfinished work, unrequited love, and erotic tension.

Gnessin wrote short stories, poetry, sketches, and literary criticism, but his reputation rests mainly on his four short novels, entitled *Hatsidah* (*Sideways*), *Beynatayyim* [In the Meantime], *Beterem* [Beforehand], and *Etsel* [By the Way], whose titles alone evoke the theme of alienation and of struggling to forge a life between worlds. These four works are very similar in their style, themes, and characters. Their protagonists closely resemble the author as wandering Jewish intellectuals who are comfortable neither in small-town Jewish life nor in the secular sophisticated city, and while Gnessin usually writes in the third person, everything is filtered through these protagonists' perspectives.

Hatsidah tells the story of a young intellectual who leaves the large city of Vilna for a teaching post in a small town, where he hopes to find enough peace for his literary pursuits. Instead, he becomes attached to a family with three sisters with whom he builds complex relationships bordering on desire. The novella follows the peaks and valleys of the protagonist's relationship with these three women, and the reader is left with an unmistakable impression of disappointment and dislocation. The same can be said of Gnessin's other three novellas, which many critics have interpreted as variations on the same story, which for Gnessin was an autobiographical one – the wandering intellectual who always seems to be in the wrong place at the wrong time.

Gnessin also wrote short stories and poetry that use the same style as these novellas. Perhaps the best known of his shorter works is the story "Baganim" [In the Gardens]. Like the novellas, this story describes a wandering intellectual. Returning to his backward native village, he encounters two old acquaintances, both vividly portrayed – a coarse farmer and his mentally deficient daughter. Unlike much Hebrew writing at the time, the story is unromantic in the extreme. Most of the text is taken up with detailed impressions of the landscape, the village, and its people, and only at the story's horrifying conclusion does the reader realize the lurid nature of these details. While dramatic denouements are rare in Gnessin's work, this story does clearly demonstrate how he typically uses a strong aesthetic focus on exterior details to reflect the inner life of his characters.

Many modern Hebrew writers have followed in Gnessin's aesthetic path, most notably S. Yizhar and Amalia Kahana-Karmon. And nearly all modern Israeli writers owe some debt to Gnessin as one of the first and best Hebrew writers to tip the balance of Hebrew literature from polemics toward art.

DARA HORN

Goldberg, Leah

German-born Israeli poet and critic, 1911–1970

Born in Königsberg, 1911. Spent early childhood in Russia; after revolutions of 1917, moved with family to their home in Kaunas, Lithuania. Studied at Hebrew Gymnasium, Kaunas; began to write Hebrew verse; first poem published in *Hed Lita*, 1926. Studied at universities of Kaunas, Berlin, and Bonn; PhD in Semitic languages, Bonn, 1933. Emigrated to Palestine, 1935; settled in Tel Aviv; joined circle of modernist authors whose mentor was Avraham Shlonsky; began publishing poems in group's literary forum, *Turim*. Shlonsky helped her compile her first volume of verse, 1935. Worked as schoolteacher; then became theatre critic on *Davar* and, later, *Mishmar*; became editor of *Al hamishmar*'s literary supplement; worked on popular children's magazine, *Davar liyeladim*; was children's book editor, Sifriyat Poalim; served as literary adviser to Habima, national theatre of Israel. Organized Department of Comparative Literature and held professorship, from 1952, Hebrew University, Jerusalem. Died 1970. Awarded Israel Prize posthumously.

Selected Writings

Poetry
Tabaot ashan [Smoke Rings], 1935
Shibolet yerukat haayin [Green-Eyed Spike], 1940
Mibeiti hayashan [From My Old Home], 1942
Shir bekefarim [Songs in the Villages], 1942
Al haprihah, 1948; as *On the Blossoming*, translated by Miriam Billig Sivan, 1992
The Cobbler, 1950
Ahavat shimshon [Samson's Love], 1952
Barak baboker [Morning Lightning], 1955
Mukdam vemeuhar [Sooner or Later], 1959
Im halaylah hazeh [This Night], 1964
Yalkut shirim [Collected Poems], 1970
Sheerit hahayim [The Rest of Life], 1971
Light on the Rime of a Cloud, translated by Ramah Commanday, 1972
Selected Poems, translated by Robert Friend, 1976
Leket mishirei Leah Goldberg [Selected Poems], 1980
Zuta [Small], 1981
Shirim [Poems], 1986
At telkhi basadeh [You Will Walk in the Fields], 1989
Mivhar shirim [Selected Poems], 1989
Beerets ahavati [In My Beloved Country], 1997

Plays
Baalat haarmon, 1956; as *Lady of the Castle*, translated by T. Carmi, 1974
Mahazot [Plays], 1979

Fiction
Mikhtavim minesiah medumah [Letters from an Imaginary Journey], 1937
Vehu haor [He is the Light], 1946
Sipurim [Stories], 1996

For Children
Hair vehakfar [City and Countryside], 1939
Haorahat mikineret [A Visitor from Kineret], 1939
Dan vedina metaylim betel aviv [Dan and Dina Walk in Tel Aviv], 1940
Gan hahayot [The Zoo], 1941
Yedidai Mirehov arnon [My Friends from Arnon Street], 1943
Mah osot haayalot? [What Do the Does Do?], 1944
Habivar healiz [The Merry Zoo], 1947
Kah yashir olam tzair [The Song of a Young World], 1950
Beerets sin [In the Land of China], 1951
Nissim veniflaot [Nissim and Niflaot], 1954
Malkat sheva haktanah, 1956; as *Little Queen of Sheba*, 1959
Ayeh pluto? [Where is Pluto?], 1957
Dirah leaskir, 1959; as *A Flat to Let*, 1972
Maase betsayar [The Story of a Painter], 1965
Harpatkah bamidbar [Adventures in the Desert], 1966
Hamefuzar mikfar azar [The Absent-Minded Guy from Kefar Azar], 1968
Lapilah yesh nazelet [The Elephant Has a Cold], 1975
Mar gazmay habaday [Mr Fibber, the Storyteller], 1977
Vekulam haverim [And All are Friends], 1978
Shamgar hanagar [Shamgar the Carpenter], 1979
Danny vehatuki [Danny and the Parrot], 1980
Maaseh besloshah egozim [The Story of Three Nuts], 1980
Bou ananim [Come Clouds], 1982
Uri [Uri], 1983
Dov duboni ben dubim metsahtseah naalayim [Teddy Bear Shoeshine], 1987
Misipurei mar kashkash [Mr Kashkash Tells Stories], 1987
Mor hehamor [Mor the Donkey], 1987
Aleh shel zahav [A Golden Leaf], 1988
Mah nishkaf behaloni [Reflections on My Window], 1989
Halomotav shel melekh [Dreams of a King], 1994
Mi babitan? [Who is at the Pavilion?], 1997

Other
Pegishah im meshorer [Encounter with a Poet], 1952
Tsrif katan [A Little Shack], 1959
Russian Literature in the Nineteenth Century: Essays, translated by Hillel Halkin, 1976
Mikhtavim veyoman [Letters and Diary], 1978

Further Reading

Alter, Robert, *Commentary*, 49/5 (1970)
Gay, Hanoch, *Tsipor Sasgonit: Mehkar Be-Temot Uve-Simbolim Be-Shiratah Shel Leah Goldberg*, Tel Aviv: Tserikover, 1977
Rivner, Toviyah (Tuvia Ruebner), *Leah Goldberg: Monografyah*, Tel Aviv: Sifriyat Poalim, 1980
Seh-Lavan, Yosef, *Leah Goldberg*, Tel Aviv: Hotsaat Oram, 1977
Shaked, Gershon, *Moznayim*, 2nd series, 3/3 (1956)
Shaked, Gershon, *Orot*, 38 (January 1960)
Spicehandler, Ezra, *Israel* (Spring 1961)
Yoffe, A.B., *Leah Goldberg, Mivhar Maamrei Bikoret al Yetsiratah* [Leah Goldberg: A Selection of Critical Essays on Her Writings], Tel Aviv: Am Oved, 1980
Yoffe, A.B., *Leah Goldberg, Tave Demut Vi-Yetsirah*, Tel Aviv: Reshafim, 1994
Yardeni, Galia, *Sihot im Soferim*, Tel Aviv: Hakibuts hameuhad, 1961

Leah Goldberg was raised in Kaunas (Kovna), Lithuania, where she attended the Hebrew Gymnasium. She later studied at the universities of Kaunas, Berlin, and Bonn and received her PhD in Semitic studies in 1933. She emigrated to Mandatory Palestine in 1935, settling in Tel Aviv.

Kaunas was a multilingual city. Goldberg's mother language was Russian but as a schoolgirl she opted for Hebrew as her primary language. In her quasi-autobiographical novel *He Is the Light*, Nora, a budding young writer, after pondering as to what language she should write in, is advised by her mentor "to pick out a language as you do a ring". As a typical Lithuanian Jewish intellectual, she was to master Lithuanian, German, French, Italian, and English in addition to Hebrew and Russian, but Hebrew became her primary language and her literary vehicle. She was extremely well read in Hebrew and European literature and her poetry was very much influenced by the Russian Acmeist poets, particularly by Anna Akhmatova. Like the Acmeists, she rejected the symbolist poetics of early 20th-century Russian poetry and favoured the use of simple, concrete imagery written in a clear unadorned style and in traditional verse forms (quatrain, sextets, and sonnets). She also eschewed the high rhetoric and biblical prosody employed by the preceding generation of Hebrew poets, preferring a conversational style that was direct and unencumbered. Although, while still in Kaunas, she published several poems and was attracted by the then new poetry of Abraham Shlonsky and Natan Alterman, she avoided their frequently unconventional use of metaphor and radical poetic forms.

After Goldberg's arrival in Tel Aviv, Shlonsky not only assisted her in obtaining employment at a leading daily newspaper, but also arranged for the publication of *Tabaot ashan* [Smoke Rings] shortly after her arrival. Goldberg was a prolific writer and in addition to her journalistic pieces, mainly as a literary reviewer and dramatic critic, she did a great deal of translation of works by Russian, German, French, and Italian authors into Hebrew (Tolstoi, Turgenev, Gor'kii, Heinrich Mann, and Petrarch). She published numerous and very popular children's volumes of poetry and fiction and wrote several plays.

Her poetry, unlike that of most of her contemporaries, was non-ideological and apolitical. It concentrated on the personal experiences of an intellectual but sensitive artist. Her subjects mainly consisted of landscapes, nature, love (particularly unrequited love), art, and the problems of poetic expression. While at times she resorted to biblical themes (her Samson poems), she rarely touched upon contemporary Jewish themes. However, after the Holocaust, in "From My Old Home" she reminisces about Jewish Lithuania. Nevertheless, her translations or elaborations of non-Jewish Lithuanian folk poetry are more numerous than those on "Jewish" themes.

Her poems of childhood and early adulthood reflect both the personal tragedies and communal tragedies that she experienced. Her later poems, however, are often softened by her lyrical acceptance of the tragic and her unexpected discovery of solace in ordinary phenomena. Initially her landscape poetry expresses the ambivalence of the immigrant poet who was impelled to exchange the lush Lithuanian countryside and the solid permanence of cities (its parks, churches, and tall buildings) for sun-soaked Palestine and its then unsubstantial, hastily constructed architecture.

In 1952 she was invited to Jerusalem to organize the comparative literature department of the Hebrew University. She grew to love Jerusalem, its stony landscape, its special "light". "In the Hills of Jerusalem" contains some of the most powerful landscape poetry written in modern Hebrew literature. Her series of sonnets on "The Love of Therese du Meun" tells about the tragic love affair between an ageing medieval aristocrat and her young lover – expressing both the sweet pain and the assuaging resignation incurred by an ageing, tragic lover.

Her bibliography also includes the translations of the 13th-century romance *Aucassin and Nicolette*, a play by Molière, and Ibsen's *Peer Gynt* (probably from the German). In addition she published a handbook on poetics and one on prose fiction as well as a volume of critical essays on 19th-century Russian writers (*Russian Literature in the Nineteenth Century*), and a critical introductory essay to Dante's *Divine Comedy*.

EZRA SPICEHANDLER

Goldemberg, Isaac

Peruvian fiction writer, poet, and critic, 1945–

Born in Chepén, 15 November 1945. Spent first eight years of his life with maternal family in native village; raised in Catholic faith. Moved to Lima to live with his Jewish father, 1953. Studied at León Pinelo Jewish school, Lima, from 1954; joined club of young Zionists, Betar. Sent to Leoncio Prado Military Academy, 1955. Moved to Israel, where he lived on kibbutz for more than one year. Briefly returned to Peru, then moved to United States; has lived in New York since 1964. Studied at City College of New York, University of Madrid, and New York University. Taught at New York University, 1970–86; now teaches at Eugenio María de Hostos Community College, New York; director of its Latin American Writers Institute; editor of literary journal *Brújula*. Awards include Premio Nuestro, 1977; Nathaniel Judah Jacobson Award, 1996; Teatro Ediciones Estival Award, 2000.

Selected Writings

Poetry
Tiempo de silencio [Time of Silence], 1969
De Chepén a La Habana [From Chepén to Havana], 1973
Hombre de paso, 1981; as *Just Passing Through*, translated by David Unger, 1981
La vida al contado [Life Paid in Cash], 1992
Cuerpo del amor [Love's Body] 2000
Las cuentas y los inventarios [Tallies and Inventories], 2000
Peruvian Blues, 2000

Novels
La vida a plazos de don Jacobo Lerner, 1978; as *The Fragmented Life of Don Jacobo Lerner*, translated by Robert S. Picciotto, 1976
Tiempo al tiempo, 1984; as *Play by Play*, translated by Hardie S. Martin, 1985

Plays
No poseo sino muerte para expresar mi vida / To Express My Life I Have Only My Death, 1969
Hotel AmeriKKa, 2000
Golpe de gracia [Coup de Grâce], 2001

Other
El gran libro de América judía [The Great Book of Jewish America], 1998
"Life in Installments" in *King David's Harp: Autobiographical Essays by Jewish Latin American Writers*, edited by Stephen A. Sadow, 1999
Luces de la memoria [Lights of Memory], 2001

Further Reading

Barr, Lois Baer, "Unbinding the Ties: Isaac Goldemberg" in her *Isaac Unbound: Patriarchal Traditions in the Latin American Jewish Novel*, Tempe: Arizona State University, Center for Latin American Studies, 1995
Canfield Reisman, Rosemary M., *The Fragmented Life of Don Jacobo Lerner: A Study Guide*, Boston: Salem Press, 1998
Cortés Cabán, David, "Isaac Goldemberg o la pasión del cuerpo: hacia una visión poética" in *Cuerpo del amor*, New York: Digital Book Publisher, 2000
Friedman, Edward, "The Novel as Revisionist History: Art as Process in Goldemberg's *Tiempo al tiempo*", *Modern Jewish Studies Annual*, 6 (1987)
Friedman, Edward, "Theory in the Margin: Latin American Literature and the Jewish Subject" in *The Jewish Diaspora in Latin America: New Studies on History and Literature*, edited by David Sheinin and Lois Baer Barr, New York: Garland, 1996
Gazarian-Gautier, Marie-Lise, "Isaac Goldemberg" in *Interviews with Latin American Writers*, Elmwood Park, Illinois: Dalkey Archive Press, 1989
Gazarian-Gautier, Marie-Lise, prologue to *Entre rascacielos: Nueva York en nueve poetas hispanos*, edited by Gazarian-Gautier, Quito: Casa de la Cultura Ecuatoriana, 1998
Nouhaud, Dorita, "Mémoire hébraique: *La vida a plazos de don Jacobo Lerner*" in *La littérature hispano-américaine: Le roman, la nouvelle, le conte*, Paris: Dunod, 1996
Rosser, Harry, "Being and Time in *La vida a plazos de don Jacobo Lerner*", *Chasqui*, 17/1 (1988)
Schneider, Judith, "Crossing Cultures in Isaac Goldemberg's Fiction", *Folio*, 17 (1987)
Stavans, Ilan, "Judaísmo y letras latinoamericanas: entrevista a Isaac Goldemberg", *Folio*, 17 (1987)
Stavans, Ilan, introduction to *The Fragmented Life of Don Jacobo Lerner*, translated by Robert S. Picciotto, Albuquerque: University of New Mexico Press, 1999
Tittler, Jonathan, "*The Fragmented Life of Don Jacobo Lerner*: The Aesthetics of Fragmentation" in his *Narrative Irony in the Contemporary Spanish-American Novel*, Ithaca, New York: Cornell University Press, 1984

Isaac Goldemberg spent a great part of his childhood and adolescence trying to reconcile his Jewish and Peruvian heritages – dealing with them exclusively, at some times, syncretically, at others. Not surprisingly, his writing seems to oscillate between these two cultural poles. Goldemberg's creative fiction is highly autobiographical, exploring the issues of exile, marginalization, and legitimacy. His characters are often hybrid constructions, struggling for legitimacy against great odds, and ultimately realizing the futility of their search. Although Goldemberg's writings manifest a strong interest in Jewish identity, he asserts that he does not treat Judaism "as a purely historical process, but as something from which to retrieve a series of myths still latent in Judaism".

Goldemberg begins to explore Jewish themes in his second book of poems, *De Chepén a La Habana* [From Chepén to Havana]. The poems in this collection already show an inclination towards the marginal. The poetic voice emerges cautiously, yet it is strong enough to transform the soil of his personal memories into a universal setting as he searches unrelentingly for his roots. Thus Goldemberg begins remoulding the literary figure of the wandering Jew, which would become central to his writing.

His ambitious first novel, *La vida a plazos de don Jacobo Lerner*, was first published in English translation as *The Fragmented Life of Don Jacobo Lerner*. It juxtaposes the relatively brief history of the Peruvian Jewish community, several centuries of the Peruvian national experience, and over five millennia of Jewish history. The novel tells the story of Don Jacobo Lerner, a Russian Jewish immigrant in Lima, during the 1920s and 1930s. It opens with Don Jacobo on his deathbed trying to piece together his life.

Fleeing a pogrom, Jacobo Lerner arrives in Peru hoping to make his fortune and marry a Jewish woman with whom to start a family. When he hears that an old friend lives in the village of Chepén, Jacobo moves there, soon becoming prosperous enough to be somewhat regarded in the small town. When he finds out that a local (Catholic) woman is carrying his son, he flees to Lima, where he leads an ever-deteriorating existence. Ultimately, he cannot marry the Jewish woman he loves, for she is married to his brother (he marries her sister instead, which proves to be a further mistake) and he cannot marry his mistress – for she is Catholic. Having found neither love nor fortune, his tormented life comes to an end without even granting him the opportunity of reaching a reconciliation with his only son.

Paradoxically, the protagonist has no voice in the novel, and it becomes the task of the reader to reconstruct his identity from the narrations of other characters – as in the memorable testimony of his bastard son – as well as from newspaper clippings from *Alma Hebrea* [Jewish Soul], a publication of the Jewish community in Lima. Don Jacobo's voicelessness can be read as further evidence of his marginalized condition and the hostility of his environment.

The characters' monologues in *La vida a plazos de don Jacobo Lerner* suggest a certain dialectal foreignness – or what the critics claimed was "a sensibility that is foreign to Peruvian letters" – and a mode of expression that was deemed characteristically Jewish. Faced with such reactions from both his Peruvian and North American readers, Goldemberg began to ponder his newly granted attribute of "Latin American Jewish writer", a preoccupation that has since marked his poetic and narrative oeuvre.

His second novel, *Tiempo al tiempo* (*Play by Play*), seems even more autobiographical than the first. The protagonist, Marquitos Karushansky Avila, is raised by his Peruvian mother until the age of 12, by which time he moves with his father to Lima. Once there, Marquitos is sent to the very schools attended by Goldemberg in his youth, the León Pinelo Jewish school and the Leoncio Prado Catholic military academy. Marquitos is eventually expelled from the military academy, and later emigrates to Israel where we find him in the midst of the 1967 Arab–Israeli conflict. Goldemberg once again deprives the protagonist of a voice in his own story, as his ordeals are narrated by the distant voice of the narrator (mimicking an announcer at a soccer game) and by the testimony of his classmates. *Tiempo al tiempo* is, in Goldemberg's own words, "a consideration of what it means or what it could mean to be Peruvian and/or Jewish."

In *Hombre de paso* (*Just Passing Through*) Goldemberg explores his multicultural and multilingual identity through a collage of English, Spanish, Yiddish, Quechua, and Castilian words, as well as a colorful array of historical and contemporary figures, ranging from the Spanish conquistadors and Inca chieftains to Jewish peddlers and rabbis. Likewise, his fourth book of poems, *La vida al contado* [Life Paid in Cash], deals with many of the same issues of identity. It explores the equally forceful desires of finding one's roots and of merging into the foreignness that surrounds us, thereby making all movement gravitate between these seemingly opposite points.

Goldemberg's *El gran libro de América judía* [The Great Book of Jewish America] is a panoramic literary anthology of the Jewish presence in Latin America, encompassing the poems, short stories, essays, interviews, and testimony of more than 150 writers. This monumental work provides a frame in which to place Goldemberg's own writings and, above all, it bears witness to a presence of long enough standing to counter any charges of exoticism in Jewish Latin American letters.

LYDIA M. GIL

Goldfaden, Avrom

Russian poet, song writer, and dramatist, 1840–1908

Born in Staro Konstatinov, Ukraine, 12 July 1840. Wrote first poem in Hebrew, 1850; studied at government school from 1855; much influenced by one teacher, Avrom Ber Gotlober; graduated with honours from Kazyoner Jewish School, 1857; entered rabbinical seminary at Zhitomir. Gotlober and other leaders of *Haskalah* movement, such as E.Z. Zweifel and H.S. Slonimsky, encouraged him to compose his first Hebrew lyrics, published in *Hamelits*, 1862; poems also appeared in *Kol mevaser.* Graduated as teacher, 1866. Married Perele Verbl, daughter of maskilic poet Eliyahu-Mordkhe Verbl, 1868. With Yitskhok Yoel Linetski briefly published humorous magazine *Der alter yisrolik*, 1875. Moved to Romania; began writing musical plays; toured cities in Romania and Russia with singing and acting troupe, until Russian government banned Yiddish theatre, 1883. Moved to New York, London, Paris, and Lemberg, mounting productions of his plays. Returned to New York, 1903. Supported Hovevei Zion movement. Died in New York, 9 January 1908; more than 100,000 people attended funeral.

Selected Writings

Collection
Oysgeklibene shriftn [Selected Writings], edited by Shmuel Rozshanski, 1963

Yiddish Songs
Tsitsim ufrakhim [Buds and Flowers], 1865
Dos yidele [This Little Jewish Child], 1866
Di yidene [A Jewish Woman], 1869
Yisrolik [Little Israel], 1884
Shabsiel: Poeme [Little Shabtai], 1896
Yidishe natsyonal-gedikhte [Yiddish National Poems], 1898

Plays
Di mume sosye [Aunt Sosye], 1869
Shmendrik [An Awkward Person], 1876
Di bobe mitn eynikl [The Grandmother and her Granddaughter], 1877
Kaptsnson et Hungerman [Pauperson and Hungerman], 1877
Di kishef-makherin [The Sorceress], *c.*1878
Der fanatik oder di tsvey kuni lemels [The Fanatic or the Two Kuni Lemels], 1880
Shulamis, 1880
Doctor Almosada, 1882
Akeydes yitskhok [The Sacrifice of Isaac], 1887
Bar kokhba, 1887; as *Bar Kochba: or, the Last Hour of Zion: Historical Opera*, translated by E. Dorf, 1908
Meshiekhs tsaytn [The Messianic Era], 1891
Dos tsente gebot [Thou Shalt Not Covet], *c.*1895
Ben Ami, 1907

Further Reading

Goldfaden-bukh, New York: Jewish Theatre Museum, 1926
Gorin, Bernard, *Di geshikhte fun yidishn teater*, 2 vols, New York: Mayzel, 1923
Howe, Irving, *World of Our Fathers*, New York: Harcourt Brace, 1976; as *The Immigrant Jews of New York*, London: Routledge, 1976
Jeshurin, Ephim H., *Avraham Goldfaden bibliografye/Avrom Goldfaden Bibliography*, Buenos Aires: Ateneo Literario en el Iwo, 1963
Lahad, Ezra, "Makhazot Avraham Goldfaden" [Avraham Goldfaden's Works], Haifa: Music Museum and Library, 1970
Liptzin, Solomon, *The Flowering of Yiddish Literature*, New York: Yoseloff, 1963

Liptzin, Solomon, *A History of Yiddish Literature*, New York: Jonathan David, 1972
Mayzel, Nachman, *Avraham Goldfaden, 1840–1908*, New York: Kooperativer Folks Farlag fun Internatsyonaln Arbeter Ordn, 1938
Minkoff, Nochum Boruch, *Literarishe vegn*, Mexico City: Tsevi Kesel Fond, Kultur-Komisye Yidishe Tsentral Komitet, 1955
Oyslender, Nokhem and Uri Finkel, *Avrom Goldfaden: Materyaln far a biografye*, Minsk: Institute for Ukrainian Culture, 1926
Perlmutter, Sholem, *Yidishe dramaturgn un teater-kompositors*, New York: Ikuf, 1952
Rosenfeld, Lulla, *Bright Star of Exile: Jacob Adler and the Yiddish Theatre*, New York: Crowell, 1977
Sandrow, Nahma, *Vagabond Stars: A World History of Yiddish Theater*, New York: Harper and Row, 1977
Shatzky, Jacob (editor), *Arkhiv far der geshikhte fun yidishn teater un drame*, Vilna and New York: Kletskin, 1930
Shatzky, Jacob (editor), *Hundert yor Goldfadn*, New York: YIVO, 1940
Zylbercweig, Zalmen, *Leksikon fun yidishn teater*, vol. 1, New York: Elisheva, 1931
Zylbercweig, Zalmen, *Avraham Goldfaden un Zigmunt Mogulesko*, Buenos Aires: Elisheva, 1936
Zylbercweig, Zalmen, *Album of the Yiddish Theatre*, New York: Zylbercweig, 1937

Goldfaden continually explored issues of Jewish identity, history, and politics in his work. His early poetry, in the tradition of Yiddish folk poets and minstrels such as Velvl Zbarzher and Eliokum Tsunzer, demonstrates his love for the ordinary Jew. When Goldfaden began publishing books of Hebrew and Yiddish poetry in the 1860s, there was no professional Yiddish stage for which to write. Nevertheless, following the example of Jewish Enlightenment (*Haskalah*) writers such as Israel Aksenfeld (1787–1866), Solomon Ettinger (1801–56), and Goldfaden's teacher Avrom Ber Gottlober (1811–99), Goldfaden included a dramatic dialogue and a full-length comedy in his second volume of Yiddish writings, *Di yidene* [A Jewish Woman]. He also began making a name for himself as a songwriter, having learned how to set his own words to music.

After a nearly a decade of drifting from one endeavour to another following his years as a seminary student, Goldfaden and former classmate Yitskhok Yoel Linetski co-founded a Yiddish newspaper in Bukovina, Romania, which was closed by government censors after only half a year. Shortly thereafter, Goldfaden was invited to perform some of his songs at a beer garden in Jassy, Romania. He soon began writing vaudeville-like sketches for performance, and touring with a small company that would expand in the coming years.

For the rest of the 1870s, Goldfaden would churn out a steady stream of farces and melodramas, many of them attacking religious orthodoxy in the *Haskalah* manner. Most accomplished of these early works are *Di bobe mitn eynikl* [The Grandmother and her Granddaughter], *Shmendrik* [An Awkward Person], and *Der fanatik oder di tsvey kuni lemels* [The Fanatic or the Two Kuni Lemls]. Both of the latter plays, farces featuring physically repulsive title characters who embody all that is wrong with religious fanaticism, became wildly popular, and the names of their title characters became Yiddish bywords for imbeciles. The playwright found an equally successful formula for satirizing superstitious beliefs in *Di kishef-makherin* [The Sorceress], a folktale-like fantasy featuring a deliciously evil witch (traditionally played by a man) and the loveable, unscrupulous peddler Hotsmakh, another Goldfaden creation that would become an archetype in Yiddish culture.

When the Jews' situation in eastern Europe drastically changed, Goldfaden's dramaturgy would change with it. Following the assassination of Czar Alexander II in 1881, the Jews of the Russian empire faced a wave of pogroms, and a series of harsh legislation from the new czar. Goldfaden abruptly stopped writing satires that targeted Jewish institutions and figures, and began creating epics based on highlights of Jewish heroism from history and legend. Several of his most popular and accomplished operas were written in this mode, notably *Shulamis*, inspired by both a Talmudic legend and by contemporary Hebrew fiction, and *Bar kokhba* (*Bar Kochba*), a dramatization of the famous 1st-century Jewish rebellion against the Romans. Both plays remained ever-present in the Yiddish repertoire and inspired numerous adaptations and avant-garde experiments in subsequent generations. A number of Goldfaden's songs, such as "Rozhinkes mit mandlen" [Raisins and Almonds], were sung and recorded countless times, and continue to hold a privileged place in the musical repertoire.

After attempting unsuccessfully to break into the American Yiddish market in the mid-1880s, Goldfaden returned to Europe, living and working for extended periods in Warsaw, Lemberg, London, and Paris, among other cities. Several of his major works of musical theatre during this period drew upon the Bible for inspiration, including *Kenig akhashveyresh* [King Ahasuerus] and *Akeydes yitskhok* [The Sacrifice of Isaac], the latter joining the ranks of the most popular of his plays.

In spite of Goldfaden's dazzling creativity and the popularity of many of his works, he spent the last decade of his life in constant poverty and ill health. He wrote far fewer new works during these years, though he did continue to write poems and plays right up until the end of his life. His last play, *Ben Ami*, a Zionist epic, had its New York premiere under Boris Thomashefsky's direction just weeks before Goldfaden died. By then, he had long been virtually beatified as the Father of the Yiddish Theatre, and his work would continue to inspire new interpretations on Yiddish stages around the world.

JOEL BERKOWITZ

Golding, Louis

British fiction writer, scriptwriter, journalist, and essayist, 1895–1958

Born in Manchester, 19 November 1895. Studied at Manchester Grammar School; wrote poems, contributed to school magazine, and won literary awards; received scholarship to Queen's College, Oxford, 1914; studied history and classics. Studies interrupted by World War I; was refused entry to Officers' Training Corps; served briefly as hospital orderly in York; worked for YMCA in Greece and France; service cut short by bout of malaria. Returned to Oxford, 1918; edited *Queen's College Miscellany*. Began travelling abroad on medical advice to avoid another serious illness; spent half his time in London and half visiting Italy (including Capri and Sicily with Norman Douglas and D.H. Lawrence), Switzerland, Egypt, Palestine, Morocco, United States, Germany, and Russia. Married childhood friend, Annie Wintrobe, 1956. Died in London, 10 August 1958.

Selected Writings

Novels
Forward from Babylon, 1920
Seacoast of Bohemia, 1923
Day of Atonement, 1925
Luigi of Catanzaro, 1926
Store of Ladies, 1927
The Miracle Boy, 1927
The Prince or Somebody, 1929
Give Up Your Lovers, 1930
Magnolia Street, 1931
Five Silver Daughters, 1934
The Camberwell Beauty, 1935
The Pursuer, 1936
The Dance Goes On, 1937
Mr Emmanuel, 1939
No News from Helen, 1943
The Glory of Elsie Silver, 1946
Three Jolly Gentlemen, 1947
The Dark Prince: A Short Novel, 1948
Honey for the Ghost, 1949
The Dangerous Places, 1951
The Bare-Knuckle Breed, 1952
The Loving Brothers, 1952
To the Quayside, 1954
Mr Hurricane, 1957
The Little Old Admiral, 1958
The Frightening Talent, 1973

Short Stories
The Doomington Wanderer: A Book of Tales, 1934; as *This Wanderer*, 1935
Pale Blue Nightgown: A Book of Tales, 1944
The Vicar of Dunkerly Briggs and Other Short Stories, 1944
Mario on the Beach and Other Tales, 1956

Poetry
Sorrow of War, 1919
Oxford Poetry, with others, 1921
Shepherd Singing Ragtime and Other Poems, 1921
Prophet and Fool: A Collection of Poems, 1923

Travel Narratives
Sunward, 1924
Sicilian Noon, 1925
Those Ancient Lands: Being a Journey to Palestine, 1928
In the Steps of Moses the Lawgiver, 1937
In the Steps of Moses the Conqueror, 1938
Louis Golding Goes Travelling, 1945
Goodbye to Ithaca, 1955

Other
A Letter to Adolf Hitler, 1932
James Joyce, 1933
Terrace in Capri: An Imaginary Conversation with Norman Douglas, 1934
The Song of Songs (Newly Interpreted and Rendered as a Masque), 1937
The Jewish Problem, 1938
Hitler through the Ages, 1939
The World I Know, 1940
Editor, with André Simon, *We Shall Eat and Drink Again: A Wine and Food Anthology*, 1944
Epilogue in *The Future of the Jews: A Symposium*, 1945
Memories of Old Park Row, 1887–1897, 1946
Editor, *Boxing Tales: A Collection of Thrilling Stories of the Ring*, 1948
My Sporting Days and Nights, 1948

Further Reading

Fisch, Harold, *The Dual Image: A Study of the Figure of the Jew in English Literature*, London: Lincolns-Prager, 1959
Simons, J.B., *Louis Golding: A Memoir*, London: Mitre Press, 1958

Louis Golding was the successor to Israel Zangwill as the leading Anglo-Jewish novelist. One year before Zangwill's death, Golding had published *Day of Atonement* and this signalled the start of a glittering career for the writer who was quickly recognized as the one to follow in Zangwill's footsteps. Today, Golding, who also wrote a number of successful novels on non-Jewish themes, is perhaps described more correctly a popular novelist, but he was, in his day, seen as rather more than that. But he was never quite in the same class of Jewish novelists such as his American contemporaries Daniel Fuchs, Meyer Levin, and Isaac Rosenfeld.

Golding is now best remembered for his *Doomington* novels, Doomington being his fictional name for his home town of Manchester. He was born in the Jewish slum of Red Bank in the city and his father was a struggling *magid* (Hebrew teacher) recently arrived from Russia. Yiddish was the family language. Golding was bright enough to win a scholarship to the prestigious Manchester Grammar School and later another to an Oxford college. He started to write when he was quite young and some short stories on Jewish topics were published in the *Manchester Guardian* in 1919. This was soon followed by a clearly part-autobiographical novel, *Forward from Babylon*, but it was not well received, described by some critics as a strong but unpleasant book. It is an account of Philip Massel, a youth from a poor home, who won a scholarship to the local grammar school. He then abandoned his religious faith and fell in love with a Gentile girl. *Give Up Your Lovers* in 1930 continued this story some ten years later and it dealt with problems of inter-marriage, a theme to which Golding returned on several occasions.

Day of Atonement, written in 1925, was an ambitious novel and it made the strong impression that marked out Golding out as a Jewish writer of real promise. It is the tragic story of Eli, a former yeshiva student, his wife Leah, and their young son. The novel is first set in Russia and then Doomington. Eli, who used to pray with the fervour typical of Hasidism (the religious movement founded by the Baal Shem Tov in the 18th century), becomes a passionate Christian and eventually is killed by his wife when, crucifix in hand, he attempts to preach in front of the Holy Ark on Yom Kippur. This novel showed Golding to have much maturity in his prose and in his characterizations.

Magnolia Street appeared in 1931; this work, which has been translated into 20 languages and dramatized for stage and screen, firmly established his reputation. Golding used his knowledge of life in the Jewish ghetto of Manchester and he dealt with the problems faced by Jews living side-by-side with Gentiles. *Magnolia Street* is a collection of tales chronicling the lives of the residents of the street from 1910 to 1930. It is set in the Longton district of Doomington, his fictional name for the Hightown district of Manchester. The real Hightown has many street names based on trees, such as Sycamore Street and Larch Street, and Golding's streets are similarly named. In Magnolia Street, Jews and Gentiles live on opposite sides of the street and are separated by customs and mistrust, but some barriers come down when Benny Edelman saves Tommy Wright from drowning. Mixed romance also helps to bring the two sides closer. Golding goes a little too far, however, in having one of his characters go off to Salonica, a destination surely no-one in Longton or Hightown would have imagined to be possible. There are many well-crafted characters in the book, such as the spinster Miss Tregunter who is disgusted with her alien neighbours, Mr Billig who lives on his wits, Mrs Poyser who encourages gossip in her store, and the gentle Isaac Emmanuel.

The five-volume Elsie Silver saga was written over a 20-year span from 1934 to 1953. It opens in Doomington with *Five Silver Daughters.* The opening narrative involves an anarchists' meeting in the Silver home in Oleander Street. Sam Silver was modelled on a tailor to whom Golding taught English. Silver moves to an affluent part of the city but wealth does not bring him happiness. He is ruined by his partner and son-in-law, Smirnoff, who swindles him before Smirnoff kills himself by jumping out of an express train. Sam then returns to Longton to become a simple workman living in a humble home, but he and his wife became happy again. All five daughters go their separate ways. With husbands or lovers they move through many countries, but Elsie is the one on whom her creator concentrates.

Mr Emmanuel takes place before Elsie's adventures. It is the story of Isaac Emmanuel, a kindly, warm-hearted but fearless old Jew who travels from Doomington to Germany to search for the mother of a Christian German child pining for her. Golding uses this plot as the basis of his vivid picture of life in Hitler's Germany. Golding is able to contrast Mr Emmanuel's innocence with the crude ungodliness of the Nazi regime. Unsurprisingly, the fearless old man becomes entangled in the Nazi system. He is imprisoned but freed thanks to Elsie Silver, now the mistress of an important Nazi official. Mr Emmanuel was based on a real person, a teacher and Zionist, whom Golding knew in Manchester.

In *The Glory of Elsie Silver* Elsie, the wife of a Nazi general, is in the Warsaw ghetto where, in an unsuccessful effort to erase her sins and iniquities, she helps to tend the wounded. (She survives the destruction of the ghetto and then appears in *The Dangerous Places* in 1951.) This story begins in the final days of the Warsaw ghetto. Elsie has achieved widespread fame as a cabaret artist and wife of a Nazi general, but she sets out to escape the Nazis, taking a small girl, Mila, with her. *To the Quayside* opens with Elsie on her own on a beach in Adriatic Italy where she determines to go to Buenos Aires to get hold of the fortune hidden there by her husband. She decides to travel via Doomington, where her name is reviled. After Argentina she is found in the south of France helping Mila load displaced persons onto a ship for Palestine. She herself sails on *Exodus* but she is returned to Hamburg where she dies on the quayside. There was also a collection of short stories called *Doomington Wanderer* in 1934.

Golding wrote a number of novels on non-Jewish subjects and several volumes of verse. He also wrote books on boxing and a charming piece on cricket in Corfu. These non-Jewish novels are of little importance today except perhaps for *The Miracle Boy* (1927). His *Song of Songs* provides a new interpretation of the biblical narrative rendered as a masque. He travelled a great deal in the Middle East and wrote of these travels. *In the Steps of Moses the Lawgiver* and *In the Steps of Moses the Conqueror* trace Moses' travels from birth in Egypt to the Promised Land and they provide some insight into pre-1939 life in Palestine. He wrote other travel books such as *Goodbye to Ithaca* which showed his love of the classical world.

Despite a lifestyle in which his friends included such distinguished literary figures as Compton Mackenzie and D.H. Lawrence, and which belied much Jewish activity (he was not a Zionist), he was a committed Jew and in 1938 he wrote *The Jewish Problem* which traced the progress of anti-Semitism in Europe. The influence of German propaganda beyond Germany itself was a particular concern of his. One other work is worth mentioning: *The World I Know* was not really an autobiography, but it disclosed much about the man.

Golding once wrote that his intention in his Elsie Silver books was to "render the adventures and passion of the Jewish people in our time", but in this he only partly succeeds; the job has been done far more effectively by American and Israeli writers. *Day of Atonement* and *Magnolia Street* may meet his aim but the Elsie Silver stories are trivial books, merely romances, although they do highlight some of the trauma suffered by the Jewish people.

CECIL BLOOM

Goloboff, Gerardo Mario

Argentine fiction writer, 1939–

Born in Carlos Casares, 1939, an agricultural colony established by Jewish Colonization Association. Trained as a lawyer, but devoted himself to literature; began to write poetry and literary criticism in early 1960s. Founded literary journal *Nuevos Aires*, 1970. Self-exiled to France, 1973; taught literary theory and the literature of Latin America at universities of Toulouse and Paris-Nanterre. Returned for brief visits to Argentina as it moved towards democracy; took up permanent residence again, 1999. Frequent contributor to newspapers; leads literary workshops in several Argentinian universities.

Selected Writings

Poetry
Entre la diáspora y octubre [Between the Diaspora and October], 1966
Lettres [Letters; bilingual collection in French and Spanish], 1982
Toujours encore [Forever More], 1982
Los versos del hombre pájaro [Poems of the Birdman], 1994

Novels
Caballos por el fondo de los ojos [Horses in the Depths of Our Eyes], 1976
Criador de palomas [Dove Breeder], 1984
La luna que cae [The Falling Moon], 1989
El soñador de Smith [The Dream Man from Smith], 1990
Comuna verdad [Truth Commune], 1995

Short Story
"La pasión según San Martín", 1979; as "The Passion According to Saint Martin", translated by Ilan Stavans, 1994

Other
Leer Borges [Reading Borges], 1978
"Nuestra Babel" [Our Babel], 1987
Genio y figura de Roberto Arlt [Robert Arlt: The Writer and his World], 1988
"Las lenguas del exilio" [The Languages of Exile], 1989
Literatura e identidad en América latina: Carpentier, Borges, Vallejo, with Jeanine Potelet and Osvaldo Fernández Diaz, 1991
"Una experiencia literaria de la identidad judía" [A Literary Experience of Jewish Identity], 1992
Julio Cortázar: la biografía [Julio Cortazar: A Biography], 1998

Further Reading

Aizenberg, Edna, "The Writing of the Disaster: Gerardo Mario Goloboff's *Criador de palomas*", *Inti*, 28 (1988): 67–73
Barr, Lois Baer, review of *La luna que cae*, *Noaj*, 4/5 (1990): 113–15
Barr, Lois Baer, "Noah in the Pampas: Syncretism in Goloboff's *Criador de palomas*" in *Tradition and Innovation: Reflections on Latin American Jewish Writing*, edited by Robert DiAntonio and Nora Glickman, Albany: State University of New York Press, 1993
Barr, Lois Baer, "Noah in the Pampas: A Trilogy: Gerardo Mario Goloboff" in her *Isaac Unbound: Patriarchal Traditions in the Latin American Jewish Novel*, Tempe: Arizona State University Center for Latin American Studies, 1995
"Entrevista a Gerardo Mario Goloboff", *Noaj*, 2/2 (1988): 96–100
Farré, Adela, "Goloboff segueix la seva recerca del perquè de la decadència", *Mirador Catalán* (19 April 1990)
Gilberto de León, Olver, "Un mítico viaje hacia la infancia", *La Prensa* (8 December 1985): suplemento dominical 3
Glickman, Nora, review of *El soñador de Smith*, *World Literature Today*, 66/1 (Winter 1992): 96–97
Glickman, Nora, "Discovering Self in History: Aída Bortnik and Gerardo Mario Goloboff" in *The Jewish Diaspora in Latin America: New Studies on History and Literature*, edited by David Sheinin and Lois Baer Barr, New York: Garland, 1996
Gutiérrez Girardot, Rafael, "La tierra prometida: la trilogía novelística de Gerardo Mario Goloboff", *Hispamérica*, 21/62 (1992): 111–26
Isod, Liliana, "No sería quien soy y no escribiría como escribo si no fuese judío", *Mundo Israelita* (22 May 1987): 6
Moreno, Fernando, "La escritura, nido de ausencias: una aproximación a la obra de Gerardo M. Goloboff", *Cahiers du CRIAR* [Publications de l'Université de Rouen], 11 (1991): 71–77
Renard, Maria Adela, review of *Criador de palomas*, *La Prensa* (3 February 1985): section 1, 11
Senkman, Leonardo, *La identidad judía en la literatura argentina*, Buenos Aires: Pardés, 1983
Senkman, Leonardo, "Escribir para buscar los orígenes de los enigmas que nos acosan", *Nueva Sion*, 598 (20 July 1984): 23–24
Senkman, Leonardo, "Goloboff: The Creation of a Mythical Town", *Yiddish*, 9/1 (1993): 105–10
Sosnowski, Saúl, "Gerardo Mario Goloboff: hacia el décimo mes en la diáspora" in *La orilla inminente: escritores judíos argentinos*, Buenos Aires: Legasa, 1987
Taffetani, Oscar, "El poder de la ficción", *La Razón*, (13 October 1985): Cultura 10–11
Weinstein, Ana E. and Miryam E. Gover de Nasatsky, *Escritores judeo-argentinos: bibliografía 1900–1987*, 2 vols, Buenos Aires: Milá, 1994

Goloboff's life and oeuvre have been deeply marked by exile. His birth in one of the Jewish agricultural colonies in Argentina made him heir to the tension between integration and assimilation. When the Argentine government considered fostering Jewish European immigration to the Pampa in the late 19th century, the project was clearly designed with the aim of repopulating the remote province with white European immigrants. Government officials were convinced that, in time, the newcomers would assimilate seamlessly into Argentine society. West European Jewish leaders, on the other hand, saw this willingness on the part of the Argentine government as the answer to their concerns for Jews living in pogrom-infested eastern Europe. Therefore, under the patronage of the Baron de Hirsch and the Jewish Colonization Association, thousands of east European Jews moved to the Argentine Pampa, a proclaimed haven for these predominantly devout Jewish communities. Consequently, a conflict of interests erupted: while the Argentine government pushed for the swift assimilation of the newcomers, the Jewish settlers sought integration into Argentine society without having to give up their Jewish identity. This conflict, which has marked Jewish-Argentine letters to this day, is central to Goloboff's work.

The suspension between exile and integration is evident in the title of his first collection of poetry, *Entre la diáspora y octubre* [Between the Diaspora and October]. The critic Saúl Sosnowski considers the "entre" [in between] of the title as "transition". According to Sosnowski, "Diaspora" and "October" are the two poles of a journey, which can be read respectively as "problem" and "solution", as "oppression" and "redemption". Although sprinkled with the biblical imagery of Exodus, the Diaspora of Goloboff's text is not exclusively Jewish; it encompasses all the dispossessed. Their lack is not only of a homeland, but also of the ability to participate in "History". If Goloboff seems overly optimistic about the redemptive powers of socialism, as some critics have suggested, it must be remembered that, ultimately, the poet remains suspended in the "in between" of the title. Goloboff's caution to place himself indefinitely "in between" can be read as further evidence of the Utopian character of his verses.

In his first novel, *Caballos por el fondo de los ojos* [Horses in the Depths of Our Eyes], Goloboff seems to have shed the hopefulness of *Entre la diáspora y octubre*. This novel can be read as a literary compendium of the various doctrines and programmes embraced by Argentine Jews, such as socialism, populism (Peronism), Zionism, and psychoanalysis, among others, which were thought to facilitate Jewish-Argentine participation in national life. These postures are reviewed within the span of three generations of a Jewish-Argentine family. The protagonist is forced to deal with a compound history – that of his great-grandfather in the Russia of the pogroms, his own rather recent history as an Argentine Jew, and his son's fervent Argentinity that leads him to join an anti-government group. As the protagonist looks at his son's corpse, executed by the military Junta, it becomes evident that none of the alluring dogmas would ultimately serve him to deal effectively with the dilemma of assimilation versus integration.

Goloboff's subsequent four novels, *Criador de palomas* [Dove Breeder], *La luna que cae* [The Falling Moon], *El soñador de Smith* [The Dream Man from Smith], and *Comuna Verdad* [Truth Commune], constitute the tetralogy known as "The Saga of Algarrobos", for all them take place in the town of Algarrobos, province of La Pampa.

Criador de palomas is the story of an unnamed orphaned Jewish boy, known only as El Pibe [The Kid]. Although the time frame of the novel is deliberately vague, it seems to suggest that El Pibe's childhood and adolescence took place during the 1950s and 1960s, decades marred by Peronist and anti-Peronist hostilities. Goloboff weaves the painful disappointments characteristic of the *Bildungsroman* with the lyrical imagery of the biblical story of the Flood. As the critic Lois Baer Barr has noted, this adds a touch of irony for "there seems to be no covenant with God, nor any justice for random evil acts". The death of his beloved Tío Negro – the uncle who had raised him – and the butchered remains of his doves suggest the increasing violence in Argentina in a poetic, yet deeply disturbing fashion, reminiscent of René Clément's 1951 French film *Les Jeux interdits* [The Forbidden Games].

La luna que cae brings El Pibe back to Algarrobos, after a long and unexplained absence. His return was motivated by a sudden desire to learn more about his past and his uncle's death. He seeks the soothsayer from Smith, who will reappear in the third novel of the saga. The insertion in the novel of a heap of corpses discovered in the town of Algarrobos allows Goloboff to ponder the violence and extortion instigated by the military and the tacit complicity of its inhabitants.

El soñador de Smith focuses on the dialogue between El Pibe and the soothsayer as the former continues to investigate his past and, above all, the circumstances surrounding his uncle's death. The "Dream Man" tells him Gauchesque tales of rural life, an oddity in a time when the only remains of the Gaucho are to be found in books. This is all part of the El Pibe's apprenticeship. While learning about his uncle's death, he will also learn about the town's history and how to embrace it, even if marked by treason and violence.

While not related to the story of El Pibe, *Comuna Verdad* is based on a rather obscure historical event in the same town of Algarrobos. This event predates the story of El Pibe, as it concludes with the onset of the Perón era in 1943. This is the story of an anarchist commune set by Italian and Jewish immigrants on the outskirts of Algarrobos. The short-lived experiment comes to a violent end with the military coup of 1943. Goloboff details the sources of his novel in an epilogue, thereby substantiating the historical validity of an otherwise highly lyrical text.

Goloboff's latest work, *Julio Cortázar: la biografía* [Julio Cortazar: A Biography], is the first extended biographical study of this important Argentine writer. The text is centred on "Cortázar the writer", linking his literary texts to specific events of his life. Goloboff sought to write "the biography of a man of letters", placing Cortázar's literary preoccupations within the context of his life.

Goloboff's recent – yet permanent – return to his native Argentina may signal a new consideration of the dilemma that has been at the core of his oeuvre: how to participate fully in Argentine national life, how to claim a part of that history, without giving up that other history, his Jewish identity.

LYDIA M. GIL

Goodman, Allegra

US fiction writer, 1967–

Born in Brooklyn, New York, 5 July 1967. Studied at Harvard University, BA 1989, and at Stanford University, PhD in English 1997. Married; three children. Awarded Whiting Writer's Award, 1991.

Selected Writings

Short Stories
Total Immersion, 1989
The Family Markowitz, 1996

Novels
Kaaterskill Falls, 1998
Paradise Park, 2000

Other
"Writing Jewish Fiction In and Out of the Multicultural Context" in *Daughters of Valor: Contemporary Jewish American Women Writers*, edited by Jay L. Halio and Ben Siegel, 1997

In "Writing Jewish Fiction In and Out of the Multicultural Context", a paper originally given at the annual convention of the Modern Language Association of America in December 1994 and later published in *Daughters of Valor*, Allegra Goodman briefly surveyed past and current writing by Aleichem, Grade, Singer, Bellow, and Roth, and then asked, "Where do I stand as I look for strategies and models?" She answered, "I write about Jewish culture, but not merely Jewish culture. I write about religion as well." In an autobiographical piece that was also in part a literary manifesto, she went on to proclaim that "Jewish American writers must recapture the spiritual and the religious dimension of Judaism." In much of her fiction, and especially in her first full-length novel, *Kaaterskill Falls*, Allegra Goodman has done just that.

She began writing and publishing short stories about growing up Jewish in Hawaii. Her first story, "And Also Much Cattle", describes a breakaway Orthodox high holiday service on the lanai of a private home in Honolulu. Although many of the incidents are hilarious, as the family's pets race through the rooms and some of the children refuse to conform in appropriate dress, Goodman captures the longing for spiritual communion with the deity on the part of many who attend the service. Similarly in other stories, the urge to find God and thereby one's own identity becomes emphatic. This is particularly true in "Onionskin", written as a letter by a non-traditional student, Sharon, to her philosophy professor to explain, if not excuse, her behaviour in walking out of his class, because she felt his discussion of St Augustine was beside the point of her main interest: "to learn about religion – God, prayer, ritual, the Madonna mother-goddess figure, forgiveness, miracles, sin, abortion, death, the big moral concepts". Goodman does not preach or directly teach about those "big moral concepts," but they underlie her fiction very profoundly.

Not all of her stories involve predominantly Jewish characters ("Fait'"), and many of her stories are more deeply concerned with universal issues, such as family loyalties ("Retrospective"), growing old ("Fannie Mae"), and female aspirations in a male-dominated world ("Sarah"), than with the superficial aspects of daily life, though these become the vehicle, as they must, for conveying those issues. While her first volume of short stories, *Total Immersion*, is a heterogeneous collection, her second book, *The Family Markowitz*, focuses, as the title indicates, on the various members of one family and their relationships with each other. As a matter of fact, Goodman began writing about this family in *Total Immersion*, in "Young People" and "Wish List", but she became so interested in them that she continued writing about them in a succession of stories that first appeared in the *New Yorker* and *Commentary*. Taken together, they almost succeed as a novel, with Rose as the matriarch of the family, and Henry and Ed as her two sons. Ed is married to an aspiring writer, Sarah, and they have four children, whom Goodman introduces at various stages of their development in various stories. Ed is a professor of political science at Georgetown University and a rather acerbic personality. Henry, who may have begun as a closet homosexual, moves to England and marries a good English woman as both approach their middle age. The interactions among these family members bring out the themes of family responsibility, caring, and, as one of Ed's children becomes more and more orthodox, the tensions that arise when families do not share the same religious convictions.

That is not the main theme of *Kaaterskill Falls*, however, which also focuses directly on family relationships of differing kinds. Kaaterskill Falls is the name of a small town in upstate New York that has become the summer retreat for the followers of Rav Kirshner, a very strict Orthodox rabbi but not a Hasidic rebbe. While Goodman devotes most of the novel to Elizabeth and Isaac Shulman and their five daughters, all loyal followers of Rav Kirshner, other families of greater or less religious observance also appear, such as that of Andras Melish, his Argentine wife, Nina, and their daughter Renée. Like Sarah, Ed's wife in the Markowitz stories, Elizabeth has aspirations beyond her position as a housewife and mother and tries to open a little store in Kaaterskill Falls, only to have her growing success as a shopkeeper stifled by Elijah Kirshner after he succeeds his father as leader of the sect. Renée Melish, forced to practice the piano by her mother, would much rather cavort with Stephanie, her Gentile friend, than serve as a counsellor at the day camp where all the other Jewish children spend their summer days.

These tensions are reflected, indeed magnified, in the characters and actions of Rav Kirshner's two sons, Jeremy and Isaiah, the first a brilliant professor of humanities, the other a more plodding but devoted Talmudic scholar. The tensions between them and their father recall those that Chaim Potok portrayed so admirably in novels such as *The Chosen* and *My Name is Asher Lev*, that is, between a family's religious tradition and the secular attractions of contemporary life. Indeed, Goodman's fiction recalls the work of both Potok and Cynthia Ozick, but as a stylist of English prose, she surpasses both of them. Hers is a more graceful and at times even lyrical prose style that harbingers even greater things to come.

Jay L. Halio

Gordimer, Nadine

South African fiction writer and essayist, 1923–

Born in Springs, near Johannesburg, 20 November 1923. Studied at convent school and for one year at University of the Witwatersrand, Johannesburg; became full-time writer. Married, first, G. Gavron, 1949; second, Reinhold Cassirer, 1954; one son, one daughter. Visiting lecturer, Institute of Contemporary Arts, Washington DC, 1961, Harvard,

Princeton, and Northwestern universities, 1969, University of Michigan, 1970; Adjunct Professor of Writing, Columbia University, 1971. Presenter, *Frontiers* (television series), 1990. Many awards, including W.H. Smith Literary Award, 1961; Thomas Pringle Award, 1969; James Tait Black Memorial Prize, 1972; Booker Prize, 1974; Grand Aigle d'Or (France), 1975; CNA Award, 1974, 1975, 1980; Scottish Arts Council Neil Gunn Fellowship, 1981; Commonwealth Prize for Distinguished Service to Literature, 1981; Modern Languages Association Award (United States), 1981; Malaparte Prize (Italy), 1985; Royal Society of Literature Medal, 1990; Nobel Prize for Literature, 1991.

Selected Writings

Fiction
Face to Face, 1949
The Soft Voice of the Serpent and Other Stories, 1952
The Lying Days, 1953
Six Feet of the Country, 1956
A World of Strangers, 1958
Friday's Footprint and Other Stories, 1960
Occasion for Loving, 1963
Not for Publication and Other Stories, 1965
The Late Bourgeois World, 1966
A Guest of Honour, 1970
Livingstone's Companions, 1971
The Conservationist, 1974
Selected Stories, 1975; as *No Place Like*, 1978
Some Monday for Sure, 1976
Burger's Daughter, 1979
A Soldier's Embrace, 1980
Town and Country Lovers, 1980
July's People, 1981
Something Out There, 1984
A Sport of Nature, 1987
My Son's Story, 1990
Crimes of Conscience, 1991
Jump and Other Stories, 1991
Why Haven't You Written? Selected Stories 1950–1972, 1993
None to Accompany Me, 1994
The House Gun, 1998
The Pickup, 2001

Television Plays and Documentaries: *A Terrible Chemistry*, 1981; *Choosing for Justice: Allan Boesak*, with Hugo Cassirer, 1985; *Country Lovers*, *A Chip of Glass Ruby*, *Praise*, *Oral History* (all in The Gordimer Stories series), 1985

Other
"A South African Childhood: Allusions in a Landscape", *New Yorker* (16 October 1954)
Editor, with Lionel Abrahams, *South African Writing Today*, 1967
The Black Interpreters: Notes on African Writing, 1973
On the Mines, 1973
What Happened to Burger's Daughter; or, How South African Censorship Works, with others, 1980
Lifetimes: Under Apartheid, 1986
The Essential Gesture: Writing, Politics, and Places, edited by Stephen Clingman, 1988
Writing and Being, 1995
Living in Hope and History: Notes from Our Century, 1999

Further Reading

Bazin, Nancy Topping and Marilyn Dallman Seymour (editors), *Conversations with Nadine Gordimer*, Jackson: University Press of Mississippi, 1990
Clingman, Stephen, *The Novels of Nadine Gordimer: History from the Inside*, London and Boston: Allen and Unwin, 1986
Cooke, John, *The Novels of Nadine Gordimer: Private Lives, Public Landscapes*, Baton Rouge: Louisiana State University Press, 1985
Driver, Dorothy *et al.*, *Nadine Gordimer: A Bibliography*, Grahamstown, South Africa: National English Literary Museum, 1993
Ettin, Andrew Vogel, *Betrayals of the Body Politic: The Literary Commitments of Nadine Gordimer*, Charlottesville: University Press of Virginia, 1993
Haugh, Robert F., *Nadine Gordimer*, New York: Twayne, 1974
Head, Dominic, *Nadine Gordimer*, Cambridge and New York: Cambridge University Press, 1994
Newman, Judie, *Nadine Gordimer*, London and New York: Routledge, 1988
Oliphant, Andries Walter (editor), *A Writing Life: Celebrating Nadine Gordimer*, London: Viking, 1998
Pettersson, Rose, *Nadine Gordimer's One Story of a State Apart*, Uppsala, Sweden: Uppsala University Press, 1995
Smith, Rowland (editor), *Critical Essays on Nadine Gordimer*, Boston: G.K. Hall, 1990
Stein, Pippa and Ruth Jacobson, *Sophiatown Speaks*, Johannesburg: Junction Avenue Press, 1986
Temple-Thurston, Barbara, *Nadine Gordimer Revisited*, New York: Twayne, 1999
Wade, Michael, *Nadine Gordimer*, London: Evans, 1978
Wagner, Kathrin M., *Rereading Nadine Gordimer: Text and Subtext in the Novels*, Bloomington: Indiana University Press, 1994

Nadine Gordimer occupies a pre-eminent position in South African letters and was the first South African writer to receive a Nobel Prize (1991). Her work has been translated into many languages and her reputation as a craftswoman, and especially as a literary interpreter of South Africa, is worldwide.

She grew up in a small mining town 30 miles from Johannesburg. From the age of 15 she published regularly in local journals. "A Watcher of the Dead", a story which deals with Jewish custom, was published in *Jewish Affairs* in 1948 and later reprinted. During her long writing career she has published more than 200 short stories and 14 novels, and has made important contributions to South African writing on culture and politics.

Her father was a Jewish immigrant from Lithuania who was trained as a watchmaker. Her mother came from a more assimilated English Jewish family. Most readers and critics are either unaware of her Jewish background or disregard it. She herself asserts that she was not raised in the Jewish tradition but rather as an agnostic. "I never had much sense of identity with the Jewish community", she said in an interview with Pippa Stein and Ruth Jacobson in 1986. In an article published in the *New Yorker* in 1954, Gordimer recorded that her mother distanced herself from the Jewish section of the community and worked for charity sales in aid of the Presbyterian Church. Gordimer identified with her mother and felt alienated from her father who paid his dues to the "ugly little synagogue". Here she applies a key anti-Semitic epithet, "ugly", to the synagogue. Noteworthy too is her use of "ugly" in relation to the Jewish characters of her early fiction. The portraits of Jewish store keepers at the mines in *The Lying Days* and in her short story, "The Defeated" are unsympathetic and repeat the stereotypes of racial difference.

Generally, there are few Jewish characters in Gordimer's writing. The most memorable is Joel Aaron in *The Lying Days*. He is cultured, bookish, and caring, but is nevertheless presented as seen through the eyes of the Gentile narrator and her parents as other. In a much later novel, *A Sport of Nature*, the main character is, surprisingly, a Jewish girl, Hillela, who marries two black revolutionaries. Although in many respects it is an anti-realist text, dealing with political resolution and transformation, it yet perpetuates, in some minor characters, typical South African Jewish stereotypes. Gordimer said in an interview with Alan Ross in 1965, "I have no religion, no political dogma – only plenty of doubts about everything except my conviction that the colour-bar is wrong and utterly indefensible. This I have found the basis of a moral code that is valid for me." Indeed, most of her life has been a commitment to the liberation movement and to social transformation. But, despite her enduring anti-racialism, the evidence of her fiction seems to suggest that her tolerance does not always extend to Jews.

In a story written as late as 1991, "My Father Leaves Home", a Jew (seemingly closely based on Gordimer's father), stigmatized on racial grounds, becomes, himself, a racist and a bully. She explains:

> my father had, during his childhood, suffered from a form of apartheid. But he never drew the parallel between the two situations [Russian and South African]. Born a Lithuanian Jew, he had . . . lived under Russian domination, which denied Jewish children the right to go to the same schools as others or to attend university . . . My father quickly forgot that he had arrived in South Africa in very humble circumstances, that he did not at first speak English . . . [and] did not hesitate to adopt the biases of the South African society.

The story can be read as an illustration of the Jew's fear of social slippage. But the tone suggests that this complex is not entirely overcome by the narrator and, one assumes, despite her protestations, by the author.

In 1994 Gordimer responded to the suggestion that she had denied or suppressed her Jewish origins by claiming: "I have never denied that I'm Jewish and have no desire to deny it. For me, being Jewish is like being black: you simply are. To want to deny it is disgusting." But she has also made it clear that, as she says, "[Jewishness has] played no part at all in my life . . . I'm conscious of the fact that I am Jewish, but it hasn't had anything much to do with the formation of my attitude to life, with my philosophy, or with my moral attitudes." Moreover she does not she regard herself as a feminist or "woman writer". For her, "the formative thing has been being a white African". "You begin with human life and you begin with the mystery of life. Where I live the mystery of life is very political."

When South Africa was politically and culturally ostracized by the rest of the world, Gordimer's work was internationally acclaimed as a window on the troubled situation under apartheid. She has been hailed by Oliphant as "a voice of conscience during the years of silence and repression", reflecting not only political but also psychological tensions, and recording what it feels like to live through the events of South African history in the second half of the 20th century. Stephen Clingman calls her work "writing history from the inside".

Her fiction and essays demonstrate most amply her rigorous intelligence and impeccable artistry. She is best known as a realist. With an unerring eye for detail she has charted not only the urban landscape but also the inner reality. A significant aspect of her art is the method of what she calls "let(ting) the general seep up through the individual", and of presenting insight through the intensity of psychological epiphany. Until the 1990s her work was habitually read by critics as a chronological development, as an increasingly sophisticated treatment of gender, sexual, colonial, and racial themes, and as a movement away from chronicle to prophecy. During the 1990s she has commented on South African life after apartheid. Recent criticism of her work has been broadened by a poststructuralist approach. Some detractors see her apparent detachment and coldness as a fault, but none deny the massive importance of her contribution to South African letters and the centrality of her vision of the complex and troubled world of South Africa.

MARCIA LEVESON

Gordin, Yankev

Russian dramatist, 1853–1909

Born in Mirgorod, Ukraine, 1 May 1853. Educated by private tutors and in both traditional and secular schools. Married; 14 children. Failed in business; worked in a variety of manual trades; journalist; actor. Settled in Elizavetgrad (now Kirovohrad); taught in Russian-Jewish school. Attracted by ideas of the Narodniki and by Ukrainian nationalism. Set up agricultural commune guided by Tolstoyan principles, the Spiritual Biblical Brotherhood, 1880; commune suppressed, 1891; fled to New York with family. Application to Baron de Hirsch for funds to establish communal farm rejected. Became Yiddish journalist, then popular Yiddish dramatist. Died in New York, 10 June 1909.

Selected Writings

Plays
Sibirye [Siberia], 1891
Der pogrom in rusland [The Pogrom in Russia], 1891
Der yidisher kenig lir [The Jewish King Lear], 1892
Medea, 1897
Mirele efres, 1898
Got, mentsh un tayvl [God, Man, and the Devil], 1900
Der vilder mentsh [The Wild Man], 1907
Ale shriftn, 4 vols, 1910
Yankev gordins dramen, 2 vols, 1911
Yankev gordins eynakters, 1917
Dray drames, edited by Shmuel Rozhanski, 1973

Further Reading

Clifford, Dafna, "The Devil and Beethoven: Convergent Themes in Yiddish Film and Literature" in *When Joseph Met Molly: A Reader on Yiddish Film*, edited by Sylvia Paskin, Nottingham: Five Leaves Press, 1999
Kahan, A., *Bleter fun mayn lebn*, vol. 3, New York: Forverts Association, 1928
Lahad, Ezra, "Undzer literarisher repertuar: bibliografye" in *Yidisher teater in eyrope tsvishn beyde velt-milkhomes*, edited by Itsik Manger, Yonas Turkov, and Moyshe Pernson, vol. 2, New York: Alveltlekher Yidisher Kultur-Kongres, 1971
Marmor, K., *Yankev Gordin* (with bibliography), New York: IKUF, 1953
Prager, Leonard, "Of Parents and Children: Jacob Gordin's *The Jewish King Lear*", *American Quarterly*, 18/3 (Fall 1966): 506–16
Waldinger, Albert, "Jewish Groundlings, Folk Vehemence and King Lear in Yiddish", *Yiddish*, 10/2–3 (1996): 121–39
Zylbercweig, Zalmen (editor), *Leksikon fun yidishn teater*, vol. 1, New York: Elisheva, 1931: columns 392–461
Zylbercweig, Zalmen, *Di velt fun yankev gordin*, Tel Aviv: Elisheva, 1964

If it was Avrom Goldfadn who gave birth to modern Yiddish theatre, it was Yankev Gordin who became its reformer and lifted it to a higher level. Some of the high-minded reformist ideals that had animated the sectarian colony permeate the dramatic writings that he created after arriving in New York. At that time the New York Yiddish stage was still dominated by the meretricious vaudeville of Yoysef Latayner, Moyshe Hurvits, and Shomer. Gordin's *Sibirye* [Siberia] which opened in November 1891 and *Der pogrom in rusland* [The Pogrom in Russia] put on two months later (neither of which was ever published) brought a purer Yiddish as well as more serious and realistic content to the Yiddish stage. In his prolific output he frequently contented himself with openly avowed, free adaptations from classical English, German, and Russian drama. He adopted plots from Gerhart Hauptmann, Schiller, Gogol', Gor'kii. Sudermann, Grillparzer, Ibsen, Lessing, Karl Gutzkow, and others. His work, which was more naturalistic in character than Goldfadn's generally romantic style, tends to suffer, however, from stereotyped characters and tendentious pathos. Only about a quarter of his plays has been published. Among his most successful works was *Der yidisher kenig lir* (performed 1892) which was based on Shakespeare. The theme of the conflict of generations was topical at the time as the result of Americanized children rebelling against their immigrant parents. Gordin's opposition to both Orthodoxy and Hasidism is reflected here in the struggle between on the one hand parental authority based on tradition and on the other children influenced by modern society. At the *purim* festival the stubborn Dovid Hersheles divides his property among his children before setting out for the Promised Land, but soon returns to Vilna (Vilnius) when his money runs out. Two of his daughters are married to Hasidic or Orthodox husbands and deceive their father. His enlightened daughter, who is a medical student and has genuine affection for her father, tells him the unadorned truth and is rejected by him. But at the time of her marriage to a maskil, whom her father had previously regarded as an apostate, a reconciliation is effected. The play established Gordin's reputation and that of Yankev Adler who played the leading role. What was perhaps the most popular and powerful drama in the whole Yiddish repertoire, *Mirele efres* (staged in 1898) reworked the same theme with a female protagonist. Mirele, one of the most impressive female figures in Yiddish literature and a kind of latter-day Glikl Haml, has rebuilt the business of her bankrupt, suicide husband, but at the time of the marriage of her son Yosele to Sheyndele, who comes from a distinguished but impoverished family, Mirele's daughter-in-law and her parents impose such severe financial conditions that Mirele is inclined to call off the match. She gives in, however, out of love for her son who has in the meantime set his heart on Sheyndele. The clash between the two strong-headed women reaches such a pitch of intensity that Mirele is driven from her home by the arrogance of her daughter-in-law. Eventually a reconciliation is achieved at the time of the bar-mitsvah of her grandson, Shloymele. One of the most notable performances of *Mirele efres* was in 1909 with Ester Rokhl Kaminska in the title role. *Medea* (published and performed in New York in 1897) is based on Grillparzer's *Die Argonauten*. *Got, mentsh un tayvl* was loosely adapted from Goethe's *Faust* and staged by David Kessler in 1900, while *Der umbakanter* [The Stranger] owed much to Stanisław Przybyszewski's *Złote Runo* [The Golden Fleece]. During the two decades of Gordin's dominance of the New York Yiddish stage he wrote more than 70 plays (at a steady rate of approximately four a year), many of which were successfully adapted for the cinema after his death. *Mirele efres* was three times given cinematic treatment, in two silent versions in 1912 and most effectively by Joseph Berne in 1939 with screenplay by Osip Dimov and with Berta Gersten in the title role. In fact more of Gordin's works were filmed than those of any other single Yiddish writer and included: *Der vilder foter* [The Wild Father] (1911), *Got, mentsh un tayvl* (1912, 1949), *Khasye di yesoyme* [Khasye the Orphan] (1912), *Yom hakhupe* [Wedding Day] (1912), *Di shkhite* [The Slaughter] (1913), *Der umbakanter* [The Stranger] (1913), *Gots shtrof* [God's Punishment] (1913), *Di shtifmuter* [The Stepmother] (1914), *Der yidisher kenig lir* (1935) and *On a heym* [Homeless] with screenplay by Alter Katsizne (1939). During his lifetime

Gordin was spectacularly successful, despite a bitter campaign waged against him by Abe Kahan, and a quarter of a million Jews followed his funeral cortège.

HUGH DENMAN

Grade, Chaim

Russian-born US fiction writer, poet, and lecturer, 1910–1982

Born in Vilna (Vilnius), 4 April 1910, to Shloyme-Mote Grade, teacher of Hebrew, and Vella (née Blumenthal), a fruit seller. Studied in various Polish yeshivas, including *musar* yeshiva in Navaredok. Joined "Young Vilna" literary movement in 1930s; published first poems in *Vilna Tog*, 1932. Refugee in Soviet Union, 1941–46; wife, Frume-Libe Grade, and mother both killed in Holocaust. Returned briefly to Poland, then moved to Paris, 1946. Married, second, Inna Hecker Grade. Attended Jewish Culture Congress in United States, 1948; settled in New York; became US citizen, 1960. Worked for *Jewish Morning Journal*. Many awards, including Leyvik Prize for Yiddish literature; William and Janice Epstein Fiction Award from Jewish Book Council of the National Jewish Welfare Board, 1968; Remembrance Award of World Federation of Bergen–Belsen Associations, 1969; award from American Academy for Jewish Research; award for excellence from B'nai B'rith; Jewish Heritage Award (for excellence in literature), 1976. Died in New York, 26 June 1982.

Selected Writings

Poetry

Yo [Yes], 1936
Musernikes: poeme [Musarists or Musar Students], 1939
Doyres: lider un poemes [Generations], 1945
Farvoksene vegn: lider un poemes [Overgrown Paths], 1947
Oyf di khurves [On the Ruins], 1947
Pleytim [Refugees], 1947
Der mame's tsavoe [My Mother's Will], 1949
Shayn fun farloshene shtern: lider un poemes [The Glow of Extinguished Stars], 1950
In *The Golden Peacock: A Worldwide Treasury of Yiddish Poetry*, edited by Joseph Leftwich, 1961
Der mentsh fun fayer: lider un poemes [The Man of Fire], 1962
In *Anthology of Modern Yiddish Poetry*, edited by Ruth Whitman, 1966
Parmetene erd [Parchment Earth], 1968
Oyf mayn veg tsu dir: bedarki elaykh [On My Way to You], 1969

Novels and Short Fiction

"Mayn krig mit hersh raseyner: esey", 1951; as "May krig mit hersh reseyner", 1969; as "My Quarrel with Hersh Rasseyner", translated by Milton Himmelfarb, 1954; as *The Quarrel*, film adaptation by David Brandes, 1992
Der shulhoyf [The Courtyard of the Synagogue], 1958; a story in this volume "Der Brunem" as *The Well*, translated by Ruth Wisse, 1967
Di agune [The Abandoned Wife], 1961; as *The Agunah*, translated by Curt Leviant, 1974
Tsemakh atlas: di yeshive [Tsemakh Atlas: The Yeshiva], 2 vols, 1967–68; as *The Yeshiva*, translated by Curt Leviant, 1976–77
Milhemet hayetser [The Moralists], 1970
Di kloyz un di gas: dertseylungen, 1974; as *Rabbis and Wives*, translated by Harold Rabinowitz and Inna Hecker Grade, 1982
Der shtumer minyen [The Silent Minyen], 1976

Other

Der mames shabosim [My Mother's Sabbaths], 1955; the last segment as *The Seven Little Lanes*, translated by Curt Leviant, 1972; as *My Mother's Sabbath Days: A Memoir*, translated by Channa Kleinerman Goldstein and Inna Hecker Grade, 1986

Further Reading

Alexander, Edward, "A Dialogue of the Mind with Itself: Chaim Grade's Quarrel with Hersh Rasseyner", *Judaism*, 21–22 (1972–73)
Konvitz, Milton, "Chaim Grade's Quarrel", *Midstream*, 41/8 (November 1995)
Moskowitz, Moshe, "Chaim Grade and the Jewish Ego", *Judaism*, 25 (1976)
Moskowitz, Moshe, "Contra Musar" (review of Grade's *The Yeshiva*), *Judaism*, 27 (1978)
Pinsker, Sanford, "Chaim Grade: The Yiddish Writer as Agunah", *Yiddish*, 8/2 (1992)
Ribalow, Harold, "A Conversation with Chaim Grade", *Congress Monthly*, 42/2 (February 1975)
Shepard, Richard, "The World of Chaim Grade", *Moment*, 5/8 (1980)
Slotnick, Susan, "Chaim Grade's Central Concern", *Jewish Book Annual*, 37 (1979–80)
Szeintuch, Yechiel, "Chaim Grade as Poet of the Holocaust", *Jewish Book Annual*, 48 (1990–91)
Wisse, Ruth, "In Praise of Chaim Grade", *Commentary*, 63/4 (April 1977)
Wisse, Ruth, "Religious Imperatives and Mortal Desires", *New York Times* (14 November 1982)

Chaim (Khayim) Grade, unique among Yiddish writers of his generation in the depth of his traditional learning and command of classical Jewish texts, was the product of a rigorous yeshiva education, most importantly as a student of *musar* – an ascetic religious sect that combined Torah learning with a strict programme of personal introspection, self-abnegation, and the study of ethical tracts. Although he left the yeshiva world in 1932 to begin his career as a Yiddish poet, he is one of few Yiddish writers who captured the ideas, debates, and texture of traditional Jewish culture in Poland in the inter-war period. His Yiddish is a rich pastiche drawn from the earthy language of the Vilna masses (Grade's mother was an impoverished fruit peddler), and from the Hebrew-Aramaic cadences of religious high culture. Much of Grade's postwar writing remained fixed on portraying the secular and religious sweep of Jewish Vilna in all its richness and conflict. "I cannot escape, so to speak, the

[Vilna] synagogue courtyard . . . Not that I don't desire to. I simply *cannot*." Grade was often compared to the Hebrew poet Hayyim Nahman Bialik because of his self-positioning as a national Jewish writer. In 1978 he attracted an audience of more than 400 guests to hear him deliver the first-ever lecture in Yiddish at Harvard University. Elie Wiesel suggested that he was the "most authentic" of Yiddish novelists.

Grade's first collection of poetry, *Yo* [Yes], betrayed its optimistic title with poems of gloom and unrest that explored the dire material conditions of Vilna Jewry in the 1930s. The poet also expressed his own guilt at having abandoned a life of Jewish learning for secular literary pursuits: "And I see in my weakness the pain of my generation and its shame . . .". In the volume's title poem, the speaker groped through self doubt to assert that the inner transition from an inherited tradition of religious observance to a moral and spiritual posture independent of formal religion must be willed with an entirely new vocabulary: "Yes! – that is the answer of my youth/ When it needs to escape from its own skin./ Yes! – that means: My destiny is my virtue/ My fate is the milky-way to my greatness." The volume concluded with the poetic cycle "Ezekiel", an apocalyptic vision delivered in a prophetic national voice that captured the despair of European Jewry under Nazi threat. In a 1939 lecture in Vilna, Grade affirmed his understanding of the connection between the biblical prophets and the modern Yiddish writer: "The poet . . . must learn from the prophets who in times of impudence warned of impending danger, and times of destruction, when all lay waste, foretold the resurrection of the dead."

Grade was a master at dramatizing ideas. He captured the flavour of intellectual and moral debate within Jewish culture. Grade was so persuaded by the dramatic intensity of his former *musar* milieu that he explored it in three distinct literary genres – his pre-war, book-length narrative poem *Musernikes* [Musarists], his philosophical essay "My Quarrel with Hersh Rasseyner", and his two-volume novel *The Yeshiva*. In these works, Grade examined the spiritual and ethical struggles of *musar* students and their teachers, and their interactions with the wider community. *Musernikes* is a melancholy portrait of the anxieties Grade experienced and witnessed as a former student at the Navaredok *musar* yeshiva. He explored his characters' struggle towards a life of moral perfection even as they contended with individual lusts, vanities, and doubts about the level of their own faith. Through the eyes of the semi-autobiographical figure Chaim Vilner, Grade portrayed the corrupting effects of a religious and moral training that provided little room for moderation. When Chaim is caught reading forbidden secular books, the full zeal of his teacher is unleashed against him: "There is only one truth/ . . . Torah and the world – they cannot co-exist/ don't be the dog who wants to show himself at both weddings."

In "My Quarrel with Hersh Rasseyner" and *The Yeshiva* Grade intensified the argument between religious faith and scepticism in a world in which historic events presented serious challenges to the traditional believer and progressive secularist alike. "My Quarrel with Hersh Rasseyner", according to Curt Leviant "perhaps the finest story of ideas in Jewish literature", positioned two survivors of World War II – the *mussar* instructor Hersh Rasseyner and the former *mssarist* turned Yiddish writer, Chaim Vilner – in a pitched philosophical battle for each others' souls. Hersh rejects the Godlessness and vanity inherent in the secular Jewish writer, as represented by Chaim. He suggests that in their thirst for critical recognition, secular artists portray licentiousness and wickedness, thereby transforming human evil into aesthetic idolatry. He is bolstered in his arguments by the recent German murder of European Jewry, attacking those who would put their faith in reason and art to expand the soul of humanity: "A man should choose between good and evil only as the Law [Torah] chooses for him . . . Reason is like a dog on a leash who follows sedately in his mater's footsteps – until he sees a bitch." For his part, Chaim attacks Hersh's rigid traditionalism for its unwillingness to recognize the cultural value of Jewish non-believers: "You didn't discover the truth, you received it ready made . . . If we have abandoned Jewish tradition, it is because of you. You barricaded yourself and let no one go out into the open." In *The Yeshiva*, Grade created one of the most memorable characters in all of Yiddish fiction, the tortured *musar* teacher Tsemakh Atlas. Atlas is at permanent war with himself, consumed by his spiritual vacillations, and by his obsession to eradicate sin from both himself and society. The novel provided a compassionate Talmudic master (modelled on Grade's former teacher, the renowned *Khazon Ish*) to serve as a humane religious counterpoint to Atlas's moral extremism.

Grade's fiction was consumed with the moral pitch of Jewish life in pre-war Vilna. In *The Well* – a novel about an impoverished porter who undertakes a campaign to repair the communal well – the author explored how an act of simple charity captured the imagination of an entire community, regardless of religious or ideological divisions. *The Agunah* is a tragic tale of a woman whose husband is presumed killed in battle, but is forbidden from remarrying because the rabbinic authorities lack sufficient evidence to provide her with a legal divorce. The novel shows how the tension between strict *halakhic* legalism and the need for a compassionate interpretation of the Law permeated all areas of society, from the rabbinic courts down to the simple Jews of the marketplace. In the short story "The Rebbetsin" Grade exposed the complicated, pre-war world of rabbis and competing religious factions, showing how such human traits as ambition, vanity, and the pursuit of status sometimes corrupted the noble values at the root of Torah scholarship. Ruth Wisse concluded that Grade, "more than any monument or commemoration, . . . pays Eastern European Jews the ultimate respect of recalling them as they lived, not as they died, with all their energy and complexity."

Grade's poetry and fiction occupy a significant place in the literature of Jewish catastrophe and renewal. *My Mother's Sabbath Days* is Grade's memoir of the great, tragic divide caused by the Holocaust. The memoir movingly describes his mother and Vilna on the eve of World War II, then charts his years as a refugee in the Soviet Union, and concludes with a searing account of the guilt that consumed the survivor upon his return to a destroyed home in 1946. In his famous "Elegy for the Soviet Yiddish writers", Grade paid homage to those talented colleagues who put their faith in the promise of communism, only to be eliminated in Stalinist purges: "I weep for you with all the letters of the alphabet/ that made your hopeful songs." *On My Way to You* (appearing after Grade's visit to Israel) probed Grade's redemptive vision of the Jewish state, suggesting that the Jewish writer's longing for *Erets Israel* "becomes a prayer to a love that is eternal."

JUSTIN CAMMY

Greenberg, Uri Zvi ("Tur Malka")

Polish-born Israeli poet, 1896–1981

Born in Bialykmien, 1896, into leading Hasidic family. Earliest poems, in Hebrew and Yiddish, published in important periodicals, 1912. Drafted into Austro-Hungarian army, 1915; served on Serbian front; deserted, 1917; returned to L'viv, where he witnessed pogroms against Jews, 1918. Published further poems in Hebrew and Yiddish; became leader of group of Yiddish Expressionist poets; edited shortlived avant-garde periodical, *Albatros*, 1922–23. Lived in Warsaw (1921–22) and Berlin (1923). Immigrated to Palestine, 1923. Became regular columnist on Labour daily newspaper *Davar*; broke with Labour after Arab riots, 1929; joined Zionist Revisionist movement. Adopted Hebrew pen-name Tur Malka ("King's Mountain"), referring to ancient hilltop settlement in Jerusalem, 1931. Lived in Warsaw where he edited newspapers of the Revisionist movement, *Di velt* and *Der moment*, 1931–39. Supported Irgun Zeva'i Le'ummi during War of Independence. Member of Knesset (Israeli legislature), representing Herut party, 1949–51. Married Aliza (known as Ayin Tur Malka), Jerusalem-born poet, 1950; five children. Awarded Bialik Prize, 1948, 1955, 1977; Israel Prize, 1957. Died 1981.

Selected Writings

Collections
Gesamelte verke [Collected (Yiddish) Work], 1979
Kol ketavav [Complete Works], 1990

Poetry in Yiddish
Ergets oyf felder [Somewhere in the Fields], 1915
In tsaytens roysh [In the Tumult of Time], 1919
Farnakhtengold [Dusk Gold], 1921
Mefiste [Mephistopheles], 1921
Krig oyf der erd [War on Earth], 1923
Undzere oysyes glien [Our Letters Glow], 1978

Poetry in Hebrew
Eimah gedolah veyareah [Great Fear and the Moon], 1925
Hagavrut haolah [Manhood on the Rise], 1926
Anakreon al kotev haitsavon [Anacreon at the Pole of Sorrow], 1928
Hazon ahad haligyonot [A Vision of One of the Legions], 1928
Kelev bayit [House Dog], 1929
Eizor Magen uneum ben hadam [Defence Zone and the Speech of the Son-of-Blood], 1930
Sefer hakitrug vehaemunah [The Book of Denunciation and Faith], 1937
Sefer haamudim [The Book of Pillars], 1945–56
Sefer haigul [The Book of the Circle], 1947–53
Leseif sela eitam [By their Vulture's Rock-Fissure], 1950s–1970s
Rehovot hanahar [Streets of the River], 1951
Shirei aspaklar / behaalma [Poems of a Looking-Glass / In this World], 1954–61
Al daat hazman vedaat hamakom [In Accordance with Time and Heaven], 1956–75

Poetry in English Translation
Jerusalem: yerushalayim shel matah, translated by Charles A. Cowen, 1939
Modern Hebrew Poetry: A Bilingual Anthology, edited and translated by Ruth Finer Mintz, 1966
Tri-Quarterly, special issue, "Contemporary Israeli Literature" (Spring 1977)
The Penguin Book of Hebrew Verse, edited and translated by T. Carmi, 1981
The Literature of Destruction: Jewish Responses to Catastrophe, edited by David Roskies, 1989

Further Reading

Bahat, Ya'aqov, *Uri Zvi Greenberg: Heqer Ve'iyun Beshirato Uvehaguto* [A Critical Examination of the Poetry and Thought of Uri Zvi Greenberg], Tel Aviv: Yahdav, 1983
Barzel, Hillel, "Uri Zvi Greenberg: Hagevanim Shebamihlol" [Uri Zvi Greenberg: The Nuances in the Whole] in *Uri Zvi Greenberg: Bibliografiyah Shel Mif'alo Hasifruti Umah Shenikhtav Aalav 1912–1978* [Uri Zvi Greenberg: A Bibliography of his Literary Work and Criticism on It 1912–1978], edited by Yohanan Arnon, Tel Aviv: Adi Moses, 1980
Burnshaw, Stanley, T. Carmi and Ezra Spicehandler (editors and translators), *The Modern Hebrew Poem Itself*, New York: Holt, Rinehart and Winston, 1965
Friedlander, Yehuda, *Uri Zvi Greenberg – Iyunim Beshirato* [Uri Zvi Greenberg – A Study of his Poetry], Jerusalem: Schocken, 1973
Geldman, Mordechai, "Ohel Eish Shoteh Eish" [Eats Fire Drinks Fire], *Haaretz sefarim* (10 May 1995)
Goodblatt, Chanita, " 'From Back Street to Boulevard': Directions and Departures in the Scholarship on Uri Zvi Greenberg", *Prooftexts*, 16 (1996)
Hever, Hannan, *Uri Tsvei Grinberg Bimlot Lo Shemonim* [Uri Zvi Greenberg on his Eightieth Birthday], catalogue of the exhibition at the Jewish National and University Library, Jerusalem: Bet hasefarim, 1977
Hever, Hannan, *Peiytanim Ubiryonim: Tsemihat Hashir Hapoliti Haivri Be'erets Yisrael* [Poets and Zealots: The Rise of Political Hebrew Poetry in Erets Yisrael], Jerusalem: Bialik Institute, 1994
Hever, Hannan, *Bishvi Ha'otopiyah: Masah 'al Meshihiyut Vepolitiqah Bishirah Ha'ivrit Be'erets Yisrael Bein Shetei Milhamot Ha'olam* [Captives of Utopia: An Essay on Messianism and Politics in Hebrew Poetry in Erets Yisrael between the Two World Wars], Beer Sheva: Ben-Gurion University Press, 1995
Kurzweil, Baruch, *Bein Hazon Levein Ha'absurdi* [Between Vision and the Absurd], Jerusalem: Schocken, 1966

Lindenbaum, Shalom, *Shirat Uri Zvi Greenberg: Qavei Mit'ar* [The Poetry of Uri Zvi Greenberg: An Outline], Tel Aviv: Hadar, 1984
Mintz, Alan, "Streets of the River" in *Hurban: Responses to Catastrophe in Hebrew Literature*, New York: Columbia University Press, 1984
Miron, Dan, "Uri Zvi Grinberg's War Poetry" in *The Jews of Poland Between Two World Wars*, edited by Y. Gutman *et al.*, Hanover, New Hampshire: University Press of New England, 1989
Shoham, Reuven, *Seneh Basar Vedam: Poetica Verhetoriqa Beshirato Ha-Modernistit Veha-Arhitipit shel Uri Zvi Greenberg* [Burning Bush of Flesh and Blood: Poetics and Rhetoric in the Modernist and Archetypal Poetry of Uri Zvi Greenberg], Sede Boqer: Ben-Gurion University of the Negev Press, 1997
Weiss, Hillel *et al.* (editors), *Ha'matkonet Ve'Ha'dmut: Mehqarim Ve'iyunim Beshirat Uri Zvi Greenberg* [Ha'matkonet Ve'Ha'dmut: Studies on the Poetry of Uri Zvi Greenberg], Ramat-Gan: Bar-Ilan University Press, 2000

According to Mordechai Geldman, Uri Zvi Greenberg is a writer "whose situation in Jewish time – preceding and following the Holocaust, and close to the beginning days of the Jewish state – bestows on his powerful voice, terrible at times in the violence of its simplification and its simplified violence, a superior motive and an absolute justification". His career spanned 60 years of poetic and journalistic writings, evoking complex and always passionate responses from all parts of the literary and political establishments.

He began as a Yiddish poet, establishing himself, in the view of Dan Miron, as a "late and minor romanticist" with the publication of three collections of verse between 1915 and 1922. In an additional volume, however, titled *Mefiste* [Mephistopheles] and published in 1921, he adopted the expansive, rhetorical style of Expressionist poetics with its unconventional long lines, the speaker's "thundering I", and the hymns to land and body. Greenberg's embrace of the Expressionist movement is carried into his first verse collections in Hebrew. These were published in various Zionist and socialist newspapers and journals in the years 1925 and 1926. They reveal his concern about the Zionist enterprise of the Third Aliyah (1917–23), expressing the terror of an individual and a nation living in exile, yearning for redemption from destruction and ruin.

Greenberg thus transformed himself from a Yiddish into a Hebrew poet, as well as from a Romantic into an Modernist writer. With the publication at the end of the 1920s of four further volumes of verse, Greenberg establishes two primary areas of poetic concern. One defines the genre of political poetry in Erets Yisrael, which begins with *Hazon ahad haligyonot* [A Vision of One of the Legions], while the other is heralded by the more delicate and personal lyric style of *Anakreon al kotev haitsavon* [Anacreon at the Pole of Sorrow].

Greenberg's political poetry of the 1920s and 1930s responds to contemporary events such as the diminishing British support for Zionism, as well as the mounting violence between Arab and Jew, and among the different camps within the Zionist movement. The later poems depict Greenberg's political-national view in the face of the events that preceded the establishment of the state, as well as relating to the Sinai Campaign, the Six Day War, and the Yom Kippur War. In contrast to these poems of national revival, there are the personal and lyrical-metaphysical poems. Many of these poems, as Dan Miron notes, derive from early visions and from childhood memories, while others shift from such enchanted and distant landscapes to the existence of life and death in this world.

Finally one must take special note of *Rehovot hanahar* [Streets of the River], which comprises Greenberg's response to the Holocaust. This is a magnificent dirge on the destruction of European Jewry, and contains three imaginative movements in which the poet attempts to come to terms with what is both a personal and a national tragedy: "a description of the procession of Jewish victims; the loss of self-confidence and engulfment by feelings of guilt and impotence; and a return to the messianic hope and the vision of the Kingdom of Israel", as Alan Mintz has seen it.

The distinguishing issues and themes of Greenberg's poetry revolve around conceptions of Judaism and the political realm. Kurzweil identifies what he terms "five theoretical and spiritual circles: the poet's election, the national myth, the world of childhood, the relationship between the Jewish and Christian worlds, and the religious issue" (page 10). Barzel for his part focuses on additional themes and structures (page xii), including:

> Zion as the sole, the only possible answer . . . belief in a living divinity, [and] rebellion against the failure to act . . . the realization of the image, the open metaphor, the multiplicity of the metaphors of death, the synoptic aspect that joins scenes of place and connects times . . . [and] a vocabulary of key terms . . . and characters [moon, musical instruments, Jesus, David].

One also finds in Greenberg's works a redrawing of the boundaries between lyric and political genres. His intertwining of the literary and the political is already evident in his Hebrew Expressionist collections, in which he supports a conception of poetry that is both rhetorical and engagé. In his political poetry, he subsequently turns the poem into a "political instrument that activates poetic means, and also a literary text that arouses and creates political action", in the words of Hannan Hever. What is more, in his radical development of the concept of messianism, Greenberg aestheticizes the political, with the consequence that his "poetic text almost completely ceased asking moral and practical questions . . . the aesthetic view marks out his boundaries and directions without attaching real significance to the moral accounts of the individual and his fate; much attention is given to the great structures of national history" (Hever, 1995).

Greenberg's poetry thus moves through a wide poetic, political, and emotional range, catalyzing public opinion and personal loyalties while demonstrating a deep involvement with the central experiences and issues of contemporary Jewish history.

CHANITA GOODBLATT

Grossman, David

Israeli fiction writer, dramatist, and journalist, 1954–

Born in Jerusalem, 25 January 1954. Worked for Israel Radio, 1963–88. Studied at Hebrew University, Jerusalem, BA 1979. Military service, 1971–75. Married; three children. Many awards, including Prime Minister's Prize for Hebrew Literature, 1984; Israel Publishers Association Prize, 1985; Israel's Best Journalist, 1988; Italian Literary Critics Prize, 1989; Nelly Sachs Award, 1991; Shalom Aleichem Prize, 1993; Messina Award, 1995; Premio Mondello Award, 1996; Chevalier de l'Ordre des Arts et des Lettres, 1998; Vittorio de Sica Award, 1999; Sappir Prize for Literature, 2001.

Selected Writings

Fiction

Hiyukh hagdi, 1983; as *The Smile of the Lamb*, translated by Betsy Rosenberg, 1990
Rats: sipurim [The Jogger: Stories], 1983
Ayen erekh: ahavah, 1986; as *See Under: Love*, translated by Betsy Rosenberg, 1989
Sefer hadikduk hapenimi, 1991; as *The Book of Intimate Grammar*, translated by Betsy Rosenberg, 1994
Yesh yeladim zigzag, 1994; as *The Zigzag Kid*, translated by Betsy Rosenberg, 1997
Shetehi li ha-sakin, 1998; as *Be My Knife*, translated by Vered Almog and Maya Gurantz, 2002
Mishehu laruts ito [Someone to Run With], 2000

Play

Gan riki [Riki's Kindergarten], 1988

Other

Itamar metayel al kirot [Itamar Walks on Walls], 1986
Hazeman hatsahov, 1987; as *The Yellow Wind*, translated by Haim Watzman, 1988
Itamar mikhtav [Itamar of the Letter], 1988
Itamar pogesh arnav [Itamar Meets a Rabbit], 1988
War Diaries, 1991
Nokhekhim nifkadim, 1992; as *Sleeping on a Wire*, translated by Haim Watzman, 1993
The Puz Book of World Records, 1994
Once Upon a Time, You Had Been Two Monkeys, 1996
Don't Worry, Ruthie, 1999
Good Night, Giraffe, 1999

Further Reading

Ramras-Rauch, Gila, *The Arab in Israeli Literature*, Bloomington: Indiana University Press, and London: Tauris, 1989
Sokoloff, Naomi B., *Imagining the Child in Modern Jewish Fiction*, Baltimore: Johns Hopkins University Press, 1992
Yudkin, Leon I., "Holocaust Trauma in the Second-Generation: The Hebrew Fiction of David Grossman" in *Breaking Crystal: Writing and Memory after Auschwitz*, edited by Efraim Sicher, Urbana: University of Illinois Press, 1998

Grossman became the most prominent Hebrew fiction writer of the 1980s. His was a voice that was fresh, fluent, daring, and original, adapting to the tones of the fictional figures, and unafraid to mix Israeli argot with high language in a joyous celebration of the possibilities of linguistic expression. He continued the experimentation in fictional presentation, moving from straight chronological narrative to a collage of styles, points of view, literary methods, and shock tactics.

He has written in a variety of media: children's fiction, short stories, novels, and reportage. But sometimes too, he has attempted a synthesis, for example, inserting fiction in a collection of essays, or basing a fictional work on nose-to-the-ground reporting. So what emerges is sometimes hard to categorize in a unitary fashion, and the emergent work can be a dazzling display of postmodern pyrotechnics. But one of the sources of the author's popularity may be the rootedness of the whole opus in the immediate Israeli scene, as it changes, and as it exposes its shifting contours. The subject too is large: Israeli society, with its roots and branches. The topics and sources of tension remain the major issues, such as the Holocaust and its continuing residue in the second and further generations, and the struggle in Israel between Arabs and Jews for control of the Land. These are well-worn topics, and they have naturally preoccupied creative writers as well as historians and commentators. But Grossman has added a fresh dimension to the view of the whole in sometimes adopting the perspective of a child. Although the topics may seem to be routine and even wearisome to the adult reader, the child happens on them for the first time. The articulated rendering can then be startling, and can also overwhelm the adult reader with an apparently first-time view. Socioeconomic reality can grind down simply by its vocabulary. But here the child, naturally through the author's intervention, invests what he sees afresh and discovers for himself, with his own vocabulary and imagery, thus creating an original portrait.

The first collection of stories, *Rats* [Jogging], is of the traditional mode. But his first novel, *Hiyukh hagdi* (*The Smile of the Lamb*) of the same period, is already experimental in narration. The very contemporary setting is the occupied West Bank, the characters are Arabs and Jews, the political views differ, and the unfolding plot is seen and narrated by the various characters in turn. So we read the story from different points of view, and cannot then easily ascribe any particular standpoint to the author behind the various narratorial voices. The later novel, *Ayen erekh: ahavah* (*See Under: Love*), is even more technically innovative, as it is divided into sections, not just telling the story from various standpoints, but using variant stylistic and narrative methods. It goes from the memoir mode as relayed by a nine-year-old child, newly discovering the fact of the concentration camp world, to fantastic fiction as told in the strangely distanced Hebrew of the inmate, then to the world of myth, and further to the cold, factual account of the encyclopaedia, when we indeed look under "love". Subsequent work by the author brings the worlds even closer together by offering us autobiography, but mediated by fiction: an approach akin to Joyce's in *Portrait of the Artist as a Young Man* is used in *Sefer dadikduk hapnimi* (*The Book of Intimate Grammar*), and Grossman no doubt turned to Joyce for a literary model. Another central aspect of Grossman's work has been his constant and questioning reporting of the Israeli scene, brought together in several collections of essays.

The influences and sources for Grossman's work are clear. The title story of the first collection of stories is very close in spirit and mood to Alan Sillitoe's *The Loneliness of the Long-Distance Runner*. His novel, *The Smile of the Lamb*, however, adopted the multi-focused spectrum that has been a familiar feature in the fiction of A.B. Yehoshua, and the use of faction has been a constant in Israeli prose generally. So many of Israel's authors have commented on issues of public life, and a significant number of them have also brought their comments together in published book form. Amos Oz, for example, has regularly collected his journalism in book form around a particular theme, sometimes a public concern, and sometimes on personal and literary matters. But he has always insisted on separating out the spheres of political, social comment, and fiction. Grossman however has deliberately closed the spaces between the genres, perhaps creating a new mixed-media genre that does not recognize such separation.

Common to all the works is a concern with the theme of domination. So here we have not so much a distinction between public, journalistic writing on the one hand and fiction on the other, as between the domination exercised by groups and nations in one line of experience, and between individuals on the other. One clear distinction that does necessarily come through between the author's political writing and his fiction is that in the former, his own personal view and opinions are not only expressed, but become the centre and point of the work. In the fiction, the voices all retain their own ground, and the author does not mediate between them to decide who is right, or even who is telling the truth. Nor does he insert an omniscient narrator, or one who can be identified with the author. This sort of self-identification, becoming disclosure, might seem to betray the function of writer as creator of an autonomous world. Grossman is a tragedian, a writer for whom the human condition is beyond the control of the individual, dealing with the very painful subject of man's domination by his fellows. In politics we try to play down this element. But in fiction, which might be closer to the eternal truths of poetry (in Aristotelian terms), it persists in the created life that the writer manufactures.

LEON I. YUDKIN

Grossman, Vasilii Semenovich

Russian fiction and non-fiction writer, 1905–1964

Born in Berdichev, Ukraine, 12 December 1905. Attended secondary school in Kiev, 1914–19; Institute of Higher Education, Kiev, 1921; studied chemistry, Moscow University, 1924–29. Chemical analyst in the Donbass coal mining area until tuberculosis diagnosed, 1932. Worked in Moscow pencil factory. Married twice. Second wife, Ol'ga Mikhailovna, arrested in 1937; Grossman wrote to Ezhov requesting her release; released 1938. Nominated for Stalin prize; denounced as "Menshevist" by Stalin, deleted from nominees. Joined military newspaper, *Krasnaia zvezda*, August 1941. Served on Briansk and Central Fronts. Reported Battle of Stalingrad, sketches widely read. Detailed account of Nazi atrocities published as *Treblinskii ad* [The Hell of Treblinka], 1944. Grossman's only play published, 1946; attacked for non-materialist interpretation of history. *Za pravoe delo* nominated by Aleksandr Fadeev for Stalin Prize; during campaign against so-called Doctors' Plot, at height of anti-Semitism, Grossman again attacked. Sequel, *Zhizn' i sud'ba*, finished 1960, published in west, 1980. Awarded medal "For Valour"; Red Banner of Labour for services to Soviet literature, 1955. Member Soviet Writer's Union, 1954–64. Died in Moscow, 14 September 1964.

Selected Writings

Collections

Rasskazy, 1937
Stalingrad Hits Back, translated by A. Fineberg and D. Fromberg, 1942
Stalingradskaia bitva [The Battle of Stalingrad], 1943
Gody voiny, 1946; as *The Years of War*, translated by Elizabeth Donnelly and Rose Prokofiev, 1946
Zhizn', Rasskazy [Life, Short Stories], 1947
Povesti i rasskazy, 1950
Povesti, Rasskazy, Ocherki, 1958
Staryi uchitel'. Povesti i rasskazy [The Old Teacher], 1962
Dobro vam! [Peace Be To You!], 1967
Neskol'ko pechal'nykh dnei [Several Sad Days], 1989
Gody voiny [The Years of the War], 1989
Vse techet: pozdnaia proza [Everything Flows: Late Prose], 1994

Fiction

"Glück auf!", *God XVII, Al'manakh*, 4 (1934)
Schast'e [Happiness], 1935
Chetyre dnia [Four Days], 1936
Stepan Kol'chugin, 1937–40; as *Kol'chugin's Youth, A Novel*, translated by Rosemary Edmonds, 1946
Kukharka [The Cook], 1938
Narod bessmerton, 1943; as *The People Immortal*, translated by Elizabeth Donnelly, 1943; as *No Beautiful Nights*, 1944
"Za pravoe delo" [For a Just Cause], *Novyi mir*, 7–10 (1952); as separate edition, 1956
Vse techet, 1970; as *Forever Flowing*, translated by Thomas P. Whitney, 1972
Zhizn' i sud'ba, 1980; as *Life and Fate*, translated by Robert Chandler, 1985

Play

"Esli verit' pifagoreitsam" [If You Believe the Pythagoreans], *Znamia*, 7 (1946)

Other

Treblinskii ad [The Hell of Treblinka], 1945
With the Red Army in Poland, translated by Helen Altschuler, 1945
"Poezdka v Kirgiziiu" [Trip to Kirgizia], *God XXXI, Al'manakh Pervyi* (1948)
"V znakomykh mestakh" [In Familiar Places], *Ogonek*, 45 (1953)
Editor, with Il'ia Erenburg, *Chernaia kniga*, 1980; as *The*

Complete Black Book of Russian Jewry, translated by David Paterson, 2001
"Vasilii Grossman, iz zapisnykh knizhek voennykh let" [Vasilii Grossman, From His Wartime Notebooks], *Voprosy literatury*, 6 (1987)

Further Reading

Eberstadt, Fernanda, "Suppressed Epic of Stalingrad", *Washington Post* (6 April 1986)

Ellis, Frank, "Vasilii Grossman: The Challenge to Ideology", in *Perestrojka und Literatur*, edited by Eberhard Reissner, Berlin: Arno Spitz, 1990

Garrard, John, "A Conflict of Visions, Vasilii Grossman and the Russian Idea", in *The Search for Self-Definition in Russian Literature*, edited by Ewa M. Thompson, Amsterdam: John Benjamins, 1991

Lipkin, Semen, *Stalingrad Vasiliia Grossmana*, Ann Arbor, Michigan: Ardis, 1986

Markish, Shimon, "A Russian Writer's Jewish Fate", *Commentary* (April 1986)

Pirani, Simon, "Unsung Genius among Great Modern Russian Novelists", *Jewish Chronicle* (18 February 2000)

A recognized member of the Soviet literary establishment for most of his career, praised for his stories, sketches, and epic novels that reflected the ideals of the Communist party, Vasilii Grossman became a victim of the savage anti-Semitism of the Stalinist period, characterized by campaigns against "rootless cosmopolitans" (Jews) and the "Jewish Doctors' Plot". This caused his work to be deemed ideologically unacceptable; his "subversive" writing was suppressed and then confiscated by Soviet officials, but posthumously praised when it was eventually smuggled out and published in the west.

Vasilii Semenovich Grossman was born in the quintessentially Jewish Ukrainian town of Berdichev (called "our kike capital" by Isaak Babel'). His family was an assimilated one, Russian rather than Jewish. According to Semen Lipkin's memoir, his Jewish consciousness was largely "gastronomic", but he possessed a set of the Russian *Jewish Encyclopedia*. Grossman's first literary attempts were about Berdichev ("Berdichev in All Seriousness", 1928 and the 1934 story "V gorode Berdicheve" [In the Town of Berdichev], the latter winning the approval of Maksim Gor'kii who offered the young writer his support. The story tells the story of a female commissar who gives birth to a child, abandoning it and leaving it for safe-keeping to a Jewish family. The perseverance and dignity of the Jewish family is contrasted with the foolish romanticism of the revolutionaries. Literary historian Shimon Markish points out that Grossman was not ashamed of shtetl life and did not attempt to distance himself from his Jewish heritage (as did Osip Mandel'shtam and Eduard Bagritskii).

Having taken a degree in physics and mathematics, he worked as a chemical engineer in the Donbass coal mining area until tuberculosis was diagnosed in 1932. His story "Glück auf!" was about Soviet miners of this period. In stories like "Chetyre dnya" [Four Days], "Tovarisch Fedor" [Comrade Fyodor] and *Kukharka* [The Cook] he described struggles against the czarist regime and the suffering endured during the Civil War and the building of the new Soviet state.

Grossman won widespread national acclaim for his journalistic coverage of the World War II. He spent four years at the front for the military newspaper *Krasnaia zvezda* [Red Star] writing about the shame, despair, and horror of defeat, and the rapture and triumph of victory. He wrote as a Russian about the wartime suffering and heroism of the Russian people. Representative of this time are the stories "Napravlenie glavnogo udara" [Direction of the Main Strike] and *Narod bessmerten* (*The People Immortal*), and his play, published in 1946, "Esli verit' pifagoreitsam" [If You Believe the Pythagoreans].

Grossman, however, was to lose his mother in the Berdichev ghetto in 1941. As a war correspondent he was among the first Russian witnesses to the atrocities of the Holocaust. He was indeed the first writer to tell about the horrors of the Treblinka death camp (in the sketch "The Treblinka Hell", August 1944). Earlier, he had worked with Il'ia Erenburg on a "Black Book" about the destruction of Russian Jewry in German-occupied territory. Grossman went to Berdichev looking for witnesses to the final minutes of Ekaterina Grossman, writing a poignant letter to her ten years after her death, imagining the face of her Nazi killer, the last person to see her.

Grossman was becoming increasingly critical of the Soviet establishment during the "black years" of Stalin's postwar regime, and his Stalingrad novel *Za pravoe delo* [For a Just Cause], published in 1952 in four issues of *Novyi Mir*, was attacked by party officials for its Jewish content, and provoked the wrath of Malenkov. Despite being an orthodox Soviet epic narrative, Grossman presented a harsh commentary on the totalitarianism of both Nazi and Stalinist regimes, equating the two. Facing deportation or execution in the 1950s, Grossman was undoubtedly spared by the death of Stalin in 1953.

A 900-page epic about the siege of Stalingrad, the novel *Za pravoe delo* was rehabilitated and its author given a medal for his services to Soviet literature on his 50th birthday. Grossman continued working on the project for ten years, finishing the sequel in 1960 as *Zhizn' i sud'ba* (*Life and Fate*). The Central Committee decided to "arrest" the novel and let the author go free. In 1961, two KGB functionaries confiscated all copies they could find, and told Grossman it would not be published for 250 years! The microfilm was smuggled to Switzerland where a Russian edition was published in 1980.

The plot forms a whole with *Za pravoe delo*. It concerns Mostovskoy, an old Bolshevik imprisoned in a German concentration camp, who, when called into the SS, argues that there is no difference between Communism and National Socialism. The novel is also about Victor Shtrum, a Jewish physicist evacuated to Kazen, "a mediocrity full of petty passions" and his sister-in-law Yevgenia, torn between her love for a tank commander at Stalingrad and her loyalty to her ex-husband who has been arrested on a charge of espionage.

Despite Grossman's excoriation of evil, he offers hope in the small, selfless acts of individuals. Among the various digressions in the book are two chapters about anti-

Semitism. Shtrum's mother writes a troubling yet uplifting letter to him on the eve of her death in a Nazi-run ghetto. "I never felt like a Jew. I grew up with Russian girlfriends, my favourite poets were Pushkin and Nekrasov . . . But now, in these terrible days I have been overcome by a mother's tenderness for the Jewish people." There is another moment of epiphany when the elderly spinster Sonya Leviton discovers in the gas chambers that she is "linked with the whole nation". "This is me"; she recognizes herself as a Jew, as part of something that "never changes". Grossman's own experience of injustice opened his eyes to others' pain.

After the arrest of the novel, Grossman lived only three and a half years, suffering at the end from cancer. In these years he rewrote an expanded version of *Vse techet* (*Forever Flowing*) (published in West Germany in 1970), several stories and a travel sketch about Armenia, "Peace Be With You" (1962–63). At the end of the sketch he describes a wedding celebration of Armenian peasants, "who spoke about the suffering of the Jews".

Grossman began writing *Forever Flowing* in 1955, telling the story of Ivor Grigoryevich's return to Moscow after 30 years in a Siberian labour camp for making a speech that differed from official Communist doctrine. He attempts to comprehend everything that has occurred, to understand the nature of Marxist-Leninist ideology and the Stalinist system that succeeded it. The novel is deeply subversive, a bitter indictment of Soviet society. Grossman argues that Leninism laid the foundations of Hitler's "new order". Ivor's friends and relatives are embarrassed at the disparity between their comfortable lifestyles as established intelligentsia and the suffering Ivor has endured in the camp. Despite his acerbic view of Soviet society, Grossman reiterates his belief in the small kindnesses of ordinary individuals, the frailty and strength of human goodness.

SORREL KERBEL

Gur, Batya

Israeli fiction writer, 1947–

Born in Tel Aviv, 1947. Married; three children. Educated at Hebrew University of Jerusalem; MA in Hebrew literature. Taught Hebrew literature in high school for nearly 20 years. Began writing fiction, late 1980s. Writes weekly column on literature for *Haaretz*. Lectures on scriptwriting at the Israel Film School. Edits series of classic books, published in Hebrew by Am Oved. Awarded Krimi Preis (Germany) and WIZO Prize (France).

Selected Writings

Novels

Retsah beshabat baboker, 1988; as *The Saturday Morning Murder: A Psychoanalytic Case*, translated by Dalya Bilu, 1992

Mavet bahug lesifrut, 1989; as *Literary Murder: A Critical Case*, translated by Dalya Bilu, 1993

Linah meshutefet, 1991; as *Murder on a Kibbutz: A Communal Case*, translated by Dalya Bilu, 1994

Lo kakh tiarti li [I Didn't Imagine It Would be This Way], 1994

Hamerhak hanakhon, 1996; as *Murder Duet: A Musical Case*, translated by Dalya Bilu, 1999

Even tahat even [Stone for Stone], 1998

Meragel betokh habayit [A Spy in the House], 1999

What Happened to Benji, 2000

Other

Mikvish hara av semola [Next to the Hunger Road] (essays), 1990

Requiem to Modesty: Or Living in Jerusalem, 2001

Batya Gur popularized the detective genre in the Israeli literary canon. For Gur the appearance of the detective genre is a symptom of a nation's maturity.

There are two major traditions in the police procedural. The tradition made famous by authors such as John Creasey has a heroic sleuth, invincible, unbribable, happily married with children – the pursuit is all. The other tradition is more modern. The sleuth is vulnerable, often at odds with his or her superiors, usually divorced, and with problematic relationships. The essence of this tradition is the relationship between characters – forensic detail and attention to alibis are secondary. Often, the sleuth is an outsider or is made to feel an outsider.

Gur's Moroccan-born intellectual Chief Inspector Michael Ohayon is firmly in the latter tradition. He is divorced, and attempting to maintain a relationship with his son from that marriage. His love life is problematic. Gur invariably sets her murders in self-contained insular societies. In *Retsah beshabat baboker* (*The Saturday Morning Murder*) Ohayon gradually solves both the murder and the riddle of the enigmatic self-contained world of the Psychoanalytic Society. The novel is a spell-binding detective story, as well as an examination of a microcosm of Israeli society that reveals some basic truths about human nature. *Publishers Weekly* notes that "with sly, affectionate humour and acute insight" this is a flawless mystery with "a complex, fully satisfying resolution".

Mavet bahug lesifrut (*Literary Murder: A Critical Case*) investigates the deaths of a professor of literature and his junior colleague. Ohayon raises profound ethical questions about the relationship between the artist and his creation, and between the artist and a moral code. The book brings the detective into contact with the social problems and differing perspectives of the academic elite, and with problems of plagiarism and literary theory, constructing an unusual milieu that is liberally interspersed with allusions and literary quotations.

The setting for *Linah meshutefet* (*Murder on a Kibbutz: A Communal Case*) is the complex, closed society of the kibbutz. As Ohayon delves deep into the investigation to uncover the secrets of the kibbutz, Gur exposes the contradictions of this "ideal" way of life. Ohayon maintains an inscrutable facade, even as he sits in judgement on the character and personality of the person he is examining and cross-examining. Gur also gives us their view of events, so that we know what they think of him. Ohayon even has his own philosophy: to "enter the essence of things". This business of the "essence of things" is often mentioned with a smile in all the investigating teams he works with, and is his personal contribution to an unusual style of detective work. He needs to become part of the environment that he is investigating, to sense the subtle nuances of the murdered person's world.

The fourth Ohayon mystery, *Hamerhak hanachon* (*Murder Duet: A Musical Case*) is set in the Jerusalem Symphony Orchestra, as Ohayon investigates the murders in a famous musical family, the van Geldens. Newly returned to the police after a two-year sabbatical to study law, Ohayon appears particularly vulnerable and alone on the eve of Rosh Hashana, and finds an abandoned infant crying in a bomb shelter. Ohayon forms a relationship with Nita van Gelden, the daughter of the murder victim, who is a cellist. Her brother Theo is a conductor, while another brother, Gabriel, is a violinist. Gur excels at exploring their psychological motivations in an interesting tale, complete with musical digressions.

Lo kakh tiarti li [I Didn't Imagine It Would be This Way], is an extremely realistic novel about a prominent Jerusalem gynaecologist, infused with psychological insights. *Even tahat even* [Stone for Stone] is loosely based upon a true incident in Israel and retells the story of a woman whose son is killed playing a form of Russian roulette while serving in the Israeli army. In all Gur's novels we get glimpses of Jerusalem. The beautiful views over the Old City, the architecture, old and new, the Mahane Yehuda market along the Jaffa Road. Gur places Jerusalem under the feet of her characters, in front of their eyes, over their heads, reminds them constantly of climate and weather and how it affects individuals. Smell, touch, sight, sound are all part of the story – even as it slows down for the cross-examination of witnesses.

Michael Ohayon, however, has his weaknesses, his vulnerabilities. He often feels the need to parade his academic knowledge (he has an unfinished doctoral paper on medieval guilds). He still feels pride in his humble background and rejoices in his conquests. There are times when he admits to himself that he has not seen the truth (but gets to it later). His greatest failure seems to be in his love life, where, great detective that he is, he fails to see the evidence in front of his eyes.

Batya Gur's first young adult mystery, *What Happened to Benji*, is about adolescent love and torment in a neighbourhood school in Jerusalem. When the friendship of two young boys begins to disintegrate, the older boy sets out to investigate what's happening to Benji.

Requiem to Modesty; or, Living in Jerusalem is Gur's personal observation of the small introverted town that grew – following the Six Day War – into a megalomaniac, pseudo-glorified metropolis. She details the price of this transfiguration with all its economic, political, and social tensions. The book questions the possibility of living a normal life in Jerusalem, and illuminates the mythologies permeating all religious and secular life on both sides of the city.

It is not enough for a crime novel merely to amuse, entertain, beguile. It must have an "extra", something for us to think about when the journey is over and the book has been put away. This is where Gur excels. She has a sharp ear for the things that are not said, and her creativity and sense of fun shine throughout.

Alex Auswaks

Gurevitch, Zali

US-born Israeli poet, 1949–

Born in California, 25 May 1949; moved to Israel with his parents same year. Began publishing poetry, 1967. Received PhD from Hebrew University in Jerusalem. Married; two children. Teaches in Department of Sociology and Anthropology, Hebrew University. Received Hershon Award, 1979; Akum Prize, 1984; Kugel Prize, 1996.

Selected Writings

Poetry

Ketaim mehalom patuah [Excerpts from an Open Dream], 1980
Shurah psukah [Broken Line], 1984
Yabashah [Land], 1989
Hevel [The Book of the Voice], 1990
Ha veda [This and That], 1996
Sefer hayareah [The Book of the Moon], 1999
In *Found in Translation: A Hundred Years of Modern Hebrew Poetry*, translated by Robert Friend, edited by Gabriel Levin, 1999

Other

Translator, *Self-Portrait in a Convex Mirror*, by John Ashbery, 1982
"Distances and Inner Distances: An Invitation to Hebrew Poetry", *Poetry from Israel 1970–1980: The Literary Review*, guest-edited by Gurevitch and Gabriel Levin, 26/2 (1983)
"Poetry Conversation and Culture", *Studies in Symbolic Interaction*, 14 (1993)
"The Tongues Break Dance: Theory, Poetry and the Critical Body", *Sociological Quarterly*, 40 (1999)
"Eternal Loss", afterword to *Revealment and Concealment: Five Essays*, by H.N. Bialik, 2000
"The Serious Play of Writing", *Qualitative Inquiry*, 6/1 (2000)

Further Reading

Levin, Gabriel, "The Breath of Speech", *Modern Hebrew Literature*, Fall/Winter, 7 (1991)

The restless, dialectical motion of Zali Gurevitch's thought already suggests itself in the title of his first collection of poems, *Ketaim mehalom patuah* [Excerpts from an Open Dream], for in Hebrew "dream", *halom*, and "window", *halon*, are near homonyms, and playfully announce the poet's continued exploration of the seam or the thin "broken line" of consciousness separating the inner, solitary life of dream and the imagination, from an outer, shared reality on the "the outskirts of the mind".

This is conveyed in Gurevitch's early poems by short, brooding lyrics in which glimpses of everyday life – a bare, mundane reality stripped of any romantic appeal, and yet at the same time darkly alluring – blend with the poet's inner musings: "The dream's shudder still grips my back though it already/ dropped out of memory, the breath on my face/ of a man who just brushed past me; what is real,/ the changing seasons, or/ the leash that ties and leads my life beside me/ like a house-trained dog? . . ." The poet's terse, syncopated rhythms and a jarring music embody the poetry's underlying sense of urgency and latent violence. Such irregular rhythms and rough handling of Hebrew can be traced to the work of Gurevitch's immediate predecessors, David Avidan, Meir Wieseltier and Yona Wallach, and perhaps most of all to the poetry of Avot Yeshurun. But Gurevitch's developing poetics was shaped as well by contemporary American poetry, particularly the projective verse of Charles Olson, which plays a key role – along with the French modernist poet Francis Ponge – in the poet's later work.

In 1986 Gurevitch spend a year in California where he wrote his third collection of poems, *Yabashah* [Land], a volume that marks a turning point in the poet's writing. Eschewing the traditional, self-contained lyric, Gurevitch experimented in *Land* with the short-lined, bare-boned, book-length poetic sequence, a form that had been previously introduced into Hebrew by Aharon Shabtai. Formal innovations dovetail with the widening of thematic concerns as Gurevitch's private reflections are conjoined with a prodding inquiry into the nature of the poet's relationship to the Land of Israel – *Erets Yisrael* – that takes on mythic proportions. Nothing is quite what it seems. Is it possible to apprehend the land as plain fact, divorced of its religious and historic significance? Do we inhabit the land, or the word, and particularly the Hebrew tongue, which envelops our lives and is at the root of our identity? Gurevitch's temporary displacement in the United States ("how relinquish/ America, rich broad, every/ one's plaything/ far from the place/ where the single peg of our life is driven . . .") is the trigger for an emotionally charged series of meditations on the nature of dispersion exile, and return. Though here too dream and reality, myth and history, slip in and out of the poet's mind in a rapid succession of images:

Watch your tongue

each
word
flares

the thought on fire

memory
shudders
beast-like

blood (behind
them) they
had to leave, how many

left
carted away
with them
their imagination

their language jogged from its place

on the dense
page
of earth "Land extending to the shores
of raging sea . . ."

(begins Graetz) etc.
landmass
a sacred fact

shaking themselves
like
animals

wading out (from the belly
of shipwreck)
of
the water

go forth
&
behold

burning
to drink gold of the earth
to grasp the jug . . .

In as much as Gurevitch sets out in search of land in *Yabashah*, the poet's next volume, *Hevel* – Hebrew for breath or vapour, as in Ecclesiastes, *hevel hevelim*, "vanities of vanieties" – is Gurevitch's dark descent into a world void of meaning and solid ground. What remains, the poet's only certainty, is a voice, the tracing of sounds in the air, and here too Gurevitch offers a vertical rush of words in 52 untitled sections that form a carefully orchestrated whole: "Listen// in breath/breath// in fire/fire// in the voice/ a voice shattering in air/ 'lionlike'// the heart// is all mud/ all/ from nothing, from the dark, vanishing throat, from/ the void". Thus the opening lines of *Hevel*, in which a Hebrew reader cannot help hearing in its vocative *Shema*, "Listen", at once the biblical prayer "Hear, O Israel", and the easy buttonholing familiarity of "listen" (to me). This is the vantage point from where the poet would have us listen, standing as it were along the faultline where modern, colloquial Hebrew and its ancient, aural counterpart, collapse into each other. Biblical imagery of creation is repeatedly evoked in describing a personal, inner quest for the confirmation of selfhood – and its correlate, that the self "is an other" – through a language that can never be completely fathomed and which conceals, as H.N. Bialik wrote in his seminal essay "Revealment and Concealment in Language", more than it reveals.

Gurevitch's debt to Hebrew literature's first modern poet, whose major poems were written on the cusp of the 20th century, may hover in the background of *Hevel*, but is made explicit in the poet's most recent volumes, *Ha veda* [This and That] and *Sefer hayareah* [The Book of the Moon], in which Gurevitch returns to the traditional lyric with a vengeance: word repetition, end-rhymes and sprung rhythms recall the simple, catching tunes of children's poetry. Yet the startling emotive power of these poems lies precisely in the tension between the surface "lightness" of the poems – their seeming childlike innocence – and the continued thematic testing of the limits of the self:

I'm the only beast
and the lonely beast

I'm the riddle
and the gist

I'm the flare
and I'm the snare

I'm the beast
lost in the glare

I'm the hasp
and I'm the task

all sweat and tear
or madness and fear

I'm all nerves
and sharp sight

one memory
rent from the start

one race
and one face

and if I love these songs
I'll love my soul

my distant soul
my only, my whole

Gurevitch's rhythms and images are steeped in the language of Israeli pre-school cradlesongs and nursery rhymes, and in particular in the many songs written by Bialik after he had moved to Palestine and settled in Tel Aviv in the 1920s. Recognizing that the deepest truths may be couched in the lightest of airs, Gurevitch offers through the prism of his own poems, among other things, a rereading, and reorienting, of Bialik's children's verse, which the latter poet wrote late in life in the crisp, native accents of Israeli Hebrew. But above all the poems return to Gurevitch's own childhood, to the infancy of the state of Israel, to the *alpha-bet* – the building blocks of language – and to the primacy of love, in their relentless yearning for wholeness in a divided world.

GABRIEL LEVIN

Guri, Haim

Israeli poet, 1923–

Born in Tel Aviv, 9 October 1923. Served in Palmach and Israeli army, 1941–49; organized Jewish youth movements, recruited immigrants, and trained commandos and paratroopers in Hungary, Austria, and Czechoslovakia, 1947. Studied at Hebrew University, Jerusalem, BA in Hebrew and French literature and philosophy 1952; also at the Sorbonne. Married Aliza Becker, 1952; three children. Columnist, *La Merhav*, 1954–70, and *Davar*, from 1970. Headed army brigade in Jerusalem, 1967; army education officer, Sinai, 1973. Has been a member of the Israeli Film Censorship Board. Many awards including Ussishkin Prize, 1961; Sokolov Prize, 1962; Bialik Prize, 1975; Akum Prize, 1979; Walenrode Prize; Israel Prize, 1987.

Selected Writings

Poetry
Pirhei esh [Flowers of Fire], 1949
Ad alot hashahar [Until Dawn Rises], 1950
Shirei hotam [Seal Poems], 1954
Shoshanat haruhot [Lily of the Winds], 1960
Tenuah lemaga [Movement to Contact], 1968
Dapim mimahazor nesher [Pages from the Cycle of the Eagle], 1974
Marot gehazi [Visions of Gehazi], 1974
Ad kav nesher, 1949–1975 [To the Eagle Line], 1975
Mivhar shirim [Selected Poems], 1975
Ayumah [Terrible], 1979
Veod rotseh otah [And Still He Wants Her], 1987
Heshbon over: mivhar shirim 1945–1987, 1988
Mahbarot elul [Notebooks of Elul], 1988
Milim bedami haholeh ahavah, 1995; as *Words in My Lovesick Blood*, translated by Stanley F. Chyet, 1996

Fiction
Iskat hashokolad, 1965; as *The Chocolate Deal*, translated by Seymour Simckes, 1968
Hasefer hamshuga [The Crazy Book], 1971
Mi makir et yosef g.? [Who Knows Joseph G.?], 1980
Hahakirah: sipur reuel [The Interrogation: Reuel's Story], 1981

Other
Mul ta hazekhukhit [The Glass Cage: The Jerusalem Trial], 1963
Dapim yerushalmiyim [Jerusalem Years], 1968
Mishpahat hapalmah: yalkut alilot vezemer [The Family of the Palmach: A Collection of Songs and Deeds], with Chayim Chefer, 1976
Translations of French plays, songs, and stories into modern Hebrew.

Further Reading

Burnshaw, Stanley, T. Carmi and Ezra Spicehandler (editors and translators), *The Modern Hebrew Poem Itself*, New York: Holt, Rinehart, 1965
Seh-Lavan, Yosef, *Hayim Guri*, Tel Aviv: Or'am, 1977
Vardi, Dov, "Property of a Non-Believer: The Poetic Visions of Hayim Guri", *Modern Hebrew Literature*, 2 (1975)

Born in Tel Aviv, Haim Guri (or Hayim Gouri) became the archetypal representative of the so-called Palmach literature, i.e. the new Hebrew literature specifically characteristic of the infant Hebrew State. Guri matured with the foundation of independent Israel; he wrote of it and to it. He was its spokesman, and became an icon of the times. He seemed to fit the bill precisely; young, male, sabra (Israeli-born), strong, and committed to a powerful Jewish country, the very antithesis, as it seemed, of Diaspora existence.

His first poem was published in *Mishmar* (edited by the famous poet, Avraham Shlonsky), in 1945, "Masa yam" [Sea Voyage], and his first complete volume of poetry, *Pirhei esh* [Flowers of Fire] appeared immediately in the wake of the War of Independence, and became its most representative expression. What may be his best known poem, "Hineh mutalot gufotenu" [See Our Corpses are Laid Out] appeared in that volume. The poem opens with the statement that all "our" corpses are laid out, row by row. For these people, life had ceased. But the final stanza contradicts that assumption. Opening with the identical phrase, it continues: "But the wind is strong in the mountains and breathes./ And morning is born, morning dew sings out./ We shall meet again and return as red flowers/ . . . Then we shall flower when the last shout of the shot is silenced." In this poem of measured rhythm, the narrator identifies with the dead. But he also envisions a possible resurrection when the terrible war ends. Together, man and writer could stand for the new country.

A later poem takes up the theme of the Binding of Isaac. In "Yerushah" [Heritage] from *Shoshanat haruhot* [Lily of the Winds] in 1960, he writes more prosaically about both Abraham and Isaac. But Isaac, the apparently minor figure of the biblical story, is the key. The poem has it that he lived for many days and prospered. But the crucial moment of what was apparently to be the imminent sacrifice, suddenly thwarted, was transmitted to the descendants: "They are born with a knife in their hearts." The Jewish Fate, recognized in the Holocaust and in the struggle for the Israeli State, is a perpetual presence.

Writers often become fixated on the one formative period or episode in their lives, a point to which they keep returning, and which retains the power of a magnet. For Guri, that formative period was clearly the War of Independence, and, more specifically, the association with the Palmach. Both his earlier and his later writing return to this point, which he seeks to perpetuate and to recreate both in poetry and in prose. In *Ad alot hashahar* [Until Dawn Arises] he writes in the preface that his aspiration is to relate the history of a Palmach squadron. He is removed from the scene, at this point, by two years. But he is of one body with those who fought, and he recognizes that together they form a unit that will always hold together: "For out of one pit have we been scraped, and one heart has borne us in its beat." The Palmach clearly constituted a small, inner circle of familiars, young, fit, independent Hebrews, committed to the cause of Israeli independence, all of whom seemed to know each other, and whose fates and lives were to become inextricably entwined to the end. Now, only a few months after the awesome events of the fighting, all seems so distant, and yet significant, as though enshrined in mythical terms. The battle for the control of Beer Sheva, capital of the Negev, is invoked, the crucial struggle for control of the centre of the Land: "Surely, here, in the heart of this drought, in view of the scorn of the eagle and the primal landscape – we were born." For this group, the Palmach became indeed a substitute parent, as it reared a radically different generation. It was a new land, a new cohort, a new language, a new situation, and a new culture. Although this State of Israel was created for the Jewish people, it also represented a radical breach with the recent past, as well as a shift from the Diaspora, even a reversal of its values. The poet writes about their move into the southern Negev: "We moved a great deal in this land. The Palmach, our father, taught us the work." And so the myth was created. The foundation myth of modern Israel is the figure of the Palmachnik, which Guri helped to create, and of which he was also the incarnation. In the final poem of a series that comes after the long prose section describing the activities of the group, the author seeks to immortalize its activities, even though individually they may be anonymous:

> Who is for the fire, to the fire, the gold is beaten here
> Of those nameless squads engraving their flaming
> inscription.
> Here laughs out from the belly of time the taught beast
> of the nation.
> Do you see, my beauty, how the words flower on the
> stone?

There they remain, unnamed and permanently mounted.

Guri has written prose as well as poetry, some reportage, and some experimental novels. *Hasefer hamshuga* [The Crazy Book] of 1971 is a venture into the picaresque, a revisitation of the Palmach myth after 20 years. He seeks through a collage of words to recreate the time and place of foundation and activity. Prose is succeeded by poetry, or is interspersed with verses. The author is enraptured by the Israeli slang of the period, which we must remember is the primal Israeli argot, the very first of the new, spoken Hebrew, revelling in its newness and authenticity, the first form of the Hebrew language of modern times to be a mother tongue, not derived from European sources. The author is constantly in search of the classic form and statement. His poetry adopts the classic contours of Natan Alterman, a poet often invoked there, and the consciousness of the Hebrew tradition.

LEON I. YUDKIN

H

Halkin, Shmuel

Russian poet, 1897–1960

Born in Rogashev, Belorussia, 5 December 1897. Fled devastation of Rogashev during World War I; moved to Kiev. Began to write in Yiddish; first poems published in journal *Shtern*. Moved to Moscow, 1922; poems attacked by communist press, 1929; obliged to recant. Worked as translator. Joined Jewish Anti-Fascist Committee during World War II; contributed to newspaper *Eynikayt*. Committee liquidated, 1948; Halkin arrested and exiled to Siberia, 1949; released, 1955; rehabilitated, 1958. Died in Moscow, 1960. Street in Rogashev named in his honour, 1961.

Selected Writings

Poetry
Lider [Poems], 1922
Vey un mut [Pain and Courage], 1929
Far dem nayem fundament [For the New Foundation], 1932
Kontakt [Contact], 1935
Erdishe vegn [Worldly Ways], 1945
Mayn oytser [My Treasure], 1966

Plays
Bar kokhba, 1939
Arn fridman, 1939
Shulamis, 1940
Umshterblekhkayt [Immortality], 1940
Der shpilfoygl [Songbird], 1942
Of toyt un of lebn [On Death and On Life] or *Oyfshtand in geto* [Uprising in the Ghetto], 1944

Further Reading

Gurshtein, Aron, *Izbrannye stat'i*, Moscow: Sovetskii pisatel, 1959
Mayzel, Nakhman, *Dos yidishe shafn un der yidisher shrayber in Sovetnfarband* [Jewish Creative Activity and the Jewish Writer in the Soviet Union], New York: Yidisher Kultur Farband, 1959
Shmeruk, Chone, "Yiddish Literature in the USSR" in *The Jews in Soviet Russia since 1917*, edited by Lionel Kochan, London and New York: Oxford University Press, 1970

"Among the Soviet Yiddish writers", wrote the American Yiddish literary critic Nakhman Mayzel in 1958, "Shmuel Halkin has remained the most complex and sophisticated, the most profound and the most Jewish." Aron Gurshtein, a noted Soviet Yiddish literary critic, agreed, noting that Halkin's poems "strongly strived toward the threads of old Jewish culture, toward the metaphorical imagery of ancient Jewish literature, among which the Bible is given the first place." This was a remarkable description of a Jewish writer who made his career in Soviet Russia.

Halkin was born in the Belorussian town of Rogashev; his father, a lumber inspector, taught him a love of nature and philosophical appreciation for physical labour that would permeate much of his early writing. As a youth, Halkin began writing Hebrew poetry on the theme of nature. Fleeing the wartime devastation of Rogachev, he moved to Kiev, where he was introduced to a thriving Yiddish literary culture. It was in Kiev that he began to write in Yiddish, publishing his first poems in the Minsk literary journal *Shtern* in 1921. A collection of his poetry was published the following year under the title, *Lider* [Poems]. While the majority of Soviet Yiddish writers of the time painted portraits of contemporary Jewish life in the shtetl, Halkin instead drew inspiration from biblical and historical themes.

In 1922 Halkin moved to Moscow, where he became enamoured with the progress of the revolution. His 1929 collection, *Vey un mut* [Pain and Courage], reflects his distaste for the excesses of capitalism and his admiration for the working man and woman. He retained his earlier penchant, however, for imagery drawn from nature and for motifs borrowed from biblical and Judaic lore. As a result, his poetry was attacked by the communist press in 1929 for displaying counter-revolutionary and nationalist traits, forcing Halkin to recant his work. In 1932 Halkin released his third collection, *Far dem nayem fundament* [For the New Foundation], and in 1935 published a fourth volume, *Kontakt* [Contact]. Despite his recantation, Halkin continued to draw inspiration from Jewish lore. His poetry continued to champion the simple folk, but his refusal to embrace socialist realism ensured that he remained out of favour with the authorities.

New attacks soon appeared against Halkin in the press, accusing him of using nationalist themes. Halkin, however, found that his creative impulse was integrally linked to a national stimulus. Deprived of Hebraic motifs, he had difficulty composing. Although he continued sporadically to publish poetry in various anthologies and journals after 1935, he, like many other Soviet writers who fell out of favour with the regime, began to support himself with translation work. He translated into Yiddish Russian works by Aleksandr Pushkin, Vladimir Maiakovskii, Sergei Esenin, Aleksandr Blok, Dmitrii Furmanov, and others. His most important translation work, though, came in 1935 when he was commissioned to translate Shakespeare's *King Lear* into Yiddish for its performance at the Moscow State Yiddish Theatre. Five years later, Halkin translated Shakespeare's *Richard III* into Yiddish as well.

In addition to translations, Halkin adapted two Yiddish plays by Avrom Goldfaden for the Soviet stage: *Shulamis* (first performed 1937, published 1940) and *Bar kokhba* (first performed 1938, published 1939). Although Halkin publicly maintained that the plays demonstrated the international struggle of the working class, they can both be counted among the most nationalist works of Soviet Yiddish writing. Both plays, set in ancient Judaea, glorified the halcyon days of Jewish statehood in Palestine and demonstrated the perseverance of the Jewish people in times of crisis and oppression.

Halkin's work on the drama of Shakespeare and Goldfaden inspired him to try writing original plays for the stage. His first effort at original writing since 1935 came with his 1939 play *Arn fridman*. This socialist realist depiction of the collective farm movement helped Halkin reinvent himself as a loyal Soviet writer. The play follows Arn Fridman, a young teacher who abandons his shtetl to join a newly-established collective farm. There he learns that together the collective can triumph over all obstacles. The play ends as Arn's son joins the Red Army, fulfilling his father's ultimate dream. The play's message that a new Jewish life can be built on collective farms in the Soviet Union appealed to Halkin's communist enemies. His next two dramatic efforts, *Umshterblekhkayt* [Immortality] and *Der shpilfoygl* [Songbird] also followed contemporary Soviet styles.

During World War II Halkin joined the Jewish Anti-Fascist Committee, and served as a contributor to the committee's newspaper, *Eynikayt*. After the war Halkin took advantage of what he believed was a relaxed official attitude toward national themes in literature, and returned to poetry and dramatic writing. His first postwar play, *Of toyt un of lebn* [On Death and On Life] or *Oyfshtand in geto* [Uprising in the Ghetto], was another play about Jewish heroism, this time set in a ghetto in Poland under Nazi rule. The story of a ghetto uprising was reminiscent of his earlier adaptation of *Bar kokhba* – both argued for resistance to oppressive authorities. His first collection of poetry published after the war, *Erdishe vegn* [Worldly Ways], also dealt with Soviet heroism during the war.

In 1949 Halkin was arrested and his literary works were repressed in connection with the Soviet campaigns against Jewish culture. He was spared execution due to severe illness, but was instead sentenced to ten-years imprisonment. During his time in prison, Halkin continued writing. He was released from prison in 1955 and rehabilitated as part of the de-Stalinization campaigns. He died in Moscow in 1960. His last collection, *Mayn oytser* [My Treasure], which included many of his prison writings, was released posthumously in 1966.

JEFFREY VEIDLINGER

Halpern, Moyshe-Leyb

Polish-born US poet, 1886–1932

Born near Zlochev, 2 January 1886; studied at kheder and Polish-Jewish school. Sent by father for training in applied arts, 1898; participated in first Yiddish Language Conference, Czernowitz, 1908. Emigrated to United States, 1908. Lived mostly in New York, but spent brief periods in Montreal, and in Los Angeles, 1927–29. Member of literary group *Di yunge* (the Young Ones). Married Royzele Baron, 1919; one son. Died after heart attack, 31 August 1932.

Selected Writings

Poetry

In nyu-york, 1919; as *In New York: A Selection*, translated by Kathryn Hellerstein, 1982
Di goldene pave [The Golden Peacock], 1924
Moyshe-Leyb Halpern, edited by Eliezer Greenberg, 2 vols, 1934
In *The Golden Peacock: An Anthology of Yiddish Poetry*, translated by Joseph Leftwich, 1939
In *A Treasury of Yiddish Poetry*, translated by Irving Howe and Eliezer Greenberg, 1969
In *American Yiddish Poetry*, translated by Benjamin Harshav and Barbara Harshav, 1986
In *The Penguin Book of Modern Yiddish Verse*, translated by Irving Howe, Ruth R. Wisse, and Khone Shmeruk, 1987
In *An Anthology of Modern Yiddish Poetry*, translated by Ruth Whitman, 3rd edition, 1995

Further Reading

Greenberg, Eliezer, *Moyshe Leyb Halpern: in ram fun zayn dor*, New York: M.L. Halpern Arbeter Ring Brentsh, 1942
Harshav, Benjamin, "American Yiddish Poetry and Its Background" in *American Yiddish Poetry*, edited by Benjamin Harshav and Barbara Harshav, Berkeley: University of California Press, 1986
Hellerstein, Kathryn, introduction to *In New York*, by Moshe-Leyb Halpern, translated by Hellerstein, Philadelphia: Jewish Publication Society of America, 1982
Jeshurin, Ephim H., *Moshe-Leyb Halpern bibliografye*, New York: Matones, 1954
Kronfeld, Chana, "David Vogel and Moyshe Leyb Halpern: Liminal Moments in Hebrew and Yiddish Literary History" in *On the Margins of Modernism: Decentering Literary Dynamics*, Berkeley: University of California Press, 1996
Weinper, Zishe, *Moyshe-Leyb Halpern*, New York: Oyfkum, 1940
Wisse, Ruth R., *A Little Love in Big Manhattan*, Cambridge, Massachusetts: Harvard University Press, 1988
Wolitz, Seth, "Structuring the World View in Halpern's *In New York*", *Conference on Modern Jewish Studies Annual*, 1 (1977) (special issue of *Yiddish*)

When Warsaw's weekly *Literarishe bleter* conducted a survey among its readers asking them to choose their favourite Yiddish poet, Moyshe-Leyb Halpern's international popularity was confirmed when his name appeared more frequently than any of his contemporaries. Halpern was the great rebel of American Yiddish poetry. He crafted for himself an uncompromising, original poetic voice that wove together an earthy, colloquial idiom, and a hyper-critical eye for the most topical social and political issues, with a tenderness and philosophical posture born out of the Jew's and the immigrant's experience of longing and social alienation. His writing reveals the anxiety of the Yiddish writer in a foreign world that he can never entirely possess. While, in some places, this is expressed through a playful, ironic self-posture (as in the self-deprecating refrain to his "*Memento Mori*" – "Will anyone believe Moyshe-Leyb?"), elsewhere this tension is enunciated through thinly veiled autobiographical speakers who are consumed by a web of chaotic internal contradictions: "My restlessness is like a wolf's, my rest is like a bear's,/ Wildness shrieks in me, and boredom listens./ I am not what I want, I am not what I think,/ I am the magician and I'm the magic trick./ I am the riddle that tortures itself . . ."

Halpern's informal literary education was conducted in the German cultural sphere. During his young adulthood in Vienna in a commercial arts apprenticeship, he sat in on German literature evening classes at the university, and published his first poems in the local German-Jewish press. When he returned to home to Zlochev thoroughly assimilated in 1907, he came under the influence of several local Yiddish writers who convinced him to try his hand at Yiddish. Weary of the anti-Semitism he encountered in Vienna, too cosmopolitan to re-accustom himself to life at home, and fearful that he would be drafted into the army, Halpern left for America. Once in New York, he became an associate of *Di yunge* (the Young Ones), that generation of immigrant writers in America who introduced new standards of literary sophistication to Yiddish writing. Halpern straddled the worlds of high and popular Yiddish culture. In his early years, he published both in *Di yunge*'s journals, and in local humour magazines.

Halpern could not be contained within *Di yunge*'s programme of high aestheticism. The crowded struggle of Jewish immigrant life on the Lower East Side of Manhattan intruded into his creative work. In early poems such as "The Street Drummer" he cast an artistic identity for himself as the lowest embodiment of the creative performer – a wild, earthy, socially marginal noise-maker who would sooner drown out the challenges of life in the big city with his rhythmic banging than submit to the falsity of affected refinement. "I will play –/ Drum until the drum explodes!/ Beat upon the cymbals!/ Round and round I whirl and spin./ Jin, jin, boom-boom-boom./ Boom boom jin!" As "the rascal Moyshe-Leyb" he mocked those who preferred to see Yiddish poetry serve as a quiet sanctuary against the tumult of daily existence. Elsewhere, he struck out at the genteel snobbery of nativist Americans who, in their criticism of immigrant coarseness, glossed over their desperate physical conditions: "That is why I'll never go on bragging/ That it's not nice to crowd around a wagon/ With onions, cucumbers and plumbs . . ."

Halpern's first poetic volume, *In New York*, took as its subject the immigrant Jew's disorientation and disillusionment at his unfamiliar existence in America. As Mani Leyb, a leading writer of *Di yunge*, commented: "We, his friends, were like all other Jewish immigrants, afraid of this wondrous unknown called America. But somehow we gave in, we learned to adapt ourselves, we 'ripened', and eventually we became real Americans. Not Moyshe-Leyb. He couldn't compromise or bend." The volume's opening poem, "Our Garden", ironically undermines the immigrant's fantasy of America as the new, collective Eden through its speaker's sober encounter with the reality of existence in New York. Halpern's city park is a diminished, almost pathetic Eden: its single tree has scarcely any leaves, its grass is so sparse that one needs a magnifying glass just to see it, and its watchman is cruel to those looking for rest. Even the garden's bird subverts its function as the symbol of both nature and poetry by forgetting to feed it chicks and refusing to sing. By the time the speaker reaches his refrain, all he can do is answer his own rhetorical question with a response that shows resigned acceptance to the realities of this new Jewish world: "Can this be our garden, then,/ Just as is, in light of dawn?/ Sure, it's our garden. What, not our garden?"

In New York provided a moving, if harrowing "soulscape"(Wolitz) that functioned simultaneously as an expression of Halpern's personal experience of alienation and dislocation, and of the generational condition of exile and destruction. Both elements are at work in the book's long verse narratives "On Alien Soil" and "A Night". "On Alien Soil" was the first significant American Yiddish poem to explore the permanence of the immigrant Jew's internal mood of isolation in a Christian universe. As the speaker recalls a childhood in which his Polish classmates made him kiss a small gold cross and painted a crucifix on his body, he realizes that he will never be able to find "a spark of love" for their religious brethren, the dancing Irishmen whom he encounters on the ship with him to America. New York is envisioned as a "steel city" in which solace from the "unhappiness of my childhood" will prove elusive.

"A Night" is one of the most disturbing visions of the destruction of Jewish life in eastern Europe in all of modern Yiddish literature. Halpern interwove vivid, apocalyptic images of death and desecration (such as dangling bodies, the severed head of a rabbi, and a blood splattered prayer shawl) with a subversion of all former dreams. In the mocking figure of the *mentshele* (the little man), Halpern provided a counter-voice to the mournful tones of the survivor: "Your own brother, poor thing,/ Lost both his hands at war./ Now he doesn't sleep at night./ Since he can't scratch himself anymore." Halpern's nihilistic vision proved so persuasive that even its speaker chose to erase himself from the experience at the poem's end: "I was never here." The Yiddish literary critic A.B. Tabachnik called Halpern's *In New York* "one of the few epoch-making books in Yiddish literature."

In Halpern's subsequent books, *Di goldene pave* [The Golden Peacock] and his posthumous *Moyshe-Leyb Halpern*, his verse grew more philosophical, aggressive, and involved with national political and cultural battles. In poems such as "Sacco-Vanzetti", "We the Revolutionaries or

This America", and "Salute" (about the lynching of an innocent young black man), he consciously expanded the territory of Yiddish beyond "Jewish" themes, exposing simmering social tensions. From 1922 to 1925, he emerged as "the King of Freiheit" (Wisse), the featured poet of the New York communist Yiddish daily, only to be dismissed from its pages at the peak of his success for his unwillingness to conform to its ideological demands.

At the same time that Halpern was becoming more of an "American" writer, his poems re-focused attention on the Jewish internalization of homelessness. Yet Halpern denied his readers the opportunity to soothe themselves with the false idealization of their eastern Europe past. In "Zlochev, My Home", he crafted a devastating mockery of the familiar Yiddish ode of nostalgia. He reminded his readers of the church steeple that cast a constant shadow over their lives, and of the moral hypocrisy of his town's Jewish inhabitants. While Halpern himself may never have felt himself comfortable as either Jew or Yiddish poet in New York, at the very least life in America allowed him the freedom to explore the sources of his disillusionment: "And this, indeed, is my only consolation/ That they will not bury me in you –/ My home, my Zlochev." Despite the anger and gloom that characterized much of Halpern's writing, in the end his darkest anxieties are mitigated by his rediscovery of hope through moments of human intimacy. Perhaps the ending of a verse letter to his wife best captures the paradoxical tone of Halpern's relationship to his environment: "Give my regards to New York – lousy town/ But not too bad, if you have someone there."

JUSTIN CAMMY

Halter, Marek

Polish-born French writer, artist, and editor, 1936–

Born in Warsaw, 27 January 1936, to Salomon Halter, member of long line of printers and publishers, and wife Perl, poet. Spent early childhood in ghetto but fled with family to Soviet Union, 1941. Returned to Poland with family after war ended. Emigrated to France, 1950. Lived for a time as artist in Argentina; worked as mime artist in pantomime in Paris, then studied at École des Beaux-Arts, Paris. Showed work in Tel Aviv, Buenos Aires, and New York. Married Clara. After Six Day War he and wife tried to promote Arab–Jewish dialogue, 1967 onwards. Founding editor of *Elements*, magazine exploring possibilities of peace in Middle East. Worked as illustrator.

Selected Writings

Novels

La Vie incertaine de Marco Mahler [The Uncertain Life of Marco Mahler], 1979
La Mémoire d'Abraham, 1983; as *The Book of Abraham*, translated by Lowell Bair, 1986
Les Fils d'Abraham, 1989; as *The Children of Abraham*, translated by Lowell Bair, 1990
Le Messie [The Messiah], 1996
Les Mystères de Jérusalem [The Mysteries of Jerusalem], 1999

Other

Le Fou et les Rois, 1976; as *The Jester and the Kings: A Political Autobiography*, translated by Lowell Bair, 1989
Un Homme, un cri [A Man, A Cry], 1991 (autobiography)
Les Fous de la paix: Histoire Secrète d'une Négociation [The Madmen for Peace], with Eric Laurent, 1994
Tzadek [The Righteous], 1994
La Force du bien [The Force for Good], 1995; as *Stories of Deliverance: Speaking with Men and Women who Rescued Jews from the Holocaust*, translated by Michael Bernard, 1998

Further Reading

Los Angeles Times Book Review (13 April 1986; 3 September 1989; 23 December 1990)
New York Times (3 April 1986; 27 December 1990)
New York Times Book Review (6 April 1986)
Publishers Weekly (4 April 1986)
Time (5 May 1986)
Washington Post Book World (6 April 1986)
World Literature Today (Spring 1984)

Marek Halter takes rank in a special lineage of French intellectuals which includes writers such as Jean-Paul Sartre and Simone de Beauvoir. Like them Halter has made a name for himself based on his daring political stances, his public involvement with various political figures, and his courageous campaigning for causes he believes in. Like them, he has travelled to countries embroiled in social and political conflict in order to show support for leaders he approves of, and like them he has written widely on these topics in French left-wing newspapers and reviews. But his role as a writer is a more ambiguous and murky domain to define because, unlike Sartre or de Beauvoir, who wrote novels and plays that owe more to their philosophical than to their political convictions, Halter has chosen not to separate his political and cultural identity from his fiction.

Born in 1936 to Polish Jews in the Warsaw ghetto, Halter escaped with his family to Russia in 1941, where they faced conditions almost as horrifying as the ghetto. His little sister died of hunger during the family's desperate flight. At the end of the war the family returned to Poland. Halter came to Paris in 1950 at the age of 14, and eventually returned there after living for a time in Argentina as an artist and allying himself with Argentinean President Juan Perón. The substance of his fiction is drawn, if not entirely from his own personal experience as a Jew in World War II, at least from rich family folklore about the Holocaust, as well as about the years that preceded it.

While Halter was not the only Jewish artist to survive the Warsaw ghetto and then to seek refuge and fortune in a superpower nation before leading a brilliant artistic and intellectual life in Paris (one thinks of Roman Polanski's trajectory as well), he is perhaps the only one to have consecrated his artistic energy so entirely to the development of the history of the Holocaust. There are in fact two themes that characterize Halter's work and help to frame it within cultural and literary context: his devotion to history as a way of protecting future generations against disasters like the Holocaust, and his vociferous denunciation of what is, in his own words, *evil*: "The problem with Evil . . . is that it is in each of us, just as in each of us there resides a great capital of generosity", Halter told an interviewer in 1996, after having been refused a literary award in France because of his Jewishness. His having been stripped of the prize by the extreme right-wing mayor of Toulon scandalized the entire country, but Halter, whose award was subsequently offered to Brigitte Bardot (she tactfully refused), didn't dwell on his slight. His notion of evil is in fact, not limited to anti-Semitism. In 1994 he wrote, along with a friend, *Les Fous de la paix* [The Madmen for Peace], in which he recounts his own role in peace talks between two of his friends, Yitzhak Rabin and Yasser Arafat. He has also written on the tragedy of Algeria, the politics of Pope John-Paul II, and even on the sex scandal that nearly destroyed the Clinton administration.

But probably the most surprising aspect of the work of this daringly political writer is the degree to which Halter succeeds in fictionalizing events. His novels read like suspense classics that would once have led to movie scripts haggled over by the likes of Clouzot or Hitchcock. In *Les Fils d'Abraham* (*The Children of Abraham*) the opening scene ends in a bloodbath whose meaning we spend the rest of the novel discovering. But Halter never strays far from his subject. Even though his novels read like bestsellers (and some of them have been), his material is invariably taken from Jewish cultural or political history. His 1996 novel *Le Messie* [The Messiah] tells the story of a Jewish prince from the 16th century who crusades for an independent Israeli state in Palestine (based on a true story) before the European monarchs of his day.

And Halter, true to his image as an energetic intellectual roaming freely among various genres, has refused to rest within the parameters of the written word, exploiting a number of media to promulgate the two themes that interest him the most, history and evil. In 1994, while American and European audiences were watching Liam Neeson as Oskar Schindler make his life-saving list on movie screens everywhere, French TV audiences were learning all about the real Berthold Beitz, another young German industrial magnate who hired (and thus saved) 800 Jews during the war. Beitz was one of the 36 men and women chosen by Halter to be interviewed for a four-hour documentary directed by himself and wife Clara, *Tzadek* [The Righteous]. This documentary, perhaps more than any other single work of Halter's, illustrates his devotion and constancy to his lifelong leitmotivs. His reasons for making the film, he says, were motivated by his denial of evil: "I could not accept philosophically that there was no good, no generosity left in the world." So he began his own search for "the righteous" – Gentiles who risked their lives to protect Jews during World War II. In doing so, Halter has provided us with a precious document for history. These "righteous" are men and women never interviewed before, and their testimony goes a long way to proving Halter's thesis: good can survive even in the most evil of circumstances.

Halter's role as writer, despite the success of his novels and the sheer artistic energy of his works, will no doubt continue to perplex those in France who believe that the writer cannot mix art and politics in such a way. In fact one of the persistent images of literature is typified by Roland Barthes's *Le Degré zéro de l'écriture* and posits an absolute separation of art and politics. As long as there are writers like Marek Halter, its authority will always be questioned.

JANE BLEVINS

Hareven, Shulamith ("Tal Yaari")

Polish-born Israeli fiction writer and journalist, 1930–

Born in Warsaw, 14 February 1930. Emigrated to Palestine, 1940. Graduated from Rehavia Secondary School, 1947. Served in Haganah as combat medic in War of Independence, 1948. Among founders of Israel defence forces broadcasting station Galei Tsahal, 1949. Worked with new immigrants from Arab countries in refugee camps, early 1950s. Married Alouph Hareven, 1954; one son, one daughter. Military correspondent for press in later wars. Became first woman member of Academy of Hebrew Language, 1979. Spokesperson for Peace Team; went twice into Arab refugee camps and reported on them in Israeli press during first Intifada. Author in residence, Ohio State University, 1974; Hebrew University, Jerusalem, 1989–90; Oxford Centre for Postgraduate Hebrew, 1994. Awards include Prime Minister's Creativity Prize, 1971; Wallenrod Prize, 1973.

Selected Writings

Short Stories
Bahodesh haaharon [In the Last Month], 1966
Reshut netunah [Permission Granted], 1970
Bedidut [Loneliness], 1980
Hahuliyah [The Link], 1986
Twilight and Other Stories, translated by Miriam Arad, 1992
Habalon shehalakh lemakom aher [The Balloon That Went Away], 1994

Novels
Ir yamim rabim, 1972; as *City of Many Days*, translated by Hillel Halkin, 1993
Sone hanisim, 1983; as *The Miracle Hater*, translated by Hillel Halkin, 1988
Navi, 1989; as *Prophet*, translated by Hillel Halkin, 1990
Acharei hayaldut, 1994; as *After Childhood* in *Thirst*, the trilogy containing *The Miracle Hater* and *Prophet*, translated by Hillel Halkin, 1996

Poetry
Yerushalayim dorsanit [Jerusalem, the Predator], 1962
Mekomot nifradim [Separate Places], 1969
Ani ohev lehariah [I Love to Smell], 1976
Mah ani ashem sheani gadol? [Is It My Fault I'm All Grown Up?], 1999

Essays
Tismonet dulcinea [Dulcinea Syndrome], 1981

Massiah O Knesset, 1987
Ivrim beazah [Eyeless in Gaza], 1991
Otsar hamilim shel hashalom, 1991; as *The Vocabulary of Peace: Life, Culture and Politics in the Middle East*, 1995

Further Reading

Domb, Risa, introduction to *New Women's Writing from Israel*, edited by Domb, London: Vallentine Mitchell, 1996
Farhi, Moris, "Shulamit Hareven: Voice of the Levant", *Jewish Quarterly*, 144 (Winter 1991–92)
Feldman, Yael S., *No Room of their Own: Gender and Nation in Israeli Women's Fiction*, New York: Columbia University Press, 1999; Hebrew edition, Tel Aviv: Hakibuts hameuhad, 2001
Weill, Asher (editor), *The Best of Ariel: A Celebration of Contemporary Israeli Prose, Poetry and Art*, vol. 2 (1993): 77–88

Honoured by the World Jewish Women's Organization as one of "Israel's 11 most outstanding woman", listed by the French journal, *L'Expres*, as "one of a hundred women of our times who make the world move", a writer who has been translated into 20 languages, Shulamith Hareven has been a towering figure both in literature and politics.

In many ways her life chronicles the formative years of her country: medic in the Haganah during the siege of Jerusalem, 1947–8; IDF officer in charge of the welfare of 11 camps of immigrants from Arab countries; frontline correspondent in the Wars of Attrition and Yom Kippur; reporter from Palestinian refugee camps during the Intifada. First-hand knowledge of warfare – "the total failure of common sense", as she defines it – made her, for many years, a passionate spokesperson for the Peace Now! Movement.

Hareven's most famous political pronouncement may well prove to be "I am a Levantine!", a declaration that seeks to elucidate the true perspectives of the Israeli identity: a country and a people rooted, spiritually, linguistically, and geographically, in the Middle East. Though she acknowledges that Levantinism can manifest "the moral principles of an alleycat", Hareven believes its virtues outweigh its shadows. Levantinism, she states, is "the colour-blind pluralism that sees no racial, ethnic or religious differences", that nurtures people who distrust powers and cultures "that speak one language only". Above all, identifying the "institutionalized brutality" of totalitarianism as the legacy of a Christianity cynically misused by Europe, she champions Levantinism as a humanism that, knowing that "not everything has a solution", is wise enough to exercise "great patience", yet strong enough "to carve signs in stones".

Reflections of these views can be found in almost all her essays and short stories. Her famous novel, *City of Many Days*, set during the British Mandate years, is an early wistful consideration of all that she later defines as Levantinism. The city in question is Jerusalem, transformed by iniquitous colonial rule and the possessive demands of Jews and Arabs into "a duplicitous city in which everything is its own looking glass". However, this is also a city where the old Ottoman tolerance for pluralism prevails, where strife brings wisdom, where grief – even despair – somehow nurtures hope. The novel has many memorable characters – Sara, the protagonist; her eccentric family; Subhi and Faiza, their close Arab friends whose son, Taleb, embraces Palestinian nationalism; Crowther, the English Captain; Matti, Sara's boyfriend who becomes a leading figure in the Jewish underground; Elias, Sara's husband, Haganah's lawyer who is also sympathetic to Arab aspirations; Dr Barzel, an immigrant from Germany, who builds up a hospital for all the city's inhabitants; his mother, oppressive with her "superior" Germanic ways. The story unfolds in impressionistic vignettes; as the characters interpret or misinterpret events, we sense rather than witness the changes. Hareven's portrait of Jerusalem, with a spirit as vibrant as Durrell's Alexandria, Kazantzakis's Crete, and García Lorca's Andalusia, further enhances the subtlety of the narrative.

Another Levantine characteristic that dominates Hareven's work is "that quality which knows there is no great art, no serious literature, without a hidden theology". However, her "theology" is not institutionalized; it is, quite simply, the innate awareness of God, the Supreme, but Incomprehensible Creator, with whom we can deal directly, praise or curse as we used to when we trusted our spirituality.

This Creator is heavily present in "the Desert trilogy", *Thirst*. The three novellas, *The Miracle Hater*, *Prophet*, and *After Childhood*, possess, despite their brevity, great density; and Hareven's austere imagery, such a feature of her poetry, elevates them to scriptural lyricism.

The trilogy, chronicling the early times of the Hebrews, is at its core a stark study of solitude, not only of the individual, but of a people, indeed of mankind. *The Miracle Hater* narrates the Exodus from Egypt with the story of Eshkhar, a new-born, entrusted by his mother to a five-year-old girl, Baita. In the wilderness, Baita, forced into marriage, abandons her husband for Eshkhar, but dies in fear of the punishment she will incur. Thereafter, Eshkhar drifts in and out of the ancestral lands. Only when he comes upon a young woman, Dina, and accepts her illegitimate child as his own, does he choose to settle in the Promised Land.

In *Prophet* a hilltop city panics upon rumours of an approaching enemy. The city's prophet, Hivai, having caused his daughter's death with a wrongful prophecy, attaches himself to the Hebrews to study their ways. One day, he asks to see the Hebrew God. When told that God has no body or form, Hivai, disbelieving them, scours the camp. Discovered and expelled from the settlement, he proceeds to the river Jordan. There, cultivating his patch, he meets a mute boy; through this attachment, he regains some of his prophetic gifts.

In *After Childhood* Salu, a solitary youth – one who has survived his father's attempt to sacrifice him – commissions a caravan leader to find him a wife. The latter brings Moran, a free-spirited maiden from a mountain settlement. They prove compatible. Moran gives birth to a boy. Salu, declaring that Moran can have many more children, takes their son to an old paramour, a barren Hittite. The Hittites force the woman to send the boy back. But Moran is unforgiving; though she bears Salu other sons, she refuses to talk to him. Salu, seeking distraction in an abandoned fort, is killed when the Egyptians return. Moran lives on in another kind of solitude. "God . . . had given and taken as always, but he took far more than he gave."

It is impossible not to draw parallels, in these intense stories, between the ancient Hebrews struggling to settle in ancestral lands and the Israel of today, endeavouring to build a future in the same lands. Many questions are posed. Is justice on the side of the strong? Can we accept this premise for an Israel that strives, sometimes brutally, to stay strong? Are we living through Israel's years in the wilderness? Does Israel's intransigence in certain areas suggest arrogance like that of Moses who extracts water from the rock by striking it not *once*, as God had told him, but *twice*?

One message is clear: solitude, notwithstanding occasional communion, is mankind's fare, possibly a fare necessary to forge the requisite strength for survival. Could the corollary to this be that "everything can still happen, the good or the bad; for nothing is predestined", as is suggested in "Portrait of a Terrorist" in *The Vocabulary of Peace*? Might humanism, Levantinism, the miracle of diversity, given the chance, lead to peace, the true salvation?

MORIS FARHI

Harwood, Ronald

South African-born British dramatist, 1934–

Born Ronald Horwitz in Cape Town, South Africa, 9 November 1934. Educated at Sea Point Boys' High School, Cape Town; Royal Academy of Dramatic Art, London. Married Natasha Riehle in 1959; one son and two daughters. Joined Donald Wolfit's Shakespeare Company in London, 1953; actor, 1953–59; presenter, *Kaleidoscope* radio programme, 1973, and television series *Read All about It*, 1978–79, and *All the World's a Stage*, 1984. Chairman, Writers Guild of Great Britain, 1969; member of the Literature Panel, Arts Council of Great Britain, 1973–78; artistic director, Cheltenham Festival, 1975; visitor in theatre, Balliol College, Oxford, 1986. Awards include the Royal Society of Literature prize, 1974; *Evening Standard* award, 1980; Drama Critics Circle award, 1980. Fellow, Royal Society of Literature, 1974. President, International PEN, 1993.

Selected Writings

Plays
Country Matters, 1969
One Day in the Life of Ivan Denisovich, 1970
The Good Companions, 1974
The Ordeal of Gilbert Pinfold, 1977
A Family, 1978
The Dresser, 1980
A Night of the Day of the Imprisoned Writer, with Christopher Hampton, 1981
After the Lions, 1982
Tramway Road, 1984
The Deliberate Death of a Polish Priest, 1985
Interpreters: A Fantasia on English and Russian Themes, 1985
J.J. Farr, 1987
Another Time, 1989
Reflected Glory, 1990
Home, 1993
Poison Pen, 1993
The Collected Plays of Ronald Harwood, 1993
Taking Sides, 1995
The Handyman, 1996
Equally Divided, 1999
Quartet, 1999
Goodbye Kiss, 2000
The Guests, 2000
Mahler's Conversion, 2001

Screenplays: *The Barber of Stamford Hill*, 1962; *Private Potter*, with Casper Wrede, 1962; *A High Wind in Jamaica*, with Denis Cannan and Stanley Mann, 1965; *Drop Dead Darling* (*Arrivederci Baby!*), with Ken Hughes, 1966; *Diamonds for Breakfast*, with N.F. Simpson and Pierre Rouve, 1968; *Cromwell*, with Ken Hughes, 1970; *Eyewitness*, 1970; *One Day in the Life of Ivan Denisovich*, 1972; *Operation Daybreak*, 1975; *The Dresser*, 1984; *The Doctor and the Devils*, 1986

Radio Play: *All the Same Shadows*, 1971

Television Plays: *The Barber of Stamford Hill*, 1960; *Private Potter*, with Casper Wrede, 1961; *Take a Fellow Like Me*, 1961; *The Lads*, 1963; *Convalescence*, 1964; *Guests of Honour*, 1965; *The Paris Trip*, 1966; *The New Assistant*, 1967; *All the Same Shadows*, 1971; *Long Lease of Summer*, 1972; *The Guests*, 1972; *A Sense of Loss*, with John Selwyn, 1978; *The Way up to Heaven*, 1979, *Parson's Pleasure*, 1986, and *The Umbrella Man*, 1986 (all in *Tales of the Unexpected* series); *Evita Perón*, 1981; *Breakthrough at Reykjavik*, 1987; *Mandela*, 1987; *Countdown to War*, 1989

Novels
All the Same Shadows, 1961; as *George Washington September, Sir!*, 1961
The Guilt Merchants, 1963
The Girl in Melanie Klein, 1969
Articles of Faith, 1973
The Genoa Ferry, 1976
César and Augusta, 1978

Short Stories
One. Interior. Day. Adventures in the Film Trade, 1978

Other
Sir Donald Wolfit, CBE: His Life and Work in the Unfashionable Theatre, 1971
Editor, with Francis King, *New Stories 3*, 1978
Editor, *A Night at the Theatre*, 1982
All the World's a Stage, 1984
Editor, *The Ages of Gielgud: An Actor at Eighty*, 1984
Mandela, 1987
Editor, *Dear Alec: Guinness at Seventy-Five*, 1989
Editor, *The Faber Book of Theatre*, 1993

In recent years Harwood's oeuvre has undergone a metamorphosis. His earlier plays were largely concerned with the theatre. *After the Lions*, *Reflected Glory*, *Tramway Road*, and *The Dresser* all have theatrical backgrounds. *The Dresser*, probably his most successful play, which later transferred to the screen, describes the relationship between an ageing actor-manager and his dresser. This was a world well known to Harwood, who came to London from South Africa as a 19-year-old, joining Donald Wolfit's travelling Shakespeare Company, where he worked as both actor and dresser.

Pivotal to *Tramway Road* is the hateful situation, so common in pre-Mandela South Africa, where a young boy is "re-classified" as " Coloured", while he "tries for White". He is having speech lessons from an English couple in order to try for the stage in London. Harwood's moral sensibilities are finely tuned to the horrors of the Apartheid regime.

Harwood has commented: "My stand [the condemnation of South Africa] was honourable, and it was certainly fashionable at the time. But it is easy to pontificate when one is six thousand miles away." But his social conscience translated into theatre is powerful and true.

Another Time, dedicated to his brother Ralph Horwitz, seems drawn from personal experience. Set in Cape Town in the early 1950s, the first act is dominated by Ike Lands, an émigré Lithuanian Jew, a kind of *luftmensch*, who has gone to pieces after his mother's death, shortly after his son Leonard's birth. His stressed and exhausted wife, Belle, has been the breadwinner since then. The play captures the rhythms of agitated family life, as Ike and Belle stake out territory in different rooms (a cramped and crowded domain, in Saul Radomsky's set for the first production), and communicate largely through other people – her brother, the moral philosopher, her librarian sister, and son Leonard.

The dilemma facing the family is whether they have the money to send their prodigy son overseas to further his musical career. Much of the humour is derived from the Jewish idiomatic speech, "From your mouth into God's ear"; "So, what else is new?"; "You take my meaning . . ."; "It's better than having an enema but the results will be the same"; "Touch wood, I'm going" (ironical since wood symbolizes the cross); "God forbid he wants to be a chauffeur". When Rose declares she needs to be near her books or she will die (she lives above the library), her brother quips, "So instead of a shroud they'll wrap you in a dust jacket". In scene 4, when Ike dies, the mirrors are covered, a custom of traditional Jewish families.

Act 2 takes place in London 35 years later, in a recording studio. The family is visiting the now famous pianist. Belle is the archetypal guilt-inducing Jewish mother ("You eat properly?" Leonard asks. "Who eats?" she replies). She tries to persuade him by moral blackmail that he should perform in racist South Africa, something he refuses. Yet Harwood suggests that to endorse the cultural boycott is to take the easy way out, also a problematic option.

Taking Sides is Harwood's masterwork. It was first performed in Chichester, 18 May 1995, and on the same day in Poland. The central figure is ambivalent: Wilhelm Furtwängler, the chief conductor of the Berlin Philharmonic during the Third Reich. At the height of his powers when Hitler became Chancellor, Furtwängler decided to stay on in Germany, rather than leave as an act of protest, as others were doing. Two Denazification Tribunals in 1946 found him innocent of serving the Reich. Yet the Nazi stench remained, and a dark shadow was cast over his reputation. Once he had conducted at a birthday concert for Hitler. Furtwängler's defence was that he felt he had to keep alive the spirit of German music in barbarous times. He loved his country and people, and remained to guard the glorious musical tradition so that it was intact when the nightmare was over. He also claimed to have helped several Jewish musicians to flee to safety, a claim verified in the play by Tamara Sachs, who reveals how the conductor helped her Jewish husband escape. What is particularly disturbing is the thought that this great music was especially enjoyed by those very Nazis who sent Jews to their deaths in the camps. What does that say about the spiritual or redemptive quality of great art?

Taking Sides is set in the American zone of Berlin in 1946 when the great conductor is ignominiously hauled before, and interrogated by, an American officer. The bullying Major Arnold, so hostile to the conductor, has come fresh from the horrors of Bergen-Belsen two days after its liberation. "I've seen things with these eyes . . .". The humour is telling when Arnold describes the Viennese cleaning up bomb damage, scavenging for rotten food, and remembers how a million of them came out to welcome the Führer. His driver responds bitterly with the view, "Oh not these people, Major. These people were all at home hiding Jews in their attics."

The American takes the adversarial "bad cop" role, while the British Lieutenant Wills, a Jew, is more tempered and decent, thanking Furtwängler for opening up a musical world to him. But when Furtwängler's anti-Semitic remarks about Jewish musicians are quoted, Wills responds bitterly, "Show me a non-Jew who hasn't made anti-Semitic remarks and I'll show you the gates of paradise."

The play asks what any of us would have done in those circumstances. To leave Germany would have meant abandoning much of his musical career; so he stayed, believing he was merely a pawn. Could the action of one conductor, in leaving, have altered much in the general scheme of things? It is a morally complex arena, with no clear-cut answers. As Harwood says, "It all depends on the side you take." The play resonates powerfully especially when we consider that the Americans, so hard on Furtwängler, were then taking high-ranking Nazi scientists to work for them to make missiles and rocket fuels.

The subject matter of Harwood's next play, *The Handyman*, is another topical war-crimes trial. When the play opens, we see Romka, the handyman, an aged family retainer, in the garden with his employers burying their cat. The peaceful interlude is disrupted by police inquiring into the handyman's past, when he had allegedly taken part in the murder of 817 Jews as a member of the SS in Ukraine in 1941. Themes of justice and vengeance emerge but, unlike *Taking Sides*, where a verdict was never clear, the balance here is weighed to assume Romka's guilt.

The rather feeble Catholic employers, the Fields, attempt to hire a Jewish lawyer to defend their handyman, but the solicitor turns out only to be married to one. The Fields are outraged that British law has been altered to allow it to pursue old men for crimes committed more than 50 years before, and believe it to be immoral, unjust, and Old Testament revenge. Can he have a fair trial? Can you trust the memories of elderly witnesses? The lawyer thinks it a moot point that anyone would murder Jews nowadays, and recalls the Holocaust deniers who call the Holocaust a "Jewish fantasy". She has taken on the case, not because Romka is evil but, she suggests, because he is human and needs to be defended well.

But it is the evidence of a nun, who was a friend of Romka's family, that testifies to his crimes. Sister Sophia believes that it is because the Jews rejected Christ that they have been persecuted, and wishes for Romka's incarceration and consequent suffering because it will lead to everlasting redemption. The play ends with his employer denying the Holocaust. "It never happened. None of it. Ever."

It is interesting that Harwood's earliest novels were similarly concerned with complex moral issues. His powerful first novel, *All the Same Shadows*, is the story of a few days in the life of George Washington September, a young Cape Town Zulu, torn between hating and admiring the overbearing racist White world, and driven by loneliness and fear to find a way out. Harwood's second novel, *The Guilt Merchants*, sees Hyman Sidnitz on a special mission to trace a former Nazi to an American town, El Pueblo. His presence in the town disturbs and threatens a former Nazi doctor, a Spanish-Jew living in the town, and a victim of Nazism. Like *The Handyman* this novel uncovers the painful and terrible workings of perverted racial hatred and guilt.

Mahler's Conversion explores the composer's marriage to Alma Schindler (a noted anti-Semite), his conversion from Judaism to Catholicism (a cynical conversion of convenience in order to qualify for the position of conductor at the Vienna State Opera, where only Catholics could be employed), and his meeting with Sigmund Freud (to whom he admits his guilt at having forsaken his Jewish roots, his tormented feeling that he has been punished by the deaths of his beloved children, and by his sexual impotency). The atmosphere of fin-de-siècle Vienna, with its virulent anti-Semitism, is well drawn; the newspaper reviews at the time of Mahler's appointment at the State Opera House reveal that he was still reviled as a Jew notwithstanding his conversion. Professor Freud tells him a joke about two poor Jews outside a church where it is advertised that a huge sum of money will be given to those converting. After the first man comes out, his friend asks anxiously if he has been paid, to be told "Oh, you Jews, only interested in the money". Freud explains how quickly and easily the first Jew has acquired and assimilated the prevailing anti-Jewish attitudes – a salutary lesson.

Sorrel Kerbel

Hazaz, Hayim ("H. Zevi")

Russian-born Israeli fiction writer, 1898–1973

Born in Kiev, 1898; received both religious and secular education. Moved to Kharkov, then Moscow; worked in Moscow for Hebrew daily *Haam*. Moved to Istanbul, 1921. Emigrated to France, 1921; settled in Paris. Emigrated to Palestine, 1931; settled in Jerusalem. Awarded Israel Prize, 1953; American Academy Prize for Jewish Research. Died in Jerusalem, 1973.

Selected Writings

Fiction

Beyishuv shel yaar [A Settlement in the Woods], 1930
Rehayim shevurim [Broken Millstones], 1942
Hayoshevet baganim [Thou That Dwellest in the Garden], 1944; as *Mori Sa'id*, translated by Ben Halpern, 1956
Avanim rotehot [Seething Stones], 1946
Ya'ish, 4 vols, 1947
Daltot nehoshet, 2 vols, 1956; as *Gates of Bronze*, translated by S. Gershon Levi, 1975
Hagorat mazzalot [Zodiac Lights], 1958
The Gallows, 1963
Sundial, 1973
Paamon verimon [Bell and Pomegranate], 1974
Stories of the Revolution, 1980

Play

Bekets hayamim, 1950; as *The End of Days*, translated by Dalya Bilu, 1982

Other

Contributor to *In These Great Days: Words of Hebrew Writers*, translated by I.M. Lask, 1967
Kol kitvei Hayim Hazaz [Collected Works], 8 vols, 1968
The Right of Redemption, 1977

Further Reading

Bargad, Warren, "Character, Idea, and Myth in the Works of Hayim Hazaz" (PhD dissertation), Brandeis University, 1970
Bargad, Warren, *Ideas in Fiction: The Works of Hayim Hazaz*, Chico, California: Scholars Press, 1981
Barzel, Hillel, *Hazon vehizayon: Kafka, Shofman, Hazaz, Alterman, Apelfeld, Yehoshua* [Message and Vision], Tel Aviv: Hotsaat Yahdav, 1987
Morris, Elaine I., "Key Motifs in the Writings of Hayyim Hazaz" (PhD dissertation), New York University, 1968
Weiser, Rafa'el, *Bibliografyah mu-eret shel kitvei Haim Hazaz* [An Annotated Bibliography of the Writings of Haim Hazaz], Jerusalem: University of Jerusalem Press, 1992
Yudkin, Leon I., *1948 and After: Aspects of Israeli Fiction*, Manchester: Manchester University Press, 1984

Hayim Hazaz was one of the formative influences on Palestinian Hebrew fiction, or, put another way, on the renaissance of Hebrew literature in the Land of Israel. Devoted to the cause of Hebrew literature from the time of his early youth in Ukraine where he was born, he attempted to thread together all the sources of the Hebrew language which was undergoing a singular revival, and bring them to bear on a fictional construction of panoramic Jewish history, over time and space, and a portrait of the Jewish situation of his time, including the Israeli phase.

One of the special contributions Hazaz made to Modern

Hebrew literature was the augmentation, the sifting and the creation, of a new Hebrew as an appropriate vessel for sophisticated fictional expression across a broad range of themes and character types. He is a true inheritor of the tradition of Mendele Moykher Sforim, in Bialik's formulation, the initial creator of the modern literary Hebrew, bringing together the disparate elements of traditional language over the centuries, with the colloquial supplements of Aramaic and calques from Yiddish, the spoken tongue of the Jewish majority. He also added to that a portrait of the range of Jewish communities, not just from his own region and background, the Ashkenazim, but those from Yemen, the old settlement of Jerusalem, and Sephardim of various origins. If modern Israel was to be regarded as a melting pot, it was up to the chronicler to record the profiles of the disparate elements that went into this pot. But although Hazaz was indeed a chronicler in this sense, attempting to etch a portrait for his time and unique in his time, he was also a sort of historian, recording the changes that were taking place even before his eyes. Part of the picture was the ideology that offered some sort of sense to the fact. Not only was Jewry the way that it was, but it was also being transformed. And the question arose as to whether this was to be a transformation into a different element, or whether the agent of change would not render the Jew in the modern world an anachronism. In much of his fiction, Hazaz allows ideas to pitch themselves against each other, and the characters of his stories often act as vessels for the transmission of ideas, specifically of views of Jewish history.

One of the great agents for change in the Jewish history of past and present is the Messiah. The Messiah indeed can be seen as the *deus ex machina* of Jewish history, conferring meaning on this strange presence in the world. Much of Hazaz's writing is concerned with the figure of the Messiah. We can see this in his play, *Bekets hayamim* (*The End of Days*), which, as the title suggests, concerns itself with an apocalyptic view of history. Hazaz not only lived through difficult times – World War I, the Bolshevik Revolution, the destruction of the shtetl, the rise of Nazism and the Holocaust and the emergence of the State of Israel – he also recorded them, and attempted to make sense of them. He conducted this enterprise in the light of an attempted understanding of Jewish history. In this sense, he thought of his own period, that immediately preceding our own, as being Messianic. The times of the Messiah would represent a historical crux, in which nothing following would remain as it had been before. Whether the Messiah should be understood literally as a single figure bringing redemption, or, metaphorically, as a series of cataclysmic events, ushering in a new era, we were still to expect an unprecedented wave of changes. The events itemized seemed to fit this bill, and 1935, the date of the original composition of the play, seemed to reverberate with the harrowing experiences of the events recorded in the play surrounding the life and times of the Messianic or pseudo- Messianic figure of Shabbetai Tsvi. As there were multiple pogroms at the time of the Khmielnitski pogroms of 1648–49, so in the 1930s, there were Nazi gangs threatening Jewish life and existence. And just as the Messianic cult came in the wake of those distant events, even seeking to nullify Jewish law and practice, so in the mid-20th century there was a movement seeking to revolutionize, radicalize, transform, and perhaps even annul current Jewish existence. The name of this new movement was Zionism, and Hazaz writes much, fictionally of course, about the meaning and implications of Zionism. Is Zionism a fulfilment or a negation? Hazaz is not a historian, nor is he a philosopher of history. But he does allow his characters to represent different views, to articulate opposing theses. Hazaz thus becomes a fictional dialectician, or a novelist of ideas, whether he sets his stories in revolutionary Russia, in Yemen, or in Israel, whether his characters are enlightened but despairing Westerners or naive and expectant Easterners.

Hazaz brings to bear his linguistic virtuosity in the deployment of the Hebrew language on the situation of Jews fighting either for a cause or simply for enlightenment in his writing about his present circumstances, his contemporary situation over a long literary life, or in his confrontation with the past, whether "here" (in Israel) or "there" (in exile). The literary output of his lifetime was considerably supplemented by the posthumous publications, which chronicle a consciously broad range of experience, as in *Paamon verimon* [Bell and Pomegranate]. He is not afraid to present the arguments that offer the most radical challenge to the idea of the very existence of the Jewish people and their continuation. But his own work also constitutes a refutation of those arguments, and is in itself an unarticulated antithesis. There is also an argument in progress in his work over the function of fiction itself, and whether there has to be an authorial standpoint or not. But that again is the difference between fiction and journalism.

LEON I. YUDKIN

Heijermans, Herman

Dutch dramatist, journalist, and fiction writer, 1864–1924

Born in Rotterdam, 3 December 1864. Worked as dealer in old clothes and scrap metal before following father into journalism, starting in Rotterdam, later in Amsterdam. Edited *De Jonge Gids*, 1897–1901. Used many pseudonyms: best known are Samuel Falkland and K. Habbema. Married, first, Marie Peers, 1898; divorced 1918; one daughter; second, Annie Jurgens; one daughter, one son. Travelled to Berlin; contributed to *Berliner Tageblatt*. Died in Zandvoort, 22 November 1924.

Selected Writings

Plays

Ahasverus, 1886

Dora Kremer, 1893

Ghetto, 1899

Op Hoop van zegen, 1901; as *Dayagim* (in Hebrew), translated by Abraham Shlonsky, 1927; as *The Good Hope: a Drama of the Sea*, translated by Harriet Gampert Higgins, 1912, and by Lillian Saunders and Caroline Heijermans-Houwink, 1928

'n Jodenstreek? [a Jew Trick], 1904
Bloeimaand [Bloom Month], 1905
Schakels [Links], 1905
De opgaande zon, 1911; as *The Rising Sun*, translated by Christopher St John, 1925
De wijze kater [The Wise Tomcat], 1917
Eva Bonheur, 1919
Toneelwerken [Complete Plays], 3 vols, edited by S. Carmiggelt *et al.*, 1965

Novels
Kamertjeszonde [The Sin Indoors], 1897
Sabbath, 1903
Diamantstad [Diamond City], 1904
Droomkoninkje [Little Dreamer King], 1924
Vuurvlindertje [Little Fire Butterfly], 1925
Duczika, 1926

Other
Stories (as Samuel Falkland) in *Het Algemeen Handelsblad*, 13 vols, 1896–1915
Kleine verschrikkingen [Little Horrors], 1904
Wat niet kon en andere verhalen [What Could Not and Other Stories], 1908
Joep's wonderlijke avonturen [Joep's Miraculous Adventures], 1909
Levensschetsen [Sketches], 1922–25
Stories in *Great Stories of All Nations: One Hundred and Fifty-Eight Stories from All Periods and Countries*, edited by Maxim Lieber and Blanche Colton Williams, 1927
Stories in *Ysröel: The First Jewish Omnibus*, edited by Joseph Leftwich, 1933

Further Reading

Flaxman, Seymour Lawrence, *Herman Heijermans and His Dramas*, The Hague: Nijhoff, 1954
Goedkoop, Hans, *Geluk: Het leven van Herman Heijermans*, Amsterdam: Arbeiderspers, 1996
Heijermans, Hermine, *Mijn vader Herman Heijermans: Leven naast roem door zijn oudste dochter*, Amsterdam: De Bezige Bij, 1973
Jong, Evert de, *Herman Heijermans en de vernieuwing van het Europese drama*, Groningen: Wolters, 1967
Schilp, C.A., *Herman Heijermans*, Amsterdam: Moussault, 1967
Yoder, Hilda van Neck, *Dramatizations of Social Change: Herman Heijermans' Plays as Compared with Selected Dramas by Ibsen, Hauptmann and Chekhov*, The Hague: Nijhoff, 1978

In 1907 the famous British actress Ellen Terry went on a tour of the United States. She was the leading lady in *Op Hoop van zegen* (*The Good Hope*) by a certain Herman Heijermans, a Dutch playwright. The successful tour was sensational in more than one way, for never since has a Dutch playwright had such an international success as Heijermans. And never before were the classical rules of tragedy broken so completely as in *Op Hoop van zegen*, a tragedy in a fiercely realistic style about poverty-stricken fishermen in a village on the Dutch coast.

Op Hoop van zegen, first performed on Christmas eve of 1900 in Amsterdam, made Heijermans immortal in Dutch literature. The play is about a fisherman's widow who, driven by dire need, lets her last remaining son sail on the unseaworthy ship of a corrupt ship owner. Every Dutchman, whether or not he has ever been to the theatre, knows the expression "I paid dearly for that fish", Mother Kniertje's lament after hearing that her youngest son has drowned. Audiences all over the world have identified with the universal aspect of her situation; from St Petersburg to San Francisco, people have reached for their handkerchiefs. The play was made into a film twice, the last time in 1986.

The fisherman's play is a good example of Heijermans's social conscience, one of the foundations of his career as a writer. Although he tried many literary styles during his more than 30-year-long literary career, and even dabbled in symbolism, his readers loved his realistic style above all. He was generally mentioned in the same breath as Balzac, Dickens, and Zola.

Heijermans was born into a Jewish family in which Judaism played practically no role in daily life. His father, Herman Heijermans, Sr, worked as journalist for a newspaper in Rotterdam. Although he was a freethinker, he nevertheless was a member of the Jewish religious community of Rotterdam. However, his children did not attend religious school. In 1877 Herman Jr turned 13, bar mitzvah, but no attention was paid to his religious coming-of-age.

All his life Heijermans had a difficult relationship with Judaism and Dutch Jews. Like many people of his generation, he felt that Jews had to take advantage of the possibilities for integration that were offered by the changing Dutch society. He himself suffered from being different which, he felt, was linked to being a Jew. He married twice; both times his wives were not Jewish. Being different was the subject of many of his early works, such as the play *Ghetto*, about a Jewish socialist who wants to marry a non-Jewish housemaid but is pressured by his father to drop her. It is also the theme of his first novel, *Kamertjeszonde* [The Sin Indoors], a fiercely realistic tale that was considered so filthy by his contemporaries that he could publish it only under a pseudonym.

All his life he remained a Jew who didn't want to be a Jew, was very eager to assimilate, and above all wanted to be accepted by the non-Jews around him. In his work as well as in his personal life, he was driven by the urge to be considered as an equal. When his early play *Dora Kremer* did not receive the favourable reviews that he had expected, he wrote his next play under a pseudonym in order to play a nasty trick on the critics. He loved to show that he belonged in society and to that end spent money that he didn't have, then earned that money by writing: another play, another newspaper article. Early in his career he had borrowed the journalistic form of the regular newspaper column from his father. The senior Heijermans introduced the short narrative sketch into Dutch daily newspapers; in addition to the column form, Herman Jr also took his father's pseudonym Samuel Falkland. To this day the column is a much used and very popular literary form in which many a Dutch writer prefers to express himself.

Like almost every intellectual of his generation,

Heijermans was by nature a fervent socialist. His social conscience bursts forth in all his writing, whether a novel, newspaper article, play, or short story. He once wrote to a colleague:

> Go to the old Jewish quarters where our people lies trampled, trampled in dreck, in mud. Go to Marken and Uilenburg, to the slums. Long ago the Jews crucified their Messiah, then that Messiah rose up. Go there and if you leave other than an emotional socialist (it is in your character), other than completely horror-stricken, other than swearing that you will help and that you will sacrifice yourself for others, then you're utterly lost, no matter how many beautiful verses you write.

The unequalled success of *Op Hoop van zegen* made it possible for Heijermans to be invited to come and work in Berlin, the cultural centre of Europe before World War I. After a number of prosperous years, he returned to the Netherlands with his wife and daughter. In Amsterdam he started his own theatre company. The new company led to an expensive failure that brought him to the edge of bankruptcy (he had been there many times before). In this tumultuous time, he met his second wife, the actress Annie Jurgens. For the two children from this second marriage he wrote two novels of a type that we would now call fantasy: *Droomkoninkje* [Little Dream King] and *Vuurvlindertje* [Little Fire Butterfly]. Heijermans did not enjoy his new family for long; in 1924 he died of cancer.

In hindsight, his work has the openness of a Jew who did not have to experience the Holocaust. His very firm belief in assimilation seems rather naïve in retrospect. Heijermans wrote as easily about non-Jewish as about Jewish characters. The novels, short stories, and plays were often set in a Jewish workers' milieu but he portrayed the non-Jewish neighbours just as easily. During his lifetime, Heijermans enjoyed immense public acclaim as a writer. A century on, he has not been forgotten. Most of his novels and stories are no longer in print, although the occasional short story or Falkland newspaper sketch still finds its way into an anthology. After a century, they are still fresh and readable. Heijermans's plays are still performed regularly. No theatre season in the Netherlands and Flanders goes by without at least one play by Heijermans, although present-day directors usually cut out most supporting parts and streamline the text, to make for a modern adaptation.

DAPHNE MEIJER
translated by Jeannette Ringold

Heller, Joseph

US fiction writer, 1923–1999

Born in Brooklyn, New York, 1 May 1923. Studied at Abraham Lincoln High School, New York; University of Southern California, Los Angeles, 1945–46; New York University, BA 1948; Columbia University, MA 1949; Oxford University (Fulbright Scholar), 1949–50. Served in air force during World War II: lieutenant. Married, first, Shirley Held, 1945; one son, one daughter; second, Valerie Humphries. Instructor in English, Pennsylvania State University, 1950–52; advertising writer, *Time*, New York, 1952–56, *Look*, New York, 1956–58; promotion manager, *McCall's*, New York, 1958–61. Awarded American Academy grant, 1963; Prix Médicis, 1985; Interallie Prize (France), 1985. Member, American Academy of Arts and Letters, 1977. Died in New York, 12 December 1999.

Selected Writings

Novels
Catch-22, 1961
Something Happened, 1974
Good as Gold, 1979
God Knows, 1984
Picture This, 1988
Closing Time, 1994
Portrait of the Artist, as an Old Man, 2000

Plays
We Bombed in New Haven, 1967
Catch-22, 1973
Clevinger's Trial, 1974

Screenplays: *Sex and the Single Girl*, with David R. Schwarz, 1964; *Casino Royale* (as Max Orange), 1967; *Dirty Dingus Magee*, with Tom Waldman and Frank Waldman, 1970

Other
No Laughing Matter, with Speed Vogel, 1986
Now and Then: A Memoir from Coney Island to Here, 1998

Further Reading

Dodd, Burr, "Joseph Heller's *Catch-22*" in *Approaches to the Novel*, edited by John Colmer, Edinburgh: Oliver and Boyd, 1967
Kiley, Frederick T. and Walter MacDonald (editors), *A Catch-22 Casebook*, New York: Crowell, 1973
Merrill, Robert, *Joseph Heller*, Boston: Twayne, 1987
Nagel, James (editor), *Critical Essays on Catch-22*, Encino, California: Dickenson, 1974
Nagel, James (editor), *Critical Essays on Joseph Heller*, Boston: G.K. Hall, 1984
Pinsker, Sanford, *Understanding Joseph Heller*, Columbia: University of South Carolina Press, 1991
Potts, Stephen W., *From Here to Absurdity: The Moral Battlefields of Joseph Heller*, San Bernardino, California: Borgo Press, 1982
Protherough, Robert, "The Sanity of *Catch-22*", *Human World*, 3 (May 1971)
Searles, George J., "Something Happened: A New Direction", *Critique*, 18/3 (1977)
Seed, David, *The Fiction of Joseph Heller: Against the Grain*, London: Macmillan, and New York: St Martin's Press, 1989

The phrase "Catch 22" has entered the language and is employed by many who do not know of its origin and have never heard of Joseph Heller. This is precisely the kind of paradoxical irony that would have appealed to the author of that ground-breaking book. Particularly as the very title was not his: when Heller proposed "Catch 18", the alternative was suggested by his publisher in order to avoid confusion with Leon Uris's *Mila 18* which was published the same year.

By breaking the conventions of war novels *Catch-22* rapidly achieved cult status despite early critical puzzlement. The book is a literary *tour de force*, and its time shifts, its apparent irreverence, its deadly serious comedy, anticipated much of what came to be regarded as postmodernist techniques. It was also, as was much of Heller's subsequent work, a howl of rage against post-industrial American consumerist society as much as it was an anti-war novel. And, also in common with his later work, it drew on classical Greek and Roman models.

Despite the fact that in his most famous novel there is no Jewish character (although in an early draft the Yossarian character was meant to be a Jew), and although Heller had a totally secular upbringing in Brighton Beach, which he has referred to as a neighbourhood with no "Jewish hangups", and taking into account that he was never bar-mitzvahed, he is nonetheless an essentially Jewish writer. When Leo Rosten wrote in *The Joys of Yiddish* that Yiddish "loves the ruminative, because it rests on a rueful past; it favors paradox, because it knows that only paradox can do justice to the injustices of life; adores irony, because the only way the Jews could retain their sanity was to view a dreadful world with sardonic, astringent eyes", he could have been describing the Heller style and approach.

Heller has explained that when writing *Catch-22* he:

> . . . wanted somebody who would seem to be *outside* the culture in every way – ethnically as well as others. I wanted to get an extinct culture, somebody who could not be identified either geographically, or culturally, or sociologically – somebody who has a capability of divorcing himself completely from all emotional and psychological ties.

Hence Yossarian the Armenian. In this way Heller broke the mould of previous war novels (even when those novels, like his, were as much comments on the America of the postwar years in which they were written), for instance, Mailer's *The Naked and the Dead* with its gallery of representative ethnic types, or Hemingway's *A Farewell to Arms*, where a romantic attachment results in a rejection of conventional patriotism. Fundamentally, his work is mordant, describing with satire, irony, and paradox a lousy world full of pain, disease, corruption, and suffering, where there are no saints or angels only "people cashing in on every decent impulse and every human tragedy". It is a viewpoint that was barely modified in what turned out to be a considerable body of work.

Though the viewpoint was retained it was expressed with greater specificity, both of location and character. In Heller's next novel, *Something Happened*, his protagonist, Slocum, exists in a recognizable context (the world of publishing and advertising) and reacts to its values with recognizable discontent, boredom, and ambivalence. In representing the flatness of Slocum's life some feel that Heller's prose was too mimetic, producing a similar effect on its readers.

With *Good as Gold*, his third novel, Heller introduces specifically Jewish characters in a particularly Jewish situation – the attempt to assimilate and take on the values of an essentially WASP culture. The novel contrasts Gold's private life, in a family descended from immigrants, with his public life in the Washington corridors of power. Typically he finds humorous paradox in the behaviour of the family – proud of their Jewish cookery but eating pork in Chinese restaurants, the father scrupulously observing the High holidays while proudly declaring himself an atheist, and so on. But it is in Gold's attempts to break into the Washington establishment and absorb its values that Heller depicts both the emptiness of those values and the ultimate barrenness of the Jews embracing, and assimilating into, the American way of life. To emphasize the Jewish specificity of the theme Heller has Gold writing a book using his experiences as a paradigm of the Jewish experience in America, including his confrontation with the anti-Semitism of his putative WASP father-in-law.

God Knows, Heller's next novel, is a rewriting of the Old Testament story of David told in the first person. It was initially poorly received by most American reviewers who thought it too flippant for the theme it tried to carry, but with the passing years Heller's ability to deal with serious topics through outrageous humour has come to be seen for what it is – like so much Jewish humour an attempt to express what would otherwise be inexpressible. David is constantly questioning God's authority, his omniscience, and his omnipotence, until God himself is led to expostulate "If you want to have sense, you can't have a religion", and in response to David's complaint that it all makes no sense, God asks "Where is it written it should make sense?" Another device Heller employs is to give David a particularly Yiddish voice when he is undermining especially fundamental aspects of the biblical story – such as the idea of a covenant.

Fundamentally these techniques – based as has been said on an essentially Yiddish tradition – underlay all Heller's fiction, including his plays, and his last two novels. *Picture This*, written after he had recovered from his battle with the Guillain-Barre Syndrome, draws parallels between three civilizations at the height of their power – Greece in the time of Aristotle, the Netherlands in the time of Rembrandt, and contemporary America – and illustrates the ubiquity and consistency of human greed and self-interest, and the elites' manipulation of social institutions. In much the same way as he did with the Old Testament in *God Knows*, Heller manipulates famous texts in order to question their conclusions. This time the sources include Plato, Plutarch, Thucydides, and Xenophon. The book also contains many of Heller's trademark insights expressed as apparent paradox – "Peace on earth would mean the end of civilization as we know it."

Closing Time is a sequel to *Catch-22* in so far as it explores what has happened to some of the main characters from the earlier novel (especially Yossarian and Minderbinder) in the intervening 33 years. And what has happened is compromise. Yossarian has now joined with Minderbinder, accepting that if the dire fate of most is to be avoided, and even a half-way good life achieved, money is essential. Not that Heller's mordancy has modified. As in the first novel he draws a Dantesque portrait of the hell of modern city life in sections that are positively apocalyptic. By introducing characters not in the first book he is also able to enter Philip Roth territory and portray the lives of second-generation American Jews.

To the end paradox was a prime constituent of Heller's work and even of reactions to it. In 1999 he published a poorly received (with some exceptions) autobiographical work, *Now and Then*, and his last novel, *Portrait of an Artist, as an Old Man*, traces the agonies and difficulties of an ageing novelist (Eugene Pota) faced with the loss of creative energy and inspiration. While the autobiography presented an unconvincing, self-satisfied portrait of the artist settling contentedly into an old age enhanced by past achievements, the novel's protagonist, who might be part-Jewish and is the same age as Heller, is haunted by the fact that appreciation of his work has always been limited by comparison with his first outstanding success. He now wishes to write one final acclaimed bestseller but can only come up with titles, fragments, or ideas which either he or others have already mined out. Many feel that Eugene Pota is closer to Heller than the subject of the autobiography. While by no means Heller's best work *Portrait of an Artist, as an Old Man* is entertaining, thought-provoking, and has many typical tropes, such as the rewriting from a new point of view of biblical and classical stories.

If Heller never departed from his view that the human predicament was hopeless, he also maintained that we can still have a lot of laughs on our pointless journey, and supplied more than his share of them. Like his fictional Eugene Pota his body of work has often been overshadowed by the remarkable achievement of *Catch-22*, and one would like to believe that his reported response when being charged with never having written any thing as good – "Who has?" – was another example of his sardonic irony. In truth he produced a body of work which in its innovations, its perceptions, and its literary skills, stands comparison with that of the very best of his contemporaries.

GERALD DE GROOT

Hellman, Lillian

US dramatist and fiction writer, 1906–1984

Born in New Orleans, 20 June 1906, to Max Bernard Hellman, businessman, and wife Julia (née Newhouse). Studied at New York University and Columbia University. Married Arthur Kober, writer, 1925; divorced, 1932. Worked as reader, Horace Liveright publishers, New York, 1924–25; theatrical play reader, New York, 1927–30. Began long relationship with crime novelist and screenwriter Dashiell Hammett, 1930. Scenario reader, Metro-Goldwyn-Mayer, Hollywood, 1930–31; part-time play reader for producer Harold Shulman, 1932. Directed plays in New York, including *Another Part of the Forest*, 1946, and *Montserrat*, 1949. Taught at Yale University, 1966, and at Harvard University, Massachusetts Institute of Technology, and University of California. Contributed articles to *Collier's*, *New York Times*, *Travel and Leisure*, and other publications. Member, American Academy of Arts and Sciences, 1960; Vice-President, National Institute of Arts and Letters, 1962. Numerous awards, including New York Drama Critics Circle Award, 1941, 1960; Brandeis University Creative Arts Medal in Theater, 1960; American Academy Gold Medal, 1964; National Book Award 1970; Paul Robeson Award and MacDowell Medal, both 1976. Died in Martha's Vineyard, Massachusetts, 30 June 1984.

Selected Writings

Plays
The Children's Hour, 1934
Days to Come, 1936
The Little Foxes, 1939
Watch on the Rhine, 1941
Four Plays, 1942
The Searching Wind, 1944
Another Part of the Forest, 1947
Montserrat, 1949
Regina, 1949
The Autumn Garden, 1951
The Lark, 1955
Candide, 1957 (first performed 1956)
Six Plays, 1960
Toys in the Attic, 1960
My Mother, My Father and Me, 1963
The Collected Plays, 1972

Screenplays: *Dark Angel*, with Mordaunt Shairp, 1935; *These Three*, 1936; *Dead End*, 1937; *The Little Foxes*, 1941; *The North Star*, 1943; *Watch on the Rhine*, with Dashiell Hammett, 1943; *The Searching Wind*, 1946; *The Chase*, 1966

Other
An Unfinished Woman, 1969
Pentimento: A Book of Portraits, 1972
Scoundrel Time, 1976
Three (includes *An Unfinished Woman*, *Pentimento: A Book of Portraits*, *Scoundrel Time*), 1979
Maybe: A Story, 1980
Eating Together: Recollections and Recipes, with Peter Feibleman, 1984

Further Reading

Adams, Timothy Dow, *Telling Lies in Modern American Autobiography*, Chapel Hill: University of North Carolina Press, 1990
Adler, Jacob Henry, *Lillian Hellman*, Austin, Texas: Steck Vaughn, 1969
Adler Jacob Henry, "Modern Southern Drama" in *The History of Southern Literature*, edited by Louis D. Rubin, Jr *et al.*, Baton Rouge: Louisiana State University Press, 1985
Austin, Gayle, "The Exchange of Women and Male Homosocial Social Desire in Arthur Miller's *Death of a Salesman* and Lillian Hellman's *Another Part of the Forest*" in *Feminist Rereadings of Modern American*

Drama, edited by June Schlueter, Rutherford, New Jersey: Fairleigh Dickinson University Press, 1989
Dick, Bernard F., *Hellman in Hollywood*, Rutherford, New Jersey: Fairleigh Dickinson University Press, 1982
Dillon, Ann and Cynthia Bix, *Theater*, Minneapolis: Dillon Press, 1978 (*Contributions of Women* series)
Estrin, Mark W. (editor), *Critical Essays on Lillian Hellman*, Boston: G.K. Hall, 1989
Falk, Doris V., *Lillian Hellman*, New York: Ungar, 1978
Feibleman, Peter S., *Lilly: Reminiscences of Lillian Hellman*, New York: Morrow, 1988
Gassner, John, *Dramatic Soundings*, edited by Glenn Loney, New York: Crown, 1968
Gellhorn, Martha, "On Apocryphism", *Paris Review*, 79 (Spring 1981): 280–301
Georgoudaki, Ekaterini, "Women in Lillian Hellman's Plays, 1930–1950" in *Women and War: The Changing Status of American Women from the 1930s to the 1950s*, edited by Maria Diedrich and Dorothea Fischer-Hornung, New York: Berg, 1990
Gilman, Sander L., *Jewish Self-Hatred: Anti-Semitism and the Hidden Language of the Jews*, Baltimore: Johns Hopkins University Press, 1986
Glazer, Nathan, "An Answer to Lillian Hellman", *Commentary*, 61/6 (June 1976)
Goodman, Charlotte, "The Fox's Cubs: Lillian Hellman, Arthur Miller, and Tennessee Williams" in *Modern American Drama: The Female Canon*, edited by June Schlueter, Rutherford, New Jersey: Fairleigh Dickinson University Press, 1990
Graver, Lawrence, *An Obsession with Anne Frank: Meyer Levin and The Diary*, Berkeley: University of California Press, 1995
Griffin, Alice and Geraldine Thorsten, *Understanding Lillian Hellman*, Columbia: University of South Carolina Press, 1999
Horn, Barbara Lee, *Lillian Hellman: A Research and Production Sourcebook*, Westport, Connecticut: Greenwood Press, 1998
Howe, Irving, "Lillian Hellman and the McCarthy Years", *Dissent*, 23/4 (Autumn 1976)
James, Clive, "It is of a Windiness: Lillian Hellman" in his *At the Pillars of Hercules*, London and Boston: Faber, 1979
Kempton, Murray, "Witnesses: *Scoundrel Time* by Lillian Hellman", *New York Review of Books* (10 June 1976)
Lederer, Katherine, *Lillian Hellman*, Boston: Twayne, 1979
Lenker, Lagretta Tallent, "The Foxes in Hellman's Family Forest" in *The Aching Hearth: Family Violence in Life and Literature*, edited by Sara Munson Deats and Lenker, New York: Insight, 1991
Lyons, Bonnie, "Lillian Hellman: 'The First Jewish Nun on Prytania Street' " in *From Hester Street to Hollywood: The Jewish-American Stage and Screen*, edited by Sarah Blacher Cohen, Bloomington: Indiana University Press, 1983
McCracken, Samuel, "'Julia' and Other Fictions by Lillian Hellman", *Commentary*, 77/6 (June 1984)
Mahoney, Rosemary, *A Likely Story: One Summer with Lillian Hellman*, New York: Doubleday, 1998
Mellen, Joan, *Hellman and Hammett: The Legendary Passion*, New York: HarperCollins, 1996
Melnick, Ralph, *The Stolen Legacy of Anne Frank: Meyer Levin, Lillian Hellman, and the Staging of the Diary*, New Haven, Connecticut: Yale University Press, 1997
Moody, Richard, *Lillian Hellman, Playwright*, New York: Pegasus, 1972
Newman, Robert P., *The Cold War Romance of Lillian Hellman and John Melby*, Chapel Hill: University of North Carolina, 1989
Ozick, Cynthia, "Who Owns Anne Frank?", *New Yorker* (6 October 1997)
Podhoretz, Norman, *Ex-Friends: Falling Out with Allen Ginsberg, Lionel and Diana Trilling, Lillian Hellman, Hannah Arendt, and Norman Mailer*, New York: Free Press, 1999
Rollyson, Carl Edmund, *Lillian Hellman: Her Legend and Her Legacy*, New York: St Martin's Press, 1988
Triesch, Manfred (editor), *Lillian Hellman Collection at the University of Texas*, Austin: University of Texas, 1966
Wright, William, *Lillian Hellman: The Image, The Woman*, New York: Simon and Schuster, 1986

Lillian Hellman was equally famed for left-wing politics and commercial success in theatre and film. Both her parents were assimilated Jews from families who had immigrated to the American South from Germany in the mid-19th century. The world of her Southern childhood is revisited in her best-selling memoirs, *An Unfinished Woman* and *Pentimento*, and in some of her most successful plays, also adapted for film, *The Little Foxes*, *Another Part of the Forest*, *The Autumn Garden*, and *Toys in the Attic*.

She began her literary career as script reader for MGM studios during the Depression era when the flourishing movie industry enticed American writers and artists to Hollywood. Her 30-year relationship with the communist novelist and screenwriter Dashiell Hammett influenced her writing and politics.

In *The Children's Hour*, later filmed as *We Three*, a resentful schoolgirl accuses two teachers of lesbianism. Hellman's acclaimed portrait of the adolescent liar recalls her precocious curiosity about adult sexuality in *An Unfinished Woman*. The tough, outspoken servant present as chorus in most of Hellman's plays is based on her adored nurse Sophronia Mason, who curbed her temper and jealousy. Hellman's abiding need for external controls may have attracted her to Hammett's aloof style of mentorship, and to the discipline of the Communist Party.

The 1952 revival directed by Hellman turned *The Children's Hour* into a powerful allegory of the McCarthy era. Hellman's emphasis on the adult characters' weakness and lack of self-knowledge foreshadowed her accusation in *Scoundrel Time* that liberal intellectuals caved in to childish pranksters.

The political and psychological currents of *The Children's Hour* are echoed in Arthur Miller's *Crucible*. In both plays wayward, manipulative adolescents challenge repressive adults in a primal power struggle coloured by guilt. Children lie to get out of trouble, while adults confront the loss of innocence. In a melodramatic finale, delayed recognition of forbidden desire for Karen destroys Martha. Miller's protagonist has time to resolve his dual struggle against political injustice and personal unworthiness.

As a dramatist, Hellman gained more from analysis than from Marxism. *Days to Come* and *The Searching Wind* were "mechanical thesis drama[s]". In *Days to Come* the liberal factory owner and his loyal workers delude themselves that friendship and decency can prevail during a strike. A cynical labour organizer resembling Hammett forecasts the historically determined outcome.

Watch on the Rhine, a dated propaganda play encouraging American entry into World War II, was a popular success. Hostile reviews by the Communist Party (which backtracked after Germany invaded Russia) support Hellman's argument that she was "nobody's girl", i.e. too much of a maverick to be a party member. However both her biographers, Rollyson and Wright, found evidence of her membership. *Watch on the Rhine* reflects Hellman's reading of Henry James's novels *The Europeans* and *The American*. German resistance leader Kurt Miller cold-bloodedly murders a blackmailer in the home of his liberal American in-laws, confronting them with hard wartime choices. In supporting Kurt, they commit to the anti-fascist cause. Hellman's usual contempt for liberals is deflected to the decadent aristocratic blackmailer, a Romanian diplomat whose "neutrality" is a cover for profiteering.

The hero, Miller, is explicitly not Jewish. Fearing an anti-Semitic backlash, most Allied propaganda conspicuously avoided any hint of a "Jewish war". Hellman also displays the Marxist preference for universalizing oppression. A single obscure reference to "the tailor in Lodz" slotted among victims of all races and nationalities, is the closest she gets to mentioning the Holocaust in *Watch on the Rhine*. In *The Searching Wind* a vividly evoked offstage pogrom in 1923 Berlin is blamed on German big business and worked into her thesis that US neutrality encouraged the rise of European fascism.

Hellman had a role in the 1950s stage and screen adaptation of Anne Frank's diary. Blacklisted by Hollywood, Hellman feared her authorship could damage the play, instead nominating and assisting comedy writers Frances Goodrich and Albert Hackett. The Zionist author Meyer Levin blamed Hellman's ideology for the "feel-good" revisionism of the authorized stage version, which consistently minimized Anne's strong Jewish identification and the particularity of Jewish persecution.

Apart from her politics, Hellman was noted for the perfectionism of her craft. In the 1930s she gave Ibsen's naturalistic form contemporary currency as black comedy or melodrama with sophisticated dialogue and daring characterizations, especially of women. *The Little Foxes*, staged with Tallulah Bankhead and filmed with Bette Davis, was one of the biggest theatre and screen hits of that era. It was based on her observation of her mother's wealthy business and banking family. Initially scandalized, Hellman later found their "greed and . . . cheating . . . comic as well as evil and . . . began to enjoy the family dinners with the talk of who did what to whom". In *The Little Foxes* the Hubbards were of the ruthless Southern nouveau riche business class. But their exploitation of the defeated aristocracy and the black Americans was secondary to their internal power struggles. Regina Giddens schemed against her no-good brothers and her dying husband to escape suffocating small-town life. She denied her husband life-saving medicine, but according to Hellman's biographer, William Wright, audiences adored her because she was "smart, goodlooking, and funny". Descended from Ibsen's Nora and Hedda Gabler, she was one of the strong, sexual women of 1930s noir film and fiction.

Hellman's later plays experimented stylistically. *The Autumn Garden* was full of retrospective Chekhovian melancholy. The mix of incestuous possessiveness, sex, and violence in *Toys in the Attic* was closer to the Southern Gothic of Tennessee Williams. In response to new Jewish writing (Bellow, Malamud, Philip Roth), Hellman wrote a crude, shortlived Jewish farce, *My Mother, My Father and Me*, in 1963 with Walter Matthau in the lead role.

In the 1960s and early 1970s, Hellman's popularity and public stature grew. In 1970 she mobilized her remarkable social network to create an influential, broadly based political organization: the Committee for Public Justice sponsored important conferences on the FBI and on Watergate.

The mannered throwaway style of Hellman's memoirs, *An Unfinished Woman*, *Pentimento*, and *Scoundrel Time*, derived from Hemingway and Hammett (James). A skilled raconteur, she took dramatic liberties in quirky, celebrity-studded vignettes of friendships, fights, and affairs in the turbulent 1930s. Her political adventures included visiting the Spanish Civil War; Russia in 1937 and again in 1944; an undercover mission to her friend "Julia" in the German resistance, filmed with Vanessa Redgrave, Jane Fonda, and Jason Robards in 1976; and her ordeal in the McCarthy era.

Both political and personal anecdotes were subsequently discredited as unreliable, fantastic, self-serving, and meanly disparaging of others. (Gellhorn, James, McCracken, Howe *et al.*) Like the Julia story, her nightmare visit to Maidanek concentration camp on the Russian front line was fictitious posturing. Controversy intensified when Hellman blamed American liberals for McCarthyism, the Vietnam War, and Watergate in *Scoundrel Time*. Her admired defiance of the House Unamerican Activities Committee ("I cannot and will not cut my conscience to fit this year's fashions") and her subsequent Hollywood blacklisting and financial problems were not as unusual as she claimed.

Her accusation that Hollywood studio bosses cooperated with McCarthy because they were "children of timid immigrants", or "born in foreign lands" with "inherited foreign fears", and that (unlike herself) these Jews didn't see themselves as "American citizens with inherited rights and obligations" verged on anti-Semitism. While implying that Jews were more compromised by McCarthyism than others, her own well-documented support for the "sins of Stalin communism", long after other 1930s radicals had repented, was airbrushed in a couple of nonchalant asides.

Maybe, a slight autobiographical work reflecting on the blurred boundaries of memory, fantasy, and truth, was published shortly after Hellman sued Mary McCarthy for defamation for stating on *The Dick Cavett Show* that every word Hellman had written was a lie including "and" and "the". By then Hellman was ailing and nearly blind and the case lapsed with her death. It was an ironic finale for an author whose career was launched by a play about the destructiveness of lies.

FELICITY BLOCH

Hendel, Yehudit

Polish-born Israeli fiction writer, 1926–

Born in Warsaw, 1926, into rabbinic family. Emigrated to Palestine, 1930; settled in Haifa, moved to Kibbutz Gesher, then returned to Haifa. Married Zvi Meirovitz; two children. Awarded many literary prizes, including Jerusalem Prize, Prime Minister's Prize, Bialik Prize.

Selected Writings

Stories

Anashim aherim hem: sipurim [They Are Different], 1950

Kesef katan [Small Change], 1988

"Tapuhim bidvash", as "Apples in Honey", translated by Barbara Harshav, in *Ribcage: Israeli Women's Fiction*, edited by Carol Diament and Lily Rattok, 1994

"The Letter That Came in Time" in *Stories from Women Writers of Israel*, 1995

Aruhat boker temimah [An Innocent Breakfast], 1996

"A Story with No Address" in *The Oxford Book of Hebrew Short Stories*, edited by Glenda Abramson, 1996

"My Friend B's Feast" in *New Women's Writing from Israel*, edited by Risa Domb, 1996

Novels

Rehov hamadregot, 1956; as *Street of Steps*, translated by Rachel Katz and David Segal, 1963

Hahamsin Haaharon or *Hahatser shel momo hagedolah* [The Last Hamsin or The Yard of Momo the Great], 1969; as *Hahamsin haaharon* [The Last Hamsin], 1993

Hakoah Haaher [The Other Power], 1984

Har hatoim [The Mountain of Losses], 1991

Plays

The Street of Steps, 1958

Small Change, 1990

Other

Leyad kefarim shketim [Near Quiet Places], 1987

12 Days in Poland (series of radio programmes), 1987

Further Reading

Hoffman, Anne, "The Private, The Mundane, The Banal", *Modern Hebrew Literature*, new series, 13 (Autumn 1994)

Litwin, Rina, "The Subtext of Bereavement, The Mountain of Losses", *Modern Hebrew Literature*, new series, 8 (Spring–Autumn 1992)

Peninah, Shirav, *Ketivah Lo Tamah: 'Emdat Siha Vi-Yitsuge Nashiyut Bi-Yetsirotam Shel Yehudit Hendel, 'Amalyah Kahana-Karmon Ve Rut Almog* [Non-Innocent Writing: Discourse, Position and Female Representations in Works by Yehudit Hendel, Amalia Kahana-Carmon and Ruth Almog], Tel Aviv: Hakibuts hameuhad, 1998

Samuel, Rina, in *New York Times Book Review* (8 December 1963)

Wallenrod, Reuben, *The Literature of Modern Israel*, New York: Abelard Schuman, 1956

Yehoshua, Abraham B., "On the Other Power", *Modern Hebrew Literature* (Summer 1986)

Born in Warsaw, Yehudit Hendel moved to Israel in 1930 and grew up in Haifa. She now lives in Tel Aviv. Her first stories emerged at a time in Israel's literary history when women's writing was a barely known phenomenon. She was among the first women writers to become known after the establishment of the State of Israel. At every stage her writing examines the uncomfortable issues of society, from cultural tensions to the feminist struggle for autonomy and self-esteem. The theme of bereavement pervades her writing, and accounts for its sometimes grotesque, sometimes disturbing representation of women's plight.

Themes of alienation and difference appear in Hendel's work written from the early 1950s in the form of conflict within Israeli society. She presents the misunderstandings between people from Ashkenazi (western) and Sephardi (eastern) backgrounds. She looks closely at clashes of expectation and approach between the new immigrants in Israel, who are frequently survivors of the Holocaust bringing with them their burdens of trauma, and the sabras, those born in Israel and possessing a different collective awareness. Her literary heritage can be traced back both to Yosef Hayyim Brenner, with his self-deprecating realism, and to Mendele Moykher Sforim, with his moral tales of the grotesque. She captures the dialogue of the different social and cultural groups with skilful use of heteroglossia.

Although there have been some long gaps in the course of Hendel's writing, at each phase she re-emerges with her focus firmly on contemporary concerns. Thus she moves from her earlier persona as a writer within the Palmach generation to take her place as a significant feminist writer. She first explores the issues confronting the new state as it moves from great collective idealism towards a certain disillusionment, and later shifts her focus to the individual. Her second novel, *The Yard of Momo the Great* (republished later as *The Last Hamsin*), explores the difficulties in forging personal connections. Men are portrayed with great hostility, breaking off relationships and escaping responsibility, leaving behind women unfulfilled, damaged.

Two major events in her private life form a thread running through Hendel's work: her mother's death when Hendel was a young adolescent, and much later, the loss of her husband Zvi Meirovitch. The theme of absent mother is presented in various ways, accompanied by a sense of loss and profound sadness. One key image is the young protagonist looking at her reflection in the mirror, imagining a fleeting glimpse of her mother and struggling to recollect her clear likeness. In a second recurring demonstration the author explores the complex oedipal relationship between father and daughter. The mother figure is either absent, or present and constrained, silenced, as in the eponymous story from the collection *Small Change*. In this particularly grotesque story passions and relationships are twisted, fraught with Expressionist angst. Male cruelty and dispassion for women are presented in nightmarish sequences. The result throughout her work is an overwhelming absence of female self-esteem.

In the book *The Other Power* Hendel pays homage to her beloved husband, through this biographical tribute developing an autobiographical self-awareness. Hendel's next novel *The Mountain of Losses* transfers the intensity of personal bereavement onto a national scale while retaining the intimacy of individual experience. In a country founded on the sacrifice of so many lives, the bereaved families often have to repress the pain of their loss. This work looks at life in the shadow of the death of loved ones, especially parents losing their sons in war. It opens up the Akeda Complex, parents "sacrificing" their children, the unnatural death of the young, plus the recurring effort to find meaning or responsibility for it all. The strength of this work is that Hendel finds a language to express this experience with sensitivity and complexity.

Hendel juxtaposes relentless inner motion with a static plot: she portrays the conversations and activities of those who meet at the military cemetery. The novel is organized around a central lyrical format and a complex set of images: legends, myth, fragments of memory, midrashic quotations on the enigma of human destiny, of life after death. This is a shared experience for Israeli society, indivisible by social, economic, or cultural differences. Bereavement is unifying in its awe and profound sadness. The story "Tapuhim bidvash" ("Apples in Honey") from the collection *Aruchat boker temimah* [An Innocent Breakfast] spotlights the widow of a fallen soldier, tending his grave once a year. The desire for living contact among those bereaved by war is sublimated: distracted and frenetic gardening creates a substitute bond with the gravestone and all it denotes.

Hendel returns to the theme of female desolation in many of her short stories. Women are manipulated and undermined by their male partners, struggling through domestic rituals that barely conceal an empty existence, a living death. "There are lots of synonyms for Hell" shouts the protagonist B in "My Friend B's Feast". B, dying of cancer, persists in frantically observing all the details of a full final dinner at home, with her husband's new lover already deliberately in place. The first-person narrator, the observer of these appalling rituals, cannot properly remember the conversations. "I didn't know what to say", is her refrain to most of B's comments in the face of such pain. Even B's full name is already lost, communication is dislocated, all is in the gesture, the unspoken effort.

"The Letter That Came in Time" reinforces the sense of nightmare. Michaela is seen determined to continue the details of the repast after the death of her husband. But as Michaela tries to repress her pain and deny her vulnerability, their intensity overwhelm her. The narrator presents the accumulation of events, her "perfect behaviour", her "strength" in the face of death, her determination to answer everyone's physical needs, leading to the inevitable tragic conclusion. Hendel adds here a postmodern touch with the narrator questioning "I don't know why I'm telling the details . . . the story after all everyone knew . . . only in different versions". A woman's life is defined by her husband's achievements, and without him she too is lost.

In "A Story with No Address" Hendel tells a modern tale of the absurd. Here the theme is centred on sheer dislocation and loneliness. Disembodied voices shriek, a grotesque cacophony of hollow communication fills the air. Both in death and in life the characters seem to be quite alone with their possessions, devoid of meaningful human contact. This impression is heightened when only the dog feels any sense of attachment to the unnamed woman "with no address". Through the technique of free association the narrator paints a leitmotif of sudden and unexplained death. First the poet Paul Celan is remembered, and then the theme of absent mother is repeated, as she recalls her mother's last conversations, and ethereal passing away. "I remembered my mother once told me there is no need to be afraid of the dead". Yet in this story death seems unfathomable, disjointed, without bringing a sense of closure or completeness.

Hendel's literature presents her world view as expressively bleak and angry. She subverts any romantic myth of female fulfilment in love. Quotidian life continues relentlessly in the face of rejection. Often the love affair itself is communicated without dialogue, an ephemeral memory, leaving women with destabilized lives, tainted by suspicions and premonitions. Their search for personal self-worth is defeated by shameful silence.

TAMARA LEVINE

Herzberg, Judith

Dutch poet and dramatist, 1934–

Born in Amsterdam, 4 November 1934, daughter of lawyer and writer Abel Herzberg. Went into hiding during World War II. Studied at Montessori Lyceum, graduated 1952. Divorced; two children. Became teacher at film schools in Amsterdam, in Jerusalem, and at University of Leiden. Has lived alternately in Ramat Gan, Israel, and in Amsterdam since 1983. Awarded Jan Campert Prize 1980, 1981; Bayerische Filmpreis, 1980; Theatre Critics Prize, 1981; Joost van den Vondel Prize, 1984; Charlotte Kohler Prize, 1988; Cestodaprijs, 1988; Nederlands–Vlaamse Toneelschrijfprijs, 1989; Constantijn Huygens Prize, 1995; P.C. Hooft Award (for poetry), 1997.

Selected Writings

Poetry
Zeepost [Slow Boat], 1963
Beemdgras [Meadow Grass], 1968
Vliegen [Flies], 1970
Strijklicht [Grazing Light], 1971
27 liefdesliedjes [27 Love Songs], 1971
Botshol [Hit and Run], 1980
Dagrest [Remains of the Day], 1984
Twintig gedichten [Twenty Poems], 1984
But What: Selected Poems, translated by Shirley Kaufman and Judith Herzberg, 1988

Zoals [As], 1992
Doen en laten [Doings], 1994
Wat zij wilde schilderen [What She Meant to Paint], 1998
Bijvangst [Small Catch], 1999
In *The Shape of Houses: Women's Voices From Holland and Flanders*, translated by Manfred Wolf, 1974; *Quartet: An Anthology of Dutch and Flemish Poetry*, edited by Konrad Hopkins and Ronald van Roekel, 1978; *Nine Dutch Poets*, 1982; *Dutch Interior: Postwar Poetry of the Netherlands and Flanders*, edited by James S. Holmes and William Jay Smith, 1984; *The Defiant Muse: Dutch and Flemish Feminist Poetry from the Middle Ages to the Present: A Bilingual Anthology*, edited by Maaike Meijer, 1998

Plays
Naar Archangel [To Archangel], 1971
De deur stond open [The Door was Open], 1972
Het is geen hond [It is Not a Dog], 1973
Dat het's ochtends ochtend wordt [That Day May Dawn], 1974
Cranky Box, 1975
Leedvermaak [Gloating], 1982; as *The Wedding Party*, translated by Rina Bergano, 1997
De val van Icarus [The Fall of Icarus], 1983
En/Of [And/Or], 1985
Die kleine Zeemeermin [The Little Mermaid], 1986
Merg [Marrow], 1986
De Caracal, 1988; as *The Caracal*, translated by Rina Bergano, 1997
De tijd en het vertrek [Time and Departure], 1989
Kras, 1989; as *Scratch*, translated by John Rudge, 1995
Lulu: de doos van Pandora [Lulu: Pandora's Box], 1989
Het Zuiden [The South], 1990
De zomer van Aviya [Aviya's Summer], 1991
Een goed hoofd [A Good Head], 1991
Teksten voor toneel en film, 1972–1988 [Texts for the Stage and Film, 1972–1988], 1991
Rijgdraad [Sewing Thread], 1995
De Nietsfabriek [The Nothing Factory], 1997

Screenplays: *Rooie Sien* [Red Sien], 1975; *Een vrouw als Eva* [A Woman like Eva], 1979; *Twee vrouwen* [Two Women], 1979; *Charlotte* [Charlotte], 1980; *Leedvermaak* [Gloating], 1989; *Qui Vive* [On Your Guard], 2002

Television Plays: *Het Hooglied* [Song of Songs], 1971; *Lieve Arthur* [Dear Arthur], 1976

Other
Het maken van gedichten en het praten daarover [The Making of Poems and the Talking about Them], 1977
Charlotte: dagboek bij een film [Charlotte: Diary with a Film], 1981
Dat Engels geen au heeft [That English has No Word For], 1985
Hoe de oorlog is verdwenen [How the War Disappeared], 1986
Tussen Amsterdam en Tel Aviv: artikelen en brieven [Between Amsterdam and Tel Aviv: Articles and Letters], 1988
Brief aan wie niet hier is [Letter to Someone Who is Not Here], 1996

Translator of books by Henrik Ibsen, Peter Vos, Uri Orlev, among others

Further Reading
Balk-Smit Duyzentkunst, Frida, "Getransformeerde directe rede en toch geen indirecte rede: over de grammatica en poética van Judith Herzberg", *Forum der Letteren*, 24 (1983)
Coninck, Herman de, *Over de troost van pessimisme*, Antwerp: Manteau, 1983
Fokkema, R.L.K., in *Kritisch lexicon van de Nederlandstalige literatur na 1945*, edited by Ad Zuiderent, Alphen aan den Rijn: Samson, 1980
Guépin, J.P., *In een Moeilijke Houding Geschreven Opstellen*, The Hague: Baaker/Daamen, 1969
Kunkeler, J., "Judith Herzberg: het blijft Gaan Om Het Weefsel Van de Taal" (interview), *De Tijd* (29 September 1979)
Moeyart, Bart "Sober: over Judith Herzberg", *De Gids: Nieuwe Vaderlandsche Letteroefeningen*, 161/5 (1998)
Poll, K.L., *De eigen vorm: essays over poezie*, Amsterdam: Meulenhoff, 1967
Ritsma, Anneke, "Medeplichege aan het Leven: niewe poëzie van Judith Herzberg", *Ons Erfdeel*, 40/2 (1997)
Zuiderent, Ad (editor), *Jan Campert Prijzen 1994*, Baarn, Netherlands: Uitgeverij De Prom, 1994

Dutch children learn in school that poetry is a question of reading between the lines: just read, it doesn't say what it says, in the words of the famous poet Martinus Nijhoff. This statement seems particularly applicable to the work of Judith Herzberg. Her literary trademark is a seemingly simple observation of something in ordinary life. Her poetry resembles nothing more elaborate than thoughts that come to her about things she sees around her. So deceptively simple, and on closer consideration so incredibly subtle.

She herself says about her poetic talent that she learned to observe so carefully during the time that she spent with host families. A greater euphemism seems impossible. It is the mimicry of a Jewish child who has to adapt continually to new hiding parents, brothers and sisters, new customs, and new surroundings. Survival may depend on it.

Herzberg does not talk much about her work, and preferably not at all with journalists. "It is not my intention to show myself in my poems, but rather to show what I see. I don't have the need to put everything in poetry. There are certain things that present themselves as poetry, and others don't. I don't consider myself a poet. I still don't have the feeling that I'm a poet. I'm simply myself, and once in a while I write a poem. But it isn't my identity or anything."

Herzberg was born in Amsterdam in 1934, the youngest daughter of Abel and Thea Herzberg. Her father was a lawyer and a well-known Zionist who by himself managed to fill many a Zionist magazine with his writings. After the war, Abel Herzberg became a well-known and loved author of novels and essays. In 1943, the Herzberg family was torn apart; the children went into hiding, the parents landed in

Westerbork and then Bergen-Belsen where they survived the war.

Judith drifted from one hiding family to the next. She was 11 years old when she had to part from her hiding parents to return to her real parents, a traumatic experience. In 1945, her older brother and sister left for Palestine; Judith remained behind with her parents in shattered postwar Jewish Amsterdam. In the 1950s she married and had two children, and, under the shadow cast by her well-known father, she cautiously began publishing poems here and there. In 1963 her first volume of poetry, *Zeepost*, was published and was followed by many more. Herzberg's poetry can be read on many levels. The simple comments about day-to-day worries in and around a house with family and friends often contain strange paradoxes that unsettle quick conclusions about the meaning of the poems.

In the 1970s she began writing scenarios for television, film scripts, and plays, with increasing success. The 1980 script for *Charlotte* was awarded the Bayerische Film Preis. The play *Leedvermaak* (*The Wedding Party*) received an absorbing production in 1982; in the Netherlands it is considered to be the best play of the 1980s. Herzberg won critical acclaim and the director Leonard Frank was also much honoured. The performance – in which there is much singing in addition to the spoken text – has the structure of a wedding party. During the evening, a dozen guests are celebrating the marriage of Lea with Nico, her third and his second marriage. Both of them experienced World War II as children, just like their friends and contemporaries. Her parents, his father, her hiding mother, and his stepmother are also marked by the war. The party degenerates into emotional chaos during which Lea and Nico cannot but conclude that their marriage will never work. Meanwhile, all the family members, friends, and exes give their opinions: conversations and monologues – sometimes sung – in which the dilemmas of two generations of Dutch Jews and Christians are revealed. "They don't know how they should live and they cover that with lox", says one of the characters about those present, an apparently simple observation that resonates in one's memory – vintage Herzberg.

The play was also performed in Germany. In the Netherlands it was made into a film by Frans Weisz, the director with whom Herzberg had in 1980 made *Charlotte*, a film about the life and work of the German painter Charlotte Salomon. There followed other successful performances of plays: *En/Of* [And/Or], a play about the hypocrisy of an eternal triangle; and *Kras* (*Scratch*), about an old lady who thinks that someone is continually breaking into her house. Like many of her generation, she chooses – consciously or not – not to write solely about Jewish themes and Jewish characters.

In 1995 Herzberg wrote *Rijgdraad* [Sewing Thread], a sequel to *The Wedding Party*, with the same director and actors. The world premiere in Amsterdam was a cultural event that even made the German press. A journalist from *Die Zeit* was present and noted that Herzberg had not lost her special talent for putting the Zeitgeist into words. *Rijgdraad* is also a reunion of the characters from *Leedvermaak* in situations that take place years later, but still in a Jewish milieu in which the memory of the Holocaust is present as a matter of course. It is in *Rijgdraad* that for the first time Herzberg puts Jews on the stage who assert their Jewishness, with yarmulke and all. Like *Leedvermaak* 10 years previously, *Rijgdraad* too was made into a film by Herzberg and her regular collaborator, director Franz Weisz. *Qui Vive* [On Your Guard] premiered in February 2002 in Dutch cinemas. The film was subject to mixed reviews.

At present Herzberg has created the best of two worlds for herself. She lives by turns in Amsterdam and in Israel. She regularly writes about her experiences in Israel for Dutch weeklies. These very personal observations have also been collected and published in books. In one of the very few interviews that she has ever permitted, she said that the distance from the Dutch language keeps her sharp as a poet. In Israel she hears no Dutch around her; a greater concentration on the right word and the right phrase takes the place of the natural presence of language.

DAPHNE MEIJER
translated by Jeannette Ringold

Herzl, Theodor

Austrian essayist, dramatist, and Zionist activist, 1860–1904

Born in Pest, 2 May 1860. Studied law in Vienna, 1878–84; worked as legal clerk in Vienna and Salzburg, 1884–85. Plays produced at Burgtheater, Vienna, from 1885. Turned to journalism; Paris correspondent for *Neue Freie Presse*, including coverage of trial of Alfred Dreyfus, 1891–95; returned to Vienna to join feuilleton section of *Neue Freie Presse*. Founded weekly Zionist newspaper, *Die Welt*, 1897; convened First World Zionist Congress, Basel, 1897; instituted yearly world Zionist congresses; President, World Zionist Organization. Died in Edlach, Austria, 3 January 1904

Selected Writings

Plays
Tabarin, 1884
Die Wilddiebe [The Poachers], 1887
Der Flüchtling [The Refugee], 1888
Seine Hoheit [His Highness], 1888
Die Glosse [The Commentary], 1894
Das neue Ghetto, 1895; as *The New Ghetto*, translated by Heinz Norden, 1955
Unser Käthchen [Our Little Katy], 1898

Fiction
Altneuland, 1902; as *Old-New Land*, translated by Jacob de Haas in *The Maccabaean*, 1902–03; translated by Lotta Levensohn, 1941; translated by Paul Arnold, 1960
Philosophische Erzählungen [Philosophical Tales], 1919

Essays
Der Judenstaat, 1896; as *The Jewish State: An Attempt at a Modern Solution of the Jewish Question*, translated by Sylvie d'Avigdor, 1896; translated by Harry Zohn, 1970

Der Baseler Congress, 1897; as *The Congress Address*, translated by Nell Straus, 1917
Theodor Herzls Zionistische Schriften, edited by Leon Kellner, 2 vols, 1905; as *Zionist Writings: Essays and Addresses*, translated by Harry Zohn, 1973–75
Feuilletons, 2 vols, 1911
Gesammelte zionistische Werke, 5 vols, 1934–35

Other
Theodor Herzls Tagebücher, 1895–1904, 3 vols, 1922–23; as *Complete Diaries of Theodor Herzl*, translated by Harry Zohn, 5 vols, 1960
Theodor Herzl: Briefe und Tagebücher, edited by Alex Bein, 7 vols, 1983–96

Further Reading

Avineri, Shlomo, *The Making of Modern Zionism*, New York: Basic Books, 1981
Bein, Alex, *Theodore Herzl: A Biography*, translated by Maurice Samuel, Philadelphia: Jewish Publication Society of America, 1940
Beller, Steven, *Herzl*, London: Halban, 1990; New York: Grove Weidenfeld, 1991
Berkowitz, Michael, *Zionist Culture and West European Jewry before the First World War*, Cambridge and New York: Cambridge University Press, 1993
Brude-Firnau, Gisela, "The Author, Feuilletonist, and Renowned Foreign Correspondent Theodor Herzl Turns toward Zionism and Writes the Manifesto *The Jewish State*" in *The Yale Companion to Jewish Writing and Thought in German Culture, 1096–1996*, edited by Sander L. Gilman and Jack Zipes, New Haven, Connecticut and London: Yale University Press, 1997
Bunzl, Matti, "The Poetics of Politics and the Politics of Poetics: Richard Beer-Hofmann and Theodor Herzl Reconsidered", *German Quarterly*, 69/3 (1996)
Elon, Amos, *Herzl*, New York: Holt Rinehart, 1975
Gelber, Mark H., "Theodor Herzl, Martin Buber, Berthold Feiwel, and the Young-Jewish Viennese Poets" in *Turn-of-the-Century Vienna and Its Legacy: Essays in Honor of Donald G. Daviau*, edited by Jeffrey B. Berlin *et al.*, Vienna: Atelier, 1993
Robertson, Ritchie, "The Problem of 'Jewish Self-Hatred' in Herzl, Kraus and Kafka", *Oxford German Studies*, 16 (1985)
Stolow, Jeremy, "Utopia and Geopolitics in Theodor Herzl's Altneuland", *Utopian Studies*, 8/1 (1997)
Zohn, Harry, "Herzl Draws International Attention to Zionism, and the Young Vienna Circle Flourishes" in *The Yale Companion to Jewish Writing and Thought in German Culture, 1096–1996*, edited by Sander L. Gilman and Jack Zipes, New Haven, Connecticut and London: Yale University Press, 1997

Theodor Herzl, as the founder of the modern political Zionist movement, established the World Zionist Organization in 1897, which in turn led the way to the establishment of the State of Israel in 1948. However, Herzl was first and foremost a writer and journalist who came late to Jewish political activity. Following his entry into Jewish political life in 1896, he continued to use his literary talents in two separate contexts. First, he carried on his editorial and journalistic work at Vienna's most prestigious newspaper, the *Neue Freie Presse*, until his early death in 1904. Second, he worked as a writer and journalist in the service of the Zionist idea. In 1897 he founded *Die Welt*, originally conceived as an organ that would help lay the groundwork for the technical organization of the First Zionist Congress. Soon *Die Welt* became the Zionist movement's primary journalistic instrument. Herzl contributed literary work to it, recruited editors and other writers to do the same, and thus he put his personal stamp on the nature and quality of the paper. In these ways, he was able to attract to Zionism many young and promising literary and journalistic talents by virtue of his own standing and reputation as an important man of letters in central Europe.

Herzl's literary and journalistic output from the period before he embraced the Zionist cause has receded from cultural memory. After he finished his university studies in jurisprudence and then abandoned the idea of pursuing a legal career, his ambition was to become a successful playwright. He wrote more than a dozen dramatic works in his pre-Zionist phase. Furthermore, he enjoyed certain success, and some of his plays were accepted for performance at the Burgtheater in Vienna and on Prague and Berlin stages as well. His work for the theatre was mostly based on French models of social comedy and satire. Yet, given the subsequent rise of naturalist and expressionist modes of theatre and the hegemony of modernism in terms of canon formation in the 20th century, Herzl's light and witty, but mostly shallow, and ultimately unengaging, comedies have been forgotten. Since he enjoyed only limited success as a dramatist, he decided to change course and devote his energies full time to journalism. During the 1880s and 1890s he wrote travel pieces, short stories, cultural criticism, and essays for several central European newspapers. He adopted the feuilleton style, which Heinrich Heine and Ludwig Börne had popularized earlier in the century. This writing projected an urbane, cosmopolitan, and witty authorial voice which freely and ironically, yet personally, critiqued various aspects of political life, the theatre, local mores, current events, developments in literature and the arts, foreign customs, and the like. His appointment in 1891 as Paris correspondent for Vienna's *Neue Freie Presse* is clear evidence of his growing prestige as a journalist.

Herzl's Zionist writings and numerous speeches have receded from Jewish memory, although the idea and the movement they served succeeded in realizing Herzl's prophecy of the establishment of a Jewish state. Herzl's Zionist writings range from his proto-Zionist drama, *Das neue Ghetto* (*The New Ghetto*), to his Zionist manifesto, *Der Judenstaat* (*The Jewish State*) to his numerous shorter Zionist essays and vignettes, to his utopian novel, *Altneuland* (*Old-New Land*) in 1902. Also, his many Zionist speeches, especially those delivered as major events at the annual Zionist congresses, were subsequently published, and they figure importantly in the Zionist literary canon.

Das neue Ghetto represents an early stage in the playwright's coming to Jewish-national consciousness, before he embraced the Zionist cause. The protagonist, Jakob

Samuel, is killed in a duel in the name of Jewish honour, and his dying words are: "I want a way out! Out of the Ghetto!" Within the context of the drama, these words express the desire to transform radically the problematical and reprehensible forms of Jewish existence in anti-Semitic Europe at the end of the 19th century. While the Zionist solution is not yet explicit, the notion of Jewish honour became central in Herzl's scheme of things as he gravitated towards a Jewish-national ideology.

Herzl's Zionist brochure *Der Judenstaat* argued forcefully for Jewish nationalism and the establishment of a Jewish state, as countermeasures to the perniciousness of modern anti-Semitism. Still, many of the features of the work, especially those that appear to be lacking in Jewish sensibility, have been repressed or forgotten. For example, although Herzl credited the Jewish religion with helping to maintain the nation during centuries of persecution and duress, there would nevertheless be only a very limited and minor role for the rabbis and religion in the modern secular State of the Jews. Herzl envisioned the state not as a democracy, but rather as an aristocratic republic with the old Venetian republic serving as its model. The state would be composed of cantons, where Jews continued to speak and function in the various different languages from their home countries before their immigration. They would preserve and develop their own educational and cultural institutions in these different languages in separate cantons. Herzl opposed the idea of introducing Hebrew as the Jewish national language. He did not consider a national language essential for the state. The national flag of the state would not contain any Jewish symbolism. Rather it would be white with seven gold stars, representing the seven-hour work-day, which Herzl favoured.

Some of Herzl's short Zionist prose pieces, published in *Die Welt*, touched on sensitive Jewish issues of the time, especially the issue of assimilation. In his short piece entitled "Die Menorah" ("The Menorah") he depicted poignantly the return of the assimilated Jew to his people, employing the festival of Hanukah and the lights of the Menorah to provide graphic historical colouration, a widely recognizable image, and sentimentality to explicate this process. In a sense it is a modern Jewish-national version of the parable of the prodigal son. In "Mauschel" in 1897 he excoriated bitterly the assimilated Jew, who failed to acknowledge the cogency of Zionism. He delimited this pitiful self-denying type in great detail, in order to buttress his argument that the Jewish enemy within was just as pernicious, if not more dangerous to the Jewish cause, than the anti-Semitic enemy without.

Herzl's utopian Zionist novel *Altneuland* attempted to present readers with his concrete idea of what life in the proposed State of the Jews would be like. The work is divided chronologically into two parts. The first is set in the present of turn-of-the-century Vienna and is comprised of a cast of Jewish characters, ranging from the "Mauschel", the self-hating western type, to the proud but impoverished and desperate east European Jew. The second part takes place 20 years later in the already established, technologically advanced, politically stable, and economically sound State of the Jews. In the novel, the despairing and aimless, acculturated western Jewish protagonist of the first part finds his way back to his people and to the possibility of a meaningful existence within the framework of Jewish nationalism in the second part. There are numerous warm evocations of Jewish life, like the depiction of the celebration of the Passover Seder in Tiberius or the welcoming of the Sabbath in Jerusalem. However, the work has a pronounced internationalist orientation. For example, the centre of activity in the rebuilt old city of Jerusalem is the Peace Palace, a kind of international emergency aid and relief centre. The fantastic process by which a state on the scale depicted in the novel might be established within a 20-year period is only vaguely intimated. Given its internationalist orientation and certain lack of verisimilitude, the novel was quite controversial and it elicited scathing criticism upon publication, especially from Cultural Zionists such as Ahad Ha'am. Whether it was able to galvanize Jewish readers and help win them over to Zionism, similar to the success of *Der Judenstaat*, is difficult to document.

MARK GELBER

Heym, Stefan

German fiction writer 1913–2001

Born Helmut Flieg in Chemnitz, 10 April 1913. Studied at University of Berlin, but forced to flee to Prague after Nazi seizure of power and then emigrated to United States, 1933. Studied at University of Chicago, MA 1935. Clerk, Carson Pirie Scott department store, Chicago, 1936; editor, *Deutsches Volksecho*, New York, 1937–39; salesman, New Union Press printing company, from 1939. Became US citizen, 1943; name legally changed to Stefan Heym, 1943. Served in US Army, 1943–46. Married, first, Gertrude Peltyn, 1944; she died, 1969; second, Inge Hohn, 1971. Returned to Germany, 1952; settled in (East) Berlin. Expelled from Writers Union of German Democratic Republic, 1977; fined for publishing abroad without official permission, 1979. Awards include Heinrich Mann Prize, 1953; National Prize (German Democratic Republic); Jerusalem Prize, 1993. Elected member of Bundestag, 1994; resigned, 1995. Died in Jerusalem, 16 December 2001.

Selected Writings

Fiction

Hostages, 1942; as *The Glasenapp Case*, 1962; as *Der Fall Glasenapp*, 1958

Of Smiling Peace, 1944

The Crusaders, 1948; as *Kreuzfahrer von heute*, 1950; as *Der bittere Lorbeer*, 1950

The Eyes of Reason, 1951; as *Die Augen der Vernunft*, 1955

Die Kannibalen und andere Erzählungen, 1953; as *The Cannibals and Other Stories*, 1957

Goldsborough, 1953; in German, 1954

Schatten und Licht: Geschichten aus einem geteilten Lande, 1960; as *Shadows and Lights: Eight Short Stories*, 1963

Die Papiere des Andreas Lenz, 1963; as *Lenz; oder, Die Freiheit*, 1965; as *The Lenz Papers*, 1964
Lassalle, 1969; as *Uncertain Friend*, 1969
Die Schmähschrift oder Königin gegen Defoe, 1970; as *The Queen against Defoe and Other Stories*, 1974
Der König-David-Bericht, 1972; as *The King David Report*, 1973
5 Tage im Juni, 1974; as *Five Days in June*, 1977
Erzählungen [Stories], 1976
Die richtige Einstellung und andere Erzählungen [The Right Attitude and Other Stories], 1977
Collin, 1979; in English, 1980
Ahasver, 1981; as *The Wandering Jew*, 1984
Gesammelte Erzählungen [Collected Stories], 1984
Schwarzenberg, 1984
Auf Sand gebaut: sieben Geschichten aus der unmittelbaren Vergangenheit [Built on Sand: Seven Stories from the Immediate Past], 1990
Filz: Gedanken über das neueste Deutschland [Felt: Thoughts on the Latest Germany], 1992
Radek, 1995
Immer sind die Weiber weg und andere Weisheiten [The Women Are Always Off Somewhere and Other Wise Insights], 1997
Pargfrider, 1998

Play
Tom Sawyers grosses Abenteuer [Tom Sawyer's Great Adventure], with Hanuš Burger, 1952

Other
Nazis in USA: An Exposé of Hitler's Aims and Agents in the USA, 1938
Forschungsreise ins Herz der deutschen Arbeiterklasse [Voyage of Discovery into the Heart of the German Working Class], 1953
Offene Worte: So Liegen die Dinge [Speaking Plainly: That's How Things Are], 1953
Im Kopf sauber: Schriften zum Tage [Sound in Mind: Writings for Today], 1954
Reise ins Land der unbegrenzten Möglichkeiten [Journey to the Land of Limitless Possibilities], 1954; as *Keine Angst vor Russlands Bären*, 1955
Offen Gesagt: Neue Schriften zum Tage [Speaking Plainly: New Writings for Today], 1957
Das kosmische Zeitalter, 1959; as *A Visit to Soviet Science*, 1959; as *The Cosmic Age: A Report*, 1959
Translator, *King Leopold's Soliloquy*, by Mark Twain, 1961
Casimir und Cymbelinchen: zwei Märchen [Casimir and Little Cymbeline: Two Fairytales], 1966
Editor, *Auskunft 1-2: Neue Prosa aus der DDR*, Munich, Verlag der Autoren, 2 vols, 1974–78
Cymbelinchen; oder, Der Ernst des Lebens: vier Märchen für kluge Kinder [Little Cymbeline; or, The Serious Side of Life: Four Fairytales for Clever Children], 1975
Das Wachsmuth-Syndrom, 1975
Erich Hückniesel, und das fortgesetzte Rotkäppchen [Eric Hückniesel, and Red-Riding-Hood Continued], 1977
Wege und Umwege: Streitbare Schriften aus fünf Jahrzehnten [Directly and Indirectly: Controversial Writings from Five Centuries], edited by Peter Mallwitz, 1980
Atta Troll: Versuch einer Analyse [Atta Troll: An Attempt at an Analysis], 1983
Münchner Podium in den Kammerspielen '83: Reden über das eigene Land Deutschland, 1983
Märchen für kluge Kinder [Fairytales for Clever Children], 1984
Reden an den Feind [Speeches to the Enemy], 1986
Nachruf [Obituary], 1988
Meine Cousine, die Hexe und weitere Märchen für kluge Kinder [My Cousin the Witch and Further Fairytales for Clever Children], 1989
Einmischung: Gespräche, Reden, Essays [Interference: Conversations, Speeches, Essays], 1990
Editor, with Werner Heiduczek, *Die sanfte Revolution*, 1990
Stalin verlässt den Raum: politische Publizistik [Stalin Leaves the Room: Political Journalism], 1990

Further Reading

Dorman, M., "The State vs. the Writer: Recent Developments in Stefan Heym's Struggle against the GDR's Kulturpolitik", *Modern Languages*, 62/3 (September 1981)
Fisher, Rodney W., "Stefan Heym's *Ahasver*: Structure and Principles", *Seminar*, 22/3 (September 1986)
Graves, Peter J., "Authority, the State and the Individual: Stefan Heym's Novel *Collin*", *Forum for Modern Language Studies*, 23/4 (October 1987)
Hutchinson, Peter, "Problems of Socialist Historiography: The Example of Stefan Heym's *The King David Report*", *Modern Language Review*, 81/1 (January 1986)
Hutchinson, Peter, *Stefan Heym: The Perpetual Dissident*, Cambridge and New York: Cambridge University Press, 1992; as *Stefan Heym: Dissident auf Lebenszeit*, Würzburg: Könighausen und Neumann, 1999
Lauckner, Nancy A., "Stefan Heym's Revolutionary Wandering Jew: A Warning and a Hope for the Future" in *Studies in GDR Culture and Society, IV: Selected Papers from the Ninth New Hampshire Symposium on the German Democratic Republic*, edited by Margy Gerber, Lanham, Maryland: University Press of America, 1984
O'Doherty, Paul, *The Portrayal of Jews in GDR Prose Fiction*, Amsterdam: Rodopi, 1997
Pender, Malcolm, "Popularising Socialism: The Case of Stefan Heym" in *Socialism and the Literary Imagination: Essays on East German Writers*, edited by Martin Kane, Oxford and New York: Berg, 1991
Petr, Pavel, "Stefan Heym and the Concept of Misunderstanding", *AUMLA: Journal of the Australasian Universities Language and Literature Association*, 48 (1977)
Tait, Meg, "Stefan Heym's Radek: The Conscience of a Revolutionary," *German Life and Letters*, 51/4 (1998)
Zachau, Reinhard, *Stefan Heym*, Munich: Beck, 1982

Although born into a practising German Jewish family, Stefan Heym never regarded himself as a believer. A slightly troubled conscience in this regard betrays itself on a small number of occasions in his autobiography, *Nachruf* [Obituary] from 1988; it is also striking that he should have turned in his later, semi-biographical fiction increasingly towards figures who are Jews, and that these should be presented consistently favourably. Although Jewish themes as such play a relatively small role in his work – and are regularly subordinate to political and social concerns – Jewish characters, their harassment, their resilience, are a constant. Heym lost an illegitimate child in a concentration camp (although he did not learn of this until years after the event), and, as a journalist, he covered part of the Lüneberg War Trials; the Holocaust as such never featured in his fiction, however, even though his concern with the fascist mentality was particularly strong in his early period.

Heym began as a poet and journalist while at Berlin University. His first pieces date from 1931, and from that point onwards he proved a prolific and compulsive writer, especially after his escape from Nazi Germany to Prague, and then to the USA on a scholarship awarded by the Jewish university fraternity Phi Sigma Delta. Jewish issues are treated rarely in these years, and only light-heartedly (as in the short story "Golem Anno 35") or briefly (as in the brief article "Fünf Jahre Bücherverbrennung" [Five Years of Book Burning]).

Owing to this period in American exile, Heym's early novels are written in English; his later ones are in German. (Most of his works he translated himself, and he proved to be one of the most successful self-translators of our age.) His fiction is almost exclusively in the realist tradition and owes much to his experience as a journalist. His preferred subject is the struggling, often idealistic, intellectual, who is used as a focus for broad questions on the nature of truth, power, and forces in history, and Heym regularly depicts the reactions of individuals in crisis or in revolutionary situations. The perspective is always socialist: problems of socialism, as well as taboo moments in socialist history, constantly recur.

Jewish figures feature in minor roles in several of Heym's novels of the 1940s and 1950s. Formative influences during this period had been his work in "psychological warfare" for the US army during World War II, and then the threat of McCarthyist persecution for his undisguised left-wing sympathies. The latter drove him back to Europe, finally to the German Democratic Republic, where he was soon to become a leading dissident. It is not, however, until the 1960s that a prominently Jewish figure appears, that of the banker Einstein and his beautiful daughter Lenore in the novel *The Lenz Papers*. The portrayal here is slightly clichéd, with the banker as wise, wealthy, compassionate, but despised for his race, and his daughter as caring, brave, and prepared to abandon father and faith for the man she loves.

Heym's fictional investigation of problematic socialist figures, who are also Jews, begins properly with Lassalle, first president of the German Workers' Party, the figure with whom the undemocratic, tyrannical structure of later communist societies and the "cult of personality" can be first associated. Lassalle's Jewishness is not a focal point of *Uncertain Friend* in 1969, but instances of anti-Semitism are seen throughout and they are seen as a spur to Lassalle's desire for success. Interestingly, his origins as a poor Jew from the eastern provinces are regarded by others as a reason for his actions, whether desire for Prussian women, or lust for power and recognition. Heym's portrayal is ambivalent. In his autobiography he confessed certain parallels between himself and this figure, and although there is no evidence that Heym's Jewishness was a particular spur to his own success, he was keenly aware of it in others.

Heym's most successful novel, *The King David Report*, is based on the Old Testament, an indictment of the almost Stalinist practices adopted by King Solomon in the brutal running of ancient Israel, and, especially the (re-)writing of history (in this case the story of his father, King David). The choice of subject arose from the author's avid reading of the Bible after the death of his first wife, but there is little specifically Jewish in the novel apart from its setting.

The figure of the Jew is, however, proclaimed in the very title of *Ahasver* (*The Wandering Jew*), a complex and bitterly humorous novel containing Heym's most consistent analysis of Jewish persecution throughout the ages. Using an old legend to interpret features of modern and earlier societies, the author explores anti-Semitism alongside questions of religious and secular order, bigotry, ruthless adherence to dogma, and idealistic dissent. The work appeared as the GDR was preparing itself for the "Luther Year" (1983), preparing to overlook aspects of the reformer's career in order to claim him as a progressive antecedent of modern socialism. In that part of his novel set at the time of the Reformation, however, Heym emphasizes the vicious anti-Semitism in Luther (a point he was to emphasize in a speech to the International Council of Christians and Jews in 1982) and points to the survival of anti-Semitism even in the GDR. But he also hints at dangerous Zionist tendencies in Israel.

Karl Radek was a leading German communist, a Jew who joined Lenin after the Russian Revolution and played an important role in the Kremlin; he finally fell victim to Stalin, a clear anti-Semite, in one of the first show trials. Although posterity has rarely seen him positively, the massive novel *Radek*, 1995, portrays him in a remarkably sympathetic light, depicting him from the first line as a victim of religious bigotry ("The eternal Polish Jew . . ."); his Jewish origins occasionally flashing back to him, offering solace in moments of despair. The outsider Pargfrider, central character of the eponymous novel published in 1998, is also seen favourably, for all his contradictions, his coldness and his calculations. More aware of his origins than most of Heym's characters, he is determined to have his revenge on an Austrian aristocracy which has ostracized him because he is the illegitimate child of a Jewish actress, whose lover may have been the Emperor.

One can detect varying degrees of self-identification in the sad fate of all these figures, whose Jewishness may be seen as a principal cause of their tragedy.

PETER HUTCHINSON

Hilsenrath, Edgar

German fiction writer and satirist, 1926–

Born in Leipzig, 2 April 1926. Escaped to Sereth, Romania, with mother and brother, 1938; deported to ghetto of Moghilev-Podelsk, Ukraine, 1941; returned to Bucharest, 1944. Emigrated to Palestine, and eventually to United States, 1951; relocated to Berlin, 1975. Awards include Alfred Döblin Prize, 1989; Galinski Prize, 1993; Hans-Erich Nossak Prize, 1994; Hans Sahl Prize, 1998. Honorary member, Neue Gesellschaft für Literatur (New Association for Literature), 1988; American PEN Club; PEN Center of Federal Republic of Germany.

Selected Writings

Novels

Nacht, 1964; as *Night*, translated by Michael Roloff, 1966

Der Nazi und der Friseur, 1977; as *The Nazi and the Barber*, translated by Andrew White, 1971

Gib acht, Genosse Mandelbaum [Beware, Comrade Mandelbaum], 1979

Bronskys Geständnis [Bronsky's Confession], 1980

Das Märchen vom letzten Gedanken, 1989; as *The Story of the Last Thought*, translated by Hugo Young, 1990

Jossel Wassermanns Heimkehr [Jossel Wassermann's Return], 1993

Moskauer Orgasmus [Moscow Orgasm], 1997

Die Abenteuer des Ruben Jablonski: ein autobiographischer Roman [The Adventures of Ruben Jablonski], 1997

Other

Zibulsky, oder, Antenne im Bauch [Zibulski; or, Antenna in the Stomach], 1983

Das Unerzählbare erzählen [Telling the Unspeakable], 1996

Further Reading

Bauer, Karin, "Erzählen im Augenblick höchster Gefahr: Zu Benjamins Begriff der Geschichte in Edgar Hilsenraths Jossel Wassermans Heimkehr", *German Quarterly*, 71/4 (1998)

Gilman, Sander L., "Jüdischer Literaten und deutsche Literatur: Antisemitismus und verborgene Sprache der Juden am Beispiel von Jurek Becker und Edgar Hilsenrath", *Zeitschrift für Deutsche Philologie*, 107/2 (1988)

Lorenz, Dagmar C.G., "Social Darwinism in Edgar Hilsenrath's Ghetto Novel *Nacht*" in *Insiders and Outsiders: Jewish and Gentile Culture in Germany and Austria*, edited by Lorenz and Gabriele Weinberger, Detroit: Wayne State University Press, 1994

Moeller, Susann, "Politics to Pulp a Novel: The Fate of the First Edition of Edgar Hilsenrath's Novel *Nacht*" in *Insiders and Outsiders: Jewish and Gentile Culture in Germany and Austria*, edited by Dagmar C.G. Lorenz and Gabriele Weinberger, Detroit: Wayne State University Press, 1994

Rosenthal, Bianca, "Autobiography and the Fiction of the I: Edgar Hilsenrath" in *The Fiction of the I: Contemporary Austrian Writers and Autobiography*, edited by Nicholas J. Meyerhofer, Riverside, California: Ariadne Press, 1999

Stenberg, Peter, "Memories of the Holocaust: Edgar Hilsenrath and the Fiction of Genocide", *Deutsche Vierteljahrsschrift für Literaturwissenschaft und Geistesgeschichte*, 56/2 (1982)

Stenberg, Peter, "Edgar Hilsenrath and Jakov Lind Meet at the Employment Office in Netanya, Palestine, Discuss Literature, and Contemplate Their Recent Past" in *Yale Companion to Jewish Writing and Thought in German Culture, 1096–1996*, edited by Sander L. Gilman and Jack Zipes, New Haven, Connecticut and London: Yale University Press, 1997

Taylor, Jennifer L., "Writing as Revenge: Jewish German Identity in Post-Holocaust German Literary Works: Reading Survivor Authors Jurek Becker, Edgar Hilsenrath, and Ruth Klüger" (PhD dissertation), Cornell University, 1995

The Holocaust and the survivor's trauma are central to Hilsenrath's work. His first novel *Nacht* (*Night*) is set in a Romanian ghetto and describes the ordeal of the deported Jews from the perspective of an adult man. In contrast, the voice of the later picaresque autobiographical novel *Die Abenteuer des Ruben Jablonski* [The Adventures of Ruben Jablonski] is that of a youngster. The latter more detached narrative traces the adventures of a boy who, aided by cunning and good fortune, manages to survive the ghetto and post-liberation chaos. However, despite his resilience Ruben suffers irreversible damage. Ruben's life is characterized by multiple disruptions: his formal education and family life come to an end; growing up in the ghetto he becomes accustomed to give free rein to his impulses and thus remains an outsider to bourgeois culture. Like Hilsenrath, who returned to Germany after 20 years in New York, Ruben deals with the legacy of the Shoah through writing, his tool to make sense of the past that shaped his present. An important aspect in Hilsenrath is exploring the genocides and state-sanctioned brutality in different ages and cultures. In *Nacht* the burnt-out ghetto epitomizes the horrors of the Holocaust: the men and women left to starve are firmly in the grip of an all-pervasive cruelty that causes them to victimize each other. Hilsenrath's satirical strategy in *Der Nazi und der Friseur* (*The Nazi and the Barber*) allows the randomness of the roles of victims and perpetrator to become apparent. Max Schulz, a Nazi killer, turns into an upstanding Israeli. In *Bronskys Geständnis* [Bronsky's Confession] and *Gib acht, Genosse Mandelbaum* [Beware, Comrade Mandelbaum] the author employs black humour and the grotesque to portray the exasperating American experience of disenfranchised male Jewish immigrants in New York in the 1950s.

Hilsenrath explores the absurd and tragic fates of men and women marginalized because they are perceived as other. Forcibly cut off from their cultural roots, his German-Jewish characters vacillate between permanent alienation and a sense of being at home everywhere in the world. Like other post-Shoah writers, Hilsenrath has nothing but disregard for German high culture and integrates street language and obscenities into his texts. His body-centred writing – he foregrounds metabolic functions and physical sensations caused by hunger, torture, and sexual desires – undermines conventional identity constructs. In his texts sensations, feelings, and thoughts are inseparably intertwined. In *Nacht* the extreme deprivation imposed by the Nazis becomes the leveller among persons of different class and education, in *Das Märchen vom letzten Gedanken* (*The Story of the Last Thought*) it is the atrocities committed against the Armenians by the Turks. Hilsenrath's textual strategies reflect the realization that human beings are anything but fundamentally good or benign.

Despite the fact that German Nazism had forced him into exile, Hilsenrath does not view anti-Semitism as unique to the German mentality, and it did not interfere with his lifelong dream of becoming a German author in Berlin. In addition, traditional rural Jewish life, which he encountered for the first time in Romania, left a deep impression on him. *Jossel Wassermanns Heimkehr* [Jossel Wassermann's Return] calls to mind the world of the shtetl, as do the descriptions of rural Armenia in *Das Märchen vom letzten Gedanken*. The simple patriarchal structures portrayed in these novels celebrate lost worlds that fell victim to genocide. To depict them it took Hilsenrath several decades. From his liberation in 1944 until the 1960s Hilsenrath was obsessed with the Holocaust of which the physical, intellectual, and moral demise of his Jewish protagonist Ranek (*Nacht*) is paradigmatic. In the absence of food, material goods, and shelter, Nazi victims are shown to perish without the direct involvement of concentration camp guards or SS. Men are the first to abandon peacetime values. Unrestrained by religious and moral considerations they take advantage of women, children, and weaker men. The overt portrayal of humans dominated by their instincts and the absence of philosophical or religious perspectives set Hilsenrath's writing apart from the humanistic or conciliatory tendency prevalent in much German Holocaust literature. Moreover, Hilsenrath insists on Jewish agency and creates protagonists capable of the full range of emotions and actions. *Nacht* challenged the stereotype of Jews as victims perpetuated by non-Jewish writers. The focus on the body and the instrumentalization of sexuality to assert power and establish identity was undoubtedly seen as a transgression against the dominant West German discourse. Kindler, Hilsenrath's first publisher, prevented a larger distribution of *Nacht* by producing an exceedingly small edition. The English translation, *Night*, was more successful, but only after the sensation caused by *Der Nazi und der Friseur* was *Nacht* published again in German by the Literarischer Verlag Braun.

Der Nazi und der Friseur and the stories in *Zibulsky; oder, Antenne im Bauch* [Zibulski; or, Antenna in the Stomach] continue the tradition of Jewish satire. In the former work the perpetrators of the Holocaust are satirized. After 1945 many of them, like Hilsenrath's protagonist Max Schulz, posed as Nazi victims. An adherent of the ethos of pre-war Jewish pacifism, Hilsenrath criticizes the Zionist ideal of the heroic Jew by transforming Schulz, the Nazi murderer, into a Jewish fighter and a Zionist. Hilsenrath's narrative is critical of the representation of the Nazi past by prominent German postwar authors such as Günter Grass. Revealing that even progressive mainstream writers fail to come to terms with the Holocaust, Hilsenrath exposes the rift between Jewish and Gentile memory.

Hilsenrath's narrative voice in general resists co-optation by the dominant culture, be it in *Bronskys Geständnis* which thematizes the marginality of German-Jewish exiles in New York or *Das Märchen vom letzten Gedanken* which associates the Holocaust with the genocide perpetrated by the Young Turks against the Armenians. Hilsenrath draws parallels between the vanishing of the stories of persecuted minorities, so for instance in *Jossel Wassermanns Heimkehr.* Here he exposes the discrepancy between the average person's experience and the sanitized legal and academic discourses that obliterate the individual fate. Hilsenrath's priority is the plight of the oppressed. Disregarding official versions of history he explores aspects of domination: lust, sexual gratification, and greed, all merging into the ecstasy of power. Few other writers have so candidly exposed the ties between sadism, politics, war, and genocide. Ultimately, Hilsenrath's works call for a re-examination of "human nature". His portrayal of human behaviour, particularly of men, suggests that humans are mistaken to ascribe "humane" qualities to their own species. Hilsenrath's profoundly pessimistic insights are imparted in narratives of fairytale-like simplicity and irony that call to mind the *muser*, the storyteller of Ashkenazic popular culture.

DAGMAR C. G. LORENZ

Hirshbein, Perets

Polish dramatist, fiction writer, and travel writer, 1880–1948

Born in Kleszczele, 1880. Left home to study in various yeshivas, 1894. Began to write stories in Yiddish and poems in Hebrew, 1898. Moved to Warsaw, 1904; associated with H.N. Bialik, Y.L. Perets, and Sholem Asch. Moved to Vilna (Vilnius); became teacher of Hebrew; organized illegal study circle for young workers. Moved to Odessa; with Bialik's help, formed drama group, Hirshbein Troupe, 1908; travelled with troupe throughout Russian empire, 1904–06. Married poet Esther Shumiatcher, 1920. Travelled around world with wife, 1920–22; travel reports serialized in Yiddish daily *Der tog*. Lived mainly in United States from 1930; from 1940 in Los Angeles. Died in Los Angeles, 1948.

Selected Writings

Plays
Miriam, 1905
Oyf yener zayt taykh [On the Other Side of the River], 1905
Di erd [The Earth], 1907
Der tkies-kaf [The Handshake], 1908
A farvorfn vinkl [A Far-flung Corner], 1912
Di puste kretshme [The Destitute Inn], 1912
A lebn far a lebn [A Life for a Life], 1915
Bebele, 1915
Eliyohu hanovi [Elijah the Prophet], 1915
Gezamlte dramen [Collected Plays], 1916
Deramot [Dramas], translated into Hebrew by the author, 1921

Grine felder trilogy [Green Fields], 1923 (includes *Tsvey shtet* [Two Towns], 1919 and *Levi yitskhok*, 1923); as a film, 1941
Mahazot [Plays], translated into Hebrew by the author, 1923
Der ershter melekh in yisroel [Saul, The First King of Israel], 1934

Fiction
Gaguim [Yearnings], 1901
Royte felder [Red Fields], 1935
Bovl [Babylon] (trilogy), 1942

Other
Arum der velt [Around the World], 1927
Erets Israel, 1929
Mayne kinder-yorn [My Childhood Years], 1932
Monologn [Monologues], 1939

Further Reading

Landis, Joseph C. (translator and editor), *The Dybbuk and Other Great Yiddish Plays*, New York: Bantam, 1966
Leksikon fun der nayer yidisher literatur [Biographical Dictionary of Modern Yiddish Literature], vol. 3, New York: World Jewish Culture Congress, 1960
Lifson, David S. (translator and editor), "*Farvorfen vinkel* by Peretz Hirschbein" in *Epic and Folk Plays of the Yiddish Theater*, Rutherford, New Jersey: Fairleigh Dickinson, University Press, 1975
Madison, Charles A., *Yiddish Literature: Its Scope and Major Writers*, New York: Ungar, 1968
Rozhanski, Shmuel (editor), *Peretz Hirschbein: teater, veltrayzes zikhroynes*, Buenos Aires: YIVO, 1967
Segal, Yisroel, "Peretz Hirschbeins *grine felder* in Vilner Ghetto", *Di tsukunft* (October 1948)

Perets Hirshbein's early childhood was spent in his father's mill, surrounded by nature and in an atmosphere of fear and superstition. His mother lost seven of her 11 children, and versions of her appear in his work, e.g. the deranged mother in *A farvorfn vinkl* [A Far-flung Corner], and the pregnant mother in *Bebele* who fears that her future child will die. His own childhood sweetheart, Sheyndl, was accidentally poisoned, and it took him years to recover from this loss. His relationship with Sheyndl provided the model for his depiction of romance in his plays and novels. She appears in varying forms, including as the daughter in *Bebele*, as the key figure, Kreyndl in *Bovl* [Babylon], and as the strong-minded Lena in *Royte felder* [Red Fields].

Hirshbein's early literary influences were Bialik in Hebrew and Tolstoi and Gor'kii in Russian and, from the point of view of drama, Ibsen, Strindberg, and Maeterlinck. In Vilna, he became a Hebrew teacher and organized an illegal study circle for young workers. He was already writing stories and poetry in Hebrew (*Gaguim* [Yearnings] was published in 1901) when a chance meeting with a young Jewish prostitute led him to produce his realistic drama *Miriam*. With no professional Hebrew theatre in prospect, Hirshbein was to turn to Yiddish. His first drama, written originally in Yiddish, was *Oyf yener zayt taykh* [On the Other Side of the River], a symbolist play full of riddles and mysteries. In Berlin, he wrote *Di erd* [The Earth], a bizarre drama involving a village girl who burns down her father's pine forest to drive away the city people and cleanse the earth of the countryside. The theme prefigures Hirshbein's later concern with village life, but most of his writing during this period – the "cellar dramas" – was concerned with urban poverty. When he was in St Petersburg for the publication of a volume of his plays in Russian, he wrote *Der tkies-kaf* [The Handshake], the plot of which was very similar to that of An-ski's *The Dybbuk*. While in Łódź for a production of the play in spring 1908, Hirshbein conceived his idea of a new Yiddish theatre on a more artistic level. Among writers and critics in general, there was a view that Yiddish theatre was sullied by commercially orientated and a poorly written plays (*shund* – rubbish), and characterized by a style of performance that focused on the personality of the actor rather than on the character in the play. After returning to Odessa for a Russian production of *Oyf yener zayt taykh*, the Hirshbein Troupe was established. A wide range of productions were undertaken, including translations from the European repertoire. Though financial security was never achieved, the troupe did encounter a successful reception in western Russia. But not in Warsaw: here, they received particularly devastating reviews, and shortly afterwards the company collapsed. Clearly, whatever their immediate success or failure, their role as a prototype and their influence on later Yiddish theatre, such as the Vilna troupe or the Yiddish Art Theatre of New York, was profound. Hirshbein's own influence on the Yiddish theatre was considerable. His plays launched the Yiddish Art Theatre, and remained within the repertoire of leading Yiddish theatre companies throughout the Jewish world. The most popular, *Grine felder* [Green Fields] was made into one of the finest Yiddish films in 1941.

Hirshbein's earlier dramas had struck false notes, because he was trying so hard to make himself into a particular kind of writer, and the personality of the author was lost under the layers of literary style and flowery expression. With the *Di puste kretshme* [The Destitute Inn], and on a new continent, Hirshbein embarked on a new style of writing. America seems to have brought out in him a new outburst of creativity, perhaps because it gave him sufficient distance come to terms with his own rural background. A series of plays, including *A farvorfn vinkl*, *Eliyohu hanovi* [Elijah the Prophet], and *A lebn far a lebn* [A Life for a Life] culminated in *Grine felder*. Here, he was able to recreate the village life of his youth, with its sturdy and straightforward Jews, full of fear and superstition, religious but with little learning, in touch with nature and, unlike the town Jews, able to enjoy their environment and to feel themselves fully a part of it.

After revealing the sources of his creativity in his autobiography, *Mayne kinder-yorn* [My Childhood Years] in 1932, Hirshbein left the theatre behind and worked on *Royte felder* [Red Fields], the fictional version of his experiences with the Jewish agricultural settlers in the Crimea, where he had spent ten months between 1928 and 1929. The continuity of the writing is revealed in the title itself, now red rather than green fields. On the wider canvas of the novel, the emotional drama is painted within the framework of an atavistic class struggle and a contemporary cultural and social clash between town and village, between proletarian and peasant, before the brutal effects of Stalinist collectivization were to make themselves felt.

Shortly after the publication of *Royte felder*, Hirshbein began his American trilogy, *Bovl*, which took him seven years to complete. This was an extensive novel, which covered the fates of two contrasting immigrant families in New York City, the Babylon of the title, from 1883, until the beginning of the 1930s. Hirshbein was exploring what is now seen as a very familiar and obvious contrast between old and new values, with assimilation and the loss of faith and of Jewish culture in general. While in the Soviet Union the process of change was revolutionary, in the United States it was more organic and more insidious. The luxuries and freedoms offered by American society removed much of the external agony from Jewish lives, though naturally the internal, psychological ones remained.

Hirshbein's restlessness found an outlet in his extensive world travel, which included journeys to South America, Australasia, South Africa, China, India, and Palestine, and a long period in the Soviet Union. From all of this came his travel writing, with its combination of portraiture and reportage, and Hirshbein occupies a unique position in this genre of Yiddish literature. His account of the Crimea, "Shvartsbrukh" [Black Ploughed Earth] remains an exceptional historical document of a fascinating social experiment for the Jews of the Soviet Union, and was the basis for *Royte felder*.

Hirshbein was a lonely soul, but a social animal. The restlessness in his nature was embedded in the experience of the Jews and, of course, ended up as part of the contemporary experience. Though *Grine felder* presented an image of idyllic stability, the effect of change was stronger in the other two parts of the trilogy (*Tsvey shtet* [Two Towns], and *Levi yitskhok*) and, of course, in the novels. In the end, change was cataclysmic. Yisroel Segal recalled the intensity of feeling among the audience, when *Grine felder* was performed in the Vilna Ghetto in 1942. They were aware that, at that moment, the Nazis were trampling on those "Grine felder" which had belonged to the Jews.

BARRY DAVIS

Hoffman, Yoel

Israeli fiction writer, 1937–

Born in Hungary, 1937, to a Jewish-Austrian family. Family moved to Palestine a year later. Father, Abraham, was an insurance executive; mother died early. Boarded with family members and in children's home until father's second marriage. Spent two years in Buddhist monastery. Studied at University of Kyoto, Japan, 1970–74; received doctorate. Translator of Japanese poetry. Professor of Far Eastern Philosophy at Haifa University. Awarded Koret Jewish Book Award, 1999, Neumann Prize for Hebrew Literature, 1999. Lives in Haifa.

Selected Writings

Short Stories

Sefer yosef, 1988; as *The Book of Joseph*, translated by Alan Treister with *Katschen*, translated by David Kriss, 1998

Novels

Befebruar kedai liknot pilim [It's a Good Idea to Buy Elephants in February: for children], 1988

Bernhard, 1989; translated as *Bernhard*, by Alan Treister, 1998

Kristus shel hadagim, 1991; as *The Christ of Fish*, translated by Eddie Levenston, 1999

Gutapersha, 1993

Mah shlomekh dolores? [How Do You Do Dolores?], 1995

Lev hu katmandu; as *The Heart Is Katmandu*, translated by Peter Cole, 2001

Other

Translator, *The Sound of the One Hand: 281 Zen Koans with Answers*, 1975

Translator, *Every End Exposed: The 100 Koans of Master Kido*, 1977

Translator, *Radical Zen: The Sayings of Joshu*, 1978

The Idea of Self, East and West: A Comparison between Buddhist Philosophy and the Philosophy of David Hume, 1980

Editor, *Japanese Death Poems*, 1986

Further Reading

Hadassah Magazine (February 1999)

Publishers' Weekly (30 March 1998)

Review of Contemporary Fiction (Summer 1999)

The Forward (22 May 1998)

The New Leader (4–18 May 1998)

World Literature Today (Spring 1999)

From a poetic point of view, Yoel Hoffman is the most interesting, prolific, and innovative writer in Israel today. He is the author of six books that can be described as novels, yet it would be best to describe them as poetry in prose. Although not an experimental writer in a strict sense, he is well known for his stylistic and poetic innovations and inventiveness. The main thematic characteristics of his work were defined in *Sefer yosef* (*The Book of Joseph*). An impressive debut, it is a collection of four stories that deal with existence, writing, and history in a quite unique way. The formal aspects, now typical of his writing, were formed and perfected in his second, and by far best work, *Bernhard*.

Hoffman was born in 1937 to Austrian Jews who emigrated to Palestine in the late 1930s due to the rise to power of the Nazis. His mother's early death and the existential alienation of growing up in a rather collectivist society mark his work heavily. In a rare public statement (Hoffman refuses media interviews) he marked being an orphan as the formative experience and the defining abyss that affects his work. The expressions of this are manifold, beginning with the fact that Hoffman's work is first and foremost a phenomenological account of the mind, the character, and our way of conceiving the world and its events. This poetic vision is further extended by Hoffman's work as a professor of Japanese poetry, Buddhism, and philosophy, at Haifa University; in fact, the first three books he published were translations of Eastern philosophy and poetry. Israeli critics tend to picture Hoffman as a "Zen Jewish writer". That is not necessarily a mistaken view, though the relations between the different influences in Hoffman's work are complex and sometimes undecipherable.

As a writer Hoffman was born mature. In 1986 he published his first story, "Katschen", in *Igra*, a shortlived but influential literary magazine, edited by the senior poet Nathan Zach and the critic Dan Miron. "Katschen" is a boy whose mother dies, whose father is institutionalized, and who is taken care of by a series of well-meaning and badly-adjusted immigrant relatives. Katschen (cat) is taken from home to home and ends up in a kibbutz, as happened frequently in those days. This place is intolerable to his independent mind, and Katschen runs away from this collective existence. After a series of encounters he finally finds his "krank" (sick) father who explains: "'You must choose, small and important or big and worthless?' That moment Katschen clearly knew that if he makes the wrong choice, he will lose his father again." Katschen chooses correctly and they escape out the window.

The main mechanisms of this story are two: one is that of translation. The Hebrew narrative does not suppress the different languages spoken by the different characters and they emerge as focal points of linguistic and consciousness *difference*. (Translations are provided in the text.) Second is an unbreachable gap between Katschen's narrative and the way the world perceives him. Through a unique narrative voice Hoffman manages to present a story of a child whose beautifully intelligent inner monologue is mistaken for madness. This creates an interesting portrait of the young artist and art itself, as though stories were just such eruptions of an otherwise silent inner monologue, bound to be misunderstood.

Hoffman's stylistic and poetic breakthrough came in *Bernhard*, his first full-length novel. It is the story of a widower, Bernhard, proprietor of a unique and remarkable mind; it is tempting to say that the novel is about a person who experiences the most extreme loss and slowly regains the world. As is the case with Hoffman himself, Bernhard's writing is about something but it is more about everything else. The narrative is quite loose, alternating between Bernhard's story and a story he is telling. All this happens while World War II goes on, and the reaction between the historical and the phenomenology of the private mind is enlightening. Graphically the "Hoffman mode" was created – the story is divided into mini-chapters like the "inner text"' in the Talmud and on one side of the page. All his books since have been written in this form. Yet important as form may be, the most exciting feature in Hoffman's writing was the perfection of the rhythmic interplay between the different layers of Hebrew, the different languages, and the delicate balance between prose and poetry that create the textual texture. Although all of these were present to begin with, in *Bernhard* they reached perfection, creating one of the most important Hebrew novels of our time. This also makes Hoffman's writing extremely difficult to translate as can be seen from the first page:

> After his wife died Bernhard thought: "the world
> Is infinite. Beyond each galaxy lies
> Another galaxy" he tried to picture for himself
> How Paola, her flesh pale, uniting with the
> Large-scale order of the universe. But
> The death of Paola was not such a simple matter.
> "Where", thought Bernhard to his heart, "is Paola
> Now?"

After *Bernhard* Hoffman proceeded to write *Kristus shel hadagim* (*The Christ of Fish*), which was close enough to *Bernhard* in themes and form to give some the feeling that the "Hoffman mode" was nothing more than a mannerism. *Gutapersha*, the less communicative novel, and *Mah shlomekh dolores?* [How Do You Do Dolores?], the female-voice novel that followed, did little to change this opinion. Hoffman's writing continued to be beautiful, touching, smart, and culturally enlightening. His most recent novel, *Lev hu katmandu* (*The Heart is Katmandu*), demonstrates how Hoffman has established his own poetic terms, style, and discourse within which even the most common tale of love turns into a philo-poetic voyage into beauty, grace, and all other things that language will allow.

URI COHEN

Hollander, John

US poet, 1929–

Born in New York City, 28 October 1929. Studied at Columbia University, BA 1950, MA 1952; Indiana University, Bloomington, PhD 1959. Married, first, Anne Loesser, 1953; divorced 1977; two daughters; second, Natalie Charkow, 1981. Junior Fellow, Society of Fellows, Harvard University, 1954–57; lecturer, Connecticut College, New London, 1957–59; instructor, 1959–61, assistant professor, 1961–64, and associate professor of English, 1964–66, Yale University; professor of English, City University of New York, 1966–77; professor of English, 1977–86, and A. Bartlett Giamatti Professor of English, 1986–95, Yale University. Gauss lecturer, Princeton University, 1962, 1965; visiting professor, Indiana University, 1964; lecturer, Salzburg Seminar in American Studies, 1965; Overseas Fellow, Churchill College, Cambridge, 1967–68; Fellow, Ezra Stiles College, Yale University, since 1977. Member of poetry board, Wesleyan University Press, 1959–62; editorial assistant for poetry, *Partisan Review*, 1959–65; contributing editor, *Harper's*, New York, 1969–71. Awards include Yale Series of Younger Poets Award, 1958; American Academy grant, 1963; National Endowment for the Arts Fellowship, 1973; Levinson Prize, 1974; Guggenheim Fellowship, 1979; Modern Language Association Shaughnessy Medal, 1982; Bollingen Prize 1983; MacArthur Fellowship, 1990; Ambassador Book Award of English-speaking Union, 1994; Cleanth Brooks–Robert Penn Warren Award, 1997. Chancellor, Academy of American Poets; member, American Academy of Arts and Letters.

Selected Writings

Poetry
A Crackling of Thorns, 1958
A Beach Vision, 1962

Movie-Going, and Other Poems, 1962
A Book of Various Owls, 1963
Visions from the Ramble, 1965
Philomel, 1968
Types of Shape, 1969; expanded edition, 1991
The Night Mirror, 1971
Selected Poems, 1972
The Immense Parade on Supererogation Day and What Happened to It, 1972
Town and Country Matters: Erotica and Satirica, 1972
The Head of the Bed, 1974
Tales Told of the Fathers, 1975
Reflections on Espionage: The Question of Cupcake, 1976
In Place, 1978
Spectral Emanations: New and Selected Poems, 1978
Blue Wine and Other Poems, 1979
Looking Ahead, 1982
Powers of Thirteen, 1983
A Hollander Garland, 1985
In Time and Place, 1986
Some Fugitives Take Cover, 1986
Harp Lake, 1988
Selected Poetry, 1993
Tesserae and Other Poems, 1993
Figurehead and Other Poems, 1999

Play
An Entertainment for Elizabeth, Being a Most Excellent Princely Maske of the Seven Motions or Terpsichore Unchain'd, 1972

Other
The Untuning of the Sky: Ideas of Music in English Poetry 1500–1700, 1961
The Quest of the Gole (for children), 1966
Images of Voice: Music and Sound in Romantic Poetry, 1970
Vision and Resonance: Two Senses of Poetic Form, 1975
Rhyme's Reason: A Guide to English Verse, 1981
The Figure of Echo: A Mode of Allusion in Milton and After, 1981
Dal Vero, 1983
Melodious Guile: Fictive Pattern in Poetic Language, 1988
The Death of Moses: Libretto for an Oratorio by Sir Alexander Goehr, 1992
"The Question of Jewish American Poetry" in *What is Jewish Literature*, edited by Hana Wirth-Nesher, 1994
The Gazer's Spirit: Poems Speaking to Silent Works of Art, 1995
The Work of Poetry, 1997
The Poetry of Everyday Life, 1998

Also editor of many collections of poetry and prose

Further Reading
Bloom, Harold, "The White Light of Trope" in his *Agon: Towards a Theory of Revisionism*, New York and Oxford: Oxford University Press, 1982
Corn, Alfred, "God's Spies" in *The Metamorphoses of Metaphor*, edited by Corn, New York: Viking, 1987
Gemmett, Robert J. and Philip L. Gerber, "The Poem as Silhouette: A Conversation with John Hollander", *Michigan Quarterly Review*, 9/4 (1970): 253–60
Giorcelli, Cristina, "I carmina figurata di John Hollander", *Arte e letteratura: Scritti in ricordo di Gabriele Baldini*, Rome: Storia e Letteratura, 1972
Giorcelli, Cristina, "John Hollander: 'Powers of Thirteen'", *Letture anglo-americane in memoria di Rolando Anzilotti*, Pisa: Nistri-Lischi, 1986
Hammer, Langdon, interview with Hollander, *Southwest Review*, 80 (1995)
Howard, Richard, *Alone with America*, New York: Atheneum, 1969; London: Thames and Hudson, 1970
Jackson, Richard, interview with Hollander, *Poetry Miscellany*, 8 (1978)
Jackson, Richard, *The Dismantling of Time in Contemporary Poetry*, Tuscaloosa: University of Alabama Press, 1988
Lehman, David, "Virtuosity and Virtue: A Profile of John Hollander", *Columbia College Today* (Spring 1983)
Lehman, David, "The Sound-and-Sense of the Sleight-of-Hand Man" in *Contemporary Poets*, edited by Harold Bloom, New York: Chelsea House, 1986
McClatchy, J.D., "Speaking of Hollander", *American Poetry Review*, 11/5 (September–October 1982)
McClatchy, J.D., "John Hollander's *In Time and Place*" in his *White Paper on Contemporary American Poetry*, New York: Columbia University Press, 1989
Prunty, Wyatt, *Fallen from the Symboled World*, Oxford and New York: Oxford University Press, 1990: chapter 5

While there is a complex relationship between John Hollander's poetic commitments and his Jewish interests, these are never exclusive nor singularly determinative. Judaic elements in Hollander's work are persistent rather than consistent. Hollander gives a particular shape to the (in my opinion) correct tautology that a Jewish writer is a writer who is Jewish. To be Jewish, in Hollander's case – which is the case of a certain generation of American – is to have had certain exposures to Jewish culture, which however then rattle around alongside and among other no less important cultural investments. Hollander in this is quintessentially American-Jewish: Jewish as within a range of other cultural opportunities and commitments, in a banquet-like array that is less competitive than syncretic, less focusing than prismatic. This cultural libertarianism has positioned Hollander to spot and invoke elements of mystery in the Judaic cultural heritage – as textual, as sacral, as revelatory – without having to submit to the disciplines which in many ways bind those more immersed in its exclusive realms. One resource among others, Judaism enters into his work in complex interaction with a diversity of impulses, as another dimension, another reference, another attitude.

Hollander's Judaic alignments can be discovered, first, through references, scattered throughout both his poetry and prose. There is a recurrent turning to biblical texts and figures, as also, although to a lesser extent, to rabbinic ones. "The Head of the Bed" (as Harold Bloom, Hollander's best commentator, has pointed out in his essay "Nebuchadnezzar's Dream") has its striking sequence of female figures in canto 4 – Vashti, Hagar, Orpah, Lillith, also Martha – recalling work on the Bible by women poets. Genesis scenes veritably haunt Hollander's writings, as in, for example, his widely anthologized "Adam's Task" on the originary naming ("Thou paw-paw-paw"); or his to my mind even more witty and impelling "The Lady's-Maid's Song" which figures the war between the sexes through the bone of contention of Adam's rib. The Golem lurches large in "Letter to Jorge Luis Borges: Apropos of the Golem"; but enters subtle and arcane into "Violet", where "truth is one letter away from death" – a play on the destruction of the Golem by removing the E from EMET (truth) to get MET (death). Likewise, the Shekhinah – the feminine presence of God in the world – graces "The Head of the Bed" as Lady Evening, or "Yellow" as the Queen of the Peaceful Day. The rich and light-handed Judaic web ranges from details to large organizing figures, such as the "Seven Branches in Lieu of a Lamp" of *Spectral Emanations* to the Galilee sea of Kinneret in *Harp Lake*.

But there is more to this matter than reference or even grand figural structure. In fundamental ways Hollander's very notions of poetry are themselves deeply grounded in Judaic textuality. When Hollander answers his own "Question of American Jewish Poetry" by quoting Paul Celan quoting Marina Tsvetaeva: "All Poets are Jews", he is proposing poetry and Jewishness as figures for each other, with an added clue to the ways this can work in the very chain of quotation through which he expresses himself. That is, poetry, like Jewish textual practice, is woven out of chains of reference, allusion, quotation, invocation, memory, commentary, words responding to and generating other words. Such figural generation and transfiguration among (and within) words forms the heart of Hollander's theorizing in a book such as *The Figure of Echo*, as well in essays such as "Originality" (where originality is itself an enmeshed term for chains of generation), and in the notions of poetic misunderstanding and translation in both "Hearing and Overhearing the Psalms" and "The Question of American Jewish Poetry". The Hebrew Bible and its modes of interpretation emerge as both example and model: "True poetry . . . partakes of what Rabbi Ben Bag Bag said of Torah itself: 'Turn it and turn it over again, for everything is in it'" (from "Question"). Like Scripture, poetry is inexhaustible. It is the very nature of poetic language always to mean more, to conjure further levels of sense, further possibilities of meaning. But such extensions and transfigurations never let go of the shapes of the words that make up, in very radical senses, the substance of poetry. The materials of poetic creation are the letters and grammars of words, how they carry within them their histories through etymologies, how they generate patterns through repetitions and variations (*Vision and Resonance* brilliantly charts this through classical metrical study), how suggestion comes from, yes, misunderstandings that anchor in the words' sounds and shapes in generative "misconstruings and reconstructions" (from "Psalms"): notions grounded, as Hollander hints, in the (syncretist) experience of the Bible itself, "the complex relations between the Hebrew Bible, the strange and powerful tendentious reading of it called the Old Testament, and the various vernacular translations". Hollander's interests in nonsense, in shape poems, as well as his metrical studies and allusive literary histories all intersect in this focus on the word and its letters, the very fabric of Hebraic interpretative method, as these generate further figures.

But Hollander's syncretism is not seamless (as syncretism never is). Conflicts lurk and erupt between Hebrew and English traditions, between the Jewish and the American. Just how inextricably conflict is bound with commitment is especially vivid in Hollander's translations of the Yiddish poet, Moyshe-Leyb Halpern. Translation is, like misunderstanding, a core figure in Hollander's senses of poetic generation from word to word and figure to figure. But if this is rooted in his Judaic experience, it also measures his distances and resistances from it. Yet is this resistance not itself typical to Jewish exilic life of a certain type? Halpern's "The Bird" pits brother against brother, possession against claim, independence against attachment, all with irreverence and speed and wit. Hollander's translation of this Yiddish predicament binds him no less within its own wars and worlds of words.

SHIRA WOLOSKY

I

Ionesco, Eugène

Romanian-born French dramatist, 1912–1994

Born in Slatina, 26 November 1912. Studied at Sfantul Sava college in Bucharest and secondary school in Craiova, baccalaureate, 1928. Made debut as poet in daily newspaper *Bilete de papagal*, 1928. Studied French at University of Bucharest, 1929–33. Published first article in *Zodiac Review*, 1930. Married Rodica Burileanu, 1936; one daughter. Emigrated to France. Returned to Romania, 1939; taught French at Sfantul Sava college. Returned to France, 1942; granted French citizenship, 1950. Awarded Tours Festival Prize, 1959; Italia Prize, 1963; Society of Authors Theatre Prize (France), 1966; National Grand Prize for Theatre (France), 1969; Monaco Grand Prize, 1969; Austrian State Prize for European Literature, 1970; Jerusalem Prize, 1973; T.S. Eliot Award, 1985; Monte Carlo International Prize for Contemporary Art, 1985. Member, Académie française, 1970; Chevalier, Légion d'Honneur, 1970. Died in Paris, 28 March 1994.

Selected Writings

Plays (dates of first performance)

La Cantatrice chauve, 1950; as *The Bald Soprano*, translated by Donald Allen, 1958; as *The Bald Prima Donna*, 1961

La Leçon, 1951; as *The Lesson*, translated by Donald Allen, 1958

Les Chaises, 1952; as *The Chairs*, translated by Martin Crump, 1957

Sept Petits Sketches, 1953: *Les Grandes Chaleurs*; *La Jeune Fille à marier*, as *Maid to Marry*, translated by Richard N. Coe, 1960; *Le Maître*, as *The Leader*, translated by Richard N. Coe, 1960; *Le connaissez-vous?*; *La Nièce-Épouse*, as *The Niece-Wife*, translated by Richard N. Coe, 1971; *Le Rhume onirique*; *Le Salon de l'automobile*, as *The Motor Show*, translated by Donald Watson, 1963

Victimes du devoir, 1953; as *Victims of Duty*, translated by Donald Watson, 1958

Amédée; ou Comment s'en débarrasser, 1954; as *Amédée*, translated by Donald Watson, 1955

Jacques; ou, La Soumission, 1955; as *Jack*, translated by Donald Watson, 1958

Le Nouveau Locataire, 1955; as *The New Tenant*, translated by Donald Watson, 1956

Le Tableau, 1955; as *The Picture*, translated by Donald Watson, 1969

L'Impromptu de l'Alma; ou La Caméléon du berger, 1956; as *Improvisation; or, The Shepherd's Chameleon*, translated by Donald Watson, 1960

L'Avenir est dans les oeufs; ou, Il faut tout pour faire un monde, 1957; as *The Future is in Eggs, or, It Takes All Sorts to Make a World*, translated by Donald Watson, 1960

L' Impromptu pour la Duchesse de Windsor [Improvisation for the Duchess of Windsor], 1957

Rhinocéros, 1959; as *Rhinoceros*, translated by Derek Prouse, 1960

Scène à quatre, 1959; as *Foursome*, translated by Donald Watson, 1970

Tueur sans gages, 1959; as *The Killer*, translated by Donald Watson, 1960

Apprendre à marcher, 1960; as *Learning to Walk*, translated by Donald Watson, 1973

Délire à deux, 1962; as *Frenzy for Two*, translated by Donald Watson, 1965

Le Piéton de l'air, 1962; as *A Stroll in the Air*, translated by Donald Watson, 1965

Le Roi se meurt, 1962; as *Exit the King*, translated by Donald Watson, 1963

La Soif et la faim, 1964; as *Hunger and Thirst*, translated by Donald Watson, 1968

La Lacune, 1965; as *The Oversight*, translated by Donald Watson, 1971

Leçons de Français pour Américains [French Lessons for Americans], 1966

Les Salutations, 1966; as *Salutations*, translated by Donald Watson, 1968

Pour Préparer un Oeuf dur [Hard-Boiling an Egg], 1966

Jeux de massacre, 1970; as *Killing Game*, translated by Helen G. Bishop, 1974; as *Here Comes a Chopper*, 1990

La Vase, 1970

Macbett, 1972; as *Macbett*, translated by Charles Marowitz, 1973

Ce Formidable Bordel, 1973; as *A Hell of a Mess*, translated by Helen G. Bishop, 1975; as *Oh What a Bloody Circus*, 1976

L'Homme aux Valises, 1975; as *Man with Bags*, translated by Israel Horovitz, 1977; as *The Man with the Luggage*, 1979

Voyages chez les morts, 1980; as *Journeys among the Dead*, translated by Barbara Wright, 1985

Théâtre complet [Complete Plays], edited by Emmanuel Jacquart, 1 vol., 1991

Fiction
La Photo du Colonel, 1962; as *The Colonel's Photograph*, translated by Jean Stewart and John Russell, 1967
Le Solitaire, 1973; as *The Hermit*, translated by Richard Seaver, 1975

Other
Elegii pentru fiinte mici, 1931
Nu! 1934; as *Non*, translated by Marie France Ionesco, 1986
Notes et Contre-notes, 1962; as *Notes and Counter-Notes*, translated by Donald Watson, 1964
Entretiens avec Claude Bonnefoy, 1966; as *Conversations with Ionesco*, translated by Jan Dawson, 1970
Journal en miettes, 1967; as *Fragments of a Journal*, translated by Jean Stewart, 1968
Conte numéro 1–4 pour enfants, 1967–71; as *Story Number 1–4 for Children*, translated by Calvin K. Towle, 1968–73
Présent passé, passé présent, 1968; as *Present Past, Past Present*, translated by Helen R. Lane, 1971
Découvertes [Discoveries], 1969
Mise en train: première année de français [Getting Started: French Year One], with Michel Benamou, 1969
Monsieur Tête [Mister Head], 1970
Discours de réception à l'Académie française [Speech on Being Received into the Académie française], 1971
Antidotes, 1977
Entre la vie et la rêve: entretiens avec Claude Bonnefoy [Between Life and Dreams: Conversations with Claude Bonnefoy], 1977
Un Homme en question, 1979
Le Noir et le blanc [Black and White], 1980
Hugoliade, 1982; as *Hugoliad: or, The Grotesque and Tragic Life of Victor Hugo*, translated by Yara Milos, 1987 (originally written in Romanian, 1935–36)
Pourquoi j'écris [Why I Write], 1986
La Quête intermittente [The Intermittent Quest], 1987
Ruptures de silence: rencontres avec André Coutin [Breaking Silence: Meetings with André Coutin], 1995

Further Reading
Coe, Richard N., *Ionesco: A Study of His Plays*, London: Methuen, 1971
Gaensbauer, Deborah B., *Eugène Ionesco Revisited*, New York: Twayne, and London: Prentice Hall, 1996
Grossvogel, David I., *The Blasphemers: The Theatre of Brecht, Ionesco, Beckett, and Genet*, Ithaca, New York: Cornell University Press, 1965
Hayman, Ronald, *Eugène Ionesco*, London: Heinemann, 1972
Jacobsen, Josephine and William R. Mueller, *Ionesco and Genet: Playwrights of Silence*, New York: Hill and Wang, 1968
Kluback, William, *The Clown in the Agora: Conversations about Eugène Ionesco*, New York: Peter Lang, 1998
Lamont, Rosette C., *Ionesco: A Collection of Critical Essays*, Englewood Cliffs, New Jersey: Prentice Hall, 1973
Lamont, Rosette C. and Melvin J. Friedman (editors), *The Two Faces of Ionesco*, Troy, New York: Whitston, 1978
Lane, Nancy, *Understanding Ionesco*, Colombia: University of South Carolina Press, 1994
Lazar, Moshe (editor), *The Dream and the Play: Ionesco's Theatrical Quest*, Malibu, California; Undena, 1982
Website <www.ionesco.org>, compiled by Søren Olsen, contains comprehensive bibliography, list of performances, and other information

Being Jewish was never one of Ionesco's priorities. As a matter of fact, one has to question whether he was Jewish or not. In his *Fragments of a Journal*, he talks about Jews only twice with lines like:

> But nowadays, since it's become quite easy, since nobody objects, since at one time it was forbidden to oppose Fascism and now it's approved of, I see plays that show how the Nazis massacred Jewish women and children and old men, I am moved to indignation and of course I want revenge, I become the Jew.

Later in the journal he writes, "The Jews invented love, the love of others, fatherly love, divine love. That's the reason why they have been accused of hatred." He never actually associates himself with being Jewish nor is it alluded to. What he does address himself to is living a life of leaden existence. His plays are self-plays for they are dramatic presentations of his own apprehensions, anxieties, and frustrations within an awesomely heavy world. It is through the proliferation and multiplication of words and material objects, whether they are banalities or chairs or cadavers that Ionesco manifests the heavy, laden, hopeless, depressive states of consciousness. The proliferation of matter expresses the concretization of solitude and the victory of anti-spiritual forces.

Ionesco's *Les Chaises* (*The Chairs*) presents certain subjective themes that are his obsessions. *Les Chaises* is a concomitant expression of the emptiness and heaviness of the human condition. This tragic farce, as Ionesco refers to the play, expresses the incommunicability of a lifetime of experience; futility and failure of human existence made bearable only by self-delusion and the proliferation of banal conversation; the mechanical exchange of platitudes. Throughout the play there is an expression of unreality, of the search to find some essential reality, nameless and forgotten, which the characters demonstrate by their incoherent drifting; their anguish, remorse, and failure; and the vacuity of their lives. The heaviness and emptiness of existence is represented by the continual multiplication of unoccupied chairs. The multiplication of *Les Chaises* continues throughout the play and we are not assured, even with the death of the protagonists, that the death of *Les Chaises* and their subsequent disappearance is also imminent. The death of the elderly couple does not preclude the possibility of a continued existence for *Les Chaises*. For Ionesco, the chairs will continue to multiply forever.

In *Amédée; ou Comment s'en débarrasser* (*Amedée; or, How To Get Rid of It*) Ionesco dramatizes the proliferation of a cadaver and its effect on the protagonists. The corpse is that of Madeleine's ex-boyfriend who 15 years earlier, before her marriage to Amedée, had been her lover. The corpse has been in their bedroom and has been growing ever since Amedée's marriage began and has spread throughout the apartment. Accordingly, it has been the ruination of their marriage: *Amedée* represents a failed and barren marriage, a nostalgic desire to return to a utopian past, and, in the character of the corpse, a victory for death. Moreover, the implication behind Amedée's arrival at Torco Square, with the omnipresent and proliferating corpse beside him, continues to verify May's love-death principle. The incident at Torco Square points out the irony of the title because Amedée cannot get rid of the corpse nor is there any way to get rid of it since death is too large, too proliferating, and too heavy. Death is ubiquitous for Amedée as well as Ionesco.

Early in *Victimes du devoir* (*Victims of Duty*), Choubert alludes to the fact that the only way to understand the problems of economics and existence is to "detach" ourselves from existence, to relieve ourselves of individuality, to sink and die. Choubert states that the "Government urges" this loss of individuality. It is an authority that regulates how one should live. This authority constitutes heaviness of authority. It is not coincidental that the policeman, who is representative of authority and, therefore, weight, causes Choubert to think of mud and of sinking into the mud – an image that can be closely related to sinking into anxiety, despair, depression, and death. The authority and the mud are both representative of the heaviness with which Ionesco is so profoundly preoccupied.

In *Rhinocéros* (*Rhinoceros*) the proliferation of collective ideology and idiocy is represented by animals. *Rhinoceros* illustrates both the heaviness of existence, embodied in the sheer weight and proliferation of animals, and the heaviness inherent in political dogma, authority, and collective irrationality. While *Rhinoceros* is "an anti-Nazi play, it is also, and mainly, an attack on collective hysteria and the epidemics that lurk beneath the surface of reason and ideas, but are nonetheless serious collective diseases passed off as ideologies." *Rhinoceros* concerns itself with the guilt and monster in each of us that can rise to the surface and control our being. The beasts of which Ionesco speaks, were men once dedicated to the resistance of Nazism, but the conforming political ideologies of the day caused these men to give up their humanity and sensitivity and opt for the monster within. Berenger, the main character, is a human among monsters, but as a human he is a monster among monsters. To be a rhinoceros is to be normal, to be human is not. To be a conformist is to be normal, to maintain one's individuality is not. To be insensitive to the political horrors of Nazism is normal, to transcend those horrors is not. Berenger is humanity being put to the test of existence among those demonic forces that, unless controlled, opt for the conforming nausea of collective ideology.

What might be called the most depressing archetype of contemporary man's condition may also be the most exemplary play of proliferation in the catalogue of Ionescan drama. In *Le Nouveau Locataire* (*The New Tenant*) a gentleman arrives at an empty flat devoid of any furniture and possessing a single window. The furniture movers begin to arrive and carry into the apartment enough furniture to fill every inch of space, block the window, and obstruct the doors. The stairway becomes cluttered, streets become crowded, traffic becomes stopped, the subway becomes paralysed, and even the Seine has stopped flowing. The protagonist has willingly imprisoned himself in the midst of endless pieces of furniture. This endless flooding of furniture is symbolic of the material pressures inherent in a bourgeois existence. *The New Tenant* is devoted exclusively to the fallen state of humankind. It presents a character that is already devoid of humanity, he has no name or personhood as the play opens, who does not even possess a memory of more propitious times, and who remains the same at the end of the play as he does in the beginning without any concern for a possible release from his entombed existence. It is the final dissolution of communication: the preference for a safe, secure world of objects. The tenement in which the new tenant resides is that of the material world and the furniture represents the pressure in existing in that world as well as the elimination of communication within it.

MARK AXELROD

J

Jabès, Edmond

Egyptian-born French fiction writer and poet, 1912–1991

Born in Cairo, 16 April 1912, son of Isaac Jabès, banker, and wife Berthe (née Arditi). Studied at Collège Saint-Jean Baptiste de la Salle and Lycée français, 1920s; at the Sorbonne, 1930–31. Married Arlette Sarah Cohen, biologist, 1935; two children. Emigrated to France, 1957; became French citizen, 1967. Many awards, including Prix des Critiques from Éditions du Pavois, 1970; Prix des Arts, des Lettres et des Sciences of Foundation for French Judaism, 1982; Pasolini Prize, 1983; Citadella Eurotechnic Prize, 1987; Grand Prix National de la Poésie, 1987; Officier, Légion d'honneur; Commander, Ordre des Arts et des Lettres. Died in Paris, 2 January 1991.

Selected Writings

Préface aux lettres de Max Jacob à Edmond Jabès [Introduction to Max Jacob's Letters to Edmond Jabès], 1945
Chansons pour le repas de l'ogre [Songs for the Ogre's Meal], 1947
Le Fond de l'eau [The Far End of the Water], 1947
Trois Filles de mon quartier [Three Girls of My Quarter], 1948
La Voix d'encre [The Ink Voice], 1949
La Clef de voûte [The Key of the Vault], 1950
Paul Éluard, 1953
Je bâtis ma demeure: poèmes, 1943–1957 [I Build My Dwelling], 1959; new edition, 1975; selected poems published as *A Share of Ink*, translated by Anthony Rudolf, 1979
Le Livre des questions: vol. 1, 1963; as *The Book of Questions*, translated by Rosmarie Waldrop, 1976; vol. 2, *Le Livre de Yukel*, 1964; vol. 3, *Le Retour au livre*, 1965, as *The Book of Yukel* and *Return to the Book*, translated by Rosmarie Waldrop and published together, 1978; vol. 4, *Yaël*, 1967; vol. 5, *Elya*, 1969; vol. 6, *Aely*, 1972; as *Yaël, Elya, Aely*, translated by Rosmarie Waldrop and published together, 1983; vol. 7, *.El; ou Le Dernier Livre*, 1973, as *.El; or, The Last Book*, translated by Rosmarie Waldrop, 1984
Answer to a Letter, translated by Rosmarie Waldrop, 1973
Ça suit son cours [It Follows Its Course], 1975
Le Livre des marges, 1975; as *The Book of Margins*, translated by Rosmarie Waldrop, 1993
L'Imprononçable: l'écriture nomade [The Unpronouncable: Nomadic Writing], with others, 1975
Le Livre des ressemblances: vol. 1, *Le Livre des ressemblances*, 1976; as *The Book of Resemblances*, translated by Rosmarie Waldrop, 1990; vol. 2, *Le Soupçon, le désert* [The Suspicion, The Desert], 1978; vol. 3, *L'Ineffaçable, l'inaperçu* [The Indelible, The Unnoticed], 1980
The Death of God, translated by Rosmarie Waldrop, 1979
Du Désert au livre: entretiens avec Marcel Cohen, 1980; as *From the Desert to the Book: Conversations with Marcel Cohen*, translated by Pierre Joris, 1990
Le Petit Livre de la subversion hors de soupçon [The Little Book of Subversion Unsuspected], 1982
Obsidiane, 1982
Récit [Poems], 1983
Le Livre du dialogue, 1984; as *The Book of Dialogue*, translated by Rosmarie Waldrop, 1986
Dans la Double Dépendance du dit [The Double Dependence of the Said], 1984
Le Parcours [The Journey], 1985
Le Livre du partage, 1987; as *The Book of Shares*, translated by Rosmarie Waldrop, 1989
Le Livre lu en Israël [The Book Read in Israel], 1987
La Mémoire et la main [The Memory and the Hand], 1987
If There Were Anywhere but Desert: The Selected Poems of Edmond Jabès, translated by Keith Waldrop, 1988
Un Étranger avec, sous le bras, un livre de petit format, 1989; as *A Foreigner Carrying in His Arm a Tiny Book*, translated by Rosmarie Waldrop, 1993
La Mémoire des mots: comment je lis Paul Celan [The Memory of Words: How I Read Paul Celan], 1990
Le Seuil; le sable: poésiés complètes, 1943–1988 [The Threshold; The Sand: Complete Poems, 1943–1988], 1990
From the Book to the Book: An Edmond Jabès Reader, translated by Rosmarie Waldrop with additional translations by Pierre Joris, Anthony Rudolf and Keith Waldrop, 1991
Intimations, The Desert, translated by Rosmarie Waldrop, 1991
Le Livre de l'hospitalité [The Book of Hospitality], 1991
Cela a eu lieu [It Happened], 1993
Bâtir au quotidien [Building Daily], 1997

Further Reading

Bounoure, Gabriel, *Edmond Jabès: La demeure et le livre*, Montpellier: Fata Morgana, 1984

Cahen, Didier, *Edmond Jabès*, Paris: Belfond, 1991
Caws, Mary Ann, *Edmond Jabès*, Amsterdam: Rodopi, 1988
Change, 22 (March 1975)
Comparative Literature, 27/4 (1975)
Denver Quarterly, 15/2 (Summer 1980)
Derrida, Jacques, "Edmond Jabès and the Question of the Book" and "Ellipsis" in *Writing and Difference*, translated by Alan Bass, Chicago: University of Chicago Press, 1978
Fernandez Zoila, Adolfo, *Le Livre, recherche autre d'Edmond Jabès*, Paris: Place, 1978
Gould, Eric (editor), *The Sin of the Book: Edmond Jabès*, Lincoln: University of Nebraska Press, 1985
Guglielmi, Joseph, *La Ressemblance impossible: Edmond Jabès*, Paris: Les Éditeurs Français Réunis, 1978
Kluback, William, *Edmond Jabès: The Poetry of the Nomad*, New York: Peter Lang, 1998
Laifer, Miryam, *Edmond Jabès: un Judaïsme après Dieu*, New York: Peter Lang, 1986
Mole, Gary D., *Levinas, Blanchot, Jabès: Figures of Estrangement*, Gainesville: University Press of Florida, 1997
Motte, Warren F., *Questioning Edmond Jabès*, Lincoln: University of Nebraska Press, 1990
Saint-Germain, Christian, *Écrire sur la nuit blanche: l'éthique du livre chez Emmanuel Levinas et Edmond Jabès*, Sillery, Québec: Presses de l'Université du Québec, 1992
Shillony, Helena, *Edmond Jabès: une rhétorique de la subversion*, Paris: Lettres Modernes, 1991
Stoddard, Roger E., *Edmond Jabès: "Du blanc des mots et du noir des signes": A Preliminary Record of the Printed Books*, Paris: Lettres Modernes Minard, 1997
Studies in 20th Century Literature, 12/1 (Autumn 1987)

Although Edmond Jabès was born into a Jewish family of Italian origin, and lived in Cairo, French was his mother tongue and he received a French education. His early poetry, published in France and Egypt from the 1930s onwards, reflected the influence of Mallarmé, Paul Éluard, and Max Jacob.

Jabès lived in Palestine during World War II, working for the British and continuing to write poetry. He returned to Egypt after the war and made regular trips to Paris until he was expelled from Egypt following the Suez Crisis and moved to Paris. He retracted his earliest poems, but in 1959 his main works from 1943 onwards were published under the title *Je bâtis ma demeure: poèmes, 1943–1957* [I Build My Dwelling: Poems 1943–1957].

One of the most striking differences between the early poetry and the poetic prose of *Le Livre des questions* (*The Book of Questions*), the first work he published after moving to France, is the emergence in the latter of Jewishness as a central preoccupation of his writing. Indeed, one could describe the seven-volume *Book of Questions* (published between 1963 and 1973) as a prolonged meditation on Jewishness. The book can equally be described as a meditation on writing and there would be no contradiction between the two claims; for Jabès the Jew and the writer share the same condition, each suffering the "torment of an ancient word":

> I brought you my words. I talked to you about the difficulty of being Jewish, which is the same as the difficulty of writing. For Judaism and writing are but the same waiting, the same hope, the same wearing out.

After moving to France Jabès began to study Jewish texts, particularly the Talmud and Kabbalah, and each of these influences is apparent in *The Book of Questions*, which is populated with imaginary rabbis who, like the rabbis of the Talmud, are made to speak to each other across the boundaries of time and space. Jabès's rabbis are given names, but are not described or in any way located temporally or geographically. They are disembodied voices whose existence is limited to their authorship of the remarks they make.

The Book of Questions, and its continuation in the three-volume *The Book of Resemblances*, are Jabès's best-known works, written in his own unique style of poetic prose. The books are composed of fragments of writing from a variety of genres, including letters, journal entries, songs, narrative, aphorism, and quotations, among many others. The typography and layout of the text contribute to the sense of a fragmentary work, with frequent use of italics, quotation marks, parentheses, and large white spaces constantly interrupting the flow of reading.

At the centre of the first volume of the septology is a simple story about Sarah and Yukel, two young Jewish lovers separated during the Nazi deportations. Sarah is sent to a concentration camp; she survives, but returns insane. The story is not directly narrated in the text. Rather it is commented upon by various rabbis who are the "privileged readers" we meet "at the threshold" of the book:

> "What is going on behind this door?"
> "A book is shedding its leaves."
> "What is the story of the book?"
> "Becoming aware of a scream."
> "I saw rabbis go in."
> "They are privileged readers. They come in small groups to give us their comments."
> "Have they read the book?"
> "They are reading it." [. . .]
> "Where is the book set?"
> "In the book."

Jabès understands the condition of the Jew as that of perpetual exile. ("'I have been wandering for 2,000 years' "). Indeed, his interest in Judaism's sacred texts was initially sparked by the realization that, as a writer living in enforced exile, he was repeating the Jewish experience. Uprooted from his homeland, he found that "The Book" had become the unifying force in his life, and the source of its meaning; the Book had, in a sense, become his home. Although the Book that dominated Jabès's life was the one he was struggling to write, while the Jews' book is an already existing book, the Torah, which they must interpret, this difference, for Jabès, is much less important than the concerns shared by writer and Jew. For both are compelled, more than anyone else, to enquire into the nature of language, meaning, reading, writing, and the Book.

For Jabès, exile is not simply a historical contingency; rather, it is an ontological description of the Jew and indeed of the world. In *.El; or, The Last Book* (the seventh book of the septology) Jabès draws on the Kabbalistic idea of *zimzum* (withdrawal), portraying the absence of God as necessary for the process of creation. According to Lurianic Kabbalah, if the Infinite were not somehow to contract Himself, there would be no room for creation. The first stage in creation was therefore the withdrawal of God from a "point", and the image of God appearing in a circle or point occurs several times in *The Book of Questions*, including the title of the final book (*.El; or, The Last Book*). Jabès thus traces exile to the moment of creation itself.

Exile is linked with other recurrent, negative images and themes in the book, including the wound, wandering, suffering, and the scream, which, we are told, is the story of the book ("becoming aware of a scream"). The scream is the cry of the madwoman, Sarah ('"I do not hear the scream," said Sarah. "I am the scream."'), but through the commentary of the imaginary rabbis, it also conveys thousands of years of Jewish suffering: "*The light of Israel is a scream to the infinite.*" "And Reb Louel: 'The Jewish soul is the fragile casket of a scream.' "

Exile, however, is also a positive condition for Jabès. Precisely because they are homeless, Jews turn to the Book. "The Jew's fatherland is a sacred text amid the commentaries it has given rise to." The book is not a repository of certainties, but a text to be questioned, interpreted, and in the process of reading, re-written. ("– Is there a book hidden in the one I am reading? – The one you are writing.").

Despite the focus on exile and the suffering that has accompanied it, Jabès's writing is ultimately hopeful; indeed, hope is one of the recurrent motifs in the book.

> "I have turned all the pages of the book without finding hope."
> "Perhaps hope is the book."

TAMRA WRIGHT

Jacob, Max

French poet, 1876–1944

Born in Quimper, 12 July 1876. Studied at École Coloniale, 1894. Moved to Paris, 1897; gave piano lessons and attended art courses. Art critic, *Le Gaulois*, Paris, 1898; resigned and returned to Quimper; had a variety of jobs. Returned to Paris, 1901; became clerk and labourer at department store, Entrepôt Voltaire. Closely associated with Guillaume Apollinaire and Pablo Picasso, who became his godfather after Jacob's conversion to Catholicism, 1915. Settled at Benedictine monastery, St-Benoît-sur-Loire, after 1921. Returned to Paris, 1928; associated with Jean Cocteau; lived in poverty. Member, Légion d'honneur, 1932. Arrested as Jew by Nazis, 1944. Died in Drancy concentration camp, 5 March 1944.

Selected Writings

Collections
Théâtre, 1953
The Wonderful World of Max Jacob, translated by Cora Harding, 1980
Hesitant Fire: Selected Prose, translated by Moishe Black and Maria Green, 1991

Poetry
La Côte: recueil de chants celtiques inédits [The Coast: Collection of Unpublished Celtic Songs], 1911
Saint Matorel, 1911
Les Oeuvres burlesques et mystiques de Frère Matorel, mort au couvent de Barcelone, 1912
Les Alliés sont en Arménie: Poème [The Allies in Armenia], 1916
Le Cornet à dés: Poèmes en prose, 1917; translated as *The Dice Cup: Selected Prose Poems*, edited by Michael Brownstein, translated by John Ashbery *et al.*, 1979
La Défense de Tartufe: extases, remords, visions, prières, poèmes, et méditations d'un juif converti, 1919
Le Voyage en autobus [Coach Journey], 1920
Le Laboratoire central, 1921
Visions infernales: poèmes en prose, 1924
Les Pénitents en maillots roses [The Penitents in Pink Vests], 1925
Fond de l'eau, 1927
Le Sacrifice impérial, 1929
Rivage, 1931
Cinq poèmes, 1932
Chemin de croix infernal [Way of the Infernal Cross], 1936
Ballades, 1938
L'Homme de cristal [Man of Glass], 1939
Derniers poèmes en vers et en prose [Last Poems], 1945
Les Poèmes de Morvan le Gaëlique, 1953
Trois quatrains, 1953
À poèmes rompus, 1960
Selections translated by Judith Morganroth Schneider in *The Play of the Text*, 1981
Double Life: Thirty Prose Poems, translated by Michael Bullock, 1989

Fiction
L'Histoire du roi Kaboul Ier et du Marmiton Gauwain [The Story of King Kabul I and the Kitchen-Boy Gawain], 1903
Le Géant du soleil, 1904
Le Siège de Jérusalem: drame céleste, 1914
La Phanérogame, 1918
Cinématoma, 1919
Le Roi de Béotie, 1921
Wenceslas, ancien cocher, 1921
Filibuth; ou, La Montre en or, 1922
Isabelle et Pantalon, 1922
Le Cabinet noir, 1922; enlarged edition, 1928
La Couronne de Vulcain, 1923
Le Terrain bouchaballe, 2 vols, 1923
L'Homme de chair et l'homme reflet, 1924
Le Bal masqué, 1932

Other
Translator, with A. de Barrau, *Le Livre de l'ami et de l'aimé,* by Raymond Lulle, 1919
Dos d'Arlequin, 1921
Matorel en province, 1921
Ne coupez pas, mademoiselle; ou, Les Erreurs des PTT: plaquette de grand luxe, 1921
Art poétique, 1922
Le Chien de pique, 1928
Visions des souffrances et de la mort de Jésus, fils de Dieu, 1928
Tableau de la bourgeoisie, 1929
Bourgeois de France et d'ailleurs, 1932
Morceaux choisis, edited by Paul Petit, 1936
Conseils à un jeune poète, conseils à un jeune étudiant, 1945; as *Advice to a Young Poet*, translated by John Adlard, 1976
Lettres à Edmond Jabès, 1945
Méditations religieuses, 1945
Lettres inédites du poète à Guillaume Apollinaire, 1946
En février 1942, Max Jacob écrivait, 1947
Le Symbolisme de la face, 1948
Choix de lettres de Max Jacob à Jean Cocteau (1919–1944), edited by André Fraigneau and Jean Denoël, 1949
Miroir d'astrologie, with Claude Valence, 1949
Drawings and Poems, edited and translated by Stanley J. Collier, 1951
Lettres à un ami: correspondance 1922–1937, with Jean Grenier, 1951
Lettres à Bernard Esdras-Gosse (1924–1944), 1953
Correspondance, edited by François Garnier, 2 vols, 1953–55
Lettres aux Salacrou (août 1923–janvier 1926), 1957
Lettres à Marcel Béalu, 1959
Quatre problèmes à résoudre, 1962
Max Jacob and Les Feux de Paris, edited by Neal Oxenhandler, 1964
Lettres, 1920–41, edited by S.J. Collier, 1966
Lettres à Michel Levanti, suivies des poèmes de Michel Levanti, edited by Lawrence A. Joseph, 1975
Lettres à René Villard, suivies du Cahier des Maximes, edited by Yannick Pelletier, 1978
Lettres à Marcel Jouhandeau, edited by Anne S. Kimball, 1979
Lettres à Liane de Pougy, with Salomon Reinach, 1980
Lettres à René Rimbert, edited by Christine Andréucci and Maria Green, 1983
Lettres mystiques, 1934–1944, à Clotilde Bauguion, 1984
Lettres à Michel Manoll, edited by Maria Green, 1985
Méditations religieuses: derniers cahiers 1942–1943, 1986
Chroniques d'art 1898–1900, with Léon David, edited by Lawrence A. Joseph, 1987
Lettres à Pierre Minet, edited by Anne S. Kimball, 1988
Lettres à Nino Frank, edited by Anne S. Kimball, 1989
Lettres à Florent Fels, edited by Maria Green, 1990

Further Reading

Andreu, Pierre, *Vie et mort de Max Jacob*, Paris: La Table Ronde, 1982
Béalu, Marcel, "Circonstances" in *Conseils à un jeune poète*, by Max Jacob, Paris: Gallimard, 1945
Belaval, Yvon, "Max Jacob" in *Encyclopaedia Universalis*, new edition, vol. 12, Paris: Encyclopedia Universalis, 1995
Green, Maria, *Bibliographie et documentation sur Max Jacob*, Paris: En vente à le Librairie le pont traversé, 1988
Hermans, Theo, "Max Jacob: Style, Situation" in his *The Structure of Modernist Poetry*, London: Croom Helm, 1982
Hubert, Renée Riese, "Max Jacob's Bourgeois Voices", *Folio*, 9 (1976)
Kamber, Gerald, *Max Jacob and the Poetics of Cubism*, Baltimore: Johns Hopkins University Press, 1971
Lagarde, Pierre (editor), *Max Jacob, mystique et martyr*, Paris: Baudinière, 1944
Lévy, Sydney, *The Play of the Text: Max Jacob's Le Cornet à dés*, Madison: University of Wisconsin Press, 1981
Lockerbie, S.I., "Realism and Fantasy in the Work of Max Jacob: Some Verse Poems" in *Order and Adventure in Post-Romantic French Poetry*, edited by Ernest M. Beaumont *et al.*, Oxford: Blackwell, 1973
Oxenhandler, Neal, *Looking for Heroes in Post-War France: Albert Camus, Max Jacob, Simone Weil*, Hanover, New Hampshire: University Press of New England, 1996
Poulenc, Francis, "Max Jacob" in *My Friends and Myself*, translated by James Harding, London: Dobson, 1978
Schneider, Judith Morganroth, *Clown at the Altar: The Religious Poetry of Max Jacob*, Chapel Hill: University of North Carolina Press, 1978

Poet, painter, novelist, frequent essayist, and Christian mystic, Max Jacob is almost as difficult to place in an historical context as his work is. Reputed master of the prose poem and conjurer of tales involving strange objects that take on personal, even endearing traits, Jacob was nevertheless not an active surrealist. His familiar profile haunting the Montmartre quarter of Paris included a butcher boy's vest, a monocle, and an enigmatic smile that reminded his friends vaguely of Baudelaire. He was an intimate friend of Picasso's, yet also the subject of a few decidedly unflattering and ironical portraits done by the Spanish painter, even while they were still rooming together in Paris in the early 1900s. Picasso was nevertheless sure that Jacob was exceptionally gifted and of all the poets and artists in his circle in the early 1900s, Jacob was apparently something of a spiritual brother to him. Amedeo Modigliani once reported that of all the artists in the Paris School, Max Jacob and Picasso were the only ones he did not detest. Yet Paul Claudel was apparently incapable of referring to Jacob without adding the perfunctory "poor Max" in an ever so slightly degrading fashion. Jacob's personal relationships (outside of the complex ties with Picasso) are just as riddled with contradiction. "Friendship has been the nail on which my life is hung", he was quoted as saying at the end of his life, yet there are few artists who felt themselves to be more maligned and mistreated by his "friends" than Max Jacob.

So where to begin drawing a profile of a man who provoked such contradictory impressions? The secret lies at least in part in Jacob's complex personality. Always playful and ready with pun, word play, or other such lingual amusement (this comes through in his poetry) he enjoyed making others laugh, often by indulging in a fair amount of self deprecation. But he was also subject to fears about his friends' loyalties, and this sensitivity led to easily provoked resentment and hair-trigger mood swings that could make all his good intentions sour instantly. His *Conseils à un jeune poète* (*Advice to a Young Poet*) is a good example of the effusive goodwill and subsequent disappointment that characterized what might have passed for romantic sensitivity a century earlier. This poetic treatise was the result of Jacob's desire to instruct a newly made friend, only 18 years old, in the art of poetry. He wrote the treatise in 1941 (three years before his death) in a little notebook on which he had inscribed "Notebook belonging to J.E." (the boy's initials). The dialogue was cut short however by the young man's tardy response (delayed probably by exams) and by what Jacob considered a misplaced question, "What is sentiment?"

His spiritual convictions however, remained unwavering from the time of his conversion to Catholicism in 1915 to his death in 1944 at the age of 68. Returning from the National Library one day in 1909 to his miserable quarters in Paris, Jacob saw a divine apparition on the wall of his room. This was the beginning of his identification with Christianity and his departure from Jewish cultural and spiritual identity. He had come to Paris from Quimper, Brittany (one of the most Catholic of regions in France) almost 12 years before (1897), having stolen money from his mother to fund the trip. Since then, he had been holding down odd jobs, frequenting the major artistic personalities of his day, and making a literary debut in the great capital where he had witnessed the Dreyfus affair and the rise of a new Catholic spirituality with thinkers such as Henri Bergson (also Jewish) and Paul Claudel.

In 1921 Jacob retired to a monastery where he would remain for long periods off and on until he was apprehended by the Gestapo in 1944. In the 40 some odd years that elapsed between his flight from his hometown in 1897 to his final arrest at St Benoît-sur-Loire, he composed more than 40 works, was counted as one of the most brilliant literary figures of his day along with friends Apollinaire and Salmon, and gained a reputation as an almost compulsively generous and self-giving friend, as well as being a consummate storyteller and an indefatigable correspondent.

Because of his tragic death in a concentration camp in Drancy, one of the Nazi holding camps in France for those destined for the gas chambers, it is easy to forget Jacob's achievements and to make of him something of a martyr, a man misunderstood by his readers, betrayed by his friends, and finally by his country. While much of this is true, it would be a shame to remember the poet only for his end or for the fact that he was a Jew turned Christian. It is also true that Jacob lived at a time when Jewish culture and spirituality had been driven to atrophy by a growing tide of anti-Semitism. For men and women like Jacob, Catholicism seemed to provide an alternative to spiritual needs that the besieged Jewish community no longer provided. Jacob's leaving of his cultural roots in any case, did not entail total abandonment of his heritage. He never felt the need to change his name or to cut ties with his family: he went back for frequent visits in his later years and maintained a certain identity with both worlds, Christian and Jewish.

In fact, the greatest tragedy in Jacob's life is not perhaps in what he left behind but what he kept, quite stubbornly, until the very end. Known for his willing innocence and trusting nature, Jacob was probably unaware of the sinister fate that was swallowing up his entire people until the very end, and with his characteristic optimism, he probably imagined that his friends would eventually come to his aid. It is just this trusting nature that gives to much of his work a light, youthful energy with just a touch of the irony that so often came to his aid when momentarily disappointed or disabused.

JANE BLEVINS

Jacobson, Dan

South African-born British fiction writer, 1929–

Born in Johannesburg, 7 March 1929. Studied at University of the Witwatersrand, Johannesburg, BA 1949. Public relations assistant, South African Jewish Board of Deputies, Johannesburg, 1951–52; correspondence secretary, Mills and Feeds Ltd, Kimberley, 1952–54. Married Margaret Pye, 1954; three sons, one daughter. Fellow in creative writing, Stanford University, 1956–57; visiting professor, Syracuse University, New York, 1965–66; visiting fellow, State University of New York, Buffalo, 1971, and Australian National University, Canberra, 1980; lecturer, 1976–80, reader, 1980–88, and Professor of English, since 1988, University College, London (Emeritus since 1994). Vice Chairman of Literature Panel, Arts Council of Great Britain, 1974–76. Awards include Rhys Memorial Prize, 1959; Somerset Maugham Award, 1964; *Jewish Chronicle* H.H. Wingate Award, 1978; Society of Authors Travelling Scholarship, 1986; J.R. Ackerley Award for Autobiography, 1986. Fellow, Royal Society of Literature, 1974.

Selected Writings

Novels
The Trap, 1955
A Dance in the Sun, 1956
The Price of Diamonds, 1957
The Evidence of Love, 1960
The Beginners, 1966
The Rape of Tamar, 1970
The Wonder-Worker, 1973
The Confessions of Josef Baisz, 1977
Her Story, 1987
Hidden in the Heart, 1991
The God-Fearer, 1992

Short Stories
A Long Way from London, 1958
The Zulu and the Zeide, 1959
Beggar My Neighbour, 1964
Through the Wilderness and Other Stories, 1968

Penguin Modern Stories 6, with others, 1970
A Way of Life and Other Stories, edited by Alix Pirani, 1971
Inklings: Selected Stories, 1973; as *Through the Wilderness: Selected Stories*, 1977

Play
The Caves of Adullan, 1972

Other
No Further West: California Visited, 1959
Time of Arrival and Other Essays, 1963
The Story of the Stories: The Chosen People and Its God, 1982
Time and Time Again: Autobiographies, 1985
Adult Pleasures: Essays on Writers and Readers, 1988
The Electronic Elephant: A Southern African Journey, 1994
Security Concerns: Insights from the Israeli Experience, 1998
Heshel's Kingdom, 1999

Further Reading

Bayley, John, "Stories", *London Review of Books* (October 1987)
Bell, Pearl K., "The Gift of Metamorphosis", *New Leader* (April 1974)
Decter, Midge, "Novelist of South Africa" in her *The Liberated Woman and Other Americans*, New York: Coward McCann, 1971
Driver, C.J., "A Somewhere Place", *New Review* (October 1977)
Lansdown, Richard, "Dan Jacobson", *Critical Review*, 34 (1994)
Roberts, Sheila, *Dan Jacobson*, Boston: Twayne, 1984
Roberts, Sheila, "Her Story", *Current Writing: Text and Reception in Southern Africa*, 5/1 (1993): 36–47
Wade, Michael, "Apollo, Dionysus, and Other Performers in Dan Jacobson's Circus", *World Literature Written in English* (April 1974)
Wade, Michael, "Jacobson's Realism Revisited", *Southern African Review of Books* (October 1988)
Winegarten, Renee, "The Novels of Dan Jacobson", *Midstream*, 12/2 (May 1966)

Dan Jacobson is a superb stylist, whose sentences flow with faultless rhythm and whose words are perfectly judged and perfectly placed. Another key characteristic of his work is an unflinching search for what seems truthful though hidden within disjunctions and ambiguities. He grew up very conscious of being a Jew in a country, South Africa, of implacable antagonisms both racial and cultural, and his early fiction explores with the sharpest perception the contradictions and ambivalences arising from group animosity and private alienation, probing seemingly mutually exclusive emotions, such as shame indistinguishable in its roots from pride. The application is universal but, according to Jacobson in an interview in *New Moon*, "it is only by being more intensely true to the specificity of your own experience that you are ever likely to reach, to speak to, the experience of other peoples."

Jacobson spent most of his childhood in the bleak mining town of Kimberley. Both his parents had emigrated, in separate family groups, from Lithuania around the turn of the century. His active and ambitious father, virtually without religious belief, still "dragged his unwilling children to synagogue services and Hebrew lessons" (see *Time and Time Again*). He was both devoted to South Africa and a passionate Zionist. Jacobson's novel-reading mother was hostile to the Jewish religion. She tried to impart to her children a "gentle liberalism and goodwill-to-all-mankindism"; however, Jacobson comments on his own conflict "between my inclination towards liberal-rationalist politics on the one hand, and a Nietzchean excitement in the idea of never-ending struggles and overcomings on the other."

During the 1950s Jacobson published a considerable number of striking short stories set in South Africa, often about Jews painfully conscious of being a minority group among powerful Afrikaners and persecuted blacks. The naturalistic prose and frequent first-person narration create great intensity, and ironic reversals move the tales far beyond the danger of any stereotyping. "The Zulu and the Zeide" is deservedly well-known and anthologized, but many other stories have a similar cumulative impact of pain, grief, and guilt. His two novellas, *The Trap* and *A Dance in the Sun*, set in bleak South African landscapes, share the themes of uncovering of crimes and consequent different acts of betrayal. Ideas of betrayal and self-betrayal almost become a leitmotiv in much of Jacobson's later work. For example, *The Confessions of Josef Baisz*, set in the mythical totalitarian state of Sarmeda, very like apartheid South Africa, is a brilliant fictional creation of tormented ambition, political thuggery, and ultimate self-betrayal.

Other earlier novels set in South Africa were the humorous and ironic *The Price of Diamonds*, about two Jewish business partners; *The Evidence of Love*, delineating a "mixed-race" relationship, then forbidden by law in South Africa; and finally the long and ambitious novel, *The Beginners*. Central to this work is the Jewish experience in the lives of Joel Glickman, his family and his friends, in mid-century South Africa. Its panoramic scope encompasses such themes, among others, as prejudice, assimilation, intermarriage, the effect of the new State of Israel, and the cultural pull of Britain.

The Rape of Tamar was an innovative breakthrough in terms of its inspiration (a few lines from the Bible) and its technique. The narrator is the disconcertingly modern and scheming Yonadab, King David's nephew; by drawing the reader into some sort of complicity, this cynical observer (and participator) allows Jacobson a sharper voice and a greater expression of moral complexity than hitherto. His initial fascination was with the actual story of the rape and its consequences, but "Nothing in my own career has surprised me more than my continuing preoccupation with the Scriptures; especially, perhaps, as this preoccupation has not led from or towards anything a believer would call belief" (see *Adult Pleasures*).

This "continuing preoccupation" led to *Her Story*, which was derived very loosely from the Christian scriptures. It moves skilfully in time from the future of the year 2296, back to 2007 to the birth of a novelist whose only novel is set in the distant (but very familiar) past. This layered and deeply moving story is also a most intriguing puzzle of identity.

Sandwiched between these two scripturally inspired novels came a critical book, *The Story of the Stories*, which is a daring scrutiny of "The Chosen People and Its God" – daring because God is taken seriously "only as a fiction, as a fantasy, as an imaginative creation". It presents an historical scheme in which favour is followed by disfavour, chosenness by rejection, in what Jacobson describes as a kind of "primitive dialectic" which will come to an end only in the Messianic age. The Hebrew Bible is one of the greatest formative myths of mankind, the Hebrew and Christian scriptures do form an ever-changing yet coherent narrative, but it is "the *un*truth of the prophetic interpretation of the history of Israel which ensured its survival . . ."

For someone of Jacobson's deeply reflective and creative introspection, essays have proved an unsurprisingly fruitful genre. *Time of Arrival and Other Essays* gives a thoughtful account of his experience in coming to London and living alone in it, well before he settled there in 1954. *Time and Time Again* was subtitled "Autobiographies" (in the plural) in order to produce only selected narratives, with a sort of fictive shape and meaning. Half of these vivid and meditative pieces return to South Africa for significant personal episodes, and Part Two is set in London and includes an account of his meeting with F.R. Leavis.

Throughout his writing career Jacobson has written serious and penetrating literary reviews, and from 1976 to 1984 he taught English at University College, London. Both his creative and critical powers are brought to bear on a range of writers, including Disraeli, Herzl, and Isaak Babel' in *Adult Pleasures: Essays on Writers and Readers*. Illuminating linkages are made between groups of writers, and there are also speculative, general essays, the most profound of which might well be "Fantasy and Ethics", in which Jacobson explores the complex inter-relations of fantasy and moral consciousness in life and in the literary work.

From the earlier "autobiographies" Jacobson has moved into a genre that combines memoir, travel-writing, and history. *The Electronic Elephant* in 1994 describes, among much else, his journey along "the missionary road" through some of the more arid regions of southern Africa. The intensely sombre yet multi-faceted *Heshel's Kingdom* speculates on the life of Jacobson's unknown grandfather, who died in Lithuania in 1919. His widow and children (Jacobson's mother was one of them) joined relatives in South Africa, but three generations of Lithuanian Jews, including all his mother's remaining family, were murdered within a matter of months by the Nazis and their local helpers. Jacobson and his son travelled to Lithuania to search for graves, to search for the past. Sheila Roberts comments in *Current Writing*: "The dreams Jacobson records, both during his quest and as a final longing but hopeless reassembling of his lost family, are not fantasies but the profound responses of his inner life to a misery and horror previously unimagined."

After such dreams, perhaps only poetry has the condensed power to harness the feelings engendered – not by the "What-If" of *The God-Fearer*, but the actuality of prejudice and persecution. In Jacobson's ironically entitled poem, "Cultural Studies", the representations of treachery as Fagin-like in appearance, "misplaced among the Aryan disciples" in certain European cathedrals, are described with savage wit.

MARGE CLOUTS

Jacobson, Howard

British fiction writer, critic, and travel writer, 1942–

Born in Manchester, 25 August 1942. Studied at Stand Grammar School, 1953–60; Downing College, Cambridge, 1961–64 (under F.R. Leavis), BA in English 1964. Married Rosalind Sadler, 1978; one son from previous marriage. Lecturer, University of Sydney, New South Wales, 1965–68; supervisor, Selwyn College, Cambridge, 1969–72; senior lecturer, Wolverhampton Polytechnic, 1974–80. Writer and presenter, *Traveller's Tales* (television series), 1991–93; free-lance writer for the *Independent* and the *Sunday Times*, London. Awarded *Jewish Quarterly* Prize, 1999.

Selected Writings

Novels
Coming from Behind, 1983
Peeping Tom, 1984
Redback, 1986
The Very Model of a Man, 1992
No More Mister Nice Guy, 1998
The Mighty Walzer, 1999
Who's Sorry Now?, 2002

Other
Shakespeare's Magnanimity: Four Tragic Heroes, Their Friends and Families, with Wilbur Sanders, 1978
In the Land of Oz, 1987
Roots Schmoots: Journeys among Jews, 1993
Seeing with the Eye: The Peter Fuller Memorial Lecture, 1993
Seriously Funny: From the Ridiculous to the Sublime, 1996
Editor, *The Picador Book of Spleen*, 1996

Further Reading

Brauner, David, *Post-War Jewish Fiction: Ambivalence, Self-Explanation and Transatlantic Connections*, London and New York: Palgrave, 2001
Cheyette, Bryan, "Moroseness and Englishness", *Jewish Quarterly*, 42 (1995)
Cheyette, Bryan (editor), *Contemporary Jewish Writing in Britain and Ireland: An Anthology*, London: Halban, and Lincoln: University of Nebraska Press, 1998
Lehrer, Natasha, "Howard Jacobson meets his Métier", *Jewish Quarterly*, 46 (1999)

As Bryan Cheyette has noted, Jacobson began by writing robust novels that were less about being Jewish than they were about Jewishness defined in opposition to the mainstream, dominant English culture in which he was steeped at Cambridge: "*Coming from Behind* and *Peeping Tom* are not, strictly, 'Jewish' novels. More accurately, they are 'anti-Gentile novels' in which his protagonists define themselves as the opposite of English gentility". It is clear that English literature is extremely precious to Jacobson, and the 19th-century novel is an influence writ large on his novels. In *Peeping Tom*, for example, Barney Fugelman finally discovers that he needs Thomas Hardy and his "goyische greenery" to exist. Jacobson applies himself with some ferocity to the comedy of deprivation and of difference, however, and is extremely funny about Cambridge in a thread that runs from the interview process undergone by Sefton Goldberg in *Coming from Behind* to the reserve so acute that dons and undergraduates prefer to fall off their bicycles than to undergo the torment of having to greet one another in *The Mighty Waltzer.* Thus Jacobson epitomizes the Anglo-Jewish writer who holds both parts of this identity in equally unhappy juxtaposition.

Jacobson is essentially a writer of the family drama, the story of growing up in a family, leaving home, discovering the possibilities of sexual relationships, and being able to return home, armed with that discovery. Corollaries of the theory of family drama are that all the characters within this traditional narrative, apart from the idealized sexual partner, are father-figures, mother-figures, or "splits" and "repeats" of the narrator. In *Redback*, a novel that rewrites the 19th-century plot of the young man who is sent out to the colonies, Jacobson begins with childhood, the loss of the father, and life with a mother and three further mother-figures in the shape of aunts. Jacobson audaciously pushes the family drama to its logical limits in a tender and moving sequence which culminates in the hero's spending the night with and making love to his step-mother, Trilby, following his father's funeral, in the knowledge that his father had never managed to fathom Trilby's mysteries, and push her over the cliff of orgasm.

Sexual and familial relationships are truly Jacobson's subject. He writes both comically and movingly again and again about fathers and sons. In *The Mighty Waltzer* the father is big and square, he has a big heart and is built like a "brick shithouse"; in *Redback* the father is tiny:

> In my early post-pram days when he carried me around on his little back and shoulders . . . it was silently acknowledged between us that for all the difference it would have made as far as speed, comfort or elevation was concerned, I might just as well have carried him.

Both of these parental portraits reveal the influence of Dickens; most particularly, I think, of the opening of that quintessential family drama *David Copperfield*. The father-son connection is one that Jacobson cannot leave alone: in a telling moment in *In the Land of Oz* Jacobson and his wife encounter a road-accident victim. Jacobson notes that a taxi driver who stops to help orders him to rummage in the boot of the taxi for a warm coat, "he being as much the habitual father as I am the habitual son". This exploration reaches its apogee in *The Very Model of a Man* in which, as Eric Korn notes in his review of the novel, we find a family displaying the prototypical psychoanalytical constellation; "the typical, prototypical family, for the father here is Adam and the narrator is Cain". The revisioning of the biblical story in this novel considers the impossibility of family life when there are no outsiders; Cain, for example, meditates on Abel's beauty:

> Such precious perishability is wasted on mere family. You wonder why your brother doesn't have a healthier appetite, why he is looking quite so translucent, then you go about your business. You have to be a perfect stranger to appreciate it perfectly. It was Abel's bad luck to have been born before there were strangers.

By contrast *No More Mister Nice Guy* looks only at the sexual odyssey; omitting the original family, it deals only with the gaining of sexual experience.

The family drama is most fully realized in the complex *Peeping Tom*, the main preoccupation of which, as Alan Franks notes in a review, is "an individual's gradual self-release from the accretions of genealogy, cultural or familial". Here the narrator's neighbour, Monty Frankel, is part of the poorest Jewish family in the neighbourhood. Monty's family is racked by illness and poverty, and he regularly seeks solace by hanging himself from a gallows in his garden until he froths at the mouth. It is clear that Monty is a repeat of the protagonist Barney Fugelman, a possible alternative self, and Barney is dismayed by Monty's ending up working for London Underground: "No one in my family knew another Jew with such a job". Jacobson weaves a complicated web of sexual secrets and complications so that at the point at which his protagonist begins fully to live the outer reaches of his sexual self, he goes home to discover, inevitably, that that is what his parents have been doing all along. Jacobson makes much, in this novel, of the way in which Barney cannot look at his mother without seeming to merge with her, and how he cannot spend time with his family without feeling as if he is losing his identity. Thus he offers us a clue to how hard-won that identity is, a clue followed up in *Roots Schmoots* at the climactic moment of Jacobson's arrival with his wife, in Israel: "But as we came off the plane, she clasped my hand and whispered 'Welcome home, Howard.' We could feel each other shiver. This is how deep the idea of return runs. This is how much of a foreigner she thinks I have been in England."

LOUISE SYLVESTER

Jhabvala, Ruth Prawer

German-born US fiction writer, 1927–

Born in Cologne, of Polish parents, 7 May 1927. Sister of writer S.S. Prawer. Emigrated to Britain as refugee, 1939; became British citizen, 1948; now US citizen. Studied at Hendon County School, London; Queen Mary College, London, from 1945, MA in English literature 1951. Married Cyrus Jhabvala, 1951; three daughters. Lived in India, 1951–75; in New York City from 1975. Awards include Booker Prize, 1975; Guggenheim Fellowship, 1976; Neil Gunn International Fellowship, 1978; MacArthur Fellowship, 1984.

Selected Writings

Fiction
To Whom She Will, 1955; as *Amrita*, 1956
The Nature of Passion, 1956
Esmond in India, 1958
The Householder, 1960
Get Ready for Battle, 1962
Like Birds, Like Fishes and Other Stories, 1963
A Backward Place, 1965
A Stronger Climate: Nine Stories, 1968
An Experience of India, 1971
A New Dominion, 1972; as *Travelers*, 1973
Heat and Dust, 1975
How I Became a Holy Mother and Other Stories, 1976
In Search of Love and Beauty, 1983
Out of India: Selected Stories, 1986
Three Continents, 1987
Poet and Dancer, 1993
Shards of Memory, 1995
East into Upper East: Plain Tales from New York and New Delhi, 1998

Plays
Shakespeare Wallah: A Film, with James Ivory, 1973
Autobiography of a Princess, Also Being the Adventures of an American Film Director in the Land of the Maharajas, with James Ivory and John Swope, 1975

Screenplays: *The Householder*, 1963; *Shakespeare Wallah*, with James Ivory, 1965; *The Guru*, 1969; *The Bombay Talkie*, 1970; *Autobiography of a Princess*, with James Ivory and John Swope, 1975; *Hullabaloo over Georgie and Bonnie's Pictures*, 1977; *Roseland*, 1977; *The Europeans*, 1979; *A Call from the East*, 1981; *Quartet*, 1981; *Heat and Dust*, with Saeed Jaffrey and Harish Khare, 1983; *The Bostonians*, 1984; *A Room with a View*, 1985; *Madame Sousatzka*, with John Schlesinger, 1988; *Howards End*, 1992; *The Remains of the Day*, 1993; *Jefferson in Paris*, 1995

Other
Meet Yourself at the Doctor, 1949

Further Reading

Agarwal, Ramlal G., *Ruth Prawer Jhabvala: A Study of Her Fiction*, New York: Envoy Press, 1990
Bailur, Jayanti, *Ruth Prawer Jhabvala: Fiction and Film*, New Delhi: Arnold, 1992
Chakravarti, Aruna, *Ruth Prawer Jhabvala: A Study in Empathy and Exile*, New Delhi: BR, 1998
Crane, Ralph J., *Ruth Prawer Jhabvala*, New York: Twayne, 1992
Gooneratne, Yasmine, *Silence, Exile and Cunning: The Fiction of Ruth Prawer Jhabvala*, New Delhi: Orient Longman, 1983
Shahane, Vasant Anant, *Ruth Prawer Jhabvala*, New Delhi: Arnold Heinemann, 1976
Shepherd, Ronald, *Ruth Prawer Jhabvala in India: The Jewish Connection*, New Delhi: Chanakya, 1994
Sucher, Laurie, *The Fiction of Ruth Prawer Jhabvala*, New York: St Martin's Press, and London: Macmillan, 1989

To many of her readers, Ruth Prawer Jhabvala is equated with the silks and spices of *Heat and Dust*. In appending her husband's even more exotic name, she has been able to overshadow her own alien origins, and her Jewish descent is a surprisingly little known fact, especially in India, where it is enough that she is a westerner in Delhi, presuming to comment on Indian country and culture. Nevertheless, perhaps by its very absence, it is central to her writing.

Jhabvala was, in her own words, "practically born a displaced person" (quoted in Gooneratne). In the spring of 1939, when she was 12 years old, she and her family were among the last to escape from Nazi Germany to England. In all, they lost some 40 relatives in the Shoah, and many more besides: "My father's entire family, part of my mother's family, the children I went to school with, and most of my parents' family friends – in fact, our entire social circle."

She rarely speaks of this or of her childhood, but a rare public lecture, given in 1979, she said of the years 1933–36:

> They should have been my most formative years, and maybe they were, I don't know. Together with the early happy German-Jewish bourgeois family years – 1927–1933 – they should be that profound well of memory and experience (childhood and ancestral) from which as a writer I should have drawn. I never have . . . I don't know why not. I do know that they were the beginning of my disinheritance – the way they are for other writers of their inheritance.

While she has yet to write directly about this "moment of disinheritance", her work set in the West is peopled by German-Jewish characters who lead dislocated, albeit comfortable existences, far from home. Of these, "A Birthday in London" perhaps comes closest yet to describing her own adolescent years in England. There, Sonia Wolff, a widowed German-Jewish émigré, hosts a birthday party. As dusk falls, she and her friends sit over *apfel strudel* and coffee and try not to talk about the old times. It is a melancholy but spirited gathering. At one point Sonia's son Werner breezes in, but while he is fully at ease in London, for his mother and her friends it has not been easy to start over in a country where no one knows your name or what it stood for. As Mrs Gottlob bravely reflects: "'Yes, there we were all different people . . . Still, here we all are, no bones broken, eh, Lumbik?'" Jhabvala's father committed suicide in London in the 1950s and, like Bruno in *In Search of Love and Beauty*, Sonia's husband Otto has simply wasted away.

Jhabvala's passage to India was an inversion of the immigrant's move from east to west, but while the country's poverty and corruption rankled with her sense of social justice (India remains for her a "great animal of poverty and backwardness" as she explains in "Myself in India"), she found life there "much closer to the Jewish world I knew than the Anglo-Saxon world", and came across very Jewish attitudes towards, for example, the ritual of food, which often features in her writing. But even by marriage Jhabvala was an outsider, since her husband was a Parse, a member of a generally well-educated and prosperous ethnic group whose position in Indian society is not dissimilar to that of the Jews in Europe.

While Sonia and her friends drink strong coffee in continental cafes and sit in dark apartments full of heavy furniture, their children ponder their disinheritance. In *In Search of Love and Beauty*, Bruno's daughter Marianna adopts a Jewish baby, Natasha, in an attempt to tune into her heritage. But Natasha, with her "pale ghetto complexion, her dark inward-looking eyes", is not what she expects, and it turns out that Marianna has confused her image of a Jewish child with that of a Russian one. Later in the novel, Marianna's son, Tim, takes up his own search for the WASP landscape he feels he should rightfully have inherited from the father he barely knew.

In "Myself in India" Jhabvala writes, "I'm absolutely passive, like blotting paper", explaining elsewhere: "Not really having a world of my own, I made up for my disinheritance by absorbing the worlds of others". Just as she captured the Anglo-Indian experience so comprehensively in *Heat and Dust*, so her many successful screenplays, including *Howards End* and *A Room with a View*, written for Merchant-Ivory, evoke an England more English than ever it was. Her characters are often animated by a desire to absorb and appropriate the better qualities of others. In *In Search of Love and Beauty*, Leo Kellerman, typical of Jhabvala's messianic male figures, draws a harem of searchers in his wake, while Boy in "A Summer by the Sea" exercises a similar, albeit less manipulative, fascination over both men and women, and in "Great Expectations", a career woman's careful, solitary life is turned upside down by a golden-haired, fairy-like trio.

As one who espouses James Joyce's view that writing is all about "silence, exile and cunning", Jhabvala's disinheritance has been as productive as any inheritance. To quote Yasmine Gooneratne, hers are "novels of expatriation" in all its various guises: national, cultural, emotional, familial. Her multiple exile has left her with an ambivalent identity: early blurbs described her as a Polish writer; she is a Westerner in the East, and an Easterner in the West; and just when we might have got the measure of her, she added another layer to her camouflage by moving back west to spend half her time in New York, a transition she has recently chronicled in *East into Upper East*.

In a personal letter written in 1991, Jhabvala claimed to be able to trace no influence of her Jewish background in herself or her writing, but for the informed reader, an unmistakably Jewish sensibility shines through – in her social conscience, in her characters' constant questing for spiritual and emotional enlightenment, in the compassion and pathos that flesh out her otherwise crisp, Austenesque prose. After all, silence, cunning, and exile are, as Gooneratne points out, not so far removed from "silence, omission, and the wish to forget" – sadly, more Jewish precepts altogether.

HEPHZIBAH ANDERSON

Jong, Erica

US fiction writer and poet, 1942–

Born Erica Mann in New York City, 26 March 1942. Studied at High School of Music and Art, New York; Barnard College, New York, 1959–63, BA 1963; Columbia University, MA 1965; Columbia School of Fine Arts, 1969–70. Married, first, Michael Werthman, 1963; divorced 1965; second, Allan Jong, 1966; divorced 1975; third, Jonathan Fast, 1977; divorced 1983; one daughter; fourth, Kenneth David Burrows, 1989. Lecturer in English, City College, New York, 1964–70, and at University of Maryland European Division, Heidelberg, 1967–68; instructor in English, Manhattan Community College, 1969–70; instructor in poetry, YM–YWHA Poetry Center, New York, since 1971. President, 1991–93, and since then member of advisory board, Authors Guild; member of advisory board, National Writers Union. Many awards, including Academy of American Poets Award, 1963; New York State Council on the Arts grant, 1971; National Endowment for the Arts grant, 1973; Creative Artists Public Service grant, 1973; International Sigmund Freud Prize, 1979; United Nations Award of Excellence for Literature, 1998.

Selected Writings

Novels
Fear of Flying, 1973
How to Save Your Own Life, 1977
Fanny, Being the True History of the Adventures of Fanny Hackabout-Jones, 1980
Parachutes and Kisses, 1984
Serenissima: A Novel of Venice, 1987; as *Shylock's Daughter*, 1995
Any Woman's Blues, 1990
Inventing Memory: A Novel of Mothers and Daughters, 1997

Poetry
Fruits and Vegetables, 1971
Half-Lives, 1973
Here Comes and Other Poems, 1975
Loveroot, 1975
The Poetry of Erica Jong, 1976
Selected Poems, 2 vols, 1977–80
At the Edge of the Body, 1979
Ordinary Miracles, 1983
Becoming Light: Poems, New and Selected, 1991

Other
Four Visions of America, with others, 1977
Witches, 1981
Megan's Book of Divorce: A Kid's Book for Adults, 1984; revised edition, as *Megan's Two Houses*, 1996
The Devil at Large: Erica Jong on Henry Miller, 1993
Fear of Fifty: A Midlife Memoir, 1994
What Do Women Want? Bread, Roses, Sex, Power, 1998

Further Reading

Bannon, Barbara A., "*Publishers Weekly* Interviews Erica Jong", *Publishers Weekly*, 211 (14 February 1977)
Fishkin, Shelley Fisher, "Erica Jong", *American Writers*, supplement 5, edited by Jay Parini, New York: Scribner, 2000
Frankfort, Ellen, "Erica Jong: An Intimate Conversation", *Viva* (September 1977)

Henderson, Bruce, "Erica Jong", *Jewish American Women Writers: A Bio-Bibliographical and Critical Sourcebook*, edited by Ann R. Shapiro *et al.*, Westport, Connecticut: Greenwood Press, 1994

Interviews in *New York Quarterly*, 16 (1974); *Playboy* (September 1975)

Miller, Henry, "Erica Jong's *Tropic*", *New York Times* (20 August 1974)

Reardon, Joan, "Fear of Flying: Developing the Feminist Novel", *International Journal of Women's Studies*, 1/3 (1978)

Ruth, Julie Anne, "Isadora and Fanny, Jessica and Erica: The Feminist Discourse of Erica Jong", *Australian Women's Book Review* (September 1990)

Showalter, Elaine and Carol Smith, "Interview with Erica Jong", *Columbia Forum*, new series, 4/2 (1975)

Stoffman, Judy, "Portnoy, Stop Your Complaining: Writer Erica Jong Fights Stereotypes of Jewish Women", *Toronto Star* (2 November 1997)

Templin, Charlotte, "That Mispronounced Poet: An Interview with Erica Jong", *Boston Review*, 17 (March–April 1992)

Templin, Charlotte, *Feminism and the Politics of Literary Reputation: The Example of Erica Jong*, Lawrence: University Press of Kansas, 1995

Toth, Emily, entry in *Twentieth-Century American-Jewish Fiction Writers*, edited by Daniel Walden, Detroit: Gale, 1984 (Dictionary of Literary Biography, vol. 28)

Walker, Nancy, A., *Feminist Alternatives: Irony and Fantasy in the Contemporary Novel by Women*, Jackson: University Press of Mississippi, 1990

With the publication of Erica Jong's first novel, *Fear of Flying*, in 1973, a new kind of Jewish-American heroine entered the literary landscape. Isadora Wing (like Jong, her creator) was a Barnard-educated, middle-class, nice Jewish girl from Manhattan's Upper West Side trying to "find herself". She was unafraid to break the rules: she was open about her body, candid about her sexual fantasies, honest about male sexual performance, and unafraid to express herself frankly in four-letter words. Appearing just as the women's movement was beginning profoundly to transform American society, Jong's novel became an instant icon, a cultural document. It wasn't so much that it contained four-letter words or was candid about sexual gratification and the lack thereof. It was that all this sex-talk happened inside a woman's head and was told from a woman's point of view. The sex object – the role into which women had traditionally been cast in literature in the US – was talking back. What's more, she was talking back assertively and aggressively. She was taking the initiative and suiting herself; no matter that her results were decidedly mixed. What mattered was the audacity of the venture. Conflicted, confused – much as her readers probably were – Isadora nonetheless broke out of the role society cast her in and gave birth to a new self.

That new self lived inside of a Jewish American woman who was both more interesting and appealing than the stereotypical devouring Jewish mother that Jong's older contemporary, Philip Roth, had created four years earlier in *Portnoy's Complaint*, a book in which sex had also been central. *Portnoy's Complaint*, which aspired to be more than pornography, foregrounded a Jewish man's candidly described sexual obsessions. Can a writer pack a book with sex and four-letter words and still get taken seriously as literature? Roth proved it could be done. If you were male. Jong found out when she wrote a novel that tried to do the same thing from a woman's point of view that the same rules didn't apply. Roth evoked titillation where Jong provoked outrage; Roth was celebrated for breaking the rules, while Jong was castigated (two prominent critics called the book hopelessly "vulgar"). Jong found herself at the barricades of the sexual revolution, poster-girl for an Equal Rights Amendment for writers.

Like her heroine, Isadora, Jong had grown up in a family of painters in a middle-class Jewish home in Manhattan. Her father, Seymour Mann (né Samuel Weisman), the child of Polish Jews, was a musician. Her mother, Eda Mirsky, the child of Russian Jews who had settled in England before moving to New York, followed the example of her own father (a successful portrait painter and commercial artist), and became a painter. The pair met in the Catskill Mountains when they were teenagers.

While Jong's most recent novel, *Inventing Memory: A Novel of Mothers and Daughters*, foregrounds issues of Jewish history and Jewish identity more prominently than any of her earlier works, Jewish concerns and themes have, in fact, been central to Jong's fiction from the start. In *Fear of Flying*, for example, Isadora often thinks about the residues of the Holocaust in modern Germany, and holds forth on modern German amnesia about the Nazi past. She is also aware of the role her "exotic" Jewishness plays in her non-Jewish lover's attraction to her. Isadora's sense of herself as a Jew surfaces again in *Parachutes and Kisses*, where she makes a pilgrimage when in Russia to Babi Yar. But even when she's not visiting the sites of anti-Semitic atrocities, Isadora is uncomfortably aware of anti-Semitic stereotypes in all of the novels in which she is a central figure. She is also prone to pepper her observations in all of these volumes with apt Yiddish phrases. A selfconscious awareness of Jewish history, humour, and language surface throughout Jong's novels. One might even argue that her decision as an artist to reject any reticence about the pleasures of the flesh may owe something to the traditionally Jewish acceptance of the earthy vitality of the body in all its robust physicality. After all, the daily morning prayer prescribed by Jewish tradition makes a point of thanking God quite specifically for having created pores, orifices, hollows, holes, openings, cavities, channels, and ducts which open and close according to a brilliant Divine plan.

Inventing Memory tracks four generations of Jewish women from the end of the 19th century to the early years of the 21st century, reprising a number of the themes that have animated Jong's earlier novels – particularly the challenge of forging a viable identity as an artist, a woman, a daughter, and a mother. If Jewish issues have been germane to Jong's writing from the start, in *Inventing Memory* they often take centre stage. A pogrom – described in all its brutal rawness – propels matriarch Sarah Solomon, born in Russia in the 1880s, to flee to America around 1905, where she will move in and out of the downtown world of Jewish anarchists and bohemians. Four generations later, her great granddaughter, Sara, born in 1978, researches family histories at New York's Council on Jewish History, searching for a "usable past" that she can both discover and invent. The narrative is punctuated with quotes from the Talmud, wry Yiddish proverbs, and comments on Jews and Jewishness from figures including Tolstoi, Emma Lazarus, and Gershom Sholem. The novel lovingly savours, in all its sensuous concreteness, the texture of a past the legacies of which reach into the present. The four women whose lives Jong chronicles have much in common with previous Jong heroines: they are honest, libidinous, and all-too-human in their imperfections, and they aspire to forging new ways of being a woman in the modern world.

Ambitious, inventive, honest, erudite, and wonderfully funny, Jong's poetry, fiction, and essays depict a particularly robust version of "having it all": bread and roses; work and love; poetry and prose; children and career; lust and laughter. She has managed to populate the literary landscape with Jewish American women determined to settle for nothing less. Millions of readers around the world who have encountered their journeys of self-discovery have found the experience engaging, entertaining, and, ultimately, empowering.

SHELLEY FISHER FISHKIN

Josipovici, Gabriel

French-born British fiction writer, dramatist, and critic, 1940–

Born in Nice, 8 October 1940, to Jean Josipovici, writer, and wife Sacha (née Rabinovitch), poet and translator. Studied at Victoria College, Cairo, 1950–56; Cheltenham College, 1956–57; St Edmund Hall, Oxford, 1958–61, BA in English 1961. Lecturer, 1963–74, reader, 1974–84, Professor of English, 1984–99, University of Sussex; Northcliffe Lecturer, University College, London, 1981; Lord Weidenfeld Professor of Comparative Literature, University of Oxford, 1996–97. Fellow, Royal Society of Literature, 1997. Fellow of the British Academy, 2001. Received *Sunday Times* Award, 1970; South East Arts Prize, 1978.

Selected Writings

Novels
The Inventory, 1968
Words, 1971
The Present, 1975
Migrations, 1977
The Echo Chamber, 1980
The Air We Breathe, 1981
Conversations in Another Room, 1984
Contre-Jour: A Triptych after Pierre Bonnard, 1986
The Big Glass, 1991
In a Hotel Garden, 1993
Moo Pak, 1994
Now, 1998
Goldberg: Variations, 2002

Short Stories
Mobius the Stripper: Stories and Short Plays (includes the plays *One*, *Dreams of Mrs Fraser*, *Flow*), 1974
Four Stories, 1977
In the Fertile Land, 1987
"Goldberg", 1990
"Can More Be Done?", 1992
"A Modern Fairytale", 1993
"The Hand of God", 1996
"Geheimnisse" [Secrets], 1998
"Hearts Wings", 2000

Plays
Evidence of Intimacy, 1969
Dreams of Mrs Fraser, 1972
Flow, 1973
Echo, 1978
A Moment, 1979
Marathon, 1980

Radio Plays: *Playback*, 1973; *A Life*, 1974; *Ag*, 1976; *Disappearance of a Physicist*, with Sacha Rabinovitch, 1981; *Vergil Dying*, 1981; *The Seven*, with Jonathan Harvey, 1983; *Metamorphosis*, 1985; *Ode for Saint Cecilia*, 1986; *Mr Vee*, 1988; *A Little Personal Pocket Requiem*, 1990; *Memorials of LS*, 1996

Other
The World and the Book: A Study of Modern Fiction, 1971; 2nd edition 1979
Editor, *The Modern English Novel: The Reader, the Writer and the Work*, 1976
The Lessons of Modernism and Other Essays, 1977; 2nd edition, 1979
Editor, *The Sirens' Song: Selected Essays*, by Maurice Blanchot, translated by Sacha Rabinovitch, 1982
Writing and the Body: The Northcliffe Lectures 1981, 1982
The Mirror of Criticism: Selected Reviews 1977–1982, 1983
The Book of God: A Response to the Bible, 1988
Steps: Selected Fictions and Drama, 1990
Text and Voice: Essays 1981–1991, 1992
Editor, *Collected Stories*, by Franz Kafka, 1993
Touch: An Essay, 1996
"Thirty-Three Variations on a Theme of Graham Greene" in *Real Voices: On Reading*, edited by Philip Davis, 1997
"Borges and the Plain Sense of Things" in *Borges and Europe Revisited*, edited by Evelyn Fishburne, 1998
Introduction to *Trilogy*, by Samuel Beckett, 1998
"Kierkegaard and the Novel" in *Kierkegaard: A Critical Reader*, edited by Jonathan Ree and Jane Chamberlain, 1998
"Memory: Too Much/Too Little" in *The German-Jewish Dilemma*, edited by Edward Timms and Andrea Hammel, 1999
On Trust: Art and the Temptations of Suspicion, 1999
A Life, 2001

Further Reading
Fludernik, Monika, *Echoes and Mirrorings: Gabriel Josipovici's Creative Oeuvre*, New York: Peter Lang, 2001
Hansford, James, *Prospice*, Portree, Isle of Skye: 1985
Hyman, Timothy, interview with Josipovici, *Jewish Quarterly* (1985)
Josipovici, Gabriel, "True Confessions of an Experimentalist", *Books and Bookmen* (1982)
Josipovici, Gabriel, essay in *Contemporary Authors Autobiography Series*, 8, edited by Mark Zadrozny, Detroit: Gale, 1988
Kapitanchik, Maurice, interview with Josipovici, *Books and Bookmen* (1982)
Sharratt, Bernard, interview with Josipovici, *Orbit* (December 1975)

The temptation might be to seek the origins of Gabriel Josipovici's sense of himself as a writer, especially as a Jewish writer, in his experience of hiding from the Nazis with his mother in occupied France during World War II; or in the uprootedness that accompanied his subsequent emigration to Egypt, thence to England, where he attended university, and where he has, since the 1960s, been a professor of literature; or indeed in the anti-parochial, broadly international perspective this early experience enjoined upon him. Yet it would be equally fruitful to seek these origins not in such biographical evidence but in other writers' work, for if Josipovici is so fine a critic, it is precisely because reading can itself be the most intense and transforming of experiences. It is when viewed alongside the writers Josipovici most admires that the lineaments of his literary and critical works become clearer, when these two strains are in fact inextricable: such Jewish writers as Franz Kafka, Aharon Appelfeld, and Georges Perec; such part-Jewish writers as Marcel Proust and Muriel Spark; and such excoriating commentators on anti-Semitism as Gert Hofmann and Thomas Bernhard.

Josipovici is an example of the increasingly rare writer-critic, currently perhaps Britain's finest (if Britain may indeed lay claim to him). From the start of his career, fictions have regularly alternated with critical studies, common to both being the endeavour to reveal the mystery and wonder of the world as it is, when faith has been lost in the conventions or traditions that might make this world interpretable. How to achieve acceptance, simplicity, directness, the startled joy of the child, all the virtues and wisdom Josipovici finds in Homer and in Dante, when contemporary culture (Jewish culture frequently included) is so in thrall to simulacra, sentimentality, as well as grand or melodramatic gestures? As the novel *Moo Pak* cites its protagonist:

> The whole history of language and of human culture, he said, is to be found in the decision to renounce the immediate pleasure for the long-term benefit. Aaaaah to Ma-Ma, as Roman Jakobson has so well described it. The task of art, on the other hand, he said, is to find a way of returning to the Aaaah! But in such a way that it can be grasped by others, that it enters the sphere of the social.

From his first critical book, *The World and the Book*, Josipovici has seen this "task of art" as best fulfilled in work from the medieval and modernist periods, work that avoids the pitfalls of romanticism and realism (two constant antagonists). In these preferred periods Josipovici locates an art not of invention *ex nihilo* but of craft within tradition, or in search of a lost tradition; in either case an art that refuses to make man or self the measure of all. The insight of the early book has become more explicitly linked to Jewish themes in *The Book of God*, where Josipovici reads the Bible through a lens offered as much by Marcel Proust and Samuel Beckett, as by the established exegetes; in *Touch*, where he militates against the dominance of vision and sight in our culture; and in *On Trust*, where he tries to show what has been lost to our understanding of art and the world in our Age of Suspicion.

Josipovici's critical work is an ideal counter to that of George Steiner or Harold Bloom. For where Steiner inflates and attitudinizes, Josipovici deals with many of the same issues and writers, but quietly, modestly, and with much greater discernment. Where Bloom proposes the writer's relation to tradition as being that of an "anxiety of influence", Josipovici tries continually to reveal the writer's indebtedness to tradition, citing Lucien Freud's remark: "When I lose faith in my work a visit to the National Gallery restores me". In an age of increasing specialization of the academic critic, Josipovici is an unashamed *generalist*, determined to wrench his honoured writers from the hands of the theory-anxious professionals.

The sense of the present, of the now, of the phenomenal world divested of extravagant imagination and myth, is as central to Josipovici's fiction as it is to his criticism (*The Present* and *Now* are both among his novel-titles, while the "phenomenal" is reflected in his interest in both Wittgenstein and Merleau-Ponty). Yet once again this sense is not merely given, rather has to be won, against the incursions of culture with its noise and distortions, as well as the incursions of more private trauma. Certain of Josipovici's protagonists are trying unsuccessfully to capture life through a monumental *magnum opus* (as in *The Big Glass* or *Moo Pak*). Others are suffering from the invasions of just such ambitious artists (*The Air We Breathe*, *Contre-Jour*). Others again are trying to free themselves of their past (*The Echo Chamber*, *In a Hotel Garden*), when that past is cluttered by chatter and superficially consoling advice. For the present is, of course, the hardest thing to find; which is where the uprooted Jewish subjects often at the centre of his fictions have a paradoxically privileged place, being impervious to many of the prevailing comforts and distractions, hence more attuned to what Georges Perec calls the "infraordinaire".

It is in a fragile, quiet, in-between space, that, along with his beloved Kafka, Josipovici seeks to make his voice heard, a thousand miles from more bold pronouncements on Jewishness and tragedy. "If there is anything I loathe more than calls for the murderers to be brought to book", states the protagonist of *Moo Pak*, "it is the anguished debates about the theology of Auschwitz that so-called intellectuals go in for these days". Far from the quasi-theological doctrine of "Real Presence" promulgated by Steiner, Josipovici's real presence (in *Touch*) is that of a child reaching up and clasping his mother's hand – though even this simple gesture, like the statement against "the theology of Auschwitz" which is itself ever at risk of becoming a theory, cannot simply be assumed, but requires a whole literary context to bring it fully alive and make it resonate. As the protagonist of *Moo Pak* puts it – and again it will require the entire surrounding fiction first to undercut then to embody the statement:

The barking of dogs and the communal praise of God, the murder of millions and the individual's joy at the play of sunlight on leaves, the utter pointlessness of life and thanksgiving for being alive. Our art must reflect both or it is worthless and less than worthless, a hindrance to joy and understanding.

DAN GUNN

K

Ka-Tzetnik 135633

Polish-born Israeli fiction writer, before 1917–2001

Born Yechiel Feiner in Sosnowiec into Hasidic family. He gave his date of birth as 1917 but it was certainly earlier. Studied in yeshiva in Lublin; became rabbi, early 1930s. Started publishing poems in Yiddish; began abandoning Orthodox Judaism. Deported to Auschwitz; survived Auschwitz death march and escaped, February 1945. Wandered through ruins of Europe; after arrival in Italy was hospitalized by members of Jewish Brigade of British army. Settled in Palestine and changed his name to Dinur. Wrote as "Ka-Tzetnik 135633" ("I was born in 1943"). Testified in camp uniform at trial of Adolf Eichmann, 1961. Collaborated with wife Nina on early and ongoing attempts to bring Arabs and Jews together in "dialogue groups" for mutual understanding. Lived a reclusive life in northern Tel Aviv. Died 19 July 2001.

Selected Writings

Prose

Salamandra, 1946; as *Sunrise over Hell*, translated by Nina Dinur, 1977
Beit habubot, 1953; as *House of Dolls*, translated by Moshe M. Kohn, 1955
Hashaon asher meal harosh [The Clock Overhead], 1960
Karu lo pipl [They Called Him Piepel], 1961; as *Piepel*, translated by Moshe M. Kohn, 1961; as *Atrocity*, 1963
Kokhav haefer, 1966; as *Star Eternal*, translated by Nina Dinur, 1972
Kahol miefer, 1966; as *House of Love*, translated by Nina Dinur, 1971
Nidon lahayim [Judgement of Life], 1974
Haimut [The Confrontation], 1975
Ahavah balehavot, 1976; as *Love in the Flames*, translated by Nina Dinur, 1977
Hadimah [The Tear], 1978
Daniella [Daniella], 1980
Nakam [Revenge], 1981
Hibutei ahavah [Struggling with Love], 1984
Shivitti: A Vision, translated by Eliyah Nike Dinur and Lisa Herman, 1989
Madrich, 1993
Kaddish (contains *Star Eternal* plus essays written in English or Yiddish), 1998

Poems and short prose texts, translated by Anthony Rudolf and the author, published in various journals, including *Jewish Chronicle* (28 February 1997); *Jewish Quarterly*, 165 (Spring 1997); *Stand Magazine*, 39/4 (Autumn 1998); also in *Voices of Conscience: Poetry from Oppression*, edited by Hume Cronyn, Richard McKane and Stephen Watts, 1995

Further Reading

Bartov, Omer, "Kitsch and Sadism in Ka-Tzetnik's Other Planet: Israeli Youth Imagine the Holocaust", *Jewish Social Studies*, new series, 3/2 (1997)
Caspi, Mishael, *Nehar Dinur: Shirat ha-nefesh ba-shirah ha-ivrit be-Teman le-or mekorot yenikata behagut uva-shirael*, Tel Aviv: Afikim, 1978
Rudolf, Anthony, "Katzetnik 135633", *Stand*, 14/4 (1973)

I have burned in all the crematoria,
fire without end, fire without end,
I have burned for one, two, three, four years,
all my family gathered in a heap,
fire, burn!, fire, rape!, oh God, the ravages!

All but one of Ka-Tzetnik 135633's books are fictionalized chronicles rather than novels as such. Based on or derived from real events, many of them are accounts of the terror and cruelty experienced or witnessed by the author and other Jews during World War II, both inside and outside camps and ghettos. There is sometimes an over-the-top element in the writing ("kitsch, sadism and what initially appears as outright pornography", wrote Omer Bartov in 1997) and, in this respect, Ka-Tzetnik's work stands at the opposite pole to the understated prose of his contemporary, Primo Levi, for whom "Piotr Rawicz is too literary, Ka-Tzetnik not literary enough". Ka-Tzetnik and Levi both began writing *before* the war. But, unlike Levi, Ka-Tzetnik actually completed a book pre-war: his Yiddish poems, published without his permission in 1931.

Ka-Tzetnik's books leave the reader reeling. But his obsessional and stylized descriptions of cruelty recollected in emotion have the ring of truth not only because he was *there*, but because he shapes his material through a mythic and poetic imagination. His sometimes frenzied prose, bypassing intellectual rationalization, is often mesmerizing; his words, neither euphemistic nor voyeuristic, are vatic emanations of a remembrancer returned from the dead. His populist shock-horror tendencies have meant that not only has he not received the critical acclaim of Levi or Appelfeld, he is completely ignored by scholars and critics outside Israel, with the exemplary exception of Omer Bartov. Uncontrolled and uncontrollable, Ka-Tzetnik embarrasses the experts.

Piotr Rawicz, no understater himself, has stated that Ka-Tzetnik is "hysterical, but authentically hysterical". In the years before his death Ka-Tzetnik was writing an ongoing and endless work, his noble and hopeless ambition being to convey in words the look in the eyes of those on "Planet Auschwitz" who knew they had been selected for the gas chambers by the man they themselves called the angel of death, Dr Mengele. Ka-Tzetnik himself survived several selections, by a hair's breadth. Latterly, writing all night, he destroyed most of his work next morning, perhaps fearing that the dead will say that even he could not know what they knew, for somehow he cheated death . . .

Ka-Tzetnik 135633, Yechiel Dinur, is one of the most significant writers, certainly the strangest, to have emerged from the camps and ghettos. His pen [tattoo needle . . .] name is, in its ineffable anonymity, the ultimate disguise imaginable, for it embraces, in mocking and savage irony, the abstract imposition of an enemy whose aim was to destroy individuality before killing the individual. In other words, Ka-Tzetnik 135633 – his given name on the other planet – is not a pen name at all.

At the centre of his work are the descriptions of perpetrators' cruelty and victims' pain, and yet the hard-won lesson Ka-Tzetnik eventually brings to the world from "Auschwitz of night" is neither hate nor cynicism, but a positive and universal one concerning tolerance for the stranger in a strange land, in this instance a passionate belief in the need to work for mutual understanding between Jew and Arab in the shared homeland. At the end of *Shivitti: A Vision* he goes further. "Auschwitz of night" is transcended by his awareness of the nuclear danger facing us all – "the mushroom-shaped cloud of Auschwitz of day" – and by the obligation to fight this danger.

Ka-Tzetnik's identity was revealed to the world when he made a powerful and widely reported speech at the Eichmann trial in Jerusalem, before collapsing in court. The speech had a great impact, equal to that of his books, and told the same story.

Ka-Tzetnik's alter ego is his character, Harry Preleshnik. Preleshnik survives – whether by luck or by judgement – to become a witness. Having reached Palestine (see *House of Love*), he will tell the history, the story, of a bleak and unredemptive journey, whose ending is dependent upon eventual reconciliation between enemies.

House of Dolls, based on the tragic life of the author's own sister, recounts the experiences of young Daniella Preleshnik in a German army officers' brothel. The book's descriptions of cruelty and degradation are exceeded only in *Piepel* (*Atrocity*), which is the story of Daniella's fictional younger brother Moni, in a place where human identity was systematically dislocated and torn asunder. Moni, aged around 11, is the "lover" of each of the block chiefs in turn, then cast out and all but destroyed by a combination of starvation, flogging, and despair. Moni's mistaken belief that Harry and Daniella are in Palestine sustains him until the end of the book, when he commits suicide in a final burst of instinctive heroism, in order to cheat the gas chambers.

Ka-Tzetnik is the most obsessive of the Holocaust writers. Certain themes and images, like the daily cycle of murder and fear, occur time and again, such as the "darting tongues" of the skeletal figures. He conveys powerfully the hopeless bravado of a *musselman*'s cunning theft of a turnip, unseen, or so he imagines. It is the desperate man's last action before, inevitably, he is discovered and murdered. Each chapter of *Star Eternal* is organized like a poem, with variations played on a key word, a phrase or a motif. The very structure dramatizes the degradation and hopelessness of Auschwitz inmates.

Ka-Tzetnik's only explicitly autobiographical book is *Shivitti*, although *Kaddish* also contains additional material as well as the complete text of *Star Eternal*. *Shivitti* is a remarkable account of the controversial treatment used by the Dutch psychiatrist Bastiaans – involving the use of the drug LSD under which the patient relives the past in the company of the therapist – for what Bastiaans has called the Concentration Camp Syndrome, in this instance Ka-Tzetnik's nightly dreams of Auschwitz. The book is a telling reminder of the high price paid by all survivors of traumatic cruelty, active remembrancers or not.

In *House of Love*, Harry, a broken vessel, is put together by the love of a sabra woman who awaits him, having spent all night reading his anonymous first book about the camps (*Sunrise over Hell*, written in Yiddish in Italy after the death march and before the author reached Palestine). "El Molé Rahamim", the prayer for the dead, is played at their wedding. Galilea takes on Harry's suffering and attempts to exorcise his demons. They have two children, named for Moni and Daniella. Now she must promote reconciliation between Jew and Arab. For Harry: love and writing; for Galilea: love and politics. "A direct line ran within her from the suffering of the Jews in Europe to the humiliation of these Arabs."

Robert Antelme insisted that we can judge the Nazi perpetrators not because they were monsters but because they too were human. Among other crimes, they created a system which set Jewish victim on Jewish victim, for example the murderous Chief Orderly Fruchtenbaum in *Piepel*. Jewish suffering in the Diaspora is no excuse for improper behaviour towards Arabs in or by the Jewish state. We understand from the books of Ka-Tzetnik that writing shall incarnate memory and truth, love shall incarnate children and personal survival, political action shall incarnate peace and justice.

"Like drifting smoke, the lesson of Auschwitz will disappear if man does not learn from it. And if Auschwitz is forgotten, man will not deserve to exist." Harry and Galilea conflate the songs of innocence and experience in a synthesis that is the knowledge they bring to bear on action when art and love and politics come together.

When Ka-Tzetnik died, he weighed 30 kilos. In mind and body, he had returned to Auschwitz.

ANTHONY RUDOLF

Kafka, Franz

Czech-Austrian fiction writer, 1883–1924

Born in Prague, 3 July 1883. Studied at Staatsgymnasium, Prague, 1893–1902; studied law at Karl Ferdinand University, Prague, from 1901, qualified in law, 1907. Unpaid work in law courts, 1906–07; clerical work, Assicurazioni Generali insurance company, 1907–08, Workers Accident Insurance Institute, 1908–22. Learned about Zionism from friend Max Brod; befriended Yiddish theatrical troupe; interested in Hasidism through Jiří Langer; studied Hebrew; attended lectures at Hochschule für die Wissenschaft des Judentums, Berlin. Considered settling in Palestine with Dora Dymant, who nursed him in his final illness; also had relationship with Milena Jesenska, his first Czech translator; corresponded intensively with Felice Bauer; twice engaged. Tuberculosis diagnosed, 1917; undertook various cures. Died in Sanatorium Kierling, near Vienna, 3 June 1924. Fragmentary novels and other works of fiction published posthumously, largely owing to Brod's editorial efforts.

Selected Writings

Collections

Gesammelte Werke [Collected Works], edited by Max Brod *et al.*, 11 vols, 1950–74
Sämtliche Erzählungen [Complete Stories], edited by Paul Raabe, 1970
The Complete Stories, edited by Nahum N. Glatzer, 1971
Shorter Works, edited and translated by Malcolm Pasley, 1973
Stories 1904–1924, translated by J.A. Underwood, 1981
Schriften, Tagebücher, Briefe [Writings, Diaries, Letters], edited by Jürgen Born *et al.*, 1982–
The Penguin Complete Novels, translated by Edwin Muir and Willa Muir, 1983
Collected Stories, edited by Gabriel Josipovici, translated by Edwin Muir, 1993

Fragmentary (Unfinished) Novels

Der Prozess, 1925; edited by Max Brod, 1925; as *Der Process*, edited by Malcolm Pasley, 1990; as *The Trial*, translated by Edwin Muir and Willa Muir, 1937; translated by Douglas Scott and Chris Waller, 1977; translated by Idris Parry, 1994
Das Schloss, 1926; edited by Malcolm Pasley, 1982; as *The Castle*, translated by Edwin Muir and Willa Muir, 1930; translated by Mark Harmon, 1998
Der Verschollene [The One Who was Never Heard from Again]; as *Amerika*, 1927; translated by Edwin Muir and Willa Muir, 1938

Short Fiction

Die Verwandlung, 1915; as *Metamorphosis*, translated by Eugène Jolas, *Transition* (Paris), 1936–38; translated by A.L. Lloyd, 1946; as *The Metamorphosis*, translated by Willa Muir and Edwin Muir in *The Penal Colony: Stories and Short Pieces*, 1948; edited and translated by Stanley Corngold, 1972; translated by Joachim Neugroschel in *The Metamorphosis and Other Stories*, 1993
Das Urteil, 1916; as *The Judgement*, translated by Willa and Edwin Muir, included in *The Penguin Complete Novels*, 1983
Ein Bericht vor Einer Akademie, 1917; as *A Report to an Academy*, translated by Willa Muir and Edwin Muir, included in *The Penguin Complete Novels*, 1983
Ein Landarzt: Klein Erzählungen, 1919; as *A Country Doctor*, translated by Willa Muir and Edwin Muir, 1962
In der Strafkolonie, 1919; as *In the Penal Settlement: Tales and Short Prose Works*, translated by Ernst Kaiser and Eithne Wilkins, 1949
Ein Hungerkünstler, 1924; as *The Hunger Artist*, translated by Kevin Blahut, 1996
Beim Bau der chinesischen Mauer, edited by Max Brod and Hans Joachim Schoeps, 1931; as *The Great Wall of China, and Other Pieces*, translated by Edwin Muir and Willa Muir, 1933
Parables in German and English, translated by Edwin Muir and Willa Muir, 1947
The Penal Colony: Stories and Short Pieces, translated by Edwin Muir and Willa Muir, 1948 (includes *Josephine die Sängerin; oder, Das Volk der Mäuse*, 1924; as *Josephine the Singer; or, The Mice-Folk*)
Wedding Preparations in the Country and Other Stories, translated by Ernst Kaiser and Eithne Wilkins, 1954; also published as *Dearest Father: Stories and Other Writings*, 1954
Parables and Paradoxes: Parabeln und Paradoxe (bilingual edition), 1958
Metamorphosis and Other Stories, translated by Edwin Muir and Willa Muir, 1961
Description of a Struggle and Other Stories, translated by Willa Muir *et al.*, 1979
The Transformation and Other Stories, edited and translated by Malcolm Pasley, 1992

Other

Tagebücher 1910–23, 1949; edited by Hans Gerd Koch, Michael Müller, and Malcolm Pasley, 1990; as *The Diaries of Franz Kafka*, edited by Max Brod, translated by Joseph Kresh and Martin Greenberg, 2 vols, 1948–49
Briefe an Milena, edited by Willy Haas, 1952; as *Letters to Milena*, translated by Tania Stern and James Stern, 1953; translated by Philip Boehm, 1990
Briefe 1902–24, edited by Max Brod, 1959; as *Letters to Friends, Family and Editors*, translated by Richard Winston and Clara Winston, 1977
Briefe an Felice, edited by Erich Heller and Jürgen Born, 1967; as *Letters to Felice*, translated by James Stern and Elisabeth Duckworth, 1973
Briefe an Ottla und die Familie, edited by Klaus Wagenbach and Hartmut Binder, 1974; as *Letters to Ottla and the Family*, translated by Richard Winston and Clara Winston, 1982
Max Brod, Franz Kafka: Ein Freundschaft, 2 vols, 1987–89
Briefe an die Eltern aus den Jahren 1922–1924, edited by Josef Cermák and Martin Svatos, 1990

Further Reading

Alter, Robert, *Necessary Angels: Tradition and Modernity in Kafka, Benjamin, and Scholem*, Cambridge, Massachusetts: Harvard University Press, 1991

Anderson, Mark (editor), *Reading Kafka: Prague, Politics and the Fin de Siècle*, New York: Schocken, 1989

Beck, Evelyn Torton, *Kafka and the Yiddish Theater: Its Impact on His Work*, Madison: University of Wisconsin Press, 1971

Canetti, Elias, *Kafka's Other Trial*, translated by Christopher Middleton, New York: Schocken, 1974 (German original 1969)

Gilman, Sander L., *Franz Kafka, the Jewish Patient*, New York: Routledge, 1995

Hayman, Ronald, *K: A Biography of Kafka*, London: Weidenfeld and Nicolson, 1981; New York: Oxford University Press, 1982

Jofen, Jean, *The Jewish Mystic in Kafka*, New York: Peter Lang, 1987

Mailloux, Peter Alden, *A Hesitation before Birth: The Life of Franz Kafka*, Newark: University of Delaware Press, 1989

Northey, Anthony, *Kafka's Relatives: Their Lives and His Writing*, New Haven, Connecticut: Yale University Press, 1991

Oppenheimer, Anne, "Franz Kafka's Relation to Judaism" (dissertation), Oxford University, 1977

Politzer, Heinz, *Franz Kafka: Parable and Paradox*, Ithaca, New York: Cornell University Press, 1962

Robertson, Ritchie, *Kafka: Juadaism, Politics, and Literature*, Oxford: Clarendon Press, and New York: Oxford University Press, 1985

The career of Franz Kafka has attracted an entire industry of various types of critical attention, and it is fair to say that he has become recognized as one of the towering figures in 20th-century western literary history. What is odd and ironical about this status is that he published precious little during his lifetime, certainly when compared to other major writers. What he did publish, he, in retrospect, mostly rejected. His last will stipulated that his unfinished literary manuscripts be burned and that all of the available copies of his published works also be destroyed, in order that his name be forgotten totally from the annals of literary history. Thanks to the tireless efforts of his dedicated friend and fellow Prague writer, Max Brod, Kafka's great unfinished novels, including *The Trial*, *The Castle*, and *America*, in addition to other writings and fragments, were published posthumously. Even so, a good amount of Kafka's reputation today rests on his substantial correspondence, especially with Felice Bauer and Milena Jesenska, as well as on his extensive diaries, which contain literary sketches also.

Whereas there are few explicit references in his fiction to Jews or to Jewish-related issues, his letters and diaries are replete with such references. Kafka lived most of his adult life within a circle of relations and friends who were either interested in or committed to understanding modern Judaism or who were quite prominent in Zionist activity in Prague. He was fascinated by the Yiddish theatre and the life of east European Jews; he read avidly about Jewish history and developments in modern Jewish life; he learned Hebrew intensively and visited the Zionist Congress in Vienna in 1913; late in life, he planned to move to the Land of Israel. This apparent discrepancy between his life and writings within a Jewish context has occasioned a certain split among commentators. On one hand, there is an enormous corpus of interpretive writing about Kafka that focuses on the universal topics that emerge directly from the texts, such as isolation, guilt, and existential alienation from modern life, the loneliness and loss of self in the bureaucratic mazes and the technological jungles of modernity, the oedipal conflict and the structure of the family, the conundrum of authentic expression in art, or the impossibility of discovering truth or finding human salvation. On the other hand, Jewish readings of Kafka have had to piece together convincing Jewish contexts for the fiction, in order to formulate interpretations that may be seen to pertain specifically to Jewish issues. Kafka's work has been viewed as extraordinarily polysemic, and its open-ended qualities have allowed for an extremely wide range of possible readings. In this connection a good amount of attention has been directed to his literary language and style, as well as his humour and treatment of the gothic and grotesque.

Kafka's breakthrough short story, *Das Urteil* (*The Judgement*) may be read as a tale that explores the problem of guilt and the psychological complexities of the father–son relationship, especially in face of the impending prospect of marriage and the inevitability of dual loyalties, including faithfulness to the deceased mother as well as to the distant friend. In the plot, the Jewish businessman Georg Bendemann neglects his ageing father, hides the truth of his impending marriage from his friend in Russia, and is also accused by his father of disloyalty to the memory of his dead mother. The text does not contain a single explicit reference to Jews, Judaism, or Jewish issues. However, Evelyn Torton Beck has demonstrated how Kafka's fascination with the Yiddish theatre can be related directly to *Das Urteil*. In fact, without the impact of the Yiddish theatre, she claims, Kafka could never have achieved the breakthrough he did by penning this tale, especially regarding its dramatic elements, its style, but also its literary motifs. It is precisely at the time of the beginning of his intense preoccupation with Yiddish, Yiddish theatre, and Jewish history that he wrote the story. Ritchie Robertson has viewed *Das Urteil* as Kafka's fictive exploration of Judaism, by arguing that the text is a fictional answer to a situation presented in a novel of his close friend, Max Brod. In Brod's novel, *Arnold Beer: Das Schicksal eines Juden* (*Arnold Beer: The Fate of a Jew*) the Jewish protagonist's encounter with his elderly, Yiddish-speaking grandmother encourages his turn away from modern decadence and confusion towards a future life of journalistic engagement. It may be presumed that a commitment to a more Jewishly pronounced form of life is also in the offing in this context. However, in Kafka's story, the encounter with the father only leads to the condemnation, ruination, and death of the protagonist. Unlike Brod's novel, Kafka's story offers no possibility of gaining strength from an encounter with the Jewish past. Furthermore, Robertson cites a lecture that Kafka attended in the Jewish city hall in Prague before he wrote *Das Urteil* on the topic of how the commercial spirit was leading to the dissolution of traditional Jewish communities, particularly in the West. Since Georg Bendemann is depicted in *Das Urteil* as a very successful businessman, the consequences of the depiction for Jewish life may be registered within the contextualized Jewish framework, although they are missing from the work of fiction. Other observers have pointed out hidden allusions in *Das Urteil* to the Beilis blood libel affair, as if to suggest that the anti-Semitism endemic to Prague and Kafka's personal experience of the city also find their way into the text. One last Jewish contextualization would be Kafka's budding relationship with Felice Bauer, whom he had met about one month before writing the story. He dedicated this story to her, and her initials are the same as those of the fiancée, Frieda Brandenfeld, in *Das Urteil*. During their first encounter, Kafka and Felice discussed the possibility of their visiting Palestine together. Thus, the erotic and love motifs in the text correspond to and blend with the Jewish and Zionist dimensions of their new relationship.

Usually, Jewish readings of Kafka's texts help shed light on very difficult passages or aspects of his writings, which have not been illuminated sufficiently by other readings. For example, Jewish readings of *In der Strafkolonie* (*In the Penal Settlement*), which piece together bits of references in and outside of the text, see this agonizing work as a harsh critique of traditional Jewish life. Jewish readings of "Vor dem Gesetz" ("Before the Law"), which first appeared in the Prague Zionist newspaper *Selbstwehr*, emphasize its relationship to, and possibly its parody of, Hasidic life and Hasidic tales, as well as criticism of the labyrinth of Talmudic reasoning. This latter aspect can be fully appreciated when the text is viewed within the larger framework of its place in *Der Prozess* (*The Trial*). Stories in the collection *Ein Landarzt* (*A Country Doctor*) may also be seen to draw on the world of Hasidic storytelling made popular in the collections of Martin Buber. Two of Kafka's animal stories, "Ein Bericht vor einer Akademie" ("A Report to an Academy") and "Schakale und Araber" ("Jackals and Arabs") first appeared in Martin Buber's *Der Jude*, and the external Jewish contextualization that is forged by the simple fact of publication in a leading Jewish journal, gives certain credibility to Jewish readings. Max Brod viewed "Ein Bericht vor einer Akademie" as the most brilliant and scathing analysis of the problematical process of Jewish acculturation and assimilation ever penned. Other animal tales, like "Forschungen eines Hundes" or "Josephine die Sängerin" ("Josephine the Singer"), have been read Jewishly as well, despite the lack of specific Jewish publication contexts. Jewish readings of Kafka often focus on issues of community, that is, on the possibility or impossibility of forging a sense and building structures of Jewish community, which might alleviate the painful loneliness of modern life.

Walter Benjamin suggested that Kafka's writings are a kind of code, and accordingly, in the Jewish sense, the writings paradoxically develop a critique of assimilation and Zionism, as possibly valid directions for Jewry. There appear to be no easy answers, if there are answers at all, in terms of Kafka's code. As he himself wrote to Buber, his stories were not parables, that is, texts that sought to devise some kind of message or lesson. In the last year of his life, Kafka, although quite ill, succeeded in leaving his family and the Prague environment which have left their marks or scars in different ways on his literary production. He joined his last love, the young Dora Dymant in Berlin, which was to serve, perhaps, as a way station on the path to Palestine. But, ultimately, there was no true escape for Kafka from what he perceived and lived as the difficult conditions of human and Jewish existence. Similarly, there is no escape for his emaciated hunger artist, the subject of the title story in his last published collection. He is abandoned by the world and left to die in his cage. In the end, that is the way Kafka would have had it as well.

MARK GELBER

Kahana-Carmon, Amalia

Israeli fiction writer, 1930–

Born Amalia Kahana on Kibbutz Ein Harod, 1930. Studied at School of Librarianship, Hebrew University, Jerusalem, BA in literature and librarianship. Served in Negev Brigade during War of Independence, 1948. Married Aryeh Carmon, 1951; one daughter, two sons. Assistant to military attaché; worked for BBC, London, 1950; lived in West Germany, 1951–58; librarian, Tel Aviv University Central Library; chief librarian, Israeli Petroleum Institute. Writer in residence, Tel Aviv University, 1974–75, and Oxford Centre for Postgraduate Hebrew Studies, 1978–79; participated in International Writers Program, University of Iowa; has lectured at many universities in United States. Member of executive board, Hebrew Writers Association, 1977–79, 1982–84. Many awards, including Ammot Award, 1964; Bnai Brith Award for Librarianship, 1964; Bamachaneh Writer of the Year, 1964–65; S.D. Steinberg award (Zürich), 1967; Prime Minister's Creative Writing Award, 1971; Aricha Award, 1981; Brenner Prize, 1985; Bialik Prize, 1994.

Selected Writings

Fiction
Bikhefifah achat [Under One Roof], 1966
Veyareah beemek ayalon [And Moon in the Valley of Ayalon], 1971
Sadot magnetiyim [Magnetic Fields], 1977
Lemaalah bemontifer [Up in Montifer], 1984
Liviti otah baderekh leveytah [With Her on Her Way Home], 1991
Kan nagur; hamesh novelot [Here We'll Live], 1996

Play
Keta lebamah betaam hasignon hagadol [A Piece for the Stage in the Grand Manner], 1976

Further Reading

Feldman, Yael S., *No Room of their Own: Gender and Nation in Israeli Women's Fiction*, New York: Columbia University Press, 1999; Hebrew edition, Tel Aviv: Hakibuts hameuhad, 2001
Fuchs, Esther, "Gynographic Re-Visions: Amalia Kahana-

Carmon" and "Self-Conscious Heroism: *And Moon in the Valley of Ayalon*" in *Israeli Mythogynies: Women in Contemporary Hebrew Fiction*, Albany: State University of New York Press, 1987
Fuchs, Esther, "Amalia Kahana-Carmon and Contemporary Hebrew Women's Fiction", *Signs*, 13/2 (1988)
Grober, Sonia, "A Re-Reading: 'First Axioms': A Writer's Attempt at Self-Definition", *Modern Hebrew Literature*, 13/3–4 (1988)
Yudkin, Leon I., "Amalia Kahana-Carmon and the Plot of the Unspoken" in his *1948 and After: Aspects of Israeli Fiction*, Manchester: University of Manchester Press, 1984

Amalia Kahana-Carmon is a native product of Israel, born on Kibbutz Ein Harod and raised in Tel Aviv, producing fiction that is both local and introverted. Her first collection of stories, *Bikhefifah achat* [Under One Roof], marked out her fictional path, and has become the most representative volume in her output of stories, novellas, and novels. But she continues to plough her own very specific furrow, with her idiosyncratic prose, her analyses of the principal fictional figures in her stories (female), and her dramatic accounts of passion and disappointment.

Unlike so many of her peers, Kahana-Carmon is concerned with the individual, and the feminine individual at that, rather than with the public events of the Israeli State. She started to produce stories in the 1960s, at the time when Israeli writers, through their fiction, were beginning to react against collectivization, the sense that the writer represented a point of view that was associated with public and joint concerns. The Israeli literature of the period of the State usually echoed the predominant thrust of public life, the ingathering of exiles, the war situation, Israel and the Diaspora, Israel and the Arabs, the aspiration towards the creation of a new type of society, the kibbutz, and the collective future. The individual emerging against this backdrop began to be increasingly portrayed as escaping from this sense of "us" into a more assertive "me". Kahana-Carmon, though, is distinct even within the terms of this new tendency in focusing on the private, emotional life of the female. And this is brought into sharper relief by the plotting of many of the stories, which chart a moment of crisis, brought about by a love that has mystical contours.

Her work is intensely concerned with the analysis of interpersonal relationships and their refraction on a particular individual. She portrays the intensity of the moment, as contrasted with whatever preceded that moment. That moment takes its meaning, often inexpressible in words, from the contrast with the mundane, and then transcends the common moment. But the mystical moment can not be achieved by the individual in isolation. She requires the catalyst of the other, the man through whom that moment has come about, the man who serves as the spark that ignites the flame. This love, then, is a form of mystical union. However, this sense is perceived only by one of the two parties to the union, and so what follows, in the prosaic world of the everyday, is inevitable disappointment. Kahana-Carmon's writing is romantic, offering a sharply pointed contrast between the actual and the ideal, a fact with which the heroine must come terms, and take her subsequent being. The frustration is also inevitable, and turns into poignant sadness.

So the writer's plots are the framework allowing the expression of the emotion. The instrument for the achievement of this effect is her language. Kahana-Carmon's literary Hebrew language is quintessential, quite different from that of her contemporaries. The new subject is couched in a new language. Now we can say that this writing is specifically feminine. Not only is she one of the few women to forge a distinct path in the Israeli literary landscape and to become a prominent writer, but her writing is unmistakably of another order, which is also indubitably feminist. The whole view embodied is feminine; the way that the consciousness is brought to bear on the world, as well as the nature of the subjects selected, brings about a new charge in Hebrew literature from the 1960s onwards. It is indeed from this point that women writers come more and more to the fore in the literature of the country.

Any prosaic paraphrasing of her work would certainly sound precious and even sentimental, perhaps overdramatic and limited. So precarious is the link that she establishes with external reality that special demands are made upon the creative power of the word. The word has to conjure up its own credibility, because the view of the material invoked is not often confirmed by other participants in the story nor by the events described. It is her own unique universe, and in order to achieve the credibility of the word, the author builds up that universe by a special language. This language, even as it represents dialogue, departs from the prevalent vernacular and from the dominant convention. These departures permeate the whole text, and create a specific tone, and it is this tone that then becomes the reality. The register of the Hebrew is what we would call generally "high", not just in the recording of special moments, and not just in the descriptive passages that surround speech (where we might normally expect common colloquial language in imitation of the argot patterns generally employed), but throughout. We are aware in a Kahana-Carmon story that it is recorded in this distinct, often dreamlike language.

This language can also be regarded as a form of mimesis, as the world that the author seeks to present is itself an imitation. The stories become novellas, and sometimes novels. The characters generally appear under different names, but not always, as we sometimes have a recurrence of the same name. We also find the point of focus moving in the various stories, and, as we might expect, that focus is often of a woman becoming older. The preoccupations of an adolescent girl and middle-aged divorcée may share a good deal, but there still remains an adjustment of perspective, for all the romance, and for all the regrets. Sometimes too, the narrator shifts the perspective from the central character to another, so that she can then test the reality from the outside. But another test can also be applied. This time, not the shifting of focus from one individual to another, but removing the individual to another time, and then looking back as from a distance, and, as it were, to another reality. This is carried out in all her books, and in both shorter and longer fiction. The male perspective is also occasionally tested, but the author behind the narrator discloses herself, as the voice that comes over is distinctly feminine.

LEON I. YUDKIN

Kaniuk, Yoram

Israeli fiction writer and journalist, 1930–

Born in Tel Aviv, 2 May 1930. Fought and was wounded in the War of Independence, 1948; went to United States, initially for medical treatment; lived in New York, 1951–61 Married; two children. Began to write in Hebrew, paying to have work translated into English, 1959; began publishing prose, 1961. Became theatre and film critic, *Davar* and *Lamerhave*; contributor to periodicals including *Devar hashavua*. Many literary prizes, including Prix des Droits de l'Homme, Paris, 1997; President's Prize (Israel), 1998; Prix Méditerranée étranger, 2000. Now lives in Tel Aviv.

Selected Writings

Novels

The Acrophile, translated by Zeva Shapiro, 1961; published in Hebrew as *Hayored lemala*, 1963
Himmo melekh yerushalayim, 1965; as *Himmo, King of Jerusalem*, translated by Yosef Shachter, 1969
Adam ben kelev, 1968; as *Adam Resurrected*, translated by Seymour Simckes, 1969
Susets, 1974; as *Rocking Horse*, translated by Richard Flantz, 1977
Hasipur al dodah shlomtsion hagedolah, 1976; as *Aunt Shlomzion the Great*, translated by Zeva Shapiro, 1978
Hayehudi haaharon, 1982; as *The Last Jew*, translated by Riva Rubin, 1990
Aravi tov, 1983; as *Confessions of a Good Arab*, translated by Dalya Bilu, 1987
Bito, 1987; as *His Daughter*, translated by Seymour Simckes, 1988
Ahavat david [The Second Book of David], 1990
Post mortem, 1992
Taygerhil [Tigerhill], 1995
Od sipur ahavah [Another Love Story], 1996
Nevelot hasipur haamiti [Assholes – A Real Story], 1997
Hasaga shel mefaked haexodus, 1999; as *Exodus: The Odyssey of a Commander*, translated by Seymour Simckes, 2000

Short Stories

Mot haayir [Death of a Donkey], 1973
Afar veteshukah [Soil and Desire], 1975
Kemo sipurim [Like Stories], 1983
4 Sipurim veshir [Four Stories and a Poem], 1985
Sipurei sof shavua [Weekend Stories], 1986

For Children

Habayit shebo metim hadzhukim miseivah tovah [The House Where the Cockroaches Lived to a Ripe Old Age], 1976
Haganav ha nadiv [The Generous Thief], 1980
Wasserman, 1988
Yovi, haluk nahal vehapil [Yovi, the Pebble and the Elephant], 1993

Further Reading

Fish, Harold, "On *Adam Resurrected* by Yoram Kaniuk", *Commentary*, 54 (1972)
Fuchs, Esther, *Encounters with Israeli Authors*, Marblehead, Massachusetts: Micah, 1982
Shaked, Gershon, *Ha-Siporet Ha'ivrit, 1880–1970* [Hebrew Narrative Fiction], 5 vols, Jerusalem: Keter, and Tel Aviv: Hakibuts hameuhad, 1977–98
Shaked, Gershon, "Waves and Currents in Hebrew Fiction in the Past Forty Years", *Modern Hebrew Literature*, new series, 1 (Autumn–Winter 1988)

Most Israeli writers let themselves be inspired by the beauty and spirituality of Jerusalem. Novelist Yoram Kaniuk is more interested in that other Israeli city: Tel Aviv. Kaniuk is a Tel Avivnik by birth and choice. His love of the city and what it stands for is a constant in his writing; his work is deeply rooted in the secular tradition of contemporary Israel, the society that was created by non-religious immigrants who wanted to build a new world.

Kaniuk was born in 1930, as the son of eastern European immigrants who had at that time spiritually barely unpacked their bags in their new homeland. Yoram's father Mosche, who originally came from Tarnopol in Ukraine, had been spending some time in Berlin's cafe-society before embarking for Palestine. Berlin transformed Mosche; his father's nostalgia for the lost world of pre-Nazi Germany influenced Yoram, who was brought up on a diet of German *Bildung*. As well as giving him a treasure-trove of memories and anecdotes that would eventually lead to his autobiographical novel *Post mortem* of 1992, this upbringing triggered Kaniuk's literary sensitivity.

Straight out of his Tel Aviv high school Kaniuk joined the Israeli Haganah, the defence force of the Jewish settlements in Palestine. During the 1948 War of Independence he participated in the siege of Jerusalem. Physically he came out of prolonged military battle in one piece, but the fighting and the death of many friends changed him.

In 1951 he left the country for the United States. He lived in New York and worked as a painter before trying his hand at writing fiction. He went back to Israel in 1961 and published his first novel *Hayored lemala* (*The Acrophile*). In 1965 *Himmo melekh yerushalayim* (*Himmo, King of Jerusalem*) appeared, a love story with a cruel twist, set in Jerusalem after the War of Independence.

He since has written more than ten novels, some collections of short stories, and a few children's books. His body of work has been highly acclaimed, in Israel as well as abroad, with translations of many of his novels into 20 foreign languages, including Chinese. In comparison to his contemporaries on the Israeli literary scene, however, Kaniuk has not become the general public's pet. He is a writer's writer; his novels are complex examples of highly evolved literary craftsmanship, nonlinear in structure and full of metaphor.

Yet his work is very humorous and almost frivolous in its insolence; in this respect there is a connection between his writing and the works of many masters in the European tradition of the absurd and surreal. Or just simply as a accurate naturalist of Israeli daily life, as the Israeli reviewer Leon I. Yudkin wrote in *Hebrew Literature Today* (Fall 1988): "Since his early work in the sixties Kaniuk has put his stamp on Hebrew fiction with a succession of jagged, outlandish images whose polarized metaphorical representation tries to capture the edge of Israeli experience." And in the same article, a review of Kaniuk's *Bito* (*His Daughter*) of 1987: "A characterization of the essence of Israelism emerges in this as in the rest of Kaniuk's single-minded novels: the hero as a tragic failure, the Israeli as non-human, the striving for life as the attainment of death."

Kaniuk has never shied away from controversy, be it political or personal. Already in 1968 he wrote a bitter, yet very funny novel about the post-Holocaust world: *Adam ben kelev* (*Adam Resurrected*). Structurally it is probably his most complex work of fiction: a literary evocation of how postwar life in Israel turns into a surreal nightmare in the eyes of a Holocaust survivor, the former clown Adam.

Equally controversial was his search into the heart of darkness of apartheid Israeli-style: in his playful yet painful novel *Aravi tov* (*Confessions of a Good Arab*) of 1983, the son of a rather odd couple – a Jewish immigrant from Germany and a Palestinian from Acre – experiences the body politic of the Arab–Israeli conflict. Kaniuk has never stopped trying to change Israeli public opinion. He has strong views, which he expresses in his novels and stories, as well as in his direct actions. In the 1980s he co-founded a binational committee of intellectuals for human rights.

In the 1990s Kaniuk began to explore other literary genres. He published the thriller *Taygerhil* [Tigerhill] in 1995, about a woman photographer in Tel Aviv. In 1999 the biographical *Hasaga shel mefaked haexodus* (*Exodus: The Odyssey of a Commander*) came out, a book about Yossi Harel, the Haganah commander on the famous 1947 immigrant-ship *Exodus*. He has also collaborated with his Palestinian colleague and friend Emile Habibi on *The Land of Two Promises*, a forthcoming series of letters about the need of further-reaching co-existence between Israelis and Palestinians.

In 1987 *Himmo melekh yerushalayim* was made into a feature film by the Israeli director Amos Guttman. *Adam ben kelev* got a new lease on life after the Gesher Theatre in Tel Aviv adapted it in the early 1990s. The successful stage production, with which Gesher toured the world's theatre festivals, was itself the object of a fake documentary by Israeli film director Lili Hanoch. Her rebellious rendering of novel and play made for avant-garde cinema and an autonomous work of art, albeit almost incomprehensible, and as such quite befitting Kaniuk's oeuvre of non-naturalistic storytelling and poetic metaphor.

DAPHNE MEIJER
translated by Jeanette Ringold

Karpinovich, Avrom

Lithuanian-born Israeli short story writer, 1918–

Born in Vilna (Vilnius), 1918. Studied at Vilna Realgymnasium, under teachers including Moyshe Kulbak and Max Erik. Left Vilna for Birobidjan Jewish Autonomous Area, 1937; returned to Vilna, 1944. Emigrated to Palestine, after period of internment in Cyprus by British, 1947. Administrator, Israel Philharmonic Orchestra; frequent contributor to *Di goldene keyt* and *Letste nayes*; co-editor, second volume of *Almanakh fun di yidishe shrayber in Isroel*, 1967. Member of group of Yiddish writers, Yung Isroel.

Selected Writings

Fiction
Der veg keyn sdom [The Way to Sodom], 1959
Baym vilner durkh-hoyf [At the Courtyard in Vilna], 1967
A tog fun milkhome [A Day of War], 1973
Af vilner gasn [On Vilna's Streets], 1981
Af vilner vegn [On Vilna's Paths], 1987
Di geshikhte fun vilner ger-tsedek graf valentin pototski [The Story of Vilna's Convert, Graf Valentin Pototski], 1990
Vilne, mayn vilne [Vilna, My Vilna], 1993
Sipurei vilne [Stories of Vilna], 1995
Die phantastische Theorie vom Schuster Prenzik [The Fantastic Theory of the Cobbler Prenzik], translated into German by Johannes Brosi, 1996
Geven, geven amol vilne [Once, Once There was Vilna], 1997

Further Reading

Abramovicz, Dina, *Yiddish Literature in English Translation*, New York: Yivo Institute for Jewish Research, 1967; 2nd edition, 1968
Karpinovich, Meylekh (editor), *Vilner Pinkes* (periodical devoted to history of Vilna, 7 issues, 1969)
Karpinovitch, Avrom, interview in *Di Pen* (February 1995)
Leftwich, Joseph (editor), *An Anthology of Modern Yiddish Literature*, The Hague: Mouton, 1974
Liptzin, Solomon, *A History of Yiddish Literature*, New York: Jonathan David, 1972
Roback, Abraham Aaron, *Contemporary Yiddish Literature: A Brief Outline*, London: Lincolns Prager, 1957
Rothenberg, Joshua and Robert Szulkin (editors), *Gleanings from Yiddish Literature*, Waltham, Massachusetts: Brandeis University Press, 1968
Sokoloff, Naomi B. *et al.*, *Gender and Text in Modern Hebrew and Yiddish Literature*, New York: Jewish Theological Seminary of America, 1992

Avrom Karpinovich has devoted himself to Yiddish literature and culture since settling in Tel Aviv after World War II. He is one of the few remaining living Yiddish authors who was totally immersed in the rich Yiddish-speaking culture of pre-war Vilna. Despite a half century in Israel, his short stories microscopically examine the city that he knew so well. They are imbued with a deep sadness for the cruel obliteration of a lost world and yet they resonate with a compassion and vibrancy that bring Vilna's past inhabitants to life. Although Karpinovich's medium is fiction, he performs the function of an oral historian for the modern reader by continually enlarging a perspective of Yiddish culture in a given place and time.

Karpinovich has always written exclusively in Yiddish although some of his work has been translated into Hebrew. He has also written stories that revolve around life in contemporary Israel and that touch on human problems in the face of larger events. But Vilna is always at the heart of his work.

The well-known Yiddish poet Avrom Sutskever (Abraham Sutzkever) was a childhood friend of Karpinovich who also settled in Tel Aviv and became editor of *Di goldene keyt*. He once said that many authors would write about life in Israel but that there was no one like Karpinovich (after Chaim Grade) who could write about Vilna. There wasn't anyone who could still remember every stone and corner, the characters and vendors, the reality of daily life as it was. Karpinovich's precise recollection of Vilna's topography is comparable to Isaac Bashevis Singer's memory of Warsaw.

Karpinovich was one of six children. Their father Moishe ran a Yiddish theatre, and organized the building of a new Yiddish folk theatre on a former circus site. His dream was to have balcony space, which would enable cheaper seating for the poor. When this was achieved, there were complaints that the Yiddish intellectuals were frequenting the Polish theatre. Moishe Karpinovich engaged the famous Vilna Troupe to vary the repertoire and to coax the intellectuals back to the Yiddish theatre. When the Germans occupied Vilna, they tore down the balcony and transformed the venue into a garage for tanks. Karpinovich writes about this in a story titled "Zikhroynes fun a farshnitener teater heym" [Memoirs of an Annihilated Theatre Home]. With the Yiddish theatre as a major influence in Karpinovich's life, it is not surprising that many short stories include characters who are actors. Other stories weave a narrative around well-known actors, actresses, and theatre people. Velfke Usian's restaurant, where many actors, musicians, and artists congregated, is frequently mentioned in the stories. The elation of success and the difficulty of failure on stage are sensitively woven into the tales, with an insider's knowledge. In 1995 Karpinovich returned to Vilna where a marble plaque was installed to commemorate his father's Yiddish folk theatre.

In all of Karpinovich's stories, characters, vendors, and their particular trades are authentically named. Embedded in a fictional form, the author chooses to maintain this feature in order to offer a small memorial for those who perished without trace (which included his parents and one sister at Ponar). By naming names and providing small details, characters are brought to life with an intimacy that is both warming and disturbing. Karpinovich details the lives of ordinary people and presents an array of the Yiddish speaking "underworld" which includes pick-pockets, kidnappers, prostitutes, thieves, and political activists. Educated, well-connected Jews also feature and are united with the rest in a common humanity. The author has described unsuccessfully attempting to superimpose his Vilna characters upon a Tel Aviv landscape.

Throughout his career, Karpinovich has been an active supporter and campaigner for Yiddish language and culture. He believes that as part of a broader Jewish heritage Yiddish should be promoted and that doing so does not conflict with Hebrew language and culture, the State of Israel, or any other aspects of Jewish culture.

Karpinovich's long involvement with the Israel Philharmonic Orchestra also feeds into his fiction. Like actors, musicians figure in the stories and descriptions of instruments and musical performance are rendered with accuracy and sensitivity.

Many stories include mention of characters who feature in other stories, Karpinovich thereby enlarging the characters themselves as well as injecting a sense of realism into his picture of Vilna's bustling life. Culture and idealism transcend poverty in the stories. Writing in his native Lithuanian dialect, Karpinovich uses a language that is rich and natural. Characters speak an authentic language appropriate to their situation and spiced with wonderful idioms. In the author's own words, "Men volt gedarft brengen keyn vilne hunderte un hunderte gedenk-tovlen, kedey dos amolike lebn dort zol nit fargesn vern" [one would need to bring hundreds and hundreds of memorial plaques to Vilna, so that the life from before should not be forgotten].

The stories are beautifully crafted, they are romantic, humane yet realistic. Karpinovich is a masterly storyteller and in a limited space, his characters come to life with great subtlety and sensitivity. In recent years, Karpinovich has frequently visited Vilna, a difficult undertaking because so little remains that resembles the place he knew and loved. He brings his memories of Vilna back to Vilna where he says there remains only the tiniest spark of Jewish life.

Some of the Vilna stories have been translated into German, Lithuanian, and Russian. Translations into Polish are currently being prepared.

HELEN BEER

Katz, Menke

Russian-born US poet, 1906–1991

Born in Svencionys (Tsvintsyan), 7 June 1906. Emigrated to United States, 1920; became US citizen, 1925. Married, first, Haske Bliacher, 1926; daughter, Troim and son, Noah (deceased); second, Rivke (Ruth) Feldman, 1950; one son, Hirshe-Dovid. In 1920s was a regular contributor to Yiddish literary journals under the pseudonym "Elchik Hiat". Co-founded and co-edited literary journal *Mir* (1944–47) and founded and edited poetry magazine *Bitterroot* (1962–1991). Appointed honorary Poet Laureate of Ferdinand Marcos's Philippines, 1967; Steven Vincent Benet Award, 1969 and 1973; nominated for Pulitzer Prize, 1972. Died in Spring Glen, New York, 24 April 1991.

Selected Writings

Poetry
Dray shvester [Three Sisters], 1932
Der mentsh in togn [Dawning Man], 1935
Brenendik shtetl, 2 vols, 1938; as *Burning Village*, 1972
S'hot dos vort mayn bobe moyne [My Grandmother Moyne Speaks], 1939
Tsu dertseyln in freydn [Tales of Joy], 1941
Der posheter kholem [The Simple Dream], 1947
Inmitn tog [In the Middle of the Day], 1954
Land of Manna, 1965
Rockrose, 1970
Tsfas [Safed], 1979
Two Friends, with Harry Smith, 1981
A Chair for Elijah, 1985
Nearby Eden, 1990
Menke sonetn [Menke Sonnets], 1996

Fiction
Forever and Ever and a Wednesday, with Harry Smith, 1980

Further Reading

Kinsman, Clare D. (editor), entry in *Contemporary Authors Autobiography Series*, 9, Detroit: Gale, 1988

Although many believe him to have been born in Michalishek, Lithuania, Menke Katz was born in Svencionys on 7 June 1906. Though he spent only two years there as a youth during World War I, it was in Michalishek, surrounded by the Viliya River and reached only by ferry, that he claims he first confronted Jewish mysticism and the inspiration to write poetry. He was an intensely romantic storyteller who merged reality and fiction into a fascinating Menke mythology of his own life. The fantastic, superstitious folktales and songs heard in childhood, that explained life and its mysteries, remained with him and formed the basis of his thinking and writing. He believed in the power of dreams. His first love was the imaginary Paragoolt, who revealed herself to him in erotic dreams. She appears throughout his poetry, and *Nearby Eden*, in which he makes peace with his life, ends with the lines: "Come Paragoolt, we shall love/ forever and a moonbow". In *A Chair for Elijah* Katz has dreamed of his own great-grandson, also a poet named Menke. His last book, published posthumously, was based on a dream in which, not long before his death, his mother, Badana appeared to him and commanded him to write again in Yiddish. *Menke sonetn* is the result.

A knowledge of Katz's biography is essential to an understanding of his poetry, in which his homes, family, friends, and lovers, past, present and future, predominate. *Burning Village* depicts the desperate plight of the Jews in Europe through the experiences of his own family. When Katz was eight, his father left for America to seek his fortune, but World War I broke out before his ship reached New York, and the family did not hear from him again until 1920, when he sent for them from Passaic, New Jersey. He was an impoverished factory worker and the young Menke had to join him in the factory to support the family. At 18 Katz married Haske, several years his senior, who was pregnant with their daughter Troim. Feeling stifled by the relationship and life in Passaic, he ran off to New York. Following a brief return visit, Haske became pregnant with their son, Noah, whom Katz did not see after the age of eight, but he met Troim again on a bus in New York when she was 16. He did not recognize her, but she confronted him as her father. In later life, Menke and Troim were reconciled and became close friends.

In New York, the Depression left Katz both unemployed and homeless. It was also the location of another catastrophic relationship: Ethel, his married lover, the woman who literally kissed the ground beneath his feet, committed suicide, jumping from the window of an apartment block, when her husband threatened to harm Katz. She haunts his later poetry. Having virtually lived the life of a bachelor until he was 44, he met the artist and teacher, 28-year-old Rivke (Ruth) Feldman. They married within ten days, and lived happily until his death. In 1954–56 and 1959–60, they lived in Safed, Israel, after which he named his eighth Yiddish collection of poems. In Israel, he was appalled by the hostility he encountered towards Yiddish and decided to return to the United States. Then in 1978, Katz and his wife moved with their only son from New York City to settle in a simple "forest house" in Spring Glen, upstate New York, where Katz lived until his death. Here, in the mountains, he gained the freedom for which he yearned. He had lived for 30 years in Rivke's mother's house in Borough Park, Brooklyn, where the attic was his artistic garret and escape. In Spring Glen, the couple thrived in their isolation. Katz wrote his poems, strummed the old Yiddish folksongs on his mandolin and Rivke painted, and served up vegetarian fare. From 1962 until his death Katz edited and distributed his own poetry journal entitled *Bitterroot*. Rivke provided most of the illustrations. The kitchen table at Spring Glen was covered with buff envelopes brushed to one side at mealtimes that would be stuffed by hand with the latest edition of the journal, addressed in Rivke's distinctive handwriting, driven down to the tiny village post office and mailed all over the world. As an editor Katz would ruthlessly hack and hone down poems to his satisfaction, without consulting the authors. But he received hundreds of submissions for each issue that went to press without a break for some 30 years. Towards the end of his life Katz taught poetry in maximum security prisons. He wrote the foreword to a book of poems entitled *Waves and License* written on death row by Stephen Todd Booker, to whom Katz referred as "a talented poet".

Katz experimented with poetic form and came up with his own, including a new sonnet form: "I know most poets and lovers of poetry will not agree with me, will wonder why I call [it] a sonnet. It is not a Petrarchan, Spenserian or Shakespearean fourteen-line sonnet, in iambic pentameter. It is an unrhymed fourteen-line Menke-sonnet. I only took the name and the number fourteen". He was vehemently against rhyme asserting: "I believe it is about time to leave the rhymes in the nursery". In "Against Lock and Rhyme", in *A Chair for Elijah*, he complains of the constriction of rhyme to subject matter: "A chased deer in panic of the forest does/ not race in rhyme, a grieved stone does not mourn in rhyme", yet the Menke sonnet is no less constraining, and the iambic pentameter, which he rejects, does after all echo the human heartbeat, whereas the artificial construction of his own sonnets, that he also calls "Menke triangles" are geared towards a physical shape that often takes no account of a corresponding emphasis of meaning: "my Chant Royal", he explains, "consists of fifty-five unrhymed, unrefrained lines with a five-line unrhymed envoy (see "Elchik and Dverke"). The strict confines of his forms are echoed in the controlled environment in which he preferred to live his life, and the familiar, unconditional supporters with whom he peopled it. Linguistically, Katz is most at home in Yiddish, in spite of the power of some of his English poetry. The Yiddish rhythms and lexicon are natural to him and echo his everyday speech. Yiddish words are employed throughout his English poetry, but not the other way round. Even his representation of Kabbalism is a naive magic. It is the work he produces in rhyme and in Yiddish, under the constraints of the traditional forms he rejects, such as "Der zeyger geyt" [The Clock Ticks] in *Tsfat*, commemorating the 25th anniversary of his father's death, and "Yiddish", the didactic dialogue between mother and child advocating the eternal existence of Yiddish as part of nature, that capture the essence of the oral tradition in which he was raised and which influenced everything he wrote. These poems, though sentimental, have a strength and power often lacking in the artificially expanding and contracting lines of the sonnets.

Katz was never politically comfortable among the leftist Yiddish literati in New York. He co-founded in 1944 the literary journal *Mir*, which opposed political meddling in literature, but when news of Stalin's murder of Yiddish writers was confirmed in 1953 he severed his ties with the Yiddish left wing for ever. The break led to his literary isolation and the rest of his career was characterized by an unchecked freedom that has yet to be assessed in relation to his writing. His poetry has been translated into many diverse languages including French, Greek, Hebrew, Italian, Japanese, and Kannada.

DEVRA KAY

Katz, Steve

US fiction writer, poet, and dramatist, 1935–

Born in Bronx, New York, 14 May 1935. Studied at Cornell University, BA 1956; University of Oregon, MA 1959. Has taught at Cornell University, University of Iowa, Brooklyn College, Queens College, New York; writer in residence, 1970–71, co-director of Projects in Innovative Fiction, 1971–73, Associate Professor of English, Notre Dame University, Indiana, 1976–78; taught at University of Colorado, Boulder, 1978. Awards include PEN grant, 1972; Creative Artists Public Service grant; 1976; National Endowment for the Arts grant, 1976, 1982.

Selected Writings

Fiction
The Lestriad, 1962
The Exagggerations of Peter Prince, 1968
Creamy and Delicious: Eat My Words (In Other Words), 1970
Posh (as Stephanie Gatos), 1971
Saw, 1972
Moving Parts, 1977
Stolen Stories, 1984
Wier and Pouce, 1984
Florry of Washington Heights, 1987
43 Fictions, 1992
Swanny's Ways, 1995

Poetry
The Weight of Antony, 1964
Cheyenne River Wild Track, 1973
Journalism, 1990

Further Reading

Grant, J. Kerry, "Fiction and Facts of Life: Steve Katz' *Moving Parts*", *Critique: Studies in Modern Fiction*, 24 (Summer 1983)
Klinkowitz, Jerome "Steve Katz" in his *The Life of Fiction*, Urbana: University of Illinois Press, 1977
McCaffery, Larry, "An Interview with Steve Katz" in *Anything Can Happen: Interviews with Contemporary American Novelists*, edited by Tom LeClair and McCaffery, Urbana: University of Illinois Press, 1983
McCaffery, Larry, "Steve Katz" in *Postmodern Fiction*, edited by McCaffery, New York: Greenwood Press, 1986

Born and raised in the Washington Heights section of New York City, Steve Katz has spent his personal life in flight from the urban reality of his Jewish-American neighbourhood and his writer's career in a love-hate relationship with traditions in the novel. At Cornell University, where Vladimir Nabokov taught literature, Katz studied animal husbandry in the agricultural college (where tuition was free). He has lived in the intermountain West, in an undeveloped area of Nova Scotia, and in Boulder, Colorado, where he became a professor of English. At the same time his fiction pushed innovations farther than any of his contemporaries. Yet as his work matured it began looking back to the city life of his childhood and adolescence, partially recovering his Jewish-American background. He included materials that older Jewish-American writers such as Bernard Malamud and Philip Roth had explored, and became at least apparently realistic – although his work was in fact addressing itself to formal experiments with rules derived from the novel's masters.

In an age when literary conventions seemed to exist only to be broken, Katz associated himself with several other Jewish-American writers from New York – Jonathan Baumbach, Peter Spielberg, and Ronald Sukenick – in the founding of the Fiction Collective, a writer-controlled publishing house devoted to fiction too experimental for commercial houses. Unlike these others, Katz was able to succeed for a time with conventional publishers, launching his career with the most radical looking novel of all, *The Exagggerations of Peter Prince*. The three g's of its title signal Katz's first anti-illusionistic gesture: that his story is not a representation of something in the world but rather an addition to that world, with its primary reality located right there on the printed page, where even a word such as "exaggerations" can be written in a selfconsciously exaggerated way. While the action itself is little more than a *Bildungsroman*, tracing its protagonist's adventures toward maturity, this novel's form is anything but traditional. Typefaces vary, as do layouts on the page; some pages are crossed out, while others bifurcate into dual columns of actions advancing in parallel. The author's intent is to have his novel reflect not so much the world as how the world is received: discontinuous, interrupted, unstable.

What *is* stable in the world? It's mythologies, as Katz demonstrates in *Creamy and Delicious: Eat My Words (In Other Words)*. Whether from popular culture (including comic book and adventure heroes) or history, mythological figures invite writers to locate experience in the realm of timelessness. To disrupt this convention Katz keeps his own mythologies short and sweet, mixed together abruptly so that their artifice appears in even higher profile. A similar plan informs *Saw*; for an age in which America's space programme provided ready-made heroes in the form of astronauts, Katz reverses the process with an alien astronaut visiting Earth, where conditions belie the ideals of any civilization reaching beyond itself. A mirror image of this experience is formed in *Cheyenne River Wild Track*, a cycle of poems that forms a narrative about postmodern filmmakers encountering Sioux culture and its ancient, shamanistic traditions.

In *Moving Parts* Katz returns to the metafictive dimensions of his first novel, but here is less interested in action on the page than in the interplay between imagination and documentable reality. In one section, the author receives a parcel of wrists mailed from Iron City, Tennessee – an obvious fabrication that is mocked by the photograph of his own wrists in a dozen and a half replications. Then, as if to test the grounding of his fantasy, he travels by bus to the actual town of Iron City, Tennessee, where adventures (documented by photographs) just as novel await him. Throughout, the emphasis remains on the act of writing and the search for workable material, with the search becoming its own story.

While in *Stolen Stories* and *43 Fictions* Katz continues his experiments with offbeat, borderline magical situations (in which realistic settings and offhand manners of narration are disrupted by radically uncompliant materials, materials the presence of which demands a life of their own), his subsequent novels flow smoothly from start to finish. *Wier and Pouce* establishes a rhythm between good and evil that recalls the playful reference to *War and Peace* in its title. Dusty Wier and E. Pouce are old college friends who pursue opposed lifestyles: the former mindfully good, the latter irrationally bad. Despite Dusty's good intentions, his life goes bad; even worse, as Pouce takes control of the narrative it seems that the initial good experiences in Dusty's life may have never happened at all. At this point short, interlocking stories become the characteristic form, indicating how no master narrative, whether good or evil, can be adequate. Yet the novel's progress continues, now propelled by its cleverness of invention and overwhelming sympathy for its characters.

Dusty Wier's experiences in Italy contrast with Katz's treatment of a similar world in 1962, in the short novel *The Lestriad* (reprinted by Bamberger Books in 1987). An even greater contrast is evident in what must be considered Katz's breakthrough novel to urban realism, *Florry of Washington Heights*. Written in the form of a memoir about growing up amid the influences of neighbourhood life, this narrative spoken by the half-Jewish, half-Irish protagonist Swanny Swanson appears thoroughly conventional, a *Bildungsroman* with none of the metafictive selfconsciousness that typified Katz's earlier work. Yet the novel's real action is in its subtext. "Whoever tells you he knows everything about his own neighbourhood you can be sure is fooling himself", Swanny begins, and even as the action progresses – largely centred on how the hero's nostalgia-filled world of candy, movies, and comic books is unsettled by the first dawning of sexual interest and threatened by the intrusions of a rival gang of older kids – readers surmise that something of much greater importance is bothering the narrator. In time, we learn what these matters are: sexuality as an intimation of adult responsibilities, and the rival gang as a suggestion of how postwar politics is influenced by communist aggression (in Korea) and American response (via the Korean War and McCarthyism at home). Yet these latter events are never directly portrayed. Instead, they remain effective as an undercurrent in the adolescent narrator's consciousness, a consciousness whose formation is the novel's true action.

That Katz would continue with this theme is evident from both his poetry collection, *Journalism*, and his 550-page masterwork of a novel, *Swanny's Ways* in 1995. This last book is an homage to Proust in its attempt to recover lost time, but also honours the *Thousand and One Nights* by choosing storytelling rather than memory as its enabling device. Here Swanny is an adult, living in the 1990s but still obsessed with Florry's murder. Because the recipient of Swanny's therapeutic narratives is Jack Ryan, who years ago led the rival gang that disrupted Swanny's adolescence, Katz is able to incorporate reader response into the novel's actions.

JEROME KLINKOWITZ

Katzir, Yehudit (Judith)

Israeli fiction writer and dramatist, 1963–

Born in Haifa, 1963. Studied general literature and cinema at Tel Aviv University. Currently a reader for publishers Hakibuts hameuhad and teaches creative writing at Tel Aviv University. Has also worked in research department of Israel Television. Began publishing short stories in the Israeli press in the 1980s. Individual stories and her collection *Closing the Sea* have been awarded literary prizes.

Selected Writings

Stories

Sogrim et hayam, 1990; as *Closing the Sea*, translated by Barbara Harshav, 1992

Migdalorim shel yabasha [Inland Lighthouses], 1999

Novel

Lematisse yesh et hashemesh babeten [Matisse Has the Sun in His Belly], 1995

Play
Devorah Baaron [A Bee in the Closet], produced 2000

For Children
Hapiknik shel amaliah [Amalia's Picnic], 1994

Further Reading

Diament, Carol, and Lily Rattok, introduction to *Ribcage: Israeli Women's Writing*, New York: Hadassah, 1994
Rattok, Lily, "Since the Murder Everything's been Collapsing on our Heads", *Modern Hebrew Literature* (Spring–Summer, 2000)

Yehudit Katzir has said, "For me, writing is exorcism, a battle with my fear of having missed out on anything". She delivered an impassioned speech at the President's Residence for Israeli Book Week, revealing what it meant to be a woman writer in the year 2000. She spoke about her burning need to write

> the enchanted consciousness that forges characters, the lust to create the universe and the human soul with words, to capture the arbitrary and that which passes, and to give them life by putting them in words, the aspiration to leave a mark in this world . . .

She noted that while male writers are privileged to enjoy a dialogue with continuity and thus have a legitimacy in writing, she and other female writers of her generation have had to create their own alternative canon.

Influenced by Jossl Birstein and Yakov Shabtai, her writing reveals a coherent world in which nothing happens merely by coincidence, or occurs in a vacuum. Since the publication of four novellas in *Closing the Sea*, this gifted writer has left her imprint on Israeli narrative fiction. Katzir combines fine sober writing with comic–grotesque images to describe a sharply drawn reality, mingling past and present, fantasy and mundane reality. A central theme of the writing is the disappointment of love and trust – these are not romances that end conventionally in happiness. Somehow her women are not destroyed in the process, but seem to be renewed as they emerge from their chrysalis. They gain independence and move on to what promises to be a better future. She takes us into the psyche of each central character, allowing us also a more distanced pleasure in her writer's craft.

Through the protagonist Rivi in her second book *Lematisse yesh et hashemesh babeten* [Matisse Has the Sun in His Belly] Katzir tells of a special love between two people. The flowing openness of style, the fearless sexual language, and the local Tel Aviv vocabulary, result in a remarkable book. One is swept away by the story (of disappointed love) and beguiled by a text that is laden with literary allusions and quotations, and by the sheer technical ability of a skilled contemporary writer.

Migdalorim shel yabasha [Inland Lighthouses] purports to be "three stories of journeys". Each novella has an original structure. Together, the three coalesce into a contemporary, detailed Israeli version of the Odyssey. Parallels between Odysseus returning home and the male hero of the first novella serve to remind us of the value of family ties and strengthened family relationships. Each story describes a journey in space – between cities or countries – and a journey in time – to faraway times. The traveller journeys to lost realms where a life of passion or love is revealed, a golden time for which he later longs throughout life. Each protagonist decides "to bet on the right horse", choosing the stable love that will yield a decent, peaceful existence. Yet the choice of a safe relationship, rather than the risk of emotional upheaval results in shallow mundanity. Each pays a high price for their choice, feeling that "in this way, there's no point, there's no longer any point". Only a terminal illness or the loss of bonds with family members can lead them to prefer suicide to a life devoid of feeling. In "And the Clouds Sail On", Aunt Ruth decides to end her life because of old age and mental and physical suffering; yet she clings to the young woman who helps her, out of love, to commit suicide. "I want another child . . . to put one more thing between me and death", the heroine explains. She wants to give birth again despite hardships, "because that's what you can do with your body before it grows old". In the end she chooses family life and forgets the tempestuous emotions of past dreams. This is the message for our generation, the importance of safeguarding the lives of children born and yet to be born. (See Lily Rattok in *Modern Hebrew Literature*.)

Each story revolves around types of letting go: letting go of dreams, letting go of complete devotion to creativity, and letting go of romantic love in exchange for a stable, secure life. Ayelet Negev, writing in *Yediot aharonot,* describes the way in which, "on dry land, without the raging sea storms, without the dangers of the sea, even without the adventures or the freedom of the sea, yet these lighthouses shed their light".

Lily Rattok talks of the recurring theme of crisis, personal and national. Each of the three protagonists in the three novellas in the collection feels that "something inside him is broken and can never be mended". Similar feelings exist on the national level, reflecting the crisis with great precision. "Since Rabin's assassination, he feels as if he were in a dream, in which everyone was behaving normally, and in fact under the thin crust of sanity, horrible things were happening, and everything was deteriorating, and becoming debased". These words by the protagonist of *Inland Lighthouses* exemplify the psychological distress of many Israelis whose world was drastically altered by the murder. Rattok believes this may also be seen as an indirect explanation for the shift in Katzir's writing. Previously personal and intimate, in this publication her work assumes a pronounced political orientation. Katzir has her main character hope that in the elections Netanyahu's government, "conceived and born in sin", will be replaced by a government that will realize the vision of peace.

A character called Judith (the author's own name) describes the horrible Israeli reality as a nightmare. In a dream she sees a city whose inhabitants teach their children to play "war games" and they also "sacrifice them on the altar of gods and eat their flesh". This nightmarish reality exists because "they know no other reality". Her criticism of the continuous state of conflict serves to explain why the high towers of the Peace Centre are represented as "lighthouses on dry land", and function to light the way.

In the third novella in the collection, "Letters to Emanuel – A Family Etude", Katzir includes letters from her own family archives, mingling fact and fiction. She imaginatively creates the story of a relationship between her grandfather and grandmother. In all three novellas, there is a clinging to life despite the odds. Each protagonist has enjoyed a time of great happiness in love. But after betrayal from the loved one, ending a time of isolation, separation and alienation, each one manages to rebuild her life in varying ways, succeeding in finding new directions. Katzir writes of individual lives, not the grand issues of a reborn nation, but succeeds in describing the painful difficulties of a believable contemporary Israel.

SORREL KERBEL

Kenaz, Yehoshua

Israeli fiction writer, 1937–

Born in Petah Tikvah, 1937. Studied philosophy and Romance languages at Hebrew University, Jersualem, and French literature at the Sorbonne. Works as translator of French classics into Hebrew and as editor at Am Oved Publishers; has been on editorial staff of daily newspaper *Haaretz*. Awarded Bialik Prize, 1995; commended by Israel Publishers Association, 1997. Now lives in Tel Aviv.

Selected Writings

Novels

Aharei hahagim, 1964; as *After the Holidays*, translated by Dalya Bilu, 1987

Haisha hagedolah mehahalomot [The Great Woman of the Dreams], 1973

Hitganvut lehidim [Heart Murmur], 1986

Baderekh la hatulim, 1991; as *The Way to the Cats*, translated by Dalya Bilu, 1994

Mahzir ahavot kodmot, 1997; as *Returning Lost Loves*, translated by Dalya Bilu, 2001

Short Stories

Moment musikali, 1980; as *Musical Moment and Other Stories*, 1995

Further Reading

Hertsig, Hanah, *Ha-Shem Ha-Perati: Masot 'Al Ya'Akov Shabtai, Yehoshu'a Kenaz, Yo'el Hofman*, Tel Aviv: Hakibuts hameuhad, 1994

Levy, Nili, *Me-Rehov Ha-Even Ha-Hatulim: 'Iyunim Ba-Siporet Shel Yehoshua Kenaz*, Tel Aviv: Hakibuts hameuhad, 1997

Yehoshua Kenaz deals with very delicate issues in a very sensitive and lyrical manner. The first of these is the complex transition from childhood to adulthood, which is represented both in "Moment musikali" ("Musical Moment") and in "The Three Legged Chicken". In the former, the protagonist describes this transition via his relationship to music and more specifically, his violin lessons. These violin lessons also play an important part in reflecting the protagonist's relationship to his parents, who are the ones to either forbid or allow these lessons. The story shows with beautiful imagery the insecurity and confusion of a young boy who must deal with the expectations, or what he perceives as expectations, of his peers and of his parents, and the gradual recognition that adulthood is often achieved only after a certain amount of inner struggle. At first the child feels hopelessly inferior as a violinist in comparison to a certain other student. The fact that this other student can express great beauty and heights of emotion through playing only serves to emphasize the artistic and personal impotence of the child protagonist. Indeed the episode at the concert when the child fears the unwanted and disruptive entrance of a street beggar reveals how uncomfortable and afraid he feels in the presence of such beauty. In addition to this, the contrast between sensitivity to music and sensitivity to humans is also looked at in "Musical Moment". The child rejects the pleas of another student named Eitan and it is only when it is too late that he realizes how insensitive he has been. Finally, the more concrete representation of the transition from childhood to adulthood can be found in the protagonist's habit of blinking, which is a distressing issue for both himself and his family. However, the story ends with the blinking stopping. The fact that it is this which ends the story rather than some other part of the plot underlines the fact that it is the transition that is important rather than how it was achieved.

"The Three Legged Chicken" deals with similar issues as well as that of loss and death and how these contribute to growing up. The loss of innocence is also a strong feature in this particular tale. The child protagonist, known only as "the boy", tells the story of a child who has recently lost his beloved grandfather. The sense of alienation from the world around him is movingly portrayed in a scene where he is lying in his bed and listening to a woodworm. In this description it is as if the boy and the woodworm are completely alone in the world, and both are struggling. It is almost as if there is some sort of a dialogue.

Alongside this coping with loss, "The Three Legged Chicken" also shows the boy's loss of innocence which occurs with his confrontation with human cruelty, when he is talked into spending his money to attend a meaningless freak show. The fact that the protagonist chooses wrong for the first time and doesn't fulfil the tasks set him by his family is significant. Also significant is the fact that he feels that he should be amused by the spectacle, and not being so makes him feel different. On one level the "secret" that would enable him to be amused has to do with sexual awareness, since the chicken's third leg arouses crude thoughts and consequent jeering. On another level the lack of amusement is to do with the boy's kind personality. Therefore his embarrassment of not knowing the "secret" is amusing to the reader. His understanding of human nature also alters subtly with regards to his friend Molko. Molko encourages the "boy" to pay for the freak show and promises him all sorts of favours afterwards. He promises to look after him, to let him play on his swing, to protect him etc. However, after the brutal display of human greed and cruelty inherent at the freak show the boy leaves, understanding that Molko will be just as mean as before and that nothing has really changed between them. However, the boy no longer cares and accepts perhaps rather cynically the fickleness of human nature.

The Way to the Cats is also about rites of passage, but this time those endured by the old and the sick. It is a third-person narrative that tells the story of Yolanda Moscowitz, a 76-year-old schoolteacher living in an old people's home. Here Kenaz demonstrates how the life of an old person about to die is just as rich, in fear and in learning, as that of any other age group. Yolanda not only forms friendships with those around her but also falls in love and experiences an awakening desire, while struggling to come to terms with her decaying body and mind. Certain things such as physical appearances or mind games, usually associated with the young, play a crucial part in her life. However, Kenaz never lets the reader forget that his protagonist is also desperately trying to hold onto her life, and not let herself become greyed out by the mortality around her. Unfortunately this desire to hold on leaves Yolanda vulnerable to those stronger than she. Her constant paranoia, coupled with her wish to form genuine friendships, is beautifully captured by Kenaz whose attention to detail makes his characters very believable and very real. Kenaz also demonstrates that a person's feelings and hopes do not lessen with age and that the tragedy is that people often disregard the needs of the aged. The subject of the geriatric is an original one to tackle and Kenaz does so without being patronizing or unrealistic.

GIULIA MILLER

Kertész, Imre

Hungarian novelist, 1929–

Born in Budapest, 9 November 1929 to an assimilated Jewish family. Deported to Auschwitz, 1944, then to Buchenwald; liberated, May1945. Worked for various Budapest newspapers; dismissed from *Világosság* after the Communists took power, 1951. Military service, 1952–3. Worked as translator of German authors into Hungarian (Nietzsche, Hofmannsthal, Schnitzler, Freud and Canetti), as well as writing musical light theatre. Many awards including the *Brandenburger Literaturpreis*, 1995, *Liepziger Buchpreis*,1997, *Welt- Literaturpreis*, 2000, and the Nobel Prize for Literature, 2002.

Selected Writing

Novels

Sorstalanság , 1975; as *Fateless*, translated by Christopher C. Wilson and Katherina M. Wilson, 1992.

A Kudarc [Fiasco], 1988

Kaddis a meg nem születetett gyermekért, 1990; as *Kaddish for a Child Not Born* , translated by Christoher C. Wilson and Katherina M. Wilson, 1997

Other

A nyomkereő: Két regény [The Pathfinder], 1977

Az angol lobogó [The English Flag], 1992

Gályanapló [Galley Diary], 1992

A holocaust mint kultúra: három eloadás [The Holocaust as Culture], 1993

Valaki más: változás krónikája [I — Another Chronicle of a Metamorphosis], 1997

A gondolatnyi csend, amíag kivégz?oztag újratölt [Moments of Silence While the Execution Squad Reloads],1998

A számuzött nyelv [The Exiled Language], 2001

Further Reading

Nagy, M. M., editor, *A Journey into History: Essays on Hungarian Literature,* New York: P. Lang, 1990

Riding, Alan,"Hungarian Novelist Wins Nobel Prize", *The New York Times*, 10 October 2002

Skakun, Michael, "Imre Kertesz, Hungarian Jewish Survivor, Awarded 2002 Prize in Literature", *Jewish Press*, 23 October 2002

Szirtes, George, "Who is Imre Kertész?", *The Times Literary Supplement,* 18 October 2002

The Nobel Prize for Literature 2002 was awarded to Kertész for upholding "the fragile experience of the individual against the barbaric arbitrariness of history". "Both perpetrators and victims were preoccupied with insistent practical problems, the major questions did not exist", the Swedish Academy says in its citation. "Kertész' message is that to live is to conform. The capacity of the captives to come to terms with Auschwitz is one outcome of the same principle that finds expression in everyday human existence."

Fateless (1975), Kertész' first novel, is told in the first person and recounts how fifteen year-old Gyorgy Köves, like Kertész himself, is sent to Auschwitz, then Buchenwald, and accepts the normality of life in the camps, "I continue to live my unlivable life (because) there is no absurdity that one cannot live quite naturally." There are no ready-made answers, neither moral indignation nor metaphysical protest, to the atrocities he encounters. What intrigues him is the language that he needs to define his condition. He is unable to reconcile the vocabulary that awaits him on his liberation, entering as he does a society moving from one form of totalitarianism to another. "One cannot start a new life, you can only continue the old one." His second novel *A Kudarc* [Fiasco] continues to use Köves' voice; now an older man he experiences frustration, unable to find a publisher for his memoirs of Auschwitz. The book is a meditation on this helpless situation.Yet when it is eventually published, he feels revulsion at having his innermost thoughts exposed. He still searches for an appropriate language with which to comprehend the evil that resulted in the Holocaust, which "does not have a language because it has no homeland." The third of this semi-autobiographical trilogy, *Kaddish for a Child Not Born*, is about a middle-aged survivor looking back on his life. His *kaddish* (prayer for the dead) is said for the child he refuses to bring into a world which has tolerated Auschwitz.

Kertész explains that his Judaism is "problematic". "I am a non-believing Jew. Yet as a Jew I was taken to Auschwitz, as a Jew I was in the death camps, and as a Jew I live in a society that does not like Jews . . . I am Jewish, I accept it, but to a large extent it is also true that it was imposed on me." Visiting Jerusalem in 2002, he believes, reinforced his Jewish identity. "I am not impartial and, cannot be . . . I leave that to . . . intellectuals. They have never bought a ticket for a bus ride from Jerusalem to Haifa."

SORREL KERBEL

Kiš, Danilo

Yugoslav fiction writer, 1935–1989

Born in Subotica, Serbia, 22 February 1935. Father died in Auschwitz. Brought up by an uncle in Cetinje, Montenegro. Educated in Cetinje Grammar School. Published first short story "Juda" [Judas] in *Omladinski list* [The Youth Newspaper], 1953. Graduated 1954. Studied at University of Belgrade, BA in comparative literature 1958. Editor, *Vidici*. Worked at Centre for Theory of Literature and Art in Belgrade after completing graduate work in 1960. Lecturer in Serbo-Croat, universities of Strasbourg, 1961–63, Bordeaux, 1973–76, and Lille, 1979–83. Lived and worked in Paris from 1979. Awarded NIN Prize, 1973; Ivan Goran Kovacic Award, 1977; Grand Aigle d'Or, from the city of Nice, 1980; Ivo Andrić Award, 1984; PEN Bruno Schulz Prize, 1989. Died of cancer, 15 October 1989.

Selected Writings

Novels
Mansarda [The Garret], 1962
Psalam 44 [Psalm 44], 1962
Bašta, Pepeo, 1965; as *Garden, Ashes*, translated by William J. Hannaher, 1975
Peščanik, 1972; as *Hourglass*, translated by Ralph Manheim, 1990

Short Stories
Rani jadi: za decu i osetljive, 1970; as *Early Sorrows: For Children and Sensitive Readers*, translated by Michael Henry Heim, 1998
Grobnica za Borisa Davidoviča, 1976; as *A Tomb for Boris Davidovich*, translated by Duška Mikić-Mitchell, 1978
Enciklopedija mrtvih, 1983; as *The Encyclopedia of the Dead*, translated by Michael Henry Heim, 1989
Lauta i Oiziljci, 1994
Skladiste, 1995

Plays
Elektra, 1969
Noć i magla [Night and Mist] (includes *Papagaj* [The Parrot]; *Drveni Sanduk Tomasa Vulfa* [The Wooden Chest of Thomas Wolfe]; *Mehanički lavovi* [The Mechanical Lions]), 1983

Other
Po-etika [Poetics], 2 vols, 1972–74
Caš anatomije [The Anatomy Lesson], 1978
Homo poeticus, 1983; *Homo Poeticus: Essays and Interviews*, edited by Susan Sontag, translated by Michael Henry Heim, 1995
Sabrana dela [Collected Works], 10 vols 1983
Consejos a un joven escritor, 1990
Gorki talog iskustva (interviews), with Mirjana Miočinović, 1990
Pesme i preperi, edited by Predrag Čudić, 1992
"On Nationalism", 1996

Further Reading

Bankovic-Rosul, Jelena S., "The Awakening of Sleepers in Danilo Kiš's *Encyclopedia of the Dead*", *Serbian Studies* (Spring 1990)
Birnbaum, Marianna D., "History and Human Relationships in the Fiction of Danilo Kiš", *Cross Currents*, 8 (1989)
Bynum, David, "Philosophical Fun and Merriment in the First Fiction of Danilo Kiš", *Serbian Studies*, 2/4 (1984)
Czarny, Norbert and Catherine Vincent, "Imaginary-Real Lives: On Danilo Kiš", *Cross Currents*, 3 (1984)
Eekman, Thomas, *Thirty Years of Yugoslav Literature, 1945–1975*, Ann Arbor: Michigan Slavic Publications, 1978
Gorjup, Branko, "Danilo Kiš: From 'Enchantment' to 'Documentation' ", *Canadian Slavonic Papers*, 29/4 (1987)
Hawkesworth, Celia, "Silk, Scissors, Gardens, Ashes: The Autobiographical Writing of Irena Vrkljan and Danilo Kiš", in *Literature and Politics in Eastern Europe*, London: Macmillan, and New York: St Martin's Press, 1992
Longinovic, Tomislav Z., *Borderline Culture: The Politics of Identity in Four Twentieth-Century Slavic Novels*, Fayetteville: University of Arkansas Press, 1993
Matvejevic, Predrag, "Danilo Kiš: *Encyclopedia of the Dead*", *Cross Currents*, 7 (1988)
Review of Contemporary Fiction, special issue, 15/1 (1994)
Shishkoff, Serge, "Kosava in a Coffee Pot; or, A Dissection of a Literary Cause Célèbre", *Cross Currents*, 6 (1987)
Spiro, Gyorgy, "Danilo Kiš, 1935–1989", *New Hungarian Quarterly*, 31/119 (1990)

Poet, translator, essayist, and novelist, Danilo Kiš is one of the best-known modern Serbian writers. He was born in 1935 to a Jewish Hungarian father and a Montenegrin Orthodox mother. In 1942, following the massacre of Serbs and Jews by Hungarian fascists, his family escaped from Novi Sad to the countryside on the Yugoslav–Hungarian border. Kiš's father was arrested in 1944, deported, and died in Auschwitz with many of his family. In response to anti-Semitic legislation, Kiš and his sister had been given Orthodox baptisms in 1939, and survived to be repatriated to Cetinje, Yugoslavia, after the war. Kiš lived for many years in Belgrade, and later in Paris where he died in 1989.

Kiš's work is permeated by his childhood experiences of having been a witness to the humiliation of his own father, the massacre of Novi Sad, and the deportation of his father. He writes of his "obsession" with the totalitarian wars, regimes, and extermination camps of the 20th century, and the ways in which the horrors of Nazism and the terrors of Stalinism threatened our very humanity. His documentary narratives offer a unique blend and balance of fiction and fact. He utilizes literary sources, real and imagined, in his attempts to re-personalize history by focusing on the "unheroic" lives lost to official histories – ". . . what does it mean, six million, if we cannot see one single man and his face, his body, his years and his personal story". Kiš acknowledged the influence of Kafka, Borges, and Joyce on the form of his work.

The loss of his father is the principal theme of his three volumes of autobiographical writing (*Garden, Ashes*, *Early Sorrows*, *Hourglass*). *Garden, Ashes* is a novel told by the narrator, Andreas Scham, Kiš's fictional self, and describes the experiences of a child whose world is torn apart by brutality, hunger, and war, his family seeking refuge, and the loss of a disturbed, wonderful, and erratic father taken away by strangers. *Early Sorrows*, a series of connected stories again told by Andreas, relates the departure of E.S., his father, never to return, and the collapse of an already fragile family and social order. One of the stories ("The Pogrom") gives a graphic account of a crowd caught up in the looting of a Jewish store, and another ("The Game") has Andreas playing at being his Jewish grandfather, a feather merchant, to the anxiety of his mother and the delight of father. A number of the stories evoke the beauty of nature and the seasons, this more fundamental order beneath the human world. The book climaxes with his aunt returned from the camps lighting a candle, prompting him to picture the details of his father's death. In the trilogy Kiš explores the multilayered processes that give significance to the events that form us.

Hourglass, a novel, ends with an actual letter written by Kiš's father and from this point is expanded backwards, as the context in which the letter was written and the events to which it refers are presented. Using the anchor of the letter and a number of imagined documentary sources, the 67 sections chart the mental disintegration of the hounded E.S. in the final months leading up to his fatal and, it seems, inevitable deportation, disappearance, and death. The fragmentary literary form composed of intuitions, gaps, and guesses reflects the indeterminate and inconclusive reality of complex and confused motivations and knowledge amid the swirling and engulfing chaos of Nazism.

Kiš is perhaps best known for his book of imaginary anti-Stalinist case histories, *A Tomb for Boris Davidovich*. In these tales the narrator painstakingly pieces together the truth ("The story that I am about to tell, a story born in doubt and perplexity, has only the misfortune (some call it fortune) of being true . . .") from obscure fictional documents hidden in libraries and archives. Although published in 1976, long before the 1989 end of state socialism in eastern Europe, Kiš writes as if looking back on an empire already gone. These tales of murder, terrorism, assassination, conspiracy, Comintern intrigue, torture, true and false confessions, disillusionment, disappearance, and death, celebrate the silenced individual victims of the Soviet and all oppressive institutional systems of evil.

In order to create a sense of literary authenticity, Kiš incorporated actual and fictional documents and the work of other writers in these stories, in particular, the form and feel of his narratives draw on the work of Borges. Although this was conscious, and his intention is clearly to challenge the "universal infamy" of Borges's pirates and gangsters with the much more comprehensive infamy of the gulag and the death camps, the Belgrade literary establishment charged him with plagiarism. This very public attack on a "European", successful, and subversive writer appears to have been driven by anti-Semitism, jealousy, and the climate of political fear. Kiš's reply to his accusers, *Cas anatomije* [The Anatomy Lesson], offers his understanding of the task and responsibilities of a writer, and includes his famous and prescient essay, "On Nationalism".

In 1983 Kiš published a collection of haunting stories, *The Encyclopedia of the Dead*. Here slight and seemingly insignificant events form connections that do have consequences and serve to shape our lives and destinies. Kiš's interest again is in exposing hidden histories and those lost to formal historical records. In the title story he reports of an encyclopedia that has entries only for the non-famous and that can be accessed only in dreams. In "The Book of Kings and Fools" Kiš traces the insane genesis of the notorious forgery of a world Jewish conspiracy, based on *The Protocols of the Elders of Zion*, and the huge impact of this book on the 20th century as its readers created the death camps. Kiš's "Postscript" authenticates the stories by giving details of the history and his sources.

Many of Kiš's characters are Jewish, and the name Boris Davidovich in the title of his book clearly indicates a Jewish identity. His own identification with Jews and Judaism is complex. In *Garden, Ashes* Kiš's portrayal of "his" Jewish father is as the Christian archetype of the wandering Jew, or as one of the Hebrew prophets, or Moses, or even as Christ. His own "Jewishness" here appears as shadowy as his image of his father. His writings, from his second book, *Psalam 44*, to his posthumously published short story, about a suicidal Auschwitz survivor ("Jurij Golec", 1994), are centred on anti-Semitism and the Holocaust. In his essay "Judaism" Kiš notes the influence of Arthur Koestler's "cruel theory of assimilation" and reports that in later life he was less convinced by the Hungarian's stark choice between Israel and cultural disappearance. The "Jew" appears often to be a literary device that allows the writer to construct himself as an outsider, what Kiš calls "de-familiarization". He writes about his father, "He became mythical to me when I realized that he had an exceptional destiny and that my own destiny was marked by his Jewishness".

PAUL MORRIS

Kisch, Egon Erwin

Czech-Austrian journalist and fiction writer, 1885–1948

Born in Prague, 29 April 1885. Briefly studied engineering at technical high school, Prague; one year of voluntary military service; undertook private study of journalism in Berlin. Journalist on *Prager Tagblatt*, 1904–05; *Deutsche Zeitung Bohemia*, 1906–13; *Berliner Tageblatt*, 1913; made sensational revelations in affair of espionage by Colonel Redl, 1913. Served on Serbian front during World War I; joined press corps of military staff in Vienna. Active as leader of revolutionary Red Guard in Vienna; imprisoned briefly, 1919; later joined Communist Party of Germany. Travelled widely in Europe and North Africa; visited Soviet Union, 1925; made illicit visit to United States using false papers. Expelled from Germany after Nazi seizure of power, 1933; moved to Prague; visited Melbourne as delegate to World Committee against War and Fascism, 1933; refused entry to Australia as "undesirable alien" and threw himself overboard in Perth harbour, 1934; lived in Paris, 1934–37; served in International Brigade during Spanish Civil War, 1937–38. Married Gisella Lyner, 1938. Fled Spain, reaching New York, 1939, and Mexico, 1940; lived in Mexico until 1946. Undertook intense anti-Nazi activity in Freies Deutschland movement during World War II; brothers Arnold and Paul murdered in Theresienstadt, 1944. Returned to Prague, 1947; became honorary President of Prague Jewish Community. Died in Prague after heart attack, 31 March 1948.

Selected Writings

Fiction

Aus Prager Gassen und Nächten [From Prague Alleys and Nights], 1912
Prager Kinder [Prague Children], 1913
Der Mädchenhirt [The Shepherd of Girls], 1914
Die gestohlene Stadt [The Stolen City], 1922
Der Fall des Generalstabschefs Redl [The Downfall of Chief of General Staff Redl], 1924
Wagnisse in aller Welt [Exploits throughout the World], 1927
Geschichten aus sieben Ghettos, 1934; as *Tales from Seven Ghettos*, translated by Edith Bone, 1948
Die drei Kühe, 1938; as *The Three Cows*, translated by Stewart Farrar, 1939
Marktplatz der Sensationen, 1941; as *Sensation Fair*, translated by Guy Endore, 1941

Other

Die Abenteuer in Prag [Adventures in Prague], 1920
Soldat in Prager Korps [Soldier in the Prague Brigade], 1922; as *Schreib das Auf, Kisch!*, 1929
Klassischer Journalismus [Classic Journalism], 1923
Der rasende Reporter [The Raging Reporter], 1924
Hetzjagd durch die Zeit [Hunting through Time], 1925
Zaren, Popen, Bolschewiken [Czars, Popes, Bolsheviks], 1927
Egon Erwin Kisch beehrt sich darzubieten: Paradies Amerika [Egon Erwin Kisch Has the Honour to Present: Paradise America], 1930
Prager Pitaval, 1931
Asien gründlich verändert, 1932; as *Changing Asia*, translated by Rita Reil, 1935
China Geheim, 1933; as *Secret China*, translated by Michael Davidson, 1935
Abenteuer in fünf Kontinenten [Adventures in Five Continents], 1936
Landung in Australien, 1937; as *Australian Landfall*, translated by John Fisher, Irene Fitzgerald, and Kevin Fitzgerald, 1937
Soldaten am Meeresstrand [Soldiers on the Beach], 1938
Entdeckungen in Mexiko [Discoveries in Mexico], 1945
Karl Marx in Karlsbad, 1968
Egon Erwin Kisch, the Raging Reporter: A Bioanthology, edited and with an introduction by Harold B. Segel, 1997

Further Reading

Geisler, Michael, *Die literarische Reportage in Deutschland*, Königstein im Taunus, Germany: Scriptor, 1982
Geissler, Rudolf, *Die Entwicklung der Reportage Egon Erwin Kischs in der Weimarer Republik* [The Development of Egon Erwin Kisch's Reporting in the Weimar Republic], Cologne: Pahl Rugenstein, 1982
Hofman, Fritz, *Egon Erwin Kisch, der rasende Reporter* [Egon Erwin Kisch, the Raging Reporter], Berlin: Neues Leben, 1988
Lewis, Ward B., "Egon Erwin Kisch beehrt sich darzubieten: *Paradies Amerika*", *German Studies Review*, 13/2 (1990)
Prokosch, Erdmute, *Egon Erwin Kisch: reporter einer rasenden Zeit*, Bonn: Keil, 1985
Schlenstedt, Dieter, *Egon Erwin Kisch: Leben und Werk*, Berlin: Volk und Wissen, 1985
Utitz, Emil, *Egon Erwin Kisch, der klassische Journalist*, Berlin: Aufbau, 1956

Kisch was non-observant and, like the majority of Czech Jews, his first language was German and his cultural identification wholly with that language area. Jewish subjects, among others, caught his attention as sources of colourful literary material, and he ranged throughout the world, delving into the past and seizing upon the present to construct fascinating accounts from village and metropolis of the famous and the obscure.

The most significant literary contribution of Kisch to his time was the conception and development of reportage, a style born of the marriage between journalism and creative writing. Motivated by a curiosity, which in *Sensation Fair* he termed his "most violent" quality, he focused upon an initial real event, which then spurred his fantasy as this was spun into literature. Or in the alternative, he might serve up the germinal concept accompanied by "such details and such an association of ideas that reality becomes at least as interesting as any product of the imagination".

Kisch explains his innovative approach to the creation of literature. The creative imagination requires that a balance be achieved and maintained between fantasy and fact in order to attain credibility. One's fancy, Kisch notes, must "confine herself to the strait and narrow path that leads from fact to fact; she can range only so far as the rhythmic harmony with these facts will allow". "Logical fantasy" is exercised in order to combine and supplement these facts within the limits of probability and the creative imagination.

A characteristic sketch illustrates the author's style and technique. "Indiodorf unter dem Davidstern" [Indian Village under the Star of David] from *Entdeckungen in Mexiko* is one of nearly three dozen pieces generated by Kisch's interest in, and affection for, the country of his exile refuge. In this collection the author's tone is by turns sophisticated and cosmopolitan, professorial, witty, sarcastic, ironic, simple, and reminiscent. The reader is served geography, history, fairy tales, and fantasy.

An account consisting incipiently of reportage is transformed by the creative literary imagination into a stirring tribute to the dignity and perseverance of humankind, when the narrator visits the outlying village of Venta Prieta on a Saturday morning. The settlement is occupied by some 37 Jews, not unlike a lost tribe living among the indigenous mestizos. Characteristically, Kisch recalls the historical role of Hispanic Jews and their necessity to conceal their beliefs. The villagers observe their rites, after their fashion, as an indulgent Jehovah looks down.

A factual description assumes greater dimensions while the narrator stands before the altar in a prayer for the dead, recalling the members of his family. He has found safety in Mexico, a brother the same in India via China, and two others found death in a concentration camp. Millions are recalled in this prayer, and the scene is transformed as his thoughts expand to include all the victims of Hitler, devoted as they were to achieving a better mankind.

A vision reveals smoke rising from a chimney as rows of humans move towards the source of death by gas. Futility and resignation prevail. It is as if humanity had no meaning, as if there had been no striving towards wisdom, truth, justice, beauty, love, and happiness.

WARD B. LEWIS

Kishon, Ephraim

Hungarian-born Israeli satirist, dramatist, and fiction writer, 1924–

Born Ferenc Hoffman in Budapest, in 1924, to David Hoffman, clerk, and wife Elizabeth (née Steiner). Studied painting, sculpture, and history of art at University of Budapest, 1945–48. Married, first, Ava Klamer, 1946; divorced; one son; second, Sara Lipovitz, 1959; two children. Began writing for stage and publishing humorous essays. Emigrated to Israel, 1949. Began to publish in Hebrew, 1951; wrote political and social satire, and humorous essays, for daily newspaper *Maariv*, Tel Aviv, from 1952. Many awards, including Nordau Prize, 1953; Sokolov Prize (for outstanding journalism), 1958; Golden Globe Award (for best foreign film, *Sallah Shabbati*), 1965; Herzl Prize, 1970; Jabotinsky Prize, 1970; Israeli Broadcasting Service Prize, 1970.

Selected Writings

Novels
Haoleh hayored lehayenu [Immigrant upon Us], 1952
Elef gadyiah vegadyiah [A Thousand and One Kids], 1954
Ein kemunim, 1955; as *The Fox in the Chicken Coop: A Satirical Novel*, translated by Jacques Namiel, 1971; as *Hashual belul hatamegolot*, 1972
Hinta-palinta: Humoresekek [See-Saw], 1956
Lo norah [Never Mind], 1957; as *Look Back Mrs Lot*, translated by Yohanan Goldman, 1961
Hakol talui [It Depends], 1961
Beehad haemeshim [One of Those Yesterdays], 1962
Shminiot baavir [Bending over Backwards], 1965
Etsem bagaron [A Pain in the Neck], 1967
Bead [In Favour], 1970
Kishon X 25 [25 X Kishon], 1973
Sliha shenitsahnu, with Kariel Gardosh, 1967; as *So Sorry We Won*, translated by Yohanan Goldman, 1967
Oy lamenatshim, with Kariel Gardosh, 1969; as *Woe to the Victors*, translated by Yohanan Goldman, 1969
Hor bamasakh [A Hole in the Curtain], 1973; as *Nuts Hams and Prompters*, translated by Yohanan Goldman, 1975
Partaha ahuvati [Half-Assed Forever], 1974
Hiukh babatsoret [A Smile in the Drought], 1978
Sefer mishpahti [A Family Book], 1980
Sefer hamasaot [Travel Log], 1988
Arbinka, 1991
Hakippah haserugah [The Knitted Kippah], 1993
Sair, laazazel [The Bald Truth], 1998

For Children
Dodim al hutim [Uncles on Strings], 1981
Mastik im pasim [Stripped Chewing Gum], 1981
Hagavia hu shelanu [We Won the Trophy], 1981
Ele masaot yonaton [Those Were Jonathan's Travels], 1981
Haharpatkah habilti gemurah [The Unfinished Adventure], 1981
Millhemet hanemalim [The War of the Ants], 1981
Iluf hakalbah hasoreret [The Taming of the Shrewish Dog], 1995
Hercules veshivat hagamadim [Hercules and the Seven Dwarfs], 1995

Plays
Shmo holekh lefanav [His Name Precedes Him], 1953
Shahor al gabei lavan [Black on White: A Comedy Fantasy in Three Acts], 1956
Haketuvah [The Marriage Contract], 1961
Hu vehi [He and She], 1963
Totsi et hashteker, hamayim rotehim [Pull out the Plug, the Water is Boiling: A Satirical Farce in Six Scenes], 1965
Ho, ho, iulia [Oh, Oh Juliet], 1974; as *Oh Romeo*, translated by Lucienne Hill, 1984
Tealat blaumilch [The Blaumilch Canal], 1974 (based on an earlier film, 1969)
Sallah shabbati, 1988 (based on an earlier film, 1964)

Further Reading

Christian Science Monitor (25 October 1962)
London, Yaron, *Kishon Du-Siah Biographi* [Biographical Dialogue with Kishon], Tel Aviv: Sifriyat Maariv, 1993
Nesvisky, Matt, "Tales of Hoffmann", *Jerusalem Post* (11 August 1989)
New York Times Book Review (21 October 1962; 14 April 1968)
Silberschlag, Eisig, *From Renaissance to Renaissance, vol. 2: Hebrew Literature in the Land of Israel: 1870–1970*, New York: Ktav, 1977
Ziv, Avner, "Psycho-Social Aspects of Jewish Humour in Israel and the Diaspora" in *Jewish Humor*, edited by Ziv, Tel Aviv: Papyrus, 1986; New Brunswick, New Jersey: Transaction, 1998

Ephraim Kishon is a peculiar figure in modern Hebrew literature. The prodigiously productive author of countless sketches, essays, short stories, novels, plays, filmscripts, and works of nonfiction is far and away the most popular and successful of Israeli authors. Yet while his accomplishments are widely acknowledged, while many of his characters have become the stuff of Israeli folklore, while his coinages and tropes have fixed themselves in everyday Israeli speech, Kishon himself lacks status, not to say honour, within Israel's literary establishment. He is regularly passed over for the kinds of awards the cultural mandarins present to each other, is rarely mentioned in critical discussions of Israeli letters. Eisig Silberschlag is hardly alone among critics in dismissing Kishon as an "entertainer" rather than an authentic "literary figure". In a word, Ephraim Kishon is not taken seriously.

Not being viewed seriously of course is the fate of many comic writers. In the specific case of Israel's tightly constrained, highly politicized, and fiercely competitive cultural and literary establishment, the dismissal of the popular comic writer is sorry but perhaps understandable. Jealousy no doubt has played a role in keeping Kishon outside of the inner circles. In a small nation in which virtually no writer can make a living solely by his pen, Kishon wrote the longest-running Hebrew play in history (*The Marriage Contract*), wrote and directed the most successful Israeli film of all time (*Sallah Shabbati*) and has sold far more books than any other Israeli writer. And where only a handful of Israeli writers has ever achieved the renown and economic reward that come with breaking the bonds of Hebrew by being translated into other languages, Kishon has piled up royalties in scores of countries. He reports that his books have appeared in hundreds of editions in nearly 50 languages, that he has had plays running simultaneously in 10 different countries, that he's been in the *Guinness Book of World Records* as the best-selling author in German of all time.

Seeing his books frequently top Germany's bestseller lists is what Kishon wryly refers to as "Kishon's revenge". Born Ferenc Hoffman in Budapest in 1924, Kishon was one of the few members of his family to survive the Nazi era. Today, as he once told the *Jerusalem Post*, he finds "considerable gratification that so many children and grandchildren of Nazis read – not so much my books, but stories originally written in Hebrew for the people of the Jewish state".

In the same interview Kishon confirmed the widely circulated story that when he arrived in Israel in 1949 he knew "not a single letter of Hebrew" and taught himself the language by memorizing the dictionary. Forty years later, he would teach himself German by studying translations of his own works, and now he can write directly in that language as well.

In the intervening years Kishon churned out newspaper columns six days a week and produced a steady stream of books, films, and plays. Virtually all of this production is marked by crackling dialogue, clever wordplay, cunning plotlines, and an exuberant sense of fun. His heroes include the confidence man and small-time crook Ervinke, the crafty immigrant underdog Sallah, the cafe kibitzers, the mental gymnasts, the loveable luftmenschen of Jewish folklore. His villains are petty bureaucrats, pompous politicos, and anyone unsympathetic to the Zionist enterprise. Kishon films like *Sallah Shabbati* (later staged as a successful musical comedy) and plays such as *Oh, Oh Juliet*, in which Shakespeare's star-crossed lovers survive into marriage and midlife crisis, are as neatly turned out as any classic French farce. *The Blaumilch Canal* is a bureaucracy fantasia that blends Franz Kafka and Groucho Marx. Kishon once even applied his ingenious imagination to the surreal frustrations of clearing a package through Israeli customs and made this the basis of a popular Hebrew boardgame.

Kishon is often a satirist, but his satire is more comforting than cruel; he is less concerned with the attack, more concerned with reaffirming established values. The Israeli psychology professor and humour expert Avner Ziv maintains that Kishon's "social satire is mingled with love for the characters he describes". Often as not Kishon's wit is predicated on the timeless, the domestic, the foible and the folly – as Kishon has said: "Humor that arises out of losing your spectacles on your forehead". Overall, Kishon's human comedy is clearly more apt to appeal to the European-born Israelis of his generation, and less to the younger, native-born members of a "post-Zionist" society whose comic writers and playwrights more often than not indulge in scatology, sarcasm, and cynicism – things never manifest in Kishon's work.

It is no exaggeration to say that Israeli society, which has developed and changed at a dizzying pace, has largely passed Ephraim Kishon by. Yet this observation must be weighed against the fact that even while he was long a master at entertaining his compatriots, he never went out of his way to ingratiate himself with his audience. In a resolutely political country where even the sports organizations – not to mention the literary establishment – are apt to have party backing, Kishon studiously avoided any political label. In a nation where for generations socialism was promoted on an equal footing with Zionism, Kishon remained fiercely independent. He says his experience with Nazism has made him suspicious of all ideology. In the same vein he has said that he got his sense of humour from Adolf Hitler.

> He taught me early on that mankind is insane, absurd, ludicrous. It's the only way I could comprehend a world in which a blond, blue-eyed youth who had done no one any harm, was turned into a hunted animal by Aryan racists. It's true that my work is in the tradition of the Central European cabaret. But my understanding of psychology, which I see as thoroughly irrational, was shaped by the madness of the Nazi era.

Kishon's independent-mindedness is often perceived as crankiness – or even as reactionary. But he shows no more regret for writing a book-length attack on modern art (*Picasso Was No Charlatan*) than he has for writing a book on computers and chess – or for anything else that has tumbled from his tireless pen.

MATTHEW NESVISKY

Klein, A.M.

Russian-born Canadian poet and fiction writer, 1909–1972

Born Abraham Moses Klein in Ratno, Ukraine, 14 February 1909. Emigrated with family to Montreal, 1910. Studied at Baron Byng High School, Montreal, graduated 1926. Editor, Zionist periodical, *The Judaea,* and educational director, Young Judaea, 1928–32. Studied at McGill University, BA 1930; founding editor, *McGilliad* magazine; University of Montreal, law degree 1933. Called to Quebec Bar, 1933; lawyer in Montreal, 1934–36, Rouyn, Quebec, 1937–38, then Montreal again. Married Bessie Kozlov, 1935; three children. Associate director, Zionist Organization of Canada, 1936; editor, *Canadian Zionist*, 1936–37, and *Canadian Jewish Chronicle*, Montreal, 1938–55; wrote speeches for, and gave advice on public relations to, Samuel Bronfman, President of Canadian Jewish Congress, from 1939 on. Visiting lecturer in poetry, McGill University, 1945–48. Unsuccessful as Cooperative Commonwealth Federation candidate for federal Parliament, 1949. Suffered nervous breakdown, 1954; withdrew from public life by 1955. Awarded Edward Bland Fellowship, 1947; Governor-General's Award, 1949; Quebec Literary Prize, 1952; Kovner Memorial Award, 1952; Lorne Pierce Medal of Royal Society of Canada, 1956. Died in Montreal, 20 August 1972.

Selected Writings

Poetry
Hath Not a Jew . . ., 1940
Poems, 1944
The Hitleriad, 1944
Seven Poems, 1947
Huit Poèmes canadiens (en anglais), 1948
The Rocking Chair and Other Poems, 1948
Collected Poems, edited by Miriam Waddington, 1974
Complete Poems, 2 vols, edited by Zailig Pollock, 1990

Plays
Hershel of Ostropol, 1939
Conscience, translated by Claude Vincent, 1952

Novel
The Second Scroll, 1951

Short Stories
Short Stories, edited by M.W. Steinberg and Usher Caplan, 1983

Other
Translator, *From Palestine to Israel*, by Moishe Dickstein, 1951
Translator, *Of Jewish Music, Ancient and Modern*, by Israel Rabinovitch, 1952
Beyond Sambation: Selected Essays and Editorials 1928–1955, edited by M.W. Steinberg and Usher Caplan, 1982
Literary Essays and Reviews, edited by M.W. Steinberg and Usher Caplan, 1987

Further Reading

Broad, M.I., "Art and the Artist: Klein's Unpublished Novella", *Journal of Canadian Fiction*, 30 (1980)
Caplan, Usher, *Like One that Dreamed: A Portrait of A.M. Klein*, New York: McGraw Hill Ryerson, 1982
Cavell, Richard, "Nth Adam: Dante in Klein's *The Second Scroll*", *Canadian Literature*, 106 (Autumn 1985)
Collin, William Edwin, "The Spirit's Palestine" in *The White Savannahs*, by Collin, Toronto: Macmillan, 1936
Dudek, Louis, "A.M. Klein", *Canadian Forum*, 30 (April 1950)
Edel, Leon, "Abraham M. Klein", *Canadian Forum*, 12 (May 1932)
Fischer, Gretl Keren, *In Search of Jerusalem: Religion and Ethics in the Writings of A.M. Klein*, Montreal: McGill–Queen's University Press, 1975
Fisher, E.S., "A.M. Klein: Portrait of the Poet as Jew", *Canadian Literature*, 79 (Winter 1978)
Fuerstenberg, Adam, "From Yiddish to 'Yiddishkeit': A.M. Klein, J.I. Segal and Montreal's Yiddish Culture", *Journal of Canadian Studies*, 19/2 (1984)
Golfman, N., "Semantics and Semitics", *University of Toronto Quarterly*, 51 (Winter 1981–82)
Greenstein, M., "History in *The Second Scroll*", *Canadian Literature*, 76 (Spring 1978)
Journal of Canadian Studies, special issue, 19 (Summer 1984)
Marshall, Tom (editor), *A.M. Klein*, Toronto: Ryerson, 1970
Nadel, Ira, "The Absent Prophet in Canadian Jewish Fiction", *English Quarterly*, 5 (Spring 1972)
Pacey, Desmond, "A.M. Klein" in his *Ten Canadian Poets*, Toronto: Ryerson, 1958
Pollock, Zailig, "Sunflower Seeds: Klein's Hero and Demagogue", *Canadian Literature*, 82 (Autumn 1979)
Pollock, Zailig *et al.*, *A.M. Klein: An Annotated Bibliography*, Toronto: ECW Press, 1993
Rome, David, *Jews in Canadian Literature: A Bibliography*, Montreal: Canadian Jewish Congress and Jewish Public Library, 1962
Russell, K.C., "Blasphemies of A.M. Klein", *Canadian Literature*, 72 (Spring 1977)
Seymour, Mayne (editor), *The A.M. Klein Symposium, 1974*, Ottawa: University of Ottawa Press, 1975
Smith, A.J.M., "Abraham Moses Klein", *Les Gants du Ciel*, 11 (Spring 1946)
Steinberg, M.W., "A Twentieth Century Pentateuch", *Canadian Literature*, 2 (Autumn 1959)
Steinberg, M.W., "Poet of a Living Past", *Canadian Literature*, 25 (Summer 1965)
Steinberg, M.W., "The Conscience of Art: A.M. Klein on Poets and Poetry" in *A Political Art: Essays and Images in Honour of George Woodcock*, edited by William H. New, Vancouver: University of British Columbia Press, 1978
Steinberg, M.W., "A.M. Klein as Journalist", *Canadian Literature*, 82 (Autumn 1979)
Waddington, Miriam, *A.M. Klein*, Toronto: Copp Clark, 1970

In 1936, when the American critic Ludwig Lewisohn dubbed A.M. Klein the "first contributor of authentic Jewish poetry to the English language", he signalled not only the inception of a particular Jewish contribution to literature in English; he also unwittingly ushered in the era in which Canada's sense of its literary life would be not only bicultural, but multicultural. The idea of a Canadian tradition with many unique voices is now commonplace, and a host of writers whose cultural resources blend specifically south Asian or Caribbean or Cherokee concerns with Canadian issues are among the best read and most carefully critiqued of Canada's literary artists. Klein's vision of a polyglot literary culture is affirmed again and again in his early poetry and fiction. Montreal became the landscape on which he imagined this culture's richest possibilities, and it was often in response to the city's variety that he strove to conjure such a multicultural tradition for Canadian readers before they knew what such a thing might mean. In a 1948 pamphlet printed by the Canadian Jewish Congress Klein employs a poetic method in which these concerns are addressed in a poetic diction he calls "un 'langage bilingue'": with the exception of articles and auxiliaries, his vocabulary is meant to resonate for both English and French readers.

Into this bicultural smorgasbord Klein inserted his own Jewish language and yearnings – a mix of Yiddish, Zionism, his love of the Montreal Jewish "ghetto", and a melancholy sense of the lost European world of his parents. Klein straddled old world and new like no other Canadian writer in English. He was Talmudist and modernist, Hebraist and journalist, a chronicler of the upheavals of modern Jewish history who earned a side income writing speeches for the head of the Bronfman liquor dynasty. This breadth, and the concomitant dividedness it created in Klein's pursuits, may have contributed to his ultimate withdrawal from public life. But in his active years he was a true representative man – striving to sing the particularity of his city, his nation, his tribal record, just as Whitman offered a song of his people in his own characteristic voice. In "Montreal" (in *The Rocking Chair*) Klein wrote:

> Never do I sojourn in alien place
> But I do languish for your scenes and sounds,
> City of reverie, nostalgic isle,
> Pendant most brilliant on Laurentian cord!
> The coigns of your boulevards – my signiory –
> Your suburbs are my exile's verdure fresh,
> Your parks, your fountain'd parks –
> Pasture of memory!

Klein's output was substantial in a range of genres, but his poetry has proved his most lasting work. His sonnets on themes "Semitic", his highly personal odes to Montreal – its treed mountain and its "ghetto streets" – resonate with bold imagery and a unique voice of almost ecstatic praise. His most enduring volume is *The Rocking Chair*, which won Canada's then-nascent Governor General's Award for its portraits of iconic Canadian scenes – the prairie grain elevator, the Québecois rocking chair counting time on a farmer's porch, the Frigidaire of a cold water flat. *The Rocking Chair* closes with what many think of as Klein's masterpiece, a Joycean parable of artistic sacrifice called "Portrait of the Poet as Landscape". Oddly enough, this bleak poem of the writer's meaninglessness in modern society, his eclipse by "the local tycoon", is often taught to bright-eyed university newcomers. In it we find lines that may also presage the oncoming collapse of Klein's poetic energy:

> We are sure only that from our real society
> he has disappeared; he simply does not count,
> except in the pullulation of vital statistics –
> somebody's vote, perhaps . . .

Klein's single novel, *The Second Scroll*, retains its freshness and provocative character. It is a short narrative that addresses questions related to the Holocaust, exile, and the declaration of the State of Israel. It is also an exemplary modernist text – a narrative fractured into five main parts, the shape and motifs of which mimic that of the Torah. Appended to these chapters are a set of what Klein called "glosses", poems, prayers, and a play that comment on and interpret the foregoing text. The resonances and intertextual strategies of *The Second Scroll* are a stylistic triumph. The novel's investigation of religion, history, and poetry presents the reader with a stunning array of thematic concerns. And the details of the narrator's life – his religious parents, the family left behind in pogrom-ridden Russia, the ardour for the newly declared State of Israel – also provide the reader with a veiled autobiography of the novelist himself.

Many Canadian poets after him cite Klein as their forefather – Irving Layton, Leonard Cohen, David Solway, and Miriam Waddington have all paid tribute to him as a central influence. His eventual withdrawal has proved haunting as well, as an example of the risks inherent in a creative public life. In "Song for Abraham Klein", Leonard Cohen wrote:

> The weary psalmist paused
> His instrument beside
> Departed was the Sabbath
> And the Sabbath Bride.

In the musings of others Klein has been transformed into an almost mythic presence in Canadian letters, one of the few precursors who truly haunts the ephebes of later generations.

NORMAN RAVVIN

Klíma, Ivan

Czech fiction writer, 1931–

Born in Prague, 14 September 1931 to assimilated Jewish parents. Spent over three years in concentration camps at Terezín as a child. Educated at Charles University, Prague, graduated 1956. Married social psychologist Helena Klíma in 1958; one son, one daughter. Editor of periodicals, 1956–59; deputy editor-in-chief *Literární noviny* [Literary Journal], 1964–68; Visiting Professor, University of Michigan, Ann Arbor, 1969–70; also worked as an ambulance man, messenger, and surveyor's assistant. Returned to Prague, 1970.

Writings banned in Czechoslovakia, 1970–89. Member of Charter 77 (human rights movement); President, Czech PEN, since 1990. Awards include the Hostovsky award, 1986.

Selected Writings

Fiction
Bezvadný den [The Wonderful Day], 1960
Hodina ticha [Hour of Silence], 1963
Milenci na jednu noc [Lovers for One Night], 1964
Kokrhací hodiny a jiné příběhy z Vlaských Kloboúk a podobných Tramtárii, 1965
Lod' jménem naděje, 1969; as *A Ship Named Hope: Two Novels (The Jury; A Ship Named Hope)*, translated by Edith Pargeter, 1970
Markétin zvěřinec, 1973
Malomocní [The Lepers], 1974
Stojí, stojí, šibenička, 1976; as *Soudce z milosti*, 1986; as *Judge on Trial*, translated by A.G. Brain, 1991
Má veselá jitra, 1978; as *My Merry Mornings*, translated by George Theiner, 1985
Milostné léto, 1979; as *A Summer Affair*, translated by Ewald Osers, 1987
Moje první lásky, 1985; as *My First Loves*, translated by Ewald Osers, 1986
Láska a smetí, 1986; as *Love and Garbage*, translated by Ewald Osers, 1990
Moje zlatá řemesla, 1990; as *My Golden Trades*, translated by Paul Wilson, 1992
Milenci na jeden den, 1992; as *Lovers for the Day*, translated by Gerald Turner, 1999
Ostrov mrtvých králů [The Island of the Dead Kings], 1992
Čekání na t'mu, čekání na světlo, 1993; as *Waiting for the Dark, Waiting for the Light*, translated by Paul Wilson, 1994
Poslední stupeň důvěrnosti, 1996; as *The Ultimate Intimacy*, translated by A.G. Brain, 1997

Plays
Zámek, 1965; as *The Castle*, 1968
Cukrárna Myriam, with *Klára a dva páni*, 1967; as *A Sweetshop Myriam*, 1968
Klára a dva páni, with *Cukrárna Myriam*, 1967; as *Klára and Two Men*, 1968
Mistr, 1967; as *The Master*, 1968
Ženich pro Marcelu, 1968; as *Bridegroom for Marcela*, 1969
Porota [The Jury], 1968
Theaterstücke (in German; includes *Zámek*, *Klára a dva páni*; *Cukrárna Myriam*, *Ženich pro Marcelu*; *Pokoj pro dva*), 1971
Pokoj pro dva a jiné hry (includes *Pokoj pro dva*; *Hromobití*; *Ministr a anděl*) [The Double Bedroom; The Thunderstorm; The President and the Angel], 1973
Hry, 1974; as *Games*, 1981
Franz a Felice, 1983; as *Kafka and Felice*, 1986

Radio Plays: *Porota*, 1968; as *The Jury*; *Ženich pro Marcelu*, 1969 (banned; original recording broadcast Prague, 1990); *Minstr a anděl*, 1984; as *The President and the Angel*, 1985; *Hromobití* [The Thunderstorm], 1990

Television Plays
Pokoj pro dva [The Double Bedroom], 1990; *Franz a Felice* [Franz and Felice], 1992; *Markétin zvěřinec*, 1993

Other
Mezi třemi hranicemi [Between Three Borders], 1960
Karel Čapek, 1962
Návštěva u nesmrtelné tetky: Polské zápisky [Visit to an Immortal Auntie], 1965
Už se blíží meče [The Swords Are Approaching], 1990
The Spirit of Prague, translated by Paul Wilson, 1994
Fictions and Histories, with others, 1998
Between Security and Insecurity, translated by Gerry Turner, 1999

Further Reading

Czech Center of International PEN, *Literature and Tolerance*, Prague: Readers International, 1994
Goetz-Stankiewicz, Marketa, *The Silenced Theatre: Czech Playwrights without a Stage*, Toronto: University of Toronto Press, 1979
Goetz-Stankiewicz, Marketa (editor), *Czechoslovakia: Plays by Milan Kundera, Václav Havel, Pavel Kohout, Milan Uhde, Pavel Landovský, and Ivan Klíma*, New York: Performing Arts Journal, 1985
Hájek, Igor, "Profile: Ivan Klíma", *Index on Censorship*, 12/2 (1983)
Klíma, Ivan, "A Christmas Conspiracy" in *The Writing on the Wall: An Anthology of Contemporary Czech Literature*, edited by Peter Kussi and Antonin Liehm, New York: Karz Cohl, 1983
Lopate, Phillip, "Czechs, But Not My Mates", *Newsday* (24 September 1995)
Roth, Philip, "A Conversation in Prague", *New York Review of Books*, 37/6 (12 April 1990)
Schapiro, Mark, "Fading Czech Velvet: Interview with Ivan Klíma", *Nation*, 268/8 (17 May 1999)
Schubert, Peter Z., "My Golden Trades (Book Review)", *World Literature Today*, 69 (Summer 1995)
Spafford, Peter (editor), *Interference: The Story of Czechoslovakia in the Words of Its Writers*, Gloucester, UK: New Clarion Press, 1992
Welch, Frances, "My Faith Grew under the Nazis, Then Died Me and My God", *Sunday Telegraph* (7 December 1997)

"Writing enables you to enter places inaccessible in real life, even the most forbidden spaces", says Ivan Klíma in his essay "A Rather Unconventional Childhood". The unconventionality on which Klíma principally meditates in this essay is his incarceration as child prisoner in Terezín, a Nazi concentration camp in occupied Czechoslovakia. Klíma was born in Prague in 1931. His parents were Jewish (his mother's family by conversion), but they were not interested in – "they rejected" – Jewish faith and identity. Klíma's father, an engineer by trade, was a Marxist thinker and a rationalist who believed above all in technology – "he thought that technology knew no borders and therefore he was at home anywhere in the world". His mother had Klíma baptized in 1939 in a futile attempt to evade the Nazi war machine. Klíma's first sense of himself as Jewish came through Nazi racial edicts. Suddenly, former playmates and neighbours avoided him, and, in some cases, harassed him outright.

Klíma retreated from the outdoors, and began to read books – Homer, Dickens, Jules Verne. He continued reading those same books (he smuggled them in), and began writing essays and poetry in Terezín. Klíma explains that while he certainly recalls hunger, and wrote in the barracks "liberating" essays about trees, mountains, a tower on a hill in Prague (places he was not free to experience), the distinguishing feature of his childhood "was the constant presence of death." Klíma writes of being surrounded by death, and the deathly stillness left in the wake of transports. Against this constant presence, he believes he constructed an "inner wall" as defence from the continual partings and separations. Further, this inner wall, a self-protective mechanism developed during childhood, is the same wall one must deconstruct as an adult in the world after Terezín.

> If you construct such an inner wall when you are still a child, you must then spend the rest of your life tearing it down, and the question is, can you ever manage to destroy it completely . . . Endless lines of ignominiously branded and doomed people accompanied by a handful of armed men stretch throughout my childhood. The image of those lines, whose length can be calculated in kilometers, but the sum of whose despair is beyond measure, has stayed with me all my life and often determines the circle of ideas and themes that attract me.

As with other survivor-writers, Klíma feels that he has been given a responsibility to "become their voice", the voice of the endless line, "their cry of protests against a death that had erased their lives from this world". Klíma and his immediate family did survive the war – but the questions to which his novels, short stories, and essays return are original to childhood, to the imposed conflict of forming an inner life that resists intimacy with the outer, that preserves a sense of self against the continual presence of death.

Klíma's subjects are intimacy, disappointment, hope, justice, and work – private considerations in coordination with the communal. Klíma's country was liberated, then almost immediately surrendered to another repressive (Soviet communist) system. Once again, his education as a writer was shaped by a force that necessitated subversion. His writings, as a collective narrative body, seem to move from an analysis of the condition of living under the Nazi, and then Soviet regimes, in nonfiction, to a fictional (often semi-autobiographical) animation of the inner life of a man straddling that exact divide. Critics, including John Updike, have complained at Klíma's heavy hand; and Klíma himself confesses that his wife is one of his best readers because she questions when his fictional characters act as sounding boards to ethical and humanist questions. For Klíma, fidelity to the real in writing – and especially in fiction – is crucial if one wishes to avoid making literature a self-referential commodity. Literature must do work, he insists in a recent collection of essays, not in service to a government or ideology, but to the body of readers, to the "public". Narrative must not "abdicate" the responsibility to interpret and make meaning in "its eager pursuit of novelty and originality". Klíma is arguing for a conscience, it appears, an aesthetic destruction of anything that might constitute a wall between the artist and, as he names it, "the public".

This posture is consistent with his opposition to the kind of social realism favoured, monied, and plundered by the Soviet party ruling Czechoslovakia until 1989. Klíma was integral to the *samizdat*, an underground publishing circle of writers, where manuscripts were circulated not by printing press, but privately. Writers of this period, from 1968 to 1989, reproduced and circulated illegally stories and essays, novels, and dramatic works without the official endorsement of, and in direct violation of, the ruling authorities. Klíma was himself interrogated and followed, though never imprisoned (Václav Havel was the only of his immediate circle to be incarcerated). Many Czech writers of this period, including Bohumil Hrabal (a fellow Czech writer Klíma much admires) wrote against the false realism the government funded and mandated because it was forwarding a self-serving ideology. Soviet Realism was intended for one purpose only: the glorification of its own presence in power. As with the Nazi Party, the Soviet Communist Party sought the construction of an aesthetic that sought to fashion a reality out of ideology.

The kind of realism Klíma writes for, therefore, can be considered absurd, unrealistic, fantastic. The absurd tradition in Czech literature does not belong to Klíma alone of course – it is shared by Jaroslav Seifert, Jaroslav Hašek, Hrabal and others – but Klíma's place in it is made unique by his own preoccupation with betrayal. Whether the betrayals happen in marriage (many of his novels explore infidelity) or in religion (as in *The Ultimate Intimacy*, where a priest has an affair) they investigate the shaky contract between the individual and a society. Klíma is again trying to dismantle the wall his childhood erected, and in doing so working against his own experience of betrayal – by the outside world against the private.

Klíma is not, like his father, a Marxist, nor does he consistently ally with any organized religious or philosophical body. But he is fascinated by the meaning of labour, of the identity specific to one's work. He sees his father's belief in Marxism as a kind of religion, indicative of a need for faith, a faith that did not manifest as a strict adherence to his Jewish heritage. During the Nazi occupation, European intellectuals and thinkers were murdered; during the Soviet reign, remaining intellectuals and writers in Czechoslovakia either had to emigrate (a complicated matter), cooperate with the state, or take on jobs requiring manual labour to survive. He wrote a collection of stories translated into English as *My Golden Trades*: each story bears a different occupation – the painter, the courier, the smuggler – reflecting the specific condition of labour and the artist in Czechoslovakia. Klíma continues his father's intellectual pro-labour posture, believing that work, in Klíma's own case the work of literature, has transcendent possibilities. He is concerned, as always, with the stress of the untrue, the false on the real, or of the real on something that was never or is no longer true.

JEANIE M. TIETJEN

Koestler, Arthur

Hungarian-born British novelist, dramatist, and nonfiction writer, 1905–1983

Born in Budapest, 5 September 1905. Studied at Polytechnic High School, Vienna; University of Vienna, 1922–26. Married, first, Dorothy Asher, 1935; divorced, 1950; second, Mamaine Paget, 1950; divorced, 1953; third, Cynthia Jefferies, 1965; one daughter. Became private secretary to Zionist leader, Vladimir Jabotinsky, *c.*1925; worked as labourer in Jezreel Valley kibbutz, lemonade vendor in Haifa, assistant to Arab architect, and editor of Cairo weekly, 1926–29. Middle East correspondent, 1927–29, Paris correspondent, 1929–30, and member of editorial board, 1930–32, Ullstein Newspapers, Berlin; also science editor, *Vossische Zeitung*, and foreign editor, *BZ am Mittag*, 1930; sole journalist aboard *Graf Zeppelin* Arctic expedition, summer 1931. Member of Communist Party, 1931–38; travelled through Soviet Central Asia, 1932–33; freelance journalist in Paris, London, and Zürich, 1933–36; Spanish Civil War correspondent, London *News Chronicle*, 1936–37; imprisoned by Nationalists in Malaga and Seville, sentenced to death, then released after three months, 1937. Editor, *Zukunft*, Paris, 1938. Detained as anti-fascist refugee and imprisoned at Le Vernet, October 1939 to January 1940; member of French Foreign Legion, under assumed name Albert Dubert, 1940–41; escaped to Britain, jailed for having false papers, 1941; member, British Pioneer Corps, 1941–42; worked for Ministry of Information, for BBC, and as night ambulance driver until 1944. Palestine correspondent, London *Times*, 1945–47; Palestine war correspondent, *Manchester Guardian* and New York *Herald Tribune*, 1948. Became British citizen, 1948; full-time writer from 1950. Fellow, Center for Advanced Study in the Behavioral Sciences, Stanford University, 1964–65. Vice President, Exit (British voluntary euthanasia society), 1981–83. Fellow, Royal Society of Literature, 1958, and Companion of Literature, 1974; CBE (Commander of the British Empire), 1972; honorary member, American Academy of Arts and Sciences, 1977. Died in suicide pact with wife Cynthia at their home in Montpelier Square, London, 1 March 1983.

Selected Writings

Fiction
The Gladiators, translated by Edith Simon, 1939
Darkness at Noon, translated by Daphne Hardy, 1940
Arrival and Departure, 1943
Thieves in the Night: Chronicle of an Experiment, 1946
The Age of Longing, 1951
The Call-Girls: A Tragi-Comedy with Prologue and Epilogue, 1972

Autobiography
Spanish Testament, 1937; excerpt, as *Dialogue with Death*, translated by Trevor Blewitt and Phyllis Blewitt, 1942
Scum of the Earth, 1941
Arrow in the Blue, 1952
The Invisible Writing, 1954
Stranger on the Square, with Cynthia Koestler, 1984

Plays
Black Gallery series; *Protective Custody* (radio plays), 1942
Lift Your Head, Comrade (screenplay), 1944
Twilight Bar: An Escapade in Four Acts, 1945

Other
Encyclopédie de la vie sexuelle (as Alfrède Costler), with Ludwig Léry-Lenz and A. Willey, 1934; as *Encyclopedia of Sexual Knowledge*, edited by Norman Haire, 1934; 2nd edition, 1952
Von weissen Nächten und roten Tagen [Of White Nights and Red Days], 1934
Sexual Anomalies and Perversions: A Summary of the Works of Magnus Hirschfeld, 1936 (published anonymously)
Menschenopfer unerhört [Incredible Human Sacrifice], 1937
The Yogi and the Commissar and Other Essays, 1945
Insight and Outlook: An Inquiry into the Common Foundations of Science and Social Ethics, 1949
Promise and Fulfilment: Palestine 1917–1949, 1949
The God that Failed: Six Studies in Communism, with others, edited by Richard Crossman, 1950
The Trail of the Dinosaur and Other Essays, 1955
Reflections on Hanging, 1956
Réflexions sur la peine capitale, with Albert Camus, 1957
The Sleepwalkers: A History of Man's Changing Vision of the Universe, 1959; section published as *The Watershed: A Biography of Johannes Keppler*, 1960
The Lotus and the Robot, 1960
Hanged by the Neck: An Exposure of Capital Punishment in England, with C.H. Rolph, 1961
Editor, *Suicide of a Nation? An Enquiry into the State of Britain Today*, 1963
The Act of Creation, 1964
The Ghost in the Machine, 1967
Drinkers of Infinity: Essays 1955–1967, 1968
Editor, with J.R. Smythies, *Beyond Reductionism: New Perspectives in the Life Sciences*, 1969
The Case of the Midwife Toad, 1971
The Roots of Coincidence, 1972
The Challenge of Chance: Experiments and Speculations, with Alister Hardy and Robert Harvie, 1973
The Lion and the Ostrich, 1973
The Heel of Achilles: Essays 1968–1973, 1974
The Thirteenth Tribe: The Khazar Empire and Its Heritage, 1976
Janus: A Summing Up, 1978
Bricks to Babel: Selected Writings with Comments, 1980
Kaleidoscope, 1981

Further Reading

Atkins, John Alfred, *Arthur Koestler*, London: Spearman, 1956
Cesarani, David, *Arthur Koestler: The Homeless Mind*, London: Heinemann, 1998; New York: Free Press, 1999
Day, Frank, *Arthur Koestler: A Guide to Research*, New York: Garland, 1987
Harris, Harold (editor), *Astride the Two Cultures: Arthur Koestler at 70*, London: Hutchinson, 1975; New York: Random House, 1976

Koestler, Mamaine, *Living with Koestler: Mamaine Koestler's Letters 1945–51*, edited by Celia Goodman, New York: St Martin's Press, and London: Weidenfeld and Nicolson, 1985
Levene, Mark, *Arthur Koestler*, New York: Ungar, 1984
Mikes, George, *Arthur Koestler: The Story of a Friendship*, London: André Deutsch, 1983
Pearson, Sidney A., *Arthur Koestler*, Boston: Twayne, 1978
Reed, Merrill and Thomas Frazier (editors), *Arthur Koestler: An International Bibliography*, Ann Arbor, Michigan: Ardis, 1979
Smyth, Susan J. (editor), *The Koestler Archive in Edinburgh University Library*, Edinburgh: Edinburgh University Library, 1987
Sperber, Murray A. (editor), *Arthur Koestler: A Collection of Critical Essays*, Englewood Cliffs, New Jersey: Prentice Hall, 1977

Arthur Koestler survived imprisonment during the Spanish Civil War and the fall of France to become one of the most original thinkers of the 20th century. His prodigious literary output included memorable novels, philosophy, sociology, psychology, and politics, and served as a record for his own turbulent life. Born in Budapest, he acquired a keen interest in science and mathematics, and later attended the University of Vienna, but failed to complete his course of studies. Koestler's personality varied between contemplative and enthusiastic phases, and one of his first enthusiasms was Zionism. A rational sceptic with a scientific background, he was unimpressed by Orthodox Judaism and what he saw as the ghetto mentality of his more traditionalist fellow Jews; on the other hand, he was greatly influenced by the Zionist Vladimir Jabotinsky, who convinced him that an independent homeland in Palestine was the answer to the ills of his people. In 1926 Koestler made his way to Palestine and worked on the Kuvtsa Heftseba, a remote Zionist settlement in the Jezreel Valley. Although he later grew disillusioned with what he felt was narrow traditionalism and the imposition of an east European ghetto lifestyle on the new country, he never lost his belief in the importance of the Jewish homeland. Koestler visited Israel several times in later years, and celebrated it in his writing. His novel *Thieves in the Night: Chronicle of an Experiment* draws on personal experience to give a "documentary"-style fictional treatment to the events behind the founding of the Jewish state. In *Promise and Fulfilment: Palestine 1917–1949*, he declared that the newly-formed Israel owed its existence to the early pioneer settlements, and expressed his hopes for the future of the infant nation.

> Now that the mission of the Wandering Jew is completed, he must discard the knapsack and cease to be an accomplice in his own destruction . . . The fumes of the death chambers still linger over Europe; there must be an end to every calvary.

Unlike some of Koestler's enthusiasms, his love for Israel remained constant throughout his life.

Returning to Europe, he converted to another faith, that of communism. In the late 1920s, with fascism a threat and Europe's democracies proving ineffectual, communism seemed the one way forward, and in 1931 Koestler joined the Communist Party. His first doubts came on a visit to the Soviet Union, where he witnessed the famine caused by forced collectivization, but it was Stalin's Terror and the show trials of the mid-1930s that finally convinced him of his mistake. Koestler, who left the party in 1938, later denounced the communist system with other former party members in *The God that Failed; Six Studies in Communism*. The drift towards war, and the conflict in Spain led him to believe that communism still had a positive role to play in opposing the Nazis, and he served as a Comintern agent. Arrested as a spy, he was imprisoned and sentenced by Franco, but later reprieved. *Spanish Testament*, written at this time, is notable for the section entitled "Dialogue with Death", where Koestler set down his thoughts and feelings as he awaited execution. Released, he was in France when the Nazis invaded, and found himself interned as a refugee at the notorious Le Vernet prison. In *Scum of the Earth*, Koestler noted the anti-Semitism that was rife in French society at this time, and the approval many had for Hitler's genocidal policies. Escaping under the assumed identity of a *legionnaire*, he made his way to England, where he was imprisoned in Pentonville while his credentials were confirmed. Koestler was later to recall that, "At a conservative estimate, three out of every four people whom I knew before I was thirty were subsequently killed in Spain, or hounded to death at Dachau, or gassed at Belsen, or deported to Russia, or liquidated in Russia".

During this time he had written *The Gladiators* and *Darkness at Noon*, two of his trilogy of novels on the nature and ethics of revolution; the trilogy was completed with *Arrival and Departure*. In these novels Koestler examines the early idealism that gives rise to revolutions, and contrasts it with the later corruption and subversion of those ideals. All three are memorable works of fiction, but *Darkness at Noon* stands out from the others. Based on his knowledge of the Stalinist purges, it describes the last days of the old Bolshevik Rubashov and his dialogues with the Stalinist interrogators who intend to force him to "confess" to crimes he never committed. Once a hard-line revolutionary himself, Rubashov reflects on his complicity in the web of tyranny and mass murder that now reaches out to include him as a victim. Koestler presents Rubashov without excuses, but enlists the reader's sympathy for him as "confession" is made and death approaches; his portrayal is given added force by Rubashov's name, which is itself Jewish, Koestler doubtless reliving his own experience of prison and impending death through this fictional character. His most accomplished work of fiction, *Darkness at Noon*, remains one of the most important novels of modern times.

Koestler made his home in Britain, taking British citizenship, and after 1940 all his books (hitherto written in German) appeared in English. This didn't prevent him from taking issue with his adopted country over capital punishment with *Reflections on Hanging*, or predicting its downfall in *Suicide of a Nation? An Enquiry into the State of Britain Today*. In the years that were left him his writings explored a wide array of subjects that demonstrated the reach of his formidable intellect. Of particular significance were his writings on the psychology of the creative mind, where he was able to suggest unexpected links between art, science, religion, and the supernatural. In *The Sleepwalkers: A History of Man's Changing Vision of the Universe*, Koestler pays tribute to the great pioneers of science who aroused his admiration as a young boy. *The Act of Creation* explores the creative process at work in science and art, while in *The Ghost in the Machine* Koestler examines the self-destructive urges inherited from our prehistoric brain and their threat to man's continued existence. (His solution was to suggest the use of "mind-controlling" drugs, in order to ensure "the transformation of *homo maniacus* into *homo sapiens*".) *The Lotus and the Robot* contrasts the automated lifestyle of the West with the Eastern systems of Yoga and Zen Buddhism, while in *The Case of the Midwife Toad* Koestler indicates the dangers of scientific oppression. Two volumes of autobiography, *Arrow in the Blue* and *The Invisible Writing* described his own eventful life up to 1949; later experiences were detailed in a posthumous volume, *Stranger on the Square*. His death was to prove as dramatic as his life had been. Learning that he had a terminal illness, Koestler and his wife ended their lives in a suicide pact in March 1983.

Often controversial, always stimulating, Koestler impresses with the range of his vision, and the unexpected sharpness of his perceptions. Although he spurned Judaism, his feeling for the Jewish homeland was genuine and deep, and his writings attest to his pride in his Jewish heritage.

GEOFF SADLER

Kolmar, Gertrud

German poet, dramatist, and fiction writer, 1894–1943

Born Gertrud Käthe Chodziesner in Berlin, 12 October 1894; cousin of the philosopher and critic Walter Benjamin. Graduated from Klockow school for girls, Berlin, 1911; studied home economics, Leipzig, 1911; also studied Russian, Czech, Spanish, Flemish, Hebrew. Worked in daycare centres and enrolled in seminars on language teaching, 1914–15; diploma in French and English, 1916. Censored mail and served as interpreter in prisoner-of-war camp, Döberitz, 1917–18. Governess and private tutor in Peine, Berlin, and Hamburg, 1919–27; summer courses in Dijon, France, 1927; returned to Berlin to manage parents' household. Evicted from her family home in Finckenkrug, she was compelled to live in ghetto created by Nazis in Berlin; forced labour at Epeco, 1941; father, Georg, deported to Theresienstadt, 1942; Kolmar deported to Auschwitz, 1943. Died in Auschwitz, 2 March 1943.

Selected Writings

Poetry
Gedichte [Poems], 1917
Preussische Wappen [Prussian Coats of Arms], 1934
Die Frau und die Tiere [The Woman and the Animals], 1938
Welten [Universes], 1947
Das lyrische Werk, edited by Friedhelm Kemp, 1960
Tag- und Tierträume [Day and Animal Dreams], 1963
Die Kerze von Arras: ausgewählte Gedichte [The Candle of Arras: Selected Poems], 1968
Selected Poems of Gertrude Kolmar, translated by David Kipp, 1970
Dark Soliloquy: The Selected Poems by Gertrud Kolmar, translated by Henry A. Smith, 1975
Das Wort der Stummen [The Word of the Mute], 1978
Weibliches Bildnis: sämtliche Gedichte [Female Image: Collected Poems], 1980
Gedichte [Poems], 1983
The Shimmering Crystal: Poems from Das Lyrische Werk by Gertrud Kolmar (first bilingual edition), translated by Elizabeth Spencer, 1995

Fiction
Eine Mutter, edited by Friedhelm Kemp, 1965
Eine jüdische Mutter, edited by Berndt Balzer, 1981; as *A Jewish Mother from Berlin*, translated by Brigitte Goldstein, 1997
Susanna, edited by Thomas Sparr, 1993; as *Susanna*, translated by Brigitte Goldstein, 1997

Letters
Briefe an die Schwester Hilde [Letters to Sister Hilde], edited by Johanna Zeitler, 1970
Briefe, edited by Johanna Woltman, 1997

Further Reading

Blumenthal, Bernhardt, *Gertrud Kolmar: Love's Service to the Earth*, Philadelphia: American Association of Teachers of German, 1969
Eichmann-Leutenegger, Beatrice, *Gertrud Kolmar: Leben und Werk in Texten und Bildern*, Frankfurt: Jüdischer Verlag, 1993
Frantz, Barbara C., *Gertrud Kolmar's Prose*, New York: Peter Lang, 1997
Hammer, Stephanie, "In the Name of the Rose: Gertrud Kolmar, Hélène Cixous, and the Poerotics of Jewish Femininity" in *Transforming the Center, Eroding the Margins: Essays on Ethnic and Cultural Boundaries in German-Speaking Countries*, edited by Dagmar C.G. Lorenz and Renate Posthofen, Columbia, South Carolina: Camden House, 1998
Lorenz, Dagmar C.G., "The Unspoken Bond: Else Lasker-Schüler and Gertrud Kolmar in their Historical and Cultural Context", *Seminar: A Journal of Germanic Studies*, 29/4 (1993): 349–69
Lorenz-Lindemann, Karin (editor), *Widerstehen im Wort: Studien zu den Dichtungen Gertrud Kolmars*, Göttingen: Wallstein, 1996
Shafi, Monika, *Gertrud Kolmar: eine Einführung in das Werk*, Munich: Iudicium Verlag, 1995

Gertrud Kolmar, an accomplished poet of the Weimar Republic, has often been compared to Else Lasker-Schüler and Nelly Sachs. After the Nazi takeover Kolmar played a central role in the Berlin *Kulturbund*, the Jewish cultural association, until in 1938 all venues for Jewish cultural activity were dismantled. Kolmar was born to privilege. She was a daughter of the defence attorney and German patriot Ludwig Chodziesner, whose family had come from Poznań, and his wife Elise, daughter of the prominent Schönflies family from the Mark Brandenburg. Kolmar, a teacher for children with disabilities, a poet, and translator, was the favourite cousin of Walter Benjamin and the sister-in-law of Hilde Benjamin, later Minister of Justice of the German Democratic Republic. In 1938 Kolmar's sister Hilde Wenzel took exile in Switzerland, but Kolmar seems to have underestimated the risk of staying. She was relocated together with her father from their suburban home into a ghetto house (*Judenhaus*) and forced to work in a factory producing packaging materials for grenades. In 1939 she tried to emigrate but was too late to secure a visa. In 1943, a few months after her 81-year-old father's deportation to Theresienstadt, she was among the last Jewish workers to be taken from Berlin to Auschwitz. Hilde Benjamin saved her poetry cycle *Das Wort der Stummen*, Hilde Wenzel kept her sister's letters from Berlin and later she took charge of Kolmar's estate.

German language and culture represented the basis of Kolmar's identity as a writer. At the same time she was proud of her Jewish heritage. As the Nazi repression intensified so did her interest in Judaism and the Hebrew language. Throughout her career a Jewish perspective is implied in her writing. It became more forceful in the poetry cycle *Preussische Wappen* in 1934 which reclaims "German" territory for the Jewish poet, and in the novellas *Eine jüdische Mutter* and *Susanna*, both written in the 1930s. The fates of Kolmar's protagonists, Jewish women, reveal how superficial the relationships between Jews and non-Jews actually are, and they expose divisiveness among Jews. Filtered through the eyes of outsiders Kolmar shows the position of Jews in Germany and in eastern Europe to be untenable both from a psychological and a social point of view. She links the marginality of Jewishness with those of gender and species and makes transparent the multiple oppressive structures and dynamics within central European society.

Kolmar was a certified translator of French, English, and Russian and combined in her approach to writing extreme linguistic sensitivity with directness and clarity. Her works reflect the sobriety of post-World War I Weimar *Neue Sachlichkeit* [New Objectivity], the influences of German classical, romantic, and realist literature – an integral part of the high school curriculum – and elements from the Bible, Jewish mysticism, and fairy tales. The fusion of these discourses in her highly poetic texts is paradigmatic of the achievement of 1920s German-Jewish high culture. Kolmar lived in Berlin except for short-term assignments as a private tutor, her studies in France, and brief trips such as the one with Karl Josef Keller in 1934 to Hamburg and the Baltic Sea. The scope of her works reflects the limited but intense spheres of experience marked by spatial confinement, thwarted love, foiled motherhood, and her work as a governess and her father's housekeeper. Her writing emerges from torment about being the "other" rather than the "only" woman, remorse over an abortion, the humiliation of never being the mistress of her own house, and the anguish over bigotry and racism. Her partiality to the oppressed – women, Jews, the poor, the homeless, and animals – derives from her agony and despair. Female desire, sensuality, and femininity as a social construct are major issues in her poetry. Although in the 1930s Kolmar faced mounting hardship, she was extremely productive during that period. She published collections of poetry, contributed to journals, magazines, and anthologies including *Herz zum Hafen*, *Die literarische Welt*, *Der Weisse Rabe*, and *Jüdische Lyrik der Zeit*. Her two novellas, not published until after the Shoah, "Das Bildnis Robespierres", *Welten*, the four-act drama *Cécile Renault*, and the letters to her sister were written within a decade. Her last volume of poetry, *Die Frau und die Tiere*, appeared in the autumn of 1938.

Critical of the binary and hierarchical thinking of the extreme right and National Socialism, Kolmar rejects the categories of "Man" and "Humanity". Her texts are an indictment of the bias against the Jewish and female body and psyche in the dominant culture of early 20th-century Germany. There are parallels between her assessments of Christian and secular European culture and Walter Benjamin's cultural criticism. Kolmar portrays civilization as the product of barbarism and disparages a historiography informed by the victors' ideology. In *Robespierre,* written in 1933/4, Kolmar revises the image of one of the central figures of the French Revolution. Foregrounding Robespierre's humanity, she portrays him as the victim of intrigue and injustice. In other texts Kolmar, a precursor of modern human rights discourses, casts humans as a species of predators.

Kolmar's changing views of German culture to which Jews of former generations had aspired are shaped by the cataclysmic events of World War I and the rise of National Socialism. Kolmar, herself a victim of middle-class morality who in her younger years appears to have been coerced to have an abortion for the sake of her family's reputation, articulates the destructive effects of secular Christian morality on women. The loss of a child and the violent destruction of the bond between mother and daughter are recurring themes throughout her work. Kolmar links women's issues and Jewish concerns. *Eine jüdische Mutter* portrays a Jewish woman's loss of identity as the result of internalized anti-Semitism and the woman's isolation in a patriarchal society.

Whereas Kolmar's poems assume the standpoint of those who suffer, her narratives explore also the psyche of the aggressors and trace the process by which Jews and women identify with their oppressors. Martha Wolg (*Eine jüdische Mutter*) mistakenly assumes that her non-Jewish neighbours will support her in her search for her kidnapped daughter, and that her Gentile lover will help her to take revenge on the sex offender who traumatized the child. Realizing that she is left to fend for herself, the distraught mother kills her daughter. Martha's life is void of a positive support network. She is alienated from her family and the Jewish community. Deeply affected by the ideology of the day, she is convinced that she is right in performing a mercy-killing. *Susanna*, on the other hand, validates the archaic, sensuous, and poetic universe of a young woman who is taken for insane by those around her. The east European Jewish community, Susanna's sphere, no less than that of the modern metropolis in *Eine jüdische Mutter*, fails the young woman as well as all of its members by adapting to secular and even proto-Nazi ideas. Kolmar points toward a complicity between National Socialism and Jews who relinquish their traditional values, thereby becoming accomplices of those intent on destroying them.

DAGMAR C. G. LORENZ

Konrád, György

Hungarian fiction writer and essayist, 1933–

Born in Debrecen, 2 April 1933. Educated at Debrecen Reform College; Madách Gymnasium, Budapest, 1947–51; Lenin Institute, Budapest; Loránd Eötvös University, Budapest, degree in teaching literature 1955. Married Judit Lakner; three sons, one daughter. Teacher, general gymnasium, Csepel, 1956; editor, *Életképek*, 1956, and *Magyar Helikon*, 1960–66; social worker, Budapest, 1959–65; sociologist, City Planning Research Institute, 1965–73. Arrested and imprisoned for six days, Budapest, 1974. Also worked at Institute for Literary Scholarship for several years. Visiting Professor of Comparative Literature, Colorado Springs College, 1986. Former President, International PEN. Corresponding member, Bayerische Academy. Many awards, including Herder Prize, 1984; Veillon Prize, 1986; Fredfonden (Peace Foundation) Prize (Copenhagen), 1986; German Critics Prize, 1986; Kossuth Prize, 1990.

Selected Writings (in English published as George Konrád)

Fiction

A látogató, 1969; as *The Case Worker*, translated by Paul Aston, 1974
A városalapító, 1977; as *The City Builder*, translated by Ivan Saunders, 1977
The Loser, translated by Ivan Saunders, 1982; as *A cinkos*, 1983
Kerti mulatság, 1989; as *A Feast in the Garden*, translated by Imre Goldstein, 1992
Melinda és Dragomán, 1991
Kőóra, 1994; as *Stonedial*, translated by Ivan Sanders, 2000
Hazatérés [Homecoming], 1995
A hagyaték [The Remains], 1998

Other

Editor, *A francia "új regény"*, 1967
Az új lakótelepek szociológiai problémái [Sociological Problems in the New Housing Development], with Iván Szelényi, 1969
Az értelmiség útja az osztályhatalomhoz: esszé, with Iván Szelényi, 1978; as *The Intellectuals on the Road to Class Power*, translated by Andrew Arato and Richard E. Allen, 1979
Az autonómia kísértése: kelet-nyugati utigondolatok 1977–1979 [The Temptation of Autonomy], 1980
Antipolitics, translated by Richard E. Allen, 1984; as *Antipolitika*, with *Az autonómia kísértése*, 1989
"Our Galut Island", 1989
Európa köldökén: esszék 1979–1989 [At the Navel of Europe], 1990
Az ujjászületés melankóliája, 1992; as *The Melancholy of Rebirth*, translated by Michael Henry Helm, 1995
The Invisible Voice: Meditations on Jewish Themes, translated by Peter Reich, 1999
"Aphorism on the Durability of Jews", 2000

Further Reading
Heron, Elizabeth, "György Konrád: On the Front Line", *Index on Censorship*, 14/2 (1985)
Sanders, Ivan, "Freedom's Captives: Notes on George Konrád's Novels", *World Literature Today*, 57/2 (1983)
Varnai, Paul, "György Konrád's Novel *A látogató*", *International Fiction Review*, 1/1 (1974)

"I was born in 1933, the year of the seizure of power and the book burnings. Many members of my family and most of my Jewish classmates fell victim to the Holocaust in Hungary. It was circumstances which made me politically conscious, even as a child." This is how Konrád himself describes his background and the description is an apt one: Konrád began his literary career as a political writer. His first novels, *A látogató* (*The Case Worker*) and *A városalapitó* (*The City Builder*), deal with the disintegrating social fabric of the Hungarian capital. At this time, Konrád was himself employed as a social worker and *The Case Worker* is the powerful indictment of a state employee no longer able to deal with the human misery he encounters. Both these early novels are the works of a political rebel disillusioned with socialism. Konrád's Jewishness is peripheral here and the issue does not even arise in these works.

This may be less to do with the chosen themes of the novels than Konrád's political convictions of the time. As a left-winger by conviction, he accorded matters such as Jewishness little or no importance. He shared with his left-wing friends the view that, in a society striving to achieve equality, differences of origin and belief deserved to be levelled out in the same way as social inequalities.

Konrád's Jewish past first emerged as a central theme in his literary work in the novel *Kerti mulatság* (*A Feast in the Garden*), published in 1989. In this book he becomes the angry yet sad chronicler of his extended Jewish family and indeed of the entire rural Jewish population of eastern Hungary, which had been wiped out. His father's ironmonger's shop in Berettyóújfalu and the fate of his parents, who were transported to the camps and returned home as if by a miracle, are described in the same way as the occupation and war atrocities in the small town. He mourns the death of his deported classmates in the same way as that of his first great love. Konrád interweaves the highly personal Jewish history of his family with the history of Hungary and defines his mission thus: "The father must live on in the son, the murdered in those still living."

The fact that Konrád's Jewish origin begins to play an important role only at a relatively late stage is linked to his political development: from being a left-winger by conviction, he evolved over the course of time into a liberal of equal conviction. Even a year before the collapse of socialism, which he himself worked actively towards within the democratic opposition, he claimed that the way in which the Hungarian majority dealt with the 100,000 or so Jews remaining in the country would be a touchstone of the new Hungarian democracy.

In his essay "Our Galut Island" in 1989, he asks himself the question, "To what shall I commit myself, having been born into two communities? . . . Christian and Jewish Hungary – two strong identities." Konrád finally decided to be a Jewish Hungarian. He was never a devout Jew; the ritual means nothing to him and is in fact alien to him, making it all the more important for him to feel at home with the Hungarian language and literature. Konrád is a politico-cultural Jew, for whom the Hungarian identity is of great importance.

Unquestionably, a slight change is present in the body of his work: his interest in Judaism and in his own Jewish roots appears to grow with age. In his late works, *Melinda és Dragomán* [Melinda and Dragoman] and the rather unsuccessful *A hagyaték* [The Remains], Jewish life stories once again come into play. In 1995 he dedicated another story to his Jewish childhood. In the book *Hazatérés* [Homecoming], perhaps his most beautiful work, he describes in tones which are light but all the more vivid for being so, how he and his sister experienced the Russian invasion and the collapse of fascist rule in Budapest, how they made their way back to their small home town, overcoming many obstacles and experiencing many adventures. The book is not only the literal history of their homecoming but is itself a type of spiritual homecoming.

Konrád continues this theme of a spiritual homecoming to one's roots in the essay "Aphorism on the Durability of Jews", published in 2000. In the essay he attempts to answer the question of what characterizes a worldly, non-believing Jew. The fragments read like a self-description, a spiritual autobiography:

> Jews generally bring liveliness, the initiate, identities in friction are productive. They see from outside, not just from inside. The consciousness of Jews is generally paradoxical, other's is too, but that of Jews is in any case, as a rule. Contrary impulses exist, and they do not want to suppress either.

What Konrád is describing in these aphorisms are his ideals of the politically committed central European Jew: "A transnational people in nation-states!" To whom could this sentence better apply than the cosmopolitan Konrád, who has lived in New York and Berlin as well as Budapest and who with the same naturalness was president of PEN and chairman of the German Academy of the Arts?

> Worldly Jews select what to keep out of the prescriptions . . . they believe they have more important things to do in the spring than to burn the home. They give religious discrimination no room on their bookshelf. There is more to life than being Jewish, Christian or Muslim. Being human means more than any sub-group identity. The task of Jews is to practice their humanity, to understand and appreciate the other person in their own particularity.

This is a summary not just of his own perceptions of Judaism but a representation of the majority of the Jewish intellectuals living today in central and eastern Europe. With his liberal, cosmopolitan views rooted in Judaism, Konrád has done much for the democratization of Hungarian society which, for centuries, has been encrusted in nationalism. Whether this will be enough to secure the continuation of the Jewish tradition in Hungarian literature is, however, doubtful. His readiness to assimilate is too great, his affection for the milieu too small.

KRISZTINA KOENEN
translated by Karen Goulding

Kops, Bernard

British dramatist, fiction writer, and poet, 1926–

Born in London, 28 November 1926, to working-class Jewish parents of Dutch origin. Attended London elementary schools, 1931–39. Married Erica Gordon, 1956; four children. Has worked as docker, chef, salesman, waiter, lift man, and barrow boy. Writer in residence, London Borough of Hounslow, 1980–82; lecturer in drama, Spiro Institute, 1985–86; writer in residence, Polka Theatre, London, 1991–92. Awards include Arts Council of Great Britain bursaries, 1957, 1979, 1985, 1990, 1991; C. Day Lewis Fellowship, 1981–83; London Fringe Award, 1993; Writers Guild Award, 1995.

Selected Writings

Plays
The Hamlet of Stepney Green, 1958
Goodbye World, 1959
Change for the Angel, 1960
The Dream of Peter Mann, 1960
Stray Cats and Empty Bottles, 1961
Enter Solly Gold, 1962
Home Sweet Honeycomb, 1962
The Lemmings, 1963
Four Plays, 1964
The Boy Who Wouldn't Play Jesus, 1965
David, It is Getting Dark, 1970
Just One Kid, 1974
It's a Lovely Day Tomorrow, with John Goldschmidt, 1975
Moss, 1975
Rocky Marciano is Dead, 1976
More Out than In, 1980
Ezra, 1981
Simon at Midnight, 1982
Night Kids, 1983
Some of These Days, 1990; as *Sophie! Last of the Red Hot Mamas*, 1990
Playing Sinatra, 1991

Androcles and the Lion, 1992
Dreams of Anne Frank, 1992
Who Shall I Be Tomorrow?, 1992
Call in the Night, 1995
Golem, 1998
Jacob and the Green Rabbi, 1998
Café Zeitgeist, 1999
Plays, 2 vols, 1999–2000
Riverchange, 2001

Novels
Awake for Mourning, 1958
Motorbike, 1962
Yes from No-Man's Land, 1965
The Dissent of Dominick Shapiro, 1966
By the Waters of Whitechapel, 1969
The Passionate Past of Gloria Gaye, 1971
Settle Down Simon Katz, 1973
Partners, 1975
On Margate Sands, 1978

Poetry
Poems, 1955
Poems and Songs, 1958
An Anemone for Antigone, 1959
Erica, I Want to Read You Something, 1967
For the Record, 1971
Barricades in West Hampstead, 1988
Grandchildren and Other Poems, 2000

Other
The World is a Wedding, 1963
Editor, *Poetry Hounslow*, 1981
Neither Your Honey nor Your Sting: An Offbeat History of the Jews, 1985
Shalom Bomb, 2000

Further Reading

Cheyette, Bryan, "Way Out in No Man's Land", *Times Literary Supplement* (18 August 2000)
Dace, Tish, "Ezra", *Masterplots II: Drama Series*, edited by Frank N. Magill, Pasadena, California: Salem Press, 1990
Dace, Tish, entry on Bernard Kops in *Contemporary British Dramatists*, edited by K.A. Berney, London and Detroit: St James Press, 1994
Demastes, Williams W. (editor), *British Playwrights, 1956–1995: A Research and Production Sourcebook*, Westport, Connecticut: Greenwood Press, 1996
Kustow, Michael, "Fresh as New Paint" in *Plays Two* by Kops, London: Oberon, 2000
Leigh, Mike, introduction to *Plays One* by Kops, London: Oberon, 1999

Because Bernard Kops regards the family as so important, he typically selects domestic settings for his fiction, poetry, and plays, and he usually evokes realistic details of real Jewish lives that make us laugh or cry – or both. Yet he often incorporates presentational elements. Thus he puts Sam Levy's ghost into *The Hamlet of Stepney Green*, he has the house in *Dreams of Anne Frank* talk to the family, and Hugo in *Call in the Night* interacts at once with his past and his present. Regardless of the style he employs, Kops's humanism embraces humanity, even those he indicts, such as anti-Semite Ezra Pound.

Surreal yet playful, *Ezra* creates the poet's mad mind jumping around in a demented vaudeville encompassing Mussolini, Vivaldi, and Pound's anti-Semitic tirades. Pound is physically imprisoned as a traitor by the Allies for his broadcasts on behalf of fascism, and his mind also appears fettered by prejudice and a naivety which cannot comprehend that he has helped kill individuals he liked and admired. In a feat that demonstrates the size of his own soul, Kops asks us to condemn but also pity Pound, and writer Kops balks at approving censorship of another author. The play leaves us with the image of the poet summoning the Jews in Venice's ghetto. He calls, but, since they died in the gas chambers, no one remains to respond; only the wind replies to his entreaties. This provides a chilling conclusion to a deeply disturbing play that struggles to comprehend how such a poetic genius could have espoused such dangerous bigotry.

Although *Ezra*'s genocide represents Kops's largest-scale evocation of death, repeatedly this writer considers our mortality. *Yes from No-Man's Land* depicts an elderly Jew who lies dying in a Catholic hospital. *Just One Kid* dramatizes the illness of a boy whose father and sister die, while another teleplay, *Moss*, portrays an East-End Jew who hoards his money until he loses his beloved grandson; when the boy perishes at a playground, the old man appreciates life is more precious than wealth. In *Home Sweet Honeycomb*, death, in the form of a firing squad, comes for those who won't relinquish their individuality. *Change for the Angel* dramatizes a boy who prays for his hateful father's death but who instead loses his mother, whereas its predecessor, *Goodbye World*, concerns a would-be suicide. In *The Lemmings* Kops satirizes such a death wish. The playwright locates the source of the dysfunction of the protagonist in *Call in the Night* in the Holocaust deaths of his parents and sister and his own survivor guilt. *It's a Lovely Day Tomorrow* reprises the Bethnal Green tube disaster, when several hundred people were crushed to death while entering a shelter; Kops's parents survived this tragedy.

Despite his obsession with death, Kops conveys a clear imperative to live. He creates such survivors as the former boxer-manager, Harry Marcus, in *Rocky Marciano is Dead*, or the idealistic title character of *Simon at Midnight*. *The Dream of Peter Mann* rejects materialism and embraces life, and the con man in the black-comic satire *Enter Solly Gold* spreads joy among the victims he fleeces and helps them to reject stultifying convention and lifesapping greed. Although death's threnody sings through poem after poem, he urges us to dance. Even in "First Poem", his life force helped him harness life and death's inherent contradictions; he adjures us "let's dance upon the desolation". "Shalom Bomb", the poem that supplied the title for Kops's second autobiography, describes his search for the paradoxical "live long and die happy bomb". Although Kops's grandfather and cousins in Amsterdam died, the victims of genocide, Kops insists, in "Neither Your Honey nor Your Sting", "I really must continue to resist / the temptation of ceasing to exist".

As he castigates materialism, Kops counsels compassion. *David, It is Getting Dark* depicts a successful right-wing writer who plagiarizes the work of an impoverished Jewish author. *The Boy Who Wouldn't Play Jesus* complains that Christians don't live by Christian values. *Who Shall I Be Tomorrow?* dramatizes the travails of a middle-aged actress, once successful, who has fallen on hard times, and *Night Kids* touches us with its treatment of teenage runaways who prostitute themselves and try to shelter from the cold in discarded boxes.

One of many works by Kops that explore the psyche's fragility, *By the Waters of Whitechapel* inspires compassion for an unhinged Jew who has failed to escape the Whitechapel area of Stepney Green for the more affluent districts of northwest London. *Partners* traces successful businessman Daniel Klayman's descent into madness. A third novel, *On Margate Sands*, and its stage version, *More Out than In*, depict the consequences of de-institutionalizing the mentally ill. *Call in the Night* concerns a man teetering on the edge of cracking up. Some Kops poems likewise reflect a tenuous hold on sanity; the persona in "Breakdown" says he rushes out "through the wallpaper" and pleads with his mother to see "how ill I am".

Kops indicts conformity in, for example, his study of an elderly Jewish con man, *Settle Down Simon Katz*. Yet he also mocks his own early bohemianism with his 1960s antihero, the young title character in *The Dissent of Dominick Shapiro*, Kops's answer to Salinger's *The Catcher in the Rye*. Kops contrasts rebellion and conformity here, finding a certain absurdity in each.

Often Kops selects 20th-century icons as his subjects – Sophie Tucker in *Sophie! Last of the Red Hot Mamas*, Anne in *Dreams of Anne Frank*, Ezra Pound in *Ezra*. While rooting for survival, he deplores characters' destructive or self-destructive obsessions – for example, their fixations on Ol' Blue Eyes in *Playing Sinatra*; here he permits Sandra to escape the trap of the stifling Streatham house. Much as Kops admires Anne's diary, he focuses on making us experience anew the anguish of her death; he would prefer for us to have lost the book but for Anne to have survived. Here, as always, Kops chooses life.

TISH DACE

Korczak, Janusz

Polish children's writer, broadcaster, and educator, 1878–1942

Born Henryk Goldszmit in Warsaw, on 22 July 1878, to Józef Goldszmit, lawyer, and wife Cecylia (née Gebicka). Father died, after long mental illness, 1896; family suffered financial hardship; gave private lessons in order to support mother and sister while at high school and university. Began studying for medical degree in Warsaw, 1898. Adopted pen name Janusz Korczak. Travelled to Zürich to learn about work of the educator J.H. Pestalozzi; graduated as paediatrician, 1905; further study and training, Berlin, 1907; also made study visits to Paris and London. Worked as physician in Jewish children's hospital, Warsaw, 1904–05 and 1907–10; served on hospital train in China during and after Russo–Japanese War, 1905–06; counsellor in summer camps for boys, 1907–10. Briefly imprisoned after criticizing hospital management, 1909. Co-founder, with Stefania Wilczyńska, and director, orphanage for Jewish children, Warsaw, 1911–42. Served as physician in Russian imperial army on Eastern front during World War I; paediatrician in Kiev, 1917–18. Co-founder, with Maryna Falska, of public orphanage for Christian children, Warsaw, 1918–36. Lecturer, Warsaw Institute for Special Pedagogy. Fought in Polish–Soviet War, 1920. Contracted typhus and infected mother, who died of disease, 1920. Pedagogic director, Nasz Dom orphanage, Warsaw. Founding editor, children's magazine *Mały Przegląd*, supplement to Jewish magazine *Nasz Przegląd*, 1926–30. Hosted popular Polish Radio broadcasts, as "The Old Doctor", 1930s. Visited Palestine several times between 1934 and 1938. Awarded Golden Laurel Award, Polish Academy of Literature, 1937; posthumously awarded German Book Trade's Peace Prize, 1972. Arrested with about 200 Jewish orphans and taken to Treblinka extermination camp. Died in Treblinka, 1942. Unesco declared 1978–79 "Year of Korczak", coinciding with "Year of the Child".

Selected Writings

Fiction

Dzieci ulicy [Street Children], 1901
Dziecko salonu [Salon Child], 1906
Mośki, Jośki i Srule, 1910
Józki, Jáśki i Franki, 1922
Król Maciuś na wyspie bezludnej, 1923; as *Little King Matty and the Desert Island*, translated by Adam Czasak, 1990
Król Maciuś Pierwszy, 1923; as *Matthew: The Young King*, adapted by Edith and Sydney Sulkin, 1945; as *King Matt the First*, translated by Richard Lourie, 1986
Bankructwo małego Dżeka [The Bankruptcy of Little Jack], 1924
Trzy wyprawy Herszka, 1930
Kajtuś czarodziej [Confessions of a Butterfly], 1934/35
Ludzie są dobrzy, 1938
Big Business Billy, translated by Cyrus Brooks, 1939
Tajemniczy przyjaciel [Mysterious Friend], 1957
Wybór pism [Selected Writings], 4 vols, 1957–58
Kiedy znów będę mały, 1961
Dzek Hakatan (in Hebrew), 1963
Mały człowiek [Little Man], 1965
Klucz do Berlina, 1966
Yotam hakasam (in Hebrew), 1966
Selected Works of Janusz Korczak, edited by Martin Wolins, translated by Jerzy Bachrach, 1967
Noc w Quedlinburgu; opowiadnia, 1971
Pożegnanie z Bekiem Martyna: wybór opowiadan, 1974
Wysoki Krzyz, 1974
Yaldut shel kavod (in Hebrew), 1976
Dat hayeled (in Hebrew), 1978
Fragmenty utworów, edited by Danuta Stępniewska, 1978
Pisma wybrane [Selected Writings], 1978; vol. 1: *Wielka*

Synteza Dziecka, oto co mi się śnilo; vol. 2: *Praktyka to Moje Życie*; vol. 3: *Otwórzmy Wrota Szkoły Szeroko*; vol. 4: *Jestem Człowiekiem Samotnej Drogi*
Cożeś Ty Za Pani, 1979
Myśl Pedagogiczna Janusza Korczaka: Nowe Źródła, 1983
Blaszane Nieśmiertelniki, 1989
Dzieła [Works], 16 vols, 1992–
Janusz Korczak w Getcie: Nowe Źródła, 1992
Misja Ostatniej Nadziei, 1992
Ketavim (in Hebrew), 1996

Other
Momenty wychowawcze [Moments of Educational Observation], 1924
Prawo dziecka do szacunku [A Manifesto for Children's Rights], 1929
Wybór pism pedagogicznych [Selected Writings on Education], 2 vols, 1957
Ghetto Diary, translated from the original Polish manuscripts, *Pamiętnik z getta*, 1978; as *The Warsaw Ghetto Memoirs of Janusz Korczak*, translated by E.P. Kulawiec, 1979; as *The Ghetto Years, 1939–1942*, 1980
When I am Little Again; and The Child's Right to Respect, translated by E.P. Kulawiec, 1992 [*Kiedy znów będę mały* and *Prawo dziecka do szacunku*]

Further Reading

Arnon, Josef, *Who Was Janusz Korczak?*, Tel Aviv: World Federation of Polish Jews, 1977
Child Education (Autumn 1989)
Cohen, Adir, *The Gate of Light: Janusz Korczak, The Educator and Writer Who Overcame the Holocaust*, Rutherford, New Jersey: Fairleigh Dickinson University Press, 1994
Education Leadership (May 1986)
Gutman, Israel (editor), *Encyclopedia of the Holocaust*, 4 vols, New York: Macmillan, and London: Collier Macmillan, 1990
Jaworski, Marek, *Janusz Korczak*, Warsaw: Interpress, 1978
Lifton, Betty Jean, *The King of Children: A Biography of Janusz Korczak*, New York: Farrar Straus, and London: Chatto and Windus, 1988
Mortkowicz-Olczakowa, Hanna, *Mister Doctor: The Life of Janusz Korczak*, translated by Romuald Jan Kruk and Harold Gresswell, London: Peter Davies, 1965
New Republic (6 June 1988)
Newerly, Igor, *Żywe Wiązanie*, Warsaw: Czytelnik, 1966
Pörzgen, Rainer, *Janusz Korczak: Bibliographie*, Munich: Saur, 1982
Szlązkowa, Alicja, *Janusz Korczak w legendzie poetyckiej*, Warsaw: Interlibro, 1992
Wołoszyn, Stefan, *Korczak*, Warsaw: Wiedza Powszechna, 1978

The extensive work of Janusz Korczak, who as a doctor, educator, and writer devoted his life to the welfare and rights of the child, is now more topical than ever, as his children's books, novels, essays, humorous writings and stories, poems, prayers, and treatises on child psychology translated into many languages testify. Korczak is considered "the poet among the pedagogues and the pedagogue among the writers of his time". Both practically and in terms of literature, he began to commit himself at an early stage to the interests of children, above all the "proletariat on little feet", from the lowest strata of society, the abandoned and orphaned among them. He did this as the director of two orphanages – one for Christian children in Bielany, the other in Krochmalna-Strasse for Jewish children – where he applied the best ideas of the newly emerging reformed style of pedagogy in Europe, and he gave these children a home and all his love.

"I have a researching spirit, not an inventing spirit", he wrote in his memoirs late in life. And so he used the ideas of modern pedagogy from J.H. Pestalozzi via Maria Montessori to F.W. Foerster in the service of his "applied love of children" and went still further because "I direct my questions at people (small children and old men), at facts, events, fates". Korczak himself was a quiet, imaginative child; a dreamer. When his father became ill with a nervous disorder, this placed an emotional burden on the son too, and he suffered from depression at various times in his life. His material situation after the death of his father became precarious, such that the young man was obliged to provide for his family with the meagre fees he earned as a private tutor and from working on the satirical weekly *Kolce*. On his extended tours through the poor quarters of the town, he encountered the total misery of the population. Here he experienced the ragged proletariat of his time and the poverty and disease of the children in particular made a lasting impression on him; he noted in his diary: "I understand now, why the children here have the earthy skin of a prisoner, inflamed eyelids and crooked little legs, and why only four out of ten survive . . .". In order to alleviate their fate, he taught and treated them, without payment of course, and this is where his vocation took form: "I have made a promise and will keep to it: I am committed to the welfare of the child." His novel *Dziecko salonu* about privileged children, as a counterpoint to his *Dzieci ulicy* about under-privileged children, made him famous.

Coming from an assimilated parental home had made Korczak aware of being a Jew and a Pole, although it must be remembered here that at the time Poland was still divided and Warsaw was part of the Russian empire. However, the intelligentsia became politically conscious and formed an opposition to the regime. Korczak wrote about his work with the Jewish children in the summer camp in his book *Mośki, Jośki i Srule* and about the Polish children in *Józki, Jáśki i Franki*. These titles are among a whole series of famous books for children and young people which Korczak wrote, above all the novels *Król Maciuś Pierwszy* (*Matthew: The Young King*), *Bankructwo małego Dżeka* [The Bankruptcy of Little Jack], and *Kajtuś czarodziej* [Confessions of a Butterfly], as well as the last pre-war works *Ludzie są dobrzy* and *Trzy wyprawy Herszka*. In all his writings, including these, he takes as his theme the fate of children who are mostly sad and disillusioned, while always appealing to the good in man. Korczak was accused of propagandizing paedocracy, because his childlike hero Maciuś reigns as king over adults. Today, with children's parliaments and war declared on child labour, it seems obsolete, yet the children in his orphanages were allowed to criticize their teachers. He himself had to go before such a children's court on five occasions for behaving unfairly or thoughtlessly. As an author, too, he sought the opinion of the children, who listened attentively to his stories, but he rejected anti-authoritarian teaching and a certain discipline and order prevailed in his houses, which was beneficial to the personality of the pupils, because at the same time he indulged in a "cheerful pedagogy": he viewed the children on the same level as small individuals and was convinced that they would develop into kind, wise and responsible adults as a result. The failure of Maciuś's government and his condemnation on account of the – revolutionary – defence of the rights of children is a reflection of Korczak's own disappointment that, like the medieval children's crusades – his Magna Carta of children's rights was not generally accepted.

The Geneva Declaration of 1924 on the Rights of the Child had failed to protect Jewish children in the Nazi period. Korczak and his Jewish pupils were forced to realize that men were not good. Despite his fascination with the pioneer life in Palestine, he returned to Warsaw because, as he wrote in 1939, "I would like to safeguard their future [that of his children], so that the worst and the most diabolical person does not spit in the face of a good person just because he is a Jew." In the Warsaw ghetto he continued to dream of life in Israel, but it was too late. Igor Newerly offered him the opportunity of leaving the ghetto using forged papers but Korczak refused – he would not leave his children in the lurch in the face of death. And so on 5 August 1942 he went with them from the deportation point to the gas chambers of Treblinka. The last pages of his diary contains the following note: "I wish no man evil. I cannot; I know not how . . ."

Leon Harari, one of Korczak's pupils and a contributor, as a child, to *Mały Przegląd*, called him "Tzaddik Hador", one of the 36 hidden righteous men, thanks to whom the world remains intact, while Pope John Paul II proclaimed Korczak to be "a symbol of religion and morality for the modern world".

ELVIRA GROEZINGER
translated by Karen Goulding

Kosinski, Jerzy

Polish-born US fiction writer and dramatist, 1933–1991

Born in Łódź, 14 June 1933. Studied at University of Łódź, BA 1950, MA (history) 1953, MA (political science) 1955; doctoral candidate and graduate assistant in sociology, Polish Academy of Sciences, 1955–57; researcher, Lomonosov University, Moscow, 1957. Worked as writer and photographer, ski instructor in Zakopane, winters 1950–1956. Emigrated to United States, 1957; naturalized US citizen, 1965. Doctoral study in sociology, Columbia University, 1958–63; graduate study, New School for Social Research, 1962–66. Worked as paint scraper of excursion-line boats, truck driver, chauffeur, and cinema projectionist. Married, first, Mary Hayward Weir, 1962; she died, 1968; second, Katherina von Fraunhofer, 1987. Resident Fellow in English, Center for Advanced Studies, Wesleyan University, 1967–68; visiting lecturer in English and resident senior fellow of Council of Humanities, Princeton University, 1969–70; professor of English and resident fellow, Davenport College and School of Drama, 1970–73, and fellow, Timothy Dwight College, 1986–91, Yale University. President, American Foundation for Polish–Jewish Studies, 1987–91. Played Grigory Zinoviev in film *Reds*, 1981; one-man exhibitions of photographs, including at State's Crooked Circle Gallery, Warsaw, 1957. President, American PEN, 1973–75; Director, International League for Human Rights, 1973–79. Many awards, including Ford Foundation Fellowship, 1958–60; Prix du Meilleur Livre Étranger (France), 1966; Guggenheim Fellowship, 1967–68; National Book Award, 1969; National Institute of Arts and Letters and American Academy of Arts and Letters Award in Literature, 1970; Brith Shalom Humanitarian Freedom Award, 1974; American Civil Liberties Union First Amendment Award, 1978; Best Screenplay of the Year Award from Writers Guild of America, 1979, and from British Academy of Film and Television Arts, 1981; Polonia Media National Achievement Perspectives Award, 1980; Spertus College of Judaica International Award, 1982. Committed suicide in New York, 3 May 1991.

Selected Writings

Fiction
The Painted Bird, 1965
Steps, 1968
Being There, 1971
The Devil Tree, 1973
Cockpit, 1975
Blind Date, 1977
Passion Play, 1979
Pinball, 1982
The Hermit of 69th Street: The Working Papers of Norbert Kosky, 1986

Screenplays: *Being There*, 1979; *Passion Play*, 1987

Other
Dokumenty walki o Czlowieka: Wspominenia Proletariatczykow [Documents Concerning the Struggle of Man: The Reminiscences of the Members of "Proletariat"], 1954–55
Program Rewolucji Jakoba Jaworskiego [The Programme of the People's Revolution of Jakob Jaworski], 1954–55
The Future is Ours, Comrade: Conversations with the Russians (as Joseph Novak), 1960
No Third Path: A Study of Collective Behaviour (as Joseph Novak), 1962
Editor, *Socjologia Amerykanska: Wybór Prac, 1950–1960* [American Sociology: Translations of Selected Works, 1950–1960], 1962
Notes of the Author on "The Painted Bird", 1965
The Art of Self: Essays à Propos "Steps", 1969

Passing By: Selected Essays, 1962–1991, 1992
Conversations with Jerzy Kosinski, edited by Tom Teicholz, 1993

Further Reading

Bruss, Paul, *Victims: Textual Strategies in Recent American Fiction*, Lewisburg, Pennsylvania: Bucknell University Press, 1981
Cronin, Gloria L., *Jerzy Kosinski: An Annotated Bibliography*, New York: Greenwood Press, 1991
Everman, Welch D., *Jerzy Kosinski: The Literature of Violation*, San Bernardino, California: Borgo Press, 1991
Haydn, Hiram Collins, *Words and Faces*, New York: Harcourt Brace, 1974
Hicks, Jack, *In the Singer's Temple: Prose Fictions of Barthelme, Gaines, Brautigan, Piercy, Kesey, and Kosinski*, Chapel Hill: University of North Carolina Press, 1981
Karl, Frederick Robert, *American Fictions 1940–1980*, New York: Harper and Row, 1983
Klinkowitz, Jerome, "Jerzy Kosinski" in *The New Fiction: Interviews with Innovative American Writers*, edited by Joe David Bellamy, Urbana: University of Illinois Press, 1974
Klinkowitz, Jerome, *Literary Disruptions: The Making of a Post-Contemporary American Fiction*, Urbana: University of Illinois Press, 1975
Klinkowitz, Jerome, *Keeping Literary Company: Working with Writers since the Sixties*, Albany: State University of New York Press, 1998
Langer, Lawrence, L., *The Holocaust and the Literary Imagination*, New Haven, Connecticut: Yale University Press, 1975
Lilly, Paul R., Jr, *Words in Search of Victims: The Achievement of Jerzy Kosinski*, Kent, Ohio: Kent State University Press, 1988
Lupack, Barbara Tepa, *Plays of Passion, Games of Chance: Jerzy Kosinski and His Fiction*, Bristol, Indiana: Wyndham Hall Press, 1988
Lupack, Barbara Tepa (editor), *Critical Essays on Jerzy Kosinski*, New York: G.K. Hall, and London: Prentice Hall, 1998
Plimpton, George (editor), *Writers at Work: The "Paris Review" Interviews*, vol. 5, New York: Viking Press, 1981
Sloan, James Park, *Jerzy Kosinski: A Biography*, New York: Dutton, 1996
Sweeney, Terrace A., *God &*, Minneapolis: Winston Press, 1985

Jerzy Kosinski's career was bedevilled by alternate, contrary, and essentially untrue assumptions: first, that his novel *The Painted Bird* was not fiction but rather autobiography, and second that what he did present as his own life and work were in fact utter fabrications, the events falsified and his accounts in fact ghost-written by others. A decade after his own death (in 1991) researchers have sorted out historical details and critics have placed his work in a larger context. Though his childhood as a Polish Jew during World War II consisted more of being sheltered in disguise than suffering, his imaginative confrontation with the terrors of both Nazi aggression and native superstition yielded valuable fictive work. As for the work itself, its author was so aware of the powers of language that he felt obliged to test its effects among various speakers, provoking suspicions but in fact providing a range of editorial styles from which he could choose his final writing product.

As a postwar student in communist Poland, Kosinski undertook the work that would appear in his first two books, written in English after his emigration to America (in 1957) and published as *The Future is Ours, Comrade* and *No Third Path* under the pseudonym of Joseph Novak. Patterned after the lyrical, somewhat fictive sociology of C. Wright Mills of Columbia University (where Kosinski pursued but did not complete a doctorate in the subject), these books convey the same theme of his fiction: that collectivism operates with the same force in both socialist and capitalist economies, in both totalitarian dictatorships and more open democracies. In each case, the pressure is against the individual, who can best survive by privileging the imagination. *The Painted Bird* celebrates the survival of a young boy abandoned as the Germans invaded Poland; yet the narrative also has its chilling dimensions, as the boy learns to admire power in all its manifestations, whether in the guise of a Nazi officer or a Russian sharpshooter. Kosinski's second novel, *Steps*, follows its author's life as somewhat of a postwar sequel, the protagonist first fighting off the pressures of Soviet-enforced collectivism and then making his way against similar forces (although differently expressed as a mass-market economy) after his escape to the United States. This latter cultural condition generates the action of what stands as a minor masterpiece, the short novel *Being There*, in which a retarded illiterate with virtually no experience of the outside world wanders into it and within days becomes the leading candidate for Vice-President of the United States.

Although set entirely in America, *Being There* is told in the manner of an Old Country fable; scholars would find its source in a popular Polish folktale made famous as a novel and eventually as a Polish television series. Yet its imaginative currency is that of the mass media that controls the popular imagination, and hence the novel serves as a cautionary tale for a young world from an older, more sophisticated viewpoint. From here Kosinski would move on to a more comfortably American perspective. *The Devil Tree* is a novel that explores the powers of American industrial capitalism and its deleterious human effect in the form of inherited wealth, a lesson its author observed firsthand when married to Mary Hayward Weir, heir to the Republic Steel fortune and a victim of debilitating alcoholism through marriage, divorce, and eventually death. *Cockpit*, as its title suggests, is a novel that places its protagonist in control but also thrown into the middle of a fray; as a retired secret agent, the character Tarden is a master of self-protection, of control, and eventually of revenge, all of which is achieved at the cost of hideous isolation. *Blind Date* extends this theme farther, letting its hero range across the world as a speculative investor, in the meantime experiencing adventures similar to those Kosinski had not only been sharing but recounting to television audiences as a frequent guest on *The*

Tonight Show. Well known was the author's friendship with film director Roman Polanski; after Polanski's wife, Sharon Tate, was murdered with a group of her friends by the Charles Manson gang, Kosinski spread the story that only as a last minute no-show at the party was he spared a similar fate. This scene is fictionalized in *Blind Date*, but with the added shock of having the Kosinski-like protagonist show up and commit retaliatory murders of his own, far more brutal than anything Manson's cohorts did. With matters such as these, Kosinski was effecting a public personhood as fictively manipulative as anything a writer could manage – Ernest Hemingway's precedent pales by comparison. The intent was to challenge distinctions between life and art, showing how the action of one's imagination was the key factor in each (and more important than either by itself).

Passion Play and *Pinball* mark Kosinski's personal excesses as a novelist – excesses for which he would soon be called to task – while *The Hermit of 69th Street* signals his unsuccessful attempt to recapture high regard. His protagonists in these first two novels reflect his own fame as a novelist, Fabian doing much the same in playing (and writing about) polo, Patrick Domostroy mirroring Kosinski's passion for life by seeking it in its most challenging depths. Yet each book seems uncomfortably self-taken and at times repulsively self-indulgent, its heroes using women in ways well beyond any complaints against political correctness. When the author used his friendship with New York's publishing elite and Hollywood's world of stars in order to publicize himself even more so, reaction set in. Investigative reporters for the *Village Voice* claimed Kosinski had been promoted by neo-conservatives for their own self-interests, while the author himself had paid to have his novels ghost-written. *The Hermit of 69th Street* is Kosinski's answer to these charges, with its protagonist beset by similar charges at the same time that Kosinski himself writes a Joycean word-salad of language to display his command of the art.

Beset by criticism and suffering from the depression which would finally drive him to take his own life, Kosinski spent his last years working on the collection of essays published in 1992 as *Passing By*. The most characteristic of these pieces would be "Hosana to What?", in which he accused contemporary Jewish culture of committing a second Holocaust by almost totally ignoring the artistic contributions of the postwar generation in favour of mourning the loss of all that died in the war. As a way of taking an active role, he was involving himself in the rebirth of Jewish culture in Poland following the political success of the Solidarity movement, helping establish a Jewish cultural centre in Kraków and a banking network in Warsaw. These activities represented a complete turnaround from the attitude he had maintained since coming to America in 1957, a long period in which he refused to discuss his native land at all. Some commentators believed he was trying to rebuild his damaged American reputation back in Poland, but his suicide in 1991 prevented any of these matters from being resolved.

JEROME KLINKOWITZ

Kovner, Abba

Russian-born Israeli poet, fiction writer, and essayist, 1918–1987

Born in Sebastopol, 1918. Grew up in Vilna (Vilnius); studied in Hebrew Gymnasium, but did not graduate; left school, 1935; took external examinations. Became head of Vilna branch of Ha-Shomer Ha-Zair Pioneering Youth Movement. After Soviet and then Nazi invasions of Lithuania, nuns hid him and 30 other Jews in convent outside Vilna. Among initiators of Jewish resistance to genocide, 1942; member of resistance leadership, commanding four Jewish battalions in partisan fighting in forests, until 1943. First poems, in Hebrew and Yiddish, published in Vilna. Life companion Vitka Kemper, fellow partisan. Started and led first "Brihah line", helping Jews from central and eastern Europe to enter British-ruled Palestine illicitly. Went to Palestine, seeking poison to be used in revenge on German people, 1945; arrested by British authorities because of false papers and detained until March 1946. Joined Kibbutz Ein Hachoresh. Enlisted in the Givati Brigade, and wrote daily news sheet for troops, 1948. Became spiritual father of Beit-Hatefutzot (Diaspora Museum). Awarded Israel Prize and elected Chairman of Hebrew Writers Association of Israel, 1970. Died in Kibbutz Ein-Hachoresh, 25 September 1987.

Selected Writings

Poetry
Ad loor [While There is Still Night], 1947
Peridah mehadarom [Parting from the South], 1949
Hamafteah tsalal [The Key Sank], 1950
Admat hahol [Sandy Ground], 1961
Mikol haavot [Of All the Loves], 1965
Ahoti ketanah, 1967; as *My Little Sister and Selected Poems*, translated by Shirley Kaufman, 1986
Hupah bamidbar, 1970; as *A Canopy in the Desert*, translated by Shirley Kaufman with Ruth Adler and Nurit Orchan, 1973
Abba Kovner and Nelly Sachs: Selected Poems, translated by Shirley Kaufman and Nurit Orchan, 1971
Lehakat haketsev mofrah al har gerizim [On Mount Grizim], 1972
Hasefer hakatan [The Small Book], 1973
Tatspiot [Observation Points], 1977
El [To], 1980
Sloan-Kettering, 1986
Shirat rosa [Songs of Rosa], 1987
Kol shirei Abba Kovner [Collected Poems], 3 vols, 1996–97

Poetry for Children
Masah el erets hamilim [A Journey to the Land of Words], 1981
Mashehu al leviatanim [Something About Whales], 1989
Hamalakh hakatan michael [The Little Angel Michael], 1989

Prose
Panim el panim [Face to Face], part 1: *Sheat haefes* [Zero Time], 1953; part 2: *Hatsomet* [Junction], 1955
Megilot haesh [The Scrolls of Testimony], 1981

Essays
Al hagesher hatsar [On the Narrow Bridge], 1981
Mishelo vealav [From His Own and about Him], 1988
Leakev et hakeryiah [Beyond Mourning], 1998

Further Reading

Ben-Yosef Ginor, Tzvia, *Ad kets habedayah: iyun beshirat Abba Kovner* [Beyond the Legend: A Study of Abba Kovner's Poetry], Tel Aviv: Hakibuts hameuhad, 1995
Lurya, Shalom (editor), *Aba Kovner: Mivhar maamre bikoret al yetsirato* [Abba Kovner: A Selection of Critical Essays on His Writings], Tel Aviv: Hakibuts hameuhad, 1988
Porat, Dina, *Beyond the Reaches of Our Souls: The Life and Times of Abba Kovner*, Tel Aviv: Am Oved, 2000

The life and times of Abba Kovner are, perhaps inevitably, interwoven in his literary works and in his publicist writing. Kovner, an original and unique man of letters and thought, who exercised a deep influence on historiography and public thought in Israel, created his own venues in his artistic expression. Therefore, in order to fathom these venues, one should be thoroughly acquainted with his stormy life story and with his concepts of Jewish and Zionist history, and not only with the literary tools he chose to use. Hence, the analysis proposed here is an attempt to follow the main themes in his work – the individual in the collective experience of the Jewish people, sorrow as universal tenet of one's life, and land as a source of religious and national continuity. In most of his writing and planning he stood alone, in opposition to the general consensus of the time.

The two great works of prose he wrote, *Face to Face*, on Israel's 1948 War of Independence, and *The Scrolls of Testimony*, on the Holocaust, embody his ideas on Jewish history, first and foremost the unity of the Jewish people and the equal role of every one of its members in its history. Having grown up in Vilna, Jerusalem of Lithuania, where the Jewish community functioned as a unit despite the chasm between Orthodox and atheists, communists and right-wing Zionists, among others, he fostered the notion of unity in every later encounter with a Jewish public: in the underground in the ghetto, in the partisans' forests, among the survivors streaming down to the ports of the Mediterranean on their way to the Land of Israel, among the soldiers of the "Givati" brigade and in his kibbutz, Ein-Hachoresh. When he wrote *Face to Face*, his war novel, he broke the conventional rules of the genre, placing no hero at the centre of the story. He described a long line of soldiers, from every corner of the country and the globe, every age and origin, each one of them and his story, each as important as the other, gaining victory altogether. This novel was his way of objecting to the Israeli notion of "The Silver Platter", coined by Natan Alterman's poem on the Hebrew lad and lass whose sacrifice created the state: every one, including survivors and newcomers, had a share.

The Scrolls of Testimony too, does not have a central hero. Each scroll carries the story of the Holocaust, along countries, ghettos, camps and killing sites, describing – again – Jews of every type and reaction, thereby saying that the distinction made in Israel between those who fought back and the majority that did not is unfair and non-relevant to the situation during World War II. The Holocaust experience and the suffering is not to be divided – it is a common one, and every one stood up to the test as much as he could, and far more respectably than did other nations. When Kovner wrote the texts for the Diaspora Museum in Tel Aviv, he added yet another dimension to the same idea: the visitor is confronted, upon entering the exhibition, with a wall covered with photos of changing faces. "And they are one people", says Kovner to the visitor, a unique and united people, whose contribution to the world cultural treasures is the summary of all individual efforts. In the texts he suggested for other museums he went on to develop the same notions of unity, common fate, and contribution, reverence for every Jew in any period and place.

> My true message is not the [description of the] event which happened in the past, but rather the sorrow in life, any kind of life. This sorrow was epitomized, in the deepest sense, in the Holocaust [. . .], but I have never seen life not based on sorrow.

Thus, in a letter to his daughter, Kovner tried to define himself not as a "Holocaust author", a term he detested, but rather as a poet who can detach himself from the past, no matter how painful. But the Holocaust does cast a shadow on much of his writing, especially his poems. He was the only Hebrew poet of his time to choose the poem as his main vehicle, perhaps wishing to use the space and breath this genre offers in order to convey the complexities he witnessed. At the centre of most of his poems stands the event he could never shake off: a mother – his mother, whom he left behind in the ghetto while leaving with the underground members for the forests. It is she in "The Key Sank", the poem about the ghetto's dead-end situation; it is she at the closing of "My Little Sister", the poem about his first love, Hadassa, who chose to go with her mother to the killing pit, instead of hiding with him in the monastery – a long life reproach of his own choice. And it is to her that his last book, *Shirat rosa* [Songs of Rosa] is dedicated – so he wished on his deathbed: with her he began and ended his life, and with her, and the sorrow she embodied, he wrote almost every line.

Kovner's strong sense of place, and the religious, national or personal attachment to it, gave birth to his partisan forest poems ("Until No Light" and "Black Angel"), to his Brazil-inspired "Soil of Sand" and to his "The Rhythm Band Dancing on Mount Grizim". In each the protagonists' actions or beliefs stem from their being part and parcel of their place. In his kibbutz, Ein-Hachoresh, to which he referred as "a place I have", he wrote or adapted plays, poems, religious texts, columns in the local newspaper, and commemoration ceremonies – all expressions of his vision: to see Judaism integrated into Zionism and creating a new way to live in an old-new place, and to see the members of his place and of the country in general form a true community. Judaism, he used to say, is the culture of togetherness. Therefore he signed or gave his name to his poetry and prose, and refrained from signing or even adding his name to the texts that originated between him and a public he felt part of and mentor to.

DINA PORAT

Kraus, Karl

Austrian journalist, poet, dramatist, and satirist, 1874–1936

Born in Jičín, Bohemia, 28 April 1874, to Jakob Kraus, paper bag manufacturer, and wife Ernestine (née Kantor). Moved with family to Vienna, 1877. Studied at Franz-Josefs Gymnasium, Vienna; at University of Vienna, initially law, then philosophy and German literature, 1894; left without degree, 1898. Made unsuccessful acting debut in Schiller's *Die Räuber*, 1893; contributed to many journals; founded and edited satirical journal *Die Fackel*, 1899–1936; gave public readings of his own and others' literary works. Abandoned Judaism, and detached himself from family after father's death, 1899, but continued to receive allowance from family; baptized into Catholic Church, 1911; abandoned Catholicism, 1922. First met Baroness Sidonie Nádherny von Borutin, 1913; proposed marriage to her many times, in vain, but maintained affectionate relationship until his death. Died in Vienna, 12 June 1936.

Selected Writings

Collections
Werke [Works], 14 vols, edited by Heinrich Fischer, 1952–67
Frühe Schriften 1892–1900 [Early Writings], 2 vols, edited by Johannes J. Braakenburg, 1979
Schriften, 20 vols, edited by Christian Wagenknecht, 1986–94

Poetry
Worte in Versen [Words in Verse], 9 vols, 1916–30
Die Ballade vom Papagei: Couplet Macabre [The Ballad of the Parrot: Macabre Couplet], 1919
Ausgewählte Gedichte [Selected Poems], 1920
Poems, edited and translated by Albert Bloch, 1930
Zeitstrophen [Timely Verses], 1931

Plays
Die letzten Tage der Menschheit: Tragödie in fünf Akten mit Vorspiel und Epilog [The Last Days of Mankind: Tragedy in Five Acts with Preamble and Epilogue], published in parts, 1918–19; excerpts as *The Last Days of Mankind*, translated by Alexander Gode and Sue Ellen Wright, edited by Frederick Ungar, 1974
Die letzte Nacht: Epilog zu der Tragödie Die letzten Tage der Menschheit [The Last Night: Epilogue to the Tragedy The Last Days of Mankind], 1918
Literatur; oder, Man wird doch da sehn: Magische Operette in zwei Teilen [Literature: or, We'll See about That: A Magic Operetta], 1921
Traumstück [Dream Play], 1923
Wolkenkuckucksheim [Cloudcuckooland], 1923
Traumtheater [Dream Theatre], 1924
Die Unüberwindlichen: Nachkriegsdrama in vier Akten [The Unconquerables: Post-War Drama in Four Acts], 1928

Books and Pamphlets
Die demolirte Literatur [Demolished Literature], 1897
Eine Krone für Zion [A Crown for Zion], 1898
Maximilian Harden: Eine Erledigung [Maximilian Harden: Finishing Him Off], 1907
Maximilian Harden: Ein Nachruf [Maximilian Harden: An Obituary], 1908
Sittlichkeit und Kriminalität [Morality and Criminal Justice], 1908
Sprüche und Widersprüche [Sayings and Contradictions], 1909
Die chinesische Mauer [The Chinese Wall], 1910; revised edition, 1930
Heine und die Folgen [Heine and the Consequences], 1910
Nestroy und die Nachwelt: Zum fünfzigsten Todestage [Nestroy and Posterity: For the Fiftieth Anniversary of his Death], 1912
Pro domo et mundo [For Home and for the World], 1912 (aphorisms)
Nachts [At Night], 1918
Peter Altenberg, 1919
Weltgericht [Last Judgement], 1919
Untergang der Welt durch schwarze Magie [The End of the World through Black Magic], 1922
Epigramme [Epigrams], 1927
Offenbach-Renaissance, 1927
Literatur und Lüge [Literature and Lie], 1929
Adolf Loos: Rede am Grab, 25 August 1933 [Adolf Loos: Speech at the Grave], 1933
Die Sprache [Language], 1937
Die Dritte Walpurgisnacht [The Third Night of St Walpurgis], 1952

Other
Editor, *Die Fackel* [The Torch], 1–37 (April 1899–February 1936)
Editor, *Peter Altenberg: Auswahl aus seinen Büchern* [Selections from his Works], 1932
Shakespeares Dramen: Für Hörer und Leser bearbeitet teilweise sprachlich erneuert [Shakespeare's Dramas: For Listeners and Readers Revised Linguistically in Part], 1934
Translator of works by Offenbach and Shakespeare

Letters and Selections
Briefe an Sidonie Nádherny von Borutin, 1913–1936 [Letters to Sidonie Nádherny of Borutin], 2 vols, edited by Heinrich Fischer, Michael Lazarus, and Friedrich Pfäfflin, 1974
Half-Truths and One-and-a-Half Truths: Selected Aphorisms, edited and translated by Harry Zohn, 1976
In These Great Times: A Karl Kraus Reader, edited by Harry Zohn (includes translations by Joseph Fabry, Max Knight, Karl F. Ross, and Zohn), 1976
No Compromise: Selected Writings of Karl Kraus, edited by Frederick Ungar, 1977

Further Reading

Benjamin, Walter, "Karl Kraus" in *Reflections*, New York: Harcourt Brace, 1978
Daviau, Donald G., "Language and Morality in Karl

Kraus's *Die Letzten Tage der Menschheit*", *Modern Language Quarterly*, 22/1 (March 1961): 46–54
Field, Frank, *The Last Days of Mankind: Karl Kraus and His Vienna*, London: Macmillan, and New York: St Martin's Press, 1967
Fischer, Heinrich, "The Other Austria and Karl Kraus" in *In Tyrannos: Four Centuries of Struggle against Tyranny in Germany*, edited by Hans J. Rehfisch, London: Drummond, 1944
Grimstad, Kari, *Masks of the Prophet: The Theatrical World of Karl Kraus*, Toronto: University of Toronto Press, 1982
Heller, Erich, "Karl Kraus" in his *The Disinherited Mind: Essays in Modern German Literature and Thought*, Cambridge: Bowes and Bowes, and Philadelphia: Dufour and Saifer, 1952; 4th edition, London: Bowes and Bowes, and New York: Harcourt Brace, 1975
Heller Erich, "Karl Kraus" in his *In the Age of Prose*, Cambridge and New York: Cambridge University Press, 1984
Iggers, Wilma Abeles, *Karl Kraus: A Viennese Critic of the Twentieth Century*, The Hague: Nijhoff, 1967
Janik, Allan and Stephen Toulmin, "Language and Society: Karl Kraus and the Last Days of Vienna" in their *Wittgenstein's Vienna*, New York: Simon and Schuster, and London: Weidenfeld and Nicolson, 1973
Modern Austrian Literature, 8/1–2 (1975): special Kraus issue, edited by Donald G. Daviau
Rosenfeld, Sidney, "Karl Kraus: The Future of a Legacy", *Midstream*, 20 (April 1974): 71–80
Simons, Thomas W., Jr, "After Karl Kraus" in *The Legacy of the German Refugee Intellectuals*, edited by Robert Boyers, New York: Schocken, 1972
Snell, Mary, "Karl Kraus' *Die Letzten Tage der Menschheit*: An Analysis", *Forum for Modern Language Studies*, 4/3 (July 1968): 234–47
Stern, Joseph Peter, "Karl Kraus's Vision of Language", *Modern Language Review*, 61 (January 1966): 71–84
Timms, Edward, *Karl Kraus, Apocalyptic Satirist: Culture and Catastrophe in Habsburg Vienna*, New Haven, Connecticut: Yale University Press, 1986
Williams, Cedric E., "Karl Kraus: The Absolute Satirist" in his *The Broken Eagle: The Politics of Austrian Literature from Empire to Anschluss*, London: Elek, and New York: Barnes and Noble, 1974
Zohn, Harry, "Krausiana, 1: Karl Kraus in English Translation", *Modern Austrian Literature*, 3/2 (Summer 1970): 25–30
Zohn, Harry, *Karl Kraus*, New York: Twayne, 1971

Karl Kraus was born in Jičín in Bohemia in 1874, one of nine children of a well-to-do Jewish manufacturer, who moved to Vienna in 1877. In 1899 Kraus founded *Die Fackel* [The Torch], which appeared until his death in 1936 and which after 1911 he wrote without other contributors. His main theme was the press, mainly in Vienna and particularly *Die Neue Freie Presse*. He accused it of being greedy, pretentious, unscrupulously profiteering and as time went on, of creating a mood that led up to World War I. Much of his journal consisted of texts reprinted from the press which, sometimes with the aid of "glosses", revealed the sloppy thinking or the immorality of the writer. His tirades were echoed by an enthusiastic following which in the 36 years during which *Die Fackel* was published diminished only gradually.

Kraus is primarily thought of as a social, but sometimes also as a literary critic. His life differed from those of his peers from similar backgrounds in so far as he was allowed to follow his interests in attending lectures at the university without a particular aim, to break off his studies, to write articles for various publications and, most importantly, to publish his own journal with financial support from his father. Thus he was able to write and accept contributions without financial considerations and without printing advertisements.

Although there is no evidence that he ever inwardly identified with any religion, he left the Jewish community, was baptized a Catholic in 1899, and left the Catholic church in 1922, in protest against what he felt were violations by the Catholic church of its own principles.

His observations during the war resulted in the gigantic play, *Die letzten Tage der Menschheit* (*The Last Days of Mankind*), which consisted of hundreds of scenes showing unscrupulous politicians, journalists, industrialists, primitive persons from various social strata, society ladies and gentlemen in Austria and Germany, all spreading or succumbing to war propaganda. Among the many characters who were identified by name were the two emperors, the editor in chief of the *Neue Freie Presse* (Moritz Benedikt), and Alice Schalek who as a war reporter interviewed dying soldiers in the trenches.

Despite protests by Krausians, there is no question that his attacks against Jews – Jewish journalists, businessmen, socialites, etc. – were more frequent than those against others. Well known anti-Semites such as Houston Stewart Chamberlain and Jörg Lanz von Liebenfels were contributers to *Die Fackel*, and Leopold Liegler, his first biographer, made no effort to hide his anti-Jewish feelings even in his book on Kraus. Kraus even defended Otto Weininger, who in his book *Geschlecht und Charakter* [Sex and Character] presented a scheme according to which good and bad characteristics were distributed in such a way that men and non-Jews had the good ones while women and Jews had the bad ones. Thus it should not be surprising that Theodor Lessing in his book on Jewish self-hatred pointed to Kraus as one of his prime examples.

Before the turn of the century there were two anti-Semitic "affairs" which attracted much attention internationally, and in both cases Kraus sided with the prosecutors of the Jewish victims: the Dreyfus affair in France and the Hilsner affair in Bohemia where a poor, probably mentally subnormal Jew was falsely accused of ritual murder.

Kraus was no political thinker; after vaguely identifying with liberalism, he supported the Social Democrats for a while after the turn of the century and again, more emphatically in the early years of the Austrian Republic. When Hitler became chancellor of Germany, Kraus must have come to realize that in much of the anti-Semitic propaganda he now heard there was a similarity to his own often repeated themes. When he came out in favour of the Austrofascist chancellor Dollfuss, to whom he referred as "the little savior from great distress", many of his followers abandoned him. From then on, Kraus was increasingly isolated.

In Kraus's lifetime his audiences and readership consisted largely of young intellectuals, in many cases from Jewish backgrounds similar to his own, many of whom were enabled to live comfortably by the fathers who were part of the society Kraus criticized. The enthusiasm about Kraus among his followers amounted to a cult not unlike other cults one finds in the German-speaking world: the Goethe, Nietzsche, and Stefan George cults and many others. Contrary to often repeated predictions that he could be understood only by readers familiar with his world and its languages, the Kraus cult survived his death and the deaths of his contemporaries.

The Kraus renaissance – which began more than 20 years after his death – in Germany, Austria, and among Germanists internationally, may be attributed to a liking for his anti-rationalism, his antimilitarism, his antinationalism, his concern for the environment, his attacks against the media, his early advocacy of sexual freedom, and ironically but plausibly, his Jewishness. And finally there was his "Sprachmystik", the conviction that language leads to thought, rather than that thoughts need to be expressed in language, which also has found modern followers. To him, language was not a means of communication. He felt that the breakdown of morality begins with the minutest neglect of language, even of a comma or of an individual letter. Kraus, whose mastery of the German language was unquestionable, considered himself the ultimate judge in matters concerning it. Although it is fairly certain that he knew no other language even fairly well, he considered the German language the profoundest, and believed that it was through his efforts that the German language, which had been misused, had become pure again.

It is astonishing that many women idealized him as much as men did, despite the fact that he considered it their only mission in life to bring joy to men, and admired prostitutes because only they had the courage to be "totally women".

Among writers who lived before his time, Kraus attacked Heine most frequently, especially for affecting the German language in a way that is usually seen positively: making it more facile and less plodding. In Kraus's language: he "so loosened the bodice of the German language – he often spoke of language as female – that any little salesman can finger her breasts." Most readers of course recognize easily the many similarities between Kraus and Heine, but also the basic differences.

Kraus was conservative in temperament. He idealized Biedermeier culture, rejected with few exceptions new trends in literature, innovative styles of acting, and modern technology. He glorified "the good old days", especially the Burgtheater of his childhood days, and resented changes and developments in many areas. He often wrote nostalgically of *Ursprung* (origin), meaning the time before the corruption of the world set in.

WILMA IGGERS

Kreitman, Esther

Polish fiction writer, 1891–1954

Born Hinde Esther Singer in Bilgoray, 31 March 1891, to Pinkhos Menakhem Singer, rabbi, and wife Basheve, daughter of rabbi; sister of writers I.J. Singer and I.B. Singer. Brought up in village of Leoncin, town of Radzymin, and then in Warsaw. Suffered continual mental and physical ill-health from 1903 to death. Was first in family to take up writing; persuaded to destroy stories written in Warsaw before leaving for Berlin and arranged marriage. Married Avraham Kreitman, diamond cutter; one son, Maurice. Lived in Antwerp; fled to London when Germans invaded, 1914, but husband, conscripted into Russian imperial army, was deported from Britain. Took son to Warsaw to escape unhappy marriage, 1926; stayed only three months, with I.J. Singer; was made to return home to Hampstead, London. Took up writing again. Died 13 June 1954.

Selected Writings

Novels

Der sheydim tants, 1936; as *Deborah*, translated by Maurice Carr (Kreitman's son), 1946

Brilyantn [Diamonds], 1944

Short Stories

Yikhes [Ancestry], 1949

Further Reading

Forman, Frieda *et al.* (editors), *Found Treasures: Stories by Yiddish Women Writers*, with an introduction by Irena Klepfisz, Toronto: Second Story Press, 1994

Hadda, Janet, *Isaac Bashevis Singer: A Life*, New York and Oxford: Oxford University Press, 1997

Sinclair, Clive, *The Brothers Singer: A Life*, London: Allison and Busby, 1983

Esther Kreitman, the now almost proverbial "forgotten sister" of Yiddish literature, has nevertheless been fortunate in that one of her novels, *Der sheydim tants* (*Deborah*), is one of the few complete works by Yiddish women prose writers to have been translated. Apart from this novel, a handful of her short stories have appeared in English translation.

This is actually a remarkable achievement – to a large extent thanks to the efforts of the author's son, Maurice Carr – considering that her total literary output comprises not more than two novels and a collection of short stories. A lack of talent does not seem to have been the reason keeping Kreitman away from a prolific writing career. "I do not know of a single woman in Yiddish literature who wrote better than she did", her brother I.B. Singer would say about her. Weak physical and mental health, as well as material hardships adding strain to an altogether unhappy married life in exile, made it hard for Kreitman to devote herself to writing the way her brothers did.

The single most decisive factor crippling Kreitman's literary aspirations, or any claims to intellectual self-fulfilment whatsoever, can be found in her family background. The sense of confinement and confusion it engendered in the young Ester are vividly described in Kreitman's autobiographical novel *Deborah*. When young Deborah asks her father what she can be when she grows up, he replies "What are *you* going to be one day? Nothing, of course!" As Janet Hadda points out, the family home was simultaneously both typical and exceptional. It was indeed a home "filled with piety and learning, as well as with the grinding poverty that epitomized Polish Jewry", but most of the family members somehow deviated from the norms laid out for them.

At the basis of this lay the problematic relationship between the parents, who "would have been a well-mated couple if she had been the husband and he the wife", in the words of her other brother I.J. Singer. Although both parents were equally pious, the cool-headed rationalism of the mother, Basheve, clashed with the gentle Hasidic fervour of father Pinkhos Menakhem. Neither the mother, embittered by her own thwarted intellectualism, nor the father, deeply rooted in tradition, could provide a role model for a daughter who was eager to "make her own life", as Kreitman calls it in *Deborah*.

> Ever since childhood she had longed to receive an education, to cease being the nonentity of the family. She would learn things, gain understanding, and then not only would papa be a great Talmudist, not only would her mother possess a boundless store of knowledge, not only would Michael [the fictional counterpart of I.J. Singer] be a brilliant student, but she, Deborah [. . .] would be a person of real consequence.

Deprived of a formal education, she found a means of escape in voracious reading. In this respect she reminds the reader of that other tragic heroine of Yiddish literature, Mirl Hurvitz in Dovid Bergelson's *When All is Said and Done*, who like Deborah, gradually descends into neurosis, as she is unable to find her place in a changing society.

Referring to the gender difficulties the example of her parents caused Esther, I.B. Singer aptly described her as a "Hasid in skirts". In Kreitman's fiction we find many examples of confusion over gender roles or simply manly women and men with female traits, as in the title story of the collection *Yikhes* [Ancestry], where the bridegroom's mother is described as a "cossack" and the boy himself as having "girlish red lips" and "small white hands".

I.B.Singer may have been mistaken, though, in attributing a "Hasidic fire" to his sister. Despite the lack of love and support from Basheve's side, Esther would eventually resemble her more than either of them realized. An example of this is Basheve's contempt for the Hasidic ways, which is echoed in Kreitman's gently ridiculing description of the Hasidic in-laws in the same story.

> They were a little tipsy as they were getting ready to dance. The women from the bridegroom's side dried their eyes and smacked their lips contentedly. The mother of the bridegroom even got into a loud fit from sheer exultation. Khaye Beyle looked at them and didn't say a word. But deep inside she couldn't stand the bridegroom's mother and her Hasidic whims.

Kreitman's own in-laws found their way into *Deborah*, where they get their share of wry and sometimes even grotesque descriptions. "Tertsa-Roisa and Baila began to undress, unlacing their corsets at the back, undoing the clasps at the front, removing cotton wool padding from their hips and taking more pads off their buttocks, substantial though these were." Her other novel, *Brilyantn* [Diamonds], is entirely based on the diamond milieu of Antwerp to which her in-laws belonged.

In the collection of short stories and sketches *Yikhes*, her last work of fiction, which appeared five years before her death, Kreitman draws on two worlds. There are stories like "An atlesene kapote" [A Satin Coat] and "Yikhes" [Ancestry], in which she recounts the lives of Jews in a Polish shtetl, and stories such as "Zeygers" [Clocks] and "Opgefast zikh" [Broken the Fast] that tell about Jewish immigrants in London during and after World War II. Irrespective of time and place, Kreitman confronts the reader with carefully balanced pictures of different paths taken by the characters, often family members, in each of the stories, e.g. the choice between a traditionally arranged match and romantic love, in "Yikhes", or the decision whether or not to hide in a London shelter during the Nazi bombardments, in "Zeygers". Especially in the characterization of both older and more recent immigrants, Kreitman proves to be an astute observer, capturing a few moments in their transition from the old Jewish traditions to a new life in London, the Yiddish very tellingly interlaced with English words and phrases.

Dorothée van Tendeloo

Kulbak, Moyshe

Russian poet, fiction writer, and dramatist, 1896–1940

Born in Smorgon, near Vilna (Vilnius), 1896. Traditional Jewish education. Father in lumber trade and mother's family Jewish farmers in Jewish agricultural colony in Vilna region. During World War I, while in Kovno, began writing poetry, first in Hebrew (influenced by Ahad Ha'am's Zionism) and then in Yiddish. Poem "Shterndl" in Vilna journal, *Literarishe heftn*, 1916. Lived in Berlin, 1920–23, published several significant poems, including "Raysn". Wrote first play, *Yankev frank*, 1922; first novel, *Moshiakh ben efraim*, 1924. Settled again in Vilna, 1923–28; active in Yiddish cultural scene, taught literature at Yiddish Teacher's Seminary. Mentor to Vilna students, group known as Yung Vilna. Returned to Minsk, 1928, participated in Minsk group. Arrested by the secret police, 1937, served in a prison camp in Siberia until his death in 1940. "Rehabilitated" in 1956 along with many of the other Yiddish writers murdered in Stalin's purges of Yiddish culture.

Selected Writings (in Yiddish)
Shirim [Songs], 1920
Lider [Poems], 1922
Naye lider [New Poems], 1922

Yankev frank [Jacob Frank] (play), 1923
Moshiakh ben efraim [The Messiah of the House of Efraim] (novel), 1924
Montik [Monday] (novel), 1929
Ale verk [Complete Works], 1929
Lider un poemen 1917–1928 [Songs and Poems], 1929
Zelmenyaner [The Zelmenyaner Clan] (novel), 1931–35
Disner tshayld harold [The Childe Harold of Disna] (epic poem), 1933

Selected Writings (in English)
"Munie the Bird Dealer" in *A Treasury of Yiddish Stories*, edited by Irving Howe and Eliezer Greenberg, 1953
Poems in *Onions and Cucumbers and Plums*, edited by Sarah Betsky-Zweig, 1958
"Childe Harold" and "Vilna" in *A Treasury of Yiddish Poetry*, edited by Irving Howe and Eliezer Greenberg, 1969
Zelmenyaner, in *Ashes Out of Hope: Fiction by Soviet-Yiddish Writers*, edited by Irving Howe and Eliezer Greenberg, 1977
Monday in *The Shtetl: A Creative Anthology of Jewish Life in Eastern Europe*, edited by Joachim Neugroschel, 1979
The Messiah of the House of Efraim and "The Wind Who Lost His Temper" in *Great Tales of Jewish Fantasy and the Occult*, edited by Joachim Neugroschel, 1987
Poems in *The Penguin Book of Yiddish Verse*, edited by Irving Howe, Ruth Wisse, and Khone Shmeruk, 1987
Poems in *An Anthology of Modern Yiddish Poetry*, edited by Ruth Whitman, 1995

Further Reading
Altshuler, Mordechai (editor), *Briv fun yidishe sovetishe shraybers* [Letters from Soviet Yiddish Writers], Jerusalem: Hebrew University Press, 1980
Hoffman, Matthew, "Reclaiming Jesus and the Construction of Modern Jewish Culture" (PhD dissertation), Graduate Theological Union, University of California, Berkeley, 2000
Howe, Irving and Eliezer Greenberg, introduction to *A Treasury of Yiddish Stories*, New York: Viking, 1953
Howe, Irving and Eliezer Greenberg, introduction to *Ashes Out of Hope: Fiction by Soviet-Yiddish Writers*, New York: Schocken, 1977
Hrushovski, B., Kh. Shmeruk, and A. Sutskever (editors), *A shpigl af a shteyn* [A Mirror on a Stone], Tel Aviv: Di goldene keyt, 1964
Kats, Daniel, *Na krawedzi zycia: Mojsze Kulbak: zydowski poeta, prozaik, dramaturg*, Warsaw, 1993
Kronfeld, Chana, *On the Margins of Modernism: Decentering Literary Dynamics*, Berkeley: University of California Press, 1996
Mayzel, Nachman, *Dos Yidishe Shafn un Der Yidisher Shrayber in Sovetfarband* [Yiddish Works and the Yiddish Writer in the Soviet Union], New York: YKUF, 1959
Roskies, David G., *Against the Apocalypse: Responses to Catastrophe in Modern Jewish Culture*, Cambridge, Massachusetts: Harvard University Press, 1984

The work of the Yiddish poet, novelist, and dramatist Moyshe Kulbak stands out for incorporating traditional elements of Jewish life such as mysticism, messianism, and folklore along with powerful new currents in Jewish life such as revolutionary idealism and literary modernism. Kulbak created a distinctive literary voice as he drew from Jewish sources such as Kabbalah and folklore, as well as from European modernist literary trends such as German Expressionism and Russian Symbolism. Kulbak was thus able to preserve and subvert tradition simultaneously, creating new legends from the cloth of the old. For this creative fusion, he was criticized and rebuked by Soviet "Proletarian" Yiddish critics, who criticized many modernist writers in the late 1920s for not writing in the evolving form of Soviet literature, socialist realism. This criticism reveals the perpetual tension in Kulbak's work between the old and the new, the traditional and the revolutionary. The American Yiddish critic Shmuel Niger recognized this tension in his review of Kulbak's last novel, *Zelmenyaner*, when he wrote: "It is hard [for the party-liners] to rely on him . . . Kulbak strives honestly to orient himself toward Minsk [the center of the proletarian Yiddish critics] . . . yet there remains about him an aroma of Vilna [the center of traditional Jewish learning and Yiddish culture]" (cited in Howe and Greenberg, 1977). Kulbak's dual orientation toward Minsk (Revolution) and Vilna (Tradition) resulted in a richly creative and dynamic body of work.

In much of his poetry, as well in as his novels, Kulbak portrays Jews who are like peasants, connected to the soil and to nature, toiling in the forest or under the hot sun. He creates a neoromantic mood through his idyllic portraits of these simple country Jews. Kulbak's long poem "Raysn" ("Byelorussia") exemplifies this sort of elegy to the rugged and rustic lifestyle of his White Russian forbears, "As common as the clay are all/ My sixteen uncles and my father . . . They toil the livelong day like ordinary peasants". Kulbak just as aptly romanticizes Jewish urban life in his ode to Vilna, "Vilna", in which he lyrically depicts the rhythms of traditional Jewish life as well as the emerging secular Jewish culture in that city. In Kulbak's last long poem cycle, *Disner tshayld harold*, he satirically depicts the seething cultural ferment of cosmopolitan Berlin during the early 1920s, deftly and colourfully capturing all of the tempestuousness and adventure of those years, wryly observing: "It is a confusing age./ Uneasy voices clamor".

Kulbak's first novel, *The Messiah of the House of Efraim*, is an allegorical tale full of Kabbalistic symbolism, biblical allusions, messianic motifs, and mythical characters. It also contains apocalyptic images of cosmic sweep, and seems especially enamoured of rustic, ascetic characters, such as Benye the Miller, Simkhe Plakhte (a character from Yiddish folklore), and Gimpl the philosopher-idiot, who are all *lamed-vovniks* – hidden holy men, who according to popular Jewish lore appear as simpletons but are actually quasi-redemptive figures. Moreover, the title, which also refers to the role of the central character, draws on a particular strand in Jewish tradition that speaks of a secondary Messiah figure: the Messiah son of Joseph (*ben yosef*) also known as son of Ephraim (*ben efraim*). In his often esoteric, richly symbolic narrative, Kulbak weaves together these various legends and popular traditions in creating a modernist redemption tale that is more tragic than heroic. The text conveys a fundamental ambivalence about messianic redemption by presenting the old, pathetic bumpkin, Benye the Miller as the Messiah. Kulbak also incorporates Christian messianic motifs in establishing the story's apocalyptic theme. Benye, as the Messiah son of Efraim, closely parallels Jesus; they both share the distinction of symbolizing redemption through death, and they both die violently at the hands of those whom they are trying to redeem. Kulbak thus draws freely from both Christian and Jewish legends in constructing his own modernist, dystopian messianic farce in which simpletons and charlatans compete to redeem the world, and both fail miserably.

In Kulbak's second novel, *Monday*, he depicts the effects of the Russian revolution on an eccentric cast of characters in an unnamed shtetl. In typical expressionist style, Kulbak juxtaposes the realistic and the surrealistic, the physical and the metaphysical, the traditional and the revolutionary, in exploring the impact of the revolution on Jewish shtetl life. He intermingles mundane scenes of shtetl life with bursts of revolutionary chaos, mayhem, and violence. A grotesque aesthetic and sense of the absurd persist throughout the novel. Kulbak's narrative style is richly metaphorical and esoteric, using poetic bursts of description to convey mood, sensation, and emotion, rather than following a linear narrative sequence. His images are often jarring and disjointed as he moves fluidly from comic depictions of quirky characters to rambling discourses on existential philosophy and fantastic treatments of the revolution as a tumultuous storm cloud, or a giant bear in the sky. The novel revolves primarily around Mordechai Marcus, a reclusive shtetl intellectual who rejects traditional Jewish piety, but also opposes the revolution. Marcus champions poverty and the life of the itinerant Jewish beggar, proclaiming that Monday – which represents the profane, ordinary "everyday Jew" – is the "day of salvation". He also frequently engages in bouts of metaphysical contemplation on the nature of Being and Existence along with ten "holy men" who sit in the synagogue discussing the "pure world" and the world of illusion. In contrast to Marcus and the synagogue sages, the revolution is represented by a character Kulbak terms "the mass", implying the mob mentality associated with the supporters of the revolution. The mass talks about "class warfare" while inundating the shtetl in a nightmarish, topsy-turvy world of violence and chaos. Although clouded in allegory, and veiled by a freely associative narrative of images and metaphors, *Monday* explores the fundamental tension between Jewish and Communist notions of salvation: redemption versus revolution.

In Kulbak's last novel, *Zelmenyaner*, he further explores how the Bolshevik Revolution transformed traditional Jewish life in telling the family saga of the Zelmenyaner clan. The Zelmenyaner are depicted as simple working Jews – "plain like a piece of bread" – who represent that certain type of traditional, shtetl Jews who so fascinated Kulbak. Using a more conventional narrative style than in his previous novels, reflecting the more straightforward narrative strategies of socialist realism, Kulbak tells a story of generational conflict in which the youngest generation of Zelmenyaner gradually introduces the ideals of the revolution and "Soviet progress" to their traditional elders. At first, the elders are disdainful of such "rubbish", deriding it as "current foolishness" and initially rejecting such symbols of progress as electricity and the radio. Eventually, the elders accept, and even embrace, the new realities of Soviet life. However, Kulbak treats his subject rather ironically, mildly mocking the communist youth along with their traditional forebears, and bathing the whole tale in a comically absurdist tone. From his first to his last work, through the waves of modernist trends, and through socialist realism, Kulbak maintained a commitment to fusing traditional Jewish life and the new ways of modernity.

MATTHEW HOFFMAN

Kunitz, Stanley

US poet, 1905–

Born Stanley Jasspon Kunitz in Worcester, Massachusetts, 29 July 1905 to immigrant Jews from Ukraine. Mother worked as seamstress. Educated at Worcester Classical High School; Harvard University, BA 1926, MA 1927. Married, first, Helen Pearce, 1930 (divorced 1937); second, Eleanor Evans, 1939 (divorced 1958), one daughter; third, Elise Asher, 1958. Editor, Wilson Library *Bulletin*, New York, 1928–43. Member of Faculty, Bennington College, Vermont, 1946–49; Professor of English, Potsdam State Teachers College (now State University of New York), 1949–50, and summers, 1949–53; Lecturer, New School for Social Research, New York, 1950–57; Visiting Professor, University of Washington, Seattle, 1955–56; Queens College, Flushing, New York, 1956–57; Brandeis University, 1958–59; Yale University, 1970–72; Rutgers University, 1974; Princeton University, 1978; Vassar College, 1981. Director, YM-YWHA Poetry Workshop, New York, 1958–62; Danforth Visiting Lecturer, 1961–63; Lecturer, 1963–67, and Adjunct Professor of Writing, 1967–85, Columbia University. Since 1968 associated with Fine Arts Center, Provincetown, Massachusetts. Editor, Yale Series of Younger Poets, 1967–77. Consultant in Poetry, Library of Congress, Washington, DC, 1974–76. Cultural Exchange lecturer, USSR, Poland, Senegal, Ghana, Israel, and Egypt. Senior Fellow in Humanities, Princeton University, 1978. Since 1969, Fellow, Yale University. Since 1985 president, Poets House, New York. Many awards, including Guggenheim Fellowship, 1945; Amy Lowell Travelling fellowship, 1953; Harriet Monroe award, 1958; Pulitzer Prize, 1959; Ford Grant, 1959; American Academy grant, 1959; Academy of American Posts fellowship, 1968; National Endowment for the Arts Senior Fellowship, 1984; Bollingen Prize, 1987; Walt Whitman award, 1987; National Book Award, 1995. Member, and since 1985, secretary, American Academy; Chancellor, Academy of American Poets, 1970. Poet Laureate of United States, 2001.

Selected Writings

Poetry
Intellectual Things, 1930
Passport to the War: A Selection of Poems, 1944
Selected Poems 1928–1958, 1958
The Testing-Tree, 1971

The Terrible Threshold: Selected Poems 1940–1970, 1974
The Coat without a Seam: Sixty Poems 1930–1972, 1974
The Lincoln Relic, 1978
The Poems of Stanley Kunitz 1928–1978, 1979
The Wellfleet Whale and Companion Poems, 1983
Next-to-Last-Things, 1985
The Ageless Spirit, 1992
Passing Through: The Later Poems New and Selected, 1995
The Wild Card: Selected Poems, Early and Late, 1998
Collected Poems of Stanley Kunitz, 2000

Other
Editor, *Poems by John Keats*, 1964
Translator, *Stolen Apples*, by Evgenii Evtushenko, 1971
Robert Lowell, Poet of Terribilità, 1974
Editor and translator, *Poems of Akhmatova*, 1974
Translator, *Story under Full Sail*, by Andrei Voznesenskii, 1974
A Kind of Order, A Kind of Folly: Essays and Conversations, 1975
From Feathers to Iron, 1976
Editor and co-translator, *Orchard Lamps*, by Ivan Drach, 1978
A Celebration for Stanley Kunitz: On his Eightieth Birthday, 1986
Editor, *The Essential Blake*, 1987
Interviews and Encounters with Stanley Kunitz, 1993

Also edited many library reference works

Further Reading

Boyers, Robert, " Imagine Wrestling with an Angel", *Contemporary Poetry in America*, edited by Boyers, New York: Schocken, 1974
Hagstrom, James, "The Poetry of Stanley Kunitz" in *Poets in Progress*, edited by Edward Hungerford, Evanston, Illinois: Northwestern University Press, 1962
Henault, Marie, *Stanley Kunitz*, Boston: Twayne, 1980
Moss, Stanley, "Man with a Leaf in his Head", *Nation* (20 September 1971)
Moss, Stanley, "The Darkness of the Self", *Times Literary Supplement* (30 May 1980)
Moss, Stanley, *The Art of Poetry: Interviews with Stanley Kunitz*, New York: Sheep Meadow Press, 1989
Orr, Gregory, *Stanley Kunitz: An Introduction to the Poetry*, New York: Columbia University Press, 1985
Ostroff, Anthony, *The Contemporary Poet as Artist and Critic*, Boston: Little Brown, 1964
Vine, Richard, "The Language that Saves", *Salmagundi* (Winter 1977)

"I have no religion – perhaps that is why I think so much about God". This terse statement, from "Seedcorn and Windfall", accurately conveys Stanley Kunitz's attitude toward organized religion. It is characteristic, in many ways, of his solitary way as a person and as a poet. And one looks in vain for any significant statement about his religious association or background, although, like many Jews in the 20th century, that identity occasionally plagued him. As noted in one of the great postmodernist poems, "The Testing-Tree", being a Jew meant that as a young boy he could not play on the grounds of Worcester Academy, a traditional New England prep school. Later, after graduating magna cum laude and completing an MA degree at Harvard, Kunitz was told that he could not hope to teach there because "Anglo-Saxons would resent being taught English by a Jew". And in that splendid "song", "An Old Cracked Tune", its hero a 15th-century rabbi and poet, one hears the voice of a person who has survived similar displacements and rejection, but with characteristic bravado, even pride: "My name is Solomon Levi/ the desert is my home,/ my mother's breast was thorny,/ and father I had none./ The sands whispered, Be separate,/ the stones taught me, Be hard/ I dance, for the joy of surviving,/ On the edge of the road."

Identity for Kunitz, in other words, lies somewhere other than with religion and race – singular, solitary, alone. In an early poem, "The Words of the Preacher", for example, the speaker says, "my soul rejected the sweet snare/ Of happiness; declined/ That democratic bait, set in the world/ By fortune's old and mediocre mind". And in a later poem, "The Guilty Man", the speaker says: "I stand within myself, myself my shield". It is clear from his poems and essays that Kunitz's identity resembles that of many modern writers, the artist and intellectual linked to no particular history or religious heritage. Though a descendant of Sephardic Jews, as we learn from "My Mother's Story (Yetta Helen Dine, 1866–1952)", Kunitz repeatedly made choices that distinguished him from his contemporaries. For many years he lived apart from the literary world, "in rural isolation", as he described it. Theodore Roethke was his only close literary friend. During World War II, he chose to serve in the army as a conscientious objector (1-A-O), not because he was a member of the Fellowship of Reconciliation or War Resister's League, but because he refused to carry a gun. That theme of isolation informs a later poem, "Passing Through – on My Seventy-ninth Birthday": "The way I look at it, I'm passing through a phase: nothing is truly mine except my name. I only borrowed this dust". At the same time, Kunitz treasures community, particularly his friendship with painters and his commitment to a literary tradition that includes Dante, the Metaphysical Poets, Blake, Hopkins, and Yeats. In a foreword to *Passing Through: The Later Poems New and Selected*, he acknowledged the essential moral thrust of his art: "The craft that I admire most manifests itself not as an aggregate of linguistic or prosodic skills, but as a form of spiritual testimony, the sign of the inviolable self consolidated against the enemies with and without that would corrupt or destroy human pride and dignity." Regarding his religious background, Kunitz once responded to an interviewer's saying that "Insofar as your poems are morally conscious they may be construed to be Jewish". Although "Jewish cultural aspiration and ethical doctrine entered into my bloodstream", Kunitz said, "in practice I am an American freethinker, a damn stubborn one . . . Moses and Jesus and Lao-tse have all instructed me. And all the prophets as well, from Isaiah to Blake." But it's also true, he added, "that three of the poets who most strongly influence me – Donne, Herbert, Hopkins – happen to have been Christian churchmen." So is the subject of one of Kunitz's most powerful lyrics, "Around Pastor Bonhoeffer", the German Lutheran clergyman implicated in a plot to kill Hitler.

As with many artists and intellectuals in recent history, established religion seems to function as an impediment rather than as an encouragement to being "religious". A single inheritance is apparently too narrow or exclusionary to include the heroes, "the saints", of his religious pantheon. Once asked if the God that he was contending with in "King of the River" was a Christian God, for example, Kunitz answered, "Call Him the God of all gods. I have no sectarian faith."

Named Poet Laureate at 95, after being honoured frequently for his art, including the Pulitzer, National Book, and Bollingen awards, Kunitz recently published his collected poems, with the collected essays soon to follow. Newer poems are as strong and carefully made as always, but with the simplicity and natural rhythms that characterize his work since the publication of *The Testing-Tree* in 1971, rather than the clotted, "metaphysical" verse of earlier collections. A theme throughout is the search for the father, explored in two signature poems, "Father and Son" and later "The Portrait", beginning: "My mother never forgave my father for killing himself especially at such an awkward time and in a public park, that spring when I was waiting to be born".

Recent poems include "The Layers", "Touch Me" – beginning "Summer is late my heart", and "My Mother's Pears", looking back to his childhood in Worcester, Massachusetts. A longer poem, its setting a summer beach at Cape Cod, near Kunitz's summer residence. Entitled "The Wellfleet Whale", it conveys the essentially tragic vision for his early poems, in a tribute to that great voyager, "chief of the pelagic world", in his final hour. Dying on a beach among a crowd of sun worshipers, the whale, like us, "Disgraced and mortal", is given a final salute, then prayed over: "you turned, like a god in exile, out of your wide primeval element, delivered to the mercy of time. Master of the whale-roads, let the white wings of the gulls spread out their cover".

MICHAEL TRUE

Kushner, Tony

US dramatist, 1956–

Born in New York City, 16 July 1956. Grew up in Lake Charles, Louisiana. Studied at Columbia University, BA, 1978; New York University, MFA in theatre directing, 1984. Guest artist, New York University Graduate Theater Program, Yale University, and Princeton University, since 1989; Director, Literary Services, Theater Communications Group, New York, 1990–91; playwright in residence, Juilliard School of Drama, New York, 1990–92. Many awards, including National Endowment for the Arts Directing Fellowship, 1985; Princess Grace Award, 1986; John Whiting Award, 1990; Kennedy Center/American Express Fund for New American Plays Award, 1990, 1992; National Arts Club Kesselring Award, 1991; *Evening Standard* Drama Award, 1992; Lifetime Achievement Award of the National Foundation for Jewish Culture, 1999.

Selected Writings

Plays

Yes, Yes, No, No, 1985
A Bright Room Called Day, 1987
Hydriotaphia, 1987
Stella, 1987
The Illusion, 1988
Angels in America, Part One: The Millennium Approaches, 1991
Widows, with Ariel Dorfman, 1991
Angels in America, Part Two: Perestroika, 1992
Slavs! Thinking about the Longstanding Problems of Virtue and Happiness, 1995
A Dybbuk, 1998
Death and Taxes: Hydrioptaphia and Other Plays, 2000
Homebody/Kabul, 2001

Other

The Persistence of Prejudice: Antisemitism in British Society during the Second World War, 1989
The Holocaust and the Liberal Imagination: A Social and Cultural History, 1994
Refugees in an Age of Genocide, with Katharine Knox, 1999

Also editor or co-editor of several other volumes of sociological historical studies.

Further Reading

Geis, Deborah R. and Steven F. Kruger (editors), *Approaching the Millennium: Essays on Angels in America*, Ann Arbor: University of Michigan Press, 1997
The Holocaust Needs a Liberal Imagination: A Critique of Kushner's Chutzpah, London: Anglo-Hebrew Publishing, 1995
Vorlicky, Robert (editor), *Tony Kushner in Conversation*, Ann Arbor: University of Michigan Press, 1998

At one time, Kushner's description of his massive two-part play, *Angels in America*, as "a gay fantasia on national themes", might have appeared grandiose; after both plays had been staged it was clearly seen to be modest. There is so much more to them than a view of American life seen from the point of view of members of a subculture, even one that permeates all levels of society. They are also infused with an unflagging dramatic energy that maintains momentum over the whole seven-hour 20-minute length of the work.

"When I first started", said Kushner (interviewed by this writer for the London *Jewish Chronicle* on 28 November 1993):

> the brief I gave myself was to write about being gay in the middle 1980s in America. Roy Cohn came into it as a character; I didn't intend to address him specifically as a Jew.
>
> But there's a sort of play within a play that has become an almost private event, something that happens among the Jewish characters.

Mormons, WASPS, Catholics and Jews; angels and ghosts; fantasy, realism, surrealism and McCarthyism; guilt with a Puritan and Jewish provenance, dreams and hallucinations are all present in Part One, subtitled *The Millennium Approaches*. Louis Ironson, in a panic of revulsion, deserts his WASP lover, Prior Walter, and takes up with Joe, a married Mormon in whom religion and homosexuality battle for supremacy. His sexual preference wins, helped by close contact, not only with Louis, but with Roy Cohn, the McCarthy aide and homophobic, homosexual racist who was later to die of AIDS. Cohn becomes the play's dynamic, representing all that is evil, both politically and socially. He refuses to be labelled a homosexual on the grounds that gays do not possess power and he does; therefore he is merely a man who has sex with other men. He cracks any illusion there might exist of a gay brotherhood crossing all barriers. The first play closes with an angel crashing through the ceiling to visit the dying Prior with the assurance that he will become a prophet.

In *Perestroika*, the second of the plays, Cohn, by now dying of AIDS, is visited by the ghost of Ethel Rosenberg whom he helped to send to the electric chair for spying for the USSR. He begs her to sing the lullaby *Tumbalalaika* for him and, touched by his distress, she does. At which point he cackles in triumph and shouts that at last he has got her to sing. Cohn's mockery of Ethel Rosenberg, his abuse of a gay black male nurse, his exultation over his private stock of AZT, the AIDS drug, make him powerfully odious. Which is where forgiveness, described as the place where love and justice meet, comes in. It is important to Kushner and he has Ethel Rosenberg persuading the protesting, secular Louis to say a halting *Kaddish* for the dead Cohn.

"One of the keys to the second half of the play", said Kushner, "came when I was reading an introduction by Harold Bloom to a book called, *Musical Variations on Jewish Thought*. He relates the Hebrew word for blessing to the concept of life. I found that very moving."

Prior wrestles with the Angel for a blessing and visits heaven, which is not unlike San Francisco. The Angel tells Prior that God abandoned the world on 18 April 1906, the night of the San Francisco earthquake, having become tired of mankind ceaselessly rushing around trying to improve itself. People should stay still and be quiet, instructs the Angel, telling Prior to spread the word. But Kushner rejects the idea and the play ends with a thundering affirmation of man's insatiable need to try to improve the world.

Kushner's parents were classical musicians who settled in Lake Charles, Louisiana, when they started a family and could no longer tour. They taught music and there was also a family timber business. His father is conductor of two Louisiana orchestras. There aren't many Jews in Lake Charles.

> As a result, [said Kushner] we defined ourselves very strongly. My parents grew up in the shadow of the Holocaust . . . that had a big impact on the way I came to understand my gay identity. I doubt if Jews are more homophobic than anyone else, but there is a particular quality in Jewish homophobia that is difficult for gay Jews to accept.

Not surprisingly, neither his earlier plays nor his subsequent theatre work had the same impact as *Angels in America*. *A Bright Room Called Day*, first seen at the Eureka Theatre, San Francisco, later at the Bush, London, had a split set. On one side was a dinner party in Hitler's Germany in 1932; on the other sat Zillah, a paranoid Jewess in Thatcher's Britain who likened the Conservative prime minister to Hitler.

Slavs connects the collapse of communism with the greater visibility of homosexuality and studies the stiffening geriatric leadership of the USSR. It is set in a laboratory where the brains of dead leaders are examined, and is suffused with the sad questioning of a socialist baffled by the spectacular failure of the great experiment. More successful was *Homebody/Kabul*. It is a complex play in which a woman setting out to buy some Afghan hats in a junkshop somehow gets to survey a strife-wrecked nation in which yesterday's national treasurers become tomorrow's garbage.

Kushner is reaching the end of ten years work on a play about Henry Box Brown, a former slave who toured the textile towns of Britain during the American Civil War. It was commissioned by Richard Eyre, former director of the Royal National Theatre. He has also written screenplays, a children's book, and two opera libretti.

In May 1999, Kushner received the Lifetime Achievement Award of the National Foundation for Jewish Culture. "It makes me an officially approved Jew", he said.

DAVID NATHAN

L

Langer, Jiří

Czech-Austrian poet, 1894–1943

Born Jiří Mordecai Langer in Prague, 1894; younger brother of dramatist and novelist František Langer. Rebelled against assimilated upbringing; lived within Hasidic environment in Belz, Poland, 1913; returned to Prague, 1914. Taught Hebrew to Franz Kafka and Max Brod. Conscripted into Austro-Hungarian army 1914, but released because of religious "inflexibility". Emigrated illicitly to Palestine, 1939. Died in Tel Aviv, 1943.

Selected Writings

Poetry
Piyutim veshire jedidut [Songs of Praise and Friendship], 1929
Zpevy zavrzenych [Songs of the Rejected], 1937
Meat tsori [A Little Balsam], 1942

Other
Die Erotik der Kabbala [The Eroticism of the Kabbalah], 1923
Zur Funktion der juedischen Tuerpfortenrolle [On the Function of the Jewish Doorpost Sign], 1928
Die juedischen Gebetriemen-Phylakterien [Jewish Phylacteries], 1931
Devet bran, 1937; as *Nine Gates to the Chasidic Mysteries*, translated by Stephen Jolly, 1961

Further Reading

Bloom, Cecil, "Kafka's Hassid", *Midstream* (January 1996)
Brod, Max, *Der Prager Kreis*, Stuttgart: Kohlhammer, 1966
Dagan, Avigdor *et al.* (editors), *The Jews of Czechoslovakia*, Philadelphia: Jewish Publication Society of America, 1968
Dror, Miryam (editor), *Me'at tsori: asupat ketavav: Mordekhai Giorgio (Dov) Langer*, Tel Aviv: Aguda hasofrim ha'Ivrim bebedinat Yisrael ve-Ekad, 1984
Gottlieb, F., "The Hassid from Prague", *Jewish Quarterly* (Spring/Summer 1976)
Langer, František, introduction to *Nine Gates to the Chasidic Mysteries*, by Jiří Langer, translated by Stephen Jolly, New York: Behrman House, 1975
Oppenheimer, Anne, "Franz Kafka's Relation to Judaism" (dissertation), Oxford University, 1977: 297–304
Robertson, Ritchie, *Kafka: Judaism, Politics, and Literature*, Oxford: Clarendon Press, and New York: Oxford University Press, 1985

Jiří Langer's main claim to fame is as a friend of Franz Kafka and as the person mainly responsible for acquainting Kafka with Orthodox Jewish life and legend and especially Hasidism (the religious movement founded by the Baal Shem Tov in the 18th century). Kafka became deeply interested in the Hasidic movement after Langer took him to meet Hasidic rabbis; first, in September 1915, the "wonder rabbi" (as described by Kafka) of Goodeck who was then living in Prague, and the Belzer rabbi, who was taking the cure in Marienbad, in 1916. These meetings are clearly described in Kafka's fiction and, although none of Kafka's fictional works contain the word "Jew", other Jewish aspects detected in his fiction can also be attributed to Langer. Langer was responsible for teaching Kafka Hebrew and he probably appears in Kafka's *The Castle* as the chief secretary Erlanger who wore a black fur coat not dissimilar to the Hasidic dress at one time worn by Langer. Max Brod, who introduced Langer to Kafka, has declared that some of Kafka's works would not have been written without Langer's help.

Langer's father came from a deeply Orthodox family, but in Prague, where he became a shopkeeper, his life took on a modern style similar to that of the Kafka family. His son Jiří started to become interested in religion when he was 16. He studied Hebrew and the Talmud and to his author and playwright brother, František, he became a "dreamer of the ghetto". When he was 19 he left home and joined the court of the Belzer rabbi attracted by a society "living in a state of unending ecstasy, entirely beyond time, space and matter". He believed in the spiritual nature of all matter, and found most beautiful the Hasidic doctrine which insisted that all matter is full of supernatural "sparks" of the holiness of God. Ordinary human functions such as eating and drinking, sleeping, and sexual activity were dematerialized and were considered to be the most sublime actions in the service of the Almighty.

Langer then returned to Prague in Hasidic dress sporting a red beard and *peyyot* (long ringlets of hair worn in front of the ears). When war broke out in 1914, he was called up for army service and was court-martialled for refusing army food and not working on the Sabbath. Thanks to his brother's intercession, he was eventually discharged on the grounds that he was mentally disturbed.

For the remainder of the war he was at the Belzer rabbi's court, but his attitude changed somewhat and he returned to Prague less extreme in habit and dress. After the war, Langer taught at the Jewish College in Prague when Freudian philosophy became an important interest and he began to analyse the essential meaning of Jewish ritual practice. This led to *Die Erotik der Kabbala* [The Eroticism of the Kabbalah] in 1923. In this book he applied Freudian methods in order to examine the meaning of these practices and to try to find the subconscious sources of Jewish mysticism. He wrote papers in the Freudian journal *Imago* on the ritual of *Tefillin* (phylacteries) and on the function of *Mezzuzot* (doorpost parchment scrolls) and their connection, as he saw them, to primitive ideas in the form of sexual symbols. In his essays he attempted to attribute erotic features to many of the deeply held practices of Orthodox Jewish beliefs. Further articles were published in Prague Jewish newspapers.

He then took an interest in Hebrew poetry and he published a collection in 1929 called *Piyutim veshire jedidut* [Songs of Praise and Friendship] which was the first book of Hebrew to be printed in Prague for over a hundred years. This work has been praised by critics who consider it to be an expression of a colourful, many-sided, and exceptionally gifted personality seeking relief from personal distress. One poem in this collection, "Lamot hameshorer" ["On the Death of the Poet"], was written in Kafka's memory and he saw the latter's death as the union of a pure soul with the infinite. In 1937 Langer published *Zpevy zavrzenych* [Songs of the Rejected], a collection of Czech translations of Hebrew poetry from 11th-century Spain to 18th-century Prague, and he also wrote in Czech a popular book about the origins of the Talmud.

Langer's literary reputation, however, rests largely on *Nine Gates to the Chasidic Mysteries* which was written in Czech under the title *Devet bran* in 1937. It was translated into English in 1961. This book is a collection of stories about some of the *tsaddikim* (righteous men of faith and piety) who lived in the Hasidic world and it deals with their lives, practices, and teachings. It tells also of their miracles. The book has no timeframe and the reader travels to many countries as its author reverts to the mysticism and ecstasy of the Hasidic courts. Langer claimed he learned these stories orally and that they had never previously appeared in print. His objective was to entertain and not to present a philosophical analysis.

When Czechoslovakia was invaded by the Germans, Langer escaped to Palestine through Istanbul and settled in Tel Aviv. There, he wrote a memoir of his friendship with Kafka for the Hebrew newspaper *Hege* and in 1942 he published another collection of poems, *Meat tsori* [A Little Balsam], which includes his poem of appreciation of Kafka. He also wrote about the Palestinian countryside, which fascinated him. Shortly before he died, he wrote a nostalgic poem in Hebrew about Prague and its *Altneushul* (the Old-New synagogue built in the 13th century).

One Langer scholar believes that his work represents an expression of a colourful and many-sided, exceptionally gifted personality seeking relief from his distress as a man and a Jew against the background of his time. František Langer, who believed that *Nine Gates* had the atmosphere of a Hasidic *Thousand and One Nights*, claimed that his brother combined deft naivety with simplicity, a characteristic gift of great Jewish artists, and this is a most appropriate epitaph for a man whose narrative was laced throughout with the smiling scepticism of an adult who tells children of the rabbis' miracles and with the over-incredibility of the child who believes all he is told.

CECIL BLOOM

Lapid, Shulamit

Israeli fiction writer, poet, and dramatist, 1934–

Born in Tel Aviv, 1934. Studied oriental studies at Hebrew University, Jerusalem, 1956–57. Married Joseph Lapid, member of Knesset (Israeli legislature); three children (one deceased). Has been Chair, Hebrew Writers Association. Awarded Newman Prize (for her oeuvre); Prime Minister's Award for Literature.

Selected Writings

Short Stories
Mazal dagim [Pisces], 1969
Shalvat shotim [The Calm of Fools], 1974
Kadahat [Fever], 1979
Mah mesameah akavishim [Happy Spiders], 1990

Novels
Gai oni, 1982
Kaheres hanishbar [As a Broken Vessel], 1984
Mekomon [Local Paper], 1989
Pitui [Bait], 1992
Hatakhshit [The Jewel], 1993
Hol baeinayim [Sand in your Eyes], 1997
Etsel babou [Chez Babou], 1998
Pilegesh begivah [Concubine on the Hill], 1999

Novella
Hasafsal [The Bench], 2000

Poetry
Shirei halon [Window Poems], 1988

Plays
Rekhush natush [Abandoned Property], 1987
Rehem pundaki [Surrogate Mother], 1991
Mifal hayav [His Life's Work], 1992
Haflagot [Sailings], 1994

For Children
Shpits, 1971
Naarat hahalomot [The Girl of Dreams], 1985
Hatanin mitsrayim [Egypt the Crocodile], 1987
Oded hamelukhlakh [Dirty Oded], 1988
Oreah [The Visitor], 1988
Hasmikhah zehavah [Zehavah the Blanket], 1998

Further Reading

Feldman, Yael S., *No Room of Their Own: Gender and Nation in Israeli Women's Fiction*, New York: Columbia University Press, 1999; Hebrew edition, Tel Aviv: Hakibuts hameuhad, 2001

After several collections of short stories, Lapid first gained readers' attention with her popular novel, *Gai oni*, which was the first Israeli book to be labelled "feminist". Its feminism is displaced though, taking place in Palestine of the 1890s, thereby establishing a precedent in Israeli fiction for masking feminist protest by historical distancing. Framed in a narrative about first-settlers struggling with a harsh motherland, in a culture that kept gender roles distinct and separate, Lapid's heroine, Fania, stands out in her attempt to cross boundaries. She is both mother and merchant, venturing out on the road alone, even defending herself against armed Arab horsemen when attacked.

Yet at the end of a romance plot that borders on the melodramatic, Lapid does not allow Fania to go it alone, despite her "androgynous" qualities and her long training toward independence. This ambivalence about feminist liberation was reflected at the time also by the author's public pronouncements: she did not consider herself a feminist, nor believed in "women writing" per se. At the same time, she has mostly limited herself to "women's subjects". Except for one historical novel, *Kaheres hanishbar* [As a Broken Vessel] all her subsequent work features female protagonists. Her first play, *Rekhush natush* [Abandoned Property], explored the psychological dynamics between mother and daughters in a broken family on the margins of the social system, while her second play, *Rehem pundaki* [Surrogate Mother], engaged the contemporary issue of surrogate mothering by deftly rewriting the biblical model (Abraham, Sarah, and Hagar). By 1989, however, in an interview outside Israel, this "happily married mother" (by her own admission) described herself as "small, delicate, and becoming more and more aggressive" at her "ripe 54".

By the end of the decade, Lapid had "resolved" her ambivalence by shifting from the "canonic" historical narrative and the female euphoric text (the romantic betrothal plot), to a different genre – the spinster detective story. In a series of popular thrillers (1989–2000), all set in a contemporary provincial town (Beer Sheva), she has constructed a "New *Israeli* Woman", a lower middle-class journalist whose first priority is work, and for whom love is divorced from matrimony. Thirty-some years old and single, Lizzie Badihi, who is proud of her "professionalism" and work ethic, is not a descendent of the "New Hebrew Woman" of the Zionist revolution (Fania and her like); rather, she is a throwback to the turn-of-the-century spinster detective of English literature. In Lapid's version of this genre, motherhood is rejected first hand ("I have seen my sisters", Lizzie explains), and masculine autonomy is appropriated without any equivocation. The first novel's final question, repeated twice, "What do you want, Lizzie?", reads like a wry parody of Freud's notorious question, "What does a woman want?" What this woman wants is apparently work and a new kind of romance (male-modelled, of course: no strings attached . . .). The latter makes its appearance only at the close of the story: a tawny, handsome, rich, and worldly divorcé, whose timely offered "information" rescues Lizzie from the imminent danger of losing her job. It is hard to determine whether the simplicity with which sexual difference is overcome in these plots is an indicator of naive conceptualization, or of a projection of a collective fantasy. Whatever the case, it is clear that the feminist romance produced here is an essentialist mirror image of its masculinist counterpart.

The same goes for some of Lapid's later short stories in which romance is replaced by aggression. A straightforward reversal of roles in a violent rape scene, for example, is the subject of "Nehitat oness" (published in English as "The Bed", but better rendered as "Forced Entry"). The painful experience of what I would call "counter rape" is focalized through the eyes of the victim – a young *man* whose bewildered incomprehension is utterly ignored by his female attacker. Gender difference is again turned upside down: here the female grotesquely "redeems" her alterity by donning the dark face of masculine subjectivity, aggression.

While her earlier stories (*Mazal dagim* [Pisces] in 1969 and five later collections), were much more traditional, her recent work is marked by both social and feminist consciousness, e.g. the plays mentioned above, and the recent novel *Etsel babou* [Chez Babou], in which she tackles the painful topic, rarely addressed in Israeli literature, of the foreign, mostly illegal, labourers and the subhuman conditions of their work and life. Lapid has also published poems and children's books.

YAEL S. FELDMAN

Lasker-Schüler, Else

German poet, prose writer, and dramatist, 1869–1945

Born Else Schüler in Elberfeld, 11 February 1869. Claimed that she began suffering from St Vitus's dance, 1880, and could not go to school; taught by private tutors, including her brother Paul (who died aged 20, 1882). Deeply affected by mother's death, 1890. Married, first, Jonathan Berthold Lasker; divorced. One child, Paul, born 1899; father's identity unknown. Strongly influenced by poet Peter Hille. Married, second, George Levin (also known as Herwarth Walden); divorced, 1912. Edited Walden's magazine *Der Sturm* for first three years. Influenced by Martin Buber's writings and by Expressionist painting. Moved in Expressionist circles in and around Berlin after 1912; work published in major magazines and books of the Expressionists. Awarded Kleist Prize for Literature, 1932. Forbidden to publish her works after Nazi seizure of power and emigrated to Switzerland, 1933; travelled to Egypt; emigrated to Palestine, 1937; settled in Jerusalem. Died in Jerusalem, in poverty and isolation, 22 January 1945.

Selected Writings

Collections

Gesammelte Werke [Collected Works], 3 vols, 1959–61
1. *Gedichte 1902–1943* [Poems], edited by Friedhelm Kemp, 1959
2. *Prosa und Schauspiele* [Prose and Plays], edited by Friedhelm Kemp, 1962
3. *Verse und Prosa aus dem Nachlass* [Unpublished Verse and Prose], edited by Werner Kraft, 1961

Sämtliche Gedichte [Complete Poems], edited by Friedhelm Kemp, 1966

Gesammelte Werke in Acht Bänden [Collected Works in Eight Volumes], 1986
Werke und Briefe [Works and Letters], 4 vols, 1997– (vol. 1 not yet published)
2. *Dramen* [Plays], 1997
3. *Prosa. 1903–1920* [Prose 1903–1920], 1998
4. *Prosa 1921–1945, Nachgelassene Schriften* [Prose 1921–1945, Unpublished Writings], 2001

Poetry
Styx, 1902
Der Siebente Tag [The Seventh Day], 1905
Die Nächte Tino von Bagdads [The Nights of Tino of Bagdad], 1907; revised as *Die Nächte der Tino von Bagdad*, 1919
Meine Wunder: Gedichte [My Miracles], 1911
Hebräische Balladen, 1913; as *Hebrew Ballads and Other Poems*, translated by Audri Durchslag and Jeanette Litman-Demeestère, 1980
Die Gesammelten Gedichte [Collected Poems], 1920
Die Kuppel: Der Gedichte Zweiter Teil [The Cupola: Poems Part Two], 1920
Theben: Gedichte und Lithographien [Thebes: Poems and Lithographs], 1923
Mein blaues Klavier: Neue Gedichte [My Blue Piano], 1943

Prose
Mein Herz [My Heart], 1912
Der Malik: Ein Kaisergeschichte mit Bildern und Zeichnungen [The Malik: A King's History with Pictures and Drawings], 1919

Plays
Die Wupper [The Wupper River], 1909
"Plumm-Pascha: Morgenländische Komödie" [Plumm-Pascha: Oriental Comedy] in *Das Kinobuch*, edited by Kurt Pinthus, 1914
Arthur Aronymus und seine Väter (Aus Meines Geliebten Vaters Kinderjahren): Schauspiel in fünfzehn Bildern [Arthur Aronymus and His Forefathers: From My Beloved Father's Childhood Years. Play in Fifteen Scenes], first produced 1936
Ich und Ich: Eine theatralische Tragödie in sechs Akten, einem Vor- und einem Nachspiel, written 1940–41; first produced, 1979; published 1980; as *I and I*, translated by Beate Hein Bennet in *The Divided Home/Land: Contemporary German Women's Plays*, 1992

Prose with some Poetry
Das Peter Hille-Buch [The Peter Hille Book], 1906
Gesichte: Essays und Andere Geschichten [Visions: Essays and Other Tales], 1913; reprinted 1973
Der Prinz von Theben: Ein Geschichtenbuch [The Prince of Thebes: A Storybook], 1914
Der Wunderrabiner von Barcelona: Erzählung [The Miracle Rabbi of Barcelona: A Story], 1921
Ich räume auf! Meine Anklage gegen meine Verleger [I'm Cleaning Up! My Accusation Against My Publishers], 1925
"Etwas von Mir" [Something of Myself] in *Führende Frauen Europas: In 25 Selbstschilderungen. Neue Folge*, edited by Elga Kern, 1930
Arthur Aronymus: Die Geschichte meines Vaters [Arthur Aronymus: My Father's Story], 1932
Konzert [Concert], 1932
Das Hebräerland [The Land of the Hebrews], 1937
Dichtungen und Dokumente: Gedichte, Prosa, Schauspiele, Briefe, Zeugnis und Erinnerung [Literary Works and Documents: Poems, Prose, Plays, Letters, Literary Evidence and Memoirs], edited by Ernst Ginsberg, 1951

Other
Gesamtausgabe [Complete Works], 10 vols, 1919–20

Further Reading

Alker, Ernst, *Profile und Gestalten der deutschen Literatur nach 1914*, Stuttgart: Kroner, 1977
Bauschinger, Sigrid, *Else Lasker-Schüler: Ihr Werk und ihre Zeit*, Heidelberg: Stiehm, 1980
Blumenthal, Bernhardt George, "Aspects of Love in the Life and Works of Else Lasker-Schüler" (dissertation), Princeton University, 1965
Brauneck, Manfred (editor), *Autorenlexikon deutschsprachiger Literatur des 20. Jahrhunderts*, Reinbek, Hamburg: Rowohlt, 1984; 5th edition, 1995
Closs, August (editor), *Twentieth Century German Literature*, New York: Barnes and Noble, 1969
Cohn, Hans W., *Else Lasker-Schüler: The Broken World*, London: Cambridge University Press, 1974
Hedgepeth, Sonja M., *Überall blicke ich nach einem heimatlichen Boden aus: Exil im Werk Else Lasker-Schülers*, New York: Lang, 1994
Heizer, Donna K., *Jewish-German Identity in the Orientalist Literature of Else Lasker-Schüler, Friedrich Wolf, and Franz Werfel*, Columbia, South Carolina: Camden House, 1996
Hessing, Jakob, *Else Lasker-Schüler: Biographie einer deutsch jüdischen Dichterin*, Karlsruhe: Loeper, 1985
Klüsener, Erika, *Else Lasker-Schüler*, Reinbek, Hamburg: Rowohlt, 1980
Lattmann, Dieter (editor), *Die Literatur der Bundesrepublik Deutschland*, Munich: Kindler, 1973
Lorenz, Dagmar C.G., "Else Lasker-Schüler Becomes Permanently Exiled in Jerusalem" in *Yale Companion to Jewish Writing and Thought in German Culture 1096–1996*, edited by Sander L. Gilman and Jack Zipes, New Haven, Connecticut: Yale University Press
Newton, Robert P. (editor), *Your Diamond Dreams Cut Open My Arteries*, Chapel Hill: University of North Carolina Press, 1982
Robertson, Ritchie, *The "Jewish Question" in German Literature, 1749–1939*, Oxford and New York: Oxford University Press, 1999
Schmid, Michael (editor), *Else Lasker-Schüler: Ein Buch zum 100. Geburtstag der Dichterin*, Wuppertal: Hammer, 1969
Valencia, Heather, *Else Lasker-Schüler und Abraham Nochem Stenzel. Eine Unbekannte Freundschaft*, Frankfurt and New York: Campus, 1995
Yudkin, Leon I., *Else Lasker-Schüler: A Study in German Jewish Literature*, Northwood, Middlesex: Science Reviews, 1991

Else Lasker-Schüler's exile did not begin in 1933; alienation is the keynote of her persona and her poetry, and is expressed in her voluminous correspondence with acquaintances among the German intellectual and artistic avant-garde of the Weimar Republic. In her literary work this alienation manifests itself clearly in three principal themes: the poeticized dream of childhood and of the father–protector figure, the search for mystical–erotic fulfilment in love, and the quest for a Jewish identity. These are interwoven themes, and in her poetic imagery the erotic and religious impulses are inextricably linked; the human lover and God melt into each other.

Sigrid Bauschinger describes Lasker-Schüler's relationship to Judaism as "an instinctive and emotional one . . ., mystical and ecstatic". Lasker-Schüler rejected bourgeois assimilated Jewish society but, like many young Jewish intellectuals between the wars, she pursued a vision of a genuine *whole* Judaism; she was influenced by Buber's retelling of the Hasidic tales and by contact with eastern European Yiddish writers whom she met in the Romanische Cafe. It is a commonly held misapprehension that Else Lasker-Schüler despised Yiddish and the *Ostjuden*; in fact she was fascinated by the world of the eastern European Jews which in her eyes embodied an uncorrupted, unbroken Jewish identity. Her vision of Judaism combines eastern European tradition, her own eclectic oriental fantasy, and an ideal of Judeo-Christian symbiosis.

The search for a true homeland led to the creation of an inner world or fanatasy biography which had more reality for her than her "factual" biography, as in her description of herself for Kurt Pinthus's 1920 anthology *Menschheitsdämmerung* [Twilight of Humankind]: "I was born in Thebes in Egypt, even though I came into the world in Elberfeld in the Rhineland". More often the inner reality took precedence over mundane fact. She created fabulous personae for herself – Tino of Baghdad, Jussuf, Prince of Thebes – and for those she loved, and incorporated these in her writings as part of her search for a truer reality.

Else Lasker-Schüler has been called an Expressionist poet but she cannot be so easily pigeonholed. The ferment of Expressionist activity in Berlin coloured her earlier life and poetry – she published in Herwarth Walden's periodical *Der Sturm* [The Storm] and in Karl Kraus's *Die Fackel* [The Torch]. The predominant affinities are rather with Expressionist painting and symbolist poetry: she developed a language of vibrant colour reminiscent of the work of her friend Franz Marc, of key symbols – the colours blue and gold, the moon, stars, angels – which she invested with her own particular meaning, and of evocative neologisms and intricate semantic structures to express her intense vision. In her love poetry the gender roles are blurred and in poems addressed to many lovers, real or imagined, she strives for union with the beloved transcending time and space as in "Ein alter Tibetteppich" [An Old Tibetan Rug], where the souls of the lovers are woven together in the colours of the rug:

Deine Seele, die die meine liebet.
Ist verwirkt mit ihr im Teppichtibet.
Strahl in Strahl, verliebte Farben,
Sterne, die sich himmellang umwarben
[Your soul, which mine loves/ is woven with it in the rug-Tibet/ Ray within ray, infatuated colours/ Stars which wooed each other heaven-long]

In the *Hebrew Ballads* the poet, according to Ritchie Robertson, "manages to combine and universalize her various preoccupations": here the lover and the God-figure merge – in the poem "Zebaoth" the Lord of Hosts becomes a tender "Gottjüngling" [God-youth] – and both the idealized Orient and the figures of the Hebrew Bible are interpreted according to her personal vision. At the same time the ambivalent relationship of Lasker-Schüler to her Jewish identity emerges, especially in the opening poem of the cycle "Mein Volk" [My People], where the "I" is a rivulet springing from the "crumbling rock" which is the Jewish people. She cannot free herself and reach the sea because of the eternal echo within her of her people screaming to God.

The poeticization of the Jewish Orient is most vivid in *Das Hebräerland*: her Palestine is a combination of the Zionist dream and a mystical land in which romanticized Arab, Jew, and Christian live in harmony. Significantly she was unable to write when she was there, only expressing this vision from the distance of Switzerland after her first visit to Palestine.

This most sensitive of poets was also extremely perceptive to political realities, sensing earlier and with more horrifying clarity than many German Jews what lay in wait for them. Thus the story and play centred on the figure of Arthur Aronymus, her father as a child, combine fantasy with shocking brutality: the poeticized biography of her ancestors and a vision of Jewish–Christian symbiosis contrast with the pogrom and the medieval witchhunt, grotesquely acted out by children. A year later the poet fled from Nazi Germany and eventually reached the yearned for "Land of the Hebrews": the gulf between her vision of this land and the reality of exile there embittered the end of her life and gave her last poems their terrible poignancy.

The title poem of the collection *Mein blaues Klavier* [My Blue Piano], written in 1937 before Lasker-Schüler finally left Germany, is a prophetic poem of exile: the mourned homeland is seen as a world of childhood and poetry, symbolized by the blue piano which was formerly played by "Sternenhände" [star-hands], but now stands in the deserted cellar, crumbling and rat-infested. *Mein blaues Klavier* was Lasker-Schüler's first new collection of poetry for more than 20 years and in it "the great lover was slowly transformed into the great mourner". The poems are a last intense flaring of erotic passion and at the same time an elegy for her lost identity and country, though with moments towards the end where inner harmony is attained, particularly in the last lines of the poem that was read at Else Lasker-Schüler's funeral, "Ich weiss" [I know]:

Mein Odem schwebt über Gottes Fluss
Ich setze leise meinen Fuss
Auf den Pfad zum ewigen Heime.
[My breath floats over God's river -/ Quietly I place my foot/ On the path to my eternal home].

HEATHER VALENCIA

Layton, Irving

Romanian-born Canadian poet, short story writer, and essayist, 1912–

Born Irving Peter Lazarovitch in Neamtz, 12 March 1912, to Moshe Lazarovitch, scholar, and wife Keina, grocer. Emigrated with family to Canada, 1913. Studied at Baron Byng High School, Montreal, 1925–30; MacDonald College, Ste Anne de Bellevue, BSc in agriculture 1939; McGill University, MA in economics and political science 1946. Served in Canadian army, 1942–43. Married, first, Faye Lynch, 1938; divorced; second, Betty Francis Sutherland, 1946; divorced; one son, one daughter; third, Aviva Cantor, 1961; divorced; one son; fourth, Harriet Bernstein, 1978; divorced; one daughter; fifth, Anna Poitter, 1984. Lecturer, Jewish Public Library, Montreal, 1943–59; teacher, Herzaliah High School, Montreal, 1945–60; part-time lecturer, 1949–65, and poet in residence, 1965–69, Sir George Williams University, Montreal; writer in residence, University of Guelph, Ontario, 1968–69; professor of English literature, York University, Toronto, 1970–78; poet in residence, University of Ottawa, 1978, Concordia University, Montreal, 1978–81, and University of Toronto, 1981; adjunct professor and writer in residence, Concordia University, 1988–89. Co-founder and co-editor, *First Statement*, later *Northern Review*, Montreal, 1941–43; associate editor, *Contact*, and Contact Press, Toronto, 1952–54, and *Black Mountain Review*. Many awards, including Canadian Foundation Fellowship, 1957; Canada Council Award, 1959, 1963, 1967, 1968, 1973, 1979; Governor General's Award, 1959; Centennial Medal, 1967; Officer, Order of Canada, 1976; Francesco Petrarca Premio Letterario Nazionale (Italy), 1993.

Selected Writings

Poetry

Here and Now, 1945
Now is the Place: Poems and Stories, 1948
The Black Huntsman, 1951
Cerberus, 1952
Love the Conqueror Worm, 1953
In the Midst of My Fever, 1954
The Long Pea-Shooter, 1954
The Blue Propeller, 1955
The Cold Green Element, 1955
The Bull Calf and Other Poems, 1956
Music on a Kazoo, 1956
The Improved Binoculars: Selected Poems, 1956
A Laughter in the Mind, 1958; augmented edition, 1959
A Red Carpet for the Sun: Collected Poems, 1959
The Swinging Flesh, 1961
Balls for a One-Armed Juggler, 1963
The Laughing Rooster, 1964
Collected Poems, 1965
Anvil: A Selection of Workshop Poems, 1966
Periods of the Moon, 1967
The Shattered Plinths, 1968
Selected Poems, 1969
The Whole Bloody Bird (obs, aphs and pomes), 1969
Five Modern Canadian Poets, with others, edited by Eli Mandel, 1970
Collected Poems, 1971
Nail Polish, 1971
Lovers and Lesser Men, 1973
Seventy-Five Greek Poems 1951–1974, 1974
The Pole-Vaulter, 1974
Selected Poems: The Darkening Fire 1945–1968, preface by Wynne Francis, 1975
The Unwavering Eye 1969–1975, 1975
For My Brother Jesus, 1976
The Uncollected Poems, 1936–1959, 1976
Selected Poems, edited by Wynne Francis, 1977
The Covenant, 1977
The Poems of Irving Layton, edited and introduced by Eli Mandel, 1977
The Love Poems, 1978
The Tightrope Dancer, 1978
Droppings From Heaven, 1979
The Tamed Puma, 1979
There Were No Signs, 1979
For My Neighbours in Hell, 1980
The Love Poems of Irving Layton, 1980; as *With Reverence and Delight: The Love Poems of Irving Layton*, 1984
Europe and Other Bad News, 1981
A Wild Peculiar Joy: Selected Poems 1945–1982, 1982; revised edition *1945–1989*, 1989
Shadows on the Ground, 1982
The Gucci Bag, 1983
A Spider Danced a Cozy Jig, edited by Elspeth Cameron, 1984
Love Poems, 1985
Where Burning Sappho Loved, 1985
Dance with Desire: Love Poems, 1986
Final Reckoning: Poems 1982–1986, 1987
Fortunate Exile, 1987
Fornalutx: Selected Poems 1928–1990, introduced by Brian Trehearne, 1992
Il Cacciatore Sconcertato [The Baffled Hunter], translated by Francesca Valente, 1993

Play

A Man Was Killed, with Leonard Cohen, *Canadian Theatre Review*, 14 (Spring 1977)

Other

Editor, with Louis Dudek, *Canadian Poems 1850–1952*, 1952; revised edition, 1953
Editor, *Pan-ic: A Selection of Contemporary Canadian Poems*, 1958
Editor, *Poems for 27 Cents*, 1961
Editor, *Love Where the Nights Are Long: Canadian Love Poems*, 1962
Editor, *Anvil: A Selection of Workshop Poems*, 1966
Editor, *Poems to Colour: A Selection of Workshop Poems*, 1970
Editor, *I Side Up*, 1971
Engagements: The Prose of Irving Payton, edited by Seymour Mayne, 1972
Editor, *Anvil Blood: A Selection of Workshop Poems*, 1973
Editor, *New Holes in the Wall*, 1975
Editor, *Shark Tank*, 1977

Taking Sides: The Collected Social and Political Writings, edited by Howard Aster, 1977
Editor, *Handouts from the Mountain*, 1978
An Unlikely Affair: The Irving Layton–Dorothy Rath Correspondence, 1980
Translator, with Greg Gatenby and Francesca Valente, *Selected Poems*, by Georgio Bassani, 1980
Waiting for the Messiah, with David O'Rourke, 1985
Editor, *Rawprint: Concordia Poetry Workshop Collection, 1989*, 1989
Wild Gooseberries: The Selected Letters of Irving Layton, 1989
Irving Layton/Robert Creeley: The Complete Correspondence, 1990

Further Reading

Bennet, Joy and James Polson, *Irving Layton: A Bibliography 1935–1977*, Montreal: Concordia University Libraries, 1979
Cameron, Elspeth, *Irving Layton: A Portrait*, Toronto: Stoddart, 1985
Carruth, Hayden, "The Heaven-Sent Lively Ropewalker, Irving Layton", *Tamarack Review* (Spring 1966)
Doyle, Mike, "The Occasions of Irving Layton", *Canadian Literature*, 54 (Autumn 1972): 70–83
Dudek, Louis, "Layton on the Carpet", *Delta*, 9 (October–December 1959)
Francis, Wynne, "Irving Layton" in *Canadian Writers and their Works*, edited by Robert Lecker *et al.*, Toronto: ECW Press, 1985
Layton, Aviva, *Nobody's Daughter*, Toronto: McClelland and Stewart, 1982
Lund, K.A., "Satyric Layton", *Canadian Author and Bookman* (Spring 1967)
Mansbridge, Francis, *Irving Layton: God's Recording Angel*, Toronto: ECW Press, 1995
Mayne, Seymour (editor and introduction), *Irving Layton: The Poet and his Critics*, Toronto and New York: McGraw Hill Ryerson, 1978
Rizzardi, Alfredo (editor), *Italian Critics on Irving Layton: A Symposium*, Padua: Piovan, 1988
Ross, A., "The Man Who Copyrighted Passion", *Maclean's* (15 November 1965)
Skelton, Robin, "The Personal Heresy", *Canadian Literature*, 23 (Winter 1965)
Woodcock, George, "A Grab at Proteus: Notes on Irving Layton", *Canadian Literature*, 28 (Spring 1966): 5–21

To write about Irving Layton means initiating a series of endlessly deferred beginnings since no end, no final understanding or definitive summation is possible. The analysis of the poems has been long undertaken by a host of perceptive critics. The novel has been written (Aviva Layton's *Nobody's Daughter*). The biography by Elspeth Cameron, skewed and controversial, has generated the predictable flap, and Layton's autobiography, *Waiting for the Messiah*, compensates more than adequately while contributing to the memorial parallax that bedevils the "Life" of any great writer, turning it into a sequence of perpetual adjustments. The *Encyclopedia Britannica* has accomplished its work of canonization. Nobel nominations have added to the reputation. And an arsenal of revisionary estimates will be massively deployed in the coming years as time performs its work of editorial sifting, disengaging the core of truly remarkable work from the 40 to 50 volumes of Layton's prolific output.

The quality of the essential work is complex and manifold. There is the property of paradoxical candour one finds in lines like "and when I write my lying poems know I am using/ an anodyne from which the fastidious man recoils". There is the sheer magnitude of the oeuvre, which differentiates it from that of our "North American Poet[s]" easing "self-contempt by writing verse". There is the pathos of "I want to climb the highest rooftop/ in the village/ and announce to all/ that no one in it will ever die". There is the rich and empathetic Jewish sense of moral fervour mixed with compassion for suffering humanity that we find in his elegy for his mother, "For Keine Lazarovitch", or in the unforgettable "O Jerusalem", which concludes with the central question Judaism poses to its God:

> And how may we walk upon this earth
> with forceful human stir
> unless we adore you and betray?

The definitive quality of Layton's work involves what another Jew, Jacques Derrida, borrowing a term from plainsong, calls the *neume*, that species of vocalization that whiffles "between cry and speech, animal and man", a language that, in Derrida's phrase, is "uncontaminated by supplementarity", retaining in its momentum and inevitability a trace of some original plenitude that constantly recedes, eluding the critic and the imitator. It is a language that takes its origin not in contract or agreement, in the prose of our quotidian transactions, but in the irruption of the sense of festival and adoration, the "pure presence" of joy, rage, and celebration, the plunge into the conjugal amalgam of the Creation. Therefore it is, paradoxically, not a fully finished language in the sense of a medium hospitable to logical discriminations, a mere disruptive accuracy, but a language that is constantly *being born*, a pure vocalization which, as Derrida claims, "is inspired in us by God and may address only Him", uncorrupted by interval and discontinuity.

The voice of the neume, diffracted into the myriad articulations of grim lament and pure doxology, is the language of restoration, of the discovery and recovery of all that suffers the attrition of an increasingly worried, mundane, and banausic age. Layton's pivotal awareness is that we are living in a thin, demythologized time that lacks, for all its technological aplomb and its conquest of the natural world, a sense of mythic grandeur, sustaining heroism, and biblical vitality: "Runts are the problem,/ runts who long for the stride and stature/ of giants . . ." It is precisely these deficits that Layton's Muse has determined to remedy and supply. The lineage he honours and redeems goes back to Amos who confronts the monstrosities of human corruption, and to Jeremiah who resists the violent and idolatrous temper of the age in which he lives. Thus Layton deploys the neumic language of genuine poetry, which sings and curses in its festival of revival. This is

Layton's gift and calling, the source of his authority as a poet, accounting for the tone of prophetic exuberance that animates his work as it alienates a progressively empirical audience.

Irving Layton must finally be approached as a religious poet in the tradition of the Hebrew prophets, a poet nourished in the Old Testament who is self-defined in various poems as a "cringing semite" with a "hot Hebrew heart", as a "quiet madman never far from tears", as the transcendent scribe mentioned by Ezekiel who, clothed with linen and with an inkhorn at his side, accompanies the group of men with slaughter weapons in their hands. It is, after all, the scribe who is commanded to go in between the wheels of the cherubim and fill his hands with coals of fire. As Layton writes in "Esthetique", "poems that love the truth tell/ All things have value being combustible". And the source of that immense vitality lies in a kind of pluralistic élan, like his own Jehovah or "Artist-God who shapes and plays with . . . infinite variety". In Layton, the word and the event in all their multiplicity have coincided and merged to become one and the same thing, which is, after all, the meaning of the Hebrew term *davar*. Word and event, work and life struggle to encompass the entire body of the world.

Troubling as his declamatory presence may sometimes appear, no other Canadian poet has written such vital, elegiac, and comminatory poems as these, poems to discomfit "the pragmatic vegetables in their stands", poems which, for all their lyric exuberance, pack a *political* wallop, attacking both our consensual anonymity and the arrogance of ignorance. They are, finally, poems that have probed to the Schikelgruber depths of all of us, victor and victim alike.

DAVID SOLWAY

Leśmian, Bolesław

Polish poet, 1877/78–1937

Born Bolesław Lesman in Warsaw, 22 January 1877 or 12 January 1878. Mother died in his childhood; raised in Kiev. Studied at Classical Gymnasium, Kiev, until 1897; then trained as a lawyer in Kiev, graduating 1901. First poem published in *Wędrowiec*, 1895; awarded prize by Kraków modernist group Życie. Imprisoned for six months as result of membership of secret oppositional organization Oświata. Employed as clerk on Vienna–Warsaw Railway, Warsaw, 1901–03; pursued literary activities as journalist for *Chimera*, journal of *Young Poland* group. Travelled widely in Europe, especially to Paris. Married (in Paris) Zofia Wiesława Chilinska; two daughters. Made contact with Russian artistic colony formed around Konstantin Balmont. Returned to Warsaw, 1907. Co-founder, manager, and director of experimental Teatr Artystyczny, from 1911. In France again, 1912–14. Dramatic adviser to Teatr Polski, Łódź, 1916; published writings under pseudonyms "Felicjan Kostrycki" and "Jerzy Ziembolowski" in journal *Myśl Polska*. Notary in province of Hrubieszów, 1918–35; co-owner of kilim mill in Gorzeń Górny, from 1922; financial problems for remaining years, largely as result of embezzlement by employee, 1929. Elected to membership of Polish Academy of Literature, 1933. Returned to Warsaw, 1935. Died in Warsaw after heart attack, 5 April 1937.

Selected Writings

Poetry
Pieśni przemądrej Wasylisy [The Songs of Wise Vasilissa], 1906, in Russian
Sad rozstajny [The Widespread Orchard], 1912
Łąka [The Meadow], 1920
Ballady [Ballads], 1926
Napój cienisty [A Shadowy Drink], 1936
Dziejba Leśna [The Wood Fable], 1938
Mythematics and Extropy I: Selected Poems of Bolesław Leśmian, translated by Sandra Celt, 1984
W malinowym chruśniaku [In the Raspberry Bushes], 1990
Samotność i inne wiersze [Loneliness and Other Poems], 1992
Dwoje ludzieńków [Two Little People], 1993

Prose
Klechdy sezamowe [The Sesame Folktales], 1913
Przygody Sindbada Żeglarza [The Adventures of Sindbad the Sailor], 1915
Klechdy polskie [Polish Folktales], 1956
Szkice literackie z pism Bolesława Leśmiana [Literary Sketches from the Writings of Bolesław Leśmian], edited by Jacek Trznadel, 1959
Utwory rozproszone, listy [Selected Works, Letters], edited by Jacek Trznadel, 1962
Mythematics and Extropy II: Selected Literary Criticism of Bolesław Leśmian, translated by Alexandra Chciuk-Celt, 1992

Plays
Pierrot i Kolombina [Pierrot and Columbine], 1985
Skrzypek opętany [The Possessed Violinist], 1985

Translation
Edgar Allan Poe, *Niesamowite opowieści* [Weird Tales], 1914

Further Reading

Pankowski, Marian, *Leśmian: La révolte d'un poète contre les limites*, Brussels: Presses Universitaires de Bruxelles, 1967
Stone, Rochelle Heller, *Bolesław Leśmian: The Poet and His Poetry*, Berkeley: University of California Press, 1976
Trznadel, Jacek, *Twórczość Leśmiana: Próba przekroju*, Warsaw: Panstwowy Instytut Wydawniczy, 1964

Not recognized as one of the most original Polish writers of the 20th century until late in life, Bolesław Leśmian is now considered in the study of literature to be the most important symbolic poet of his country and indeed as one of the most important symbolists in world literature. He ranks alongside C. Norwid, W.B. Yeats, T.S. Eliot, P. Valéry, and R.M. Rilke.

Leśmian's literary beginnings were indeed under the aegis of modernist *Młoda Polska* [Young Poland], yet he soon moved and remained outside all the dominant literary currents, including the subsequent *Skamander* group with its rebellious city and everyday lyrics, or futurism with its language frequently detached from the rules of grammar, the "anti-poetic misbirth" (to quote Bruno Jasieński in a futurist manifesto). This is no surprise because Leśmian professed a mythopoetic conception of language, made heavy demands of the purity of the poetic word (the "holy dance" of sound and rhythm) and used the traditional verse form. Literary theory engaged Leśmian for many years, starting from the essays on rhythm, "Rhythmus als Weltanschauung" [Rhythm as a World View] in 1910 and "Bei den Quellen des Rhythmus" [At the Source of Rhythm], right to his "Traktat o poezji" [Treaty on Poetry]. Leśmian's unique linguistic art, full of neologisms, archaisms, and dialectisms and based on Ukrainian, Polish, and Russian folk literature, combines fairy-tale fantasy, dream visions, and Polish, Ukrainian, and Jewish folklore with elements of occidental philosophy from Spinoza to Heidegger. Leśmian's writing, which matured slowly and is often compared with the painting of Marc Chagall, also draws on the Kabbalistic tradition of Hasidim and is inspired by Russian symbolism and the Polish *art nouveau* of the painter S. Wyspiański. Although he could not be considered as belonging to a particular school, the links with Impressionism, Expressionism, and – in anticipation – Existentialism, i.e. to the most important intellectual currents of his time, are apparent. Alongside Leśmian's many elegiac works, his sensual lyricism, comparable to that of Adam Mickiewicz with its recurring grotesque, humouristic, and self-ironic overtones, is a surprise. He also revived the Polish style of personal, i.e. erotic poetry, for example in his cycle of poems *W malinowym chruściaku* [In the Raspberry Bushes], which reflects the experiences of his numerous love affairs.

Leśmian's literary talent clearly ran in the family: the poet and popular children's author Jan Brzechwa and the versatile man of letters Antoni Lange numbered among his relatives. One of the main themes of his poetry manifested itself even in his early volume of poetry, *Sad rozstajny* [The Widespread Orchard] – the idea of infinity, which pervades everything, and the contrast of civilization and nature. For a time, man close to nature appeared to him the ideal synthesis; yet he went further, in the tracks of Bergson's "*élan vital*", Schopenhauer, or Nietzsche, for example in his poem "Nieznanemu bogu" [The Unknown God], in which he picked out the theme of the problem of creation without God and the problem of a creator without creation: he was the "highest but yet also the poorest of all gods". Yet man too is poor and in no way omnipotent. Leśmian also examined the question of life after death in depth. Death for him is not final, and the boundaries of the realm of the dead are permeable, as in Greek and Roman mythology.

In Leśmian's works, which embrace the whole spectrum of occidental culture, Slavic tradition plays an important role. In his play *Skrzypek opętany* [The Possessed Violinist], printed posthumously, a reworking of a work previously printed under the title *Pierrot i Colombina* [Pierrot and Columbine], he replaced the figures of *Commedia dell'arte* with figures from Slavic mythology such as the forest nix (Rusałka leśna). Another feature specific to Leśmian is his dualism of purity and impurity, specifically in art. In *Skrzypek opętany*, it is the violinist Alaryel who is inspired by the nix to produce absolute music. Here, instrumental music represents purity, while the representational painting, embodied by Alaryel's lover, the portrait painter Chryza, represents impurity and indeed crime, as she murders the nix. Yet Rusałka rises from the grave to return to the realm of the dead, to where Alaryel, now playing absolute music, follows her after a snakebite. The violin, according to Leśmian, is the ideal musical instrument of symbolism.

Yet Leśmian did not remain only in the "higher" regions of literature – essays on theatre criticism, treatises on linguistic theory and poetry – but successfully incorporated material from oriental fairy tales, such as in the fantasy novel *Przygody Sindbada Żeglarza* [The Adventures of Sindbad the Sailor] or in *Klechdy sezamowe* [The Sesame Folktales]; these achieved a somewhat greater success but still did not make a breakthrough for a long time. The leading literary journals had boycotted him for many years and so he remained virtually unknown to the public at large. This only changed when, shortly before his death, he was elected to the Polish Academy of Literature together with the "Icon of Polish literature", Leopold Staff. Perhaps it was because he was highly productive in literary terms, yet was little concerned in his lifetime with making his work public, that most of his stage works have remained missing or have never been printed to this day. For this reason, Leśmian as a writer is still far from being a subject of international research.

In linguistic theory, Leśmian is linked to the "Polish Kafka", the writer Bruno Schulz. Like Schulz, Leśmian sees the word as the generative core of creation, as this distinguishes between the pure and the impure. Leśmian and Schulz are both successors to the east European Jewish tradition and it is here that the key to their work must be sought. Leśmian's work is rich in association and enigmatic; with imaginary worlds subject to constant metamorphosis on the one hand and full of miserable, tragic, misformed figures, punished by life, on the other. He identified with these, and particularly towards the end of his life, on the eve of World War II, when his pessimism gained the upper hand, Leśmian's poems revolved almost exclusively around the uncertainty and the illusory nature of earthly existence and resembled a dance of death: from the dreams came nightmares. For Czesław Miłosz, Leśmian's song is "a code, and if it is deciphered, it reveals itself in a diverse wealth of meanings", yet only a few readers outside Poland will experience this because, unfortunately, the greater part of the poetry of this writer of genius is untranslatable due to his experimental use of language.

ELVIRA GROEZINGER
translated by Karen Goulding

Levi, Carlo

Italian fiction writer, essayist, and artist, 1902–1975

Born in Turin, 29 November 1902. Studied medicine at University of Turin; graduated 1924, but never formally practised. Turned to painting (work shown in the

Expressionist "Six Painters of Turin" exhibition, 1929), literature, and politics. Helped to found and organize *Giustizia e libertà* movement, early 1930s; founded and was active in group *Oneg Shabbat*; co-editor, underground anti-fascist publication *Lotta politica*. Arrested, 1934; exiled to Grassano and Gagliano, both in Lucania, 1935–36; freed under general amnesty, 1936. Emigrated to France; returned to Italy to work with resistance movement in Florence, 1942; rearrested. Co-editor, *La Nazione del popolo*; editor, Action Party's journal *L'Italia libera*, Rome, 1945–46; frequent contributor to *La stampa*, Turin. Independent deputy, on Communist Party list, in lower house of Parliament, 1963–72. Died in Rome, 4 January 1975.

Selected Writings

Fiction

Cristo si è fermato a Eboli, 1945; as *Christ Stopped at Eboli*, translated by Frances Frenaye, 1947

L'orologio, 1950; as *The Watch*, translated by John Farrar, 1952

Other

Paura della libertà, 1946; as *Of Fear and Freedom*, translated by Adolphe Gourevitch, 1950

Le parole sono pietre: tre giornate in Sicilia, 1955; as *Words Are Stones: Impressions of Sicily*, translated by Angus Davidson, 1958

Il futuro ha un cuore antico: viaggio nell'Unione Sovietica [The Future Has an Old Heart: A Voyage in the Soviet Union], 1956

La doppia notte dei tigli, 1959; as *The Linden Trees*, translated by Joseph M. Bernstein, 1962; also as *The Two-Fold Night: A Narrative of Travel in Germany*, 1962

Un volto che ci somiglia: Ritratto dell'Italia, 1960

Tutto il miele è finito [All the Honey is Finished], 1964

Contadini e Luigini: Testi e disegni, edited by Leonardo Sacco, 1975

Coraggio dei miti: Scritti contemporanei, edited by Gigliola De Donato, 1975

Editor, *Amicizia: Storia di un vecchio poeta e di un giovane canarino*, by Umberto Saba, 1976

Carlo Levi 1928–1937, edited by Mario De Micheli, 1977

I monotipi di Carlo Levi, 1977

Levi si ferma a Firenze, edited by Carlo Ludovico Ragghianti, 1977

Quarderni a cancelli, 1979

Disegni 1920–1935, 1980

In Lucania con carlo Levi, commentary by Gino Melchiorre, 1980

L'altro mondo è il Mezzogiorno, edited by Leonardo Sacco, 1980

Carlo Levi e la Lucania: Dipinti del confino 1935–1936, 1990

È questo il "carcer tetro"?: Lettere dal carcere 1934–1935, edited by Daniela Ferraro, 1991

Further Reading

Bollettino, Vincenzo, "Carlo Levi: The Pursuit of the Essential in *Christ Stopped at Eboli*", *La Fusta*, 8/1 (1990)

De Donato, Gigliola, *Saggio su Carlo Levi*, Bari: De Donato, 1974

Falaschi, Giovanni, *Carlo Levi*, Florence: La Nuova Italia, 1978

Miccinesi, Mario, *Come leggere Cristo si è fermato a Eboli di Carlo Levi*, Milan: Mursia, 1979

Moss, Howard, "The Politics of *Cristo si è fermato a Eboli*", *Association of Teachers of Italian Journal* (Spring 1988)

Napolillo, Vincenzo, *Carlo Levi: Dall'antifascismo al mito contadino*, Cosenza: Brenner, 1984

Sirovich, Ghislana, *L'azione politica di Carlo Levi*, Rome: Il Ventaglio, 1988

Carlo Levi belonged by birth and education to the enlightened Jewish middle class of Italy: his mother was the sister of Claudio Treves, a first rank exponent of Piedmontese socialism and among the major antagonists of Mussolini within the Socialist Party. Carlo Levi thus came into contact when a child with the heart of the local socialist movement, and from his city, Turin, he absorbed – in decades which were both restless and passionate – a good deal of its anti-fascist ferment. This was the context in which Carlo Levi finished his university medical studies. He began to paint, following an inclination that was to become a career, as he had made painting the main expression of his protean personality. His political activities, which he never neglected, became progressively more intense as the fascist regime consolidated its power: as an assiduous frequenter of the anti-fascist exiles in Paris, Levi was connected with opponents of the regime like Carlo and Nello Rosselli (assassinated by hired killers in 1937), Leone Ginzburg with whom he founded and organized the movement *Giustizia e libertà* [Justice and Freedom], and various exponents of the young Jewish Turin intelligentsia and the group *Oneg Shabbat*, a Jewish organization with an anti-fascist standpoint.

The fact that he belonged to the Jewish minority was the very aspect which the fascist regime stressed when they first arrested Carlo Levi and other militants of *Giustizia e libertà*, in March 1934, and, with clear derogatory intent, spoke of "the Jewish race" and "the Jewish and Masonic demo-pluto-liberal congregation". Released in May of the same year, Levi was again arrested on 15 May 1935 and sentenced to three years' confinement in a small village, Lucania, in an isolated and backward region of southern Italy. The birth of his first book, *Cristo si é fermato a Eboli*, translated as *Christ Stopped at Eboli* in 1947, his masterpiece, is linked to this experience. It is the transfigured account of his stay in Gagliano, which he basically wrote from December 1943 to July 1944 in Florence, where he was in hiding to escape the Germans occupying the city. (The six years that had elapsed between the end of his confinement and his stay in the hiding place in Florence had been taken up by his exile in France, his joining the *Partito d'Azione* [Action Party] – an anti-fascist organization – his return to Italy and another arrest.) Thanks to a characteristic of making something positive out of every experience, however uncomfortable or painful it might be, Levi lived his state of confinement with curiosity and passion. If the years of his youth were the years of friendship with the best of the anti-fascist intellectual avant-garde, those of his confinement represented for him the beginning of his maturity: he was no longer in contact with the suffering of the politically persecuted, of the socialists whom he had helped to look for safety outside fascist Italy, but rather with an ancient suffering, that of the peasant farmers of Lucania, representatives of a civilization outside the confines of history, immobile in its backwardness because of the narrow-mindedness and disinterest of the rural petty bourgeoisie and of the state. The book is devoid of any Jewish characters, but Levi describes the role of thaumaturge or miracle worker that the farmers had assigned to him for his medical knowledge, converting him to their magic code, and he himself uses the Yiddish word *rofè*, sacred healer. In truth, in line with a rather common characteristic of Italian middle-class Jews, Levi's involvement in Judaism is rather overshadowed by his political and artistic involvement, nor has he ever spoken of himself as a Jewish writer or artist. Nevertheless, although references to his original culture are in a strict sense absent from the greater part of his books, this is not true for all of them, and above all it is difficult to trace in him any neurotic denial of his own Jewish identity. Indeed if *Paura della libertà*, translated as *Of Fear and Freedom* in 1950 – an essay in which Levi, even though he does not ever name it, produces an acute analysis of the birth of Nazi totalitarianism – is not recognizable as a Jewish book, and if in *L'orologio* (*The Watch*) – a reconstruction of the political climate the day after the liberation – the two Jewish characters make only sporadic appearances, something bluntly personal can be traced in *Il futuro ha un cuore antico: viaggio nell'Unione Sovietica* [The Future Has an Old Heart: A Voyage in the Soviet Union], and *La doppia notte dei tigli* (*The Two-Fold Night: A Narrative of Travel in Germany*). These two volumes – both accounts of travel – narrate "special" stays, while those described in *Le parole sono pietre: tre giornate in Sicilia* (*Words Are Stones: Impressions of Sicily*) and *Tutto il miele è finito* [All the Honey is Finished] stay with the theme of the South, and betray a more intimate involvement. In *The Two-Fold Night*, Levi, speaking of his travels in postwar Germany, fails to find his characteristic empathetic tone: the country remains something external for him. In his account of his journey across Russia during the era of de-Stalinization, however, he opens up in more than one passage towards an autobiography which might be termed familiar, "ethnic". Accompanied on his visit by a young Ukrainian Jew, the writer – having arrived in Kiev – informs himself about Hebrew and Yiddish literature, and wants to know if newspapers or books are printed in these languages; without being put off by the reticence of his interlocutor, he insists on asking about the old Jewish customs. But it is during lunch at the house of his guide that Levi, when he sees the food, the very same food of his childhood, *griban* (a mushroom dish), same in taste and name in Kiev as in Turin, rediscovers the full meaning of what it is to belong to something that goes back centuries: "I was thus in my own family, in my family of fifty or perhaps a hundred years earlier, or perhaps two hundred, or a thousand years earlier, who knows?"

CLARA CORONA

Levi, Primo

Italian fiction writer and essayist, 1919–1987

Born in Turin, 31 July 1919, to Cesare Levi, engineer, and wife Ester (née Luzzati). Studied at Liceo-Ginnasio D'Azeglio from 1934; University of Turin, degree in chemistry, 1941. Joined partisans in Valle D'Aosta to fight German invaders, 1943; arrested and sent to Carpi-Fossoli internment camp near Modena. Deported to Auschwitz, February 1944; worked as slave labourer at rubber factory of Buna-Monowitz (I.G. Farben, Auschwitz III). Liberated by Soviet army, 1945; after long journey through central and eastern Europe, reunited with family in Turin, October 1945. Married Lucia Morpurgo, teacher, 1947; two children. Worked as industrial chemist for SIVA (paints, enamels, synthetic resins), Settimo, Turin; retired to write full-time, 1975. Regular contributor to *La stampa*. Many awards, including Premio Campiello, 1963, 1982; Premio Bagutta, 1967; Premio Strega, 1979; Premio Viareggio, 1982; co-recipient, with Saul Bellow, of Kenneth B. Smilen Fiction Award of Jewish Museum, New York, 1985; Present Tense/Joel H. Cavior Literary Award, 1986; Prato Prize (for resistance work). Died after fall down stairwell, some postulate a suicide attempt, Turin, 11 April 1987.

Selected Writings

Collection

Opere [Complete Works], 1987–90

Fiction

Storie naturali (as Damiano Malabaila), 1967; parts translated by Raymond Rosenthal, in *The Sixth Day and Other Tales*, 1990

Vizio di forma [Structural Defect], 1971; as *The Sixth Day*, selected stories translated by Raymond Rosenthal, in *The Sixth Day and Other Tales*, 1990

Il sistema periodico, 1975; as *The Periodic Table*, translated by Raymond Rosenthal, 1984

La chiave a stella, 1978; as *The Monkey's Wrench*, translated by William Weaver, 1986; as *The Wrench*, translated by Weaver, 1987

Lilìt e altri raconti, 1981; as *Moments of Reprieve*, translated by William Weaver, 1986; also translated by Ruth Feldman, 1986

Se non ora, quando?, 1982; as *If Not Now, When?*, translated by William Weaver, 1985

Poetry

L'osteria di Brema [Brema's Inn], 1975; as *Shemà: Collected Poems*, translated by Ruth Feldman and Brian Swann, 1976

Ad ora incerta, 1984; as *At An Uncertain Hour*, in *Collected Poems*, 1988

Collected Poems, translated by Ruth Feldman and Brian Swann, 1988; revised edition, 1992 (contains previously uncollected or untranslated poems which are translated by Ruth Feldman alone)

Plays

Se questo è un uomo [If This is a Man], with Pieralberto Marché, 1966

Intervista aziendale, with Carlo Carducci, 1968

Other

Se questo è un uomo, 1947; as *If This is a Man*, translated by Stuart Woolf, 1959; as *Survival in Auschwitz: The Nazi Assault on Humanity*, translated by Woolf, 1961

La tregua, 1963; as *The Reawakening*, translated by Stuart Woolf, 1965; as *The Truce: A Survivor's Journey Home from Auschwitz*, translated by Woolf, 1965; in *If This is a Man; The Truce*, translated by Stuart Woolf, 1979; also in *Survival in Auschwitz; The Reawakening: Two Memoirs*, translated by Woolf, 1986

La ricerca della radici: antologia personale, 1981

Translator, *Il processo*, by Franz Kafka, 1983

Dialogo, with Tullio Regge, 1984; as *Conversations*, translated by Raymond Rosenthal, 1989

Translator, *Lo squalo da lontano*, by Claude Lévi-Strauss, 1984

Introduction by Levi, *Uomini ad Auschwitz*, by Hermann Langbein, 1984

Preface by Levi, *Comandate ad Auschwitz*, by Rudolf Höss, 1985

Translator, *La via della maschere*, by Claude Lévi-Strauss, 1985

L'altrui mestiere, 1985; as *Other People's Trades*, translated by Raymond Rosenthal, 1989

I sommersi e i salvati, 1986; as *The Drowned and the Saved*, translated by Raymond Rosenthal, 1988

Racconti e saggi, 1986; as *The Mirror Maker: Stories and Essays*, translated by Raymond Rosenthal, 1989

"The Memory of Offence" in *Bitburg in Moral and Political Perspective*, edited by Geoffrey H. Hartman, 1986

Autoritratto, edited by Ferdinando Camon, 1987; as *Conversations with Primo Levi*, with Ferdinando Camon, translated by John Shepley, 1989

Further Reading

Cannon, JoAnn, "Canon-Formation and Reception in Contemporary Italy: The Case of Primo Levi", *Italica*, 69/2 (1992): 30–44

Cicioni, Mirna, *Primo Levi: Bridges of Knowledge*, Oxford and Washington, DC: Berg, 1995

Epstein, Adam, "Primo Levi and the Language of Atrocity", *Bulletin for the Society of Italian Studies*, 20 (1987): 31–38

Frassica, Pietro (editor), *Primo Levi as Witness: Proceedings of a Symposium Held at Princeton University*, Fiesole: Casalini Libri, 1990

Gilman, Sander L., "Primo Levi: The Special Language of the Camps and After", *Midstream*, 35 (October 1989): 22–30

Klein, Ilona, "Primo Levi: The Drowned, The Saved, and the 'Grey Zone'", *Simon Weisenthal Annual*, 7 (1990): 77–89

Kremer, Roberta S. (editor), *Memory and Mastery: Primo Levi as Writer and Witness*, Albany, New York: SUNY, 2001

Levi-Montalcini, Rita, "Epilogue: Primo Levi's Message" in *In Praise of Imperfection: My Life and Work*, translated by Luigi Attardi, New York: Basic Books, 1988: 212–14

Murawski, John, "In Order to Tell: Primo Levi and the Subversion of Literary Language", *Prose Studies*, 14 (1991): 81–96

Ozick, Cynthia, "Primo Levi's Suicide Note" in *Metaphor and Memory*, New York: Knopf, 1989: 34–48

Patruno, Nicholas, "Primo Levi: Science and Conscience", *Italian Culture*, 10 (1992): 159–66

Patruno, Nicholas, *Understanding Primo Levi*, Columbia: University of South Carolina Press, 1995

Rudolf, Anthony, *At an Uncertain Hour: Primo Levi's War Against Oblivion*, London: Menard, 1990

Schehr, Lawrence R., "Primo Levi's Strenuous Clarity", *Italica*, 66 (1989): 429–43

Sodi, Risa, "An Interview with Primo Levi", *Partisan Review*, 54/3 (Summer 1987): 355–66

Sodi, Risa, "Primo Levi: A Last Talk", *Present Tense*, 15/4 (1987–88): 40–45

Sodi, Risa B., *A Dante of Our Time: Primo Levi and Auschwitz*, New York: Lang, 1990

Sowell, Madison U., "Survival Poetics: Primo Levi's Remembering of Dante's Ulysses", *Literature and Belief*, 18/2 (1998): 1–19

Tarrow, Susan (editor), *Reason and Light: Essays on Primo Levi*, Ithaca, New York: Center for International Studies, Cornell University, 1990

Wilde-Menozzi, Wallis, "A Piece You've Touched is a Piece Moved: On Primo Levi", *Tel Aviv Review*, 2 (Winter 1989–90): 149–65

Woolf, Judith, *The Memory of the Offence: Primo Levi's "If This is a Man"*, Market Harborough, Leicestershire, and Hull: University Texts, 1995

In his flawless and thought-provoking writing, the secular Italian Jew and scientist, Primo Levi, successfully married the sciences with the humanities. He is an author of international status for his works are universal in conception, reaching far beyond the themes of Italian Jewry. One does not do justice to Primo Levi if he is remembered exclusively as a Holocaust author because the breadth of his vision and of his knowledge cover autobiography, science-fiction, poetry, philosophical/ethical essays, realistic short stories, hypothetical-futuristic scenarios, novels, and an undying passion for chemistry.

He was born the son of a well-to-do assimilated urban Jewish family. From an early age, the boy was fascinated by the facts of science. He explained this interest later in life as probably a reaction to the fascist rhetoric which so pervaded academic studies of that time with perhaps the exception of the sciences, chemistry in particular. Thus, he chose to study chemistry to be free from the political literary demagogy that surrounded him as a young Jew during Mussolini's regime. Levi realized the extent of his Jewishness only after the infamous Italian anti-Semitic racial laws were promulgated in 1938, here accounted in *The Periodic Table*:

> In truth, until precisely those months it had not meant much to me that I was a Jew: . . . I had always considered my origin as an almost negligible but curious fact, a small amusing anomaly, like having a crooked nose or freckles.

He received his doctorate in chemistry at age 22 from the University of Turin "maxima cum laude": his degree also indicated that he was "of the Jewish race". Unable to find a job due to racial discrimination, he joined a small group of young, unskilled partisan fighters in northern Italy. They were soon betrayed and Levi was deported to Auschwitz in February 1944. During the last months of internment in the camp, he reported as a slave worker inside the rubber factory of Buna-Monowitz (I.G. Farben, Auschwitz III). Primo Levi's first published book, *Se questo è un uomo* (*If This is a Man*), recounts his ordeal in the camp. He attributed his survival to mere coincidence ("fortuna", as he puts it in Italian), to a smattering of German learned at school – which enabled him to a certain extent to understand orders barked in German, and to the help of the civilian Italian worker, Lorenzo Perrone, who unselfishly and at great personal risk smuggled food into the camp for Levi and other prisoners.

Primo Levi's prose and style reflect his training as a scientist: his sentences are crystalline, terse, concise, focused. He bears unbiased testimony to the events witnessed in Auschwitz with emotional detachment and dispassionate descriptions, detailing minute events. It might be this aspect of Levi's writing that makes him such a powerful author. Levi's biographical works are memorable because, being objectively narrated, they ask for implicit judgement. In his later works, Levi becomes somewhat more explicit in assessing specific political and moral culpability, notably in *The Drowned and the Saved*. Some 40 years after his concentration camp ordeal, this volume examines the aftermath of some of the most difficult traumas facing a camp survivor: "The Memory of the Offence", "Useless Violence", "Shame", the hardships of "The Intellectual in Auschwitz", and a brilliant analysis of what Levi defines as "The Grey Zone", treating the role of small-fish Nazi officers vs. so-called privileged Jewish prisoners within the camp's hierarchical structure.

Notable among Levi's other works is *The Truce*, Levi's own narrative of the long journey which brought him home to Turin after being liberated from Auschwitz. Unlike *If This is a Man*, written by Levi's own admission in "order of urgency" to recount his story, *The Truce* was penned in the vein of a picaresque novel for autobiographical literary enjoyment. Levi's third book is the collection of science-fiction short stories written under the pseudonym of Damiano Malabaila (*Storie naturali*). Some of these short stories have been translated into English and can be found in *The Sixth Day and Other Tales*. With futuristic acumen, Levi describes technology which today is commonly used (word processors, for instance, or virtual-reality visual caps) but which was unheard of in the 1960s. His volume of short stories and essays *Vizio di forma* [Structural Defect] looks at the world and at humankind as an ecosystem which holds a dark side to it, a resigned (but not necessarily pessimistic) overview of life's dynamics.

Until 1975, Primo Levi managed a varnish factory (Siva) near Turin during the day and spent his evenings writing. After retirement, he fulfilled his dream of becoming a full-time author. His first work published after retiring is *The Periodic Table*. Together with *If This is a Man* and *The Drowned and the Saved*, *The Periodic Table* established international readership for Primo Levi. The book moves chronologically, following in a general manner Levi's own life experience. The titles of its chapters were taken from chemical elements of Mendeleev's chemical periodic table. In the chapter entitled "Iron", Primo Levi equated the chemical periodic table to a literary solemn poem containing its own rhyme scheme. One only needs to learn how to read it to fully appreciate it.

The 1970s were politically particularly dishevelled times for Italy (Red Brigades, extreme-right terrorist attacks, "historical compromise" between the demo-Christians and the communists, the assassination of Prime Minister Aldo Moro) with the trade unions acquiring much power. In 1978, Levi published *The Monkey's Wrench*, recounting the imaginary vicissitudes of skilled blue-collar Libertino (Tino) Faussone, an Italian worker specializing in cranes and giant derricks, who enjoys the precision required in his trade. Levi's novel partially reflects the economic and demographic complexities of the working-class vindications of the time. Levi's first novel proper, *If Not Now, When?*, required that he study Yiddish and the history of Jewish eastern European Ashkenazi partisans during World War II. In this book, Levi described in vivid detail the hopes and defeats of these underground fighters, a life which he himself never experienced, having been arrested after his own brief stint with an Italian partisan group.

A literary portrait of Primo Levi cannot be complete until one reads his volume of poetry *Ad ora incerta*. Unlike his prose, which is reporter-like, dispassionate, equanimous, and emotionally detached, his verse is pessimistic, dark, haunting ghosts suffocating him. His terror coming to the surface, Levi the poet shows a completely different literary persona, that of a man deeply wounded by life's events. Whether Levi took his own life or whether he accidentally fell to his untimely death on the morning of 11 April 1987, posterity will never know. The truth is, the circumstances of his death are simply too ambiguous to tell one way or another.

When Primo Levi died, the world lost a magnificent writer, a man of great moral integrity who bridged the purported gap between science and literature, an intellectual whose skilled authorship was recognized worldwide, a Jew for whom the microcosm was never more important than humanity's overall macrocosmic vision. Primo Levi remains one of the few true humanists of the 20th century.

ILONA KLEIN

Levin, Hanoch

Israeli dramatist, satirist, short story writer, and poet, 1943–1999

Born in Tel Aviv, 18 December 1943 to an immigrant Polish Jewish family. Studied Philosophy and Hebrew Literature at Tel Aviv University. First success with 1968 cabaret, *You and Me and the Next War*. Resident playwright at Cameri Theatre, Tel Aviv, for ten years. Married three times; four children. Worked with Habima, Israel's National Theatre. Received numerous theatrical awards in Israel and abroad, including first prize at 1978 Edinburgh Festival for *Ya'akobi and Leidental*; Leah Porat Prize, 1983; Meskin Prize, 1984; Bialik Prize, 1995. Died in Tel Aviv, 18 August 1999.

Selected Writings

Plays
At vaani vehamilhamah habaah [You and Me and the Next War], 1968
Ketchup, 1969
Solomon Grip, 1969
Malkat ambatiah [The Queen of the Bathtub], 1970
Hefetz, 1972; translated as *Hefetz*, 1980
Yaakovi veleidental, 1972; as *Ya'akobi and Leidental: A Play with Songs*, translated by Dennis Silk and Shimeon Levy, 1979
Neurei vardale [Vardale's Youth], 1974
Shits, 1974
Krum, 1975
Popper, 1977
Soharei hagumi, 1978; translated as *The Rubber Merchants*, 1983
Halvayah horpit [Winter Funeral], 1978
Hotsaa lahoreg [The Execution], 1979
Yesurei yov [Job's Passion], 1981; translated as *The Sorrows of Job*, 1993
Hapatriot [The Patriot], 1982
Hazonah hagdolah mibavel [The Great Whore of Babylon], 1982
Orzei mizvadot, 1982; as *The Suitcase Packers*, translated by the Israeli Centre of International Theatre Institute, 1984
Yakish vepuptshe [Yakish and Poupche], 1982
Hanashim haavudiot mitroya [The Lost Women of Troy], 1983
Kulam rotsim lihiot [Everybody Wants to Live], 1985
Nikhna umenutsakh [Beaten and Defeated], 1988
Mlekhet hahayim [The Labour of Life], 1988
Hefetz veaherim [Hefetz and Other Plays], 1988
Mahazot [Plays], 1988
Soharei hagumi veaherim [The Rubber Merchants and Other Plays], 1988
Yesurei yov veaherim [Job's Passion and Other Plays], 1988
Hagigolo mikongo [The Gigolo of the Congo], 1989
Hamitlabet [The Hesitator], 1990
Hops vehopla [Hops and Hopla], 1991
Mlekhet hahayim veaherim [The Labour of Life and Other Plays], 1991
Hayeled holem [The Child Dreams], 1993
Haishah hamuflaa betokhenu [The Wonderful Woman Inside Us], 1994
Peurei peh [Mouth Open], 1995
Hazonah miohaio veaherim [The Whore from Ohio and Other Plays], 1995
Kritat rosh [Beheading], 1996
Mishpat ones veaherim [Rape Trial and Other Plays], 1997
Retsah [Murder], 1998
Haholkhim bahoshekh [Those Who Walk in the Darkness], 1998
Hashkavah [Requiem], 1999
Hamitabel lelo kets veaherim [The Perpetual Mourner], 1999
Haneehazim veaherim [To Hold On and Never Let Go], 1999
Haholkhim bahoshekh veaherim [Those Who Walk in the Darkness and Other Plays], 1999
Hashkavah veaherim [Requiem and Other Plays], 1999
The Whiners, produced posthumously, 2000

Short Stories
Haholeh hanitshi vehaahuvah [The Eternal Invalid and the Beloved], 1986
Ish omed meahorei ishah yoshevet [A Man Stands behind a Seated Woman], 1992
Hagigolo mikongo vetipusim aherim [The Gigolo from Congo and Other Characters], 1994

Poetry
Hayaldah haiutah roah mamutah [The Happy, Cheerful Cock], 1999
Shirei hametim [Songs of the Dead], 1999

Other
Masah hadod max [Uncle Max's Journey], 1982
Ma ikhpat latsipor [What Does the Bird Care: satire], 1987
Collected Works (in Hebrew) 16 vols, 1988

Further Reading

Abramson, Glenda, *Drama and Ideology in Modern Israel*, Cambridge and New York: Cambridge University Press, 1998
Handelzalts, Mikhael, *Hanokh Levin:'al-pi darko*, Tel Aviv: Yediot Ha-aharonot, Sifre hemed, 2001
Laor, Yitzhak, *Anu Kotvim Otakh Moledet*, Tel Aviv: Hakibuts hameuhad, 1995
Oz, Avraham, "Dried Dreams and Bloody Subjects: Body Politics in the Theatre of Hanoch Levin", *JTD*, 1 (1995)
Taub, Michael (editor), *Modern Israeli Drama in Translation*, Portsmouth, New Hampshire: Heinemann, 1993

Hanoch Levin began his career as a playwright shortly after the 1967 war, writing bitter political reviews that attacked Israeli politics and national euphoria following the occupation of the territories (for example, *You and Me and the Next War* (1968); *Ketchup* (1969); *The Queen of the Bathtub* (1970) The latter, especially, shocked the public so much, that the Cameri Theatre stopped its run following fierce attacks in the press and physical assaults on the actors.

Except for one later political review (*The Patriot*, 1982, following the Israeli invasion to Lebanon), Levin reverted in the second phase of his dramatic work to full-length plays, exposing grotesquely the vain ambitions underlying human conduct, the absurdity of human existence. His heroes are normally small people who mercilessly compete with others on the portions of success bourgeois life allows them: marriage, own apartment and (especially) sexual conquests (notably *Hefetz*; *Ya'akobi and Leidental*; *Shits*; *Krum*; *Popper*; *The Rubber Merchants*; *The Suitcase Packers*; *The Labour of Life*; and *The Hesitator*). The aspirations and desires of Levin's characters are mostly visually located rather than temporal: from possessing a marital status or obtaining another version of possession, through the discharge of sexual tension according to the routine decreed by one's hierarchical position ("stinking in bed" with the wife, going to a prostitute, masturbating with a magazine), to dreaming to "roll like a ball under the cupboard". Time, grasped in its age-old metaphorical capacity as an instrument of decay and ruin, has no positive function for human existence. Its working is accounted for in the bodily terms usually appropriated in Levin's work to expel any romantic shade from sexual touch: "time kneads". The only potential progression reserved for humanity is a move on the scale of hierarchy, the spatial aspect of social life, a move the major property of which is topographical rather than dynamic. Hierarchy is the desired disparity of the social phases of material existence, measured by calculated units of social prestige, which is why Levin's characters permanently engage in social and ontological gerrymandering. Being placed somewhere within the recognized span of hierarchy is what keeps man going in the world: whatever that place may be, it is one's token of identity, the fulfilment of the major strife in which humanity is engaged. It is the awareness of this placement that is the antidote for anarchy, and since Levin does not care much for the dividing line between the conscious and the unconscious in constructing his dramatic subjects, anarchy counters all forms of subjective orientation. It is, therefore, that kind of shattering anarchy that forms the greatest danger for Levin's subjects, threatening to exclude them from any kind of order which would safeguard their stable position (whether happy or pitiful) in the hierarchy. Temporal changes threaten the constancy of placement. Therefore they are willingly transformed into bodily cycles, be they related to the corporeal body or the communal one. The body is all, for it is the signifier of place informed by hierarchical value. Since the power relations informing the Levinian universe are never manifestly governed by any providential overseer, the binarities furnishing them are exclusively appropriated by human struggles, involving winners and losers, rich and poor, man and woman. It is this latter relation that predominates in most of Levin's plays, and it is of a complex structure in the deployment of its victor–victim binary. Levin's bodily discourse is not produced from a point of indifference representing an ungendered humanity. Rather it is heavily bound to distinctly male perspectives on subjectivity. Women may be accorded a high position on the hierarchical scale of power in the plays, but there is always a higher male link in the chain of command, whether present on the scene, or assumed. One notable property of culture and the world as constituted from the male point of view is an overriding desire for totality, whether in happiness or at least in utter misery. It is in totality, the highlight point of hierarchy, where utmost pleasure lies, and whose humblest qualification is the minimalist dictum coyly, yet emphatically, pronounced by the humiliated Floch: "I do exist!" – the least assertion of identity. Woman, from that vantage, represents the ritual enactment of external danger: she threatens man by reminding him of his own vulnerable nature as inscribed first and foremost in his fallible body. Devoid of the domineering phallic agency of sexual desire, woman is the eternal other, the object of male erotic fantasies.

Although often accused by critics of turning almost apolitical after abandoning his early political cabarets, both historically and structurally, Levin's lifelong dramatic strategy originated in his early satirical practice. His satirical idiom was considered the highlight of his original and influential contribution to the Hebrew theatre. From the early stages of his dramatic work, Levin was an ardent critic of the heightened rhetoric and imagery produced by Zionist ideology to adorn reality by heroic narratives, and worship the myth of the "new Jew", the Israeli-born "tsabar". It was that tradition onto which Levin's post-1967 satire intruded. Levin responded fiercely to the aestheticization of politics by ideological romanticism from the very start of his theatrical writing by displacing objects of national pride (cannons and military aircraft, set biographies and privileged individuals, the halo of warriors and rejection of unbecoming, "squeamish" sentiments) and disintegrating their pretence. Rather than adopting the set strategies of characterization and narrative construction developed by his predecessors, Levin's satirical method combines subversive parody with black humour, a palpable hit at the soft belly of an entire myth. In a combination of a biting parody and a frightening image of the callous, nightmarish travesty the Zionist dream of the "new Jew" has become by ignoring the other, Levin produces a devastating critique of what may be regarded as "the white mythology" of Zionist subjectivity. In a powerful reversal of the mythmaking of the Zionist project, Levin reverts the "tsabar" into his allegedly squeamish diasporic predecessors.

A third phase of Levin's work carries his theatre of cruelty to the cosmic dimensions of mythological parables, in which humans are squeezed into their bodily and spiritual elements by the painful presence of imminent destruction and death, notably: *The Execution*; *The Sorrows of Job*; *The Great Whore of Babylon*; *The Lost Women of Troy*; *Everybody Wants to Live*; *Beaten and Defeated*; *The Child Dreams*; *Mouth Open*; *Beheading*; *Those Who Walk in the Darkness*. In *Murder* he enhances his perspective on 30 years of bloodshed in the Middle East since his dramatic writing began, into a shuddering political parable. *Requiem*, written and produced while a terminal disease was conquering his body, is, like his last book of poetry published in the same year, a sad, passionate, and powerful account of, and resignation to, imminent death. Levin's fame as Israeli theatre's greatest satirist remains, with 50 plays, 34 of which were performed on stage.

AVRAHAM OZ

Leyvik, H.

Russian-born US poet and dramatist, 1888–1962

Born Leyvik Halpern in Igumen, Belorussia, 1888. Became active in Jewish socialist movement, the Bund; arrested, freed, and rearrested during first Russian revolution, 1906; refused defence counsel at trial; two years hard labour in Butyrka transit prison, Moscow, 1906–08; then exiled to Siberia for life. Escaped and settled in United States, 1913. Married Sara Sulman, 1916; two sons. Worked in sweatshop and as paperhanger. Returned to Europe, 1925. Contracted tuberculosis, beginning of 1930s; in sanatorium for four years. Issued literary anthologies, *Zamlbikher*, with Joseph Opatoshu, 1936; published poems and articles in Yiddish daily *Der tog*. Spent three months in Palestine, 1937. Awarded honorary doctorate of Yiddish literature, Hebrew Union College, 1958. Received Medal of Honor of National Jewish Welfare Board, for services to American Jewish culture, 1961. Died in 1962.

Selected Writings

Poetry
Di keytn fun meshiakh [The Chains of the Messiah], 1907–08
Hintern shlos [Behind the Lock], 1918
Der volf [The Wolf], 1920
Dortn, vu di tseder [There, Where the Cedars], 1938
Ergets vayt [From Somewhere Afar], 1940
Oyf di vegn sibires [On the Roads of Siberia], 1940
Ikh bin nisht geven in treblinka [I Was Not in Treblinka], 1945
A blat af an eplboym [A Leaf on an Apple Tree], 1953
Lider tsum eybikn [Poems to Eternity], 1959

Plays and Verse Dramas
Der goylem [The Golem], 1921
Shmates [Rags], 1921 (published 1922)
Andersh [Different] (in manuscript), *c.*1922
Bankrot [Bankrupt], 1923 (published 1927)
Di oreme melukhe [The Poor Kingdom], 1923 (published 1927)
Shap [Shop], 1926 (published 1928)
Keytn [Chains], 1929
Hirsh lekert, 1931
Sdom [Sodom], written 1933–36 (published 1937)
Di geule komedie–der goylem khulemt [The Redemption Comedy–The Golem Dreams], 1934
Hitler nekht-motivn [Hitler Night-Motifs], 1937
Der poet iz gevorn blind [The Poet Became Blind] in *Zamlbikher*, vol. 3, 1938
Der nes in geto [The Miracle in the Ghetto] (in manuscript), 1940
The MaHaRaM of Rothenburg, 1944
Khasene in fernvald [Wedding in Fernwald], 1949
In di teg fun yoyv [In the Days of Job], 1953

Other
Mit der sharis-hapleyte [With the Saved Remnant], 1947

Further Reading

Leksikon fun der nayer yidisher literatur [Biographical Dictionary of Modern Yiddish Literature], vol. 5, New York: Alveltlekhn Yidishn Kultur-Kongres, 1963
Liptzin, Solomon, *A History of Yiddish Literature*, New York: Jonathan David, 1972
Madison, Charles A., *Yiddish Literature: Its Scope and Major Writers*, New York: Ungar, 1968
Vayner, Gershon (editor), *Shtudies in Leyvik* [Studies in Leivick], Ramat Gan: Bar Ilan University, 1992
Waldman, Moshe-Shim'on (compiler), *H. Leyvik zamlbukh* [Leyvik Anthology], Paris: World Jewish Cultural Congress in France, 1963
Waxman, Meyer, *A History of Jewish Literature*, vol. 4, New York: Yoseloff, 1960

Leyvik was hailed as a prophet, but as he himself quoted: "*Nibah, veainu yadah mah nibah*" [He prophesied, and did not know what he prophesied]. Described as the conscience of his generation, he had an uncompromising honesty and a willingness to accept suffering. This was clearly demonstrated in his refusal in 1906 to deny his desire to overthrow the czarist system, in order to lighten his prison sentence. He saw his poems as a direct reflection of all the conflicts within his personality as well as of the conflicts between the Jew and the world. Briefly, in New York, he flirted with the *Inzikhistn* (the Introspectivists), who sought to reject national and social themes, in favour of the purely personal in their poetry, but this was clearly alien to his sensibility. Yet, the grinding poverty of his own childhood was to remain fixed in his poetic imagination, bringing with it a deep personal wound and sense of humiliation. As a child, he bore an intense sense of compassion for the suffering of the silent, which he described in *A blat af an eplboym* [A Leaf on an Apple Tree]. His four-year-old sister, two years younger than him, endured a painfully slow death in her cradle-grave (*keyver-vigl*), after she was accidentally burned.

The messianic idea was the hope to escape from Jewish suffering in exile, and was at the centre of the Jewish religious imagination. It was also at the centre of his poetry. His messiah was in chains (see *Di keytn fun meshiakh* [Chains of the Messiah] written 1907–08 while he himself was in chains in Minsk), and this proved an apt metaphor for the Jewish condition as he depicted it. Though not traditionally religious, for him writing a poem was like praying, and traditional religious themes were staples of his poetry. The pogroms in Ukraine after World War I, described in the poem *Der volf* [The Wolf] in 1920, were contemporary manifestations of the destruction of Jerusalem. The poet, himself, was the burning bush:

> The world enfolds me with barbed fingers
> and carries me to the fire, and carries me to the pyre;
> I burn and I burn and I am not consumed —
> I raise myself up again and I stride on.

A key theme for Leyvik was the reversal of roles, when the oppressed became the oppressor, the area where ideals become corrupted, and goodness and evil seem to merge. *Der goylem* [The Golem] has to be destroyed by his creator, Rabbi Löw, when the attempt to create a better world ends in a nightmare. All this starts with rebellion against an unjust world or, as with his play *In di teg fun yoyv* [In the Days of Job] against an unjust God. In *Di keytn fun meshiakh*, the Angel Ezriel rejects his role as God's messenger and seeks to become human. He cannot praise God while there is so much human suffering, and he wants to go to earth to work there for its salvation. In difficult times, the patience of the Jews evaporates and leads to the false Messiah (*kemo meshiakh*). The resurrected golem in *Di geule komedie–der goylem khulemt* [The Redemption Comedy–The Golem Dreams], loosely based on Dante's *Divine Comedy*, replaces the true Messiah, who retreats from the world in self-disgust. The reference to the Soviet Union is made clear here, as in the earlier *Der goylem*. It took his visit there in 1925 to clarify his disillusion. Nevertheless, Leyvik did not stop writing for the communist newspaper, *Der frayhayt* [Freedom] until 1929, when he labelled the communists who defended the Arab attacks on the Jews of Hebron as "*fareter*" [traitors], and wrote his drama *Keytn* [Chains]. Leyvik's commitment to the left had remained consistent in plays such as *Shmates* [Rags], *Bankrot* [Bankrupt], *Di oreme melukhe* [The Poor Kingdom], and *Shap* [Shop]. These realistic dramas, concerned with issues of social justice, were staged in New York fairly soon after they were written, but the symbolic poetic drama *Der goylem*, surely Leyvik's most famous work, which is still performed in repertoire, had to wait ten years for its first performance there.

In the 1930s, the rise of the Nazis displaced the preoccupation with the Soviet Union. In *Sdom* [Sodom], the city dedicated to evil is clearly Nazi Germany, and in *Hitler nekht-motivn* [Hitler Night-Motifs] Leyvik foresaw slaughter. For Leyvik, there had been a continuity, a familiarity in Jewish suffering until the Holocaust, and it was clear that he was trying to come to terms with an unprecedented experience. In his play, *The MaHaRam of Rothenburg*, Leyvik sought to invoke the Talmudist, Rabbi Meir ben Barukh of Rothenburg (imprisoned by Holy Roman Emperor in 1286), to give moral support to Daniel, a Jewish inmate of Dachau. Yet, the Emperor deprived the MaHaRaM of his freedom, while the Nazis deprived the Jews of their humanity. To make the comparison more viable in his play, the Duke who imprisons the MaHaRam tortures him to death.

So haunted was Leyvik by his sense of the inadequacy of words to express the tragedy of human suffering, and in particular that of the Holocaust, words which seemed to him to distort reality, that he strove to make his poetry less smooth, less aesthetically satisfying. The poet who had not directly suffered could not adequately describe the event and, moreover, lacked the moral right to do so. In *Ikh bin nisht geven in treblinka* [I Was Not in Treblinka], he wrote: "I know that now is not the time for sonnets, now is the time for canons and tanks", but silence was no alternative, since there were even more silent victims to whom a voice would have to be given. After visiting displaced persons camps Europe in 1946, he published his diary, *Mit der sharis-hapleyte* [With the Saved Remnant], and portrayed this experience in *Khasene in fernvald* [Wedding in Fernwald, 1949].

While embracing the idea of the return to Zion, Leyvik could not identify with the physical Land of Israel. Real, as opposed to ideological, homelessness was central to his creative identity. He made a positive attempt to identify with the Land during his three visits in 1937, 1950 and in 1957, when he was acclaimed on all sides. But, in his cycle of poems written after the first visit, *Dortn, vu di tseder* [There, Where the Cedars] there is a reticence at the Western Wall in Jerusalem: "I want to touch you with my fingers/ - and/ I don't touch". His honesty prevented him from uttering false notes, and on his last visit to Israel he warned against feelings of moral superiority by Israelis over Jews of the Diaspora, and against negative views of Yiddish.

Nevertheless, in his last collection of poems, *Lider tsum eybikn* [Poems to Eternity] there was a note of reconciliation towards Israel, and also towards God, and finally, perhaps, with himself:

> I don't say that my life is a mistake
> It's just that I talk like a tightrope walker
> Talking and singing to himself over the deep abyss,
> As if there was a bridge under his feet.

BARRY DAVIS

Liberman, Serge

Soviet-born Australian short story writer, editor, essayist, translator, and bibliographer, 1942–

Born in Fergana, Uzbekistan, 14 November 1942, to Abram Jacob Liberman, maker of kvass, and wife Regina (née Minski), seamstress; both later fruiterers and delicatessen owners. Spent year in Ziegenhain displaced persons camp, 1946. Moved to Paris, 1947. Emigrated to Australia, 1951; settled in Melbourne; naturalized, 1956. Studied at Melbourne University, from 1962, MBBS 1967. First story published in *Speculum*, medical students' journal; youth leader in Ichud Habonim movement; editor of *Situations*, 1964, *Venture*, 1965. Married Eva Matzner, 1969; divorced, 1991; three children. Junior doctor at Prince Henry's Hospital, Melbourne, and Tel Hashomer Hospital, Israel, 1968–71; registrar, Prince Henry's Hospital, 1971–74. Private medical practice in Melbourne since 1974. Life companion Anna Mow, from 1995. Editor, English section of bilingual (English and Yiddish) literary journal, *Melbourne Chronicle*, 1977–84 and 1991–96; literary editor, *Menorah: Journal of the Australian Association of Jewish Studies*, 1984–87; associate editor, later corresponding editor, *Outrider: Journal of Australian Multicultural Literature*; member of editorial board, *Australian Jewish Historical Society Journal*, 1985–96; literary editor, *Australian Jewish News*, 1987–99; member of editorial committee, *Gesher: The Journal of the Victorian Council of Christians and Jews* since 1992. Vice President, PEN Melbourne Centre, 1986–87. Many awards, including Zionist Federation of Australia Short Story Award, 1975; Alan Marshall Manuscript Award, 1978, 1979, 1981; New South Wales Premier's and New South Wales Ethnic Affairs Commission Literary Award, 1985.

Selected Writings

Short Stories
On Firmer Shores, 1981
A Universe of Clowns, 1983
The Life That I Have Led, 1986
The Battered and the Redeemed, 1990
Voice From the Corner, 1999

Other
A Bibliography of Australian Judaica, 1987; revised and updated edition, 1991

Essays
"Australian Jewish Fiction Since World War Two", *Jewish Book Annual: The American Year Book of Jewish Literary Creativity*, 42 (1984–85)
"Jewish Writing in Australia", *Writing in Multicultural Australia 1984: An Overview*, 1985
"Gentile Companions of Jews in Australia" in *Jews in the Sixth Continent*, edited by W.D. Rubinstein, 1987
"Alongside the Education, the Learning: Jewish Literacy – One Perspective" in *Reinventing Literacy: The Multicultural Imperative*, edited by David Myers, 1995
"Pan Populi: Multicultural Writing in Australia in the 1990s", *Lesen und Schreiben: Literatur, Kritik, Germanistik: Festschrift für Manfred Jurgensen zum 55. Geburtstag*, edited by Volker Wolf, 1995
"Koheleth – A Secular View", *Gesher: The Official Journal of the Council of Christians and Jews*, 2/2 (1999)

Further Reading

Ballyn, Susan, "How Firm the Shores?, Serge Liberman and the Migrant Experience", address presented at *Modern Jewish Literature Symposium*, Perth, July 6–9, 1998
Berger, Alan L., "'From Theology to Morality', Post-Auschwitz *Tikkun Olan* in the Stories of Serge Liberman", *Australian Journal of Jewish Studies*, 9/1–2 (1995)
Corkhill, Annette Robyn, *Australian Writing: Ethnic Writers 1945–1991*, Melbourne: Academia Press, 1994
Hart, Alexander, "Writing the Diaspora: A Bibliography and Critical Commentary on Post-Shoah English-Language Jewish Fiction in Australia, South Africa, and Canada" (PhD dissertation), University of British Columbia, 1996
Houbein, Lolo (editor), *Ethnic Writings in English from Australia: A Bibliography*, Adelaide: University of Adelaide, 1984
Lumb, Peter and Anne Hazell, *Diversity and Diversion: An Annotated Bibliography of Australian Ethnic Minority Literature*, Richmond, Victoria: Hodja Educational Resources Cooperative, 1983
Morera de al Vaal, Elisa, "The Elusive Land of Milk and Honey" in *A Spanish Sampler of Australian Studies*, edited by Susan Ballyn, Barcelona: Promociones y Publicaciones Universitarias, 1996
Pierce, Peter (editor), *The Oxford Literary Guide to Australia*, Melbourne and New York: Oxford University Press, 1987
Rubinstein, Hilary L., *Chosen: The Jews in Australia*, Sydney and Boston: Allen and Unwin, 1987
Rubinstein, Hilary L., *The Jews in Australia: A Thematic History*, vol. 2, Port Melbourne, Victoria: Heinemann, 1991

Serge Liberman is one of Australia's finest Jewish writers, and an important voice in contemporary Australian literature more generally. The stories focus on a very specific ethnic constituency, yet the best of them – and many are very fine – possess the philosophical breadth and the emotional range of formidable literary art. Liberman is an accomplished narrative craftsman. He has an urgent, sinewy prose style that is particularly attuned to the expression of intense emotional states and flights of metaphysical speculation. The stories contain a rich array of memorable human figures, the overwhelming majority of them Jews who have come to an uneasy accommodation with their pasts and with their adoptive Australian culture. Liberman is a master of dramatic tempo. The typical rhythm of the tales is one in which a pained but ethically sentient protagonist arrives at a moment of transformative crisis or recognition. Many of the endings are grim; but some are profoundly affirmative. In these a state variously characterized as "prayer", "love", or "understanding" – a kind of secular Jewish equivalent of grace – comes to suffuse the consciousness of the central character. Liberman's signature narrative mode, unique in Australian writing, is a form of speculative but sociologically grounded and psychologically penetrating realism – a mode indebted to Chekhov, Dostoevskii, Sholem Aleichem, Y.L. Perets, Nahman of Bratslav, Isaac Bashevis Singer, Saul Bellow, Bernard Malamud, and others. In another, though related, register Liberman writes a type of allegory that is reminiscent of Nathaniel Hawthorne.

"The Story Teller" charts some of the main lines of Liberman's artistic development. In particular, it identifies the ethnic constituency about which he generally writes: middle, lower middle, and working class Australian Jews of eastern European origin who have survived or fled the Holocaust, and who, "battered" and traumatized, have sought a new life in, as one of his characters puts it, "this paradise that in your atlas is called Australia". In fact, the Australia of Liberman's stories, while offering "firmer shores" in some respects, is often a lot less than paradisal: parents experience the anxieties of adjustment; children encounter anti-Semitism. In a pattern that is all too familiar in post-Holocaust Jewish writing, the children of Holocaust survivors take on an immense legacy of pain: pain as the knowledge of the Holocaust dawns; pain at the anguish they see in their parents, whether because the parents (and others) speak of the past, or because they do not; pain at having to balance loyalty to their eastern European Jewish heritage, on the one hand, and the need – the yearning – to assimilate, on the other. There are other familiar patterns: distress at the prospect of children "marrying out"; the enormous difficulty of maintaining faith – in particular, traditional religious belief – "after Auschwitz"; difficulties in being able to give, to trust, to connect present and past manifestations of the self, to forgive, to love.

And yet, there *is* a redemptive dimension in many of the stories. In "Messiah in Acland Street", a man pays a writer a compliment that applies equally well to Liberman's writings:

> What is constant in your work, though . . . what is constant is how man stands always at the centre of your world, how it is in man that you place your highest trust, and how it is his sanctity that you prize, and his genius, his innate goodness, his diversity and great potential.

Liberman's work expresses a form of post-Holocaust Jewish humanism: chastened by the knowledge of evil, rationalistic in its drive to understand and intervene in an immensely threatening world, chary of orthodox transcendental belief, yet committed to the value and the virtue of the human individual, to the salving power of cultural tradition, and to a spiritual dimension in which the ordinary is transfigured, infused with heightened significance. In some of these stories the spiritual intensity of the shtetl, and many of its traditional literary character types, are transplanted to the suburbs of Melbourne. The principal article of faith in this humanistic creed is the notion of love. Not an unworldy, ethereal love; rather, the tougher kind that comes through yearning, pain, experience, emotional openness, forgiveness, the soul's troubled ascension to a higher ethical plane. Many of his characters come to know "the grandeur and the helplessness, the ecstasy and the brutality, the exultation and the devastation of love".

The ethical impulse, the drive to know how a life should be lived in the here and now, that runs so deep in Jewish sensibility, is everywhere apparent in these stories. They are seldom prescriptive or reductive about personal conduct. The best of them open out complex moral situations in a way that deeply engages the heuristic powers of art. "The Promise" is a case in point. An Australian Jew returns to Warsaw and meets his former fiancée from whom he was separated at the time of the uprising. They meet in the city square, but 50 years after their promise to meet there had been thwarted by the chaos of the uprising. The man, Shimen, would have the woman, Hana, come to Australia with him now, after all these years. She refuses, saying, among other things: "I have what I have . . . and what I have I have". In the aftermath of the Holocaust she has settled into a modest but meaningful way of life. The now distant promise is annulled by what has happened, and the commitments, the promises, that structure her present life. The story is a profound and profoundly moving creative inquiry into the nature of one of human kind's most distinctive and necessary ethical practices – promising. "The Promise" is fine narrative art by any standard.

In Liberman's stories the Holocaust is both historical fact and symbol of a metaphysical condition. It epitomizes the terrors and the limits, but also, in its tales of heroism and survival, the redemptive aspects of the human estate. Liberman's exploration of this condition is many-faceted (the stories often render powerfully the woman's point of view). A doctor by profession, his stories often deal with illness, death, and the frailties of the body; a creative metaphysician by temperament, the tales explore central philosophical issues: determinism, free will and chance, accident, structure, and meaning; "the hard God called anonymity" and the puzzles of human identity; the nature of good and evil. This is Jewish art which, like Judaism itself, speaks of universal human concerns.

RICHARD FREADMAN

Liebrecht, Savyon

German-born Israeli fiction writer and dramatist, 1948–

Born Sabina Sosnowic in Munich, 1948, to parents who were Holocaust survivors from Poland. Emigrated with family to Israel, 1949. Changed first name to "Savyon", 1966. Began to write while doing military service on kibbutz, 1966. Studied at Tel Aviv University, BA in philosophy and literature. Married, 1974; one daughter, one son; now separated from husband. Awarded Alterman Award, 1987; received awards for two television scripts.

Selected Writings

Stories

Tapuhim min hamidbar, 1986; translated as *Apples from the Desert*, 1998, by Marganit Weinberger-Rotman *et al.* under the direction of the Institute for Translation of Hebrew Literature

Susim al kvish geah [Horses on the Highway], 1988

Sinit ani medaberet elekhah [It's All Greek to Me], 1992

Tsarikh sof lesipur ahavah [On Love Stories and Other Endings], 1995

Nashim mitokh katalog [Women from a Catalogue], 2000

Novels

Ish veishah veish [A Man and a Woman and a Man], 1998; excerpt translated by Yael Lotan in *Modern Hebrew Literature*, 23 (1999–2000)

Other

"The Influence of the Holocaust on My Work" in *Hebrew Literature in the Wake of the Holocaust*, edited by Leon I. Yudkin, 1993

Further Reading

Rattok, Lily, introduction to *Apples from the Desert*, New York: Feminist Press, City University of New York, 1998

Yudkin, Leon I., *Beyond Sequence: Current Israeli Fiction and its Context*, Northwood, Middlesex: Symposium Press, 1992

Yudkin, Leon I., *A Home Within: Varieties of Jewish Expression in Modern Fiction*, Northwood, Middlesex: Symposium Press, 1996

Savyon Liebrecht was born in Germany, moving to Israel as a young child. Her early collections of short stories established her literary reputation and her remarkable popularity in Israel. She writes plays and television scripts and has published one novel. Both her parents were Holocaust survivors who had lost their entire families during the war. This background provided her with the creative impetus to write, to fill in the silences that her parents imposed in her home life and the gaps in her family history. She attests that "the influence of the Holocaust on my work cannot be separated from the influence of the Holocaust on my life". Liebrecht's experiences as a second generation survivor led to her explore that resonance within the family unit of people haunted by the trauma of their past. She is among the most significant contributors to this field of Israeli literature, which emerged as the full psychological impact of the war in Europe on its refugees was acknowledged.

Liebrecht portrays more than a simple feminist viewpoint. Her female characters may work from a position of weakness but their quiet determination leads them to explore the conflict and shift boundaries surrounding them.

Significantly her stories include the child in the family dynamic, thereby enlarging the male-female relationships. Lily Rattok shows that Liebrecht rejects the romantic myth of courtship as the defining moment in a woman's life (see her Introduction to *Apples from the Desert*). The triangle of father–mother–child allows a more complex set of female roles and responsibilities to be explored.

Her first collection of short stories shows the themes that develop in her writing. In the title story "Apples from the Desert" the wife/mother figure, Victoria, tries to break the bonds of the patriarchal structure to which she is tied. She is forced to reappraise her role as dutiful wife when her daughter Rivka leaves the suffocating religious world of arranged marriages, moving to a kibbutz and living out of wedlock but very much in love with her partner. The symbolism is effective: the apples Victoria takes with her on her journey from Jerusalem are rotten at the core, while those grown in the freedom of the kibbutz are sharp and crisp. Within Hebrew literature the apple has loaded significance, representing both fruitfulness and knowledge. Rivka will not be constrained by the bonds of marriage, as she physically moves outside the realm of her father's power. This self-assertion is successful for the daughter; while for Victoria it is nuanced. She gains self-awareness of her own sacrifices, colluding with her daughter's needs, yet returning to her life in Jerusalem. Liebrecht's protagonist subverts male authority and dominance from within the story, while the author achieves this by painting many of the male characters as one-dimensional.

This is true of the Israeli husband Yoel in "Room on the Roof". Against his advice the protagonist (never named) decides to hire Arab workers to construct a room for her. The story plays out the development of new respect and sensibility for the Arab workers alongside gnawing questions about their intentions, political and personal. Liebrecht's strength is that she examines broad philosophical questions of stereotype and individual within an intimate landscape. Here, as in "The Road to Cedar City" from her next collection, women are seen as able to cross accepted boundaries of a society wracked by national and patriarchal suspicions to achieve small steps towards reconciliation. Both women and Arabs have been marginal to the mainstream ethos of society; Liebrecht illustrates mutual yet guarded understanding. She deftly sketches out the locale that brings the immediate struggle of each story into sharp focus. In "The Road to Cedar City" it is the deafening commercialism and superficiality of America blaring out from the radio that foregrounds the profound hostility between the protagonists in the car. Since both families are "in exile" from Israel in this story, it makes the rapprochement between the women more striking.

Savyon Liebrecht's particular insight of Holocaust survivors, the emotional toll their past trauma exacts on them and their family, radiates in many of her stories and in her essay "The Influence of the Holocaust on my Work". Through the prism of Holocaust memories and their continuing destructive power, Liebrecht explores family dynamics. She looks at the intensity and closeness between parent and child, between grandparent and grandchild. She uses the past as a separate protagonist in her stories, latching on as a dybbuk to tormented characters. The conspiracy of silence that these characters feel forces the demon to burst out in unfortunate situations, causing devastation to those the survivor most wants to protect. In "Hayuta's Engagement Party", Grandpa Mendel cannot abstain from recalling his most grim memories at times of celebration and plenty. This causes anguish for family members and it is their responses that Liebrecht discusses in her essay. His granddaughter, in anticipation of her party, attempts to deal with his probable outburst with kind pragmatism. As the third generation she exhibits some understanding but no empathy for his pain. Shifra, Mendel's daughter-in-law, is intolerant of his outbursts and reacts harshly. As the outsider to the family group she introduces quite different viewpoints, confusing his need for personal testimonial with the public commemoration of Memorial Day and Holocaust Day, assigned days in the Israeli calendar. The persona of in-law acts as messenger of dissent, seeking to change accepted patterns of behaviour. Yet Mendel's daughter Bella, speaking perhaps for the author, can understand the infinite sadness Mendel feels, and how little the formal memorials alleviate his pain. She finds some relief in his outbursts; for her they clarify his years of silence. Liebrecht's work cannot simply be categorized as postmodern or highly individual, for the Holocaust survivor syndrome, while always intensely personal, is a collective phenomenon in Israel society.

In her collection of stories *Tsarikh sof lesipur ahavah* [On Love Stories and Other Endings] she continues to use the past as a vigorous protagonist, needing to be acknowledged and responded to. In "The Last Meal" there is even a place set for Gershon's deceased wife by his new companion, to acknowledge her importance in his life. By recognizing past events and people Liebrecht wishes to hand the baton of choice to her protagonists. Although they cannot change history, they have the responsibility to re-explore its burdens and ameliorate the effects for the future.

In her novel *Ish veisha veish* [A Man and a Woman and A Man] the backdrop of an old people's nursing home draws the protagonists together, while exposing fundamental questions relating to choice and self-determination in life. She exposes that juncture where the fabric of love, dreams, and life interweave, and choice has to be exercised. Again she delineates the richness of the family configuration as the protagonist Hammutal's thoughts wander: "Now I've managed to drag them all into this bed – Arnon and Hillah and Shaul Inlander's father and mother and his father's mistresses." The author's technique is compelling: while her use of dialogue is sensitive and nuanced, she is master of the unspoken word, of intuition and gesture.

Liebrecht works gently with her protagonists compared with the angry or abrasive tone expressed by some of her contemporary Israeli women writers – Yehudit Hendel and Orly Castel-Bloom for example. Her characters operate in an intimate arena yet are able to show radical resolve. In her writing Liebrecht presents characters with whom her readers can connect, and this must account in part for her popular success. Her objective for these characters is to consider the options they face, and thereby rewrite the endings of their own love – and life – stories.

TAMARA LEVINE

Lind, Jakov

Austrian-German fiction writer, 1927–

Born Heinz Landwirth in Vienna, 10 February 1927. One of four children (only son) of Simon, a merchant (died 1948) and Rosa Landwirth, née Birnbaum (died in Tel Aviv during the World II), assimilated Jews. Attended Academy of Dramatic Art, Vienna, for two years. Escaped to Holland after Anschluss, 1938. Parents went to Palestine, 1941. Obtained false papers under name Jan Overbeek. Went to Germany as deckhand on a Rhine barge to escape round-ups of Jews in the Netherlands. Worked for Ministry of Air as courier. Boss there a British spy. Went illegally to Palestine as Jakov Chaklan, 1945. Returned to Europe after five years. Studied acting at Max-Reinhardt-Seminar, Vienna. Came to London, 1954. Married Faith Henry, 1955; two children. Writer in residence, Long Island University, Brooklyn Centre, 1966–67 and Boulder, Colorado, 1975.

Selected Writings

Short Stories
Eine Seele aus Holz, 1962; as *Soul of Wood*, translated by Ralph Manheim, 1964
The Stove, 1983

Novels
Landschaft in Beton, 1963; as *Landscape in Concrete*, translated by Ralph Manheim, 1967
Ergo, 1966; adapted for the stage in New York, 1968
Travels to the Enu: Story of a Shipwreck, 1982
The Inventor, 1987

Plays
The Pagans, 1964
Irgo, 1968
The Kitlauer Affair, 1970
Bulan King of the Kazars, 1972

Radio Plays: *Anna Laub*, 1965; *The Silver Foxes are Dead*, 1965; *Hunger*, 1968; *Angst*, 1968; *Voices*, 1970; *The Message*, 1975

Autobiography
Counting My Steps, 1969
Numbers: A Further Autobiography, 1972
Crossing: The Discovery of Two Islands, 1991

Other
The Trip to Jerusalem, 1973

Further Reading

Hammel, Andrea, Silke Hassler and Edward Timms, *Writing After Hitler: The Work of Jakov Lind*, Cardiff: University of Wales Press, 2001
Rosenfeld, Alvin, "Jakov Lind and the Trials of Jewishness", *Midstream*, 20 (February 1974)
Stella Rosenfeld, "Jakov Lind: Writer at the Crossroads", *Modern Austrian Literature*, 4/4 (1971)
Stenberg, Peter, "Edgar Hilsenrath and Jakov Lind Meet at the Employment Office in Netanya, Palestine, Discuss Literature, and Contemplate Their Recent Past" in *Yale Companion to Jewish Writing and Thought in German Culture, 1096–1996*, edited by Sander L. Gilman and Jack Zipes, New Haven, Connecticut and London: Yale University Press, 1997

Jakov Lind's importance as a Jewish writer derives from the particular circumstances of his upbringing in Vienna, the singular pattern of his survival during World War II, his decision to leave Israel after the founding of the State, and his ability to construct a literary career for himself first in German and then in English, based on a unique supranational, multi-perspectival and multilingual orientation. A fair amount of Lind's overall literary output is autobiographical. This feature tends to lead to a thematization of the issue of his identity or multiple identities, although some observers have claimed that Lind gave up or lost his identity during the War. He was not able merely to hide his identity and resume it later on. After the War, according to these same observers, a series of poses and assumed identities have had to substitute for any genuine or authentic identity he may have once possessed. This unhappy process of recurring identity formation or repeated posturing is discernible in his writings, which have provided sobering challenges to his readers.

Lind was born and spent his formative years in Vienna, a city he later described as "not just a town, it was a philosophy of mutual tolerance of the most varied kind of people." (*Counting My Steps*). Having joined the local Zionist youth organization, Barak, he spent the summer of 1936 at its summer camp in Burgenland. During these formative years he developed an idealized view of the Zionist movement, and he planned to emigrate to Palestine to realize his Zionist dream. However, the Anschluss of Austria and the Nazification of the country dictated otherwise. In order to secure his safety, Lind was sent by his parents to the Netherlands on a *Kindertransport* while they and his sisters found other ways to leave Vienna. Later, with the Nazi invasion of the Netherlands, Lind went underground and emerged with a new Gentile identity. He survived the war working on river boats on the Rhine and in 1945 he came to Palestine, in order to be reunited with his family, which had made its way there in the interim. Lind took on a new Jewish-Zionist identity for a few years, as he sought odd jobs and began to write and entertain the notion of developing a career as a writer. He initially wrote in German, since his Hebrew was insufficient in this regard.

He published his first story, *The Diary of Hanan Malinek*, in installments in late 1949 and early 1950 in Hebrew translation in *Ashmoret*, an Israeli literary journal. It is the grim tale of a young Holocaust survivor, who is subsequently killed in the Israeli War for Independence shortly after his arrival in the promised land. The gruesome background of the Shoah and the terse depiction of the rigors of the escape from Europe and the illegal arrival in Palestine help establish a thoroughly sober framework for the fragmented account of drab military experiences, difficult religious and philosophical meditations, restrained love letters, together with uneasy depictions of army chat and awkward encounters with women. There is no idealism or conviction in ideology or purpose in the cause, for which this war and battle are being waged. Death, insanity, corruption, the impossibility of authentic human communication, the senselessness of life, and the bitter nature of the particular Jewish fate are all thematized. There is no celebration of homecoming and no sense of physical or spiritual rebirth or their very possibility.

This rather bleak assessment of the human condition, which has its sources in the Holocaust, is characteristic of most of Lind's subsequent literary output over the years, whether Jewish-related or not. However, when the context is Holocaust-related, as it is in his most successful work, *Soul of Wood*, the results are extremely macabre and grotesque. The characters in *Soul of Wood* form a brotherhood of the sick, the crippled, and the refuse of society, who offer a brutal, merciless commentary on western society and on the human condition at large. As Lind summed it up in his novel *Landscape in Concrete*: "There is a disease; it is called mankind". Complimenting this vision is his compact, unsparing literary style, which Alvin Rosenfeld compared to the writings of Kafka and Günter Grass. Like these writers, Lind tends to ironize the nightmarish aspects, or treat them with a type of restrained, black humour, or dour commentary, in order to make them barely palatable.

In the autobiographical writings, Lind thematizes several Zionist issues. It may be that the bleak literary depiction in his first published story is related to his subsequent description of himself as an outsider in his own country. As he wrote in retrospect: "When I lived there (between 1945 and 1950) I couldn't find my place. I belonged there yet I didn't. I probably belonged to the Palestine of my childhood dreams and didn't know how to live in its reality." Zionism functioned in this sense as a form of pschoanalysis. Actually Lind changed his mind about his relationship to Zionism and Israel. In *Crossing* (1991), he wrote: I had my emotional roots – and an unshaken belief —in the ideas of Zionism, the most revolutionary of Jewish ideas to date. Beyond this, I loved the sheer beauty of my ancestral country, which never lost its mystical hue for me and never will. But, talking about cultural isolation, I had neither a German, nor an Austrian, nor a Dutch, nor an Israeli, nor a specifically Jewish identity." His depiction of his lack of a nation can be tied to his statement that he is a writer without a language. Loss, confusion, and disorientation are the inevitable fate of the Jew who has experienced what Lind has lived through. As he wrote: "I have an Austrian passport and residences in London and Majorca. I speak Hebrew fluently and lived five years in this country. I am a Zionist by education, a Jew by choice; I am not an Israeli, I am not a Zionist, I don't know what Jew really means."

Still, there is a mystical, spiritual element to his writings, which lends a sense of hope, perhaps, to the general despair. In *The Trip to Jerusalem*, for example, he described his interest in mysticism in general and his meeting with Gershom Sholem. When he was asked once in Paris about his occupation, he described the dialogue as follows: "What do you do? I repair the universe. It fell to pieces and I am picking them up . . ." (*Numbers*). It is the sense of a broken universe that is conveyed so poignantly and insistently by Jakov Lind in his writings. If sometimes his writing is conceived and perceived as a possible way to repair it, that is about the most optimistic tone he ever strikes.

MARK GELBER

Lispector, Clarice

Soviet-born Brazilian fiction writer, 1925–1977

Born in Tchetchelnik, Ukraine, 10 December 1925. Emigrated with family to Brazil, 1926; settled in Recife. 1927. Began to write, 1932. Studied at Ginásio Pernambuco, 1935–36; Colégio Sílvio Leite, 1937; Colégio Andrews; National Faculty of Law, Rio de Janeiro, from 1941, law degree, 1944. Edited and contributed to *Agência Nacional* and *A Noite*, 1941–44. Married Mauri Gurgel Valente, diplomat, 1943; two sons. Accompanied husband on postings in Europe, mainly in Naples and Berne, until 1952, and in United States, 1952–59. Separated from husband and returned to Brazil, 1959. Awards include Graça Aranha Foundation Prize, 1944; São Paulo Carmen Dolores Barbosa Prize, 1962; Golfinho de Ouro Prize, 1969. Died 9 December 1977.

Selected Writings

Novels

Perto do coração selvagem, 1944; as *Near to the Wild Heart*, translated by Giovanni Pontiero, 1990
O lustre [The Chandelier], 1946
A cidade sitiada [The Besieged City], 1949
A maçã no escuro, 1961; as *The Apple in the Dark*, translated by Gregory Rabassa, 1967
A paixão segundo G.H., 1964; as *The Passion According to G.H.*, translated by Ronald W. Sousa, 1988
Uma aprendizagem ou o livro dos prazeres, 1969; as *An Apprenticeship, or The Book of Delights*, translated by Richard A. Mazzara and Lorri A. Parris, 1986
Água viva, 1973; as *The Stream of Life*, translated by Elizabeth Lowe and Earl E. Fitz, 1989
A hora da estrela, 1977; as *The Hour of the Star*, translated by Giovanni Pontiero, 1986
Um sopro de vida: pulsações [A Breath of Life: Pulses], 1978

Short Fiction

Alguns contos [Some Stories], 1952
Laços de família, 1960; *as Family Ties*, translated by Giovanni Pontiero, 1972
A legião estrangeira, 1964; as *The Foreign Legion: Stories and Chronicles*, translated by Giovanni Pontiero, 1986
Felicidade clandestina: contos [Clandestine Happiness: Stories], 1971
A via crucis do corpo [A Via Crucis of the Body], 1974
Onde estivestes de noite [Where You Were at Night], 1974
A bela e a fera, 1979; as *Beauty and the Beast, or the Wound Too Great*, translated by Earl E. Fitz, in *Scents of Wood and Silence: Short Stories by Latin American Women Writers*, 1991

For Children

O mistério de coelho pensante (uma estória policial para crianças) [The Mystery of the Coelho Pensante], 1967
A mulher que matou os peixes, 1968; as *The Woman Who Killed the Fish*, translated by Earl E. Fitz, *Latin American Literary Review*, 11/21 (July–December 1988)
A vida íntima de Laura [The Intimate Life of Laura], 1974
Quase de verdade [Almost True], 1978

Other
Para não esquecer [In Order Not to Go Mad], 1978
A descoberta do mundo, 1984; as *Discovering the World*, translated by Giovanni Pontiero, 1992 (newspaper articles published between 1967 and 1976)

Anthology in Translation
Soulstorm: Stories, translated by Alexis Levitin, 1989

Further Reading
Barbosa, Mario José Somerlate, *Clarice Lispector: Spinning the Webs of Passion*, New Orleans: University Press of the South, 1997
Castillo, Debra A., "Negation: Clarice Lispector" in *Talking Back: Toward a Latin American Feminist Literary Criticism*, Ithaca, New York: Cornell University Press, 1992
Cixous, Hélène, "Reading Clarice Lispector's *Sunday Before Going to Sleep*" in *Modern Latin American Fiction*, edited by Harold Bloom, New York: Chelsea House, 1990
Cixous, Hélène, *Reading with Clarice Lispector*, edited, translated, and introduced by Verena Andermatt Conley, Minneapolis: University of Minnesota Press, and London: Harvester/Wheatsheaf, 1990
Cixous, Hélène, *"Coming to Writing" and Other Essays*, edited by Deborah Jenson, translated by Sarah Cornell, Cambridge, Massachusetts: Harvard University Press, 1991
Douglass, Ellen H., "Myth and Gender in Clarice Lispector: Quest as a Feminist Statement in 'A imitacão da rosa'", *Luso-Brazilian Review*, 25/2 (Winter 1988)
Fitz, Earl E., "Freedom and Self-Realization: Feminist Characterization in the Fiction of Clarice Lispector", *Modern Language Studies*, 10/3 (1980)
Fitz, Earl E., *Clarice Lispector*, Boston: Twayne, 1985
Galvez-Breton, Mara, "Post-Feminist Discourse in Clarice Lispector's *A hora da estrela*" in *Splintering Darkness: Latin American Women Writers in Search of Themselves*, edited by Lucia Guerra Cunningham, Pittsburgh: Latin American Literary Review Press, 1990
Lindstrom, Naomi, "Clarice Lispector: Articulating Women's Experience" in *Women's Voice in Latin American Literature*, Washington, DC: Three Continents Press, 1989
Lowe, Elizabeth, "Liberating the Rose: Clarice Lispector's *Água viva* as a Political Statement" in *Splintering Darkness: Latin American Women Writers in Search of Themselves*, edited by Lucia Guerra Cunningham, Pittsburgh: Latin American Literary Review Press, 1990
Marting, Diane E. (editor), *Clarice Lispector: A Bio-Bibliography*, Westport, Connecticut: Greenwood Press, 1993
Patai, Daphne, "Clarice Lispector and the Clamour of the Ineffable", *Kentucky Romance Quarterly*, 27/2 (1980)
Patai, Daphne, "Clarice Lispector: Myth and Mystification" in *Myth and Ideology in Contemporary Brazilian Fiction*, Rutherford, New Jersey: Fairleigh Dickinson University Press, and London: Associated University Presses, 1983
Peixoto, Marta, *Passionate Fictions: Gender, Narrative, and Violence in Clarice Lispector*, Minneapolis: University of Minnesota Press, 1994
Pontiero, Giovanni, "Clarice Lispector: An Intuitive Approach to Fiction" in *Knives and Angels: Women Writers in Latin America*, edited by Susan Bassnett, London and Atlantic Highlands, New Jersey: Zed, 1990
Schiminovich, Flora, "Two Modes of Writing the Female Self: Isabel Allende's *The House of Spirits* and Clarice Lispector's *The Stream of Life*" in *Redefining Autobiography in Twentieth-Century Women's Fiction*, edited by Janice Morgan and Colette T. Hall, New York: Garland, 1991
Schiminovich, Flora, "Lispector's Rethinking of the Biblical and Mystical Discourse" in *Tradition and Innovation: Reflections on Latin American Jewish Writing*, edited by Robert DiAntonio and Nora Glickman, Albany: State University of New York Press, 1993
Vieira, Nelson H., "Clarice Lispector: A Jewish Impulse and a Prophecy of Difference" in *Jewish Voice in Brazilian Literature: A Prophetic Discourse of Alterity*, Gainesville: University Press of Florida, 1995

Although there is no argument that Lispector came from a Ukrainian-Jewish background, there is also no argument that she identified completely with Brazil and, most of all, with that part of the poorest north-east, Recife. And although she seems not to have written anything specifically Jewish, there is something in the alienation of her characters that recalls a kind of diasporic writing. Chief among that writing is the novella *The Hour of the Star*, published one month before her death. Certainly the main protagonist of the novel, Macabéa, a "nordestina" whose quest for a better life takes her from provincial squalor to a more metropolitan squalor, is much like Lispector herself. However, even though the prevailing social conditions are important in *The Hour of the Star*, what is patently clear about the novel is that it functions on two distinct levels: first, as a quasi-biographical novel and implicit in that autobiography, a testament to her life; and, secondly, as a novel about the act of novel writing. The novella's "Author's Dedication" is devoted not just to music, but also to meditation, presumably, Zen meditation. This notion of meditating, and especially of Zen meditation, fits very nicely into the presumably ambiguous patterns that one reads in *The Hour of the Star*, patterns that lend themselves directly to this kind of Zen thought in which the whole notion of truth is called into question. The novella is replete with allusions to being and non-being, a state of humanness that is a fundamental part of the Zen (non)philosophy.

But Lispector also writes: "we must never forget that if the atom's structure is invisible, it is none the less real". In that statement we not only have a Zen refrain, but a Kabbalistic one as well. As a Jew, Lispector would doubtlessly have been familiar with the Kabbalah and would certainly have been familiar with the Zohar. The Zohar states that human beings are composed of spirit, soul, and of a coarser spirit that is closely related to the soul. Lispector begins the novel by writing that "Everything in the world began with a yes. One molecule said yes to another molecule and life was born", and so begins a Zoharic connection between the "coarser spirit" and molecular biology. But the Kabbalah is a means for education, for one's quest, one's journey in life that, among many things, is clearly a trial and the trial is Macabéa's, a name that is infused with a certain amount of irony as is her boyfriend's name, Olímpico: Olímpico from Mt Olympos, the residence of the gods, and Macabéa after Judas Maccabeus who recovered the temple in 165 BCE, or after one of the family of Maccabees who, because they were obedient to the commandments of God, had been given victory over those who would undermine the teachings of Torah. Clearly, the character of Olímpico as "one who inhabits Olympos" is irony enough since he came from the backwoods of Paraíba with a tin of perfumed vaseline and a comb. Clearly, Olímpico is not a character whose name revivifies times and heroes of a nobler age. One could make a case that Lispector's novella is forging a relationship between the Jews and the Hellenistic tradition out of which the Maccabean uprising occurred, since inherent in the Hellenistic culture was the challenge to the culture of the Torah, but Lispector was not after that kind of dynamic. What she was after was the distinctly ironic way in which she uses the process of (un)naming and in the role Fortune plays, especially in the case of Macabéa.

With regard to the former, one discovers that Macabéa had no name at birth, and names, of course, relate to identity. So from birth, she had no identity, no way of knowing who she was or what she was. In an odd state of affairs, when she does discover who she is, she is an ugly virgin who drinks Coke and listens to the radio; who doesn't know she is impoverished, who's always thinking about who or what she is as mediated by the narrator, Rodrigo S.M., who is also constantly thinking about who or what she is. Lispector even writes:

> Forgive me if I add something more about myself since my identity is not very clear, and when I write I am surprised to find that I possess a destiny. Who has not asked himself at some time or other: am I a monster or is this what it means to be a person?

This, of course, relates to the writer Rodrigo S.M., the facile alias of Lispector herself, clearly implicated in the destiny of the Dedication. But Lispector also goes on to talk about Macabéa in identical terms.

> First of all, I must make it clear that this girl does not know herself apart from the fact that she goes on living aimlessly. Were she foolish enough to ask herself "Who am I?", she would fall flat on her face. For the question "Who am I?" creates a need. And how does one satisfy that need? To probe oneself is to recognize that one is incomplete.

Such an attitude towards incompleteness seems to imply a kind of duality between body and other. The Hegelian resolution would be to recognize the other as the spirit, though Hegel would contend that the spirit would usurp the body and, therefore, be one spiritual being. But Macabéa has no Hegelian credentials. For Macabéa, who was born without a name and hence without an immediate identity, spirituality gains no parcel. The fact that Macabéa is nameless at birth and that as an adult she hardly exists for those around her is tied in with the notion of her name. The use of the name Macabéa, after one of the heroes of the Jews, is doubly ironic in that Macabéa has no leadership capabilities at all and she is more a product of the "fickleness" of Fortune than was Maccabeus whose Fortunes smiled kindly on the leader of "the chosen people".

The novella ends where it began with a "yes" and, perhaps, that closed the circle on Lispector and her poetics of mortality. One can divide the novel into sections, quadrants, portions, as one wishes, which highlight a number of interdependent subjects: novel writing, God, death, allusions to Jewishness, Fortune, etc., all of which form a kind of nexus of creation. It is incumbent on a reader to negotiate with these issues in a way that renders them novel yet at the same time renders the text a kind of homage to a life lost. Certainly *The Hour of the Star* is an autobiographical novel, but what gives it a different posture to other novels is the immediacy of the immanent moment, that as she writes the story of the rise and fall of Macabéa she writes the rise and fall of herself, her life, and the history of her being. The novel is, in fact, an epitaph for Lispector, her poetics of mortality.

MARK AXELROD

Litvinoff, Emanuel

British fiction writer, dramatist, and poet, 1915–

Born in London, 30 June 1915, one of nine children. Educated at Wood Close Elementary School; left at 14. Worked in tailoring, cabinet-making, and the fur trade; experienced unemployment and destitution. Served in British Army in Royal West African Frontier Force, 1940–46, in Ulster, West Africa and the Middle East: left with rank of major. Married Cherry Marshall, 1942 (divorced); four children. After World War II worked as journalist and broadcaster; founded the journal *Jews in Eastern Europe*, London. Edited the journals *Insight: Soviet Jews* and *Soviet Anti-Semitism*. Director, Contemporary Jewish Library, London 1958–89. Awarded Wingate Award, 1979.

Selected Writings

Novels
The Lost Europeans, 1960
The Man Next Door, 1968
A Death Out of Season, 1973
Blood on the Snow, 1975
The Face of Terror, 1978
Falls the Shadow, 1983

Autobiography
"Children of Two Inheritances: How It Worked Itself Out", 1953
Journey through a Small Planet, 1972
"They Made a Jew of Me", 1973

Play
Magnolia Street Story, 1951

Television Plays: *Another Branch of the Family*, 1967; *Marriage and Henry Sunday*, 1967; *A Dream in the Afternoon*, 1967; *Foxhole in Bayswater*, 1968; *A Foot in the Door*, 1969 (in *Armchair Theatre* series), *The Kazmirov Affair*, 1969 (in *Special Branch* series); *The World in a Room*, 1970 (in *Armchair Theatre* series); *Warm Feet, Warm Heart*, 1970 (in *Armchair Theatre* series); *Find the Lady*, 1971 (in *The Mind of Mr J.G. Reeder* series)

Poetry
Conscripts: A Symphonic Declaration, 1941
The Untried Soldier, 1942
A Crown for Cain, 1948
Poems for a Survivor, 1973

Other
Editor, *Penguin Modern Short Stories, 2*, 1969
Editor, *Soviet Anti-Semitism: The Paris Trial*, 1974
Editor, *The Penguin Book of Jewish Short Stories*, 1979

Further Reading

Abse, Dannie, "Portrait of a Jewish Poet", *Jewish Quarterly*, 1/4 (1954)
"Children of Two Inheritances", *Commentary*, 15/3 (March 1953)
The Guardian, 27 March 1993 (profile)
Lawson, Peter (editor), *Passionate Renewal: Jewish Poetry in Britain since 1945*, Nottingham: Five Leaves, 2001

One of the "East End" Anglo-Jewish writers, Emanuel Litvinoff has written poetry, short stories, and novels that explore Jewish identity and survival in the aftermath of the Bolshevik Revolution, Stalinism, and the Holocaust. His atmospheric, autobiographical *Journey through a Small Planet* powerfully evokes the smells, squalor, desperation, anti-Semitism, street fascism, and the hopes of the Jews of London's now vanished "ghetto". This rich portrayal of adolescent longings and confusion in a disintegrating immigrant culture between the wars ends when then the young author experiences liberation as a writer with the penning of his first poem.

Litvinoff's two published volumes of "war" poetry focus on the futility and frustrations of war. A number of poems dwell on the ambivalence of the Jewish soldier fighting to save the very civilization that renders him an outsider and oppresses him as a Jew. He also entertains the choice between a fragmented, dislocated, and problematic Jewish identity and the appealing, apparently uncomplicated freedom and normality of assimilation into English society. Litvinoff returns to these themes of "civilized" anti-Semitism and assimilation in his 1951 poem "To T.S. Eliot" and in his 1960 novel *The Lost Europeans*. In the poem he identifies with Eliot's crass stereotype of Jews – "Bleistein is my relative, and I share the protozoic slime of Shylock" and calls for an open recognition of anti-Jewish prejudice. His reading of the poem at the Institute of Contemporary Arts in London led to calls for an apology and silence from the literary establishment about Eliot's portrayal of Jews. In the meticulously researched novel, the English-educated Jewish protagonist, Martin Stone, travels after the war to a shattered Berlin to find that a now hidden but still active anti-Semitism prevents him from returning "home" to Germany. These deliberations lead him to acknowledge that it is the same anti-Semitism that prevented him from ever being at home in England too. The triumphant war against fascism was never a war against, nor a victory over, a deeply embedded and enduring European Christian anti-Semitism. As a survivor Stone meets other Jewish survivors, in particular Hugo Krantz, and shares the growing recognition that assimilation can never be a real possibility as he discovers his deeper identity as a Jew. It is a mere accident of fate that leads to a Jew living, or dying, in Whitechapel, Riga, Odessa, Berlin, Treblinka, or Auschwitz. The Jew as outsider is equally exiled from the premature universality of the Left and the blood and soil of the Right – a Jew is only at home in his "rootlessness".

Litvinoff's next novel, *The Man Next Door*, deepens his exploration of English racism. Harold Bollam, ex-army and public schoolboy, middle-manager and unhappy husband and father, comes to his mid-life crisis by seeing his new Jewish next door neighbours, the Winstons (née Weinstein) as the cause of all his woes. The novel offers a plausible psychopathological account of the birth and growth of a middle-class English anti-Semite amid the threatening transformations of late 1960s Britain.

Litvinoff labels his "ancestors" East End anarchists and describes their clandestine meetings, their perpetual fear of exposure, and their plans for symbolic action to further their cause. This background provides the scene for the first volume of his "The Faces of Terror" trilogy. This is Litvinoff's most extensive work (*A Death Out of Season*, *Blood on the Snow*, and *The Face of Terror*). The novels span the period from 1910 and the Jewish anarchist and revolutionary plots against the monarchs of Europe, via the Bolshevik victory of 1917, to the covert actions and internal politics of the Communist Party and its secret services under Stalin. The thrillers trace the action from Warsaw and London to Moscow, Berlin, and Paris. Litvinoff delineates the competing ideologies of revolution, the commitment to freedom and belief in the cause of justice, followed by disillusion and despair at the new, equally repressive forms of power. He writes of love, loyalty, and betrayal in a world of spies and double agents, a world that ends in the terror of Stalin's purges of the 1930s.

Falls the Shadow, Litvinoff's 1983 novel, returns to the theme of the Holocaust and survival with an intriguingly twisted tale. It seems that a murdered man shot by a camp survivor in Tel Aviv might have been a Nazi SS officer who had escaped Europe and taken on the identity of a Jewish victim. It appears that he lived as a Jew, a believing Jew, for nearly 40 years in suburban Tel Aviv, raised a family and was buried as a Jew in a Jewish cemetery. The author asks us to consider whether this life could constitute an adequate penance.

Litvinoff was also a television playwright, the editor of the successful *The Penguin Book of Jewish Short Stories*, and continued to publish poetry in the *Jewish Quarterly* and elsewhere, with a fourth volume, *Poems for a Survivor*, published in 1973.

In his novels and poems Litvinoff wrote about the Holocaust and totalitarian terror before many other writers. Likewise, he sought to address the anti-Semitism of Eliot and others decades before this became a public issue. His writings offer a series of sustained deliberations on the fragmenting of European Jewish identity and the tensions and realities of Jewish assimilation into wider society in the context of the unprecedented disruptions of the last century. He reports that his writing is haunted by the Holocaust and in a sense his Jewish protagonists are all dislocated survivors of the lost worlds of European Jewry. Litvinoff's portrayals rarely focus on the religious dimensions of Jewish identity and his characters are non-religious and find neither identity nor solace in religious belief, practice, or community. Jewish identity, strong and natural, is often rejected or minimized only to return strengthened by the experiences of exclusion and prejudice. This damaged sense of self is often reinforced by Jews themselves. His English Jew, poet and novelist, escapee from the East End and communal life now at the edge of the "host culture" with its many limitations clearly seen, cannot yet conceive, as a later generation of writers would insist, that these very peculiarities of Anglo-Jewry be a cause for celebration.

PAUL MORRIS

Further Reading

Cheyette, Bryan, introduction to *Contemporary Jewish Writing in Britain and Ireland: An Anthology*, London: Peter Halban, and Lincoln: University of Nebraska Press, 1998

Louvish, Simon

British fiction writer, film-maker, and biographer, 1947–

Born in Glasgow, 6 April 1947. Emigrated with family to Israel, 1949; served in Six Day War as military cameraman, 1967. Returned to Britain, 1968; studied at London School of Film Technique, 1968; freelance documentary film producer and director, 1970–76; tutor and lecturer, London International Film School, 1978–86. Married Mairi Macdonald, 1979.

Selected Writings

Novels

A Moment of Silence: Journeys Through a Counterfeit Mezuza, 1979
The Therapy of Avram Blok, 1985
The Death of Moishe-Ganef, 1986
City of Blok, 1988
The Last Trump of Avram Blok, 1990
Your Monkey's Shmuck, 1990
The Silencer, 1991
The Resurrection, 1994
What's Up God?, 1995
The Days of Miracles and Wonders, 1997

Other

It's a Gift, 1994
Man on the Flying Trapeze: The Life and Times of W.C. Fields, 1997
Monkey Business: The Lives and Legends of the Marx Brothers, 1999
Stan and Ollie: The Roots of Comedy, 2001

Simon Louvish was born in Glasgow in 1947 and was taken to Israel at the age of two. He was educated in Israel, serving in the Six Day War as a military cameraman, and returned to Britain in 1968 where he has lived since then. His is a hybrid cross-cultural voice whose literary influences range from the South American novel to North American science fiction and Israeli popular satire. His uncategorizable writing not only eschews the conventional forms that stifle much fiction in Britain but also challenges the boundaries of what supposedly constitutes literary fiction. *The Therapy of Avram Blok* is the first of his "Blok-busters" akin in structure (Blok is Louvish's alter ego) to Philip Roth's Zuckerman quintet. Louvish's fiction is an endlessly mobile hotch-potch of memory, fantasy, history, graffiti, parody, and Israeli street humour. All of Louvish's Blok novels have the same exuberant overflowing expansiveness and a central figure, Avram Blok, who seeks to contain multiple cultures and histories and find a much needed sense of place.

In *The Therapy of Avram Blok*, a lunatic asylum in Jerusalem has become a metaphor for a world where the line between fantasy and political reality has become increasingly blurred. By the end, the novel revolves around the pun of whether Israel remains an asylum – that is a refuge – or is just plain lunatic. Louvish refuses to use a linear narrative and therefore structures his Blok novels in terms of historical cycles that encompass World War I, World War II, the Shoah, and the Israeli Wars. In this way, Louvish both leaps about in time while still, depressingly, dealing with the same themes. As well as transgressing temporal boundaries, where dead figures come back to life, Louvish also crosses ever-changing spatial boundaries. His *alter ego*, Avram Blok, thus travels throughout the globe in a desperate but failed bid to obtain some kind of rational perspective. While Louvish's plural contexts, temporal fluidity, and cinematic technique characterize him as a postmodern author *par excellence* this would be a reductive reading of his fiction. His fiction is a roller-coaster ride through the fundamentalist politics of the post-war and, in these terms, Louvish remains a Swiftian political satirist whose aim is to subvert the moral certainties that have led to war and bloodshed in the first place.

His second Blok novel *City of Blok*, which spans the election of Menachem Begin in 1977 and the Lebanon War of 1982, has Louvish's protagonist pursued by the shadowy Department of Apocalyptic Affairs. At one point the fragmented, restless, perpetually mobile Blok sums up his desperation when he states that he does not care about the future as "the past has taken over the present". And yet, like an inverted Dorian Gray, Blok succeeds in remaining pure and innocent while all around him become corrupt. Forced into the maelstrom of Middle Eastern politics, Blok encounters Jewish fascists, Palestinian resistance, and Israeli Peaceniks, in a world "composed of a thousand splinters". His most recent Blok books, *The Last Trump of Avram Blok* and *The*

Days of Miracles and Wonders, range from the Gulf War to the London literary establishment and, not unlike the later fiction of Salman Rushdie, have an increasingly global reach.

To show that he has the courage of his convictions Louvish has recently published *What's Up God?*, a satirical account of what the apocalyptic age might look like after the Messiah has arrived. He has also written comic thrillers, such as *The Death of Moishe-Ganef* and *The Silencer*, to give his themes a more recognizable form. These two self-consciously formulaic novels have Joe Dekel as their anarcho-religious hero. Dekel, an Israeli journalist, has been "silenced" in America by a far right blacklister. After meeting his "silencer" at a conference on Jewish-Palestinian peace in New York, the "certified paranoid" Dekel finds himself (not just in his darkest imaginings) the object of various state security apparatuses. Dekel discovers a body in Manhattan whose dying words prove to be the clue to an attempt by a fanatical group of American Christian fundamentalists to fatally destabalize the Middle East. Whether it be apocalyptic Christians, the FBI, Mossad, or extreme Israeli nationalists, Louvish's *schlemiel*-protagonist becomes unwittingly involved with a series of bizarre competing interests.

Once thrown into the maelstrom of Levantine politics, Dekel thinks of himself as "an old ragged whore. The ebb and flow of the traumas of my battered country, the blistering, jagged, sandy winds of circumstance have carved their mark on my soul". It is this painful sense of helplessness in the face of insuperable odds that enables Louvish to transcend the thriller genre. Louvish is particularly good at exploiting the staple questions of any formulaic thriller – "Who is the murderer? Who is blamed? For what?" – so as to show their geopolitical implications. He also neatly incorporates actual Israeli newspaper headlines into his fiction which – although they might appear completely bizarre to the non-cognoscenti – are, in fact, true. As Dekel finally realizes: "the awful truth: we had not been paranoid enough". Both Louvish's Blok novels and his more accessible thrillers reveal that only the insane really understand the madness of the world. In this way, his diasporic sensibility extends the range and vocabulary of the novel in English to encompass both global concerns and a sense of morality beneath the rubble of geopolitical conflict.

Louvish, in recent years, has become an acclaimed biographer, publishing *Man on the Flying Trapeze: The Life and Times of W. C. Fields* and *Monkey Business: The Lives and Legends of the Marx Brothers*. These books return Louvish to an abiding interest in the history of film and film-making in general, which have always fed into his fiction. In 1968 he attended the London School of Film Technique where he began a series of political documentaries including *End of the Dialogue* about apartheid in South Africa, *Greece of the Christian Greeks* on the Colonels' regime in Greece, and *To Live in Freedom*, a documentary about the Israeli-occupied West Bank and Gaza Strip. He has also published *A Moment of Silence: Journeys Through a Counterfeit Mezuza*, an autobiographical account of his life in Israel, and various collections of shorter fiction.

BRYAN H. CHEYETTE

Lunel, Armand

French fiction writer, 1892–1977

Born in Aix-en-Provence, 9 June 1892. Descended from old Provençal Jewish family of rabbis and the poet of 18th-century Carpentras, author of the *Tragédie provençale de la reine Esther*, which would inspire Lunel's own *Esther de Carpentras*. Educated at Lycée Mignet in Aix and Lycée Henri IV in Paris. Studied law and philosophy in Monaco. Taught philosophy in Monaco for some 30 years. Served in World War I; called up in 1939–40. In 1940, affected by the "Jewish Statute" of the Vichy government, dismissed from his teaching post; thanks to patronage of princely family of Monaco he escaped deportation to the Polish extermination camps. Married Suzanne Messiah, 1920; two daughters. Wrote libretti for his childhood friend Darius Milhaud. Awarded Renaudot Prize. Invited to Israel by Israeli government to organize with Darius Milhaud a performance of the opera *David* to celebrate Jerusalem's third millennium, 1952. Chevalier de la Légion d'honneur; Grand Prix National des Lettres, 1977. Died in Monaco, 7 November 1977.

Selected Writings

Novels
L'Imagerie du cordier [The Ropemaker's Pictures], 1924
Occasions, 1926
Nicolo-Peccavi; ou, L'Affaire Dreyfus à Carpentras [Nicolo Peccavi; or, The Dreyfus Affair at Carpentras], 1926
Noire et grise [Black and Grey], 1930
Le Balai de sorcière [The Witch's Broomstick], 1935
La Maison de la femme peinte [The House of the Painted Lady], 1946
Les Amandes d'Aix [The Almond Trees of Aix], 1949
La Belle à la Fontaine [The Lady of the Fountain], 1959

Short Stories
Et s'il n'en reste qu'une [And if Only One Woman is Left], 1937
Le Banquier du Village [The Village Banker], 1937
Jérusalem à Carpentras [Jerusalem in Carpentras], 1938

Musical Libretti
Les Malheurs d'Orphée [The Sorrows of Orpheus], music by Darius Milhaud, 1924; English version by Charles C. Cushing, 1959
Esther de Carpentras [The Esther of Carpentras], music by Darius Milhaud, 1925
La Chartreuse de Parme, music by Henri Sauguet, 1926–36
Maximilien, music by Darius Milhaud, 1930
Un petit peu d'exercice: Jeu Pour Enfants [A Little Bit of Exercise: A Game for Children], music by Darius Milhaud, 1937
Barba Garibo, 1949
David, music by Darius Milhaud, 1952; English version by R. Meyers, 1956

Other
Par d'étranges chemins: souvenirs de mai–juin, 1940; as *Along Strange Paths: Memories of May–June*], 1940
J'ai vu vivre la Provence [I Have Lived in Provence], 1962
Sénégal, atlas de voyage [Senegal: A Traveller's Atlas], 1966

Juifs du Langudoc, de la Provence et des États français du Pape [Jews of the Languedoc, Provence and the French States of the Pope], 1975
Mon ami Darius Milhaud [My Friend Darius Milhaud], 1992
Les Chemins de mon judaïsme et divers inedits [The Path of My Judaism and Unpublished Pieces], 1993

Further Reading

Astro, Alan (editor), *Discourses of Jewish Identity in Twentieth Century France*, New Haven, Connecticut: Yale University Press, 1994
Horn, Pierre, *Modern Jewish Writers of France*, Lewiston, New York: Mellen Press, 1997
Iancu, Carol (editor), *Armand Lunel et les Juifs du Midi: Actes du Colloque International du Centre Regional d'Histoires des Mentalites, 14–16 Juin 1982*, Montpellier: Centre du Recherches et d'Études Juives et Hébraïques–Centre Régional d'Histoire des Mentalités, 1986
Iancu, Danièle and Carol Iancu, *Les Juifs du Midi: Une histoire millénaire*, Avignon: Éditions A. Barthélémy, 1995
Marks, Elaine, *Marrano as Metaphor: The Jewish Presence in French Writing*, New York: Columbia University Press, 1996
Spire, André, *Quelques juifs et demi-juifs*, Paris: Societé du Mercure de France, 1928

Judaism and Provence feature everywhere in Lunel's work – here we consider only aspects of his Judaism in the writings concerned with the "four holy communities" that were under papal jurisdiction until 1789, and with their inexorable decline in the 19th and 20th centuries. In the house of his maternal grandfather at Carpentras, Lunel learned about the "surprising, dreamy" Jewish world, with its own language, *chouadit*, Judeo-Provençal, a mixture of Provençal and Hebrew. This occurs in his writings as *quimfaros*, a tall hat, also called a *décalitre* (two-gallon hat); *tarafsalim*, a frock-coat; *farfudo*, in Provençal *panturlo* (tart, whore); *rhalambouilleur*, a term of contempt; *freskun* or *frahun*, the whiff of popery; *mohof*, housekeeping money; *coudoles*, unleavened bread (Hebrew: *matza*); *méfekin*, hooligans, like those who threw stones at Jewish shops at the time of the Dreyfus affair; *catamarret*, "rotten Cathar", an ancient insult in Provence. This last expression occurs in the rhyme Catholic children used to shout at the gates of the Jewish quarter before the French Revolution, quoted by Lunel in the novel *Nicolo-Peccavi, ou, L'Affaire Dreyfus à Carpentras*: "Catamarray! he made me shout".

Pride in being a member of the Jewish community and scorn for converts constitute another important aspect of the Jewishness of Lunel's work. It is seen in *Nicolo-Peccavi* where grievances between Jews and Christians, and the hostility of a long-marginalized minority are illustrated by a character who is a descendant of converted Jews. Augustin Nicolo, a maker of church vestments, is conscience-stricken when Dreyfus is found guilty, and to show his goodwill, knocks at the door of his neighbour, Lunel's grandfather. In an unforgettable scene the author evokes the rebuff that greets the turncoat:

> "Hypocrite! bigot! priest's spy! renegade!"
>
> "Renegade?", I echoed, appalled and mystified. Nicolo Peccavi in our house! was it possible? I was more likely to see the bishop there, or the Holy Sacrament! Mamette, Abranet's wife, stays on her guard, she could tell by the whiff of popery on him, the *freskun* or *frahun*, as it was called in their Hebraico-Provençal patois by our good maiden aunts Anna and Sara, who would take to their heels at the mere sight of a priest's cassock in the offing.

Another aspect of Judeo-Christian relations in the papal enclave was constituted by the "conversion carols", short poems composed at Christmas by priests and folk singers. Lunel knew the conversion carols and used them as the basis for *Esther de Carpentras*. Three characters representing the ghetto of Carpentras, wait for the Cardinal's permission to stage the story of Esther for Purim. It so happens that the hobby of Vaucluse, the Cardinal's manservant, is composing conversion carols. Vaucluse's efforts to convert the three Jews fall on deaf ears, but the Cardinal promises that there will be a mass conversion of *all* the town's Jews and agrees to the Jewish delegation's request, intending to carry out his plan during the play.

The Bible story and Judeo-Comtat history merge. Just as Esther is about to plead with Ahasuerus to save her people, the Cardinal appears on the stage. He announces unless they convert immediately, the Jews of Carpentras will be banished. This key scene turns into surprise and confusion. The fair Esther, a daughter of the Carpentras ghetto, defends Judaism and argues cleverly in support of the refusal to convert. As in the Bible story, she wins her case. The work ends with two choruses, one of Jews giving thanks to the Eternal, the other of the Christians come to fetch their Cardinal. Here are the voices of the Old and the New Testaments "resounding under the southern sky".

Lunel recreates Jewish life in the Comtat Venaissin. Witness the fine description of the feast of Purim in *Esther de Carpentras*:

> Households still celebrate the happy anniversary by giving one another various kinds of sweets, in the shape of [Haman's] ears. In the days of the ghettos, Purim was not only a religious occasion but an actual street gala with fairground stalls, open-air feasts, dancing at the crossways, bands playing on wooden platforms, and all the wild capers of the masquerade . . . Some Jewish districts got up popular re-enactments of Bible legends in front of the Synagogue.

Neither in the novels nor in his history of the Jews of Languedoc, Provence, and the French territories of the Pope, is the portrayal of the old Jewish communities idyllic. Lunel does not overlook tensions and crises, and highlights the ostracization of the inhabitants of the ghetto, as well as certain degrading practices, the defamatory oath "more judaico", and finally the distinguishing badges – the yellow hat for men, the small yellow rosette for women. The problem of discriminatory dress crops up in his first novel, *L'Imagerie du cordier* in which Labri is asked about the yellow "*capéou*" that the Pope forced Jews to wear.

Lunel also reminds us that their daily life had its pleasures. They played *boule* and skittles, they danced the galliard and the branle to the sound of the tambourine and the three-holed flute. Lunel understands celebration and the joy of living; he brings out both tragic and positive aspects of Jewish–Christian relations.

After emancipation and the break-up of the ghettos, we see a progressive disintegration of the Jewish communities and the integration of Jews into the towns of the Midi. It is from the picturesque world of the small folk who used to live in the old-time ghettos, whose survivors he knew, that Lunel wrote the framework of most of his novels. His works show that the declaration of emancipation was not followed immediately by integration. Thus there were pious Jews in Carpentras who refused to give up wearing the yellow hat! On the other hand there was "persecution by *capo*": up until the middle of the 19th century, children meeting a Jew in the street would throw stones at him, shouting "capo! capo!", until he took his hat off. It was the miserable Nicolo Peccavi mentioned earlier who at the time of the Dreyfus affair wrote to the *Veilleur du Comtat* under a patriotic pseudonym to call for the resumption of the practice.

Lunel also paints a stern picture of the decline of Provençal Judaism, of a whole way of life disappearing, torn between conformism and tradition. This Judaism is represented above all by women. Religious Judaism preserved by women – is that the only reason Lunel grants them unusual prominence in most of his novels? This feminine world is often sterile, closed, oppressive, and superstitious. Aunt Sara in *Nicolo Peccavi*, kept her nail-parings and "could have taught Leon of Modena a thing or two about Hebrew rituals and peculiarities". In Lunel's novels the great myths and stories of the Bible are transposed into feminine mode. When her daughter Anna runs away to her father, Régine in *Le Balai de sorcière* punishes her by shaving her head (Samson's hair was the source of his vital force) and shutting her in her room for months. Unlike the sacrifice in the story of Abraham and Isaac, which does not take concrete form, Régine's madness kills her daughter and estranges her husband.

Jewish women are the guardians of Jewish memory, religion, the law. Lunel sees the problem as the encounter with modernity. How can one preserve one's identity in a world that is growing more liberal and permissive? That is the challenge facing descendants of the Pope's Jews. In Lunel those who abandon family and faith pay the penalty. Émilienne, in *Noire et grise* escapes her family, returns humiliated. "In these little towns women lived intimately, narrowly, behind moral walls that were really the last vestiges of the high walls of the old legal ghetto".

Armand Lunel, "the Israel Zangwill of the Midi", remains the supreme bard of the Jewish universe in Provence.

CAROL IANCU
translated by Olive Classe

Lustig, Arnošt

Czechoslovak-born US fiction writer and dramatist, 1926–

Born in Prague, 21 December 1926. Held in concentration camps of Theresienstadt, Auschwitz, and Buchenwald during World War II: escaped, spring 1945. Studied at College of Political and Social Sciences, Prague, MA 1951. Married Věra Weislitzová, 1949; one son, one daughter. Correspondent for Radio Prague in Middle East, Europe, Asia, and North America, 1948–50; worked for Czechoslovak Radio Corporation, 1950–68; correspondent for literary magazines, 1950–58; editor, *Mladý svět* magazine, 1958–59; scriptwriter, Barandov Film Studios, Prague, 1960–68; head of Czechoslovak film delegation to San Sebastian Film Festival, 1968; member of jury, Karlovy Vary International Film Festival, 1968; scriptwriter, Jadran Film Studio, Zagreb, 1969–70. Emigrated to United States, 1970; naturalized US citizen, 1979. Member of International Writers Program, 1970–71, and visiting professor, 1971–72, University of Iowa; visiting professor, Drake University, 1972–73; professor of literature and film, American University, Washington, DC, since 1973. Honorary President, Kafka Society of Prague, since 1990. Many awards, including Mladá Fronta Prize, 1962; Locarno Film Festival Prize, 1963; Mannheim Prize (for film), 1964; Monte Carlo Film Festival Prize, 1966; Czechoslovak Radio Corporation Prize, 1966, 1967; Gottwald Prize, 1967; B'nai B'rith Prize, 1974; National Jewish Book Award, 1980, 1986; Emmy, 1986; Karel Capek Award for Literary Acheivement, 1996. Honorary doctorate in Hebrew letters, Spertus College of Judaica, Chicago, 1986.

Selected Writings

Fiction

Můj známý Vili Feld [My Acquaintance Willi Feld], 1949
Ulice ztracených bratří, 1949; as *Street of Lost Brothers*, translated by Jonathan Brent, 1990
Noc a naděje, 1958, as *Night and Hope*, translated by George Theiner, 1962
Démanty noci, 1959; as *Diamonds of the Night*, translated by Jeanne Němcová, 1962
Dita Saxová, 1962; as *Dita Sax*, translated by George Theiner, 1966
Noc a den (includes *Noc a naděje*; *Démanty noci*; *Můj známý Vili Feld*), 1962
Nikoho neponížíš [Nobody Will Be Humiliated], 1963; as *Indecent Dreams*, translated by Jeanne Němcová, 1988 (including also *Blue Day* and *The Girl with the Scar*)
Modlitba pro Kateřinu Horovitzovou, 1964; as *A Prayer for Katerina Horovitzova*, translated by Jeanne Němcová, 1973
Vlny v řece [Waves in the River], 1964
Bílé břízy na podzim [The White Birches in September], 1966
Hořká vůně mandlí [The Bitter Smell of Almonds], 1968
Miláček [Darling], 1969
Tma nemá stín, as *Darkness Casts No Shadow*, translated by Jeanne Němcová, 1976

Nemilovaná: z deníku sedmnáctileté Perly Sch., 1979; as *The Unloved: From the Diary of Perla S.*, 1985
Porgess, 1995

Screenplays: *Transport z ráje* [Transport from Paradise], from his stories *Noc a naděje* (*Night and Hope*), 1962; *Diamonds of the Night*, 1964; *Dita Saxová*, 1968; *The Precious Legacy*, 1984

Radio Plays: *Prague Crossroads*, 1966; *A Man the Size of a Postage Stamp*, 1967

Television Plays: *Names for Which There Are No People*, 1960; *The Blue Day*, 1960; *A Prayer for Katerina Horovitzova*, 1965; *Theresienstadt* (*Terezin*), with Ernest Pendrell, 1965; *Stolen Childhood*, 1966

Other
První stanice štěstí: reportáže [The First Stop of Happiness: Reportage], 1961
Children of the Holocaust: The Collected Works of Arnost Lustig, translated by Jeanne Němcová and George Theiner, 2 vols, 1976

Further Reading

Cargas, Harry James, "Arnošt Lustig" in *Voices from the Holocaust*, Lexington: University Press of Kentucky, 1993
French, A., *Czech Writers and Politics 1945–1969*, Boulder, Colorado: East European Monographs, 1982
Lustig, Arnošt and Josef Lustig, "Return to Czechoslovakia: Snapshots of a Revolution", *The Kenyon Review*, 2nd series, 12/4 (Fall 1990)
Milk, Leslie, "Now My Father Was Smoke", *The Washingtonian*, 28/7 (April 1993)
Townsend, Charles, "Dita Saxová", *Slavic Review*, 54/2 (Summer 1995)
Trucks, Rob, "A Conversation with Arnošt Lustig", *New England Review*, 20/4 (Fall 1999)
Young, Jeffrey, interview with Arnošt Lustig and Miroslav Holub, *Trafika: An International Literary Review*, 1 (Autumn 1993)

"Literature itself is the emotional memory of man", reflects Czech author Arnošt Lustig, and writing itself is a process of discovery whereby the memory of experience is continuously transformed. Memory, whether it is individual or collective, is not a fixed event, he believes, but an interpretative human capacity which simultaneously forms our recollection and is itself transformed by current and living desires. Literature, constructed from memory, is not an historical account therefore, but a manifestation of a dynamic force by which we discern the *meaning* of our personal and collective histories.

For Lustig, the Holocaust is the central event. In nearly 20 works of fiction, half of which has been translated into English, the Nazi concentration camp is the primary setting, the given universe in relation to which all characters have their being. Born in 1926 in Prague, Lustig spent his adolescence in camps – Theresiendstadt, Auschwitz-Birkenau, Bergen-Belsen. He escaped in 1945 by throwing himself from a transport train, returned to Prague, and joined the Czech Resistance. He started writing because when he recounted what he had experienced in the camps, and what horrors he had seen and survived, people thought he had gone mad. Because they were unable to understand Auschwitz, because he was "exploding with experiences" which rendered him senseless to his listeners, Lustig explains, he was compelled to write.

Writing has thus always been directly connected to and a consequence of his experience as a Jewish prisoner in Nazi death camps. His novels, short stories, and screenplays narrate from this *Lager* – as in the works of Primo Levi, Tadeusz Borowski, and other survivor-writers, the camp is the condition in and against which the human world is revealed. By means of dialogue and precise, physical detail, Lustig conveys the acute and perilous maintenance of life in an environment comprehensively devoted to annihilation. The presence of human detail works against the authority of genocidal death by its mere existence. That a young girl, for example, could contrive an adolescence out of Nazi incarceration is the subject of *The Unloved* (winner of the National Jewish Book Award for Fiction). It is written as a diary, a private document narrated by young Perla. She is a prostitute at Theresienstadt, and readers are privy to the smallest, most intimate details of her life – conversations with other girls and also from so-called lovers, an inventory of things like barrettes and bread as "gifts" in exchange for sex, and letters to the rat with whom she shares a room. Lustig presents this world as self-referential, self-contained, and in doing so he creates a text which seeks to reconcile Auschwitz with the world into which he survived. The "madness" of Auschwitz is the condition of existence in story after story – and so it becomes the certain realm, the normalized state. The denial that Lustig (and other survivors) encountered in life, the sheer inability of listeners to conceive of the unbelievable state of the *Lager*, and especially in the first postwar years, is simply not possible in fiction because the camp *is* the world.

But Lustig's stories take shape not so much from the offence itself (that is the absolute, the given), as from the daily emotions and decisions of the oppressed. In this radical suffering, Lustig's figures are yet characterized by recognizable traits – innocence, loneliness, hope – ordinary, human traits which continue in an inhumane world. This persistence of the human contextualizes and amplifies the depth of the Nazi assault and genocide. At the same time, Auschwitz in fiction is rendered less absolute – for while Lustig's characters are nearly always murdered, the vivid evidence of their fictionalized lives reports past death. Perla's death is inevitable, but it is her life which is documented, made manifest. And perhaps because Lustig's characters are most often children or adolescents, this proximity of annihilation and anticipation of a life yet to be defined and claimed is an especially grievous pairing.

Because there are so many autobiographical elements in his work, it might seem logical to presume that, now in his seventies, Lustig would feel a sense of finally having spoken, of having been heard and understood – that he would believe he has reported to the best of his ability the truth of Auschwitz. But he does not. Though he has written from the experiences of his adolescence his whole life, he maintains that "Auschwitz will never be written" because "the living cannot speak for the dead". Like Primo Levi, who refers to the camp as a world of those drowned and saved, Lustig reminds us that the vast majority of Nazi prisoners were murdered. History and literature as instruments of memory serve the living, Lustig writes, and "it is not in the power of the living to give voice to the dead". For him as for many other survivor-writers, the despair at the catastrophe (Lustig prefers *catastrophe* to *Holocaust*) is compounded by the impossible distance between the living and the dead.

Lustig acknowledges this loss (this "betrayal" on the part of language towards the dead) in his fiction by employing symbols which demonstrate the authority and permanence of the Nazi genocide. In *A Prayer for Katerina Horovitzova*, a prize-winning novel also adapted to screen, the central character is a beautiful Polish dancer caught in a hopeless charade to bargain for her life with Nazi authorities. Her death is certain from the beginning, and the novel is a dramatization of the corrupt, teasing dance between the powerless and the despotic. This novel is remarkable because the murder occurs in the text, onstage and present. The dancer, Katerina, upsets the balance near the end of her life is a dramatic fashion, performing a strip tease for a Nazi official in an anteroom to the gas chamber, in order that she might distract him, steal his gun, and shoot him. This story of the dancer has been reported by other writers who survived Auschwitz, so the tale is significant not so much for its presence alone as for how it is described. Lustig's dancer is heroic in that she sacrifices her own life to act against the oppressor. Lustig employs the ordinary (non-Auschwitz) measure of a brave or heroic act in this novel (powerless as she is, she shoots the soldier), demonstrating a courage that, without the story, would never be known – and inscribing this resistance seems wilful, optimistic, brave. Co-existent with this heroism, however, is the presence of ash in the air. Unnatural and indestructible death is everywhere in the air, in the freezeless ashes, indestructible evidence of the lost millions. The ashes are like the feathers of Bialik's pogrom in the "City of Slaughter", resonant of the catastrophe of hatred, weightless evidence of millions murdered; "contained in the milk that will be drunk by babies yet unborn", Lustig writes, "contained in the breath and statement of every one of us . . . the nagging ashes" of those who "died in innocence". This pairing of innocence and slaughter are the irreconcilable markers of Lustig's own life as survivor, and the tension to which he is always speaking in his work.

JEANIE M. TIETJEN

M

Mailer, Norman

US fiction and nonfiction writer, 1923–

Born Norman Kingsley Mailer in Long Branch, New Jersey, 31 January 1923. Studied at Harvard University, SB in aeronautical engineering 1943; the Sorbonne, 1947. Served in US Army, 1944–46. Married, first, Beatrice Silverman, 1944; divorced 1951; second, Adèle Morales, 1954; divorced 1961; third, Lady Jeanne Campbell, 1962; divorced 1963; fourth, Beverly Bentley, 1963; divorced 1979; fifth, Carol Stevens, 1980; divorced 1980; sixth, Barbara Norris (Norris Church), 1980; nine children. Co-founder, 1955, and columnist, 1956, *Village Voice*, New York; columnist ("Big Bite"), *Esquire*, New York, 1962–63, and *Commentary*, New York, 1962–63. Member of executive board, 1968–73, and President, 1984–86, PEN American Center. Many awards, including *Story* Prize, 1941; American Academy grant, 1960; National Book Award (for nonfiction), 1969; Pulitzer Prize, 1969, 1980; MacDowell Medal, 1973; National Arts Club Gold Medal, 1976. Member, American Academy of Arts and Letters, 1985.

Selected Writings

Novels
The Naked and the Dead, 1948
Barbary Shore, 1951
The Deer Park, 1955
An American Dream, 1965
Why Are We in Vietnam?, 1967
A Transit to Narcissus: A Facsimile of the Original Typescript, edited by Howard Fertig, 1978
Ancient Evenings, 1983
Tough Guys Don't Dance, 1984
Harlot's Ghost, 1991

Short Stories
New Short Novels 2, with others, 1956
Advertisements for Myself (includes essays and poetry), 1959
The Short Fiction of Norman Mailer, 1967
The Short Fiction of Norman Mailer, 1981

Plays
The Deer Park, 1960
DJ, 1967; as *A Fragment from Vietnam* in *Existential Errands*, 1972
Maidstone: A Mystery, 1971

Screenplays: *Beyond the Law*, 1968; *Wild 90*, 1968; *Maidstone*, 1971; *The Executioner's Song*, 1982; *Tough Guys Don't Dance*, 1987

Poetry
Deaths for the Ladies and Other Disasters, 1962

Other
The White Negro, 1957
The Presidential Papers, 1963
Cannibals and Christians, 1966
The Bullfight, 1967
Miami and the Siege of Chicago: An Informal History of the Republican and Democratic Conventions of 1968, 1968
The Armies of the Night: The Novel as History, History as a Novel, 1968
The Idol and the Octopus: Political Writings on the Kennedy and Johnson Administrations, 1968
King of the Hill: On the Fight of the Century, 1971
Of a Fire on the Moon, 1971; as *A Fire on the Moon*, 1971
The Long Patrol: 25 Years of Writing from the Works of Norman Mailer, edited by Robert F. Lucid, 1971
The Prisoner of Sex, 1971
Existential Errands, 1972
St. George and the Godfather, 1972
Marilyn: A Novel Biography, 1973
The Faith of Graffiti, with Mervyn Kurlansky and John Naar, 1974; as *Watching My Name Go By*, 1975
The Fight, 1975
Genius and Lust: A Journey through the Major Writings of Henry Miller, with Henry Miller, 1976
Some Honorable Men: Political Conventions 1960–1972, 1976
The Executioner's Song: A True Life Novel, 1979
Of Women and Their Elegance, 1980
Pieces and Pontifications, 1982
The Essential Mailer, 1982
Huckleberry Finn: Alive at 100, 1985
Conversations with Norman Mailer, edited by J. Michael Lennon, 1988
How the Wimp Won the War, 1992
Oswald's Tale: An American Mystery, 1995
Portrait of Picasso as a Young Man, 1995
The Gospel According to the Son, 1997
The Time of Our Time, 1998

Further Reading

Bernstein, Mashey, "The Heart of the Nation: Jewish Values in the Fiction of Norman Mailer", *Studies in American Jewish Literature*, 2 (1982)

Braudy, Leo (editor), *Norman Mailer: A Collection of Critical Essays*, Englewood Cliffs, New Jersey: Prentice Hall, 1972

Dearborn, Mary V., *Mailer: A Biography*, Boston: Houghton Mifflin, 1999

Leigh, Nigel, *Radical Fictions and the Novels of Norman Mailer*, London: Macmillan, 1989; New York: St Martin's Press, 1990

Lennon, J. Michael, "Norman Mailer," *Contemporary Authors Bibliographical Series*, 3 vols, Detroit: Gale, 1986–89

Lennon, J. Michael (editor), *Critical Essays on Norman Mailer*, Boston: G.K. Hall, 1986

Manso, Peter (editor), *Mailer: His Life and Times*, New York: Simon and Schuster, and London: Viking, 1985

Merrill, Robert, *Norman Mailer*, Boston: Twayne, 1978

Podhoretz, Norman, *Ex-friends: Falling Out with Allen Ginsberg, Lionel and Diana Trilling, Lillian Hellman, Hannah Arendt, and Norman Mailer*, New York: Free Press, 1999

Poirier, Richard, *Norman Mailer*, New York: Viking, and London: Collins, 1972

Solotaroff, Robert, *Down Mailer's Way*, Urbana: University of Illinois Press, 1974

Norman Mailer, in his long and varied career, has been perhaps more notorious for his pronounced and controversial presence on America's cultural scene – his marriages, his politics, his fights, his parties, his personality – than praised for the prose he has produced. Born in New Jersey, raised in Brooklyn, Mailer has said, famously, that the one self-image he finds intolerable is that of the "nice Jewish boy from Brooklyn". Though most of his critics and biographers agree that he rejected Judaism thoroughly, Mailer did join his parents every week for Friday night dinners while they were alive, is said to have considered writing a novel about a concentration camp, featured some Jewish characters and themes in his writing, and at one point declared that it was the task of "sons of immigrants" to "explain America" to itself (*Cannibals and Christians*).

After his graduation from Harvard, Mailer served in the Pacific at Leyte and Luzon during World War II, and published his first novel, *The Naked and the Dead*, in 1948. This extraordinarily successful first novel, an account of a campaign for a fictional Pacific island, Anapopei, features an panoramic array of characters, including the fascistic General Cummings, his embattled aide (and by some accounts the "hero" of the novel) Lieutenant Hearn, and in a mirror plot, the members of a platoon led by Sergeant Croft. The novel also includes two Jewish characters: the neurotic, agnostic, "Jewish looking" Roth, and the gentle, morose, blond, and handsome Goldstein, who peppers his speech with Yiddishisms and is obsessed with the Nazi slaughter of European Jews. The anti-Semitic slurs made by other members of the platoon throughout the novel prompt one conversation between the two characters, in which Goldstein tells Roth, "When the time comes, they won't ask you what kind of Jew you are." The novel features interludes for each character that describe their lives before the war; Goldstein remembers a boyhood in Brooklyn, modelled, perhaps, on Mailer's own, in which his grandfather comforts him after neighbourhood boys call him a "sheenie", by explaining:

> We are a harried people, beset by oppressors. We must always journey from disaster to disaster, and it makes us stronger and weaker than other men, makes us love and hate the other Juden more than other men. We have suffered so much that we know how to endure. We will always endure.

Goldstein (and perhaps Mailer), however, rejects the meaningfulness of Jewish suffering: "All the ghettoes, all the soul cripplings, all the massacres and pogroms, the gas chambers, the lime kilns – all of it touched no one, all of it was lost."

The work that placed Mailer once again squarely in the public eye after *The Naked and the Dead* was *Advertisements for Myself*, a miscellany of short stories, excerpts from his novels, his columns from the *Village Voice* (the alternative paper which he had helped to found in 1955), political essays, and arguably his most famous piece, "The White Negro", which had first appeared two years before in *Dissent*, edited by Irving Howe. The collection was held together by the author's running commentary set in italics, a performance piece in itself, which provided a frank account of Mailer's bouts with drug use, depression, and bad writing. His rejection of the persona of the "nice Jewish boy from Brooklyn" is also voiced in this work. "The White Negro" dealt with the influence of black culture, the increasing alienation of bohemian youth, and the violence of the "hipster", who Mailer equated with the psychopath and the black, and whose morality is "to do what one feels whenever and wherever it is possible".

Mailer's reputation as a pugnacious provocateur was established with this work. "The White Negro" was also significant in shaping his conflicted relationship with the New York intellectuals, who, in the 1950's with *The Partisan Review*, had established themselves as the most active, serious, and passionate critics of American culture. They were also predominantly Jewish. Politically and culturally, however, Mailer was a maverick: he wasn't interested in Jewish issues as they were, nor did he assert his Judaism as they did. He was not as passionately anti-communist. Although he and Norman Podhoretz were good friends for a while, Podhoretz is reported to have commented more recently that Mailer had never circumcised his sons and had never been to Israel. "The White Negro", however, initiated a longstanding preoccupation with the status of minority groups in America. Mailer's *Presidential Papers* includes a section entitled "Minorities", in which he calls minorities "the artistic nerve of a republic". In 1963 Mailer wrote three articles for *Commentary* on Buber and mystical Judaism. He had become fascinated by Hasidism, and had even convinced Podhoretz to take him to a Hasidic Yom Kippur service. Those Jews, he said later admiringly, were "a bunch of crazy motherfuckers, hard core and mean and tough". His novel *An American Dream*, whose hero is part Jewish, has been read as incorporating certain Jewish mystical principles, namely, the union of opposites, the mutuality of God and Man, and the mystical transcendence of the sex act.

Mailer continued to be a prolific and unpredictable writer. His major achievements of the 1960s and 1970s were in the realm of nonfiction, or rather in what Truman Capote called the "nonfiction novel". *Armies of the Night* grew out of his experiences marching on the Pentagon in 1967 (in it, Mailer describes how each of his wives represents a particular culture, Jewish, Latin, and English, up to his current wife, who is an "American girl"). *Miami and the Siege of Chicago* concerns the Democratic and Republican presidential primaries and conventions, and was nominated for a National Book Award. *The Prisoner of Sex*, a response to the women's movement, and *Marilyn*, about Marilyn Monroe, are notable for the storm of protest they inspired. *The Executioner's Song*, about executed murderer Gary Gilmore, won another Pulitzer Prize. The 1980s saw less critically successful novels: *Ancient Evenings*, designed to be Mailer's magnum opus, about a family in ancient Egypt (Leslie Fiedler read the book as anti-Jewish in its preoccupation with the pagan), and *Tough Guys Don't Dance*, a noir detective novel.

Mailer's prodigious cultural output has crossed genres: he has written and acted in films, has written poetry, has even run for mayor of New York. He has always resisted being called a Jewish writer, and indeed, it is difficult to tease out Jewish themes in his work. His overwhelming desire to be American, to represent the American cultural scene, to write with the spirit of his time, and his abilities as a cultural and literary chameleon, all, perhaps, mark his Jewishness. Mailer has transformed himself from Brooklynite into Harvard man, from bohemian hipster into conservative, from filmmaker into politician, and the list goes on. Perhaps no Jewish cultural figure in America has represented so unwittingly the experience of the Jew in America; as Mailer himself writes, "[Minority groups] are both themselves and the mirror of the culture as it reflects upon them".

RACHEL RUBINSTEIN

Malamud, Bernard

US fiction writer, 1914–1986

Born in Brooklyn, New York, 26 April 1914. Studied at Erasmus Hall High School, New York; City College of New York, BA 1936; Columbia University, MA 1942. Married Ann de Chiara, 1945; one son, one daughter. Teacher, New York high schools, evenings, 1940–49; instructor, later associate professor of English, Oregon State University, 1949–61; member of Division of Languages and Literature, Bennington College, Vermont, 1961–86; visiting lecturer, Harvard University, 1966–68. President, PEN American Center, 1971–81. Many awards, including Rosenthal Award, 1958; Daroff Award, 1958; Ford Foundation Fellowship, 1959, 1960; National Book Award, 1959, 1967; Pulitzer Prize, 1967; O. Henry Award, 1969, 1973; Jewish Heritage Award, 1979; Brandeis University Award, 1981; Bobst Award; Mondello Prize (Italy), 1985. Member, American Academy of Arts and Letters, 1964; American Academy of Arts and Sciences, 1967. Died 18 March 1986.

Selected Writings

Short Stories
The Magic Barrel, 1958
Idiots First, 1963
Rembrandt's Hat, 1973
Two Fables, 1978
The Stories of Bernard Malamud, 1983
The People, and Uncollected Short Stories, edited by Robert Giroux, 1989

Novels
The Natural, 1952
The Assistant, 1957
A New Life, 1961
The Fixer, 1966
Pictures of Fidelman: An Exhibition, 1969
The Tenants, 1971
Dubin's Lives, 1979
God's Grace, 1982

Other
A Malamud Reader, 1967
Conversations with Malamud, edited by Lawrence Lasher, 1991

Further Reading

Abramson, Edward A., *Bernard Malamud Revisited*, New York: Twayne, 1993
Alter, Iska, *The Good Man's Dilemma: Social Criticism in the Fiction of Bernard Malamud*, New York: AMS Press, 1981
Astro, Richard and Jackson J. Benson (editors), *The Fiction of Bernard Malamud*, Corvallis: Oregon State University, 1977
Avery, Evelyn, *Rebels and Victims: The Fiction of Richard Wright and Bernard Malamud*, Port Washington, New York: Kennikat Press, 1979
Avery, Evelyn (editor), *The Magic Worlds of Bernard Malamud*, Albany: State University of New York Press, 2001
Bloom, Harold (editor), *Bernard Malamud*, New York: Chelsea House, 1986
Cohen, Sandy, *Bernard Malamud and the Trial by Love*, Amsterdam: Rodopi, 1974
Ducharme, Robert, *Art and Idea in the Novels of Bernard Malamud*, The Hague: Mouton, 1974
Field, Leslie A. and Joyce W. Field (editors), *Bernard Malamud and the Critics*, New York: New York University Press, 1970
Field, Leslie A. and Joyce W. Field (editors), *Bernard Malamud: A Collection of Critical Essays*, Englewood Cliffs, New Jersey: Prentice Hall, 1975
Helterman, Jeffrey, *Understanding Bernard Malamud*, Columbia: University of South Carolina Press, 1985
Hershinow, Sheldon J., *Bernard Malamud*, New York: Ungar, 1980

Lasher, Lawrence M., *Conversations with Bernard Malamud*, Jackson: University Press of Mississippi, 1991
Meeter, Glenn, *Bernard Malamud and Philip Roth: A Critical Essay*, Grand Rapids, Michigan: Eerdmans, 1968
Rajagopalachari, M., *Theme of Compassion in the Novels of Bernard Malamud*, New Delhi: Prestige, 1988
Richman, Sidney, *Bernard Malamud*, New Haven, Connecticut: College and University Press, 1966
Salzberg, Joel (editor), *Critical Essays on Bernard Malamud*, Boston: G.K. Hall, 1987
Soloratoff, Robert, *Bernard Malamud: A Study of the Short Fiction*, Boston: Twayne, 1989

Bernard Malamud was one of the foremost American Jewish writers, a term he disliked, thinking it reductive: "I'm an American, I'm a Jew, and I write for all men." However, it is the case that his best writing focuses upon Jews. When he turns to other groups – Italians, African Americans, WASPS – a certain edge is missing: an awareness of a long, often suffering-laden past, with the folklore and bittersweet humour that accompany this. He uses Jews and Jewishness as metaphors for humanity: "I handle the Jew as a symbol of the tragic experience of man existentially. I try to see the Jew as universal man. Every man is a Jew though he may not know it." His major concern in what may be seen as morality plays is with what a character must do to develop from selfishness to altruism and love. If the character learns correctly from suffering, acceptance of responsibility for others and a moral obligation to humanity ensues, and a type of secular redemption can be achieved.

Malamud's first novel, *The Natural*, gives a muted sense of these future concerns. The book is heavily weighted with mythological allusions and has no Jewish content. Baseball is only a backdrop for a tale of tortuous and stunted personal development that leaves the protagonist unfulfilled and unsaved.

In *The Assistant*, probably Malamud's best novel, Frank Alpine succeeds in the journey to moral involvement. There is a strong prison motif, with the outer prison of the store mirroring the inner one, "the blind or blinded self". Malamud succeeds in creating a sense of unreality and timelessness. Grocer Morris Bober provides the moral force imbued from his understanding of Judaism, his experience of poverty, and his Russian past to transform Frank into a disciplined, selfless person.

A New Life is a college novel in which Seymour Levin's Jewishness is not particularly relevant to his achievement of the self-sacrificial new life he accepts at the end. It is Malamud's first politically aware novel, with the effects of McCarthyism prominent. *The Fixer* received both a Pulitzer Prize and National Book Award for its fictionalization of the events surrounding the arrest and prosecution of Menahem Mendel Beilis, in czarist Russia (1911–13). Malamud is concerned with Yakov Bok's moral development in what is a very Jewish novel, despite the protagonist's not being religious. Bok develops a strong sense of responsibility for the Jewish people, which leads him to a realization that all people suffer, Jewish or not, and a righteous person must fight injustice. The focus is upon the inner man, who must break through his own prisons of ignorance and necessity. Malamud creates his most impressive novels in *The Fixer* and *The Assistant*.

Pictures of Fidelman: An Exhibition marks a departure as the six stories form chapters of a novel but stand on their own – a short-story cycle. It is a comic work that deals with the nature of art, as seen through visual arts; the Jewish content is largely limited to "Last Mohican", the first story. In this piece, Arthur Fidelman has his Jewish consciousness and sense of human responsibility restored by beggar / con-man / teacher, Shimon Susskind, who combines harsh reality with fantasy. In *The Tenants* Malamud is again concerned with art, this time writing. He relates African American anti-Semitism through the confrontation between two writers: black Willie Spearmint and Jewish Harry Lesser. This is the first novel in which Malamud is concerned with clearly contemporary issues, in his pursuit of the tragedy of black–Jewish confrontation. There are three endings that highlight the possible outcomes.

Dubin's Lives sees a return to a traditional plot structure, relating the mid-life crisis of a biographer who has little Jewish awareness. However, there is a dramatic change in Malamud's last completed novel, *God's Grace*, which returns to fantasy and literary experimentation, here with talking monkeys. Jewishness is an important theme as, after God destroys the world because of humankind's wickedness, Calvin Cohn attempts to create a new society with the surviving monkeys through inculcating values that are both cooperative and religious, and which have a strong Jewish flavour. Discussions with God, allusions to the Hebrew Bible, and a gorilla who says *Kaddish* for the sacrificed Cohn are part of this beast fable.

When Malamud died in 1986, he was working on chapter 17 of a novel to be called *The People*, about a Jewish peddler and carpenter who becomes the chief of an Indian tribe and tries to save it from annihilation at the hands of a rapacious government. Parallel with *The Fixer* in its theme of a single man trying to save a people, it was left incomplete and unrevised at Malamud's death.

Malamud wrote more than 50 short stories and was a master of the form. These stories were collected in four volumes, some of the best being brought together in the 1983 collection *The Stories of Bernard Malamud*. Some of his most moving insights into the human condition, presented through the plight of poor Jewish immigrants, are seen in tales such as "The First Seven Years", "The Mourners", "The Magic Barrel", and "Angel Levine". The first two are written within a realistic convention, the latter two illustrate Malamud's skill in the use of fantasy. These were collected in *The Magic Barrel*, for which he received the National Book Award. He also wrote many tales having Italian characters. These explore many of the same themes as his Jewish tales, but the ambience is different, even if the suffering and sense of imprisonment in the past is the same. These can be seen in the Fidelman stories and in such tales as "Behold the Key" and "The Maid's Shoes"; in "The Lady of the Lake" he brings together Italian and Jewish milieus. There are also socio-political tales having a strong Jewish content ("The German Refugee", "The Man in the Drawer").

Malamud presented Jewishness as liberal humanism, seeing in Jewish history and struggle ("the very stuff of drama") a paradigm for humanity.

EDWARD A. ABRAMSON

Mamet, David

US dramatist, 1947–

Born David Alan Mamet in Flossmoor, Illinois, 30 November 1947. Studied at Rich Central High School; Francis W. Parker School; Goddard College, Plainfield, Vermont, BA in English 1969; Neighborhood Playhouse School, New York, 1968–69. Married, first, Lindsay Crouse, 1977; divorced; two daughters; second, Rebecca Pidgeon, 1991; one daughter. Actor in summer stock, 1969; stage manager, *The Fantasticks*, New York, 1969–70; lecturer in drama, Marlboro College, Vermont, 1970; artist in residence, Goddard College, 1971–73; founder and artistic director, St Nicholas Company, Plainfield, Vermont, 1972, and St Nicholas Players, Chicago, 1974–76; faculty member, Illinois Arts Council, 1974; visiting lecturer, University of Chicago, 1975–76 and 1979, and New York University, 1981; teaching fellow, Yale University School of Drama, 1976–77; associate artistic director, Goodman Theater, Chicago, 1978–84; associate director, New Theater Company, Chicago, 1985; associate professor of film, Columbia University, since 1988. Contributing editor, *Oui* magazine, 1975–76. Awards include Joseph Jefferson Award, 1974; Obie, 1976, 1983; Rockefeller Foundation grant, 1976; CBS–Yale University Fellowship, 1977; New York Drama Critics Circle Award, 1977, 1984; Outer Circle Award, 1978; Society of West End Theatre Award (London), 1983; Pulitzer Prize, 1984; Dramatists Guild Hull–Warriner Award, 1984; American Academy Award, 1986; Tony, 1987.

Selected Writings

Plays
Lakeboat, 1970
Duck Variations, 1972
Mackinac, 1972
Marranos, 1972
Sexual Perversity in Chicago, 1974
Squirrels, 1974
The Poet and the Rent: A Play for Kids from Seven to 8.15, 1974
American Buffalo, 1975
Reunion, 1976
A Life in the Theatre, 1977
All Men Are Whores, 1977
Dark Pony, 1977
The Revenge of the Space Pandas; or, Binky Rudich and the Two-Speed Clock, 1977
The Water Engine: An American Fable, 1977
The Woods, 1977
Mr Happiness, 1978
Prairie du Chien, 1978
Lone Canoe; or The Explorer, 1979
Shoeshine, 1979
The Sanctity of Marriage, 1979
A Sermon, 1981
Short Plays and Monologues, 1981
Edmond, 1982
Film Crew, 1983
Five Unrelated Pieces, 1983
4 A M, 1983
Glengarry Glen Ross, 1983
Red River, 1983
The Disappearance of the Jews, 1983
The Dog, 1983
The Frog Prince, 1984
Vermont Sketches, 1984
Cross Patch, 1985
Dramatic Sketches and Monologues, 1985
Goldberg Street: Short Plays and Monologues, 1985
Speed-the-Plow, 1985
The Cherry Orchard, 1985
The Shawl, 1985
The Spanish Prisoner, 1985; screenplay, 1998
Vint, 1985
Three Children's Plays, 1986
Things Change, with Shel Silverstein, 1988
Where Were You When It Went Down?, 1988
Bobby Gould in Hell, 1989
House of Games, 1989
Five Television Plays, 1990
Uncle Vanya, 1990
We're No Angels, 1990
Homicide, 1991
Oh Hell: Two One-Act Plays, 1991
Three Sisters, 1991
Oleanna, 1992
No One Will Be Immune, 1994
Death Defying Acts: Three One-act Comedies, 1995
The Cryptogram, 1995
Fruitful and Multiplying: Nine Contemporary Plays, 1996
The Duck and the Goat, 1996
The Old Neighborhood: Three Plays, 1998
Boston Marrriage, 2001

Fiction
The Village, 1994
The Old Religion, 1997
Bar Mitzvah, 1999
Wilson: A Consideration of the Sources, 1999

Poetry
The Hero Pony, 1990
The Chinaman, 1999

Other
Writing in Restaurants, 1986
The Owl (for children), with Lindsay Crouse, 1987
Warm and Cold (for children), with Donald Sultan, 1988
Some Freaks, 1989
On Directing, 1991
The Cabin: Reminiscences and Diversions, 1992
Make Believe Town: Essays and Remembrances, 1996

True and False: Heresy and Common Sense for the Actor, 1997
Jafsie and John Henry: Essays, 1999

Further Reading

Bigsby, C.W.E., *David Mamet*, London and New York: Methuen, 1985
Carroll, Dennis, *David Mamet*, London: Macmillan, and New York: St Martin's Press, 1987
Kane, Leslie (editor), *David Mamet: A Casebook*, New York: Garland, 1992
Kane, Leslie, *Weasels and Wisemen: Ethics and Ethnicity in the Work of David Mamet*, London: Macmillan, and New York: St Martin's Press, 1999
King, Kimball, *Ten Modern American Playwrights*, New York: Garland, 1982
Norman, Geoffrey and John Rezek, interview with David Mamet, *Playboy* (April 1995)

The atrophying of domestic aspirations, the elevation of individual desires over communal necessities, the substitution of inter-personal communication for commercial transaction, the loss of self in a culture of assimilation. David Mamet mines a rich seam of postmodern discontent and utilizes a wide variety of critical media to apply his theories. Mamet is known for his violent, often obscene language, and his dry, ironic humour has made him one of postwar America's most prolific authors and heir to Arthur Miller's drama of social concern.

The moral and ethical inconsistencies writ large in the press and on television each day in the Western world evoke a network of dark, internalized contradictions that usually defy articulation. Mamet implies that a polemical tone is the optimum means of communication for a generation whose culture is built on ever shifting sands. Self-deceit may have become the most essential means of preserving a connection to society and Mamet's work is determined to reveal the sacrifice of strong personal identities this has meant.

He first came to public attention with a series of dramas about the construction of male life in urban America, particularly in Chicago, where he spent his childhood. His work reaches from the arrogant misogyny and gender miscommunications of *Sexual Perversity in Chicago*, to the focus on mutual exploitation and self-delusion of petty criminality and corporate business in *American Buffalo*, from *Glengarry Glen Ross*, which concentrates on real estate salesmen, to *Speed-the-Plow*, a satire on Machiavellian antics in Hollywood. In all, Mamet's characters speak with a highly stylized staccato delivery, richly laced with extravagant obscenity. In addition, as an extension of his muse of the criminal underworld, Mamet has shown a considerable interest in the confidence game. The plots of two films he has both written and directed – *House of Games* and *The Spanish Prisoner* – have dwelt exclusively on the illusions created by this twilight hinterland.

Mamet appears convinced of the penetrating inroads that the metaphor of the confidence game has made into personal and professional life in postwar society: "The con game is what most people do, most of the time, with few exceptions. After we reach a certain economic level, we try to say that we're no longer trying to talk you out of your money, we're doing 'investment banking' or we've got a film 'in development'" (from Norman and Rezek, 1995). Dennis Carroll emphasizes Mamet's fetish for ambivalence: "Dichotomies, paradoxes and dialectical tensions are central to his work, and apparent in the personality he projects." For Carroll such ambiguities are symptomatic of the expression of the isolation of the individual in the face of an increasingly fractured social structure inherent in much of Mamet's work.

Ascertaining what is true, what is false, and crucially what is neither true nor false but merely simultaneously evident, appears to be at the heart of understanding Mamet. The ease of uncovering their boundaries is clouded by the author himself. The careful control of information received by the audience is a central mechanism in Mamet's work. He shows a concern that his audience should not be aware that they are in receipt of information, but that it should be consciously "planted by the author" (according to Norman and Rezek). The most appropriate medium for Mamet to demonstrate this authorial control is film, through the particular adoption of an Eisensteinian montage-style editing procedure. Contrary to a more linear editing style which ensured a smoothly evolving narrative, Eisenstein favoured a more combative process that relied on the juxtaposition of individual shots in a sequence which demanded the viewer consciously draw certain conclusions which unconsciously affected their emotional and psychological state. He argued on behalf of confrontational editing which evoked the Hegelian dialectic, with each shot representing a thesis and an antithesis, and the viewer's conclusion acting as the synthesis. In his introduction to the screenplay of *House of Games*, Mamet recognizes his debt to the Russian master: "The shot should stand as one unemotional term of a sequence, the totality of which should create in the mind of the audience a new idea." He provided a classic example of this desired effect in a later essay: "a windlashed beach and a woman looking out of a window create the idea of apprehension". For Mamet this provides an unparalleled power to manoeuvre an idea into the mind of his audience. It is a policy he adopts in all of his drama, stage or screen.

In recent years the issue of Jewish identity has entered the personal realm of his life, infusing it with a previously rejected dimension. Of the home in which he grew up, he has written: "My parent's generation was, in the rabid pursuit, first of education, and then of success, greatly assimilationist." More recently he has remarked: "It's in the nature of human beings to say I want to give my kids what I didn't have. In the case of my parents that was economic stability. In the case of myself it's community and identity." In his one-act play *The Disappearance of the Jews* two characters nostalgically talk of their childhood and the absence of any lasting value in their lives since distancing themselves from their community: "everything is so far from us today. And we have no connection." The world of their fathers they invoke so longingly is long gone and nostalgia cannot replace the fact that their ideas of a Jewish life devoid of the compromises they've both made is a fact of the past not their present. *Homicide*, a film Mamet wrote and directed, offers a Jewish protagonist, Bobby Gold, caught between self-hatred and revived Jewish identity, between commitment to his friends and colleagues in a racist police force and his efforts to help a Jewish anti-fascist terrorist cell. Choosing neither, Mamet places Gold in limbo, isolated and in crisis from the decay of identity. *The Old Religion*, a *roman à clef* about Leo Frank, the Jewish factory owner accused of rape and murder in Alabama in 1915. Mamet constructs the entire novel on Frank's inner thoughts, in particular his contradictory relationship, of suspicion and attraction, with his Jewishness. Consumed with the obligations of genteel society and the hope of maintaining his positive relations with the townsfolk who ultimately lynch him, Frank chooses to deny the implication of ethnic membership in a culture which alienates and punishes difference. These three major works on Jewish identity have reflected Mamet's concern for the way in which the rampant pursuit of the American melting pot has engineered a society without any lasting value.

For Mamet corruption and illusion are thus key components of the American condition, be it commercial or personal. It is therefore reasonable to read Mamet's works as intimately self-referential, his plays operating alongside his films as a body of interconnecting texts, rather than independent and unrelated material. The repetition in Mamet's work of both commercial corruption and the nature of Jewishness in America is indicative of a barely concealed obsession. Certainly in the case of the latter, his increased involvement in the activities of the Jewish community over the last 15 years, from worship at synagogue to sending his children to Jewish schools, coincides with the increase in the number of major artistic works and prose essays that focus on that very subject. Conservative by nature, Mamet longs for the stability of the community, yet recognizes this as fantasy and instead religiously inspired ethics prompt him to expose the neglect of identity and commercial corruption at the heart of American culture.

ALEX GORDON

Mandel'shtam, Osip

Polish-born Russian poet, prose writer, and literary critic, 1891–1938

Born Osip Emil'evich Mandel'shtam in Warsaw, 15 January 1891, into middle-class Jewish family. Spent childhood and youth in St Petersburg and Pavlovsk; studied at Tenishev School, St Petersburg, 1900–07; trained for rabbinate and was forbidden secular books. Went to Berlin, 1905; there studied at school of higher Talmudic studies, but also read works by Friedrich Schiller; went to Paris, 1907–08; returned to Germany, 1908. First poems published in *Apollon*, 1908. Studied Old French literature, University of Heidelberg, 1909–10. Returned to Russia to study philosophy, University of St Petersburg, 1911; left without graduating, 1917. Member of Poets' Guild, 1911; developed close personal ties with Anna Akhmatova and her husband, Nikolai Gumilev. After Bolshevik Revolution, 1917, worked for People's Commissariat of Education, Moscow, 1918. Moved to Kiev and worked on journal *Hermes*, 1919. Married Nadezhda Iakovlevna Khazin, 1922. Poem critical of Josef Stalin led to three years in exile, initially in Cherdinki, from 1934; attempted suicide, 1934; following intercession of Akhmatova and Boris Pasternak, transferred to exile in Voronezh; returned to Moscow, 1937. Arrested again, 2 May 1938. Died in transit camp near Vladivostok, 27 December 1938.

Selected Writings

Collections

Sobranie sochinenii [Collected Works], edited by G.P. Struve, 1 vol., 1955
The Prose of Osip Mandelstam, edited and translated by Clarence Brown, 1965; as *The Noise of Time*, 1986; as *The Noise of Time and Other Prose Pieces*, 1988
Sobranie sochinenii [Collected Works], edited by G.P. Struve and B.A. Filippov, 2nd edition, 4 vols, 1967–81
The Complete Critical Prose and Letters, edited by Jane Gary Harris, translated by Harris Link and Constance Link, 1979; as *The Collected Critical Prose and Letters*, 1991; as *The Complete Critical Prose*, 1997
Sochineniia [Works], edited by P.M. Nerler, 2 vols, 1990
Izbrannoe [Selection], edited by P.M. Nerler, 1991
Stikhotvoreniia; Izbrannaia proza [Poetry; Selected Prose], 1991
Sobranie sochinenii [Collected Works], 4 vols, 1993–97

Poetry

Kamen', 1913; as *Pervaia kniga stikhov*, 1923; as *Stone*, translated by Robert Tracy, 1981
Tristia, 1922; as *Vtoraia kniga*, 1923; as *Tristia*, translated by Bruce McClelland, 1986
Stikhotvoreniia [Poetry], 1928; reprinted 1984
Complete Poetry, translated by Burton Raffel and Alla Burago, 1973
Selected Poems, translated by Clarence Brown and W.S. Merwin, 1973
Selected Poems, translated by David McDuff, 1973
Stikhotvoreniia [Poetry], edited by A.L. Dymshits and N.I. Khardzhiev, 1973
Octets, translated by John Riley, 1976
50 Poems, translated by Bernard Meares, 1977
Poems, translated by James Greene, 1977; as *The Eyesight of Wasps*, 1989; as *Selected Poems*, 1991
Otklik neba [The Response of the Sky], 1989
Medlennyi den' [Slow Day], 1990
Poems from Mandelstam, translated by R.H. Morrison, 1990
Stikhi [Poems], edited by Iu.L. Freidin, 1990
Vypriamitel'nyi vzdokh [Rectifying Deep Breath], 1990
Izvozchik i Dant [The Coach Driver and Dante], 1991
Moskovie tetradi, written 1930–34; as *The Moscow Notebooks*, translated by Richard McKane and Elizabeth McKane, 1991
A Necklace of Bees: Selected Poems, translated by Maria Enzensberger, 1992
Sobranie proizvedenii: Stikhotvoreniia [Collected Poems], edited by S.V. Vasilenko and Iu.L. Freidin, 1992
Polnoe sobranie stikhotvorenii, edited by A.G. Mets, 1995

Fiction
Shum vremeni, 1925; as *The Noise of Time*, translated by Clarence Brown, in *The Prose of Osip Mandelstam*, 1965
Egipetskaia marka, 1928; as *The Egyptian Stamp*, translated by Clarence Brown, in *The Prose of Osip Mandelstam*, 1965
Chernyi karlik [Black Dwarf], 1992

Other
Primus, 1925
Dva tramvaia [Two Streetcars], 1926
Kukhnia [The Kitchen], 1926
Shary [Balloons], 1926
O poezii [On Poetry], 1928
Puteshestvie v Armeniiu, 1933; as *Journey to Armenia*, translated by Clarence Brown, 1973
Razgovor o Dante, 1967; as "Conversations about Dante", translated by Jane Gary Harris, in *The Complete Critical Prose and Letters, 1967*
Selected Essays, edited and translated by Sidney Monas, 1977
Voronezhkie tetradi [The Voronezh Notebooks], 1980
Slovo i kul'tura [The Word and Culture], 1987
Stikhotvoreniia; Proza; Zapisnye knizhki [Poetry; Prose; Notebooks], 1989
I Ty, Moskva, sestra moia, legka . . . [And You, Moscow, My Sister, Light . . .], 1990
Stikhotvoreniia; Perevody; Ocherki; Stat'i [Poetry; Translations; Essays; Articles], 1990
Chetvertaia proza: Ocherki, sbornik [Fourth Prose: Essays, Notebook], 1991

Further Reading

Aizlewood, Robin and Diana Myers (editors), *Mandelstam Centenary Conference, 1991*, Tenafly, New Jersey: Hermitage, 1994
Baines, Jennifer, *Mandelstam: The Later Poetry*, Cambridge: Cambridge University Press, 1976
Broyde, Steven, *Osip Mandelstam and His Age: A Commentary on the Themes of War and Revolution in the Poetry 1913–1923*, Cambridge, Massachusetts: Harvard University Press, 1975
Cavanagh, Clare, *Osip Mandelstam and the Modernist Creation of Tradition*, Princeton, New Jersey: Princeton University Press, 1995
Doherty, Justin, *The Acmeist Movement in Russian Poetry: Culture and the Word*, Oxford: Clarendon Press, and New York: Oxford University Press, 1995
Isenberg, Charles, *Substantial Proofs of Being: Osip Mandelstam's Literary Prose*, Columbus, Ohio: Slavica, 1987
Mandel'shtam, Nadezhda, *Hope against Hope: A Memoir*, translated by Max Hayward, New York: Atheneum, 1970; London: Harvill Press, 1971
Mandel'shtam, Nadezhda, *Hope Abandoned: A Memoir*, translated by Max Hayward, New York: Atheneum, and London: Harvill Press, 1974
Pollak, Nancy, *Mandelstam the Reader*, Baltimore: Johns Hopkins University Press, 1995
Przybylski, Ryszard, *God's Grateful Guest: An Essay on the Poetry of Osip Mandelstam*, translated by Madeline G. Levine, Ann Arbor, Michigan: Ardis, 1987
Shentalinsky, Vitaly, *The KGB's Literary Archive*, translated by John Crowfoot, London: Harvill Press, 1995
Taranovski, Kiril, *Essays on Mandelstam*, Cambridge, Massachusetts: Harvard University Press, 1976
West, Daphne M., *Mandelstam: The Egyptian Stamp*, Birmingham: University of Birmingham, 1980
Zeeman, Peter, *The Later Poetry of Osip Mandelstam: Text and Context*, Amsterdam: Rodopi, 1988

Mandel'shtam was a many-faceted poet and writer. It was not only the sheer scope of his work: poetry, books, reviews, essays, the whole gamut of literary endeavour. It was the semantic complexity, the literary images from different epochs of history and especially poetry, the influence of Egypt, classical Greece, Rome . . . and Jewish influences, that mark his works throughout. The attitude towards his own Jewishness was as complex and as many-sided as the rest of his creativity. He never denied his Jewishness, nor did he fail to affirm it. But the entry in *A Biographical Dictionary of Russian Authors of the XXth Century* maintains that he was received into the Protestant Church at Viborg in 1911. The source is cited as Nikita Struve's *Osip Mandel'stam*.

In attempting to determine the extent and depth of Mandel'shtam's Jewishness, researchers have paid particular attention to his early life, his being forced to study for the rabbinate and being forbidden to read secular books, and the autobiographical *Shum vremeni* (*The Noise of Time*). In it, with painful openness, he remembers the embarrassment of being Jewish in a Russian environment (coming from a dysfunctional Jewish family hardly helped), and the hypocrisy in carrying out empty rituals which he foreswore early (as did two other great Jewish literary contemporaries – Mark Aldanov and Vladimir Jabotinsky).

The passage most cited as revealing Mandel'shtam's disenchantment with his Jewish background is one chapter in *Shum vremeni*. It is pejoratively called "Haos Iudeiskii" [Judaic Chaos, rather than Jewish Chaos]. He refers to Yiddish as a language that both amazed and disenchanted him. As for being taken to synagogue, he felt as if he wasn't in a Jewish atmosphere, but in the enlightened ghetto of 17th- or 18th-century Hamburg. When he was taken to visit his grandfather, he was frightened of the Talith flung over him and being made to repeat strange words. But he is carried away by the sounds of a Jewish orchestra playing Tchaikovsky and Scriabin in a filthy Jewish cesspit! Mandel'shtam thought his love of symphonic music began there. On several occasions he mocks what he describes as the correct but lifeless and artificial-sounding speech of various Russian Jews, including his own father. He is allergic to Jewish smells and to the sound of Jewish jargon. His mother regarded herself a member of the intelligentsia, while his father was not fluent in any language. But in concentrating on Mandel'shtam's early life and on *Shum vremeni*, researchers may have overlooked that any person, but especially a sensitive and creative person, grows and matures and changes the outlook of early years. In the poem "This Night Cannot be Repaired", suffused with the death of his mother, Mandel'shtam introduces two grim symbols in the form of two suns. One is black and one is yellow. Some interpret the black one as total rejection, displaying an absence of light from the source (following Euripides). Others consider these symbols to be in opposition, the yellow light above the Temple being replaced by the black sun of apocalyptic Christianity, rising above the gates of Jerusalem. Were these suns representing black and yellow Sabbath candles (yellow brass candleholders). Were they the old black and yellow stripes of the tallit ("Yellow-black ritual")? When he writes, "how painful it is for a tribe to gather alien grass", is this his alienation from Soviet reality, or perhaps the Russian national / nationalistic environment? Hardly. He didn't greet the revolution with great ecstasy. Was it then a general reflection on Jewish fate?

In 1926, a year after Mandel'shtam's critical / negative evaluation of Judaism and Jewishness in *Shum vremeni*, in the sketch "Kiev", in the introduction to a novel by B. Lekash, and in an article on Sh. Mickhoels, he writes warmly of his own people, Jewish family cohesiveness, and "Judaic contemplativeness", he delights in the "inner plasticity/ pliant nature of the ghetto", and maintains that "there is a great creative force inside it" which will "flower only then when the ghetto is destroyed". This is also where Mandel'shtam notes the melodic nature and beauty of the Yiddish language, as well as the logical balance, steadiness, and composure of Ivrit. His journey to Armenia he saw as meeting with "the younger sister of Judea", a "biblical" "Sabbath-worshipping" country.

Mandel'shtam's many-sidedness and the cultural influences that pervade his works may be seen in a series of poems that he wrote in *Kamen'* [Stone]. In 1912 he wrote, among others, "The Lutheran", in which he gives his thoughts on running into a Lutheran funeral. The last stanza is enigmatic. Is he referring to being an atheist or a Jew? In "Aia-Sophia" he asks what the builder meant by having aisles and apses running east and west! This is followed by "The Old Man", in which a drunken old man is going home for the Sabbath, and the drunken Socrates is met by his sour wife! In the same anthology, in "The American Girl", he scoffs at the youthful American tourist.

Did he never abandon his Jewish roots or did he abandon and then return? If he did return, was it in the maturity of his years or his creativity? Was it in answer to personal persecution and rejection or sympathy with the persecuted and rejected Jews of his time and earlier times? Other than Jewish themes, there are plenty of Jewish symbols in his later work. As with so many Russian Jews, Judaism was a matter of culture, *not* religion, or rather, not religious worship. Today, when Judaism is defined according to religious criteria, it is difficult to appreciate Mandel'shtam's essential Jewishness, or how dangerous it was in the context of his times.

In assessing the extent of his Jewishness, the *Russian Jewish Encyclopedia* says that one detects an interest towards matters Jewish in his works. No more than an interest is the implication. The *Shorter Jewish Encyclopedia* considers his Jewishness to go deeper and to be more complex. In her memoirs, *Hope against Hope*, his wife Nadezhda, Jewish but baptized early, refers to their Judaeo-Christian beliefs. She died hoping that his work had been preserved by being in the hands of admirers and collectors, and would yet see the light of day. Preserving manuscripts was indeed a major concern of Russian poets and writers. The Soviet state was merciless. Not only were writers and poets eliminated, their unpublished manuscripts were destroyed. According to Nadezhda, his name was obliterated from all Soviet periodicals after 1923. She poignantly describes the subterfuges that were employed to save his published and unpublished works from the authorities. And then, in a matter-of-fact manner she says that until she was 56, she learned his poetry and prose by heart, but after that, with advancing age, she was no longer able to remember everything.

Several generations of doctoral students with a good command of Russian and the Soviet history of Mandel'shtam's times will have to dig wide and deep, and pose the right questions before the extent of his Jewishness will be assessed properly. A million arrivals in Israel from the former USSR may have raised in the eyes of locals the question of "Who is a Jew?" But eventually, the issue of "What is a Jew?" will also have to be examined. A close examination of Mandel'shtam's creativity and attitude to his Jewishness may help with an answer.

ALEX AUSWAKS

Manger, Itsik

Romanian-born poet, 1901–1969

Born in Czernowitz, 30 May 1901, to Hillel, master tailor, and wife Khave (née Voliner). Attended kheder, folkshul, and Gymnasium; expelled from last of these and apprenticed to tailor, 1915. Began writing poetry in Yiddish, 1918; first poem published in Romanian Yiddish journal *Kultur*, 1921; gave lectures on literary topics and recited own work. Moved to Poland; wrote lyrics and worked on scripts for films in Yiddish; worked with Yiddish theatres in 1930s. Married, first, Golde Trauring; second, Rokhl Auerbakh. Second wife remained in Warsaw when Manger left for Paris, 1938. Moved to Britain, 1940; settled in London with Margaret Waterhouse. Father and younger brother Notte died in concentration camps. Moved to United States, 1951; settled in New York; married, third, Genia Nadir, widow of Yiddish comic writer Moishe Nadir. Moved to Israel, 1967. Poems included in Unesco anthology of world poetry, 1961. Died in Israel, February 1969.

Selected Writings

Collections
Gezamlte shriftn [Collected Writings], 1959
Oysgeklibene shriftn: lider, proze, essayen, memuarn [Selected Writing], edited by Shmuel Rozhanski, 1970

Poetry
Shtern oyfn dakh [Stars on the Roof], 1929
Lamtern in vint [Lantern in the Wind], 1933

Khumesh lider [Pentateuch Songs], 1935
Felker zingen [Peoples Sing], 1936
Megile-lider [Songs from the Book of Esther], 1936
Demerung in shpigl, lid un balade [Twilight in the Mirror], 1937
Far yugnt [For Youth], 1937
Velvl zbarzszer shraybt briv tsu malkele der sheyner [Velvl Zbarzszer Writes a Letter to Malkele the Beautiful], 1937
Volkns ibern dakh [Clouds over the Roof], 1942
Hotsmakh shpil [Hotsmakh Play], 1947
Der shnayder-gezeln note manger zingt [The Tailor-Lad Notte Manger Sings], 1948
Lid un balade [Songs and Ballads], 1952
Shtern in shtoyb [Stars in the Dust], 1967

Selected Translations in:
Onions and Cucumbers and Plums, edited by Sarah Zweig, 1958
The Golden Peacock, edited by Joseph Leftwich, 1961
A Treasury of Yiddish Poetry, edited by Irving Howe and Eliezer Greenberg, 1969
The Penguin Book of Modern Yiddish Verse, edited by Irving Howe *et al.*, 1987

Novel
Dos bukh fun gan-eydn: di vunderlekhe lebnsbashraybung fun shmuel abe abervo, 1939; as *The Book of Paradise*, translated by Leonard Wolf, 1965

Short Story
"The Adventures of Herschl Summerwind" in *A Treasury of Yiddish Stories*, edited by Irving Howe and Eliezer Greenberg, 1954

Plays
Hotsmakh shpil, 1942 (adaptation of Avrom Goldfaden's *Di kishef-makherin* [The Witch])

Other
Getseylte verter, 1929–30
Noente geshtaltn [Close Personalities], 1938
Medresh Itsik [Midrash Itsik], 1980
Shriftn in proze [Writings in Prose], 1980

Further Reading

Bickl, Shloyme, *Shrayber fun Mayn Dor* [Writers of My Generation], vol. 1, New York: Matones, 1958
Biletsky, Israel, *Itsik Manger, Pirke Masah* [A Critical Essay], Tel Aviv: Yisro'el-Bukh, 1976
Davin, Dan, *Closing Times*, London and New York: Oxford University Press, 1975
Glatstein, Jacob, *In Tokh Genumen*, vol. 2, New York: Matones, 1956
Hofer, Yekhiel, *Itsik Manger*, Tel Aviv: Hotsa'at Y.L. Perets, 1979
Kagan, Berl, Itsik Manger in *Leksikon fun yidish-shraybers*, New York: Ilman-Kohen, 1986
Kazdan, Khayim S., *Itsik Manger*, New York: Tsiko, 1968
Liptzin, Solomon, *The Maturing of Yiddish Literature*, New York: Jonathan David, 1970
Meisl, Nakhman, *Forgeyer un Mitsaytler*, New York: Ikuf, 1946
Niger, Shmuel and Jacob Shatzky (editors), *Leksikon fun der nayer yidisher literatur*, 8 vols, New York: Alveltlekhn Yidishn Kultur-Kongres, 1956–81
Ravitch, Melech, *Mayn leksikon*, Montreal: Komitet, 1945
Roskies, David G., *A Bridge of Longing: The Lost Art of Yiddish Storytelling*, Cambridge, Massachusetts: Harvard University Press, 1995
Segal, Hersch, *Tshernovitser Yidishe Po'etn: Itsik Manger, Ya'akov Fridman, Me'ir Harats*, Tel Aviv: Y.L. Perets, 1991

Itsik Manger, who is best known as a poet, began to write poetry as a teenager. His earliest work has never been published. He also wrote essays, literary vignettes, some short stories, several plays, a single humorous novel, and provided lyrics and dialogue for several Yiddish films (*Yidl mitn fidl*, *Der purimshpiler*). He was an extremely popular poet during his lifetime. Even after his death and with the serious decline of a Yiddish readership after World War II, he continued to be widely read.

At the time of Manger's birth, Czernowitz was under Austro-Hungarian rule; by 1918 it had become a part of Romania. Both German and Romanian language and culture were to influence Manger's writing, and his life mirrors the political and cultural upheaval of 20th-century Europe. After spending a decade in Poland, he reached France from where he tried unsuccessfully to reach Palestine and the United States. From London, he eventually went to America in 1951 and lastly moved to Israel where he died. A complex and restless character, he perceived of himself as a romantic itinerant; his sense of homelessness intensified throughout his life though it must be said that the time in Poland was his happiest and most productive.

Manger attended a kheder, and later a folkshul and there was a brief spell in a gymnasium before he was expelled. His father Hillel came from eastern Galicia and was a bohemian character, a humorist and expert rhymester who earned a meagre living as a tailor. His mother Khave was illiterate but knew many stories and folksongs that she recounted to her children. She features in the poetry as do mothers in general. Attempts were made to teach Itsik a tailor's trade, but he showed preference for reading literature and for writing. His younger brother Notte did become a master tailor, albeit with a passion for literature. Notte exerted a great influence on Manger and he features in many poems.

Manger wrote a large number of ballads. He focused on the ballad genre in an unprecedented way for a Yiddish poet. He developed his own vision of the ballad that he spoke about at lectures and discussed in newspaper articles. He was passionate about folksong and theatre and was a wonderful storyteller, but at the same time he sought to express the tragic in life ("ikh zukh dos tragishe in der velt un in lebn"/ I seek the tragic in the world and in life). The ballad with its stress on narrative, dramatic, and lyric elements was a suitable medium for Manger's interests and tendencies. His ballads were initially influenced by German folk and literary ballads and he incorporated Christian subjects and symbols as an expression of universal suffering. As conditions worsened for the Jews in Poland in the 1930s and with the intensification of anti-Semitism, the Christian elements disappeared from the writing which became more consciously Jewish.

Manger was a great collector of folksongs and stories, he claimed inspirational lineage from folk bards who had preceded him such as the Broder singers, Velvl Zbarzher, Elyukem Zunser; he also paid tribute to the playwright Avrom Goldfadn. Until his departure for Poland, Manger participated in the developing Yiddish literary life in Romania (his first volume of poems was published in Bucharest). Like many Yiddish writers he was drawn to Warsaw, which was a major centre for Yiddish culture, with great opportunities for audiences, exchanges with fellow artists, publishing houses, and newspaper outlets. Manger was at his most prolific in Poland; with the outbreak of war and his own subsequent moves from place to place, he was never able to recapture the vibrant Yiddish milieu of Warsaw. He lost his father and brother Notte during the war and he became more despairing. His poetry collections perceptibly trace this development with an increasingly pessimistic tone.

Manger is probably best remembered for his poetical adaptations of biblical material which reveal his humour and his skill and originality as a poet. His *Khumesh lider* draw upon narrative material from the five books of Moses, but he translates events to a period, setting, and speech environment that is east European rather than biblical. His *Megile-lider*, drawn from the Book of Esther, satirize biblical events and characters. The *Megile-lider* were set to music and performed as a musical in Israel in the 1960s, to great acclaim.

Manger's writing is lyrical and folksy; he makes use of popular Jewish figures and legends (Elijah, the Bal Shem Tov, Hershele, Chelm stories) and turns them to his own style. His verse frequently makes mention of travellers, wanderers, and gypsies. Through his poetry he also addresses difficult issues of Jew and Gentile and Polish–Jewish tensions. Some of the writing is expressionistic and surreal, much of it is romantic and folk-like. Boundaries between dream and reality are often blurred. Language is simple and richly idiomatic. The sheer musicality of his verse is stunning. An east European landscape features in the writing and specific places in Galicia are often mentioned. Tailors are a frequent subject.

Manger exhibited great interest in all literatures. He was extremely knowledgeable, and with his impeccable memory he could recite poetry in many languages. With a penchant for drink, Manger was a difficult and enigmatic character. Gossip and scandal stories about him still circulate. Many Yiddish writers experienced disagreements with him. He became very disillusioned with Yiddish literary circles after the war and often felt that others were conspiring against him.

Manger was a neo-romantic poet with a belief in his own worth, who succeeded in conveying the essence of a Jewish and Yiddish folk spirit and in fashioning tradition to a contemporary reality. After Manger's death, Sholem Rosenfeld, who was both friend and mentor to Manger, established the Manger Archive at the Hebrew University, Jerusalem, which is said to house 80 per cent of his work.

HELEN BEER

Mani Leyb (Leib)

Russian-born US poet, 1883–1953

Born Mani Leyb Brahinsky in Niezhin, Ukraine, 20 December 1883. Involved in revolutionary socialist movements in his youth, and imprisoned. Fled to London, 1904, to avoid re-arrest; started writing poetry. Went to New York, 1905. Worked as bootmaker; frequent periods of financial hardship and ill health. Separated from his wife; lived with Yiddish poet Rochelle Weprinski from 1917 until his death. Leading member of group *Di yunge* (the Young Ones); wrote for the *Forverts* (*Jewish Daily Forward*) and for a short time for the communist *Frayhayt*. Died in the sanatorium of the Workmen's Circle, in Liberty, New York, 4 October 1953.

Selected Writings

Poetry

Baladn [Ballads], 1918
Lider [Poems], 1918
Yidishe un slavishe motivn [Jewish and Slav Motifs], 1918
Yingl-tsingl-khvat [Little Boy-Little Tongue-Little Rascal], 1918
Vunder iber vunder: lider, baladn, mayselekh [Miracle of Miracles: Poems, Ballads, Stories], 1930
A maysele in gramen: fun dray zin mit a mamen [A Story in Rhyme: Of Three Sons and a Mother], 1937
Lider un baladn [Poems and Ballads], 2 vols, 1955
Sonetn [Sonnets], 1961
In *A Treasury of Yiddish Poetry*, edited by Irving Howe and Eliezer Greenberg, 1976
Lider un baladn [Poems and Ballads], 1977
In *The Penguin Book of Modern Yiddish Verse*, edited by Irving Howe, Ruth Wisse, and Khone Shmeruk, 1987

Other

Dertseylungen [Stories], 1920
Mendele Moykher Sforim: biografye far kinder [Mendele Moykher Sforim: A Biography for Children], 1936
Briv 1918–1953: Mani Leyb tsu Roshel Veprinski [Letters 1918–1953: Mani Leyb to Rochelle Weprinski], 1980

Further Reading

Glatstein, Jacob, *In tokh genumen: eseyen* [Sum and Substance: Essays], New York: Matones, 1947
Iceland, Reuben, *Fun undzer friling* [About our Springtime] New York: Indzl, 1954
Jeshurin, Ephim H., "Mani Leyb: bibliografye" in *Lider un baladn* by Leyb, vol. 2, New York: Komitet baym Altveltlekh Yidish Kultur Kongress, 1955
Kramer, Aaron, *A Century of Yiddish Poetry*, New York and London: Cornwall, 1989
Pat, Jacob, *Shmuesn mit yidishe shrayber* [Conversations with Yiddish Writers], New York: Marstin, 1954
Wisse, Ruth R., "*Di Yunge*: Immigrants or Exiles?", *Prooftexts*, 1 (1981)
Wisse, Ruth R., *A Little Love in Big Manhattan. Two Yiddish Poets*, Cambridge, Massachusetts: Harvard University Press, 1988

The remark of the poet Reuben Iceland that Yiddish poetry should no longer be merely "the verse department of the Jewish labour movement" pinpoints the essential motivation of the New York group *Di yunge* (The Young Ones), of which Mani Leyb was a key figure. These young poets wanted to distance themselves from the didactic socialist verse of the earlier American "sweat-shop" poets. *Di yunge* – the most important of whom were Zisha Landau, Iceland, and Mani Leyb – came from traditional east European backgrounds but developed their creativity in the United States. Influenced by modern European literature, particularly by the German Romantics and the Russian Symbolists, they strove for a poetry in Yiddish arising out of the inner sensibilities of the individual; a project that was suspect to Yiddish editors and publishers, and to many older writers. Previously, Yiddish poetry had been wedded to ideas of community and social relevance. This poetry of individual sensibility demanded a mode of expression in Yiddish that had to be created, and the richness of Yiddish as a poetic language in the work of poets as diverse as Uri Zvi Greenberg and Abraham Sutzkever owes much to the innovations of *Di yunge* and their contemporaries.

Mani Leyb came to be regarded as the most important of the group. In his early phase of striving for modernity he deliberately shied away from traditional Jewish themes in order to evoke the inner world of the *ikh* and the isolation of the immigrant in the turmoil of the city. The short lyric poems of this period are suffused with gentle melancholy, and a panoply of Romantic images: mist and snow, the atmosphere of evening and the pale light of the moon, the wanderer and the storm-tossed ship as a metaphor of the self cast adrift:

To what harbour will the wind carry us?
The waves rise up before our ship like stairs,
Like stairs leading to chasms. And heavy mists hang low
On our bowed heads.
(translated by Heather Valencia)

Mani Leyb's language is relatively simple but the musicality of the verse, its synaesthesia, alliterative nuances, and onomatopoeic effects, combine to create poetry of great luminosity and emotional intensity.

The shock of World War I, when many American Jews were in anguish about the fate of loved ones in Europe, contributed to the emergence of a strong Jewish identity in Mani Leyb's work. Folk motifs became a key strand in his poetry, and he re-embraced the Jewish religious tradition with its messianic longing, returning to the notion that the poet is a representative of his people. In his most frequently anthologized poem the poet exhorts the people, or perhaps his fellow poets, to await the coming of the mysterious stranger:

Hush and hush – no sound be heard.
Bow in grief but say no word.
Black as pain and white as death,
Hush and hush and hold your breath.
Heard by none and seen by none,
Out of the dark night will he,
Riding on a snow-white steed,
To our house come quietly.
(translated by Marie Syrkin, in Howe and Greenberg, 1976)

There is no certainty, though, that the Messiah will come, and the poem ends with a repetition of the first stanza: the people's bowed heads and silent holding of breath are frozen for eternity; the quietude epitomizes the new inward-looking poetry of *Di yunge*.

Mani Leyb's socialism did not, however, vanish, and the theme of the impoverished immigrant is by no means absent from his poetry: the difference between Mani Leyb and socialist and anarchist poets such as David Edelshtadt, Moris Winchevsky, and Moris Rosenfeld is exemplified in their different treatment of these subjects. In the poem "On Fifth Avenue", Mani Leyb takes up the theme of the exploited seamstresses in the sweatshop, but here the social message, rather than being categorically stated, emerges through evocative imagery and mellifluous verse:

White silk, rose silk, violet and blue,
And the thin needles, thinly, deafly weeping,
And the sun in the window, pale with sorrow,
Among the hot pillars of green dust creeping.
(translated by Heather Valencia)

Mani Leyb wrote many ballads that are based on Slav and Jewish motifs, but also show the influence of the German Romantic folklore revival. In effortlessly rhyming verse the anonymous narrator spins tales of magic and miracles, ostensibly for children; often, however, they are dark and disturbing. Jews lost in the snow are deceived by illusory visions of hospitable inns conjured up by evil spirits, the bride weeps for her vanished lover, evil brothers snatch lost children wandering in dark woods: in most of the ballads, however, good triumphs over evil. The principal Jewish folklore motif is that of Elijah who wanders, disguised as a traveller, through Jewish markets and shtetls, providing miraculous succour for the poor before disappearing again. Mani Leyb vividly recreates the mood and form of the folk-ballad, but though apparently artless, these ballads are sophisticated compositions with intricate varied metrical patterns and rhyme schemes, and dramatic use of assonance. Itsik Manger, the master of the ballad form in Yiddish, expressed his delight in the "lyrical pearls" that Mani Leyb created "with the sound of the *folkslid* in his ears".

In the late 1920s Mani Leyb suffered a crisis caused partly by his difficult private life, partly by the decline of New York's pre-eminence as a centre of Yiddish literature, and partly by criticism of the lack of development in his work. In the early 1930s he emerged from this crisis to create the work of his maturity: the sonnets that he wrote from then until his death. In the stringent sonnet form he found his ideal poetic mode, which was "intimate enough for his soft voice yet powerful enough for the summary of a life" (Wisse, 1988). The 60 or so sonnets gather together all the strands of his life and thought in clarity and simplicity, attributes that Mani Leyb constantly strove to achieve. In two of the sonnets he confronts the Holocaust for the first time. In one he evokes in the quatrains the abundant life of traditional Jewish communities, in the tercets their destruction, after which only a few remain stubbornly standing "a tsvey-dray beymer fun an oysgehaktn vald" [two or three trees from a demolished forest]. In the other sonnet the ancient Jewish theme of longing for the redeemer – now more poignant than ever – is combined with the poet's guilt as a survivor ("a tiny Jew/ who avoided the ovens and the fire"). Here and in the other sonnets the potential of this economical form to encompass the essence of a vast theme is powerfully realized by Mani Leyb. Increasingly the focus of attention becomes his own mortality. In his best-known sonnet he writes his own inscription on his gravestone:

> Here lies Hersh Itzi's son with shards upon his eyes,
> Buried in shrouds, as a good Jew should be.
> (translated by Heather Valencia)

In death he returns to the world of his fathers, and in the remainder of the poem, with gentle irony, he sums up his life: a peddler of air, of which, however, some traces remain as his testament to the next generation. This sonnet was read aloud at Mani Leyb's funeral.

HEATHER VALENCIA

Mankowitz, Wolf

British dramatist, fiction writer, and poet, 1924–1998

Born Cyril Wolf Mankowitz in London, 7 November 1924. Studied at East Ham Grammar School, London; Downing College, Cambridge, MA in English 1946. Served as volunteer coalminer and in army during World War II. Married Ann Margaret Seligmann, 1944; four sons. Produced plays and films, with Oscar Lewenstein, 1955–60, independently, 1960–70, with Laurence Harvey, 1970–72. Emigrated to Irish Republic, 1971. Adjunct professor of English, since 1982, and adjunct professor of theatre arts, 1987–88, University of New Mexico, Albuquerque. Many awards, including Society of Authors Award (for poetry), 1946; Venice Film Festival Prize, 1955; British Academy of Film and Televsion Arts Award, 1955, 1961; Oscar for Best Screenplay, 1957; Film Council of America Golden Reel, 1957; *Evening Standard* Drama Award, 1959; Cork Film Festival International Critics Prize, 1972; Cannes Film Festival Grand Prix, 1973. Died 20 May 1998.

Selected Writings

Plays
Make Me an Offer, 1952
The Bespoke Overcoat, 1953
The Baby, 1954
The Boychik, 1954
Five One Act Plays, 1955
It Should Happen to a Dog, 1955
The Last of the Cheesecake, 1956
The Mighty Hunter, 1956
Expresso Bongo, with Julian More, 1958
Belle; or, The Ballad of Dr Crippen, with Beverley Cross, 1961
Pickwick, 1963
Passion Flower Hotel, 1965
Jack Shepherd, 1972; as *Stand and Deliver*, 1972
The Samson Riddle, 1972; as *Samson and Delilah*, 1972
Dickens of London, 1976
The Hebrew Lesson, 1976
The Irish Hebrew Lesson, 1978
Iron Butterflies, 1985

Screenplays: *Make Me an Offer*, with W.P Lipscomb, 1954; *A Kid for Two Farthings*, 1955; *Expresso Bongo*, 1955; *The Bespoke Overcoat*, 1955; *Trapeze*, 1955; *The Millionairess*, with Ricardo Aragno, 1960; *The Two Faces of Dr Jekyll*, 1960; *The Day the Earth Caught Fire*, with Val Guest, 1961; *The Long and the Short and the Tall*, with Willis Hall, 1961; *Waltz of the Toreadors*, 1962; *Where the Spies Are*, with James Leasor and Val Guest, 1965; *Casino Royale*, with others, 1967; *La Vingt-cinquième Heure*, 1967; *The Assassination Bureau*, with Michael Relph, 1969; *Bloomfield*, with Richard Harris, 1970; *Black Beauty*, with James Hill, 1971; *The Hebrew Lesson*, 1972; *The Hireling*, 1973; *Treasure Island*, with Orson Welles, 1973; *Almonds and Raisins*, 1983

Novels
Make Me an Offer, 1952
A Kid for Two Farthings, 1953
Laugh till You Cry: An Advertisement, 1955
My Old Man's a Dustman, 1956; as *Old Soldiers Never Die*, 1956
Cockatrice, 1963
The Biggest Pig in Barbados: A Fable, 1965
Raspberry Reich, 1979
Abracadabra!, 1980
The Devil in Texas, 1984
Gioconda, 1987
The Magic Cabinet of Professor Smucker, 1988
Exquisite Cadaver, 1990
A Night with Casanova, 1991

Short Stories
The Mendelman Fire and Other Stories, 1957
The Blue Arabian Nights: Tales of a London Decade, 1973
The Day of the Women and the Night of the Men: Fables, 1977

Poetry
XII Poems, 1971

Other
The Portland Vase and the Wedgwood Copies, 1952
Wedgwood, 1953
Majollika and Company, 1955
ABC of Show Business, 1956
A Concise Encyclopedia of English Pottery and Porcelain, with R.G. Haggar, 1957
Expresso Bongo: A Wolf Mankowitz Reader, 1961
The Penguin Wolf Mankowitz, 1967
The Extraordinary Mr Poe: A Biography of Edgar Allan Poe, 1978

The Day God Laughed: Sayings, Fables, and Entertainments of the Jewish Sages, commentary with Hyam Maccoby, edited and translated by Maccoby, 1978
Mazeppa: The Lives, Loves, and Legends of Adah Isaacs Menken: A Biographical Quest, 1982

Born in London in 1924 of Russian-Jewish descent, Wolf Mankowitz was the first pupil from his local grammar school to win a scholarship to Cambridge, where he was taught by the likes of F.R. Leavis. Soon after graduating he won a Society of Authors prize for poetry, but it is for his early fables of life in the Jewish East End of his childhood that he is most fondly remembered.

His much-loved novella *A Kid for Two Farthings* and his play *The Bespoke Overcoat* (the screenplay of which won Mankowitz an Oscar), were penned within a year of each other. The first tells the story of Joe, a six-year-old boy, and Africana, the one-horned kid he buys off the market and keeps in a box in the back yard of Mr Kandinsky the tailor. Mankowitz captures perfectly a time and a place that had more in common with the Old Country shtetls than the rest of London, with its *schvitzes* (bath-houses), its bare-knuckle boxing tournaments, and teeming markets.

The Bespoke Overcoat is Mankowitz's Jewish reworking of a Russian tale by Gogol, in which Fender, an elderly clerk who has spent his life working in Rantings' stone cold warehouse, comes back as a ghost. Before he died, Fender had taken his old overcoat to Morry the tailor in the hope that he could mend it. With more holes than fabric, the coat is beyond repair, even for Morry with a "needle like Paganini", so instead Morry offers to make him a new, bespoke overcoat at cost, though he can ill afford it. As the author's note explains, this play is "a sustained, typically over-long Jewish joke – than which there is no funnier and no sadder story."

These are people who have very nearly hit rock bottom but manage to carry on, saved by an ability to accept each new setback with humour and humility. Moreover, even in the humblest of settings, there is magic. Fender, for instance, dreams a poetic, sublimely surreal dream of flying overcoats, their pockets filled with hot, tasty soup that never spills; the dream compounds his simple desires, lifting them to a new level. Similarly, in *A Kid for Two Farthings* the small, sickly kid bought off the market becomes, in Joe's eyes at least, a real unicorn as it lives out its final days in Mr Kandinsky's back yard. Images kaleidoscope out of the figure of the kid, just as is in Chad Gadya, the traditional children's Passover song, from which the story takes its title. These East End stories also reveal a debt to Yiddish masters such as Sholom Aleichem; as Mankowitz himself notes in his introduction to a treasury of Yiddish stories: "For the Yiddish writer mysticism touches the earthiest existence, the most simple and common life contains a moment of the highest meaning . . . life was funny, or tragic, but never merely decorative".

While Mankowitz believed Jewishness to be dependent on far more than religious observance, he caught from his father the habit of "quite unreligious biblical study", and his robust, argumentative attitude is given full rein in his reworkings of biblical stories such as *The Samson Riddle* and *It Should Happen To A Dog*, plays based on Samson and Jonah. He also published, together with the scholar Hyam Maccoby, *The Day God Laughed*, a selection of sayings and fables of the sages with a commentary. Mankowitz was an ardent commentator on his own work, too often adding notes and introductions. Elsewhere, in his riddling poems and fables, many a mere half page long, he displays an almost Talmudic turn of mind and appreciation of the interconnectedness of the world and life. Notably, he later in life devoted some of his energies to publicizing the Hasidic sect of the Lubavich.

Mankowitz's early writing spawned hopes that he might become a British Bernard Malamud. "One cannot talk oneself out of being a Jew", he wrote in the essay that accompanies *The Samson Riddle*, but while he did return to the East End in his fiction, he was never going to confine himself to chronicling Anglo-Jewish life in London. His were an immigrant's aspirations, and although he maintained a strong sense of origin, he was proud to have come so far from the crowded two-room home in which he was raised, and was wary of sentimentalizing the old days. Writing in 1972 in the introduction to *The Blue Arabian Nights: Tales of a London Decade*, he explained: "For the children of the war, who had known no childhood, there were too many interesting parts available for the play itself to have much of a plot." He went on to satirize the pop culture of 1950s Britain with *Expresso Bongo*, and captured the public fear of nuclear war with his screenplay for *The Day the Earth Caught Fire*. He became a specialist in Wedgwood pottery, that most genteel English creation, and he brought to life a charismatic world of personalities in his fiction and non-fiction: Dickens, Poe, Casanova, and Duchamp.

At the outbreak of the Six Day War, Mankowitz briefly threw his weight behind the Zionist cause, but he left Israel feeling that "though England had not entirely made me, I had done nothing to make Israel and therefore had no permanent place there" (*The Samson Riddle*).

If anything, Mankowitz was a man who wore his talent too lightly; by his own account, he was:

> a shopkeeper and a gallery owner, a film writer and theatrical producer, an impresario and a television performer, a night-club owner and an inveterate night-walker, a musical librettist, and a newspaper columnist, a restaurateur, a ceramic encyclopaedist and a Wedgwood historian.

Add to that Visiting Professor at the University of New Mexico and sometime Honorary Consul to the Republic of Panama in Dublin, and one can at least partly appreciate the breadth of Mankowitz's sprawling talent.

Ultimately, his lasting achievement is his ability to capture an East End that even during his lifetime was fading into rose-tinted memory; his humorous, anecdotal tales, with their sharp edge of pathos are a rare portrait of one of the most vibrant, significant chapters in Anglo-Jewish history, and as such they are without rival.

HEPHZIBAH ANDERSON

Margolin, Anna

Lithuanian-born US poet and journalist, 1887–1952

Born Rosa Lebensboym in Brisk, Lithuania, 21 January 1887. Under guidance of father, Hasid turned maskil, received secular education. Lived briefly in Königsberg and Odessa; moved with father, after parents' divorce, to Warsaw. Sent by father to United States, 1906. Began writing, 1906; worked as secretary to Yiddishist Chaim Zhitlovsky, then as journalist for Yiddish press; first piece of fiction appeared in *Fraye arbeter shtime* [Free Workers' Voice]; published short stories under pseudonyms Khave Gros and Khane Barut. Travelled to London, Paris, and Warsaw. Married, first, Hebrew writer Moshe Stavski; one son. Emigrated to Palestine; unhappy in marriage and stifled by lack of intellectual stimulation in Tel Aviv, returned alone to Warsaw. Settled permanently in New York, 1914. Joined newly established Yiddish daily *Der tog*, 1914; member of its editorial board until 1920; wrote weekly column for women, "In der froyen velt" [In the Woman's World]; travelled in Europe as correspondent on women's issues; wrote articles supporting suffrage movement. Married, second, Hirsh Leyb Gordon, fellow journalist on *Der tog*; became estranged when he left to serve in US army, 1917. Published some articles under pseudonyms Sofia Brandt and, later, Clara Lenin. Met Yiddish writer Reuben Iceland (Reuven Ayzland); they became lifelong companions. Last poems appeared, 1932; no longer allowed her works to be published; suffered from severe depression and chronic minor ailments; became recluse in final years. Died in New York, 29 June 1952.

Selected Writings

Poetry

Lider [Poems], 1929; edited and translated by Abraham Novershtern, 1991

Translations of Selected Poems in

The Golden Peacock: An Anthology of Yiddish Poetry, translated by Joseph Leftwich, 1939

The Penguin Book of Modern Yiddish Verse, edited by Irving Howe *et al.*, 1987

The Tribe of Dina: A Jewish Women's Anthology, revised edition, edited by Melanie Kaye-Kantrowitz and Irena Klepfisz, 1989

An Anthology of Modern Yiddish Poetry, 3rd edition, edited and translated by Ruth Whitman, 1995

Other

Editor, *Dos yidishe lid in amerika: antologye* [The Yiddish Poem in America: Anthology], 1923

Further Reading

Ayzland, Reuven, *Fun unzer friling: literarishe zikhroynes un portretn* [From Our Spring: Literary Memoirs and Portraits], New York: Inzl, 1954

Cooper, Adrienne, "About Anna Margolin" in *The Tribe of Dina: A Jewish Women's Anthology*, edited by Melanie Kaye-Kantrowitz and Irena Klepfisz, revised edition, Boston: Beacon Press, 1989

Cooperman, Jehiel B. and Sarah H. Cooperman (editors and translators), *America in Yiddish Poetry: An Anthology*, New York: Exposition Press, 1967

Hellerstein, Kathryn, "A Question of Tradition: Women Poets in Yiddish" in *Handbook of American-Jewish Literature*, edited by Lewis Fried, New York: Greenwood Press, 1988

Hellerstein, Kathryn, "From 'Ikh' to 'Zikh': A Journey from 'I' to 'Self' in Yiddish Poems by Women" in *Gender and Text in Modern Hebrew and Yiddish Literature*, edited by Naomi B. Sokoloff *et al.*, New York: Jewish Theological Seminary of America, 1992

Korman, Ezra (editor), *Yidishe dikhterins* [Yiddish Female Poets], Chicago: Stein [Shtayn], 1928

Kramer, Aaron (editor and translator), *A Century of Yiddish Poetry*, New York: Cornwall, 1989

Leksikon fun der nayer yidisher literatur [Biographical Dictionary of Modern Yiddish Literature], vol. 5, New York: Alveltlekhn Yidishn Kultur-Kongres, 1963

Novershtern, Abraham, "Ana Margolin: materialn tsu ir poetisher geshtalt", *Yivo bleter*, new series, 1 (1991)

Novershtern, Abraham, "'Who Would Have Believed that a Bronze Statue Can Weep?': The Poetry of Anna Margolin", introduction to *Anna Margolin: Lider*, Jerusalem: Magnes, 1991

Pratt, Norma Fain, "Culture and Radical Politics: Yiddish Women Writers, 1890–1940", *American Jewish History*, 70/1 (September 1980)

Pratt, Norma Fain, "Anna Margolin's *Lider*: A Study in Women's History, Autobiography, and Poetry", *Studies in American Jewish Literature*, 3 (1983)

Reyzen, Zalman, *Leksikon fun der yidisher literatur, prese un filologye* [Dictionary of Yiddish Literature, Prose and Philology], 3rd edition, 4 vols, Vilna: Kletskin, 1928–29

Zucker, Sheva, "Ana Margolin un di poezye funem gesholtenem ikh" [Anna Margolin and the Poetry of Torn Self], *Yivo bleter*, new series, 1 (1991)

While there has yet to appear a full volume of Anna Margolin's poetry in English translation, she has long been recognized by Yiddish readers and scholars as a leading modernist poet of the generation that marked the golden age of Yiddish poetry in America. Although she cited both "the more general character of Russian and German poetry, and perhaps the America of the Imagists" and "the minds and hearts of women I have encountered, never men" as her strongest poetic influences, Margolin's poetry reveals a conscious effort both to react against and carve out her own creative space among the predominantly male writers of the leading Yiddish literary movements of her time in New York, *Di yunge* (the Young Ones) and the *Inzikhistn* (Introspectivists). Margolin resisted the stereotype, advocated by Yiddish critic Shmuel Niger in his 1928 article on poetry by women writers, "Froyen-lirik", that "it gives expression to the feminine disposition . . . that element of feeling and intimate tone". Rather, her ironic voice, her use of different masks and worldly personae, her careful avoidance of sentimentality, and her groping for textual "hardness" (Abraham Novershtern) redefined readers' expectations of the female writer. Consequently, though she published only a single volume of poetry in her lifetime,

Margolin figures alongside Rokhl Korn, Celia Dropkin, Malka Heifetz Tussman, and Kadye Molodovski, as the most important female poets of 20th-century Yiddish literature.

Prior to her emergence as the poet Anna Margolin, Rosa Lebensboym led an unsettled life of frequent moves and fleeting romances. Her father, a lapsed Hasid turned maskil and Zionist, attended to her Jewish and European education by enrolling her at a Gymnasium in Odessa, and providing her with tutors in Hebrew, German, and Russian. As a young woman, she was attracted to radical intellectual and literary circles. When she first came to the US in 1906, she began her life's work as a journalist, contributing articles to New York's *Fraye arbeter shtime* [Free Workers' Voice], and short stories under various pseudonyms. It was during this period that she grew close to the Diaspora nationalist philosopher, Dr Chaim Zhitlovsky, and then in London to Prince Piotr Kropotkin, the theoretician of anarchism, who noted in a letter that she was the only person who had ever made him think about the Jewish problem. When she settled permanently in America in 1914, Lebensboym joined the editorial staff of *Der tog* [The Day], where she edited a weekly column under her own name, "In der froyen velt" [In the Woman's World], and, from 1920, a weekly woman's column under the pseudonym Clara Levin. Her choice of Anna Margolin (Hebrew for "pearl" or "jewel") as poetic pseudonym may have something to do with her effort to efface the Old World echoes of her birth name with one that connoted American contemporaneity and literary sophistication. The refinement of her early verse led some fellow writers to assume initially "that these poems are written by an experienced hand. And a woman can't write like that". Margolin never quite recovered from the cool reception she felt from the male poetic circles. In 1923 she expressed her frustration at those in control of Yiddish literary culture by putting together her own private selection of the best poetry of the year in her Yiddish anthology, *The Yiddish Poem in America*. She would later write in "Epitaph" about "... how in her hours of bravado,/ she struggled hard with God,/ how her blood sang deep,/ and how small men destroyed her."

As part of her modernist project, Margolin was fascinated with poetic self-concealment and re-invention. She sought to undermine and complicate the relationship between her autobiographical self and the poetic "I" by merging the confessional form with first-person speakers whose identities clouded or negated aspects of her biography. In "Ikh bin geven a mol a yingling" [Once I Was Young] – the opening poem of *Lider* – she upset all expectations of Yiddish woman's poetry as self-portraiture by creating a first-person speaker who was her exact opposite – neither female, Jewish, heterosexual, nor modern. The poem's pagan, drunken speaker, living unbeknownst in the twilight of Greco-Roman civilization, dismisses faint rumours about ". . . the weakling from Nazareth/ and the wild exploits of the Jews" that would change the course of human history. The poem's vision of a pre-Christian world in which the Jews are perceived as a primitive and diminutive people provided an unexpected, startling point of view to Yiddish readers. In "Forgotten Gods", a poem about the Greek deities of the ancient world, she suggested that the existence of any god is vulnerable to the fickleness of human memory and the vagaries of historical change.

In another cycle of poems, Margolin developed the poetic persona of "Mary". Although her "Mary" is too complex a figure to conclude that she ought to be read as a creative interpretation of the Christian Mary, the cycle does contain Christological overtones. For instance, the title to "Mari's tfile" [Mary's Prayer] yokes its speaker's foreign sounding name with the Hebrew word for Jewish prayer, thereby (re)claiming Mary's Jewish roots. Its contents conjure a shockingly intimate and erotic relationship between Mary and her God that hints toward the violent personal experience of conception, immaculate or otherwise:

I built you a nest out of love
and a temple out of silence.
I am your guardian, your servant, and beloved,
and I've never seen your face.
And I lie on the edge of the world,
and you pass through me like the hour of death
you pass like a broad, glistening sword.

Margolin's resistance to being labelled a purely "Jewish" or "female" poet led her to explore the shifting landscapes of individual and historical perspective.

Margolin's poetry resisted the saccharine treatments of eastern Europe that might satisfy the Jewish immigrant's thirst for nostalgia. Although poems such as "Brisk", "Odessa", and "My Home", when read alongside those set in America such as "Broadway", "The Bridge", and "Fifth Avenue, Evening" provided poetic settings that correspond to the historical trajectory of Jewish dislocation and emigration around the turn of the 20th century, she refused to be a chronicler for a national, collective condition. In "Mayn shtam redt" [My Ancestry Speaks], she undercut the familiar genre of the warm Yiddish elegy to the old world by drawing attention to the oppressive burden of culture. The poem charts the disintegration of Jewish tradition in the modern period. Although it opens with a familiar portrait of tender men who "caress the yellowed [holy] books,/ Deep in the night they converse with God", the intrusion of bourgeois, modern values slowly transforms them into cigar-smoking merchants who are so culturally assimilated that all they possess is "*Gemora* jokes and German manners". The poem's women – strapping Jewish "grand dames" with "snide little smiles" – are far removed from the modest valour of the idealized Jewish woman of the traditional Jewish world. This complicated, diminished cultural inheritance passes through the poem's speaker "as through a darkened house" to the point where "I don't know my own voice./ My ancestors speak." In contrast to Y.L. Perets's notion of *Di goldene keyt* – that "golden chain" of Jewish tradition that extends proudly from generation to generation – Margolin defiantly establishes a genealogy of language and culture so oppressive that it smothers individual self-expression.

Margolin brought a thoroughly cosmopolitan texture to Yiddish poetry. Her poems convey the apprehensive mood of contemporary life in the cafés and salons of the big city where "all faces are like masks in the smoke./ A joke, a shrug, a weary stare./ False words flare up, then fade./ Have I offended you, my dear?" She highlighted the masquerade of social refinement where interlocutors disguise true feeling under the protective shield of intelligent banter and smiling masks. She even questioned the veracity of her own writing, lamenting its affected literariness: "Beautiful words of marble and gold,/ you were not what I wanted./ In fact, these were not the poems I wanted." By way of the epitaph she asked to be engraved on her tombstone in Queens, New York, Anna Margolin continues to stun passers-by with her insistence that she squandered her poetic gift by ". . . pouring out life's holy wine,/ on shit, on nothing".

JUSTIN CAMMY

Markfield, Wallace

US fiction writer, 1926–2002

Born Wallace Arthur Markfield in Brooklyn, New York, 12 August 1926. Studied at Abraham Lincoln High School, New York; Brooklyn College, BA 1947; New York University, 1948–50. Married Anna May Goodman, 1949; one daughter. Film critic, *New Leader*, New York, 1954–55; worked as publicist and in public relations for several years. Awards include Guggenheim Fellowship, 1965; National Endowment for the Arts grant, 1966. Died 23 May 2002.

Selected Writings

Novels
To an Early Grave, 1964
Teitlebaum's Window, 1970
You Could Live If They Let You, 1974
Radical Surgery, 1991

Short Story
Multiple Orgasms, 1977

Further Reading

Review of Contemporary Fiction, 2/1 (1982): issue on Wallace Markfield (including interview with John O'Brien)
Shatzky, Joel and Michael Taub (editors), *Contemporary Jewish-American Novelists: A Bio-Critical Sourcebook*, Westport, Connecticut: Greenwood Press, 1997
Solomon, Eric, "Childhood or Childishness: Wallace Markfield and Jewish Nostalgia/Sentimentalism", *Studies in American Humor*, new series, 7 (1989): 67–73

Arguably the funniest modern American Jewish writers are Woody Allen, Philip Roth, and Wallace Markfield. The first two of course are household names. The third is known only to a few cognoscenti. How to account for this?

Markfield's career got off to a spectacular beginning in 1964 when his first novel, *To an Early Grave*, earned ecstatic reviews. The book sold well and was made into a film (under the title *Bye Bye Braverman*) directed by the estimable Sidney Lumet. Markfield even earned a nod from Philip Roth a few years later as one of the few contemporary writers mentioned in *Portnoy's Complaint*. A second Markfield novel, *Teitlebaum's Window*, was well received in 1970. But the two that followed – at increasing intervals – were increasingly ignored. These were *You Could Live If They Let You* and *Radical Surgery*. By the end of the 20th century the entire Markfield canon, aside from some uncollected short stories, consisted of these four works, a fraction of Allen's or Roth's prodigious outputs. And except for a special Dalkey Archive paperback edition of *Teitlebaum's Window* that appeared in 1997, all of Markfield's work was long out of print.

Certainly Markfield's glacial productivity – *Radical Surgery* took a full decade and a half to write – did not help his career. The Depression-era Brooklyn and the Yiddish-inflected humour that feature so prominently in his work are also somewhat problematic: that lost Jewish world has been exploited by numerous other Jewish writers and comedians, the style of humour by now has largely gone the way of the Borscht Belt and the audience for whom Brooklyn and Borscht Belt resonate has inevitably dwindled. Moreover, with the exception of his first novel, Markfield's books offer little satisfaction in the way of plot development or narrative drive. In truth, Markfield's prose more often resembles the free-associative riffs and rants of the stand-up Jewish comics (Lenny Bruce, Buddy Hackett, Jackie Mason, etc.) whom he so admired.

Beyond the apparent shapelessness of their stories, Markfield's fictions make additional demands on readers. Markfield is as intellectual and as erudite as Allen and Roth, and his literary and cultural references fly as thick and fast as his punchlines and Yiddishisms. *To an Early Grave*, for example, focuses on four protagonists who live in the rarefied world of intellectual quarterlies. *You Could Live If They Let You* is presented as a hall-of-mirrors ragbag of notes and tape transcripts made by a Gentile literature professor named Chandler Van Horton ("Is that a name or an intersection?") who is researching the cultural significance of an especially acerbic Jewish comedian named Jules Farber. *Teitlebaum's Window* is a stylistically experimental *Bildungsroman* with more than a passing resemblance to *Portrait of the Artist as a Young Man*. (Joyce in fact is invoked both directly and indirectly in all three of these novels.)

By contrast, *Radical Surgery* presents its own set of problems: in a determined but evidently ill-conceived effort to break with his earlier work, Markfield this time tried his hand at a political thriller. The book has some fine writing and quite wonderful set-pieces, like an encounter with Josef Stalin. But the novel's central concept, which has the President of the United States secretly sanctioning assassinations of prominent Americans and blaming the Soviet Union simply to keep the Cold War hot, just doesn't work. While enriched by a fair helping of social satire, the novel is heavy-handed and, as might be suspected after some 16 years of writing, quite laboured. Nor did it help that *Radical Surgery* was published just as the Soviet Union collapsed, reality rendering moot the book's Cold War paranoia.

Yet Markfield's trio of earlier books contains a richness of language, wit and specificity that combines to evoke a certain American Jewish character and culture to a degree that should be the envy of Philip Roth, of Woody Allen, of any writer of that ilk. The humour, the rhythm, the timing, the imaginative leaps make for prose not only worth quoting but worth reading aloud at parties. Examples:

> Did Levine have a lawyer? A specialist in accident cases? If not, he recommended Coniff, on Court street. Coniff the *Goniff*. Out of a cracked sidewalk, a rusty nail, a cigarette burn, a piece of bad wiring, he mounted claims for thousands. Let two A&P shopping carts collide and a son went through medical school.
>
> *To an Early Grave*

> Then in June, 1932, on the second Saturday, a year exactly till Teitlebaum would start in with his signs ("President Roosevelt had a hundred days but you only got till this Monday to enjoy such savings on our Farm Girl pot cheese"), not long after the Workman's Circle took out space in the *Coney Island Bulletin* urging total membership to stay away from French wines and perfumes until Leon Blum was restored to his parliament; also the same week Luna Park finished off a lousy season with a nice fire; a day after Ringelman, the Dentist, got his glasses broken by Mrs. Weigholtz for proposing certain advanced oral-hygiene treatments; around the time Harry the Fish Man's daughter, Fat Rosalie, gave away her father's beautiful little Schaeffer pen for a Suchard, the semisweet . . .
>
> (*Teitlebaum's Window*)

> You take my pop – and he had partners who took him for plenty. Who needed we should be companions by the hunt? He wasn't Killdeer? So he was Killjoy. He wasn't Spencer Tracy? So I wasn't Mickey Rooney. Did I care? I didn't care. He batted me no balls, I shagged him no flies. We didn't go off on safaris? All right, twice a year he'd *schlepp* me to the Lower East Side for two dented cans of Gillette Foamy discards and an unlabeled half-gallon of after-shave lotion you could use to pickle herrings. And on *Simchas Torah* we'd share a Chiclet together in his den, he had himself a lovely den, my mom had fixed up a special shelf in the linen closet and there he'd give out, he'd lay on me his special wisdom: "Kiddo, sonny, don't be fooled like I was fooled for half my life. Because they'll try, oh how they'll try and work hard and from all sides they'll want to put it over on you. Only hear me, believe: Let them charge a dime, let them charge a dollar, let them grind it fine and let them grind it coarse – but sonny, kiddo, all . . . talcum powder . . . is the SAME!'"
>
> (*You Could Live If They Let You*)

But such samples – and they can be harvested from virtually any page Markfield wrote – can only hint at the rewards of this vastly gifted and vastly under-appreciated novelist.

MATTHEW NESVISKY

Markish, Perets

Russian poet, 1895–1952

Born in Volhynia, 1895. Traditional Jewish education; began writing in Russian aged 15. Contributed poetry to modernist journals *Eygns* and *Baginen*. With Dovid Hofshteyn and Leyb Kvitko, formed Kiev Group poets. Moved to Moscow after occupation of Kiev, 1919. Worked for Communist Party Yiddish paper, *Der emes*, as contributor and translator. Participated in Moscow Circle of Jewish Writers with Shmuel Charney, Der Nister, and Hofshteyn. Lived in Warsaw 1921–26; contributed to journal *Albatros* and participated in group Khalyastre. Co-founder of the Warsaw *Literarishe bleter*, 1924. Returned to USSR, 1926; settled Moscow. Welcomed by several Soviet Jewish cultural groups, 1927. By mid-1930s, highest paid Yiddish poet in USSR; founding member of Jewish section of Union of Soviet Writers. Awarded Order of Lenin, 1939. Joined Communist Party, 1942. During World War II, participated in Jewish Anti-fascist Committee, with Itsik Fefer and Solomon Mikhoels. Arrested together with other Yiddish writers, 1949. Executed 12 August 1952. "Rehabilitated" after Stalin's death.

Selected Writings

Shveln [Threshold], 1919
In mitn veg [On the way], 1919
Shtiferish [Mischievous], 1919
Nokhn telerl fun himl [Seeking the Impossible], 1919
Stam [For No Good Reason], 1920
Pust un pas [Idle], 1920
Volin [Volyhnia], 1921
Farbaygeyendik [Passing By], 1921
Radio [Radio], 1922
Nakht-royb [Night Prey], 1922
Di kupe [The Heap], 1922
Der galaganer hon [The Rogue Rooster], 1922
Ovnt-shoen [Evening Hours], 1922
Zang-gezang [Corn Song], 1923
Azriel un shloyme ber [Azriel and Sholyme Ber], 1927
Dor oys, dor eyn [Generations], 1929
Brider [Brothers], 1929
Farklepte tsiferblatn [Sealed Dials], 1929
Vokhnteg [Days of the Week], 1931
Nit gedayget [Don't Worry] in *Piesn*, 1933
Lider [Poems], 1933
Eyns af eyns [One Plus One], 1934
Anshl zaliaznik [Anshl Zaliaznik] in *Dem balegufs toyt* [Death of the Bourgeois], 1935
Ufgang afn dniepr [Sunrise over the Dnieper], 1937
Foterlekhe erd [Paternal Land], 1938
Lider vegn shpanie [Poems about Spain], 1938
Di melkern marfa [The Milkmaid Marfa], 1938
Dertseylungen [Tales], 1939
Roytarmeyishe balades [Red Army Ballads], 1940
Poeme vegn stalinen [An Epic Poem about Stalin], 1940
A toyt di kanibaln [Death to the Cannibals], 1941
Kol nidre, 1941
Far folk un heymland [For People and for Homeland], 1943
Tsum zig [Towards Victory], 1944
Milkhome [War], 2 vols, 1948

Archives:
State Archives of the Russian Federation (GARF); Russian State Archive for Social and Political Research (RGASPI); Charney Papers, YIVO Archives

Further Reading

Altshuler, Mordechai (editor), *Briv fun yidishe sovetishe shraybers* [Letters from Soviet Yiddish Writers], Jerusalem: Hebrew University Press, 1980
Hoffman, Matthew, "Reclaiming Jesus and the Construction of Modern Jewish Culture" (PhD dissertation), Graduate Theological Union, University of California, Berkeley, 2000
Hrushovski, B., Kh. Shmeruk and A. Sutskever (editors), *A shpigl af a shteyn* [A Mirror on a Stone], Tel Aviv: Di goldene keyt, 1964
Kronfeld, Chana, *On the Margins of Modernism: Decentering Literary Dynamics*, Berkeley: University of California Press, 1996
Mayzel, Nachman, *Dos Yidishe Shafn un Der Yidisher Shrayber in Sovetfarband* [Yiddish Works and the Yiddish Writer in the Soviet Union], New York: YKUF, 1959
Oyerbakh, Efraim, Yitskhok Kharlash, and Moyshe Shtarkman (editors), "Perets Markish" (contains bibliography of critical material) in *Leksikon fun der nayer yidisher literatur* [Biographical Dictionary of Modern Yiddish Literature], vol. 5, New York: Tsiko, 1981
Roskies, David G., *Against the Apocalypse: Responses to Catastrophe in Modern Jewish Culture*, Cambridge, Massachusetts: Harvard University Press, 1984
Wolitz, Seth, "A Yiddish Modernist Dirge: *Di Kupe* of Perets Markish", *Yiddish*, 6/4 (1987)

Although Markish's first published work in Yiddish was in the socialist journal *Der kemfer*, he began his career as a poet in 1918–19 with his contributions to the modernist Kiev journals, *Eygns* and *Baginen*. The journals' literary critics, who disagreed over almost everything, concurred that Markish stood out as the writer who was best at bringing modern aesthetics and politics to Yiddish literature. What made Markish different from the rest was his creative admixture of German Expressionism and Russian Futurism – both popular artistic movements during and after the war – to create a new, explosive Yiddish poetry for the revolutionary generation. Until this point, modern Yiddish literature, like that of other minor languages, was dominated by symbolism and impressionism, especially that of the New York group *Di yunge* and, in eastern Europe, by Dovid Hofshteyn and Dovid Bergelson. Combining the self-reflexivity and darkness of expressionism with the expansiveness, the time-play, and the creativity with words of futurism, Markish inaugurated an era in which the modernist poem became the most important medium for literary experimentation in Yiddish.

Two of his most cited poems deal with the explosion of the boundaries of time and space, between self and other. In "I Encounter You", Markish addresses time as three separate entities: past, present, and future, each one personified with different characteristics, although each one is also a part of the speaker. Most interesting is the present, which is always transient, time that is always and simultaneously dying and being born. Markish's other well-known early poem, "Don't Know If I'm at Home", is his poetic credo. It contains the same futurist fluidity of time and space, but Markish makes time and space reflections of the speaker, thereby taking an explicitly expressionist stance in this poem. The poem presents the general theme of the poet-versus-the-world through a modernist metonymy by focusing on the speaker's eyes and hands. The overriding image of the poem is "wildness" or "abandonment" (*hefker*), a celebration of the anarchic and revolutionary times in which Markish was crafting a new poetry. After his debut in the Kiev Group journals, in 1919 he published his first book of poetry, *Shveln* [Threshold]. Through this collection Markish sealed his reputation as the poet of the new, revolutionary generation that, to quote one of his poems, "had no beginning and no end".

Very few Yiddish writers ever associated themselves with a single modernist ideology, such as expressionism or futurism, Markish included. The closest he ever came was during his Warsaw years, with the publication of his 1922 Yiddish expressionist manifesto, "The Aesthetics of Struggle in Modern Poetry". In the same year, he participated in the journal, *Albatros*, and the group, Khalyastre, which included its leader, Uri Zvi Greenberg, I.J. Singer, Melekh Ravitch, and Esther Shumyacher, who wrote the poem, *Albatros*, from which the journal's title came. Although the group took an explicitly expressionist stance, each poet's vision of expressionism took a different turn. Greenberg's was an in-your-face iconoclasm while Shumyacher favoured minimalism. Markish was somewhere in between.

Like many other modernist Yiddish writers, Markish incorporated arresting Christological symbolism, especially when treating such expressionist themes as death, sorrow, and decline. Allusions to Jesus and to Christian customs and folklore pervade his bleak *poema* (long narrative poem) "Veyland" [Woeland], an excerpt of which appears as the first poem in the inaugural issue of *Albatros* in 1922. Markish's "Veyland" portrays contemporary (eastern) Europe as a civilization in decline, a place of destruction and despair where "sadness grows on trees". At the center of the *poema*, the speaker depicts scenes of desecration and wanton behavior, as Europe's Christians – the addressees of the speaker – turn in violence against their own sacred figures and texts. Like most Yiddish expressionist poetry, Markish's "Veyland" represents the conjunction of modernist aesthetics and social critique, including anti-Christian polemic.

One of Markish's most important literary works is his 1922 *poema*, *Di kupe* [The Heap], an epic poem that commemorated and lamented the 1921 pogroms that swept Ukraine. The *poema* is one of many modernist works in Yiddish and Hebrew from the early 1920s that reflect on the destruction of the pogroms, the worst wave of anti-Jewish violence to strike eastern Europe since the Khmelnitsky massacres of 1648–49. The poem is quintessentially expressionist in that the outside world exists only to the extent that it is reflected within the poet himself. Moreover, the poem has an earthy, grotesque physicality with images of decomposing bodies, blood, and harsh colours and smells. More recently, *Di kupe* has become Markish's most analysed work, receiving critics' attention for its connections to traditional forms of Jewish lamentation and for its radical overturning of such forms.

Markish's adjustment to the new literary and political scene upon his return to the Soviet Union in 1926 was quick, although writers who had stayed in the Soviet Union throughout the 1920s always reminded him of his self-imposed "exile" in Warsaw. One Soviet Jewish writer specifically mentioned *Di kupe* in suggesting that Markish's aesthetic past might not fit with the evolving form Soviet literature was taking. Despite his previous commitment to modernism, Markish very quickly found his place in the Soviet Jewish literary establishment as his writing style evolved.

If the revolutionary era was dominated by a new Yiddish poetry, by the late 1920s, Yiddish prose had become the most important medium for producing Soviet Jewish literature. This shift in genres reflected a more general movement away from the modernist experimentation of the 1920s toward a more rigid definition of Soviet literature in the 1930s that came to be known as socialist realism. Soviet Yiddish writers, who participated in this shift, began producing literature in this new model, a move to realism in a socialist key, one that portrayed the "reality" of Soviet life through the rose-colored prism of triumphalism and heroism. Markish's own literary career reflected this more general shift, as evidenced by the 1929 publication of his first novel, *Generations*, which centred on a Jewish family living during the revolution. Several Soviet Yiddish critics criticized it for its "nationalistic apologetics", because of its focus on Jewish characters alone. In the 1930s, in addition to producing poetry, Markish began writing plays, many of which were produced for Soviet Jewish theatres.

In response to the German invasion of Poland in 1939, Markish wrote the well-known poem "For a Jewish Dancer", and in 1941, the play *Kol nidre*, showing Markish's total shift away from modernism's internationalism toward socialist realism's focus on the epic, on folk cultures, and, during the war, on national themes. Markish's last major work was his 1948, two-volume *poema*, *Milkhome* [War], in which he chronicles a wide spectrum of wartime experiences, focusing particularly on the plight of the Jews. He depicts an array of Jewish characters, each of whom represents a particular theme, such as fighting, resistance, martyrdom, and sacrifice. Markish does not present one continuous narrative, but rather a series of vignettes; but unifying the narrative is the suffering of war and the evil of the Germans.

One critic has claimed that in his post-modernist/socialist realist works, Markish endows all of his Jewish protagonists with a certain air of Jewish heritage and tradition, presenting them as links in the thousand-years long chain of Jewish tradition and peoplehood, which many critics claimed that Soviet Yiddish writers had failed to do. Markish's legacy, then, is as the one who, in his early career, brought modernism and radicalism to Jewish literature and, later, brought Jewish imagery and Jewish themes to Soviet literature.

DAVID SHNEER

Matalon, Ronit

Israeli journalist and fiction writer, 1959–

Born in new immigrant town near Tel Aviv, 1959, to Jewish Egyptian parents. Studied literature and philosophy, Tel Aviv University. Journalist, at Israeli Television and *Haaretz* (covering Gaza and West Bank during first Intifada); critic and book reviewer for *Haaretz*; faculty member Department of Hebrew and Comparative Literature, Haifa University, Camera Obscura School of the Arts, Tel Aviv. Member, Council for Culture and Art at Ministry of Education, and Culture Forum of Mediterranean Culture at Van Leer Institute.

Selected Writings

Fiction

Sipur shemathil belevayah shel nahash [A Story that Starts with a Snake's Funeral], 1989

Zarim Babayit [Strangers at Home], 1992

Zeh im hapanim eleynu, 1995; as *The One Facing Us*, translated by Marsh Weinstein, 1996

Sarah, Sarah, 2000

Other

Kro uktov [Read and Write: Essays], 2001

Further Reading

Gleick, Elizabeth, "Stories of the Elders", *New York Times* (9 August 1998)

Greif, Mark, "A New Twist on the Roots Myth", *Boston Globe* (10 July 1998)

Hever, Hannan, "Kol Ehad Tzarih Ladaat et Hamakom Shelo" [Everyone Should Know His Place], *Haaretz* (2 February 2000)

Linfield, Susie, "An Egyptian Jewish Family Retraces its Personal Diaspora", *Los Angeles Times* (22 July 1998)

Ratok, Lily, "Stranger at Home: The Discourse of Identity in Ronit Matalon's *The One Facing Us*" in *Discourse on Gender – Gendered Discourses in the Middle East*, edited by Boaz Shoshan, Westport, Connecticut: Praeger, 2000

Ronit Matalon began publishing her stories in the early 1980s, particularly in the major literary periodical *Siman kriyah* [Exclamation Mark]. In her stories she has developed a "Mizrahi voice", which is recurrently involved in constituting itself through the problematization of ethnicity. Through the agency of initiation stories she has inquired into the process of revelation whereby the world is discovered, especially by girls and young women.

Her first book, a collection of short stories named *Zarim babayit* [Strangers at Home], is characterized by the proliferation of dualistic situations, featuring a high degree of intimacy together with an external, foreign view that is nonetheless unalienated. The story "Hatunah bamisperah" [A Wedding at the Hairdresser's], for example, revolves around a female Mizrahi character who is sensitive to the world and perceives it in all its participatory and compassion-filled intensity. The family space is the site where the young woman constitutes herself and the place where she locates her identity. Towards this end she manufactures a dualistic view – both internal and external – which reaches its climax in the representation of the bride's father, who delivers an impassioned Mizrahi political speech. On the one hand the speech reveals him in all his pathetic wretchedness, but on the other the irony is softened and the narrator listens to and has compassion for him. A pivotal device that demonstrates the dualistic and conflicting representation of identities is the act of taking pictures at the wedding. The photograph – even if there's no film in the camera – is the moment of self-representation, but also the moment of pretense, which is an integral part of constituting the Mizrahi identity in the story. The intimacy, which carries with it hiding from cruel and shameful external surroundings, is given its dualistic expression in the photo: a withdrawal inside and the external threat coexisting.

In 1995 Matalon published her book *Zeh im hapanim eleynu* (*The One Facing Us*), in which the device of photography has become the structural axis of the book. The initiation story of Esther, the young girl, is presented in the book from various perspectives, the central one of which brings the act of telling the story and the act of taking pictures into confrontation. The novel develops through confrontation and the development of the representation of family photographs, thus cleaving a divide between the visual and verbal/narrative representation. In this way it exposes the conflict and especially the violence involved in constituting the identity of the young woman in the face of her family and in the face of the Africans in Cameroon, where her relatives live. In the book the nationalist narrative unfolds across vast geographic expanses by means of which the Mizrahi story of immigration to Israel is presented as yet one more possible story, undermining the exclusivity of the dominant – and ostensibly natural – Ashkenazi immigration story. In this way Mizrahi destiny is represented at a proper and calculated distance from the dominance of the western Zionist narrative. Matalon's achievement in this novel is in the proposal it makes utterly to recast the chart of identities within Israeli prose of the 1990s while exposing the structure of the identities and the mechanisms that constitute them, and offering alternative possibilities as well in which fringe identities can tell their story.

In 2000 Matalon published her novel *Sarah, Sarah*, in which she combined two story-lines: one about the relations between two young women in Tel Aviv against the background of the Israeli occupation of Palestinian territories; the other concerned with the funeral of a relative in a suburb of Paris which the heroine of the novel attends. The politics of resistance to the occupation and the alternating closeness and distance between the two women, the narrator Ofri and her friend Sarah, are intertwined in a story that searches after the dynamics of the political and the intimate. Once again photography – Sarah's profession – enables Matalon to represent reality through critical eyeglasses and by this means to manufacture a contemplation distanced from reality. In this way Matalon eventually exposes the mechanism of closeness and distance as one based on violence – the collective violence of the Israeli occupation towards the Palestinians on the one hand, and the violence which percolates into the fabric of private life on the other. People's blind spots are described as the reason for the violent clashes between them, whether in politics in general or in the ruination of a family's life. The voice of Ofri the narrator is designed as an ongoing negotiation between the contemplation of reality and its active generation. Her flexible and composite identity enables her to judge reality from a different moral aspect, one which is not necessarily subject to predetermined categories. The politics of violence inside the family and outside it are consistently involved with the obliteration of any distinction between the domestic and the public. Violence breaks out in the home just as it does in the public and national space. But Matalon does more than draw a metaphorical parallel between them: she shows how the home or the public space turns, as a result of blindness towards "others", into a violent space. The novel's basic stance – examining the parallel between the (private) murder of the cat Lily and the (public) assassination of Prime Minister Yitzhak Rabin – interprets the assassination and localizes it as an integral, inseparable part of the home. Therefore the political assassination of the private person Yitzhak Rabin provides the fatal connection between the personal and national dramas; the injury to the personal body, which constitutes an injury to the national body as well, is a conclusion derived from the aesthetic structure of the novel, which links the private to the public. It is also the moral lesson of the novel, formulated by Uncle Henri as he talks about Rabin's assassination in terms that are both personal and familial, declaring: "They did this to you: they murdered your Rabin."

HANNAN HEVER

Maurois, André

French fiction writer and biographer, 1885–1967

Born Émile Salomon Wilhelm Herzog in Elbeuf, 6 July 1885. Educated at high schools in Elbeuf and Rouen. Studied at the University of Caen, BA in philosophy. Spent ten years in father's factory; liaison officer and interpreter in World War I. Married, first, Janine de Szymkiewicz (died 1924); second, Simone de Caillevet. Lectured at Trinity College, Cambridge, 1926; fled to US, 1940; taught at Princeton in early 1940s. Left US for service with Allied Forces in North Africa, 1943; returned to France, 1946. Elected to Académie Française, 1938. Died 9 October 1967.

Selected Writings

Novels

Les Silences du Colonel Bramble, 1918; as *The Silence of Colonel Bramble*, translated by Thurfrida Wake, 1919

Les Discours du docteur O'Grady, 1922; as *The Return of Doctor O'Grady*, translated by Gerard Hopkins, 1951; as *The Discourses of Doctor O'Grady*, translated by Jules Castier and Ronald Boswell, 1965
Bernard Quesnay, 1926; as *Bernard Quesnay*, translated by B.W. Downs, 1927
Climats, 1928; as *Atmosphere of Love*, translated by Joseph Collins, 1929
Le Cercle de famille, 1932; as *The Family Circle*, translated by Hamish Miles, 1932
L'Instinct du bonheur [The Instinct of Happiness], 1934
Les Roses de septembre, 1956; as *September Rose*, translated by Gerard Hopkins, 1958

Biographies
Ariel; ou, La vie de Shelley, 1923; as *Ariel: The Life of Shelley*, translated by Ella D'Arcy, 1924
Un Essai sur Dickens, 1927; as *Dickens*, translated by Hamish Miles, 1934
Vie de Disraeli, 1927; as *Disraeli: A Picture of the Victorian Age*, translated by Hamish Miles, 1927
Don Juan; ou, vie de Lord Byron, 1930; as *Byron*, translated by Hamish Miles, 1930
Lyautey, 1931; as *Marshal Lyautey*, translated by Hamish Miles, 1931
Edouard VII et son temps, 1933; as *The Edwardian Era*, translated by Hamish Miles, 1933
Tourguéniev, 1934
Chateaubriand, 1938; as *Chateaubriand: Poet, Statesman, Lover*, translated by Vera Frazer, 1938
Frédéric Chopin, 1942; as *Frédéric Chopin*, translated by Ruth Green Harris, 1942
Eisenhower le libérateur, 1945
Alain, 1949
À la recherche de Marcel Proust, 1949; as *The Quest for Proust*, translated by Gerard Hopkins, 1950
Lélia; ou, la vie de George Sand, 1952; as *Lelia: The Life of George Sand*, translated by Gerard Hopkins, 1953
Olympio; ou, la vie de Victor Hugo, 1952; as *Olympio: The Life of Victor Hugo*, translated by Gerard Hopkins, 1956
Les Titans; ou, les trois Dumas, 1957; as *The Titans: A Three-Generation Biography of the Dumas*, translated by Gerard Hopkins, 1957
Le Vie d'Alexander Fleming, 1959; as *The Life of Alexander Fleming, Discoverer of Penicillin*, translated by Gerard Hopkins, 1959
Napoléon, 1964; as *Napoleon: A Pictorial Biography*, translated by D.J.S. Thomson, 1964
Prométhée; ou, la vie de Balzac, 1965; as *Prometheus: The Life of Balzac*, translated by Norman Denny, 1965

Other
Dialogues sur le Commandement, 1924
Études anglaises, 1928
Aspects de la biographie, 1929; as *Aspects of Biography*, translated by S.C. Roberts, 1929
L'Instinct du bonheur, 1934
La Machine à lire les pensées, 1937; as *The Thought-Reading Machine*, translated by James Whitall, 1938
L'Histoire d'Angleterre, 1937; as *A History of England*, translated by Hamish Miles, 1937
Patapoufs et Filifers, 1940; as *Fatapoufs and Thinifers*, translated by Rosemary Benet, 1940; as *Fattypuffs and Thinifers*, translated by Norman Denny, 1968
Cinq Visages de l'amour, 1942
Mémoires, 2 vols, 1942; as *I Remember, I Remember*, translated by Denver Lindley and Jane Lindley, 1942
Histoire des États-Unis, 2 vols, 1943–44; as *The Miracle of America*, translated by Denver Lindley and Jane Lindley, 1944
Histoire de la France, 1947; as *History of France*, translated by Hamish Miles, 1963
De Proust à Camus, 1963; as *From Proust to Camus: Profiles of Modern French Writers*, translated by Carl Morse and Renaud Bruce, 1966
De Gide à Sartre, 1965
The Collected Stories of André Maurois, translated by Adrienne Foulke, 1967
Mémoires, 1885–1967, 1970

Further Reading
Droit, Michel, *André Maurois*, Paris: Éditions Universitaires, 1953
Fillon, Amélie F., *André Maurois, romancier*, Paris: Société Française d'Éditions Littéraires et Techniques, 1937
Keating, Louis Clark, *André Maurois*, New York: Twayne, 1969
Kolbert, Jack, *The Worlds of André Maurois*, Selinsgrove, Pennsylvania: Susquehanna University Press, 1985
Larg, David Glass, *André Maurois*, London: Shaylor, 1931
Lemaître, Georges Édouard, *André Maurois*, London: Oxford University Press, and Stanford, California: Stanford University Press, 1939

With his first novel, *Les Silences du Colonel Bramble*, Émile Salomon Wilhelm Herzog took on the pseudonym André Maurois, the first name being that of a cousin who was killed in World War I and the second that of a French village near to which he was stationed in that war. In 1947 he adopted André Maurois as his legal name. His father, an Alsatian Jewish textile manufacturer, left Mulhouse for Elbeuf after the Franco-Prussian War of 1870. Among Maurois's teachers at the Lycée of Rouen was Alain the philosopher, whose rationalism had a lasting effect on all of Maurois's thinking and writing. After his university studies, although working in his father's business, he showed a greater inclination for literature. Soon after the outbreak of war in 1914, he was first attached to the British Army as an interpreter and later as a liaison officer. At this time he discovered his vocation as a writer together with the opportunity to write. In 1918 his first novel, *Les Silences du Colonel Bramble*, based on war experiences, met with great success. This was followed by a most prolific career. At his death in 1967 (19 days after completing the preface of his memoirs, *Mémoires*), he left almost 80 completed works. These included a number of novels, among which were several, including his first and *Les Discours du docteur O'Grady* (*The Return of Doctor O'Grady*), in which he succeeded in teaching the French about the English mentality and vice versa. His great passion for English literature and culture was also reflected in many of his other works, and although much esteemed in France, Maurois's writings were probably even more appreciated in Anglophone countries.

After World War I he started to work as a journalist and initially contributed to journals, as well as writing novels, literary criticism, essays, historical works, and biographies. In 1925, the year of his father's death, he gave up the family business. Today he is best known for historical biographies of illustrious persons, often British and French literary figures of the 19th century. Many consider that *À la recherche de Marcel Proust* (*The Quest for Proust*) is his finest biography. Maurois's second wife, Simone de Caillevet, daughter of very good friends of Marcel Proust, collaborated in his research, which led to his lives of George Sand, Victor Hugo, the three Dumas (*Les Titans*), and Balzac. All his writing, in harmonious prose written with finesse and sensitivity, was imbued with the acute observations of a talented moralist. Maurois always resisted aspects of various modern-"isms", including Bergsonism, psychoanalysis, and existentialism. This is exemplified in *La Machine à lire les pensées* (*The Thought-Reading Machine*), an amusing satire on both psychoanalysis and, especially, surrealism, in which Maurois gives more weight to the impulsive vagaries of the unconscious than to rational thought.

Of his other novels *Climats* (*Atmosphere of Love*) and *Le Cercle de famille* (*The Family Circle*) are among the best known, the former being usually acknowledged his fictional masterpiece. He treated a variety of social situations in his novels, including viewpoints of both members of the working and industrialist classes, gleaned from his own ten years' industrial experience, in *Bernard Quesnay*; perspectives of life experienced by both members of a married couple in *Climats*, so gaining him very many women readers; and the generation gap in *Le Cercle de famille*. In *L'Instinct du bonheur* [The Instinct of Happiness] and *Les Roses de septembre* (*September Rose*), he mixes psychological realism with descriptions of a bourgeois milieu. These and other novels were often used by Maurois as a vehicle to express his opinions on moral questions from the point of view of a social conservative. In spite of his limpid prose, these were his chief attributes as a novelist, rather than describing new worlds, atmospheres, and experiences for his readers.

Maurois is remembered as an essayist and literary critic, rather than a novelist, for his *Dialogues sur le Commandement*, *Études anglaises*, *Aspects de la biographie* (*Aspects of Biography*), *Cinq Visages de l'amour*, *Alain*, *De Proust à Camus*, *De Gide à Sartre*, and other volumes. However his historical works and biographies have so far proved a valued legacy. The considerable impact of his book on Edward VII and his histories of England, the USA, and France depended on their being precisely crafted and also most useful for the general public to which they were addressed.

Maurois's biographies are his most noteworthy creations. He was particularly interested in persons whom he believed had modelled their lives on their dreams and his biographies of Shelley, Disraeli, Byron, Lyautey, and Chateaubriand bear witness to this. The first three of these and his work on Turgenev, followed the fashion of the time and their form resembled that of romantic novels. In subsequent biographical works, romanticism was diminished and he continued to research his material meticulously, developing and analysing the influential themes in the lives of his subjects. Yet these works are imbued with wit, irony, finesse, and intuition. The range of subjects for these biographies was very broad, from Sir Alexander Fleming to Charles Dickens and Napoleon. These biographical works have proved important (and frequently unacknowledged) sources for many later authors. He also wrote books for children, including biographies of Chopin, and Eisenhower. There were few literary forms that he did not use, apart from poetry and the theatre.

There are virtually no overtly Jewish themes or characters in his works, except in one sense Disraeli and Proust, and Maurois always believed that Jews should assimilate. Immediately after the armistice of 1940 he even supported the Vichy regime of Pétain. He had been elected to the Académie Française – the second Jew after Henri Bergson – thanks to the support of Pétain, who thought that membership to this prestigious body should be based solely on merit (interview with R. Naquet, Maurois's son-in-law, July 2001). But later he violently opposed this regime and its subservience to Hitler and, when the Germans occupied France, he fled to the USA, where he taught at Princeton University. In 1943 he left the USA for service with the Allied Forces in North Africa, returning to France in 1946. Maurois never agreed to his wife's wishes that he convert to Roman Catholicism and invariably retained an interest in his Jewish identity, in particular praising the Jewish contributions to French literature. Also he always gave moral and financial support to Jewish movements, both before and after World War II (R. Serazin, grand-nephew of Maurois, 1993, private communication).

ANNY WYNCHANK

Megged, Aharon

Polish-born Israeli fiction writer and dramatist, 1920–

Born in Włocławek, 10 August 1920, to Moshe, teacher, and wife Leah (née Reichgot). Emigrated with family to Palestine, 1926. Studied at Hertzlia Gymnasium, graduated 1937. Married Eda Zoritte, writer and painter, 1944; two children. Member of Kibbutz Sdot Yam, 1938–50; worked in farming, fishing, and on docks in Haifa. Served in Israeli army during War of Independence, 1948. Editor, literary biweekly *Massa*, 1952–55; editor, literary supplement of daily newspaper *Lamerhav*, 1955–68; cultural attaché, Israeli Embassy, London, 1968–71; columnist, daily newspaper *Davar*, 1971–85; writer in residence, Haifa University, and Oxford University. President, Israeli PEN Club, 1980–87; member, Hebrew Academy, 1982. Numerous awards, including Ussishkin Prize, 1955, 1966; Brenner Prize, 1957; Shlonsky Prize, 1963; Fichman Prize, 1973; Prime Minister's Prize, 1973; Bialik Prize, 1974; Present Tense Award, 1983; Newman Prize, 1991; Efrat Prize, 1992; Agnon Prize, 1997; Wizt-Paris Prize, 1998.

Selected Writings

Stories
Ruah yamim [Spirit of the Seas], 1950
Yisraeliim haverim [Israeli Folk], 1955
Habrihah [The Escape], 1962
Hayom hasheni [The Second Day], 1967
Hatsot hayom [Midday], 1973
Maaseh meguneh [Indecent Act], 1986
Mivhar sipurim [Selected Stories], 1989

Novels
Hedva veani [Hedvah and I], 1955
Mikreh haksil, 1960; as *Fortunes of a Fool*, translated by Aubrey Hodes, 1962
Hahay al hamet, 1965; as *The Living on the Dead*, translated by Misha Louvish, 1970
Hahayim haketsarim, 1972; as *The Short Life*, translated by Miriam Arad, 1980
Mahbarot evyatar [Evyatar Notebooks], 1973
Al etsim veavanim [Of Trees and Stones], 1974
Haatalef [The Bat], 1975
Heinz ubno veharuah haraah [Heinz, His Son, and the Evil Spirit], 1975
Asahel, 1978; as *Asahel*, translated by Robert Whitehill and Susan C. Lilly, 1982
Masah beav [Journey in the Month of Av], 1980
Hagamal hameofef vedabeshet hazahav [The Flying Camel and the Golden Hump], 1982
Foiglman, 1988
Yom haor shel anat [Anat's Day of Illumination], 1992
Gaaguim leolga [Longing for Olga], 1994
Avel [Iniquity], 1996
Dudayim min haarets hakedoshah [Mandrakes from the Holy Land], 1998

For Children
El hayeladim beteiman [To the Children in Yemen], 1946
Ahavat neurim [Young Love], 1980
Nadav veimo [Nadav and his Mother], 1988

Plays
Inkubator al hassela [Incubator on the Rock], 1950
Baderekh leeilat [On the Road to Eilat], 1951
Hevdah veani [Hevdah and I], 1955
Hannah senesh, 1958
Hamesh hamesh [Tit for Tat], 1960
I Like Mike, 1960
Haonah haboeret [The High Season], 1967
El hatsippor [To the Bird], 1974
Bereshit [Genesis], 1989; as *The First Sin*, 1989

Other
Masah hayeladim laarets hamuvtahat [The Children's Journey to the Promised Land], 1984
Ezor haraash [The Turbulent Zone], 1985
Shulhan haketivah [The Writing Desk], 1989

Further Reading

Books Abroad, 45 (Spring 1971)
Commentary (August 1972)
Contemporary Authors Autobiography Series, vol. 13, Detroit: Gale, 1991
Contemporary Literary Criticism, vol. 9, Detroit: Gale, 1978
Daedalus (Autumn 1966)
Fuchs, Esther, *Encounters with Israeli Authors*, Marblehead, Massachusetts: Micah, 1982
Modern Fiction Studies, 22/2 (Summer 1976)
Modern Hebrew Literature (Summer 1983)
Yudkin, Leon I., *Escape into Siege: A Survey of Israeli Literature Today*, London and Boston: Routledge and Kegan Paul, 1974
Yudkin, Leon I., *Beyond Sequence: Current Israeli Fiction and Its Context*, Northwood, Middlesex: Symposium Press, 1992

Aharon Megged's work is concerned with three main issues. The first is the inherent and often disturbing disharmony in community life, especially in that of the kibbutz. The second is the problems that arise between different generations as portrayed in "Hashem" [The Name]. The third is the relationship between imagination, creativity and reality.

As regards the first issue, two short stories may be used as appropriate examples, "Bella Bella" and "Demaot" [Tears]. In "Bella Bella" the protagonist is a strict and industrious woman who works hard to keep everything in order, both in terms of work and socially. That is, she keeps an eye on all possible chores within the kibbutz and also concerns herself with the lives of individual members. Despite this diligence she is much disliked on the kibbutz because her apparent perfection makes everyone feel uneasy. On the surface everything is running smoothly, and yet the one person who seems to keep everything together is disliked. Members try to analyse this dislike and yet no one can quite put their finger on it. This simmering situation is brought to the boiling point by the arrival of a new French volunteer – Jeanette. Jeanette is sunny and charming and vivacious and readily accepted by the kibbutz. Unfortunately, the joy she brings subversively undermines the efficiency of the kibbutz. Bella is made to feel that all her efforts have been disregarded and that Jeanette has encouraged a light-hearted yet poisonous work ethic into the community. Suddenly, the volunteers seem happier and chirpier and Bella has become an object of complete indifference. No longer is she scorned and thus able to feel virtuous, she is actually ignored. Of course, Jeanette being genuinely kind and sweet is completely unaware of the bitterness she has caused. Her innocence is underlined when Jeanette chooses Bella as the one person to whom to confide her greatest secret. The end of the story has a slight twist, however, for what the reader originally perceives to be the great secret also reveals an even bigger secret, thus emphasizing the complex nature of a community that is in fact made up of completely unique individuals.

In "Demaot" the protagonist Mirtel is also an unpopular member of a kibbutz. Not unlike Bella, this man is very competent in his job and is therefore tolerated. However, he is regarded not so much with dislike as with indifference and indeed he is described as being like old rusty tools for which one has no need but which one doesn't have the energy or the initiative to throw away. Mirtel's character is described in such a way that the reader understands him to be not only different as regards the other kibbutz members, but also as regards people in general. His fanatical upkeep of the supplies room, his exaggerated maintenance of his donkey, all contribute to his unapproachable nature. The fact that the most unlikely of women, a kibbutz member called Heddi, chooses him as her lover arouses confusion and suspicion in the kibbutz. Certainly Megged does not disclose to the reader her reasons, leaving the reader equally perplexed. Mirtel and Heddi have a son named Yosi, and when Heddi finally leaves she abandons both the father and the son. The relationship between the two is the focus of the story since Yosi, like his father, is a complete outsider and yet there is gossip that he might even be the son of one of Heddi's other lovers. The two have an exclusive and intense relationship, which finally proves destructive. Mirtel is obliged to leave the kibbutz with his son. Yosi's reaction is powerfully described by Megged who shows the reader that despite his loneliness and unpopularity, Yosi is attached to his life on the kibbutz and is curiously dependent upon it.

The problems that arise from the generation gap is another important theme in Megged's work. In "The Name" a young couple cannot decide which name to give to their newborn son. Their grandfather chooses the name Mendele in memory of another grandson who died tragically when very young. The couple do not like the name Mendele because of its historical connotations. That is, it is a name which was popular in the ghettos of eastern Europe. The couple consider it to be backwards and therefore inappropriate for a young Israeli. However, the grandfather attaches great significance to this name and sees it symbolizing the lamentable loss of the Jewish people and an Israel that can never be redeemed.

Megged explores the gap between reality and imagination by contrasting the reality as lived by the protagonist and the imaginary life lived by the fictional characters created by the protagonist. These fictional ideals often represent ideological stereotypes. In the novel *Hahay al hamet* (*The Living on the Dead*), Jonal Rabinovitch is a writer composing the biography of Abraham Davidov, a famous leader of the resistance movement during the years of mandatory Palestine. *The Living on the Dead* thus becomes a two-level novel since Jonal's character is revealed through his biography of Davidov. The obvious parallelism in the novel enhances the significance of the fact that the biography is never completed and the life of the biographer never fulfilled. On the other hand, Davidov's life was real, whereas that of Rabinovitch is largely imaginary because of his fleeing from the real world into the world of fiction. In this way, Rabinovitch is dependent on the character he is writing about, someone who is dead: hence the title of the novel.

Similarly, in *Hahayim haketsarim* (*The Short Life*) the protagonist is also a writer, named Dr Elisheva Tal-Blumfeld whose problematic life manifests itself in the form of a novel.

GIULIA MILLER

Memmi, Albert

Tunisian novelist, poet, and nonfiction writer, 1920–

Born in Tunis, 15 December 1920. Studied at Lycée Carnot, Tunis; University of Algiers, licence ès philosophie 1943; École Pratique des Hautes Études, Paris, Docteur ès lettres, 1970. Interned in labour camp, 1942–43. Married Germaine Dubach, 1946; two sons, one daughter. Taught at technical college, 1949–53; philosophy teacher, Lycée Carnot, Tunis, 1953–56; director, Centre for Educational Research, Tunis, 1953–57; researcher, National Centre for Scientific Research, Paris, 1957; maître de conférence, École Pratique des Hautes Études, Paris, since 1958; professor of cultural studies, École des Hautes Études Commerciales, Paris, since 1958; maître de conférence, 1970, then professor of sociology, University of Paris–Nanterre; Walker Ames Professor, University of Seattle, 1972. Vice President, PEN (France), 1976–79, and International Federation of Francophone Writers, 1985. Many awards, including Carthage Prize, 1953; Fénéon Prize, 1954; Simba Prize. Commandeur, Ordre de Nichan Iftikhar (Tunisia); Officier, Légion d'honneur (France); Officier, Ordre de la République Tunisienne, 1984.

Selected Writings

Fiction

La Statue de sel, 1953; as *The Pillar of Salt*, translated by Edouard Roditi, 1955

Agar, 1955; as *Strangers*, translated by Brian Rhys, 1958

Le Scorpion; ou, la confession imaginaire, 1969; as *The Scorpion, or, The Imaginary Confession*, translated by Eleanor Levieux, 1971

Le Désert; ou, la vie et les aventures de Jubaïr Ouali El-Mammi [The Desert; or, The Life and Adventures of Jubair Ouali El-Mammi], 1977

Le Pharaon [The Pharoah], 1988

Poetry

Le Mirliton du ciel [Mirliton of the Sky], 1985

Other

Portrait du colonisé, précédé du portrait du colonisateur, 1957; as *The Colonizer and the Colonized*, translated by Howard Greenfield, 1965

Portrait d'un Juif (includes *L'Impasse*; *La Libération d'un juif*), 2 vols, 1962; as *Portrait of a Jew*, translated by Elisabeth Abbott, 1962; vol. 2 published separately as *The Liberation of the Jew*, translated by Judy Hyun, 1966

Editor, *La Poésie algérienne de 1830 à nos jours: approche socio-historique* [Algerian Poetry from 1830 to the Present Day: A Socio-Historical Approach], by Jean Dejeux, 1963

Editor, *Anthologie des écrivains maghrébins d'expression française* [Anthology of North African Writers in the French Language], 2 vols, 1964

Editor, *Bibliographie de la littérature nord-africaine d'expression française, 1945–1962* [Bibliography of North African Literature in the French Language, 1945–1962], by Jacqueline Arnaud, 1965

Les Français et le racisme [The French and Racism], with Paul Hassan Maucorps and J.F. Held, 1965

L'Homme dominé, 1968; as *Dominated Man: Notes towards a Portrait*, 1968

Juifs et arabes, 1974; as *Jews and Arabs*, translated by Eleanor Levieux, 1975

Albert Memmi: un entretien avec Robert Davies, suivi de Itinéraire de l'expérience vécue à la théorie de la domination, 1975
La Terre intérieure: entretiens avec Victor Malka, 1976
La Dépendance: esquisse pour un portrait du dépendant, 1979; as *Dependence*, 1984
Le Racisme: description, définition, traitement [Racism: Description, Definition, Treatment], 1982
Ce que je crois [What I Believe], 1985
Editor, *Écrivains francophones du Maghreb* [French-speaking Writers of North Africa], 1985
L'Écriture colorée; ou, je vous aime en rouge [Coloured Writing; or, I Love You in Red], 1986
Editor, *Le Roman maghrébin de langue française* [The North African Novel in French], 1987
Bonheurs [Joys], 1992
À Contre-Courants [Against the Tide], 1993
L'Exercice du bonheur [The Exercise of Happiness], 1995
Le Buveur et l'amoureux: le prix de la dépendance [The Drinker and the Lover: The Price of Dependence], 1998

Further Reading

Cohen, Mitchell, "The Zionism of Albert Memmi", *Midstream* (November 1978)
Hornung, Alfred and Ernstpeter Ruhe (editors), *Postcolonialisme et autobiographie*, Amsterdam: Rodopi, 1998
Roumani, Judith, "Memmi's Introduction to History: *Le Désert* as Folktale, Chronicle and Biography", *Philological Quarterly* (Spring 1982)
Roumani, Judith, *Albert Memmi*, Philadelphia: Celfan, 1987
Yetiv, Isaac, "Du *Scorpion* au *Désert*: Albert Memmi Revisited", *Studies in 20th-Century Literature* (Fall 1982)
Yetiv, Isaac, "Ethics and Aesthetics in Albert Memmi's *Le Scorpion*", *Africana Journal*, 13/1–4 (1982)

The diverse, rich culture and experience of Jews long established in North Africa, Greece, Turkey, Iraq, Syria and Iran is only beginning to be heard on a wider stage. Out of these *Maghrebi*, *Mizrachi* and *Sephardi* Jewish worlds Memmi is one of the few so far accessible to those who know only western languages.

Memmi's major work is the largely autobiographical *La Statue de sel* (*The Pillar of Salt*). This engrossing, startling book is the story of a young man growing up between Arab, Berber, Jewish, and Franco-European traditions in mid-20th-century Tunis, and reveals the living complexity of the Mediterranean civilization that existed in North Africa until the early 1960s. We follow the painful trajectory of a survivor of that world during the period of its dissolution by the effects of a combination of colonialist, Arab nationalist, and Zionist forces and ideologies.

The book's protagonist, like Memmi, had a tribal Jewish Berber mother, an urban Jewish father, was born in Tunis and educated at a school of the "Alliance Israelite Universelle" set up by French Jews to assimilate their North African co-religionists to "European civilization". Emerging from this diversity he says "I cannot be simplified", even if this is exactly the demand made in the 20th century of so many individuals all over Europe and the Mediterranean.

Movingly, the book shows us a conscious and intelligent youngster forced continually to renounce old parts of himself in exchange for others. While the Lycée inducts him into the super-rational world of French high culture, he returns to the crowded home that exists in a quite other cultural universe – bringing his Prof home to meet Ma: "(she) was not accustomed to shaking hands and caught hold of Poinsot's fingers, much as one grasps a kitchen utensil". Exotic as Memmi's background may seem, the book has universal qualities as it explores, sometimes tenderly, sometimes angrily, the common but often painful experience of cultural displacement, of a member of an ethnic minority and of someone individually "travelling" from one cultural strata to another. It is very much a common Jewish experience – particularly over the preceding two centuries – but rarely as honestly explored as here. Aside from Memmi's personal trajectory the other side of his story is as a report from the violated multi-cultural lands of the southern shore of the Mediterranean – particularly Algeria, Tunisia, and Egypt – that were ethnically "simplified" after independence by Arab Nationalists not ready or able to make a space for non-Arab, non-Muslim populations and who provoked the emigration of minorities. After *Pillar of Salt* Memmi published *Agar* in 1955, translated as *Strangers* in 1957 – a rather sad account of a Tunisian Jew who marries a young woman from Lorraine. In similar vein in the subsequent *Le Scorpion* (*The Scorpion*) on a Christmas visit to Strasbourg the protagonist finds it to be "une autre planète" where the people speak German among themselves but there is a mutual incomprehension that is more than linguistic. In his preface to the rambling, anecdotal *Portrait d'un Juif* (*Portrait of a Jew*), Memmi spells out more of his actual biography, an initial Jewish-centredness and a youthful Zionism transmuted into the generalized leftist universalism of the 1930s with the fight against fascism in Spain. After 1945 he supported Tunisian independence but in the 1956 Suez war finds himself with other Tunisian Jews supporting Israel while the newspaper he works for is fiercely pro-Egypt and the Arab cause. No doubt this procession of historical miseries, parallel to yet different from the Jewish experience in Europe (in Tunisia his grandparents still trembled with stories of anti-Semitism in the time of the Bey of Tunis, rather than that of the Czar of all the Russias) leads him to start his book with the line "I do not believe I have ever rejoiced in being a Jew". This and the subsequent "The Jewish fate, as I have lived it, is first of all one of misfortune", is honest and representative of a generation that witnessed the destruction of their Jewish world, with all that is left to them – which is something of the role Memmi has taken on – is to be a kind of token and unthreatening "Voice of the Other" within the literary and intellectual realm of the majoritarian culture. It is a very Jewish fate, like "the Wandering Jew", eternal witness to misfortune for the edification of the Christian. In later novels such *The Scorpion*, *le Désert*, and *Le Pharaon*, he examines further his North African heritage, including, in *Le Désert*, the adventures of an ancestor at the time of the conqueror Tamburlane. A series of essayistic works have focused on the fashionable 1960s theme of the complex relations of colonizer and colonized and "dependence", which he attempted to extend to almost all kinds of relationships, personal and otherwise, in *La Dépendance* (*Dependence*) in 1979. However it is Memmi's *Pillar of Salt*, which emerged directly from the time when he lived through an extraordinary set of contradictions between Jew and Arab and colonized and metropolitan, the world of his family and that of the intellectual elite, that presents us with an unforgettable and thought-provoking account of the existential situation of Jew as outsider. He concludes with a message as apposite today as Jewish (and most other) culture lives out a dialectic between extinction, continuation, and (perhaps) transformation:

> Travel if you wish, taste strange dishes, gather experience in dangerous adventures, but see that your soul remains your own. Do not become a stranger to yourself, for you are lost from that day on; you will have no peace if there is not, somewhere within you, a corner of certainty . . . where you can take refuge.

RAY KEENOY

Mendele Moykher Sforim

Russian fiction writer, 1836–1917

Born Sholem Yankev Abramovitsh in Kapuli, near Minsk, Belorussia, 1836, into rabbinical family. Received traditional Jewish education at various yeshivas; began to write poetry. Left Kapuli, aged 13, after death of father; wandered throughout Lithuania, Volhynia, Ukraine, and Podolia. Settled in Kamenets Podolsk; completed education and became partisan of *Haskalah* (Jewish Enlightenment). Married, first, 1854, divorced 1855; second, Pessie Levin, 1858. Began to publish articles in Hebrew periodicals; adopted pen name by which he is now known (meaning Mendele the Bookpeddler); wrote mainly in Yiddish, creating influential literary form of language, 1868–86; then wrote mainly in Hebrew. Lived in Berdichev, 1858–69; Zhitomir, 1869–81; Odessa, 1881–1917, apart from residence in Geneva, 1905–07, following pogroms. Principal of Talmud Torah Hebrew school in Odessa. Collaborated with H.N. Bialik and Y.H. Ravnitzky on Yiddish translation of Torah (Pentateuch). Died 8 December 1917.

Selected Writings

Collections

Ale verk fun Mendele Moykher Sforim [Collected Works of Mendele Moykher Sforim], 1928

Kol kitvei Mendele Moykher Sforim [Collected Works of Mendele Moykher Sforim], 1947

Autobiographical Works

Reshimot letoledotai [My Life Story] in *Sefer zikkaron* [The Book of Memory], 1889

Bayamin hahem (Hebrew), *Shloyme reb hayims* (Yiddish) [In Those Days], 1903

Fiction

Limmedu heitev [Learn Well], 1862

Dos vintshfingerl [The Magic Ring], 1865; in Hebrew as *Beemek habakha* [In the Vale of Tears], 1897

Haavot vehabanim [Fathers and Sons], 1868

Fishke der krumer, 1869; in Hebrew as *Sefer hakabbetsanim* [Book of Beggars], 1909; translated as *Fishke the Lame*, translated by Gerald Stillman, 1960

Di klyatshe, 1873; as *The Nag*, translated by Moshe Spiegel, 1955

Kitser masoes binyomin hashlishi, 1878 (Yiddish); in Hebrew, 1896; as *The Travels and Adventures of Benjamin the Third*, translated by Moshe Spiegel, 1949

Dos kleyne mentshele, 1879; as "The Little Man" in *Selected Works of Mendele*, 1991

Beseter raam [The Secret Place of Thunder], 1887

Dray ertseylungen: an alte mayse; a nakht in tsores; in yener tsayt [Three Stories: An Old Story; A Night of Troubles; In That Time], 1908

Play

Di takse [The Tax], 1869

Poetry

Yudel, 1875

Translations and Adaptations

Perek shirah [Chapter of Poetry], 1875

Zemirot yisrael [Songs of Israel], 1875

Other

Mishpat shalom, 1860

Toledot hateva [Natural History], 3 vols, 1862–73

Ein mishpat, 1867

Der nitslikher kalendar, 1875–85

Selected Works of Mendele Moykher Sforim, edited by Marvin Zuckerman, Gerald Shelman, and Marion Herbst, 1991

Further Reading

Frieden, Ken, *Classic Yiddish Fiction*, Albany: State University of New York Press, 1995

Liptzin, Solomon, *The Flowering of Yiddish Literature*, New York: Yoseloff, 1963

Miron, Dan, *A Traveler Disguised: A Study in the Rise of Modern Yiddish Fiction in the Nineteenth Century*, New York: Schocken, 1973

Rabinovich, Isaiah, *Major Trends in Modern Hebrew Fiction*, translated by M. Roston, Chicago: University of Chicago Press, 1968

Roback, Abraham Aaron, *The Story of Yiddish Literature*, New York: Yiddish Scientific Institute, American Branch, 1940

Spiegel, Shalom, *Hebrew Reborn*, New York: Macmillan, 1930; reprinted Cleveland, Ohio: World, 1962

Sholem Yankev Abramovitsh, often referred to as Mendele Moykher Sforim (Mendele the Bookpeddler) or simply Mendele, although this is in fact the name of one of his characters, is universally considered to be the founding genius of modern Yiddish literature and was a part of the triumvirate of Abramovitsh, Sholem Aleichem, and Y.L. Perets who between them made possible a fascinating and diverse literature especially strong in short stories, monologues, theatre, and poetry. Abramovitsh translated many of his Yiddish originals into Hebrew and represents the stage of Ashkenazi literature before the "language war" which polarized literary expression between (a usually left-leaning) Yiddishism and the Zionist protagonists of Modern Hebrew language and literature.

Of his considerable oeuvre in both languages the key work today is probably the early *Dos kleyne mentshele* (*The Little Man*), a ferocious satire of provincial life that follows the progress of a young man born in Tsvuatshits ("Hyenaville") from schooldays at the Talmud-Torah or elementary religious school ("everyone knows what a Talmud-Torah is, so that it is really unnecessary to describe it. It is a grave in which poor Jewish children are buried, where their minds are mutilated.") He matures as the very model of the *Maskilic* (the *Maskilim* were the militants of the Jewish Enlightenment who sought to awaken eastern Europe's Jews to modernity and rationalism) stereotype of a corrupted, ignorant individual – he cheats a defenceless young woman into marrying him (by getting her fiancé and protector conscripted) and makes money by aiding the rabbis in their profitable manipulation of superstition: "they decided that large roosters were a variety of eagle and consequently *treyf*" (non-kosher). This sharp satire on "the great and the good" of the Jewish communities of the time, along with the earlier play *Di takse* [The Tax] about the exploitation of poor Jews by a government-enforced communal tax on Kosher meat, made Abramovitsh unpopular with the powers that be but loved by his readers. Interestingly, Mendele's father was himself a communal tax collector.

The assault on what Mendele saw as a benighted, enclosed, and corrupted Jewish world continues in *Fishke der krumer* (*Fishke the Lame*), the story of a troupe of beggars travelling around the shtetls of Ukraine. Fascinatingly, *Fishke* is autobiographically-based – as a poor but adventurous youth Abramovitsh spent a year in the hands of such a troupe, when he was thrust forward as a presentable young fellow to cadge and *shnorr* (beg) on their behalf. As in *Dos kleyne mentshele* the book is full of the most despicable and immoral behaviour on the part of Jews. In fact the later Yiddish writers Y.L. Perets and Yankev Glatsteyn felt that Mendele's obsession with Jewish poverty – "the great beggar's sack of the House of Israel" – constituted a negative and depressing view of Jewish life. Although he intended to encourage the reform of Jewish institutions (he eventually became director of a modernized, Talmud-Torah in Odessa for example), his books might also have encouraged assimilation and the abandonment of a hopelessly corrupt, narrow, and dark *Yidishkayt*.

For this reason his last significant work *Kitser masoes binyomin hashlishi* (*The Travels and Adventures of Benjamin the Third*) is particularly interesting as it can be seen as throwing a more positive light on the "ghetto personality". A very highly developed satire, *The Travels and Adventures of Benjamin the Third* is a literary parody of a genre of older Hebrew "travel writing" where imaginary characters recount their visits to mythical places; such as the river Sambatyon over which the lost or "Red" Jews live, an impassable river of wind and stones that ceases to flow only on the Sabbath, when a pious Jew may not of course cross it. The Quixote-like Benjamin and his escape from little Tuneyadevke ("Idlersville"), his traversal of an actual and sometimes hostile landscape of Ukrainian peasants and czarist officials and his encounters with other equally ignorant and wrong-headed Jewish citizens in the town of Glupsk or "Idiotsville", his head stuffed with a fabulistic vision of the world are often both heartrending and hilarious. Fellow Jews trick him into the czarist army's military draft from which he is lucky to escape. However the book does at least show a traditional Jew prepared to attempt to break out of his immemorial provincial ignorance and seclusion.

In general though, Abramovitsh's characters escape the "Jewish darkness" only when alone in the world of nature, as he had himself as a youth spending time at his stepfather's watermill.

It would be the writers who followed Abramovitsh, Sholem Aleichem and particularly Y.L. Perets, who would take the literary possibilities Abramovitsh created to produce a more morally positive and hopeful vision of the shtetl Jew. However the terrific humour in the language of his books and his exhilarating play between different registers of Jewish speech and texts, between highly colloquial beggar's Yiddish and the biblically flavoured Hebrew citations in his introduction or *hagdome* in *Fishke der krumer* for example – both sadly rather difficult to transmit in translation – was an enormous founders' gift to Yiddish literature, helping to create the enthusiastic audience for Yiddish fiction later enjoyed by Sholem Aleichem, Perets, Sholem Asch, and the Singer brothers, Isaac Bashevis and Israel Joshua.

Other works by Abramovitsh include *Di klyatshe* (*The Nag*), an allegory of the Jewish people, and the novel *Dos vintshfingerl* [The Magic Ring] and we should note that as well as translating his Yiddish works into Hebrew versions he often revised and expanded his major works over time. His career as a writer of fiction and theatrical adaptations was accompanied by activity as translator of popular scientific works into Modern Hebrew and running a reformist school in Odessa. In fact his important pioneering role in Hebrew started when he was only 21 with a letter on pedagogy published in a Berlin magazine which created a stir for its clarity of expression. Abramovitsh was clearly a linguistic and literary prodigy in both these Jewish languages, cherishing and improving both Yiddish and Hebrew expression, albeit often with a didactic and polemical outlook on the Jewish world he observed. However he found ways to continue the line of Jewish narrative, even if satirically, and carry it into the harsh present of czarist Russia where many Jews still lived in a cut-off and oppressive medieval atmosphere and in dire poverty. Out of these unlikely conditions and in the face of competition from the "modern" literary languages of his day, particularly Russian and Polish, Abramovitsh forged a literary culture that would essentially and organically express the genius of the Ashkenazi world.

RAY KEENOY

Michael, Sami

Iraqi-born Israeli fiction writer, 1926–

Born in Baghdad, 15 August 1926, into large *hamulah* (extended family). Studied at Jewish schools, matriculated, 1945. Largely in response to Iraqi military regimes' support for Nazi Germany, became active member of Communist Party while at high school; joined leftist underground group, 1939; activities discovered, fled to Iran, 1948. Emigrated to Israel, 1949. Served in Israeli army, 1950–52. Married Malka, 1953; two children; separated from wife, 1997; new life partner, Rachel Yonah. On editorial staff of Arabic weekly *Al-Ittihad* in Haifa, writing mostly for literary section, 1951–55; field worker for Ministry of Agriculture, mainly near Israeli–Syrian border, where he surveyed water sources, 1955–82. Studied Arabic literature and psychology at Haifa University, BA, 1970. Many awards, including Ze-ev Prize, 1975, 1992; Koguel Prize, 1977; Petah-Tikvah Prize, 1979; Prime Minister's Prize, 1981, 1998; International Board on Books for Young People Prize, 1992; Am-Oved Prize, 1993; Agnon Prize, 1993; Israeli Literature Prize, 1994.

Selected Writings

Novels
Shavim veshavim yoter [All Men Are Equal, but Some Are More], 1974
Hasut, 1977; as *Refuge*, translated by Edward Grossman, 1988
Hofen shel arafel [A Handful of Fog], 1979
Hatsotsrah bawadi [A Trumpet in the Wadi], 1987
Victoria, 1993; as *Victoria*, translated by Dalya Bilu, 1995
Hakanaf hashlishit [The Third Wing], 2000
Mayim noshkim lemayim [Water Kissing Water], 2001

For Young Readers
Sufah bein hadekalim [Palm Trees in the Storm], 1975
Pahonim vehalomot [Tin Shacks and Dreams], 1979
Ahavah bein hadekalim [Love among the Palms], 1990
Shedim humim [Brown Devils], 1993

Plays
Hasud [Refuge], 1980
Shedim bamartef [Demons in the Basement], 1983
Teomim [Twins], 1988
Hatsotsrah bawadi [A Trumpet in the Wadi], 1988

Other
Translator, *The Cairo Trilogy*, by Naguib Mahfouz, 1981, 1984, 1987
Eleh shivtei israel [These Are the Tribes of Israel], 1984
Gvulot harovah [Unbounded Ideas], 2000
Havayah israeli [Israeli Experience], 2001

Further Reading

Ben Shitrit, David, *Samir* (documentary film), 1996
Farhi, Moris, "Sami Michael's *Refuge*", *Jewish Quarterly*, 138 (Summer 1990)
Goldstein, Imre, "On Being an Iraqi-Jewish Writer in Israel", *Prooftexts*, 4 (1984)
Ramras-Rauch, Gila, *The Arab in Israeli Literature*, London: Tauris, and Bloomington: Indiana University Press, 1989
Yudkin, Leon I., *Beyond Sequence: Current Israeli Fiction and Its Context*, Northwood, Middlesex: Symposium Press, 1992

A progeny of a Jewry which, until the 1950s, stretched back to antiquity and which, through active involvement in the region's cultural and political aspirations, considered itself indisputably Iraqi, Michael is one of Israel's finest novelists and the most "Arab" of Israel's writers. His different usage of Hebrew, so strongly imbued with Middle Eastern ethos, places him, as he puts it, "in an abandoned area of Israeli literature". This is too modest an appraisal. He is a role model for emerging writers of Oriental descent. If Israeli literature is to attain that unique voice which will harmonize its extraordinary blend of Occidental and Oriental heritage – as opposed to favouring western conventions – the foundations will have been laid by Michael.

Michael started his literary career in Israel by writing for the Israeli Communist Party's Arabic weekly, *Al-Ittihad* and its cultural monthly, *Al-Jadid*. His attempt to recapture the idealistic times in Iraq waned as he found himself integrating, particularly spiritually, with the dreams and aspirations of the young state. After a few years, he left the Communist Party. He describes his disenchantment thus: "Whereas in Iraq, Jews embraced communism because they were Iraqi patriots, in Israel, communist Jews looked to the USSR as their sacred and mysterious motherland and sought to become her satellite." His swift acquisition of Israeli identity owed much to his fieldwork for the Ministry of Agriculture's Hydrography department. (Since most of Israel's water resources were on her borders, this travail was not without considerable danger.) He gave up this work, reluctantly, some 27 years later, because of the demands of his literary career.

Integration led, quite naturally, to the compulsion to write in Hebrew. Having arrived to the country "mute" and "illiterate", it took him some 15 years to master the language. "Giving up one language for another is like losing a limb; another limb takes over to compensate. Maybe my special Hebrew with its Arabic flavour is this compensation."

The dual reality of an immigrant's life – memories of a lost world riding in tandem with a new existence – serve as important themes in most of Michael's works. His first novel, *All Men Are Equal, but Some Are More*, describes life in the *maabarot*, the temporary dwellings that housed the new arrivals during the mass Aliyah of the 1950s. The autobiographical, *Palm Trees in the Storm*, narrates the maturation of a Jewish teenager, in Iraq, during World War II. *A Handful of Fog*, while recounting the activities of Jewish and Iraqi revolutionaries, evokes hauntingly the twilight years of Baghdad's Jewish community, which could trace its origins all the way to the destruction of the First Temple in 586 BCE. The international bestseller, *Victoria*, inspired by the eventful life of Michael's own mother, almost serves as a biblical account of the history of Iraqi Jews in the 20th century.

A third dimension in Michael's writing is his political

vision. Endowed with both Arab and Israeli minds, he has become, over the years, one of the most astute analysts of the Middle East conflict and of Israel's turbulent political, social, and cultural realities. Moreover, having maintained contact with Arab comrades despite his resignation from the Communist Party, he has a particularly good understanding of the aspirations of Israeli Palestinians. As a result of this disposition, his views are much respected. He has lectured widely in Israel and in various universities in Germany, the USA, Argentina, and Chile.

Refuge, one of Michael's finest works, set in the early days of the Yom Kippur War, specifically explores the raw feelings engendered by that traumatic confrontation. Indeed, one of this novel's great achievements is its empathy for the despair of Israeli Arabs at the discrimination inflicted on them by the Jewish state, a despair that leads them to espouse the Communist Party. He elaborates on this thus:

> They were like the Jews of Iraq. They joined the Party not for ideology but because it was the only party that accepted them and undertook to work for their rights . . . Consequently, even as I criticised them for advocating Palestinian nationalism, I understood them. Had I been Arab, I would have acted the same way.

His empathy is all the more poignant when he points out the impasse that faced the Israeli Arabs:

> They wanted brotherhood, emancipation and communist rule. Yet they knew that should they succeed, there would not be a secular state for Jews and Palestinians, but an Islamic one where, as western orientated intellectuals, they themselves would be in danger – like Salman Rushdie.

A Trumpet in the Wadi, a later but equally powerful novel – and latterly a very successful play – further examines the impasse facing Israelis and Palestinians. Moreover, by recounting a hopeless love story between a young Palestinian woman and a new immigrant from Russia, it also reflects on the mutable nature of Israel's demography and the conflicts – as well as the blessings – change always engenders.

Michael now believes that Palestinians and Israel must develop separately until such time when the mutual hatred and distrust that govern their politics will have been soothed. His recent work, *Unbounded Ideas*, a compilation of lectures, talks and interviews, elucidates these views by analysing the full spectrum of the Arab–Israeli discord: immigration and emigration, religiosity and secularism, democracy and communism, ecology and the arts, the State of Israel and her future. In many ways, this collection serves as a retrospective companion to *These Are the Tribes of Israel*, Michael's 1984 collection of 12 interviews with Knesset members, journalists, and public figures, on social integration in Israel.

Michael compares the writing of a novel to the composition of a symphony, an endeavour that has the capacity to weave together the textures and developmental range of a complex culture. His latest novel, *Water Kissing Water*, chronicles the birth and development of Israel by "orchestrating" his experiences as a guardian of her water resources.

Michael's works have been translated into Russian, German, Dutch, English, Arabic, French, and Greek.

MORIS FARHI

Michaels, Anne

Canadian poet and fiction writer, 1958–

Born in Toronto, 15 April 1958, to Isaiah Michaels, Russian immigrant, and wife Rosalind Michaels. Studied at University of Toronto, BA in English 1980. Teacher of creative writing, University of Toronto; writer in residence, University of New Brunswick, 1995. Many awards, including Epstein Award, 1980; Commonwealth Prize for the Americas, 1986; Canadian Authors' Association Award for Poetry, 1991; National Magazine Award (Gold) for Poetry, 1991; and (for first novel, *Fugitive Pieces*) Martin and Beatrice Fischer Award, Lannan Literary Award, *Guardian* Fiction Award, Orange Prize, and Trillium Book Award, all 1997; as well as Harold Ribalow Award and *Jewish Quarterly* Prize, both 1998.

Selected Writings

Poetry
The Weight of Oranges, 1986
Miner's Pond, 1991
The Weight of Oranges / Miner's Pond, 1997
Skin Divers, 1999

Novel
Fugitive Pieces, 1999

Further Reading

Bentley, D.M.R., "Anne Michaels' *Fugitive Pieces*", *Canadian Poetry: Studies, Documents, Reviews*, 41 (1997)

Bringhurst, Robert, "Everywhere Being is Dancing, Knowing is Known", *Poetry Canada Review*, 14/3 (1994)

Brown, Mick, "A Labour of Love", *Daily Telegraph Magazine* (31 January 1998)

Cook, Meira, "At the Membrane of Language and Silence: Metaphor and Memory in *Fugitive Pieces*", *Canadian Literature*, 164 (Spring 2000)

Gladstone, Bill, "Harbourfront Authors Festival", *Canadian Jewish News*, 38/31 (1997)

Gladstone, Bill, "Michaels Creates Extraordinary Piece", *Canadian Jewish News*, 39/3 (1998)

Hillger, Annick, "'Afterbirth of Earth': Messianic Materialism in Anne Michaels' *Fugitive Pieces*", *Canadian Literature*, 160 (Spring 1999)

Jones, Manina, "Letters in Canada: 1996 Fiction", *University of Toronto Quarterly*, 67/1 (1997–98)

King, Nicola, " 'We Come After': Remembering the Holocaust" in *Literature and the Contemporary: Fictions and Theories of the Present*, edited by Roger Luckhurst and Peter Marks, Harlow and New York: Longman, 1999: 94–108

Morrissey, Stephen, review of *The Weight of Oranges*, *Poetry Canada Review*, 8/1 (1986)
Morrissey, Stephen, review of *Miner's Pond*, *Poetry Canada Review*, 12/3–4 (1992)
Panofsky, Ruth, review of *Skin Divers*, *Quill and Quire*, 65/10 (1999)
Parry, Ann, "'to Give . . . Death a Place': Rejecting the 'ineffability' of the Holocaust: The Work of Gillian Rose and Anne Michaels", *Journal of European Studies*, 30/4 (December 2000)
Rampton, David, review of *The Weight of Oranges*, *Journal of Canadian Poetry*, 2 (1987)
Ravvin, Norm, "Unfinished Still Life: Canadians Write the Holocaust", *Books in Canada*, 28/6 (1999)
Schneider, Wendy, "Images of War Haunted Author of *Fugitive Pieces*", *Canadian Jewish News*, 38/9 (1997)
Tregebov, Rhea, "Letters in Canada 1993: Poetry", *University of Toronto Quarterly*, 64/1 (1994)
Turbide, Diane, "Anne Michaels", *Maclean's*, 110/51 (1997)
Vaisius, Andrew, review of *Miner's Pond*, *Prairie Fire*, 13/4 (1992–93)
Verwaayen, Kimberly, "Re-Membering the (W)holes: Counter-Memory, Collective Memory, and Bergsonian Time in Anne Michaels' *Miner's Pond*", *Canadian Poetry: Studies, Documents, Reviews*, 46 (2000)

Born to Jewish parents – her father was a Russian immigrant – Michaels examines the subjects of history, memory, and identity in her works, with particular attention paid in her novel, *Fugitive Pieces*, to the trauma of the Holocaust. Her poetry, though not always overtly concerned with Judaism, does explore questions of loss and longing, often using words to attempt to restore or at least pay tribute to that absence. Her first two books of poetry, *The Weight of Oranges* and *Miner's Pond*, reissued in a combined volume in 1997 by McClelland and Stewart, showcase her elegant and complex lyric style, in poems that usually take the forms and themes of love poems, elegies, or dramatic monologues. The love poems are often quite brief, lyrical, and concerned primarily with the private world created by lovers themselves, whereas the longer poems tend to examine the loss of such intimacy through sensual language and powerful imagery. In poems such as "Memoriam" and "What the Light Teaches," Michaels addresses her Jewish heritage indirectly by depicting the attempts of the speaker to go back in time and remember the stories and languages that have been lost. "Memoriam" recalls the pain of individuals who have been unable to bury their memories of the dead or the horrors of their own experiences, even decades later. As Michaels' speaker notes in the middle of the poem, "The dead leave us starving with mouths full of love". Similarly, in "What the Light Teaches," Michaels recalls her father's family roots in Russia and laments the loss of language and story that accompanied the Holocaust. Yet, her speaker also asserts the fact that despite this tragedy, "Language remembers./ Out of obscurity, a word takes its place/ in history. Even a word so simple/ it's translatable: number. Oven". The parallels between the loss of language and the loss of life create resonant and powerful images of both but the creation of poetry also asserts a legacy that survives and carries this history forward.

Her latest book of poetry, *Skin Divers*, also reflects this belief in, according to Ruth Panofsky, "the redemptive quality of language to transform —even radically alter – experience". In this collection, love remains powerful and mysterious but also becomes a tool for deferring loneliness, as is demonstrated by "The Hooded Hawk", dedicated to Adele Wiseman, a Jewish Canadian writer who lost her beloved mother. Part of the poem explores the refugee legacy of Wiseman's mother and the way in which history remains part of a person, through the power of memory, long after the event has occurred: "History: the silver spoon/ in your kitchen drawer,/ swastika on its handle. The 'tulips and daffodils'/ escaping children who were told to run to, who/ remembered instead 'bloodhounds and rats'". For Michaels, love presents a viable alternative to this sense of abandonment and pain.

Fugitive Pieces, Michaels's internationally acclaimed first novel, depicts the impact of the Holocaust on several generations of Jews. It tells the story of Jakob Beer, who is saved from the Nazi genocide of the Polish Jews by an archaeologist, and Ben, a Jewish Canadian professor whose parents survived the death camps. Shifting between Greece and Toronto, these two interrelated first-person narratives explore the personal struggle both characters face in trying to come to terms with the horrors of the past and their attempts to claim a present for themselves. As Michaels explains, the Holocaust has a personal significance for her: "The war was in the house. I was aware of it from very early on". Though her father's immediate family left Poland in 1931, many relatives were lost during the Holocaust. In writing her novel about the effects of this mass genocide on the Jewish population in Europe, Michaels describes the profound effect the topic had on her: "Images of war haunted me. There was such a deep incomprehension of what I was looking at. There were basic philosophical questions that I couldn't, as a human being, ask myself or try to answer". Despite the centrality of the Jewish experience to *Fugitive Pieces*, Michaels insists that the book is not specifically Jewish and usually prefers not to dwell on her own Jewishness in interviews. Instead, she argues that the subject matter of *Fugitive Pieces* is universal and that the book could have been written by anyone.

Nonetheless, her writing "carries strong Judaic philosophical elements" and offers a poetic vision of a historical event that both challenges and pays homage to Theodor Adorno's assertion that there can be "No poetry after Auschwitz". In fact, when asked about Adorno's claim, Michaels argues that the time has come to write about the Holocaust:

> the participants in these events are dying. And the questions remain . . . and the moral imperative is shifting. Whereas they used to say, "I must not speak it because I have not lived it," now they say, "I must speak about it because I have not lived it."

JENNIFER ANDREWS

Mikes, George

Hungarian-born British travel writer and humorist, 1912–1987

Born György Mikes in Siklós, 15 February 1912, to Alfred Mikes, lawyer, and wife Margit Alice (née Gal). Studied law at University of Budapest, doctorate, 1933. Became journalist; sent to Britain as correspondent, 1938; settled in Britain. Correspondent for Hungarian-language service of BBC, 1939–51. Married Lea Hanak, 1948; two children. President of PEN in Exile, 1973–80. Converted to Catholicism, but maintained links with Jewish community. Died in London, 30 August 1987.

Selected Writings

Sketches and Travel Writing
The Epic of Lofoten, 1941
Darlan: A Study, 1943
We Were There to Escape: The True Story of a Yugoslav Officer, 1945
How to be an Alien: A Handbook for Beginners and More Advanced Pupils, 1946
How to Scrape Skies: The United States Explored, Rediscovered and Explained, 1948
Milk and Honey: Israel Explored, 1950
Talicska: Humoreszkek, Essek, Sohajtasok, 1950
Wisdom for Others, 1950
Down with Everybody! A Cautionary Tale for Children over Twenty-One, and Other Stories, 1951
Shakespeare and Myself, 1952
Über Alles: Germany Explored, 1953
Eight Humorists, 1954
Leap through the Curtain: The Story of Nora Kovach and Istvan Rabovsky, 1955
Little Cabbages, 1955
Italy for Beginners, 1956
The Hungarian Revolution, 1957
East is East, 1958
A Study in Infamy: The Operations of the Hungarian Secret Police, 1959
As Others See You, 1961
How to be Inimitable: Coming of Age in England, 1961
Tango: A Solo across South America, 1961
Switzerland for Beginners, 1962
The Best of Mikes, 1962
How to Unite Nations, 1963
Mortal Passion, 1963
Eureka! Rummaging in Greece, 1965
Germany Laughs at Herself: German Cartoons since 1848, 1965
The Duke of Bedford's Book of Snobs, 1965
How to be Affluent, 1966
Not by Sun Alone, 1967
Boomerang: Australia Rediscovered, 1968
Coat of Many Colours: Israel, 1969
The Prophet Motive, 1969
Humour in Memoriam, 1970
The Land of the Rising Yen: Japan, 1970
Laughing Matter, 1971
Any Souvenirs?, 1972
How to Run a Stately Home, with the Duke of Bedford, 1972
The Spy Who Died of Boredom, 1973
Charlie: A Novel, 1976
How to be Decadent, 1977
Tsi-tsa: The Biography of a Cat, 1978
English Humour for Beginners, 1980
How to be Seventy: An Autobiography, 1982
How to be Poor, 1983
How to be a Brit: A Mikes Minibus, 1984
How to be a Yank and More Wisdom, 1987
The Riches of the Poor: Who's WHO: A Journey round the World Health Organisation, 1987

Other
Editor, *Prison: A Symposium*, 1963
Arthur Koestler: The Story of a Friendship, 1983

Further Reading

Books and Bookmen (December 1968)
Christian Science Monitor (18 January 1968)
New Statesman (17 March 1967)
New York Times (4 September 1987)
Observer Review (20 October 1968)
Punch (18 March 1970)
The Listener (31 December 1970)
The Times (3 September 1987)
Times Literary Supplement (27 April 1967)

During the 1956 October days of the Hungarian revolution, Arthur Koestler and George Mikes were drinking at Mikes's London home. The house was easily identifiable, since Mikes had fashioned a blue plaque stating "George Mikes lives here". As a protest, Koestler suggested throwing bricks at the Hungarian embassy, but Mikes refused, saying the police would arrest them and deport them as undesirable aliens. As the author of *How to be an Alien*, Mikes knew something about the British mentality and their dour ways of dealing with strangers. In his writings about his friendship with Koestler, and in the brilliant texts about the Hungarian uprising, about his return to Budapest, and particularly in his "Letter from Budapest" in *Encounter*, these issues are dealt with in detail. Still, the humour and inventiveness of his many books could conceal as well as reveal his confrontations with a Europe which he scrutinized in so many ways. In some ways, it was a pity that *How to be an Alien* was such a sensational, long-lasting bestseller. It pushed him into a category of a critic who was viewed with benign fondness and not considered a serious thinker. Few realized that he had received his doctorate in law at the University of Budapest. At one point, he broke with his Jewish family tradition, converting to Catholicism and becoming a governor of a Catholic school. At the same time, an awareness of his Jewish roots remained within his social and personal life. The experience of German Jewish refugees coming to his home in Hungary for help after 1933 had left an abiding impression upon him.

Mikes felt himself part of the English scene. Melvin Lasky, the editor of *Encounter*, remembers a long tennis match at the Hurlingham Club with Mikes, Milton Shulman, himself, and Peregrine Worsthorne – long, because after almost every point they had to sit down and debate the current political scene. Mikes delighted in bringing the European dimension to the English provincial consciousness, not only in his writings but also in his popular BBC radio broadcasts. He, Koestler, and André Deutsch were the "Hungarian mafia" of their time, and the world of English letters was enriched by their presence. It was Deutsch's publishing house that promoted Mikes as a writer. What troubled Mikes throughout his life was that his readers could laugh along with him and fail to note the bitterness under the light text.

Mikes could be considered the "Jewish outsider" who tried to be a Socratic gadfly to society. His most revealing book was *English Humour for Beginners*, in which he tried to give his readers a view of humour from the inside, in the tradition of Sigmund Freud and Theodor Reik.

He linked his jokes to social and economic circumstances, and used humour as self defence or as attack. As Mikes put it: "Humour is philosophy, the trouble is that everyone nowadays tries to make money out of it." His book contains the mandatory collection of Jewish jokes – jokes *by* Jews and not *about* Jews. Here, Mikes makes an interesting claim:

> "English and Jewish humour possess the same element of self mockery, the ability to laugh at themselves. But I thought understatement was not a conspicuously Jewish characteristic. I was put right about that in Israel. An Israeli was boasting about his country and its achievements, and then said something about typical Jewish understatement."
>
> "How," asked Mikes, "can you say that Israel is the greatest of all nations, and then talk about Jewish understatement?" "Because that *is* an understatement", said the Israeli.

Mikes wrote two books about Israel. The first, *Milk and Honey*, was a travel book. It is interesting that Mikes always remains the observer, never identifying himself with the country he describes with much sympathy and understanding. He begins by describing himself at the age of six, in a small Hungarian town, learning in school about the founding of Hungary by "our father, Arpad", feeling guilty about the way Hungary was "founded", but yearning to see this rare founding of a state in his own time. And then came Israel. Mikes went there determined to write about Israelis without according them a special status: "The Jews had the right to be treated as any other nation in the world – no better and no worse."

His readership read this book as they had read the others, as an amusement. Few realized that it was a serious and intelligent presentation of the birth of a new nation. When he returned to this topic, two decades later, in *The Prophet Motive*, after the Six Day War, he visited a land with many problems which he saw clearly.

Mikes celebrates the movement from a divided to a united city where Orthodox Jews and Arabs view one another in friendly amazement. Mikes points out that

> Jerusalem *always* – even in Ottoman times, had a Jewish Majority. East Jerusalem never became part of Jordan and Jordan has no proper claim to the city. Israelis fail to see why Christians should be happier to see the holy places in Moslem than in Jewish hands. Jerusalem is a holy city of three great religions each of which has held it in turns. The Jews were deprived of Jerusalem for about 2,000 years; it's their turn now, they feel.

The text still sparkles with anecdotes and with sarcastic descriptions of the new type of American Jewish tourists ("They think they own Jerusalem – well, perhaps they do"). In *How to Scrape Skies* Mikes describes the United States with good humour. There may be acidity in the text; but it was acclaimed by Americans. He wanted them to gain some self-knowledge from his cheerful criticism. The moral indignation and pain felt by Mikes make one realize that a book of humour can also be a moral tract. It is most apparent when Mikes writes about Germany in *Über Alles: Germany Explored*:

> I went to Germany to write a humorous book but did not find my subject any too humorous. So I must apologise to the reader who looks forward to finding "a laugh on every page". He will not find it. I must also apologise to the serious student; he, in turn, will find my account superficial and altogether too light.

The book may be written humorously, but Mikes describes Germany after the Holocaust. Still, the *Sunday Times* comments, "his innocently startling logic and his poker-faced humour . . . are crossed with acumen and good sense to breed wisdom." Mikes describes German humour with all its heaviness and obtuseness. Yet this book is a solid analysis of the political mistakes made by the Allies after the war, and his approach was fair to a Germany in which he recognized all the flaws of a land shaped by Hitler:

> Being anti-German is just as stupid a prejudice as being anti-semitic, anti-negro or anti-American.
>
> The right policy is to forgive but not to forget. And I also knew the policy followed by the West was to forget but not to forgive.

Mikes talked to ex-Nazis – he noted how rare it was to find anyone who knew that Nazis had existed in Germany, let alone to find one who admitted the past – and to those who did feel some guilt. The book deserves to be taken seriously; sadly, it is seen as humorous literature. His writings reveal a scholar, a serious observer of world politics, giving advice under the cloak of the humorist; only a few see beneath the surface. Mikes was an observer of the human comedy, and he described it with brilliance and insight. In so doing, he encountered the darkness of the human soul.

ALBERT H. FRIEDLANDER

Miller, Arthur

US dramatist and fiction writer, 1915–

Born in New York City, 17 October 1915. Studied at Abraham Lincoln High School, New York, graduated 1932; University of Michigan from 1934, Hopwood Award, 1936 and 1937, AB 1938. Married, first, Mary Slattery, 1940; divorced 1956; one son, one daughter; second, Marilyn Monroe, 1956; divorced, 1961; third, Inge Morath, 1962; one daughter; wife died 2002. Worked in automobile supply warehouse, 1932–34; member of Federal Theatre Project, 1938; writer for CBS and NBC Radio Workshops. Associate professor of drama, University of Michigan, 1973–74. International President, PEN, London and New York, 1965–69. Many awards, including Theatre Guild Award, 1938; New York Drama Critics Circle Award, 1947, 1949; Tony, 1947, 1949, 1953; Pulitzer Prize, 1949; National Association of Independent Schools Award, 1954; American Academy Gold Medal, 1959; Brandeis University Creative Arts Award, 1969; Peabody Award (for television play), 1981; Bobst Award, 1983; National Arts Club Medal of Honor, 1992; City University of New York Edwin Booth Award, 1992; Commonwealth Award, 1992. Member, American Academy of Arts and Letters, 1981.

Selected Writings

Plays
Honors at Dawn, 1936
No Villain (They Too Arise), 1937
Listen my Children (with Norman Roster), 1939
The Pussycat and the Expert Plumber Who Was a Man, 1941
William Ireland's Confession, 1941
The Half-Bridge, 1943
That They May Win, 1944
The Man Who Had All the Luck, 1944
Grandpa and the Statue, 1945
All My Sons, 1947
Death of a Salesman: Certain Private Conversations, 1947
The Guardsman, 1947
The Story of Gus, 1947
Three Men on a Horse, 1947
An Enemy of the People, 1950
The Crucible, 1954
A View from the Bridge, 1955
The Memory of Two Mondays, 1955
Collected Plays (includes *All My Sons*, *Death of a Salesman*, *The Crucible*, *A Memory of Two Mondays*, *A View from the Bridge*), 1957
After the Fall, 1964
Incident at Vichy, 1964
The Price, 1968
Fame, and The Reason Why, 1970
The Creation of the World and Other Business, 1972; as *Up from Paradise*, 1974
The Archbishop's Ceiling, 1977
The American Clock, 1979
Playing for Time, 1980
Collected Plays 2 (includes *The Misfits*, *After the Fall*, *Incident at Vichy*, *The Price*, *The Creation of the World and Other Business*, *Playing for Time*), 1981
Eight Plays (includes *All My Sons*, *Death of a Salesman*, *The Crucible*, *A Memory of Two Mondays*, *A View from the Bridge*, *After the Fall*, *Incident at Vichy*, *The Price*), 1981
Two-Way Mirror (includes *Elegy for a Lady* and *Some Kind of Love Story*), 1982
Danger! Memory! (includes *I Can't Remember Anything* and *Clara*), 1987
Speech to the Neighborhood Watch Committee in *Urban Blight*, 1988
Plays 3 (includes *The American Clock*, *The Archbishop's Ceiling*, *Two-Way Mirror*), 1990
The Last Yankee, 1991
The Ride down Mount Morgan, 1991
The American Clock: A Vaudeville, 1992
Broken Glass, 1994
Focus, 1997

Screenplays: *The Story of G.I. Joe*, 1945; *The Witches of Salem*, 1958; *The Misfits*, 1961; *Everybody Wins*, 1990; *The Crucible*, 1992

Radio Plays: *The Pussycat and the Expert Plumber Who Was a Man*; *William Ireland's Confession*; *Grandpa and the Statue*; *The Story of Gus*; *The Guardsman*; *Three Men on a Horse*, early 1940s; *The Golden Years*, 1987

Television Play: *Playing for Time*, 1980

Novels
Focus, 1945
The Misfits, 1961
Homely Girl, 1995; as *Plain Girl*, 1995

Short Stories
I Don't Need You Any More, 1967

Other
"Hitler's Quarry", *Jewish Survey*, 1 (May 1941): 8–9, 21
Situation Normal, 1944
Jane's Blanket, 1963
In Russia, 1969
The Portable Arthur Miller, edited by Harold Clurman, 1971
In the Country, 1977
Chinese Encounters, 1979
"Salesman" in Beijing, 1984
Timebends, 1987
The Theater Essays of Arthur Miller, revised edition edited by Steve Centola and Robert A. Martin, 1996

Further Reading

Bigsby, C.W.E. (editor), *A Critical Introduction to Twentieth-Century American Drama*, vol. 2, Cambridge and New York: Cambridge University Press, 1984
Bigsby, Christopher (editor), *The Cambridge Companion to Arthur Miller*, Cambridge and New York: Cambridge University Press, 1997
Carson, Neil, *Arthur Miller*, London: Macmillan, and New York: Grove Press, 1982

Centola, Steve, *Arthur Miller in Conversation*, Dallas: Northouse and Northouse, 1993
Centola, Steve (editor), *The Achievement of Arthur Miller: New Essays*, Dallas: Contemporary Research Press, 1995
Corrigan, Robert Willoughby (editor), *Arthur Miller: A Collection of Critical Essays*, Englewood Cliffs, New Jersey: Prentice Hall, 1969
Ferres, John H., *Arthur Miller: A Reference Guide*, Boston: G.K. Hall, 1979
Griffin, Alice, *Understanding Arthur Miller*, Columbia: University of South Carolina Press, 1996
Hayman, Ronald, *Arthur Miller*, London: Heinemann, 1970; New York: Ungar, 1972
Huftel, Sheila, *Arthur Miller: The Burning Glass*, London: W.H. Allen, and New York: Citadel Press, 1965
Martin, Robert A., introduction to *The Theater Essays of Arthur Miller*, edited by Martin, New York: Viking, 1978
Moss, Leonard, *Arthur Miller*, New York: Twayne, 1967
Nelson, Benjamin, *Arthur Miller: Portrait of a Playwright*, London: Peter Owen, and New York: McKay, 1970
Roudané, Matthew, C. (editor), *Conversations with Arthur Miller*, Jackson: University Press of Mississippi, 1987
Schlueter, June and James K. Flanagan, *Arthur Miller*, New York: Ungar, 1987
Welland, Dennis, *Arthur Miller the Playwright*, London and New York: Methuen, 1983

Although widely recognized as one of America's most accomplished, prolific, and best known playwrights, it is often forgotten that Arthur Miller is also Jewish. This is perhaps a result of his life-long concern with the universal lessons that can be derived from events such as the Depression and the Holocaust. Nonetheless, his Jewishness was a primary factor in defining his artistic and political development, which manifested itself primarily through a fear of anti-Semitism, and how to prevent it.

Miller's use of his Jewishness was complex, fluid, and shifted over time according to differing circumstances. He grew up in an Orthodox Jewish environment. His grandfather was the president of the synagogue, and Miller read and understood a measure of Hebrew. Like many other second-generation Jewish-American youngsters of his time Miller was embarrassed of his ethnic origins and he showed an early desire to become an American like Frank Merriwell or Tom Swift. Later in his life, possibly after much reflection, Miller began to acknowledge the impact of his Jewish upbringing. In 1966 he felt that the Jewish tradition in which he was brought up had indeed influenced him. Later he stated that his ethnic background had been vital for him as a writer, particularly in America. By the 1980s, he was more certain of the role of his Jewishness than he was in the 1950s, as expressed in his autobiography, *Timebends*. Certainly, more overtly Jewish content appeared in Miller's plays from the 1960s onwards, but this should not be allowed to overshadow the explicit and implicit Jewish influences in Miller's art and politics throughout his life.

Miller may have attempted to deny his Jewishness but he was constantly reminded of it by anti-Semitism. His parents and grandparents transmitted memories of discrimination and persecution to him and these inherited memories were built upon by his own experiences of discrimination at the University of Michigan, then at the Brooklyn Navy Yard where he worked during World War II, and finally by the Holocaust. Miller recalled how these experiences ended his "innocence". Christopher Bigsby wrote that the "fierce anti-semitism" that Miller encountered at work, "did something to shape his social and political views and explains why it is a major, if submerged, theme of his work".

Miller's early works articulated a leftist anti-fascism. The Depression had destroyed any notion of equality for Jews under capitalism, so Miller turned to universalism, in particular socialism, struggling to identify himself "with mankind rather than one small tribal fraction of it". He wrote a series of plays and other works that fused his secular Jewishness with communism's emphasis on egalitarianism and opposition to all forms of fascism and Nazism. These included *No Villain*, which was revised as *They Too Arise*, *Honors at Dawn*, *Listen My Children*, *Hitler's Quarry*, *The Half-Bridge*, *Situation Normal*, and *The Man Who Had All the Luck*. Perhaps his most important response to anti-Semitism came in a rather unusual form, namely his first novel, *Focus*, which was reputedly the first postwar novel written about anti-Semitism in America.

The Holocaust had an immediate impact on Miller. Thereafter, he struggled with "the problem with identifying the universals in the Nazi condition", believing it was important to "memorialize the Holocaust lest it fade away". Yet, paradoxically, Miller admitted to turning away from Jews as material for his work after 1947. He did this out of a fear of exacerbating what he perceived to be an already rampant anti-Semitism. So while concerned with preventing the repetition of another Holocaust, Miller downplayed any openly Jewish content in his next plays. *All My Sons*, *Death of a Salesman*, *An Enemy of the People*, *The Crucible*, *A Memory of Two Mondays*, and *A View from the Bridge* were all concerned with the destruction of the close-knit bonds of community and its consequences. Taken together most of these works are now considered to be classic works of American rather than Jewish literature, having transcended their particularistic roots. Many of them have been produced around the world in very different times and circumstances. Nonetheless, in all of them, an ill-concealed Jewishness resides just beneath the surface, barely submerged beneath a series of metaphors and analogies. Close examination reveals that it is scarcely hidden and that Miller never gave up Jews as his subject matter despite his claims to the contrary.

There seems to be some weight to the argument that Miller desired to hide his ethnic origins while striving for universality; that he would never be accepted as an American playwright if he stuck to his Jewish roots. Furthermore, Miller feared the continuation of anti-Semitism after the war's end and was thus averse to mentioning Jews openly. It was not until 1964 when Miller was sufficiently established and when his fears had receded after the decline of McCarthyism that he felt able to refer overtly to Jewish material in his work. He began with *After the Fall*, which explored his relationship with Marilyn Monroe and his ordeal with the House Un-American Activities Committee, beneath the central, dominating signifier of the Holocaust – a watchtower. From then on Miller dealt with

Jewish themes more openly in his next plays: *Incident at Vichy*, *The Creation of the World and Other Business*, *Playing for Time*, and *Broken Glass*. In these plays, he was particularly concerned with the responsibility of the individual, the role of the intellectual, the problem of evil, the universal lessons of the Holocaust, and "man's inhumanity towards man".

Although he is best known for his plays, Miller is not just a playwright. In addition to his dramatic works, he has written scores of articles, short stories, and several novels, as well as an extensive autobiography, which have combined to form a vast oeuvre.

NATHAN ABRAMS

Millin, Sarah Gertrude

Lithuanian-born South African fiction writer and diarist, 1888–1968

Born Sarah Gertrude Liebson, in Zagar, Lithuania, March 1888. Emigrated with family to South Africa, August 1888; settled in Barkly West in diamond-mining area. Studied at schools in Kimberley, matriculating 1904. Obtained music teacher's certificate; never taught. Married Philip Millin, 1912; husband died 1952; no children. Moved with husband to Johannesburg. Died 6 July 1968.

Selected Writings

Fiction
The Dark River, 1919
Middle Class, 1921
Adam's Rest, 1922
The Jordans, 1923
God's Step-Children, 1924
Mary Glenn, 1925
An Artist in the Family, 1928
The Coming of the Lord, 1928
The Fiddler, 1929
Men on a Voyage, 1930
The Sons of Mrs Aab, 1931
Three Men Die, 1934
What Hath a Man?, 1938
The Herr Witchdoctor, 1941; as *The Dark Gods*, 1941
King of the Bastards, 1949
The Burning Man, 1952
Two Bucks without Hair and Other Stories, 1957
The Wizard Bird, 1962
Goodbye, Dear England, 1965

Other
Rhodes, 1933
The South Africans, 1934
General Smuts, 1936
The Night is Long, 1941
War Diary
  World Blackout, 1944
  The Reeling Earth, 1945
  The Pit of the Abyss, 1946
  The Sound of the Trumpet, 1947
  Fire Out of Heaven, 1947
  The Seven Thunders, 1948
The People of South Africa, 1951
The Measure of My Days, 1955
White Africans are Also People, 1966

Further Reading

Braun, Lavinia, "Not Gobineau but Heine – Not Racial Theory but Biblical Theme: The Case of Sarah Gertrude Millin", *English Studies in Africa*, 34/1 (1991)
Clayton, Cherry, "Women Writers and the Law of the Father: Race and Gender in the Fiction of Olive Schreiner, Pauline Smith and Sarah Gertrude Millin", *English Academy Review*, 7 (1990)
Kossick, Shirley, "Writing with Heart: Some South African Jewish Novelists", *Jewish Affairs*, 48/2 (1993)
Levy, Fanelle, *The Works of Sarah Gertrude Millin 1952–1968: A Bibliography*, Johannesburg: University of the Witwatersrand Press, 1969
Rubin, Martin, *Sarah Gertrude Millin: A South African Life*, Johannesburg: Donker, 1977
Whyte, Morag, *Bibliography of the Works of Sarah Gertrude Millin*, Cape Town: University of Cape Town Press, 1952
Zander, Horst, "Millin's Step-Children and Her Grandchildren: Miscegenation in Some Southern African Novels" in *Current Themes in Contemporary South African Literature*, edited by Elmar Lehmann and Erhard Reckwitz, Essen: Die Blaue Eule, 1989

In her autobiography Sarah Gertrude Millin wrote, "the end of myself may very well be the end of all concerning myself. For to whom but myself do we really matter?" Once considered the greatest of South African writers, Millin now no longer matters. A prolific writer who published more than 30 books, she outlived her fame and reputation to become an example of colonial paternalism and outdated racism, which is now an embarrassment to the reader.

She is remembered primarily as the author of *God's Step-Children*, which enjoyed many translations and editions and won a French prize. Its theme is the shame caused over four generations by miscegenation, which she regarded as a sin against the White race. Kenneth Parker writes that she "occupies a unique place among the ranks of writers in English in that she makes racism a respectable topic in the novel". Millin describes blacks as primitive and disease-ridden. Interracial sex is associated with degeneracy; this theme appears in at least eight of her novels. Nowhere does she suggest that the unhappiness felt by mixed offspring is caused by the prejudice and racial animosity shown by the white South African.

Her ideas were moulded by a childhood spent on the Vaal River near Kimberley on remote alluvial diamond diggings, where her father had trading and ferry concessions. One of the few white families, the Liebsons were surrounded by impoverished diggers, frequently drunk and violent, whose children Sarah was not allowed to invite home. Her formative years had a formidable impact on her attitudes, and are described in her first book, *The Dark River*, as well as in *Adam's Rest* and *The Sons of Mrs Aab*. The irrational fears which seem to lie deep in her childhood are connected with a sense of shame at her own Lithuanian immigrant background, and her sensitivity to the social exclusion this caused.

Her belief in white racial superiority was allied to an equally strong belief in Jewish superiority. She had a Jewish identity, without being a practising Jew, and was a keen Zionist and friend of Chaim Weizmann. However there is no mention of Jewishness in her earlier novels. Marcia Leveson has said that it is a recurrent phenomenon in the literature of the early part of this century that Jewish writers defensively blur the religion of their protagonists. In *The Dark River* the heroine says, "the Jews were an extraordinary race. Apparently they were either shamefully dejected or shamelessly opulent." Millin herself became a socially ambitious snob who enjoyed an opulent lifestyle. *The Coming of the Lord* is her only book that deals with the problem of a Jewish minority in South Africa, and describes the Jews as socially and professionally insecure in an environment of Gentile distrust. She links Jewish suffering with that of a black religious sect. The evenhandedness of the book is spoiled by the racial views that overshadow her writing. When the son of the Jewish protagonist dies for the sect, "it was his most awful regret that it had been for black savages that Saul had given his life".

Despite her sensitivity to anti-Semitic intolerance, to the extent of walking out of social gatherings if she suspected any, Millin was unable to see any inconsistency between this and her own racial ideas. She was angry when *God's Step-Children* became a pirated bestseller in Germany as an example of the evils of race mixing. She used her political influence in South Africa and England in the 1930s to campaign against Nazi Germany, and wrote *The Herr Witchdoctor* for this reason.

Her writings are not concerned with the feelings of people as men or as women, but with universal responses of human beings in the world in which they live. She focuses with aloof clarity on failures and pettiness. "Though I am against humanity, I can't help liking human beings", she wrote. Katherine Mansfield called her pessimistic and often fatalistic view of life, "a low throbbing note which is never stilled . . . running through" her novels. Millin's novels have strong story lines, and were always written around a theme using simple and flexible vocabulary, terse sentences, irony and penetrating observations. She thought in categories and stereotypes, her portrayals of black characters being particularly shallow. Marriage was the only secure life for women, and spinsterhood a dreaded fate. *Mary Glenn*, which was made into a play, shows the struggle of a gifted woman to rise above her situation, and depicts the mother–child relationship as destructive.

Later Millin considered herself to be a political writer, gaining fame for her biographies of Cecil John Rhodes and General Jan Smuts, and her popular book, *The People of South Africa*, remains an important document on colonialism, and its effects on black and white. The works she took most pride in were her *War Diary*, which has much detail and insight. The final volume contains her impressions of the Nuremberg trial, which she attended. Her frank autobiographies, *The Night is Long* and *The Measure of My Days*, include her views on Israel.

Rubin writes that after 1948 Millin found herself rejected on all fronts. In South Africa she had lost political status, in America she had lost her literary reputation, and in Israel she found herself disregarded. After the death of her husband in 1952, she became increasingly eccentric and racist. Her book championing Rhodesia's independence, *White Africans are Also People*, finally destroyed any measure of respect in literary and intellectual circles.

Sociopolitical judgement can obscure the ways in which texts may be read. Clayton believes that Millin's accurately rendered world of South African class phobias has not been adequately discussed. By providing an insight into the attitudes prevalent in racial South Africa, *God's Step-Children* remains interesting: so Sarah Gertrude Millin may still matter.

GWYNNE SCHRIRE

Minco, Marga

Dutch fiction writer, 1920–

Born Sara Menco in Ginneken, near Breda, 31 March 1920, into Orthodox Jewish family. Reporter for daily newspaper *Bredase Courant* until dismissal shortly after Nazi occupation of Netherlands began, 1940; went into hiding and assumed false identity; parents and two older siblings arrested and died during occupation. Married Bert Voeten, poet and translator of Shakespeare, 1945; husband died, 1992; two daughters. Awarded Mutator Prize, 1957; Vijverbergprijs van de Jan Campertstichting, 1958; Annie Romein Award, 1999.

Selected Writings

Novels

Het bittere kruid: een kleine kroniek, 1957; as *Bitter Herbs: A Little Chronicle*, translated by Roy Edwards, 1960
Het huis hiernaast [The House Next Door], 1965
Een leeg huis, 1966; as *An Empty House*, translated by Margaret Clegg, 1990
De val, 1983; as *The Fall*, translated by Jeannette Kalker Ringold, 1990
De glazen brug, 1986; as *The Glass Bridge*, translated by Stacey Knecht, 1988
Nagelaten dagen [Posthumous Days], 1997

Short Stories

De andere kant, 1959; as *The Other Side*, translated by Ruth Levitt, 1994
Meneer Frits en andere verhalen uit vijftiger jaren [Mr Frits and Other Stories about the 1950s], 1974
Verzamelde verhalen [Collected Stories], 1982
Short stories in *Triquarterly*, 61 (1984)

Other

De zon is maar een zeepbel [The Sun is Only a Soap Bubble: Twelve Dream Reports], 1990

Further Reading

Devereaux, Elisabeth, "No Way Out: Marga Minco's War and Remembrance", *Village Voice* (20 August 1991)

Middledorp, A. Synthese, *Over het proza van Marga Minco*, Amsterdam: Wetenschappelijke Uitgeverij, 1981

Snapper, Johan P., *De wegen van Marga Minco*, Amsterdam: Bakker, 1999

Taylor, Jolanda, "Bitter Herbs, Empty Houses, Traps and False Identities: The (Post) War World of Marga Minco", *Canadian Journal of Netherlandic Studies*, 11 (1990)

All of the Netherlands has grown up with Marga Minco. For decades she has been one of the favourite authors of Dutch students. In all probability this has something to do with the small size of her novels and short stories and the requirement in the Netherlands that all students in the last grade of high school must read a certain number of Dutch literary texts. Although most Dutch today, Jews and non-Jews, were born after World War II and have no first-hand experience of the period, they still have a great interest in books about the war and the persecution of the Jews. Minco's writing meets their need to know and to understand. Thematically, her oeuvre is limited; her work is about what happened to Jews in World War II and how the survivors cope with that for the rest of their lives. All of her work has an autobiographical basis, although the relationship between Minco's work and her private life is not one-to-one.

Marga Minco was born Sara Menco. Her nickname was Selma. She was the youngest in a traditional Jewish family living in a small city in the south of the Netherlands. Right before the outbreak of the war, she got her first job as apprentice journalist at a newspaper in Breda. After the capitulation, she was dismissed because she was Jewish. She moved to Amersfoort with her parents. Later they were forced to move to Amsterdam because of German anti-Jewish regulations. When her parents were picked up at home and put on transport to Westerbork and then to eastern Europe, Sara managed to escape by fleeing to the neighbours via the garden. She went into hiding and was given a false identity. From then on her first name was Marga, a name that she continued using after the war. After the liberation of the Netherlands, Minco turned out to be the only surviving member of her family. During her time in hiding she met up again with her future husband Bert Voeten, whom she had already met before the war in Breda. Together they became part of the circle of artists and writers in Amsterdam. In the 1950s she began to publish in literary magazines that were being started all around her. The events of the war are worked into her first novel, *Het bittere kruid: een kleine kroniek* (*Bitter Herbs: A Little Chronicle*), published in 1957. Pure chance, which can sometimes be the basis of survival (like the leap over the garden gate), resonates in her later work. It appears in her 1983 novel, *De val* (*The Fall*), in which old Mrs Borgstein realizes every day that it was pure chance that spared her life. She happened to be upstairs in one of the bedrooms when the police van arrived, taking away her husband and her two children. In many of the short stories this theme is important as well.

During the first few years after liberation, the energy of the Dutch went into postwar reconstruction; little attention was given to the plight of the Jewish survivors. The difficulty of adjusting to the postwar Netherlands is the theme of Minco's second novel, *Een leeg huis* (*An Empty House*), published in 1966.

In addition to significant postwar Jewish themes, Minco's work is remarkable for its strikingly restrained style. Another distinguishing feature in her work is the symbolic meaning given to mementos. Her characters are attached to the possession of small objects such as a photo, a tea set, or a shawl. These possessions have little material value, but they are of invaluable emotional importance because they represent the only link to a loved one who was murdered. By holding on to these objects, the survivor tries to hold on to the memory of the past. But in vain, because the memory fades and holding on to the past turns out to be impossible.

In his study of Minco's work Johan Snapper, a professor of Dutch literature at the University of California in Berkeley, noted that the material object of the house itself is a central theme in her stories and novels. For most people a house is a symbol of security and love, but in Minco's work the spaces that count are those that do not, or do no longer, belong to the domain of security. She prefers the attic or the cellar, not accidentally the places where Jews were in hiding. In *An Empty House* the theme of the house is developed most clearly. Several days after liberation, the main character Sepha meets Yona, a fellow-sufferer. Both women have been in hiding in the countryside. Together they travel to Amsterdam where they stay in touch. While Sepha manages to rebuild her life somewhat, Yona can't cope with the total destruction of her pre-war existence. For her the destruction is symbolized by her parental home, a stately residence on a canal in Amsterdam that was dismantled inside and out during the last year of the war. Even the floorboards were taken out and were used as fuel by people living nearby. Yona commits suicide on the day that Sepha and her husband move to a new house in another neighbourhood.

Minco has never lacked for enthusiastic readers, although many of them identify her too strongly with her characters. On the occasion of the publication of *Nagelaten dagen* [Posthumous Days] in 1997, Minco was the guest of honor on a popular Dutch television talkshow about art. During this programme, the author mentioned that she had been extremely surprised to hear that her brother-in-law's sister turned out to be alive. The journey to this woman, who lived in Santa Barbara, California, is one of the story-lines of this novel. Minco stated that she is a much happier person than many of her readers seem to think. She explained that she once received a letter from a reader who wrote that she had great compassion for her. Minco thought that was a bit excessive. "I'm really not sad every day", she said, "when I finish writing, I close the door of my study and then I'm usually quite cheerful."

Her work has been translated into many languages and is constantly reprinted in the Netherlands. Her short stories continue to appear with some regularity. In 1985 a movie was made of *Het bittere kruid*, but the filmmakers did not stick to the original story: they added a romance between the main character and an SS officer. Minco was furious – and rightfully. Her own adaptation of *Een leeg huis* for the stage in 1991 was much more successful. This wasn't really surprising since she had already written several screenplays for television dramas that have been shown on Dutch and Belgian television.

DAPHNE MEIJER
translated by Jeannette Ringold

Modiano, Patrick

French fiction writer, 1945–

Born in Boulogne-sur-Seine, 30 July 1945. Educated at the Collège Saint-Joseph, Thônes; Lycée Henri-IV, Paris. Married Dominique Zehrfuss, 1970; two daughters. Many awards including the Nimier Prize, 1968; Fénéon Prize, 1969; Académie Française Grand Prize, 1972; French Booksellers Prize, 1976; Goncourt Prize, 1978; Monaco Prize, 1984; Prix Relais H du Roman d'Évasion, 1990.

Selected Writing

Fiction
La Place de l'étoile [The Place of the Star], 1968
La Ronde de nuit, 1969; as *Night Rounds*, translated by Patricia Wolf, 1971
Les Boulevards de ceinture, 1972; as *Ring Roads*, translated by Caroline Hillier, 1974
Villa Triste, 1975; as *Villa Triste*, translated by Caroline Hillier, 1977
Livret de famille [Family Record], 1977
Rue des boutiques obscures, 1978; as *Missing Person*, translated by Daniel Weissbort, 1980
Memory Lane, 1981
Une Jeunesse [Young Lives], 1981
Quartier perdu, 1984; as *A Trace of Malice*, translated by Anthea Bell, 1988
Dimanches d'août [Sundays in August], 1986
Vestiaire de l'enfance [The Cloakroom of Childhood], 1989
Voyage de noces, 1990; as *Honeymoon*, translated by Barbara Wright, 1992
Fleurs de ruine [Flowers of Decay], 1991
Chien de Printemps, 1993
Du Plus Loin de l'Oubli, 1996; as *Out of the Dark*, translated by Jordan Stump, 1998
La Petite Bijou [The Small Jewel], 2001

Plays
La Polka, 1974
Lacombe Lucien (screenplay), with Louis Malle, 1974
Poupée blonde, with Pierre Le-Tan, 1983

Other
Emmanuel Berl interrogatoire, with *Il fait beau, allons au cimetière*, by Emmanuel Berl, 1976
Une Aventure de Choura, 1986
Editor, *Paris*, 1987
Une Fiancée pour Choura, 1987
Catherine Certitude, 1988
Paris tendresse, with photographs by Brassaï, 1990
Dora Bruder, 1997; as *Dora Bruder*, 1999, and *The Search Warrant*, 2000, translated by Joanna Kilmartin

Further Reading

Golsan, Richard J., "Collaboration, Alienation, and the Crisis of Identity in the Film and Fiction of Patrick Modiano" in *Film and Literature*, edited by Wendell Aycock and Michel Schoenecke, Lubbock: Texas Tech University Press, 1988
Nettelback, C.W. and P.A. Hueston, "Anthology as Art: Modiano's *Livret de famille*", *Australian Journal of French Studies* (May–August 1984)
O'Keefe, Charles, "Patrick Modiano's *La Place de l'étoile*: Why Name a Narrator 'Raphaël Schlemilovitch'?", *Literary Onomastics Studies*, 15 (1988)
Prince, Gerald, "Re-Membering Modiano, or Something Happened", *Sub-Stance*, 49 (1986)
Warehime, Marja, "Originality and Narrative Nostalgia: Shadows in Modiano's *Rue des boutiques obscures*", *French Forum* (September 1987)

Patrick Modiano is a novelist obsessed with the problem of personal identity. His father was Jewish, his mother was half-Belgian, half-Hungarian, and his childhood, by his own account, was insecure. These circumstances helped shape both the obsessive nature of his fiction and its retrospective slant. Fascinated by the German Occupation of France, in which he located a metaphorical setting for the uncertainties he felt driven to explore, Modiano acquired such mastery of a period of which he had no personal knowledge that his first three novels convey an uncanny impression of lived rather than vicarious experience. His apparent ability to remember, rather than recast, places and events led to his being credited with pioneering the *mode rétro* (the upsurge of interest in the "black years" of the Occupation) of the 1970s. His association with the trend was confirmed by his collaboration on the script of Louis Malle's much remarked film, *Lacombe Lucien*.

La Place de l'étoile was prefaced by an anecdote that captures the playful seriousness of Modiano's first, highly-acclaimed novel. In June 1942 a German officer asks a young man to point out the famous Paris landmark; the young man indicates the place, over his heart, where Jews were required to display the star of David. The ambiguity raises both a smile and a wince and sets the tone for the freewheeling story of Raphaël Schlemilovitch who sets out to discover the nature of his Jewishness. He assumes various roles, guises, and identities and moves unimpeded through time and space. He plays the Jewish snob, the servile Jew, the Jewish wartime collaborator, and even catches tuberculosis because Kafka had suffered from the disease. He tries out both anti-French attitudes and anti-Semitism, and from his many theatrical incarnations acquires a clearer view of "the Jewish question". Yet he never ceases to be a wanderer and his unfruitful search for roots is a cipher for his equally anchorless creator, whose biography he shares. Swing Troubadour, the hero of *La Ronde de nuit* (*Night Rounds*; the title contains an allusion to Rembrandt's *The Night Watch*), is a *gestapiste* who is ordered to join the

Resistance which in turn sends him to infiltrate the Gestapo. As a double agent, he is uncertain of who he is. Unable to be a traitor, he cannot be a hero and is doomed to be the victim of his tenuous hold on his identity. The world of wartime collaboration also provides the setting of *Les Boulevards de ceinture* (*Ring Roads*) which shows how, through imagined memories, Serge Alexandre travels in time in search of his father, who might be a black market trafficker or possibly a hunted Jew. His quest proves to be both fruitless and illusory, for its object is not his absent father but himself.

Modiano has indicated that his first three novels may be taken as a loose trilogy, a triple mirror reflecting the same images. His wartime Paris is not a real place, in spite of the striking immediacy with which it is evoked, but an imaginary landscape ideally suited to explorations of the themes that fascinate him: personal identity, time, memory, and the vanity of autobiography. But his fictions also embody the search for lost values, authority, and morality, and tell us more about the present than about the past. Yet the obsessiveness with which Modiano returned to the same themes and mechanisms in these early fictions clearly indicates their role as exercises in self-exorcism.

Villa Triste, set in Switzerland in the 1960s, sends Victor Chmara in search of family ties. The tale seems uncomplicated until a wrong name or a memory lapse casts doubt upon the truth of what is remembered, the perception of the past, and the reality of the quest. The less unified *Livret de famille* [Family Record] also casts doubts on the reality of "Switzerland" as a satisfying destination but strikes a more optimistic note in the reality of family ties. The excellent *Rue des boutiques obscures* (*Missing Person*) features an amnesiac detective who sets his professional skills the task of finding out who he is. More than a successful pastiche of a popular genre, it offers a more relaxed meditation on the uses of the past, and signals a lowering of the intensity of Modiano's compulsive preoccupation with identity. By the time *Une Jeunesse* [Young Lives] appeared in 1981, Modiano had a family of his own and in his subsequent work has continued to explore the same themes – interchangeable places, retrospection, searches for missing persons which turn out to be quests for the self – in a mood of greater detachment. *Dimanches d'août* [Sundays in August] is a slightly ghostly tale of a man and a woman who are simultaneously running away and pursuing. The novelist hero of *Vestiaire de l'enfance* [The Cloakroom of Childhood] again shares Modiano's biography and, in what might be Mexico or North Africa, can neither jettison the past nor accept the present.

Modiano's eternally tumescent fiction – the play of time and memory recurs with variations in *Fleurs de ruine* [Flowers of Decay] – asserts that the truth about ourselves exists somewhere, in a continuum that may be glimpsed through the real or false memories of a past that we can never possess fully enough to let us be who we are. His heroes work out their obsessions in a process of perpetual self-discovery that is much less "difficult" than at first appears. It is true that Modiano's early work, in the manner of the New Novel, abandoned conventional chronology, linear plots, and palpable "characters". Yet such techniques did not signal allegiance to experimental fiction, which Modiano dismisses: "What I dislike about the 'nouveau roman' is that it lacks both tone and life. I am opposed to disembodied literature." Hence the absence of formal and linguistic experiment in a body of work which now, less anguished but no less challenging, has acquired the sobriety and elegance of the classic tradition.

DAVID COWARD

Molodovski, Kadye

Russian-born US poet, dramatist, and fiction writer, 1894–1975

Born in shtetl Bereza Kartuska, Belorussia, 1894, into family influenced by *Haskalah* (Jewish Enlightenment). Taught to read Yiddish by paternal grandmother, Bobe Shifre; studied Torah and Gemara under father; studied Russian language, geography, and philosophy under private tutors. Obtained teaching certificate, Bereza, 1912. Taught in schools in Sherpetz and Bialystok; joined group seeking revival of Hebrew language; studied teaching of Hebrew under Yehiel Halperin, Warsaw, 1913–14. Taught in schools in Poltave, Romny, and Saratov, 1914–16. Settled in Odessa, 1916–17. After Bolshevik revolution, 1917, private tutor, Kiev, and worker in home for displaced Jewish children. Published first poem after surviving Kiev pogrom, 1920. Married Simkhe Lev, 1920. Teacher in children's home, Brest-Litovsk, 1923. Lived in Warsaw, teaching Yiddish by day at elementary school of Central Yiddish Schools Organization (Tshisho), and Hebrew by night at Jewish community school, until 1935; active in Yiddish Writers' Union. Emigrated to United States, 1935; settled in New York. Wrote column, "Great Jewish Women", for *Forverts* (*Jewish Daily Forward*), using pseudonym Rivke Zilberg; edited journal *Svive*, from 1943. Lived in Tel Aviv, 1950–52; edited journal for Pioneer Women's Organization, *Heym* [Home]. Awards include Manger Prize, 1971. Died in Philadelphia, 23 March 1975.

Selected Writings

Poetry

Kheshvndike nekht: lider [Nights of Heshvan: Poems], 1927

Geyen shikhlekh avek: mayselekh [Little Shoes Go Away], 1930

Dzshike gas: lider [Dzshike Street: Poems], 1933

Freydke: lider [Freydke: Poems], 1935

In land fun mayn gebeyn [In the Country of My Bones], 1937

Afn barg [On the Mountain], 1938

Yidishe kinder [Jewish Children], 1945

Der melekh dovid aleyn iz geblibn [Only King David Remained], 1946

In yerushalayim kumen malokhim [In Jerusalem, Angels Come], 1952

Likht fun dornboym [Lights of the Thorn Bush], 1965

Martsepanes: mayselekh un lider far kinder [Marzipan: Tales and Poems for Children], 1970

In English translation in
Onions and Cucumbers and Plums, translated by Sarah Betsky-Zweig, 1958
An Anthology of Modern Yiddish Poetry, translated by Ruth Whitman, 1966
A Treasury of Yiddish Poetry, edited by Irving Howe and Eliezer Greenberg, 1969
The Penguin Book of Modern Yiddish Verse, edited by Irving Howe *et al.*, 1987
A Century of Yiddish Poetry, edited and translated by Aaron Kramer, 1989
Paper Bridges: Selected Poems of Kadye Molodowsky, translated and edited by Kathryn Hellerstein, 1999

Fiction
"Meydlekh, froyen, vayber, un . . . nevue", *Literarishe bleter* (3 June 1927)
Fun lublin biz nyu-york: togbukh fun Rivke Zilberg [From Lublin to New York: Diary of Rivke Zilberg], 1942
A shtub mit zibn fentster [A House with Seven Windows], 1957
Baym toyer: roman fun dem lebn in yisroel [At the Gate: Novel about Life in Israel], 1967

In English translation in
The Tribe of Dina, revised edition, edited by Melanie Kaye/Kantrowitz and Irena Klepfisz, 1989
Found Treasures: Stories by Yiddish Women Writers, edited by Frieda Forman *et al.*, 1994

Plays
Ale fentster tsu der zun: shpil in elef bilder [All Windows Open to the Sun: Play in 11 Images], 1938
Nokhn got fun midber: drame [Toward the God of the Desert: Drama], 1949
A hoyz af grand strit [A House on Grand Street], 1953

Other
Af di vegn fun tsion [On the Roads of Zion], 1957
Editor, *Lider fun khurbm: antologye* [Poems of the Holocaust], 1962
Mayn elter-zeydns yerushe [My Great-Grandfather's Legacy], *Svive* (March 1965–April 1974)

Further Reading

Hellerstein, Kathryn, "A Question of Tradition: Women Poets in Yiddish" in *Yiddish Handbook of American-Jewish Literature*, edited by Lewis Fried, New York: Greenwood Press, 1988
Hellerstein, Kathryn, "Kadya Molodowsky's *Froyen-lider*: A Reading", *AJS Review*, 13 (1988)
Hellerstein, Kathryn, "The Subordination of Prayer to Narrative in Modern Yiddish Poems" in *Parable and Story in Judaism and Christianity*, edited by Clemens Thoma and Michael Wyschogrod, New York: Paulist Press, 1989
Hellerstein, Kathryn, "Hebraism as Metaphor in Kadya Molodowsky's Froyen-Lider!" in *The Uses of Adversity: Failure and Accommodation in Reader Response*, edited by Ellen Spolsky, Lewisburg, Pennsylvania: Bucknell University Press, 1990
Hellerstein, Kathryn, "In Exile in the Mother Tongue: Yiddish and the Woman Poet" in *Borders, Boundaries, and Frames: Essays in Cultural Criticism and Cultural Studies*, edited by Mae G. Henderson, New York and London: Routledge, 1995
Hellerstein, Kathryn, "A Yiddish Poet's Response to the *Khurbm:* Kadya Molodowsky in America" in *Freedom and Responsibility: Exploring the Challenges of Jewish Continuity*, edited by Rela Mintz Geffen and Marsha Bryan Edelman, New York: Ktav, 1998
Klepfisz, Irena, "Di Mames, dos loshn/The Mothers, the Language: Feminism, Yidishkayt, and the Politics of Memory", *Bridges*, 4/1 (Winter–Spring 1994)
Peczenik, F., "Encountering the Matriarchy: Kadya Molodowsky's Women Songs", *Yiddish*, 7/2–3 (1988)
Pratt, Norma Fain, "Culture and Radical Politics: Yiddish Women Writers in America, 1890–1940" in *Women of the Word: Jewish Women and Jewish Writing*, edited by Judith R. Baskin, Detroit: Wayne State University Press, 1994
Zucker, Sheva, "Kadya Molodowsky's 'Froyen Lider'", *Yiddish*, 9/2 (1994)

And why should this blood without blemish
Be my conscience, like a silken thread
Bound upon my brain
And in my life, a page plucked from a holy book
The first line torn?

These lines from Kadye Molodovski's 1927 sequence "Froyen-Lider!" [Women-Poems] pose a crucial question. How can a Yiddish writer reconcile her art with Judaism's definition of a woman's role? Molodovski's answer to that question in her poems, children's poems, novels, short stories, plays, autobiography, and journalism, published between 1927 and 1974, evolved into even broader questions about the very survival of Jews in the modern world.

In 1927, Molodovski published her first book of poetry, *Kheshvndike nekht* [Nights of Heshvan], under the imprint of a prestigious Vilna (Vilnius) and Warsaw Yiddish publisher, B. Kletskin. The book's narrator, a woman in her thirties, moves through the landscape of Jewish eastern Europe. Molodovski contrasts the narrator's modernity with the roles decreed by Jewish tradition for women, according to law, custom, or history. *Nights of Heshvan* received approximately 20 reviews in the Yiddish press, nearly all of them laudatory.

As a teacher in Warsaw during the 1930s, Molodovski was deeply aware of the poverty in which many of her students lived. She wrote poems for and about these young children in order to nurture their imaginations against the limits imposed by hunger and need. Her second book, *Geyen shikhlekh avek: mayselekh* [Little Shoes Go Away], was awarded a prize by the Warsaw Jewish Community and the Yiddish Pen Club.

Molodovski's third book of poems, *Dzshike gas* [Dzshike Street], published in 1933 by the press of the leading Warsaw literary journal, *Literarishe bleter*, was reviewed negatively on political grounds, for being too "aesthetic", despite

Molodovski's work for the poor among whom she lived. In the title poem, "Dzshike gas", Molodovski quotes the criticism of her own poetry:

And I-they point at me with their fingers:
'There she is – the lady singer,
The devil take her mother, —
She hangs around her all the time
And braids our misery into rhymes.

In response, Molodovski's fourth book, *Freydke*, features a 16-part narrative poem about a heroic, Jewish, working-class woman.

Molodovski emigrated to the United States in 1935. She settled in New York City, where her husband joined her in 1937 or 1938. Her fifth book, *In land fun mayn gebeyn* [In the Country of My Bones], contains fragmented poems that represent an internalization of exile.

Molodovski's literary endeavours then branched out in several directions. In 1938 she published a new edition of her children's poems, *Afn barg* [On the Mountain]. In 1942, she published *Fun lublin biz nyu-york: togbukh fun Rivke Zilberg* [From Lublin to New York: Diary of Rivke Zilberg], a novel about a young immigrant woman. At this time, Molodovski also wrote a series of columns on "Great Jewish Women" for the Yiddish daily *Forverts*, using Rivke Zilberg, the name of the novel's protagonist as her pseudonym.

Fearful for her brother and other family still in Poland in 1944, Molodovski put aside her editorship of the literary journal *Svive*, which she had co-founded in 1943, publishing seven issues, and began to write the poems of *Der melekh dovid aleyn iz geblibn* [Only King David Remained]. This contains many *khurbm-lider* (destruction-poems), which draw upon traditional Jewish literary responses to catastrophe, as in her famous lines from "Eyl khanun" [Merciful God]: "Merciful God,/ Choose another people,/ Elect another./ We are tired of death and dying,/ We have no more prayers./ Choose another people,/ Elect another./ We have no more blood/ To be a sacrifice." Despairing in the wake of the Holocaust, Molodovski appeals to the God of traditional Jewish prayer. Paradoxically as these lines claim to sever God's covenant with the Jewish people, in the same breath, they reaffirm a desire to believe in God.

From 1950 through 1952, Molodovski and Simkhe Lev lived in Tel Aviv. There, Molodovski edited a journal for the Pioneer Women Organization, *Heym* [Home], which portrayed life in Israel. In Israel, Molodovski also began work on a novel, *Baym toyer: roman fun dem lebn in yisroel* [At the Gate: Novel about Life in Israel]. After her return to New York, she revived the literary journal *Svive* and began to write her autobiography, *Mayn elter-zeydns yerushe* [My Great-Grandfather's Legacy], which appeared serially in *Svive* between 1965 and 1974.

Published in Buenos Aires in 1965, Molodovski's last book of poems, *Likht fun dornboym* [Lights of the Thorn Bush] includes dramatic monologues in the voices of legendary personae from Jewish and non-Jewish traditions and contemporary characters. For example, "Ikh bin a viderkol" [I am an Echo] expresses the despair, responsibility, and inspiration of the Jewish poet after the Holocaust:

I am an echo
Of a vanished symphony.
My voice is a marvel,
Whether it's prayer or blasphemy.

A fiddler appears,
Saying, I've come from yesterday.
He raises his fiddle —
His pallid fingers:

Soon I will play
The prescribed melody
That they played long ago
By the walls of Jericho.

Soon I will play
By the walls of Jericho.

The book concludes with a section of poems on Israel from the 1950s, which, like the ending of her autobiography, express Molodovski's Zionism, her vision of hope.

Kadye Molodovski was one of the few women Yiddish poets able to sustain and develop her writing throughout her life in several genres. Her works reflect the vast cultural and historical crises that the Jews experienced in the 20th century.

KATHRYN HELLERSTEIN

Morante, Elsa

Italian fiction writer, 1912–1985

Born in Rome, 18 August 1912. Married Alberto Moravia, 1941; divorced 1962. Lived in Anacapri, 1941–43. After German invasion, 1943, went into hiding with Moravia in Fondi, near Cassino, until 1944. Contributor, *Il Mondo*, from 1951; travelled extensively after 1957. Awards include Viareggio Prize, 1948; Strega Prize, 1957; Zafferana Prize, 1968; Séguier Prize, 1977; Médicis Foreign Book Prize (France), 1984. Died 25 November 1985.

Selected Writings

Collection

Opere, 2 vols, edited by Carlo Cecchi and Cesare Garboli, 1988–90

Fiction

Le bellissime avventure di Caterì dalla trecciolina, 1941; as *Le straordinarie avventure di Caterina* [The Wonderful Adventures of Cateri with the Plaited Hair], 1959

Il gioco segreto [The Secret Game], 1941

Menzogna e sortilegio, 1948; as *House of Liars*, translated by Adrienne Foulke, 1951

L'isola di Arturo, 1957; as *Arturo's Island*, translated by Isabel Quigly, 1959

Botteghe oscure [The Dark Little Shop], 1958

Lo scialle andaluso [The Andalusian Shawl], 1963

La storia, 1974; as *History: A Novel*, translated by William Weaver, 1977

Aracoeli, 1982; as *Aracoeli*, translated by William Weaver, 1984

Poetry
Alibi, 1958
Il mondo salvato dai ragazzini e altri poemi [The World Saved by Little Boys and Other Poems], 1968

Other
Translator, *Il libro degli appunti*, by Katherine Mansfield, 1945; as *Quaderno appunti*, 1979
Translator, with Marcella Hannau, *Il meglio di Katherine Mansfield* [The Best of Katherine Mansfield], 1957

Further Reading

Blelloch, Paola, "Elsa Morante's Use of Dream", *La Fusta* (Spring–Fall 1990)
Briziarelli, Susan, "Cassandra's Daughters: Prophecy in Elsa Morante's *La storia*", *Romance Languages Annual* (1990)
Capozzi, Rocco, "Elsa Morante's *Aracoeli*: The End of a Journey" in *Donna: Women in Italian Culture*, edited by Ada Testaferri, Ottawa: Dovehouse, 1989
Capozzi, Rocco, "Elsa Morante: The Trauma of Possessive Love and Disillusionment" in *Contemporary Women Writers in Italy*, edited by Santo L. Aricò, Amherst: University of Massachusetts Press, 1990
Kalay, Grace Zlobnicki, *The Theme of Childhood in Elsa Morante*, University, Mississippi: Romance Monographs, 1996
Parks, Tim, "The Experience of Separation: The Novels of Elsa Morante", *PN Review*, 14 (1987–88)
Wood, Sharon, "The Bewitched Mirror: Imagination and Narration in Elsa Morante", *Modern Language Review*, 86/2 (1991)

Elsa Morante, who can be counted among the most original and outstanding figures of 20th-century Italian letters, was born in Rome on 18 August 1912, the daughter of Irma Poggibonsi and Francesco Lo Monaco, although her legal father was a Sicilian reform-school teacher, Augusto Morante. Her mother, who worked as an infant school teacher in a working-class area of Rome, came from a Jewish family in the city of Modena. Although her family background was evidently lower-middle class, Morante spent her childhood moving up and down the social scale, among both working-class and patrician families via a close relationship with her godmother, a well-off noblewoman with whom she often stayed. In fact her subsequent sympathetic understanding of very different social strata in Italian society was one of the strongest elements in her make-up and a factor that protected her from a narrow and conformist mindset.

Similarly fundamental to Morante's work was her deep religiosity and sense of literary vocation. Starting early as a writer she simultaneously displayed an interest and curiosity in religion despite her secular family background and developed a strong if unconventional Catholic faith, insisting on a church wedding when she married Alberto Moravia in 1941. The fact that Moravia himself was also of Jewish descent indicates the high and even paradoxical degree of assimilation among Italy's long-established Jewish communities after the founding of modern Italy in the second half of the 19th century.

For Morante the practice of literature was a religious impulse that had the aim of reflecting the human being back to him or herself to create a beneficial and healing self-comprehension. In all her novels Morante expressed a perception of the alienated quality of normal existence; "real life" for her was the domain of simple souls, little children, the mentally subnormal, the same people that history conspired to crush and that only literature could restore through its utopian possibilities and its evasive mechanisms. After publishing a short story collection *Il gioco segreto* [The Secret Game] and the fable *Le bellissime avventure di Caterì dalla trecciolina* [The Wonderful Adventures of Caterì with the Plaited Hair] in 1941, but which had been written many years before while still an adolescent, her novel *Menzogna e sortilegio* [Lies and Sorcery] caught the attention of the critics. Here what Morante felt to be the troubling distance between reality and the impenetrable depths of human subjectivity emerges in the shocking story of the decay of a noble southern Italian family told by a female protagonist who lives closed up in her room. Told in the first person its story is prefigured – in the adoption of the narrative I, in the long gap between events and their outcomes, and in some of its minor characters – in "Il ladro dei lumi" [The Lamp-thief] in *Lo scialle andaluso* [The Andalucian Shawl], a story from 1935 set in a Jewish milieu, a story that shows the thematic rather than stylistic influence of Kafka on Morante's writing. The narrator, a woman looking back to a childhood event, tells the story of Jusvin, a synagogue beadle whom she sees from her window overlooking the ghetto surprised in the act of stealing oil from the *shul*. Punished with an awful death, Jusvin finds no mercy either before God Himself whose judgement is silent and implacable. Another case of "apartness" from the everyday world is found in the unchanging landscape of Procida, an island in the Gulf of Naples, setting for *L'isola di Arturo* (*Arthur's Island*). It is the story of a child's difficult growing-up, told by its protagonist as an adult. The theme is the pitilessness of history, "a scandal that has lasted ten thousand years", and of the simple, defenceless ones that are its principal victims but at the same time those that maintain an authentic relationship with life. The same theme prevails in *Il mondo salvato dai ragazzini* [The World Saved by Little Boys] in which the *ragazzetti celesti* ("heavenly" or "sky-blue boys") are shown as the bearers of the only possible happiness, an innocence that exists outside any real history. It finds, though, its most extensive and successful expression in the long, epic novel *La storia* (*History*) which in its proof stage was entitled *Senza i conforti della religione* [Without the Consolations of Faith]. This book, product of a long gestation and of epic scope, is reminiscent of the great realist novels of the 19th century, relinquishing the narrative "I" for the traditional omniscient author-narrator. The odyssey of World War II is traced through the microcosm of the family of Ida Ramundo, her strong and vigorous son Nino, and little Useppe, a charming and cheerful creature born from Ida's rape by a German soldier. This act of violence opens the book and is followed by a detailed (and partly autobiographical) reconstruction of the life of Ida, the primary schoolteacher terrified by the Jewish heritage which she sees as a dark curse, a feeling she inherits from her mother. Against a background of bombing raids, ruins, and psychological and material devastation Morante takes her characters through six years, from 1941 to 1946, and then to a dramatic epilogue – Nino dies in a traffic accident, Useppe dies from his epilepsy, and Ida survives for a few years but has gone mad and is in an asylum. Another major figure in the novel is David Segre, also Jewish, who escapes from a concentration camp and conceals his identity until the end of the war, joining Nino who is with the partisans.

Segre, however, becomes a drug addict, incapable of transcending the mental restrictions of his bourgeois upbringing, and dies miserably. A figure caught between an original existential sense of innocence and the corruption of his upbringing, he exists precisely on the frontier between Morante's polarities of (moral) utopia and actual history. Morante gives Segre the task of expressing what she felt to be the inner unity of things, an unreachable mystery, putting into his mouth what she saw as the world's secret: "God is the intimacy of all things that exist and he reveals that secret with beauty. Beauty is the modesty of the divine."

Morante's strange trajectory – a devotee of the Cult of the Madonna and yet powerfully returning to (generally tragic) Jewish figures in her work – is suggestive of the plight of Italian Jews in 20th-century Italy; often well-established in the liberal professions, business, and the arts, and even among prominent early supporters of fascism – and yet this did not protect them from the "Racial Laws" enacted by Mussolini in 1938 or eventual deportation and mass murder.

CLARA CORONA

Moravia, Alberto

Italian fiction writer, dramatist, and essayist, 1907–1990

Born Alberto Pincherle in Rome, 28 November 1907. Studied privately because of tuberculosis, contracted 1916; received high school equivalency diploma, 1917. Published first novel, 1929, using pseudonym Alberto Moravia, referring to family's country of origin; also used pseudonym Pseudo, 1938. Foreign correspondent, *La Stampa*, Milan, and *Gazzetta del Popolo*, Turin, in 1930s; travelled extensively, with long periods in France, Britain, United States, Mexico, Greece, and China. Married, first, Elsa Morante, 1941; divorced 1962. Lived in Anacapri, 1941–43. After German invasion, 1943, went into hiding with Morante in Fondi, near Cassino, until 1944. Film critic, *La Nuova Europa*, 1944–46; co-editor, with Alberto Carocci, *Nuovi Argomenti*, Milan, from 1953; film critic, *L'Espresso*, Milan, from 1955; State Department lecturer, United States, 1955; travelled extensively, 1958–70. Married, second, Dacia Maraini, 1963; third, Carmen Llera, 1986. President, International PEN, 1959. Awards include Corriere Lombardo Prize, 1945; Strega Prize, 1952; Marzotto Prize, 1954; Viareggio Prize, 1961. Honorary member, American Academy of Arts and Letters; Chevalier, 1952, and Commandeur, 1984, Légion d'Honneur. Died 26 September 1990.

Selected Writings

Fiction

Gli indifferenti, 1929; as *The Indifferent Ones*, translated by Aida Mastrangelo, 1932; as *The Time of Indifference*, translated by Angus Davidson, 1953

Le ambizioni sbagliate, 1935; as *The Wheel of Fortune*, translated by Arthur Livingston, 1937; as *Mistaken Ambitions*, translated by Arthur Livingston, 1955

La bella vita [The Beautiful Life], 1935

L'imbroglio [The Swindle], 1937

I sogni del pigro [The Dreams of the Lazy Man], 1940

La mascherata, 1941; as *The Fancy Dress Party*, translated by Angus Davidson, 1947

L'amante infelice [The Unhappy Lover], 1943

L'epidemia: racconti surrealistici e satirici [The Epidemic: Surreal and Satirical Stories], 1944

Agostino, 1945; as *Agostino*, translated by Beryl de Zoete, 1947

Due cortigiane; Serata di Don Giovanni [Two Courtesans; The Evening of Don Giovanni], 1945

La romana, 1947; as *The Woman of Rome*, translated by Lydia Holland, 1949

La disubbidienza, 1948; as *Two Adolescents: The Stories of Agostina and Luca*, translated by Angus Davidson, 1952

L'amore coniugale e altri racconti, 1949; selection as *Conjugal Love*, translated by Angus Davidson, 1951

Il conformista, 1951; as *The Conformist*, translated by Angus Davidson, 1951

I racconti, 1952; as *I racconti 1927–1951*, 2 vols, 1983; selections as *Bitter Honeymoon and Other Stories*, translated by Bernard Wall *et al.*, 1954, and *The Wayward Wife and Other Stories*, translated by Angus Davidson, 1960

Il disprezzo, 1954; as *A Ghost at Noon*, translated by Angus Davidson, 1955

Racconti romani, 1954; selection as *Roman Tales*, translated by Angus Davidson, 1956

Five Novels (includes *Mistaken Ambitions*; *Agostino*; *Luca*; *Conjugal Love*; *A Ghost at Noon*), translated by Arthur Livingston *et al.*, 1955

La ciociara, 1957; as *Two Women*, translated by Angus Davidson, 1958

Nuovi racconti romani, 1959; selection as *More Roman Tales*, translated by Angus Davidson, 1963

La noia, 1960; as *The Empty Canvas*, translated by Angus Davidson, 1961

L'automa, 1962; as *The Fetish and Other Stories*, translated by Angus Davidson, 1964

Cortigiana stanca [The Tired Courtesan], 1965

L'attenzione, 1965; as *The Lie*, translated by Angus Davidson, 1966

Una cosa è una cosa, 1967; selection as *Command and I Will Obey You*, translated by Angus Davidson, 1969

Il paradiso, 1970; as *Paradise and Other Stories*, translated by Angus Davidson, 1971, as *Bought and Sold*, 1973

Io e lui, 1971; as *Two: A Phallic Novel*, translated by Angus Davidson, 1972, as *The Two of Us*, 1972

Un'altra vita, 1973; as *Lady Godiva and Other Stories*, translated by Angus Davidson, 1975

Boh, 1976; as *The Voice of the Sea and Other Stories*, translated by Angus Davidson, 1978
La vita interiore, 1978; as *Time of Desecration*, translated by Angus Davidson, 1980
1934, 1982; as *1934*, translated by William Weaver, 1983
Storie della preistoria [Stories from Prehistory: Fables], 1982
La cosa e altri racconti, 1983; as *Erotic Tales*, translated by Tim Parks, 1985
L'uomo che guarda, 1985; as *The Voyeur*, translated by Tim Parks, 1986
Il viaggio a Roma, 1988; as *Journey to Rome*, translated by Tim Parks, 1990

Plays
Gli indifferenti [The Indifferent Ones], with Luigi Squarzini, in *Sipario* [Curtain], 1948
Il provino [The Test Tube], 1955
Non approfondire [Don't Go Deeper], 1957
Teatro, 1958
Beatrice Cenci in *Teatro*, 1958; as *Beatrice Cenci*, translated by Angus Davidson, 1965
La mascherata [The Fancy Dress Party], 1958
Il mondo è quello che è [The World is That Which Is], 1966
Il dio Kurt [Kurt the God], 1968
La vita è gioco [Life's a Game], 1969

Screenplays: *Un colpo di pistola*, 1941; *Zazà*, 1942; *Sensualità*, 1951; *Ultimo incontro*, 1951; *La provinciale* (*The Wayward Wife*), 1952; *Tempi nostri*, 1952; *Villa Borghese*, 1953; *La donna del fiume*, 1954; *La romana* (*The Woman of Rome*), 1955; *Racconti romani* (*Roman Tales*), 1956; *Racconti d'estate* (*Love on the Riviera*), 1958; *I delfini* (*The Dauphins*), 1960; *La giornata balorda* (*From a Roman Balcony*), 1960; *Una domenica d'estate*, 1961; *Agostino*, 1962; *Ieri oggi domani* (*Yesterday, Today, and Tomorrow*), 1963; *Le ore nude*, 1964; *L'occhio selvaggio* (*The Wild Eye*), 1967

Other
Opere complete [Complete Works], 16 vols, 1952–76
La speranza: ossia cristianesimo e comunismo [Hope: Or Rather Christianity and Communism], 1944
Un mese in USSR [A Month in the USSR], 1958
I moralisti moderni [The Modern Moralists], with Elemire Zolla, 1960
Editor, with Elemire Zolla, *Saggi italiani* [Italian Essays], 1960
Women of Rome, 1960
Un'idea dell'India [An Idea of India], 1962
Claudia Cardinale, 1963
L'uomo come fine e altri saggi, 1964; as *Man as an End: A Defence of Humanism*, translated by Bernard Wall, 1965
La rivoluzione culturale in Cina ovvero il convitato di pietra, 1967; as *The Red Book and the Great Wall: An Impression of Mao's China*, translated by Ronald Strom, 1968
A quale tribù appartieni?, 1972; as *Which Tribe Do You Belong To?*, translated by Angus Davidson, 1974
Al cinema: centoquarantotto film d'autore [The Cinema: 148 Films d'auteur], 1975
La mutazione femminile: conversazione con Alberto Moravia sulla donna [The Female Mutation: Conversations with Alberto Moravia on Women], with Carla Ravaiola, 1975
Preface to Giacomo Debenedetti's *16 October 1943*, 1976
Intervista sullo scrittore scomodo [Interview with the Uncomfortable Writer], edited by Nello Ajello, 1978
Quando Ba Lena era tanto piccola [When Ba Lena was Very Small], 1978
Cosima e i briganti [Cosima and the Brigands], 1980
Impegno controvoglia: saggi, articoli, interviste [The Unwilling Obligation: Essays, Articles, Interviews], edited by Renzo Paris, 1980
Lettere del Sahara [Letters from the Sahara], 1981
Lettere [Letters], with Giuseppe Prezzolini, 1982
Passeggiate africane [African Walks], 1987
Io e il mio tempo: Conversazioni critiche con Ferdinando Camon [Me and My Time: Critical Conversations with Ferdinando Camon], 1988

Further Reading
Alexander, Foscarina, *The Aspiration toward a Lost Natural Harmony in the Work of Three Italian Writers: Leopardi, Verga and Moravia*, Lewiston, New York: Mellen Press, 1990
Alfonsi, Ferdinando, *An Annotated Bibliography of Moravia Criticism in Italy and in the English-Speaking World (1929–1975)*, New York: Garland, 1976
Capozzi, Rocco and Mario B. Mignone (editors), *Homage to Moravia*, Stony Brook, New York: Forum Italicum, 1993
Cottrell, Jane E., *Alberto Moravia*, New York: Ungar, 1974
Dego, Giuliano, *Moravia*, New York: Barnes and Noble, and Edinburgh: Oliver and Boyd, 1966
Freed, Donald and Joan Ross, *The Existentialism of Alberto Moravia*, Carbondale: Southern Illinois University Press, 1972
Heiney, Donald W., *Three Italian Novelists*, Ann Arbor: University of Michigan Press, 1968
Slaymaker, William, "The Forensics of Freedom: Dialogues and Dialectics in Moravia's Seventies Novels", *Italian Culture*, 66/2 (1989)
Wood, Sharon, "For Better, for Worse: Elements of Irony and Reversal in Alberto Moravia's *L'Amore coniugale*", *Italianist*, 7 (1987)
Wood, Sharon, "Gender and Structure in Moravia's *1934*", *Bulletin of the Society for Italian Studies*, 20 (1987)
Wood, Sharon, "Crossing Frontiers: Some Reflections on Moravia", *Association of Teachers of Italian Journal*, 52 (1988)
Wood, Sharon, "Religion, Politics and Sexuality in Moravia's *Il conformista*", *Italian Studies*, 44 (1989)
Wood, Sharon, *Woman as Object: Language and Gender in the Work of Alberto Moravia*, London: Pluto Press, and Savage, Maryland: Barnes and Noble, 1990

Alberto Pincherle was born in Rome on 28 November 1907, the third child of Gina De Marsanich and Carlo Pincherle. His mother was a lower middle-class Catholic; his father descended from an illustrious Venetian Jewish family. Among Alberto's four paternal uncles and aunts, Gabriele was an Italian senator – the result of the struggle for national unity in which the Jewish minority was actively engaged – and Amelia was a writer and the mother of Carlo and Nello Rosselli, figures in the liberal-democratic opposition to fascism. Alberto's education does not, however, reveal any trace of his Jewish heritage – and the author always stressed the non-denominational nature of his education, notwithstanding his baptism – not even as a tradition. On the contrary, he displayed total indifference towards it, if not intolerance. Speaking of his grandparents, for example, he said that, having seen a portrait of them – they died before his birth – they left "an archaeological, depressing impression of a past which was tedious and obsolete". On the other hand, the adolescent Moravia shows the same indifference towards the anti-fascism of his cousins Carlo and Nello, whom he judged "deluded and nineteenth century, with their heads full of generous but scarcely practical ideas". Although he undoubtedly had no affinity with the fascist regime in terms of sensibility and ideas, he nonetheless felt that "the anti-Fascists were losers" and initially kept his distance. The trauma of his cousins' death, murdered at the hands of the regime's hired assassins in 1937 in France, was to lead eventually, in 1951, to the novel *Il conformista* (*The Conformist*), later successfully filmed by Bertolucci.

The central event in Moravia's life is perhaps disease, a bone tuberculosis which first appeared when he was nine years old and which confined him to a long period of immobility and to extended stays in the sanatorium. His ill-health favoured his vocation for reading – he read Dostoevskii, Kafka, Proust, Joyce, etc. – but noticeably left its mark on his emotional development, increasing his adolescent turmoil, including that linked to the discovery of sexuality, described subsequently in his short novel *Agostino*. Indeed his debut novel, after collaboration on the review *900*, was published at his father's expense in 1929, but he had begun writing it in 1925, when he was barely 18 years old.

His first novel *Gli indifferenti* (*The Time of Indifference*) was a merciless portrait of the Italian bourgeoisie in the early fascist years. In the young Michele's inability to react as he witnesses his sister's involvement in an affair with his mother's lover in an atmosphere of moral corruption, Moravia's most characteristic motifs already appear: ineptitude, the failure to come out of oneself (only in *La disubbidienza*, translated in *Two Adolescents* in 1952, does Luca, the adolescent main character, find redemption for his own anxiety in sexual experience – before that sex was reduced to the mere venting of a pressing urge), indifference, boredom. These themes recur more or less explicitly in the whole of Moravia's work, even in the so-called neo-realist novels *La romana* (*The Woman of Rome*), *La ciociara* (*Two Women*), and the *Racconti romani* (*Roman Tales*), where, instead of the usual well-off bourgeois characters, we find the lower and lower middle classes pictured against the background of the war and the Resistance. Significantly, in 1960 Moravia was to entitle one of his novels, *La noia*, translated as *The Empty Canvas*, but whose title means literally "boredom" – the story of the bourgeois Dino who, unable to find self-fulfilment through art, tries to establish a relationship with reality through love with the young Cecilia, failing once again – and, even in the span of his long career as a storyteller capable of self-renewal by measuring himself successively against Marxism, feminism, and psychoanalysis, he was to remain anchored to his own themes and style. If, in an internal association with Italian literature, the themes of failure and ineptitude immediately recall the work of Italo Svevo, who called himself a "dissimulated" [dissimulato], that's to say hidden, Jew, these are nonetheless the guiding motifs of a large part of 20th-century European literature and, for Moravia at least, it is quite difficult to trace them back to a Jewish milieu. Rather it is the very absence in the writer's pages of any reference to Jewish characters or contexts that is significant, even where it would normally be inevitable to expect them, as he set a good part of his work in Rome, the Italian city where the Jewish presence is most immediately felt. Nor does *Il dio Kurt* [Kurt the God] belie this assertion: this play in two acts dedicated to the theme of the Nazi death camps is based on the Moravian motif of the family and only as a pretext on that of the Shoah. Of further significance is Moravia's reticence in recognizing his own Jewishness, which is hardly admitted. In reality he suffered, as Jew, the consequences of the anti-Jewish campaign and the racial laws promulgated in Italy 1938: he was forced to publish under a pseudonym (he chose the transparent "Pseudo") and to change his own surname to Piccinni; he escaped in 1943 with Elsa Morante, whom he had married two years prior to the German round-ups. Generally, though, Moravia saw the racial policy as being relatively benign (in comparison with the Teutonic thoroughness of Italy's Nazi ally) because Italians were not strict or thorough in their application. However occasionally the wall of reticence cracked, as in his preface to the 1976 edition of Giacomo Debenedetti's *16 October 1943* (the date the Germans rounded up the inhabitants of the ghetto in Rome): Moravia here re-evokes his own story as a Jew, through a reiterated "I too" which conveys his direct personal involvement, and although he does so in reference to an extreme catastrophe, he agrees here to measure himself against Jewishness: to do otherwise, he maintains:

> . . . would in some way be the equivalent, even after twenty-five years, of denying my solidarity with the unfortunate people whom Kappler's SS arrested on that distant October morning in order to send them to their deaths in the death camp gas chambers.

CLARA CORONA

Möring, Marcel

Dutch fiction writer, 1957–

Born in Enschede, 5 September 1957, to Jewish mother and Protestant father. Studied Dutch literature at polytechnic; left after two years to become writer. Theatre critic, *Drents-Groningse Pers*. Married; two children. Awards include Geertjan Lubberhuizen Prize, 1990; AKO Literary Prize, 1994; Aga Khan Prize of the literary magazine *Paris Review*, 2001.

Selected Writings

Fiction

Mendels erfenis [Mendel's Heritage], 1990

Het grote verlangen, 1992; as *The Great Longing*, translated by Stacey Knecht, 1995

Bederf is the weg van alle vlees [Decay is the Way of all Flesh], 1994

In Babylon, 1997; as *In Babylon*, translated by Stacey Knecht, 1999

Modelvliegen, 2000; as *The Dream Room*, translated by Stacey Knecht, 2002

Further Reading

Carstens, Daan, "Reiziger door de tijd: over het wek van Marcel Möring" [Traveller through Time: About Marcel Möring's Work], *Ons Erfdeel*, 40 (1997)

Isler, Alan, "Wandering through Hellish Images", *Jewish Quarterly* (Spring 1985)

Marcel Möring was born in 1957 in Enschede, the son of a Jewish mother and a Protestant father. At home all the holidays were celebrated. In the 1960s the family moved to Assen in the northern part of the Netherlands. As a 12-year-old in Assen, Möring already knew he wanted to be a writer. Therefore, when he finished high school in the mid-1970s he decided that going to university would be a waste of time.

Möring spent the next years reading philosophy and doing various jobs. For a time he worked as theatre critic for a regional newspaper in the northern part of the Netherlands. In 1985 he read that Oek de Jong, a well-known Dutch author at the time, was giving a course in fiction writing. Marcel took the train from Assen to Amsterdam and signed up. Oek de Jong, enthusiastic about the work of his unassuming pupil, suggested that Möring should let his first novel be read by his publisher.

A few years later, Möring surpassed his mentor in popularity and critical attention. His first book, *Mendels erfenis* [Mendel's Heritage], was immediately recognized by the critics as a special book by a talented author and received a prize for best first novel. The main character in the novel, Mendel Adenauer, doesn't know what to do with himself after high school. Mendel, who is Jewish, is all alone: his mother and grandparents on his mother's side have died. He never knew his father. His grandfather told Mendel about an overwhelming event during World War II when he was picked up to be sent to Westerbork. He was the man with the yellow star on his coat who was driven like an animal to the train while the neighbours watched. Mendel has internalized the isolation of his grandfather. The only person with whom he has any contact is a girlfriend from school who is also an outsider, but for another reason: she is blamed for the fact that her parents were collaborators during the war.

The characters in Möring's novels are always the last ones left of their family. In the world of his novels, families are always torn apart, albeit not necessarily because of the war. In his second novel, *Het grote verlangen* (*The Great Longing*), Sam van Dijk loses his parents when he is 12 years old; they are killed in a car accident. He is placed in a foster family, just like his brother Ralph and his twin sister Lisa. For years there is no contact between the children. When Sam is old enough to be independent, he goes looking for his sister and his brother. This is an emotional as well as a physical journey. All his memories are gone; all he has is a desire for security in a family context. A part of the book is a road-movie on paper, a trip of two brothers who want to get to know each other.

Like many of his generation, Möring doesn't want to be pegged as a Jewish writer. He says himself that he is a writer and that's that. Nevertheless his novels are rich in themes and symbols that arise from Jewish themes and traditions. About this he says: "Your themes are inside you; you get them from your upbringing. In my books there is often a question of absence; people have disappeared. I don't put that in consciously, but it's still there." Möring's main characters are continuously searching for the vanished past.

The search for the past by a young Jew who has not experienced persecution himself is a constant in Möring's work. He reflects about this: "In Helmut Kohl's words, through the luck of late birth this is not your physical history, but through the whim of fate which caused you to be born a Jew, you are part of that psychological history." Sam van Dijk digs in his memory for traces of his own early life. Only his sister Lisa, who still remembers many details about their family life, can set his mind to rest.

In 1994 *The Great Longing* won the AKO prize, the Dutch equivalent of Britain's Booker Prize. The novel has been translated into many languages. The London *Times* felt that *The Great Longing* was a particularly northern European book, about "the necessity of travelling enormous emotional distances to reach even members of your own family." In the *Jewish Quarterly*, Alan Isler noted that the book "is curiously hopeful in its hopelessness. We must grow up: that is the answer to the human condition."

The main characters of Möring's third novel, *In Babylon*, are also family members who try to elicit images of the past from each other. In this novel, which is much more complex in thematic layers and structure, Möring turns the longing for security upside down. Nathan and Nina Hollander are together physically, snowed in at the hunting lodge of their deceased relative Herman Hollander; the isolation forces them to a profound reflection on their family's past. They are, once again, the last remaining members of a large Jewish family which has been scattered over all the continents.

With *In Babylon* Möring again attracted much attention in the Netherlands, Europe, and in the English-speaking world. Paul Binding of the British *Times Literary Supplement* wrote about *In Babylon*: "It is a Jewish history, and it evokes a deep sense of loss and impermanence, together with a courageous facing up to restlessness. The novel is a moving and convincing testimony to the continuing tension between the desire for assimilation and the awareness of separateness." Möring was called "beyond doubt one of the most imaginative and perceptive novelists writing today." The London *Times* also thought "this fat, rich novel, wide-ranging, adaptable, learned and clever" was worthy of much praise.

DAPHNE MEIJER
translated by Jeannette Ringold

Mulisch, Harry

Dutch fiction writer, poet, dramatist, and essayist, 1927–

Born in Haarlem, 29 July 1927, to Kurt Mulisch, Hungarian immigrant, and his Jewish wife Alice (née Schwarz). Mother's family died in concentration camps; father imprisoned after World War II for collaborating with Nazis. Studied at Haarlem Lyceum. Married Sjoerdje Woudenberg, 1971; two daughters; also has one son. Founding editor, *Randstad* magazine; member of board, De Bezige Bij publishers, Amsterdam. Many awards, including Reina Prinsen Geerligs Prize, 1951; Bijenkorf Prize, 1957; Anne Frank Prize, 1957; Visser Neerlandia Prize, 1960; Athos Prize, 1961; Constantijn Huygens Prize, 1977; State Prize, 1977; P.C. Hooft Prize, 1980; Prijs van de Nederlands Letteren for Dutch Literature, 1995. Knight, 1977, and Officer, 1992, Order of Orange-Nassau.

Selected Writings

Fiction

Archibald Strohalm [Archibald Strohalm], 1952
Tussen hamer en aambeeld [Between Hammer and Anvil], 1952
Chantage op het leven [Blackmailing Life], 1953
De diamant [The Diamond], 1954
De sprong der paarden en de zoute zee [The Horses' Leap and the Salt Sea], 1955
Het mirakel [The Miracle], 1955
Het zwarte licht [The Black Light], 1956
De versierde mens, 1957; as "The Decorated Man", translated by Adrienne Dixon in *Writing in Holland and Flanders*, 1973
Het stenen bruidsbed, 1959; as *The Stone Bridal Bed*, translated by Adrienne Dixon 1962
Quauhquauhtinchan in den vreemde: een Sprookje [Quauhquauhtinchan Abroad: A Fairytale], 1962
De verteller [The Narrator], 1970
Wat gebeurde er met sergeant Massuro?, 1972; excerpts translated as "What Happened to Sergeant Massuro" in *The Modern Image: Outstanding Stories from the Hudson Review*, edited by Frederick Morgan, 1965
De grens [The Limit], 1975
Twee vrouwen, 1975; as *Two Women*, translated by Els Early, 1980
Oude lucht: drie verhalen [Stale Air: Three Stories], 1977
Verzamelde verhalen 1947–1977 [Collected Stories], 1977
De aanslag, 1982; as *The Assault*, translated by Claire Nicolas White, 1985
Symmetrie en andere verhalen [Symmetry and Other Stories], 1982
De gezochte spiegel [The Sought Mirror], 1983
De kamer [The Room], 1984
Hoogste tijd, 1985; as *Last Call*, translated by Adrienne Dixon, 1987
De pupil [The Pupil], 1987
De elementen [The Elements], 1988
Het beeld en de klok [The Picture and the Clock], 1989
Voorval: variatie op een thema [Incident: Variation on a Theme], 1989
De ontdekking van de hemel, 1992; as *The Discovery of Heaven: A Novel*, translated by Paul Vincent, 1996
Ik Bubanik [I Bubanik], 1994
Twee opgravingen [Two Excavations], 1994
De procedure, 1998; as *The Procedure*, translated by Paul Vincent, 2001
Siegfried, 2001

Plays

Tanchelijn: kroniek van een ketter [Tanchelijn: Chronicle of a Heretic], 1960
De knop: gevolgd door Stan Laurel & Oliver Hardy [The Button: Followed by Stan Laurel and Oliver Hardy], 1961
Reconstructie [Reconstruction], with others, 1969
Oidipous Oidipous [Oedipus Oedipus], 1972
Bezoekuur [Visiting Time], 1974
Volk en vaderliefde: een koningskomedie [The People and Paternal Love: A Royal Comedy], 1975
Axel, 1977
Theater 1960–1977 [Theatre 1960–1977], 1988

Poetry

Woorden, woorden, woorden [Words, Words, Words], 1973
De vogels: drie balladen [The Birds: Three Ballads], 1974
Kind en kraai [Kinfolk], 1975
Tegenlicht [Light in the Eyes], 1975
De wijn is drankbaar dank zij het glas [The Wine is Drinkable Because of the Glass], 1976
Wat poëzie is: een leerdicht, 1978; as *What Poetry Is*, translated by Claire Nicholas White, 1981
De taal is een ei [Language is an Egg], 1979
Opus gran, 1982
Egyptisch [Egyptian], 1983
De gedichten 1974–1983 [The Poems 1974–1983], 1987

Other

Manifesten [Manifestos], 1958
Voer voor psychologen [Fodder for Psychologists], 1961
Wenden voor de bescherming van uw gezin en uzelf, tijdens de jongste dag [Tips for the Protection of Your Family and Yourself, at the Day of Judgement], 1961
De zaak 40/61: een reportage [The Eichmann Case: A Report], 1962
Bericht aan de rattenkoning [Report to the King Rat], 1966
Wenken voor de jongste dag [Tips for the Day of Judgement], 1967
Het woord bij de daad: getuigenissen van de revolutie op Cuba [Words After Deeds: Testimony on the Cuban Revolution], 1968
Israel is zelf een mens [Israel is Human Too], 1969
Paralipomena Orphica [Paralipomena Orphica], 1970
Over de affaire Padilla [On the Padilla Affair], 1971
De verteller verteld [The Story of the Narrator], 1971
De toekomst van gisteren [The Future of Yesterday], 1972
Soep lepelen met een vork [Eating Soup with a Fork], 1972
Het sexuele bolwerk [The Sexual Bastion], 1973

Mijn getijdenboek [My Book of Hours], 1975
Het ironische van de ironie: over het geval G.K. van het Reve [The Irony of Irony: On the Case of G.K. van het Reve], 1976
Vergrote raadsels: verklaringen, paradoxen, mulischesken [Magnified Riddles: Explanations, Paradoxes, Mulischesques], edited by Gerd de Ley, 1976
Paniek der onschuld [Panic of Innocence], 1979
Der compositie van de wereld [The Composition of the World], 1980
De mythische formule: dertig gesprekken 1951–1981 [The Mythical Formula: Thirty Conversations 1951–1981], 1981
De toekomst van het boek [The Future of the Book], with others, 1984
Het boek [The Book], 1984
Het ene: Huizinga-Lezing 1984 [The One: Huizinga-Reading 1984], 1984
Vaders en toverballen [Fathers and Magic Balls], 1984
Wij uiten wat wij voelen, niet wat past [We Say What We Feel, Not What is Appropriate], 1984
Aan het woord: zeven toespraken [On the Word: Seven Speeches], 1986
Bijlage bij de eerste druk van "De compositie van de wereld" [Appendix to the First Impression of "The Composition of the World"], 1986
Grondslagen van de mythologie van het schrijverschap [Foundations of the Mythology of Writing], 1987
Het licht [The Light], 1988
Oedipus als Freud: naar aanleiding van Jung [Oedipus as Freud], 1988
De Zuilen van Hercules [The Pillars of Hercules], 1990
Op de drempel van de geschiedenis [On the Threshold of History], 1992
Spookgeshiedenis [A Ghost Story], 1993
Bij gelegenheid [On Occasion], 1995
De oer-Aanslag [The First Draft of The Assault], 1996
Het zevende land [The Seventh Country], 1998

Further Reading

Janssens, Marcel, "The Prolog in Mulisch's *Aanslag*: A Novel in a Nutshell" in *The Berkeley Conference on Dutch Literature 1987: New Perspectives on the Modern Period*, edited by Johan P. Snapper and Thomas F. Shannon, Lanham, Maryland: University Press of America, 1989
Mathijsen, Marita, *Harry Mulisch: een bibliografie*, The Hague: BZZTÔH, 1979
Michielsen, John, "Coming to Terms with the Past and Searching for an Identity: The Treatment of the Occupied Netherlands in the Fiction of Hermans, Mulisch and Vestdijk", *Canadian Journal of Netherlandic Studies*, 7/1–2 (1986)
Paardt, R. van der, "A Unity of Opposites: The Paradoxical Oeuvre of Harry Mulisch" in *The Low Countries: Arts and Society in Flanders and the Netherlands: A Yearbook 1994–1995*, edited by Jozef Deleu, Rekkem, Belgium: Stichting Ons Erfdeel, 1994
Raskin, Jonah, article in *International Herald Tribune* (14 May 1987)
Sazaki, Kristina R., "An Interview with Harry Mulisch", *New German Review*, 2 (1986)
Spender, Stephen, review of *The Assault*, *New York Times* (5 December 1985)

In his 1998 novel *De procedure* (*The Procedure*), Harry Mulisch says through his narrator: "I'm not a writer of words, nor a writer of sentences, but a writer of an oeuvre." There is a lot of truth in that.

Mulisch's work is exceptionally varied; it consists of novels, poetry, short stories, theatre, histories of our time, studies, and essays. Yet a reader of Mulisch will experience the unity and the coherence of his work as its most important characteristics. Within Mulisch's work every detail does indeed have meaning for the whole; everything is connected with everything else, but two constants are very much felt: World War II and Harry Mulisch the person. Mulisch's life and work cannot be separated because he considers his life as a source of insight, and from his very first novel, *Archibald Strohalm*, Mulisch himself has been the undisputed centre of his work.

Mulisch sees his work as a new, self-created body, a living organism that has to survive him because of a personal and human longing for eternity and immortality. The act of writing is central in his esoteric view of the profession of letters because according to him the author exists only in the written word. The other constant, World War II, has strongly influenced Mulisch's thinking. His father was an Austro-Hungarian army officer in World War I; his mother was a Belgian Jew. In the Netherlands during World War II, Mulisch's father collaborated with the enemy, among other things to protect his family. These circumstances, heartbreaking for the young Mulisch, explain his later statement: "I *am* the Second World War."

Mulisch considers the history of his time as an extension of his existence. Consequently, his novels can be read as documents of historical interest. He prefers to choose utopian moments from "his" history. He considers World War II as a horrific universal point of reference – starting from the thought that "Auschwitz" should never happen again. In his most successful novel, *De aanslag* (*The Assault*), in which one evening in World War II is the basis of a whole life, he manages to link wartime with two moments that he considers utopian: the Hungarian uprising of 1956 and the massive peace demonstration of 1981 in Amsterdam.

But his work offers more than a reflection of the present – the essence of a Mulisch novel is that it can be read and studied in many ways. *The Assault*, for example, is a metaphysical novel constructed like a classic tragedy that can also be read as an engrossing war story, a probing psychological novel, and a poetic novel. Only a small part of *The Assault* is about the assassination of a Dutch collaborator during the occupation and the direct consequences of this on the Steenwijk family, which is murdered except for the youngest son, Anton. The rest of the book is about the effect World War II seems to have had on the survivor, Anton Steenwijk, and on Dutch society in general. Psychologically it is the story of Anton's development: the way in which he tries to sort out this dramatic event of his youth. Philosophically, the central question is about the relevance of guilt and responsibility.

This philosophical tendency is typical of Mulisch's work which is on the borderline between literature, philosophy, and para-philosophy. Mulisch is exclusively interested in humanity; for him everything revolves around understanding what inspires humankind – not a unique individual. He prefers to show the awareness and acceptance of mythical patterns, such as the Oedipus complex, as the psychological motivation of mankind. But above all Mulisch is a philosophical author who doesn't shy away from asking the great (metaphysical) questions about life. In *De ontdekking van de hemel* (*The Discovery of Heaven: A Novel*), a work of more than 900 pages, he raises the question of the erosion of religion because of advancing technological developments and their harmful consequences for mankind. Whoever is not yet convinced that Mulisch is pre-eminently the writer of an oeuvre will have to capitulate before *De procedure* (*The Procedure*). Not only does it contain countless reminiscences of his earlier work, but all prose genres imaginable are present: from a poetry manual, a psychological novel in diary form, a boyish adventure story, an essay, and a thriller like the one in *De diamant* [The Diamond]. But didn't Mulisch have his oeuvre culminate in *The Discovery of Heaven*? Yes, but in *The Procedure* he takes one additional step: in it he analyses his profession as author.

It is not unusual for an author to create an oeuvre and then round it off with a magnum opus. For Anthony Powell it was his saga *A Dance to the Music of Time*, for Mulisch it was *The Discovery of Heaven*. I am not arbitrarily linking these two authors whose work is so different. Although in their old age both could look back on a complete oeuvre, they continued writing. It would have been easy to write a light book, but Powell published *The Fisher King* and Mulisch, *The Procedure*. Both chose an identical solution: they each wrote a novel which can only be understood if you know their whole oeuvre. *The Procedure* is a meta-novel of *The Discovery of Heaven*.

The Procedure is the grand finale of Mulisch's work. Its conclusion is sombre: now that God with his Word has disappeared and technology has free rein, mankind surrenders language and with it, its soul. This dark and layered novel is about nothing less than *creatio ex nihilo*. From Mulisch's point of view, every form of creation is connected to the Word – and with a method that should be followed. For him, the building materials for creation consist of language. And with language Mulisch doesn't mean the sounds but the formulas. As if saying "Open Sesame" the author knocks at the door of creation.

The pseudo-disdain regarding his own profession as writer (and his workmanship) shows in the quasi-facile writing in this novel. This makes *The Procedure* a soaring book, soaring above his authorship. It is a book about literary theory, but at the same time its proof: the creative process takes place during writing. Not only does this book write itself and does the reader experience it, but the reader also experiences the author. Mulisch doesn't write a novel but instead his profession as author. Where *The Discovery of Heaven* is a giant monument, *The Procedure* is a virtual floor plan, a glass cathedral.

JEROEN VULLINGS

N

Nathansen, Henri

Danish dramatist and fiction writer, 1868–1944

Born in Hjørring, 1868. Moved with family to Copenhagen. Studied at Copenhagen University, law degree, 1892. Practised law, 1892–1902. Married Johanne Jørgensen, 1899. Stage director, Royal Theatre, Copenhagen, 1909. Made public speech in protest against persecution of Polish Jewry, 1918. Called for solidarity in Copenhagen Jewish community to counteract influence of Nazi anti-Semitism, 1930. Fled to Sweden, with majority of Danish Jews, October 1943. Committed suicide in Lund, Sweden, 1944.

Selected Writings

Plays
Daniel Hertz, 1908
Indenfor Murene [Within the Walls], 1912
Affæren, 1913
Dr Wahl, 1915

Novels
En Sommernat [A Summer's Night], 1899
Floden [The River], 1902
Af Hugo Davids Liv [From Hugo David's Life], 1917
Mendel Philipsen og Søn, 1932

Other
Georg Brandes, 1929
Portrætstudier, 1930

Further Reading

Arnheim, Louise, "Henri Nathansens forhold til zionismen", *Tidskrift for dansk jødisk historie*, 30 (1990): 42–54

Wamberg, Niels Birger, "Københavner-forfattere" in *Danske digtere i det 20. århundrede*, edited by Torben Brostrøm and Mette Winge, 5 vols, Copenhagen: Gad, 1980–82

Henri Nathansen's first novel *En Sommernat* [A Summer's Night] is about a sensitive wife in a seemingly happy marriage who finds her true soulmate in the quiet, shy male friend of the family. The underlying themes of isolation and elegiac disillusion reappear in some of Nathansen's later works. In his next novel *Floden* [The River] Nathansen introduced "the Jewish problem", which was to become the central theme in his major works. The young Jewish woman Selma Hertz discards her traditional, oppressive Jewish home for a relationship with a Christian man, only to find that "freedom" leads to "homelessness", and she returns "home".

The Jews became naturalized Danish subjects in 1814, but strong anti-Semitic feelings led to riots and attacks on Jewish homes in 1819. Nathansen was not the first writer to deal with the dilemma of the Jewish "outsider", that of being a Dane and an Orthodox Jew simultaneously. His admired model was the writer Meïr Aron Goldschmidt (1819–87), whose first novel *En Jøde* [A Jew] in 1845 opens with a description of the 1819 riots and focuses on the painful experience of trying to belong to two rival cultures. While other contemporary Danish artists, e.g. the poet and playwright Henrik Hertz (1797–1870) and the actress Johanne Louise Heiberg (1812–90), distanced themselves from their Jewish background, Goldschmidt openly displayed his. In 1844 Goldschmidt made a public speech, beginning with the words, "I am a Jew. What do I want among you?" and gave the bitter, ironic answer, "I will teach you to hate!"

Another important influence was the literary critic Georg Brandes, who came from a non-orthodox, intellectual Jewish family but considered himself Danish (and European) rather than Jewish. He did not think that "Jewishness" was a worthy topic for literary treatment and criticized Nathansen for returning to "Goldschmidt's old Jewish soup", snarling, "Why do we need this Jewish stuff in literature?"

Undeterred, Nathansen pursued this theme in several of his plays, notably in *Daniel Hertz*, *Indenfor Murene* [Within the Walls], and *Dr Wahl*. *Daniel Hertz* combines a social class conflict (employers versus workers) with a cultural conflict (Christians/Danes versus Jews). In his youth Daniel Hertz broke with his father (a wealthy factory owner) and married Valborg (one of his father's factory girls) instead of the love of his youth, his Jewish cousin Gerda. Daniel has been the workers' political leader for 20 years when a major industrial dispute brings him into direct conflict with his father. At the same time Gerda, recently widowed after a meaningless marriage, suddenly turns up. Attempting to reach a compromise, the old father makes a direct approach to his ostracized son, using Gerda as an intermediary, and this plus the fecklessness of Valborg and her brother Victor makes Daniel realize the futility of his marriage and the worthlessness of the values he has fought for. He rejects both and "returns" to his family and racial roots.

Indenfor Murene represents Nathansen's most affectionate and charming portrayal of an Orthodox Jewish family home, at a time of changing attitudes. Here the "rebel" is the youngest child, Esther, a modern young woman who snubs the traditional Sabbath meal in favour of public lectures and has become engaged to the university lecturer, Dr Herming, the son of her father's old anti-Semitic enemy. The conflict follows the usual pattern. Esther distances herself from her "claustrophobic" background ("the Dead Sea"), but when her parents are humiliated in the home of Councillor of State Herming by hearing that Esther has agreed to a Christian wedding and to having her children christened, she is overcome by remorse and hurries home to apologize. Her fiancé follows her, and together they envisage a time of reconciliation between the races. The conflict is unresolved, but the play ends with a hope for a happier future, also "outside the walls". The detailed characterization of this loveable, if at times narrow-minded, Jewish family and the brilliance of Nathansen's dialogue helped to further a greater understanding among Danes for life "inside the walls" and to make this one of the most popular and frequently performed plays at The Royal Theatre in Copenhagen.

The protagonist in *Dr Wahl* is modelled on Georg Brandes. Nathansen condemns the shabby treatment and deceitful behaviour to which Dr Wahl is exposed, as was the real-life Brandes who was shamefully denied the Chair at Copenhagen University at least as much because his Jewish background as for his controversial ideas.

Nathansen's greatest work is the long *Bildungsroman Af Hugo Davids Liv* [From Hugo David's Life]. The protagonist's life often mirrors that of Nathansen: the Jewish childhood in small town in Jutland, the move to Copenhagen, the law studies and the important step to pursue his artistic inclinations, in Hugo's case as an actor. However, he soon finds himself caught between "the two worlds". First, he discards a safe career in his uncle's business in favour of the stage, but later he is frozen out of the theatre for being "outlandish", i.e. Jewish. When his marriage also fails, he feels "homeless" and leaves the country. In Berlin the famous but mysterious Jewish actor Goldfeld gives him a new belief in himself, and when he is invited back to The Royal Theatre in Copenhagen, he achieves a successful acting career and becomes reconciled with his dying wife. But on a visit to his parental home, he suddenly falls ill and dies. His life has followed the familiar circular movement: home—homeless—home again.

The lack of critical acclaim gradually made Nathansen very disillusioned, and he turned to writing short biographies and character sketches, mainly of actors and theatre directors. His most important biography, however, was about his old "sparring partner" Georg Brandes, published two years after Brandes's death. Brandes even appears as himself in Nathansen's last novel, *Mendel Philipsen & Søn*, which portrays a Jewish family in Copenhagen through three generations. The main contrast is between two brothers, the quiet-living, Orthodox Semmy and the ambitious Frederik, who dreams of becoming integrated into the higher circles of Danish society, but ends up bankrupted, both financially and morally. The focus moves on to Semmy's daughter Sofie and later to her son Aron, whose cousin Julius, an aspiring writer, at times becomes Nathansen's mouthpiece. Thus in a heated discussion at the student club following the German attack on Belgium in 1914, after the ageing Brandes has declared himself to be neither Jew nor Dane, Julius gets up and proclaims himself a Jew, using exactly the same words about his own "persecuted people" that Nathansen uttered in his protest speech against the persecution of the Polish Jewry in 1918.

On hearing that Semmy Philipsen has died, an elderly Jew exclaims spontaneously, "He was a good Jew". Such value judgements are found throughout Nathansen's works, e.g. in *Indenfor Murene* when Jacob dismisses an argument by his humanist brother with the words, "You are a bad Jew". For most of his life, Nathansen himself struggled to overcome the conflict between being Jewish and being an ordinary member of Danish society, while preserving his own identity and culture. When forced into exile in Sweden in 1943, his long-held Zionist dreams must have been crushed, and the following year he took his own life. It has often been pointed out that he deserves Semmy Philipsen's epitaph: "He was a good Jew".

TOM LUNDSKÆR-NIELSEN

O

Odets, Clifford

US dramatist, 1906–1963

Born in Philadelphia, 18 July 1906. Grew up in New York; formal education ended after two years at Morris High School, New York. Acted with various theatre groups, including Drawing Room Players, 1924–29; first lead role, Group Theater, 1933. Joined Communist Party, 1930. Married, first, Luise Rainer, 1937; divorced 1941; second, Betty Grayson, 1943; two children. Group Theater dissolved, 1941; moved to Hollywood, writing filmscripts, 1955–63. Called before House of Representatives Committee on Un-American Activities, 1952. Awards include New Theater League Prize, and Yale Drama Prize, both 1935; American Academy of Arts and Letters Award, 1961. Died in Los Angeles, 14 August 1963.

Selected Writings

Plays
Awake and Sing!, 1935
Paradise Lost, 1935
Till the Day I Die, 1935
Waiting for Lefty, 1935
I Can't Sleep, 1936
Golden Boy, 1937
Rocket to the Moon, 1938
Night Music, 1940
Clash By Night, 1941
Humoresque, 1942
Deadline at Dawn, 1943
Lonely Heart, 1943
The Big Knife, 1949
The Country Girl, 1951
The Flowering Peach, 1955
Winter Journey, 1955

Screenplays: *None But the Lonely Heart*, 1944; *Deadline at Dawn*, 1945; *The Sweet Smell of Success*, 1957; *The Story on Page One*, 1959; *Wild in the Country*, 1960

Radio Plays: *At the Water-Line*, 1926; *Dawn*, 1926; *The Show Must Go On*, 1939

Other
The Time is Ripe: The 1940 Journal of Clifford Odets, 1988

Further Reading

Brenman-Gibson, Margaret, *Clifford Odets: American Playwright: The Years from 1906 to 1940*, New York: Atheneum, 1981
Cantor, Harold, *Clifford Odets, Playwright-poet*, Metuchen, New Jersey: Scarecrow, 1978
Clurman, Harold, *The Fervent Years: The Story of the Group Theater and the Thirties*, New York: Knopf, 1945
Cooperman, Robert, *Clifford Odets: An Annotated Bibliography, 1935–1988*, Westport, Connecticut: Meckler, 1989
Demastes, William W., *Clifford Odets: A Research and Production Sourcebook*, New York: Greenwood Press, 1991
Mendelsohn, Michael J., *Clifford Odets, Humane Dramatist*, Deland, Florida: Everett/Edwards, 1969
Miller, Arthur, *Timebends: A Life*, New York: Grove Press, and London: Methuen, 1987
Miller, Gabriel, *Clifford Odets*, New York: Continuum, 1989
Murray, Edward, *Clifford Odets: The Thirties and After*, New York: Ungar, 1968
Shuman, Robert Baird, *Clifford Odets*, New York: Twayne, 1962
Weales, Gerald Clifford , *Clifford Odets, Playwright*, New York: Pegasus, 1971

Clifford Odets, son of a print shop worker in the Philadelphia ghetto, was imbued with the doctrine of aspiration and betterment, inculcated by his father, a man with the wit and humour of the natural entertainer. Odets the dramatist exploited the family and community around him for much of his material in the first phase of his writing up to the success of the Group Theater, and notably *Waiting for Lefty* and *Awake and Sing!*, the plays that made his reputation. He was something of an all-rounder in the entertainment business, but scriptwriting was his metier and the culture and language of Yiddish in America was his springboard to art.

His critical neglect is somewhat puzzling. He is not represented in the latest (fifth edition) of the *Norton Anthology of American Literature*, and in the *Penguin Guide to American Literature* (volume 9) he merits only a grudging mention. But in the 1970s he was the focus of much attention, and the revisionary view was often that his communism, his agit-prop view of drama, and his tendency towards melodrama in the representation of the Jewish working class were distancing him from universal acceptance in the postmodern cultural frame. Nevertheless, he was always part of American realism, and his ability to link broader social and economic tensions to family, microcosmic disorder was a potent literary brew.

The social messages of the early plays are perhaps to blame for this negative perspective; notably, the view that the working class have aspirations other than material wealth, and that idealism may be found there, along with celebration and joy, is difficult to take for modern audiences. Yet, the sheer dynamism of his Jewish characters and the powerfully authentic dialogue often raises comparisons with J.M. Synge and his heightening of the Aran Island workers' language into poetry. Odets was called the "poet of the Jewish middle class" and the richness of his colloquial base in writing has encouraged comments such as, "the idiomatic, bluntly-explosive Yiddish American language would be experienced by the audience as authentic, fresh, and even lyrically uplifting" (here according to Margaret Brenman-Gibson). In comparison with, for instance, Wasserstein or Mamet at the end of the millennium, Odets's language seems unduly stretched and hyperbolic, but that distortion has only emerged with the dissolution of a certain social context. That context is only accessible perhaps, through an effort of historical imagination.

Awake and Sing! provides evidence that Odets made a significant contribution to American Jewish literature. One reason for this is his version of realism in his early phase; again, according to Brenman-Gibson: "Odets was substituting for the consolatory spectacles and sentimentality in the Yiddish theatre the first deeply-felt and formally achieved realism in America." Certainly his best work merits comparison with Grace Paley in its representation of the Jewish family given with the candour achieved of a mix of love and criticism. Clearly, at the time of the inception of the Group Theater, Odets was theorizing in depth about his place and ambition as an artist, and his note about form, after using musicians as his yardstick, is revealing: "But acceptance of a social form does something else, informs the artist's work with a sense of life and love, gives him a sense of building up".

It is hard to deny that Odets had a considerable influence on how the forms of off-Broadway theatre could accommodate the personal aesthetics and vision of individual playwrights. But Arthur Miller condenses the reservations felt with hindsight: "I was troubled by a tendency in his plays to over-theatricalised excess – lines sometimes brought laughter when there should have been outrage."

Arguably, the ongoing interest in reading Odets is the dialectic he constructs concerning the ethic of the American parable of material success and the disappearance or transmutation of the Yiddish *goldene medine* in the minds of the immigrants. The condition of being almost in pre-identity we find in the stories of Anzia Yezierksa and Abraham Cahan is present in Odets's characters, at one more stage towards assimilation. He also understands the situation of the dispossessed and the young in a society that only notices obvious signs of influence and status. In terms of his overall impact on American-Jewish writing, a true perception of his contribution is only established when his argot of the modern city is registered. That was the locus of transformation for the Jew: the handcart to business roots story is both a short story and an epic, depending on how we read it. Odets's work monitors that transformation with a ruthless honesty.

STEPHEN WADE

Olsen, Tillie

US fiction writer, 1912 or 1913–

Born Tillie Lerner in Nebraska, 14 January 1912 or 1913, to Samuel Lerner and wife Ida (née Berber), both Russian immigrants. Married Jack Olsen; four daughters. Worked in service, warehouse, and food-processing industries, and as office typist. Creative writing fellow, Stanford University, 1956–57; fellow, Radcliffe Institute for Independent Study, Cambridge, Massachusetts, 1962–64; writer in residence, Amherst College, 1969–70; Visiting professor, Stanford University, Spring 1971; writer in residence, Massachusetts Institute of Technology, 1973; visiting professor, University of Massachusetts, 1974; visiting lecturer, University of California, San Diego, 1978; visiting scholar, Norway, 1980; Hill Professor, University of Minnesota, 1986; writer in residence, Amherst College; writer in residence, Kenyon College, Ohio, 1987; Regents' Professor, University of California, Los Angeles, 1988. Many awards, including Ford Foundation grant, 1959; O. Henry Award, 1961; American Academy Award, 1975; Guggenheim Fellowship, 1975; Unitarian Women's Federation Award, 1980; National Endowment for the Humanities grant, 1966 and 1984; Bunting Institute Fellowship, 1986; Rea Award (for distinguished contribution to the short story), 1994. "Tillie Olsen Day" observed in San Francisco, 1981.

Selected Writings

Novel

Yonnondio: From the Thirties, 1974; new edition, 1980

Short Stories

Tell Me a Riddle: A Collection, 1961; new edition, edited and introduced by Deborah Silverton Rosenfelt, 1995

"Requa-I", in *The Best American Short Stories 1971*, edited by Martha Foley and David Burnett, 1971

Other

Editor and biographical interpreter, *Life in the Iron Mills and Other Stories*, by Rebecca Harding Davis, 1972; revised edition, 1985

Silences, 1978; reprinted 1989

The Impact of McCarthyism on the Family, 1980

Editor, *Mother to Daughter, Daughter to Mother: Mothers on Mothering*, 1984

The Word Made Flesh, 1984

Mothers and Daughters: That Special Quality: An Exploration in Photographs, with Julie Olsen-Edwards and Estelle Jussim, 1987

Further Reading

Coiner, Constance, *Better Red*, Oxford and New York: Oxford University Press, 1995

Dawahare, Anthony David, "American Proletarian Modernism and the Problem of Modernity in the 30s: Meridel Le Sueur, Tillie Olsen and Langston Hughes" (PhD dissertation), University of California, Irvine, 1994

Faulkner, Mara, *Protest and Possibility in the Writing of Tillie Olsen*, Charlottesville: University Press of Virginia, 1993

Frye, Joanne S., *Tillie Olsen: A Study of the Short Fiction*, New York: Twayne, and London: Prentice Hall, 1995
Hedges, Elaine and Shelley Fisher Fishkin (editors), *Listening to Silences*, Oxford and New York: Oxford University Press, 1994
Martin, Abigail, *Tillie Olsen*, Boise, Idaho: Boise State University, 1984
Nelson, Kay Hoyle and Nancy Huse (editors), *The Critical Response to Tillie Olsen*, Westport, Connecticut: Greenwood, 1994
Orr, Elaine Neil, *Tillie Olsen and a Feminist Spiritual Vision*, Jackson: University Press of Mississippi, 1987
Roberts, Nora Ruth, *Three Radical Women Writers: Class and Gender in Meridel Le Sueur, Tillie Olsen and Josephine Herbst*, New York: Garland, 1996
Werlock, Abby H.P. and Mickey Pearlman, *Tillie Olsen*, Boston: Twayne, 1991

Tillie Olsen was born in Wahoo, Omaha, or Mead, Nebraska on 14 January 1912 or 1913. She was the second of six children of Samuel and Ida (Beber) Lerner, immigrants from czarist Russia after the 1905 rebellion. For 20 years during which she raised four children and held various jobs, she writes in *Silences*, "the simplest circumstances for creation did not exist". These are the words of a nationally prominent writer whose published work consists of five short stories, one unfinished novel, the nonfiction book *Silences*, and two edited collections.

Tillie Olsen is the quintessential writer of silences. One of her two most anthologized stories, "I Stand Here Ironing", is a long monologue of a mother without privilege, who is responsible for making a living and caring for her children. The first-person narrator speaks to a school official about her troubled daughter Emily, who, according to the educator, "needs help".

The opening line is the controlling metaphor of the story. "I stand here ironing, and what you asked me moves tormented back and forth with the iron". The iron frames the story, for at the end the mother pleads "Only help her to know – help make it so there is cause for her to know – that she is more than this dress on the ironing board, helpless before the iron." The iron and the dress represent the overpowering routines of motherhood that have caused such problems for mother and daughter, limiting their ability to live full and happy lives.

Olsen's most ambitious and celebrated work is the novella-length story "Tell Me a Riddle". Eva, the main character, is near the end of her life and can only rise above her tragic circumstances when she remembers her youth in Russia and finds, according to two critics, "the music and song long buried within her", until she "can hear the 'song' of the child within her".

The story is marked by the conflict between Eva and David, her husband of 47 years. While David wants to leave their family home and move to a retirement lodge, Eva desires only to be alone. "Never again to be forced to move to the rhythms of others." She can only find peace in solitude after giving her life to her family. Finally, David convinces Eva to visit with their children and grandchildren, who live in different parts of the United States. As she travels, Eva's mind roams back to her past. In some of her best writing, Olsen captures Eva's mental experience in a stream-of-consciousness style that has the compression and music of poetry. The story concludes in southern California where Eva and David are looked after by their granddaughter Jeannie. As Eva moves closer to death from cancer, her past sings through her: "While from floor to balcony to dome a bare-footed sore-covered little girl threaded the sound-throned tumult, danced her ecstasy of grimace to flutes that scratched at a cross-roads village wedding".

It is Jeannie who sees and sketches David and Eva lying on adjoining beds, holding each other's hand. Finally, after Eva dies, Jeannie consoles David:

> Granddaddy, Granddaddy, don't cry. She is not there, she promised me. On the last day, she said she would go back to when she first heard music, a little girl on the road of the village where she was born. She promised me. It is a wedding – and they dance while the flutes so joyous and vibrant tremble in the air. Leave her there, Granddaddy. It is all right. She promised me. Come back, come back and help her poor body to die.

In this great conclusion to Olsen's justly famous work, her prose has the depth and clarity of truth.

The third story of *Tell Me a Riddle*, "Hey Sailor, What Ship?" describes Whitey, an alcoholic sailor, and his unsuccessful attempt to re-establish a bond with his friends Lennie and Helen, and their three children. At the conclusion, he is called back for one last time to his life on the sea. In the other story in the volume, "O Yes", Helen and Carol, white mother and daughter, attend the baptism of Carol's black friend Parry at her mother Alva's Baptist church. The story dramatizes the racial tension that comes between the two girls.

In a note that introduces Olsen's unfinished novel *Yonnondio*, the author explains the unusual and disturbing facts of its publication:

> Thought long since lost or destroyed, some of its pages were found intermixed with other old papers last winter, during the process of searching for another manuscript. A later, more thorough, search turned up additional musings: odd tattered pages, lines in yellowed notebooks, scraps. Other parts, evidently once in existence, seem irrevocably lost.

Yet out of silences comes the powerful story of a Depression era family that moves from coal mining town to farm to city, looking for a better life. Anna Holbrook, mother of the family and the main character, is heroic in her endurance. To Deborah Rosenfelt, Olsen's treatment shows her "sense of the deepest, most intractable contradiction of all: the unparalleled satisfaction and fulfillment combined with the overwhelming, all-consuming burden of motherhood".

In *Yonnondio* Olsen's communist leanings surface as she reveals the terrible vicissitudes that plague the oppressed proletariat during the 1930s. Again, according to Rosenfelt: "Few other American novels ... reveal so starkly the destructive interactions of class and sex under patriarchal capitalism". Yet the question remains. Why did drafts of the novel remain unfinished for 40 years? If we are to believe the author, the answer is silences. Tillie Olsen has become famous, especially in feminist circles, because in Abby Werlock's and Mickey Pearlman's opinion:

> she has forced us to pay attention to the influence of economic circumstance and social class; the meaning of limited time, money, energy, and space on the productivity of women; the nature and pain of imposed silence; and the often debilitating effect of "otherness" in a society that equates difference with disability, sameness with safety.

Her survival as a writer is a triumph over silences.

GARY PACERNICK

Opatoshu, Joseph (Yoysef)

Polish-born US fiction writer and journalist, 1886–1954

Born near Mlave, 1886, to Dovid Opatoshu, wood merchant and noted maskil, and wife Nantshe. Emigrated to United States, 1907; settled in New York. Studied civil engineering in evening classes at Cooper Union, graduated 1914; worked in shoe factory, sold newspapers, taught in Hebrew schools. Began publishing stories, 1910; edited anthology of his own stories, *Di naye heym*, including "Fun nyu yorker geto", 1914. Joined staff of Yiddish daily *Der tog* at its foundation, 1914; contributed stories, sketches, and serials, most reprinted in books, until death. Married Adele Wolf, 1917; one son. Died, 1954.

Selected Writings

Novels and Novellas

A roman fun a ferd ganev un andere ertsehlungen [Romance of a Horse Thief and Other Stories], 1917 ("Romance of a Horse Thief" in *A Shtetl and Other Yiddish Novellas*, edited by Ruth R. Wisse, 1986)
Trilogy (*In poylishe velder*)
In poylishe velder, 1921; as *In Polish Woods*, translated by Isaac Goldberg, 1938
1863, 1926
Aleyn [Alone], 1919
Farloyrene mentshn [Lost People], 1922
Di tentserin [The (female) Dancer], 1930
Ven poyln iz gefaln [When Poland Fell], 1943
Der letstn oyfstand: roman in tsvey bikher, 2 vols, 1948–55; as *The Last Revolt: The Story of Rabbi Akiba*, translated by Moshe Spiegel, 1952

Short Stories

A tog in regensburg, 1933; as *A Day in Regensburg*, translated by Jacob Sloan, 1968
Mentshn un khayes [Men and Beasts], 1938
Yidn-legende un andere dertseylungen [The Legend of the Jew and Other Stories], 1951
In *Yiddish Stories Old and New*, edited by Irving Howe and Eliezer Greenberg, 1974

Other

Gezamlte verk [Collected Works], 14 vols, 1926–36
Yidish un yidishkayt: eseyen, 1949

Further Reading

Bickel, Shlomo, *Shrayber fun mayn dor* [Writers of My Generation], vol. 1, New York: Matones, 1958
Freilich, Charles A., *Yosef Opatoshus shafung-veg* [The Creative Strategy of Joseph Opatoshu], Toronto: Gershon Pomerants, 1951
Glatstein, Jacob, *In tokh genumen* [In Essence], New York: Matones, 1956
Leksikon fun der nayer yidisher literatur [Biographical Dictionary of Modern Yiddish Literature], vol. 1, New York: Alveltlekhn Yidishn Kultur-Kongres, 1956
Liptzin, Solomon, *The Maturing of Yiddish Literature*, New York: David, 1970
Madison, Charles A., *Yiddish Literature: Its Scope and Major Writers*, New York: Ungar, 1968
Mayzel, Nachman, *Yosef Opatoshu: zayn lebn un shafn* [Joseph Opatoshu: His Life and Work], Warsaw: Literarishe Bleter, 1937
Opatoshu bibliografie, 2 vols, New York, 1937–47
Rivkin, B., *Yosef Opatoshus Gang*, Toronto: Gershon Pomerants Esey Bibliotek, 1948

Joseph (Yoysef) Opatoshu was a wide-ranging contributor to Yiddish prose literature, creating at least one major work about his native Poland *In poylishe velder* (*In Polish Woods*), and many stories and sketches of Jewish immigrant life in America, as well as some bold attempts at novels and short stories set at important moments of Jewish history.

While his *Der letstn oyfstand* (*The Last Revolt*) seems laboured and rather "Ben-Hur-ish" today, it treats the fascinating period of Jewish Palestine, 58 years after the destruction of the temple, living under Roman domination but with important stirrings of national resistance that will eventually lead to Bar-Kochba's revolt. Its detailed focus on a widespread, pragmatic Jewish accommodation to the languages and practices of the Empire is no doubt to be taken as a comment on the rampant cultural assimilationism of US Jews at the time it was written, particularly painful perhaps to a Yiddish writer seeing an ever-shrinking audience.

Much more successful and enjoyable is the collection of historically-set pieces *A tog in regensburg* (*A Day in Regensburg*). Opatoshu gives us an overview of the history of Ashkenazi Jews in Europe from the early Middle Ages through the 16th century and into the 20th century. The title piece, the novella "A Day in Regensburg", is a tale of Jewish life in the ancient city of that name around the 12th century, a fascinating glimpse into an interesting period. "A Sabbath Afternoon" shows Jews in the process of being forced out of Germany a few centuries later and captures the tense and overheated atmosphere of a people under siege. Its protagonists are preparing to sell up and move to harbour towns in readiness for a messianic transference to *Erets Isroel* – the Land of Israel. Opatoshu also sets a story ("Ben Sira's Grandson") in ancient Alexandria, then one-third Jewish in its population. There are stories set in 17th-century Poland, "In the Jewish District of Vienna" set in late-medieval

Vienna (then a considerable centre for Talmudic studies), and in the Polish-Russian borderlands shortly after the Russian Revolution and showing the grave disruption to traditional Jewish culture this created. "The Mute Hungarian" is a grim story of Jewish partisans fighting the German mass-murderers in World War II. Also treating this period is the excellent "Meyer Balaban", brief but burning-hot in its anger at the destruction of Jewish Poland and where Opatoshu takes us, in the person of an elderly Jewish historian, to the smoking ruins of the Warsaw Ghetto in 1944.

As well as historical breadth there is a sociological dimension to much of Opatoshu's work. In his notorious "Roman fun a ferd ganev" ("Romance of a Horse Thief" in an anthology entitled *A Shtetl and Other Yiddish Novellas*), he gives us racy subject matter and a racing narrative with the story of the bold young Zanvl and his horse-stealing and horse-smuggling activities. Although Zanvl is humanized for the more respectable reader by his tender feelings for the good Rachel, Opatoshu captures well the excitement and exhaustion of a criminal's high-adrenaline lifestyle. Zanvl's pure but impossible passion (Rachel's father won't hear of an alliance with a *ferd-ganev* or rustler) is transmuted through the beds of various loose women and climaxes in a pink-bedecked chamber of the local brothel, "Victoria's". It is, though, an understanding vision of marginal existence, parallel with Opatoshu's sketches of immigrant working-class life, an example of which, "The Machine" was translated for the anthology *Yiddish Stories Old and New*. There we witness the confrontation of modern industrial exigencies and old-fashioned *yidishkayt* in Brodsky's shoe factory – the kind of place that Opatoshu had himself worked in for several years – with the interesting twist that both Sephardi and Ashkenazi immigrants are portrayed.

However, Opatoshu's major literary legacy is the impressive *In poylishe velder* (*In Polish Woods*). The main focus of this trilogy (*In Polish Woods*, *1863*, and *Aleyn*) is the decadence of the Hasidic culture, so we move from the early pages which describe a community of simple but pious forest-dwelling Jews in a lyrical, rolling style with asides, to related rural Polish themes such as an evocation of the old pagan Poland of Slavic tribes. As the virgin forest is thinned out and consumed by man's activities and greed so the old stock of Hasidism is eaten away by the avaricious descendants of genuine spiritual leaders and their ignorant and fanatic followers. Opatoshu entertains us with a terrific array of "Hasidic colour"; "Every few minutes a quorum of ten would be formed in this corner or that, they would don prayer-shawl and phylacteries, rush through the prayers, remove prayer-shawl and phylacteries almost at once, and then pass the brandy from mouth to mouth". Various larger-than-life figures are brought in like Wanda the Queen of the Forest who, as legend has it, refused Prince Rittyer the German or Berek Yoselovitch who ferociously fought the Russians with a whole regiment of Jewish soldiers in 1790. Although Opatoshu was very aware of Polish anti-Semitism he also displays a great reverence for the land. In "Before the Storm", the final part of the book *In Polish Woods*, the figure of Kahane looms large, a Jewish agitator for Polish freedom through whom the difficulties of Jewish assimilation are rehearsed. Aside from Slavic Poland, Opatoshu's attitude to Hasidism displays a similar mixture of regret and respect; "Kahane compared the Hasidim with the Essenes, beheld in them the protest of the Jewish spirit against the petrified letters of the Torah." An untranslated sequel to *In Polish Woods* followed entitled *1863*, chronicling the Polish uprising of that year. Among much other untranslated work of interest is a book about the persecution of black people in the American South.

Although Joseph Opatoshu was sometimes more of a worthy craftsman than a great artist, the breadth of his visions of Jewish history in Europe, Egypt, and America over more than a thousand years makes his work an important resource, and, at his best he is well able to transmit the emotional reality of his rich material.

RAY KEENOY

Oppen, George

US poet, 1908–1984

Born in New Rochelle, New York, 24 April 1908. Studied at public schools in California. Married Mary Colby, 1928; one daughter. Founder and publisher, with wife, of To Publishers, Paris, 1930–33; founder and publisher, Objectivist Press Co-op, New York, 1934–36. Member of Worker's Alliance, Brooklyn, New York, and Utica, New York, from 1935; joined Communist Party, 1936. Military service in army, 1942–45; wounded in combat; received standard decorations. Under investigation by House of Representatives Committee on Un-American Activities, 1950; moved to Mexico; worked as furniture maker in Mexico City. Returned to United States, 1958. Awarded Pulitzer Prize, 1969, American Academy and Institute of Arts and Letters Award, 1980. Died in California, 7 July 1984.

Selected Writings

Poetry
Discrete Series, 1934
The Materials, 1962
This is Which, 1965
Of Being Numerous, 1968
Alpine: Poems, 1969
Collected Poems, 1972
Seascape: Needle's Eye, 1973
The Collected Poems of George Oppen, 1929–1975, 1975
The Forms of Love, 1975
Primitive, 1978
Poems of George Oppen, 1908–1984, 1990

Other
Foreword, *Communion*, by Paul Vangelisti 1970
The Selected Letters of George Oppen, edited by Rachel Blau DuPlessis, 1990

Further Reading

Dembo, L.S., "The Objectivist Poet: Four Interviews", *Contemporary Literature*, 10 (1969)

Griffin, Jonathan *et al.*, *Not Comforts, but Vision: Essays on the Poetry of George Oppen*, Budleigh Salterton, Devon: Interim Press, 1985

Hamburger, Michael, *Art as Second Nature: Occasional Pieces*, Manchester: Carcanet New Press, 1975

Hatlen, Burton and Julie Courant, "Annotated Chronological Bibliography of Discussion of George Oppen's Work: Reviews, Articles and Books" in *George Oppen: Man and Poet*, edited by Hatlen, Orono, Mexico: National Poetry Foundation, 1981

Heller, Michael, *Conviction's Net of Branches: Essays on the Objectivist Poets and Poetry*, Carbondale: Southern Illinois University Press, 1985

Ironwood, 26 (1985): George Oppen: A Special Issue

Kenner Hugh, *The Pound Era*, Berkeley: University of California Press, 1971

Kenner, Hugh, *A Homemade World: The American Modernist Writers*, New York: Knopf, 1974

Oppen, Mary, *Meaning a Life: An Autobiography*, Santa Barbara, California: Black Sparrow Press, 1978

Taggart, John, "Walk Out: Rereading George Oppen", manuscript, Mandeville Special Collections Library, University of California, San Diego (several versions), 1995

The entire corpus of George Oppen is contained in two slender volumes, his *Collected Poems* and *Primitive*, both spartan and sparse. At the beginning of this desert-like career, Oppen was an original member of the Objectivism movement in American poetry inaugurated in the February 1931 issue of *Poetry* magazine. As the term implies, Objectivist poetry attempts to encounter reality *as it is*, unfettered by a controlling poetic imagination or unencumbered with ornamental language. This austere, minimal poetics was indebted to the influence of Ezra Pound, whose Imagist dicta (i.e. use absolutely no word that does not contribute to the presentation) served as a model for the group of younger, mostly Jewish, poets which also included Charles Reznikoff, Carl Rakosi, and Louis Zukofsky. Although this group did not cohere as an organized movement, the affiliation did provide for Oppen a lifelong camaraderie and a shared aesthetic "objective". In 1934 he published his first volume of poetry, *Discrete Series*, which included a mere 32 pages of poetry along with a preface by Pound and a review in *Poetry* by William Carlos Williams.

The role of Oppen's Judaism in his poetic composition is complex and controversial, although little has been published about it. Poet John Taggart, Oppen's friend and correspondent, writes that:

> insofar as Oppen's work may be considered Jewish, the product of a Jewish imagination, it is a heterodox/heteronomic Jewishness, a differing Jewishness. Its ground is not the covenant experience, but rather that experience reread and inverted so that what is revealed is the undeniable and finally unreadable physical universe.

Where this puts Oppen, Taggart claims, is in a Jewishness of "between": between objectivist realism and avant garde experimentation, between self-chosen and self-exiled, between Roman and barbarian, between secular and sacred. Ultimately, this is an experience of otherness or outsiderness. According to his niece, Diane Meyer, Oppen returned from a 1975 trip to Israel a "shaken man", one of the ways in which he expressed his ambivalence toward his Judaism. In a letter to Donald Davie circa October 1972, Oppen remarks, "I feel myself the American and the Jew – Semite, nomad, no islander, unable to feel myself included in that tone or ever possibly included. Alien? Alien?" He then laments: ". . . being Jewish, I am not quite American . . . being not quite American since I am a Jew, I am the MOST American". Yet in an 1968 interview with L.S. Dembo, Oppen states that the Jewish poetry of "Reznikoff has been the most important to me". In spite of the problems with his heternomic Jewishness, it is, as Taggart points out, a Jewishness nonetheless.

This heterodox experience of otherness that marks Oppen's Judaism also makes him an ethical poet *par excellence*. Indeed, his life itself was an example of a man struggling with how to be/think/write ethically. Taking a 25-year absence from writing of any kind, Oppen felt in 1934 "[t]hat poetry was not the most important thing in the world at that time". What was important during that time was becoming a craftsman, a carpenter, and metal worker; organizing labour and leading with his wife Mary the Farmers' Union milk strike in Utica; joining the Communist Party whose later Stalinist leanings disillusioned them; having a daughter, Linda, in 1940, a source of inspiration for many of his poems; fighting in the 411th Infantry of the 103rd American Division against fascism in the Battle of the Bulge where he was gravely wounded a few weeks before the war ended. Yet, after service to his country for which he won the Purple Heart, Oppen and his wife were harassed by the FBI and HUAC for refusing to name fellow members of the Party and were subsequently forced to flee to Mexico where they remained in exile for eight years. In 1958, however, when the climate of the country had begun to change, Oppen began to write again and four years later had published *The Materials*.

In his poetry as in his life, Oppen seems to be taking on responsibility for the entire world and its history or, at least, he does not shy away from the idea of inescapable obligation. The 1968 *Of Being Numerous*, for which Oppen won the Pulitzer Prize, examines the ways in which humans relate to urbanized technology as well as to each other. In its lines are issues concerning Vietnam and World War II, the women's and hippie movements, and the undeterred rise of capitalism. Even the shape of Oppen's poems – shape being important to an Objectivist poet who believed that a poem should be sculpted like an object – have an ethical resonance. For example, in his later, more experimental work such as *Seascape: Needle's Eye*, Oppen comes to emphasize the heternomic experience of his own Judaism in his work by putting gaps in the very middle of lines. For instance, in "Exodus" the gaps and disrupted syntax truly add to the exposure of the poem to responsibility:

> When she was a child I read Exodus
> To my daughter   "The children of Israel . . .

Pillar of fire
Pillar of cloud

We stared at the end
Into each other's eyes   Where
She said hushed

Were the adults

Each gap seems to enact a space that at once signals a bond of relationship and at the same time points to the otherness that pervades relationship. The poem not only describes a dialogue between Oppen and his daughter who asked "Where were the adults?", but calls attention to the language itself, of history and human relations, that "children" could stand for all of Israel. The gap between "eyes" and "Where" sets up a tension in which the face-to-face relation of the father and daughter becomes itself the site of language. The gap (in poem and in presence) opens the possibility of conversation in language where the "eyes", the face itself, do the talking. In addition to conversation, this is the space of the Other and Oppen's own unsayable Judaism.

G. MATTHEW JENKINS

Orpaz, Yitzhak

Russian-born Israeli fiction writer, dramatist, and poet, 1923–

Born in Zinkov, 15 October 1923, into Hasidic family. Studied in yeshivas. Married, later divorced; four children. Emigrated to Palestine, 1938. Member of Jewish Brigade of British army during World War II; member of Israeli defence forces, 1948–62. Studied philosophy and literature at Tel Aviv University, BA. Lived for some years on kibbutz; worked in building, diamond-cutting, editing, and teaching; night editor and columnist, *Al hamishmar*, 1962–85. Guest professor, 1986, and teacher of creative writing, 1981–94, Tel Aviv University. Awards include Pichman Prize, 1976; Efrat Prize, 1985; Bialik Prize, 1986; Creativity Prize, 1976 and 1990.

Selected Writings

Novels
Or bead or [Skin for Skin], 1962
Mot lysanda, 1964; as *The Death of Lysanda*, translated by Richard Flint, 1970
Nemalim [Ants], 1968
Masa daniel [The Voyage of Daniel], 1969
Shalosh novelot [Three Novellas], 1972
Bayit leadam [A House for One], 1975
Hagvirah [The Mistress], 1983
Haelem [A Charming Traitor], 1984
Hakalah hanitshit [The Eternal Bride], 1988
Lifnei harash [Age of Treason], 1999

Short Stories
Esev pere [Wild Grass], 1959
Tseyd hatsveyah [The Hunting of the Doe], 1966
Ir sheeyn bah mistor [A City with No Shelter], 1973
Rehov hatomozhenna [Tomozhenna Street], 1979; new edition 1989
Ahavot ketanot, tirufim ketanim [Loves and Follies], 1992
Laylah besanta paulina [A Night in Santa Paulina], 1997

Poetry
Litsloah et hameah [Cruising the Century], 1993
Radio Plays: *The Death of Lysanda*, 1969; *Haseder Hakatan* [The Small Seder], 1983; *The Trial*, 1985

Other
Hatsalyan habiloni [The Secular Pilgrim], 1982

Further Reading

Abarbanell, Nitza, *Eve and Lilith*, Ramat-Gan: Bar-Ilan University, 1994
Bartana, Orzion, *Fantasy in Israeli Literature*, Tel Aviv: Papirus, 1989
Barzel, Hillel, *The Best in Hebrew Prose*, Tel Aviv: Yahdav, 1981
Bibliography of Orpaz's work at the "Gnazim" Institute, Beit Hasofer, Tel Aviv
Moked, Gavriel, "Harechov Ha'pilee Shel Hayaldut", *Haaretz* (6 July 1979)
Navot, Amnon, "Ma'amad Hainkvizitor Mul Inud Hatodaa", *Maariv* (8 January 1988)
Shaked, Gershon, *Wave After Wave in Hebrew Narrative Fiction*, Jerusalem: Keter, 1985
Yudkin, Leon I., *Escape into Siege: A Survey of Israeli Literature Today*, London and Boston: Routledge and Kegan Paul, 1974

The writing of Orpaz is as diverse as the man himself, who has gone through a range of experiences and work fields. He has emerged as one of Israel's most adventurous and experimental novelists, not content with a single mode or voice, but always ready to try out new forms, new approaches, and a variety of fictional settings.

He has developed into a writer of allegories, fantasies, and exercises in surrealism. The overall tendency, for all that it is difficult to pin down, confirms a move away from Naturalism as a major trend in Israeli fiction. He has been able to do this as a response to the extreme situations in which Israel has found herself; the literature, to be true to its own function as reflecting the ultimately reality of its context, has to match the extreme situation with an appropriate expression of the extreme. So Orpaz's work is a constant search for the special expression, for the specific form, which may be peculiar, and will also be somewhat estranged from the commonplace. This is a tendency that we find in Hebrew fiction somewhat removed from that generally regarded as the New Wave – that of Oz, Yehoshua, and Grossman. This tendency is the surrealism of Yoram Kaniuk, David Shahar, and Yitzhak Orpaz.

We can see the attempt of the author to come to terms with the great events of his time and place in a novel such as *Masa daniel* [The Voyage of Daniel], written soon after the traumatic Six Day War, and also in response to it. The story revolves around the eponymous hero, Daniel. Daniel had fought in the war, and he returns home, exhausted. The expectations generated in the reader arising from this experience might be a mixture of relief, exaltation, pride, and satisfaction. A victory was apparently achieved convincingly, massively, and speedily, with relatively small losses, against what seemed at the time to be enormous odds. But Daniel, who was himself of course a player in the great events, does not share this feeling. Immediately, the narrator, through the personage of Daniel, thwarts and undermines the expectation, and raises further questions. And the questions that Daniel puts are only partly related to the events as external events, as an expression of the collective. What Daniel has to do is to find himself; this is a metaphysical search. The book is in three parts: first, Daniel's return home to his seaside town, and to his mother; second, Daniel's escape from home to the sea; and third, Daniel's return home once more, presumably enriched with the sense of the new possibilities in life, and his sudden realization of wonder in the slogan, "What matters is to be happy." From the massive, public euphoria, Daniel has moved into a private sphere, the only one that may offer some satisfaction and personal reward. There are different levels of reality, and they are counterpointed here. There is the war, and Israel's everyday life. And then there is the sea. The latter is clearly the "other" place, eternity, also a reality, but not sharing the concerns of shopping, jobs, weddings, and the things that invade the space of an individual such as Daniel. What Daniel will learn is to look intensively at every detail of the world, and to discover the truth there in a concentrated version of itself. Daniel's father has disappeared. Some think that he is dead, but Daniel believes that he has gone out to the sands, and the son must search for him out there. The sea then becomes his father, and there he can be born anew, like Aphrodite. There is a community too at the sea, through which he can be revitalized and find new life for his return home. He returns as a sort of Messiah.

Orpaz had earlier experimented with the formalism of the Modern in such surrealistic works as *Or bead or* [Skin for Skin], which displays metaphysical and religious predilections, *Mot lisanda* [Death of Lysanda], *Tseyd hatsveyah* [The Hunting of the Doe], and *Nemalim* [Ants]. These novellas and novels are surrealistic, speculative and anti-Naturalist. In *Masa daniel*, Daniel is not a realized character, but rather serves as a symbol. In later works, such as the novel, *Haelem* [The Charming Traitor], he returns more to the space of the everyday reality. The narrative is conveyed from the point of view of a young man (as the title suggests) about to enter the army. He bears all the accepted characteristics of adolescents, cut off from his parents, discontented with himself and the world, and uncertain of his future. As he himself is fundamentally incommunicado, so the Jerusalem of the novel's setting is seen by Yoav (the hero's name) as physically and geographically cut off; to the west there is green, and to the east, very suddenly, there is desert. The great city does not inspire love in him, but awe. This is also a source of distancing, and his total stance is detached and alienated. Orpaz offers symbols in pursuit of the meaning of contact, as presumably the surface description would be insufficient to capture the undercurrent that is otherwise not discernible to the naturalistic word. Symbols, which stand for more than the words themselves actually articulate, and radiate beyond the limitations of the text, are dangerous elements, and may be uncontrollable. Allegories, such as are conveyed in *Nemalim*, act as one for one substitutes, and may be more easily interpreted. We have the feeling that Orpaz is a writer of enormously ambitious scale, whose imagination has run ahead of his achievement, and who is constantly running to push out the frontiers and possibilities of narrative. This is by no means the end of the story.

LEON I. YUDKIN

Oz, Amos

Israeli fiction writer and essayist, 1939–

Born in Jerusalem, 4 May 1939. Studied at Hebrew University, Jerusalem, BA in Hebrew literature and philosophy, 1963. Served in Israeli army, 1957–60; reserve soldier in tank corps in Sinai, 1967, and in Golan Heights, 1973. Married Nily Zuckerman, 1960; two daughters, one son. Teacher of literature and philosophy, Hulda High School, Kibuts Hulda, and Regional High School, Givat Brenner, 1963–86; also tractor driver, youth instructor, Kibuts Hulda. Visiting fellow, St Cross College, Oxford, 1969–70; Hebrew University, Jerusalem, 1975; University of California, Berkeley, 1980; Colorado College, Colorado Springs, 1984–85; Boston University, 1987; Hebrew University, 1990; professor of Hebrew literature, Ben Gurion University, Beer Sheva, since 1987. Many awards, including Holon Prize, 1965; Israel–American Cultural Foundation Award, 1968; B'nai B'rith Award, 1973; Brenner Prize, 1976; Ze'ev Award (for children's books), 1978; Bernstein Prize, 1983; Bialik Prize, 1986; H.H. Wingate Award, 1988; Prix Femina Étranger (France), 1988; German Publishers Union International Peace Prize, 1992. Chevalier, Ordre des Arts et des Lettres, 1984. Member, Catalan Academy of the Mediterranean, Barcelona, 1989; Academy of the Hebrew Language, 1991.

Selected Writings

Fiction
Artsot hatan, 1965; as *Where the Jackals Howl, and Other Stories*, translated by Nicholas de Lange and Philip Simpson, 1981
Makom aher, 1966; as *Elsewhere, Perhaps*, translated by Nicholas de Lange, 1973
Michael sheli, 1968; as *My Michael*, translated by Nicholas de Lange, 1972
Ahavah meuheret, 1971; as *Unto Death*, translated by Nicholas de Lange, 1975
Lagaat bamayim, lagaat baruah, 1973; as *Touch the Water, Touch the Wind*, translated by Nicholas de Lange, 1974
Anashim aherim [Different People], 1974
Har haetsah haraah, 1976; as *The Hill of Evil Counsel*, translated by Nicholas de Lange, 1978
Menuhah nekhonah, 1982; as *A Perfect Peace*, translated by Hillel Halkin, 1985
Kufsah shehorah, 1987; as *Black Box*, translated by Nicholas de Lange, 1988
Ladaat ishah, 1989; as *To Know a Woman*, translated by

Nicholas de Lange, 1991
Hamatsav hashelishi, 1991; as *Fima*, translated by Nicholas de Lange, 1993
Al tagidi laylah, 1994; as *Don't Call It Night*, translated by Nicholas de Lange, 1995
Panter bamartef, 1994; as *Panther in the Basement*, translated by Nicholas de Lange, 1997
Oto hayam, 1999; as *The Same Sea*, 2001, translated by Nicholas de Lange

Other
Soumchi, 1978; in English, translated by Penelope Farmer, 1980
Beor hakelet heazah, 1979; as *Under This Blazing Light: Essays*, 1995
Poh vesham beerets yisrael, 1983; as *In the Land of Israel*, translated by Maurie Goldberg-Bartura, 1983
Editor, with Richard Flantz, *Until Daybreak: Stories from the Kibbutz*, 1984
Mimordot halevanon, 1987; as *The Slopes of Lebanon*, translated by Maurie Goldberg-Bartura 1989
Al matsavah shel yisrael [Report on the Situation in the State of Israel], 1992
Shtikat hashamayim, 1993; as *The Silence of Heaven*, translated by Barbara Harshav, 2000
Hagorem haamiti lemot savati [The Real Cause of My Grandmother's Death], 1994
Israel, Palestine and Peace, translated by Nicholas de Lange, 1994
Mathilim sipur, 1996; as *The Story Begins: Essays on Literature*, translated by Maggie Bar-Tura, 1999

Further Reading

Anderson, Elliot, *Contemporary Israeli Literature*, Philadelphia: Jewish Publication Society, 1977
Balaban, Abraham, *Between God and Beast: An Examination of Amos Oz's Prose*, University Park: Pennsylvania State University Press, 1993
Barzilai, Shuli, "Amos Oz in Arad: A Profile", *Southern Humanities Review*, 21/1 (1987)
Chertok, Chaim, "Amos Oz: Off the Reservation" in *We Are All Close: Conversations with Israeli Writers*, New York: Fordham University Press, 1989
Cohen, Joseph, *Voice of Israel: Essays on and Interviews with Amichai, Yehoshua, Carmi, Appelfeld and Oz*, Albany: State University of New York Press, 1990
Fuchs, Esther, "Amos Oz: The Lack of Conscience" in her *Israeli Mythogynies: Women in Contemporary Hebrew Fiction*, Albany: State University of New York Press, 1987
Gertz, Nurit, "*My Michael* – from Jerusalem to Hollywood via the Red Desert" in *Modern Hebrew Literature in English Translation*, edited by Leon I. Yudkin, New York: Wiener, 1987
Grossman, Susan A., "An Interview with Amos Oz", *Partisan Review*, 53/3 (1986)
Silberschlag, Eisig, *From Renaissance to Renaissance II: Hebrew Literature in the Land of Israel, 1870–1970*, New York: Ktav, 1977
Vardi, Dov, "On Amos Oz: Under the Blazing Light", *Modern Hebrew Literature*, 5/4 (1979)
Wachtel, Eleanor, "Amos Oz" (interview), *Queen's Quarterly*, 98/2 (1991)
Yerushalmi, Y., *Amos Oz: Bibliography, 1953–1981*, Tel Aviv: Am Oved, 1984
Yudkin, Leon I., "The Jackal and the Other Place: The Stories of Amos Oz" in *1948 and After: Aspects of Israeli Fiction*, Manchester: Manchester University Press, 1984

When he began publishing his short stories and novels in the early 1960s, the young Amos Oz all but embodied what the critic Gershon Shaked called the "New Wave" of Israeli fiction – the writing that followed the nation-building socialist-Zionist literature of the State's founding generation. Indeed, with his rugged good looks and his muscular but pensive prose, Amos Oz in many ways personified his entire native-born generation. These were the sunburnt sabras, tough young Israelis widely perceived as sensitive soldiers and confident but contemplative rebuilders of the land. His very name combines that of a prophet with the Hebrew word for strength. Today of course a new generation of Israeli writers has established itself, and Amos Oz must now be relegated to what we might call Israel's "Middle Wave". Yet even in middle age Amos Oz continues to be a vigorous contributor to his nation's literature.

Popular as he was at home, Amos Oz also became the best-known writer of Israeli fiction to the world at large and arguably still holds that distinction today. His high visibility however has not been unattended by criticism and controversy, a fate he shares with Israel itself. At home Amos Oz is as widely known as a political polemicist as he is a novelist. An early supporter of Peace Now, a movement founded by young reserve army officers and dedicated to accommodation with Israel's Arab neighbours, Oz remains a foremost spokesman for the country's political left and a perennial target of its political right. More recently, by his public alignment with the Reform religious movement, Oz has drawn the wrath of Israel's politically powerful Orthodox establishment. In both instances, what seems to be motivating Oz is less an attachment to any particular ideology than a determined opposition to any form of fanaticism, especially that generated by messianic ideals. This is a theme readily seen in his fiction as well.

An early work like *Unto Death* (first published in Hebrew in 1971) is a good example. Each of the book's two novellas demonstrates how ideological conviction can bleed into self-destructive paranoia. The first story, "Crusade", is set in the 11th century and concerns a motley collection of European fanatics set on liberating Jerusalem. The second story, "Late Love", is about an aged Zionist ideologue fixated on the evils of the Soviet regime. These stories, along with several in the early collection *Where the Jackals Howl*, and in the kibbutz novels *Elsewhere, Perhaps* and *A Perfect Peace*, are readily interpreted by many of Oz's critics, both friendly and unfriendly, as warnings against blinkered ideology in general, and against expansionist political and military thinking in Israel in particular.

Even an ostensibly psychological character study like *My*

Michael, which is probably Oz's most popular novel, has not been free of political interpretation. Daringly told from the point of view of a restless young Israeli wife and mother who is given to fantasies of violence and eroticism, *My Michael* has been read as an allegory of Zionist aggrandizement and self-delusion. In the words of critic Nurit Gertz, for example, the novel's narrator is a "symbolic representation of Israel, which has 'gone mad' in its attempt to realize messianic and nationalistic dreams of redemption through violence". While acknowledging that many of his novels are inevitably "full of politics", Oz nevertheless insists he has "never written a story or novel to make a political point". To do the latter, he says, he simply addresses his nation through the medium of the newspaper column or article. (Three collections of such pieces, *Under This Blazing Light*, *In the Land of Israel*, and *The Slopes of Lebanon* have been translated into English.)

But even if Amos Oz manages to wriggle his fiction off the political hook, his work has been pierced by other critical barbs. Feminist critics, for example, have eagerly subjected the handsome former armoured corps officer's depiction of female characters to the sort of hostile interpretation usually reserved for the likes of Philip Roth. Women protagonists like *My Michael's* Hannah Goren or the women who ride away – or at least dream of doing so – in such tales as *The Hill of Evil Counsel* and *Elsewhere, Perhaps* have been interpreted at worst as morally obtuse and at best as unhealthily romantic, if not downright traitorous to their men, to their heritage, to their society and to their nation.

All such critical analysis of course threatens to lead readers astray from what Amos's Oz's fiction has chiefly been about, which is very human characters in conflict with themselves and with those closest to them. This is seen perhaps most acutely in the writer's most recent novels, such as *Fima*, *Don't Call It Night*, and *The Same Sea*. These books are much less politically charged – or at least less open to political or ideological charges – and more concerned with such enduring matters as human nature, family relationships, and the vicissitudes of love.

This is not to suggest the later Amos Oz is any less an engaged novelist. But it does perhaps suggest an engagement now more focused on character, story-telling and style, three of literary fiction's chief components. A good example is *The Same Sea*, which appeared in English in 2001. This highly acclaimed novel concerns the aching hearts of a father and son, is related entirely in poetic stanzas, and is totally devoid of politics. Moreover, in recent years Oz has been supplementing his output of fiction not so much with political writing as with literary analysis. Whatever the cause of this, in such critical studies as *The Silence of Heaven* and *The Story Begins* Amos Oz proves himself an especially perceptive, wide-ranging and original literary critic.

Nor must we overlook yet another facet of this remarkable writer, and that is his novels for children. From the early *Soumchi* to *Panther in the Basement*, Amos Oz has shown that he can write with uncommon intelligence and deep feeling for young readers. But of course, this is what he has always done for all of his readers.

MATTHEW NESVISKY

Ozick, Cynthia

US fiction writer and essayist, 1928–

Born in New York, 17 April 1928. Studied at New York University, BA in English 1949; Ohio State University, Columbus, MA 1950. Married Bernard Hallote, 1952; one daughter. Taught at New York University, 1964–65; Indiana University, Bloomington, 1972; distinguished artist in residence, City College, New York, 1981–82. Many awards, including O. Henry Short Story Award (four times); National Endowment for the Arts Fellow, 1968; Wallant Award for Fiction, 1972; American Academy of Arts and Letters Award, 1973; Guggenheim Fellowship, 1982. Honorary degrees from 11 institutions.

Selected Writings

Short Stories
The Pagan Rabbi and Other Stories, 1971
Bloodshed and Three Novellas, 1976
Levitation: Five Fictions, 1982

Novels
Trust, 1966
The Cannibal Galaxy, 1984
The Messiah of Stockholm, 1987
The Puttermesser Papers, 1997

Essays and Related Prose
Art and Ardor, 1983
Metaphor and Memory, 1989
What Henry James Knew, and Other Essays on Writers, 1993
Portrait of the Artist as a Bad Character, and Other Essays on Writing, 1996
Fame and Folly, 1996
A Cynthia Ozick Reader, edited by Elaine M. Kauver, 1996
Quarrel and Quandary: Essays, 2000

Other writings include poetry and a play.

Further Reading

Currier, Susan and Daniel J. Cahill, "A Bibliography of Writings by Ozick", *Texas Studies in Literature and Language* (Summer 1983)
Epstein, Joseph, "Cynthia Ozick, Jewish Writer", *Commentary*, 77/3 (March 1984): 64–69
Friedman, Lawrence S., *Understanding Cynthia Ozick*, Columbia: University of South Carolina Press, 1991
Pinsker, Sanford, *The Uncompromising Fictions of Cynthia Ozick*, Columbia: University of Missouri Press, 1987
Strandberg, Victor H., *Greek Mind/Jewish Soul: The Conflicted Art of Cynthia Ozick*, Madison: University of Wisconsin Press, 1994

Cynthia Ozick is descended from a Litvak (Lithuanian) tradition of scepticism, rationalism, and anti-mysticism (her father was a scholar of Yiddishized Hebrew, her uncle the Hebrew poet Abraham Regelson). Yet she has succeeded in creating her own distinctive blend of mystical and often idiosyncratic tragi-comic personae. Her public appearances draw large audiences; 2500 people attended her lecture at the Lincoln Center in June 1984. Ozick rejects the notion that Jewish writers are parochial, insisting this is a charge made essentially only against Jewish writers. "The entire planet", she asserts, "is founded on Jewish literary tradition, on Torah. The world ought to be reassimilated into the Jewish tradition. To be a Jew is the opposite of parochial. To be a Jew is the expression of universalism." Ozick feels that to ignore one's history is to perform "a kind of cultural autolobotomy". She sees nothing in the least antithetical, much less adversarial, between "American" and Jewish", and believes that the writer has a serious ethical function.

Her short story, "Envy; or, Yiddish in America" is a lamentation for the murder of Yiddish, the mother-tongue of a thousand years, by the Nazis. An immigrant Yiddish poet searches in anguish for a translator. Essays on Judaism include "Toward a New Yiddish", "Bialik's Hint", and "Sholem Aleichem's Revolution".

Her early novels and stories are concerned with the "Pan versus Moses" theme (as a character in *Trust* calls it). In the title story of *The Pagan Rabbi*, the rabbi is seduced by and couples with a dryad (forbidden in Mosaic law) and hangs himself from her tree. The narrator, a classmate in the rabbinic seminary, visits the rabbi's widow and learns how the rabbi became a pagan. Ozick enunciates the paradox of the Jewish artist. "The single most serviceable description of a Jew . . . is someone who shuns idols, yet to create literature is to put oneself in competition, like a god, with the Creator so that (art) too is turned into an idol."

The short story "Bloodshed" tells of the inner transformation in Bleilip who visits a Hasidic community. He meets the Rebbe, a camp-survivor who carries physical scars, and is surrounded by other Holocaust survivors. Bleilip hears the Rebbe give a lecture on ritual sacrifice and the idea of the scapegoat; Bleilip admits to carrying a gun, contemplates suicide; he is forced (and the reader too) to re-evaluate his idea of himself as a Jew as he realizes that " despair must be earned".

In "The Shawl", a harrowing Holocaust tale, a baby is thrown onto an electrified fence by a Nazi soldier. The mother, Rosa, has to fight her maternal instinct, and stuffs into her own mouth the shawl which was the baby's wrap, "swallowing up the wolf's screech . . . tasting the cinnamon and almond depth of Magda's saliva until it dried." "Rosa" is not merely a sequel to "The Shawl". The two stories were published independently in the *New Yorker* in 1980 and 1983. But once we have read both, we read differently, so that the second becomes a kind of Talmudic commentary on the first and vice versa. Here Rosa is seen 35 years later in New York and Miami. With her background of Polish-Jewish intelligentsia she attempts to assert her integrity over what she sees as a degraded Jewish-American culture. "My Warsaw is not your Warsaw" she tells the kindly but vulgar former button manufacturer. Persky's philosophy is different, "For everything there's a bad way of describing." So for Persky, Rosa is "no ordinary button" but a unique individual. Rosa calls upon magical powers to invoke the spirit of her infant daughter murdered at Auschwitz. She is also a writer, composing letters that are fictions, fictions that help to endow the past with meaning.

After a visit to Jerusalem in 1980 to the profound student of mysticism, Gershom Scholem, Ozick wrote two somewhat "mystical" novels, *The Cannibal Galaxy* and *The Messiah of Stockholm*. The central theme of both is the state of physical and spiritual exile that defines the Jewish post-Holocaust experience. Joseph Brill, an astronomy student and son of a pious fishmonger, survives the Holocaust by hiding in the cellar of a convent in Paris. There he reads the work of Edmond Fleg, a French-Jewish philosopher. This inspires the curriculum for the school in the American Midwest that Brill establishes after the war; a school founded on the fusion of two civilizations, Western and Jewish. The problem for Brill is that by "consorting with the middle", in merging the two cultures, he destroys the very heritage he hoped to preserve. In *The Messiah of Stockholm*, the Swedish hero Lars Andemening believes he is the son of Bruno Schulz, the Polish-Jewish writer who was murdered in the street by a Nazi SS agent in 1942. Lars learns Polish and obsessively attempts to find his roots. In the conflict between past and present East and West, and the lives of Jews and Gentiles, Lars suffers because he lives "between cultures".

Ruth Puttermesser of *The Puttermesser Papers* lives in New York City. She yearns for a daughter, and creates one from the earth in a pot plant. This is the world's first recorded female "golem" (the benevolent robot of legend, one of the most famous being the creation of Rabbi Loew of Prague, which later ran amok). Puttermesser dreams of reforming the city and, with the efficient help of her golem, manages to be elected mayor, but problems wittily follow.

In many of Ozick's novels and short stories, there is a sprinkling of untranslated Yiddish, and the flavour of idiomatic Yiddish expression in the dialogue. Nonetheless, her writing is easily accessible. Hers is a powerful expression of a Jewish ethos. Most critics are agreed that Ozick contributes importantly to the larger American literary tradition; she indeed allows it "to become reassimilated into the Jewish tradition". This may be the effect of her own writing when she comments in an essay in *Art and Ardor*, 1983, about a "liturgical literature" that has the "configuration of a ram's horn". "You give your strength to the inch-hole, and the splendor spreads wide."

SORREL KERBEL

P

Pagis, Dan

Romanian-born Israeli poet and medievalist, 1930–1986

Born in Bukovina, 1930. Interned for three years during World War II. Arrived in Palestine, 1946; became schoolteacher on kibbutz. Began writing in Hebrew only four years after arrival. Enrolled in the Hebrew University in 1962, PhD in medieval Hebrew literature; professor of Hebrew literature, 1972–86. Died in Jerusalem, 1986.

Selected Writings

Poetry
Shaon hahol [The Shadow Dial], 1959
Sheut meuheret [Late Leisure], 1964
Gilgul [Transformation], 1970
Poems, translated by Stephen Mitchell, 1972
Moah [Brain], 1975
Selected Poems of T. Carmi and Dan Pagis, translated by Stephen Mitchell, 1976
Points of Departure, translated by Stephen Mitchell, introduced by Robert Alter, 1981
Shneim asar panim [Twelve Faces], 1981
Milim nirdafot [Double Exposure], 1982
Shirim aharonim [Last Poems], 1987
Variable Direction: The Selected Poetry of Dan Pagis, translated by Stephen Mitchell, 1989
Kol hashirim [Collected Poems], 1991
The Selected Poetry of Dan Pagis, translated by Stephen Mitchell, introduced by Robert Alter, 1996

Other
Editor, *Kol hashirim*, by David Fogel, 1966
Shirei levi ibn alatabban [The Poems of Levi Ibn Al-Tabban], 1967
Shirat hahol vetorat hashir le moshe eben ezra uvnei doro [The Secular Poetry and the Poetics of Moses Ibn-Ezra and his Contemporaries], 1970
Habeitsah shehithapsah [The Egg's Disguises] (for children), 1973
Hidush umasoret beshirat hahol haivrit, sefarad veitalyah [Change and Tradition in Secular Hebrew Poetry, Spain and Italy], 1976
Editor, *Kehut hashani* [The Scarlet Thread: Hebrew Love Poems from Spain, Italy, Turkey and the Yemen], 1979
Editor, with Ezra Fleischer, *A Bibliography of the Writing of Professor Jefim Schirmann 1904–1981*, 1983
Al sod hatum [A Secret Sealed], 1986
Hebrew Poetry of the Middle Ages and the Renaissance, 1991
Hashir davur al ofanav [Poetry Aptly Explained: Studies and Essays on Medieval Hebrew Poetry], 1993

Further Reading

Baruch, Robert Karl, "Return and Repression: Defensive Gestures in the Poetic Language of Dan Pagis" (dissertation), 1994
Hirschfield, Ariel, "Al shirato shel Dan Pagis" [On the Poetry of Dan Pagis] in *Lev pitomi* [Sudden Heart], by Ada Pagis, Tel Aviv: Am Oved, 1995
Pagis, Ada, *Lev pitomi* [Sudden Heart], Tel Aviv: Am Oved, 1995

Dan Pagis was born in Bukovina, which before it was ceded to Romania in 1918 had been part of the Austro-Hungarian empire. His father, Josef, emigrated to Palestine in 1934 seeking employment in that country so that he could settle his family there. Unfortunately, Pagis's mother, Julie, died during that very year. Josef agreed to permit Dan to be raised by his wife's parents who like many Bukovinian Jews were German speakers and admirers of German culture.

In 1941 Romania joined the Rome–Berlin axis and under German pressure transferred the bulk of Bukovinian Jewry to German forced labour camps. The 11-year-old Pagis was shipped to a camp where he spent three years. In 1946 his father arranged for Dan's emigration to Palestine. Having remarried, his father sent him to a youth centre in Kibbutz Merhaviah. Dan, who knew very little Hebrew at the time, rapidly acquired an extraordinary fluency in that language and by 1949 began publishing his first Hebrew poems.

Pagis published five volumes of Hebrew verse: *The Shadow Dial*, *Late Leisure*, *Transformation*, *Brain*, and *Double Exposure*. *Last Poems*, a selection from his literary remains, appeared in 1987. The full edition of his poems, *Collected Poems*, followed in 1991.

The trauma of the death of his mother and his abandonment by his father which occurred when he was four years old could hardly be assuaged by his aged grandparents, who subjected him to the discipline imposed upon every "properly raised child" of the time. As a means of escape, he immersed himself in the classic volumes of German literature he found in the family library and in the rich world of his imagination.

His first volume of verse is influenced by the German poetry of the 18th and 19th centuries – by Hölderlin and particularly by Rilke. It contains a long section of "Dingedichte à la Rilke" [Little Songs of Praise, in *Collected Poems*]. One of its better poems is "Falling from Rock to Rock" (for a discussion of this poem, see Hirschfield):

The water's life falls from rock to rock,
The brook's streams are swallowed by the cascade,
The sky's halo sheds its lights.

The water's life falls from rock to rock
Whose soul seeks its depths
[Flowing] From the frost mountain peeks to the lap of
 its sources.
But the capering light
Captures it and creates a rainbow within it.
The water lives in all the colors of the sky.

Here Pagis reserves the pessimistic conclusion of the Hölderlin poem: light triumphs. However, in *Late Leisure*, the shadows of Pagis's sombre life darken his horizons. The devastating experiences of early orphanhood, abandonment, and all the dreadful years spent in Nazi labour camps, now slowly surface. Like many survivors of the Nazi terror, Pagis preferred to avoid recalling this period of his life, both privately and in his poetry. According to his wife, Ada Pagis:

> Dan would put me off with a rather indefinite shrug, the corners of his mouth would curl in a distorted grimace of disgust. It is difficult to assess how the days of expulsion and escape marked Dan's soul and to gauge their relationship to the despairs and depression that attacked him . . . that grew stronger a few years before his death.

Nevertheless, in *Transformation* he devoted several poems to the Holocaust. "Written in Pencil on a Sealed Box-Car" and "The Line-up" are extremely moving Holocaust poems. In "Testimony" he describes the concentration camp guards:

No, no. They are absolutely
Were human beings: uniforms, boots.
How to explain: they were created in the image [Hebrew
 tselem]

I was a shadow [Hebrew *tsel*]. I had another Creator.

And He in His mercy, did not leave anything in me that
 could die
And I fled to Him
Rose lightly, blue
Reconciled (placated) I would say: Apologetic
Smoke to Omnipotent smoke
Who has neither body or form.

The Nazi views himself as a whole man (*tselem:* a man created in God's image); the inmate is only partially human – *tsel* (Hebrew: a shadow). Like a Holocaust offering (Leviticus) he must be consumed entirely by fire. *Qalil* is the Hebrew for weighing lightly but the poet is punning; *kalil* means entirely. *Ashan* smoke refers to the smoke of the sacrifice on the altar; but *ashan* harks back to *amud ashan*, the pillar of smoke, the sign of God's Presence. But God was not present at the extermination camps – "he has neither body or form".

The victims live in "nothingness", non-existence in the eyes of their tormentors, more tragic in the eyes of the persecuted themselves. They had become zeros with no identity except the numbers tattooed on their arms. Clearly Pagis's personal history was a history of non-identity; he was overwhelmed by a sense of hopelessness and ultimate nothingness. Yet, as his poetic vision grew clearer, he learned to view the nothingness that is death as the source of life. And that the living must realize that their lives are temporal and must reconcile themselves to the truth of death in order to attain "the light".

In the eighth canto of *Brain* Pagis alluded to the opening lines of Dante's *Commedia*, but gave them a Pagisian twist:

In the middle of half my death, in the grief
Over the middle of my life, while I am still gripped in
 the tangle of veins. In the darkness of the forest
. . . Suddenly there emerged, breaking a path for himself

This blood my servant, my master.
Why have I spoken. And to whom: no, no
I didn't really wish to leave a message. Hello, who is
 there? Who is listening? Hello.

Pagis seems to be suggesting that "nothing" is metaphysically present; that the ultimate discovery of the self is the awareness of the great nothingness that awaits all mortals: death.

The last canto of *Brain* closes with the death of the brain. "For a short time it [the brain] tarries: There was certainly something here,/ Very near disturbing. What was it?/ Afterwards/ It is forgotten/ And this is the light".

Pagis, then, realizes that death, non-being, is the light that overcomes the dark fear of death.

EZRA SPICEHANDLER

Paley, Grace

US short story writer and poet, 1922–

Born Grace Goodside in New York City, 11 December 1922, to Isaac Goodside, photographer and physician, and wife Manya (née Ridnyik), both socialist immigrants from Ukraine. Studied at Evander Childs High School, New York; Hunter College, New York, 1938–39. Married, first, Jess Paley, 1942; divorced; one daughter, one son; second, Robert Nichols, dramatist, 1972. Taught at Columbia University and Syracuse University; Sarah Lawrence College, Bronxville, New York, 1966–88; City College, New York, 1983–95; short courses at Stanford, Johns Hopkins, and Dartmouth universities. Has become prominent in community action in Manhattan on environmental and civic issues. Many awards, including Guggenheim Fellowship, 1961; National Endowment for the Arts grant, 1966; American Academy Award, 1970; American Institute of Arts and Letters Award, 1970; Edith Wharton Award, 1988, 1989.

Selected Writings

Short Stories
The Little Disturbances of Man: Stories of Men and Women in Love, 1959
Enormous Changes at the Last Minute, 1974
Later the Same Day, 1985
The Collected Stories of Grace Paley, 1994

Poetry
Leaning Forward, 1985
New and Collected Poems, 1992
Begin Again: Collected Poems, 2000

Other
365 Reasons Not to Have Another War, 1989
Long Walks and Intimate Talks, 1991
Just as I Thought, 1998

Further Reading

Arcana, Judith, *Grace Paley's Life Stories: A Literary Biography*, Urbana: University of Illinois Press, 1993
Bach, Gerhard and Blaine H. Hall (editors), *Conversations with Grace Paley*, Jackson: University Press of Mississippi, 1997
Barthelme, Donald, William Gass, Grace Paley, and Walker Percy, "A Symposium on Fiction", *Shenandoah*, 27 (1976): 3–31
Baumbach, Jonathan, "Life Size", *Partisan Review*, 42/2 (1975): 303–06
Blake, Nancy, "Grace Paley's Quiet Laughter", *Revue Française d'Études Américaines*, 4 (November 1977): 55–58
DeKoven, Marianne, "Mrs Hegel-Shtein's Tears", *Partisan Review*, 48/2 (1981): 217–33
Gelfant, Blanche, "Fragments for a Portrait in Collage", *New England Review*, 3/2 (Winter 1980): 276–93
Halfmann, Ulrich and Philipp Gerlach, "Grace Paley: A Bibliography", *Tulsa Studies in Women's Literature*, 8 (1989): 339–62
Hiemstra, Anne, "Grace Paley" in *Modern American Women Writers*, edited by Elaine Showalter, New York: Scribner, 1991
Isaacs, Neil David, *Grace Paley: A Study of the Short Fiction*, Boston: Twayne, 1990
Kaplan, Cora, *Writing Lives: Conversations between Women Writers*, edited by Mary Chamberlain, London: Virago, 1988
Levy, Barbara, *Grace Paley's Wit; or, The Ear is Smarter than the Eye*, Wellesley, Massachusetts: Wellesley College, Center for Research on Women, 1990
Lidoff, Joan, "Clearing Her Throat: An Interview with Grace Paley", *Shenandoah*, 32 (1981): 3–26
Michaels, Leonard, "Conversation with Grace Paley", *Threepenny Review*, 1 (Autumn 1980): 4–6
Mickelson, Anne Z., *Reaching Out: Sensitivity and Order in Recent American Fiction by Women*, Metuchen, New Jersey: Scarecrow Press, 1979
Shapiro, Harriet, "Grace Paley: 'Art is on the Side of the Underdog'", *Ms.*, 2/11 (May 1974): 43–45
Sorkin, Adam J., "'What Are We, Animals?': Grace Paley's World of Talk and Laughter", *Studies in American Jewish Literature*, 2 (1982)
Taylor, Jacqueline, *Grace Paley: Illuminating the Dark Lives*, Austin: University of Texas Press, 1990

Most critics comment that the generative basis of Grace Paley's fictional art is the voice: the spoken word. The oral tradition is invoked when her work is assessed. Certainly, her refined and economical small-scale works have an appeal founded on the colloquial, and her early work has the quality of the comic monologue at times (e.g. the story of Rosie and Vlashkin in "Goodbye and Good Luck"). However, there is considerable literary sophistication in her stories, and the art that hides art so essential to the form. "Her stories always carry the past within their present, even as both turn amazingly to the future. Every story, she has said, is at least two stories . . .", according to Judith Arcana. In an era in which the short story became the most prestigious and notably experimental fictional form in the USA, a time in which Cheever, Carver, and Coover emerged, Paley made a profound impact with her first collection, and much of the strength of this was due to that Yiddish culture, the *heimisch* integuments of the immigrants and their family values.

She has said that she wished to write to tell the stories of hidden lives, and certainly her fiction gives us in Anne Hiemstra's words "the way language emerges from the mouths of real people". But at the heart of her achievement is the chronicling of the journey towards assimilation of the Jewish immigrants since the first generation from Russia and eastern Europe at the turn of the century. Again Hiemstra, "The dialectic of Jewish and American attitudes forms an almost paradoxical synthesis in the attitudes of a number of her most fully realized characters – a Jewish memory of the past, the consciousness of oppression, and the resultant 'ancestral grief'". In this sense her work may be representative of a central line of development in American Jewish writing, one that concentrated on the microcosmic issues of living together rather than in post-Holocaust issues and the supposed grievous loss of a Judaic faith.

In her poetry, Paley has been quite open in her sarcastic and ironical statements about assimilation. In "A Warning" she rhetorically uses the line "One day I forgot Jerusalem" to telling ironical effect, working to the crescendo of "Even my lover, a Christian with pale eyes and the barbarian's foreskin has left me." Nevertheless, in the stories she is closer to Woody Allen and Philip Roth in her depiction of the "little disturbances" that provide a fictional terrain somewhere on the cusp between comedy of manners and serious satire. Her faultless sense of point of view and creation of the innocent narrator fuels a sense of simple understanding, typified in the closure of "The Loudest Voice": "I had prayed for everybody: my talking family, cousins far away, passers-by, and all the lonesome Christians. I expected to be heard . . ."

In her later writing the subjects are more overtly political, reflecting her lifestyle of a committed individual against the establishment injustices of urban, consumer-led America. Through the character of Faith Darwin Ashbury, called a "co-worker in the mother trade" we follow the progress of a politicized being in the suburbs. Though there may be a didactic element, as in the purposeful inclusion of a wider sweep of reference, notable in "Faith in a Tree", it is never clumsy and always embedded in a human frame of reference seeped in Jewish consciousness. But the discussions of identity become more direct and percipient: "Her grandmother pretended she was German in just the same way that Faith pretends she is an American" (from *Enormous Changes at the Last Minute*).

Paley's special contribution to Jewish-American writing, politics, and feminism, will be her attitude to the generational distance created by those differentiated perceptions based on degrees of accommodation to American centrality, and to the acquisition of "happiness" given by the acculturated ideology of optimism and media-defined contentment. Her characters' levels of change and Americanization often relate to the more postmodern issues of global and universal erosion of difference, so that in an ironical way, her stories of communities assailed by social change and political neglect take on a fresh importance as demographic change inevitably reshuffles the USA and all its immigrant constituents.

On a human plane, Paley's stories always insist on the centrality of humour, wit, and survival, on eccentricity and the social comedy of role-play and parent power. Though politics came to matter more and more as the fiction developed, the still and stable centre of Paley's aesthetics has always been rooted in the oral tradition, and its transmutation among the tower blocks and apartments where loneliness might be the greatest enemy.

STEPHEN WADE

Parker, Dorothy

US fiction writer, dramatist, and poet, 1893–1967

Born Dorothy Rothschild in West End, New Jersey, 22 August 1893, to mother who died when she was young. Father remarried; bad relationship developed with him and stepmother. Expelled from Blessed Sacrament Convent school, New York, after confusing "Immaculate Conception" and "spontaneous combustion"; studied at Miss Dana's girls' school, New Jersey, graduated 1911. Father died, leaving family without money, 1912. Caption writer, *Vogue* magazine; fashion writer, *Vanity Fair*, from 1914; drama critic, *Vanity Fair*, from 1918; dismissed after writing caustic reviews of productions by three of magazine's backers, 1920; drama and book critic, *Ainslee's*, 1920–33, and *New Yorker*, from 1931, for latter under pen name "Constant Reader". Joined "Round Table" at Algonquin Hotel, New York; became alcoholic. First short story published, in *Smart Set*, 1922; published poems and short prose in *Life*, *Saturday Evening Post*, *Everybody's*, and *Ladies' Home Journal*. Married, first, Edwin Pond Parker II, Wall Street broker, 1917; attempted suicide after abortion, 1923; divorced 1928; liaison with Alan Campbell, bisexual actor, from 1928; married, Campbell, 1933; divorced, 1947; remarried, 1950; Campbell died, 1963. Supported many radical causes, including Spanish Republic against Franco; reporter for *New Masses* in Spain, 1937; helped found Screen Writers Guild and Anti-Nazi League; blacklisted by Hollywood studios during "Red scare". Distinguished visiting professor of English, California State College, Los Angeles, 1963–64. Awarded Marjorie Peabody Waite Award by American Academy of Arts and Letters, 1958; member of Academy, 1959. Found dead at Hotel Volney, New York, 7 June 1967. Left estate, copyrights, and royalties to Martin Luther King, Jr, to be passed after his death to National Association for the Advancement of Colored People.

Selected Writings

Fiction and Sketches

Men I'm Not Married To published with *Women I'm Not Married To*, by Franklin P. Adams, 1922
Laments for Living, 1930
After Such Pleasures, 1933
Soldiers of the Republic, 1938
Here Lies: Collected Stories, 1939; as *The Collected Stories of Dorothy Parker*, 1942
The Viking Portable Library Dorothy Parker, 1944; as *The Indispensable Dorothy Parker*, 1944; as *Selected Short Stories*, 1944; revised and enlarged as *The Portable Dorothy Parker*, 1973; as *The Collected Dorothy Parker*, 1973
The Best of Dorothy Parker, 1952
Constant Reader, 1970; as *A Month of Saturdays*, 1971

Poetry

Enough Rope, 1926
Sunset Gun, 1928
Death and Taxes, 1931
Not So Deep as a Well, 1936; as *The Collected Poetry of Dorothy Parker*, 1944

Plays

Chauve-Souris, with others, 1922
Nero, with Robert Benchley, 1922
Close Harmony, or The Lady Next Door: A Play in Three Acts, with Elmer Rice, 1924
Round the Town, 1924
Shoot the Works, 1931
The Coast of Ilyria, with Ross Evans, 1949
The Ladies of the Corridor: A Play, with Arnaud D'Usseau, 1953

Film Writing: *Business is Business*, with George S. Kaufman, 1925; *Here is My Heart*, 1932; *Big Broadcast of 1936*, 1935; *Hands across the Table*, 1935; *Mary Burns, Fugitive*, 1935; *One Hour Late*, 1935; *Paris in Spring*, 1935; *Lady, Be Careful*, with Alan Campbell and Harry Ruskin, 1936; *Suzy*, with Alan Campbell, Horace Jackson, and Lenore Coffee, 1936; *The Moon's Our Home*, with Alan Campbell, 1936; *Three Married Men*, with Alan Campbell, 1936; *A Star is Born*, with Alan Campbell and Robert Carson, 1937; *Woman Chases Man*, with Joe Bigelow, 1937; *Sweethearts*, with Alan Campbell, 1938; *Trade Winds*, with Alan Campbell and Frank R. Adams, 1938; *Weekend for Three*, with Alan Campbell, 1941; *Saboteur*, with Peter Viertel and Joan Harrison, 1942; *Smash Up: The Story of a Woman*, with Frank Cavett, 1947; *The Fan*, with Walter Reisch and Ross Evans, 1949; *Queen for a Day*, 1950

Television Writing: *The Lovely Leave*, *A Telephone Call*, and *Dusk Before Fireworks*, 1962

Other
Editor, *The Portable F. Scott Fitzgerald*, 1945
Editor, with Frederick B. Shroyer, *Short Story: A Thematic Anthology*, 1965

Further Reading

Bunkers, Suzanne L., "'I am Outraged Womanhood': Dorothy Parker as Feminist and Social Critic", *Regionalism and the Female Imagination*, 4/2 (Autumn 1978)
Calhoun, Randall, *Dorothy Parker: A Bio-Bibliography*, Westport, Connecticut: Greenwood Press, 1993
Capron, Marion "Dorothy Parker", *Paris Review*, 13/4 (1956)
Cooper, Wyatt, "Whatever You Think Dorothy Parker Was, She Wasn't", *Esquire* (July 1968)
Crowninshield, Frank, "Crowninshield in the Cub's Den", *Vogue* (15 September 1944)
Gaines, James R., *Wit's End: Days and Nights of the Algonquin Round Table*, New York: Harcourt Brace, 1977
Gill, Brendan, introduction to *The Portable Dorothy Parker*, New York: Viking Press, 1973
Hellman, Lillian, *An Unfinished Woman*, Boston: Little Brown, and London: Macmillan, 1969
Keats, John, *You Might as Well Live: The Life and Times of Dorothy Parker*, New York: Simon and Schuster, 1986
Kinney, Arthur F., *Dorothy Parker*, Boston: Twayne, 1978
Meade, Marion, *Dorothy Parker: What Fresh Hell is This?*, New York: Villard, 1988
Melzer, Sondra, *The Rhetoric of Rage: Women in Dorothy Parker*, New York: Peter Lang, 1997
Toth, Emily, "Dorothy Parker, Erica Jong and New Feminist Humor", *Regionalism and the Female Imagination*, 32–3 (Autumn 1977/Winter 1977–78)
Walker, Nancy, "'Fragile and Dumb': The 'Little Woman' in Women's Humour, 1900–1940", *Thalia*, 5 (Autumn/Winter 1982–83)
Woollcott, Alexander, "Our Mrs Parker" in his *While Rome Burns*, New York: Viking, and London: Barker, 1934

Dorothy Parker's life was long but her fame and creative peak were concentrated into relatively few years. Although she continued writing well into the 1960s, her best work was done in, and was about, New York in the 1920s and 1930s, a period and place which, in many ways, she came to symbolize.

Born as Dorothy Rothschild ("We'd never *heard* of *those* Rothschilds") to a Jewish father and Scottish mother she was therefore, by the rules of Halachah, not Jewish. But she considered herself, ethnically, not religiously, Jewish, and seems to have been considered so by those around her and virtually all who wrote about her. And this was not a source of comfort or pride to her. On the contrary, she regarded her "Jewishness" as one of her many reasons, some would say excuses, for self-demeaning and seemingly masochistic low self-esteem.

That she was somewhat ambivalent about her heritage is evidenced by the fact that she gave the impression to her Round Table acquaintances that her father had been a famous Talmudic scholar – he had in fact been a relatively successful garment manufacturer – though this may also have resulted from her self-consciousness at having not received a university education and being to a large extent an autodidact.

More telling perhaps is that according to her biographer, Marion Meade, she blamed the breakdown of her marriage to Edwin Pond Parker II not to his alcoholism, but to her a failure as a Jew not to have realized that marriage to a high-born Gentile was striving above her station. Though the marriage ended in divorce, she certainly preferred and continued to use the name "Parker" to her own given name. She also penned at least one poem in which she portrays her own people as dark "devil-gotten sinners", although she did not include it in her selection for the Portable Viking edition of her works in 1944. Nonetheless her ambivalence is manifest by her strong involvement in left-wing and anti-Nazi movements during her Hollywood years of the late 1930s, leading the FBI in 1947 to attempt to establish, unsuccessfully, that she had been a member of the Communist Party.

All this may well be a specific expression of her generally pessimistic and morbid view of life. Parker was justifiably known as a wit: her wit and her writing were mordant and the mordancy was rooted in the inevitable fact of death, which appeared to render meaningless romantic and sanguine approaches. "People ought to be one of two things, young or old. No; what's the use of fooling? People ought to be one of two things: young or dead." And again:

> Accursed from their birth they be
> Who seek to find monogamy,
> Pursuing it from bed to bed-
> I think they would be better dead.

or:

> If wild my breast and sore my pride,
> I bask in dreams of suicide;
> If cool my heart and high my head,
> I think, "How lucky are the dead!".

She particularly admired the way Hemingway dealt with this problem in his work as well as in his life. She lost her mother in infancy and appears to have been unhappy at school and with her family (her father married again) and left both as soon as she could. Her alcoholism, her disastrous relationships with men, and her lonely old age have all been well documented and even made the subject of a Hollywood biopic. But it was from these elements in her own life and in the lives of the people she socialized with that she crafted her poems and stories.

Parker painted on a small canvas, and within a restricted landscape, but she reproduced it with unerring skill and accuracy. She drew entirely from her own life and experiences and on the lives and experiences of those around her. All her stories are *romans à clef*. Her characters and situations were not imaginatively contrived, and her poems, often in a tone of stoical self-pity, are commentaries on the illusion of love and friendship and the ubiquity of death.

She came to the notice of Frank Crowninshield, the editor of *Vogue*, in 1916; having read some of her verses he gave her an editorial post writing captions for fashion photographs and drawings. Within a year she had been promoted to *Vanity Fair*, where she met, and shared an office with, Robert Benchley and Robert Sherwood, leading to the establishment of the famous Algonquin Round Table and her coronation as its sharpest wit. Although much quoted in its day the members of this clan did not include the true literary heavies of the time who were, presumably, more engaged in getting it down on paper than expending energy on ephemeral badinage. The connection proved fruitful in that it led another member, Harold Ross, to employ her when he founded *The New Yorker* in 1925. Her work appeared in the magazine from 1926 to 1955 and the earlier stories played a considerable role in giving that publication its distinctive tone.

She had, rather than enjoyed, fame and financial success, becoming friends with literary luminaries such as Hemingway and the Fitzgeralds. With her second husband, Alan Campbell (also half-Jewish and half-Scottish) she became a successful and highly paid Hollywood screenwriter, but it was the stories and poems of the 1920s and 1930s documenting and commenting on that sophisticated New York milieu that gave her such a high literary reputation among her peers. Many contemporary readers find the very specificity of her focus too limiting for the reputation she appears to have enjoyed. If her work has a certain superficiality it is superbly crafted, and is evidence of the seriousness with which she took it and the dedication with which she laboured over it. Other aspects of her life may have been disorganized and chaotic, but never her writing, and she remains one of the most insightful, wittiest, and from time to time, moving, chroniclers of a unique time and place in the second and third decades of the 20th century.

GERALD DE GROOT

Pasternak, Boris

Russian poet, fiction writer, and dramatist, 1890–1960

Born Boris Leonidovich Pasternak in Moscow, 10 February 1890. Studied at Moscow Fifth Gymnasium, 1901–08; University of Moscow, 1909–13; also at University of Marburg, 1912. Manager in chemical factories in Urals, 1915–17; librarian, People's Commissariat of Enlightenment, 1918. Married, first, Evgeniia Vladimirovna Lourie, 1922; divorced 1931; one son; second, Zinaida Nikolaevna Neigauz, 1934; one son. Attended first Conference of Soviet Writers, 1934. Lived in Peredelkino, 1936–40; evacuated to Chistopol, 1941–43; returned to Moscow, 1943; in Peredelkino again, 1944–60. Translator, 1940–60. Expelled from Writers Union, 1958. Awarded Medal for Valiant Labour, 1946; Nobel Prize for Literature (forced to decline), 1958. Died in Peredelkino, 30 May 1960.

Selected Writings

Collections

Sochineniia [Works], edited by Gleb Struve and Boris Filippov, 3 vols, 1961
Stikhotvoreniia i poemy [Poetry and Narrative Verse], edited by L.A. Ozerov, 1965
Stikhi [Poems], edited by Z. Pasternak and E. Pasternak, 1966
Izbrannoe [Selection], edited by E.V. Pasternak and E.B. Pasternak, 2 vols, 1985
Sobranie sochinenii [Collected Works], edited by E.B. Pasternak and K.M. Polivanova, 5 vols, 1989–92
Izbrannye proizvedeniia [Selected Works], edited by E.B. Pasternak, 1991

Poetry

Bliznets v tuchakh [Twin in the Clouds], 1914
Poverkh bar'erov [Above the Barriers], 1917
Sestra moia zhizn': Leto 1917 goda, 1922; as *Sister My Life: Summer, 1917*, translated by P.C. Flayderman, 1967; complete version, as *My Sister, Life*, translated by Mark Ruderman and Bohdan Boychuk, 1983
Temy i variatsii [Themes and Variations], 1923
"Leitenant Shmidt", 1926, 1927
Deviat'sot piaty god, 1927; as *The Year Nineteen Five*, translated by Richard Chappell, 1989
Spektorskii, 1931
Vtoroe rozhdenie [Second Birth], 1932
Poemy [Narrative Verse], 1933
Stikhotvoreniia [Poetry], 1933
Na rannikh poezdakh [On Early Trains], 1943
Zemnoi prostor [Earth's Vastness], 1945
Selected Poems, translated by J.M. Cohen, 1946
Stikhi o Gruzii [Poems about Georgia], 1958
Poems, translated by Eugene M. Kayden, 1959
Kogda razguliaetsia: Poems 1955–1959 [When the Weather Clears] (bilingual edition), translated by Michael Harari, 1960; reprinted with *An Essay in Autobiography*, 1990
Poeziia [Poetry], 1960
The Poetry of Boris Pasternak 1914–1960, translated by George Reavey, 1960
Stikhotvoreniia i poemy [Poetry and Narrative Verse], 1961
In the Interlude: Poems 1945–1960, translated by Henry Kamen, 1962
Fifty Poems, translated by Lydia Pasternak Slater, 1963
The Poems of Doctor Zhivago, translated by Donald Davie, 1965
Selected Poems, translated by Jon Stallworthy and Peter France, 1983
Svobodnyi krugozor [Free Horizon], 1987
Kogda razguliaetsia [When It's on the Loose], 1989
Stikhotvoreniia; Poemy; Perevody [Poetry; Narrative Verse; Translations], 1989
Poems (in translation), edited by Evgenii Pasternak, 1990
Second Nature: Forty-Six Poems, translated by Andrei Navrozov, 1990

Fiction

Detstvo Liuvers, 1922; as *Childhood*, translated by Robert Payne, 1941; as *The Childhood of Luvers* in *Collected Prose Works*, 1945

Rasskazy [Stories], 1925; as *Vozdushnye puti* [Aerial Ways], 1933
Povest' [A Tale], 1934; as *The Last Summer*, translated by George Reavey, 1959
Doktor Zhivago, 1957; as *Doctor Zhivago*, translated by Max Hayward and Manya Harari, 1958
Vozdushnye puti: Proza raznykh let [Aerial Ways: Prose of Various Years], edited by C.B. Pasternak and E.V. Pasternak, 1982
Zhenia's Childhood and Other Stories (includes "The Childhood of Luvers"; "Il Tratto di Apelle"; "Letters from Tula"; "Ariel Routes"), translated by Alec Brown, 1982

Play
Slepaia krasavitsa, edited by Christopher J. Barnes and Nicholas J. Anning, 1969; as *The Blind Beauty*, translated by Max Hayward and Manya Harari, 1969

Other
Karusel [The Carousel], 1925
Zverinets [The Menagerie], 1929
Okhrannaia gramota, 1931; as *The Safe Conduct* in *Collected Prose Works*, 1945
Knizhka dlia detei [Little Book for Children], 1933
Editor and translator, with Nikolai Tikhonov, *Gruzinskie liriki* [Georgian Lyric Poetry], 1935
Izbrannie perevody [Selected Translations], 1940
Translator, *Gamlet prints datskii* [Hamlet], by William Shakespeare, 1941
Translator, *Romeo i Dzhul'etta* [Romeo and Juliet], by William Shakespeare, 1943
Translator, *Antonii i Kleopatra* [Antony and Cleopatra], by William Shakespeare, 1944
Collected Prose Works, edited by Stefan Schimanski, translated by Beatrice Scott and Robert Payne, 1945
Translator, *Otello, venetsii anskii maur* [Othello], by William Shakespeare, 1945
Gruzinskie poety [Georgian Poets], 1947
Translator, *Genrikh chetverty* [Henry IV, parts 1 and 2], by William Shakespeare, 1948
Translator, *Stikhotvoreniia* [Poems], by N.M. Baratashvili, 1948
Translator, *Korol' Lir* [King Lear], by William Shakespeare, 1949
Safe Conduct: An Early Autobiography, and Other Works, edited by Robert Payne, translated by Payne *et al.*, 1949
Selected Writings, 1949
Vil'iam Shekspir v perevode Borisa Pasternaka [William Shakespeare in Translation], 1949
Translator, *Faust* (part 1), by Johann Wolfgang von Goethe, 1950
Translator, *Vitiaz ianoshch* [John the Hero], by Sándor Petőfi, 1950
Translator, *Makbet* [Macbeth] in *Tragedii*, by William Shakespeare, 1951
Translator, *Mariia Stiuart*, by Friedrich von Schiller, 1958
An Essay in Autobiography, translated by Manya Harari, 1959; as *I Remember*, edited and translated by David Magarshack, 1959; partial Russian text, as *Liudi i polozheniia* in *Novyi mir* (January 1967)
Prose and Poems, edited by Stefan Schimanski, 1959
Translator, *Zvezdnoe nebo* [The Celestial Sphere], 1966
Letters to Georgian Friends, edited and translated by David Magarshack, 1968
Boris Pasternak: Voices of Prose, edited by C.J. Barnes, 1977
Marina Cvetaeva, Boris Pasternak, Rainer Maria Rilke: Lettere 1926, edited by Yevgeny Pasternak *et al.*, 1980; as *Letters, Summer 1926: Correspondence between Boris Pasternak, Marina Tsvetaeva and Rainer Maria Rilke*, translated by Margaret Wettlin and Walter Arndt, 1985
Perepiska s Olga Freidenberg [Sketches with Olga Freidenberg], edited by Elliott Mossman, 1981; as *Correspondence with Olga Freydenberg*, translated by Mossman and Margaret Wettlin, 1982
Pasternak on Art and Creativity, edited by Angela Livingstone, 1985
Iz pisem raznykh let [Letters from Various Years], 1990
Moi vzgliad na iskusstvo [My View on Art], 1990
Ob iskusstve [On Art], 1990
Perepiska Borisa Pasternaka [Sketches of Boris Pasternak], 1990
Selected Writings and Letters, translated by Catherine Judelson, 1990
Zarubezhnaia poeziia v perevodakh B.L. Pasternaka [Foreign Poetry Translated by B.L. Pasternak], 1990
Ne ia pishu stikhi . . . [I Don't Write Poetry . . .], 1991

Further Reading
Cornwell, Neil, *Pasternak's Novel: Perspectives on Doctor Zhivago*, Keele: Keele University Press, 1986
Davie, Donald and Angela Livingstone (editors), *Pasternak: Modern Judgements*, London: Macmillan, 1969; Nashville, Tennessee: Aurora, 1970
Erlich, Victor (editor), *Pasternak: A Collection of Critical Essays*, Englewood Cliffs, New Jersey: Prentice Hall, 1978
Fleishman, Lazar, *Boris Pasternak: The Poet and His Politics*, Cambridge, Massachusetts: Harvard University Press, 1990
Gifford, Henry, *Boris Pasternak: A Critical Study*, London and New York: Cambridge University Press, 1977
Gladkov, A.K., *Meetings with Pasternak: A Memoir*, translated by Max Hayward, New York: Harcourt Brace, and London: Collins Harvill, 1977
Hayward, Max, *Writers in Russia, 1917–78*, San Diego: Harcourt Brace, and London: Harvill Press, 1983
Hingley, Ronald, *Pasternak: A Biography*, New York: Knopf, and London: Weidenfeld and Nicolson, 1983
Hughes, Olga Raevsky, *The Poetic World of Boris Pasternak*, Princeton, New Jersey: Princeton University Press, 1974
Ivinskaya, Olga Vsevolodovna, *A Captive of Time: My Years with Pasternak*, translated by Max Hayward, New York: Doubleday, and London: Collins Harvill, 1978
Levi, Peter, *Boris Pasternak*, London: Hutchinson, 1990
Mallac, Guy de, *Boris Pasternak: His Life and Art*, Norman: University of Oklahoma Press, 1981
O'Connor, Katherine Tiernan, *Boris Pasternak's "My Sister-Life": The Illusion of Narrative*, Ann Arbor, Michigan: Ardis, 1988

Pasternak, E.B., *Boris Pasternak: The Tragic Years, 1930–1960*, translated by Michael Duncan, London: Collins Harvill, 1990
Sendich, Munir and Erika Greber, *Pasternak's "Dr Zhivago": An International Bibliography of Criticism 1957–1985*, East Lansing, Michigan: Russian Language Journal, 1990
Sendich, Munir, *Boris Pasternak: A Reference Guide*, New York: G.K. Hall, 1994

One of the greatest Russian poets, Boris Pasternak is better known in the West as the author of *Doctor Zhivago*. He was born in Moscow to Jewish parents, his painter father Leonid being descended from an 18th-century Sephardic family. As a boy Pasternak met Scriabin, Rachmaninov, Tolstoi, and Rilke. He received a broad classical education and studied at Moscow and Marburg universities, pursuing career choices in music and philosophy before settling on literature. Pasternak's parents were not religious, but as a child he accompanied his nurse to Orthodox church services which had a lasting effect on him. He read the Bible, taking from early Jewish and Christian teachings elements for his own philosophy of life, which found mature expression in his writing. Pasternak welcomed the Revolution of 1905, but saw early reforms swept away by World War I and the turmoil of 1917. During this time he made his poetic debut with *Twin in the Clouds*, followed by *Above the Barriers*.

Pasternak's writing was distinct and individual, distinguished by an elusive personal quality, but rooted in the business of everyday life. His poems display an exultant joy in the use of language, crammed with unusual metaphors where elements, seasons and inanimate objects take on human characteristics – a door sings, a garden "scatters beetles", besotted humans drink "The gleam of stars, pulsing on ice." "From Superstition" praises a lover, who "took down my life from the shelf/ And blew the dust from my name." Fame arrived in 1922 with *My Sister, Life*, a unified cycle of poems whose arrangement suggests a novel in verse. The same year produced *The Childhood of Luvers*, the first of many attempts at a prose record of past experiences, whose simplicity contrasts with the subtle precision of his poems.

Ever the individualist, Pasternak refused to commit himself to any one party. A close friend of the socialist Maiakovskii, he also supported former "White" Marina Tsvetaeva. While acknowledging the need for change and social justice, he was troubled by the chaos and suffering that followed the Revolution. In the late 1920s he wrote *The Year Nineteen Five* and "Leitenant Shmidt", narrative poems praising the first, "democratic revolution", but these are the only real examples of his "political" poetry.

1931 saw radical changes in Pasternak's life. A new love, Zinaida Neigauz, and a rejuvenating visit to Georgia where he befriended the poets Yashvili and Tabidze, brought fresh inspiration which he celebrated in *Second Birth*, but Stalin's tyranny dashed any hopes of freedom. The terror that ensued with show trials and arrests dismayed Pasternak, and he actively opposed it. He called Stalin direct in a vain attempt to save Mandel'shtam from imprisonment, refused to sign the denunciation of Marshal Tukhachevski, and made an impassioned speech for artistic freedom at the Minsk Writers' Conference in 1936. While he survived, others perished; the deaths of Tabidze, Yashvili, and Tsvetaeva left him devastated. Restricted by censorship, Pasternak worked as a translator from the late 1930s onwards. His translations from Shakespeare, Goethe, and Schiller are held by many to be the finest in the Russian language, and from them he drew confirmation of his own beliefs. Denied publication, Pasternak determined to speak out and bear witness. Alexander Gladkov, who met the poet at this time, recalls that he was determined to speak out against the regime once the war ended.

The postwar period saw a return to rigid authoritarian rule and the brutal suppression of dissent, and Pasternak began work on the novel whose theme had occupied him from the early 1920s. From Jewish and Christian teachings he formed the belief that was to sustain him, and which found expression in *Doctor Zhivago*. Mankind's experience of lived time was through history, which began with Christ, and which was surrounded by the greater, mysterious time known as eternity, glimpsed by man only in brief revelations. Within this framework the artist, and his fellow men, must endure with integrity, and sacrifice themselves for the good of others. The figure of Hamlet, who in Pasternak's interpretation takes on his tragic role from a sense of duty, adapted well to this concept. Inspiration also came from his love affair with Olga Ivinskaya, from whom the character of Lara is partly derived.

For *Doctor Zhivago* Pasternak avoided the oblique style of his poetry, choosing a simpler, direct prose. The novel was his masterpiece, a breathtaking vision of the "flood of events" that formed modern Russia. In a succession of fragmented, interlinked scenes Pasternak brings home the impact of revolution, famine, and civil war. At the heart of the maelstrom is Iurii Zhivago, the idealistic healer struggling to serve the common good but troubled by tyranny and tormented by illicit love. Pasternak's combination of the cosmic and the personal is masterly throughout, his Christian-based philosophy expressed by Zhivago while describing the day-to-day problems of finding potatoes or firewood in a starving land. Heroism and tragedy walk hand in hand with everyday routine, and the blend is unforgettable. The Jewish origins of Pasternak's beliefs are acknowledged by Zhivago, who reflects on the persecution of the Jews and their rejection of a Saviour they themselves produced. Pasternak saw the Jewish people as an isolated, oppressed nation who mistakenly rejected the liberating gospel of Christ, and in the sequence of "Zhivago's poems" at the end of the book, Christ and Hamlet combine to express Pasternak's own beliefs and the perils of the defiant stand he had taken. "A thousand opera-glasses level/ The dark, point-blank, at me./ Abba, Father, if it be possible/ Let this cup pass from me."

Suppressed in Russia, *Doctor Zhivago* was published abroad, and made a profound impression in the West. Pasternak was awarded the Nobel Prize, but the award sparked a political storm. Pasternak was forced to decline the prize and expelled from the Writers Union. Living in exile at Peredelkino, his health declined and he suffered several heart attacks. In his final years he worked on further translations, the poetic cycle "When the Weather Clears", and his play *The Blind Beauty*. He died of lung cancer in 1960.

A Jewish artist who rejected separation in favour of a Christ-based gospel of integrity and sacrifice, Pasternak became an icon for many Russians. Lines from "When the Weather Clears" sum up his attitude to life and art. "In everything I want to reach/ The very essence:/ In work, in seeking a way,/ In passion's turbulence . . .// "Always catching the thread/ Of actions, histories,/ To live, to think, to feel, to love,/ To make discoveries".

GEOFF SADLER

Perec, Georges

French fiction writer, dramatist, and essayist, 1936–1982

Born in Paris, 7 March 1936, to André Perec (Icek Judko Peretz), metal worker, and wife Cyrla (née Szulewicz), both Yiddish-speaking immigrants from Poland. Father, having joined French army, 1939, killed on day of French surrender to Nazi Germany, 16 June 1940; mother died in concentration camp, 1943. Adopted by father's sister; brought up in foothills of Alps and then in Paris. Studied at Collège d'Étampes, state boarding school, then Lycée Claude-Bernard and Lycée Henri IV, left school, 1954; registered for arts degree at the Sorbonne but did not complete course. Compulsory service in army, 1958–59. Married Paulette Petras, 1960. Public opinion pollster, 1959–61; research librarian in neurophysiology, Centre Nationale de la Recherche Scientifique, 1962–79. Contributed crossword puzzles to weekly magazine *Le Point*, 1976–82. Member, L'Ouvroir de Littérature Potentielle (Workshop of Potential Literature, or OuLiPo), from 1967. Awarded Prix Renaudot, 1965; Prix Médicis, 1978. Died of lung cancer, 3 March 1982.

Selected Writings

Novels

Les Choses: une histoire des années 60, 1965; as *Les Choses: A Story of the Sixties*, translated by Helen R. Lane, 1968; as *Things: A Story of the Sixties*, translated by David Bellos, 1990

Quel Petit Vélo à guidon chromé au fond de la cour?, 1966; as *Which Moped with Chrome-plated Handlebars at the Back of the Yard?*, translated by Ian Monk, 1996

Un homme qui dort, 1967; as *A Man Asleep*, translated by Andrew Leak, 1990

La Disparition, 1969; as *A Void*, translated by Gilbert Adair, 1994

Les Revenentes [Spectres], 1972

La Vie, mode d'emploi, 1978; as *Life A User's Manual*, translated by David Bellos, 1987

Un cabinet d'amateur, 1979

"53 jours", edited by Harry Mathews and Jacques Roubaud, 1989; as *"53 Days"*, translated by David Bellos, 1992

Film and Television: *Un Homme qui dort*, 1973; *Récits d'Ellis Island. Histoires d'errance et d'espoir*, 1980

Plays

L'Augmentation [The Raise], 1970

La Poche Parmentier, 1974

Théâtre (includes *L'Augmentation* . . . and *La Poche Parmentier*), 1981

Poetry

Alphabets, 1976

La Clôture et autres poèmes [The Fence and Other Poems], 1980

Ulcérations, 1986

Other

Die Maschine, 1968, translated into German by Eugen Helmle, 1972

La Boutique obscure: 124 rêves, 1973

Espèces d'espace, 1974; as *Species of Spaces and Other Pieces*, edited and translated by John Sturrock, 1997

W; ou, Le Souvenir d'enfance, 1975; as *W; or, The Memory of Childhood*, translated by David Bellos, 1988

Je me souviens [I Remember], 1978

Les Mots croisés I [Crossword Puzzles], 1979

Récits d'Ellis Island: histoires d'errance et d'espoir, with Robert Bober, 1980; as *Ellis Island*, translated by Harry Mathews, 1995

Tentative d'épuisement d'un lieu parisien, 1982

[Les] Mots croisés II [Crossword Puzzles 2], 1986

Penser/Classer, 1985

Further Reading

American Book Review (September–October 1981)

Bellos, David, "Perec in English: Perec's Titles; Secondary Sources in English", *Review of Contemporary Fiction* (Spring 1993): 135–41

Bellos, David, *Georges Perec: A Life in Words*, London: Harvill, and Boston: Godine, 1993

Bloomsbury Review (March–April 1988): 16

Burgelin, Claude, *Georges Perec*, Paris: Seuil, 1988

Cahiers Georges Perec, 1985–

L'Arc, special issue on Perec, 76 (Summer 1979)

Littératures, special issue on Perec, 7 (Spring 1983)

Magazine Littéraire, special issue on Perec, 193 (March 1983)

MLN (September 1987): 867–76

Motte, Warren F., Jr., *The Poetics of Experiment: A Study of the Work of Georges Perec*, Lexington, Kentucky: French Forum Monographs, 1984

New Republic (8 February 1988): 38–40

New York Review of Books (16 June 1988): 34–37

Oulipo, *À Georges Perec*, Paris: Bibliothèque Oulipienne, 1984

Pedersen, John, *Perec; ou, Les textes croisés*, Copenhagen: Revue Romane, 1985

Raynaud, Jean-Michel, *Pour un Perec lettré, chiffré*, Lille: Presses Universitaires de Lille, 1987

Schwartz, Paul, *Georges Perec: Traces of His Passage*, Birmingham, Alabama: Summa, 1988

Half way into *Life A User's Manual*, Perec's longest and perhaps greatest work, we meet Cinoc, who works at the dictionary-publisher Larousse: "while other compilers sought out new words and meanings, his job was to make room for them by eliminating all the words and meanings that had fallen into disuse". Cinoc is a "word-killer", who eliminates thousands of objects, people, cities, events, all of which are "swept by his hand into eternal obscurity". Yet even as his work progresses apace, in his free time Cinoc is mustering a formidable erudition to enable him to compile a "dictionary of forgotten words", thereby replacing what has been extinguished elsewhere: word-killer become word-saver.

Cinoc is just one of the hundreds of eccentrics encountered in what many consider to be *the* major postwar French novel. Yet his dual activity is emblematic of his fellow-inhabitants of the apartment building whose contents and activities the novel describes in painstaking detail, as it is of Perec's entire literary venture: murder and revival, writing as eradication, recovery, and testament to loss. It is here, more than in any explicit addressing of Jewish identity, that Perec's writing aligns itself with other major postwar European Jewish writers. As he puts it in *W; or, The Memory of Childhood* (the second pillar of the Perec canon, and one of the great books in the entire autobiographical fiction genre), speaking here of his parents and their brutal premature deaths – father killed in 1940 during the German invasion of France, mother deported, "destination Auschwitz": "I write because they left in me their indelible mark, whose trace is writing. Their memory is dead in writing; writing is the memory of their death and the assertion of my life".

Born in Paris of Jewish Polish parents, Perec (original family name Peretz) was evacuated to the Vercors in 1941 by his mother, who was due to join him there when she was captured and deported. Perhaps partly to provide extra protection, the young Georges was baptized during his stay in Villard-de-Lans. After the Liberation, he returned to Paris an orphan, and was raised principally by his aunt and uncle, who were fully assimilated into French civic life, such that the young Georges received little in the way of specifically Jewish teaching or culture. Despite visiting relatives in Israel, Perec never adopted Jewish causes or chose to stress his Jewish identity, though towards the end of his tragically short life – he died when he was only 45 – he was increasingly setting his personal tragedy and its incumbent traumas within the context of the suffering of Jewish people. As his biographer, David Bellos, puts it:

> Perec's feelings about Jewishness were awkward and contradictory . . . Jewishness was the subject that Perec tackled with the least spontaneity in his own writing until he was past the age of forty: for much of his life he was stuck with impulses of assertion and denial, which nearly cancelled each other out and left him largely silent on the issue.

However, Perec did treat themes dear to late 20th-century Jewish writers, and was foremost in finding new forms for expressing the loss and trauma suffered as a result of anti-Semitic hatred. What characterizes Perec's work is its reluctance to remain with the purely personal, and its extreme formal inventiveness in finding ways to situate tragedy, blankness, or what Maurice Blanchot has called "le désastre". In his early work, *Things: A Story of the Sixties*, the proto-yuppie couple at the centre of the novel lead lives enthralled by commodities. Yet to the specificities of their consumerist fantasies corresponds Perec's resistance to yield any inner life at all to his protagonists, or even to distinguish them by individualized personal pronouns, so they remain almost irremediably "they", representatives of an entire generation and class. In *A Man Asleep* the depressed protagonist tries to reach a state of utter passivity, yet is constantly being harangued by the pronoun with which he is designated throughout, "you"; the novel being that rare thing, a "second person" fiction.

It is in this context of the attempt to find a form for loss that Perec's engagement with the OuLiPo is best understood. This group was devoted to experiments with arbitrary rules, and literary constraints and games, which they saw as generative of new potentialities for literature. Perec, who excelled at all forms of crosswords, acrostics, and puzzles, wrote his later novel, *La Disparition* (*A Void*), without what is by far the most common letter in the French language, the letter *e*. Yet the sheer virtuosity of the feat does not cover the violence of the excisions, as well as the novel's attempt to make something meaningful, even beautiful, not despite but even because of the very violence of these elisions.

With his mentor, Raymond Queneau, Perec was surely the most versatile of recent French writers. He stated his wish to write four fairly discrete types of literary texts: "sociological", "autobiographical", "ludic", and "fictive". In *W; or, The Memory of Childhood*, written around the time of Perec's psychoanalysis, it is the autobiographical which dominates, as the author finds strategy after strategy to show how his entire past is rooted in the unnameable trauma of his childhood. The work combines memories and forgettings with an oddly truncated detective story about a man in search of a child whose name he has borrowed, which then leads into a horrifying account (combining Sade, Kafka, and Primo Levi) of an island society devoted to sport and ruled by merciless unknowable overlords. The book concludes by making explicit the connection between Perec's fantasy island and the Camps, with a quotation from David Rousset's book *L'Univers concentrationnaire*.

Even in the novel which most fully combines Perec's four types of writing, *Life A User's Manual*, loss is not only thematized but also structurally present: in the projects of Bartlebooth, Winckler, and Valène, the three presiding spirits of the building which is so minutely described; as it is in the missing room in the basement, and the missing 100th chapter. Like his other less renowned works, Perec's most dazzling achievement is founded upon the defeat of any totalizing plan or scheme, as it is in some measure devoted to a humanizing acceptance of indigence and failure.

DAN GUNN

Perelman, S.J.

US humorist, 1904–1979

Born Sidney Joseph Perelman in Brooklyn, New York, 1 February 1904. Spent childhood in Providence, Rhode Island; studied at Brown University, 1921–25. Married Laura West, sister of Nathanael West, 1929; one son and one daughter; wife died 1970. Contributed to humorous magazines *Judge* and *College Humor*; regular contributor to the *New Yorker* from 1934. Moved to London, 1970. Awards included Oscar and New York Critics Award for Best Screen Writer, 1956; Oscar, for screenplay, 1957. Died 17 October 1979.

Selected Writings

Essays and Sketches
Dawn Ginsbergh's Revenge, 1929
Strictly from Hunger, 1937
Look Who's Talking, 1940
Crazy like a Fox, 1944
Keep It Crisp, 1946
Acres and Pains, 1947
Westward Ha!, 1948
Listen to the Mocking Bird, 1949
The Swiss Family Perelman, 1950
The Ill-tempered Clavichord, 1952
Hold That Christmas Tiger!, 1954
Perelman's Home Companion, 1955
The Road to Miltown; or, Under the Spreading Atrophy, 1957
The Rising Gorge, 1961
Chicken Inspector No. 23, 1966
Baby, It's Cold Inside, 1970
Vinegar Puss, 1975
Eastwood Ha!, 1977
The Saucier's Apprentice and Other Stories, 1983
Don't Tread on Me: The Selected Letters of S. J. Perelman, edited by Prudence Crowther, 1987

Plays
One Touch of Venus, with Ogden Nash, 1943
The Beauty Part, 1963

Screenplays: *Monkey Business*, 1931; *Horsefeathers*, 1932; *Florida Special*, 1936; *Ambush*, 1938; *Sweethearts*, 1938; *Boy Trouble*, 1939; *Around the World in 80 Days*, 1956

Further Reading

Cooke, Alistair, *The American in England: Emerson to S. J. Perelman*, Cambridge and New York: Cambridge University Press, 1975
Fowler, Douglas, *S. J. Perelman*, Boston: Twayne, 1983
Gale, Steven H., *S. J. Perelman: An Annotated Bibliography*, New York: Garland, 1985
Gale, Steven H., *S. J. Perelman: A Critical Study*, New York: Greenwood Press, 1987
Gale, Steven H. (editor), *S. J. Perelman: Critical Essays*, New York: Garland, 1992
Herrman, Dorothy, *S .J. Perelman: A Life*, New York: Putnam, 1986
Lister, Eric, *Don't Mention the Marx Brothers: Reminiscences of S. J. Perelman*, Lewes, Sussex: Book Guild, 1985
Wilk, Max, *And Did You Once See Sidney Plain? A Random Memoir of S.J. Perelman*, New York: Norton, 1986

S.J. Perelman, forever associated in the public mind with the Marx Brothers, in fact worked on only two of their films, *Monkey Business* and *Horsefeathers*. The irony is that he and the Brothers did not get on and he declared that nothing would ever impel him to work for them again. It is the close relationship between Groucho's rhythms and some aspects of Perelman's prose, their common acerbity in interviews, and a certain physical resemblance which all contribute to this confusion. But confusion it is, and does Perelman less than justice.

The author of one novel, 560 short prose pieces (most of which appeared in the *New Yorker* and were subsequently published in 23 collections), eight plays, 11 film scripts and at least four television plays, was manifestly more than a scriptwriter for the Marx Brothers. Moreover, as a prose stylist he was admired by, among others, such luminaries as Dorothy Parker, Harold Pinter, T.S. Eliot, John Updike, and Kurt Vonnegut. As a humorist he was envied by Robert Benchley and is the admitted model for Woody Allen.

Although he found his early film writing experiences distasteful and forever after vilified Hollywood, he continued working there, presumably for the money, and collected an Oscar for his script for *Around the World in Eighty Days*. He even contributed to a Nelson Eddy piece of nonsense, *Sweethearts*. These adventures did, nonetheless, furnish him with material which he mined consistently for his prose pieces, and it was from working on *Monkey Business* that he emerged with his distinctive voice.

Perelman combined an encyclopedic mind, a deep love and appreciation of the Western literary canon and an objective eye with a profoundly rational temperament. These elements coalesced into one of the most distinctive literary styles of 20th-century America. It is at its most recognizable in the short prose pieces for which he is best remembered. In a 1981 essay Tom Wolfe elucidated eight devices of the Perelman style:

i) Parodying the grandiloquence of late 19th-century prose,
ii) Puncturing slang,
iii) Subverting cliché,
iv) Employing ironically elegant foreign words,
v) Using distinctive puns ("My choler wilted"),
vi) Extending similes ("Like walking through a room full of absorbent cotton"),
vii) Employing micro-metonymy ("Humma listened to the veins throbbing in my head"), and
viii) Extrapolating cliché into a metaphor.

To this list he might have added the imaginative use of Yiddish, a Jonsonian or Dickensian genius for granting characters names which illuminated their personality (Dudley Nightshade, Louella Grope, Downey Couch, Clay Modelling, Olaf Hasholem) and an equal way with titles (*Nothing but the Tooth, To Sleep, Perchance to Steam, Swing Out, Sweet Chariot*).

On the other hand Perelman himself was dubious about academic approaches to the analysis of humour. In a *Paris Review* interview of 1963 he said:

> Humour is purely a point of view, and only the pedants try to classify it. For me its chief merit is the use of the unexpected, the glancing allusion, the deflation of pomposity, and the constant repetition of one's helplessness in a majority of situations.

Despite the fact that after his wife's death he did live for a couple of years in London, Perelman is essentially American, and one necessary attribute to appreciating his work is a deep knowledge of the American scene (specifically that of New York and Hollywood) in the period of the late 1920s to the 1960s. Another necessary ingredient is a high level of cultural, and specifically, literary understanding.

Perelman's art is not deep, but neither is it superficial. With consummate reason he attacks, through ridicule, the debasement of language, political paranoia, the superficiality of a world dominated by commercialism and advertising, the values of Hollywood, and so on. But he does not seem to be concerned to advocate remedies or change. His social satire restricts itself to relatively trivial targets. Although he wrote some extended pieces (including one novel), he is at his best and most typical in the short prose piece of around 2000 words. The relentless word play on which he mainly relies can become tiresome in longer versions.

He had some success as a dramatist, but his short prose pieces are his main and most distinctive work. The extent to which his Jewishness contributed to their uniqueness is debatable. Certainly he used Yiddish to great effect. But this is at one with his general love of language. He commented on Yiddish words, "I like them for their invective content. There are nineteen words in Yiddish which convey gradations of disparagement from a mild, fluttering helplessness to a state of downright, irreconcilable brutishness." He also, in common with other Jewish-American writers, develops the absurdities of his world to outlandish comic proportions. This is often seen as a typically Jewish response to unbearable realities. But Perelman's targets are rarely the serious issues towards which other literate Jews, his brother-in-law Nathanael West, for instance, aimed their shafts. Unlike many of his coevals he was not brought up on the Lower East Side but in the relative prosperity of Providence, Rhode Island, and it is stretching a point, as some critics have, to see in one who considered the Circe episode of Joyce's *Ulysses* the greatest comic writing in English, a love of words and word play based on his Jewish background.

There is little doubt that today much of Perelman seems dated. His humour is anchored in language, not in character, and language changes. The world too has changed since Perelman's time, and much of today's reality exceeds in absurdity his most extreme images. A different type of comic writer has emerged with a darker vision. Nonetheless his influence is pervasive and he will always give some delight to those who consider language among their paramount concerns.

GERALD DE GROOT

Perets, Yitskhok-Leyb

Polish poet, short-story writer, dramatist, and editor, 1851–1915

Born in Zamość into a well connected strictly mitnagdic family, 25 May 1851. Privately tutored in Hebrew grammar, German, and Russian. Read voraciously from a library of Polish and German books, but had no systematic secular education. Began to write at age 14. Arranged marriage, 1869. Moved to Warsaw where he met and was influenced by R.A. Braudes, 1875. Divorced, 1876. Returned to Zamość. Passed law exams, 1877; practised for 10 years. Married, second, Helena Ringelheim, 1878. Published Hebrew verse with former father-in-law, 1877. Wrote in Polish, 1870–78; after 1881 pogroms, attitude towards Yiddish and Hebrew became more positive. Visited Warsaw, 1886; renewed contacts with Jewish literary circles. Lost right to practise law as the result of a false accusation, 1888. Moved to Warsaw; became official of the Jewish Communal Bureau. Made literary début in Yiddish with "Monish" in *Di yidishe folks-bibliotek*, 1888. Joined statistical survey, financed by Jan Bloch, 1890; visited villages and *shtetlekh* in Tomaszów province. Results not published; raw material for his writing. Permanent official in charge of burial sites of Warsaw's Jewish community, 1891–1915. Edited influential *Di yidishe bibliotek*, 1891–95. *Yontev bletlekh* appeared, 1894–96. Attended illegal socialist meeting, imprisoned for three months, 1899. Died of a heart attack, 3 April 1915; funeral procession followed by thousands.

Selected Writings

Collections

Ale verk, 18 vols, edited by Shmuel Niger, 1944; partially reproduced as: *Ale verk*, 8 vols, 1947–48

Kol kitḇei y.l. perets: ha'iḇrim vehameturgamim meyidiš, 10 vols, 1948–60

Other

Ha'ugaḇ: širei 'ahaḇah [The Harp: Love Poems], 1894

Bay nakht oyfn altn mark [Night on the Old Market], 1907

Khsidish [Hasidic Tales], 1908

Folkstimlekhe geshikhtn [Popular National Stories], 1908

Y.l. perets: briv un redes [Correspondence and Speeches], edited by N. Mayzl, 1929

Y.l. perets in 20stn yorhundert, lider, dertseylungen, eseyen, edited by Shmuel Rozhanski, 1962

Peretses yiesh-vizye: interpretatsye fun y.l. peretses "bay nakht oyfn altn mark" un kritishe oysgabe fun der drame, edited by Khone Shmeruk, 1971

Translations

Bontshe the Silent, translated by A.S. Rappoport, 1927; reprinted 1971

Peretz, bilingual edition, edited and translated by Solomon Liptzin, 1947

As Once We Were: Selections From the Works of I.L. Peretz, translated by Elly T. Margolis, 1951

The Book of Fire: Stories by I.L. Peretz, translated by Joseph Leftwich, 1959

My Memoirs, translated by Fred Goldberg, 1964

Selected Stories, edited by Irving Howe and Eliezer Greenberg, 1974
The I. L. Peretz Reader, edited with an introduction by Ruth R. Wisse, 1990
Geklibene dertseylungen/Selected Stories, bilingual edition, edited by Eli Katz, 1991
Selected Works of Isaac Leib Peretz, edited by Marvin S. Zuckerman and Marion Herbst, 1996

Further Reading

Frieden, Ken, *Classic Yiddish Fiction Abramovitsh, Sholem Aleichem, and Peretz*, Albany, New York: SUNY Press, 1995
Madison, Charles A., *Yiddish Literature: Its Scope and Major Writers*, New York: Ungar, 1968
Mayzl, Nakhmen, *Yitskhok-leybush perets un zayn dor shrayber*, New York: IKUF, 1951
Niger, Shmuel, *Y.l. perets, zayn lebn, zayn firndike perzenlekhkayt, zayne hebreishe un yidishe shriftn, zayn virkung*, Buenos Aires: Alveltlekher Opteyl fun Kultur-Kongres, 1952
Roskies, D.G., "The Conjuror: I.L. Peretz", in D.G. Roskies, *A Bridge of Longing: The Lost Art of Yiddish Storytelling*, Cambridge, Massachusetts: Harvard University Press, 1995
Samuel, Maurice, *Prince of the Ghetto*, Philadelphia: Jewish Publishing Society of America, 1948
Weinreich, Uriel, "Guide to English Translations of Yitskhok Leybush Peretz", *The Field of Yiddish*, New York: Linguistic Circle of New York, 1954
Wisse, Ruth R., *I.L. Peretz and the Making of Modern Jewish Culture*, Seattle: University of Washington Press, 1991

Together with Mendele Moykher-Sforim and Sholem Aleykhem, Yitskhok-Leyb Perets (Isaac Leib Peretz) was one of three major classical writers in Yiddish literature. Perets was the most influential of all Yiddish writers, dominating the Jewish literary and intellectual scene. His house in Warsaw became the focal point for the younger generation of Yiddish writers on whom he had a profound influence. Perets is justly remembered for the encouragement that he gave to Pinski, Bergelson, Reyzn, Der Nister, and many others. During the 1870s Perets believed that education, technology, and productive labour would lead to autonomous cultural identity and an atmosphere of reciprocal respect between the communities living side by side on Polish soil. However, in common with An-ski and other Jewish intellectual figures of this period, his attitudes became less maskilic and more nationalist following the pogroms of 1881 and he took an increasingly favourable attitude towards writing in Yiddish.

While steeped in the traditions of the past, he was also the first truly modern Yiddish writer in the sense that he was sensitive to the disintegrative pressures of his times and developed a truly individual voice. The more he distanced himself from Jewish religious observance, the more he emphasized the development of national consciousness through a strengthened Jewish culture. In 1888 he contributed a major mock-epic poem to Sholem Aleykhem's *Di yidishe folks-bibliotek* entitled "Monish". With its deliberate ambiguity of narrative perspective this was the first verse novel in Yiddish literature. Monish is a Talmud student so gifted that his learning represents a threat to the power of Satan. He is tempted by the love of Maria, swears blasphemous oaths and is carried away to Gehenna by triumphant demons. The style of Itsik Manger is adumbrated by the humorously anachronistic description of the feasting in hell. The irony underlying the work is the disparity between the damnation of Monish, the naive yeshive-bokher (rabbinical academy students), and the survival of the narrator whose deviations from tradition are by implication much more far-reaching. This work also broke new ground by drawing attention to deficiencies in the ability of Yiddish to capture nuances of individual feeling while at the same time attempting to transcend these limitations. Between 1891 and 1895, Perets edited *Di yidishe bibliotek*, a publication which lacked the literary lightness of touch of *Di yidishe folks-bibliotek*, but for all its ponderousness was more influential. In the introduction to "Bildung", Perets calls for a literature in Yiddish, the language of the people, while advocating the study of Hebrew and Polish. *Di yidishe bibliotek* gradually became the focal point of contemporary Yiddish literature with Perets as its leader. The second volume (1892) included his own "Bilder fun a provints-rayze in tomashover povyat in yor 1890" which reflects the experiences of the statistical survey. We find graphic and unsentimental descriptions of the poverty endured by the Jewish inhabitants of the *shtetlekh* and of the petty crime to which they may be driven by their circumstances; yet the narrator's bona fides is called in question by a succession of vividly drawn figures. He realizes that he cannot hope to fathom the Jewish condition using the methodology of the social sciences alone. This readiness to question the premises of his own rationalism sets him aside from earlier maskilic optimists. The statistician covertly sympathizes with the poverty-stricken Jews whose wary answers frustrate his work. The scepticism of the informants vis-à-vis the urban intellectual are shown to be well-founded. Disillusionment with the power of reason to right social evils revived his appreciation of traditional culture. Perets's impoverished Hasidim have much greater moral stature than the familiar maskilic caricature would have us believe.

A popular brochure *Ver es vil nisht, shtarbt nisht oyf kholyere* [One does not need to die of cholera if one does not wish to], 1892, represents an attempt to rationalize the laws of ritual cleanliness as principals of hygiene and typifies Perets's work as a disseminator of contemporary scientific thinking. In 1894 Perets published in *Literatur un lebn* what was to become perhaps his best-known work, a story entitled "Bontshe shvayg" (*Bontshe the Silent*). The story is that of a long-suffering simple Jew who can only think of a buttered roll when invited by the celestial court to chose his reward for a lifetime of self-abnegation and was intended to satirize the passivity of the Jewish worker. However, the loving depiction of the central character tends to subvert the underlying moral. Typical of this misconception was the reaction of Zangwill who wrote that the story exemplified Jewish and Christian ideals of humility. After the renaissance of Hebrew letters towards the turn of the century, Perets resumed writing in Hebrew in 1894. Inter alia he published

Ha'ugab: širei 'ahabah [The Harp: Love Poems], a slim volume of Hebrew verse in the style of Heine. In 1904 he contributed to *Hašiloah* his Hebrew drama *Ḥurban bet ẓadiq* [The Destruction of the Rebe's Court], which in 1907 he reworked in Yiddish as *Di goldene keyt* [The Golden Chain]. The dwindling of the Rebe's spiritual power anticipates Anski's handling of the same theme in *Der dibek*. The image of the golden chain came to epitomize the continuity of essential Jewish values across the centuries. As the years went by Perets became increasingly attracted by neo-romantic and symbolist currents in Western literature and especially to the use of folklore. Under this influence he gave new expressive force to the Yiddish language in numerous stories such as his celebrated "Oyb nisht nokh hekher" [If Not Higher] which concerns a sceptic who sets out to investigate the belief that the rabbi of Nemirov ascends to heaven between Rosh Hashanah and Yom Kippur. In fact the rabbi disguises himself as a woodcutter in order to perform anonymous acts of charity. The sceptic becomes the rabbi's disciple and whenever anyone speaks of the rabbi's "ascent" he adds under his breath "if not higher", thus attributing higher value to earthly goodness than to traditional piety. Such secular revaluations of traditional material were typical of the stories collected as *Khsidish* [Hasidic Tales] and *Folkstimlekhe geshikhtn* [Popular National Stories] (both 1908) in which Hasidic material is viewed from the standpoint of a secular literary intellect.

Once seen as a radical, Perets became increasingly anxious about the revolutionary aims of the left. With extraordinary prescience he gave expression to these fears in an address to Jewish socialists published in *Der veg* [The Way] in 1906 as "Hofenung un shrek" [Hope and Alarm] and voiced his apprehension lest the forces of reform stifle rather than promote individual liberty. He was also worried by the rigidities and intolerance concerning literary questions among the younger generation. Although attracted by aspects of socialism he was nonetheless appalled by simplistic egalitarianism and class politics and left-wing radicals came to see him as a traitor to their cause. Among Perets's dramatic works special mention should be made of *Bay nakht oyfn altn mark* [Night on the Old Market] (1907), a verse-drama and dream-play encompassing a wide spectrum of Polish Jewish culture in which the living and the dead, material reality, and the life of the spirit are conflated in a manner betraying the influence of the symbolist dramas of Stanislaus Wyspiański. In August 1908 Perets was Deputy-Chairman of the Czernowitz Yiddish Language Conference. Despite his own inconsistency and doubts, he dominated the conference and used his influence to ensure that Yiddish was declared *a* national language of the Jewish people rather than *the* national language. He was saddened that Yiddish, which he had regarded as a unifying force, should now have become a cause of internal conflict. He continued to stress the cultural values of the folk in a multilingual environment and to look optimistically for a decline in the importance of the nation-state at a time when these views were being confounded by events. In 1914 Perets, like An-ski, was caring for Jewish refugees in Warsaw who had been expelled from their *shtetlekh* by the czarist government. On the eve of his death he was writing poems for children. With unintentional irony one of his last poems expressed the idea that political adversity might serve to strengthen the Jews. History has cruelly disappointed Perets's noble aspirations, but it would be difficult to overestimate the powerful cultural impact that he exerted upon his era.

HUGH DENMAN

Perry, Lily

Israeli fiction writer, 1953–

Born in Hadera, 1953. Studied philosophy, Jewish philosophy, and Hebrew literature, Tel Aviv University. Has contributed articles on famous women in history to several Hebrew newspapers; editor of textbooks for Open University, Tel Aviv, since 1988; also editor, Yediot Aharonot Publications.

Selected Writings

Novels
Eynayim yehefot [Bare Eyes], 1974
Golem bemaagal [Golem in the Circle], 1986
Rikud al hamayim [Dancing on the Water], 1994
Bikur hatalyan [The Executioner's Visit], 1999

Further Reading

Yudkin, Leon, *Public Crisis and Literary Response: The Adjustment of Modern Jewish Literature*, Paris: Suger, 2001

Lily Perry began her novel writing at an early age, publishing her first novel, *Eynayim yehefot* [Bare Eyes], in 1974. Her work presents personal life from the vantage point of a 24-year-old woman engaged in the search for significance and satisfaction. She is angry at a God who, instead of working for the good of what is supposedly His people, allows them to suffer. Since He is, by definition, omnipotent, He apparently must even will this situation. He seems to take delight in this arbitrary and even sadistic exercise of absolute power, and our heroine enters a plea that her special lover should be spared in what is now a very tense military situation. The story is situated in the immediate wake of the 1973 Yom Kippur war, and so has a very specific and localized colour. It is told in colloquial Hebrew, and the monologue is humorous as well as painful. What she demands is her apparently natural entitlement to a peaceful life, with her own man, in a world without the war that others have brought about. The monologue is an ongoing protest, a protest at the dreadful fighting that has interrupted the purest love and the unique experience that the two of them have created for each other. Then, the inevitable occurs, and Danny's tank is hit by a rocket. She goes to the Syrian front, confronting ultimate horror constantly. Even her driver is shot to pieces while she is in the vehicle. The writing takes the form of a retreat from the great arena of constant conflict, deprivation, unnecessary suffering, injury, and death. She addresses two people in the book, herself and her lover, so it takes the form of letters (unsent of course), and reflections on life and death.

She is apparently a rampant individualist, who despises imposed frameworks, and asserts her own values and being as one who embraces peace and love. But when Danny goes missing from the front, she finds it hard to know how to react within the uncertain space between life and death. When she finally ascertains that he was indeed killed, she falls into a catatonic despair. She can find no point in anything, and sees herself as death itself; in her own words, she is a "grave". In order to recover, she urges herself to get a life, and begins to see her own writing as therapy. Finally, after the departure of Danny's friend Doron, who had been boarding with her, she becomes reconciled to the residual presence of Danny.

The novel *Golem bemaagal* [Golem in the Circle] is for some reason generally accounted in the bibliographies to be Perry's first. Like *Eynayim yehefot*, it is also a monologue, transmitted by Miki Stav, a loner, seeking her way through to love and significance. She deploys the image of a cat, an animal whose attachments are unpredictable as well as maybe fickle, to illustrate her own relationship to others. These others, whom she had so loved, are like cats, attractive but unreliable. It is here that a connection is established between the current reality of Israel, through the person of the narrator, and the catastrophe of European Jewry. The narrative is conveyed from the point of view of one whose contact with the external world is very fragile.

Perry's following work, *Rikud al hamayim* [Dancing on the Water], was written some 20 years after her first. It adopts an unusual but striking theme. This is a first-person account of one Leni Avni, a relatively young woman who recalls that some eight years earlier, in 1976, she had abandoned her home, following the death of her daughter, Ruthie, at the age of six and a half (she had been born with a defective right lung). Now, at the age of 37, she enters an old age home, ostensibly as a house mother, but, subliminally, in order to do nothing other than await a quiet and orderly death. This decision, following estrangement from her already distant husband, Alex, is a turning back on life as well as on her son, Michael, then 17 years old. Retirement to a home in Netanya, by the sea, represents a statement of acceptance of death. This use of the sea image is frequently associated with death; the novel poses the question of whether such a retreat can be accepted.

The narrative takes place on different time scales. One level is the present, Leni's final stretch at the institution. Another is the history of her marriage, her family, her relations with her tempestuous, ideologically Marxist husband, and, more painfully than anything else, with little Ruthie. A recurrent theme in the novel is the impulse towards death, a death that would take her away stealthily, inconspicuously, and painlessly. To that end she seeks relief through her affair with her ex-dancing teacher, Moshe Kushnir, mentor and lover, whose wife owned the institution. We should not forget that Leni had been a fine dancer in her youth, a fact that is both reflected in the title of the novel, and in the memories of her associates. This is not the only irony in the story of an institution that can only achieve financial success through failure, that is, by the demise of those who fill it.

In her next novel, *Bikur hatalyan* [The Executioner's Visit], the author again visits the margin between history, the external event, and personal crisis. The family conflict is treated as though it is a subject for a significant public chronicle, with necessary recourse to the most relevant sources. The primary source in this case is the telephone, and the evidence of auditors to conversations conducted in this medium, whether they be immediately involved, or random neighbours who happen to be within earshot. Perry deploys the traditional terminology of Jewish historiography, such as "prophets", "elders", "kings", and, as the principal motif, "the destruction of the house" (the Hebrew word for house also means temple). This is her now familiar technique of monologue, whose aim here is the clarification and explication of family history. The narrator is a young member of the Halevi family, Daniel, much affected by the family saga, although he tries to keep its significance in proportion. As in her earlier work, the narrative voice creates a gap between the characters and their parents by a process of distancing nomenclature. The father in the novel is referred as the "head of the family", for example, and he speaks also of the father's wife, i.e. Daniel's mother, as the "mother of his offspring", although what is described is an atmosphere of conflict and distress bordering on abuse. The narrator himself is a witness from early childhood, the principal witness to a situation where the adults deteriorate constantly and rapidly, and require assistance and support more than the children. The novel follows a recent trend in Israeli fiction in its attempt at resurrecting recent family history; the recording of the events, by any means available. (In the novel *My First Sony* by Benny Barbash the medium of representation is the Sony recorder.) The means involved act as a corrective and support to the frailties of human memory. And the novel itself, the produced work, is the monument to that past, so active in the present.

Perry's novels are studies in human suffering, with a specifically feminine take on lived reality, and related not only realistically, but also through a network of metaphors. The narratives are concerned with the personal issues of women, not specifically located in the political or social reality of Israel, but rather those of fears, phobias, and aspirations of the individual. We find loneliness, desolation, pain, and withdrawal from life. The condition can border on insanity, as it is so remote from the perceived world of others. But there is also an eventual acceptance of the changed and still changing reality. The fictions, so close to the bone, constitute studies, in varying modes, of emotional deadness and turmoil.

LEON I. YUDKIN

Perutz, Leo

Czech-Austrian fiction writer, 1882–1957

Born in Prague, 2 November 1882, into assimilated family. Father's textile plant burned down, 1899; moved with family to Vienna, 1901. Studied at Erzherzog Rainer-Real Gymnasium, Vienna; formed literary club, Freilicht, with friends; after cheating in mathematics test, expelled from school and rendered unable to enter university, 1902. Began voluntary military service, but discharged as incapable of bearing arms, 1902. Studied actuarial theory, applied economics, and probability theory; became insurance actuary; developed widely used Perutz equalization formula; actuary, Assicuranzioni Generali, Trieste, 1907–08, and Der Anker life insurance company, Vienna, 1908–23. Joined Austro-Hungarian army, 1915; shot in lung at Burkanow, 1916; censor and decoder, war press headquarters, Vienna; military correspondent, Ukraine and Romania, to 1918. Married, first, Ida Weil, 1918; she died in childbirth, 1928; three children; after attempting contact with her through medium, had affairs with rich young women; married, second, Grete Humburger, 1935. Emigrated to Palestine, 1938. Refused to join literary groups or contribute to literary magazines. Maintained summer residence in St Wolfgang on Wolfgangssee, Austria, after World War II. Died, after heart attack, at Bad Ischl, 25 August 1957.

Selected Writings

Novels

Die dritte Kugel [The Third Bullet], 1915

Zwischen neun und neun, 1918; as *From Nine to Nine*, translated by Lily Lore, 1926

Der Marques de Bolibar, 1920; as *The Marquis de Bolibar*, translated by Graham Rawson, 1926

Der Meister des jüngsten Tages, 1923; as *The Master of the Day of Judgement*, translated by Hedwig Singer, 1929; new translation by Eric Mosbacher, 1994

Turlupin, 1924; as *Turlupin*, translated by John Brownjohn, 1996

Der Kosak and die Nachtigall [The Cossack and the Nightingale], with Paul Frank, 1927

Wohim Rollst du Äpfelchen, 1928; as *Where Will You Fall?*, translated by Hedwig Singer, 1930

Flammen auf San Domingo: Roman nach Victor Hugo's Bug-Jargal [Flames on San Domingo: A Novel after Victor Hugo's *Bug-Jargal*], 1929

St Petri-Schnee, 1933; as *The Virgin's Brand*, translated by E.B.G. Stamper and E.M. Hodgson, 1934; as *St Peter's Snow*, translated by Eric Mosbacher, 1990

Der schwedische Reiter, 1936; as *The Swedish Cavalier*, translated by John Brownjohn, 1992

Nachts unter der steinernen Brücke: ein Roman aus dem alten Prague, 1953; as *By Night under the Stone Bridge: A Novel of Old Prague*, translated by Eric Mosbacher, 1989

Der Judas des Leonardo, 1959; as *Leonardo's Judas*, translated by Eric Mosbacher, 1989

Short Stories and Novellas

Das Mangobaumwunder: eine unglaubwürdige Geschichte [The Mango Tree Wonder: An Implausible Story], with Paul Frank, 1916

Das Gasthaus zur Kartätsche: eine Geschichte aus dem alten Österreich [The Inn of the Grapeshot: A Story of Old Austria], 1920

Die Geburt des Antichrist [The Birth of the Antichrist], 1921

Herr, Erbarme dich Meiner! [Lord, Have Mercy on Me!], 1930

Plays

Die Reise nach Pressburg [The Journey to Pressburg], 1930

Morgen ist Feiertag [Tomorrow is a Holiday], 1936

Other

Editor and translator, with Oswald Levett, *Das Jahr der Guillotine* [The Year of the Guillotine], 1925

Mainacht in Wien: Romanfragmente; Klein Erzahlprosa; Feuilletons; aus dem Nachlass Leo Perutz [May Night in Vienna: Novel Fragments, Short Stories; Essays; from the Unpublished Work of Leo Perutz], 1996

Further Reading

Adler, Jeremy, "Voices in a Metaphysical Madhouse", *Times Literary Supplement* (7–13 October 1988)

Engel, Peter and Hans-Harald Müller (editors), Perutz issue, *Modern Austrian Literature*, 21/1 (1988)

F.T., "Leo Perutz (1882–1957), ein Romancier aus Österreich" [Leo Perutz (1882–1957), a Novelist from Austria], *Forum*, 4 (1957)

Luth, Reinhard, *Drommetenrot und azurblau: Studien zur Affinität von Erzähltechnik und Phantastik in Romanen von Leo Perutz und Alexander Lernet-Holenia*, Meitingen: Corian, 1988

Mandelartz, Michael, *Poetik und Historik: christliche und jüdische Geschichtstheologie in den historischen Romanen von Leo Perutz*, Tübingen: Niemeyer, 1992

Müller, Hans-Harald and Wilhelm Schernus, *Leo Perutz: eine Bibliographie*, Frankfurt and New York: Lang, 1991

Müller, Hans-Harald, *Leo Perutz*, Munich: Beck, 1992

Neuhaus, Dietrich, *Erinnerung und Schrecken: die Einheit von Geschichte, Phantastik und Mathematik im Werk Leo Perutz*, Frankfurt: Lang, 1984

Panter, Peter (Kurt Tucholsky), "Die Geburt des Antichrist", *Die Weltbühne*, 18/2 (1922)

Serke, Jürgen, *Böhmische Dörfer: Wanderungen durch eine verlassene literarische Landschaft*, Vienna: Zsolnay, 1987

Terrile, Cristiana, *La Crise de la volonté ou le romanesque en question Borgese, Green, Perutz, Pirandello, Kafka*, Paris: Champion, 1997

Torberg, Friedrich, "Wenn der Boden schwankt", *Die Welt* (3 April 1975)

Tschertkow, Leonid, "Gustav Meyrink und Leo Perutz in Russland", *Literatur und Kritik*, 10 (1975)

Ueding, Gert, "Triebkraft ist die Furcht: Gelegenheit, den Romancier Leo Perutz wiederzuentdecken", *Frankfurter Allgemeine Zeitung* (24 May 1975)

Weinzierl, Ulrich, "Frohnatur und manche Leiche: *Die Dritte Kugel* von Leo Perutz", *Frankfurter Allgemeine Zeitung* (7 November 1978)

Although Perutz came from Prague, he had no direct contact at that time with the "Prague Circle", which developed around Max Brod and Franz Kafka. His literary talent blossomed in Vienna after the turn of the century; from 1901 to 1904 in the "Freilicht" society, a group of assimilated Jews, he met writers who would later become important figures: Ernst Weiss, Bertolt Viertel, Richard A. Bermann. He was particularly fascinated by E.T.A. Hoffmann and his imaginative and romantic view of the world, but took care to imitate these elements less in his style than in the construction of his works. Stylistically, he was influenced instead by the more reserved Arthur Schnitzler, although he rejected Schnitzler's psychological representation. Perutz was a difficult personality and rejected the habitual literary cliquishness of Vienna. Nevertheless, in the 1920s he became a successful writer, with the newspapers fighting for the rights to serialize his works before publication. In 1938, after the Nazi invasion of Austria, friends shielded him from arrest but he was legally obliged to emigrate. Ignoring the advice of his friends, in Palestine he did nothing to adjust his literary activities to the new circumstances: "So I am, as far as my work is concerned, a foreign body in this country and shall remain so." After 1945 he was no longer able to re-create his past successes.

In contrast to his brother Hans, who became a passionate Zionist, Leo Perutz could not bring himself to accept either Zionism or the "Jewish Renaissance". As a writer he lived in the past; his works were "historical novels", behind which the author disappeared as a person. There was "no room for intellectual meditations and personal confessions" (Shalom Ben-Chorin). Nevertheless, many of his novels can be read as a sharp criticism of Europe's Christian and rationalist traditions, for example his very first novel *Die dritte Kugel* [The Third Bullet], which picked out Cortez's destruction of the Aztec kingdom as its central theme. Even in this early novel, the realms of reality and imagination become blurred in fairy-tale form: the devil appears and changes the outcome of a game of dice, which was already lost, by splitting the dice in an unforeseeable and unpredictable event – Perutz's "daily bread" corresponded fully to his interest not in penetrating the complexity of fate and necessity but rather in portraying it as impenetrable. The predictable necessity in everyday life appears as fate, simple fate as the necessity of a reality concealed behind the everyday, which regularly shows itself to be cryptic and diabolical in a non-theological sense. Perutz never alluded to self-interpretation; his frequent prologues and epilogues in the novels, which appear as such, serve the sole purpose of rendering the levels of realities ever more complex. The hero of the story is struck down by a bullet before he can fire the "third bullet", which it was foretold would hit him. All the details of this are narrated by a man who also appears to be the hero. Nowhere in the novels is the suspension between the levels of reality resolved; it frequently remains impossible to decide whether the story was a dream or a deluded fantasy or not, and it often remains unclear whether a person is himself or merely a "returner", a type of reincarnation of historical figures.

Like Kafka, with whom he had much in common, Perutz did not have an optimistic image of man, and with all due caution, a passage from *Der Meister des jüngsten Tages* (*The Master of the Day of Judgement*) can serve as a statement of self: "We are all images which have failed the mighty will of the Creator. We carry a terrible enemy within us and do not realize it. He does not arouse himself; he sleeps, he lies as if dead. Woe if he should come to life!" It is never stated clearly but the main figures in his novels are often broken figures, who have made themselves guilty of a wrong by wanting to intervene with specific targets in history but achieving the opposite. In *Der Meister des jüngsten Tages* a character wishes to achieve liberation using a drug but meets instead with death, like all those who seek to explain his mysterious death. In his *Aesthetic Theory* Theodor W. Adorno called this novel a "thriller of genius". Jürgen Serke used a quotation from Gershom Sholem to explain the Perutzian view of the world: "Sin, the offence of the Divine Will by man, is what brings anger to life and diverts every spark of holiness, which actually belongs elsewhere, to the wrong side." There is no doubt that an atmosphere of Kabbalistic intrigue pervades the novels, but Perutz would scarcely have subscribed to the Kabbalists' view that this world as a whole is the "wrong one" and the other world is the "right one". It was not the debasement of history by the other world he portrayed but the reciprocal questioning, the "perhaps, but perhaps not". Serke also quotes Perutz: "What are we fighting for? What are we bleeding for? For the love of God? We are all blind moles on the earth and know not what is the true Will of God." Perutz saw the chasms of being less in world affairs than in man: "What do we know then one of another? Each of us carries his Last Judgment within him."

There are two reasons for the powerful impact of Perutz's novels. On the one hand, they are plot oriented; almost like films, often with short scenes which do not follow a narrative but reveal new aspects with "counter-cuts": events are evaluated quite differently by different persons, and later these persons too are portrayed in a new and transforming light. The action is frequently driven forward by dialogue. It is not by chance that Hollywood was quick to buy up the film rights to the novel *Zwischen neun und neun* (*From Nine to Nine*) – although the film was never made – and in 1925 the famous director F.W. Murnau enquired whether Perutz could write a screenplay for him. In the 1930s Perutz was involved in minor film projects for financial reasons. The second reason for his impact is the artistic and complex construction of his novels. There are often frame stories, giving a pretence of security that, ultimately, is destroyed because a logical resolution to the contradictions contained in the events proves impossible. Friedrich Torberg was right when he called Leo Perutz "the result of an indiscretion between Agatha Christie with Franz Kafka".

After his major successes, of which mention should also be made here of *Der Marques de Bolibar* (1920; *The Marquis de Bolibar*) and *Der schwedische Reiter* (1936; *The Swedish Cavalier*), it was not until 1953 that Perutz published the novel which is now considered his best, *Nachts unter der steinernen Brücke* (*By Night under the Stone Bridge*). His old publisher Paul Zsolnay did not want to publish the manuscript, which Perutz had begun no later than 1938, because it was "too Jewish". This cycle of 14 stories, woven around medieval legendary Prague in the time of Emperor Rudolf II, incorporates old Jewish Sippurim legends. The old Jewish quarter in Prague, which he had known, comes to life here with the great Rabbi Löw at its heart. This book is rightly considered one of the best Prague novels. Hilde Spiel wrote: "This is a rich and beautiful book, the tone of which is reminiscent of the fairy tales of the Brothers Grimm both in its simplicity and in its sweetness – the book of a storyteller in the truest, oldest sense."

MANFRED VOIGTS
translated by Karen Goulding

Piercy, Marge

US poet and fiction writer, 1936–

Born in Detroit, Michigan, 31 March 1936. Studied at University of Michigan, BA 1957; Northwestern University, MA 1958. Married, third, Ira Wood, 1982. Instructor, Indiana University, Gary, 1960–62; poet in residence, University of Kansas, Lawrence, 1971; visiting lecturer, Thomas Jefferson College, Grand Valley State Colleges, Allendale, Michigan, 1975; visiting faculty, Women Writers' Conference, Cazenovia College, New York, 1976, 1978, 1980; staff member, Fine Arts Work Centre, Provincetown, Massachusetts, 1976–77; writer in residence, College of the Holy Cross, Worcester, Massachusetts, 1976; Butler Professor of Letters, State University of New York, Buffalo, 1977; Elliston Professor of Poetry, University of Cincinnati, 1986; DeRoy Distinguished Visiting Professor, University of Michigan, 1992. Member, advisory board, HILAI, Israeli Centre for the Arts, 1989–95; editor, Leapfrog Press, since 1997. Many awards, including Borestone Mountain Award, 1968, 1974; National Endowment for the Arts grant, 1978; Carolyn Kizer Prize, 1986, 1990; Shaeffer–Eaton PEN New England Award, 1989; Shalom Centre Brit Ha-Dorot Award, 1992; Arthur C. Clarke Award (for best science fiction novel published in UK), 1993; Paterson Poetry Prize (for *The Art of Blessing the Day*), 2000.

Selected Writings

Poetry
Breaking Camp, 1968
Hard Loving, 1969
A Work of Artifice, 1970
4-Telling, with others, 1971
To Be of Use, 1973
Living in the Open, 1976
The Twelve-Spoked Wheel Flashing, 1978
The Moon is Always Female, 1980
Circles on the Water: Selected Poems, 1982
Stone, Paper, Knife, 1983
My Mother's Body, 1985
Available Light, 1988
Mars and her Children, 1992
Eight Chambers of the Heart, 1995
What are Big Girls Made Of?, 1997
Early Grrrl: The Early Poems of Marge Piercy, 1999
The Art of Blessing the Day: Poems with a Jewish Theme, 1999

Novels
Going down Fast, 1969
Dance the Eagle to Sleep, 1970
Small Changes, 1973
Woman on the Edge of Time, 1976
The High Cost of Living, 1978
Vida, 1980
Braided Lives, 1982
Fly away Home, 1984
Gone to Soldiers, 1987
Summer People, 1989
He, She and It, 1991; as *Body of Glass*, 1992
The Longings of Women, 1994
City of Darkness, City of Light, 1996
Storm Tide, with Ira Wood, 1998
Three Women, 1999

Play
The Last White Class: A Play About Neighborhood Terror, with Ira Wood, 1978

Other
The Grand Coolie Damn, 1969
Parti-Coloured Blocks for a Quilt, 1982
Editor, *Early Ripening: Young Women's Poetry Now*, 1987
The Earth Shines Secretly: A Book of Days, 1990
So You Want to Write, 2001
Sleeping with Cats, 2002

Further Reading

Doherty, Patricia, *Marge Piercy: An Annotated Bibliography*, Westport: Connecticut: Greenwood Press, 1997
Keulen, Margarete, *Radical Imagination: Feminist Conceptions of the Future in Ursula Le Guin, Marge Piercy and Sally Miller Gearhart*, New York: Peter Lang, 1991
Lauter, Estella, *Women as Mythmakers: Poetry and Visual Art by Twentieth-Century Women*, Bloomington: Indiana University Press, 1984
Rainwater, Catherine and William J. Scheick (editors), *Contemporary American Women Writers: Narrative Strategies*, Lexington: University Press of Kentucky, 1985
Rosenbaum, Jean, "You Are Your Own Magician: A Vision of Integrity in the Poetry of Marge Piercy", *Modern Poetry Studies*, 8 (1977)
Shands, Kerstin W., *The Repair of the World: The Novels of Marge Piercy*, Westport, Connecticut: Greenwood Press, 1994
Thielmann, Pia, *Marge Piercy's Women: Visions Captured and Subdued*, Frankfurt: Fischer, 1986
Walker, Sue and Eugenie Hamner (editors), *Ways of Knowing: Critical Essays on Marge Piercy*, Mobile, Alabama: Negative Capability Press, 1991
Wynne, Edith J., "Imagery of Association in the Poetry of Marge Piercy", *Publications of the Missouri Philological Association*, 10 (1985): 57–73
Zee, Nancy Scholar, "Marge Piercy: A Collage", *Oyez Review*, 9/1 (1975)

In her poem "The Ram's Horn Sounding", Piercy speaks of being a Jewish poet in metaphorical terms: "A woman and a Jew, sometimes more/ of a contradiction than I can sweat out,/ yet finally the intersection that is both/ collision and fusion, stone and seed." As Piercy shows in her poetry, there can be a reciprocal relationship between Judaism and feminism. They can reinforce and grow out of each other, but this cannot take place within the closed canon of traditional Judaism. Piercy's Jewish poetry renders religious meaning within nature and contributes to a new feminist vision of Judaism.

In Piercy's poems of "The Lunar Cycle", the pagan moon goddess and other goddesses predominate, but there is at least the implicit influence of the Jewish lunar calendar and beyond that the impact of her Jewish mother and grandmother and remembrance of Jewish rituals and worship. In her cover statement concerning "The Lunar Cycle", she reveals, "I first heard of the lunar calendar in childhood, when I asked why Passover falls on a different date each year and was answered that it falls on Nisan 14 – the fourteenth day of the lunar month of Nisan."

The only poem in the cycle that has explicit Jewish references is "At the Well". In this poem, the poet creates her own version or midrash of the biblical encounter between Jacob and the angel of the lord. The female protagonist, who practises sorcery and resembles a shaman, encounters an androgynous angel who strikes her, and they wrestle throughout the night. After the angel speaks in vague and cynical terms, the narrator rejects her advances, but suddenly there is a revelation: "I spat/ and she gathered her tall shuddering wings/ and scaled the streaks of the dawn/ a hawk on fire soaring . . ." This passage foreshadows the poet's later depiction of the Shekinah as hawk. Here the words evoke the force of the mystical experience.

"Crescent Moon like a Canoe" is Piercy's poem for Fearn, the last month of the lunar cycle, and her birth month. The poet says that this "is the time when the mysteries commemorated the return of Persephone from the underworld to reunite with her mother Demeter . . ." Here she goes beyond myth and symbol to invoke the maternal life force that shaped her:

> You taught me to see the scale on the bird
> leg, the old woman's scalp pink as a rose
> under the fluff, the golden flecks in the iris
> of your eye, the silver underside of leaves
> blown back. I am your poet, mother.

The protagonist inherits maternal love and sensitivity but also rage and frustration at the oppression of women, including her own mother: "The life you gave me burns its acetylene/ of buried anger, unused talents, rotted wishes,/ the compost of discontent, flaring into words/ strong for other women under your waning moon."

Because of her empathy with her mother, she senses that the latter had "wanted" "to birth a witch, a revenger, a sword." In the complex quilt of Piercy's poems, we see how she weaves feminist, mystical, and traditional Jewish strands with the influence of her mother and grandmother to create her personal imaginative response to Judaism.

In recent years, Piercy has written liturgical poems in the tradition of piyyutim. But her most powerful and original Jewish poems are contained in *Available Light*. Here the complex interweaving of feminist, Jewish, and autobiographical sources comes to fruition within the unity of nature. Poem after poem in this volume shows the way nature contains and unifies the diverse forces in Piercy's poetry. In the title poem "Available Light", the poet-narrator says she is learning Hebrew at 50, showing her renewed interest in the texts of her Jewish tradition, but the vision that she seeks is centred in the surrounding winter landscape teeming with life that "seethes with more/ than I can ever live to name and speak."

"A Candle in the Glass" describes the poet's associations that come with the lighting of the yahrzeit candle, burning in memory of her mother during Passover. As she recites the words of the *Kaddish* prayer, she is surrounded by the "dark tidal shifts/ of the Jewish calendar of waters and the moon", linking Jewish and secular associations in nature's fertility and its sensuous cycles.

In "The Garden as Synagogue", the poet envisions a female figure in various forms. She is the earth goddess, the female force that connects humanity and nature. The narrator sees her also as hawk and falconwoman, who represents a rootedness to the earth that modern civilization has lost touch with. Then the narrator invokes this "goddess/ rooted in animal power and grace, the sacred/ that connects us to the green flesh/ of the grass." This holy earth mother, who is also the Shekinah, this sacred force rooted in nature, breaks through the binaries of flesh and spirit, body and soul, male and female. As in "At the Well", the instrument of unifying vision is the female hawk that flies above the earth and yet represents its mystical powers.

Nature is the synagogue; the Passover Seder feast takes place in the garden (Eden, paradise) where the participants eat the lamb (memory of ancient temple sacrifices as well as a symbol of mourning for the lost temple in Jerusalem), the bitter herbs (the bitterness of slavery), the apples and almonds (the bricks and mortars the Jews used in building as slaves in Egypt). And so the narrator says, "I am healed/ to the sprouting earth that bears them all in me." During the traditional Seder feast as she eats nature's foods, she knows that she is of the earth, her mother, and thus is herself holy.

Piercy's "Wellfleet Sabbath" is a hymn to the divine spirit on this Sabbath evening when the moon floats over the ocean. The poem begins with the hawk, the poet's symbol of the fierce power of mystical possession, and it also evokes the Shekinah: "Here on this piney sandspit, the Shekinah/ comes on the short strong wings of the seaside/ sparrow raising her song and bringing/ down the fresh clear night." For Piercy, the Jewish-feminist-mystic, Sabbath observation opens the door to oneness and brings back the exiled Shekinah.

"The Ram's Horn Sounding", the last poem in the volume, begins and ends with animal life, but also probes the poet's Jewishness. To one who questions the sentimentality of her Judaism, she speaks of her identity with relatives who survived Hitler and her commitment to them. Then she articulates the contradiction of being woman and Jew, but it is her duty as poet to "serve the word/ I cannot have" within nature's congregation: "Coming to the new year, I am picked/ up like the ancient ram's horn to sound/ over the congregation of people and beetles,/ of pines, whales, marshhawks and asters." The ram's horn is the shofar used to proclaim the new year and freedom throughout the land (Leviticus 25:9–10). The sounding of the ram's horn is connected with the sacrifice of Isaac, the story of which is the Torah reading for the second day of Rosh Ha Shanah, the Jewish New Year. The earliest history of Rosh Ha Shanah may be related to the monthly celebration of the new moon, when the sounding of horns accompanied the special sacrifice of the day.

Although she serves the word like the shofar, the poet can

only "wrestle the holy name" and knows she cannot contain or control the divine voice, yet she appears to be an oracle for the "fierce/ voice whose long wind lifts my hair/ chills my skin and fills my lungs/ to bursting". So for a time she is religiously inspired or feels the wish to be so consummated. Then she comes back to mundane reality "into the factory of words" and back to "piece work again".

She concludes by praying to the Shekinah to use her for "telling and naming". Again, Piercy's protagonist acts as an instrument for the divine voice. She is the prophetess inspired and penetrated by the hawk-like presence "stooping on hawk wings prying into my heart/ with your silver beak; floating down/ a milkweed silk dove of sunset . . ."

In this mystical moment, the contradiction that she feels as woman, Jew, and poet is reconciled in the oneness of nature and the word. Thus she creates a unifying circle of her central influences and sources: moon goddess, Shekinah, the lunar calendar of the Jewish year, grandmother, and her mother from whose body she was born. Now she and we are transformed by the poetic vision "aligning everything into a new pattern."

GARY PACERNICK

Pinski, Dovid

Russian-born dramatist, fiction writer, and critic, 1872–1959

Born in Mohilev, 5 April 1872; grew up in Mohilev, Moscow, and Vitebsk. Studied briefly in Vienna, settled in Warsaw. Contributed to Y.L. Perets's *Literatur un lebn* and *Yontev bletlekh*. Founded publishing house, Tsaytgayst, 1896. Married Hodl Koyfman. Emigrated to USA, 1899. Contributed to New York daily *Abend blat*, becoming its literary editor in 1899. Coedited *Der arbeter*, 1904–11. Became editor of the Labour Zionist *Idisher kemfer* in 1916 and of *Di tsayt* in 1920, and also served as first president of the Yiddish division of PEN. Contributed to the periodicals *Arbeter tsaytung*, *Yud*, *Fraynd*, *Tog*, *Tsukunft*, and *Morgen zhurnal*. Settled in Israel, 1949. Died in Haifa, 11 August 1959.

Selected Writings

Plays

Yesurim, 1899; as *Sorrows*, translated by Bessie F. White, 1932
Isaac Sheftel, 1904–05
Di muter [The Mother], 1904
Di familye tsvi [The Family Zvi], 1905
Der oytser, 1906–07; as *The Treasure*, translated by Nahma Sandrow, 1999
Der eybiker yid [The Eternal Jew], 1906
Gabri un di froyen [Gabri and the Women], 1908
Yankl der shmid [Yankl the Blacksmith], 1910
Der shtumer meshiekh [The Mute Messiah], 1912
Dovid hamelekh un zayne vayber, 1914–16; as *King David and His Wives*, translated by Joseph Landis, 1966
Six Plays of the Yiddish Theatre, translated by Isaac Goldberg, 1916 (includes Pinski's *Forgotten Souls* and *Abigail*)
Three Plays, translated by Isaac Goldberg, 1918 (includes *The Dumb Messiah*, *The Last Jew* [*Di familye Tsvi*], *Isaac Sheftel*)
Dramen [Plays] 1918–20
Der tzerisener mentsh, 1920; as *Arnold Levenberg*, translated by Isaac Goldberg, 1930
Ten Plays, translated by Isaac Goldberg and others, 1920 (includes *Little Heroes*, *A Dollar!*, *The Stranger* [or *The Eternal Jew*], *Poland – 1919*, *The Beautiful Nun*, *The God of the Newly Rich Wool Merchant*, *Cripples*, *The Inventor and the King's Daughter*, *The Phonograph*, *Diplomacy*)
The Final Balance, translated by Isaac Goldberg, 1926
Meshikhim [Messiahs], 1930
Rabi Akiva [Rabbi Akiva], 1930
Laid Off, translated by Anna K. Pinski, 1932

Fiction

Temptations: A Book of Short Stories, translated by Isaac Goldberg, 1919
Dos hoyz fun noyekh edon [The House of Noah Edon], 1931
Bruriya, un andere dertseylungen [Bruriah and Other Stories], 1938
A fremde neshome un andere dertseylungen [A Foreign Soul and Other Stories], 1938
Er lebt! un andere dertseylungen [He Lives! and Other Stories], 1946

Other

Dos idishe drame [The Yiddish Drama], 1909
Der tserisener mentsh [The Person Torn to Pieces], 1928
Rayzebukh [Travelogue], 1938

Further Reading

Bass, Hyman (editor), *Di yidishe drame fun tsvantsikstn yorhundert*, vol. 1, New York: Congress for Jewish Culture, 1977
Landis, Joseph, introduction to *The Dybbuk and Other Great Yiddish Plays*, edited by Landis, New York: Bantam, 1966
Leksikon fun der nayer yidisher literatur, vol. 7, New York: CYCO, 1968
Lifson, David S., *The Yiddish Theatre in America*, New York: Yoseloff, 1965
Perlmutter, Sholem, *Yidishe dramaturgn un teater-compositors* [Yiddish Playwrights and Theatre Composers], New York: YKUF, 1952
Sandrow, Nahma (editor), *Vagabond Stars: A World History of Yiddish Theater*, New York: Harper and Row, 1977
Sandrow, Nahma, introduction to *God, Man, and Devil: Yiddish Plays in Translation*, edited and translated by Sandrow, Syracuse, New York: Syracuse University Press, 1999
Shtarkman, Moyshe and L. Rubinshtayn (editors), *Dovid Pinski: tsum tsentn yortsayt*, New York: Yiddish natsyonale arbeter farband, 1969
Zylbercweig, Zalmen, *Leksikon fun yidishn teater*, vol. 3, New York: Elisheva, 1959

While Dovid Pinski is best known today as a dramatist – a leader of the "art theatre" movement in Yiddish – his literary and cultural activities were as varied as they were long-lived. He served as editor on many newspapers and literary journals; wrote fiction and criticism; and took an active role in Jewish affairs – particularly the socialist and Zionist movements.

As a boy, Pinski received a traditional Jewish education, but his father also took him to the Yiddish and Russian theatre in Mohilev. Pinski read widely in Hebrew, Yiddish, and Russian, and sensed his own "literary" ability even in his early letters to his father. But it was a literary father figure who brought him into the Yiddish fold. When Pinski sought out Yitskhok-Leyb Perets in Warsaw, he was received warmly, and Perets encouraged the young man's literary pursuits.

Pinski began making a name for himself with writings that have been considered among the first works to bring proletarian issues into Yiddish literature. Unlike the work of many of his contemporaries, however, he focused not on the mass proletariat, but on the individual worker's impulse to revolt against oppression. His early stories were published in such journals as Mordkhe Spektor's *Hoyz fraynd* and Perets's *Literatur un lebn* and *Yontev bletklekh*. In the late 1890s Pinski wrote for a variety of publications under several pseudonyms, and founded a publishing house, Tsaytgayst. He also married Spektor's sister-in-law, Hodl Koyfman, whose input would have a profound impact on her husband's work throughout their long life together.

After his emigration to New York City in 1899, Pinski added to his early dramatic efforts with a long list of one-act and full-length plays, many of which would become international sensations. Much of the content is sombre: grim family dramas in which ordinary people are ground down by economic and/or political oppression. The one-act drama *Sorrows* shows the anguish of a mother unable to pull her daughter away from revolutionary activities in Russia; the daughter narrowly escapes – though perhaps only for a while – the police who enter the home as the curtain falls. The title character of *Isaac Sheftel* is a poor but talented inventor whose employer steals his ideas and becomes rich off them. And *To Each His Own God* depicts new immigrants struggling to make an honest living and a decent life in New York, but driven to desperate measures by their circumstances.

Pinski's writings in various genres explore countless facets of the Jewish experience. Novels such as *The House of Noah Edon* depict an emptiness in the lives of assimilated modern Jews, while in his dramas, he often turned to historical events as the basis for his inquiries into the Jewish condition. Notable among these works is his six-play cycle *Meshikhim* [Messiahs], each drama turning to messianic figures over the course of Jewish history, from days of the Temple to the rise of Hasidism.

Like his contemporary Sholem Asch, Pinski was also famous for his frank examination of sexual matters. Whether exploring the lives of historical or contemporary figures, Pinski often looked at the ways in which sex drives human actions, bringing people together or driving them apart. One of his best-known works on this theme is the drama *Yankl the Blacksmith*, which became a popular film starring Moyshe Oysher as the eponymous charming rogue. He applied his treatment of sexuality to historical figures as well, in such works as the drama *King David and His Wives* and the novel *King Solomon's Thousand Wives*.

Serious as the tone of much of his work tends to be, Pinski had a keen satirical eye; indeed, arguably his best work is the comic masterpiece *The Treasure*. Like Sholem Aleichem's *Gold Diggers*, written in the same year, *The Treasure* traces a comic spiral into chaos when a town goes mad with greed over the belief that a substantial treasure lies buried in its midst. Pinski's handling of the subject proved immensely popular; it was first performed in German under Max Reinhardt's direction, and was later staged by Egon Brecher in Vienna and the Theatre Guild in New York in 1920, in addition to many productions in Yiddish. The play shows Pinski's ability to draw finely delineated characters in outrageous comic situations, ultimately imbuing the whole affair with a strong scent of social satire.

Pinski also took an active role in Jewish affairs. To cite just a few examples, he was a founding member of the Yidisher teater-gezelshaft in New York and of its publication, *Tealit*; president of the Yidisher kultur-gezelshaft; among the founders of CYCO and the World Jewish Culture Congress; and first president of the Yiddish division of PEN, the international writers' organization.

Shortly after the founding of the State of Israel, Pinski emigrated to Haifa, where he had bought land in the 1930s. He had anything but a quiet retirement, as he continued writing plays, fiction, and regular reportage on daily life in Israel for such newspapers as the New York-based *Morgen zhurnal* and *Tog*. He succumbed to a long illness on 11 August 1959, just five months after the death of his wife Hodl. So respected was he in Israel that a street on his adopted Mount Carmel was named after him.

JOEL BERKOWITZ

Pinsky, Robert

US poet, essayist, and translator, 1940–

Born Robert Neal Pinsky, Long Branch, New Jersey, 20 October 1940. Studied at Rutgers University, BA 1962; Stanford University, MA 1966. Married Ellen Bailey, 1961; three daughters. Taught at various universities; professor of English, Wellesley College, Massachusetts, 1968–80; University of California, Berkeley, 1980–89, and Boston University since 1988. Poetry editor, *New Republic*, Washington, DC, 1978–87, *Slate*, since 1996. Many awards: Oscar Blumenthal Prize, 1978; American Academy Award, 1980; Saxifrage Prize, 1980; Guggenheim Fellowship, 1980; William Carlos Williams Award, 1985; American Academy of Arts and Sciences, 1993; London Prize in Translation, 1995; US Poet Laureate, 1997–2000.

Selected Writings

Poetry
Sadness and Happiness, 1975
An Explanation of America, 1979

Five American Poets, with others, 1979
History of My Heart, 1984
The Want Bone, 1990
The Inferno of Dante, 1995
The Figured Wheel: New and Collected Poems 1966–1996, 1996
Jersey Rain, 2000

Novel
Mindwheel, 1985

Other
Landor's Poetry, 1968
The Situation of Poetry: Contemporary Poetry and Its Traditions, 1977
Translator, with Robert Hass, *The Separate Notebooks*, by Czesław Miłosz, 1984
Poetry and the World, 1988
Translator, *The Inferno of Dante*, 1994
The Sounds of Poetry: A Brief Guide, 1999

Further Reading

Longenbach, James, "On Robert Pinsky", *Salmagundi*, 103 (Summer 1994)
Spiegelman, Willard, *The Didactic Muse*, Princeton, New Jersey: Princeton University Press, 1989

There is a consistent ground rule for Robert Pinsky's poems, early to recent, which has the searching Talmudic querulousness: he assumes that apparent simplicity is the invitation to troubling complexity. It is an attractive movement of the mind: finding exceptions to simple rules, unexpected textures to smooth surfaces, division and ambivalence to simple feelings, confusion where you expect clarity. And the strategies are abundance, surprise, and variations on a theme. In the first poem, "Poem about People", in his first book, *Sadness and Happiness*, what begins as genial and compassionate people-watching, turns to a friend's painful divorce, to a movie clip that in turn leads to a burning vision of desperate personal shame: ". . . the sensitive/ Young Jewish soldier nearly drowns/ Trying to rescue the thrashing/ Anti-semitic bully, swimming across/ The river raked by nazi fire,/ The awful part is the part truth:/ *Hate my whole kind*, but me,/ Love me for myself." Not a predictable sequence. The most ambitious poems in the book are meditative sequences that are in the form of theme and variations.

Pinsky's commitment to discursive poetry is seen in his collection, *History of My Heart*, where he adopts his method defiantly, in the face of the dominant current approach to his subject, which is the shaping of his feelings. Yet the explanatory and discursive mode has not eliminated lyricism. It has restored to the lyric the modes of discourse that have been rare in this century. This strategy is continued in "The Unseen". Set in a tour of a concentration camp, he addresses the absent God in the voice of the defiantly secular Jew facing his contradictory and unwilling servitude to God:

> O discredited Lord of Hosts, your servant gapes
>
> Obediently to swallow various doings of us, the most
> Capable of all your former creatures – we have no shape,
> We are poured out like water, but still
> We try to take in what won't be turned from in despair.

This is not cold exposition but intelligent discourse about the heart's history in History. In his poem "The Cold" Pinsky retrieves that exhausted fashionable word and moves the philosophical cold outdoors, as weather, where it belongs: "Or like me,/ working in a room alone,/ Watching out from a window . . . / . . . not having been out in hours/ I come up close idly to feel the cold,/ Forgetting for a minute what I was doing." His rhythms are inventive and formal without being insistent – he is one of the most sophisticated technicians of his generation and may well prove one of its finest poets.

The new poems in *The Figured Wheel: New and Collected Poems*, extend this mastery, and contain poems that may well become American classics, particularly a poem central to a sequence about cities, "Avenue", and an elegy for Elliot Gilbert, called "Impossible to Tell", built around two Jewish jokes. The new poems in the volume are not a random assortment. In a note on "Avenue", in reference to the explanation of Yom Kippur as the day of "at-one-ment", he says: "All, one: a play of unity and diversity that in turn makes me think of the fragmented, plural American city, held together visibly by words, by the signs and spoken or sung syllables of its streets, where all our 'they' is somehow 'one'." This motif is woven through the new poems in the volume, many of them dealing with the city as the figure for the multiplicity and "numerousness" of the soul.

Pinsky includes a poem composed for a Halloween celebration, "The Rhyme of Reb Nachman", among his selection of translations, and a poem by Miłosz, "Incantation", among his own poems, in part at least because his poem "The World" was rejected as a translation by Miłosz, and is an English poem in its own right, and not sufficiently subordinated to the Polish. An odd justification enabling an odd situation indeed, and yet entirely appropriate to the overlapping boundaries that Pinsky's new work celebrates.

Pinsky accepted his elevation to the Poet Laureateship of the United States with deep seriousness, and he took on the task of establishing some record of "best loved poems" of the American people. His approach was to exclude the customary canon shapers, the poets and scholars, in order to discover a popular demotic consensus. This is part of a somewhat quixotic overall project of recovering or discovering or defining the historical memory of a pluralist culture of improvised traditions that is separable from the commercial project of pop culture. His presence on the Public Broadcasting *Newshour* every week has made poetry present to a wide audience.

The Sounds of Poetry is a guide to prosody for students that focuses on accent and sound pattern and does not begin with scansion or the customary classifications of accentual-syllabic poetry. The starting point is vocal reality rather than traditional prosody, although discussion of metre and the sounds it explains runs throughout. However it is restricted, and gives way to a non-technical empirical approach. Pinsky is, in effect, paraphrasing technical prosody for technophobes, at the same time that his sustained attention to sound reveals patterns that were not attended to before.

The recent *Jersey Rain* reflects in its turn Pinsky's determination once again to expand his art. The move in this case is toward a high style, a solemnity, a high seriousness in the Arnoldian sense. It was not absent from his previous work, but there it was accompanied by a subversive metaphysical wit, like the jokes in his elegies, and his sly satirical flashes. These qualities are rarer in this book. The poems are still rooted in his vernacular strength that flourishes in delicate tension with his formality, which is itself subtle and not self-assertive, and might be missed by young, infatuated readers, as they might not have noticed the loosened formality of Yeats, Bishop, Lowell, or Stevens.

"Ode to Meaning" is an elegy with no jokes: its reach is straightforwardly metaphysical, and its tone and music elevated. It begins: "Dire one and desired one,/ Savior and sentencer—" and concludes: "If I/ Dare to disparage/ Your harp of shadows/ I taste/ Wormwood and motor oil, I pour/ Ashes on my head. You are the wound. You/ Be the medicine."

We can look on this poem, fruitfully, as a struggle with the meaning of the *Kaddish*. The "meaning" invoked here has become deeply interwoven with death and the struggle against the threat of its meaninglessness. The poem is very different from the improvisational and digressive prose piece "An Alphabet of My Dead" – one of the few works in this collection that points backward towards his earlier work. It is nostalgic and full of a sense of real loss, but lacks the grief-driven desperation for meaning of the "Ode". It is this latter quality that characterizes this book.

BARRY GOLDENSOHN

Pinter, Harold

British dramatist, 1930–

Born in Hackney, London, 10 October 1930. Educated at Hackney Downs Grammar School, 1943–47; Royal Academy of Dramatic Art, London, 1948. Married, first, Vivien Merchant, 1956 (divorced, 1980); one son; second, Antonia Fraser, 1980. Professional actor, director; associate director, National Theatre, London, 1973–83; director, United British Artists, 1983; from 1988, editor and publisher, Greville Press. Awards include *Evening Standard* Award, 1960; Newspaper Guild of New York Award, 1962; Italia Prize, for television play, 1962; Berlin Film Festival Silver Bear, 1963; Screenwriters Guild Award, for television play, 1963, for screenplay, 1963; New York Film Critics Award, 1964; BAFTA Award, 1965, 1971; CBE (Commander, Order of the British Empire), 1966; Tony Award, 1967; Whitbread Award, 1967; New York Drama Critics Circle award, 1967, 1980; Shakespeare Prize (Hamburg), 1970; Writers Guild Award, 1971; Cannes Film Festival Golden Palm, 1971; Austrian State Prize, 1973; Pirandello Prize, 1980; Commonwealth Award, 1981; Donatello Prize, 1982; British Theatre Association Award, 1983, 1985; Olivier Award for Lifetime Achievement, 1995; David Cohen British Literature Prize for Lifetime Achievement, 1995; S.T. du Pont Golden Pen Award for Lifetime Distinguished Service to Literature, 2001. Fellow, Royal Society of Literature; honorary member, American Academy and Institute of Arts and Letters, 1984, and American Academy of Arts and Sciences, 1985.

Selected Writings

Plays
The Room, 1957
The Birthday Party, 1958
Sketches in *One to Another*, 1959
Sketches in *Pieces of Eight*, 1959
A Slight Ache, 1959
The Dumb Waiter, 1959
The Dwarfs, 1960
The Birthday Party and Other Plays, 1960
The Caretaker, 1960
Night School, 1960
A Night Out, 1960
A Slight Ache and Other Plays, 1961
Three Plays, 1962
The Lover, 1963
The Collection, and The Lover (includes the prose piece *The Examination*), 1963
The Compartment (unreleased screenplay), 1963
Dialogue for Three, 1963
Tea Party, 1965
The Homecoming, 1965
The Dwarfs and Eight Revue Sketches, 1965
The Basement, 1967
Tea Party and Other Plays, 1967
The Lover, The Tea Party, The Basement, 1967
Early Plays: A Night Out, Night School, Revue Sketches, 1968
Landscape, 1968
Sketches by Pinter, 1969
Silence, 1969
Night, 1969
Old Times, 1971
Monologue, 1973
No Man's Land, 1975
Plays 1–4, 1975–81
The Proust Screenplay: À la recherche du temps perdu, 1977
Betrayal, 1978
The Hothouse, 1980
Family Voices, 1981
The French Lieutenant's Woman (screenplay), 1981
Other Places, 1982
Precisely (sketch), 1983
One for the Road, 1984
Mountain Language, 1988
The Heat of the Day, from the novel by Elizabeth Bowen, 1989
The Comfort of Strangers and Other Screenplays, 1990
The New World Order, 1991
Party Time, 1992
Moonlight, 1993
Ashes to Ashes, 1996
Recreation, 1998

Many radio and television plays, and screenplays

Novel
The Dwarfs, 1990

Poetry
Poems, edited by Alan Clodd, 1968
I Know the Place, 1979
Ten Early Poems, 1992

Other
Mac, 1968
Poems and Prose 1949–1977, 1978
Conversations with Pinter, 1994
Collected Poems and Prose, 1996
Various Voices: Prose, Poetry, Politics, 1998

Further Reading

Armstrong, Raymond, *Kafka and Pinter: Shadow-Boxing: The Struggle between Father and Son*, London: Macmillan, and New York: St Martin's Press, 1999
Billington, Michael, *The Life and Work of Harold Pinter*, London: Faber, 1996
Bold, Alan (editor), *Harold Pinter: You Never Heard Such Silence*, London: Vision, and Totowa, New Jersey: Barnes and Noble, 1984
Cahn, Victor L., *Gender and Power in the Plays of Harold Pinter*, New York: St Martin's Press, 1993; London: Macmillan, 1994
Esslin, Martin, *The Peopled Wound: The Plays of Harold Pinter*, London: Methuen, and New York: Doubleday, 1970; revised edition, as *Pinter: A Study of His Plays*, London: Methuen, 1973; 6th edition as *Pinter: The Playwright*, London: Methuen, 2000
Eyre, Richard (editor), *Harold Pinter: A Celebration*, London: Faber, 2000
Gordon, Lois (editor), *Harold Pinter: A Casebook*, New York: Garland, 1990
Gussow, Mel, *Conversations with Pinter*, London: Nick Hern, and New York: Limelight, 1994
Hall, Ann C., *"A Kind of Alaska": Women in the Plays of O'Neill, Pinter, and Shepard*, Carbondale: Southern Illinois University Press, 1993
Klein, Joanne, *Making Pictures: The Pinter Screenplays*, Columbus: Ohio State University Press, 1985
Knowles, Ronald, *Understanding Harold Pinter*, Columbia: University of South Carolina Press, 1995
Merritt, Susan, *Pinter in Play*, Durham, North Carolina, Duke University Press, 1990
Peacock, D. Keith, *Harold Pinter and the New British Theatre*, Westport, Connecticut: Greenwood, 1997
Regal, Martin S., *Harold Pinter: A Question of Timing*, London: Macmillan, and New York: St Martin's Press, 1995
Silverstein, Marc, *Harold Pinter and the Language of Cultural Power*, Lewisburg, Pennsylvania: Bucknell University Press, 1993

Harold Pinter is considered one of the leading dramatists of the second half of the 20th century. His style is noted for its charged ambiguities, understatements, and contradictions, as well as pregnant pauses and silences. All of these contribute to a very personal blend of poetic realism. His plays are also considered to be related to the Theatre of the Absurd (notably by critics such as Martin Esslin and Walter Kerr).

The only son of a lower-middle-class Jewish tailor, Pinter (the name, according to family tradition, was originally de Pinta, of Jewish-Portuguese roots) grew up in the East End of London, in a working-class neighbourhood. His grandparents had emigrated to western Europe from Poland and Ukraine. From an early age he wrote poetry and prose for small-circulation magazines. His father encouraged his writing, but the former's Zionist views were in opposition to Pinter's rejection of the Jewish religion. This, among other things, may have initiated in him a non-conformist attitude from the very outset of his career. He was a conscientious objector and refused national service. He started to study acting at the Royal Academy of Dramatic Art in 1948, but left to join a touring company in Ireland and various provincial repertory companies, including Sir Donald Wolfit's company. His experience as an actor may have been responsible for the way that his characters behave on stage, by subtle means where no spoken communication has taken place.

After completing a novel, *The Dwarfs*, whose characters were drawn from a group of Jewish male boyhood friends, the focus of Pinter's writing was for the stage. A recurring theme in his early dramatic writing is that of intrusion: a set of balanced, routine relations maintained between a couple, family or another kind of group, is disrupted by the sudden appearance of a foreign element, bringing in the menacing presence of some outside power, which shakes the group's stability and brings to the surface old rivalries and jealousies, repressed fears, and terror of the unknown. Pinter himself has noted that this may have some connection with his fear of German invasion as a boy in Hackney during the bombing. This sense of menace is notable from his first one-act plays. *The Room* (1957) is a symbolic play about an elderly couple, a chattering wife and a reticent husband, living as recluses in their one-room apartment, apparently protecting themselves from the unknown outside, which eventually penetrates their shelter in the shape of a blind black man who brings the woman an obscure message from her (dead?) father, only to be beaten harshly by the enraged husband. In *The Dumb Waiter* (1959) two hired killers, awaiting a victim in a basement room, are provoked and shaken by the straining demands of some mysterious agency upstairs, sent through a mechanical dumb waiter. Later Pinter began to accommodate the menacing characters more with common reality (he later referred to the blind black man of *The Room*: "if I were writing the play now I'd make him sit down, have a cup of tea").

His first full-length play, *The Birthday Party* (1958), concerns two strangers, Goldberg and McCann, who intrude on a small boarding-house and its sole tenant, Stanley Webber, and insist on having a party to mark his birthday. They then brainwash him through an inexorable interrogation and take him away to treat his alleged nervous breakdown. Apart from the surname Goldberg, there is no ostensible Jewish content.

The radio play *A Slight Ache* (1959), adapted for the stage, once more personified intrusion, this time in the silent presence of a matchseller bringing out the conflicting sides of a married couple. *The Caretaker* (1960), Pinter's second full-length play, established his reputation as one of the most intriguing young playwrights to emerge on the British stage. Here, a dirty old tramp, brought from the street and made a caretaker at the home of two neurotic brothers, upsets the balance between the brothers until they have to throw him out. Two more one-act plays, *The Collection*, produced for television, and *The Lover* paved the way for Pinter's next major play.

The Homecoming is an enigmatic play about the old rage, rivalry, and sexual confusion caused by the visit to a London family of their passive, detached elder brother, Teddy, and Ruth, his wife. Ruth, newly introduced to the family, not only accepts sexual overtures and interference in her marital relations, but eventually stays in London, despite her husband's muted and ineffectual protests, to become the family's prostitute/mother/provider. (This play, whose characters, says the playwright, do not act "arbitrarily, but for very deep-rooted reasons", was inspired, according to Michael Billington, by the life story of a boyhood friend, a university professor in Canada, who had concealed his marriage to a Gentile woman from his Jewish family.)

Betrayal is considered one of Pinter's most accessible plays, yet is full of subtle nuances of feeling in depicting backwards a narrative of a love triangle. In *A Kind of Alaska* (part of *Other Places*, 1982) the major character, Deborah, awakens after 29 years of sleep to find that she has become an adult and missed a good part of her life. The play is a version of the Pygmalion myth inspired by Oliver Sacks's "Awakenings", in which Pinter, as Anne Hall argues, expresses the idea that the male-signified "place of the other, this 'kind of Alaska', has some cracks".

Since the 1970s, Pinter has directed many plays, both his own and others'. He has continued to act occasionally, and has published and republished his poetry (growing ever more overtly political, culminating in "Poem", where he states: "The world's about to break", or "God", where God discovers "he had no blessing to bestow"). He has also written essays on literary and political matters.

Although the author of *The Birthday Party* or *The Hothouse* (the latter written in 1958, but not staged until 1980) was never oblivious to the political dimension informing his plots, Pinter's increasingly public role as a political activist, in the late 1970s and early 1980s, is reflected in his dramatic work. Since the 1980s, Pinter's dramatic writing often takes a more directly political turn, as in *One for the Road*, an account of a political investigation by a state security apparatus. "There's only one reality", Pinter argues in his introduction to the play, "You can interpret reality in various ways. But there's only one. And if that reality is thousands of people being tortured to death at this very moment . . . It has to be faced." This new proclivity was continued in plays such as *Mountain Language*, in which citizens are prevented from speaking their native language, suppressed by the state (in a locus that mysteriously hovers between Britain and some remote third-world domain), and in *The New World Order* (1991), a satiric discussion between two torturers about what pain to inflict upon their victim – who is present in the room, blindfolded and silent, almost reconciled to the cruel logic of the situation. *Party Time* is a menacing futuristic vision of a fascist Britain.

Ashes to Ashes is a one-act play relating sadomasochistic marital cruelty and political oppression. The play opens with Rebecca recounting for Devlin a story of sadomasochistic sex. It gradually emerges that her lover was not merely dominating but a high-level Nazi functionary. Pinter provides a few clues – "train", "factory", "baby", "guilt", "atrocity". Rebecca is one of his victims, a mother whose baby was taken from her as she boarded a train to the camps. Pinter shows that "the personal and the political are ultimately indivisible" (Michael Billington).

In 1993 he produced a late masterpiece, *Moonlight*, in which civil servant Andy's dying scene is informed by the rhetoric and politics of domestic power struggles with his wife Bel attending his deathbed, his sons Fred and Jake who fail to show up, their daughter Brigit whose absence may allude to her already being dead, and the invocation of the couple's respective lovers. All this is wrapped by a series of short poetic scenes haunted by death imagery, hovering through the liminal space between past and present, the dead and the living.

AVRAHAM OZ

Potok, Chaim

US fiction writer, 1929–2002

Born Herman Harold Potok in the Bronx, New York, 17 February 1929. Studied at Orthodox Jewish schools; Yeshiva University, New York, from 1946, BA in English 1950; Jewish Theological Seminary, New York, from 1950, MHL and rabbinic ordination 1954; University of Pennsylvania, Philadelphia, from 1959, PhD in philosophy 1965. Military service as army chaplain, Korea, 1955–56; lieutenant. Married Adena Sara Mosevitsky, 1958; two daughters, one son. National director, Leaders Training Fellowship, Jewish Theological Seminary, 1954–55; director, Camp Ramah, Ojai, California, 1957–59; instructor, University of Judaism, Los Angeles, 1957–59; scholar in residence, Har Zion Temple, Philadelphia, 1959–63; faculty member, Teachers' Institute, Jewish Theological Seminary, 1964–65; managing editor, *Conservative Judaism*, New York, 1964–65; editor in chief, 1966–74, and special projects editor, since 1974, Jewish Publication Society, Philadelphia. Lived in Israel, 1973–77. Visiting professor of philosophy, University of Pennsylvania, 1983, and Bryn Mawr College, Pennsylvania, 1985. Awarded Wallant Award, 1968; Atheneum Award, 1969; National Jewish Book Award for Fiction 1990; Jewish Cultural Achievement Award, 1997; O. Henry Award, 1999. Died in Merion, Pennsylvania, 23 July 2002.

Selected Writings

Novels
The Chosen, 1967
The Promise, 1969
My Name is Asher Lev, 1972

In the Beginning, 1975
The Book of Lights, 1981
Davita's Harp, 1985
The Gift of Asher Lev, 1990
I am the Clay, 1992

Other
Jewish Ethics (pamphlets), 14 vols, 1964–69
The Jew Confronts Himself in American Literature, 1975
Wanderings: Chaim Potok's History of the Jews, 1978
Ethical Living for a Modern World, 1985
Theo Tobiasse: Artist in Exile, 1986
The Tree of Here, 1993
The Sky of Now, 1994
The Gates of November: Chronicles of the Slepak Family, 1996

Further Reading

Abramson, Edward A., *Chaim Potok*, Boston: Twayne, 1986
Forbes, Cheryl, "Judaism Under the Secular Umbrella" (interview with Chaim Potok), *Christianity Today* (8 September 1978): 14–21
Kauver, Elaine M., "Interview with Chaim Potok", *Contemporary Literature*, 27/3 (Fall 1986)
Kremer, S. Lilian, Potok entry in *Twentieth-Century American-Jewish Fiction Writers*, edited by Daniel Walden, Detroit: Gale, 1984 (*Dictionary of Literary Biography*, vol. 28)
Potok, Chaim, "Cultural Confrontation in Urban America: A Writer's Beginnings" in *Literature and the American Urban Experience*, edited by Michael C. Jaye and Ann Chalmers Watts, New Brunswick, New Jersey: Rutgers University Press, and Manchester: Manchester University Press, 1981

Chaim Potok built a formidable reputation as a novelist. He also wrote nonfiction, including a history of the Jewish people, as well as plays, short stories, and children's books. Whereas most American Jewish writers have been committed to a cultural/historical approach to Jewishness, Potok, a conservative rabbi, raised cultural issues from within the religious tradition. He presented Judaism as relevant in the modern world, through moral protagonists who must contend with American society, usually through a demanding faith and tightly knit Jewish community. They must cope with the "culture confrontation" between Judaism and the larger "umbrella civilization". His novels have been best-sellers and stress good versus good, eschewing physical violence and sexuality.

His first novel is also one of his best. *The Chosen* is concerned with conflicts between Jewish fundamentalism, as seen in Reb Saunders's Hasidic sect, and liberal Orthodoxy, or Conservatism, seen in David Malter's approach. These views are dramatized in the fraught friendship between the sons, who stress the father/son theme, which parallels God's historical relationship to Israel. Potok's optimism can be seen in that all problems are resolved for the major characters.

The Promise is a sequel depicting the results of the choices made in *The Chosen*, and focusing upon commitment to different interpretations of Jewish law and practice. Revolving around study, Potok dramatizes the excitement generated when people pursue important subjects. Several approaches to Judaism conflict, with Potok preferring the middle way between Orthodoxy and Reconstructionism. There is much didacticism, but the reader is immersed in issues central to Jewish belief.

My Name is Asher Lev concerns the commandment against the use of graven images and the consequent low status of the artist within Jewish culture. The protagonist is a child prodigy in art, who is also a Hasidic Jew. Not wishing to hurt his parents or leave his community, he nonetheless finds that he cannot reconcile his artistic gift with the demands of his father and local society. The influences of the secular society are crucial, as to be an artist forces Asher into the world of Christian art and secular values. Finally, he must leave home, but Potok is unwilling to cut him off totally from Judaism and places him in a more "understanding" Jewish community in Paris.

In the Beginning concerns anti-Semitism and the scholarly protagonist's decision to fight it through defending Jewish values against the "higher biblical criticism" that emanated from Germany and was used by some scholars to attack Judaism. Anti-Semitism is seen as an import to America from Europe, with the novel set in the 1930s and 1940s. As in the previous novels, the protagonist is highly gifted and committed to positive values. The stress is on the importance of Jews being active in their defence by whatever means necessary.

Potok wrote two novels based upon his experiences as an army chaplain in the Korean War. In the impressive *The Book of Lights*, he turns to Kabbalah, Jewish mysticism, with the protagonists placed in a culture that has never heard of Judaism. The "lights" refer to those of the *En-Sof* and *Sefiroth* in Kabbalistic lore, and to that of the atomic bomb. The two adult protagonists are rabbis, one a budding Kabbalist, the other a physicist who has rejected science because of the "death light" it created. Here Potok depicts adults, not adolescents, and for the first time his characters engage in sexual thoughts and activities. There are still teachers and students, a constant in Potok's writings, and a reflection of his view of an important aspect of Judaism. *I am the Clay* is Potok's first novel wherein Jews barely appear at all. The characters are Korean and have to cope with the upheavals of the Korean War, which test their survival skills and compassion.

Potok's first female protagonist appears in *Davita's Harp*, where we see Davita's problems in an Orthodox community. Davita is denied the Akiva Award given to the best student at her school, which cannot admit that girls are capable of better academic performance than boys. It is clear that Orthodoxy is only an acceptable spiritual home for those not willing to question certain ideas. She also must learn to cope with her parents' communism and their fight against fascism in the Spanish Civil War, world events being important here as they have been in all of Potok's novels. This novel contains Potok's widest range of "religious" beliefs: Orthodox Judaism, Christianity, communism, and a type of humanism. Davita will probably leave Orthodoxy for the "spiritual" truths of literature.

In *The Gift of Asher Lev* Potok returns to his exiled artist, now famous and living in France. Upon the death of his uncle in Brooklyn, Asher returns to his childhood home and confronts the legacy of his past. His son Avrumel is his gift to the rebbe, his father, and the Ladover community. Avrumel will become the Hasid that Asher could not.

Of Potok's nonfiction writings, two of the most interesting are *Wanderings: Chaim Potok's History of the Jews* and *The Gates of November: Chronicles of the Slepak Family*. In the former, he attempts to combine a scholarly and popular Jewish history, and largely succeeds. He shows the effects on Judaism and Jewish culture of exposure to different civilizations, and treats pagan and other non-Jewish cultures with great understanding. In the latter text, Potok focuses upon the true story of the Slepak family, whose generations include a high-ranking communist officer and a son who is a "refusenik", against everything his father stood for. As in *Wanderings*, the real people dramatize the history through which they pass.

Potok's deep knowledge of Judaism gave his work an authority lacking in that of many other American-Jewish writers, while his more progressive approach to the faith made his work accessible to a wide audience and allowed him an understanding of the larger society.

EDWARD A. ABRAMSON

Preil, Gabriel Yehoshua

Russian-born US poet, 1911–1993

Born in Tartu, Estonia, 1911. Studied at yeshiva in Lithuania. Following father's death, emigrated with mother to United States, 1922. Studied at Isaac Elchanan Rabbinical School and its College of Liberal Arts. Awards include New York University Newman Award; Bialik Prize. Died in Jerusalem, 1993.

Selected Writings

Poetry
Nof shemesh ukefor [Landscape of Sun and Frost], 1944
Ner mul kokhavim [A Candle Opposite the Stars], 1954
Mappat erev [Map of Evening], 1961
"Lakes", translated by Robert Alter in *The Modern Hebrew Poem Itself*, edited by Stanley Burnshaw, T. Carmi, and Ezra Spicehandler, 1965
Lider, 1966
Fire and Silence, 1968
Of Time and Place, 1972
Poems from End to End, 1976
Autumn Music: Selected Poems of Gabriel Preil, translated by Laya Firestone, 1979
Courteous to Myself, 1980
Sunset Possibilities, translated by Robert Friend, 1985
Fifty Poems in the Wilderness, 1987
Collector of Autumns, 1992
To be Recorded, 1992

Further Reading

Feldman, Yael S., *Modernism and Cultural Transfer: Gabriel Preil and the Tradition of Jewish Literary Bilingualism*, Cincinnati: Hebrew Union College Press, 1986
Miron, Dan, "Two Connections" in *Gabriel Preil: Asfan setavim/Collector of Autumns*, Jerusalem: Mosad Bialik, 1993

Gabriel Preil was the last of a small school of Hebrew poets writing in the United States during the first half of the 20th century. Like their more numerous Yiddish-writing colleagues, they belonged to the generation of east European Jewish immigrants which had settled in the United States between 1905 and 1925. For decades an important Yiddish literary centre flourished in New York and a more modest Hebrew writing community. However, by the 1940s, it became clear that the dream of Jewish bilingualism in America could not be sustained. English had replaced Yiddish as the spoken and literary language of American Jews and even fewer had acquired Hebrew as either a spoken or literary language. By the 1950s the remaining American Hebrew poets who were not too old moved to Israel where Hebrew had become the vernacular and the language of a dynamic literary renaissance. Preil, although one of the youngest American Hebrew poets, chose to remain in New York and soon was called "the last Mohican of Hebrew literature in America".

Born in Estonia, a scion of a scholarly rabbinic family, he was brought to New York in 1922 where he received his secular and religious education at the Isaac Elchanan Rabbinical School and its College of Liberal Arts. (Both are now part of the Yeshiva University.) He became well versed not only in Jewish literature but also in Anglo-American literature. Unlike his older colleagues who arrived in the United States as adults and whose acquaintance with American literature was generally limited to 19th-century authors, Preil was familiar with modern American poetry and was influenced by some of its poets. To quote the Israeli critic Dan Miron, Preil's work was "modern, urban, secular . . . unmetered, unrimed, private and almost conversational . . . [with] traces of post symbolist poetic modes. It is focused upon everyday experiences . . . and shuns symbolism, mysticism, nationalist pathos . . . Its language is discursive and at times ironic".

The Hebrew "establishment" in New York reacted to the young Preil's poetry ambivalently. On the one hand, he was viewed as the heir for whom they had hoped: a young, almost native American who had chosen to be a Hebrew poet. On the other, his modernist, conversational low-key poetry sharply contrasted with the nationalist romantic, neo-symbolist poetry of the great Russian Hebrew poets who had served as the mentors of the older poets. Fortunately Preil proved not to be confrontational; he displayed the proper deference to the American Hebrew establishment and was open to their overtures of friendship. He simply continued writing his new poetry without flaunting its divergence from the older accepted norms.

It was only in the 1950s that he was discovered by a new generation of Israeli poets who had broken with the neosymbolist poetics of Avraham Shlonsky and Natan Alterman, the two leading poets of the 1930s and 1940s. Nathan Zach, the major polemicist of the new poetics, attempted to counter the accusation that the new poets were rootless and imitators of "foreign" European models by arguing that the new poets were simply continuing an alternative tradition that had existed in Hebrew letters but had been ignored by the older generation. He pointed to the works of David Fogel, Ber Pomerantz, and Hayyim Lensky as examples. This alternative tradition had stressed the individual and his personal existential milieu and had shunned advocating the national-communal message of the old poetry, its pathos, and its prophetic posing. It had rejected its metaphysical transcendentalist views, concentrating upon the concrete, existential human experience. The new poets preferred the metonym to the colourful metaphor and a discursive and conversational tone rather than high rhetoric. They were open to the new trends of European literature. Preil's "American" poetry was viewed as the precursor of these new trends. The new Israeli criticism crowned him as one of the first poets who represented this alternative tradition.

Yael Feldman has called attention to the fact that Preil began as a Yiddish poet and was influenced by the school of the introspective Yiddish *In zikh* [Within Yourself] poets led by Yankev Glatshteyn. Whether his early involvement with the *In zikh* school was the determining factor that led to Preil's "modernism" has been questioned by Dan Miron who, without ignoring the effects of Yiddish modernism on Preil, correctly claims that the main "mentors" of Preil were rather Ber Pomerantz, David Fogel, and Hayyim Lensky themselves – a "triumvirate" that Preil described as being "more serious than seriousness". Yet perhaps because he did not suffer the tragic fate of these three poets: poverty, familial tragedies, and ultimately victimization by either the Holocaust (Pomerantz and Fogel) or Stalinist purges (Lensky) and lived a comparatively care-free life in New York, his introspective, ironic poetry frequently is less pessimistic. His perception of the condition of modern man has compelled him to view the world through an anti-romantic and ironic prism, but he was able to yearn for a more romantic era. In one of his few quasi-autobiographical poems he writes:

> Each man has his own manna in his own times
> This is an autobiographical pill
> approved for consumption until the dawning of the last quarter of the twentieth century.
> The days from then on – clown
> skating warily on thin ice
> It is hard to imagine what Grandpa would have said about them —
> at any rate I would have liked to have lived in his time.
> But I do see myself standing
> in the center of a city ringed in barbed wire
> whose skies are a cold stubborn flame
> while Eden near or far
> remains an open-shut question.
> But my ear does catch the music
> which is beyond listening; I
> draw closer then to Grandpa —
> soon I shall live in his time.

Dan Miron gives us a final comment about Preil's work:

> Preil's poetry rather than being confrontational (one of his early books of verse is called *A Candle Opposite the Stars*) is a poetry of compromise and resolution. It converts situations of confrontation to the possibility of an existential continuity. At times it lights starry candles in the house of Hebrew poetry and at times it lights stars that are candle-like. In either case, he endows Hebrew poetry with a unique twilight: a light of sobriety that does not eliminate intoxication, a light of secular days in which a holiday is imbedded.

EZRA SPICEHANDLER

Pressburger, Giorgio

Hungarian-born Italian fiction writer, filmmaker, and theatre director, 1937–

Born in Budapest, 1937. Emigrated to Italy, 1956. Studied at Accademia d'Arte Drammatica di Roma, diploma in directing; also studied biological science at University of Rome. Taught directing and acting at Accademia d'Arte Drammatica, 1968–76; history of theatre at University of Lecca, 1971, and at University of Rome, 1974; now director of Institute of Italian Culture, Budapest. Has written for newspapers *Corriere della Sera* and *La Repubblica*, and for periodicals including *Granta*. Many awards, including Premio Selezione Campiello, 1989; Premio Basilicata, 1989; Premio San Vidal, 1991; *Independent* Foreign Fiction Award, 1992; Premio Stafnelli di Caserta, 1993; Premio Viareggio, 1998.

Selected Writings

Stories

Storie dell'ottavo distretto, with Nicola Pressburger, 1986; as *Homage to the Eighth District*, translated by Gerald Moore, 1990

La legge degli spazi bianchi, 1989; as *The Law of White Spaces*, translated by Piers Spence, 1992

La nieve e la colpa, 1998; as *Snow and Guilt*, translated by Shaun Whiteside, 2000

Novels

L'elefante verde, with Nicola Pressburger, 1988; as *The Green Elephant*, translated by Piers Spence, 1994

Il sussurro della grande voce [Murmuring of the Great Voice], 1990

La conscienza sensibile [The Tender Conscience], 1992

Denti e spie, 1994; as *Teeth and Spies*, translated by Shaun Whiteside, 1999

I due gemelli [The Two Twins], 1996

Other

Esecuzione [Performance], 1963

La parabola [The Parable], 1972

La partita [The Game], 1974
Eroe di scena, fantasma d'amore [Stage Hero, Spectre of Love], 1986
Le tre Madri [The Three Mothers], 1995

Pressburger has also translated works by Heinrich von Kleist, Georg Kaiser, Karl Valentin, Arpád Göncz, Balázs-Bartók, Kodály, and István Orkény. He has directed works by Goldoni, Kleist, Peter Shaffer and others. He has developed works by others and produced original pieces for radio, winning several prizes. He has also directed television shows, films, and operas.

Further Reading

Abelman, Kim Gardi, "From Diversity to New Identity: Illness as Process in Giorgio Pressburger", *Identity and Diversity in Italian Culture: Pretoria 1998* (Association of Professional Italianists Conference 10) www.unisa.ac.za/dept/rom/api

Until Nicola's death in 1985 Giorgio and Nicola Pressburger were a writing team, twin brothers who left their native Hungary for Italy in 1956. They produced two widely acclaimed and translated books *Storie dell'ottavo distretto* (*Homage to the Eighth District*) and *L'elefante verde* (*The Green Elephant*). The Eighth District of Budapest was "thronged with Jews and Gypsies, those two rejected minorities of the Austro-Hungarian Empire" and in a few spare but vivid stories the Pressburgers recreate the intense and insecure energy of its markets and streets. This is largely the Budapest of the poor with its "aristocracy" of wealthy goose-dealers like the queenly, brutal, and vast-bodied Selma Grün, filled with grotesque vitality (and survival-instinct). Although the Holocaust looms over these stories, their focus is much more on the life of Jewish Budapest before and after World War II, told through the evocation of various extravagant characters; the gross Selma; the exceptionally beautiful Ilona Weiss who inspires suicide and a popular song and "had once been like that music, lovely, tender, ephemeral"; sly and cynical cousin Tibor who tells the young narrator "life is like Rákòczy Avenue: to begin with it's all theatre, in the middle it's a hospital, and at the end a cemetery"; or in the final story named after its protagonist, Nathan, an assimilated Budapest Jew who eventually rediscovers his *yidishkayt* in Venice, devoting many hours to studying the Zohar and giving the authors the opportunity to muse "I see a time when the Jews, descendants of those who were tortured and exterminated, will be fertile once more. The Eighth District . . . will be repopulated, flowers will burst forth and minds will be illuminated with wisdom."

The Green Elephant, like *Homage to the Eighth District*, emerges from memories of a poor Jewish Budapest, here in the period from the end of World War I to the end of World War II. A charming novella, told mainly through a child's eyes, it is also an essay on a strand that has deeply marked exceptional Jews throughout the last few centuries; the messianic, utopian, far-seeing urge that often possesses them; something born out of the combination of the notion of a Chosen People, their relative sophistication in a world of ignorant peasants and feckless aristocrats, and the actual limitation on what Jews were allowed to do in a universe of hostility and discrimination. A yearning for a better, holier, richer, wider life thus became deeply ingrained and the dream of the "Green Elephant" that is the keynote of this book seems to be a beautiful literary reflection of the rich and felicitously mad idea many Jews have had that the world will/can/must change for the better. Written in a peculiarly exalted vein, it develops into a *Kaddish* (the Jewish prayer for the dead) for Europe's Lost Tribe, an elegiac, fanciful, and beautiful tribute.

After his brother's death, Giorgio Pressburger produced *La legge degli spazi bianchi* (*The Law of White Spaces*), five stories, set mainly again in the poverty-stricken, sometimes chaotic Budapest of before and just after World War II, which form a series of reflections on illness and their resonances in our feelings. The title piece shows a doctor afflicted with a disease that makes his memory slip away from him literally word by word until he comes to believe that meaning really resides not in words but in the white spaces between words. The strange tale "Vera" illustrates a similar disturbance of outer and inner worlds. As in much of Pressburger's writing, a lot of the main action takes place out of frame. In this sense Pressburger's work is like that of S.Y. Agnon, another Jewish writer also originally from *Mitteleuropa*. Agnon was described as having "a deliberately restrained tone of narration"; this restraint, this delicacy in the face of individual tragedy and the general loss of war and social dislocation also marks Pressburger's tone. Both writers' work is set against the background of a world that no longer exists; their writing and their memories are, practically speaking, all that remains of it. This great sadness, indirectly reflected in their stories, makes the stories more than they appear to be at first glance.

Most of Giorgio Pressburger's subsequent works, such as *Il sussurro della grande voce* [Murmuring of the Great Voice] or *La nieve e la colpa* (*Snow and Guilt*) have been much less explicitly Jewish although featuring Jewish protagonists. In *Denti e spie* (*Teeth and Spies*) there is something of a return to the quasi-medical themes of *Law of White Spaces* in its format of stories around the loss or inflammation of a man's teeth, one by one, and each accompanied by a story or sketch. Within this conceit there is a strange intimacy, a turning upon the self in an oppressive world, and a physical claustrophobia that seem either Mediterranean or Jewish in intensity. There is also the trademark European Jewish pessimism; "Our son returned safe and sound from that demented war: . . . he had learned to play the guitar and to suffer the anguish of a constant and invisible menace. He had understood the essence of life." The protagonist, who we are told is the son of a *shoykhet*, a ritual slaughterer, is constantly, Jewishly, we might say, in movement and succeeds in finding a Central European Jewish dentist in almost every city he visits (probably not such an unlikely feat). In a typically oblique Pressburger way, perhaps the way of the assimilated Jew – and Pressburger is doubly-assimilated as a Hungarian-speaker who has become an Italian writer – he evokes a Jewish-populated world but hardly comments on and never celebrates its Jewishness. He expresses well the unease of his generation of European Jews, not so far from older culturally distinct and separate Jewish worlds but with no safe way openly to express that Jewish residue, except perhaps in books like these.

RAY KEENOY

Proust, Marcel

French fiction writer, 1872–1922

Born Valentin Louis Georges Eugène Marcel Proust in Auteuil, 10 July 1872. Contracted asthma, 1881, remaining subject to attacks for rest of life. Studied at Lycée Condorcet but suffered periods of ill health. Military service, 1889–90; qualified as lawyer, 1893. Wrote for *Revue Blanche*; graduated in philosophy. Lived as semi-recluse on Boulevard Haussmann, Paris. Awarded the Prix Goncourt and the Légion d'honneur, 1919. Died in Paris, 18 November 1922.

Selected Writings

Fiction

À la recherche du temps perdu, 8 vols, 1913–27; as *Remembrance of Things Past*, translated by C.K. Scott Moncrieff, 1922–31; Scott Moncrieff's traslation revised by Terence Kilmartin, 3 vols, 1981; 1981 translation revised by D.J, Enright as *In Search of Lost Time*, 6 vols, 1992

Du côté de chez Swann, 1913; as *Swann's Way*, translated by C.K. Scott Moncrieff, 2 vols, 1922

À l'ombre des jeunes filles en fleurs, 1919; as *Within a Budding Grove*, translated by C.K. Scott Moncrieff, 1924

Le Côté de Guermantes, 1920–21; as *The Guermantes Way*, translated by C.K. Scott Moncrieff, 1925

Sodome et Gomorrhe, 1921–22; as *Cities of the Plain*, translated by C.K. Scott Moncrieff, 2 vols, 1929; as *Sodom and Gomorrah* in Enright translation, 1992

La Prisonnière, 1923; as *The Captive*, translated by C.K. Scott Moncrieff, 1929

Albertine disparue, 1925; as *The Sweet Cheat Gone*, translated by C.K. Scott Moncrieff, 1930; as *Albertine Gone*, in Kilmartin translation, 1981; as *The Fugitive* in Enright translations, 1992

Le Temps retrouvé, 1927; as *Time Regained*, translated by Stephen Hudson, 1931; translated by Andreas Mayor, 1970

Jean Santeuil, 1952; as *Jean Santeuil*, translated by Gerard Hopkins, 1955

Other

Les Plaisirs et les jours, 1896; as *Pleasures and Regrets*, translated by Louise Varèse, 1948

Pastiches et mélanges [Pastiches and Miscellanies], 1919

Chroniques [Chronicles], 1927

Correspondance générale, 6 vols, 1930–36; selection as *Letters*, edited by Mina Curtiss, 1950

A Selection, edited by Gerard Hopkins, 1948

Letters to a Friend, translated by Alexander Henderson and Elizabeth Henderson, 1949

Letters of Marcel Proust to Antoine Bibesco, translated by Gerard Hopkins, 1953

Contre Sainte-Beuve, 1954; as *On Art and Literature 1896–1919*, translated by Sylvia Townsend Warner, 1958 (as *By Way of Sainte-Beuve*, 1958); as *Against Sainte-Beuve and Other Essays*, translated by John Sturrock, 1988

Letters to His Mother, translated and edited by George D. Painter, 1957

Textes retrouvés, edited by Philip Kolb and Larkin B. Price, 1968

Correspondance, edited by Philip Kolb, 1970–

Le Carnet de 1908, edited by Philip Kolb, 1976

Selected Letters 1880–1903, edited by Philip Kolb, 1983

Further Reading

Ellison, David R., *The Reading of Proust*, Baltimore: Johns Hopkins University Press, 1984

Hayman, Ronald, *Proust: A Biography*, London: Heinemann, and New York: HarperCollins, 1990

Hughes, Edward Joseph, *Marcel Proust: A Study in the Quality of Awareness*, New York and Cambridge: Cambridge University Press, 1983

Kasell, Walter, *Marcel Proust and the Strategy of Reading*, Philadelphia: Benjamins, 1980

Kilmartin, Terence, *A Guide to Proust*, London: Chatto and Windus, 1983, as *A Reader's Guide to Remembrance of Things Past*, New York: Random House, 1983; revised by Joanna Kilmartin and included in *Time Regained* by Proust, revised translation by D.J. Enright, Chatto and Windus, 1992; New York: Modern Library, 1993

Kristeva, Julia, "Marcel Proust: In Search of Identity" in *The Jew in the Text*, edited by Linda Nochlin and Tamar Garb, London and New York: Thames and Hudson, 1995

Painter, George D., *Marcel Proust: A Biography*, 2 vols, London: Chatto and Windus, 1959

Seymour, Gabriel N., *Marcel Proust's Combray*, translated by C.K. Scott Moncrieff, Salisbury, Connecticut: Lime Rock Press, 1979

Thody, Philip, *Marcel Proust*, London: Macmillan, 1987; New York: St Martin's Press, 1988

Proust was born to a Catholic father and a Jewish mother, Jeanne Weil, daughter of a wealthy Paris stockbroker. Although christened, Marcel and his younger brother were taken occasionally to a synagogue, as when his mother's cousin was married. Proust was compelled into Jewishness in 1894 over the Dreyfus affair, and broke with his high Catholic friend, Robert de Montesquiou, who was an anti-Dreyfusard: "If I am a Catholic, like my father and brother, my mother is Jewish", he wrote in a letter to Montesquiou (19 May 1896). With his friends Bizet, Yeatman, and the two brothers Halévy, Proust organized the *Manifeste des cent quatre*, which collected 13,000 signatures in support of Alfred Dreyfus who had been unfairly accused of treason and sent to Devil's Island. It was eventually revealed that the documents on which the affair hinged had been forged; Dreyfus was re-tried, declared guilty, but then pardoned and allowed to return to France.

After his mother's death, Proust agreed to contribute to a Catholic journal only anonymously, because "I would be afraid it might look disrespectful towards Mamma that I should write for a paper whose objective is nothing but anti-Semitism". Initially a Dreyfusard identifying with the fate of the condemned and exiled Jew, the disillusioned Proust was revolted by the anti-clericalism expressed by his side, and continued to feel ambivalent about social commitment.

The Paris of the Third Republic was a highly anti-Semitic society. Catholic conservatives held the Jews responsible for the death of Christ, yet at the same time tolerated some few rich Jews within high society. There were also popular Marxist groupings which blamed Jewish capitalism for causing local poverty.

In the novel, *À la recherche du temps perdu* (*Remembrance of Things Past*), the sensitive boy growing up remembers Charles Swann, who lived nearby, "like certain other Jews, my parents' old friend had contrived to illustrate in turn all the successive stages through which those of his race had passed, from the most naive snobbery and the crudest vulgarity to the most exquisite good manners". Swann has an unpleasant odour and "punchinello nose, absorbed for years within a pleasant face, now seemed enormous, tumid, crimson, the nose of an old Hebrew"; "a prophet's beard beneath a huge nose". The novel conveys the small treacheries of Parisian society. Despite being an assimilated and very marginal Jew, Swann is turned away from the salon of the Prince de Guermantes, then later from that of the Duc de Guermantes. When the boy/narrator brings home Jewish school friends, his grandfather disapprovingly hums a theme from *La Juive* or else " Israel, break thy chains". One of the most unsympathetic characters in the novel is Jewish – Bloch, the blundering boor, "a bad egg, one of the very worst, a pretty detestable specimen". Bloch, with his "hooked nose", is not invited to the house again, despite the fact that the narrator is fond of him.

Julia Kristeva notes that throughout the novel red and pink are systematically associated with Jews and Judaism. The Jewish redness of Gilberte; Odette, the woman in pink; the red dress and shoes of Oriane, contrasted with the virginal whiteness and purity of the Church. Yet Kristeva also comments on the way in which Proust ironically fuses Judaism with homosexuality. Sodom and Zionism become dual singularities.

The controversies of the Dreyfus affair appear at various stages of the novel, illustrating the peculiarities of anti-Semitism in France and its effects on French society. Swann, as a Jew, is a Dreyfusard. He is described as "comically blind". The Duc de Guermantes cannot quite understand how "this man who yearly sends me the best port in the world" and who is "so cultured and respected" can fall into the "aberration" of supporting Dreyfus. On another occasion Mme Verdurin denies the Baron status as a member of the French community, "What is his nationality exactly, isn't he an Austrian?" She concludes that he is a spy and has "wormed" his way into her house. As both Jew and Catholic, Proust can see both points of view, allowing him to be an astute social commentator. Yet at the end of *À la recherche du temps perdu*, the narrator believes that "every public event, be it the Dreyfus case, be it the war, furnishes the writer with a fresh excuse for *not* attempting to decipher this book."

In his great novel, now more accurately rendered in English as *In Search of Lost Time*, involuntary memory and time play an important role. The brilliance and subtlety of Proust's descriptive writing, the sardonic depth, and the variety of psychological analyses makes this one of the great novels of the 20th century.

Critics such as Beatrice Aaronson have commented on his Talmudic "serpentine" style, those long meandering sentences that enwrap you and pertain to every aspect of life, from the most mundane to the most elevated and spiritual. And then there is the aspect of Proust's obsession with details, like Talmudic "pilpulim", debating first this way and then that. The remembrance power of his creativity is part of the ethos of Zakhor (the importance of remembering), and the ultimate Jewish quality of textual identity as the People of the Book. For Proust, writing, the book, becomes his life.

Although awarded the Prix Goncourt, Proust was denied membership of the French Academy. According to Ronald Hayman (*Proust*, p.476), when the anti-Semitic L'Action française refused to acknowledge the name of the "dirty Jew" (Proust) who had written the article that they had published anonymously, Proust accepted the phrase "dirty Jew" as "a Homeric epithet in the household".

SORREL KERBEL

R

Raab, Esther

Israeli poet, 1894–1981

Born in Petah Tikvah agricultural settlement, 1894, to Judah Raab, one of its founders, and wife Leah. Lived, worked, and studied in a variety of agricultural settlings including Kibbutz Degania. Began working as teacher and writing first poems, 1919. Lived in Cairo. Married Yitzhak Green; no children. Lived in Paris. Eventually settled in Tel Aviv; home became centre for writers and painters. Died 1981.

Selected Writings

Poetry
Kimshonim [Thistles], 1930
Shirei [Poems], 1964
Tefilah aharonah [Last Prayer], 1972
Yalkut shirim [Anthology of Poems], 1982
Gan sheharav [A Destroyed Garden], 1983
Kol hashirim [Collected Poems], 1988
Esther Raab – kol haprozah [Esther Raab – Collected Prose], 1994

Further Reading

Ehud, Ben'Ezer, *Yamin Shel La'anah U-Devash: Sipur Hayeha Shel Ha-Mishorevet Esther Raab* [Days of Gall and Honey: The Biography of the Poet Esther Raab], Tel Aviv: Am Oved, 1998

Lapidus Lerner, Anne, "The Naked Land: Nature in the Poetry of Esther Raab" in *Women of the Word: Jewish Women and Jewish Writing*, edited by Judith Baskin, Detroit: Wayne State University Press, 1994

Luz, Zvi, *Shirat Esther Raab* [Poetry of Esther Raab], Tel Aviv: Hakibuts hameuhad, 1997

Mann, Barbara, "Framing the Native: Esther Raab's Visual Poetics", *Israel Studies* (Winter 1999)

Miron, Dan, "Why Was There No Women's Poetry in Hebrew before 1920?" in *Gender and Text in Modern Hebrew and Yiddish Literature*, edited by Naomi B. Sokoloff, Anne Lapidus Lerner, and Anita Norich, New York: Jewish Theological Seminary of America, 1992

Esther Raab is considered the first native Modern Hebrew poet, the first poet for whom Hebrew was a vernacular language. She was born in Palestine to a Hungarian family who were among the founders of Petah Tikvah – an agricultural settlement established in the late 19th century that resembled traditional, religious Jewish communities of eastern Europe, but was at the same time committed to physical labour and a Zionist "redemption" of the land. Most Hebrew writers of this period were born in eastern and central Europe, and their initial exposure to the Mediterranean landscape derived from traditional Jewish texts, including biblical descriptions of the Land of Israel. Raab, however, from a young age, was surrounded by the Middle Eastern landscape, and its sensual details of plant life and seasonal change permeate her work. For example, the invention of names for the natural environment was one of the achievements of modern Hebrew in Palestine during the early decades of the 20th century. The blend of these new botanical terms, with elements of traditional Jewish prayers she had learned as a child, distinguished Raab's poetic style from that of Hebrew writers of her generation who were raised in Europe. At the same time, Raab was also influenced by modern European literature, and has commented on the particular importance of French symbolist poetry. Her earliest poems appeared in 1922 in the literary journal *Hedim*, edited by Asher Barash. Her first and perhaps signature volume *Kimshonim* [Thistles] contained mostly short lyrics, whose dense imagism and often obscure syntax also distinguished Raab's from other Hebrew poetry of the period. An intense and seemingly unmediated treatment of the natural landscape would remain a defining feature of Raab's poetry: "My heart is with your dews, homeland,/ at night above fields of [nettles], and the scent of pines and moist [thistle], I will unfold a hidden wing."

Raab was one of a number of Hebrew women writers active in Palestine during this period, including Dvora Baron, Rachel (Bluwstein), Yocheved Bat-Miriam, and, somewhat later, Leah Goldberg. Like other Hebrew women writers, Raab had a special relation to Jewish tradition, particularly to Hebrew's linguistic authority and weight. In an interview published at the end of her life, she claimed to feel less "burdened" by Hebrew's prestige as an ancient, sacred language. Despite her linguistic experimentation, Raab's lyrics are also indebted to biblical sources and their archaic linguistic forms. One of her early poems addresses a group of poetic matriarchs – "holy grandmothers of Jerusalem" – asking them, in the tradition of Yiddish *tkhines* (petitionary or supplicatory prayers), to protect and inspire her. The same poem takes as its hero the biblical figure of Deborah, with whom the poet imagines herself drinking coffee and discussing military strategy. Other poems display a subversive sense of sexual politics though their use of inverted or ambiguous grammatical constructions, such as the feminizing of a noun which is conventionally gendered male. The word for land in Hebrew is grammatically gendered female, and the paradigmatic discursive relation between poet and land in this period was the male poet celebrating the fertility of a feminized land. Raab's landscape poems capitalize on this figuration of the land in sexual terms, but celebrate the land's simplicity, the barrenness of its sands, often describing it in a wild or even derelict, weed-ridden state: "Upon your nakedness, a white day celebrates/ you – so [meager] and so rich."

Raab's home became a centre of the newly-developing Hebrew culture in Tel Aviv during the 1930s, and she was associated with the coterie of artists and writers surrounding the literary journal *Ktuvim*. Her poem "Tel Aviv" borrows the language of Lamentations and Isaiah to personify "the first Hebrew city" as a barren and rebellious young woman, whose newly sprouted cement structures choke its sandy "skinny chest". Again, Raab's evocation of the damage incurred through encroaching urbanization went against the grain of much Hebrew poetry celebrating the city. Though her later years were marked by long poetic silences, Raab's work became an example to poets who began publishing in the 1960s, and whose more individualized, personal voices went against the grain of Hebrew literature in the early state period. Since her death in 1981, Raab's work has received extended critical attention in Hebrew literary histories, and in more theoretical studies of gender and Israeli culture.

BARBARA MANN

Rachel (Bluwstein, Blaustein)

Russian-born poet, 1890–1931

Born in Vyatka, 1890. Arrived in Palestine 1909; lived in agricultural school for girls on shores of the Kinneret (Sea of Galilee) until 1913. Went to France to study agronomy and drawing. Returned to Russia at outbreak of World War I. Worked in educational institutions for refugee children. Contracted tuberculosis. Returned to live on Kibbutz Degania, 1919. Unable to work with children because of illness, left kibbutz. Settled in one-room apartment in Tel Aviv, where she lived from 1927 until she died, 1931. Published under first name only.

Selected Writings

Poetry
Safiah [Aftergrowth], 1927
Mineged [Across From], 1930
Nevo [Nevo], 1932
Shirat Rachel [Poems], 1982
Kehakot Rachel [As Rachel Waited], 1982
Begani netaatikha [In My Garden], 1985
Hatishmah koli [Will You Hear My Voice], 1986
Flowers of Perhaps: Selected Poems, translated by Robert Friend, 1994
Shirei Rahel [Rachel's Poems], 1997

For Children
Babayit ubahuts [Inside and Outside Home], 1974

Other
Shirim, mikhtavim, reshimot [Poems, Letters, Writings], 1985

Further Reading

Chachlili, Binyamin, *For You and About You*, Tel Aviv: Hakibuts hameuhad, 1987
Gluzman, M., "The Exclusion of Women from Hebrew Literary History", *Prooftexts* (September 1991)
Kritz, Reuven, *On Rahel's Poetry*, Tel Aviv: Pura-Books, 1987
Milstein, Uri, *Rachel*, Tel Aviv: Zmora Bitan, 1985
Snir, Mordecai and Shimon Kushnir, *Rachel and her Poetry*, Tel Aviv: Davar, 1971

Rachel was the first Hebrew woman poet. Hers was the first voice in a cycle of four women poets – the others being Elisheva, Yocheved Bat-Miriam, and Esther Raab – who published their work in an entirely male landscape; each one of them presents a different poetic statement.

Rachel published her first poem, "Mood", in 1920 in the newspaper *Davar*. This poem prefigures the composition that she introduces to the landscape of Hebrew poetry. It is brief, of balanced and precise construction, but it rages with a pervasive emotional storm. The general audience read Rachel's poems as articulations of their yearning to possess the land, defining the physical and ideological-Zionist aspect as one. This interpretation missed the distinctive style arising in her poetry. Rachel goes to the heart of the conversation between the poet and *the* native land and changes it into a dialogue between the poet and *her* native land. This change of speaker causes a permutation in the quality and character of the dialogue. This in itself becomes an act of pioneering. In contrast to the longing and love directed towards the land of Israel in the poetry of male poets, a closer intimacy arises between the spokeswoman and her land.

In the poem "To My Land", for example, Rachel joins the national discussion about the land and the cultivating of the soil, but she declares her distance from it and from the alternative option she has: she wants to win the heart of the land not by heroic conquest, but as a mother deals with her home, carefully and with an intrinsically unique tenderness:

> I didn't sing to you, my land, and I didn't glorify your name, with the falsity of heroism, with the spoils of battles; just a tree – my hands have planted, the shores of the Jordan are peaceful. Just a path – my feet have subdued, on the surface of fields . . . I knew that, the mother, very wretched, indeed, from the repose of her daughter . . . in the day the light will become bright, just the mysterious cry, upon your eyes.

In her poetry Rachel creates a new category of relations between the writer and the earth, which is based upon the ties of a mother and daughter who are co-dependent and maintain a mutual system of giving.

The Kinneret is a recurring theme in Rachel's poems. For many years the conventional interpretation of the Kinneret poems was seen to be the promotion of the concept of settlement and love of the land. Yet in Rachel's poetry, the Kinneret symbolizes yearnings for the more wondrous period in her life – a time of realization and usefulness – that culminated in disillusionment and rejection (she was asked to leave the kibbutz after only two years because of her illness). Kinneret symbolizes a period of nature and integration in the collective and creative experience of the kibbutz, and at the same time a split with the collective path and passage through the urban landscape to independent life and dedication to writing.

Rachel is involved with the image of the woman in many of her poems; she defines femininity, and she wraps the essence of this quality in an interlacing of strength and ability on the one hand and fragility and dependence on the other. In the poem "Your Hands Are Tender", she writes, "Behold a woman, I am just a woman"; this modest phrasing conceals within itself an attribution of great strength to the same "just a woman"; she compares herself to a twig that wants to reach the top of the tree, but "without support – sad and pallid, I will fall to the earth". The mighty female presence and the longing for exaltation are intertwined, step-by-step with the deeply submerged need rooted in woman.

The image of the beloved in Rachel's poems is also two-faced – she is drawn to the existence of a romantic connection on the one hand, and she recoils from it on the other. Rachel has two poems that conduct a kind of dialogue one with another and represent the dual face of the image of the woman – "Rebellion" and "Surrender".

The image of the woman in Rachel's poetry identifies with stereotypical female roles; one of which is the wife who hopes for the achievement of motherhood. Indeed, this component is common in her poetry, but it does not resonate well with the place it occupies in her writing. One of her most contemplative poems is "Barren", which deals with this yearning for the maternal experience. This has led to the impression that the subject of barrenness echoes in her poetry, yet she deals with it only in this poem.

Rachel the poet defines herself as a descendant of Rachel, "mother of mothers". Both guard the functioning of the subject in accordance with the masculine conventions – apparently – but in practice they break them and rebel against them. Rachel suggests a poetic alternative, a female contribution, in a way pretentious and definitely not transparent. Rachel brings a dialectic practice; short and minimalist poems that appear to be simple and absorb within them complexities, orderly poetry, symmetrical and strictly organized from the point of view of *prose* – but engaged with the contents of emotional conflict, pain and confusion, using silence and the absence of the word in order to express things with greater strength and in a novel way.

The poem "Expectation", for example, expresses a sense of distress. In light of her loneliness and her bitter pain, the speaker asks to be grasped by a little hope, a shadow of comfort by which to be reinforced. Her difficult fate results in deep sorrow, yet this experience is wrapped in great despair, is embodied in a symmetrical and exact poetic structure (constant rhyme, repetitious syntactical structure, and uniform metre). "And to seek refuge in the lap of my past shadow, in compassionate contiguity, in pure contact, to tremble from choked tears, and until the day becomes light, to reward phrases of the pain and its strange confection . . ." This tension between the content and its form, and the dialect of chaos and order, stands at the poetic heart of Rachel's poetry.

In the poem, "Idiom" she declares, "I have known any number of words – therefore, I shall keep quiet". In this way she emphasizes the choice of speaking in silence. Because of the endless words that are available to her, she prefers the silence. The absence is not empty but a contrasting strength to the words used.

In the article "On the Sign of the Time", published in 1927, Rachel describes simplicity as a category of sophistication and declares the conscious choice of a poetry of economy: "It is clear to me: a sign of the time in the art of the poem is the simplicity of expression, simple expression, that is to say: the first fluttering of the lyrical emotion, an instantaneous expression, before it manages to cover its nakedness in festive garments of silk and golden ornaments."

Her poems and pen name are characterized by economy – from a figurative to a literal aspect. Through the simple and apparently innocent poetry, Rachel demands an attentive ear to listen to her recitations that establish a female presence of a degree not recognized by Hebrew poetry. By way of the short poem, she breaks through its boundaries, by her seemingly delicate turning to the reader to whom she directs her poems straight at the heart. By the design of her private world alongside both the ancient and contemporary Hebrew culture she penetrates the most highly guarded cultural assets.

TALI ASHER
translated by Rachel M. Paul

Rakosi, Carl

German-born US poet, 1903–

Born in Berlin, 6 November 1903; emigrated to United States, 1910. Educated at University of Wisconsin, BA 1924, MA 1926; University of Pennsylvania, Philadelphia, MSW 1940; University of Chicago; University of Texas, Austin. Married Leah Jaffe, 1939; one daughter and one son. Instructor, University of Texas, 1928–29; social worker, Cook County Bureau of Public Welfare, Chicago, 1932–33; supervisor, Federal Transient Bureau, New Orleans, 1933–34; field work supervisor, Graduate School of Social Work, Tulane University, New Orleans, 1934–35, and Jewish Family Welfare Society, Brooklyn, 1935–40; case supervisor, Jewish Social Service Bureau, and Bellefaire, both Cleveland, 1943–45; executive director, Jewish Family and Children's Service, Minneapolis, 1945–68; writer in residence, Yaddo Colony, 1968–75, University of Wisconsin, 1969–70, and Michigan State University, East Lansing, 1974. Psychotherapist, Minneapolis, 1958–68; since 1986 senior editor *Sagetrieb*, Orono, Maine. Awarded National Endowment for the Arts Award, 1969; and fellowship, 1972, 1979; Fund for Poetry Award, 1988; National Poetry Association Award, 1988.

Selected Writings

Poetry
Two Poems, 1933
Selected Poems, 1941
Amulet, 1967
Ere-VOICE, 1971
Ex Cranium, Night, 1975
My Experiences in Parnassus, 1977
Droles de Journal, 1981
History, 1981
Spiritus I, 1983
Meditation, 1985
The Collected Poems, 1986
The Beast, 1994
Poems, 1923–1941, edited by Andrew Crozier, 1995
The Earth Suite, 1997
The Old Poet's Tale, 1999

Other
Collected Prose, 1984

Further Reading

Codrescu, Andrei, "Carl Rakosi, A Warm, Steady Presence", *Baltimore Sun* (1 April 1984)
Crozier, Andrew, "Found: A Modern Masterpiece", introduction to *Carl Rakosi: Poems 1923–1941*, edited by Crozier, Los Angeles: Sun and Moon Press, 1995
Dembo, L.S., "The Objectivist Poet: Interviews with Oppen, Rakosi, Reznikoff and Zukofsky", *Contemporary Literature*, 10/2 (1981)
Dembo, L.S., "The Poetry of Carl Rakosi", *Iowa Review*, 2/1 (1981)
Heller, Michael, "Heaven and the Modern World", *New York Times* (8 March 1987)
Heller, Michael (editor), *Carl Rakosi: Man and Poet*, Orono: University of Maine Press, 1993
Marshall, Jack, "An Objectivist Speaks", *Poetry Flash* (March 1987)
Rosenblum, Martin J., "Unexpected Arrangement", *Wisconsin Review*, 22/1 (1988)
Sharp, Tom, "Objectivists 1927–1934: A Critical History of the Work and Association of Zukofsky, Williams, Reznikoff, Pound, Rakosi and Oppen" (dissertation), Stanford University, 1982

Carl Rakosi was a member of a group of poets (Louis Zukofsky, Charles Reznikoff, George Oppen) who, in the 1930s, called themselves the Objectivists. Though many interpretations of this label have been offered, all agree that it was a philosophy of verse in the context of Modernism, via Pound and Williams, that eschewed sentimentality. A strong sense of historicity balanced in the poetic imagination and the embrace of new language and the affect of contemporary culture were some of its characteristics. In 1941 James Laughlin's New Directions published a very slim volume of Rakosi's work, called *Selected Poems*, in the multi-publisher Poet of the Month series. The short prosy poems bear titles such as "Early American Chronicle", "The People", and "To an Anti-Semite", which begins with this stanza: "So you fought for the Jews/ in the last war/ and have become a patriot again!"; and ends: "And now I find you/ trying to drive the Jews/ and Communists out of America!"

They are poems of social conscience, though not partisan in any political or religious sense. This early period of Rakosi's literary life, from about 1923 through 1932, was active and energetic, but intertwined with his writing, publishing, and engaging in literary correspondence was a growing dilemma of how to earn a living, which less and less seemed possible as a poet. His production diminished through the 1930s as he first trained himself to be a social worker, then attempted to become a doctor, but could not afford to complete medical school, instead returning to what became his lifetime profession: social work.

Carl Rakosi wrote under his own name and was always so-published, but when he became a social worker he changed his professional name to Callman Rawley, fearing the great anti-Semitism he believed dominated the public sector. Despite this heightened awareness of his Jewishness, his early work, rather than being either religious or political, is more a poetry of cultural awareness, emphasizing a kind of Whitmanian democratic vision. After the publication of his *Selected Poems* in 1941, he more or less stopped writing, or at least publishing, for almost 25 years.

The second half of Rakosi's poetry life was active, following a similar kind of silence which his fellow Objectivist poet, George Oppen, had also assumed in his career. Many critics believe that both poets held strong beliefs about the need for change in society and felt that poetry was a distraction or irrelevance to this. Rakosi broke his silence in 1967 with a collection of poems called *Amulet*, published by New Directions, 26 years after his first book from that same publisher.

By 1975, when Black Sparrow Press published a later selection of poems (*Ex Cranium, Night*), and from then onward, Rakosi was far more preoccupied with the subject of what it means to be a poet or the place of poetry in the world than with social issues per se. An example of this might be demonstrated in his poem "Poetry": "Its nature is to look/ both absolute and mortal/ as if a boy had passed through/ or the imprint of his foot/ had been preserved/ unchanged/ under the ash of Herculaeneum."

In 1986 The National Poetry Foundation issued *The Collected Poems of Carl Rakosi*. This collection, arranged by Rakosi himself, though not chronological, gives the reader a strong sense of the shape of his lifetime work. Despite the fact that he was never a religious poet, he poignantly opens the collection with a prayer, "Lord, What is the Shape of Man", and ends with a group of early poems called "Exercises in Scripture Writing" that imitate various Hebrew religious poets. Thus, while his Judaic self is seldom a subject for Rakosi, his awareness of his heritage and how it meshes with American democracy is clearly significant to him in this latest presentation of his oeuvre.

Most of Rakosi's poems are short and spritely, filled with pithy and succinct observations. As a poet, he is a sort of gadfly, stinging and buzzing about everything, a reminder that to live intelligently is never to relax or leave unnoticed any slightly foolish thing. He assumes as his role the philosopher-poet, commentator on all of life. For instance, "The Weight Lifter": "When a man's/ sweat/ is strong/ enough to repel/ mosquitoes,/ boy,/ that's character." His Objectivist idealism transcends simple politics, social, or religious awareness, and to quote Karl Young introducing him in 1985 at Woodland Pattern Book Center in Milwaukee, "Rakosi's unadorned verse radiates open good humor, playful irony, untroubled powers of precise observation, sly exuberance, unresentful disregard for authority and trendiness, judicious respect for proportion and scale in human activities, a direct jocularity rare in contemporary poetry, and, rarer still, unalloyed horse-sense".

DIANE WAKOSKI

Raphael, Frederic

US-born British fiction writer, 1931–

Born Frederic Michael Raphael, in Chicago, 14 August 1931. Educated at Charterhouse School, Surrey; St John's College, Cambridge, 1950–54; MA 1954. Married Sylvia Betty Glatt, 1955; two sons, one daughter. Awards include British Screen Writers award, 1965, 1966, 1967; British Academy award, 1965; Oscar, for screenplay, 1966; Royal Television Society Writer of the Year Award, 1976. Fellow, Royal Society of Literature, 1964.

Selected Writings

Novels
Obbligato, 1956
The Earlsdon Way, 1958
The Limits of Love, 1960
A Wild Surmise, 1961
The Graduate Wife, 1962
The Trouble with England, 1962
Lindmann, 1963
Darling, 1965
Orchestra and Beginners, 1967
Like Men Betrayed, 1970
Who Were You with Last Night?, 1971
April, June and November, 1972
Richard's Things, 1973
California Time, 1975
The Glittering Prizes, 1976
Heaven and Earth, 1985
After the War, 1988
The Hidden I: A Myth Revised, 1990
A Double Life, 1993
Old Scores, 1995
Coast to Coast, 1999

Short Stories
Sleeps Six, 1979
Oxbridge Blues and Other Stories, 1980
Think of England, 1986
The Latin Lover and Other Stories, 1994
All His Sons, 1999

Plays
Lady at the Wheel, with Lucienne Hill, music and lyrics by Leslie Bricusse and Robin Beaumont, 1958
A Man on the Bridge, 1961
The Island in *Eight Plays 2*, edited by Malcolm Stuart Fellows, 1965
An Early Life, 1979
The Serpent Son: Aeschylus: Oresteia (television play), with Kenneth McLeish, 1979
From the Greek, 1979

Screenplays: *Bachelor of Hearts*, with Leslie Bricusse, 1958; *Nothing but the Best*, 1963; *Darling*, 1965; *Two for the Road*, 1967; *Far from the Madding Crowd*, 1967; *A Severed Head*, 1970; *Don't Bother to Knock* (*Why Bother to Knock*), with Denis Cannan and Frederic Gotfurt, 1971; *Daisy Miller*, 1974; *Richard's Things*, 1981; *The Man in the Brooks Brothers Shirt*, 1990; *Eyes Wide Shut: A Screenplay* (with Stanley Kubrick), 1999

Radio Plays: *The Daedalus Dimension*, 1979; *Death in Trieste*, 1981; *The Thought of Lydia*, 1988

Television Plays: *The Executioners*, 1961; *The Trouble with England*, 1964; *The Glittering Prizes*, 1976; *Something's Wrong*, 1978; *Of Mycenae and Men*, with Kenneth McLeish, 1979; *School Play*, 1979; *The Best of Friends*, 1980; *Byron: A Personal Tour* (documentary), 1981; *Oxbridge Blues*, 1984; *After the War* series, 1989

Other
Editor, *Bookmarks*, 1975
W. Somerset Maugham and His World, 1977
Translator, with Kenneth McLeish, *The Poems of Catullus*, 1978
Cracks in the Ice: Views and Reviews, 1979
A List of Books: An Imaginary Library, with Kenneth McLeish, 1981
Byron, 1982
The Necessity of Anti-Semitism, 1989
Eyes Wide Open: A Memoir of Stanley Kubrick and Eyes Wide Shut, 1999
Popper: The Great Philosopher, 1999
Personal terms: the 1950s and 1960s, 2001

Further Reading

McDowell, Frederick P.W., "The Varied Universe of Frederic Raphael", *Critique* (Fall 1965)
"Strictly Personal: Frederic Raphael on Jews, Himself and England", *Prospect* (June 1996)

Frederic Raphael is best known as one of Britain's leading novelists, although he is also a playwright, screenwriter, Classics scholar, and translator. Born in the United States, he went to an English public school where he suffered "squalid little public-school Jew-bait(ing)". He has an ambivalent relationship with the country of his education and formation and lives both in London and abroad. Raphael's novels have been acclaimed, and he won an Oscar as a screenwriter.

Raphael writes of the aspirations, relationships in formation and disintegration, infidelities, and trials of the educated, suburban middle class. Many of his characters are Jewish and struggle to make sense of their "unchosen" backgrounds and lives shaped by external factors. In his novel *The Limits of Love* the camp survivor Otto Kahane, comes to north London to his only remaining family, and brings the Shoah into the Jewish home of the Adlers. The Adler children represent a number of options facing British Jews in the postwar world. Colin, an architect, after the army tries to keep his head down, work steadily, and forget that he is Jewish. He suffers anti-Semitism silently at work and at the golf club, and his attempt at assimilation leaves him empty and unfulfilled but without any real idea why. Susan marries an East End Jewish communist with a very definite sense of identity and commitment, but her background make it difficult for her fully to share these, and she comes to the brink of leaving him. Julie meets the main protagonist, Paul Reisman, the son of assimilated Jews.

Reisman's school days of humiliation, when he is "exposed" as being a Jew are powerfully recalled. He resists confirmation as an Anglican in response to officially sanctioned anti-Semitism. At Cambridge, Reisman, a clever and angry young man, reasons away all faith and the need for a Jewish identity, but he marries Julie in a synagogue, for the sake of her parents. He comes to think of his Jewishness as a difficulty to be overcome, allowing him to become a writer. All three of the Adler children test and find the "limits of [their] love". Colin meets again a Jewish architect working on development projects in Israel and elsewhere, and rediscovers himself and a passion for living. Susan supports her husband against all the odds, and Julie and Paul, after Paul's discovery of the East End, decide that they will have a child, as Otto says, as an antidote to Hitler's plans. Each of them, albeit in different ways, comes to the necessary recognition of themselves as Jews, finding meaning and sufficient integrity to want to carry on.

The Holocaust is again the shadowy background to *Lindmann*. A British civil servant, responsible for the sinking of a refugee ship and the loss of 600 Jewish lives, adopts the identity of a survivor as an act of penance, and dedicates "his" life to trying to find some meaning in selfless human kindness. The truth of this life too is called into question when a Jewish director plans to make a film of the tragedy of the *SS Broda*. This strange psychological study of a man's attempt to overcome guilt demands that we ask what sort of life is valuable after the Holocaust.

The Glittering Prizes traces a group of Cambridge friends into their relationships, marriages, and careers. The central character, Adam Morris, is successfully working in the mass media but with little satisfaction. Adam was a public school boy hounded for being Jewish and continues to encounter English anti-Semitism. He is intelligent with a biting wit and aspirations to be a great novelist. His condemnation of the seemingly empty pieties of suburban Jewish life are telling and harsh, and his own Jewish identity is ever present but without form – his wife is not Jewish and yet he circumcises his son. It is as if the mere knowledge of the concentration camps somehow undermines the meaning of his life. Adam cannot clearly feel and it takes the grossly premature death of his fellow student to bring him to the beginning of a path back to himself, a path that is open to his writing and more accepting of his background.

These Jewish dilemmas of identity are also explored in *A Wild Surmise*, *Orchestra and Beginners*, and in the recent collection, *All His Sons*. In *A Double Life* the main character is a repressed homosexual French diplomat, accused of being a Jew, and raped by a Nazi officer amid daily denunciations of Jews by French men and women. Again, the brutality perpetrated upon the outsider renders him lost to himself.

Raphael's experience of working with Stanley Kubrick on the script for the film *Eyes Wide Shut* is recorded in his, *Eyes Wide Open: A Memoir of Stanley Kubrick*. The two reworked the novel *Traumnovelle*, by the Viennese-Jewish writer Arthur Schnitzler, into a script set in contemporary New York. Raphael writes that Kubrick insisted that the lead couple be non-Jews, and that the director's Jewish identity, although seemingly suppressed, is an integral part of the man and his filmmaking.

A number of Raphael's essays and articles were published as *The Necessity of Anti-Semitism*. He describes himself as middle-class, Anglo-American, a liberal, and a "sceptical Jew". Acknowledging that we cannot merely carry on as if the past had not happened, Raphael asks how we can make sense of a world that evidently does not easily make any sense at all? He contends that each of us must resist tyranny, and that the written word and the writer have a vital role to play in that resistance. Raphael considers that his "kind of Jewishness" is to "feel myself alien from everyone". He is the most marginal of Jews, estranged from communal life, ritual, and practice, and yet his experiences as a Jew, forged in the anti-Semitism of an English education, and reinforced at all levels of European culture, have been central to his writing. His fiction examines the limits of our freedom to construct our selves, and the recognition of a necessary dimension to our identities. Being a Jew entails not being at home in England, for example, and not becoming an Englishman, but equally not being able to return easily, if at all, to a existing "community". But this broken personal integrity must be addressed. Raphael explores perceptively and with honesty how post-Holocaust Jews do make sense of their lives, and how they live between the lure of losing themselves in the wider culture and the realities of difference and prejudice.

PAUL MORRIS

Ratosh, Yonatan

Polish-born Israeli poet, 1908–1981

Born Uriel Halperin in Warsaw, 18 November 1908. Hebrew-speaking family emigrated to Palestine, 1921. Published his first poem in 1926. Studied law for a year in Jerusalem. Attended lectures casually at the Hebrew University and the Sorbonne. Edited Revisionist movement's newspaper *Hayarden* and was active in right-wing underground organizations, mid-1930s. Founded Canaanite movement, 1939, which rejected religion and Jewish nationalism and promoted the theory of a shared cultural heritage for the entire Middle East. Changed his name in early 1940s.

Founded and co-edited *Alef*, a widely translated literary journal which included the works of Camus, O'Neill, Shaw, and Stendhal. Died 25 March 1981.

Selected Writings

Poetry
Lekever yishmael [The Tomb of Yishmael] (as Uriel Halperin), 1932
Hupah shehorah [Black Canopy], 1941
Yohemed [Yohemed], 1942
Tsela [Rib], 1959
Shirei heshbon [Songs of Accounting], 1963
Shirei mamash [Real Songs], 1965
1967 Umah haleah: shalom ivri, [1967 – And What's Next], 1967
Shirei herev [Songs of the Swords], 1969
Shirim [Poems], 1974
Yalkut shirim [Collected Poems] 3 vols, 1974–75
Ahavat nashim [Women's Love], 1975
Shirei nearah [Songs of a Maiden], 1975
Shirei prat [Individual Poems], 1975
Shirei ahavah [Love Poems], 1983
Yalkut shirim [Collected Poems], 1991
Haholkhim bahoshekh: poemah [Walkers in the Dark: Poem] date unknown

Other
Translator, *Cyrano de Bergerac*, by Edmond Rostand, 1965
Translator, *Torat hagifrut*, by Rene Wellek and Austin Warren, 1967
Editor, *Minitsahon lemapolet* [From Victory to Defeat], 1976
Reshit hayamim: petihot ivriyot [Early Days: Hebrew Introductions], 1982
Sifrut yehudit balashon haivrit: petihot bevikoret uviveayot halashon [Jewish Literature in the Hebrew Language: Introductory Notes in Literary Criticism and Linguistics], 1982
Mikhtavim 1937–1980 [Letters 1937–1980], 1986

Further Reading

Diamond, James S., *Homeland or Holy Land? The "Canaanite" Critique of Israel*, Bloomington: Indiana University Press, 1986
Porath, Yehoshua, *Shelah Ve-'et Be-Yado: Sipur Hayav Shel Uriel Shelah (Yonathan Ratosh)*, Tel Aviv: Mahberot Le-Sifrut, 1989
Shamir, Ziva, *Le-Hathil Me-Alef: Shirat Ratosh, Mekoriyut U-Mekoroteha*, Tel Aviv: Hakibuts hameuhad, 1993
Shavit, Jacob, *The New Hebrew Nation: A Study in Israeli Heresy and Fantasy*, London: Frank Cass, 1987

Yonatan Ratosh, founder of a new modernistic movement in Hebrew poetry between the two world wars, emerged on the scene of Hebrew poetry as a revolutionary artist, whose primeval poems seemed to grow autonomously, independent of precedents in Hebrew verse, or paradigms derived from the literature of the world. Many critics ask whether his work constitutes "a continuity or a revolution". Ratosh himself claimed that he had never become familiar with any other poetry and was unaware of any direct influence by foreign sources on his art.

As the father of the Canaanite group, Ratosh believed that Hebrew literature needed to sever itself sharply and finally from the contents and values of the Hebrew literature created in foreign lands. He believed, with the extremism of an utopian-revolutionary, that literature created in Israel after the revolution and instigated by the native Hebrew would be able to preserve from the past only those few isolated texts that were not contaminated by the values generated by the existence of the Jews in the Diaspora. In other words: it was necessary to reduce the existing literature, reject the old in favour of the new, to create space for those innovations in the realms of ideas, themes, forms and typology, etc., associated with the renewed experience in Israel. It is not surprising then, that he attempted to present his poetry as a primeval creation – detached from roots and cuttings suckled by Western culture, including the Jewish culture throughout its two thousand years of Diaspora. These cultures represented for him all the distorted values that he attempted to discard and leave behind.

In order to understand the essence of Ratosh's novelty against the background of modernism in Israel, one needs to examine, first, from which characteristics he abstained when searching for a modernistic paradigm. He rejected Russian-Jewish metre and rhyme, as employed by the school of Avraham Shlonsky: Ratosh often relied in his work on grammatical rhyme, characteristic of early Piyut (liturgical Hebrew poems) and resorted to extreme metre arrangements, reminiscent of the ritualistic rhythms of a primitive tribe. In this way he renounced the wide array of material of expressionistic poetry, in the style of Uri Zvi Greenberg, and chose a concise and crystallized style, chiselled in stone. Ratosh also felt an aversion to the excessive sentimentalism of Shlonsky's poetry describing the shtetl – and saw them as signifiers of the Diaspora; in their place, the artist's quill described landscapes of primordial deserts, with rocky stones and dry treacherous rivers. It is noteworthy that, even though he stressed the connection to the native reality, he maintained a distance from any specific signifiers of locality, and preferred the archetypal, detached in time and place. Naturally, he was not attracted in his earliest period to the stylized urbanism of Natan Alterman. The tumultuous colourfulness of this poetry was equally alien to Ratosh. By contrast, he chose the "simple" and "raw" phenomena of primal cultures. (In his poem cycle *Black Canopy* he tried to recreate the sounds and sights of the ancient pagan world, while raising essentially modern problems.) In comparison to a "primitivist" such as Avot Yeshurun, he chose a very pure, minimalist language. His early poetry appears and sounds like a symbolist Hebrew *niggun* (tune) – archaic, or beyond time – yet one can notice extreme ideological messages, characteristic to the circles of the political Right, within which the poet grew up.

Over the years, Ratosh's poetry underwent several reversals in its direction, oscillating between extreme polarities, totally rejecting earlier trends, which by then had became popular and famous. The first revolution took place before he became known as a Canaanite, prior to World War II, when he left his underground career, which as a young poet he had regarded as the essence of his life. This change was expressed by the reversal of all the hierarchies that had been established in his poetry: up to that point, his poetry had been mainly political and did not pay attention to details of beauty of expression; yet now, it had become principally aesthetic, while hiding its political content. In his new poems, dating from the beginning of the 1940s, Ratosh presented a persona different from the one expressed in his political poetry: from a writing that was propagandist in nature, directed towards a wide public of readers, his work turned to "art for art's sake", a new hermetic poetry, poetry intended for a small public of cognoscenti. Moving away from unsophisticated allegorical writing, Ratosh began to write in an obscure and foggy style, where the signifier and the signified merged and became one entity; from journalistic writing, often embellished by humour and satire, his poetry changed and became sombre and sad, the expression of a tragic challenge and provocation of fate.

The second revolution in his art, which seemed even more extreme and drastic than the former one, occurred at the beginning of the 1950s, after Ratosh had written the love songs of the cycle *Yohemed*, which were composed after several long years of silence, around the time of the foundation of the State of Israel and the establishment of the periodical *Alef*. This revolution, which came to light for the first time in its entirety in the collection *Tsela*, apparently expressed itself again by a complete reversal, discarding all those qualities that the critics had identified in his earlier work, qualities that had made his art popular with its readers. Rhythmical and melodic poetry was displaced by a free, unravelled style. Instead of poetry of an archaic nature, which refrained from using biblical derivatives, emerged poetry that contained a plenitude of expressions and forms borrowed from the language of the sages, which did not seem to agree with the Canaanite credo. (This work was simultaneously embellished with contemporary slang, in distinction to the archaic impression created by his early poetry.) Lofty and ornate poems were displaced by poetry that was ironic and sarcastic. Instead of a poetry of heroic pathos, surfaced mundane subjects, lacking lustre and radiance. Colours of purple and black, fierce and impressive, were replaced by a "grey" poetry, lacking vigour and joy, mirroring a "distorted" and castrated world, the expression of a man who had experienced difficult trials and tribulations, and was left hurt and desolate. As a consequence, these poems disappointed the readers, who had become used to his heroic, forceful, colourful, and sophisticated poetry.

These two revolutions demonstrated complete reversals, where Ratosh turned his back on his previous poetic stance, and were drastic, sudden, and surprising steps, which cannot be defined as "developments", but as provocation. Ratosh's political poems written in the 1960s, at the same time as his editorship of *Alef* after the Six Day War, are to a large degree a return to the poetry and political thought of the 1930s, particularly in the cycle *Songs of the Swords* in which Ratosh re-wrote some of his dissent poems from the days of the underground movement. Quite a few lines from his "later" work *Walkers in the Dark* were composed during the time of the British Mandate, 30 years prior to their actual publication. The cultivation of a single ideological concept over the course of a generation, and beyond, is the ultimate witness to a consistent stance, stubborn and monolithic, which a life of upheaval did not manage to uproot.

The monolithic and unchanging position of Ratosh was also expressed in the static self-image that he maintained throughout his life: the poet never sought to free himself from his self perception as a rejected and ostracized artist, and made absolutely no effort to get closer to his admirers. His attempt to skip over "two thousand and more, years of Diaspora", in an endeavour to build a linking bridge to primal Hebrew traditions, dating from before monotheism, forced Ratosh to restrict the scope and range of his art, and to include in it only those elements that did not interfere by their presence with such poetry. In his generation Ratosh had many followers, and even those poets who did not join the Canaanite movement adopted, to a certain degree, its ethical and aesthetic values. Today, when the Canaanite fashion has long passed, and the Anglo-American version of Modernism has replaced the Russian–Jewish Modernism of the Shlonsky–Alterman school, one can discern the influence of Ratosh through his follower Nathan Zach. Zach learned from the late poems of Ratosh the unmediated vernacular version; he learned that the meagreness of Ratosh's material was a matter of choice, not something enforced.

ZIVA SHAMIR
translated by Miriam Pedatsur

Ravikovitch, Dalia

Israeli poet, 1936–

Born in Ramat-Gan, 17 November 1936. Has one son. Teacher, 1959–63; journalist.

Selected Writings

Poetry
Ahavat tapuah hazahav [The Love of an Orange], 1959
Mivhar shirim udevarim al yetsiratah [Selected Poems and Comments on Her Work], 1962
Hahalil vahahets [The Flute and the Sorrow], 1963
Horef kasheh [Hard Winter], 1964
Hasefer hashlishi [The Third Book], 1969
Kol mishbarekhah vegalekhah [All Thy Breakers and Waves], 1972
A Dress of Fire, translated by Chana Bloch, 1976
Tehom kore [Deep Calleth unto Deep], 1976
Ahavah amitit [Real Love], 1986
The Window: New and Selected Poems, translated by Chana Bloch and Ariel Bloch, 1989

Other
Mavet bamishpahah [Death in the Family], 1976
Mealilot dedi hamufla [The Deeds of Dedi the Wonderful], 1977
Editor, *The New Israeli Writers: Short Stories of the First Generation*, 1990

Further Reading

Burnshaw, Stanley, T. Carmi, and Ezra Spicehandler (editors and translators), *The Modern Hebrew Poem Itself*, New York: Holt Rinehart and Winston, 1965

Gamzu, Yossi, "Closing Distances: Three Modern Hebrew Poets", *Poetry Australia*, 66 (1978)

Hess, Tamar, and Hamutal Tsamir, "Two Studies in Dahlia Ravikovitch's Early Poetry," *Mikan-Journal for Hebrew Literary Studies*, 1 May 2000

Mazor, Yair, "Besieged Feminism: Contradictory Rhetorical Themes in the Poetry of Daliah Rabikovitz", *World Literature Today*, 58/3 (1984)

Dalia Ravikovitch is a truly lyrical poet. Her work revolves around personal feelings, expressed with a bright intensity, where words are sought for their metaphorical appropriateness. The outer world, that of the Hebrew Bible, classical mythology, or external calamities and wars, are the mirrors of her own mental mechanisms. They reflect her own critical situations.

Her first volume, *Ahavat tapuah hazahav* [The Love of an Orange], appeared in 1959, and set the scene for all her subsequent work. The title poem brings up the image of incorporation of the orange itself, entering its consumer, then entering his skin, and itself consuming the consumer's flesh. An ambiguity is suggested here in the apparently divergent roles of eater and eaten, and in other poems, that ambiguity is taken further in the view of the dead taking over the living. She invokes a rabbinic passage, where it is said that 613 commandments were given to "Israel", seven were handed to the "sons of Noah", i.e. non Jews, and one to the dead. So the dead are still alive, and they live inside those who mourn them. In that same volume, in a sonnet, she images herself in the first person, and so directly, as a "mechanised doll". She has been a mechanical doll, dropped and broken, and then subsequently repaired. She seems to function, but only in an artificial state and in very precarious circumstances. She is so fragile that she might soon be utterly shattered. Her apparent freedom of movement is illusory, controlled from the outside.

Ravikovitch's second collection, *Horef kasheh* [Hard Winter], accentuates the mournful tone, still melodious, full of refrains of assonance. The nightmare is never assuaged, as the narrator craves some assurance of what will be ". . . when our youth ends." But no such assurance is forthcoming, as that scenario is certain and is the fate of all. For her, the subsequent existence will be populated by frightful sea monsters. She herself can only take refuge in a world of dreams, distanced from the earthly reality that condemns her to increasing torment. In "Hamaarav hakahol" [The Blue West], she writes:

> I want to reach out beyond the hill
> Want to reach
> Want to come.
> I want to get loose from the heavy earth.
> I want to reach out to the end of thought
> Where even its suggestion cuts like a knife.
> I want to go up to the edges of the sun
> Where I will not be consumed by fire.

This is the longing of the individual to reach out, a longing of a dream, of a love that cannot be properly uttered. She addresses her love in the poem, "Halomotekhah shel tirtsah" [Tirzah's Dreams]: "My beloved, my beloved,/ All my love/ I could not relate." So the need for love is part of this reaching out. But that love is so delicate that it can hardly be grasped, let alone contained. It floats, and it may indeed float away. In the poem "Agur" [Crane] she tries to capture the sense of the longing of the individual for love, as she images herself as floating above her beloved: "I shall be able to wing beyond him like feathers,/ I shall be able to shine like a peacock's mane."

The volume which the author herself entitled "The Third Book", *Hasefer hashlishi*, the longing for love seems to move further into an aspiration to isolation, "to be alone with poems". In the poem, "Atah bevaday zokher" [You Must Remember], she writes: "After they have all gone/ I remain alone with the poems./ Then everything will disappear, and you'll become be pure crystal./ And then love." The possibility of ultimate love is held out when all the dross of existence is removed, and just the pure element is retained. The individual's isolation is radical, although there is God in another poem, who ". . . knows the end of the fall." Otherwise there is an empty space. This almost empty universe is even more frightening, as, although there may be the presence of God, this is a God who is afraid to intervene to protect the creature that He cherishes. This creature is a helpless child, and we see in another poem, "Habeged" [The Garment], that apparently protective clothing is also illusory. There is a dialogue between the narrator and others, who tell her that she has been granted a cloak of fire, as in the Greek myth of Jason. The dialogue becomes an argument, and then a hysterical screech as she describes her terrifying ordeal. She says: "I am not wearing any clothes at all. It is I who am burning." There is no barrier between the self and the destructive, oppressive, and tormenting elements. The poems here offer an account of the agony of being in the most transparent way possible.

Ahavah amitit [Real Love] is paradoxical. The suggestion of the title is that the subject matter is the poet's true vocation, the love that she has always been seeking out, and that has always eluded her. It is the true love between herself and the free spirit of her beloved, unimpeded by the constraints of prosaic reality. But more than in earlier volumes, here the eternal world is very much a presence, specifically the horrible war in the Lebanon, and Israel's own part in it, as well as a view of some of the most dreadful revelations of horrific cruelty. Here the fantasy extends to a longing for a peaceful territory, as articulated in "Shnei iyim linyu ziland" [New Zealand has Two Islands]. An escape is the order of the day, far from the ravaging fighting in Israel, and distant too from Asia and Africa, where other acts of mass cruelty and destruction are taking place. New Zealand, although of course it is a concrete, geographical reality, represents here a haven of peace and a fantasy of escape: "Everywhere there is too much murderousness . . . In New Zealand/ On grassy lawns and by the water/ Good people/ will offer me of their food." The myths of individual flight and yearning for peace here meet up with a political world. The internal is now acting upon the external, and the two are becoming intertwined. But this is all expressed in the lyrical language of unfettered emotionalism.

LEON I. YUDKIN

Rawicz, Piotr

Polish/Ukrainian fiction writer and journalist, 1919–1982

Born in Lwów (L'viv), 12 July 1919. Studied law and orientalism at University of Lwów, 1937–40. Evaded capture for some time during World War II, then detained as political prisoner in Auschwitz and Leitmeritz; liberated, 1945. Wrote poems and wandered around Poland, 1945–47. Emigrated to France, 1947; settled in Paris; degrees in Hindi and Sanskrit. Received Prix Rivarol, 1962. Wrote influential articles on Aleksandr Solzhenitsyn and other Slavic writers for *Le Monde*, Paris. Committed suicide, 21 May 1982.

Selected Writings

Novel

Le Sang du ciel, 1961; as *Blood from the Sky*, translated by Peter Wiles, 1964

Memoir

Bloc-notes d'un contre-revolutionnaire; ou, La Gueule de bois [Writing-pad of a Counter-revolutionary; or, The Hangover], 1969

Further Reading

Alexander, Edward, *The Resonance of Dust: Essays on Holocaust Literature and Jewish Fate*, Columbus: Ohio State University Press, 1979

Kauffmann, Judith, "Language de la violence et violence du language: la Shoah dans *Le Sang du ciel* de Piotr Rawicz", *Hebrew University Studies in Literature and the Arts* (1993)

Kiš, Danilo, "Youri Goletz", *La Règle du jeu*, 9 (1993)

Mitgang, Herbert, "Portrait of Helen Wolff", *New Yorker* (2 August 1982)

Rudolf, Anthony, *Engraved in Flesh: Piotr Rawicz and his Novel Blood from the Sky*, London: Menard Press, 1996

Piotr Rawicz published only two books, although he left a journal written in many languages which his friends hope will one day be edited into what will undoubtedly prove to be a fascinating and singular work. In addition, his essays, meditations, and poetical texts deserve to be collected. But his reputation necessarily rests on one great book: his only novel – metaphysical and apocalyptic – which was written in his sixth language, French. His other published book, a highly personal investigation of the May 1968 "events" in Paris is a fascinating work, and well worth reading for the light it sheds both on that "continuous carnival" (Miłosz's phrase in his review of the book) and on a classic Bohemian's response to it. This Bohemian also cultivated a persona of Oblomov, causing some people to feel that it was something of a miracle he wrote a great novel, or indeed anything at all. But appearances were deceptive and Rawicz found time to write what he had to write.

Blood from the Sky is a magnificently indirect, ontologically complex, darkly humorous, surrealistically disjunctive, and deeply troubling book: "a wantonly brilliant novel", in the words of Irving Howe. Angus Wilson found it "fierce in its impact and often horrifyingly funny". On the strength of this one book Rawicz will survive, along with a handful of other writers, as an enduring witness of the Shoah. Long out of print in the United Kingdom and the United States, the book remains, despite many efforts by its supporters, the only major Holocaust novel already in English translation not to have found a paperback publisher.

The novel tells the story of Boris, a Jewish poet and lover of women, who survives life on the run in occupied Poland by pretending not to be Jewish. He does not sound or look Jewish. Except, that is, for his circumcision, engraved in his flesh. The sign of the Jewish covenant, which wrote him into a community of fate at eight days old, had always signalled life for Boris, always empowered the man. But in these dire circumstances it could be the death of him . . . Thus death and life merge in the penis. Boris's job as a character is to survive mental and physical extremity, and for one reason only: to remember. Rawicz's job as a writer was to render the process of survival possible in literary form, freeing himself to live less intensely outside the difficult freedom of the highest art.

We understand from hints dropped at the end of the book that Boris will be deported to Auschwitz-Birkenau, but although the author transposes Auschwitz experiences from his own life to settings outside the camp, he does not write about the camp itself. In real life Rawicz had a medical certificate explaining his circumcision and was deported not as a Jew but as a Ukrainian political prisoner. Boris, however, does not have a certificate. The amazing interrogation scene, presided over by an SS officer in occupied Poland, in which Boris out-argues a Ukrainian nationalist and "proves" himself not to be Jewish, is one of the great set-piece tableaux in European literature – there are five others in *Blood from the Sky* – and brings to mind Dostoevskii.

Blood from the Sky is a picaresque philosophical poem in prose in which the existential self-awareness of Boris, poet and saloon-bar philosopher, is central to the process of writing and thus of the way we read the book. The frame narrative, set in postwar Paris, includes poems, dialogues, digressions, footnotes and quotations, and does its best to confuse our reading of the broken tale told by Boris. The author deploys a classic "alienation" technique. The narrative, often baroque, hallucinatory, and phantasmagorical, is at war with itself. Boris's story moves in and out of synch with its alleged provenance: the frame narrator's record of Boris's conversations and writings.

Blood from the Sky is a very early example of the self-referential postmodern novel, with desire, mind, writing, the body, all merging, collapsing kaleidoscopically. Not solipsistic, it is necessarily self-referential because of its ontological preoccupations. Even in a world of putrefaction, cockroaches, bedbugs, and rats, mind can transcend body, and memory can salvage a town and its people. In a historical and experiential territory – genocide – where metaphor is overwhelmed by reality, where documentation risks flooding or suffocating even well-wishers through its ever-increasing weight, it is the architectonic structure of a complex literary work that, in the long term, may well bear the burden of commemoration most effectively.

Boris, aware of the deportations, knows there is no hope at all for the Jews of Nazi-occupied Europe. Indeed he understands this even before the occupation and the setting up of ghettos. As Rawicz wrote in his second book: "I consider myself to be an expert in defeats, a specialist in humiliations undergone". *Blood from the Sky* is not a book for the squeamish or the lazy or the optimistic. But even one reading of it changes the reader and the reader's perception of the world we have all inherited: against the small hope generated by Rawicz's having written the book at all, stands the large despair of the *tremendum* (in Arthur Cohen's word), that which we cannot comprehend, our minds on fire in the burning bush of a historical caesura which cannot be transcended, let alone redeemed. The book is a gift to the post-Holocaust world, a world rendered a little less unbearable because Rawicz bore the burden of history and suffering, because he saw clearly, because he agreed "to keep watch over absent meaning", in the remarkable formulation of Maurice Blanchot.

Rawicz filters the omnipresent disaster through the mind of the main character, an intellectual man, a sexual man, a literary man, a Jewish man: in short, an archetypal geometry of forces. The author's apparent detachment is the only objective correlative available to incarnate the terrible and unbearable reality, the reality of impending genocide. Boris is free only on the margins of the absolute, and he learns that there is more to life than philosophical disgust and sexual love. His commitment to remember becomes a passion. Remembrance, indeed, not understanding is the key to survival. Nothing in Boris's existential philosophy or symbolist poetry equips him to understand, but native intelligence demands that he remember, that he witness, that he carry his community's past into a future, at least on paper.

Blood from the Sky in its own high Modernist way is an expression of deep spirituality. The Ukraine/Poland of the novel is a late mutation of the world of Hasidism and the shtetl. Boris and others are put through the mill. The beauty and hurt of the writing in the scene involving the torture of children as well as certain other scenes, scenes in which all the dams of hopeless hope are flooded, are extreme in their power, but they completely and designedly avoid *frisson*. Technique is ethical.

Overall, the book's architectonic and rhetorical complexity has been built up to enable the author *to think atrocity*. Rawicz's anger is displaced and projected onto a character whose survival gives us reason to believe that the passion to remember, informed by intelligence, is a necessity for all of us. Without it, Boris would die, and along with him the story of his people. This extraordinary novel, as singular as its author, cannot by itself give meaning to a crazy universe, but it renders the absence of meaning less meaningless.

ANTHONY RUDOLF

Reyzen, Avrom

Russian-born US poet and short-story writer, 1876–1953

Born in Koydenev, 1876, son of Hebrew-Yiddish poet, Kalman Reyzen. Brother Zalmen was literary historian; sister, Sarah, poet. Served in Russian army. First poem published in *Yidishe biliotek*, anthology, 1891. Regular contributor to *Yidishes folksblat*, St Petersberg. Taught in Minsk. Settled in Warsaw; worked as editor of literary journals and as translator of medieval and modern poetry. Attended Czernowitz Yiddish Conference, 1908. Visited US, 1911; settled in New York, 1914; continued to work as editor of journals and Yiddish textbooks. Died in New York, 1953.

Selected Writings

Poetry
Tsayt-lider [Contemporary Poems], 1902
In *A Treasury of Jewish Poetry*, edited and translated by Nathan and Marynn Ausubel, 1957

Fiction
In *Yiddish Tales*, edited and translated by Helena Frank, 1912
In *Yiddish Short Stories*, edited and translated by Isaac Goldberg, 1923
In *The Jewish Caravan*, edited and translated by Leo W. Schwarz, 1935
In *A Treasury of Yiddish Stories*, edited and translated by Irving Howe and Eliezer Greenberg, 1954
The Heart-Stirring Sermon and Other Stories, edited and translated by Curt Leviant, 1992

Plays
Brothers in *One-Act Plays from the Yiddish*, 2nd series, translated by Etta Block, 1929

Other
Complete Works, 12 vols, 1917
Epizodn fun mayn lebn [Episodes of My Life], 3 vols, 1929–35
In *A Golden Treasury of Jewish Literature*, edited and translated by Leo W. Schwarz, 1937

Further Reading

Liptzin, Solomon, *Flowering of Yiddish Literature*, New York: Yoseloff, 1963
Madison, Charles A., *Yiddish Literature: Its Scope and Major Writers*, New York: Ungar, 1968
Minkoff, N.B., *Avrom Reyzen: der dikhter fun lid*, New York: Bodn, 1936
Rogoff, Harry, *Nine Yiddish Writers*, New York: Forward, 1916(?)

Born in Koydenev, White Russia in 1876, Avrom Reyzen, the Yiddish poet and story writer, was the son of a poor wheat merchant who wrote poems in both Hebrew and Yiddish. Talent abounded in the family. His younger brother, Zalmen, a literary historian, compiled the authoritative 1-volume, and later, the 4-volume, lexicon of Yiddish writers. His sister, Sarah, was a poet.

In his childhood Reyzen received a traditional Hebrew education. He also learned Russian and German. By the age of 14 he had begun to write in earnest, while he tutored local children in order to earn extra money for the family. In 1890, aged only 15, he sent samples of his writing to Y.L. Perets in Warsaw. Perets may be considered to be the chief architect of Jewish modernism in eastern Europe, and his influence was such that he held court to young writers who would travel for miles in order to present him with their writings. They sought his opinion with trepidation, fearing his condemnation. To Reyzen's delight, Perets published one of his poems, "Ven dos lebn is farbitert" [When This Life is Embittered], in *Yidishe bibliotek* [The Yiddish Library] and placed him on the ladder of literary success. Reyzen's first short story was published a year later, when he was 16.

Five years later he was drafted into the Russian army for four years, but was released from the most arduous of military duties when he joined the regimental band.

In 1902, a 48-page volume of his poems entitled *Tsaytlider* [Contemporary Poems] was published. It was well received, which led to its publication in New York, where an enthusiastic review appeared in the daily Yiddish newspaper *Forverts*. Reyzen had become an internationally renowned poet at the age of 26.

Six years later, in 1908, Reyzen was one of a group of Yiddish writers and scholars who attended the First Yiddish Language Conference in Czernowitz. One issue of the conference, which provoked hostility between the European-based supporters of Yiddish and the predominantly Zionist, Hebrew factions, and which continued for decades, was the decision as to whether Hebrew or Yiddish should be established as the Jewish national language. While the conference finally decided on a compromise – that Yiddish was "a" rather than "the" national Jewish language – Yiddish was acknowledged with a new sense of pride as a language, and not a jargon or dialect as it had been viewed even by its own speakers. This view was endorsed by the linguistic treatises of a new wave of Yiddish linguists such as Max Weinreich and Ber Borokhov, also present at the conference. It was also seen as a language in which great literary works could be written by authors such as Reyzen. Together with other writers including Perets, Sholem Asch and H.D. Nomberg, Reyzen toured Jewish settlements to win support for the political, cultural, and social equality of Yiddish and to establish it as a literary and scholarly language as well as the everyday language of the masses.

It was in 1911 that Reyzen first visited the United States where he edited a new literary weekly *Dos naye land* [The New Country] for several months. He finally settled in New York at the outbreak of World War I, where he remained for the rest of his life. He contributed regularly to Yiddish newspapers and magazines and many of his works were published in periodicals in Europe and the United States.

Reyzen crafted a literary Yiddish style that retains a natural, flowing, idiomatic language. His poems are written in simple quatrains. The central figures of his poems and stories are the poor and rejected: the members of society about whom nobody cares. To Reyzen, all members of the community are worthy of having their story told. His pathos is instilled with dignity. The children dream of the freedom of the natural world that lies beyond the stifling indoor life of prayer and learning imposed on them that fails to provide the spiritual richness so sought after by a community deprived of worldly comforts.

In New York, more than half a century after he had proffered his own work to Perets in Warsaw, it was Reyzen himself who held court to a steady stream of literary hopefuls. He could be found most days sipping coffee with other Yiddish literary figures in the Europa Cafe on East Broadway, a favourite haunt of the Yiddish literati. There, new Yiddish writers would approach Reyzen and read their poetry or prose to him, hoping for a positive response. But unlike Perets, who was known to reduce his victims to the deepest despair, Reyzen received all comers with patience, kindness, and good humour.

Though not easy in the often volatile climate of the Yiddish literary world, he was popular among his peers as an author and as an amiable man.

DEVRA KAY

Reznikoff, Charles

US poet, fiction writer, and dramatist, 1894–1976

Born Ezekiel Rezmikoff in Brownsville, Brooklyn, New York, 31 August 1894, to Russian immigrants; called "Charlie" or "Charles" from childhood. Studied at Boys' High School, Brooklyn, graduated 1909; School of Journalism, University of Missouri, 1910–11; New York University, LL.B 1915; Columbia University, postgraduate law courses. Admitted to Bar of State of New York, 1916; practised law only briefly. Member, Columbia University Reserve Officers' Training Corps, 1917–18. Married Marie Syrkin, Zionist activist and, later, professor at Brandeis University, 1930. Varied employment, 1930s, including working for family hat-making business; contributor to encyclopedias, particularly *Corpus Juris*; legal writer, freelance editor, translator, and writer; personal assistant to producer at Paramount Studios, Hollywood. Journalist on Labor Zionist monthy *Jewish Frontier* from mid-1950s. Awarded Jewish Book Council of America Kovner Memorial Award, 1963; National Institute of Arts and Letters Zabel Award, 1971. Died 22 January 1976.

Selected Writings

Poetry
Rhythms, 1916
Poems, 1920
Uriel Acosta: A Play and a Fourth Group of Verse, 1921
Five Groups of Verse, 1927
In Memoriam: 1933, 1934
Jerusalem the Golden, 1934
Separate Way, 1936
Going To and Fro and Walking Up and Down, 1941
Inscriptions: 1944–1956, 1959
By the Waters of Manhattan: Selected Verse, 1962
Testimony: The United States 1885–1890: Recitative, 1965
Testimony: The United States 1891–1900: Recitative, 1968

By the Well of Living and Seeing and the Fifth Book of the Maccabees, 1969
By the Well of Living and Seeing: New and Selected Poems, 1918–1973, 1974
Holocaust, 1975
Poems 1918–1936, edited by Seamus Cooney, 1976 (Complete Poems, vol. 1)
Poems 1937–1975, edited by Seamus Cooney, 1977 (Complete Poems, vol. 2)
Testimony: The United States, 1885–1915, 1979

Plays
Chatterton, the Black Death and Meriwether Lewis: Three Plays, 1922
Coral and Captive Israel: Two Plays, 1923
Nine Plays, 1927

Novels
By the Waters of Manhattan, 1930
The Lionhearted: A Story about the Jews in Medieval England, 1944
The Manner Music, 1977

Other
Testimony, 1934
Early History of a Sewing Machine Operator, with Nathan Reznikoff, 1936
The Jews of Charleston: A History of an American Jewish Community, with Uriah Z. Engelman, 1950
Translator, *Stories and Fantasies from the Jewish Past*, by Emil Cohn, 1951
Translator, *Three Years in America, 1859–1862*, by Israel Joseph Benjamin,1956
Editor, *Louis Marshall, Champion of Liberty: Selected Papers and Addresses*, 1957
Family Chronicle, with Sarah Reznikoff and Nathan Reznikoff, 1963
Selected Letters of Charles Reznikoff 1917–1976, edited by Milton Hindus, 1997

Further Reading
Bernstein, Charles, "Reznikoff's Nearness", *Sulfur*, 32 (Spring 1993)
Davidson, Michael, *Ghostlier Demarcations: Modern Poetry and the Material World*, Berkeley: University of California Press, 1997
Dembo, L.S., "The Objectivist Poet: Four Interviews: Charles Reznikoff", *Contemporary Literature*, 10/1(Spring 1969)
Finkelstein, Norman, "Tradition and Modernity, Judaism and Objectivism: The Poetry of Charles Reznikoff" in *The Objectivist Nexus: Essays in Cultural Poetics*, edited by Rachel Blau DuPlessis and Peter Quartermain, Tuscaloosa: University of Alabama Press, 1999
Fredman, Stephen, *A Menorah for Athena: Charles Reznikoff and the Jewish Dilemmas of American Objectivist Poetry*, Chicago: University of Chicago Press, 2001
Hatlen, Burton (editor), Charles Reznikoff special issue, *Sagetrieb*, 13/1–2 (Spring/Autumn 1994)
Heller, Michael, "Charles Reznikoff", *New York Times Book Review* (16 May 1976): 47
Hindus, Milton (editor), *Charles Reznikoff: Man and Poet*, Orono: University of Maine, 1984
Hindus, Milton, "Charles Reznikoff" in *The "Other" New York Jewish Intellectuals*, edited by Carole S. Kessner, New York: New York University Press, 1994
Omer, Ranen, "The Stranger and the Metropolis: Partial Visibilities and Manifold Possibilities of Identity in the Poetry of Charles Reznikoff", *Shofar: An Interdisciplinary Journal of Jewish Studies*, 16/1 (Fall 1997)
Omer, Ranen, "'Palestine was a Halting Place, One of Many': Transnationalism and the Poet", *Melus*, 25/1 (Spring 2000)
Omer Sherman, Ranen, *Diaspora and Zionism in Jewish-American Literature: Lazarus, Syrkin, Reznikoff, and Roth*, Hanover, New Hampshire: University Press of New England, 2002
Oppen, Mary, *Meaning a Life: An Autobiography*, Santa Barbara, California: Black Sparrow Press, 1978
Pinsker, Sanford, "On Charles Reznikoff", *Jewish Spectator*, 43 (Spring 1978)
Reed, John R., "A Review of *Poems 1918–1936*", *Ontario Review*, 6 (Autumn–Winter 1976–77)
Schimmel, Harold, "Historical Grit and Epic Gestation", *Sagetrieb*, 1 (Autumn 1982)
Shevelow, Kathryn, "History and Objectification in Charles Reznikoff's Documentary Poems, *Testimony* and *Holocaust*", *Sagetrieb*, 1/2 (Autumn 1982)
Sternburg, Janet, and Alan Ziegler, "A Conversation with Charles Reznikoff", *Montemora*, 2 (Summer 1976)
Zukofsky, Louis, "Sincerity and Objectification, with Special Reference to the Work of Charles Reznikoff", *Poetry*, 37/5 (February 1931)

Charles Reznikoff was born to Russian immigrant parents in Brooklyn in 1894. As a poet and writer, he would tell the tale of their struggle in Russia and in the challenging and highly competitive world of the New York rag trade, in illuminating and unsparing detail in highly praised nonfiction (*Early History of a Sewing Machine Operator*) as well as verse. But Reznikoff was also drawn to the struggle of other dislocated Americans, whose stories of hardship in both the industrial and agricultural American landscapes constitute the scrupulous and informative narratives gathered together in *Testimony*. A general indebtedness to Ezra Pound's Modernist experimentation, as well as the unique, almost uninterrupted milieu of Reznikoff's urban environment, combined to shape what has become known as "urban imagism". A wide range of contemporary poets (Jewish and non-Jewish) – Charles Bernstein, Robert Duncan, Robert Creeley, to name a few – were profoundly influenced by Reznikoff's incisive arrangement of detail, lyrical understatement, and ethical vision. In the late 1920s he became acquainted with the poets Louis Zukofsky and George Oppen. Together, with Carl Rakosi and William Carlos Williams (the only non-Jewish member), they formed a group whose label, the Objectivists, suggests a school of poetry, more than the mutual interest and support group they really were. In 1928 Pound demonstrated his support by publishing poems by Williams, Zukofsky, and Rakosi, as well as Reznikoff. By 1934 Reznikoff, Zukofsky, and Oppen founded the Objectivist Press, which published the initial installment of Reznikoff's *Testimony*, with an introduction by Kenneth Burke.

In the Depression, Reznikoff worked briefly as editor for the *Corpus Juris* law encyclopedia, but was fired for being too slow and meticulous. Nevertheless, Reznikoff's study of the law fired his passion for the "plainspoken" possibilities of language, a paradigm that had increasing influence, according to Michael Davidson, on his poetic mission to "redirect modernism's emphasis on the materiality of aesthetic language to the materiality of social speech". Moreover, this experience also inspired his poetic disavowal of a monolithic national identity during the years of America's most nativist and xenophobic period. As he later recalled:

> Reading cases from every state and every year (since this country became a nation) . . . it seemed to me that out of such material the century and a half during which the U.S. has been a nation could be written up, not from the standpoint of an individual, as in diaries, nor merely from the angle of the unusual, as in newspapers, but from every standpoint – as many standpoints as were provided by the witnesses themselves.

In 1930, Reznikoff married Marie Syrkin, the daughter of Nachman Syrkin, an important theoretician and ideologue of Labor Zionism. Though the two remained married until Reznikoff's death, their personalities often clashed. Her Zionism and his exilic sensibility and unwillingness to sacrifice his poetry for the practical demands of supporting a family, often caused marital antagonism and periods of separation during the years Syrkin taught at Brandeis University. As Reznikoff enigmatically remarked in later life, when Syrkin took one of her increasingly frequent trips to Palestine (later Israel), he was unwilling to accompany her because he "had not yet explored Central Park to the full". But this gentle jest masks Reznikoff's resolutely diasporic identity, which these lines from "Black Death", a verse-play, eloquently affirm:

> Palestine was a halting place,
> One of many. Our kin, the Arabs,
> Wander over their desert. Our desert
> Is the Earth. Our strength
> Is that we have no land.
> Nineveh and Babylon, our familiar cities,
> Become dust; but we Jews have left
> for Alexandria and Rome.
> When the land is impoverished, as lands become,
> The tree dies. Israel is not planted,
> Israel is in the wind.

Alive to his family origins in the Russian-Jewish Diaspora, Reznikoff wrote lyrics that consistently explore the Jewish historical experience with remarkable effect, particularly in the epic cycle *In Memoriam: 1933*. But they also bear witness to the displacements, traumas, and cosmopolitan identities of other city dwellers in America; Jews, blacks, Puerto Ricans, and others. Reznikoff's intimate knowledge, even affection, for the urban environment is juxtaposed with an acute sense of never quite being at home.

Reznikoff's poetry and prose are haunted by the ghost of this grandfather, a poet whose entire body of Hebrew lyrics was burned by his illiterate widow, who feared that the writing might contain subversive elements that might prove dangerous to her family. This burnt manuscript, emblematic of greater catastrophes in Jewish history, lived with Reznikoff in the present moment, as a sign that he must take responsibility for printing his own work, even if there was no market for it. For years his poems appeared only in limited editions of hand-set books that Reznikoff privately typeset, printed, and distributed from his parents' basement. For a brief time (1938–39) Reznikoff laboured at a $75-a-week job as writer and script-consultant for Paramount Pictures in Hollywood, one of his rare ventures outside the city of New York. This period of self-loathing is acerbically described in the lyrical series "Autobiography/Hollywood."

Reznikoff's work failed to make the kind of commercial impact in his lifetime that other modernist Jewish-American artists such as Mike Gold and Henry Roth enjoyed. But his early works were well reviewed by critics such as Leonard Ehrlich and Lionel Trilling, and attracted the attention of many younger poets. Allen Ginsberg, who often praised Reznikoff's neglected oeuvre to his own audiences, dedicated his *Plutonian Ode* "After Whitman and Reznikoff", fitting company for a poet who had struggled to mediate between his Jewish and American identities. In an important sense his poetry helped to create the very possibility of the Jewish-American poetic tradition that has evolved from Karl Shapiro to Jerome Rothenberg. His poetry is replete with the historical consciousness of the Jewish writer, with dramatic monologues set in times of crisis: Samaria of 722 BCE, Spain of 1492, Russia of 1905. Finally, after decades of preoccupation with the Shoah, Reznikoff published *Holocaust*, a condensation of court records from the Nuremberg and Eichmann trials and the most thorough American literary exploration of the European catastrophe to date.

Public recognition for his gifts came late. At the age of 76 he received an award for his poetry from the National Institute of Arts and Letters which simply read:

> To Charles Reznikoff, born by the waters of Manhattan. Mr. Reznikoff was educated for the law but has instead dedicated his life to giving sworn testimony in the court of poetry against the swaggering injustices of our culture and on behalf of its meek wonders.

Thanks to Black Sparrow Press, a rush of publications followed and after a lifetime of self-publishing and obscurity, Reznikoff lived to see the publication of several volumes of his poetry: *By the Well of Living and Seeing: New and Selected Poems 1918-1973*, and *Holocaust*, as well as the first volume of his Complete Poems. On the evening of 22 January 1976, Reznikoff remarked to Syrkin that, "You know, I never made money but I have done everything that I most wanted to do" and died of a heart attack. Reznikoff was buried in the Old Mount Carmel Cemetery, Brooklyn, where his epitaph (from *Separate Way*) reads: "And the day's brightness dwindles into stars".

RANEN OMER-SHERMAN

Rich, Adrienne

US poet, 1929–

Born Adrienne Cecile Rich in Baltimore, 16 May 1929, to Arnold Rice Rich, Jewish professor of pathology at Johns Hopkins Medical School, and wife Helen, Protestant. Studied at Radcliffe College, BA 1951. Married Alfred Haskell Conrad, 1953; husband died, 1970; three children. Conductor of workshops, YM–YWCA Poetry Center, New York City, 1966–67; visiting lecturer, Swarthmore College, Pennsylvania, 1967–69; adjunct professor in writing division of Graduate School of the Arts, Columbia University, 1967–69; instructor in creative writing programme, 1970–71, then assistant professor of English, 1971–72 and 1974–75, City College of the City University of New York; Fannie Hurst Visiting Professor of Creative Literature, Brandeis University, 1972–73; Lucy Martin Donnelly Fellow, Bryn Mawr College, Pennsylvania, 1975; professor of English, Douglass College, Rutgers University, 1976–78; A.D. White Professor at Large, Cornell University, 1981–86; Clark Lecturer and Distinguished Visiting Professor, Scripps College, California, 1983; visiting professor, San Jose State University, 1984–86; Burgess Lecturer, Pacific Oaks College, California, 1986; professor of English and feminist studies, Stanford University, 1986–92. Founding co-editor of *Bridges: A Journal for Jewish Feminists and Our Friends.* Many awards, including Yale Series of Younger Poets Award, 1951; Guggenheim Fellowship, 1952 and 1961; National Institute of Arts and Letters Award, 1961; Amy Lowell Travelling Fellowship, 1962; Bollingen Foundation translation grant, 1962; Poetry Society of America Shelley Memorial Award, 1971; Ingram Merrill Foundation grant, 1973–74; National Book Award, 1974; National Gay Task Force Fund for Human Dignity Award, 1981; Modern Poetry Association–American Council for the Arts Ruth Lilly Poetry Prize, 1986; Brandeis University Creative Arts Medal (for poetry), 1987; National Poetry Association Award, 1987; Commonwealth Award in Literature, 1991; Academy of American Poets Fellowship, 1992; Lambda Literary Award, 1992; Publishing Triangle Bill Whitehead Award, 1992; MacArthur Fellowship, 1994–1999; Lannan Foundation Lifetime Achievement Award, 1999.

Selected Writings

Poetry
A Change of World, 1951
The Diamond Cutters and Other Poems, 1955
Snapshots of a Daughter-in-Law: Poems, 1954–1962, 1963
Necessities of Life, 1966
Selected Poems, 1967
Leaflets: Poems, 1965–1968, 1969
The Will to Change: Poems, 1968–1970, 1971
Diving into the Wreck: Poems, 1971–1972, 1973
Poems: Selected and New, 1950–1974, 1974
Adrienne Rich's Poetry: Texts of the Poems; The Poet on Her Work; Reviews and Criticism, edited by Barbara Charlesworth Gelpi and Albert Gelpi, 1975; revised edition, as *Adrienne Rich's Poetry as Prose: Poems, Prose, Reviews, and Criticism*, 1993
Twenty-One Love Poems, 1977
The Dream of a Common Language: Poems, 1974–1977, 1978
A Wild Patience Has Taken Me This Far: Poems, 1978–1981, 1981
Sources, 1983
The Fact of a Doorframe: Poems Selected and New, 1950–1984, 1984
Your Native Land, Your Life, 1986
Time's Power: Poems, 1985–1988, 1989
An Atlas of the Difficult World: Poems, 1988–1991, 1991
Collected Early Poems, 1950–1970, 1992
Dark Fields of the Republic: Poems, 1991–1995, 1995
Midnight Salvage: Poems, 1995–1998, 1999
Fox: Poems, 1998–2000, 2001

Other
Translator, with Aijaz Ahmad *et al.*, *Ghazals of Ghalib*, edited by Aijaz Ahmad, 1971
Of Woman Born: Motherhood as Experience and Institution, 1976; new edition 1986
On Lies, Secrets and Silence: Selected Prose, 1966–1978, 1979
"Split at the Root: An Essay on Jewish Identity" in *Nice Jewish Girls: A Lesbian Anthology*, edited by Evelyn Torton Beck, 1982; revised edition, 1989
Blood, Bread and Poetry: Selected Prose, 1979–1986, 1986
"The Genesis of Yom Kippur 1984" in *Adrienne Rich's Poetry and Prose*, edited by Barbara Charlesworth Gelpi and Albert Gelpi, 1993
What is Found There: Notebooks on Poetry and Politics, 1993
Arts of the Possible: Essays and Conversations, 2001

Further Reading

Birkle, Carmen, *Women's Stories of the Looking Glass: Autobiographical Reflections and Self-Representations in the Poetry of Sylvia Plath, Adrienne Rich and Audre Lorde*, Munich: Fink, 1996
Cooper, Jane Roberta (editor), *Reading Adrienne Rich: Reviews and Re-Visions, 1951–1981*, Ann Arbor: University of Michigan Press, 1984
Diaz-Diocaretz, Myriam, *The Transforming Power of Language: The Poetry of Adrienne Rich*, Utrecht: HES, 1984
Kalstone, David, *Five Temperaments: Elizabeth Bishop, Robert Lowell, James Merrill, Adrienne Rich, John Ashbery*, New York: Oxford University Press, 1977
Keyes, Claire, *The Aesthetics of Power: The Poetry of Adrienne Rich*, Athens: University of Georgia Press, 1986
McDaniel, Judith Adair, *Reconstituting the World: The Poetry and Vision of Adrienne Rich*, Argyle, New York: Spinsters Ink, 1978

Markey, Janice, *A New Tradition? The Poetry of Sylvia Plath, Anne Sexton and Adrienne Rich: A Study of Feminism and Poetry*, New York: Peter Lang, 1985
Martin, Wendy, *An American Triptych: Anne Bradstreet, Emily Dickinson, Adrienne Rich*, Chapel Hill: University of North Carolina Press, 1984
Montenegro, David, interview with Adrienne Rich in *Points of Departure: International Writers on Writing and Politics*, Ann Arbor: University of Michigan Press, 1991
Ostriker, Alicia, *Writing like a Woman*, Ann Arbor: University of Michigan Press, 1983
Ratcliffe, Krista, *Anglo-American Feminist Challenges to the Rhetorical Traditions: Virginia Woolf, Mary Daly, Adrienne Rich*, Carbondale: Southern Illinois University Press, 1996
Spender, Dale, *Women of Ideas and What Men Have Done to Them: From Aphra Behn to Adrienne Rich*, London and Boston: Routledge and Kegan Paul, 1982
Templeton, Alice, *The Dream and the Dialogue: Adrienne Rich's Feminist Poetics*, Knoxville: University of Tennessee Press, 1994
Werner, Craig Hansen, *Adrienne Rich: The Poet and Her Critics*, Chicago: American Library Association, 1988
Yorke, Liz, *Adrienne Rich: Passion, Politics and the Body*, London and Thousand Oaks, California: Sage, 1997

Adrienne Rich, a prolific American poet and essayist, proves that the political is also poetic. Much of her work responds to the political and social oppression of minorities – people of colour, women, Jews, and homosexuals – that has plagued American history. As a Jewish lesbian feminist, her poetic explorations of political issues are also extremely personal; the alienation, confusion, and suffering of the oppressed are also her own.

And yet, Rich is aware that her outsider status is precarious. Born in Baltimore in 1929 to a Jewish father and a white southern Protestant mother, Rich was urged to conform to middle-class Christian values, "to speak quietly in public, to dress without ostentation, [and] to repress the vividness and spontaneity" that would mark her as other. Rich's father, Arnold Rich, employed this same tactic with much success: he taught at the elite Johns Hopkins University Department of Pathology at a time when few Jews even attended the university. Thus, Rich learned early on that the southern white Protestant woman was always available to "peel back into" should the social ostracization frequently foisted on Jews become too overwhelming. In the poem "Readings of History" Rich defines herself as "Split at the root, neither Gentile nor Jew,/ Yankee nor Rebel". The recurrence of mutilated natural imagery in Rich's work articulates those identity struggles she sees as unique to American Jews who are encouraged to assimilate through intermarriage, self-hatred, and denial.

Although Rich recognizes women, lesbians, Jews, and people of colour as social outcasts, victims of a conservative, capitalist America, her work on Jewishness expresses an ambivalence absent in her feminist and lesbian poems. American Jews, Rich seems to suggest, are complicit in their own oppression because they either willingly subscribe to assimilationist values that demand the suppression of difference, or adhere to stringent patriarchal religious laws that command the inferiority of Jewish women. In "Split at the Root: An Essay on Jewish Identity", Rich argues that "one message of assimilation – of America – [is] that the unlucky or the unachieving want to pull you backward, that to identify with them is to court downward mobility, lose the precious chance of passing, of token existence". The desire for the privileged, unmarked status of American fosters anti-Semitic attitudes within the Jewish community.

Poems such as "Prospective Immigrants Please Note" and "Living Memory" explore the cost of embracing the American Dream in general terms. "Prospective Immigrants" abstractly warns new immigrants that "much will blind you,/ much will evade you" in America, while "Living Memory" confronts "Jews following yankee footprints,/ prey to many myths but most of all/ that Nature makes us free". In these poems Rich demythologizes the frontier, the land of freedom and opportunity, by revealing the high price it exacts from those who subscribe to it – their heritage. In "After Dark" and "Sources", Rich personalizes the destructiveness of assimilationist values by positioning her father as audience in order directly to accuse him of stifling the Jew in them both.

Because Rich was forced to learn Jewish culture, history, and religion on her own, many of her Jewish-oriented poems serve as tools for self-discovery. The conflict between social and religious definitions of "Jew" is a recurring theme. Traditionally, Jewish law would not recognize Rich as a Jew because religious affiliation follows the maternal line. And yet, the anti-Semitism and self-hatred implicit in her father's choices and the inescapable presence of the Holocaust during Rich's adolescence suggest that, to those in power, Rich is Jewish. As Rich states in "Split at the Root", her two Jewish grandparents rendered her "*Mischling, first-degree* – nonexempt from the Final Solution". The poems "Eastern War Time", "The Burning of Paper Instead of Children", "Food Packages", "Sources", and "Jews", among others, address the confused sense of loyalty, debt, kinship, and anger that assimilated American Jews harboured toward the European Jews who perished in the Holocaust. In "Jews" Rich talks of the pressure of survival that is manifested, in part, in the "burden for anyone/ to be fascinating, brilliant/ after the six million". Rich suggests that the burden for many American Jews is twofold: (1) They must prove themselves worthy of the comfort and security they enjoy as integrated Americans; and (2) They must find a connection between themselves and the six million to legitimate the sense of loss and oppression they feel in America after the Holocaust.

Ultimately, Rich suggests, we must focus on the experiences that bind the disparate communities to which we belong. "The Genesis of Yom Kippur 1984" outlines the three current events that served as impetus for the poem of the same name: a series of rapes and murders of women in the Santa Cruz Mountains; the drowning of a gay man in Maine; and the shooting of a black college student, Edmund Perry, by police. In the poem, these brutal snapshots serve to amalgamate the often contradictory facets of herself – Jew, Gentile, feminist, lesbian, successful artist, and scholar – in the solitude of exile. During Yom Kippur, the Day of Atonement, Jews reconcile themselves with their community before asking God to forgive their sins. For Rich, the difficulty of the task rests in finding the community that will accept her unconditionally. As feminist, she cannot fail to recognize "the laws of her exclusion,/ the men too holy to touch her hand" that render the Jewish community neither completely "us" nor "them". The common experience of isolation creates a more global community of diverse individuals. We can find strength in solitude.

Rich's work provides insight into many of the identity crises facing contemporary American Jews who simultaneously desire the privilege promised by melting pot ideology, and feel inextricably linked to a minority community they do not fully understand. It becomes painfully clear throughout Rich's work that there is no simple solution. But, as Rich tells her deceased ex-husband in "Sources", we may take comfort in the dignity of the struggle: "no person, trying to take responsibility for her or his identity, should have to be so alone. There must be those among whom we can sit down and weep, and still be counted as warriors."

JENNIFER LEVI

Richler, Mordecai

Canadian fiction writer and dramatist, 1931–2001

Born in Montreal, 27 January 1931; father, Moses Isaac Richler, was scrap metal merchant. Studied at Montreal Hebrew Academy; Baron Byng High School, Montreal, 1944–49; Sir George Williams College, Montreal, from 1949; left without degree, 1950. Lived in Paris, 1951–54, and London, 1954–72; otherwise lived mainly in Montreal. Worked for Canadian Broadcasting Corporation, 1952–53; columnist, "Books and Things", *Gentlemen's Quarterly/ GQ*, New York. Married Florence Wood, 1959; three sons, two daughters. Writer in residence, Sir George Williams University, 1968–69; visiting professor, Carleton University, Ottawa, 1972–74. Judge, Book of the Month Club, 1972–88. Awards include Canada Council Junior Arts Fellowship, 1959, 1960, and Senior Arts Fellowship, 1966; Guggenheim Fellowship, 1965; Governor General's Award, 1971, 1972; Writers Guild of America Award (for screenplay), 1974; Berlin Film Festival Golden Bear (for screenplay), 1974; Schwartz Award (for children's book), 1976; *Jewish Chronicle* Wingate Award, 1981; Commonwealth Writers Prize, 1990; Giller Prize, 1997; International Festival of Authors Award, 2000. Died, of cancer, in Montreal, 2 July 2001.

Selected Writings

Novels
The Acrobats, 1954; as *Wicked We Love*, 1955
Son of a Smaller Hero, 1955
A Choice of Enemies, 1957
The Apprenticeship of Duddy Kravitz, 1959
The Incomparable Atuk, 1963; as *Stick Your Neck Out*, 1963
Cocksure, 1968
St Urbain's Horseman, 1971
Joshua Then and Now, 1980
Solomon Gursky Was Here, 1989
Barney's Version, 1997

For Children
Jacob Two-Two Meets the Hooded Fang, 1975
Jacob Two-Two and the Dinosaur, 1987
Jacob Two-Two's First Spy Case, 1995

Film and Television Plays: *Paid in Full*, 1958; *No Love for Johnnie*, with Nicholas Phipps, 1959; *The Trouble with Benny*, 1959; *The Fall of Mendel Crick*, 1963; *The Bells of Hell*, 1974; *The Apprenticeship of Duddy Kravitz*, 1975; *Joshua Then and Now*, 1985

Other
Hunting Tigers under Glass: Essays and Reports, 1968
Editor, *Canadian Writing Today*, 1970
Shovelling Trouble, 1972
The Street, 1972
Notes on an Endangered Species and Others, 1974
Creativity and the University, with André Fortier and Rollo May, 1975
Images of Spain, 1977
The Great Comic Book Heroes and Other Essays, edited by Robert Fulford, 1978
Editor, *The Best of Modern Humour*, 1983
Home Sweet Home: My Canadian Album, 1984
Broadsides: Reviews and Opinions, 1990
Editor, *Writers and World War Two: An Anthology*, 1991
Oh Canada! Oh Quebec! Requiem for a Divided Country, 1992
This Year in Jerusalem, 1993
Belling the Cat: Essays, Reports and Opinions, 1998

Further Reading

Brenner, Rachel Feldhay, *Assimilation and Assertion: The Response to the Holocaust in Mordecai Richler's Writings*, New York: Peter Lang, 1989
Craniford, Ada, *Fiction and Fact in Mordecai Richler's Novels*, New York: Mellen Press, 1992
Darling, Michael, "Mordecai Richler: An Annotated Bibliography" in *The Annotated Bibliography of Canada's Major Authors*, vol. 1, edited by Robert Lecker and Jack David, Downsview, Ontario: ECW Press, 1979
Darling, Michael (editor), *Perspectives on Mordecai Richler*, Toronto: ECW Press, 1986
Davidson, Arnold E., *Mordecai Richler*, New York: Ungar, 1983
McSweeney, Kerry, *Mordecai Richler and His Works*, Toronto: ECW Press, 1984
Ramraj, Victor J., *Mordecai Richler*, Boston: Twayne, 1983
Sheps, G. David (editor), *Mordecai Richler*, Toronto and New York: Ryerson, 1971
Woodcock, George, *Mordecai Richler*, Toronto: McClelland and Stewart, 1970
Woodcock, George, *Introducing Mordecai Richler's The Appenticeship of Duddy Kravitz*, Toronto: ECW Press, 1990

A third-generation Canadian Jew, Mordecai Richler was born in 1931 in Montreal, where his grandfather settled after venturing to Canada in 1904 to escape the eastern European pogroms. Richler grew up in a self-contained world circumscribed by orthodoxy and by fear and ignorance of French and English Canadians. He attended Jewish parochial school, studied the Talmud, and was expected to become a rabbi. At Baron Byng High School (the Fletcher's Field of his fiction), a Protestant school, he began to ease away from orthodoxy and to conceive of himself as both Jewish and Canadian, though this was not always an easy complementary conception of himself. "The minority man", he points out, quoting Norman Mailer, "grows up with a double-image of himself, his own and society's."

Of his Montreal Jewish community of the 1930s and 1940s, Richler stated, "that was my time, my place and I have elected myself to get it right". His early novels *Son of a Smaller Hero* and *The Apprenticeship of Duddy Kravitz* vividly recreate the Montreal community of his youth, the first providing an incisive study of the growth of a sensitive, intense Jewish youth, Noah Adler, in this environment. The many evident parallels between Noah's life and Richler's obliged him to include a prefatory note disclaiming any autobiographical intention. Richler's later novels range in setting from London to Jerusalem to Paraguay, but he continued to focus on his Montreal community, showing the socioeconomic and cultural changes that have taken place in subsequent decades. Though most of his fiction is set in Jewish communities and is peopled by Jews, and though he raises many ethnic issues, he looks beneath the racial to the human, and, like Bernard Malamud, he uses the Jewish world as a metaphor for human experience. His novels try to transcend time, place, and ethnicity and are at once Jewish, Canadian, and universal.

Particularly in his later novels, Richler examines the Jewish experience more inclusively, going beyond the Montreal community. In *St Urbain's Horseman*, he ambitiously employs the metaphor of the horseman to create a myth for the contemporary Jew who, having "not gone like sheep to the slaughterhouse" in Auschwitz and being "too fastidious to punish Arab villages with napalm", did not fit a mythology. Jake shares in his people's collective memory of persecutions and injustices which scream for an avenger and a defender. And initially he believes in the possibility of the Jews becoming assertive and heroic, shedding their image as a people who accept unprotestingly persecution and exploitation as their lot. The Horseman is the symbol of this aspiration. He avenges the wrongs against the Jews in Montreal, Israel, and Germany, and his current task in the novel is hunting down the archenemy of the Jews, Dr Mengele, the butcher of Auschwitz. For Jake, the Horseman astride his magnificent Pleven stallion, "Galloping, thundering, planning fresh campaigns, more daring manoeuvres", is the image of dignity and courage.

Richler's portrayal of the Jewish community is imbued oftentimes by an ambivalence. He and his protagonists simultaneously praise and criticize it. Noah of *Son of a Smaller Hero*, for instance, discovers that though his extended family lived in a cage, "that cage, with all its faults, had justice and safety and a kind of felicity" and he begins to question his supercilious view of it. Some reviewers have interpreted Richler's criticism as undue authorial coldness. Richler himself inadvertently gave rise to this censure with a brash youthful comment that he later regretted making:

> I now recall with embarrassment [that I did not] wish to be classified as a Jewish writer. No, no. I was, as I pompously protested to an interviewer, a writer who merely happened to be Jewish.
>
> Fortunately for me, a Yiddish newspaper in Montreal saw the interview and swiftly cut me down to size: "The oven is big, the loaf is small."

In a later interview, Richler unhesitatingly acknowledges that he is a thoroughly Jewish writer. He contends that the very fact that he is writing about a minority group from within makes his criticism suspect by his community. Such a problem does not exist for writers who belong to the mainstream:

> A Gentile, in my position, can ridicule the pretensions of the middle class and their clergy with a degree of impunity. He has, it's true, to face the tests of accuracy and artistic worth, but never will be called an anti-Gentile. My people, unfortunately are still so insecure here that they want their artists to be publicists, not critics.

A dedicated novelist, Richler, as his novels demonstrate, shunned the publicist function, affirming that "any serious writer is a moralist".

A prolific journalist, Richler published more than 600 pieces in such popular and prestigious journals and magazines as *Punch*, *New Statesman*, *Commentary*, *Atlantic Monthly*, *New York Times Book Review*, *Saturday Night*, *Playboy*, and *Life*. His topics tend to be primarily Canadian and Jewish issues. Not unexpectedly for one who wrote so much and in such a range of publications, his journalism is uneven in quality. Some articles were written simply to startle or to be controversial, some were hasty opinions evidently written to be discarded and forgotten, and some were very serious, written with great deliberation over matter and style. Richler himself selected and edited the pieces important to him in several collections. His journalistic tone tends to have a satirical edge, which, in most of his novels, is generally muted by his narrators' ambivalent perception of experience. Richler was also a scriptwriter with many film and television scripts to his credit. However, while he dismissed scriptwriting as a means of buying time for his novels, journalism is another matter: "I like journalism," he stated frankly; "I take as much care of my journalism as anything I write."

VICTOR J. RAMRAJ

Riding, Laura

US poet, fiction writer, and critic, 1901–1991

Born Laura Reichenthal in New York City, 16 January 1901. Studied at Girls' High School, Brooklyn; Cornell University, 1918–21. Married, first, Louis Gottschalk, 1920; divorced 1925. Adopted surname Riding, 1927. Moved to Deyá, Mallorca, 1929; later lived in Britain, Switzerland, and France; returned to United States, 1939. Associated with Fugitive group of poets; co-founded, with Robert Graves, Seizin Press, 1928, and *Epilogue* magazine, 1935. Married, second, Schuyler B. Jackson, 1941; husband died 1968. Awarded Mark Rothko Appreciation Award, 1971; Guggenheim Fellowship, 1973; National Endowment for the Arts Fellowship, 1979; Bollingen Prize, 1991. Died in Wabasso, Florida, 2 September 1991.

Selected Writings

Poetry
The Close Chaplet, 1926
Voltaire: A Biographical Fantasy, 1927
Love as Love, Death as Death, 1928
Poems: A Joking Word, 1930
Though Gently, 1930
Twenty Poems Less, 1930
Laura and Francisca, 1931
Poet: A Lying Word, 1933
The First Leaf, 1933
The Life of the Dead, 1933
Americans, 1934
The Second Leaf, 1935
Collected Poems, 1938
Selected Poems: In Five Sets, 1970
The Poems, 1980
First Awakening: The Early Poems of Laura Riding, edited by Elizabeth Friedmann, Alan J. Clark, and Robert Nye, 1992
A Selection of the Poems of Laura Riding, edited by Robert Nye, 1996

Fiction
Experts Are Puzzled, 1930
No Decency Left, with Robert Graves, 1932
14A, with George Ellidge, 1934
Progress of Stories, 1935; revised edition, 1982
Convalescent Conversations, 1936
A Trojan Ending, 1937
Lives of Wives, 1939
Description of Life, 1980

Other
Translator, *Anatole France at Home*, by Marcel Le Goff, 1926
A Survey of Modernist Poetry, with Robert Graves, 1927
A Pamphlet against Anthologies, with Robert Graves, 1928; as *Against Anthologies*, 1928
Anarchism is Not Enough, 1928
Contemporaries and Snobs, 1928
Four Unposted Letters to Catherine, 1930; new edition 1993
Editor, *Everybody's Letters*, 1933
Pictures, 1933
Editor, *Epilogue 1–3*, 3 vols, 1935–37
Translator, with Robert Graves, *Almost Forgotten Germany*, by Georg Schwarz, 1936
Len Lye and the Problem of Popular Films, 1938
Editor, *The World and Ourselves: Letters about the World Situation from 65 People of Different Professions and Pursuits*, 1938
The Covenant of Literal Morality, 1938
The Left Heresy in Literature and Life, with others, 1939
The Telling, 1972
"It Has Taken Long" (selected writings) in Laura Riding Issue, *Chelsea*, 35 (1976)
How a Poem Comes to Be, 1980
Some Communications of Broad Reference, 1983
The Word "Woman" and Other Related Writings, 1993
Letters to Ken (1917–1961), with Robert Graves, edited by Harvey Sarner, 1997
Rational Meaning: A New Foundation for the Definition of Words and Supplementary Essays, with Schuyler B. Jackson, 1997

Further Reading

Adams, Barbara Block, "Riding's Poems: A Double Ripeness", *Modern Poetry Studies*, 11 (1987)
Adams, Barbara Block, *The Enemy Self: Poetry and Criticism of Laura Riding*, Ann Arbor, Michigan: UMI Research Press, 1990
Baker, Deborah, *In Extremis: The Life of Laura Riding*, New York: Grove Press, and London: Hamish Hamilton, 1993
Christiensen, Peter G., "Women as a Spiritual Force in Laura Riding's *Lives of Wives*", *Focus on Robert Graves and his Contemporaries*, 1/13 (Winter 1992)
Ciani, Daniela M., "Laura Riding's Truthfulness to the Word and to the Self", *Revue française d'études américaines*, 61 (August 1994)
Matthews, Thomas Stanley, *Under the Influence: Recollections of Robert Graves, Laura Riding and Friends*, London: Cassell, 1979
Rosenthal, M.L., "Riding's Poetry", *Southern Review* 21/1 (Winter 1985)
Schultz, Susan M., "Riding's Essentialism and the Absent Muse," *Arizona Quarterly* (Spring 1992)
Temes, Peter S., "Code of Silence: Laura (Riding) Jackson and the Refusal to Speak", *Publications of the Modern Language Association of America*, 109/1 (January 1994)
Wexler, Joyce Piell, *Laura Riding's Pursuit of Truth*, Athens: Ohio University Press, 1979
Wexler, Joyce Piell, *Laura Riding: A Bibliography*, New York: Garland, 1981

The daughter of an immigrant tailor, Laura Reichenthal was raised on the Lower East Side of Manhattan in the shadow of the garment district. Nathan Reichenthal had come to America with his father and mother in 1884 in flight from anti-Jewish riots in eastern Europe. By the time Laura was born in 1901, Nathan was involved with the "Jewish socialism" movement flourishing among the sweatshops of New

York City. For intellectual stimulation, the young girl was encouraged to read the newspaper. Indeed, her father's political and economic views overshadowed any traditional expression of the Reichenthal family's social and religious heritage, and Laura embarked on a lifelong spiritual search. "I was born in New York City", she once wrote, "of Jewish (but not religiously so) parents." In 1916 she embraced poetry both as an outlet for her creativity and as a path to enlightenment, and she rejected outright her father's socialism. When she moved in with her older half-sister Isabel, she adopted the name Laura Riding, taken formally by deed poll in England in 1927. Critic Barbara Adams has questioned whether this gesture too was intended as a renunciation of her Jewish heritage. Indeed, some of Riding's earliest poetry, like the poem "Jews" for example, seeks to position herself outside any cultural allegiance. "Hapless and unmysterious they thrive/ Like flowers by themselves torn out of earth", she writes, "Martyrs and stubborn miracles alive/ Upon the spiteful victory of pain." The effect of Riding's childhood is reflected most vividly in her later short story "Socialist Pleasures". Here, she explores a flight from paternal politics and religion as illustrated by her protagonist, Fanny. "Fanny's family was a Jewish family," Riding writes, "but they did not live as Jews lived or think of themselves as Jews. They were Socialists." While Fanny seeks eventually to escape the limitations of socialism, such an escape is not facilitated by embracing her Jewish heritage. While she notices with envy that "some Jewish girls had holes in their ears and wore ear-rings," she acknowledges that "Spanish girls in pictures also had holes in their ears with long ear-rings in them, but they were Catholics." Thus, she begins longing for the exotic. As an adult, Fanny the psychologist occasionally feels melancholy in her staid life, and she resorts to having costume pictures of herself taken with "ear-rings that could be screwed on". Injured during a trip to Spain, she recasts her childhood in the care of Catholic nuns, even going so far as acquiring a pet and buying her own ear-rings. Upon returning to the United States, she quits her job and teaches Spanish dance, eventually taking a job in a cabaret. Feigning Spanish blood, she never embraces her Jewish roots, and her father's conversion to communism confirms her suspicion that all the dogmatic teachings that coloured her background are woefully superficial.

In 1920, Laura Riding married Louis Gottschalk, her Cornell University history professor. Her faith in the power of poetry, and her faith in her aptitude for it, was boosted when she received the Nashville Prize from the little magazine the *Fugitive* in 1924; the next year, she divorced Gottschalk and returned to New York, attuning herself to the city's artistic circles. But by the end of 1925, she had sailed to England to collaborate with Robert Graves. While her unconventional romance with the married Graves would result in a suicide attempt in 1929, their collaboration gave rise to her clearest critical voice, resulting in *A Survey of Modernist Poetry* and *A Pamphlet against Anthologies*. Her emerging secular morality was developed in *Four Unposted Letters to Catherine*, and her creative work was influenced heavily by another secular Jew, Gertrude Stein. Stein's concern with language and purity of meaning can be read in the reductionism that framed Riding's poetry. While religion in a conventional sense played no role in Riding's life, in her work she used to great effect fragments drawn from the tenets of Judaeo-Christian faith. The unreliability of words is evident in poems such as "The Last Covenant" that employ religious imagery. "And those pledges," Riding writes, "Which between man and heaven held/ By rapt contrivance, stumblings, stutterings/ And the visions of wan, rheumy eyes?/ And those infatuated ordinances/ Scratched on the stubborn tablets of persuasion." In "The Readers", Riding uses scripture itself as a metaphor when she writes, "The Bible and the other books –/ The books beginning with the Bible/ Ending with the Bible which the Bible/ In its fear of words, the word was not . . ." The irony here, of course, is that she is questioning the unquestioned word to underline the limitations of all language. God himself appears in "Then Follows": "It came about by chance/ I met God/ 'What,' he said, 'you already?'/ 'What,' I said, 'you still?'" At the end of the poem, Riding admits to having invented here a God that does not exist, but she eventually elevates the poet to take His place.

In October 1929 Riding moved to Deyá, Mallorca to live with Graves. Much of the 1930s were in turn productive and tempestuous, with a great deal of writing emerging from the distractions of a small colony of artists who came to work with Riding there. Although Riding's biographer Deborah Baker describes her as "anti-Jewish", Riding's criticism in this period bristled against the intellectual laziness of anti-Semitism, and she was shocked by the manifestation of this hatred in fascism. The Spanish Civil War chased Riding and Graves from Deyá in 1936; over the next two years they lived in England, Switzerland, and France. Riding returned to the United States in 1939, and she soon met and married Schuyler Jackson. Her lack of faith in words led her to abandon poetry, for the most part, and she spent much of the last 50 years of her life pursuing her interest in philology. She undertook a variety of unfinished dictionary projects with her husband, and in the years before his death in 1968 she began to use publicly the name Laura (Riding) Jackson. There was a renewed interest in her work in the 1970s and 1980s, and before her death in 1991 she undertook revisions of some of her earlier writing.

CRAIG MONK

Rosenberg, Isaac

British poet, 1890–1918

Born in Bristol, 25 November 1890, to Barnard and Anna Rosenberg, Russian immigrants. Moved with family to Whitechapel, London, 1897. Studied at kheder until 1903; Baker Street School, Stepney, 1899–1904; evening classes at London County Council School of Photo-engraving and Lithography, 1907–10, and Birkbeck School of Art, London; Slade School of Art, London, 1911–14. Apprentice engraver, Carl Hentschel Company, London, 1904–07. Visited South Africa, to see sister, Minnie Horvitsch, and for health, 1914–15. Served in British army from 1915; killed in action near Arras on the Somme, 1 April 1918.

Selected Writings

Collections
The Collected Works of Isaac Rosenberg: Poetry, Prose, Letters, and Some Drawings, edited by Gordon Bottomley and Denys Harding, 1937; revised edition of poetry section as *The Collected Poems of Isaac Rosenberg*, 1949
Collected Works: Poetry, Prose, Letters, Paintings, and Drawings, edited by Ian Parsons, 1979

Poetry
Night and Day, 1912
Youth, 1915
Poems, edited by Gordon Bottomley, 1922

Play
Moses: A Play, 1916

Further Reading

Bergonzi, Bernard, *Heroes' Twilight: A Study of the Literature of the Great War*, London: Constable, 1965; New York: Coward McCann, 1966
Cohen, Joseph, *Journey to the Trenches*, London: Robson, 1975
Graham, Desmond, *The Truth of War: Owen, Blunden, and Rosenberg*, Manchester: Carcanet, 1984
Liddiard, Jean, *Isaac Rosenberg: The Half Used Life*, London: Gollancz, 1975
Maccoby, Deborah, *God Made Blind: Isaac Rosenberg, His Life and Poetry*, Northwood, Middlesex: Symposium, 1999
Moorcroft Wilson, Jean, *Isaac Rosenberg, Poet and Painter: A Biography*, London: C. Woolf, 1975
Silkin, Jon, and Maurice de Sausmarez, *Isaac Rosenberg 1890–1918: A Catalogue of an Exhibition Held at Leeds University, 1959, Together with Text of Unpublished Material*, Leeds: University of Leeds, 1959
Silkin, Jon, *Out of Battle: The Poetry of the Great War*, 2nd edition, Basingstoke: Macmillan, and New York: St Martin's Press, 1998
Tomlinson, Charles, *Isaac Rosenberg of Bristol*, Bristol: Bristol Branch of the Historical Association, 1982

Isaac Rosenberg was the first important poet to emerge from Anglo-Jewry, and he remains a poet of major significance. In 1937, his *Collected Works* was published posthumously with a foreword by Siegfried Sassoon, who hailed the "fruitful fusion between English and Hebrew culture" in this fine poet. Known today primarily as a war poet, Rosenberg is above all a Jewish poet, transposing many biblical images in a subtle and unique way to illustrate his poetry, tussling with ideas of God, and introducing for the first time into the 20th century the idea of the deracinated, tormented Jew, caught hanging. We see Rosenberg's energy and poignancy in the "Trench Poems", including the robust yet tender "Break of Day in the Trenches", "Marching", "Dead Man's Dump", and "Daughters of War" (which Rosenberg believed to be one of his best poems). His interest in Jewish themes may be seen in his poems from the earliest, "Zion" and "Creation", in the privately published pamphlets of verse, *Night and Day* and *Youth*, in *Moses: A Play*, and in his last poems.

His individual voice responds to the vitality of the countryside that he visits in "Night and Day":

> I lay upon the sparkling grass
> And God's own mouth was kissing me.
> And there was nothing that did pass
> But blazèd with divinity.

The first poem in *Youth* is "None Have Seen the House of the Lord", in which twilight waits for night; God is desired but feared, and is indeed elusive. The creative powers of the poet begin to challenge the Creator's, a concept enunciated in "The Blind God" and "God". Rosenberg wrote most of the manuscript of the play *Moses* before enlisting in the 12th (Bantam) Battalion of the Suffolk Regiment in 1915. He later transferred to the 11th Battalion, The King's Own, with whom he embarked for France on 2 June 1916.

Born in Bristol, Rosenberg had grown up in London's East End, where his impoverished Yiddish-speaking father struggled to make a living as a peddler. Barnard Rosenberg had fled from Dvinsk to avoid forced conscription in the Czar's army. Rosenberg's artistic talent led to his years at the Slade School of Art, sponsored by three wealthy Jewish ladies (immortalized in the short story "Rudolph") and a grant from the Jewish Educational Aid Society, with contemporaries such as David Bomberg and Mark Gertler. After a year in South Africa, visiting his sister and recuperating from weak lungs, Rosenberg enlisted. He delayed telling his parents because he knew they would be upset. The son had volunteered for what the father had rejected. ("My parents are Tolstoyans – nothing can justify war.")

Unlike other war poets such as Wilfred Owen or Rupert Brooke, Rosenberg went to war as a private soldier, not an officer, and saw the war from a ruder, rougher perspective. He wrote to Sydney Schiff about his military experience: "It is most revolting . . . Besides my being a Jew makes it bad amongst these wretches. I am looking forward to a bad time altogether . . ." And in a letter to Lascelles Abercrombie: "nobody but a private in the army knows what it is to be a slave." As Jon Silkin's essay "An Idea of Moses" demonstrates, the issues discussed in the play *Moses* and the image of enslaved Jews in Egyptian captivity, although mostly written before Rosenberg joined up, remained with him in the trenches, and it is a play "infected . . . by the War, its hovering imminence, and its outbreak". Rosenberg explained his play to R.C. Trevelyan: "Moses symbolises the fierce desire for virility, and original action in contrast to slavery of the most abject kind." In the following passage, Rosenberg identifies with Moses: "Moses, from whose loins I sprung,/ Lit by a lamp in his blood/ Ten immutable rules, a moon/ For mutable lampless men".

The play concerns Moses, caught between two cultures, tending his sheep over the fumes of a burning bush, while famine grips Egypt. The Jews are seeking a leader to free them from captivity, thus providing the way for Moses' evolution from Egyptian prince to Jewish hero. He yearns for Abinoah's beautiful daughter but his crisis of conscience is ended when he kills Abinoah, the cruel overseer, and is arrested. "Fine! Fine!/ See in my brain/ What madmen have rushed through,/ And like a tornado/ Torn up the tight roots/ Of some dead universe . . .".

The image of the root, which F.R. Leavis has shown Rosenberg to use frequently, like an archetype, "to yield different meanings in different contexts while retaining its 'root' significance, as it does in Hebrew where the root meaning of a word will be retained even if the prefix or suffix modifies it". Here the "root" of the "dead universe" must be torn, the old order changed, before Egyptian society based on slavery can change, and lead to Jewish freedom. The awakening Moses chooses to redeem his people's destiny, his brain in torment as he makes the decision, and then commits the act of murder as he challenges Abinoah: "The roots hid secrecy, old source of race,/ Unreasoned reason of the savage instinct". In "unreasoned reason", Rosenberg reveals the duality of instinct and reason, the merging of opposites in strength and delicacy.

Included in the published *Moses* are three "God" poems, including the poem "Chagrin", where Rosenberg articulates his mixed feelings about the war, and describes the deracinated rootless state of the alienated Jew:

> Caught still as Absalom
> Surely the air hangs from the swayless cloud-boughs
> Like hair of Absalom, caught and hanging still.
> From the imagined weight of spaces in a sky of mute
>   chagrin, my thoughts
> Hang like branch-clung hair . . .
> We are lifted of all we know
> And hang from implacable boughs.

Rosenberg uses the figure of Absalom, favoured son of King David who betrayed him, and who was killed on horseback when his long hair was caught in overhanging branches, as a delicate metaphor for his own dilemma. The tree is "swayless" – no air to sway the boughs: "cloud-boughs" – a duality of air and living tree, held still, "hanging", dangling in the suspense of the moment. With economy and assurance, Rosenberg presents a very different figure from the dashing Moses freeing himself and the slaves from bondage.

After *Moses,* Rosenberg considered writing other plays using biblical themes: "I have thoughts of a play round our Jewish hero, Judas Maccabeus . . ." and "a most gorgeous play about Adam and Lilith" (which survives in fragments as "The Amulet" and "The Unicorn"). His last three poems were on Old Testament themes: "The Burning of the Temple", "The Destruction of Jerusalem by the Babylonian Hordes", and his poignant yearning for the pools of Hebron and a dream of "Lebanon's summer slope" in "Through These Pale Cold Days". This last poem was enclosed in a letter in which he wrote of his wish "to write a battle song for the Judains [sic] but can think of nothing strong and wonderful enough yet."

Rosenberg died on active service, near Arras, on 1 April 1918; his body was never found. As he wrote in "Dead Man's Dump", "We heard his weak scream/ We heard his very last sound/ And our wheels grazed his dead face".

SORREL KERBEL

Rosenfarb, Chava

Polish-born Canadian poet and fiction writer, 1923–

Born in Łódź, 9 February 1923, to Abraham Rosenfarb and wife Sima (née Pinczewska). Survived Łódź ghetto, and Auschwitz and Bergen-Belsen camps, during World War II. Emigrated to Belgium, settled in Brussels. Emigrated to Canada. Married, first, Henry Morgentaler; divorced; second, Bono Weiner; husband died 1976; two children. Studied at Jewish Teachers Seminary, Montreal. Awarded J.J. Segal Prize, 1972; Niger Prize, 1973; Manger Prize (for life's work), 1979.

Selected Writings

Poetry

Di balade fun nekhtikn vald un andere lider [The Ballad of Yesterday's Forest and Other Poems] (includes *Nokhmilkhome lider* [Post-War Poems]), 1948

Dos lid fun dem yidishn kelner avram [The Song of Abraham the Waiter], 1948

Geto un andere lider: oykh fragmentn fun a togbukh [Ghetto and Other Poems with Fragment from a Diary], 1948

Aroys fun gan-edn [Out of Paradise], 1965

Play

Der foygl fun geto [The Ghetto Bird], 1958

Novels

Der boym fun lebn, 3 vols, 1972; as *The Tree of Life: A Novel about Life in the Lodz Ghetto*, translated and abridged by Rosenfarb with Goldie Morgentaler, 1985

Botshani, 1983; as *Bociany* and *Of Lodz and Love*, translated by Rosenfarb, 2 vols, 2000

Briv tsi abrashen [Letter to Abrashen], 1992

Novella

Edgia's Revenge, translated in *Found Treasures: Stories by Yiddish Women Writers*, edited by Frieda Forman *et al.*, 1994

Other

In *Canadian Yiddish Writings*, edited by Abraham Boyarsky and Lazar Sarna, 1976

Further Reading

Rosenfarb, Chava, "Feminism and Yiddish Literature: A Personal Approach" in *Gender and Text in Modern Hebrew and Yiddish Literature*, edited by Naomi B. Sokoloff *et al.*, New York: Jewish Theological Seminary of America, 1992

Sharlet, Jeffrey, "More Objective than Tears. A Portrait of Chava Rosenfarb", *Pakn Treger* (National Yiddish Book Center) (Summer 1997): 50–65

Although Chava Rosenfarb always saw herself as a poet, she tells us, in a paper published in 1990, that on a fateful day in August 1944 she stood, after surviving the selection ramp at Auschwitz, "naked, with my head shaved, but my life spared" and decided to write a novel about the Łódź ghetto, recently "liquidated" with a mass deportation.

She felt that "the brutal reality of the ghetto demanded the dry precision of words" to be found in prose rather than the "song" of verse. After establishing herself in Canada she wrote that book, the tremendous *Der boym fun lebn* (*The Tree of Life*). She had worked on it for 13 years, under tremendous physical and psychological difficulties; weighed down with family responsibilities, she rose at 4am to write and to struggle with the pain of recalling the nightmarish period she spent as a teenager in the Łódź ghetto. Given its length – three large volumes in Yiddish, more than 1000 small-type pages in the abridged English version – its highly autobiographical nature, and Rosenfarb's astonishingly calm and detailed recall of this dark period it is both a major document of ghetto life and a major artistic achievement in itself. As well as evoking the unspeakably cruel situation of the Jews herded into the ghetto's confines – perhaps the worst moment being the round-up of all children under 12 years of age who are sent off, as their parents then suspected, and as we now know, to be murdered by the Germans – Rosenfarb lets us taste the complexity of the life lived and suffered there. With the character of young Rachel we attend classes (pre-ghetto) in the Jewish Girls' Gymnasium and learn of the fierce assimilationism of its Polish-speaking teachers and their disdain for Yiddish and *yidishkayt* and, later, when the ghetto has been set up and sealed we share something of both the particular bitterness felt by the youngsters trapped within it, as well as their hopeful, heroic loves, their thirst for learning and their adolescent idealism. Peculiar and particular rhythms and repetitions special to the ghetto-world emerge and establish themselves in our consciousness; the petty struggle for survival – often bought, for a while, by serving the ghetto's (Jewish) administration headed by the ambiguous figure of Chaim Rumkowski, "Eldest of the Jews" – such as the constant counting, exchanging, and measuring of soups which become the real currency inside the ghetto as starvation and exhaustion close in. As the book progresses through a compressed, relentless four years, the very fullness and variety of characters Rosenfarb describes, set against the fact that we know almost all of them will die, is intensified by this ghastly reality. Her focus often falls on artists and writers in the ghetto, creating work, as she did both during and after the war, in difficult and seemingly hopeless circumstances. She thus throws a light on what could be considered the highest achievement of the contemporary Jewish contribution to civilization; its fidelity to the values of culture, the word, and memory even, literally, in the face of the abyss. There is also here an unsentimental portrayal of various rich and selfish individuals; magnates or rather former magnates come under the lash of Rosenfarb's leftist politics. This is not a ghetto of "plaster saints", but the real people she knew. Largely a book waiting to become better known and better and more widely translated, *Tree of Life* will stand as one of the real monuments to the victims of the Holocaust.

In 1948 Rosenfarb published *Di balade fun nekhtikn vald un andere lider* [The Ballad of Yesterday's Forest and Other Poems], her poems written in a labour camp late in the war called *Geto-lider* [Ghetto Poems] and some immediately afterwards, *Nokh-milkhome lider* [Post-War Poems]. There is poignant prison-talk of green fields and freshly-baked bread, a weeping mother's dialogue in "Vu bistu zuneniu?" [Where are you my little son?] with her murdered child while "Tey-bey-tsey-balade" [TB-ballad] is a poem dedicated to a friend, Jacob, "taken on the first winter transport 1940-1" and the moving "Mir kumen um" [We Perish] "Who will remember the father's last groan/ who will remember the mother's last cry?"

A 1992 novel, *Briv tsi abrashen* [Letter to Abrashen] also deals with the terrible moment of extermination, reminding us in a period where a great deal of literature about the Holocaust is being written that in Rosenfarb we have a talented writer who had the unusual fortune to survive these events, a real Polish-Jewish witness whose great importance has been overlooked.

Rosenfarb also wrote about an earlier period preceding the war with the marvellous *Botshani* (*Bociany* and *Of Lodz and Love*), which follows Yacov and Binele in their journey from the picturesque *kleynshtetl* (small Jewish-inhabited town) of Bociany, where storks roost on every roof, to the energetic and corrupt textile centre, Łódź. These are beautiful, enjoyable rich-textured works, enabling us to share some of the cultural wealth and emotional depth of this "drowned world". In an autobiographical epilogue that reflects Rosenfarb's own brief trip back to postwar Poland in 1947, when the border policeman stamps her passport asking her how long she has been in the country she wants to answer "about a thousand years", and in fact Rosenfarb's work, her profound and detailed celebration, her excavation of Łódź is a worthy tribute to Jewish Poland, heartland of the Ashkenazi world.

Another "epilogue" is *Edgia's Revenge*, translated in the anthology *Found Treasures*, where the question of the guilt feelings of survivors and of those who survived through privileges ultimately granted by the German murderers is argued in a complex and disturbing way.

Apart from her poetry and novels, and her activity travelling and speaking about Yiddish literature as a living and still-productive symbol of this threatened tradition, Rosenfarb wrote a play, *Der foygl fun geto* [The Ghetto Bird]. This relates the real-life drama of the night of 16 July 1943 in the Vilna (Vilnius) ghetto when the leader of the United Partisan Organization, Itzik Wittenberg, was arrested by the Germans and freed by partisans. The Germans threatened to liquidate the ghetto immediately if he wasn't handed over. Wittenberg's eventual decision to give himself up to preserve Jewish unity symbolizes the narrow, terrible choices open to this trapped and abandoned people.

RAY KEENOY

Rosenfeld, Isaac

US fiction writer and critic, 1918–1956

Born in Chicago, 10 March 1918. Lost mother at 22 months; alienated from father and stepmother. Yiddish was his first language. Attended Sholem Aleichem Schools for several years; Tuley High School; University of Chicago, MA 1941; New York University, PhD. Married Vasiliki Sarantakis,

1941; divorced, 1951. Contributor to *New Republic*, 1941–45. After 1945, contributor to *Partisan Review*, *Commentary*, *New Leader*, and *Nation*. Taught at University of Minnesota, 1951–53; University of Chicago, 1953–56. Received John Billings Fisk Prize, 1937. Died of heart attack, 15 July 1956.

Selected Writings

Fiction and Essays
Passage from Home, 1946
An Age of Enormity: Life and Writing in the Forties and Fifties (collection of short stories and reviews), edited by Theodore Solotaroff, foreword by Saul Bellow, 1962
Alpha and Omega: Stories by Isaac Rosenfeld, 1966
Preserving the Hunger: An Isaac Rosenfeld Reader, edited by Mark Shechner, foreword by Saul Bellow, 1988

Further Reading

Atlas, James, "Golden Boy", *New York Review of Books*, 36/11 (1989)
Atlas, James, *Saul Bellow: A Biography*, New York: Random House, and London: Faber, 2000
Bell, Daniel, "A Parable of Alienation" in *Mid-Century: An Anthology of Jewish Life and Culture in Our Times*, edited by Harold U. Ribalow, New York: Beechhurst Press, 1955
Bellow, Saul, "Zetland: By a Character Witness" in his *Him with His Foot in His Mouth and Other Stories*, New York: Harper and Row, and London: Secker and Warburg, 1984
Bluestein, Gene, "Prufrock-Schmufrock", *Yiddish*, 7/1 (1987)
Howe, Irving, *A Margin of Hope: An Intellectual Autobiography*, San Diego, California: Harcourt Brace Jovanovich, 1982; London: Secker and Warburg, 1983
Kazin, Alfred, *New York Jew*, New York: Knopf, and London: Secker and Warburg, 1978
Lyons, Bonnie, "Isaac Rosenfeld: A Reappraisal", *Studies in American Jewish Literature*, 1 (Spring 1975)
Phillips, William, "Four Portraits", *Partisan Review*, 5/4 (1983)
Rifkind, Donna, "Hunger Artist", *New Criterion*, 7/3 (1988)
Shechner, Mark, "The Journals of Isaac Rosenfeld", *Salmagundi* (1980)
Shechner, Mark, "From Isaac Rosenfeld's Journals", *Partisan Review*, 47 (1980)
Shechner, Mark, "Yiddish Fables", *Prooftexts*, 2 (1982)
Shechner, Mark, introduction to *Preserving the Hunger: An Isaac Rosenfeld Reader*, edited by Shechner, Detroit: Wayne State University Press, 1988
Solotaroff, Theodore, introduction to Rosenfeld's *An Age of Enormity: Life and Writing in the Forties and Fifties*, Cleveland: World, 1962
Solotaroff, Theodore, *A Few Good Voices in Your Head*, New York: Harper and Row, 1983
Zipperstein, Steven J., "The First Loves of Isaac Rosenfeld", *Jewish Social Studies: History, Culture, and Society*, 5/1–2 (1998–99)

Inevitably, Isaac Rosenfeld gets remembered as a footnote to the life and career of Saul Bellow. Try as we will, we can't make the separation. In the early 1930s, Bellow and Rosenfeld were schoolmates at Tuley High School, in the Humboldt Park neighbourhood of Chicago. Many years later, Bellow would eulogize their youth together in a portrait of Rosenfeld – everyone called him Isaac – that played up the qualities of intellectual passion and boyish precocity that, along with a winking sense of mischief, would characterize his intellectual life throughout. The following passage is from Bellow's preface to a collection of Rosenfeld's essays, *An Age of Enormity*:

> It is late afternoon, a spring day, and the Tuley Debating Club is meeting on the second floor of the old building, since destroyed by fire. The black street doors are open, the skate wheels are buzzing on the hollow concrete and the handballs strike the walls with a taut puncturing sound. Upstairs, I hold the gavel. Isaac rises and asks for the floor. He has a round face, somewhat pale, glasses, and his light hair is combed back with earnestness and maturity. He is wearing short pants. His subject is *The World as Will and Idea*, and he speaks with perfect authority. He is very serious. He has read Schopenhauer.

That Bellow would live to memorialize so many of his friends in portraits like this has been his fate, particularly as he would outlive them all. But the place of Rosenfeld in his life, and in his writing, was special: they were boys together and rivals as well, constantly taking the measure of each other. Bellow would at one point begin a novel about Rosenfeld titled "Zetland". He could never finish it, though a fragment of it – a sketch for it, really – did reach print in "Zetland: By a Character Witness". In bold verbal strokes it outlined Rosenfeld's childhood, the discord of family life under the disapproving reign of a bullheaded patriarch ("Ozymandias" Bellow calls him), his marriage to his "Macedonian" wife (in actuality, Vasiliki Sarantakis), and his life in Greenwich Village as an ascetic Dostoevskian in the 1940s: an underground man suffering grave illnesses while feathering his "Zet habitat", a paradise for cockroaches with the agreeable dimness of a chapel. "Believe me", Rosenfeld wrote in a short story, "chaos is the mother of knowledge." Exalted and bereaved, Bellow's sketch describes Isaac/Zetland as an adolescent, "somewhat between the stout boy and the nearsighted young man with odd ideas and exotic motives. Loving, virtually Franciscan, a simpleton for God's sake, easy to cheat. An ingenue. At the age of nineteen he had a great deal of Dickensian heart." Between them, Bellow and Rosenfeld would divide up the world of emotions: "We decided that we were the tender-minded and tough-minded of William James, respectively."

None of this would have mattered had Rosenfeld not also been a writer, whose career, languishing in the shadow of Bellow's as it did, boasted a novel, a brace of stories, and a handful of essays, and reviews that resonated far beyond the subject at hand. Rosenfeld's promise, though troubled and erratic, was genuine, but it was cut short by his death in 1956, at the age of 38. He was the only Jewish writer of his generation to write fiction in both Yiddish and English. In

1946 he published a story in Yiddish titled "Dos Meser" ("The Knife") and published it in English as "Red Wolf" two years later. He also wrote "Dray fabeln far Yidn" ("Three Stories for Jews") some time in the 1940s, though they would not see print until three years after his death. While the accumulated harvest of writing in both languages was small, the freshness and penetration of Rosenfeld's mind blaze through in all of it. He left behind the one novel, *Passage from Home*, and several collections edited posthumously by friends and admirers, including *An Age of Enormity* and *Alpha and Omega*. Rosenfeld's career was a flash of light, and it is still capable of surprising and warming those who come upon it.

Passage from Home was an auspicious debut for a young writer, just 28 in 1946. A postwar disenchantment novel, typical of its time, it was a public exhibition of the wounds that festered in Rosenfeld's heart, and with the solemnity of David at psalms he wrote passionately about his childhood, as if by doing so he could exorcize its miseries and cleanse his spirit. It was virtually a Passover service, as it detailed the plagues of his childhood: relatives instead of locusts. The hero, Bernard Miller, is Isaac Rosenfeld in all but name, and his struggles with his father were the very same that had driven Rosenfeld from the home of Ozymandias. The Jewish family in *Passage from Home* is a decomposed institution, in which the father's tyranny has been divorced from any semblance of religious authority. An American, Chicago born, Bernard Miller has learned – to borrow a formula from Abraham Joshua Heschel – the danger and gloom of this world but not the infinite beauty of heaven or the holy mysteries of piety.

Afterwards, Rosenfeld would start, and soon abandon, a longer novel, an allegory titled *The Enemy*. He was at his best in short forms, including some vivid stories, which were collected in *Alpha and Omega*. Among them was the much-anthologized "King Solomon", which transported the fabled king to a realm that sounded like New York City. Rosenfeld's King Solomon is a foppish old Jew, an overweight, cigar-smoking, pinochle-playing monarch who can barely recall his former wisdom but is still beloved by young girls who come from all over Judea – or is it Brooklyn? – to lie beside him and place their hands upon his breast. Other memorable stories included a Depression-romance spawned in the waiting room of the WPA Writers' Project, "The Hand that Fed Me"; a Dostoevskian parable of humiliation in love, "Wolfie"; and a political satire, "The Party." The latter is about a political party that collapses when its members grow bored; it is yawned to death by a caucus of younger comrades – the Ennui Club – who nod off during the national chairman's speeches. Unnamed, the Workers Party and its chairman, Max Shachtman, are clearly the targets of Rosenfeld's broad satire.

Rosenfeld had broken in as a poet and fiction writer with the *New Republic* in 1942, at the age of 24, and was soon a regular contributor there and to *Partisan Review*, *Commentary*, *Kenyon Review*, *Harper's*, *New Leader*, and the *Nation*. The apartment he and Vasiliki shared on Barrow Street was an ongoing salon, and he was, for an instant, a master of ceremonies for those young writers and intellectuals who gathered in Greenwich Village during the 1940s, before the migration uptown shattered their brief bohemian/luftmensch soiree. If one totals up all the stories and reviews published between 1942 and 1956, Rosenfeld seems a marvel of productivity, though the great novel eluded him, while Saul Bellow soldiered his way through book after book. Most of his achievements were unpremeditated triumphs of occasion, book reviews stretched into proclamations. However, what he lacked in amplitude he possessed in fire and acuteness. His judgements do not fade with time. They remain contemporary. Reviews and essays such as "Farewell to Hemingway", "The Fall of David Levinsky", "Isaac Leib Peretz: The Prince of the Ghetto", and "Simone Weil as Saint" remain among the best essays ever written about their subjects.

Give Bellow the last word.

> Singlemindedly, Isaac was out for the essential qualities. He believed that heart and truth were to be had. He tried to fix them within himself. He seemed occasionally to be trying to achieve by will, by fiat, the openness of heart and devotion to truth without which a human existence must be utterly senseless.

MARK SHECHNER

Rosenfeld, Moris

Polish-born US poet, 1862–1923

Born Moyshe Yankev Alter in Bokshe, near Sejny, 1862. Studied at kheder. Left to join parents in London, 1882; moved to United States, 1886. Tailor, sweatshop worker, poet; co-edited satirical weekly, *Der ashmeday*, 1894. Son died, 1905; suffered partial paralysis and near-blindness; health later improved. Wrote for Yiddish daily newspaper *Forverts* and numerous other periodicals. Toured eastern Europe and attended Czernowitz Yiddish Conference as delegate, 1908. Died 1923.

Selected Writings

Poetry
Di gloke [The Bell], 1888
Dos lider bukh, 1897; as *Songs from the Ghetto*, translated by Leo Wiener, 1898
Shriftn [Writings], 6 vols, 1908–10
Geveylte shriftn [Selected Writing], 3 vols, 1912
Dos bukh fun libe [The Book of Love], 1914
Songs of Labor and Other Poems, translated by Rose P. Stokes and Helena Frank, 1914
Grine tsores, 1919
Teardrop Millionaire and Other Poems, translated by Aaron Kramer, 1955
Poems of Morris Rosenfeld, translated by Mortimer T. Cohen, 1979

Other
Heinrich Heine, 1906
Judah Halevi, 1907

Further Reading
Goldenthal, Edgar J., *Poet of the Ghetto: Morris Rosenfeld*, Hoboken, New Jersey: Ktav, 1998
Jeshurin, Ephim H., *Morris Rosenfeld Bibliografye*, Buenos Aires, 1962
Leftwich, Joseph (editor and translator), *The Golden Peacock: A Worldwide Treasury of Yiddish Poetry*, New York: Yoseloff, 1961
Madison, Charles A., *Yiddish Literature: Its Scope and Major Writers*, New York: Ungar, 1968
Meisl, N. (editor), *Tsum Hundertstn Geboyrntog fun Moris Rozenfeld*, New York: YKUF, 1962
Tabachnik, Abraham Baer, "Moris Rosenfeld" in *Dikhter un Dikhtung*, New York: Tabachnik, 1949

Moris Rosenfeld came from a traditional family. He attended kheder and later studied *gemara*. He read Hebrew, studied German and Polish, and learned English. He began to write poetry at the age of 15. Although best known as a poet (many of his poems were set to music), Rosenfeld also wrote prose, satirical pieces, plays, philosophical essays, travel sketches, theatre criticism, and aphorisms. For most of his working life he was a tailor and a presser, but for a time he made a living as a published poet who performed his own work. He was reputed to be a fine singer and a dynamic reader of verse. He also became a journalist, working both as editor and contributor to Yiddish papers and journals.

Rosenfeld is identified with the earliest group of modern Yiddish poets which emerged in the United States known as the "labour", "sweatshop" or "proletarian" poets. The others in this group are Dovid Edelshtat, Yosef Bovshover, and Morris Vinchevsky. All are part of the large wave of immigrants that arrived from eastern Europe late in the 19th century.

Rosenfeld's poetry addressed the working class, the poor and struggling Jewish masses, by exploring the hardships of immigrant life. He offered a forceful voice to the Jewish collective by chronicling their suffering in the old world and their struggles in the new. Identifying with both the Jew and the worker, he wrote as one of their kind. Against a backdrop of socialist ideology, Rosenfeld's work, though bleak, offered hope for a better life. He focused on schisms between the old and new worlds and presented a generally pessimistic view of Jewish life in the Diaspora. Social and political change could offer redemption but equally, Zion could serve as its symbol. Although many of Rosenfeld's themes are universal, the Jewish experience is central to his work.

Rosenfeld's parents had moved to London where he joined them in 1882, working in tailoring and enduring great poverty and hardship. He became acquainted with anarchists and began to write *arbeter lider* (workers' poems/songs). Rosenfeld moved to New York in 1886 where he worked long hours in a sweatshop and continued his writing at night, and he began to publish socialist and propagandist poems which were immediately popular among Jewish workers. In the 1880s and 1890s his work was published in a variety of American and European Yiddish papers (*Varheit*, *Yidishes folksblat*, *Morgnshtern*, and *Arbeiter tsaytung* among others), by which time his poems were being recited and sung in the "shops", at meetings of socialists and union members, and at concerts of workers. Rosenfeld, encouraged by the popular response to his work tried unsuccessfully to leave the sweatshop which was adversely affecting his health.

The best of his work has endured and the most successful poems and songs continue to be republished in Yiddish poetry and song anthologies. The popular "Mayn yingele" ("My Little Boy") describes a father's sadness when he realizes that his small son is asleep when he leaves for work and again when he returns. The child repeatedly asks the whereabouts of his father and the poem ends with the father musing that one day the child may find his father gone. In other words, extreme working conditions may bring about his early death. Many of Rosenfeld's poems describe the minutiae of an industrialized world, and whereas the rhythm in "Dos lid fun mashinen" ("The Song of Machines") mimics the sounds made by machines, in "Di svet shop", human forms are actually transformed into machines – "mayn ikh vert dort botl, ikh ver a mashin" [my self is obliterated, I become a machine]. In "Mayn rue plats" ("My Resting Place"), the harsh reality of the workplace is contrasted with images of nature. The poetic persona addresses a lover, listing all the inaccessible spots of natural beauty which do not constitute his resting place.

Rosenfeld's first two published books of poetry were unsuccessful. The publication of *Dos lider bukh* marked a change in fortune and established his international reputation. Leo Wiener, Professor of Slavic Languages at Harvard, translated the book into English under the title *Songs from the Ghetto*. This led to Rosenfeld's engagement for readings in American universities and precipitated the translation of his work into many European languages (German, French, Czech, Polish, and Russian). This fame meant that Rosenfeld was finally able to leave sweatshop tailoring and he became a Yiddish journalist.

When Rosenfeld's 15-year-old son died in 1905, he became partly paralysed and he was almost blind. By 1908, with his health much improved, Rosenfeld toured eastern Europe and Galicia performing his work. He also attended the Czernowitz Yiddish Conference as a delegate in the same year.

Despite being the first Yiddish poet to receive such international acclaim, Rosenfeld lost his place of honour in Yiddish literary circles. Literary sensibilities were changing and he came to be criticized by a younger generation of Yiddish poets. He started to be undermined and isolated, an object of ridicule, as can be seen in cartoons in the satirical paper *Der groyser kundes* [The Prankster]. By 1910 Rosenfeld was an angry and bitter man. The sweatshop poets came to be seen as naive, coarse, and unsophisticated. There was a development away from poetry as a conduit for the expression of collective struggle and more towards the utterance of an individual, lyric voice; art for art's sake that did not favour political and social realism.

By all accounts Rosenfeld was pushed out of his work as a regular correspondent for *Forverts* in 1913. He did not enjoy and was dismissed from his subsequent job as correspondent for the Orthodox *Yiddishes tageblat*. His bitterness grew and he was in constant conflict with Yiddish writers and editors. Following the change in career from "scissors" to "pen", Rosenfeld complained that the interference from editors was comparable to the sweatshop experience under enslaving bosses. When he died in 1923 his funeral was attended by thousands and he is buried next to Sholem Aleichem.

Some of Rosenfeld's work justifiably deserves the criticism of being overstated, clichéd, repetitive, lacking in subtlety, and with an abundance of predictable rhymes. His work is characterized by its direct invocations, declamatory style, clear social commentary, and accentual-syllabic versification. He addresses injustice and inequality and promotes a striving for freedom. National and folk motifs are imbued with Jewish symbols and allusions. His work also incorporates a quieter, lyric voice. His Yiddish language contains American-English and German elements. Rosenfeld played a considerable role in recording a moment in the history of Jewish America and in contributing to the growth of American Yiddish poetry.

HELEN BEER

Rosten, Leo

Polish-born US fiction writer and dramatist, 1908–1997

Born Leo Calvin Rosten in Łódź, 11 April 1908. Emigrated with family to United States, 1910. Studied at University of Chicago, BA 1930, PhD 1937; London School of Economics and Political Science, 1934. Married, first, Priscilla Ann Mead, 1935; wife died; one son, two daughters; second, Gertrude Zimmerman, 1970. English teacher in Chicago, 1930–32; writer of screenplays, 1937–38; special consultant, National Defense Commission, 1939–40; director, Motion Picture Research Project, 1939–41; chief, Motion Picture Division, Office of Facts and Figures, Washington, DC, 1941–42; Deputy Director, Office of War Information, Washington, 1942–43; special consultant, US Secretary of War, 1945; colonel, US Army, 1945; member, Senior Staff, RAND Corporation, 1947–49; editorial adviser, *Look* magazine, New York, 1949–71. Lecturer, Columbia University, from 1955. Ford Visiting Professor of Political Science, University of California, Berkeley, 1960–61. Member of National Board, Authors League of America. Many awards, including Rockefeller Foundation grant, 1940; George Polk Memorial Award, 1955; Freedom Foundation Award, 1955. Member, American Academy of Arts and Sciences. Died on 3 March 1997.

Selected Writings

Novels
The Education of Hyman Kaplan (as Leonard Q. Ross), 1937
Dateline: Europe (as Leonard Ross), 1939; as *Balkan Express*, 1939
Adventure in Washington (as Leonard Ross), 1940
The Dark Corner, 1945
Sleep, My Love, 1946
The Return of Hyman Kaplan, 1959
Captain Newman, M.D., 1961
A Most Private Intrigue, 1967
Dear "Herm" – With a Cast of Dozens, 1974
O Kaplan! My Kaplan!, 1976
Silky: A Detective Story, 1979
King Silky!, 1980

Screenplays: *All through the Night*, with Leonard Spigelgass and Edward Gilbert, 1942; *The Conspirators*, with Vladimir Pozner and Jack Moffitt, 1944; *Lured*, 1947; *Sleep, My Love*, with others, 1947; *The Velvet Touch*, with others, 1948; *Where Danger Lives*, with Charles Bennett, 1950; *Whistle at Eaton Falls*, with others, 1951; *Double Dynamite*, with Mel Shavelson and Harry Crane, 1952; *Walk East on Beacon*, with others, 1952

Other
The Washington Correspondents, 1937
The Strangest Places (as Leonard Ross), 1939
Hollywood: The Movie Colony, the Movie Makers, 1941
112 Gripes about the French, 1944
Editor, *A Guide to the Religions of America*, 1955; as *Religions of America*, 1957; as *Religions in America*, 1963
The Story behind the Painting, 1962
The Many Worlds of Leo Rosten, 1964; as *The Leo Rosten Bedside Book*, 1965
The Joys of Yiddish, 1968
A Trumpet for Reason, 1970
People I Have Loved, Known, or Admired, 1970
Leo Rosten's Treasury of Jewish Quotations, 1972
Rome Wasn't Burned in a Day: The Mischief of Language, 1972
Editor, *The "Look" Book*, 1975
The 3:10 to Anywhere, 1976
The Power of Positive Nonsense, 1977
Passions and Prejudices; or, Some of My Best Friends Are People, 1978
Editor, *Infinite Riches: Gems from a Lifetime of Reading*, 1979
Hooray for Yiddish: A Book about English, 1982
Leo Rosten's Giant Book of Laughter, 1985; as *Leo Rosten's Book of Laughter*, 1986
The Joys of Yinglish, 1989

Further Reading

Obituary, *University of Chicago Magazine* (June 1997)

Active and highly productive as journalist, author, and academic, Leo Rosten is nevertheless largely remembered for just two of his many books, both wildly successful; the humorous novel *The Education of Hyman Kaplan* in 1937, and the work of popular etymology and anecdote *The Joys of Yiddish* in 1968.

In *The Education of Hyman Kaplan* the sustained situation humour of the twitchy WASP teacher Mr Parkhill, trapped in an inescapable relationship with Bolshie Hyman Kaplan and various other adult immigrants who are trying to get their English up to speed in a New York classroom, belies the subtlety of its arguments about the complex interactions of languages and cultures. Whether counterposing the essentially passionate mien of the Jewish Kaplan and his Mediterranean and Slavic cohorts to the dry reason of Mr Parkhill in countless, generally absurd conflicts over grammar, vocabulary, and pronunciation, or presenting the spectacle of the adult infantilized by lack of knowledge and the authoritarianism of the classroom situation, there is always the sense of the outsider ironically questioning the strong but naive sense of superiority of the established American confronting the newcomer.

What makes the book so satisfying is that "the joke" is on both Hyman Kaplan and his teacher, on both immigrant culture and American culture. The quick-witted and verbally adept Kaplan is forever coming up with splendidly creative reprises on American English, produced by the subtle operation of his ever-so-slightly untuned ear, so that "a kit is anyone under twenty-one" while foods are to be avoided that cause "high blood pleasure". Kaplan is also equipped with a superior but not normative linguistic logic demonstrated by his privately-coined but instantly comprehensible English verb conjugations; "die, dead, funeral" or "fail, failed, bankrupt".

The proud and self-confident Kaplan, although forced by history and economics to seek a life in the New World, would rather like to re-write America to fit better his own sense of self and national identity, therefore he transforms an all-American icon into "Abram Lin-cohen". Beyond the humour, though, one senses the fact that America in the 1930s had little time for the culture and languages of its newcomers and that all Kaplan achieves, even in the face of the ineffectual Mr Parkhill, is a mere nostalgic coda to the rich language dying on his own lips as American English is born there, although the reader also glimpses a marvellous English potentially improved and deepened by the influence of millions of Kaplans. *The Education of Hyman Kaplan* was followed by two later sequels, *The Return of Hyman Kaplan* and *O Kaplan! My Kaplan!* which do not have its classic quality.

It is also in a nostalgic vein that *The Joys of Yiddish* operates. This is a book written in a necessarily New World genre: "immigrant-folkloric"; a celebration of the good old, curious, and quaint ways of our parents, grandparents, etc. As a book about the Yiddish language – and it is the only well-known one ever produced – its curiosities include an emphasis on American Yiddish and what Rosten calls "Yinglish", and a disregard, partly corrected in the later *Hooray for Yiddish,* of contemporary Yiddish literature, which had much to say about the immigrant experience and the transition to urban modernity that is part of Rosten's subject matter. Nevertheless, Rosten brings his years of journalistic experience to bear, alongside his comic sense, to assemble a highly readable selection of short items around Yiddish and Jewish immigrant life and Jewish life in America. He gathers up, apart from his "Yinglishisms", word definitions that illuminate the particularity of Jewish culture, proverbial sayings, and plenty of jokes. Where the jokes partly depend on linguistic knowledge he tries to fill the reader in on some very basic Yiddish.

Like *Hyman Kaplan*, *The Joys of Yiddish* is a much-loved book that refuses to go away, however much contemporary proponents of Ashkenazi culture and language might find it sentimental and ahistorical. The present revival of interest in Yiddish and "Ashkenaz" (as the destroyed homeland of east European Jews is now called) will no doubt bear Rosten's book along with it. He followed it with *Hooray for Yiddish* in 1982 and *The Joys of Yinglish* in 1989, but the best jokes had already been used up.

An insight into the Jewishness that Rosten felt had (or should have?) established itself in that mainstream America that essentially took immigrant culture and Yiddish as an outdated joke can be gained from his *Treasury of Jewish Quotations*. The book is a huge compendium of one-line quotes – 4352 of them – such as "The provision is scant and the road is long" (Kethuboth from the Talmud); many are from the Talmud, others from Jewish sages: Hillel, Rabbi Nahman of Bratslav, etc. and it is a book that, rather in the Zionist mode, jumps directly from the distant glorious past to the present, mostly eliding the modern period. For Rosten Jewish thought and ideas seem to have ended with the end of "tradition" and what he offers are "timeless maxims". Nevertheless his two most popular works spoke, and spoke to many, of a language, a tradition and an ironic way of seeing the world at the time when Jewish cultural amnesia was at its very height.

RAY KEENOY

Roth, Henry

Austrian-born fiction writer, 1906–1995

Born in Tysmienica, Galicia, 8 February 1906. Emigrated with family to United States, 1908. Studied at DeWitt Clinton High School, New York, graduated 1924; City College, New York, BS 1928. Married Muriel Parker, 1939; two sons. Employed by Works Progress Administration, 1939; teacher, Roosevelt High School, New York, 1939–41; precision metal grinder in New York, Providence, Rhode Island, and Boston, 1941–46; teacher, Montville, Maine, 1947–48; attendant, Maine State Hospital, 1949–53; waterfowl farmer, 1953–62; private tutor, 1956–65. Awards included American Academy grant, 1965. Died in Alberquerque, New Mexico, 13 October 1995. Posthumously awarded Hadassah Harold Ribalow Lifetime Achievement Award; honoured by Museum of the City of New York, 29 February 1996 being named "Henry Roth Day"; awarded first *Forward* Foundation Isaac Bashevis Singer Prize in Literature, 1997.

Selected Writings

Novels
Call It Sleep, 1934
Mercy of a Rude Stream
  A Star Shines over Mt Morris Park, 1994
  A Diving Rock on the Hudson, 1995
  From Bondage, 1996
  Requiem for Harlem, 1998

Other
Nature's First Green, 1979

Shifting Landscape: A Composite 1925–1987, edited by Mario Materassi, 1987

Further Reading

Alter, Robert, "The Desolate Breach between Himself and Himself", review of *A Star Shines Over Mt Morris Park*, *New York Times* (16 January 1994)
Dickstein, Morris, "Call It an Awakening", *New York Times* (29 November 1987)
Fiedler, Leslie A., "Henry Roth's Neglected Masterpiece", *Commentary*, 30/2 (August 1960)
Goodman, Allegra, "About Time", review of *Requiem for Harlem*, *New York Times* (5 April 1998)
Gordon, Mary, "Confession, Terminable and Interminable", review of *A Diving Rock on the Hudson*, *New York Times* (26 February 1995)
Halkin, Hillel, "Henry Roth's Secret", *Commentary*, 97/5 (May 1994)
Kazin, Alfred, foreword to *Call It Sleep*, New York: Farrar Straus, 1991
Kermode, Frank, "Holistic Rendering of My Lamentable Past", review of *From Bondage*, *New York Times* (14 July 1996)
Kleederman, Frances, "Bilingual Markers of a Culture in Translation" (dissertation), New York University, 1974
Lyons, Bonnie, *Henry Roth: The Man and His Work*, New York: Cooper Square, 1976
Michaels, Leonard, "The Long Comeback of Henry Roth: Call It Miraculous", *New York Times* (15 August 1993)
Nicholls, Richard E., obituary, *New York Times* (15 October 1995)
Pogrebin, Robin, "A Deep Silence of 60 Years, and an Even Older Secret", *New York Times* (16 May 1998)
Rosen, Jonathan, "Lost and Found: Remembering Henry Roth", *New York Times* (10 December 1995)
Roth, Henry, "Weekends in New York: A Memoir", *Commentary*, 78/3 (September 1984)
Weil, Robert, "Editor's Afterword" and "About the Author" in *Requiem for Harlem*, New York: St Martin's Press, 1998
Wirth-Nesher, Hana, "Between Mother Tongue and Native Language: Multilingualism and Multiculturalism in Henry Roth's *Call It Sleep*", *Prooftexts*, 10/1 (Spring 1990)

The work of US author American Henry Roth spans 20th-century literature. *Call It Sleep* in 1934, his searing, highly crafted novel about New York Jewish immigrants, was inspired by the early modernists, T.S. Eliot and James Joyce. Then, after a silence of 60 years, he caused another literary sensation with *Mercy of a Rude Stream*, a four-volume autobiographical sequence in which Roth's rambling, paralysing quarrels with himself unlocked his past.

The modernists revealed to Roth the poetry of the urban wasteland, as evidenced in this passage from *From Bondage*:

> *Ulysses* . . . showed . . . how to address whole slagheaps of squalor, and make them available for . . . art. . . . the sorcery of language . . . to fluoresce, to electrify the mood . . . the Chicago packing houses . . . used every part of the pig except the squeal. Joyce elucidated ways to use even the squeal.
>
> Ira sensed that he was a *mehvin* of that same kind of world . . . of that same kind of pocked and pitted reality.
>
> Hell, of nastiness, of sordidness, perversity, and squalor – compared to anyone in *Ulysses*, he had loads, he had droves, he had troves. But it was language . . . that could magically . . . free him from this depraved exile . . . this . . . bondage . . . the raw material of literature . . . he was rich beyond compare: his whole world was a junkyard.

Joyce's *Ulysses* pointed the direction Roth was to take in *Call It Sleep*. A young troubled child, David Schearl, is a barometer of Jewish immigrants' struggle, confusion, and loneliness in the teeming city slums. At an age before experience crystallizes into language, Oedipal family tensions split his world into apocalyptic light and shadow.

Both Joyce and Roth shared a facility for and fascination with language itself. The inner babble of a lost, fearful child, the raucous ebullience of Yiddish, "Yinglish", parroted kheder Hebrew, sundry slum dialects, and highly crafted literary English contribute to the brilliant linguistic mosaic of *Call It Sleep*. In *World of Our Fathers*, the critic Irving Howe suggested that a "new and astonishing American prose style" emerged from the "bi-lingualism of Englished Yiddish and Yiddished English" in Roth and later Jewish writers.

Like many Jews and intellectuals of his generation, Roth joined the Communist Party. Ironically a communist journal condemned the "introspective and febrile" style of *Call It Sleep* as a betrayal of Roth's proletarian origins. After abandoning efforts to write a second novel in an approved proletarian mould, he worked in poorly paid, mostly blue-collar, jobs.

The successful first edition of *Call It Sleep* sold 4000 copies. Thirty years later the 1964 paperback edition was hailed by Irving Howe as a masterpiece of 20th-century American literature, selling more than a million copies. Belated recognition and financial security encouraged Roth to begin writing again. The 1967 Arab–Israeli war dispelled his lingering communist allegiances and renewed his identification with Jews and Jewish culture. He began, then abandoned, a novel about Spanish *conversos* (forced Jewish converts to Christianity). Then in 1979 he started *Mercy of a Rude Stream* which picked up the story of the young David Schearl, renamed Ira Stigman.

The narrative is framed by the commentary and self-questioning of the older Ira, to all intents and purposes the elderly author himself. Like Roth, Ira, now crippled with arthritis, has retired to a mobile home in Albuquerque. His ironic broodings over early success and failure, and the futility of belated insight are mingled with effusive gratitude for a long happy marriage to M (Muriel Parker), a promising composer who sacrificed her career to support the family as a teacher.

The first volume, *A Star Shines over Mt Morris Park*, recalls how anti-Semitism, encountered when he moves from the Jewish Lower East Side to white, Irish-dominated, Harlem, made Ira question and despise his Jewishness:

Bar Mitzvah brought the realization he was only a Jew because he *had* to be a Jew: he hated being a Jew; he didn't want to be one . . . and realized he was caught, imprisoned . . . The kid who had once been like a drop of water in the pool of water that was the East Side, indistinguishable from the homogeneity about him, who had wept and wailed to be allowed to return and felt the tears of separation rise in his throat . . . wanted none of it now.

In the second volume, *A Diving Rock on the Hudson*, non-Jewish friendships offer tantalizing glimpses of a wholesome, idealized American boyhood of outdoor adventures and working your way through college, the route not taken. His dysfunctional immigrant family transmits problems of guilt and failure.

A terrifying childhood sexual assault by a stranger triggers precocious sexual experimentation in which he is the victimiser. His incestuous abuse of his sister and cousin continues for years. As Roth claimed in a *Vanity Fair* interview, *Portnoy's Complaint* seems tame by comparison. His namesake Philip might indeed envy Henry Roth's black, taboo-violating, sexual comedy of forbidden cravings and satisfactions. But Roth's handwringing over adolescent sins that blighted his entire life seems overwrought, particularly as Ira/Roth spares little concern for the youthful partners or victims of his lust.

In college, his feelings of exclusion and marginalization by institutional anti-Semitism are offset by joining an avant-garde circle which includes Hart Crane, Louise Bogan, Margaret Mead, Kenneth Burke, and the poet and English professor, Eda Lou Walton, to whom Roth dedicated *Call It Sleep*.

In the last two posthumous volumes, *From Bondage*, and *Requiem for Harlem*, Ira's growing intimacy with Edith (Walton) helps him escape from destructive domestic and sexual tensions. The lusted after sister and fat cousin who have just been counters in his inner world begin emerging in their own right. Fat aunts, kindly uncles, and Zaida, the selfish self-pitying Orthodox patriarch, are viewed with comic empathy. With growing detachment there is also pity for his parents. However his emotional and financial dependence on the older woman clearly continues the oedipal pattern of his childhood.

The gritty, moody New York streetscapes, the radiant precision of domestic and public settings, are Roth at his best. As poetry of the urban junkyard, it is unbeatable. But his self-centred confessions almost vindicate the hardline communist criticism of his youthful writing as "introspective and febrile". Despite the dual perspective of elderly narrator and youthful protagonist Roth continues to have difficulty seeing beyond his adolescent self. Snapshots of extended family, neighbours, school and college life, just whet the appetite for the comic epic of Jewish immigrant society that Roth never wrote. In interviews, Roth conceded that he still shared the messianic temperament of the tortured child in *Call It Sleep*. As a writer, he fits Isaiah Berlin's distinction between the fox who knows many things and the hedgehog who knows one big thing.

Irving Howe suggested that education and creativity uprooted the immigrant writer: "Tradition as discontinuity – this is the central fact in the cultural experience of the American Jewish writers." The four volumes of *Mercy of a Rude Stream* record Ira's painfully won enlightenment, a liberation by tiny increments from his dysfunctional family and their shreds of ghetto culture. As in Ralph Glasser's roughly contemporary masterpiece, *Growing Up in the Gorbals*, and Isaac Bashevis Singer's earlier *Love and Exile*, the journey begins with a lonely slum boy drawn like a magnet to the great 19th-century urban institution of the public reading rooms and lending library. *Mercy of a Rude Stream* is distinguished by its confessional intensity and exuberant, self-consciously modernist style. At the same time it is an archetypal story of secularization and social mobility created by mass Jewish migration to the slums of great cities – Glasgow, Warsaw, New York – in the early 20th century.

FELICITY BLOCH

Roth, Joseph

Austrian fiction writer, 1894–1939

Born in Brody, Galicia, 2 September 1894. Suffered from poor health most of his life. Studied at Baron-Hirsch-Schule, Brody, 1901–05; Imperial-Royal Crown Prince Rudolph Gymnasium, 1905–13; University of Lemberg, Vienna, 1913; studied German literature, University of Vienna, 1914–16. Married Friederike Reichler, 1922. Served in Austro–Hungarian army, 1916–18; may have spent months as prisoner of war in Russia. Journalist, Vienna, 1919–23. Emigrated to Germany, 1923; settled in Berlin. Staff member, Berlin, 1923–25, cultural correspondent, Paris, 1925, Soviet Union, 1926, Albania, 1927, and Poland, 1928, for *Frankfurter Zeitung*. Emigrated to France after Nazi seizure of power in Germany, 1933; settled in Paris. Visited Poland, on lecture tours for PEN, 1933 and 1937. Died in Paris, 27 May 1939.

Selected Writings

Collections

Werke, edited by Hermann Kesten, 3 vols, 1956

Werke, edited by Klaus Westermann and Fritz Hackert, 6 vols, 1989

Fiction

Das Spinnennetz, 1923 (newspaper publication); as *The Spider's Web*, translated by John Hoare, with *Zipper and His Father*, 1988

Die Rebellion, 1924; as *Rebellion*, translated by Michael Hofmann, 1999

Hotel Savoy, 1924; in *Hotel Savoy; Fallmerayer the Stationmaster; The Bust of the Emperor*, translated by John Hoare, 1986

April: Die Geschichte einer Liebe [April: The History of a Love], 1925

Der blinde Spiegel [The Blind Mirror], 1925

Die Flucht ohne Ende, 1927; as *Flight without End*, translated by Ida Zeitlin, 1930; translated by David Le Vay and Beatrice Musgrave, 1977

Zipper und sein Vater, 1928; as *Zipper and His Father*,

translated by John Hoare, with *The Spider's Web*, 1988
Rechts und Links, 1929; as *Right and Left*, translated by Michael Hofmann, 1991
Hiob: Roman eines einfachen Mannes, 1930; as *Job: The Story of a Simple Man*, translated by Dorothy Thompson, 1931
Radetzkymarsch, 1932; as *The Radetzky March*, translated by Geoffrey Dunlop, 1933; translated by Eva Tucker, 1974; translated by Joachim Neugroschel, 1995
Der Antichrist, 1934; as *Antichrist*, translated by Moray Firth, 1935
Le Buste de l'Empereur, 1934; translated as *Die Büste des Kaisers*, 1964; as *The Bust of the Emperor*, translated by John Hoare, with *Hotel Savoy* and *Fallmerayer the Stationmaster*, 1986
Tarabas: ein Gast auf dieser Erde, 1934; as *Tarabas: A Guest on Earth*, translated by Winifred Katzin, 1934
Beichte eines Mörders, erzählt in einer Nacht, 1936; translated as *Confessions of a Murderer, Told in One Night*, translated by Desmond L. Vesey, 1938
Die hundert Tage, 1936; as *The Ballad of the Hundred Days*, translated by Moray Firth, 1936; as *The Story of the Hundred Days*, 1936
Das falsche Gewicht, 1937; as *Weights and Measures*, translated by David Le Vay, 1982
Die Kapuzinergruft, 1938; as *The Emperor's Tomb*, translated by John Hoare, 1984
Die Geschichte von der 1002. Nacht, 1939; as *The Tale of the 1002nd Night*, translated by Michael Hofmann, 1998
Die Legende vom heiligen Trinker, 1939; as *The Legend of the Holy Drinker*, translated by Michael Hofmann, 1989
Der Leviathan [The Leviathan], 1940
Romane, Erzählungen, Aufsätze [Novels, Stories, Essays], 1964
Der stumme Prophet, 1966; as *The Silent Prophet*, translated by David Le Vay, 1979
Die Erzählungen [The Stories], 1973

Other
Für Gott und Vaterland [For God and Fatherland], 1925
Juden auf Wanderschaft, 1927; as *The Wandering Jews*, translated by Michael Hofmann, 2001
Die Flucht ohne Ende, 1927; as *Flight without End*, translated by Ida Zeitlin, 1930; translated by David Le Vay and Beatrice Musgrave, 1977
Das Moskauer Jüdische Akademische Theater [The Moscow Jewish Academic Theatre], 1928
Panoptikum: Gestalten und Kulissen [The Curio Collection: Figures and Scenery], 1930
Zwischen Lemberg und Paris [Between Lemberg and Paris], edited by Ada Erhart, 1961
Briefe 1911–1939 [Letters 1911–1939], edited by Hermann Kesten, 1970
Der neue Tag: unbekannte politische Arbeiten 1919 bis 1927, Wien, Berlin, Moskau [The New Day: Little Known Political Works 1919 to 1927, Vienna, Berlin, Moscow], edited by Ingeborg Sültemeyer, 1970
Perlefter: die Geschichte eines Bürgers [Perlefter: The History of a Citizen], edited by Friedemann Berger, 1978
Berliner Saisonbericht: unbekannte Reportagen und journalistische Arbeiten 1920–39 [Berlin Season Report: Little Known Reports and Journalistic Works 1920–39], edited by Klaus Westermann, 1984

Further Reading
Bronsen, David, "The Jew in Search of a Fatherland: The Relationship of Joseph Roth to the Hapsburg Monarchy", *Germanic Review* (Spring 1979): 54–61
Butler, Geoffrey, "Short Weight in Full Measure: Joseph Roth's *Das falsche Gewicht* in English", *Quinquereme: New Studies in Modern Languages*, 6 (1983)
Chambers, Helen (editor), *Coexistent Contradictions: Joseph Roth in Retrospect*, Riverside, California: Ariadne Press, 1991
Eggers, Frank Joachim, *Ich bin ein Katholik mit judischen Gehirn: Modernitätskritik und Religion bei Joseph Roth und Franz Werfel*, Frankfurt: Peter Lang, 1996
Koester, Rudolf, *Joseph Roth*, Berlin: Colloquium, 1982
Mathew, Celine, *Ambivalence and Irony in the Works of Joseph Roth*, Frankfurt and New York: Peter Lang, 1984
Siegel, Rainer-Joachim, *Joseph Roth: Bibliographie*, Morsum, Sylt: Cicero, 1995

Was Joseph Roth Jewish? There have been some doubts about whether he was or not. He wrote only one book that can unequivocally be considered to be "Jewish", although Jews consistently occupy the pages of his other novels. He is a difficult writer to categorize and is as enigmatic a character as the biblical Job whose name he chose for his great masterpiece.

There are many misconceptions about Roth. He was supposedly uncertain about his origins, being unsure whether his mother was of Ukrainian or Jewish stock, but his paternal grandfather was a Yiddish speaker and was Orthodox in faith. Roth served in the Austrian army in the 1914–18 war and was a great patriot. He may have been taken prisoner on the Russian front although, again, this is uncertain; but what is clear is that he never recovered from the collapse of the Hapsburg empire and Austria's subsequent annexation by Nazi Germany. He came to see himself as a Roman Catholic but, ironically, all his literary work demonstrated his Jewish sensibilities. Inner conflicts between his love of Austria and the ghetto orthodoxy of the Jew were never resolved. He wrote *Juden auf Wanderschaft* (*The Wandering Jews*), which has a realistic description of a shtetl and is based on his home town of Brody in eastern Galicia.

Roth was described as the "most musical and graceful writer in the German tongue in our day" and he was notable for being able to depict his characters and his situations in simple terms and without ornament. He had an "illuminated simplicity" and has been favourably compared with such dissimilar writers as Dostoevskii, Knut Hamsun, and Hans Christian Andersen. From 1923 until his death in 1939, Roth wrote 15 novels the themes of which stressed the decadence of modern society; these established him as a major writer.

"Jews in the Diaspora" was written in 1927 soon after he returned from Russia (he went there as a newspaper correspondent) and it contradicted his rejection of Judaism. It drew on his personal experiences as well as on his observations on Judaism, and it clearly showed that his Roman Catholicism was thin and that he had not lost his Jewish consciousness. His Jewish origins had not been forgotten and the essay shows much sympathy for and understanding of Jewish life in eastern Europe. Roth berated western Jews who conducted mechanical services in boring temples and he showed much affection for the simple traditional prayer houses where Jews really came into contact with their Maker. In the essay he proclaimed that "no matter how superficial assimilation is, it is an attempt to reconcile the irreconcilable".

One of Roth's early works, *Das Spinnennetz* (1923 in instalments in a newspaper; published in English in 1988 as *The Spider's Web*), takes a real person as the central character. This was Arthur Trebitsch, an Austrian Jew who abandoned his faith, became a notorious anti-Semite, and collaborated with the Austrian Nazi movement. In this novel, Trebitsch is depicted as the leader of a secret anti-Semitic organization. Roth's next novel was *Hotel Savoy* which, like so many of his other works, is set in the early postwar years in eastern Europe. A returning Austrian soldier stops at a town in eastern Europe, a town that is shabby but boasts a magnificent and splendid hotel. The lower floors are occupied by rich people; poor wretches occupy the upper floors and these wretches are known not by name but by room number. This plot provides Roth with the opportunity of showing where his sympathies lie, especially when an industrial dispute splits the town.

Die Flucht ohne Ende (*Flight without End*) is a Jewish story but without Jews, and it presents the meaning of disillusionment in postwar Europe in a positive and bold manner. The hero is an Austrian lieutenant captured by the Russians who escapes and wanders from country to country seeking an identity as he becomes fully aware of the injustices associated with the established order. The book ends on a note of complete disillusionment on its author's part and it may be a complete rehash of Roth's own experiences. *Der stumme Prophet* (*The Silent Prophet*) was written in 1929 but was published posthumously in 1966 and, again, it is based on failure, being the tale of a revolutionary activist who fails. It predicts a totalitarian society.

Roth's early life in Brody is vividly described in *Radetzkymarsch* (*The Radetsky March*). This book, now considered to be one of his greatest works, is a study of the disintegration of an empire; one critic has described it as "the perfect formula for the historical novel". In it, Roth's cry was one of despair and the book's theme is one that obsessed him throughout his life. As well as his skill in developing characters, Roth could develop themes, well illustrated in *Tarabas: ein Gast auf dieser Erde* (*Tarabas: A Guest on Earth*). Set on the Polish–Russian border during World War I and the following few years, the story is one of sin and repentance and in it Roth dealt with the inability of humankind to control history. The characters in the novel, soldiers and long-suffering Jews, are all confused by the problems of war. Tarabas is feared by his soldiers and by the Jews until his moment of truth arrives.

Many of Roth's novels are autobiographical, none more so than *Die Legende vom heiligen Trinker* (*The Legend of the Holy Drinker*), his last novel. This work tells us a great deal about Roth himself – his poverty, unhappiness, solitude, his failures. Not long after completing it, he died from excessive drinking. *Das falsche Gewicht* (*Weights and Measures*) is set in Galicia and Roth's usual themes of evil, justice and suffering are explored. The main character is the inspector of weights and measures who is ultimately destroyed by a hostile world. There are many Jews in the story. *Beichte eines Mörders, erzählt in einer Nacht* (*Confessions of a Murderer, Told in One Night*) is about a man's search for his identity, clearly mirroring Roth's obsession with his own origins. The inner life of an indeterminate soul is pitilessly described.

But Roth's reputation as a Jewish writer is based mainly on *Hiob: Roman eines einfachen Mannes* (*Job: The Story of a Simple Man*). A quintessentially Jewish story, it is the tale of the Wandering Jew and again is partly autobiographical. Like the story of the biblical Job, it is the drama of a human soul and its theme is that of the trial and eventual cleansing of a man through suffering. Mendel Singer is a *melamed*, a Hebrew teacher, with only a handful of pupils to whom he teaches Torah and Talmud in his kitchen in Zuchnow in Russia. His eldest son becomes a Cossack and eats the flesh of the pig. His daughter gave herself freely in the fields to soldiers and his third son Menuchim was born a cripple. His second son Shemariah went to the United States where he became a soldier and Mendel then decides to follow him there, partly in order to save his daughter from sexual disaster, but he has to leave Menuchim at home. At first Mendel fails and flounders in the US and is unable to adjust to life there, but his story is a credible one of human distress. The wrath of God follows him to the New World and, like his biblical namesake, he turns on Him. But all comes out well in the end and Mendel is rehabilitated. *Job* is a very "Jewish" novel which moved Stefan Zweig to tears and Marlene Dietrich, incredibly, was so taken by it that she turned it into a film script. This novel is a first-class example of Jewish "angst".

CECIL BLOOM

Roth, Philip

US fiction writer, 1933–

Born Philip Milton Roth in Newark, New Jersey, 19 March 1933. Studied at Weequahic High School, Newark; Newark College, Rutgers University, 1950–51; Bucknell University, Pennsylvania, 1951–54, BA 1954; University of Chicago, 1954–55, MA 1955. Served in army, 1955–56. Married, first, Margaret Martinson, 1959; separated, 1962; she died, 1968; second, the actress Claire Bloom, 1990; divorced 1995. Instructor in English, University of Chicago, 1956–58; visiting writer, University of Iowa, 1960–62; writer in residence, Princeton University, 1962–64; visiting writer, State University of New York, Stony Brook, 1966, 1967, and University of Pennsylvania, 1967–80; Distinguished Professor, Hunter College, New York, since 1988. General editor, Writers from the Other Europe series, Penguin Books,

1975–80. Many awards, including Guggenheim Fellowship, 1959; National Book Award for Fiction, 1960, 1995; Daroff Award, 1960; American Academy grant, 1960; O. Henry Award, 1960; Ford Foundation grant (for drama), 1965; Rockefeller Fellowship, 1966; National Book Critics Circle Award, 1988, 1992; National Jewish Book Award, 1988; PEN/Faulkner Award for Fiction, 1993; Pulitzer Prize, 1998. Member, American Academy of Arts and Letters, 1970.

Selected Writings

Novels
Letting Go, 1962
When She Was Good, 1967
Portnoy's Complaint, 1969
Our Gang (Starring Tricky and His Friends), 1971
The Breast, 1972
The Great American Novel, 1973
My Life as a Man, 1974
The Professor of Desire, 1977
Zuckerman Bound, 1985
The Ghost Writer, 1979
Zuckerman Unbound, 1981
The Anatomy Lesson, 1983
The Prague Orgy, 1985
The Counterlife, 1987
Deception, 1990
Operation Shylock: A Confession, 1993
The Professor of Desire, 1994
Sabbath's Theater, 1995
American Pastoral, 1997
I Married a Communist, 1998
The Human Stain, 2000
The Dying Animal, 2001

Short Stories
Goodbye, Columbus, and Five Short Stories, 1959
Penguin Modern Stories 3, with others, 1969
Novotny's Pain, 1980

Television Play: *The Ghost Writer*, with Tristram Powell, 1983

Other
Reading Myself and Others, 1975
A Philip Roth Reader, 1980
The Facts: A Novelist's Autobiography, 1988
Patrimony: A True Story, 1991
Conversations with Philip Roth, edited by George J. Searles, 1992
Sleep Talk: A Writer and His Colleagues and Their Work, 2001

Further Reading

Appelfeld, Aharon, *Beyond Despair: Three Lectures and a Conversation with Philip Roth,* translated by Jeffrey M. Green, New York: Fromm, 1994
Baumgarten, Murray and Barbara Gottfried, *Understanding Philip Roth*, Columbia: University of South Carolina Press, 1990
Cooper, Alan, *Philip Roth and the Jews*, Albany: State University of New York Press, 1996
Danziger, Marie A., *Text/Countertext: Postmodern Paranoia in Samuel Beckett, Doris Lessing and Philip Roth*, New York: Peter Lang, 1996
Halio, Jay L., *Philip Roth Revisited*, New York: Twayne, 1992
Meeter, Glenn, *Bernard Malamud and Philip Roth: A Critical Essay*, Grand Rapids, Michigan: Eerdmans, 1968
Pinsker, Sanford, *The Comedy That "Hoits": An Essay on the Fiction of Philip Roth*, Columbia: University of Missouri Press, 1975
Pughe, Thomas, *Comic Sense: Reading Coover, Elkin, and Philip Roth*, Basel and Boston: Birkhäuser, 1994
Shechner, Mark, "Jewish Writers" in *The Harvard Guide to Contemporary American Writing*, edited by Daniel Hoffman, Cambridge, Massachusetts: Harvard University Press, 1979
Wade, Stephen, *The Imagination in Transit: The Fiction of Philip Roth*, Sheffield: Sheffield Academic Press, 1996

Philip Roth has been producing stories, novels, memoirs, and essays for nearly half a century. When his first book, *Goodbye, Columbus, and Other Stories* appeared in 1959 and won the National Book Award, he was recognized, along with Saul Bellow and Bernard Malamud, as one of the three best Jewish American writers to emerge in the post-World War II period. Since that time the ethnic qualifier, though still relevant, is no longer necessary: specializing in the infinite varieties of human comedy, although comedy typically populated by Jews, he is simply one of the best fiction writers in America today.

His oeuvre may be divided into roughly three periods. The first begins with the novella and stories in *Goodbye, Columbus* and culminates in the novel for which he is most famous, *Portnoy's Complaint* in 1969. With the exception of *When She Was Good*, a novel set in the American heartland without a Jewish character in it, the fiction in this ten-year period mainly focuses on Jewish family relationships and the problems that young Jewish men had in defining their identity and establishing a satisfying and fruitful relationship with a woman. Usually, the setting is Newark, New Jersey, where Roth was born and grew up. The honesty and candour with which he presented this fiction aroused the ire of many in the middle-class Jewish establishment, and the writer was roundly criticized for his treatment of Jews. In his defence, Roth claimed that as a writer he could not and should not be concerned with what was "good for the Jews". His integrity as a writer lay in treating his subjects with the truth they deserved and indeed demanded. If his initial response to the attacks on him was to vow never to write about Jews again, he overcame that reluctance and in *Portnoy's Complaint* deliberately provided his critics with greater provocation than ever. The often raw language he used in the novel, moreover, he defended as an attempt to raise the nature of language in fiction to the level of a subject.

The second period starts with *My Life as a Man* and continues into the 1990s, reaching its first apex in *The Counterlife* and again in *Operation Shylock*. It is in these novels that Roth began playing with his conception of the counterlife, alternative treatments of characters either by the author or, as it were, by the characters themselves. In *My Life as a Man* Nathan Zuckerman first appears, not as Roth's surrogate, but as Peter Tarnopol's, although Tarnopol is clearly himself a Roth surrogate. In the two stories, called "Useful Fictions", that preface the novel proper, Tarnopol fictionalizes aspects of his earlier life, much as Roth does with Tarnopol and later with Zuckerman as his own surrogate, as in the trilogy *Zuckerman Bound* and *The Counterlife*. Here Roth reveals himself as a postmodern novelist deeply concerned with the aspects of subjectivity in fiction and the ways autobiography may be used to provide the substance for fiction. For example, in *Zuckerman Unbound*, the second in the trilogy, Nathan has achieved great notoriety for his scandalous novel, *Carnovsky*, which bears a very close resemblance to *Portnoy's Complaint*, just as Zuckerman's experiences bear a close but far from exact resemblance to Roth's own experiences after the publication of his novel. In *The Counterlife* Roth produced a tour de force of counterlives, taking Nathan and his brother Henry and interchanging with each of them various experiences, including their deaths, only to resurrect one or the other of them later in the novel. As a measure of Roth's skill, at no time is the reader confused by these counterlives, which are carefully developed and explained by Nathan after his "death" for what they are.

In *Deception* and more fully in *Operation Shylock* Roth abandons Zuckerman, at least for the purposes of these novels, and appears first as "Philip" and then as "Philip Roth". The experimentation that has been evident in his previous work, particularly in the confessional novel *Portnoy's Complaint* and the postmodernism of *The Counterlife*, continues in full force here. *Deception* is written almost entirely in dialogue, much in the manner of Ivy Compton-Burnett (although no one would otherwise confuse it with one of her novels), and uses the game of "reality shift", which "Philip" and Maria (a character from *The Counterlife* who was Nathan's wife) play to develop further the concept of counterlives. In *Operation Shylock* Roth goes still further and invents a double of himself, living in Israel and advocating a policy of reverse immigration, which he calls "Diasporism". In this novel Roth probes more deeply than ever into the novelist's preoccupation with subjectivity, subtitling the book "A Confession", and in public statements printed in the *New York Times* and elsewhere proclaiming that what happened actually did happen. But the novel ends with the absence of a promised chapter and a simple statement that the "confession is false".

Meanwhile, to complicate matters still further, Roth produced two memoirs: *The Facts*, subtitled *A Novelist's Autobiography*, and *Patrimony*, an account of his father's last years, when he suffered from an inoperable brain tumour, and of his son's care of him. In *The Facts* Zuckerman again appears, first as the recipient of the author's letter prefixed to the book, and then in his reply to Roth. Zuckerman advises Roth against publication, insisting that he is an impersonator, not an autobiographer, that he does his best work through him. *Deception* and *Operation Shylock* appear to be attempts to discredit Zuckerman's argument, but the way Roth treats both "Philip" and "Philip Roth" in those books tends, if anything, to confirm Zuckerman's position. *Patrimony* does not appear to play these kinds of identity games. It is one of the most moving tributes a son has ever paid to his father, presenting the man as he was, refusing to sentimentalize in any way either the man or father–son relationship.

The third period commences thereafter with *Sabbath's Theater* and continues with what Roth has called his thematic trilogy: *American Pastoral*, *I Married a Communist*, and *The Human Stain*. For some, Mickey Sabbath is an Alexander Portnoy grown older, abandoning his respectable life altogether and becoming a puppeteer and roué. The language in this novel exceeds anything and everything in *Portnoy's Complaint*, but Roth has not seemed to feel the need to rise to its defence. As James Mellard has shown, it is connected through the death of Sabbath's family to *Patrimony*; indeed, the book, whose epigraph is from Shakespeare's *The Tempest* ("Every third thought shall be my grave"), is drenched in death. In the next three novels, Zuckerman returns, but chiefly as the narrator of other men's stories, some of whom he knew as a boy or young man growing up, like Portnoy or Roth himself, in Newark, New Jersey, in the 1930s and later. Roth is here developing a fiction chronicle of the America he knew and grew up with or later experienced as a mature adult: the communist enthusiasms in the 1930s, the red-baiting in the 1950s, traumatic involvement of the United States in the Vietnam war in the 1960s and 1970s, the sanctimonious hypocrisies of the Clinton era in the 1990s. The narration, especially in *American Pastoral*, which focuses partly on the Vietnam period, is among the most beautifully rendered and moving prose Roth has yet achieved. It harbingered further fiction chronicles of this kind, as in *I Married a Communist* and *The Human Stain*. Since Roth has always sought new ways of writing novels, new modes of artistic development, his subsequent work is again bound to be different, full of surprises and unexpected kinds of intellectual appeal.

JAY L. HALIO

Rothenberg, Jerome

US poet and dramatist, 1931–

Born in New York, 11 December 1931. Studied at City College of New York, BA 1952; University of Michigan, MA 1953. Married Diane Brodatz, 1952; one son. Served in army in Germany, 1954–55. Founder, Hawk's Well Press, New York, 1958. Lecturer, City College of New York, 1959–60; Mannes College of Music, New York, 1961–70; University of California, San Diego, 1971; visiting lecturer in anthropology, New School for Social Research, New York, 1971–72; visiting professor at various universities, 1974–88, including University of Wisconsin, Milwaukee, University of California, San Diego, and State University of New York, Albany; Professor of Visual Arts and Literature, University of California, San Diego, from 1988. Has edited and contributed to many literary journals. Received American Book Award, 1982.

Selected Writings

Poetry
White Sun, Black Sun, 1960
The Seven Hells of Jigoku Zoshi, 1962
Sightings I-IX, with *Lunes* by Robert Kelly, 1964
The Gorky Poems, 1966
Between: Poems 1960–1963, 1967
Conversations, 1968
Offering Flowers, with Ian Tyson, 1968
Poems 1964–1967, 1968
Sightings I-IX & Red Easy a Color, with Ian Tyson, 1968
Poland/1931, 1969
The Directions, with Tom Phillips, 1969
Polish Anecdotes, 1970
A Book of Testimony, 1971
Net of Moon, Net of Sun, 1971
Poems for the Game of Silence 1960–1970, 1971
A Valentine No a Valedictory for Gertrude Stein, 1972
Poems for the Society of the Mystic Animals, with Ian Tyson and Richard Johnny John, 1972
A Poem of Beavers: Seneca Journal I, 1973
Three Friendly Warnings, with Ian Tyson, 1973
Esther K Comes to America, 1931, 1974
The Cards, 1974
Poland/1931 (complete edition), 1974
A Poem to Celebrate the Spring and Diane Rothenberg's Birthday, 1975
Book of Palaces: The Gatekeepers, 1975
I Was Going through the Smoke, with Ian Tyson, 1975
Seneca Journal: Midwinter, with Philip Sultz, 1975
The Pirke and the Pearl, 1975
A Vision of the Chariot in Heaven, 1976
Rain Events, 1976
The Notebooks, 1976
Narratives and Realtheater Pieces, with Ian Tyson, 1977
Seneca Journal: The Serpent, with Philip Sultz, 1978
*B*R*M*Tz*V*H*, 1979
Letters and Numbers, 1979
Vienna Blood and Other Poems, 1980
For E.W.: Two Sonnets, 1981
Altar Pieces, 1982
Imaginal Geography 9: Landscape with Bishop, 1982
That Dada Strain, 1982
The History of Dada as My Muse, 1982
15 Flower World Variations, with Harold Cohen, 1984
A Merz Sonata, 1985
New Selected Poems 1970–1985, 1986
Gematria 5, 1987
Further Sightings and Conversations, 1989
Khurbn and Other Poems, 1989
The Gematria, 1990
The Lorca Variations (1-8), 1990
An Oracle for Delfi, 1994
A Poem in Yellow after Tristan Tzara, 1995
Seedlings and Other Poems, 1996
Delight/Délices and Other Gematria, 1997
At the Grave of Nataheva Chuya, 1998
The Leonardo Project, 1998
A Paradise of Poets: New Poems, 1999
Poems for the Millennium, with Pierre Joris, 2000

Plays
The Deputy, 1965
That Dada Strain, 1987
Poland 1931, 1988

Further Reading

Castro, Michael, *Interpreting the Indian: Twentieth-Century Poets and the Native American*, Albuquerque: University of New Mexico Press, 1983
Gitenstein, R. Barbara, *Apocalyptic Messianism and Contemporary Jewish-American Poetry*, Albany: State University of New York Press, 1986
Paul, Sherman, *In Search of the Primitive: Rereading David Antin, Jerome Rothenberg and Gary Snyder*, Baton Rouge: Louisiana State University Press, 1986
Perloff, Marjorie, "Soundings: Zaum, Seriality and the Discovery of the 'Sacred'", *American Poetry Review*, 15/1 (January–February 1986): 37–46
Polkinhorn, Harry (editor), *Jerome Rothenberg: A Descriptive Bibliography*, Jefferson, North Carolina: McFarland, 1988

Rothenberg's first collection of poems, *White Sun, Black Sun* gave little indication of the rich intellectual feast that was to follow. The poems are vivid, small imagistic works, some of which, like the title poem, were inspired by William Blake's *Songs of Innocence*, but all held a surrealist promise of uncovering the dream world and the world of the unconscious, not necessarily an intellectual journey. However, one might have guessed the immense possibilities for him by reading his essay on the concept of "deep image", written in the early 1960s, in which he talks about poetry "as a natural structure arising at once from the act of emotive vision". He tells us that "The power of the deep image is its ability to convey a sense of two-worlds-in-one: directly: with no concept to come between the inner experience and its meaning."

It is clear now that Rothenberg through his translations of primitive poetry, his elaborate exploration of cultural anthropology and the extensions of his "deep image" poetry into the realm of ethnopoetics, is a pioneer of a new approach to poetry itself. Like Gary Snyder and other poets who wish to move away from an anthro-centred universe, and his Native American brothers who wish to abolish the Euro-centred way of thinking that has altered non-white peoples, Rothenberg hopes to expand and diversify poetry so that it will represent the bigger vision of the world.

There is a tradition in American letters which shows that some of the country's best writers must go abroad to find their true recognition. Europeans were touting Walt Whitman for his revolutionary and refreshing manner of writing himself into his poems while Americans were still hemming and hawing. Poe had to be translated by Baudelaire, and during his lifetime Charles Bukowski found his greatest audience in Germany, Italy, France, and Sweden. Jerome Rothenberg also, because of his involvement with avant garde performance and theatre, has a larger audience in Europe than America.

What has become apparent in recent years is the immense

intellectual energy that has gone into Rothenberg's poetry and even more, his aesthetic explorations and writings. So-called "anthologies" edited by Rothenberg are not merely collections of books full of poems. Each one is an exercise in studying the possibilities of poetry. Not only his selections, but his editorial writing and essays continue to show us how superficial our readings and definitions of poetry have become. In this sense he is part of that great movement in letters created by Ezra Pound and carried on by Charles Olson, to search for the connections between past and the present in art and history.

Rothenberg's recent work has been evolving from a personal mythology that includes his sense of himself as an American Jew, born in Brooklyn in 1931 of east European ancestors, as well an inheritor of the Native American traditions which he has come to revere and feel part of by study and adoption into one of the tribes of the Seneca. In *That Dada Strain* he acknowledges other origins and resonances, in particular a use of the Dadaist's sense of 20th-century language collapsing in on itself and needing to be reconstructed by all who wish to make language serve new purposes other than to reinforce old (often obsolete) values.

In *Vienna Blood* Rothenberg concluded the book with a tour de force, "Abulafia's Circles", a homage to Tristan Tzara, founder of the Dada movement. It is a poem written for performance, as well as being a ritual presentation of all of Rothenberg's own secret ideas about poetry, and after reading it (or preferably, hearing him perform it) one must be overwhelmed by the wideness of the spectrum of possibilities Rothenberg takes into the poem. He uses incantation. He uses catalogues. He uses historical perspective and narrative devices for presenting that perspective. He uses both surrealist and realist imagery. He uses ritual, song, and even analytical discussion. All these techniques are for showing the complexity of any identity once we consider all its possible origins.

In his 1989 collection *Khurbn and Other Poems* Rothenberg offers another overwhelmingly powerful dramatic, oral poem, this one a meditation on the Holocaust of the Jews during the Nazi regime in Germany. In the introduction to the book he says:

> When I was writing *Poland/1931*, at a great distance from the place, I decided deliberately that that was not to be a poem about the holocaust. There was a reason for that I think, as there is now for allowing my uncle's khurbn to speak through me. The poems I first began to hear at Treblinka are the clearest message I have ever gotten about why I write poetry.

The various parts of this poem move through a kind of requiem for the human race, presenting the unusual combination of ferocity, black but playful arabesque language, and dark vision that readers have come to associate with Rothenberg and his mythic treatment of big subjects.

Because Rothenberg writes large-purposed works, never concentrating his poems into political messages, "Khurbn" is far more than a poem about this terrible episode in recent human history. For Rothenberg, in the tradition of Pound and Olson, political concerns and aesthetic concerns are the same, or at least interacting realities. He says in "Der Vidershtand":

> began with this in Olson's words it was
> the pre/face so much fat for soap
> superphosphate for soil filings & shoes for sale
> each fragmentation delivered by whatever means
> the scrolls of Auschwitz buried now brought to light
> again

DIANE WAKOSKI

Rubens, Bernice

British fiction writer and film-maker, 1928–

Born Bernice Ruth Rubens in Cardiff, 26 July 1928. Studied at Cardiff High School for Girls; University College of South Wales and Monmouthshire, Cardiff, 1944–47, BA in English 1947. Married Rudi Nassauer, 1947; two daughters. English teacher, Handsworth Grammar School for Boys, Birmingham, 1948–49. Documentary film writer and director, for United Nations and others, since 1950. Awards include American Blue Ribbon Award, 1968; Booker Prize, 1970; Welsh Arts Council Award, 1976; Wingate Prize, 1990.

Selected Writings

Novels
Set on Edge, 1960
Madame Sousatzka, 1962
Mate in Three, 1965
The Elected Member, 1969; as *Chosen People*, 1969
Sunday Best, 1971
Go Tell the Lemming, 1973
I Sent a Letter to My Love, 1975
The Ponsonby Post, 1977
A Five Year Sentence, 1978; as *Favors*, 1979
Spring Sonata, 1979
Birds of Passage, 1981
Brothers, 1983
Mr Wakefield's Crusade, 1985
Our Father, 1987
Kingdom Come, 1990
A Solitary Grief, 1991
Mother Russia, 1992
Autobiopsy, 1993
Yesterday in the Back Lane, 1995
The Waiting Game, 1997
I, Dreyfus, 1999

Play
I Sent a Letter to My Love, 1978

Screenplays: *One of the Family*, 1964; *Call Us by Name*, 1968; *Out of the Mouths*, 1970

Television Play: *Third Party*, 1972

Further Reading

Abrams, Rebecca, "Autobiopsy", *Guardian* (28 September 1993)

"Our Father", *Times Literary Supplement* (27 March 1987)
Shrapnel, Norman, "A Solitary Grief", *Guardian* (9 May 1991)
"Spring Sonata", *Times Literary Supplement* (7 December 1979)
"The Waiting Game", *Times* (2 August 1997)
Williamson, Malcolm, "Mother Russia", *Guardian* (8 March 1992)

The author of some 20 novels, winner of the Booker Prize and the Jewish Quarterly/Wingate Award, Bernice Rubens is invariably described by interviewers as, to quote one from the *Evening Standard*, "Exotically swarthy, gypsily beringed, small, plump . . . at one remove from the seemly, London-Library circuit of modern letters". She looks very Jewish, and in her writing she has never shied away from that which she knows best: life in the tight-knit, immigrant Lithuanian-Jewish community in Cardiff where she grew up.

Her first novel, *Set on Edge*, is based on the life of her maternal grandmother, and describes the mixed blessings of parental expectation, and although she has gone on to write about everything from the trials and tribulations of a male, Gentile transvestite (in the first person) to sinister goings on aboard a cruise ship full of genteel widows, she frequently returns to Jewish themes and characters; as she explains it: "Everything that happens in family is more so in a Jewish family. In a Gentile family someone may have a cold. In a Jewish family, it has to be consumption."

Nowhere is this more poignantly demonstrated than in the Booker-winning *The Elected Member*, in which Norman Zweck, a rabbi's son and the apple of his parents' eyes, becomes a drug addict aged 41. As a child, Norman had shown an extraordinary ability to pick up languages, but to highlight his genius, his mother lies about his age and even delays his bar mitzvah by three years. Saddened and shamed by what he sees as his son's failure, Rabbi Zweck muses that to be driven mad by one's own genius would not be so bad – "an inverted *nachus* almost" – but drugs . . .?

Herself number three in a family of four, and the only one not to play a musical instrument as a child (her sister and two brothers all went on to become professional musicians), Rubens was designated the "listener" from an early age. Her own favourite novel, *A Five Year Sentence*, is all about solitude, and if family and relationships constitute one theme in her work, solitude – whether the result of exile or of alienation – is another. *Yesterday in the Back Lane* tells the tale of Bronwen Davies, who too is afraid to admit to having stabbed a man who flashed at her as a teenager. Bronwen guards her guilty secret even as an innocent man is sent to the gallows, and so after 50 years of yesterdays, she is still serving her own, secret life sentence, just as Harley Street psychiatrist Alastair will have to in *A Solitary Grief*.

Rubens is first-generation British; her mother was born in Poland and her father was just 16 when he arrived in Cardiff from Lithuania which, thanks to an unscrupulous ticket salesman, he took to be New York for a full week. It quickly became apparent just how lucky they were to have escaped at all, and during Rubens's childhood the family home was a refuge for some of the last Jews to flee the continent. One boy from Austria, whose name her mother picked from the long lists that filled the Jewish press in those days, stayed for five years, and they were eventually able to get his parents out too. All this had its impact, as did her father's awareness of his own "guest" status in Britain, and many of her female characters are stunted by irrepressible feelings of gratefulness. In *Birds of Passage*, for example, Alice, a widow on a well-earned cruise with her neighbour, desperately feels the need to be grateful to the dapper Mr Bowers: "for each bowing and scraping of Mr Bowers' feet, she felt the need to offer him at least her body, if not her spirit." Writing in the *Sunday Telegraph Magazine* in 1987, Rubens explained how the "guest syndrome" she picked up from her father stayed with her right up until his death. "On that day, I ceased to be a guest. With my father's grave, I could claim entitlement to roots."

I, Dreyfus is Rubens's most polemical novel to date. Its protagonist, Sir Alfred, has lived life as a "count me in Jew", belting out hymns louder than anyone else in church and gleefully exposing his uncircumcised member at the urinals. Ultimately, this offers no protection, and his Jewishness still screams out to all but himself. Gradually, he realizes that by denying his Jewish identity, he has been living in a wilderness, and it is only when he can accept himself for who he is that he is truly released from his cell.

The novel offers a bleak prognosis of anti-Semitism; as Rubens explains in the author's note: "This novel makes no attempt to update the Dreyfus story. Rather it is concerned with the Dreyfus syndrome, which alas needs no updating." *Brothers*, her epic of survival, tells the tale of six generations of the Bindel family, chased halfway round the world by the Russian army, pogroms, and the Nazis, only to return to Russia to find prejudice as rife and virulent as ever. In *Mother Russia*, a tumultuous tale of that country's passage through the 20th century, Sonya's husband divorces her because her Jewishness will hinder his party career; soon will come a time when such things will not matter, he opines, to which she replies: "There has never been such a time. Nowhere in the world." Elsewhere, Mrs Feinberg, the "token Jew" at the exclusive Hollyhocks nursing home of *The Waiting Game*, is welcomed by Matron with an over-understanding that "bordered on racism". Rubens's finely tuned ear for the unspoken truths that hide behind even the most inane social banter is crucial in pinpointing that particularly British brand of anti-Semitism.

Rubens's work often reflects a concern for social injustice, the motivation behind her other career as a documentary filmmaker, but there is nothing soft about her work, and retribution ranks far higher than forgiveness; it is her acerbic brand of menace and tragi-comedy that has won her such a broad and loyal readership, and allowed her to escape marginalization.

HEPHZIBAH ANDERSON

Rudnicki, Adolf

Polish fiction writer, 1912–1990

Born in Warsaw, 19 February 1912, into middle-class family. Graduated from commercial school and began work as bank clerk. After Nazi and Soviet invasions of Poland, 1939, fought against and was taken prisoner by Germans; escaped into Soviet-occupied zone; stayed in L'viv (Lwów), 1940–41; contributed to communist literary monthly *Nowe Widnokręgi*. After Nazi attack on Soviet Union, 1941, returned to Warsaw, 1942; lived outside Nazi-created ghetto, using false papers; active in clandestine publishing; fought in Warsaw Uprising, 1944. After liberation, 1945, settled in Łódź; joined Marxist literary group Kuźnica and wrote for its weekly journal, *Kuźnica*; also began writing for *Świat*. Moved to Warsaw, 1950. Column in *Świat* suppressed during anti-Semitic campaign, 1968. Moved between Paris and Warsaw from 1971. Awarded State Prize (second class), 1955; New York Jurzykowski Foundation Prize, 1966; Prix Médicis Étranger (France), 1976; State Prize, 1987. Died in Warsaw, 14 November 1990.

Selected Writings

Novels
Szczury [Rats], 1932
Żołnierze [Soldiers], 1933
Niekochana [The Unloved], 1937
Lato [Summer], 1938
Doświadczenia [Experiences], 1939; as *Profile i Drobiazgi Żołnierskie* [Profiles and Soldiers' Trifles], 1946

Stories
Epoka pieców [Time of the Gas Chambers], 1948
Szekspir [Shakespeare], 1948
Żywe i martwe morze [The Dead Sea and the Living Sea], 1952
Młode cierpienia [Young Suffering], 1954
Złote okna [Golden Windows], 1954
Krowa, 1957
Kupiec Łódzki, 1963

Play
Manfred, 1954

Other
Ucieczkaz z jasnej Polany, 1949
Ślepe lustro tych lat [The Blind Mirror of These Years], 1956
Prześwity [Afterglows], 1957
Narzeczony Beaty, 1960
Niekochana, 1961
Obraz z Kotem i Psem, 1962
Niebieskie kartki [Blue Pages], 1963
Pył Miłosny, 1964
Weiss Wpada Do Morza, 1965
Wspólne Zdjęcie [The Group Photograph], 1967
Niekochana i Inne Opowiadania, 1969
Teksty Małe i Mniejsze, 1971
Noc Będzie Chłodna, Niebo w Purpurze, 1977
Daniela Naga, 1978
Zabawa ludowa, 1979
Rogaty Warszawiak, 1981
Sto Jeden, 1984
Krakowskie Przedmieście pełne deserów, 1986
Teatr zawsze grany, 1987
Sercem Dnia Jest Wieczór, 1988
Sto Lat Temu Umarł Dostojewski, 1989
Dżoker Pana Boga, 1989
Niekochana: Szczury, 1996

Further Reading

Czerwinski, E.J. (editor), *Dictionary of Polish Literature*, Westport: Greenwood Press, 1994
Krzyzanowski, Julian, *A History of Polish Literature 1892–1976*, translated by Doris Ronowicz, Warsaw: PWN, 1978
Miłosz, Czesław, *The History of Polish Literature*, 2nd edition, Berkeley: University of California Press, 1983
Shenfeld, Ruth, *Adolf Rudnitski: Sofer Ben Shene 'Olamot*, Jerusalem: Hotsa'at Sefarim 'a Sh. Y.L. Magnes, Ha-Universitah H'a-Ivrit, 1991

As the author of five novels prior to World War II, Adolf Rudnicki was among the most gifted and productive of Poland's young prose writers, whose first books, *Szczury* [Rats] and *Żołnierze* [Soldiers], belonged to the genre of the documentary novel. Later works such as *Niekochana* [The Unloved] and *Lato* [Summer] earned him the reputation of a psychological writer in the tradition of Dostoevskii and provided him with a passport to the drawing rooms of Warsaw society. The novel *Doświadczenia* [Experiences] appeared in 1939 and brought an end to the Jewish Rudnicki's hitherto relatively uncomplicated and highly promising existence. Even during the war he had embarked on a testimony to the "Nation of Polish Jews" and their murder. The works of this "tragic and lyrical cantor of Polish Judaism", as the critics called him, were translated into several languages.

Before the war Rudnicki was a regular contributor to various journals, which played a part in his popularity. After being the first author in Poland to use the technique of "stream of consciousness", in *Żołnierze*, paving the way for the *nouveau roman*, in particular Nathalie Sarraute's *Portrait d'un inconnu*, and achieving a considerable *succès d'estime*, he recorded his greatest publishing success with the novella *Niekochana*. *Żołnierze* offers a masterly study of the psyche of a young, indecisive man, who does not have his life under control. The military camp is depicted with almost photographic accuracy and this relentless portrayal provoked loud protests from fascist and reactionary circles in Poland. In *Niekochana* Rudnicki describes with the enormous empathy he developed for his weak and suffering characters the crisis-ridden relationship of a couple where the woman loves "too much" and the man "too little", leading to a tragic end. Love as a force that explodes morals and conventions is one of the three major themes in Rudnicki's works.

After the war, the Holocaust became Rudnicki's second major theme. He created a cycle, which gave this period the name "Time of the Gas Chambers", *Epoka pieców*, comprising the volumes of stories *Szekspir* [Shakespeare], *Żywe i martwe morze* [The Dead Sea and the Living Sea], *Młode cierpienia* [Young Suffering] and *Złote okna* [Golden Windows], in which he recounts the fate of the Polish Jews doomed to death. He says that something happened in this era that changed all the basic conditions of human life. The way he depicts the degradation and murder of the Polish Jews, and Jewish intelligence, is particularly moving in these stories and novellas. In the story "Czysty nurt" he writes: "Before sending these people into the smoke of the crematoria, they were first transformed into dirt and soot." He says that art too, the most fragile and threatened of all human expressions of being, has fallen victim to barbarity. The language of Rudnicki's stories of this period is tailored to the subject, full of breaks and tears, creating a powerful lamentation but simultaneously highly authentic. Yet the "ideological spectacles" through which Rudnicki viewed society allowed him, as Miłosz commented, always to portray the Jewish proletariat as noble and the Jewish bourgeoisie as bad. This is what Rudnicki writes in the story "Kupiec Łódzki" about the chairman of the Jewish council in Łódź:

> It is not Hitler who was dreadful but the apothecary from the small town who immediately discovered the Hitler within himself and played him in daily life. A tyrant with power is a caricature. A caricature with power is a tyrant. He was called Mordche Chaim Rumkowski and with German grace he exercized power over the Jews enclosed in the Łódź ghetto.

In *Ucieczka z jasnej Polany* he also writes about National Socialism, but in particular about what he regards as the moral fiasco of Thomas Mann, namely that he did not want to return to the "new (East) Germany", where National Socialism, according to Rudnicki, then an enthusiastic communist, would finally be eradicated. At the time he could not know that this was a tragic historical error on the part of many of his contemporaries, although he later recognized it. Rudnicki's inclination towards psychology benefits these stories of extreme situations because they replicate the feelings of people, both the negative and the heroic character traits, moral conflicts too, not only the historical events. In Rudnicki's preface to the commemorative volume he edited on the subject of Auschwitz, *Wieczna Pamięć*, he offers the following challenge to his contemporaries and, of course, also to those born later:

> It is my firm conviction that – among other things – the reading and dissemination of books which offer the naked truth about the concentration camps and not the avoidance of these books, as some people want . . . that the reading of these books may arouse in people a new and powerful hatred of atrocities, hatred of war, of fascism, and that they can teach patience and goodwill . . .

Not until many years later was Rudnicki able to write about subjects other than the "debris literature", and if he now wrote about the Holocaust, then he also portrayed the obliterated Jewish community poetically, as in the volume of short stories *Krowa*. But the Jewish theme stayed with him to the end, for example in *Rogaty Warszawiak* where he portrayed the Polish-Jewish writer and companion of Julian Tuwim, Antoni Słonimski, or *Teatr zawsze grany*, in which he described the life story of Ida Kamińska, for many years director of the Jewish theatre in Warsaw.

The third main theme in Rudnicki's later phase, during which he no longer wrote novels, but concentrated on short forms such as essays, diaries, and reportage, is the artist and his role in society, which was suggested in *Ucieczka z jasnej Polany* and in the anthologies *Ślepe lustro tych lat* [The Blind Mirror of These Years], *Narzeczony Beaty*, and *Kupiec Łódzki*, until *Zabawa ludowa* created a new myth of the writer as a higher moral being. As he makes higher moral demands of artists, their failings are all the more serious. Rightly or wrongly, his criticism of many of them is severe, although he never subjected himself to the same criticism and as a result was accused of egomania, conceit, and injustice. In one of his last collections of essays, *Krakowskie Przedmieście pełne deserów*, he portrayed the writers Jerzy Andrzejewski, Witold Gombrowicz, and S.J. Lec. The same themes are dealt with in the feuilletons and sketches of the cycle *Niebieskie kartki* [Blue Pages], in which he reflects in a more relaxed manner on culture – literature, film, and theatre. As before, he is no diagnostician of the spirit of the time, but an admonisher, a less detached observer, because he is a committed, emotional fighter to whom irony and scepticism are alien. Yet Rudnicki, who had experienced the anti-Semitic agitation of 1968, made no comment on it, which is hard to understand. He had indeed become familiar with existence in emigration, yet, unlike other exiles, he was never barred from returning. In his later writings, he analyses the differences between Poland and other countries from this situation, demonstrating the same stylistic brilliance but tempered now with a greater degree of sobriety.

One can largely agree with Miłosz when he says that Rudnicki:

> . . . has created an immortal memorial to the victims of the gas chambers . . . Compared with his, almost all the works which have been written on this subject in so many languages sound as though they are being related secondhand. Only one person, who was so very conscious of his duality as a Jew and a Pole, was able to express the complex relations between Jews and Jews, Jews and Poles, victims and executioners, so well.

ELVIRA GROEZINGER
translated by Karen Goulding

Rukeyser, Muriel

US poet and political activist, 1913–1980

Born in New York City, 15 December 1913, to Lawrence Rukeyser and wife Myra (née Lyons). Studied at Fieldston School, 1919–30; Vassar College; Columbia University, 1930–32. Married briefly; one son by another man; raised him alone. Vice President, House of Photography, New York, 1946–60; teacher, Sarah Lawrence College, Bronxville, New York, 1946 and 1956–57. Member of Board of Directors, Teachers–Writers Collaborative, New York, from 1967; President, PEN American Center, 1975–76. Jailed after protesting against Vietnam War on steps of US Capitol, Washington, DC. Many awards, including Harriet

Monroe Award, 1941; American Academy Award, 1942; Guggenheim Fellowship, 1943; American Council of Learned Societies Fellowship, 1963; Swedish Academy Translation Award, 1967; Copernicus Award, 1977; Shelley Memorial Award, 1977. Member, American Academy of Arts and Letters. Died 12 February 1980.

Selected Writings

Poetry
Theory of Flight, 1935
Mediterranean, 1937
U.S. 1, 1938
A Turning Wind, 1939
The Soul and Body of John Brown, 1940
Wake Island, 1942
Beast in View, 1944
The Children's Orchard, 1947
The Green Wave, 1948
Elegies, 1949
Orpheus, 1949
Selected Poems, 1951
Body of Waking, 1958
Waterlily Fire: Poems 1935–1962, 1962
The Outer Banks, 1967
The Speed of Darkness, 1968
29 Poems, 1972
Breaking Open: New Poems, 1973
The Gates, 1976
The Collected Poems of Muriel Rukeyser, 1978
Out of Silence: Selected Poems, 1992

Plays
The Middle of the Air, 1945
The Colours of the Day: A Celebration for the Vassar Centennial, 10 June 1961, 1961
Houdini, 1973

Fiction
Orgy, 1965

For Children
Come Back Paul, 1955
I Go Out, 1961
Bubbles, 1967
Mazes, 1970
More Night, 1981

Other
Willard Gibbs, 1942
"Under Forty", *Contemporary Jewish Record*, 7 (February 1944): 4–9
The Life of Poetry, 1949
One Life, 1957
Translator, with others, *Selected Poems of Octavio Paz*, 1963; revised edition, 1973
Translator, *Sun Stone*, by Octavio Paz, 1963
"Double Dialogue: Homage to Robert Frost", *Saturday Review*, 48/9 (29 February 1964)
Translator, with Leif Sjöberg, *Selected Poems of Gunnar Ekelöf*, 1967
Translator, *Three Poems by Gunnar Ekelöf*, 1967
Poetry and Unverifiable Fact: The Clark Lectures, 1968
The Traces of Thomas Hariot, 1971
Translator, with others, *Early Poems 1935–1955*, by Octavio Paz, 1973
A Muriel Rukeyser Reader, edited by Jan Heller Levi, 1994

Further Reading

Barber, David S., "Finding Her Voice: Muriel Rukeyser's Poetic Development", *Modern Poetry Studies*, 11/1 (1982): 127–38
Barber, David S., " 'The Poet of Unity': Muriel Rukeyser's Willard Gibbs", *CLIO: A Journal of Literature, History and the Philosophy of History*, 12 (Fall 1982): 1–15
Bernikow, Louise, "Muriel at 65: Still Ahead of Her Time", *Ms.*, 7/7 (January 1979): 14–16
Daniels, Kate, "Searching/Not Searching: Writing the Biography of Muriel Rukeyser", *Poetry East* 16/17 (Spring/Summer 1985): 70–93 (Special Issue on Muriel Rukeyser)
Gardinier, Suzanne. "'A World That Will Hold All the People': On Muriel Rukeyser", *Kenyon Review*, 14 (Summer 1992): 88–105
Herzog, Anne F. and Janet E. Kaufman (editors), *How Shall We Tell Each Other of the Poet? The Life and Writing of Muriel Rukeyser*, New York: St Martin's Press, 1999
Hume-George, Diana, "Who is the Double Ghost Whose Head is Smoke? Women Poets on Aging" in *Memory and Desire: Aging, Literature, Psychoanalysis*, edited by Kathleen Woodward and Murray M. Schwarz, Bloomington: Indiana University Press, 1986
Jarrell, Randall, *Poetry and the Age*, New York: Knopf, 1953; London: Faber, 1955
Kertesz, Louise, *The Poetic Vision of Muriel Rukeyser*, Baton Rouge: Louisiana State University Press, 1980
Madden, David (editor), *Proletarian Writers of the Thirties*, Carbondale: Southern Illinois University Press, 1968
New York Quarterly, "Craft Interview with Muriel Rukeyser" in *The Craft of Poetry: Interviews from the New York Quarterly*, edited by William Packard, New York: Doubleday, 1974
Pacernick, Gary, "Muriel Rukeyser: Prophet of Social and Political Justice" in *Memory and Fire: Ten American Jewish Poets*, New York: Peter Lang, 1989
Rich, Adrienne, "Beginners", *Kenyon Review*, 15 (Summer 1993): 12–19
Rosenthal, M.L., "Muriel Rukeyser: The Longer Poems", *New Directions in Prose and Poetry*, 14 (1953): 202–29
Solotaroff, Ted, "Rukeyser: Poet of Plenitude", *Nation*, 230/9 (8 March 1980): 277–78
Turner, Alberta, "Muriel Rukeyser" in *American Poets, 1880–1945*, 2nd series, edited by Peter Quartermain, Detroit: Gale, 1986 (*Dictionary of Literary Biography*, vol. 48): 370–75
Ware, Michele S., "Opening 'The Gates': Muriel Rukeyser and the Poetry of Witness", *Women's Studies: An Introductory Journal*, 22/3 (1993): 297–308

Very little of Muriel Rukeyser's poetry is overtly "Jewish" in content; seldom does it employ traditional Judaic symbols and themes. In its understanding of history, its expansiveness, and its desire for justice, Rukeyser's voice is committed to and participates in a mode of oracular poetry that ends with Whitman and Blake and begins with Isaiah, Joel, and Ezekiel.

Rukeyser found her love for the Bible's "clash and poetry and nakedness, its fiery vision of conflict", on her own. There was not a trace of Jewish culture in her childhood home, with the exception of a silver Kiddush cup and a legend that Rukeyser's mother was a direct descendant of Rabbi Akiba. Rukeyser grew up among Reform Jews whose desire for assimilation left them spiritually and politically starved. As a Jewish poet, Rukeyser opposes herself to Reform Jews whom she characterizes as those who "read Sokolsky's column at breakfast, and agreed with him every time he said that Jews should be quiet and polite . . . who told van Paassen he was crazy to worry about the Jews in Germany and Poland". Rukeyser laments that while Pierre von Paassen, a non-Jewish, non-American writer, warned and demanded action from the world about Hitler and the Jews, the majority of American Jews themselves remained silent. Moreover, she uses the New York journalist George Sokolsky as a foil, because he ultimately espouses passive resistance to anti-Semitism in his book *We Jews*.

For Rukeyser, social protest is a powerful means to dignity. In "Letter to the Front", Rukeyser calls being a Jew in the 20th century a gift. Those who refuse this gift choose "death of the spirit, the stone insanity", while those who accept it "take full life". The scale of "full life", however, is all encompassing, requires the "guarantee/ for every human freedom", and thus may cause suffering for the individual who defends it: "The gift is torment. Not alone the still/ Torture, isolation; or torture of the flesh./ That may come also." For Rukeyser, this kind of suffering is more than worth it, so long as it results in a community that is responsible for itself and for others, similar and different. Daring to suffer is why she was arrested while covering the second Scottsboro trial, attended the hearings on a silicon mining disaster in Gauley, West Virginia, traveled to Hanoi on an unofficial peace mission, was arrested and jailed in Washington, DC for protesting the Vietnam War, and travelled to Korea to protest the incarceration of poet Kim Chi-Ha.

Throughout her writing, Rukeyser strives to renew her community by transforming its received traditions in both form and content. "Traditional Tune" exemplifies her unorthodox use of time, for within nine lines it weaves together moments as disparate as World War II, the crucifixion of Jesus, the exodus from Egypt, and the Crusades. In its leaps through history and shifts in poetic diction, the poem's structure recapitulates its thematic struggle to grasp the meaning of historical transition (its potential and its violence), and thus illustrates Rukeyser's respect for tradition; she treats the past, not as an inert object, but as a living force.

One of Rukeyser's heroes of suffering is Rabbi Akiba, about whom she wrote a full-length "life" poem, "Akiba", and later recalled in two poems ("Trinity Churchyard" and "The Gates") of her final collection, *The Gates*. Written in five sections, "Akiba" memorializes the great scholar's commitment to study and teaching, his faithfulness to the holy word as well as his capacity to interpret it freshly (he encouraged the canonization of the Song of Songs). Most importantly, the poem seeks to resurrect for society Akiba's willingness to fight for belief, his refusal to compromise, and his ultimate acceptance of suffering and martyrdom: "Does the old man during uprising speak for compromise?/ In all but the last things. Not in the study itself./ . . . / Prepare yourselves for suffering."

"Akiba" is a poem of witnessing. Its first section, "The Way In", depicts the Israelites in the desert wandering from "I to opened Thou", and its final section, "The Witness", beckons the reader to accept and transmit to a new generation the signs and wonders of the world. Testimonial is the predominant style of Rukeyser's poetry, from the poems of *U.S. 1*, which incorporate within them excerpts of courtroom depositions, to "The Speed of Darkness", where the poet asks "Who will speak these days,/ if not I,/ if not you?"

It is ironic that, given the centrality of witnessing to her oeuvre, and to "Akiba" itself, Rukeyser attributes a detail from the life of Rabbi Jochanan ben Zakkai to Akiba's. Rukeyser noted her mistake in the serial publication of "Akiba" in *American Judaism* (1960–61), but failed to revise the poem for subsequent publications. For some readers Rukeyser's willingness to allow "stories handed down, vague, unprovable, and marvelous" into her poetic testimonials may risk voiding the act of witnessing itself. Indeed, in "Miriam: Red Sea", a section of "Searching / Not Searching", Rukeyser's desire to sing a universal song endangers the unique qualities of the specific characters and events of the Bible. "For My Son" may in one sense be the gift of a richly textured, capacious genealogy, but in another it erases distinction, leaves one nearly as undefined as the Reform Jews against whom Rukeyser sets herself.

There are, then, limits to Rukeyser's poetic endeavour. Yet in the end, in the strong poems, they are more than made up for by her awareness of the struggle, her refusal to submit. Though she never refers to the midrash in which Akiba, walking through the ruins of Jerusalem and the Temple, smiles because the prophecy of redemption cannot be too distant, in this quality Rukeyser most resembles her ancestor – steadfast faithfulness, even at the darkest hour: "But night in this country,/ is deep promise of day,/ is busy with preparations and awake for fighting/ and there is no time for leavetaking and regretting."

MICHAEL J. SCHWARTZ

S

Saba, Umberto

Italian poet, 1883–1957

Born Umberto Poli in Trieste, 9 March 1883, to Jewish mother abandoned by Catholic husband before birth of their son. Studied at Ginnasio Dante Alighieri, Trieste; Imperial Academy of Commerce and Nautical Science; University of Pisa, 1903–04. Abandoned commercial studies to join merchant marine and, later, infantry regiment, Salerno, 1908. Married Carolina (Lina) Woelfler, 1909; wife died 1957; one son, one daughter. Businessman; secretary, Taverna Rossa cabaret, Milan; assigned briefly to Ministry of War, Rome, 1916; technical official, Taliedo Airport, 1917; publicity writer, Leoni Films, Trieste, 1919; owner and manager, Libreria Antiquaria bookshop, Trieste, 1919–40. As tribute to mother's grandfather, S.D. Luzzatto, legally adopted surname Saba (Hebrew for "grandfather"), 1920. Member, Solaria artistic circle, from 1926. Fled Trieste with family, 1943; moved to Paris, then Florence; in hiding in Florence until Liberation, 1944; moved to Rome, then Milan; returned to Trieste in last years of life. Received Taormina Prize, 1951; Novaro Foundation Prize, 1951; Viareggio Prize, 1951. Died in Gorizia, 25 August 1957.

Selected Writings

Collections
Tutte le opere [Complete Works], 6 vols, 1949–59
Opere [Works], edited by Linuccia Saba, 1964
Tutte le poesie [The Collected Poems], edited by Arrigo Stara, 1988

Poetry
Il mio primo libro di poesie [My First Book of Poetry], 1903; as *Poesie* [Poetry], 1911
Coi miei occhi [With My Eyes] 1912; edited by Claudio Milanini, 1981
Cose leggere e vaganti [Light and Wondering Things], 1920
La serena disperazione [The Serene Despair], 1920
Il canzoniere (1900–1921) [The Songbook], 1921; 1st revised edition as *Il canzoniere (1900–1945)*, 2 vols, 1945; 2nd revised edition as *Il canzoniere (1900–1947)*, 2 vols, 1948; complete edition as *Il canzoniere (1900–1954)*, 1961, corrected 1965; original edition as *Il canzoniere 1921*, edited by Giordano Castellani, 1981
L'amorosa spina [The Loving Thorn], 1921
Preludio e canzonette [Prelude and Little Songs], 1923
Autobiografia [Autobiography], 1924
Figure e canti [Images and Songs], 1926
Preludio e fughe [Prelude and Fugues], 1928
Tre poesie alla mia balia [Three Poems to My Nanny], 1929
Ammonizione ed altre poesie 1900–1910 [Warning and Other Poems], 1932
Tre composizioni [Three Compositions], 1933
Parole [Words], 1934
Ultime cose [Last Things], 1944
Mediterranee [Mediterranean], 1947
Poesie dell'adolescenza e giovanili 1900–1910 [Adolescent Poetry and Juvenilia], 1949
Trieste e una donna [Trieste and a Woman], 1950
Uccelli: quasi un racconto [Birds: Almost a Story], 1950
Epigrafe: ultime prose [Epigraphs: Last Prose], 1959
Il piccolo Berto 1929–1931 [Little Berto], 1961
Parole, Ultime cose 1933–1943 [Words, Last Things], 1961
Antologia del "Canzoniere" [Anthology of the Songbook], 1963
Cuor morituro e altre poesie [Dying Heart and Other Poems], 1964
Poesie scelte [Selected Poetry], 1976
Umberto Saba: Thirty-one Poems, translated by Felix Stefanile, 1978
The Dark of the Sun: Selected Poems, translated by Christopher Millis, 1994
La terza stagione: poesie e prose dal 1933–1946 [The Third Season: Poems and Prose from 1933–1946], 1997
History and Chronicle of the Songbook, translated by Stephen Sartarelli, 1998
Songbook: Selected Poems from the Canzoniere of Umberto Saba, translated by Stephen Sartarelli, 1998

Fiction
Ernesto, 1975; as *Ernesto*, translated by Mark Thompson, 1987

Play
Il letterato Vincenzo: dramma inedito in un atto [Vincenzo, Man of Letters: Unpublished Drama in One Act], 1989

Other
Scorciatoie e raccontini [Short Cuts and Short Stories], 1946
Storia e cronistoria del canzoniere [Story and Chronicle of the Songbook], 1948
Amicizia: storia di un vecchio poeta e di un giovane canarino [Friendship: Story of an Old Poet and a Young Canary], edited by Carlo Levi, 1951; as *Il vecchio e il*

giovane: carteggio 1930–1957 [The Old and the Young: Letters 1930–1957], edited by Linuccia Saba, 1965

Ricordi-Racconti [Recollections and Short Stories], 1956 (includes *Gli Ebrei*)

Quello che resta da fare ai poeti (Trieste-Febbraio 1911) [What Remains to Do to the Poets], edited by Anna Pittoni, 1959

Prose, edited by Linuccia Saba, 1964

Lettere a un'amico [Letters to a Friend], 1966

Saba, Svevo, Comisso: lettere inedite [Saba, Svevo, Comisso: Unpublished Letters], edited by Mario Sutor, 1968

L'adolescenza del Canzoniere, e undici lettere [The Adolescence of the Collection of Lyrics and Eleven Letters], 1975

Lettere a un amico vescovo [Letters to a Bishop Friend], edited by Rienzo Colla, 1980

Per conoscere Saba [To Know Saba], edited by Mario Lavagetto, 1981

La spada d'amore: lettere scelte 1902–1957 [The Sword of Love: Selected Letters], edited by Aldo Marcovecchio, 1983

Atroce paese che amo: lettere famigliari (1945–1953) [Atrocious Country That I Love: Intimate Letters], 1987

The Stories and Recollections of Umberto Saba, translated by Estelle Gilson, 1993

Lettere a Sandro Penna 1929–1940 [Letters to Sandro Penna], 1997

Further Reading

1983 Anno di Umberto Saba: Celebrazioni per il Centenario Della Nascita, Trieste: Tipografia-Litografia Moderna, 1983

Anceschi, Luciano, "Cultura poetica novencentesca", *Letteratura Italiana*, 4 (1979): 3069–83

Ara, Angelo and Claudio Magris, *Trieste*, Turin: Einaudi, 1982

Aymone, Renato, *Saba e la psicoanalisi*, Naples: Guida, 1971

Baldi, Nora, *Il paradiso di Saba*, Milan: Mondadori, 1958

Baldi, Nora, *Immagini per Saba*, Trieste: Comitato per le Celebrazioni dell Anno Di Umberto Saba, 1983

Baroni, Giorgio, *Umberto Saba e dintorni*, Milan: Istituto Propaganda Libraria, 1984

Caccia, Ettore, *Lettura e storia di Saba*, Milan: Bietti, 1967

Cary, Joseph, *Three Modern Italian Poets: Saba, Ungaretti, Montale*, 2nd edition, Chicago: University of Chicago Press, 1993

Cimmino, Nicola Francesco, *La poesia di Saba*, Rome: Elia, 1976

Debenedetti, Giacomo, "Saba ebreo e il melodramma", *Letteratura Italiana*, 4 (1979)

Favretti, Elvira, *La prosa di Umberto Saba: dai racconti Giovanili a "Ernesto"*, Rome: Bonacci, 1982

Ferrata, Giansiro, *Classici*, Milan: Garzanti, 1995

Ferri, Teresa, *Poetica e stile di Umberto Saba*, Urbino: QuattroVenti, 1984

Guagnini, Elvio (editor), *Il punto su Saba*, Rome: Laterza, 1987

Guarneri, Sandro, *Umberto Saba e la critica*, Pasian di Prato (Udine): Campanotto, 1998

Lavagetto, Mario, *La gallina di Saba*, Turin: Einaudi, 1974

Lavagetto, Mario (editor), *Per conoscere Saba*, Milan: Mondadori, 1981

Magrini, G., "Saba: un testo di persecuzione", *Paragone*, 458 (1988): 143–51

Maier, Bruno, *Umberto Saba, Poesia e Teatro*, Modena: Mucchi, 1991

Majorino, G., "La Poesia Onesta", *Paragone*, 194 (1966)

Mattioni, Stelio, *Storia di Umberto Saba*, Milan: Camunia, 1989

Montale, Eugenio, "Ragioni di Saba", *Letteratura Italiana*, 4 (1980)

Morelli, Giovanni, *Umberto Saba: la poesia tra "latenza" e atto poetico*, Manduria (Taranto): Capone, 1999

Muscetta, Carlo, *Pace e guerra nella poesia contemporanea: da Alfonso Gatto a Umberto Saba*, Rome: Bonacci, 1984

Muzzioli, Francesco (editor), *La critica e Saba*, Bologna: Cappelli, 1976

Pinchera, Antonio, *Saba*, Florence: La Nuova Italia, 1974

Polato, Lorenzo, *L'aurea anello: saggi sull'opera poetica di Umberto Saba*, Milan: FrancoAngeli, 1994

Portinari, Folco, *Umberto Saba*, Milan: Mursia, 1963

Raimondi, Piero, *Invito alla lettura di Umberto Saba*, Milan: Mursia, 1974

Savarese, Gennaro, *Umberto Saba*, Milan: Marzorati, 1976

Savoca, Giuseppe and Maria Caterina Paino, *Concordanza del "Canzoniere 1921" di Umberto Saba: testo, concordanza, liste di frequenza, indici*, Florence: Olschki, 1996

Solmi, Sergio, *Scrittori negli anni*, Rome: Il Saggiatore, 1963

Tordi, Rosita (editor), *Convegno "Umberto Saba, Trieste e la cultura Mitteleuropea 1984"*, Milan: Fondazione Mondadori, 1986

Venaille, Franck, *Umberto Saba*, Paris: Seghers, 1989

Saba often declared, "I always felt an Italian among Italians. Everything else, before men's insanity and despair turned it all into tragedy, was for me – I repeat it willingly – nothing more than a note of (cultural) colour." This "note of colour" had, however, strong and long-lasting implications in his life and work: it resulted in an internal "race-conflict", traceable to his being "mixed", that permeates his entire poetic and fictional oeuvre. In the collection *Autobiografia* the poet, recalling his non-Jewish, frivolous, vagabond, carefree father, and his gloomy Jewish mother who "felt all the weight of life", tackles this distressful tension. The same is true of "Fugues", written during the oppressive years of fascism when Saba, forced into silence, confronted the two internal voices, paternal and maternal, the two lives he had not managed to merge into some sort of unity.

Although he came from a Jewish background, remembered with loving description and a pressing rhythm in the collection of short stories *Gli Ebrei* [The Jews], Saba never fully recognized himself in the world of his ancestors, in the family of his mother. This ambivalence is well disclosed in one of the stories where, of the main character Anna, he declares: "She belonged, not without prideful proclamation, to that religion which, says Heinrich Heine, is not a religion but a misfortune". The poet, however, also looked upon that world with affectionate curiosity clearly evident in the unforgettable ironic evocations of some of the family members, such as his famous great-grandfather Samuel Davide Luzzatto.

As soon as Saba began to write poetry, he felt the need to find his own path by getting rid of "everything deformed they (his eyes) have seen/ of too much Jewishness". The conflict with his Jewishness was also intensified by his mother's and aunt's full disapproval of his becoming a poet. Saba did nevertheless devote himself to poetry, but with a strong sense of guilt and transgression. To redeem himself, he tried to make of poetry something "honest, solid, sincere" by observing with a ritual sense of duty the severe laws of prosody, of strophe and the recurrence of rhythm. He also did something completely contrary to the times, he chose to follow in the tradition of metric poetry and composed his most important work, *Il canzoniere* [Songbook], a collection of lyrical poems. These lyrics are to a certain extent interdependent and recall, in their structure and psychological unity, Heine's "Buch der Lieder". Adhering to literary tradition meant for Saba, who lived in Trieste, a peripheral city as far as national literary currents were concerned, but still a central European province, recovering both Italian and central European culture from Heine down to Nietzsche and Freud. In the Italian framework – in the midst of D'Annunzio's triumphalism, of Futurism, and of the spreading movement of hermetic poetry – *Il canzoniere* differs completely from all other poetic production. Here the poet-protagonist takes upon himself, quite differently from the Symbolist and Decadent poets, who took into consideration only the solitude of man in time and space, a responsible and positive social position. The poet places himself in Trieste among the people, depicting himself in conversations with his wife Lina, with strangers in a coffee house, with his daughter, with soldiers. The Trieste drama becomes an absolute parable of the human condition, and Trieste, no less than Kafka's Prague, a symbolic city.

The often-stated aim of Saba was to make this world "more habitable". At the basis of his poetry – his most famous critic, Debenedetti, defined it "cathartic" – lies an unmistakably Jewish ethic: the sense of responsibility, of commitment towards the reality in which one operates and lives. With this in mind, one should read the long poetic composition "L'uomo" [The Man], where the poet compresses some typical situations, almost symbolical of human life. It is therefore significant that Saba considered it his most Jewish poem, the one which most kept alive "the memory of his maternal blood", more so than the often-quoted "La capra" [The Goat]. His concern was not so much with the aesthetic outcome; what really mattered to him was the creation of a homogeneous character, a paradigmatic one tied to ethics and destiny. In other words a quasi-biblical figure.

The end of World War II marked for Saba – in the poem "Old Hearth" he calls himself a "survivor" – a breach. He decided, but was not able to keep his promise, to abandon poetry and write only prose, a much more suitable means for a direct analysis of burning matters such as racism, nationalism, concentrations camps, the Shoah. Once again Saba, sustained by his deeply felt adherence to the theories of Freud, confirmed his ethical commitment to make this world "more habitable", to advance, as he declared in the collection *Il piccolo Berto* [Little Berto], a new world.

"The world needs more clarity than obscurity" claimed the poet in explaining his non-adherence to the fashion of hermetic poetry. And it was this same commitment to clarity that led him to write *Storia e cronistoria* [History and Chronicle], a work completely at odds with the prevailing criteria of poetic interpretation, and above all an extraordinary example of Jewish self-exegesis.

ELVIRA LATO VINTI

Sachs, Nelly

German-born Swedish poet and translator, 1891–1970

Born Nelly Leonie Sachs in Berlin, 10 December 1891, into the artistic and literary family of a wealthy assimilated industrialist. Began correspondence with Swedish poet Selma Lagerlöf, 1906. Emigrated from Nazi Germany to Sweden, with assistance of Lagerlöf and others, 1940; settled in Stockholm. Awarded Nobel Prize for Literature, shared with S.Y. Agnon, 1966. Died in Stockholm, 12 May 1970.

Selected Writings

Collections
Gedichte [Poems], edited by Hilde Domin, 1977

Poetry
In den Wohnungen des Todes [In the Homes of the Dead], 1947
Sternverdunkelung [Darkening of the Stars], 1949
Und niemand weiss weiter [And No One Knows Any More], 1957
Flucht und Verwandlung [Flight and Transformation], 1959
Fahrt ins Staublose [Dust-free Journey], 1961
Ausgewählte Gedichte [Selected Poems], 1965
Späte Gedichte [Late Poems], 1965
O the Chimneys: Selected Poems, Including the Verse Play, Eli, translated by Michael Hamburger *et al.*, 1967
The Seeker and Other Poems, translated by Ruth Mead, Mathew Mead, and Michael Hamburger, 1970
Suche nach Lebenden [Search for the Living], edited by Margaretha Holmqvist and Bengt Holmqvist, 1971
Teile dich Nacht: die lezten Gedichte [Open up Night: The Last Poems], edited by Margaretha Holmqvist and Bengt Holmqvist, 1971

Other
Legenden und Erzählungen [Legends and Stories], 1921
Eli: Ein Mysterienspiel vom Leiden Israels, 1951; as *Eli: A Mystery Play of the Sufferings of Israel* in *O the Chimneys*, translated by Michael Hamburger *et al.*, 1967
Zeichen im Sand: Die szenischen Dichtungen der Nelly Sachs [Signs in the Sand: The Dramatic Works of Nelly Sachs], 1962

Verzauberung: Späte szenische Dichtungen [Enchantment: Later Dramatic Works], 1970
Briefe der Nelly Sachs [The Letters of Nelly Sachs], 1984

Further Reading

Bahr, Ehrhard, *Nelly Sachs*, Munich: Beck, 1980
Bahti, Timothy and Marilyn Sibley Fries (editors), *Jewish Writers, German Literature: The Uneasy Examples of Nelly Sachs and Walter Benjamin*, Ann Arbor: University of Michigan Press, 1995
Beil, Claudia, *Sprache als Heimat: jüdische Tradition und Exilerfahrung in der Lyrik von Nelly Sachs und Rose Ausländer*, Munich: Tuduv Studien, 1991
Berendsohn, Walter A., *Nelly Sachs: Einführung in das Werk der Dichterin jüdischen Schicksals*, Darmstadt: Agora, 1974
Guida, Patrizia, *La lirica di Nelly Sachs*, Bari: Levante, 1986
Holmqvist, Bengt (editor), *Das Buch der Nelly Sachs*, Frankfurt: Suhrkampf, 1977
Kessler, Michael and Jürgen Wertheimer (editors), *Nelly Sachs: Neue Interpretationen*, Tübingen: Stauffenburg, 1994
Klingmann, Ulrich, *Religion und Religiosität in der Lyrik von Nelly Sachs*, Frankfurt: Peter Lang, 1980
Lehmann, Annette Jael, *Im Zeichen der Shoah: Aspekte der Dichtungs- und Sprachkrise bei Rose Ausländer und Nelly Sachs*, Tübingen: Stauffenburg, 1999
Michel, Peter, "Mystische und literarische Quellen in der Dichtung von Nelly Sachs" (dissertation), University of Freiburg im Breisgau, 1981
Rudnick, Ursula, *Post-Shoa Religious Metaphors: The Image of God in the Poetry of Nelly Sachs*, Frankfurt and New York: Peter Lang, 1995
Schütze, Hans J., *Juden in der Deutschen Literatur*, Munich: Piper, 1992
Spender, Stephen, "Catastrophe and Redemption", *New York Times Book Review* (8 October 1967)
Zampieri, Stefano, *Il Flauto d'osso*, Florence: Giuntina, 1996

Nelly Sachs disowned all her early literary production, strongly indebted to the German Romantic tradition, and recognized only the work born out of the human catastrophe she lived through: the Shoah. Writing became an existential necessity, a way to survive, "to express the inexpressible", to give voice to the victims and keep their memory alive. "Zakhor" (remember), the most recurrent biblical imperative, becomes her guiding strength, the ancestral ethical duty to be fulfilled, of all things, in the language of the persecutors. In a letter to a friend she states:

> The terrible events which brought me close to death and darkness were my teachers. If I could not have written, I would have not survived. Death was my teacher. How could I have been occupied with anything else? My metaphors are my wounds.

In light of this fact, all the endless discussions about her being or not the poet of the Shoah reveal their banality and deceptiveness. Her work is understandable only in light of this historical event that pervades her entire oeuvre. Together with Celan's, Sachs's poetry remains the strongest reply to Adorno's dictum, later retracted, "After Auschwitz writing poetry is barbaric". As the critic Ehrhard Bahr points out, Sachs not only wrote after Auschwitz but also about Auschwitz, managing to translate the verity of horror into the language of art without escaping from nor aestheticizing reality.

Since the 1970s critics have tended to consider her poetic production a monolithic oeuvre ranging from poems inspired by the devastating reality of the genocide to a poetry where the poet reaches a certain detachment and ventures upon a journey towards a new reality. Hardly recognized is her dramatic work the main theme of which is the link between the Jewish destiny in the Shoah and the long history of persecution of the Jews. The use of a-logical, highly subjective, multivalent, and polysemantic images, as well as the adoption of various levels of communication, make those works almost impossible for theatrical production. An exception is the widely acclaimed miracle play *Eli*, broadcast in West Germany as a radio play.

The first verses of the initial poem, "In der Wohnungen der Tod" [In the Houses of Death], set the poetic prospective of her entire poetic journey: "O die Schornsteine/ Auf den sinnreich erdachten Wohnungen des Todes/ . . . O ihr Finger." [Oh the chimneys/ on the cunning houses of death/ . . . Oh the fingers]. Both the chimneys and the fingers – elements of ordinary reality – refer here to another reality: the crematoria and the selective pointing of the executioners. By a reductive use of synecdoches, by concentrating on a few real elements, Sachs creates a new poetic language capable of presenting and suggesting what defies comprehension and is beyond any form of imagination. Her recurrent metaphors – "Staub" (dust), "Sand" (sand), "Rauch" (smoke), "Aschen" (ashes) – as Hans Magnus Enzensberger points out, remain, above all, concrete realities; only later do they assume a universal symbolic dimension of the Shoah and the Diaspora.

This first collection presents the point of view of the victims: they speak of how they died, of what they felt while being killed: their deaths regain thereby an individual process that allows the victims to recover some personal dignity. In this same book Sachs states a fundamental ethical commitment: not to submit to the overwhelming grief but to live through it in order to reveal the "false death", to face the horror of this reality and look for a meaning beyond this shattered world. A line from "Überall Jerusalem" [Jerusalem Everywhere] reads: "There in the madness gold is hidden"; only in the framework of pain and suffering can there be partial relief, only in facing the truth can we break the conspiracy of silence, tell the truth to ourselves and face God.

Sachs had always been strongly drawn towards mysticism, but her religion entails primarily the personal experience of transcendence without constituting a religious system. Much has been written about her mysticism and its various sources – Kabbalist and Hasidic thought, Christian and Asian mysticism, Romantic thought – and Bahr's definition, "syncretic mysticism", seems most appropriate to describe her case. An important aspect of it is the vision of death regarded as a passage to a divine reality. The recurrent butterfly symbolizes the metamorphosis of a spiritual creature that awaits reunion with God. From the Kabbalah she inherits the concept of language: the word as a healing power that can transform reality. The duty of the poet, therefore, is to restore the letters of the alphabet to their light, to let them live again and to remind us of their divine origin.

These insights, already present in her second volume *Sternverdunkelung* [Darkening of the Stars] change her perspective: the atrocities of the Shoah are now set in a larger context of the recurrent theme of persecutors and persecuted, yet they do not altogether mitigate her deep-seated anxiety and devastating suffering. The victims continue to torture themselves and the poet in her sleepless nights; their sadness becomes unbearably heavier even in the collection *Flucht und Verwandlung* [Flight and Metamorphosis] that contains various themes well condensed in one of her most famous poems: "In der Flucht" [In the Flight]. Here the lyrical "I" states: "Anstelle von Heimat/ Halte ich die Verwandlung der Welt" [Instead of home/ I hold to the transformations of the world]. This position explains the following statement: "I am not a Zionist in the sense in which it is understood these days. I believe that our home (Heimat) is any place where there are sources of eternity".

Her ethical refusal to lapse into nihilism or despair, to succumb to silence, led her to write until the very end of her life; yet many of her late poems express the difficulty of speaking and manifest a tendency towards silence. Language becomes fragmented: paradox and enallage (interchange) dominate, many poems do not consist of complete sentences but lack verbs and punctuation and often end with hyphens, leading readers to finish the sentences themselves. Capturing the destruction and the fragmentation caused by the Shoah inevitably meant englobing "speechlessness": evil cannot be understood, it is a mystery to be endured.

ELVIRA LATO VINTI

Sadeh, Pinhas

Polish-born Israeli fiction writer and poet, 1929–1994

Born in Lwów (L'viv), 1929. Emigrated with family to Palestine, 1934. No formal education. Night watchman; shepherd in Jezreel Valley. Awarded Bialik Prize. Died in 1994.

Selected Writings

Fiction
Hahayim kemashal, 1958; as *Life as a Parable*, translated by Richard Flantz, 1966
Al matsavo shel haadam [On Man's Condition], 1967
Mot avimelekh [The Death of Abimelech], 1969

Poetry
Massah dumah [Burden of Dumah], 1951
Sefer hashirim 1947–1970 [Book of Poems], 1970
Al shtei naarot nekhbadot [To Two Honourable Young Ladies], 1977
Sefer haagasim hatsehubim [The Book of Yellow Pears], 1985
Shirim 1985–1988 [Poems 1985–1988], 1988
Ikh zing vi a feygele [I Sing Like a Bird], 1993

Other
Nesiah [Journey], 1971
Nesiah beerets israel [Journey in the Land of Israel], 1974
Odot hahayim kemashal [The Diary of the Writing of Life as a Parable], 1980
Shiva hartsaot al Bialik [Seven Lectures on Bialik], 1985
Haganav [The Thief], 1988
Jewish Folktales, translated by Hillel Halkin, 1989
A Man in a Closed Room. His Heart is Broken. Darkness Falls Outside, 1992

Further Reading

Mundy, Josef, *Sihot ba-Hazot-Laylah im Pinhas Sadeh* [Conversations at Midnight with Pinhas Sadeh], Tel Aviv: Alef, 1969

A great deal of Israeli fiction has naturally enough been concerned with the immediate environment, with Israel's geopolitical situation, with the absorption of new populations, with war, with aspects of the new State, and with the changed situation of the Jewish world, and even the meaning of Jewishness. In such turbulent times, when it was not just a new political entity that was being created, but a whole new population, with the massive and revolutionary turmoil and transformation on all fronts, it would seem understandable that literature in the country should primarily reflect all this, and address itself to it. That was indeed generally the case. But Sadeh was a different sort of writer, and he was determined that his writing and his concerns should not be carved out and determined by these outside events. Indeed, he regarded all such as trivial, and his writing, prose and poetry, was occupied with other realms, those of ultimate concern, not with the transient.

Sadeh's writing is thinly disguised autobiography, and his principal work, *Hahayim kemashal* (*Life as a Parable*) is a sort of *Confessions* for his time and place (although the specific locus is of little concern to the author). The principal, virtually the only, figure in his writing is the I of the narrative. But there are also his observations of the passing scene, where he rejects that which preoccupies almost everyone else. His is the search for the ultimate, for God and His word, for the final truth, for the permanent rather than the temporary. In this respect, Sadeh's writing stands out as singular in the Israeli literary scene. We can divide up Modern Hebrew literature into public writing, even in the sphere of belles lettres, and private writing. The former tendency predominates, and it pronounces, in one way or another, on the Jewish polity, on the revival of Hebrew culture, on the situation of the Jews, on the return to the Land of Israel, on the changes in society, and on the world. The latter confines itself more to the psychology of the individual, and to his/her private world, often expressed in lyrical terms. The public predominates, as might be expected in Hebrew literature, where the very act of writing in that language constitutes a declaration. To the second category belong such writers as U.N. Gnessin, David Vogel, and, in the Israeli period, Amalia Kahana-Carmon, Nathan Zach, and Yoel Hoffman. Sadeh belongs here too: he adds transparently metaphysical and autobiographical elements to the lyrical aspects of his work.

Life as a Parable introduces the subject, and the dialectic. I versus the masses, isolated man vis-à-vis the others. The narrator sees himself as the only one who can really hear the "silence of the earth", because everyone else is so deafened by the day-to-day. Perhaps Sadeh's work is unique on the Israeli scene in being authentically theological; his books resemble the biblical books of prophecy, written in the language and mode of those texts. The title of the novel carries the symbolic nature of the material, as "life", as we know it, is only the carrier for other, more profound messages. He writes that it is only in relation to God that life can have any significance. Suffering is also important, as it is the true cloak of the spirit. What is going on outside, as he continues his autobiographical account, has no bearing on his life. He had, as he claims, no family, and as for the war (the 1948 War of Independence) raging outside, that "[h]ad no meaning for me, and I could see nothing to fight for." Why? Because:

> [M]y real enemies were lying in wait in another place in the dark recesses of the soul. It didn't matter to me who would rule over the city. It didn't matter to me whose soldiers would parade in a band for public view . . . It didn't matter who were to be the ministers and satraps of the State, whether circumcised or uncircumcised. After all, what is a State and what is Exile? The fact of this existence is the real Exile.

The implication is that there is an ultimate truth, whereas his outer body, his husk, is the peel of trash. Our necessary function is to discover the kernel, the nucleus within, which we can call the soul. That "[i]s the parable and God is the object of the parable. This, as I understand it, is what it means to be religious." The function of the writer, the true writer, not the myriad routine pen pushers, is to be a "voice crying in the wilderness". And this is what Sadeh tries to render in highly individual work.

Al matsavo shel haadam [On Man's Condition], as well as other of his works, continues this theme, although its tone is rather more worldly. The first-person narrator is a more subdued figure, placing himself in the background of his narrative. In some respects, the tone is less prophetic, dwelling on the small issues that dominate the lives of his characters: "Things that take place quietly, in the dark, between a person and himself." The narrator comes to the conclusion that the "condition" of which he speaks is complex, many sided, and therefore difficult to present. The principal character in the novel, Jonah Ben-David, is a shadowy, undistinguished figure, not one of the great shakers, but one who rather waits for things to happen. Jonah is accustomed to looking at things from the side, and is so desperate that he contemplates suicide. It is the thought of his mother, with whom he cannot communicate, that saves him from this. But the narrator's own attitude may be gathered from what he attributes to Jonah in the final words of the novel: "The condition, he suddenly murmurs to himself, is even worse than I thought." From what is presented in the texts, it would seem that Sadeh is not an optimistic writer.

LEON I. YUDKIN

Salinger, J.D.

US fiction writer, 1919–

Born Jerome David Salinger in New York City, 1 January 1919, to Sol, meat and cheese importer, and wife Miriam (née Jillich). Studied at McBurney School, New York, 1932–34; Valley Forge Military Academy, Pennsylvania (editor, *Crossed Sabres*), 1934–36; New York University, 1937. Lived in Europe, mainly Vienna, studying importing business, 1937–38. Studied, further, at Ursinus College, Pennsylvania, 1938; Columbia University, 1939, where attended evening class on writing short stories under Whit Burnett, editor of *Story* magazine. Served in US army, 1942–45: staff sergeant. Married, first, Sylvia, French physician, 1945; divorced 1946; second, Claire Douglas, 1955; divorced 1967; one daughter, one son; third, Colleen O'Neill. Has lived in seclusion in Cornish, New Hampshire, since 1953.

Selected Writings

Novel
The Catcher in the Rye, 1951

Short Stories
Nine Stories, 1953; as *For Esme – With Love and Squalor and Other Stories*, 1953
Raise High the Roof Beam, Carpenters, and Seymour: An Introduction, 1959
Franny and Zooey, 1961
The Complete Uncollected Short Stories of J.D. Salinger, 2 vols, 1974

Further Reading

Alsen, Eberhard, *Salinger's Glass Stories as a Composite Novel*, Troy, New York: Whitston, 1983
Bloom, Harold (editor), *J.D. Salinger: Modern Critical Views*, New York: Chelsea House, 1987
Bloom, Harold (editor), *Holden Caulfield*, New York: Chelsea House, 1990
Buitenhuis, Peter, *Five American Moderns: Mary McCarthy, Stephen Crane, J.D. Salinger, Eugene O'Neill, H.L. Mencken*, Toronto: Ascham Press, 1968
French, Warren, *J.D. Salinger Revisited*, Boston: Twayne, 1988
Grunwald, Henry Anatole (editor), *Salinger: A Critical and Personal Portrait*, New York: Harper, 1962; London: Peter Owen, 1964
Hamilton, Ian, *In Search of J.D. Salinger*, London: Heinemann, and New York: Random House, 1988
Kumar, Anil, *Alienation in the Fiction of Carson*

McCullers, J.D. Salinger and James Purdy, Amritsar: Guru Nanak Dev University Press, 1991
Kurian, Elizabeth N., *A Religious Response to the Existential Dilemma in the Fiction of J.D. Salinger*, New Delhi: Intellectual Publishing House, 1992
Lundquist, James, *J.D. Salinger*, New York: Ungar, 1979
Miller, James. E., Jr., *J.D. Salinger*, Minneapolis: University of Minnesota Press, 1965
Pinsker, Sanford, *"The Catcher in the Rye": Innocence under Pressure*, New York: Twayne, 1993
Rosen, Gerald, *Zen in the Art of J.D. Salinger*, Berkeley, California: Creative Arts, 1977
Salzberg, Joel, *Critical Essays on Salinger's "The Catcher in the Rye"*, Boston: G.K. Hall, 1990
Salzman, Jack (editor), *New Essays on "The Catcher in the Rye"*, New York and London: Cambridge University Press, 1991
Stashower, Daniel M., "On First Looking into Chapman's Holden: Speculation on a Murder", *American Scholar*, 52/3 (Summer 1983)
Steiner, George, "The Salinger Industry", *Nation*, 189 (14 November 1959)
Sublette, Jack R., *J.D. Salinger: An Annotated Bibliography 1938–1981*, New York: Garland, 1984
Wenke, John Paul, *J.D. Salinger: A Study of the Short Fiction*, Boston: Twayne, 1991

The famously reclusive Salinger, who has not published for more than 30 years, has seen his literary reputation slump from its one time dominant position. Based as it was on one novel and a selection of short stories, most of which chronicled the fortunes of one family, the Glasses, its fragility was always apparent. He is not included in the latest edition of the *Norton Anthology of American Literature*.

The great fame he enjoyed was secured by the popularity of his novel *The Catcher in the Rye*, whose protagonist Holden Caulfield gave voice and style to a whole generation of disillusioned postwar college students, with much the same force, but nothing like the longer-term literary influence, of Hemingway's lost generation's stoical hard-boiled utterance.

Serious critical appraisal of Salinger's work was always inhibited by the popular response to his brilliant mimetic ability and narrative skill, which for some years obscured the search for a religious position which is present from the first of the Glass stories, such as "A Perfect Day for Banana Fish" (which appeared in the *New Yorker* in 1948), to his last published story "Hapworth 16, 1924" (also in *The New Yorker* in 1965). It is also deeply embedded in the symbolism and synecdochical elements of the famous novel.

Salinger was born into a New York Jewish family though his early experiences exposed him to wider, and for most Jewish men of his generation, somewhat unusual influences. Thus, in his 15th year he attended Valley Forge Military Academy in Pennsylvania, graduating and then spending time travelling in Europe.

His first published story appeared in 1940 just after he attended a short-story writing course, and this was followed by another in the *Saturday Evening Post* in 1943 when he was in the United States Army, and in the years following his discharge (1945) he began to publish regularly in *Esquire* and the *New Yorker* as well as the *Post*. Yet it is with the first of the Glass stories, "A Perfect Day for Banana Fish", that the individual voice starts to appear, and is consolidated in his long and special relationship with that magazine.

His most famous character has been seen to be in the tradition of other famous first-person American narrators such as Huckleberry Finn, Nick Carraway, and even Jake Barnes. Certainly there are influences – Finn's colloquialism, Carraway's detachment, Barnes's objectivity – but Caulfield has a unique and individual spiritual sensibility.

Similarly some have found Salinger's style confined by the urbane sophistication of the *New Yorker*, but this is to ignore the unique employment of contemporaneous demotic as well as the underlying spiritual/mystical content. Salinger's involvement with Zen is evident in his work, and is overtly signalled by the Buddha-like withdrawal from society of his ten-year-old character in the story, "Teddy", who has a mystical revelation, and by his affixing to "Nine Stories" the Zen *koan* in which the disciple is questioned about the sound of one hand clapping.

Salinger's spiritual journey incorporating Judaeo-Christian as well as Buddhist elements has been the mainspring of all his major fiction, and it would appear of his private life as well. The catcher in the rye, as Holden Caulfield famously explains to his sister Phoebe, is the saviour. He knowingly changes the Burns's line from "meet a body comin' through the rye" to "catch a body" because that is what Holden wishes to do. He wants to catch the little children before they fall over the cliff – to be their saviour. Caulfield does, of course, appear to be in revolt against many of the values and mores of contemporary society and is trying to withdraw from it. For many readers this is the main thrust of the novel. What is often overlooked is that finally Holden ends up *missing* everybody, even the characters of whom he seems to have been critical. The Zen philosophy of acceptance of all things non-judgmentally and of love may be deeply buried in the famous novel, but it is there. There, too, is the Buddhist belief that in order truly to participate in the world one must withdraw from it. This is Holden's odyssey.

The Zen message is more overt in the Glass family stories and especially in the characters of Seymour and his brother Buddy, and in the story "Teddy", when Teddy explains that if he were in charge of education he would try to empty children's minds of all they acquired from others, including parents, and show them how to meditate, how to find out who they are. It is the conflict between being simultaneously repelled and tempted by society that is common to all Salinger's heroes with, for some, the solution being found in the Buddhist concept of withdrawal in order to participate. Some have seen in this indications of psychological or spiritual sickness, and indeed the obsession with consistency and the desire for an impossibly ordered universe (Holden, Seymour, and Buddy) does have elements in common with autism.

There is little specific Jewish reference in Salinger's work, although, of course, the Glass family is half Jewish and in the story "Down at the Dingy" he does use anti-Semitism as a paradigm for the world's brutality and in "Raise High the

Roof Beam, Carpenters" Bessie does offer chicken soup as a cure-all. The Glass family's various religious explorations seem to parallel Salinger's own, from Judaism, through Catholicism, to Buddhism.

Salinger's own withdrawal, his reclusiveness, and his refusal to publish are also cited as evidence of imbalance or creative impotence. But he has produced a literature that has left its mark, and his Zen beliefs inevitably lead to a rejection of ego and the acceptance of a way of life which would seem, for him, to have more significance than producing any more words on paper.

GERALD DE GROOT

Samuel, Maurice

Romanian-born US novelist and nonfiction writer, 1895–1972

Born in Macin, 8 February 1895, into traditional Jewish family. Emigrated with family, first to France, 1901; lived in Paris; then to Britain, 1902; lived in Manchester. Self-declared socialist from 1908. Studied at Victoria University, Manchester, 1911–14. Emigrated to United States, 1914. Served in US army, 1917–18; sergeant. Interpreter for US government commission investigating pogroms in Poland, 1919. Married, first, Gertrude Kahn, 1921; divorced; second, Edith Brodsky; one daughter, one son. Naturalized US citizen, 1921. Worker for Zionist Organization of America, 1921–28. Guest on numerous radio and television programmes, including *Words We Live By*, 1953–71. Many awards, including Anisfield–Wolf Award, 1943; *Saturday Review of Literature* Award, 1944; Stephen B. Wise Award, 1956; B'nai B'rith Award, 1967; Manger Prize (Israel), 1972. Died in New York, 4 May 1972.

Selected Writings

Fiction
The Outsider, 1921
Whatever Gods, 1923
Beyond Woman, 1934
Web of Lucifer, 1947
The Devil That Failed, 1952
The Second Crucifixion, 1960

Other
You Gentiles, 1924
I, the Jew, 1927
What Happened in Palestine: The Events of August 1929, 1929
Jews on Approval, 1931
King Mob: A Study of the Present-day Mind, 1931
On the Rim of the Wilderness: The Conflict in Palestine, 1931
The Great Hatred, 1941
The World of Sholom Aleichem, 1943
Harvest in the Desert, 1944
Prince of the Ghetto, 1948
The Gentleman and the Jew, 1950
Level Sunlight, 1953
Certain People of the Book, 1955
The Professor and the Fossil: Some Observations on Arnold Toynbee's "A Study of History", 1956
Little Did I Know, 1963
Blood Accusation: The Strange History of the Beiliss Case, 1966
Light on Israel, 1968
In Praise of Yiddish, 1971
In the Beginning, Love: Dialogues on the Bible, with Mark van Doren, edited by Edith Samuel, 1973
The Book of Praise: Dialogues on the Psalms, edited by Edith Samuel, 1975
The Worlds of Maurice Samuel, edited by Milton Hindus, 1977

Translated 22 books, including works of Sholem Asch, I.J. Singer, and H.N. Bialik.

Further Reading

Alter, Robert, *Commentary* (March 1964)
Christian Century (11 January 1961; 26 May 1971)
Harper's (October 1966)
Jewish Quarterly (Spring 1968)
Liptzin, Solomon, *Generation of Decision: Jewish Rejuvenation in America*, New York: Bloch, 1958
Liptzin, Solomon, *The Jew in American Literature*, New York: Bloch, 1966
Nation (16 October 1943; 17 October 1966)
New York Times (4 April 1943; 13 August 1966)
New York Times Book Review (18 September 1966; 2 June 1968)
Saturday Review (18 May 1968)
Times Literary Supplement (26 May 1961; 6 April 1967)

As Robert Alter wrote in *Commentary*, Maurice Samuel was "a kind of one-man educational movement in American Jewish life". His subjects ranged from anti-Semitism to Zionism, from the Bible to Sholem Aleichem, and his audience ranged from "sisterhood ladies to intellectuals ignorant of Judaism and curious non-Jews". Samuel's mission was to recreate the world of the little people in the citadels of Jewish life in eastern Europe before the Holocaust destroyed them – to describe their faith and its savour and colour, their capacity to draw hope from sorrow, and to respond with character to adversity. He recreated this world with his unique gifts of spirit and style – not with the acid satire of Dickens, or the macabre aloofness of Balzac, but with the tender humour of Sholem Aleichem and Mendele. It required almost an act of necromancy, he realized, but it had to be done. For he wanted the children of the shtetl, and their children, to know their grandparents, not as an act of curiosity, but as an act of decency. They were a remarkable lot, and he was determined they would not become a mystery to their own posterity. He was an interpreter of Jewish values and culture, making manifest an unfamiliar world to Western readers.

Samuel recreated this world with a style that was linked to discipline. Every sentence, every phrase, every word, had to be unerring in tone as well as meaning, no matter how much effort that required. His style flowed from this emphasis on undeviating standards, a dedication to immaculate craftsmanship.

Considered by many critics to be his best work, *The World of Sholom Aleichem* demonstrated his skill in recreating, not merely Sholem Aleichem and his writing, but the shtetl world in which he lived. He depicted "how the Kasrielevkites lived, married, brought up children, earned their bread, sorrowed, rejoiced and died", as a *New York Times* reviewer put it. He is credited with introducing Sholem Aleichem to the English-speaking world. He did this too for another great Yiddish writer, Y.L. Perets, in *Prince of the Ghetto. In Praise of Yiddish* was hailed as a highpoint in his career "as translator and Jewish cultural mediator". As Lucy S. Dawidowicz puts it, the book is not merely a study of the Yiddish language, but "constitutes a kind of discursive Yiddish–English dictionary of over a thousand words, idioms and phrases". These are defined, with appropriate examples. Curt Leviant noted in the *Saturday Review*, that he describes Yiddish, "from its birth nearly a millennium ago".

Samuel's fiction includes *The Outsider*, *Whatever Gods*, *Beyond Woman*, *Web of Lucifer*, *The Devil That Failed*, and *The Second Crucifixion*. *The Web of Lucifer* was described in the *New Yorker* as "a brilliant closeup of life in the service of the Borgias during the reign of Alexander VI in Rome". The story of a young Italian peasant's search for his brother's murderer, the novel was especially praised for what R.E. Danielson in *Atlantic Monthly* called its "careful reconstruction and presentation of an amazingly rich and varied scene". As P.J. Searles wrote in the *New York Herald Tribune Weekly Book Review*, "the author, whose knowledge of the times seems prodigious, has woven a tapestry of history, complete and accurate in detail". Samuel spent ten years painstakingly researching the past before writing *The Second Crucifixion*; the *Times Literary Supplement* called the novel " a notable and sober feat of historical reconstruction". *Christian Century* described the novel as "a vivid recreation of a dramatic period in the early history of the Church". The novel concerns a Jewish girl in Hadrian's Rome who is at first adopted by an aristocratic Roman family, but returns to her Jewish roots after a disastrous marriage.

From the first, Samuel's non-fiction writing in *You Gentiles* and *I, the Jew* was provocative, his thesis being that Jewish and Gentile approaches to ultimate issues were contrary and irreconcilable. Samuel provided a dual perspective. Alter notes in *Commentary* that he placed many of his books within an autobiographical framework. As a result, his subject emerges not as "a set of ideas, lives or events" but as "his own discovery of them". On the other hand, Samuel "continually viewed the idea of being a Jew against the background of eternity". The basis of his work was religious, supporting the conviction, in Alter's words, "that the moral aspirations of Jewish tradition reflect a divine will and purpose".

Jews on Approval, *The Great Hatred*, and *The Gentleman and the Jew* continued this theme. Anti-Semitism is not a Jewish malaise, but an affliction of the Gentiles, to which Jews need to be accustomed; it was contained in Samuel's title, a "great hatred". Samuel compared the Jewish and Gentile ideal of man in *The Gentleman and the Jew*.

Samuel was an influential and popular Zionist; his convictions arose from his friendship with Chaim Weizmann, whom he met at Manchester University, and with whom he maintained a lasting personal, political, and literary bond. Having visited for many years in what was then Palestine, he believed that Jews would succeed in building a moral commonwealth there. He called upon American Jews to help realize this dream in *Harvest in the Desert* and *Level Sunlight*, maintaining that Zionism went beyond the mere building of a state. It extended to the regeneration of the Jewish people all over the world, and American Jewry had an important role to play.

Other works of Zionist interest include *On the Rim of the Wilderness: The Conflict in Palestine*, an exploration of attitudes in the conflict between Palestinian Arabs and the Zionist movement, a subject also tackled in *What Happened in Palestine: The Events of August 1929*. In *Light on Israel*, a discussion of the history of Arab–Jewish relations in the run-up to Palestine, and in modern Israel, the author states, "I'm not writing to persuade or convince anyone. I am writing to testify." In his review of the book, Curt Leviant notes, "For the constant intelligence, urbanity, and grace of his writing, Maurice Samuel has earned an honored role in Jewish literature. American literary critics have been remiss in not properly evaluating the place in English letters of one of the master stylists in the language."

Samuel exposed the iniquities of the Beiliss trial in *Blood Accusation*. This book scrupulously details events as they occurred in 1911, when a Jew, Mendel Beilis, was falsely accused of killing a Ukrainian boy, and using the blood for ritual purposes. He also wrote several books on his thoughts about being a Jew, a fine example being *Little Did I Know*.

Samuel wrote for 50 years in a steady succession of interesting volumes, bringing his message to thousands, accompanied by much travel. A brilliant orator and conversationalist, he reached a wide audience through his broadcast discussions with the poet and critic Mark van Doren. Neither physical weariness nor even serious illness weakened his resolve. He completed *In Praise of Yiddish* between spasms of angina, but the integrity of the volume does not reflect the pain of creation. Samuel's last work, which he did not complete, was to expose the betrayal of the disciples of Jesus who had destroyed the heritage of their teacher.

JUANITA ROTHMAN

Sarraute, Nathalie

Russian-born French fiction writer, dramatist, and literary critic, 1900–1999

Born Nathalie Tcherniak in Ivanovo, 18 July 1900, into assimilated family. After parents divorced, 1902, early childhood divided between mother and father, and between France and Russia; from age eight, with father in Paris. Studied at Lycée Fénelon, Paris; the Sorbonne, degree in English, 1920; history, University of Oxford, 1921; philosophy and sociology, University of Berlin, 1921–22; Faculty of

Law, Paris, law degree, 1925. Married Raymond Sarraute, 1925; three daughters. Member of French Bar, 1926–41. Joined resistance group formed by Jean-Paul Sartre and others, and spent long periods using false papers, during World War II. Signatory, Manifesto of the 121, protesting against French state policy towards Algeria, 1960. Awards include Prix International de Littérature, 1964; Grand Prix National des Lettres, 1982; Grand Prix de la SACD, 1996. Died in Paris, 19 October 1999.

Selected Writings

Fiction

Tropismes, 1939 (revised 1957); as *Tropisms*, with *The Age of Suspicion*, translated by Maria Jolas, 1963
Portrait d'un inconnu, 1948 (revised 1956); as *Portrait of a Man Unknown*, translated by Maria Jolas, 1958
Martereau, 1953; as *Martereau, a Novel*, translated by Maria Jolas, 1959
Le Planétarium, 1959; as *The Planetarium*, translated by Maria Jolas, 1960
Les Fruits d'or, 1963; as *The Golden Fruits*, translated by Maria Jolas, 1964
Entre la vie et la mort, 1968; as *Between Life and Death*, translated by Maria Jolas, 1969
Vous les entendez?, 1972; as *Do You Hear Them?*, translated by Maria Jolas, 1973
"disent les imbéciles", 1976; as *"fools say"*, translated by Maria Jolas, 1977
L'Usage de la parole, 1980; as *The Use of Speech*, translated by Barbara Wright with the author, 1980
Enfance, 1983; as *Childhood*, translated by Barbara Wright with the author, 1984
Tu ne t'aimes pas, 1989; as *You Don't Love Yourself: A Novel*, translated by Barbara Wright with the author, 1990
Ici, 1995; as *Here: A Novel*, translated by Barbara Wright with the author, 1997
Ouvrez [Open], 1997

Plays

Le Silence, suivi de Le Mensonge, 1967; as *Silence, and The Lie*, translated by Maria Jolas, 1969
Isma, 1970; as *Izzum*, translated by Maria Jolas, in *Collected Plays*, 1980
C'est beau, 1975; as *It's Beautiful*, translated by Maria Jolas, in *Collected Plays*, 1980
Elle est là, 1978; translated as *It is There*, translated by Maria Jolas, in *Collected Plays*, 1980
Théâtre (includes *Elle est là*, *C'est beau*, *Isma*, *Le Mensonge*, *Le Silence*), 1978
Collected Plays (includes *It is There*, *It's Beautiful*, *Izzum*, *The Lie*, *Silence*), translated by Maria Jolas and Barbara Wright, 1980
Pour un oui ou pour un non, 1982; as *For No Good Reason*, 1985

Other

L'Ère du soupçon, 1956; as *The Age of Suspicion: Essays on the Novel*, translated by Maria Jolas, 1963; with *Tropisms*, 1963
Paul Valéry et l'Enfant d'Éléphant; Flaubert le précurseur [Paul Valéry and the Elephant's Child; Flaubert the Forerunner], 1986
Nathalie Sarraute, qui êtes-vous? Conversations avec Simone Benmussa [Nathalie Sarraute, Who Are You? Conversations with Simone Benmussa], 1987
Oeuvres complètes [Complete Works], Pléiade edition, 1996

Further Reading

Angrémy, Annie (editor), *Nathalie Sarraute: portrait d'un écrivain* (exhibition catalogue), Paris: Bibliothèque Nationale, 1995
Asso, Françoise, *Nathalie Sarraute: une écriture de l'effraction*, Paris: Presses Universitaires de France, 1995
Bell, Sheila M., *Nathalie Sarraute: A Bibliography*, London: Grant and Cutler, 1982
Bell, Sheila M., "The Conjuror's Hat: Sarraute Criticism since 1980", *Romance Studies*, 23 (Spring 1994)
Besser, Gretchen Rous, *Nathalie Sarraute*, Boston: Twayne, 1979
Boué, Rachel, *Nathalie Sarraute: La Sensation en quête de parole*, Paris: L'Harmattan, 1997
Clayton, Alan J., *Nathalie Sarraute; ou, Le tremblement de l'écriture*, Paris: Lettres Modernes, 1989
Foutrier, Pascale (editor), *Éthiques du Tropisme*, Paris: L'Harmattan, 1999
Gleize, J. and A. Leoni, *Nathalie Sarraute, un écrivain dans le siècle*, Aix-en-Provence: Publications de l'Université de Provence, 2000
Jefferson, Ann, *The Nouveau Roman and the Poetics of Fiction*, Cambridge: Cambridge University Press, 1980
Jefferson, Ann, *Nathalie Sarraute, Fiction and Theory*, Cambridge and New York: Cambridge University Press, 2000
Minogue, Valerie, *Nathalie Sarraute and the War of the Words: A Study of Five Novels*, Edinburgh: Edinburgh University Press, 1981
O'Beirne, Emer, *Reading Nathalie Sarraute: Dialogue and Distance*, Oxford: Clarendon Press, 1999
Pierrot, Jean, *Nathalie Sarraute*, Paris: Corti, 1990
Raffy, Sabine (editor), *Autour de Nathalie Sarraute*, Annales Littéraires de l'Université de Besançon, Paris: Belles Lettres, 1995
Rykner, Arnaud, *Nathalie Sarraute*, Paris: Seuil, 1991
Tadié, Jean-Yves, introduction to *Nathalie Sarraute, Oeuvres complètes*, Paris: Gallimard, 1996; with *Notices* [critical commentaries] by A. Jefferson, V. Minogue and A. Rykner

Special Issues

L'Arc, 95 (1984)
Critique (Jan–Feb 2000)
Digraphe, 32 (March 1984)
L'Esprit créateur, 36/2 (Summer 1996)
Magazine littéraire, 196 (June 1983)
"Nathalie Sarraute: Portrait d'un inconnu et tu ne t'aimes pas", *Roman 20–50*, 25 (June 1998)
Revue des Sciences Humaines, 217 (1990–91)

Born Nathalie Tcherniak, Russian Jew by birth, French by education, and European by culture, Sarraute was always intensely aware of, and resistant to the reductive powers of categorizing language: she refused to be described as a "woman writer", and would equally refuse the label "Jewish writer". Growing up in Paris in the highly cultured milieu of her free-thinking father, Sarraute never felt any sense of difference in status between men and women, and Jewishness was never an issue.

While Jewishness in itself was not a salient feature of Sarraute's life, it became a very serious issue with the German occupation of France. As a Jew, she was no longer allowed to practise at the Bar, and in 1942, when the yellow star was imposed, she collected hers but decided not to wear it. Living in the provinces under a false name, she was denounced by a local baker, but got away just in time. The Nazi occupation and the hideous revelations of the Holocaust had a profound impact on Sarraute, reinforcing a horror of which she had had early intimations, growing up among Russian émigrés who had experienced the czarist regime, and having been appalled by the atmosphere of terror and oppression she encountered on her visit to Russia in 1935. The totalitarian world of censorship, fear, prisons, and secret police haunts Sarraute's work, despite the fact that history as such has no place within it. Her work is focused not on external but on internal events.

She was vividly aware of Jewish suffering and, with her husband Raymond, co-edited an anthology on Jewish experience of the Occupation. She does not deal in her work with the matter of being Jewish, nor with anti-Semitism, but the thrust of all her work is against every sort of racism, terrorism, and tyranny. At the end of an essay of 1947 Sarraute makes one explicit and passionate reference to the infamies of Nazism, with an explosion of rage, contempt, and something that goes beyond all these emotions: "a huge blank stupefaction, a definitive and total bafflement".

Sarraute's entire oeuvre is dedicated to the exploration of minute, ephemeral movements of feeling at the very limits of consciousness. These she called "tropisms", a term that provided the title of her first book of short sketches or prose poems. In the works that followed, Sarraute showed the tropisms at work in the wider scope of the novel form, creating slow-motion close-ups that dramatize and enormously enlarge – often with comic effect – the virtual dramas latent in ephemeral flickers of feeling. In her pursuit of the tropisms, characterization and conventional plot were discarded, in defiance of the most hallowed traditions of the novel, traditions she explicitly challenged in the seminal critical essays of *The Age of Suspicion*. This radical questioning of the novel form made her a major player in the "new novel" movement which, in the 1950s, allied her with such very different writers as Alain Robbe-Grillet, Michel Butor, and Claude Simon in a common rebellion against what were felt to be the outdated constraints of traditional realism.

For Sarraute, personality is a fundamentally artificial invention, and the very notion of "character" is called in question. The beings in her novels remain undefined and nameless. *The Planetarium*, exceptionally, has named "characters", but they are shown to be artificial social constructs – false planets in the false sky of the Planetarium. Names, and even common nouns such as those indicating family relationships or professions, are seen as imprisoning, freezing people into fixed roles. Sarraute shows language to be a powerful weapon; not merely names and nouns, but even pronouns can have petrifying effects: if "we" produces a cosy togetherness for "us", it chills the excluded, while a plural "you" can seem to convict and irrevocably sentence. The milieu Sarraute presents throughout her work is one with which she is familiar – the world of the Parisian bourgeois intellectual, though her interest lies not in any specific social group, but in the tropismic sub-surface, the level at which we are all, in Sarraute's view, alike.

Sarraute's natural mode is hesitancy, and her mood interrogative; her refusal of definition and closure is everywhere evident – in the frequent trails of dots that bestrew her pages, the avoidance of social or historical context, the rejection of characterization, and the refusal of all certainty. Art itself, literary values, aesthetic values of every kind, are all put to the question – whether in *The Golden Fruits*, which recounts with a great deal of wit and perspicacity the way a novel soars and plummets in critical estimation, or in *Between Life and Death*, which takes the reader into the very quick of literary composition with its anguish and doubts. *Do You Hear Them?*, unfolding the dramas latent in a father's reaction to the laughter of his children, continues the questioning, weighing the civilized (conformist? moribund?) culture of age against the barbarous (original? vital?) culture of youth. Even when dealing with complex or abstract subjects, Sarraute's writing remains securely anchored in the most inward realities of human interactions.

Throughout Sarraute's work, there is a growing insistence on the *inter*personal – a view of the self not as an individual and separate entity confronting the world of others, but as the habitation of a multitude of virtual selves. In *Childhood*, Sarraute uncovers the tropisms underlying various fragments of her own childhood memories, creating, in the process, at the age of 85, her first bestseller. In *You Don't Love Yourself*, every personal pronoun – and especially the first-person singular – becomes a question-mark, while in Sarraute's penultimate book, *Here*, the "I" is replaced by a simple location – the "here" of the title.

The very inwardness of Sarraute's writing would seem to be inimical to the theatre, but in the 1960s, she was persuaded to provide a radio play, *Silence*, for Radio Stuttgart. Three other radio plays followed – all later successfully produced on stage. *It is There* was the first to be actually written for the stage and this was followed by the best-known of her plays, *For No Good Reason*. In the plays, as in Sarraute's other works, characters are virtually nonexistent; names are rare, and plot is minimal. Drama, however, is sustained, as the multifarious impulses and conflicts of the subconversation become the spoken dialogue, in a turning inside out of the normal process.

Sarraute's strength lies above all in her rich ironic humour and her poetic ability to translate sensation into language, articulating the tropisms through images and rhythm, not defining nor analysing, but making her readers experience them for themselves. In 1996 Sarraute had the rare accolade of having her works published during her lifetime in the classic Pléiade collection. Her production of a further (well-named!) volume, *Open*, one year after the publication of her *Complete Works*, rather splendidly underlined her characteristic refusal of closure.

VALERIE MINOGUE

Schindel, Robert

Austrian poet and fiction writer, 1944–

Born in Bad Hall, near Vienna, 1944, to parents deported soon after; kept in hiding until World War II ended, 1945. Studied philosophy. Abandoned studies to become politically active, late 1960s. Founder, *Hundsblume* literary journal. Appeared in Ruth Beckermann's film *Die papierene Brücke*, 1987.

Selected Writings

Poetry

Ohneland: Gedichte vom Holz der Paradeiserbäume 1979–1984 [Landless: Poems from the Wood of the Tomato Trees 1979–1984], 1986

Geier sind pünktliche Tiere: Gedichte [Vultures are Punctual Creatures: Poems], 1987

Im Herzen die Krätze: Gedichte [A Heart of Scabies], 1988

Ein Feuerchen im Hintennach: Gedichte 1986–1991 [A Small Fire Beyond: Poems 1986–1991], 1992

Fiction

Gebürtig, 1992; as *Born Where?*, translated by Michael Roloff, 1995

Die Nacht der Harlekine: Erzählungen [Night of the Harlequins: Stories], 1994

Other

Gott schütz uns vor den guten Menschen: Jüdisches Gedächtnis-Auskunftsbüro der Angst [God Protect Us from Good People: The Jewish Memorial Information Bureau of Fear], 1995

Further Reading

Bormann, Alexandre von, "Die Dinge, die Menschen – Auge und Herz: Zu Gedichten von Bernd Wagner und Robert Schindel", *Die Horen*, 34/1 (1989)

Kernmeyer, Hildegeard, "Gebürtig Ohneland: Robert Schindel: Auf der Suche nach der verlorene Idenität", *Modern Austrian Literature*, 27/3–4 (1994)

Konzett, Matthias, "The Politics of Recognition in Contemporary Austrian Jewish Literature", *Monatshefte*, 90/1 (1998)

Lappin, Elena (editor), *Jewish Voices, German Words: Growing Up Jewish in Postwar Germany and Austria*, North Haven, Connecticut: Catbird Press, 1994

Lorenz, Dagmar C.G. (editor), *Contemporary Jewish Writing in Austria: An Anthology*, Lincoln: University of Nebraska Press, 1999

Spork, Ingrid, "1992: Robert Schindel's Novel Gebürtig Continues the Development of Jewish Writing after the Shoah" in *Yale Companion to Jewish Writing and Thought in German Culture, 1096–1996*, edited by Sander L. Gilman and Jack Zipes, New Haven, Connecticut: Yale University Press, 1997

Literary insiders knew Robert Schindel mainly as a Viennese poet until his novel *Gebürtig* (*Born Where?*) won him international attention. His success, which coincided with a revival of Jewish literature in Germany and Austria, made him one of the outstanding exponents of emerging ethnic literatures in the 1990s. However, it should be kept in mind that Schindel's treatment of ethnicity is highly nuanced, much like that of his Austrian Jewish contemporaries Elfriede Jelinek, Robert Menasse, Ruth Beckermann, Georg Tabori, and Doron Rabinovici. No easy definitions of ethnicity and Jewish identity can be found throughout the plurivocal novel *Born Where?* that foregrounds the multiple negotiations in which subjective and cultural identities are formed. Unlike the more explicitly ethnic Jewish novels of Raphael Seligmann, Barbara Honigmann, and Esther Dischereit, Schindel draws on the cosmopolitan setting of Vienna in which collective definitions are at best tentative and exploratory.

Reflecting, nevertheless, a provocative and distinctly Jewish point of view, the novel takes a highly critical view of Austria's dubious normalization, belying a climate of enforced harmonized consensus: "Your fathers have pushed our people into the ovens, your mothers have prayed the rosary and the sons generously want to incorporate us, disregard the past, and, untarnished, want to be the victims themselves." Yet, even in light of this persistent denial of the past, Schindel emphasizes the possibility of cultural rebirth through genuine engagement with history. With a sympathetic perspective, Schindel's multiplot novel shows most of his characters (Jewish and non-Jewish) struggling for more viable forms of cultural identity in which difference and commonality can coexist and in which the past is acknowledged but is not necessarily the single determining avenue to Jewish identity: "Is it permissible for our Jews to remain occasionally dead or must their bones and ashes always remained sharpened?"

The centrality of social and cultural co-dependence is emphasized by the twin characters Sascha Graffito and Danny Demant, who are symbiotically connected to each other as passive observer-narrator and acting character, respectively producing together a narrated life or story. This symbiotic model subsequently plays itself out in a series of other paired characters whose lives intersect with Danny and Sascha's. At the outset, the novel depicts patterns of interaction typical of Austria's amnesiac society: "He emphasized his Jewish heritage; she said that she could do little with that, she wasn't interested in politics." The work further highlights generational conflicts between survivors and their descendants, such as Emmanuel Katz, who becomes the indirect victim of his mother's traumatic memory, or Susanne Ressel, who questions her father's fond memories of communist activism and comradeship during the Spanish civil war. Eventually, however, the novel presents more positive transformations, such as the public outing of a repressed Jewish identity (Katz and Adel) or a hidden Nazi past (Konrad Sachs), the commitment to confront once again a traumatic past as a witness in a Nazi trial (Gebirtig), and the approximation of the Shoah experience, albeit highly ironized, as stand-ins in a Holocaust movie set.

The novel's flippant tone, admittedly not without its own problems, resists a sanctimonious quality that lately has become a cliché in the treatment of the Holocaust, turning critical reflection into iconic reverence for events claimed to be beyond human comprehension. Like his German colleague Maxim Biller, Schindel attempts to break this spell of unquestioning awe and reticence by means of irreverent satire to allow for a continued inquiry into Jewish history and identity. In addition, Schindel's more easygoing cosmopolitan perspective, critically grounded in distinct regional settings, does not attempt to universalize the various cultural encounters between Jews and non-Jews. Indeed, each of the novel's encounters produces a unique negotiation of Jewish identity from within uniquely interpreted cultural settings. Schindel's collection of short stories *Die Nacht der Harlekine* [Night of the Harlequins] similarly underscores such a regional emphasis in its grotesquely Viennese and regionally coloured characters and language.

In a follow-up collection of public lectures *Gott schütz uns vor den guten Menschen* [God Protect Us from Good People], Schindel continues his work of cultural memory that runs from his poetry of the 1980s through his prose works of the 1990s. Exploring his own biography as the son of a mother who had survived Auschwitz and a father executed at Dachau, Schindel delves into his communist family background that, on closer analysis, betrays disturbing anti-Semitic tendencies in its abstract universality that cancels out any specific ethnic identity. For Schindel, however, the recovery of his Jewish heritage in a maze of overlapping ideologies of nationhood, assimilation, and political orientation does not imply a mere return to the religious traditions of Judaism. As the child of atheist Jews, he is cut off from this tradition and views himself more linked to a modern diasporic tradition of European Jews interested in the restoration of a context of solidarity with other oppressed groups.

The work of Schindel, it can be said, reflects the shift from inherited traditions of Judaism to a post-Shoah construction of secular Jewishness. Renewing the significance of Jewish identity and its public visibility, Schindel ultimately manages to avoid a facile pluralism and a dogmatic politics of identity obliging every Jew to be Jewish in the same manner. Because Jewishness, as Schindel realizes, overlaps with other private and public identities, it recedes or presses into the foreground in accordance with changing subject positions influenced by age, gender, generation, community, region, and language. Its visibility, although desirable in Austria's all too homogeneous cultural landscape, cannot be reduced to any single strategy or form of public disclosure.

MATTHIAS KONZETT

Schneour, Zalkind-Zalmen

Russian poet and fiction writer, 1887–1959

Born in Shklov, Belorussia, 1887; left for Odessa, 1900, befriended by H.N. Bialik; moved to Warsaw, 1902; employed at Tushiyyah publishing house. Published first poems in *Olam katan*, 1902. Returned to Shklov, 1903. Moved to Vilna (Vilnius) to work on Hebrew daily *Hazman*, 1904; left for Switzerland, 1905; moved to Paris, 1907, studied literature, philosophy, and natural sciences at Sorbonne. Travelled throughout Europe and North Africa, 1908–13; interned in Germany, 1914. During war years, studied medicine at University of Berlin, and worked in a hospital. Visited United States, 1919; returned to Berlin. Founded Hasefer publishing house, Berlin, 1920. Abandoned medical studies to settle in Paris, 1924. Escaped via Spain to United States, 1940. Lived in New York, 1941–49, emigrated to Israel, 1949. Died in New York, 1959; buried in Israel next to Bialik and Saul Tchernichovski, 1960.

Selected Writings

Collections
Kitvei [Works], 1958
Restless Spirit: Selected Writings, translated by Moshe Spiegel, 1963

Poetry
Im shekiat hahammah, 2 vols, 1906–07
Beharim, 1908
Im tselilei hamandolinah, 1912
Yemei habeinayim mitkarevim, 1913
Hezionot, shirim upoemot, 1923
Fertsiker lider un poemen, 1903–1944, 1945
Luhot genuzim, 1948
Mishirei erets israel, 1948

Fiction
Mavet, 1906
A toyt: shriftn fun a zelbstmerder a tiref, 1910
Shklover yidn: noveln, 1929
Noyekh pandre, 1936; as *Song of the Dnieper*, translated by Joseph Leftwich, 1945 (abridged translation as *Noah Pandre*, 1936)
Tzurik fun astrog, 1939
Di vant, 1939
Anshei shklov, 1944
Kayzer un rebe [The Emperor and the Rabbi], 5 vols, 1944–52
Hadod zyame, 1945
Di meshumedeste [The Baptized Jewess], 1948
Shklover kinder: dertseylungen, 1951
Der mamzer [The Bastard], 1957

Further Reading

Klausner, Joseph, *Zalman Shne'ur, ha-meshorer veha-mesafer*, Tel Aviv: Hotsaat Yavne, 1947

Zalkind-Zalmen Schneour, the Hebrew and Yiddish writer of poetry and prose, was born in Shklov, Belorussia in 1887, into the famous Hasidic Schneerson family. His literary talent was evident from early childhood when, at the age of eight, he was writing poems in both Hebrew and Yiddish. Schneour had a great zest for life and learning and was endowed with the mind and ability to succeed in a diversity of ambitions. Unlike those artists and writers who must create their works in isolation, Schneour actively sought out the company of the most flourishing and prestigious literary circles and became part of them. Attaining his Jewish adulthood with his bar mitzvah at 13, he left Shklov and journeyed to Odessa, which was a thriving centre of Jewish literature and Zionism. There he was warmly received by the great Hebrew writer, H.N. Bialik, and he met other literary figures including Mendele Moykher Sforim (Mendele the Bookpeddler) the first of the three great modern Yiddish classicists (the other two being Sholem Aleichem and Y.L. Perets). Two years later, he moved to Warsaw, where Jewish literary projects were flourishing, and there, on the recommendation of Bialik, was hired by the Tushiyyah publishing house and for a short while worked for Perets as his personal secretary. He also published his first poems. In 1903 he returned to his family in Shklov, but in the following year, aged 17, the literary circles of Vilna tempted him to leave home again. He found work on a Hebrew daily newspaper and also published his first collection of poetry, his first novel, and his first collection of stories. Schneour's poems were a great success, and several editions were published. Two years later he was on the move once more, living first in Switzerland and then Paris, where he studied philosophy, literature, and natural sciences at the Sorbonne, while continuing with his literary work. From 1908 until 1913 he travelled throughout Europe and also visited North Africa. He was in Germany when World War I broke out, and was interned along with all Russian subjects who were trapped in Germany at that time. During the war years he studied medicine at the University of Berlin, and worked in a hospital. In 1919 he made his first trip to the United States, but soon after he decided to return to Berlin to continue his studies. In 1924 he moved to Paris and remained there until Hitler's troops invaded in 1940, when he fled first to Spain, and then to New York.

Several times between 1925 and 1936 he attempted to emigrate to Israel, but failed to receive the help he sought from the Zionist organizations. He felt he was being treated unfairly, and he became embittered against them. At the end of 1949 he finally arrived in Tel Aviv. He later settled in the Orthodox town of Ramat Gan, back among his Hasidic roots. He stayed in Israel for six years but returned to Europe due to his failing health, and then to America where he died in New York in 1959. At the end of 1960 his remains were flown from America to Israel and interred in a final resting place in the old cemetery in Tel Aviv.

Between the wars, Schneour wrote almost exclusively in Yiddish for the American Yiddish press and became one of the most widely read Yiddish authors. In the 1950s he wrote for several Israeli newspapers, revised his Hebrew poetry and prose which were printed in various publications, and he adapted his story *Pandre hagibor* (*Pandre the Hero*) into a stage drama that was performed by the prestigious Habima company in Tel Aviv. Some of his poems set to music in a folk style, such as "Margaritkelekh" [Daisies], "Karshn" [Cherries] and "Friling" [Spring], are among the best known and best loved of Yiddish folksongs, and are still sung today. His ironic lyrics highlight human folly.

In the United States, at the end of World War II, many Jewish writers chose as the themes for their fiction the Holocaust and the period preceding it. But some, Schneour among them, steered away from explicit reference to the raw pain of the immediate past, and cultivated a vogue for the Yiddish historical novel, in which Jewish suffering could be reconstructed in the remoteness of the distant past. Schneour's *Kayzer un rebe* [The Emperor and the Rabbi] appeared in five volumes between 1944 and 1952.

Like his earliest mentors, Mendele, Bialik and others, Schneour was successful in bridging the gulf that existed in Israel between Hebrew and Yiddish. He wrote with equal skill in both Jewish languages: the newly-established Hebrew of the Zionist movements and Israel, in which he is thought to have written his best poetry, and Yiddish, the language of the Diaspora and eastern European socialism, in which he is most admired for his prose. He wrote of the shtetl, the small Jewish communities in eastern Europe, but on different themes and of other characters from Sholem Aleichem. The fragility of the balance of the self-contained, mutually supportive, God-fearing, but pitifully poor community and the tiny changes in circumstance of one of its members that can entirely rock that balance are among his themes. He studied human frailty with the best intentions and neither glorified nor patronized his characters, but portrayed them as possessing great fortitude in difficult circumstances.

DEVRA KAY

Schnitzler, Arthur

Austrian dramatist and fiction writer, 1862–1931

Born in Vienna, 15 May 1862. Studied medicine at University of Vienna from 1879–85, MD 1885. Voluntary service in military hospital, 1885, then assistant doctor in Vienna; opened private surgery, 1893. Member of Jung Wien literary circle. Married Olga Gussmann, 1903; separated, 1921; one son and one daughter. Awards included Bauernfeld Prize, 1899, 1903; Grillparzer Prize, 1908; Raimund Prize, 1910; Vienna Volkstheater Prize, 1914. Died 21 October 1931.

Selected Writings

Collections

Gesammelte Werke [Collected Works], 7 vols, 1912; enlarged edition, 9 vols, 1922

Gesammelte Werke [Collected Works], edited by Robert O. Weiss, 5 vols, 1961–67

Plays and Stories, edited and translated by Egon Schwarz, 1982

Illusion and Reality: Plays and Stories, translated by Paul F. Dvorak, 1986

Plays

Anatol (cycle of seven one-act plays; produced as a cycle 1910), 1893; edited by Ernst L. Offermann, 1964; as *Anatol: A Sequence of Dialogues*, translated by H. Granville-Barker, 1911; as *The Affairs of Anatol*, 1933; translated by Charles Osborne, in *The Round Dance and Other Plays*, 1982; translated by Frank Marcus, 1982

Liebelei, 1895; as *Light-o'-Love*, translated by Bayard Quincy Morgan, in *The Drama*, 1912; as *Playing with Love*, translated by P. Morgan Shand, 1914; as *Love Games*, translated by Charles Osborne, in *The Round Dance and Other Plays*, 1982; as *Flirtations*, translated by Arthur S. Wensinger and Clinton J. Atkinson, in *Plays and Stories*, 1982; as *Dalliance*, translated by Tom Stoppard, with *Undiscovered Country*, 1986

Freiwild, 1897; as *Free Game*, translated by Paul Grummann, 1913

Das Vermächtnis, 1898; as *The Legacy*, translated by Mary L. Stephenson, in *Poet Lore*, 1911

Der grüne Kakadu, Paracelsus, Die Gefährtin, 1899; as *The Green Cockatoo and Other Plays* (includes *Paracelsus* and *The Mate*), translated by Horace B. Samuel, 1913; *The Green Cockatoo* and *Paracelsus* in *Paracelsus and Other One-Act Plays*, translated by G.J. Weinberger, 1995

Der Schleier der Beatrice, 1900

Reigen, 1900; scenes 4–6 produced 1903; complete production, 1912; as *Hands Around*, translated by L.D. Edwards and F.L. Glaser, 1920; as *Couples*, translated by Lily Wolfe and E.W. Titus, 1927; as *Merry-Go-Round*, translated by Frank Marcus and Jacqueline Marcus, 1953; as *La Ronde*, translated by Eric Bentley, in *From the Modern Repertoire*, edited by Bentley, 1954; as *The Round Dance*, translated by Charles Osborne, in *The Round Dance and Other Plays*, 1982

Lebendige Stunden (includes *Die Frau mit dem Dolche*; *Die letzten Masken*; *Literatur*; *Lebendige Stunden*), 1902; as *Living Hours: Four One-Act Plays* (includes *The Lady with the Dagger*; *Last Masks*; *Literature*; *Living Hours*), translated by Paul H. Grummann, 1913

Der einsame Weg, 1904; as *The Lonely Way*, translated by Edwin Björkman, 1904; as *The Lonely Road*, 1985

Zwischenspiel, 1906; as *Intermezzo*, translated by Edwin Björkman, in *Three Plays*, 1915

Die Verwandlung des Pierrot, 1908; as *The Transformation of Pierrot*, translated by G.J. Weinberger, in *Paracelsus and Other One-Act Plays*, 1995

Komtesse Mizzi; oder, Der Familientag , 1909; as *Countess Mizzie*, translated by Edwin Björkman, in *Three Plays*, 1915; as *Countess Mitzi; or, The Family Reunion*, revised translation by Egon Schwarz, in *Plays and Stories*, 1982

Der Schleier der Pierrette, 1910; as *The Veil of Pierrette*, translated by G.J. Weinberger, in *Paracelsus and Other One-Act Plays*, 1995

Das weite Land, 1911; as *Undiscovered Country*, translated by Tom Stoppard, 1980

Professor Bernhardi, 1912; edited by Martin Swales, 1972; as *Professor Bernhardi*, translated by Kate A. Pohli, 1913; translated by Hetty Landstone, 1927; translated by Louis Borell and Ronald Adam, in *Famous Plays of 1936*, 1936

Fink und Fliederbusch, 1917

Komödie der Verführung, 1924; as *Seduction Comedy*, translated by G.J. Weinberger, in *Three Late Plays*, 1992

Der Gang zum Weiher, 1926; as *The Way to the Pond*, translated by G.J. Weinberger, in *Three Late Plays*, 1992

Im Spiel der Sommerlüfte, 1929; as *Summer Breeze*, translated by G. J. Weinberger, in *The Final Plays*, 1996

The Round Dance and Other Plays, translated by Charles Osborne, 1982

Three Late Plays, translated by G.J. Weinberger, 1992

Paracelsus and Other One-Act Plays, translated by G.J. Weinberger, 1995

The Final Plays, translated by G.J. Weinberger, 1996

Fiction

Sterben, 1895; as *Dying*, translated by Harry Zohn, in *The Little Comedy and Other Stories*, 1977

Die Frau des Weisen: Novelletten [The Wife of the Wise Man: Novellas], 1898

Frau Bertha Garlan, 1901; as *Bertha Garlan*, translated by Agnes Jacques, 1913, also translated by J.H. Wisdom and Marr Murray, 1914; as *Berta Garlan*, translated by G.J. Weinberger, 1987

Leutnant Gustl, 1901; as *None but the Brave*, translated by Richard L. Simon, 1926 (reprinted as *Lieutenant Gustl*, 1993)

Die griechische Tänzerin: Novellen [The Greek Dancing Girl: Novellas], 1905

Dämmerseelen: Novellen [Twilight Souls: Novellas], 1907

Der Weg ins Freie, 1908; as *The Road to the Open*, translated by Horace B. Samuel, 1923

Masken und Wunder: Novellen [Masks and Miracles], 1912

Frau Beate und ihr Sohn, 1913; as *Beatrice*, translated by Agnes Jacques, 1926

Doktor Gräsler, Badearzt, 1917; as *Dr. Graesler*, translated by E.C. Slade, 1923

Casanovas Heimfahrt, 1918; as *Casanova's Homecoming*, translated by Eden Paul and Cedar Paul, 1921

Der Mörder [The Murderer], 1922

The Shepherd's Pipe and Other Stories, translated by O.F. Theis, 1922

Fräulein Else, 1924; as *Fräulein Else*, translated by Robert A. Simon, 1925; translated by F.H. Lyon, 1925

Die Frau des Richters, 1925; as "The Judge's Wife", translated by Peter Bauland, in *The Little Comedy and Other Stories*, 1977

Traumnovelle, 1926; as "Fridolin and Albertine", translated by Erich Posselt, *Vanity Fair* (October 1926); as *Rhapsody: A Dream Novel*, translated by Otto P. Schinnerer, 1927

Spiel im Morgengrauen, 1927; as *Daybreak*, translated by William A. Drake, 1927

Therese: Chronik eines Frauenlebens, 1928; as *Theresa: The Chronicle of a Woman's Life*, translated by William A. Drake, 1928

Flucht in die Finsternis, 1931; as *Flight into Darkness*, translated by William A. Drake, 1931

Viennese Novelettes, translated by W.A. Drake *et al.*, 1931

Vienna 1900: Games with Love and Death, translated by Robert Muller, 1973

Other

Buch der Sprüche und Bedenken: Aphorismen und Fragmente [The Book of Sayings and Reflections: Aphorisms and Fragments], 1927

Der Geist im Wort und der Geist in der Tat, 1927; as *The Mind in Words and Action: Preliminary Remarks Concerning Two Diagrams*, translated by Robert O. Weiss, 1972

Über Krieg und Frieden [On War and Peace], 1939

Briefwechsel [Correspondence], with Otto Brahm, edited by Oskar Seidlin, 1953

Briefwechsel [Correspondence], with Georg Brandes, edited by Kurt Bergel, 1956

Briefwechsel [Correspondence], with Hugo von Hofmannsthal, edited by Therese Nickl and Heinrich Schnitzler, 1964

Jugend in Wien: eine Autobiographie, edited by Therese Nickl and Heinrich Schnitzler, 1968; as *My Youth in Vienna*, translated by Catherine Hutter, 1971

Liebe, die starb vor der Zeit: Ein Briefwechsel [Love That Died Prematurely: Correspondence], with Olga Waissnix, edited by Therese Nickl and Heinrich Schnitzler, 1970

Briefwechsel [Correspondence], with Max Reinhardt, edited by Renate Wagner, 1971

Correspondence, with Raoul Auernheimer, edited by Donald G. Daviau and Jorun B. Johns, 1972

Letters of Arthur Schnitzler to Hermann Bahr, edited by Donald G. Daviau, 1978

Briefe 1875–1912 [Letters 1875–1912], edited by Therese Nickl and Heinrich Schnitzler, 1981

Tagebuch 1909–1912 [Diary 1909–1912], edited by Peter M. Braunworth *et al.*, 1981; further volumes: *1913–1916*, 1983; *1917–1919*, 1985; *1879–1892*, 1987

Briefe 1913–1931 [Letters 1913–1931], edited by Peter M. Braunworth *et al.*, 1984

Beziehungen und Einsamkeiten: Aphorismen [Relationships and Solitudes: Aphorisms], edited by Clemens Eich, 1987

Further Reading

Allen, Richard H., *An Annotated Arthur Schnitzler Bibliography: Editions and Criticisms in German, French, and English 1879–1965*, Chapel Hill: University of North Carolina Press, 1966

Berlin, Jeffrey B., *An Annotated Arthur Schnitzler Bibliography 1965–1977*, Munich: Fink, 1978

Boetticher, Dirk von, *Meine Werke sind lauter Diagnosen: über die ärztliche Dimension im Werk Arthur Schnitzlers*, Heidelberg: Winter, 1999

Botstein, Leon, "The Jews of Vienna in the Age of Franz Joseph", *New York Times Book Review* (14 January 1990)

Farese, Giuseppe, *Arthur Schnitzler: una vita a Vienna 1862–1931*, Milan: Mondadori, 1997

Keiser, Brenda, *Deadly Dishonor: The Duel and the Honor Code in the Works of Arthur Schnitzler*, New York: Peter Lang, 1990

Kuttenberg, Eva, *The Tropes of Suicide in Arthur Schnitzler's Prose*, New York: Peter Lang, 2000

Perlmann, Michaela L., *Der Traum in der literarischen Moderne: Untersuchungen zum Werk Arthur Schnitzlers*, Munich: Fink, 1987

Roberts, Adrian Clive, *Arthur Schnitzler and Politics*, Riverside, California: Ariadne Press, 1989

Swales, Martin, *Arthur Schnitzler: A Critical Study*, Oxford: Clarendon Press, 1971

Tax, Petrus W. and Richard H. Lawson (editors), *Arthur Schnitzler and His Age: Intellectual and Artistic Currents*, Bonn: Bouvier, 1984

Thompson, Bruce, *Schnitzler's Vienna: Image of a Society*, London and New York: Routledge, 1990

Tweraser, Felix W., *Political Dimensions of Arthur Schnitzler's Late Fiction*, Columbia, South Carolina: Camden House, 1998

Weinberger, G.J., *Arthur Schnitzler's Late Plays: A Critical Study*, New York: Peter Lang, 1997

Weiner, Marc A., *Arthur Schnitzler and the Crisis of Musical Culture*, Heidelberg: Winter, 1986

Yates, William Edgar, *Schnitzler, Hofmannsthal and the Austrian Theatre*, New Haven, Connecticut: Yale University Press, 1992

Within the context of literature at the turn of the century, Arthur Schnitzler's work takes up a middle position between aestheticism and naturalism. Whereas his early plays, such as *Anatol* in 1893, can be interpreted as a typical 1890s work of art, the protagonist Anatol is at the same time a perfect example of the turn-of-the-century dandy.

As a son of a famous medical professor, Schnitzler at first followed his father's footsteps, though his father blamed him for his "mangelhaftes wissenschaftliches Gewissen" [lack of scientific conscience]. Schnitzler himself felt a strong "Abneigung gegen die Medizin, die sich in erschreckendem Maße gesteigert hatte" [aversion to medicine, which has increased in an alarming way]. Nonetheless, scientific observations play an important role in his writings. Although he finally gave up his job as a medical doctor to work as a freelance writer, Schnitzler extended his knowledge both in the psychological and the psychoanalytical field. On 5 May 1906 Freud wrote to him: "Seit vielen Jahren bin ich mir der weitreichenden Übereinstimmung bewußt, die zwischen Ihren und meinen Auffassungen besteht." [For many years I have been aware of the similarities of our opinions.] Traces of Freudian psychology can be found throughout his work, especially in *Lieutenant Gustl*, *Fräulein Else*, and *Traumnovelle* ("Fridolin and Albertine"). All three prose works provide a deep insight in the protagonists' characters, wishes, and fears. In *Lieutenant Gustl* Schnitzler combines individual psychology with an analysis of society: Gustl's aggressive psychological disposition is linked to the imperialistic state of the Austro-Hungarian empire, unveiling the perfidiousness of the military code. This is achieved by a special narrative technique, called *Innerer Monolog* (inner monologue), which was also used by James Joyce. Like many of Schnitzler's figures, neither Gustl nor Else are consistent characters in the old-fashioned sense. According to late 19th-century philosophical beliefs, as maintained for example by Ernst Mach, the "I" is not coherent anymore. Even though the protagonists believe themselves to be normal, Schnitzler peels their personalities like layers of an onion, displaying how far the dissolution of their psychological condition has already proceeded. A recurrent topic in his work is the existential crisis of an individual, a crisis that very often leads to suicide.

In addition, Schnitzler is a chronicler of intrigues and social events of the middle and upper strata of Viennese society in the first decades of the 20th century. One of his best-known plays, *Professor Bernhardi* reveals the anti-Semitic currents in Vienna that finally lead to the expelling and humiliation of Bernhardi, who is painted as a noble Jew. Like many of Schnitzler's characters, he believes in his own free will and the freedom to chose, rejecting the behavioural norms of the powerful institution he is working in. As the play was perceived to be a harsh criticism of the Vienna of that time, it was soon censored and every performance was forbidden until the end of World War II. Together with the later plays *Der einsame Weg* (*The Lonely Way*) and *Das weite Land* (*Undiscovered Country*) it can be seen as a discussion of the disintegration of society before World War I. *Der einsame Weg* unveils a society that is falling apart because it lacks traditional values: family bonds as well as the ties of love and affection become meaningless. Everybody pursues his own way, regardless of the possible advantage or disadvantage of others.

Der grüne Kakadu (*The Green Cockatoo*) is a play within a play: while the French revolution is taking place outside, a mime troupe is performing a play about a revolution in a pub named Der grüne Kakadu. Deliberately ignoring reality, the actors go on playing until the revolutionaries enter the scene. Apart from experiments like this, Schnitzler was all his life concerned with the growing anti-Semitism in Austria. In *Professor Bernhardi*, *Der Weg ins Freie* (*The Road to the Open*) and in his autobiography *Jugend in Wien* (first edited 1968) anti-Semitism plays an important role. *Fink und Fliederbusch* is a comedy about journalists that shows the frailty of truth: the arguments between a conservative and the liberal journalist become completely absurd, because both turn out to be the same person in the end. Thus, both the rites and habits of an outdated epoch, in this case the duel, are rendered ridiculous.

Today Schnitzler is regarded as one of the most important Austrian writers of the turn of the 20th century. In a unique way, he combined Freudian psychoanalysis with fiction and an awareness of anti-Semitism, preparing the path for many writers to follow.

BIRGIT HAAS

Schulz, Bruno

Polish fiction writer, 1892–1942

Born in Drohobycz, 1892. Youngest child of Jakub and Henrietta Schulz. Educated at grammar school in Drohobycz, 1902–10; studied architecture in Lwów, 1910–11. Moved to Vienna, 1917; returned to Drohobycz after three months. Art teacher in Drohobycz, 1924–39; illustrated own works and *Ferdydurke* by Witold Gombrowicz. Polish Academy of Letters Golden Laurel award, 1938. Shot in Drohobycz ghetto by Gestapo officer, 19 November 1942.

Selected Writings

Collections

Proza, edited by Artur Sandauer and Jerzy Ficowski, 1964; revised edition, 1973

The Complete Fiction, translated by Celina Wieniewska, 1989

Fiction

Księga bałwochwalcza, 1922; as *The Booke of Idolatry*, edited by Jerzy Ficowski, translated by Bogna Piotrowska, 1988(?)

Sklepy cynamonowe, 1934; translated by Celina Wieniewska as *The Street of Crocodiles*, 1963; as *Cinnamon Shops and Other Stories*, 1963; as *The Fictions of Bruno Schulz*, 1988

Sanatorium pod klepsydrą, 1937; as *Sanatorium under the Sign of the Hourglass*, translated by Celina Wieniewska, 1978

Other

Księga listów [A Book of Letters], edited by Jerzy Ficowski, 1975

Listy, fragmenty, wspomnienia o pisarzu [Letters, Fragments, and Reminiscences about Writing], edited by Jerzy Ficowski, 1984

Letters and Drawings, with Selected Prose, edited by Jerzy Ficowski, translated by Walter Arndt and Victoria Nelson, 1988

Opowiadania, wybór esejów i listów [Stories, Selections, Essays, and Letters], edited by Jerzy Ficowski, 1989

The Drawings of Bruno Schulz, edited by Jerzy Ficowski, 1990

Ilustracje do własnych utworow, edited by Jerzy Ficowski, 1992

Further Reading

Brown, Russell E., "Metamorphosis in Bruno Schulz", *Polish Review*, 30 (1985)

Brown, Russell E., "Bruno Schulz: The Myth of Origins", *Russian Literature*, 22 (1987)

Brown, Russell E., "Schulz's Sanatorium Story: Myth and Confession", *Polish Perspectives*, 30 (1987)

Brown, Russell E., "Bruno Schulz and Franz Kafka: Servant Girls and Other Temptations", *Germano-Slavica*, 6/1(1988)

Brown, Russell E., "Bruno Schulz and World Literature", *Slavic and East European Journal* (Summer 1990)

Brown, Russell E., *Myths and Relatives: Seven Essays on Bruno Schulz*, Munich: Sagner, 1991

Budurowycz, Bohdan, "Galicia in the Work of Bruno Schulz", *Canadian Slavonic Papers*, 28 (1986)

Drozdowski, Piotr J., "Bruno Schulz and the Myth of the Book", *Indiana Slavic Studies*, 5 (1990)

Ficowski, Jerzy, *Regiony wielkiej herezji*, Kraków: Wydawnictwo Literackie, 1967

Goldfarb, David, "Czytając Schulza" [Reading Schulz], *Kresy*, 13 (1993): 17–18
Jastrzębski, Jerzy, *Schulz*, Wrocław: Wydawnictwo Dolnośląskie, 1999
Kuryluk, Ewa, "The Caterpillar Car; or, Bruno Schulz Drives into the Future of the Past", in *The Drawings of Bruno Schulz*, edited by Jerzy Ficowski, Evanston: Northwestern University Press, 1990
Lukashevich, Olga, "Bruno Schulz's *The Street of Crocodiles*: A Study in Creativity and Neurosis", *Polish Review*, 13 (1968)
Miron, Dan, *The Image of the Shtetl*, Syracuse, New York: Syracuse University Press, 2000
Panas, Władysław, *Księga blasku* [The Book of Lustre], Lublin: Towarzystwo Naukowe KUL, 1997
Polonsky, Antony and Monika Adamczyk-Garbowska, introduction to *Contemporary Jewish Writing in Poland*, Lincoln: University of Nebraska Press, 2001
Prokopczyk, Czeslaw (editor), *Bruno Schulz: New Documents and Interpretations,* New York: Peter Lang, 1999
Robertson, Theodosia S., "Time in Bruno Schulz", *Indiana Slavic Studies*, 5 (1990)
Shmeruk, Chone, "Isaac Bashevis Singer on Bruno Schulz", *Polish Review*, 36/2 (1991): 161–67
Stala, Krzysztof, *On the Margins of Reality: The Paradoxes of Representation in Bruno Schulz's Fiction*, Stockholm: Almqvist och Wiksell, 1993
Taylor, Coleen M., "Childhood Revisited: The Writings of Bruno Schulz", *Slavic and East European Journal*, 13 (1969)
Wegrocki, Henry, "Masochistic Motives in the Literary and Graphic Art of Bruno Schulz", *Psychoanalytical Review*, 33 (1946)

Dan Miron, while discussing the concept of "Jewish literature" in *The Image of the Shtetl*, poses a very significant question about the limits of its scope. Namely, does it include the literary output of Jewish writers who wrote in the languages of European and American cultures and for those audiences? Furthermore, does it include only the works with so-called "Jewish essence" and how could this essence be defined? Bruno Schulz, the assimilated Polish-Jewish writer and artist from the inter-war Drohobycz (before World War II in Poland, now Ukraine), serves as a perfect example of this ambiguity, the question of his "Jewishness" arousing many controversies. As Jerzy Jastrzębski notices, some critics underline his dependence on Judaism, its philosophy and mysticism, claiming that the main plots and motifs of Schulz's prose can be explained by them. Others emphasize the writer's cross-cultural creative background – Jewish, Polish, and German – arguing that Judaism and Jewish culture are only one of the elements of this background.

Thus, Schulz's literary world of *Sklepy cynamonowe* (*Cinnamon Shops*) and *Sanatorium pod klepsydrą* (*Sanatorium under the Sign of the Hourglass*) and its integral mythology seem to be permeated with the traces of Jewish tradition although they are never straightforward, and demand a deeper insight into the writer's imagery.

One of the main ideas dominating Schulz's mystical prose is the myth of the beginning of the world. Schulz uses the biblical metaphor of God and His Word with its creative power as a perfectly united being. Their separation becomes the cause of the whole creation and its subsequent enormous, stunning diversity as well as unavoidable departure from the initial idealistic state. Therefore, Schulz focuses in his prose on the tendency of people and nature to return to their origins, to look for the perfect order of the beginning, the so called "splendid epoch of childhood" on the one hand and the need for expansion, searching for something new on the other. *Cinnamon Shops* and Schulz's letters, especially the one to Andrzej Pleśniewicz were the basis of Władysław Panas's theory presented in *Księga blasku* [The Book of Lustre]. He discovered the similarity between Schulz's motifs and the Kabbalistic theory of Isaac Luria. According to the latter the world is emanated by God, who as infinite and powerful Creator has to retreat into himself to make space for his creation. Therefore, Schulz's longing for childhood, symbolically presented in his fiction as "The Book", "The Authentic", constitutes at the same time longing for the absolute beginning of the universe, the original though never realized divine plan of creation.

This eschatological plot leads to another recurring motif of Schulz's prose, so characteristic for Jewish beliefs – the arrival of the Messiah. Schulz's Messiah, however, is not the liberator of Israel, the missing step in the world's history. His arrival, as suggested in "Belle Epoque", would correlate in time with the return to the original purity and unity of the world, its "splendid epoch", symbolic childhood. With that, as Panas reveals, the whole history, the chaos and imperfections of the creation, so vividly presented in Schulz's works, would disappear. Redemption would become a completed act. This theme was to be developed in Schulz's unfinished and lost novel *Messiah*, which according to Jerzy Ficowski, one of Schulz's most devoted critics, was meant to have been the essence of the writer's career.

The important element of Schulz's mythology is the concept of time. Seemingly rhythmical, it still has its strange insubordinate byways and branches – unusual periods of dream or the border of dream and reality when everything is possible. Schulz compares these periods to, among other things, a freak month. (For a detailed analysis of Schulz's concept of time see Goldfarb (1993) and Jastrzębski (1999).) The idea of such a month can be traced within the Jewish calendar which periodically adds the 13th month to cover the discrepancy between the lunar and solar systems of the year. Such a "freak" time seems to be equally important for Schulz's world as the moment of real artistic creation possessing a redemptive function.

The descriptions of the weird protagonists of *Cinnamon Shops* are a perfect occasion for Schulz to resort to biblical metaphors. This is the case with one of Schulz's main motifs – the figure of the narrator's father, Jacob, presented as a patriarch of the family, the merchant governing his assistants like an ancient prophet, leader of the nation. The child narrator equates him to Noah among birds, the sage unraveling the philosophical, metaphysical ideas, or the biblical Jacob fighting with the Angel. But even he does not escape the ironic fate of Schulz's protagonists – finally degraded to the position of a lusty old man slowly changing into a cockroach.

Schulz's drawings and paintings are also significant artistic creations. The majority of these black and white graphics, including the writer's self-portraits and the famous series *Księga bałwochwalcza* (*The Booke of Idolatry*) touch upon the erotic sphere, presenting grotesque scenes with beautiful lofty naked women and dwarf-like men humiliated at their feet (see Kuryluk, 1990). Another aspect of his art is his portraits of Drohobycz Jews during their traditional holidays or gatherings. The best of Schulz's surviving paintings, *The Meeting*, shows two young women passing by a Hasid against the dim panorama of Drohobycz. Thus, in Schulz's graphic works, as in his writing, Jewish life is a natural picturesque part of the presented world, bearing a mystery worth pursuing.

Searching for the roots of Schulz's artistic creation requires acknowledging the integral mystery of his prose. Although the writer draws from different cultures and traditions, including the Jewish one, their elements merge and never escape the power of his transforming imagination. I.B. Singer's comments on Schulz's prose are perfect evidence of the indirect character of its "Jewishness":

> Nazi bullets killed a man who embodied the powers and whims of a master. If Schulz weren't or didn't want to be alienated from the Jewish environment, uprooted from Judaism, he wouldn't have lost so much energy on mocking, parodying, he wouldn't have to create literature on the basis of other literature (see Shmeruk).

But was Schulz really alienated? Wasn't he rather a visitor to the most mysterious spheres of Jewish culture?

KATARZYNA WIECLAWSKA

Schütz, David

German-born Israeli fiction writer and scriptwriter, 1941–

Born in Berlin, 5 August 1941. Emigrated to Israel with his brother at age seven. Served in Israeli army as a captain in the artillery, 1960–63. Studied history and philosophy at the Hebrew University, Jerusalem, 1963–68, BA and MA; studied history in Heidelberg, 1970–72. Divorced; two children. Documentary film producer for Israeli Film Service, Jerusalem; scriptwriter and novelist. Awarded Agnon Prize, 1992; Prime Minister's Prize, 1979, 1993.

Selected Writings

Novels
Haesev vehahol [The Grass and the Sand], 1978; revised version, with afterword by Yigal Schwartz, 1991
Ad olam ahakeh [I Shall Wait Forever], 1987
Shoshan lavan shoshan adom [White Rose, Red Rose], 1988
Avishag, 1990
Sheva nashim [Seven Women], 1995
Kemo nahar [Like a River], 1997

Short Stories
Hahizdamnut haaharona [The Last Chance], 1980

For Children
Yoman zahav [The Golden Diary], 1991

Further Reading

Holtzman, Avner, "The Memory as Kaleidoscope, an Examination of David Schütz's *White Rose, Red Rose*", *Alei Siach*, 26 (1999)
Navot, Amnon, "The Novel in its Own Chains", *Massa* (21 July 1987)

David Schütz emigrated to Israel in 1948 with the youth movement (*Aliyat HaNoar*). In Israel, he lived with foster families, and later in youth institutions. He was never raised by his mother and, although he met her a few times as an adult, he never came to understand the mystery of his childhood and his family.

Schütz entered the consciousness of Israeli culture in 1978 when his first book, *Haesev vehahol* [The Grass and the Sand], was published. This book became a bestseller and was an object of great interest both on the part of the critics who offered either lavish praise or complete censure, and on the part of the readers. In an interview, Schütz noted that he tried to write a mythical, fictional biography. In fact, his books contain extensive biographical elements, and the central focus of this one was the attempt to come to terms with his childhood and his mother's abandonment of him. In order to understand this, the narrator Immanuel goes back four generations and examines the course of a family curse through the biography of the women in the family. The first character in the chain is his grandmother, who was born of adultery, and sexually abused by her father as punishment. After running away from her village, she marries a Jew and converts to Judaism, and at the beginning of World War II she abandons her daughter, Lotta Miriam, in her parents' home. The sins of adultery and abandonment become the driving force in the life of Lotta Miriam and her family. She bears four children to three separate men, and abandons them, one by one, at the home of her neighbours: a non Jewish woman and her husband, a member of the Nazi party. The children grow as weeds, untended, and each carries differently the consequences of the mother's betrayal.

The Grass and the Sand explores in a magnified manner the central themes of Schütz's later creations. Feminine strength, in its various layers (the mother, the wife, the lover, the whore), and its influence on the protagonist, who is completely under its force, comprises a powerful issue in Schütz's work, one to which he returns again and again, perhaps because it contains the answer to his questions. It is also possible that this is the reason that many of his works are written from a feminine perspective. The delving into the past is also a fixed motif in his stories, arising from the same desperation to understand, and in that delving into the past and the memories, he always returns to the parents' betrayal. A common motif in his books is the picture of the child, lying in his bed, hearing his parents whispering their plans to strangle or murder him one way or another.

In a manner similar to Aharon Appelfeld, Schütz describes in his books the fate of the immigrant children, Holocaust survivors, who arrived in Israel from Europe upon the establishment of the State of Israel, and met with a reality hostile to their foreignness, in which the admission ticket is the assimilation and the erasing of the past. This theme is common also to stories written by Oriental immigrants, such as Shimon Ballas, Eli Amir, and others, who describe the difficult and humiliating encounter with veterans in Israel, and the difficulty in finding and establishing their place and identity there.

Stylistically, Schütz belongs to an expressionistic writing movement, which is guided by empowerment and emotional expression. The reality that is magnified in a text does not demand to be logically realistic, but to expose the soul, the internal, empowered self, and the majority of literary elements (confession, letters, diaries, a network of points-of-view) are thus subject to the expression of the human, emotional situation, the longing, the desire to end the mysteries and miseries that are embedded in his life story. Yet along with the hyperbolic expression of the soul, Schütz brings a moderating perspective, which avoids direct contact with the soul's exposed nerves. In his style, Schütz is close to Yoram Kaniuk, who is considered an expressionistic writer, as well as the hyper-realistic German writing tradition represented by Gunther Grass, and Jerzy Kosinski, the Pole.

Schütz's second book, *Hahizdamnut haaharona* [The Last Chance], a collection of short stories and novellas, in a somewhat surrealistic allegorical style, did not earn the critics' approval. In the majority of the stories, the supposedly orderly world is upset by some kind of madness, murder, sexual promiscuity, and abandonment. The feeling of decay, which is cutting at the roots of human existence, is sharpened by the motif of the axe, which appears again and again in the various stories.

After the book's failure, Schütz settled into seven years of silence, following which two books were published in fairly close sequence: *Ad olam ahakeh* [I Shall Wait Forever] in 1987 and *Shoshan lavan shoshan adom* [White Rose, Red Rose] in 1988. *I Shall Wait Forever* appears to be a characteristic Israeli novel, describing the non-religious experience in Jerusalem of the 1980s. It is, however, actually the story of Peretz, the son of European immigrants, who arrived in Israel at the end of the 1930s and settled in a *moshav* (an agricultural settlement). Here, too, the unloved child is abandoned by his parents, who return to Europe, the land of the longing, and the boy is left with his step-uncle, Yedidiah. After the uncle breaks the law, the child is sent to a juvenile facility, where he must contend with groups of violent youths, and learn to survive. It is no wonder then, that the driving force in the plot is the longing of Peretz, the detached child who grew up, for a home, a family, and a normal relationship that will satisfy his hunger for warmth and love. But the novel opens at the shattering of the dream: Peretz is aware of the fact that his wife, Raheli, is betraying him. The story carries him through his futile attempts to hold onto these fragments, to try to mend the pieces. Other characters also experience betrayal, and are unable to fulfil in their adult life the ultimate love that was denied them as children.

As in *The Grass and the Sand*, this novel and those that follow it are remarkable for their complex architecture, in the multiplicity of standpoints from which the various parts of the plot are presented, sometimes illuminating or giving another perspective to a portion of the story already told. Particularly of note are the expressionistic elements.

White Rose, Red Rose tells the story of six displaced children. The children arrive in Israel from Europe, and are sent to foster families in a pastoral village. In each of the three parts of the book a variation of forbidden, dark, and destructive love is presented: the erotic love story of Lily and Nehemiah, who are raised as brother and sister; the story of the handsome Goldin's love for the whore Margo, love that leads him to a murder considered as patricide; and finally the story of the sexual relationship between Felix, the immigrant boy, and the woman who adopted him in his youth.

In the forefront of these stories of transplantation, Schütz gives expression to the voices of the immigrants and the refugees, the same characters who are generally pushed to the margins and through whose stories, the desperate search for identity and belonging is described. Additionally, he describes difficult encounters with Israeli society, which ignores the difficulties of the immigrant.

The novel *Avishag* again expresses Schütz's almost compulsive need to decipher femininity and its power. The main characters are dark, dramatic, powerful women, who choke their male victims. It seems that his constant musing about female power expresses the painful absence of the great mother, an absence for which he seeks to compensate in his various female characters.

Also of note is *Yoman zahav* [The Golden Diary] from 1991, a children's book describing a summer in a Youth Centre. Here, clear autobiographical elements enter the story from Schütz's own childhood in such an institution. One of the more interesting elements is the manner in which the main character succeeds in surviving among other violent and powerful youths. The child becomes a sought-after storyteller, and the ability to tell a story is perceived as power both by the child and by his environment. Here we return to *The Grass and the Sand* as a starting point, the book that tries to make order of memory, to create a memory that doesn't exist, to create an identity, but also to come to terms with characters who hurt the narrator. Immanuel, the "historian", keeps a red book of judgement, in which he lists those from whom he must seek revenge. It seems that in writing the novel the narrator realizes the book of judgement, and closes accounts with those who harmed him. Thus, the book itself becomes an act of power, power to remember what does not exist in memory, to create an identity, to attempt to understand, and further, to avenge, all of which provide a cleansing element in this modern story of misery.

BATYA SHIMONY

Schwartz, Delmore

US poet, dramatist, and short story writer, 1913–1966

Born in Brooklyn, New York, 8 December 1913, to Harry Schwartz and wife Rose (née Nathanson), Romanian immigrants. Studied at Townsend Harris High School and George Washington High School, New York (first published poems in *Poet's Pack of George Washington High School*, 1929), graduated 1931; University of Wisconsin, Madison, 1931–32; New York University, 1933–35, BA in philosophy 1935; Harvard University, 1935–37. Married, first, Gertrude Buckman, 1938; separated, 1943, divorced, 1944; second, Elizabeth Pollet, 1949; separated, 1955. Briggs–Copeland instructor in English composition, 1940, instructor in English, 1941–45, and assistant professor of English, 1946–47, Harvard University; lecturer, New School for Social Research and New York University, late 1940s; Gauss Lecturer, 1949, and visiting professor, 1952, Princeton University; professor of English, Syracuse University, 1962–66. Poetry editor, 1939, editor, 1943–47, and associate editor, 1947–55, *Partisan Review*; poetry editor and film critic, *New Republic*, Washington, DC, 1955–57. Many awards, including Guggenheim Fellowship, 1940, 1941; American Academy of Arts and Letters Award in Literature, 1953; Bollingen Prize, 1960; Shelley Memorial Award, 1960. Died 11 July 1966.

Selected Writings

Poetry

In Dreams Begin Responsibilities (includes short story and play), 1938
Genesis: Book One, 1943
Vaudeville for a Princess and Other Poems, 1950
Summer Knowledge: New and Selected Poems 1938–1958, 1959; revised as *Selected Poems 1938–1958: Summer Knowledge*, 1967
What is To Be Given: Selected Poems, edited by Douglas Dunn, 1976
Last and Lost Poems, edited by Robert Phillips, 1979

Plays

Choosing Company in *The New Caravan*, edited by Alfred Kreymborg, 1936
Shenandoah; or, The Naming of the Child, 1941
Shenandoah and Other Verse Plays, edited by Robert Phillips, 1992

Fiction

The World is a Wedding and Other Stories, 1948
Successful Love and Other Stories, 1961
In Dreams Begin Responsibilities and Other Stories, edited by James Atlas, 1978

Other

Translator, *A Season in Hell*, by Arthur Rimbaud, 1939; revised edition 1940
American Poetry at Mid-Century, with John Crowe Ransom and John Hall Wheelock, 1958
Editor, *Syracuse Poems 1964*, 1965
Selected Essays, edited by Donald A. Dike and David H. Zucker, 1970
I am Cherry Alive, the Little Girl Sang, 1979
Letters, edited by Robert Phillips, 1984
Portrait of Delmore: Journals and Notes 1939–1959, edited by Elizabeth Pollet, 1986
The Ego is Always at the Wheel: Bagatelles, edited by Robert Phillips, 1986
Delmore Schwartz and James Laughlin: Selected Letters, edited by Robert Phillips, 1993

Further Reading

Ashbery, John, *The Heavy Bear: Delmore Schwartz's Life versus His Poetry*, Tokyo: English Literary Society of Japan, 1996
Atlas, James, *Delmore Schwartz: The Life of an American Poet*, New York: Farrar Straus, 1977
Barrett, William, *The Truants: Adventures among the Intellectuals*, New York: Doubleday, 1982
Bawer, Bruce, *The Middle Generation: The Lives and Poetry of Delmore Schwartz, Randall Jarrell, John Berryman and Robert Lowell*, Hamden: Connecticut: Archon, 1986
Grayson, Richard, *I Brake for Delmore Schwartz: Stories*, Somerville, Massachusetts: Zephyr Press, 1983
Labuz, Ronald, "Delmore Schwartz: A Bibliographical Checklist", *American Book Collector* (July–August 1983)
McDougall, Richard, *Delmore Schwartz*, New York: Twayne, 1974
New, Elisa, "Reconsidering Delmore Schwartz", *Prooftexts*, 5 (1985)

Publishing his debut collection at the age of 24 to exuberant acclaim, Delmore Schwartz quickly established a reputation as a leader in a new generation of American poets, a generation that came to include Robert Lowell, Randall Jarrell, and John Berryman. "The pathos and controlled intensity of his style", writes his biographer James Atlas, "fused the language of the Jewish immigrants among whom Schwartz had grown up with a Modernist weariness that echoed Baudelaire." Perhaps the tragedy of Schwartz's life – dissipation, madness, early death – has overshadowed the body of poetry, prose, and criticism he left behind, texts that can be regarded as exemplars of high modernism as well as poignantly and self-consciously Jewish-American.

Perhaps Schwartz's most famous short story is the brilliant "In Dreams Begin Responsibilities", which appeared as the lead piece in the first issue of *Partisan Review* in 1937, and again one year later in the collection of the same name. The protagonist of the story finds himself in a darkened movie theatre where he watches, on a silent screen, his young parents re-enact their courtship. The narrator, increasingly distressed as his parents move closer towards what he knows will be a disastrous marriage, begins to shout. He is escorted out of the theatre by an usher, and at that moment wakes up to the morning of his 21st birthday. Inspired, no doubt, by Delmore's own parents' unhappy marriage, the story is a keen portrait of a generation and its peculiar mixture of cultural anxiety and pride. In introducing Schwartz's stock protagonist, the alienated Jewish son who nevertheless cannot seem to escape his parents, the story also introduces, in the words of Elisa New, the "specifically Jewish symbiosis and paralysis, a conflation of generations" that Schwartz would continue to dramatize. The story also foregrounds the cinema – long an obsession of Schwartz's – and in particular the role of American mass culture in scripting and mediating the experience of Jewish immigrants and their children.

Schwartz wrote that his Jewishness became "available to me as a central symbol of alienation, bias, point of view, and certain other characteristics which are the peculiar marks of modern life, and, as I think now, the essential ones". In *Shenandoah*, Schwartz's verse play, the Jewish poet Shenandoah Fish (a cognate of "Delmore Schwartz") witnesses, from off stage, the drama of his naming. Elsie Fish picks the name out of a society page account of a Shenandoah Valley estate; family arguments ensue, and the child is finally named after Walter Fish's Irish-Catholic attorney gives his blessing. The play ends with the infant's *bris*, and the adult Shenandoah glosses: "A Jew forever! quickly taught the life/ That he must lead, an heir to lasting pain:/ Do I exaggerate, do I with hindsight see/ The rise of Hitler?"

Genesis, Schwartz's long poem that he worked on for over a decade, fuses blank verse with what Schwartz called "Biblical prose", and documents the history of "Hershey Green's" family (an analogue for Schwartz's own) from eastern Europe to America, in biblical, epic proportions. The poem is a type of *Bildungsroman*, documenting the development of Hershey Green's consciousness in episodes from Schwartz's own autobiography, and was heavily influenced by Schwartz's reading of Freud. Originally planned as the first instalment in a sweeping epic that was intended to rival Pound's *Cantos*, the poem's tepid critical reception made Schwartz abandon the project. Schwartz returned to biblical themes in his collection *Summer Knowledge*, with such poems as "Abraham," "Sarah", "Jacob", published alongside older poems such as "Abraham and Orpheus" and "Starlight like Intuition Pierced the Twelve". The themes persistent in these poems are alienation and exile, memory and inheritance. In "Abraham", for instance, the patriarch struggles with the command to sacrifice his son, and concludes: "An alien to myself until at last the caste of the last/ alienation/ The angel of death comes to make the alienated and/ indestructible one a part of his famous society."

Shenandoah Fish reappears in several stories in Schwartz's collection *The World is a Wedding* , notably in "America, America!" Based on Rose Schwartz's (Delmore's mother's) stories about their neighbours, the Salomons, the story records Mrs Fish's long narrative about the Baumanns, told to her son Shenandoah, a young, stagnated writer. Schwartz captures the intonations and mannerisms of his parents' generation in the voice of Mrs Fish, and in the portrait of the Baumann family describes the vulgarity and ambition of two generations of Jewish Americans. The collection, James Atlas writes, "really constituted a portrait of two generations: Delmore's parents and those second-generation Jews known as the New York intellectuals (many of whom could recognize themselves in these stories) . . . His sense of the frailty of people . . . is forgiving but unsparingly critical." The title story of the collection is a thinly veiled and cuttingly satirical portrait of the poet Paul Goodman and his circle; "New Year's Eve" describes the members of the *Partisan Review* crowd with whom Goodman was associated, including Dwight MacDonald, Lionel Abel, William Barrett, and Schwartz himself, as, once again, Shenandoah Fish. Delmore's own family – the uncle who died young, his handsome, philandering father, the battles between his parents, and his ne'er-do-well uncle – is the subject of "The Child is the Meaning of This Life". Schwartz chronicles the tensions of unfulfilled ambition, the claustrophobia of his and his parents' sphere, and personal and cultural paralysis.

Schwartz was a true intellectual poet, schooled in Western philosophy, an avid reader of Pound, Eliot, and Joyce, a translator of Rimbaud, a distinguished and thoughtful literary critic in the pages of numerous publications. In contrast, however, to the Jewish-American heroes of Saul Bellow and Philip Roth, peripatetic and freewheeling protagonists in the style of Huck Finn, Schwartz's protagonists (all versions of himself) all seem, as Elisa New notes, to "linger in their mother's kitchens through middle age, eating late breakfasts and rehashing petty quarrels". The failure of Schwartz's protagonists to "take off" is paralleled by the interruptedness of his own career, his descent into manic depression, paranoia, insanity, and a premature heart attack.

RACHEL RUBINSTEIN

Schwarz-Bart, André

French fiction writer, 1928–

Born in Metz, 23 May 1928, to Polish immigrant parents, both deported and killed by 1941. Reportedly taught himself to read and write French from library books; studied at the Sorbonne. Member, French resistance, and later prisoner in German concentration camp, during World War II. Mechanic, salesman, miner, librarian, foundry labourer; left foundry to write, 1959. Married Simone Bruman, Guadeloupean writer, 1960; two sons. Awarded Prix Goncourt, 1959; Jerusalem Prize, 1967.

Selected Writings

Novels

Le Dernier des Justes, 1959; as *The Last of the Just*, translated by Stephen Becker, 1961

Un Plat de porc aux bananes vertes [A Plate of Pork with Green Bananas], with Simone Schwarz-Bart, 1967

La mulâtresse Solitude, with Simone Schwarz-Bart, 1972; as *A Woman Named Solitude*, translated by Ralph Manheim, 1973

Further Reading

Atlantic Monthly (March 1973)

Commentary (May 1973)

Gyssels, Kathleen, *Filles de solitude: essai sur l'identité antillaisé dans les (auto)biographies fictives de Simone et André Schwarz-Bart*, Paris: L'Harmattan, 1996

Kahn, Lothar, *Mirrors of the Jewish Mind: A Gallery of Portraits of European Jewish Writers of Our Time*, New York: Yoseloff, 1968

Lehrmann, Chanan, *The Jewish Element in French Literature*, translated by George Klin, Rutherford, New Jersey: Fairleigh Dickinson University Press, 1971 (French version, 1961)

National Review (16 March 1973)

New Statesman (10 February 1961)
New York Review of Books (22 March 1973)
New York Times (19 February 1967)
New York Times Book Review (16 April 1967; 11 February 1973)
Yudkin, Leon I., *A Home Within: Varieties of Jewish Expression in Modern Fiction*, Northwood, Middlesex: Symposium Press, 1996

André Schwarz-Bart's major work, for which he was awarded the prestigious Goncourt prize in 1959, is entitled *The Last of the Just*. It is a powerful, epic tale which traces the history of the fictional character Ernie Levy, the "Last of the Just" of the title, from his birth in the small German town of Stillenstadt to the gas chambers of Auschwitz-Birkenau. Ernie is one of the 36 just men or *tzaddikim* who, in each generation, in Schwarz-Bart's interpretation of this Talmudic legend, take the sufferings of the world on their shoulders. As Schwarz-Bart states, the Lamed-vavs (literally, "36s") are the "hearts of the world multiplied, into which all our griefs are poured, as into one receptacle", without which "the sufferings of mankind would poison even the souls of the new-born".

Through the fate of the ascendants of Ernie Levy, Schwarz-Bart presents us with a chronicle of the spectacular cruelties of Christian anti-Judaism in Europe, starting with the martyrdom of Rabbi Yom Tov Levy who led the community of York at the time of the York massacre of 1185 and from whom Ernie is supposedly descended. The history proceeds via accusations of ritual murder, of well-poisoning, witchcraft and spreading plague to forced conversions, expulsions, inquisition, mass drownings, and more. With the life-story of Ernie Levy himself, we are to learn the terrible tale of anti-Semitism in Europe in the second quarter of the 20th century.

In tracing Ernie's lineage, it evolves that each of the Just is not always aware of his awesome role, and it is with delicate irony that Schwarz-Bart depicts the surprising figures who emerge among the descendants of the Levys of York. A Chaim Levy immediately refutes that he possesses miraculous powers, "except perhaps, *perhaps*, he emphasised, the power of tears", has little interest in the study of Talmud and prefers the company of children for whom he secretly leaves little piles of raisins and nuts to nibble. The tale of the lineage of the Levys is thus by no means a tale of glory and glorious martyrdom, and Schwarz-Bart's characterizations never lose their idiosyncrasy and gentleness.

It is after the pogroms by the Cossack White Guards, which "passed unremarked among hundred of others", that the remnants of the Levy family are forced for the first time in generations to leave Zemyock, a pious shtetl in the province of Bialystok in Poland, and to settle in Germany where Jews, fatefully, "considered themselves 'almost' more German than Jewish". Stillenstadt, where Ernie is born, is a little town of cobblers and textile dyers in the Rhenish plains which feels and looks like some "secretion of that old Germanic sentimentality which penetrates and binds all things intimately, as the spittle of the swallow holds the twigs of its nest by an invisible thread". In the midst of this apparent tranquillity, the three generations of Levys feel displaced and tired: Old Mordecai moves "with that kind of heavy regret expressed in the tread of an old elephant, each step seemingly torn from a vast stretch of stillness". At the same time, the descriptions of new life are full of hope: the pale and fragile Ernie comes into the world, his head poised on his thin neck "with the inimitable grace of a bird", the colour of his eyes deepening to a midnight blue "sprinkled with brilliant, stellar sparks".

Through the experiences of Ernie Levy, initiated from a young age by his grandfather into the legend of the Lamed-vav, the reader witnesses the rising tide of anti-Semitism in this not untypical small German town. Throughout, Schwarz-Bart shows a particular feel for children, their world of imagination, joy, cruelty, seriousness, and confusion. And it is through a children's game that Schwarz-Bart suggests the changing social and political climate, a "trial of Jesus" game which culminates in hysterical violence which the children themselves do not quite understand (Ernie is assigned the role of the Jew). After several other vertiginous episodes where, with Hitler youth on the streets and in the school, Ernie suffers intense childhood desolation and confusion, the family succeeds in emigrating to France. Schwarz-Bart gives us some of his most cutting prose from this point on, alluding to the hostility and indifference of which the Jews of Europe were victim. For example, as the *Saint-Louis* (with Jewish refugees aboard) sails around the world and is refused anchorage:

> . . . the democracies refrained from any vulgar show of emotion. After a pleasant cruise, the whole group returned by way of Hamburg to end its days in the motherland. Never in history had an embargo been so admirably observed. And long live democracy, cried the democracies.

Ernie's bleak experiences and the passionate questioning which emerges for him of how to be a Jew (his father's remark, as the situation worsens in France: "*To be a Jew is impossible*") lead him into self-negation in order to survive, calling himself "the late Ernie". At the same time, he always harbours the tormented consciousness of his true self. Finally, his fate is the transit camp of Drancy, north of Paris, from which he is deported to his death in the gas chambers of Auschwitz-Birkenau, a figure of Jewish suffering and persecution in the Shoah and across the ages: Ernie Levy, "dead six million times".

Schwarz-Bart's later works, one of which he co-authored with his Guadeloupean wife Simone, are concerned with the excluded and maltreated members of society, but do not have a specific Jewish theme. *A Woman Named Solitude* is set in the French colony of Martinique in the late 18th century, the Solitude of the title being the daughter of a slave mother and a white sailor. Solitude's mixed parentage is such that she is rejected by the black slaves but treated as nothing but an ornamental puppet by the white slave-owners; however, in a final gesture of revolt, she attains a heroic stature despite her destitution.

There is a value put on suffering in Schwarz-Bart's works which may seem more Christian than Jewish in its sacrificial and redemptive overtones; indeed, Schwarz-Bart's interpretation of the legend of the Just is highly tendentious, since traditionally each Just remedies evil in this world – so that the existence of ten just men, or even one, would have saved Sodom and Gomorrah from destruction – with no suggestion that a Just should offer himself as sacrificial victim. However, the intensity and poetry of *The Last of the Just* make it a powerful work, without pathos, and with an implicit questioning of the martyrology into which it nevertheless inscribes the short life of Ernie Levy.

SASKIA BROWN

Schwob, Marcel

French essayist, critic, and fiction writer, 1867–1905

Born in Chaville, 23 August 1867, into liberal republican family. Tutored privately; learned to speak English and German; studied at high school in Nantes; living with uncle, studied at Lycée Louis-le-Grand, Paris. Voluntary military service, Vannes, 1885–86. Studied at the Sorbonne, L ès L (BA). Undertook research in National Archives, Paris, and published study of French argot, 1889; journalist, *L'Echo de Paris* and *L'Événement*, 1890–91; joined literary life of Paris, associating with Jules Renard, Paul Claudel, Anatole France, Edmond de Goncourt, and Paul Valéry. Met actress Marguerite Moreno, 1895. Contracted severe illness; underwent five operations but health remained poor. Visited Britain; married Marguerite Moreno there, 1900. Returned to Paris; visited Jersey, 1901; also visited Australia, New Zealand, and Pacific islands. Lectured on François Villon, the Sorbonne, 1904. Died in Paris, 26 February 1905.

Selected Writings

Collection

Les Oeuvres complètes [The Complete Works], 10 vols, 1927–30

Novel

Le Livre de Monelle, 1894; as *The Book of Monelle*, translated by William Brown Meloney, 1929

Short Stories

Coeur double [Double Heart], 1891
Le Roi au masque d'or, 1893; in *The King in the Golden Mask and Other Writings*, edited and translated by Iain White, 1982
Mimes 1893; as *Mimes*, translated by A. Lenalie, 1901
La Croisade des enfants, 1896; as *The Children's Crusade*, translated by Henry Copley Greene, 1907
Spicilège [Spice-essence], 1896
Vies imaginaires, 1896; as *Imaginary Lives*, translated by Lorimer Hammond, 1924; translated by Harry Hives, 1991
Vie de Morphiel, démiurge: une vie imaginaire oubliée [The Life of Morphiel, Demiurge: A Forgotten Imaginary Life], 1985

Other

Étude sur l'argot français [Study of French Slang], with others, 1889
Translator, *Moll Flanders*, by Daniel Defoe, 1895
La Porte des rêves [The Door of Dreams], 1899
Translator, with Eugène Morand, *Hamlet*, by William Shakespeare, 1900
Translator, *Francesca da Rimini*, by F.M. Crawford, 1902
La Lampe de Psyché [Psyche's Lamp], 1903
Les Mœurs des diurnales, 1903
La Guerre commerciale [The Trade War], 1904
Le Parnasse satyrique du quinzième siècle [Satyric Parnassus of the 15th Century], 1905
Le Petit et le grand testament de Villon [The Small and the Great Testament of Villon], 1905
François Villon: rédactions et notes [François Villon: Essays and Notes], 1912
R.L.S. An Essay (on Robert Louis Stevenson), translated by A. Lenalie, 1920
Mélanges d'histoires littéraire et de linguistique: L'argot, Villon, Rabelais [Miscellany of Literary and Linguistic Histories: Slang, Villon, Rabelais], 1928
Chroniques [Chronicles], 1981
The King in the Golden Mask and Other Writings, edited and translated by Iain White, 1982
Correspondance inédite [Unpublished Correspondence], 1985
François Rabelais, 1990 (from *Mélanges*)

Further Reading

Champion, Pierre, *Marcel Schwob et son temps*, Paris: Grasset, 1927
De Meyer, Bernard, "Le Conte de Marcel Schwob: sur les antécédents", *French Studies in Southern Africa*, 24 (1995)
Jutrin, Monique, *Marcel Schwob, coeur double*, Lausanne: De L'Aire, 1982
Lisse, Michel, "Machine parlante, machine à parler, machine à écrire: entre Schwob et Heidegger", *Les Lettres Romaines*, 48/3–4 (August and November 1994)
Tremblay, George, *Marcel Schwob: faussaire de la nature*, Geneva: Droz, 1969
Wynchank, Anny, "Marcel Schwob; ou, La Porte des rêves", *French Studies in Southern Africa*, 7 (1978)

Marcel Schwob was descended from a family of literary figures on his father's side. His mother was born Mathilde Cahun (Cohen) from a long line of rabbis and one of her ancestors allegedly saved the life of the Crusader, Le Sieur de Joinville. This and other legends of his family history made Schwob very proud of his Jewish ancestry. His uncle, Léon Cahun had collected many Jewish legends and published a remarkable book, entitled *Jewish Life*, and Schwob learned much of Jewish culture from this uncle. However in later life Schwob shunned the company of his co-religionists and was concerned principally with French and European culture. When he started writing towards the end of the 1880s, the French public, tiring of realism and naturalism, was beginning to be attracted by the imaginative and the fantastic, by stories of adventures and dreams. Schwob's writing began to leave the realities of the external world and of his surroundings, because this world fell short of his ideals and through his stories he escaped into a dream world.

He also explored the mysteries of ancient cultures and civilizations.

What are the key elements that shaped his inspiration? First, he was proficient in both spoken German and its literature, and even more so in English. At the age of eight he read *Treasure Island* in English and at 11 Poe's *Tales*. Later important influences were Daniel Defoe, Shakespeare, D.G. Rossetti, Thomas De Quincey, Mark Twain, and others. Schwob, being gifted with keen powers of analysis and absorption, retained much from this literature, especially its fantasy and violence. Another influence on Schwob's writings was his rich knowledge of classical literature, life, and thought. In his teens he read Petronius, Anacreon, Apuleius, and Catullus and studied the city of ancient Rome, its daily life, slavery, magic, and thieves. He often evoked in his short stories the classical world with its prostitutes, poverty, and beliefs. Similarly he used material gained from studies of the travellers of the 14th and 15th centuries, especially pilgrims. An additional important influence was his Jewish heritage, which caused him to be ever conscious of man's obligations to his fellow man and the ideals of pity and mercy.

Schwob's deep knowledge and erudition were the foundations of his imaginative writings. "It is necessary", he said, "to be the counterfeiter of nature". He often offered as real the narratives of imaginary witnesses, which he had created from authentic sources. Reality triggered this visionary man's vision in *Vies imaginaires* (*Imaginary Lives*). Schwob's tormented mind and dreams tended towards the bizarre and violent. In his short stories he achieves a harmonious balance between realism and symbolism.

Terror and pity formed the two poles of Schwob's inspiration for his penetration into the world of dreams. Terror can be triggered by exterior elements, outside normal human experience, for instance by magical powers in the short story "Les Striges", or a concourse of extraordinary circumstances, with the intrusion of unreality in the context of real life, in "Le Train 081". Horror can also arise from sources within a person, such as a dual personality in "L'Homme double", from external suggestion in "L'Homme voilé", madness in "Arachné", and even as a consequence of seeking strong sensations such as the quintessence of love in "Béatrice", of literature in "Lilith", or of the bizarre in "Les Portes de l'opium". By all these means Schwob plunged more deeply into horror, to examine its many aspects. But Schwob can also give us humorous stories such as "Spiritualisme" and "Un Squelette", in which terror mocks itself and shows that familiarity with terror can lead to indifference and irony.

Poe's pessimism and Villiers de l'Isle Adam's bitter irony remain unalleviated in their writings, in contrast to Schwob, whose works are suffused with humanism. He states, "As soon as [a man] tries to project in others misery, suffering, fear, . . . he chases away all the terrors within and outside himself and knows nothing more than pity". Pity for others lightens Schwob's otherwise gloomy stories. In "La Mort d'Odjigh" and "L'Incendie terreste" he demonstrates his hopes for a better world and his love of mankind. The first work describes the dawn of humanity, when an ice age threatens to destroy all life, and in the second a fiery, cataclysmic end menaces everything on earth. Such scenes of devastation and desolation conjure up similar biblical depictions. But these tales end with glimmers of hope and human love.

How can this optimism be explained? Together with Schwob's deep erudition, his Jewish heritage shaped the style of his writings. This is particularly evident in *Le Livre de Monelle*, the style of which evokes the Psalms of David. Schwob's perception of humanity is Jewish, hence the doctrine of original sin is absent and there is a belief that pity, innocence, and love can save humanity on earth. In *Le Livre de Monelle*, an elegant and idealistic, though obscure, work, he conceives of a superior form of love. Monelle, an enigmatic prostitute, has eerie nocturnal excursions to communicate with a poet, finally vanishing mysteriously. Monelle was based on a real person, Louise, a childish, consumptive, and illiterate prostitute, beloved by Schwob. After her death in 1893 he was despondent and found refuge in his dream world, writing the symbolist work, *Le Livre de Monelle*: Louise became the evanescent child-woman, who spurred on illusion, evasion, oblivion, and mystification and also portrays a form of sublime love and mercy.

At least once in his life, Schwob attempted to live one of his dreams. He tried to experience the romantic aspects of the life of a seafaring figure, such as Captain Kidd, or the pirate Kennedy, whose portrait he had painted. So in 1901, though very weak, he set out on a five-month voyage to Samoa. He wished to honour the tomb of his "friend", Robert Louis Stevenson, whom he had never met, but whose magical writing had bewitched him. Unhappily this voyage proved to be a great disappointment. He far preferred dreaming and recording his dreams in words, to action. His great interest in the past, his power of analysis and his fundamental belief in man's humaneness and benevolence, which together permeated his writings, are the clearest indication of his Jewishness.

ANNY WYNCHANK

Scliar, Moacyr

Brazilian fiction writer, 1937–

Born in Porto Alegre, 23 March 1937, into Russian immigrant family. Studied at Jewish School in Porto Alegre; studied medicine, graduated 1962; degree in public health; joined Public Health Department in native state of Rio Grande do Sul. Married; one son. Contributor to several newspapers, including *Jornal do Brasil* and *Frankfurter Rundschau*; columnist. *Zero Hora*, Porto Alegre, and *Folha de São Paulo*. Writer in residence, Department of Portuguese and Brazilian Studies, Brown University, 1997, and Department of Spanish and Portuguese, University of Texas, Austin. Numerous awards, including Academia Mineira de Letras Award, 1968; Brasilia Prize, 1977; Guimarães Rosa Prize, 1977; Associação Paulista de Criticos de Arte Prize, 1989; Casa de las Américas Prize, 1989; PEN Clube do Brasil Prize, 1990; Academia Brasileira de Letras Award, 1998.

Selected Writings

Short Stories
O carnaval dos animais, 1968; as *The Carnival of the Animals*, translated by Eloah F. Giacomelli, 1985
A balada do falso mesias, 1976; as *The Ballad of the False Messiah*, translated by Eloah F. Giacomelli, 1987
Os melhores contos de Moacyr Scliar [The Best Stories of Moacyr Scliar], 1984
O olho enigmático: contos, 1986; as *The Enigmatic Eye*, translated by Eloah F. Giacomelli, 1989
A orelha de Van Gogh: contos [Van Gogh's Ear], 1989
"Inside My Dirty Head – The Holocaust", translated by Eloah F. Giacomelli, in *Tropical Synagogues: Short Stories by Jewish-Latin American Writers*, edited by Ilan Stavans, 1994
Contos reunidos [Collected Short Stories], 1995
O amante da Madonna e outras historias [The Lover of the Madonna and Other Stories], 1997
The Collected Stories of Moacyr Scliar, translated by Eloah F. Giacomelli, introduction by Ilan Stavans, 1999

Novels
Histórias de un médico em Formação, 1962
A guerra no Bom Fim [The War of Bom Fim], 1972
O exército de um homem só, 1973; as *The One-Man Army*, translated by Eloah F. Giacomelli, 1986
Os deuses de Raquel, 1975; as *The Gods of Raquel*, translated by Eloah F. Giacomelli, 1986
O ciclo das aguas [The Cycle of Waters], 1976
Os voluntários, 1979; as *The Volunteers*, translated by Eloah F. Giacomelli, 1988
O centauro no jardim, 1980; as *The Centaur in the Garden*, translated by Margaret A. Neves, 1984
Max es os felinos, 1981; as *Max and the Cats*, translated by Eloah F. Giacomelli, 1990
A estranha nação de Rafael Mendes, 1983; as *The Strange Nation of Rafael Mendes*, translated by Eloah F. Giacomelli, 1987
Cenas da vida minuscula [Scenes of a Minuscule Life], 1991
Sonhos tropicais [Tropical Dreams], 1992
A majestade do Xingu [The King of Xingu], 1997
A mulher que escreveu a Bíblia [The Woman Who Wrote the Bible], 1999
Os leopardos de Kafka [Kafka's Leopards], 2000

Other
A condição Judaica [The Jewish Condition], 1985
Do mágico ao social: a trajetória da saúde pública [From Magic to Social Theory: Pathways of Public Health], 1987
Do Edén ao divã: humor Judaico [From Eden to the Couch: Jewish Humour], with Eliahu Toker and Patricia Finzi, 1990
Caminhos da esperança: a presença Judaica no Rio Grande do Sul / Pathways of Hope: The Jewish Presence in Rio Grande do Sul, translated by Vânia L.S. de Barros Falcão, 1991
Se eu fosse Rothschild: citações que marcaram a trajetória do povo Judeu [If I Were Rothschild], 1993
Judaismo: dispersao e unidade [Judaism: Dispersion and Unity], 1994
A paixão transformada: história da medicina na literatura [Passion Transformed: History of Medicine in Literature], 1996
Meu filho o doutor: Judaismo e medicina [My Son the Doctor: Judaism and Medicine], 2000

Further Reading

Barr, Lois Baer, "Navigators without a Compass and Builders without a Plan: Moacyr Scliar" in *Isaac Unbound: Patriarchal Traditions in the Latin American Jewish Novel*, Tempe: Arizona State University Center for Latin American Studies, 1995
Barr, Lois Baer, "The Jonah Experience: The Jews of Brazil According to Scliar" in *The Jewish Diaspora in Latin America: New Studies on History and Literature*, edited by David Sheinin and Lois Baer Barr, New York: Garland, 1996
Baumgarten, Murray "Urban Life and Jewish Memory in the Tales of Moacyr Scliar and Nora Glickman" in *Tradition and Innovation: Reflections on Latin American Jewish Writing*, edited by Robert E. DiAntonio and Nora Glickman, Albany: State University of New York Press, 1993
DiAntonio, Robert E., "Aspects of Contemporary Judeo-Brazilian Writing: Moacyr Scliar's *O centauro no jardim*: Ethnicity, Affirmation, and a Unique Mythic Perspective" in *Brazilian Fiction: Aspects and Evolution of the Contemporary Narrative*, Fayetteville: University of Arkansas Press, 1989
DiAntonio, Robert E., "The Brazilianization of the Yiddishkeit Tradition", *Latin American Literary Review*, 34 (1989)
Glickman, Nora, "*Os voluntários*: A Jewish-Brazilian Pilgrimage", *Yiddish* 4/4 (1982)
Igel, Regina, "Jewish Component in Brazilian Literature: Moacyr Scliar", *Folio*, 17 (1987)
Lindstrom, Naomi, "Oracular Jewish Tradition in Two Works by Moacyr Scliar", *Luso–Brazilian Review*, 21/2 (1984)
Vieira, Nelson H., "Judaic Fiction in Brazil: To Be and Not to Be Jewish", *Latin American Literary Review*, 14/2 (1986)
Vieira, Nelson H., "Moacyr Scliar: Difference and the Tyranny of Culture" in *Jewish Voices in Brazilian Literature: A Prophetic Discourse of Alterity*, Gainesville: University Press of Florida, 1995

Moacyr Scliar is a prolific Portuguese-language Jewish fabulist, novelist, short-story writer, essayist, anthologist, and newspaper columnist, as well as professional physician. With an oeuvre translated into more than half a dozen languages, Scliar is responsible for bringing Jewish-Latin American literature to the global stage with books such as *The Centaur in the Garden.*

Scliar (pronounced in English *Mwa seer Skleer*) is recognized as a major Brazilian writer of the 20th century, but has also spent considerable time pursuing his career as doctor. His characters always explore the fragile tension between their ethnic and their national identities. What distinguishes Scliar from other Jewish-Latin American authors is his humour, which is allegorical, never sarcastic. Two forces coloured his upbringing: ideology and culture – and the two emanated from a single source: his Jewishness. "I have lived my life among Jews", he said in an interview, "and my Jewish world view circumscribes everything I do, for I am the child of Eastern European immigrants. Socialism was their principle and Yiddish was their tongue."

His first book, *Histórias de un médico em Formação*, published in 1962, even if Scliar would later reject it as unworthy, announces a theme that permeates his vast oeuvre: medicine not as a mere enhancer of Western civilization and a repository of modernity, but as a way to mend the world. His talent to invent a cast of pathetic characters, always in search for some cure for the miseries of society, is astounding. At times his protagonists are radicals from Europe seeking to establish an egalitarian Promised Land in the Amazon forest. Others are Jews born and raised in the pampa who are involved in voodoo. Or they might be disoriented mystics and false messiahs. Scliar incorporates into his literature elements of mythology and folklore, and also inserts in unlikely landscapes historical figures such as Vincent Van Gogh, Karl Marx, James Cagney, Leon Trotskii, Sigmund Freud, and Sabbethai Zevi. None of his characters ever finds redemption in these faiths, and the acts of embracing and then renouncing them are equally appealing to Scliar. Salvation, he suggests, is only a subterfuge, a lie we like to repeat to ourselves. Their Jewishness is a condition they cannot escape, one that carries within itself the strength to endure.

When Scliar began his literary career, Brazil had no well-established cadre of Jewish writers. Not that the stage was empty. In 1973, in *Musteverke*, Shmuel Rodzansky included a volume, entitled *Antologie Brasilianish*, with tales by Moyshe Lockietsh, Meir Kutshinsky, Pinye Polotnik, and Itzjak Guterman. But Scliar knew nothing about them, for their readership was a minuscule group of immigrants. Sure, Porto Alegre had an excellent library of Yiddish classics, frequented by Yiddish-speaking intellectuals. Only when, decades later, Jacó Guinzburg, the father of non-religious secular Jewish culture in Brazil, translated these and countless other Jewish stories from Yiddish into Portuguese, did Scliar feel less shaky.

In his formative years, the only writer he was acquainted with was Marcos Lolovitch, a lawyer whose memoir, *Numa clara manhã de Abril*, is a valuable, if undistinguished chronicle of immigration. Also Clarice Lispector, of Jewish descent, known as "Brazil's Virginia Woolf", already had a solid following. But her Jewish themes are so eclipsed, so buried in allegorical fantasies that it takes heavy critical tools to unearth them.

Not finding role models at home, Scliar read Jewish writers from Europe and the United States, such as Sholem Aleichem, Y.L. Perets, and Michael Gold, as well as Kafka and Isaak Babel. Humour, he quickly learned from Kafka, is the most efficient response to catastrophe. Along this line, he makes his characters laugh constantly at themselves and their circumstance. Of these heroes, Babel is unequivocally adored. "His portrait of childhood remains unparalleled", Scliar said in an interview:

> I could easily see myself reflected in his Odessa. Kafka, of course, is an ambivalent figure, but so is Babel. His ambivalence toward the Jews and his idolatry of the Cossacks [are inspiring]. His Jews are ugly, even monstrous, whereas the Cossacks are imposing and muscular. One could even go so far as to suggest a certain dose of anti-Semitism in *Red Cavalry*.

Scliar's most famous book is *The Centaur in the Garden*. A delightful meditation "so powerful, so enchanting", claims critic Alberto Manguel, "that it succeeds in imposing its own magic on sceptical readers, convincing us that [the] centaur's world is ours, unfathomable and overwhelming." The novel describes the physical and existential journey of a monstrous creature, a centaur born to Russian immigrants in Brazil that is half Jewish and, obviously, also half human, in his quest for a place of his own in society. The tale is told through comic episodes that address alienation but that ultimately allow him to overcome his limitations.

As a novelist, Scliar has grown more adventurous with age. He is comfortable in historical novels set in medieval and early 20th-century Europe, featuring landscapes not offered regularly to a Latin American audience. He often explores Ashkenazic traditions, but Sephardic traditions, and traditions that incorporate Indian elements, are also present in volumes such as *The Strange Nation of Rafael Mendes*. Among the most popular are *A majestade do Xingu* [The King of Xingu], in which Scliar follows the path of a legendary doctor in Rio Grande do Sul known during the Getúlio Vargas dictatorship for fleeing his private patients and moving to the Amazon jungle to help its Indian population. In *A mulher que escreveu a Bíblia* [The Woman Who Wrote the Bible] Scliar takes to the limit Harold Bloom's idea that it was a female author who wrote the Bible. And in *Os leopardos de Kafka*, set in 1916 and in the vein of espionage literature of Ian Fleming, Scliar envisions a plot – with Leon Trotskii as a protagonist – wherein the political stability of Europe depends on a coded message from Kafka.

Scliar's essays and newspaper columns are comparatively light. By offering comments on Brazil's political, economic, and social reality, they serve as a window to his fiction. It is in the short stories that he shines the brightest: his microfiction, the length of some of his tales might be a single paragraph, is not based on character development but on sharp anecdotes that have the quality of myth. He has produced more than 120 stories. His most widely known collections are *The Carnival of the Animals*, *The Ballad of the False Messiah*, and *Van Gogh's Ear*. The majority of the stories are not cerebral but anecdotal. Their value is in their long-lasting impact. Long after they have ended, their texture and message continues to linger in the reader's mind.

It is through these stories, and also through his novels, that Scliar has exercised an influence over a generation of successors. He has managed to be truthful to his central theme – *mestizaje*, the assimilation of Jews to the South American milieu – by enlightening those unfamiliar with it and offering a mirror of recognition to those who are part of it. He is simultaneously entertaining and openly political. Successive writers, myself included, see Scliar as a role model.

Ilan Stavans

Self, Will

British fiction writer, 1961–

Born William Woodard Self in London, 26 September 1961. Educated at Exeter College, Oxford, BA. Married, first, K. Chancellor, two children; second, D.J. Orr, one son. Freelance cartoonist, 1982–88; publishing director, Cathedral Publishing, 1988–90; contributing editor, *Evening Standard* magazine, 1993–95; columnist, *The Observer*, 1995–97; *The Times*, 1998–99; *Independent on Sunday*, from 1999. Awards include Geoffrey Faber Memorial Prize, 1993.

Selected Writings

Fiction
Cock and Bull, 1993
Grey Area and Other Stories, 1994
My Idea of Fun: A Cautionary Tale, 1994
The Quantity Theory of Insanity: Together with Five Supporting Propositions, 1995
The Sweet Smell of Psychosis, 1996
Great Apes, 1997
Tough, Tough Toys for Tough, Tough Boys, 1998
How the Dead Live, 2000

Essays
Junk Mail, 1995
Perfidious Man (with David Gamble), 2000
Sore Sites, 2000
Feeding Frenzy, 2001

Further Reading

Barker, Lynn, "Self Control", *The Guardian* (11 June 2000)
Harbord, Janet, "Performing Parts: Gender and Sexuality in Recent Fiction and Theory", *Women: A Cultural Review*, 7 (Spring 1996)
Heller, Zoe, "Self Examination", *Vanity Fair* (June 1993)
Henchman, Anna, "Will Self: An Enfant Terrible Comes of Age", *Publishers Weekly* (8 September 1997)
Lyall, Sarah, "Tale of Recovery from a Bad Boy of Letters", *New York Times* (16 October 2000)
Morace, Robert A., "The Quantity Theory of Insanity", *Literary Annual 1996*, Pasadena, California: Salem, 1996
Morace, Robert A., "How the Dead Live", *Literary Annual 2001*, Pasadena, California: Salem, 2001
Sender, Katherine, "To Have and to Be: Sex, Gender and the Paradox of Change", *Women and Language*, 20 (Spring 1997)

"I don't write fiction for people to identify with, and I don't write a picture of the world they can recognize. I write to astonish people." And astonish Will Self has: for his well-publicized use of heroin and cocaine, his irreverent journalism in which he takes on everyone from Princess Diana to Irvine Welsh, and above all for his fiction: stories, novellas, and novels. Anointed early by *Granta* magazine as one of the "Best of the Young British Novelists" (before he had even published his first novel or novella), Self quickly earned a reputation as the bad boy of contemporary British literature, the London literati's very visible (at 6 feet 5 inches tall) addict-in-residence. However, Self does more than astonish, or appal. Even as it oozes excess and drips disgust, his writing combines moral outrage and outrageous prose in equal measure, each rendered in the same deadpan tone as he goes about his self-appointed task of keeping his readers human despite their best efforts to be anything but. For he is, at heart, a satirist and therefore a moralist in the tradition of Swift, Voltaire, Rabelais, Kesey, Heller, and Vonnegut, with touches of O'Connor ("for the near blind you have to write large"), Kafka (the terrifying and terrifically comical logic of the irrational), Terry Gilliam's post-Orwellian dystopian satire, *Brazil*, and the three writers that Self himself has singled out: Alasdair Gray, J.G. Ballard, and Woody Allen (as much for his insights into the situation of the deracinated Jew as for his comic genius). Because the targets of his satires are so numerous and often so vaguely defined and because his prose is often so self-regarding and seemingly detached from any real-world referents, it is easy to misread Self's satirical bent as just another sign of the "sophisticatedly nihilistic", postmodern-*Pulp Fiction* times, delighting those who take pleasure in stylish debunking for its own sake. In "License to Hug" (*Esquire*, November 1995), for example, Self proves just as adept at skewering by mimicry the stiff upper lip style and macho substance of Ian Fleming's James Bond books as he is at pillorying the brave new world of political correctness (with its very own thought police) in which the "Therapeutic Hug and Stroke" is the weapon of choice.

As a writer of surrealist prose, Self does not lose himself in metafiction's funhouse. His sensibility is closer to Ballard's and indeed, like Ballard, he is preoccupied with the "problem of scale", especially as it manifests itself in the "built environment". For Self, whose father was a professor of urban planning at the London School of Economics, the built environment includes both all planned communities such as The Hampstead Garden Suburb in North London where he grew up and abstract theories of various kinds that Self finds similarly "soulless and institutional". Working in the "grey area" where the mundane and the absurdly phantasmagoric meet, he deconstructs the "incantatory hum" of contemporary life in order to expose both the artifice and irrationality of much of what passes for everyday existence and the perniciousness of what is assumed to be either common sense or professional expertise. Self effects this exposure by creating parallel worlds in which men and women, humans and apes, and therapists and patients all trade places, anthropologists take on the characteristics of those they observe, and analysands fabricate dreams and experiences to match their theories.

Self's style is itself a selfconsciously wrought "built environment" that everywhere declares itself as artifice (most obviously in Self's love of unusual words). Playfully pedantic, furiously funny, riotously excessive and anything but self-effacing, it is a style well suited to the author's imaginative grotesquerie although also open to the change of being self-indulgent, undisciplined, and "striking rather than illuminating". The digressiveness for which Self is often criticized is no less intentional and well-suited, both as a reflection of the author's "mindlessly peripatetic life" and as a response to the arbitrarily imposed order of urban planners, psychological theorists, and others. Self's mode of characterization is similarly unconventional and appropriate. Not the rounded people of realistic fiction, his characters more closely resemble the stick figures found in the dream-like stories of Kafka and Schulz or of Self's own published cartoons. "The prototypical Will Self character", Craig Seligman has noted (*New Yorker*, 11 April 1995), "has no will and . . . has no self". Many are grotesquely banal and terminally passive; some are like Woody Allen's portrait of the assimilated Jew in *Zelig*, social chameleons; a few possess not a will but "a whim of iron"; while others impose their wills (and theories) on others: the utterly effaced and subjugated wife who grows a penis and rapes her husband to death; the Fat Controller, a "personified id"; and especially dispensers of pharmaceutical cures and psychological theories such as the R.D. Laing-like Dr Zack Busner, a recurrent figure in Self's fiction, the very personification of "theory in the face of real distress".

Self's withering critique of utopian social and psychological theories and of the sheer banality and absurdity of contemporary British life made in theory's therapeutic and Margaret Thatcher's entrepreneurial images is especially effective in his first two collections of short fiction, *The Quantity Theory of Insanity* and *Grey Area*. The paired novellas *Cock and Bull*, which he wrote to express his "anger at the way gender-based sexuality is so predetermined", represents Self at his most structurally disciplined and grotesquely and perversely imaginative. *My Idea of Fun* is Self's most ambitious, narratively complex, and intertextually rich work. Drawing on De Quincey, Nietzsche, Singer, Freud, Bret Easton Ellis, the Rev. W.V. Awdry (author of the *Thomas the Tank Engine* stories), and others, the novel is narrated by a direct marketer aptly named Ian Wharton and set at a time when "People had begun to feel less ashamed about being greedy and of wanting more than their share of fairness". Self's next three works – the novella *The Sweet Smell of Psychosis*, the novel *Great Apes*, and the story collection *Tough, Tough Toys for Tough, Tough Boys* – did little to advance either his art or his reputation. *Great Apes*, which received some withering reviews, is Self's longest and weakest book, a one-idea joke belaboured over 404 pages. Published following his second marriage and successful rehabilitation for drug and alcohol addiction, *How the Dead Live* represents not only Self at his best but a surprising and significant advance. Oddly enough, it is an advance that involved his returning to one of his earliest stories, "The North London Book of the Dead", and its autobiographical subtext, Self's troubled relationship with his deeply troubled Jewish American mother. There has always been a Stanley Elkin-like quality to Self's fiction, but in this novel about "the awful karmic outcomes of having lived a materialist, self-obsessed life", it is most effectively apparent. In his fictionalized mother, Lily Bloom, Self has found his most human face and most appealing voice, at once scathingly, ragingly funny and elegiac. Where the early story was a variation on the Jewish mother joke, *How the Dead Live* is the author's most ambiguously affirmative and emotionally affecting work to date, a work that represents less a change in direction in Self's furious art than a breakthrough to a deeper level of engagement with his material and his audience.

ROBERT A. MORACE

Sendak, Maurice

US writer and illustrator, 1928–

Born Maurice Bernard Sendak in Brooklyn, New York, 10 June 1928, to immigrants from Poland; grandson of rabbis. Studied at Lafayette High School, New York (cartoonist, *Lafayette News*), graduated 1946; Art Students' League, New York, 1949–51. Illustrator, *Mutt and Jeff* comic strip, All American Comics, New York, 1944–45; window display designer, Timely Service, New York, 1946–48, and F.A.O. Schwarz, New York, 1948–51. Instructor in children's literature, Yale University, 1974–75; instructor, Parsons School of Design, New York, 1974–79. Founder, The Night Kitchen, theatre specializing in productions for children. Designer of opera sets in Houston, Brussels, London, New York, and Glyndebourne. Animator, *Seven Monsters* and *Bumbl-Ardy* (*Sesame Street* television series), 1970. Individual exhibitions at Gallery of Visual Arts, New York, 1964; Rosenbach Foundation, Philadelphia, 1970, 1975; Trinity College, Hartford, Connecticut, 1972; Galerie Daniel Keel, Zürich, 1974; Ashmolean Museum, Oxford, 1975; American Cultural Center, Paris, 1978. Many awards, including American Library Association Caldecott Medal, 1964; Laura Ingalls Wilder Award, 1983; Hans Christian Andersen International Medal, 1970; University of Southern Mississippi Award, 1981; Boston *Globe–Horn Book* Award, 1981; American Book Award, 1982; National Medal of Arts Award, 1997; Jewish Cultural Achievement Award in Visual Arts, 1998.

Selected Writings

For Children

Fiction
Kenny's Window, 1956
Very Far Away, 1957
The Sign on Rosie's Door, 1960
Where the Wild Things Are, 1963
Higglety Pigglety Pop! or, There Must Be More to Life, 1967
In the Night Kitchen, 1970
Outside over There, 1981
Swine Lake, 1999

Plays
Really Rosie, 1975; revised version, 1978
Where the Wild Things Are, 1980

Poetry
The Nutshell Library (*Alligators All Around, Chicken Soup with Rice, One Was Johnny, Pierre: A Cautionary Tale*), 4 vols, 1962
Seven Little Monsters, 1976
We Are All in the Dumps with Jack and Guy: Two Nursery Rhymes with Pictures, 1993

Other
The Acrobat, 1959
Pictures, 1971
The Magician: A Counting Book, 1971
Some Swell Pup; or Are You Sure You Want a Dog?, with Matthew Margolis, 1976

For Adults
Fantasy Sketches, 1970
Questions to an Artist Who is Also an Author: A Conversation between Virginia Haviland and Maurice Sendak, 1972
A Conversation with Maurice Sendak, 1975
Collection of Books, Posters and Original Drawings, 1984
Posters, 1987
Caldecott and Co.: Notes on Books and Pictures, 1989
"Visitors from My Boyhood" in *Worlds of Childhood: The Art and Craft of Writing for Children*, edited by William Zinsser, 1990

Illustrator of more than 80 books by other authors, including works by Isaac Bashevis Singer, the Grimm Brothers, Tolstoi, and Else Minarik.

Further Reading

Alderson, Brian (editor), *Catalogue for an Exhibition of Pictures by Maurice Sendak at the Ashmolean Museum, Oxford, 16 December–29 February 1975–1976*, London: Bodley Head, 1975
Cech, John, *Angels and Wild Things: The Archetypal Poetics of Maurice Sendak*, University Park: Pennsylvania State University Press, 1995
Hanrahan, Joyce Y., *Works of Maurice Sendak, 1947–1994: A Collection with Comments*, Portsmouth, New Hampshire: P.E. Randall, 1995
Lanes, Selma G., *The Art of Maurice Sendak*, New York: Abrams, 1980; London: Bodley Head, 1981
Sendak at the Rosenbach (exhibition catalogue), Philadelphia: Rosenbach Museum and Library, 1995
Sendak in Asia: Exhibition and Sale of Original Artwork, Kingston, New York: Battledore, 1996
Sonheim, Amy, *Maurice Sendak*, New York: Twayne, 1991

With the publication of *Where the Wild Things Are* and its subsequently receiving the American Library Association's Caldecott Medal, Maurice Sendak became one of the most important figures in the field of children's literature. In addition to receiving critical acclaim, *Where the Wild Things Are* is a best-selling children's book.

Sendak began his career in children's literature as an illustrator and continues to illustrate others' books as well as his own. One of the first works he illustrated was Marcel Aymé's *The Wonderful Farm*, published in 1951. In 1952 he illustrated *A Hole is to Dig* by Ruth Krauss, a book that received critical acclaim and that made enough money for Sendak eventually to leave his job working with window displays at the F.A.O. Schwarz toy store and to get his own apartment in Greenwich Village in New York. He went on to illustrate more than 80 children's books.

In 1956, with *Kenny's Window*, he began to write as well as illustrate books. The third book he wrote and illustrated, *The Sign on Rosie's Door*, is supposedly drawn from sights he saw outside his window in the late 1940s. It involves a very forceful, imaginative young girl who shares her fantasies with other children in her neighbourhood.

Among the works he both illustrated and wrote are the extremely popular and highly praised Nutshell Library and the Wild Things trilogy. The Nutshell Library consists of four slim books, *Alligators All Around*, *Chicken Soup with Rice*, *One Was Johnny*, and *Pierre*. Central to his early works is the idea of children dressing up or disguising themselves, an idea that remains part of Sendak's later works, especially his Wild Things trilogy. Of the works in the Nutshell Library, *Pierre* is the most controversial. A kind of Little Red-Riding Hood tale, it is about a boy named Pierre who constantly says he does not care until a lion asks whether it can devour him. Pierre says that he does not care, so the lion eats him up. When his parents rescue him, he discovers that he really does care.

The trilogy consists of *Where the Wild Things Are*, *In the Night Kitchen*, and *Outside over There*. All three are controversial, even being called inappropriate for children. Some critics have found the first book too scary. The second is attacked for its illustrations of Mickey nude. The third is called too confusing. Still, most critics agree that in these three works we see Sendak at his best. Each treats imaginary lands in which the protagonists work out problems central to their real-life existences. In them Sendak seems to have plumbed his own psyche, seeking and finding the child within himself and drawing upon it to recreate and work through some of the fears and anxieties that children experience.

In the first Max comes to grips with the Wild Things inside himself. One night, he wears his wolf suit and creates terrible "mischief", including putting a crack in the wall with a hammer and nail and chasing his dog with a fork. After his mother sends him to his room without supper, he journeys to the land of the Wild Things, becomes their king, and sends them to bed without their suppers. But he grows "lonely" and wants to be "where someone loved him best of all". So he returns home to find his warm dinner waiting for him. On a deeper level, Max becomes much more content with his role as a civilized little boy rather than a wild thing.

In the second book in the trilogy Mickey journeys into the Night Kitchen where he makes it possible for the bakers to bake the morning bread. He then, like Max, returns to his bedroom. On a deeper level, he comes to grips with the disturbing noises in the night and with his anxiety about food.

In the third, Ida is left by her absent father and distracted mother to take care of her baby sister. When goblins snatch the sister, Ida heroically rescues her. On a deeper level Ida works through her feelings of sibling rivalry and learns that she loves her baby sister.

At their best Sendak's books work on multiple levels, exploring the darker parts of the human psyche, especially the child's psyche. And the child, he claims, is something we all carry within. That is probably part of the reason he insists that many of his books are for adults as well as children. Even his illustrations in books by others can often be read on multiple levels. For example, his 1995 illustrations of *The Miami Giant*, by Arthur Yorinks, allude to popular culture, especially movies such as *King Kong* and *The Mighty Joe Young*, fairy tales such as *Jack and the Beanstalk*, books such as *Gulliver's Travels*, and legendary American history, including the idea that Christopher Columbus was Jewish and that the Native Americans are lost tribes of Israel.

The pictures of the people who inhabit his books are, he says, based on children he knew growing up in his largely immigrant neighbourhood and on his own relatives. Some appear to be self-portraits, sharing many of the Sendak's facial and physical characteristics. Sendak's illustrations often receive more critical attention than his words, but even in the works he illustrates for others, the words and pictures are inseparable.

Sendak works in art forms other than picture books. He put together material from *The Sign on Rosie's Door* and the Nutshell Library to produce *Maurice Sendak's Really Rosie: Starring the Nutshell Kids*, which appeared on network television and later evolved into the off-Broadway musical, *Really Rosie*. He helped transform several of his works into operas, including *Where the Wild Things Are*. He also designed sets for operas, including *The Magic Flute* and *The Nutcracker*.

Sendak has illustrated a number of folk fairy tales, and in ways familiar to readers of Bruno Bettelheim's *The Uses of Enchantment*, Sendak's works draw heavily on the darker parts of the unconscious mind. In his often controversial works Sendak embodies his own fears and hopes, thus making his creations of interest to children and adults.

RICHARD TUERK

Shabtai, Yaakov

Israeli fiction writer and dramatist, 1934–1981

Born in Tel Aviv, 1934. Joined Kibbutz Merhavia after completing military service, 1957; returned to Tel Aviv, 1967. Married; two daughters. Awarded Kenneth B. Smilen Literary Award, 1986; Kinor David Prize for Plays, 1978; Bernstein Prize, 1978. Agnon Prize awarded posthumously, 1982. Died after heart attack, 1981. Street in Tel Aviv named after him, 1999.

Selected Writings

Fiction
Hamasa hamuflah shel hakarpad [The Wondrous Journey of the Toad], 1964
Hadod perets mamri [Uncle Peretz Takes Off], 1972
Zikhron dvarim, 1977; as *Past Continuous*, translated by Dalya Bilyu, 1985
Sof davar, 1984; as *Past Perfect*, translated by Dalya Bilyu, 1987

Plays (in Hebrew)
The Life of Caligula, 1975
The Chosen, 1976
Don Juan and His Friend Shipel, 1978
The Spotted Tiger, 1985
Crowned Head and Other Plays, 1995
The Spotted Tiger and Other Plays, 1995
Eating, 1999

Other
Shirei hazemer [Poems and Ballads], 1992

Further Reading

Hertsig, Hanah, *Hashem Ha-Perati: Masot al Shabtai, Kenaz, Hofman*, Tel Aviv: Hakibuts hameuhad, 1994
Yudkin, Leon I., *1948 and After: Aspects of Israeli Fiction*, Manchester: Manchester University Press, 1984

At his death in 1981, at the age of 47, Shabtai was already recognized as one of the most innovative writers of his generation. In his novels he combines stylistically bold writing – interior monologue recorded in the third person, and a prose that is driven by a kind of compulsive energy – with an acute analysis of Israeli society and its transformations.

Past Continuous is an epic of lives and deaths in Tel Aviv in the 1970s, narrated with Shabtai's extraordinary richness of precision, humour, and imagination, in the "hypnotically rhythmic" (according to Yudkin) prose which is his singular hallmark. The story follows the lives of three friends in their forties – Goldman, Caesar, and Israel – starting with a funeral in the scorching sun and ending precisely nine months later on Goldman's suicide and on the birth of an unwanted child from Israel's lover Ella: the interweaving of life and death, the intensity of life in the face of (always imminent) death is one of Shabtai's key themes. Life is, as Caesar puts it, a "'swinging suicide' ".

Goldman, Caesar, and Israel live restless and unfulfilled lives: Caesar, a photographer, has given up on everything except sex; Israel never quite bestirs himself into doing anything with his considerable musical gifts, and Goldman never quite manages to devote himself to any of his various interests in psychology, cosmology, dietetics, Taoism, and body-building. All three have disastrous relationships and their lives are a mixture of metaphysical despondency and edgy activity.

However, these three key figures generate innumerable others in the novel – friends, relatives, lovers, great-uncles, mothers, second cousins – and the reader is plunged into an extraordinary analysis of interwoven lives, showing a quite different Tel Aviv, before the city "grew like a crazy creature over the sand dunes and the vineyards and the melon patches", and showing also the chequered lives of Jews born in Europe: Uncle Lazar, whose childhood was spent in a luckless village which changed hands from Poland to Russia to Germany, leaves Germany for Eretz Israel as an impassioned Zionist, becomes a communist and returns to fight in the Spanish Civil War, from there going to the then USSR out of communist conviction, where he is summarily exiled to freezing Yakut on trumped-up charges of anarchism and Trotskyite sympathies, returning half a life later to Israel.

This older generation suffers a different kind of disillusion from that of the younger one, social and political this time: the rise of the right wing (Menachem Begin came to power in 1977, the year of publication of *Past Continuous*), speculation, rising land prices, and the socialist ideals of the State trampled underfoot. This perception of how Israel is changing is summed up in one of Shabtai's many and memorable diatribes, Caesar's uncle Zvi complaining that:

> . . . the government was allowing all kinds of parasites to make easy profits at the public's expense and widening the social gap in a total blindness which would lead to catastrophe, and that the country was sinking into mindless nationalism and undergoing a process of fascisization and increasing brutalization under the cloak of religion or other irrational theories . . .

Zvi's fierce condemnation reflects the dismay and disillusion of a whole generation.

Past Perfect is focused exclusively through the eyes of one character, the engineer Meir. Meir's consciousness of mortality, around his 40th birthday, is sudden and overwhelming, and takes the form of a realization that he can now very probably calculate how many pairs of shoes he will buy before he dies. One of the last straws is a doctor's diagnosis of slight hypertension, which Meir takes as a sure sign of life's pleasure in heaping arbitrary injustices upon him. Narrated, like *Past Continuous*, entirely in the third person, the novel follows Meir's restless thoughts, oscillating between childlike enthusiasm and hope, and feelings of despondency and regret. The trivial and the essential slip into each other without transition (suddenly overwhelmed by remorse at not having paid more attention to his eccentric friend Gavrouch while he was still alive, Meir simultaneously muses on his mother's butter biscuits and will he take a detour via the seafront and up Hayarkon St or will he carry straight on . . . ?), producing both an extremely funny and an unnerving tale of angst, instability, and obsession. The narrative moves forward in one unbroken paragraph, like the rush of life itself, never letting up.

These are novels about an Israel that has, for better or for worse, lost an encompassing sense of purpose. The more mature novel has as central character a "model" family man, who loves and appreciates his wife, visits his parents, has a "proper job", and so forth. Yet Meir nevertheless has all the characteristics associated in Israeli literature with the Diaspora Jew: neurotic, absorbed in the everyday, guilty, and egotistic. Meir's mid-life crisis can be seen, in this respect, as a crisis also of a certain Israeli identity, and a crisis of self-confidence: nothing can be placed beyond doubt or beyond question.

The short stories in *Uncle Peretz Takes Off* are, again, stylistically innovative, written in an understated and allusive style. The collection is composed of sometimes melancholy, sometimes very funny but always suggestive tales of lives in Tel Aviv: the narrator remembers the arrival of plastics and stainless steel which replace chipped porcelain brought all the way from Europe, and the special set for Pesach is never replaced; the rivalry between different Zionist movements as reflected in the flags hung out on 1 May; the terror of an approaching bar mitzvah; and a haunting tale of exile, wandering and international neglect ("Journey to Mauritius") ending, eventually, on the shores of Tel Aviv. These are powerful tales, with the same fierce, precise and uncompromising vision that makes all of Shabtai's writing so gripping.

Saskia Brown

Shaffer, Peter

British dramatist, 1926–

Born Peter Levin Shaffer in Liverpool, 15 May 1926; twin brother of Anthony Shaffer, also dramatist. Studied at preparatory school in Liverpool; Hall School, London; St Paul's School, London; Trinity College, Cambridge, 1947–50; BA in history 1950. Conscript coalminer, Chislet colliery, Kent, 1944–47. Lived in New York, 1951–54, working in Doubleday bookstore, airline terminal, Grand Central Station, Lord and Taylor department store, and New York Public Library. After returning to Britain, on staff of Boosey and Hawkes, music publishers, 1954–55; literary critic, *Truth*, 1956–57; music critic, *Time and Tide*, 1961–62. Many awards, including *Evening Standard* Drama Award, 1958, 1980, 1988; New York Drama Critics Circle Award, 1960, 1975; Tony, 1975, 1981; Outer Critics Circle Award, 1981; Vernon Rice Award, 1981; New York Film Critics Circle Award, 1984; Los Angeles Film Critics Association Award, 1984; Oscar for Best Screenplay, 1985; Hamburg Shakespeare Prize, 1989. Commander, Order of the British Empire, 1987; knighthood, 2001.

Selected Writings

Plays
Five Finger Exercise, 1958
The Private Ear, and The Public Eye, 1962
Sketch in *The Establishment*, 1963
The Merry Roosters' Panto, 1963; as *It's about Cinderella*, 1969
The Royal Hunt of the Sun: A Play Concerning the Conquest of Peru, 1964
Black Comedy, 1965
White Lies, 1967; as *White Liars*, 1968
Black Comedy, Including White Lies: Two Plays, 1967; as *White Liars, Black Comedy: Two Plays*, 1968
Shrivings, 1970; as *The Battle of Shrivings*, 1970
Equus, 1973
Amadeus, 1979
The Collected Plays of Peter Shaffer (includes *Five Finger Exercise, The Private Ear, The Public Eye, The Royal Hunt of the Sun, White Liars, Black Comedy, Equus, Shrivings, Amadeus*), 1982
Black Mischief, 1983
Yonadab, 1985
Lettice and Lovage, 1987
Whom Do I Have the Honour of Addressing?, 1989
The Gift of the Gorgon, 1992

Screenplays: *Lord of the Flies*, with Peter Brook, 1963; *The Public Eye (Follow Me!)*, 1972; *Equus*, 1977; *Amadeus*, 1984

Radio Plays: *Alexander the Corrector*, 1946; *The Prodigal Father*, 1957; *Whom Do I Have the Honour of Addressing?*, 1989

Television Plays: *The Salt Land*, 1955; *Balance of Terror*, 1957

Novels
The Woman in the Wardrobe (as Peter Antony), 1951
How Doth the Little Crocodile? (as Peter Antony, with Anthony Shaffer), 1952
Withered Murder, with Anthony Shaffer, 1955

Further Reading

Cooke, Virginia and Malcolm Page (editors), *File on Shaffer*, London: Methuen, 1987
Gianakaris, C. J. (editor), *Peter Shaffer: A Casebook*, New York: Garland, 1991
Gianakaris, C.J., *Peter Shaffer*, London: Macmillan, 1992
Klein, Dennis A., *Peter Shaffer*, Boston: Twayne, 1979
Klein, Dennis A., *Peter and Anthony Shaffer: A Reference Guide*, Boston: G.K. Hall, 1982
MacMurraugh-Kavanagh, Madeleine K., *Peter Shaffer: Theater and Drama*, New York: St Martin's Press, 1998
Plunka, Gene A., *Peter Shaffer: Roles, Rites and Rituals in the Theater*, Rutherford, New Jersey: Fairleigh Dickinson University Press, 1988
Taylor, John Russell, *Peter Shaffer*, London: Longman, 1974
Thomas, Eberle, *Peter Shaffer: An Annotated Bibliography*, New York: Garland, 1991

Peter Shaffer stepped into the centre of theatrical attention when he was in his early thirties. Ever since the 1958 premiere of his first stage play, *Five Finger Exercise*, he has been one of the most acclaimed playwrights in Britain and America. Almost all his plays have been immensely successful, with both critics and audiences. Shaffer's work has won numerous major awards, as have film versions of his plays.

Born into an Orthodox Jewish family in Liverpool, Shaffer attended school in London. Following three years as a conscript coalminer in Kent, he went on to read history at Cambridge. After frustrating years in New York, he returned to England and ended up working for a music publisher. This, along with his early training as a pianist, has given Shaffer a musical background that he has utilized ingeniously in many plays. Shaffer's writing career started in the genre of the detective novel, collaborating with his twin brother Anthony Shaffer, author of the play *Sleuth*. Peter Shaffer next wrote plays for television and radio, a medium to which he returned in 1989 with *Whom Do I Have the Honour of Addressing?*, a monologue that sheds light on Shaffer's ambiguous relationship with America, for many years his second home.

In his first television play, *The Salt Land*, Shaffer investigates the situation in Israel in the years immediately following the birth of that nation. The play's exploration of the antagonism between strict belief in the Scriptures and purely mercenary interests, a battle waged between two brothers, foreshadows themes in Shaffer's later writing. However, with the exception of *Five Finger Exercise*, it was not until *The Royal Hunt of the Sun* that Shaffer again approached such serious issues as the role of religion in modern society, conforming to traditions, and living an authentic life.

In *Five Finger Exercise*, set in the country home of a middle-class family, the latent tensions within the family finally turn against the daughter's tutor, a young refugee named Walter. Trying to settle down after running away from Germany because of his parents' involvement in the Nazi state, Walter unsuccessfully attempts suicide to avoid the loss of yet another family. Two further motifs of Shaffer's writing are already fully developed here: manipulation and deceit as common phenomena in much human interaction, as well as the troubles of love between parents and their children, tainted as such relations are by questions of truth, trust, and power.

In the one-act plays that followed, Shaffer maintains some of these interests, but mostly presents witty and satirical comedies, most successfully in *Black Comedy*. Acting in complete darkness (presented to the audience as bright light), the sculptor Brindsley is host to both a Jewish art-dealer and the father of his fiancée. The unexpected return of his neighbour, whose cherished antiques Brindsley had secretly borrowed to impress his guests, as well as the reappearance of his former lover Clea, set the scene for hilarious encounters.

The epic drama *The Royal Hunt for the Sun* is the first play in which Shaffer staged a large-scale theatrical spectacle. Set in the Inca empire at the time of the Conquistadors, the play portrays the destruction of the native culture through certain European attitudes: lust for gold, inability to trust and hope, and Christian hypocrisy. The variously rewritten *Shrivings* takes place in an English mansion, home to Sir Gideon and two of his young fellow anti-violence protesters. On his arrival, the poet Mark Askelon involves his former mentor Gideon in a dangerous competition. Mark challenges his hosts by claiming that his own behaviour will cause them to send him away forcefully, thus violating their pacifism. Years earlier Mark had exiled his own son, now one of the residents at Shrivings, sensing in him a Dionysian capacity to believe and feel that his own Apollonian self lacked. Finally, touched by the love of his son, the poet admits defeat. But while Mark is reconciled with both his son and Sir Gideon's philosophy, the ideal of pacifism has suffered severely by the violence that has taken place, ending the play without a definite conclusion.

In *Equus*, Shaffer takes on psychoanalysis, personified by the impotent and professionally disillusioned Dr Dysart. The play circles around the analyst's sessions with Alan, a boy who has brutally blinded six horses. Dysart assumes that tensions in Alan's family – originating in his mother's strict Catholicism and class-snobbery as well as his father's materialism and hypocrisy – have caused Alan to escape into his own world of equestrian worship. Until the horrible incident, Alan used to experience religious and sensual bliss in the company of horses. Dr Dysart is at first enviously fascinated by Alan's unconventional psyche, but eventually works to transform Alan into an adapted member of mainstream society, albeit only after sensing the shortcomings of his own life and profession.

To date, *Amadeus* is Shaffer's masterpiece. The temporal setting – ranging from Mozart and Salieri's Vienna to the present day – often changes in mid-sentence, making the play technically demanding yet fascinating. This postmodern, cinema-inspired technique, combined with narrative framing, is a device that Shaffer uses in many of his plays, with the greatest dexterity in *The Gift of the Gorgon*. In *Amadeus* the religious theme centres on one man's confrontation with a merciless God. Salieri functions as the mediocre opponent of the genial, yet unappreciated Mozart. Having devoted his entire life to writing sacred music and leading a moral life, Salieri must accept the fact that true aesthetic perfection is granted to a giggling and immoral lout. He henceforth plots to silence Mozart's divine talent, embarking on a battle with God that, with Mozart's death, he seemingly wins. Only later does Salieri understand that his punishment is to live and see his music and name become forgotten, finally claiming for himself the status of "Patron Saint of Mediocrities."

Given Shaffer's unfavourable view of any form of orthodox belief or absolute truth, it comes as no surprise that in *Yonadab* he does not shrink from presenting a rather unflattering view of King David and his family. With the incestuous rape of Tamar as a general theme taken from the Scriptures, Shaffer develops a tale of violence and betrayal, combined with Yonadab's own battle with an unjust God, reminiscent of Salieri in *Amadeus*.

Peter Shaffer's plays have managed to bridge the gap between successful entertainment and philosophical questioning. While this dual status has earned him criticism from many different directions, Shaffer remains committed to drama as a means of addressing profound issues, ranging from psychoanalysis to violence and religion. Issues of Jewishness only rarely appear in Shaffer's work.

GERD BAYER

Shaham, Nathan

Israeli fiction writer, 1925–

Born in Tel Aviv, 29 January 1925. Member, Kibbutz Beit Alfa, since 1945. Served in the army during War of Independence, 1948. Israeli cultural attaché, New York, 1977–80; has also been vice-chairman, Israeli Broadcasting Authority; now editor in chief, Sifriyat Poalim publishing house. Awards include Bialik Prize, 1988; National Jewish Book Award for Fiction (United States).

Selected Writings

Novels
Dagan veoferet [Grain and Lead], 1948
Haelim atselim [The Gods Are Lazy], 1949
Tamid anahnu [Always Us], 1952
Even al pi habeer [A Stone on the Well's Mouth], 1956
Hokhmat hamisken [The Wisdom of the Poor], 1960
Reah hadarim [Citrus Scent], 1962
Guf rishon rabim [First Person Plural], 1968
Halokh veshov [Round Trip], 1972
Daber el haruah [Talk to the Wind], 1975
Ed hamelekh [Witness for the King], 1975
Kirot ets dakim, 1978; as *The Other Side of the Wall*, translated by Leonard Gold, 1983
Etsem el atsmo, 1981; as *Bone to the Bone*, translated by Dalya Bilu, 1993
Demamah dakah [Still Silent Voice], 1983
Hutsot ashkelon [The Streets of Ashkelon], 1985
Reviyat rosendorf, 1987; as *The Rosendorf Quartet*, translated by Dalya Bilu, 1991
Sidra [Series], 1992
Lev tel aviv [The Heart of Tel Aviv], 1996

Short Stories
Shikun vatikim [Veteran's Housing], 1958
"Coming Home" in *Firstfruits*, edited by James A. Michener, 1973
Sipurim [Stories], 1978
Stav yarok [Green Autumn], 1979
Naknikiot hamot [Hot Dogs], 1993
Mikhtav baderekh [Expect a Letter], 1999

Plays
Hem yagyu mahar, 1949; as *They'll Be Here Tomorrow*, translated by Israel Schen, 1957
Kra li siomka [Call Me Siomka], 1950
Heshbon hadash [New Account], 1989

Other
Yohanan bar hama: hizayon min heavar [Vision from the Past], 1952
Kevar mutar legalot [It's Already Been Allowed to Reveal], 1959
Masa leerets kush [The Journey to the Land of Kush], 1962
Kav lidemut: zeev havatselet mipi reav [An Outline: A Wolf, a Flower from the Mouth of Hunger], 1963
Zeh biglal [Because], 1964
Masa beerets yisrael, 1966; as *Journey in the Land of Israel*, translated by I.M. Lask, 1966
Masa beerets nodaat [A Journey to a Familiar Country], 1968
Sefer hadiokanaot [The Book of Portraits], 1968
Shishah yamin, 1968; translated as *Israel Defence Forces: The Six Day War*, 1968
This Land We Love, 1970
Hahar ve habayit [Mountain and Home], 1984
Arba beteivah ahat [Four in One Bar], 1987
Sefer hatum [Sealed Book], 1988
Dor hamidbar [The Desert Generation], 1991
Dor hapalmah basifrut uvashirah: bimelot 50 shanim ledor hapalmah [A Generation of the Palmach in Literature and Poetry], 1994

Further Reading

Silberschlag, Eisig, *From Renaissance to Renaissance II: Hebrew Literature in the Land of Israel, 1870–1970*, New York: Ktav, 1977

Nathan Shaham is one of a multitude of Israeli writers who is widely respected and admired in his Hebrew-speaking homeland but is little known abroad. Still, in this regard he has fared better than most; he is among the handful of contemporary Israeli writers who has had at least some of his work translated into English. And while Shaham has by no means earned the international repute of Aharon Appelfeld, Amos Oz, A.B. Yehoshua or David Grossman, he arguably deserves his place in that first rank of Israeli writers.

Shaham was born in 1925 and came of age in Israel's War of Independence as a member of the "Palmach generation" of novelists that included S. Yizhar, Moshe Shamir, Aharon Megged, Hanokh Bartov and Yigal Mossinsohn. In addition, he is a longtime kibbutz member. It is not surprising, therefore, that much of Shaham's writing has been devoted to exploring such matters as the impact of statehood and collective living on the Jewish soul. To be sure, each of these subjects has been well mined by numerous hands, and by now interest in both the struggle for independence and the kibbutz has understandably waned – both in Israel and elsewhere. But Shaham has repeatedly demonstrated his ability to fashion lasting literature from such materials.

Shaham's most acclaimed novel is *The Rosendorf Quartet*, which appeared in Hebrew in 1987 and which was subsequently translated into English, German, Russian, and Chinese. The story concerns the struggles of four musicians who have emigrated from Europe to Palestine in the 1930s to achieve some measure of harmony – not only in music making but in reconciling themselves spiritually and psychologically to the harsh and uncertain new environment of pre-state Israel. One character in the novel quotes Bronislaw Huberman, founder of the Palestine Symphony Orchestra, as insisting that "unless they adhered to European values, the Jewish minority in Palestine was liable to slide into Levantinism in the confines of a messianic ghetto, which would be no less dangerous than the ghettos of Eastern Europe." Yet what point is there, Shaham asks, in attempting to transplant "European values" into the Middle East when those very values are being trampled upon in Europe itself? As the quartet's second violinist agonizes:

> My theory teacher . . . That good man, who saw himself as the keeper of the flame of pure German tradition, imagined that preserving the exact traditional measurements of tempo and volume was in itself a guarantee of the survival of a civilization.
>
> But after he was set upon by S.S. men in the street on his way to the concert hall and heard his heart beating more than a hundred times a minute, he understood that what was moderato in Haydn's day was no longer so in the days of Hitler.

Beyond serving as an obvious metaphor, Shaham's quartet comprises four distinct individuals. Each of them, along with a fifth character, a writer, narrates a section of the novel, and each in his or her way illuminates the tribulations of reinvention, renewal and integrity of self that attend such a momentous experience as the forging of a new nation. Like the music that figures at its heart, *The Rosendorf Quartet* is an unusually rich book, full of surprising counterpoints of melancholy and irony.

Melancholy and irony also envelop the life of Avigdor Berkov, the sorry hero of Shaham's novel *Bone to the Bone*. Berkov is one of that unhappy number of Russian Jews who came to Palestine as pioneers and then, once the Bolsheviks had seized power in Russia, went back to help foster the workers' paradise and the worldwide revolution. Ironically, most of these revolutionary dreamers were swallowed up in labour camps and never heard of again. Berkov himself underwent imprisonment, torture, and endless deprivations and humiliations. But somehow he survived. Now at age 70, he leaves the shambles of his personal and political life behind him in Russia and joins the new wave of Soviet immigration to Israel. Here he revisits the life he had made before he abandoned Zionism for Communism. In an old-age home a one-time fellow pioneer tells Berkov: "'All that tremendous experience . . . An apocalyptic experience . . . The most profound trauma suffered by humanity in the twentieth century . . . The rupture which split the globe and tore subterranean currents from the bowels of the earth – all this passed over your head without your learning or understanding a thing. The poison fed you in your youth is still seething in your bones. You're incorrigible.'"

Incorrigible – or perhaps just a fool. Or perhaps in a more compassionate view, this one Berkov's own: "Unknowingly, I performed a classical Jewish role: the chosen people. The revolution has chosen us to be the Jesus of our times. Although we said 'Render unto the revolution what is the revolution's' – they crucified us."

For further evidence of Shaham's ability to write philosophical fiction in deeply human terms, one only need consider *The Other Side of the Wall*. Here we have three novellas that deal with characters' political ideals put to the test by the unexpected and disruptive intrusion of emotional life. In "S/S Cairo City" a pioneer from Palestine attends an international Zionist congress in 1939 only to suffer the twin agonies of the looming war in Europe and the love of a much younger girl who insists on remaining in Poland. In "The Salt of the Earth" a 70-year-old kibbutz veteran travels for the first time to the United States and falls victim both to the lures of capitalist achievement and to the charms of a delightful widow. And in the title story a city-bred woman who elects kibbutz life finds herself consumed by erotic fever because of the sounds of lovemaking coming from the room next door. As in all of Shaham's work, ideology looms large in the lives of these characters, but they are no less credible – or absorbing – for that.

Shaham maintains his steady creative output in the 21st century, as evidenced by his latest collection of deeply felt short stories *Mikhtav baderekh* [Expect a Letter]. He also continues to serve as editor in chief of Sifriyat Poalim, one of Israel's most prestigious publishing houses, where he continues to exercise considerable influence on the literary life of his country.

MATTHEW NESVISKY

Shahar, David

Israeli fiction writer, 1926–1997

Born in Jerusalem, 1926. Studied at yeshiva and secular secondary school, Jerusalem; Hebrew University, Jerusalem, graduate in philosophy. Fought in wars of 1948, 1956, and 1967. Lived in Paris, 1962–64 and 1971. Former chairman, Hebrew Writers Association. Many awards, including Prime Minister's Award, 1969 and 1978; Agnon Prize, 1973; Prix Médicis Étranger (France), 1981; Bialik Prize, 1984; Newman Prize, 1987. Commandeur, Ordre des Art et des Lettres. Died in Paris, 1997.

Selected Writings

Short Stories
Al hahalomot [On Dreams], 1956
Caesar, 1960
News from Jerusalem, translated by Dalya Bilu *et al.*, 1974; as *Stories from Jerusalem*, 1976
Shaloshot sipurim [Three Stories], 1974
Sipurim ketsarim, 1979
Moto shel haelohim hakatan [The Death of the Little God], 1982
Sfamo shel haafifor [The Pope's Moustache], 1982
Al ner veal ruah [On Candles and Winds], 1994
El har hazeytim [To the Mount of Olives], 1998

Novels
Yareah hadevash vehazahav [Moon of Honey and Gold], 1959
Magid haatidot [The Fortune Teller], 1966
Heikhal hakelim hashevurim, 1969–91; as *The Palace of Shattered Vessels*, translated by Dalya Bilu, 1975–93
Kayits bederekh haneviim, 1969; as *Summer in the Street of the Prophets*, 1975
H-massa leur kasdim, 1971; as *A Voyage to Ur of the Chaldees*, 1975
Yom arozenet, 1976; as *Day of the Countess*, 1976
Nin-gal, 1983; as *Nin-Gal*, 1985
Yom harefaim, 1986; as *Day of the Ghosts*, 1989
Halom leyl tammuz, 1989; as *A Tammuz Night's Dream*, 1989
Leylot lutetsia, 1991; as *Nights of Lutetia*, 1993
Sokhen hamelekh [His Majesty's Agent], 1979

Other
Sodo shel ricky [Ricky's Secret], 1974

Further Reading

Morahg, Gilead, "Piercing the Shimmering Bubble: David Shahar's *The Palace of Shattered Vessels*", *AJS Review*, 10/2 (Fall 1985): 211–34
Sokoloff, Naomi, "Metaphysics and Metanarrative in the Stories of David Shahar", *Hebrew Annual Review* (1982)
Telpaz, Gideon, *Israeli Childhood Stories of the Sixties*, Chico, California: Scholars Press, 1983

David Shahar's novels and short stories are mostly set in Jerusalem, a city that serves as a metaphysical and mythical source as well as a physical setting for the part-fictional and part-autobiographical worlds that he describes.

The Palace of Shattered Vessels, Shahar's major work, takes its title from the "shattered vessels" by which the 16th-century Kabbalist Isaac Luria, born in Jerusalem, describes the world in which we live. The order of the material world, into which God has breathed life, is incompatible with the order of the divine; the world, and each of us in it, is a broken vessel. Writing, as Shahar states in an interview, is one way of repairing this splintered reality: "I attempt to gather up these fragments."

Shahar's extraordinary fresco in the seven volumes of this work, written from 1969 to 1991, develops principally out of his childhood memories of Jerusalem in the 1930s. The work is constructed of interwoven tales, where characters take on form, intersect with other characters, fade into the background, disappear and re-emerge in new contexts. In these shifting sands, there is a touchstone in the form of Gabriel Luria whom the narrator is fascinated by as a child (and who bears the same name as the 16th-century mystic of the "shattered vessels"). The narrator's family and the Luria family share the same courtyard and well in the Street of the Prophets, and across the work we gradually piece together Gabriel's life, the worlds of his wealthy Spanish Sephardi father and poor Ashkenazi mother, Gabriel's loves and disappointments, his hopes and quests and experiences in Jerusalem, Paris, and Brittany.

Besides the key figure of Gabriel to guide us, Shahar presents us with a network of lives criss-crossing through key places in Jerusalem (the Bnei Brit library, the Paramount Café) or gathering around certain events such as the repeated motif of the arrival of the Emperor Haile Selassie at the then Abyssinian Consulate in Jerusalem, accompanied by Coptic monks and imperial eunuchs and protected by British police, an episode that recurs across the work, with different perspectives at different points. Fish-packers, "Galician thiefs", former Officers of the Ottoman Empire, Scottish aristocrats and more mingle in the streets of Jerusalem; love songs from Arab cafés vie with Chopin walzes in the evening air, Mrs Luria screams curses at her husband, the "old adulterous Turk", as she calls him when annoyed, reflecting that Moses wandered for 40 years in the desert with the Hebrews because he was "ashamed to appear in public with them"; Anastasia Wissotsky, a romantic and impressionable woman fresh from Europe dances in the empty courtyard on Lag-Ba'omer in the arms of a Kurdish taxi driver, while Bukharan women peek through the fence and curse these "Ashkenazi women, wild whores". It is a colourful, indulgent, and humorous view of Jerusalem, where faiths, languages, empires, and personalities battle it out in a more or less tolerant way, and where surprises are as common as they are magical.

As the narrative shifts from first to third person, jumps back and forth from one time frame to another, follows up strands and comes back to the point of departure, the reader is plunged into the stories in a way that has a timeless quality to it. Reflections on the relation of body and soul in different religions, on reincarnation and on the uncanny or mystical moments that are lived and relived through memory or chance also contribute to the mythical feel, revealing the "insubstantiality of this world which is founded on the nothingness of the senses and bursts like a bubble and rises again with all its illusions and mirages".

A key source of these extraordinary lives and experiences is the narrator's memory. For Shahar, memory is the basis of everything: "Without it, there is nothing . . . we are tissues of memory", he says. It is perhaps for this reason that Shahar has been compared to Proust, in his emphasis on the creative and redemptive role of memory, triggered by small details as much as by major events. In Shahar, the past is preserved in a complex layered present, both timeless and timebound, gathering and preserving the traces of former times. Jerusalem has a privileged position in this respect, its stones described as a "time-reserve in space". Unlike Proust, however, Shahar's expression is simple, and there is an intriguing evenness to the tone of the writing. This tone endows the descriptions of everyday lives and everyday events with a visionary quality, especially when these are infused with biblical rhythms and references. The overall vision conveyed by *The Palace of Shattered Vessels* can be summarized in Shahar's description of the tree of life itself, its roots "embedded in all the generations that had gone before [them] and whose branches waved in the breezes blowing over all the generations to come".

The collection of short stories *News from Jerusalem* again takes its inspiration in the main from the narrator's childhood memories of Jerusalem, and we find in condensed form some of the features that make the mystery of Shahar's longer works: stories twist and turn, jumping 20 years or concentrating on a few hours of an afternoon, and characters undergo sudden and strange transformations. For example, an Uncle Zemach, after a ruthless rise in the world of law, suddenly, at the death of his wife, begins to hear voices, to be overcome by inexplicable bursts of anger and despair, and finally reverts to a life of dreamy inactivity. The stories also abound in uncanny repetitions – another uncle, the respected Uncle Zerach, is shamed publicly by a prostitute, Reizale, and takes refuge in a neighbouring café, only to find himself drawn to the young student Eva. Shahar's writing in these stories is at its most delicate and suggestive, leaving the powerful forces behind these transformations and inversions to the imagination of the reader, preserving the calm and measured surface that also characterizes his longer works.

SASKIA BROWN

Shalev, Meir

Israeli fiction writer, dramatist, and columnist, 1948–

Born in agricultural cooperative of Nahalal, 29 July 1948; father, poet Itzhak Shalev. Studied at Hebrew University, Jerusalem, BA in psychology 1972. Military service in army, 1966–68. Married Rina; one daughter, one son. Writer in residence, Hebrew University, 1994. Producer and host of radio and television programmes; regular columnist in Israeli press. Awarded Prime Minister's Prize, 1989; Shalom Aleichem Prize, 1994; Entomological Society Prize, 1989; WIZO Prize, 1992.

Selected Writings

Novels

Roman russi, 1988; as *The Blue Mountain*, translated by Hillel Halkin, 1991

Esav, 1991; as *Esau*, translated by Barbara Harshav, 1993

Keyamim ahadim, 1994; as *The Loves of Judith*, translated by Barbara Harshav, 1999

For Children

Hayeled hayim ve hamifletset miyerushalayim, 1982; as *Michael and the Monster of Jerusalem*, 1990

Gumot hahen shel zohar [Zohar's Dimples], 1987

Aba oseh bushot, 1988; as *My Father Always Embarrasses Me*, 1990

Hakinah nehamah [Nehamah the Louse], 1990

Other

Mishkav letsim [Sofa for Clowns], 1982

Tanakh akhshav, 1985; as *Bible Now*, 1999

Rewriting History in the Bible: The Book of Ruth vs The Book of Chronicles, 1988

Beikar al ahavah [Mainly about Love], 1995

Bebeyito bamidbar [His House in the Desert], 1998

Sod ahizat haenayim [Elements of Conjuration], 1999

Further Reading

Shiffman, Smadar, *Tevi 'At Etsba 'o Shel Ha-Mahaber: Ha-'Olamot Ha-po'etiyim Shel Faulkner, Hemingway U-Meir Shalev*, Tel Aviv: Hakibuts hameuhad, 1999

There are many elements to take into consideration when reading the works of Meir Shalev. The first of these is Zionism, or the myth of Zionism as portrayed in *Roman Russi* (*The Blue Mountain*). Here the entire text seems to emphasize the rise and fall of Zionist ideology. This emphasis is first demonstrated at the start of the novel, and involves a description of how tourists flock each year to visit the "creation" of the founding fathers, namely the orchards and crops. This visit ends in the renowned cemetery, which is aptly named Pioneer Home. Consequently, this guided tour that begins in the orchards and ends in the much visited and lucrative graveyard actually chronicles the Zionist dream as it falls prey to commercialism and thus to capitalism. This description of the guided tour therefore encapsulates that which occurs during the novel.

The second cynical portrayal of the Zionist dream is shown via the protagonist's role as both narrator and owner of Pioneer Home. Baruch claims that his cemetery is exclusively for those pioneers who reached Palestine during the Second Aliyah and who are considered cornerstones of the Zionist movement and thereby respected. However, Baruch ends up burying many Jews who, although they arrived at the right time, left after a few weeks to seek their fortune elsewhere. Thus in burying such people Baruch is in fact recreating history. He is ignoring their unimpressive contribution to the Zionist cause and maintaining the integrity of the cemetery. The reason being, of course, money.

The fact that most of the characters Baruch describes end up in his cemetery explains why it is appropriate that he should look backwards and tell us, the reader, about their lives up until the moment when they are buried. In other words, the entire narration serves to justify the burial of certain characters. This bias obviously subverts the value of the entire narration, since Baruch's descriptions are pointed and deliberate and therefore reductive.

This reductive narration also explains the mythical element of history. That is, Baruch, in his attempt to mould the past, seems to rely heavily on oral history, stories and legends that he has heard or supposedly heard from other people in his village. This oral history often seems quite fantastical, as is the case with Jean Valjean, or quite exaggerated, as is the case with the antics of the Feyge Circle. The line between myth and reality is therefore almost impossible to decipher in *The Blue Mountain*. This reductive retelling of the past can also be found in *Keyamim ahadim* (*The Loves of Judith*) where Zayde's task is to gather together stories and information in order to explain to the implied reader his own tragic yet inevitable role in the death of his mother Judith. Hence Zayde's narrative technique of switching from story to story and perspective to perspective is merely a way of weaving together a story that will eventually appear consistent in its line of causation. "Man Makes Plans and God Laughs" is the Yiddish dictum that should show itself both to Zayde and the reader. The narrative in *The Loves of Judith* is therefore as unreliable as that of Baruch's in *The Blue Mountain*.

In addition to the Zionist element and to the element of retelling the past, Shalev also employs techniques used to portray the magically real. Amaryll Chanady describes magical realism as a combination of two worlds, namely fantasy and reason. That which is considered fantastical seems feasible to the reader. This is achieved via the style of narration. The narrator who is otherwise shown to be a rational being, relates events that are in fact irrational. However, he or she does this in such a way as to seem quite natural to the reader. Thus it is the style that dictates the reaction of the implied reader. The content on the other hand, however fantastical, is irrelevant to the implied reader's reaction to the text. This reaction is of course crucial in determining whether a text is magically real or not.

In the case of *The Blue Mountain* this technique is quite apparent. The most obvious example is that of Zeister the mule. Not only does Zeister amuse a little child by imitating different birds and animals, and not only does he commit suicide, but he also knocks politely on doors using one hoof as well as making the decision that kibbutz life is incompatible with his family ideals. It is obviously against the natural laws of the universe that a mule could do or think such things. However Baruch describes them in such a detached and non-judgemental manner that the reader is made to understand that such things are perfectly natural in Baruch's mind. Since Baruch is otherwise a person to whom a reader can relate, his descriptions of supernatural or fantastical events are accepted without question.

Similarly, in *The Loves of Judith*, Zayde describes his encounter with the Angel of Death:

> A heap of dust rose and beyond it I saw the Angel of Death, his notebook in his hand, his eyes fixed on me. "What's your name?" he asked me. "Zayde" I answered, not letting go of the rope. The Angel of Death recoiled as if stunned by an invisible slap. He moistened his fingers and leafed through the notebook.

This passage contains no element of disbelief, or doubt on the part of the protagonist that such an encounter could have taken place. Consequently the reader accepts the story as part of Zayde's life. If, of course, it were understood that Zayde's inner thought processes were significantly different to those of the implied reader, then the real reader would be more sceptical.

GIULIA MILLER

Shamir, Moshe

Israeli fiction writer, dramatist, literary critic, and journalist, 1921–

Born in Safed, 15 September 1921. Studied at Herzalia High School, Tel Aviv, 1935–39. Lived on Kibbutz Mishmar Ha-Emek, 1941–47. Member, Haganah, Palmach, and Israeli forces, 1937–50. Married Zvia Frumkin, 1946; three children. Founder and first editor, Israeli army weekly *Bamahane*; visiting professor, Technion, Haifa, 1962–63; literary editor, *Maariv* daily, Tel Aviv, 1963–76. Director, Land of Israel Movement, Tel Aviv, 1967–80; director, Jewish Agency, London, 1969–71; Likud member of Knesset (Israeli legislature), 1977–81. Awarded Brenner Prize, 1953; Bialik Prize, 1955; New York University Newman Prize, 1980; Baratz–Govinska Drama Prize, 1985; Israel Prize, 1988.

Selected Writings

Novels
Hu halakh basadot [He Walked Through the Fields], 1947
Tahat hashemesh [Under the Sun], 1950
Bemo yadav, 1951; as *With His Own Hands*, translated by Joseph Schachter, 1970
Melekh basar vadam, 1954; as *The King of Flesh and Blood*, translated by David Patterson, 1958
Kivsat harash [Poor Man's Lamb], 1957; as *David's Stranger; or, The Hittite Must Die*, translated by Margaret Benaya, 1965
Ha galgal hahamishi, 1958; as *The Fifth Wheel*, translated by Aubrey Hodes, 1961
Ki erom atah [That You Are Naked], 1959
Hagvul [The Border], 1966
Trilogy
Yona mihatser aher [From a Different Yard], 1973
Hinumat hakalah [The Bridal Veil], 1985
Ad hasof [To the End], 1991
Yaldei shaashuim [Playboys], 1986

Stories
Nashim mehakot bahuts [Women Waiting Outside], 1952
Hahut hameshulash [The Threefold Cord], 1957
Sipurim [Short Stories], 1974
Ve afilu lirot kokhavim [And Even to See Stars], 1993
Abraham baboker [Abraham in the Morning], 1997

Plays
Hu halakh basadot, 1947; as *He Walked through the Fields*, translated by Aubrey Hodes, 1959
Kilometre 56 [Kilometre 56], 1949
Beit hillel [The House of Hillel], 1950
Sof haolam [The End of the World], 1954
Milhemet benei haor, 1955; as *The War of the Sons of Light*, 1956
Meagadot lod [Legends of Lydda], 1958
Hamishah maarakhonim [Five One Act Plays], 1959
Hayoresh [The Heir], 1989
Yehudit shel hametsurayim [Judith of the Lepers], 1989

Poetry
Kimat [Almost], 1991

For Children
Yedidav hagdolim shel gadi [Gady's Big Friends], 1947
Ehad efes letovatenu [One Nil for Us], 1951
Kulam beyahad [All Together], 1959
Hagalgal hahamishi [The Fifth Wheel], 1966
Bemo libo [With His Own Heart], 1976
Manhigim veshoftim [Leaders and Judges], 1976
Hamamlakhah hameuhedet [The United Kingdom], 1977
Malkhei beit david [The Kings of David's House], 1977
Sipurim beshalosh kolot [Stories in Three Voices], 1977
Malkhei yisrael [The Kings of Israel], 1978

Other
Translator, *El Resplandor*, by Mauricio Magdaleno, 1948
Portsei derekh leyerushalayim [Breaking through to Jerusalem], 1948
Ad eilat [On the Way to Eilat], 1950
Co-editor, *Yevul*, 1950
Bekulmus mahir [With a Quick Pen], 1960
Beikvot lohamei sinai: anashim venofim bemivtsa kadesh [In the Footsteps of the Sinai Warriors], 1967
Nes lo karah lanu [No Miracle Happened to Us], 1967
Translator, *Waiting for Godot*, by Samuel Beckett, 1968
Hayai im ishmael, 1968; as *My Life with Ishmael*, translated by Rose Kirson, 1970
El mul pnei hamilhamah hahazakah [In the Forefront of the Hottest Battle], 1974
Lo rehokim min haets [Not Far from the Tree], 1983
Inyan ishi [A Personal Matter], 1987
Kehut hashani [The Crimson Cord], 1987
Habead ve haneged [For and Against], 1988
Natan Alterman: ha meshorer kemanhig [Natan Alterman: The Poet as a Leader], 1988
Nosei hemshekh [The Seed Carriers], 1989
Hamakom hayarok [The Green Place], 1991
Protokol shel mapolet [A Report of Debacle], 1991
Co-editor, *Sefer yalkut hareyim*, 1992
Reuben Hecht, agadat hayim [Reuben Hecht, the Legend of a Life], 1994
Zarkor laomek [A Searchlight to the Depth], 1996
Haomdin bapirtsah:al sifrut vesofrim [Filling the Gap: Literary Essays], 1999

Further Reading
Golan, Ornah, *Ben Bidyon le-Mashmaut: Sugim Ba-Sipur Ha-Yisraeli*, vol. 2, Tel Aviv: Everyman's University, 1984
Miron, Dan, *Arbaah Panim Ba Sifrut Ha-Ivrit Be-Yameinu*, Jerusalem: Schocken, 1962
Oren, Yosef, *Zehuyot ba-siporet ha-Yisre'elit*, Rishon le-Tsiyon: Yahad, 1994
Ramras-Rauch, Gila, *The Arab in Israeli Literature*, Bloomington: Indiana University Press, and London: Tauris, 1989
Sadan, Dov, *Bein Din Leheshbon*, Tel Aviv: Dvir, 1963
Seh-Lavan, Yosef, *Moshe Shamir*, Tel Aviv: Oram, 1978
Shaked, Gershon, *Hebrew Narrative Fiction*, vol. 4, Jerusalem: Keter, 1993
Shenfeld, Ruth, *From King Messiah to King of Flesh and Blood: The Hebrew Novel in the Twentieth Century*, Tel Aviv: Papyrus Publishing House, 1986
Shoham, Chaim, *Etgar U-Metsi'ut Ba-Dramah Ha-Yisre'elit: Iyunim Be-Mahazot, Shamir, Shoham, Meged, Mosinzo, Aloni Ve Ha'ezrahi*, Ramat Gan: Bar Ilan University, 1975
Silberschlag, Eisig, "The Historical Novel" in his *From Renaissance to Renaissance*, vol. 2, New York: Ktav, 1977
Yudkin, Leon I., "Flight of the Hero in Israeli Fiction", in his *Escape into Siege: A Survey of Israeli Literature Today*, London and Boston: Routledge and Kegan Paul, 1974
Yudkin, Leon I., *1948 and After: Aspects of Israeli Fiction*, Manchester: University of Manchester, 1984
Yudkin, Leon I. (editor), *Israeli Writers Consider the "Outsider"*, Rutherford, New Jersey: Fairleigh Dickinson University Press, and London: Associated University Presses, 1993

Moshe Shamir is one of the main representatives of the 1948, or the Palmach, generation of writers, who, born in Israel and educated in Hebrew, generally shared a collective biography and reached their literary consciousness at the time of the War of Independence. These authors, following the uprooted pioneer fathers, who rejected the European Diaspora, remained committed to the values of the collective. The new social and political circumstances demanded a new kind of identity, one that would contrast the image of the Diaspora Jew. Thus the figure of the new Israeli, the sabra, emerged and with it the devotion to the group and to social duty in the new country.

Shamir's works are primarily concerned with the new social and political reality and present arguably the best portrayal of the idealized sabra. In terms of literary techniques and language, his novels are traditional, rather than innovative. The language is standard literary Hebrew, commonly used in the 1940s, although it often becomes vernacular, with many idiomatic and slang expressions. The literary techniques employed by Shamir do not present the same sense of innovation or experimentation that could be observed in the works of some writers of the late 19th century, such as Uri Nissan Gnessin or Yosef Hayyim Brenner. The descriptions are straightforward, with some flashbacks and occasional reflections. There is a pervading sense of distance from the past – the characters, the new country, and its institutions are disconnected from the former experiences of the Jewish people. As the author himself said, his novels aspire to be adequate to the revolutionary situation that is their subject, rather than to be revolutionary themselves, and as such are committed to the collective values of their time.

The hero of *He Walked through the Fields*, Uri Cahana (already an Israeli name) is a young man, born in the Land of Israel who, as many of Shamir's protagonists, exemplifies the ideology of the author and the group portrayed by him. Strong, well built, attractive, with the hair style characteristic of the early Zionist pioneers (*blurit* [cowlick]), even in his appearance he represents the ideal of the new Israeli, totally opposed to the image of the Diaspora Jew, generally perceived then as awkward, dressed in black, weak, and unattractive. The protagonist's loyalty and devotion to the collective responsibilities always take priority over his individual needs. The difficult conditions he has to face demand just that kind of dedication, and Shamir's hero takes his sense of responsibility as a part of a group even further, always following the collective and never questioning the decisions made by it, nor considering any alternatives:

> Uri was not enamoured of thinking for its own sake. He would take it up for a moment when something would trouble him or was so significant that it allowed him no rest; but thinking out of the habit of the power of thought itself, original and independent life of feeling, reaction and analysis, these were symptoms of an unfortunate sickness.

Thus the protagonist's main priority is his participation in the building of the physical environment, and his intellectual faculties are used for just that, rather than in any theoretical, emotional, or ideological context, which is associated with life in the Diaspora, an existence considered "overspiritualized". The will to become a sacrifice epitomizes the character's devotion to the Land with its sociopolitical demands. Uri fantasizes about his death, which would ultimately prove his dedication to the group and further compensate for what he had received both from the collective and from his parents, who were the creators of the ideology that Uri embodies. Indeed, the protagonist meets premature death, announced by the narrator (the father) in the beginning of the novel, thus sacrificing not only his individuality but also himself for the common cause.

With His Own Hands was originally intended to be a tribute to the author's brother, Elik Shamir, who died in 1948. As in *He Walked through the Fields*, the protagonist of the novel is a young man, who epitomizes the ideal sabra. The novel begins with a sentence "Elik was born from the sea", a remark that stresses the protagonist's closeness to nature and, above all, the mystery of his origins. He symbolizes the discontinuity, a break from the Diaspora, a new beginning in the new environment, which is completely natural to him – his unquestionable habitat is geographically and historically unproblematic. From the very beginning there is a strong, almost physical link between nature and the protagonist. The novel is written from the point of view of Elik's younger brother, who sees the protagonist as the embodiment of the collective ideals of the time. Never divided or introspective, Elik believes everything should be done by himself, "with his own hands", assuming the responsibility expected of him. Killing is considered as an act necessary for the achievement of the collective purpose and, as was the case with Uri Cahana, the group is of primary significance and that includes, above all, those under the protagonist's command in Palmach. Despite his loneliness, Elik never isolates himself from his peers because of the responsibility towards the collective and because he himself was part of that collective. At the moment of the United Nations vote, the protagonist becomes the Nation, as he feels the excitement both in the streets, in the people around him and in his blood, thus experiencing his own, individual joy as well as that of the group he belongs to: his family, the Palmach, and the nation.

The idea of premature death is again present throughout the novel, and despite momentary doubts, Elik, the commander of Palmach, sees no alternative but to accept his predicament. He asks himself who would pay the price for the creation of the State of Israel. He replies, "We will pay" and thus accepts the necessity of the sacrifice he has to make.

On the whole, Shamir's novels are moral tales, which depict the reality of the early days of the State of Israel and whose heroes are individuals with a strong sense of belonging within a larger group. Although recent literary analysis has been critical, they are representations of the collective values of the time and Shamir is writing for the group, of which he himself is a representative.

Shamir's later novels (*The King of Flesh and Blood* and *David's Stranger*) focus on earlier Jewish history that offers parallels with the more current Israeli circumstances. *My Life with Ishmael* is a political commentary on the modern Israeli situation and *Dove from Another Garden* is a novel tracing back the history of the *yishuv*, the pre-State Jewish community in Palestine. Shamir also wrote literary criticism, e.g. *The Seed Carriers*, and many critical essays.

MARTA MARZANSKA

Shapiro, Karl

US poet, 1913–2000

Born Karl Jay Shapiro in Baltimore, Maryland, 10 November 1913. Studied at the University of Virginia, 1932–33; Johns Hopkins University, 1937–39; Pratt Library School, Baltimore, 1940. Clerk in family business, mid-1930s. Served in US Army, 1941–45. Married, first, Evalyn Katz, 1945 (divorced 1967), two daughters, one son; second, Teri Kovach, 1967 (died 1982); third, Sophie Wilkins, 1985. Associate Professor, Johns Hopkins University, 1948–50; Visiting Professor, University of Wisconsin, 1948; Loyola University, 1951–52; University of California, 1955–56; and Indiana University, 1956–57; Professor of English, University of Nebraska, 1956–66; University of Illinois, 1966–68; and University of California, Davis, 1968–84. Editor, *Poetry*, 1950–56; *Newberry Library Bulletin*, 1953–55, and *Prairie Schooner*, 1956–66. Consultant in Poetry, 1946–47, and Whittall Lecturer, 1964, 1967, Library of Congress, Washington, DC. Lecturer, Salzburg Seminar in American Studies, 1952; State Department Lecturer, India, 1955; Elliston Lecturer, University of Cincinnati, 1959. Many awards, including American Academy grant, 1944; Guggenheim Fellowship, 1944, 1953; Pulitzer Prize, 1945; Shelley memorial award, 1946; Kenyon School of Letters Fellowship, 1956, 1957; Bollingen prize, 1969; Los Angeles Times Kirsch Award, 1989. Member, American Academy of Arts and Sciences, and American Academy, 1959. Died in New York, 14 May 2000.

Selected Writings

Poetry
Poems, 1935
Five Young American Poets, 1941
The Place of Love, 1942
Person, Place and Thing, 1944
V-Letter and Other Poems, 1945
Essay on Rime, 1945
Trial of a Poet and Other Poems, 1947
The Thin Bell-Ringer, 1948
Poems 1940–1953, 1953
Poems of a Jew, 1958
The Bourgeois Poet, 1964
Selected Poems, 1968
There Was That Roman Poet Who Fell in Love at Fifty Odd, 1968
White-Haired Lover, 1968
Auden (1907–1973), 1974
Adult Bookstore, 1976
Collected Poems 1940–1978, 1978
Love and War, Art and God, 1984
Adam and Eve, 1986
New and Selected Poems 1940–1986, 1987
The Old Horsefly, 1992

Novel
Edsel, 1971

Plays
The Tenor, 1957
The Soldier's Tale, 1968

Other
English Prosody and Modern Poetry, 1947
A Bibliography of Modern Prosody, 1948
Poets at Work, 1948
Beyond Criticism, 1953; as *A Primer for Poets*, 1965
Editor, *Modern American and Modern British Poetry*, 1955
Editor, *American Poetry*, 1960
In Defense of Ignorance, 1960
Start with the Sun: Studies in Cosmic Poetry, 1960
Editor, *Prose Keys to Modern Poetry*, 1962
The Writer's Experience, 1964
A Prosody Handbook, 1965
Randall Jarrell, 1967
To Abolish Children and Other Essays, 1968
The Poetry Wreck: Selected Essays 1950–1970, 1975
Poet: An Autobiography in Three Parts (includes *The Younger Son* and *Reports of My Death*), 2 vols, 1988–90

Further Reading

Bartlett, Lee, *Karl Shapiro: A Descriptive Bibliography 1933–1977*, New York: Garland, 1979
Reino, Joseph, *Karl Shapiro*, Boston: Twayne, 1981
Riva, Valerio, *Prefaces to the Tropics: Henry Miller, Karl Shapiro and Others*, Milan: Fettrinelli, 1962

Karl Shapiro's identity as a Jew informed his early work from "University" in 1940 beginning "To hurt the negro and avoid the Jew is the curriculum", through his collection, *Poems of a Jew* in 1958. And his ever-changing attitude toward the world is evident in another early poem entitled simply "Jew": "A language itself that is whispered and hissed/ Through the houses of ages, and ever a language the same,/ And ever and ever a blow on our heart like a fist."

In 1948, after voting to award the Bollingen Prize for Poetry to Ezra Pound's *Pisan Cantos*, in agreement with W.H. Auden, Louise Bogan, T.S. Eliot, Allen Tate, Katherine Anne Porter, Robert Penn Warren, and Robert Lowell, Shapiro changed his vote, in favour of William Carlos Williams's "Paterson", saying that "he could not endorse an anti-Semite for the Prize".

"Recapitulations," a biographical poem in rhyming quatrains, tells about his birth in a Catholic hospital: "downtown on a wintry day/ And under the roof where Poe expired:/ At one week all my family prayed,/ Stuffed wine and cotton in my craw;
The rabbi blessed me with a blade/ According to the Mosaic Law./ The white steps blazed in Baltimore/ And cannas and white statuary./ I went home voluble and sore influenced by Abraham and Mary."

His early initiation into Judaism and Christianity is a theme in "The Crucifix in the Filing Cabinet" and "The Missal", a prose poem from *The Bourgeois Poet*, a radical departure from his earlier "classical" verse. Set in New Guinea during World War II, it begins:

> Priests and Freudians will understand . . . Lying in mud or in soaked hammocks the soldiers stew and joke and empty their dead minds. Deprived of love and letters and the sight of woman, the dead mind rots. I seek the chaplain in the tent. Father, convert me. He looks at me and says: You must excuse me, sergeant. I have a furlough coming up. When I say the Hail Mary I get an erection. Doesn't that prove the existence of God?

At one point, Shapiro actually considered becoming a Catholic. So what is Shapiro's true identity as a religious person? Perhaps he strides across multiple personae, including the person whose voice we hear throughout *The Bourgeois Poet*: "I am an atheist who says his prayers. I am an anarchist, and a full professor at that . . . I am a mystic. I will take an oath that I have seen the Virgin."

Although his nationality and religion inform his work, Shapiro was a cultivated citizen of many cultures and literatures. In a poetic career and public life that spanned five decades, from 1945, when he received the Pulitzer Prize ("the golden albatross", as he called it) for *V-Letter and Other Poems*, until his retirement as a professor at the University of California, Davis, in 1984, he was constantly on the move.

As poet, critic, novelist, editor, teacher, memoirist, sometime ambassador for American poetry abroad and enfant terrible at home, Shapiro frequently challenged the status quo – out of pique or devotion to craft or a hatred of pretension or maybe just for fun. Along the way, he wrote poems that many readers read or learned by heart at school, particularly "University", "The Fly", "Auto Wreck", "The Dirty Word", "Lower the Standard". One of the best ways of understanding American social history – what it felt like to live during Shapiro's lifetime – is to read the poems, such as "Drug Store" from the late 1930s: "It baffles the foreigner like an idiom,/ And he is right to adopt it as a form Less serious than the living-room or bar; For it disestablishes the café,/ Is a collective, and on basic country". Similarly, poems written during his military service in the South Pacific – "Troop Train" and "The Leg" – convey the tragedy and loneliness of wartime, as well as the joy of "Homecoming". Though a soldier himself, he wrote eloquently about those who refused to kill in "The Conscientious Objector": "Well might the soldier kissing the hot beach/ Erupting in his face damn all your kind./ Yet you who saved neither ourselves nor us/ Are equally with those who shed the blood/ The heroes of our cause. Your conscience is/ What we come back to in the armistice".

After the appearance of Ginsberg's *Howl* in 1956, which Shapiro greatly admired, he turned away from regular metrical patterns and the style admired by T.S. Eliot and the dominant critics of the time toward the style of William Carlos Williams. He nonetheless wrote with affection and praise of Eliot and "his mythic poetry that has stunned the world". Shapiro's poems about other poets provide insights into literary history as well, especially those about his contemporaries – Auden ("Without him many of us would have never happened"), Theodore Roethke, and Randall Jarrell.

Although he wrote several beautiful love poems, and two long poems, "Adam and Eve" and "The Rape of Philomela", indicating his command of classical and religious mythology, Shapiro's most representative work often combines a lyrical and at the same time sceptical attitude toward his subject. These conflicting emotions are evident in "The Fly", beginning: "O hideous little bat, the size of snot,/ With polyhedral eye and shabby clothes,/ To populate the stinking cat you walk/ The promontory of the dead man's nose/ Climb with the fine leg of a Duncan-Phyfe/ The smoking mountains of my food/ And in a comic mood In Mid-air take to bed a wife". At the end of the poem, standing triumphant over the pathetic creature, he then pities the insect "that falls/ stunned, stone blind, and deaf,/ Buzzes its frightful F/ And dies between three cannibals". In "Nebraska", about the region where Shapiro lived and taught for ten years, he is both affectionate and sardonic: "I love Nowhere where the factories die of malnutrition./ I love Nowhere where there are no roads, no rivers, no interesting Indians,/ Where history is invented in the History Department and there are no centennials of anything".

Any discussion of Shapiro would be incomplete without attending to his achievements in prose as well as poetry that reflect intelligence, wit, and immense learning, although characteristically, "the bourgeois poet" wore his learning lightly. *Essay on Rime* from 1945, a 2000-line poem in iambic pentameter, discusses "confusions" in prosody, language, and belief that he thought characterized much contemporary verse. In addition to the novel, *Edsel*, he wrote three remarkable memoirs, direct and clear, "in love and anger, sadness and hope", according to Reed Whittemore, who "read no living poet whose account of the state of American poetry is more credible and trustworthy." This praise by Shapiro's contemporary suggests the need for a revaluation of a body of work that, after considerable popularity and serious critical attention, is less well known among readers in the new century than it deserves to be.

MICHAEL TRUE

Shapiro, (Levi Joshua) Lamed

Russian short-story writer, 1878–1948

Born in Rzhishchev, near Kiev, 1878. Traditional Jewish education; taught himself Russian and secular subjects. Went to Warsaw, 1896, met Y.L. Perets. Returned, 1898, supported himself by tutoring. Returned to Warsaw, 1903. Emigrated to the United States, 1905 (via London for a year). Wrote for the American Yiddish press, 1906–09, especially *Forverts* (*Jewish Daily Forward*); earned serious recognition in the Yiddish literary community. Returned to Warsaw for a few years where he worked as a reporter and translator for the paper, *Der fraynt*. In Warsaw, published two collections of stories, 1910. Returned permanently to the United States, 1911, living in New York and Los Angeles for the rest of his life. Numerous attempts to make a living as an inventor. Returned from Los Angeles to New York after the deaths of his wife and mother, 1928. Edited *Di vokh*; founded a Yiddish literary quarterly, *Studio*, producing only three issues (1933–35) before the journal folded. Worked for the WPA Federal Writers Project, 1937–38. In 1930s worked on a novel set in United States, *Der amerikaner sheyd* [The American Ghost]; never finished. Returned to Los Angeles, 1939. Died in Los Angeles, 1948.

Selected Writings

Fiction
Afn yam [At the Sea], 1910
Novelen [Novellas], 1910
Di yidishe melukhe un andere zakhn [The Jewish Government and Other Things], 1919
Nyu-yorkish un andere zakhn [New York and Other Things], 1931
Fun korbn minkhe [From the Afternoon Offering], 1941
Der shrayber geyt in kheyder [The Writer Goes to School], 1945
Ksovim [Works], 1949
The Jewish Government and Other Stories, edited and translated by Curt Leviant, 1971

Further Reading

Frank, Esther, "An Analysis of Four Short Stories by Lamed Shapiro", *Working Papers in Yiddish and East European Jewish Studies* (January 1978)

Leviant, Curt, "Lamed Shapiro: Master Craftsman of the Yiddish Short Stories" (MA thesis), Columbia University, 1957
Roskies, David G., *Against the Apocalypse: Responses to Catastrophe in Modern Jewish Culture*, Cambridge, Massachusetts: Harvard University Press, 1984

Throughout his literary career Lamed Shapiro forged a distinctive style and crafted a unique voice, securing for himself an important place in the canon of 20th-century Jewish writers. Although he was one of the least prolific prose writers of the second generation of Yiddish authors, Shapiro made his mark in the world of Yiddish literature with a number of stylistically complex and thematically daring short stories dealing with the effects of pogroms on Jewish society and the individual psyche. Every aspect of his writing is infused with various modernist styles that effectively allowed him to treat such grave subjects in chillingly graphic and boldly innovative ways, shattering conventions and taboos. Shapiro depicted the pogrom not solely as a social-historical factor in Jewish life, but rather as a window through which to view the complexities of the human psyche in relation to such brutal and traumatic experiences. Shapiro thereby effectively rendered Jewish collective tragedies in individual, psychological, and even universal terms; the personal trauma, emotional chaos, and insanity of his pogrom victim protagonists reflected and, to a degree, eclipsed the communal collapse of Jewish life in the wake of pogroms and war.

His explicit portrayals of violence and in-depth psychological character studies bring a modernist tone and sensibility to his writings that starkly set them apart from those of the Yiddish masters: Mendele Moykher Sforim, Sholem Aleichem, and Y.L. Perets – "*di klasiker*." These factors are especially salient in Shapiro's trademark pogrom stories: "Der tseylem" [The Cross], "Der kush" [The Kiss], "In der toyter shtot" [In the Dead Town], and "Shfoykh khamoskho" [Pour Out Thy Wrath], all written in 1909, as well as "Di yidishe melukhe" [The Jewish Government] and "Vayse khale" [White Challah], which were written in 1918. Howe and Greenberg refer to him as "one of the first 'art' writers in Yiddish prose" and claim that he modelled himself "after such masters of European Impressionism as Chekhov and Flaubert", while the Yiddish author Isaiah Spiegel dubbed him the "Yiddish Kafka". Shapiro incorporated aspects of impressionism, expressionism, naturalism, decadence, and psychological realism into much of his writing.

Shapiro favoured the short story over other genres such as poetry and journalism, although he dabbled in those as well. He never finished his one attempted novel, *Der amerikaner sheyd* [The American Ghost] (published in his posthumous *Ksovim*), because, as his friend and editor, S. Miller posited, "the novel was not his genre". Shapiro, commenting on his inability to complete the novel, mentioned that he wrote "Der tseylem" in three days because he had the whole story conceived in his mind beforehand, but with a novel, it was impossible to conceive the whole in one's mind. He could not maintain the "mood" of the narrative for the entire length of the novel. This demonstrates the importance of mood for Shapiro: it was a dominant feature in all of his short stories, often more than plot or even character development. Shapiro used mood and tone to sustain his short sketches; he crafted richly evocative descriptions of feelings, atmosphere, and nature rather than focusing on dialogue. He conveyed mood through vivid, almost personified images of the natural elements or inert objects, having them take part in speechless conversations. Shapiro often featured nature, in the form of dark storms, rays of sun, or a rippling river, as his protagonist.

In this respect, Shapiro's narrative world and the characters inhabiting it differ profoundly from the more folksy narratives of earlier Yiddish writers. The Yiddish poet and critic, Yankev Glatshteyn, observed that in all of his work, Shapiro attempted to break from Sholem Aleichem's trademark *baredevdikayt* (chattiness), replacing it instead with narrative silences. Indeed, Shapiro established silence as one of the prevalent motifs in his fiction, especially in his so-called pogrom stories, such as his masterful novella "The Jewish Government".

Among his several dozen short stories, "The Cross" stands out not only for its shockingly vivid depiction of violence and gore, but especially for Shapiro's bold use of the primary Christian symbol as its indispensable axis. Shapiro painted a gruesome picture of apocalyptic chaos in the form of a violent pogrom in Russia in which the pogromists carve the mark of the cross on their Jewish victim's forehead in an attempt to "save his Yid soul from hell". Instead of symbolizing Christian brotherly love, Shapiro's cross stands for a world of violence and anarchy, as the Jewish pogrom victim branded with the cross becomes transformed into an "iron man", a brutal rapist and murderer. Shapiro addresses the most primitive, animalistic human drives that are triggered through primal eruptions of violence, such as the pogrom at the story's centre. As in his other pogrom stories, "The Cross" conveys the power of nature to liberate humans from the shackles of morality, ideology, and community that bind them. Shapiro uses the image of the cross as the cohesive device that drives his narrative along and brings these various themes to the surface.

The publication of "The Cross" gained Shapiro much renown, and remained his signature story and major claim to fame for years, a fact that he came to regret later in his career. In the short story "Dak", included in Shapiro's 1931 collection *Nyu-yorkish un andere zakhn*, the protagonist, Izzi Fishler, laments the state of American Yiddish writers, including Shapiro himself, saying: "Lamed Shapiro lives off of the merit of his old story "The Cross", which has always been a false, bombastic work, written in falsetto". Toward the end of his life, Shapiro even claimed that his use of the cross as central symbol of the story was "forced and contrived". Despite the author's own later misgivings, "The Cross", along with "White Challa" and "The Jewish Government", remain some of the most aesthetically nuanced and psychologically complex treatments of the pogrom theme in modern Jewish literature.

MATTHEW HOFFMAN

Sherman, Martin

US dramatist, 1938–

Born in Philadelphia, 22 December 1938. Studied at Boston University, 1956–60, BFA 1960. Playwright in residence, Playwrights Horizons, New York, 1976–77. Awards include Wurlitzer Foundation grant, 1973; National Endowment for the Arts Fellowship, 1980; Dramatists Guild Hull–Warriner Award, 1980; Rockefeller Fellowship, 1985.

Selected Writings

Plays
We Love Adventure, 1961
A Solitary Thing, 1962
Fat Tuesday, 1966
Next Year in Jerusalem, 1968
The Night before Paris, 1970
Things Went Badly in Westphalia, 1971
Passing By, 1974
Cracks, 1975
Soaps, 1975
Rio Grande, 1976
Blackout, 1978
Bent, 1979
Messiah, 1982
When She Danced, 1985
A Madhouse in Goa (includes *A Table for a King* and *Keeps Rainin' All the Time*), 1989
Some Sunny Day, 1996
Rose, 1999
The Boy from Oz, 2002
A Passage to India, 2002

Screenplays: *Alive and Kicking*, 1997; *Bent*, 1997; *Caught between Two Worlds*, 1997; *Children of the Heart*, 1997; *Callas Forever*, 2002

Television Plays: *The Clothes in the Wardrobe*, 1993; as *The Summer House*, 1993; *The Roman Spring of Mrs Stone*, 2002

Further Reading

Dace, Tish, "Signs from God", *New York Native* (14–27 January 1985)
Dace, Tish, "Between Two Cultures: Playwright Martin Sherman Talks about Messiah", *New York Native* (28 January–10 February 1985)
Dace, Tish, "Tish Dace at Rose", *Plays International*, 14/12 (September 1999)
Morley, Sheridan, "The Gift of Big Writing", *The Times* (11 February 1983)
Rees, Jasper, "Telling the Tale of a Lifetime", *Daily Telegraph* (10 June 1999)

Although famous as a gay playwright, Martin Sherman believes Judaism figures more centrally in his work than does sexual orientation. Certainly his plays and screenplays often reflect his Ashkenazi heritage. Even when they do not, they dramatize the view of an outsider who appreciates and respects those who are in some way – by religion, race, gender, sexuality, or disability – different. As an expatriate American living in London, this offspring of immigrants from the shtetl of Ultishka cherishes those among us who fail to measure up as able-bodied, straight, white, Protestant men.

Sherman always writes about those different from the norm as conceived by right-wing American orthodoxy: he evokes women, a black man, a gay man, a Jewish writer, and his eccentric parents in *Fat Tuesday*; gay men in *Passing By*, *Bent*, and *Alive and Kicking*; a singer mother and dancer daughter in *Rio Grande*; the bohemian dancer Isadora Duncan, her poet husband, and gay pianist friend in *When She Danced*; the gay, Jewish David / Daniel character in *A Madhouse in Goa*; foreigners in 1942 Cairo, one a disguised Jew trying to escape to Palestine, in *Some Sunny Day*. So emphatically does Sherman dramatize this theme of the "other" or alien that he literally embodies creatures from outer space in two scripts.

The dramatist wrote *Next Year in Jerusalem*, the earliest of his explicitly Jewish plays, in 1967. The 25-year-old David and his parents, Aaron and Deborah – the latter barely able to walk because she suffers from a degenerative disease – visit a ruined temple in Israel's Negev Desert. David wants to institutionalize Deborah. Aaron, suffering from denial, refuses to acknowledge the gravity of his wife's condition. Although it depends too much on exposition, *Next Year in Jerusalem* nevertheless dramatizes a compelling domestic confrontation and prefigures the studies of disability later given more mature form in *Messiah*'s Rebecca, *A Madhouse in Goa*'s Daniel, and *Rose*'s Sonny.

Throughout his career Sherman has exhibited fascination with folklore concerning a dybbuk, that is, the soul of a dead person which possesses and speaks through one still living. Shloyme An-ski had dramatized this subject in its traditional folkloric setting in his turn-of-the-century play *The Dybbuk*, but Sherman has explored more contemporary manifestations of a dead man's spirit entering the body of his living lover.

A few pages survive of an early untitled Sherman manuscript employing this premise. Here, in a contemporary New York setting, Toby, a painter who depicts demons, witches, and flying dragons, tries to get his lover Daniel out of his apartment because Toby's sister is arriving. Toby wants to keep Daniel from discovering that a dybbuk has possessed Rachel. Sherman abandoned this script, but again made comic use of a dybbuk in his 1975 satiric farce *Cracks*, which uses the structure of Agatha Christie's *Ten Little Indians* to ring the death knell on the 1960s. In this play a female analyst's dybbuk possesses a female client, creating richly comic scenes in which the same actress, employing two distinct voices, converses with herself.

Two decades later Sherman finally seized the opportunity to create a serious, romantic dybbuk. In his 1997 screenplay *Caught between Two Worlds*, the dramatist transposes An-ski's plot to 1953 Atlantic City, where Channon, 19 and newly arrived from Poland, obtains a job as busboy at the Majestic Hotel. There he falls in love with his boss's daughter Leah, who is engaged to a young attorney. Convinced he and Leah are destined for each other, Channon turns to Kabbalah for assistance. The spell he puts on her intensifies their love, which frightens her into immediate marriage to her fiancé. Having starved himself to win Leah's love, Channon drops dead, then merges with her at the altar and prevents the wedding.

Possessed, Leah shares Channon's memories, most vividly of the peasants in Yultishka burned to death by the Nazis, a conflagration from which only Channon escaped. Leah's father, learning the young man was from his own shtetl, recognizes him as the son of his closest friend, and therefore pledged to marry Leah before either was born. The father and Channon, not altogether of either world, old or new, confront each other, and an elderly rabbi exorcises Channon, but the bond between the two young lovers cannot be broken: Leah dies as her spirit soars away with her beloved's, from the living world into the realm of the dead. A powerful love story, *Caught between Two Worlds* proves more accessible today than the old An-ski play.

This film script which evokes both the old country and mid-century America draws upon materials that Sherman has also employed in two plays, *Messiah*, set in 17th-century Ultishk (i.e. Ultishka), and *Rose*, which covers the journey of the 80-year-old title character all the way from childhood in Ultishka to retirement in Miami Beach. These scripts both comically and dramatically consider issues of religious faith and religious fanaticism, and both take as their central characters heroic women, female Jobs who endure horrendous suffering but survive. To paraphrase Rose, they skip over quicksand.

Although *Messiah* begins on the Ukrainian border of Poland, Rachel's spiritual journey takes her to Turkey, where she seeks a Sephardic rabbi named Sabbatai Sevi, reputed to be the Messiah. Sherman focuses on Rachel; Sevi himself never appears. Rich in eroticism, brooding mysticism, and earthy humour, *Messiah* dramatizes a courageous, resilient, autonomous woman experiencing metaphysical conflicts often reserved for male heroes. By the end, bereft of every vestige of her former life, Rachel still talks to the God whose existence she questions.

Also blessed with an ironic sensibility, Rose likewise loses those she holds dear. She sees her most cherished beliefs flouted, paradoxically, in the name of Judaism. The title – and only – character throughout sits Shiva on a wooden bench for a little girl killed in Israel. We learn her identity and who killed her only in the closing minutes, when the information surprises, shocks, and devastates us.

This wandering Jew Rose epitomizes Sherman's exiles. A displaced person, she moves from shtetl, to Warsaw, to the sewers, to the ship *Exodus*, to Palestine, to Atlantic City, to Miami, with sojourns in such spots as an ashram, the Arizona desert, and Israel. At the end of her journey Rose – and Sherman – lament the erosion in extremist Israeli Judaism of the old obligation "to be better", replaced by a convert from Kansas praising the Jew who exterminated Arabs in the Hebron mosque massacre.

That sort of action, plus the separate shootings of two little girls, fuel Rose's fierce ethical fires. All these victims, deemed different, died because of their outsider status. Rose rejects such distinctions and, by a ritual act of defiance, embraces the feared "alien".

During his 40-year career, Sherman has not deviated from his own embrace of difference. Despite his diversity of style or locale, he has achieved an impressive thematic consistency. The millennium piece *Rose*, at once hilarious and chilling, celebrates a century of Judaism, laments dying Jewish moral imperatives, and says *Kaddish* for Yiddish culture. At the beginning of the 21st century, *Rose* takes its place among the finest and most provocative works of Jewish literature.

TISH DACE

Shimoni, Yuval

Israeli fiction writer, 1955–

Born in Jerusalem, 1955. Studied cinema at Tel Aviv University.

Selected Writings

Novels
Maof hayonah [The Flight of the Dove], 1990
Heder [Room], 1999

Short Story
"Omanut hamilhamah" [The Art of War], 1990

Further Reading

Balaban, Avraham, *A Different Wave in Israeli Fiction: Postmodern Israeli Fiction*, Jerusalem: Keter, 1995 (in Hebrew)
Ben, Menachem, "Review of *A Room*", *Tel Aviv Weekly* (23 April 1999)
Oren, Yosef, "The Disappointment of the Art and Victims of Life", *Moznaim* (July 1999)
Ron, Moshe, "Towards the Crumbs", *Siman Kriah* (21 December 1999)
Schwartz, Yigal, "On Another Place for Dolly City: Illustrations of Man and Place in Hebrew Literature", *Haaretz* (16 June 1995)
Tzur, Shai, "A Transparent Universe, Tiny as a Marble", *Haaretz Sefarim* (25 August 1999)

Shimoni has published thus far a short story, a novella and a novel, but in spite of the relatively limited scope of his work, he has won great critical acclaim; his writings have been recognized as "genius, uncommon, lyrical and sophisticated"; and his novel as one of the most important in Hebrew literature.

His first story, "Omanut hamilhamah" [The Art of War], already contains many of the motifs and subjects that are to engage Shimoni in his writing. He describes the commander who trains his elite military unit in an unknown territory in preparation for a complex military operation in an enemy city, and tries to reconstruct the scene of the future battle. The attempt at reconstruction goes on ad absurdum. Eventually he arrives at the construction of an actual city identical to the city of the enemy, populated by citizens; even the implementation of the construction becomes an actual military offensive inside the city. "The Art of War", which demands perfection, defers the time of battle indefinitely and creates a circuitous and never-ending story line of an imaginary experience. Shimoni deals with questions of representation and its potential; of the original versus imitation, the role of the art and the stand of the artist versus life, not lacking irony and criticism. Yet Shimoni abounds with warmth and humanity, and his precise descriptions depict characters that try to understand the moment in which their dreams have slipped away from them. The attempt at reconstruction is liable to fail, but there is someone who records the essence of this experience.

His novella, *Maof hayonah* [The Flight of the Dove] is exceptional in its format: page opposite page, it presents alternately two different plots, wherein pagination not only forces the reader to choose the way he will read them, but also to understand the arbitrary and symbolical connections between them. The two stories happen in Paris and in an identical and restricted span of time of less than 24 hours, but their plots are different. One story is written in the style of "the new novel" and describes realistically and precisely a pair of average, middle-aged American tourists who are spending their second "honeymoon" in Paris. The second story, written in the style of the "stream of consciousness", describes a young French girl who decides to commit suicide by jumping from Notre Dame Cathedral. Ironically, the only encounter between the two plots, as well as the only actual significant contact in the book, is violent and devastating. The two plots combine at the conclusion when, due to a whim of fate, the young French girl falls to the very same spot where the American tourist is positioned so that his wife can photograph him at the historic site; this encounter apparently also leads to his death. The confrontation between the two plots contrasts two existential alternatives – one of loneliness and the yielding of intimacy, against a tired relationship and a lost passion that leaves closeness and similarity between the two spouses.

Shimoni makes sophisticated use of observation points, and plays with perspectives. He provokes and tests the two generic styles through the encounter between them while unravelling the "threads" of the literary tale and raising basic artistic questions. He describes the American tourists in great detail, yet points to their fictitiousness and is uncertain what characteristics to attribute to them. Similarly, he enters the depths of consciousness of the young French girl, but then integrates within this description thoughts and memories of the storyteller himself, and blurs the distinction between his own lost beloved and the heroine of the story. Critics complain that the story that unites the two plots and gives them their ontological strength is the mingled story of the narrator himself who casts the image of his beloved upon the French girl and thus tries to examine existential issues and perspectives. Here the span of memory has a significant role – both of the protagonists and the narrator – which becomes more inflated with the development of the story. For the Americans it is memories of their first honeymoon in Italy; for the girl her childhood memories of abandonment at a circus, and for the narrator memories of lost companionship in a foreign country. These memories, whose verity is placed in doubt, try in vain to justify the present, connect it with the past and give it meaning. The experiment in reconstruction therefore is done on a number of levels: reconstruction by the narrator of the story lines emanating from a small item that he found in a newspaper; reconstruction of his story with his beloved French girl; and the reconstruction of memories. Despite the failure, it appears that, towards the conclusion, in the presence of the enlarged memory, there is a momentary option of delight and kindness before disaster.

Shimoni's description drifts between heaven and earth; between the desire of his heroes to hover by means of an artistic act or death and the dreary, lonely and disintegrating life on earth. He follows his heroes closely, so that just at the end some great heavenly flight takes place with great symbolic presence (the dove), as with the leap of the woman from atop the cathedral. The heroes are followed by cameras, images, chance transparencies, and create locally focused representations and small metonymies. The novel ends with the hope for a share of down-to-earth mercy that happens to those who can reveal beauty in everyday life.

In the novel *Heder* [Room], all these elements reach exhaustion. The first two parts of the book, "The Candelabra" and "The Drawer", are within the scope of a novel and the third part, "The Throne", within the scope of a short story. In the first, the enquirer tries to find the causes for a fire in which a man is burnt to death at a military base. Together with him is the reader who is an observer in the film that is shot by chance from an arbitrary angle, and documents the experience of eight men filming a short training film for the airforce in which there is a flashback to the Gulf War. In the second, a frustrated Israeli painter in Paris tries to produce an homage to a Mantegna drawing in which the crucified is seen from the height of his bare feet by means of three homeless people and a prostitute in a morgue (in the two incidents the artistic teams are locked in a small room, cut off from the outside). In the third (which reminds one of "The Art of the War"), a priest tries to express his thanks to the God Juan for helping his king to victory in war by finding a suitable representation for his greatness in the form of a huge statue. These three experiments fail. These wretched "artists", who place art above life and ask to be redeemed and exalted by it, suffer a reverse which at times leads to disaster. Nevertheless, here too the protagonists are all described with exactitude and humanity, and their memories are brought forward parenthetically, taking control over the expanse of the text, just as their hidden dreams attain representation filled with mercy. They too try to burrow into their past, to grasp a small promise in a magical moment from the distant past that will give justification and meaning to the present and to locate in vain the reason for the disruption.

Shimoni's novel arouses a debate in regard to its classification as modernist or postmodernist. It must be said that the questions that he awakens in his writings are great questions, nearly all of the order of metaphysical existence, like the great yearning to create connections at different levels, likely to facilitate the relationship to modernism. Nevertheless, the acceptable answers are small, partial, and fragmentary and the vessels in which they are inspected are clearly postmodernist. The postmodernist ingredients are apparent, such as an amalgamation of perspectives and styles; the arbitrary mechanical exposure; the repeated and recurrent intervention of the narrator in the text; the emphasis on the "threads" of the act of craftsmanship and the fictitiousness of the story; the difficulty of composing a clear narrative that links the present with the past; questions of artistic representation and its possibility; and direct and indirect references to literary creations and craftsmanship in general.

Shimoni's use of Hebrew hovers between rich poetic lyricism and different forms of slang and common language used for the purpose of characterizing his characters and the different human experiences. Likewise, he hovers between foreign locales to those that are clearly Israeli and between human descriptions of universal character to different uses unique to the Hebrew language, making maximum use of it for the purpose of the artistic act.

SHAI TZUR
translated by Rachel M. Paul

Shlonsky, Avraham

Russian-born Israeli poet, 1900–1973

Born in Karyokov, Ukraine, into a Habad Hasidic family. Sent to Palestine aged 13 to study at the Herzlia High School. Returned to Russia 1914; continued studies at Jewish secular high school, Yekaterinoslav. Emigrated to Palestine, 1922. Worked on road building, and at Kibbutz Ein Harod; later worked as journalist. Studied in Paris, 1924. Staff member of newspaper, *Haaretz*, 1928–43. Editor of *Mishmar*, 1943. Founded weekly *Turim*; first literary editor of *Al hamishmar*, and of quarterly *Orlogin*, 1950–57. Headed many delegations to world peace conferences and maintained contact with Soviet writers. Died in Israel, 1973.

Selected Writings

Collection
Kitvei Avraham Shlonsky [The Complete Works of Avraham Shlonsky] (ten vols), 1972–73

Poetry
Devay [Distress], 1924
Leaba-ima [To Father-Mother], 1927
Bagalgal [In a Wheel], 1927
Beeleh hayamim [In These Days], 1930
Lo tirtsah [Thou Shalt Not Kill], 1930
Avnei bohu [Stones of Void], 1934
Shirei hamapolet vehapius [Poems of Collapse and Reconciliation], 1938
Shirei hayamim [Poems and Days], 1946
Al milet [Inlaid With Jewels], 1947
Shirim [Poems] (two vols), 1954
Ketavim nivharim [Selected Writing], 1955
Yalkut shirim [Selected Poems], 1967
Avnei gvil [Rough Stones], 1968
Mishirei haprozdor haarokh [Poems From the Long Corridor], 1968
Ketavim [Selected Works], 1971
LeAvraham Shlonsky ben hashivim [To Seventy Years Old Avraham Shlonsky], 1973
Sefer hasulamot [The Book of Ladders], 1973
Mul hayeshimon [Facing the Desert], 1973
Pirkei yoman [Chapters of a Diary], 1981

For Children
Alilot miki mahu [Mickey Who?], 1947
Ani vetali beerets halama [Me and Tali in Llama Country], 1957
Utzli Gutzli [Utzli Gutzli] (play), 1966

Further Reading

Barzel, Hillel, *Shirat Erets Yisrael*, Tel Aviv: Sifriyat Poalim, 2001
Hagorni-Green, Avraham, *Shlonski ba-avitot Byalik*, Tel Aviv: Oram, 1985
Halperin, Hagit, *Me-agvaniyah 'ad simfoniah*, Tel Aviv: Sifriyat Poalim, 1997
Kena'ani, Yaakov, *Milon hidushe Shlonski*, Tel Aviv: Sifriyat Poalim, 1989
Tsur, Reuven, *Yesodot romantyim ve-antiromantiyum*, Tel Aviv: Papirus, 1985
Yudkin, Leon I., *Isaac Lamdan: A Study in Twentieth Century Hebrew Poetry*, Ithaca, New York: Cornell University Press, 1971

Shlonsky was born in Karyokov, Ukraine, into a Habad Hasidic family, deeply rooted in Jewish tradition and much attracted to Zionist ideology. At the age of 13, he was sent to Palestine where he studied at the Herzlia High School, and thus, is some sense, he constituted a part of the Second Aliyah (wave of immigration to the Land). But this was only a brief episode, as he returned in the following year to the Russian Empire, and continued his studies at a secular Jewish school in Yekaterinoslav. He made his adult decision to emigrate to Palestine in 1922, thus now becoming an element in the Third Aliyah. He was not only an ideological pioneer, but also an active labourer, as a road builder, and a member of the newly formed Kibbutz Ein Harod. But his principal interest and activity was writing, and as a journalist, and later, poet, he contributed to the journals, *Hapoel hatsair*, *Hedim*, *Davar*, and *Ketuvim*, in all of which he played a major part as shaper of policy and propagandist poet. In 1924, he studied in Paris, which became the scene of some of his early poetry, focus of both delight and alienation. Back in Palestine, he worked on the staff of the newspaper, *Ha'arets* from 1928 to 1943. He was an editor of *Mishmar* in 1943, and founded the weekly, *Turim*. He became the first literary editor of *Al hamishmar*, as well as literary editor of the quarterly, *Orlogin*, from 1950 to 1957. He always remained a prolific poet and a translator of world authors, such as Shakespeare (indirectly, through the medium of other translations), Pushkin, and Babel'.

Shlonsky kept up constant contact with the Soviet Union, and always remained close to the Communist ideology. This is reflected not only in his opinions and thus his journals, but also in his poetry, which took on the doctrines of Russian Futurism. As he saw it, he was the child of two revolutions, the Bolshevik world revolution that heralded the Soviet

Union, and the Labour Zionist revolution, which he saw as bringing about a Workers' Hebrew State. The poetry also deals with this change, a revolution in the language, in the nature of Hebrew, and in aesthetics. By the time that he came on to the literary scene in Palestine, the newly arrived H.N. Bialik (1873–1934), the preeminent Hebrew voice, regarded as the "National Poet" and setter of the tone, had almost stopped writing poetry, and was to die within a decade. Shlonsky, like his co-editor, Eliezer Steinmann, was conscious of opening up a new Hebrew poetics, and adopted the slogan from Ecclesiastes; "A generation goes, and a generation comes", i.e. times, they are a'changing, as they argue in a 1927 issue of *Ketuvim*. What may have been appropriate for the previous era, that of exile and Diaspora, is no longer so for the new times, that of the Hebrew homeland. Now, he argued, we need new rhythms, new metres, new rhyme schemes, new images, and even new words. The actual language of poetry interested Shlonsky a good deal, the status of neologisms, the fact that, for his own generation, unlike that of Bialik, Hebrew was now a spoken language. It had also become for the first time the tongue of a new Hebrew working class, that of the *halutz*, the pioneer. The work of translation also assisted in the production of an up-to-date lexicon, flexible and modern, not one exclusively rooted in the classical sources.

In his literary opus overall, Shlonsky stressed the need for the worlds of poetry and journalism to move towards each other, and that otherwise the latter would be debased. He maintained that journalism should observe the highest literary standards, and poetry should reciprocate by dealing with questions of the moment. Each would then benefit. The implications for poetry are far reaching. Poetic imagery must reflect the reality of the contemporary world, its machinery, its technology, and also its violence. Each aspect of book production, too, takes on the character and appearance of an unmistakably modern nature; the jagged line, the striking print, the strangled syntax, the unexpected sounds, and strange assonances. The subject matter too differs, and moves from the classically removed, cosy world and from the emotionally located romantic world, into an atmosphere of shock, change, and revolution. The poet as much as the journalist greeted the fusion of socialism and nationalism, here, specifically Hebrew nationalism. Like the other Expressionist Hebrew poets of his generation, Shlonsky's effort is concentrated on the articulation of the pain of the unaccustomed confrontation with the new land, the climate, the environment, and the conditions. The new literary journals, in which Shlonsky played such a central role, were created as a conscious breakaway movement from the existing literary platforms. Paradoxically, their "credo" might be: "I do not believe."

Shlonsky's earliest poetry, collected in the volume *Devay*, tells of man's disease and the failure of religion. The traditional images, taken from the ancient texts, are urgently manifest indeed in the poetry. But they take on a new sense and context. From the section there entitled "Gilboa" we read: "Dress me, O excellent mother, in a striped cloak for splendour, and bring me at morn to toil." The pioneering work of building takes on the religious aura and power of the ancient sources of salvation. It is the early revolutionary poetry which adopts the greatest intensity and proliferation of traditional images, now reset in a different context, and recharged in the current ideology: "My country is wrappped in light like a prayer shawl. Houses stand erect like totems. And like phylactery straps do roads, that human palms erected, glide down." Building has become creative work, work of the highest order, associated with the divine. And he, the poet, reminds the reader of his namesake, our father Abraham of the biblical story, founder of the nation. Now, there is a new nation.

For all Shlonsky's revolutionary tendencies, both in sentiment and in technique, this Modernist phase in his work, as with so many other Expressionist and Futurist writers and artists in various media, was shortlived. The poet passed on to a quieter and more conventional mode in his later work, readopting traditional rhyme schemes, and particularly searching out musicality and the articulation of a more personal emotion. The initial shock of the New was increasingly modified, and Shlonsky himself ceased to be regarded as one of the vanguard of the Hebrew poetry in the period of Israeli Statehood.

LEON I. YUDKIN

Sholem Aleichem (Sholem Rabinovitsh)

Russian fiction writer, dramatist, and humorist, 1859–1916

Born in Pereyaslav, Ukraine, 1859; father innkeeper; mother died, 1872. Moved with family to Voronkov, model for his Kasrilevke. Studied at kheder until 1873; Russian Gymnasium of Pereyaslav, graduated 1876. Teacher of Russian and other subjects, Pereyaslav and surrounding district; tutor to Olga Loyev, Kiev, until love for Olga discovered, 1877; returned to Pereyaslav, 1879. Began to publish items in Hebrew weekly *Hatsefirah* and *Hamelits*. Government-appointed rabbi, Lubny, 1880–83. Married Olga Loyev, 1883. Switched to writing in Yiddish and adopted pseudonym, 1883. Lost money inherited from father-in-law in speculation on stock market; moved to Kiev (Yehupets in his stories) and spent summers in resort town of Boira (Boyberik). Founded literary annual, *Di yidishe folks-bibliotek*, 1888. Declared bankrupt; moved to Odessa, 1890; returned to stock speculation, Odessa and Kiev, 1893. Wrote propaganda pamphlets for first Zionist Congress. Contributed to *Der yid*, 1899; published in Yiddish dailies of Warsaw and St Petersburg, 1900–1906. Lived in Kiev; witnessed pogrom, 1905; lived in Lwów (L'viv), 1906. Moved to United States, 1906; settled in New York; began to write for Yiddish theatres of Lower East Side. Returned to Europe, 1907; took part in 8th Zionist Congress, The Hague, 1907, as representative of Federation of American Zionists of New York. Travelled in Russia; contracted tuberculosis; spent summers in health resorts in Switzerland, Germany, and France, 1909–14; health improved, despite relapse in 1913. Lecture tour of Russian empire, Spring 1914; went to Berlin after start of World War

I and sent family to Denmark. Returned to United States; undertook exhausting reading tours. Died 13 May 1916. Funeral in New York attended by hundreds of thousands of people.

Selected Writings

Collections
Folksfond oysgabe [Popular Subscription Edition], 28 vols, 1917–25
Oysgeveylte verk [Selected Works], 1935–41
The Best of Sholem Aleichem, edited by Irving Howe and Ruth R. Wisse, 1979
Selected Works of Sholem Aleichem, edited by Marvin Zuckerman and Marion Herbst, 1994

Short Stories
Tsvey shteyner [Two Stones], 1883
Di ibergekhapte briv oyf der post [Letters Stolen from the Post Office], 1883–84
Kontor gesheft [Shop Counter], 1885
First series of the letters of *Menakhem mendl*, 1892 (these stories were expanded and developed until 1913)
First monologue of *Tevye der milkhiker* [Tevye the Dairyman], 1894 (these stories were expanded and developed until 1916)
Second series of the letters of *Menakhem mendl*, 1895
Der ferkishefter shnayder, 1901; as *The Bewitched Tailor*, translated by Bernard Isaacs, n.d.
Dos naye kasrilevke [The New Kasrilevke], 1901
Dos tepl [The Pot], 1901
Finf un zibetsig toyznt [Seventy-five Thousand], 1902
Gents [Geese], 1902
Kleyne mentshelekh mit kleyne hasoges [Little People with Little Ideas], 1902–04
Oyf pesekh aheym [Home for Passover], 1903
Kasrilevker nisrofim [The Burnt-Out People of Kasrilevke], 1903–10
Motl peyse dem khazns, 1909; as *The Adventures of Mottel, the Cantor's Son*, translated by Tamara Kahana, 1953
The Old Country, translated by Julius Butwin and Frances Butwin, 1946
Inside Kasrilevke, translated by Isidore Goldstick, 1948 (translation of the Kasrilevke cycle)
Tevye's Daughters, translated by Frances Butwin, 1949
Selected Stories of Sholem Aleichem, introduction by Alfred Kazin, 1956
Stories and Satires, translated by Curt Leviant, 1959
Stories of Sholem Aleichem, translated by Charles Cooper, 1964
Old Country Tales, edited and translated by Curt Leviant, 1966
Some Laughter, Some Tears: Tales From the Old World and the New, translated by Curt Leviant, 1968
Hanukah Money, translated by Uri Shulevitz and Elizabeth Shub, 1978 (for children)
Holiday Tales of Sholem Aleichem, edited and translated by Aliza Shevrin, 1979
The Adventures of Menahem-Mendl, translated by Tamara Kahana, 1979
Tevye the Dairyman and the Railroad Stories, translated by Hillel Halkin, 1987
Tevye the Dairyman and Other Stories, translated by Miriam Katz, 1988
Around the Table: Family Stories of Sholem Aleichem, edited and translated by Aliza Shevrin, 1991
Nineteen to the Dozen: Monologues and Bits and Bobs of Other Things, edited by Ken Frieden, translated by Ted Gorelick, 1998

Novels
Natasha, later as *Taybele*, 1884
Sender-blank un zayn gezindl [Sender Blank and His Household], 1888
Stempeniu, 1889; as *Stempeniu: A Jewish Romance*, in *The Shtetl*, edited and translated by Joachim Neugroschel, 1979
Yosele solovey, 1890; as *The Nightingale; or, The Saga of Yosele Solovey the Cantor*, translated by Aliza Shevrin, 1985
First part of *Moshiekhs* [The Times of the Messiah], 1898
Der mabl [The Deluge], later as *In shturm*, 1906–08 (published in instalments); as *In the Storm*, translated by Aliza Shevrin, 1984
Blondzhende shtern, 1909–11 (published in serial form); as *Wandering Star*, translated by Frances Butwin, 1952
Maryenbad, 1911; as *Marienbad*, translated by Aliza Shevrin, 1982
Der blutiker shpas, 1912–13; as *The Bloody Hoax*, translated by Aliza Shevrin, 1991
Funem yarid, 1913; as *From the Fair: The Autobiography of Sholem Aleichem*, edited and translated by Curt Leviant, 1985
The Great Fair: Scenes from My Childhood, translated by Tamara Kahana, 1955

Plays
Tsezeyt un tsershpreyt [Scattered and Dispersed], 1905
Stempeniu, 1907
Di goldgreber [The Gold Diggers], also known as *Der oytser* [The Treasure], 1908
Shver tsu zayn a yid [It's Hard to be a Jew], 1914
Dos groyse gevins, 1915; as *The Jackpot: A Folk Play in Four Acts*, translated by Kobi Weitzner and Barnett Zumoff, 1989

For Children
Dos meserl [The Pocketknife], 1886
Oyfn fidl [Playing the Fiddle], 1902

Other
Di yidishe folks-bibliotek [The Yiddish Popular Library], 2 vols, 1888–90
Jewish Children, translated by Hannah Berman, 1922
Why Do the Jews Need a Land of Their Own?, translated by Joseph Leftwich and Mordechai S. Chertoff, 1984
The Song of Songs, translated by Curt Leviant, 1996

Further Reading

Borochov, Ber, *Shprakh Forshung un Literatur Geshikhte*, Tel Aviv: Y.L. Perets, 1966
Brenner, J.H., "Le-Shalom Aleikhem", *Ketavim*, 3 (1967)

Frieden, Ken, *Classic Yiddish Fiction: Abramovitsh, Sholem Aleichem and Peretz*, Albany: State University of New York Press, 1995
Frieden, Ken, *Century in the Life of Sholem Aleichem's Tevye*, Syracuse, New York: Syracuse University Press, 1997
Goodman, Saul (editor), *Our First Fifty Years: The Sholem Aleichem Folk Institute, A Historical Survey*, New York: Sholem Aleichem Folk Institute, 1972
Malkin, Dov Ber, *Ha-Universali Be-Shalom Aleikhem*, Tel Aviv: Y.L. Perets, 1970
Miron, Dan, *Sholem Aleykhem: Person, Persona, Presence*, New York: YIVO Institute for Jewish Research, 1972
Weitzner, Jacob, *Sholem Aleichem in the Theatre*, Northwood, Middlesex: Symposium Press, and Madison, New Jersey: Fairleigh Dickinson University Press, 1994
Wisse, Ruth R., *Sholem Aleichem and the Art of Communication*, Syracuse, New York: Syracuse University, 1980

Sholem Aleichem ("Peace be with you", a Hebrew and Yiddish greeting) was the pen-name and literary alter ago of Sholem Rabinovitsh, a writer who both in his own writing and as founding editor of the influential periodical the *Di yidishe folks-bibliotek* [The Yiddish Popular Library] launched Yiddish literature as a popular but at the same time serious and socially concerned enterprise with a mass audience. It is no accident that his character Tevye the Dairyman is the most famous single persona in Yiddish literature as Rabinovitsh, to an extent building on Mendele Moykher Sforim's pioneering work, developed a literary form (the wistfully comic monologue) ideally suited to its task and to its primary audience: an urbanized Jewish population already looking back to the long years of the shtetl civilization.

David Roskies calls Rabinovitsh "the great comedian of Jewish dissolution" and in fact his extensive writings trace a fascinating trajectory of a traditional society rapidly unravelling. In his early novel *Stempeniu* we still have a romantic view of the shtetl and its denizens with their traditional values, embodied by his heroine Rochel, an unhappy young wife who is courted by the Jewish outsider, the musician Stempeniu. Although her traditional values stand the test of temptation, significantly it is only away in the big city, escaping her oppressive relatives, that she achieves a happy married life. The city hoves into view again in *Menakhem mendl* (*The Adventures of Menahem Mendl*) where the urbanized Jews of Kiev are satirized. However it is with the appearance of his character Tevye, a sympathetic, nostrum-spouting, half-educated village dairyman that Rabinovitsh found an ideal vantage-point on the increasingly problematic situation of rural Jews in the Russian Empire.

As a caring Jewish father Tevye has a primary responsibility to get his daughters married, but every eventual wedding (or elopement) reflects one or other of the dissolutionary forces acting on Jewish life. When Tevye's daughter Hodel in the story of the same name marries a political militant, we witness the ideological conflicts between rabbinic Jewish custom and morality and the enlightened and even revolutionary ideas rapidly disseminating in the shtetl at the turn of the century. We also encounter the challenge of assimilation (in "Chava", when a daughter marries a Christian youth) and then, in "Modern Children", the new democratic notions appear that claim, to the chagrin of Tevye's wife, that a mere tailor might marry "a descendant of rabbis and scholars" – Tevye's daughter Tseitl.

Written after the Tevye cycle of stories (which have been translated and published in innumerable languages, collections, and editions) are the less well-known, often chilling – but still frequently humorous – "Ayznban geshikhtes" (in *Tevye the Dairyman and the Railroad Stories*). It may be that the harder edge of the late *Railroad Stories* will be the "Sholem Aleichem" future generations will admire most.

In these stories Tevye's green woods and his sympathetic if often hungry horse, are far away. A group of travelling salesmen meet on "the Jewish train" which cuts through a heavily Jewish area and they swap desperate stories of anti-Semitic attacks, of the struggle to get a child educated when quotas are applied, of suicidal or rebellious youngsters, of various tricksters and swindlers including, notoriously, in "A mensh fun Buenos-Ayres" [Man from Buenos Aires], a white-slaver who seems to represent the total collapse of Judaic ethics.

Other particularly interesting works by Rabinovitsh include the "Kasrilevke cycle" about a run-down small town, translated as *Inside Kasrilevke* and *Motl peyse dem khazns* (*The Adventures of Mottel, the Cantor's Son*). The stories about Kasrilevke (based on Voronkov where he grew up) include a cod guidebook extolling the supposed modern improvements such as a sad and freezing Jewish tram with passengers who refuse to cough up their few kopkes (kopecks) of fare money, a hilarious and dreadful hotel where the author is besieged by itinerant sock-peddlers, and the caterwauling "yactors" of a Yiddish theatre company – everywhere there is a picture of poverty and beggary, including "a livid-faced Jew . . . holding out a small, shrivelled hand, expressly fashioned for begging". Subsequent stories tell us of the town's inhabitants – burnt-out by fires which impecunious citizens would start for insurance gain – appealing to their rich cousins in Kiev for aid and receiving pretty short shrift.

In *The Adventures of Mottel* we get a racy narrative of life at the lower end of the social scale with vivid descriptions of market days, another hilarious description of an inn where Mottel encounters one of his many disasters provoking his refrain "even to be unlucky one must have luck", the trials and tribulations of emigrating to America which involve sneaking across the Russian border at the mercy of thieves who prey on clandestine emigrants. Mottel in fact is Rabinovitsh's faux-naïf witness to the historical epic of Russian Jewish life and emigration and through his marvellously-imagined child's vision he turns the travails of Jewish existence at this time into humour, to produce one of Rabinovitsh's best-loved characters.

No doubt partly accounting for his great popularity was a strain of robust egalitarianism in Rabinovitsh's work. Although his characters tend to be, like Tevye, struggling salt-of-the-earth types, there are frequent irruptions of prosperous citified Jews who generally have a baleful influence.

One of Tevye's daughters (Shprintze in the story of the same name) has her honour ruined by the rich city widow's playboy son Aronchik, whose name tellingly combines Jewish and Russian elements. In his strange and fragmentary fictionalized autobiography *Funem yarid* (*From the Fair*), Rabinovitsh tells us he was drawn to the vital and imaginative life of poor and marginal Jews even as a child, although he came himself from a respectable, well-off family. This in fact is emblematic of his role in Yiddish letters; Yiddish literature, as espoused in his work and in *Di yidishe folks-bibliotek*, was to be a literature for the masses of Jews who did not participate, through their lack of modern education, in the major literatures of that time and place; Russian, French, and German. This gives us a key to the rather special (and vulnerable) position Yiddish moved into in the 20th century, valued only by either very religious Jews who ignored secular culture, or conversely, by those who saw it as a vehicle for various left-wing philosophies.

RAY KEENOY

Shpigl, Yeshayohu (Shaye) (Isaiah Spiegel)

Polish-born Israeli poet and fiction writer, 1906–1990

Born in Balut, suburb of Łódź 1906. Taught in Yiddish schools, 1926–33; wrote for Yiddish journals. Married Renya; one child; Renya Shpigl died of hunger in Łódź ghetto during World War II; Yeshayohu Shpigl sent to Auschwitz, later to labour camp in Saxony. Returned to Łódź, 1945; taught in Jewish school there, 1946–48. Emigrated to Israel, 1951. Died in Tel Aviv, 1990.

Selected Writings

Poetry
Mitn ponem tsu der zun [Facing the Sun], 1930
Un gevorn iz likht [And There Was Light], 1949
Tsvishn tof un alef: gezamlte lider [Between Z and A: Collected Poems], 1978
In *A Treasury of Yiddish Poetry*, edited by Irving Howe and Eliezer Greenberg, 1969

Fiction
Malkhes geto, 1947; as *Ghetto Kingdom: Tales of the Lodz Ghetto*, translated by David Hirsch and Rosalyn Hirsch, 1954
Shtern ibern geto [Stars over the Ghetto], 1948
Mentshn in tom [People in an Abyss], 1949
Likht funem opgrunt [Light from the Precipice], 1952
Vint un vortslen [Wind and Roots], 1955
Di brik [The Bridge], 1963
Flamen fun der erd [Flames from the Earth], 1966
Shtign tsum himl [Stairs to Heaven], 1966
Di kroyn: dertseylungen [The Crown: Stories], 1973
Shtern laykhten in tom [Stars Shine in the Abyss], 2 vols, 1976
Tsvey dertseylungen [Two Stories], 1978
Himlen nokhn shturem [Skies after a Storm], 1984

Other
Mayn yidish bukh [My Yiddish Book], 1948
Geshtaltn un profiln: literarishe eseyen [Figures and Profiles: Literary Essays], 2 vols, 1971
Sutskevers lider fun togbukh [Sutzkever's "Poems from a Diary"], 1979

Further Reading

Fuks, Khayim-Leyb, "Dos yidishe literarishe lodzh", *Fun Noentn Over* (1957)
Glatstein, Jacob, *In tokh genumen, eseyen*, vol. 2: *1948–1956*, New York: Matones, 1956
Gris, Noyekh, *Fun fintsternish tsu likht: Yeshayohu Shpigl un zayn verk*, Tel Aviv: Yisroel-Bukh, 1974
Gris, Noyekh, "Shpigl, Yeshayohu", *Leksikon fun der nayer yidisher literatur*, vol. 8, New York: Congress for Jewish Culture, 1981
Prager, Leonard, "Sipurey hageto – hagirsa hamiyadit vehatiudit", *Dapim lekheker tekufat hashoa*, 13 (1996)
Spiegel, Isaiah (editor), *Briv tsu yeshayohu shpigl fun a farloshener velt*, Tel Aviv: Y.L. Perets, 1990
Sutskever, Avrom, "Der kinstler fun malkhes geto", *Di goldene keyt*, 55 (1966)
Szeintuch, Yechiel, "The Corpus of Yiddish and Hebrew Literature from Ghettos and Concentration Camps and Its Relevance for Holocaust Studies", *Studies in Yiddish Literature and Folklore*, 7 (1986): 186–207
Szeintuch, Yechiel (editor), *Yeshayahu Shpigl: proza sifrutit migeto lodzh*, Jerusalem: Magnes, 1995
Yungman, Moyshe, "Yeshayohu shpigls flamen fun der erd", *Di goldene keyt*, 64 (1968)

Malkhes geto (*Ghetto Kingdom*), the first Yiddish book to be published in post-World War II Poland, fell upon the Yiddish world like a meteor. Here were stories by a relatively unknown Yiddish poet and prose writer who had survived the Łódź ghetto, Auschwitz, and slave-labour camps, and had returned after his liberation to recover buried manuscripts. Yiddish critics praised *Malkhes geto* and subsequent collections of Shpigl's Holocaust writings (e.g. *Shtern ibern geto* [Stars over the Ghetto] and *Mentshn in tom* [People in an Abyss]). Through stories of ordinary people he had chronicled a national calamity with tact and restraint. Shpigl was seen as both Holocaust witness and artist.

As late as 1981, Noyekh Gris could state in his entry on Shpigl in the *Lexicon of Modern Yiddish Literature* that "zayne ershte aroysgegebene bikher nokhn khurbm zaynen di oyfgegrobene ksovim in geto" [His first published books after the Holocaust were the writings he had dug up in the ghetto]. Gris is not to be blamed for this mistaken notion, one that was fostered by editors, publishers, and the author himself. In his two-volume collection of Holocaust fiction, *Shtern laykhten in tom* [Stars Shine in the Abyss], Shpigl himself dates the stories as work of the ghetto years. But these stories were substantially revised from the manuscript texts on which they are based.

In his *Isaiah Shpigl: Literary Prose from the Lodz Ghetto*, Yechiel Szeintuch boldly asserted that, "Almost everything in the category of literature from the Holocaust period that has appeared in print in Hebrew and Yiddish has not been published in the language of the preserved original." Szeintuch claimed that the textual changes from Shpigl's original manuscripts were so extensive as to express a different set of thoughts and feelings. He exhumed Shpigl's manuscripts from archives and published them in a critical edition, placing before the public the 16 manuscript-based stories recovered by the author. These were all penned in proximity to specific events in the isolated world of the Łódź ghetto. The post-Holocaust author wrote from a quite different perspective from the ghetto writer.

The extent of revision of the manuscript versions differs from story to story and is nowhere greater than in the widely anthologized "Niki", originally titled "Der toyt fun Anna Yakovlevna Temkin" [The Death of Anna Yakovlevna Temkin]. The principal characters, their relationship, and the heroine's end differ radically in the ghetto and post-liberation versions – a result of the altered consciousness of the author, who no longer documents but memorializes. "Holocaust literature" may mean literature created in the Holocaust, post-Holocaust imaginative writings about the Holocaust, or pre-Holocaust writing of a prophetic nature. Szeintuch has turned our eyes to works written in the Holocaust, a separate genre of fictive documentation, which is both art and historiography.

In "Fir vos zenen gegangen" [Four Who Went] the differences between the stark manuscript text and the three-times longer story published as late as 1978 are palpable. Shpigl's ghetto stories all deal with hunger, murder, death, or alienation but are constructed around specific events in the life of one or several ordinary individuals. The manuscript of "Four Who Went" shows the typical Shpigl "resistance" to Nazi brutality in small expressions of respect for human life, in this instance the physical tenderness of four men carrying the body of a woman suicide. The historical events enveloping the story but by no means stressed are the "Bloody Thursday" of March 1940 when hundreds of Jews were killed to terrorize them into moving into the ghetto area, and the trauma of settling in new, generally mean quarters. The ghetto manuscript was written a day or two after the events in the story took place. It has greater immediacy, is more authentic as document, and yet is not less effective as fiction than the expanded version.

The partly autobiographical novel, *Flamen fun der erd* [Flames from the Earth], begun in the Łódź ghetto in 1943 and completed in Tel Aviv in 1954, was finally published in 1966. Each of its 18 chapters is virtually independent – Shpigl admits to having chosen the novel form when a critic suggested he could broaden his canvas by interconnecting separate episodes. Chapter 3, "The Dead Stradivarius", for example, radically revises a story of the same name in the collection *Likht funem opgrunt* [Light from the Precipice]. Set in the ghetto's fourth fierce winter, the novel explores the large themes of physical resistance, the behaviour of neighbouring Gentiles, and love in the shadow of death. The author uncovers isles of humanity in the ghetto morass of want and desperation. The Katshmarik brothers and sister ravenously profit from the spoliation of their Jewish neighbours, but the old church bell-ringer, Nikodem Zalutski, loses his life for hiding a Jew. Shpigl refuses to linger on scenes of violence and degradation; he eschews sentimentality, stereotypes and cheap heroics. Yet modulated though it be, this is a harrowing work. Noyekh Gris called it "a memorial written in blood, which like the Sambatyon cannot rest even on the Sabbath".

Like his beloved Sholem Abramovitsh [Mendele Moykher Sforim], Shpigl was a keen observer of nature, even in bleak Balut, and also wrote with great charm and perception of his childhood. *Shtign tsum himl* [Stairs to Heaven] is a too-little known autobiographical novel whose hero, Shayele, is followed through his seventh year. Written during a difficult decade (1955–65) in the writer's life in Israel, it perhaps replaces in some respects his novel of the life of poor Jewish weavers in Balut that was lost in the war (together with a volume of verse and a translation of Byron's *Cain*). Shpigl described *Shtign tsum himl*, dedicated to the memory of his daughter, as one of "autobiographical truth and imagination". The child's experiences as he is moved about among family members while his father is in prison for a political crime are deftly filtered through the adult author's heightened awareness.

In the Łódź ghetto, following the death of his daughter, Shpigl wrote the words and suggested the basic melody (Dovid Beyglman wrote the music) for the lullaby, "Makh tsu di eygelekh" [Shut Your Little Eyes], which was subsequently widely sung. Sung, however, at a concert attended by the Łódź *Judenrat* head, Rumshowski, its performance was forbidden and its author was punished, barely escaping with his life.

LEONARD PRAGER

Shrayer-Petrov, David

Russian poet and fiction writer, 1936–

Born David Peisakhovich Shraer in Leningrad, 28 January 1936. Evacuated to village in Urals following Nazi invasion of Soviet Union, 1941, and during siege of Leningrad. Studied at First Medical School from 1953, graduated 1959; Leningrad Institute of Tuberculosis, PhD, 1966. Research scientist, Gamaleya Institute of Microbiology, Russian Academy of Sciences, 1967–78; microbiologist, Crimea cholera epidemic, 1970. Married Emilia Polyak; one son. Poetry collection derailed after trial of Joseph Brodsky; ostracized and persecuted after seeking official permission to emigrate; dismissed from Gamaleya Institute; expelled from Soviet Writers Union, 1980. Refusenik, 1979–87. Emigrated to United States, 1987. Medical researcher at Brown University and resident of Providence, RI since 1987. Awards include All-Russia Prize for Poetry Translation, 1977.

Selected Writings

Poetry
Kholsty [Canvases], 1967
Pesnia o golubom slone [Song about a Blue Elephant], 1990
Villa Borgeze, 1992
Propashchaia dusha [Lost Soul], 1997
Piterskii dozh [Petersburg Doge], 1999
Barabany sud'by [Drums of Fortune], 2002

Novels
Gerbert i Nèlli [Herbert and Nelly], 1992
Frantsuzskii kottedzh [The French Cottage], 1999
Zamok v Tystemaa [The Töstemaa Castle], 2001

Other
Poèziia i nauka [Poetry and Science], 1974
Druz'ia i teni [Friends and Shadows], 1989
Moskva zlatoglavaia [Gold-Domed Moscow], 1994

Many translations into Russian, including works by Robert Frost, Hugh MacDiarmid, Salomeja Neris, Alfonsas Maldonis, Dragutin Tadijanovic.

Further Reading

Bobyshev, Dmitri, "Shraer-Petrov, David" in *Slovar' poetov russkogo zarubezh'ia*, edited by Vadim Kreid *et al.*, St Petersburg: Izdatel'stvo russkogo khristianskogo gumanitarnogo instituta, 1999
Gandel'sman, Vladimir, "Roman s uchastiem vremeni", *Vestnik*, 13 (29 December 1992)
Kukulin, Il'ia, "Anfilada povtorov", *ExLibris-Nezavisimaia gazeta* (15 November 2001)
Luksic, Irena, "Razgovor: David Srajer-Petrov. Zivot u tri dimenzije", *Vijenac* (20 May 1999)
Mashinskaia, Irina, "Zimniaia pesnia", *Novyi zhurnal*, 211 (1998)
Sonin, Iurii, "Dzazovaia poèziia", *Evreiskaia gazeta*, 3 (1998)
Terras, Victor, "Roman ob otkaznikakh" [Novel about Refuseniks], *Novoe ruskoe slovo* (28 December 1992)
Terras, Victor, "*Moskva zlatoglavaia* [Gold-Domed Moscow] by David Shrayer-Petrov", *World Literature Today*, 69/2 (Spring 1995)

The dual name of David Shrayer-Petrov betokens his literary career. Born David Peisakhovich Shraer (Shrayer is an anglicized spelling), and descended from Lithuanian rabbis and Podolian millers, he heard Yiddish in the traditional home of his grandmother. Evacuated from his native Leningrad during the Nazi siege, Shrayer-Petrov spent three years in a Russian village in the Urals. Peasant dialects and rituals left an imprint on the writer's imagination. A Mediterranean-looking youth growing up in a working-class district of Leningrad, Shrayer-Petrov formulated the questions that his writings continue to probe: Do Jews belong in Russia? Is assimilation impossible? In 1985–86, working on the first volume of his memoirs, *Friends and Shadows*, Shrayer-Petrov would apply these questions directly to himself as a Russian-Jewish writer: "Why do I not quote great Jews? I don't know the language. I only know Russian . . ." Shrayer-Petrov started medical school in 1953, the year of Stalin's death, and entered the literary scene as a poet during Khrushchev's Thaw. He adopted the pen-name Petrov, derived from a russianized first name of his father. This assimilatory gesture hardly eased the publication of Shrayer-Petrov's poetry in Russia, and during his Soviet years he made a name for himself largely as a translator.

Following his marriage in 1962 to Emilia Polyak, Shrayer-Petrov moved to Moscow, where his son Maxim was born in 1967. By the early 1970s the relations between Jews and Gentiles became Shrayer-Petrov's principal concern. In 1975–76 he composed poems where the disharmonies of his aching Russian and Jewish selves adumbrate the writer's conflict with the Soviet system. In "Chagall's Self-Portrait with Wife", the poet asks the levitating Bella: "Isn't there space enough/ In that one-room hut to press/ Your tired wings/ Against his seething brushes,/ And love this country painlessly/ All your life?" In "My Slavic Soul", unable to cope with the anxieties of a Jew who is culturally Russian, a Slavic soul abandons a poet's body here described as "a Jewish, typical, such a barren wrapping." Poems from Shrayer-Petrov's period of unsettlement circulated in *samizdat* (they were later published in the West) adding to the writer's publishing difficulties. In January 1979 Shrayer-Petrov and his family applied for exit visas. Expelled from the Union of Soviet Writers (three of his books were derailed) and fired from his academic position, Shrayer-Petrov became a Refusenik.

In 1979–80, while driving an illegal cab at night and working in an emergency room lab, Shrayer-Petrov conceived of and wrote the first part of a panoramic novel about the mutilated destinies of Jewish Refuseniks. *Herbert and Nelly* is the most significant and artistically compelling work to explore the massive exodus of Soviet Jews. The novel exhibits a Tolstoian sense of epic proportions in painting the lives of Jews from different walks of life sharing the plight of being Refuseniks and outcasts. The protagonist, Dr Herbert Levitin, is a Moscow professor of medicine. His Jewishness evolves in the course of the novel from a prohibitive ethnic garb to a historical and spiritual mission. Levitin is married to Tatiana, a Russian woman of peasant stock, and their decision to emigrate ultimately results in the killing of their son in Afghanistan and Tatiana's own death of grief. In documenting with remarkable honesty the unbreachable contradictions of a mixed Russian-Jewish marriage, Shrayer-Petrov also treats the story of Dr Levitin as an allegory of Russian-Jewish history. The Jews' marriage to Russia is doomed, the novel suggests to its Jewish readers. Emigrate or die! In book two of the novel, Palestinian drug dealers, chess, and sex fuel the plot as Dr Levitin finds transcendent fulfilment and love in his new beloved Nelly but eventually perishes in his struggle with the Soviet system.

In spite of persecution and arrest by the KGB, Shrayer-Petrov's last Soviet decade was strikingly prolific. The Refuseniks' isolation from the rest of Soviet society, coupled as it was with the pervasive sense of the absurdity of being a Jewish writer who is both silenced by and shackled to Russia, led to Shrayer-Petrov's discovery of the prose form he calls *fantella* (decipherable as "fantastic novella"). In the fantellas love, talent, and magic oppose (and sometimes vanquish) totalitarianism and philistinism. In "Dismemberers" a feminized typewriter continues to type subversive stories even after her owner has left Russia for good (the fantella was composed while a CBS crew was filming a fragment about Shrayer-Petrov for the special *Seven Days in May*).

Leaving for the USA on 7 June 1987, Shrayer-Petrov carried with him a manuscript of the first of the two books of memoirs he would publish abroad. The writer insists on calling them "novels with the participation of the author", and they offer fascinating opinions about the making of

Jewish writers in the Soviet Union (including a discussion of Joseph Brodsky's Jewishness). Of *Friends and Shadows*, Victor Terras wrote that "in its intellectual honesty and emotional ingenuousness [Shrayer-Petrov's] is indeed an 'open book'." Emigration and outwardly unturbulent life in New England afforded Shrayer-Petrov both distance and perspective. Among the most celebrated works emerging from Shrayer-Petrov's American years is the poem "Villa Borgeze" (1991), part dirge, part confession of a Jew's expired love for Russia. Putting aside these tortuously nostalgic recollections, the poet confesses that "For you and us, Russia, no closeness survives,/ We sons of Yehudah who used to be yours." Marriages between Jews and Gentiles continue to fascinate Shrayer-Petrov the belletrist. Gently ironic short stories about Russian-Jewish émigrés in America have become his most popular form, and he contributes to periodicals on both sides of the Atlantic, including the Russian edition of the *Forward* (New York). As with other doctor-writers, such as Chekhov in Russian literature, and William Carlos Williams in Anglo-American, the writings of Shrayer-Petrov are characterized by analytical qualities and passionate humanism. In a number of his works, scientific interests dovetail with those a fictionist. Shrayer-Petrov's lifelong research on bacteriophage and his investigation of the life of the great microbiologist Félix d'Herelle have informed his 1999 novel, *The French Cottage*.

Jews and Russians are the "two peoples [who] are the closest to me in flesh (genes) and spirit (language)," Shrayer-Petrov wrote in *Friends and Shadows*. Rooting into his adopted land and its culture, he increasingly inscribes non-Russian characters into the worlds of his fiction. Might he not, miraculously, wake up one day equipped to write in English about his (Russian-Jewish) America?

MAXIM D. SHRAYER

Silkin, Jon

British poet, 1930–1997

Born in London, 2 December 1930. Studied at Wycliffe College; Dulwich College; University of Leeds, BA in English 1962. Sergeant Instructor in Royal Army Education Corps, 1949–50. Married writer Lorna Tracy, 1974; three sons (one deceased), one daughter. Lavatory cleaner, 1952; teacher of English to foreign students, 1956–58; tutor in adult education, University of Leeds, 1960–65; University of Newcastle, 1965–90; also University of Durham, between 1970 and 1985. Founding co-editor, *Stand Magazine*, Newcastle upon Tyne, 1952–97; co-founder and editor, Northern House publishers, Newcastle upon Tyne, 1964–97. Beck Visiting Lecturer of Writing, Denison University, Ohio, 1965; visiting lecturer, writers' workshop, University of Iowa, 1968–69; teaching fellow and visiting lecturer, Australian Arts Council and University of Sydney, 1974; College of Idaho, 1978; visiting writer, Mishkenot Sha'ananim, Jerusalem, 1980; Bingham Poet, University of Louisville, 1981; Elliston Poet, University of Cincinnati, 1983; distinguished writer in residence, American University, Washington, DC, 1989; Literary Fellow, Dumfries and Galloway Arts Association, 1990; writer in residence, Carisbrooke School, Isle of Wight, 1990; foreign professor of literature, Tsukuba National University, Japan, 1991–94. Awarded Northern Arts Award, 1965; Geoffrey Faber Memorial Prize, 1966; C. Day Lewis Fellowship, 1976–77. Fellow, Royal Society of Literature, 1986. Died 25 November 1997.

Selected Writings

Poetry

The Portrait and Other Poems, 1950
The Peaceable Kingdom, 1954
The Two Freedoms, 1958
The Re-ordering of the Stones, 1961
Flower Poems, 1964
Nature with Man, 1965
Poems New and Selected, 1966
Three Poems, 1969
Vernon Watkins and Jon Silkin: Poems, 1969
Pergamon Poets 8, with Vernon Scannell, edited by Dennis Butts, 1970
Amana Grass, 1971
Killhope Wheel, 1971
Caring for Animals, 1972
Air That Pricks Earth, 1973
South Africa's Bird of Paradise Flower, 1974
The Principle of Water, 1974
A "Jarapiri" Poem, 1975
The Little Time-Keeper, 1976
Two Images of Continuing Trouble, 1976
Jerusalem, 1977
Into Praising, 1978
The Lapidary Poems, 1979
The Psalms with Their Spoils, 1980
Selected Poems, 1980; enlarged edition, 1988, 1993
Autobiographical Stanzas, 1984
Footsteps on a Downcast Path, 1984
The Ship's Pasture, 1986
The Lens-Breakers, 1992
Watersmeet, 1994
Testament without Breath, 1998

Play

Gurney: A Play in Verse, 1985; as *Black Notes*, 1986

Other

Isaac Rosenberg 1890–1918: A Catalogue of an Exhibition Held at Leeds University, 1959, Together with the Text of Unpublished Material, with Maurice de Sausmarez, 1959
Editor, *Living Voices: An Anthology of Contemporary Verse*, 1960
Editor, with Anthony Cronin and Terence Tiller, *New Poems 1960*, 1960
Translator, *Against Parting*, by Nathan Zach, 1967
Out of Battle: The Poetry of the Great War, 1972; revised edition, 1987
Editor, *Poetry of the Committed Individual: A "Stand" Anthology of Poetry*, 1973

Editor, with Peter Redgrove, *New Poetry 5*, 1979
Editor, *The Penguin Book of First World War Poetry*, 1979; revised edition, 1981, 1989, 1996
Editor, with Lorna Tracy and Michael Blackburn, *Stand One: Winners of Stand Magazine Short Story Competition*, 1984
Editor, *The War Poems of Wilfred Owen*, 1985; revised edition, 1994
Editor, with Lorna Tracy and John Wardle, *Best Short Stories from Stand Magazine*, 1988
Editor, with Jon Glover, *The Penguin Book of First World War Prose*, 1989
Editor, *An Anthology of Twentieth Century English Poetry*, 1994
Making a Republic, 1997
The Life of Metrical and Free Verse in Twentieth-Century Poetry, 1997

Further Reading

Abley, Mark, "The Hand That Erases", *Oxford Literary Journal* (Spring 1977)
Baker, William, "Reflections on Anglo-Jewish Poetry", *Jewish Quarterly* (Autumn–Winter 1978–79)
Brown, Merle E., "Stress in Silkin's Poetry and the Healing Emptiness of America", *Contemporary Literature*, 18 (Summer 1977)
Brown, Merle E., *Double Lyric: Divisiveness and Communal Creativity in Recent English Poetry*, London: Routledge, and New York: Columbia University Press, 1980
Cluysenaar, Anne, "Alone in a Mine of Reality: A Matrix in the Poetry of Jon Silkin" in *British Poetry since 1960*, edited by Michael Schmidt and Grevel Lindop, Oxford: Carcanet, 1972
Fuller, John, *London Magazine* (October 1966)
Halter, Aloma, "Poetry and Poezak", *Jerusalem Post Magazine* (15 May 1987)
Hill, Geoffrey, "The Poetry of Jon Silkin", *Poetry and Audience*, 2 (1962)
Glover, Jon, "Jon Silkin: The Voice in the Peaceable Kingdom", *Bananas* (20 April 1980)
Glover, Jon, "Jon Silkin at Sixty: 'But Why?'", *Stand*, 32/1 (1990)
"John Silkin: A Bibliography", *Poetry Review*, 69 (1980): 75–76
Klein, Holger, "Jon Silkin's 'The Coldness'", *Stand*, 27/3 (1986)
Meiners, R.K., "Mourning for Ourselves and for Poetry: The Lyric after Auschwitz", *Centennial Review*, 35/3 (Autumn 1991)
O'Donoghue, Bernard, "Death of a Moth", *Times Literary Supplement* (4 August 1992)
Parry, Lloyd, "Interview with a Committed Individual", *Isis*, 1 (1989)
Relich, Mario, "The Struggle against Brutality", *Lines* (September 1988)
Sail, Lawrence, "Conflict and Calm: A Reading of Two of the Flower Poems", *Poetry Review*, 69 (1980)
Schmidt, Michael, *An Introduction to Fifty Modern British Poets*, London: Pan, 1979
Sicher, Efraim, *Beyond Marginality: Anglo-Jewish Literature after the Holocaust*, Albany: State University of New York Press, 1985
Silkin, Jon, "The First Twenty-Four Years" in *Contemporary Authors Autobiography Series*, vol. 5, Detroit: Gale, 1987
Times Literary Supplement (19 July 1976)

Jon Silkin's work has been said to have followed "a trajectory of its own" (Edward Lucie-Smith in 1987), and this is justified when Silkin's poetic sources and influences are considered. He was always aware of himself as a Jewish writer, and his conceptions of Jewishness were often expressed both *in extremis* and in quite difficult, abstract terms. At times this material reflected his reading of the Old Testament and its impact on the sinews of his style and language; at other times it had a historical focus, as in his poems on anti-Semitism in English history. But this notably individual note established in his work an elaborate patterning of Jewish themes juxtaposed with other universal and profound ideas about how we should live and how we should live together.

One of the recurrent preoccupations in his impressive body of poetry is with being an outsider. His experience of xenophobia in his English schooling, and his removal to Wales as a child, intensified this, and his writing is enriched by feelings of exclusion and difference. His many volumes contain hard and direct poetry about the Shoah, but often these themes are integrated into his own life experience, notably in the long narrative poem "The People" in *The Principle of Water*, in which he uses documented autobiography touching on his own trauma at the death of his one-year-old son.

The Jewish element in Silkin's work also has a more elemental, philosophical dimension; this is sometimes related to World War I and its effect on his perception of self and reality. He said that his background was "a mixture of rationalist agnosticism and dilute Orthodox Judaism" (*The Little Time-Keeper*) and in his interest in the poet Isaac Rosenberg (who died near Arras in 1918) he found a symbolic figure for the poet-Jew whose life he could explore creatively as well as critically. Here, Silkin's questions are about love in its broadest applications, and the texture of his poetry is often sensuous and disturbing at once, seeking to find redemptive love post-Auschwitz. (see "The Lapidary Poems" in *The Psalms with Their Spoils*).

Silkin's work was always rooted in nature and the complexity of the presence of the political in the world made by God in harmony. The clash between power and the flux of history came to interest him increasingly in the later work. At times, he uses his well established Imagist technique to search universal notions in Judaism such as memory and its resonance in his faith ("The Wanderer"), but also at times explicit and located in specific events, notably in "Resting Place" (in *The Psalms with Their Spoils*) in which he mixes his northern English consciousness and sense of belonging with the call of his race. The focus is on the massacre of the Jewish population in York in 1190 when they were immolated in Clifford's Tower. With his usual restraint, Silkin weaves a tapestry of imagery and suggestion by the deftest of strokes: "the Jewish child, the gentile sword, earth/ sells itself to us." But he also, rather ambitiously, interlinks the mediation of the Warsaw Ghetto and Jerusalem into the text. If there is a weakness, it is in this reaching for multi-layered meanings and references in a tight and taut syntax.

Ever-present in Silkin's poetry is the sense of perplexity at the inhumanity of man and the aggression shown towards nature. Also in the centre is his wish to reveal autobiographical truths in an alien world. In his early poetry nature offered solace and perhaps a pattern of meanings to apply to man. But his later writing confronted extremity and his foundation and referential texts (Benjamin, Brecht, Rosenberg) used as epigraphs to the poems, hint at a darkening shadow over the themes of selfhood and history which were always a principal concern.

As an editor and critic, Silkin showed that sense of exactitude and rigour that underpinned his poetry, and that was constructed with the belief that in making visions and images, we also make the words which force meanings on our inchoate mass of life-data. His own comment was that reducing and compressing thought was the basis of his writing, and that, "The dangers of sensuous art are . . . repetition, over-abundance and prolixity". No-one can accuse Silkin of these, and in achieving a poetry of minimal form but maximum emotional reference, his Jewishness was expressed as integral to his sense of being, and of being a poet.

STEPHEN WADE

Simon, Neil

US dramatist, 1927–

Born Marvin Neil Simon, in the Bronx, New York, 4 July 1927. Studied at New York University, 1944–45; University of Denver, 1945–46. Served in air force, 1945–46: corporal. Married, first, Joan Baim, 1953; wife died 1973; two daughters; second, the actress Marsha Mason, 1973; divorced 1983; third, Diane Lander, 1987. Writer for radio and television, 1948–60. Many awards, including Emmy (for television writing), 1957, 1959; Tony, 1965, 1970, 1985, 1991; *Evening Standard* Drama Award, 1967; Shubert Award, 1968; Writers Guild of America West Award (for screenplay), 1969, 1971, 1976; New York Drama Critics Circle Award, 1983; Outer Circle Award, 1983, 1985; Pulitzer Prize, 1991.

Selected Writings

Plays
Sketches, 1952
Sketches, with Danny Simon, in *Catch a Star!* 1955
Sketches, with Danny Simon, in *New Faces of 1956*, 1956
Adventures of Marco Polo: A Musical Fantasy, with William Friedberg, 1959
Heidi, with William Friedberg, 1959
Come Blow Your Horn, 1960
Barefoot in the Park, 1962; as *Nobody Loves Me*, 1962
Little Me, 1962
The Odd Couple, 1965
The Star-Spangled Girl, 1966
Sweet Charity, 1966
Plaza Suite (includes *Visitor from Mamaroneck*; *Visitor from Hollywood*; *Visitor from Forest Hills*), 1968
Promises, Promises, 1968
Last of the Red Hot Lovers, 1969
The Gingerbread Lady, 1970
The Prisoner of Second Avenue, 1971
The Sunshine Boys, 1972
The Comedy of Neil Simon (includes *Come Blow Your Horn*; *Barefoot in the Park*; *The Odd Couple*; *The Star-Spangled Girl*; *Plaza Suite*; *Promises, Promises*; *Last of the Red Hot Lovers*), 1972
The Good Doctor, 1973
God's Favorite, 1974
California Suite (includes *Visitor from New York*; *Visitor from Philadelphia*; *Visitor from London*; *Visitor from Chicago*), 1976
Chapter Two, 1977
The Goodbye Girl (screenplay), 1977; stage version, 1992
They're Playing Our Song, 1978
Collected Plays 2 (includes *The Sunshine Boys*; *Little Me*; *The Gingerbread Lady*; *The Prisoner of Second Avenue*; *The Good Doctor*; *God's Favorite*; *California Suite*; *Chapter Two*), 1979
I Ought to Be in Pictures, 1980
Fools, 1981
Brighton Beach Memoirs, 1982
Actors and Actresses, 1983
Biloxi Blues, 1984
Broadway Bound, 1986
Jake's Women, 1990
Rumors, 1990
Lost in Yonkers, 1991
Collected Plays 3 (includes *Sweet Charity*; *They're Playing Our Song*; *I Ought to Be in Pictures*; *Fools*; *The Odd Couple* [female version]; *Brighton Beach Memoirs*; *Biloxi Blues*; *Broadway Bound*), 1992
Laughter on the 23rd Floor, 1995
London Suite, 1996

Screenplays: *After the Fox*, with Cesare Zavattini, 1966; *Barefoot in the Park*, 1967; *The Odd Couple*, 1968; *The Out-of-Towners*, 1970; *Plaza Suite*, 1971; *The Heartbreak Kid*, 1972; *The Last of the Red Hot Lovers*, 1972; *The Prisoner of Second Avenue*, 1975; *The Sunshine Boys*, 1975; *Murder by Death*, 1976; *The Goodbye Girl*, 1977; *California Suite*, 1978; *The Cheap Detective*, 1978; *Chapter Two*, 1979; *Seems like Old Times*, 1980; *I Ought to Be in Pictures*, 1982; *Only When I Laugh*, 1982; *Max Dugan Returns*, 1983; *The Lonely Guy*, with Ed Weinberger and Stan Daniels, 1984; *The Slugger's Wife*, 1985; *Brighton Beach Memoirs*, 1987; *Biloxi Blues*, 1988; *The Marrying Man*, 1991

Television Writing: *Phil Silvers Show*, 1948; *Tallulah Bankhead Show*, 1951; *Your Show of Shows*, 1956; *Sid Caesar Show*, 1956–57; *Jerry Lewis Show*, *Jacky Gleason Show*, *Red Buttons Show*, and *Sergeant Bilko* series, 1958–59; *Garry Moore Show*, 1959–60; *The Trouble with People*, 1972; *Happy Endings*, with others, 1975; *Broadway Bound*, 1992

Other
Rewrites: A Memoir, 1996
The Play Goes On: A Memoir, 1999

Further Reading

Johnson, Robert K., *Neil Simon*, Boston: Twayne, 1983
King, Kimball, *Ten Modern American Playwrights*, New York: Garland, 1982
Konas, Gary (editor), *Neil Simon: A Casebook*, New York: Garland, 1997
McGovern, Edythe M., *Neil Simon: A Critical Study*, New York: Ungar, 1979

Neil Simon has perhaps paid the price, in terms of critical standing, of sheer popularity and a tendency to entertain before he instructs. But, arguably, Simon's impressive body of work proves he has nothing to fear from criticism's tendency to categorize and list by league table. On the contrary, he began as a sketch writer, notably for Sid Caesar and Jerry Lewis, and he learned the nature of humour at the base, where humanity is a vulnerable target. If this means that his work may seem light when compared with that of, say, Woody Allen, then that is only because Simon chooses to let the more profound statements about man steal in unnoticed, subject to deflation.

Perhaps the classic scene that exemplifies this, and that defines Simon's particular strength of creating profundity through bathos, is in *Last of the Red Hot Lovers*, where Barney finally gives his apologia for the daytime trysts in his mother's apartment. His heart-felt confessional, his detestation of being "nice" to his grave, leads only to the woman's perfunctory snub and the flatness of his poetic impact.

This writing compares to Pinter's in Act 2 of *The Caretaker*, and shows that Simon could extend the role of the Jewish Nebbish into the highest tragi-comedy. We feel for the little man, his humanity as universal as the desire to eat and to be heard. In fact, in that play Simon places a reference to his protagonist's Jewish history early in the play, and this awareness of the specific New York Jewish humour of the self-negating one-liner is a virtue and perhaps a source of disquiet. Commentaries have noted the focus of his humour on middle-class New York Jews, and complained that his humour does not travel to other states or ethnic groups.

The only riposte here is to mention Simon's tendency to do what all great writers do: extend their microcosm into poetry and the passion of friendship and belonging. Together with Woody Allen and the foundation texts of Jewish humour and philosophy, he has given the world a popularized but valid textualization of the Absurd. In some ways, this places much of his theatre with that of Pinter, Beckett, and Allen but only in the sense of an undercurrent of the angst of the uprooted, the alienated and the quiet persistent rebellion of the helpless. If one had to make a comparison of genuine substance, it would have to be with Philip Roth's woe-begone and lost personae.

The early phase of his career was imbued with the television sketch quip and the comedy of situation and character. But the first successes in mainline theatre, his two hits *Barefoot in the Park* and *The Odd Couple*, meant that he began to have lucrative offers for both musical writing and screenwriting. Simon's memoirs constantly discuss the deals, the men of power in the arts, and the personality clashes around the fundamental nature of the jobbing writer: at least, that is how he presents himself, as a talented man who happened to meet the current demand.

This ability to survive and to have antennae out for the Zeitgeist gave him a deep source of aesthetic sense and creative power in the middle period which produced a flood of hits, and his much-discussed attempts at "serious drama" (as in the adaptation of Chekhov stories in *The Good Doctor* and in *The Gingerbread Lady*). According to some reference surveys, the ubiquitous temptation of the pun and the ironic aside spoils the attempt at handling a serious subject sensitively. But the point is that Simon was writing about the world he knew: that of theatrical artists and producers, with all the stresses and strains involved.

There is no doubt that *Brighton Beach Memoirs*, with its switch to straight autobiographical memoir and use of a narrator along with the protagonist, proved a major success, as did *Biloxi Blues,* a play exploring his US Air Force service years. In *Jake's Women* and *Chapter Two* Simon makes creative use of the personal loss he felt at the death of his first wife, and again demonstrates the depth and complexity he could handle from his basis of writerly skill and seemingly effortless professional ease in writing. This last point is not supported by his memoirs, which explain in detail his nature as a re-writer rather than a writer, and the book is rich in material about the relationship of the man to the persona in the art and in the writer-craftsman, learning all the time, and from everyone. Arguably, his subjects are central Jewish ones: notably the family and the hooks and bonds of friendship. His plays often show a world of caring and loss inextricably mixed with the shudders of modernity in accelerated progress in the broader context. His people dream and become lyrical; they are creatively self-deluded, and above all, they can be articulate even in their taciturnity.

Simon's triumph in winning the Pulitzer Prize for *Lost in Yonkers* brought with it undoubted critical praise also, and there are signs that his position in modern American drama may be reappraised and a task of revisionism begun. But whatever happens in terms of placing Simon's work in a broader context, there are undeniably outstanding qualities in his writing: a consummate sense of structure, a mastery of authentic dialogue, and a sense of characterization that goes far beyond the mechanical "surface" writing of much contemporary plot-driven narrative. In this perspective, Simon's stagecraft will always be exemplary of that specific variety of instinctive theatrical insight so rarely found in social comedy. His social comedy often aspires to a human comedy with unexpected perceptions and easily overlooked wisdom and an acute understanding of the human predicament.

STEPHEN WADE

Sinclair, Clive

British fiction writer and journalist, 1948–

Born in London, 19 February 1948, to David Sinclair and wife Betty (née Jacobovitch). Studied at University of East Anglia, 1966–69, BA in English and American literature 1969; University of California, Santa Cruz, 1969–70; University of Exeter, 1976–77; University of East Anglia from 1978, PhD 1983. Married Frances Redhouse; wife died, 1994; one son. Teaching assistant, University of California, Santa Cruz, 1969–70; copywriter, Young and Rubicam, 1973–76; teaching assistant, University of Exeter, 1976–77; visiting lecturer, University of California, Santa Cruz, 1980–81; literary editor, *Jewish Chronicle*, London, 1983–87; British Council writer in residence, University of Uppsala, Sweden, 1988; visiting lecturer, University of East Anglia, 1995 and 1997. Has contributed numerous book reviews, interviews with writers, travel pieces, and columns to *Times Literary Supplement*, *Guardian*, *Observer*, *Independent*, *Sunday Times*, and *Jewish Quarterly*. Many awards, including British Council Bicentennial Arts Fellowship, 1980; Somerset Maugham Award, 1981; Centre for the Book (British Library) Penguin Writer's Fellowship, 1996; *Jewish Quarterly* Fiction Prize, 1997; PEN Silver Pen Award, 1997.

Selected Writings

Novels
Bibliosexuality, 1973
Blood Libels, 1985
Cosmetic Effects, 1989
Augustus Rex, 1992

Short Stories
Hearts of Gold, 1979
Bedbugs, 1982
For Good or Evil: Collected Stories, 1991
The Lady with the Laptop and Other Stories, 1996

Other
The Brothers Singer, 1983
Diaspora Blues: A View of Israel, 1987
A Soap Opera from Hell: Essays on the Facts of Life and the Facts of Death, 1998

Further Reading

Abramson, Glenda (editor), *Blackwell Companion to Jewish Culture: From the Eighteenth Century to the Present*, Oxford: Blackwell, 1989
Bradbury, Malcolm, "Sinclair's Spectrum" in *No, Not Bloomsbury*, London: Deutsch, 1987
Cheyette, Bryan, "On the Edge of the Imagination", interview with Clive Sinclair, *Jewish Quarterly*, 31 (1984): 26–29
Cheyette, Bryan, "Philip Roth and Clive Sinclair: Representations of an 'Imaginary Homeland' in Postwar British-Jewish and American-Jewish Literature" in *Forked Tongues? Comparing Twentieth-Century British and American Literature*, edited by Ann Massa and Alistair Stead, New York: Longman, 1994
Cheyette, Bryan, "Moroseness and Englishness", *Jewish Quarterly*, 46 (Spring 1995): 22–26
Cheyette, Bryan (editor), *Contemporary Jewish Writing in Britain and Ireland: An Anthology*, London: Halban, and Lincoln: University of Nebraska Press, 1998
Hanson, Clare, *Short Stories and Short Fictions, 1880–1980*, London: Macmillan, 1985
Woolf, Michael, "Negotiating the Self: Jewish Fiction in Britain since 1945" in *Other Britain, Other British: Contemporary Multicultural Fiction*, edited by A. Robert Lee, London: Pluto Press, 1995

Sinclair's fiction seems demonically energetic, a quality derived from his astonishing facility with language. Bryan Cheyette speaks of the "battery of puns, puzzles, wisecracks, recurring images, motifs and linguistic games" that characterize Sinclair's writing, and James Young of the "layer upon layer of playful puns, extended metaphors, and words doubling back on themselves". Equally, Sinclair's writing is strictly for adults: he is not interested in the child within himself, nor in childishness in his readers. The distinctive tone of urbanity mingled with a sometimes frightened humanity, is maintained throughout.

From the early novel *Blood Libels* onwards Sinclair questions causes and imagines alternative historical outcomes: "I am convinced that if Rabbi Nathan hadn't tried to rape Helga, our German au pair, during the course of my barmitzvah celebrations . . . things would have turned out very differently". Sander Gilman notes of *Augustus Rex* that Sinclair "wants to test the thesis that history is merely context and that given a different context, different directions would necessarily be taken". Sinclair has nevertheless indicated that he is acutely aware of the dangers of transposing a model of existence from one generation onto another. Discussing his story "Bedbugs" in which the narrator, asked to teach the poetry of World War I to German teenagers, responds by reading the ghetto diary of a Warsaw Jew, Sinclair says "The narrator figure at the end thinks he's killing the German girl and uses the language, completely hypocritically, of a Jew who did have the moral right to use that language".

Sinclair's fictions explore alternatives that strain beyond the realistic into fantasy. In his story "Ashkenazia", for example, Sinclair imagines a Yiddish-speaking country in central Europe. The time-scheme is occasionally anachronistic within its own seeming terms, but the implications of this story about diaspora and statelessness are clear. Elsewhere Sinclair plays on the difficulty for his readers of determining what is real and what is not, turning the problem into an arresting comic effect.

Sinclair's writing is uncompromisingly concerned with issues raised by being Jewish in the post-Holocaust world. He is especially concerned with notions of guilt and innocence, with victimhood and the immunities it seems to confer. Jews cannot be guilty because of what was done to them, but Sinclair interrogates the implications of this cherished notion for a Jewish state which engages in *realpolitik* on the world stage, and in particular with the Palestinian population around and within it. For Sinclair the responsibilities of survival and statehood are inextricably intertwined: "I used to thank God for the holocaust", says the old

Yiddish writer in "The Luftmensch". "You want to know why? I'll tell you for nothing. Because it gave us Jews the right to sit in judgement on this stinking world. But now I am not sure. Why? On account of Israel that's why. In our own country we Jews are also not perfect." Israeli politics and its implications for a national morality are the basis of Sinclair's most fully realized novel, *Cosmetic Effects*, in which the narrator, Jonah Isaacson, is unwittingly made to carry a bomb and its detonator by his mistress who is collaborating with his Palestinian doctor. Finally, Sinclair's commitment to Zionism is deeply serious and sometimes movingly expressed, as in his discussion in *Diaspora Blues* of the carpenter's sign painted by Yosl Bergner depicting two shoes floating in the blue sky: Sinclair comments, "that is how it was in the diaspora: two shoes but no ground".

Questions of choice find expression too in Sinclair's concern with personal morality. His fictions are very sexy, and sometimes pornographic; necessarily so since his interest lies in eroticism and infidelity, in how far we allow our desires to dictate our behaviour and in the role played by an active conscience in these matters. In *Cosmetic Effects* Jonah Isaacson loses his memory and muses on the implications of this for his relationship with his wife: "Drunk on the smells of her overheated libido I wanted her all right, but for her generality not her particularity; I wanted her like an animal wants its opposite number."

This interest in responsibility is reflected in a concern with the processes of writing. In *The Brothers Singer*, Sinclair notes the "demanding dybbuk that compels a writer to make choices for the sake of the story which may go against his natural inclination" and in *Blood Libels* the narrator asks Jerry Unger (a doppelganger for Philip Roth): "Did you never feel a conflict between your religion and your talent . . . given the direction of the latter?" In a sense this forecloses the argument, claiming for the writer a natural inclination that does not run in the direction of sadistic sexuality or terrifying political revenge. Sinclair's later work reveals him at the sharp end of these issues. Several of the stories in the collection *The Lady with the Laptop* portray recently widowed husbands sometimes wondering whether their conduct is becoming to their state. In the companion volume, *A Soap Opera from Hell*, this aspect of Sinclair's life is addressed in detail. At one point he tells his son about a dream in which his late wife visits him and he holds back from making love to her: "You miss Mummy", his son announces, "But for some reason you also feel guilty." Sinclair's response is "That goes without saying", but he continues, characteristically, "Why guilty? Because I am a writer. Had I surrendered to the succubus you would have read all about it."

Ultimately, Sinclair preserves a strong detachment from the well-springs of his writing. The fictions take him where they must, often to places that are shocking to his characters and to the reader, perhaps to the writer too: diffident lovers turn into rapists, a woman has her tongue cut out; the outcome is usually surprising and violent. But Sinclair is a complex writer who never relinquishes his control over his material: his work is not reducible to its autobiographical elements (though there are many) nor to its philosophies.

LOUISE SYLVESTER

Singer, Isaac Bashevis

Polish-born US fiction writer and writer for children, 1904–1991

Born Icek-Hersz Zynger in Leoncin, 14 July 1904; son and grandson of rabbis; brother of Israel Joshua Singer. Moved with family to Warsaw, 1908; spent three years in grandfather's village of Bilgoray in adolescence. Studied at Tachkemoni Rabbinical Seminary, Warsaw, 1921–22. Proofreader and translator, *Literarishe Bleter*, Warsaw, 1923–33; co-editor, *Globus*, Warsaw, 1933–35. Lived with, but never married, Rokhl (Ronye) Shapira, from 1926; one son. Emigrated alone to United States, 1935. Married Alma Haimann Wasserman, 1940. Naturalized US citizen, 1943. Journalist, *Forverts* (*Jewish Daily Forward*), New York, from 1935. Numerous awards, including Louis Lamed Prize, 1950, 1956; American Academy grant, 1959; Epstein Fiction Award, 1963; Daroff Memorial Award, 1963; Foreign Book Prize (France), 1965; two National Endowment for the Arts grants, 1966; Bancarella Prize (Italy), 1967; National Book Award (for children's literature), 1970, (for fiction), 1974; S.Y. Agnon Gold Medal, 1975; Nobel Prize for Literature, 1978; Handel Medallion, 1986; American Academy Gold Medal, 1989. Member, American Academy of Arts and Letters, 1965. Died 24 July 1991.

Selected Writings (in English)

Short Stories

Gimpel the Fool and Other Stories, translated by Saul Bellow *et al.*, 1957
The Spinoza of Market Street and Other Stories, translated by Martha Glicklich *et al.*, 1961
Short Friday and Other Stories, translated by Mirra Ginsburg *et al.*, 1964
Selected Short Stories, edited by Irving Howe, 1966
The Séance and Other Stories, translated by Roger H. Klein *et al.*, 1968
A Friend of Kafka and Other Stories, translated by Isaac Bashevis Singer *et al.*, 1970
A Crown of Feathers and Other Stories, translated by Isaac Bashevis Singer *et al.*, 1973
Passions and Other Stories, translated by Isaac Bashevis Singer *et al.*, 1975
Old Love, translated by Isaac Bashevis Singer *et al.*, 1979
The Collected Stories of Isaac Bashevis Singer, 1982
The Image and Other Stories, translated by Isaac Bashevis Singer *et al.*, 1985
The Death of Methuselah and Other Stories, translated by Isaac Bashevis Singer *et al.*, 1988

Novels

The Family Moskat, translated by A.H. Gross *et al.*, 1950
Satan in Goray, translated by Jacob Sloan, 1955
The Magician of Lublin, translated by Elaine Gottlieb and Joseph Singer, 1960
The Slave, translated by Isaac Bashevis Singer and Cecil Hemley, 1962
The Manor, translated by Elaine Gottlieb and Joseph Singer, 1967

The Estate, translated by Elaine Gottlieb, Joseph Singer, and Elizabeth Shub, 1969
Enemies: A Love Story, translated by Aliza Shevrin and Elizabeth Shub, 1972
Shosha, translated by Isaac Bashevis Singer and Joseph Singer, 1978
Reaches of Heaven, 1980
The Penitent, translated by Joseph Singer, 1983
The King of Fields, translated by Isaac Bashevis Singer, 1988
Scum, translated by Rosaline Dukalsky Schwartz, 1991
The Certificate, translated by Leonard Wolf, 1992
Meshugah, translated by Isaac Bashevis Singer and Nili Wachtel, 1994
Shadows on the Hudson, translated by Joseph Sherman, 1997

Fiction for Children (translated by Isaac Bashevis Singer and Elizabeth Shub)
Zlateh the Goat and Other Stories, 1966
Mazel and Shlimazel; or, The Milk of a Lioness, 1967
The Fearsome Inn, 1967
When Shlemiel Went to Warsaw and Other Stories, 1968
Elijah the Slave: A Hebrew Legend Retold, 1970
Joseph and Koza; or, The Sacrifice to the Vistula, 1970
Alone in the Wild Forest, 1971
The Topsy-Turvy Emperor of China, 1971
The Wicked City, 1972
The Fools of Chelm and Their History, 1973
Why Noah Chose the Dove, 1974
A Tale of Three Wishes, 1975
Naftali the Storyteller and His Horse, Sus, and Other Stories, 1976
Reaches of Heaven: A Story of the Baal Shem Tov, 1980
The Power of Light: Eight Stories for Hanukkah, 1980
The Golem, 1982
Collected Stories for Children, 1984

Other
In My Father's Court, translated by Channah Kleinerman-Goldstein, Elaine Gottlieb, and Joseph Singer, 1966
A Day of Pleasure: Stories of a Boy Growing Up in Warsaw, translated by Channah Kleinerman-Goldstein *et al.*, 1969
An Isaac Bashevis Singer Reader, 1971
The Hasidim, with Ira Moskowitz, 1973
Love and Exile
A Little Boy in Search of God: Mysticism in a Personal Light, 1976
A Young Man in Search of Love, translated by Joseph Singer, 1978
Lost in America, translated by Joseph Singer, 1981
Nobel Lecture, 1979
Singer on Literature and Life: An Interview, with Paul Rosenblatt and Gene Koppel, 1979
The Meaning of Freedom, 1981
My Personal Conception of Religion, 1982
Conversations with Singer, with Richard Burgin, 1985
Conversations: Singer, edited by Grace Farrell, 1992

Selected Writings (in Yiddish)

Novels
Der sotn in goray, 1935, 1943
Di familye mushkat, 2 vols, 1950
Der knekht, 1967
Der kuntsnmahker fun lublin, 1971
Der bal-tshuve, 1973

Collections of Short Stories
Gimpl tam un andere dertseylungen, 1963
Der shpigl un andere dertseylungen, 1975
Mayses fun hintern oyvn, 1982

Memoirs
Mayn tatns bezdn-shtub, 1979
Mayn tatns bezdn-shtub (hemshekhim-zamlung), 1996

Translations into Yiddish
Di vogler [The Vagabonds], by Knut Hamsun, 1928
Pan, by Knut Hamsun, 1928
In opgrunt fun tayve [In Passion's Abyss], by Gabriele D'Annunzio, 1929
Mete trap [Mette Trap], by Karen Michaelis, 1929
Roman Rolan [Romain Rolland], by Stefan Zweig, 1929
Viktorya [Victoria], by Knut Hamsun, 1929
Der tsoyberbarg [The Magic Mountain], by Thomas Mann, 4 vols, 1930
Oyfn mayrev-front keyn nayes [All Quiet on the Western Front], by Erich Maria Remarque, 1930
Der veg oyf tsurik [The Road Back], by Erich Maria Remarque, 1931
Araber: folkshtimlekhe geshikhtn [Arab Folk Stories], by Moshe Smilansky, 1932
Fun moskve biz yerusholayim [From Moscow to Jerusalem], by Leon S. Glaser, 1938

Further Reading

Alexander, Edward, *Isaac Bashevis Singer*, Boston: Twayne, 1980
Alexander, Edward, *Isaac Bashevis Singer: A Study of the Short Fiction*, Boston: Twayne, 1990
Allentuck, Marcia (editor), *The Achievement of Isaac Bashevis Singer*, Carbondale: Southern Illinois University Press, 1969
Allison, Alida, *Isaac Bashevis Singer: Children's Stories and Memoirs*, New York: Twayne, and London: Prentice Hall, 1996
Biletzky, Israel Ch., *God, Jew, Satan in the Works of Isaac Bashevis Singer*, Tel-Aviv: Sifriyat Poalim, 1979; Lanham, Maryland: University Press of America, 1995
Buchen, Irving H., *Isaac Bashevis Singer and the Eternal Past*, New York: New York University Press, 1968
Christensen, Bonnie Jean M., *Bulletin of Bibliography*, 26 (January–March 1969)
Farrell, Grace (editor), *Critical Essays on Isaac Bashevis Singer*, New York: G.K. Hall, 1996
Farrell Lee, Grace, *From Exile to Redemption: The Fiction of Isaac Bashevis Singer*, Carbondale: Southern Illinois University Press, 1987
Fiedler, Leslie, "Isaac Bashevis Singer; or, The American-

ness of the American Jewish Writer", *Studies in American Jewish Literature*, 1 (1981): 124–31
Friedman, Lawrence S., *Understanding Isaac Bashevis Singer*, Columbia: University of South Carolina Press, 1988
Gibbons, Frances Vargas, *Transgression and Self-Punishment in Isaac Bashevis Singer's Searches*, New York: Peter Lang, 1995
Goran, Lester, *The Bright Streets of Surfside: The Memoir of a Friendship with Isaac Bashevis Singer*, Kent, Ohio: Kent State University Press, 1994
Hadda, Janet, *Isaac Bashevis Singer: A Life*, New York: Oxford University Press, 1997
Howe, Irving, introduction to *Selected Short Stories* by Isaac Bashevis Singer, New York: Modern Library, 1966
Joseloff, Samuel H., "Isaac Bashevis Singer", *Jewish Spectator* (November 1971): 14–16
Kresh, Paul, *Isaac Bashevis Singer: The Magician of West 86th Street*, New York: Dial Press, 1979
Kresh, Paul, *Isaac Bashevis Singer: The Story of a Storyteller*, New York: Dutton, 1984
Landis, Joseph C. (editor), *Aspects of I.B. Singer*, New York: Queens College Press, 1986
Malin, Irving (editor), *Critical Views of Isaac Bashevis Singer*, New York: New York University Press, 1969
Malin, Irving, *Isaac Bashevis Singer*, New York: Ungar, 1972
Miller, David Neal, *A Bibliography of Isaac Bashevis Singer, January 1950–June 1952*, New York: Max Weinreich Center for Advanced Jewish Studies, YIVO Institute for Jewish Research, 1979
Miller, David Neal, *A Bibliography of Isaac Bashevis Singer 1924–1949*, New York: Peter Lang, 1983
Miller, David Neal, *Fear of Fiction: Narrative Strategies in the Works of Isaac Bashevis Singer*, Albany: State University of New York Press, 1985
Miller, David Neal (editor), *Recovering the Canon: Essays on Isaac Bashevis Singer*, Leiden: Brill, 1986
Prescott, Peter S., "Singer the Magician", *Newsweek*, 92 (16 October 1978): 97–98
Rosenblatt, Paul and Gene Koppel, *A Certain Bridge: Isaac Bashevis Singer on Literature and Life*, Tucson: University of Arizona Press, 1971
Sanders, Ronald, *The Americanization of Isaac Bashevis Singer*, Syracuse, New York: Syracuse University Press, 1989
Siegel, Ben, *Isaac Bashevis Singer*, Minneapolis: University of Minnesota Press, 1969
Sinclair, Clive, *The Brothers Singer*, London: Allison and Busby, 1983
Telushkin, Dvorah, *Master of Dreams: A Memoir of Isaac Bashevis Singer*, New York: Morrow, 1997
Tuszynska, Agata, *Lost Landscapes: In Search of Isaac Bashevis Singer and the Jews of Poland*, translated by Madeline G. Levine, New York: Morrow, 1998
Wolitz, Seth L. (editor), *The Hidden Isaac Bashevis Singer*, Austin: University of Texas Press, 2001
Zamir, Israel, *Journey to My Father Isaac Bashevis Singer*, New York: Arcade, 1995

Isaac Bashevis Singer weighs what the Jewish people gained from the Emancipation against what they lost by surrendering their faith. Singer regards loss of faith as spiritual death, a condition potentially more destructive of continued Jewish survival than the Holocaust itself. Through shifting fictional settings, Singer makes his readers adjust the perspectives from which they view modern problems of Jewish identity and survival. We are made to value what has been lost, but must also ask how we can recover it.

All Singer's work is translated from Yiddish. Only ten of his books have been published in Yiddish; there are more than 50 in English. Singer deliberately set up two separate corpuses of his work, helping to prepare the English versions himself. The English texts water down the specific Jewish content of the problems Singer explores. Although Singer's command of literary English was never fluent, he repeatedly insisted that he was a "bilingual" writer. During his lifetime, international translations of his published novels could be made only from their authorized English versions. Since his death, however, translators world-wide are free to make translations of unpublished material directly from their Yiddish texts.

Singer uses biblical quotation and paradigms, and emblematic descriptions, to universalize the events he portrays. He memorializes a destroyed Jewry through allusion and analogy. Numerous published interviews with Singer reveal how far he is personally present in much of his fiction.

In *The Family Moskat* its members are a metaphor for all the Jews of eastern Europe. Their lives depict complex shifts in the nature of Jewish identity, and question Jewish survival in the face of genocide. The English version of the novel ends with the Nazi bombardment of Warsaw, and the despairing cry of one of its assimilated Jews: "I think Death is the only Messiah!"

The Manor and *The Estate* complete Singer's historical survey of the national-cultural crises of modern Jewish life. This two-volume novel tracks the decline of the family of Calman Jacoby, a wealthy and pious Polish Jew who witnesses the destruction of all he has lived for. *Satan in Goray*, a novel set in 17th-century Jewish Poland after the murderous pogroms of Bogdan Chmielnicki, exposes the folly of Jews who seek to force the coming of the Messiah. The hysteria provoked in Poland's devastated Jewish communities by the claims of the false messiah, Sabbatai Zevi, makes an encoded critique of all false promises of a messianic redemption for the Jewish people.

Yasha Mazur, a worldly Jewish circus artist who is the hero of *The Magician of Lublin*, finds every avenue of advancement into the Gentile world of power closed to him. Yasha returns to a rigorous observance of Jewish Orthodoxy by bricking himself up in a penitential cell. This solution, repeated in *The Penitent* and *Shadows on the Hudson*, disturbingly though unintentionally suggests that if its observance can be practised only in a prison, Orthodox Judaism is no longer viable for modern people.

In *The Slave* Jacob becomes the bondsman of a Polish peasant after the Chmielnicki pogroms, and is exiled from the Jewish communal life of his native village. By name and nature, Jacob is a paradigm of his biblical namesake, reenacting the age-old struggle of the Jewish people for identity and survival in a hostile environment. For love of Jacob, his master's daughter Wanda converts to Judaism and dies in giving birth to Jacob's son. The Chmielnicki massacres – like those of Hitler of which they are metaphors – demand that Jews make a conscious effort to give their survival meaning. Singer pursues this theme in *Enemies: A Love Story*. Herman Broder, a Holocaust survivor, can find no peace in his reconstructed life in America. His Polish Christian wife insists on converting to Judaism because she wishes to bear a Jewish child. Another version of this paradigm of the biblical figure of Ruth, a Gentile woman whose children will be brought up as Jews, appears in *Shadows on the Hudson*, suggesting Singer's belief that the Holocaust's devastation of the Jewish people can only be repaired by the new blood of pious Gentile converts.

In *Shosha* Singer reworks events from his own life. This novel suggests that the sterile and impotent lifestyle of the characters of pre-war Warsaw is the spiritual dead-end into which the *Haskalah* has led. Singer attached great significance to his autobiographical writing, a major component of his literary output. These works become simultaneously confessional and self-exculpatory, as fictionalized characters articulate Singer's guilt at having survived the Holocaust. Although Singer consistently refused to speak openly about the Holocaust, three "fictionalized autobiographies" he published between 1976 and 1981 – *A Little Boy in Search of God*, *A Young Man in Search of Love*, and *Lost in America* – can be read as literary acts of atonement.

Three things above all tormented Singer – his abandonment of his parents' strict religious observance, his sexual promiscuity, and his escape from Hitler's genocide, which destroyed Yiddish. Since Singer wrote in Yiddish all his life, superficially it might seem that his work preserved both the Yiddish language and its culture. *In My Father's Court*, a series of vignettes showing his rabbi father conducting his duties as a Jewish *dayan* (judge), Singer presents an elegiac if romanticized portrait of a vanished world of Orthodox pieties. However, as the number of Yiddish readers attenuated, Singer found himself writing not only of, but also for, the dead. He reversed this situation by establishing his international fame through English translations of his work.

The King of the Fields, the last novel Singer published in English in his lifetime, was a thematically strange departure. Set in the pagan world of old Poland and peopled by primitives groping towards some concept of ethics, the novel questions whether or not murderous human nature can be tamed. Judaism appears unable to accomplish this, for the novel's single Jewish character makes little impression on the feral people he encounters.

The first three of the ten collections of short stories Singer published – *Gimpel the Fool*, *The Spinoza of Market Street*, and *Short Friday* – are among his most brilliant achievements. Seven subsequent volumes of stories followed, but their quality is uneven, combining weak subject matter and shaky narrative technique with poor English.

After Singer's death in 1991, his publishers commissioned translations of novels hitherto serialized only in Yiddish. To date, four posthumous novels have appeared: *Scum*, *The Certificate*, *Meshugah*, and *Shadows on the Hudson*. Only the last displays Singer at his best. Given his desire to please his non-Jewish readership, it would mean that Singer refused to publish an English translation of *Shadows on the Hudson* during his lifetime because this novel mounts his most sustained attack on American materialism. Through the eyes of its characters, all survivors of the destroyed world of eastern Europe, we are brutally shown the decadence and immorality that Singer believes lies at the heart of modern civilization.

Singer's enormous popularity enabled him to revivify for both Jews and Gentiles the world Hitler destroyed. He made Jewish readers conscious of their need to seek a meaningful identity in a secular world. And he made the world at large aware of the valuable body of modern Yiddish literature to which he contributed so significantly.

JOSEPH SHERMAN

Singer, Israel Joshua

Polish-born US fiction writer and journalist, 1893–1944

Born Yisroel-Yeshue Zinger in Bilgoray, 1893; son and grandson of rabbis; brother of Isaac Bashevis Singer. Moved with family to Leoncin, 1895; and to Warsaw, 1908. Studied at Jewish school, under father, and in secular schools. Began trying to make living as painter, 1911; began contributing stories on Hasidic life to Warsaw Yiddish newspaper *Dos yiddishe vort* [The Yiddish Word], 1915. Moved to Kiev, 1918; proofreader for Kiev daily *Di naye tsayt* [The New Times], and for miscellanies *Oyfgang* [Ascent] and *Baginen* [Dawn]. Returned to Warsaw, 1921. Married Genya Kuper, 1922; two sons. Polish correspondent, 1923–28, writer of reports from Soviet Union, 1926, contributor on various topics (often using pseudonym G. Kuper) until 1944, New York *Forverts* (*Jewish Daily Forward*); co-editor, *Di yidishe velt* [The Yiddish World], 1928. Emigrated to United States, 1933. Died in New York, 10 February 1944.

Selected Writings

Novels

Shtol un ayzn, 1927; as *Blood Harvest*, translated by Morris Kreitman, 1935; as *Steel and Iron*, translated by Joseph Singer, 1969

Yoshe kalb, 1932; as *The Sinner*, translated by Maurice Samuel, 1933; as *Yoshe Kalb*, translated by Maurice Samuel, 1965

Di brider ashkenazi, 1936; as *The Brothers Ashkenazi*, translated by Maurice Samuel, 1936; translated by Joseph Singer, 1980

Khaver nakhmen, 1938; as *East of Eden*, translated by Maurice Samuel, 1939

Di mishpokhe karnovski, 1943; as *The Family Carnovsky*, translated by Joseph Singer, 1969

Short Stories

Perl un andere dertseylungen [Pearls and Other Stories], 1922

Af fremder erd [On Alien Soil], 1925

Friling [Spring], 1937

The River Breaks Up, translated by Maurice Samuel, 1938
Dertseylungen [Stories], 1949

Play
Erdvey: drama in dray bilder [Earth Pangs: A Play in Three Scenes], 1922

Other
Translator, *Der sof fun meshiekh* [The End of the Messiah], by Y. Zulawski, 1923
Nay-rusland: bilder fun a rayze [New Russia: Impressions of a Journey], 1928
Fun a velt vos iz nishto mer, 1946; as *Of a World That is No More*, translated by Joseph Singer, 1970

Further Reading

Bickel, Shlomo, *Zamlbikher* [Anthologies], 6 (1945): 444–48
Bickel, Shlomo, *Shrayber fun mayn dor* [Writers of My Generation], vol. 1, New York: Matones, 1958
Howe, Irving and Eliezer Greenberg (editors), *A Treasury of Yiddish Stories*, New York: Viking, 1954; London: Deutsch, 1955
Howe, Irving, "The Other Singer", *Commentary*, 31/3 (1966): 76–82
Howe, Irving, introduction to *The Brothers Ashkenazi*, London: Allison and Busby, 1983
Madison, Charles Allan, *Yiddish Literature: Its Scope and Major Writers*, New York: Ungar, 1968
Mayzel, Nachman, *Noente un vayte*, vol. 2, Vilna: Kletskin, 1926
Mayzel, Nachman, *Forgeyer un mittseytler*, New York: Ikuf, 1946
Norich, Anita, *The Homeless Imagination in the Fiction of Israel Joshua Singer*, Bloomington: Indiana University Press, 1991
Rivkin, B. (Weinrib, Baruch Abraham), *Undzere prozaiker*, New York: Ikuf, 1951
Sinclair, Clive, *The Brothers Singer*, London: Allison and Busby, 1983
Singer, Isaac Bashevis, introduction to *Yoshe Kalb*, New York: Harper and Row, 1965
Singer, Isaac Bashevis, *In My Father's Court*, New York: Farrar Straus, 1966; London: Secker and Warburg, 1967
Zeitlin, A., in *Fun a velt vos iz nishto mer*, by I.J. Singer, New York: Matones, 1946

Israel Joshua Singer's greatest strength as a writer was his ability to render in stark, powerful prose his perception of the stultifying conservatism of traditional Jewish life in mid-20th-century Poland, and to depict with ruthless severity and biting irony the limitations of a world that refused to move with the times.

Brought up in a strict rabbinical home, he was expected, as the family's eldest son, to prepare himself for the rabbinate, but at the age of 17 he rebelled and turned to the secular world. Enamoured of the ideals of the Russian Revolution, he rushed to Kiev in 1918 to participate in the dawn of what he believed would be a new age for the Jews of eastern Europe. Instead he was appalled by the vicious bloodshed and Jew-hatred he witnessed there. Bitterly disillusioned, Singer returned to Warsaw four years later, where he published his first collection of short stories, *Perl un andere dertseylungen* [Pearls and Other Stories]. Abraham Cahan, the highly influential editor of New York's largest circulation Yiddish daily, *Forverts*, was so impressed with the uncompromising realism of Singer's fiction that in 1923 he engaged him as his Warsaw correspondent, establishing a connection between them that lasted until Singer's premature death in 1944.

Singer's powerful personality made him a leading figure in Warsaw's Yiddish cultural life. He became associated with what was pejoratively called *Di khaliastre* [The Gang], a radical group of Yiddish writers opposed to both social realism and romanticism, and was deeply involved with the editing of Warsaw's Yiddish literary journals. In 1925, Singer published his second volume of short stories, *Af fremder erd* [On Alien Soil], exposing the brutality of the Red Army as much as the endemic Jew-hatred of the Poles. At Cahan's invitation in late 1926, Singer made an extensive tour through the new Soviet Union to record his impressions. These appeared regularly in *Forverts* between March and June 1927, and Singer then collected and published them in a volume entitled *Nay-rusland* [New Russia] in 1928.

Singer's visit to the Soviet Union had confirmed his fiercely anti-Bolshevik attitude, and when it appeared, his book made him highly unpopular among Warsaw's radical Jewish Left who believed passionately in "proletarian brotherhood". The repeated attacks made on Singer's anti-communist attitudes embittered him, and after the appearance of his first novel, *Shtol un ayzn* (*Steel and Iron*), a harshly realistic depiction of the effect of the German occupation of Poland during World War I, he gave up writing fiction for five years.

In 1931, at Cahan's urging during their meeting in Berlin, Singer returned to fiction, and in 1932 he published a spectacular and dramatic novel, *Yoshe kalb*, a searing critique of corruption at the heart of a Hasidic rabbinical court. Dealing boldly with lust, transgression, and deceit in the context of hypocrisy and repressed sexuality, *Yoshe kalb* was an instant success, being dramatized for the stage in 1932 by the great Yiddish actor and impresario Maurice Schwartz.

Financially secure and resentful at the continuing hostility to him from the Yiddish world of Warsaw, Singer accepted Cahan's invitation to emigrate to America, and in 1933, following the tragic death of his elder son Jacob (Yasha), he, his wife Genya, and their younger son Joseph, settled in New York, where Singer became a senior member of the staff of *Forverts*. In the first major work he published in America, the family novel *Di brider ashkenazi* (*The Brothers Ashkenazi*), Singer tried to examine individual fate in relation to both Jewish and world history. Tracking the intense rivalry of two brothers in the mercantile Polish city of Łódź, the novel is a chronicle of greed and betrayal, laying bare the impotence of generosity in a world governed by self-interest.

In 1937 Singer published a collection of five longer short stories under the title *Friling* [Spring], in which for the first time he introduced tales with an American setting and revealed a capacity for gentler satire, treating his characters with good humour and some tolerance. Still bitterly disenchanted with the failure of the Bolshevik Revolution and the way it mercilessly used and discarded individuals, Singer had previously treated it with biting irony, but only in passing; now he made it the central subject of his next major work, *Khaver nakhmen* (*East of Eden*). Neither the Poles nor the Russians escape the biting lash of Singer's savage exposure, and the novel is characterized by a claustrophobic intensity of rage.

The rise of Hitler and ferocious Nazi Jew-hatred affected Singer as deeply as all other Jewish writers, and he made it the subject of what was to be his last novel, *Di mishpokhe karnovski* (*The Family Carnovsky*). This "saga" novel traces through three generations the problem of Germany's assimilated Jews, dismissing the promises of the Enlightenment and all the hopes Jews entertained about being able to integrate into the modern world. The novel reasserts in the bleakest terms the inescapability of a Jewish identity, however unwanted it may be. Like all Singer's major works, this novel is permeated with an uncompromising despair and bleakness of vision. As always his style is clear, cold, and precise, powerful in understatement and austere realism.

By the time his last novel appeared, Singer was at the height of his fame, being widely read both in Yiddish and in English translation. Singer had been fortunate to acquire the services of the gifted Maurice Samuel as his English translator, and equally fortunate in having Maurice Schwartz adapt and stage four of his novels – *Yoshe kalb* (*The Sinner*), *Di brider ashkenazi*, *Khaver nakhmen*, and *Di mishpokhe karnovski* – which proved immensely successful in the Yiddish theatre. Yet Singer remained a deeply discontented and embittered man, finding no satisfaction from his reconstructed life in America. Witnessing with disillusionment and frustration the failure of all modern ideologies, he now looked back with mixed nostalgia to his youth in his father's pious Hasidic household and turned to writing a memoir of the youth he had rejected. The result was his autobiographical memoir, *Fun a velt vos iz nishto mer* (*Of a World That is No More*) that was being serialized in *Forverts* at the very time he died suddenly of a heart attack in New York in 1944. The memoir appeared posthumously in one volume in 1946; a further posthumous volume of short stories, under the general title *Dertseylungen* [Stories], appeared in 1949.

Although his work in English has never regained the wide appeal it enjoyed in his lifetime – reissues of some of his novels in the 1960s were not big sellers – Singer remains one of the leading exponents of realist Yiddish fiction, and his depiction, in surgically clean prose, of society at its most "nasty, brutal, and short" remains unsurpassed. His exacting sense of the sentimental and the false in literature made him a powerful and influential literary critic as well, and his work deserves renewed attention.

JOSEPH SHERMAN

Slutskii, Boris Abramovich

Soviet poet, 1919–1986

Born in Slaviansk, Ukraine, 7 May 1919. Studied at school in Kharkov; Moscow Institute of Jurisprudence, 1937–41; Gor'kii Literary Institute, Moscow, graduated 1941. Volunteered for active service, 1941; wounded; became political instructor; grandmother among group of Ukrainian Jews executed by Nazis and their collaborators. Joined Communist Party of the Soviet Union, 1943. Married Tat'iana Dashkovskaia; wife died 1977. Worked for All-Union Radio, 1948–52. Died 22 February 1986.

Selected Writings

Collections
Stikhi raznykh let: iz neizdannogo, 1988
Stikhotvorenniia, 1989
Sobranie sochinenii, 3 vols, 1991

Poetry
Pamiat [Memory], 1957
Vremia [Time], 1959
Segodnia i vchera [Today and Yesterday], 1961
Rabota [Work], 1964
Izbrannaia lirika, 1965
Sovremennye istorii [Contemporary Stories], 1969
Godovaia strelka [The Year Hand], 1971
Dobrota dnia [The Kindness of Day], 1973
Prodlennyi polden' [A Prolonged Midday], 1975
Neokonchennye spory [Unfinished Quarrels], 1978
Ruka i dusha [Hand and Soul], 1981
Unizhenie vo sne [Humiliation in a Dream], 1981
Sroki [Times], 1984
Ia istoriiu izlagaiu [I Set Forth a Story], 1990
"Iz poslednei zapisnoi knizhki" [From the Last Notebook], *Znamia*, 5 (1994)
Zapiski o voine: Stikhotvoreniia i ballady [Notes on the War], 2000

Other
Editor, *Poety Izraelya*, 1963
"Zarubki pamiati (iz knigi *Zapiski o voine*)" [Notches of Memory (from the Book Notes on the War)], *Voprosy literatury*, 3 (1995)
Things That Happened, edited and translated by G.S. Smith, 1999

Further Reading

Falikov, I., "Krasnorechie po-Slutski", *Voprosy literatury*, 2 (2000)
Lazarev, L., "Kogda proza stanovitsia poeziei", *Voprosy literatury*, 1 (1967)
Prussakova, Inna, "B.A. Slutskii: Kharakter i sud'ba", *Neva*, 4 (1994)
Samoilov, David, "Drug i sopernik", *Oktiabr'*, 9 (1992)

Since his death, Boris Slutskii has come to be acknowledged as the most important Russian poet of his generation. During his lifetime he was regarded by the Soviet authorities as a worthy individual whose war experience gave his poetry on that subject particular authority and authenticity. As a member of the Communist Party and the Union of Writers he censored himself and tried to prevent the unauthorized circulation of his writings. His loyalty was demonstrated when in 1958 he spoke and voted for the expulsion of Boris Pasternak from the Union of Writers, an act that was honest and sincere, but which tormented Slutskii for the rest of his life.

As a result of Slutskii's circumspection, an estimated 60 per cent of his poetry was left unpublished when he died. The situation was even more drastic with his prose memoirs. This previously unknown material began to be released soon after his death, and together it constituted one of the most important revelations of the Gorbachev period. The representation and interpretation of Soviet society that accumulates from these hundreds of short poems and something like a dozen prose memoirs is the most comprehensive we have by a single author.

As people who on the whole believed enthusiastically in the cause of Communism, the Russian Jews of Slutskii's generation almost all chose the path of assimilation – that is, they aimed to become Soviet citizens – an identity that in theory transcended ethnic, linguistic, economic, and social categories. The endemic anti-Semitism of Russian society, however, constantly gave the lie to this ideal and reinforced their consciousness of their origins. In respect of this factor, as in general, Slutskii's life followed a trajectory that started with a rising curve during the 1930s, peaked with the victory of 1945, and was soon followed by crushing humiliation. Slutskii's Jewishness was undoubtedly a major factor in his postwar disillusionment and his keeping a low public profile; and it certainly added an extra dimension of horror to his participation in the Pasternak affair. As a highly decorated survivor of World War II who had lost many of his relatives during the occupation of Ukraine, Slutskii soon found himself victimized by the same evil he had fought to destroy. Slutskii's first direct confrontation with official anti-Semitism came when he was dropped as a feature writer for Radio Moscow, the occasional work he had settled into while recovering from the physical trauma of his four years of active service. He soon began to discuss anti-Semitism explicitly in his poetry, one of very few Soviet intellectuals to do so in any branch of literature. The poems concerned form a small island in the ocean of Slutskii's collected works, but their power is quite disproportionate to their number. Only one of these poems was deemed to be publishable as it stood: "How They Murdered My Grandmother", a harrowing account of this old woman being shot out of hand because she would not go quietly to her death with the rest of the Jews of her village.

About ten other poems directly address this subject, all of them destined for "the drawer" and unthinkable in the pages of the Soviet press. Several of them became famous nonetheless. Despite the fact that it was first published in Russia only in 1987, "About the Jews" is one of Slutskii's best-known poems; it escaped his surveillance and soon "became folklore", with relatively few people knowing that he was the author. The poem was published abroad without authorization or attribution in 1961. Its first two stanzas rehearse some of the most frequently encountered clichés of Russian anti-Semitism: "Jews don't plant any crops,/ Jews do deals in their shops . . .", and then the poem moves into Slutskii's indignant rebuttal: "Not a single deal have I pulled,/ never stolen, and always paid,/ but I bear this accursed blood/ within me like the plague.// From the war I came back safe/ so as to be told to my face:/ 'No Jews got killed, you know! None!/ They all came back, every one!' " His other poems on the subject are equally pungent. "Patria and Patronymic" is about anti-Semitism among the literary intelligentsia, and it ends with Slutskii's defiant declaration of loyalty to his Jewish father and Jewish patronymic, which he would no more betray, he says, than he would his fatherland. "The Pale's Impaled . . ." is a lament for the Jewish communities of eastern Europe that were expunged in the Holocaust. The published poem "Uncles and Aunts" concerns this same theme, incidentally; it was acceptable because it does not mention the Jewishness of the people concerned, presenting them simply as close relatives of the poet who fell victim to unspecified historical forces.

Slutskii's most powerful piece on this subject was published only in 2000, 55 years after it was written. This is one of his "Notes on the War", entitled simply "The Jews". It begins by retelling the story of a certain Private Gershelman from Kharkov, who was captured along with his unit, escaped, lived on the run in Nazi-occupied Ukraine and encountered mainly gloating repudiation but sometimes wary protection from his former friends and neighbours, before finally crossing the front line and rejoining the Red Army in order, as he sees it, to take revenge or make acknowledgement, as appropriate to the way he was treated in his hour of desperate need. Slutskii then provides further accounts of the Jewish experience during wartime – in Austria, in the ranks of the multinational Red Army, and in occupied Europe; the attitude of non-Soviet Jews to the ostensibly assimilated Soviet Jewish soldiers is constantly at the forefront of Slutskii's attention. All this is set down in the dry, laconic, and factual style that is as characteristic of Slutskii's prose as of his poetry. The impact of the events and life stories he narrates – ineluctably horrendous, often sordid, but with occasional flashes of the noble and heroic – is all the more powerful as a result.

GERALD S. SMITH

Sobol, Yehoshua

Israeli dramatist, 1939–

Born in Tel Mond, 1939. Studied first at Tikhon-Chadash, Tel Aviv; then at the Sorbonne, from 1965, degree in philosophy, 1970. Member, kibbutz military service, Kibuts Shamir, 1957–65. Journalist, *Al hamishmar* newspaper; founder of theatre company dedicated to producing Israeli plays, 1977; teacher of aesthetics and workshop director, Tel Aviv University, Seminar Hakibutsim, and Beit Tzvi Drama Schools; artistic director, Haifa Municipal Theatre, 1984–88. Many awards, including Aharon Meskin Prize, 1983; German Critics' Poll Award, 1985; *Evening Standard* Drama Award, 1989; London Theatre Critics Award, 1990.

Selected Writings

Plays
Hayamim habaim [The Days to Come], 1971
Status Quo Vadis, 1973
Sylvester 1972 [New Year's Eve 1972], 1974

Hajoker [The Joker], 1975
Krisa [Nerves], 1976
Leyl haesrim, 1976; as *The Night of the Twentieth*, translated by Chana Hoffman, 1978
The Last of the Labourers, 1977
Gog vemagog [Gog and Magog Show], 1977
Dayarim [The Tenants], 1978
Beit kaplan [The House of Kaplan] (trilogy), 1978
The Wars of the Jews, 1981
Halaylah haaharon shel oto vaininger [The Last Night of Otto Weininger], 1982; as *Nefesh yehudi*, 1982; as *The Soul of a Jew*, translated by the Tel Aviv Institute for the Translation of Hebrew Literature, 1983
Ghetto, 1984; translated by the Tel Aviv Institute for the Translation of Hebrew Literature, 1986
Hapalestinait [The Palestinian], 1985
Sindrom yerushalayim [Jerusalem Syndrome], 1987
Adam [Man], 1989
Bamartef [In the Cellar], 1990
Solo, 1991
Girls of Toledo, lyrics by Sobol, music by Shosh Reisman, 1992
Ayin Beayin [An Eye for an Eye], 1994
Kfar [Village], 1996
Dvash [Honey], 1997
Ma-Ni-Ma-Mimah, 1998
Alma, 1999
The Masque Ball, 2000

Novel
Shetika [Silence], 2000

Further Reading

Feldman, Yael S., "Zionism: Neurosis or Cure? The 'Historical' Drama of Yehoshua Sobol", *Prooftexts*, 7/2 (1987)
Langworth, Douglas, "When Choosing Good is Not an Option: An Interview with Joshua Sobol", *Theater*, 22/3 (1991)
Sinclair, Clive, interview with Sobol, *Index on Censorship*, 14/1 (1985)

Sobol began his playwriting career in the early 1970s as the author of documentaries on social and political issues for the Haifa Municipal Theatre (for example, *The Days to Come*, 1971). He later wrote full-fledged realistic plays such as *Sylvester 1972* and *The Joker* (1975)

His first major play, *The Night of the Twentieth*, takes the form of a soul-searching confessional session carried out by a group of Jewish pioneers on the eve of their settling in a new spot in Galilee, and is based on authentic diaries of the period. The various characters range from the self-assured activist, Ephraim, whose perspective on the Zionist project of agricultural settlement is so pragmatic that even his sexual attraction to Miriam is regarded as part of the "production agenda" of new Jewish life, to the moral thinker, Moshe, who argues that no deed is to be implemented before profound confession will put it to the test of the ideal, namely the building of a Jewish society based on moral values. This led to *The Last of the Labourers*, a clown show focusing on the Tolstoyan figure of early 20th-century socialist thinker and nationalist pioneer A.D. Gordon.

Sobol's realistic trilogy, *Beit kaplan* [The House of Kaplan], about the foundation of the State of Israel, loosely modelled on the *Oresteia*, was less than successful. He then embarked on a series of historical-dramatic investigations into the lives of major Jewish historical figures who left their marks on the life of the nation.

In the years during which Israeli drama flourished at the Haifa Municipal Theatre, with the involvement of both Jewish and Arab actors, Sobol widened his questioning of national myths. First in this group of plays is *The Last Night of Otto Weininger* (also called *The Soul of a Jew*) about the life and death of the Viennese Jewish philosopher against the background of nascent Zionism. Sobol's purpose in journeying to the cradle of Zionism is not to find Herzl, its founder (who does not appear in the play, unlike historical figures such as Freud or Strindberg). Instead he focuses on Weininger, who appears as a despairing charlatan, a prisoner of his own rhetoric and haunted by an uncontrollable death wish. His teaching reproaches Judaism and femininity as being weak when confronted with the superior values of the Aryan and masculinity. He is presented as the spiritual double of the Zionist subject, materializing almost a century later in the frighteningly racist figure of Meir Kahane, a Zionist fascist and member of the Knesset, who was exerting his menacing influence while Sobol wrote the play. Zionism, with its tendency to virility and muscular supremacy, Weininger maintains, could serve as an ideal had it not been entrusted to the Jews.

Ghetto reconstructs the story of the Jewish theatre in the Vilna (Vilnius) ghetto during the Holocaust, basing his story on the diary of Kruk, the librarian. In this play Gens, the ardent Zionist head of the Jewish police in the ghetto, in his total submission to the logic of survival at every cost, finds himself collaborating with the psychotic Nazi officer Kittel in devising lists of Jews to be transported to the extermination camps, but barters with him to keep as many Jews alive as he can. Gens confronts Kruk, the non-Zionist socialist who criticizes Gens's nationalism as leading to moral annihilation. Included in the ensemble of fascinating characters is Srulik, a ventriloquist and actor whose bravery comes from the mouth of his dummy, Hayyah, a famous singer and actress before the war whom Srulik saves and who becomes the leader of the troupe, and Weiskopf, the entrepreneurial tailor who uses Jews to keep mending and repairing Nazi uniforms. The Jews struggle to create this theatre which allows them to retain humanity and some sense of culture until the unavoidable and tragic end.

Sobol openly criticizes the deteriorating Zionist dream in the political reality of Israel as a nightmare of violence and racism in *The Palestinian*. The opening night in 1987 of his *Jerusalem Syndrome* (a reworking of his earlier *The Wars of the Jews* from 1981), an elusive historical parable alluding to the topical political situation, was physically interrupted by members of right-wing groups. The incident led to Sobol's resignation from his joint artistic directorship of the Haifa Municipal Theatre, and his following plays (*Adam*, a less successful sequel to *Ghetto*; *Solo*, on the life of Spinoza) were produced elsewhere.

In the late 1980s several of Sobol's plays (especially *Ghetto*, named London's Play of the Year in 1989) were discovered internationally and produced extensively in Europe and the USA. Sobol's dramatic writing during the last decade of the century was rather eclectic: his most successful play in the 1990s, *Village*, a nostalgic depiction of his native village during his childhood in the 1940s, produced by the Russian immigrants' Gesher theatre, won great local and international success, but its ideological consistency with his earlier writing is, at best, questionable. Later themes were varied. *Honey* depicts the dismantling of the kibbutz idea by capitalist urges; *Ma-Ni-Ma-Mimah* is a brilliant short gibberish play, depicting a semi-Becketian situation between three homeless; *Alma* is a study of the life of Alma Mahler; while *The Masque Ball* is a parable on Israel as a traffic jam. Sobol's first novel *Silence* was published in 2000.

AVRAHAM OZ

Sontag, Susan

US fiction writer, critic, and essayist, 1933–

Born in New York City, 16 January 1933. Studied at University of California, Berkeley, 1948–49; University of Chicago, 1949–51, BA 1951; Harvard University, 1954–57, MA 1955; St Anne's College, Oxford, 1957; the Sorbonne. Married Philip Rieff, 1950; divorced, 1958. Has one son. Has taught at Oxford, Harvard, and Rutgers universities. Editor, *Commentary*, New York, 1959 and 1964–65. President, PEN American Center, 1987–89. Many awards, including American Association of University Women Fellowship, 1957; Rockefeller Fellowship, 1965 and 1974; Guggenheim Fellowship, 1966, 1975; American Academy Award, 1976; Ingram Merrill Foundation Award, 1976; National Book Critics Circle Award, 1977; Academy of Sciences and Literature Award (Germany, 1979); National Book Award, 2000; Jerusalem Prize, 2001. Member, American Academy of Arts and Letters, 1979; Officier, Ordre des Arts et des Lettres (France), 1984.

Selected Writings

Novels
The Benefactor, 1963
Death Kit, 1967
The Volcano Lover, 1992
In America, 2000

Short Stories
I, etcetera, 1978
The Way We Live Now, 1991

Screenplays: *Duet for Cannibals*, 1969; *Brother Carl*, 1971; *Alice in Bed*, 1993

Other
Against Interpretation and Other Essays, 1966
Trip to Hanoi, 1969
Styles of Radical Will, 1969
Editor, *Selected Writings of Artaud*, translated by Helen Weaver, 1976
On Photography, 1977
Illness as Metaphor, 1978
Under the Sign of Saturn, 1980
A Susan Sontag Reader, 1982
Editor, *A Barthes Reader*, 1982; as *Barthes: Selected Writings*, 1983
Aids and Its Metaphors, 1989
Cage, Cunningham, Johns: Dancers on a Plane: In Memory of Their Feelings, 1990

Further Reading

Dessaix, Robert, "Death to Art: Reflections on Aids, Art, and Susan Sontag", *Republica*, 4 (1999)
Hardwick, Elizabeth, introduction to *A Susan Sontag Reader*, New York: Farrar Straus, 1982; London: Penguin, 1983
Kennedy, Liam, *Susan Sontag: Mind as Passion*, Manchester: Manchester University Press, and New York: St Martin's Press, 1995
Poague, Leland (editor), *Conversations with Susan Sontag*, Jackson: University Press of Mississippi, 1995
Poague, Leland A., *Susan Sontag: An Annotated Bibliography (1948–1992)*, New York: Garland, 2000
Sayres, Sohnya, *Susan Sontag: The Elegiac Modernist*, New York and London: Routledge, 1990
Showalter, Elaine *et al.* (editors), *Modern American Women Writers*, New York: Scribner, 1991

Susan Sontag's father, Jack Rosenblatt, had a fur-trading business in China, and died when she was five years old. She kept the surname of her mother's second husband, Nathan Sontag, and this is somehow indicative of the presence (or lack of it) of Jewishness in her work. Subject to anti-Semitism at school, she admits that it did no harm to discard the name Rosenblatt. Yet, despite other subjects and preoccupations taking over her vision of the world as a writer, the intellectual in Sontag is very much representative of that incisive, deeply-read, and vibrant tradition of the New York intellectual of the 1960s, in which context she first made her name.

That first impact came after years of studying a variety of subjects, and she was a polymath with a profound interest in European culture when she wrote her first two novels, *The Benefactor* and *Death Kit*. However, her rate of publication was phenomenal, and within a decade of her first novel, she had also published influential works on critical theory and cultural studies. *Against Interpretation* is partly a defence of the subjective, intuitive relation of user to artefact; "A work of art is a thing *in* the world, not just text or commentary *on* the world", she wrote. This has particular interest when one recalls that Sontag is also responsible for much of the dissemination of thought about the work of Roland Barthes. It is entirely typical of her capacious and original mind that she should argue in response to what is pressing and urgently contemporary around her.

As a teacher, Sontag taught religion, philosophy, and literature; she is widely-travelled, and her cosmopolitan sensibility and intellect have added a certain potency and edge to her critiques of her own country. As with Ken Kesey, Scott Fitzgerald, and Joseph Heller, Sontag's basis for writing is one of finding the "worm in the apple" in American self-confidence and autonomy. Having seen other cultures and felt their spirit and identity, she looked again at her own and found it wanting.

In this way, her sensibility fastened onto whatever impinged on her intellect as significant, and her writing is fearlessly polymathic in a world of specialist academics. Her *On Photography* developed her notion of *transparency*, the act of experiencing the thing itself, not a construct of secondary language and ideas attached to it by cultural and aesthetic factors. Similarly, when she developed cancer, her questioning and acute observation of fellow patients eventually led to her ground-breaking book, *Illness as Metaphor*. Here, she wrote something that would prove to be one of the first influential works on that aspect of cultural studies concerned with the self and the body in the postmodern world of simulacra, reproductions, and replicas.

Sontag's writing has always ignored the constrictions of genre. In this she resembles intellectuals and artists in European literatures, despite her American stance on such topics as the literary canon and the nature of immigrant societies. As she noted in a recent interview, she has left the essay behind but tends to use her fiction as a space in which essay style may be integrated into the whole work. She has been much concerned with experimental Modernist fiction, and her latest two novels have been historical (as is her planned next novel, to be set in 1930s Japan) and she has said that this is because the past is a clear way of looking at and understanding the present. *The Volcano Lover* is set in the late 18th century, and concerns Emma Hamilton and Sir William Hamilton, and of course, Lord Nelson; but it is primarily concerned with revolution and with historical process and the individual. If one had to seek out Jewish preoccupations or habits of thought in her work, it might be in her abiding interest in the psyche of transitory, unsettled people, the idea of arrival and settlement.

Sontag has become increasingly preoccupied with the capitalist society around her, and with the effects of materialist behaviour. Her latest work, a novel, *In America*, is mostly about the actress Maryna Zalewska and her Polish friends in America. The theme of establishing a sub-society within a dominant ideological process is important here, and the book is also an outstanding metaphorical exploration of the mind and culture of the Jewish Europeans who came to the United States in the 19th century, and their transmutation into Americans. In this, it could be argued that, in spite of the diversity of her work, there is a unifying, organic element in her writing which has been an organizing principle: the expressions of political ideology and its human repercussions in modernity. In *Volcano Lover* we have the statement that "She would never be seduced into forgetting herself" and this could be a motif for Sontag's adoption of writing the personal, the individuated experience in a world in which we are increasingly alienated by corporate doublespeak and division of labour. The collapse of community, the dissolution of true communication and the bland acceptance of power have been preoccupations in her work, throughout the many phases and turning-points.

Undeniably, Sontag's writing has provided American literature with a range of focal points for cultural criticism; her books have mostly been influential, innovative texts; the common ground in the diversity of subjects and forms has been in that iconoclasm which is perhaps a specialism of the Jewish artist: the extension of a kvetch into a world-picture, and a gut-feeling into a philosophy. It would be hard to find another modern American writer who has had such an influence on so many disparate disciplines of thought since the 1960s: Susan Sontag continues to be a presence, and her writing has never lost its power and acerbity. But people are at the centre, and out of the rhetoric with herself (to paraphrase Yeats) she has made her art. In returning to the novel, Sontag has apparently found that the postmodern moment in fiction accommodates her free-flow enquiry, her intellectual range, and her fascination with human aspirations, questionings, and delusions.

STEPHEN WADE

Spark, Muriel

British fiction writer, poet, and literary critic, 1918–

Born Muriel Sarah Camberg in Edinburgh, 1 February 1918. Studied at James Gillespie's School for Girls and Heriot Watt College, both in Edinburgh. Lived in Bulawayo, Southern Rhodesia (now Zimbabwe), 1937–44. Married S.O. Spark, 1937; marriage dissolved; one son. Returned to Britain, 1944; worked for Political Intelligence Department, Foreign Office, London, 1944–45; General Secretary, Poetry Society, and editor, *Poetry Review*, London, 1947–49. Converted to Roman Catholicism, 1954. Now lives in Italy. Many awards, including *Observer* Story Prize, 1951; Italia Prize (for radio play), 1962; James Tait Black Memorial Prize, 1966; FNAC prize (France), 1987; Bram Stoker Award, 1988; Royal Bank of Scotland–Saltire Society Award, 1988. Fellow, Royal Society of Literature, 1963; Honorary Member, American Academy of Arts and Letters, 1978. Officer, Order of the British Empire, 1967; Officier, Ordre des Arts et des Lettres (France), 1988; Dame, Order of the British Empire, 1993; David Cohen British Literature Prize, 1997.

Selected Writings

Novels
The Comforters, 1957
Robinson, 1958
Memento Mori, 1959
The Ballad of Peckham Rye, 1960
The Bachelors, 1961
The Prime of Miss Jean Brodie, 1961
The Girls of Slender Means, 1963
The Mandelbaum Gate, 1965
The Public Image, 1968
The Driver's Seat, 1970
Not to Disturb, 1971
The Hothouse by the East River, 1973
The Abbess of Crewe, 1974
The Takeover, 1976
Territorial Rights, 1979
Loitering with Intent, 1981

The Only Problem, 1984
A Far Cry from Kensington, 1988
Symposium, 1990
Reality and Dreams, 1996
Aiding and Abetting, 2000

Short Stories
The Go-Away Bird and Other Stories, 1958
Voices at Play (includes the radio plays *The Party through the Wall*; *The Interview*; *The Dry River Bed*; *The Danger Zone*), 1962
Collected Stories I, 1968
Bang-Bang You're Dead and Other Stories, 1981
The Collected Stories of Muriel Spark, 1994
Open to the Public, 1997

Plays
Doctors of Philosophy, 1962
The Prime of Miss Jean Brodie: A Drama in Three Acts, 1969

Radio Plays: *The Party through the Wall*, 1957; *The Interview*, 1958; *The Dry River Bed*, 1959; *The Ballad of Peckham Rye*, 1960; *The Danger Zone*, 1961

Poetry
Out of a Book (as Muriel Camberg), 1933
The Fanfarlo and Other Verse, 1952
Collected Poems I, 1967
Going Up to Sotheby's and Other Poems, 1982

Other
Editor, with Derek Stanford, *Tribute to Wordsworth: A Miscellany of Opinion for the Centenary of the Poet's Death*, 1950
Child of Light: A Reassessment of Mary Wollstonecraft Shelley, 1951; revised edition as *Mary Shelley: A Critical Biography*, 1987
Editor, *A Selection of Poems*, by Emily Brontë, 1952
Emily Brontë: Her Life and Work, with Derek Stanford, 1953
John Masefield, 1953
Editor, with Derek Stanford, *My Best Mary: The Selected Letters of Mary Wollstonecraft Shelley*, 1953
Editor, *The Brontë Letters*, 1954; as *The Letters of the Brontës: A Selection*, 1954
Editor, with Derek Stanford, *Letters of John Henry Newman: A Selection*, 1957
The Very Fine Clock, 1968
Editor, *The Essence of the Brontës: A Compilation with Essays*, 1993

Further Reading

Bold, Alan, *Muriel Spark*, London and New York: Methuen, 1986
Cheyette, Bryan, *Muriel Spark*, Tavistock: Northcote House, 2000
Edgecombe, Rodney Stenning, *Vocation and Identity in the Fiction of Muriel Spark*, Columbia: University of Missouri Press, 1990
Hynes, Joseph, *The Art of the Real: Muriel Spark's Novels*, Rutherford, New Jersey: Fairleigh Dickinson University Press, 1987
Hynes, Joseph (editor), *Critical Essays on Muriel Spark*, New York: G.K. Hall, 1992
Kane, Richard C., *Iris Murdoch, Muriel Spark and John Fowles: Didactic Demons in Modern Fiction*, Rutherford, New Jersey: Fairleigh Dickinson University Press, 1988
Little, Judy, *Comedy and the Woman Writer: Woolf, Spark, and Feminism*, Lincoln: University of Nebraska Press, 1983
McQuillan, Martin (editor), *Theorizing Muriel Spark: Gender, Race, Deconstruction*, London: Palgrave, 2002
Page, Norman, *Muriel Spark*, London: Macmillan, 1990
Randisi, Jennifer Lynn, *On Her Way Rejoicing: The Fiction of Muriel Spark*, Washington, DC: Catholic University of America Press, 1991
Rees, David, *Muriel Spark, William Trevor, Ian McEwan: A Bibliography of Their First Editions*, London: Colophon Press, 1992
Sproxton, Judy, *The Women of Muriel Spark*, New York: St Martin's Press, and London: Constable, 1992
Tominaga, Thomas T. and Wilma Schneidermeyer, *Iris Murdoch and Muriel Spark: A Bibliography*, Metuchen, New Jersey: Scarecrow Press, 1976

Born in 1918, Dame Muriel Spark was nearly 40 years of age when she completed *The Comforters*, her first novel. Over the next five decades, she published 21 novels, three volumes of short stories, and the occasional play, collection of poetry and children's work. The phenomenal success of Spark's sixth novel, *The Prime of Miss Jean Brodie* – as a stage-play, feature film, and television series – has ensured that she retains a popular appeal. After gaining several literary prizes and academic awards, she is now widely considered to be one of the most engaging and tantalizing writers of her generation. What is extraordinary about Spark's achievement is that as well as having a large international readership she manages to engage with many of the most serious intellectual issues of her time. It is typical of her work that it both gestures towards and acknowledges many of the debates and concerns of the age without, ever, being wholly reliant on them.

Spark gained a good deal from avant-garde movements such as the French *nouveau roman* of Alain Robbe-Grillet and the British "experimentalism" of B.S. Johnson and Christine Brooke-Rose in the 1950s and 1960s; feminist writing of the 1970s; and postmodern and magical realist fiction of the 1980s and 1990s. At the same time, she has continued the long tradition of English social realism and literary satire in much of her work and has placed these more conventional modes alongside the avant-garde. But what is clear from even a cursory reading of Spark's dazzling and cunning fictions is that she only ever engages with these various literary modes in so far as they can be subsumed by her essentially singular vision. Spark's quirky and playful voice refuses to be contained by any one doctrine. Her abiding doubleness, above all, places a sense of history, tradition, and the avant-garde next to an irreverent and whimsical sense of the absurdity of all human philosophies.

Spark's ability to subsume the larger cultural questions of her day is in part a consequence of her formative years as a literary critic. Along with a collection of poetry, her books in the early 1950s consisted of a tribute to William Wordsworth; a reassessment of Mary Shelley and selection of her letters; editions of the poems and letters of Emily Brontë; and an account of John Masefield. Spark might well have continued as a critic and occasional poet if it were not for the publication of "The Seraph and the Zambesi" which won the *Observer* short-story prize. This story made such a profound impact that it literally transformed Spark's life. After it was published, she was immediately introduced to the editor and staff of the *Observer* and began writing occasionally for the newspaper. Because she was poverty-stricken and unwell at the time, Graham Greene offered to support her financially and was an influential patron. More importantly, "The Seraph and the Zambesi" attracted the attention of Alan Maclean, the fiction editor of Macmillan, who commissioned her to write a novel and collection of short stories which subsequently became *The Comforters* and *The Go-Away Bird and Other Stories*. Such was Spark's meteoric rise as a writer of fiction.

Her 21 novels reflect Spark's competing fictional identities as both an unchanging moralist who also happens to be playfully anarchic. The reason that she is equally well known as a Scottish-Jewish writer, Catholic convert, and poetic modernist is that she has managed to defy all the categories. Her fictions are tantalizing precisely because they are able to sustain such radically different readings. The key to understanding Spark's fiction is to recognize that it is constantly in dialogue with itself and that each of her novels, or groups of novels, zigzags between her converted and unconverted selves. After initially descending into the world of her private emotions and unconverted history in her first two novels, she eventually finds refuge behind an impersonal and God-like narrator in her neoclassical third novel, *Memento Mori*. This was a pattern that she was to continue throughout her career.

Her early didactic tales such as *Memento Mori* or *The Girls of Slender Means* are quickly followed by more unruly books such as *The Ballad of Peckham Rye* or *The Prime of Miss Jean Brodie*. If her novels become too impersonal – as in *The Driver's Seat* or *Not to Disturb* – she writes anarchic works such as *The Abbess of Crewe* or *The Takeover*, or ostensibly autobiographical books such as *Loitering with Intent* or *A Far Cry from Kensington*. Spark's abundant gifts are such that she refuses to rest on her laurels. Always shifting in time, from the 1940s to the 1990s, her fiction has encompassed Rhodesia, Edinburgh, and Jerusalem and has rotated between London, New York, and Rome. But no one time, place or culture has been allowed to delimit Spark's imagination.

Spark's self-confessed "Gentile Jewishness" can be placed in the context of the self-questioning and doubleness that characterise her best works. Clearly an aspect of her unconverted self, her part-Jewishness is dealt with at length in *The Mandelbaum Gate*, set in Jerusalem in the early 1960s, and the story that came out of this novel, "The Gentile Jewesses". Both her novel and story are instances of Spark at her most exuberant and playful, although she has subsequently rejected the novel (but not the story) because it remained outside of her narrative control. Given its unrestrained form and Jewish subject matter, it is fitting that *The Mandelbaum Gate* should continue to disturb Spark long after it was written. While many of her critics marginalize Spark as a "Catholic Writer", it is clear that the wit, intelligence, and subversiveness of her fiction are driven not by an unchanging morality but by a radical singularity (which includes her Gentile Jewishness). Far from smoothing over her sense of difference, Spark's conversion to Catholicism in 1954 places her many contradictions in a sustained, and abundantly creative, dialogue.

BRYAN H. CHEYETTE

Spiegelman, Art

Swedish-born US writer and artist, 1948–

Born in Stockholm, 15 February 1948, to Vladek and Anja (née Zylberberg). Emigrated to US and brought up in Queens, New York. Became naturalized citizen. Educated at Harpur College (now State University of New York at Binghamton), 1965–68. Married Françoise Mouly (a publisher); two children. Worked as a freelance artist and writer from 1965. Instructor in studio class on comics, San Francisco Academy of Art; instructor in history and aesthetics of comics at New York School of Visual Arts. Co-founder and editor of *RAW*, the avant-garde comics magazine. Many awards, including Annual *Playboy* award for best comic strip, 1982; Yellow Kid Award (Italy) for best comic strip author, 1982; Joel M. Cavior Award for Jewish Writing, 1986; Inkpot Award, San Diego Comics Convention, 1987; Stripschappenning Award (Netherlands) for best foreign comics album, 1987; Special Pulitzer Prize, National Book Critics Circle Award, *Los Angeles Times* Book Prize, and Before Columbus Foundation Award, all 1992.

Selected Writings

Comics
The Complete Mr Infinity, 1970
The Viper Vicar of Vice, Villainy and Vickedness, 1972
Zip-a-Tune and More Melodies, 1972
Editor, *Douglas Comix*, 1972
Ace Hole, Midget Detective, 1974
Language of Comics, 1974
Breakdowns: From Maus to Now, Anthology of Strips, 1977
Work and Turn, 1979
Every Day Has Its Dog, 1979
Two-Fisted Painters Action Adventure, 1980
Maus: A Survivor's Tale, 1986; revised edition, as *Maus I: A Survivor's Tale: My Father Bleeds History*, 1992
Editor, with Françoise Mouly, *Raw: Open Wounds from the Cutting Edge of Commix*, 1989
Maus II: A Survivor's Tale: And Here My Troubles Began, 1991
Illustrator, *The Wild Party: The Lost Classic*, by Joseph Moncure, 1994
I'm a Dog!, 1997

Strange Stories for Strange Kids, with Françoise Mouly, 2001

Further Reading

Bosmajian, Hamida, "The Orphaned Voice in Art Spiegelman's *Maus* I and II", *Literature and Psychology*, 44/1–2 (1998): 1–22

Comics Journal, August 1981: 98–125; December 1986: 43–45; April 1989: 110–117

Doherty, Thomas, "Art Spiegelman's *Maus:* Graphic Art and the Holocaust", *American Literature*, 68/1 (March 1996): 69–84

Liss, Andrea and Jill Snyder (editors), *Impossible Evidence: Contemporary Artists View the Holocaust: Melissa Gould, Ellen Rothernberg, Nancy Spero, Art Spiegelman*, Reading, Pennsylvania: Freedman Gallery, 1994 (exhibition catalogue)

New York Times Book Review, 3 November 1991: 1, 35–36

Reform Judaism, Spring 1987: 22–23, 32

Rolling Stone, 20 November 1986: 103–106, 146–148

Rothberg, Michael, "'We Were Talking Jewish": Art Spiegelman's *Maus* as 'Holocaust' Production", *Contemporary Literature*, 35/4 (Winter, 1994): 661–87

Tabachnick, Stephen E., "Of *Maus* and Memory: The Structure of Art Spiegelman's Graphic Novel of the Holocaust", *Word and Image*, 9/2 (April–June 1993): 154–62

Witek, Joseph, *Comic Books as History: The Narrative Art of Jack Jackson, Art Spiegelman and Harvey Pekar*, Jackson: University Press of Mississippi, 1989

The aesthetics of Holocaust literature has always been paradoxical and the subject of censure, burdened with emotions of guilt, shame, revulsion, and horror. The writers and defenders of Holocaust literature must delicately respond to those who feel that, after Auschwitz, there can be no poetry. Holocaust writing has, additionally, a complex generic weaving of autobiography and memoir, of fiction based on history, or of fiction by survivors. Because of its "authenticity", is the fiction by a survivor necessarily better aesthetically than some fiction created by a professional writer who has no personal first-hand experience with the Holocaust? Is the Holocaust memoir or survivor fiction subject to aesthetic judgement at all?

The "graphic novel", a relatively new genre, has its own set of reader prejudices: a narrative in the form of the comic strip, with the illustration not refined but purposely crude and "raw", usually in black-and-white, the graphic novel in the United States descends from the daily newspaper comic strip, *Mad* magazine, R. Crumb's *Fritz the Cat*, and Jules Feiffer. Only since the 1980s has it been the subject of scholarly attention, following such serious book-length "fact-based" experiments as Jack Jackson's *Comanche Moon* and *Los Tejanos* (1979 and 1982, respectively), and Harvey Pekar's *American Splendor* (1986) (see Tabachnick and Witek).

Despite the conflicts of genres and expectations, Art Spiegelman's 2-volume graphic novel, *Maus: A Survivor's Tale*, about his parents' experiences during the Holocaust, and about the traumatic aftermath of that experience for the entire family, received the 1992 Pulitzer Prize, and has been the basis of museum exhibitions and a CD with all of the taped interviews that were the basis of the work.

Maus is a serious and profoundly moving work. It has numerous claims to historical accuracy and narrative authenticity, as Spiegelman, the son of two Polish-Jewish survivors of Auschwitz, Vladek and Anja, having grown up "Americanized" in Rego Park, Queens, New York, with vacations in the Catskills, decides to interview his father formally about his wartime experiences for a comic book. Volume I, *My Father Bleeds History*, takes the story from the mid-1930s to late 1944, from increasing fears, to stratagems to avoid trouble, through betrayals, hiding, the ghetto life, and, finally, removal to Auschwitz. Volume II, *And Here My Troubles Began*, focuses on the death camps and their workings, the eventual end of the war and the residual anti-Semitism in Europe, the move to New York, and Vladek's death in 1982. Interwoven with the Holocaust narrative are the stories of the Anja's depression and suicide; Vladek's nasty treatment of his second wife, Mala, another survivor; his father's obsessions with food and frugality, held over from the period of deprivation; many stories of other victims of Hitler; Vladek's and Anja's relationships with Spiegelman; and Spiegelman's own mental breakdown (interpolating an earlier independently published comic about his mother's suicide called "Prisoner on the Hell Planet").

The tone of the work, and the emotional direction, change frequently. We have the scenes of mass arrests and the failed attempts to escape in Europe juxtaposed with Vladek's pettiness and eccentricities in Rego Park, examples of heroism and treachery, Nazis and anti-Semitic Poles, but also Jews who sometimes acted against other Jews. Vladek's profound love for Anja is in sharp contrast to his miserliness, bad treatment, and verbal abuse of Mala, who eventually feels that she has become Vladek's prisoner in the period before his death. There are some darkly humorous allusions (such as before the war, when Vladek and other Jews in the Polish army are freezing in tents while the Polish soldiers are in warm cabins, they are shown saying the daily prayers, reciting in untranslated Hebrew "How goodly are your tents, Jacob, your dwelling places, Israel").

Besides the structural complexity of the story, there is rich graphic complexity, providing illustrations that are not merely accurate depictions (and there are many diagrams and maps, and even family photographs), but the at-first shocking depiction of the characters as animals. The epigraph in volume I quotes Hitler: "The Jews are undoubtedly a race, but they are not human." Here the Jews are mice but in human clothing and with very believable actions, motives, and dialogue; the Germans are drawn as cats, the Poles are drawn as pigs, and the Americans as dogs. Broadly the work depicts processes of dehumanization, techniques of reduction to the animal.

In addition to being a graphic novel about the Holocaust, Spiegelman's *Maus* is a harrowing work of self-examination, determination, and self-doubt. It must be read in the context of the works of Elie Wiesel, Primo Levi, Aharon Appelfeld, and Tadeusz Borowski, while noting

Spiegelman's statement in a 1992 interview that he resists becoming "the Elie Wiesel of the comic book" (quoted in Rothberg, p. 665). The self-portrait of the author in the flap of the second volume, shows Art Spiegelman wearing a mouse mask, holding his head glumly while he stares at his drawing board, while outside his apartment window in New York there is an electrified barbed wire fence and a cat in a German uniform aiming a rifle from a guard tower. There is no actual liberation from the camps for the Holocaust survivors and their families, even for the next generation.

LEONARD ORR

Spire, André

French poet and Zionist activist, 1868–1966

Born in Nancy, 28 July 1868, into wealthy family. Studied literature, law, and political science, law degree 1890. Moved to Paris, 1891. Second lieutenant, army reserve, 1891. Employed by Conseil d'État, 1893. Doctorate in law, 1895. Created charity organization, Société des Visiteurs, taking care of workers, 1896; inspector general, Ministry of Agriculture, 1902–26. Co-founder, with Israel Zangwill, of Jewish Territorial Organization, based in London, finding homes for persecuted Jews; attended Zionist Congess, 1911; founder, Association des Jeunes Juifs, 1912; founder, Ligue des Amis du Sionisme, 1917; represented French Zionists at Paris Peace Conference, 1919; joined delegation to Palestine to negotiate Syrian–Palestinian frontier, 1920. Withdrew from active Zionism following rift with Chaim Weizmann; created organizations to place Jewish refugees as agricultural labourers in southern France, 1925–33; helped numerous Jewish families to escape from Nazi-controlled Germany and Austria through Comité Français pour les Immigrants Juifs, from 1933. First wife died, 1936; remarried, 1940; one daughter. Went to New York, 1941; lectured on French culture and verse at various universities in United States. Returned to France, June 1946. Died 29 July 1966. André Spire Committee established in Jerusalem to commemorate centenary of his birth, 1968.

Selected Writings

Poetry
La Cité présente [The Present City], 1903
Et vous riez! [And You're Laughing!], 1905
Versets [Verses], 1908
Vers les routes absurdes [Towards Ridiculous Roads], 1911
Et j'ai voulu la paix [And I Wanted Peace], 1916
Le Secret [The Secret], 1919
Poèmes juifs [Jewish Poems], 1919
Tentations [Temptations], 1920
Samaël: poème dramatique [Samaël: A Dramatic Poem], 1921
Fournisseurs [Tradesmen], 1923
Poèmes de Loire [Poems of the Loire], 1929
Instants [Moments], 1936
Poèmes d'ici et de là-bas [Poems from Here and There], 1944
Poèmes d'hier et d'aujourd'hui [Poems of Yesterday and Today], 1953

Other
Israël Zangwill, 1909
J'ai trois robes distinguées [I Have Three Elegant Gowns], 1910
Quelques Juifs [Some Jews], 1913
Refuges [Refuges], 1926
Quelques Juifs et demi-juifs [Some Jews and Half-Jews], 1928
Le Rabin et la sirène, 1931; as *The Rabbi and the Siren*, in *Yisroel*, edited by Joseph Leftwich, 1933
Souvenirs à bâtons rompus [Memories of This and That], 1962

Literary Criticism
"Le Vers français d'après la phonétique expérimentale" [French Verse According to Experimental Phonetics], *Mercure de France* (1914)
"Elie Faure: machinisme et judaïsme" [Elie Faure: Mechanization and Judaism], *Revue juive de Genève* (January–February 1934)
"Langage, image et ressentiment" [Language, Image, and Resentment], *Cahiers juifs* (June–July 1934)
"Rime et rythme" [Rhyme and Rythme], *Les Cahiers du Journal des poètes* (1936)
"Ponctuation et poésie" [Punctuation and Poetry], *Mercure de France* (1937)
"Georges Lote, les origines du vers français" [Georges Lote, the Origins of French Verse], *Aix-en-Provence* (1940)
"L'Ancien testament dans la littérature française" [The Old Testament in French Literature], *Revue de la pensée juive* (October 1949)
"De la poésie pure au balancement palestinien" [From Pure Poetry to Palestinian Balance], *Evidence* (1949)
"Goethe et Israël" [Goethe and Israel], *Cahiers du Sud* (1950)
"Romain Rolland fut-il antisémite?" [Was Romain Rolland Antisemitic?], *Revue française*, (1951)
"Paul Éluard et le vers libre" [Paul Éluard and Free Verse], *Europe* (April 1952)
"Rythme et personalité" [Rhythm and Personality], *Mélanges* (1956)
"Baudelaire esthéticien et précurseur du symbolisme" [Baudelaire as an Aesthetician and Forerunner of Symbolism], *Europe* (April–May 1967)

Social Issues
"Le Sweating System", *Pages libres* (June 1903)
Sous la tente: un essai de vacances ouvrières [Under the Tent: An Essay on Workers' Holidays], 1908
Le Sionisme [Zionism], 1918
Le Peuple juif [The Jewish People], 1919
Théodore Herzl et le judaisme français [Théodore Herzl and French Judaism], 1932
Les Sionistes devant la Conférence de la Paix [The Zionists before the Peace Conference], 1953

Further Reading

Burnshaw, Stanley, *André Spire and His Poetry*, Philadelphia: Centaur Press, 1933

Cassou, Jean, "André Spire, Max Jacob", *Nouvelles littéraires* (5 September 1936)
Chavannes, Pierre, "Un poète juif: André Spire", *Foi et Vie* (16 April 1920)
Franck, Henri, "André Spire", *Nouvelle revue française* (1910)
Meschonnic, Henri, "Poésie du cour, poésie familière", *Centenaire d'André Spire: Europe* (1967): 176–265

The mentor of Paul Éluard and Apollinaire, André Spire was among the first poets to vindicate the spoken language as material for poetry. Against eloquence and heavy rhetoric, Spire renewed poetical language, introducing conversational style and liberating prosody from its stiff yoke of rules and dead marble gods. There are no empty concepts or empty words in his poetry. Within this rejuvenated language, a double movement articulates the poet's thoughts: the raging satire against corruption and injustice, as well as a delicious pleasure in sensual life on earth.

Spire was also one of the precursors of a Jewish renaissance that took place at the beginning of the 20th century and that expressed itself through a composite literature represented by Edmond Fleg, Henri Franck, Jean-Claude Block, Armand Lunel, Albert Cohen, and Marcel Proust among others. European anti-Semitism, the discovery of the existence of a Jewish working class, and the work of the English author Israel Zangwill inspired Spire to think of a mode of Jewish integration within the fabric of French society. One dimension of this integration is the use of language. Prose or poetry, Spire's language is both a medium and a mediator that propels one's consciousness towards a future filled with life, emotion, and justice. For Spire, poetry is a form of life, a "special way of thinking" aimed at transforming men.

Throughout his long life Spire fought for justice and against hypocrisy. The poet and the man of action are inseparable. In his second collection of poems, *Et vous riez!*, one can feel the anxiety of the poet as he confronts his social mission. He addresses the poor, the rich, women and children to end with the simple and poignant lines: "Qu'est-ce que j'ai à vous dire?/ Il y a trop de baisers pas donnés entre nous. [What do I have to say to you?/ There are too many kisses not given between us.]

Nurtured by Nietzsche and Tolstoi, Spire is a social poet. He is also a Jewish poet who never denies the great voice of the prophets. But the Bible is a point of departure, a language, never a terminology. In "Encore", Spire writes of the "somnolence sans rêves du Shéol" [the dreamless somnolence of the Shéol] giving God the Kabbalistic name of "Trône" [Throne]. In "Cinq prières" Spire's anxiety, doubt and faith mingle in a resonating prayer where he momentarily loses his ability to speak.

Like his soulmate Heinrich Heine, Spire can be painful and sarcastic. He knows how to weave a terrible irony within his seemingly harmless "little songs":

Tu es content, tu es content,
Ton nez est presque droit, ma foi,
Et puis tant de chrétiens ont le nez un peu courbe.
Tu es content, tu es content,
Tes cheveux frisent à peine, ma foi

[You're happy, you're happy,
Your nose is almost straight, my lord,
Yet, so many Christians have a hooked nose.
You're happy, you're happy,
Your hair does not curl so much, my lord]

Spire vindicates Jewishness. Spurred by the reawakening of the Dreyfus affair, his *Poèmes juifs* show a passionate burning defense of Judaism. Like a manifesto, they project Spire's energy and his thirst for justice, but like an elegy of exile they also sing the intense consciousness of Jewish pain. In "Rêves juifs" he writes with empathy: "Oh mon ami ouvre les yeux!/ Notre chambre s'emplit d'une foule douloureuse" [Oh my friend open your eyes!/ Our room is full of people in pain].

Spire's poetry is a call to action made incarnate in a poetry of verbs. He does not find sufficient energy in nouns, because the substance of a noun is static and speaks of isolation. Verbs always involve the other. Spire was a man of action, and his poetry is all movement. Summing up *Samaël*, he speaks of some "contrées ouvertes où l'on s'élance, s'emporte, se défie, s'affronte, triomphe et tombe, pleure, rit, chante en travaillant. C'est ça la Création!" [open lands one thrusts upon, bolts, distrusts, fights for, where one triumphs and falls, cries and laughs, sings while working. That is Creation!]. Spire needs a cascade of verbs. Sometimes his lines are just an accumulation of verbs as in "Art poétique" from his *Poémes de Loire*: "Regarde, écoute, flaire, goûte, mange!" [Look, listen, smell, taste, eat].

The motivation of his poetry is to take on the world, to dialogue with nature.

In *Poèmes juifs*, he says "tu" to the whole of nature, and the landscape answers him, also using the familiar form of "you". Spire, the social and Jewish poet, is also a nature poet. He loved hunting in the French countryside. Earth, rivers, winds, and seas, the leaves of trees and the sky were his soulmates. He spoke to them. In *Souvenirs à bâtons rompus*, he calls upon sparrows: "Cris de moineaux: en virgule" [sparrows's squawkings: commas]; ducks become "floating leaves on a pond", "the sun is a blind eye." Spire did not fear death because death is part of nature, just another change:

je ne m'occupe pas de la mort.
Elle viendra quand elle voudra.
Tant qu'elle n'est pas là je fais comme si je devais vivre
Éternellement: J'aime, j'agis, je travaille.
[I do not worry about death
She will come whenever she wants.
As long as she is not here I will *live* as if
Eternally: I love, I act, I work.]

Together with his love of life, justice, and nature, women also inspire him. A wild sensuality pulsates through this man. Yet, when he speaks, a distance of modesty and restraint keeps the reader at bay. In "Nudités" Spire invokes the Talmud: "Les cheveux sont une nudité" [hair is a form of nakedness], and speaks of those chaste women who cover their hair, of the birth of their neck, yet sees them naked:

Femme, tu es nue.
Les cheveux de ton cou sont frais comme une coupe;
Ton chignon qui s'écroule palpite comme un sein;
[Woman, you are naked.
Your hair by your neck is fresh like a cup;
Your bun is undone and pulsates like a breast;]

It is no exaggeration to say that Spire's poems form a constant search for the other. Without the other, there is no life and no future. Spire's poetry is nourished by the same humanist sap as the philosophy of Emanuel Lévinas. An avid reader of Spinoza, Spire, like Lévinas, nurtures his words with ethics. We could easily speak of Spire's "poethics"!

Spire is a total poet. His life is a long poem of love, anger, and fight. From the simple popular country song to the mystical exhortation, from childhood innocence to sensual jubilation, from life's exacerbating projections of joy to bitter accents of prophetic vision, from political anger to humane softness and vulnerability, Spire touched all subject matter, all tones and all styles. He harmonized this diverse multiplicity within his thirst for life and justice. Spire lived 98 years. His literary output is considerable not only in quantity but also in quality. Yet, he is never mentioned, let alone studied, in French schools or lycées, not even acknowledged as the force behind Joyce's French *Ulysses*. It is after all thanks to Spire that James Joyce met Sylvia Beach, at his home in Neuilly. On all accounts, the recognition of this extraordinary man whom Paul Éluard and Apollinaire regarded as their spiritual father, is long overdue.

BÉA AARONSON

Stavans, Ilan (Zuri Balkoff)

Mexican-born US anthologist, essayist, and fiction writer, 1961–

Born Ilan Stavchansky Slomiansky in Mexico City, 7 April 1961. Served in army, 1977–78; theatre director, Mexico City, 1980–84; writer for television, 1982–84. Studied at Universidad Nacional Autonóma de México and Universidad Nacional Metropolitana, BA 1984. Emigrated to United States, 1985. Translator, New York City, 1985–90; library clerk, Jewish Theological Seminary, 1985–87. Studied at Jewish Theological Seminary, MA 1987; Columbia University, MA 1988, PhD 1990. Married Alison Baker, 1988; one son. Teacher of courses on literature of Latin America, Columbia University, 1988–90; associate professor, Baruch College, City University of New York, 1990–93; associate professor and, from 1993, professor, Amherst College; named Lewis Sebring Professor of Latin American and Latino Cultures, 2001. Member, PEN American Center. Founding editor, *Hopscotch: A Cultural Review*, from 1999. Awarded Latino Literary Prize, 1992; Gamma Prize, 1992; National Endowment for the Humanities Fellowship, 1991–92; Littauer Foundation Fellowship, 1992, 1994, 1996; Guggenheim Fellowship; Amherst College Foundation Fellowship, 1999, 2000.

Selected Writings

Essays

Manual del (im)perfecto resenista [Manual of the (Im)perfect Reviewer], 1989
Prontuario [Agenda], 1992
Imagining Columbus: The Literary Voyage, 1993
Anti-Heroes: Historia de la novela policiaca en Mexico, 1993; as *Anti-Heroes: Mexico and Its Detective Novel*, translated by L.H. Lytle and J.A. Mattson, 1997
La pluma y la mascara [The Pen and the Mask], 1993
Art and Anger: Essays on Politics and the Imagination, 1986–1995, 1995
The Hispanic Condition, 1995
Bandido: Oscar "Zeta" Acosta and the Chicano Experience, 1996
Felipe Alfau: A Literary Biography, 1996
Julio Cortázar: A Study of the Short Fiction, 1996
The Riddle of Cantinflas: Essays on Hispanic Popular Culture, 1998
The Stranger Within: Reflections on Hispanic Culture, 1999
The Essential Ilan Stavans, 2000
On Borrowed Words: A Memoir of Language, 2001
The Inveterate Dreamer: Essays and Conversations on Jewish Literature, 2001
Octavio Paz: A Meditation, 2002

Novel

Talia y el cielo; o, El libro de los ensueños [Talia in Heaven; or, The Book of Dreams] (as Ilan Stavans and Zuri Balkoff), 1977

Short Stories

La pianista manca, 1992; as *The One-Handed Pianist and Other Stories*, 1995

Other

Genesis 2000, 1979
Vals Triste, 1992
Editor, with Harold Augenbraum, *Growing Up Latino: Memoirs and Stories*, 1993
Editor, *Antología de cuentistas judíos* [Anthology of Jewish Short Stories], 1994
Editor, *Antología de cuentos de misterio y horror* [Anthology of Mystery and Horror Stories], 1994
Editor, *El Alienista y otros cuentos* [The Psychiatrist and Other Stories], 1994
Editor, with Flora Schiminovich, *La pluma magica: doce cuentos de Latin America* [The Magic Pen: Twelve Tales from Latin America], 1994
Editor, *Tropical Synagogues: Short Stories by Jewish Latin-American Writers*, 1994
Editor, *Oscar Zeta Acosta: The Uncollected Works*, 1996
Editor, *New World: Young Latino Writers*, 1997
Editor, *The Oxford Book of Latin American Essays*, 1997
Editor, *Prospero's Mirror: A Translator's Portfolio of Latin American Short Fiction*, 1998
Editor, *The Collected Stories of Calvert Casey*, 1998
Editor, *The Oxford Book of Jewish Stories*, 1998
Editor, *The Urban Muse: Stories on the American City*, 1998

Editor, *Mutual Impressions: Writers from the Americas Reading One Another*, 1999
The Jewish-Hispanic Reader: Before 1492 to the Present, 2001

Further Reading

Agosin, Marjorie, "Ilan Stavans: Inside the Theater of Words", *Americas* (August 1998)
Carbajo, Juan A., "Ilan Stavans: Filologo", *El Pais* (2 January 2000)
Heller, Scott, "Life on the Hyphen", *Chronicle of Higher Education* (9 January 1998)
Pakravan, Saideh, "The Writer in Exile: An Interview with Ilan Stavans", *Literary Review*, 37 (1993)
Richardson, Linda, "How to be an Outsider and an Insider", *New York Times* (13 November 1999)
Summer, Doris, "Ilan Stavans: El Jose entre sus hermanos", *Revista Iberoamericana*, 66 (2000)

"I write in English for Americans about topics they know little about", Ilan Stavans told an interviewer for the *Literary Review*, "and I write in Spanish for Mexicans about topics they are unacquainted with." Born in Mexico City in 1961, Stavans, who moved to the United States in 1985, is a vital intermediary between several cultures – Latin American and North American, Jewish and Gentile, academic and popular. He has paid tribute to Carlos Fuentes as a literary "puente", but Stavans himself performs the role of cultural bridge across the Rio Grande / Rio Bravo more effectively than anyone else of his generation. He organized his 1999 collection *Mutual Impressions: Writers from the Americas Reading One Another* into two sections: "South Reading North" (e.g. José Martí on Walt Whitman, Jorge Luis Borges on Nathaniel Hawthorne, Pablo Neruda on Robert Frost) and "North Reading South" (e.g. John Updike on Augusto Roa Bastos, Thomas Pynchon on Gabriel García Márquez, William Kennedy on Ernesto Sábato). But to read Ilan Stavans himself is to observe the South reading the North reading the South reading . . . Reading and translating himself, Stavans has made his own composite sensibility into a theatre of multiple identities.

Stavans's output has been precocious and prodigious – two dozen books by his 40th year. As an essayist, editor, translator, and fiction writer, Stavans is a figure of immense curiosity and enormous energy. Throughout his writings, he calls for the sort of polymath public intellectual missing since the death of Edmund Wilson, a voice capable of articulating complex issues in a manner that can engage non-specialists without condescension or caricature. Unlike Wilson, Stavans is a tenured professor, yet he chafes at the constraints of the merely academic. He reviews widely for a wide variety of non-specialist publications, including the *Nation*, the *Washington Post*, and the *New Republic*. *Hopscotch*, the journal he founded as a provocative forum on Hispanic culture, is representative of Stavans's ambitions to engage the general, educated reader. In his autobiography *On Borrowed Words*, as in many of his other writings, the intellectual and the personal are inseparable.

A major work of scholarship and criticism, *Tropical Synagogues* might serve as a fitting example of Stavans's aims and accomplishments. The 1994 collection is a literary reclamation project that, on a smaller scale, bears comparison with the pioneering work of Irving Howe in retrieving from oblivion the literature of North American Jews. A model of judicious and informed advocacy, the book offers North American readers acquaintance with Alberto Gerchunoff, Moacyr Scliar, Clarice Lispector, and other neglected Latin American Jews. By recouping unfamiliar texts and careers, *Tropical Synagogues* is not only an important work of cultural archaeology, but, by assembling within one volume authors who worked largely in isolation, from their national literatures and from one another, the anthology actually creates a tradition that is a revelation and an inspiration. Stavans continues his project of recovering Latin American Jewish texts in his editorship of *The Jewish-Hispanic Reader* and of the book series "Jewish-Latin America" for the University of New Mexico Press.

The grandson of immigrants from central Europe and the son of an actor in Yiddish theatre, Stavans, whose paternal surname was changed from Stavchansky, describes his Mexican birthright as accidental. His family ended up landing at Veracruz when the immigration quota to the United States was full. Yet he published his first novel, *Talia y el cielo* [Talia in Heaven], and many subsequent works, in Spanish. He has emerged as one of the most visible and vocal commentators on Latin American literature and culture, even, through his work on Spanglish, its lexicographer. Stavans's editorship of *The Norton Anthology of Latino Literature* has endowed him with authority over a tradition to which he, a Jew, feels marginal. Yet, though he was educated in Yiddish schools and wrote his first play in Yiddish, the native of Mexico seems to some an odd choice to edit the canonical *The Oxford Book of Jewish Stories*. A sense of exile – geographical, linguistic, cultural – pervades much of his own writing and accounts for his particular affinity with other marginal figures: not just Latin American Jews like himself but also other translinguals, authors including Felipe Alfau, Hector Bianciotti, Ariel Dorfman, Rosario Ferré, Franz Kafka, and Fernando Pessoa, who live both in and between languages and whom he has called "tongue snatchers". Stavans is active as a translator, especially of his own work, from Spanish into English and from English into Spanish. Even after marrying a North American and becoming a citizen of the United States, he embraces his hybrid identity. "I am divided into two hemispheres, two personas", he contends. "The injury between the two will never heal – but that doesn't scare me. I must find happiness in a divided self."

In Stavans's most characteristic fiction, written as philosophical speculation in the style of Latin American fantastical literature, a puzzled narrator is often forced to try to understand a bizarre phenomenon. The enigma is sometimes associated with another character, who, though grotesque, is essentially the narrator's doppelganger. In "The Death of Yankos", for example, a story Stavans translated from his 1992 collection *La pianista manca* (*The One-Handed Pianist and Other Stories*), an accountant named Noam recalls his acquaintance with a man who suffers from "the metaphysical distortion of measurement". Yankos is convinced that the ceiling to his apartment is descending and that it will eventually crush him. Noam, who has embraced ordinariness as a way of insulating himself from absurdity, is both puzzled and sceptical. But Yankos, who speaks for his author's own partiality for the plural, explains: "Altitude is individual. We are on one planet but in multiple worlds."

Contrasting the written word to his father's art, the theatre, which, he noted in an interview, lives only in the present, Stavans contends: "Literature is a way to say, I was here, this is what I thought, this is what I perceived. This is my signature, this is my name." Ilan Stavans has made lively use of languages to establish a distinctive name.

STEVEN G. KELLMAN

Stein, Gertrude

US fiction writer, art critic, and autobiographer, 1874–1946

Born in Allegheny, Pennsylvania, 3 February 1874, to Amelia and David Stein, wealthy immigrants from Germany. Lived with family in Vienna, Paris, and Oakland, California. Studied philosophy under William James at Harvard University, BA 1897; medicine at Johns Hopkins University, 1897–1901. Emigrated to France, 1903; lived with brother Leo, then with Alice B. Toklas from 1909. Apartment on rue de Fleurus became centre of artistic life; associated with Pablo Picasso, Henri Matisse, Ernest Hemingway, and F. Scott Fitzgerald. Lived in Mallorca, 1914–16. Worked with American Fund for French wounded, 1917–18. Founder, Plain Edition, Paris, 1930–33. Lectured in United States, 1934–35. Left Paris and lived in Belignin, southern France, 1942–45. Died 27 July 1946.

Selected Writings

Collections

The Yale Edition of the Unpublished Writings of Gertrude Stein, 8 vols, 1951–58

Writings and Lectures 1911–1945, edited by Patricia Meyerowitz, 1967; as *Look at Me Now and Here I Am*, 1971

Selected Operas and Plays, edited by John Malcolm Brinnin, 1970

The Previously Uncollected Writings of Gertrude Stein, edited by Robert Bartlett Haas, 1973

The Yale Stein: Selections, edited by Richard Kostelanetz, 1980

Really Reading Gertrude Stein: A Selected Anthology, with essays by Judy Grahn, 1989

Writings 1903–1932, 1998

Writings 1932–1946, 1998

Short Stories

Three Lives: Stories of the Good Anna, Melanctha, and the Gentle Lena, 1909

Mrs Reynolds, and Five Earlier Novelettes, edited by Carl Van Vechten, 1952

Novels

The Making of Americans, Being a History of a Family's Progress, 1925; abridged as *The Making of Americans: The Hersland Family*, 1934

A Book Concluding with As a Wife Has a Cow: A Love Story, 1926

Lucy Church Amiably, 1931

Ida: A Novel, 1941

Brewsie and Willie, 1946

Blood on the Dining Room Floor, 1948

Things as They Are: A Novel in Three Parts, 1950

A Novel of Thank You, edited by Carl Van Vechten, 1958

Lifting Belly, edited by Rebecca Marks, 1989

Plays

Geography and Plays, 1922

A Village: Are You Ready Yet Not Yet, 1928

Operas and Plays, 1932

Four Saints in Three Acts, 1934

A Wedding Bouquet: Ballet, 1936

Daniel Webster: Eighteen in America, 1937

In Savoy; or, Yes is for a Very Young Man, 1946

The Mother of Us All, 1947

Last Operas and Plays, edited by Carl Van Vechten, 1949

In a Garden, 1951

Lucretia Borgia, 1968

D. Faustus, Lights the Lights, 1984

Operas and Plays, 1987

Poetry

Tender Buttons: Objects, Food, Rooms, 1914

Have They Attacked Mary. He Giggled, 1917

If You Had Three Husbands, 1922

Before the Flowers of Friendship Faded Friendship Faded, 1931

Prothalamium for Bobolink and His Louisa: A Poem, 1939

Two (Hitherto Unpublished) Poems, 1948

Stanzas in Meditation and Other Poems, edited by Carl Van Vechten, 1956

I Am Rose, 1971

Five Short War Poems, 1988

Other

Portrait of Mabel Dodge, 1912

Composition as Explanation, 1926

Descriptions of Literature, 1926

An Elucidation, 1927

Useful Knowledge, 1928

An Acquaintance with Description, 1929

Dix Portraits, 1930

How to Write, 1931

Matisse, Picasso and Gertrude Stein, with Two Shorter Stories, 1933

The Autobiography of Alice B. Toklas, 1933

Chicago Inscriptions, 1934

Portraits and Prayers, 1934

Everybody's Autobiography, 1937

Picasso, 1938

Prothalamium, 1939

The World is Round, 1939

Paris France, 1940

What are Masterpieces, 1940

Wars I Have Seen, 1945

Four in America, 1947

Kisses Can, 1947

Literally True, 1947
Painted Lace and Other Pieces (1914-1937), 1955, edited by Carl Van Vechten
Fernhurst, Q.E.D. and Other Early Writings, 1971, edited by Leon Katz
Dear Sammy: Letters from Stein to Alice B. Toklas, 1977, edited by Samuel M. Steward

Further Reading

Chessman, Harriet Scott, *The Public is Invited to Dance: Representation, the Body, and Dialogue in Gertrude Stein*, Stanford, California: Stanford University Press, 1989
Dubnick, Randa, *The Structure of Obscurity: Gertrude Stein, Language and Cubism*, Urbana: University of Illinois Press, 1984
Fifer, Elizabeth, *Rescued Readings: A Reconstruction of Gertrude Stein's Difficult Texts*, Detroit: Wayne State University Press, 1992
Gygax, Franziska, *Gender and Genre in Gertrude Stein*, Westport, Connecticut: Greenwood Press, 1998
Kostelanetz, Richard (editor), *Gertrude Stein Advanced: An Anthology of Criticism*, Jefferson, North Carolina: McFarland, 1990
Liston, Maureen R., *Gertrude Stein: An Annotated Critical Bibliography*, Kent, Ohio: Kent State University Press, 1979
Moore, George B., *Gertrude Stein's The Making of Americans*, New York: Peter Lang, 1998
Ryan, Betsy Alayne, *Gertrude Stein's Theatre of the Absolute*, Ann Arbor, Michigan: UMI Research Press, 1984
Souhami, Diana, *Gertrude and Alice*, London: Pandora, 1991
Steiner, Wendy, *Exact Resemblance to Exact Resemblance: The Literary Portraiture of Gertrude Stein*, New Haven, Connecticut: Yale University Press, 1978
Walker, Jayne L., *The Making of a Modernist: Gertrude Stein from Three Lives to Tender Buttons*, Amherst: University of Massachusetts Press, 1984
White, Ray Lewis, *Gertrude Stein and Alice B. Toklas: A Reference Guide*, Boston: G.K. Hall, 1984
Wilson, Robert A., *Gertrude Stein: A Bibliography*, Rockville, Maryland: Quill and Brush, 1994
Wineapple, Brenda, *Sister Brother: Gertrude and Leo Stein*, New York: Putnam, 1996

Little read today because of the impenetrability of her idiosyncratic syntax and the tedium of her repetitious style, Gertrude Stein nevertheless had considerable influence on the development of 20th-century American literature. In 1952 Katherine Anne Porter named her as next to James Joyce the greatest influence on the younger literary generation.

Part of this influence was attributable as much to her personality and connections as it was to her literary output. Even during her lifetime she was more noted for her lifestyle, her pronouncements, or alleged pronouncements, and her Salon at 27 rue de Fleurus in Paris, attended by all the famous and soon to be famous painters, musicians, and writers of the day, than she was for her poems, plays, or novels. But posturing and self-promotion notwithstanding, she was a serious artist with a definite, if, in the end, mainly barren mission.

In attempting to understand Stein it is important to remember that she studied psychology under William James, who declared her to be the most brilliant woman student he had ever had. And it is the practice of rigid objective scientific observation she developed under James that she carried over to her literary experiments. At Radcliffe she conducted experiments into automatic writing and although the experiments proved nothing, she began to see character revealed in the way students reacted to the testing process, revealing itself in words and gestures, which grouped in patterns indicative of basic personality types.

The attempt to reduce all human kind to a limited number of defined types, plus her belief, also founded on her early experiences as a student of psychology, that the type is revealed directly in the rhythms and especially the *repetitions* of language, is at the heart of her linguistic experiments. Before Joyce she attempted, albeit much less successfully, to use prose as a means of depicting consciousness moving naturally. Her fundamentalist streak is revealed by her final classification of all humans into one of two types – "the independent dependent" or "the dependent independent". And she expressed this with typical Kleinian syntax and, for most readers, obscurity, in her second major novel *The Making of Americans*: "It is true then that always every one is of one kind or the other kind of them the independent dependent or the dependent independent kind of them."

Endlessly experimental, she developed and intensified her attempts to find in words values separate from their accumulated meaning, rapidly arriving at a stage where her repetitious prose became tediously somnambulistic. Her ego was massive – "Think of Homer, think of Shakespeare, think of me". She saw herself as the redeemer of language. Because of overuse, language, for her, had lost its primordial function of accurate representation, and it was she who was to restore its vitality. In explaining her famous phrase "A rose is a rose is a rose is a rose" to a student in her seminar at the University of Chicago she said:

> Can't you see that when language was new – as it was with Chaucer and Homer – the poet could use the name of a thing and the thing was really there? He could say "O moon", "O sea", "O love", and the moon and the sea and love were really there. And can't you see that after hundreds of years had gone by and thousands of poems had been written, he could call on those words and find they were just worn out literary words? . . . to write poetry in a late age . . . you have to put some strangeness, something unexpected into the structure of the sentence in order to bring back vitality to the noun . . . Now listen! I'm no fool. I know that in daily life we don't go around saying "is . . . is a . . . is a . . ." Yes, I'm no fool: but I think that in that line the rose is red for the first time in English poetry for a hundred years.

It seems nobody pointed out to her that roses come in a variety of colours.

Although born of wealthy German Jewish immigrants,

and receiving an Orthodox religious education Stein never appears to have made much of her Jewishness, although she did once declare, "I have the failing of my tribe. I believe in the sacred rites of conversation even when it is a monologue." Despite this, her massive *The Making of Americans*, based on her own family's history, is the story of two German Jewish immigrant families who make it big in the New World. But it is not the ethnic origins, or even their experiences as a paradigm of the American experience that inform the work. Rather it is her obsessive attempt to pin down character through words and syntax that provides the unifying, and, finally, amphigoric and tautological outcome. Reading a thousand closely printed pages of stuff like: "In the middle of their living they are always repeating, everybody always is repeating in all of their whole living but in the middle of the living of most men and many women it is hard to be sure about them about just what it is they are repeating" is liable to try the patience of even the most dedicated close reader.

Perhaps more significantly Stein's first published work, *Three Lives*, reveals an interest in the "other" in society. The second life, "Melanctha", especially reveals this trait. It is one of the first, if not the first, American work in which the protagonist is black and is treated simply as a human being, without condescension or patronage. It is, of course, impossible to say to what extent Stein's Jewishness, or her lesbianism, or both, influenced this approach, but the possibility must be considered.

Finally it is true to say that without Stein, we might not have had Hemingway, and much modern prose would not have developed.

GERALD DE GROOT

Steiner, George

French-born US literary critic and fiction writer, 1929–

Born Francis George Steiner in Paris, 23 April 1929. Emigrated to United States, 1940; naturalized US citizen, 1944. Studied at the Sorbonne, Bachelier-ès-Lettres 1947; University of Chicago, BA 1948; Harvard University, MA 1950; Balliol College, Oxford (Rhodes Scholarship), DPhil 1955. Married Zara Shakow, 1955; two children. Writer, *The Economist*, London, 1952–56. Member, Institute for Advanced Study, 1957–59, and Gauss Lecturer in Criticism, 1959–60, Princeton University; Fellow, since 1961, and Extraordinary Fellow, since 1969, Churchill College, Cambridge; Schweitzer Professor, New York University, 1966–67; T.S. Eliot Lecturer, University of Kent at Canterbury, 1971; Regents Professor, University of California, 1974; Professor of English and Comparative Literature, University of Geneva, 1974–94; Lord Weidenfeld Professor of Comparative Literature, University of Oxford, 1994; Fellow of St Anne's College, Oxford, 1994–95; F.E.L. Priestley Memorial Lecturer, University of Toronto, 1995; Professor Emeritus, University of Geneva, and Pensioner Fellow, Churchill College, Cambridge. President, English Association, 1975–76. Many awards, including O. Henry Award, 1958; *Jewish Chronicle* Book Award, 1968; National Institute of Arts and Letters Zabel Award, 1970; Guggenheim Fellowship, 1971; Cortine Ulisse Prize, 1972; Prix du Souvenir, 1974; Truman Capote Award (for lifetime services to literature), 1999. Fellow, Royal Society of Literature, 1964; Fellow, British Academy; Honorary Fellow, Royal Academy of Arts; Officier, Légion D'Honneur.

Selected Writings

Novel

The Portage to San Cristóbal of A.H., 1981; with a new afterword, 1999

Poetry

(Poems), 1953

Short Stories

Anno Domini: Three Stories, 1964
Proofs and Three Parables, 1992
The Deeps of the Sea and Other Fiction, 1996

Other

Malice: Chancellor's English Essay Prize, 1952
Tolstoy or Dostoevsky: An Essay in the Old Criticism, 1959; as *Tolstoy and Dostoevsky: An Essay in Contrast*, 1960
The Death of Tragedy, 1961
Editor, with Robert Eagles, *Homer: A Collection of Critical Essays*, 1962
Editor, *The Penguin Book of Modern Verse Translation*, 1966
Language and Silence: Essays on Language, Literature and the Inhuman, 1967
Editor, *Poem into Poem: World Poetry in Modern Verse Translation*, 1970
Extraterritorial: Papers on Literature and the Language Revolution, 1971
In Bluebeard's Castle: Some Notes towards the Redefinition of Culture, 1971
The Sporting Scene: White Knights at Reykjavik, 1973; as *Fields of Force: Fischer and Spassky at Reykjavik*, 1974
Nostalgia for the Absolute, 1974
After Babel: Aspects of Language and Translation, 1975; 3rd edition, 1998
Why English?, 1975
Heidegger, 1978, revised 1992; as *Martin Heidegger*, 1979
"Critic/Reader", *New Literary History*, 10 (1979)
On Difficulty and Other Essays, 1980
Antigones, 1984
George Steiner: A Reader, 1984
A Reading against Shakespeare: The W.P. Ker Lecture for 1986, University of Glasgow, 1986
Real Presences, 1986
Dialogues: sur le mythe d'Antigone, sur le sacrifice d'Abraham [Dialogues: On the Myth of Antigone, on the Sacrifice of Abraham], with Pierre Boutang, 1994
What is Comparative Literature: An Inaugural Lecture Delivered before the University of Oxford, 1995
Editor, with Aminadav Dykman, *Homer in English*, 1996
No Passion Spent: Essays 1978–1996, 1996
Errata: An Examined Life, 1997

Further Reading
Burke, Kenneth, "Above the Over-Towering Babel", *Michigan Quarterly Review*, 15 (1976)
Butler, Christopher, "George Steiner and the Critical Performance", *Sewanee Review*, 87 (1979)
Howe, Irving, "Auschwitz and High Mandarin" in his *The Critical Point: On Literature and Culture*, New York: Horizon Press, 1973
Scott, Nathan A., Jr, and Ronald A. Sharp (editors), *Reading George Steiner*, Baltimore: Johns Hopkins University Press, 1994
Simon, John, "The Theatre Critic and His Double" in *Acid Test*, New York: Stein and Day, 1963

George Steiner is important as a Jewish writer in two senses: for what he has written directly about the European Jewish situation, and as a representative – even a stereotypical – "Jewish intellectual". In England in particular he appears as a lofty late representative of that group of central European Jews harried to its island shores by the racial Inquisition of the Nazis. He seems too like the perfect model of the assimilated intellectual Jew; a leader in his field (literary criticism), a polyglot, and a thinker who both argues and embodies a European cultural perspective. While the glories of European cultural achievements – modern science, the novel, orchestral music, printing, liberal democracy etc. – seemed to augur at the turn of the 20th century for a great European civilization, the reality of course was betrayed by gross crimes against humanity carried out using some of these same achievements. Particularly in his fiction and his autobiography Steiner has tried to find ways of coming to terms with, or perhaps just exploring this sad fact.

He has done this most dramatically in the novel *The Portage to San Cristóbal of A.H.* (successfully adapted in 1983 for the stage), where the "A.H." of the title is Adolf Hitler. Steiner imagines him as hiding out for years in deepest South America and then being tracked down by Israeli commandos. Steiner puts here, in the mouth of the elderly Hitler, his own provocative contention that anti-Semitism is a reaction to the impossible moral standards and altruism originating from Judaism in the teachings of Moses, Jesus, and Karl Marx. Whatever one thinks of this rather theological explanation, Steiner makes manifest, physical, and real some of the players and victims of the Nazi period. There are related stories in the collection *Anno Domini*. In "Return no More", for example, a German officer returns in 1950 to the French village where he had served and had ordered the execution of a young partisan. He returns because "the stench of forgetting is so strong in Germany that I came back here to breathe real air." He then tries to marry the partisan's younger sister. The offended villagers eventually kill him. Here Steiner (most of whose Jewish school-friends in Paris were murdered by Germans) seems to suggest that the actual German unresponsiveness, the passive reaction to having committed the greatest crimes of a century of crimes is the result of the very enormity of those crimes. The easiest, the only "reasonable" thing for them to do is to sit back and breathe in "the stench of forgetting".

"Cake" too is set in the aftermath of World War II and attempts to let out some of the foetid air of occupied Europe from the sealed casket where it was kept for many years. Some of the foetid air of England is released in "Sweet Mars", which carries out a Jewish outsider's psychoanalysis on the rather school-boyish psychology of the upper-middle class Englishmen whom Steiner has encountered. While his "war aftermath" stories were written in the early 1960s and are about the long-term impact of World War II on a generation, *Proofs and Three Parables* deals largely with the impact of the collapse of communism. Communism is a proper European-Jewish theme for Steiner to get his teeth into, as its form of secular messianism attracted great numbers of Jews in both eastern and western Europe. More expertly written than the earlier stories, with delicious phrases such as (describing the East German frontier guards the day the Berlin Wall was breached) "Border guards grinned vacantly and reached for cigarettes as do the bears in a bankrupt circus", Steiner's clever take on communism is to compare it to Christianity; both share the same somehow ever-deferred glorious millennium . . .

He also remembers Stalin's 25 million victims, ultimately, in the Steiner view, the result of an idealistic over-estimation of the human spirit. Similar themes appear in his autobiography, the at times interesting, at times pompous and oracular, *Errata*. Tracing a heritage from his father's Vienna to Paris, New York (during the war) and latterly a career in the US, Switzerland, and England as teacher of comparative literature, book-reviewer, and essayist, he tells us that his cultivated tri-lingualism (English, French, German) is at the heart of his intellectual enterprises. In *Errata* and the essays collected in *Language and Silence* and *No Passion Spent*, he develops a portrait of himself and of the Jewish personality as pan-European, at home (and not at home) in many cultures, languages, and places. However the unacknowledged starting-point for Steiner's theory of Jewishness ("All of us obviously have something in common . . . But each of us must hammer it out for himself. That is the real meaning of the Diaspora . . .") is assimilation. The languages and cultures he celebrates and interrogates are not Jewish ones but ones where Jews have, latterly, participated. In a world-view rather recognizably Austrian or German Jewish, the Ashkenazi (Yiddish-speaking) or Sephardi Ladino and Mizrachi Judaeo-Arabic traditions are hardly on his map. Steiner always interrogates "Jewishness" rather than *Yidishkayt*. Is he a *deraciné* or a Universal Man?

On the other hand among his essays he admits that of *his* tradition – "Central European Humanism" – "almost nothing . . . survives", that like the (postwar, post-Shoah) German language (*vide* "The Hollow Miracle" in *Language and Silence*) it is utterly polluted by the uses to which it was put. He tell us in his introduction to *No Passion Spent* that, "It will not, I believe, be possible for European culture to regain its inward energies, its self-respect, so long as Christendom is not made answerable to its own seminal role in the preparation of the Shoah." He rejects the, particularly German and Austrian, "miracle of amnesia" about the cruelty, extent, participation in, and indifference to the Holocaust while nevertheless striving to establish the bridge between Christendom and the Jewish experience, particularly in writings about the role of that essential link, the partially Jewish Christian Bible in, inter alia, "A Preface to the Hebrew Bible" in *No Passion Spent.*

RAY KEENOY

Stoppard, Tom

Czechoslovak-born British playwright, 1937–

Born Tomas Straussler in Zlin, 3 July 1937; father, Eugene Straussler, company physician. Moved with family to Singapore, 1939; father killed during Japanese invasion; escaped with mother and brother to Darjeeling, India, 1942. Mother married, second, Kenneth Stoppard, officer in British army. Moved with family to Britain, 1946. Attended schools in Nottinghamshire and Yorkshire, 1946–54. Journalist, *Western Daily Press*, Bristol, 1954–58, and *Bristol Evening World*, 1958–60; freelance journalist and writer; drama critic, *Scene*, London 1962–63. Married, first, Jose Ingle, 1965; divorced, 1971; two sons; second, Miriam Moore-Robinson, 1972; divorced, 1992; two sons. Member of board, (Royal) National Theatre, London, since 1989. Many awards, including Ford Foundation grant, 1964; John Whiting Award, 1967; *Evening Standard* Drama Award, 1967, 1973, 1975, 1979, 1983; Italia Prize (for radio play), 1968; Tony, 1968, 1976, 1984; New York Drama Critics Circle Award, 1968, 1976, 1984, 1995; Hamburg Shakespeare Prize, 1979; Outer Circle Award, 1984; Drama Desk Award, 1984; Venice Film Festival Prix D'Or (for screenplay), 1990; Oscar for screenplay (for *Shakespeare in Love*), 1999. Fellow, Royal Society of Literature; Commander, Order of the British Empire, 1978; knighthood, 1997; Officier, Ordre des Arts et des Lettres (France), 1997; Order of Merit, 2000.

Selected Writings

Plays

A Walk on the Water, 1963; as *The Preservation of George Riley*, 1964; as *Enter a Free Man*, 1968
The Gamblers, 1965
A Separate Peace, 1966
If You're Glad I'll Be Frank, 1966
Rosencrantz and Guildenstern Are Dead, 1966
Tango, 1966
Albert's Bridge, 1967
Another Moon Called Earth, 1967
Teeth, 1967
Neutral Ground, 1968
The Real Inspector Hound, 1968
After Magritte, 1970
Where Are They Now?, 1970
Dogg's Our Pet, 1971
Artist Descending a Staircase, 1972
Jumpers, 1972
The House of Bernarda Alba, 1973
Travesties, 1974
Dirty Linen, and New-found-land, 1976
The Fifteen Minute Hamlet, 1976
Albert's Bridge and Other Plays (includes *Artist Descending a Staircase*; *If You're Glad I'll Be Frank*; *A Separate Peace*; *Where Are They Now?*), 1977
Every Good Boy Deserves Favour: A Play for Actors and Orchestra, 1977
"M" is for Moon among Other Things, 1977
Professional Foul, 1977
Albert's Bridge Extended, 1978
Night and Day, 1978
Dogg's Hamlet, Cahoot's Macbeth, 1979
Undiscovered Country, 1979
On the Razzle, 1981
The Dog It Was That Died, 1982
The Real Thing, 1982
The Dissolution of Dominic Boot, 1983
The Dog It Was That Died and Other Plays (includes *The Dissolution of Dominic Boot*; *"M" is for Moon among Other Things*; *Teeth*; *Another Moon Called Earth*; *Neutral Ground*; *A Separate Peace*), 1983
The Love for Three Oranges, 1983
Four Plays for Radio (includes *Artist Descending a Staircase*; *Where Are They Now?*; *If You're Glad I'll Be Frank*; *Albert's Bridge*), 1984
Rough Crossing, 1984
Squaring the Circle: Poland 1980–1981, 1984
Dalliance, 1986
Largo Desolato, 1986
Brazil (screenplay), in *The Battle of Brazil*, by Jack Mathews, 1987
Hapgood, 1988
Stoppard: The Plays for Radio, 1964-1983, 1990; expanded edition, as *Stoppard: The Plays for Radio, 1964-1991*, 1994
In the Native State, 1991
The Boundary, with Clive Exton, 1991
Arcadia, 1993
The Television Plays, 1965-1984, 1993
Indian Ink, 1995
Plays One–Five, 1996–99
The Seagull, 1997
The Invention of Love, 1998
The Coast of Utopia
Voyage, 2002
Shipwreck, 2002
Salvage, 2002

Screenplays: *The Romantic Englishwoman*, with Thomas Wiseman, 1975; *Despair*, 1978; *The Human Factor*, 1980; *Brazil*, with Terry Gilliam and Charles McKeown, 1985; *Empire of the Sun*, 1986; *The Russia House*, 1989; *Billy Bathgate: A Screenplay*, 1990; *Rosencrantz and Guildenstern Are Dead*, 1990; *Shakespeare in Love*, with Marc Norman, 1998; *Enigma*, 2000

Radio Plays: *The Dissolution of Dominic Boot*, 1964; *"M" is for Moon among Other Things*, 1964; *If You're Glad I'll Be Frank*, 1966; *Albert's Bridge*, 1967; *Where Are They Now?*, 1970; *Artist Descending a Staircase*, 1972; *The Dog It Was That Died*, 1982; *In the Native State*, 1991

Television Plays: *A Walk on the Water*, 1963, revised version, as *The Preservation of George Riley*, 1964; *A Separate Peace*, 1966; *Another Moon Called Earth*, 1967; *Teeth*, 1967; *Neutral Ground*, 1968; *The Engagement*, 1970; *One Pair of Eyes*, 1972; *The Boundary*, with Clive Exton, 1975; *Three Men in a Boat*, 1975; *Professional Foul*, 1977; *Squaring the Circle*, 1984

Novel
Lord Malquist and Mr Moon, 1966

Short Stories
Introduction 2, with others, 1964

Further Reading

Andretta, Richard A., *Tom Stoppard: An Analytical Study of His Plays*, New Delhi: Vikas, 1992
Bareham, Tony (editor), *Tom Stoppard: Rosencrantz and Guildenstern Are Dead, Jumpers, Travesties: A Casebook*, London: Macmillan, 1990
Billington, Michael, *Stoppard the Playwright*, London and New York: Methuen, 1987
Bloom, Harold (editor), *Tom Stoppard*, New York: Chelsea House, 1986
Brassell, Tim, *Tom Stoppard: An Assessment*, London: Macmillan, and New York: St Martin's Press, 1985
Corballis, Richard, *Stoppard: The Mystery and the Clockwork*, Oxford: Amber Lane Press, and New York: Methuen, 1984
Dean, Joan Fitzpatrick, *Tom Stoppard: Comedy as a Moral Matrix*, Columbia: University of Missouri Press, 1981
Delaney, Paul, *Tom Stoppard: The Moral Vision of the Major Plays*, London: Macmillan, and New York: St Martin's Press, 1990
Delaney, Paul (editor), *Tom Stoppard in Conversation*, Ann Arbor: University of Michigan Press, 1994
Easterling, Anja, *Shakespearean Parallels and Affinities with the Theatre of the Absurd in Tom Stoppard's Rosencrantz and Guildenstern Are Dead*, Umea, Sweden: Umea Universitetsbibliothek, 1982
Gabbard, Lucina Paquet, *The Stoppard Plays*, Troy, New York: Whitston, 1982
Gussow, Mel, *Conversations with Stoppard*, London: Hern, and New York: Limelight, 1995
Harty, John (editor), *Tom Stoppard: A Casebook*, New York: Garland, 1988
Hayman, Ronald, *Tom Stoppard*, London: Heinemann, and Totowa, New Jersey: Rowman and Littlefield, 1977; 4th edition, Heinemann, 1982
Hu, Stephen, *Tom Stoppard's Stagecraft*, New York: Peter Lang, 1989
Hunter, Jim, *Tom Stoppard's Plays*, London: Faber, and New York: Grove Press, 1982
Jenkins, Anthony, *The Theatre of Tom Stoppard*, London and New York: Cambridge University Press, 1987
Jenkins, Anthony (editor), *Critical Essays on Tom Stoppard*, Boston: G.K. Hall, 1990
Kelly, Katherine E., *Tom Stoppard and the Craft of Comedy: Medium and Genre at Play*, Ann Arbor: University of Michigan Press, 1991
Londré, Felicia Hardison, *Tom Stoppard*, New York: Ungar, 1981
Page, Malcolm (editor), *File on Stoppard*, London and New York: Methuen, 1986
Sammells, Neil, *Tom Stoppard: The Artist as Critic*, London: Macmillan, and New York: St Martin's Press, 1988
Tan, Peter K.W., *A Stylistics of Drama: With Special Focus on Stoppard's Travesties*, Singapore: Singapore University Press, 1993
Whitaker, Thomas R., *Tom Stoppard*, London: Macmillan, and New York: Grove Press, 1983

During his childhood, Tom Stoppard moved from his native Czechoslovakia to Singapore (where his father Eugene Straussler died), to India, and finally to England, home of his mother's second husband, whose family name Stoppard bears. Despite these diasporic beginnings, Stoppard seems to be both personally and intellectually very much at ease in England. After years as a drama critic and journalist in Bristol, and after his first television plays had been broadcast, Stoppard entered the literary world in 1966 with the publication of his only novel, *Lord Malquist and Mr Moon*. Written in the meta-fictional tradition of John Fowles and Iris Murdoch, this novel has Stoppard probing the role of the artist and of the work of art, in a manner much indebted to Oscar Wilde's positions and aphoristic language. With the figure of a donkey-rider believing to be the risen Christ, the novel also features one of the rare Jewish characters in Stoppard's plays. In the same year Stoppard made a powerful debut at the Edinburgh Festival with his immensely successful *Rosencrantz and Guildenstern Are Dead*. Transferred the following year to the National Theatre in London, the play presents two minor characters from Shakespeare's *Hamlet* as lost among the royal plotting and courtly power battle. With its emphasis on the fragile relationship between words and meaning, the play sets the theme for much of Stoppard's later writing. Although reminiscent of the Theatre of the Absurd (in particular Samuel Beckett's *Waiting for Godot*), the play is not so much concerned with the absence of sense as with the incapability of the two protagonists to understand what is happening to them, and thus to react appropriately to their environment; exhausted and frustrated, they finally welcome their imminent execution.

Stoppard's dramatic influences span from Shakespeare to Beckett, often in the form of a postmodern pastiche rich in literary allusions and quotations. However, what makes Stoppard a unique playwright is not only his inclusion of literary pre-texts, but also his frequent use of such diverse fields as, for example, Dadaistic art (*Travesties*), philosophy (*Jumpers*), physics (*Arcadia*), history and colonialism (*Indian Ink*), biography (*The Invention of Love*), as well as many other areas of contemporary cultural and academic life.

A particular feature of Stoppard's work is the regularity with which his plays have appeared in different versions, mostly due to his close involvement with stage productions of his work. Stoppard's preference of the stage over the page also makes him an outspoken critic of such academic writing as reverses this order by neglecting the theatrical aspect of live drama and performance.

Stoppard's early plays have been criticized for being too cerebral and for lacking in ethical motivation and responsibility. Indeed, much of his work is more closely concerned with fast-paced comedy, dazzling word play and, as in *The Real Inspector Hound* and *The Real Thing*, with intriguing meta-theatre, that is, the thematization of and (in the Brechtian sense) emphasis on the dramatic act *per se*. Thus, theatricality itself is a major concern of his plays. Many of Stoppard's characters also repeatedly express views that are congruent with postmodernity's overall cultural discontent and the accompanying deterioration of formerly existing guidelines and paradigms (see *Jumpers*). Both the structure and the language of Stoppard's plays draw attention to the dichotomy of chaos and order, leaving the audience looking for answers long after the end of the play. However, what may at first appear to be nonsensical often proves to have a perfectly sensible explanation, once looked at from a different angle (as in *After Magritte*). Stoppard's fascination with and creative use of language might be influenced by the fact that English for him is a second language, which possibly contributes to a detached and critical awareness of semantic arbitrariness.

While his early work was located between linguistic frivolities, postmodern meta-theatre, and theoretical moral-philosophical questioning, Stoppard in the late 1970s wrote a series of plays that deal with more humanitarian and politically committed issues. The imprisonment of critical Soviet writers (and the opportunity to write a play that would include a complete orchestra) inspired *Every Good Boy Deserves Favour*; academic freedom and censorship in Czechoslovakia, rolled into one play with an international football game and a philosophy conference, find their way into *Professional Foul*; and *Squaring the Circle* follows the political history of Solidarity in Poland. Already including one of Stoppard's future themes, romantic love, *Night and Day* probes the issues of human rights and freedom of the press as challenged by closed-shop unionization. Stoppard has also been associated with various organizations that support human rights and freedom of the press, as well as with those criticizing the imprisonment of writers. In interviews he regularly professes that he does not believe that art can have a serious impact on political life, hence his personal involvement outside the theatre.

In more recent years Stoppard has returned to full-length stage plays that combine his skill for witty dialogue with his curiosity in more remote themes. *Arcadia* is set both in the present and around the early 19th century, giving a rather amusing view of a Byron scholar and academia in general. The temporal structure of *Indian Ink* likewise oscillates between colonial India and the present, as well as freely floats between the two localities of England and the subcontinent. In both of these plays, and in *The Invention of Love*, which deals with the scholarly life and homosexuality of A.E. Housman, as well as with the Oxford of the 1890s, Stoppard also focuses on the romantic entanglements of his characters.

In addition to his numerous plays for the stage, radio, television, and screen, Stoppard has also written and staged adaptations of foreign-language plays by, among others, Johann Nestroy, Arthur Schnitzler, Federico García Lorca, and Anton Chekhov. Most recently, his screenplay for *Shakespeare in Love* contributed to the international success of the film.

The influence of Stoppard's Jewish background on his writing is, if at all present, rather faint. With as wide a range of sources as he uses for his art, hardly any one source can be said to predominate, with the possible exception of T.S. Eliot for his sense of language and Samuel Beckett for his theatricality.

GERD BAYER

Stryjkowski, Julian

Polish fiction writer, 1905–1996

Born Pesach Stark in Stryj (basis of pseudonym), 27 April 1905. Joined Zionist youth movement, but later switched to pro-Soviet Communist Party of Western Ukraine (pro-Soviet group active inside pre-war Poland). Obtained school-leaving certificate, 1924; studied Polish language and literature, University of Lwów, PhD. High school teacher in Płock. Imprisoned for Communist activity, 1935–36; assistant in academic bookshop in Warsaw. Returned to Lwów after its incorporation into Soviet Ukraine (as L'viv), 1939; became member of editorial committee, *Czerwony Sztandar* (Communist journal), and broadcaster; forced labour convict in Tergan, Soviet Union, 1941–43; editor of *Wolna Polska*, journal of (Soviet-sponsored) Union of Polish Patriots, 1943–46. Returned to Poland, 1946; director of branch of state press agency, in Katowice, 1946–49, then Rome, 1949–52; member of editorial committee, *Twórczość* (literary journal). Awarded State Prize, first class, 1951, and Officer's Cross, Polonia Restituta. Disillusioned with Stalinism by late 1960s; began writing in favour of democratic opposition and publishing works in clandestine (*samizdat*) form. Died in Warsaw, 1996.

Selected Writings

Fiction

Bieg do Fragalà [Run to Fragalà], 1951
Pożegnanie z Italią [Farewell to Italy], 1954

Trilogy
Głosy w ciemności [Voices in the Dark], 1956
Austeria, 1966; as *The Inn*, translated by Celina Wieniewska, 1971
Sen Azrila [Asril's Dream], 1975

Imię własne [First Name], 1961
Czarna róża [The Black Rose], 1962
Na wierzbach . . . nasze skrzypce [On the Willows . . . Our Harpsichords], 1974
Przybysz z Narbony [The Stranger from Narbonne], 1978
Wielki strach [The Great Awe], 1979
Odpowiedź [The Answer], 1982
Tommaso del Cavaliere, 1982
Martwa fala [The Dead Wave], 1983
Król Dawid żyje! [King David is Alive!], 1984
Juda Makabi [Judas Maccabaeus], 1986
Echo, 1988

Play
Sodoma [Sodom], 1963

Other
Ocalony na Wschedzie [Saved in the East], interview with Piotr Szewc, 1991
Translated works by Louis-Ferdinand Céline and L.M. Leonov into Polish.

Further Reading

Coulter, Kirkley S., *Polish Literature Recently Translated: A Bibliography*, Falls Church, Virginia: Quarterly Review of Polish Heritage, 1977
Czerwinski, E.J. (editor), *Dictionary of Polish Literature*, Westport, Connecticut: Greenwood Press, 1994
Gillon, Adam and Ludwik Krżyżanowski (editors), *Introduction to Modern Polish Literature*, 2nd edition, New York: Hippocrene, 1982
Polonsky, Antony and Monika Adamczyk, editorial introduction to *Contemporary Jewish Writing in Poland*, Lincoln: University of Nebraska Press, 2001

The prose writer and essayist Julian Stryjkowski, whose most important models, after distancing himself from the previously admired Romain Rolland and Theodore Dreiser "because of their naivety", were Thomas Mann and Leo Tolstoi, attempted in his epic work, like Isaac Bashevis Singer, to create "a monument" to the annihilated Jewry of eastern Europe, in particular to his Galician shtetl home. Although he had been a communist since his student days, but had simultaneously remained closely connected with the Jewish religion and tradition, he did not shrink from translating in 1937 *Mort à crédit* by the fascist writer Louis-Ferdinand Céline, whose relentless disclosure of human weaknesses he found fascinating. Yet human weaknesses that lead to destruction or self-destruction are rejected by the older Stryjkowski as novelist and story-teller; fought against, even, with a moral impetus that not all his readers and critics could appreciate.

After the publication of his novel *Bieg do Fragalà* [Run to Fragalà], which was less social realism than neo-realism, he was expelled from Italy in 1952. In this book, considered his official literary debut, he portrayed a Calabrian village of the postwar years, poor and backward, where the communists are fighting against the big landowners and the clergy. Italy was also the subject of the novella *Tommaso del Cavaliere*; the book ostensibly dealt with the favourite pupil of Michelangelo Buonarotti but was in fact about the great Florentine master himself, artistic creation, rivalry between artists, dramatic life and death – and homosexual love and friendship, which in Poland were considered taboos and had scarcely been addressed in literature before then.

Stryjkowski, who in the early 1930s became a member of the illegal Communist Party of the West Ukraine, as a result of which he was imprisoned in 1935, hoped, like so many young Polish Jews, that this would serve as a defence against the anti-Semitism and a protection from the emergent fascism. However, it seems it was in Soviet-occupied Lwów that the first doubts about communism developed, although he did not discuss this until the end of the 1970s in his book dedicated to the then prominent opposition politician Adam Michnik, *Wielki strach* [The Great Awe], the first edition of which was published underground. This work also described the Stalinist terror and the mass deportations of that time. After Hitler's invasion of the Soviet Union, Stryjkowski fled with the Red Army to the interior and was forced to labour in a battalion of convict workers loading cotton, which experience he also did not write about until much later in his book *Ocalony na Wschodzie* [Saved in the East]. He had survived thanks to the help of a Polish communist and favourite of Stalin's, Wanda Wasilewska, who had got him a job on the Moscow weekly *Wolna Polska* [Free Poland], published by the Polish communists loyal to Moscow. After returning to Poland in 1946, he had the status of an "exemplary Jew" and was a so-called "travelling specialist", allowed to travel to France, Israel, the USA, and Spain in order to gather material for his books. Yet in his literature too he had now begun gradually to distance himself from communism, for example in his novel *Czarna róża* [The Black Rose], whose hero is imprisoned, as he himself once was, in 1930s Lwów for communist activities in the name of the "Black Rose", a dogmatic factory-owner's daughter. Stryjkowski's novel is an attempt to level coded criticism at the Party, symbolized by the heroine of the novel.

Stryjkowski's works have been translated into many languages, but the best known are those that deal with the destroyed world of the Polish Jews, with their customs and traditions, the more or less loveable characters, the threat and persecution that they suffer, culminating in the mass murders carried out by the National Socialists. After experiencing the 1943 uprising in the Warsaw ghetto, he wrote his first great novel *Głosy w ciemności* [Voices in the Dark], the first part of a trilogy based on the life of the Jews before the Holocaust. The book, written as early as 1944, could not be published until after the post-Stalinist "Polish thaw" of 1956, but then went into several editions and was widely praised by literary critics for its "enormous moral and philosophical perspectives" and its "complexity and richness". In the later novels of the trilogy, *Austeria* and *Sen Azrila* [Asril's Dream], he describes the world of the Jewish shtetl of east Galicia at the end of the 19th century prior to the outbreak of World War I and ultimately World War II, a world which would have seemed exotic to the Polish postwar reader. Yet this effect was not intentional, quite the contrary: despite the irony and the grotesque and comic elements he uses to avoid pathos, he conveys a respect for the independent culture of the traditional Polish Jews and traces the history of their existence, which, whether under communism, Zionism or assimilation, was full of defeats and in the process of failing.

The fate of the Jewish family in *Głosy w ciemności* was continued in *Echo*, set in 1912. The author of the novel is now more painfully aware than before that he is one of the last surviving witnesses of the period. And so he dedicated the novel *Przybysz z Narbony* to the rebels of the Warsaw ghetto, and in so doing completed the circle to *Głosy w ciemności*. In this novel the Jewish hero Eli travels from Narbonne in the south of France to Spain, in order to make an attempt on the life of the Grand Inquisitor and to help the persecuted Jewish community of Toledo, but he dies himself. However, it is not the Jewish local colour that dominates; in this novel Stryjkowski investigates the ever effective mechanisms of oppression: the unstoppable destruction of the Jewish community inwards as a result of mistrust, conflicts, lack of solidarity, an excessive readiness to compromise, and, above all, the relinquishment of traditional Jewish values, which he bemoans.

In the stories in the collection *Na wierzbach . . . nasze skrzypce* [On the Willows . . . Our Harpsichords] he examines the fates of the rescued Polish Jews who have settled in the USA and become estranged from Judaism. Stryjkowski increasingly becomes one of the moralists condemning those who have lost and therefore betrayed their Judaism. The biblical prophets and kings and post-biblical heroes become leading figures for him, particularly in the so-called biblical triptych of the 1980s: *Odpowiedź* [The Answer], *Król Dawid żyje!* [King David is Alive!], and *Juda Makabi* [Judas Maccabaeus].

Stryjkowski has been compared with Proust in that he succeeded in retaining "time past and lost" in the same way. His works allow Polish Judaism, over which the shadow of the Holocaust hovers, to rise again. The Holocaust, "The Time of the Gas Chambers", is also dealt with in literature by Adolf Rudnicki as well as a number of Poland's younger Jewish writers such as Henryk Grynberg and Hanna Krall. Yet, perhaps also thanks to Stryjkowski, who features intermittently on school reading-lists, younger Polish non-Jewish writers are increasingly interested in the Polish Judaism that no longer exists; a phenomenon recently designated in Poland as "the Jewish current in literature".

ELVIRA GROEZINGER
translated by Karen Goulding

Sukenick, Ronald

US fiction writer, 1932–

Born in Brooklyn, New York, 14 July 1932. Studied at Cornell University, established campus magazine *The Cornell Writer*, BA 1955; Brandeis University, MA 1957, PhD 1962. Lecturer, Brandeis University, 1956–61, and Hofstra University, New York, 1961–62. Married, first, Lynn Luria, writer, 1961; divorced 1984; second, Julia Frey. Part-time teacher, 1963–66; assistant professor of English, City College of New York, 1966–67, and Sarah Lawrence College, New York, 1968–69; writer in residence, Cornell University, 1969–70, and University of California, Irvine, 1970–72; professor of English and director of Publications Center, since 1975, and director of creative writing programme, 1975–77, University of Colorado, Boulder; taught at Université Paul Valéry, Montpellier, France, Autumn 1979; Butler Professor of English, State University of New York, Buffalo, Spring 1981. Contributing editor, *Fiction International*, Canton, New York, 1970–84; founding member and co-director, Fiction Collective, New York, since 1974; founding publisher, *American Book Review*, New York, since 1977; editor, *Black Ice*, New York, since 1989. Awards include Fulbright Fellowship, 1958, 1984; Guggenheim Fellowship, 1977; National Endowment for the Arts Fellowship, 1980, 1989; Coordinating Council of Literary Magazines Award (for editing), 1985; Before Columbus Foundation Award, 1988.

Selected Writings

Novels
Up, 1968
Out, 1973
98.6, 1975
Long Talking Bad Conditions Blues, 1979
Blown Away, 1986
Doggy Bag, 1994
Mosaic Man, 1999

Short Stories
The Death of the Novel and Other Stories, 1969
A Postcard from "The Endless Short Story", 1974
The Endless Short Story, 1986

Other
Wallace Stevens: Musing the Obscure, 1967
In Form: Digressions on the Act of Fiction, 1985
Down and In: Life in the Underground, 1987
Editor, with Mark Amerika, *Degenerative Prose: Writing beyond Category*, 1995
Editor, with Curtis White, *In the Slipstream: A Fiction Collective Two Reader*, 1999
Narralogues: Truth in Fiction, 2000

Further Reading

Abady-Nagy, Zolton, "A Talk with Ronald Sukenick", *Hungarian Studies in English*, 16 (1983)
Bellamy, Joe David, "Ronald Sukenick" in *The New Fiction: Interviews with Innovative American Writers*, Urbana: University of Illinois Press, 1974
Caramello, Charles, *Silverless Mirrors: Book, Self and Postmodern American Fiction*, Tallahassee: University Presses of Florida, 1983
Cornis-Pope, Marcel, "Narrative Innovation and Cultural Rewriting: The Pynchon–Morrison–Sukenick Connection" in *Narrative and Culture*, edited by Janice Carlisle and Daniel R. Schwarz, Athens: University of Georgia Press, 1994
Cowley, Julian, "Ronald Sukenick's New Departures from the Terminal of Language", *Critique*, 28 (Winter 1987)
Friedman, Melvin, "Reading Out", *Fiction International*, 1 (Autumn 1973)
Hornung, Alfred, "Absent Presence: The Fictions of Raymond Federman and Ronald Sukenick", *Indian Journal of American Studies*, 14 (1984): 17–31
Kawin, Bruce, "Interview with Ronald Sukenick", *Arts at Santa Cruz*, 1/1 (1981)
Klinkowitz, Jerome, "Getting Real: Making It (Up) with Ronald Sukenick", *Chicago Review* (Winter 1972)
Klinkowitz, Jerome, "Ronald Sukenick and Raymond Federman" in *Literary Disruptions: The Making of a Post-Contemporary American Fiction*, Urbana: University of Illinois Press, 1975
Klinkowitz, Jerome, "Persuasive Account: Working It Out with Ronald Sukenick" in *Seeing Castaneda*, edited by Daniel C. Noel, New York: Putnam, 1976

Klinkowitz, Jerome, *The Life of Fiction*, Urbana: University of Illinois Press, 1977
Kutnik, Jerzy, *The Novel as Performance: The Fiction of Ronald Sukenick and Raymond Federman*, Carbondale: Southern Illinois University Press, 1986
McCaffery, Larry, "Interview with Ronald Sukenick" in *Anything Can Happen: Interviews with Contemporary American Novelists*, edited by Tom LeClair and Larry McCaffery, Urbana: University of Illinois Press, 1983
McHale, Brian, *Postmodernist Fiction*, New York: Methuen, 1987
Nagel, James, "A Conversation in Boston" in *American Fiction*, Boston: Northeastern University Press, 1977
Noel, Daniel, "Tales of Fictive Power: Dreaming and Imagining in Ronald Sukenick's Postmodern Fiction", *Boundary 2*, 5 (Fall 1976): 117–35
Olsen, Lance, *Circus of the Mind in Motion: Postmodernism and the Comic Vision*, Detroit: Wayne State University Press, 1990
Pearce, Richard, *The Novel in Motion*, Columbus: Ohio State University Press, 1983
Seed, David, "Interview with Ronald Sukenick", *Over Here* (Summer 1990)
Thiher, Allen, *Words in Reflection: Modern Language Theory and Postmodern Fiction*, Chicago: University of Chicago Press, 1984

It is an irony of American literary history that Ronald Sukenick, born in Brooklyn of Jewish-American parents, would be criticized during much of his career for preferring anti-mimetic innovation to conventional storytelling in his fiction, and then near the end address the key elements of Judaic narrative style in his novel *Mosaic Man*. Sukenick's justification for this latter development would be that Judaic culture had always been wary of attempting representation, and that his own work steadfastly avoided any worship of the Golden Calf. Only with *Mosaic Man*, and his complementary literary essays collected as *Narralogues*, does this connection become clear, yet perceptive readers will see hints from the very start.

As a doctoral graduate from Brandeis University, Sukenick began his writer's career with critical and fictive volumes, the study *Wallace Stevens: Musing the Obscure* and the novel *Up*. Each work poses similar questions about how the imagination does best not by presenting the real world but rather making it relevant: "Adequate adjustment to the present can only be achieved through ever fresh perception of it", Sukenick writes in the Stevens book, and in *Up* he goes on to show how traditional manners of perception in the novel have lost their freshness by becoming literary, a condition the protagonist (himself named Ronald Sukenick who is writing a novel called *Up*) resolves by following the advice the real Ronald Sukenick offered in his doctoral dissertation on Wallace Stevens. At the same time the author was crafting the materials collected as *The Death of the Novel and Other Stories*, the first examples of Sukenick's belief that fiction is not about experience but is more experience, presented in an aesthetically refined way only in so far as its vitalistic elements are more apparent.

Art as experience defines Sukenick's countercultural work of the next decade, the novels *Out*, *98.6*, and *Long Talking Bad Conditions Blues*. The first provides several strategies to help the reader: a coast-to-coast journey from New York to California that replaces urban clutter with open space, a run-on style of narrative that keeps the action (like the sentences themselves) rushing forward, and a count-down of chapters in which paragraphs appear on the page with successively fewer lines of print and more lines of space (so that pages are turned faster as the narrative action speeds up). Character itself proves fluid in these circumstances, being much like a cloud that changes as it goes. Paralleling Sukenick's own move from New York to California (where he taught for a time at the University of California, Irvine), the novel exhausts the American landscape much as *Up* eclipses the entire history of the novel. *98.6* then becomes a rebuilding of sorts, a three-part structure that begins with a nightmare reality, is countered by a cultural response more geared to dreams, and is finally resolved in a mental state – the State of Israel, as the author names it, drawing on utopian schemes that employ more natural forms of human energy. The most personally accessible answer to life's problems, however, is found in the uniquely American art form known as the blues, sung by the narrator in the last pages of *98.6* and used as a structuring device in *Long Talking Bad Conditions Blues*, a transformation of the author's occasional expatriate life in Paris into a synthesis of his whole life's existence.

By the 1980s Sukenick was established as a professor of English at the University of Colorado, from where he published *American Book Review* and helped direct the Fiction Collective. Of his four books from this decade, two are critical: the literary essays *In Form*, and the study of alternative culture in Greenwich Village over the past three decades, *Down and In*. Both studies complement his novel, *Blown Away*, and his collection *The Endless Short Story*. The novel is set entirely within the world of film production, and serves as a telling indictment of how commercial manipulation results when audiences let someone else do their imagining for them. Sukenick's stories from this period offer alternatives, such as an appreciation of Simon Rodia's Watts Towers, in which the true artistic production is as quirky as the weather yet just as inevitable a part of history.

With *Doggy Bag* and *Mosaic Man* Sukenick discards such narrative distinctions as "novel" and "short story" in favour of what he calls a "law of mosaics", in which aspects of experience are assembled less in distinctive pieces than as a contribution to the larger whole. Each draws heavily on the author's own experience. Much of *Doggy Bag* looks back to Sukenick's postgraduate travels to Europe, an experience he feels replicates the attempts made by Henry James, Gertrude Stein, and others to find there a solution to problems that were in fact indigenously American. "If Europe doesn't work write, why not fix it?" he asks as an approximation of their position. "No problem. Just rearrange history a bit, jiggle some geography, and everything comes out the way you want". In the meantime, though, Sukenick has learned how a strategy like that is in fact the same illusion European colonizers had about what was to become the United States. A more complete view can be found in *Mosaic Man* – as its title implies, a composite of all the imaginative factors in three decades of Ronald Sukenick's work. Here is where the author addresses his full range of experiences as a Jewish American, from childhood memories in Brooklyn to adult visits to Israel. In the former, he is still a writer-to-be, yet he can share a full artistic experience by following innocent fancies (of the comic book and cinema adventure variety) out into the real world of Nazi aggression and the Holocaust. In the latter, he is a mature and influential writer, who can now have his idealistic beliefs made accountable to the present day reality of a truly Jewish state (where someone of his beliefs is no longer the outsider).

Narralogues describes the form of composition Sukenick has always favoured, one that he now calls rhetorical. It involves not logical preparation but rather a facility for "thinking in the moment of composition". By avoiding the linear he can let himself evolve within the situational flow, letting his senses feed his emotions rather than having mind restrict what can be drawn from experience. This is the narrative thinking that, after rejecting convention in *Up* and exhausting countercultural alternatives in *Out* and *98.6*, can begin fashioning a true mosaic – such as an American blues musician can sing and a Jewish American novelist such as Sukenick write in a work like *Mosaic Man*.

JEROME KLINKOWITZ

Sutzkever, Abraham

Lithuanian-born Israeli poet and fiction writer, 1913–

Born in Smorgon, near Vilna (Vilnius), 15 July 1913. Fled with family from fighting between German and Russian troops to Omsk, Siberia, 1915; after father's death, 1920, family resettled in Vilna. Studied at Vilna University. Following Nazi invasion, held in Vilna ghetto, 1941–43. Worked for "Rosenberg-Stab" collecting Jewish material (also hiding material and smuggling arms into the ghetto); then with partisan groups in Narotsh forests, 1943–44. Airlifted to Soviet Union, through auspices of Jewish Anti-Fascist Committee, March 1944. Testified at Nuremberg war crimes trials, 1946. Emigrated to Palestine, 1947. Married to Freydl Sutzkever; two daughters. Editor, Yiddish literary journal *Di goldene keyt*, Tel Aviv, 1949–95. Many awards, including Association of Yiddish Writers in Vilna Ghetto Prize, 1942; World Jewish Congress Prize, 1950, 1956; *Le Petit Parisien* Prize, 1950; Manger Prize, 1969; Shalom Aleichem Prize; Yakov Fichman Prize; New York Culture Congress Prize; Zvi Kessel Prize (Mexico); Shmuel Niger Prize; B'nai B'rith Prize, 1979; Israel Prize, 1985; David Hofshteyn Prize, 1987. Freeman, City of Tel Aviv.

Selected Writings

Poetry

Lider [Poems], 1937
Valdiks [From the Forest], 1940
Di festung [The Fortress], 1945
Lider fun geto [Poems from the Ghetto], 1946
Geheymshtot [Secret Town], 1948
Yidishe gas [The Jewish Ambiance], 1948
In fayer-vogn [In the Fiery Chariot], 1952
Sibir, 1952; as *Siberia*, translated by Jacob Sonntag, 1961
Ode tsu der toyb [Ode to the Dove], 1955
In midber sinay [In the Sinai Desert], 1957
Oazis [Oasis], 1960
Gaystike erd [Spiritual Earth], 1961
Poetishe verk [Poetic Works], 2 vols, 1963
Firkantike oysyes un mofsim [Square Letters and Magical Signs], 1968
Lider fun yam-hamoves [Poems from the Dead Sea], 1968
Tsaytike penemer [Mature Faces], 1970
Di fidlroyz [The Fiddle Rose], 1974
Lider fun togbukh [Poems from a Diary], 1977
Di ershte nakht in geto [The First Night in the Ghetto], 1979
Burnt Pearls: Ghetto Poems of Abraham Sutzkever, translated by Seymour Mayne, 1981
Fun alte un yunge ksav-yadn [From Old and Young Manuscripts], 1982
Tsviling-bruder [Twin Brother], 1986
The Fiddle Rose: Poems 1970–1972, edited and translated by Ruth Whitman, 1990
A. Sutzkever: Selected Poetry and Prose, translated by Barbara Harshav and Benjamin Harshav, 1991
Der yoyresh fun regn [The Heir of the Rain], 1992

Fiction

Griner akvariyum [Green Aquarium], 1975
Dortn vu es nekhtikn di shtern [Where the Stars Spend the Night], 1979
Di nevue fun shvartsaplen [Prophecy of the Inner Eye], 1989

Other

Vilner geto 1941–1944 [Vilna Ghetto 1941–1944], 1946

Further Reading

Harshav, Benjamin, "Sutzkever: Life and Poetry", introduction to *A. Sutzkever: Selected Poetry and Prose*, translated by Barbara Harshav and Benjamin Harshav, Berkeley: University of California Press, 1991
Leftwich, Joseph, *Abraham Sutzkever, Partisan Poet*, New York and London: Yoseloff, 1971
Novershtern, Abraham, *Avrom Sutskever bibliografiye*, Tel Aviv: Yisroel-bukh, 1976
Novershtern, Abraham (editor), *Avrom Sutskever: Tsum vern a ben-shivim*, Jerusalem: Jewish National and University Library, 1983
Roskies, David G., chapter on Sutzkever in *Against the Apocalypse*, Cambridge, Massachusetts: Harvard University Press, 1984
Sadan, Dov, Zalman Shazar, and M. Gros-Tsimerman (editors), *Yoyvl-bukh tsum fuftsikstn geboyrn-tog fun Avrom Sutskever*, Tel Aviv: Yoyvl-komitet, 1963
Sadan, Dov *et al.* (editors), *Yikhes fun lid/yikhuso shel shir: lekoved Avrom Sutskever*, Tel Aviv: Yoyvl-komitet, 1983
Valencia, Heather, "The Poetry of Abraham Sutzkever", *Lines Review*, 102 (1987)
Valencia, Heather, "Avrom Sutskever's Ode tsu der toyb", *Oksforder Yidish: A Yearbook of Yiddish Studies*, 1 (1990)
Valencia, Heather, "Changing Perspectives on Two Poems by Sutzkever" in *The History of Yiddish Studies*, edited

by Dov-Ber Kerler, Chur, Switzerland, and Philadelphia: Harwood, 1991
Valencia, Heather, "Sibir b'shtey poemot shel Avraham Sutskever", *Chulyot*, 2 (1994)
Valencia, Heather, "Gezang fun a jidischn dichter in 1943: Wort als Schutz und Widerstand in der Lyrik von Abraham Sutskever" in *Kriegserlebnis und Legendenbildung: das Bild des modernen Krieges in Literatur, Theater, Photographie und Film*, edited by Thomas F. Schneider, Osnabrück: Universitätsverlag Rasch, 1999
Wisse, Ruth, introduction to Sutzkever's *Burnt Pearls*, translated by Seymour Mayne, Oakville, Ontario: Mosaic Press, 1981
Wisse, Ruth, "Abraham Sutskever the Storyteller", introduction to Sutzkever's *Di nevue fun shvartsaplen*, Jerusalem: Magnes Press, 1989
Wisse, Ruth, introduction to *The Fiddle Rose: Poems 1970–1972*, translated by Ruth Whitman, Detroit: Wayne State University Press, 1990

Abraham Sutzkever's oeuvre spans more than 70 years and encompasses three main literary genres: shorter lyrical poems (*lider*), longer epic poems (*poemes*), and short prose pieces which he called stories or "descriptions", but which, in their poetic, often surrealist language and flowing form, can be seen as prose poems. Only once, in the account of his experiences in the Vilna ghetto between 1941 and 1944, did he turn to autobiographical narrative.

From the beginning Sutzkever's work is an exploration of the nature of poetry: for him there are no boundaries between physical existence and the reality of the poetic word, and it is this centrality of the word in his universe that most deeply defines his Judaism. The early poems are essentially aesthetic and solipsistic, exploring through anthropomorphic nature imagery the emergence of the poetic self and its relationship to the world. The poet feels himself to be the creator of the universe:

Brilyantene shtilkayt. Es gafn
di oygn in vaytkayt gevendt:
hob ikh es aleyn itst bashafn, -
aleyn, mit di eygene hent?
[Diamond stillness. My eyes
Gaze into the far distant lands:
Have *I* created this world,
Alone, with the power of my hands?]

The seminal work of the earlier years is the poem-cycle *Sibir*, which Sutzkever began writing in 1936, published in an earlier version, revised throughout the war years, and published in its definitive form in 1953. The family home in Siberia is reinvented as a magical world in which the young child discovers his true identity as a poet. This voyage of discovery is represented in the poem by a movement outward and upwards: from the warm secluded cabin the child goes out into the miraculous landscape. He experiences the death of his father whose fiddle music was his earliest aesthetic inspiration, and the music and dance of the wild Kirghizian tribesmen. The poem culminates in the child-poet's soaring above the landscape and walking with the North Star. The developing awareness of the *ikh* is evoked by images of poetic awakening – the "snowsounds" of his father's fiddle, the wolf which is drawn to the music, the dove which the child carries in his bosom and which, in a decisive moment, draws him upward from his father's coffin into new poetic life. The strange figure of the snowman, "the god of children and of winds", and the North Star, come together in the final stanza, as the poet experiences a magical transfiguration: "Tsofn-shtern, shpanst mit mir in eynem,/ kh'bin dayn shneymentsh in a kleyd fun hoyt. [North Star, you and I stride along together,/ I am your snowman in a cloak of skin.] In *Sibir* we see the foundation of a network of key images that change and combine in ever new and astonishing forms, unifying his whole poetic oeuvre.

Siberia, Vilna, and Israel are the three symbolic places that define Sutzkever's work. Vilna is the focus of the poetry which he never ceased writing during the years in the ghetto and woods, under circumstances of unimaginable hardship. During this period the aestheticism of the early poetry is deepened by Sutzkever's awakening conviction that his role as a poet is to speak to the Jewish people, affirming the eternal value of art and culture even in the face of the unprecedented bestiality surrounding them. Sutzkever later expressed his belief in the magical power of the poetic word: "When the sun itself seemed to have turned to ashes – I believed with complete faith: as long as the poem does not forsake me, the bullet will not destroy me". The equivalence of word and spirit, metaphor and reality leads to an intense complex of images arising naturally out of the situation of hunger and death: images of swallowing and burying are inextricably linked with the idea of preservation and rebirth and the continuation of the "golden chain" of human existence. This receives its most extraordinary expression in his poem to his murdered child:

Ikh hob gevolt dikh aynshlingen, mayn kind.
Kedey tsu filn dem geshmak
fun mayn gehofter tsukunft.
Efshr vestu blien vi a mol
in mayn geblit.
[I wanted to devour you, my child,
So that I might feel the taste
Of my hoped for future.
It may be you will blossom in my blood
As once you did.]

In the end the poet gives the beloved child to the snow of Siberia, his central image of poetic awakening. The problem of death and regeneration is resolved through poetry.

In the early years in Israel the poet struggles to find a new identity and to integrate memory and experience with the new life in the ancient "volcanic land in childbirth". This he achieves through imagery that fuses the Siberian snow and the streets of Vilna with the fiery heat of Israel and draws on the *Tanakh* and ancient Jewish tradition. In the early 1950s a visit to Africa brought renewed awareness of nature and of the great cycle of life, death, and regeneration: the African poems "Helfandn bay nakht" [Elephants at Night] are unique in Yiddish writing in their paganistic celebration of the savage primordial forces of nature.

Sutzkever's mature work draws together and develops all the strands of his previous experience, which he has absorbed into the realm of poetry. The poems of *Di fidlroyz* [The Fiddle Rose] and the majestic *Lider fun togbukh* [Poems from a Diary] convey Sutzkever's vision of the poet who is both seer, able to communicate with the dead and those unborn, and magician (*kishufmakher*), through playful self-irony and – as throughout his work – breathtaking linguistic and stylistic virtuosity. He probes the nature of the word and tries to penetrate beyond it to the "living silence" that he sees as the genesis of poetry. In the course of his paradoxical quest to reach this by means of words he enriches and renews the Yiddish language through a web of symbolic affinities and evocative neologisms.

In giving expression to the Jewish Holocaust and the trauma of exile, in his rootedness in Jewish culture, his passionate love of the Yiddish language and his perception of the almost magical power of the word, Abraham Sutzkever is a great Jewish poet. In his affinities with the European Romantics, with Symbolist and Metaphysical poetry, in the scope of his concerns and modernism of his forms and language, he is one of the great European poets of the 20th century.

HEATHER VALENCIA

Svevo, Italo

Italian fiction writer and dramatist, 1861–1928

Born Ettore Aron Schmitz in Trieste, 19 December 1861. Studied at Jewish schools in Trieste to 1873; Brüsselische Handels- und Erziehungsinstitut, Segnitz am Main, 1873–78; Istituto Superiore Commerciale Revoltella, Trieste, 1878–80. Clerk, Trieste branch of Unionbank of Vienna, 1880–99; instructor in French and German commercial correspondence, Istituto Superiore Commerciale Revoltella, 1893–1900. Married Livia Veneziani, 1895; one daughter. Partner in wife's family's manufacturing firm, Ditta Veneziani, from 1899. Took English lessons from James Joyce in Trieste, from 1907. Wrote all literary works under pseudonyms, mainly Italo Svevo but also Erode Samigli or Ettore Samigli. Died in Motta di Livenza, Treviso, 13 September 1928.

Selected Writings

Collections
Opere di Italo Svevo [Works of Italo Svevo], edited by Bruno Maier, 1954
Opera omnia [Complete Works], edited by Bruno Maier, 4 vols, 1966–69
The Works, translated by L. Collison-Morley *et al.*, 5 vols, 1967–80
Edizione critica delle opere di Italo Svevo [Critical Edition of the Works of Italo Svevo], edited by Bruno Maier, 1985–

Fiction
L'assassinio di via Belpoggia [Murder in Via Belpoggio], 1890
Una vita, 1892; as *A Life*, translated by Archibald Colquhoun, 1963
Senilità, 1898; as *As a Man Grows Older*, translated by Beryl de Zoete, 1932
La coscienza di Zeno, 1923; as *The Confessions of Zeno*, translated by Beryl de Zoete, 1930
Una burla riuscita, 1928; as *The Hoax*, translated by Beryl de Zoete, 1929
La novella del buon vecchio e della bella fanciulla, 1930; as *The Nice Old Man and the Pretty Girl and Other Stories*, translated by L. Collison-Morley, 1930
Corto viaggio sentimentale e altri racconti inediti, edited by Umbro Apollonio, 1949; as *Short Sentimental Journey and Other Stories*, translated by Beryl de Zoete *et al.*, 1967
The Further Confessions of Zeno, translated by Ben Johnson and P.N. Furbank, 1969
Il vegliando [The Awakening], 1987

Plays
Terzetta spezzato [The Broken Trio], 1927
Commedie [Comedy] (includes *Terzetta spezzato* [The Broken Trio]; *Un marito* [A Husband]; *L'avventura di Maria* [Maria's Adventure]; *Una commedia inedita, La verità, Inferiorità* [An Unpublished Comedy, The Truth, Inferiority]; *Le ire di Giuliano* [The Anger of William]; *Le teorie del conte Alberto* [The Theory of Count Albert]; *Il ladro in casa* [The Thief in House]; *Primo del ballo* [The First of Dance]; *Atto unico* [The Only Act]; *Con la penna d'oro* [With a Golden Pen]; *La rigenerazione* [The Regeneration]), edited by Umbro Apollonio, 1960

Other
Carteggio inedito Italo Svevo, James Joyce [Unpublished Correspondence of Italo Svevo, James Joyce], 1949
James Joyce, translated by Stanislaus Joyce, 1950
Corrispondenza con Valery Larbaud, Benjamin Crémieux e Marie Anne Comnène [Correspondence with Valery Larbaud, Benjamin Crémieux and Marie Anne Comnène], 1953
Saggi e pagine sparse [Essays and Scattered Pages], edited by Umbro Apollonio, 1954
Diario per la fidanzata [Diary for the Fiancé], edited by Bruno Maier and Anita Pittoni, 1962
Lettere alla moglie [Letters to the Wife], edited by Anita Pittoni, 1963
Lettere: Eugenio Montale–Svevo [Letters: Eugenio Montale–Svevo], 1966
Saba, Svevo, Comisso: lettere inedite [Saba, Svevo, Comisso: Unpublished Letters], edited by Mario Sutor, 1968
Carteggio con gli scritti di Montale su Svevo [Correspondence with the Writings of Montale on Svevo], edited by Giorgio Zampa, 1976
Carteggio con James Joyce, Valery Larbaud, Benjamin Crémieux, Marie Anne Comnène, Eugenio Montale, Valerio Jahier [Correspondence with James Joyce, Valery Larbaud, Benjamin Crémieux, Marie Anne Comnène, Eugenio Montale, Valerio Jahier], edited by Bruno Maier, 1978
Scritti su Joyce [Writings on Joyce], edited by Giancarlo Mazzacurati, 1986

Further Reading

Furbank, P.N., *Italo Svevo: The Man and the Writer*, London: Secker and Warburg, and Berkeley: University of California Press, 1966

Lebowitz, Naomi, *Italo Svevo*, New Brunswick, New Jersey: Rutgers University Press, 1978

Maier, Bruno, in *Opera omnia*, vol. 2, Milan: Dall'Oglio, 1969

Moloney, Brian, *Italo Svevo: A Critical Introduction*, Edinburgh: Edinburgh University Press, 1974

Moloney, Brian, *Italo Svevo and the European Novel*, Hull: University of Hull Press, 1977

Staley, Thomas F. (editor), *Essays on Italo Svevo*, Tulsa, Oklahoma: University of Tulsa, 1969

Van Voorhis, J.W., "Criticism of Italo Svevo: A Selected Checklist", *Modern Fiction Studies*, 18 (1972)

Weiss, Beno, *An Annotated Bibliography on the Theatre of Italo Svevo*, University Park: Pennsylvania State University Libraries, 1974

Ettore Aron Schmitz was born in Trieste, part of the Austro-Hungarian empire until 1918, and a famously cosmopolitan and trilingual city with its Italian, German, and Slav citizenry. It was also the site of a Jewish community comparable in size to that of other major centres of the empire, important in the professions and in business. The Triestine Jews were from various geographical and cultural origins, were far from being homogenous and were largely supporters of the Italian irredentist movement that demanded that Trieste become part of Italy. Their Italian nationalism encouraged the adoption of Italian as their everyday speech and often the abandonment of the Mosaic faith, generally becoming completely secular or Freemasons.

This was the complex cultural and national context from which Svevo drew both his strength and his sense of insecurity. After attending Jewish schools in Trieste he was sent by his father to Germany to perfect his German and attend a noted school of commerce, but on his return he had to find work in a bank because of family economic problems. Things improved, though, on his marriage to a distant cousin, Livia Veneziani, in 1895; her family owned a successful marine paint company where Svevo was employed. Becoming a person with a certain economic and social status, he was now under pressure to relegate his writing – little appreciated among the mercantile classes – to an unofficial night-time activity. The critics didn't appreciate his first efforts either: the novella *L'assassinio di via Belpoggio* [Murder in Via Belpoggio] and the novel *Una vita* (*A Life*) were published at his own expense. His literary vocation seemed as problematic as his Jewishness; here, too, his marriage confirmed an interior conflict that was already present. His new family were converts, and Livia, as a fervent Catholic, pushed him to be baptized. Italian and German, Jew and apostate, industrialist and writer: Svevo lived between these contradictions, in a self-concealment evidenced by his adoption of a pen-name, the first symptom of a problematic relationship with his own identity. In fact he was to use three pseudonymous camouflages, "Italo Svevo", which was the final and definitive one that signalled the double influence of Italian (Italo) and German (Svevo, Italian for Swabian, a region of Germany) culture on the writer, while the earlier Erode (Herod) or Ettore Samigli was a reference to Jewish history and a word-play on *Shlemiel*, Yiddish for ne'er-do-well, and a reference to a denied identity. Despite the pressures in his life hostile to his writing, Svevo continued to write and in 1898 published his second novel *Senilità* (*As a Man Grows Older*). Its protagonist, Emilio Brentani, a failed author, lives with his sister Amalia and is resigned to a humdrum existence. Falling in love with the young and vivacious Angiolina, he nevertheless completely fails to understand her (and she him) and the relationship runs aground. Angiolina instead falls for Balli, Emilio's friend and entirely opposite to him in character. Sister Amalia has also fallen for Balli and tries to forget him by taking ether and dies, poisoned.

Emilio Brentani is the typical Svevian antihero, the sad protagonist of a life lived badly, sick of his own ineptness, destined to fail and spending his days in a "senile" inertia – rather different though to Alfonso Nitti, the urbanized country fellow disappointed in his hopes who in *Una vita* killed himself.

As a Man Grows Older was followed by *La coscienza di Zeno*, published 1923, again at the author's expense and translated as *The Confessions of Zeno* in 1930. This could be considered as the third part of a long trilogy in which Svevo moves from the tragic through the pathetic to the ironic. The protagonist of *Confessions of Zeno* is another anti-hero, Zeno Cosini, a businessman who, plagued by various neuroses and incapable of giving up smoking, tries psychoanalysis. Asked to keep a diary by his analyst – the book is in diary form – Zeno writes there the salient points of his life; the father who in his dying moments shook his fist at him, the misunderstanding that leads him to marry his least favourite of three sisters; the suicide of Guido the friend of whom he had felt jealous, etc. Unable to quit smoking or overcome the many neurotic symptoms that afflict him, Zeno nevertheless gets by with irony and mitigates with good-humouredness his basic pessimism about the human condition.

It was James Joyce, who had had Svevo as his student of English in Trieste and had read his novels (and consulted him about his Jewish character Leopold Bloom) who got Svevo's work known in Europe, which is how it was "reintroduced" to Italy, giving Svevo an unexpected late success.

Some critics have emphasized in Svevo the supposed characteristics of the assimilated Jew, seeing in his protagonists a feminine passivity that the (mysogynistic and anti-Semitic) Otto Weiniger accused Jews of and that Svevo was trying to escape from. However there is little explicitly Jewish in his works: the novels, plays and short stories, even his diaries and letters, are reticent on this point. The Jewish elements in Svevo are subterranean, complex, and elusive. Undoubtedly as in the case of many turn-of-the-century Jews, an original ethnic identity and coherence have been lost in the pursuit of easier social acceptance in a Gentile world. Svevo's writing, though, continued, despite the disdain of the world of commerce, and can be understood as a compensation for the denial of this repressed part of himself.

CLARA CORONA

T

Tammuz, Benjamin

Russian-born Israeli fiction writer, journalist, and sculptor, 1919–1989

Born Benjamin Kammerstein in Kharkov, 11 July 1919. Emigrated with family to Palestine, 1924; settled in Tel Aviv. Studied at yeshiva; Herzlia College, 1936; law and economics at Tel Aviv University; history of art at the Sorbonne, 1950–51. Changed name legally, 1939. Married Miriam Solberg, 1946; two children. Leading figure in unsuccessful Canaanite Movement, which advocated cooperation with Arabs. Sculptor, 1938–39; member of Palmach underground movement against British Mandate authorities, 1942–43; military liaison officer in Middle East, 1944–45; newspaper censor, 1946–47; editor, daily newspaper *Yom-yom*, Tel Aviv, 1948–50; editor, weekly newspaper *Haaretz Shelana*, Tel Aviv, 1950–65; editor of literary supplement, daily newspaper *Haaretz*, Tel Aviv, 1965–78; cultural attaché, Israeli Embassy in London, 1971–75. Visiting writer, University of Oxford, 1970–83. Member, Israel Writers Association, and Painters and Sculptors Association. Several awards, including Talpir Literary Prize, 1966; Ministry of Culture Literary Prize, 1968; Prime Minister's Prize, 1977; Jena Literary Prize (Mexico), 1979. Died in Jerusalem, July 1989.

Selected Writings

Stories and Novellas

Holot hazahav [Golden Sands], 1950
Taharut sehiyah [The Swimming Race], 1952
Gan naul [A Garden Enclosed], 1957
Sipuranton haarmeni [The Story of Anton the Armenian], 1960
Angioxyl: terufah nedirah [Angioxyl: A Rare Cure], 1973; as *A Rare Cure*, translated by Joseph Schachter, 1981
Mishlei bakbukim [Bottle Parables], 1976
Reiho hamar shel hageranium [The Bitter Scent of Geranium], 1980
Sipurim [Stories], 1987
Mivhar sipurim [Selected Stories], 1990

Novels

Hayei elyakum [The Life of Elyakum], 1963
Besof maarav, 1966; as *Castle in Spain*, translated by Joseph Schachter, 1973
Elyakum: sefer haazayot [Hallucinations], 1969
Yaakov, 1971
Hapardes, 1976; as *The Orchard*, translated by Richard Flantz, 1984
Requiem lenaaman, 1978; as *Requiem for Na'aman*, translated by Mildred Budhy and Yehuda Safran, 1982
Minotaur, 1980; as *Minotaur*, translated by Kim Parfitt and Mildred Budhy, 1981
Pundako shel yirmiahu [Jeremiah's Inn], 1984
Elyakum: trilogiyah [Elyakum: Trilogy], 1988
Hazikit vehazamir [Chameleon and Nightingale], 1989

Play

Kat shel klavim [A Sect of Dogs], 1968

For Children

Alilot kapu vedish [The Adventures of Kapu and Dish], 1958
Laylah al hagadah hamaaravit [A Night on the West Bank], 1961
Laylah beroma [A Night in Rome], 1964
Dugit mafligah layam [A Raft Sails to the Sea], 1970
Haye hakelev rizi [Rizi the Dog], 1971
Hamelekh yashen arbaa paamim beyom [The King Sleeps Four Times a Day/David's Song], 1978
Hamelekh vehagitara habilti hashmalit [The King and the Not-Electric Guitar], 1980
Mah yoter kedai, lakahat o latet [What's Better, Giving or Taking], 1980
Haneshamah hashniah [The Second Soul], 1981

Other

Editor, with Max Wykes-Joyce, *Art in Israel*, 1966
Editor, with Leon Yudkin, *Meetings with the Angel: Seven Stories from Israel*, 1973

Further Reading

Chicago Tribune (21 July 1989)
Diamond, James S., *Homeland or Holy Land? The Canaanite Critique of Israel*, Bloomington: Indiana University Press, 1986
Los Angeles Times (22 July 1982; 22 July 1989)
New York Times (21 July 1989)
New York Times Book Review (9 August 1981; 1 August 1982)
The Times (28 April 1983)
Washington Post (21 July 1989)
Washington Post Book World (27 June 1982)
Yudkin, Leon I., *Escape into Siege: A Survey of Israeli Literature Today*, London and Boston: Routledge and Kegan Paul, 1974

Benjamin Tammuz was a Hebrew writer whose fictional scope spans from the time of Israel's founding to its complex developments as a modern state. His short stories and novels reflect the development in Modern Hebrew literature away from didacticism and toward aestheticism. Unlike his more heavy-handed predecessors, Tammuz used fiction to describe life in both pre-1948 Palestine and post-1948 Israel without forcing political concerns into its centre. Instead, his fiction tackles interpersonal relationships, and particularly the peculiarities of fate, with a carefully controlled touch. A sculptor by avocation, Tammuz seems to have created his fiction in a manner similar to an artist working in clay or stone: rather than writing stories driven by plot or morals, he forges his characters out of an accumulation of small impressions formed by the atmospheres in which they find themselves, the people with whom they come in contact, and the accidents of fate that come to delineate their lives. What is unique about his work in world literature is that he was among the first to apply this understated style to the overstated concerns of Israel's short history.

Tammuz began his literary career as part of the short-lived Canaanite Movement, a group of artists and writers during the early years of Israel's statehood who denied the Zionist narrative that saw Israel as the ingathering of Jewish exiles into their yearned-for homeland. Instead, these artists saw themselves as the revivalists of ancient Near Eastern culture, an entirely new form of civilization that based itself less on the rabbinic legalism of Jewish religion than on the unmediated spirituality of the biblical period. Canaanites saw Jewish life as it had developed in the Diaspora as an unnecessary psychological burden best replaced by a new Hebrew, rather than Jewish, culture. Later in his career, however, like many Canaanite artists, Tammuz re-evaluated this standpoint with the new diversity of Israeli culture and began to see the centrality of Jewish history in the Diaspora to the development of the Israeli state, undermining the myth of the invincible sabra.

Tammuz first secured his reputation with *Holot hazahav* [Golden Sands], a collection of short stories and sketches set in mandatory Palestine and in the newly established State of Israel. While some critics classified it as mere sentimentalism, these stories are among the earliest in modern Israeli literature to express, in a simple and understated style, the struggles and passions of those living in Israel whose experiences are motivated less by politics than by relationships. Most of the stories and sketches in this collection are told from the point of view of a young child raised in Israel, for whom the complications of life in the new land are filtered through his personal shames and fears in his limited daily encounters with his Arab and Jewish neighbours. The story "An Enigma" is perhaps the strongest in the series entitled "Golden Sands". In this story, a young boy stays with two older children, the brother and sister of neighbours, while their parents go out for the evening. The neighbour's boy is a boorish beast of a young man, while the girl, a delicate and responsible beauty with whom the child promptly falls in love, dies the following year of an unspecified illness. The accidents of fate in the story are delicately described, and while political statements can be drawn from the characters' destinies (the idea, for example, that life in Israel does not alone provide redemption), ideas are secondary to the story's identity as a work of art.

The longer story "Zaki and Julia", also in this collection, particularly reflects Tammuz's light touch in depicting political issues. Zaki and Julia are a North African Jewish couple who emigrate to Israel to escape problems in their native country – one of which was a hostile Jewish man in their neighbourhood who constantly threatened Julia. Soon after their arrival in their poor but habitable refugee camp in Israel, however, they find that the man from their old neighbourhood will soon be moving to their very same refugee camp, thanks to the Israeli government's policy of placing new immigrants near those from their places of origin in order to make them more comfortable. As a result, the man rapes Julia and she becomes pregnant with his child. But instead of making this story into a polemic about treatment of refugees – a topic that many writers seized upon, including most famously Yosef Hayyim Brenner – Tammuz instead focuses the reader's attention on the reaction of the couple to this tragedy, demonstrating how good and evil are not always so clearly defined. Tammuz's refusal to assign simple blame to characters or institutions is what makes his characters not only realistic but searingly memorable.

While many Israeli writers of his era focused on shorter forms, Tammuz wrote many full-length novels. *Hapardes* (*The Orchard*) is perhaps his best-known novel. The book tells the story of two half-brothers, one Arab and one Jewish, and of the developments in their lives and families during the course of Israel's conflicts with its Arab neighbours. The allusions and symbolism are quite obvious: the half-brothers mirror the biblical story of Isaac and Ishmael, who respectively become patriarchs of the Jewish and Arab nations. Even the title suggests mythical origins, as "pardes", etymologically related to the English "paradise", can also mean paradise, suggesting the peace that is possible when those who have forgotten their brotherhood remember it again.

Tammuz's later work deals less with life within Israel than with life outside the country, particularly on the subjects of how Israelis abroad struggle to find their own identities and how Israel has developed as part of a Mediterranean culture, rather than exclusively a Middle Eastern or European culture. His best-known novel on this subject is *Minotaur*, which unfolds as a love affair between a middle-aged secret agent and a young British woman, who never meet. The secret agent, who comes from an unnamed country closely resembling Israel, scouts out the woman and sends her mysterious letters, to which she replies by following his cryptic instructions. Meanwhile the novel traces developments in her life, including a love affair with a man from Alexandria who dreams of a resurgent Mediterranean civilization. Later we are told the seemingly unrelated story of a boy raised in Israel during the British mandate and its early years of statehood, the child of cosmopolitan European parents who has trouble finding a place for himself in the coarse and cultureless colony. The connections between the two plot lines become evident only late in the novel, but the novel's themes are united from start to finish: the difficulty of constructing a cultural identity in a country as young as Israel, coupled with the desperate need to hide this difficulty when facing the rest of the world.

DARA HORN

Taylor, C.P.

British dramatist, 1929–1981

Born Cecil Philip Taylor in Glasgow, 6 November 1929, son of Russian Jewish immigrants. Educated at Queen's Park Secondary School; left at 14; variety of jobs including travelling salesman, electrical engineer, charity worker, and record company employee. Married, first, Irene Diamond, 1956, two children; second, Elizabeth Screen, 1967, two children. Wrote extensively for radio and television, several plays for children. Literary adviser, Northumberland Youth Theatre Association, from 1968; Tyneside Theatre Trust, Newcastle, from 1971, and Everyman Theatre, Liverpool, from 1971. Involved with Traverse Theatre, Edinburgh. World Jewish Congress Playwriting Prize, 1954; Arts Council Playwright's bursary, 1965; Scottish Television Theatre Award, 1969. Died in Northumberland, 9 December 1981.

Selected Writings

Plays
Aa Went te Blaydon Races, 1962
Happy Days Are Here Again, 1964
Of Hope and Glory, 1965
Allergy, 1965
Bread and Butter, 1966
Who's Pinkus? Where's Chelm? 1966
Traverse Plays, 1966
The Ballachulish Beat: A Play with Songs, 1967
Fable, 1967
Mister David, 1967
What Can a Man Do? 1968
Lies about Vietnam / Truth about Sarajevo, 1969
Thank You Very Much, 1969
Brave, 1969
Making a Television Play, 1970
Bloch's Play, 1971
Passion Play, 1971
The Cleverness of Us, 1971
The Grace Darling Show, 1971
Em'n Ben, 1971
Me, 1971
Ginger Golly and the Fable Men, 1972
The Black and White Minstrels, 1972
Happy Anniversary, 1972
You Are My Heart's Delight, 1973
Gynt, 1973
Next Year in Tel Aviv, 1973
The 5p Opera, 1973
Oil and Water, 1973
Apples, 1973
Columba, 1973
Carol O.K., 1974
So Far, So Bad, 1974
The Spital Tongues Plays, 1974
Pilgrim, 1975
The Killingworth Play, 1975
Plumber's Progress, 1975
And a Nightingale Sang, 1979
Bandits, 1979
Happy Lies, 1981
Good, 1981
Live Theatre, 1981

Many television and radio plays, and adaptations

Further Reading

Gow, Gordon, review of "And a Nightingale Sang", *Plays and Players* (August 1979)
Grant, Steve, review of "Bandits", *Plays and Players* (October 1979)
Mortimer, Peter, "C P Taylor: An Appreciation of His Work and Life", *Drama* (Autumn 1982)
Nightingale, Benedict, "Good Man", *New Statesman* (8 June 1982)
Rich, Frank, " 'Good' on Becoming a Nazi", *New York Theater Critics' Reviews*, 43 (18 October 1982)
Simon, John, "All's Well That Ends Good", *New York Magazine* (25 October 1982)
Taylor, John Russell, *Anger and After: A Guide to the New British Drama*, London: Methuen, 1962; as *The Angry Theatre: New British Drama*, New York: Hill and Wang, 1962
Taylor, John Russell, *The Second Wave: British Drama for the Seventies*, London: Methuen, and New York: Hill and Wang, 1971

C.P. Taylor was one of the most versatile and prolific British dramatists of the 1960s; he was also much undervalued. In his dedication to his father, Max George Taylor in the play *Good*, he describes him as "a refugee from anti-Semitism in Czarist Russia". C.P. Taylor left school at 14 and had many jobs, including that of travelling salesman. He married in 1956 and moved to Newcastle; later, on remarriage, he settled in Longhorsley, near Morpeth. Many of his plays are set in Northumberland and the northeast of England. Taylor wrote more than 50 plays for major companies such as the Royal Shakespeare Company, community theatre, and television. Many were first performed at the Traverse Theatre, Edinburgh; others were written for the Live Theatre Company in Newcastle, a community theatre with which he was closely associated.

Despite undeserved marginality as a playwright during most of his lifetime, the play *Good* (1981) brought his dramatic work to the fore in the very year of his death. It was undoubtedly also his most remarkable artistic achievement. An ironic fable about what Hannah Arendt called "the banality of evil", it traces the downward progress of a "good" man, Johnny Halder, through compromise, conformity, and a chain of moral rationalizations. Halder becomes a Nazi monster, and a personal assistant to Adolf Eichmann. At the start of the play, set in 1933 when the Nazis seized power, Halder is professor of literature at the

University of Frankfurt and author of a fictional novel advocating euthanasia; he is also haunted by an obsession with music. Addressed by the SS (in the name of the Führer himself, who later appears in person in the shape of a grotesque caricature), Halder is first asked to serve as the humanist cover for the extermination programme of the terminally ill and mentally disabled. This he is able to rationalize because of his experience in "assisting" his own strong-willed mother with her pains. Halder's egotistic individualism dislocates his ability to depend on the two major supporting frameworks he has leaned on until now – the myth of the family and the myth of friendship. In succumbing to an ironic reversal of values he clings to the one myth that destroys his individuality: the myth of the nation. He joins the SS and leaves his incompetent wife (who had ironically encouraged him to join the Nazi Party). He also betrays his Jewish psychoanalyst who asks his patient for help to buy train tickets to escape to Switzerland. The psychoanalyst is shattered when he realizes that the "Bourgeois contract" (whereby he considers himself as a native German and not primarily Jewish), is no more. Halder leaves his wife for Anne, a student whose relationship to him does not depend on raising a family, and betrays his genuine friendship with his analyst, for a sentimental friendship with Freddie, a Major in the SS, whose relationship to him is founded on a vulgar version of the myth of nation. Halder then takes part in the burning of so-called "subversive" books on campus; finally, he dons the SS uniform on Kristallnacht, and goes as Eichmann's emissary to explore the extermination possibilities in a remote Nazi camp called Auschwitz. There the haunting music that has been playing in his mind since the Nazis came to power, suddenly materializes in the shape of a Jewish inmates' orchestra at the gates playing Schubert's "An Die Musik".

The play has been criticized for its representation of extreme evil as stemming from a humanist, enlightened background rather than (as Taylor puts it) "a simple conspiracy of criminals and psychopaths". Taylor says he intended to write a play on the final solution "not as a Jew, wanting to add my wreath to those already piled high at the graves of the Six Million, but as my own little gesture to revive their memory in our consciousness . . . there are lessons to be learned if we can examine the atrocities of the Third Reich as the result of the infinite complexity of contemporary human society".

At the time of his premature death, on 9 December 1981, Taylor was putting final touches to his version of *The Dybbuk*. *And a Nightingale Sang* was posthumously adapted for television by Jack Rosenthal and produced in 1991. In 1992, the Edinburgh Festival devoted a retrospective season to Taylor's work.

AVRAHAM OZ

Tchernichovski, Saul

Russian-born poet and translator, 1875–1943

Born in Mikhailovka, Crimea, 3 January 1875, into family open to *Haskalah* (Jewish Enlightenment) and Zionism. Studied at modern Hebrew school, 1882–85; state school from 1885; studied German, French, English, Greek, and Latin at commercial school in Odessa, 1890–99; failed to gain admission to university; studied medicine in Heidelberg and Lausanne, 1899–1906. Returned to Russia, 1907; wandered, doing various jobs, until foreign degrees recognized in St Petersburg, 1910. Conscript physician in imperial army during World War I. Returned to Odessa, 1919; meagre living as physician. Emigrated, 1922; brief residence in Constantinople; moved to Berlin. Translated works by Sophocles, Goethe, Molière, Shakespeare, and others into Hebrew; editor, *The Book of Medical and Scientific Terms* (in Latin, Hebrew, and English), 1931–34. Emigrated to Palestine, 1931; settled in Tel Aviv. Physician, municipal schools in Tel Aviv, from 1934. Moved to Jerusalem, 1936. Awarded Bialik Prize. Died in Tel Aviv, 14 October 1943. Tchernichovski Prize (Israel) awarded biennially for outstanding translations into Hebrew.

Selected Writings

Collections
Kitvei Shaul Tchernichovsky [Collected Works], 10 vols, 1929–34
Kol kitvei Shaul Tchernichovsky [Collected Works], 7 vols, 1990–98

Poetry
Hezyonot vemanginot alef [Melodies and Liturgy 1], 1898
Hezyonot vemanginot beit [Melodies and Liturgy 2], 1901
Shirim [Poems], 1911
Lashemesh [To the Sun], 1919
Mahberet sonetot [Sonnets], 1922
Sefer haidilyot [Book of Idylls], 1922
Al hadam [On the Blood], 1923
Shirim hadashim [New Poems], 1924
Sefer habaladot [Ballads], 1930
Kol shirei Shaul Tchernichovsky [Collected Poems], 1937
Ho adamah [You See, O Earth], 1940
Amma dedehava [The Golden People], 1943
Shirim [Poems], 1943
Kokhevei shamayim rehokim [Stars of Distant Skies], 1944
Selected Poems (mainly in English), various translators, 1944

Stories
Sipurim [Stories], 1922
Shloshim veshlosshah sipurim [Thirty-three Stories], 1941

For Children
Shirim leyaldei israel [Poems for the Children of Israel], 1907
Hehalil [The Flute], 1923
Shirei Tchernichovsky leehav hatseirim [Poems by Tchernichovski for His Young Brothers], 1936
The Threshing Floor, 1936
Asher hayah velo hayah [That Which Never Was], 1942
In *Anthology of Modern Hebrew Poetry*, selected by Shemuel Yeshayahu Penueli and A. Ukhmani, 1966
In *Modern Hebrew Poetry: A Bilingual Anthology*, edited and translated by Ruth Finer Mintz, 1966
In *An Anthology of Modern Hebrew Poetry*, edited by Abraham Birman, 1968

Further Reading

Alter, Robert, "Saul Tschernichovsky" in *The Modern Hebrew Poem Itself*, edited and translated by Stanley Burnshaw, T. Carmi and Ezra Spicehandler, Cambridge, Massachusetts: Harvard University Press, 1989

Arpaly, Boaz (editor), *Saul Tchernichovski: Studies and Documents*, Jerusalem: The Bialik Institute, 1994 (in Hebrew)

Barzel, Hillel, *A History of Hebrew Poetry*, vol. 3: *The Poetry of Saul Tchernichovski*, Tel Aviv: Sifriyat Poalim, 1993

Friedlander, A.H. and Fred S. Worms (editors), *Meir Gertner: An Anthology*, London: B'nai B'rith and the Jewish Book Council, 1978

Ha'efrati, Yosef (editor), *Saul Tchernichovski: A Selection of Critical Essays of His Writings*, Tel Aviv: Am Oved, 1976

Klausner, J., *Saul Tschernichowsky: The Man and the Poet*, Jerusalem: Hebrew University Press Association, 1947

Kurzweil, Baruch, *Bialik and Tschernichowsky*, Tel Aviv: Schocken, 1960

Silberschlag, Eisig, *Saul Tschernichowsky: Poet of Revolt*, with translations by Sholom J. Kahn *et al.*, Ithaca, New York: Cornell University Press, 1968

Tsemach, Edi, *Yalkut Messot*, Tel Aviv: Ha-Poel Ha-Tsair, 1966

Saul Tchernichovski, with H.N. Bialik, is considered one of the most important poets of the "Renaissance Generation" of Hebrew writers active in Odessa in the 1890s. Born into a secular family of *maskilim*, Tchernichovski was educated in Russian and received private tutorials in biblical Hebrew, the Talmud, and modern Hebrew texts. His knowledge of Greek, Latin, German, and French enabled him to broaden the scope of Hebrew poetry linguistically, structurally, and contextually. In his attempt to combine elements from different cultures and religions, Tchernichovski linked pagan motifs with the Jewish context. His fascination with mythology included that of the Greeks, Babylonians, Egyptians, Slavs, and Finns. Although foreign cultures and their pagan roots exerted considerable influence over his works, Tchernichovski also devoted his attention to Canaanite and Semitic myths. He called for a return to the times of the "conquerors of Canaan", because they were an example of freedom from the limitations of Judaism. The traditional Jewish life in the Diaspora, *heder* and Synagogue-bound, offered, according to Tchernichovski, no room for artistic inspiration, nor would such environment be beneficial for the Zionist goals.

Tchernichovski's experimentation with genre and metre has earned him the title of the "master of form" in Modern Hebrew poetry. The cycles *On the Blood* and *To the Sun* are good examples of Tchernichovski's sonnets. The idylls (e.g. "Baruch of Mayence", "Circumcision") are the most characteristic of his creation, and the poet's innovation lies in his combining classical Greek metric devices, an introduction of which into Modern Hebrew poetry is in itself innovative, with Jewish content, namely reflections on rural Jewry. Tchernichovski is also regarded as the innovator of the ballad in Hebrew poetry – whether using traditional Jewish subjects, as in "On the Eve of Sabbath", focusing on the theme of beauty, as in "Three Crowns", or concentrating on the motif of martyrdom, as he did in "Ballads of Worms".

Hellenism signified joy, beauty, and affirmation of life for Tchernichovski, and he gave expression to such sentiments in "Before the Statue of Apollo". The poem was the first expression of the poet's interest in the pagan world and earned him the epithet "Greek". Significantly, the metre used is the dactylic hexameter, the oldest metre in Greek poetry, which became one of the accepted metres in Modern Hebrew poetry. The speaker addresses the ancient god, admiring his beauty, vigour, youth, and strength and introduces himself as the Jew, the ancient enemy of Greek culture and religion. There is a clear, dramatic historical division between the "Torah of my fathers", or the Jewish religion and tradition, and "your adorers' cult", or the pagan religion, based on beauty and strength. The speaker returns to the forgotten god and rejects the limitations of his own tradition, which is here associated with death. The beauty and vitality of Apollo contrast with that tradition and are approximated with life and light. Moreover, Judaism is portrayed as a religion that suppresses human passion and strength, as an old, inadequate tradition, which restrains one's desire for life. Apollo symbolizes the good and the sublime in creation, whereas the Jewish people are compared to "human corpses and the rotten seed of man". The God of Tchernichovski is the Nietzschean god of life and the speaker recounts the splendour of this God in connection with the ancient Canaan: "God, Lord of the wondrous deserts,/ God, Lord of the conquerors of Canaan by storm – / And they bound him in phylactery thongs." For Tchernichovski, the pagan world symbolizes the freedom of the natural existence before it was constrained by repression and inhibition. It would be false, however, to presume that Tchernichovski advocated idolatry or asserted that Greek culture was superior to Hebrew, as the Greek content of his poems is placed within a wider Hebrew context.

To the Sun is composed in the difficult form of the sonnet corona, the first in Hebrew literature, where in the cycle of 15 Petrarchan sonnets the last verse of each poem is also the first verse of the following poem and the 14th poem ends with the first verse of the first poem and the final poem is made up of the first verses of all the previous sonnets. The cycle should be read together with *On the Blood*, where the poet suggests art as a solution to violence and opposes the balance and structure of the corona against the moral chaos that surrounded him. The central theme of *To the Sun* is the speaker's adoration of the sun and its different incarnations.

The first sonnet recalls the motifs of the Song of Songs, and celebrates the life-giving qualities of the sun, which are emphasized also in the second sonnet, where the speaker compares himself to an ear of grain, fully sustained by and dependent on the sun. Already here there is a sense of the speaker's double sense of self; as a complete creature, rooted in the earth and nourished by the timeless sun, and at the same time as an alienated man, faced with brutality of the modern times, an exile unsuited for the days he lives in.

The third poem praises the beauty and magnificence of the sun, and the fourth its mystery. In the fifth, the speaker focuses on the timelessness of the sun, recounting the ancient nations that worshipped fire, one of the sun's embodiments. The motif of battle in this poem, in the context of the speaker's attempt to undermine the traditional Jewish idea of God, is extended into the next sonnet, where the speaker is an army doctor in an underground operating room on the front line. The speaker's dual sense of self is again emphasized here in the first and last line of the poem, where he stands "between the living and the already dying" (a quote from Numbers 17:13) and poses the question "Had I come too soon, or perhaps my Creator had waited too long?" The 14th sonnet shows that ultimately, everything that exists is an embodiment of the sun with its many incarnations: light, warmth, colour, and life. Therefore the 15th and final poem is the speaker's credo, in which his God is the god of light and life: "I am seized by a vanished world's gods – / or an image, in the kingdom of idols, of its last age not yet done?"

Tchernichovski's contribution to Modern Hebrew literature is immense, as his fascination with foreign cultures and religions allowed him to build bridges and to bring innovation into the form, language, and content of Hebrew poetry. He stands between Hebraic, Hellenic, and European civilizations both as a poet and a translator. He is considered to be one of the most important Hebrew poets, one who stands at the beginning of a new era.

MARTA MARZANSKA

Torberg, Friedrich

Austrian fiction writer, essayist, and critic, 1908–1979

Born Friedrich Ephraim Kantor in Alsergrund, Vienna, 16 September 1908, to Alfred Kantor and Therese Kantor (née Berg). Moved with family to Prague, 1922; poems published in *Jung-Juda*, 1926. Journalist and theatre critic, *Prager Tagblatt*, 1929; performer in the cabaret Literatur am Naschmarkt, together with satirists Peter Preses and Jura Soyfer, 1930s; contributed to *Arbeiter-Zeitung*, Vienna. Went into exile, in Switzerland and France, 1938; volunteer in Czechoslovak army in France, 1939. Escaped to United States, via Spain and Portugal, 1940; scriptwriter in Hollywood; worked for *Aufbau*, New York, 1944. Returned to Austria; honorary professorship, 1951; co-founder and editor, monthly *Forum*, from 1954. Awarded Great Austrian State Prize, 1979. Died in Vienna, 10 November 1979.

Selected Writings

Collections
Gesammelte Werke in Einzelausgaben, 19 vols, 1962–91

Novels
Der Schüler Gerber hat absolviert, 1930; as *The Examination*, translated by F.A. Voight, 1932
— und glauben, es wäre die Liebe [— and Believe It is Love], 1932
Die Mannschaft: Roman eines Sport-Lebens [The Team: A Novel about a Life Devoted to Sport], 1935
Abschied [Last Farewell], 1937
Die zweite Begegnung [The Second Encounter], 1940
Mein ist die Rache [Vengeance is Mine], 1943
Hier bin ich, mein Vater [Here I Am, My Father], 1948
Golems Wiederkehr [Golem's Return], 1968
Süsskind von Trimberg [Süsskind of Trimberg], 1972
Auch das war Wien [Also This Was Vienna], 1984

Satires and Essays
Almanach: das vierundsechzigste Jahr: 1886–1950, 1950
P.P.P.: Pamphlete, Parodien, Post Scripta [Pamphlets, Parodies, Postscripts], 1964
Mit der Zeit, gegen die Zeit [With Time, against Time], 1965
Die Tante Jolesch; oder, Der Untergang des Abendlandes in Anekdoten [Aunt Jolesch; or, The Demise of the Occident Told in Anecdotes], 1975
Mensch, Maier! Sagte der Lord: kleines kritisches Welttheater, 1975
Die Erben der Tante Jolesch [The Heirs of Aunt Jolesch], 1978
Wo der Barthel die Milch holt [Where Bartel Gets the Milk], 1981
Auch Nichtraucher müssen sterben [Even Non-Smokers Must Die], 1985
Wien oder Der Unterschied: ein Lesebuch, 1998

Letters
Kaffeehaus war überall: Briefwechsel mit Käuzen und Originalen [Everywhere was Coffeehouse: Correspondence with Eccentrics and Oddballs], 1982
Pegasus im Joch: Briefwechsel mit Verlegern und Redakteuren [Pegasus in the Yoke], 1983
Liebste Freundin und Alma: Briefwechsel mit Alma Mahler-Werfel [Dearest Friend and Alma: Correspondence with Alma Mahler-Werfel], 1987
Eine tolle, tolle Zeit: Briefe und Dokumenta aus den Jahren der Flucht 1938-1945: Zürich, Frankreich, Portugal, Amerika [A Crazy, Crazy Time: Letters and Documents from Refugee Years 1938-1941], 1988
Svoreingenommen wie ich bin: von Dichtern, Denkern und Autoren [Biased as I Am: About Poets, Thinkers, and Authors], 1991

Poetry
Lebenslied [Song of Life], 1958

Further Reading

Axmann, David (editor), *Und Lächeln ist das Erbteil meines Stammes: Erinnerung an Friedrich Torberg*, Vienna: Atelier, 1988
Beckermann, Ruth, "1938: During the Austrian Anschluss to the Third Reich, Friedrich Torberg Escapes from Prague, First to Zurich and Then to Paris" in *Yale Companion to Jewish Writing and Thought in German Culture, 1096–1996*, edited by Sander L. Gilman and Jack Zipes, New Haven, Connecticut: Yale University Press, 1997
Strelka, Josef (editor), *Der Weg war schon das Ziel: Festschrift für Friedrich Torberg zum 70. Geburtstag*, Munich: Langen Müller, 1978
Tichy, Frank, *Friedrich Torberg: ein Leben in Widersprüchen*, Vienna: Müller, 1995

Zohn, Harry, "*. . . ich bin ein Sohn der deutschen Sprache nur . . .": Jüdisches Erbe in der österreichischen Literatur*, Vienna: Amalthea, 1986

Friedrich Torberg, born Friedrich Ephraim Kantor in Vienna, was the son of a Prague liquor merchant. In elementary school he wrote his first poems expressing both Austrian patriotism and the pride of being a Jew. He grew up a believer in the Austrian-Jewish symbiosis and, like Freud and Bertha Pappenheim, in a future for Jewish life within German culture. Even after 1945 he continued to consider himself a modern urban Jew and a son of the Danube monarchy whose past imperial glory he celebrated as well as the diverse culture of inter-war central Europe, e.g. his nostalgic and satirical tales about the Jewish coffeehouse culture in *Die Tante Jolesch* [Aunt Jolesch] and *Die Erben der Tante Jolesch* [The Heirs of Aunt Jolesch]. While a student at the predominantly Jewish Wasagasse college preparatory school Torberg fought against anti-Semitism. He was a successful sportsman, a soccer and waterball player, a prominent member of the Jewish sports club Hagibor in Prague, and a fan of the Viennese HAKOAH soccer team. He endorsed the Jewish-Maccabean ideal calling for active, physically fit men and women. The autobiographical novel *Die Mannschaft* [The Team] underscores these views.

In 1922 the Kantors moved back to Prague, and Torberg came in conflict with a rigid educational system that lacked the liberalism of "Red", Social Democratic, Vienna. In 1926 he started writing poetry for the magazine *Jung-Juda*. However, he soon discovered that his penchant for satire coupled with an interest in topical issues were better suited to journalistic writing and narrative prose. In his first novel, *Der Schüler Gerber hat absolviert* (*The Examination*), Torberg addresses issues that he confronted at the time of his high school graduation. The work ends with the protagonist's suicide and is an outcry against an outdated pedagogy. Soon thereafter Torberg started working for a major paper, the *Prager Tagblatt*. He wrote short stories, reviews, and reported on sports events. His narratives were often dismissed for being sentimental, even trivial. His romantic stories, *– und glauben, es wäre die Liebe* [– and Believe It is Love] and *Abschied* [Last Farewell] were found to be out of keeping with the social and political upheavals of the time.

In the 1930s Torberg performed in the cabaret Literatur am Naschmarkt under the pseudonym Prokop with Peter Preses and the socialist satirist Jura Soyfer. He took a public stand against the opportunistic position of the Austrian PEN Club concerning Hitler's rise to power and protested the persecution of intellectuals. He spoke out against Thomas Mann and Gottfried Benn for their conciliatory attitude toward Nazi Germany. At the same time, despite his connections with the Social Democratic *Arbeiter-Zeitung*, Torberg repudiated Brecht, Feuchtwanger, and anyone he considered a communist "fellow traveller". In the second Austrian republic his wholesale rejection of "totalitarianism" was almost proverbial. Personally he remained on friendly terms with prominent Social Democrats, namely, Bruno Kreisky and Christian Broda.

Torberg was a major player among Austrian exiles and based his career on the legacy of the inter-war avant garde. His circle of friends included intellectuals, writers, and actors from Prague, Vienna, and Budapest – Anton Kuh, Alfred Polgar, Ernst Pollak, Hermann Broch, Fritz von Herzmanovsky-Orlando, Alma Mahler-Werfel, Joseph Roth, Hilde Spiel, Marlene Dietrich, and Erich Maria Remarque. The posthumously published novel *Auch das war Wien* [Also This Was Vienna] evokes the rich fabric of the world of a Viennese-Praguer journalist, a culture Torberg portrays on the eve of its destruction, revealing the instability of Jewish / non-Jewish relationships as well as the opportunism of some and the loyalty of others. Torberg's culture ended in 1938. The only identity he did not question during the years of exile and thereafter was his Jewishness.

After leaving Austria Torberg tried to rescue family members and associates, including the cabaretist Fritz Grünbaum. Appalled by the pro-Nazi sentiments in Switzerland he moved to France where he wrote for the exile journal *Die Österreichische Post*, published by Austrian monarchists. In 1939 he joined the Czech exile army. Designated an "Outstanding German Anti-Nazi Writer", Torberg managed to escape to the United States. His works at that time reflect the preoccupation with the Jewish tragedy. His protagonists try to find their bearings in a reality alien to them, as in *Mein ist die Rache* [Vengeance is Mine] and *Hier bin ich, mein Vater* [Here I Am, My Father], both of which address generational and political issues, particularly the topic of Jewish ethics in the context of National Socialism and the Holocaust, and the question how to reconcile one's own survival with the rights of others. *Die zweite Begegnung* [The Second Encounter] explores several topical issues, communism, homosexuality, and politics at the beginning of the Cold War.

In New York Torberg connected Austrian cabaret artists, including Hermann Leopoldi, Armin Berg, and Hans Kolitscher, and intellectuals around the weekly *Aufbau*. His hopes for a movie career in Hollywood came to naught. Dismayed about the susceptibility of certain segments of American society to radical right- and left-wing ideologies, Torberg decided to leave and take a part in shaping the new Austrian identity. Aided by his closest associates and with the support of the CIA he founded the Congress for Cultural Freedom. In 1951 he returned to Vienna where he wrote for the *Wiener Kurier* and the radio station *Rot-Weiss-Rot*, setting forth an uncompromisingly pro-Western programme. In 1954 he founded the cultural-political magazine *Forum*. These activities and his connections with prominent personalities made him visible and highly controversial.

Torberg's most significant contribution to postwar central European was keeping the legacy of German-Jewish culture and Vienna Jewry alive. He raised the awareness of Austria's Jewish history and the destroyed Ashkenazic culture. He became a model and mentor for the post-Shoah generation of Jewish intellectuals. His confidence in a European Jewish future is best expressed in the novella *Golems Wiederkehr* [Golem's Return]. Speaking from a distant future when the Nazis will have been forgotten, the narrator reveals that Jews have survived and emerged victorious. Conversely, *Süsskind von Trimberg* [Süsskind of Trimberg], emphasizes the bleak conditions of medieval

Jewish life. The cultural information conveyed in his fiction, the decidedly Jewish point of view, made Torberg one of the strongest Jewish voices in post-Shoah Austria.

DAGMAR C.G. LORENZ

Trilling, Lionel

US fiction writer and literary critic, 1905–1975

Born Lionel Mordecai Trilling in New York, 4 July 1905; studied at Columbia University, BA 1925, MA 1926, PhD 1938. Instructor, University of Wisconsin, 1926–27; Hunter College, 1927–32; assistant professor, 1939–45, associate professor, 1945–48, professor, 1948–65, George Edward Woodberry Professor of Literature and Criticism, 1964–70, and University Professor, 1970–74, Columbia University; George Eastman Visiting Professor, University of Oxford, 1964–65; Charles Eliot Norton Professor of Poetry, Harvard University, 1969–70; visiting fellow, All Souls College, Oxford, 1972–73. Married Diana Rubin, 1929; one son. Member, National Institute of Arts and Letters, 1951; American Academy of Arts and Sciences, 1952. Died in New York, 5 November 1975.

Selected Writings

Fiction
The Middle of the Journey, 1948
Of This Time, of That Place and Other Stories, edited by Diana Trilling, 1979

Other
Matthew Arnold, 1939
E.M. Forster, 1944
Editor, *The Portable Matthew Arnold*, 1949
Editor, *Selected Letters of John Keats*, 1950
The Liberal Imagination, 1950
The Opposing Self, 1955
A Gathering of Fugitives, 1956
Beyond Culture, 1965
Editor, with others, *The Experience of Literature*, 1967
Sincerity and Authenticity, 1972
Editor, with Harold Bloom, *Romantic Poetry and Prose*, 1973
Editor, with others, *The Oxford Anthology of English Literature*, 1973
Editor, with Harold Bloom, *Victorian Prose and Poetry*, 1973

Further Reading

Anderson, Quentin *et al.* (editors), *Art Politics and Will: Essays in Honor of Lionel Trilling*, New York: Basic Books, 1977
Boyers, Robert, *Lionel Trilling: Negative Capability and the Wisdom of Avoidance*, Columbia: University of Missouri Press, 1977
Chace, William M., *Lionel Trilling: Criticism and Politics*, Stanford, California: Stanford University Press, 1980
French, Philip, *Three Honest Men: Edmund Wilson, F.R. Leavis and Lionel Trilling: A Critical Mosaic*, Manchester: Carcanet New Press, 1980
Krupnick, Mark, *Lionel Trilling and the Fate of Cultural Criticism*, Evanston, Illinois: Northwestern University Press, 1986
Leitch, Thomas M., *Lionel Trilling: An Annotated Bibliography*, New York: Garland, 1993
O'Hara, Daniel T., *Lionel Trilling: The Work of Liberation*, Madison: University of Wisconsin Press, 1988
Rodden, John (editor), *Lionel Trilling and the Critics: Opposing Selves*, Lincoln: University of Nebraska Press, 1999
Shoben, Edward Joseph, *Lionel Trilling*, New York: Ungar, 1981
Tanner, Stephen L., *Lionel Trilling*, Boston: Twayne, 1988
Trilling, Diana, *The Beginning of the Journey: The Marriage of Diana and Lionel Trilling*, New York: Harcourt Brace, 1993

Lionel Trilling's first published writing appeared in a Jewish magazine, the *Menorah Journal*. Beginning when he was just 20, Trilling was one of a circle of Jews from comfortable middle-class backgrounds who proposed to write about Jewish authors and topics without the defensiveness or chauvinism that were the continuing traces of Jewish unease in America. Trilling wrote reviews of new books by Jewish writers such as Charles Reznikoff, Louis Untermeyer, and Ludwig Lewisohn, and a long essay, not published until after his death, on stereotypes of the Jew in English writing from Chaucer to George Eliot.

After the 1929 economic crash, the young contributors to the *Menorah Journal*, who had not previously been much concerned with political issues, moved to the political left. They quit the *Menorah Journal* and took their direction from Eliot E. Cohen, the magazine's former editor. They now involved themselves to one degree or another in communist activism. Trilling's formal involvement with the communists was very brief, lasting only about one year. In 1939, declaring his post-Marxist position in a symposium published by *Partisan Review*, he said flatly that he was centrally concerned as a critic not with the working class but with the attitudes of the group he referred to as the "educated middle class".

In 1947 Trilling published a novel, *The Middle of the Journey*, about some middle-class Stalinists facing a crisis of political belief in the late 1930s. In those years the Communist Party had become immensely more popular by playing down revolutionism and embracing certain American writers (such as Walt Whitman, Mark Twain, and John Steinbeck) who they recast as champions of the common man as celebrated in Soviet literature. Trilling's characters, except for Maxim Gifford, who was modelled on the real-life Whittaker Chambers, were all instantly recognizable as Jewish intellectuals. But Trilling made his drama seem unreal by staging it as a pastoral in summer-time Connecticut, rather than as a political-cultural melodrama in an Upper West Side (New York) apartment. One witty critic of the novel remarked on its "Episcopalian aroma".

Trilling's distaste for Jewish culture in America became explicit and unmistakable the next year. He had been asked by a journal, the *Contemporary Jewish Record*, to discuss the influence of the Jewish heritage on his work. It was clear from the unqualified certitude of his reply that Trilling had long been thinking out his position. "As the Jewish community now exists", he wrote, "it can give no sustenance to the American artist or intellectual who is born a Jew. And so far as I am aware it has not done so in the past." It's important to see that by "Judaism" or "Jewishness", Trilling was limiting his focus to what might be called the Jewish-American symbiosis. That relationship was so much more successful in terms of success and survival than the Jewish-German symbiosis, but so much inferior, Trilling would have said, in terms of achieved thought and sensibility.

In that CJR symposium, Trilling went on to comment on one particular manifestation of Jewish-American culture that he had known well. Trilling was especially eager to reject the *Menorah Journal*'s programme of "positive Jewishness", its ideal of a specifically Jewish self-realization. As Trilling now believed, the *Menorah Journal* had "fostered a willingness to accept exclusion . . . a willingness to be provincial and parochial." Trilling's case against Jewish parochialism appeared in February 1944. Inevitably, given the date, Trilling's anxiety about being provincial must itself seem provincial in the larger context of the destruction of Europe's Jews.

Trilling made a kind of peace with his own Jewishness in the curious essay "Wordsworth and the Rabbis". He began with a question: Why is Wordsworth not more attractive to the contemporary literary sensibility? (It happens that scholars and critics such as M.H. Abrams and Geoffrey Hartman were already at that time launched on studies that would bring about a revaluation of Wordsworth in the next generation.)

Trilling offers a reason for Wordsworth's being out of fashion. It is his Christianity. But after five pages Trilling suddenly puts aside this hypothesis in favour of one more radical: Wordsworth's feeling for ordinary life, his grave simplicity, and so on make him akin to the rabbis of Trilling's title. These were the rabbis of the early common era who composed the maxims that were published as the *Pirke Aboth*, or in translation the *sententiae* or Sayings of the Fathers. Readers familiar with Trilling's critical writing must have been astonished. After his mid-twenties he had written no major essay in which his Jewishness is even acknowledged. Readers of this critic, who had placed himself so selfconsciously in the secular liberal-humanist tradition of Matthew Arnold and E.M. Forster, can hardly have been ready for this dip into a tractate from a text, the Mishnah, that is composed mainly of rabbinical decisions.

Trilling tries to establish many affinities between the ancient rabbis and this Romantic poet with whom he describes himself as feeling a strong connection. But perhaps the most germane aspect of this essay as regards Trilling's Jewishness is his affectionate, nostalgic recall of his Hebrew school teacher and his devoted reading, as a boy, of the *Pirke Aboth*. If readers had known more about the family background of Lionel Mordecai Trilling, they might not have been as surprised. His own father, back in Russia, had prepared himself to be a rabbi, and Lionel himself became a rabbi of sorts, a rabbi of culture. In this fascinating essay, if nowhere else in Trilling's work, he found a way to integrate Judaism into his critique of modernity.

After 1950 Jews and Judaism appear infrequently in Trilling's writing. One reason no doubt is that anti-Semitism in American life and especially in higher education figured less importantly in the 1950s and especially the 1960s than when Trilling had been starting out. But there is one essay, on the Russian-Jewish writer Isaak Babel', that is worth reading insofar as it clarifies the Jewish resonance, as Trilling experienced it, of the conflict noted by Freud between civilization – Babel' as intellectual Jew – and instinctual life – the wild Cossack horsemen of the Ukraine whom Babel' admired and about whom he wrote in some of his best short stories.

MARK KRUPNICK

Tussman, Malka Heifetz

Russian-born US poet, 1893?–1987

Born Malke Kheyfets (Heifetz) in Volhynia, 1893, 1895, or 1896. Educated at home, then in Russian schools in Norinsk and Korostyen. Emigrated to Chicago, 1912. Married Shloyme Tussman at age 18; two sons. Lived in Milwaukee, Wisconsin. Taught in Yiddish secular school, 1924. Studied at University of Wisconsin and, briefly, University of California, Berkeley. Moved to Los Angeles, 1924; taught Yiddish to high school students at Workmen's Circle School, Boyle Heights. Instructor in Yiddish language and literature at University of Judaism, 1949. After husband's death in 1971, lived for year in Israel. Returned to Berkeley, 1972. Awarded Manger Prize, 1981. Died in Berkeley, 1987.

Selected Writings

Poetry
Lider, 1949
Mild mayn vild: lider [Mild My Wild], 1958
Shotns fun gedenkn [Shadows of Remembering], 1965
Bleter faln nit [Leaves do Not Fall], 1972
Unter dayn tseykhn: lider [Under Your Sign], 1974
Eating an Apple, translated by Marcia Falk, 1975
In *The Other Voice: Twentieth Century Women's Poetry in Translation*, edited by Joanna Bankier *et al.*, 1976
Am I Also You?, translated by Marcia Falk, 1977
Haynt iz eybik: lider, 1977
In *American Yiddish Poetry: A Bilingual Anthology*, edited by Benjamin Harshav and Barbara Harshav, 1986
In *The Penguin Book of Modern Yiddish Verse*, edited by Irving Howe, Ruth R. Wisse, and Khone Shmeruk, 1987
With Teeth in the Earth: Selected Poems, translated and edited by Marcia Falk, 1992

Further Reading

Diamant, Zeynvl, "Kheyfets-Tusman, Malke", *Leksikon fun der nayer yidisher literatur*, 3 (1960)
Hellerstein, Kathryn, "A Question of Tradition: Women Poets in Yiddish" in *Handbook of American-Jewish Literature*, edited by Lewis Fried, New York: Greenwood Press, 1988
Hellerstein, Kathryn, "From Ikh to Zikh: A Journey from I

to Self in Yiddish Poems by Women" in *Gender and Text in Modern Hebrew and Yiddish Literature*, edited by Naomi B. Sokoloff, Anne Lapidus Lerner, and Anita Norich, New York: Jewish Theological Seminary, 1992
Litvine, M., "Dos poetishe verk fun malke kheyfets-tuzman", *Di goldene keyt*, 89 (1976)
Sutskever, Avrom, "Haynt iz eybik (tsum toyt fun malke khetfets tuzman)", *Di goldene keyt*, 122 (1987)

Although she declared the natural rhythms of speech and breath as her poetic credo, at the peak of her powers the Yiddish poet Malka Heifetz Tussman introduced into Yiddish one of the most rigid verse forms, the triolet, and mastered another, the sonnet corona. A teacher of Yiddish language and literature in the US midwest and the west, Tussman published her six books of poetry relatively late in life, between 1949 and 1977. Tussman's mature poetry is characterized by a juxtaposition of sensuality and devotion that brings the poet close to the edge of blasphemy. In "Thunder My Brother" the poet identifies her voice with the thunder, a force of nature that challenges the order of things established by God's creation in Genesis and His giving of the Ten Commandments:

Thunder my brother,
My powerful brother,
Stones rolling on stones-your voice.
Like a forest, forceful, your voice.
What pleasure you take in making mountains rattle,
How happy you feel
When you bewilder creeping creatures in the valley.

Once,
Long ago
The storm-my father-
Rode on a dark cloud,
And stared at the other side of the Order-of-the-Universe,
Across to the chaos.
I, too,
Have a voice —
A voice of fearsome roaring
In the grip of my muteness.
And there are commandments
Forbidding me:
"Thou shalt not,
Thou shalt not"
O thunder,
My wild unbridled brother.

Born around the holiday of Shevuot, Tussman herself disputed the exact year, stating it variously as 1893, 1895, and 1896. She considered 15 May her American birthday. Her father was the third generation of the Hasidic Heifetz family to manage an estate in the village of her birth, Khaytshe or Bolshaya-Chaitcha, in the Ukrainian province of Volhynia. Tussman was the second of eight children; she and her siblings were educated in Hebrew, Yiddish, Russian, and English, initially by private tutors and later in the Russia schools in the nearby towns of Norinsk and Korostyen. As a young child, Tussman began to write poems in Russian about the poverty of the neighbouring peasants.

She came to the United States in 1912 and joined family members in Chicago. "Under terrible conditions she pursued her learning", as Tussman once wrote about herself. Her first Yiddish short story appeared in 1918, and her first poem in 1919. She also wrote in English for the Chicago anarchist publication, *Alarm*, in 1914.

Although she lived far from the centres of Yiddish letters, Tussman's poems, short stories, and essays appeared in the leading Yiddish newspapers and journals from 1918 onward. These publications included the New York papers *Fraye arbeter shtime* and *Der vokh*, as well as the journals *Oyfkum*, *Inzikh*, *Yidisher kemfer*, *Sviva*, *Kinder zhurnal*, and *Di tsukunft*; the Warsaw weekly *Literarishe bleter*; the Toronto literary magazine *Tint un feder*; and the Tel Aviv quarterly, *Di goldene keyt*. Her poems were represented in collections of Yiddish poetry, such as *Antologye – Mitvest-Mayrev* [From Midwest to North Pacific] and *Amerike in yidishn vort* [America in Yiddish Literature]. Until her death Tussman continued to work on a seventh volume of poetry, *Un ikh shmeykhl* [And I Smile], which has not been published.

Throughout her career as a poet, Tussman sustained literary friendships and extensive correspondence with Yiddish writers in the United States, Canada, Poland, France, and Israel, including the poets Kalman Marmor, Yankev Glatshteyn, H. Leyvik, Rokhl Korn, Kadye Molodovski, Melekh Ravitsh, and Abraham Sutzkever. She read poetry of many languages, modern and ancient, and exercised her poetic voice by translating poems by writers as various as Yeats, Rossetti, Auden, and Tagore into Yiddish. By maintaining a ferocious poetic independence from any school or movement, Tussman achieved a compressed lyrical style noted by the critic M. Litvine for its elliptical syntax and free verse rhythms that render the strophe inconspicuous but dense. Sutzkever praised her poetry for asserting an ever more flexible, youthful voice, the older the poet herself grew, as in "I Say":

I say to the Almighty:
You, eternal wanderer —
If my heart were pure,
I would invite
You for the night.

Tussman is important as a woman poet in Yiddish. Although she did not believe that poetry should be read or written in terms of gender, her poems are fuelled by an explicitly female sensuality. Denying any feminist orientation, she nonetheless acknowledged the difficulties that women writing poetry in Yiddish had, even in the heyday of Yiddish poetry in America, to publish their poems in periodicals or to find sponsors for the publication of their books. In an interview she once expressed her sense that women who excelled in writing poems for children, such as Molodovski, were often categorized by the Yiddish literary establishment as "merely children's poets" so that their other work remained unacknowledged. A poem written soon after the Holocaust, "I Am Woman", catalogues heroic women throughout Jewish history to establish a lineage for the Yiddish woman poet and to defy the Nazi destruction of Diaspora Jewry.

In her later years she taught informally and befriended a number of younger poets, many American-born and writing in English, who helped disseminate her poetry through their translations, including Eli Katz, Marcia Falk, Kathryn Hellerstein, and Daniel Marlin. She also served as a mentor for some younger Yiddish poets, of whom an Israeli recipient of the Manger Prize, Rokhl Fishman (1935–84) was the best known. Tussman thus served as a bridge between the generations of Yiddish poets who emigrated from eastern Europe and of those American-born Jewish poets who have taken up the task of making Yiddish poetry known to a readership that knows little Yiddish.

KATHRYN HELLERSTEIN

Tuwim, Julian

Polish poet and translator, 1894–1953

Born in Łódź, 13 September 1894, to a bank clerk and assimilationist wife. Made literary debut with poem "Prośba", *Kurier Warszawski*, 1913. Moved to Warsaw, 1916. Briefly studied law and philosophy at Warsaw University. Poems published in journal *Pro Arte et Studio*, founded 1916. Artistic director and co-writer of literary cabarets, Warsaw, 1917–32; one of five poets associated with monthly journal *Skamander* from 1920; also contributor, *Wiadomości Literackie* journal, from 1924, as well as satirical magazines. Following Nazi invasion, 1939, escaped to France by way of Romania; later moved to Portugal, Brazil, and United States; lived in New York and wrote for *Nowa Polska*, London, and other Polish-language publications, 1942–46. Returned to Poland, 1946. Participated in official literary and cultural activities under Communist regime; collector of books; editor of several anthologies; writer of musicals, librettos, songs, and monologues. Numerous awards, including Literary Prize of City of Łódź, 1928 and 1949; PEN Prize (for translation of works by Aleksandr Pushkin), 1935; State Literary Prize, first class, 1951. Supported Hebrew University, Jerusalem. Died after long illness in Zakopane, 27 December 1953.

Selected Writings

Collection
Dzieła [Works], 5 vols, 1955–64

Poetry
Czyhanie na Boga [Lying in Wait for God], 1918
Sokrates tańczący [Socrates the Dancer], 1920; as *The Dancing Socrates and Other Poems*, edited and translated by Adam Gillon, 1968
Siódma jesień [The Seventh Autumn], 1922
Wierszy tom czwarty [The Fourth Book of Poems], 1923
Słowa we krwi [Words in Blood], 1926
Do prostego człowieka [To the Simple Man], 1929
Rzecz Czarnoleska [The Czarnoles' Case], 1929
Biblia Cygańska [The Gypsy Bible], 1933
Jamark rymów [A Market of Rhymes], 1934
Treść gorejąca [Burning Matter], 1936
Bal w Operze [Ball at the Opera], 1946 (written 1936)
Kwiaty polskie [Polish Flowers], 1949 (written 1940–44; contains *Modlitwa*)
In *Voices within the Ark: The Modern Jewish Poets*, edited by Howard Schwartz and Anthony Rudolf, 1980
Wiersze wybrane [Selected Poems], 4th edition, 1986

For Children
Lokomotywa, Rzepka, Ptasie radio: napisal Julian Tuwim, 1938; as *Locomotive, the Turnip, the Birds' Broadcast: Rhymes, by Julian Tuwim*, 1939
Słoń Trąbalski [Trąbalski Elephant], 1938

Other
Pracowita Pszczółka: Kalendarz encyklopedyczno-informacyjny na rok [The Little Diligent Bee: An Encyclopedic-Informative Calendar for the Year], 1921
Czary i czarty polski; oraz, Wypisy czarnoksięskie [Devils and Polish Witchcraft; or, Witchcraft Anthology], 1923
Polski słownik pijacki i Antologia bachiczna [The Polish Drunkards' Dictionary and the Bacchus Anthology], 1935, 1959
My, Żydzi polscy [We Polish Jews], 1944
W oparach absurdu [In the Clouds of the Absurd], with Antoni Slonimski, 1958
Cicer cum caule, czyli groch z Kapustą [Cicer Cum Caule, or Peas with Cabbage or Topsy Turvy], 3 vols, 1958–63

Further Reading

Carpenter, Bogdana, *The Poetic Avant-Garde in Poland, 1918–1939*, Seattle: University of Washington Press, 1983
Jedlicka, Wanda and Marian Toporowski (editors), *Wspomnienia o Julianie Tuwimie*, Warsaw: Czytelnik, 1963
Matuszewski, Ryszard, *Literatura po wojnie*, 2nd edition, Warsaw: Książka i Wiedza, 1950
Matuszewski, Ryszard, *Literatura Polska lat 1918–1956*, Warsaw: Państwowe Zakłady Wydawnictw Szkolnych, 1958
Matuszewski, Ryszard and Seweryn Pollak (editors), *Poezja polska, 1914–1939*, Warsaw: Czytelnik, 1962; 3rd edition, 2 vols, 1984
Matuszewski, Ryszard, *Literatura polska, 1939–1991*, Warsaw: Wydawnictwo Szkolne i Pedagogiczne, 1992; 2nd edition 1995
Ratajczak, Józef, *Julian Tuwim*, Poznań: Rebis, 1995
Sawicka, Jadwiga, *Julian Tuwim*, Warsaw: Wiedza Powszechna, 1986
Stradecki, Janusz, *Julian Tuwim: Bibliografia*, Warsaw: Państwowy Instytut Wydawniczy, 1959
Tuwim, Irena, *Łódzkie pory roku* [Łódź Seasons], Kraków, 1956; 2nd edition, Warsaw: Czytelnik, 1958

Tuwim, who published nine volumes of poetry in the period up to 1939, is known as the "renewer of 20th-century Polish poetry" and as probably the most popular lyric poet in the Poland of the inter-war years, while at the same time being considered difficult to translate on account of his coinages and his immense linguistic range. In his language experiments, this "discoverer of the musicality of the Polish language", as a critic called him in 1936, is akin to Bolesław

Leśmian. His cabaret texts also set new standards, and, together with Konstanty Ildefons Galczynski, he was considered the father of this genre in postwar Poland. After his return to Poland, where the epic *Kwiaty polskie* [Polish Flowers], which he had written in exile, was published in 1949, he never returned to his old form and concentrated mainly on translation and published anthologies.

Tuwim's rise began with the restoration of the Polish state after World War I, when a new mood of enthusiasm prevailed. Alongside his poetry cycles, it was his satirical and historical prose (e.g. *Pracowita Pszczółka: Kalendarz encyklopedyczno-informacyjny na rok* [The Little Diligent Bee: An Encyclopedic-Informative Calendar for the Year] or *Polski słownik pijacki* [The Polish Drunkards' Dictionary]) and his children's books (*Lokomotywa* [The Locomotive] and *Słoń Trąbalski* [Trąbalski Elephant] etc.), which had made him widely known and loved. Tuwim owed his fame to his early writings, risqué in expression, about desires as in "Wiosna" and peripheral social groups such as whores or drunks in "Chrystus Miasta" [Christ of the City] (from the cycle *Czyhanie na Boga* [Lying in Wait for God] of 1918). These provoked many indignant reactions (even to the point of Tuwim being called the "Jewish pornographer") but heralded at the same time the "beginning of a new era" in the history of Polish lyric poetry, to which until then the "Apollonian" poetry of Młoda Polska [Young Poland], particularly Leopold Staff, had paid homage. Instead of the hitherto mystical sadness, the glorification, in an escapist fashion, of rural life and of modernism, a "Dionysian and Epicurean" and increasingly socially critical lyricism with elements of futurism and German Expressionism emerged. The new themes with which the Skamandrites as a group dealt, such as the progress of civilization and technology, the feverishness of city life and politics, demanded a new language that did not shy from "unpoetic" expression and was influenced by Bergson, Rimbaud, Bal'mont, Whitman, and Maiakovskii, as well as Pushkin and Heine. Tuwim, an outstanding connoisseur of world literature, embraced these influences.

Tuwim was an assimilated Jew and had grown up in the humanistically enlightened atmosphere of a family which felt itself to be Polish but never denied its Jewish roots, without being religious. In his industrial home town of Łódź, the "Polish Manchester", Poles, Germans, and Jews lived side-by-side relatively peacefully. Tuwim, a professed pacifist, who had already caricatured the madness of World War I and the prevailing petit-bourgeois militarism prevalent in Poland in the ironic-reflective poem "Do generałów" of 1923, and in his bitingly derisive poem "Pif Paf" of 1931, seems to have anticipated the emergence of fascism at an early stage. "Pif Paf" is about a fair where people amuse themselves at a shooting gallery, which joyfully "revives" the spectre of Verdun and the millions of dead.

One of the millions of dead of the next World War was Tuwim's mother. While he sat helplessly worrying about her in New York, she was shot by the Germans in 1942 or 1943 in a sanatorium in Otwock because she was a Jew. After his return to Poland, Tuwim established a foundation in his mother's name, which supported the municipal library in Inowłódź, the summer haven where he had spent childhood holidays with his mother and sister. He also dedicated a poem to his mother and for the rest of his life seems to have suffered from the fact that he, like his sister, was able to escape and survive, while she had to die, and he mourned "my Jewish, my Polish mother".

In the pre-war period, he had tended to the left and always identified with the outcasts of society, which included both the exploited proletariat and the Jewish minority living in a climate of anti-Semitism in Poland. His sentimental poem "Żydek" of 1926 from the cycle *Słowa we krwi* [Words in Blood] bears witness to this. Here is a small, mad, Jewish youth, who begs in the backyards of the town and to whom the poet, instead of coins, throws down from the window his own heart wrapped in a newspaper as a gesture of brotherly support. At this time, however, the Jewish theme scarcely entered into Tuwim's work, other than as a polemic response to the anti-Semites, occasionally of an almost self-hating nature in texts that emphasize his great distance from the "haggling Jew" or "caftan Jew" so foreign to him. The political nationalist right felt provoked by Tuwim nevertheless and frequently subjected him to bitter attacks in their pages. They accused his poems of exuding the "talmudic spirit" and being "foreign" and "permeated by Semitism". These attacks were stepped up in the 1930s and depressed Tuwim greatly, something that found expression sometimes in sarcasm but increasingly in a resigned mood in his writing – as evidenced as early as 1930 by one of his best-known poems "Mieszkańcy" [Inhabitants]. In this he expresses his complete loathing of a "terrible" reactionary, bourgeois, nouveau riche stratum, which complacently and sanctimoniously clings to its absurd principles. In 1932 he wrote the poem "Et arceo" with the programmatic opening lines "Odi profanum vulgus", denouncing the vulgarity of Polish society of the time, a society in which he feels alienated and sad. In 1936 Tuwim finally wrote the visionary poem "Bal w operze", which could not be published in full until after the war. Here he portrays an abominable waxworks of an ailing society, where the fascists have seized power after the death of Marshal Józef Piłsudski. Originally, he prefaced the poem with a motto from the Revelation of St John and, at the end, Satan takes over command, which probably represents the end of the world. Since Tuwim was a Polish patriot with a deep love for his homeland and Polish culture, the spectres of destruction, which he already sensed so clearly at that time, pained him greatly.

Tuwim himself was able to evade the destruction, but his world was destroyed and during the troubled years, learning of the murder of European Jews while in exile in America, he professed his Jewish faith anew. In 1944 he wrote the manifesto *My, Żydzi polscy* [We Polish Jews] in which he declares his affiliation to the Polish landscape and Polish culture, because "Mickiewicz and Chopin meant more to him than Shakespeare and Beethoven". At the same time he declares that he accepts his membership of the "Jewish church" and his "anguished brotherhood with the Jews" through the "baptism of blood". Despite the Christian vocabulary, which appears inappropriate here, Tuwim had never taken the step of being baptized, unlike many of his contemporaries.

ELVIRA GROEZINGER
translated by Karen Goulding

Tzara, Tristan

Romanian-born French poet and Dadaist, 1896–1963

Born Samuel Rosenstock in Moineste, 4 April 1896. Studied at schools in Moineste and at French-language school in Bucharest; studied philosophy and mathematics at Bucharest University, 1914–15; continued studies in Zürich, 1915. Became habitué of Cabaret Voltaire, Zürich; with Hugo Ball, Richard Helsenbeck, and Hans Arp founded Dada movement, 1916; wrote exclusively in French from this time. Emigrated to France, 1919. Settled in Paris; associated with Francis Picabia, Paul Éluard, Louis Aragon, and André Breton, in Dada activities, 1920; following collapse of Dada and period of isolation, joined Surrealists, 1929; expelled from Surrealists, largely because of pro-Soviet views, 1935; joined Communist Party, 1936. Spent World War II in unoccupied southern France, writing for clandestine Resistance publications. Naturalized French citizen, 1945. Lectured on poetry in various European cities, 1946 onwards. Ceased to be militant Communist after Soviet repression of Hungarian Uprising, 1956. Awarded Taormina International Grand Prix for Poetry, 1961. Died in Paris, 24 December 1963.

Selected Works

Poetry

La Première Aventure céleste de Monsieur Antipyrine, 1916; as *The First Celestial Adventure of Mister Benzedrine*, translated by Elmer Peterson, 1996
Vingt-cinq poèmes [Twenty-Five Poems], 1918
De Nos Oiseaux [Of Our Birds], 1923
L'Homme approximatif, 1931; as *Approximate Man*, translated by Mary Ann Caws, 1973
L'Antitête, 1933
Grains et issues [Seeds and Outlets], 1935
Midis gagnés [Middays Won], 1939
Terre sur terre [Earth upon Earth], 1946
La Fuite: poème dramatique en quatre actes et un épilogue, 1947
Parler seul [Speaking Alone], 1950
13 Poems, translated by Franklin Rosemont, 1969
Destroyed Days: A Selection of Poems 1943–55, translated by Lee Harwood, 1971
Cosmic Realities Vanilla Tobacco Dawnings, translated by Lee Harwood, 1975
Selected Poems, translated by Lee Harwood, 1975
Primele poeme / First Poems, translated by Michael Impey and Brian Swann, 1976
Chansons Dada: Selected Poems, translated by Lee Harwood, 1987

Play

Le Coeur à gaz, 1921; as *The Gas Heart*, translated by Michael Benedikt in *Modern French Theatre*, edited by Benedikt and George E. Wellwarth, 1964

Other

Cinéma, calendrier du coeur abstrait, maisons, 1920
Sept manifestes Dada, 1924; reprinted in *Lampisteries, précédées des Sept manifestes Dada*, 1963; as *Seven Dada Manifestos and Lampisteries*, translated by Barbara Wright, 1977
Essai sur la situation de la poésie [Essay on the State of Poetry], 1931
"Memoirs of Dadism" in *Axel's Castle*, by Edmund Wilson, 1931
"Poems and Prose Extracts" in *Surrealism*, by Julien Levy, 1936
Le Surréalisme et l'après-guerre, 1947
Zürich, Dadaco, Dadaglobe: The Correspondence between Richard Huelsenbeck, Tristan Tzara and Kurt Wolff, 1916–1924, edited by Richard Sheppard, 1982

Further Reading

Browning, Gordon Frederick, *Tristan Tzara: The Genesis of the Dada Poem; or, From Dada to Aa*, Stuttgart: Akademischer Verlag Heinz, 1979
Caws, Mary Ann, *The Poetry of Dada and Sur-realism*, Princeton, New Jersey: Princeton University Press, 1970
Caws, Mary Ann, *The Inner Theatre of Recent French Poetry: Cendrars, Tzara, Peret, Artaud, Bonnefoy*, Princeton, New Jersey: Princeton University Press, 1972
Hackett, Cecil Arthur, *Anthology of Modern French Poetry*, Oxford: Blackwell, and New York: Macmillan, 1952
Harwood, Lee, *Tristan Tzara: A Bibliography*, London: Aloes, 1974
Hulten, Pontus, *The Surrealists Look at Art: Eluard, Aragon, Soupault, Breton, Tzara*, Venice, California: Lapis Press, 1990
Ko, Won, *Buddhist Elements in Dada: A Comparison of Tristan Tzara, Takahashi Shinkichi and Their Fellow Poets*, New York: New York University Press, 1977
Lemaître, Georges Edouard, *From Cubism to Surrealism in French Literature*, Cambridge, Massachusetts: Harvard University Press, 1941
Levy, Julien, *Surrealism*, New York: Black Sun Press, 1936
Lindsay, Jack, *Meetings with Poets*, London: Muller, and New York: Ungar, 1968
Peterson, Elmer, *Tristan Tzara: Dada and Surrational Theorist*, New Brunswick, New Jersey: Rutgers University Press, 1971

It has always been questionable whether Tzara was actually the "founder" of the word "Dada" or not. Both André Breton and Francis Picabia suggested that Tzara did not discover the word at all, but it was Hans Arp, and Arp suggested as much in a 1949 confession to Robert Motherwell. However, Eugène Jolas suggested it was neither Arp nor Tzara, but rather both he and Hugo Ball discovered the word by perusing a German–French dictionary. So the distinction of being the progenitor of the word may belong to Tzara and may not. Likewise, if one looks through books attesting to be works on French writers of the 20th century, one is apt not to find Tzara among them or, if he is, he is there in scant supply. These two items, Tzara's alleged founding of "Dada" and his marginal association with French letters, are significant in relation to his Jewishness since, like his Jewishness, he was somehow disenfranchised from the community in which he lived.

It's certainly not surprising that the sole purpose of Dada

was, in effect, to "humiliate" art and, as Tzara himself said, to assign it to "a subordinate place in the supreme movement measured only in terms of life". It would seem that just as he was himself a member of a disenfranchised society (i.e. a Jew) he would be eager to disenfranchise himself from any well-founded, easily recognized art movement and to ally himself with something completely unconventional, something that advocated "gratutitousness", something whose focus was to undermine the mundane and render valorous that which denigrated the pedestrian. For example:

> To make a Dadaist poem:
> Take a newspaper.
> Take a pair of scissors.
> Choose an article as long as you are planning to make your poem.
> Cut out the article.
> Then cut out each of the words that make up this article and put them in a bag.
> Shake it gently.
> Then take out the scraps one after the other in the order in which they left the bag.
> Copy conscientiously.
> The poem will be like you.
> And here you are a writer, infinitely original and endowed with a sensibility that is charming though beyond the understanding of the vulgar.

This philosophy can be seen in his major works. Tzara was a prolific writer whose literary talents spanned the writing of narrative fiction and nonfiction, theatre and poetry, but throughout his oeuvre what is clearly seen are his poetic sensibility and his poetic imagination. What re-emerges in his writing, like a poetry of leitmotifs, are such themes as the polarized play of sun and shade, motion and rest, perfection and imperfection, themes that, in a way, reflect the notion of a "wanderer," someone caught in between the poles of Zen and Kabbalah.

In his *Sept manifestes Dada* Tzara writes that Dada is the meeting place of contradiction, "the point where the *yes* and the *no* meet, not solemnly in the castles of human philosophies, but very simply on street corners like dogs and grasshoppers", a position that sounds very Zen in and of itself since Zen is not a doctrine, nor a set of ideas nor a position.

> It is not subsumable under any sort of 'ism'. It cannot be classified as either theism, atheism, or agnosticism. It is affiliated with no particular school of philosophy; it is no closer to idealism than to materialism. It has no view about the nature of reality; it formulates no system of ethics, propounds no political ideology . . . Zen will be found not in the words themselves, but only in penetrating the living source from which come these words and from which an infinity of other wordings could come. (in the words of Suzuki)

The work is replete with allusions to being and non-being, a state of humanness that is a fundamental part of the Zen (non) philosophy. In his *Midis gagnés* he writes of "a more luminous life . . . which will dazzle us by the lightness and facility of its understanding of things and of beings".

Whether conscious or not of those luminous images so indicative of his early work, Tzara is indebted to the Kabbalists and masters of Jewish mysticism and although Tzara never directly addresses the notions of Kabbalah, they are everywhere apparent. Even when he pays homage to poets such as Apollinaire, Reverdy, Rimbaud, and Corbière, Tzara always refers to their work in terms of this notion of luminosity and as late as 1953 he speaks of the "poetic fields which are electrically charged by certain conduit images . . ."

According to Kabbalah, the soul strives to play a role in the completion of the universe and to contemplate the miracle that is Creation, in order to achieve an awareness of itself and its beginnings; and, eventually, to return to the source without becoming entirely identified with it. The return is to that inexhaustible source of light and life that the Jewish masters called "divine thought".

In a way, Tzara's poetry was a reflection of his life's pursuit, his quest, for "the light" and for a kind of completion, a wholeness that, in his masterpiece, *L'Homme approximatif*, renders him incomplete since that 19-part poem is often laden with incompleteness. Just as the entire poem strives to achieve a kind of completion with two sets of ten chapters, it does not. Just as each line strives to achieve a kind of completion with an end point, it does not. Just as each stanza strives to achieve a kind of completion without typographical intrusion, it does not. It is, in fact, a poem that is in a state of constantly achieving without quite attaining and through it all there are the allusions to "the clockface of the hour alone living in the sun", or "lives repeating themselves to infinity to atomic sparseness", or "dazzling whirlwinds", or celestial longings or, as in the end, the panoply of "slow furnaces" and fires that brighten and grow and climb and bark and flee all of which end in the "unshakable advent of its flame". Of course, none of this directly reflects his Jewish religiosity, but all of it reflects a kind Jewish mysticism that becomes more than a mere parcel of his writing.

MARK AXELROD

U

Uris, Leon

US fiction writer and dramatist, 1924–

Born Leon Marcus Uris in Baltimore, 3 August 1924. Studied at schools in Baltimore. Served in Marine Corps, 1942–45. Married, first, Betty Beck, 1945; divorced 1965; second, Margery Edwards, 1968; wife died, 1969; third, Jill Peabody, 1970; three children. Deliveryman, San Francisco *Call-Bulletin*, late 1940s; full-time writer since 1950. Awards include Daroff Memorial Award and American Academy grant, both 1959.

Selected Writings

Novels
Battle Cry, 1953
The Angry Hills, 1955
Exodus, 1959
Mila 18, 1961
Armageddon: A Novel of Berlin, 1964
Topaz, 1967
Q B VII, 1970
Trinity, 1976
The Haj, 1984
Mitla Pass, 1988
Redemption, 1995
A God in Ruins, 1999

Plays
Ari, 1971

Screenplays and documentaries: *Battle Cry*, 1955; *Gunfight at the OK Corral*, 1957; *Israel*, 1959

Other
Exodus Revisited, 1960; as *In the Steps of Exodus*, 1962
Ireland, a Terrible Beauty: The Story of Ireland Today, with Jill Uris, 1975
Jerusalem: Song of Songs, with Jill Uris, 1981

Further Reading

Cain, Kathleen Shine, *Leon Uris: A Critical Companion*, Westport, Connecticut: Greenwood Press, 1998
Hill, Mavis M. and L. Norman Williams, *Auschwitz in England: A Record of a Libel Action*, London: MacGibbon and Kee, and New York: Stein and Day, 1965

From his first novel, *Battle Cry*, to his last to come out during the 20th century, *A God in Ruins*, Leon Uris's works have repeatedly been on bestseller lists. His blockbuster, *Exodus*, was a run-away bestseller and was made into an extremely popular movie. However, few critics take him seriously as an author.

Uris's works are usually classified as historical fiction, although the history he writes about occurred for the most part during his own lifetime. His works are carefully researched, so much so that some reviewers label some of them nonfiction novels. In *Battle Cry* he treats in fictional form his own experiences in the United States Marine Corps in the Pacific during World War II. *The Angry Hills* is set during the Nazi occupation of Greece in World War II; the story is supposedly based on the exploits of one of Uris's relatives in the Greek underground. In *Topaz* and *Armageddon: A Novel of Berlin* he deals with aspects of the Cold War: the Cuban missile crisis and a Soviet spy ring in France in the former and the Berlin airlift in the latter. In *Exodus* he examines the founding of and early history of Israel, including parts of the Holocaust and events before the Holocaust that eventually led to the formation of the State of Israel. He returns to the history of Israel in *The Haj* and *Mitla Pass* and returns to the Holocaust in *Mila 18*, a story set for the most part in the Warsaw ghetto during the uprising against the Nazis, and *QB VII*, a novel about a trial held in Queen's Bench VII: a libel suit Adam Kelno brings against a writer named Abe Cady for exposing Kelno's actions during the Holocaust.

Trinity and *Redemption* concern the struggle for independence in Ireland, going into great detail about the horrors of English rule. Only *A God in Ruins*, a tale about a man who eventually becomes president of the United States, cannot be classified as historical fiction; in fact, it is set in the beginning of the 21st century, ending 19 January 2009, so it could loosely be treated as futuristic fiction.

Central to Uris's fiction is the larger-than-life hero, a strong but gentle and intelligent man capable of enduring tremendous hardship and of achieving magnificent feats in the service of a just cause. Critics often credit Uris with trying to destroy the stereotype of the male Jew as a weak intellectual afraid of anything physical. In its place, however, other critics say that Uris combines the more usual intellectual stereotype with another kind of stereotypical Jew, the strong man of the sort Ernest Hemingway uses in his portrayal of Robert Cohen in *The Sun Also Rises*, Daniel Fuchs uses in his portrayal of the hoodlums in *Summer in*

Williamsburg, and Philip Roth parodies in his portrait of Ron Patimkin and the whole Patimkin family in *Goodbye, Columbus*. Critics also often mention the one-sidedness of Uris's treatments. In *Exodus* and *The Haj*, especially, critics say that his Jews are supermen and his Arabs are demonized. Others claim that the portraits of both are fairly realistic.

At the centre of Uris's works on Jewish themes, especially *Exodus*, is the heroic Jew. Yet in *Topaz* he has the same kind of hero, André Devereaux, who is not Jewish but helped Jews escape from the Nazis in occupied France during World War II; and in *Trinity* and *Redemption* he has a similar kind of hero, Conor Larkin, only Conor is Irish-Catholic. In *A God in Ruins* he brings together his Jewish and Irish-Catholic supermen in the person of Quinn Patrick O'Connell, who is adopted by an Irish-Catholic couple and brought up believing he is Irish-Catholic but, as he runs for president, discovers that his biological parents are Jewish.

Exodus is Uris's best known work. In it he treats the heroic efforts to create and maintain a Jewish nation in the Middle East. In his vision the Jews survive Russian, Polish, and Arab pogroms, the Holocaust, British betrayal, and Arab invasions to forge a state in a hostile land. Barak Ben Canaan and his son, Ari Ben Canaan, are instrumental in creating that state. Barak is a diplomat who helps get the United Nations to vote for Israeli independence and get arms for the fledgling state. Ari serves in the Haganah (the Jewish defence force) before World War II and fights for Britain – really against the Nazis – during World War II. Then, ironically, he has to fight against Britain, trying to transport Jewish refugees who are interned on Cyprus to Israel and helping Israel gain its independence. Sometimes he works by subterfuge, as he does on Cyprus, and through non-violent resistance, as he does once he has the children aboard the ship *Exodus*. He engages in actual combat when he rescues from prison his uncle Akiva and Dov Landau, a young Holocaust survivor who has joined the Maccabees, a terrorist Jewish group. In this action he gets terribly wounded, and Kitty Fremont, an American Gentile, nurses him back to health.

Ari also fights heroically in the Israeli War for Independence. Kitty, who loves him and whom he loves, says that Ari "comes from a breed of supermen" and for that reason she can never have a love affair with him; but when she sees him crying, thus showing that he is really human, she becomes his lover.

Throughout his writings, then, Uris concentrates on ways in which strong individuals, almost always male, influence the course of history and influence those around them. His books glorify the strong individual at the same time that they show the kinds of loneliness that often plague that individual. They also glorify certain causes, including, of course, the desire for and reality of Israeli independence, the desire for and reality of Irish independence, and the need to continue to work for independence and freedom for all Jews and Irishmen as well as a just settlement to the problems of Northern Ireland and the Middle East.

RICHARD TUERK

V

Viertel, Berthold

Austrian poet, essayist, and film director, 1885–1953

Born in Vienna, 28 June 1885. Studied philosophy and drama. Writer and actor for Cabaret Simplizissimus; contributor, *Die Fackel*, 1912–14. Served in Austro-Hungarian army, 1914–18. Married Salomea Steuermann, 1918 (actress, as Salka Viertel; died 1978); son, Peter Viertel, novelist and dramatist. Stage director in Dresden, Berlin, Düsseldorf, 1918–23; founder and director, Die Truppe, Expressionist theatre group, Berlin, 1923; director and dramaturg (dramatic adviser), Freie Volksbühne theatre company, 1919–28; drama critic and editor of literary section, *Prager Tagblatt*; film director, Berlin, 1925–28, Hollywood and various British studios, 1928–47. Broadcast anti-Nazi programmes on BBC, 1939; home in Hollywood became centre for German and Austrian exile community during World War II. Moved to Switzerland, 1947; stage director in Zürich, 1947–53, Salzburg, 1949–53, Akademietheater and Burgtheater, both in Vienna, 1949–53. Died in Vienna, 24 September 1953.

Selected Writings

Poetry
Die Bahn [The Track], 1921
Fürchte dich nicht! neue Gedichte [Don't Be Afraid], 1941
Der Lebenslauf [The Curriculum Vitae], 1946
Dass ich in dieser Sprache schreibe: gesammelte Gedichte, edited by Günther Fetzer, 1981
Das graue Tuch: Gedichte, edited by Konstantin Laiser and Eberhard Frey, 1994

Novel
Das Gnadenbrot [Charity], 1927

Play
Die schoene Seele [The Beautiful Soul], 1925

Essays
Theaterwirkung [The Effect of the Theatre], 1913
Karl Kraus: ein Character und die Zeit [Karl Kraus: A Character and His Time], 1921
Die schöpferische Tätigkeit des Regisseurs [The Creative Work of the Stage Director], 1925
Regie: Interpretation [Stage Directing: Interpretation], 1925
Schriften zum Theater [Writings on Theatre], edited by Gerd Heidenreich, 1970
Tribüne und Aurora: Briefwechsel 1940–1949 / Wieland Herzfelde und Berthold Viertel, edited by Friedrich Pfäfflin, 1990
Kindheit eines Cherub: autobiographische Fragmente, 1991
Translated Tennessee Williams's *The Glass Menagerie*, *A Streetcar Named Desire*, *Camino Real*, and *The Rose Tattoo*; also *All My Sons*, by Arthur Miller.

Further Reading

Ginsberg, Ernst (editor), *Berthold Viertel: Dichtungen und Dokumente: Gedichte, Prosa, autobiographische Fragmente*, Munich: Kösel, 1956
Heidenreich, Gerd (editor), appendix to Viertel's *Schriften zum Theater*, Munich: Kösel, 1970
Jansen, Irene, *Berthold Viertel: Leben und künstlerische Arbeit im Exil*, New York: Peter Lang, 1992
Viertel, Salka, *The Kindness of Strangers*, New York: Holt Rinehart, 1969

Viertel's first literary activities began in Vienna where he regularly wrote for Karl Kraus's *Die Fackel* and the cabaret Simplizissimus. In addition, he wrote Expressionist poems, such as "Die Spur" or "Die Bahn" [The Track]. In 1911 he began his theatre career as dramatic adviser and stage director.

All his life Viertel was entirely committed to the theatre: "Jede Inszenierung beginnt als grosse Liebe. Wie schlecht das Stück auch sein mag." [Every staging begins as a great love, no matter how bad the play may be.] In 1922 Viertel moved to Berlin, where he was employed by the Deutsches Theater and the Volksbühne. One year later he established his own collective theatre group "Jenseits von Trust und Startum, Betrieb und Organisation" [Beyond stardom and trusts, business and organization]. The project only lasted for six months before it failed because of financial problems. During the following years Viertel worked as a freelance director in Berlin and Düsseldorf. It was in the work of Expressionist playwrights such as Sternheim and Kaiser that Viertel discovered "the drama of feeling" he was looking for. Apart from contemporary dramatists, he always considered Shakespeare to be one of the greatest dramatists of all times. Disillusioned with society, Viertel and his contemporaries fought for a revolution, believing that it must first take place in the human soul. The focus on the extreme subjectivism, however, left little foothold for political thought or constructive action. Like his contemporaries, Viertel at that time followed the radical vision of an integrated, total theatre.

In late 1927 the well-known film director F.W. Murnau invited him to work in Hollywood. Viertel accepted the offer and emigrated to America in 1928, together with his wife Salka. From then on he worked as a successful stage and film director, both in the USA and Europe. During the following years, he directed several films and wrote scripts for Fox, Warner Brothers, and Paramount. Crucial for his later film experiments was the encounter with Serge Eisenstein in 1930, with whom he continued to stay in close contact.

Back in Berlin in 1933, he was asked to adapt Hans Fallada's successful novel *Kleiner Mann – was nun?* [Little Man – What Now?] for the screen. After the Nazis came to power, he had to emigrate and temporarily lived in Vienna, Prague, Paris, and London. In 1939 he emigrated to the USA, but this time stayed in New York, where he contributed to various exile journals and helped to found the Aurora Press. It was during the 1940s that he resumed his work as stage director, now with the focus on anti-fascist plays, especially Bertolt Brecht's *The Private Life of the Master Race*.

The poems of his American exile are extremely bitter, as for example "Das anständige Leben": "Das anständige Leben ist es heute,/ im Gefängnis verwahrt zu sein;/ Im Konzentrationslager eingesammelt;/ In der Folterkammer verköstigt;/ Oder auf der Flucht begriffen" [The decent life of today is to be kept in prison, herded in a concentration camp, fed in the torture-chamber, or to be forced to flee]. The National Socialists' crimes are the major topic in his poems. His writing also reflects the exile that rendered him a stranger: "Nirgendwo war ich daheim, mich einzureihen vermochte ich nicht" [I was nowhere at home, unable to adapt].

After a production of Karl Kraus's *Die letzten Tage der Menschheit* he returned to Europe. Zürich was his first stop, where, contemplating the problems of staging in 1949, Viertel made a few observations on the offputtingly aggressive language that dominated the European stage:

> Aber nicht nur schaltete diese Art Pathetik das selbständige Denken des Zuhörers aus, wenn es sich darum handelte, ihm bestimmte Gedankengänge durch herausgeschmetterte, kolbenschlagartig wiederholte Begründungen beizubringen und ihm gewisse Texte und Formulierungen beizubringen und ihm gewisse Texte und Formulierungen einzuhämmern, sie beinträchtigte auch das Gefühl, indem sie es überrumpelte, überbot und überdröhnte.
>
> [But that pathetic kind of speech did not only eliminate the spectator's ability to think, trying to impose upon him certain reasons, texts and formulas, it also took away the spectator's freedom by attacking, exaggerating, and drowning his feelings.]

After an epoch which had deprived the individual of his thoughts and critical faculties, Viertel strove to restore the spectator's right to feel. From 1949 until his death Viertel worked in Vienna, Berlin, and Salzburg, directing plays by Gor'kii, Kleist, Ibsen, and others.

The most important feature of Viertel's work was his absolute commitment to the work of art, a commitment that respected the author's intentions instead of forcing the play into a different shape. He was never merely tempted to invent techniques or devices to cover up deficiencies of the plays. All his life he was concerned with the faithful rendition of the play he was going to stage, or as one of his best friends, Brecht, put it: he was a "fanatic of the stage".

BIRGIT HAAS

Vigée, Claude

French poet and essayist, 1921–

Born Claude Strauss in Bischwiller, Alsace, 3 January 1921. Learned to speak French, western Yiddish, and Alsatian. Following Nazi invasion, evacuated with family from Bischwiller, then expelled from Alsace, 1940. Participant in Jewish resistance in Toulouse, using nom de guerre "Vigée" ("J'ai vie / chai ani"), 1940–42. Emigrated to United States, 1943. Married cousin, Evelyne, 1947; two children. Studied at Ohio State University, PhD 1945. Taught at Ohio State University, and Wellesley College; Chairman, Department of European Literature, Brandeis University. Emigrated to Israel, 1960. Professor of French and Comparative Literature, Hebrew University, Jerusalem, 1963–83. Awards include Prix des Lettres de la Fondation du Judaisme français, 1994; Grand Prix de Poésie de l'Academie française, 1996.

Selected Writings

Poetry

L'Été indien [Indian Summer], 1957
Moisson de Canaan [Canaan Harvest], 1967
La Lune d'hiver [Winter Moon], 1970
Le Soleil sous la mer [The Sun beneath the Sea], 1972
Délivrance du souffle [Freeing the Breath], 1977
Les Orties noires [Black Nettles], 1984
Le Feu d'une nuit d'hiver [Fire of a Winter Night], 1989
Apprendre La Nuit [Learning the Night], 1991
Dans Le Silence de l'Aleph [In the Aleph's Silence], 1992
Flow Tide: Selected Poetry and Prose, translated by Anthony Rudolf, 1992
Aux Portes du labyrinthe [At the Gates of the Labyrinth], 1996
La Lucarne aux étoiles [Skylight to the Stars], 1998

Other

Les Artistes de la faim [The Hunger Artists], 1960
Révolte et Louanges [Revolt and Praise], 1962
L'Art et le démonique [Art and the Demonic], 1978
L'Extase et l'errance [Ecstasy and Wandering], 1982
Pâque de la parole [Passover of Words], 1983
Le Parfum et la cendre [Perfume and Ash], 1984
La Faille du regard [Fault in the Gaze], 1987
Le Puits d'eaux vives [The Well of Living Waters], with Victor Malka, 1993
Un Panier de houblon [A Basket of Hops], 2 vols, 1994–95
Treize Inconnus de la Bible [Thirteen Unknowns in the Bible], with Victor Malka, 1996

Vision et Silence dans la poétique juive [Vision and Silence in Jewish Poetics], 1999

Translations of Rainer Maria Rilke, 1950, 1957, 1989; David Seter, 1965; David Rokeah, 1968; Yvan Goll, 1971, 1988; T.S. Eliot's *Four Quartets*, 1992

Further Reading

Lartichaux, Jean-Yves, *Claude Vigée*, Paris: Seghers, 1978
Peras, Hélène and Michèle Finck (editors), *La Terre et le Souffle: recontre autour de Claude Vigée*, Paris: Michel, 1992
Rudolf, Anthony, "Interview with Claude Vigée", *London Magazine*, 35/7–8 (October–November 1995)
Silverman, G.E., *Jerusalem Post* (11 December 1970)

Slowly but surely Claude Vigée has become one of the most important living *Jewish* writers (as opposed to writers who happen to be Jewish) in any language. Vigée grew up in a relatively settled situation, Jewish, French and Alsatian, on the shores of the Rhine, but his world was irrevocably shattered by Hitler, whose imperial policies and genocidal ambitions forced the young poet to leave his homeland. Always deeply rooted in Jewish history and myth and drawn ineluctably to meditate on origins and roots, Vigée by force of circumstance emerged as a great writer of exile, indelibly marked by loss.

There are historical convolutions and ironical twists involved in Vigée's existential status as exile: while the Jewish man may in one sense be said to have returned home from exile when he made Aliyah (came up, i.e. emigrated) to Jerusalem in 1960, the French poet inevitably found himself exiled from his intellectual and cultural community as configured in the language he wrote in, although the nature of the exile was, of course, quite different from the one he endured in the United States.

Educated in the French language, he also grew up speaking Yiddish and Alsatian (the last named, his mother's tongue, banned in schools by the French authorities), and his early world was that of a Jewish community which had been established for three centuries in a province caught between two rival nations, two world cultures. Sadly Vigée may well be the last living speaker of Rhineland or western Yiddish, the original Yiddish. In America, his solitary life as a French writer was bound to dominate his psyche, against a monolingually anglophone cultural and linguistic background. For all his struggle to secure words in his mind, Vigée, like Primo Levi and unlike Paul Celan, has always trusted language to deliver.

In Israel, however, the tension between his diasporic language and the religious reality, quotidian and oneiric, of pre-Messianic – hence exilic – Jerusalem surrounded by the inscape of his beloved Judaean hills, has given rise to a manifold eloquence in verse, lyrical or narrative, and prose, meditative and/or autobiographical. It has yielded a dialectical complexity and inwardness drawn from lived experience. A beneficial outcome of his wanderings has been his brilliance as a translator, of German, Hebrew, and English poetry (including Eliot and Rilke). His biblical commentaries and critical studies of writers as opposite to each other as Kafka ("artiste de la faim") and Goethe ("artiste de l'énergie démonique") are also germane to our understanding of the structure of his thought as incarnated in his binary concerns (see below).

While one dimension or modality of his work is undoubtedly traditional Jewish lamentation – a dual expression of collective grief and personal anguish – this is frequently counterpointed by joy, or at least by hope: the age-old Jewish messianic optimism found even in the lower depths. In one Bible commentary he reminds us that even the Book of Lamentations, a poem of sorrow to equal Jeremiah if not Job, ends with an expression of hope. Though Messiah tarry, Vigée believes with more or less perfect faith that his people will survive exile, destruction, and failure of nerve concerning the Jewish mission.

This positive religious heritage inoculates Vigée's language against the ravages and torments found in the work of another major Jewish poet, one perhaps more in "tune" with the times ("Wozu Dichter in dürftiger Zeit?" asked Hölderlin, "What use are poets in a time of dearth?"), Vigée's exact contemporary Paul Celan. Neither sun nor milk is black in Vigée's eyes, despite a world whose horrors would suggest even to the man in the street that a permanent state of mourning is not a crazy response to life on earth. The French language is, of course, a *datum* for Claude Vigée, but it is not *fated*. Vigée, like many French poets before him, wrestles with its rule-bound perfections and centralized demands. The patriarch Jacob, limping victorious at Phanuel springs to mind, as an image of battle. And, indeed, it is Jacob, even more than Isaac (favoured ancestor for modern Hebrew poets, as Ruth Karton-Blum has shown), who speaks to Vigée's imaginings in manifold ways. Jacob's or Vigée's *agon*, one is tempted to say, is not merely anti-Jacobin: angelic resistance is ubiquitous.

If Vigée's main theme is exile, then the "pressure of history on experience" (Miłosz's phrase) has conferred a unity of utterance on his work which many writers would envy, despite the price paid in uprootedness. A highly distinctive feature of many of his books is that they contain poetry *and* prose, beginning with *L'Été indien*, accepted by Camus at Gallimard. For more than 60 years, in poem after poem, essay after essay, we find a kaleidoscopic variety of structured interplay, even binary opposition: silence and utterance, Israel and Diaspora, Jew and man, physicality and mind, spirit and place, plenitude and emptiness, holy and secular, anguish and joy, man and woman, sun and water, to name only ten.

Significantly, it is the poems which trigger the prose rather than the other way round, though the extraordinarily sensual prose glimmers on its own terms, not "poetically". Unlike Cavafy, famously standing at a slight angle to the universe, Vigée confronts it head (and heart) on. The matrix of Israel has yielded a radix of artistic freedom. It would be interesting to explore Vigée's spiritual journey "against" that of an important Hebrew-language poet of the Diaspora such as Gabriel Preil.

Vigée is a modest, even austere, man, but his work radiates generosity and passion. No longer alienated by the radical deeps of Europe's historical situation and the surface breadth of America's geographical bearings, Vigée, free at last, grounds his ecstasy and mythologizes his anguish, sings his memories and speaks his perceptions, all the while hoping that a secure Israel, albeit pre-Messianic, will arise in his lifetime. Which is not to say that this Zionist (born in Resistance Toulouse rather than his ancestral Alsace) rejects the idea of a creative Diaspora. The warmth of his literary and personal relations not with France but with Alsace (to the extent of writing poetry in the local dialect in later life, countering the exile that is mortality) testify to an awareness of the extent to which Jewish mythography and art have been nourished in and through Diaspora, just as he is equally concerned to explain the power of the Jewish word in Western civilization as a whole. The ear of Jerusalem counters the eye of Athens (or Paris).

ANTHONY RUDOLF

Vogel, David

Russian-born Austrian poet, 1891–1944

Born in Satanov, 1891. Spent youth in Vilna (Vilnius); began writing verse in Hebrew. Emigrated to Austria, 1912; settled in Vienna; detained as enemy alien, 1914–16. Emigrated to France, 1925; settled in Paris. Went to Palestine, 1929; moved to Berlin, 1930; returned to Paris, 1932. Detained as enemy alien in detention camps in France; deported to concentration camp. Died February 1944.

Selected Writings

Fiction

Beveit hamarpe [In the Sanatorium], 1928

Hayei nissuim, 1929; as *Married Life*, translated by Dalya Bilu, 1988

Lenokhah hayam, 1932; as *Facing the Sea* in *Eight Great Hebrew Short Novels*, edited by Alan Lelchuk and Gershon Shaked, 1983

Tahanot kavot : novelot, roman, sipur, yoman, 1990

Poetry

Lifnei hashaar haafel, 1923; as *The Dark Gate: Selected Poems*, translated by A.C. Jacobs, 1976

Kol hashirim David Vogel [Complete Poems], 1966

Further Reading

Alter, Robert, "Fogel and the Forging of a Hebrew Self", *Prooftexts*, 13/1 (January 1993)

Feldman, Yael S., *Modernism and Cultural Transfer: Gabriel Preil and the Tradition of Jewish Literary Bilingualism*, Cincinnati: Hebrew Union College Press, 1986

Gluzman, Michael, "Unmasking the Politics of Simplicity in Modernist Hebrew Poetry: Rereading David Fogel", *Prooftexts*, 13/1 (January 1993)

Kronfeld, Chana, "Fogel and Modernism: A Liminal Moment in Hebrew Literary History", *Prooftexts*, 13/1 (January 1993)

Luz, Zvi, "Before the Dark Gate: A Study of David Fogel's Poetry", *Molad*, 22 (1964)

Mazor, Yair, *Vogel, David – Not by Poem Only: The Narrative Art of David Vogel*, Tel Aviv: University Publishing Projects, 1987 (in Hebrew)

Miron, Dan, "When Will We Stop 'Discovering' Fogel?", *Yedi'ot Aharonot* (2 June 1987)

Moked, Gavriel, "More around *Married Life*", *Yedi'ot Aharonot* (19 June 1987)

Shaked, Gershon, "David Vogel: A Hebrew Novelist in Vienna" in *Austrians and Jews in the Twentieth Century*, edited by Robert S. Wistrich, London: Macmillan, and New York: St Martin's Press, 1992

Zach, Natan, "The Bitter Fate of a Gloomy Poet", *Ha'Olam Hazeh* (1 June 1987)

David Vogel came to be known posthumously as the pioneer of Modernist Hebrew poetry and an innovative Hebrew prose writer. Throughout his literary career in Europe, Vogel used Hebrew as his tool for artistic expression. However, unlike other Hebrew authors of the early decades of the 20th century, Vogel was not a Zionist, and generally apolitical. In his prose writings he therefore turned beyond the bounds of any specifically Jewish experience and instead portrayed native, European characters, whose Jewish origin is revealed only after closer introspection. Vogel's poetry is difficult to classify: as a Jewish poet writing in Hebrew in the 1920s, he is neither religious nor Zionist; as a Viennese he rejected German; and his poems have been described as neo-romantic, impressionist, decadent, and expressionist. For the public of the time, when poems of Avraham Shlonsky, Natan Alterman, and U.Z. Greenberg were particularly popular, Vogel's lack of Zionist definition caused him to be marginalized and only later discovered, although many argue for still greater acknowledgement of the poet's aesthetic talent.

Hayei nissuim (*Married Life*) is the only novel Vogel wrote. His other prose fictional writings include two novellas, *Beveit hamarpe* [In the Sanatorium] and *Lenokhah hayam* [Facing the Sea]. *Married Life* was written in Hebrew, which the author often adapted to the depicted environment; Vogel's own neologisms are frequent, as are German and Yiddish idioms and expressions. Thus the language here is thoroughly secular, rid of Hebrew symbolic and cultural undertones. The work can be related to the Viennese neo-romantic tradition, as the protagonist, Rudolf Gurdweill, experiences humiliation and degradation in the hands of his wife, Baroness Thea von Takow and it is his suffering that is the focus of the novel. The protagonist is an anti-hero, an intellectual spending his days wandering aimlessly around the streets of Vienna, its coffee houses and bars. From this point of view, the book is a metropolitan novel, a story of city life. Vogel's depiction of the city focuses on the atmosphere of the places, rather than their exact description, as many of these areas and institutions serve the purpose of adding depth to the plot of the story, symbolizing madness, conflicts, and terror.

The centre of the novel is the married life of Gurdweill, which gradually develops into a hateful, sado-masochistic relationship. Despite his love for his wife, she escalates the degrees of humiliation and pain she can cause her husband. Gurdweill, who is described as physically and emotionally weak and dependent, accepts the abuse at an increasing cost to his mental health. Thea, seeing his devotion to her, takes pleasure in recounting to him her infidelities. When they have a child, to whom Gurdweill becomes particularly attached, she hints he is not the boy's father and wilfully neglects the baby, pursuing her amorous affairs with increased relish. The child's death is an important factor contributing to Gurdweill's isolation and mental deterioration, but to the Baroness it is only another stage in brutalizing her husband. Rudolf rejects Lotte Bodenheim's love when she reveals it to him, making himself believe that his marriage with Thea is irrevocable, and that they stand a chance of reaching an understanding. Subsequently, when Lotte commits suicide, Thea sees this as another opportunity to cause him more pain, while he is at his most vulnerable. Her cruelty comes to its peak as she makes love to a strange man in front of her husband, at which point Gurdweill, seeing no other solution, despairing and crazed, murders her.

The sadistic cruelty is not, however, seen as a unique experience of an unhappy individual, but rather as a universal predicament, as the interpersonal relations described in the various subplots parallel those of Gurdweill and Thea. It is also possible to interpret this marriage as a more general reflection of the relationship between the Jewish intellectual and the Austrian-Christian culture.

Vogel's style is unique in Hebrew poetry. His first published volume of poetry, *The Dark Gate*, is closely linked with central European Modernism and stands in opposition to the Hebrew canon of poetry of the time in its simplicity, individualism, and lack of Zionist conviction. Generally interpreted as a personal expression of pain and desire, his short poems are usually free verse, loosely linked by common images, laconic in diction, avoiding decorative figurative language, and with frequent, deliberately ambiguous grammatical forms. His poetic style, and what was at the time construed as simple imagery, were criticized by his contemporaries as naive and oversimplistic. Vogel's deliberate ambiguities, subjectivity, indeterminacy, and lack of political involvement went against the Hebrew literary standards and the "correct" values of the pre-Statehood mainstream poets, as well as the prevalent view on the role of the poet in constructing a national identity. Vogel's attack on Shlonsky's poetry, presented in the lecture *Language and Style in Our Young Literature*, was not fully published until 1974. Shlonsky's subsequent response is symptomatic of the attitude of the Hebrew mainstream poets of the time towards the individualistic tone of Vogel's writings. It was only in the 1950s, when the national identity and language were unquestionably stable, that Vogel's poetry received more attention from poets such as Nathan Zach. However, the description of his artistic achievement as "minor" is prevalent even in more recent literary criticism, despite attempts by some critics to make his poetry more widely known.

Vogel's recently discovered diaries allow more insight into his life and fiction, and present an interesting study of his use of Hebrew, as well as his insights into emotional and erotic experiences. His uniqueness and individuality lie in the fact that he chose to write in Hebrew on themes unrelated with Jewish history, but universally relevant. His insight into human emotions and his literary and linguistic sensitivity show that what has previously been considered as simplistic proves to be endowed with complexity and deserves re-evaluation.

MARTA MARZANSKA

W

Wallach, Yona

Israeli poet, 1944–1985

Born in Kfar Ono, 1944, to immigrants from Bessarabia (now Moldova). Father killed during War of Independence, 1948: grew up on street named after him; mother, Esther Wallach, co-owner of cinema. Did not finish high school; studied art at Avni Institute of Art, Tel Aviv. First poems published, 1964. Committed herself to psychiatric hospital and experimented there with LSD, 1965. Active in circle of Tel Aviv poets associated with journals *Akhshav* and *Siman Kriah*, 1960s; frequent contributor to literary periodicals. Hospitalized again following suicide attempt, 1972. Wrote lyrics for, and performed and recorded with Israeli rock group, 1982. Awards included Prime Minister's Prize, 1978. Lived with and cared for mother, Esther, who had Parkinson's disease (died 1985). Died of breast cancer 1985.

Selected Writings

Poetry
Devarim [Things], 1966
Shene ganim [Two Gardens], 1969
Shirah [Collected Poems], 1976
Or pere [Wild Light], 1983
Mofa [Appearance], 1985
Tsurot [Forms], 1985
Tat hakarah niftahat kemo menifah [Selected Poems 1963–1985], 1992
Wild Light: Selected Poems of Yona Wallach, translated by Linda Zisquit, 1997

Further Reading

Cohen, Zafrira Lidovsky, "Loosen' the Fetters of Thy Tongue Woman: A Study in the Poetics of Yona Wallach" (PhD dissertation), New York University, 1997
Rattok, Lily, *Mal 'akh Ha-esh: Al Shirat Yonah Volakh*, Tel Aviv: Hakibuts hameuhad, 1997
Sarna, Igal, *Yonah Volakh: Bibliografya*, Jerusalem: Keter, 1993
Zilberman, Dorit, *Ha-Ivrit Hi Ishah Mitrahetset: 3 Perakim 'al Shirat Yonah Volakh*, Tel Aviv: Yaron Golan, 1990

In Israel Yona Wallach is considered a major "cultural hero" and an "iconoclastic poet". A dissenting persona and an innovative writer, she wrote tantalizing poems that captured the hearts and the imagination of the literary world as soon as they began to appear in magazines and periodicals in the early 1960s. Reinventing an authentic female voice in Hebrew literature and unceasingly preoccupied with language and cultural norms, her poetry – fragmentary, uncontrolled, wild, and incoherent – challenges all boundaries. It seeks to unmask and displace deterministic structures inherent in culture and society and to define new spaces of individuality and personal freedom.

Wallach's earliest poems – featuring astounding lines such as "wrapped women/ shedding their skin like a snake"; "in the pink areas passed/ me Cecilia/ dropping blue bells"; "with a wrench Lota combs/ her hair is springs" – is marked by peculiar characters with exotic names, predominately women, who find themselves on the margins of society rejected and dejected. Presented mostly in quasi-realistic situations and rendered casually in an impassive tone of voice, the poems create an initial impression that soon begins to crumble; an unexpected scenario is introduced turning an imagined common affair into a terrifying nightmare ("I'm running on the bridge/ and the kids are after me/ Jonathan/ Jonathan they call out/ a little blood/ just a little blood to cleanse the honey"). Burdened by linguistic and textual peculiarities ("I agree to a tack hole/ but the kids want/ and I'm Jonathan/ they cut off my head with a branch of/ gladiola and gather my head/ with two branches of gladiola and package/ my head with a rustling paper . . ."), the reader soon realizes extra layers of signification that link Jonathan to spiritually superior martyrs such as Jesus Christ, John the Baptist, and the mythological bard Orpheus. In other poems, further elaborated composites of symbols and poetic allusions turn a docile maiden named Cornelia, "who lacks initiative and must", from an innocent victim of the devil's sexual urging into a "she-devil" with far greater sexual strengths than his, or Nizeta, from an ostensibly mere object of sexual desire ("something/ that you burn to devour in tension") into a shrewd noblewoman. And yet, in some of Wallach's early poems one can begin to notice what would become the hallmark of her poetic legacy, that is, a deep-rooted impulse within a "woman that lives by a different rhythm" to rid herself of a stifling earthy existence and "jump into a feathers pillow/ at least marbled with stars." Vividly able to see a celestial brilliance beyond her terrestrial surroundings ("I see beyond/ the cypress trees the splendor") and ready to "experience new concepts", Wallach proceeds to "loosen the fetters" on her tongue and her ensuing poetry examines every imaginable "wedge" or "crack in time" from which her dazzling vision comes forth.

Experimenting with a wide variety of poetic structures and themes, some of Wallach's later poems are very long while others are extremely short. Some are fully rhymed, while in others the lines flow freely, sometimes even breaking in the middle of a word. Some of the poems are awe inspiring, while in others the tension between the splendour of the words and their implications produce startling effects ("the beautiful dead was already in my garden/ blossoming, doused in golden-light"). Her increasingly free employment of "hard materials" such as expletives, profanity, simulation of sexual acts, and detailed sexual fantasies reveals Wallach's independence and candour on one hand and her feminist revolt on the other. In a series of poems that begins boldly with the words "come to lie with me" (as a policeman, judge, God, and my father . . .), she challenges the myth of male physical and/or spiritual superiority. Scorning bourgeois sanctimonious morality ("a doctor of morality/ a doctor of philosophy/ knows what's bad/ what's wrong/ what's right"), she exposes the repressive powers of social systems ("the superego walks around freely/ opens windows slams doors whistles/ shrills and tells you what to do") and dismantles the authority of language ("Hebrew is a sexmaniac/ unjustly shows favor or disfavor/ grants rights and privileges"), literature ("the sleeping beauty/ opened her eyes for the one hundredth time"), history ("everybody is afraid of this voice/ this is the historical voice until/ they imitate him and become him"), and religion ("a Jew/ess enters the kitchen/ a conditioned reflex . . . everything is forbidden because everything is/ an ancient Pavlovic reflex").

Moving beyond victimization and oppression and acknowledging the associational creativity inherent in language and poetry ("let the words act in you/ let them be free/ they will enter you inside/ making forms upon forms . . .), a large part of Wallach's latest poetry appears as obsessive exploration of personal identity. Employing "free association" as a preferred method of documenting that probing, many of these poems, increasingly lengthy, sometimes appear like an elusive babble of a mind wholly controlled by words that are ceaselessly streaming from the unconscious ("the unconscious unfolds like a fan"). Displaying what students of mysticism describe as a state of semiconsciousness, or "heightened consciousness", it seems that Wallach, who in her early poetry designs mythological and semimythological characters and renders her poetry in a symbolically terse language, in her later poems undermines memory, culture, and common knowledge, at once renouncing all concepts of poetic design ("I don't feel/ how I write/ it's like a state of faint"). Allowing "life [to] plunge into the unconscious" and conversely "the unconscious [to] float to life", these poems mark Wallach's desperate and final attempt to "loose what is not nature and/ find nature's way" in the depths of her psyche. Letting "the masks that come off the face fall down" and "speech befall", her poetry embraces and exalts volumes of primordial emotions representing a movement away from the abstractions of representational thinking toward the full concreteness, "the onefoldness of the manyfold", of actual life experiences.

Yona Wallach was a unique artist for whom life was poetry and poetry was life. She was a "speaking poet" who used her creative consciousness to constitute a world of meaning in language all the while showing how language that flows out of consciousness and is spoken genuinely is inherently poetic.

ZAFRIRA LIDOVSKY COHEN

Wallant, Edward Lewis

US fiction writer, 1926–1962

Born in New Haven, Connecticut, 19 October 1926. Served in the US navy in Europe during World War II. Spent two semesters at University of Connecticut, 1944 and 1946; studied commercial art, Pratt Institute, New York, graduated 1950; modern American literature, Hunter College, New York, 1951; attended evening writing workshops, New School for Social Research, New York, 1954 and 1955. Married Joyce Fromkin, 1948; one son, two daughters. Worked in art departments of various advertising agencies in New York, 1950–62; art director, McCann Erickson. Travelled in Italy and Spain, 1962. Awards included Daroff Memorial Fiction Award, 1960; Guggenheim Fellowship, 1962; Jewish Book Council Fiction Award. Died 5 December 1962.

Selected Writings

Novels
The Human Season, 1960
The Pawnbroker, 1961
The Tenants of the Moonbloom, 1963
The Children at the Gate, 1964

Further Reading

Baumbach, Jonathan, *The Landscape of Nightmare: Studies in the Contemporary American Novel*, New York: New York University Press, 1965

Benson, Nancy, "When This World is Enough: The Vision of Edward Lewis Wallant", *Cross Currents*, 24/3 (1984)

Berger, Alan L., "Symbolic Judaism: Edward Lewis Wallant" in his *Crisis and Covenant: The Holocaust in American Jewish Fiction*, Albany: State University of New York Press, 1985

Cronin, Gloria L. *et al.* (editors), *Jewish American Fiction Writers: An Annotated Bibliography*, New York: Garland, 1991

Galloway, David D., *Edward Lewis Wallant*, New York: Twayne, 1979

Lorch, Thomas M., "The Novels of Edward Lewis Wallant", *Chicago Review*, 19/2 (1967)

Mesher, David R. "Con Artist and Middleman: The Archetypes of Wallant's Published and Unpublished Fiction", *Yale University Library Gazette*, 56/1–2 (1981)

Edward Lewis Wallant died at the age of 36 having written four novels, the last two published posthumously. His father died when he was six, and his mother, who never remarried, raised him with the help of two aunts in an assimilated household. Although he was prepared for and celebrated a bar mitzvah, his chief personal link to a Jewish past was through stories told him by his Russian-born grandfather. Connected as an adult to Reform Judaism, this youthful writer nevertheless composed a body of work that challenges the idea of the Judaeo-Christian tradition.

Wallant transforms the magical thinking implicit in pagan and Christian symbols of suffering, death, and rebirth into an enlightened, though biblically rooted, Judaism. A few themes recur in all the novels: a vitalizing anger (voiced or repressed) directed more often toward the dead than the living, a suffering that illuminates one's memories and dreams, and a redemption that is rooted in the life of a community. His characters are biblical in spirit, and, with the exception of the last, Norman Moonbloom, also in name: Joseph Berman (*The Human Season*), Solomon Nazerman (*The Pawnbroker*), Samuel Abel Kahan and Angelo DeMarco (*The Children at the Gate*). The moral lesson they are asked to learn is that evil is a part of our character, not an instrument of some separate, satanic force. Compassion becomes possible because anger and guilt are endured and transformed, rather than eradicated. While Wallant was deeply attracted to the idea of moral salvation through sacrifice, his portrayal of loss and redemption is profoundly human and earthbound.

The ambivalent moral life between generations is the form through which Wallant expresses these ideas, as if he were addressing the irony of an old French proverb – *Ce sont les morts qu'il faut qu'on tue* – and saying, over and over again, that it is with just these ancestral spectres one need learn to live.

In *The Human Season* Joseph Berman is possessed by a vital anger that breaks forth with the sudden death of his wife. Characteristic of Wallant's method, he passes his days of grief moving in and out of a series of daydreams that meld into night, and through which "he could delve into himself, carve with an exquisite pain the tender organ of his memory." Thus does he learn to renew his own health, and come to resemble his curious biblical ancestor Joseph, the interpreter of dreams.

Sol Nazerman is the suffering hero of Wallant's second, and most widely read novel, *The Pawnbroker*. Nazerman, whose name reminds us of the Nazerene prophet, is his family's sole survivor of Nazi destruction. A former professor of philosophy, he has mournfully burrowed himself in the pawnshop he runs in the postwar American ghetto of New York City. He is hard-hearted in the face of his wretched clientele and their pawned dreams. His own nights are haunted by nightmares recalling his dead wife and the crematorium that consumed her: "the smell of burning flesh . . . as though he ate the most forbidden food." His suffering, like Berman's, is seen as a kind of crucifixion, an internal riving of the flesh – the inward bite of the moral masochist.

At the novel's climax, Nazerman witnesses the sacrifice of his stock-boy Jesus Ortiz in their Harlem pawnshop during a robbery that the boy himself helped to plan. This sacrifice is redeemed as Nazerman, like Berman, comes to recognize the true nature of his profound rage toward himself and his dead. Forging in his conscience a new covenant with the living, Sol is able to break bread with those around him in a way he was unable to do with the tormented Ortiz.

The isolation that Wallant's characters painfully bear, the widowed men of his first two novels and the orphans of his last two, *The Children at the Gate* and *The Tenants of Moonbloom*, is a solitariness that springs from either the vindictive dialogue they have with their dead, or from a fear of death and grief that insulates them from the living. If it is ironic that a fear of separation can so interfere with genuinely attaching oneself to others, then there is a corresponding irony in the fact that memories of the dead may redeem us for the living. Such is the emotional path each of Wallant's characters travels.

Samuel Abel Kahan (*The Children at the Gate*) is a hospital orderly offering a strange form of priestly care to the sick and forgiveness to the wretched. His ghastly death repeats the pitiful suicide of his father, but gives meaning to the embittered youth, Angelo DeMarco, by allowing the young man to grieve finally for his own dead father. Angelo is insulated by his anger as if it were, like his obsession with science, a talisman against feeling pain – his or anyone else's. That murderous anger is at once his mark of Cain and his bond with the boundlessly feeling Sammy. Together they represent a model of Wallant's idea of revitalizing anger and a biblical, Jewish form of redemption. Neither divine nor human sacrifice may redeem us from sin or rescue us from death.

Norman Moonbloom, ostensibly the least Jewish of Wallant's people, is raised mostly by his grandmother, spends 14 years as a professional student lost in study, and wraps himself always in a cocoon of numbing fear. Like the suffering pawnbroker Sol Nazerman, Moonbloom's source of livelihood as a slum-lord is drawn from the lore of anti-Semitism. He remains profoundly isolated from the people whose rent he collects on behalf of his elder brother, until feverish memories of his earliest, orphaned years crack him open. What most distinguishes him from the earlier characters is his discovery of humour. From Berman to DeMarco the wit is always sardonic and angry. Like the others he returns to the community from which he has been estranged. Unlike them, he recognizes the connection between pain and joy, and wilfully chooses to live by a comic spirit. "For it occurred to him that joy resembled mourning and was, if anything, just as powerful and profound." The entirely assimilated Moonbloom is reborn in his 33rd year, the purported age of Jesus at his crucifixion. He, of all Wallant's men, most fully acts out the terms of the Sinai covenant by challenging his brother's authority and addressing the troubles of the desperate tenants he has always ignored or treated with a sleepwalker's contempt.

This ideal communion runs throughout Wallant's work, but the author adopts the symbols of the Passion and the Eucharist only to transform them. Anti-Semites periodically associate these rites with the supposed magical power of Jews signified by the term Juden-fresser and explicit in the charges of blood-libel. Wallant tends to emphasize the need to give up the magical form of redemption that is always linked to punishment and the sacrifice of the innocent. In these novels, communion is always a reunion with the living evoked by a change in one's memoirs of the dead. Indeed, Wallant's entire oeuvre can be read as the author's fierce struggle to understand how humanity can find redemption from sin without the shedding of blood. It is as if Wallant understood the biblical covenant in a way some of his Jewish critics had forgotten. In one way or another, Berman, Nazerman, DeMarco, and Moonbloom learn what it means to "Circumcise therefore the foreskin of your heart, and be no more stiff-necked . . . [so that you may] exercise justice for the fatherless and widow, and love . . . the stranger in giving him food and raiment" (Deuteronomy 10:16–19).

STEPHEN KARPOWITZ

Wassermann, Jakob

German fiction writer, autobiographer, and essayist, 1873–1934

Born in Fürth, 10 March 1873, to minor businessman; mother died, 1882; poor relationship with stepmother. Literary debut in *Fürther Tageblatt*, 1886. Sent by father to Vienna to work in uncle's business, 1889; military service, Würzburg, 1891–92; insurance clerk; dismissed by anti-Semitic employer in Freiburg; wandered destitute around Black Forest and on to Zürich; settled in Munich, 1894; secretary to the writer Ernst Ludwig von Wolzogen and editor of satirical journal *Simplizissimus*. Returned to Vienna; correspondent and theatre critic, *Frankfurter Zeitung*, from 1898; contributor, *Neuen Rundschau*, from 1899. Married, first, Julie Speyer, 1901; divorced 1926; met Marta Karlweis, 1919; one son, 1924; married Marta Karlweis, 1926. Member, Prussian Academy of Arts, 1926; resigned membership after Nazi seizure of power and banning of his writings, 1933. Died after heart attack at second home in Altaussee, 1 January 1934.

Selected Writings

Collections
Gesammelte Werke, 7 vols, 1944–48

Novels
Melusine: Liebesroman [Melusine: A Love Story], 1896
Die Juden von Zirndorf, 1897; as *The Jews of Zirndorf*, translated anonymously, 1918; as *The Jews of Zirndorf*, translated by Cyrus Brooks, 1933; Brooks's translation republished as *The Dark Pilgrimage*, 1933
Die Geschichte der jungen Renate Fuchs [The Story of the Young Renata Fox], 1900
Der Moloch [The Moloch], 1903; revised 1921
Alexander in Babylon, 1905
Caspar Hauser; oder, Die Trägheit des Herzens, [Caspar Hauser: The Inertia of the Heart], 1908; as *Caspar Hauser*, translated by Caroline Newton, 1928
Die Masken Erwin Reiners [The Masks of Erwin Reiners], 1910
Faustina: ein Gespräch über die Liebe [Faustina: A Discourse on Love], 1912
Der Mann von vierzig Jahren [The Man of Forty Years], 1913
Das Gänsemännchen, 1915; as *The Goose Man*, translated by Allen W. Porterfield and Ludwig Lewisohn, 1922
Christian Wahnschaffe, 2 vols, 1919; revised edition 1932; as *The World's Illusion*, translated by Ludwig Lewisohn, 1920
Der Wenderkreis [The Turning Circle], 4 vols, 1920–24; part of vol. 1 as *World's End: Five Stories*, translated by Lewis Galantière, 1927; vol. 2 as *Oberlin's Three Stages*, translated by Allen W. Porterfield, 1925; vol. 3 as *Gold*, translated by Louise Collier Wilcox, 1924; vol. 4 as *Faber; or, The Lost Years*, translated by Harry Hansen, 1925
Geronimo de Aguilar [Geronimo de Aguilar], 1923
Laudin und die Seinen, 1925; as *Wedlock*, translated by Ludwig Lewisohn, 1925; as *The Triumph of Youth*, translated anonymously, 1927
Das Amulett [The Amulet], 1927
Der Fall Maurizius, 1928; as *The Maurizius Case*, translated by Caroline Newton, 1929
Christoph Columbus: der Don Quichote des Ozeans: Ein Porträt, 1929; as *Christopher Columbus: Don Quixote of the Seas*, translated by Eric Sutton, 1930
Etzel Andergast, 1931; as *Dr Kerhoven*, translated by Cyrus Brooks, 1932; translation republished as *Etzel Andergast*, 1932
Joseph Kerkhovens dritte Existenz, 1934; as *Joseph Kerkhoven's Third Existence*, translated by Eden Paul and Cedar Paul, 1934
Olivia, 1937
Engelhart; oder, Die zwei Welten [Englehart; or, The Two Worlds], 1973

Novellas
Die Schaffnerin; Die Mächtigen: Novellen [The Conductress; The Powerful: Novellas], 1897
Schläfst Du, Mutter? Ruth: Novellen [Are You Sleeping Mother? Ruth: Novellas], 1897
Der niegeküsste Mund; Hilperich: zwei Novellen [The Mouth Never Kissed: Two Novellas], 1903
Die Schwestern: drei Novellen [The Sisters: Three Novellas], 1906

Short Stories
Der goldene Spiegel: Erzählungen in einem Rahmen [The Golden Mirror: Stories in a Frame], 1912
Der Geist des Pilgers: drei Erzählungen [Pilgrim Spirit: Three Stories], 1923
Der Aufruhr um den Junker Ernst [The Revolt Surrounding Squire Ernst], 1926
Tagebuch aus dem Winkel: Erzählungen und Ausätze aus dem Nachlass [Diary from the Recesses: Posthumous Stories and Essays], 1935

Plays
Die ungleichen Schalen: Fünf Dramen [Unequal Vessels: Five Dramas], 1912
Lukardis, 1932

Other
Die Kunst der Erzählung [The Art of Story-Telling], 1904
Der Literat; oder, Mythos und Persönlichkeit [The Man of Letters; or, Myth and Personality], 1910
Deutsche Charaktere und Begebenheiten [German Characters and Events], 2 vols, 1915–24
Imaginäre Brücken: Studien und Aufsätze [Imaginary Bridges: Studies and Essays], 1921

Mein Weg als Deutscher und Jude, 1921; as *My Life as German and Jew*, translated by S.N. Brainin, 1933
Gestalt und Humanität: zwei Reden [Personality and Humanity: Two Speeches], 1924
In Memoriam Ferrucio Busoni [In Memoriam Ferrucio Busoni], 1925
Lebensdienst: gesammelte Studien, Erfahrungen und Reden aus drei Jarzehnten [Life Service: Collected Studies, Experiences, and Speeches from Three Decades], 1928
Hofmannsthal, der Freund [Hofmannsthal, the Friend], 1930
Bula Matari: das Leben Stanleys [Bula Matari: The Life of Stanley], 1932; as *H.M. Stanley, Explorer*, translated by Eden Paul and Cedar Paul, 1932; as *Bula Matari: Stanley, Conqueror of a Continent*, 1933
Rede an die Jugend über das Leben im Geiste [Speeches to Youth about Life and Thought], 1932
Selbsbetrachtungen [Self-Contemplation], 1933
The Letters of Jakob Wassermann to Frau Julie Wasserman, edited by V. Grubwieser, translated by Phyllis Blewitt and Trevor Blewitt, 1935; as *Briefe an Seine Braut und Gattin Julie, 1900–1929*, 1940
Geliebtes Herz: Briefe [Beloved Heart: Letters], edited by A. Beranek, 1948
Bekenntnisse und Begegnungen: Porträts und Skizzen zur Literatur und Geistesgeschichte [History of Thought], edited by Paul Stöcklein, 1950
Jakob Wassermann, Deutscher und Jude: Reden und Schriften, 1904–1933 [Jacob Wasserman, German and Jew: Speeches and Writings], edited by Derek Rodewald, 1984

Further Reading

Bing, Siegmund, *Jakob Wassermann: Weg und Werk des Dichters*, Nuremberg: Frommann, 1929
Blankenagel, John C., *The Writings of Jakob Wassermann*, Boston: Christopher, 1942
Frankle, Eleanor, "Dostoievsky et Wassermann", *Revue de littérature comparée*, 19 (1939)
Garrin, Stephen H., *The Concept of Justice in Jakob Wassermann's Trilogy*, Bern and Las Vegas, Nevada: Lang, 1979
Jakob Wassermann: ein Beitrag der Stadt Fürth zu seinem 100. Geburtstag am 10. März 1973, Fürth: Stadtverwaltung, 1973
Journal of English and Germanic Philology (October 1925; April 1951; July 1951)
Karlweis, Marta, *Jakob Wassermann: Bild, Kampf und Werk; Mit einem Geleitwort von Thomas Mann*, Amsterdam: Querido, 1935
Koch, Franz, "Wassermanns Weg als Deutscher und Jude", *Forschungen zur Judenfrage*, 1 (1937)
Koester, Rudolf, *Jakob Wasserman*, Berlin: Morgenbuch, 1996
Literature and Psychology, 14/3–4 (Summer/Autumn 1964)
Mann, Thomas, *Letters of Thomas Mann: 1889–1955*, edited by Richard Winston and Clara Winston, 2 vols, London: Secker and Warburg, 1970; New York: Knopf, 1971
Martini, Fritz, "Nachwort" in Wassermann's *Der Fall Maurizius*, Munich: Langen-Müller, 1971
Mendelssohn, Peter de, "Nachwort" in Wassermann's *Schläfst Du, Mutter? Meistererzählungen*, Munich: Langen-Müller, 1984
Miller, Henry, *Maurizius Forever*, San Francisco: Colt Press, 1946
Miller, Henry, *Reflections on The Maurizius Case: A Humble Appraisal of a Great Book*, Santa Barbara, California: Capra Press, 1974
Neubauer, Martin, *Jakob Wassermann: ein Schriftsteller im Urteil seiner Zeitgenossen*, Frankfurt: Peter Lang, 1994
Rodewald, Dierk (editor), *Jakob Wassermann, 1873–1934: ein Weg als Deutscher und Jude*, Bonn: Bouvier,1984
Voegeli, Walter, *Jakob Wassermann und die Trägheit des Herzens*, Winterthur: Keller, 1956
Wassermann-Speyer, Julie, *Jakob Wassermann und sein Werk*, Vienna and Leipzig: Deutsch–Österreichischer Verlag, 1923
Wolff, Rudolf (editor), *Jakob Wassermann: Werk und Wirkung*, Bonn: Bouvier, 1987
Zahnow, Holger, "'Der Fall Maurizius': Jakob Wassermanns analytische Erzählkkunst", *Archiv für das Studium der Neueren Sprachen und Literaturen*, 221 (1984)
Zweig, Stefan, "Jakob Wassermann", *Die Neue Rundschau*, 23 (1912)

Jakob Wassermann was one of the most important novelists of his time; Thomas Mann called him a "world star of the novel". *Caspar Hauser*, *Christian Wahnschaffe* (*The World's Illusion*), and *Der Fall Maurizius* (*The Maurizius Case*) achieved great critical and popular acclaim. After 1945 he was considered no more than a second-rate author, not only because he belonged to the outdated realistic-psychological style of literature, but also because no-one could dispute his "Germanness", although he himself had insisted he was a Jew.

Probably no other writer of his time tackled the problem of German Jewishness as intensively and as self-tormentingly as Wassermann. Jews appear in many of his novels; most famously in the "prologue" to *Die Juden von Zirndorf* (*The Jews of Zirndorf*), which describes the impact of the false Messiah Shabbetai Tzevi in Fürth. The figure of Ahasuerus, around which he is said to have wanted to create a separate work in 1933, although he was never able to complete it, makes an early appearance here. Strangely, *Die Juden von Zirndorf* is dedicated to "The memory of my Father"; his father was largely assimilated but had nevertheless introduced his son to the community way of life. In *Mein Weg als Deutscher und Jude* (*My Life as German and Jew*), Wassermann described this in the darkest tones: the community comprised "the remainders of an earlier world" and, after his father's second marriage, the family no longer observed the Sabbath laws.

> One was only specifically regarded as a Jew according to one's name and as a result of hostility to, foreignness to

> or rejection of the Christian environment . . . So why was one still a Jew, and what was the sense of it? This question became increasingly irrefutable for me and no-one could answer it.

And yet Wassermann *felt* Jewish. He explained that he had started writing at an early age, fantastic stories of an intense, childlike imagination, but his stepmother forbade it. His youngest brother learned of his secret book-buying but was bribed into silence by evening stories. This is when he first experienced the "power of story-telling", that story-telling "was surely in my blood like an oriental instinct". Here he found an identity of his existence as a writer and a Jew, but it was a highly problematic identity: "The Jew as a European, as a cosmopolitan, is a man of letters; the Jew as an Oriental, not in the ethnographic but in the mythical sense, with the *power to metamorphose* to the present, which he must possess, can be a creator." This, written in 1909, marks his position in the age: rejection of the "men of letters" and "culture", which he described in terms that took up anti-Semitic stereotypes, and proximity to the "oriental myth", on which alone he conferred originality and history-making creativity:

> We know them and we suffer from them, these thousands of so-called modern Jews, who gnaw at the foundations because they have no foundations themselves; . . . The Jew, on the other hand, who I call the Oriental – he is of course a symbolic figure; I could just as well call him the Fulfilled, or the legitimate Successor – is sure of himself, sure of the world and mankind. He cannot lose himself, because a noble consciousness, an innate consciousness, links him to the past and demands an immense responsibility to the future.

For Wassermann there was no "Jewish nation", only Jewish individuals, hence his rejection of Zionism. Nevertheless, there was scarcely another writer who battled so openly and consistently against anti-Semitism – the murder of his friend Walter Rathenau was a signal to him.

With *Die Juden von Zirndorf* Wassermann sought to enter the literary life, but also sought to keep his work on this subject quiet. His literary work forms almost a unified whole; figures from earlier novels re-appeared later: *Laudin und die Seinen* (*Wedlock*) hints at the basic idea of *Der Fall Maurizius*, *Etzel Andergast* introduces persons who assume main roles in *Joseph Kerkhovens dritte Existenz* (*Joseph Kerkhoven's Third Existence*). *Der Wendekreis* [The Turning Circle] contains a cycle of four novels. He depicted the complete history of Europe from *Alexander in Babylon* via *Christoph Columbus* and ending with *Bula Matari*. If these works dealt with the borders and border experience of Europe, then the other novels traced the inner dichotomy of western European man. In broad and comprehensive portraits, he presents not only the different and contradictory levels of society but also the dubiousness of Western society as a whole. The counter-side of this for Wassermann was fate, which cannot be "made" and "mastered". His theme was the landscape and man bound up with it. Finally, he dealt with:

> the inner landscape, which brings souls from their condition before birth into the world, which determines the manner and the colour of the dream, the dream in the broadest sense, like the secret and unconscious paths of the spirit, which are its climate, its actual home. But the inner landscape means more than just imagination; rather it is the crystal of the true life itself, the place where its laws are dictated and where its real fate is engendered, of which what is reflected in so-called reality is but a reflection.

Wassermann never made a decision as to whether he was Jewish or German, but the German, or rather the German landscape, took precedence. In 1915, one year after the outbreak of war, Wassermann published an anthology of descriptions of great Germans: *Deutsche Charaktere und Begebenheiten* [German Characters and Events]; in this he wrote:

> The German has found the type of politics appropriate to him; . . . the politics of development, of knowledge and of determination. [It is based] on the natural rights of the intellect and the heart, not on arbitrary intrigues but on a necessity and a world-historical idea.

In the German, in the good German, for which he hoped, he saw the Jew. In *Das Gänsemännchen* (*The Goose Man*), he writes of the painter Anselm Feuerbach: "What a life the man has led! And what a death he has died! . . . A German life, a German death. He reaches out his hand to give and it is spat upon." As a Jew, Wassermann may himself have experienced this.

Wassermann's autobiographical work *Mein Weg als Deutscher und Jude* is rightly considered an important document of the age. It expounds the indissoluble clasp, the clutch, even, of the German and Jewish aspects: "I am a German and I am a Jew, each as much and as completely as the other; neither can be separated from the other." His life story shows the incessant oppression and disparagement suffered by Jews, and there is evidence that many readers were profoundly moved by this account. Wassermann testified here "that in the end I suffer more for the Germans than for the Jews. Does not one always suffer most where one loves most deeply, even if most in vain?"

MANFRED VOIGTS
translated by Karen Goulding

Weiss, Ernst

Austrian fiction writer, 1882–1940

Born in Brünn (Brno), 28 August 1882; father, textile merchant, died 1886. Studied at universities of Prague and Vienna; medical doctorate, 1908. In Berlin, 1910. Returned to Vienna, 1911; worked at Wiedener hospital. Contracted mild tuberculosis. Ship's physician, M.S. *Austria*, visiting Japan, China, and India, 1912–13. Met Johanna Bleschke, 1913; she became his protegée and lover until her death,

1936. Settled in Berlin (but often visited Franz Kafka and others in Prague). Physician in Austro-Hungarian army, on eastern front, 1914–18. Returned to Prague, 1918; some critics made anti-Semitic remarks about his play *Tanja*, 1920; returned to Berlin, 1921. Awarded Olympic Silver Medal for Prose Fiction, Amsterdam, 1928. Returned to Prague to care for dying mother, 1933. Moved to Paris, 1934. Awarded monthly stipend by American Guild for German Cultural Freedom, 1938. Following Nazi invasion of France, committed suicide in Paris, 15 June 1940.

Selected Writings

Collection

Gesammelte Werke [Collected Works], edited by Peter Engel and Volker Michels, 16 vols, 1982

Novels

Die Galeere [The Galley], 1913; revised 1919
Der Kampf [The Struggle], 1916; revised as *Franziska*, 1919
Tiere in Ketten [Animals in Chains], 1918
Mensch gegen Mensch [Man against Man], 1919
Stern der Dämonen [Star of the Demons], 1921
Nahar, 1922
Die Feuerprobe [Trial by Fire], 1923; revised edition, 1929
Hodin [Hodin], 1923
Der Fall Vukobrankovics [The Vukobrankovics Case], 1924
Männer in der Nacht [Men in the Night], 1925
Boëtius von Orlamünde, 1928; as *Der Aristokrat Boëtius von Orlamünde*, 1966; as *The Aristocrat Boëtius von Orlamünde*, translated by Martin Chalmers, 1994
Das Unverlierbare [That Which Cannot Be Lost], 1928
Georg Letham, Arzt und Mörder [Georg Letham, Doctor and Murderer], 1931
Der Gefängnisarzt; oder, Die Vaterlosen [The Prison Doctor; or, The Fatherless Children], 1934
Der arme Verschwender [The Poor Spendthrift], 1936
Der Verführer [The Seducer], 1938
Ich, der Augenzeuge, 1963, as *Der Augenzeuge*, 1982; as *The Eyewitness*, translated by Ella R.W. McKee, 1977
Der zweite Augenzeuge [The Second Eyewitness], edited by Klaus-Peter Hinze, 1978
Jarmila: eine Liebesgeschichte aus Böhmen [Jarmila: A Love Story from Bohemia], 1998

Stories

Atua: Drei Erzählungen [Atua: Three Stories], 1923
Daniel, 1924
Dämonenzug: fünf Erzählungen [Procession of Demons: Five Stories], 1928

Poetry

Das Versöhnungsfest: eine Dichtung in vier Kreisen [The Feast of Reconciliation], 1920

Play

Tanja, 1920
Olympia: Tragikomödie, 1923

Other

Translator, *Das Buch über Mich Selbst (Jahre des Kampfes)*, by Theodore Dreiser, 1932
Die Kunst des Erzählens: Essays, Aufsätze, Schriften zur Literatur [The Art of Storytelling: Essays, Writings on Literature], 1982

Further Reading

Adler, Sabine, *Vom "Roman Experimental" zur Problematik des wissenschaftlichen Experiments: Untersuchungen zum literarischen Werk von Ernst Weiss*, Frankfurt: Peter Lang, 1990
Delfmann, Thomas, *Ernst Weiss: Existenzialistisches Heldentum und Mythos des Unabwendbaren*, Münster: Kleinheinrich, 1989
Ehrenstein, Albert, "Ernst Weiss", *Berliner Tageblatt* (11 July 1925)
Elfe, Wolfgang, *Stiltendenzen im Werk von Ernst Weiss unter besonderer Berücksichtigung seines expressionistischen Stils*, Bern: Peter Lang, 1971
Engel, Peter (editor), *Ernst Weiss: Materialien*, Frankfurt: Suhrkamp, 1982
Engel, Peter (editor), *Internationales Ernst Weiss Symposium 1990 Hamburg*, Bern: Peter Lang, 1992
Golec, Janusz, *Die Idee des "Menschlichsten Menschen": Untersuchungen zur Sexualität und Macht im Werk von Ernst Weiss*, Lublin: Wydawnictwo Uniwersytetu, Marii Curie-Sk_odowskiej, 1994
Haas, Franz, *Der Dichter von der traurigen Gestalt: Zu Leben und Werk von Ernst Weiss*, Frankfurt: Peter Lang, 1986
Hinze, Klaus-Peter, "Ernst Weiss" in *Austrian Fiction Writers 1875–1913*, edited by James Hardin and Donald G. Daviau, Detroit: Gale, 1989 (Dictionary of Literary Biography, vol. 81)
Hinze, Klaus-Peter, "Ernst Weiss" in *Major Figures of Austrian Literature: The Interwar Years 1918–1938*, edited by Donald G. Daviau, Riverside, California: Ariadne Press, 1995
Längle, Ulrike, *Ernst Weiss, Vatermythos und Zeitkritik: Die Exilromane am Beispiel des "Armen Verschwenders"*, Innsbruck: Institut für Germanistik, Innsbruck University, 1981
Lattmann, Dieter, "Posthume Wiederkehr: Ernst Weiss, Arzt und Schriftsteller" in his *Zwischenrufe und Andere Texte*, Munich: Kindler, 1967
Mielke, Rita, *Das Böse als Krankheit: Entwurf einer neuen Ethik im Werk von Ernst Weiss*, Frankfurt: Peter Lang, 1986
Pazi, Margarita, *Fünf Autoren des Prager Kreises*, Bern: Peter Lang, 1978
Pazi, Margarita, *Ernst Weiss: Schicksal und Werk eines jüdischen mitteleuropäischen Autors in der ersten Hälfte des 20. Jahrhunderts*, Frankfurt: Peter Lang, 1993
Steinke, Angela, *Ontologie der Lieblosigkeit: Untersuchungen zum Verhältnis von Mann und Frau in der frühen Prosa von Ernst Weiss*, Frankfurt: Peter Lang, 1994
Streuter, Manuel, *Das Medizinische im Werk von Ernst Weiss*, Herzogenrath: Murken-Altrogge, 1990
Taylor, Harly U., "Ernst Weiss: Fortune's Stepchild", *West Virginia Philology Papers*, 25 (1960)
Text + Kritik, 76, special Weiss issue, edited by Heinz Ludwig Arnold (October 1982)

Versari, Margherita, *Ernst-Weiss-Individualität zwischen Vernunft und Irrationalismus: ein Werk zwischen "Mythologie" und "Aufklärung"*, Frankfurt: Peter Lang, 1984

Wollheim, Mona, *Begegnung mit Ernst Weiss, Paris 1936–1940*, Munich: Kreisselmeier, 1970

Wondrak, Eduard, *Einiges über den Arzt und Schriftsteller Ernst Weiss, mit einer autobiographischen Skizze von 1927*, Munich: Kreisselmeier, 1968

Ernst Weiss was a novelist who enjoyed a high reputation in Germany between the wars. He was also, apart from a period of estrangement, a friend of Kafka, who described him as a "Jew of the kind that is closest to the type of the Western European Jew and to whom one therefore immediately feels close". He was largely forgotten after 1945 until the publication in 1963 of his last novel – in which Hitler plays a significant role – led to a renewal of interest; a modest critical renaissance followed the publication of his complete prose works in 1982.

Weiss was born in 1882 in Brünn / Brno, the capital of Moravia in the Austro-Hungarian empire. His father died when he was four. Although his grandfather had been a teacher in a Jewish school, Weiss was educated at German-speaking primary and secondary schools. He was brought up assimilated to the local German culture and the Jewishness of his upbringing amounted to little more than the formal requirements of religion and some instruction in Hebrew.

Weiss was a doctor and served in the Austrian medical corps during World War I, finally giving up medicine for full-time writing in 1920. Despite his sympathy for Czech aspirations, he felt increasingly alien as a German-speaker in the new republic and went to Berlin in 1921, though retaining his Czech passport. He returned to Prague when Hitler came to power in 1933 and then moved to Paris after the death of his mother in 1934. It was there that he committed suicide after the entry of the German army in June 1940.

Like many of his generation, Weiss was deeply shocked by his experiences in World War I, and the impact intensified his already somewhat pessimistic outlook. In novels published shortly after the war – for example *Mensch gegen Mensch* [Man against Man] and *Die Feuerprobe* [Trial by Fire] – and above all in his one volume of poetry, *Das Versöhnungsfest* [The Feast of Reconciliation], he expressed a dualistic view of existence: God is absent from the world, which is the province of an "Anti-God", who drives mankind to evil. Both, it should be added, are for Weiss symbols of human possibilities rather than transcendental beings.

The works, both prose and poetry, of this period also reveal the stylistic influence of Expressionism. Later in the 1920s he returned to the sober, precise prose of his first novel, *Die Galeere* [The Galley], and rewrote three of his Expressionist novels. Most of Weiss's major works from the mid-1920s onwards are novels of development, following the life of the hero from childhood onwards, usually with a first-person narrator. Four – *Georg Letham, Arzt und Mörder* [Georg Letham, Doctor and Murderer]; *Der Gefängnisarzt* [The Prison Doctor]; *Der arme Verschwender* [The Poor Spendthrift]; *Ich, der Augenzeuge* (*The Eyewitness*) – have an autobiographical connection in that the main characters are doctors. Another feature they have in common is the centrality of the father–son relationship, in particular the way in which the son remains emotionally fixated on his father even though clearly perceiving his faults, even betrayal. Since Weiss's own father died when he was four, the prominence of the father–son theme has been much discussed, without any one interpretation being entirely convincing. For the fictional characters, however, the strong tie to the father is the reason none of them manages to form deep emotional relationships with others, in particular with their wives and children. The parallel to Kafka has been frequently pointed out.

In the dominance of this theme there seems to be both a personal aspect – despite a number of love affairs, Weiss never settled down or married – and a reflection of a generation which lacked the robustness of their parents and whose lives were emotionally and physically disrupted by the war and the postwar break-up of the stable social and political environment in Europe. A specifically Jewish element is almost completely absent from Weiss's work. He did write an article, "Adliges Volk", for Buber's journal *Jude* in which he praises the Jews' abiding sense of identity, but the essay is remarkably detached in tone. His one story on a Jewish subject, "Daniel", written in a rich, exotic language, is a portrait of Daniel's imagined childhood and youth as an exile who has been abandoned by his father and whose mother deliberately withdraws from his life. It is clearly closer, in theme if not in style, to Weiss's other novels than to the Old Testament chronicle.

One story, "Familiengeschichte", deals with the daughter of a Jewish–Christian marriage, but otherwise Jewish protagonists are conspicuous by their absence. Indeed, in *Der arme Verschwender* and *Ich, der Augenzeuge* the Christian upbringing of the main characters is emphasized, though they both eventually lose their mother's faith. It is the loss of religious faith and its replacement by a more general commitment to humanity that is more important for Weiss than the specific religion involved. In two of his later novels Weiss did, however, confront the phenomenon of Nazism. The doctor hero of *Der arme Verschwender* cures an old school-friend who then develops into a political leader with a pseudo-Nietzschean philosophy.

A similar situation plays a more extended role in *Ich, der Augenzeuge*. At the end of the war the hero cures a Corporal A.H. of hysterical blindness (scholars are divided over whether Weiss actually saw the case-notes of the doctor who treated Hitler) only to witness his rise as a demagogue and even, at a political meeting, to feel his attraction. After Hitler comes to power the doctor is tortured in a concentration camp by the Nazis, who want his case-notes. His Jewish wife, who has fled to Switzerland, hands them over, which the hero feels as a betrayal and which leads to an estrangement between them. In a way characteristic of Weiss's heroes, his love for his wife comes second to what he sees as his duty to the world, even if, as he is aware, his actions are unlikely to achieve much.

A touching, though minor, episode is the way their children, who during the initial years of exile have been brought up by their grandparents in Germany, have absorbed the prevalent anti-Semitism and are completely alienated from their mother. In the main, however, Weiss concentrates on Hitler and the acceptance of his person and ideas by the Germans, rather than on the victims of Nazism.

Weiss suffered from the rootlessness characteristic of a number of German-speaking Jewish writers from Bohemia and Moravia. He felt he "belonged" to the German language, but not to the German people, and in the two autobiographical pieces he wrote he makes no mention of his Jewish background. In fact, he was suspicious of any strong attachment to race, to what he called the "love gathered in the safe storehouses of racial and linguistic kinship". A few days before his suicide he claimed, doubtless under the stress of events, to have become an "orthodox" Jew, but his novels and stories are the expression of a humanism beyond race, religion, and nation which, as the hero of *Ich, der Augenzeuge* comes to realize, is no match for the intoxicating appeal of the "blood", but which remains as a testimony to the nobler aspirations of mankind.

MICHAEL MITCHELL

Weissbort, Daniel

British poet and translator, 1935–

Born in London, 30 April 1935. Studied at Queens' College, Cambridge, BA 1956; London School of Economics and Political Science. Married Jill Anderson, 1961; divorced, 1979; two daughters, one son. Director, Albion Knitwear, 1957–61. Founding co-editor, with Ted Hughes, *Modern Poetry in Translation*, London, 1965–83. Advisory director, Poetry International, London, 1970–73. Visiting professor of comparative literature, 1974–75, director, Translation Workshop, since 1975, professor of English and comparative literature, 1980–2000, acting director, International Writing Program, 1986, and Chair, Comparative Literature, 1987, University of Iowa, Iowa City; visiting professor, King's College, London, 1995, 1997. Member of General Council, Poetry Society, London, 1972–74; member of Executive Board, American Literary Translators Association, 1982–86; member of board, British Centre for Literary Translation, University of East Anglia, 2000. Many awards, including Arts Council of Great Britain bursary, 1971, 1972; Glatstein Memorial Prize, 1978; National Endowment for the Arts Translation Fellowship, 1981; Art Council of Great Britain Literature Award, 1984.

Selected Writings

Poetry
The Leaseholder, 1971
In an Emergency, 1972
Soundings, 1977
Leaseholder: New and Collected Poems 1965–1985, 1986
Fathers, 1991
Inscription, 1993
Lake: New and Selected Poems, 1993; as *Nietzsche's Attaché Case: New and Selected Poems*, 1993
What Was All the Fuss About?, 1998

Other
Translator, *The Soviet People and Their Society*, by Pierre Sorlin, 1968
Translator, *Guerrillas in Latin America: The Technique of the Counter-State*, by Luis Mercier Vega, 1969
Translator, *A History of the People's Democracies: Eastern Europe since Stalin*, by François Fetjo, 1971
Translator, *Scrolls: Selected Poems of Nikolai Zabolotsky*, 1971
Translator, *The Trial of the Four: A Collection of Material in the Case of Galanskov, Ginzburg, Dobdovolsky and Lashkova*, 1971
Translator, *Natalya Gorbanevskaya: Selected Poems, with a Transcipt of Her Trial, and Papers Relating to Her Detention in a Prison Psychiatric Hospital*, 1972
Translator, *Nose! Nose? No-se! And Other Plays*, by Andrei Amalriki, 1973
Translator, *The Rare and Extraordinary History of Holy Russia*, by Gustave Doré, 1973
Editor and translator, *Post-War Russian Poetry*, 1974
Translator, *East-West and Is Uncle Jack a Conformist?*, by Andrei Amalrik, 1976
Translator, with Anthony Rudolf, *The War is Over: Selected Poems*, by Evgeny Vinokurov, 1976
Translator, *From the Night and Other Poems*, by Lev Mark, 1978
Editor and translator, with John Glad, *Russian Poetry: The Modern Period*, 1978
Translator, *Ivan the Terrible and Ivan the Fool*, by Evgeny Evtushenko, 1979
Translator, *Missing Person*, by Patrick Modiano, 1980
Translator, *The World about Us*, by Claude Simon, 1983
Editor, *Translating Poetry: The Double Labyrinth*, 1989
Editor, *The Poetry of Survival: Post-War Poets of Central and Eastern Europe*, 1990
Editor and translator, with Tomislav Longinovic, *Red Knight: Serbian Women's Songs*, by V. S. Karad_i_, 1992
Editor and translator, with John Glad, *Twentieth Century Russian Poetry*, 1992
Editor, with Arvind Krishna Mehrotra, *Periplus: Poetry in Translation*, 1993
Editor and translator, with Albert C. Todd and Max Hayward, *Twentieth Century Russian Poetry: Silver and Steel: An Anthology*, 1993
Editor and translator, with Girdhar Rathi, *An Experience and an Experiment in Translating Modern Hindi Poetry*, 1994
Editor and translator, with Ted Hughes, *Selected Poems of Yehuda Amichai*, 1994
Translator, *The Jews of Germany*, by Enzo Traverso, 1995
Theme and Version: Plath and Ronsard, with Yves Bonnefoy and Audrey Jones, edited by Anthony Rudolf, 1995
Translator, *Nikolay Zabolotsky: Selected Poems*, 1999

Further Reading

Coates, Jenefer, "Profile: Daniel Weissbort", *In Other Words*, 13/14 (Autumn–Winter 1999–2000)
Firchow, Peter E., "Review of *Leaseholder*", *World Literature Today*, 61/2 (Spring 1987)

Heaney, Seamus, "Something to Protest: A Review of *Nikolay Zabolotsky: Selected Poems*", *Parnassus: Poetry in Review*, 25 (2001)
Jenning, Elizabeth, "New Poetry", *Scotsman* (2 February 1971)
Rudolf, Anthony, "Selflessly Considering the Self: A Review of *Nietzsche's Attaché Case*", *Jewish Chronicle* (30 July 1993)
Steiner, George, "Breaking the Language Barrier: A Review of *Translating Poetry: The Double Labyrinth*", *Sunday Times* (3 December 1989)

Daniel Weissbort is probably best known for his work in the field of literary translation, being the founder editor with the late Ted Hughes of *Modern Poetry in Translation*, which, for instance, introduced to an English public the poetry of Yehuda Amichai. George Steiner has remarked of this journal: "At a time of frequent provincialism and narrowing, it has opened windows on landscapes of feeling, of insight otherwise inaccessible." Weissbort's internationalism stems, to a large extent, from his origins. As Jenefer Coates notes: "As in all matters translational, a natural cosmopolitanism was a prerequisite. In this case it was provided by the mixed blessing of being born into a Jewish family whose hasty movements across Europe traced the major tragedies of the 20th century." Curiosity about his Jewishness characterizes a number of Weissbort's own poems, unsurprisingly since he writes predominantly out of his life experience. At the same time, he is unsure about the validity of so doing, his desire to penetrate the mystery of his own existence being allied to an acute awareness of his insignificance in the scheme of things.

His first publication, *The Leaseholder*, starts at home, home being not that of his Jewish parents, but the Jewish home that he himself created. Home is perceived as a dangerous, even explosive place, under perpetual threat. In "Walking Home at Night" for instance, "I finger the bunch of keys in my pocket . . . / I home on the lock/ and my life explodes about me." Weissbort's tentativeness is engaging. For example, in "Yom Kippur at the British Museum", finding himself inadvertently working in the Round Reading Room on the holiest day of the Jewish year, Yom Kippur, prompts rueful reflections on what it means to be a Jew: "The trouble is that,/ while I would not return to the tyranny of the old lion,/ I am no emancipated Jew . . . / yet belief does not flower."

The more Weissbort delves into his life, the fact of a Jewishness he can neither embrace nor reject, the more uncertain the legacy seems. His father, a businessman who was himself a classical and biblical scholar, made sure that his son had a "good education". He went to prep school and then public school. The Englishness of these institutions (although both institutions had substantial contingents of Jewish students) only reinforced his sense of alienation, as a Jew with non-English-speaking parents. He has explored this area in a number of poems, describing it in quite literal terms, another characteristic of his work being plainness of description which, with its reliance on the word rather than the image, he has construed as Jewish.

An early review referred to Weissbort's "domestic poems" as being "warm and masculine, overshadowed by his Jewish birthright and the historical facts of Nazi brutality." Yehuda Amichai, in an interview with Weissbort, said that for poets "a great bliss is to be like other people, just to go to work and go home to the children . . ." This observation applies to Weissbort's poems of domestic life. Family life was a source of amazement. But if his domestic poems struck one critic as "warm", another felt that they lacked a "longer perspective".

Agonizing over his role as father, Weissbort also puzzled obsessively over his own father, who had died in 1958. In a booklet, *Fathers*, he gathers a number of these poems. It is his father's Jewishness, rather than his own, that he tries particularly hard to fathom. But his father belongs to an earlier world, one that he did not try to convey to his own progeny. Weissbort's sense of a lack of identity is not unconnected with his father's remoteness and reluctance to pass on this heritage. Still, while the father was remote he was also peculiarly vulnerable. His father, dying, comes to typify the Holocaust victim, if only by contrast: "My father/ his fleshless legs, tottering/ to the bathroom, but/ it was in his own home, from his own bed/ not bare ground, tiered bunks . . ." It is almost as if, for Weissbort, who in this same book has a sequence of rather midrashic poems on "The Origins of Death", death itself is Jewish!

His more direct meditations on the Holocaust, however, seem somewhat forced. Saved by his parents' migration from the deadly blast, Weissbort tried defiantly but ultimately unsuccessfully to find a way of alluding to the historical facts: "The tide of death stopped short,/ well short, of us,/ and then retreated,/ as it had to,/ as it surely had to/ so I might grow into myself,/ the self that waited for me." In "A Family Recitative", included in a chapbook *Inscription*, he attempts to personify the historical experience, re-telling his mother's family story, literally in her own words, drawing apparently on the transcription of taped conversations with her in the last years of her life.

A volume, published simultaneously in the US and UK, also in 1993, entitled *Lake* (*Nietzsche's Attaché Case* in the UK), groups poems in sequences. A poem on his father's death is included in the title sequence "Lake". On the shores of lake Michigan, distanced from his father's European world, Weissbort evokes the latter's "Jewish" death over there. In general, in this book, an attempt is made to set Jewishness in a wider context. "Lake" includes a poem which discusses the poet's relationship to nature. His early poems were often much concerned with nature, which they celebrated in a manner not uninfluenced by G.M. Hopkins, Dylan Thomas, and D.H. Lawrence, and later by Ted Hughes. But the verbal prodigality veiled a sense of exclusion from nature, a reluctance to engage metaphorically with natural beauty, being associated by Weissbort evidently with his Jewishness.

In a sequence, "Words", he agonizes over the problems of language, returning obsessively to the theme of somehow not quite possessing English. One may speculate that his engagement with translation is a way of penetrating, working at close hand with the language. "Strange Evidence" is a narrative sequence that directly confronts the poet's sense of alienation: "I never learnt the ropes, . . . / No one explained what had gone wrong./ No one told me where I was, or where I'd been./ Were it not for the evidence/ that strange evidence,/ I would not know."

In his most recent book, *What Was All the Fuss About?*, however, Weissbort's return to England, after nearly 30 years in America, seems to be prompting somewhat more philosophical reflections. Nevertheless, the poems still mostly start from specific memories or incidents and again Weissbort tells stories from his own life, returning to the theme of his Jewishness or foreignness "in this green and Christian land". His verse continues to strive for ever greater plainness, but without either poeticizing the prose or prosaicizing the poetry.

Weissbort's concerns are familiar enough and yet his approach is untypical of Anglo-Jewish poetry. This may have something to do with the degree of his detachment from the English "scene" as such, while at the same time being intimately linked, through translation and his editorship of *Modern Poetry in Translation*, to a wider world of literature.

VALENTINA POLUKHINA

Weissenberg, Isaac Meier

Polish fiction writer and dramatist, 1881–1938

Born in Zelechow, 1881. Limited formal education; workman in Warsaw and Łódź. Married, first, Molye Zilberman; divorced; two daughters; second, Bayltshe Nadler. Associated with Y.L. Perets; editor, *Yidishe zamlbikher*, the literary organ of Yiddish-speaking intellectuals in Warsaw, 1918–20; later associated with younger novelists including Oyzer Varshavsky and Simon Horenczyk, and editor of *Indzer hofenung*; struggled to achieve realistic literary style. Visited United States, 1923. Died 1938.

Selected Writings

Collections
Geklibene shriftn [Selected Writings] (contains *A shtetl*, *Dor hoylekh ve-dor bo*, *Tsum eydem oyf kest*, *A khoyv*, *A tate mit bonim*, *Di meshugene in dorf*, *R. yoel*, *a geneyve*, *A mayse mit a tsig*, *A shlekhte froy*), 1950
Geklibene verk [Selected Works], vol. 1, 1959

Fiction
"Dor hoylekh ve-dor bo" [One Generation Passeth Away and Another Generation Cometh] and "Der kitl" [The White Robe] in *Di yidishe bibliotek*, edited by Y.L. Perets, 1904
"A shtetl" [A Townlet], supplement to *Der veg* [The Way], 1906
Di meshugene in dorf [The Village Madmen], 1907
"Di bobeshe's ophitn" [Looked After By Granny] in *Yudish*, edited by Y.L. Perets, 1910; as "Di bobe un dos eynikl" [Granny and Grandchild], 1939
Kine un tayve un andere ertseylungen [Jealousy and Desire and Other Stories], 1911
Ertseylungen un bilder [Stories and Sketches], 1912
"Zelner" [Soldier] in *Shul bibliotek*, 1919
"A hayser shabes-tog" [A Hot Sabbath Day] in *Yidishe zamlbukh*, edited by Weissenberg, 1920
A shlekhte froy un andere ertseylungen [A Bad Woman and Other Stories], 1921–22
"Gebrengt a sod" [Brought a Secret], *Indzer hofenung* [Our Hope], bi-weekly journal, edited by Weissenberg (April 1926)
"Nisht dos" [Not This], *Indzer hofenung* (September 1926)
"Finf shreklekhe mayses" [Five Terrible Tales], *Indzer hofenung* (April 1927)
Der ibergang fun kindhayt tsu dervaksung [The Transition from Childhood to Adulthood], 1927
"Fervandlung" [Transformation], *Indzer hofenung* (October 1928)
"Ayfer un gevisn" [Zeal and Conscience], *Indzer hofenung* (April 1929)
Der moderner shed [The Modern Demon], 1930
Dos bukh fun libe [The Book of Love], 1930
Shtarker fin toyt [Stronger than Death], 1931
In der tifer eybikayt [In Deep Eternity], 2 vols, 1937
"A dertrunkener" [A Drowned Man], *Haynt* (September 1938)
"Der orimer yung" [The Poor Youth], *Der moment*, 1939
"Khasene makhn" [Making a Wedding], *Der moment*, 1939
Dertseylungen [Short Stories], 1954
"A farbisener" [Embittered] in *Svive*, edited by K. Molodovsky, 1966

Stories with unknown publication date: "A rekrutnik" [A Recruit]; "Berek pod kockem" [Berek near Kock], *Haynt*; "Bunem feldsher" [Bunem the Barber-Surgeon]; "Der blinder aron" [The Blind Aaron]; "Khayiml" [Khayiml]; "Malgoshe" [Malgoshe], *Der moment*; "Nigunim" [Melodies]; "Tsu hakofes" [At the Torah Circuit]; "Vide" [Confession]; "Vos kon trefn" [What Can Happen]

Plays
Kasper, 1910
Kine un tayve [Jealousy and Desire], 1911

Other
Gezamlte shriftn [Collected Writings], 1909
Geklibene shriftn [Selected Writings], 1911
Editor, *Yidishe zamlbikher* [Yiddish Almanacs], 5 vols, 1918–20
Gezamlte shriftn [Collected Writings], 1919
Toyznt un ayn nakht [A Thousand and One Nights], 1922
Geklibene verk [Selected Works], 6 vols, 1925–38
Kholem un beshayd, 1926
Geklibene verk [Selected Works], 1930
I.M. Weissenberg far yugnt [I.M. Weissenberg for the Youth], 1938

Further Reading

Glatstein, Jacob, *In Tokh Genumen*, vol. 2, New York: Matones, 1956
Howe, Irving and Eliezer Greenberg (editors), *A Treasury of Yiddish Stories*, New York: Viking, 1954

Leksikon fun der nayer yidisher literatur [Biographical Dictionary of Modern Yiddish Literature], vol. 3, New York: World Jewish Culture Congress, 1960
Ravitsh, Melekh, *Mayn leksikon*, vol. 1, Montreal: Komitet, 1945
Rejzen, Zalman, *Leksikon fun der yidisher literatur: prese un filologie* [Biographical Dictionary of Yiddish Literature: Press and Philology], vol. 1, Vilna: Vilner Farlag fun B. Kletskin, 1926; reprinted Berkeley: University of California Press, 1984
Roback, Abraham Aaron, *The Story of Yiddish Literature*, New York: Yiddish Scientific Institute, American Branch, 1940
Weissenberg-Akselrod, Pearl, *Y.M. Vaysenberg: Zayn Lebn un Shafn, 1878–1938* [I.M. Weissenberg: His Life and Works], Montreal: Aroysgegebn fun Y.M. Vaysenberg bukhfond, 1986

Weissenberg wanted to see the creation of a modern Jewish culture, with Yiddish playing a vital role. He argued that the Polish landscape and the history of Polish Jews, particularly the conditions in which they lived, had created a special genius in their language, which was rich, soft, warm, multicoloured, and nuanced. Hence, a first-class Yiddish literature was possible in Poland. What was missing, however, were dedicated writers rather than the self-serving ones who formed the literary establishment, the *meklers* (brokers) of the literary stock exchange, whom he satirized in *Der moderner shed* [The Modern Demon]. To this end, he created a series of journals to propagate his own views. He demonstrated early promise, but critics differ over why this was not fulfilled. Was it because he put too much effort into his various campaigns – that against the Litvaks (Lithuanian Jews) or for his new orthography of Yiddish? Was he too ambitious in the literary tasks he set himself and was he too much ruled by his emotions? Ravitsh called him the "Don Quixote of Yiddish literature". Weissenberg did not mince his words: he felt that vigour and honesty were a part of living, even if they involved pain. Passion could not exist without truth and truth could not exist without passion. The writer who was timid was no real writer at all. A wrong attitude was like a blister; you had to pierce it and get the pus out, otherwise it would poison the whole body. Personally courageous, he would stand up to Polish anti-Semitic hooligans and risk arrest to harbour a political fugitive, yet that same courage created the vein of insult which he visited on friend and foe alike. His first marriage broke down because his wife could not deal with his ferocious temper.

Weissenberg's treatment of Sholem Asch was characteristic of his attitude to successful writers, who must surely have sold out. Asch, with his all too obvious search for fame and fortune and his self-advertisement was, probably, too easy a target. Weissenberg wrote his novella *A shtetl* in reaction to what he saw as the sentimentalism of Asch's own book, *Dos shtetl*. As Perets wrote: "Asch's *Shtetl* is beautiful, but Weissenberg's *Shtetl* is deep". *A shtetl* is valuable because it places the 1905 revolution in the context of changing social realities of that shtetl society. A portrait of a year in the life of a Jewish community, it is a well crafted and, indeed, innovative piece of literature. Weissenberg's sympathies, of course, lay with the poor struggling workers he describes. He does not show them in a glamorous light, he does not neglect to reveal the cruelty that was a part of the class struggle and the starkness of that struggle. When the revolution is faltering, there is a call in the synagogue for "arms instead of psalms!" Though the work is not primarily concerned with the life of individuals, but rather that of the community, it is a community of flesh and blood. Though Weissenberg believed that the purpose of literature was to change society and was, himself, from the working class, he was not politically committed to its struggle. His subject-matter was not that of class, but all human beings. His natural sympathies lay with the underdog. This human concern was not just manifested on the literary level, but in his day-to-day behaviour. He was an instinctive and intensely passionate writer, and some have viewed him as uncontrolled by an intellectual or rational sense. It is true, that in some of his writing, reason is not in evidence. Weissenberg abhorred the prevalence of the Lithuanian system of orthography, as codified by YIVO in Vilna (Vilnius). His essay of 1926 in his journal *Indzer hofenung* [Our Hope] is so extreme and so problematical – the assertion that there was "no lust in Lithuania" and therefore no creativity, is typical – that it must undermine his argument. His orthographical rules were seen as far too narrowly based on the dialect of his own shtetl, Zelechow.

Weissenberg was a supreme technician of the descriptive art, a sculptor of characters, whose vigorous attack on words with hammer and chisel formed his staccato style, especially in *A shlekhte froy* [A Bad Woman] which inaugurated a revolution in Yiddish literature and, perhaps, prefigured Hemingway. He was considered the supreme realist writer, a master at describing the debased and the crude. In a story from the (unpublished) second volume of *In der tifer eybikayt* [In Deep Eternity], not dissimilar to *Animal Farm*, a group of dogs strive to make their way to the land of "Eternal Spring" but are overcome with greed and rivalry, and in the end they are reduced to fighting over the fur of the dead dogs, so as to keep themselves warm in the freezing conditions of the far north. But the brutalism was often restrained, because there was the passionate identification with the characters. As Weissenberg wrote in the first volume of *In der tifer eybikeyt*: "No one is truly guilty, for there are always reasons for their behaviour". In *Der ibergang fun kindhayt tsu dervaksung* [The Transition from Childhood to Adulthood], a semi-autobiographical novel, a sister murders her epileptic brother, because she foresees only an empty life for him. In another episode, a woman falls in love with her brother-in-law and her sister commits suicide. Weissenberg also had his lyrical side, and Glatsteyn, one of the leading Yiddish poets, described him as "a great poet". Weissenberg also wrote many satirical pieces and a number of short stories and plays. But the great novel eluded him. The achievement of this was to be the great test of Yiddish literature, its entry on to the European scene. He was working on a long novel before he died, but most of the manuscript was lost when Warsaw was bombed by the Germans in September 1939. Weissenberg's writing contained flashes of brilliance, and some marvellous writing, which was unmatched in its ability to depict Polish-Jewish life, but was seen as lacking a unifying thread.

Weissenberg could write with great humour. In "Fun rebns shtub" [From the Rebbe's House] a greedy mother believes that the clanging of her "geltinyu" [dear little money] must surely be sweeter than the singing of the angels in heaven. In "Khayim-Aron", the character's wife falls into a well, and while in Chelm-like fashion the whole town tut-tuts around the well waiting for a practical-minded Gentile to hook her out, her husband Khayim-Aron can't even be bothered to get out of bed. Despite his humour, his artistic and ideological outlook was extremely pessimistic: he saw a world of blatant injustice and endless suffering, where God simply was not bothered to intervene. Fate insults his heroes, laughs at them ("Goyroles vos lakhn"), human existence is a tragi-comedy, an eternal *tayku*, a question which it is impossible to resolve, and time and again redemption proves impossible. He realized, sometimes, that his message was too unadorned. His last words to his daughter Pearl were: "Have I said too much truth to people?"

BARRY DAVIS

Werfel, Franz

Czech-Austrian fiction writer, dramatist, and poet, 1890–1945

Born in Prague, 10 September 1890; father owner of glove-making business. Studied at Prague Gymnasium until 1908; University of Prague, 1909–10; University of Leipzig; University of Hamburg. Volunteer in Austro-Hungarian army, 1911–12. Reader for Kurt Wolff, publishers, Leipzig, 1912–14; co-founder and editor, Expressionist periodical *Der jüngste Tag*, 1913–21. Military service on eastern front, then in military press office, Vienna, during World War I. Participated in revolutionary movement in Vienna, 1919. Married, first, name untraced, 1918; set up home with Alma Gropius (widow of Gustav Mahler, wife of Walter Gropius), 1920; they married, 1929. Visited Capri, Locarno, and Ischl during 1920s; visited Palestine, 1925. Member, Prussian Academy of Arts, 1926 (expelled after Nazi seizure of power in Germany, 1933). Received Grillparzer Prize, 1926; Czechoslovak State Prize and Schiller Prize, 1927; Austrian Distinguished Service Cross for Art and Science, first class, 1937. Emigrated to France after absorption of Austria into Nazi Germany, 1938. President, Austrian PEN in Exile, from 1939. Escaped to Spain after Nazi invasion of France, 1940; emigrated with Heinrich Mann to United States; settled first in Los Angeles, 1940, then in Beverly Hills, 1942. Died in Beverly Hills, 26 August 1945.

Selected Writings

Collection

Gesammelte Werke [Collected Works], edited by Adolf D. Klarmann, 14 vols, 1948–75

Plays

Die Versuchung: ein Gespräch des Dichters mit dem Erzengel und Luzifer [The Temptation: A Conversation between the Poet and the Archangel and Lucifer], 1913
Die Troerinnen [The Trojan Women], 1915
Der Gerichtstag [The Day of Judgement], 1919
Die Mittagsgöttin [The Afternoon Goddess], 1919
Der Besuch aus dem Elysium: romantisches Drama [The Visit from Elysium: Romantic Drama], 1920
Spiegelmensch [Mirrorman], 1920
Bocksgesang, 1921; as *Goat Song*, translated by Ruth Langner, 1926
Schweiger: ein Trauerspiel [Silent One: A Mournful Play], 1922
Juarez und Maximilian: dramatische Historie in 3 Phasen und 13 Bildern, 1924; as *Juarez and Maximilian: A Dramatic History in Three Phases and Thirteen Pictures*, translated by Ruth Langner, 1926
Paulus unter den Juden, 1926; as *Paul among the Jews*, translated by Paul P. Levertoff, 1928
Das Reich Gottes in Böhmen: Tragödie eines Führers [The Kingdom of God in Bohemia], 1930
Der Weg der Verheissung: ein Bibelspiel, 1935; as *The Eternal Road*, translated by Ludwig Lewisohn, 1936
In Einer Nacht [In A Single Night], 1937
Jacobowsky und der Oberst: Komödie einer Tragödie in Drei Akten, 1944; as *Jacobowsky and the Colonel: Comedy of a Tragedy in Three Acts*, translated by Gustave O. Arlt, 1944
Die Dramen [The Dramas], 2 vols, edited by Adolf D. Klarmann, 1959

Fiction

Der Dschin: ein Märchen; Gedichte aus Der Gerichtstag; Blasphemie eines Irren; Fragmente [Der Dschin – The Jinn: A Fairy Tale; Poems from the Day of Judgement; Blasphemy of a Madman; Fragments], 1919
Nicht der Mörder, der Ermordete ist schuldig: eine Novelle [Not the Murderer, but the Victim is Guilty], 1920
Spielhof: eine Phantasie [Playground: A Fantasy], 1920
Arien [Arias], 1921
Verdi: Roman der Oper, 1924; as *Verdi: A Novel of the Opera*, translated by Helen Jessiman, 1925
Der Tod des Kleinbürgers, 1927; as *The Man Who Conquered Death*, translated by Clifton P. Fadiman and William A. Drake, 1927 (as *The Death of a Poor Man*, 1927)
Geheimnis eines Menschen [Saverio's Secret] (includes *Die Entfremdung* [Estrangement], *Geheimnis eines Menschen* [Secret of a Person], *Die Hoteltreppe* [The Staircase], *Das Trauerhaus* [The House of Mourning]), 1927
Der Abituriententag: die Geschichte einer Jugendschuld, 1928; as *Class Reunion*, translated by Whittaker Chambers, 1929
Barbara; oder, Die Frömmigkeit [Barbara; or, Piety], 1929; as *The Pure in Heart*, translated by Geoffrey Dunlop, 1931 (as *The Hidden Child*, 1931)
Die Geschwister von Neapel [The Sisters of Naples], 1931; as *The Pascarella Family*, translated by Dorothy F. Tait-Price, 1932
Kleine Verhältnisse [Poor People], 1931
Die vierzig Tage des Musa Dagh, 2 vols, 1933; as *The Forty Days of Musa Dagh*, translated by Geoffrey Dunlop, 1934 (as *The Forty Days*, 1934)

Höret die Stimme, 1937; as *Hearken unto the Voice*, translated by Moray Firth, 1938; as *Jeremias*, 1956
Twilight of a World, translated by H.T. Lowe-Porter, 1937
Der Veruntreute Himmel: die Geschichte einer Magd, 1939; as *Embezzled Heaven*, translated by Moray Firth, 1940
Das Lied von Bernadette, 1941; as *The Song of Bernadette*, translated by Ludwig Lewisohn, 1942
Eine Blassblaue Frauenschrift [Pale Blue Female's Handwriting], 1941
Die wahre Geschichte vom wiederhergestellten Kreuz [The True Story of the Restored Cross], 1942
Stern der Ungeborenen, 1946; as *Star of the Unborn*, translated by Gustave O. Arlt, 1946
Erzählungen aus zwei Welten [Stories from Two Worlds], edited by Adolf D. Klarmann, 3 vols, 1948–54
Meisternovellen [The Master Novels], 1972
Cella; oder, Die Überwinder [Cella; or, The Conqueror], 1982
Die Schwarze Messe: Erzählungen [The Black Mass: Stories], 1989
Die Entfremdung: Erzählungen [The Estrangement: Stories], 1990
Die Tanzenden Derwische: Erzählungen [The Dancing Dervishes: Stories], 1990
Weissenstein, der Weltverbesserer: Erzählungen [Weissenstein, the World Improver: Stories], 1990

Poetry
Der Weltfreund [The Philanthropist], 1911
Wir Sind: neue Gedichte [We Are: New Poems], 1913
Einander: Oden, Lieder, Gestalten [Each Other: Odes, Songs, Forms], 1915
Gesänge aus den drei Reichen: Ausgewählte Gedichte [Songs of Three Realms: Selected Poems], 1917
Beschwörungen [Entreaties], 1923
Gedichte [Poems], 1927
Neue Gedichte [New Poems], 1928
Dramatische Dichtungen [Dramatic Poems], 1929
Schlaf und Erwachen: neue Gedichte [Sleep and Awakening: New Poems], 1935
Gedichte aus Dreissig Jahren [Poems of Thirty Years], 1939
Poems, translated by Edith Abercrombie Snow, 1945
Gedichte aus den Jahren 1908–1945 [Poems From the Years 1908–1945], edited by Ernst Gottlieb and Felix Guggenheim, 1946
Das Lyrische Werk von Franz Werfel [The Lyrical Works of Franz Werfel], edited by Adolf D. Klarmann, 1967

Other
"Die christliche Sendung" [The Christian Mission], *Die Neue Rundshau*, 28 (January 1917): 92–105
Editor, *Briefe*, by Giuseppe Verdi, 1926; as *Verdi: The Man in His Letters*, translated by Edward Downes, 1942
Gesammelte Werke [Collected Works], 8 vols, 1927–36
"Begegnungen mit Rilke" [Encounters with Rilke], *Das Tagebuch*, 8/4 (1927): 140–44
Translator, *Simon Boccanegra*, by Verdi and F.M. Piave, 1929
Realismus und Innerlichkeit [Realism and Inwardness], 1931
Translator, *Don Carlos*, by Verdi, 1932
Können Wir ohne Gottesglauben Leben? [Can We Live without Belief in God?], 1932
Reden und Schriften [Speeches and Writings], 1932
Von der Reinsten Glückseligkeit des Menschen [About the Purest Bliss of Man], 1938
Between Heaven and Earth, translated by Maxim Newmark, 1944; as *Zwischen Oben und Unten*, 1946
Translator, *Die Macht des Schicksals* [La Forza del Destino], by Verdi and F.M. Piave, 1950
Das Franz Werfel Buch [The Franz Werfel Book], edited by Peter Stephan Jungk, 1986
Leben Heisst, Sich Mitteilen: Betrachtungen, Reden, Aphorismen [Life Means Communication: Reflections, Speeches, Aphorisms], 1992

Further Reading

Abels, Norbert, *Franz Werfel: Mit Selbstzeugnissen und Bilddokumenten*, Reinbek bei Hamburg: Rowohlt, 1990
Arlt, Gustave O. (editor), *About Franz Werfel*, New York: Rinehart, 1948
Arlt, Gustave O., "Franz Werfel and America", *Modern Language Forum*, 36 (March–June 1951): 1–7
Bentley, Eric, "Franz Werfel's Open Secret", *New Republic*, 114 (18 February 1946): 259–60
Braselmann, Werner, *Franz Werfel*, Wuppertal: Müller, 1960
Edman, Irwin, "What Price Mysticism?", *Saturday Review of Literature*, 27 (18 November 1944): 9–11
Eggers, Frank Joachim, *Ich bin ein Katholik mit judischen Gehirn: Modernitätskritik und Religion bei Joseph Roth und Franz Werfel*, Frankfurt: Peter Lang, 1996
Foltin, Lore B. (editor), *Franz Werfel 1890–1945*, Pittsburgh: University of Pittsburgh Press, 1961
Foltin, Lore B. and John M. Spalek, "Franz Werfel's Essays: A Survey", *German Quarterly*, 42/1 (March 1969): 172–203
Foltin, Lore B., *Franz Werfel*, Stuttgart: Metzler, 1972
Haas, Willy, *Die literarische Welt: Erinnerungen*, Munich: List, 1958
Heizer, Donna K., *Jewish-German Identity in the Orientalist Literature of Else Lasker-Schüler, Friedrich Wolf, and Franz Werfel*, Columbia, South Carolina: Camden House, 1996
Huber, Lothar (editor), *Franz Werfel: An Austrian Writer Reassessed*, Oxford and New York: Berg, 1988
Jungk, Peter Stephan, *Franz Werfel: A Life in Prague, Vienna and Hollywood*, translated by Anselm Hollo, New York: Grove Weidenfeld, 1990; as *A Life Torn by History: Franz Werfel 1890–1945*, London: Weidenfeld and Nicolson, 1990
Kirby, Rachel, *The Culturally Complex Individual: Franz Werfel's Reflections on Minority Identity and Historical Depiction in The 40 Days of Musa Dagh*, Lewisburg, Pennsylvania: Bucknell University Press, 1999
Klarmann, Adolf D., "Franz Werfel's Eschatology and Cosmogony", *Modern Language Quarterly*, 7/4 (December 1946): 385–410
Lea, Henry A., "Prodigal Sons in Werfel's Fiction", *Germanic Review*, 40 (1965)

Lea, Henry A., "The Failure of Political Activism in Werfel's Plays", *Symposium*, 22 (Winter 1968)
Mahler-Werfel, Alma and E.B. Ashton, *And the Bridge is Love*, New York: Harcourt Brace, 1958; London: Hutchinson, 1959
Mahler-Werfel, Alma, *Mein Leben*, Frankfurt: Fischer, 1960
Michaels, Jennifer E., *Anarchy and Eros: Otto Gross' Impact on German Expressionist Writers*, New York: Peter Lang, 1983
Nehring, Wolfgang and Hans Waggener (editors), *Franz Werfel im Exil*, Bonn: Bouvier, 1992
Pell, David L., "Franz Werfel: A Bibliography of Works and Criticism", *West Virginia University Philological Papers*, 18 (1971)
Politzer, Heinz, "Prague and the Origins of Rainer Maria Rilke, Franz Kafka and Franz Werfel", *Modern Language Quarterly*, 16/1 (March 1955): 49–62
Rolleston, James, "The Usable Future: Franz Werfel's *Star of the Unborn* as Exile Literature" in *Protest-Form-Tradition: Essays on German Exile Literature*, edited by Joseph P. Strelka *et al.*, University: University of Alabama Press, 1979
Slochower, Harry, "Franz Werfel and Alfred Döblin: The Problem of Individualism in *Barbara* and in *Berlin Alexanderplatz*", *Journal of English and German Philology*, 33 (1944–46): 73–82
Smith, Jeremy, *Religious Feeling and Religious Commitment in Faulkner, Dostoyevsky, Werfel and Bernanos*, New York: Garland, 1988
Sokel, Walter, *The Writer in Extremis: Expressionism in Twentieth-Century German Literature*, Stanford, California: Stanford University Press, 1959
Spalek, John M. and Robert Bell (editors), *Exile: The Writers' Experience*, Chapel Hill: University of North Carolina Press, 1982
Specht, Richard, *Franz Werfel: Versuch einer Zeitspiegelung*, Berlin: Zsolnay, 1926
Stamm, Israel, "Religious Experience in Werfel's *Barbara; oder, Die Frommigkeit*", *Publications of the Modern Language Association of America*, 54 (1939): 332–47
Steiman, Lionel B., *Franz Werfel: The Faith of an Exile, from Prague to Beverly Hills*, Waterloo, Ontario: Wilfrid Laurier University Press, 1985
Williams, C.E., *The Broken Eagle: The Politics of Austrian Literature from Empire to Anschluss*, London: Elek, and New York: Barnes and Noble, 1974
Zahn, Leopold, *Franz Werfel*, Berlin: Colloquium, 1966

When Werfel was elected to the Prussian Academy of the Arts in 1926 he was one of the most popular writers of his time. His books went into several editions, his public readings overflowed. He was popular without being a writer of light fiction.

Despite his largely assimilated parental home, Werfel was introduced into the Jewish community, although his upbringing was entrusted to an affectionate and devoutly Catholic nursemaid, whom in 1928 he portrayed in *Barbara* (*The Pure in Heart*). Right from his schooldays he had a number of acquaintances who would later become important writers; in 1908 he met Max Brod and in 1909 visited the famous Cafe Arco, meeting place of the "Prague Circle": Franz Kafka, Walter Hasenclever, Willy Haas, Oskar Baum, and others. In 1911 in Berlin Max Brod recited poems from Werfel's first volume of poetry *Der Weltfreund* [The Philanthropist], which soon brought him to public attention and is considered the start of his literary Expressionism. Werfel, whose life until then had been divided between the world of commercial realities and the world of introspection and imagination, found here a concordance of life and art that was a revolutionary contrast to *l'art pour l'art*. His directness of expression and sensitivity to the currents of the time made him one of the most widely read of the Expressionists. In 1913, while working as a reader at the Kurt Wolff publishing house, he published the most important series of writings of the Expressionist movement, *Der jüngste Tag*. His declaration: "The new poet will be free of constraints, and shall start from the beginning . . . The world starts anew with each second – let us forget literature!!"

Even before the war, Werfel had become a committed pacifist in the face of heightened social and political conflicts. Martin Buber asked him to join a circle including Gustav Landauer and Max Scheler which wanted to fight against militarism. His experiences on the Galician front had profoundly affected Werfel and moved him to participate in the October Revolution in Vienna, but his Christian and religious beliefs meant that he was against any form of violence. In 1919 in Prague, he became a member of the Socialist Council of Intellectual Workers. In the period 1919–20 he worked his experiences and life story into the plays *Spiegelmensch* [Mirrorman], *Bocksgesang* (*Goat Song*), and his first novel (designated as a novella) *Nicht der Mörder, der Ermordete ist schuldig* [Not the Murderer, but the Victim is Guilty]. Alongside autobiographical passages, here he began to portray friends and acquaintances in his works. The novel deals with the problem of patricide, a central theme in Expressionism. *Verdi: Roman der Oper* (*Verdi: A Novel of the Opera*) heralded the transition to a new phase in his life, incorporating his lifelong love of opera and Verdi in particular.

Werfel's relationship with Alma Mahler, who was still married to the architect Walter Gropius, strengthened his connections with Catholicism, and in the mid-1920s, he outgrew Expressionism and turned to historical subjects. When the play *Paulus unter den Juden* (*Paul among the Jews*) appeared in 1926, many believed that he had entered the Catholic church. He wrote in a letter:

> I wanted to do everything but "explain Christianity". Quite the opposite! I wrote this play as a Jew. And no moment for Judaism seemed to me "more dialectic", "more tragic", than when the antinomian views of the Torah and the Nation fall apart.

His view of the world was changing at this time; it was decisive for him that the political axis was no longer "right–left" but "between above and below" (i.e. between heaven and earth): for him the drama of life, according to the title of a book of confessions published while Werfel was in exile in the USA in 1944, was played out between God and the world.

In one of his most successful novels, *Der Abituriententag* (*Class Reunion*), the world of his youth is critically revived in this orientation and the destructive violence of the age portrayed in the annihilation of the Jewish pupil Adler.

After his first visit to Palestine in 1925, Werfel increasingly concerned himself with the tense relationship between Judaism and Christianity, without being able to find an unequivocal answer. In Jerusalem he visited Hugo Bergmann, the schoolfriend of Kafka, who had died in 1924, and Gershom Scholem. His early abhorrence of the eastern European Jews and the soulless Judaism of assimilation and his rejection of the Zionism supported within his circle of friends remained unchanged after 1917 when he published "Die christliche Sendung" [The Christian Mission], attracting the sharp criticism of his friend Brod. In 1929 he left the Jewish community, as Alma Mahler had made this a condition of marriage, but did not enter the Catholic church. Only under the pressure of fascism did he write two works, *Der Weg der Verheissung* (*The Eternal Road*) and *Höret die Stimme* (*Hearken unto the Voice*) which dealt more positively with Judaism. In the face of the threat to the very existence of the Jews, he took up their side, but without ever betraying his Catholic side.

For Werfel himself, the problem of Judaism and Christianity, however agonizingly he dealt with it and however insistently it was brought to him, was masked by the problem of the "upper" and "lower" world. "Without introspection there is no external world, without imagination no reality." A world without introspection but full of destructive anger was, for him, civilization.

The result was the loss of man as a vehicle of his fate, and the transformation of man into material. In 1930 Werfel was confronted by the extermination of the Armenian nation by the Turks and he wrote the novel *Die vierzig Tage des Musa Dagh* (*The Forty Days of Musa Dagh*), an indictment of genocide, almost in the form of documentation taken from multiple files, but also against the "Vampirism of the apparatus which sucks these people dry, whom it should serve". Back in 1932 Werfel had written to his parents that the subject of the book, "oppression, annihilation of minorities by nationalism", had acquired a "symbolic topicality". Although in March 1933 he signed a loyal address to the Prussian Academy of the Arts, he was expelled from the Academy before the letter was officially processed; on 10 May his books were burnt by the Nazis and in 1934 his new novel was banned in Germany.

Werfel directly experienced the turn towards fascism in Vienna and repeatedly described the events in his subsequent writings. Against this political background he said at a speech in 1937 in memory of the temples in Luxor and Karnak: "Then it became clear to me: art is the opposite of passing time. It is capturing time. It is dispelling death." And: "Archaic man lived and thought uniquely and only in the form of allegory. It is in this respect that we are most profoundly different from him. For us, things merely are but they mean nothing." At the 15th International Congress of PEN in Exile in Zürich, Werfel's critical attitude to civilization brought him into severe conflict with Lion Feuchtwanger, who supported the Soviet Union. In 1940 Werfel fled via France to the unloved USA – first to Los Angeles, later Santa Barbara – where he first wrote the novel *Das Lied von Bernadette* (*The Song of Bernadette*), in which he finally portrayed his closeness to Catholicism. In *Jacobowsky und der Oberst* (*Jacobowsky and the Colonel*) he employed great irony in incorporating his experiences of exile; in his last great novel, *Stern der Ungeborenen* (*Star of the Unborn*), he wrote a type of anti-Utopia of a humanity fully civilized and repressing death. Shortly before his death, he learned of the concentration camps in Germany and of Hiroshima. He hoped for a return to "the world of humanity".

MANFRED VOIGTS
translated by Karen Goulding

Wesker, Arnold

British dramatist, 1932–

Born in Stepney, London, 24 May 1932. Studied at Upton House Technical School, Hackney, London, 1943–48; London School of Film Technique, 1955–56. Served in Royal Air Force, 1950–52. Furniture-maker's apprentice and carpenter's mate, 1948; bookseller's assistant, 1949 and 1952; plumber's mate, 1952; seed sorter on farm, 1953; kitchen porter, 1953–54; pastry cook, London and Paris, 1954–58. Married Doreen Bicker, 1958; two sons, two daughters. Founder and director, Centre 42, 1961–70; Chair, British Centre, 1978–83, and President, Playwrights Permanent Committee, 1981–83, International Theatre Institute. Many awards, including Arts Council of Great Britain grant, 1958; *Evening Standard* Drama Award, 1959; Marzotto Prize, 1964; Best Foreign Play Award (Spain), 1979; Goldie, 1987; Last Frontier Lifetime Achievement Award (for distinguished service to theatre), 1999. Fellow, Royal Society of Literature, 1985.

Selected Writings

Plays
The Kitchen, 1957
The Wesker Trilogy, 1960
  Chicken Soup with Barley, 1958
  Roots, 1959
  I'm Talking about Jerusalem, 1960
Chips with Everything, 1962
The Nottingham Captain: A Moral for Narrator, Voices and Orchestra, 1962
Menace, 1963
The Four Seasons, 1965
Their Very Own and Golden City, 1965
The Friends, London, 1970
The Old Ones, 1972
The Wedding Feast, 1974
The Journalists, 1975
Love Letters on Blue Paper, 1976
The Merchant, 1976; revised as *Shylock*, 1990
Caritas, 1981
Mothers: Four Portraits, 1982; as *Four Portraits of Mothers*, 1984

Annie, Anna, Annabella, 1983; as *Annie Wobbler*, 1983
Sullied Hand, 1984
Yardsale, 1984
Bluey, 1985
One More Ride on the Merry-Go-Round, 1985
Whatever Happened to Betty Lemon?, 1986
Little Old Lady, 1988
Beorhtel's Hill, 1989
Shoeshine, 1989
One Woman Plays: Yardsale, Whatever Happened to Betty Lemon?, Four Portraits of Mothers, The Mistress, Annie Wobbler, 1989
The Kitchen and Other Plays (includes revised version of *The Four Seasons, The Kitchen, Their Very Own*, and *Golden City*), 1990
Chips with Everything and Other Plays (includes *The Friends, The Old Ones, Love Letters on Blue Paper*), 1990
Shylock and Other Plays (includes *The Journalists, The Wedding Feast, The Merchant as Shylock*), 1990
Lady Othello and Other Plays: One More Ride on the Merry-Go-Round, Caritas, When God Wanted a Son, Lady Othello, Bluey, 1990
Blood Libel, 1991
The Mistress, 1991
Letter to a Daughter, 1992
Three Woman Talking, 1992
Wild Spring and Other Plays, 1994

Screenplay: *The Kitchen*, 1961

Radio Plays: *Annie, Anna, Annabella*, 1983; *Yardsale*, 1984; *Bluey*, 1985

Television Plays: *Menace*, 1963; *Love Letters on Blue Paper*, 1976; *Diary of a Good Neighbour*, 1989; *Letter to a Daughter*, 1992

Short Stories
Love Letters on Blue Paper, 1974
Said the Old Man to the Young Man: Three Stories, 1978
Love Letters on Blue Paper and Other Stories, 1980
The King's Daughters: 12 Erotic Stories, 1998

Other
Labour and the Arts: II; or, What, Then, Is to be Done?, 1960
The Modern Playwright; or, "O Mother, Is It Worth It?", 1961
Fears of Fragmentation, 1970
Six Sundays in January, 1971
Say Goodbye – You May Never See Them Again: Scenes from Two East-End Backgrounds, 1974
Words as Definitions of Experience, 1976
Journey into Journalism, 1977
Fatlips, 1978
The Journalists: A Triptych (includes the play *The Journalists, A Journal of the Writing of "The Journalists"*, and *Journey into Journalism*), 1979
Distinctions, 1985
Caritas, 1991
As Much as I Dare: An Autobiography, 1994
The Birth of Shylock and the Death of Zero Mostel, 1997

Further Reading

Brown, John Russell, *Theatre Language: A Study of Arden, Osborne, Pinter, and Wesker*, London: Penguin, and New York: Taplinger, 1972
Dornan, Reade W., *Arnold Wesker Revisited*, New York: Twayne, 1994
Dornan, Reade W. (editor), *Arnold Wesker: A Casebook*, New York: Garland, 1998
Drabble, Margaret, article, *New Review* (February 1975)
Hayman, Ronald, *Arnold Wesker*, London: Heinemann, 1970; New York: Ungar, 1973
Itzin, Catherine, *Stages in the Revolution: Political Theatre in Britain since 1968*, London: Eyre Methuen, 1980
Leech, Clifford, "Two Romantics: Arnold Wesker and Harold Pinter" in *Contemporary Theatre*, edited by John Russell Brown and Bernard Harris, London: Arnold, 1962; New York: St Martin's Press, 1963
Leeming, Glenda, *Wesker the Playwright*, London and New York: Methuen, 1983
Leeming, Glenda (editor), *Wesker on File*, London and New York: Methuen, 1985
O'Connor, Garry, "Production Casebook 2: Arnold Wesker's *The Friends*", *Theatre Quarterly* (April 1971)
Wilcher, Robert, *Understanding Arnold Wesker*, Columbia: University of South Carolina Press, 1991

Arnold Wesker, considered one of the leading figures in postwar English drama, is the author of more than 30 plays, four volumes of short stories, two volumes of essays, children's literature, poetry, a book on journalism, and an extensive array of other writings including many letters. His plays have been translated into 17 languages and performed worldwide.

An autodidact, he received his education through the medium of BBC radio which he studied and listened to avidly, to be followed later by "higher education" at London's fabled Royal Court Theatre, the venue which was virtually to become his Alma Mater. Personal experience has frequently formed the basis of much of his work. His birth into a family of East End "cockney Jews" has been the cornerstone on which a great deal of his writing is based, although not all of his work is autobiographical. His National Service in the Royal Air Force as a lowly conscript in the early 1950s forms the background of one of his most commercially successful plays, *Chips with Everything*, in which two airmen, one an aristocrat and the other a working-class boy, form a relationship which develops despite the English ethic of class. As Harold Hobson of the Sunday Times put it "This is . . . the first anti-Establishment play of which the Establishment has cause to be afraid."

The Wesker family were true-blue socialists of the 1930s, a period in the UK when the bogeys of fascism and anti-Semitism were on the rise. The East End was rife with political passions and Wesker's family were right in the midst of it. Oswald Mosley, a friend and proponent of the Third Reich, was staging marches right through Jewish areas with his well-dressed blackshirts yelling ugly slogans. Wesker's vivid recollections of his family's reaction to such events are illustrated with insight and humour in *Chicken Soup with Barley*. This first success was directed by John Dexter at the avant-garde Belgrade theatre in Coventry in 1958.

Chicken Soup with Barley is the first part of *The Wesker Trilogy*. This work has done more than any other to gain Wesker international recognition despite an at times guarded respect from the literary establishment. *Roots*, in the words of the playwright himself, "explores the theme of self-discovery". The play is problematic to stage outside England as a great deal of its impact comes from the use of a strong Norfolk brogue. The character of "Jew-boy" Ronnie from *Chicken Soup with Barley* never actually arrives, although his influence is heard throughout. In the third part of *The Wesker Trilogy*, *I'm Talking about Jerusalem*, the reader may be surprised to find that it is not about the Holy City itself but is based on the English hymn / anthem that extols the idea of a New Jerusalem in which England itself is portrayed in idealistic terms. When the trilogy was published in its entirety it received rave reviews. The poet Ted Hughes summed up a very long critique thus: "... Wesker's 'Socialism' is something close to a poetic intuition, a concern with the life at the root of all parties and opinions." Margaret Drabble remarks that "Wesker's reputation has survived the vicissitudes of fashion . . ." while Bernard Levin in the *Times* states that "The passion of Mr Wesker's themes is matched by the living fire in his writing . . ." More than 400,000 copies of the trilogy in the Penguin paperback edition have been sold.

Although Wesker is an open and partisan Jew, very little of this is evident in the bulk of his work. Although intermarriage is found throughout his private and family connections and religion plays little part, Wesker is a "Jewish" writer. His oeuvre is eclectic, covering many diverse subjects such as providing the text for a book on the old East End with illustrations by an old schoolfriend, the artist John Allin, *Say Goodbye – You May Never See Them Again*, to a play based on the life of an actress, *Wild Spring*, premiered in Tokyo in October 1994. Yet other styles were undertaken when in 1991 he wrote both the libretto for the opera *Caritas* with Robert Saxton (also Jewish) on the fate of a medieval nun and, one of his very rare Judaic works, *Blood Libel*, the play commissioned by the Norwich Playhouse to commemorate the accusation of ritual child murder in that city in 1144.

In Wesker's case the label "Jewish writer" is difficult to interpret: is he a writer who is Jewish or can his work truly be defined as Jewish? His autobiography, *As Much as I Dare*, is very revealing. His origins are a source of pride told with great openness. As a chronicler of the history of London Jewry he has no equal, his youth as a member of Habonim (the Hebrew term for the Builders) illustrates unequivocally his socialist and Zionist tendencies, yet apart from this there is virtually nothing else. He has held on to his loyalty to the State of Israel, although an occasional foray into sympathy for the Palestinian ideal has led to some antagonism in the Jewish press. Yet, considering his age, he seems to have lost the Holocaust, both in his writing and his life. This dichotomy between his Englishness and his origins have led to a "them and us" attitude, not at all unusual among Anglo-Jewish writers, but one that has led to an uncomfortable relationship between English-born Jews and other European intellectuals.

The book that has had the greatest influence in the USA has probably been *The Birth of Shylock and the Death of Zero Mostel*. This book has become a piece of theatrical history describing the heartbreak of attempting to interest national theatres in a new reading of the Shylock story, the eventual production bringing with it the destruction of old friendships and the complete breakdown of the production when the great Zero Mostel died after one performance. As the actor Simon Callow wrote in his review for the *Sunday Times*, it is "a totally authentic and powerfully moving account of how plays are made – or broken." The battle between a director (in this case Wesker's old mentor and friend John Dexter) and writer have rarely been described with such passion, but Wesker has been deeply wounded by the failure of *Shylock* to find a place in the theatrical repertoire. However the diaries themselves have been widely read and highly praised.

Arnold Wesker continues to write prolifically and his plays continue to be performed worldwide. To quote the distinguished television producer and writer Michael Kustow, "Just when you think you've got him pinned down as a Jew, along he comes with *Caritas*, a story soaked in Christian mysticism . . ."

SALLY WHYTE

West, Nathanael

US fiction writer and dramatist, 1903–1940

Born Nathan Weinstein in New York City, 17 October 1903, to Max Weinstein and wife Anna (née Wallenstein), immigrants from Lithuania. Studied at DeWitt Clinton High School, New York; Tufts College, Massachusetts, 1921; Brown University, from 1922–24, PhB 1924. Worked for father in real estate business, 1924–25. Changed name, 1926. Lived in Paris, 1926–27. Night manager, Kenmore Hall Hotel and Suffolk Club Hotel, New York, 1927–31. Associate editor, working with William Carlos Williams, *Contact: An American Quarterly*, 1931–32; scriptwriter in Hollywood, for Columbia Studios, 1933, 1938; Republic, 1936–38; Universal, 1938; RKO, 1938–40. Married Eileen McKenney, 1940. Died with wife in car crash, 22 December 1940.

Selected Writings

Collections
The Complete Works, 1 vol., 1957
Novels and Other Writings, 1997

Fiction
The Dream Life of Balso Snell, 1931
Miss Lonelyhearts, 1933
A Cool Million: The Dismantling of Lemuel Pitkin, 1934
The Day of the Locust, 1939

Play
Good Hunting: A Satire, with Joseph Shrank, 1938

Screenplays: *Follow Your Heart*, with Lester Cole and Samuel Ornitz, 1936; *President's Mystery*, with Lester Cole, 1936; *Ticket to Paradise*, with Jack Natteford, 1936; *It Could Happen to You*, with Samuel Ornitz, 1937; *Rhythm in the Clouds*, 1937; *Born to be Wild*, 1938; *Gangs of New York*, 1938; *Orphans of the Street*, 1938; *Five Came Back*, with Jerry Cady and Dalton Trumbo, 1939; *I Stole a Million*, with Lester Cole, 1939; *Spirit of Culver*, with Whitney Bolton, 1939; *Let's Make Music*, 1940; *Men against the Sky*, with John Twist, 1940

Further Reading

Barnard, Rita, *The Great Depression and the Culture of Abundance: Kenneth Fearing, Nathanael West and Mass Culture in the 1930s*, Cambridge and New York: Cambridge University Press, 1995
Bloom, Harold (editor), *Nathanael West*, New York: Chelsea House, 1986
Bradbury, Malcolm, *The Modern American Novel*, Oxford and New York: Oxford University Press, 1992
Cramer, Carter M., *The World of Nathanael West: A Critical Interpretation*, Emporia: Kansas State Teachers' College, 1971
Fiedler, Leslie, "Master of Dreams", *Partisan Review*, 34 (Summer 1967): 339–56
Fiedler, Leslie, *Love and Death in the American Novel*, revised edition, New York: Stein and Day, 1966; London: Jonathan Cape, 1967
Galloway, David, "Nathanael West's Dream Dump", *Critique*, 6 (Winter 1963–64)
Hyman, Stanley Edgar, *Nathanael West*, Minneapolis: University of Minnesota Press, 1962
Light, James F., *Nathanael West: An Interpretative Study*, Evanston, Illinois: Northwestern University Press, 1961
Long, Robert Emmet, *Nathanael West*, New York: Ungar, 1985
Madden, David (editor), *Nathanael West: The Cheaters and the Cheated*, De Land, Florida: Everett Edwards, 1973
Malin, Irving, *Nathanael West's Novels*, Carbondale: Southern Illinois University Press, 1972
Raban, Jonathan, "A Surfeit of Commodities: The Novels of Nathanael West" in *The American Novel and the 1920s*, edited by Malcolm Bradbury and David Palmer, London: Edward Arnold, and New York: Crane Russak, 1971
Reid, Randall, *The Fiction of Nathanael West*, Chicago: University of Chicago Press, 1967
Ross, Alan, "The Dead Centre: An Introduction to Nathanael West", *Horizon*, 18 (October 1948)
Scott, Nathan A., *Nathanael West: A Critical Essay*, Grand Rapids, Michigan: Eerdmans, 1971
Sharma, R.K., *Contemporary Black Humour American Novels from Nathanael West to Thomas Berger*, Delhi: Ajanta, 1988
Siegel, Ben (editor), *Critical Essays on Nathanael West*, New York: G.K. Hall, 1994
Vannatta, Dennis P., *Nathanael West: An Annotated Bibliography of the Scholarship and Works*, New York: Garland, 1976
Volpe, Edmund, "The Waste Land of Nathanael West", *Renascence*, 13 (Winter 1961)
White, William, *Nathanael West: A Comprehensive Bibliography*, Kent, Ohio: Kent State University Press, 1975
Widmer, Kingsley, *Nathanael West*, Boston: Twayne, 1982
Wisker, Alistair, *The Writing of Nathanael West*, New York: St Martin's Press, and London: Macmillan, 1990

Nathanael West, originally Nathan Weinstein, constructed a series of masks and identities both in life and literature. He was admitted to university on fictional grades and the purposeful confusion of his name. His literary pseudonym, Nathanael West, was partly self-invention into the traditions of New England (Nathanael Hawthorne), while his surname implied the ethnically anonymous, yet boundless openings of America. This secularizing mask over his Jewish origins was perhaps a response to anti-Semitic exclusions suffered in early life. It was also a mask for licensing cruelty, violence, and sordidity in his fictions as satiric vehicles for an attack on modern American life.

It could be argued that his internalized anti-Semitism was the source of his bitterness and satiric vehemence, or he might be understood in the tradition of Swift and Voltaire, satirically commenting on contemporary life via the thwarted progress of his various beleaguered Everymen facing up to self-deluding escapes. From Leslie Fiedler's perspective he is an American Kafka, an outsider, writing fictional parables on religious topics. Although his appeal was limited in the 1930s, West became appreciated in the 1960s as an American literary model for ironic "black humour". In his four short novels, West's style is marked by terse poetic description, satiric humour, brief conversational exchanges, violence as subject, and method contained within concise forms.

His first publication, *The Dream Life of Balso Snell*, often dismissed as immature student humour, attempts to rubbish the whole human cultural enterprise. Part of its failure is that in 60 pages it covers an array of artistic figures as merely the butts of jokes. Concision leads to an undeveloped series of spoofs. *The Dream Life of Balso Snell* parodies Joyce's *Ulysses* by echoing *The Iliad* instead of *The Odyssey*, the "hero" entering the Trojan Horse through the anus. The putative first and greatest work of Western literature diminished to an excremental joke.

Balso is taken on a Virgil-like tour of the Underworld guided by a comic Jew. In this Hell he meets surreal characters such as St Pace, the flea on Jesus' armpit, John Raskolnikov, and Beagle Hamlet Darwin. A range of Modernist writers are mocked, but the finale is Balso's sexual encounter with Miss McGeeney, a Penelope figure who gabbles like Molly in *Ulysses* and shockingly turns into a female man. As that of a Jewish outsider, West's strategy could be identified as the constant subversion of mainstream society's norms and icons.

Arguably his most coherent work, *Miss Lonelyhearts* is a fast tempo, modern "faithless Pilgrim's Progress" (according to Alan Ross) where the eponymous Christ-like schlemiel of the title is the male agony aunt of the *New York Post-Dispatch*. The columnist viewed through the function of his mask can no longer deliver his Christo-Humanistic panaceas for dealing with the grotesque sufferings of those who sign themselves "Broad Shoulders", "Broken-hearted", and "Sick-of-it-all." Miss Lonelyhearts becomes enmeshed socially and sexually with the plights of correspondents and the unfulfilled longings of his editor's wife. Yet the cynical realism of Lonelyhearts' editor, Shrike, and the satiric reduction of human beings to objects undercut all possibilities of geographical, emotional, or spiritual escape from the impossible horrors of urban living. The accumulation of shocking deformities, Doyle's enlarged foot or "Desperate's" noseless face, is the suffering of a world for which Lonelyhearts' human sacrifice is inadequate. In running to help all the victims of life's tragedies, the columnist is led to an absurd and useless death.

Although overtly Christological with few Jewish references, *Miss Lonelyhearts* is underpinned by several characteristically Jewish themes. West polarizes Messianic hope against gritty realism. There is a subversion of mainstream Christianity, an anti-hero small man is set against the overwhelming problems of modem urban life. West again adopts the outsider's perspective of, in Fiedler's expression, the "unchurched".

A Cool Million is a Swiftian satire on American dream capitalism. West reverses the Horatio Alger myth of Ragged Dick's struggle to success through a series of Lemuel Gulliver-like episodic travels. The failures of Lemuel Pitkin are reduced through the Yiddish resonance of his diminutive surname. These involve the hero's "dismantling" or loss of teeth, eye, thumb, leg, then scalping, finally being shot to become a martyr for an American fascist party. The American good boy's home in New England is bought by an interior decorator as the basis for a brothel that miniaturizes all world cultures. Lem's girlfriend, Betty, is raped and set up as a prostitute in this establishment. Lem turns to ex-president of the USA, "Shagpole" Whipple, the current owner of the Rat River National Bank, who enrols him in the National Revolutionary Party. The party's aims are to purge America of Marxism and international capitalism, both of which are associated with Jewish interests.

Negative stereotypes and diminution of Jewish characters are modulated through a series of "mock styles" (Bradbury's term). West could be accused of Jewish self-hate, but these attitudes were a worrying norm of America in the 1930s and West's humour about Jewish stereotypes is counterbalanced by his highly politicized satire aimed against American versions of fascism.

West's finest and last work, *The Day of the Locust*, is about the plague of parasites in Hollywood who feed off the news and films of "lynchings, murder, sex crimes, explosions . . . miracles, revolutions, wars". The anti-heroes of this novel are crowds of failures who have come to Los Angeles to die, but have a degenerate interest in brothels, vicious cock-fighting, or the dubious glamour of being a studio extra. These are the frenzied crowds of embittered dreamers, like Abe Kusich, the pugnacious dwarf, Harry Greener, "bedraggled harlequin", and his daughter, the hopeful starlet Faye (fairy-like, as in Scott Fitzgerald's Daisy Faye) Greener (pastures?), whose invitation to love is "closer to murder". At the centre are the unhealthy, "reject" Homer Simpson and the minor artist Tod Hackett, whose apocalyptic picture, *The Burning of Los Angeles* is enacted when a mob, awaiting a premiere, breaks loose to burn and loot the city.

West often has a lack of sympathy for his characters, but this is a function of satire; the more empathy or development of individuals, the less poignant the attack. His surreal humour could be identified with immigrant defensiveness or the smart wisecracks of his brother-in-law S.J. Perelman.

West's early death, however, prevented his development from major satiric talent into a more substantial novelist.

MERVYN LEBOR

Wiesel, Elie

Romanian-born US fiction writer, dramatist, and journalist, 1928–

Born Eliezer Wiesel, in Sighet, 30 September 1928. Interned in concentration camps Auschwitz, 1944–45, and Buchenwald, 1945. Studied at the Sorbonne, 1948–51. Foreign correspondent, *L'Arche*, Paris, from 1949, *Yedioth Ahronoth*, Tel Aviv, from 1952, and *Forverts* (*Jewish Daily Forward*), New York, from 1957. Naturalized US citizen, 1963. Married Marion Esther Rose, 1969; one son. Professor of Judaic studies, City College of City University of New York, 1972–76; Andrew Mellon Professor in the Humanities since 1976, and professor of philosophy since 1988, Boston University; Henry Luce Visiting Scholar in the Humanities and Social Thought, Yale University, 1982–83. Chair, US Holocaust Memorial Council. Many awards, including Rivarol Prize, 1963; Remembrance Award, 1965; Epstein Award, 1965; Jewish Heritage Award, 1966; Médicis Prize (France), 1969; Bordin Prize, 1972; Eleanor Roosevelt Memorial Award, 1972; American Liberties Medallion, 1972; Cohen Award, 1973; Martin Luther King, Jr, Award, 1973; Joseph Prize for Human Rights, 1978; Shazar Award, 1979; Prix Livre International, 1980; Jabotinsky Award, 1980; Shcharansky Humanitarian Award, 1983; Royal Academy of Belgium International Literary Prize for Peace, 1983; Congressional Gold Medal of Achievement, 1984; Anne Frank Award, 1985; Medal of Jerusalem, 1986; Nobel Peace Prize, 1986; Edelman Award, 1989; Weil Award, 1990. Grand Officier, Légion d'Honneur (France), 1990.

Selected Writings

Fiction

Un di velt hot geshvign [And the World Has Remained Silent], 1956; revised and abridged edition, as *La Nuit*, 1958; as *Night*, translated by Stella Rodway, 1960

L'Aube, 1960; as *Dawn*, translated by Frances Frenaye, 1961

Le Jour, 1961; as *The Accident*, translated by Anne Borchardt, 1962

La Ville de la chance, 1962; as *The Town beyond the Wall*, translated by Stephen Becker, 1964

Les Portes de la forêt, 1964; as *The Gates of the Forest*, translated by Frances Frenaye, 1966

Le Mendiant de Jérusalem, 1968; as *A Beggar in Jerusalem*, translated by Lily Edelman, 1970

Vingt Ans après Auschwitz (includes *Zalmen, Le Mendiant de Jérusalem*), 1968
Night, Dawn, The Accident: Three Tales, 1972; as *The Night Trilogy*, 1987
Le Serment de Kolvillàg, 1973; as *The Oath*, translated by Marion Wiesel, 1973
Le Testament d'un poète juif assassiné, 1980; as *The Testament*, translated by Marion Wiesel, 1981
Le Cinquième Fils, 1983; as *The Fifth Son*, translated by Marion Wiesel, 1985
Le Crépuscule au loin, 1988; as *Twilight*, translated by Marion Wiesel, 1988
L'Oublié, 1989; as *The Forgotten*, translated by Stephen Becker, 1992

Plays
Zalmen; ou, La Folie de Dieu, 1968; as *Zalmen; or, The Madness of God*, translated by Nathan Edelman, 1974
Ani Maamin: un chant perdu et retrouvé, 1973; as *Ani Maamin: A Song Lost and Found Again*, 1973
Le Procès de Shamgorod tel qu'il se déroula le 25 février 1649: pièce en trois actes, 1979; as *The Trial of God (as It Was Held on February 25, 1649, in Shamgorod)*, translated by Marion Wiesel, 1988
The Haggadah, 1980
A Song for Hope, 1987

Other
Le Chant des morts, 1966; as *Legends of Our Time*, translated by Lily Edelman, 1968
Les Juifs du silence, 1966; as *The Jews of Silence: A Personal Report on Soviet Jewry*, translated by Neal Kozodoy, 1966
And the Sea is Never Full, 1969; translated by Marion Wiesel, 1999
Entre Deux Soleils, 1970; translated as *One Generation After*, translated by Lily Edelman, 1970
Célébration hassidique: portraits et légendes, 1972; as *Souls on Fire: Portraits and Legends of Hasidic Masters*, translated by Marion Wiesel, 1972
Célébration biblique: portraits et légendes, 1975; as *Messengers of God: Biblical Portraits and Legends*, translated by Marion Wiesel, 1976
Un Juif aujourd'hui: récits, essais, dialogues, 1977; as *A Jew Today*, translated by Marion Wiesel, 1978
Four Hasidic Masters and Their Struggle against Melancholy, 1978
Images from the Bible, 1980
Contre la mélancolie: célébration hassidique II, 1981; as *Somewhere a Master: Further Hasidic Portraits and Legends*, translated by Marion Wiesel, 1982
Five Biblical Portraits, 1981
Inside a Library; and, The Stranger in the Bible, 1981
Paroles d'étranger, 1982
The Golem: The Story of a Legend as Told by Elie Wiesel, translated by Anne Borchardt, 1983
Against Silence: The Voice and Vision of Elie Wiesel, edited by Irving Abrahamson, 3 vols, 1985
Signes d'exode, 1985
Job; ou, Dieu dans la tempête, with Josy Eisenberg, 1986
The Nobel Address: Hope, Despair and Memory, 1986; as *Discours d'Oslo*, 1987
Le Mal et l'exil, with Philippe-Michaël de Saint-Cheron, 1988; as *Evil and Exile*, translated by Jon Rothschild and Jody Gladding, 1990
The Six Days of Destruction: Meditations towards Hope, with Albert H. Friedlander, 1988
A Journey of Faith, with John Cardinal O'Connor, 1989
Silences et mémoire d'hommes, 1989
From the Kingdom of Memory: Reminiscences, 1990
Célébration talmudique, 1991
Sages and Dreamers, 1991
Memoirs
All Rivers Run to the Sea, 1995
And the Sea is Never Full, 1999
Hope against Hope: Johann Baptist Metz and Elie Wiesel Speak Out on the Holocaust, interviews with Ekkehard Schuster and Reinhold Boschert-Kimmig, translated by J. Matthew Ashley, 1999

Further Reading

Abramowitz, Molly, *Elie Wiesel: A Bibliography*, Metuchen, New Jersey: Scarecrow Press, 1974
Berenbaum, Michael, *The Vision of the Void: Theological Reflections on the Works of Elie Wiesel*, Middletown, Connecticut: Wesleyan University Press, 1979
Cargas, Harry James, *Harry James Cargas in Conversation with Elie Wiesel*, New York: Paulist Press, 1976
Cargas, Harry James (editor), *Responses to Elie Wiesel*, New York: Persea, 1978
Cargas, Harry James (editor), *Telling the Tale: A Tribute to Elie Wiesel*, St Louis, Missouri: Time Being Books, 1993
Estess, Ted L., *Elie Wiesel*, New York: Ungar, 1980
Fine, Ellen S., *Legacy of Night: The Literary Universe of Elie Wiesel*, Albany: State University of New York Press, 1982
Friedman, Maurice S., *Abraham Joshua Heschel and Elie Wiesel: You are My Witnesses*, New York: Farrar Straus, 1987
Greenberg, Irving and Alvin H. Rosenfeld (editors), *Confronting the Holocaust: The Impact of Elie Wiesel*, Bloomington: Indiana University Press, 1978
Kaufmann, Henry and Gene Koppel (editors), *Elie Wiesel: A Small Measure of Victory* (interview), Tucson: University of Arizona Press, 1974
Patterson, David, *In Dialogue and Dilemma with Elie Wiesel* (interview), Wakefield, New Hampshire: Longwood, 1991
Rittner, Carol, *Elie Wiesel: Between Memory and Hope*, New York: New York University Press, 1990
Rosen, Alan (editor), *Celebrating Elie Wiesel*, Notre Dame, Indiana: University of Notre Dame Press, 1998
Roth, John King, *A Consuming Fire: Encounters with Elie Wiesel and the Holocaust*, Atlanta: John Knox Press, 1979
Walker, Graham B., *Elie Wiesel: A Challenge to Theology*, Jefferson, North Carolina: McFarland, 1988

Wiesel received the Nobel Peace Prize in 1986, an award that caused some surprise. While it was fully deserved in terms of his tireless work for many persecuted minority groups, the victims of state terror from Kosovo to Cambodia, he had been proposed and is still being nominated for the Nobel Prize in Literature. Behind all his writings and activities there stands a unique person, a teacher of humanity, who has now also published a two-volume autobiography. In it, he gives us some insights into the total, incomprehensible darkness of the 20th century, and records his encounters with great leaders as well as with those who bear the scars of this century of brutality.

Since Wiesel has now emerged from behind his work, it is quite understandable that he is now being attacked by fanatic anti-Zionists, failed jealous authors, and by those who deny the Holocaust. The most vicious among them, who have clearly not read his work, claim that he would not have been so honoured had he not taken the Holocaust as his theme in order to profit from it. Wiesel, who has always channelled the income of these books into charitable causes, is deeply saddened by this: "They say we reap dividends from Auschwitz and Buchenwald, as though these awful places had anything to do with dividends. What they really mean is that we should keep silent. But that is impossible and immoral." It seems contradictory to say this, but Elie Wiesel is *not* the recorder of the Holocaust. He describes the fate of suffering humanity in its totality, and is the great theologian and midrashic teacher of Judaism from the first pages of the Bible to the new paradigms of thought of the 21st century. He has actually written more about the Bible, the Talmud, the rabbinic teachers of past centuries, and about Hasidism and contemporary Jewish thought than about the death camps. The famous trilogy *Night*, *Dawn*, and *The Accident* brought a stunned world into full awareness of Auschwitz. The readers did not realize that Wiesel was describing a world in which the Holocaust remained an integral part. *A Beggar in Jerusalem* was a majestic piece of literature, rightly receiving the Médicis Prize as a poetic vision where past and present mingled. At the time, André Schwarz-Bart rightly noted: "For many years, Elie Wiesel, through his life and his books, has been for us as source of light and a legend; now, with *A Beggar in Jerusalem*, the young survivor from Auschwitz becomes this generation's only prophet."

Prophets speak about God, even in denial and in challenge. At the beginning, in *Night*, Wiesel's description of the three gallows of Auschwitz, with a small child hanging between two adults, became a key text for Christian theologians, who related it to Calvary; others used it for a "death of God" theology. At a conference in New York where it was discussed by critics as a novel, Wiesel protested vehemently. First of all, they had to realize that behind the text there was a grim reality: there *was* a real child who had died in Auschwitz. And while the text: "Where is God? There He is, hanging on the gallows" expressed a belief in the absence of God, it was also a reminder that God was in the camp along with the victims – but not with the perpetrators. In his own life, Wiesel has always been part of the Hasidic tradition, and he moved from the despair of that time into an often questioning, questing faith.

Wiesel's work moves towards the understanding of a Suffering God, a theme that the rabbis after the destruction of Jerusalem developed in some detail. More than that, the loneliness of God rises out of his anguished understanding of humans fashioned in God's image, caught up in their own loneliness and far away from God. In one novel (*Twilight*) the inmates see themselves as biblical figures. One of them is "God" and the narrator is asked to cry for God. One rabbinic view sees Ecclesiastes as referring to God: "For all my days are but sorrow!" That is not man howling, but God. "What?" asks Wiesel. "Cry not to God, but for God? God needs us too?" Here, the texture of religious life is interwoven with the awareness of the Divine suffering within humanity. Human solitude depicts God's loneliness. Faith in our time, he feels, must break through the wall dividing us from God: there must be the freedom to challenge God with this. And so, in one of his plays, *Zalmen*, the "chairman" points to the rabbi's loneliness:

> Do you know what it means to be the last teacher, the last messenger, the last believer? What it means to realize that one's truth will be lost and one's ideals forgotten? Do you know what it means to witness silently, day after day, week after week, the disappearance – worse, the distortion – of one's faith, one's image, one's past in front of one's very eyes?

Wiesel's struggle to be a witness for those who died in the camps is matched by his awareness of the traditions of Judaism being distorted and misused. His great texts on Hasidism are different from Buber's radical editing, but also from the work of the sober historians of that time. Wiesel *is* a Hasid, joyously celebrating that life and showing the complexity and anguish of figures like the Kotzer rebbe and the Seer of Lublin where darkness and fear are part of the religious life. He writes:

> Hasidism is a movement out of despair, away from despair – a movement against despair. Only Hasidism? Judaism too. Who is a Jew? A Jew is he – or she – whose song cannot be muted, whose joy cannot be killed by the enemy – ever.

One reads Wiesel's biblical commentaries and encounters these figures in all their complexity, from Cain and Abel to Saul and David. Wiesel touches the very stones of the Holy Land (which also reach out to his awareness of the Israel of today), and his words contain Hebrew cadences – but also Yiddish, French, and American English. Seen in its totality, Elie Wiesel's work contains all variations of literature: plays, cantatas, prayers, novels, factual reports, poetry, and parable. At the same time, the work is linked to the rabbinic writings of 2000 years of Jewish life and becomes a total testimony of Jewish life. It is an attempt to communicate both darkness and light, letters addressed to humanity and to God.

ALBERT H. FRIEDLANDER

Wieseltier, Meir

Russian-born Israeli poet and translator, 1941–

Born in Moscow, 1941. Emigrated with family, 1947; visited Poland, Germany, and France; settled in Israel, 1949. Studied at Hebrew University, Jerusalem, BA. Active in circle of Tel Aviv poets associated with journals *Akhshav* and *Siman Kriah*, 1960s; co-founder and co-editor of several issues of literary magazine *Siman Kriah*; poetry editor, Am-Oved publishing house. Divorced; two children. Awarded Israel Prize for Literature, 2000.

Selected Writings

Poetry
Perek alef, perek beit [Chapter One, Chapter Two], 1967
Meah shirim [100 Poems], 1969
Kakh [Take], 1973
Davar optimi, asiyat shirim [An Optimistic Thing, The Making of Poems], 1976
Pnim vahutz [Interior and Exterior], 1977
Motsah el hayam [Exit into the Sea], 1981
Kitsur shnot hashishim [The Concise Sixties], 1984
Yi yevani [Greek Island], 1985
Mihtavim veshirim aherim [Letters and Other Poems], 1986
Mahsan [Warehouse], 1994
Shirim itiim [Slow Poems], 2000

Further Reading

Laor, Yitzchak, *Anu Cotvim Otach Moledet* [Narratives with No Natives], Tel Aviv: Hakitbutz HaMeuhad, 1995

Meir Wieseltier began publishing his poetry in the mid-1960s. Recognizable even in his early work was a dissent from the primary voice of the poetry of "the generation of statehood" led by Nathan Zach. Together with other poets such as Yair Horowitz, Yona Wallach, and Aaron Shabtai, Wieseltier offered an alternative to the ironic, detached and abstract voice of Nathan Zach and his generation. Already in his early poems there was a degree of concrete corporeality that gave shape to a biting and committed moralistic voice. In "Min leyeladim" [Sex for Children], one of his early poems, he depicts sexual activity from a moral standpoint and judged through moralistic categories as a savage and brutal act:

> My child, when you see a dog
> On top of a bitch, a rooster
> On top of a hen, a bird
> Leaping on a bird, don't learn from this about the ways
> of men . . .
> But when you see a bull
> On top of a heifer, a cat on top of a cat,
> Or the face of a hunted-down rapist, in the newspaper,
> Don't translate their gaze, coarse
> And blunted, into something softer
> And more refined, rich
> And desirous, this is the way it is
> With all of mankind.

The speaker in these poems is a harsh and judgemental "I" who assumes a moral social tone. It is a different voice, almost contrary to the stance of distance and detachment from society and morality that was typical of the Israeli poets in the period prior to it.

In 1973 Wieseltier published his book *Kakh* [Take], which he began with an appeal to the reader to take the book as a material object and apply violence to it:

> Take the poems, and don't read
> Do violence to this book:
> Spit on it, crush it
> Kick it, pinch it . . .
> This book is a rag of paper
> And letters like flies, whereas you are
> A rag of meat, eater of dust and dripping blood,
> Staring at it half asleep.

The morality of literature is gauged in relation to literature's place in reality. Poetry has become an instrument of action in the real world, action that must obey moral injunctions.

Wieseltier's primary effort is to expose the moral foundation hidden behind cultural representations. In the poem "Leningrad: geluyat nof" [Leningrad: A Picture Postcard] he exposes the horror of the Soviet regime behind the representation of Leningrad in a picture postcard. A penetrating moral judgement is handed down by exposing the hidden truth:

> Leningrad full of rivers and canals
> And plazas and palaces and monuments:
> A history seemingly stylized
> In gray-purple light like a postage stamp; . . .
> And truly, like Florence, like Paris
> But a cardboard movable scenery
> For the distress of men
> Short, clear and desperate
> Drawn in all the colors of the rainbow
> But mainly in blood.

Wieseltier deconstructs familiar cultural representations and exposes their political and moral foundations. In 1976 he published *Davar optimi, asiyat shirim* [An Optimistic Thing, The Making of Poems], which included a group of poems titled "Sirtutim tel aviviim" [Tel Aviv Sketches] featuring a fascination with the repugnant, the wretched, and the drab as the very essence of human existence in Tel Aviv: "A desolate abandoned seaside yard with no shade with no hammock/ On a beach hostile to the longings of the crazy heart". In a group of poems titled "Elegiyot al-yad hahushim" [Elegies beside the Senses], a crude and direct sensuality is accompanied by a sublime elegiac stance: "Once again a grayish khaki light descends/ Upon the wine we poured into cups/ And we crouched towards its living purple/ And the memory of its taste of the year before." In this book Wieseltier continued in the vein of the Tel Aviv poems that had already appeared in the volume *Kakh*, in which he contemplates urban human wretchedness and accords it a central place in the human representation in the poems.

In 1982, at the time of the Lebanese War, Wieseltier wrote some of his harshest condemnations. These were included in

Mihtavim veshirim aherim [Letters and Other Poems], which appeared in 1986. Literary genres and accepted channels of communication become for him the target of political critique: "Come I shall regale you with patriotic songs;/ Why do you tremble?/ I shall regale you with all songs brought from all homelands,/ All the words which have dressed themselves in the destined melodies." It is an already widely accepted description of the voice that speaks in Wieseltier's poetry as one which is at odds with reality, which it decries in an authoritative and coherent manner. He attacks reality, he describes it, but most of all he establishes the poetic voice in opposition to it as a complete and prepotent voice, usually with a moralistic strength to it. In all of his books up to and especially including the volume *Mahsan* [Warehouse], published in 1994, Wieseltier continued to wage his cultural project as the producer of a clear and prominent voice in Hebrew poetry.

This is usually a musical voice that finds its place in and forms the map of Hebrew poetry by means of its rich linguistic texture, which is organized and has an internal hierarchy. It is a voice that offers models of representation for private worlds; mainly, however, as his central stance, Wieseltier writes poetry that judges reality, manufactures a moral attentiveness to it, and sketches mediating paths within it between the personal and the collective.

In the recent *Shirim itiim* [Slow Poems], Wieseltier remains true to his constant effort to produce a prominent voice, in which the political and the universally human coexist side by side. All the same, these poems display a great sensitivity to the immense cultural difficulty of formulating – at the start of the new millennium, with a situation of cultural disintegration in Israel – a prominent place and stance in reliance on fixed poetic apparatuses. They therefore propose a change in the apparatus which constitutes the poetic voice. In contrast to the great closeness between the contemplative gaze and the poetic voice which had been typical of Wieseltier's poetry, *Shirim itiim* divides between the two: the spectator and the speaker. Now it is possible to point to his poetry as having turned its attention from the question "Who is talking?" to the question "Where is he / she talking from?" In this book Wieseltier pursues a consistent poetic course that draws its strength not so much from the presence of the voice as from its placing. The poems in *Shirim itiim* are less subject to the rhythm of the speaker's voice than to the space represented in them; less to time and its speed than to the slowness of movement through space. Thus, in the poem "Tsillum avir tsolel" [Diving Aerial Photo], Tel Aviv – the well-known symbolic place of the moralistic Wieseltieran speaker – turns into a large catalogue of statements that compartmentalize it and identify it by means of a rich and unfocused space. All the same, the moral view not only has not been abandoned or dropped, it has been shaped in a dynamic manner very sensitive to its spatial condition (an aerial photo in freefall).

Wieseltier's moral subject, then, is one that does not obey any clear-cut story; it delivers its moral judgement at each point in space, from moment to moment in time.

HANNAN HEVER

Winter, Léon de

Dutch fiction writer and film producer, 1954–

Born in Hertogenbosch, 24 February 1954, into an Orthodox Jewish family. Moved to Amsterdam, 1974; studied at Dutch Film Academy there. First film released, 1979. Married to the writer Jessica Durlacher, daughter of Gerhard Durlacher; two children. Works as film producer in Hollywood.

Selected Writings

Fiction

The Day before Yesterday: Six Stories, translated by Scott Rawlins, 1985
Kaplan, 1986
Eergisteren, overmorgen, 1990
Hoffman's honger, 1990; as *Hoffman's Hunger*, translated by Arnold Pomerans and Erica Pomerans, 1995
Een Abessijnse woestijnkat, 1991
Supertex, 1991
De ruimte van Sokolov, 1992
De verhalen, 1993
Serenade, 1995
Zionoco, 1995
Lady Di in een bevallige pose, 1996
De hemel van Hollywood, 1997

Further Reading

Bakker, Siem, *Leon de Winter: Hoffman's honger*, Laren, Netherlands: Walvaboek, 1996
Peeters, Carel, *Houdbare Illusies*, Amsterdam: Harmonie, 1984

The most important character in the novel *Kaplan* is the writer Leo Kaplan, a caricatured alter ego of Léon de Winter's. A critic tells Kaplan: "For you, your material is not only your own imagination . . . but also your parents' experiences and everything that you have read and that you run across in the newspapers. You would really like to be a classic village storyteller." Starting from such an approach, an author has of course more than enough material; and that is certainly true for de Winter. *Kaplan* is the book that contains the most representative subjects from his oeuvre: constant themes such as the profession of writing and Jewish identity; also the diplomatic milieu and the relationship with the father. De Winter's later novels, *Hoffman's honger* and *Supertex*, are more concentrated elaborations – also in form – of material from *Kaplan*.

In all three novels the main characters are in a crisis because they are wrestling with the war experiences of their parents. In *Kaplan*, the theme of Jewish identity has been pushed from the margin to the centre. Even in his earliest work – he debuted in 1976 – the subject was the guilt feelings of the survivors of the Holocaust, but not until after *Kaplan* did this confrontation with the Jewish past lead to reconciliation. In his native city Leo Kaplan finally reconciles himself with his dead father and his Jewish past which he has always denied and avoided.

In de Winter's most important book, *Hoffman's honger*,

the 56-year-old Felix Hoffman is ambassador of the Kingdom of the Netherlands to Prague. His life is a failure; his marriage is dead. Hoffman cannot cope with his past; he knows the shame of survival: unlike his parents, he did survive the war. The death of his children has taken away any further belief in life. He feels that he doesn't have the right to live, but he can't put an end to his life either. If he did that, he would throw away as worthless something that was taken away from his children. Tormented by continual sleeplessness, Hoffman throws himself into excessive eating; a secret way to end life with an unavoidable heart attack. This hunger for food, tenderness, and youth caused by permanent feelings of guilt is called "Hoffman's hunger" by his wife. The story covers the period between June and September 1989, during the upheavals in the Eastern Bloc which are commented on by Hoffman with his cynical view of humanity and politics. At that time, at the end of his career, he takes stock and decides to risk everything that he has reached in life in a risky affair with a Czech double agent.

Although *Hoffman's honger* opens like spy novel by John le Carré, the real subject is the crisis of the older diplomat who is Jewish. Even though the plot is grafted onto the conventions and the ingredients of the spy novel, the genre seems to have been chosen primarily as the most suitable way to develop Hoffman's world. That world is a grotesque labyrinth in which nothing is what it seems – just as Hoffman is outwardly the conformist diplomat and inside, in head and guts, chaos. As a diplomat he embodies the professional outsider par excellence, a modern version of the Wandering Jew. The philosophical component of the story must be seen in that light. Hoffman is constantly absorbed in Spinoza's book *Treatise on the Improvement of the Understanding*. Because Spinoza carried out a secret mission during wartime, he fits superficially into the world of espionage. But the importance of Spinoza's sacred texts in *Hoffman's honger* lies in their contrast with Hoffman's profane behaviour. What fascinates Hoffman is Spinoza's detachment, the search for happiness in the world of ideas – a comforting answer to boundless consumerism.

Although de Winter's themes are original, his style is imitative, used to create strong scenes, and is often cheap, especially in the images used. Everything is in the service of realism, even though this pushes him in the direction of pulp literature as in *Kaplan*. In his earlier books he used a somewhat elevated style; after *Kaplan* the voice of the (coarse) principal character dominates to such an extent that the characters determine the genre: content always dictates form.

In *Kaplan*, *Hoffman's honger*, and especially in *Supertex*, it becomes clear that in de Winter's view it is impossible to write about an emotionally charged subject such as "Jewish identity" without hamming it up. *Supertex* seems to have been intended as de Winter's Great Jewish Novel: almost all the characters are members of the same Jewish family. Sephardic Jews, eastern European Jews, small-town Jews, Israeli Jews, Jews from Arab countries, all sorts and groups of people who are called or call themselves Jewish, with all the customs and characteristics ascribed to them, appear in the novel. Every character in *Supertex* is ultimately concerned about tradition and continuity – not surprising for a people with such a history. Using kitschy contrasts and playing with clichés, de Winter really writes about the endless puzzle of being Jewish. In *De ruimte van Sokolov* he goes even further. This thriller is set in Israel, during the Gulf War. The alcoholic street-sweeper Sasha Sokolov, a former Russian missile expert, sees his boyhood friend Lev commit a murder in broad daylight; that is the start of a story about friendship, morality, and opportunistic amorality, and the meaning of being Jewish in the most diverse circumstances: clandestinely in the Soviet Union and openly in Israel. Sokolov's moral dilemmas reflect those of Israel's national politics: when can you kill someone? At what point does the preservation of life prevail over your principles? *De ruimte van Sokolov* truly breaks taboos in its picture of Israel as a super-capitalistic country that houses brave souls as well as rock-hard gangsters.

De Winter is the kind of writer whose stories stay with you long after you've read them. The headlong pace of his narrative, the speed with which the intrigue branches out, and the excessive anecdotes emphasize his themes even more. De Winter has clearly chosen to change course for this purpose and seeks contact with forms of writing that are outside the literary canon. He does this so that he can tell his own story in every genre; in this way de Winter creates his own chameleon-like tradition. "Just continue telling stories . . . As long as stories are being told about recognizable characters who experience their own more or less necessary development, we hold on to the idea of autonomous consciousness." This pronouncement by a character from de Winter's 1997 novel, *De hemel van Hollywood*, shows the vigorous attitude of the writer himself.

JEROEN VULLINGS

Wiseman, Adele

Canadian fiction writer, 1928–1992

Born Adele Waisman in Winnipeg, 21 May 1928. Parents, Chaika (née Rosenberg) and Pesach Waisman immigrants from Ukraine. Studied at St John's Technical High School; University of Manitoba, Winnipeg, 1944–49, BA in English and psychology 1949. Married Dmitry Stone; one daughter. Member of Department of English, University of Manitoba, 1949. Social worker, Stepney Jewish Girls' Hospital, London, 1950; teacher, Overseas School of Rome, 1951–52. Laboratory technician, Winnipeg, and executive secretary, Royal Winnipeg Ballet, 1952–55. Lived in London, 1956 and 1961–63; New York, 1957–60. Lecturer, Sir George Williams University, and Macdonald College, McGill University, both Montreal, 1964–69; writer in residence, University of Toronto, 1975–76; head of writing programme, Banff School of Fine Arts, Alberta, 1987–91. Several awards, including Governor-General's Award, National Conference of Christians and Jews Brotherhood Award, and Guggenheim Fellowship, all 1957; Canada Council Senior Arts Award, 1975. Died in Toronto, 1992.

Selected Writings

Novels
The Sacrifice, 1956
Crackpot, 1974

Plays
The Lovebound: A Tragi-Comedy, 1960
Testimonial Dinner, 1978

Other
Old Markets, New Worlds, 1964
Old Woman at Play, 1978
Memoirs of a Book Molesting Childhood and Other Essays, 1987
Kenji and the Cricket, 1988
Selected Letters of Margaret Laurence and Adele Wiseman, edited by John Lennox and Ruth Panofsky, 1997

Further Reading

Greene, Elizabeth (editor), *We Who Can Fly: Poems, Essays and Memories in Honour of Adele Wiseman*, Dunvegan, Ontario: Cormorant, 1997
Greenstein, Michael, *Adele Wiseman and Her Works*, Toronto: ECW Press, 1983
Panofsky, Ruth, *Adele Wiseman: An Annotated Bibliography*, Toronto: ECW Press, 1992

"My consciousness is Jewish . . . part of my strong feeling of the need to express my Jewishness stems from the fact that I feel we are so distorted in other people's eyes . . . So I'm singing me. I'm singing us." Adele Wiseman recognized her vocation as a Jewish writer "very early". Almost all her central characters are Jewish; their language is peppered with Yiddish rhythms and idioms; many bear biblical names and uphold Jewish values such as the importance of family, work, humour, and knowledge; and they bear witness to the horror of relentless anti-Semitism, pogroms, forced exile, loss, suffering, death, the Holocaust. Some perish. Others heroically reclaim "defiance and . . . dignity as their birthright".

Wiseman's parents, Chaika (née Rosenberg) and Pesach Waisman, immigrated to Winnipeg, fleeing pogroms in the Ukraine. Chaika also escaped the domestic abuse of her mother by her father, becoming a pillar of female strength and practicality, her motto "One gives oneself a solution." Schooled in the grinding hardships and poverty of immigrant life in the Depression, Wiseman grew up with *attitude*, with "a Judaism which is life-oriented, which celebrates life, because it's all we've got, because beyond life is somebody else's responsibility. We have to do the best we can with life, after which no amount of whining or prayer will make very much difference."

Wiseman was part of a postwar "literary greening" in Canada, which included Jewish writers A.M. Klein, Mordecai Richler, and Leonard Cohen; she became the country's first celebrated Jewish woman novelist. She notes in *Memoirs of a Book Molesting Childhood* that this carried responsibility. "I had more dead than I could ever count . . . I did not feel guilt because I survived; I felt the responsibility, rather, in some sense to make the dead survive through me."

The Holocaust, Jewish moral ideas, and the occurrence of the first murder in Manitoba to be committed by a Jew, together inspired Wiseman to write *The Sacrifice*. Reviewing the novel, Miriam Waddington recorded the influence of Yiddish writer Sholem Aleichem, judged *The Sacrifice* as much superior to Herman Wouk's *Marjorie Morningstar* and Mordecai Richler's *Son of a Smaller Hero*, and praised Wiseman as "the first Jewish novelist writing in English that I know of, who has understood and combined both the secular and the religious traditions in Jewish life." The fictional Abraham and Sarah immigrate to Winnipeg with Isaac, their one remaining son, his two brothers having been killed in a pogrom in the Ukraine. Whereas Sarah sinks passively under her burden of grief, Abraham is depicted much like Wiseman's own father, "determined to conquer the new world for his children" by sheer hard work. The climactic event – his rash murder of the prostitute Laiah – ultimately yields the central truth that "when a human being cries out to you, no matter who it is, don't judge him, or you turn away God himself."

Wiseman's plays, privately printed and unperformed, explore Jewish identity as both reality and symbol. *The Lovebound* concerns the tragedy of a shipload of unwanted Jewish refugees. *Testimonial Dinner* explores the problem of rootlessness and the relationship of past to present. In 19th-century Canada, Métis rebel leader Louis Riel, according to Wiseman, "made the equation with Judaism when he was mad", renaming himself "David Mordecai". "That was one of the things that validated my own intuition that by using the development of the Jew in Canadian society, I could get very close to something that was very real in our whole social concept." Jewishness thus becomes a metaphor for social exclusion.

Elsewhere Wiseman clusters "Jews, women, blacks, and others who find themselves fixed as inferior breeds." Beginning with a mission to right the anti-Semitic image of the Jew, she developed a parallel, feminist consciousness with respect to negative stereotypes of women. Her second novel, *Crackpot*, paints an iconoclastic portrait of female independence in the prostitute Hoda, whom Wiseman describes as "an enlarged version of something in myself", a woman who, despite all odds, "was strong because she knew who she was". Overcoming ignorance, poverty, marginalization, loss, and even incest with her unsuspecting "orphan" son, the outcast Hoda is linked in the end, through Lazar, to the Holocaust itself. Wiseman sums up, "Essentially, the two of them are survivors."

The autobiographical *Old Woman at Play* celebrates female ingenuity and creativity (Chaika's doll-making) as it documents the joys and sorrows of a deeply loving mother–daughter–granddaughter relationship. Despite suffering, disinheritance, and death, the Wiseman women affirm community, compassion, nurturance, and humour as the means to survival. "When we were strangers in the land we made our own welcome and warmed ourselves with our own laughter and created our own belonging", she writes in *Memoirs of a Book Molesting Childhood*.

Summoning up "the cumulative power of her best

writing", Wiseman's final short story, "Goon of the Moon and the Expendables", calls for compassionate acceptance of extreme difference and the almost unbridgeable "otherness" caused by severe disability. The institutionalized children Lucinda, Joshua, and Gordon, declared "alien and sent away to live with other strangers", long for reinstatement as "True human beings! With rights, and maybe even something to contribute." As if speaking for Wiseman's lifetime cast of the dispossessed, Josh addresses his "fellow expendables", in heroic words:

> All he knew was that even the maimed, the incomplete, the scattered, the mistaken, even those who had had every promise broken in the molecule, retained the dream of particle and multiverse. It stirred in him even now, irrepressibly, straining against his loneliness and misery, the dream of a life of great beauty.

Wiseman set out as a Jewish writer with a mission, which became progressively more comprehensive and broadly humanitarian to include a host of marginalized and outcast "others". At her finest, she surely reaches her dream "that I may yet be able to create my own true magic model for the spirit of a more humane world."

WENDY ROBBINS

Woolf, Leonard Sidney

British fiction writer and journalist, 1880–1969

Born in London, 25 November 1880. Educated at St Paul's School, London, and Trinity College, Cambridge. Married Virginia Stephen (the writer Virginia Woolf), 1912 (she died 1941). Worked in the Colonial Service, Ceylon, 1904–11, and as journalist and writer until his death. Co-founder with his wife, Hogarth Press, 1917. Literary editor, *The Nation*, 1923–30; co-founder and joint editor, *Political Quarterly*, 1931–59. Died in Lewes, Sussex, 14 August 1969.

Selected Writings

Fiction
The Village in the Jungle, 1913
The Wise Virgins, 1914
"Three Jews" in *Two Stories*, 1917
Stories of the East, 1921
The Hotel, 1939

Autobiography
Sowing, 1960
Growing, 1961
Beginning Again, 1964
Downhill All the Way, 1967
The Journey Not the Arrival Matters, 1969

Other
International Government, 1916
The Framework of a Lasting Peace, 1917
Co-operation and the Future of Industry, 1919
Empire and Commerce in Africa, 1919
Mandates and Empire, 1920
Economic Imperialism, 1921
Socialism and Co-operation, 1921
Fear and Politics, 1925
Essays on Literature, History and Politics, 1927
Hunting the Highbrow, 1927
Imperialism and Civilisation, 1928
After the Deluge: A Study of Communal Psychology, 2 vols, 1931–39
Quack! Quack!, 1935
The League and Abyssinia, 1936
Barbarians at the Gate, 1939; as *Barbarians Within and Without*, 1939
Principia Politica, 1953
Diaries in Ceylon 1908–1911, 1962

Further Reading

Adamson, Judith (editor), *Love Letters: Leonard Woolf and Trekkie Ritchie Parsons, 1941–1969*, London: Chatto and Windus, 2001
Alexander, Peter F., *Leonard and Virginia Woolf: A Literary Partnership*, London: Harvester Wheatsheaf, and New York: St Martin's Press, 1992
de Silva, M.C.W. Prabhath, *Leonard Woolf: A British Civil Servant as a Judge in the Hambantora District of Colonial Sri Lanka, 1908–1911*, Sri Lanka: de Silva, 1996
Meyerowitz, Selma S., *Leonard Woolf*, Boston: Twayne, 1982
Rosenfeld, Natania, *Outsiders Together: Virginia and Leonard Woolf*, Princeton, New Jersey: Princeton University Press, 2000
Spotts, Frederic (editor), *Letters of Leonard Woolf*, London: Weidenfeld and Nicolson, and San Diego: Harcourt Brace Jovanovich, 1989
Wilson, Duncan, *Leonard Woolf: A Political Biography*, London: Hogarth Press, and New York: St Martin's Press, 1978

Publisher, editor, journalist, novelist, and political commentator and activist, Leonard Woolf is perhaps best known for his literary partnership with his wife, Virginia. Together they founded the Hogarth Press and were central members of the influential "Bloomsbury" group of authors, artists, and intellectuals.

Woolf was the third of nine children. His mother's family came from the Netherlands, and his father's from London; she was a regular Sabbath worshipper while he attended synagogue only on high holidays. The children had a Hebrew tutor and were taught the rudiments of the language and a number of prayers. Sidney Woolf, his father, was a successful barrister and QC, and the family was comfortable until Sidney's early death when Leonard was 11. Thereafter the family was subject to considerable financial pressures.

Educated at St Paul's School and Trinity College, Cambridge, where he read Classics, Woolf was a member of the "Apostles" at university, and was part of a group of students and fellows influenced by the philosopher, G.E. Moore, a number of whom later became part of the Bloomsbury set. After graduating he joined the Ceylon Civil Service as an assistant government agent. His official *Diaries in Ceylon 1908–1911* are a fascinating record of the issues facing a colonial official in the Hambantota district. Woolf later wrote that his lifelong anti-imperialism began with his questioning of the morality of the empire, although de Silva (1996) paints Woolf as an inflexible and stern disciplinarian. His novel *The Village in the Jungle* and his *Stories of the East* reflect his experiences in Ceylon. The novel, which powerfully evokes the ruling presence of the jungle itself, sympathetically portrays the hard and uncertain life of rural peasantry. The iniquities of an alien legal system in a foreign language are noted, even if the judge remarks, "there is almost certainly something in this case that has not come out", and then he finds the accused guilty anyway.

Returning to England in 1911, he renewed his acquaintance with Virginia Stephen and they were married the following year. The place and reception of the Jew in English society was a major concern of Woolf's at this time. In his witty novel *The Wise Virgins* he explores the position of a young educated Jewish "gentleman" living in a society that is openly and covertly anti-Semitic, and which appears to have no clear or comfortable place for this young English Jew. The protagonist, Harry Davis (Woolf) is alienated from the Jewish world of his family as it assimilates into the pretentious, suburban middle class life of South London, nor is he at home in the more elevated world of the Lawrence family, whose daughter Camilla (Virginia) he has fallen in love with. Woolf explores the different possibilities facing an English Jew, although Jewish communal life is never even considered, and when Camilla rejects him, the novel ends with the final act of imaginary assimilation – unhappily marrying Gwen, "the girl next door", in the local Anglican church.

His mother was unhappy that the book was published at all and it was reprinted only after Leonard's death. The book has a bitter edge, employs negative anti-Semitic prejudicial descriptions of Mr and Mrs Davis, offers a rather jaundiced view of Jewish family life, and reports the antipathy to Jews on the part of different English classes.

In 1917 Virginia and Leonard established the Hogarth Press and published their first work, *Two Stories*, consisting of "The Mark on the Wall" by Virginia and "Three Jews" by Leonard. His didactic short story focuses on a dialogue, between two Jews who meet on a park bench, about the loss of their faith and the fact that they go to synagogue on the high holidays out of mere "habit". The third Jew is the cemetery keeper ("even he has lost his faith") who is equally estranged from Jewish beliefs and practices. These three Jews share the predicament of having assimilated to the "universal disbelief" of their day and yet still recognize each other ("We're Jews only externally now") and are linked to those who went before them and to each other, but somehow not to the future. The story includes crude racial stereotypes, particularly of facial features ("a nose like an elephant trunk") and discusses faith in a fashion more Protestant than Jewish. The Hogarth Press, whose authors included Katherine Mansfield, T.S. Eliot, E.M. Forster, and Robert Graves, and which published translations of Freud's papers and Gor'kii and Dostoevskii, went on to play a major role in British publishing.

World War I transformed Woolf from an aesthete into a political activist and advocate for socialism and international peace. He was invited to join the Fabian Society and commissioned to write a report, later published as *International Government* (1916), which influenced British government views and was part of the theoretical foundations of the League of Nations. As a member of the Labour Party's Advisory Committee on International Questions he did much to raise international issues on the party's agenda. He was literary editor of *The Nation* (1923–30), co-founder and joint editor of the *Political Quarterly* (1931–59), editor of *International Review*, and a regular contributor to the Fabian journal, *New Statesman*. In addition to his political editing and journalism, Woolf wrote a three-volume study of modern political thought, *After the Deluge*, the third volume of which was published as *Principia Politica*, and is probably best known for his five volumes of autobiography (1960–69).

Woolf's identity as an assimilated Jew was somewhat ambivalent. Being a Jew he likened to being part of a family, a matter that generated both pride and shame. In spite of being a self-declared atheist at 14 and counting himself out of the "synagogue" community, he continued to identify himself as Jewish. Woolf lived with the standard negative Jewish epithets, from his Sri Lankan biographer who noted that he was Jewish and was mean with money, to his new wife, Virginia, who wrote to her friends that she had just married a "penniless Jew". He was, however, concerned about public anti-Semitism and argued that the Dreyfus case was the touchstone for liberty and justice in modern Europe. Although he did not write directly about the Holocaust, he and Virginia seem to have been very worried about a German victory, and Woolf had arranged for his brother-in-law to give them two lethal doses of morphine so that they could commit suicide in the event of a Nazi invasion.

Although Woolf included being Jewish (under "race") in his list of loyalties, he considered that, "I have always felt in my bones, and brain, and heart English, and more narrowly as a Londoner, but with a nostalgic love of the city and civilisation of ancient Athens".

PAUL MORRIS

Wouk, Herman

US fiction writer and dramatist, 1915–

Born in New York City, 27 May 1915. Studied at Townsend Harris Hall, New York, 1927–30; Columbia University, New York, BA 1934. Radio writer, 1935; scriptwriter for comedian Fred Allen, 1936–41; consultant, US Treasury, 1941. Served in naval reserve, 1942–46: Lieutenant. Married Betty Sarah Brown, 1945; three sons (one deceased). Visiting professor of English, Yeshiva University, New York, 1952–58; scholar in residence, Aspen Institute, Colorado, 1973–74. Many awards, including Pulitzer Prize, 1952; *Washingtonian* Award, 1986; American Academy of Achievement Golden Plate, 1986; US Navy Memorial Foundation Award, 1987; Katzetnik Award, 1990.

Selected Writings

Novels
Aurora Dawn, 1947
The City Boy, 1948
The Caine Mutiny, 1951
Marjorie Morningstar, 1955
Slattery's Hurricane, 1956
Youngblood Hawke, 1962
Don't Stop the Carnival, 1965
The Lomokome Papers, 1968
The Winds of War, 1971
War and Remembrance, 1978
Inside, Outside, 1985
The Will to Live On, 1985
The Hope, 1993
The Glory, 1994

Plays
The Traitor, 1949
Modern Primitive, 1951
The Caine Mutiny Court-Martial, 1953
Nature's Way, 1957

Television Series: *The Winds of War*, 1983; *War and Remembrance*, 1986

Other
The Man in the Trench Coat, 1941
This is My God: The Jewish Way of Life, 1959

Further Reading

Beichman, Arnold, *Herman Wouk: The Novelist as Social Historian*, New Brunswick, New Jersey: Transaction, 1984
Mazzeno, Laurence W., *Herman Wouk*, New York: Twayne, 1994
Wouk, Herman, "You, Me and the Novel", *Saturday Review-World* (29 June 1974)

The descendant of east European immigrants, Herman Wouk has achieved international fame through his novels and television screenplays, most of which draw heavily on the Jewish experience and religious tradition. Wouk's fiction is notable for its epic length and firm defence of establishment values. Respect for parents, chastity before marriage, obedience to authority, are recurrent themes in his work, and his writings acknowledge 19th-century models such as Dickens and Tolstoi. Foremost of Wouk's beliefs is his commitment to the Jewish faith; he was the grandson of a rabbi, and his novels celebrate the Torah and the Talmud, and faithful adherence to the traditional ceremonies. *The City Boy*, set in the Jewish Bronx, follows Herbie Bookbinder in his youthful journey to manhood and responsibility. Wouk's vivid portrayal of the young Jewish boy and his community is enriched by an impressive gift for humour, tinged with wistful sadness at the passing of childhood, but here as elsewhere in his fiction the need for obedience and straight dealing is emphasized. Wouk's affection for his characters is evident, and *The City Boy* remains a significant affirmation of his Jewish heritage.

The Caine Mutiny won Wouk both lasting fame and the Pulitzer Prize, and is justly celebrated. The novel describes the unpredictable tyranny of Captain Queeg, the discontent of the crew that erupts into mutiny, the trial and its aftermath. Queeg's unstable behaviour, his rolling of the two steel balls during questioning is now part of popular folklore, but in the end he is vindicated. Jewish defence lawyer Barney Greenwald successfully defends the mutineers but afterwards spoils their celebration dinner by putting them straight. Queeg defended the country against Hitler and "kept Mama out of the soap dish"; sane or insane, he should have been obeyed. Wouk's insistence on authority receiving its due, while in this case hard to swallow, results in a startling shift of focus for the novel's climax. Against this affirmation of traditional values he places sailor / novelist Tom Keefer, whose gutless, shifty behaviour fuels the mutiny, and who later ducks out of responsibility. Keefer, rather than Queeg, emerges as the villain here, and his treatment sets the pattern for Wouk's portrayal of intellectuals.

Parents also know best in *Marjorie Morningstar*, where young Marjorie Morgenstern changes her name in an effort to make it as a show business star. "Honour thy father and thy mother" is a central theme, the mundane views of Marjorie's parents wiser than her own dreams of stardom. Her glamorous lover Noel Airman (formerly Saul Ehrmann) also proves a phoney, his plans and self-justifications failing to hide his lack of substance. Both he and Marjorie are trying to escape their Jewish heritage, signified by the changing of their names, but the attempt is vain. Airman becomes a third-rate nobody, while Marjorie finds happiness by returning to the fold as the dutiful wife of a lawyer. Once more Wouk refutes arty idealism in favour of life in "the real world".

This is My God: The Jewish Way of Life is Wouk's credo, and his most important venture into non-fiction. In it he explains the Jewish faith, its history, and his own commitment to it, and defends the young State of Israel. Brief and to the point, Wouk delivers a forthright defence of his beliefs which is strong without being strident.

Wouk's "middle period" novels are somehow less satisfying than those before and after. *Youngblood Hawke*, an ambitious but uneven study of a writer's personal tragedy, lacks the cohesiveness of his best work, while *Don't Stop the Carnival*, in spite of several lively comic passages and a few neat character portraits, falls some distance short of *The City Boy*. Similarly *Slattery's Hurricane*, though an effective adventure story, cannot be ranked with his earlier novels.

The last 30 years have seen Wouk at work as fictional chronicler of the 20th century, presenting World War II and the Holocaust (*The Winds of War*; *War and Remembrance*) and the emergence of the State of Israel (*The Hope*; *The Glory*) in the style of a Tolstoian epic. Here he handles his large cast with considerable skill, the narrative shifting from frontline action and the sufferings of the Jewish Jastrow family at Nazi hands to the overview of Bible-reading Commander "Pug" Henry as he flits from one theatre of war to the other. Both novels have been bestsellers and the televised version drew a record-breaking viewing audience. The later sequence follows a similar pattern, soldier / envoy Zev Barak in the "Pug" Henry role and action viewed through the eyes of the Barak, Luria, and Nitzan families. These volumes provide a fitting sequel to the previous chronicle, the Jew as victim replaced by the Jew as heroic victor. Wouk has described these later novels as "a single task of bearing witness", and his role as fictional chronicler is given detailed assessment by Beichman in his 1984 study.

Inside, Outside is narrated by Israel David Goodkind, who combines in his multi-faceted career most aspects of the American Jewish experience. Talmudic scholar, joke-writer, defence lawyer, and adviser to President Nixon, Goodkind takes time off during the Watergate crisis to recall his past life. His lively account crackles with quickfire humour as he describes his Bronx childhood, his rabbinical heritage, and his "outside" encounters with writers, entertainers, and glamorous showgirl Bobbie Webb. The book abounds with memorable characters, wonderful dialogue exchanges, and some probing social insights, including a sympathetic portrayal of Nixon through Jewish eyes. Poignant and hilarious, *Inside, Outside* shows Wouk at his most Jewish, and is one of his finest achievements.

GEOFF SADLER

Y

Yehoshua, A.B.

Israeli fiction writer and dramatist, 1936–

Born Abraham Yehoshua in Jerusalem, 9 December 1936. Studied at Jerusalem Hebrew Gymnasium; Hebrew University, Jerusalem, BA 1961; Teachers College, graduated 1962. Served in army, 1954–57. Married Rivka Kirsninski, 1960; one daughter, two sons. Teacher, Hebrew University High School, Jerusalem, 1961–63. Lived in Paris, 1963–67; director, Israeli School, Paris, 1963–64; Secretary General, World Union of Jewish Students, 1963–67. Dean of Students, 1967–72, and professor of comparative literature since 1972, Haifa University; Visiting Fellow, St Cross College, Oxford, 1975–76; guest professor, Harvard University, 1977, University of Chicago, 1988, and Stanford University, 1990. Many awards, including Akum Prize, 1961; Municipality of Ramat-Gan Prize, 1968; University of Iowa Fellowship, 1969; Prime Minister's Prize, 1972; Brenner Prize, 1983; Alterman Prize, 1986; Bialik Prize, 1989; National Jewish Book Award (United States), 1990; Israel Prize, 1995.

Selected Writings

Fiction

Mot hazaken [Death of the Old Man], 1962
Mul hayearot, 1968; as *Facing the Forests*, translated by Miriam Arad, 1970
Sheloshah yamim veyeled, 1969; as *Three Days and a Child*, translated by Miriam Arad, 1970
Tishah sipurim [Nine Stories], 1970
Shenei sipurim, 1970–71
Bithilat kayits 1970, 1972; as *Early in the Summer of 1970*, translated by Miriam Arad and Pauline Shrier, 1977
Ad horef 1974: mivchar, 1975
Hameahev, 1977; as *The Lover*, translated by Philip Simpson, 1978
Gerushim meuharim, 1982; as *A Late Divorce*, translated by Hillel Halkin, 1984
Molcho, 1987; as *Five Seasons*, translated by Hillel Halkin, 1989
The Continuing Silence of a Poet: The Collected Stories of A.B. Yehoshua, translated by Miriam Arad and Pauline Shrier, 1988
Mar mani, 1990; as *Mr Mani*, translated by Hillel Halkin, 1992
Hashivah mehodu, 1994; as *Open Heart*, translated by Dalya Bilu, 1996
Masa el tom haelef, 1997; as *A Journey to the End of the Millennium*, translated by Nicholas de Lange, 2000

Plays

Laylah bemay, 1969; as *A Night in May*, in *Two Plays*, translated by Miriam Arad, 1974
Tipolim aharonim, 1973; as *Last Treatment*, in *Two Plays*, translated by Miriam Arad, 1974
Hafetsim [Possessions], 1986
Tinokot laylah [Children of the Night], 1992

Screenplays: *Sheloshah yamim veyeled* [Three Days and a Child], 1967; *Hameahev* [The Lover], 1986

Other

Bizekhut hanormaliyut, 1980; as *Between Right and Right*, translated by Arnold Schwartz, 1981
Israel, with Frederic Brenner, translated by Philip Simpson, 1988
Hakir vehahar: metsiuto hasifrutit shel hasofer beyisrael [The Wall and the Mountain: The Literary Reality of the Writer in Israel], 1989

Further Reading

Anderson, Elliott, *Contemporary Israeli Literature*, Philadelphia: Jewish Publication Society, 1977
Aschkenasy, Nehama, "Yehoshua's 'Sound and Fury': *A Late Divorce* and Its Faulknerian Model", *Modern Language Studies*, 21/2 (1991)
Berg, Nancy E., "Sephardic Writing: From the Margins to the Mainstream" in *The Boom in Contemporary Israeli Fiction*, edited by Alan Mintz, Hanover, New Hampshire: University Press of New England, 1997
Chertok, Haim, "A.B. Yehoshua: Dismantler" in *We Are All Close: Conversations with Israeli Writers*, New York: Fordham University Press, 1989
Cohen, Joseph, *Voices of Israel: Essays on and Interviews with Amichai, Yehoshua, Carmi, Appelfeld and Oz*, Albany, New York: State University of New York Press, 1990
Feinberg, Anat, "A.B. Yehoshua as Playwright", *Modern Hebrew Literature*, 1 (1975)
Fuchs, Esther, "Casualties of Patriarchal Double Standards: Old Women in Yehoshua's Fiction", *South Central Bulletin*, 43/4 (1984)
Fuchs, Esther, "The Sleepy Wife: A Feminist Consideration of A.B. Yehoshua's Fiction", *Hebrew Annual Review*, 8 (1984)

Horn, Bernard, *Facing the Fires: Conversations with A.B. Yehoshua*, Syracuse, New York: Syracuse University Press, 1997

Jerushalmi, Joseph, *A.B. Yehoshua; A Bibliography 1953–1979*, Tel Aviv: Sifriyat Poalim, 1980

Kurzwel, Baruch, "An Appraisal of the Stories of Avraham B. Yehoshua", *Literature East and West*, 14/1 (1970)

Ofrat, Gideon, "Possessions as a Death Wish", *Modern Hebrew Literature*, 12/1–2 (1986)

Pfefferkorn, Eli, "A Touch of Madness in the Plays of A.B. Yehoshua", *World Literature Today*, 51 (1977)

Ramras-Rauch, Gila, "A.B. Yehoshua" in *The Arab in Israeli Literature*, Bloomington: Indiana University Press, and London: Tauris, 1989

Ramras-Rauch, Gila, "A.B. Yehoshua and the Sephardic Experience", *World Literature Today*, 65/1 (1991)

Shaked, Gershon, "A Great Madness Hides Behind All This", *Modern Hebrew Literature*, 8/1–2 (1982–83)

Shoham, Haim, "Distress and Constriction", *Ariel*, 41 (1976)

Yudkin, Leon I., "Multiple Focus and Mystery", *Modern Hebrew Literature*, 3 (1977)

Like his lifelong friend Amos Oz, A.B. Yehoshua is one of a handful of Israeli novelists to have won international renown. Like Oz, Yehoshua is also a prominent public figure at home, frequently writing articles and speaking out on Israel's contentious political, religious, and cultural issues. Not surprisingly, the two writers share some common concerns that surface in their novels and short stories. But the similarities largely end there, and few readers would mistake the work of one writer for the other.

Yehoshua was born in Jerusalem in 1936 ("three years earlier than Oz but just two streets away") and like Oz he left that city fairly early on to live in more open and secular parts of Israel. But while Oz opted for life in the southern desert region, Yehoshua migrated north, and today is a literature professor at Haifa University. More significantly, Oz is the son of European immigrants, while Yehoshua comes from a Sephardic family long rooted in Jerusalem. This distinction is evident in much of the two writers' work.

As part of the "New Wave" or "Second Generation" of Israeli writers, Yehoshua came to prominence in the 1960s with collections of well-crafted and often cunningly symbolic short stories. (Many of these would eventually be published in English in 1988 in a retrospective collection called *The Continuing Silence of a Poet*.) Yehoshua was also drawn to Haifa's lively theatre life and began writing a series of well-received plays, beginning in 1969 with the politically provocative *A Night in May*. By the mid-1970s, with the publication of his first novel, *The Lover*, Yehoshua was established as a major writer of his generation.

Virtually all of Yehoshua's writing is densely detailed, lyrical, and meditative. He also delights in such literary techniques as multiple points of view, interior monologue, and shifts in time. These devices, not to mention the frequent climactic flashpoints of violence in his early stories, reflect Yehoshua's acknowledged debt to William Faulkner. His concern with existential isolation, however, shows influences of Albert Camus and other French modernists. (Yehoshua has spent several years in France.) Yet despite these heady antecedents, his narratives, especially in his most recent novels, are usually anchored in domestic matters such as troubled relationships, thwarted love, and other conflicts of the heart.

To be sure, Yehoshua's first fictions easily lent themselves to political interpretation. His shocking short story, "Death of an Old Man", in which neighbours simply do away with a troublesome old-timer, was widely read as an allegory about the new generation of Israelis overthrowing the European-born founders of the State. Similarly, "Facing the Forest", in which a confused and aimless young student helps an Arab incinerate a Jewish National Fund forest planted over the remains of the Arab's destroyed village, was seen as a parable of self-destructive political obtuseness and ideological malaise.

Yehoshua has said that many Israeli writers of the first generation explored in their fiction the "Israeli condition" just as Tolstoi, Dostoevskii, and Chekhov examined the "Russian condition", and clearly in his early work Yehoshua was continuing in this vein. It is of course a mistake to view every pensioner who appears in Israeli literature as a stand-in for the founding Zionist fathers, every troubled marriage as an allegory of uneasy Israeli identity. Many readers nonetheless gleefully continue to mine political and ideological symbols out of Yehoshua's later writing. Thus an old automobile that fascinates a garage mechanic in *The Lover* becomes for critic Joseph Cohen "the symbol of the 1948 War of Independence and the resulting freedom it brought to the Jews in Israel" – this even though the car in question is a Morris, built in Britain in 1947. Still, readers must be free to interpret an ostensible domestic melodrama like *The Lover*, with its multi-generational and multi-ethnic characters, as an overview of Israel; or *A Late Divorce*, with its tensions over a family inheritance, as an examination of the erosion of the Israeli soul; or *Five Seasons* (published in Hebrew in 1987 as *Molcho*), a lugubrious tale of a Sephardic Israeli striving to come to grips with the death of his German-Jewish wife (in the process he becomes a virtual wandering Jew) as an emblematic view of "post-Zionist" Israel.

Yehoshua's novels of the 1990s, however, call for different kinds of interpretation. *Mr Mani* is a bold if uneven look at a Sephardic family set in several different eras and countries and narrated in a series of different voices. *Open Heart* (published in Israel as *The Return from India*) is a compelling story of obsessive love, not to mention a tour de force for its depiction of the subcontinent, which the author has never visited. And *A Journey to the End of the Millennium* is another tour de force, this time for its lavish evocation of both North African and European Jewry on the brink of the year 1000 CE.

With its minutely detailed description, its leisurely pace, and its relentlessly focused style (the book's 300 pages contain virtually no dialogue), *A Journey to the End of the Millennium* seems like yet another stylistic experiment and thematic departure for the ever innovative Yehoshua. Yet for all its apparent newness of direction, the novel rests comfortably within his canon. Its plot is driven by familial conflict, this time between the bigamous North African Jewish merchant Ben Attar and his European relatives and business partners. A troubled love affair also entangles the central characters. Underlying all of the action is the cultural and spiritual disharmony between Sephardic and Ashkenazic Jews. All of these concerns are subjects that Yehoshua has to greater or lesser degree touched on before. In this regard, the apparently uncharacteristic *A Journey to the End of the Millennium* is in fact as quintessential a Yehoshua work as this ever inventive and individualistic author has produced.

MATTHEW NESVISKY

Yeshurun, Avot

Russian-born Israeli poet, 1904–1992

Born Yechiel Perlmutter in Volhynia, 1904, into Hasidic family. Raised in shtetl of Krasnystaw; studied at yeshiva. Emigrated to Palestine, 1925; worked in Jewish and Arab villages, dredging swamps, picking fruit, and working as watchman and construction worker. First poems published in *Turim*, 1934. Relatives remaining in Europe killed in Holocaust. Regular contributor to literary journal *Siman Kriah*. Awarded Israel Prize, 1992. Died 1992.

Selected Writings

Poetry
Al hokhmat drakhim [On the Wisdom of Roads] (as Yechiel Perlmutter), 1942
Pesah al kukhim [Passover on Caves], 1952
Reem, 1960
Shoshim amud shel Avot Yeshurun [Thirty Pages of Avot Yeshurun], 1964
Zeh shem hasefer [This is the Name of the Book], 1970
Hashever hasuri-afrikani, 1974; as *The Syrian–African Rift*, translated by Harold Schimmel, 1980
Kapella kolot [A Capella Voices], 1977
Shaar knisah, shaar yetsiah [Entrance Gate, Exit Gate], 1981
Homograph [Homograph], 1985
Adon menuha [Master of Rest], 1990
Ein li akhshav [I Have No Now], 1992
Kol shirav [Complete Poems], 1995

Further Reading

Avraham, Gidon, "A Bridge of Words: A Term List Based on the Study and Classification of Compounding Operations in Avot Yeshurun's Later Poetry (1974–1992): Concerning the Notion of Bayit [home/house]", *Studia Semitica Upsaliensia*, 15 (1999)
Gluzman, Michael, "Pesach al kukhim" [Passover on Caves], *Teoria u-bikoret*, 12–1 (1999)
Lachman, Lilach, "I Manured the Lawns with My Mother's Letters : Avot Yeshurun and the Question of the Avant-Garde", *Poetics Today*, 21/1 (2000)
Openhaimer, Yohai, *Tenu li ledaber kemo she-ani: Shirat Avot Yeshurun*, Tel Aviv: Hakibuts hameuhad, 1997
Yeshurun, Helit, "Ani hoekl el ha-kol" [I Walk towards Everything: An Interview with Avot Yeshurun), *Chadarim*, 3 (1982–83)
Zoritte, Eda, *Shirat ha-pere ha-atsil: Biografiyah shel ha-meshorer Avot Yeshurun* [The Song of the Noble Savage: A Biography], Tel Aviv: Hakibuts hameuhad, 1995

Born in 1904 as Yechiel Perlmutter, Avot Yeshurun was raised in the Polish shtetl Krasnystaw and emigrated to Palestine in 1925. His first volume of poetry, *Al hokhmat drakhim* [On the Wisdom of Roads], which appeared in 1942 under his original name, made little impact at the time of its publication. However, during the 1950s and 1960s Yeshurun's idiosyncratic use of Hebrew and far left-wing political views outraged the Israeli reading public and made him a highly controversial poet.

Yeshurun's initial marginality was due to his stylistic preferences. In the 1940s and early 1950s, the *moderna* coterie led by Avraham Shlonsky, Natan Alterman, and Leah Goldberg dominated Hebrew letters. Influenced by Russian Symbolism, *moderna* poets highly favoured figurative language, as well as regularized metre and rhyme. Although initially embraced by the coterie leaders, Yeshurun's wild, "broken" language flagrantly violated the *moderna*'s poetic norms. Consequently, Yeshurun was assigned a liminal and precarious position among *moderna* poets. However, with the rise of the Statehood Generation in the late 1950s, poets such as Yehuda Amichai, Nathan Zach, Moshe Dor, and Dalia Ravikovitch turned against the poetics of the *moderna* and embraced previously peripheral poets such as David Vogel and Yeshurun. The new generation's rejection of the quatrain and regularized rhyme allowed Yeshurun further to revolutionize his poetic language. From then on, when he was already in his fifties, Yeshurun entered the most prolific phase of his poetic career. Until his death in 1992, he published numerous volumes of poetry and enjoyed the increasing admiration of readers and critics alike.

The most distinctive characteristic of Yeshurun's poetry is precisely its "broken" Hebrew. Like the vast majority of Hebrew poets in the first half of the 20th century, Yeshurun was an immigrant whose native languages were Yiddish and Polish. Unlike other Hebrew poets who suppressed their mother tongue – and who wrote their poems in a seamless Hebrew – Yeshurun brought this biographic and linguistic rift into his poetic language. His poems echo the languages of his childhood and those he encountered in Palestine, including Arabic, thus creating a poetic language marked by hybridity, fragmentation, and ungrammaticality. As critic Shimon Sandbank has already observed, Yeshurun turns the biographic trauma of immigration into the organizing principle of his language. Unlike other modernist writers who attempted to assimilate into a new language, Yeshurun made a conscious effort to retain the broken, polyglot nature of the immigrant linguistic experience. As he said in an interview with Helit Yeshurun, "Woe to him, the one who betrays, who abandons his mother tongue!"

Yeshurun's refusal to deny his European past had not only linguistic but also thematic ramifications. His contemporaries, for the most part, embraced the Zionist negation of exile, and participated in the cultural attempt to create a New Jew free of Diaspora ills. In Zionist culture, Europe and Palestine came to represent two diametrically opposed geographical, political, and cultural sites: the former emblematized the despised diasporic past, while the latter promised a Jewish return to history. At precisely that time, Yeshurun fiercely challenged this dichotomy and refused to ignore the legacy of his forefathers. In a symbolic act, he changed his name to Avot Yeshurun, literally meaning "Our fathers are looking at us", as an indication of his emotional and cultural attachment to his European Jewish past.

More than any other Hebrew writer, Yeshurun created a poetic space shaped by memory in which past and present, Krasnystaw and Tel Aviv, are fused and intertwined. Obsessed by what he terms "the work of longing", he continuously portrays the coexistence of these two distinct worlds. However, this coexistence is not seamless or harmonious, for Yeshurun is ceaselessly haunted by the absence of the Jewish world of his childhood which exists only through memory and language.

While Yeshurun's position vis-à-vis his diasporic past has gradually gained legitimacy, his views on the Israeli–Arab conflict remained, and perhaps still remain, outside of the Israeli consensus. Very early on, Yeshurun objected to what he viewed as Hebrew literature's disregard for the Arab. In his own words:

> A strange relationship has settled between me and Hebrew literature. She did not attract me. I have a major gripe against her: she did not fulfil her fundamental role to bring us closer to the Arab question and to the Arab people of the land . . . Hebrew literature brought us to Zion and she had to say the truth about who lived in the land, not to say that it was empty.

Although other writers and critics have advanced a critique of Zionism's disregard for the Arab, Yeshurun went as far as creating an analogy between the Jewish Holocaust and the expulsion of the Arabs from Palestine during the 1948 war. He often talked about "the crisis of two holocausts: the holocaust of the Jewish people there and the holocaust of the Arab people here", an analogy that infuriated the world of Hebrew letters. In a bold, long poem of 1952, *Pesah al kukhim* [Passover on Caves], he advanced a fierce critique of Zionist perceptions of the Arab as a national Other and called for a Jewish–Arab brotherhood. The critical reception of this poem was extraordinarily hostile and Yeshurun was regarded as "ex-centric" in both senses of the word.

With the passage of time, however, he became highly regarded, and during the 1980s and 1990s he came to be acknowledged as one of Israel's truly great poets. Before his death in 1992, he was awarded the Israel Prize – together with the Israeli-Arab writer, Emil Habibi.

MICHAEL GLUZMAN

Yezierska, Anzia

Russian-born US fiction writer, *c.*1885–1970

Born in mud hut in Plinsk around 1885. Emigrated with family to United States before 1900. Settled in Lower East Side, New York City; worked in sweatshops and at other menial jobs by day; studied English at night school; scholarship to study domestic science at Columbia University, 1903. Teacher of domestic science for short time. First marriage, *c.*1910, annulled after few months; married, second, Arnold Levitas; one daughter; left husband and daughter. First short story published, 1915. Met John Dewey, 1917; relationship lasted till Dewey's departure on extended travels abroad, 1918. Collection of stories, *Hungry Hearts*, published 1920: film rights bought by Sam Goldwyn. Settled in California but, unable to write away from familiar milieu, returned to Lower East Side. Employed by Works Progress Administration Writers Project, cataloguing trees in Central Park. Using legacy from acquaintance, moved briefly to New Hampshire but returned to New York City. Died in California, 21 November 1970.

Selected Writings

Collection
The Open Cage: An Anzia Yezierska Collection, 1979
How I Found America: Collected Stories of Anzia Yezierska, introduction by Vivian Gornick, 1991

Novels
Salome of the Tenements, 1923
Bread Givers: A Novel: A Struggle between a Father of the Old World and a Daughter of the New, 1925
Arrogant Beggar, 1927
All I Could Never Be, 1932
Red Ribbon on a White Horse, 1950; revised edition 1987

Short Stories
Free Vacation House, 1915
Fat of the Land, 1919
Hungry Hearts, 1920
Children of Loneliness: Stories of Immigrant Life in America, 1923
Take Up Your Bed and Walk, in *Chicago Jewish Forum* (1964)

Further Reading

Auden, W.H. (introduction) and Louise Levites Henriksen (afterword) in Yezierska's *Red Ribbon on a White Horse*, New York: Persea, 1987
Burstein, Janet Handler, *Writing Mothers, Writing Daughters: Tracing the Maternal in Stories by American Jewish Women*, Urbana: University of Illinois Press, 1996
Dearborn, Mary V., *Love in the Promised Land: The Story of Anzia Yezierska and John Dewey*, New York: Free Press, 1988
Dearborn, Mary V., "Anzia Yezerska and the Making of an Ethnic American Self" in *The Invention of Ethnicity*, edited by Werner Sollors, New York and London: Oxford University Press, 1989
Gelfant, Blanche H., introduction to Yezierska's *Hungry Hearts*, New York: Penguin, 1997
Harris, Alice Kessler, introduction to Yezierska's *Bread Givers*, New York: Persea, 1975
Harris, Alice Kessler (introduction) and Louise Levitas Henriksen (afterword) in *The Open Cage: An Anzia Yezierska Collection*, New York: Persea, 1979

Henriksen, Louise Levitas and Jo Ann Boydston, *Anzia Yezierska: A Writer's Life*, New Brunswick, New Jersey: Rutgers University Press, 1988

Inglehart, Babette, "Daughters of Loneliness: Anzia Yezierska and the Immigrant Woman Writer", *Studies in American Jewish Literature*, 1/2 (Winter 1975): 1–10

Levin, Tobe, "How to Eat without Eating: Anzia Yezierska's Hunger" in *Cooking By the Book*, edited by Mary Anne Schofield, Bowling Green, Ohio: Bowling Green State University Popular Press, 1989

Neidle, Cecyle S., *America's Immigrant Women*, Boston: Twayne, 1975

Schoen, Carol B., *Anzia Yezierska*, Boston: Twayne, 1982

Stubbs, Katherine, introduction to Yezierska's *Arrogant Beggar*, Durham, North Carolina: Duke University Press, 1996

Wexler, Laura, "Looking at Yezierska" in *Women of the Word: Jewish Women and Jewish Writing*, edited by Judith R. Baskin, Detroit: Wayne State University Press, 1994

Wilentz, Gay, introduction to Yezierska's *Salome of the Tenements*, Urbana: University of Illinois Press, 1995

Much of Yezierska's fiction dramatizes the conflicts Jewish immigrant women faced in adapting to American culture. In her early stories, collected in *Hungry Hearts*, and subsequent novels, such as *Salome of the Tenements*, *Bread Givers*, and *Arrogant Beggar*, Yezierska translates the dreams, disappointments, and successes of immigrants, women, and members of the working class for a broad American audience. Her sometimes realistic, sometimes melodramatic portrayals of Jewish life in the Lower East Side of Manhattan offer critiques of class prejudice, anti-Semitism, institutional philanthropy, patriarchy, and Orthodox Judaism. Her work focuses on Jewish immigrant women's struggles to achieve social and economic mobility, attain independence from shtetl traditions, and define new ways of expressing Jewish identity in America. The passionate language of her fiction helps illustrate the way in which immigrants experienced America as a *farkerte velt* (a perverse or upside down world). Their expectations of a promised land, with streets paved in gold, were turned upside down by the realities of working-class, tenement life – a life represented vividly in Yezierska's fiction. In later years, as Yezierska aged, the focus of her writing turned to themes of ageing.

The young women of Yezierska's fiction long to escape the dirt and squalor of the Lower East Side ghetto with hopes of locating the "real" America beyond the tenements. Their opportunities to find this America are circumscribed by poor education, poverty, prejudice against the working class, and Orthodox religious values.

Finding America's riches proves difficult for Hannah Breineh, the protagonist of Yezierska's best-known story, "The Fat of the Land". When she haggled with pushcart peddlers for potatoes a penny cheaper, she longed for the happiness and peace accompanying wealth. With her children's material and cultural success (one child is a socially conscious playwright), Hannah no longer yearns for a full stomach, but for the human connections among members of the ghetto. The painful conflicts between first-generation immigrants and their rich, successful children underscore Hannah's relocation from Delancey Street to Riverside Drive. Hannah complains to an old neighbour, "What have I from all my fine furs and feathers when my children are strangers to me?" Tobe Levin sees Hannah as one of Yezierska's "hungry" characters; she hungers not only for food, but for the mythic, ever-elusive America flowing with "milk and honey".

The unnamed protagonist in "Soap and Water" also hungers for the riches of America and confronts obstacles in her quest for social mobility. She has worked long hours in a laundry to support herself as she attended college. Upon the culmination of her degree, the Dean (strikingly named Miss Whiteside) threatens to withhold her diploma owing to her unkempt appearance. "Soap and Water are cheap", she scolds. "Anyone can be clean." The Dean's warnings about her appearance prove prophetic: with diploma in hand, the protagonist cannot find work because her unclean appearance excludes her from the middle-class profession of teaching.

The feminist rediscovery of *Bread Givers* in the 1970s drew attention to themes underscored by the book's subtitle, "A struggle between a father of the Old World and a daughter of the New." Sara Smolinsky's desire for independence and mobility is as much a struggle against the limitations of ghetto life as it is against the tyranny represented by her father's Orthodox Judaism. Sara leaves home, puts herself through night school and college, and "makes herself for a person" by becoming a teacher. Yezierska's protagonists long to become educated and work for themselves, even though most immigrant women were expected to hand over their wages to support the family economy. Her characters, therefore, resist hostility from members of the Jewish community and derision from the larger, American culture which promoted male professionalism and female domestication. Sara's return to the ghetto as a teacher dramatizes her struggle to free herself from ghetto constraints. This struggle becomes poignant when Sara's mother dies, and she refuses to tear "her only suit" in accordance with Jewish custom.

Bread Givers, like much of Yezierska's fiction, does not provide a straightforward ending. While it is easy to recognize the fairy-tale qualities in her fiction, her endings are always bittersweet – with characters meditating on both the pleasures and pains of Jewish-American identity. Sara's impending marriage and happiness with Hugo Seelig, at the end of the novel, are undercut by the prospect of her father coming to live with them. "I felt the shadow still there, over me. It wasn't just my father, but the generations who made my father whose weight was still upon me." Yezierska suggests that Jewish women's escape from the Old World is not as easy or complete as they might hope.

If *Bread Givers* contests women's roles in Jewish family economies, then institutionalized charity is at the centre of Yezierska's critique in *Arrogant Beggar*. Adele Lindner enters the Hellman Home for Working Girls with hopes of transcending the drudgery of her working-class, tenement life. She soon learns that the Home provides charity in order to maintain distinctions among classes, rather than to encourage mobility. When Adele loses her job, Mrs Hellman enrols her in a domestic science course and puts her to work as a servant. Yezierska revises *tzedakah* (literally "charity" and "righteousness") in the American economy by contrasting the heartless, condescending philanthropy of the Hellman House with the charitable ethos of Muhmenkeh's Coffee Shop. Adele opens the coffee shop in the ghetto to give back to the community and allows customers to pay what and when they can afford: "Giving my people the most for the least money was my way of working out the hungers I had suffered." For Adele, giving is a way of living, and it is through this lifestyle that she enjoys the riches of America.

Yezierska's Jewish contemporaries did not always welcome her biting critiques. To some, she aired the dirty laundry of the Jewish community – exposing ghetto conditions and ethnic tensions among American Jews. For others, she inscribed the "living life" of Jewish immigrant experience in America.

WENDY H. BERGOFFEN

Yizhar, S.

Israeli fiction writer, 1916–

Born Yizhar Smilansky in Rehovot, 1916. Taught at Ben Shemen youth village. Fought in War of Independence, 1948. Member of Knesset (Israeli legislature), 1948–67. Professor of literature, Tel Aviv University. Awards include Brenner, Bialik, and Israel prizes.

Selected Writings

Fiction
Ephraim Goes Back to Alfalfa, 1938
Befatei negev [On the Edge of the Negev], 1945
Hahorshah bagivah [The Forest on the Hill], 1947
Sippur hirbet hizah [The Story of Hirbet Hizah], 1949
Midnight Convoy, 1950
Yamei tsiklag [The Days of Ziklag], 1958
Stories of a Plain, 1964
"The Runaway" in *The Bantam Book of Hebrew Stories*, edited by Ezra Spicehandler, 1967
Midnight Convoy and Other Stories, translated by Institute for the Translation of Hebrew Literature, 1969
Seven Stories, 1971
"The Prisoner" in *Modern Hebrew Literature*, edited by Robert Alter, 1975
"Hauling the Water-Tank", *Jerusalem Quarterly*, 12 (Summer 1979)
Mikdamot, 1992
Tzalhavim, 1993

Other
Six Summer Stories, 1950
Barefoot, 1959
Reading a Story, 2 vols, 1980
Two Polemics, 1990

Further Reading

Alter, Robert (editor), *Modern Hebrew Literature*, New York: Behrman House, 1975
Avigur-Rotem, Gabriela, "The Fountain", *Modern Hebrew Literature*, new series 18 (Spring–Summer 1997)
Ben, Menahem, "Journey to the Sources of the Spirit", *Modern Hebrew Literature*, new series 18 (Spring–Summer 1997)
Golan, Ornah, *Ben Bidyon le-Mamashut: Sugim ba-Sipur ha-Yisraeli*, vol. 2, Tel Aviv: Everyman's University, 1984
Miron, Dan, *Arba' Panim baSifrut halvrit Bat-Yamenu*, Jerusalem: Schocken, 1962
Miron, Dan, "S. Yizhar: Some General Observations" in *Midnight Convoy and Other Stories*, Jerusalem: Institute for the Translation of Hebrew Literature, 1969
Nagid, Chayim (editor), *S. Yizhar: A Selection of Critical Essays on His Writing*, Tel Aviv: Am Oved, 1972
Oz, Amos, "A Letter to S. Yizhar", *Modern Hebrew Literature*, new series 18 (Spring–Summer 1997)
Ramras-Rauch, Gila, *The Arab in Israeli Literature*, Bloomington: Indiana University Press, and London: Tauris, 1989
Ratner, Tzila, "Preserving the Hopes and Fears of a Generation", *Jewish Chronicle* (27 February 1998)
Telpaz, Gideon, *Israeli Childhood Stories of the Sixties*, Chico, California: Scholars Press, 1983
Yudkin, Leon I., *Escape into Siege: A Survey of Israeli Literature Today*, London and Boston: Routledge and Kegan Paul, 1974
Yudkin, Leon I., *1948 and After: Aspects of Israeli Fiction*, Manchester: Manchester University Press, 1984

S. Yizhar (pen name for Yizhar Smilansky) comes from a family of pioneers, farmers, and writers, who came to Erets Israel from Russia in 1890. Continuing this family tradition, Yizhar combined his literary career with teaching and political activity (he was a member of Israel's first six parliaments). He is the first novelist, both chronologically and in terms of quality of writing, of the Palmach or the 1948 generation of Israeli-born writers. The authors of this generation, cut off from their historical roots of European Diaspora, educated in Hebrew, and committed to the ethos of pioneering labour in the Land of Israel, generally shared a collective biography.

On the whole, Yizhar's contribution to the canon of Hebrew literature can be considered from two perspectives: the aesthetic and the linguistic innovation. Continuing the Hebrew literary tradition of authors such as Uri Nissan Gnessin and Yosef Hayyim Brenner, Yizhar often employed the technique of internal monologue, used the descriptions of sensory impressions as an expression of his protagonists' emotions, and extended the characters' personal, moral issues into general, existential dilemmas. While the majority of the Palmach generation authors focused their attention on the ethos of work in the Land of Israel, the priority of the values of the collective over the needs of the individual and the idealized figure of the new Israeli, the sabra, Yizhar depicted characters who voiced some doubts as to these values and distanced themselves from the "stream-of-the-collective-consciousness". His protagonists are generally sensitive, ambivalent individuals, who strive to define themselves outside the collective and question the prevalent system of values, inherited from the pioneer fathers. Linguistically, Yizhar expanded the extent of the descriptive mode of Hebrew prose, coining new phrases and combining the elements of the older literary Hebrew with colloquialisms, often juxtaposing the high register of language with specific military or agricultural expressions, which are particularly discernible in his descriptions of nature.

The first publication, a short story *Ephraim Goes Back to Alfalfa*, is recognized as marking the beginning of the first Israeli-born generation's period of Hebrew literature. Here, as in many of his other works, Yizhar employed the stream-of-consciousness technique, where the protagonist/narrator withdraws into himself by long interior monologues. As in his later works, the plot revolves around the alienated protagonist, who, although a part and participant of his community (kibbutz), remains an outsider, observing his peers with distance and ambivalence, often presenting very sharp and critical remarks on the individuals within the collective.

Ephraim (the protagonist) longs to leave his work at the fodder and change his working environment to a more comfortable labour in an orange grove, where he could be alone, away from the unbearable heat and monotony of everyday, mundane tasks and conversations, and to have the privacy and time to define his individuality. Ephraim's existence within the collective, with its strenuous routine, deadens his sense of life and causes him to rebel. The tension between the individual and the group is extended into man's relationship with the landscape: nature is initially a source of frustration, as Ephraim strives to subjugate it to his own needs, and eventually he finds it impossible to conquer. On the other hand, Yizhar's poetic description of nature (which led to his being described as "the greatest poet of landscape in Israeli literature") reveals Ephraim's love for the wild, uncultivated landscape, which here comes to symbolize the freedom he yearns for and is never able to realize. Yizhar's hero, when finally given the opportunity to follow his needs, decides to remain within the collective and to continue the routine of everyday tasks. He remains the outsider, never quite merging with the group, but at the same time not being able to break away from it, and thus submitting himself to a meaningless existence, nullifying the individual will.

"The Prisoner" was written in 1948, during the War of Independence, and published in 1949 together with the controversial work, *The Story of Hirbet Hizah*. Both stories depict the shock of the sensitive protagonist at the brutality and senselessness of war. This is contrasted with the poetic descriptions of the tranquil landscape and pastoral life of Arab villagers, who are seen as the natural inhabitants of such scenery. *The Story of Hirbet Hizah* is an account of the evacuation of an Arab village, whereas in "The Prisoner" the anonymous protagonist/narrator, a soldier, participates in the capture of an Arab shepherd, who is subsequently interrogated and driven to the Israeli Army headquarters. The story can be divided into three parts. In the first, the lyrical description of the ancient, peaceful landscape is often interrupted by the laconic exclamations of the manoeuvring military unit, increasing the ironic gap between the invaders and the local inhabitants. The second part of the story reveals the protagonist as part of the group, depicting his peers with sarcastic clarity as a thoughtless crowd. Interestingly, the narration verges between the "I" and the "we", emphasizing the fact that the protagonist, although critically distant from the group, remains a participant in all the actions and decisions. This notion is taken further in the third part of the story, where the "we" is totally replaced by the "I" of the narrator in his internal dialogue and inner struggle, where he is split into two voices: the voice of moral values and individual conscience, dictating that he set the prisoner free, in the second person, and the voice of the protagonist's weakness, answering the accusations with conventional collective excuses in the first person. This shift of vision beyond "us" enables the narrator to question the group and the collective order. However, as he remains one of many in the circle around the prisoner, group values take over individual convictions and the protagonist fails to perform any action that would go against the collective.

The stream-of-consciousness technique is also employed in Yizhar's novel *The Days of Ziklag*, which is considered by some to be the most important of its time. The narrative focuses on the shifts within the protagonists, soldiers in a small commando unit, rather than the external plot, which is confined to seven days of a battle over an Arab village. Here, as in the two previous stories, Yizhar's innovation lies not only in his use of language, his neologisms, and portraying ambivalent individuals within a collective, but also in the fact that the author gives voice to the enemy at a time of political crisis.

Yizhar's latest, autobiographical novels, *Mikdamot* and *Tzalhavim*, were written after 30 years of silence. He describes life in Israel in its early days, showing compassion and understanding towards the pioneering fathers from the point of view of a young boy.

S. Yizhar is one of the best Israeli writers and certainly one of the most innovative. In his poetic descriptions he reached beyond the linguistic boundaries of Hebrew and in his choice of themes he countered prevailing viewpoints, not only questioning accepted collective values but also giving voice to Israel's enemies.

Marta Marzanska

Z

Zach, Nathan

German-born Israeli poet, 1930–

Born in Berlin, 1930. Emigrated with family to Palestine, 1935. Studied at Hebrew University, Jerusalem. Repertory director, Ohel trade union theatre; adviser, Chambre Theatre, Tel Aviv. Lived in Britain, 1967–79; studied at University of Essex, 1967–70; PhD. London news editor, Jewish Telegraphic Agency. Professor of comparative literature, Haifa University. Co-editor, *Likrat* and *Yohani* literary journal; co-founder, Achshav publishing house. Awards include Bialik Prize, 1981; Israel Prize, 1995.

Selected Writings

Poetry
Shirim rishonim [First Poems], 1955
Shirim shonim [Various Poems], 1960
Natan Zach, mivhar shirim [Selected Poems], 1962
Bimkom halom [Instead of a Dream], 1966
Kol hehalav vehadvash [All the Milk and Honey], 1966
Against Parting, translated by Jon Silkin, 1967
Dekalim utemarim [Palms and Dates: Arab Folksongs], 1967
Shirim shonim [Various Poems], 1968
Mivhar [The Best], 1974
Tsefonit mizrahit [North Easterly], 1979
The Static Element: Selected Poems, translated by Peter Evermine and Schulamit Yasny-Starkman, 1982
Anti-mehikon [Hard to Remember], 1984
Beit sefer lerikudim: album kolot [Dancing School], 1985
Shirim al kelev vekalbah [Poems about a Dog and a Bitch], 1990

Other
Translator, *Dominoes*, by Chanoch Levine, 1974
Editor, with Moshe Dor, *The Burning Bush: Poems from Modern Israel*, 1977
Kave avir: al haromantikah basiporet hayisreelit veal nosim aherim: sihot miluim [Lines in the Air: On Romanticism in Israeli Literature and Other Topics], 1983
Editor and Translator, *Kadish veshirim aherim*, by Allen Ginsberg, 1988

Further Reading

Baruch, Miri, "Aspects in the Poetics of Nathan Zach" (dissertation), Los Angeles: University of California, 1977
Burnshaw, Stanley, T. Carmi and Ezra Spicehandler (editors and translators), *The Modern Hebrew Poem Itself*, New York: Holt Rinehart and Winston, 1965
Levy, Shimon, "Elements of Poetic Self-Awareness in Modern Poetry", *Modern Hebrew Literature*, 3 (1976)
Milman, Yoseph, *Opacity in the Writings of Robbe-Grillet, Pinter, and Zach*, Lewiston, New York: Mellen Press, 1991

Born in Berlin, Zach has been one of the leading Hebrew poets of Israel's post-State period. His first poems were published in the 1950s, and augured a major shift of poetics from what he regarded as the rhetorical formalism of the mainly Russian-reared Hebrew poets, with their tight metres, rhyme schemes, and high literary language, as represented by H.N. Bialik in his generation (although he too broke with the predominant poetic conventions), and by Natan Alterman from the 1930s onwards. Zach is a modernist poet, minimalist in language, allusive rather than explicit, spare and reflective, whose poetry reflects natural, idiomatic speech. But he still shapes that speech into units that are recognizably poetry, although they break with traditional metre, rhyme schemes, and expected poetic closure.

One of the themes of his writing is the consideration of the question of how poetry comes about. This is a significant issue, as one might sometimes wonder, as the poet himself does, whether a specific set of words is a poem at all. In a poem from *Kol hehalav vehadvash* [All the Milk and Honey] he speculates on the genesis of poetry: "When loneliness is not fear/ Poetry is born." It seems that poetry is produced by the poet within himself, writing to and for himself. But this stems from a sense of daring, a movement that is also a challenge. The poem is a consciously intellectual activity, although it may derive from an unconscious need. No necessary distinction is made between emotion and intellect here, as intellect is itself emotional. Thought is integral and requisite, and the poem that is formed is based on the rhythms of thought, the movement in one direction, the challenge and opposition, the reaction, the hesitation, and then, if not the conclusion, at least the abandonment of the line. Zach breaks the regular and inherited, the very "literary" patterns and prosodic schemes to produce another type of model, this one based on mental patterns. He attempts to locate precise definitions of states of mind, of love, of attachment, to people, to places, sometimes through a rejection of inappropriate yardsticks. So a Zach poem can become an argument with himself, or with the imagined other.

Zach's *Shirim rishonim* [First Poems] in 1955 sets the tone and the theme. Some of the poems are not foreclosed, in the sense that they may lack a full stop. This may also suggest that the line could be carry over and continue. The poem is made up of pithy lines, of refrains and echoes, and assonance rather than rhyme to reproduce normal conversational patterns. The subject is the individual who notes and records his own changing mood and sense impressions. This represents an attempt to confront reality, which is multivalent and constantly shifting, unstable and uncertain, subject to shafts of light and shade, thought and perception of varying strengths and modifications. But he places the instruction, as a kind of motto, at the head of a poem: "Al tira" [Do Not Be Afraid]. The cliché of inevitable suffering and death is cited here in the words of the biblical Psalms and Job: "Mankind's days are as grass" and "Man is born to suffering as the sparks fly upwards". But the only possible reaction that the poet (through the poetic statement) can offer is the refrain, "Do not be afraid", which concludes each of the three stanzas in this short poem.

Zach's poems often reflect on their own capacity and shape. In "Yeridat kosher harikuz shel hameshorer" [The Declining Concentration of the Poet] he speculates on the poet's capacity and production in the third person, as though outside himself. He (again the anonymous poetic voice) notes a weakening of perception, a tendency towards repetition bringing about a loss of poetic talent, and raising the question of whether what is written is poetry at all. He opens: "His poems are no longer so much on target". The anonymous narrator and the instructions offered to an unknown audience are intercut with the voice of the I, concluding only that: "You have indeed to take care of your limbs".

There is in Zach's poems a lack of specificity. But this too is a noted feature of normal conversation, where thoughts are left uncompleted, suggest more than they actually articulate, and allow for ambiguity. What is known can be grasped more immediately and certainly than stated. Here is a poem about (presumably) the end of a relationship (the title is the first line):

> When you rang your voice trembled
> And I knew that I was in mourning because of you
> And I had no need to hear what you said
> Because when you rang your voice trembled
> And I knew that I was in mourning because of me
> And you had no need to hear my voice
> Because when you rang your voice trembled
> And I knew that you were no longer there.

Desperate echoes move from sound to silence.

The persons in a Zach poem consist of an I in the centre, a you, which is unpredictable, and a he/she, who is either preoccupied, does not notice, or attempts to interpret, but does so differently. Questions are left unanswered, as in "I Sit at the Edge of the Road":

> I sit at the edge of the road
> And look at people.
> They do not know
> That I am looking at them.
> Is it in this way that God looks at us,
> Without our noticing, without our understanding,
> Without our being asked?
> I don't know.
> There are many things that I ask.
> For the time being
> I sit by the edge of the road
> And look.

Here is the concatenation: the observer, the observed, the possible observer of the observer, and the speculation on the meaning of the interaction, all these receive no answer, and the picture remains. This is what becomes the poem, and this is what is retained by the reader.

LEON I. YUDKIN

Zangwill, Israel

British fiction writer, journalist, and dramatist, 1864–1926

Born in Whitechapel, London, 21 January 1864. Studied at schools in Plymouth and Bristol; Jews' Free School, Spitalfields, London; University of London, BA 1884. Teacher, Jews' Free School; journalist from 1888; editor, humorous periodical *Ariel*. Met Theodor Herzl, 1895, and became active in Zionist movement; President, Jewish Territorial Organization for the Settlement of Jews within the British Empire, Jewish Historical Society, and Jewish Drama League. Married Edith Ayrton, 1903; two sons, one daughter. Died 1 August 1926.

Selected Writings

Collection
The Works of Israel Zangwill, edited by Alfred A. Wolmark, 14 vols, 1925; reprinted 1969

Fiction
Motza Kleis [Matzoh Balls], with Louis Cowen, 1882
The Premier and the Painter: A Fantastic Romance (with Louis Cowen, as J. Freeman Bell), 1888
The Bachelors' Club, 1891
The Old Maids' Club, 1892
The Big Bow Mystery, 1892
Children of the Ghetto, Being Pictures of a Peculiar People, 3 vols, 1892; reprinted in part as *Grandchildren of the Ghetto*, 1914
Ghetto Tragedies, 1893
Merely Mary Ann, 1893
The King of Schnorrers: Grotesques and Fantasies, 1894
Joseph the Dreamer, 1895
The Master, 1895
Dreamers of the Ghetto, 1898
They That Walk in Darkness: Ghetto Tragedies, 1899
The Mantle of Elijah, 1900
The Grey Wig: Stories and Novelettes, 1903
The Celibates' Club, 1905

Ghetto Comedies, 1907
Jinny the Carrier: A Folk Comedy of Rural England, 1919

Plays
The Great Demonstration, with Louis Cowen, 1892
Aladdin at Sea, 1893
Six Persons, 1893
The Lady Journalist, 1893
Threepenny Bits, 1895
Children of the Ghetto, 1899
The Moment of Death; or, The Never, Never Land, 1900
The Revolted Daughter, 1901
Merely Mary Ann, 1903
The Mantle of Elijah, 1904
The Serio-Comic Governess, 1904
Jinny the Carrier, 1905
The King of Schnorrers, 1905
Nurse Marjorie, 1906
The Melting-Pot, 1908
The War God, 1911
The Next Religion, 1912
Plaster Saints: A High Comedy, 1914
The Moment Before: A Psychical Melodrama, 1916
Too Much Money, 1918
The Cockpit, 1921
We Moderns, 1922
The Forcing House; or, The Cockpit Continued, 1923

Poetry
Blind Children, 1903

Other
"English Judaism", *Jewish Quarterly Review* (1989)
A Doll's House Repaired, with Eleanor Marx Aveling, 1891
Hebrew, Jew, Israelite, 1892
The Position of Judaism, 1895
Without Prejudice, 1896
The People's Saviour, 1898
The East African Question: Zionism and England's Offer, 1904
What Is the ITO?, 1905
A Land of Refuge, 1907
One and One Are Two, 1907
Talked Out!, 1907
Be Fruitful and Multiply, 1909
Old Fogeys and Old Bogeys, 1909
Report on the Purpose of Jewish Settlement in Cyrenaica, 1909
The Look on the Ladies, 1909
Italian Fantasies, 1910
Sword and Spirit, 1910
The Hithertos, 1912
The Problem of the Jewish Race, 1912
Report of the Commission for Jewish Settlement in Angora, 1913
The War and the Women, 1915
Zangwill in the Melting-Pot: Selections, edited by Elsie E. Morton, 1915
The War for the World, 1916
The Principle of Nationalities, 1917
The Service of the Synagogue, with Nina Davis Salaman and Elsie Davis, 3 vols, 1917
Chosen Peoples: The Hebraic Ideal "versus" the Teutonic, 1918
Hands Off Russia, 1919
The Jewish Pogroms in the Ukraine, with others, 1919
The Voice of Jerusalem, 1920
Watchman, What of the Night?, 1923
Translator, *Selected Religious Poems of Ibn Gabirol, Solomon ben Judah, Known as Avicebron, 1020?–1070?*, edited by Israel Davidson, 1923
Is the Ku Klux Klan Constructive or Destructive? A Debate between Imperial Wizard Evans, Zangwill, and Others, 1924
Now and Forever: A Conversation with Zangwill on the Jew and the Future, 1925
Our Own, 1926
Speeches, Articles, and Letters, edited by Maurice Simon, 1937

Further Reading

Adams, Elsie Bonita, *Israel Zangwill*, New York: Twayne, 1971
Fisch, Harold, *The Dual Image: A Study of the Figure of the Jew in English Literature*, London: Lincolns-Prager, 1959
Leftwich, Joseph, "Israel Zangwill", *Transactions of the Jewish Historical Society of England*, 18 (1953–55): 77–88
Leftwich, Joseph, *Israel Zangwill: A Biography*, New York: Yoseloff, 1957
Peterson, Annamarie, "Zangwill: A Selected Bibliography", *Bulletin of Bibliography* (September–December 1961)
Schilling, Bernard Nicholas, *The Comic Spirit: Boccaccio, Dickens, Fielding, Zangwill and Thomas Mann*, Detroit: Wayne State University Press, 1965
Udelson, Joseph H., *Dreamer of the Ghetto: The Life and Works of Israel Zangwill*, Tuscaloosa: University of Alabama Press, 1990
Winehouse, Bernard, "Zangwill's *Children of the Ghetto*: A Literary History of the First Anglo-Jewish Best-Seller", *English Literature in Transition*, 16/2 (1973)
Wohlgelernter, Maurice, *Israel Zangwill: A Study*, New York: Columbia University Press, 1964
Wolf, Lucien, "Israel Zangwill 1864–1926", *Transactions of the Jewish Historical Society of England*, 11 (1924–27): 252–60

There were Jews in Britain writing in English on Jewish themes before Israel Zangwill – Amy Levy and Grace Aguilar were the two foremost – but Zangwill was the first to be recognized as a major force on the English literary scene. On his death he was acknowledged as a writer with "profound and original thought" and he was the first Jew of stature to write in English (Disraeli cannot be considered because he had converted to Christianity; the American pioneer Abraham Cahan started to write only in the last decade of the 19th century). A number of Americans have since emulated Zangwill, but he remains the most important

British figure to write in English of Jewish life, especially immigrant life. His reputation in the US was so high that in 1897, it was reported, a small town in Oklahoma was named in his honour.

Zangwill was a prolific writer. In addition to his novels, he wrote short stories, poems, plays, and essays. His great masterpiece, *Children of the Ghetto*, appeared in 1892, but he had been active for some time before that. He had been known primarily as a member of the "New Humour" group of writers, led by Jerome K. Jerome. He edited a *Punch*-like magazine called *Ariel* and in 1891 had written two books, *The Bachelors' Club* and *Old Maids' Club* (later published together as one novel *The Celibates' Club*), which were full of humour.

In the 1880s Zangwill began writing stories on Jewish themes. The first was a pamphlet *Motsa Kleis* [Matzoh Balls], a satire on Anglo-Jewry, which was later lifted in its entirety into *Children of the Ghetto*. He also edited an annual called *Purim*. One powerful story, "Satan Mekatrig", is based on the Faust legend, but set in a Jewish context. He followed this with articles in the *London Jewish Standard* (this newspaper appears in *Children of the Ghetto* as the *Flag of Judah*) and he wrote an impressive paper for the prestigious *Jewish Quarterly Review* entitled "English Judaism: A Criticism and a Classification" in 1889. This was a sociological study of Anglo-Jewry that contended that there were major differences in class, origins, and religious beliefs in the community; it was at least partially responsible for bringing him to the attention of the Jewish Publication Society of America, which commissioned him to write *Children of the Ghetto*.

Zangwill's first novel, *The Premier and the Painter*, was written jointly with a friend, Louis Cowen. It was a political satire and a comedy and was published under the pseudonym J. Freeman Bell. He wrote many other novels and short story collections but his literary reputation now rests largely on *Children of the Ghetto*. It is a combination of comedy and tragedy and raises many questions on the nature of Judaism. The history of the central characters, the Ansell family, is a study of Zangwill's own, and Esther Ansell is clearly a stand-in for the author himself. The Jewish Publication Society of America wanted him to write the "Jewish *Robert Elsmere*". The popular Victorian novelist Mrs Humphry Ward's novel is the story of the spiritual crisis of a young clergyman, but Zangwill's novel was to be quite a different one. With its subtitle "Pictures of a Peculiar People", it is about the trials and tribulations of Jews who emigrated from eastern Europe to London, settling first in the Whitechapel ghetto. Zangwill skillfully and sympathetically lays bare the heart and soul of these people. There is no standard plot; the book is essentially a series of sketches of characters, although the narrative is continuous. The book focuses on Esther Ansell and her father Moses, but Zangwill's talent was in his ability to portray a wide range of personalities – the better-off relatives, the exploiter of workers, the saintly rabbi who gives his last coins to others and the rabbi who left his pulpit because of his doubts about his faith, all of whom are clearly delineated. A number of Anglo-Jewish figures are represented in this novel, but the most famous real figure is Naphtali Herz Imber, the author of "Hatikvah". Melchitzedek Pinchas, the Hebrew poet, was based on Imber and is one of the most celebrated characters in all Jewish fiction. Pinchas was depicted in a derisive manner and was viewed by Zangwill as unsavoury a person as he saw Imber to be. The final part of the novel is set ten years after the first when respectability enters the story as it moves to the Bayswater and Kensington neighbourhoods. This section was later published separately as *Grandchildren of the Ghetto*.

Dreamers of the Ghetto is a collection of biographical sketches in story form of famous Jews from the Middle Ages onwards. The dreamers range from Uriel Acosta and Solomon Maimon to Sabbatai Zevi, Heine, Spinoza, Disraeli, and Lassalle, all of whom were unable to find peace within or without the ghetto. Zangwill was the first to introduce Hasidism (the religious movement founded by the Baal Shem Tov in the 18th century) into English literature with his portrait of its founder.

The King of Schnorrers is a hilarious book consisting of tales of Jewish life in 18th-century London. Its hero is Menasseh Buena Abidu de Costa, a Portuguese beggar who carried all before him through effrontery and impudence (*chutzpah*) beyond belief, and which left his victims almost speechless. Menasseh pitted his wits against a number of people as well as one institution – the *Mahamad* governing body of the Sephardi congregation. Menasseh has been compared to Falstaff and Micawber for his humorous disposition.

They That Walk in Darkness (also called *Ghetto Tragedies*) and *Ghetto Comedies* are collections of short stories. They go beyond London and include occurrences and events of Jewish life all over the world. The titles of both works are somewhat misleading because comedy and tragedy appear in the stories in both. As in *Children of the Ghetto*, Zangwill's characterizations are memorable and reveal him as a writer with much compassion and humanity.

Zangwill was also a productive playwright, and some of his plays fix on Jewish subjects. *The Melting-Pot* was performed in Washington in front of President Theodore Roosevelt who called out "That's a great play, Mr Zangwill!" But it was not. It lacked drama. The hero of the play is a "handsome youth of the Russo-Jewish type" called David Quixano who emigrated to the US and fell in love with a Christian girl. The message was that in America there existed the great Melting Pot where all European peoples could combine together and discard hate and vengeance. This was followed by *The Next Religion* in 1912 which pointed the way to a fresh religion where international brotherhood and tolerance would be important. The Lord Chamberlain initially banned it from the stage because of its "heretical views" and it received its first performance in 1924.

In 1920 Zangwill published a collection of articles on Jewish subjects under the title *The Voice of Jerusalem*. One critic has written that this book is "one of the finest apologetic works in the entire Jewish literature". It is in two parts, with the first part condemning the way Christian society has treated the Jews. Zangwill's message was that Judaism could cure the world's ills. He also dealt with Zionism. Zangwill had been an early supporter of Herzl but he left the Zionist organization over the Uganda issue (the plan that a portion of East Africa could serve as a Jewish homeland) to found the Jewish Territorial Organization (ITO), which was in favour of seeking a Jewish home anywhere in the world. The second part of the book is an attack on anti-Semitism.

Zangwill also wrote poetry. One collection, *Blind Children*, contains "The Hebrew's Friday Night" in which he argued on the immortality of Jewish life. He also translated some of Ibn Gabirol's Hebrew poetry.

Two other books, *The Master* and *The Mantle of Elijah*, have some slight Jewish interest. The former is about an immigrant child from Canada who became a famous artist, and the latter is a political novel about the Boer War that attacks jingoism. Zangwill also wrote some travel sketches in *Italian Fantasies*. His last, unfinished work was *Baron Offenbach*, which was intended to be a historical novel on a Jewish theme.

CECIL BLOOM

Zelda

Russian-born Israeli poet, 1914–1984

Born Zelda Shneiurson in Yekaterinoslav, Ukraine, 1914, into Hasidic family. Moved with parents to Chernigov, Ukraine, 1918. Emigrated with family to Palestine, 1926; settled in Jerusalem; studied at religious seminary for teachers; studied art, Tel Aviv. Moved to Haifa; worked with handicapped children. Married Hayyim Mishkovsky, 1950. After husband's death, 1971, returned to Jerusalem; taught at religious elementary school, Jerusalem. Awards include Brenner Prize, 1971; Prime Minister's Prize, 1974; Bialik Prize, 1977. Died 1984.

Selected Writings

Poetry

Pnay [Leisure], 1967

Hakarmel haineireh [The Non-visible Carmel], 1971

Al tirhak [Be Not Far], 1975

Halo har halo esh [Behold, a Mountain! A Fire!], 1977

In *Contemporary Israeli Literature*, edited by Elliott Anderson, 1977

Zelda: shirim [Zelda: Poems], 1979

Hashoneh hamarhev [The Amazing Difference], 1981

In *The Penguin Book of Hebrew Verse*, edited by T. Carmi, 1981

In *The Stones Remember: Native Israeli Poetry*, edited by Moshe Dor and Barbara Goldberg, 1991

In *A Jewish Book of Comfort*, edited by Alan K. Kay, 1993

In *The Book of Blessings*, edited by Marcia Falk, 1996

In *After the First Rain: Israeli Poems on War and Peace*, edited by Moshe Dor and Barbara Goldberg, 1997

In *The Defiant Muse*, edited by Shirley Kaufman *et al.*, 1999

She nivdelu meekol merhak [Who Were Separated from Any Distance], 1984

Shirei Zelda [Zelda's Poems], 1985

Further Reading

Bar-Yosef, Hamutal, *Al shirat Zelda* [On Zelda's Poetry], Tel Aviv: Hakibuts hameuhad, 1988

Bar-Yosef, Hamutal, "Interpretations of Three Poems by Zelda" in *The Modern Hebrew Poem Itself, Part Two*, edited and translated by Stanley Burnshaw, Ezra Spicehandler, Susan Glassman, and Ariel Hirschfeld, Detroit, Michigan: Wayne State University Press, 2002

Moris, B., "Ultra-Orthodox Jewish Poet", *Present Tense*, 10/1 (1982)

Sharoni, Edna, "Luminous Mirror of the Human Spirit", *Modern Hebrew Literature*, 10/1–2 (Winter 1984)

Tsamir, Hamutal, "Nation's Place and Other's Places: Zelda's Dead Bird and Old House", *Discourse on Gender / Gendered Discourse in the Middle East*, edited by Boaz Shoshan, Westport, Connecticut: Praeger, 2000

Waldman, Nahum, "Revelations: The Poetry of Zelda", *Reconstructionist*, 50/3 (December 1984)

Zwi, Aza, "The Poetry of Zelda", *Ariel*, 65 (1986)

Zelda was a descendent of two aristocratic Jewish dynasties: her father was Rabbi Shalom Shlomo Shneiurson, a descendant of the Shneiurson Habbadic dynasty and the uncle of the famous New York Rabbi Menahem Mendel Shneiurson ("The Messiah"). Her mother, Rachel Chen, daughter of Rabbi David Zvi Chen, the rabbi of Chernigov, was a descendant of the Chen-Gracian dynasty, which from the 11th century included famous rabbis, philosophers, exegetes, physicians, and Jewish leaders. In the late 18th century the Chen family became close to the Habbadic circle in the Ukraine and had close contacts with the Shneiursons. As a child Zelda lived with her parents at her grandfather Rabbi David Zvi Chen's home, where she absorbed Hasidic tales, sayings, and concepts. Habbadic terminology and symbolism is inlaid throughout her poetry. Zelda's mother and aunts read Russian literature, and one of her uncles studied at the Academy of Arts in St Petersburg. Zelda herself was also a painter. A Russian literary background is common to her and to poets such as H.N. Bialik and Abraham Shlonsky, not to Israeli poets of the 1960s–80s.

The Hasidic idea of art, sacred melody (*nigun*), and joy as ways of God-worship (*avodat hashem*) and mystical correction of the world (*tikkun*) seem to have inspired her both as a poet and as a painter. In her allegoric long poem "A Strange Weeping", from *Al tirhak* [Be Not Far], the poet is a violinist (the violin being a traditional symbol of Jewish music) whose soul, after recovering from bereavement, is lit by heavenly light. His tune of wonder and admiration for the elements of nature is stopped by scepticism, criticism, and refusal to accept the difference between different creatures, expressed by the "swamp" around him. Most of Zelda's poems, even when they criticize or complain, have the therapeutic effect characteristic of mystical texts written by very wise spiritual leaders.

At the age of six Zelda refused her mother's request to change her Jewish name into Russian, a common habit among Jews after the Bolshevik Revolution. She kept this unpopular, non-Israeli name, even after her emigration to Erets Israel, where change of names into Hebrew was the rule. Was it her way of expressing her respect for her Jewish identity? Later she wrote a poem under the title "Every One Has a Name", beginning with the lines "Every one has a name/ which God gave him/ and his parents gave him", which have become an Israeli song.

Zelda's family was not Zionist, but the murder in a pogrom of her uncle, Rabbi Mendel Chen, the young and brilliant rabbi of Niezhin, as well as Soviet persecutions of Orthodox Jews, motivated the small family to leave Ukraine. A few months after their arrival at Jerusalem Zelda's grandfather died, and her father died a few weeks later. Having no male relative to say the *Kaddish* after them, Zelda, who was then 12 years old, received a special permission from the Georgian synagogue, where she said the *Kaddish* on her father and grandfather every morning for 11 months. These traumatic experiences, and especially the inner battle against the grief of bereavement, death wishes, and acute feelings of loneliness and helplessness, are dominant themes in Zelda's poetry. In her autobiographical long poem "Betor hayaldut pri hadash" [In the Season of Childhood New Fruit] in *Hakarmel hainireh* [The Non-visible Carmel] she describes her experiences of immigration, bereavement, and the energies of spiritual maturation that brought her back to life.

The appearance of Zelda's poetry in the late 1960s signalled a change in Israeli poetry: after more than a decade of an ironic, pessimistic, anti-heroic, prose-like poetry, cultivated by Nathan Zach, Yehuda Amichai, Dan Pagis and David Avidan, Zelda's poetry opened the gates of return to mysticism and colourful legend. This direction was followed by Rivka Miriam, Yona Wallach, Ya'ir Hurvitz, Mordechai Geldman, Admiel Kossman, and others in the 1970s, 1980s, and 1990s. Zelda also marked the return of the long poem, which in the first half of the 20th century was a dominant genre in Hebrew poetry, but was purged from Israeli poetry during the 1950s and the 1960s. In fact, Zelda's first literary works from the mid-1930s and the 1940s were prose poems, while narrative and dramatic elements continued to dominate her early poetry. The prose aspect of Zelda's poetry shows also in her tendency to describe in her poems portraits of characters, not only to express her own lyrical "I".

At the centre of her long poem "The Bad Neighbour" in *Pnay* [Leisure] is a scene of conflict between a non-religious woman and the Orthodox neighbourhood where she lives, reconstructing a dramatic, imaginative subtext of speech which only the lyrical "I" can hear. While in the prologue the poet recalls her childish reaction of contempt to her grandfather's "too careful" morning prayer, which includes the words "and save us from a bad neighbour", she now sees the neighbourhood's indifference and her own passive reaction to the neighbour's aggressive expression of loneliness as a failure to stand up to a simple everyday trial (*amidah benissayon*). Many of Zelda's poems deal with her and others' failure to get out of their own ivory tower ("enchanted circle", in Zelda's words, which echo Hasidic terminology) and to enter a soul of the other when he/she is in a state of deep emotional suffering, "to touch his inner spot".

Zelda's poetry is more often lyrical and mystical than political. Her early poetry includes many poems where religious rites (the lighting of the Shabbat candles, for example) are described as experiences of great inner freedom, or even as wild outbursts of bravery (Zelda greatly appreciated freedom and bravery in everyday life), in contrast to the accepted non-religious opinion according to which religious life limits personal freedom. In her "A Place of Fire", written a short time after the Six Day War, Zelda depicts Jerusalem as a place of fear and madness, lying like a beast on the life of "the little soldier" in his grave. At the same time she expresses deep sadness when "an alien king/ impures our belongingness to the city/ on whose neck a loving prophet/ hanged sapphires, rubies and jacinths." In other poems, Jerusalem, the city where Zelda lived most of her life, is an ocean of mystery, where the poet drowns or is paralysed to death.

Although Modern Hebrew poetry has never disconnected itself from Judaism and especially from Jewish mysticism, Orthodox poets were very rare in pre-Israeli poetry (the exceptions were Y.Z. Rimmon and M.G. Langer). Zelda's appearance upon the Israeli scene was in many ways extraordinary – she was an Orthodox woman in her late fifties. This scene was greatly changed during the last quarter of the 20th century: now many Israeli writers and poets belong to different religious circles. From this point of view as well Zelda was an important pioneer of Israeli-Jewish literature and culture.

HAMUTAL BAR-YOSEF

Zukofsky, Louis

US poet, literary critic, and translator, 1904–1978

Born in New York City, 23 January 1904. Studied at Columbia University, MA 1924. Married Celia Thaew, 1939; one son. Teacher of English, University of Wisconsin, 1930–31, and Polytechnic Institute of Brooklyn, 1947–66; visiting assistant professor, Colgate University, 1947; poet in residence, San Francisco State College, 1958. Many awards, including Lola Risge Memorial Award, 1949; Longview Foundation Award, 1961; Union League Civic and Arts Foundation Prize, 1964; Oscar Blumenthal–Charles Leviton Prize, 1966; National Endowment for the Arts grant, 1967, 1968; American Academy Award, 1976. Died in Port Jefferson, New York, 12 May 1978.

Selected Writings

Poetry
First Half of "A"–9, 1934
55 Poems, 1941
Anew, 1946
Some Time, 1956
Barely & Widely, 1958
"A" 1–12, 1959
Louis Zukofsky: 16 Once Published, 1962
I's, 1963
After I's, 1964
Found Objects: 1962–1926, 1964
An Unearthing, 1965
Finally a Valentine: A Poem, 1965

I Sent Thee Late, 1965
Iyyob, 1965
All: The Collected Short Poems, 2 vols, 1965–66
"A"–9, 1966
"A"–14, 1967
"A" 13–21, 1969
The Gas Age, 1969
Initial, 1970
"A"–24, 1972
"A"–22 & 24, 1975
"A" (complete version), 1978
80 Flowers, 1978
Complete Short Poetry, 1991

Fiction
It Was, 1959
Little: A Fragment for Careenagers, 1967; complete version, 1970
Ferdinand, Including "It Was", 1968
Collected Fiction, 1990

Play
Arise, Arise, 1973

Other
Editor, *An "Objectivists" Anthology*, 1932
Le Style Apollinaire, with René Taupin, 1934
A Test of Poetry, 1948
5 Statements for Poetry, 1958
Bottom: On Shakespeare, with Celia Zukofsky, 2 vols, 1963
Prepositions: The Collected Critical Essays of Louis Zukofsky, 1967
Translator, with Celia Zukofsky, *Catullus*, 1969
Translator, with Celia Zukofsky, *Catullus Fragmenta*, 1969
Autobiography, 1970

Further Reading

Ahearn, Barry, *Zukofsky's "A": An Introduction*, Berkeley: University of California Press, 1983
Carson, Luke, *Consumption and Depression in Gertrude Stein, Louis Zukofsky and Ezra Pound*, New York: St Martin's Press, 1999
Fredman, Stephen, *A Menorah for Athena: Charles Reznikoff and the Jewish Dilemmas of Objectivist Poetry*, Chicago: University of Chicago Press, 2001
Gilonis, Harry (editor), *Louis Zukofsky or Whoever Someone Else Thought He Was: A Collection of Responses to the Work of Zukofsky*, Twickenham: North and South Press, 1988
Heller, Michael, *Conviction's Net of Branches: Essays on the Objectivist Poets and Poetry*, Carbondale: Southern Illinois University Press, 1985
Pound, Ezra, *Polite Essays*, London: Faber, 1937; Norfolk, Connecticut: New Directions, 1940
Quartermain, Peter, *Disjunctive Poetics: From Gertrude Stein and Louis Zukofsky to Susan Howe*, New York and Cambridge: Cambridge University Press, 1992
Scroggins, Mark, *Louis Zukofsky and the Poetry of Knowledge*, Tuscaloosa: University of Alabama Press, 1998
Stanley, Sandra Kumamoto, *Louis Zukofsky and the Transformation of a Modern American Poetics*, Berkeley: University of California Press, 1994
Zukofsky, Celia, *A Bibliography of Louis Zukofsky*, Los Angeles: Black Sparrow Press, 1969

Louis Zukofsky is arguably the most important "unknown" poet in American literary history and may even be called the consummate poet of his century. Most famous for coining the short-lived "Objectivist" movement of the 1930s, Zukofsky acted as contact and point man between the older Modernists, particularly Ezra Pound and William Carlos Williams, and younger poets, such as fellow Objectivists Carl Rakosi and George Oppen, who sought ways to adapt Modernist poetics to a rapidly changing America. The only member of his family to be born in the 20th century, Zukofsky adapted the Modernist poetics of his mentors, Pound and Williams (both born in the 19th century), and provided a focus on the importance of material particulars that galvanized his generation and influenced generations to come. Critic and biographer Carroll F. Terrell perceives these influential aspects of Zukofsky's work in six apt keywords: "love, intensity, discipline, simplicity, music, and poetry".

Born of Yiddish-speaking Russian immigrants, Zukofsky did not learn English until he began public school on New York's Lower East Side, in a mostly Jewish neighbourhood known as "Hell's Kitchen". But little is definitively known about Zukofsky the man because of his dismissive notions about (auto)biography: "As a poet", Zukofsky once wrote, "I have always felt that the work says all there needs to be said of one's life". This explains why his brief *Autobiography* is composed mostly of his poetry set to musical scores written by his wife, Celia. Aside from the snapshots we get in the poetry, most of the details we know about Zukofsky's Jewish heritage come not from his *Autobiography*, but from letters, especially ones he wrote to Lorine Niedecker, Pound, and Rakosi, and interviews with people who knew him, particularly Celia. True to his attitude about personal data, the letters he wrote to one-time lover, lifelong friend, and fellow poet, Lorine Niedecker, were highly edited by her at Zukofsky's request before the Harry Ransom Center at the University of Texas in Austin bought them. All of Zukofsky's papers are now housed there.

Even more rare than basic biographical data is an account by Zukofsky of his Jewish heritage. According to Celia, Zukofsky was bar mitzvahed at the Tifereth Jerusalem synagogue on East Broadway in Manhattan, but apparently it was a perfunctory ceremony and seemed to establish his secular detachment from the religion. "Assimilation is not hard", Zukofsky writes in his 1926 "Poem beginning 'The,'", "And once the Faith's askew/ I might as well look Shagetz just as much as Jew". He was, however, indirectly steeped in Judaic tradition. The *Autobiography* does mention that his first exposure to literature came in Yiddish theatres and Yiddish translations of Longfellow, Shakespeare, and Aeschylus. Using this background, he eventually translated the Yiddish poet Yehoash into English, and bits and pieces of that translation appear in "Poem beginning 'The'", an ironic send-up of T.S. Eliot's *The Waste Land* that established Zukofsky's reputation as fashioner of Modernist collage when it was published in Pound's little magazine, *The Exile*. In addition to Yiddish being his first language, Zukofsky studied the Bible throughout his life, New Testament and Old, while his family's literary tradition, if not its religious practices, had a profound influence on him. His father, a garment worker, was an ardent student of Spinoza, whose philosophy, particularly the *Ethics*, seeps into Zukofsky's work as well in such poems as *"A"1–12* and *"A"–9*:

An eye to action sees love bear the semblance
Of things, related is equated, – values
The measure all use who conceive love, labor
Men see, abstraction they feel, the resemblance.

In addition to Spinoza, one might notice in this poem a Marxist analysis of surplus value. Although unlike many of his contemporaries he was never a member of the Communist Party, Zukofsky was committed to a study of Marx's philosophy. Zukofsky's writings, particularly his long critical work written in 1961, *Bottom: On Shakespeare*, engage the thought of Wittgenstein, Hegel, Charles Sanders Peirce, and Henry Adams, among other philosophers.

In fact, most of Zukofsky's poetic response to the world has a philosophical basis. Witness his article that inaugurated the 1931 issue of *Poetry* magazine featuring "Objectivist" poetry. The article, entitled "Sincerity and Objectification", was a revision of an earlier work rejected by the *Menorah Journal* with a subtitle, "With Special Reference to the Work of Charles Reznikoff" (Fredman). In this article, he sets out the terms that reflect the shared poetics of the contributors to the issue. Using a visual analogy, Zukofsky describes the goal or "objective" of his new poetics: "An Objective: (Optics) – The lens bringing the rays from an object to a focus. That which is aimed at. (Use extended to poetry) – Desire for what is objectively perfect, inextricably the direction of historic and contemporary particulars."

Zukofsky implies that a poem is to be written in such a way as to focus on an object or particular, defined as "a thing or things as well as an event or a chain of events", in order to "desire what is objectively perfect". From this "Objective", Zukofsky extrapolates his two primary terms: "Sincerity", as a shape in the form of a combination of words, "is the detail, not mirage, of seeing, of thinking with things as they exist, and of directing them along the line of melody". In other words, sincerity in writing does not shape reality but follows the shape of an existence outside the poem, like a melody follows the rise and fall of pitch, evoking a certain trueness to reality in the seeing of particulars. "Objectification", on the other hand, involves the "objectively perfect" through the achievement of "rested totality". This rest, defined in terms of a mental state, is a "perfect rest, complete appreciation" and is "the resolving of words and their ideation into structure", conceivably the placement of words and the concepts to which they refer into the structure of a poem. This last idea, that words themselves and, thus, the poem, become objects, is one of Zukofsky's most enduring legacies. Equating poetry somewhat to sculpture, this concept of language has influenced many contemporary poets, particularly the school of Language poets, for whom the materiality of the word and the materiality of the world are inextricably related.

That this "Objectivist" movement was composed mainly of four Jewish poets (Reznikoff, Zukofsky, Oppen, and Rakosi) is not mentioned in the "Objectification and Sincerity" article, but the Jewish flavour of their poetry is unmistakable. Reznikoff's work is often explicitly about Jewish history, while Zukofsky grapples with the problem of tradition by dramatizing the lineage from his Russian poet grandfather, Maishe Afraim, to his virtuoso violinist son, Paul. *"A"*, the book-length long poem that was written over the course of his 50-year poetic career, deals with this tradition. The family tradition, in turn, is linked to Zukofsky's place in the American poetic tradition, as well as in the long line of philosophers, some Jewish, that have had a marked effect on history.

After decades of neglect, a neglect based mostly on claims that Zukofsky's work was "arcane" and "obscure", the poetry of Zukofsky is finally being taken seriously. Such charges disheartened him throughout his career because he saw clarity and directness as his main objective. Mark Scroggins argues for the greatness of Zukofsky's work by appealing to those very things that have kept Zukofsky from due recognition as one of America's greatest poets: Zukofsky's poetry is "prickly, obdurate, resistant both to our commonsense expectations of precisely how a poem means and to our conventional notions of what pleasures a poem should afford." Mostly, he continues, the poetry is great because of its *music*, the raw sound of language and meaning. Zukofsky's poetry, from the brilliant, gem-like short poetry to the complex, symphonic long poem *"A"*, is a feast for the mind and music for the eye, Eye Music. This sound, where poetry and music meet, is the clarion call for a new way of conceiving the poetic enterprise.

G. MATTHEW JENKINS

Zweig, Arnold

German fiction writer and dramatist, 1887–1968

Born in Glogau, 10 November 1887. Studied German literature, modern languages, philosophy, history, psychology, history of art, and economics in Breslau, Munich, Berlin, Göttingen, Rostock, and Tübingen. Volunteered for German army, 1915; fought in trenches on western front. Freelance writer, Bavaria and Berlin; editor, Zionist periodical *Jüdische Rundschau*. After Nazi seizure of power, 1933, emigrated to Palestine via Czechoslovakia, Switzerland, and France; contributor to numerous émigré magazines; co-editor, *Orient*, Haifa. Returned to Germany, 1948; settled in (East) Berlin; President, Academy of Arts, German Democratic Republic, 1950–53. Awarded Lenin Peace Prize (Soviet Union), 1958. Died in Berlin, 26 November 1968.

Selected Writings

Collections

Ausgewählte Werke in Einzelausgaben [Selected Works in Separate Editions], 16 vols, 1957–67
Essays, 2 vols, 1959–67
Novellen 1907–1955 [Novellas 1907–1955], 2 vols, 1961

Novels

Der Streit um den Sergeanten Grischa, 1927; as *The Case of Sergeant Grischa*, translated by Eric Sutton, 1928
Junge Frau von 1914, 1931; as *Young Woman of 1914*, translated by Eric Sutton, 1932
De Vriendt kehrt heim, 1932; as *De Vriendt Goes Home*, translated by Eric Sutton, 1933
Erziehung vor Verdun, 1935; as *Education before Verdun*, translated by Eric Sutton, 1936
Einsetzung eines Königs, 1937; as *The Crowning of a King*, translated by Eric Sutton, 1938
Versunkene Tage, 1938
Das Beil von Wandsbeck [The Axe of Wandsbeck], 1947
Die Feuerpause [The Lull in the Fighting], 1954
Die Zeit ist reif [The Time is Ripe], 1957

Novellas and Shorter Prose

Vorfrühling [Early Spring], 1909
Aufzeichnungen über eine Familie Klopfer [Sketches of the Klopfer Family], 1911
Novellen um Claudia, 1912; as *Claudia*, translated by Eric Sutton, 1930
Geschichtenbuch [Story Book], 1916
Die Bestie [The Beast], 1919
Das zweite Geschichtenbuch [The Second Story Book], 1920
Drei Erzählungen [Three Stories], 1920
Gerufene Schatten, 1923
Söhne [Sons], 1923
Frühe Fährten [Early Journeys], 1925
Regenbogen [Rainbow], 1925
Pont und Anna, 1928
Mädchen und Frauen [Girls and Women], 1930
Knaben und Männer [Boys and Men], 1931
Spielzeug der Zeit [Time's Plaything], 1933
Abschied vom Frieden [Farewell to Peace], 1949
Allerleirauch, 1949
Stufen [Steps], 1949
Über den Nebeln [Above the Fog], 1950
Der Elfenbeinfächer [The Ivory Fan], 1952

Plays

Abigail und Nabal, 1912
Ritualmord in Ungarn [Ritual Murder in Hungary], 1914; produced as *Die Sendins Semaels* [The Mission of Semael]
Die Umkehr der Abtrünnigen [Return of the Deserters], 1925
Laubheu und keine Bleibe, 1930
Bonaparte in Jaffe, 1939
Soldatenspiele: Drei Dramatische Historien [Soldiers' Games: Three Dramatic Histories], 1956

Essays

Das ostjüdische Antlitz [The East European Jewish Face], 1920
Das neue Kanaan: eine Untersuchung über Land und Geist [The New Canaan: A Study of Land and Spirit], 1925
Lessing, Kleist, Büchner, 1925
Brennendes Bilderbuch [The Burning Picturebook], 1926
Caliban; oder, Politik und Leidenschaft [Caliban; or, Politics and Passion], 1927
Juden auf der deutschen Bühne [Jews on the German Stage], 1927
Herkunft und Zukunft [Origin and Future], 1929
Bilanz der deutschen Judenheit, 1933; as *Insulted and Exiled: The Truth about the German Jews*, translated by Eden Paul and Cedar Paul, 1937
Die Aufgabe des Judentums [The Task of the Jews], with Lion Feuchtwanger, 1933
Baruch Spinoza, 1961

Other

Sigmund Freud–Arnold Zweig Briefwechsel, 1968; as *Letters of Sigmund Freud and Arnold Zweig*, edited by Ernst L. Freud, translated by Elaine and William Robson-Scott, 1971

Further Reading

Ascheim, Steven E., "The Cult of the Ostjuden" in his *Brothers and Strangers: The East European Jew in German and German Jewish Consciousness*, Madison: University of Wisconsin Press, 1982
Cohen, Robert, "Arnold Zweig's War Novellas of 1914 and Their Versions: Literature, Modernity, and the Demands of the Day" in *War, Violence, and the Modern Condition*, edited by Bernd Hüppauf, Berlin and New York: De Gruyter, 1997
Goldstein, Moritz, "Arnold Zweig" in *Juden in der deutschen Literatur*, edited by Gustav Krojanker, Berlin: Welt, 1922
Isenberg, Noah, *Between Redemption and Doom: The Strains of German-Jewish Modernism*, Lincoln: University of Nebraska Press, 1999
Kahn, Lothar, *Mirrors of the Jewish Mind: A Gallery of Portraits of European Jewish Writers of Our Time*, New York: Yoseloff, 1968
Liptzin, Solomon, "Arnold Zweig: From Zionism to Marxism" in his *Germany's Stepchildren*, Philadelphia: Jewish Publication Society of America, 1944
Salamon, George, *Arnold Zweig*, New York: Twayne, 1975
Weissberg, Liliane, "Arnold Zweig" in *German Fiction Writers, 1885–1913*, edited by James Hardin, Detroit: Gale, 1988 (Dictionary of Literary Biography, vol. 66)
White, Ray Lewis, *Arnold Zweig in the USA*, New York: Peter Lang, 1986

Arnold Zweig was born in Germany where he lived until Hitler came to power. He then fled to Palestine via Czechoslovakia in 1933 settling in Haifa, but his strong communist beliefs led him to return in 1948 to spend the rest of his life in East Berlin. In Palestine he saw no conflict between his Jewish nationalism and his emphatic antagonism towards nationalism in general, but his Jewish nationalism was tempered by his following the Jewish communist line in Palestine which favoured a bi-national Jewish–Arab state. He did, however, refuse to join the East German condemnation of Israel after the Six Day War. He became president of the East German Academy of Arts and was a member of the parliament of the German Democratic Republic. In 1958 he received the Lenin Peace Prize for his anti-war novels.

His first novella was written in 1911 when he was 22 and it was semi-autobiographical. In some ways it was prophetic because *Aufzeichnungen über eine Familie Klopfer* [Sketches of the Klopfer Family] is the story of an ardent young Zionist writer who finally emigrated to Palestine. This book does suggest that Zweig had an early interest in Zionism but it attracted little attention. His next book was, however, noticed. *Novellen um Claudia* (*Claudia*) consisted of some short stories about a young woman, a hypersensitive girl full of inhibitions, which deal with her courtship and unhappy marriage to a bashful professor. The stories have no real Jewish themes, although the heroine has many Jewish attributes. In 1912 Zweig wrote a biblical drama *Abigail and Nabal* and two years later came a play, *Ritualmord in Ungarn* [Ritual Murder in Hungary], which dealt with an actual ritual libel in Hungary – the notorious *Tisza Eszlar* blood libel. The theme of this play, which was first banned and then renamed *Die Sendins Semaels* [The Mission of Semael] when permission was given for it to be performed, was that Jews must defend themselves. Pro-Zionist sentiments came from Heaven in the words of Rabbi Akiva and the Baal Shem Tov. Max Reinhardt produced the play in Berlin.

After this, Zweig used few Jewish themes in his fiction but he wrote many essays on Jewish subjects. He came under the influence of Martin Buber and his Zionist beliefs were thereby strengthened. He wrote many articles for Buber's *Der Jude* and, for a time, he edited *Jüdische Rundschau*, the newspaper of the German Zionist movement. Zweig also produced a number of articles supporting Zionism and socialism and with other German-Jewish writers cast his eyes benevolently on his eastern European Jewish cousins as a result of his experiences as a private soldier in the war. *Das ostjüdische Antlitz* [The East European Jewish Face] is a vivid description of Jewish life in eastern Europe and is a warm and sympathetic portrait of Polish and Russian Jewry. *Das neue Kanaan* [The New Canaan] was an attempt to justify a Jewish socialist society in Palestine if typical Jewish standards were to be maintained. Other essays that show Zweig's thinking on Jewish problems include *Bilanz der deutschen Judenheit* (*Insulted and Exiled*).

Caliban; oder, Politik und Leidenschaft [Caliban; or, Politics and Passion] led Zweig to a long association with Sigmund Freud. Here he used the teachings of Freud to develop an exposition of the meaning of anti-Semitism. His extensive correspondence with Freud was eventually published in 1968; an English edition appeared in 1971.

But *De Vriendt kehrt heim* (*De Vriendt Goes Home*) is Zweig's major fictional work using a Jewish theme. Based on real events that took place in Palestine, it demonstrates Zweig's strong concern for justice and humanity. The character De Vriendt is based on Jacob Israel De Haan, a Dutch poet and journalist, who became spokesman for the Agudist organization (an anti-Zionist international organization of Orthodox Jews) in Jerusalem. He used to send anti-Zionist and pro-Arab reports to the press, the League of Nations, and to the British Mandatory authorities; he was killed in 1924, probably by Haganah (the pre-1948 underground military organization). Despite his orthodoxy, he was a homosexual and this was probably exploited by the Arabs. Zweig set the scene in 1929 because he wanted to portray life in a year when Arab attacks on Jews were extensive. In the novel Zweig expounded on his opinions of both Zionists and non-Zionists as well as those on the British attitudes towards Jew and Arab. Zweig tried to explain the motives of De Haan, whose personality clearly fascinated him. The novel shows De Vriendt to have a young Arab lover. Although this boy's brother was determined to kill De Vriendt, he was beaten to this by a left-wing Zionist. A British secret-service agent friend of De Vriendt then determined to see justice (as he viewed it) done and he tracked down this assailant and attempted unsuccessfully and bizarrely to drown him in – of all waters – the middle of the Dead Sea. The novel can be labelled as a psychological thriller of sorts, but it does hold attention as a portrait of the Palestine of the time, with its disturbances, feuds, and bloodshed. Zweig went on record to say that the murder in Tel Aviv of Chaim Arlossorof, a member of the Jewish Agency, motivated this book. In actual fact, Arlossorof was believed to have been assassinated by a member of Jabotinsky's Revisionist Organization (although this was never proved), but Zweig's reason is a curious one given the different politics and lifestyle of Arlossorof and the fictional character.

Zweig's main claim to literary fame rests on his anti-World War I novels. His greatest and most famous book is *Der Streit um den Sergeanten Grischa* (*The Case of Sergeant Grischa*), which deals with the plight of an insignificant, wretched, ordinary Russian peasant who was captured as a prisoner-of-war and who became the victim of militarism and politics. Grischa escaped from his prison under the assumed name of a dead deserter and, although his innocence was finally established, he was executed by the Germans on a judicial pretext. This novel, which some critics consider to be superior to Remarque's *All Quiet on the Western Front* and to be the finest to emerge from the 1914–18 conflict, shows Zweig's concern about man's inhumanity to man. The book has been translated into some 20 languages. Two other novels, *Erziehung vor Verdun* (*Education before Verdun*) and *Einsetzung eines Königs* (*The Crowning of a King*), were attached to *Grischa* to form a trilogy. Zweig later wrote a number of novels exposing the rise of German nationalism of which *Das Beil von Wandsbeck* [The Axe of Wandsbeck] was the most important. Its central character was a simple man who believed in Hitler, but the novel was an indictment of educated people who were taken in by the Nazis. *Junge Frau von 1914* (*Young Woman of 1914*) exposed rising German nationalism. On his return to Berlin after the war, Zweig combined these latter two novels with a third, *Die Feuerpause* [The Lull in the Fighting], and his earlier trilogy to form a cycle of six works entitled *Der grosse Krieg der weissen Manner*.

CECIL BLOOM

Zweig, Stefan

Austrian essayist, poet, fiction writer, and dramatist
1881–1942

Born in Vienna, 28 November 1881, into wealthy family. Studied at University of Vienna, 1899–1904; University of Berlin, 1901; doctorate 1904. Worked with Theodor Herzl in Zionist movement; *feuilleton* editor of *Neue Freie Presse*. Travelled extensively prior to 1914. Declared unfit for front-line service, 1914; worked in Austro-Hungarian War Archive, Vienna, writing and revising press releases during World War I. Set up home with Friderike Maria Burg (then wife of another man), 1919; married, 1920. Lived in Salzburg, 1919–34. Travelled to Russia, 1928; Italy, 1930, 1932; France, 1932. Helped to found Reichner Verlag publishing house, Vienna, 1934. Emigrated to Britain, 1934; settled in London. Had affair with Charlotte (Lotte) Elisabeth Altmann; divorced Friderike and married, second, Lotte Altmann, 1939. Given special permission (as enemy alien) to speak at Sigmund Freud's cremation, London, 1939. Naturalized British subject, 1940. Left England, 1940; travelled to New Haven and New York. Settled in Petrópolis, Brazil, 1941. Depressed by war news, committed suicide there with Lotte, 23 February 1942.

Selected Writings

Collection
Gesammelte Werke [Collected Works], 10 vols, edited by Knut Beck, 1982

Poetry
Silberne Saiten: Gedichte [Silver Strings], 1901
Die Frühen Kranze [Early Wreaths], 1906
Die Gesammelten Gedichte [The Collected Poems], 1924
Ausgewählte Gedichte [Selected Poems], 1931

Plays
Tersites: ein Trauerspiel [Tersites], 1907; revised 1919
Das Haus am Meer [The Seaside House], 1912
Der verwandelte Komödiant: ein Spiel aus dem deutschen Rokoko [The Transformed Actor], 1912
Jeremias, 1917; as *Jeremiah*, translated by Eden Paul and Cedar Paul, 1922
Legende eines Lebens [Legend of a Life], 1919
Das Lamm des Armen [Lamb of the Poor], 1929
Drei Dramen [Three Dramas], 1964

Fiction
Die Liebe der Erika Ewald: Novellen [The Love of Erika Ewald: Novellas], 1904
Erstes Erlebnis: vier Geschichten aus Kinderland [First Experience: Four Stories from Childhood], 1911; as *Die Kette: Ein Novellenkreis*, vol. 1, 1923
Brennendes Geheimnis: Eine Erzahlung, 1913; as *The Burning Secret*, translated by Zweig using the pseudonym Stephen Branch, 1919
Angst: Novelle [Fear: Novella], 1920
Der Zwang: eine Novelle [The Compulsion: A Novella], 1920
Amok: Novellen einer Leidenschaft [Amok: Novellas of a Passion], 1922; as *Amok: A Story*, translated by Eden Paul and Cedar Paul, 1931
Die Augen des ewigen Bruders: eine Legende [Eyes of the Eternal Brother: A Legend], 1922
Passion and Pain, translated by Eden Paul and Cedar Paul, 1924
Verwirrung der Gefühle: drei Novellen, 1927; translated as *Conflicts: Three Tales*, translated by Eden Paul and Cedar Paul, 1927
Die unsichtbare Sammlung [The Invisible Collection], 1929
Kleine Chronik [Little Chronicle], 1929
Rahel Rechtet mit Gott: Legende [Rachel Argues with God], 1930
Die Kette [The Chain], 1936
Kaleidoskop [Kaleidoscope], 1936
Der begrabene Leuchter, 1937; as *The Buried Candelabrum*, translated by Eden Paul and Cedar Paul, 1937
The Old Book Peddler and Other Tales for Bibliophiles, translated by Theodore W. Koch, 1937
Ungeduld des Herzens, 1939; as *Beware of Pity*, translated by Phyllis Blewitt and Trevor Blewitt, 1939
Stories and Legends, translated by Eden Paul, Cedar Paul, and Constantine FitzGibbon, 1955
Novellen der Leidenschaft [Novellas of Passion], 1966
Meisternovellen, 1970
Clarissa: ein romanentwurf [Clarissa: Outline of a Novel], edited by Knut Beck, 1990

Biography
Verlaine, 1905; as *Paul Verlaine*, translated by O.F. Theis, 1913
Emile Verhaeren, 1910; translated by Jethro Bithell, 1914
Drei Meister: Balzac-Dickens-Dostojewski, 1921; as *Three Masters: Balzac, Dickens, Dostoeffsky*, translated by Eden Paul and Cedar Paul, 1930
Romain Rolland: der Mann und das Werk, 1921; as *Romain Rolland: The Man and His Work*, translated by Eden Paul and Cedar Paul, 1921
Der Kampf mit dem Dämon: Hölderlin, Kleist, Nietzsche, 1925; as "The Struggle with the Daimon" in *Master Builders*, translated by Eden Paul and Cedar Paul, 1939
Marceline Desbordes-Valmore: das Lebensbild einer Dichterin [Marceline Desbordes-Valmore: The Biography of a Poet], 1927
Drei Dichter ihres Lebens: Casanova, Stendhal, Tolstoi, 1928; as *Adepts in Self-portraiture*, translated by Eden Paul and Cedar Paul, 1928
Joseph Fouché: Bildnis eines politischen Menschen, 1929; as *Joseph Fouché: The Portrait of a Politician*, translated by Eden Paul and Cedar Paul, 1930
Die Heilung durch den Geist: Franz Anton Mesmer, Mary Baker-Eddy, Sigmund Freud, 1931; as *Mental Healers*, translated by Eden Paul and Cedar Paul, 1932
Marie Antoinette: Bildnis eines mittleren Charakters, 1932; as *Marie Antoinette: The Portrait of an Average Woman*, translated by Eden Paul and Cedar Paul, 1933
Triumph und Tragik des Erasmus von Rotterdam, 1934; as *Erasmus of Rotterdam*, translated by Eden Paul and Cedar Paul, 1934
Mary Stuart, 1935; as *Mary, Queen of Scotland and the Isles*, translated by Eden Paul and Cedar Paul, 1935 (as *The Queen of Scots*, 1935)

Amerigo: Die Geschichte eines historischen Irrtums, 1944; as *Amerigo: A Comedy of Errors in History*, translated by Andrew St James, 1942
Balzac: Der Roman seines Leben, 1946; as *Balzac: A Biography*, translated by William and Dorothy Rose, 1946

Other
Castellio gegen Calvin; oder, ein Gewissen gegen die Gewalt, 1936; as *The Right to Heresy: Castellio against Calvin*, translated by Eden Paul and Cedar Paul, 1936
Georg Friedrich Händels Auferstehung: eine historische Miniatur, 1937: as *George Frederick Handel's Resurrection*, translated by Eden Paul and Cedar Paul, 1938
Die Welt von Gestern: Erinnerungen eines Europäers, 1942; as *The World of Yesterday*, translated by Eden Paul and Cedar Paul, 1943
Stefan Zweig, Joseph Gregor, Correspondence 1921–1936, edited by Kenneth Birkin, 1992

Further Reading
Gelber, Mark H. and Klaus Zelewitz (editors), *Stefan Zweig: Exil und Suche nach dem Weltfrieden*, Riverside, California: Ariadne, 1995
Klawiter, Randolph J., *Stefan Zweig: An International Bibliography*, Riverside, California: Ariadne, 1991; Addendum I, 1999
Modern Austrian Literature, 14, 3/4 (1981): special Zweig issue
Prater, Donald A., *European of Yesterday: A Biography of Stefan Zweig*, Oxford: Clarendon Press, 1972
Prater, Donald A. and Volker Michels (editors), *Stefan Zweig: Leben und Werk im Bild*, Frankfurt: Insel, 1981
Sonnenfeld, Marion (editor), *Stefan Zweig: The World of Yesterday's Humanist Today*, Albany: State University of New York Press, 1983
Turner, David, *Moral Values and the Human Zoo: The Novellen of Stefan Zweig*, Hull: Hull University Press, 1988
Zelewitz, Klaus, "1901: Nineteen-year-old Stefan Zweig Publishes His First Volume of Poetry" in *Yale Companion to Jewish Writing and Thought in German Culture, 1096–1996*, edited by Sander L. Gilman and Jack Zipes, New Haven, Connecticut and London: Yale University Press, 1997
Zohn, Harry, "Stefan Zweig and Contemporary European Literature", *German Life and Letters*, 5 (1952): 202–12
Zweig, Friderike Maria, *Stefan Zweig*, translated by Erna McArthur, New York: Crowell, and London: W.H. Allen, 1946

In his posthumously published memoirs, *Die Welt von Gestern* (*The World of Yesterday*), Stefan Zweig characterized himself "as an Austrian, as a Jew, as a writer, as a humanist, and pacifist." Each of these designations has value and a justification. Zweig, who was one of the most popular European writers between the world wars, has been regularly celebrated since his death as a great European humanist. While his reputation in academic and scholarly circles has declined over the last few decades, he continues to be read in translation throughout the world. In fact, his prestige outside of central Europe remains extremely high, and his popularity is intact in numerous countries around the globe, especially in France, Russia, China, Japan, Brazil, and elsewhere.

His humanism came to expression in his writings in several areas. First, by means of his work as a mediator between cultures, especially between French literature and culture and central European, German-language readers, Zweig sought to realize his idea of European intellectual and artistic unity. Some observers, such as Harry Zohn, have viewed Zweig's activity in this regard as Jewish in its own right. Throughout his career, Zweig promoted the translation, publication, and dissemination of French writing in central Europe. As a teenager he translated poetry into German, including that of Verlaine, Baudelaire, Rimbaud, and others. His important literary biographies of Romain Rolland and the Belgian poet Emile Verhaeren, as well as his literary-biographical studies of Stendahl, Balzac, Montaigne, and others form the core of his accomplishment in this area. His biographical-historical studies of Marie Antoinette, Joseph Fouché, Napoleon's Minister of Police, and others compliment the more literarily oriented studies. Zweig also mediated work from other world literatures and cultures into central Europe, advising publishers, writing introductions, arranging for translations and for publication in German.

Second, Zweig was an inveterate traveller, who wrote an extensive and intellectually lively travel literature, documenting the encounter of the enlightened European observer with foreign landscapes, peoples, and cultures. He travelled to India and to central America before World War I, and he wrote about his travels to these exotic locations, as well as about his journeys throughout Europe and Russia. This same type of encounter can also be found as a theme throughout his short fiction.

Third, his humanism was marked by a commitment to pacifism, and his pacifist activities can be documented from 1914, despite his short-lived enthusiasm for the Austrian cause at the outbreak of World War I. In his biblical drama *Jeremias* (*Jeremiah*), written and first produced during the war, Zweig gave expression to his beliefs in the spiritual superiority of the vanquished and the ultimate triumph of the spirit over political and military force. While the drama was received as evidence of the writer's pacifist and internationalist outlook, it was also read and viewed in terms of his faith in the Jewish mission in the world, defined precisely in these same terms. In the eighth part of the play, Jeremiah, in a trance-like state, prophesies ecstatically in the midst of the destruction of Jerusalem, the rebirth of Israel and the return of the Jewish people to Zion. After coming out of his trance, he reformulates this vision, clarifying that the eternal Jerusalem and the Temple will be built in Jewish hearts and in the Jewish spirit, not in the real land of Israel. By choosing the biblical prophetic material for dramatic treatment, Zweig was able to unite the Jewish and the general humanist themes. In a letter to Martin Buber from the time of the genesis of the play, Zweig referred to the drama as a "tragedy and hymn of the Jewish people, the chosen/ ones/

. . . The end of the play proclaims in the exile from Jerusalem the eternally rebuilt Jerusalem." As Zweig explained in a letter to Abraham Schwadron from the same time, "the greatness of the Jewish people is that it strives towards a spiritual homeland, an eternal Jerusalem . . . The greatness of Jewry is its desire to be international, a fermenting and unifying force for all nations." In 1929 and later, this play was produced successfully in a Hebrew version with a more pronounced Jewish-national tendency, by the Ohel Theatre in Tel Aviv, and it was lauded on a grand tour of Europe after the rise of the Nazis. Although Zweig did not understand Hebrew, he took great pleasure in seeing the Hebrew production and witnessing its great success in London.

Zweig had developed an early interest in Zionism. He felt indebted throughout his life to Theodor Herzl, who as a literary editor of the *Neue Freie Presse*, Vienna's prestigious newspaper, accepted for publication an early prose work prose penned by the aspiring teenager. Despite maintaining a certain distance from the Zionist organization, Zweig expressed solidarity with cultural Zionism over the years. When he sensed the eventual dissolution of his household in Salzburg with the ascendancy of Nazism in Germany, he secretly came to an agreement with the Jewish National Library in Jerusalem to establish a Zweig archive where he could send his private correspondence and autograph collection for safe-keeping. In British exile in 1936, he wrote *Der begrabene Leuchter* (*The Buried Candelabrum*) a Jewish legend, set in the Middle Ages, which follows the fate of the holy vessels from the Jewish Temple, as they wander through the Diaspora, emblematic of the wandering of the Jewish people themselves. A dual perspective, characteristic of exile-literature, is interwoven in this text, allowing for Zionist and Diaspora-oriented readings of the work.

Eventually, Zweig left the Europe which seemed to him to have betrayed the very humanist values he treasured and which formed the core of his existence and work as a man of letters. He sought refuge in the United States and later in Brazil, a country that fascinated him as the land of the future. Nevertheless, as World War II dragged on, he despaired that there was no place left for him, and he committed suicide with his second wife in Petrópolis.

MARK GELBER

Zwicky, Fay

Australian poet, 1933–

Born Julia Fay Rosefield in Melbourne, 4 July 1933. Educated at University of Melbourne, 1950–54, BA. Married, first, Karl Zwicky, 1957, divorced, one son and one daughter; second, James Mackie, 1990. Concert pianist, 1950–65; senior lecturer in English, University of Western Australia, Perth, 1972–87. Member of literature board, Australia Council, Sydney, 1978–81; poetry editor, *Westerly*, Perth, and *Patterns*, Fremantle, 1974–83; writer in residence Macquarie University, Sydney, 1982; Rollins College, Florida, 1984; and LaTrobe University, Melbourne, 1985; associate editor, since 1988, *Overland*, Melbourne, and since 1989, *Southerly*, Sydney. Awarded New South Wales Premier's Award, 1982; Western Australian Literary Award for non-fiction, 1987; Western Australian Premier's Award for poetry, 1991.

Selected Writings

Poetry
Isaac Babel's Fiddle, 1975
Kaddish and Other Poems, 1982
Ask Me, 1990
A Touch of Ginger, with Dennis Haskell, 1991
Poems 1970–1992, 1993
The Gatekeeper's Wife, 1998

Short Stories
Hostages, 1983

Other
Editor, *Quarry: A Selection of Western Australian Poetry*, 1981
Editor, *Journeys: Judith Wright, Rosemary Dobson, Gwen Harwood, Dorothy Hewett*, 1982
The Lyre in the Pawnshop: Essays on Literature and Survival 1974–1984, 1986
Editor, *Procession: Youngstreet Poets Three*, 1987
"The Deracinated Writer: Another Australia" in *Crisis and Creativity in the New Literatures in English*, edited by Geoffrey Davis and Hena Maes-Jelinek, 1990

Further Reading

Indyk, Ivor, "Fay Zwicky: The Poet as Moralist", *Southerly*, 54/3 (September 1994)
Kirkby, Joan, "Finding a Voice in 'This Fiercely Fathered and Unmothered World': The Poetry of Fay Zwicky" in *Poetry and Gender*, edited by David Brooks and Brenda Walker, St Lucia: University of Queensland Press, 1989
Linguanti, Elsa, "On the Shifting Sands of Our Experience: Fay Zwicky's Poetry", *Southerly*, 54/3 (September 1994)
Page, Geoff, "Fay Zwicky" in *A Reader's Guide to Contemporary Australian Poetry*, St Lucia: University of Queensland Press, 1995
Sant, Andrew, editor, *Toads: Australian Writers: Other Work, Other Lives*, Sydney: Allen and Unwin, 1992
Willbanks, Ray, "A Conversation with Fay Zwicky", *Antipodes*, 3/2 (1989)
Willbanks, Ray, "Interview with Fay Zwicky" in his *Australian Voices: Writers and Their Work*, Austin: University of Texas Press, 1991; as *Speaking Volumes: Australian Writers and Their Work*, Ringwood, Victoria: Penguin, 1992

Essayist, literary critic, academic, journalist, and concert pianist, Fay Zwicky is a noted Australian poet. She was born in suburban Melbourne into a fourth generation Australian family and educated at an Anglican school (see *Hostages*). Descended from European Jews, she studied literature and music and describes herself as an "outsider", alienated ("I was ashamed of my foreign interloper status") from an "Anglo-Saxon dominated" Australian culture. Zwicky's writings are an attempt to give a voice to the "other Australians", to be an articulate antidote to "silent colonial (male) Australia", a "misogynist nation" cut off from the traditions and cultures of her peoples – "Our present remains unconnected to the main history of human suffering". Her profound deliberations on Australian identity are found in her poetry, and in her collection of critical writings, *The Lyre in the Pawnshop: Essays on Literature and Survival 1974–1984*. In "Influence and Independence", "Language or Speech: A Colonial Dilemma", and "Speeches and Silences", Zwicky traces the ways in which the construction of an Australian literature has served to marginalize minority writers and women. Her autobiographical essays, "Disinterested Motives?" and "Democratic Repression: The Ethnic Strain", further discuss the Jewish writer with specific reference to the absence, until very recently, of any place for a Jewish writer in Australian literature – "Living and growing up in this country has been an exercise in repression". Zwicky is a selfconscious poet who understands the "word" to have great power ("poets tell more than most") and the poet's task and responsibilities to be likewise great (see "Poets and Critics: What Price Survival?", "Rumours of Morality: The Poet's Part", and "Love and Language", also the poet series in *Kaddish and Other Poems*, and the recent "Poems and Things").

Zwicky's poetry is personal, direct, frequently didactic, carefully crafted, economical, honest – sometimes brutally so, brave, ironic, and often in free verse form. Her first book of poetry, *Isaac Babel's Fiddle* (1975) includes a number of poems about her Russian grandfather and his cultural displacement in Australia, a displacement that meant that he – and his descendants – survived the Holocaust ("Summer Pogrom", "Totem and Taboo"). She writes of her own alienation, in spite of her being "whiter than Persil", and offers a wicked picture of a new immigrant in "An Australian". In 1982 she published *Kaddish and Other Poems*; the title poem is a wonderful evocation of her "nine years dead" father who drowned in the Tasman Sea. Liberated by Allen Ginsberg's *Kaddish*, she reports that she could complete her own poem. "Kaddish" is the name of the traditional Aramaic prayer for the dead recited by Jewish mourners. Zwicky's father died without the Kaddish being recited, as he had only daughters and no son, and here Zwicky puts this aright by using the Aramaic phrases to frame her own memorial prayer detailing her fraught and complex relationship with her father. She draws on the *Haggadah*, the Passover Seder night liturgy, the four sons become the three daughters of her family, and the cadences, resonance, and form of "Chad Gadya", the final song of the Passover Seder service, are used to convey something of those family gatherings. "Kaddish" also uses the Lord's Prayer and invokes the goddess. There are bitter notes to her memories, threats, and a father seemingly already irrevocably separated from his children. In the same collection, Zwicky's humour is evident in "Ark Voices" which details the trials of Mrs Noah keeping the ark clean, and in "Identity" she forges a stark contrast between Jewish "memory" and "gentile" nature, a distinction that separates her from the Australian literary veneration of the Australian landscape.

Ask Me, Zwicky's third book of poetry, has clusters of poems on China, America, and a series of religious poems on the deities of the Hindu pantheon ("Ganesh", "Vishnu", "Siva", and the goddess "Devi"). These lyrical portrayals reveal a new religious sensibility, evident also in "Broadway Vision" and the earlier "Kali". Her cynicism about cheap religion is relayed in "New Age" and "Maharishi Consolator" from the 1970s. There are also rich portraits of friends ("The Call") and literary figures ("Casting the Die"). Her most recent book of poetry is *The Gatekeeper's Wife*. In the title poem, Zwicky, now a widow, writes of the devastating loss of her husband, and recalls that Jewish custom of lighting a memorial candle – "Severed from my ancestors, I light a candle for you". Painfully honest, she writes, "You'd hardly believe, the woman I grew to be, watching you, turning away". These poems are about death, dying, aging, grief, loneliness, and lament ("Orpheus"). In the deeply spiritual poem "Losing Track", for example, the death of her husband is likened to the tragic Jewish loss of Zion, Jerusalem. The collection includes a powerful elegy, "Banksia Blechifolia", for Primo Levi, and "Groundswell for Ginsberg" an homage to Allen Ginsberg,

Describing herself as "too much of a Jew to be a Christian and too much of a Christian to be a Jew", Zwicky recalls that her parents' Judaism was one of "that dark day of fasting and repentance for a year's sin" but not of the "feasts of joyful celebration". While always aware of her Jewishness ("Besides, we were Jews"), and the way in which this identity was intensified negatively, as it were, by the war, she had only the loosest links to Jews, Judaism, or the Jewish community – "lacking both knowledge and allegiance". It was only much later in the aftermath of her father's death that Zwicky began exploring systematically her latent Jewish identity, via her reading of the American Jewish novelists, Philip Roth, Bernard Malamud, and Saul Bellow. It was here that she discovered a "community" of Jews – of Jewish writers. Zwicky is part of the international community of Jewish writers, and has been a major influence on the current generation of Australian poets. She is clearly not religious in any traditional sense, but her poetry is both intensely spiritual ("not sacred, not profane but different you might say getting closer to god without god") and intensely Jewish, reflecting on her experiences in "our twentieth century/ darkness".

PAUL MORRIS

TITLE INDEX

This index lists all the titles in the Poetry, Fiction (Novels, Short Stories), and Plays sections of the Selected Writings lists. The name in parentheses directs the reader to the appropriate entry, where fuller information is given.

4 A M (Mamet), 1983
4 Sipurim veshir (Kaniuk), 1985
4-Telling (Piercy), 1971
5 Tage im Juni (Heym), 1974
5p Opera (Taylor), 1973
14A (Riding), 1934
15 Flower World Variations (Rothenberg), 1984
23 Pat O'Brien Movies (Friedman), 1966
36 Gerechte (Ausländer), 1975
43 Fictions (S. Katz), 1992
53 Days (Perec), 1992
53 jours (Perec), 1989
80 Flowers (Zukofsky), 1978
98.6 (Sukenick), 1975
99 (Abish), 1990
100 Gedichte ohne Vaterland (Fried), 1978
100 Poems without a Country (Fried), 1978
$1200 a Year (Ferber), 1920
1863 (Opatoshu), 1926
1934 (Moravia), 1982
1946 (Applefeld), 1980
1948 (Ben-Yehuda), 1981
1967 Umah haleah (Ratosh), 1967

A (Aub), 1933
A (Zukofsky), 1978
A gondolatnyi csend, amíag kivégzőoztag újratölt (Kertész), 1998
A holocaust mint kultúra: három eloadás (Kertész), 1993
À la découverte du monde connu (Bloch), 1924
À la recherche de Marcel Proust (Maurois), 1949
À la recherche du temps perdu (Proust), 1913–27
À l'ombre des jeunes filles en fleurs (Proust), 1919
A Kudarc (Kertész), 1988
A nyomkereő: Két regény (Kertész), 1977
À poèmes rompus (Jacob), 1960
A számuzött nyelv (Kertész), 2001
Aa Went te Blaydon Races (Taylor), 1962
Aanslag (Mulisch), 1982
Aba oseh bushot (Shalev), 1988
Abba Kovner and Nelly Sachs (Kovner), 1971
Abbess of Crewe (Spark), 1974
Abenteuer des Ruben Jablonski (Hilsenrath), 1997
Abenteuer in Japan (Brod), 1938
Abenteuer Napoleons und andere Novellen (Brod), 1954
Abigail und Nabal (A. Zweig), 1912
Abituriententag (Werfel), 1928
About Harry Towns (Friedman), 1974
Abracadabra! (Mankowitz), 1980
Abraham baboker (Shamir), 1997
Abschied (Torberg), 1937
Abschied vom Frieden (A. Zweig), 1949
Abschied von der Jugend (Brod), 1912
Abundant Dreamer (Brodkey), 1989
Acapulco (Berkoff), 1986
Accident (Wiesel), 1962
Ace Hole, Midget Detective (Spiegelman), 1974
Acharei hayaldut (Hareven), 1994
Acılı Bitimler (Gerez), 1960
Acres and Pains (Perelman), 1947
Acrobats (Richler), 1954
Acrophile (Kaniuk), 1961
Actors and Actresses (Simon), 1983
Actual (Bellow), 1997
Ad alot hashahar (Guri), 1950
Ad hasof (Shamir), 1991
Ad heinah (Agnon), 1952
Ad horef 1974 (Yehoshua), 1975
Ad kav nesher, 1949–1975 (Guri), 1975
Ad loor (Kovner), 1947
Ad nefesh (Applefeld)
Ad olam ahakeh (Schütz), 1987
Ad ora incerta (P. Levi), 1984
Ad sheyaaleh amud hashahar (Applefeld), 1995
Adam (Sobol), 1989
Adam and Eve (K. Shapiro), 1986
Adam ben kelev (Kaniuk), 1968
Adam Resurrected (Kaniuk), 1969
Adam's Rest (Millin), 1922
Adieu Gary Cooper (Gary), 1969
Admat hahol (Kovner), 1961
Adnei hanahar (Applefeld), 1971
Adolf Loos (Kraus), 1933
Adon menuha (Yeshurun), 1990
Adult Bookstore (K. Shapiro), 1976
Adventure in Washington (Rosten), 1940
Adventures of Augie March (Bellow), 1953
Adventures of Herschl Summerwind (Manger), 1954
Adventures of Marco Polo (Simon), 1959
Adventures of Menahem-Mendl (Sholem), 1979
Adventures of Mottel, the Cantor's Son (Sholem), 1953
Advertisement (Ginzburg), 1969
Advertisements for Myself (Mailer), 1959
Aely (Jabès), 1972
Af fremder erd (Israel Singer), 1925
Af Hugo Davids Liv (Nathansen), 1917
Af vilner gasn (Karpinovich), 1981
Af vilner vegn (Karpinovich), 1987
Afar veteshukah (Kaniuk), 1975
Affæren (Nathansen), 1913
Affairs of Anatol (Schnitzler), 1933
Afn barg (Molodovski), 1938
Afn yam (L. Shapiro), 1910
Afsnay (Fefer), 1948
After Childhood (Hareven),1996
After Every Green Thing (Abse), 1948
After I's (Zukofsky), 1964
After Magritte (Stoppard), 1970
After Such Pleasures (Parker), 1933
After the Fall (Miller), 1964
After the Fox (Simon), 1966
After the Holidays (Kenaz), 1987
After the Lions (Harwood), 1982
After the War (Raphael), 1988
Ag (Josipovici), 1976
Agada hayah (Bartov), 1989
Agadat hasofer (Agnon), 1929
Again, Forever (Ben-Ner), 1985
Against Parting (Zach), 1967
Agamemnon (Berkoff), 1971
Agar (Memmi), 1955
Agav-orha (D. Baron), 1960
Age of Enormity (I. Rosenfeld), 1962
Age of Longing (Koestler), 1951
Age of Suspicion (Sarraute), 1963
Age of Wonders (Applefeld), 1981
Ageless Spirit (Kunitz), 1992
Aggadat shloshah vearbaah (Bialik), 1930
Agostino (Moravia), 1945
Água viva (Lispector), 1973
Agujero en la tierra (Dujovne Ortiz), 1983
Agunah (Grade), 1974
Agune (Grade), 1961
Agunot (Agnon), 1908
Aharei hageshem (Ben-Ner), 1979
Aharei hahagim (Kenaz), 1964
Aharei tu bishvat (Almog), 1979
Ahasver (Heym), 1981
Ahasverus (Heijermans), 1886

Ahat hi li (Carmi), 1985
Ahavah amitit (Ravikovitch), 1986
Ahavah balehavot (Ka-Tzetnik 135633), 1976
Ahavah bein hadekalim (Michael), 1990
Ahavah meuheret (Oz), 1971
Ahavat david (Kaniuk), 1990
Ahavat nashim (Ratosh), 1975
Ahavat neurim (Megged), 1980
Ahavat shaul (Amir), 1998
Ahavat shimshon (Goldberg), 1952
Ahavat tapuah hazahav (Ravikovitch), 1959
Ahavot ketanot, tirufim ketanim (Orpaz), 1992
Ahot rehokah (Bartov), 1973
Ahoti ketanah (Kovner), 1967
Aiding and Abetting (Spark), 2000
Air That Pricks Earth (Silkin), 1973
Air We Breathe (Josipovici), 1981
Airone (Bassani), 1968
Airplane Dreams (Ginsberg), 1968
Akeydes yitskhok (Goldfaden), 1887
Akhshav baraash (Amichai), 1968
Akhshav ubeyamim haakherim (Amichai), 1955
Akhzar mikol hamelekh (Aloni), 1953
Al daat hazman vedaat hamakom (Greenberg), 1956–75
Al etsim veavanim (Megged), 1974
Al hadam (Tchernichovski), 1923
Al hagesher hatsar (Kovner), 1981
Al hahalomot (Shahar), 1956
Al haprihah (Goldberg), 1948
Al hokhmat drakhim (Yeshurun), 1942
Al kapot hamanul (Agnon), 1922
Al kol hapeshaim (Applefeld), 1989
Al matsavo shel haadam (Sadeh), 1967
Al milet (Shlonsky), 1947
Al ner veal ruah (Shahar), 1994
Al shtei naarot nekhbadot (Sadeh), 1977
Al tagidi laylah (Oz), 1994
Al tirhak (Zelda), 1975
Aladdin at Sea (Zangwill), 1893
Alain (Maurois), 1949
Alba ai vetri (Bassani), 1963
Albert's Bridge (Stoppard), 1967
Albert's Bridge Extended (Stoppard), 1978
Albertine disparue (Proust), 1925
Albertine Gone (Proust), 1981
Ale fentster tsu der zun (Molodovski), 1938
Ale shriftn (Gordin), 1910
Aleh shel zahav (Goldberg), 1988
Alex and the Gypsy (Elkin), 1977
Alexander in Babylon (Wassermann), 1905
Alexander the Corrector (Shaffer), 1946
Alexanderplatz, Berlin (Döblin), 1931
Aleyn (Opatoshu), 1919
Alibi (Morante), 1958
Alice (Allen), 1990
Alice in Bed (Sontag), 1993
Alilot kapu vedish (Tammuz), 1958
Alilot miki mahu (Shlonsky), 1947
Alive and Kicking (Sherman), 1997
All (Zukofsky), 1965–66
All His Sons (Raphael), 1999
All I Could Never Be (Yezierska), 1932
All Men Are Whores (Mamet), 1977
All My Sons (Miller), 1947
All Our Yesterdays (Ginzburg), 1985
All the Same Shadows (Harwood), 1971
All through the Night (Rosten), 1942
All You Need (Feinstein), 1989
Aller Welt Freund (Becker), 1982
Allergy (Taylor), 1965
Allerleirauch (A. Zweig), 1949
Alliés sont en Arménie (Jacob), 1916
Alma (Sobol), 1999
Almanach (Torberg), 1950
Almonds and Raisins (Mankowitz), 1983
Alone in the Wild Forest (Isaac Singer), 1971
Alpha and Omega (I. Rosenfeld), 1966
Alphabetical Africa (Abish), 1974
Alphabets (Perec), 1976
Alpine (Oppen), 1969
Altar Pieces (Rothenberg), 1982
Altered States (Brookner), 1996
Altneuland (Herzl), 1902
Altra libertà (Bassani), 1951
Altra vita (Moravia), 1973
Am I Also You? (Tussman), 1977
Am Rand unsere Lebenszeit (Fried), 1987
Amadeus (Shaffer), 1979
Amana Grass (Silkin), 1971
Amanda herzlos (Becker), 1992
Amandes d'Aix (Lunel), 1949
Amante da Madonna e outras historias (Scliar), 1997
Amante infelice (Moravia), 1943
Amazonas, 1988
Amberstone Exit (Feinstein), 1972
Ambizioni sbagliate (Moravia), 1935
Ambush (Perelman), 1938
Amédée (Ionesco), 1954
Amen (Amichai), 1978
Amer Eldorado (Federman), 1974
America (Asch), 1918
American Beauty (Ferber), 1931
American Buffalo (Mamet), 1975
American Clock (Miller), 1979
American Dream (Mailer), 1965
American Pastoral (P. Roth), 1997
American Princess (Aloni), 1980
Americans (Riding), 1934
Amerika (Asch), 1911
Amerika (Kafka), 1927
Amerikaner (Feuchtwanger), 1921
Amerikaner dertseylungen (Asch), 1918
Amerike un ikh (Glants-Leyeles), 1963
Amma dedehava (Tchernichovski), 1943
Ammonizione (Saba), 1932
Amnon un Tamar (Asch), 1907
Amok (S. Zweig), 1922
Among the Beasts (Federman), 1967
Amore coniugale (Moravia), 1949
Amorosa spina (Saba), 1921
Amour d'une délicatesse (Cixous), 1982
Amrita (Jhabvala), 1956
Amulet (Rakosi), 1967
Amulett (Wassermann), 1927
Anakreon al kotev haitsavon (Greenberg), 1928
Anankè (Cixous), 1979
Anaseh lagaat betabbur bitni (Bejerano), 1997
Anashim aherim (Oz), 1974
Anashim aherim hem (Hendel), 1950
Anatol (Schnitzler), 1893
Anatomy Lesson (P. Roth), 1983
Ancient Evenings (Mailer), 1983
And a Nightingale Sang (Taylor), 1979
... and Co. (Bloch), 1929
Andere kant (Minco), 1959
Andere Zeichen (Ausländer), 1974
Andersh (Leyvik), *c.*1922
Androcles and the Lion (Kops), 1992
Anemone for Antigone (Kops), 1959
Anew (Zukofsky), 1946
Anfechtungen (Fried), 1967
Ange au secret (Cixous), 1991
Angels in America, (Kushner), 1991-92
Angioxyl (Tammuz), 1973
Angoisse du roi Salomon (Gary), 1979
Angry Hills (Uris), 1955
Angst (Cixous), 1977
Angst (Lind), 1968
Angst (S. Zweig), 1920
Ani Maamin (Wiesel), 1973
Ani ohev lehariah (Hareven), 1976
Ani vetali beerets halama (Shlonsky), 1957
Ankor Wat (Ginsberg), 1968
Anna Laub (Lind), 1965
Annerl (Brod), 1936
Annie, Anna, Annabella (Wesker), 1983
Annie Hall (Allen), 1977
Annie Wobbler (Wesker), 1983
Anno Domini (Steiner), 1964
Anoblissement en France au temps de François Ier (Bloch), 1934
Another Branch of the Family (Litvinoff), 1967
Another Full Moon (Fainlight), 1976
Another Moon Called Earth (Stoppard), 1967
Another Part of the Forest (Hellman), 1947
Another Time (Harwood), 1989
Another Woman (Allen), 1988
Anshei shklov (Schneour), 1944
Anshl zaliaznik (Markish), 1935
Answer to a Letter (Jabès), 1973
Antichrist (J. Roth), 1934
Antigone (Carmi), 1969
Anti-Heroes (Stavans), 1993
Anti-mehikon (Zach), 1984
Antitête (Tzara), 1933
Antologia del Canzoniere (Saba), 1963
Anvil (Layton), 1966
Any Souvenirs? (Mikes), 1972
Any Woman's Blues (Jong), 1990
Apariciones (Glantz), 1996
Apocalypse (Fleg), 1938
Apostle (Asch), 1943
Apparition (Alvarez), 1971
Appius und Virginia (Feuchtwanger), 1918
Apple in the Dark (Lispector), 1967
Apples (Taylor), 1973
Apples from the Desert (Liebrecht), 1998
Apples in Honey (Hendel), 1994
Apprendre à marcher (Ionesco), 1960
Apprendre La Nuit (Vigée), 1991
Apprenticeship (Lispector), 1986
Apprenticeship of Duddy Kravitz (Richler), 1959
Approximate Man (Tzara), 1973
Aprendizagem ou o livro dos prazeres (Lispector), 1969
April (J. Roth), 1925

April, June and November (Raphael), 1972
Aracoeli (Morante), 1982
Aravi tov (Kaniuk), 1983
Arayış İçinde (Gerez), 1967
Arbinka (Kishon), 1991
Árbol de la gitana (Dujovne Ortiz), 1997
Arbre de la gitane (Dujovne Ortiz), 1990
Arcadia (Stoppard), 1993
Arcadia, One Mile (Abse), 1998
Archbishop's Ceiling (Miller), 1977
Archibald Strohalm (Mulisch), 1952
Ari (Uris), 1971
Ariel (Maurois), 1923
Arien (Werfel), 1921
Arise, Arise (Zukofsky), 1973
Aristocrat Boëtius von Orlamünde (Weiss), 1994
Aristokrat Boëtius von Orlamünde (Weiss), 1966
Arlekino (Aloni), 1963
Armageddon (Uris), 1964
Arme Verschwender (Weiss), 1936
Armer Cicero (Brod), 1955
Arn fridman (Halkin), 1939
Arnold Beer (Brod), 1912
Arnold Levenberg (Pinski), 1930
Around the Table (Sholem), 1991
Around the World in 80 Days (Perelman), 1956
Aroys fun gan-edn (Rosenfarb), 1965
Arrival and Departure (Koestler), 1943
Arrivederci Baby! (Harwood), 1966
Arrogant Beggar (Yezierska), 1927
Arrow in the Blue (Koestler), 1952
Art and Anger (Stavans), 1995
Art and Ardor (Ozick), 1983
Art of Blessing the Day (Piercy), 1999
Arthur Aronymus (Lasker-Schüler), 1932
Articles of Faith (Harwood), 1973
Artist Descending a Staircase (Stoppard), 1972
Artist in the Family (Millin), 1928
Artsot hatan (Oz), 1965
Arturo's Island (Morante), 1959
Aruhat boker temimah (Hendel), 1996
Arum vakzal (Bergelson), 1909
As a Man Grows Older (Svevo), 1932
As Once We Were (Perets), 1951
As Others See You (Mikes), 1961
Asahel (Megged), 1978
Aschensommer (Ausländer), 1977
Ash on a Young Man's Sleeve (Abse), 1954
Ashab mebagdad (Ballas), 1970
Asher hayah velo hayah (Tchernichovski), 1942
Asher lemlekh (Glants-Leyeles), 1927
Ashes out of Hope (Bergelson), 1977
Ashes to Ashes (Pinter), 1996
Ashtoret (Aini), 1999
Ask Me (Zwicky), 1990
Ask the Bloody Horse (Abse), 1986
Assassination Bureau (Mankowitz), 1969
Assassinio di via Belpoggia (Svevo), 1890
Assault (Mulisch), 1985
Assenza (Ginzburg), 1934
Assistant (Malamud), 1957
At An Uncertain Hour (P. Levi), 1988
At telkhi basadeh (Goldberg), 1989
At the Edge (Feinstein), 1972
At the Edge of the Body (Jong), 1979
At the Grave of Nataheva Chuya (Rothenberg), 1998
At the Stone of Losses (Carmi), 1983
At the Water-Line (Odets), 1926
At vaani vehamilhamah habaah (Levini), 1968
Atalia (Ben-Ner), 1986
Atemwende (Celan), 1967
Atlas of the Difficult World (Rich), 1991
Atmosphere of Love (Maurois), 1929
Atrocity (Ka-Tzetnik 135633), 1963
Atsabim (Brenner), 1910
Attenzione (Moravia), 1965
Atua (Weiss), 1923
Aube (Wiesel), 1960
Auch das war Wien (Torberg), 1984
Auch Nichtraucher müssen sterben (Torberg), 1985
Au-delà de cette limite votre ticket n'est plus valable (Gary), 1975
Auden (1907–1973) (K. Shapiro), 1974
Auf Sand gebaut (Heym), 1990
Aufbruch nach Deutschland (Biller), 1993
Aufforderung zur Unruhe (Fried), 1972
Aufgabe des Judentums (A. Zweig), 1933
Aufruhr um den Junker Ernst (Wassermann), 1926
Aufzeichnungen über eine Familie Klopfer (A. Zweig), 1911
Augen der Vernunft (Heym), 1955
Augen des ewigen Bruders (S. Zweig), 1922
Augenzeuge (Weiss), 1982
Augmentation (Perec), 1970
August Nachreiters Attentat (Brod), 1921
Augustus Rex (Sinclair), 1992
Aunt Rachel's Fur (Federman), 2001
Aunt Shlomzion the Great (Kaniuk), 1978
Aurora Dawn (Wouk), 1947
Aus den Augen verlieren / Desaparecer (Dorfman), 1979
Aus der Luft gegriffen (Broch), 1981
Aus Prager Gassen und Nächten (Kisch), 1912
Austeria (Stryjkowski), 1966
Autobiografia (Saba), 1924
Autobiographical Stanzas (Silkin), 1984
Autobiography of a Princess (Jhabvala), 1975
Autobiopsy (Rubens), 1993
Auto-da-Fé (E. Canetti), 1946
Automa (Moravia), 1962
Autumn Garden (Hellman), 1951
Autumn Music (Preil), 1979
Autumn to Autumn (Alvarez), 1978
Aux Portes du labyrinthe (Vigée), 1996
Available Light (Piercy), 1988
Avanim rotehot (Hazaz), 1946
Avel (Megged), 1996
Avenir est dans les oeufs (Ionesco), 1957
Avidanium 20 (Avidan), 1987
Avishag (Schütz), 1990
Avnei bohu (Shlonsky), 1934
Avnei gvil (Shlonsky), 1968
Awake and Sing! (Odets), 1935
Awake for Mourning (Kops), 1958
Axel (Mulisch), 1977
Ayalah ashalah otakh (Gilboa), 1973
Ayeh pluto? (Goldberg), 1957
Ayen erekh (D. Grossman), 1986
Ayfer un gevisn (Weissenberg), 1929
Ayin Beayin (Sobol), 1994
Ayumah (Guri), 1979
Az angol lobogó (Kertész), 1992
Azriel un shloyme ber (Markish), 1927

*B*R*M*Tz*V*H* (Rothenberg), 1979
Baalat haarmon (Goldberg), 1956
Babayit ubahuts (Rachel), 1974
Baby (Mankowitz), 1954
Baby, It's Cold Inside (Perelman), 1970
Babylonische Wandrung (Döblin), 1934
Bachelor of Hearts (Raphael), 1958
Bachelors (Spark), 1961
Bachelors' Club (Zangwill), 1891
Back to China (Fiedler), 1965
Backward Place (Jhabvala), 1965
Bad Man (Elkin), 1967
Bad Man from Bodie (Doctorow), 1961
Badenheim 1939 (Applefeld), 1980
Badenheim, ir nofesh (Applefeld), 1979
Baderekh la hatulim (Kenaz), 1991
Baderekh leeilat (Megged), 1951
Badlands (Feinstein), 1986
Bagalgal (Shlonsky), 1927
Baganim (Gnessin), 1909
Bahn (Viertel), 1921
Bahodesh haaharon (Hareven), 1966
Bahoref (Brenner), 1904
Bair hataḥtit (Ballas), 1979
Bal masqué (Jacob), 1932
Bal w Operze (Tuwim), 1946
Balada do falso mesias (Scliar), 1976
Balade fun nekhtikn vald un andere lider (Rosenfarb), 1948
Balai de sorcière (Lunel), 1935
Balance of Terror (Shaffer), 1957
Bald Prima Donna (Ionesco), 1961
Bald Soprano (Ionesco), 1958
Balkan Express (Rosten), 1939
Ballachulish Beat (Taylor), 1967
Ballad of Peckham Rye (Spark), 1960
Ballad of the False Messiah (Scliar), 1987
Ballad of the Hundred Days (J. Roth), 1936
Ballade vom Papagei (Kraus), 1919
Ballades (Jacob), 1938
Ballady (Leśmian), 1926
Balls for a One-Armed Juggler (Layton), 1963
Bal-tshuve (Isaac Singer), 1973
Balut hapele shel kamila (Almog), 1999
Bam dnieper (Bergelson), 1932–36
Bamaagal (Alterman), 1971
Bamartef (Sobol), 1990
Bambini (Ginzburg), 1934
Bananas (Allen), 1971
Bandido (Stavans), 1996
Bandits (Taylor), 1979
Bang-Bang You're Dead (Spark), 1981
Bankrot (Leyvik), 1923
Bankructwo małego Dżeka (Korczak), 1924
Banquier du Village (Lunel), 1937
Bar kokhba (Goldfaden), 1887
Bar kokhba (Halkin), 1939
Bar Mitzvah (Mamet), 1999
Barabany sud'by (Shrayer-Petrov), 2002
Barak baboker (Goldberg), 1955
Barba Garibo (Lunel), 1949
Barbara (Broch), 1973

Barbara (Werfel), 1929
Barbary Shore (Mailer), 1951
Barber of Stamford Hill (Harwood), 1962
Barefoot in the Park (Simon), 1962
Bare-Knuckle Breed (Golding), 1952
Barely & Widely (Zukofsky), 1958
Barney's Version (Richler), 1997
Barricades in West Hampstead (Kops), 1988
Bartfus ben almavet (Applefeld), 1983
Baruch Spinoza (A. Zweig), 1961
Baseler Congress (Herzl), 1897
Basement (Pinter), 1967
Basic Training (Barbash)
Bašta, Pepeo (Kiš), 1965
Bat yaana (Bejerano), 1978
Bataille d'Arcachon (Cixous), 1986
Bâtir au quotidien (Jabès), 1997
Battered and the Redeemed (Liberman), 1990
Battle Cry (Uris), 1953
Battle of Brazil (Stoppard), 1987
Battle of Shrivings (Shaffer), 1970
Bay nakht oyfn altn mark (Perets), 1907
Bay of Angels (Brookner), 2001
Bayamin hahem (Mendele Moykher Sforim), 1903
Bayit leadam (Orpaz), 1975
Baym fus fun barg (Glants-Leyeles), 1957
Baym opgrunt (Asch), 1937
Baym toyer (Molodovski), 1967
Baym vilner durkh-hoyf (Karpinovich), 1967
Be My Knife (D. Grossman), 2002
Be Seated, Thou (Abse), 2000
Beach Vision (Hollander), 1962
Bead (Kishon), 1970
Beast (Rakosi), 1994
Beast in View (Rukeyser), 1944
Beatrice (Schnitzler), 1926
Beatrice Cenci (Moravia), 1958
Beautiful Losers (L. Cohen), 1966
Beauty and the Beast (Lispector), 1991
Beauty Part (Perelman), 1963
Beayot ishiot (Avidan), 1957/59
Bebele (Hirshbein), 1915
Becoming Light (Jong), 1991
Bedbugs (Sinclair), 1982
Bederf is the weg van alle vlees (Möring), 1994
Bedidut (Hareven), 1980
Beehad haemeshim (Kishon), 1962
Beeld en de klok (Mulisch), 1989
Beeleh hayamim (Shlonsky), 1930
Beemdgras (Herzberg), 1968
Beemek habakha (Mendele Moykher Sforim), 1897
Beemtsa haroman (Bartov), 1984
Beerets ahavati (Goldberg), 1997
Beerets gezirah (Almog), 1970
Beerets sin (Goldberg), 1951
Beet uveonah ahat (Applefeld), 1985
Befatei negev (Yizhar), 1945
Befebruar kedai liknot pilim (Hoffman), 1988
Before the Flowers of Friendship Faded Friendship Faded (Stein), 1931
Befreiung von der Flucht (Fried), 1968
Befristeten (E. Canetti), 1964
Begani netaatikha (Rachel), 1985
Beggar in Jerusalem (Wiesel), 1970
Beggar My Neighbour (D. Jacobson), 1964
Begin Again (Paley), 2000
Beginah hatsiburit (Amichai), 1959
Beginners (D. Jacobson), 1966
Beginning Again (Woolf), 1964
Begrabene Leuchter (S. Zweig), 1937
Beharim (Schneour), 1908
Behind the Door (Bassani), 1972
Beichte eines Mörders, erzählt in einer Nacht (J. Roth), 1936
Beiden Freudinnen und ihr Giftmord (Döblin), 1925
Beikvot maveer hasadot (Ben-Ner), 1967
Beil von Wandsbeck (A. Zweig), 1947
Beim Bau der chinesischen Mauer (Kafka), 1931
Beinahe ein Vorzugsschüler oder Pièce Touchée (Brod), 1952
Beine der Grösseren Lügen (Fried), 1969
Being Busted (Fiedler), 1969
Being There (Kosinski), 1971
Beit habubot (Ka-Tzetnik 135633), 1953
Beit hillel (Shamir), 1950
Beit kaplan (Sobol), 1978
Beit sefer lerikudim (Zach), 1985
Bekets hayamim (Hazaz), 1950
Bekomat hakarka (Applefeld), 1968
Bela e a fera (Lispector), 1979
Beliebteste Familiengeschichte (Becker), 1992
Bella vita (Moravia), 1935
Bellarosa Connection (Bellow), 1989
Belle (Mankowitz), 1961
Belle à la Fontaine (Lunel), 1959
Belle du Seigneur (A. Cohen), 1968
Bellissime avventure di Caterì dalla trecciolina (Morante), 1941
Bells and Trains (Amichai), 1966
Bells of Hell (Richler), 1974
Bemerhak shetey tikvot (Amichai), 1958
Bemo libo (Shamir), 1976
Bemo yadav (Shamir), 1951
Ben Ami (Goldfaden), 1907
Ben Preserve Us (Bermant), 1965
Benefactor (Sontag), 1963
Benia Krik (Babel'), 1926
Benmussa Directs (Cixous), 1979
Bent (Sherman), 1979
Benya Krik (Babel'), 1935
Beorhtel's Hill (Wesker), 1989
Berazim arufei sefatayim (Avidan), 1954
Berek pod kockem (Weissenberg)
Bereshit (Megged), 1989
Berge, Meere und Giganten (Döblin), 1924
Bergroman (Broch), 1969
Bericht vor Einer Akademie (Kafka), 1917
Berl Make Tea (Bermant), 1965
Berlin Alexanderplatz (Döblin), 1929
Bernard Quesnay (Maurois), 1926
Bernhard (Hoffman), 1989
Berta Garlan (Schnitzler), 1987
Bertha Garlan (Schnitzler), 1913
Beruah hanoraah hazot (Amichai), 1961
Beschwörungen (Werfel), 1923
Beseter raam (Mendele Moykher Sforim), 1887
Beshuvah vanahat (Agnon), 1935
Besod yesharim (Agnon), 1921
Besof maarav (Tammuz), 1966
Bespoke Overcoat (Mankowitz), 1953
Best of Ariel (Castel-Bloom), 1995
Best of Friends (Raphael), 1980
Bestie (A. Zweig), 1919
Besuch aus dem Elysium (Werfel), 1920
Bête (Fleg), 1910
Beterem (Gnessin), 1909
Betrayal (Pinter), 1978
Betrothed (Agnon), 1966
Between (Rothenberg), 1967
Between Life and Death (Sarraute), 1969
Beunruhigungen (Fried), 1984
Beveit hamarpe (Vogel), 1928
Beware of Pity (S. Zweig), 1939
Bewitched Tailor (Sholem), n.d.
Beyishuv shel yaar (Hazaz), 1930
Beynatayyim (Gnessin), 1906
Beyond the Law (Mailer), 1968
Beyond Woman (Samuel), 1934
Bezoekuur (Mulisch), 1974
Bezvadný den (Klíma), 1960
Biblia Cygańska (Tuwim), 1933
Bibliosexuality (Sinclair), 1973
Bieg do Fragalà (Stryjkowski), 1951
Big as Life (Doctorow), 1966
Big Bow Mystery (Zangwill), 1892
Big Broadcast of 1936 (Parker), 1935
Big Business Billy (Korczak), 1939
Big Glass (Josipovici), 1991
Big Knife (Odets), 1949
Bigdei hamelekh hahadashim (Aloni), 1961
Biggest Pig in Barbados (Mankowitz), 1965
Bijvangst (Herzberg), 1999
Bikhefifah achat (Kahana-Carmon), 1966
Bikur hatalyan (Perry), 1999
Bilanz der deutschen Judenheit (A. Zweig), 1933
Bílé břízy na podzim (Lustig), 1966
Billy Bathgate (Doctorow), 1989
Billy Bathgate (Stoppard), 1990
Biloxi Blues (Simon), 1984
Bilvav yamim (Agnon), 1935
Bimkom halom (Zach), 1966
Biography of Lenin (Esther), 1925–26
Birds of Passage (Rubens), 1981
Birebidzshaner (Bergelson), 1934
Birobidzhaner lider (Fefer), 1939
Birthday Party (Pinter), 1958
Bithilat kayits 1970 (Yehoshua), 1972
Bito (Kaniuk), 1987
Bitter Herbs (Minco), 1960
Bitter Honeymoon (Moravia), 1954
Bittere kruid (Minco), 1957
Bittere Lorbeer (Heym), 1950
Bixby Canyon Ocean Path Word Breeze (Ginsberg), 1972
Black and White Minstrels (Taylor), 1972
Black Angels (Friedman), 1966
Black Beauty (Mankowitz), 1971
Black Box (Oz), 1988
Black Comedy (Shaffer), 1965
Black Gallery (Koestler), 1942
Black Huntsman (Layton), 1951
Black Mischief (Shaffer), 1983
Black Notes (Silkin), 1986
Blackout (Sherman), 1978
Blake's Therapy (Dorfman), 2001

Blasphemie eines Irren (Werfel), 1919
Blassblaue Frauenschrift (Werfel), 1941
Blaszane Nieśmiertelniki (Korczak), 1989
Blat af an eplboym (Leyvik), 1953
Blaubart und Miss Ilsebill (Döblin), 1923
Blaue Frau (Almog), 1992
Blaue Tiger (Döblin), 1938
Blendung (E. Canetti), 1936
Bleter faln nit (Tussman), 1972
Blind Beauty (Pasternak), 1969
Blind Children (Zangwill), 1903
Blind Date (Kosinski), 1977
Blinde Spiegel (J. Roth), 1925
Blinder aron (Weissenberg)
Blinder Sommer (Ausländer), 1965
Bliznets v tuchakh (Pasternak), 1914
Bloch's Play (Taylor), 1971
Bloc-notes d'un contre-revolutionnaire (Rawicz), 1969
Bloeimaand (Heijermans), 1905
Blondzhende shtern (Sholem), 1909–11
Blood from the Sky (Rawicz), 1964
Blood Harvest (Israel Singer), 1935
Blood Libel (Wesker), 1991
Blood Libels (Sinclair), 1985
Blood on the Dining Room Floor (Stein), 1948
Blood on the Snow (Litvinoff), 1975
Bloodshed (Ozick), 1976
Bloody Hoax (Sholem), 1991
Bloomfield (Mankowitz), 1970
Blown Away (Sukenick), 1986
Blue Arabian Nights (Mankowitz), 1973
Blue Day (Lustig), 1960
Blue Mountain (Shalev), 1991
Blue Propeller (Layton), 1955
Blue Wine (Hollander), 1979
Bluey (Wesker), 1985
Blutiker shpas (Sholem), 1912–13
Bluzhdaiushchie zvezdy (Babel'), 1926
Bobby Gould in Hell (Mamet), 1989
Bobe mitn eynikl (Goldfaden), 1877
Bobe un dos eynikl (Weissenberg), 1939
Bobeshe's ophitn (Weissenberg), 1910
Bociany (Rosenfarb), 2000
Bocksgesang (Werfel), 1921
Body of Glass (Piercy), 1992
Body of Waking (Rukeyser), 1958
Body Parts of Margaret Fuller (Broner), 1976
Boëtius von Orlamünde (Weiss), 1928
Bog sokhraniaet vse (Brodsky), 1991
Boh (Moravia), 1976
Boker shel shotim (Ben-Ner), 1992
Bombay Talkie (Jhabvala), 1970
Bonaparte in Jaffe (A. Zweig), 1939
Bone to the Bone (Shaham), 1993
Bontshe the Silent (Perets), 1927
Book Concluding with As a Wife Has a Cow (Stein), 1926
Book of Abraham (Halter), 1986
Book of Daniel (Doctorow), 1971
Book of Dialogue (Jabès), 1986
Book of Fire (Perets), 1959
Book of Intimate Grammar (D. Grossman), 1994
Book of Joseph (Hoffman), 1998
Book of Lights (Potok), 1981
Book of Margins (Jabès), 1993
Book of Mercy (L. Cohen), 1984
Book of Monelle (Schwob), 1929
Book of Palaces (Rothenberg), 1975
Book of Paradise (Manger), 1965
Book of Promethea (Cixous), 1991
Book of Questions (Jabès), 1976
Book of Resemblances (Jabès), 1990
Book of Shares (Jabès), 1989
Book of Testimony (Rothenberg), 1971
Book of Various Owls (Hollander), 1963
Book of Yukel (Jabès), 1978
Book that was Lost (Agnon), 1995
Booke of Idolatry (Schulz), 1988
Boomerang (Mikes), 1968
Border (Feinstein), 1984
Borghesia (Ginzburg), 1977
Born to be Wild (West), 1938
Born Where? (Schindel), 1995
Boston Marrriage (Mamet), 2001
Bostonians (Jhabvala), 1984
Boswell (Elkin), 1964
Botshani (Rosenfarb), 1983
Botshol (Herzberg), 1980
Botteghe oscure (Morante), 1958
Bou ananim (Goldberg), 1982
Bought and Sold (Moravia), 1973
Boulevards de ceinture (Modiano), 1972
Boundary (Stoppard), 1991
Bourgeois Poet (K. Shapiro), 1964
Bovl (Hirshbein), 1942
Boxer (Becker), 1976
Boy from Oz (Sherman), 2002
Boy Prophet (Fleg), 1928
Boy Trouble (Perelman), 1939
Boy Who Wouldn't Play Jesus (Kops), 1965
Boychik (Mankowitz), 1954
Boym fun lebn (Rosenfarb), 1972
Braided Lives (Piercy), 1982
Brass Serpent (Carmi), 1964
Brauchen wir eine neue Gruppe 47? (Biller), 1995
Brave (Taylor), 1969
Bravo! (Ferber), 1948
Brazil (Stoppard), 1985
Bread and Butter (Taylor), 1966
Bread Givers (Yezierska), 1925
Bread of Exile (Gershon), 1985
Breakdown and Bereavement (Brenner), 1971
Breakdowns (Spiegelman), 1977
Breaking Camp (Piercy), 1968
Breaking Open (Rukeyser), 1973
Breakthrough at Reykjavik (Harwood), 1987
Breast (P. Roth), 1972
Brenendik shtetl (M. Katz), 1938
Brenendiker dorn (Asch), 1946
Brennendes Bilderbuch (A. Zweig), 1926
Brennendes Geheimnis (S. Zweig), 1913
Brewsie and Willie (Stein), 1946
Bridal Canopy (Agnon), 1967
Bride and the Butterfly Hunter (Aloni), 1998
Bridegroom for Marcela (Klíma), 1969
Brider (Markish), 1929
Brider ashkenazi (Israel Singer), 1936
Brief Lives (Brookner), 1990
Briefe an die Schwester Hilde (Kolmar), 1970
Brigade (Bartov), 1968
Bright Room Called Day (Kushner), 1987
Brighton Beach Memoirs (Simon), 1982
Brik (Shpigl), 1963
Brilyantn (Kreitman), 1944
Briv tsi abrashen (Rosenfarb), 1992
Broadway Bound (Simon), 1986
Broadway Danny Rose (Allen), 1984
Broken Glass (Miller), 1994
Bronskys Geständnis (Hilsenrath), 1980
Bronstein's Children (Becker), 1988
Bronsteins Kinder (Becker), 1986
Brother Carl (Sontag), 1971
Brothers (Reyzen), 1929
Brothers (Rubens), 1983
Brothers Ashkenazi (Israel Singer), 1936
Broyt mil (Bergelson), 1930
Brüder Lautensack (Feuchtwanger), 1944
Brunem (Grade), 1967
Bruriya, un andere dertseylungen (Pinski), 1938
Bubbles (Rukeyser), 1967
Buch der Liebe (Brod), 1921
Buenas intenciones (Aub), 1954
Bukh fun gan-eydn (Manger), 1939
Bukh fun libe (M. Rosenfeld), 1914
Bukh fun libe (Weissenberg), 1930
Bulan King of the Kazars (Lind), 1972
Bull Calf (Layton), 1956
Bullets over Broadway (Allen), 1994
Bunem feldsher (Weissenberg)
Bunten Getüme (Fried), 1978
Bürger und Soldaten 1918 (Döblin), 1939
Burger's Daughter (Gordimer), 1979
Buria (Erenburg), 1948
Buried Candelabrum (S. Zweig), 1937
Burla riuscita (Svevo), 1928
Burn Helen (Gershon), 1980
Burnaia zhizn' Lazika Roitshvanetsa (Erenburg), 1928
Burning Man (Millin), 1952
Burning Secret (S. Zweig), 1919
Burning Village (M. Katz), 1972
Burnt Pearls (Sutzkever), 1981
Business is Business (Parker), 1925
Bust of the Emperor (J. Roth), 1986
Buste de l'Empereur (J. Roth), 1934
Büste des Kaisers (J. Roth), 1964
But What (Herzberg), 1988
Buttered Side Down (Ferber), 1912
Büyük Güzel (Gerez), 1969
Buzón de la esquina (Dujovne Ortiz), 1977
By Night under the Stone Bridge (Perutz), 1989
By the Waters of Manhattan (Reznikoff), 1930
By the Waters of Whitechapel (Kops), 1969
By the Well of Living and Seeing (Reznikoff), 1969
Byron (Maurois), 1930
Byron (Raphael), 1981

Ça suit son cours (Jabès), 1975
Caballos por el fondo de los ojos (Goloboff), 1976
Cabinet d'amateur (Perec), 1979
Cabinet noir (Jacob), 1922
Cacaouettes et bananes (Bloch), 1929
Cacciatore Sconcertato (Layton), 1993
Caesar (Shahar), 1960
Café Zeitgeist (Kops), 1999

Cage aux Folles (Fierstein), 1983
Cages (Fainlight), 1966
Caine Mutiny (Wouk), 1951
Caine Mutiny Court-Martial (Wouk), 1953
Calf of Paper (Asch), 1936
Caliban (A. Zweig), 1927
California Suite (Simon), 1976
California Time (Raphael), 1975
Call from the East (Jhabvala), 1981
Call in the Night (Kops), 1995
Call It Sleep (H. Roth), 1934
Call Us by Name (Rubens), 1968
Callas Forever (Sherman), 2002
Calle de Valverde (Aub), 1961
Call-Girls (Koestler), 1972
Camberwell Beauty (Golding), 1935
Campo abierto (Aub), 1951
Campo cerrado (Aub), 1943
Campo de los almendros (Aub), 1968
Campo de sangre (Aub), 1945
Campo del moro (Aub), 1963
Campo francés (Aub), 1965
Can More Be Done? (Josipovici), 1992
Candide (Hellman), 1957
Cannibal Galaxy (Ozick), 1984
Cannibals (Heym), 1957
Canopy in the Desert (Kovner), 1973
Cantatrice chauve (Ionesco), 1950
Canzoniere (Saba), from 1921
Captain Newman, M.D. (Rosten), 1961
Captive (Proust), 1929
Cara y cruz (Aub), 1948
Caracal (Herzberg), 1988
Carambole (Avidan), 1965
Cards (Rothenberg), 1974
Careless Love (Ginsberg), 1978
Caretaker (Pinter), 1960
Caring for Animals (Silkin), 1972
Caritas (Wesker), 1981
Carnaval dos animais (Scliar), 1968
Carnaval est mort (Bloch), 1920
Carnival of the Animals (Scliar), 1985
Caro Michele (Ginzburg), 1973
Carol O.K. (Taylor), 1974
Casa al mare (Ginzburg), 1937
Casanovas Heimfahrt (Schnitzler), 1918
Casanova's Homecoming (Schnitzler), 1921
Case of Sergeant Grischa (A. Zweig), 1928
Case Worker (Konrád), 1974
Casino Royale (Heller, Mankowitz), 1967
Caspar Hauser (Wassermann), 1908
Castle (Kafka), 1930
Castle (Klíma), 1968
Castle in Spain (Tammuz), 1973
Catch-22 (Heller), 1961
Catcher in the Rye (Salinger), 1951
Caught between Two Worlds (Sherman), 1997
Caves of Adullan (D. Jacobson), 1972
Ce Formidable Bordel (Ionesco), 1973
Čekání na t'mu, čekání na světlo (Klíma), 1993
Cela a eu lieu (Jabès), 1993
Celebrants (Feinstein), 1973
Celebrity (Allen), 1998
Celibates' Club (Zangwill), 1905
Cella (Werfel), 1982
Celluloid Closet (Fierstein), 1996
Celui que ne parle pas (Cixous), 1984
Cenas da vida minuscula (Scliar), 1991
Centaur in the Garden (Scliar), 1984
Centauro no jardim (Scliar), 1980
Cerberus (Layton), 1952
Cercle de famille (Maurois), 1932
Cerco (Aub), 1968
Cerfs-volants (Gary), 1980
Certificate (Isaac Singer), 1992
César and Augusta (Harwood), 1978
C'est beau (Sarraute), 1975
Chaim Lederer's Return (Asch), 1938
Chair for Elijah (M. Katz), 1985
Chairs (Ionesco), 1957
Chaises (Ionesco), 1952
Change (Ginsberg), 1963
Change for the Angel (Kops), 1960
Change of World (Rich), 1951
Chansons Dada (Tzara), 1987
Chansons pour le repas de l'ogre (Jabès), 1947
Chant nouveau (Fleg), 1971
Chantage op het leven (Mulisch), 1953
Chantez avec nous! (Bloch), 1945
Chapter Two (Simon), 1977
Charlie (Mikes), 1976
Charlotte (Herzberg), 1980
Chartreuse de Parme (Lunel), 1926–36
Chase (Hellman), 1966
Chasses de Renaut (Bloch), 1927
Chast' rechi (Brodsky), 1980
Chateaubriand (Maurois), 1938
Chatterton, the Black Death and Meriwether Lewis (Reznikoff), 1922
Chauve-Souris (Parker), 1922
Cheap Detective (Simon), 1978
Cheerful, By Request (Ferber), 1918
Chekhov, Stendhal (Erenburg), 1962
Chemin de croix infernal (Jacob), 1936
Chernaia kniga (Erenburg), 1980
Chernyi karlik (Mandel'shtam), 1992
Cherry Orchard (Mamet), 1985
Chetyre dnia (V. Grossman), 1936
Cheyenne River Wild Track (S. Katz), 1973
Chiave a stella (P. Levi), 1978
Chicken Inspector No. 23 (Perelman), 1966
Chicken Soup with Barley (Wesker), 1958
Chien de Printemps (Modiano), 1993
Childe Harold (Kulbak), 1969
Childhood (Pasternak), 1941
Childhood (Sarraute), 1984
Childhood and Youth (Erenburg), 1962
Childhood of Luvers (Pasternak), 1945
Children and Fools (Fried), 1992
Children at the Gate (Wallant), 1964
Children of Abraham (Asch), 1942
Children of Abraham (Halter), 1990
Children of Loneliness (Yezierska), 1923
Children of the Ghetto (Zangwill), 1892
Children of the Heart (Sherman), 1997
Children of the Rainbow (Farhi), 1999
Children of the Rose (Feinstein), 1975
Children of Two Inheritances (Litvinoff), 1953
Children's Crusade (Schwob), 1907
Children's Hour (Hellman), 1934
Children's Orchard (Rukeyser), 1947
Chinaman (Mamet), 1999
Chinesische Mauer (Kraus), 1910
Chip of Glass Ruby (Gordimer), 1985
Chips with Everything (Wesker), 1962
Chocolate Deal (Guri), 1968
Choice of Enemies (Richler), 1957
Choosing Company (Schwartz), 1936
Choosing for Justice (Gordimer), 1985
Chosen (Potok), 1967
Chosen (Shabtai),1976
Chosen People (Rubens), 1969
Choses (Perec), 1965
Christ of Fish (Hoffman), 1999
Christ Stopped at Eboli (C. Levi), 1947
Christian Wahnschaffe (Wassermann), 1919
Christoph Columbus (Wassermann), 1929
Christopher Columbus (Wassermann), 1930
Ciclo das aguas (Scliar), 1976
Cidade sitiada (Lispector), 1949
Cimarron (Ferber), 1930
Cinématoma (Jacob), 1919
Cinkos (Konrád), 1983
Cinnamon Shops (Schulz), 1963
Cinque romanzi brevi (Ginzburg), 1964
Cinque storie ferraresi (Bassani), 1956
Cinquième Fils (Wiesel), 1983
Ciociara (Moravia), 1957
Circle (Feinstein), 1970
Circles on the Water (Piercy), 1982
Cité présente (Spire), 1903
Cities of the Plain (Proust), 1929
Città di pianura (Bassani), 1940
Città e la casa (Ginzburg), 1984
City and the House (Ginzburg), 1987
City Boy (Wouk), 1948
City Builder (Konrád), 1977
City Music (Feinstein), 1990
City of Blok (Louvish), 1988
City of Darkness, City of Light (Piercy), 1996
City of Glass (Auster), 1985
City of God (Doctorow), 2000
City of Many Days (Hareven), 1993
Civil War (Bergelson), 1977
Clarissa (S. Zweig), 1990
Clash By Night (Odets), 1941
Class Queen (Ben-Ner), 1988
Class Reunion (Werfel), 1929
Claudia (A. Zweig), 1930
Clef de voûte (Jabès), 1950
Cleverness of Us (Taylor), 1971
Clevinger's Trial (Heller), 1974
Climates (Fainlight), 1983
Climats (Maurois), 1928
Clínica del Dr Mefistófeles (Gerchunoff), 1937
Close Chaplet (Riding), 1926
Close Harmony (Parker), 1924
Closed Eye (Brookner), 1991
Closed Place (Ayalon), 1998
Closing the Sea (Katzir), 1992
Closing Time (Heller), 1994
Clothes in the Wardrobe (Sherman), 1993
Clôture (Perec), 1980
Coast of Ilyria (Parker), 1949
Coast of Utopia (Stoppard), 2002
Coast to Coast (Raphael), 1999
Coat of Many Colours (Mikes), 1969
Coat without a Seam (Kunitz), 1974

Cobbler (Goldberg), 1950
Cock and Bull (Self), 1993
Cockatrice (Mankowitz), 1963
Cockpit (Kosinski), 1975
Cockpit (Zangwill), 1921
Cocksure (Richler), 1968
Coeur à gaz (Tzara), 1921
Coeur double (Schwob), 1891
Coffee Room (Elkin), 1987
Coi miei occhi (Saba), 1912
Cold Green Element (Layton), 1955
Collection (Pinter), 1963
Collector of Autumns (Preil), 1992
Collin (Heym), 1979
Colonel Higginson (Broner), 1968
Colonel's Photograph (Ionesco), 1967
Colours of the Day (Rukeyser), 1961
Colpo di pistola (Moravia), 1941
Columba (Taylor), 1973
Come and Get It (Ferber), 1935
Come Back Paul (Rukeyser), 1955
Come Blow Your Horn (Simon), 1960
Comedy of Vanity (E. Canetti), 1983
Comfort of Strangers (Pinter), 1990
Comforters (Spark), 1957
Coming Back from Babylon (Gershon), 1979
Coming from Behind (H. Jacobson), 1983
Coming Home (Shaham), 1973
Coming of the Lord (Millin), 1928
Command and I Will Obey You (Moravia), 1969
Commencements (Cixous), 1970
Companion (Bermant), 1988
Company of Men (Gary), 1950
Compartment (Pinter), 1963
Complete Black Book of Russian Jewry (Erenburg), 2001
Complete Mr Infinity (Spiegelman), 1970
Comuna verdad (Goloboff), 1995
Confessions of a Good Arab (Kaniuk), 1987
Confessions of a Murderer, Told in One Night (J. Roth), 1938
Confessions of Josef Baisz (D. Jacobson), 1977
Confessions of Zeno (Svevo), 1930
Conflicts (S. Zweig), 1927
Conform or Die (Abse), 1957
Conformist (Moravia), 1951
Conformista (Moravia), 1951
Congress Address (Herzl), 1917
Conjugal Love (Moravia), 1951
Connaissez-vous? (Ionesco), 1971
Conscience (Klein), 1952
Conscienza sensibile (Pressburger), 1992
Conscripts (Litvinoff), 1941
Conservationist (Gordimer), 1974
Conspirators (Rosten), 1944
Constant Reader (Parker), 1970
Continuing Silence of a Poet (Yehoshua), 1988
Contre-Jour (Josipovici), 1986
Convalescence (Harwood), 1964
Convalescent Conversations (Riding), 1936
Conversations (Rothenberg), 1968
Conversations in Another Room (Josipovici), 1984
Conversion (Applefeld), 1998
Cool Million (West), 1934
Coral and Captive Israel (Reznikoff), 1923
Cormorano (Ginzburg), 1991
Cornet à dés (Jacob), 1917
Cortigiana stanca (Moravia), 1965
Corto viaggio sentimentale (Svevo), 1949
Cosa (Moravia), 1983
Cosa è una cosa (Moravia), 1967
Coscienza di Zeno (Svevo), 1923
Cose leggere e vaganti (Saba), 1920
Cosmetic Effects (Sinclair), 1989
Cosmic Realities Vanilla Tobacco Dawnings (Tzara), 1975
Cosmopolitan Greetings (Ginsberg), 1994
Côte (Jacob), 1911
Côté de Guermantes (Proust), 1920–21
Countdown to War (Harwood), 1989
Counterlife (P. Roth), 1987
Countess Mitzi (Schnitzler), 1982
Countess Mizzie (Schnitzler), 1915
Counting My Steps (Lind), 1969
Country Doctor (Kafka), 1962
Country Girl (Odets), 1951
Country Lovers (Gordimer), 1985
Country Matters (Harwood), 1969
Couples (Schnitzler), 1927
Couronne de Vulcain (Jacob), 1923
Courteous to Myself (Preil), 1980
Courting of Essie Glass (Abse), 1975
Covenant (Layton), 1977
Cożeś Ty Za Pani (Korczak), 1979
Crackling of Thorns (Hollander), 1958
Crackpot (Wiseman), 1974
Cracks (Sherman), 1975
Cranky Box (Herzberg), 1975
Crazy like a Fox (Perelman), 1944
Creamy and Delicious (S. Katz), 1970
Creation of the World and Other Business (Miller), 1972
Crépuscule au loin (Wiesel), 1988
Cría ojos (Dorfman), 1979
Criador de palomas (Goloboff), 1984
Criers and Kibitzers, Kibitzers and Criers (Elkin), 1968
Crimes and Misdemeanors (Allen), 1989
Crimes of Conscience (Gordimer), 1991
Cristo si è fermato a Eboli (C. Levi), 1945
Croisade des enfants (Schwob), 1896
Cromwell (Harwood), 1970
Cross Patch (Mamet), 1985
Cross the Border — Close the Gap (Fiedler), 1972
Crossing (Lind), 1991
Crown for Cain (Litvinoff), 1948
Crown of Feathers (Isaac Singer), 1973
Crowned Head (Shabtai),1995
Crowning of a King (A. Zweig), 1938
Crucible (Miller), 1954
Crusaders (Heym), 1948
Cryptogram (Mamet), 1995
Crystal Garden (Feinstein), 1974
Cuentas y los inventarios (Goldemberg), 2000
Cuentos ciertos, Ciertos cuentos (Aub), 1955
Cuentos de ayer (Gerchunoff), 1919
Cuentos mexicanos (con pilón) (Aub), 1959
Cuentos para militares (Dorfman), 1986
Cuerpo del amor (Goldemberg), 2000
Cukrárna Myriam (Klíma), 1967
Cuor morituro e altre poesie (Saba), 1964
Current Climate (Friedman), 1990
Curse of the Jade Scorpion (Allen), 2001
Cyrano de Bergerac (Carmi), 1986
Czarna róża (Stryjkowski), 1962
Czyhanie na Boga (Tuwim), 1918

D. Faustus, Lights the Lights (Stein), 1984
Daber el haruah (Shaham), 1975
Daedalus Dimension (Raphael), 1979
Dagan veoferet (Shaham), 1948
Dagrest (Herzberg), 1984
Daisy Miller (Raphael), 1974
Dalliance (Schnitzler, Stoppard), 1986
Daltot nehoshet (Hazaz), 1956
Dämmerseelen (Schnitzler), 1907
Dämonenzug (Weiss), 1928
Dan vedina metaylim betel aviv (Goldberg), 1940
Dance Goes On (Golding), 1937
Dance in the Sun (D. Jacobson), 1956
Dance of Gengis Cohn (Gary), 1969
Dance the Eagle to Sleep (Piercy), 1970
Dance with Desire (Layton), 1986
Dancing Bear (Bermant), 1984
Dancing Socrates (Tuwim), 1968
Danger! Memory! (Miller), 1987
Danger Zone (Spark), 1961
Dangerous Places (Golding), 1951
Dangling Man (Bellow), 1944
Dani mehunani benyu york (Avidan), 1993
Daniel (Doctorow), 1983
Daniel (Weiss), 1924
Daniel Daniel (Ayalon), 1988
Daniel Hertz (Nathansen), 1908
Daniel Webster (Stein), 1937
Daniella (Ka-Tzetnik 135633), 1980
Danny vehatuki (Goldberg), 1980
Dans la Double Dépendance du dit (Jabès), 1984
Dans Le Silence de l'Aleph (Vigée), 1992
Danse de Gengis Cohn (Gary), 1967
Dapim mimahazor nesher (Guri), 1974
Daraçılar (Gerez), 1965
Dark Angel (Hellman), 1935
Dark Corner (Rosten), 1945
Dark Fields of the Republic (Rich), 1995
Dark Gate (Vogel), 1976
Dark Gods (Millin), 1941
Dark Inheritance (Feinstein), 2000
Dark of the Sun (Saba), 1994
Dark Pilgrimage (Wassermann), 1933
Dark Pony (Mamet), 1977
Dark Prince (Golding), 1948
Dark River (Millin), 1919
Dark Soliloquy (Kolmar), 1975
Darkness at Noon (Koestler), 1940
Darkness Casts No Shadow (Lustig), 1976
Darlan (Mikes), 1943
Darling (Raphael), 1965
Dass ich in dieser Sprache schreibe (Viertel), 1981
Dat hayeled (Korczak), 1978
Dat het's ochtends ochtend wordt (Herzberg), 1974
Dateline (Rosten), 1939
Dauphins (Moravia), 1960

Davar aher (Carmi), 1970
Davar optimi, asiyat shirim (Wieseltier), 1976
David (Lunel), 1952
David August (Ben-Ner), 1983
David, It is Getting Dark (Kops), 1970
David Rëubeni in Portugal (Brod), 1927
David's Stranger (Shamir), 1965
Davita's Harp (Potok), 1985
Dawn (Odets), 1926
Dawn (Wiesel), 1961
Dawn Ginsbergh's Revenge (Perelman), 1929
Dawn O'Hara (Ferber), 1911
Day before Yesterday (Winter), 1985
Day in Regensburg (Opatoshu), 1968
Day of Atonement (Alvarez), 1991
Day of Atonement (Golding), 1925
Day of the Countess (Shahar), 1976
Day of the Ghosts (Shahar), 1989
Day of the Locust (West), 1939
Day of the Women and the Night of the Men (Mankowitz), 1977
Day the Earth Caught Fire (Mankowitz), 1961
Day Will Come (Feuchtwanger), 1944
Dayagim (Heijermans), 1927
Dayarim (Sobol), 1978
Daybreak (Schnitzler), 1927
Daylife and Nightlife (Fainlight), 1971
Daylight (Feinstein), 1997
Days of Miracles and Wonders (Louvish), 1997
Days to Come (Hellman), 1936
De algun tiempo a esta parte (Aub), 1949
De Chepén a La Habana (Goldemberg), 1973
De la France trahie à la France en armes (Bloch), 1949
De Nos Oiseaux (Tzara), 1923
De Vriendt Goes Home (A. Zweig), 1933
De Vriendt kehrt heim (A. Zweig), 1932
Dead End (Hellman), 1937
Dead Yesterdays (Ginzburg), 1956
Deadline at Dawn (Odets), 1943
Dean's December (Bellow), 1982
Dear Herm (Rosten), 1974
Dear Michael (Ginzburg), 1975
Dearest Father (Kafka), 1954
Death (Allen), 1975
Death and Fame Poems (Ginsberg), 1999
Death and Taxes (Kushner), 2000
Death and Taxes (Parker), 1931
Death and the Maiden (Dorfman), 1991
Death Defying Acts (Mamet), 1995
Death in the Rain (Almog), 1993
Death in Trieste (Raphael), 1981
Death Kit (Sontag), 1967
Death of a Ladies' Man (L. Cohen), 1977
Death of a Lady's Man (L. Cohen), 1978
Death of a Poor Man (Werfel), 1927
Death of a Salesman (Miller), 1947
Death of God (Jabès), 1979
Death of Lysanda (Orpaz), 1969
Death of Methuselah (Isaac Singer), 1988
Death of Moishe-Ganef (Louvish), 1986
Death of the Novel (Sukenick), 1969
Death of Virgil (Broch), 1945
Death Out of Season (Litvinoff), 1973
Deaths for the Ladies and Other Disasters (Mailer), 1962
Deborah (Kreitman), 1946
Debut (Brookner), 1981
Decadence (Berkoff), 1981
Deception (P. Roth), 1990
Deconstructing Harry (Allen), 1997
Decorated Man (Mulisch), 1973
Dedans (Cixous), 1969
Deeps of the Sea (Steiner), 1996
Deer Park (Mailer), 1955
Défense de Tartufe (Jacob), 1919
Dekalim utemarim (Zach), 1967
Del amor (Aub), 1960
Delfini (Moravia), 1960
Deliberate Death of a Polish Priest (Harwood), 1985
Délices (Rothenberg), 1997
Delight (Rothenberg), 1997
Délire à deux (Ionesco), 1962
Délivrance du souffle (Vigée), 1977
Déluge (Cixous), 1992
Dem tatns shotn (Glatshteyn), 1953
Demamah dakah (Shaham), 1983
Démanty noci (Lustig), 1959
Demerung in shpigl, lid un balade (Manger), 1937
Demo (Abse), 1969
Democracy (Brodsky), 1990
Démocratie (Brodsky), 1990
Demokratiia (Brodsky), 1990
Demolirte Literatur (Kraus), 1897
Den' vtoroi (Erenburg), 1934
Denn wo ist Heimat (Ausländer), 1994
Denti e spie (Pressburger), 1994
Deputy (Rothenberg), 1965
Derevo (Erenburg), 1946
Dernier des Justes (Schwarz-Bart), 1959
Dernier Empereur (Bloch), 1927
Derniers poèmes en vers et en prose (Jacob), 1945
Dertrunkener (Weissenberg), 1938
Dertseylungen (Israel Singer), 1949
Descent (Bergelson), 1999
Desconfiado prodigioso y otras obras (Aub), 1971
Description of a Struggle (Kafka), 1979
Description of Life (Riding), 1980
Deseada (Aub), 1950
Désert (Memmi), 1977
Desiat' loshadinykh sil (Erenburg), 1929
Despair (Stoppard), 1978
Destin du siècle (Bloch), 1931
Destin du théâtre (Bloch), 1930
Destroyed Days (Tzara), 1971
Detstvo (Babel'), 1979
Detstvo Liuvers (Pasternak), 1922
Deur stond open (Herzberg), 1972
Deuses de Raquel (Scliar), 1975
Deutschland (Fried), 1944
Devarim (Wallach), 1966
Devay (Shlonsky), 1924
Deviat'sot piaty god (Pasternak), 1927
Deviatyi val (Erenburg), 1951
Devil in Texas (Mankowitz), 1984
Devil That Failed (Samuel), 1952
Devil Tree (Kosinski), 1973
Devorah Baaron (Katzir), 2000
Di là dal cuore (Bassani), 1984
Dialogo (Ginzburg), 1990
Dialogue for Three (Pinter), 1963
Dialogue with Death (Koestler), 1942
Diamant (Mulisch), 1954
Diamantstad (Heijermans), 1904
Diamond Cutters (Rich), 1955
Diamonds for Breakfast (Harwood), 1968
Diamonds of the Night (Lustig), 1962
Diario de Djelfa (Aub), 1944
Diary of a Good Neighbour (Wesker), 1989
Diary of an Old Man (Bermant), 1966
Dice Cup (Jacob), 1979
Dick (Friedman), 1970
Dick Gibson Show (Elkin), 1971
Dickens (Maurois), 1934
Dickens of London (Mankowitz), 1976
Dietro la porta (Bassani), 1964
Dimanches d'août (Modiano), 1986
Dimdumin (Bergelson), 1946
Dinner at Eight (Ferber), 1932
Dio Kurt (Moravia), 1968
Diokan (Aini), 1988
Dirah leaskir (Goldberg), 1959
Direct Flight to Allah (Gary), 1975
Directions (Rothenberg), 1969
Dirty Dingus Magee (Heller), 1970
Dirty Linen (Stoppard), 1976
Disappearance of a Physicist (Josipovici), 1981
Disappearance of the Jews (Mamet), 1983
Disappearances (Auster), 1988
Discours du docteur O'Grady (Maurois), 1922
Discourses of Doctor O'Grady (Maurois), 1965
Discovery of Heaven (Mulisch), 1996
Discrete Series (Oppen), 1934
disent les imbéciles (Sarraute), 1976
Disner tshayld harold (Kulbak), 1933
Disparition (Perec), 1969
Disprezzo (Moravia), 1954
Disraeli (Maurois), 1927
Dissent of Dominick Shapiro (Kops), 1966
Dissolution of Dominic Boot (Stoppard), 1964
Disubbidienza (Moravia), 1948
Dita Sax (Lustig), 1966
Dita Saxová (Lustig), 1962
Divided Home/Land (Lasker-Schüler), 1992
Diving into the Wreck (Rich), 1973
Diving Rock on the Hudson (H. Roth), 1995
Diyun vehesbbon ishi al masa LSD (Avidan), 1968
DJ (Mailer), 1967
Do prostego człowieka (Tuwim), 1929
Do You Hear Them? (Sarraute), 1973
Dobro vam! (V. Grossman), 1967
Dobrota dnia (Slutskii), 1973
Doctor Almosada (Goldfaden), 1882
Doctor and the Devils (Harwood), 1986
Dr Clock's Last Case (Fainlight), 1994
Doctor Detroit (Friedman), 1983
Dr. Graesler (Schnitzler), 1923
Dr Kerhoven (Wassermann), 1932
Dr Wahl (Nathansen), 1915
Doctor Zhivago (Pasternak), 1958
Doctors of Philosophy (Spark), 1962
Dodim al hutim (Kishon), 1981
Doen en laten (Herzberg), 1994

Dog (Mamet), 1983
Dog It Was That Died (Stoppard), 1982
Dogg's Hamlet, Cahoot's Macbeth (Stoppard), 1979
Dogg's Our Pet (Stoppard), 1971
Doggy Bag (Sukenick), 1994
Dogs of Pavlov (Abse), 1969
Doktor Gräsler, Badearzt (Schnitzler), 1917
Doktor Zhivago (Pasternak), 1957
Dolly City 1992
Domenica d'estate (Moravia), 1961
Don Juan (Maurois), 1930
Don Juan and His Friend Shipel (Shabtai),1978
Don't Bother to Knock (Raphael), 1971
Don't Call It Night (Oz), 1995
Don't Call it Suicide (Ezekiel), 1993
Don't Drink the Water (Allen), 1966
Don't Go Away Mad (Ginsberg), 1968
Don't Stop the Carnival (Wouk), 1965
Don't Tread on Me (Perelman), 1987
Donna del fiume (Moravia), 1954
Doomington Wanderer (Golding), 1934
Doppelspiel (Ausländer), 1977
Dor hoylekh ve-dor bo (Weissenberg), 1904
Dor oys, dor eyn (Markish), 1929
Dora Kremer (Heijermans), 1893
Dorando la pildora (Dorfman), 1985
Dortn vu es nekhtikn di shtern (Sutzkever), 1979
Dortn, vu di tseder (Leyvik), 1938
Doscientas ballenas azules (Glantz), 1979
Doświadczenia (Rudnicki), 1939
Double Dynamite (Rosten), 1952
Double Life (Jacob), 1989
Double Life (Raphael), 1993
Double or Nothing (Federman), 1971
Double, Double, Toil and Trouble (Feuchtwanger), 1943
Dov duboni ben dubim metsahtseah naalayim (Goldberg), 1987
Dovid hamelekh un zayne vayber (Pinski), 1914–16
Down with Everybody! (Mikes), 1951
Downhill All the Way (Woolf), 1967
Doyres (Grade), 1945
Dray hoyptshtet (Der Nister), 1934
Dray shvester (M. Katz), 1932
Dream in the Afternoon (Litvinoff), 1967
Dream Life of Balso Snell (West), 1931
Dream of a Common Language (Rich), 1978
Dream of Peter Mann (Kops), 1960
Dream Room (Möring), 2002
Dreamers (Feinstein), 1994
Dreamers of the Ghetto (Zangwill), 1898
Dreams of Anne Frank (Kops), 1992
Dreams of Mrs Fraser (Josipovici), 1972
Drei angelsächsische Stücke (Feuchtwanger), 1927
Drei Kühe (Kisch), 1938
Drei Sprünge des Wang-lun (Döblin), 1915
Drenkeling (Durlacher), 1987
Dress of Fire (Ravikovitch), 1976
Dresser (Harwood), 1980
Drinks before Dinner (Doctorow), 1979
Dritte Kugel (Perutz), 1915
Dritte Walpurgisnacht (Kraus), 1952
Driver's Seat (Spark), 1970
Droles de Journal (Rakosi), 1981
Droomkoninkje (Heijermans), 1924
Drop Dead Darling (Harwood), 1966
Droppings From Heaven (Layton), 1979
Drowning (Durlacher), 1993
Dry Heart (Ginzburg), 1949
Dry River Bed (Spark), 1959
Dschin (Werfel), 1919
Du côté de chez Swann (Proust), 1913
Du Désert au livre (Jabès), 1980
Du Plus Loin de l'Oubli (Modiano), 1996
Dubim vayaar (Ben-Ner), 1995
Dubin's Lives (Malamud), 1979
Duck and the Goat (Mamet), 1996
Duck Variations (Mamet), 1972
Duczika (Heijermans), 1926
Dudayim min haarets hakedoshah (Megged), 1998
Due cortigiane (Moravia), 1945
Due gemelli (Pressburger), 1996
Duel Site (Abish), 1970
Duel-l (Federman), 1991
Duet for Cannibals (Sontag), 1969
Dugit mafligah layam (Tammuz), 1970
Duke of Bedford's Book of Snobs (Mikes), 1965
Duma pro Opanasa (Bagritskii), 1932
Dumb Waiter (Pinter), 1959
Durchbruch ins Wunder (Brod), 1962
Dusk Before Fireworks (Parker), 1962
Dutch Merchant (Feuchtwanger), 1934
Dvash (Sobol), 1997
Dwarfs (Pinter), 1960
Dwelling Place of My People (Agnon), 1983
Dwoje ludzieńków (Leśmian), 1993
Dybbuk (An-ski), 1926
Dybbuk (Kushner), 1998
Dying (Schnitzler), 1977
Dying Animal (P. Roth), 2001
Dzek Hakatan (Korczak), 1963
Dzieci ulicy (Korczak), 1901
Dziecko salonu (Korczak), 1906
Dziejba Leśna (Leśmian), 1938
Dzshike gas (Molodovski), 1933

È stato così (Ginzburg), 1947
Earlsdon Way (Raphael), 1958
Early Chapters (D. Baron), 1988
Early Grrrl (Piercy), 1999
Early in the Summer of 1970 (Yehoshua), 1977
Early Life (Raphael), 1979
Early Sorrows (Kiš), 1998
Earth Suite (Rakosi), 1997
Earwitness (E. Canetti), 1979
East (Berkoff), 1975
East into Upper East (Jhabvala), 1998
East is East (Mikes), 1958
East of Eden (Israel Singer), 1939
East River (Asch), 1946
Eastwood Ha! (Perelman), 1977
Eating (Shabtai),1999
Eating an Apple (Tussman), 1975
Eccentric (Abse), 1961
Echo (Josipovici), 1978
Echo (Stryjkowski), 1988
Echo Chamber (Josipovici), 1980
Eclipse (Auster), 1977
Eclipse Fever (Abish), 1993
Écoute Israël (Fleg), 1913–21
Ecstasy of Dr Miriam Garner (Feinstein), 1976
Ed hamelekh (Shaham), 1975
Eddy king (Aloni), 1975
Edgia's Revenge (Rosenfarb), 1994
Edmond (Mamet), 1982
Edo and Enam (Agnon), 1966
Edouard VII et son temps (Maurois), 1933
Edsel (K. Shapiro), 1971
Education before Verdun (A. Zweig), 1936
Éducation Européenne (Gary), 1945
Education of Hyman Kaplan (Rosten), 1937
Edward II (Feuchtwanger), 1966
Edwardian Era (Maurois), 1933
Een Abessijnse woestijnkat (Winter), 1991
Een goed hoofd (Herzberg), 1991
Een leeg huis (Minco), 1966
Een vrouw als Eva (Herzberg), 1979
Eergisteren, overmorgen (Winter), 1990
Egipetskaia marka (Mandel'shtam), 1928
Egyptian Stamp (Mandel'shtam), 1965
Egyptisch (Mulisch), 1983
Ehad efes letovatenu (Shamir), 1951
Ehe (Döblin), 1931
Eight Chambers of the Heart (Piercy), 1995
Eight Humorists (Mikes), 1954
Eimah gedolah veyareah (Greenberg), 1925
Einander (Werfel), 1915
Einblicke, Durchblicke (Fried), 1993
Einen Drachen reiten (Ausländer), 1980
Einsame Weg (Schnitzler), 1904
Einsamen (Feuchtwanger), 1903
Einsetzung eines Königs (A. Zweig), 1937
Einverständnis (Ausländer), 1980
Eisenhower le libérateur (Maurois), 1945
Eizor Magen uneum ben hadam (Greenberg), 1930
El (Jabès), 1973
El (Kovner), 1980
El erets aheret (Carmi), 1977
El erets hagomeh (Applefeld), 1986
El har hazeytim (Shahar), 1998
El hatsippor (Megged), 1974
El hayeladim beteiman (Megged), 1946
Eldest (Ferber), 1925
Ele masaot yonaton (Kishon), 1981
Elected Member (Rubens), 1969
Elef gadyiah vegadyiah (Kishon), 1954
Elefante verde (Pressburger), 1988
Elegies (Rukeyser), 1949
Elegy to John Donne (Brodsky), 1967
Elektra (Kiš), 1969
Elektrik tsher (Asch), 1923
Elementen (Mulisch), 1988
Elfenbeinfächer (A. Zweig), 1952
Elijah the Slave (Isaac Singer), 1970
Eliyohu hanovi (Hirshbein), 1915
Elle est là (Sarraute), 1978
Elsewhere, Perhaps (Oz), 1973
Elu veelu (Agnon), 1932
Elya (Jabès), 1969
Elyakum (Tammuz), 1969
Em'n Ben (Taylor), 1971
Embezzled Heaven (Werfel), 1940
Emet vehovah (Carmi), 1993

Emil un Karl (Glatshteyn), 1940
Emma McChesney and Co (Ferber), 1915
Emperor's Tomb (J. Roth), 1984
Empire of the Sun (Stoppard), 1986
Empty Canvas (Moravia), 1961
Empty House (Minco), 1990
Empty Mirror (Ginsberg), 1961
En Sommernat (Nathansen), 1899
En/Of (Herzberg), 1985
Enchanters (Gary), 1975
Enchanteurs (Gary), 1973
Enciklopedija mrtvih (Kiš), 1983
Encounters (Abse), 2001
Encyclopedia of the Dead (Kiš), 1989
End of Days (Hazaz), 1982
End of It (Alvarez), 1958
End of the Season is the End of the World (Avidan), 1962
End to Innocence (Fiedler), 1955
Endless Short Story (Sukenick), 1986
Enemies (Isaac Singer), 1972
Enemy of the People (Miller), 1950
Enemy Scope (Ben-Ner), 1999
Energia meshurbetet (Avidan), 1979
Energy of Slaves (L. Cohen), 1972
Enfance (Sarraute), 1983
Enfant prophète (Fleg), 1926
Engagement (Stoppard), 1970
Engelhart (Wassermann), 1973
English Humour for Beginners (Mikes), 1980
Enigma (Stoppard), 2000
Enigmatic Eye (Scliar), 1989
Enormous Changes at the Last Minute (Paley), 1974
Enough Rope (Parker), 1926
Enter a Free Man (Stoppard), 1968
Enter Solly Gold (Kops), 1962
Entertainment for Elizabeth (Hollander), 1972
Entfremdung (Werfel), 1990
Entre la diáspora y octubre (Goloboff), 1966
Entre la vie et la mort (Sarraute), 1968
Entsühnung (Broch), 1934
Ephraim Goes Back to Alfalfa (Yizhar), 1938
Epic of Lofoten (Mikes), 1941
Epidemia (Moravia), 1944
Epigrafe (Saba), 1959
Epigramme (Kraus), 1927
Epitaffio (Bassani), 1974
Epoka pieców (Rudnicki), 1948
Equally Divided (Harwood), 1999
Equus (Shaffer), 1973
Er lebt! (Pinski), 1946
Erben der Tante Jolesch (Torberg), 1978
Erd (Asch), 1910
Erd (Hirshbein), 1907
Erdishe vegn (Halkin), 1945
Erdvey (Israel Singer), 1922
Erets rehokah (Ben-Ner), 1981
Ere-VOICE (Rakosi), 1971
Erfolg (Feuchtwanger), 1930
Ergets oyf felder (Greenberg), 1915
Ergets vayt (Leyvik), 1940
Ergo (Lind), 1966
Erica, I Want to Read You Something (Kops), 1967
Ermordung einer Butterblume (Döblin), 1913
Ernesto (Saba), 1975
Erotic Tales (Moravia), 1985
Ershte nakht in geto (Sutzkever), 1979
Ershter melekh in yisroel (Hirshbein), 1934
Erstes Erlebnis (S. Zweig), 1911
Erzählungen aus zwei Welten (Werfel), 1948–54
Erziehung vor Verdun (A. Zweig), 1935
Es bleibt noch viel zu sagen (Ausländer), 1978
Es ist alles anders (Ausländer), 1977
Es ist was es ist (Fried), 1983
Esau (Shalev), 1993
Esav (Shalev), 1991
Esev pere (Orpaz), 1959
Esli verit' pifagoreitsam (V. Grossman), 1946
Esmond in India (Jhabvala), 1958
Espagne, Espagne! (Bloch), 1936
Espejo de avaricia (Aub), 1935
Essai sur Dickens (Maurois), 1927
Essay in Autobiography (Pasternak), 1990
Essay on Rime (K. Shapiro), 1945
Estate (Isaac Singer), 1969
Ester hamalka (Alterman), 1966
Esther de Carpentras (Lunel), 1925
Esther K Comes to America, 1931 (Rothenberg), 1974
Estranha nação de Rafael Mendes (Scliar), 1983
... et Cie (Bloch), 1918
Et hazar vehaoyev (Almog), 1980
Et j'ai voulu la paix (Spire), 1916
Et s'il n'en reste qu'une (Lunel), 1937
Et Tu Aimeras l'Éternel (Fleg), 1948
Et vous riez! (Spire), 1905
Été indien (Vigée), 1957
Eternal Road (Werfel), 1936
Éternel est Notre Dieu (Fleg), 1940
Éternel est Un (Fleg), 1945
Étranger avec, sous le bras, un livre de petit format (Jabès), 1989
Etsel (Gnessin), 1913
Etsel babou (Lapid), 1998
Etsem bagaron (Kishon), 1967
Etsem el atsmo (Shaham), 1981
Etwas von Mir (Lasker-Schüler), 1930
Etzel Andergast (Wassermann), 1931
Eureka! (Mikes), 1965
Europa (Gary), 1972
Europe and Other Bad News (Layton), 1981
European Education (Gary), 1960
Europeans (Jhabvala), 1979
Eva Bonheur (Heijermans), 1919
Eve of War, 1933–41 (Erenburg), 1963
Even a Fist Was Once an Open Palm with Fingers (Amichai), 1991
Even al pi habeer (Shaham), 1956
Even tahat even (Gur), 1998
Every Day Has Its Dog (Spiegelman), 1979
Every Good Boy Deserves Favour (Stoppard), 1977
Every One Had Six Wings (Bartov), 1971
Everybody Wins (Miller), 1990
Everyone Says I Love You (Allen), 1996
Everything You Always Wanted to Know about Sex (Allen), 1972
Evidence of Intimacy (Josipovici), 1969
Evidence of Love (D. Jacobson), 1960
Evita Perón (Harwood), 1981
Evreiskie rasskazy (Babel'), 1927
Ex Cranium, Night (Rakosi), 1975
Exact Time (Ezekiel), 1965
Exagggerations of Peter Prince (S. Katz), 1968
Examination (Torberg), 1932
Executioners (Raphael), 1961
Executioner's Song (Mailer), 1982
Exército de um homem só (Scliar), 1973
Exil (Feuchtwanger), 1940
Exit the King (Ionesco), 1963
Exodus (Kaniuk), 2000
Exodus (Uris), 1959
Experience of India (Jhabvala), 1971
Experimente (Brod), 1907
Experts Are Puzzled (Riding), 1930
Explanation of America (Pinsky), 1979
Expresso Bongo (Mankowitz), 1958
Exquisite Cadaver (Mankowitz), 1990
Extraordinary Adventures of Julio Jurenito and His Disciples (Erenburg), 1930
Eybiker yid (Pinski), 1906
Eyes of Reason (Heym), 1951
Eyes Wide Shut (Raphael), 1999
Eyesight of Wasps (Mandel'shtam), 1989
Eyewitness (Harwood), 1970
Eyewitness (Weiss), 1977
Eyn perahim shehorim (Carmi), 1953
Eynayim yehefot (Perry), 1974
Eyns af eyns (Markish), 1934
Ezra (Kops), 1981

Faber (Wassermann), 1925
Fable (Taylor), 1967
Fábula verde (Aub), 1932
Fabyus lind (Glants-Leyeles), 1937
Face of Terror (Litvinoff), 1978
Face to Face (Gordimer), 1949
Facing the Forests (Yehoshua), 1970
Facing the Music (Auster), 1980
Facing the Sea 1983
Fact of a Doorframe (Rich), 1984
Fadensonnen (Celan), 1968
Fahrt ins Land ohne Tod (Döblin), 1937
Fahrt ins Staublose (Sachs), 1961
Fall (Minco), 1990
Fall des Generalstabschefs Redl (Kisch), 1924
Fall Glasenapp (Heym), 1958
Fall Maurizius (Wassermann), 1928
Fall of America (Ginsberg), 1972
Fall of Mendel Crick (Richler), 1963
Fall of Paris (Erenburg), 1942
Fall of the House of Usher (Berkoff), 1974
Fall Vukobrankovics (Weiss), 1924
Falling Slowly (Brookner), 1998
Falls the Shadow (Litvinoff), 1983
Falsche Gewicht (J. Roth), 1937
Falsche Nero (Feuchtwanger), 1936
Fälscher (Brod), 1920
Fame and Folly (Ozick), 1996
Fame, and The Reason Why (Miller), 1970
Famiglia (Ginzburg), 1977
Famiglia Manzoni (Ginzburg), 1983
Family (Ginzburg), 1988
Family (Harwood), 1978
Family and Friends (Brookner), 1985
Family Carnovsky (Israel Singer), 1969

Family Circle (Maurois), 1932
Family Markowitz (Goodman), 1996
Family Mashber (Der Nister), 1948
Family Moskat (Isaac Singer), 1950
Family Romance (Brookner), 1993
Family Sayings (Ginzburg), 1967
Family Ties (Lispector), 1972
Family Tree (Glantz), 1991
Family Voices (Pinter), 1981
Familye mushkat (Isaac Singer), 1950
Familye tsvi (Pinski), 1905
Fan (Parker), 1949
Fanatik (Goldfaden), 1880
Fancy Dress Party (Moravia), 1947
Fanfarlo (Spark), 1952
Fanny (Jong), 1980
Fanny Herself (Ferber), 1917
Far Cry from Kensington (Spark), 1988
Far dem nayem fundament (Halkin), 1932
Far folk un heymland (Markish), 1943
Far from the City of Class (Friedman), 1963
Far from the Madding Crowd (Raphael), 1967
Far Land (Ben-Ner), 1992
Far over the Sea (Bialik), 1939
Far yugnt (Manger), 1937
Farbaygeyendik (Markish), 1921
Farbisener (Weissenberg), 1966
Farewell, Baghdad (Amir), 1993
Farklepte tsiferblatn (Markish), 1929
Farloyrene mentshn (Opatoshu), 1922
Farn mabl (Asch), 1929
Farnakhtengold (Greenberg), 1921
Farvoksene vegn (Grade), 1947
Farvorfn vinkl (Hirshbein), 1912
Fast alles Mögliche (Fried), 1975
Fat of the Land (Yezierska), 1919
Fat Tuesday (Sherman), 1966
Fathers (Weissbort), 1991
Father's Kisses (Friedman), 1996
Faustina (Wassermann), 1912
Favors (Rubens), 1979
Favourite Game (L. Cohen), 1963
Fear of Flying (Jong), 1973
Fearsome Inn (Isaac Singer), 1967
Feast in the Garden (Konrád), 1992
Feast of Euridice (Feinstein), 1980
Feeding Frenzy (Self), 2001
Feldzeugmeister Cratz (Döblin), 1926
Felicidade clandestina (Lispector), 1971
Felipe Alfau (Stavans), 1996
Felker zingen (Manger), 1936
Femme Couleur Tango (Dujovne Ortiz), 1998
Ferdinand (Zukofsky), 1968
Ferkishefter shnayder (Sholem), 1901
Fertsiker lider un poemen, 1903–1944 (Schneour), 1945
Fervandlung (Weissenberg), 1928
Feste Burg ist unser Gott (Feuchtwanger), 1911
Festtag in Manhattan (Ausländer), 1987
Festung (Sutzkever), 1945
Fetisch (Feuchtwanger), 1907
Fetish (Moravia), 1964
Feu d'une nuit d'hiver (Vigée), 1989
Feuerchen im Hintennach (Schindel), 1992
Feuerpause (A. Zweig), 1954
Feuerprobe (Weiss), 1923
Feuilletons (Herzl), 1911
Fiancée juive (Cixous), 1995
Fiddle Rose (Sutzkever), 1990
Fiddler (Millin), 1929
Fidlroyz (Sutzkever), 1974
Fifteen Minute Hamlet (Stoppard), 1976
Fifteen to Infinity (Fainlight), 1983
Fifth Generation (Gershon), 1987
Fifth Son (Wiesel), 1985
Fifth Wheel (Shamir), 1961
Fifty Poems in the Wilderness (Preil), 1987
Figure e canti (Saba), 1926
Figured Wheel (Pinsky), 1996
Figurehead (Hollander), 1999
Filibuth (Jacob), 1922
Film Crew (Mamet), 1983
Fils d'Abraham (Halter), 1989
Filz (Heym), 1992
Fima (Oz), 1993
Final Balance (Pinski), 1926
Final Reckoning (Layton), 1987
Finally a Valentine (Zukofsky), 1965
Find the Lady (Litvinoff), 1971
Finf shreklekhe mayses (Weissenberg), 1927
Finf un zibetsig toyznt (Sholem), 1902
Fink und Fliederbusch (Schnitzler), 1917
Fire and Silence (Preil), 1968
Fire in Heaven (Abse), 1948
Firkantike oysyes un mofsim (Sutzkever), 1968
First Awakening (Riding), 1992
First Blues (Ginsberg), 1975
First Celestial Adventure of Mister Benzedrine (Tzara), 1996
First Day (D. Baron), 2001
First Days of the Year (Cixous), 1998
First Half of A–9 (Zukofsky), 1934
First Leaf (Riding), 1933
First Love and Other Sorrows (Brodkey), 1957
First Meeting (Gershon), 1974
First Offenders (Friedman), 1973
First Sin (Megged), 1989
First Years of Revolution, 1918–21 (Erenburg), 1962
Firstborn (Carmi), 1958
Fishke der krumer (Mendele Moykher Sforim), 1869
Fishke the Lame (Mendele Moykher Sforim), 1960
Five Came Back (West), 1939
Five Days in June (Heym), 1977
Five Finger Exercise (Shaffer), 1958
Five Seasons (Yehoshua), 1989
Five Silver Daughters (Golding), 1934
Five Stories of Ferrara (Bassani), 1971
Five Unrelated Pieces (Mamet), 1983
Five Year Sentence (Rubens), 1978
Fixer (Malamud), 1966
Flamen fun der erd (Shpigl), 1966
Flammen auf San Domingo (Perutz), 1929
Flat to Let (Goldberg), 1972
Flatbush Tosca (Fierstein), 1975
Fleurs de ruine (Modiano), 1991
Flight into Darkness (Schnitzler), 1931
Flight without End (J. Roth), 1930
Flirtations (Schnitzler), 1982
Floating Light Bulb (Allen), 1982
Floden (Nathansen), 1902
Florida Special (Perelman), 1936
Florry of Washington Heights (S. Katz), 1987
Flow (Josipovici), 1973
Flow Tide (Vigée), 1992
Flower Poems (Silkin), 1964
Flowering Peach (Odets), 1955
Flowers for Hitler (L. Cohen), 1964
Flowers of Perhaps (Rachel), 1994
Flucht in die Finsternis (Schnitzler), 1931
Flucht ohne Ende (J. Roth), 1927
Flucht und Verwandlung (Sachs), 1959
Flüchtling (Herzl), 1888
Fly away Home (Piercy), 1984
Focus (Miller), 1997
Foiglman (Megged), 1988
Folksfond oysgabe (Sholem), 1917–25
Folkstimlekh (Gebirtig), 1920
Folkstimlekhe geshikhtn (Perets), 1908
Folle de Chaillot (Carmi), 1979
Follow Me! (Shaffer), 1972
Follow Your Heart (West), 1936
Fond de l'eau (Jabès), 1947
Fond de l'eau (Jacob), 1927
Fools (Simon), 1981
Fools of Chelm and Their History (Isaac Singer), 1973
fools say (Sarraute), 1977
Foot in the Door (Friedman), 1979
Foot in the Door (Litvinoff), 1969
Footsteps on a Downcast Path (Silkin), 1984
For E.W. (Rothenberg), 1981
For Esme — With Love and Squalor (Salinger), 1953
For Every Sin (Applefeld), 1989
For Good or Evil (Sinclair), 1991
For My Brother Jesus (Layton), 1976
For My Neighbours in Hell (Layton), 1980
For No Good Reason (Sarraute), 1985
For the Record (Kops), 1971
For the Soul of the Planet is Wakening (Ginsberg), 1970
Forbidden Tree (Ausländer), 1995
Forces du monde (Bloch), 1927
Forcing House (Zangwill), 1923
Forecast, a Fable (Fainlight), 1958
Foreign Legion (Lispector), 1986
Foreigner Carrying in His Arm a Tiny Book (Jabès), 1993
Forest of Anger (Gary), 1944
Forever and Ever and a Wednesday (M. Katz), 1980
Forever Flowing (V. Grossman), 1972
Forget Him (Fierstein), 1988
Forgotten (Wiesel), 1992
Forma vremeni (Brodsky), 1992
Forms of Love (Oppen), 1975
Fornalutx (Layton), 1992
Fortunate Exile (Layton), 1987
Fortunes of a Fool (Megged), 1962
Forty Days (Werfel), 1934
Forty Days of Musa Dagh (Werfel), 1934
Forward from Babylon (Golding), 1920
Foter un zun (An-ski), 1906
Foterlekhe erd (Markish), 1938
Found Objects (Zukofsky), 1964

Four Portraits of Mothers (Wesker), 1984
Four Saints in Three Acts (Stein), 1934
Four Seasons (Wesker), 1965
Fournisseurs (Spire), 1923
Fourrure de ma Tante Rachel (Federman), 1996
Foursome (Ionesco), 1970
Fox (Rich), 2001
Fox in the Chicken Coop (Kishon), 1971
Foxhole in Bayswater (Litvinoff), 1968
Foygl fun geto (Rosenfarb), 1958
Fragment from Vietnam (Mailer), 1972
Fragmente (Werfel), 1919
Fragmented Life of Don Jacobo Lerner (Goldemberg), 1976
Fragments from Cold (Auster), 1977
Fragmenty utworów (Korczak), 1978
Franchiser (Elkin), 1976
Franco is Dying (A. Baron), 1977
Franny and Zooey (Salinger), 1961
Frantsuzskii kottedzh (Shrayer-Petrov), 1999
Franz a Felice (Klíma), 1983
Franzi (Brod), 1922
Franziska (Weiss), 1919
Frau Beate und ihr Sohn (Schnitzler), 1913
Frau Bertha Garlan (Schnitzler), 1901
Frau des Richters (Schnitzler), 1925
Frau des Weisen (Schnitzler), 1898
Frau, die nicht enttäuscht (Brod), 1933
Frau, nach der man sich sehnt (Brod), 1927
Frau und die Tiere (Kolmar), 1938
Fraud (Brookner), 1992
Frauenverkäufer (Feuchtwanger), 1923
Fräulein Else (Schnitzler), 1924
Fraye ferzn (Glatshteyn), 1926
Freaks (Fiedler), 1978
Freaky Pussy (Fierstein), 1973
Frédéric Chopin (Maurois), 1942
Free Agents (Apple), 1984
Free Game (Schnitzler), 1913
Free Vacation House (Yezierska), 1915
Freiheit den Mund aufzumachen (Fried), 1972
Freiwild (Schnitzler), 1897
Fremde neshome un andere dertseylungen (Pinski), 1938
French Lieutenant's Woman (Pinter), 1981
Frenzy for Two (Ionesco), 1965
Freundschaft mit der Mondin (Ausländer), 1987
Freyd fun yidishn vort (Glatshteyn), 1961
Freydke (Molodovski), 1935
Friday's Footprint (Gordimer), 1960
Fridolin and Albertine (Schnitzler), 1926
Friede (Feuchtwanger), 1917
Friend from England (Brookner), 1987
Friend of Kafka (Isaac Singer), 1970
Friends (Wesker), 1970
Frightening Talent (Golding), 1973
Friling (Israel Singer), 1937
Frog Prince (Mamet), 1984
From a Roman Balcony (Moravia), 1960
From A to Z (Allen), 1960
From Bondage (H. Roth), 1996
From Many Countries (Asch), 1958
From Nine to Nine (Perutz), 1926
From the Ashes of Thebes (Farhi), 1969
From the Book to the Book (Jabès), 1991
From the City, from the Plough (A. Baron), 1948
From the Desert to the Book (Jabès), 1990
From the Fair (Sholem), 1985
From the Greek (Raphael), 1979
From Threshold to Threshold (Celan), 1988
Frühe Fährten (A. Zweig), 1925
Frühe Gedichte (Fried), 1986
Frühen Kranze (S. Zweig), 1906
Fruitful and Multiplying (Mamet), 1996
Fruits and Vegetables (Jong), 1971
Fruits d'or (Sarraute), 1963
Füchse im Weinberg (Feuchtwanger), 1947
Fugitive (Proust), 1992
Fugitive Pieces (Michaels), 1999
Fugue in a Nursery (Fierstein), 1979
Fuite (Tzara), 1947
Fun alte un yunge ksav-yadn (Sutzkever), 1982
Fun finftn yor (Der Nister), 1964
Fun korbn minkhe (L. Shapiro), 1941
Fun lublin biz nyu-york (Molodovski), 1942
Fun mayn gantser mi (Glatshteyn), 1956
Fun mayne giter (Der Nister), 1929
Fund (V. Canetti), 2001
Funem yarid (Sholem), 1913
Funland (Abse), 1971
Fürchte dich nicht! neue Gedichte (Viertel), 1941
Further Confessions of Zeno (Svevo), 1969
Further Sightings and Conversations (Rothenberg), 1989
Future (L. Cohen), 1992
Future is in Eggs (Ionesco), 1960

Gaaguim leolga (Megged), 1994
Gabri un di froyen (Pinski), 1908
Gaguim (Hirshbein), 1901
Gai oni (Lapid), 1982
Galaganer hon (Markish), 1922
Galeere (Weiss), 1913
Galilei in Gefangenschaft (Brod), 1948
Gallows (Hazaz), 1963
Gályanapló (Kertész), 1992
Gam haegrof hayah paam yad petuhah (Amichai), 1989
Gamblers (Stoppard), 1965
Games (Klíma), 1981
Gan hahayot (Goldberg), 1941
Gan naul (Tammuz), 1957
Gan riki (D. Grossman), 1988
Gan sheharav (Raab), 1983
Gang zum Weiher (Schnitzler), 1926
Gangs of New York (West), 1938
Gänsemännchen (Wassermann), 1915
Garden, Ashes (Kiš), 1975
Garden of the Finzi-Continis (Bassani), 1965
Garry Moore Show (Simon), 1959–60
Gas Age (Zukofsky), 1969
Gas Heart (Tzara), 1964
Gasthaus zur Kartätsche (Perutz), 1920
Gatekeeper's Wife (Zwicky), 1998
Gates (Rukeyser), 1976
Gates of Bronze (Hazaz), 1975
Gates of the Forest (Wiesel), 1966
Gates of Wrath (Ginsberg), 1972
Gauchos judíos (Gerchunoff), 1910
Gaystike erd (Sutzkever), 1961
Géant du soleil (Jacob), 1904
Gebrengt a sod (Weissenberg), 1926
Geburt des Antichrist (Perutz), 1921
Gebürtig (Schindel), 1992
Gedakht (Der Nister), 1922
Gedanken un motivn (Der Nister), 1907
Gedenklider (Glatshteyn), 1943
Gedichte aus Der Gerichtstag (Werfel), 1919
Geduld bringt Rosen (V. Canetti), 1992
Gefährtin (Schnitzler), 1899
Gefängnisarzt (Weiss), 1934
Gegen das Vergessen (Fried), 1987
Gegengift (Fried), 1974
Geheimnis eines Menschen (Werfel), 1927
Geheimnisse (Josipovici), 1998
Geheymshtot (Sutzkever), 1948
Geier sind pünktliche Tiere (Schindel), 1987
Geist des Pilgers (Wassermann), 1923
Geklibende lider (Gebirtig), 1954
Geklibns (Fefer), 1940
Gelbe Strasse (V. Canetti), 1990
Gelobte Land (Brod), 1917
Gematria (Rothenberg), 1990
Gematria 5 (Rothenberg), 1987
Genealogías (Glantz), 1981
Genesis (Schwartz), 1943
Genoa Ferry (Harwood), 1976
Gentle Folk (A. Baron), 1976
Gents (Sholem), 1902
Geografía (Aub), 1929
Geography and Plays (Stein), 1922
Georg Letham, Arzt und Mörder (Weiss), 1931
George Mills (Elkin), 1982
George Washington September, Sir! (Harwood), 1961
Gerbert i Nèlli (Shrayer-Petrov), 1992
Gerichtstag (Werfel), 1919
Germany Laughs at Herself (Mikes), 1965
Geronimo de Aguilar (Wassermann), 1923
Gerufene Schatten (A. Zweig), 1923
Gerushim meuharim (Yehoshua), 1982
Gesammelte zionistische (Herzl), 1934–35
Gesänge aus den drei Reichen (Werfel), 1917
Geschichte der jungen Renate Fuchs (Wassermann), 1900
Geschichte von der 1002. Nacht (J. Roth), 1939
Geschichten aus sieben Ghettos (Kisch), 1934
Geschwister Oppermann (Feuchtwanger), 1933
Geschwister von Neapel (Werfel), 1931
Geshikhte fun vilner ger-tsedek graf valentin pototski (Karpinovich), 1990
Gesichte der Simone Machard (Feuchtwanger), 1957
Gestohlene Stadt (Kisch), 1922
Get Ready for Battle (Jhabvala), 1962
Geto un andere lider (Rosenfarb), 1948
Getting Even (Allen), 1971
Geule komedie–der goylem khulemt (Leyvik), 1934
Geut hahol (Aini), 1992
Geven, geven amol vilne (Karpinovich), 1997
Geyen shikhlekh avek (Molodovski), 1930
Gezang fun tol (Asch), 1938
Gezang un gebet (Der Nister), 1912
Gezangen fun rekhts tsu links (Glatshteyn), 1971
Gezochte spiegel (Mulisch), 1983
Ghetto (Heijermans), 1899
Ghetto (Sobol), 1984

Ghetto Comedies (Zangwill), 1907
Ghetto Kingdom (Shpigl), 1954
Ghetto Tragedies (Zangwill), 1893
Ghost at Noon (Moravia), 1955
Ghost Writer (P. Roth), 1979
Ghosts (Auster), 1986
Giant (Ferber), 1952
Giardino dei Finzi-Contini (Bassani), 1962
Gib acht, Genosse Mandelbaum (Hilsenrath), 1979
Giborei kayits (Aini), 1991
Gift of Asher Lev (Potok), 1990
Gift of the Gorgon (Shaffer), 1992
Giganten (Döblin), 1932
Gigolo (Ferber), 1922
Gilgil (Almog), 1986
Gilgil rotsa kelev (Almog), 1998
Gilgul (Pagis), 1970
Gili's Water Man (Gilboa), 1963
Gimpel the Fool (Isaac Singer), 1957
Gimpl tam un andere dertseylungen (Isaac Singer), 1963
Ginger Golly and the Fable Men (Taylor), 1972
Gingerbread Lady (Simon), 1970
Ginsberg's Improvised Poetics (Ginsberg), 1971
Gioco segreto (Morante), 1941
Gioconda (Mankowitz), 1987
Giornata balorda (Moravia), 1960
Girl in Melanie Klein (Harwood), 1969
Girls (Ferber), 1921
Girls of Slender Means (Spark), 1963
Girls of Toledo (Sobol), 1992
Giulietta (Ginzburg), 1934
Givat hahol (Agnon), 1920
Give Up Your Lovers (Golding), 1930
Gladiators (Koestler), 1939
Glasenapp Case (Heym), 1962
Glass Alembic (Feinstein), 1973
Glass Bridge (Minco), 1988
Glazen brug (Minco), 1986
Glengarry Glen Ross (Mamet), 1983
Glittering Prizes (Raphael), 1976
Gloke (M. Rosenfeld), 1888
Glory (Wouk), 1994
Glory of Elsie Silver (Golding), 1946
Glosse (Herzl), 1894
Głosy w ciemności (Stryjkowski), 1956
Glück auf! (V. Grossman), 1934
Gnadenbrot (Viertel), 1927
Go Tell the Lemming (Rubens), 1973
Goat Song (Werfel), 1926
Go-Away Bird (Spark), 1958
God (Allen), 1975
God in Ruins (Uris), 1999
God Knows (Heller), 1984
God of Vengeance (Asch), 1918
God-Fearer (D. Jacobson), 1992
Godovaia strelka (Slutskii), 1971
God's Favorite (Simon), 1974
God's Grace (Malamud), 1982
Gods of Raquel (Scliar), 1986
God's Step-Children (Millin), 1924
Gody voiny (V. Grossman), 1946
Gog vemagog (Sobol), 1977
Going down Fast (Piercy), 1969
Going To and Fro and Walking Up and Down (Reznikoff), 1941
Going Up to Sotheby's (Spark), 1982
Gold (Feinstein), 2000
Gold (Wassermann), 1924
Goldberg (Josipovici), 1990
Goldberg Street (Mamet), 1985
Golden Boy (Odets), 1937
Golden Fruits (Sarraute), 1964
Golden Princess (A. Baron), 1954
Golden Years (Miller), 1987
Goldene pave (Halpern), 1924
Goldene Spiegel (Wassermann), 1912
Goldgreber (Sholem), 1908
Goldkorn Tales (Epstein), 1985
Gold-Rimmed Eyeglasses (Bassani), 1975
Gold-Rimmed Spectacles (Bassani), 1960
Goldsborough (Heym), 1953
Golem (Kops), 1998
Golem (Isaac Singer), 1982
Golem bemaagal (Perry), 1986
Golems Wiederkehr (Torberg), 1968
Golpe de gracia (Goldemberg), 2001
Gone (Abse), 1962
Gone in January (Abse), 1977
Gone to Soldiers (Piercy), 1987
Gönülden Damlalar (Gerez), 1952
Good (Taylor), 1981
Good as Gold (Heller), 1979
Good Companions (Harwood), 1974
Good Doctor (Simon), 1973
Good Hope (Heijermans), 1912,
Good Hunting (West), 1938
Goodbye, Columbus (P. Roth), 1959
Goodbye, Dear England (Millin), 1965
Goodbye Girl (Simon), 1977
Goodbye Kiss (Harwood), 2000
Goodbye to Ithaca (Golding), 1955
Goodbye World (Kops), 1959
Goose Man (Wassermann), 1922
Gorky Poems (Rothenberg), 1966
Got fun nekome (Asch), 1907
Got, mentsh un tayvl (Gordin), 1900
Gots gefangene (Asch), 1933
Goya (Feuchtwanger), 1951
Goylem (Leyvik), 1921
Grace Darling Show (Taylor), 1971
Graduate Wife (Raphael), 1962
Graft (Berkoff), 1998
Grains et issues (Tzara), 1935
Grand Vestiaire (Gary), 1948
Grandchildren (Kops), 2000
Grandchildren of the Ghetto (Zangwill), 1914
Grandes Chaleurs (Ionesco), 1960
Grandpa and the Statue (Miller), 1945
Graue Tuch (Viertel), 1994
Great American Novel (P. Roth), 1973
Great Apes (Self), 1997
Great Demonstration (Zangwill), 1892
Great Fair (Sholem), 1955
Great Longing (Möring), 1995
Great Son (Ferber), 1945
Great Tranquillity (Amichai), 1983
Great Wall of China (Kafka), 1933
Greek (Berkoff), 1980
Green Cockatoo (Schnitzler), 1913
Green Elephant (Pressburger), 1994
Green Wave (Rukeyser), 1948
Grens (Mulisch), 1975
Grey Area (Self), 1994
Grey Wig (Zangwill), 1903
Griechische Tänzerin (Schnitzler), 1905
Grine felder trilogy (Hirshbein), 1923
Grine tsores (M. Rosenfeld), 1919
Griner akvariyum (Sutzkever), 1975
Grobnica za Borisa Davidoviča (Kiš), 1976
Gros-Câlin (Gary), 1974
Grosman un zun (Asch), 1954
Gross Intrusion (Berkoff), 1979
Grosse Wagnis (Brod), 1918
Grote verlangen (Möring), 1992
Ground Work (Auster), 1990
Growing (Woolf), 1961
Groyse gevins (Sholem), 1915
Grüne Kakadu (Schnitzler), 1899
Guardsman (Miller), 1947
Gucci Bag (Layton), 1983
Guermantes Way (Proust), 1925
Guerra de los hermanos (Glantz), 1982
Guerra no Bom Fim (Scliar), 1972
Guest for the Night (Agnon), 1968
Guest of Honour (Gordimer), 1970
Guests (Harwood), 2000
Guests of Honour (Harwood), 1965
Guf rishon rabim (Shaham), 1968
Guilt Merchants (Harwood), 1963
Guiltless (Broch), 1974
Guilty Head (Gary), 1969
Gumot hahen shel zohar (Shalev), 1987
Gunfight at the OK Corral (Uris), 1957
Gurney (Silkin), 1985
Guru (Jhabvala), 1969
Gutapersha (Hoffman), 1993
Gynt (Taylor), 1973

Ha galgal hahamishi (Shamir), 1958
Ha veda (Gurevitch), 1996
Haatalef (Megged), 1975
Haavot vehabanim (Mendele Moykher Sforim), 1868
Habaday (Bartov), 1975
Habalon shehalakh lemakom aher (Hareven), 1994
Habayit shebo metim hadzhukim miseivah tovah (Kaniuk), 1976
Habilti musariyim (Ayalon), 1996
Habivar healiz (Goldberg), 1947
Habrihah (Megged), 1962
Hadimah (Ka-Tzetnik 135633), 1978
Hadod perets mamri (Shabtai),1972
Hadod zyame (Schneour), 1945
Hadodah liza (Aloni), 1968
Haelem (Orpaz), 1984
Haelim atselim (Shaham), 1949
Haesev vehahol (Schütz), 1978
Hafetsim (Yehoshua), 1986
Haflagot (Lapid), 1994
Hagalgal hahamishi (Shamir), 1966
Hagamal hameofef vedabeshet hazahav (Megged), 1982
Haganav ha nadiv (Kaniuk), 1980
Hagavia hu shelanu (Kishon), 1981
Hagavrut haolah (Greenberg), 1926
Haggadah (Wiesel), 1980

Hagigat hakayits (Alterman), 1965
Hagigolo mikongo (Levini), 1989
Hagigolo mikongo vetipusim aherim (Levini), 1994
Hagolim (D. Baron), 1970
Hagorat mazzalot (Hazaz), 1958
Hagvirah (Orpaz), 1983
Hagvul (Shamir), 1966
Hagyaték (Konrád), 1998
Hahakirah (Guri), 1981
Hahalil vahahets (Ravikovitch), 1963
Hahamsin Haaharon (Hendel), 1969
Haharpatkah habilti gemurah (Kishon), 1981
Hahatser shel momo hagedolah (Hendel), 1969
Hahay al hamet (Megged), 1965
Hahayim haketsarim (Megged), 1972
Hahayim kemashal (Sadeh), 1958
Haheshbon vehanefesh (Bartov), 1953
Hahizdamnut haaharona (Schütz), 1980
Haholeh hanitshi vehaahuvah (Levini), 1986
Haholkhim bahoshekh (Levini), 1998
Haholkhim bahoshekh (Ratosh)
Hahom vehakor (Bejerano), 1981
Hahorshah bagivah (Yizhar), 1947
Hahuliyah (Hareven), 1986
Hahut hameshulash (Alterman), 1971
Hahut hameshulash (Shamir), 1957
Haimut (Ka-Tzetnik 135633), 1975
Hair vehakfar (Goldberg), 1939
Haish misham (Ben-Ner), 1967
Haisha hagedolah mehahalomot (Kenaz), 1973
Haishah hamuflaa betokhenu (Levini), 1994
Haj (Uris), 1984
Hajoker (Sobol), 1975
Hakalah hanitshit (Orpaz), 1988
Hakalah vetsiad haparparim (Aloni), 1967
Hakanaf hashlishit (Michael), 2000
Hakarmel haineireh (Zelda), 1971
Haketavim hayidiyim (Brenner), 1985
Haketuvah (Kishon), 1961
Hakhnasat kalah (Agnon), 1931
Hakinah nehamah (Shalev), 1990
Hakippah haserugah (Kishon), 1993
Hakoah Haaher (Hendel), 1984
Hakol holekh (Gilboa), 1985
Hakol talui (Kishon), 1961
Hakutonet vehapasim (Applefeld), 1983
Halavan (D. Baron), 1946
Halaylah haaharon shel oto vaininger (Sobol), 1982
Half Portions (Ferber), 1920
Half-Bridge (Miller), 1943
Half-Lives (Jong), 1973
Halo har halo esh (Zelda), 1977
Halokh veshov (Shaham), 1972
Halom leyl tammuz (Shahar), 1989
Halomotav shel melekh (Goldberg), 1994
Halvayah horpit (Levini), 1978
Hamaabarah (Ballas), 1964
Hamafteah tsalal (Kovner), 1950
Hamahapekhah vehatarnegolet (Aloni), 1964
Hamalakh hakatan michael (Kovner), 1989
Hamamlakhah hameuhedet (Shamir), 1977
Hamasa hamuflah shel hakarpad (Shabtai),1964
Hamasa sheli im alex (Almog), 1998
Hamatsav hashelishi (Oz), 1991
Hameahev (Yehoshua), 1977
Hamefuzar mikfar azar (Goldberg), 1968
Hamelekh vehagitara habilti hashmalit (Tammuz), 1980
Hamelekh yashen arbaa paamim beyom (Tammuz), 1978
Hamerhak hanakhon (Gur), 1996
Hamesh hamesh (Megged), 1960
Hamifrats haaharon (Avidan), 1991
Hamina lisa (Castel-Bloom), 1995
Hamishah sipurim (Applefeld), 1969
Hamitabel lelo kets (Levini), 1999
Hamitlabet (Levini), 1990
Hamlet (Döblin), 1956
Hamlet (Carmi), 1981
Hamlet of Stepney Green (Kops), 1958
Hamotsa (Brenner), 1919
Hanashim haavudiot mitroya (Levini), 1983
Hand of God (Josipovici), 1996
Hands across the Table (Parker), 1935
Hands Around (Schnitzler), 1920
Hands around the Wall (Abse), 1950
Handyman (Harwood), 1996
Haneehazim (Levini), 1999
Haneshamah hashniah (Tammuz), 1981
Hanesikhah haamerikait (Aloni), 1963
Haniftar mitparea (Aloni), 1980
Hannah and Her Sisters (Allen), 1986
Hannah senesh (Megged), 1958
Hanukah Money (Sholem), 1978
Haoleh hayored lehayenu (Kishon), 1952
Haonah haboeret (Megged), 1967
Haor vehakutonet (Applefeld), 1971
Haorahat mikineret (Goldberg), 1939
Hapalestinait (Sobol), 1985
Hapardes (Tammuz), 1976
Hapatriot (Levini), 1982
Hapgood (Stoppard), 1988
Hapiknik shel amaliah (Katzir), 1994
Happiness? (Ayalon), 1998
Happy Anniversary (Taylor), 1972
Happy Days Are Here Again (Taylor), 1964
Happy Endings (Simon), 1975
Happy Lies (Taylor), 1981
Hapsiga (Applefeld), 1982
Hapsikhiater haelektroni sheli (Avidan), 1974
Har haetsah haraah (Oz), 1976
Har hatoim (Hendel), 1991
Hard Loving (Piercy), 1969
Hard Rain (Dorfman), 1990
Hardufim o sipurim muralim al ahava (Aini), 1997
Harlem Holocaust (Biller), 1998
Harlot's Ghost (Mailer), 1991
Harp Lake (Hollander), 1988
Harpatkah bamidbar (Goldberg), 1966
Hasafsal (Lapid), 2000
Hasaga shel mefaked haexodus (Kaniuk), 1999
Hasdei halayla shel margerita (Almog), 1969
Haseder Hakatan (Orpaz), 1983
Hasefer Hahadash (Castel-Bloom), 1998
Hasefer hakatan (Kovner), 1973
Hasefer hamshuga (Guri), 1971
Hasefer hashlishi (Ravikovitch), 1969
Hashanim hatovot (Agnon), 1925
Hashaon asher meal harosh (Ka-Tzetnik 135633), 1960
Hashever hasuri-afrikani (Yeshurun), 1974
Hashivah mehodu (Yehoshua), 1994
Hashkavah (Levini), 1999
Hashoneh hamarhev (Zelda), 1981
Hashual belul hatamegolot (Kishon), 1972
Hashuk hakatan (Bartov), 1957
Hasimlah ha-kehullah vesokhen habittuah (Bejerano), 1993
Hasipur al dodah shlomtsion hagedolah (Kaniuk), 1976
Hasmikhah zehavah (Lapid), 1998
Hässliche Herzogin (Feuchtwanger), 1923
Hasud (Michael), 1980
Hasut (Michael), 1977
Hatakhshit (Lapid), 1993
Hatanin mitsrayim (Lapid), 1987
Hath Not a Jew ... (Klein), 1940
Hatishmah koli (Rachel), 1986
Hatsidah (Gnessin), 1905
Hatsoanim miyafo (Aloni), 1971
Hatsomet (Kovner), 1955
Hatsot hayom (Megged), 1973
Hatsotsrah bawadi (Michael), 1987
Ha'ugab (Perets), 1894
Hauling the Water-Tank (Yizhar), 1979
Haunikorn mistakel bamarah (Carmi), 1967
Haus am Meer (S. Zweig), 1912
Have They Attacked Mary. He Giggled (Stein), 1917
Hayaldah haiutah roah mamutah (Levini), 1999
Hayam haaharon (Carmi), 1958
Hayamim habaim (Sobol), 1971
Hayanshuf (Aloni), 1975
Haye hakelev rizi (Tammuz), 1971
Hayehudi haaharon (Kaniuk), 1982
Hayei elyakum (Tammuz), 1963
Hayei nissuim (Vogel), 1929
Hayekitsah hagedolah (Barbash), 1982
Hayeled hayim ve hamifletset miyerushalayim (Shalev), 1982
Hayeled holem (Levini), 1993
Haynt iz eybik (Tussman), 1977
Hayofi hu kaas (Bejerano), 2001
Hayom hasheni (Megged), 1967
Hayored lemala (Kaniuk), 1963
Hayoresh (Ballas), 1987
Hayoresh (Shamir), 1989
Hayoshevet baganim (Hazaz), 1944
Hayser shabes-tog (Weissenberg), 1920
Hazatérés (Konrád), 1995
Hazikit vehazamir (Tammuz), 1989
Hazon ahad haligyonot (Greenberg), 1928
Hazonah hagdolah mibavel (Levini), 1982
Hazonah miohaio (Levini), 1995
He Walked through the Fields (Shamir), 1959
He, She and It (Piercy), 1991
Head of the Bed (Hollander), 1974
Healer (Applefeld), 1990
Hearken unto the Voice (Werfel), 1938
Heart is a Clock (Ginsberg), 1968
Heart Is Katmandu (Hoffman), 2001
Heartbreak Kid (Simon), 1972
Hearts of Gold (Sinclair), 1979
Hearts Wings (Josipovici), 2000
Heart-Stirring Sermon (Reyzen), 1992
Heat and Dust (Jhabvala), 1975

Heat of the Day (Pinter), 1989
Heaven and Earth (Raphael), 1985
Hebräerland (Lasker-Schüler), 1937
Hebräische Balladen (Lasker-Schüler), 1913
Hebrew Ballads (Lasker-Schüler), 1980
Hebrew Lesson (Mankowitz), 1976
Heder (Shimoni), 1999
Ḥeder naul (Ballas), 1980
Hedva veani (Megged), 1955
Hefetz (Levini), 1972
Hefetz veaherim (Levini), 1988
Hehalil (Tchernichovski), 1923
Hei, yuli (Aini), 1995
Heidi (Simon), 1959
Heikhal hakelim hashevurim (Shahar), 1969–91
Heikhan ani nimtset (Castel-Bloom), 1990
Heimkehr des Vergil (Broch), 1937
Heine und die Folgen (Kraus), 1910
Heinz ubno veharuah haraah (Megged), 1975
Heitere Magie (Döblin), 1948
Hekher fun der erd (Der Nister), 1910
Hell of a Mess (Ionesco), 1975
Hem yagyu mahar (Shaham), 1949
Hemel van Hollywood (Winter), 1997
Henderson the Rain King (Bellow), 1959
Her Mothers (Broner), 1975
Her Story (D. Jacobson), 1987
Hercules veshivat hagamadim (Kishon), 1995
Here (Sarraute), 1997
Here and Now (Layton), 1945
Here Comes (Jong), 1975
Here Comes a Chopper (Ionesco), 1990
Here Endeth the Lesson (Bermant), 1969
Here is My Heart (Parker), 1932
Here Lies (Parker), 1939
Herkunft und Zukunft (A. Zweig), 1929
Hermit (Ionesco), 1975
Hermit of 69th Street (Kosinski), 1986
Hero Pony (Mamet), 1990
Heron (Bassani), 1970
Herr, Erbarme dich Meiner! (Perutz), 1930
Herr Puntila und sein Knecht Matti (Carmi), 1962
Herr Witchdoctor (Millin), 1941
Hers (Alvarez), 1974
Hershel of Ostropol (Klein), 1939
Herzog (Bellow), 1964
Heshbon hadash (Shaham), 1989
Heshbon over (Guri), 1988
Hesitant Fire (Jacob), 1991
Hetsi veananas (Aini), 1996
Hevdah veani (Megged), 1955
Hevel (Gurevitch), 1990
Hezionot, shirim upoemot (Schneour), 1923
Hetsits venifga (Berdyczewski), 1888
Hezyonot vemanginot alef (Tchernichovski), 1898
Hezyonot vemanginot beit (Tchernichovski), 1901
Hibutei ahavah (Ka-Tzetnik 135633), 1984
Hidden Christ (Werfel), 1931
Hidden I (Raphael), 1990
Hidden in the Heart (D. Jacobson), 1991
Hier bin ich, mein Vater (Torberg), 1948
Higglety Pigglety Pop! (Sendak), 1967
High Cost of Living (Piercy), 1978
High Wind in Jamaica (Harwood), 1965
Hill of Evil Counsel (Oz), 1978
Hilperich (Wassermann), 1903
Him with His Foot in His Mouth (Bellow), 1984
Himlen nokhn shturem (Shpigl), 1984
Himmo, King of Jerusalem (Kaniuk), 1969
Himmo melekh yerushalayim (Kaniuk), 1965
Hinta-palinta (Kishon), 1956
Hintern shlos (Leyvik), 1918
Hinumat hakalah (Shamir), 1985
Hiob (J. Roth), 1930
Hireling (Mankowitz), 1973
Hirsh Lekert (Esther), 1922
Hirsh lekert (Leyvik), 1931
His Daughter (Kaniuk), 1988
Hispanic Condition (Stavans), 1995
Histoire du roi Kaboul Ier et du Marmiton Gauwain (Jacob), 1903
Histoire terrible mais inachevée de Norodom Sihanouk, roi du Cambodge (Cixous), 1985
Historias de mala muerte (Aub), 1965
Histórias de un médico em Formação (Scliar), 1962
History (Morante), 1977
History (Rakosi), 1981
History and Chronicle of the Songbook (Saba), 1998
History of Dada as My Muse (Rothenberg), 1982
History of My Heart (Pinsky), 1984
Hitbaharut (Ballas), 1972
Hitganvut lehidim (Kenaz), 1986
Hitler nekht-motivn (Leyvik), 1937
Hitleriad (Klein), 1944
Hitnatslut hamehaber (Carmi), 1974
Hiukh babatsoret (Kishon), 1978
Hiyukh hagdi (D. Grossman), 1983
H-massa leur kasdim (Shahar), 1971
Ho adamah (Tchernichovski), 1940
Ho, ho, iulia (Kishon), 1974
Hoax (Svevo), 1929
Hochzeit (E. Canetti), 1932
Hodin (Weiss), 1923
Hodina ticha (Klíma), 1963
Hofen shel arafel (Michael), 1979
Hoffman's honger (Winter), 1990
Hoffman's Hunger (Winter), 1995
Höhe des Gefühls (Brod), 1918
Hokhmat hamisken (Shaham), 1960
Hol baeinayim (Lapid), 1997
Hold That Christmas Tiger! (Perelman), 1954
Holiday Tales (Sholem), 1979
Holländische Kaufmann (Feuchtwanger), 1923
Hollywood Ending (Allen), 2002
Holocaust (Reznikoff), 1975
Holot hazahav (Tammuz), 1950
Homage to the Eighth District (Pressburger), 1990
Hombre de paso (Goldemberg), 1981
Hombre importante (Gerchunoff), 1934
Home (Harwood), 1993
Home Sweet Honeycomb (Kops), 1962
Homebody/Kabul (Kushner), 2001
Homecoming (Pinter), 1965
Homecoming of Vergil (Broch), 1966
Homely Girl (Miller), 1995
Homicide (Mamet), 1991
Homme à la colombe (Gary), 1958
Homme approximatif (Tzara), 1931
Homme aux Valises (Ionesco), 1975
Homme de chair et l'homme reflet (Jacob), 1924
Homme de cristal (Jacob), 1939
Homme du communisme (Bloch), 1949
Homme qui dort (Perec), 1967
Homograph (Yeshurun), 1985
Honey for the Ghost (Golding), 1949
Honeymoon (Modiano), 1992
Honors at Dawn (Miller), 1936
Hooglied (Herzberg), 1971
Hoogste tijd (Mulisch), 1985
Hope (Wouk), 1993
Hops vehopla (Levini), 1991
Hor bamasakh (Kishon), 1973
Hora da estrela (Lispector), 1977
Höre, Israel! (Fried), 1974
Ḥoref aḥaron (Ballas), 1984
Horef kasheh (Ravikovitch), 1964
Höret die Stimme (Werfel), 1937
Hořká vůně mandlí (Lustig), 1968
Horsefeathers (Perelman), 1932
Hostages (Heym), 1942
Hostages (Zwicky), 1983
Hotel (Woolf), 1939
Hotel AmeriKKa (Goldemberg), 2000
Hotel du Lac (Brookner), 1984
Hotel Savoy (J. Roth), 1924
Hothouse (Pinter), 1980
Hothouse by the East River (Spark), 1973
Hotsaa lahoreg (Levini), 1979
Hotsmakh shpil (Manger), 1947
Houdini (Rukeyser), 1973
Hour of the Star (Lispector), 1986
Hourglass (Kiš), 1990
House Gun (Gordimer), 1998
House of Bernarda Alba (Stoppard), 1973
House of Cowards (Abse), 1960
House of Dolls (Ka-Tzetnik 135633), 1955
House of Games (Mamet), 1989
House of Liars (Morante), 1951
House of Love (Ka-Tzetnik 135633), 1971
House of Women (Bermant), 1983
Householder (Jhabvala), 1960
How Can you Lose your Cool, When the Kinneret is as Calm as a Pool (Castel-Bloom), 1991
How Doth the Little Crocodile? (Shaffer), 1952
How German Is It (Abish), 1980
How I Became a Holy Mother (Jhabvala), 1976
How I Found America (Yezierska), 1991
How the Dead Live (Self), 2000
How to be a Brit (Mikes), 1984
How to be a Yank and More Wisdom (Mikes), 1987
How to be Affluent (Mikes), 1966
How to be an Alien (Mikes), 1946
How to be Decadent (Mikes), 1977
How to be Inimitable (Mikes), 1961
How to be Poor (Mikes), 1983
How to be Seventy (Mikes), 1982
How to Run a Stately Home (Mikes), 1972
How to Save Your Own Life (Jong), 1977
How to Scrape Skies (Mikes), 1948

How to Unite Nations (Mikes), 1963
Howards End (Jhabvala), 1992
Howl (Ginsberg), 1956
Hoyz af grand strit (Molodovski), 1953
Hoyz fun noyekh edon (Pinski), 1931
Hromobití (Klíma), 1990
Hry (Klíma), 1974
Hu halakh basadot (Shamir), 1947
Hu vehi (Kishon), 1963
Hügel ruft (Brod), 1942
Huis hiernaast (Minco), 1965
Huit Poèmes canadiens (en anglais) (Klein), 1948
Hullabaloo over Georgie and Bonnie's Pictures (Jhabvala), 1977
Hulyot (D. Baron), 1952
Human Factor (Stoppard), 1980
Human Kind (A. Baron), 1953
Human Season (Wallant), 1960
Human Stain (P. Roth), 2000
Humboldt's Gift (Bellow), 1975
Humoresque (Odets), 1942
Humour in Memoriam (Mikes), 1970
Hundert Tage (J. Roth), 1936
Hungarian Revolution (Mikes), 1957
Hunger (Lind), 1968
Hunger and Thirst (Ionesco), 1968
Hunger Artist (Kafka), 1996
Hungeriker (a skitse) (An-ski) 1915
Hungerkünstler (Kafka), 1924
Hungry Hearts (Yezierska), 1920
Hunt (Alvarez), 1978
Hupah bamidbar (Kovner), 1970
Hupah sheborah (Ratosh), 1941
Husbands and Wives (Allen), 1992
Hutsot ashkelon (Shaham), 1985
Hydriotaphia (Kushner), 1987
Hydrogen Jukebox (Ginsberg), 1990
Hymns in Darkness (Ezekiel), 1976

I Am Rose (Stein), 1971
I am the Clay (Potok), 1992
I and I (Lasker-Schüler), 1980
I Can't Sleep (Odets), 1936
I Don't Need You Any More (Miller), 1967
I, Dreyfus (Rubens), 1999
I, etcetera (Sontag), 1978
I Go Out (Rukeyser), 1961
I Keep Recalling (Glatshteyn), 1993
I Know the Place (Pinter), 1979
I Like Mike (Megged), 1960
I Love Gootie (Apple), 1998
I Married a Communist (P. Roth), 1998
I Ought to Be in Pictures (Simon), 1980
I Sent a Letter to My Love (Rubens), 1975
I Sent Thee Late (Zukofsky), 1965
I Stole a Million (West), 1939
I Was Going through the Smoke (Rothenberg), 1975
Ia istoriiu izlagaiu (Slutskii), 1990
Ia zhivu (Erenburg), 1911
Ibbud netunim 52 (Bejerano), 1982
Ibergang fun kindhayt tsu dervaksung (Weissenberg), 1927
Ibergekhapte briv oyf der post (Sholem), 1883–84
Ice and Fire (Dworkin), 1986
Ice Fire Water (Epstein), 1999
Ice Palace (Ferber), 1958
Ich, der Augenzeuge (Weiss), 1963
Ich räume auf! (Lasker-Schüler), 1925
Ich spiele noch (Ausländer), 1987
Ich und Ich (Lasker-Schüler), 1940–41
Ich zähl die Sterne meiner Worte (Ausländer), 1983
Ici (Sarraute), 1995
Ida (Stein), 1941
Idiots First (Malamud), 1963
Ieri oggi domani (Moravia), 1963
If Not Now, When (P. Levi), 1985
If There Were Anywhere but Desert (Jabès), 1988
If You Had Three Husbands (Stein), 1922
If You're Glad I'll Be Frank (Stoppard), 1966
Ik Bubanik (Mulisch), 1994
Ikh bin nisht geven in treblinka (Leyvik), 1945
Ikh zing vi a feygele (Sadeh), 1993
Illa (Cixous), 1980
Ill-tempered Clavichord (Perelman), 1952
Illuminated Poems (Ginsberg), 1996
Illusion (Kushner), 1988
Illusion and Reality (Schnitzler), 1986
Iluf hakalbah hasoreret (Kishon), 1995
I'm a Dog! (Spiegelman), 1997
Im Atemhaus wohnen (Ausländer), 1979
Im halaylah hazeh (Goldberg), 1964
Im Herzen die Krätze (Schindel), 1988
Im shekiat hahammah (Schneour), 1906–07
Im Spiel der Sommerlüfte (Schnitzler), 1929
I'm Talking about Jerusalem (Wesker), 1960
Im tselilei hamandolinah (Schneour), 1912
I'm Your Man (L. Cohen), 1987
Image (Isaac Singer), 1985
Imagerie du cordier (Lunel), 1924
Imaginal Geography 9 (Rothenberg), 1982
Imaginary Lives (Schwob), 1924
Imagining Columbus (Stavans), 1993
Imbroglio (Moravia), 1937
Imię własne (Stryjkowski), 1961
Immense Parade on Supererogation Day and What Happened to It (Hollander), 1972
Immer sind die Weiber weg und andere Weisheiten (Heym), 1997
Immortal Bartfuss (Applefeld), 1988
Imported Bridegroom (Cahan), 1898
Imposible Sinaí (Aub), 1982
Impromptu de l'Alma (Ionesco), 1956
Impromptu pour la Duchesse de Windsor (Ionesco), 1957
Imprononçable (Jabès), 1975
Improved Binoculars (Layton), 1956
Improvisation (Ionesco), 1960
In a fargrebter shtot (Bergelson), 1919
In a Garden (Stein), 1951
In a Green Eye (Feinstein), 1966
In a Hotel Garden (Josipovici), 1993
In a konspirativer dire (An-ski), 1920–25
In a shlekhter tsayt (Asch), 1903
In America (Sontag), 2000
In an Emergency (Weissbort), 1972
In Babylon (Möring), 1997
In den Wohnungen des Todes (Sachs), 1947
In der Strafkolonie (Kafka), 1919
In der tifer eybikayt (Weissenberg), 1937
In di teg fun yoyv (Leyvik), 1953
In die Sinne einradiert (Fried), 1985
In Dreams Begin Responsibilities (Schwartz), 1938
In Einer Nacht (Werfel), 1937
In fayer-vogn (Sutzkever), 1952
In gran segreto (Bassani), 1978
In land fun mayn gebeyn (Molodovski), 1937
In Memoriam (Reznikoff), 1934
In midber sinay (Sutzkever), 1957
In mitn veg (Markish), 1919
In New York (Halpern), 1982
In nyu-york (Halpern), 1919
In Place (Hollander), 1978
In Polish Woods (Opatoshu), 1938
In poylishe velder (Opatoshu), 1921
In rima e senza (Bassani), 1982
In Savoy (Stein), 1946
In Search of Lost Time (Proust), 1992
In Search of Love and Beauty (Jhabvala), 1983
In Search of the Cobra Jewels (Fierstein), 1972
In shturm (Sholem), 1906–08
In the Beginning (Asch), 1935
In the Beginning (Potok), 1975
In the Cage (Abse), 1967
In the Country of Last Things (Auster), 1987
In the Fertile Land (Josipovici), 1987
In the Future Perfect (Abish), 1977
In the Heart of the Seas (Agnon), 1948
In the Interlude (Pasternak), 1962
In the Midst of My Fever (Layton), 1954
In the Native State (Stoppard), 1991
In the Night Kitchen (Sendak), 1970
In the Penal Colony (Berkoff), 1968
In the Penal Settlement (Kafka), 1949
In the Steps of Moses the Conqueror (Golding), 1938
In the Steps of Moses the Lawgiver (Golding), 1937
In the Storm (Sholem), 1984
In the Wilderness (Applefeld), 1965
In Time and Place (Hollander), 1986
In tsaytens roysh (Greenberg), 1919
In yerushalayim kumen malokhim (Molodovski), 1952
In-between Time (A. Baron), 1971
Incident at Vichy (Miller), 1964
Incidents in the Rue Laugier (Brookner), 1995
Incomparable Atuk (Richler), 1963
Indecent Dreams (Lustig), 1988
Indenfor Murene (Nathansen), 1912
Indiade (Cixous), 1987
Indian Ink (Stoppard), 1995
Indifferent Ones (Moravia), 1932
Indifferenti (Moravia), 1929
Indizienbeweise (Fried), 1966
Ineffaçable, l'inaperçu (Jabès), 1980
Inferno of Dante (Pinsky), 1995
Initial (Zukofsky), 1970
Inklings (D. Jacobson), 1973
Inkubator al hassela (Megged), 1950
Inmitn tog (M. Katz), 1954
Inn (Stryjkowski), 1971
Inscription (Weissbort), 1993
Inscriptions (Reznikoff), 1959
Inserzione (Ginzburg), 1968
Inside (Cixous), 1986
Inside Kasrilevke (Sholem), 1948
Inside My Dirty Head — The Holocaust (Scliar), 1994

Inside, Outside (Wouk), 1985
Instants (Spire), 1936
Instinct du bonheur (Maurois), 1934
Insulted and Exiled (A. Zweig), 1937
Intellectual Things (Kunitz), 1930
Interiors (Allen), 1978
Intermezzo (Schnitzler), 1915
International Stud (Fierstein), 1978
Interpreters (Harwood), 1985
Interview (Spark), 1958
Intervista (Ginzburg), 1989
Intervista aziendale (P. Levi), 1968
Intimations, The Desert (Jabès), 1991
Into Praising (Silkin), 1978
Inventar (Ausländer), 1972
Inventing Memory (Jong), 1997
Invention of Love (Stoppard), 1998
Inventor (Lind), 1987
Inventory (Josipovici), 1968
Inveterate Dreamer (Stavans), 2001
Invisible Writing (Koestler), 1954
Inyenei lashon (Berdyczewski), 1908
Io e lui (Moravia), 1971
Ir hayonah (Alterman), 1957
Ir sheeyn bah mistor (Orpaz), 1973
Ir yamim rabim (Hareven), 1972
Irgo (Lind), 1968
Irish Hebrew Lesson (Mankowitz), 1978
Iron Butterflies (Mankowitz), 1985
Iron Horse (Ginsberg), 1972
Iron Tracks (Applefeld), 1998
Irreführung der Behörden (Becker), 1973
I's (Zukofsky), 1963
Is geen hond (Herzberg), 1973
Is the House Shut? (Abse), 1964
Isaac Babel's Fiddle (Zwicky), 1975
Isaac Sheftel (Pinski), 1904–05
Isabelle et Pantalon (Jacob), 1922
Ish omed meahorei ishah yoshevet (Levini), 1992
Ish veishah veish (Liebrecht), 1998
Iskat hashokolad (Guri), 1965
Island (Raphael), 1965
Isma (Sarraute), 1970
Isola di Arturo (Morante), 1957
Israel (Uris), 1959
Ist River (Asch), 1946
Istoriia moei golubiatni (Babel'), 1926
It Could Happen to You (West), 1937
It is There (Sarraute), 1980
It Should Happen to a Dog (Mankowitz), 1955
It Was (Zukofsky), 1959
Italy for Beginners (Mikes), 1956
It's a Lovely Day Tomorrow (Kops), 1975
It's about Cinderella (Shaffer), 1969
It's Beautiful (Sarraute), 1980
Iugo-Zapad (Bagritskii), 1928
Ivrim beazah (Hareven), 1991
Iyyob (Zukofsky), 1965
Iz poslednei zapisnoi knizhki (Slutskii), 1994
Izbrannaia lirika (Slutskii), 1965
Izvozchik i Dant (Mandel'shtam), 1991
Izzum (Sarraute), 1980

J.J. Farr (Harwood), 1987
Jack (Ionesco), 1958
Jack Shepherd (Mankowitz), 1972
Jackpot (Sholem), 1989
Jacky Gleason Show (Simon), 1958–59
Jacob and the Green Rabbi (Kops), 1998
Jacob der Lügner (Becker), 1969
Jacob the Liar (Becker), 1975
Jacob Two-Two and the Dinosaur (Richler), 1987
Jacob Two-Two Meets the Hooded Fang (Richler), 1975
Jacob Two-Two's First Spy Case (Richler), 1995
Jacobowsky and the Colonel (Werfel), 1944
Jacobowsky und der Oberst (Werfel), 1944
Jacques (Ionesco), 1955
Jake's Women (Simon), 1990
Jamark rymów (Tuwim), 1934
Janusz Korczak w Getcie (Korczak), 1992
Jarapiri Poem (Silkin), 1975
Jarmila (Weiss), 1998
Je bâtis ma demeure (Jabès), 1959
Jean Santeuil (Proust), 1952
Jeans (Ben-Ner), 1991
Jefferson in Paris (Jhabvala), 1995
Jefta und seine Tochter (Feuchtwanger), 1957
Jephta and his Daughter (Feuchtwanger), 1958
Jepthah's Daughter (Gershon), 1978
Jeremiah (S. Zweig), 1922
Jeremias (S. Zweig), 1917
Jeremias (Werfel), 1956
Jericho Sleep Alone (Bermant), 1964
Jerry Lewis Show (Simon), 1958–59
Jersey Rain (Pinsky), 2000
Jerusalem (Greenberg), 1939
Jerusalem (Silkin), 1977
Jérusalem à Carpentras (Lunel), 1938
Jerusalem the Golden (Reznikoff), 1934
Jestem Człowiekiem Samotnej Drogi (Korczak), 1978
Jesus, raconté par le Juif errant (Fleg), 1933
Jesus, Told by the Wandering Jew (Fleg), 1934
Jeune Fille à marier (Ionesco), 1960
Jeunesse (Modiano), 1981
Jeux de massacre (Ionesco), 1970
Jew of Rome (Feuchtwanger), 1936
Jewish Gauchos of the Pampas (Gerchunoff), 1955
Jewish Government (L. Shapiro), 1971
Jewish Mother from Berlin (Kolmar), 1997
Jewish State (Herzl), 1970
Jews of Zirndorf (Wassermann), 1918
Jinny the Carrier (Zangwill), 1919
Job (J. Roth), 1931
Jodenstreek? (Heijermans), 1904
Joker (Abse), 1962
Jordans (Millin), 1923
Joseph and Koza (Isaac Singer), 1970
Joseph Kerkhoven's Third Existence (Wassermann), 1934
Joseph Kerkhovens dritte Existenz (Wassermann), 1934
Joseph Shur, The Hole through which Life Slips (Bergelson), 1977
Joseph the Dreamer (Zangwill), 1895
Josephus (Feuchtwanger), 1932
Josephus and the Emperor (Feuchtwanger), 1942
Joshua Then and Now (Richler), 1980
Jossel Wassermanns Heimkehr (Hilsenrath), 1993
Jour (Wiesel), 1961
Journalism (S. Katz), 1990
Journalists (Wesker), 1975
Journey (Fink), 1992
Journey Not the Arrival Matters (Woolf), 1969
Journey through a Small Planet (Litvinoff), 1972
Journey through the Wilderness (Farhi), 1989
Journey to Rome (Moravia), 1990
Journey to the End of the Millennium (Yehoshua), 2000
Journeys among the Dead (Ionesco), 1985
Jours de l'an (Cixous), 1990
Józki, Jáśki i Franki (Korczak), 1922
Juarez und Maximilian (Werfel), 1924
Jud Süss (Feuchtwanger), 1917
Juda Makabi (Stryjkowski), 1986
Judas des Leonardo (Perutz), 1959
Juden auf der deutschen Bühne (A. Zweig), 1927
Juden von Zirndorf (Wassermann), 1897
Judenstaat (Herzl), 1896
Judge Not (Asch), 1938
Judge on Trial (Klíma), 1991
Judge's Wife (Schnitzler), 1977
Judgement (Kafka), 1983
Jüdin von Toledo (Feuchtwanger), 1955
Jüdinnen (Brod), 1911
Jüdische Krieg (Feuchtwanger), 1932
Jüdische Mutter (Kolmar), 1981
Juego de cartas (Aub), 1964
Jugend im Nebel (Brod), 1959
Juif du Pape (Fleg), 1925
Julia Farnese (Feuchtwanger), 1915
Julio Cortázar (Stavans), 1996
Julio Jurenito (Erenburg), 1958
July's People (Gordimer), 1981
Jump (Gordimer), 1991
Jumpers (Stoppard), 1972
Junge Frau von 1914 (A. Zweig), 1931
Junk Mail (Self), 1995
Jury (Klíma), 1969
Jusep Torres Campalans (Aub), 1958
Just One Kid (Kops), 1974
Just Passing Through (Goldemberg), 1981

K incompréhensible (Cixous), 1975
Kaaterskill Falls (Goodman), 1998
Kadahat (Lapid), 1979
Kaddis a meg nem születetett gyermekért (Kertész), 1990
Kaddish (Ginsberg), 1961
Kaddish (Ka-Tzetnik 135633), 1998
Kaddish (Zwicky), 1982
Kadur hakesef (Almog), 1986
Kaffeehaus war überall (Torberg), 1982
Kafka and Felice (Klíma), 1986
Kah yashir olam tzair (Goldberg), 1950
Kaheres hanishbar (Lapid), 1984
Kahol miefer (Ka-Tzetnik 135633), 1966
Kajtuś czarodziej (Korczak), 1934/35
Kakh (Wieseltier), 1973
Kaleidoskop (S. Zweig), 1936
Kalkutta, 4 Mai (Feuchtwanger), 1925
Kamelot (Ayalon), 1995
Kamen' (Mandel'shtam), 1913
Kamer (Mulisch), 1984
Kamertjeszonde (Heijermans), 1897

Kampf (Weiss), 1916
Kan beitsim (Ayalon), 1998
Kan nagur; hamesh novelot (Kahana-Carmon), 1996
Kannibalen und andere Erzählungen (Heym), 1953
Kapella kolot (Yeshurun), 1977
Kaplan (Döblin), 1926
Kaplan (Winter), 1986
Kaptsnson et Hungerman (Goldfaden), 1877
Kapuzinergruft (J. Roth), 1938
Karine Saporta, Peter Greenaway (Cixous), 1990
Karl and Rosa (Döblin), 1983
Karl Kraus (Viertel), 1921
Karu lo pipl (Ka-Tzetnik 135633), 1961
Kasper (Weissenberg), 1910
Kasrilevker nisrofim (Sholem), 1903–10
Kat shel klavim (Tammuz), 1968
Katerina (Applefeld), 1992
Katerinah (Applefeld), 1989
Kayits bederekh haneviim (Shahar), 1969
Kayzer un rebe (Schneour), 1944–52
Kazmirov Affair (Litvinoff), 1969
Keep It Crisp (Perelman), 1946
Kefor al haarets (Applefeld), 1965
Kehakot Rachel (Rachel), 1982
Kehulim veadumim (Gilboa), 1963
Keisarit hapirion hamedumeh (Aini), 1990
Keishon haayin (Applefeld), 1973
Kelev bayit (Greenberg), 1929
Kelev chutsot (Agnon), 1950
Kemeah edim (Applefeld), 1975
Kemo nahar (Schütz), 1997
Kemo sipurim (Kaniuk), 1983
Kemunim (Kishon), 1955
Kenny's Window (Sendak), 1956
Keritut vesipurim aherim (D. Baron), 1997
Kerl muss eine Meinung haben (Döblin), 1976
Kerti mulatság (Konrád), 1989
Kerze von Arras (Kolmar), 1968
Kesef katan (Hendel), 1988
Keshepartsah hamedinah (Ben-Yehuda), 1991
Keta lebamah betaam hasignon hagadol (Kahana-Carmon), 1976
Ketaim mehalom patuah (Gurevitch), 1980
Ketanot (D. Baron), 1933
Ketatah (Gnessin), 1912
Ketavim (Korczak), 1996
Ketchup (Levini), 1969
Kette (S. Zweig), 1923
Keyamim ahadim (Shalev), 1994
Keytn (Leyvik), 1929
Keytn fun meshiakh (Leyvik), 1907–08
Kfar (Sobol), 1996
Khasene in fernvald (Leyvik), 1949
Khasene makhn (Weissenberg), 1939
Khaver nakhmen (Israel Singer), 1938
Khayim leyderers tsurik-kumen (Asch), 1927
Khayiml (Weissenberg)
Kheshvndike nekht (Molodovski), 1927
Kholmy (Brodsky), 1991
Kholsty (Shrayer-Petrov), 1967
Khorbm poyln (Asch), 1918
Khsidish (Perets), 1908
Kh'tu dermonen (Glatshteyn), 1967
Khumesh lider (Manger), 1935
Khurbn (Rothenberg), 1989
Ki erom atah (Shamir), 1959
Kid for Two Farthings (Mankowitz), 1955
Kiddush Hashem (Asch), 1926
Kidish hashem (Asch), 1919
Kiedy znów będę mały (Korczak), 1961
Killer (Ionesco), 1960
Killhope Wheel (Silkin), 1971
Killing Game (Ionesco), 1974
Killingworth Play (Taylor), 1975
Kilometre 56 (Shamir), 1949
Kimat (Shamir), 1991
Kimshonim (Raab), 1930
Kind en kraai (Mulisch), 1975
Kinder und Narren (Fried), 1965
Kindheit eines Cherub (Viertel), 1991
Kine un tayve (Weissenberg), 1911
Kine un tayve un andere ertseylungen (Weissenberg), 1911
King David and His Wives (Pinski), 1966
King David Report (Heym), 1973
King Dido (A. Baron), 1969
King in the Golden Mask (Schwob), 1982
King Matt the First (Korczak), 1986
King of Fields (Isaac Singer), 1988
King of Flesh and Blood (Shamir), 1958
King of Schnorrers (Zangwill), 1894
King of the Bastards (Millin), 1949
King of the Jews (Epstein), 1979
King Silky! (Rosten), 1980
King Solomon (Gary), 1983
Kingdom Come (Rubens), 1990
Kingdom of Love (Brod), 1930
King's Daughters (Wesker), 1998
Kinneret, kinneret (Alterman), 1962
Kirot ets dakim (Shaham), 1978
Kishef-makherin (Goldfaden), *c.*1878
Kishif-makherin fun kastilye (Asch), 1926
Kishon X 25 (Kishon), 1973
Kishona (Ben-Ner), 1978
Kitchen (Wesker), 1957
Kitl (Weissenberg), 1904
Kitlauer Affair (Lind), 1970
Kitser masoes binyomin hashlishi (Mendele Moykher Sforim), 1878
Kitsur shnot hashishim (Wieseltier), 1984
Kitvei Uri Nisan Genesin (Gnessin), 1946
Kivsat harash (Shamir), 1957
Klára a dva páni (Klíma), 1967
Klára and Two Men (Klíma), 1968
Klarissas halbes Herz (Brod), 1924
Klechdy polskie (Leśmian), 1956
Klechdy sezamowe (Leśmian), 1913
Kleine Chronik (S. Zweig), 1929
Kleine Dramen (Feuchtwanger), 1905–06
Kleine Verhältnisse (Werfel), 1931
Kleine Zeemeermin (Herzberg), 1986
Kleyne mentshele (Mendele Moykher Sforim), 1879
Kleyne mentshelekh mit kleyne hasoges (Sholem), 1902–04
Kloyz un di gas (Grade), 1974
Klucz do Berlina (Korczak), 1966
Klyatshe (Mendele Moykher Sforim), 1873
Knaben und Männer (A. Zweig), 1931
Knekht (Isaac Singer), 1967
Knock at the Manor Gate (Berkoff), 1972
Knop (Mulisch), 1961
Knot (Fainlight), 1990
Kogda razguliaetsia (Pasternak), 1960
Kokhav haefer (Ka-Tzetnik 135633), 1966
Kokhavim bahuts (Alterman), 1938
Kokhevei shamayim rehokim (Tchernichovski), 1944
Kokrhací hodiny a jiné příběhy z Vlaských Kloboúk a podobných Tramtárii (Klíma), 1965
Kol (Bejerano), 1987
Kol asher ahavti (Applefeld), 1999
Kol hehalav vehadvash (Zach), 1966
Kol mishbarekhah vegalekhah (Ravikovitch), 1972
Kol nidre (Markish), 1941
Kol'chugin's Youth, A Novel (V. Grossman), 1946
Kommentierte Werkausgabe (Broch), 1974–81
Komödie der Eitelkeit (E. Canetti), 1950
Komödie der Verführung (Schnitzler), 1924
Komtesse Mizzi (Schnitzler), 1909
Konarmiia (Babel'), 1926
Konets prekrasnoi epokhi (Brodsky), 1977
Konfidenz (Dorfman), 1994
König und die Tänzerin (Feuchtwanger), 1917
König-David-Bericht (Heym), 1972
Königin Esther (Brod), 1918
Kontakt (Halkin), 1935
Kontor gesheft (Sholem), 1885
Konzert (Lasker-Schüler), 1932
Kőóra (Konrád), 1994
Korbones (Der Nister), 1943
Korol' (Babel'), 1926
Kosak and die Nachtigall (Perutz), 1927
Kra li siomka (Shaham), 1950
Kral Majales (Ginsberg), 1965
Kras (Herzberg), 1989
Kredos (Glatshteyn), 1929
Kreuzfahrer von heute (Heym), 1950
Kriegsgefangenen (Feuchtwanger), 1919
Krig oyf der erd (Greenberg), 1923
Krisa (Sobol), 1976
Kristus shel hadagim (Hoffman), 1991
Kritat rosh (Levini), 1996
Król Dawid żyje! (Stryjkowski), 1984
Król Maciuś na wyspie bezludnej (Korczak), 1923
Król Maciuś Pierwszy (Korczak), 1923
Krone für Zion (Kraus), 1898
Krowa (Rudnicki), 1957
Kroyn (Shpigl), 1973
Krum (Levini), 1975
Księga bałwochwalcza (Schulz), 1922
Kufsah shehorah (Oz), 1987
Kukharka (V. Grossman), 1938
Kulam beyahad (Shamir), 1959
Kulam rotsim lihiot (Levini), 1985
Kuntsnmahker fun lublin (Isaac Singer), 1971
Kupe (Markish), 1922
Kupiec Łódzki (Rudnicki), 1963
Kuppel (Lasker-Schüler), 1920
Kvetch (Berkoff), 1986
Kwiaty polskie (Tuwim), 1949

La (Cixous), 1976
Labirint (Glants-Leyeles), 1918
Laboratoire central (Jacob), 1921
Lacombe Lucien (Modiano), 1974
Laços de família (Lispector), 1960
Lacune (Ionesco), 1965
Ladaat ishah (Oz), 1989
Ladies of the Corridor (Parker), 1953
Lads (Harwood), 1963
Lady at the Wheel (Raphael), 1958
Lady, Be Careful (Parker), 1936
Lady Chatterley's Confession (Feinstein), 1995
Lady Di in een bevallige pose (Winter), 1996
Lady Godiva (Moravia), 1975
Lady Journalist (Zangwill), 1893
Lady L. (Gary), 1963
Lady of the Castle (Goldberg), 1974
Lady Othello (Wesker), 1990
Lady with the Laptop (Sinclair), 1996
Lagaat bamayim, lagaat baruah (Oz), 1973
Laid Off (Pinski), 1932
Laish (Applefeld), 1994
Łąka (Leśmian), 1920
Lake (Weissbort), 1993
Lakeboat (Mamet), 1970
Lakes (Preil), 1965
Laments for Living (Parker), 1930
Lamm des Armen (S. Zweig), 1929
Lamtern in vint (Manger), 1933
Land der Väter und Verräter (Biller), 1994
Land in which God Dwells (Fleg), 1955
Land is Bright (Ferber), 1941
Land of Manna (M. Katz), 1965
Land of Promise (Fleg), 1933
Land of the Rising Yen (Mikes), 1970
Land ohne Tod (Döblin), 1947
Landarzt (Kafka), 1919
Landscape (Pinter), 1968
Landscape in Concrete (Lind), 1967
Landschaft in Beton (Lind), 1963
Language Mesh (Celan), 1988
Language of Comics (Spiegelman), 1974
Laot (Gilboa), 1942
Lapidary Poems (Silkin), 1979
Lapilah yesh nazelet (Goldberg), 1975
Largo Desolato (Stoppard), 1986
Lark (Hellman), 1955
Lashemesh (Tchernichovski), 1919
Láska a smetí (Klíma), 1986
Lassalle (Heym), 1969
Last Analysis (Bellow), 1965
Last and Lost Poems (Schwartz), 1979
Last Call (Mulisch), 1987
Last Days of Mankind (Kraus), 1974
Last Days of Or (Alterman), 1990
Last Honours (Fried), 1968
Last Jew (Kaniuk), 1990
Last Jew in America (Fiedler), 1966
Last of Days (Farhi), 1983
Last of the Cheesecake (Mankowitz), 1956
Last of the Just (Schwarz-Bart), 1961
Last of the Labourers (Sobol), 1977
Last of the Red Hot Lovers (Simon), 1969
Last Revolt (Opatoshu), 1952
Last Song of Manuel Sendero (Dorfman), 1987
Last Summer (Pasternak), 1959
Last Supper (Bermant), 1973
Last Treatment (Yehoshua), 1974
Last Trump of Avram Blok (Louvish), 1990
Last Waltz in Santiago (Dorfman), 1988
Last White Class (Piercy), 1978
Last Yankee (Miller), 1991
Late Bourgeois World (Gordimer), 1966
Late Divorce (Yehoshua), 1984
Latecomers (Brookner), 1987
Later the Same Day (Paley), 1985
Latin Lover (Raphael), 1994
Lato (Rudnicki), 1938
Látogató (Konrád), 1969
Latterday Psalms (Ezekiel), 1982
Laubheu und keine Bleibe (A. Zweig), 1930
Laudin und die Seinen (Wassermann), 1925
Laugh till You Cry (Mankowitz), 1955
Laughing Matter (Mikes), 1971
Laughing Rooster (Layton), 1964
Laughter in the Mind (Layton), 1958
Laughter on the 23rd Floor (Simon), 1995
Laura and Francisca (Riding), 1931
Lauta i Oiziljci (Kiš), 1994
Lautensack Brothers (Feuchtwanger), 1944
Law of White Spaces (Pressburger), 1992
Laylah al hagadah hamaaravit (Tammuz), 1961
Laylah bemay (Yehoshua), 1969
Laylah beroma (Tammuz), 1964
Laylah besanta paulina (Orpaz), 1997
Leaba-ima (Shlonsky), 1927
Leader (Ionesco), 1960
Leaflets (Rich), 1969
Leahar haseudah (Agnon), 1963
Leakev et hakeryiah (Kovner), 1998
Leaning Forward (Paley), 1985
Leap through the Curtain (Mikes), 1955
Learning to Walk (Ionesco), 1973
Leaseholder (Weissbort), 1971
Leben Eduards des Zweiten von England (nach Marlowe) (Feuchtwanger), 1924
Leben mit einer Göttin (Brod), 1923
Lebendige Stunden (Schnitzler), 1902
Lebenslauf (Viertel), 1946
Lebenslied (Torberg), 1958
Lebensschatten (Fried), 1981
Lebn far a lebn (Hirshbein), 1915
Leçon (Ionesco), 1951
Leçons de Français pour Américains (Ionesco), 1966
Leedvermaak (Herzberg), 1982
Leet atah (D. Baron), 1942
Legacies and Encounters (Gershon), 1972
Legacy (Alvarez), 1972
Legacy (Schnitzler), 1911
Legend of the Holy Drinker (J. Roth), 1989
Legende eines Lebens (S. Zweig), 1919
Legende vom heiligen Trinker (J. Roth), 1939
Legge degli spazi bianchi (Pressburger), 1989
Legião estrangeira (Lispector), 1964
Legs Diamond (Fierstein), 1988
Lehakat haketsev mofrah al har gerizim (Kovner), 1972
Leitenant Shmidt (Pasternak), 1926
Leket mishirei Leah Goldberg (Goldberg), 1980
Lekever yishmael (Ratosh), 1932
Lélia (Maurois), 1952
Lelia (Maurois), 1953
Lemaalah bemontifer (Kahana-Carmon), 1984
Lematisse yesh et hashemesh babeten (Katzir), 1995
Lemmings (Kops), 1963
Lenin's Writings (Esther), 1925
Lenokhah hayam (Vogel), 1932
Lens-Breakers (Silkin), 1992
Lentils in Paradise (Farhi), 1996
Lenz (Heym), 1965
Lenz Papers (Heym), 1964
Leonardo Project (Rothenberg), 1998
Leonardo's Judas (Perutz), 1989
Leopardos de Kafka (Scliar), 2000
Leseif sela eitam (Greenberg), 1950s–1970s
Lessico famigliare (Ginzburg), 1963
Lessing, Kleist, Büchner (A. Zweig), 1925
Lesson (Ionesco), 1958
Lestriad (S. Katz), 1962
Let Us Compare Mythologies (L. Cohen), 1956
Let's Hear It for a Beautiful Guy (Friedman), 1984
Let's Make Music (West), 1940
Letstn oyfstand (Opatoshu), 1948–55
Letter That Came in Time (Hendel), 1995
Letter to a Daughter (Wesker), 1992
Letterato Vincenzo (Saba), 1989
Letters and Numbers (Rothenberg), 1979
Lettice and Lovage (Shaffer), 1987
Letting Go (P. Roth), 1962
Lettres (Goloboff), 1982
Letzte Nacht (Kraus), 1918
Letzten Tage der Menschheit (Kraus), 1918–19
Leutnant Gustl (Schnitzler), 1901
Lev hakhamim (Bartov), 1962
Lev hu katmandu (Hoffman)
Lev tel aviv (Shaham), 1996
Levi yitskhok (Hirshbein), 1923
Leviathan (Auster), 1992
Leviathan (J. Roth), 1940
Levitation (Ozick), 1982
Lévy (Bloch), 1912
Lewis Percy (Brookner), 1989
Leyad even hatoim (Carmi), 1981
Leyl haesrim (Sobol), 1976
Leylot lutetsia (Shahar), 1991
Li akhshav (Yeshurun), 1992
Lichtzwang (Celan), 1970
Lid fun dem yidishn kelner avram (Rosenfarb), 1948
Lider bukh (M. Rosenfeld), 1897
Lider fun geto (Sutzkever), 1946
Lider fun togbukh (Sutzkever), 1977
Lider fun yam-hamoves (Sutzkever), 1968
Lider tsum eybikn (Leyvik), 1959
Lider vegn shpanie (Markish), 1938
Lider, balades, poemes (Fefer), 1967
Lie (Moravia), 1966
Lie (Sarraute), 1969
Liebe der Erika Ewald (S. Zweig), 1904
Liebelei (Schnitzler), 1895
Liebesgedichte (Fried), 1979
Liebling Kreuzberg (Becker), 1990
Liebste Freundin und Alma (Torberg), 1987
Lied von Bernadette (Werfel), 1941
Lies about Vietnam / Truth about Sarajevo (Taylor), 1969

Lieutenant Gustl (Schnitzler), 1993
Lieve Arthur (Herzberg), 1976
Life (Josipovici), 1974
Life (Svevo), 1963
Life A User's Manual (Perec), 1987
Life and Fate (V. Grossman), 1985
Life as a Parable (Sadeh), 1966
Life before Us (Gary), 1986
Life in the Theatre (Mamet), 1977
Life of Alexander Fleming (Maurois), 1959
Life of Caligula (Shabtai),1975
Life of Edward II of England (Feuchtwanger), 1970
Life of Moses (Fleg), 928
Life of Solomon (Fleg), 1930
Life of the Automobile (Erenburg), 1976
Life of the Dead (Riding), 1933
Life That I Have Led (Liberman), 1986
Life-Terms (E. Canetti), 1983
Lifnei harash (Orpaz), 1999
Lifnei hashaar haafel (Vogel), 1923
Lift Your Head, Comrade (Koestler), 1944
Lifting Belly (Stein), 1989
Light for Fools (Ginzburg), 1957
Light of Lost Suns (Gilboa), 1979
Light on the Rime of a Cloud (Goldberg), 1972
Light-o'-Love (Schnitzler), 1912
Like Birds, Like Fishes (Jhabvala), 1963
Like Men Betrayed (Raphael), 1970
Likht fun dornboym (Molodovski), 1965
Likht funem opgrunt (Shpigl), 1952
Lilit e altri raconti (P. Levi), 1981
Limits of Love (Raphael), 1960
Limmedu heitev (Mendele Moykher Sforim), 1862
Limonade tout était si infini (Cixous), 1982
Linah meshutefet (Gur), 1991
Lincoln Relic (Kunitz), 1978
Lindmann (Raphael), 1963
Lionhearted (Reznikoff), 1944
Lisheelat hatarbut (Berdyczewski), 1902
Listen my Children (Miller), 1939
Listen to the Mocking Bird (Perelman), 1949
Literary Murder (Gur), 1993
Literatur (Kraus), 1921
Literatur und Lüge (Kraus), 1929
Literature of Destruction (Greenberg), 1989
Litsloah et hameah (Orpaz), 1993
Little (Zukofsky), 1967
Little Cabbages (Mikes), 1955
Little Disturbances of Man (Paley), 1959
Little Foxes (Hellman), 1939
Little King Matty and the Desert Island (Korczak), 1990
Little Man (Mendele Moykher Sforim), 1991
Little Me (Simon), 1962
Little Old Admiral (Golding), 1958
Little Old Lady (Wesker), 1988
Little Personal Pocket Requiem (Josipovici), 1990
Little Queen of Sheba (Goldberg), 1959
Little Tales (Feuchtwanger), 1935
Little Time-Keeper (Silkin), 1976
Little Town (Asch), 1948
Liubka the Cossack (Babel'), 1963
Liubov' Zhanny Nei (Erenburg), 1924
Liudi, Gody, Zhizn' (Erenburg), 1961–66
Live Theatre (Taylor), 1981
Lives of the Poets (Doctorow), 1984
Lives of Wives (Riding), 1939
Living End (Elkin), 1979
Living Hours (Schnitzler), 1913
Living in the Open (Piercy), 1976
Living on the Dead (Megged), 1970
Livingstone's Companions (Gordimer), 1971
Liviti otah baderekh leveytah (Kahana-Carmon), 1991
Livre de l'hospitalité (Jabès), 1991
Livre de Monelle (Schwob), 1894
Livre de Promethea (Cixous), 1983
Livre de Yukel (Jabès), 1964
Livre des marges (Jabès), 1975
Livre des questions (Jabès), 1963
Livre des ressemblances (Jabès), 1976
Livre du dialogue (Jabès), 1984
Livre du partage (Jabès), 1987
Livre lu en Israël (Jabès), 1987
Livret de famille (Modiano), 1977
Livyatan (Bejerano), 1990
Lo bimkoma (Ballas), 1994
Lo kakh tiarti li (Gur), 1994
Lo meakhshav, lo mikan (Amichai), 1963
Lo norah (Kishon), 1957
Lo rahok Mimerkaz hair (Castel-Bloom), 1987
Lo tirtsah (Shlonsky), 1930
Lobensteiner reisen nach Böhmen (Döblin), 1917
Locked Room (Auster), 1986
Locomotive, the Turnip, the Birds' Broadcast (Tuwim), 1939
Lod' jménem naděje (Klíma), 1969
Loitering with Intent (Spark), 1981
Lokomotywa, Rzepka, Ptasie radio (Tuwim), 1938
Lomokome Papers (Wouk), 1968
London Suite (Simon), 1996
Lone Canoe (Mamet), 1979
Lonely Guy (Simon), 1984
Lonely Heart (Odets), 1943
Lonely Road (Schnitzler), 1985
Lonely Way (Schnitzler), 1904
Long and the Short and the Tall (Mankowitz), 1961
Long Lease of Summer (Harwood), 1972
Long Pea-Shooter (Layton), 1954
Long Talking Bad Conditions Blues (Sukenick), 1979
Long Way from London (D. Jacobson), 1958
Longings of Women (Piercy), 1994
Look at Me (Brookner), 1983
Look at Me Now and Here I Am (Stein), 1971
Look Back Mrs Lot (Kishon), 1961
Look Who's Talking (Perelman), 1940
Looking Ahead (Hollander), 1982
Loon Lake (Doctorow), 1980
Lorca Variations (1-8) (Rothenberg), 1990
Lord Byron kommt aus der Mode (Brod), 1929
Lord Malquist and Mr Moon (Stoppard), 1966
Lord of the Flies (Shaffer), 1963
Loser (Konrád), 1982
Lost (Alvarez), 1968
Lost Europeans (Litvinoff), 1960
Lost in Yonkers (Simon), 1991
Lost Son (Broch), 1966
Love and Death (Allen), 1975
Love and Death in the American Novel (Fiedler), 1960
Love and Garbage (Klíma), 1990
Love and War, Art and God (K. Shapiro), 1984
Love as Love, Death as Death (Riding), 1928
Love for Three Oranges (Stoppard), 1983
Love Games (Schnitzler), 1982
Love in the Flames (Ka-Tzetnik 135633), 1977
Love Letters on Blue Paper (Wesker), 1974
Love of Jeanne Ney (Erenburg), 1929
Love on the Riviera (Moravia), 1958
Love Poems (Layton), 1978
Love the Conqueror Worm (Layton), 1953
Lovebound (Wiseman), 1960
Lovely Leave (Parker), 1962
Lover (Pinter), 1963
Lover (Yehoshua), 1978
Loveroot (Jong), 1975
Lovers and Lesser Men (Layton), 1973
Lovers for the Day (Klíma), 1999
Loves (Federman), 1986
Loves of Judith (Shalev), 1999
Loving Brecht (Feinstein), 1992
Loving Brothers (Golding), 1952
Lowlife (A. Baron), 1963
Lucarne aux étoiles (Vigée), 1998
Lucretia Borgia (Stein), 1968
Lucy Church Amiably (Stein), 1931
Ludzie są dobrzy (Korczak), 1938
Luhot genuzim (Schneour), 1948
Luigi of Catanzaro (Golding), 1926
Luis Álvarez Petreña (Aub), 1934
Lukardis (Wassermann), 1932
Lulu (Herzberg), 1989
Luminous Dreams (Ginsberg), 1997
Luna que cae (Goloboff), 1989
Lunatic's Tale (Allen), 1986
Lunch (Berkoff), 1983
Lunchtime (Abse), 1974
Lune d'hiver (Vigée), 1970
Lured (Rosten), 1947
Lusitania (Döblin), 1920
Lustre (Lispector), 1946
Lyautey (Maurois), 1931
Lydia und Mäxchen (Döblin), 1906
Lying Days (Gordimer), 1953
Lynch (Ayalon), 2000

M is for Moon among Other Things (Stoppard), 1977
Ma Palestine (Fleg), 1932
Má veselá jitra (Klíma), 1978
Maase betsayar (Goldberg), 1965
Maaseh besloshah egozim (Goldberg), 1980
Maaseh meguneh (Megged), 1986
Maaseh rabi gadiel hatinok (Agnon), 1925
Mabl (Sholem), 1906–08
Maçã no escuro (Lispector), 1961
Macbett (Ionesco), 1972
Maccabaean (Herzl), 1902–03
MacGuffin (Elkin), 1991
Mächtigen (Wassermann), 1897
Mackinac (Mamet), 1972
Madame Sousatzka (Jhabvala), 1988
Madame Sousatzka (Rubens), 1962

Mädchen und Frauen (A. Zweig), 1930
Mädchenhirt (Kisch), 1914
Madhouse in Goa (Sherman), 1989
Madre (Ginzburg), 1957
Madrich (Ka-Tzetnik 135633), 1993
Mafriah hayonim (Amir), 1992
Magic Apple Tree (Feinstein), 1971
Magic Barrel (Malamud), 1958
Magic Cabinet of Professor Smucker (Mankowitz), 1988
Magic Kingdom (Elkin), 1985
Magician of Lublin (Isaac Singer), 1960
Magid haatidot (Shahar), 1966
Magnolia Street (Golding), 1931
Magnolia Street Story (Litvinoff), 1951
Mah ani ashem sheani gadol? (Hareven), 1999
Mah mesameah akavishim (Lapid), 1990
Mah nishkaf behaloni (Goldberg), 1989
Mah osot haayalot? (Goldberg), 1944
Mah shehayah (D. Baron), 1939
Mah shlomekh dolores? (Hoffman), 1995
Mah yoter kedai, lakahat o latet (Tammuz), 1980
Mahanayim (Berdyczewski), 1900
MaHaRaM of Rothenburg (Leyvik), 1944
Mahbarot elul (Guri), 1988
Mahbarot evyatar (Megged), 1973
Mahberet sonetot (Tchernichovski), 1922
Mahler's Conversion (Harwood), 2001
Mahsan (Wieseltier), 1994
Mahzir ahavot kodmot (Kenaz), 1997
Maid to Marry (Ionesco), 1960
Maidstone (Mailer), 1971
Maison de la femme peinte (Lunel), 1946
Maître (Ionesco), 1960
Majestade do Xingu (Scliar), 1997
Make Me an Offer (Mankowitz), 1952
Making a Television Play (Taylor), 1970
Making It Up (Ginsberg), 1994
Making of Americans (Stein), 1925
Making of Ashenden (Elkin), 1972
Makom aher (Oz), 1966
Malakhim baim (Ben-Ner), 1987
Malgoshe (Weissenberg)
Malheurs d'Orphée (Lunel), 1924
Malik (Lasker-Schüler), 1919
Malkat ambatiah (Levini), 1970
Malkat sheva haktanah (Goldberg), 1956
Malkhei beit david (Shamir), 1977
Malkhei yisrael (Shamir), 1978
Malkhes geto (Shpigl), 1947
Malomocní (Klíma), 1974
Mały człowiek (Korczak), 1965
Mame's tsavoe (Grade), 1949
Mamzer (Schneour), 1957
Man Asleep (Perec), 1990
Man from There (Ben-Ner), 1970
Man fun natseres (Asch), 1943
Man in the Brooks Brothers Shirt (Raphael), 1990
Man Next Door (Litvinoff), 1968
Man on the Bridge (Raphael), 1961
Man the Size of a Postage Stamp (Lustig), 1967
Man Was Killed (L. Cohen, Layton), 1977
Man Who Conquered Death (Werfel), 1927
Man Who Had All the Luck (Miller), 1944
Man with Bags (Ionesco), 1977
Man with the Luggage (Ionesco), 1979
Manas (Döblin), 1927
Mandela (Harwood), 1987
Mandelbaum Gate (Spark), 1965
Manfred (Rudnicki), 1954
Mangeclous (A. Cohen), 1938
Mangeur d'Étoiles (Gary), 1966
Mangobaumwunder (Perutz), 1916
Manhattan (Allen), 1979
Manhattan Murder Mystery (Allen), 1993
Manhigim veshoftim (Shamir), 1976
Ma-Ni-Ma-Mimah (Sobol), 1998
Mann von vierzig Jahren (Wassermann), 1913
Manna, for the Mandelstams, for the Mandelas (Cixous), 1994
Manne aux Mandelstams aux Mandelas (Cixous), 1988
Männer in der Nacht (Weiss), 1925
Manner Music (Reznikoff), 1977
Mannschaft (Torberg), 1935
Manny and Jake (Fierstein), 1987
Manor (Isaac Singer), 1967
Mansarda (Kiš), 1962
Mantle of Elijah (Zangwill), 1900
Manual del (im)perfecto resenista (Stavans), 1989
Many Loves (Ginsberg), 1984
Manzoni Family (Ginzburg), 1987
Maof hayonah (Shimoni), 1990
Mapa del olvidado tesoro (Dujovne Ortiz), 1967
Mappat erev (Preil), 1961
Mar arnav mehapes avoda (Aini), 1994
Mar gazmay habaday (Goldberg), 1977
Mar mani (Yehoshua), 1990
Marathon (Josipovici), 1980
Marbles (Brodsky), 1989
Marchand de Paris (Fleg), 1929
Märchen vom letzten Gedanken (Hilsenrath), 1989
Marianne in India (Feuchtwanger), 1935
Marianne in Indien und sieben andere Erzählungen (Feuchtwanger), 1934
Marienbad (Sholem), 1982
Mariia (Babel'), 1935
Mario on the Beach (Golding), 1956
Marjorie Morningstar (Wouk), 1955
Markétin zvěřinec (Klíma), 1973
Marktplatz der Sensationen (Kisch), 1941
Marot gehazi (Guri), 1974
Marques de Bolibar (Perutz), 1920
Marquis de Bolibar (Perutz), 1926
Marranos (Mamet), 1972
Marriage and Henry Sunday (Litvinoff), 1967
Married Life (Vogel), 1988
Marrying Man (Simon), 1991
Mars and her Children (Piercy), 1992
Marshal Lyautey (Maurois), 1931
Martereau (Sarraute), 1953
Martsepanes (Molodovski), 1970
Martwa fala (Stryjkowski), 1983
Mary (Asch), 1949
Mary Burns, Fugitive (Parker), 1935
Mary Glenn (Millin), 1925
Marya (Babel')
Maryenbad (Sholem), 1911
Masa daniel (Orpaz), 1969
Masa el tom haelef (Yehoshua), 1997
Masa leninveh (Amichai), 1962
Masah beav (Megged), 1980
Masah el erets hamilim (Kovner), 1981
Mascara (Dorfman), 1988
Máscaras (Dorfman), 1988
Mascherata (Moravia), 1941
Mashehu al leviatanim (Kovner), 1989
Mashehu bishvil mishehu (Avidan), 1964
Mashehu kiyyumi (Ayalon), 1991
Masken Erwin Reiners (Wassermann), 1910
Masken und Wunder (Schnitzler), 1912
Masot binyamin haaharon mitudelah (Amichai), 1977
Masque Ball (Sobol), 2000
Massage (Berkoff), 1987
Massah dumah (Sadeh), 1951
Massiah O Knesset (Hareven), 1987
Master (Brod), 1951
Master (Klíma), 1968
Master (Zangwill), 1895
Master of the Day of Judgement (Perutz), 1929
Mastik im pasim (Kishon), 1981
Mate in Three (Rubens), 1965
Materials (Oppen), 1962
Matters of Chance (Feinstein), 1972
Matthew (Korczak), 1945
Matzavim potentsia veimpotentsia (Barbash), 2000
Maurizius Case (Wassermann), 1929
Maus (Spiegelman), 1986
Mavet (Schneour), 1906
Mavet Bageshem (Almog), 1982
Mavet bahug lesifrut (Gur), 1989
Mavet bepurim (Bartov), 1992
Max and the Cats (Scliar), 1990
Max Dugan Returns (Simon), 1983
Max es os felinos (Scliar), 1981
Maximilian Harden (Kraus), 1907
Maximilien (Lunel), 1930
May krig mit hersh reseyner (Grade), 1969
Mayim noshkim lemayim (Michael), 2001
Mayn Fayfele (Gebirtig), 1997
Mayn krig mit hersh raseyner (Grade), 1951
Mayn oytser (Halkin), 1966
Mayn tatns bezdn-shtub (hemshekhim-zamlung) (Isaac Singer), 1996
Mayn tatns bezdn-shtub (Isaac Singer), 1979
Mayne lider (Gebirtig), 1936
Mayse Bikhl (Bergelson), 1922
Maysele in gramen (Mani Leyb), 1937
Mayselekh fun khumish (Asch), 1913
Mayses fun hintern oyvn (Isaac Singer), 1982
Mazal ayalah (Bartov), 1988
Mazal dagim (Lapid), 1969
Mazel and Shlimazel (Isaac Singer), 1967
Mazes (Rukeyser), 1970
Me (Taylor), 1971
Me Too (Federman), 1975
Meachorei kol zeh mistater osher gadol (Amichai), 1974
Meadam atah veel adam tashuv (Amichai), 1985
Meagadot lod (Shamir), 1958
Meahev mushlam (Almog), 1995
Measure for Measure (Carmi), 1979

Meat tsori (Langer), 1942
Meaz umeatah (Agnon), 1931
Medea (Gordin), 1897
Meditation (Rakosi), 1985
Mediterranean (Rukeyser), 1937
Mediterranee (Saba), 1947
Medlennyi den' (Mandel'shtam), 1990
Meemek akhor (Brenner), 1901
Meemesh (D. Baron), 1954
Meeresspiegel (Broch), 1933
Mefiste (Greenberg), 1921
Megile-lider (Manger), 1936
Megilot haesh (Kovner), 1981
Mehamat hametsik (Agnon), 1921
Mein Atem heisst jetzt (Ausländer), 1981
Mein blaues Klavier (Lasker-Schüler), 1943
Mein Herz (Lasker-Schüler), 1912
Mein ist die Rache (Torberg), 1943
Mein Venedig versinkt nicht (Ausländer), 1982
Meine Wunder (Lasker-Schüler), 1911
Meister (Brod), 1951
Meister des jüngsten Tages (Perutz), 1923
Meisternovellen (S. Zweig), 1970
Meisternovellen (Werfel), 1972
Mekomon (Lapid), 1989
Mekomot nifradim (Hareven), 1969
Melekh basar vadam (Shamir), 1954
Melekh dovid aleyn iz geblibn (Molodovski), 1946
Melinda és Dragomán (Konrád), 1991
Melkern marfa (Markish), 1938
Melting-Pot (Zangwill), 1908
Melusine (Wassermann), 1896
Memento Mori (Spark), 1959
Mémoire d'Abraham (Halter), 1983
Mémoire des mots (Jabès), 1990
Mémoire et la main (Jabès), 1987
Memoirs (Erenburg), 1964
Memorials of LS (Josipovici), 1996
Memory Lane (Modiano), 1981
Memory of Two Mondays (Miller), 1955
Men against the Sky (West), 1940
Men I'm Not Married To (Parker), 1922
Men on a Voyage (Millin), 1930
Men without Mercy (Döblin), 1937
Men, Years, Life (Erenburg), 1962
Menace (Wesker), 1963
Menakhem mendl (Sholem), 1892
Mendel Philipsen og Søn (Nathansen), 1932
Mendelman Fire (Mankowitz), 1957
Mendels erfenis (Möring), 1990
Mendiant de Jérusalem (Wiesel), 1968
Meneer Frits (Minco), 1974
Menke sonetn (M. Katz), 1996
Mensch gegen Mensch (Weiss), 1919
Mensch, Maier! Sagte der Lord (Torberg), 1975
Mensonge (Sarraute), 1967
Mentsh fun fayer (Grade), 1962
Mentsh in togn (M. Katz), 1935
Mentshn in tom (Shpigl), 1949
Mentshn un khayes (Opatoshu), 1938
Menuhah nekhonah (Oz), 1982
Menzogna e sortilegio (Morante), 1948
Meotsar haaggadah (Berdyczewski), 1913
Meragel betokh habayit (Gur), 1999
Merchant (Wesker), 1976
Mercy (Dworkin), 1990
Mercy of a Rude Stream (H.Roth), 1994–98
Merely Mary Ann (Zangwill), 1893
Merg (Herzberg), 1986
Meri (Asch), 1913
Merry Roosters' Panto (Shaffer), 1963
Merry-Go-Round (Schnitzler), 1953
Merz Sonata (Rothenberg), 1985
Meserl (Sholem), 1886
Meshiekhs tsaytn (Goldfaden), 1891
Meshikhim (Pinski), 1930
Meshugah (Isaac Singer), 1994
Meshugene in dorf (Weissenberg), 1907
Meshumedeste (Schneour), 1948
Mesilat barzel (Applefeld), 1991
Message (Fleg), 1904
Message (Lind), 1975
Message II (Ginsberg), 1968
Messengers Will Come No More (Fiedler), 1974
Messiah (Berkoff), 2000
Messiah (Sherman), 1982
Messiah of Stockholm (Ozick), 1987
Messiah of the House of Efraim (Kulbak), 1987
Messie (Cixous), 1996
Messie (Halter), 1996
Metamorphosis (Berkoff), 1968
Metamorphosis (Josipovici), 1985
Metamorphosis (Kafka), 1936–38
Metaphor and Memory (Ozick), 1989
Meydlekh, froyen, vayber, un ... nevue (Molodovski), 1927
Meyhaneden Çıkan Kıral (Gerez), 1956
Mi babitan? (Goldberg), 1997
Mi makir et yosef g.? (Guri), 1980
Mibaad leavotot (Ben-Yehuda), 1985
Mibeiti hayashan (Goldberg), 1942
Michael and the Monster of Jerusalem (Shalev), 1990
Michael sheli (Oz), 1968
Middle Class (Millin), 1921
Middle of the Air (Rukeyser), 1945
Middle of the Journey (Trilling), 1948
Mides-hadin (Bergelson), 1929
Midis gagnés (Tzara), 1939
Midnight Convoy (Yizhar), 1950
Midnight Salvage (Rich), 1999
Midsummer Night's Dream (Carmi), 1964
Midsummer Night's Sex Comedy (Allen), 1982
Mifal hayav (Lapid), 1992
Migdalorim shel yabasha (Katzir), 1999
Mighty Aphrodite (Allen), 1995
Mighty Hunter (Mankowitz), 1956
Mighty Walzer (H. Jacobson), 1999
Migrations (Josipovici), 1977
Mihvat haor (Applefeld), 1980
Mikan umikan (Brenner), 1911
Mikdamot (Yizhar), 1992
Mikhtav baderekh (Shaham), 1999
Mikhtavim minesiah medumah (Goldberg), 1937
Mikol haavot (Kovner), 1965
Mikreh haksil (Megged), 1960
Mil y una calorías (Glantz), 1978
Mila 18 (Uris), 1961
Miláček (Lustig), 1969
Mild mayn vild (Tussman), 1958
Milenci na jeden den (Klíma), 1992
Milenci na jednu noc (Klíma), 1964
Milhemet benei haor (Shamir), 1955
Milhemet hayetser (Grade), 1970
Milim bedami haholeh ahavah (Guri), 1995
Milim nirdafot (Pagis), 1982
Milk and Honey (Mikes), 1950
Milkhome (Markish), 1948
Milkhome-balades (Fefer), 1943
Millhemet hanemalim (Kishon), 1981
Millionairess (Mankowitz), 1960
Milostné léto (Klíma), 1979
Mimekor yisroel (Berdyczewski), 1930–45
Mimes (Schwob), 1893
Min hametser (Brenner), 1909
Mind Breaths (Ginsberg), 1978
Minds Meet (Abish), 1975
Mindwheel (Pinsky), 1985
Mineged (Rachel), 1930
Miner's Pond (Michaels), 1991
Minick (Ferber), 1924
Minotaur (Tammuz), 1980
Minstr a anděl (Klíma), 1984
Mio marito (Ginzburg), 1964
Mio primo libro di poesie (Saba), 1903
Mir viln lebn (Bergelson), 1946
Mira (Brod), 1958
Miracle Boy (Golding), 1927
Miracle Hater (Hareven), 1988
Mirakel (Mulisch), 1955
Mirele efres (Gordin), 1898
Mireya (Dujovne Ortiz), 1998
Miriam (Berdyczewski), 1921
Miriam (Hirshbein), 1905
Mirliton du ciel (Memmi), 1985
Misalliance (Brookner), 1986
Misaviv lanekudah (Brenner), 1904
Misfits (Miller), 1961
Misham (D. Baron), 1945
Mishehi tsricha lihiot kan (Aini), 1995
Mishehu laruts ito (D. Grossman), 2000
Mishelo vealav (Kovner), 1988
Mishirei erets israel (Schneour), 1948
Mishirei haprozdor haarokh (Shlonsky), 1968
Mishlei bakbukim (Tammuz), 1976
Mishnat hasidim (Berdyczewski), 1899
Mishpat ones (Levini), 1997
Mishpat pythagoras (Alterman), 1965
Mishpokhe karnovski (Israel Singer), 1943
Mishpokhe mashber (Der Nister), 1939
Misipurei mar kashkash (Goldberg), 1987
Misja Ostatniej Nadziei (Korczak), 1992
Miss Julie versus Expressionism (Berkoff), 1973
Miss Lonelyhearts (West), 1933
Missing (Dorfman), 1982
Missing Person (Modiano), 1980
Mistaken Ambitions (Moravia), 1955
Mister David (Taylor), 1967
Mr Emmanuel (Golding), 1939
Mr Happiness (Mamet), 1978
Mr Hurricane (Golding), 1957
Mr Mani (Yehoshua), 1992
Mr Prufrock's Songs (Berkoff), 1974
Mr Sammler's Planet (Bellow), 1970
Mr Vee (Josipovici), 1988
Mr Vertigo (Auster), 1994
Mr Wakefield's Crusade (Rubens), 1985

Mistério de coelho pensante (Lispector), 1967
Mistr (Klíma), 1967
Mistress (Wesker), 1991
Mrs Reynolds (Stein), 1952
Mrs Ted Bliss (Elkin), 1995
Mit der Zeit, gegen die Zeit (Torberg), 1965
Mitahat lamayim (Ayalon), 1983
Mitham oyev (Ben-Ner), 1997
Mitla Pass (Uris), 1988
Mitn ponem tsu der zun (Shpigl), 1930
Mittagsgöttin (Werfel), 1919
Mivhar (Zach), 1974
Mivhar shirim udevarim al yetsiratah (Ravikovitch), 1962
Miyitneni malon (Amichai), 1971
Mizmorei iyyov (Bejerano), 1993
Mlekhet hahayim (Levini), 1988
Mlekhet hahayim (Levini), 1991
Młode cierpienia (Rudnicki), 1954
Moah (Pagis), 1975
Mobius the Stripper (Josipovici), 1974
Modelvliegen (Möring), 2000
Modern Fairytale (Josipovici), 1993
Modern Primitive (Wouk), 1951
Moderner shed (Weissenberg), 1930
Modlitba pro Kateřinu Horovitzovou (Lustig), 1964
Mofa (Wallach), 1985
Mohn ist noch nicht rot (Ausländer), 1994
Mohn und Gedächtnis (Celan), 1952
Moïse raconté par les Sages (Fleg), 1928
Moisson de Canaan (Vigée), 1967
Moje první lásky (Klíma), 1985
Moje zlatá řemesla (Klíma), 1990
Molcho (Yehoshua), 1987
Mole (Bermant), 1982
Moloch (Wassermann), 1903
Moment (Josipovici), 1979
Moment (Weissenberg)
Moment Before (Zangwill), 1916
Moment musikali (Kenaz), 1980
Moment of Death (Zangwill), 1900
Moment of Silence (Louvish), 1979
Moments of Reprieve (P. Levi), 1986
Moments Return (Ginsberg), 1970
Monday (Kulbak), 1979
Mondo è quello che è (Moravia), 1966
Mondo salvato dai ragazzini (Morante), 1968
Monkey Business (Perelman), 1931
Monkey's Wrench (P. Levi), 1986
Monologue (Pinter), 1973
Month of Saturdays (Parker), 1971
Montik (Kulbak), 1929
Montserrat (Hellman), 1949
Moo Pak (Josipovici), 1994
Moon is Always Female (Piercy), 1980
Moon is Down (Barbash), 1986
Moon Palace (Auster), 1989
Moonlight (Pinter), 1993
Moon's Our Home (Parker), 1936
Mor hehamor (Goldberg), 1987
Mörder (Schnitzler), 1922
More Die of Heartbreak (Bellow), 1987
More Night (Rukeyser), 1981
More Out than In (Kops), 1980
More Roman Tales (Moravia), 1963
Morgen ist Feiertag (Perutz), 1936
Mori Sa'id (Hazaz), 1956
Morir por cerrar los ojos (Aub), 1944
Morning of Fools (Ben-Ner), 1992
Moros en la costa (Dorfman), 1973
Mortal Passion (Mikes), 1963
Mosaic Man (Sukenick), 1999
Mosby's Memoirs (Bellow), 1968
Moscou–Paris (Bloch), 1947
Moscow Notebooks (Mandel'shtam), 1991
Moses (Asch), 1951
Moses (Rosenberg), 1916
Moshiakh ben efraim (Kulbak), 1924
Moshiekhs (Sholem), 1898
Moskauer Orgasmus (Hilsenrath), 1997
Mośki, Jośki i Srule (Korczak), 1910
Moskovie tetradi (Mandel'shtam), 1930–34
Moskve (Asch), 1931
Moss (Kops), 1975
Most Private Intrigue (Rosten), 1967
Mostly Sitting Haiku (Ginsberg), 1978
Mot avimelekh (Sadeh), 1969
Mot haayir (Kaniuk), 1973
Mot hazaken (Yehoshua), 1962
Mot lysanda (Orpaz), 1964
Mother (Asch), 1930
Mother Knows Best (Ferber), 1927
Mother of Us All (Stein), 1947
Mother Russia (Rubens), 1992
Mothers (Wesker), 1982
Mother's Girl (Feinstein), 1988
Mother's Kisses (Friedman), 1964
Motke ganiv (Asch), 1916
Motl peyse dem khazns (Sholem), 1909
Moto shel haelohim hakatan (Shahar), 1982
Motor Show (Ionesco), 1963
Motorbike (Kops), 1962
Motsah el hayam (Wieseltier), 1981
Mottke the Thief (Asch), 1935
Motza Kleis (Zangwill), 1882
Mountain Language (Pinter), 1988
Movie-Going (Hollander), 1962
Moving Parts (S. Katz), 1977
Moyshe (Asch), 1951
Mramor (Brodsky), 1984
Much Ado About Nothing (Carmi), 1983
Muerte y la doncella (Dorfman), 1992
Muertos (Aub), 1971
Můj známý Vili Feld (Lustig), 1949
Mujeres en espejo (Glantz), 1985
Mujeres, memorias, malogros (Glickman), 1991
Mukdam vemeuhar (Goldberg), 1959
Mul haḥomah (Ballas), 1969
Mul hayearot (Yehoshua), 1968
Mul hayeshimon (Shlonsky), 1973
Mulâtresse Solitude (Schwarz-Bart), 1972
Mulher que escreveu a Bíblia (Scliar), 1999
Mulher que matou os peixes (Lispector), 1968
Multiple Orgasms (Markfield), 1977
Mum vehalom (Carmi), 1951
Mume sosye (Goldfaden), 1869
Munie the Bird Dealer (Kulbak), 1953
Mur des pleurs (Fleg), 1919
Murder by Death (Simon), 1976
Murder Duet (Gur), 1999
Murder on a Kibbutz (Gur), 1994
Musernikes (Grade), 1939
Music of Chance (Auster), 1990
Music on a Kazoo (Layton), 1956
Musical Moment (Kenaz), 1995
Muter (Asch), 1925
Muter (Pinski), 1904
Mutter (Kolmar), 1965
Mutterland (Ausländer), 1978
My Daughters, My Sisters (Gershon), 1975
My Experiences in Parnassus (Rakosi), 1977
My Father Always Embarrasses Me (Shalev), 1990
My First Loves (Klíma), 1986
My First Sony (Barbash), 1994
My Friend B's Feast (Hendel), 1996
My Golden Trades (Klíma), 1992
My House is on Fire (Dorfman), 1990
My Idea of Fun (Self), 1994
My Life as a Man (P. Roth), 1974
My Little Sister (Kovner), 1986
My Merry Mornings (Klíma), 1985
My Michael (Oz), 1972
My Mother, My Father and Me (Hellman), 1963
My Mother's Body (Piercy), 1985
My Name is Asher Lev (Potok), 1972
My Old Man's a Dustman (Mankowitz), 1956
My Quarrel with Hersh Rasseyner (Grade), 1954
My Sister, Life (Pasternak), 1983
My Son's Story (Gordimer), 1990
Myśl Pedagogiczna Janusza Korczaka (Korczak), 1983
Mystères de Jérusalem (Halter), 1999
Mythematics and Extropy I (Leśmian), 1984
Mythematics and Extropy II (Leśmian), 1992

Na pole chesti (Babel'), 1920
Na rannikh poezdakh (Pasternak), 1943
Na wierzbach ... nasze skrzypce (Stryjkowski), 1974
Naar Archangel (Herzberg), 1971
Naarat hahalomot (Lapid), 1985
Nach der ersten Zukunft (Becker), 1980
Nacht (Hilsenrath), 1964
Nacht der Harlekine (Schindel), 1994
Nächte der Tino von Bagdad (Lasker-Schüler), 1919
Nächte Tino von Bagdads (Lasker-Schüler), 1907
Nachts (Kraus), 1918
Nachts unter der steinernen Brücke (Perutz), 1953
Nadav veimo (Megged), 1988
Naftali the Storyteller and His Horse, Sus (Isaac Singer), 1976
Nag (Mendele Moykher Sforim), 1955
Nagelaten dagen (Minco), 1997
Nahar (Weiss), 1922
Nahash hanehoshet (Carmi), 1961
Nahe suchen (Fried), 1982
Nail Polish (Layton), 1971
Nailcruncher (A. Cohen), 1940
Naissance d'une culture (Bloch), 1936
Nakam (Ka-Tzetnik 135633), 1981
Naked and the Dead (Mailer), 1948
Nakht-royb (Markish), 1922
Naknikiot hamot (Shaham), 1993
Name of Oedipus (Cixous), 1991
Names for Which There Are No People (Lustig), 1960

Nanny and the Iceberg (Dorfman), 1999
Naphy nasikh hakarnafim (Almog), 1979
Napój cienisty (Leśmian), 1936
Napoléon (Maurois), 1964
Napoleon — hai o met (Aloni), 1967
Narod bessmerton (V. Grossman), 1943
Narratives and Realtheater Pieces (Rothenberg), 1977
Narrenweisheit (Feuchtwanger), 1952
Nashim (Almog), 1986
Nashim mehakot bahuts (Shamir), 1952
Nashim mitokh katalog (Liebrecht), 2000
Natasha (Sholem), 1884
Natural (Malamud), 1952
Nature of Passion (Jhabvala), 1956
Nature with Man (Silkin), 1965
Nature's Way (Wouk), 1957
Navi (Hareven), 1989
Naye dertseylungen (Bergelson), 1947
Naye kasrilevke (Sholem), 1901
Naye tsayt (Esther), 1909
Nazarene (Asch), 1939
Nazi and the Barber (Hilsenrath), 1971
Nazi und der Friseur (Hilsenrath), 1977
Near to the Wild Heart (Lispector), 1990
Nearby Eden (M. Katz), 1990
Necessities of Life (Rich), 1966
Necklace of Bees (Mandel'shtam), 1992
Nefesh yehudi (Sobol), 1982
Nemalim (Orpaz), 1968
Nemilovaná (Lustig), 1979
Neobychainye pokhozhdeniia Khulio Khurenito i ego uchenikov (Erenburg), 1922
Neokonchennye spory (Slutskii), 1978
Ner mul kokhavim (Preil), 1954
Nero (Parker), 1922
Nerves (Brenner), 1983
Nes in geto (in manuscript) (Leyvik), 1940
Neskol'ko pechal'nykh dnei (V. Grossman), 1989
Nestroy und die Nachwelt (Kraus), 1912
Net of Moon, Net of Sun (Rothenberg), 1971
Neue Ghetto (Herzl), 1895
Neue Kanaan (A. Zweig), 1925
Neue Urwald (Döblin), 1948
Neuner (Becker), 1991
Neurei vardale (Levini), 1974
Neutral Ground (Stoppard), 1968
Neutre (Cixous), 1972
Nevelot hasipur haamiti (Kaniuk), 1997
Nevo (Rachel), 1932
Nevue fun shvartsaplen (Sutzkever), 1989
New Assistant (Harwood), 1967
New Coin Poetry (Clouts), 1984
New Dominion (Jhabvala), 1972
New Ghetto (Herzl), 1955
New Life (Malamud), 1961
New Skin for the Old Ceremony (L. Cohen), 1974
New Step (L. Cohen), 1972
New Tenant (Ionesco), 1956
New Woman's Broken Heart (Dworkin), 1980
New Women's Writing from Israel (Hendel), 1996
New World Order (Pinter), 1991
New Year Blues (Ginsberg), 1972
New York Trilogy (Auster), 1987
New-found-land (Stoppard), 1976
News from Jerusalem (Shahar), 1974
Next Big Thing (Brookner), 2002
Next Religion (Zangwill), 1912
Next Year in Jerusalem (Sherman), 1968
Next Year in Tel Aviv (Taylor), 1973
Next-to- Last-Things (Kunitz), 1985
Nice Old Man and the Pretty Girl (Svevo), 1930
Nicht der Mörder, der Ermordete ist schuldig (Werfel), 1920
Nicolo-Peccavi (Lunel), 1926
Nidon lahayim (Ka-Tzetnik 135633), 1974
Nièce-Épouse (Ionesco), 1971
Niece-Wife (Ionesco), 1971
Niegeküsste Mund (Wassermann), 1903
Niekochana (Rudnicki), 1937
Niemandsrose (Celan), 1963
Niet verstaan (Durlacher), 1995
Nietsfabriek (Herzberg), 1997
Nietzsche's Attaché Case (Weissbort), 1993
Nieve e la colpa (Pressburger), 1998
Night (Hilsenrath), 1966
Night (Pinter), 1969
Night (Wiesel), 1960
Night and Day (Rosenberg), 1912
Night and Day (Stoppard), 1978
Night and Hope (Lustig), 1962
Night before Paris (Sherman), 1970
Night in Kurdistan (Bloch), 1931
Night in May (Yehoshua), 1974
Night Kids (Kops), 1983
Night Mirror (Hollander), 1971
Night Music (Odets), 1940
Night of the Day of the Imprisoned Writer (Harwood), 1981
Night of the Twentieth (Sobol), 1978
Night Out (Pinter), 1960
Night Rounds (Modiano), 1971
Night School (Pinter), 1960
Night Trilogy (Wiesel), 1987
Night with Casanova (Mankowitz), 1991
Nightingale (Sholem), 1985
Nights of Lutetia (Shahar), 1993
Nigunim (Weissenberg)
Nikhna umenutsakh (Levini), 1988
Nikoho neponížíš (Lustig), 1963
Nili (Ben-Ner), 1996
Nineteen to the Dozen (Sholem), 1998
Nin-gal (Shahar), 1983
Ninth Wave (Erenburg), 1955
Nisht dos (Weissenberg), 1926
Nissim veniflaot (Goldberg), 1954
Nit gedayget (Markish), 1933
No (Aub), 1952
No Beautiful Nights (V. Grossman), 1944
No Chanting in the Court! (Ginsberg), 1969/70
No Decency Left (Riding), 1932
No Love for Johnnie (Richler), 1959
No Man's Land (Pinter), 1975
No More Mister Nice Guy (H. Jacobson), 1998
No News from Helen (Golding), 1943
No One Will Be Immune (Mamet), 1994
No Place Like (Gordimer), 1978
No poseo sino muerte para expresar mi vida (Goldemberg), 1969
No pronunciarás (Glantz), 1980
No Room at the Inn (Ferber), 1941
No son cuentos (Aub), 1951
No Telegrams, No Thunder (Abse), 1962
No Villain (Miller), 1937
No Way (Ginzburg), 1974
No! In Thunder (Fiedler), 1960
Nobody Loves Me (Simon), 1962
Nobody's in Town (Ferber), 1938
Noc a den (Lustig), 1962
Noc a naděje (Lustig), 1958
Noć i magla (Kiš), 1983
Noc w Quedlinburgu (Korczak), 1971
Noch ist Raum (Ausländer), 1976
Nof shemesh ukefor (Preil), 1944
Noia (Moravia), 1960
Noire et grise (Lunel), 1930
Noise of Time (Mandel'shtam), 1965
Nokh alemen (Bergelson), 1913
Nokhn got fun midber (Molodovski), 1949
Nokhn telerl fun himl (Markish), 1919
Nom d'Oedipe (Cixous), 1978
Non approfondire (Moravia), 1957
Non-Being and Somethingness (Allen), 1978
None but the Brave (Schnitzler), 1926
None But the Lonely Heart (Odets), 1944
None to Accompany Me (Gordimer), 1994
Nonnen von Kemnade (Döblin), 1923
No-one's Rose (Celan), 1988
North Star (Hellman), 1943
Not by Sun Alone (Mikes), 1967
Not for Publication (Gordimer), 1965
Not of This Time, Not of This Place (Amichai), 1968
Not So Deep as a Well (Parker), 1936
Not to Disturb (Spark), 1971
Notebooks (Rothenberg), 1976
Notes after an Evening with William Carlos Williams (Ginsberg), 1970
Nothing but the Best (Raphael), 1963
Nothing Important Ever Dies (Gary), 1960
Notte del '43 (Bassani), 1960
Nottingham Captain (Wesker), 1962
Nous de l'Espérance (Fleg), 1949
Nouveau Locataire (Ionesco), 1955
Novel of Thank You (Stein), 1958
Novella del buon vecchio e della bella fanciulla (Svevo), 1930
Novellen aus Böhmen (Brod), 1936
Novellen der Leidenschaft (S. Zweig), 1966
Novellen um Claudia (A. Zweig), 1912
November 1918 (Döblin), 1948–50
Novi (Asch), 1955
Novotny's Pain (P. Roth), 1980
Novye stansy k Avguste (Brodsky), 1983
Now (Josipovici), 1998
Now Dowager (Bermant), 1971
Now is the Place (Layton), 1948
Now Newman was Old (Bermant), 1978
Now Then (Federman), 1992
Noyekh pandre (Schneour), 1936
Nude Croquet (Fiedler), 1969
Nudhur al-Kharīf (Ballas), 1997
Nuit (Wiesel), 1958
Nuit kurde (Bloch), 1920
Nuit miraculeuse (Cixous), 1989
Numbered (E. Canetti), 1956

Numbers (Lind), 1972
Nun Denn (Federman), 1992
Nuovi racconti romani (Moravia), 1959
Nurse Marjorie (Zangwill), 1906
Nuts Hams and Prompters (Kishon), 1975
Nutshell Library (Sendak), 1962
Nyu-yorkish un andere zakhn (L. Shapiro), 1931

O. Jones, O. Jones (Abse), 1970
O Kaplan! My Kaplan! (Rosten), 1976
O the Chimneys (Sachs), 1967
Oath (Wiesel), 1973
Oazis (Sutzkever), 1960
Obbligato (Raphael), 1956
Oberlin's Three Stages (Wassermann), 1925
Oberst und der Dichter (Döblin), 1946
Obsidiane (Jabès), 1982
Occasion for Loving (Gordimer), 1963
Occasions (Lunel), 1926
Occhiali d'oro (Bassani), 1958
Occhio selvaggio (Moravia), 1967
Octavio Paz (Stavans), 2002
Octets (Mandel'shtam), 1976
Od sipur ahavah (Kaniuk), 1996
Odd Couple (Simon), 1965
Ode for Saint Cecilia (Josipovici), 1986
Ode tsu der toyb (Sutzkever), 1955
Oded hamelukhlakh (Lapid), 1988
Odesskie rasskazy (Babel'), 1931
Odore del fieno (Bassani), 1972
Odpowiedź (Stryjkowski), 1982
Odysseus and the Swine (Feuchtwanger), 1949
Odysseus und die Schweine und zwölf andere Erzählungen (Feuchtwanger), 1950
Oedipus Wrecks (Allen), 1989
Oeuvres burlesques et mystiques de Frère Matorel (Jacob), 1912
Of Being Numerous (Oppen), 1968
Of Hope and Glory (Taylor), 1965
Of Lodz and Love (Rosenfarb), 2000
Of Mycenae and Men (Raphael), 1979
Of Smiling Peace (Heym), 1944
Of This Time, of That Place (Trilling), 1979
Of Time and Place (Preil), 1972
Of toyt un of lebn (Halkin), 1944
Offenbach-Renaissance (Kraus), 1927
Offering Flowers (Rothenberg), 1968
Offrande à la politique (Bloch), 1933
Oger (V. Canetti), 1991
Oh Hell (Mamet), 1991
Oh Romeo (Kishon), 1984
Oh What a Bloody Circus (Ionesco), 1976
Ohneland (Schindel), 1986
Ohrenzeuge (E. Canetti), 1974
Oidipous Oidipous (Mulisch), 1972
Oil and Water (Taylor), 1973
Oil Islands (Feuchtwanger), 1928
Oisgeveilte lider un poemes (Bagritskii), 1940
Old Book Peddler (S. Zweig), 1937
Old Country (Sholem), 1946
Old Country Tales (Sholem), 1966
Old Horsefly (K. Shapiro), 1992
Old Love (Isaac Singer), 1979
Old Love Story (Ginsberg), 1986
Old Maids' Club (Zangwill), 1892
Old Man Minick (Ferber), 1924
Old Neighborhood (Mamet), 1998
Old Ones (Wesker), 1972
Old Poet's Tale (Rakosi), 1999
Old Religion (Mamet), 1997
Old Scores (Raphael), 1995
Old Soldiers Never Die (Mankowitz), 1956
Old Times (Pinter), 1971
Old-New Land (Herzl), 1902–03
Oleanna (Mamet), 1992
Olho enigmático (Scliar), 1986
Olivia (Wassermann), 1937
Ölü Nokta (Gerez), 1966
Olympia (Weiss), 1923
Olympio (Maurois), 1952
Omanut hamilhamah (Shimoni), 1990
On Borrowed Words (Stavans), 2001
On Firmer Shores (Liberman), 1981
On İki Kavim / On ıki Tablo (Gerez), 1986
On Margate Sands (Kops), 1978
On ne part pas, on ne revient pas (Cixous), 1991
On New Year's Day, Next to a House Being Built (Amichai), 1979
On Pain of Seeing (Fried), 1969
On the Blossoming (Goldberg), 1992
On the Evening Road (Abse), 1994
On the Razzle (Stoppard), 1981
Onde estivestes de noite (Lispector), 1974
One Basket (Ferber), 1947
One Day in the Life of Ivan Denisovich (Harwood), 1970
One Facing Us (Matalon), 1996
One for the Road (Pinter), 1984
One Hour Late (Parker), 1935
One. Interior. Day. (Harwood), 1978
One Life (Clouts), 1966
One More Ride on the Merry-Go-Round (Wesker), 1985
One of the Family (Rubens), 1964
One Pair of Eyes (Stoppard), 1972
One Touch of Venus (Perelman), 1943
One Woman Plays (Wesker), 1989
One-Handed Pianist (Stavans), 1995
One-Legged on Ice (Abse), 1983
One-Man Army (Scliar), 1986
Onkl mozes (Asch), 1918
Only Problem (Spark), 1984
Only When I Laugh (Simon), 1982
Only Yesterday (Agnon), 2000
Ontdekking van de hemel (Mulisch), 1992
Op Hoop van zegen (Heijermans), 1901
Open Cage (Yezierska), 1979
Open Head (Ginsberg), 1972
Open Heart (Yehoshua), 1996
Open to the Public (Spark), 1997
Operation Daybreak (Harwood), 1975
Operation Shylock (P. Roth), 1993
Opgaande zon (Heijermans), 1911
Opgang (Bergelson), 1920
Opklayb (Glants-Leyeles), 1968
Oppermanns (Feuchtwanger), 1934
Opus gran (Mulisch), 1982
Opustoshaiushchaia liubov' (Erenburg), 1922
Or bead or (Orpaz), 1962
Or pere (Wallach), 1983
Oracle for Delfi (Rothenberg), 1994
Oral History (Gordimer), 1985
Oranging of America (Apple), 1976
Orchard (Tammuz), 1984
Orchestra and Beginners (Raphael), 1967
Ordeal of Gilbert Pinfold (Harwood), 1977
Ordinary Miracles (Jong), 1983
Ore nude (Moravia), 1964
Oreah (Lapid), 1988
Oreah nata lalun (Agnon), 1939
Orejas invisibles para el rumor de nuestros pasos (Dujovne Ortiz), 1966
Orelha de Van Gogh (Scliar), 1989
Oreme melukhe (Leyvik), 1923
Orgy (Rukeyser), 1965
Orimer yung (Weissenberg), 1939
Orologio (C. Levi), 1950
Orphans of the Street (West), 1938
Orpheus (Rukeyser), 1949
Orties noires (Vigée), 1984
Orzei mizvadot (Levini), 1982
Osennii krik iastreba (Brodsky), 1990
Ostanovka v pustyne (Brodsky), 1970
Osteria di Brema (P. Levi), 1975
Österreich (Fried), 1946
Ostjüdische Antlitz (A. Zweig), 1920
Ostrov mrtvých králů (Klíma), 1992
Othello (Carmi), 1991
Other Places (Pinter), 1982
Other Side (Minco), 1994
Other Side of the Wall (Shaham), 1983
Otklik neba (Mandel'shtam), 1989
Oto hayam (Oz), 1999
Otot stav (Ballas), 1992
Otsar hamilim shel hashalom (Hareven), 1991
Ottepel' (Erenburg), 1954
Otwórzmy Wrota Szkoły Szeroko (Korczak), 1978
Oublié (Wiesel), 1989
Oude lucht (Mulisch), 1977
Our Father (Rubens), 1987
Our Gang (P. Roth), 1971
Our Mrs McChesney (Ferber), 1915
Out (Sukenick), 1973
Out of a Book (Spark), 1933
Out of Chaos (Erenburg), 1934
Out of India (Jhabvala), 1986
Out of Silence (Rukeyser), 1992
Out of the Dark (Modiano), 1998
Out of the Depths (Brenner), 1992
Out of the Mouths (Rubens), 1970
Outer Banks (Rukeyser), 1967
Out-of-Towners (Simon), 1970
Outside over There (Sendak), 1981
Outsider (Samuel), 1921
Ouvrez (Sarraute), 1997
Oversight (Ionesco), 1971
Ovnt-shoen (Markish), 1922
Owl and the Pussycat (Friedman), 1971
Oxbridge Blues (Raphael), 1980
Oxford Poetry (Golding), 1921
Oy lamenatshim (Kishon), 1969
Oyf di khurves (Grade), 1947
Oyf di vegn sibires (Leyvik), 1940
Oyf mayn veg tsu dir (Grade), 1969
Oyf pesekh aheym (Sholem), 1903
Oyf yener zayt taykh (Hirshbein), 1905
Oyfn fidl (Sholem), 1902

Oyfshtand in geto (Halkin), 1944
Oytser (Pinski), 1906–07
Oytser (Sholem), 1908

P.D. Kimerakov (Epstein), 1975
P.P.P. (Torberg), 1964
Paamon verimon (Hazaz), 1974
Paamonim verakavot (Amichai), 1963
Padenie Parizha (Erenburg), 1942
Paese di mare (Ginzburg), 1973
Pagan Rabbi (Ozick), 1971
Pagans (Lind), 1964
Pahonim vehalomot (Michael), 1979
Paid in Full (Richler), 1958
Painted Bird (Kosinski), 1965
Paixão segundo G.H. (Lispector), 1964
Palace of Shattered Vessels (Shahar), 1975–93
Pale Blue Nightgown (Golding), 1944
Pamiat (Slutskii), 1957
Pandaemonium (Epstein), 1997
Panim el panim (Kovner), 1953
Pantagleize (Carmi), 1963
Panter bamartef (Oz), 1994
Panther in the Basement (Oz), 1997
Papiere des Andreas Lenz (Heym), 1963
Parables and Paradoxes (Kafka), 1958
Parables in German and English (Kafka), 1947
Paracelsus (Schnitzler), 1899
Parachutes and Kisses (Jong), 1984
Paradise (Moravia), 1971
Paradise Lost (Odets), 1935
Paradise of Poets (Rothenberg), 1999
Paradise Park (Goodman), 2000
Paradiso (Moravia), 1970
Parasites of Heaven (L. Cohen), 1966
Parcours (Jabès), 1985
Pardon wird nicht gegeben (Döblin), 1935
Pargfrider (Heym), 1998
Paris Gazette (Feuchtwanger), 1940
Paris in Spring (Parker), 1935
Paris Trip (Harwood), 1966
Parler seul (Tzara), 1950
Parmetene erd (Grade), 1968
Parmi Les Monstres (Federman), 1967
Parole (Saba), 1934
Paroles juives (A. Cohen), 1921
Parrucca (Ginzburg), 1990
Parshiyot (D. Baron), 1951
Parson's Pleasure (Harwood), 1986
Partaha ahuvati (Kishon), 1974
Partie (Cixous), 1976
Partners (Kops), 1975
Party (Bermant), 1981
Party through the Wall (Spark), 1957
Party Time (Pinter), 1992
Pascarella Family (Werfel), 1932
Pasión según San Martín (Goloboff), 1979
Passage from Home (I. Rosenfeld), 1946
Passage in the Night (Asch), 1953
Passage to India (Sherman), 2002
Passeggiata prima di cena (Bassani), 1953
Passing By (Sherman), 1974
Passing Through (Kunitz), 1995
Passion According to G.H. (Lispector), 1988
Passion According to Saint Martin (Goloboff), 1994
Passion and Pain (S. Zweig), 1924
Passion Flower Hotel (Mankowitz), 1965
Passion Play (Kosinski), 1979
Passion Play (Taylor), 1971
Passionate Past of Gloria Gaye (Kops), 1971
Passions (Isaac Singer), 1975
Passport to the War (Kunitz), 1944
Past Continuous (Shabtai),1985
Past Perfect (Shabtai),1987
Pastel de choclo (Dorfman), 1986
Patriarch (Bermant), 1981
Paul among the Jews (Werfel), 1928
Paul Éluard (Jabès), 1953
Paulus unter den Juden (Werfel), 1926
Pawnbroker (Wallant), 1961
Peaceable Kingdom (Silkin), 1954
Peeping Tom (H. Jacobson), 1984
Pegasus im Joch (Torberg), 1983
Peizazh s navodneniem (Brodsky), 1996
Penal Colony (Kafka), 1948
Penitent (Isaac Singer), 1983
Pénitents en maillots roses (Jacob), 1925
People (Malamud), 1989
People Betrayed (Döblin), 1983
People Immortal (V. Grossman), 1943
PEP (Feuchtwanger), 1928
Perechityvaia Chekhova (Erenburg), 1960
Perek alef, perek beit (Wieseltier), 1967
Perfect Peace (Oz), 1985
Perfidious Man (Self), 2000
Peridah mehadarom (Kovner), 1949
Periodic Table (P. Levi), 1984
Periods of the Moon (Layton), 1967
Perl un andere dertseylungen (Israel Singer), 1922
Person, Place and Thing (K. Shapiro), 1944
Personality Plus (Ferber), 1914
Perto do coração selvagem (Lispector), 1944
Peruvian Blues (Goldemberg), 2000
Pervaia kniga stikhov (Mandel'shtam), 1923
Pesah al kukhim (Yeshurun), 1952
Peščanik (Kiš), 1972
Pesnia o golubom slone (Shrayer-Petrov), 1990
Peter Altenberg (Kraus), 1919
Peter Hille-Buch (Lasker-Schüler), 1906
Petit Livre de la subversion hors de soupçon (Jabès), 1982
Petit peu d'exercice (Lunel), 1937
Petite Bijou (Modiano), 2001
Petroleuminseln (Feuchtwanger), 1927
Peurei peh (Levini), 1995
Pews (Bermant), 1980
Phanérogame (Jacob), 1918
Phantastische Theorie vom Schuster Prenzik (Karpinovich), 1996
Pharaon (Memmi), 1988
Phil Silvers Show (Simon), 1948
Philomel (Hollander), 1968
Philosophische Erzählungen (Herzl), 1919
Photo du Colonel (Ionesco), 1962
Pianista manca (Stavans), 1992
Piccolo Berto 1929–1931 (Saba), 1961
Pickup (Gordimer), 2001
Pickwick (Mankowitz), 1963
Picture (Ionesco), 1969
Picture This (Heller), 1988
Pictures of Fidelman (Malamud), 1969
Piepel (Ka-Tzetnik 135633), 1961
Pierrot i Kolombina (Leśmian), 1985
Pierrots Herrentraum (Feuchtwanger), 1916
Pieśni przemądrej Wasylisy (Leśmian), 1906
Piéton de l'air (Ionesco), 1962
Pilegesh begivah (Lapid), 1999
Pilgrim (Taylor), 1975
Pillar of Salt (Memmi), 1955
Pinball (Kosinski), 1982
Pinto and Sons (Epstein), 1990
Pirhei esh (Guri), 1949
Pirke and the Pearl (Rothenberg), 1975
Pirkei yoman (Shlonsky), 1981
Piterskii dozh (Shrayer-Petrov), 1999
Pithei devarim (Agnon), 1977
Pittzei bagrut (Bartov), 1965
Pitui (Lapid), 1992
Piyutim veshire jedidut (Langer), 1929
Pizmonim veshirei zemer (Alterman), 1976
Place de l'étoile (Modiano), 1968
Place of Love (K. Shapiro), 1942
Plain Girl (Miller), 1995
Planet News (Ginsberg), 1968
Planétarium (Sarraute), 1959
Planetarium (Sarraute), 1960
Plaster Saints (Zangwill), 1914
Plat de porc aux bananes vertes (Schwarz-Bart), 1967
Play by Play (Goldemberg), 1985
Play It Again, Sam (Allen), 1969
Play of the Text (Jacob), 1981
Playback (Josipovici), 1973
Playing for Time (Miller), 1980
Playing Sinatra (Kops), 1991
Playing with Love (Schnitzler), 1914
Playtexts (Federman), 1989
Plaza Suite (Simon), 1968
Pleasure of Your Death (Farhi), 1972
Pleytim (Grade), 1947
Pluma y la mascara (Stavans), 1993
Plumber's Progress (Taylor), 1975
Plumm-Pascha (Lasker-Schüler), 1914
Plutonian Ode (Ginsberg), 1982
Pnay (Zelda), 1967
Pnim vahutz (Wieseltier), 1977
Pobediteli (Bagritskii), 1932
Poche Parmentier (Perec), 1974
Podroz (Fink), 1990
Poem in Yellow after Tristan Tzara (Rothenberg), 1995
Poem of Beavers (Rothenberg), 1973
Poem to Celebrate the Spring and Diane Rothenberg's Birthday (Rothenberg), 1975
Poemas cotidianos (Aub), 1929
Poeme vegn stalinen (Markish), 1940
Poèmes d'hier et d'aujourd'hui (Spire), 1953
Poèmes d'ici et de là-bas (Spire), 1944
Poèmes de Loire (Spire), 1929
Poèmes de Morvan le Gaëlique (Jacob), 1953
Poèmes juifs (Spire), 1919
Poems All over the Place (Ginsberg), 1978
Poems and Songs (Bialik), 1933
Poems for a Survivor (Litvinoff), 1973
Poems for the Game of Silence 1960–1970 (Rothenberg), 1971
Poems for the Millennium (Rothenberg), 2000

Poems for the Society of the Mystic Animals (Rothenberg), 1972
Poems from End to End (Preil), 1976
Poems from the Hebrew (Bialik), 1924
Poems, Golders Green (Abse), 1962
Poems, Interviews, Photographs (Ginsberg), 1994
Poems of a Jew (K. Shapiro), 1958
Poems of Doctor Zhivago (Pasternak), 1965
Poems of Jerusalem (Amichai), 1987
Poems of Ten Brothers (Alterman), 1961
Poesie dell'adolescenza e giovanili 1900–1910 (Saba), 1949
Poet (Riding), 1933
Poet and Dancer (Jhabvala), 1993
Poet and the Rent (Mamet), 1974
Poet iz gevorn blind (Leyvik), 1938
Poets and Presidents (Doctorow), 1994
Pogrom in rusland (Gordin), 1891
Points of Departure (Pagis), 1981
Poison Pen (Harwood), 1993
Pokoj pro dva a jiné hry (Klíma), 1973
Poland/1931 (Rothenberg), 1969
Pole-Vaulter (Layton), 1974
Polin (Agnon), 1925
Polish Anecdotes (Rothenberg), 1970
Polka (Modiano), 1974
Polnoe sobranie sochinenii (Erenburg), 1927–28
Poltrona (Ginzburg), 1987
Ponsonby Post (Rubens), 1977
Pont und Anna (A. Zweig), 1928
Popper (Levini), 1977
Poppy and Memory (Celan), 1988
Porgess (Lustig), 1995
Porota (Klíma), 1968
Porta sbagliata (Ginzburg), 1990
Portage to San Cristóbal of A.H. (Steiner), 1981
Portes de la forêt (Wiesel), 1964
Portnoy's Complaint (P. Roth), 1969
Portrait (Silkin), 1950
Portrait d'un inconnu (Sarraute), 1948
Portrait de Dora (Cixous), 1976
Portrait du soleil (Cixous), 1974
Portrait of a Man Unknown (Sarraute), 1958
Portrait of Dora (Cixous), 1979
Portrait of the Artist as a Bad Character (Ozick), 1996
Portrait of the Artist, as an Old Man (Heller), 2000
Portrety russkikh poetov (Erenburg), 1922
Posh (S. Katz), 1971
Posheter kholem (M. Katz), 1947
Poslední stupeň důvěrnosti (Klíma), 1996
Posledniia noch' (Bagritskii), 1932
Post mortem (Kaniuk), 1992
Postcard from The Endless Short Story (Sukenick), 1974
Post-War Years, 1945–54 (Erenburg), 1966
Poupée blonde (Modiano), 1983
Pour Préparer un Oeuf dur (Ionesco), 1966
Pour un oui ou pour un non (Sarraute), 1982
Pourquoi je suis juif (Fleg), 1928
Poverkh bar'erov (Pasternak), 1917
Power (Feuchtwanger), 1926
Power of Light (Isaac Singer), 1980
Powers of Thirteen (Hollander), 1983
Pożegnanie z Bekiem Martyna (Korczak), 1974
Pożegnanie z Italią (Stryjkowski), 1954
Prager Kinder (Kisch), 1913
Prager Tagblatt (Brod), 1968
Prague Crossroads (Lustig), 1966
Prague Orgy (P. Roth), 1985
Prairie du Chien (Mamet), 1978
Praise (Gordimer), 1985
Praktyka to Moje Życie (Korczak), 1978
Prayer for Katerina Horovitzova (Lustig), 1973
Precious Legacy (Lustig), 1984
Precisely (Pinter), 1983
Préface aux lettres de Max Jacob à Edmond Jabès (Jabès), 1945
Preludio e canzonette (Saba), 1923
Preludio e fughe (Saba), 1928
Premier and the Painter (Zangwill), 1888
Première Aventure céleste de Monsieur Antipyrine (Tzara), 1916
Première journée à Rufisque (Bloch), 1926
Prénom de Dieu (Cixous), 1967
Préparatifs de noces au delà de l'abîme (Cixous), 1978
Present (Josipovici), 1975
Preservation of George Riley (Stoppard), 1964
Preserving the Hunger (I. Rosenfeld), 1988
President and the Angel (Klíma), 1985
President's Mystery (West), 1936
Pretender (Feuchtwanger), 1937
Preussische Wappen (Kolmar), 1934
Price (Miller), 1968
Price of Diamonds (D. Jacobson), 1957
Prime of Miss Jean Brodie (Spark), 1961
Primechaniia paporotnika (Brodsky), 1990
Primitive (Oppen), 1978
Primitives (Farhi), 1960
Prince of the Rhinoceri (Almog), 1976
Prince or Somebody (Golding), 1929
Principle of Water (Silkin), 1974
Prints reuveni (Bergelson), 1946
Prinz von Theben (Lasker-Schüler), 1914
Prise de l'école de Madhubaï (Cixous), 1983
Prisoner (Yizhar), 1975
Prisoner of Second Avenue (Simon), 1971
Prisoners of War (Feuchtwanger), 1934
Prisonnière (Proust), 1923
Private Ear (Shaffer), 1962
Private Potter (Harwood), 1962
Private View (Brookner), 1994
Pro domo et mundo (Kraus), 1912
Procedure (Mulisch), 1998
Procès de Shamgorod tel qu'il se déroula le 25 février 1649 (Wiesel), 1979
Process (Kafka), 1990
Prodigal Father (Shaffer), 1957
Prodlennyi polden' (Slutskii), 1975
Profane Friendship (Brodkey), 1994
Professional Foul (Stoppard), 1977
Professor Bernhardi (Schnitzler), 1912
Professor of Desire (P. Roth), 1977
Profile i Drobiazgi Żołnierskie (Rudnicki), 1946
Progress of Stories (Riding), 1935
Prométhée (Maurois), 1965
Prometheus (Maurois), 1965
Promise (Potok), 1969
Promises, Promises (Simon), 1968
Prontuario (Stavans), 1992
Proofs and Three Parables (Steiner), 1992
Propashchaia dusha (Shrayer-Petrov), 1997
Prophet (Asch), 1955
Prophet (Hareven), 1990
Prophet and Fool (Golding), 1923
Prophet Motive (Mikes), 1969
Propheteers (Apple), 1987
Prose Contribution to Cuban Revolution (Ginsberg), 1966
Prospect of Ferrara (Bassani), 1962
Proste trit (Fefer), 1924
Protective Custody (Koestler), 1942
Prothalamium for Bobolink and His Louisa (Stein), 1939
Protokol (Ben-Ner), 1983
Proud Destiny (Feuchtwanger), 1947
Proust Screenplay (Pinter), 1977
Providence (Brookner), 1982
Provinciale (Moravia), 1952
Provino (Moravia), 1955
Prozess (Kafka), 1925
Prozess Bunterbart (Brod), 1924
Pruebas al canto (Dorfman), 1980
Przybysz z Narbony (Stryjkowski), 1978
Przygody Sindbada Żeglarza (Leśmian), 1915
Psalam 44 (Kiš), 1962
Psalms with Their Spoils (Silkin), 1980
Psaume de la terre promise (Fleg), 1919
Public Eye (Shaffer), 1962
Public Image (Spark), 1968
Pull Down Vanity (Fiedler), 1963
Pundak haruhot (Alterman), 1962
Pundako shel yirmiahu (Tammuz), 1984
Pupil (Mulisch), 1987
Pupille (Cixous), 1972
Pure in Heart (Werfel), 1931
Purple Rose of Cairo (Allen), 1985
Pursuer (Golding), 1936
Pussycat and the Expert Plumber Who Was a Man (Miller), 1941
Pust un pas (Markish), 1920
Puste kretshme (Hirshbein), 1912
Puttermesser Papers (Ozick), 1997
Pythagoras (Abse), 1976
Pythagoras Smith from Row G (Abse), 1990

Q B VII (Uris), 1970
Quantity Theory of Insanity (Self), 1995
Quarantaine (Durlacher), 1993
Quarrel (Grade), 1992
Quarrel and Quandary (Ozick), 2000
Quartet (Harwood), 1999
Quartet (Jhabvala), 1981
Quartier perdu (Modiano), 1984
Quase de verdade (Lispector), 1978
Quauhquauhtinchan in den vreemde (Mulisch), 1962
Queen against Defoe (Heym), 1974
Queen for a Day (Parker), 1950
Queen of the East (A. Baron), 1956
Quel Petit Vélo à guidon chromé au fond de la cour? (Perec), 1966
Quest for Proust (Maurois), 1950
Qui Vive (Herzberg), 2002

Rabbi of Lud (Elkin), 1987
Rabbis and Wives (Grade), 1982

Rabi Akiva (Pinski), 1930
Rabota (Slutskii), 1964
Racconti d'estate (Moravia), 1958
Racconti romani (Moravia), 1954
Racines du ciel (Gary), 1956
Radek (Heym), 1995
Radetzky March (J. Roth), 1933
Radetzkymarsch (J. Roth), 1932
Radical Surgery (Markfield), 1991
Radio (Markish), 1922
Radio Days (Allen), 1987
Ragtime (Doctorow), 1975
Rahel Rechtet mit Gott (S. Zweig), 1930
Rain Events (Rothenberg), 1976
Raise High the Roof Beam, Carpenters (Salinger), 1959
Rakefet, ahavati harishonah (Almog), 1992
Rani jadi (Kiš), 1970
Rape of Tamar (D. Jacobson), 1970
Rapto de Europa o Siempre se puede hacer algo (Aub), 1946
Raquel, the Jewess of Toledo (Feuchtwanger), 1956
Rare Cure (Tammuz), 1981
Raspberry Reich (Mankowitz), 1979
Rats (D. Grossman), 1983
Ratsiti likhtov siftei yeshenim (Gilboa), 1968
Ravelstein (Bellow), 2000
Reaches of Heaven (Isaac Singer), 1980
Reader (Dorfman), 1992
Reah hadarim (Shaham), 1962
Real Inspector Hound (Stoppard), 1968
Real Thing (Stoppard), 1982
Reality and Dreams (Spark), 1996
Reality Sandwiches (Ginsberg), 1963
Really Rosie (Sendak), 1975
Reason Why (Miller), 1970
Reb shloyme nogid (Asch), 1913
Rebellion (J. Roth), 1924
Rebellische Herzen (Brod), 1957
Recetas, florecillas y otros contentos (Dujovne Ortiz), 1973
Rechts und Links (J. Roth), 1929
Récits d'Ellis Island (Perec), 1980
Reconstructie (Mulisch), 1969
Recreation (Pinter), 1998
Red Buttons Show (Simon), 1958–59
Red Carpet for the Sun (Layton), 1959
Red Cavalry (Babel'), 1929
Red Easy a Color (Rothenberg), 1968
Red Ribbon on a White Horse (Yezierska), 1950
Red River (Mamet), 1983
Redback (H. Jacobson), 1986
Redemption (Uris), 1995
Redemption of Tycho Brahe (Brod), 1928
Reem (Yeshurun), 1960
Reflected Glory (Harwood), 1990
Reflections on Espionage (Hollander), 1976
Refuge (Michael), 1988
Regaim (Alterman), 1973
Regel ahat bahuts (Bartov), 1994
Regenbogen (Ausländer), 1939
Regenbogen (A. Zweig), 1925
Regie (Viertel), 1925
Regina (Epstein), 1982
Regina (Hellman), 1949
Region's Violence (Fainlight), 1973
Rehayim shevurim (Hazaz), 1942
Rehem pundaki (Lapid), 1991
Rehov hamadregot (Hendel), 1956
Rehov hatomozhenna (Orpaz), 1979
Rehovot hanahar (Greenberg), 1951
Reich der Steine (Fried), 1963
Reich Gottes in Böhmen (Werfel), 1930
Reigen (Schnitzler), 1900
Reiho hamar shel hageranium (Tammuz), 1980
Reise nach Pressburg (Perutz), 1930
Rekhush natush (Lapid), 1987
Rekrutnik (Weissenberg)
Remains of the Day (Jhabvala), 1993
Rembrandt's Hat (Malamud), 1973
Remembrance of Crimes Past (Abse), 1990
Remembrance of Things Past (Proust), 1922–31
Renklerin Akını (Gerez), 1954
Re-ordering of the Stones (Silkin), 1961
Report to an Academy (Kafka), 1983
Requa-I (Olsen), 1971
Requiem for Harlem (H. Roth), 1998
Requiem for Na'aman (Tammuz), 1982
Requiem lenaaman (Tammuz), 1978
Reshimot letoledotai (Mendele Moykher Sforim), 1889
Reshimot shel hatul rehov (Aloni), 1996
Reshut hayahid bead harabbim (Berdyczewski), 1892
Reshut netunah (Hareven), 1970
Resistance Trilogy (Dorfman), 1998
Restless Spirit (Schneour), 1963
Resurrection (Louvish), 1994
Retour au livre (Jabès), 1965
Retrato de un general visto de medio cuerpo y vuelto hacia la izquierda (Aub), 1969
Retreat (Applefeld), 1984
Retsah (Levini), 1998
Retsah beshabat baboker (Gur), 1988
Retterin (Brod), 1914
Return of Doctor O'Grady (Maurois), 1951
Return of Hyman Kaplan (Rosten), 1959
Return of the Vanishing American (Fiedler), 1968
Return to the Book (Jabès), 1978
Returning Lost Loves (Kenaz), 2001
Rëubeni, Fürst der Juden (Brod), 1925
Rëubeni, Prince of the Jews (Brod), 1928
Reunion (Mamet), 1976
Revenentes (Perec), 1972
Revenge of the Space Pandas (Mamet), 1977
Reviyat rosendorf (Shaham), 1987
Revolted Daughter (Zangwill), 1901
Révolutions pour plus d'un Faust (Cixous), 1975
Rhapsody (Schnitzler), 1927
Rhinocéros (Ionesco), 1959
Rhinoceros (Ionesco), 1960
Rhume onirique (Ionesco), 1963
Rhythm in the Clouds (West), 1937
Rhythms (Reznikoff), 1916
Ribcage (Hendel), 1994
Richard's Things (Raphael), 1973
Riches of the Poor (Mikes), 1987
Richtige Einstellung (Heym), 1977
Riddle of Cantinflas (Stavans), 1998
Ride down Mount Morgan (Miller), 1991
Right and Left (J. Roth), 1991
Rigmarole of Contrariety (Federman), 1982
Rijgdraad (Herzberg), 1995
Rikud al hamayim (Perry), 1994
Rimskie elegii (Brodsky), 1982
Ring Roads (Modiano), 1974
Rio Grande (Sherman), 1976
Rise of David Levinsky (Cahan), 1917
Rising Gorge (Perelman), 1961
Rising Sun (Heijermans), 1925
Ritspat esh (Applefeld), 1988
Ritter Laberius schafft sich aus der Welt (Brod), 1964
Ritualmord in Ungarn (A. Zweig), 1914
Rivage (Jacob), 1931
River Breaks Up (Israel Singer), 1938
Riverchange (Kops), 2001
Road to Miltown (Perelman), 1957
Road to the City (Ginzburg), 1949
Road to the Open (Schnitzler), 1923
Roast Beef, Medium (Ferber), 1913
Robinson (Spark), 1958
Robinson juif (Bloch), 1970
Rocket to the Moon (Odets), 1938
Rocking Chair (Klein), 1948
Rocking Horse (Kaniuk), 1977
Rockrose (M. Katz), 1970
Rocky Marciano is Dead (Kops), 1976
Roi au masque d'or (Schwob), 1893
Roi de Béotie (Jacob), 1921
Roi se meurt (Ionesco), 1962
Rolls Royce (Bassani), 1982
Roman fun a ferd ganev un andere ertsehlungen (Opatoshu), 1917
Roman russi (Shalev), 1988
Roman Spring of Mrs Stone (Sherman), 2002
Roman Tales (Moravia), 1956
Romana (Moravia), 1947
Romance of a Horse Thief (Opatoshu), 1986
Romantic Englishwoman (Stoppard), 1975
Romanzo di Ferrara (Bassani), 1974
Ronde (Schnitzler), 1954
Ronde de nuit (Modiano), 1969
Rondos un andere lider (Glants-Leyeles), 1926
Rooie Sien (Herzberg), 1975
Room (Pinter), 1957
Room with a View (Jhabvala), 1985
Roommates (Apple), 1994
Roots (Wesker), 1959
Roots of Heaven (Gary), 1958
Rose (Sherman), 1999
Roseland (Jhabvala), 1977
Rosencrantz and Guildenstern Are Dead (Stoppard), 1966
Rosendorf Quartet (Shaham), 1991
Rosenkoralle (Brod), 1961
Roses are Blooming in Picardy (Bermant), 1972
Roses de septembre (Maurois), 1956
Rosh leshualim (Avidan), 1994
Rosie Hogarth (A. Baron), 1951
Rough Crossing (Stoppard), 1984
Round Dance (Schnitzler), 1982
Round the Town (Parker), 1924
Royal Family (Ferber), 1927
Royal Hunt of the Sun (Shaffer), 1964
Roytarmeyishe balades (Markish), 1940

Royte felder (Hirshbein), 1935
Ruah yamim (Megged), 1950
Rubber Merchants (Levini), 1983
Rue des boutiques obscures (Modiano), 1978
Ruimte van Sokolov (Winter), 1992
Ruka i dusha (Slutskii), 1981
Rumors (Simon), 1990
Runaway (Yizhar), 1967
Runaway Soul (Brodkey), 1991
Russia House (Stoppard), 1989
Rustic Sunset (Ben-Ner), 1998
Ruth (Wassermann), 1897
Rzecz Czarnoleska (Tuwim), 1929

Sa habaytah yonatan (Bartov), 1962
Sabbath (Heijermans), 1903
Sabbath's Theater (P. Roth), 1995
Saboteur (Parker), 1942
Sacrifice (Wiseman), 1956
Sacrifice impérial (Jacob), 1929
Sad Dust Glories (Ginsberg), 1975
Sad rozstajny (Leśmian), 1912
Sadness and Happiness (Pinsky), 1975
Sadot magnetiyim (Kahana-Carmon), 1977
Safe Sex (Fierstein), 1987
Safiah (Rachel), 1927
Sagittario (Ginzburg), 1957
Said the Old Man to the Young Man (Wesker), 1978
Saint Matorel (Jacob), 1911
St Peter's Snow (Perutz), 1990
St Petri-Schnee (Perutz), 1933
St Urbain's Horseman (Richler), 1971
Sair, laazazel (Kishon), 1998
Salamandra (Ka-Tzetnik 135633), 1946
Sallah shabbati (Kishon), 1988
Salome of the Tenements (Yezierska), 1923
Salomon (Fleg), 1930
Salon de l'automobile (Ionesco), 1963
Salt Land (Shaffer), 1955
Salutations (Ionesco), 1966
Salvage (Stoppard), 2002
Salvation (Asch), 1934
Samaël (Spire), 1921
Same Sea (Oz), 2001
Samotność (Leśmian), 1992
Samson and Delilah (Mankowitz), 1972
Samson Riddle (Mankowitz), 1972
Samukh venireh (Agnon), 1950
San Juan (Aub), 1943
Sanatorium pod klepsydrą (Schulz), 1937
Sanatorium under the Sign of the Hourglass (Schulz), 1978
Sanctity of Marriage (Mamet), 1979
Sand aus den Urnen (Celan), 1948
Sang du ciel (Rawicz), 1961
Sar ehad laazazel (Aloni), 1973
Sarah, Sarah (Matalon), 2000
Saratoga Trunk (Ferber), 1941
Satan in Goray (Isaac Singer), 1955
Saturday Morning Murder (Gur), 1992
Saucier's Apprentice (Perelman), 1983
Savrulan Zaman (Gerez), 1955
Saw (S. Katz), 1972
S'Brent (Gebirtig), 1946
Scapegoat (Amir), 1988
Scène à quatre (Ionesco), 1959
Scenes from Humanitas (Bellow), 1956
Schaffnerin (Wassermann), 1897
Schakels (Heijermans), 1905
Schast'e (V. Grossman), 1935
Schatten und Licht (Heym), 1960
Schildkröten (V. Canetti), 1999
Schlaf und Erwachen (Werfel), 1935
Schlaflose Tage (Becker), 1978
Schläfst Du, Mutter? (Wassermann), 1897
Schlafwandler (Broch), 1931–32
Schleier der Beatrice (Schnitzler), 1900
Schleier der Pierrette (Schnitzler), 1910
Schloss (Kafka), 1926
Schloss Nornepygge (Brod), 1908
Schmähschrift oder Königin gegen Defoe (Heym), 1970
Schneepart (Celan), 1971
Schoene Seele (Viertel), 1925
School Play (Raphael), 1979
Schöpferische Tätigkeit des Regisseurs (Viertel), 1925
Schriften zum Theater (Viertel), 1970
Schuldlosen (Broch), 1950
Schüler Gerber hat absolviert (Torberg), 1930
Schwarze Messe (Werfel), 1989
Schwarze Vorhang (Döblin), 1919
Schwarzenberg (Heym), 1984
Schwedische Reiter (Perutz), 1936
Schweiger (Werfel), 1922
Schwestern (Wassermann), 1906
Scialle andaluso (Morante), 1963
Scorpion (Memmi), 1969
Scorpion (Memmi), 1971
Scrap Leaves, Hasty Scribbles (Ginsberg), 1968
Scrap of Time (Fink), 1987
Scratch (Herzberg), 1995
Scuba Duba (Friedman), 1967
Scum (Isaac Singer), 1991
Scum of the Earth (Koestler), 1941
Sdom 1933
Se non ora, quando? (P. Levi), 1982
Se questo è un uomo (P. Levi), 1966
Sea Level (Broch), 1966
Seacoast of Bohemia (Golding), 1923
Seagull (Stoppard), 1997
Séance (Isaac Singer), 1968
Search (Durlacher), 1998
Searchers and Seizures (Elkin), 1973
Searching Wind (Hellman), 1944
Seascape (Oppen), 1973
Second Crucifixion (Samuel), 1960
Second Day (Erenburg), 1984
Second Leaf (Riding), 1935
Second Mrs Whitberg (Bermant), 1976
Second Nature (Pasternak), 1990
Second Scroll (Klein), 1951
Second Stone (Fiedler), 1963
Second Woman and Insecurity (Ayalon), 1998
Secret (Spire), 1919
Seduction Comedy (Schnitzler), 1992
See Under (D. Grossman), 1989
Seedlings (Rothenberg), 1996
Seeing Life (A. Baron), 1958
Seeker (Sachs), 1970
Seele aus Holz (Lind), 1962
Seems like Old Times (Simon), 1980
Sefer haagasim hatsehubim (Sadeh), 1985
Sefer haamudim (Greenberg), 1945–56
Sefer habaladot (Tchernichovski), 1930
Sefer hadikduk hapenimi (D. Grossman), 1991
Sefer haefsharuyot (Avidan), 1985
Sefer hahidot (Alterman), 1971
Sefer haidilyot (Tchernichovski), 1922
Sefer haigul (Greenberg), 1947–53
Sefer hakabbetsanim (Mendele Moykher Sforim), 1909
Sefer hakitrug vehaemunah (Greenberg), 1937
Sefer hamasaot (Kishon), 1988
Sefer hashirim 1947–1970 (Sadeh), 1970
Sefer hasulamot (Shlonsky), 1973
Sefer hayareah (Gurevitch), 1999
Sefer mishpahti (Kishon), 1980
Sefer, sofer vesipur (Agnon), 1938
Sefer yosef (Hoffman), 1988
Segodnia i vchera (Slutskii), 1961
Seine Hoheit (Herzl), 1888
Seize the Day (Bellow), 1956
Sen Azrila (Stryjkowski), 1975
Sender-blank un zayn gezindl (Sholem), 1888
Seneca Journal (Rothenberg), 1975
Seni Yaşamak (Gerez), 1963
Senilità (Svevo), 1898
Sensation Fair (Kisch), 1941
Sense of Loss (Harwood), 1978
Sensualità (Moravia), 1951
Separate Peace (Stoppard), 1966
Separate Way (Reznikoff), 1936
Sept Petits Sketches (Ionesco), 1953
September (Allen), 1987
September Rose (Maurois), 1958
Serata di Don Giovanni (Moravia), 1945
Serena disperazione (Saba), 1920
Serenade (Winter), 1995
Serenissima (Jong), 1987
Sergeant Bilko (Simon), 1958–59
Serio-Comic Governess (Zangwill), 1904
Serment de Kolvillàg (Wiesel), 1973
Sermon (Mamet), 1981
Serpent Son (Raphael), 1979
Sestra moia zhizn' (Pasternak), 1922
Set on Edge (Rubens), 1960
Settle Down Simon Katz (Kops), 1973
Seuil (Jabès), 1990
Seven (Josipovici), 1983
Seven Hells of Jigoku Zoshi (Rothenberg), 1962
Seven Little Monsters (Sendak), 1976
Seventh Column (Alterman), 1948–54
Severed Head (Raphael), 1970
Sex and the Single Girl (Heller), 1964
Sexual Perversity in Chicago (Mamet), 1974
Seymour (Salinger), 1959
Sfamo shel haafifor (Shahar), 1982
Shaar knisah, shaar yetsiah (Yeshurun), 1981
Shabbetai Zvi (Asch), 1930
Shabsiel (Goldfaden), 1896
Shadow Master (Feinstein), 1978
Shadows and Fog (Allen), 1992
Shadows and Lights (Heym), 1963
Shadows on the Ground (Layton), 1982
Shadows on the Hudson (Isaac Singer), 1997
Shahor al gabei lavan (Kishon), 1956

Shakespeare and Myself (Mikes), 1952
Shakespeare in Love (Stoppard), 1998
Shakespeare Wallah (Jhabvala), 1965)
Shaloshot sipurim (Shahar), 1974
Shalvat shotim (Lapid), 1974
Shamgar hanagar (Goldberg), 1979
Shaon hahol (Pagis), 1959
Shap (Leyvik), 1926
Shards of Memory (Jhabvala), 1995
Share of Ink (Jabès), 1979
Shattered Plinths (Layton), 1968
Shaul ufaul (Berdyczewski), 1971
Shavim veshavim yoter (Michael), 1974
Shavririm (D. Baron), 1948
Shawl (Mamet), 1985
Shayn fun farloshene shtern (Grade), 1950
Shayn un opshayn (Fefer), 1946
She nivdelu meekol merhak (Zelda), 1984
Sheat haefes (Kovner), 1953
Sheat hahesed (Amichai), 1982
Shedim bamartef (Michael), 1983
Shedim humim (Michael), 1993
Sheerit hahayim (Goldberg), 1971
Shekhol vekishalon (Brenner), 1920
Shel mi ata yeled? (Bartov), 1970
Sheleg biyerushalayim (Carmi), 1956
Sheloshah sipurim (D. Baron), 1974
Sheloshah yamim veyeled (Yehoshua), 1969
Shemà (P. Levi), 1976
Shenandoah (Schwartz), 1941
Shene ganim (Wallach), 1969
Shepherd Singing Ragtime (Golding), 1921
Shepherd's Pipe (Schnitzler), 1922
Shesh kenafayim laehad (Bartov), 1954
Shetehi li ha-sakin (D. Grossman), 1998
Shetika (Sobol), 2000
Sheut meuheret (Pagis), 1964
Sheva nashim (Schütz), 1995
Sheva rashuyot (Gilboa), 1949
Shevuat emunim (Agnon), 1943
Sheydim tants (Kreitman), 1936
Shibolet yerukat haayin (Goldberg), 1940
Shifs-Karta (Erenburg), 1922
Shikun vatikim (Shaham), 1958
Shimmering Crystal (Kolmar), 1995
Shinui arakhin (Berdyczewski), 1890s
Ship Named Hope (Klíma), 1970
Ship's Pasture (Silkin), 1986
Shipwreck (Stoppard), 2002
Shir ani, shir immah (Aini), 2000
Shir bekefarim (Goldberg), 1942
Shira (Agnon), 1989
Shirah (Agnon), 1971
Shirat hatsipporim (Bejerano), 1985
Shirat rosa (Kovner), 1987
Shirei (Raab), 1964
Shirei ahava vemin (Avidan), 1976
Shirei aspaklar (Greenberg), 1954–61
Shirei halon (Lapid), 1988
Shirei hamapolet vehapius (Shlonsky), 1938
Shirei hametim (Levini), 1999
Shirei hayamim (Shlonsky), 1946
Shirei herev (Ratosh), 1969
Shirei heshbon (Ratosh), 1963
Shirei hotam (Guri), 1954
Shirei lahats (Avidan), 1962
Shirei makot mitsrayyim (Alterman), 1944
Shirei mamash (Ratosh), 1965
Shirei milhamah vemehaah (Avidan), 1976
Shirei nearah (Ratosh), 1975
Shirei Tchernichovsky leehav hatseirim (Tchernichovski), 1936
Shirei yerushalayim (Amichai), 1987
Shirim (Carmi), 1994
Shirim 1948–1962 (Amichai), 1962/63
Shirim al kelev vekalbah (Zach), 1990
Shirim baboker, baboker (Gilboa), 1953
Shirim bilti efshariim (Avidan), 1968
Shirim ekroniim (Avidan), 1978
Shirim hitsoniim (Avidan), 1970
Shirim itiim (Wieseltier), 2000
Shirim leyaldei israel (Tchernichovski), 1907
Shirim min haazuvah (Carmi), 1988
Shirim shimushiim (Avidan), 1973
Shits (Levini), 1974
Shivitti (Ka-Tzetnik 135633), 1989
Shkiah kafrit (Ben-Ner), 1976
Shklover kinder (Schneour), 1951
Shklover yidn (Schneour), 1929
Shlekhte froy un andere ertseylungen (Weissenberg), 1921–22
Shloyme moylkhe (Glants-Leyeles), 1926
Shloyme reb hayims (Mendele Moykher Sforim), 1903
Shmates (Leyvik), 1921
Shmendrik (Goldfaden), 1876
Shminiot baavir (Kishon), 1965
Shmo holekh lefanav (Kishon), 1953
Shnayder-gezeln note manger zingt (Manger), 1948
Shneim asar panim (Pagis), 1981
Shneinu nitnaheg yafeh (Castel-Bloom), 1997
Shoes of Tanboury (Ballas), 1970
Shoeshine (Mamet), 1979
Shoeshine (Wesker), 1989
Shoot the Works (Parker), 1931
Shorshei avir (Almog), 1993
Short Friday (Isaac Singer), 1964
Short Life (Megged), 1980
Short Sentimental Journey (Svevo), 1967
Shosha (Isaac Singer), 1978
Shoshan lavan shoshan adom (Schütz), 1988
Shoshanat haruhot (Guri), 1960
Shoshim amud shel Avot Yeshurun (Yeshurun), 1964
S'hot dos vort mayn bobe moyne (M. Katz), 1939
Shotns fun gedenkn (Tussman), 1965
Show Boat (Ferber), 1926
Show Must Go On (Odets), 1939
Shower (Aini), 1992
Shpener (Fefer), 1922
Shpigl un andere dertseylungen (Isaac Singer), 1975
Shpilfoygl (Halkin), 1942
Shpits (Lapid), 1971
Shrayber geyt in kheyder (L. Shapiro), 1945
Shrinking (Almog), 1986
Shrivings (Shaffer), 1970
Shtarker fin toyt (Weissenberg), 1931
Shtern ibern geto (Shpigl), 1948
Shtern in shtoyb (Manger), 1967
Shtern laykhten in tom (Shpigl), 1976
Shtern oyfn dakh (Manger), 1929
Shtetl (Asch), 1904
Shtetl (Weissenberg), 1906
Shteyn tsu a shteyn (Fefer), 1925
Shtiferish (Markish), 1919
Shtign tsum himl (Shpigl), 1966
Shtol un ayzn (Israel Singer), 1927
Shtralendike yidn (Glatshteyn), 1946
Shtub mit zibn fentster (Molodovski), 1957
Shtumer meshiekh (Pinski), 1912
Shtumer minyen (Grade), 1976
Shturemteg (Bergelson), 1928
Shulamis (Goldfaden), 1880
Shulamis (Halkin), 1940
Shulhoyf (Grade), 1958
Shum vremeni (Mandel'shtam), 1925
Shurah psukah (Gurevitch), 1984
Shveln (Markish), 1919
Shver tsu zayn a yid (Sholem), 1914
Shylock (Wesker), 1990
Shylock's Daughter (Jong), 1995
Siberia (Sutzkever), 1961
Sibir (Sutzkever), 1952
Sibirye (Gordin), 1891
Sibyls (Fainlight), 1980
Sicilian Noon (Golding), 1925
Sid Caesar Show (Simon), 1956–57
Side Effects (Allen), 1975
Sideways (Gnessin), 1983
Sidra (Shaham), 1992
Siebente Tag (Lasker-Schüler), 1905
Siège de Jérusalem (Jacob), 1914
Siegfried (Mulisch), 2001
Siesta in Xbalba and Return to the States (Ginsberg), 1956
Sightings I-IX (Rothenberg), 1964
Sign on Rosie's Door (Sendak), 1960
Sikum beinayim (Avidan), 1960
Silberne Saiten (S. Zweig), 1901
Silence (Pinter), 1969
Silence (Sarraute), 1969
Silence of Colonel Bramble (Maurois), 1919
Silencer (Louvish), 1991
Silences du Colonel Bramble (Maurois), 1918
Silent Areas (Feinstein), 1980
Silent Prophet (J. Roth), 1979
Silky (Rosten), 1979
Silver Foxes are Dead (Lind), 1965
Silver Platter (Alterman), 1974
Simhat aniyyim (Alterman), 1941
Simon at Midnight (Kops), 1982
Simone (Feuchtwanger), 1944
Simple Story (Agnon), 1985
Sindrom yerushalayim (Sobol), 1987
Síndrome de naufragios (Glantz), 1984
Singing Book of Friendship (Alterman), 1958
Sinit ani medaberet elekhah (Liebrecht), 1992
Sink the Belgrano! (Berkoff), 1986
Sinner (Israel Singer), 1933
Siódma jesień (Tuwim), 1922
Sipario (Moravia), 1948
Sippur hirbet hizah (Yizhar), 1949
Sipur pashut (Agnon), 1935
Sipur shemathil belevayah shel nahash (Matalon), 1989

Sipuranton haarmeni (Tammuz), 1960
Sipurei ahavim (Agnon), 1931
Sipurei sof shavua (Kaniuk), 1986
Sipurei vilne (Karpinovich), 1995
Sipurim beshalosh kolot (Shamir), 1977
Sipurim bilti retsuim (Castel-Bloom), 1993
Sipurim ketsarim (Shahar), 1979
Sipurim veagadot (Agnon), 1944
Sistema periodico (P. Levi), 1975
Sister My Life (Pasternak), 1967
Sisters of Mercy (L. Cohen), 1973
Sittlichkeit und Kriminalität (Kraus), 1908
Sitton (Barbash), 1995
Six Feet of the Country (Gordimer), 1956
Six Persons (Zangwill), 1893
Sixth Day (P. Levi), 1990
Six-Year-Old Man (Elkin), 1987
Sketches (Simon), 1952
Ski Bum (Gary), 1966
Skin Divers (Michaels), 1999
Skladiste (Kiš), 1995
Sklepy cynamonowe (Schulz), 1934
Skrawek czasu (Fink), 1983
Skrzypek opętany (Leśmian), 1985
Sky in Narrow Streets (Abse), 1987
Slattery's Hurricane (Wouk), 1956
Slave (Isaac Singer), 1962
Slavs! (Kushner), 1995
Sleep, My Love (Rosten), 1946
Sleeper (Allen), 1973
Sleepless Days (Becker), 1979
Sleeps Six (Raphael), 1979
Sleepwalkers (Broch), 1932
Slepaia krasavitsa (Pasternak), 1969
Slight Ache (Pinter), 1959
Slightly Older Guy (Friedman), 1995
Sliha shenitsahnu (Kishon), 1967
Sloan-Kettering (Kovner), 1986
Słoń Trąbalski (Tuwim), 1938
Słowa we krwi (Tuwim), 1926
Slugger's Wife (Simon), 1985
Small Change (Hendel), 1990
Small Changes (Piercy), 1973
Small Desperation (Abse), 1968
Small Explosion (Abse), 1964
Small Time Crooks (Allen), 2000
Smash Up (Parker), 1947
Smell of Hay (Bassani), 1975
Smile of the Lamb (D. Grossman), 1990
Smiles on Washington Square (Federman), 1985
Snapshots of a Daughter-in-Law (Rich), 1963
Snow and Guilt (Pressburger), 2000
So Big (Ferber), 1924
So Far, So Bad (Taylor), 1974
So Forth (Brodsky), 1996
So kam ich unter die Deutschen (Fried), 1977
So Sorry We Won (Kishon), 1967
Soaps (Sherman), 1975
Sobranie sochinenii (Erenburg), 1962–67
Sodom and Gomorrah (Proust), 1992
Sodoma (Stryjkowski), 1963
Sodome et Gomorrhe (Proust), 1921–22
Sof davar (Shabtai),1984
Sof haolam (Shamir), 1954
Soft Voice of the Serpent (Gordimer), 1952
Sogni del pigro (Moravia), 1940
Sogrim et hayam (Katzir), 1990
Soharei hagumi (Levini), 1978
Söhne (A. Zweig), 1923
Söhne (Feuchtwanger), 1935
Soif et la faim (Ionesco), 1964
Sokhen hamelekh (Shahar), 1979
Sokrates tańczący (Tuwim), 1920
Solal (A. Cohen), 1930
Solal of the Solals (A. Cohen), 1933
Soldat und ein Mädchen (Fried), 1960
Soldatenspiele (A. Zweig), 1956
Soldier's Embrace (Gordimer), 1980
Soldiers of the Republic (Parker), 1938
Soldier's Tale (K. Shapiro), 1968
Soleil sous la mer (Vigée), 1972
Solitaire (Ionesco), 1973
Solitary Grief (Rubens), 1991
Solitary Thing (Sherman), 1962
Solo (Ballas), 1998
Solo (Sobol), 1991
Solomon Grip (Levini), 1969
Solomon Gursky Was Here (Richler), 1989
Some Corner of an English Field (Abse), 1956
Some Fugitives Take Cover (Hollander), 1986
Some Laughter, Some Tears (Sholem), 1968
Some Monday for Sure (Gordimer), 1976
Some of These Days (Kops), 1990
Some Sunny Day (Sherman), 1996
Some Time (Zukofsky), 1956
Some Unease and Angels (Feinstein), 1977
Somebody Like You (Carmi), 1971
Something Happened (Heller), 1974
Something Out There (Gordimer), 1984
Something to Remember Me By (Bellow), 1991
Something's Wrong (Raphael), 1978
Sommer, den man zurückwünscht (Brod), 1952
Son of a Smaller Hero (Richler), 1955
Soñador de Smith (Goloboff), 1990
Sone hanisim (Hareven), 1983
Song for Hope (Wiesel), 1987
Song of Bernadette (Werfel), 1942
Song of Deprivation (Ezekiel), 1969
Song of the Dnieper (Schneour), 1945
Song of the Valley (Asch), 1939
Songbook (Saba), 1998
Songs from a Room (L. Cohen), 1969
Songs from the Ghetto (M. Rosenfeld), 1898
Songs of Jerusalem and Myself (Amichai), 1973
Songs of Labor (M. Rosenfeld), 1914
Songs of Love and Hate (L. Cohen), 1971
Sonhos tropicais (Scliar), 1992
Sons of Mrs Aab (Millin), 1931
Sophie! Last of the Red Hot Mamas (Kops), 1990
Sopro de vida (Lispector), 1978
Sore Sites (Self), 2000
Sorrow of War (Golding), 1919
Sorrows (Pinski), 1932
Sorrows of Job (Levini), 1993
Sorstalanság (Kertész), 1975
Sotn in goray (Isaac Singer), 1935
Soudce z milosti (Klíma), 1986
Souffles (Cixous), 1975
Soul and Body of John Brown (Rukeyser), 1940
Soul of a Jew (Sobol), 1983
Soul of Wood (Lind), 1964
Soundings (Weissbort), 1977
Soupçon, le désert (Jabès), 1978
Sources (Rich), 1983
South Africa's Bird of Paradise Flower (Silkin), 1974
Sovremennye istorii (Slutskii), 1969
Sowing (Woolf), 1960
Spanische Ballade (Feuchtwanger), 1955
Spanish Prisoner (Mamet), 1985
Spanish Testament (Koestler), 1937
Spectral Emanations (Hollander), 1978
Speech to the Neighborhood Watch Committee (Miller), 1988
Speech-Grille (Celan), 1971
Speed of Darkness (Rukeyser), 1968
Speed-the-Plow (Mamet), 1985
Spektorskii (Pasternak), 1931
Spell (Broch), 1987
Spice-Box of Earth (L. Cohen), 1961
Spicilège (Schwob), 1896
Spider Danced a Cozy Jig (Layton), 1984
Spider's Web (J. Roth), 1988
Spiegelmensch (Werfel), 1920
Spiel im Morgengrauen (Schnitzler), 1927
Spielhof (Werfel), 1920
Spieltexte (Federman), 1989
Spielzeug der Zeit (A. Zweig), 1933
Spinnennetz (J. Roth), 1923
Spinoza of Market Street (Isaac Singer), 1961
Spirit of Culver (West), 1939
Spiritus I (Rakosi), 1983
Spital Tongues Plays (Taylor), 1974
Splash (Friedman), 1984
Spookhouse (Fierstein), 1982
Sport of Nature (Gordimer), 1987
Spotted Tiger (Shabtai),1985
Sprache (Kraus), 1937
Sprachgitter (Celan), 1959
Spring Sonata (Rubens), 1979
Sprong der paarden en de zoute zee (Mulisch), 1955
Sprüche und Widersprüche (Kraus), 1909
Spy Who Died of Boredom (Mikes), 1973
Squaring the Circle (Stoppard), 1984
Squire of Bor Shachor (Bermant), 1977
Squirrels (Mamet), 1974
Sroki (Slutskii), 1984
Stage Door (Ferber), 1936
Stalingrad Hits Back (V. Grossman), 1942
Stalingradskaia bitva (V. Grossman), 1943
Stam (Markish), 1920
Stand and Deliver (Mankowitz), 1972
Stanzas in Meditation (Stein), 1956
Star Eternal (Ka-Tzetnik 135633), 1972
Star is Born (Parker), 1937
Star of the Unborn (Werfel), 1946
Star Shines over Mt Morris Park (H. Roth), 1994
Stardust Memories (Allen), 1980
Star-Spangled Girl (Simon), 1966
Start in Life (Brookner), 1981
Staryi uchitel'. Povesti i rasskazy (V. Grossman), 1962
Static Element (Zach), 1982
Statue de sel (Memmi), 1953
Status Quo Vadis (Sobol), 1973
Stav yarok (Shaham), 1979
Steambath (Friedman), 1970

Steel and Iron (Israel Singer), 1969
Stefan Rott (Brod), 1931
Steinway Quintet plus Four (Epstein), 1976
Stella (Kushner), 1987
Stempeniu (Sholem), 1889
Stenen bruidsbed (Mulisch), 1959
Stepan Kol'chugin (V. Grossman), 1937–40
Steps (Kosinski), 1968
Sterben (Schnitzler), 1895
Stern (Friedman), 1962
Stern der Dämonen (Weiss), 1921
Stern der Ungeborenen (Werfel), 1946
Sternverdunkelung (Sachs), 1949
Stick Your Neck Out (Richler), 1963
Stikhi o Gruzii (Pasternak), 1958
Stikhi o voine (Erenburg), 1943
Stikhi raznykh let (Slutskii), 1988
Stir Crazy (Friedman), 1980
Stojí, stojí, šibenička (Klíma), 1976
Stolen Childhood (Lustig), 1966
Stolen Stories (S. Katz), 1984
Stone (Mandel'shtam), 1981
Stone Bridal Bed (Mulisch), 1962
Stone, Paper, Knife (Piercy), 1983
Stonedial (Konrád), 2000
Store of Ladies (Golding), 1927
Storia (Morante), 1974
Storie dei poveri amanti e altri versi (Bassani), 1946
Storie dell'ottavo distretto (Pressburger), 1986
Storie della preistoria (Moravia), 1982
Storie naturali (P. Levi), 1967
Stories from Jerusalem (Shahar), 1976
Stories in an Almost Classical Mode (Brodkey), 1988
Stories of a Plain (Yizhar), 1964
Stories of the East (Woolf), 1921
Stories of the Revolution (Hazaz), 1980
Storm (Erenburg), 1949
Storm Tide (Piercy), 1998
Stormy Life of Lasik Roitschwantz (Erenburg), 1960
Stormy Life of Laz Roitshvants (Erenburg), 1965
Story of G.I. Joe (Miller), 1945
Story of Gus (Miller), 1947
Story of the Hundred Days (J. Roth), 1936
Story of the Last Thought (Hilsenrath), 1990
Story on Page One (Odets), 1959
Story with No Address (Hendel), 1996
Stove (Lind), 1983
Strada che va in città (Ginzburg), 1942
Straight Hearts' Delight (Ginsberg), 1980
Strange Case of Dr Simmonds and Dr Glas (Abse), 2002
Strange Nation of Rafael Mendes (Scliar), 1987
Strange New Cottage in Berkeley (Ginsberg), 1963
Strange Stories for Strange Kids (Spiegelman), 2001
Stranger in Shakespeare (Fiedler), 1972
Stranger Music (L. Cohen), 1993
Stranger on the Square (Koestler), 1984
Stranger Within (Stavans), 1999
Strangers (Memmi), 1958
Straordinarie avventure di Caterina (Morante), 1959
Stray Cats and Empty Bottles (Kops), 1961
Stream of Life (Lispector), 1989
Street of Crocodiles (Schulz), 1963
Street of Lost Brothers (Lustig), 1990
Street of Steps (Hendel), 1958
Streit um den Sergeanten Grischa (A. Zweig), 1927
Strepen aan de hemel (Durlacher), 1985
Strictly from Hunger (Perelman), 1937
Strijklicht (Herzberg), 1971
Strip Jack Naked (A. Baron), 1966
Stripes in the Sky (Durlacher), 1991
Stroll in the Air (Ionesco), 1965
Stronger Climate (Jhabvala), 1968
Stück weiter (Ausländer), 1979
Stücke in Prosa (Feuchtwanger), 1936
Stücke in Versen (Feuchtwanger), 1954
Study in Infamy (Mikes), 1959
Stufen (A. Zweig), 1949
Stumme Prophet (J. Roth), 1966
Styx (Lasker-Schüler), 1902
Success (Feuchtwanger), 1930
Successful Love (Schwartz), 1961
Suche nach Lebenden (Sachs), 1971
Südlich wartet ein wärmeres Land (Ausländer), 1982
Sufah bein hadekalim (Michael), 1975
Sugar-Paper Blue (Fainlight), 1997
Suitcase Packers (Levini), 1984
Sullied Hand (Wesker), 1984
Summer Affair (Klíma), 1987
Summer Breeze (Schnitzler), 1996
Summer House (Sherman), 1993
Summer in the Street of the Prophets (Shahar), 1975
Summer is a Foreign Land (Broner), 1966
Summer Knowledge (Schwartz), 1959
Summer People (Piercy), 1989
Sunday Best (Rubens), 1971
Sundial (Hazaz), 1973
Sunrise over Hell (Ka-Tzetnik 135633), 1977
Sunset (Babel'), 1960
Sunset Gun (Parker), 1928
Sunset Possibilities (Preil), 1985
Sunshine Boys (Simon), 1972
Sunward (Golding), 1924
Supertex (Winter), 1991
Sur un cargo (Bloch), 1924
Survivors (Feinstein), 1982
Susanna (Kolmar), 1993
Susets (Kaniuk), 1974
Susim al kvish geah (Liebrecht), 1988
Süsskind von Trimberg (Torberg), 1972
Sussurro della grande voce (Pressburger), 1990
Suzy (Parker), 1936
Svivah oyenet (Castel-Bloom), 1989
Svobodnyi krugozor (Pasternak), 1987
Svoreingenommen wie ich bin (Torberg), 1991
Swann's Way (Proust), 1922
Swanny's Ways (S. Katz), 1995
Swedish Cavalier (Perutz), 1992
Sweet and Lowdown (Allen), 1999
Sweet Charity (Simon), 1966
Sweet Cheat Gone (Proust), 1930
Sweet Smell of Psychosis (Self), 1996
Sweet Smell of Success (Odets), 1957
Sweethearts (Parker), 1938
Sweethearts (Perelman), 1938
Sweetshop Myriam (Klíma), 1968
Swine Lake (Sendak), 1999
Swinging Flesh (Layton), 1961
Swinging in the Rain (Bermant), 1967
Swiss Family Perelman (Perelman), 1950
Switzerland for Beginners (Mikes), 1962
Sybilla (Bloch), 1932
Sylvester 1972 (Sobol), 1974
Symmetrie (Mulisch), 1982
Symposium (Spark), 1990
Syrian–African Rift (Yeshurun), 1980
Szczury (Rudnicki), 1932
Szekspir (Rudnicki), 1948

Taal is een ei (Mulisch), 1979
Taatuon (Ben-Ner), 1989
Tabaot ashan (Goldberg), 1935
Tabarin (Herzl), 1884
Table (Fink), 1983
Tableau (Ionesco), 1955
Tag- und Tierträume (Kolmar), 1963
Tag wird kommen (Feuchtwanger), 1940
Tagebuch aus dem Winkel (Wassermann), 1935
Tahanot kavot (Vogel), 1990
Taharut sehiyah (Tammuz), 1952
Tahat hashemesh (Shamir), 1950
Tajemniczy przyjaciel (Korczak), 1957
Take a Fellow Like Me (Harwood), 1961
Take It or Leave It (Federman), 1976
Take the Money and Run (Allen), 1969
Take Up Your Bed and Walk (Yezierska), 1964
Takeover (Spark), 1976
Takhrikh shel sipurim (Agnon), 1984
Taking Sides (Harwood), 1995
Takse (Mendele Moykher Sforim), 1869
Tale of the 1002nd Night (J. Roth), 1998
Tale of Three Wishes (Isaac Singer), 1975
Talent Scout (Gary), 1961
Tales from Seven Ghettos (Kisch), 1948
Tales of My People (Asch), 1948
Tales of Odessa (Babel'), 1955
Tales Told of the Fathers (Hollander), 1975
Talia y el cielo (Stavans), 1977
Talicska (Mikes), 1950
Tallulah Bankhead Show (Simon), 1951
Tamed Puma (Layton), 1979
Tamid anahnu (Shaham), 1952
Tammuz Night's Dream (Shahar), 1989
Tanchelijn (Mulisch), 1960
Tango (Mikes), 1961
Tango (Stoppard), 1966
Tanja (Weiss), 1920
Tante Jolesch (Torberg), 1975
Tanzenden Derwische (Werfel), 1990
Tapuhim bidvash (Hendel), 1994
Tapuhim min hamidbar (Liebrecht), 1986
Tarabas (J. Roth), 1934
Tarnegol kapparot (Amir), 1983
Tatspiot (Kovner), 1977
Taybele (Sholem), 1884
Taygerhil (Kaniuk), 1995
Te lucis ante (Bassani), 1947
Tea Party (Pinter), 1965
Tealat blaumilch (Kishon), 1974

Teardrop Millionaire (M. Rosenfeld), 1955
Teatro incompleto (Aub), 1931
Teeth (Stoppard), 1967
Teeth and Spies (Pressburger), 1999
Tefilah aharonah (Raab), 1972
Tegenlicht (Mulisch), 1975
Tehom kore (Ravikovitch), 1976
Teile dich Nacht (Sachs), 1971
Teitlebaum's Window (Markfield), 1970
Teksten voor toneel en film, 1972–1988 (Herzberg), 1991
Tel Aviv Mizraḥ (Ballas), 1998
Telephone Call (Parker), 1962
Tell Me a Riddle (Olsen), 1961
Tell-Tale Heart (Berkoff), 1985
Temol shilshom (Agnon), 1945
Tempi nostri (Moravia), 1952
Tempojahre (Biller), 1991
Temps retrouvé (Proust), 1927
Temptations (Pinski), 1919
Temy i variatsii (Pasternak), 1923
Tenants (Malamud), 1971
Tenants of the House (Abse), 1957
Tenants of the Moonbloom (Wallant), 1963
Tender Buttons (Stein), 1914
Tenor (K. Shapiro), 1957
Tentations (Spire), 1920
Tenth Chick (Alterman), 1943
Tentserin (Opatoshu), 1930
Tenuah lemaga (Guri), 1968
Teomim (Michael), 1988
Tepl (Sholem), 1901
Terapia (Dorfman), 1999
Terezin (Lustig), 1965
Terrain bouchaballe (Jacob), 1923
Terre de promesses (Fleg), 1924
Terre que Dieu habite (Fleg), 1953
Terre sur terre (Tzara), 1946
Terrible but Unfinished Story of Norodom Sihanouk, King of Cambodia (Cixous), 1994
Terrible Chemistry (Gordimer), 1981
Terrible Threshold (Kunitz), 1974
Territorial Rights (Spark), 1979
Tersites (S. Zweig), 1907
Terza stagione (Saba), 1997
Terzetta spezzato (Svevo), 1927
Tesserae (Hollander), 1993
Testament (Wiesel), 1981
Testament d'un poète juif assassiné (Wiesel), 1980
Testament without Breath (Silkin), 1998
Testimonial Dinner (Wiseman), 1978
Testimony (Reznikoff), 1965
Testing-Tree (Kunitz), 1971
Tête coupable (Gary), 1968
Têtes de Stéphanie (Gary), 1974
Teviah (Carmi), 1967
Tevye der milkhiker (Sholem), 1894
Tevye the Dairyman and the Railroad Stories (Sholem), 1987
Tevye's Daughters (Sholem), 1949
Thank You Very Much (Taylor), 1969
That (Brod), 1905
That Dada Strain (Rothenberg), 1982
That They May Win (Miller), 1944
Thaw (Erenburg), 1955
Theben (Lasker-Schüler), 1923
Theft (Bellow), 1989
Their Very Own and Golden City (Wesker), 1965
Theodor Herzls Zionistische Schriften (Herzl), 1905
Theory of Flight (Rukeyser), 1935
Therapy of Avram Blok (Louvish), 1985
There Was a Young Man from Cardiff (Abse), 1991
There Was That Roman Poet Who Fell in Love at Fifty Odd (K. Shapiro), 1968
There Were No Signs (Layton), 1979
There's No Home (A. Baron), 1950
There's One Born Every Minute (Bermant), 1983
Theresa (Schnitzler), 1928
Therese (Schnitzler), 1928
Theresienstadt (Lustig), 1965
These Three (Hellman), 1936
They Brought their Women (Ferber), 1933
They Made a Jew of Me (Litvinoff), 1973
They That Walk in Darkness (Zangwill), 1899
They Too Arise (Miller), 1937
They'll Be Here Tomorrow (Shaham), 1957
They're Playing Our Song (Simon), 1978
Thieves in the Night (Koestler), 1946
Thin Bell-Ringer (K. Shapiro), 1948
Things (Perec), 1990
Things as They Are (Stein), 1950
Things Change (Mamet), 1988
Things We Used to Say (Ginzburg), 1997
Things Went Badly in Westphalia (Sherman), 1971
Think of England (Raphael), 1986
Third (Ezekiel), 1958
Third Body (Cixous), 1999
Third Party (Rubens), 1972
Thirst (Hareven), 1996
This is the Hour (Feuchtwanger), 1951
This is Which (Oppen), 1965
This Time of Year (Fainlight), 1993
This Wanderer (Golding), 1935
Thomas Wendt (Feuchtwanger), 1919
Thorny Path (D. Baron), 1969
Those Ancient Lands (Golding), 1928
Though Gently (Riding), 1930
Thought of Lydia (Raphael), 1988
Three Cities (Asch), 1933
Three Continents (Jhabvala), 1987
Three Cows (Kisch), 1939
Three Days and a Child (Yehoshua), 1970
Three Friendly Warnings (Rothenberg), 1973
Three Jews (Woolf), 1917
Three Jolly Gentlemen (Golding), 1947
Three Leaps of Wang-lun (Döblin), 1991
Three Lives (Stein), 1909
Three Loves (Brod), 1929
Three Married Men (Parker), 1936
Three Men Die (Millin), 1934
Three Men in a Boat (Stoppard), 1975
Three Men on a Horse (Miller), 1947
Three Sisters (Mamet), 1991
Three Woman Talking (Wesker), 1992
Three Women (Piercy), 1999
Threepenny Bits (Zangwill), 1895
Threshing Floor (Tchernichovski), 1936
Through the Wilderness (D. Jacobson), 1968
Ti ho sposato per allegria (Ginzburg), 1965
Ticket to Paradise (West), 1936
Tiempo al tiempo (Goldemberg), 1984
Tiempo de silencio (Goldemberg), 1969
Tiere in Ketten (Weiss), 1918
Tightrope Dancer (Layton), 1978
Tijd en het vertrek (Herzberg), 1989
Tikrah li milemata (Aini), 1994
Tikun omanuti (Almog), 1993
Tilim yid (Asch), 1934
Till the Day I Die (Odets), 1935
Timbuktu (Auster), 1999
Time (Amichai), 1979
Time of Desecration (Moravia), 1980
Time of Indifference (Moravia), 1953
Time Regained (Proust), 1931
Time to Change (Ezekiel), 1952
Time's Power (Rich), 1989
Timyon (Applefeld), 1993
Tinokot laylah (Yehoshua), 1992
Tipolim aharonim (Yehoshua), 1973
'Tis Folly to be Wise (Feuchtwanger), 1953
Tishdoret milavyan rigul (Avidan), 1976
Tismonet dulcinea (Hareven), 1981
Titans (Maurois), 1957
Titch (Bermant), 1987
Tkies-kaf (Hirshbein), 1908
Tma nemá stín (Lustig), 1976
To an Early Grave (Markfield), 1964
To Be of Use (Piercy), 1973
To be Recorded (Preil), 1992
To Express My Life I Have Only My Death (Goldemberg), 1969
To Know a Woman (Oz), 1991
To Live the Orange (Cixous), 1979
To See the Matter Clearly (Fainlight), 1968
To the Land of the Cattails (Applefeld), 1986
To the Quayside (Golding), 1954
To Urania (Brodsky), 1988
To Whom it May Concern (Federman), 1990
To Whom She Will (Jhabvala), 1955
Tochter (Biller), 2000
Tod den Toten! (Brod), 1906
Tod des Kleinbürgers (Werfel), 1927
Tod des Vergil (Broch), 1945
Todas las rosas (Glantz), 1985
Tog fun milkhome (Karpinovich), 1973
Tog in regensburg (Opatoshu), 1933
Tog un nakht (An-ski), 1920–25
Tokyo Woes (Friedman), 1985
Tolle, tolle Zeit (Torberg), 1988
Tom Sawyers grosses Abenteuer (Heym), 1952
Tomb for Boris Davidovich (Kiš), 1978
Tombe (Cixous), 1973
Tommaso del Cavaliere (Stryjkowski), 1982
Toneelwerken (Heijermans), 1965
Tönerne Gott (Feuchtwanger), 1910
Tonight Show (Allen)
Too Much Money (Zangwill), 1918
Topaz (Uris), 1967
Topsy-Turvy Emperor of China (Isaac Singer), 1971
Tor hapelaot (Applefeld), 1978
Torch Song Trilogy (Fierstein), 1981
Tortoises (V. Canetti), 2001

Total Immersion (Goodman), 1989
Totnauberg (Celan), 1968
Totsi et hashteker, hamayim rotehim (Kishon), 1965
Touch of Ginger (Zwicky), 1991
Touch the Water, Touch the Wind (Oz), 1974
Tough Guys Don't Dance (Mailer), 1984
Tough, Tough Toys for Tough, Tough Boys (Self), 1998
Toujours encore (Goloboff), 1982
Tourguéniev (Maurois), 1934
Tower of Babel (E. Canetti), 1947
Town and Country Lovers (Gordimer), 1980
Town and Country Matters (Hollander), 1972
Town beyond the Wall (Wiesel), 1964
Toyber (Bergelson),
Toys in the Attic (Hellman), 1960
Toyt (Schneour), 1910
Toyt di kanibaln (Markish), 1941
Toyt urteyl (Asch), 1923
Toyten-tants (Agnon), 1911
Trace (Fink), 1990
Trace of Malice (Modiano), 1988
Traces (Fink), 1997
Trade Winds (Parker), 1938
Traitor (Wouk), 1949
Tramway Road (Harwood), 1984
Transformation (Kafka), 1992
Transformation of Pierrot (Schnitzler), 1995
Transit to Narcissus (Mailer), 1978
Transport z ráje (Lustig), 1962
Trap (D. Jacobson), 1955
Trapeze (Mankowitz), 1955
Traum hat offene Augen (Ausländer), 1987
Traumnovelle (Schnitzler), 1926
Traumstück (Kraus), 1923
Traumtheater (Kraus), 1924
Travelers (Jhabvala), 1973
Travels (Amichai), 1986
Travels and Adventures of Benjamin the Third (Mendele Moykher Sforim), 1949
Travels of a Latter-Day Benjamin of Tudela (Amichai), 1977
Travels to the Enu (Lind), 1982
Traverse Plays (Taylor), 1966
Travesía (Dorfman), 1986
Travesties (Stoppard), 1974
Tre composizioni (Saba), 1933
Tre poesie alla mia balia (Saba), 1929
Treasure (Pinski), 1999
Treasure Island (Mankowitz), 1973
Tree of Life (Rosenfarb), 1985
Tres monólogos y uno solo verdadero (Aub), 1956
Treść gorejąca (Tuwim), 1936
Trest D E (Erenburg), 1923
Trial (Berkoff), 1971
Trial (Kafka), 1937
Trial (Orpaz), 1985
Trial of a Poet (K. Shapiro), 1947
Trial of God (as It Was Held on February 25, 1649, in Shamgorod) (Wiesel), 1988
Tribüne und Aurora (Viertel), 1990
Trieste e una donna (Saba), 1950
Trinity (Uris), 1976
Tristia (Mandel'shtam), 1922
Triumph of Youth (Wassermann), 1927
Troerinnen (Werfel), 1915
Trois Filles de mon quartier (Jabès), 1948
Trois quatrains (Jacob), 1953
Troisième Corps (Cixous), 1970
Trojan Ending (Riding), 1937
Tropical Synagogues (Scliar), 1994
Tropismes (Sarraute), 1939
Tropisms (Sarraute), 1963
Trouble with Benny (Richler), 1959
Trouble with England (Raphael), 1962
Trouble with People (Simon), 1972
Truce (Erenburg), 1963
Trust (Ozick), 1966
Trzy wyprawy Herszka (Korczak), 1930
Tsarikh sof lesipur ahavah (Liebrecht), 1995
Tsaytike penemer (Sutzkever), 1970
Tschechisches Dienstmädchen (Brod), 1909
Tsefonit mizrahit (Zach), 1979
Tsela (Ratosh), 1959
Tsemakh atlas (Grade), 1967–68
Tsente gebot (Goldfaden), *c.*1895
Tseyd hatsveyah (Orpaz), 1966
Tsezeyt un tsershpreyt (Sholem), 1905
Tsfas (M. Katz), 1979
Tsi-tsa (Mikes), 1978
Tsitsim ufrakhim (Goldfaden), 1865
Tsu der frage vegn der yidisher folkshul (Esther), 1910
Tsu dertseyln in freydn (M. Katz), 1941
Tsu hakofes (Weissenberg)
Tsum zig (Markish), 1944
Tsurot (Wallach), 1985
Tsvey dertseylungen (Shpigl), 1978
Tsvey shtet (Hirshbein), 1919
Tsvey shteyner (Sholem), 1883
Tsvey veltn (Bergelson), 1953
Tsviling-bruder (Sutzkever), 1986
Tsvishn tof un alef (Shpigl), 1978
Tsvishn tsvey veltn (der dibek) (An-ski), 1920
Tu ne t'aimes pas (Sarraute), 1989
Tueur sans gages (Ionesco), 1959
Tulipe (Gary), 1946
Turlupin (Perutz), 1924
Turning Wind (Rukeyser), 1939
Tussen hamer en aambeeld (Mulisch), 1952
Tutti i nostri ieri (Ginzburg), 1952
TV Baby Poems (Ginsberg), 1967
Twee opgravingen (Mulisch), 1994
Twee vrouwen (Herzberg), 1979
Twee vrouwen (Mulisch), 1975
Twelve-Spoked Wheel Flashing (Piercy), 1978
Twenty Poems Less (Riding), 1930
Twilight (Hareven), 1992
Twilight (Wiesel), 1988
Twilight Bar (Koestler), 1945
Twilight of a World (Werfel), 1937
Twilight of the Bums (Federman), 2001
Two (Moravia), 1972
Two Adolescents (Moravia), 1952
Two Anglo-Saxon Plays (Feuchtwanger), 1928
Two Bucks without Hair (Millin), 1957
Two Fables (Malamud), 1978
Two Faces of Dr Jekyll (Mankowitz), 1960
Two for the Road (Raphael), 1967
Two Freedoms (Silkin), 1958
Two Friends (M. Katz), 1981
Two (Hitherto Unpublished) Poems (Stein), 1948
Two Images of Continuing Trouble (Silkin), 1976
Two of Us (Moravia), 1972
Two Views (L. Cohen), 1980
Two Women (Moravia), 1958
Two Women (Mulisch), 1980
Two-Fisted Painters Action Adventure (Spiegelman), 1980
Twofold Vibration (Federman), 1982
Two-Way Mirror (Miller), 1982
Tycho Brahes Weg zu Gott (Brod), 1915
Types of Shape (Hollander), 1969
Tyranny of the Normal (Fiedler), 1996
Tzalhavim (Yizhar), 1993
Tzerisener mentsh (Pinski), 1920
Tzili, the Story of a Life (Applefeld), 1983
Tzoanim bapardes (Almog), 1986
Tzugvintn (Bergelson), 1929
Tzurik fun astrog (Schneour), 1939

U.S. 1 (Rukeyser), 1938
Uba hayareah uba halaylah (Ayalon), 1987
Über Alles (Mikes), 1953
Über den Nebeln (A. Zweig), 1950
Überlegungen (Fried), 1964
Uccelli (Saba), 1950
Ufgang afn dniepr (Markish), 1937
Ugly Duchess (Feuchtwanger), 1928
Ulcérations (Perec), 1986
Ulice ztracených bratří (Lustig), 1949
Última canción de Manuel Sendero (Dorfman), 1982
Ultimate Intimacy (Klíma), 1997
Ultime cose (Saba), 1944
Ultimi anni di Clelia Trotti (Bassani), 1955
Ultimo incontro (Moravia), 1951
Últimos cuentos de la guerra de España (Aub), 1969
Um Klarheit (Fried), 1985
Umbrella Man (Harwood), 1986
Umkehr der Abtrünnigen (A. Zweig), 1925
Umshterblekhkayt (Halkin), 1940
Un di velt hot geshvign (Wiesel), 1956
Un gevorn iz likht (Shpigl), 1949
Unambo (Brod), 1949
Unbekannte Grösse (Broch), 1933
Uncertain Friend (Heym), 1969
Uncle Moses (Asch), 1920
Uncle Vanya (Mamet), 1990
—und glauben, es wäre die Liebe (Torberg), 1932
Und niemand weiss weiter (Sachs), 1957
Und Vietnam und ... 41 Gedichte (Fried), 1966
Under the Weather (Bellow), 1966
Undiscovered Country (Schnitzler), 1980
Undiscovered Country (Stoppard), 1979
Undue Influence (Brookner), 1999
Undzer shtetl brent (Gebirtig), 1938
Undzere oysyes glien (Greenberg), 1978
Unearth (Auster), 1974
Unearthing (Zukofsky), 1965
Unfinished Man (Ezekiel), 1960
Ungeduld des Herzens (S. Zweig), 1939
Ungleichen Schalen (Wassermann), 1912

Universe of Clowns (Liberman), 1983
Unizhenie vo sne (Slutskii), 1981
Unknown Quantity (Broch), 1935
Unloved (Lustig), 1985
Unmass aller Dinge (Fried), 1982
Uno de sus Juanes y otros cuentos (Glickman), 1983
Unser Käthchen (Herzl), 1898
Unsichtbare Sammlung (S. Zweig), 1929
Unter a ployt (Der Nister), 1929
Unter dayn tseykhn (Tussman), 1974
Unter Nebenfeinden (Fried), 1970
Untergang der Welt durch schwarze Magie (Kraus), 1922
Until the Entire Guard Has Passed (Aini), 1995
Unto Death (Oz), 1975
Unto the Soul (Applefeld), 1994
Untried Soldier (Litvinoff), 1942
Unüberwindlichen (Kraus), 1928
Unverlierbare (Weiss), 1928
Unverwundenes (Fried), 1988
Unwavering Eye 1969–1975 (Layton), 1975
Uomo che guarda (Moravia), 1985
Up (Sukenick), 1968
Up from Paradise (Miller), 1974
Uraniia (Brodsky), 1987
Urba parah (Berdyczewski), 1900
Uri (Goldberg), 1983
Uri Muri (Ben-Ner), 1999
Uriel Acosta (Reznikoff), 1921
Urteil (Kafka), 1916
Usage de la parole (Sarraute), 1980
Use of Speech (Sarraute), 1980
Utzli Gutzli (Shlonsky), 1966

V dvadtsat' let (An-ski), 1892
V okrestnostiakh Atlantidy (Brodsky), 1995
V smertnyi chas (Stat'i 1918–19) (Erenburg), 1996
Val (Minco), 1983
Val van Icarus (Herzberg), 1983
Valaki más : változás krónikája (Kertész), 1997
Valdiks (Sutzkever), 1940
Valentine No a Valedictory for Gertrude Stein (Rothenberg), 1972
Valentino (Ginzburg), 1957
Valeureux (A. Cohen), 1969
Vamos a Vladivostok (Dujovne Ortiz), 1990
Van Gogh's Room at Arles (Elkin), 1993
Vant (Schneour), 1939
Various Positions (L. Cohen), 1985
Városalapító (Konrád), 1977
Varshe (Asch), 1930
Vasantasena (Feuchtwanger), 1916
Vase (Ionesco), 1970
Vaudeville for a Princess (Schwartz), 1950
Ve afilu lirot kokhavim (Shamir), 1993
Veg (Weissenberg), 1906
Veg keyn sdom (Karpinovich), 1959
Veg tsu zikh (Asch), 1914
Vegliando (Svevo), 1987
Vegn zikh un azoyne vi ikh (Fefer), 1924
Vehayah heakov lemishor (Agnon), 1912
Vehu aher (Ballas), 1991
Vehu haor (Goldberg), 1946
Veil of Pierrette (Schnitzler), 1995
Vekulam haverim (Goldberg), 1978
Velo al menat lizkor (Amichai), 1971
Velt-oys, velt-ayn (Bergelson), 1930
Velvet Touch (Rosten), 1948
Velvl zbarzszer shraybt briv tsu malkele der sheyner (Manger), 1937
Ven poyln iz gefaln (Opatoshu), 1943
Venedig (Texas) (Feuchtwanger), 1946
Veod rotseh otah (Guri), 1987
Verbotene Frau (Brod), 1960
Verdadera historia de la muerte de Francisco Franco y otros cuentos (Aub), 1960
Verdi (Werfel), 1924
Verführer (Weiss), 1938
Vergil Dying (Josipovici), 1981
Verhalen (Winter), 1993
Verlorener Sohn (Broch), 1933
Vermächtnis (Schnitzler), 1898
Vermont Sketches (Mamet), 1984
Vernost' (Erenburg), 1941
Vers le Monde qui vient (Fleg), 1960
Vers les routes absurdes (Spire), 1911
Verschollene (Kafka)
Versierde mens (Mulisch), 1957
Version of My Life (Federman), 1993
Versiones y subversiones (Aub), 1971
Versöhnungsfest (Weiss), 1920
Versos del hombre pájaro (Goloboff), 1994
Versucher (Broch), 1953
Versuchung (Werfel), 1913
Versunkene Tage (A. Zweig), 1938
Verteller (Mulisch), 1970
Vertreibung der Gespenster (Döblin), 1968
Veruntreute Himmel (Werfel), 1939
Verwandelte Komödiant (S. Zweig), 1912
Verwandlung (Kafka), 1915
Verwandlung des Pierrot (Schnitzler), 1908
Verwirrung der Gefühle (S. Zweig), 1927
Very Far Away (Sendak), 1957
Very Model of a Man (H. Jacobson), 1992
Verzauberung (Broch), 1934
Vestiaire de l'enfance (Modiano), 1989
Veter (Erenburg), 1922
Vey un mut (Halkin), 1929
Veyareah beemek ayalon (Kahana-Carmon), 1971
Via crucis do corpo (Lispector), 1974
Viaggio a Roma (Moravia), 1988
Vicar of Dunkerly Briggs (Golding), 1944
Victim (Bellow), 1947
Victimes du devoir (Ionesco), 1953
Victims of Duty (Ionesco), 1958
Victoria (Michael), 1993
Vida (Piercy), 1980
Vida a plazos de don Jacobo Lerner (Goldemberg), 1978
Vida al contado (Goldemberg), 1992
Vida conyugal (Aub), 1943
Vida íntima de Laura (Lispector), 1974
Vide (Weissenberg)
Vie d'Alexander Fleming (Maurois), 1959
Vie de Disraeli (Maurois), 1927
Vie de Morphiel, démiurge (Schwob), 1985
Vie devant soi (Gary), 1975
Vie incertaine de Marco Mahler (Halter), 1979
Vie, mode d'emploi (Perec), 1978
Vienna 1900 (Schnitzler), 1973
Vienna Blood (Rothenberg), 1980
Viennese Novelettes (Schnitzler), 1931
Vierzig Tage des Musa Dagh (Werfel), 1933
Vies imaginaires (Schwob), 1896
View from Row G (Abse), 1990
View from the Bridge (Miller), 1955
Vilder mentsh (Gordin), 1907
Villa Borgeze (Shrayer-Petrov), 1992
Villa Borghese (Moravia), 1953
Villa Triste (Modiano), 1975
Village (Mamet), 1994
Village (Stein), 1928
Village in the Jungle (Woolf), 1913
Ville de la chance (Wiesel), 1962
Vilna (Kulbak), 1969
Vilne, mayn vilne (Karpinovich), 1993
Vinegar Puss (Perelman), 1975
Vingt Ans après Auschwitz (Wiesel), 1968
Vingt-cinquième Heure (Mankowitz), 1967
Vint (Mamet), 1985
Vint un vortslen (Shpigl), 1955
Vintshfingerl (Mendele Moykher Sforim), 1865
Violencia (Friedman), 1988
Viper Vicar of Vice, Villainy and Vickedness (Spiegelman), 1972
Virgin's Brand (Perutz), 1934
Vision of the Chariot in Heaven (Rothenberg), 1976
Visions from the Ramble (Hollander), 1965
Visions infernales (Jacob), 1924
Visions of Simone Machard (Feuchtwanger), 1965
Visitors (Brookner), 1997
Vita (Svevo), 1892
Vita è gioco (Moravia), 1969
Vita interiore (Moravia), 1978
Viudas (Dorfman), 1981
Vivre l'orange (Cixous), 1979
Vizio di forma (P. Levi), 1971
V-Letter (K. Shapiro), 1945
Vliegen (Herzberg), 1970
Vlny v řece (Lustig), 1964
Vocabulary of Peace (Hareven), 1995
Voci della sera (Ginzburg), 1961
Vogels (Mulisch), 1974
Voice from the Corner (Liberman), 1999
Voice in the Closet (Federman), 1979
Voice of the Sea (Moravia), 1978
Voices (Lind), 1970
Voices at Play (Spark), 1962
Voices in the Evening (Ginzburg), 1963
Void (Perec), 1994
Voix d'encre (Jabès), 1949
Voix dans le cabinet de Debaras (Federman), 1979
Vokhnteg (Markish), 1931
Volcano Lover (Sontag), 1992
Volf (Leyvik), 1920
Volin (Markish), 1921
Volk en vaderliefde (Mulisch), 1975
Volkns ibern dakh (Manger), 1942
Voltaire (Riding), 1927
Voluntários (Scliar), 1979
Volunteers (Scliar), 1988
Von Schwelle zu Schwelle (Celan), 1955

Voorval (Mulisch), 1989
Vorfrühling (A. Zweig), 1909
Vorübungen für Wunder (Fried), 1987
Vos kon trefn (Weissenberg)
Vous les entendez? (Sarraute), 1972
Voyage (Stoppard), 2002
Voyage de noces (Modiano), 1990
Voyage en autobus (Jacob), 1920
Voyage to Ur of the Chaldees (Shahar), 1975
Voyages chez les morts (Ionesco), 1980
Voyeur (Moravia), 1986
Vozdushnye puti (Pasternak), 1933
Vrai Jardin (Cixous), 1971
Vremia (Slutskii), 1959
Vse techet (V. Grossman), 1970
Vtoraia kniga (Mandel'shtam), 1923
Vtoroe rozhdenie (Pasternak), 1932
Vueltas (Aub), 1965
Vunder iber vunder (Mani Leyb), 1930
Vuurvlindertje (Heijermans), 1925
Vypriamitel'nyi vzdokh (Mandel'shtam), 1990

W malinowym chruśniaku (Leśmian), 1990
Wächst das Rettende auch? Gedichte für den Frieden (Fried), 1986
Wadzeks Kampf mit der Dampfturbine (Döblin), 1918
Waffen für Amerika (Feuchtwanger), 1947
Wagnisse in aller Welt (Kisch), 1927
Wahre Geschichte vom wiederhergestellten Kreuz (Werfel), 1942
Waiting for Lefty (Odets), 1935
Waiting for the Dark, Waiting for the Light (Klíma), 1994
Waiting Game (Rubens), 1997
Wake Island (Rukeyser), 1942
Wales — A Visitation, July 29, 1967 (Ginsberg), 1968
Walk East on Beacon (Rosten), 1952
Walk on the Water (Stoppard), 1963
Walking under Water (Abse), 1952
Wall of Weeping (Fleg), 1929
Wall Writing (Auster), 1976
Wallenstein (Döblin), 1920
Waltz of the Toreadors (Mankowitz), 1962
Wandering Jew (Heym), 1984
Wandering Star (Sholem), 1952
Want Bone (Pinsky), 1990
War (Erenburg), 1964
War and Remembrance (Wouk), 1978
War God (Zangwill), 1911
War Goes On (Asch), 1936
War of the Sons of Light (Shamir), 1956
Wara, la petite indienne de l'Altiplano (Dujovne Ortiz), 1983
Warm Feet, Warm Heart (Litvinoff), 1970
Warngedichte (Fried), 1964
Warren Hastings, Gouverneur von Inden (Feuchtwanger), 1916
Wars of the Jews (Sobol), 1981
Wartesaal Trilogie (Feuchtwanger), 1939
Wasserman (Kaniuk), 1988
Wat gebeurde er met sergeant Massuro? (Mulisch), 1972
Wat poëzie is (Mulisch), 1978
Wat zij wilde schilderen (Herzberg), 1998
Watch (C. Levi), 1952
Watch on the Rhine (Hellman), 1941
Water Engine (Mamet), 1977
Waterlily Fire (Rukeyser), 1962
Watersmeet (Silkin), 1994
Waterworks (Doctorow), 1994
Way of Life (D. Jacobson), 1971
Way Out (Gary), 1977
Way Out in the Centre (Abse), 1981
Way to the Cats (Kenaz), 1994
Way to the Pond (Schnitzler), 1992
Way up to Heaven (Harwood), 1979
Way We Live Now (Sontag), 1991
Wayward Wife (Moravia), 1952
We Are All in the Dumps with Jack and Guy (Sendak), 1993
We Bombed in New Haven (Heller), 1967
We Love Adventure (Sherman), 1961
We Moderns (Zangwill), 1922
We Were There to Escape (Mikes), 1945
Weave of Women (Broner), 1978
Web of Lucifer (Samuel), 1947
Wedding (E. Canetti), 1986
Wedding Bouquet (Stein), 1936
Wedding Feast (Wesker), 1974
Wedding Party (Herzberg), 1997
Wedding Preparations in the Country (Kafka), 1954
Wedlock (Wassermann), 1925
Weekend for Three (Parker), 1941
Weg der Verheissung (Werfel), 1935
Weg des Verliebten (Brod), 1907
Weg ins Freie (Schnitzler), 1908
Weiberwirtschaft (Brod), 1913
Weibliches Bildnis (Kolmar), 1980
Weight of Antony (S. Katz), 1964
Weight of Oranges (Michaels), 1986
Weights and Measures (J. Roth), 1982
Weissenstein, der Weltverbesserer (Werfel), 1990
Weite Land (Schnitzler), 1911
Welcome to Hard Times (Doctorow), 1960
Well (Grade), 1967
Wellfleet Whale (Kunitz), 1983
Welsh Retrospective (Abse), 1997
Welten (Kolmar), 1947
Weltfreund (Werfel), 1911
Weltgericht (Kraus), 1919
Wenceslas, ancien cocher (Jacob), 1921
Wenderkreis (Wassermann), 1920–24
Wenn ich einmal reich und tot bin (Biller), 1990
We're No Angels (Mamet), 1990
West (Berkoff), 1980
Westward Ha! (Perelman), 1948
What are Big Girls Made Of? (Piercy), 1997
What Can a Man Do? (Taylor), 1968
What Happened to Benji (Gur), 2000
What Happened to Sergeant Massuro (Mulisch), 1965
What Hath a Man? (Millin), 1938
What Henry James Knew (Ozick), 1993
What is To Be Given (Schwartz), 1976
What Poetry Is (Mulisch), 1981
What Was All the Fuss About? (Weissbort), 1998
What Was Literature? (Fiedler), 1982
What's New, Pussycat (Allen), 1965
What's Up God? (Louvish), 1995
Whatever Gods (Samuel), 1923
Whatever Happened to Betty Lemon? (Wesker), 1986
Wheel of Fortune (Moravia), 1937
When All is Said and Done (Bergelson), 1977
When She Danced (Sherman), 1985
When She Was Good (P. Roth), 1967
When Shlemiel Went to Warsaw (Isaac Singer), 1968
Where Are They Now? (Stoppard), 1970
Where Burning Sappho Loved (Layton), 1985
Where Danger Lives (Rosten), 1950
Where the Jackals Howl (Oz), 1981
Where the Spies Are (Mankowitz), 1965
Where the Wild Things Are (Sendak), 1963
Where Were You When It Went Down? (Mamet), 1988
Where Will You Fall? (Perutz), 1930
Which Moped with Chrome-plated Handlebars at the Back of the Yard? (Perec), 1996
Whiners (Levini), 2000
Whistle at Eaton Falls (Rosten), 1951
White (Aini) 1994
White Coat, Purple Coat (Abse), 1989
White Liars (Shaffer), 1968
White Lies (Shaffer), 1967
White Shroud (Ginsberg), 1986
White Sun, Black Sun (Rothenberg), 1960
White Terror and the Red (Cahan), 1905
White-Haired Lover (K. Shapiro), 1968
Who Shall I Be Tomorrow? (Kops), 1992
Who Were You with Last Night? (Raphael), 1971
Whole Bloody Bird (Layton), 1969
Whom Do I Have the Honour of Addressing? (Shaffer), 1989
Who's Pinkus? Where's Chelm? (Taylor), 1966
Who's Sorry Now? (H. Jacobson), 2002
Whose Little Boy are You? (Bartov), 1978
Why Are We in Vietnam? (Mailer), 1967
Why Bother to Knock (Raphael), 1971
Why Haven't You Written? (Gordimer), 1993
Why I am a Jew (Fleg), 1929
Why Noah Chose the Dove (Isaac Singer), 1974
Wichita Vortex Sutra (Ginsberg), 1966
Wicked City (Isaac Singer), 1972
Wicked We Love (Richler), 1955
Widow Capet (Feuchtwanger), 1956
Widows (Dorfman), 1983
Widows (Kushner), 1991
Widows and Children First! (Fierstein), 1979
Wielka Synteza Dziecka, oto co mi się śnilo (Korczak), 1978
Wielki strach (Stryjkowski), 1979
Wien oder Der Unterschied (Torberg), 1998
Wier and Pouce (S. Katz), 1984
Wierszy tom czwarty (Tuwim), 1923
Wijn is drankbaar dank zij het glas (Mulisch), 1976
Wijze kater (Heijermans), 1917
Wild 90 (Mailer), 1968
Wild Card (Kunitz), 1998
Wild Eye (Moravia), 1967
Wild in the Country (Odets), 1960
Wild Light (Wallach), 1997
Wild Patience Has Taken Me This Far (Rich), 1981

Wild Peculiar Joy (Layton), 1982
Wild Spring (Wesker), 1994
Wild Surmise (Raphael), 1961
Wilddiebe (Herzl), 1887
Will to Change (Rich), 1971
Will to Live On (Wouk), 1985
William Ireland's Confession (Miller), 1941
Wilson (Mamet), 1999
Wind Who Lost His Temper (Kulbak), 1987
Window (Ravikovitch), 1989
Winds of War (Wouk), 1971
Wine of Etna (A. Baron), 1950
Winter Games (Ben-Ner), 1989
Winter Journey (Odets), 1955
Wir Sind (Werfel), 1913
Wir sind auch nur ein Volk (Becker), 1995
Wir ziehen mit den dunklen Flüssen (Ausländer), 1993
Wird Hill amnestiert? (Feuchtwanger), 1923
Wisdom for Others (Mikes), 1950
Wise Publications (L. Cohen), 1978
Wise Virgins (Woolf), 1914
Witches of Salem (Miller), 1958
With (Cixous), 1981
With His Own Hands (Shamir), 1970
With Hope, Farewell (A. Baron), 1952
With Reverence and Delight (Layton), 1984
With Teeth in the Earth (Tussman), 1992
Withered Murder (Shaffer), 1955
Within a Budding Grove (Proust), 1924
Without Feathers (Allen), 1972
Witwe Capet (Feuchtwanger), 1956
Wizard Bird (Millin), 1962
Wo der Barthel die Milch holt (Torberg), 1981
Woe to the Victors (Kishon), 1969
Wohim Rollst du Äpfelchen (Perutz), 1928
Wolkenkuckucksheim (Kraus), 1923
Woman Chases Man (Parker), 1937
Woman in the Wardrobe (Shaffer), 1951
Woman Named Solitude (Schwarz-Bart), 1973
Woman of Rome (Moravia), 1949
Woman on the Edge of Time (Piercy), 1976
Woman Who Gave Birth to Twins and Disgraced Herself! (Castel-Bloom), 1995
Woman Who Killed the Fish (Lispector), 1988
Woman Who Wanted to Kill Someone (Castel-Bloom), 1995
Woman Who Went Looking for a Walkie Talkie (Castel-Bloom), 1995
Women and Angels (Brodkey), 1985
Women I'm Not Married To (Parker), 1922
Women's Theater in French (Cixous), 1991
Wonderbird (Almog), 1991
Wonderings and an Absurd Shattering (Ayalon), 1998
Wonder-Worker (D. Jacobson), 1973
Woods (Mamet), 1977
Woorden, woorden, woorden (Mulisch), 1973
Words (Josipovici), 1971
Words in My Lovesick Blood (Guri), 1996
Work and Turn (Spiegelman), 1979
Work of Artifice (Piercy), 1970
World in a Room (Litvinoff), 1970
World Is a Room (Amichai), 1984
World is a Wedding (Schwartz), 1948
World is the Home of Love and Death (Brodkey), 1997
World of Strangers (Gordimer), 1958
World's End (Wassermann), 1927
World's Fair (Doctorow), 1985
World's Illusion (Wassermann), 1920
Wort der Stummen (Kolmar), 1978
Worte in Versen (Kraus), 1916–30
Wrecker (Bellow), 1956
Wrench (P. Levi), 1987
Wunderrabiner von Barcelona (Lasker-Schüler), 1921
Wupper (Lasker-Schüler), 1909
Wysoki Krzyz (Korczak), 1974

Ya'akobi and Leidental (Levini), 1979
Yaakov (Tammuz), 1971
Yaakovi veleidental (Levini), 1972
Yabashah (Gurevitch), 1989
Yaël (Jabès), 1967
Ya'ish (Hazaz), 1947
Yakish vepuptshe (Levini), 1982
Yaldei shaashuim (Shamir), 1986
Yaldut shel kavod (Korczak), 1976
Yalkut shirim (Goldberg), 1970
Yalkut shirim (Raab), 1982
Yamei tsiklag (Yizhar), 1958
Yankev frank (Kulbak), 1923
Yankl der shmid (Pinski), 1910
Yardsale (Wesker), 1984
Yareah hadevash vehazahav (Shahar), 1959
Year Nineteen Five (Pasternak), 1989
Years of War (V. Grossman), 1946
Yedidai Mirehov arnon (Goldberg), 1943
Yedidav hagdolim shel gadi (Shamir), 1947
Yedidi emanuel veani (Ben-Ner), 1979
Yehudi katan (Bartov), 1980
Yehudit shel hametsurayim (Shamir), 1989
Yekl (Cahan), 1896
Yellow Street (V. Canetti), 1990
Yemei habeinayim mitkarevim (Schneour), 1913
Yerushalayim dorsanit (Hareven), 1962
Yerushalayim mibifnokho (Ben-Yehuda), 1988
Yes from No-Man's Land (Kops), 1965
Yes, Yes, No, No (Kushner), 1985
Yesh yeladim zigzag (D. Grossman), 1994
Yeshiva (Grade), 1976–77
Yeshu ben hanan (Berdyczewski), 1958?
Yesterday in the Back Lane (Rubens), 1995
Yesterday, Today, and Tomorrow (Moravia), 1963
Yesurei yov (Levini), 1981
Yesurim (Pinski), 1899
Yi yevani (Wieseltier), 1985
Yid fun lublin (Glatshteyn), 1966
Yid oyfn yam (Glants-Leyeles), 1947
Yidele (Goldfaden), 1866
Yidene (Goldfaden), 1869
Yidishe gas (Sutzkever), 1948
Yidishe kinder (Molodovski), 1945
Yidishe melukhe un andere zakhn (L. Shapiro), 1919
Yidishe natsyonal-gedikhte (Goldfaden), 1898
Yidishe un slavishe motivn (Mani Leyb), 1918
Yidisher kenig lir (Gordin), 1892
Yidishstaytshn (Glatshteyn), 1937
Yidn-legende (Opatoshu), 1951
Yikhes (Kreitman), 1949
Yingl-tsingl-khvat (Mani Leyb), 1918
Yisraeliim haverim (Megged), 1955
Yisrolik (Goldfaden), 1884
Yo (Grade), 1936
Yo vivo (Aub), 1953
Yohemed (Ratosh), 1942
Yom arozenet (Shahar), 1976
Yom haor shel anat (Megged), 1992
Yom harefaim (Shahar), 1986
Yoman zahav (Schütz), 1991
Yona mihatser aher (Shamir), 1973
Yonadab (Shaffer), 1985
Yonnondio (Olsen), 1974
Yosele solovey (Sholem), 1890
Yoshe kalb (Israel Singer), 1932
Yotam hakasam (Korczak), 1966
You Are My Heart's Delight (Taylor), 1973
You Can't Say Hello to Anybody (Abse), 1964
You Could Live If They Let You (Markfield), 1974
You Don't Love Yourself (Sarraute), 1990
You Must Know Everything (Babel'), 1969
Young Woman of 1914 (A. Zweig), 1932
Youngblood Hawke (Wouk), 1962
Your Monkey's Shmuck (Louvish), 1990
Your Native Land, Your Life (Rich), 1986
Your Show of Shows (Allen, Simon)
Your Ticket is No Longer Valid (Gary), 1977
Your Town (Ferber), 1948
Youth (Rosenberg), 1915
Yovi, haluk nahal vehapil (Kaniuk), 1993
Yoyresh fun regn (Sutzkever), 1992
Yudel (Mendele Moykher Sforim), 1875
Yugend (Asch), 1908
Yungharbst (Glants-Leyeles), 1922

Za pravoe delo (V. Grossman), 1952
Zakat (Babel'), 1927
Zalmen (Wiesel), 1968
Zámek (Klíma), 1965
Zamok v Tystemaa (Shrayer-Petrov), 2001
Zang-gezang (Markish), 1923
Zapiski o voine (Slutskii), 2000
Zarim Babayit (Matalon), 1992
Zauberreich der Liebe (Brod), 1928
Zazà (Moravia), 1942
Zeepost (Herzberg), 1963
Zeh im hapanim eleynu (Matalon), 1995
Zeh ishi medaber (Bartov), 1990
Zeh shem hasefer (Yeshurun), 1970
Zehu gan-eden (Ayalon), 1984
Zeit ist reif (A. Zweig), 1957
Zeitfragen (Fried), 1967
Zeitgehoft (Celan), 1976
Zeitlupe (Döblin), 1962
Zeitstrophen (Kraus), 1931
Zelig (Allen), 1983
Zelmenyaner (Kulbak), 1931–35
Zelner (Weissenberg), 1919
Zemnoi prostor (Pasternak), 1945
Ženich pro Marcelu (Klíma), 1968
Zeyde (An-ski), 1920–25
Zhenia's Childhood (Pasternak), 1982
Zhizn' i sud'ba (V. Grossman), 1980

Zhizn', Rasskazy (V. Grossman), 1947
Zigzag Kid (D. Grossman), 1997
Zikhron dvarim (Shabtai),1977
Zikhronot netushim (Castel-Bloom), 1998
Zilelei hahayyim (Gnessin), 1904
Zionoco (Winter), 1995
Zip (Apple), 1978
Zip-a-Tune and More Melodies (Spiegelman), 1972
Zipper and His Father (J. Roth), 1988
Zipper und sein Vater (J. Roth), 1928
Zlateh the Goat (Isaac Singer), 1966
Złote okna (Rudnicki), 1954
Zoals (Herzberg), 1992
Zoektocht (Durlacher), 1991
Zomer van Aviya (Herzberg), 1991
Żołnierze (Rudnicki), 1933
Zolotoe serdtse (Erenburg), 1922
Zopilote y otros cuentos mexicanos (Aub), 1964
Zpevy zavrzenych (Langer), 1937
Zuckerman Bound (P. Roth), 1985
Zuckerman Unbound (P. Roth), 1981
Zuiden (Herzberg), 1990
Zulu and the Zeide (D. Jacobson), 1959
Zur Zeit und zur Unzeit (Fried), 1981
Zuta (Goldberg), 1981
Zvezda mordvina (Bagritskii), 1931
Zwang (S. Zweig), 1920
Zwarte licht (Mulisch), 1956
Zwei Erzählungen (Feuchtwanger), 1938
Zweite Augenzeuge (Weiss), 1978
Zweite Begegnung (Torberg), 1940
Zweite Geschichtenbuch (A. Zweig), 1920
Zwischen neun und neun (Perutz), 1918
Zwischenspiel (Schnitzler), 1906
Żywe i martwe morze (Rudnicki), 1952

NOTES ON CONTRIBUTORS

Aaronson, Béa. Multimedia artist, art critic, award-winning poet, and independent scholar affiliated to the University of South Carolina, Columbia. Author of *Baudelaire-Miller: Sexual Squalor in Paris* (1998). Her doctoral dissertation is entitled "A Midrashic Reading of Marcel Proust's *À la recherche du temps perdu*". **Essays:** Hélène Cixous; André Spire.

Abrams, Nathan. Lecturer, Birkbeck College, London. Author of *Studying Film* (with Ian Bell and Jan Udris, 2001). Editor of *Containing America: Cultural Production and Consumption in Fifties America* (with Julie Hughes, 2000). Currently researching the history of *Commentary* magazine. **Essay:** Arthur Miller.

Abramson, Edward A. Senior Lecturer in American Literature, University of Hull, England. Author of *The Immigrant Experience in American Literature* (1982), *Chaim Potok* (1986), and *Bernard Malamud Revisited* (1993), in addition to numerous articles and reviews on literary subjects, particularly American-Jewish literature. **Essays:** Bernard Malamud; Chaim Potok.

Agnon, Tamar. Poet/performer. **Essay:** Yehuda Amichai.

Anderson, Hephzibah. Freelance writer and a regular reviewer for the *Jewish Quarterly*. Currently researching material for a historical novel. **Essays:** Ruth Prawer Jhabvala; Wolf Mankowitz; Bernice Rubens.

Andrews, Jennifer. Assistant Professor, Department of English, University of New Brunswick and a member of the editorial board of *Studies in Canadian Literature*. Has published widely in the fields of American and Canadian literature. Co-author of forthcoming book on Thomas King. **Essay:** Anne Michaels.

Asher, Tali. Teacher of literature. Currently writing dissertation on Rachel's poetry at the Hebrew University of Jerusalem; her essay on the subject will be published in the forthcoming anthology *Woman in the Settlement and Zionism in View of the Gender*. **Essay:** Rachel.

Auswaks, Alex. Translator and editor of Russian literature into English. Reviewer of crime fiction on www.crimebuff.com. **Essays:** Batya Gur; Osip Mandel'shtam.

Axelrod, Mark. Professor of English and Comparative Literature, Chapman University, California, where he is Director of the John Fowles Center for Creative Writing. Author of *The Politics of Style in the Fiction of Balzac, Beckett and Cortázar* (1992), *The Poetics of Novels* (1999), and *Aspects of the Screenplay* (2001). Currently working on a new novel, *The Posthumous Memoirs of Blase Kubash*. He is also a screenwriter. **Essays:** Eugène Ionesco; Clarice Lispector; Tristan Tzara.

Bar-Yosef, Hamutal. Professor of Modern Hebrew Literature, Ben-Gurion University of the Negev, Beer Sheva, Israel, and at the Hartman Institute, and poet. Research interests include the Russian context of Hebrew literature as well as the Jewish aspects of Israeli literature. Author of academic publications including six books and over 200 articles, reviews, and translations. **Essay:** Zelda.

Baraitser, Marion. Playwright, most recently *The Story of an African Farm* (performed at the Young Vic, London, 2000, published 2000) and *The Crystal Den* (performed at the New End Theatre, London, 2002, published 2002). Formerly, tutor in English Literature Diploma, Birkbeck College, London. Editor of *Bottled Notes from Under ground: Contemporary Plays by Jewish Writers* (with Sonja Linden, 1998), among other works. Founder of Loki Books in 1996, which aims to publish in English the best writing in minority languages and which was nominated for the Women in Publishing Pandora Award, for peace, 2001. **Essay:** Orly Castel-Bloom.

Bayer, Gerd. Lecturer, Department of Modern Languages and Literatures, Case Western Reserve University, Cleveland, Ohio. Doctoral candidate in English, Friedrich-Alexander-Universität, Erlangen-Nürnberg, Germany. Author of " 'A sterile promontory': Jane Rogers's and Jenny Diski's Views of the Future" *Arachne* (1999), "The Band J.B.O. and Exploding the Serious Side of Pop Culture" *Journal of Popular Culture* (2000), "Representations of Political Power in African Writing" *Journal of Cultural Studies* (2001), and other publications. **Essays:** Peter Shaffer; Tom Stoppard.

Beer, Helen. Lecturer in Yiddish, University College London. Teacher at the Oxford Centre for Hebrew and Jewish Studies, 1995–99. Currently working on a biography of Itsik Manger. Interests include Modern Yiddish literature and culture. Veteran of Yiddish Summer Programmes. **Essays:** Avrom Karpinovich; Itsik Manger; Moris Rosenfeld.

Bergoffen, Wendy H. Doctoral candidate, Department of English and American Studies, University of Massachusetts, Amherst. Her dissertation explores the construction of Jewish identity (narratives through ethnic conflict) in New York, Montreal, Galveston, and Buenos Aires. **Essays:** Edna Ferber; Alberto Gerchunoff; Anzia Yezierska.

Berkowitz, Joel. Professor, Department of Judaic Studies, State University of New York at Albany. Author of *Shakespeare on the American Yiddish Stage* (2002) and *The Yiddish Theatre: New Approaches* (in preparation). **Essays:** Avrom Goldfaden; Dovid Pinski; Yiddish Writing in the 20th Century.

Blevins, Jane. Doctoral candidate in French Literature, University of Chicago and University of Paris. Has written mainly on Paul Valéry (the subject of her dissertation). Author of "Le Visage américaine de Paul Valéry" *Paul Valéry, Lettres modernes* (1999), "Edgar Poe, Paul Valéry and the Question of Genetic Criticism in America" *L'Esprit créateur* (2001), and an essay on the history of scientific writing, *Genesis 21* (2001). **Essays:** Marek Halter; Max Jacob.

Bloch, Felicity. Reviewer and writer based in Melbourne, Australia. Editor and translator from the Yiddish of her father, Mark Verstandig's memoir of interwar Polish Jewry, *I Rest My Case* (1997). **Essays:** Lillian Hellman; Henry Roth.

Bloom, Cecil. Freelance writer based in Leeds, England. Formerly, Technical Director of a major pharmaceutical company. Author of many journal articles, including "The Institution of *Halukkah*" and "The British Labour Party and Palestine 1917–1948", both *Jewish Historical Studies* (1999–2001), "Was Richard Strauss a Nazi?" *Midstream* (2000), and "Paul Ben-Haim: Father of Israeli Music" *Midstream* (2001), also the chapter "Jewish Dispersion within Britain" in *Patterns of Migration 1850–1914* edited by A. Newman and S.W. Massil (1996). **Essays:** Lion Feuchtwanger; Louis Golding; Jiří Langer; Joseph Roth; Israel Zangwill; Arnold Zweig.

Brown, Saskia. Editor for an international NGO in Paris. Formerly, Lecturer in French Studies, University of Warwick, England. Author of various articles on Jewish-French literature and thought, and on 17th-century French literature. Editor of *The Babel Guide to Jewish Fiction* (with Ray Keenoy, 1998). **Essays:** André Schwarz-Bart; Yaakov Shabtai; David Shahar.

Cammy, Justin. Instructor of Jewish Studies and Comparative Literature, Smith College, Massachusetts. Currently completing doctoral dissertation entitled " 'Yung Vilne': A Cultural History of a Yiddish Literary Group in Inter-War Poland". Author of "Tsevorfene bleter: The Emergence of Yung Vilne" *Polin: Studies in Polish Jewry* (2001). **Essays:** Chaim Grade; Moyshe-Leyb Halpern; Anna Margolin.

Cheyette, Bryan H. Professor of English Literature, University of Southampton, England. Author of *Muriel Spark: Writers and Their Work* (2000). **Essays:** British-Jewish Literature; Simon Louvish; Muriel Spark.

Clifford, Dafna. Teacher of Israeli and Jewish literature, School of Oriental and African Studies, University of London and at the Oxford Institute for Yiddish Studies. Currently working on a study of Esther Kreitman. **Essay:** Dovid Bergelson.

Clouts, Marge. Freelance reviewer and writer. Teacher of creative writing classes in Gloucestershire. **Essays:** Sydney Clouts; Dan Jacobson.

Cohen, Uri. Teacher of Hebrew literature, Hebrew University, Jerusalem on Mount Scopus. Literary critic on Israeli radio and for newspapers for over six years. **Essay:** Yoel Hoffman.

Cohen, Zafrira Lidovsky. Assistant Professor of Hebrew Language and Literature, Stern College for Women of Yeshiva University, New York. Among other works, author of "Mystical Elements in Yona Wallach's Poetry" (in Hebrew) *Alei Siah* (1999), "Back from Oblivion: The Nature of 'Word' in Yona Wallach's Poetry" *Hebrew Studies* (2000), and "Yona Wallach: An Israeli Cultural Hero" (in Hebrew) *Moznaim* (2000). **Essay:** Yona Wallach.

Corona, Clara. Teacher of Italian literature, Venice, Italy. Contributor to *Babel Guides to Fiction in English Translation* series. **Essays:** Giorgio Bassani; Natalia Ginzburg; Carlo Levi; Elsa Morante; Alberto Moravia; Italo Svevo.

Coward, David. Research Professor, Department of French, University of Leeds, England. Member of the editorial board of *Voltaire Studies*. Winner of 1996 Scott-Moncrieff Prize for the translation of *Belle du Seigneur* by Albert Cohen. Has published prolifically; his most recent book is *A History of French Literature: From Chanson de geste to Cinema* (2002). **Essays:** Albert Cohen; Patrick Modiano.

Cox, Victoria. Assistant Professor, Appalachian State University, North Carolina. Author of various articles on Latin American literature and colonial Andean literature and the forthcoming book *Guaman Poma de Ayala: entre los conceptos andino y europeo de tiempo y espacio*. **Essay:** Nora Glickman.

Crownshaw, Richard. Lecturer, Department of English, Manchester Metropolitan University, England. Currently researching British and American cultural memories of the Holocaust. Author of "Performing Memory in Holocaust Museums" *Performance Research* (2000) and "Blacking Out Holocaust Memory in Saul Bellow's *The Victim* and *Mr Sammler's Planet*" *Saul Bellow Journal* (2000). **Essay:** Paul Auster.

Cutter, William. Steinberg Professor of Human Relations and Professor of Hebrew Literature and Education, Hebrew Union College Jewish Institute of Religion, Los Angeles. Founding director of School of Education, where he still teaches modern Hebrew poetry. Currently working on the essays of Berdyczewski for a book with commentary. **Essay:** Micha Yosef Berdyczewski.

Dace, Tish. Chancellor Professor of English at the University of Massachusetts Dartmouth and winner of that university's 1997 Scholar of the Year Award. Author of nearly 200 essays, articles, and book chapters; reviews of several thousand plays; and several books, most recently *Langston Hughes: The Contemporary Reviews* (1997). **Essays:** Bernard Kops; Martin Sherman.

Dauber, Jeremy. Assistant Professor of Yiddish, Columbia University. Research interests include Yiddish and Hebrew literature of the Haskala, and Yiddish theatre. **Essay:** Yankev Glatshteyn.

Davis, Barry. Lecturer in Yiddish Literature at the Spiro Ark, Middlesex University, England. Teacher at the Oxford Institute for Yiddish Summer Programmes, and is a film consultant for Yiddish. Lecturer in History at the London Jewish Cultural Centre and at Thames Valley University. Yiddish Editor of *The Jewish Quarterly*. Author of "When Joseph Met Molly: Oz Yoshir Moyshe (Then Moyshe Sang)" (article on Yiddish film) *Manna* (2000). Contributor of essays on Sholem Asch, Y.L. Peretz, and I.J. Singer to *The Babel Guide to Jewish Fiction* edited by Ray Keenoy and Saskia Brown (1998). **Essays:** Mordkhe Gebirtig; Perets Hirshbein; H. Leyvik; Isaac Meier Weissenberg.

de Groot, Gerald. Freelance reviewer, mainly for the *Jewish Chronicle*. Author of *The Persuaders Exposed* (1980) and other publications relating to his previous full-time occupation dealing with the relationship between social science theory and survey applications. **Essays:** Alexander Baron; E.L. Doctorow; Bruce Jay Friedman; Joseph Heller; Dorothy Parker; S.J. Perelman; J.D. Salinger; Gertrude Stein.

Denman, Hugh. Benzion Margulies Lecturer in Yiddish, Department of Hebrew and Jewish Studies, University College London. Has written extensively on Yiddish literature and linguistics in numerous reference works and scholarly journals, including *Encyclopaedia Britannica* (1988) and *The Everyman Companion to East European Literature* edited by Robert B. Pynsent (1993); and recently edited *The Work and World of Isaac Bashevis Singer* (2002). **Essays:** An-ski; Yankev Gordin; Arn Glants-Leyeles; Yitskhok-Leyb Perets.

Desmarais, Claude. Teacher at York University, Toronto, Canada. Doctoral dissertation on Elias Canetti's autobiographical work at the University of Toronto. **Essay:** Elias Canetti, Veza Canetti.

Diamond-Nigh, Lynne. Associate Professor of Romance Languages, Elmira College, New York. Founding Editor of *New Novel Review* since 1993. Author of "The Twilight of the Bums" in *Journey to Chaos: A Casebook of Real and Fictitious Discourses by and about Raymond Federman* edited by L. McCaffery (1998) and *Conflagrations/Art and the New Novel* (in preparation). Editor of *Word and Image in Contemporary Literature* (in preparation). **Essay:** Raymond Federman.

Estraikh, Gennady. Lecturer in Yiddish Linguistics at the School of Oriental and African Studies, University of London, and Yiddish Research Fellow at the European Humanities Research Centre, University of Oxford. **Essay:** Itsik Fefer.

Farhi, Moris. Recipient of an MBE (2001) for "services to literature". Fellow of the Royal Society of Literature. International Vice President of PEN. Author of novels, most recently, *Children of the Rainbow* (1999). His poems have appeared in many British, European, and US publications and in the anthology of 20th-century Jewish poets, *Voices Within the Ark* (1980). **Essays:** Jozef Habib Gerez; Shulamith Hareven; Sami Michael.

Feldman, Yael S. Abraham I. Katsh Professor of Hebrew Culture and Education, New York University. Cultural Editor of the Hebrew journal *HaDoar*. Author of *No Room of Their Own: Gender and Nation in Israeli Women's Fiction* (1999), an American National Jewish Book Award Finalist, also published in Hebrew. Currently working on a book-length study on Israeli psycho-politics, *Shrinking Zionism*. **Essays:** Shulamit Lapid; Netiva Ben-Yehuda.

Fischthal, Hannah Berliner. Associate Professor, St John's University, Jamaica, New York. Book Review Editor of *Studies in American Jewish Literature*. Author of "Abraham Cahan and Sholem Asch" *Yiddish* (1998), "Uncle Moses" in *When Joseph Met Molly: A Reader on Yiddish Film* edited by S. Paskin (1999), and "Poe's Influence on I.B. Singer" *Studies in American Jewish Literature* (with Daniel Walden, 2000). Currently completing a book on Sholem Asch. **Essay:** Sholem Asch.

Fishkin, Shelley Fisher. Professor of American Studies and English, University of Texas. Author of *Lighting Out for the Territory: Reflections on Mark Twain and American Culture* (1996). Editor of *Listening to Silences: New Essays in Feminist Criticism* (with Elaine Hedges, 1994) and *People of the Book: Thirty Scholars Reflect on Their Jewish Identity* (with Jeffrey Rubin-Dorsky, 1996). Currently working on a book entitled *Taking Women Seriously: Feminist Forays into American Literature*. **Essay:** Erica Jong.

Freadman, Richard. Professor of English, and Director of the Unit for Studies in Biography and Autobiography, La Trobe University, Melbourne, Australia. Author of *Threads of Life: Autobiography and the Will* (2001). Currently working on a study of Australian Jewish autobiography and an autobiographical volume about his father. **Essay:** Serge Liberman.

Friedlander, Albert H. Recipient of an OBE (2001). Dean of the Leo Baeck College, London. Rabbi emeritus of the Westminster Synagogue. Author of *Riders Towards the Dawn* (1997). Senior Editor of *Leo Baeck: Werke* (5 volumes so far, 1996–2001). **Essays:** Erich Fried; George Mikes; Elie Wiesel.

Gelber, Mark. Professor of Comparative Literature, Ben-Gurion University of the Negev, Beer Sheva, Israel. Author of *Melancholy Pride: Nation, Race, and Gender in the German Literature of Cultural Zionism* (2000). **Essays:** Max Brod; Theodor Herzl; Franz Kafka; Jakov Lind; Stefan Zweig.

Gil, Lydia M. Assistant Professor of Spanish, SUNY College at Old Westbury, New York. Research interests include Jewish literature of Latin America and the convergence of dramatic arts and pedagogy. **Essays:** Ariel Dorfman; Margo Glantz; Isaac Goldemberg; Gerardo Mario Goloboff.

Glickman, Nora. Professor of Latin American Literature, Queens College, City University of New York. Author of *The Jewish White Slave Trade and the Untold Story of Raquel Liberman* (2000) and *Antologia de teatro de Nora Glickman* (2000). **Essays:** Max Aub; Alicia Dujovne Ortiz.

Gluzman, Michael. Assistant Professor of Hebrew Literature, Ben-Gurion University of the Negev, Beer Sheva, Israel. Author of *Lines of Resistance in Modernist Hebrew Poetry* (in preparation). **Essay:** Avot Yeshurun.

Goldensohn, Barry. Professor of English, Skidmore College, Saratoga Springs, New York. Author of, among other titles, *Dance Music* (1992) and *East Long Pond* (1997). **Essay:** Robert Pinsky.

Goodblatt, Chanita. Senior Lecturer, Department of Foreign Literatures and Linguistics, Ben-Gurion University of the Negev, Beer Sheva, Israel. Author of "From Jewish Literal Meaning to Christian Interpretation in the Sermons of John Donne" (in Hebrew) *Eit Hada'at* (2000), "In Other Words: Breaking the Monologue in Whitman, Williams and Hughes" *Language and Literature* (2000), "The Poetic Speaker and the Multiplicity of Voices in the Poetry of Walt Whitman and Uri Zvi Greenberg" *Ha'matkonet Ve'Ha'dmut: Studies on the Poetry of Uri Zvi Greenberg* (2000), and "Adding an Empirical Dimension to the Study of Poetic Metaphor" *Journal of Literary Semantics* (2001). **Essay:** Uri Zvi Greenberg.

Gordon, Alex. Visiting Lecturer in English, Goldsmiths College, University of London, and in Cultural Studies at the University of Surrey and University of North London. Author of "From Ambivalence to Contradiction: Postmodernity, Time and American-Jewish Identity" *New Voices in Jewish Thought: Volume 2* (1999). Editor of *New Voices in Jewish Thought: Volume 3* (2000). **Essay:** David Mamet.

Grant, Linda. Novelist and journalist. Second novel, *When I Lived in Modern Times*, won the Orange Prize for Fiction in 2000. **Essay:** Andrea Dworkin.

Grey, Nancy. Assistant Professor of French Language and Literature, University of South Alabama. Author of "To Be a French Jew: Identity and Loss in Jean-Richard Bloch's *Lévy*" *Contemporary French Civilization* (2001). **Essays:** Jean-Richard Bloch; Edmond Fleg.

Groezinger, Elvira. Doctor of Philosophy, academic researcher, and Lecturer at the School of Jewish Studies, University of Potsdam, Germany. Author of two books and over 100 articles, including "Das deutsch-polnisch-jüdische Dreiecksverhältnis als Thema der polnischen Gegenwartsliteratur" in *Mythen und Stereotypen auf beiden Seiten der Oder* edited by H.D. Zimmermann (2000), "Żydzi i obraz Żydów w polskiej literaturze po 1918 r." in *Lebn wil ich. To co pozostalo: Cmentarze Zydowskie w Polsce* edited by P. Blachetta-Madajczyk (2000), and "*Le juif imaginaire*: die Suche nach jüdischer Identität in Frankreich nach 1945" in *Zwischen Adaption und Exil: jüdische Autoren und Themen in den romanischen Ländern* edited by Brigitte Sändig (2001). **Essays:** Janusz Korczak; Bolesław Leśmian; Adolf Rudnicki; Julian Stryjkowski; Julian Tuwim.

Gunn, Dan. Associate Professor of Comparative Literature and English, American University of Paris. Director of the Paris Centre for the correspondence of Samuel Beckett. Author of *Psychoanalysis and Fiction* (1988), *Almost You* (1994), *Body-Language* (2002), and *Wool-Gathering or How I Ended Analysis* (2002). Regular contributor to the *Times Literary Supplement*. **Essays:** Aharon Appelfeld; Gabriel Josipovici; Georges Perec.

Haas, Birgit. Lecturer, Department of German, Bristol University, England. Author of *Das Theater des Barock* (1998), *Das "Käthchen von Heilbronn"* (1999), and *Das Theater des George Tabori* (2000). **Essays:** Maxim Biller; Hermann Broch; Arthur Schnitzler; Berthold Viertel.

Halio, Jay L. Professor of English, University of Delaware. Member of the editorial board of the University of Delaware Press, and on the advisory committees of *College Literature*, *TEXT*, and *Journal of Theater and Drama*. Author of *Philip Roth Revisited* (1992). Editor of *Daughters of Valor: Contemporary Jewish American Women Writers* (with Ben Siegel, 1997) and *Comparative Literary Dimensions* (with Ben Siegel, 2000). **Essays:** Allegra Goodman; Philip Roth.

Hellerstein, Kathryn. Senior Fellow in Yiddish and Jewish Studies, Department of Germanic Languages, University of Pennsylvania. Poetry Editor of *Kerem*. Editor of *Paper Bridges: Selected Poems of Kadya Molodowsky* (1999) and *Jewish American Literature: A Norton Anthology* (with Jules Chametzky, 2001). **Essays:** Kadye Molodovski; Malka Heifetz Tussman.

Hever, Hannan. Professor, Department of Hebrew Literature, Hebrew University, Israel. Author of *Literature Written from Here: A Short History of Israeli Literature* (in Hebrew, 1999), *Suddenly the Sight of War: Violence and*

Nationality in Hebrew Poetry of the 40s (in Hebrew, 2001), and *Producing the Modern Hebrew Canon: Nation Building and Minority Discourse* (2002). **Essays:** Amir Gilboa; Ronit Matalon; Meir Wieseltier.

Hoffman, Matthew. Postdoctoral fellow in Jewish studies, University of California, Davis. Visiting Professor, Centre for Jewish Studies at Graduate Theological Union, Berkeley, California. His doctoral dissertation was entitled "From Rebel to Rabbi: Images of Jesus and the Making of Modern Jewish Culture". **Essays:** Moyshe Kulbak; Lamed Shapiro.

Horn, Dara. Doctoral candidate in comparative literature, focusing on Hebrew and Yiddish literature, Harvard University. MPhil from the University of Cambridge, England. Freelance journalist for *American Heritage*, *Christian Science Monitor*, *Hadassah Magazine*, and *Science*. Author of a novel, *In the Image* (2002). **Essays:** Natan Alterman; Yosef Hayyim Brenner; Uri Nissan Gnessin; Benjamin Tammuz.

Hutchinson, Peter. Teaches German at the University of Cambridge, where he is Vice-Master of Trinity Hall. Author of *Stefan Heym: Dissident auf Lebenszeit* (1999) and has published widely on German literature. **Essay:** Stefan Heym.

Iancu, Carol. Professor of Contemporary History and Jewish Studies, Montpellier 3 University, France. Author of *Les Juifs du Midi: une histoire millénaire* (with Danièle Iancu, 1995); *Evreii din Romania 1866–1919: de la excludere la emancipare* (1996), published in English as *Jews in Romania, 1866–1919: From Exclusion to Emancipation* (1996); and *La Shoah en Roumanie* (1998, revised edition 2000). **Essay:** Armand Lunel.

Iggers, Wilma. Professor Emerita of German, Canisius College, Buffalo, New York. Author of *Women of Prague: Ethnic Diversity and Social Change from the Eighteenth Century to the Present* (1995), published in German as *Frauenleben in Prag: ethnische Vielfalt und kultureller Wandel seit dem 18. Jahrhundert* (2000). Editor of *Die Juden in Böhmen und Mähren* (1986), published in English as *The Jews of Bohemia and Moravia* (1992). Currently working on the Czech collective memory in the 20th century for an exhibition involving many nationalities planned by the German Historical Museum in Berlin. **Essay:** Karl Kraus.

Jaron, Steven. Received doctorate in French and comparative literature from Columbia University in 1997. Editor of *Portrait(s) d'Edmond Jabès* (1999). Author of essays on Perec, Rawicz, Kofman, and Vidal-Naquet, elements of which form a study-in-progress on autobiography and the Shoah. **Essay:** Romain Gary.

Jenkins, G. Matthew. Lecturer in English, Old Dominion University, Virginia. Having written on the ethical aspect of the American poetic tradition from Objectivism to Language poetry, he is currently working on a study of experimental black poetry since 1945. **Essays:** George Oppen; Louis Zukofsky.

Karpowitz, Stephen. Founding member of the National Association of Psychoanalytic Critics. Advisory Editor of *Literature and Psychology*. Formerly taught at the University of Pennsylvania, now retired. Author of "The Dilemma of Primo Levi — Biographical Roots" *European Judaism*. **Essay:** Edward Lewis Wallant.

Kay, Devra. First holder of the full-time lectureship in Yiddish at the University of Oxford. For some years she held a Research Fellowship in Yiddish at Queen Mary and Westfield College, University of London, where she was also Director of Yiddish and Ashkenazic Studies. Author of *Elementary Yiddish* (1992), *Haworth and the Brontës* (1996), and *The Tkhines: The Lost Women's Prayerbook* (2002). She now works by day at the House of Commons and by night she sings jazz. **Essays:** Harvey Fierstein; Menke Katz; Esther; Avrom Reyzen; Zalkind-Zalmen Schneour.

Keenoy, Ray. Series Editor of *Babel Guides to Fiction in English Translation*. Currently working on the *Babel Guide to Yiddish Fiction in English Translation*. **Essays:** Der Nister; Albert Memmi; Mendele Moykher Sforim; Joseph Opatoshu; Giorgio Pressburger; Chava Rosenfarb; Leo Rosten; Sholem Aleichem; George Steiner.

Kellman, Steven G. Professor of Comparative Literature, University of Texas at San Antonio. Author of *The Translingual Imagination* (2000). Editor of *Leslie Fiedler and American Culture* (with Irving Malin, 1999) and *Torpid Smoke: The Stories of Vladimir Nabokov* (with Irving Malin, 2000). **Essay:** Ilan Stavans.

Kerbel, Sorrel. Formerly, Lecturer in English, University of Port Elizabeth, South Africa. Her doctoral dissertation, from the University of Cape Town, was on D.H. Lawrence and Thomas Hardy. Lectured on Anita Brookner at the University of Potsdam, Germany, 1995, on behalf of the British Council. **Essays:** Isaak Emanuilovich Babel'; Anita Brookner; Vasilii Semenovich Grossman; Ronald Harwood; Yehudit Katzir; Imre Kertész; Cynthia Ozick; Marcel Proust; Isaac Rosenberg.

Klein, Ilona. Associate Professor of Italian, Brigham Young University, Utah. Book Review Editor of *Italian Culture*, 1998–2001. Author of "Primo Levi and Bruno Piazza: Auschwitz in Italian Literature" in *Remembrance, Repentance, Reconciliation: The 25th Anniversary Volume of the Annual Scholars' Conference on the Holocaust and the Churches* edited by Douglas F. Tobler (1998) and "La Science, la science-fiction et la mémoire dans l'oeuvre de Primo Levi" in *Shoah, mémoire et écriture: Primo Levi et le dialogue des savoirs* edited by Giuseppina Santagostino (1997). **Essay:** Primo Levi.

Klinkowitz, Jerome. Professor of English and University Distinguished Scholar, University of Northern Iowa, Cedar Falls. Author of *Literary Disruptions* (1975, revised edition 1980), *Structuring the Void* (1992), *Keeping Literary Company: Working with Writers Since the Sixties* (1998), *With the Tigers Over China* (1999), and 30 other books on literature, music, art, philosophy, sport, and military historiography. Editor of "Prose Since 1945", *The Norton Anthology of American Literature* (General Editor Nina Baym, 6th edition, 2002). **Essays:** Max Apple; Stanley Elkin; Steve Katz; Jerzy Kosinski; Ronald Sukenick.

Koenen, Krisztina. Studied Hungarian and German literature in Budapest, and German literature and language in Frankfurt for her masters degree. Translates Hungarian literature into German; latest publication is *Szürke Galamb* by Sándor Tar (1999). Reporter for the *Frankfurter Allgemeine Zeitung*; since 1999 senior reporter to the economics weekly *Wirtschaftswoche*. **Essay:** György Konrád.

Konzett, Matthias. Associate Professor, Yale University. Author of *The Rhetoric of National Dissent in Thomas Bernhard, Peter Handke and Elfriede Jelinek* (2000). Editor of *The Encyclopedia of German Literature* (2000) and *A Companion to Thomas Bernhard* (2002). **Essay:** Robert Schindel.

Krupnick, Mark. Professor in the Divinity School and the Committee on Jewish Studies, University of Chicago. Author of *Lionel Trilling and the Fate of Cultural Criticism* (1986). **Essay:** Lionel Trilling.

Lebor, Mervyn. Teacher of literature in adult, further, and higher education in West Yorkshire, England. Writes reviews and articles for *Jewish Quarterly, The Guardian*, and the *Times Educational Supplement*. **Essays:** Allen Ginsberg; Nathanael West.

Leveson, Marcia. Retired Associate Professor, English Department, University of the Witwatersrand, and currently an Honorary Research Fellow. Past President of the English Academy of Southern Africa. Member of the editorial board of *Jewish Affairs*. Author of *People of the Book: Images of the Jew in South African Fiction 1880–1992* (1996) and "The Enemy Within: Some South African Jewish Writers" in *Jewries at the Frontier* edited by Sander L. Gilman and Milton Shain (1999). Editor of *Roy Campbell: Collected Works* (with Peter Alexander and Michael Chapman, 1985–88). **Essay:** Nadine Gordimer.

Levi, Jennifer. Doctoral candidate and teacher in the English Department, University of Delaware, working on dissertation entitled "Ancestral Performances: Reclaiming White Ethnic Identity in Postmodern America". **Essay:** Adrienne Rich.

Levin, Gabriel. Poet and translator based in Jerusalem. Author of collection of poems *Ostraca* (1999) and forthcoming translations of the medieval Hebrew poet Yehuda Halevi. **Essay:** Zali Gurevitch.

Levine, Tamara. Librarian and researcher. Currently writing doctoral dissertation on David Grossman and his work. Interests include Israeli literature, which she teaches. Contributor to *The Babel Guide to Jewish Fiction* edited by Ray Keenoy and Saskia Brown (1998). **Essays:** Ruth Almog; Benny Barbash; Yehudit Hendel; Savyon Liebrecht.

Lewis, Ward B. Emeritus Professor of German, University of Georgia. Author of *Eugene O'Neill: The German Reception of America's First Dramatist* (1984) and *The Ironic Dissident: Frank Wedekind in the View of His Critics* (1997). Editor of *The Birds in Langfoot's Belfry* by Paul Zech (1994). **Essay:** Egon Erwin Kisch.

Lorenz, Dagmar C.G. Professor of German, University of Illinois, Chicago. Author of *Verfolgung bis zum Massenmord: Holocaust-Diskurse in deutscher Sprache aus der Sicht der Verfolgten* (1992) and *Keepers of the Motherland: German Texts by Jewish Women Writers* (1997). Editor of *Insiders and Outsiders: Jewish and Gentile Culture in Germany and Austria* (with Gabriele Weinberger, 1994) and *Contemporary Jewish Writing in Austria* (1999). **Essays:** Edgar Hilsenrath; Gertrud Kolmar; Friedrich Torberg.

Loseff, Lev. Professor, Chairman of the Russian Department, Dartmouth College, New Hampshire. Author of *Sobrannoe* [Collected Works] (2000). Editor of *Joseph Brodsky: The Art of a Poem* (with Valentina Brodsky, 2000) and *Iosif Brodskii: stikhi I poemy* [Joseph Brodsky: Annotated Poetry] (in preparation). **Essay:** Joseph Brodsky.

Lubin, Orly. Department of Poetics and Comparative Literature and Head of the section of Women and Gender Studies at the School of Humanities, Tel Aviv University, Israel. Assistant Editor of *Poetics Today*. Has published on literature, cinema, theatre, visual culture, feminist theories, reader response theories, and Israeli culture. Author of *Women Reading Women* (in Hebrew, 2002). **Essay:** Dvora Baron.

Lundskær-Nielsen, Tom. Senior Lecturer in Danish and Head of the Department of Scandinavian Studies, University College London. Author of *Prepositions in Old and Middle English* (1993), *Danish: A Comprehensive Grammar* (with R. Allan and P. Holmes, 1995), and *Danish: An Essential Grammar* (with R. Allan and P. Holmes, 2000). Editor of the section on Danish language in *The Year's Work in Modern Language Studies*. **Essay:** Henri Nathansen.

Mann, Barbara. Assistant Professor of Hebrew Literature, Princeton University. Author of "Jewish Imagism: A Few Don'ts" *Religion and Literature* (1998), "Framing the Native: Esther Raab's Visual Poetics" *Israel Studies* (1999), and "Modernism and the Zionist Uncanny: Reading the Old Cemetery in Tel Aviv" *Representations* (2000). **Essay:** Esther Raab.

Marzanska, Marta. Doctoral candidate, University of Cambridge. Interests include Israeli literature, particularly the theme of hatred, the subject of her dissertation. **Essays:** Moshe Shamir; Saul Tchernichovski; David Vogel; S. Yizhar.

Meijer, Daphne. Novelist, journalist, playwright, and documentary filmmaker, based in Amsterdam. Writes both fiction and non-fiction. Author of the novel *Het plezier van de duivel* (1995), the novella *De Bezoeking* (1999), and

Onbekende Kinderen. De laatste trein uit Westerbork (2001). Editor of the anthology *Levi in de Lage Landen: 350 jaar joodse schrijvers in de Nederlandse literatuur* (1999). **Essays:** G.L. Durlacher; Herman Heijermans; Judith Herzberg; Yoram Kaniuk; Marga Minco; Marcel Möring.

Miller, Giulia. Received masters degree from the University of Cambridge. Currently working on translations and research. **Essays:** Yitzhak Ben-Ner; Yehoshua Kenaz; Aharon Megged; Meir Shalev.

Minogue, Valerie. Emeritus Professor of French, University of Wales Swansea. Author of *Proust, 'Du côte de chez Swann'* (1973), *Nathalie Sarraute: The War of the Words* (1981), and *Zola: 'L'Assommoir'* (1996). Co-editor of Nathalie Sarraute's *Oeuvres complètes* (General Editor Jean-Yves Tadié, 1996). Founder and General Editor of *Romance Studies*. **Essay:** Nathalie Sarraute.

Mirkowicz, Tomasz. Polish novelist, critic, and translator. Author of *Lekcja geografii* (1996) and *Pielgrzymka do Ziemi Świętej Egiptu* (1999). **Essay:** Moris Farhi.

Mitchell, Michael. Freelance writer and translator. Formerly, Lecturer in German, University of Stirling, Scotland. Author of *Austria* (World Bibliographical Series, 1999), a new translation of Alfred Kubin's *The Other Side* (2000), and various articles on Austrian literature. **Essay:** Ernst Weiss.

Monk, Craig. Associate Professor, Department of English, University of Lethbridge, Alberta, Canada. Author of "*Transition* and *Merlin*: Two Generations of Little Magazines in Paris" *Journal of Modern Literature* (1996), "Eugene Jolas and the Translation Policies of *Transition*" *Mosaic* (1999), and "Modernism in *Transition*" *Miscelánea* (1999). **Essay:** Laura Riding.

Morace, Robert A. Teaches at Daemen College, New York. Author of several books and numerous articles on contemporary fiction, including a short book on Irvine Welsh's *Trainspotting* (2001). **Essay:** Will Self.

Morris, Paul. Professor of Religious Studies, Victoria University of Wellington, New Zealand. **Essays:** A. Alvarez; Chaim Bermant; Nissim Ezekiel; Elaine Feinstein; Danilo Kiš; Emanuel Litvinoff; Frederic Raphael; Leonard Sydney Woolf; Fay Zwicky.

Nathan, David. A lifetime in journalism from reporter to deputy editor, but mainly as theatre critic of *Jewish Chronicle* (from 1971). Author of biographies on Tony Hancock, John Hurt, and Glenda Jackson, two novels, a book on comedy, two radio plays, one television play, and writer for *That Was the Week That Was* in collaboration with Dennis Potter. President of Critics' Circle, 1986–88. Died 2001. **Essay:** Tony Kushner.

Nesvisky, Matthew. Associate Professor of English, Kutztown University, Pennsylvania. Formerly, editor and features writer at the *Jerusalem Post*. **Essays:** Leslie Epstein; Ephraim Kishon; Wallace Markfield; Amos Oz; Nathan Shaham; A.B. Yehoshua.

Omer-Sherman, Ranen. Assistant Professor of American Literature, Saint Louis University, Madrid. Author of " 'It is I Who Have Been Defending a Religion Called Judaism': The T.S. Eliot and Horace M. Kallen Correspondence" *Texas Studies in Literature and Language* (1997), "The Stranger and the Metropolis: The Jewish Poetics of Charles Reznikoff" *Shofar* (1997), and *Diaspora and Zionism in Jewish American Literature: Lazarus, Syrkin, Reznikoff, and Roth* (2002). **Essays:** E.M. Broner; Charles Reznikoff.

Orr, Leonard. Professor of English, Washington State University. Author of a number of books including *A Dictionary of Critical Theory* (1991) and *Problems and Poetics of the Nonaristotelian Novel* (1991). Editor of *A Joseph Conrad Companion* (with Ted Billy, 1999). Currently working on an introduction to modernism and *A Joseph Conrad Encyclopedia*. **Essays:** Walter Abish; Art Spiegelman.

Oz, Avraham. Professor of Theatre, University of Haifa and Tel Aviv University, Israel. Artistic Director of the Haifa University Theatre. Has published extensively on Shakespeare, Marlowe, and early modern English theatre. Publications include *The Yoke of Love: Prohetic Riddles in The Merchant of Venice* (1995) and collections of essays on Shakespeare and Marlowe; his most recent book is *Political Theatre* (Hebrew–English version in preparation). Trans lator into Hebrew of plays by Shakespeare, Brecht, and Pinter, among others. **Essays:** Nissim Aloni; Hanoch Levin; Harold Pinter; Yehoshua Sobol; C.P. Taylor.

Pacernick, Gary. Professor of English, Wright State University, Ohio. Author of limited edition poetry collection *Summer Psalms* (1999) and *Meaning and Memory: Interviews with Fourteen Jewish Poets* (2001). **Essays:** Tillie Olsen; Marge Piercy.

Polukhina, Valentina. Emeritus Professor of Russian Literature, Keele University, England. Author of *Joseph Brodsky: A Poet for Our Time* (1989), *Brodsky Through the Eyes of His Contemporaries* (1992), and *Dictionary of Brodsky's Tropes* (1995). Editor of *Joseph Brodsky: The Art of a Poem* (with Lev Loseff, 1998) and *Joseph Brodsky: Selected Interviews* (2001). **Essay:** Daniel Weissbort.

Porat, Dina. Professor and Head of the Department of Jewish History, of the Stephen Roth Institute for the Study of Contemporary Anti-Semitism and Racism, and Alfred P. Slaner Chair for the Study of Racism and Anti-Semitism, Tel Aviv University, Israel. Author of *Beyond the Reaches of Our Soul: The Life and Times of Abba Kovner* (2000) and some 40 articles and a number of books on various aspects of the Holocaust and anti-Semitism. **Essay:** Abba Kovner.

Prager, Leonard. Emeritus Professor, University of Haifa, Israel. Author of *Yiddish Literary and Linguistic Periodicals* *and Miscellanies: A Selective Annotated Bibliography* (with A.A. Greenbaum, 1982) and *Yiddish Culture in Britain: A Guide* (1990). Editor of the electronic journal *The Mendele Review* and the website "The World of Yiddish". **Essays:** Abraham Cahan; Yeshayohu Shpigl.

Ramraj, Victor J. Professor, Department of English, University of Calgary, Alberta, Canada. Author of *Mordecai Richler* (1985). Editor of *ARIEL: A Review of International English Literature*. **Essay:** Mordecai Richler.

Ravvin, Norman. Critic, writer, and teacher. Chair of the Institute for Canadian Jewish Studies, Concordia University, Montreal. Author of *Café des Westens* (1991), *A House of Words: Jewish Writing, Identity and Memory* (1997), *Sex, Skyscrapers, and Standard Yiddish* (1997), and *Hidden Canada: An Intimate Travelogue* (2001). Editor of *Great Stories of the Sea* (1999) and *Not Quite Mainstream: Canadian Jewish Short Stories* (2001), and General Editor of Hungry I Books. **Essays:** Leonard Cohen; A.M. Klein.

Robbins, Wendy. Professor, Department of English, and Interdisciplinary Women's Studies Program, University of New Brunswick, Canada. Author of *Ralph Gustafson* (1979), *Work in Progress: Tracking Women's Equality in Canada/Un dossier en évolution* (with Research Department of the Canadian Advisory Council on the Status of Women, 1994), and "Electronic Communications and Feminist Activism: The Experience of PAR-L" *Atlantis* (with Michèle Ollivier, 1999). Guest Editor of special issue "Women Writers of the Commonwealth" *World Literature Written in English* (with Lois C. Gottlieb, 1978). President of the Canadian Association for Commonwealth Literature and Language Studies and Vice-President of the Women's Issues Network, Humanities and Social Sciences Federation of Canada. **Essay:** Adele Wiseman.

Rock, David. Senior Lecturer in German, Keele University, England. Author of *Jurek Becker: A Jew Who Became a German?* (2000) and many articles on German Democratic Republic writers and post-unification cultural issues. Editor of *Gerhart Hauptmann: Bahnwärter Thiel* (with David Horrocks, 1992), *Jurek Becker: Five Stories* (1993), *Voices in Times of Change* (2000), *German Studies Towards the Millennium: Selected Papers from the CUTG Conference 1999* (with Chris Hall, 2000), and *Coming Home to Germany? The Integration of Ethnic Germans from Central and Eastern Europe in the Federal Republic* (with Stefan Wolff, 2002). **Essay:** Jurek Becker.

Rothman, Juanita. Publisher and editor of the journal *Hovering Craft and Hydrofoil/High Speed Surface Craft*. **Essay:** Maurice Samuel.

Rubenstein, Joshua. Northeast Regional Director, Amnesty International USA. Associate, Davis Center for Russian Studies, Harvard University. Author of *Soviet Dissidents: Their Struggle for Human Rights* (1980, revised edition 1985), *Adolf Hitler* (1982), *Tangled Loyalties: The Life and Times of Ilya Ehrenburg* (1996), and numerous articles on Soviet literature and dissent. Editor of Anatoly Marchenko's memoir *From Tarusa to Siberia* (1980) and *Stalin's Secret Pogrom: The Postwar Inquisition of the Jewish Anti-Fascist Committee* (with Vladimir P. Naumov, 2001). **Essay:** Il'ia Erenburg.

Rubinstein, Rachel. Doctoral candidate, Harvard University and resident tutor in English, Quincy House, completing dissertation on modernism in Jewish-American literature. Currently teaching at Smith College and Mount Holyoke College, Massachusetts. **Essays:** Leslie A. Fiedler; Norman Mailer; Delmore Schwartz.

Rudolf, Anthony. Writer, translator, and publisher. Author of *Wine from Two Glasses* (1991), *Engraved in Flesh: Piotr Rawicz and His Novel Blood from the Sky* (1996), *The Arithmetic of Memory* (1999), and *Mandorla* (1999). **Essays:** Ka-Tzetnik 135633; Piotr Rawicz; Claude Vigée.

Sadler, Geoff. Assistant Librarian, Local Studies, Chesterfield Public Library, England. Author of *Journey to Freedom* (with Antoni Snarski, 1990), *Shirebrook in Old Picture Postcards* (1993), *Shirebrook* (1994), *Shirebrook: A Second Selection* (1995), *Who Was Who? The Black and Whites* (2000), *Chesterfield: History and Guide* (2001), and, as "Jeff Sadler" and "Wes Calhoun", 28 Western novels. Editor of *20th Century Western Writers* (1991) and *St Nazaire to Shepperton: A Sailor's Odyssey* by Ralph Batteson (1996). Contributor of essays on Ruth Fainlight and Daniel Weissbort to *Contemporary Poets* edited by Thomas Riggs (2001). **Essays:** Dannie Abse; Ruth Fainlight; Arthur Koestler; Boris Pasternak; Herman Wouk.

Schrire, Gwynne. Trained as a social worker, she later read Jewish Studies at the University of Cape Town, South Africa. Works at the South African Jewish Board of Deputies. Author of *In Sacred Memory: Recollections of the Holocaust by Survivors Living in Cape Town* (1995), another book on local history, and many scholarly articles dealing with early 20th-century East European Jewish immigration to South Africa. **Essay:** Sarah Gertrude Millin.

Schwartz, Michael J. Assistant Professor, California State University at Chico. Received doctorate from New York University in 2002 with dissertation on the georgic mode in 18th-century Britain. Contributor of essay on Muriel Rukeyser to *Jewish Women in America: An Encyclopedia* edited by Paula E. Hyman and Deborah Dash Moore (1997). Currently writing an essay on Milton's translation of Psalms 1–8 and 80–88 for *Reassembling Truth: Twenty-First-Century Milton* edited by Charles W. Durham and Kristin A. Pruitt (in preparation). **Essay:** Muriel Rukeyser.

Shamir, Ziva. Lecturer, Department of Hebrew Literature, Tel Aviv University, Israel. **Essay:** Yonatan Ratosh.

Shechner, Mark. Professor of English, State University of New York, Buffalo. Author of *After the Revolution: Studies in Contemporary Jewish American Imagination* (1987), the Introduction to Isaac Rosenfeld's *Passage from Home*

(1988), and *The Conversion of the Jews and Other Essays* (1990). Editor of *Preserving the Hunger: An Isaac Rosenfeld Reader* (1988). Contributor of essay on Philip Roth to *Contemporary Jewish-American Novelists: A Bio-Critical Sourcebook* edited by Joel Shatsky and Michael Taub (1997). **Essays:** American-Jewish Literature; Harold Brodkey; Isaac Rosenfeld.

Sherman, Joseph. Corob Fellow in Yiddish Studies, Oxford Centre for Hebrew and Jewish Studies, University of Oxford. Author of over 40 academic articles and editor of nine books. Chief interests are the works of Isaac Bashevis Singer, whom he interviewed in 1983, and whose *Shadows on the Hudson* he translated into English (1987), and of Dovid Bergelson whose novella, *Opgang*, he translated into English as *Descent* for the Modern Language Association (1999). **Essays:** Isaac Bashevis Singer; Israel Joshua Singer.

Shimony, Batya. Doctoral candidate, Ben-Gurion University of the Negev, Beer Sheva, Israel. Her dissertation is on the relationship between the narratives of veteran Western Jewish writers and those of oriental Jews who wrote about the experience of immigration and absorption in the first years of Israel. **Essay:** David Schütz.

Shneer, David. Assistant Professor of History and Jewish Studies, University of Denver, Colorado. His doctoral dissertation, entitled "A Revolution in the Making: Yiddish and the Creation of Soviet Jewish Culture", examines the relationship between language, culture, and political power in the creation of modern Jewish cultures. **Essay:** Perets Markish.

Shrayer, Maxim D. Associate Professor of Russian and English, Boston College, Massachusetts. Author of *The World of Nabokov's Stories* (1999), *Nabokov: Temy i variatsii* [Nabokov: Themes and Variations] (2000), *Russian Poet, Soviet Jew: The Legacy of Eduard Bagritskii* (2000), and *An Anthology of Russian-Jewish Literature: Two Centuries of a Dual Identity* (forthcoming, 2004). His Russian poetry has been published in three collections and his translations, as well as English and Russian poetry and fiction, have appeared in periodicals. **Essays:** Eduard Bagritskii; David Shrayer-Petrov.

Smith, Gerald S. Professor of Russian, University of Oxford. Author of a translation with commentary of the poetry and prose of Boris Slutsky, *Things That Happened* (1999), *D.S. Mirsky: A Russian-English Life 1890–1930* (2000), and numerous books on topics in modern and 18th-century Russian literature. **Essay:** Boris Abramovich Slutskii.

Snir, Reuven. Senior Lecturer and Head of Department of Arabic Language and Literature, Haifa University, Israel. Associate Editor of *Al-Karmil: Studies in Arabic Language and Literature*. Has published extensively in English, Arabic, and Hebrew on Arabic literature and theatre, and the Hebrew literature of Oriental Jews. **Essays:** Eli Amir; Shimon Ballas.

Solway, David. Writer-in-Residence, Concordia University, Montreal. Associate Editor at *Books in Canada*. Contributing Editor to *Canadian Notes and Queries*. Author of poetry volumes *Chess Pieces* (1999), *Saracen Island* (2000), and *The Lover's Progress* (2002) and prose titles *Lying About the Wolf: Essays in Culture and Education* (1997), *Random Walks: Essays in Elective Criticism* (1997), and *The Turtle Hypodermic of Sickenpods: Liberal Studies in the Corporate Age* (2000). **Essay:** Irving Layton.

Spicehandler, Ezra. Professor Emeritus of Hebrew Literature, Hebrew Union College, Cincinnati, Ohio. Author of *Modern Hebrew Stories* (1971). Editor of *The Modern Hebrew Poem Itself* (with Stanley Burnshaw and T. Carmi, 1965, revised edition 1989). Divisional Editor of Modern Hebrew Literature, *Encyclopaedia Judaica* edited by Cecil Roth (1972). Translator of *Random Harvest: The Novellas of Bialik* (with David Patterson, 1999). **Essays:** Hayyim Nahman Bialik; T. Carmi; Leah Goldberg; Dan Pagis; Gabriel Yehoshua Preil.

Stavans, Ilan. Lewis-Sebring Professor in Latin American and Latino Culture, Amherst College, Massachusetts. Author of *The Hispanic Condition* (1995, revised edition 2001) and *The Inveterate Dreamer: Essays and Conversations on Jewish Culture* (2001). Editor of *The Oxford Book of Jewish Stories* (1998) and *The Essential Ilan Stavans* (2000). **Essay:** Moacyr Scliar.

Sylvester, Louise. Research Fellow, Kings College, London. Author of "The Feminist Struggle with Feminist Identity" *The Jewish Quarterly* (1992), *Studies in the Lexical Field of Expectation* (1994), "Reading Narratives of Rape: The Story of Lucretia in Chaucer, Gower and Christine de Pizan" *Leeds Studies in English* (2000), "Reading Rape in Medieval Literature" in *Medievalism and the Academy II: Cultural Studies* edited by David Metzger (2000), and "A Knock at the Door: Reading Judith Kerr's Picture Books in the Context of Her Holocaust Fiction" *The Lion and the Unicorn* (2002). **Essays:** Howard Jacobson; Clive Sinclair.

Tietjen, Jeanie M. Masters student and instructor at the University of Massachusetts, Amherst, teaching Holocaust studies. Author of *I Have Arrived Before My Words: The Autobiographical Writings of Homeless Women* (with Deborah Pugh, 1997). Currently researching and writing a biography of literary critic and scholar Terrence Des Pres. **Essays:** Ida Fink; Ivan Klíma; Arnošt Lustig.

True, Michael. Author of *An Energy Field More Intense Than War: The Nonviolent Tradition and American Literature* (1995) and other writings. Has taught American literature, nonviolence, and peace studies at Assumption, Holy Cross, and Colorado colleges, and Hawaii, Columbia, and Duke universities, as well as in China and India, as a Fulbright lecturer. **Essays:** Stanley Kunitz; Karl Shapiro.

Tuerk, Richard. Professor of Literature and Languages, Texas A&M University-Commerce. Member of the editorial board of the *Journal of the American Studies Association of Texas*. Past President, Texas Popular Culture Association. Author of *Central Still: Circle and Sphere in Thoreau's Prose* (1975), "The *American Spectator* Controversy: Was Dreiser Anti-Semitic?" *Prospects* (1991), "At Home in the Land of Columbus: Americanization in European-American Immigrant Autobiography" *Multicultural Autobiography* (1992), and "Michael Gold's *Hoboken* Blues" *MELUS* (1995). **Essays:** Saul Bellow; Maurice Sendak; Leon Uris.

Tzamir, Hamutal. Teaches Hebrew literature at Ben-Gurion University of the Negev, Beer Sheva, Israel. Main interests are Hebrew and Israeli poetry in the contexts of nationalism and gender. Author of "Love for the Land and a Deaf One's Talk: One Poem of Esther Raab and Its Reception in the 1960s" *Theory and Criticism* (1995), "Femininity and Utopia in Yonah Wallach's Early Poetry" *The Porter Institute Studies* (1996), "Believers and Uprooted: Daliah Rabikovitch, a Poetess and a Prophet" *Mikan* (1999), "Nation's Place and Others' Places: Zelda's Dead Bird and Old House" in *Discourse on Gender/Gendered Discourse in the Middle East* edited by Boas Shoshan (2000), " 'It Seems to Me That I Am Liked': Dalia Hertz's Poetics of Mimicry" *Theory and Criticism* (2001), and " 'The Landscape Loses Its Name': Nathan Zach's New National/Israeli Subject", *Mechkarei Yerushalayim Be-Sifrut Ivrit* (2002). **Essays:** Leah Ayalon; Maya Bejerano.

Tzur, Shai. Masters student, Hebrew University of Jerusalem, Mount Scopus, Israel. Has written much on literary criticism and post-modern Israeli literature. Currently working as editor for Yedioth Aharonot Books in Tel Aviv. **Essay:** Yuval Shimoni.

Valencia, Heather. Honorary Lecturer, Department of German, University of Stirling, Scotland, and Associate Lecturer, Open University, Milton Keynes, England. Author of *Else Lasker-Schüler und Abraham Nochem Stenzel: eine unbekannte Freundschaft* (1995), "Yiddish Writers in Berlin 1920–1936" in *The German-Jewish Dilemma: From the Enlightenment to the Shoah* edited by Edward Timms and Andrea Hammel (1995), " 'Gezang fun a jidischn dichter in 1943': Wort als Schutz und Widerstand in der Lyrik von Abraham Sutzkever" in *Kriegserlebnis und Legendenbildung: das Bild des "modernen" Krieges in Literatur, Theater, Photographie und Film* edited by Thomas F. Schneider (1999), *Sprachinseln: jiddische Publizistik in London, Wilna und Berlin 1880–1930* (with Susanne Marten-Finnis, 1999), and "The Vision of Zion from the "Kingdom of the Cross": Uri Tsvi Grinberg's *Albatros* in Berlin (1923)" in *Berlin Wien Prag: Modernity, Minorities and Migration in the Inter-war Period* edited by Susanne Marten-Finnis and Matthias Uecker (2001). **Essays:** Else Lasker-Schüler; Mani Leyb; Abraham Sutzkever.

van Tendeloo, Dorothée. London-based researcher of Jewish literature and culture, and translator of Dutch, Hebrew, and Yiddish fiction. Author of "La Pratique de l'Autre" *Études Inter-Ethniques*, issue on "Juifs des Flandres et de Hollande:1945–1995" (with Toon van Dun, 2000) and contributor to *Papieren Schatten* (2001), a Dutch anthology of Yiddish women's writing. **Essays:** S.Y. Agnon; Esther Kreitman.

Veidlinger, Jeffrey. Assistant Professor, Department of History, Indiana University, Bloomington. Author of *The Moscow State Yiddish Theater: Jewish Culture on the Soviet Stage* (2000). **Essay:** Shmuel Halkin.

Vice, Sue. Reader in English Literature, University of Sheffield, England. Author of *Introducing Bakhtin* (1997) and *Holocaust Fiction* (2000). **Essay:** Holocaust Writing.

Vinti, Elvira Lato. Reader in English, Institute of Electronic Engineering, University of Perugia, Italy. Formerly, free-lance editor at Electa Umbri Editori, Perugia, now a free-lance reader of English language literature for Deutscher Taschenbuch Verlag in Munich. Also active in various literary circles as a poetess and is currently working on her first book. **Essays:** Rose Ausländer; Umberto Saba; Nelly Sachs.

Voigts, Manfred. Lecturer for the Jewish Studies programme, University of Potsdam, Germany. Author of *Oskar Goldberg* (1992), *Jüdischer Messianismus und Geschichte* (1994), "Der Kompromiss, Plädoyer für einen umschrittenen Begriff" *Zeitschrift für Religions- und Geistesgeschichte* (1994), *Das geheimnisvolle Verschwinden des Geheimnisses* (1995), "Brecht and the Jews" *The Brecht Yearbook 21* (1996), and "Kafka und die jüdische Frau" *Aschkenas* (1998). Editor of *Franz Kafka 'Vor dem Gesetz'* (1994). **Essays:** Alfred Döblin; Leo Perutz; Jakob Wasserman; Franz Werfel.

Vullings, Jeroen. Editor and literary critic, Dutch weekly *Vrij Nederland*. **Essays:** Harry Mulisch; Léon de Winter.

Wade, Stephen. Senior Lecturer in English, University of Huddersfield, England. Author of *The Imagination in Transit: The Fiction of Philip Roth* (1996) and *Jewish American Literature Since 1945: An Introduction* (1999). **Essays:** Woody Allen; Paul Celan; Karen Gershon; Clifford Odets; Grace Paley; Jon Silkin; Neil Simon; Susan Sontag.

Wakoski, Diane. University Distinguished Professor, Department of English, Michigan State University. Author of *Towards a New Poetry* (1980), *Emerald Ice: Selected Poems 1962–1987* (1988), *The Butcher's Apron: New & Selected Poems* (2000), and, in "The Archaeology of Movies and Books" series, *Medea the Sorceress* (1991), *Jason the Sailor* (1993), *The Emerald City of Las Vegas* (1995), and *Argonaut Rose* (1998). **Essays:** Carl Rakosi; Jerome Rothenberg.

Weissman, Anat. Teacher of Hebrew literature at the Hebrew University of Jerusalem, Israel. **Essay:** David Avidan.

Whyte, Sally. Associate Editor, Coda Editions, London. Member of the Society of Authors and the International Association of Art Critics (UNESCO). Member of the editorial board of *The Dreyfus Trilogy* (1994). International features writer for *Ha'Aretz*, Israel, since 1982, and arts correspondent for *Tribune de Genève*, *Die Welt*, and *IMZ*. Author of "Theresienstadt" in *Die Musik in Geschichte und Gegenwart: allgemeine Enzyklopädie der Musik* edited by Ludwig Finscher (2000) and "Music of the Holocaust" in *Remembering for the Future* edited by John K. Roth and Elisabeth Maxwell (2001). Contributor to *Encyclopaedia Judaica: Decennial Book, 1983–1992* edited by Geoffrey Wigoder (1994) and *International Dictionary of Opera* edited by C. Steven LaRue (1993). **Essays:** Steven Berkoff; Arnold Wesker.

Wieclawska, Katarzyna. Works at the newly established Centre for Jewish Studies, Maria Curie University, Lublin, Poland. Her doctoral dissertation is on the image of the Shtetl in the fiction of Polish, Jewish-American, and Jewish writers after 1945. Delivered a paper on fantastic elements in the work of Bruno Schulz, Asch, and I.B. Singer at the conference on the Shtetl, University College London, 2001. **Essay:** Bruno Schulz.

Wolosky, Shira. Professor of English and American Literature, Hebrew University of Jerusalem, Israel, and received a Guggenheim fellowship, 2000. Author of *Emily Dickinson: A Voice of War* (1984), *Language Mysticism* (1993), *The Art of Poetry: How to Read a Poem* (2001), and "Poetry and Public Discourse" in *The Cambridge History of American Literature* volume 3, edited by Sacvan Bercovitch (in preparation). **Essay:** John Hollander.

Wright, Tamra. Holds the Bradfield Lectureship in Jewish Studies at the London School of Jewish Studies. London School of Jewish Studies Fellow of the School of Oriental and African Studies, University of London. Author of *The Twilight of Jewish Philosophy: Emmanuel Levinas' Ethical Hermeneutics* (2000). **Essay:** Edmond Jabès.

Wynchank, Anny. Associate Professor and Head of French Section, Department of Modern and Classical Languages and Literatures, University of Cape Town, South Africa. Member of the editorial board of *English Studies in Africa*, *Uniswa Research Journal*, *Literator*, and *Francophone Studies*. Editor of *Afriques imaginaires: regards réciproques et discours littéraires* (with Philippe-Joseph Salazar, 1995). Research interests include Francophone writings and film from West Africa, Jewish life and literature in the Maghreb, and various French authors, especially Marcel Schwob and André Gide, and has published almost 50 articles on all these topics. **Essays:** André Maurois; Marcel Schwob.

Yudkin, Leon I. Professor, University of Paris VIII, 200, and Lecturer in Hebrew and Comparative Literature, University College London. His ninth book is *Public Crisis and Literary Response: The Adjustment of Modern Jewish Literature* (2001). **Essays:** Lea Aini; Hanokh Bartov; David Grossman; Haim Guri; Hayim Hazaz; Hebrew Literature in the 20th Century; Amalia Kahana-Carmon; Yitzhak Orpaz; Lily Perry; Dalia Ravikovitch; Pinhas Sadeh; Avraham Shlonsky; Nathan Zach.